AF521962

THE

HOLY BIBLE

THE

HOLY BIBLE

CONTAINING THE OLD AND NEW TESTAMENTS

Words of Jesus in Red

NASHVILLE DALLAS MEXICO CITY RIO DE JANEIRO BEIJING

The Holy Bible, New King James Version
© 1982 by Thomas Nelson, Inc.

Section Introductions and Maps © 1990 by Thomas Nelson, Inc.

Concordance © 1985 by Thomas Nelson, Inc.

Published in Nashville, Tennessee, by Thomas Nelson. Thomas Nelson is a trademark of Thomas Nelson, Inc.

The text of the New King James Version (NKJV) may be quoted or reprinted without prior written permission with the following qualifications: (1) up to and including 1,000 verses may be quoted in printed form as long as the verses quoted amount to less than 50% of a complete book of the Bible and make up less than 50% of the total work in which they are quoted; (2) all NKJV quotations must conform accurately to the NKJV text.

Any use of the NKJV text must include a proper acknowledgment as follows:

> Scripture taken from the New King James Version. © 1982 by Thomas Nelson, Inc. Used by permission. All rights reserved.

However, when quotations from the NKJV text are used in church bulletins, orders of service, Sunday School lessons, church newsletters and similar works in the course of religious instruction or services at a place of worship or other religious assembly, the following notice may be used at the end of each quotation: NKJV.

For quotation requests not covered by the above guidelines, write to Thomas Nelson Publishers, Attn: Bible Rights and Permissions, P.O. Box 141000, Nashville, Tennessee 37214-1000.

All Rights Reserved
Printed in China

14 15 16 17 18 — 22 21 20

Preface

Purpose

In the preface to the 1611 edition, the translators of the Authorized Version, known popularly as the King James Bible, state that it was not their purpose "to make a new translation . . . but to make a good one better." Indebted to the earlier work of William Tyndale and others, they saw their best contribution to consist in revising and enhancing the excellence of the English versions which had sprung from the Reformation of the sixteenth century. In harmony with the purpose of the King James scholars, the translators and editors of the present work have not pursued a goal of innovation. They have perceived the Holy Bible, New King James Version, as a continuation of the labors of the earlier translators, thus unlocking for today's readers the spiritual treasures found especially in the Authorized Version of the Holy Scriptures.

A Living Legacy

For nearly four hundred years, and throughout several revisions of its English form, the King James Bible has been deeply revered among the English-speaking peoples of the world. The precision of translation for which it is historically renowned, and its majesty of style, have enabled that monumental version of the Word of God to become the mainspring of the religion, language, and legal foundations of our civilization.

Although the Elizabethan period and our own era share in zeal for technical advance, the former period was more aggressively devoted to classical learning. Along with this awakened concern for the classics came a flourishing companion in interest in the Scriptures, an interest that was enlivened by the conviction that the manuscripts were providentially handed down and were a trustworthy record of the inspired Word of God. The King James translators were committed to producing an English Bible that would be a precise translation, and by no means a paraphrase or a broadly approximate rendering. On the one hand, the scholars were almost as familiar with the original languages of the Bible as with their native English. On the other hand, their reverence for the divine Author and His Word assured a translation of the Scriptures in which only a principle of utmost accuracy could be accepted.

In 1786 Catholic scholar Alexander Geddes said of the King James Bible, "If accuracy and strictest attention to the letter of the text be supposed to constitute an excellent version, this is of all versions the most excellent." George Bernard Shaw became a literary legend in our century because of his severe and often humorous criticisms of our most cherished values. Surprisingly, however, Shaw pays the following tribute to the scholars commissioned by King James: "The translation was extraordinarily well done because to the translators what they were translating was not merely a curious collection of ancient books written by different authors in different stages of culture, but the Word of God divinely revealed through His chosen and expressly inspired scribes. In this conviction they carried out their work with boundless reverence and care and achieved a beautifully artistic result." History agrees with these estimates. Therefore, while seeking to unveil the excellent *form* of the traditional English Bible, special care has also been taken in the present edition to preserve the work of *precision* which is the legacy of the 1611 translators.

Complete Equivalence in Translation

Where new translation has been necessary in the New King James Version, the most complete representation of the original has been rendered by considering the history of usage and etymology of words in their contexts. This principle of complete equivalence seeks to preserve *all* of the information in the text, while presenting it in good literary form. Dynamic equivalence, a recent procedure in Bible translation, commonly results in paraphrasing where a more literal rendering is needed to reflect a specific and vital sense. For example, complete equivalence truly renders the original text in expressions such as "lifted her voice and wept" (Gen. 21:16); "I gave you cleanness of teeth" (Amos 4:6); "Jesus met them, saying, 'Rejoice!'" (Matt. 28:9); and "'Woman, what does your concern have to do with Me?'" (John 2:4). Complete equivalence translates fully, in order to provide an English text that is both accurate and readable.

In keeping with the principle of complete equivalence, it is the policy to translate interjections which are commonly omitted in modern language renderings of the Bible. As an example, the interjection *behold,* in the older King James editions, continues to have a place in English usage, especially in dramatically calling attention to a spectacular scene, or an event of profound importance such as the Immanuel prophecy of Isaiah 7:14. Consequently, *behold* is retained for these occasions in the present edition. However, the Hebrew and Greek originals for this word can be translated variously, depending on the circumstances in the passage. Therefore, in addition to *behold,* words such as *indeed, look, see,* and *surely* are also rendered to convey the appropriate sense suggested by the context in each case.

In faithfulness to God and to our readers, it was deemed appropriate that all participating scholars sign a statement affirming their belief in the verbal and plenary inspiration of Scripture, and in the inerrancy of the original autographs.

Devotional Quality

The King James scholars readily appreciated the intrinsic beauty of divine revelation. They accordingly disciplined their talents to render well-chosen English words of their time, as well as a graceful, often musical arrangement of language, which has stirred the hearts of Bible readers through the years. The translators, the committees, and the editors of the present edition, while sensitive to the late-twentieth-century English idiom, and while adhering faithfully to the Hebrew, Aramaic, and Greek texts, have sought to maintain those lyrical and devotional qualities that are so highly regarded in the Authorized Version. This devotional quality is especially apparent in the poetic and prophetic books, although even the relatively plain style of the Gospels and Epistles cannot strictly be likened, as sometimes suggested, to modern newspaper style. The Koine Greek of the New Testament is influenced by the Hebrew background of the writers, for whom even the gospel narratives were not merely flat utterance, but often song in various degrees of rhythm.

The Style

Students of the Bible applaud the timeless devotional character of our historic Bible. Yet it is also universally understood that our language, like all living languages, has undergone profound change since 1611. Subsequent revisions of the King James Bible have sought to keep abreast of changes in English speech. The present work is a further step toward this objective. Where obsolescence and other reading difficulties exist, present-day vocabulary, punctuation, and grammar have been carefully integrated. Words representing ancient objects, such as *chariot* and *phylactery,* have no modern substitutes and are therefore retained.

A special feature of the New King James Version is its conformity to the thought flow of the 1611 Bible. The reader discovers that the sequence and selection of words, phrases, and clauses of the new edition, while much clearer, are so close to the traditional that there is remarkable ease in listening to the reading of either edition while following with the other.

In the discipline of translating biblical and other ancient languages, a standard method of transliteration, that is, the English spelling of untranslated words, such as names of persons and places, has never been commonly adopted. In keeping with the design of the present work, the King James spelling of untranslated words is retained, although made uniform throughout. For example, instead of the spellings *Isaiah* and *Elijah* in the Old Testament, and *Esaias* and *Elias* in the New Testament, *Isaiah* and *Elijah* now appear in both Testaments.

King James doctrinal and theological terms, for example, *propitiation, justification,* and *sanctification,* are generally familiar to English-speaking peoples. Such terms have been retained except where the original language indicates need for a more precise translation.

Readers of the Authorized Version will immediately be struck by the absence of several pronouns: *thee, thou,* and *ye* are replaced by the simple *you,* while *your* and *yours* are substituted for *thy* and *thine* as applicable. *Thee, thou, thy* and *thine* were once forms of address to express a special relationship to human as well as divine persons. These pronouns are no longer part of our language. However, reverence for God in the present work is preserved by capitalizing pronouns, including *You, Your,* and *Yours,* which refer to Him. Additionally, capitalization of these pronouns benefits the reader by clearly distinguishing divine and human persons referred to in a passage. Without such capitalization the distinction is often obscure, because the antecedent of a pronoun is not always clear in the English translation.

In addition to the pronoun usages of the seventeenth century, the *-eth* and *-est* verb endings, so familiar in the earlier King James editions, are not obsolete. Unless a speaker is schooled in these verb endings, there is common difficulty in selecting the correct form to be used with a given subject of the verb in vocal prayer. That is, should we use *love, loveth,* or *lovest? do, doeth, doest,* or *dost? have, hath,* or *hast?* Because these forms are obsolete, contemporary English usage has been substituted for the previous verb endings.

In older editions of the King James Version, the frequency of the connective *and* far exceeded the limits of present English usage. Also, biblical linguists agree that the Hebrew and Greek original words for this conjunction may commonly be translated otherwise, depending on the immediate context. Therefore, instead of *and,* alternatives such as *also, but, however, now, so, then,* and *thus* are accordingly rendered in the present edition, when the original language permits.

The real character of the Authorized Version does not reside in its archaic pronouns or verbs or other grammatical forms of the seventeenth century, but rather in the care taken by its scholars to impart the letter and spirit of the original text in a majestic and reverent style.

The Format

The format of the New King James Version is designed to enhance the vividness and devotional quality of the Holy Scriptures:

- Subject headings assist the reader to identify topics and transitions in the biblical content.
- Words or phrases in *italics* indicate expressions in the original language which require clarification by additional English words, as also done throughout the history of the King James Bible.
- Verse numbers in **bold** type indicate the beginning of a paragraph.
- *Oblique type* in the New Testament indicates a quotation from the Old Testament.
- Poetry is structured as contemporary verse to reflect the poetic form and beauty of the passage in the original language.
- The covenant name of God was usually translated from the Hebrew as "LORD" or "GOD" (using capital letters as shown) in the King James Old Testament. This tradition is maintained. In the present edition the name is so capitalized whenever the covenant name is quoted in the New Testament from a passage in the Old Testament.
- Significant explanatory notes, alternate translations, and cross-references, as well as New Testament citations of Old Testament passages, are supplied in footnotes.

The Old Testament Text

The Hebrew Bible has come down to us through the scrupulous care of ancient scribes who copied the original text in successive generations. By the sixth century A.D. the scribes were succeeded by a group known as the Masoretes, who continued to preserve the sacred Scriptures for another five hundred years in a form known as the Masoretic Text. Babylonia, Palestine, and Tiberias were the main centers of Masoretic activity; but by the tenth century A.D. the Masoretes of Tiberias, led by the family of ben Asher, gained the ascendancy. Through subsequent editions, the ben Asher text became in the twelfth century the only recognized form of the Hebrew Scriptures.

Daniel Bomberg printed the first Rabbinic Bible in 1516–17; that work was followed in 1524–25 by a second edition prepared by Jacob ben Chayyim and also published by Bomberg. The text of ben Chayyim was adopted in most subsequent Hebrew Bibles, including those used by the King James translators. The ben Chayyim text was also used for the first two editions of Rudolph Kittel's *Biblia Hebraica* of 1906 and 1912. In 1937 Paul Kahle published a third edition of *Biblia Hebraica.* This edition was based on the oldest dated manuscript of the ben Asher text, the Leningrad Manuscript B19a (A.D. 1008), which Kahle regarded as superior to that used by ben Chayyim.

For the New King James Version the text used was the 1967/1977 Stuttgart edition of the *Biblia Hebraica,* with frequent comparisons being made with the Bomberg edition of 1524–25. The Septuagint (Greek) Version of the Old Testament and the Latin Vulgate also were consulted. In addition to referring to a variety of ancient versions of the Hebrew Scriptures, the New King James Version draws on the resources of relevant manuscripts from the Dead Sea caves. In the few places where the Hebrew was so obscure that the 1611 King James was compelled to follow one of the versions, but where information is now available to resolve the problems, the New King James Version follows the Hebrew text. Significant variations are recorded in the footnotes.

The New Testament Text

There is more manuscript support for the New Testament than for any other body of ancient literature. Over five thousand Greek, eight thousand Latin, and many more manuscripts in other languages attest the integrity of the New Testament. There is only one basic New Testament used by Protestants, Roman Catholics, and Orthodox, by conservatives and liberals. Minor variations in hand copying have appeared through the centuries, before mechanical printing began about A.D. 1450.

Some variations exist in the spelling of Greek words, in word order, and in similar details. These ordinarily do not show up in translation and do not affect the sense of the text in any way.

Other manuscript differences such as omission or inclusion of a word or a clause, and two paragraphs in the Gospels, should not overshadow the overwhelming degree of *agreement* which exists among the ancient records. Bible readers may be assured that the most important differences in English New Testaments of today are due, not to manuscript divergence, but to the way in which translators view the task of translation: How literally should the text be rendered? How does the translator view the matter of biblical inspiration? Does the translator adopt a paraphrase when a literal rendering would be quite clear and more to the point? The New King James Version follows the historic precedent of the Authorized Version in maintaining a literal approach to translation, except where the idiom of the original language cannot be translated directly into our tongue.

The King James New Testament was based on the traditional text of the Greek-speaking churches, first published in 1516, and later called the Textus Receptus or Received Text. Although based on the relatively few available manuscripts, these were representative of many more which existed at the time but only became known later. In the late nineteenth century, B. Westcott and F. Hort taught that this text had been officially edited by the fourth-century church, but a total lack of historical evidence for this event has forced a revision of the theory. It is now widely held that the Byzantine Text that largely supports the Textus Receptus has as much right as the Alexandrian or any other tradition to be weighed in determining the text of the New Testament. Those readings in the Textus Receptus which have weak support are indicated in the footnotes as being opposed by both Critical and Majority Texts (see "Footnotes").

Since the 1880s most contemporary translations of the New Testament have relied upon a relatively few manuscripts discovered chiefly in the late nineteenth and early twentieth centuries. Such translations depend primarily on two manuscripts, Codex Vaticanus and Codex Sinaiticus, because of their greater age. The Greek text obtained by using these sources and the related papyri (our most ancient manuscripts) is known as the Alexandrian Text. However, some scholars have grounds for doubting the faithfulness of Vaticanus and Sinaiticus, since they often disagree with one another, and Sinaiticus exhibits excessive omission.

A third viewpoint of New Testament scholarship holds that the best text is based on the consensus of the majority of existing Greek manuscripts. This text is called the Majority Text. Most of these manuscripts are in substantial agreement. Even though many are late, and none is earlier than the fifth century, usually their readings are verified by papyri, ancient versions, quotations from the early church fathers, or a combination of these. The Majority Text is similar to the Textus Receptus, but it corrects those readings which have little or no support in the Greek manuscript tradition.

Today, scholars agree that the science of New Testament textual criticism is in a state of flux. Very few scholars still favor the Textus Receptus as such, and then often for its historical prestige as the text of Luther, Calvin, Tyndale, and the King James Version. For about a century most have followed a Critical Text (so called because it is edited according to specific principles of textual criticism) which depends heavily upon the Alexandrian type of text. Most recently many have abandoned this Critical Text (which is quite similar to the one edited by Westcott and Hort) for one that is more eclectic. Finally, a small but growing number of scholars prefer the Majority Text, which is close to the traditional text except in the Revelation.

In light of these facts, and also because the New King James Version is the fifth revision of a historic document translated from specific Greek texts, the editors decided to retain the traditional text in the body of the New Testament and to indicate major Critical and Majority Text variant readings in the footnotes. Although these variations are duly indicated in the footnotes of the present edition, it is most important to emphasize that fully eighty-five percent of the New Testament text is the same in the Textus Receptus, the Alexandrian Text, and the Majority Text.

Footnotes

Significant explanatory notes, alternate translations, and cross-references, as well as New Testament citations of Old Testament passages, are supplied in footnotes to the text.

Important textual variants in the Old Testament are identified in a standard form.

The textual notes in the present edition of the New Testament make no evaluation of readings, but do clearly indicate the manuscript sources of readings. They objectively present the facts without such tendentious remarks as "the best manuscripts omit" or "the most reliable manuscripts read." Such notes are value judgments that differ according to varying viewpoints on the text. By giving a clearly defined set of variants the New King James Version benefits readers of all textual persuasions.

Where significant variations occur in the

New Testament Greek manuscripts, textual notes are classified as follows:

1. NU-Text
   These variations from the traditional text generally represent the Alexandrian or Egyptian type of text described previously in "The New Testament Text." They are found in the Critical Text published in the Twenty-sixth edition of the Nestle-Aland Greek New Testament (N) and in the United Bible Societies' third edition (U), hence the acronym, "NU-text."
2. M-Text
   This symbol indicates points of variation in the Majority Text from the traditional text, as also previously discussed in "The New Testament Text." It should be noted that M stands for whatever reading is printed in the published *Greek New Testament According to the Majority Text,* whether supported by overwhelming, strong, or only a divided majority textual tradition.

The textual notes reflect the scholarship of the past 150 years and will assist the reader to observe the variations between the different manuscript traditions of the New Testament. Such information is generally not available in English translations of the New Testament.

Table of Contents

The

OLD TESTAMENT

THE PENTATEUCH

Genesis • Exodus • Leviticus • Numbers • Deuteronomy

The Pentateuch is the first five books of the Bible, called "Torah" in the Hebrew Scriptures. Though we often call these books "The Law," *Torah* does not mean "law," but "teaching." Basic to the Torah is the idea of the covenant. A covenant is an agreement. In the Bible covenants are special, because God is one of the parties to the covenant. Biblical covenants have three parts:

(1) a statement about God's saving act (what God brings to the agreement);
(2) a statement about what God expects from humanity in response; and
(3) a sign or symbol as a reminder of the covenant.

The Torah is, in part, a record of God's covenant and the implications of the covenant for human life in society.

GENESIS begins with the Creation, setting the covenant in the context of God's rule over the entire universe. The first covenant is with Adam and Eve and, through them, with all humanity, and includes the understanding that human beings will be responsible stewards of all of creation. The second covenant is with Noah, the promise that the world will never again be destroyed by flood. Then the biblical account focuses on one particular person, Abraham, who enters into covenant with God and is given the promise that he and his descendants will become a blessing to all humanity. Through the narratives dealing with Abraham and Sarah, Isaac and Rebekah, Jacob and Leah and Rachel, and Joseph, the questions of faithfulness to the covenant and hope for the fulfillment of God's promises take concrete form.

EXODUS centers on the escape of God's people from Egypt under the leadership of Moses and the making of the great covenant at Mt. Sinai. The parts of the covenant are clear: God's gracious saving act is seen in Passover and Exodus; the expectation of human response is summarized in the Ten Commandments; and the Feast of Passover is the great sign and reminder. Moses, Aaron, and Miriam are both the leaders of God's people and the models of struggle and faith.

LEVITICUS takes its name from the Latin word for "book of the Levites." The major concern of the book is the holiness of the community of Israel. Holiness means to be set apart by God for a special purpose. Holiness is expressed in proper forms of worship and living out the love of God in the routine of daily life. The "Holiness Code" (chs. 17—27) is a good example of how worship and justice mingle together in the life of Israel.

NUMBERS is named for the census that begins the book. The narrative part of the book is the wilderness journey from Kadesh Barnea to the Promised Land. Included are the great accounts of the spies entering Canaan, the forty years of wandering, and the miracles of Moses. Finally come the conquests of the kingdoms of Sihon and Og in the Transjordan, and the story of Balaam. The book ends with Israel prepared to enter the Promised Land under the leadership of Joshua.

DEUTERONOMY is written as Moses' farewell speech before the tribes enter the Land. It reviews God's acts of salvation and the implications of salvation for life. The book itself was apparently found in the temple in the reign of Josiah (621 B.C.). The discovery sparked a great religious reform. One of the real concerns of Deuteronomy is how to make old traditions relevant for a new time. The most important statement of belief is the "Shema," found in 6:4, 5. ■

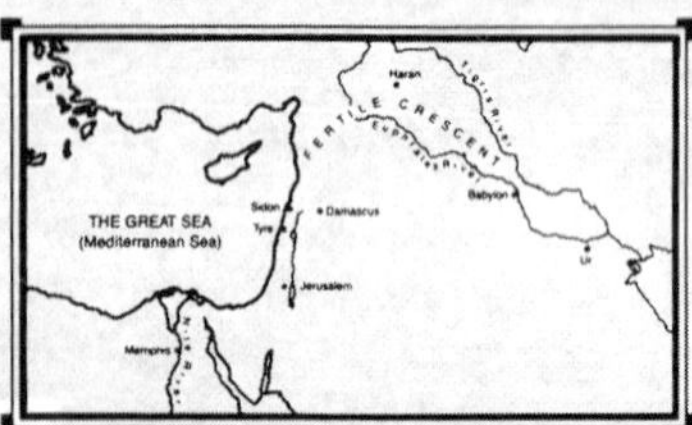

THE ANCIENT NEAR EAST

The First Book of Moses Called

GENESIS

The History of Creation

1 In the beginning God created the heavens
and the earth.
2 The earth was without form, and void; and
darkness *was*[a] on the face of the deep. And the
Spirit of God was hovering over the face of the
waters.
3 Then God said, "Let there be light"; and
there was light.
4 And God saw the light, that *it was* good;
and God divided the light from the darkness.
5 God called the light Day, and the darkness
He called Night. So the evening and the morn-
ing were the first day.
6 Then God said, "Let there be a firmament
in the midst of the waters, and let it divide the
waters from the waters."
7 Thus God made the firmament, and di-
vided the waters which *were* under the firma-
ment from the waters which *were* above the
firmament; and it was so.
8 And God called the firmament Heaven. So
the evening and the morning were the second
day.
9 Then God said, "Let the waters under the
heavens be gathered together into one place,
and let the dry *land* appear"; and it was so.
10 And God called the dry *land* Earth, and
the gathering together of the waters He called
Seas. And God saw that *it was* good.
11 Then God said, "Let the earth bring forth
grass, the herb *that* yields seed, *and* the fruit
tree *that* yields fruit according to its kind,
whose seed *is* in itself, on the earth"; and it
was so.
12 And the earth brought forth grass, the herb
that yields seed according to its kind, and the
tree *that* yields fruit, whose seed *is* in itself
according to its kind. And God saw that *it was*
good.
13 So the evening and the morning were the
third day.
14 Then God said, "Let there be lights in the
firmament of the heavens to divide the day
from the night; and let them be for signs and
seasons, and for days and years;
15 "and let them be for lights in the firma-
ment of the heavens to give light on the earth";
and it was so.
16 Then God made two great lights: the
greater light to rule the day, and the lesser light
to rule the night. *He made* the stars also.
17 God set them in the firmament of the heav-
ens to give light on the earth,
18 and to rule over the day and over the night,
and to divide the light from the darkness. And
God saw that *it was* good.
19 So the evening and the morning were the
fourth day.
20 Then God said, "Let the waters abound
with an abundance of living creatures, and let
birds fly above the earth across the face of the
firmament of the heavens."
21 So God created great sea creatures and
every living thing that moves, with which the
waters abounded, according to their kind, and
every winged bird according to its kind. And
God saw that *it was* good.
22 And God blessed them, saying, "Be fruitful
and multiply, and fill the waters in the seas,
and let birds multiply on the earth."
23 So the evening and the morning were the
fifth day.
24 Then God said, "Let the earth bring forth
the living creature according to its kind: cattle
and creeping thing and beast of the earth, *each*
according to its kind"; and it was so.
25 And God made the beast of the earth ac-
cording to its kind, cattle according to its kind,
and everything that creeps on the earth ac-
cording to its kind. And God saw that *it was*
good.
26 Then God said, "Let Us make man in Our
image, according to Our likeness; let them
have dominion over the fish of the sea, over
the birds of the air, and over the cattle, over
all[a] the earth and over every creeping thing
that creeps on the earth."
27 So God created man in His *own* image; in
the image of God He created him; male and
female He created them.
28 Then God blessed them, and God said to
them, "Be fruitful and multiply; fill the earth
and subdue it; have dominion over the fish of
the sea, over the birds of the air, and over every
living thing that moves on the earth."
29 And God said, "See, I have given you every
herb *that* yields seed which *is* on the face of
all the earth, and every tree whose fruit yields
seed; to you it shall be for food.
30 "Also, to every beast of the earth, to every
bird of the air, and to everything that creeps
on the earth, in which *there is* life, *I have given*
every green herb for food"; and it was so.
31 Then God saw everything that He had
made, and indeed *it was* very good. So the
evening and the morning were the sixth day.
2 Thus the heavens and the earth, and all the
host of them, were finished.
2 And on the seventh day God ended His
work which He had done, and He rested on the
seventh day from all His work which He had
done.
3 Then God blessed the seventh day and
sanctified it, because in it He rested from all
His work which God had created and made.
4 This *is* the history[a] of the heavens and the
earth when they were created, in the day that
the LORD God made the earth and the heavens,
5 before any plant of the field was in the
earth and before any herb of the field had
grown. For the LORD God had not caused it to
rain on the earth, and *there was* no man to till
the ground;
6 but a mist went up from the earth and wa-
tered the whole face of the ground.
7 And the LORD God formed man *of* the dust
of the ground, and breathed into his nostrils the
breath of life; and man became a living being.

1:2 [a]Words in italic type have been added for clarity. They are not found in the original Hebrew or Aramaic. **1:26** [a]Syriac reads *all the wild animals of.* **2:4** [a]Hebrew *toledoth,* literally *generations*

Life in God's Garden

8 The LORD God planted a garden eastward
in Eden, and there He put the man whom He
had formed.
9 And out of the ground the LORD God made
every tree grow that is pleasant to the sight
and good for food. The tree of life *was* also in
the midst of the garden, and the tree of the
knowledge of good and evil.
10 Now a river went out of Eden to water the
garden, and from there it parted and became
four riverheads.
11 The name of the first *is* Pishon; it *is* the one
which skirts the whole land of Havilah, where
there is gold.
12 And the gold of that land *is* good. Bdellium
and the onyx stone *are* there.
13 The name of the second river *is* Gihon; it
is the one which goes around the whole land
of Cush.
14 The name of the third river *is* Hiddekel;[a] it
is the one which goes toward the east of As-
syria. The fourth river *is* the Euphrates.
15 Then the LORD God took the man and put
him in the garden of Eden to tend and keep it.
16 And the LORD God commanded the man,
saying, "Of every tree of the garden you may
freely eat;
17 "but of the tree of the knowledge of good
and evil you shall not eat, for in the day that
you eat of it you shall surely die."
18 And the LORD God said, "*It is* not good
that man should be alone; I will make him a
helper comparable to him."
19 Out of the ground the LORD God formed
every beast of the field and every bird of the
air, and brought *them* to Adam to see what he
would call them. And whatever Adam called
each living creature, that *was* its name.
20 So Adam gave names to all cattle, to the
birds of the air, and to every beast of the field.
But for Adam there was not found a helper
comparable to him.
21 And the LORD God caused a deep sleep to
fall on Adam, and he slept; and He took one of
his ribs, and closed up the flesh in its place.
22 Then the rib which the LORD God had
taken from man He made into a woman, and
He brought her to the man.
23 And Adam said:

"This *is* now bone of my bones
And flesh of my flesh;
She shall be called Woman,
Because she was taken out of Man."

24 Therefore a man shall leave his father and
mother and be joined to his wife, and they shall
become one flesh.
25 And they were both naked, the man and
his wife, and were not ashamed.

The Temptation and Fall of Man

3 Now the serpent was more cunning than
any beast of the field which the LORD God
had made. And he said to the woman, "Has
God indeed said, 'You shall not eat of every
tree of the garden'?"
2 And the woman said to the serpent, "We
may eat the fruit of the trees of the garden;
3 "but of the fruit of the tree which *is* in the
midst of the garden, God has said, 'You shall
not eat it, nor shall you touch it, lest you die.'"
4 Then the serpent said to the woman, "You
will not surely die.
5 "For God knows that in the day you eat of
it your eyes will be opened, and you will be
like God, knowing good and evil."
6 So when the woman saw that the tree *was*
good for food, that it *was* pleasant to the eyes,
and a tree desirable to make *one* wise, she
took of its fruit and ate. She also gave to her
husband with her, and he ate.
7 Then the eyes of both of them were
opened, and they knew that they *were* naked;
and they sewed fig leaves together and made
themselves coverings.
8 And they heard the sound of the LORD God
walking in the garden in the cool of the day,
and Adam and his wife hid themselves from
the presence of the LORD God among the trees
of the garden.
9 Then the LORD God called to Adam and
said to him, "Where *are* you?"
10 So he said, "I heard Your voice in the gar-
den, and I was afraid because I was naked; and
I hid myself."
11 And He said, "Who told you that you *were*
naked? Have you eaten from the tree of which
I commanded you that you should not eat?"
12 Then the man said, "The woman whom
You gave *to be* with me, she gave me of the
tree, and I ate."
13 And the LORD God said to the woman,
"What *is* this you have done?" The woman
said, "The serpent deceived me, and I ate."
14 So the LORD God said to the serpent:

"Because you have done this,
You *are* cursed more than all cattle,
And more than every beast of the field;
On your belly you shall go,
And you shall eat dust
All the days of your life.
15 And I will put enmity
Between you and the woman,
And between your seed and her Seed;
He shall bruise your head,
And you shall bruise His heel."

16 To the woman He said:

"I will greatly multiply your sorrow and
your conception;
In pain you shall bring forth children;
Your desire *shall be* for your husband,
And he shall rule over you."

17 Then to Adam He said, "Because you have
heeded the voice of your wife, and have eaten
from the tree of which I commanded you, say-
ing, 'You shall not eat of it':

"Cursed *is* the ground for your sake;
In toil you shall eat *of* it
All the days of your life.
18 Both thorns and thistles it shall bring
forth for you,
And you shall eat the herb of the field.
19 In the sweat of your face you shall eat
bread
Till you return to the ground,
For out of it you were taken;
For dust you *are*,
And to dust you shall return."

20 And Adam called his wife's name Eve, be-
cause she was the mother of all living.

2:14 [a]Or *Tigris*

21 Also for Adam and his wife the LORD God made tunics of skin, and clothed them.

22 Then the LORD God said, "Behold, the man has become like one of Us, to know good and evil. And now, lest he put out his hand and take also of the tree of life, and eat, and live forever"—

23 therefore the LORD God sent him out of the garden of Eden to till the ground from which he was taken.

24 So He drove out the man; and He placed cherubim at the east of the garden of Eden, and a flaming sword which turned every way, to guard the way to the tree of life.

Cain Murders Abel

4 Now Adam knew Eve his wife, and she conceived and bore Cain, and said, "I have acquired a man from the LORD."

2 Then she bore again, this time his brother Abel. Now Abel was a keeper of sheep, but Cain was a tiller of the ground.

3 And in the process of time it came to pass that Cain brought an offering of the fruit of the ground to the LORD.

4 Abel also brought of the firstborn of his flock and of their fat. And the LORD respected Abel and his offering,

5 but He did not respect Cain and his offering. And Cain was very angry, and his countenance fell.

6 So the LORD said to Cain, "Why are you angry? And why has your countenance fallen?

7 "If you do well, will you not be accepted? And if you do not do well, sin lies at the door. And its desire *is* for you, but you should rule over it."

8 Now Cain talked with Abel his brother;[a] and it came to pass, when they were in the field, that Cain rose up against Abel his brother and killed him.

9 Then the LORD said to Cain, "Where *is* Abel your brother?" He said, "I do not know. *Am* I my brother's keeper?"

10 And He said, "What have you done? The voice of your brother's blood cries out to Me from the ground.

11 "So now you *are* cursed from the earth, which has opened its mouth to receive your brother's blood from your hand.

12 "When you till the ground, it shall no longer yield its strength to you. A fugitive and a vagabond you shall be on the earth."

13 And Cain said to the LORD, "My punishment *is* greater than I can bear!

14 "Surely You have driven me out this day from the face of the ground; I shall be hidden from Your face; I shall be a fugitive and a vagabond on the earth, and it will happen *that* anyone who finds me will kill me."

15 And the LORD said to him, "Therefore,[a] whoever kills Cain, vengeance shall be taken on him sevenfold." And the LORD set a mark on Cain, lest anyone finding him should kill him.

The Family of Cain

16 Then Cain went out from the presence of the LORD and dwelt in the land of Nod on the east of Eden.

17 And Cain knew his wife, and she conceived and bore Enoch. And he built a city, and called the name of the city after the name of his son—Enoch.

18 To Enoch was born Irad; and Irad begot Mehujael, and Mehujael begot Methushael, and Methushael begot Lamech.

19 Then Lamech took for himself two wives: the name of one *was* Adah, and the name of the second *was* Zillah.

20 And Adah bore Jabal. He was the father of those who dwell in tents and have livestock.

21 His brother's name *was* Jubal. He was the father of all those who play the harp and flute.

22 And as for Zillah, she also bore Tubal-Cain, an instructor of every craftsman in bronze and iron. And the sister of Tubal-Cain *was* Naamah.

23 Then Lamech said to his wives:

"Adah and Zillah, hear my voice;
Wives of Lamech, listen to my speech!
For I have killed a man for wounding me,
Even a young man for hurting me.
24 If Cain shall be avenged sevenfold,
Then Lamech seventy-sevenfold."

A New Son

25 And Adam knew his wife again, and she bore a son and named him Seth, "For God has appointed another seed for me instead of Abel, whom Cain killed."

26 And as for Seth, to him also a son was born; and he named him Enosh.[a] Then *men* began to call on the name of the LORD.

The Family of Adam

5 This is the book of the genealogy of Adam. In the day that God created man, He made him in the likeness of God.

2 He created them male and female, and blessed them and called them Mankind in the day they were created.

3 And Adam lived one hundred and thirty years, and begot *a son* in his own likeness, after his image, and named him Seth.

4 After he begot Seth, the days of Adam were eight hundred years; and he had sons and daughters.

5 So all the days that Adam lived were nine hundred and thirty years; and he died.

6 Seth lived one hundred and five years, and begot Enosh.

7 After he begot Enosh, Seth lived eight hundred and seven years, and had sons and daughters.

8 So all the days of Seth were nine hundred and twelve years; and he died.

9 Enosh lived ninety years, and begot Cainan.[a]

10 After he begot Cainan, Enosh lived eight hundred and fifteen years, and had sons and daughters.

11 So all the days of Enosh were nine hundred and five years; and he died.

12 Cainan lived seventy years, and begot Mahalalel.

13 After he begot Mahalalel, Cainan lived eight hundred and forty years, and had sons and daughters.

14 So all the days of Cainan were nine hundred and ten years; and he died.

15 Mahalalel lived sixty-five years, and begot Jared.

4:8 [a]Samaritan Pentateuch, Septuagint, Syriac, and Vulgate add *"Let us go out to the field."* **4:15** [a]Following Masoretic Text and Targum; Septuagint, Syriac, and Vulgate read *Not so.* **4:26** [a]Greek *Enos* **5:9** [a]Hebrew *Qenan*

16 After he begot Jared, Mahalalel lived eight hundred and thirty years, and had sons and daughters.
17 So all the days of Mahalalel were eight hundred and ninety-five years; and he died.
18 Jared lived one hundred and sixty-two years, and begot Enoch.
19 After he begot Enoch, Jared lived eight hundred years, and had sons and daughters.
20 So all the days of Jared were nine hundred and sixty-two years; and he died.
21 Enoch lived sixty-five years, and begot Methuselah.
22 After he begot Methuselah, Enoch walked with God three hundred years, and had sons and daughters.
23 So all the days of Enoch were three hundred and sixty-five years.
24 And Enoch walked with God; and he *was* not, for God took him.
25 Methuselah lived one hundred and eighty-seven years, and begot Lamech.
26 After he begot Lamech, Methuselah lived seven hundred and eighty-two years, and had sons and daughters.
27 So all the days of Methuselah were nine hundred and sixty-nine years; and he died.
28 Lamech lived one hundred and eighty-two years, and had a son.
29 And he called his name Noah, saying, "This *one* will comfort us concerning our work and the toil of our hands, because of the ground which the LORD has cursed."
30 After he begot Noah, Lamech lived five hundred and ninety-five years, and had sons and daughters.
31 So all the days of Lamech were seven hundred and seventy-seven years; and he died.
32 And Noah was five hundred years old, and Noah begot Shem, Ham, and Japheth.

The Wickedness and Judgment of Man

6 Now it came to pass, when men began to multiply on the face of the earth, and daughters were born to them,
2 that the sons of God saw the daughters of men, that they *were* beautiful; and they took wives for themselves of all whom they chose.
3 And the LORD said, "My Spirit shall not strive[a] with man forever, for he *is* indeed flesh; yet his days shall be one hundred and twenty years."
4 There were giants on the earth in those days, and also afterward, when the sons of God came in to the daughters of men and they bore *children* to them. Those *were* the mighty men who *were* of old, men of renown.
5 Then the LORD[a] saw that the wickedness of man *was* great in the earth, and *that* every intent of the thoughts of his heart *was* only evil continually.
6 And the LORD was sorry that He had made man on the earth, and He was grieved in His heart.
7 So the LORD said, "I will destroy man whom I have created from the face of the earth, both man and beast, creeping thing and birds of the air, for I am sorry that I have made them."
8 But Noah found grace in the eyes of the LORD.

Noah Pleases God

9 This is the genealogy of Noah. Noah was a just man, perfect in his generations. Noah walked with God.
10 And Noah begot three sons: Shem, Ham, and Japheth.
11 The earth also was corrupt before God, and the earth was filled with violence.
12 So God looked upon the earth, and indeed it was corrupt; for all flesh had corrupted their way on the earth.

The Ark Prepared

13 And God said to Noah, "The end of all flesh has come before Me, for the earth is filled with violence through them; and behold, I will destroy them with the earth.
14 "Make yourself an ark of gopherwood; make rooms in the ark, and cover it inside and outside with pitch.
15 "And this is how you shall make it: The length of the ark *shall be* three hundred cubits, its width fifty cubits, and its height thirty cubits.
16 "You shall make a window for the ark, and you shall finish it to a cubit from above; and set the door of the ark in its side. You shall make it *with* lower, second, and third *decks*.
17 "And behold, I Myself am bringing floodwaters on the earth, to destroy from under heaven all flesh in which *is* the breath of life; everything that *is* on the earth shall die.
18 "But I will establish My covenant with you; and you shall go into the ark—you, your sons, your wife, and your sons' wives with you.
19 "And of every living thing of all flesh you shall bring two of every *sort* into the ark, to keep *them* alive with you; they shall be male and female.
20 "Of the birds after their kind, of animals after their kind, and of every creeping thing of the earth after its kind, two of every *kind* will come to you to keep *them* alive.
21 "And you shall take for yourself of all food that is eaten, and you shall gather *it* to yourself; and it shall be food for you and for them."
22 Thus Noah did; according to all that God commanded him, so he did.

The Great Flood

7 Then the LORD said to Noah, "Come into the ark, you and all your household, because I have seen *that* you *are* righteous before Me in this generation.
2 "You shall take with you seven each of every clean animal, a male and his female; two each of animals that *are* unclean, a male and his female;
3 "also seven each of birds of the air, male and female, to keep the species alive on the face of all the earth.
4 "For after seven more days I will cause it to rain on the earth forty days and forty nights, and I will destroy from the face of the earth all living things that I have made."
5 And Noah did according to all that the LORD commanded him.
6 Noah *was* six hundred years old when the floodwaters were on the earth.
7 So Noah, with his sons, his wife, and his

6:3 [a]Septuagint, Syriac, Targum, and Vulgate read *abide.* **6:5** [a]Following Masoretic Text and Targum; Vulgate reads *God;* Septuagint reads *LORD God.*

sons' wives, went into the ark because of the
waters of the flood.
8 Of clean animals, of animals that *are* unclean, of birds, and of everything that creeps
on the earth,
9 two by two they went into the ark to Noah,
male and female, as God had commanded
Noah.
10 And it came to pass after seven days that
the waters of the flood were on the earth.
11 In the six hundredth year of Noah's life, in
the second month, the seventeenth day of the
month, on that day all the fountains of the
great deep were broken up, and the windows
of heaven were opened.
12 And the rain was on the earth forty days
and forty nights.
13 On the very same day Noah and Noah's
sons, Shem, Ham, and Japheth, and Noah's
wife and the three wives of his sons with them,
entered the ark—
14 they and every beast after its kind, all cattle after their kind, every creeping thing that
creeps on the earth after its kind, and every
bird after its kind, every bird of every sort.
15 And they went into the ark to Noah, two
by two, of all flesh in which *is* the breath of
life.
16 So those that entered, male and female of
all flesh, went in as God had commanded him;
and the LORD shut him in.
17 Now the flood was on the earth forty days.
The waters increased and lifted up the ark, and
it rose high above the earth.
18 The waters prevailed and greatly increased on the earth, and the ark moved about
on the surface of the waters.
19 And the waters prevailed exceedingly on
the earth, and all the high hills under the whole
heaven were covered.
20 The waters prevailed fifteen cubits upward, and the mountains were covered.
21 And all flesh died that moved on the earth:
birds and cattle and beasts and every creeping
thing that creeps on the earth, and every man.
22 All in whose nostrils *was* the breath of the
spirit[a] of life, all that *was* on the dry *land,* died.
23 So He destroyed all living things which
were on the face of the ground: both man and
cattle, creeping thing and bird of the air. They
were destroyed from the earth. Only Noah and
those who *were* with him in the ark remained
alive.
24 And the waters prevailed on the earth one
hundred and fifty days.

Noah's Deliverance

8 Then God remembered Noah, and every
living thing, and all the animals that *were*
with him in the ark. And God made a wind to
pass over the earth, and the waters subsided.
2 The fountains of the deep and the windows
of heaven were also stopped, and the rain from
heaven was restrained.
3 And the waters receded continually from
the earth. At the end of the hundred and fifty
days the waters decreased.
4 Then the ark rested in the seventh month,
the seventeenth day of the month, on the
mountains of Ararat.
5 And the waters decreased continually until the tenth month. In the tenth *month,* on the
first *day* of the month, the tops of the mountains were seen.
6 So it came to pass, at the end of forty days,
that Noah opened the window of the ark which
he had made.
7 Then he sent out a raven, which kept going
to and fro until the waters had dried up from
the earth.
8 He also sent out from himself a dove, to
see if the waters had receded from the face of
the ground.
9 But the dove found no resting place for the
sole of her foot, and she returned into the ark
to him, for the waters *were* on the face of the
whole earth. So he put out his hand and took
her, and drew her into the ark to himself.
10 And he waited yet another seven days, and
again he sent the dove out from the ark.
11 Then the dove came to him in the evening,
and behold, a freshly plucked olive leaf *was* in
her mouth; and Noah knew that the waters had
receded from the earth.
12 So he waited yet another seven days and
sent out the dove, which did not return again
to him anymore.
13 And it came to pass in the six hundred and
first year, in the first *month,* the first *day* of
the month, that the waters were dried up from
the earth; and Noah removed the covering
of the ark and looked, and indeed the surface
of the ground was dry.
14 And in the second month, on the twenty-seventh day of the month, the earth was dried.
15 Then God spoke to Noah, saying,
16 "Go out of the ark, you and your wife, and
your sons and your sons' wives with you.
17 "Bring out with you every living thing of
all flesh that *is* with you: birds and cattle and
every creeping thing that creeps on the earth,
so that they may abound on the earth, and be
fruitful and multiply on the earth."
18 So Noah went out, and his sons and his
wife and his sons' wives with him.
19 Every animal, every creeping thing, every
bird, *and* whatever creeps on the earth, according to their families, went out of the ark.

God's Covenant with Creation

20 Then Noah built an altar to the LORD, and
took of every clean animal and of every clean
bird, and offered burnt offerings on the altar.
21 And the LORD smelled a soothing aroma.
Then the LORD said in His heart, "I will never
again curse the ground for man's sake, although the imagination of man's heart *is* evil
from his youth; nor will I again destroy every
living thing as I have done.

22 "While the earth remains,
Seedtime and harvest,
Cold and heat,
Winter and summer,
And day and night
Shall not cease."

God's Promise to Noah

9 So God blessed Noah and his sons, and
said to them: "Be fruitful and multiply, and
fill the earth.[a]
2 "And the fear of you and the dread of you
shall be on every beast of the earth, on every
bird of the air, on all that move *on* the earth,

7:22 [a]Septuagint and Vulgate omit *of the spirit.* **9:1** [a]Compare Genesis 1:28

and on all the fish of the sea. They are given
into your hand.
3 "Every moving thing that lives shall be
food for you. I have given you all things, even
as the green herbs.
4 "But you shall not eat flesh with its life,
that is, its blood.
5 "Surely for your lifeblood I will demand *a
reckoning;* from the hand of every beast I will
require it, and from the hand of man. From the
hand of every man's brother I will require the
life of man.

6 "Whoever sheds man's blood,
By man his blood shall be shed;
For in the image of God
He made man.
7 And as for you, be fruitful and multiply;
Bring forth abundantly in the earth
And multiply in it."

8 Then God spoke to Noah and to his sons
with him, saying:
9 "And as for Me, behold, I establish My cov-
enant with you and with your descendants[a] af-
ter you,
10 "and with every living creature that *is* with
you: the birds, the cattle, and every beast of
the earth with you, of all that go out of the ark,
every beast of the earth.
11 "Thus I establish My covenant with you:
Never again shall all flesh be cut off by the
waters of the flood; never again shall there be
a flood to destroy the earth."
12 And God said: "This *is* the sign of the cov-
enant which I make between Me and you, and
every living creature that *is* with you, for per-
petual generations:
13 "I set My rainbow in the cloud, and it shall
be for the sign of the covenant between Me
and the earth.
14 "It shall be, when I bring a cloud over the
earth, that the rainbow shall be seen in the
cloud;
15 "and I will remember My covenant which
is between Me and you and every living crea-
ture of all flesh; the waters shall never again
become a flood to destroy all flesh.
16 "The rainbow shall be in the cloud, and
I will look on it to remember the everlasting
covenant between God and every living crea-
ture of all flesh that *is* on the earth."
17 And God said to Noah, "This *is* the sign of
the covenant which I have established between
Me and all flesh that *is* on the earth."

Noah and His Sons

18 Now the sons of Noah who went out of the
ark were Shem, Ham, and Japheth. And Ham
was the father of Canaan.
19 These three *were* the sons of Noah, and
from these the whole earth was populated.
20 And Noah began *to be* a farmer, and he
planted a vineyard.
21 Then he drank of the wine and was drunk,
and became uncovered in his tent.
22 And Ham, the father of Canaan, saw the
nakedness of his father, and told his two
brothers outside.
23 But Shem and Japheth took a garment,
laid *it* on both their shoulders, and went back-
ward and covered the nakedness of their fa-
ther. Their faces *were* turned away, and they
did not see their father's nakedness.
24 So Noah awoke from his wine, and knew
what his younger son had done to him.
25 Then he said:

"Cursed *be* Canaan;
A servant of servants
He shall be to his brethren."

26 And he said:

"Blessed *be* the LORD,
The God of Shem,
And may Canaan be his servant.
27 May God enlarge Japheth,
And may he dwell in the tents of Shem;
And may Canaan be his servant."

28 And Noah lived after the flood three hun-
dred and fifty years.
29 So all the days of Noah were nine hundred
and fifty years; and he died.

Nations Descended from Noah

10 Now this *is* the genealogy of the sons of
Noah: Shem, Ham, and Japheth. And
sons were born to them after the flood.
2 The sons of Japheth *were* Gomer, Magog,
Madai, Javan, Tubal, Meshech, and Tiras.
3 The sons of Gomer *were* Ashkenaz, Ri-
phath,[a] and Togarmah.
4 The sons of Javan *were* Elishah, Tarshish,
Kittim, and Dodanim.[a]
5 From these the coastland *peoples* of the
Gentiles were separated into their lands,
everyone according to his language, according
to their families, into their nations.
6 The sons of Ham *were* Cush, Mizraim,
Put,[a] and Canaan.
7 The sons of Cush *were* Seba, Havilah, Sab-
tah, Raamah, and Sabtechah; and the sons of
Raamah *were* Sheba and Dedan.
8 Cush begot Nimrod; he began to be a
mighty one on the earth.
9 He was a mighty hunter before the LORD;
therefore it is said, "Like Nimrod the mighty
hunter before the LORD."
10 And the beginning of his kingdom was Ba-
bel, Erech, Accad, and Calneh, in the land of
Shinar.
11 From that land he went to Assyria and
built Nineveh, Rehoboth Ir, Calah,
12 and Resen between Nineveh and Calah
(that *is* the principal city).
13 Mizraim begot Ludim, Anamim, Lehabim,
Naphtuhim,
14 Pathrusim, and Casluhim (from whom
came the Philistines and Caphtorim).
15 Canaan begot Sidon his firstborn, and
Heth;
16 the Jebusite, the Amorite, and the Girga-
shite;
17 the Hivite, the Arkite, and the Sinite;
18 the Arvadite, the Zemarite, and the Ha-
mathite. Afterward the families of the Canaan-
ites were dispersed.
19 And the border of the Canaanites was
from Sidon as you go toward Gerar, as far as
Gaza; then as you go toward Sodom, Gomor-
rah, Admah, and Zeboiim, as far as Lasha.
20 These *were* the sons of Ham, according to
their families, according to their languages, in
their lands *and* in their nations.

9:9 [a]Literally *seed* **10:3** [a]Spelled *Diphath* in 1 Chronicles 1:6 **10:4** [a]Spelled *Rodanim* in Samaritan Pentateuch and 1 Chronicles 1:7 **10:6** [a]Or *Phut*

21 And *children* were born also to Shem, the
father of all the children of Eber, the brother
of Japheth the elder.
22 The sons of Shem *were* Elam, Asshur, Ar-
phaxad, Lud, and Aram.
23 The sons of Aram *were* Uz, Hul, Gether,
and Mash.[a]
24 Arphaxad begot Salah,[a] and Salah begot
Eber.
25 To Eber were born two sons: the name of
one *was* Peleg, for in his days the earth was
divided; and his brother's name *was* Joktan.
26 Joktan begot Almodad, Sheleph, Hazar-
maveth, Jerah,
27 Hadoram, Uzal, Diklah,
28 Obal,[a] Abimael, Sheba,
29 Ophir, Havilah, and Jobab. All these *were*
the sons of Joktan.
30 And their dwelling place was from Mesha
as you go toward Sephar, the mountain of the
east.
31 These *were* the sons of Shem, according
to their families, according to their languages,
in their lands, according to their nations.
32 These *were* the families of the sons of
Noah, according to their generations, in their
nations; and from these the nations were di-
vided on the earth after the flood.

The Tower of Babel

11 Now the whole earth had one language
and one speech.
2 And it came to pass, as they journeyed
from the east, that they found a plain in the
land of Shinar, and they dwelt there.
3 Then they said to one another, "Come, let
us make bricks and bake *them* thoroughly."
They had brick for stone, and they had asphalt
for mortar.
4 And they said, "Come, let us build our-
selves a city, and a tower whose top *is* in the
heavens; let us make a name for ourselves, lest
we be scattered abroad over the face of the
whole earth."
5 But the LORD came down to see the city
and the tower which the sons of men had built.
6 And the LORD said, "Indeed the people *are*
one and they all have one language, and this
is what they begin to do; now nothing that they
propose to do will be withheld from them.
7 "Come, let Us go down and there confuse
their language, that they may not understand
one another's speech."
8 So the LORD scattered them abroad from
there over the face of all the earth, and they
ceased building the city.
9 Therefore its name is called Babel, be-
cause there the LORD confused the language
of all the earth; and from there the LORD scat-
tered them abroad over the face of all the earth.

Shem's Descendants

10 This *is* the genealogy of Shem: Shem *was*
one hundred years old, and begot Arphaxad
two years after the flood.
11 After he begot Arphaxad, Shem lived five
hundred years, and begot sons and daughters.
12 Arphaxad lived thirty-five years, and be-
got Salah.
13 After he begot Salah, Arphaxad lived four
hundred and three years, and begot sons and
daughters.
14 Salah lived thirty years, and begot Eber.
15 After he begot Eber, Salah lived four hun-
dred and three years, and begot sons and
daughters.
16 Eber lived thirty-four years, and begot
Peleg.
17 After he begot Peleg, Eber lived four hun-
dred and thirty years, and begot sons and
daughters.
18 Peleg lived thirty years, and begot Reu.
19 After he begot Reu, Peleg lived two hun-
dred and nine years, and begot sons and
daughters.
20 Reu lived thirty-two years, and begot
Serug.
21 After he begot Serug, Reu lived two hun-
dred and seven years, and begot sons and
daughters.
22 Serug lived thirty years, and begot Nahor.
23 After he begot Nahor, Serug lived two hun-
dred years, and begot sons and daughters.
24 Nahor lived twenty-nine years, and begot
Terah.
25 After he begot Terah, Nahor lived one hun-
dred and nineteen years, and begot sons and
daughters.
26 Now Terah lived seventy years, and begot
Abram, Nahor, and Haran.

Terah's Descendants

27 This *is* the genealogy of Terah: Terah begot
Abram, Nahor, and Haran. Haran begot Lot.
28 And Haran died before his father Terah in
his native land, in Ur of the Chaldeans.
29 Then Abram and Nahor took wives: the
name of Abram's wife *was* Sarai, and the name
of Nahor's wife, Milcah, the daughter of Haran
the father of Milcah and the father of Iscah.
30 But Sarai was barren; she had no child.
31 And Terah took his son Abram and his
grandson Lot, the son of Haran, and his daugh-
ter-in-law Sarai, his son Abram's wife, and
they went out with them from Ur of the Chalde-
ans to go to the land of Canaan; and they came
to Haran and dwelt there.
32 So the days of Terah were two hundred
and five years, and Terah died in Haran.

Promises to Abram

12 Now the LORD had said to Abram:
"Get out of your country,
From your family
And from your father's house,
To a land that I will show you.
2 I will make you a great nation;
I will bless you
And make your name great;
And you shall be a blessing.
3 I will bless those who bless you,
And I will curse him who curses you;
And in you all the families of the earth
shall be blessed."

4 So Abram departed as the LORD had spo-
ken to him, and Lot went with him. And Abram
was seventy-five years old when he departed
from Haran.
5 Then Abram took Sarai his wife and Lot
his brother's son, and all their possessions that

10:23 [a]Called *Meshech* in Septuagint and 1 Chronicles 1:17 **10:24** [a]Following Masoretic Text, Vulgate, and Targum; Septuagint reads *Arphaxad begot Cainan, and Cainan begot Salah* (compare Luke 3:35, 36). **10:28** [a]Spelled *Ebal* in 1 Chronicles 1:22

they had gathered, and the people whom they had acquired in Haran, and they departed to go to the land of Canaan. So they came to the land of Canaan.

6 Abram passed through the land to the place of Shechem, as far as the terebinth tree of Moreh.[a] And the Canaanites *were* then in the land.

7 Then the LORD appeared to Abram and said, "To your descendants I will give this land." And there he built an altar to the LORD, who had appeared to him.

8 And he moved from there to the mountain east of Bethel, and he pitched his tent *with* Bethel on the west and Ai on the east; there he built an altar to the LORD and called on the name of the LORD.

9 So Abram journeyed, going on still toward the South.[a]

Abram in Egypt

10 Now there was a famine in the land, and Abram went down to Egypt to dwell there, for the famine *was* severe in the land.

11 And it came to pass, when he was close to entering Egypt, that he said to Sarai his wife, "Indeed I know that you *are* a woman of beautiful countenance.

12 "Therefore it will happen, when the Egyptians see you, that they will say, 'This *is* his wife'; and they will kill me, but they will let you live.

13 "Please say you *are* my sister, that it may be well with me for your sake, and that I[a] may live because of you."

14 So it was, when Abram came into Egypt, that the Egyptians saw the woman, that she *was* very beautiful.

15 The princes of Pharaoh also saw her and commended her to Pharaoh. And the woman was taken to Pharaoh's house.

16 He treated Abram well for her sake. He had sheep, oxen, male donkeys, male and female servants, female donkeys, and camels.

17 But the LORD plagued Pharaoh and his house with great plagues because of Sarai, Abram's wife.

18 And Pharaoh called Abram and said, "What *is* this you have done to me? Why did you not tell me that she *was* your wife?

19 "Why did you say, 'She *is* my sister'? I might have taken her as my wife. Now therefore, here is your wife; take *her* and go your way."

20 So Pharaoh commanded *his* men concerning him; and they sent him away, with his wife and all that he had.

Abram Inherits Canaan

13 Then Abram went up from Egypt, he and his wife and all that he had, and Lot with him, to the South.[a]

2 Abram *was* very rich in livestock, in silver, and in gold.

3 And he went on his journey from the South as far as Bethel, to the place where his tent had been at the beginning, between Bethel and Ai,

4 to the place of the altar which he had made there at first. And there Abram called on the name of the LORD.

5 Lot also, who went with Abram, had flocks and herds and tents.

6 Now the land was not able to support them, that they might dwell together, for their possessions were so great that they could not dwell together.

7 And there was strife between the herdsmen of Abram's livestock and the herdsmen of Lot's livestock. The Canaanites and the Perizzites then dwelt in the land.

8 So Abram said to Lot, "Please let there be no strife between you and me, and between my herdsmen and your herdsmen; for we *are* brethren.

9 "*Is* not the whole land before you? Please separate from me. If *you take* the left, then I will go to the right; or, if *you go* to the right, then I will go to the left."

10 And Lot lifted his eyes and saw all the plain of Jordan, that it *was* well watered everywhere (before the LORD destroyed Sodom and Gomorrah) like the garden of the LORD, like the land of Egypt as you go toward Zoar.

11 Then Lot chose for himself all the plain of Jordan, and Lot journeyed east. And they separated from each other.

12 Abram dwelt in the land of Canaan, and Lot dwelt in the cities of the plain and pitched *his* tent even as far as Sodom.

13 But the men of Sodom *were* exceedingly wicked and sinful against the LORD.

14 And the LORD said to Abram, after Lot had separated from him: "Lift your eyes now and look from the place where you are—northward, southward, eastward, and westward;

15 "for all the land which you see I give to you and your descendants[a] forever.

16 "And I will make your descendants as the dust of the earth; so that if a man could number the dust of the earth, *then* your descendants also could be numbered.

17 "Arise, walk in the land through its length and its width, for I give it to you."

18 Then Abram moved *his* tent, and went and dwelt by the terebinth trees of Mamre,[a] which *are* in Hebron, and built an altar there to the LORD.

Lot's Captivity and Rescue

14 And it came to pass in the days of Amraphel king of Shinar, Arioch king of Ellasar, Chedorlaomer king of Elam, and Tidal king of nations,[a]

2 *that* they made war with Bera king of Sodom, Birsha king of Gomorrah, Shinab king of Admah, Shemeber king of Zeboiim, and the king of Bela (that is, Zoar).

3 All these joined together in the Valley of Siddim (that is, the Salt Sea).

4 Twelve years they served Chedorlaomer, and in the thirteenth year they rebelled.

5 In the fourteenth year Chedorlaomer and the kings that *were* with him came and attacked the Rephaim in Ashteroth Karnaim, the Zuzim in Ham, the Emim in Shaveh Kiriathaim,

6 and the Horites in their mountain of Seir, as far as El Paran, which *is* by the wilderness.

7 Then they turned back and came to En Mishpat (that *is*, Kadesh), and attacked all the country of the Amalekites, and also the Amorites who dwelt in Hazezon Tamar.

8 And the king of Sodom, the king of Gomorrah, the king of Admah, the king of Ze-

12:6 [a]Hebrew *Alon Moreh* **12:9** [a]Hebrew *Negev* **12:13** [a]Literally *my soul* **13:1** [a]Hebrew *Negev* **13:15** [a]Literally *seed*, and so throughout the book **13:18** [a]Hebrew *Alon Mamre* **14:1** [a]Hebrew *goyim*

boiim, and the king of Bela (that *is*, Zoar) went
out and joined together in battle in the Valley
of Siddim
9 against Chedorlaomer king of Elam, Tidal
king of nations,[a] Amraphel king of Shinar, and
Arioch king of Ellasar—four kings against five.
10 Now the Valley of Siddim *was full of* as-
phalt pits; and the kings of Sodom and Gomor-
rah fled; *some* fell there, and the remainder
fled to the mountains.
11 Then they took all the goods of Sodom and
Gomorrah, and all their provisions, and went
their way.
12 They also took Lot, Abram's brother's son
who dwelt in Sodom, and his goods, and de-
parted.
13 Then one who had escaped came and told
Abram the Hebrew, for he dwelt by the tere-
binth trees of Mamre[a] the Amorite, brother of
Eshcol and brother of Aner; and they *were* al-
lies with Abram.
14 Now when Abram heard that his brother
was taken captive, he armed his three hundred
and eighteen trained *servants* who were born
in his own house, and went in pursuit as far as
Dan.
15 He divided his forces against them by
night, and he and his servants attacked them
and pursued them as far as Hobah, which *is*
north of Damascus.
16 So he brought back all the goods, and also
brought back his brother Lot and his goods, as
well as the women and the people.
17 And the king of Sodom went out to meet
him at the Valley of Shaveh (that *is*, the King's
Valley), after his return from the defeat of
Chedorlaomer and the kings who *were* with
him.

Abram and Melchizedek

18 Then Melchizedek king of Salem brought
out bread and wine; he *was* the priest of God
Most High.
19 And he blessed him and said:

"Blessed be Abram of God Most High,
Possessor of heaven and earth;
20 And blessed be God Most High,
Who has delivered your enemies into
your hand."

And he gave him a tithe of all.
21 Now the king of Sodom said to Abram,
"Give me the persons, and take the goods for
yourself."
22 But Abram said to the king of Sodom, "I
have raised my hand to the LORD, God Most
High, the Possessor of heaven and earth,
23 "that I *will take* nothing, from a thread to
a sandal strap, and that I will not take anything
that *is* yours, lest you should say, 'I have made
Abram rich'—
24 "except only what the young men have
eaten, and the portion of the men who went
with me: Aner, Eshcol, and Mamre; let them
take their portion."

God's Covenant with Abram

15 After these things the word of the LORD
came to Abram in a vision, saying, "Do
not be afraid, Abram. I *am* your shield, your
exceedingly great reward."
2 But Abram said, "Lord GOD, what will You
give me, seeing I go childless, and the heir of
my house *is* Eliezer of Damascus?"
3 Then Abram said, "Look, You have given
me no offspring; indeed one born in my house
is my heir!"
4 And behold, the word of the LORD *came*
to him, saying, "This one shall not be your heir,
but one who will come from your own body
shall be your heir."
5 Then He brought him outside and said,
"Look now toward heaven, and count the stars
if you are able to number them." And He said
to him, "So shall your descendants be."
6 And he believed in the LORD, and He ac-
counted it to him for righteousness.
7 Then He said to him, "I *am* the LORD, who
brought you out of Ur of the Chaldeans, to give
you this land to inherit it."
8 And he said, "Lord GOD, how shall I know
that I will inherit it?"
9 So He said to him, "Bring Me a three-year-
old heifer, a three-year-old female goat, a
three-year-old ram, a turtledove, and a young
pigeon."
10 Then he brought all these to Him and cut
them in two, down the middle, and placed each
piece opposite the other; but he did not cut the
birds in two.
11 And when the vultures came down on the
carcasses, Abram drove them away.
12 Now when the sun was going down, a deep
sleep fell upon Abram; and behold, horror *and*
great darkness fell upon him.
13 Then He said to Abram: "Know certainly
that your descendants will be strangers in a
land *that is* not theirs, and will serve them,
and they will afflict them four hundred years.
14 "And also the nation whom they serve I
will judge; afterward they shall come out with
great possessions.
15 "Now as for you, you shall go to your fa-
thers in peace; you shall be buried at a good
old age.
16 "But in the fourth generation they shall
return here, for the iniquity of the Amorites *is*
not yet complete."
17 And it came to pass, when the sun went
down and it was dark, that behold, there ap-
peared a smoking oven and a burning torch
that passed between those pieces.
18 On the same day the LORD made a cov-
enant with Abram, saying:
"To your descendants I have given this
land, from the river of Egypt to the great river,
the River Euphrates—
19 "the Kenites, the Kenezzites, the Kadmon-
ites,
20 "the Hittites, the Perizzites, the Rephaim,
21 "the Amorites, the Canaanites, the Girga-
shites, and the Jebusites."

Hagar and Ishmael

16 Now Sarai, Abram's wife, had borne him
no *children*. And she had an Egyptian
maidservant whose name was Hagar.
2 So Sarai said to Abram, "See now, the
LORD has restrained me from bearing *children*.
Please, go in to my maid; perhaps I shall obtain
children by her." And Abram heeded the voice
of Sarai.
3 Then Sarai, Abram's wife, took Hagar her
maid, the Egyptian, and gave her to her husband

14:9 [a]Hebrew *goyim* **14:13** [a]Hebrew *Alon Mamre*

Abram to be his wife, after Abram had dwelt
ten years in the land of Canaan.
4 So he went in to Hagar, and she conceived.
And when she saw that she had conceived, her
mistress became despised in her eyes.
5 Then Sarai said to Abram, "My wrong *be*
upon you! I gave my maid into your embrace;
and when she saw that she had conceived, I
became despised in her eyes. The LORD judge
between you and me."
6 So Abram said to Sarai, "Indeed your maid
is in your hand; do to her as you please." And
when Sarai dealt harshly with her, she fled
from her presence.
7 Now the Angel of the LORD found her by
a spring of water in the wilderness, by the
spring on the way to Shur.
8 And He said, "Hagar, Sarai's maid, where
have you come from, and where are you go-
ing?" She said, "I am fleeing from the presence
of my mistress Sarai."
9 The Angel of the LORD said to her, "Return
to your mistress, and submit yourself under
her hand."
10 Then the Angel of the LORD said to her, "I
will multiply your descendants exceedingly, so
that they shall not be counted for multitude."
11 And the Angel of the LORD said to her:

"Behold, you *are* with child,
And you shall bear a son.
You shall call his name Ishmael,
Because the LORD has heard your
affliction.
12 He shall be a wild man;
His hand *shall be* against every man,
And every man's hand against him.
And he shall dwell in the presence of all
his brethren."

13 Then she called the name of the LORD who
spoke to her, You-Are-the-God-Who-Sees; for
she said, "Have I also here seen Him who sees
me?"
14 Therefore the well was called Beer Lahai
Roi;[a] observe, *it is* between Kadesh and Bered.
15 So Hagar bore Abram a son; and Abram
named his son, whom Hagar bore, Ishmael.
16 Abram *was* eighty-six years old when Ha-
gar bore Ishmael to Abram.

The Sign of the Covenant

17 When Abram was ninety-nine years old,
the LORD appeared to Abram and said
to him, "I *am* Almighty God; walk before Me
and be blameless.
2 "And I will make My covenant between Me
and you, and will multiply you exceedingly."
3 Then Abram fell on his face, and God
talked with him, saying:
4 "As for Me, behold, My covenant is with
you, and you shall be a father of many nations.
5 "No longer shall your name be called
Abram, but your name shall be Abraham; for
I have made you a father of many nations.
6 "I will make you exceedingly fruitful; and
I will make nations of you, and kings shall
come from you.
7 "And I will establish My covenant between
Me and you and your descendants after you in
their generations, for an everlasting covenant,
to be God to you and your descendants after
you.
8 "Also I give to you and your descendants
after you the land in which you are a stranger,
all the land of Canaan, as an everlasting pos-
session; and I will be their God."
9 And God said to Abraham: "As for you,
you shall keep My covenant, you and your de-
scendants after you throughout their genera-
tions.
10 "This *is* My covenant which you shall
keep, between Me and you and your descen-
dants after you: Every male child among you
shall be circumcised;
11 "and you shall be circumcised in the flesh
of your foreskins, and it shall be a sign of the
covenant between Me and you.
12 "He who is eight days old among you shall
be circumcised, every male child in your gener-
ations, he who is born in your house or bought
with money from any foreigner who is not your
descendant.
13 "He who is born in your house and he who
is bought with your money must be circum-
cised, and My covenant shall be in your flesh
for an everlasting covenant.
14 "And the uncircumcised male child, who
is not circumcised in the flesh of his foreskin,
that person shall be cut off from his people; he
has broken My covenant."
15 Then God said to Abraham, "As for Sarai
your wife, you shall not call her name Sarai,
but Sarah *shall be* her name.
16 "And I will bless her and also give you a
son by her; then I will bless her, and she shall
be *a mother of* nations; kings of peoples shall
be from her."
17 Then Abraham fell on his face and
laughed, and said in his heart, "Shall *a child*
be born to a man who is one hundred years
old? And shall Sarah, who is ninety years old,
bear *a child?*"
18 And Abraham said to God, "Oh, that Ish-
mael might live before You!"
19 Then God said: "No, Sarah your wife shall
bear you a son, and you shall call his name
Isaac; I will establish My covenant with him
for an everlasting covenant, *and* with his de-
scendants after him.
20 "And as for Ishmael, I have heard you. Be-
hold, I have blessed him, and will make him
fruitful, and will multiply him exceedingly. He
shall beget twelve princes, and I will make him
a great nation.
21 "But My covenant I will establish with
Isaac, whom Sarah shall bear to you at this set
time next year."
22 Then He finished talking with him, and
God went up from Abraham.
23 So Abraham took Ishmael his son, all who
were born in his house and all who were
bought with his money, every male among the
men of Abraham's house, and circumcised the
flesh of their foreskins that very same day, as
God had said to him.
24 Abraham *was* ninety-nine years old when
he was circumcised in the flesh of his foreskin.
25 And Ishmael his son *was* thirteen years
old when he was circumcised in the flesh of his
foreskin.
26 That very same day Abraham was circum-
cised, and his son Ishmael;
27 and all the men of his house, born in the
house or bought with money from a foreigner,
were circumcised with him.

16:14 [a]Literally *Well of the One Who Lives and Sees Me*

The Son of Promise

18 Then the LORD appeared to him by the
terebinth trees of Mamre,[a] as he was sit-
ting in the tent door in the heat of the day.
2 So he lifted his eyes and looked, and be-
hold, three men were standing by him; and
when he saw *them,* he ran from the tent door to
meet them, and bowed himself to the ground,
3 and said, "My Lord, if I have now found
favor in Your sight, do not pass on by Your
servant.
4 "Please let a little water be brought, and
wash your feet, and rest yourselves under the
tree.
5 "And I will bring a morsel of bread, that
you may refresh your hearts. After that you
may pass by, inasmuch as you have come to
your servant." They said, "Do as you have
said."
6 So Abraham hurried into the tent to Sarah
and said, "Quickly, make ready three mea-
sures of fine meal; knead *it* and make cakes."
7 And Abraham ran to the herd, took a ten-
der and good calf, gave *it* to a young man, and
he hastened to prepare it.
8 So he took butter and milk and the calf
which he had prepared, and set *it* before them;
and he stood by them under the tree as they
ate.
9 Then they said to him, "Where *is* Sarah
your wife?" So he said, "Here, in the tent."
10 And He said, "I will certainly return to you
according to the time of life, and behold, Sarah
your wife shall have a son." (Sarah was listen-
ing in the tent door which *was* behind him.)
11 Now Abraham and Sarah were old, well
advanced in age; *and* Sarah had passed the age
of childbearing.[a]
12 Therefore Sarah laughed within herself,
saying, "After I have grown old, shall I have
pleasure, my lord being old also?"
13 And the LORD said to Abraham, "Why did
Sarah laugh, saying, 'Shall I surely bear *a
child,* since I am old?'
14 "Is anything too hard for the LORD? At the
appointed time I will return to you, according
to the time of life, and Sarah shall have a son."
15 But Sarah denied *it,* saying, "I did not
laugh," for she was afraid. And He said, "No,
but you did laugh!"

Abraham Intercedes for Sodom

16 Then the men rose from there and looked
toward Sodom, and Abraham went with them
to send them on the way.
17 And the LORD said, "Shall I hide from
Abraham what I am doing,
18 "since Abraham shall surely become a
great and mighty nation, and all the nations of
the earth shall be blessed in him?
19 "For I have known him, in order that he
may command his children and his household
after him, that they keep the way of the LORD,
to do righteousness and justice, that the LORD
may bring to Abraham what He has spoken to
him."
20 And the LORD said, "Because the outcry
against Sodom and Gomorrah is great, and
because their sin is very grave,
21 "I will go down now and see whether they
have done altogether according to the outcry
against it that has come to Me; and if not, I will
know."
22 Then the men turned away from there and
went toward Sodom, but Abraham still stood
before the LORD.
23 And Abraham came near and said, "Would
You also destroy the righteous with the
wicked?
24 "Suppose there were fifty righteous within
the city; would You also destroy the place and
not spare *it* for the fifty righteous that were in
it?
25 "Far be it from You to do such a thing as
this, to slay the righteous with the wicked, so
that the righteous should be as the wicked; far
be it from You! Shall not the Judge of all the
earth do right?"
26 So the LORD said, "If I find in Sodom fifty
righteous within the city, then I will spare all
the place for their sakes."
27 Then Abraham answered and said, "In-
deed now, I who *am but* dust and ashes have
taken it upon myself to speak to the Lord:
28 "Suppose there were five less than the fifty
righteous; would You destroy all of the city
for *lack of* five?" So He said, "If I find there
forty-five, I will not destroy *it.*"
29 And he spoke to Him yet again and said,
"Suppose there should be forty found there?"
So He said, "I will not do *it* for the sake of
forty."
30 Then he said, "Let not the Lord be angry,
and I will speak: Suppose thirty should be
found there?" So He said, "I will not do *it* if I
find thirty there."
31 And he said, "Indeed now, I have taken
it upon myself to speak to the Lord: Suppose
twenty should be found there?" So He said, "I
will not destroy *it* for the sake of twenty."
32 Then he said, "Let not the Lord be angry,
and I will speak but once more: Suppose ten
should be found there?" And He said, "I will
not destroy *it* for the sake of ten."
33 So the LORD went His way as soon as He
had finished speaking with Abraham; and
Abraham returned to his place.

Sodom's Depravity

19 Now the two angels came to Sodom in
the evening, and Lot was sitting in the
gate of Sodom. When Lot saw *them,* he rose to
meet them, and he bowed himself with his face
toward the ground.
2 And he said, "Here now, my lords, please
turn in to your servant's house and spend the
night, and wash your feet; then you may rise
early and go on your way." And they said, "No,
but we will spend the night in the open square."
3 But he insisted strongly; so they turned in
to him and entered his house. Then he made
them a feast, and baked unleavened bread, and
they ate.
4 Now before they lay down, the men of the
city, the men of Sodom, both old and young,
all the people from every quarter, surrounded
the house.
5 And they called to Lot and said to him,
"Where are the men who came to you tonight?
Bring them out to us that we may know them
carnally."
6 So Lot went out to them through the door-
way, shut the door behind him,

18:1 [a]Hebrew *Alon Mamre* **18:11** [a]Literally *the manner of women had ceased to be with Sarah*

7 and said, "Please, my brethren, do not do
so wickedly!
8 "See now, I have two daughters who have
not known a man; please, let me bring them
out to you, and you may do to them as you
wish; only do nothing to these men, since this
is the reason they have come under the shadow
of my roof."
9 And they said, "Stand back!" Then they
said, "This one came in to stay *here*, and he
keeps acting as a judge; now we will deal
worse with you than with them." So they
pressed hard against the man Lot, and came
near to break down the door.
10 But the men reached out their hands and
pulled Lot into the house with them, and shut
the door.
11 And they struck the men who *were* at the
doorway of the house with blindness, both
small and great, so that they became weary
trying to find the door.

Sodom and Gomorrah Destroyed

12 Then the men said to Lot, "Have you any-
one else here? Son-in-law, your sons, your
daughters, and whomever you have in the
city—take *them* out of this place!
13 "For we will destroy this place, because
the outcry against them has grown great be-
fore the face of the LORD, and the LORD has
sent us to destroy it."
14 So Lot went out and spoke to his sons-in-
law, who had married his daughters, and said,
"Get up, get out of this place; for the LORD will
destroy this city!" But to his sons-in-law he
seemed to be joking.
15 When the morning dawned, the angels
urged Lot to hurry, saying, "Arise, take your
wife and your two daughters who are here,
lest you be consumed in the punishment of the
city."
16 And while he lingered, the men took hold
of his hand, his wife's hand, and the hands of
his two daughters, the LORD being merciful to
him, and they brought him out and set him
outside the city.
17 So it came to pass, when they had brought
them outside, that he[a] said, "Escape for your
life! Do not look behind you nor stay anywhere
in the plain. Escape to the mountains, lest you
be destroyed."
18 Then Lot said to them, "Please, no, my
lords!
19 "Indeed now, your servant has found favor
in your sight, and you have increased your
mercy which you have shown me by saving my
life; but I cannot escape to the mountains, lest
some evil overtake me and I die.
20 "See now, this city *is* near *enough* to flee
to, and it *is* a little one; please let me escape
there (*is* it not a little one?) and my soul shall
live."
21 And he said to him, "See, I have favored
you concerning this thing also, in that I will not
overthrow this city for which you have spoken.
22 "Hurry, escape there. For I cannot do any-
thing until you arrive there." Therefore the
name of the city was called Zoar.
23 The sun had risen upon the earth when Lot
entered Zoar.
24 Then the LORD rained brimstone and fire
on Sodom and Gomorrah, from the LORD out
of the heavens.
25 So He overthrew those cities, all the plain,
all the inhabitants of the cities, and what grew
on the ground.
26 But his wife looked back behind him, and
she became a pillar of salt.
27 And Abraham went early in the morning
to the place where he had stood before the
LORD.
28 Then he looked toward Sodom and Go-
morrah, and toward all the land of the plain;
and he saw, and behold, the smoke of the land
which went up like the smoke of a furnace.
29 And it came to pass, when God destroyed
the cities of the plain, that God remembered
Abraham, and sent Lot out of the midst of the
overthrow, when He overthrew the cities in
which Lot had dwelt.

The Descendants of Lot

30 Then Lot went up out of Zoar and dwelt in
the mountains, and his two daughters were
with him; for he was afraid to dwell in Zoar.
And he and his two daughters dwelt in a cave.
31 Now the firstborn said to the younger,
"Our father *is* old, and *there is* no man on the
earth to come in to us as is the custom of all
the earth.
32 "Come, let us make our father drink wine,
and we will lie with him, that we may preserve
the lineage of our father."
33 So they made their father drink wine that
night. And the firstborn went in and lay with
her father, and he did not know when she lay
down or when she arose.
34 It happened on the next day that the first-
born said to the younger, "Indeed I lay with
my father last night; let us make him drink
wine tonight also, and you go in *and* lie with
him, that we may preserve the lineage of our
father."
35 Then they made their father drink wine
that night also. And the younger arose and lay
with him, and he did not know when she lay
down or when she arose.
36 Thus both the daughters of Lot were with
child by their father.
37 The firstborn bore a son and called his
name Moab; he *is* the father of the Moabites to
this day.
38 And the younger, she also bore a son and
called his name Ben-Ammi; he *is* the father of
the people of Ammon to this day.

Abraham and Abimelech

20 And Abraham journeyed from there to
the South, and dwelt between Kadesh
and Shur, and stayed in Gerar.
2 Now Abraham said of Sarah his wife, "She
is my sister." And Abimelech king of Gerar
sent and took Sarah.
3 But God came to Abimelech in a dream by
night, and said to him, "Indeed you *are* a dead
man because of the woman whom you have
taken, for she *is* a man's wife."
4 But Abimelech had not come near her; and
he said, "Lord, will You slay a righteous nation
also?
5 "Did he not say to me, 'She *is* my sister'?
And she, even she herself said, 'He *is* my
brother.' In the integrity of my heart and inno-
cence of my hands I have done this."
6 And God said to him in a dream, "Yes, I
know that you did this in the integrity of your

19:17 [a]Septuagint, Syriac, and Vulgate read *they*.

heart. For I also withheld you from sinning against Me; therefore I did not let you touch her.

7 "Now therefore, restore the man's wife; for he *is* a prophet, and he will pray for you and you shall live. But if you do not restore *her,* know that you shall surely die, you and all who *are* yours."

8 So Abimelech rose early in the morning, called all his servants, and told all these things in their hearing; and the men were very much afraid.

9 And Abimelech called Abraham and said to him, "What have you done to us? How have I offended you, that you have brought on me and on my kingdom a great sin? You have done deeds to me that ought not to be done."

10 Then Abimelech said to Abraham, "What did you have in view, that you have done this thing?"

11 And Abraham said, "Because I thought, surely the fear of God *is* not in this place; and they will kill me on account of my wife.

12 "But indeed *she is* truly my sister. She *is* the daughter of my father, but not the daughter of my mother; and she became my wife.

13 "And it came to pass, when God caused me to wander from my father's house, that I said to her, 'This *is* your kindness that you should do for me: in every place, wherever we go, say of me, "He *is* my brother." ' "

14 Then Abimelech took sheep, oxen, and male and female servants, and gave *them* to Abraham; and he restored Sarah his wife to him.

15 And Abimelech said, "See, my land *is* before you; dwell where it pleases you."

16 Then to Sarah he said, "Behold, I have given your brother a thousand *pieces* of silver; indeed this vindicates you[a] before all who *are* with you and before everybody." Thus she was rebuked.

17 So Abraham prayed to God; and God healed Abimelech, his wife, and his female servants. Then they bore *children;*

18 for the LORD had closed up all the wombs of the house of Abimelech because of Sarah, Abraham's wife.

Isaac Is Born

21 And the LORD visited Sarah as He had said, and the LORD did for Sarah as He had spoken.

2 For Sarah conceived and bore Abraham a son in his old age, at the set time of which God had spoken to him.

3 And Abraham called the name of his son who was born to him—whom Sarah bore to him—Isaac.

4 Then Abraham circumcised his son Isaac when he was eight days old, as God had commanded him.

5 Now Abraham was one hundred years old when his son Isaac was born to him.

6 And Sarah said, "God has made me laugh, *and* all who hear will laugh with me."

7 She also said, "Who would have said to Abraham that Sarah would nurse children? For I have borne *him* a son in his old age."

Hagar and Ishmael Depart

8 So the child grew and was weaned. And Abraham made a great feast on the same day that Isaac was weaned.

9 And Sarah saw the son of Hagar the Egyptian, whom she had borne to Abraham, scoffing.

10 Therefore she said to Abraham, "Cast out this bondwoman and her son; for the son of this bondwoman shall not be heir with my son, *namely* with Isaac."

11 And the matter was very displeasing in Abraham's sight because of his son.

12 But God said to Abraham, "Do not let it be displeasing in your sight because of the lad or because of your bondwoman. Whatever Sarah has said to you, listen to her voice; for in Isaac your seed shall be called.

13 "Yet I will also make a nation of the son of the bondwoman, because he *is* your seed."

14 So Abraham rose early in the morning, and took bread and a skin of water; and putting *it* on her shoulder, he gave *it* and the boy to Hagar, and sent her away. Then she departed and wandered in the Wilderness of Beersheba.

15 And the water in the skin was used up, and she placed the boy under one of the shrubs.

16 Then she went and sat down across from *him* at a distance of about a bowshot; for she said to herself, "Let me not see the death of the boy." So she sat opposite *him,* and lifted her voice and wept.

17 And God heard the voice of the lad. Then the angel of God called to Hagar out of heaven, and said to her, "What ails you, Hagar? Fear not, for God has heard the voice of the lad where he *is.*

18 "Arise, lift up the lad and hold him with your hand, for I will make him a great nation."

19 Then God opened her eyes, and she saw a well of water. And she went and filled the skin with water, and gave the lad a drink.

20 So God was with the lad; and he grew and dwelt in the wilderness, and became an archer.

21 He dwelt in the Wilderness of Paran; and his mother took a wife for him from the land of Egypt.

A Covenant with Abimelech

22 And it came to pass at that time that Abimelech and Phichol, the commander of his army, spoke to Abraham, saying, "God *is* with you in all that you do.

23 "Now therefore, swear to me by God that you will not deal falsely with me, with my offspring, or with my posterity; but that according to the kindness that I have done to you, you will do to me and to the land in which you have dwelt."

24 And Abraham said, "I will swear."

25 Then Abraham rebuked Abimelech because of a well of water which Abimelech's servants had seized.

26 And Abimelech said, "I do not know who has done this thing; you did not tell me, nor had I heard *of it* until today."

27 So Abraham took sheep and oxen and gave them to Abimelech, and the two of them made a covenant.

28 And Abraham set seven ewe lambs of the flock by themselves.

29 Then Abimelech asked Abraham, "What

20:16 [a]Literally *it is a covering of the eyes for you* *is the meaning of* these seven ewe lambs which you have set by themselves?"

30 And he said, "You will take *these* seven ewe lambs from my hand, that they may be my witness that I have dug this well."

31 Therefore he called that place Beersheba,[a] because the two of them swore an oath there.

32 Thus they made a covenant at Beersheba. So Abimelech rose with Phichol, the commander of his army, and they returned to the land of the Philistines.

33 Then *Abraham* planted a tamarisk tree in Beersheba, and there called on the name of the LORD, the Everlasting God.

34 And Abraham stayed in the land of the Philistines many days.

Abraham's Faith Confirmed

22 Now it came to pass after these things that God tested Abraham, and said to him, "Abraham!" And he said, "Here I am."

2 Then He said, "Take now your son, your only *son* Isaac, whom you love, and go to the land of Moriah, and offer him there as a burnt offering on one of the mountains of which I shall tell you."

3 So Abraham rose early in the morning and saddled his donkey, and took two of his young men with him, and Isaac his son; and he split the wood for the burnt offering, and arose and went to the place of which God had told him.

4 Then on the third day Abraham lifted his eyes and saw the place afar off.

5 And Abraham said to his young men, "Stay here with the donkey; the lad[a] and I will go yonder and worship, and we will come back to you."

6 So Abraham took the wood of the burnt offering and laid *it* on Isaac his son; and he took the fire in his hand, and a knife, and the two of them went together.

7 But Isaac spoke to Abraham his father and said, "My father!" And he said, "Here I am, my son." Then he said, "Look, the fire and the wood, but where *is* the lamb for a burnt offering?"

8 And Abraham said, "My son, God will provide for Himself the lamb for a burnt offering." So the two of them went together.

9 Then they came to the place of which God had told him. And Abraham built an altar there and placed the wood in order; and he bound Isaac his son and laid him on the altar, upon the wood.

10 And Abraham stretched out his hand and took the knife to slay his son.

11 But the Angel of the LORD called to him from heaven and said, "Abraham, Abraham!" So he said, "Here I am."

12 And He said, "Do not lay your hand on the lad, or do anything to him; for now I know that you fear God, since you have not withheld your son, your only *son*, from Me."

13 Then Abraham lifted his eyes and looked, and there behind *him was* a ram caught in a thicket by its horns. So Abraham went and took the ram, and offered it up for a burnt offering instead of his son.

14 And Abraham called the name of the place, The-LORD-Will-Provide;[a] as it is said *to* this day, "In the Mount of the LORD it shall be provided."

15 Then the Angel of the LORD called to Abraham a second time out of heaven,

16 and said: "By Myself I have sworn, says the LORD, because you have done this thing, and have not withheld your son, your only *son*—

17 "blessing I will bless you, and multiplying I will multiply your descendants as the stars of the heaven and as the sand which *is* on the seashore; and your descendants shall possess the gate of their enemies.

18 "In your seed all the nations of the earth shall be blessed, because you have obeyed My voice."

19 So Abraham returned to his young men, and they rose and went together to Beersheba; and Abraham dwelt at Beersheba.

The Family of Nahor

20 Now it came to pass after these things that it was told Abraham, saying, "Indeed Milcah also has borne children to your brother Nahor:

21 "Huz his firstborn, Buz his brother, Kemuel the father of Aram,

22 "Chesed, Hazo, Pildash, Jidlaph, and Bethuel."

23 And Bethuel begot Rebekah.[a] These eight Milcah bore to Nahor, Abraham's brother.

24 His concubine, whose name was Reumah, also bore Tebah, Gaham, Thahash, and Maachah.

Sarah's Death and Burial

23 Sarah lived one hundred and twenty-seven years; *these were* the years of the life of Sarah.

2 So Sarah died in Kirjath Arba (that *is*, Hebron) in the land of Canaan, and Abraham came to mourn for Sarah and to weep for her.

3 Then Abraham stood up from before his dead, and spoke to the sons of Heth, saying,

4 "I *am* a foreigner and a visitor among you. Give me property for a burial place among you, that I may bury my dead out of my sight."

5 And the sons of Heth answered Abraham, saying to him,

6 "Hear us, my lord: You *are* a mighty prince among us; bury your dead in the choicest of our burial places. None of us will withhold from you his burial place, that you may bury your dead."

7 Then Abraham stood up and bowed himself to the people of the land, the sons of Heth.

8 And he spoke with them, saying, "If it is your wish that I bury my dead out of my sight, hear me, and meet with Ephron the son of Zohar for me,

9 "that he may give me the cave of Machpelah which he has, which *is* at the end of his field. Let him give it to me at the full price, as property for a burial place among you."

10 Now Ephron dwelt among the sons of Heth; and Ephron the Hittite answered Abraham in the presence of the sons of Heth, all who entered at the gate of his city, saying,

11 "No, my lord, hear me: I give you the field and the cave that *is* in it; I give it to you in the presence of the sons of my people. I give it to you. Bury your dead!"

12 Then Abraham bowed himself down before the people of the land;

13 and he spoke to Ephron in the hearing of

21:31 [a]Literally *Well of the Oath* or *Well of the Seven* 22:5 [a]Or *young man* 22:14 [a]Hebrew *YHWH Yireh* 22:23 [a]Spelled *Rebecca* in Romans 9:10

the people of the land, saying, "If you *will give*
it, please hear me. I will give you money for
the field; take *it* from me and I will bury my
dead there."
14 And Ephron answered Abraham, saying
to him,
15 "My lord, listen to me; the land *is worth*
four hundred shekels of silver. What *is* that
between you and me? So bury your dead."
16 And Abraham listened to Ephron; and
Abraham weighed out the silver for Ephron
which he had named in the hearing of the sons
of Heth, four hundred shekels of silver, cur-
rency of the merchants.
17 So the field of Ephron which *was* in Mach-
pelah, which *was* before Mamre, the field and
the cave which *was* in it, and all the trees that
were in the field, which *were* within all the
surrounding borders, were deeded
18 to Abraham as a possession in the pres-
ence of the sons of Heth, before all who went
in at the gate of his city.
19 And after this, Abraham buried Sarah his
wife in the cave of the field of Machpelah, be-
fore Mamre (that *is*, Hebron) in the land of
Canaan.
20 So the field and the cave that *is* in it were
deeded to Abraham by the sons of Heth as
property for a burial place.

A Bride for Isaac

24 Now Abraham was old, well advanced
in age; and the LORD had blessed Abra-
ham in all things.
2 So Abraham said to the oldest servant of
his house, who ruled over all that he had,
"Please, put your hand under my thigh,
3 "and I will make you swear by the LORD,
the God of heaven and the God of the earth,
that you will not take a wife for my son from
the daughters of the Canaanites, among whom
I dwell;
4 "but you shall go to my country and to my
family, and take a wife for my son Isaac."
5 And the servant said to him, "Perhaps the
woman will not be willing to follow me to this
land. Must I take your son back to the land
from which you came?"
6 But Abraham said to him, "Beware that
you do not take my son back there.
7 "The LORD God of heaven, who took me
from my father's house and from the land of
my family, and who spoke to me and swore to
me, saying, 'To your descendants[a] I give this
land,' He will send His angel before you, and
you shall take a wife for my son from there.
8 "And if the woman is not willing to follow
you, then you will be released from this oath;
only do not take my son back there."
9 So the servant put his hand under the thigh
of Abraham his master, and swore to him con-
cerning this matter.
10 Then the servant took ten of his master's
camels and departed, for all his master's goods
were in his hand. And he arose and went to
Mesopotamia, to the city of Nahor.
11 And he made his camels kneel down out-
side the city by a well of water at evening time,
the time when women go out to draw *water*.
12 Then he said, "O LORD God of my master
Abraham, please give me success this day, and
show kindness to my master Abraham.
13 "Behold, *here* I stand by the well of water,
and the daughters of the men of the city are
coming out to draw water.
14 "Now let it be that the young woman to
whom I say, 'Please let down your pitcher that
I may drink,' and she says, 'Drink, and I will
also give your camels a drink'—*let* her *be the*
one You have appointed for Your servant Isaac.
And by this I will know that You have shown
kindness to my master."
15 And it happened, before he had finished
speaking, that behold, Rebekah, who was born
to Bethuel, son of Milcah, the wife of Nahor,
Abraham's brother, came out with her pitcher
on her shoulder.
16 Now the young woman *was* very beautiful
to behold, a virgin; no man had known her.
And she went down to the well, filled her
pitcher, and came up.
17 And the servant ran to meet her and said,
"Please let me drink a little water from your
pitcher."
18 So she said, "Drink, my lord." Then she
quickly let her pitcher down to her hand, and
gave him a drink.
19 And when she had finished giving him a
drink, she said, "I will draw *water* for your
camels also, until they have finished drinking."
20 Then she quickly emptied her pitcher into
the trough, ran back to the well to draw *water*,
and drew for all his camels.
21 And the man, wondering at her, remained
silent so as to know whether the LORD had
made his journey prosperous or not.
22 So it was, when the camels had finished
drinking, that the man took a golden nose ring
weighing half a shekel, and two bracelets for
her wrists weighing ten *shekels* of gold,
23 and said, "Whose daughter *are* you? Tell
me, please, is there room *in* your father's house
for us to lodge?"
24 So she said to him, "I *am* the daughter
of Bethuel, Milcah's son, whom she bore to
Nahor."
25 Moreover she said to him, "We have both
straw and feed enough, and room to lodge."
26 Then the man bowed down his head and
worshiped the LORD.
27 And he said, "Blessed *be* the LORD God of
my master Abraham, who has not forsaken
His mercy and His truth toward my master. As
for me, being on the way, the LORD led me to
the house of my master's brethren."
28 So the young woman ran and told her
mother's household these things.
29 Now Rebekah had a brother whose name
was Laban, and Laban ran out to the man by
the well.
30 So it came to pass, when he saw the nose
ring, and the bracelets on his sister's wrists,
and when he heard the words of his sister Re-
bekah, saying, "Thus the man spoke to me,"
that he went to the man. And there he stood
by the camels at the well.
31 And he said, "Come in, O blessed of the
LORD! Why do you stand outside? For I have
prepared the house, and a place for the
camels."
32 Then the man came to the house. And he
unloaded the camels, and provided straw and
feed for the camels, and water to wash his feet
and the feet of the men who *were* with him.
33 *Food* was set before him to eat, but he said,

24:7 [a]Literally *seed*

"I will not eat until I have told about my errand." And he said, "Speak on."
34 So he said, "I *am* Abraham's servant.
35 "The LORD has blessed my master greatly, and he has become great; and He has given him flocks and herds, silver and gold, male and female servants, and camels and donkeys.
36 "And Sarah my master's wife bore a son to my master when she was old; and to him he has given all that he has.
37 "Now my master made me swear, saying, 'You shall not take a wife for my son from the daughters of the Canaanites, in whose land I dwell;
38 'but you shall go to my father's house and to my family, and take a wife for my son.'
39 "And I said to my master, 'Perhaps the woman will not follow me.'
40 "But he said to me, 'The LORD, before whom I walk, will send His angel with you and prosper your way; and you shall take a wife for my son from my family and from my father's house.
41 'You will be clear from this oath when you arrive among my family; for if they will not give *her* to you, then you will be released from my oath.'
42 "And this day I came to the well and said, 'O LORD God of my master Abraham, if You will now prosper the way in which I go,
43 'behold, I stand by the well of water; and it shall come to pass that when the virgin comes out to draw *water,* and I say to her, "Please give me a little water from your pitcher to drink,"
44 'and she says to me, "Drink, and I will draw for your camels also,"—*let* her *be* the woman whom the LORD has appointed for my master's son.'
45 "But before I had finished speaking in my heart, there was Rebekah, coming out with her pitcher on her shoulder; and she went down to the well and drew *water.* And I said to her, 'Please let me drink.'
46 "And she made haste and let her pitcher down from her *shoulder,* and said, 'Drink, and I will give your camels a drink also.' So I drank, and she gave the camels a drink also.
47 "Then I asked her, and said, 'Whose daughter *are* you?' And she said, 'The daughter of Bethuel, Nahor's son, whom Milcah bore to him.' So I put the nose ring on her nose and the bracelets on her wrists.
48 "And I bowed my head and worshiped the LORD, and blessed the LORD God of my master Abraham, who had led me in the way of truth to take the daughter of my master's brother for his son.
49 "Now if you will deal kindly and truly with my master, tell me. And if not, tell me, that I may turn to the right hand or to the left."
50 Then Laban and Bethuel answered and said, "The thing comes from the LORD; we cannot speak to you either bad or good.
51 "Here *is* Rebekah before you; take *her* and go, and let her be your master's son's wife, as the LORD has spoken."
52 And it came to pass, when Abraham's servant heard their words, that he worshiped the LORD, *bowing himself* to the earth.
53 Then the servant brought out jewelry of silver, jewelry of gold, and clothing, and gave *them* to Rebekah. He also gave precious things to her brother and to her mother.
54 And he and the men who *were* with him ate and drank and stayed all night. Then they arose in the morning, and he said, "Send me away to my master."
55 But her brother and her mother said, "Let the young woman stay with us *a few* days, at least ten; after that she may go."
56 And he said to them, "Do not hinder me, since the LORD has prospered my way; send me away so that I may go to my master."
57 So they said, "We will call the young woman and ask her personally."
58 Then they called Rebekah and said to her, "Will you go with this man?" And she said, "I will go."
59 So they sent away Rebekah their sister and her nurse, and Abraham's servant and his men.
60 And they blessed Rebekah and said to her:

"Our sister, *may* you *become*
The mother of thousands of ten
thousands;
And may your descendants possess
The gates of those who hate them."

61 Then Rebekah and her maids arose, and they rode on the camels and followed the man. So the servant took Rebekah and departed.
62 Now Isaac came from the way of Beer Lahai Roi, for he dwelt in the South.
63 And Isaac went out to meditate in the field in the evening; and he lifted his eyes and looked, and there, the camels *were* coming.
64 Then Rebekah lifted her eyes, and when she saw Isaac she dismounted from her camel;
65 for she had said to the servant, "Who *is* this man walking in the field to meet us?" The servant said, "It *is* my master." So she took a veil and covered herself.
66 And the servant told Isaac all the things that he had done.
67 Then Isaac brought her into his mother Sarah's tent; and he took Rebekah and she became his wife, and he loved her. So Isaac was comforted after his mother's *death.*

Abraham and Keturah

25 Abraham again took a wife, and her name *was* Keturah.
2 And she bore him Zimran, Jokshan, Medan, Midian, Ishbak, and Shuah.
3 Jokshan begot Sheba and Dedan. And the sons of Dedan were Asshurim, Letushim, and Leummim.
4 And the sons of Midian *were* Ephah, Epher, Hanoch, Abidah, and Eldaah. All these *were* the children of Keturah.
5 And Abraham gave all that he had to Isaac.
6 But Abraham gave gifts to the sons of the concubines which Abraham had; and while he was still living he sent them eastward, away from Isaac his son, to the country of the east.

Abraham's Death and Burial

7 This *is* the sum of the years of Abraham's life which he lived: one hundred and seventy-five years.
8 Then Abraham breathed his last and died in a good old age, an old man and full *of years,* and was gathered to his people.
9 And his sons Isaac and Ishmael buried him in the cave of Machpelah, which *is* before Mamre, in the field of Ephron the son of Zohar the Hittite,
10 the field which Abraham purchased from

the sons of Heth. There Abraham was buried, and Sarah his wife.

11 And it came to pass, after the death of Abraham, that God blessed his son Isaac. And Isaac dwelt at Beer Lahai Roi.

The Families of Ishmael and Isaac

12 Now this *is* the genealogy of Ishmael, Abraham's son, whom Hagar the Egyptian, Sarah's maidservant, bore to Abraham.

13 And these *were* the names of the sons of Ishmael, by their names, according to their generations: The firstborn of Ishmael, Nebajoth; then Kedar, Adbeel, Mibsam,

14 Mishma, Dumah, Massa,

15 Hadar,[a] Tema, Jetur, Naphish, and Kedemah.

16 These *were* the sons of Ishmael and these *were* their names, by their towns and their settlements, twelve princes according to their nations.

17 These *were* the years of the life of Ishmael: one hundred and thirty-seven years; and he breathed his last and died, and was gathered to his people.

18 (They dwelt from Havilah as far as Shur, which *is* east of Egypt as you go toward Assyria.) He died in the presence of all his brethren.

19 This *is* the genealogy of Isaac, Abraham's son. Abraham begot Isaac.

20 Isaac was forty years old when he took Rebekah as wife, the daughter of Bethuel the Syrian of Padan Aram, the sister of Laban the Syrian.

21 Now Isaac pleaded with the LORD for his wife, because she *was* barren; and the LORD granted his plea, and Rebekah his wife conceived.

22 But the children struggled together within her; and she said, "If *all is* well, why *am I like* this?" So she went to inquire of the LORD.

23 And the LORD said to her:

"Two nations *are* in your womb,
Two peoples shall be separated from your body;
One people shall be stronger than the other,
And the older shall serve the younger."

24 So when her days were fulfilled *for her* to give birth, indeed *there were* twins in her womb.

25 And the first came out red. *He was* like a hairy garment all over; so they called his name Esau.[a]

26 Afterward his brother came out, and his hand took hold of Esau's heel; so his name was called Jacob.[a] Isaac *was* sixty years old when she bore them.

27 So the boys grew. And Esau was a skillful hunter, a man of the field; but Jacob was a mild man, dwelling in tents.

28 And Isaac loved Esau because he ate *of his* game, but Rebekah loved Jacob.

Esau Sells His Birthright

29 Now Jacob cooked a stew; and Esau came in from the field, and he *was* weary.

30 And Esau said to Jacob, "Please feed me with that same red *stew,* for I *am* weary." Therefore his name was called Edom.[a]

31 But Jacob said, "Sell me your birthright as of this day."

32 And Esau said, "Look, I *am* about to die; so what *is* this birthright to me?"

33 Then Jacob said, "Swear to me as of this day." So he swore to him, and sold his birthright to Jacob.

34 And Jacob gave Esau bread and stew of lentils; then he ate and drank, arose, and went his way. Thus Esau despised *his* birthright.

Isaac and Abimelech

26 There was a famine in the land, besides the first famine that was in the days of Abraham. And Isaac went to Abimelech king of the Philistines, in Gerar.

2 Then the LORD appeared to him and said: "Do not go down to Egypt; live in the land of which I shall tell you.

3 "Dwell in this land, and I will be with you and bless you; for to you and your descendants I give all these lands, and I will perform the oath which I swore to Abraham your father.

4 "And I will make your descendants multiply as the stars of heaven; I will give to your descendants all these lands; and in your seed all the nations of the earth shall be blessed;

5 "because Abraham obeyed My voice and kept My charge, My commandments, My statutes, and My laws."

6 So Isaac dwelt in Gerar.

7 And the men of the place asked about his wife. And he said, "She *is* my sister"; for he was afraid to say, "*She is* my wife," *because he thought,* "lest the men of the place kill me for Rebekah, because she *is* beautiful to behold."

8 Now it came to pass, when he had been there a long time, that Abimelech king of the Philistines looked through a window, and saw, and there was Isaac, showing endearment to Rebekah his wife.

9 Then Abimelech called Isaac and said, "Quite obviously she *is* your wife; so how could you say, 'She *is* my sister'?" Isaac said to him, "Because I said, 'Lest I die on account of her.'"

10 And Abimelech said, "What *is* this you have done to us? One of the people might soon have lain with your wife, and you would have brought guilt on us."

11 So Abimelech charged all *his* people, saying, "He who touches this man or his wife shall surely be put to death."

12 Then Isaac sowed in that land, and reaped in the same year a hundredfold; and the LORD blessed him.

13 The man began to prosper, and continued prospering until he became very prosperous;

14 for he had possessions of flocks and possessions of herds and a great number of servants. So the Philistines envied him.

15 Now the Philistines had stopped up all the wells which his father's servants had dug in the days of Abraham his father, and they had filled them with earth.

16 And Abimelech said to Isaac, "Go away from us, for you are much mightier than we."

17 Then Isaac departed from there and pitched his tent in the Valley of Gerar, and dwelt there.

18 And Isaac dug again the wells of water which they had dug in the days of Abraham his father, for the Philistines had stopped them

25:15 [a]Masoretic Text reads *Hadad.* **25:25** [a]Literally *Hairy* **25:26** [a]Literally *Supplanter* **25:30** [a]Literally *Red*

up after the death of Abraham. He called them by the names which his father had called them.

19 Also Isaac's servants dug in the valley, and found a well of running water there.

20 But the herdsmen of Gerar quarreled with Isaac's herdsmen, saying, "The water *is* ours." So he called the name of the well Esek,[a] because they quarreled with him.

21 Then they dug another well, and they quarreled over that *one* also. So he called its name Sitnah.[a]

22 And he moved from there and dug another well, and they did not quarrel over it. So he called its name Rehoboth,[a] because he said, "For now the LORD has made room for us, and we shall be fruitful in the land."

23 Then he went up from there to Beersheba.

24 And the LORD appeared to him the same night and said, "I *am* the God of your father Abraham; do not fear, for I *am* with you. I will bless you and multiply your descendants for My servant Abraham's sake."

25 So he built an altar there and called on the name of the LORD, and he pitched his tent there; and there Isaac's servants dug a well.

26 Then Abimelech came to him from Gerar with Ahuzzath, one of his friends, and Phichol the commander of his army.

27 And Isaac said to them, "Why have you come to me, since you hate me and have sent me away from you?"

28 But they said, "We have certainly seen that the LORD is with you. So we said, 'Let there now be an oath between us, between you and us; and let us make a covenant with you,

29 'that you will do us no harm, since we have not touched you, and since we have done nothing to you but good and have sent you away in peace. You *are* now the blessed of the LORD.' "

30 So he made them a feast, and they ate and drank.

31 Then they arose early in the morning and swore an oath with one another; and Isaac sent them away, and they departed from him in peace.

32 It came to pass the same day that Isaac's servants came and told him about the well which they had dug, and said to him, "We have found water."

33 So he called it Shebah.[a] Therefore the name of the city *is* Beersheba[b] to this day.

34 When Esau was forty years old, he took as wives Judith the daughter of Beeri the Hittite, and Basemath the daughter of Elon the Hittite.

35 And they were a grief of mind to Isaac and Rebekah.

Isaac Blesses Jacob

27 Now it came to pass, when Isaac was old and his eyes were so dim that he could not see, that he called Esau his older son and said to him, "My son." And he answered him, "Here I am."

2 Then he said, "Behold now, I am old. I do not know the day of my death.

3 "Now therefore, please take your weapons, your quiver and your bow, and go out to the field and hunt game for me.

4 "And make me savory food, such as I love, and bring *it* to me that I may eat, that my soul may bless you before I die."

5 Now Rebekah was listening when Isaac spoke to Esau his son. And Esau went to the field to hunt game and to bring *it*.

6 So Rebekah spoke to Jacob her son, saying, "Indeed I heard your father speak to Esau your brother, saying,

7 'Bring me game and make savory food for me, that I may eat it and bless you in the presence of the LORD before my death.'

8 "Now therefore, my son, obey my voice according to what I command you.

9 "Go now to the flock and bring me from there two choice kids of the goats, and I will make savory food from them for your father, such as he loves.

10 "Then you shall take *it* to your father, that he may eat *it*, and that he may bless you before his death."

11 And Jacob said to Rebekah his mother, "Look, Esau my brother *is* a hairy man, and I *am* a smooth-*skinned* man.

12 "Perhaps my father will feel me, and I shall seem to be a deceiver to him; and I shall bring a curse on myself and not a blessing."

13 But his mother said to him, "*Let* your curse *be* on me, my son; only obey my voice, and go, get *them* for me."

14 And he went and got *them* and brought *them* to his mother, and his mother made savory food, such as his father loved.

15 Then Rebekah took the choice clothes of her elder son Esau, which *were* with her in the house, and put them on Jacob her younger son.

16 And she put the skins of the kids of the goats on his hands and on the smooth part of his neck.

17 Then she gave the savory food and the bread, which she had prepared, into the hand of her son Jacob.

18 So he went to his father and said, "My father." And he said, "Here I am. Who *are* you, my son?"

19 Jacob said to his father, "I *am* Esau your firstborn; I have done just as you told me; please arise, sit and eat of my game, that your soul may bless me."

20 But Isaac said to his son, "How *is it* that you have found *it* so quickly, my son?" And he said, "Because the LORD your God brought *it* to me."

21 Isaac said to Jacob, "Please come near, that I may feel you, my son, whether you *are* really my son Esau or not."

22 So Jacob went near to Isaac his father, and he felt him and said, "The voice *is* Jacob's voice, but the hands *are* the hands of Esau."

23 And he did not recognize him, because his hands were hairy like his brother Esau's hands; so he blessed him.

24 Then he said, "*Are* you really my son Esau?" He said, "I *am*."

25 He said, "Bring *it* near to me, and I will eat of my son's game, so that my soul may bless you." So he brought *it* near to him, and he ate; and he brought him wine, and he drank.

26 Then his father Isaac said to him, "Come near now and kiss me, my son."

27 And he came near and kissed him; and he smelled the smell of his clothing, and blessed him and said:

"Surely, the smell of my son
Is like the smell of a field

26:20 [a]Literally *Quarrel* 26:21 [a]Literally *Enmity* 26:22 [a]Literally *Spaciousness* 26:33 [a]Literally *Oath* or *Seven* [b]Literally *Well of the Oath* or *Well of the Seven*

Which the LORD has blessed.
28 Therefore may God give you
Of the dew of heaven,
Of the fatness of the earth,
And plenty of grain and wine.
29 Let peoples serve you,
And nations bow down to you.
Be master over your brethren,
And let your mother's sons bow down to
you.
Cursed *be* everyone who curses you,
And blessed *be* those who bless you!"

Esau's Lost Hope

30 Now it happened, as soon as Isaac had
finished blessing Jacob, and Jacob had
scarcely gone out from the presence of Isaac
his father, that Esau his brother came in from
his hunting.
31 He also had made savory food, and
brought it to his father, and said to his father,
"Let my father arise and eat of his son's game,
that your soul may bless me."
32 And his father Isaac said to him, "Who
are you?" So he said, "I *am* your son, your
firstborn, Esau."
33 Then Isaac trembled exceedingly, and
said, "Who? Where *is* the one who hunted
game and brought *it* to me? I ate all *of it* before
you came, and I have blessed him—*and* indeed
he shall be blessed."
34 When Esau heard the words of his father,
he cried with an exceedingly great and bitter
cry, and said to his father, "Bless me—me also,
O my father!"
35 But he said, "Your brother came with de-
ceit and has taken away your blessing."
36 And *Esau* said, "Is he not rightly named
Jacob? For he has supplanted me these two
times. He took away my birthright, and now
look, he has taken away my blessing!" And he
said, "Have you not reserved a blessing for
me?"
37 Then Isaac answered and said to Esau,
"Indeed I have made him your master, and all
his brethren I have given to him as servants;
with grain and wine I have sustained him.
What shall I do now for you, my son?"
38 And Esau said to his father, "Have you
only one blessing, my father? Bless me—me
also, O my father!" And Esau lifted up his voice
and wept.
39 Then Isaac his father answered and said
to him:

"Behold, your dwelling shall be of the
fatness of the earth,
And of the dew of heaven from above.
40 By your sword you shall live,
And you shall serve your brother;
And it shall come to pass, when you
become restless,
That you shall break his yoke from your
neck."

Jacob Escapes from Esau

41 So Esau hated Jacob because of the bless-
ing with which his father blessed him, and
Esau said in his heart, "The days of mourning
for my father are at hand; then I will kill my
brother Jacob."
42 And the words of Esau her older son were
told to Rebekah. So she sent and called Jacob
her younger son, and said to him, "Surely your
brother Esau comforts himself concerning you
by intending to kill you.
43 "Now therefore, my son, obey my voice:
arise, flee to my brother Laban in Haran.
44 "And stay with him a few days, until your
brother's fury turns away,
45 "until your brother's anger turns away
from you, and he forgets what you have done
to him; then I will send and bring you from
there. Why should I be bereaved also of you
both in one day?"
46 And Rebekah said to Isaac, "I am weary
of my life because of the daughters of Heth; if
Jacob takes a wife of the daughters of Heth,
like these *who are* the daughters of the land,
what good will my life be to me?"

28 Then Isaac called Jacob and blessed
him, and charged him, and said to him:
"You shall not take a wife from the daughters
of Canaan.
2 "Arise, go to Padan Aram, to the house of
Bethuel your mother's father; and take your-
self a wife from there of the daughters of La-
ban your mother's brother.

3 "May God Almighty bless you,
And make you fruitful and multiply you,
That you may be an assembly of peoples;
4 And give you the blessing of Abraham,
To you and your descendants with you,
That you may inherit the land
In which you are a stranger,
Which God gave to Abraham."

5 So Isaac sent Jacob away, and he went to
Padan Aram, to Laban the son of Bethuel the
Syrian, the brother of Rebekah, the mother of
Jacob and Esau.

Esau Marries Mahalath

6 Esau saw that Isaac had blessed Jacob and
sent him away to Padan Aram to take himself
a wife from there, *and that* as he blessed him
he gave him a charge, saying, "You shall not
take a wife from the daughters of Canaan,"
7 and that Jacob had obeyed his father and
his mother and had gone to Padan Aram.
8 Also Esau saw that the daughters of Ca-
naan did not please his father Isaac.
9 So Esau went to Ishmael and took Maha-
lath the daughter of Ishmael, Abraham's son,
the sister of Nebajoth, to be his wife in addition
to the wives he had.

Jacob's Vow at Bethel

10 Now Jacob went out from Beersheba and
went toward Haran.
11 So he came to a certain place and stayed
there all night, because the sun had set. And
he took one of the stones of that place and put
it at his head, and he lay down in that place to
sleep.
12 Then he dreamed, and behold, a ladder
was set up on the earth, and its top reached
to heaven; and there the angels of God were
ascending and descending on it.
13 And behold, the LORD stood above it and
said: "I *am* the LORD God of Abraham your
father and the God of Isaac; the land on which
you lie I will give to you and your descendants.
14 "Also your descendants shall be as the dust
of the earth; you shall spread abroad to the
west and the east, to the north and the south;
and in you and in your seed all the families of
the earth shall be blessed.
15 "Behold, I *am* with you and will keep you

wherever you go, and will bring you back to
this land; for I will not leave you until I have
done what I have spoken to you."
16 Then Jacob awoke from his sleep and said,
"Surely the LORD is in this place, and I did not
know *it*."
17 And he was afraid and said, "How awe-
some *is* this place! This *is* none other than the
house of God, and this *is* the gate of heaven!"
18 Then Jacob rose early in the morning, and
took the stone that he had put at his head, set
it up as a pillar, and poured oil on top of it.
19 And he called the name of that place
Bethel;[a] but the name of that city had been Luz
previously.
20 Then Jacob made a vow, saying, "If God
will be with me, and keep me in this way that
I am going, and give me bread to eat and cloth-
ing to put on,
21 "so that I come back to my father's house
in peace, then the LORD shall be my God.
22 "And this stone which I have set as a pillar
shall be God's house, and of all that You give
me I will surely give a tenth to You."

Jacob Meets Rachel

29 So Jacob went on his journey and came
to the land of the people of the East.
2 And he looked, and saw a well in the field;
and behold, there *were* three flocks of sheep
lying by it; for out of that well they watered the
flocks. A large stone *was* on the well's mouth.
3 Now all the flocks would be gathered
there; and they would roll the stone from the
well's mouth, water the sheep, and put the
stone back in its place on the well's mouth.
4 And Jacob said to them, "My brethren,
where *are* you from?" And they said, "We *are*
from Haran."
5 Then he said to them, "Do you know La-
ban the son of Nahor?" And they said, "We
know him."
6 So he said to them, "Is he well?" And they
said, "*He is* well. And look, his daughter Ra-
chel is coming with the sheep."
7 Then he said, "Look, *it is* still high day; *it is*
not time for the cattle to be gathered together.
Water the sheep, and go and feed *them*."
8 But they said, "We cannot until all the
flocks are gathered together, and they have
rolled the stone from the well's mouth; then we
water the sheep."
9 Now while he was still speaking with
them, Rachel came with her father's sheep, for
she was a shepherdess.
10 And it came to pass, when Jacob saw Ra-
chel the daughter of Laban his mother's
brother, and the sheep of Laban his mother's
brother, that Jacob went near and rolled the
stone from the well's mouth, and watered the
flock of Laban his mother's brother.
11 Then Jacob kissed Rachel, and lifted up
his voice and wept.
12 And Jacob told Rachel that he *was* her
father's relative and that he *was* Rebekah's
son. So she ran and told her father.
13 Then it came to pass, when Laban heard
the report about Jacob his sister's son, that he
ran to meet him, and embraced him and kissed
him, and brought him to his house. So he told
Laban all these things.
14 And Laban said to him, "Surely you *are*
my bone and my flesh." And he stayed with
him for a month.

Jacob Marries Leah and Rachel

15 Then Laban said to Jacob, "Because you
are my relative, should you therefore serve me
for nothing? Tell me, what *should* your wages
be?"
16 Now Laban had two daughters: the name
of the elder *was* Leah, and the name of the
younger *was* Rachel.
17 Leah's eyes *were* delicate, but Rachel was
beautiful of form and appearance.
18 Now Jacob loved Rachel; so he said, "I will
serve you seven years for Rachel your younger
daughter."
19 And Laban said, "*It is* better that I give her
to you than that I should give her to another
man. Stay with me."
20 So Jacob served seven years for Rachel,
and they seemed *only* a few days to him be-
cause of the love he had for her.
21 Then Jacob said to Laban, "Give *me* my
wife, for my days are fulfilled, that I may go in
to her."
22 And Laban gathered together all the men
of the place and made a feast.
23 Now it came to pass in the evening, that
he took Leah his daughter and brought her to
Jacob; and he went in to her.
24 And Laban gave his maid Zilpah to his
daughter Leah *as* a maid.
25 So it came to pass in the morning, that
behold, it *was* Leah. And he said to Laban,
"What is this you have done to me? Was it not
for Rachel that I served you? Why then have
you deceived me?"
26 And Laban said, "It must not be done so
in our country, to give the younger before the
firstborn.
27 "Fulfill her week, and we will give you this
one also for the service which you will serve
with me still another seven years."
28 Then Jacob did so and fulfilled her week.
So he gave him his daughter Rachel as wife
also.
29 And Laban gave his maid Bilhah to his
daughter Rachel as a maid.
30 Then *Jacob* also went in to Rachel, and
he also loved Rachel more than Leah. And he
served with Laban still another seven years.

The Children of Jacob

31 When the LORD saw that Leah *was* un-
loved, He opened her womb; but Rachel *was*
barren.
32 So Leah conceived and bore a son, and she
called his name Reuben;[a] for she said, "The
LORD has surely looked on my affliction. Now
therefore, my husband will love me."
33 Then she conceived again and bore a son,
and said, "Because the LORD has heard that I
am unloved, He has therefore given me this
son also." And she called his name Simeon.[a]
34 She conceived again and bore a son, and
said, "Now this time my husband will become
attached to me, because I have borne him three
sons." Therefore his name was called Levi.[a]
35 And she conceived again and bore a son,

28:19 [a]Literally *House of God* **29:32** [a]Literally *See, a Son* **29:33** [a]Literally *Heard* **29:34** [a]Literally *Attached*

and said, "Now I will praise the LORD." Therefore she called his name Judah.[a] Then she stopped bearing.

30 Now when Rachel saw that she bore Jacob no children, Rachel envied her sister, and said to Jacob, "Give me children, or else I die!"

2 And Jacob's anger was aroused against Rachel, and he said, "*Am* I in the place of God, who has withheld from you the fruit of the womb?"

3 So she said, "Here is my maid Bilhah; go in to her, and she will bear *a child* on my knees, that I also may have children by her."

4 Then she gave him Bilhah her maid as wife, and Jacob went in to her.

5 And Bilhah conceived and bore Jacob a son.

6 Then Rachel said, "God has judged my case; and He has also heard my voice and given me a son." Therefore she called his name Dan.[a]

7 And Rachel's maid Bilhah conceived again and bore Jacob a second son.

8 Then Rachel said, "With great wrestlings I have wrestled with my sister, *and* indeed I have prevailed." So she called his name Naphtali.[a]

9 When Leah saw that she had stopped bearing, she took Zilpah her maid and gave her to Jacob as wife.

10 And Leah's maid Zilpah bore Jacob a son.

11 Then Leah said, "A troop comes!"[a] So she called his name Gad.[b]

12 And Leah's maid Zilpah bore Jacob a second son.

13 Then Leah said, "I am happy, for the daughters will call me blessed." So she called his name Asher.[a]

14 Now Reuben went in the days of wheat harvest and found mandrakes in the field, and brought them to his mother Leah. Then Rachel said to Leah, "Please give me *some* of your son's mandrakes."

15 But she said to her, "*Is it* a small matter that you have taken away my husband? Would you take away my son's mandrakes also?" And Rachel said, "Therefore he will lie with you tonight for your son's mandrakes."

16 When Jacob came out of the field in the evening, Leah went out to meet him and said, "You must come in to me, for I have surely hired you with my son's mandrakes." And he lay with her that night.

17 And God listened to Leah, and she conceived and bore Jacob a fifth son.

18 Leah said, "God has given me my wages, because I have given my maid to my husband." So she called his name Issachar.[a]

19 Then Leah conceived again and bore Jacob a sixth son.

20 And Leah said, "God has endowed me *with* a good endowment; now my husband will dwell with me, because I have borne him six sons." So she called his name Zebulun.[a]

21 Afterward she bore a daughter, and called her name Dinah.

22 Then God remembered Rachel, and God listened to her and opened her womb.

23 And she conceived and bore a son, and said, "God has taken away my reproach."

24 So she called his name Joseph,[a] and said, "The LORD shall add to me another son."

Jacob's Agreement with Laban

25 And it came to pass, when Rachel had borne Joseph, that Jacob said to Laban, "Send me away, that I may go to my own place and to my country.

26 "Give *me* my wives and my children for whom I have served you, and let me go; for you know my service which I have done for you."

27 And Laban said to him, "Please *stay,* if I have found favor in your eyes, *for* I have learned by experience that the LORD has blessed me for your sake."

28 Then he said, "Name me your wages, and I will give *it*."

29 So *Jacob* said to him, "You know how I have served you and how your livestock has been with me.

30 "For what you had before I *came was* little, and it has increased to a great amount; the LORD has blessed you since my coming. And now, when shall I also provide for my own house?"

31 So he said, "What shall I give you?" And Jacob said, "You shall not give me anything. If you will do this thing for me, I will again feed and keep your flocks:

32 "Let me pass through all your flock today, removing from there all the speckled and spotted sheep, and all the brown ones among the lambs, and the spotted and speckled among the goats; and *these* shall be my wages.

33 "So my righteousness will answer for me in time to come, when the subject of my wages comes before you: every one that *is* not speckled and spotted among the goats, and brown among the lambs, will be considered stolen, if *it is* with me."

34 And Laban said, "Oh, that it were according to your word!"

35 So he removed that day the male goats that were speckled and spotted, all the female goats that were speckled and spotted, every one that had *some* white in it, and all the brown ones among the lambs, and gave *them* into the hand of his sons.

36 Then he put three days' journey between himself and Jacob, and Jacob fed the rest of Laban's flocks.

37 Now Jacob took for himself rods of green poplar and of the almond and chestnut trees, peeled white strips in them, and exposed the white which *was* in the rods.

38 And the rods which he had peeled, he set before the flocks in the gutters, in the watering troughs where the flocks came to drink, so that they should conceive when they came to drink.

39 So the flocks conceived before the rods, and the flocks brought forth streaked, speckled, and spotted.

40 Then Jacob separated the lambs, and made the flocks face toward the streaked and all the brown in the flock of Laban; but he put his own flocks by themselves and did not put them with Laban's flock.

41 And it came to pass, whenever the stronger livestock conceived, that Jacob placed the

29:35 [a]Literally *Praise* **30:6** [a]Literally *Judge* **30:8** [a]Literally *My Wrestling* **30:11** [a]Following Qere, Syriac, and Targum; Kethib, Septuagint, and Vulgate read *in fortune.* [b]Literally *Troop* or *Fortune* **30:13** [a]Literally *Happy* **30:18** [a]Literally *Wages* **30:20** [a]Literally *Dwelling* **30:24** [a]Literally *He Will Add*

rods before the eyes of the livestock in the gut-
ters, that they might conceive among the rods.
42 But when the flocks were feeble, he did
not put *them* in; so the feebler were Laban's
and the stronger Jacob's.
43 Thus the man became exceedingly pros-
perous, and had large flocks, female and male
servants, and camels and donkeys.

Jacob Flees from Laban

31 Now *Jacob* heard the words of Laban's
sons, saying, "Jacob has taken away all
that was our father's, and from what was our
father's he has acquired all this wealth."
2 And Jacob saw the countenance of Laban,
and indeed it *was* not *favorable* toward him as
before.
3 Then the LORD said to Jacob, "Return to
the land of your fathers and to your family, and
I will be with you."
4 So Jacob sent and called Rachel and Leah
to the field, to his flock,
5 and said to them, "I see your father's coun-
tenance, that it *is* not *favorable* toward me as
before; but the God of my father has been with
me.
6 "And you know that with all my might I
have served your father.
7 "Yet your father has deceived me and
changed my wages ten times, but God did not
allow him to hurt me.
8 "If he said thus: 'The speckled shall be
your wages,' then all the flocks bore speckled.
And if he said thus: 'The streaked shall be your
wages,' then all the flocks bore streaked.
9 "So God has taken away the livestock of
your father and given *them* to me.
10 "And it happened, at the time when the
flocks conceived, that I lifted my eyes and saw
in a dream, and behold, the rams which leaped
upon the flocks *were* streaked, speckled, and
gray-spotted.
11 "Then the Angel of God spoke to me in a
dream, saying, 'Jacob.' And I said, 'Here I am.'
12 "And He said, 'Lift your eyes now and see,
all the rams which leap on the flocks *are*
streaked, speckled, and gray-spotted; for I
have seen all that Laban is doing to you.
13 'I *am* the God of Bethel, where you
anointed the pillar *and* where you made a vow
to Me. Now arise, get out of this land, and
return to the land of your family.' "
14 Then Rachel and Leah answered and said
to him, "Is there still any portion or inheritance
for us in our father's house?
15 "Are we not considered strangers by him?
For he has sold us, and also completely con-
sumed our money.
16 "For all these riches which God has taken
from our father are *really* ours and our chil-
dren's; now then, whatever God has said to
you, do it."
17 Then Jacob rose and set his sons and his
wives on camels.
18 And he carried away all his livestock and
all his possessions which he had gained, his
acquired livestock which he had gained in Pa-
dan Aram, to go to his father Isaac in the land
of Canaan.
19 Now Laban had gone to shear his sheep,
and Rachel had stolen the household idols that
were her father's.
20 And Jacob stole away, unknown to Laban
the Syrian, in that he did not tell him that he
intended to flee.
21 So he fled with all that he had. He arose
and crossed the river, and headed toward the
mountains of Gilead.

Laban Pursues Jacob

22 And Laban was told on the third day that
Jacob had fled.
23 Then he took his brethren with him and
pursued him for seven days' journey, and he
overtook him in the mountains of Gilead.
24 But God had come to Laban the Syrian in
a dream by night, and said to him, "Be careful
that you speak to Jacob neither good nor bad."
25 So Laban overtook Jacob. Now Jacob had
pitched his tent in the mountains, and Laban
with his brethren pitched in the mountains of
Gilead.
26 And Laban said to Jacob: "What have you
done, that you have stolen away unknown to
me, and carried away my daughters like cap-
tives *taken* with the sword?
27 "Why did you flee away secretly, and steal
away from me, and not tell me; for I might have
sent you away with joy and songs, with timbrel
and harp?
28 "And you did not allow me to kiss my sons
and my daughters. Now you have done fool-
ishly in *so* doing.
29 "It is in my power to do you harm, but
the God of your father spoke to me last night,
saying, 'Be careful that you speak to Jacob nei-
ther good nor bad.'
30 "And now you have surely gone because
you greatly long for your father's house, *but*
why did you steal my gods?"
31 Then Jacob answered and said to Laban,
"Because I was afraid, for I said, 'Perhaps you
would take your daughters from me by force.'
32 "With whomever you find your gods, do
not let him live. In the presence of our breth-
ren, identify what I have of yours and take *it*
with you." For Jacob did not know that Rachel
had stolen them.
33 And Laban went into Jacob's tent, into
Leah's tent, and into the two maids' tents, but
he did not find *them*. Then he went out of
Leah's tent and entered Rachel's tent.
34 Now Rachel had taken the household
idols, put them in the camel's saddle, and sat
on them. And Laban searched all about the
tent but did not find *them*.
35 And she said to her father, "Let it not dis-
please my lord that I cannot rise before you,
for the manner of women *is* with me." And he
searched but did not find the household idols.
36 Then Jacob was angry and rebuked La-
ban, and Jacob answered and said to Laban:
"What *is* my trespass? What *is* my sin, that you
have so hotly pursued me?
37 "Although you have searched all my
things, what part of your household things
have you found? Set *it* here before my brethren
and your brethren, that they may judge be-
tween us both!
38 "These twenty years I *have been* with you;
your ewes and your female goats have not mis-
carried their young, and I have not eaten the
rams of your flock.
39 "That which was torn *by beasts* I did not
bring to you; I bore the loss of it. You required
it from my hand, *whether* stolen by day or sto-
len by night.
40 "*There* I was! In the day the drought con-
sumed me, and the frost by night, and my sleep
departed from my eyes.

41 "Thus I have been in your house twenty
years; I served you fourteen years for your two
daughters, and six years for your flock, and
you have changed my wages ten times.
42 "Unless the God of my father, the God of
Abraham and the Fear of Isaac, had been with
me, surely now you would have sent me away
empty-handed. God has seen my affliction and
the labor of my hands, and rebuked *you* last
night."

Laban's Covenant with Jacob

43 And Laban answered and said to Jacob,
"*These* daughters *are* my daughters, and *these*
children *are* my children, and *this* flock *is* my
flock; all that you see *is* mine. But what can I
do this day to these my daughters or to their
children whom they have borne?
44 "Now therefore, come, let us make a cov-
enant, you and I, and let it be a witness be-
tween you and me."
45 So Jacob took a stone and set it up *as* a
pillar.
46 Then Jacob said to his brethren, "Gather
stones." And they took stones and made a
heap, and they ate there on the heap.
47 Laban called it Jegar Sahadutha,[a] but Ja-
cob called it Galeed.[b]
48 And Laban said, "This heap *is* a witness
between you and me this day." Therefore its
name was called Galeed,
49 also Mizpah,[a] because he said, "May the
LORD watch between you and me when we are
absent one from another.
50 "If you afflict my daughters, or if you take
other wives besides my daughters, *although*
no man *is* with us—see, God *is* witness be-
tween you and me!"
51 Then Laban said to Jacob, "Here is this
heap and here is *this* pillar, which I have placed
between you and me.
52 "This heap *is* a witness, and *this* pillar *is* a
witness, that I will not pass beyond this heap
to you, and you will not pass beyond this heap
and this pillar to me, for harm.
53 "The God of Abraham, the God of Nahor,
and the God of their father judge between us."
And Jacob swore by the Fear of his father
Isaac.
54 Then Jacob offered a sacrifice on the
mountain, and called his brethren to eat bread.
And they ate bread and stayed all night on the
mountain.
55 And early in the morning Laban arose, and
kissed his sons and daughters and blessed
them. Then Laban departed and returned to
his place.

Esau Comes to Meet Jacob

32 So Jacob went on his way, and the an-
gels of God met him.
2 When Jacob saw them, he said, "This *is*
God's camp." And he called the name of that
place Mahanaim.[a]
3 Then Jacob sent messengers before him to
Esau his brother in the land of Seir, the country
of Edom.
4 And he commanded them, saying, "Speak
thus to my lord Esau, 'Thus your servant Jacob
says: "I have dwelt with Laban and stayed
there until now.
5 "I have oxen, donkeys, flocks, and male
and female servants; and I have sent to tell my
lord, that I may find favor in your sight." '"
6 Then the messengers returned to Jacob,
saying, "We came to your brother Esau, and
he also is coming to meet you, and four hun-
dred men *are* with him."
7 So Jacob was greatly afraid and dis-
tressed; and he divided the people that *were*
with him, and the flocks and herds and camels,
into two companies.
8 And he said, "If Esau comes to the one
company and attacks it, then the other com-
pany which is left will escape."
9 Then Jacob said, "O God of my father
Abraham and God of my father Isaac, the
LORD who said to me, 'Return to your country
and to your family, and I will deal well with
you':
10 "I am not worthy of the least of all the
mercies and of all the truth which You have
shown Your servant; for I crossed over this
Jordan with my staff, and now I have become
two companies.
11 "Deliver me, I pray, from the hand of my
brother, from the hand of Esau; for I fear him,
lest he come and attack me *and* the mother
with the children.
12 "For You said, 'I will surely treat you well,
and make your descendants as the sand of the
sea, which cannot be numbered for multi-
tude.'"
13 So he lodged there that same night, and
took what came to his hand as a present for
Esau his brother:
14 two hundred female goats and twenty
male goats, two hundred ewes and twenty
rams,
15 thirty milk camels with their colts, forty
cows and ten bulls, twenty female donkeys and
ten foals.
16 Then he delivered *them* to the hand of his
servants, every drove by itself, and said to his
servants, "Pass over before me, and put some
distance between successive droves."
17 And he commanded the first one, saying,
"When Esau my brother meets you and asks
you, saying, 'To whom do you belong, and
where are you going? Whose *are* these in front
of you?'
18 "then you shall say, 'They *are* your servant
Jacob's. It *is* a present sent to my lord Esau;
and behold, he also *is* behind us.'"
19 So he commanded the second, the third,
and all who followed the droves, saying, "In
this manner you shall speak to Esau when you
find him;
20 "and also say, 'Behold, your servant Jacob
is behind us.'" For he said, "I will appease him
with the present that goes before me, and after-
ward I will see his face; perhaps he will accept
me."
21 So the present went on over before him,
but he himself lodged that night in the camp.

Wrestling with God

22 And he arose that night and took his two
wives, his two female servants, and his eleven
sons, and crossed over the ford of Jabbok.
23 He took them, sent them over the brook,
and sent over what he had.
24 Then Jacob was left alone; and a Man
wrestled with him until the breaking of day.

31:47 [a]Literally, in Aramaic, *Heap of Witness* [b]Literally, in Hebrew, *Heap of Witness* **31:49** [a]Literally *Watch*
32:2 [a]Literally *Double Camp*

25 Now when He saw that He did not prevail
against him, He touched the socket of his hip;
and the socket of Jacob's hip was out of joint
as He wrestled with him.
26 And He said, "Let Me go, for the day
breaks." But he said, "I will not let You go
unless You bless me!"
27 So He said to him, "What *is* your name?"
He said, "Jacob."
28 And He said, "Your name shall no longer
be called Jacob, but Israel;[a] for you have strug-
gled with God and with men, and have pre-
vailed."
29 Then Jacob asked, saying, "Tell *me* Your
name, I pray." And He said, "Why *is* it *that*
you ask about My name?" And He blessed him
there.
30 So Jacob called the name of the place Pe-
niel:[a] "For I have seen God face to face, and
my life is preserved."
31 Just as he crossed over Penuel[a] the sun
rose on him, and he limped on his hip.
32 Therefore to this day the children of Israel
do not eat the muscle that shrank, which *is* on
the hip socket, because He touched the socket
of Jacob's hip in the muscle that shrank.

Jacob and Esau Meet

33 Now Jacob lifted his eyes and looked,
and there, Esau was coming, and with
him were four hundred men. So he divided
the children among Leah, Rachel, and the two
maidservants.
2 And he put the maidservants and their
children in front, Leah and her children be-
hind, and Rachel and Joseph last.
3 Then he crossed over before them and
bowed himself to the ground seven times, until
he came near to his brother.
4 But Esau ran to meet him, and embraced
him, and fell on his neck and kissed him, and
they wept.
5 And he lifted his eyes and saw the women
and children, and said, "Who *are* these with
you?" So he said, "The children whom God
has graciously given your servant."
6 Then the maidservants came near, they
and their children, and bowed down.
7 And Leah also came near with her chil-
dren, and they bowed down. Afterward Joseph
and Rachel came near, and they bowed down.
8 Then Esau said, "What *do* you *mean by*
all this company which I met?" And he said,
"*These are* to find favor in the sight of my
lord."
9 But Esau said, "I have enough, my brother;
keep what you have for yourself."
10 And Jacob said, "No, please, if I have now
found favor in your sight, then receive my
present from my hand, inasmuch as I have
seen your face as though I had seen the face of
God, and you were pleased with me.
11 "Please, take my blessing that is brought
to you, because God has dealt graciously with
me, and because I have enough." So he urged
him, and he took *it*.
12 Then Esau said, "Let us take our journey;
let us go, and I will go before you."
13 But Jacob said to him, "My lord knows
that the children *are* weak, and the flocks and
herds which are nursing *are* with me. And if
the men should drive them hard one day, all
the flock will die.
14 "Please let my lord go on ahead before his
servant. I will lead on slowly at a pace which
the livestock that go before me, and the chil-
dren, are able to endure, until I come to my
lord in Seir."
15 And Esau said, "Now let me leave with you
some of the people who *are* with me." But he
said, "What need is there? Let me find favor in
the sight of my lord."
16 So Esau returned that day on his way to
Seir.
17 And Jacob journeyed to Succoth, built
himself a house, and made booths for his live-
stock. Therefore the name of the place is called
Succoth.[a]

Jacob Comes to Canaan

18 Then Jacob came safely to the city of She-
chem, which *is* in the land of Canaan, when he
came from Padan Aram; and he pitched his
tent before the city.
19 And he bought the parcel of land, where
he had pitched his tent, from the children of
Hamor, Shechem's father, for one hundred
pieces of money.
20 Then he erected an altar there and called
it El Elohe Israel.[a]

The Dinah Incident

34 Now Dinah the daughter of Leah, whom
she had borne to Jacob, went out to see
the daughters of the land.
2 And when Shechem the son of Hamor the
Hivite, prince of the country, saw her, he took
her and lay with her, and violated her.
3 His soul was strongly attracted to Dinah
the daughter of Jacob, and he loved the young
woman and spoke kindly to the young woman.
4 So Shechem spoke to his father Hamor,
saying, "Get me this young woman as a wife."
5 And Jacob heard that he had defiled Dinah
his daughter. Now his sons were with his live-
stock in the field; so Jacob held his peace until
they came.
6 Then Hamor the father of Shechem went
out to Jacob to speak with him.
7 And the sons of Jacob came in from the
field when they heard *it*; and the men were
grieved and very angry, because he had done
a disgraceful thing in Israel by lying with Ja-
cob's daughter, a thing which ought not to be
done.
8 But Hamor spoke with them, saying, "The
soul of my son Shechem longs for your daugh-
ter. Please give her to him as a wife.
9 "And make marriages with us; give your
daughters to us, and take our daughters to your-
selves.
10 "So you shall dwell with us, and the land
shall be before you. Dwell and trade in it, and
acquire possessions for yourselves in it."
11 Then Shechem said to her father and her
brothers, "Let me find favor in your eyes, and
whatever you say to me I will give.
12 "Ask me ever so much dowry and gift, and
I will give according to what you say to me;
but give me the young woman as a wife."
13 But the sons of Jacob answered Shechem
and Hamor his father, and spoke deceitfully,
because he had defiled Dinah their sister.

32:28 [a]Literally *Prince with God* **32:30** [a]Literally *Face of God* **32:31** [a]Same as *Peniel*, verse 30 **33:17** [a]Literally *Booths* **33:20** [a]Literally *God, the God of Israel*

14 And they said to them, "We cannot do this
thing, to give our sister to one who is uncircum-
cised, for that *would be* a reproach to us.
15 "But on this *condition* we will consent to
you: If you will become as we *are*, if every male
of you is circumcised,
16 "then we will give our daughters to you,
and we will take your daughters to us; and we
will dwell with you, and we will become one
people.
17 "But if you will not heed us and be circum-
cised, then we will take our daughter and be
gone."
18 And their words pleased Hamor and She-
chem, Hamor's son.
19 So the young man did not delay to do the
thing, because he delighted in Jacob's daugh-
ter. He *was* more honorable than all the house-
hold of his father.
20 And Hamor and Shechem his son came to
the gate of their city, and spoke with the men
of their city, saying:
21 "These men *are* at peace with us. There-
fore let them dwell in the land and trade in it.
For indeed the land *is* large enough for them.
Let us take their daughters to us as wives, and
let us give them our daughters.
22 "Only on this *condition* will the men con-
sent to dwell with us, to be one people: if every
male among us is circumcised as they *are* cir-
cumcised.
23 "*Will* not their livestock, their property,
and every animal of theirs *be* ours? Only let us
consent to them, and they will dwell with us."
24 And all who went out of the gate of his city
heeded Hamor and Shechem his son; every
male was circumcised, all who went out of the
gate of his city.
25 Now it came to pass on the third day, when
they were in pain, that two of the sons of Jacob,
Simeon and Levi, Dinah's brothers, each took
his sword and came boldly upon the city and
killed all the males.
26 And they killed Hamor and Shechem his
son with the edge of the sword, and took Dinah
from Shechem's house, and went out.
27 The sons of Jacob came upon the slain,
and plundered the city, because their sister had
been defiled.
28 They took their sheep, their oxen, and
their donkeys, what *was* in the city and what
was in the field,
29 and all their wealth. All their little ones
and their wives they took captive; and they
plundered even all that *was* in the houses.
30 Then Jacob said to Simeon and Levi, "You
have troubled me by making me obnoxious
among the inhabitants of the land, among the
Canaanites and the Perizzites; and since I *am*
few in number, they will gather themselves to-
gether against me and kill me. I shall be de-
stroyed, my household and I."
31 But they said, "Should he treat our sister
like a harlot?"

Jacob's Return to Bethel

35 Then God said to Jacob, "Arise, go up
to Bethel and dwell there; and make an
altar there to God, who appeared to you when
you fled from the face of Esau your brother."
2 And Jacob said to his household and to all
who *were* with him, "Put away the foreign
gods that *are* among you, purify yourselves,
and change your garments.
3 "Then let us arise and go up to Bethel;
and I will make an altar there to God, who
answered me in the day of my distress and has
been with me in the way which I have gone."
4 So they gave Jacob all the foreign gods
which *were* in their hands, and the earrings
which *were* in their ears; and Jacob hid them
under the terebinth tree which *was* by She-
chem.
5 And they journeyed, and the terror of God
was upon the cities that *were* all around them,
and they did not pursue the sons of Jacob.
6 So Jacob came to Luz (that *is*, Bethel),
which *is* in the land of Canaan, he and all the
people who *were* with him.
7 And he built an altar there and called the
place El Bethel,[a] because there God appeared
to him when he fled from the face of his
brother.
8 Now Deborah, Rebekah's nurse, died, and
she was buried below Bethel under the tere-
binth tree. So the name of it was called Allon
Bachuth.[a]
9 Then God appeared to Jacob again, when
he came from Padan Aram, and blessed him.
10 And God said to him, "Your name *is* Jacob;
your name shall not be called Jacob anymore,
but Israel shall be your name." So He called
his name Israel.
11 Also God said to him: "I *am* God Almighty.
Be fruitful and multiply; a nation and a com-
pany of nations shall proceed from you, and
kings shall come from your body.
12 "The land which I gave Abraham and
Isaac I give to you; and to your descendants
after you I give this land."
13 Then God went up from him in the place
where He talked with him.
14 So Jacob set up a pillar in the place where
He talked with him, a pillar of stone; and he
poured a drink offering on it, and he poured
oil on it.
15 And Jacob called the name of the place
where God spoke with him, Bethel.

Death of Rachel

16 Then they journeyed from Bethel. And
when there was but a little distance to go to
Ephrath, Rachel labored *in childbirth*, and she
had hard labor.
17 Now it came to pass, when she was in hard
labor, that the midwife said to her, "Do not
fear; you will have this son also."
18 And so it was, as her soul was departing
(for she died), that she called his name Ben-
Oni;[a] but his father called him Benjamin.[b]
19 So Rachel died and was buried on the way
to Ephrath (that *is*, Bethlehem).
20 And Jacob set a pillar on her grave, which
is the pillar of Rachel's grave to this day.
21 Then Israel journeyed and pitched his tent
beyond the tower of Eder.
22 And it happened, when Israel dwelt in that
land, that Reuben went and lay with Bilhah his
father's concubine; and Israel heard *about it*.

35:7 [a]Literally *God of the House of God* **35:8** [a]Literally *Terebinth of Weeping* **35:18** [a]Literally *Son of My Sorrow* [b]Literally *Son of the Right Hand*

Jacob's Twelve Sons

Now the sons of Jacob were twelve:
23 the sons of Leah *were* Reuben, Jacob's
firstborn, and Simeon, Levi, Judah, Issachar,
and Zebulun;
24 the sons of Rachel *were* Joseph and Ben-
jamin;
25 the sons of Bilhah, Rachel's maidservant,
were Dan and Naphtali;
26 and the sons of Zilpah, Leah's maid-
servant, *were* Gad and Asher. These *were* the
sons of Jacob who were born to him in Padan
Aram.

Death of Isaac

27 Then Jacob came to his father Isaac at
Mamre, or Kirjath Arba[a] (that *is,* Hebron),
where Abraham and Isaac had dwelt.
28 Now the days of Isaac were one hundred
and eighty years.
29 So Isaac breathed his last and died, and
was gathered to his people, *being* old and full
of days. And his sons Esau and Jacob buried
him.

The Family of Esau

36 Now this *is* the genealogy of Esau, who
is Edom.
2 Esau took his wives from the daughters of
Canaan: Adah the daughter of Elon the Hittite;
Aholibamah the daughter of Anah, the daugh-
ter of Zibeon the Hivite;
3 and Basemath, Ishmael's daughter, sister
of Nebajoth.
4 Now Adah bore Eliphaz to Esau, and Base-
math bore Reuel.
5 And Aholibamah bore Jeush, Jaalam, and
Korah. These *were* the sons of Esau who were
born to him in the land of Canaan.
6 Then Esau took his wives, his sons, his
daughters, and all the persons of his house-
hold, his cattle and all his animals, and all his
goods which he had gained in the land of Ca-
naan, and went to a country away from the
presence of his brother Jacob.
7 For their possessions were too great for
them to dwell together, and the land where
they were strangers could not support them
because of their livestock.
8 So Esau dwelt in Mount Seir. Esau *is*
Edom.
9 And this *is* the genealogy of Esau the fa-
ther of the Edomites in Mount Seir.
10 These *were* the names of Esau's sons: Eli-
phaz the son of Adah the wife of Esau, and
Reuel the son of Basemath the wife of Esau.
11 And the sons of Eliphaz were Teman,
Omar, Zepho,[a] Gatam, and Kenaz.
12 Now Timna was the concubine of Eliphaz,
Esau's son, and she bore Amalek to Eliphaz.
These *were* the sons of Adah, Esau's wife.
13 These *were* the sons of Reuel: Nahath, Ze-
rah, Shammah, and Mizzah. These were the
sons of Basemath, Esau's wife.
14 These were the sons of Aholibamah,
Esau's wife, the daughter of Anah, the daugh-
ter of Zibeon. And she bore to Esau: Jeush,
Jaalam, and Korah.

The Chiefs of Edom

15 These *were* the chiefs of the sons of Esau.
The sons of Eliphaz, the firstborn *son* of Esau,
were Chief Teman, Chief Omar, Chief Zepho,
Chief Kenaz,
16 Chief Korah,[a] Chief Gatam, *and* Chief Am-
alek. These *were* the chiefs of Eliphaz in the
land of Edom. They *were* the sons of Adah.
17 These *were* the sons of Reuel, Esau's son:
Chief Nahath, Chief Zerah, Chief Shammah,
and Chief Mizzah. These *were* the chiefs of
Reuel in the land of Edom. These *were* the sons
of Basemath, Esau's wife.
18 And these *were* the sons of Aholibamah,
Esau's wife: Chief Jeush, Chief Jaalam, and
Chief Korah. These *were* the chiefs *who de-
scended* from Aholibamah, Esau's wife, the
daughter of Anah.
19 These *were* the sons of Esau, who is Edom,
and these *were* their chiefs.

The Sons of Seir

20 These *were* the sons of Seir the Horite who
inhabited the land: Lotan, Shobal, Zibeon,
Anah,
21 Dishon, Ezer, and Dishan. These *were* the
chiefs of the Horites, the sons of Seir, in the
land of Edom.
22 And the sons of Lotan were Hori and He-
mam.[a] Lotan's sister *was* Timna.
23 These *were* the sons of Shobal: Alvan,[a]
Manahath, Ebal, Shepho,[b] and Onam.
24 These *were* the sons of Zibeon: both Ajah
and Anah. This *was the* Anah who found the
water[a] in the wilderness as he pastured the
donkeys of his father Zibeon.
25 These *were* the children of Anah: Dishon
and Aholibamah the daughter of Anah.
26 These *were* the sons of Dishon:[a] Hemdan,[b]
Eshban, Ithran, and Cheran.
27 These *were* the sons of Ezer: Bilhan, Zaa-
van, and Akan.[a]
28 These *were* the sons of Dishan: Uz and
Aran.
29 These *were* the chiefs of the Horites: Chief
Lotan, Chief Shobal, Chief Zibeon, Chief
Anah,
30 Chief Dishon, Chief Ezer, and Chief Di-
shan. These *were* the chiefs of the Horites, ac-
cording to their chiefs in the land of Seir.

The Kings of Edom

31 Now these *were* the kings who reigned in
the land of Edom before any king reigned over
the children of Israel:
32 Bela the son of Beor reigned in Edom, and
the name of his city *was* Dinhabah.
33 And when Bela died, Jobab the son of Ze-
rah of Bozrah reigned in his place.
34 When Jobab died, Husham of the land of
the Temanites reigned in his place.
35 And when Husham died, Hadad the son
of Bedad, who attacked Midian in the field of
Moab, reigned in his place. And the name of
his city *was* Avith.
36 When Hadad died, Samlah of Masrekah
reigned in his place.
37 And when Samlah died, Saul of Rehoboth-
by-the-River reigned in his place.

35:27 [a]Literally *Town of Arba* **36:11** [a]Spelled *Zephi* in 1 Chronicles 1:36 **36:16** [a]Samaritan Pentateuch omits *Chief Korah.* **36:22** [a]Spelled *Homam* in 1 Chronicles 1:39 **36:23** [a]Spelled *Alian* in 1 Chronicles 1:40 [b]Spelled *Shephi* in 1 Chronicles 1:40 **36:24** [a]Following Masoretic Text and Vulgate (*hot springs*); Septuagint reads *Jamin;* Targum reads *mighty men;* Talmud interprets as *mules.* **36:26** [a]Hebrew *Dishan* [b]Spelled *Hamran* in 1 Chronicles 1:41 **36:27** [a]Spelled *Jaakan* in 1 Chronicles 1:42

38 When Saul died, Baal-Hanan the son of
Achbor reigned in his place.
39 And when Baal-Hanan the son of Achbor
died, Hadar[a] reigned in his place; and the name
of his city *was* Pau.[b] His wife's name *was* Me-
hetabel, the daughter of Matred, the daughter
of Mezahab.

The Chiefs of Esau

40 And these *were* the names of the chiefs
of Esau, according to their families and their
places, by their names: Chief Timnah, Chief
Alvah,[a] Chief Jetheth,
41 Chief Aholibamah, Chief Elah, Chief
Pinon,
42 Chief Kenaz, Chief Teman, Chief Mibzar,
43 Chief Magdiel, and Chief Iram. These *were*
the chiefs of Edom, according to their dwelling
places in the land of their possession. Esau
was the father of the Edomites.

Joseph Dreams of Greatness

37 Now Jacob dwelt in the land where his
father was a stranger, in the land of Ca-
naan.
2 This *is* the history of Jacob. Joseph, *being*
seventeen years old, was feeding the flock with
his brothers. And the lad *was* with the sons
of Bilhah and the sons of Zilpah, his father's
wives; and Joseph brought a bad report of
them to his father.
3 Now Israel loved Joseph more than all his
children, because he *was* the son of his old
age. Also he made him a tunic of *many* colors.
4 But when his brothers saw that their father
loved him more than all his brothers, they
hated him and could not speak peaceably to
him.
5 Now Joseph had a dream, and he told *it* to
his brothers; and they hated him even more.
6 So he said to them, "Please hear this
dream which I have dreamed:
7 "There we were, binding sheaves in the
field. Then behold, my sheaf arose and also
stood upright; and indeed your sheaves stood
all around and bowed down to my sheaf."
8 And his brothers said to him, "Shall you
indeed reign over us? Or shall you indeed have
dominion over us?" So they hated him even
more for his dreams and for his words.
9 Then he dreamed still another dream and
told it to his brothers, and said, "Look, I have
dreamed another dream. And this time, the
sun, the moon, and the eleven stars bowed
down to me."
10 So he told *it* to his father and his brothers;
and his father rebuked him and said to him,
"What *is* this dream that you have dreamed?
Shall your mother and I and your brothers in-
deed come to bow down to the earth before
you?"
11 And his brothers envied him, but his father
kept the matter *in mind.*

Joseph Sold by His Brothers

12 Then his brothers went to feed their fa-
ther's flock in Shechem.
13 And Israel said to Joseph, "Are not your
brothers feeding *the flock* in Shechem? Come,
I will send you to them." So he said to him,
"Here I am."
14 Then he said to him, "Please go and see if
it is well with your brothers and well with the
flocks, and bring back word to me." So he sent
him out of the Valley of Hebron, and he went
to Shechem.
15 Now a certain man found him, and there
he was, wandering in the field. And the man
asked him, saying, "What are you seeking?"
16 So he said, "I am seeking my brothers.
Please tell me where they are feeding *their
flocks.*"
17 And the man said, "They have departed
from here, for I heard them say, 'Let us go to
Dothan.'" So Joseph went after his brothers
and found them in Dothan.
18 Now when they saw him afar off, even be-
fore he came near them, they conspired
against him to kill him.
19 Then they said to one another, "Look, this
dreamer is coming!
20 "Come therefore, let us now kill him and
cast him into some pit; and we shall say, 'Some
wild beast has devoured him.' We shall see
what will become of his dreams!"
21 But Reuben heard *it*, and he delivered him
out of their hands, and said, "Let us not kill
him."
22 And Reuben said to them, "Shed no blood,
but cast him into this pit which *is* in the wilder-
ness, and do not lay a hand on him"—that he
might deliver him out of their hands, and bring
him back to his father.
23 So it came to pass, when Joseph had come
to his brothers, that they stripped Joseph *of* his
tunic, the tunic of *many* colors that *was* on
him.
24 Then they took him and cast him into a pit.
And the pit *was* empty; *there was* no water in
it.
25 And they sat down to eat a meal. Then they
lifted their eyes and looked, and there was a
company of Ishmaelites, coming from Gilead
with their camels, bearing spices, balm, and
myrrh, on their way to carry *them* down to
Egypt.
26 So Judah said to his brothers, "What profit
is there if we kill our brother and conceal his
blood?
27 "Come and let us sell him to the Ishmael-
ites, and let not our hand be upon him, for he
is our brother *and* our flesh." And his brothers
listened.
28 Then Midianite traders passed by; so *the
brothers* pulled Joseph up and lifted him out
of the pit, and sold him to the Ishmaelites for
twenty *shekels* of silver. And they took Joseph
to Egypt.
29 Then Reuben returned to the pit, and in-
deed Joseph *was* not in the pit; and he tore his
clothes.
30 And he returned to his brothers and said,
"The lad *is* no *more;* and I, where shall I go?"
31 So they took Joseph's tunic, killed a kid of
the goats, and dipped the tunic in the blood.
32 Then they sent the tunic of *many* colors,
and they brought *it* to their father and said,
"We have found this. Do you know whether it
is your son's tunic or not?"
33 And he recognized it and said, "*It is* my
son's tunic. A wild beast has devoured him.
Without doubt Joseph is torn to pieces."
34 Then Jacob tore his clothes, put sackcloth

36:39 [a]Spelled *Hadad* in Samaritan Pentateuch, Syriac, and 1 Chronicles 1:50 [b]Spelled *Pai* in 1 Chronicles 1:50
36:40 [a]Spelled *Aliah* in 1 Chronicles 1:51

on his waist, and mourned for his son many
days.
35 And all his sons and all his daughters
arose to comfort him; but he refused to be com-
forted, and he said, "For I shall go down into
the grave to my son in mourning." Thus his
father wept for him.
36 Now the Midianites[a] had sold him in Egypt
to Potiphar, an officer of Pharaoh *and* captain
of the guard.

Judah and Tamar

38 It came to pass at that time that Judah
departed from his brothers, and visited
a certain Adullamite whose name *was* Hirah.
2 And Judah saw there a daughter of a cer-
tain Canaanite whose name *was* Shua, and he
married her and went in to her.
3 So she conceived and bore a son, and he
called his name Er.
4 She conceived again and bore a son, and
she called his name Onan.
5 And she conceived yet again and bore a
son, and called his name Shelah. He was at
Chezib when she bore him.
6 Then Judah took a wife for Er his firstborn,
and her name *was* Tamar.
7 But Er, Judah's firstborn, was wicked in
the sight of the LORD, and the LORD killed him.
8 And Judah said to Onan, "Go in to your
brother's wife and marry her, and raise up an
heir to your brother."
9 But Onan knew that the heir would not be
his; and it came to pass, when he went in to his
brother's wife, that he emitted on the ground,
lest he should give an heir to his brother.
10 And the thing which he did displeased the
LORD; therefore He killed him also.
11 Then Judah said to Tamar his daughter-in-
law, "Remain a widow in your father's house
till my son Shelah is grown." For he said, "Lest
he also die like his brothers." And Tamar went
and dwelt in her father's house.
12 Now in the process of time the daughter
of Shua, Judah's wife, died; and Judah was
comforted, and went up to his sheepshearers
at Timnah, he and his friend Hirah the Adul-
lamite.
13 And it was told Tamar, saying, "Look, your
father-in-law is going up to Timnah to shear
his sheep."
14 So she took off her widow's garments, cov-
ered *herself* with a veil and wrapped herself,
and sat in an open place which *was* on the way
to Timnah; for she saw that Shelah was grown,
and she was not given to him as a wife.
15 When Judah saw her, he thought she *was*
a harlot, because she had covered her face.
16 Then he turned to her by the way, and said,
"Please let me come in to you"; for he did not
know that she *was* his daughter-in-law. So she
said, "What will you give me, that you may
come in to me?"
17 And he said, "I will send a young goat from
the flock." So she said, "Will you give *me* a
pledge till you send *it?*"
18 Then he said, "What pledge shall I give
you?" So she said, "Your signet and cord, and
your staff that *is* in your hand." Then he gave
them to her, and went in to her, and she con-
ceived by him.
19 So she arose and went away, and laid aside
her veil and put on the garments of her widow-
hood.
20 And Judah sent the young goat by the
hand of his friend the Adullamite, to receive
his pledge from the woman's hand, but he did
not find her.
21 Then he asked the men of that place, say-
ing, "Where is the harlot who *was* openly by
the roadside?" And they said, "There was no
harlot in this *place*."
22 So he returned to Judah and said, "I can-
not find her. Also, the men of the place said
there was no harlot in this *place*."
23 Then Judah said, "Let her take *them* for
herself, lest we be shamed; for I sent this young
goat and you have not found her."
24 And it came to pass, about three months
after, that Judah was told, saying, "Tamar your
daughter-in-law has played the harlot; further-
more she *is* with child by harlotry." So Judah
said, "Bring her out and let her be burned!"
25 When she *was* brought out, she sent to her
father-in-law, saying, "By the man to whom
these belong, I *am* with child." And she said,
"Please determine whose these *are*—the signet
and cord, and staff."
26 So Judah acknowledged *them* and said,
"She has been more righteous than I, because
I did not give her to Shelah my son." And he
never knew her again.
27 Now it came to pass, at the time for giving
birth, that behold, twins *were* in her womb.
28 And so it was, when she was giving birth,
that *the one* put out *his* hand; and the midwife
took a scarlet *thread* and bound it on his hand,
saying, "This one came out first."
29 Then it happened, as he drew back his
hand, that his brother came out unexpectedly;
and she said, "How did you break through?
This breach *be* upon you!" Therefore his name
was called Perez.[a]
30 Afterward his brother came out who had
the scarlet *thread* on his hand. And his name
was called Zerah.

Joseph a Slave in Egypt

39 Now Joseph had been taken down to
Egypt. And Potiphar, an officer of Pha-
raoh, captain of the guard, an Egyptian,
bought him from the Ishmaelites who had
taken him down there.
2 The LORD was with Joseph, and he was a
successful man; and he was in the house of his
master the Egyptian.
3 And his master saw that the LORD *was*
with him and that the LORD made all he did to
prosper in his hand.
4 So Joseph found favor in his sight, and
served him. Then he made him overseer of his
house, and all *that* he had he put under his
authority.
5 So it was, from the time *that* he had made
him overseer of his house and all that he had,
that the LORD blessed the Egyptian's house for
Joseph's sake; and the blessing of the LORD
was on all that he had in the house and in the
field.
6 Thus he left all that he had in Joseph's
hand, and he did not know what he had except
for the bread which he ate. Now Joseph was
handsome in form and appearance.
7 And it came to pass after these things that

37:36 [a]Masoretic Text reads *Medanites*. **38:29** [a]Literally *Breach* or *Breakthrough*

his master's wife cast longing eyes on Joseph, and she said, "Lie with me."

8 But he refused and said to his master's wife, "Look, my master does not know what *is* with me in the house, and he has committed all that he has to my hand.

9 "*There is* no one greater in this house than I, nor has he kept back anything from me but you, because you *are* his wife. How then can I do this great wickedness, and sin against God?"

10 So it was, as she spoke to Joseph day by day, that he did not heed her, to lie with her *or* to be with her.

11 But it happened about this time, when Joseph went into the house to do his work, and none of the men of the house *was* inside,

12 that she caught him by his garment, saying, "Lie with me." But he left his garment in her hand, and fled and ran outside.

13 And so it was, when she saw that he had left his garment in her hand and fled outside,

14 that she called to the men of her house and spoke to them, saying, "See, he has brought in to us a Hebrew to mock us. He came in to me to lie with me, and I cried out with a loud voice.

15 "And it happened, when he heard that I lifted my voice and cried out, that he left his garment with me, and fled and went outside."

16 So she kept his garment with her until his master came home.

17 Then she spoke to him with words like these, saying, "The Hebrew servant whom you brought to us came in to me to mock me;

18 "so it happened, as I lifted my voice and cried out, that he left his garment with me and fled outside."

19 So it was, when his master heard the words which his wife spoke to him, saying, "Your servant did to me after this manner," that his anger was aroused.

20 Then Joseph's master took him and put him into the prison, a place where the king's prisoners *were* confined. And he was there in the prison.

21 But the LORD was with Joseph and showed him mercy, and He gave him favor in the sight of the keeper of the prison.

22 And the keeper of the prison committed to Joseph's hand all the prisoners who *were* in the prison; whatever they did there, it was his doing.

23 The keeper of the prison did not look into anything *that was* under *Joseph's* authority,[a] because the LORD was with him; and whatever he did, the LORD made *it* prosper.

The Prisoners' Dreams

40 It came to pass after these things *that* the butler and the baker of the king of Egypt offended their lord, the king of Egypt.

2 And Pharaoh was angry with his two officers, the chief butler and the chief baker.

3 So he put them in custody in the house of the captain of the guard, in the prison, the place where Joseph *was* confined.

4 And the captain of the guard charged Joseph with them, and he served them; so they were in custody for a while.

5 Then the butler and the baker of the king of Egypt, who *were* confined in the prison, had a dream, both of them, each man's dream in one night *and* each man's dream with its *own* interpretation.

6 And Joseph came in to them in the morning and looked at them, and saw that they *were* sad.

7 So he asked Pharaoh's officers who *were* with him in the custody of his lord's house, saying, "Why do you look so sad today?"

8 And they said to him, "We each have had a dream, and *there is* no interpreter of it." So Joseph said to them, "Do not interpretations belong to God? Tell *them* to me, please."

9 Then the chief butler told his dream to Joseph, and said to him, "Behold, in my dream a vine *was* before me,

10 "and in the vine *were* three branches; it *was* as though it budded, its blossoms shot forth, and its clusters brought forth ripe grapes.

11 "Then Pharaoh's cup *was* in my hand; and I took the grapes and pressed them into Pharaoh's cup, and placed the cup in Pharaoh's hand."

12 And Joseph said to him, "This *is* the interpretation of it: The three branches *are* three days.

13 "Now within three days Pharaoh will lift up your head and restore you to your place, and you will put Pharaoh's cup in his hand according to the former manner, when you were his butler.

14 "But remember me when it is well with you, and please show kindness to me; make mention of me to Pharaoh, and get me out of this house.

15 "For indeed I was stolen away from the land of the Hebrews; and also I have done nothing here that they should put me into the dungeon."

16 When the chief baker saw that the interpretation was good, he said to Joseph, "I also *was* in my dream, and there *were* three white baskets on my head.

17 "In the uppermost basket *were* all kinds of baked goods for Pharaoh, and the birds ate them out of the basket on my head."

18 So Joseph answered and said, "This *is* the interpretation of it: The three baskets *are* three days.

19 "Within three days Pharaoh will lift off your head from you and hang you on a tree; and the birds will eat your flesh from you."

20 Now it came to pass on the third day, *which was* Pharaoh's birthday, that he made a feast for all his servants; and he lifted up the head of the chief butler and of the chief baker among his servants.

21 Then he restored the chief butler to his butlership again, and he placed the cup in Pharaoh's hand.

22 But he hanged the chief baker, as Joseph had interpreted to them.

23 Yet the chief butler did not remember Joseph, but forgot him.

Pharaoh's Dreams

41 Then it came to pass, at the end of two full years, that Pharaoh had a dream; and behold, he stood by the river.

2 Suddenly there came up out of the river seven cows, fine looking and fat; and they fed in the meadow.

3 Then behold, seven other cows came up

39:23 [a]Literally *his hand*

after them out of the river, ugly and gaunt, and
stood by the *other* cows on the bank of the
river.
4 And the ugly and gaunt cows ate up the
seven fine looking and fat cows. So Pharaoh
awoke.
5 He slept and dreamed a second time; and
suddenly seven heads of grain came up on one
stalk, plump and good.
6 Then behold, seven thin heads, blighted by
the east wind, sprang up after them.
7 And the seven thin heads devoured the
seven plump and full heads. So Pharaoh
awoke, and indeed, *it was* a dream.
8 Now it came to pass in the morning that
his spirit was troubled, and he sent and called
for all the magicians of Egypt and all its wise
men. And Pharaoh told them his dreams, but
there was no one who could interpret them for
Pharaoh.
9 Then the chief butler spoke to Pharaoh,
saying: "I remember my faults this day.
10 "When Pharaoh was angry with his ser-
vants, and put me in custody in the house of
the captain of the guard, *both* me and the chief
baker,
11 "we each had a dream in one night, he
and I. Each of us dreamed according to the
interpretation of his *own* dream.
12 "Now there *was* a young Hebrew man with
us there, a servant of the captain of the guard.
And we told him, and he interpreted our
dreams for us; to each man he interpreted ac-
cording to his *own* dream.
13 "And it came to pass, just as he interpreted
for us, so it happened. He restored me to my
office, and he hanged him."
14 Then Pharaoh sent and called Joseph, and
they brought him quickly out of the dungeon;
and he shaved, changed his clothing, and came
to Pharaoh.
15 And Pharaoh said to Joseph, "I have had
a dream, and *there is* no one who can interpret
it. But I have heard it said of you *that* you can
understand a dream, to interpret it."
16 So Joseph answered Pharaoh, saying, "*It
is* not in me; God will give Pharaoh an answer
of peace."
17 Then Pharaoh said to Joseph: "Behold, in
my dream I stood on the bank of the river.
18 "Suddenly seven cows came up out of the
river, fine looking and fat; and they fed in the
meadow.
19 "Then behold, seven other cows came up
after them, poor and very ugly and gaunt, such
ugliness as I have never seen in all the land of
Egypt.
20 "And the gaunt and ugly cows ate up the
first seven, the fat cows.
21 "When they had eaten them up, no one
would have known that they had eaten them,
for they *were* just as ugly as at the beginning.
So I awoke.
22 "Also I saw in my dream, and suddenly
seven heads came up on one stalk, full and
good.
23 "Then behold, seven heads, withered, thin,
and blighted by the east wind, sprang up after
them.
24 "And the thin heads devoured the seven
good heads. So I told *this* to the magicians, but
there was no one who could explain *it* to me."
25 Then Joseph said to Pharaoh, "The dreams
of Pharaoh *are* one; God has shown Pharaoh
what He *is* about to do:
26 "The seven good cows *are* seven years,
and the seven good heads *are* seven years; the
dreams *are* one.
27 "And the seven thin and ugly cows which
came up after them *are* seven years, and the
seven empty heads blighted by the east wind
are seven years of famine.
28 "This *is* the thing which I have spoken to
Pharaoh. God has shown Pharaoh what He *is*
about to do.
29 "Indeed seven years of great plenty will
come throughout all the land of Egypt;
30 "but after them seven years of famine will
arise, and all the plenty will be forgotten in the
land of Egypt; and the famine will deplete the
land.
31 "So the plenty will not be known in the
land because of the famine following, for it *will
be* very severe.
32 "And the dream was repeated to Pharaoh
twice because the thing *is* established by God,
and God will shortly bring it to pass.
33 "Now therefore, let Pharaoh select a dis-
cerning and wise man, and set him over the
land of Egypt.
34 "Let Pharaoh do *this*, and let him appoint
officers over the land, to collect one-fifth *of
the produce* of the land of Egypt in the seven
plentiful years.
35 "And let them gather all the food of those
good years that are coming, and store up grain
under the authority of Pharaoh, and let them
keep food in the cities.
36 "Then that food shall be as a reserve for
the land for the seven years of famine which
shall be in the land of Egypt, that the land may
not perish during the famine."

Joseph's Rise to Power

37 So the advice was good in the eyes of Pha-
raoh and in the eyes of all his servants.
38 And Pharaoh said to his servants, "Can we
find *such a one* as this, a man in whom *is* the
Spirit of God?"
39 Then Pharaoh said to Joseph, "Inasmuch
as God has shown you all this, *there is* no one
as discerning and wise as you.
40 "You shall be over my house, and all my
people shall be ruled according to your word;
only in regard to the throne will I be greater
than you."
41 And Pharaoh said to Joseph, "See, I have
set you over all the land of Egypt."
42 Then Pharaoh took his signet ring off his
hand and put it on Joseph's hand; and he
clothed him in garments of fine linen and put
a gold chain around his neck.
43 And he had him ride in the second chariot
which he had; and they cried out before him,
"Bow the knee!" So he set him over all the land
of Egypt.
44 Pharaoh also said to Joseph, "I *am* Pha-
raoh, and without your consent no man may
lift his hand or foot in all the land of Egypt."
45 And Pharaoh called Joseph's name Zaph-
nath-Paaneah. And he gave him as a wife Ase-
nath, the daughter of Poti-Pherah priest of On.
So Joseph went out over *all* the land of Egypt.
46 Joseph was thirty years old when he stood
before Pharaoh king of Egypt. And Joseph
went out from the presence of Pharaoh, and
went throughout all the land of Egypt.
47 Now in the seven plentiful years the
ground brought forth abundantly.
48 So he gathered up all the food of the seven

years which were in the land of Egypt, and laid up the food in the cities; he laid up in every city the food of the fields which surrounded them.

49 Joseph gathered very much grain, as the sand of the sea, until he stopped counting, for *it was* immeasurable.

50 And to Joseph were born two sons before the years of famine came, whom Asenath, the daughter of Poti-Pherah priest of On, bore to him.

51 Joseph called the name of the firstborn Manasseh:[a] "For God has made me forget all my toil and all my father's house."

52 And the name of the second he called Ephraim:[a] "For God has caused me to be fruitful in the land of my affliction."

53 Then the seven years of plenty which were in the land of Egypt ended,

54 and the seven years of famine began to come, as Joseph had said. The famine was in all lands, but in all the land of Egypt there was bread.

55 So when all the land of Egypt was famished, the people cried to Pharaoh for bread. Then Pharaoh said to all the Egyptians, "Go to Joseph; whatever he says to you, do."

56 The famine was over all the face of the earth, and Joseph opened all the storehouses[a] and sold to the Egyptians. And the famine became severe in the land of Egypt.

57 So all countries came to Joseph in Egypt to buy *grain*, because the famine was severe in all lands.

Joseph's Brothers Go to Egypt

42 When Jacob saw that there was grain in Egypt, Jacob said to his sons, "Why do you look at one another?"

2 And he said, "Indeed I have heard that there is grain in Egypt; go down to that place and buy for us there, that we may live and not die."

3 So Joseph's ten brothers went down to buy grain in Egypt.

4 But Jacob did not send Joseph's brother Benjamin with his brothers, for he said, "Lest some calamity befall him."

5 And the sons of Israel went to buy *grain* among those who journeyed, for the famine was in the land of Canaan.

6 Now Joseph *was* governor over the land; and it was he who sold to all the people of the land. And Joseph's brothers came and bowed down before him with *their* faces to the earth.

7 Joseph saw his brothers and recognized them, but he acted as a stranger to them and spoke roughly to them. Then he said to them, "Where do you come from?" And they said, "From the land of Canaan to buy food."

8 So Joseph recognized his brothers, but they did not recognize him.

9 Then Joseph remembered the dreams which he had dreamed about them, and said to them, "You *are* spies! You have come to see the nakedness of the land!"

10 And they said to him, "No, my lord, but your servants have come to buy food.

11 "We *are* all one man's sons; we *are* honest *men;* your servants are not spies."

12 But he said to them, "No, but you have come to see the nakedness of the land."

13 And they said, "Your servants *are* twelve brothers, the sons of one man in the land of Canaan; and in fact, the youngest *is* with our father today, and one *is* no more."

14 But Joseph said to them, "It *is* as I spoke to you, saying, 'You *are* spies!'

15 "In this *manner* you shall be tested: By the life of Pharaoh, you shall not leave this place unless your youngest brother comes here.

16 "Send one of you, and let him bring your brother; and you shall be kept in prison, that your words may be tested to see whether *there is* any truth in you; or else, by the life of Pharaoh, surely you *are* spies!"

17 So he put them all together in prison three days.

18 Then Joseph said to them the third day, "Do this and live, *for* I fear God:

19 "If you *are* honest *men*, let one of your brothers be confined to your prison house; but you, go and carry grain for the famine of your houses.

20 "And bring your youngest brother to me; so your words will be verified, and you shall not die." And they did so.

21 Then they said to one another, "We *are* truly guilty concerning our brother, for we saw the anguish of his soul when he pleaded with us, and we would not hear; therefore this distress has come upon us."

22 And Reuben answered them, saying, "Did I not speak to you, saying, 'Do not sin against the boy'; and you would not listen? Therefore behold, his blood is now required of us."

23 But they did not know that Joseph understood *them*, for he spoke to them through an interpreter.

24 And he turned himself away from them and wept. Then he returned to them again, and talked with them. And he took Simeon from them and bound him before their eyes.

The Brothers Return to Canaan

25 Then Joseph gave a command to fill their sacks with grain, to restore every man's money to his sack, and to give them provisions for the journey. Thus he did for them.

26 So they loaded their donkeys with the grain and departed from there.

27 But as one *of them* opened his sack to give his donkey feed at the encampment, he saw his money; and there it was, in the mouth of his sack.

28 So he said to his brothers, "My money has been restored, and there it is, in my sack!" Then their hearts failed *them* and they were afraid, saying to one another, "What *is* this *that* God has done to us?"

29 Then they went to Jacob their father in the land of Canaan and told him all that had happened to them, saying:

30 "The man *who is* lord of the land spoke roughly to us, and took us for spies of the country.

31 "But we said to him, 'We *are* honest *men;* we are not spies.

32 'We *are* twelve brothers, sons of our father; one *is* no *more*, and the youngest *is* with our father this day in the land of Canaan.'

33 "Then the man, the lord of the country, said to us, 'By this I will know that you *are* honest *men:* Leave one of your brothers *here* with me, take *food for* the famine of your households, and be gone.

41:51 [a]Literally *Making Forgetful* **41:52** [a]Literally *Fruitfulness* **41:56** [a]Literally *all that was in them*

34 'And bring your youngest brother to me; so I shall know that you *are* not spies, but *that* you *are* honest *men.* I will grant your brother to you, and you may trade in the land.' "

35 Then it happened as they emptied their sacks, that surprisingly each man's bundle of money *was* in his sack; and when they and their father saw the bundles of money, they were afraid.

36 And Jacob their father said to them, "You have bereaved me: Joseph is no *more,* Simeon is no *more,* and you want to take Benjamin. All these things are against me."

37 Then Reuben spoke to his father, saying, "Kill my two sons if I do not bring him *back* to you; put him in my hands, and I will bring him back to you."

38 But he said, "My son shall not go down with you, for his brother is dead, and he is left alone. If any calamity should befall him along the way in which you go, then you would bring down my gray hair with sorrow to the grave."

Joseph's Brothers Return with Benjamin

43 Now the famine *was* severe in the land.
2 And it came to pass, when they had
eaten up the grain which they had brought from Egypt, that their father said to them, "Go back, buy us a little food."

3 But Judah spoke to him, saying, "The man solemnly warned us, saying, 'You shall not see my face unless your brother *is* with you.'

4 "If you send our brother with us, we will go down and buy you food.

5 "But if you will not send *him,* we will not go down; for the man said to us, 'You shall not see my face unless your brother *is* with you.' "

6 And Israel said, "Why did you deal so wrongfully with me *as* to tell the man whether you had still *another* brother?"

7 But they said, "The man asked us pointedly about ourselves and our family, saying, '*Is* your father still alive? Have you *another* brother?' And we told him according to these words. Could we possibly have known that he would say, 'Bring your brother down'?"

8 Then Judah said to Israel his father, "Send the lad with me, and we will arise and go, that we may live and not die, both we and you *and* also our little ones.

9 "I myself will be surety for him; from my hand you shall require him. If I do not bring him *back* to you and set him before you, then let me bear the blame forever.

10 "For if we had not lingered, surely by now we would have returned this second time."

11 And their father Israel said to them, "If *it must be* so, then do this: Take some of the best fruits of the land in your vessels and carry down a present for the man—a little balm and a little honey, spices and myrrh, pistachio nuts and almonds.

12 "Take double money in your hand, and take back in your hand the money that was returned in the mouth of your sacks; perhaps it was an oversight.

13 "Take your brother also, and arise, go back to the man.

14 "And may God Almighty give you mercy before the man, that he may release your other brother and Benjamin. If I am bereaved, I am bereaved!"

15 So the men took that present and Benjamin, and they took double money in their hand, and arose and went down to Egypt; and they stood before Joseph.

16 When Joseph saw Benjamin with them, he said to the steward of his house, "Take *these* men to my home, and slaughter an animal and make ready; for *these* men will dine with me at noon."

17 Then the man did as Joseph ordered, and the man brought the men into Joseph's house.

18 Now the men were afraid because they were brought into Joseph's house; and they said, "*It is* because of the money, which was returned in our sacks the first time, that we are brought in, so that he may make a case against us and seize us, to take us as slaves with our donkeys."

19 When they drew near to the steward of Joseph's house, they talked with him at the door of the house,

20 and said, "O sir, we indeed came down the first time to buy food;

21 "but it happened, when we came to the encampment, that we opened our sacks, and there, *each* man's money *was* in the mouth of his sack, our money in full weight; so we have brought it back in our hand.

22 "And we have brought down other money in our hands to buy food. We do not know who put our money in our sacks."

23 But he said, "Peace *be* with you, do not be afraid. Your God and the God of your father has given you treasure in your sacks; I had your money." Then he brought Simeon out to them.

24 So the man brought the men into Joseph's house and gave *them* water, and they washed their feet; and he gave their donkeys feed.

25 Then they made the present ready for Joseph's coming at noon, for they heard that they would eat bread there.

26 And when Joseph came home, they brought him the present which *was* in their hand into the house, and bowed down before him to the earth.

27 Then he asked them about *their* well-being, and said, "*Is* your father well, the old man of whom you spoke? *Is* he still alive?"

28 And they answered, "Your servant our father *is* in good health; he *is* still alive." And they bowed their heads down and prostrated themselves.

29 Then he lifted his eyes and saw his brother Benjamin, his mother's son, and said, "*Is* this your younger brother of whom you spoke to me?" And he said, "God be gracious to you, my son."

30 Now his heart yearned for his brother; so Joseph made haste and sought *somewhere* to weep. And he went into *his* chamber and wept there.

31 Then he washed his face and came out; and he restrained himself, and said, "Serve the bread."

32 So they set him a place by himself, and them by themselves, and the Egyptians who ate with him by themselves; because the Egyptians could not eat food with the Hebrews, for that *is* an abomination to the Egyptians.

33 And they sat before him, the firstborn according to his birthright and the youngest according to his youth; and the men looked in astonishment at one another.

34 Then he took servings to them from before
him, but Benjamin's serving was five times as
much as any of theirs. So they drank and were
merry with him.

Joseph's Cup

44 And he commanded the steward of his
house, saying, "Fill the men's sacks with
food, as much as they can carry, and put each
man's money in the mouth of his sack.
2 "Also put my cup, the silver cup, in the
mouth of the sack of the youngest, and his
grain money." So he did according to the word
that Joseph had spoken.
3 As soon as the morning dawned, the men
were sent away, they and their donkeys.
4 When they had gone out of the city, *and*
were not *yet* far off, Joseph said to his steward,
"Get up, follow the men; and when you over-
take them, say to them, 'Why have you repaid
evil for good?
5 '*Is* not this *the one* from which my lord
drinks, and with which he indeed practices
divination? You have done evil in so doing.'"
6 So he overtook them, and he spoke to them
these same words.
7 And they said to him, "Why does my lord
say these words? Far be it from us that your
servants should do such a thing.
8 "Look, we brought back to you from the
land of Canaan the money which we found in
the mouth of our sacks. How then could we
steal silver or gold from your lord's house?
9 "With whomever of your servants it is
found, let him die, and we also will be my lord's
slaves."
10 And he said, "Now also *let* it *be* according
to your words; he with whom it is found shall
be my slave, and you shall be blameless."
11 Then each man speedily let down his sack
to the ground, and each opened his sack.
12 So he searched. He began with the oldest
and left off with the youngest; and the cup was
found in Benjamin's sack.
13 Then they tore their clothes, and each man
loaded his donkey and returned to the city.
14 So Judah and his brothers came to Jo-
seph's house, and he *was* still there; and they
fell before him on the ground.
15 And Joseph said to them, "What deed *is*
this you have done? Did you not know that
such a man as I can certainly practice divina-
tion?"
16 Then Judah said, "What shall we say to
my lord? What shall we speak? Or how shall
we clear ourselves? God has found out the iniq-
uity of your servants; here we are, my lord's
slaves, both we and *he* also with whom the cup
was found."
17 But he said, "Far be it from me that I
should do so; the man in whose hand the cup
was found, he shall be my slave. And as for
you, go up in peace to your father."

Judah Intercedes for Benjamin

18 Then Judah came near to him and said:
"O my lord, please let your servant speak a
word in my lord's hearing, and do not let your
anger burn against your servant; for you *are*
even like Pharaoh.
19 "My lord asked his servants, saying, 'Have
you a father or a brother?'
20 "And we said to my lord, 'We have a father,
an old man, and a child of *his* old age, *who is*
young; his brother is dead, and he alone is left
of his mother's children, and his father loves
him.'
21 "Then you said to your servants, 'Bring him
down to me, that I may set my eyes on him.'
22 "And we said to my lord, 'The lad cannot
leave his father, for *if* he should leave his fa-
ther, *his father* would die.'
23 "But you said to your servants, 'Unless
your youngest brother comes down with you,
you shall see my face no more.'
24 "So it was, when we went up to your ser-
vant my father, that we told him the words of
my lord.
25 "And our father said, 'Go back *and* buy us
a little food.'
26 "But we said, 'We cannot go down; if our
youngest brother is with us, then we will go
down; for we may not see the man's face unless
our youngest brother *is* with us.'
27 "Then your servant my father said to us,
'You know that my wife bore me two sons;
28 'and the one went out from me, and I said,
"Surely he is torn to pieces"; and I have not
seen him since.
29 'But if you take this one also from me, and
calamity befalls him, you shall bring down my
gray hair with sorrow to the grave.'
30 "Now therefore, when I come to your ser-
vant my father, and the lad *is* not with us, since
his life is bound up in the lad's life,
31 "it will happen, when he sees that the lad
is not *with us*, that he will die. So your servants
will bring down the gray hair of your servant
our father with sorrow to the grave.
32 "For your servant became surety for the
lad to my father, saying, 'If I do not bring him
back to you, then I shall bear the blame before
my father forever.'
33 "Now therefore, please let your servant re-
main instead of the lad as a slave to my lord,
and let the lad go up with his brothers.
34 "For how shall I go up to my father if the
lad *is* not with me, lest perhaps I see the evil
that would come upon my father?"

Joseph Revealed to His Brothers

45 Then Joseph could not restrain himself
before all those who stood by him, and
he cried out, "Make everyone go out from me!"
So no one stood with him while Joseph made
himself known to his brothers.
2 And he wept aloud, and the Egyptians and
the house of Pharaoh heard *it*.
3 Then Joseph said to his brothers, "I *am*
Joseph; does my father still live?" But his
brothers could not answer him, for they were
dismayed in his presence.
4 And Joseph said to his brothers, "Please
come near to me." So they came near. Then he
said: "I *am* Joseph your brother, whom you
sold into Egypt.
5 "But now, do not therefore be grieved or
angry with yourselves because you sold me
here; for God sent me before you to preserve
life.
6 "For these two years the famine *has been*
in the land, and *there are* still five years in
which *there will be* neither plowing nor har-
vesting.
7 "And God sent me before you to preserve
a posterity for you in the earth, and to save
your lives by a great deliverance.
8 "So now *it was* not you *who* sent me here,

but God; and He has made me a father to Pharaoh, and lord of all his house, and a ruler throughout all the land of Egypt.

9 "Hurry and go up to my father, and say to him, 'Thus says your son Joseph: "God has made me lord of all Egypt; come down to me, do not tarry.

10 "You shall dwell in the land of Goshen, and you shall be near to me, you and your children, your children's children, your flocks and your herds, and all that you have.

11 "There I will provide for you, lest you and your household, and all that you have, come to poverty; for *there are* still five years of famine."'

12 "And behold, your eyes and the eyes of my brother Benjamin see that *it is* my mouth that speaks to you.

13 "So you shall tell my father of all my glory in Egypt, and of all that you have seen; and you shall hurry and bring my father down here."

14 Then he fell on his brother Benjamin's neck and wept, and Benjamin wept on his neck.

15 Moreover he kissed all his brothers and wept over them, and after that his brothers talked with him.

16 Now the report of it was heard in Pharaoh's house, saying, "Joseph's brothers have come." So it pleased Pharaoh and his servants well.

17 And Pharaoh said to Joseph, "Say to your brothers, 'Do this: Load your animals and depart; go to the land of Canaan.

18 'Bring your father and your households and come to me; I will give you the best of the land of Egypt, and you will eat the fat of the land.

19 'Now you are commanded—do this: Take carts out of the land of Egypt for your little ones and your wives; bring your father and come.

20 'Also do not be concerned about your goods, for the best of all the land of Egypt *is* yours.'"

21 Then the sons of Israel did so; and Joseph gave them carts, according to the command of Pharaoh, and he gave them provisions for the journey.

22 He gave to all of them, to each man, changes of garments; but to Benjamin he gave three hundred *pieces* of silver and five changes of garments.

23 And he sent to his father these *things:* ten donkeys loaded with the good things of Egypt, and ten female donkeys loaded with grain, bread, and food for his father for the journey.

24 So he sent his brothers away, and they departed; and he said to them, "See that you do not become troubled along the way."

25 Then they went up out of Egypt, and came to the land of Canaan to Jacob their father.

26 And they told him, saying, "Joseph *is* still alive, and he *is* governor over all the land of Egypt." And Jacob's heart stood still, because he did not believe them.

27 But when they told him all the words which Joseph had said to them, and when he saw the carts which Joseph had sent to carry him, the spirit of Jacob their father revived.

28 Then Israel said, "*It is* enough. Joseph my son *is* still alive. I will go and see him before I die."

Jacob's Journey to Egypt

46 So Israel took his journey with all that he had, and came to Beersheba, and offered sacrifices to the God of his father Isaac.

2 Then God spoke to Israel in the visions of the night, and said, "Jacob, Jacob!" And he said, "Here I am."

3 So He said, "I *am* God, the God of your father; do not fear to go down to Egypt, for I will make of you a great nation there.

4 "I will go down with you to Egypt, and I will also surely bring you up *again;* and Joseph will put his hand on your eyes."

5 Then Jacob arose from Beersheba; and the sons of Israel carried their father Jacob, their little ones, and their wives, in the carts which Pharaoh had sent to carry him.

6 So they took their livestock and their goods, which they had acquired in the land of Canaan, and went to Egypt, Jacob and all his descendants with him.

7 His sons and his sons' sons, his daughters and his sons' daughters, and all his descendants he brought with him to Egypt.

8 Now these *were* the names of the children of Israel, Jacob and his sons, who went to Egypt: Reuben *was* Jacob's firstborn.

9 The sons of Reuben *were* Hanoch, Pallu, Hezron, and Carmi.

10 The sons of Simeon *were* Jemuel,[a] Jamin, Ohad, Jachin,[b] Zohar,[c] and Shaul, the son of a Canaanite woman.

11 The sons of Levi *were* Gershon, Kohath, and Merari.

12 The sons of Judah *were* Er, Onan, Shelah, Perez, and Zerah (but Er and Onan died in the land of Canaan). The sons of Perez were Hezron and Hamul.

13 The sons of Issachar *were* Tola, Puvah,[a] Job,[b] and Shimron.

14 The sons of Zebulun *were* Sered, Elon, and Jahleel.

15 These *were* the sons of Leah, whom she bore to Jacob in Padan Aram, with his daughter Dinah. All the persons, his sons and his daughters, *were* thirty-three.

16 The sons of Gad *were* Ziphion,[a] Haggi, Shuni, Ezbon,[b] Eri, Arodi,[c] and Areli.

17 The sons of Asher *were* Jimnah, Ishuah, Isui, Beriah, and Serah, their sister. And the sons of Beriah *were* Heber and Malchiel.

18 These *were* the sons of Zilpah, whom Laban gave to Leah his daughter; and these she bore to Jacob: sixteen persons.

19 The sons of Rachel, Jacob's wife, *were* Joseph and Benjamin.

20 And to Joseph in the land of Egypt were born Manasseh and Ephraim, whom Asenath, the daughter of Poti-Pherah priest of On, bore to him.

21 The sons of Benjamin *were* Belah, Becher,

46:10 [a]Spelled *Nemuel* in 1 Chronicles 4:24 [b]Called *Jarib* in 1 Chronicles 4:24 [c]Called *Zerah* in 1 Chronicles 4:24 **46:13** [a]Spelled *Puah* in 1 Chronicles 7:1 [b]Same as *Jashub* in Numbers 26:24 and 1 Chronicles 7:1 **46:16** [a]Spelled *Zephon* in Samaritan Pentateuch, Septuagint, and Numbers 26:15 [b]Called *Ozni* in Numbers 26:16 [c]Spelled *Arod* in Numbers 26:17

Ashbel, Gera, Naaman, Ehi, Rosh, Muppim,
Huppim,[a] and Ard.
22 These *were* the sons of Rachel, who were
born to Jacob: fourteen persons in all.
23 The son of Dan *was* Hushim.[a]
24 The sons of Naphtali *were* Jahzeel,[a] Guni,
Jezer, and Shillem.[b]
25 These *were* the sons of Bilhah, whom La-
ban gave to Rachel his daughter, and she bore
these to Jacob: seven persons in all.
26 All the persons who went with Jacob to
Egypt, who came from his body, besides Ja-
cob's sons' wives, *were* sixty-six persons in all.
27 And the sons of Joseph who were born to
him in Egypt *were* two persons. All the persons
of the house of Jacob who went to Egypt were
seventy.

Jacob Settles in Goshen

28 Then he sent Judah before him to Joseph,
to point out before him *the way* to Goshen.
And they came to the land of Goshen.
29 So Joseph made ready his chariot and
went up to Goshen to meet his father Israel;
and he presented himself to him, and fell on
his neck and wept on his neck a good while.
30 And Israel said to Joseph, "Now let me die,
since I have seen your face, because you *are*
still alive."
31 Then Joseph said to his brothers and to
his father's household, "I will go up and tell
Pharaoh, and say to him, 'My brothers and
those of my father's house, who *were* in the
land of Canaan, have come to me.
32 'And the men *are* shepherds, for their occu-
pation has been to feed livestock; and they
have brought their flocks, their herds, and all
that they have.'
33 "So it shall be, when Pharaoh calls you
and says, 'What is your occupation?'
34 "that you shall say, 'Your servants' occupa-
tion has been with livestock from our youth
even till now, both we *and* also our fathers,'
that you may dwell in the land of Goshen; for
every shepherd *is* an abomination to the Egyp-
tians."

47 Then Joseph went and told Pharaoh,
and said, "My father and my brothers,
their flocks and their herds and all that they
possess, have come from the land of Canaan;
and indeed they *are* in the land of Goshen."
2 And he took five men from among his
brothers and presented them to Pharaoh.
3 Then Pharaoh said to his brothers, "What
is your occupation?" And they said to Pharaoh,
"Your servants *are* shepherds, both we *and*
also our fathers."
4 And they said to Pharaoh, "We have come
to dwell in the land, because your servants
have no pasture for their flocks, for the famine
is severe in the land of Canaan. Now therefore,
please let your servants dwell in the land of
Goshen."
5 Then Pharaoh spoke to Joseph, saying,
"Your father and your brothers have come to
you.
6 "The land of Egypt *is* before you. Have
your father and brothers dwell in the best of
the land; let them dwell in the land of Goshen.
And if you know *any* competent men among
them, then make them chief herdsmen over my
livestock."
7 Then Joseph brought in his father Jacob
and set him before Pharaoh; and Jacob blessed
Pharaoh.
8 Pharaoh said to Jacob, "How old *are* you?"
9 And Jacob said to Pharaoh, "The days of
the years of my pilgrimage *are* one hundred
and thirty years; few and evil have been the
days of the years of my life, and they have not
attained to the days of the years of the life of
my fathers in the days of their pilgrimage."
10 So Jacob blessed Pharaoh, and went out
from before Pharaoh.
11 And Joseph situated his father and his
brothers, and gave them a possession in the
land of Egypt, in the best of the land, in the
land of Rameses, as Pharaoh had commanded.
12 Then Joseph provided his father, his
brothers, and all his father's household with
bread, according to the number in *their* fami-
lies.

Joseph Deals with the Famine

13 Now *there was* no bread in all the land;
for the famine *was* very severe, so that the land
of Egypt and the land of Canaan languished
because of the famine.
14 And Joseph gathered up all the money that
was found in the land of Egypt and in the land
of Canaan, for the grain which they bought;
and Joseph brought the money into Pharaoh's
house.
15 So when the money failed in the land of
Egypt and in the land of Canaan, all the Egyp-
tians came to Joseph and said, "Give us bread,
for why should we die in your presence? For
the money has failed."
16 Then Joseph said, "Give your livestock,
and I will give you *bread* for your livestock, if
the money is gone."
17 So they brought their livestock to Joseph,
and Joseph gave them bread *in exchange* for
the horses, the flocks, the cattle of the herds,
and for the donkeys. Thus he fed them with
bread *in exchange* for all their livestock that
year.
18 When that year had ended, they came to
him the next year and said to him, "We will
not hide from my lord that our money is gone;
my lord also has our herds of livestock. There
is nothing left in the sight of my lord but our
bodies and our lands.
19 "Why should we die before your eyes, both
we and our land? Buy us and our land for
bread, and we and our land will be servants of
Pharaoh; give *us* seed, that we may live and
not die, that the land may not be desolate."
20 Then Joseph bought all the land of Egypt
for Pharaoh; for every man of the Egyptians
sold his field, because the famine was severe
upon them. So the land became Pharaoh's.
21 And as for the people, he moved them into
the cities,[a] from *one* end of the borders of Egypt
to the *other* end.
22 Only the land of the priests he did not buy;
for the priests had rations *allotted to them*
by Pharaoh, and they ate their rations which
Pharaoh gave them; therefore they did not sell
their lands.
23 Then Joseph said to the people, "Indeed I

46:21 [a]Called *Hupham* in Numbers 26:39 **46:23** [a]Called *Shuham* in Numbers 26:42 **46:24** [a]Spelled *Jahziel* in 1 Chronicles 7:13 [b]Spelled *Shallum* in 1 Chronicles 7:13 **47:21** [a]Following Masoretic Text and Targum; Samaritan Pentateuch, Septuagint, and Vulgate read *made the people virtual slaves.*

have bought you and your land this day for
Pharaoh. Look, *here is* seed for you, and you
shall sow the land.
24 "And it shall come to pass in the harvest
that you shall give one-fifth to Pharaoh. Four-
fifths shall be your own, as seed for the field
and for your food, for those of your households
and as food for your little ones."
25 So they said, "You have saved our lives; let
us find favor in the sight of my lord, and we
will be Pharaoh's servants."
26 And Joseph made it a law over the land of
Egypt to this day, *that* Pharaoh should have
one-fifth, except for the land of the priests
only, *which* did not become Pharaoh's.

Joseph's Vow to Jacob

27 So Israel dwelt in the land of Egypt, in the
country of Goshen; and they had possessions
there and grew and multiplied exceedingly.
28 And Jacob lived in the land of Egypt seven-
teen years. So the length of Jacob's life was
one hundred and forty-seven years.
29 When the time drew near that Israel must
die, he called his son Joseph and said to him,
"Now if I have found favor in your sight, please
put your hand under my thigh, and deal kindly
and truly with me. Please do not bury me in
Egypt,
30 "but let me lie with my fathers; you shall
carry me out of Egypt and bury me in their
burial place." And he said, "I will do as you
have said."
31 Then he said, "Swear to me." And he
swore to him. So Israel bowed himself on the
head of the bed.

Jacob Blesses Joseph's Sons

48 Now it came to pass after these things
that Joseph was told, "Indeed your fa-
ther *is* sick"; and he took with him his two
sons, Manasseh and Ephraim.
2 And Jacob was told, "Look, your son Jo-
seph is coming to you"; and Israel strength-
ened himself and sat up on the bed.
3 Then Jacob said to Joseph: "God Almighty
appeared to me at Luz in the land of Canaan
and blessed me,
4 "and said to me, 'Behold, I will make you
fruitful and multiply you, and I will make of
you a multitude of people, and give this land
to your descendants after you *as* an everlasting
possession.'
5 "And now your two sons, Ephraim and Ma-
nasseh, who were born to you in the land of
Egypt before I came to you in Egypt, *are* mine;
as Reuben and Simeon, they shall be mine.
6 "Your offspring whom you beget after
them shall be yours; they will be called by the
name of their brothers in their inheritance.
7 "But as for me, when I came from Padan,
Rachel died beside me in the land of Canaan
on the way, when *there was* but a little distance
to go to Ephrath; and I buried her there on the
way to Ephrath (that is, Bethlehem)."
8 Then Israel saw Joseph's sons, and said,
"Who *are* these?"
9 Joseph said to his father, "They *are* my
sons, whom God has given me in this *place*."
And he said, "Please bring them to me, and I
will bless them."
10 Now the eyes of Israel were dim with age,
so that he could not see. Then Joseph brought
them near him, and he kissed them and em-
braced them.
11 And Israel said to Joseph, "I had not
thought to see your face; but in fact, God has
also shown me your offspring!"
12 So Joseph brought them from beside his
knees, and he bowed down with his face to the
earth.
13 And Joseph took them both, Ephraim with
his right hand toward Israel's left hand, and
Manasseh with his left hand toward Israel's
right hand, and brought *them* near him.
14 Then Israel stretched out his right hand
and laid *it* on Ephraim's head, who *was* the
younger, and his left hand on Manasseh's
head, guiding his hands knowingly, for Manas-
seh *was* the firstborn.
15 And he blessed Joseph, and said:

"God, before whom my fathers Abraham
and Isaac walked,
The God who has fed me all my life long
to this day,
16 The Angel who has redeemed me from all
evil,
Bless the lads;
Let my name be named upon them,
And the name of my fathers Abraham
and Isaac;
And let them grow into a multitude in the
midst of the earth."

17 Now when Joseph saw that his father laid
his right hand on the head of Ephraim, it dis-
pleased him; so he took hold of his father's
hand to remove it from Ephraim's head to Ma-
nasseh's head.
18 And Joseph said to his father, "Not so, my
father, for this *one is* the firstborn; put your
right hand on his head."
19 But his father refused and said, "I know,
my son, I know. He also shall become a people,
and he also shall be great; but truly his younger
brother shall be greater than he, and his de-
scendants shall become a multitude of na-
tions."
20 So he blessed them that day, saying, "By
you Israel will bless, saying, 'May God make
you as Ephraim and as Manasseh!'" And thus
he set Ephraim before Manasseh.
21 Then Israel said to Joseph, "Behold, I am
dying, but God will be with you and bring you
back to the land of your fathers.
22 "Moreover I have given to you one portion
above your brothers, which I took from the hand
of the Amorite with my sword and my bow."

Jacob's Last Words to His Sons

49 And Jacob called his sons and said,
"Gather together, that I may tell you
what shall befall you in the last days:

2 "Gather together and hear, you sons of
Jacob,
And listen to Israel your father.

3 "Reuben, you are my firstborn,
My might and the beginning of my
strength,
The excellency of dignity and the
excellency of power.
4 Unstable as water, you shall not excel,
Because you went up to your father's bed;
Then you defiled *it*—
He went up to my couch.

5 "Simeon and Levi *are* brothers;
Instruments of cruelty *are in* their
dwelling place.

6 Let not my soul enter their council;
Let not my honor be united to their
assembly;
For in their anger they slew a man,
And in their self-will they hamstrung an
ox.
7 Cursed *be* their anger, for *it is* fierce;
And their wrath, for it is cruel!
I will divide them in Jacob
And scatter them in Israel.

8 "Judah, you *are he* whom your brothers
shall praise;
Your hand *shall be* on the neck of your
enemies;
Your father's children shall bow down
before you.
9 Judah *is* a lion's whelp;
From the prey, my son, you have gone up.
He bows down, he lies down as a lion;
And as a lion, who shall rouse him?
10 The scepter shall not depart from Judah,
Nor a lawgiver from between his feet,
Until Shiloh comes;
And to Him *shall be* the obedience of the
people.
11 Binding his donkey to the vine,
And his donkey's colt to the choice vine,
He washed his garments in wine,
And his clothes in the blood of grapes.
12 His eyes *are* darker than wine,
And his teeth whiter than milk.

13 "Zebulun shall dwell by the haven of the
sea;
He *shall become* a haven for ships,
And his border shall adjoin Sidon.

14 "Issachar is a strong donkey,
Lying down between two burdens;
15 He saw that rest *was* good,
And that the land *was* pleasant;
He bowed his shoulder to bear *a burden*,
And became a band of slaves.

16 "Dan shall judge his people
As one of the tribes of Israel.
17 Dan shall be a serpent by the way,
A viper by the path,
That bites the horse's heels
So that its rider shall fall backward.
18 I have waited for your salvation, O LORD!

19 "Gad, a troop shall tramp upon him,
But he shall triumph at last.

20 "Bread from Asher *shall be* rich,
And he shall yield royal dainties.

21 "Naphtali *is* a deer let loose;
He uses beautiful words.

22 "Joseph *is* a fruitful bough,
A fruitful bough by a well;
His branches run over the wall.
23 The archers have bitterly grieved him,
Shot *at him* and hated him.
24 But his bow remained in strength,
And the arms of his hands were made
strong
By the hands of the Mighty *God* of Jacob
(From there *is* the Shepherd, the Stone of
Israel),
25 By the God of your father who will help
you,
And by the Almighty who will bless you
With blessings of heaven above,
Blessings of the deep that lies beneath,
Blessings of the breasts and of the womb.
26 The blessings of your father
Have excelled the blessings of my
ancestors,
Up to the utmost bound of the everlasting
hills.
They shall be on the head of Joseph,
And on the crown of the head of him who
was separate from his brothers.

27 "Benjamin is a ravenous wolf;
In the morning he shall devour the prey,
And at night he shall divide the spoil."

28 All these *are* the twelve tribes of Israel,
and this *is* what their father spoke to them.
And he blessed them; he blessed each one ac-
cording to his own blessing.

Jacob's Death and Burial

29 Then he charged them and said to them:
"I am to be gathered to my people; bury me
with my fathers in the cave that *is* in the field
of Ephron the Hittite,
30 "in the cave that *is* in the field of Mach-
pelah, which *is* before Mamre in the land of
Canaan, which Abraham bought with the field
of Ephron the Hittite as a possession for a
burial place.
31 "There they buried Abraham and Sarah
his wife, there they buried Isaac and Rebekah
his wife, and there I buried Leah.
32 "The field and the cave that *is* there *were*
purchased from the sons of Heth."
33 And when Jacob had finished command-
ing his sons, he drew his feet up into the bed
and breathed his last, and was gathered to his
people.

50 Then Joseph fell on his father's face and
wept over him, and kissed him.
2 And Joseph commanded his servants the
physicians to embalm his father. So the physi-
cians embalmed Israel.
3 Forty days were required for him, for such
are the days required for those who are em-
balmed; and the Egyptians mourned for him
seventy days.
4 Now when the days of his mourning were
past, Joseph spoke to the household of Pha-
raoh, saying, "If now I have found favor in your
eyes, please speak in the hearing of Pharaoh,
saying,
5 'My father made me swear, saying, "Be-
hold, I am dying; in my grave which I dug for
myself in the land of Canaan, there you shall
bury me." Now therefore, please let me go up
and bury my father, and I will come back.'"
6 And Pharaoh said, "Go up and bury your
father, as he made you swear."
7 So Joseph went up to bury his father; and
with him went up all the servants of Pharaoh,
the elders of his house, and all the elders of the
land of Egypt,
8 as well as all the house of Joseph, his
brothers, and his father's house. Only their lit-
tle ones, their flocks, and their herds they left
in the land of Goshen.
9 And there went up with him both chariots
and horsemen, and it was a very great gath-
ering.
10 Then they came to the threshing floor of
Atad, which *is* beyond the Jordan, and they
mourned there with a great and very solemn
lamentation. He observed seven days of
mourning for his father.
11 And when the inhabitants of the land, the

Canaanites, saw the mourning at the threshing
floor of Atad, they said, "This *is* a deep mourning of the Egyptians." Therefore its name was
called Abel Mizraim,[a] which *is* beyond the
Jordan.
12 So his sons did for him just as he had commanded them.
13 For his sons carried him to the land of Canaan, and buried him in the cave of the field
of Machpelah, before Mamre, which Abraham
bought with the field from Ephron the Hittite
as property for a burial place.
14 And after he had buried his father, Joseph
returned to Egypt, he and his brothers and all
who went up with him to bury his father.

Joseph Reassures His Brothers

15 When Joseph's brothers saw that their father was dead, they said, "Perhaps Joseph will
hate us, and may actually repay us for all the
evil which we did to him."
16 So they sent *messengers* to Joseph, saying,
"Before your father died he commanded,
saying,
17 'Thus you shall say to Joseph: "I beg you,
please forgive the trespass of your brothers
and their sin; for they did evil to you."' Now,
please, forgive the trespass of the servants of
the God of your father." And Joseph wept when
they spoke to him.
18 Then his brothers also went and fell down
before his face, and they said, "Behold, we *are*
your servants."
19 Joseph said to them, "Do not be afraid, for
am I in the place of God?
20 "But as for you, you meant evil against me;
but God meant it for good, in order to bring it
about as *it is* this day, to save many people alive.
21 "Now therefore, do not be afraid; I will
provide for you and your little ones." And he
comforted them and spoke kindly to them.

Death of Joseph

22 So Joseph dwelt in Egypt, he and his father's household. And Joseph lived one hundred and ten years.
23 Joseph saw Ephraim's children to the third
generation. The children of Machir, the son of
Manasseh, were also brought up on Joseph's
knees.
24 And Joseph said to his brethren, "I am dying; but God will surely visit you, and bring
you out of this land to the land of which He
swore to Abraham, to Isaac, and to Jacob."
25 Then Joseph took an oath from the children
of Israel, saying, "God will surely visit you,
and you shall carry up my bones from here."
26 So Joseph died, *being* one hundred and ten
years old; and they embalmed him, and he was
put in a coffin in Egypt.

The Second Book of Moses Called

EXODUS

Israel's Suffering in Egypt

1 Now these *are* the names of the children of
Israel who came to Egypt; each man and
his household came with Jacob:
2 Reuben, Simeon, Levi, and Judah;
3 Issachar, Zebulun, and Benjamin;
4 Dan, Naphtali, Gad, and Asher.
5 All those who were descendants[a] of Jacob
were seventy[b] persons (for Joseph was in Egypt
already).
6 And Joseph died, all his brothers, and all
that generation.
7 But the children of Israel were fruitful and
increased abundantly, multiplied and grew exceedingly mighty; and the land was filled with
them.
8 Now there arose a new king over Egypt,
who did not know Joseph.
9 And he said to his people, "Look, the people of the children of Israel *are* more and
mightier than we;
10 "come, let us deal shrewdly with them, lest
they multiply, and it happen, in the event of
war, that they also join our enemies and fight
against us, and *so* go up out of the land."
11 Therefore they set taskmasters over them
to afflict them with their burdens. And they
built for Pharaoh supply cities, Pithom and Raamses.
12 But the more they afflicted them, the more
they multiplied and grew. And they were in
dread of the children of Israel.
13 So the Egyptians made the children of Israel serve with rigor.
14 And they made their lives bitter with hard
bondage—in mortar, in brick, and in all manner of service in the field. All their service in
which they made them serve *was* with rigor.
15 Then the king of Egypt spoke to the Hebrew midwives, of whom the name of one *was*
Shiphrah and the name of the other Puah;
16 and he said, "When you do the duties of a
midwife for the Hebrew women, and see *them*
on the birthstools, if it *is* a son, then you shall
kill him; but if it *is* a daughter, then she shall
live."
17 But the midwives feared God, and did not
do as the king of Egypt commanded them, but
saved the male children alive.
18 So the king of Egypt called for the midwives and said to them, "Why have you done
this thing, and saved the male children alive?"
19 And the midwives said to Pharaoh, "Because the Hebrew women *are* not like the
Egyptian women; for they *are* lively and give
birth before the midwives come to them."
20 Therefore God dealt well with the midwives, and the people multiplied and grew very
mighty.
21 And so it was, because the midwives feared
God, that He provided households for them.
22 So Pharaoh commanded all his people,
saying, "Every son who is born[a] you shall cast
into the river, and every daughter you shall
save alive."

50:11 [a]Literally *Mourning of Egypt* **1:5** [a]Literally *who came from the loins of* [b]Dead Sea Scrolls and Septuagint read *seventy-five* (compare Acts 7:14). **1:22** [a]Samaritan Pentateuch, Septuagint, and Targum add *to the Hebrews.*

Moses Is Born

2 And a man of the house of Levi went and took *as wife* a daughter of Levi.

2 So the woman conceived and bore a son. And when she saw that he *was* a beautiful *child*, she hid him three months.

3 But when she could no longer hide him, she took an ark of bulrushes for him, daubed it with asphalt and pitch, put the child in it, and laid *it* in the reeds by the river's bank.

4 And his sister stood afar off, to know what would be done to him.

5 Then the daughter of Pharaoh came down to bathe at the river. And her maidens walked along the riverside; and when she saw the ark among the reeds, she sent her maid to get it.

6 And when she opened *it*, she saw the child, and behold, the baby wept. So she had compassion on him, and said, "This is one of the Hebrews' children."

7 Then his sister said to Pharaoh's daughter, "Shall I go and call a nurse for you from the Hebrew women, that she may nurse the child for you?"

8 And Pharaoh's daughter said to her, "Go." So the maiden went and called the child's mother.

9 Then Pharaoh's daughter said to her, "Take this child away and nurse him for me, and I will give *you* your wages." So the woman took the child and nursed him.

10 And the child grew, and she brought him to Pharaoh's daughter, and he became her son. So she called his name Moses,[a] saying, "Because I drew him out of the water."

Moses Flees to Midian

11 Now it came to pass in those days, when Moses was grown, that he went out to his brethren and looked at their burdens. And he saw an Egyptian beating a Hebrew, one of his brethren.

12 So he looked this way and that way, and when he saw no one, he killed the Egyptian and hid him in the sand.

13 And when he went out the second day, behold, two Hebrew men were fighting, and he said to the one who did the wrong, "Why are you striking your companion?"

14 Then he said, "Who made you a prince and a judge over us? Do you intend to kill me as you killed the Egyptian?" So Moses feared and said, "Surely this thing is known!"

15 When Pharaoh heard of this matter, he sought to kill Moses. But Moses fled from the face of Pharaoh and dwelt in the land of Midian; and he sat down by a well.

16 Now the priest of Midian had seven daughters. And they came and drew water, and they filled the troughs to water their father's flock.

17 Then the shepherds came and drove them away; but Moses stood up and helped them, and watered their flock.

18 When they came to Reuel their father, he said, "How *is it that* you have come so soon today?"

19 And they said, "An Egyptian delivered us from the hand of the shepherds, and he also drew enough water for us and watered the flock."

20 So he said to his daughters, "And where *is* he? Why *is* it *that* you have left the man? Call him, that he may eat bread."

21 Then Moses was content to live with the man, and he gave Zipporah his daughter to Moses.

22 And she bore *him* a son. He called his name Gershom,[a] for he said, "I have been a stranger in a foreign land."

23 Now it happened in the process of time that the king of Egypt died. Then the children of Israel groaned because of the bondage, and they cried out; and their cry came up to God because of the bondage.

24 So God heard their groaning, and God remembered His covenant with Abraham, with Isaac, and with Jacob.

25 And God looked upon the children of Israel, and God acknowledged *them*.

Moses at the Burning Bush

3 Now Moses was tending the flock of Jethro his father-in-law, the priest of Midian. And he led the flock to the back of the desert, and came to Horeb, the mountain of God.

2 And the Angel of the LORD appeared to him in a flame of fire from the midst of a bush. So he looked, and behold, the bush was burning with fire, but the bush *was* not consumed.

3 Then Moses said, "I will now turn aside and see this great sight, why the bush does not burn."

4 So when the LORD saw that he turned aside to look, God called to him from the midst of the bush and said, "Moses, Moses!" And he said, "Here I am."

5 Then He said, "Do not draw near this place. Take your sandals off your feet, for the place where you stand *is* holy ground."

6 Moreover He said, "I *am* the God of your father—the God of Abraham, the God of Isaac, and the God of Jacob." And Moses hid his face, for he was afraid to look upon God.

7 And the LORD said: "I have surely seen the oppression of My people who *are* in Egypt, and have heard their cry because of their taskmasters, for I know their sorrows.

8 "So I have come down to deliver them out of the hand of the Egyptians, and to bring them up from that land to a good and large land, to a land flowing with milk and honey, to the place of the Canaanites and the Hittites and the Amorites and the Perizzites and the Hivites and the Jebusites.

9 "Now therefore, behold, the cry of the children of Israel has come to Me, and I have also seen the oppression with which the Egyptians oppress them.

10 "Come now, therefore, and I will send you to Pharaoh that you may bring My people, the children of Israel, out of Egypt."

11 But Moses said to God, "Who *am* I that I should go to Pharaoh, and that I should bring the children of Israel out of Egypt?"

12 So He said, "I will certainly be with you. And this *shall be* a sign to you that I have sent you: When you have brought the people out of Egypt, you shall serve God on this mountain."

13 Then Moses said to God, "Indeed, *when* I come to the children of Israel and say to them, 'The God of your fathers has sent me to you,' and they say to me, 'What *is* His name?' what shall I say to them?"

14 And God said to Moses, "I AM WHO I

2:10 [a]Literally *Drawn Out* **2:22** [a]Literally *Stranger There*

AM." And He said, "Thus you shall say to the
children of Israel, 'I AM has sent me to you.'"
15 Moreover God said to Moses, "Thus you
shall say to the children of Israel: 'The LORD
God of your fathers, the God of Abraham, the
God of Isaac, and the God of Jacob, has sent
me to you. This *is* My name forever, and this *is*
My memorial to all generations.'
16 "Go and gather the elders of Israel together, and say to them, 'The LORD God of
your fathers, the God of Abraham, of Isaac,
and of Jacob, appeared to me, saying, "I have
surely visited you and *seen* what is done to you
in Egypt;
17 "and I have said I will bring you up out
of the affliction of Egypt to the land of the
Canaanites and the Hittites and the Amorites
and the Perizzites and the Hivites and the Jebusites, to a land flowing with milk and honey."'
18 "Then they will heed your voice; and you
shall come, you and the elders of Israel, to the
king of Egypt; and you shall say to him, 'The
LORD God of the Hebrews has met with us;
and now, please, let us go three days' journey
into the wilderness, that we may sacrifice to
the LORD our God.'
19 "But I am sure that the king of Egypt will
not let you go, no, not even by a mighty hand.
20 "So I will stretch out My hand and strike
Egypt with all My wonders which I will do in
its midst; and after that he will let you go.
21 "And I will give this people favor in the
sight of the Egyptians; and it shall be, when
you go, that you shall not go empty-handed.
22 "But every woman shall ask of her neighbor, namely, of her who dwells near her house,
articles of silver, articles of gold, and clothing;
and you shall put *them* on your sons and on
your daughters. So you shall plunder the Egyptians."

Miraculous Signs for Pharaoh

4 Then Moses answered and said, "But suppose they will not believe me or listen to
my voice; suppose they say, 'The LORD has not
appeared to you.'"
2 So the LORD said to him, "What *is* that in
your hand?" He said, "A rod."
3 And He said, "Cast it on the ground." So
he cast it on the ground, and it became a serpent; and Moses fled from it.
4 Then the LORD said to Moses, "Reach out
your hand and take *it* by the tail" (and he
reached out his hand and caught it, and it became a rod in his hand),
5 "that they may believe that the LORD God
of their fathers, the God of Abraham, the God
of Isaac, and the God of Jacob, has appeared
to you."
6 Furthermore the LORD said to him, "Now
put your hand in your bosom." And he put his
hand in his bosom, and when he took it out,
behold, his hand *was* leprous, like snow.
7 And He said, "Put your hand in your bosom again." So he put his hand in his bosom
again, and drew it out of his bosom, and behold, it was restored like his *other* flesh.
8 "Then it will be, if they do not believe you,
nor heed the message of the first sign, that they
may believe the message of the latter sign.
9 "And it shall be, if they do not believe even
these two signs, or listen to your voice, that
you shall take water from the river[a] and pour
it on the dry *land*. The water which you take
from the river will become blood on the dry
land."
10 Then Moses said to the LORD, "O my Lord,
I *am* not eloquent, neither before nor since You
have spoken to Your servant; but I *am* slow of
speech and slow of tongue."
11 So the LORD said to him, "Who has made
man's mouth? Or who makes the mute, the deaf,
the seeing, or the blind? *Have* not I, the LORD?
12 "Now therefore, go, and I will be with your
mouth and teach you what you shall say."
13 But he said, "O my Lord, please send by
the hand of whomever *else* You may send."
14 So the anger of the LORD was kindled
against Moses, and He said: "Is not Aaron the
Levite your brother? I know that he can speak
well. And look, he is also coming out to meet
you. When he sees you, he will be glad in his
heart.
15 "Now you shall speak to him and put the
words in his mouth. And I will be with your
mouth and with his mouth, and I will teach you
what you shall do.
16 "So he shall be your spokesman to the people. And he himself shall be as a mouth for
you, and you shall be to him as God.
17 "And you shall take this rod in your hand,
with which you shall do the signs."

Moses Goes to Egypt

18 So Moses went and returned to Jethro his
father-in-law, and said to him, "Please let me
go and return to my brethren who *are* in Egypt,
and see whether they are still alive." And
Jethro said to Moses, "Go in peace."
19 Now the LORD said to Moses in Midian,
"Go, return to Egypt; for all the men who
sought your life are dead."
20 Then Moses took his wife and his sons and
set them on a donkey, and he returned to the
land of Egypt. And Moses took the rod of God
in his hand.
21 And the LORD said to Moses, "When you
go back to Egypt, see that you do all those
wonders before Pharaoh which I have put in
your hand. But I will harden his heart, so that
he will not let the people go.
22 "Then you shall say to Pharaoh, 'Thus says
the LORD: "Israel *is* My son, My firstborn.
23 "So I say to you, let My son go that he may
serve Me. But if you refuse to let him go, indeed
I will kill your son, your firstborn."'"
24 And it came to pass on the way, at the
encampment, that the LORD met him and
sought to kill him.
25 Then Zipporah took a sharp stone and cut
off the foreskin of her son and cast *it* at *Moses'*[a]
feet, and said, "Surely you *are* a husband of
blood to me!"
26 So He let him go. Then she said, "*You are*
a husband of blood!"—because of the circumcision.
27 And the LORD said to Aaron, "Go into the
wilderness to meet Moses." So he went and
met him on the mountain of God, and kissed
him.
28 So Moses told Aaron all the words of the
LORD who had sent him, and all the signs
which He had commanded him.
29 Then Moses and Aaron went and gathered
together all the elders of the children of Israel.
30 And Aaron spoke all the words which the

4:9 [a]That is, the Nile **4:25** [a]Literally *his*

LORD had spoken to Moses. Then he did the
signs in the sight of the people.
31 So the people believed; and when they
heard that the LORD had visited the children
of Israel and that He had looked on their affliction,
then they bowed their heads and worshiped.

First Encounter with Pharaoh

5 Afterward Moses and Aaron went in and
told Pharaoh, "Thus says the LORD God of
Israel: 'Let My people go, that they may hold a
feast to Me in the wilderness.'"
2 And Pharaoh said, "Who *is* the LORD, that
I should obey His voice to let Israel go? I do
not know the LORD, nor will I let Israel go."
3 So they said, "The God of the Hebrews
has met with us. Please, let us go three days'
journey into the desert and sacrifice to the
LORD our God, lest He fall upon us with pestilence
or with the sword."
4 Then the king of Egypt said to them, "Moses
and Aaron, why do you take the people
from their work? Get *back* to your labor."
5 And Pharaoh said, "Look, the people of
the land *are* many now, and you make them
rest from their labor!"
6 So the same day Pharaoh commanded the
taskmasters of the people and their officers,
saying,
7 "You shall no longer give the people straw
to make brick as before. Let them go and
gather straw for themselves.
8 "And you shall lay on them the quota of
bricks which they made before. You shall not
reduce it. For they are idle; therefore they cry
out, saying, 'Let us go *and* sacrifice to our God.'
9 "Let more work be laid on the men, that
they may labor in it, and let them not regard
false words."
10 And the taskmasters of the people and
their officers went out and spoke to the people,
saying, "Thus says Pharaoh: 'I will not give
you straw.
11 'Go, get yourselves straw where you can
find it; yet none of your work will be reduced.'"
12 So the people were scattered abroad
throughout all the land of Egypt to gather stubble
instead of straw.
13 And the taskmasters forced *them* to hurry,
saying, "Fulfill your work, *your* daily quota, as
when there was straw."
14 Also the officers of the children of Israel,
whom Pharaoh's taskmasters had set over
them, were beaten *and* were asked, "Why have
you not fulfilled your task in making brick
both yesterday and today, as before?"
15 Then the officers of the children of Israel
came and cried out to Pharaoh, saying, "Why
are you dealing thus with your servants?
16 "There is no straw given to your servants,
and they say to us, 'Make brick!' And indeed
your servants *are* beaten, but the fault *is* in
your *own* people."
17 But he said, "You *are* idle! Idle! Therefore
you say, 'Let us go *and* sacrifice to the LORD.'
18 "Therefore go now *and* work; for no straw
shall be given you, yet you shall deliver the
quota of bricks."
19 And the officers of the children of Israel
saw *that* they *were* in trouble after it was said,
"You shall not reduce *any* bricks from your
daily quota."
20 Then, as they came out from Pharaoh, they
met Moses and Aaron who stood there to meet
them.
21 And they said to them, "Let the LORD look
on you and judge, because you have made us
abhorrent in the sight of Pharaoh and in the
sight of his servants, to put a sword in their
hand to kill us."

Israel's Deliverance Assured

22 So Moses returned to the LORD and said,
"Lord, why have You brought trouble on this
people? Why *is* it You have sent me?
23 "For since I came to Pharaoh to speak in
Your name, he has done evil to this people;
neither have You delivered Your people at all."
6 Then the LORD said to Moses, "Now you
shall see what I will do to Pharaoh. For with
a strong hand he will let them go, and with a
strong hand he will drive them out of his land."
2 And God spoke to Moses and said to him:
"I *am* the LORD.
3 "I appeared to Abraham, to Isaac, and to
Jacob, as God Almighty, but *by* My name
LORD[a] I was not known to them.
4 "I have also established My covenant with
them, to give them the land of Canaan, the
land of their pilgrimage, in which they were
strangers.
5 "And I have also heard the groaning of the
children of Israel whom the Egyptians keep in
bondage, and I have remembered My covenant.
6 "Therefore say to the children of Israel: 'I
am the LORD; I will bring you out from under
the burdens of the Egyptians, I will rescue you
from their bondage, and I will redeem you with
an outstretched arm and with great judgments.
7 'I will take you as My people, and I will be
your God. Then you shall know that I *am* the
LORD your God who brings you out from under
the burdens of the Egyptians.
8 'And I will bring you into the land which I
swore to give to Abraham, Isaac, and Jacob;
and I will give it to you *as* a heritage: I *am* the
LORD.'"
9 So Moses spoke thus to the children of
Israel; but they did not heed Moses, because of
anguish of spirit and cruel bondage.
10 And the LORD spoke to Moses, saying,
11 "Go in, tell Pharaoh king of Egypt to let
the children of Israel go out of his land."
12 And Moses spoke before the LORD, saying,
"The children of Israel have not heeded me.
How then shall Pharaoh heed me, for I *am* of
uncircumcised lips?"
13 Then the LORD spoke to Moses and Aaron,
and gave them a command for the children of
Israel and for Pharaoh king of Egypt, to bring
the children of Israel out of the land of Egypt.

The Family of Moses and Aaron

14 These *are* the heads of their fathers'
houses: The sons of Reuben, the firstborn of
Israel, *were* Hanoch, Pallu, Hezron, and Carmi.
These are the families of Reuben.
15 And the sons of Simeon *were* Jemuel,[a] Jamin,
Ohad, Jachin, Zohar, and Shaul the son
of a Canaanite woman. These *are* the families
of Simeon.
16 These *are* the names of the sons of Levi according
to their generations: Gershon, Kohath,

6:3 [a]Hebrew *YHWH*, traditionally *Jehovah* **6:15** [a]Spelled *Nemuel* in Numbers 26:12

and Merari. And the years of the life of Levi
were one hundred and thirty-seven.
17 The sons of Gershon *were* Libni and Shimi
according to their families.
18 And the sons of Kohath *were* Amram, Iz-
har, Hebron, and Uzziel. And the years of the
life of Kohath *were* one hundred and thirty-
three.
19 The sons of Merari *were* Mahli and Mushi.
These *are* the families of Levi according to
their generations.
20 Now Amram took for himself Jochebed,
his father's sister, as wife; and she bore him
Aaron and Moses. And the years of the life of
Amram *were* one hundred and thirty-seven.
21 The sons of Izhar *were* Korah, Nepheg,
and Zichri.
22 And the sons of Uzziel *were* Mishael, Elza-
phan, and Zithri.
23 Aaron took to himself Elisheba, daughter
of Amminadab, sister of Nahshon, as wife; and
she bore him Nadab, Abihu, Eleazar, and Ith-
amar.
24 And the sons of Korah *were* Assir, Elka-
nah, and Abiasaph. These are the families of
the Korahites.
25 Eleazar, Aaron's son, took for himself one
of the daughters of Putiel as wife; and she bore
him Phinehas. These *are* the heads of the fa-
thers' houses of the Levites according to their
families.
26 These *are the same* Aaron and Moses to
whom the LORD said, "Bring out the children
of Israel from the land of Egypt according to
their armies."
27 These *are* the ones who spoke to Pharaoh
king of Egypt, to bring out the children of Is-
rael from Egypt. These *are the same* Moses
and Aaron.

Aaron Is Moses' Spokesman

28 And it came to pass, on the day the LORD
spoke to Moses in the land of Egypt,
29 that the LORD spoke to Moses, saying, "I
am the LORD. Speak to Pharaoh king of Egypt
all that I say to you."
30 But Moses said before the LORD, "Behold,
I *am* of uncircumcised lips, and how shall Pha-
raoh heed me?"
7 So the LORD said to Moses: "See, I have
made you *as* God to Pharaoh, and Aaron
your brother shall be your prophet.
2 "You shall speak all that I command you.
And Aaron your brother shall tell Pharaoh to
send the children of Israel out of his land.
3 "And I will harden Pharaoh's heart, and
multiply My signs and My wonders in the land
of Egypt.
4 "But Pharaoh will not heed you, so that I
may lay My hand on Egypt and bring My ar-
mies *and* My people, the children of Israel, out
of the land of Egypt by great judgments.
5 "And the Egyptians shall know that I *am*
the LORD, when I stretch out My hand on
Egypt and bring out the children of Israel from
among them."
6 Then Moses and Aaron did *so;* just as the
LORD commanded them, so they did.
7 And Moses *was* eighty years old and
Aaron eighty-three years old when they spoke
to Pharaoh.

Aaron's Miraculous Rod

8 Then the LORD spoke to Moses and Aaron,
saying,
9 "When Pharaoh speaks to you, saying,
'Show a miracle for yourselves,' then you shall
say to Aaron, 'Take your rod and cast *it* before
Pharaoh, *and* let it become a serpent.' "
10 So Moses and Aaron went in to Pharaoh,
and they did so, just as the LORD commanded.
And Aaron cast down his rod before Pharaoh
and before his servants, and it became a ser-
pent.
11 But Pharaoh also called the wise men and
the sorcerers; so the magicians of Egypt, they
also did in like manner with their enchant-
ments.
12 For every man threw down his rod, and
they became serpents. But Aaron's rod swal-
lowed up their rods.
13 And Pharaoh's heart grew hard, and he
did not heed them, as the LORD had said.

The First Plague: Waters Become Blood

14 So the LORD said to Moses: "Pharaoh's
heart *is* hard; he refuses to let the people go.
15 "Go to Pharaoh in the morning, when he
goes out to the water, and you shall stand by
the river's bank to meet him; and the rod which
was turned to a serpent you shall take in your
hand.
16 "And you shall say to him, 'The LORD God
of the Hebrews has sent me to you, saying,
"Let My people go, that they may serve Me
in the wilderness"; but indeed, until now you
would not hear!
17 'Thus says the LORD: "By this you shall
know that I *am* the LORD. Behold, I will strike
the waters which *are* in the river with the rod
that *is* in my hand, and they shall be turned to
blood.
18 "And the fish that *are* in the river shall die,
the river shall stink, and the Egyptians will
loathe to drink the water of the river." ' "
19 Then the LORD spoke to Moses, "Say to
Aaron, 'Take your rod and stretch out your
hand over the waters of Egypt, over their
streams, over their rivers, over their ponds,
and over all their pools of water, that they may
become blood. And there shall be blood
throughout all the land of Egypt, both in *buck-
ets of* wood and *pitchers of* stone.' "
20 And Moses and Aaron did so, just as the
LORD commanded. So he lifted up the rod and
struck the waters that *were* in the river, in the
sight of Pharaoh and in the sight of his ser-
vants. And all the waters that *were* in the river
were turned to blood.
21 The fish that *were* in the river died, the
river stank, and the Egyptians could not drink
the water of the river. So there was blood
throughout all the land of Egypt.
22 Then the magicians of Egypt did so with
their enchantments; and Pharaoh's heart grew
hard, and he did not heed them, as the LORD
had said.
23 And Pharaoh turned and went into his
house. Neither was his heart moved by this.
24 So all the Egyptians dug all around the
river for water to drink, because they could not
drink the water of the river.
25 And seven days passed after the LORD had
struck the river.

The Second Plague: Frogs

8 And the LORD spoke to Moses, "Go to Pha-
raoh and say to him, 'Thus says the LORD:
"Let My people go, that they may serve Me.

2 "But if you refuse to let *them* go, behold, I will smite all your territory with frogs.

3 "So the river shall bring forth frogs abundantly, which shall go up and come into your house, into your bedroom, on your bed, into the houses of your servants, on your people, into your ovens, and into your kneading bowls.

4 "And the frogs shall come up on you, on your people, and on all your servants."'"

5 Then the LORD spoke to Moses, "Say to Aaron, 'Stretch out your hand with your rod over the streams, over the rivers, and over the ponds, and cause frogs to come up on the land of Egypt.'"

6 So Aaron stretched out his hand over the waters of Egypt, and the frogs came up and covered the land of Egypt.

7 And the magicians did so with their enchantments, and brought up frogs on the land of Egypt.

8 Then Pharaoh called for Moses and Aaron, and said, "Entreat the LORD that He may take away the frogs from me and from my people; and I will let the people go, that they may sacrifice to the LORD."

9 And Moses said to Pharaoh, "Accept the honor of saying when I shall intercede for you, for your servants, and for your people, to destroy the frogs from you and your houses, *that* they may remain in the river only."

10 So he said, "Tomorrow." And he said, "*Let it be* according to your word, that you may know that *there is* no one like the LORD our God.

11 "And the frogs shall depart from you, from your houses, from your servants, and from your people. They shall remain in the river only."

12 Then Moses and Aaron went out from Pharaoh. And Moses cried out to the LORD concerning the frogs which He had brought against Pharaoh.

13 So the LORD did according to the word of Moses. And the frogs died out of the houses, out of the courtyards, and out of the fields.

14 They gathered them together in heaps, and the land stank.

15 But when Pharaoh saw that there was relief, he hardened his heart and did not heed them, as the LORD had said.

The Third Plague: Lice

16 So the LORD said to Moses, "Say to Aaron, 'Stretch out your rod, and strike the dust of the land, so that it may become lice throughout all the land of Egypt.'"

17 And they did so. For Aaron stretched out his hand with his rod and struck the dust of the earth, and it became lice on man and beast. All the dust of the land became lice throughout all the land of Egypt.

18 Now the magicians so worked with their enchantments to bring forth lice, but they could not. So there were lice on man and beast.

19 Then the magicians said to Pharaoh, "This *is* the finger of God." But Pharaoh's heart grew hard, and he did not heed them, just as the LORD had said.

The Fourth Plague: Flies

20 And the LORD said to Moses, "Rise early in the morning and stand before Pharaoh as he comes out to the water. Then say to him, 'Thus says the LORD: "Let My people go, that they may serve Me.

21 "Or else, if you will not let My people go, behold, I will send swarms *of flies* on you and your servants, on your people and into your houses. The houses of the Egyptians shall be full of swarms *of flies*, and also the ground on which they *stand*.

22 "And in that day I will set apart the land of Goshen, in which My people dwell, that no swarms *of flies* shall be there, in order that you may know that I *am* the LORD in the midst of the land.

23 "I will make a difference[a] between My people and your people. Tomorrow this sign shall be."'"

24 And the LORD did so. Thick swarms *of flies* came into the house of Pharaoh, *into* his servants' houses, and into all the land of Egypt. The land was corrupted because of the swarms *of flies*.

25 Then Pharaoh called for Moses and Aaron, and said, "Go, sacrifice to your God in the land."

26 And Moses said, "It is not right to do so, for we would be sacrificing the abomination of the Egyptians to the LORD our God. If we sacrifice the abomination of the Egyptians before their eyes, then will they not stone us?

27 "We will go three days' journey into the wilderness and sacrifice to the LORD our God as He will command us."

28 So Pharaoh said, "I will let you go, that you may sacrifice to the LORD your God in the wilderness; only you shall not go very far away. Intercede for me."

29 Then Moses said, "Indeed I am going out from you, and I will entreat the LORD, that the swarms *of flies* may depart tomorrow from Pharaoh, from his servants, and from his people. But let Pharaoh not deal deceitfully anymore in not letting the people go to sacrifice to the LORD."

30 So Moses went out from Pharaoh and entreated the LORD.

31 And the LORD did according to the word of Moses; He removed the swarms *of flies* from Pharaoh, from his servants, and from his people. Not one remained.

32 But Pharaoh hardened his heart at this time also; neither would he let the people go.

The Fifth Plague: Livestock Diseased

9 Then the LORD said to Moses, "Go in to Pharaoh and tell him, 'Thus says the LORD God of the Hebrews: "Let My people go, that they may serve Me.

2 "For if you refuse to let *them* go, and still hold them,

3 "behold, the hand of the LORD will be on your cattle in the field, on the horses, on the donkeys, on the camels, on the oxen, and on the sheep—a very severe pestilence.

4 "And the LORD will make a difference between the livestock of Israel and the livestock of Egypt. So nothing shall die of all *that* belongs to the children of Israel."'"

5 Then the LORD appointed a set time, saying, "Tomorrow the LORD will do this thing in the land."

6 So the LORD did this thing on the next day, and all the livestock of Egypt died; but of the livestock of the children of Israel, not one died.

8:23 [a]Literally *set a ransom* (compare Exodus 9:4 and 11:7)

7 Then Pharaoh sent, and indeed, not even
one of the livestock of the Israelites was dead.
But the heart of Pharaoh became hard, and he
did not let the people go.

The Sixth Plague: Boils

8 So the LORD said to Moses and Aaron,
"Take for yourselves handfuls of ashes from a
furnace, and let Moses scatter it toward the
heavens in the sight of Pharaoh.
9 "And it will become fine dust in all the land
of Egypt, and it will cause boils that break out
in sores on man and beast throughout all the
land of Egypt."
10 Then they took ashes from the furnace and
stood before Pharaoh, and Moses scattered
them toward heaven. And *they* caused boils
that break out in sores on man and beast.
11 And the magicians could not stand before
Moses because of the boils, for the boils were
on the magicians and on all the Egyptians.
12 But the LORD hardened the heart of Pha-
raoh; and he did not heed them, just as the
LORD had spoken to Moses.

The Seventh Plague: Hail

13 Then the LORD said to Moses, "Rise early
in the morning and stand before Pharaoh, and
say to him, 'Thus says the LORD God of the
Hebrews: "Let My people go, that they may
serve Me,
14 "for at this time I will send all My plagues
to your very heart, and on your servants and
on your people, that you may know that *there
is* none like Me in all the earth.
15 "Now if I had stretched out My hand and
struck you and your people with pestilence,
then you would have been cut off from the
earth.
16 "But indeed for this *purpose* I have raised
you up, that I may show My power *in* you, and
that My name may be declared in all the earth.
17 "As yet you exalt yourself against My peo-
ple in that you will not let them go.
18 "Behold, tomorrow about this time I will
cause very heavy hail to rain down, such as
has not been in Egypt since its founding until
now.
19 "Therefore send now *and* gather your live-
stock and all that you have in the field, for the
hail shall come down on every man and every
animal which is found in the field and is not
brought home; and they shall die."'"
20 He who feared the word of the LORD
among the servants of Pharaoh made his ser-
vants and his livestock flee to the houses.
21 But he who did not regard the word of the
LORD left his servants and his livestock in the
field.
22 Then the LORD said to Moses, "Stretch out
your hand toward heaven, that there may be
hail in all the land of Egypt—on man, on beast,
and on every herb of the field, throughout the
land of Egypt."
23 And Moses stretched out his rod toward
heaven; and the LORD sent thunder and hail,
and fire darted to the ground. And the LORD
rained hail on the land of Egypt.
24 So there was hail, and fire mingled with
the hail, so very heavy that there was none like
it in all the land of Egypt since it became a
nation.
25 And the hail struck throughout the whole
land of Egypt, all that *was* in the field, both man
and beast; and the hail struck every herb of
the field and broke every tree of the field.
26 Only in the land of Goshen, where the chil-
dren of Israel *were*, there was no hail.
27 And Pharaoh sent and called for Moses
and Aaron, and said to them, "I have sinned
this time. The LORD *is* righteous, and my peo-
ple and I *are* wicked.
28 "Entreat the LORD, that there may be no
more mighty thundering and hail, for *it is*
enough. I will let you go, and you shall stay no
longer."
29 So Moses said to him, "As soon as I have
gone out of the city, I will spread out my hands
to the LORD; the thunder will cease, and there
will be no more hail, that you may know that
the earth *is* the LORD's.
30 "But as for you and your servants, I know
that you will not yet fear the LORD God."
31 Now the flax and the barley were struck,
for the barley *was* in the head and the flax *was*
in bud.
32 But the wheat and the spelt were not
struck, for they *are* late crops.
33 So Moses went out of the city from Pharaoh
and spread out his hands to the LORD; then the
thunder and the hail ceased, and the rain was
not poured on the earth.
34 And when Pharaoh saw that the rain, the
hail, and the thunder had ceased, he sinned yet
more; and he hardened his heart, he and his
servants.
35 So the heart of Pharaoh was hard; neither
would he let the children of Israel go, as the
LORD had spoken by Moses.

The Eighth Plague: Locusts

10 Now the LORD said to Moses, "Go in to
Pharaoh; for I have hardened his heart
and the hearts of his servants, that I may show
these signs of Mine before him,
2 "and that you may tell in the hearing of
your son and your son's son the mighty things
I have done in Egypt, and My signs which I
have done among them, that you may know
that I *am* the LORD."
3 So Moses and Aaron came in to Pharaoh
and said to him, "Thus says the LORD God
of the Hebrews: 'How long will you refuse to
humble yourself before Me? Let My people go,
that they may serve Me.
4 'Or else, if you refuse to let My people go,
behold, tomorrow I will bring locusts into your
territory.
5 'And they shall cover the face of the earth,
so that no one will be able to see the earth; and
they shall eat the residue of what is left, which
remains to you from the hail, and they shall
eat every tree which grows up for you out of
the field.
6 'They shall fill your houses, the houses of
all your servants, and the houses of all the
Egyptians—which neither your fathers nor
your fathers' fathers have seen, since the day
that they were on the earth to this day.'" And
he turned and went out from Pharaoh.
7 Then Pharaoh's servants said to him,
"How long shall this man be a snare to us? Let
the men go, that they may serve the LORD their
God. Do you not yet know that Egypt is de-
stroyed?"
8 So Moses and Aaron were brought again
to Pharaoh, and he said to them, "Go, serve
the LORD your God. Who *are* the ones that are
going?"

9 And Moses said, "We will go with our
young and our old; with our sons and our
daughters, with our flocks and our herds we
will go, for we must hold a feast to the LORD."
10 Then he said to them, "The LORD had bet-
ter be with you when I let you and your little
ones go! Beware, for evil is ahead of you.
11 "Not so! Go now, you *who are* men, and
serve the LORD, for that is what you desired."
And they were driven out from Pharaoh's pres-
ence.
12 Then the LORD said to Moses, "Stretch out
your hand over the land of Egypt for the lo-
custs, that they may come upon the land of
Egypt, and eat every herb of the land—all that
the hail has left."
13 So Moses stretched out his rod over the
land of Egypt, and the LORD brought an east
wind on the land all that day and all *that* night.
When it was morning, the east wind brought
the locusts.
14 And the locusts went up over all the land
of Egypt and rested on all the territory of
Egypt. *They were* very severe; previously there
had been no such locusts as they, nor shall
there be such after them.
15 For they covered the face of the whole
earth, so that the land was darkened; and they
ate every herb of the land and all the fruit of the
trees which the hail had left. So there remained
nothing green on the trees or on the plants of
the field throughout all the land of Egypt.
16 Then Pharaoh called for Moses and Aaron
in haste, and said, "I have sinned against the
LORD your God and against you.
17 "Now therefore, please forgive my sin only
this once, and entreat the LORD your God, that
He may take away from me this death only."
18 So he went out from Pharaoh and en-
treated the LORD.
19 And the LORD turned a very strong west
wind, which took the locusts away and blew
them into the Red Sea. There remained not one
locust in all the territory of Egypt.
20 But the LORD hardened Pharaoh's heart,
and he did not let the children of Israel go.

The Ninth Plague: Darkness

21 Then the LORD said to Moses, "Stretch out
your hand toward heaven, that there may be
darkness over the land of Egypt, darkness
which may even be felt."
22 So Moses stretched out his hand toward
heaven, and there was thick darkness in all the
land of Egypt three days.
23 They did not see one another; nor did any-
one rise from his place for three days. But all
the children of Israel had light in their dwell-
ings.
24 Then Pharaoh called to Moses and said,
"Go, serve the LORD; only let your flocks and
your herds be kept back. Let your little ones
also go with you."
25 But Moses said, "You must also give us
sacrifices and burnt offerings, that we may
sacrifice to the LORD our God.
26 "Our livestock also shall go with us; not a
hoof shall be left behind. For we must take
some of them to serve the LORD our God, and
even we do not know with what we must serve
the LORD until we arrive there."
27 But the LORD hardened Pharaoh's heart,
and he would not let them go.
28 Then Pharaoh said to him, "Get away from
me! Take heed to yourself and see my face no
more! For in the day you see my face you shall
die!"
29 So Moses said, "You have spoken well. I
will never see your face again."

Death of the Firstborn Announced

11 And the LORD said to Moses, "I will
bring one more plague on Pharaoh and
on Egypt. Afterward he will let you go from
here. When he lets *you* go, he will surely drive
you out of here altogether.
2 "Speak now in the hearing of the people,
and let every man ask from his neighbor and
every woman from her neighbor, articles of
silver and articles of gold."
3 And the LORD gave the people favor in
the sight of the Egyptians. Moreover the man
Moses *was* very great in the land of Egypt, in
the sight of Pharaoh's servants and in the sight
of the people.
4 Then Moses said, "Thus says the LORD:
'About midnight I will go out into the midst of
Egypt;
5 'and all the firstborn in the land of Egypt
shall die, from the firstborn of Pharaoh who
sits on his throne, even to the firstborn of the
female servant who *is* behind the handmill,
and all the firstborn of the animals.
6 'Then there shall be a great cry throughout
all the land of Egypt, such as was not like it
before, nor shall be like it again.
7 'But against none of the children of Israel
shall a dog move its tongue, against man or
beast, that you may know that the LORD does
make a difference between the Egyptians and
Israel.'
8 "And all these your servants shall come
down to me and bow down to me, saying, 'Get
out, and all the people who follow you!' After
that I will go out." Then he went out from Pha-
raoh in great anger.
9 But the LORD said to Moses, "Pharaoh will
not heed you, so that My wonders may be mul-
tiplied in the land of Egypt."
10 So Moses and Aaron did all these wonders
before Pharaoh; and the LORD hardened Pha-
raoh's heart, and he did not let the children of
Israel go out of his land.

The Passover Instituted

12 Now the LORD spoke to Moses and
Aaron in the land of Egypt, saying,
2 "This month *shall be* your beginning of
months; it *shall be* the first month of the year
to you.
3 "Speak to all the congregation of Israel,
saying: 'On the tenth of this month every man
shall take for himself a lamb, according to the
house of *his* father, a lamb for a household.
4 'And if the household is too small for the
lamb, let him and his neighbor next to his
house take *it* according to the number of the
persons; according to each man's need you
shall make your count for the lamb.
5 'Your lamb shall be without blemish, a
male of the first year. You may take *it* from the
sheep or from the goats.
6 'Now you shall keep it until the fourteenth
day of the same month. Then the whole assem-
bly of the congregation of Israel shall kill it at
twilight.
7 'And they shall take *some* of the blood and
put *it* on the two doorposts and on the lintel of
the houses where they eat it.
8 'Then they shall eat the flesh on that night;

roasted in fire, with unleavened bread *and*
with bitter *herbs* they shall eat it.
9 'Do not eat it raw, nor boiled at all with
water, but roasted in fire—its head with its legs
and its entrails.
10 'You shall let none of it remain until morning, and what remains of it until morning you
shall burn with fire.
11 'And thus you shall eat it: *with* a belt on
your waist, your sandals on your feet, and your
staff in your hand. So you shall eat it in haste.
It *is* the LORD's Passover.
12 'For I will pass through the land of Egypt
on that night, and will strike all the firstborn
in the land of Egypt, both man and beast; and
against all the gods of Egypt I will execute
judgment: I *am* the LORD.
13 'Now the blood shall be a sign for you on
the houses where you *are*. And when I see the
blood, I will pass over you; and the plague shall
not be on you to destroy *you* when I strike the
land of Egypt.
14 'So this day shall be to you a memorial; and
you shall keep it as a feast to the LORD throughout your generations. You shall keep it as a feast
by an everlasting ordinance.
15 'Seven days you shall eat unleavened
bread. On the first day you shall remove leaven
from your houses. For whoever eats leavened
bread from the first day until the seventh day,
that person shall be cut off from Israel.
16 'On the first day *there shall be* a holy convocation, and on the seventh day there shall
be a holy convocation for you. No manner of
work shall be done on them; but *that* which
everyone must eat—that only may be prepared
by you.
17 'So you shall observe *the Feast of* Unleavened Bread, for on this same day I will have
brought your armies out of the land of Egypt.
Therefore you shall observe this day throughout your generations as an everlasting ordinance.
18 'In the first *month*, on the fourteenth day
of the month at evening, you shall eat unleavened bread, until the twenty-first day of the
month at evening.
19 'For seven days no leaven shall be found
in your houses, since whoever eats what is
leavened, that same person shall be cut off
from the congregation of Israel, whether *he is*
a stranger or a native of the land.
20 'You shall eat nothing leavened; in all your
dwellings you shall eat unleavened bread.'"
21 Then Moses called for all the elders of Israel and said to them, "Pick out and take lambs
for yourselves according to your families, and
kill the Passover *lamb*.
22 "And you shall take a bunch of hyssop, dip
it in the blood that *is* in the basin, and strike
the lintel and the two doorposts with the blood
that *is* in the basin. And none of you shall go
out of the door of his house until morning.
23 "For the LORD will pass through to strike
the Egyptians; and when He sees the blood on
the lintel and on the two doorposts, the LORD
will pass over the door and not allow the destroyer to come into your houses to strike *you*.
24 "And you shall observe this thing as an
ordinance for you and your sons forever.
25 "It will come to pass when you come to the
land which the LORD will give you, just as He
promised, that you shall keep this service.
26 "And it shall be, when your children say to
you, 'What do you mean by this service?'
27 "that you shall say, 'It *is* the Passover sacrifice of the LORD, who passed over the houses
of the children of Israel in Egypt when He
struck the Egyptians and delivered our households.'" So the people bowed their heads and
worshiped.
28 Then the children of Israel went away and
did *so;* just as the LORD had commanded Moses and Aaron, so they did.

The Tenth Plague: Death of the Firstborn

29 And it came to pass at midnight that the
LORD struck all the firstborn in the land of
Egypt, from the firstborn of Pharaoh who sat
on his throne to the firstborn of the captive
who *was* in the dungeon, and all the firstborn
of livestock.
30 So Pharaoh rose in the night, he, all his
servants, and all the Egyptians; and there was
a great cry in Egypt, for *there was* not a house
where *there was* not one dead.

The Exodus

31 Then he called for Moses and Aaron by
night, and said, "Rise, go out from among my
people, both you and the children of Israel.
And go, serve the LORD as you have said.
32 "Also take your flocks and your herds, as
you have said, and be gone; and bless me also."
33 And the Egyptians urged the people, that
they might send them out of the land in haste.
For they said, "We *shall* all *be* dead."
34 So the people took their dough before it
was leavened, having their kneading bowls
bound up in their clothes on their shoulders.
35 Now the children of Israel had done according to the word of Moses, and they had
asked from the Egyptians articles of silver, articles of gold, and clothing.
36 And the LORD had given the people favor
in the sight of the Egyptians, so that they
granted them *what they requested*. Thus they
plundered the Egyptians.
37 Then the children of Israel journeyed from
Rameses to Succoth, about six hundred thousand men on foot, besides children.
38 A mixed multitude went up with them also,
and flocks and herds—a great deal of livestock.
39 And they baked unleavened cakes of the
dough which they had brought out of Egypt;
for it was not leavened, because they were
driven out of Egypt and could not wait, nor
had they prepared provisions for themselves.
40 Now the sojourn of the children of Israel
who lived in Egypt[a] *was* four hundred and
thirty years.
41 And it came to pass at the end of the four
hundred and thirty years—on that very same
day—it came to pass that all the armies of the
LORD went out from the land of Egypt.
42 It *is* a night of solemn observance to the
LORD for bringing them out of the land of
Egypt. This *is* that night of the LORD, a solemn
observance for all the children of Israel
throughout their generations.

Passover Regulations

43 And the LORD said to Moses and Aaron,
"This *is* the ordinance of the Passover: No foreigner shall eat it.

12:40 [a]Samaritan Pentateuch and Septuagint read *Egypt and Canaan*.

44 "But every man's servant who is bought
for money, when you have circumcised him,
then he may eat it.
45 "A sojourner and a hired servant shall not
eat it.
46 "In one house it shall be eaten; you shall
not carry any of the flesh outside the house,
nor shall you break one of its bones.
47 "All the congregation of Israel shall keep
it.
48 "And when a stranger dwells with you *and*
wants to keep the Passover to the LORD, let
all his males be circumcised, and then let him
come near and keep it; and he shall be as a
native of the land. For no uncircumcised person shall eat it.
49 "One law shall be for the native-born and
for the stranger who dwells among you."
50 Thus all the children of Israel did; as the
LORD commanded Moses and Aaron, so they
did.
51 And it came to pass, on that very same day,
that the LORD brought the children of Israel
out of the land of Egypt according to their armies.

The Firstborn Consecrated

13 Then the LORD spoke to Moses, saying,
2 "Consecrate to Me all the firstborn,
whatever opens the womb among the children
of Israel, *both* of man and beast; it is Mine."

The Feast of Unleavened Bread

3 And Moses said to the people: "Remember
this day in which you went out of Egypt, out of
the house of bondage; for by strength of hand
the LORD brought you out of this *place*. No
leavened bread shall be eaten.
4 "On this day you are going out, in the
month Abib.
5 "And it shall be, when the LORD brings
you into the land of the Canaanites and the
Hittites and the Amorites and the Hivites and
the Jebusites, which He swore to your fathers
to give you, a land flowing with milk and
honey, that you shall keep this service in this
month.
6 "Seven days you shall eat unleavened bread,
and on the seventh day *there shall be* a feast
to the LORD.
7 "Unleavened bread shall be eaten seven
days. And no leavened bread shall be seen
among you, nor shall leaven be seen among
you in all your quarters.
8 "And you shall tell your son in that day,
saying, '*This is done* because of what the LORD
did for me when I came up from Egypt.'
9 "It shall be as a sign to you on your hand
and as a memorial between your eyes, that the
LORD's law may be in your mouth; for with a
strong hand the LORD has brought you out of
Egypt.
10 "You shall therefore keep this ordinance
in its season from year to year.

The Law of the Firstborn

11 "And it shall be, when the LORD brings you
into the land of the Canaanites, as He swore to
you and your fathers, and gives it to you,
12 "that you shall set apart to the LORD all
that open the womb, that is, every firstborn that
comes from an animal which you have; the
males *shall be* the LORD's.
13 "But every firstborn of a donkey you shall
redeem with a lamb; and if you will not redeem
it, then you shall break its neck. And all the
firstborn of man among your sons you shall
redeem.
14 "So it shall be, when your son asks you in
time to come, saying, 'What *is* this?' that you
shall say to him, 'By strength of hand the LORD
brought us out of Egypt, out of the house of
bondage.
15 'And it came to pass, when Pharaoh was
stubborn about letting us go, that the LORD
killed all the firstborn in the land of Egypt,
both the firstborn of man and the firstborn
of beast. Therefore I sacrifice to the LORD all
males that open the womb, but all the firstborn
of my sons I redeem.'
16 "It shall be as a sign on your hand and as
frontlets between your eyes, for by strength of
hand the LORD brought us out of Egypt."

The Wilderness Way

17 Then it came to pass, when Pharaoh had
let the people go, that God did not lead them
by way of the land of the Philistines, although
that *was* near; for God said, "Lest perhaps the
people change their minds when they see war,
and return to Egypt."
18 So God led the people around *by* way of the
wilderness of the Red Sea. And the children of
Israel went up in orderly ranks out of the land
of Egypt.
19 And Moses took the bones of Joseph with
him, for he had placed the children of Israel
under solemn oath, saying, "God will surely
visit you, and you shall carry up my bones from
here with you."[a]
20 So they took their journey from Succoth
and camped in Etham at the edge of the wilderness.
21 And the LORD went before them by day in
a pillar of cloud to lead the way, and by night
in a pillar of fire to give them light, so as to go
by day and night.
22 He did not take away the pillar of cloud by
day or the pillar of fire by night *from* before
the people.

The Red Sea Crossing

14 Now the LORD spoke to Moses, saying:
2 "Speak to the children of Israel, that
they turn and camp before Pi Hahiroth, between
Migdol and the sea, opposite Baal Zephon; you
shall camp before it by the sea.
3 "For Pharaoh will say of the children of
Israel, 'They *are* bewildered by the land; the
wilderness has closed them in.'
4 "Then I will harden Pharaoh's heart, so
that he will pursue them; and I will gain honor
over Pharaoh and over all his army, that the
Egyptians may know that I *am* the LORD." And
they did so.
5 Now it was told the king of Egypt that the
people had fled, and the heart of Pharaoh and
his servants was turned against the people;
and they said, "Why have we done this, that
we have let Israel go from serving us?"
6 So he made ready his chariot and took his
people with him.
7 Also, he took six hundred choice chariots,
and all the chariots of Egypt with captains over
every one of them.

13:19 [a]Genesis 50:25

8 And the LORD hardened the heart of Pha-
raoh king of Egypt, and he pursued the chil-
dren of Israel; and the children of Israel went
out with boldness.
9 So the Egyptians pursued them, all the
horses *and* chariots of Pharaoh, his horsemen
and his army, and overtook them camping by
the sea beside Pi Hahiroth, before Baal Ze-
phon.
10 And when Pharaoh drew near, the chil-
dren of Israel lifted their eyes, and behold, the
Egyptians marched after them. So they were
very afraid, and the children of Israel cried out
to the LORD.
11 Then they said to Moses, "Because *there*
were no graves in Egypt, have you taken us
away to die in the wilderness? Why have you
so dealt with us, to bring us up out of Egypt?
12 "*Is* this not the word that we told you in
Egypt, saying, 'Let us alone that we may serve
the Egyptians'? For *it would have been* better
for us to serve the Egyptians than that we
should die in the wilderness."
13 And Moses said to the people, "Do not be
afraid. Stand still, and see the salvation of the
LORD, which He will accomplish for you today.
For the Egyptians whom you see today, you
shall see again no more forever.
14 "The LORD will fight for you, and you shall
hold your peace."
15 And the LORD said to Moses, "Why do
you cry to Me? Tell the children of Israel to go
forward.
16 "But lift up your rod, and stretch out your
hand over the sea and divide it. And the chil-
dren of Israel shall go on dry *ground* through
the midst of the sea.
17 "And I indeed will harden the hearts of the
Egyptians, and they shall follow them. So I will
gain honor over Pharaoh and over all his army,
his chariots, and his horsemen.
18 "Then the Egyptians shall know that I *am*
the LORD, when I have gained honor for Myself
over Pharaoh, his chariots, and his horsemen."
19 And the Angel of God, who went before
the camp of Israel, moved and went behind
them; and the pillar of cloud went from be-
fore them and stood behind them.
20 So it came between the camp of the Egyp-
tians and the camp of Israel. Thus it was a
cloud and darkness *to the one*, and it gave
light by night *to the other*, so that the one did
not come near the other all that night.
21 Then Moses stretched out his hand over
the sea; and the LORD caused the sea to go
back by a strong east wind all that night, and
made the sea into dry *land*, and the waters
were divided.
22 So the children of Israel went into the
midst of the sea on the dry *ground*, and the
waters *were* a wall to them on their right hand
and on their left.
23 And the Egyptians pursued and went after
them into the midst of the sea, all Pharaoh's
horses, his chariots, and his horsemen.
24 Now it came to pass, in the morning watch,
that the LORD looked down upon the army of
the Egyptians through the pillar of fire and
cloud, and He troubled the army of the Egyp-
tians.
25 And He took off[a] their chariot wheels, so
that they drove them with difficulty; and the
Egyptians said, "Let us flee from the face of
Israel, for the LORD fights for them against the
Egyptians."
26 Then the LORD said to Moses, "Stretch out
your hand over the sea, that the waters may
come back upon the Egyptians, on their chari-
ots, and on their horsemen."
27 And Moses stretched out his hand over the
sea; and when the morning appeared, the sea
returned to its full depth, while the Egyptians
were fleeing into it. So the LORD overthrew the
Egyptians in the midst of the sea.
28 Then the waters returned and covered the
chariots, the horsemen, *and* all the army of
Pharaoh that came into the sea after them. Not
so much as one of them remained.
29 But the children of Israel had walked on
dry *land* in the midst of the sea, and the waters
were a wall to them on their right hand and on
their left.
30 So the LORD saved Israel that day out of
the hand of the Egyptians, and Israel saw the
Egyptians dead on the seashore.
31 Thus Israel saw the great work which the
LORD had done in Egypt; so the people feared
the LORD, and believed the LORD and His ser-
vant Moses.

The Song of Moses

15 Then Moses and the children of Israel
sang this song to the LORD, and spoke,
saying:

"I will sing to the LORD,
For He has triumphed gloriously!
The horse and its rider
He has thrown into the sea!
2 The LORD *is* my strength and song,
And He has become my salvation;
He *is* my God, and I will praise Him;
My father's God, and I will exalt Him.
3 The LORD *is* a man of war;
The LORD *is* His name.
4 Pharaoh's chariots and his army He has
cast into the sea;
His chosen captains also are drowned in
the Red Sea.
5 The depths have covered them;
They sank to the bottom like a stone.

6 "Your right hand, O LORD, has become
glorious in power;
Your right hand, O LORD, has dashed the
enemy in pieces.
7 And in the greatness of Your excellence
You have overthrown those who rose
against You;
You sent forth Your wrath;
It consumed them like stubble.
8 And with the blast of Your nostrils
The waters were gathered together;
The floods stood upright like a heap;
The depths congealed in the heart of the
sea.
9 The enemy said, 'I will pursue,
I will overtake,
I will divide the spoil;
My desire shall be satisfied on them.
I will draw my sword,
My hand shall destroy them.'
10 You blew with Your wind,
The sea covered them;
They sank like lead in the mighty waters.

14:25 [a]Samaritan Pentateuch, Septuagint, and Syriac read *bound*.

11 "Who *is* like You, O LORD, among the gods?
Who *is* like You, glorious in holiness,
Fearful in praises, doing wonders?
12 You stretched out Your right hand;
The earth swallowed them.
13 You in Your mercy have led forth
The people whom You have redeemed;
You have guided *them* in Your strength
To Your holy habitation.

14 "The people will hear *and* be afraid;
Sorrow will take hold of the inhabitants of Philistia.
15 Then the chiefs of Edom will be dismayed;
The mighty men of Moab,
Trembling will take hold of them;
All the inhabitants of Canaan will melt away.
16 Fear and dread will fall on them;
By the greatness of Your arm
They will be *as* still as a stone,
Till Your people pass over, O LORD,
Till the people pass over
Whom You have purchased.
17 You will bring them in and plant them
In the mountain of Your inheritance,
In the place, O LORD, *which* You have made
For Your own dwelling,
The sanctuary, O Lord, *which* Your hands have established.

18 "The LORD shall reign forever and ever."

19 For the horses of Pharaoh went with his
chariots and his horsemen into the sea, and
the LORD brought back the waters of the sea
upon them. But the children of Israel went on
dry *land* in the midst of the sea.

The Song of Miriam

20 Then Miriam the prophetess, the sister of
Aaron, took the timbrel in her hand; and all
the women went out after her with timbrels
and with dances.
21 And Miriam answered them:

"Sing to the LORD,
For He has triumphed gloriously!
The horse and its rider
He has thrown into the sea!"

Bitter Waters Made Sweet

22 So Moses brought Israel from the Red Sea;
then they went out into the Wilderness of Shur.
And they went three days in the wilderness
and found no water.
23 Now when they came to Marah, they could
not drink the waters of Marah, for they *were*
bitter. Therefore the name of it was called Marah.[a]
24 And the people complained against Moses, saying, "What shall we drink?"
25 So he cried out to the LORD, and the LORD
showed him a tree. When he cast *it* into the
waters, the waters were made sweet. There He
made a statute and an ordinance for them, and
there He tested them,
26 and said, "If you diligently heed the voice
of the LORD your God and do what is right in
His sight, give ear to His commandments and
keep all His statutes, I will put none of the
diseases on you which I have brought on the
Egyptians. For I *am* the LORD who heals you."
27 Then they came to Elim, where there *were*
twelve wells of water and seventy palm trees;
so they camped there by the waters.

Bread from Heaven

16 And they journeyed from Elim, and all
the congregation of the children of Israel came to the Wilderness of Sin, which is
between Elim and Sinai, on the fifteenth day
of the second month after they departed from
the land of Egypt.
2 Then the whole congregation of the children of Israel complained against Moses and
Aaron in the wilderness.
3 And the children of Israel said to them,
"Oh, that we had died by the hand of the LORD
in the land of Egypt, when we sat by the pots
of meat *and* when we ate bread to the full! For
you have brought us out into this wilderness
to kill this whole assembly with hunger."
4 Then the LORD said to Moses, "Behold, I
will rain bread from heaven for you. And the
people shall go out and gather a certain quota
every day, that I may test them, whether they
will walk in My law or not.
5 "And it shall be on the sixth day that they
shall prepare what they bring in, and it shall
be twice as much as they gather daily."
6 Then Moses and Aaron said to all the children of Israel, "At evening you shall know that
the LORD has brought you out of the land of
Egypt.
7 "And in the morning you shall see the
glory of the LORD; for He hears your complaints against the LORD. But what *are* we, that
you complain against us?"
8 Also Moses said, "*This shall be seen* when
the LORD gives you meat to eat in the evening,
and in the morning bread to the full; for the
LORD hears your complaints which you make
against Him. And what *are* we? Your complaints *are* not against us but against the
LORD."
9 Then Moses spoke to Aaron, "Say to all
the congregation of the children of Israel,
'Come near before the LORD, for He has heard
your complaints.'"
10 Now it came to pass, as Aaron spoke to
the whole congregation of the children of Israel, that they looked toward the wilderness,
and behold, the glory of the LORD appeared in
the cloud.
11 And the LORD spoke to Moses, saying,
12 "I have heard the complaints of the children of Israel. Speak to them, saying, 'At twilight you shall eat meat, and in the morning
you shall be filled with bread. And you shall
know that I *am* the LORD your God.'"
13 So it was that quails came up at evening
and covered the camp, and in the morning the
dew lay all around the camp.
14 And when the layer of dew lifted, there,
on the surface of the wilderness, was a small
round substance, *as* fine as frost on the ground.
15 So when the children of Israel saw *it*, they
said to one another, "What is it?" For they did
not know what it *was*. And Moses said to them,
"This *is* the bread which the LORD has given
you to eat.
16 "This is the thing which the LORD has commanded: 'Let every man gather it according to

15:23 [a]Literally *Bitter*

each one's need, one omer for each person,
according to the number of persons; let every
man take for *those* who *are* in his tent.'"
17 Then the children of Israel did so and gath-
ered, some more, some less.
18 So when they measured *it* by omers, he
who gathered much had nothing left over, and
he who gathered little had no lack. Every man
had gathered according to each one's need.
19 And Moses said, "Let no one leave any of
it till morning."
20 Notwithstanding they did not heed Moses.
But some of them left part of it until morning,
and it bred worms and stank. And Moses was
angry with them.
21 So they gathered it every morning, every
man according to his need. And when the sun
became hot, it melted.
22 And so it was, on the sixth day, *that* they
gathered twice as much bread, two omers for
each one. And all the rulers of the congrega-
tion came and told Moses.
23 Then he said to them, "This *is what* the
LORD has said: 'Tomorrow *is* a Sabbath rest, a
holy Sabbath to the LORD. Bake what you will
bake *today*, and boil what you will boil; and
lay up for yourselves all that remains, to be
kept until morning.'"
24 So they laid it up till morning, as Moses
commanded; and it did not stink, nor were
there any worms in it.
25 Then Moses said, "Eat that today, for today
is a Sabbath to the LORD; today you will not
find it in the field.
26 "Six days you shall gather it, but on the
seventh day, the Sabbath, there will be none."
27 Now it happened *that some* of the people
went out on the seventh day to gather, but they
found none.
28 And the LORD said to Moses, "How long
do you refuse to keep My commandments and
My laws?
29 "See! For the LORD has given you the Sab-
bath; therefore He gives you on the sixth day
bread for two days. Let every man remain in
his place; let no man go out of his place on the
seventh day."
30 So the people rested on the seventh day.
31 And the house of Israel called its name
Manna.[a] And it *was* like white coriander seed,
and the taste of it *was* like wafers *made* with
honey.
32 Then Moses said, "This *is* the thing which
the LORD has commanded: 'Fill an omer with
it, to be kept for your generations, that they
may see the bread with which I fed you in the
wilderness, when I brought you out of the land
of Egypt.'"
33 And Moses said to Aaron, "Take a pot and
put an omer of manna in it, and lay it up before
the LORD, to be kept for your generations."
34 As the LORD commanded Moses, so Aaron
laid it up before the Testimony, to be kept.
35 And the children of Israel ate manna forty
years, until they came to an inhabited land;
they ate manna until they came to the border
of the land of Canaan.
36 Now an omer *is* one-tenth of an ephah.

Water from the Rock

17 Then all the congregation of the chil-
dren of Israel set out on their journey
from the Wilderness of Sin, according to the
commandment of the LORD, and camped in
Rephidim; but *there was* no water for the peo-
ple to drink.
2 Therefore the people contended with Mo-
ses, and said, "Give us water, that we may drink."
So Moses said to them, "Why do you contend
with me? Why do you tempt the LORD?"
3 And the people thirsted there for water,
and the people complained against Moses, and
said, "Why *is* it you have brought us up out
of Egypt, to kill us and our children and our
livestock with thirst?"
4 So Moses cried out to the LORD, saying,
"What shall I do with this people? They are
almost ready to stone me!"
5 And the LORD said to Moses, "Go on be-
fore the people, and take with you some of the
elders of Israel. Also take in your hand your
rod with which you struck the river, and go.
6 "Behold, I will stand before you there on
the rock in Horeb; and you shall strike the rock,
and water will come out of it, that the people
may drink." And Moses did so in the sight of
the elders of Israel.
7 So he called the name of the place Massah[a]
and Meribah,[b] because of the contention of the
children of Israel, and because they tempted
the LORD, saying, "Is the LORD among us or
not?"

Victory over the Amalekites

8 Now Amalek came and fought with Israel
in Rephidim.
9 And Moses said to Joshua, "Choose us
some men and go out, fight with Amalek. To-
morrow I will stand on the top of the hill with
the rod of God in my hand."
10 So Joshua did as Moses said to him, and
fought with Amalek. And Moses, Aaron, and
Hur went up to the top of the hill.
11 And so it was, when Moses held up his
hand, that Israel prevailed; and when he let
down his hand, Amalek prevailed.
12 But Moses' hands *became* heavy; so they
took a stone and put *it* under him, and he sat
on it. And Aaron and Hur supported his hands,
one on one side, and the other on the other
side; and his hands were steady until the going
down of the sun.
13 So Joshua defeated Amalek and his people
with the edge of the sword.
14 Then the LORD said to Moses, "Write this
for a memorial in the book and recount *it* in
the hearing of Joshua, that I will utterly blot
out the remembrance of Amalek from under
heaven."
15 And Moses built an altar and called its name,
The-LORD-Is-My-Banner;[a]
16 for he said, "Because the LORD has sworn:
the LORD *will have* war with Amalek from gen-
eration to generation."

Jethro's Advice

18 And Jethro, the priest of Midian, Moses'
father-in-law, heard of all that God had
done for Moses and for Israel His people—that
the LORD had brought Israel out of Egypt.

16:31 [a]Literally *What?* (compare Exodus 16:15) **17:7** [a]Literally *Tempted* [b]Literally *Contention* **17:15** [a]Hebrew *YHWH Nissi*

2 Then Jethro, Moses' father-in-law, took Zip-
porah, Moses' wife, after he had sent her back,
3 with her two sons, of whom the name of
one *was* Gershom (for he said, "I have been a
stranger in a foreign land")[a]
4 and the name of the other *was* Eliezer[a] (for
he said, "The God of my father *was* my help,
and delivered me from the sword of Pharaoh");
5 and Jethro, Moses' father-in-law, came
with his sons and his wife to Moses in the wil-
derness, where he was encamped at the moun-
tain of God.
6 Now he had said to Moses, "I, your father-
in-law Jethro, am coming to you with your wife
and her two sons with her."
7 So Moses went out to meet his father-in-
law, bowed down, and kissed him. And they
asked each other about *their* well-being, and
they went into the tent.
8 And Moses told his father-in-law all that
the LORD had done to Pharaoh and to the
Egyptians for Israel's sake, all the hardship
that had come upon them on the way, and *how*
the LORD had delivered them.
9 Then Jethro rejoiced for all the good which
the LORD had done for Israel, whom He had
delivered out of the hand of the Egyptians.
10 And Jethro said, "Blessed *be* the LORD,
who has delivered you out of the hand of the
Egyptians and out of the hand of Pharaoh, *and*
who has delivered the people from under the
hand of the Egyptians.
11 "Now I know that the LORD *is* greater than
all the gods; for in the very thing in which they
behaved proudly, *He was* above them."
12 Then Jethro, Moses' father-in-law, took[a] a
burnt offering and *other* sacrifices *to offer* to
God. And Aaron came with all the elders of
Israel to eat bread with Moses' father-in-law
before God.
13 And so it was, on the next day, that Moses
sat to judge the people; and the people stood
before Moses from morning until evening.
14 So when Moses' father-in-law saw all that
he did for the people, he said, "What *is* this
thing that you are doing for the people? Why
do you alone sit, and all the people stand be-
fore you from morning until evening?"
15 And Moses said to his father-in-law, "Be-
cause the people come to me to inquire of God.
16 "When they have a difficulty, they come to
me, and I judge between one and another; and I
make known the statutes of God and His laws."
17 So Moses' father-in-law said to him, "The
thing that you do *is* not good.
18 "Both you and these people who *are* with
you will surely wear yourselves out. For this
thing *is* too much for you; you are not able to
perform it by yourself.
19 "Listen now to my voice; I will give you
counsel, and God will be with you: Stand be-
fore God for the people, so that you may bring
the difficulties to God.
20 "And you shall teach them the statutes and
the laws, and show them the way in which they
must walk and the work they must do.
21 "Moreover you shall select from all the
people able men, such as fear God, men of
truth, hating covetousness; and place *such*
over them *to be* rulers of thousands, rulers of
hundreds, rulers of fifties, and rulers of tens.
22 "And let them judge the people at all times.
Then it will be *that* every great matter they
shall bring to you, but every small matter they
themselves shall judge. So it will be easier for
you, for they will bear *the burden* with you.
23 "If you do this thing, and God *so* com-
mands you, then you will be able to endure,
and all this people will also go to their place in
peace."
24 So Moses heeded the voice of his father-in-
law and did all that he had said.
25 And Moses chose able men out of all Is-
rael, and made them heads over the people:
rulers of thousands, rulers of hundreds, rulers
of fifties, and rulers of tens.
26 So they judged the people at all times; the
hard cases they brought to Moses, but they
judged every small case themselves.
27 Then Moses let his father-in-law depart,
and he went his way to his own land.

Israel at Mount Sinai

19 In the third month after the children of
Israel had gone out of the land of Egypt,
on the same day, they came *to* the Wilderness
of Sinai.
2 For they had departed from Rephidim, had
come *to* the Wilderness of Sinai, and camped
in the wilderness. So Israel camped there be-
fore the mountain.
3 And Moses went up to God, and the LORD
called to him from the mountain, saying, "Thus
you shall say to the house of Jacob, and tell the
children of Israel:
4 'You have seen what I did to the Egyptians,
and *how* I bore you on eagles' wings and
brought you to Myself.
5 'Now therefore, if you will indeed obey My
voice and keep My covenant, then you shall be
a special treasure to Me above all people; for
all the earth *is* Mine.
6 'And you shall be to Me a kingdom of
priests and a holy nation.' These *are* the words
which you shall speak to the children of Is-
rael."
7 So Moses came and called for the elders
of the people, and laid before them all these
words which the LORD commanded him.
8 Then all the people answered together and
said, "All that the LORD has spoken we will
do." So Moses brought back the words of the
people to the LORD.
9 And the LORD said to Moses, "Behold, I
come to you in the thick cloud, that the people
may hear when I speak with you, and believe
you forever." So Moses told the words of the
people to the LORD.
10 Then the LORD said to Moses, "Go to the
people and consecrate them today and tomor-
row, and let them wash their clothes.
11 "And let them be ready for the third day.
For on the third day the LORD will come down
upon Mount Sinai in the sight of all the people.
12 "You shall set bounds for the people all
around, saying, 'Take heed to yourselves *that*
you do *not* go up to the mountain or touch
its base. Whoever touches the mountain shall
surely be put to death.
13 'Not a hand shall touch him, but he shall
surely be stoned or shot *with an arrow;*
whether man or beast, he shall not live.' When
the trumpet sounds long, they shall come near
the mountain."

18:3 [a]Compare Exodus 2:22 **18:4** [a]Literally *My God Is Help* **18:12** [a]Following Masoretic Text and Septuagint; Syriac, Targum, and Vulgate read *offered.*

14 So Moses went down from the mountain
to the people and sanctified the people, and they
washed their clothes.
15 And he said to the people, "Be ready for
the third day; do not come near *your* wives."
16 Then it came to pass on the third day, in
the morning, that there were thunderings and
lightnings, and a thick cloud on the mountain;
and the sound of the trumpet was very loud,
so that all the people who *were* in the camp
trembled.
17 And Moses brought the people out of the
camp to meet with God, and they stood at the
foot of the mountain.
18 Now Mount Sinai *was* completely in
smoke, because the LORD descended upon it
in fire. Its smoke ascended like the smoke of
a furnace, and the whole mountain[a] quaked
greatly.
19 And when the blast of the trumpet sounded
long and became louder and louder, Moses
spoke, and God answered him by voice.
20 Then the LORD came down upon Mount
Sinai, on the top of the mountain. And the
LORD called Moses to the top of the mountain,
and Moses went up.
21 And the LORD said to Moses, "Go down
and warn the people, lest they break through
to gaze at the LORD, and many of them perish.
22 "Also let the priests who come near the
LORD consecrate themselves, lest the LORD
break out against them."
23 But Moses said to the LORD, "The people
cannot come up to Mount Sinai; for You warned
us, saying, 'Set bounds around the mountain
and consecrate it.'"
24 Then the LORD said to him, "Away! Get
down and then come up, you and Aaron with
you. But do not let the priests and the people
break through to come up to the LORD, lest He
break out against them."
25 So Moses went down to the people and
spoke to them.

The Ten Commandments

20 And God spoke all these words, saying:
2 "I *am* the LORD your God, who brought you
out of the land of Egypt, out of the
house of bondage.
3 "You shall have no other gods before Me.
4 "You shall not make for yourself a carved
image—any likeness *of anything* that
is in heaven above, or that *is* in the
earth beneath, or that *is* in the water
under the earth;
5 you shall not bow down to them nor
serve them. For I, the LORD your God,
am a jealous God, visiting the iniquity
of the fathers upon the children to the
third and fourth *generations* of those
who hate Me,
6 but showing mercy to thousands, to
those who love Me and keep My commandments.
7 "You shall not take the name of the LORD
your God in vain, for the LORD will not
hold *him* guiltless who takes His name
in vain.
8 "Remember the Sabbath day, to keep it
holy.
9 Six days you shall labor and do all
your work,
10 but the seventh day *is* the Sabbath of
the LORD your God. *In it* you shall do
no work: you, nor your son, nor your
daughter, nor your male servant, nor
your female servant, nor your cattle,
nor your stranger who *is* within your
gates.
11 For *in* six days the LORD made the
heavens and the earth, the sea, and all
that *is* in them, and rested the seventh
day. Therefore the LORD blessed the
Sabbath day and hallowed it.
12 "Honor your father and your mother, that
your days may be long upon the land
which the LORD your God is giving
you.
13 "You shall not murder.
14 "You shall not commit adultery.
15 "You shall not steal.
16 "You shall not bear false witness against
your neighbor.
17 "You shall not covet your neighbor's house;
you shall not covet your neighbor's
wife, nor his male servant, nor his female servant, nor his ox, nor his donkey, nor anything that *is* your
neighbor's."

The People Afraid of God's Presence

18 Now all the people witnessed the thunderings, the lightning flashes, the sound of the
trumpet, and the mountain smoking; and when
the people saw *it*, they trembled and stood afar
off.
19 Then they said to Moses, "You speak with
us, and we will hear; but let not God speak
with us, lest we die."
20 And Moses said to the people, "Do not fear;
for God has come to test you, and that His fear
may be before you, so that you may not sin."
21 So the people stood afar off, but Moses
drew near the thick darkness where God *was*.

The Law of the Altar

22 Then the LORD said to Moses, "Thus you
shall say to the children of Israel: 'You have
seen that I have talked with you from heaven.
23 'You shall not make *anything to be* with
Me—gods of silver or gods of gold you shall
not make for yourselves.
24 'An altar of earth you shall make for Me,
and you shall sacrifice on it your burnt offerings and your peace offerings, your sheep and
your oxen. In every place where I record My
name I will come to you, and I will bless you.
25 'And if you make Me an altar of stone, you
shall not build it of hewn stone; for if you use
your tool on it, you have profaned it.
26 'Nor shall you go up by steps to My altar,
that your nakedness may not be exposed on
it.'

The Law Concerning Servants

21 "Now these *are* the judgments which
you shall set before them:
2 "If you buy a Hebrew servant, he shall
serve six years; and in the seventh he shall go
out free and pay nothing.
3 "If he comes in by himself, he shall go out

19:18 [a]Septuagint reads *all the people.*

by himself; if he *comes in* married, then his
wife shall go out with him.
4 "If his master has given him a wife, and
she has borne him sons or daughters, the wife
and her children shall be her master's, and he
shall go out by himself.
5 "But if the servant plainly says, 'I love my
master, my wife, and my children; I will not go
out free,'
6 "then his master shall bring him to the
judges. He shall also bring him to the door, or
to the doorpost, and his master shall pierce his
ear with an awl; and he shall serve him forever.
7 "And if a man sells his daughter to be a
female slave, she shall not go out as the male
slaves do.
8 "If she does not please her master, who
has betrothed her to himself, then he shall let
her be redeemed. He shall have no right to
sell her to a foreign people, since he has dealt
deceitfully with her.
9 "And if he has betrothed her to his son, he
shall deal with her according to the custom of
daughters.
10 "If he takes another *wife*, he shall not di-
minish her food, her clothing, and her marriage
rights.
11 "And if he does not do these three for her,
then she shall go out free, without *paying* money.

The Law Concerning Violence

12 "He who strikes a man so that he dies shall
surely be put to death.
13 "However, if he did not lie in wait, but God
delivered *him* into his hand, then I will appoint
for you a place where he may flee.
14 "But if a man acts with premeditation
against his neighbor, to kill him by treachery,
you shall take him from My altar, that he may
die.
15 "And he who strikes his father or his
mother shall surely be put to death.
16 "He who kidnaps a man and sells him, or
if he is found in his hand, shall surely be put
to death.
17 "And he who curses his father or his mother
shall surely be put to death.
18 "If men contend with each other, and one
strikes the other with a stone or with *his* fist,
and he does not die but is confined to *his* bed,
19 "if he rises again and walks about outside
with his staff, then he who struck *him* shall be
acquitted. He shall only pay *for* the loss of his
time, and shall provide *for him* to be thor-
oughly healed.
20 "And if a man beats his male or female
servant with a rod, so that he dies under his
hand, he shall surely be punished.
21 "Notwithstanding, if he remains alive a
day or two, he shall not be punished; for he *is*
his property.
22 "If men fight, and hurt a woman with
child, so that she gives birth prematurely, yet
no harm follows, he shall surely be punished
accordingly as the woman's husband imposes
on him; and he shall pay as the judges *deter-
mine.*
23 "But if *any* harm follows, then you shall
give life for life,
24 "eye for eye, tooth for tooth, hand for hand,
foot for foot,
25 "burn for burn, wound for wound, stripe
for stripe.
26 "If a man strikes the eye of his male or fe-
male servant, and destroys it, he shall let him
go free for the sake of his eye.
27 "And if he knocks out the tooth of his male
or female servant, he shall let him go free for
the sake of his tooth.

Animal Control Laws

28 "If an ox gores a man or a woman to death,
then the ox shall surely be stoned, and its flesh
shall not be eaten; but the owner of the ox *shall
be* acquitted.
29 "But if the ox tended to thrust with its horn
in times past, and it has been made known to
his owner, and he has not kept it confined, so
that it has killed a man or a woman, the ox
shall be stoned and its owner also shall be put
to death.
30 "If there is imposed on him a sum of
money, then he shall pay to redeem his life,
whatever is imposed on him.
31 "Whether it has gored a son or gored a
daughter, according to this judgment it shall
be done to him.
32 "If the ox gores a male or female servant,
he shall give to their master thirty shekels of
silver, and the ox shall be stoned.
33 "And if a man opens a pit, or if a man digs
a pit and does not cover it, and an ox or a
donkey falls in it,
34 "the owner of the pit shall make *it* good;
he shall give money to their owner, but the
dead *animal* shall be his.
35 "If one man's ox hurts another's, so that it
dies, then they shall sell the live ox and divide
the money from it; and the dead *ox* they shall
also divide.
36 "Or if it was known that the ox tended to
thrust in time past, and its owner has not kept
it confined, he shall surely pay ox for ox, and
the dead animal shall be his own.

Responsibility for Property

22 "If a man steals an ox or a sheep, and
slaughters it or sells it, he shall restore
five oxen for an ox and four sheep for a sheep.
2 "If the thief is found breaking in, and he is
struck so that he dies, *there shall be* no guilt
for his bloodshed.
3 "If the sun has risen on him, *there shall be*
guilt for his bloodshed. He should make full
restitution; if he has nothing, then he shall be
sold for his theft.
4 "If the theft is certainly found alive in his
hand, whether it is an ox or donkey or sheep,
he shall restore double.
5 "If a man causes a field or vineyard to be
grazed, and lets loose his animal, and it feeds
in another man's field, he shall make restitu-
tion from the best of his own field and the best
of his own vineyard.
6 "If fire breaks out and catches in thorns,
so that stacked grain, standing grain, or the
field is consumed, he who kindled the fire shall
surely make restitution.
7 "If a man delivers to his neighbor money
or articles to keep, and it is stolen out of the
man's house, if the thief is found, he shall pay
double.
8 "If the thief is not found, then the master
of the house shall be brought to the judges *to
see* whether he has put his hand into his neigh-
bor's goods.
9 "For any kind of trespass, *whether it con-
cerns* an ox, a donkey, a sheep, or clothing, *or*
for any kind of lost thing which *another* claims

to be his, the cause of both parties shall come
before the judges; *and* whomever the judges
condemn shall pay double to his neighbor.
10 "If a man delivers to his neighbor a don-
key, an ox, a sheep, or any animal to keep, and
it dies, is hurt, or driven away, no one seeing
it,
11 "*then* an oath of the LORD shall be be-
tween them both, that he has not put his hand
into his neighbor's goods; and the owner of
it shall accept *that*, and he shall not make *it*
good.
12 "But if, in fact, it is stolen from him, he
shall make restitution to the owner of it.
13 "If it is torn to pieces *by a beast*, *then* he
shall bring it as evidence, *and* he shall not
make good what was torn.
14 "And if a man borrows *anything* from his
neighbor, and it becomes injured or dies, the
owner of it not *being* with it, he shall surely
make *it* good.
15 "If its owner *was* with it, he shall not make
it good; if it *was* hired, it came for its hire.

Moral and Ceremonial Principles

16 "If a man entices a virgin who is not be-
trothed, and lies with her, he shall surely pay
the bride-price for her *to be* his wife.
17 "If her father utterly refuses to give her
to him, he shall pay money according to the
bride-price of virgins.
18 "You shall not permit a sorceress to live.
19 "Whoever lies with an animal shall surely
be put to death.
20 "He who sacrifices to *any* god, except to
the LORD only, he shall be utterly destroyed.
21 "You shall neither mistreat a stranger nor
oppress him, for you were strangers in the land
of Egypt.
22 "You shall not afflict any widow or father-
less child.
23 "If you afflict them in any way, *and* they
cry at all to Me, I will surely hear their cry;
24 "and My wrath will become hot, and I will
kill you with the sword; your wives shall be
widows, and your children fatherless.
25 "If you lend money to *any of* My people
who are poor among you, you shall not be like
a moneylender to him; you shall not charge
him interest.
26 "If you ever take your neighbor's garment
as a pledge, you shall return it to him before
the sun goes down.
27 "For that *is* his only covering, it *is* his gar-
ment for his skin. What will he sleep in? And
it will be that when he cries to Me, I will hear,
for I *am* gracious.
28 "You shall not revile God, nor curse a ruler
of your people.
29 "You shall not delay *to offer* the first of
your ripe produce and your juices. The first-
born of your sons you shall give to Me.
30 "Likewise you shall do with your oxen *and*
your sheep. It shall be with its mother seven
days; on the eighth day you shall give it to Me.
31 "And you shall be holy men to Me: you
shall not eat meat torn *by beasts* in the field;
you shall throw it to the dogs.

Justice for All

23 "You shall not circulate a false report.
Do not put your hand with the wicked
to be an unrighteous witness.
2 "You shall not follow a crowd to do evil;
nor shall you testify in a dispute so as to turn
aside after many to pervert *justice*.
3 "You shall not show partiality to a poor
man in his dispute.
4 "If you meet your enemy's ox or his don-
key going astray, you shall surely bring it back
to him again.
5 "If you see the donkey of one who hates
you lying under its burden, and you would re-
frain from helping it, you shall surely help him
with it.
6 "You shall not pervert the judgment of
your poor in his dispute.
7 "Keep yourself far from a false matter; do
not kill the innocent and righteous. For I will
not justify the wicked.
8 "And you shall take no bribe, for a bribe
blinds the discerning and perverts the words
of the righteous.
9 "Also you shall not oppress a stranger, for
you know the heart of a stranger, because you
were strangers in the land of Egypt.

The Law of Sabbaths

10 "Six years you shall sow your land and
gather in its produce,
11 "but the seventh *year* you shall let it rest
and lie fallow, that the poor of your people may
eat; and what they leave, the beasts of the field
may eat. In like manner you shall do with your
vineyard *and* your olive grove.
12 "Six days you shall do your work, and on
the seventh day you shall rest, that your ox and
your donkey may rest, and the son of your
female servant and the stranger may be re-
freshed.
13 "And in all that I have said to you, be cir-
cumspect and make no mention of the name
of other gods, nor let it be heard from your
mouth.

Three Annual Feasts

14 "Three times you shall keep a feast to Me
in the year:
15 "You shall keep the Feast of Unleavened
Bread (you shall eat unleavened bread seven
days, as I commanded you, at the time ap-
pointed in the month of Abib, for in it you came
out of Egypt; none shall appear before Me
empty);
16 "and the Feast of Harvest, the firstfruits of
your labors which you have sown in the field;
and the Feast of Ingathering at the end of the
year, when you have gathered in *the fruit of*
your labors from the field.
17 "Three times in the year all your males
shall appear before the Lord GOD.[a]
18 "You shall not offer the blood of My sacri-
fice with leavened bread; nor shall the fat of
My sacrifice remain until morning.
19 "The first of the firstfruits of your land you
shall bring into the house of the LORD your
God. You shall not boil a young goat in its
mother's milk.

The Angel and the Promises

20 "Behold, I send an Angel before you to
keep you in the way and to bring you into the
place which I have prepared.
21 "Beware of Him and obey His voice; do
not provoke Him, for He will not pardon your
transgressions; for My name *is* in Him.

23:17 [a]Hebrew *YHWH*, usually translated *LORD*

22 "But if you indeed obey His voice and do
all that I speak, then I will be an enemy to your
enemies and an adversary to your adversaries.
23 "For My Angel will go before you and
bring you in to the Amorites and the Hittites
and the Perizzites and the Canaanites and the
Hivites and the Jebusites; and I will cut them
off.
24 "You shall not bow down to their gods, nor
serve them, nor do according to their works;
but you shall utterly overthrow them and com-
pletely break down their *sacred* pillars.
25 "So you shall serve the LORD your God,
and He will bless your bread and your water.
And I will take sickness away from the midst
of you.
26 "No one shall suffer miscarriage or be bar-
ren in your land; I will fulfill the number of
your days.
27 "I will send My fear before you, I will cause
confusion among all the people to whom you
come, and will make all your enemies turn
their backs to you.
28 "And I will send hornets before you, which
shall drive out the Hivite, the Canaanite, and
the Hittite from before you.
29 "I will not drive them out from before you
in one year, lest the land become desolate and
the beasts of the field become too numerous
for you.
30 "Little by little I will drive them out from
before you, until you have increased, and you
inherit the land.
31 "And I will set your bounds from the Red
Sea to the sea, Philistia, and from the desert to
the River.[a] For I will deliver the inhabitants of
the land into your hand, and you shall drive
them out before you.
32 "You shall make no covenant with them,
nor with their gods.
33 "They shall not dwell in your land, lest
they make you sin against Me. For *if* you serve
their gods, it will surely be a snare to you."

Israel Affirms the Covenant

24 Now He said to Moses, "Come up to the
LORD, you and Aaron, Nadab and Abihu,
and seventy of the elders of Israel, and worship
from afar.
2 "And Moses alone shall come near the
LORD, but they shall not come near; nor shall
the people go up with him."
3 So Moses came and told the people all the
words of the LORD and all the judgments. And
all the people answered with one voice and
said, "All the words which the LORD has said
we will do."
4 And Moses wrote all the words of the
LORD. And he rose early in the morning, and
built an altar at the foot of the mountain, and
twelve pillars according to the twelve tribes of
Israel.
5 Then he sent young men of the children of
Israel, who offered burnt offerings and sacri-
ficed peace offerings of oxen to the LORD.
6 And Moses took half the blood and put *it*
in basins, and half the blood he sprinkled on
the altar.
7 Then he took the Book of the Covenant
and read in the hearing of the people. And they
said, "All that the LORD has said we will do,
and be obedient."
8 And Moses took the blood, sprinkled *it* on
the people, and said, "This is the blood of the
covenant which the LORD has made with you
according to all these words."

On the Mountain with God

9 Then Moses went up, also Aaron, Nadab,
and Abihu, and seventy of the elders of Israel,
10 and they saw the God of Israel. And *there*
was under His feet as it were a paved work of
sapphire stone, and it was like the very heav-
ens in *its* clarity.
11 But on the nobles of the children of Israel
He did not lay His hand. So they saw God, and
they ate and drank.
12 Then the LORD said to Moses, "Come up
to Me on the mountain and be there; and I
will give you tablets of stone, and the law and
commandments which I have written, that you
may teach them."
13 So Moses arose with his assistant Joshua,
and Moses went up to the mountain of God.
14 And he said to the elders, "Wait here for
us until we come back to you. Indeed, Aaron
and Hur *are* with you. If any man has a diffi-
culty, let him go to them."
15 Then Moses went up into the mountain,
and a cloud covered the mountain.
16 Now the glory of the LORD rested on
Mount Sinai, and the cloud covered it six days.
And on the seventh day He called to Moses out
of the midst of the cloud.
17 The sight of the glory of the LORD *was* like
a consuming fire on the top of the mountain in
the eyes of the children of Israel.
18 So Moses went into the midst of the cloud
and went up into the mountain. And Moses
was on the mountain forty days and forty nights.

Offerings for the Sanctuary

25 Then the LORD spoke to Moses, saying:
2 "Speak to the children of Israel, that
they bring Me an offering. From everyone who
gives it willingly with his heart you shall take
My offering.
3 "And this *is* the offering which you shall take
from them: gold, silver, and bronze;
4 "blue, purple, and scarlet *thread,* fine linen,
and goats' *hair;*
5 "ram skins dyed red, badger skins, and aca-
cia wood;
6 "oil for the light, and spices for the anoint-
ing oil and for the sweet incense;
7 "onyx stones, and stones to be set in the
ephod and in the breastplate.
8 "And let them make Me a sanctuary, that I
may dwell among them.
9 "According to all that I show you, *that is,*
the pattern of the tabernacle and the pattern
of all its furnishings, just so you shall make *it.*

The Ark of the Testimony

10 "And they shall make an ark of acacia wood;
two and a half cubits *shall be* its length, a cubit
and a half its width, and a cubit and a half its
height.
11 "And you shall overlay it with pure gold,
inside and out you shall overlay it, and shall
make on it a molding of gold all around.
12 "You shall cast four rings of gold for it, and
put *them* in its four corners; two rings *shall be*
on one side, and two rings on the other side.

23:31 [a]Hebrew *Nahar,* the Euphrates

13 "And you shall make poles *of* acacia wood,
and overlay them with gold.
14 "You shall put the poles into the rings on
the sides of the ark, that the ark may be carried
by them.
15 "The poles shall be in the rings of the ark;
they shall not be taken from it.
16 "And you shall put into the ark the Testi-
mony which I will give you.
17 "You shall make a mercy seat of pure gold;
two and a half cubits *shall be* its length and a
cubit and a half its width.
18 "And you shall make two cherubim of
gold; of hammered work you shall make them
at the two ends of the mercy seat.
19 "Make one cherub at one end, and the
other cherub at the other end; you shall make
the cherubim at the two ends of it *of one piece*
with the mercy seat.
20 "And the cherubim shall stretch out *their*
wings above, covering the mercy seat with
their wings, and they shall face one another;
the faces of the cherubim *shall be* toward the
mercy seat.
21 "You shall put the mercy seat on top of the
ark, and in the ark you shall put the Testimony
that I will give you.
22 "And there I will meet with you, and I will
speak with you from above the mercy seat,
from between the two cherubim which *are* on
the ark of the Testimony, about everything
which I will give you in commandment to the
children of Israel.

The Table for the Showbread

23 "You shall also make a table of acacia wood;
two cubits *shall be* its length, a cubit its width,
and a cubit and a half its height.
24 "And you shall overlay it with pure gold,
and make a molding of gold all around.
25 "You shall make for it a frame of a hand-
breadth all around, and you shall make a gold
molding for the frame all around.
26 "And you shall make for it four rings of
gold, and put the rings on the four corners that
are at its four legs.
27 "The rings shall be close to the frame, as
holders for the poles to bear the table.
28 "And you shall make the poles of acacia
wood, and overlay them with gold, that the
table may be carried with them.
29 "You shall make its dishes, its pans, its
pitchers, and its bowls for pouring. You shall
make them of pure gold.
30 "And you shall set the showbread on the
table before Me always.

The Gold Lampstand

31 "You shall also make a lampstand of pure
gold; the lampstand shall be of hammered
work. Its shaft, its branches, its bowls, its *orna-
mental* knobs, and flowers shall be *of one
piece*.
32 "And six branches shall come out of its
sides: three branches of the lampstand out of
one side, and three branches of the lampstand
out of the other side.
33 "Three bowls *shall be* made like almond
blossoms on one branch, *with* an *ornamental*
knob and a flower, and three bowls made like
almond *blossoms* on the other branch, *with* an
ornamental knob and a flower—and so for the
six branches that come out of the lampstand.
34 "On the lampstand itself four bowls *shall
be* made like almond *blossoms, each with* its
ornamental knob and flower.
35 "And *there shall be* a knob under the *first*
two branches of the same, a knob under the
second two branches of the same, and a knob
under the *third* two branches of the same, ac-
cording to the six branches that extend from
the lampstand.
36 "Their knobs and their branches *shall be
of one piece;* all of it *shall be* one hammered
piece of pure gold.
37 "You shall make seven lamps for it, and
they shall arrange its lamps so that they give
light in front of it.
38 "And its wick-trimmers and their trays
shall be of pure gold.
39 "It shall be made of a talent of pure gold,
with all these utensils.
40 "And see to it that you make *them* accord-
ing to the pattern which was shown you on the
mountain.

The Tabernacle

26 "Moreover you shall make the taberna-
cle *with* ten curtains *of* fine woven linen,
and blue, purple, and scarlet *thread;* with artis-
tic designs of cherubim you shall weave them.
2 "The length of each curtain *shall be*
twenty-eight cubits, and the width of each cur-
tain four cubits. And every one of the curtains
shall have the same measurements.
3 "Five curtains shall be coupled to one an-
other, and *the other* five curtains *shall be* cou-
pled to one another.
4 "And you shall make loops of blue *yarn* on
the edge of the curtain on the selvedge of *one*
set, and likewise you shall do on the outer edge
of *the other* curtain of the second set.
5 "Fifty loops you shall make in the one cur-
tain, and fifty loops you shall make on the edge
of the curtain that *is* on the end of the second
set, that the loops may be clasped to one another.
6 "And you shall make fifty clasps of gold,
and couple the curtains together with the
clasps, so that it may be one tabernacle.
7 "You shall also make curtains of goats'
hair, to be a tent over the tabernacle. You shall
make eleven curtains.
8 "The length of each curtain *shall be* thirty
cubits, and the width of each curtain four cu-
bits; and the eleven curtains shall all have the
same measurements.
9 "And you shall couple five curtains by
themselves and six curtains by themselves,
and you shall double over the sixth curtain at
the forefront of the tent.
10 "You shall make fifty loops on the edge of
the curtain that is outermost in *one* set, and
fifty loops on the edge of the curtain of the
second set.
11 "And you shall make fifty bronze clasps,
put the clasps into the loops, and couple the
tent together, that it may be one.
12 "The remnant that remains of the curtains
of the tent, the half curtain that remains, shall
hang over the back of the tabernacle.
13 "And a cubit on one side and a cubit on the
other side, of what remains of the length of the
curtains of the tent, shall hang over the sides
of the tabernacle, on this side and on that side,
to cover it.
14 "You shall also make a covering of ram
skins dyed red for the tent, and a covering of
badger skins above that.

15 "And for the tabernacle you shall make the
boards of acacia wood, standing upright.
16 "Ten cubits *shall be* the length of a board,
and a cubit and a half *shall be* the width of
each board.
17 "Two tenons *shall be* in each board for
binding one to another. Thus you shall make
for all the boards of the tabernacle.
18 "And you shall make the boards for the
tabernacle, twenty boards for the south side.
19 "You shall make forty sockets of silver under the twenty boards: two sockets under each
of the boards for its two tenons.
20 "And for the second side of the tabernacle,
the north side, *there shall be* twenty boards
21 "and their forty sockets of silver: two sockets under each of the boards.
22 "For the far side of the tabernacle, westward, you shall make six boards.
23 "And you shall also make two boards for
the two back corners of the tabernacle.
24 "They shall be coupled together at the bottom and they shall be coupled together at the
top by one ring. Thus it shall be for both of
them. They shall be for the two corners.
25 "So there shall be eight boards with their
sockets of silver—sixteen sockets—two sockets under each of the boards.
26 "And you shall make bars of acacia wood:
five for the boards on one side of the tabernacle,
27 "five bars for the boards on the other side
of the tabernacle, and five bars for the boards
of the side of the tabernacle, for the far side
westward.
28 "The middle bar shall pass through the
midst of the boards from end to end.
29 "You shall overlay the boards with gold,
make their rings of gold *as* holders for the bars,
and overlay the bars with gold.
30 "And you shall raise up the tabernacle according to its pattern which you were shown
on the mountain.
31 "You shall make a veil woven of blue, purple, and scarlet *thread,* and fine woven linen.
It shall be woven with an artistic design of
cherubim.
32 "You shall hang it upon the four pillars of
acacia *wood* overlaid with gold. Their hooks
shall be gold, upon four sockets of silver.
33 "And you shall hang the veil from the
clasps. Then you shall bring the ark of the Testimony in there, behind the veil. The veil shall
be a divider for you between the holy *place*
and the Most Holy.
34 "You shall put the mercy seat upon the ark
of the Testimony in the Most Holy.
35 "You shall set the table outside the veil,
and the lampstand across from the table on the
side of the tabernacle toward the south; and
you shall put the table on the north side.
36 "You shall make a screen for the door of
the tabernacle, *woven of* blue, purple, and
scarlet *thread,* and fine woven linen, made by
a weaver.
37 "And you shall make for the screen five
pillars of acacia *wood,* and overlay them with
gold; their hooks *shall be* gold, and you shall
cast five sockets of bronze for them.

The Altar of Burnt Offering

27 "You shall make an altar of acacia wood,
five cubits long and five cubits wide—
the altar shall be square—and its height *shall
be* three cubits.
2 "You shall make its horns on its four corners; its horns shall be of one piece with it.
And you shall overlay it with bronze.
3 "Also you shall make its pans to receive
its ashes, and its shovels and its basins and
its forks and its firepans; you shall make
all its utensils of bronze.
4 "You shall make a grate for it, a network
of bronze; and on the network you shall make
four bronze rings at its four corners.
5 "You shall put it under the rim of the altar
beneath, that the network may be midway up
the altar.
6 "And you shall make poles for the altar,
poles of acacia wood, and overlay them with
bronze.
7 "The poles shall be put in the rings, and
the poles shall be on the two sides of the altar
to bear it.
8 "You shall make it hollow with boards; as
it was shown you on the mountain, so shall
they make *it.*

The Court of the Tabernacle

9 "You shall also make the court of the tabernacle. For the south side *there shall be* hangings for the court *made of* fine woven linen,
one hundred cubits long for one side.
10 "And its twenty pillars and their twenty
sockets *shall be* bronze. The hooks of the pillars and their bands *shall be* silver.
11 "Likewise along the length of the north
side *there shall be* hangings one hundred *cubits* long, with its twenty pillars and their
twenty sockets of bronze, and the hooks of the
pillars and their bands of silver.
12 "And along the width of the court on the
west side *shall be* hangings of fifty cubits, with
their ten pillars and their ten sockets.
13 "The width of the court on the east side
shall be fifty cubits.
14 "The hangings on *one* side *of the gate shall
be* fifteen cubits, *with* their three pillars and
their three sockets.
15 "And on the other side *shall be* hangings
of fifteen *cubits, with* their three pillars and
their three sockets.
16 "For the gate of the court *there shall be*
a screen twenty cubits long, *woven of* blue,
purple, and scarlet *thread,* and fine woven
linen, made by a weaver. It *shall have* four pillars and four sockets.
17 "All the pillars around the court shall have
bands of silver; their hooks *shall be* of silver
and their sockets of bronze.
18 "The length of the court *shall be* one hundred cubits, the width fifty throughout, and the
height five cubits, *made of* fine woven linen,
and its sockets of bronze.
19 "All the utensils of the tabernacle for all
its service, all its pegs, and all the pegs of the
court, *shall be* of bronze.

The Care of the Lampstand

20 "And you shall command the children of
Israel that they bring you pure oil of pressed
olives for the light, to cause the lamp to burn
continually.
21 "In the tabernacle of meeting, outside the
veil which *is* before the Testimony, Aaron and
his sons shall tend it from evening until morning before the LORD. *It shall be* a statute forever
to their generations on behalf of the children
of Israel.

Garments for the Priesthood

28 "Now take Aaron your brother, and his
sons with him, from among the children
of Israel, that he may minister to Me as priest,
Aaron *and* Aaron's sons: Nadab, Abihu, Eleazar, and Ithamar.
2 "And you shall make holy garments for
Aaron your brother, for glory and for beauty.
3 "So you shall speak to all *who are* gifted
artisans, whom I have filled with the spirit of
wisdom, that they may make Aaron's garments, to consecrate him, that he may minister
to Me as priest.
4 "And these *are* the garments which they
shall make: a breastplate, an ephod,[a] a robe, a
skillfully woven tunic, a turban, and a sash. So
they shall make holy garments for Aaron your
brother and his sons, that he may minister to
Me as priest.

The Ephod

5 "They shall take the gold, blue, purple, and
scarlet *thread,* and the fine linen,
6 "and they shall make the ephod of gold,
blue, purple, *and* scarlet *thread,* and fine woven linen, artistically worked.
7 "It shall have two shoulder straps joined at
its two edges, and *so* it shall be joined together.
8 "And the intricately woven band of the
ephod, which *is* on it, shall be of the same
workmanship, *made of* gold, blue, purple, and
scarlet *thread,* and fine woven linen.
9 "Then you shall take two onyx stones and
engrave on them the names of the sons of Israel:
10 "six of their names on one stone and six
names on the other stone, in order of their birth.
11 "With the work of an engraver in stone,
like the engravings of a signet, you shall engrave the two stones with the names of the
sons of Israel. You shall set them in settings of
gold.
12 "And you shall put the two stones on the
shoulders of the ephod *as* memorial stones for
the sons of Israel. So Aaron shall bear their
names before the LORD on his two shoulders
as a memorial.
13 "You shall also make settings of gold,
14 "and you shall make two chains of pure
gold like braided cords, and fasten the braided
chains to the settings.

The Breastplate

15 "You shall make the breastplate of judgment. Artistically woven according to the
workmanship of the ephod you shall make it:
of gold, blue, purple, and scarlet *thread,* and
fine woven linen, you shall make it.
16 "It shall be doubled into a square: a span
shall be its length, and a span *shall be* its width.
17 "And you shall put settings of stones in it,
four rows of stones: *The first* row *shall be* a
sardius, a topaz, and an emerald; *this shall be*
the first row;
18 "the second row *shall be* a turquoise, a
sapphire, and a diamond;
19 "the third row, a jacinth, an agate, and an
amethyst;
20 "and the fourth row, a beryl, an onyx, and
a jasper. They shall be set in gold settings.
21 "And the stones shall have the names of
the sons of Israel, twelve according to their
names, *like* the engravings of a signet, each
one with its own name; they shall be according
to the twelve tribes.
22 "You shall make chains for the breastplate
at the end, like braided cords of pure gold.
23 "And you shall make two rings of gold for
the breastplate, and put the two rings on the
two ends of the breastplate.
24 "Then you shall put the two braided *chains*
of gold in the two rings which are on the ends
of the breastplate;
25 "and the *other* two ends of the two braided
chains you shall fasten to the two settings, and
put them on the shoulder straps of the ephod
in the front.
26 "You shall make two rings of gold, and put
them on the two ends of the breastplate, on the
edge of it, which is on the inner side of the
ephod.
27 "And two *other* rings of gold you shall make,
and put them on the two shoulder straps, underneath the ephod toward its front, right at
the seam above the intricately woven band of
the ephod.
28 "They shall bind the breastplate by means
of its rings to the rings of the ephod, using a
blue cord, so that it is above the intricately
woven band of the ephod, and so that the
breastplate does not come loose from the
ephod.
29 "So Aaron shall bear the names of the sons
of Israel on the breastplate of judgment over
his heart, when he goes into the holy *place,* as
a memorial before the LORD continually.
30 "And you shall put in the breastplate of
judgment the Urim and the Thummim,[a] and
they shall be over Aaron's heart when he goes
in before the LORD. So Aaron shall bear the
judgment of the children of Israel over his
heart before the LORD continually.

Other Priestly Garments

31 "You shall make the robe of the ephod all
of blue.
32 "There shall be an opening for his head in
the middle of it; it shall have a woven binding
all around its opening, like the opening in a
coat of mail, so that it does not tear.
33 "And upon its hem you shall make pomegranates of blue, purple, and scarlet, all
around its hem, and bells of gold between them
all around:
34 "a golden bell and a pomegranate, a
golden bell and a pomegranate, upon the hem
of the robe all around.
35 "And it shall be upon Aaron when he ministers, and its sound will be heard when he
goes into the holy *place* before the LORD and
when he comes out, that he may not die.
36 "You shall also make a plate of pure gold
and engrave on it, *like* the engraving of a
signet:

HOLINESS TO THE LORD.

37 "And you shall put it on a blue cord, that it
may be on the turban; it shall be on the front
of the turban.
38 "So it shall be on Aaron's forehead, that
Aaron may bear the iniquity of the holy things
which the children of Israel hallow in all their
holy gifts; and it shall always be on his forehead, that they may be accepted before the
LORD.

28:4 [a]That is, an ornamented vest **28:30** [a]Literally *the Lights and the Perfections* (compare Leviticus 8:8)

39 "You shall skillfully weave the tunic of fine linen *thread,* you shall make the turban of fine linen, and you shall make the sash of woven work.

40 "For Aaron's sons you shall make tunics, and you shall make sashes for them. And you shall make hats for them, for glory and beauty.

41 "So you shall put them on Aaron your brother and on his sons with him. You shall anoint them, consecrate them, and sanctify them, that they may minister to Me as priests.

42 "And you shall make for them linen trousers to cover their nakedness; they shall reach from the waist to the thighs.

43 "They shall be on Aaron and on his sons when they come into the tabernacle of meeting, or when they come near the altar to minister in the holy *place,* that they do not incur iniquity and die. *It shall be* a statute forever to him and his descendants after him.

Aaron and His Sons Consecrated

29 "And this is what you shall do to them to hallow them for ministering to Me as priests: Take one young bull and two rams without blemish,

2 "and unleavened bread, unleavened cakes mixed with oil, and unleavened wafers anointed with oil (you shall make them of wheat flour).

3 "You shall put them in one basket and bring them in the basket, with the bull and the two rams.

4 "And Aaron and his sons you shall bring to the door of the tabernacle of meeting, and you shall wash them with water.

5 "Then you shall take the garments, put the tunic on Aaron, and the robe of the ephod, the ephod, and the breastplate, and gird him with the intricately woven band of the ephod.

6 "You shall put the turban on his head, and put the holy crown on the turban.

7 "And you shall take the anointing oil, pour *it* on his head, and anoint him.

8 "Then you shall bring his sons and put tunics on them.

9 "And you shall gird them with sashes, Aaron and his sons, and put the hats on them. The priesthood shall be theirs for a perpetual statute. So you shall consecrate Aaron and his sons.

10 "You shall also have the bull brought before the tabernacle of meeting, and Aaron and his sons shall put their hands on the head of the bull.

11 "Then you shall kill the bull before the LORD, *by* the door of the tabernacle of meeting.

12 "You shall take *some* of the blood of the bull and put *it* on the horns of the altar with your finger, and pour all the blood beside the base of the altar.

13 "And you shall take all the fat that covers the entrails, the fatty lobe *attached* to the liver, and the two kidneys and the fat that *is* on them, and burn *them* on the altar.

14 "But the flesh of the bull, with its skin and its offal, you shall burn with fire outside the camp. It *is* a sin offering.

15 "You shall also take one ram, and Aaron and his sons shall put their hands on the head of the ram;

16 "and you shall kill the ram, and you shall take its blood and sprinkle *it* all around on the altar.

17 "Then you shall cut the ram in pieces, wash its entrails and its legs, and put *them* with its pieces and with its head.

18 "And you shall burn the whole ram on the altar. It *is* a burnt offering to the LORD; it *is* a sweet aroma, an offering made by fire to the LORD.

19 "You shall also take the other ram, and Aaron and his sons shall put their hands on the head of the ram.

20 "Then you shall kill the ram, and take some of its blood and put *it* on the tip of the right ear of Aaron and on the tip of the right ear of his sons, on the thumb of their right hand and on the big toe of their right foot, and sprinkle the blood all around on the altar.

21 "And you shall take some of the blood that is on the altar, and some of the anointing oil, and sprinkle *it* on Aaron and on his garments, on his sons and on the garments of his sons with him; and he and his garments shall be hallowed, and his sons and his sons' garments with him.

22 "Also you shall take the fat of the ram, the fat tail, the fat that covers the entrails, the fatty lobe *attached to* the liver, the two kidneys and the fat on them, the right thigh (for it *is* a ram of consecration),

23 "one loaf of bread, one cake *made with* oil, and one wafer from the basket of the unleavened bread that *is* before the LORD;

24 "and you shall put all these in the hands of Aaron and in the hands of his sons, and you shall wave them *as* a wave offering before the LORD.

25 "You shall receive them back from their hands and burn *them* on the altar as a burnt offering, as a sweet aroma before the LORD. It *is* an offering made by fire to the LORD.

26 "Then you shall take the breast of the ram of Aaron's consecration and wave it *as* a wave offering before the LORD; and it shall be your portion.

27 "And from the ram of the consecration you shall consecrate the breast of the wave offering which is waved, and the thigh of the heave offering which is raised, of *that* which *is* for Aaron and of *that* which is for his sons.

28 "It shall be from the children of Israel *for* Aaron and his sons by a statute forever. For it is a heave offering; it shall be a heave offering from the children of Israel from the sacrifices of their peace offerings, *that is,* their heave offering to the LORD.

29 "And the holy garments of Aaron shall be his sons' after him, to be anointed in them and to be consecrated in them.

30 "That son who becomes priest in his place shall put them on for seven days, when he enters the tabernacle of meeting to minister in the holy *place.*

31 "And you shall take the ram of the consecration and boil its flesh in the holy place.

32 "Then Aaron and his sons shall eat the flesh of the ram, and the bread that *is* in the basket, *by* the door of the tabernacle of meeting.

33 "They shall eat those things with which the atonement was made, to consecrate *and* to sanctify them; but an outsider shall not eat *them,* because they *are* holy.

34 "And if any of the flesh of the consecration offerings, or of the bread, remains until the morning, then you shall burn the remainder with fire. It shall not be eaten, because it *is* holy.

35 "Thus you shall do to Aaron and his sons,

according to all that I have commanded you. Seven days you shall consecrate them.
36 "And you shall offer a bull every day *as* a sin offering for atonement. You shall cleanse the altar when you make atonement for it, and you shall anoint it to sanctify it.
37 "Seven days you shall make atonement for the altar and sanctify it. And the altar shall be most holy. Whatever touches the altar must be holy.[a]

The Daily Offerings

38 "Now this *is* what you shall offer on the altar: two lambs of the first year, day by day continually.
39 "One lamb you shall offer in the morning, and the other lamb you shall offer at twilight.
40 "With the one lamb shall be one-tenth *of an ephah* of flour mixed with one-fourth of a hin of pressed oil, and one-fourth of a hin of wine *as* a drink offering.
41 "And the other lamb you shall offer at twilight; and you shall offer with it the grain offering and the drink offering, as in the morning, for a sweet aroma, an offering made by fire to the LORD.
42 "*This shall be* a continual burnt offering throughout your generations *at* the door of the tabernacle of meeting before the LORD, where I will meet you to speak with you.
43 "And there I will meet with the children of Israel, and *the tabernacle* shall be sanctified by My glory.
44 "So I will consecrate the tabernacle of meeting and the altar. I will also consecrate both Aaron and his sons to minister to Me as priests.
45 "I will dwell among the children of Israel and will be their God.
46 "And they shall know that I *am* the LORD their God, who brought them up out of the land of Egypt, that I may dwell among them. I *am* the LORD their God.

The Altar of Incense

30 "You shall make an altar to burn incense on; you shall make it of acacia wood.
2 "A cubit *shall be* its length and a cubit its width—it shall be square—and two cubits *shall be* its height. Its horns *shall be* of one piece with it.
3 "And you shall overlay its top, its sides all around, and its horns with pure gold; and you shall make for it a molding of gold all around.
4 "Two gold rings you shall make for it, under the molding on both its sides. You shall place *them* on its two sides, and they will be holders for the poles with which to bear it.
5 "You shall make the poles of acacia wood, and overlay them with gold.
6 "And you shall put it before the veil that *is* before the ark of the Testimony, before the mercy seat that *is* over the Testimony, where I will meet with you.
7 "Aaron shall burn on it sweet incense every morning; when he tends the lamps, he shall burn incense on it.
8 "And when Aaron lights the lamps at twilight, he shall burn incense on it, a perpetual incense before the LORD throughout your generations.
9 "You shall not offer strange incense on it, or a burnt offering, or a grain offering; nor shall you pour a drink offering on it.
10 "And Aaron shall make atonement upon its horns once a year with the blood of the sin offering of atonement; once a year he shall make atonement upon it throughout your generations. It *is* most holy to the LORD."

The Ransom Money

11 Then the LORD spoke to Moses, saying:
12 "When you take the census of the children of Israel for their number, then every man shall give a ransom for himself to the LORD, when you number them, that there may be no plague among them when *you* number them.
13 "This is what everyone among those who are numbered shall give: half a shekel according to the shekel of the sanctuary (a shekel *is* twenty gerahs). The half-shekel *shall be* an offering to the LORD.
14 "Everyone included among those who are numbered, from twenty years old and above, shall give an offering to the LORD.
15 "The rich shall not give more and the poor shall not give less than half a shekel, when *you* give an offering to the LORD, to make atonement for yourselves.
16 "And you shall take the atonement money of the children of Israel, and shall appoint it for the service of the tabernacle of meeting, that it may be a memorial for the children of Israel before the LORD, to make atonement for yourselves."

The Bronze Laver

17 Then the LORD spoke to Moses, saying:
18 "You shall also make a laver of bronze, with its base also of bronze, for washing. You shall put it between the tabernacle of meeting and the altar. And you shall put water in it,
19 "for Aaron and his sons shall wash their hands and their feet in water from it.
20 "When they go into the tabernacle of meeting, or when they come near the altar to minister, to burn an offering made by fire to the LORD, they shall wash with water, lest they die.
21 "So they shall wash their hands and their feet, lest they die. And it shall be a statute forever to them—to him and his descendants throughout their generations."

The Holy Anointing Oil

22 Moreover the LORD spoke to Moses, saying:
23 "Also take for yourself quality spices—five hundred *shekels* of liquid myrrh, half as much sweet-smelling cinnamon (two hundred and fifty *shekels*), two hundred and fifty *shekels* of sweet-smelling cane,
24 "five hundred *shekels* of cassia, according to the shekel of the sanctuary, and a hin of olive oil.
25 "And you shall make from these a holy anointing oil, an ointment compounded according to the art of the perfumer. It shall be a holy anointing oil.
26 "With it you shall anoint the tabernacle of meeting and the ark of the Testimony;
27 "the table and all its utensils, the lampstand and its utensils, and the altar of incense;
28 "the altar of burnt offering with all its utensils, and the laver and its base.
29 "You shall consecrate them, that they may

29:37 [a]Compare Numbers 4:15 and Haggai 2:11–13

be most holy; whatever touches them must be
holy.[a]
30 "And you shall anoint Aaron and his sons,
and consecrate them, that *they* may minister
to Me as priests.
31 "And you shall speak to the children of
Israel, saying: 'This shall be a holy anointing
oil to Me throughout your generations.
32 'It shall not be poured on man's flesh; nor
shall you make *any other* like it, according to
its composition. It *is* holy, *and* it shall be holy
to you.
33 'Whoever compounds *any* like it, or who-
ever puts *any* of it on an outsider, shall be cut
off from his people.' "

The Incense

34 And the LORD said to Moses: "Take sweet
spices, stacte and onycha and galbanum, and
pure frankincense with *these* sweet spices;
there shall be equal amounts of each.
35 "You shall make of these an incense, a
compound according to the art of the per-
fumer, salted, pure, *and* holy.
36 "And you shall beat *some* of it very fine,
and put some of it before the Testimony in the
tabernacle of meeting where I will meet with
you. It shall be most holy to you.
37 "But *as for* the incense which you shall
make, you shall not make any for yourselves,
according to its composition. It shall be to you
holy for the LORD.
38 "Whoever makes *any* like it, to smell it, he
shall be cut off from his people."

Artisans for Building the Tabernacle

31 Then the LORD spoke to Moses, saying:
2 "See, I have called by name Bezalel
the son of Uri, the son of Hur, of the tribe of
Judah.
3 "And I have filled him with the Spirit of
God, in wisdom, in understanding, in knowl-
edge, and in all *manner of* workmanship,
4 "to design artistic works, to work in gold,
in silver, in bronze,
5 "in cutting jewels for setting, in carving
wood, and to work in all *manner of* workman-
ship.
6 "And I, indeed I, have appointed with him
Aholiab the son of Ahisamach, of the tribe of
Dan; and I have put wisdom in the hearts of all
the gifted artisans, that they may make all that
I have commanded you:
7 "the tabernacle of meeting, the ark of the
Testimony and the mercy seat that *is* on it, and
all the furniture of the tabernacle—
8 "the table and its utensils, the pure *gold*
lampstand with all its utensils, the altar of in-
cense,
9 "the altar of burnt offering with all its uten-
sils, and the laver and its base—
10 "the garments of ministry,[a] the holy gar-
ments for Aaron the priest and the garments
of his sons, to minister as priests,
11 "and the anointing oil and sweet incense
for the holy *place.* According to all that I have
commanded you they shall do."

The Sabbath Law

12 And the LORD spoke to Moses, saying,
13 "Speak also to the children of Israel, say-
ing: 'Surely My Sabbaths you shall keep, for it
is a sign between Me and you throughout your
generations, that *you* may know that I *am* the
LORD who sanctifies you.
14 'You shall keep the Sabbath, therefore, for
it is holy to you. Everyone who profanes it
shall surely be put to death; for whoever does
any work on it, that person shall be cut off
from among his people.
15 'Work shall be done for six days, but the
seventh *is* the Sabbath of rest, holy to the
LORD. Whoever does *any* work on the Sabbath
day, he shall surely be put to death.
16 'Therefore the children of Israel shall keep
the Sabbath, to observe the Sabbath through-
out their generations *as* a perpetual covenant.
17 'It *is* a sign between Me and the children
of Israel forever; for *in* six days the LORD made
the heavens and the earth, and on the seventh
day He rested and was refreshed.' "
18 And when He had made an end of speak-
ing with him on Mount Sinai, He gave Moses
two tablets of the Testimony, tablets of stone,
written with the finger of God.

The Gold Calf

32 Now when the people saw that Moses
delayed coming down from the moun-
tain, the people gathered together to Aaron,
and said to him, "Come, make us gods that
shall go before us; for *as for* this Moses, the
man who brought us up out of the land of
Egypt, we do not know what has become of him."
2 And Aaron said to them, "Break off the
golden earrings which *are* in the ears of your
wives, your sons, and your daughters, and bring
them to me."
3 So all the people broke off the golden ear-
rings which *were* in their ears, and brought
them to Aaron.
4 And he received *the gold* from their hand,
and he fashioned it with an engraving tool, and
made a molded calf. Then they said, "This *is*
your god, O Israel, that brought you out of the
land of Egypt!"
5 So when Aaron saw *it,* he built an altar
before it. And Aaron made a proclamation and
said, "Tomorrow *is* a feast to the LORD."
6 Then they rose early on the next day, of-
fered burnt offerings, and brought peace offer-
ings; and the people sat down to eat and drink,
and rose up to play.
7 And the LORD said to Moses, "Go, get down!
For your people whom you brought out of the
land of Egypt have corrupted *themselves.*
8 "They have turned aside quickly out of the
way which I commanded them. They have
made themselves a molded calf, and worshiped
it and sacrificed to it, and said, 'This *is* your
god, O Israel, that brought you out of the land
of Egypt!' "
9 And the LORD said to Moses, "I have seen
this people, and indeed it *is* a stiff-necked peo-
ple!
10 "Now therefore, let Me alone, that My wrath
may burn hot against them and I may consume
them. And I will make of you a great nation."
11 Then Moses pleaded with the LORD his God,
and said: "LORD, why does Your wrath burn
hot against Your people whom You have brought
out of the land of Egypt with great power and
with a mighty hand?
12 "Why should the Egyptians speak, and say,
'He brought them out to harm them, to kill them
in the mountains, and to consume them from

30:29 [a]Compare Numbers 4:15 and Haggai 2:11–13 **31:10** [a]Or *woven garments*

the face of the earth'? Turn from Your fierce
wrath, and relent from this harm to Your
people.
13 "Remember Abraham, Isaac, and Israel,
Your servants, to whom You swore by Your
own self, and said to them, 'I will multiply your
descendants as the stars of heaven; and all this
land that I have spoken of I give to your de-
scendants, and they shall inherit *it* forever.'"[a]
14 So the LORD relented from the harm which
He said He would do to His people.
15 And Moses turned and went down from
the mountain, and the two tablets of the Testi-
mony *were* in his hand. The tablets *were* writ-
ten on both sides; on the one *side* and on the
other they were written.
16 Now the tablets *were* the work of God, and
the writing *was* the writing of God engraved
on the tablets.
17 And when Joshua heard the noise of the
people as they shouted, he said to Moses,
"*There is* a noise of war in the camp."
18 But he said:

"*It is* not the noise of the shout of victory,
Nor the noise of the cry of defeat,
But the sound of singing I hear."

19 So it was, as soon as he came near the
camp, that he saw the calf *and* the dancing.
So Moses' anger became hot, and he cast the
tablets out of his hands and broke them at the
foot of the mountain.
20 Then he took the calf which they had
made, burned *it* in the fire, and ground *it* to
powder; and he scattered *it* on the water and
made the children of Israel drink *it*.
21 And Moses said to Aaron, "What did this
people do to you that you have brought *so* great
a sin upon them?"
22 So Aaron said, "Do not let the anger of my
lord become hot. You know the people, that
they *are set* on evil.
23 "For they said to me, 'Make us gods that
shall go before us; *as for* this Moses, the man
who brought us out of the land of Egypt, we do
not know what has become of him.'
24 "And I said to them, 'Whoever has any
gold, let them break *it* off.' So they gave *it* to
me, and I cast it into the fire, and this calf came
out."
25 Now when Moses saw that the people *were*
unrestrained (for Aaron had not restrained
them, to *their* shame among their enemies),
26 then Moses stood in the entrance of the
camp, and said, "Whoever *is* on the LORD's
side—*come* to me!" And all the sons of Levi
gathered themselves together to him.
27 And he said to them, "Thus says the LORD
God of Israel: 'Let every man put his sword on
his side, and go in and out from entrance to
entrance throughout the camp, and let every
man kill his brother, every man his companion,
and every man his neighbor.'"
28 So the sons of Levi did according to the
word of Moses. And about three thousand men
of the people fell that day.
29 Then Moses said, "Consecrate yourselves
today to the LORD, that He may bestow on you
a blessing this day, for every man has opposed
his son and his brother."
30 Now it came to pass on the next day that
Moses said to the people, "You have committed
a great sin. So now I will go up to the LORD;
perhaps I can make atonement for your sin."
31 Then Moses returned to the LORD and
said, "Oh, these people have committed a great
sin, and have made for themselves a god of
gold!
32 "Yet now, if You will forgive their sin—but
if not, I pray, blot me out of Your book which
You have written."
33 And the LORD said to Moses, "Whoever
has sinned against Me, I will blot him out of
My book.
34 "Now therefore, go, lead the people to *the
place* of which I have spoken to you. Behold,
My Angel shall go before you. Nevertheless, in
the day when I visit for punishment, I will visit
punishment upon them for their sin."
35 So the LORD plagued the people because
of what they did with the calf which Aaron
made.

The Command to Leave Sinai

33 Then the LORD said to Moses, "Depart
and go up from here, you and the people
whom you have brought out of the land of
Egypt, to the land of which I swore to Abra-
ham, Isaac, and Jacob, saying, 'To your descen-
dants I will give it.'
2 "And I will send *My* Angel before you, and
I will drive out the Canaanite and the Amorite
and the Hittite and the Perizzite and the Hivite
and the Jebusite.
3 "*Go up* to a land flowing with milk and
honey; for I will not go up in your midst, lest I
consume you on the way, for you *are* a stiff-
necked people."
4 And when the people heard this bad news,
they mourned, and no one put on his orna-
ments.
5 For the LORD had said to Moses, "Say to
the children of Israel, 'You *are* a stiff-necked
people. I could come up into your midst in one
moment and consume you. Now therefore,
take off your ornaments, that I may know what
to do to you.'"
6 So the children of Israel stripped them-
selves of their ornaments by Mount Horeb.

Moses Meets with the LORD

7 Moses took his tent and pitched it outside
the camp, far from the camp, and called it the
tabernacle of meeting. And it came to pass
that everyone who sought the LORD went out
to the tabernacle of meeting which *was* outside
the camp.
8 So it was, whenever Moses went out to the
tabernacle, *that* all the people rose, and each
man stood *at* his tent door and watched Moses
until he had gone into the tabernacle.
9 And it came to pass, when Moses entered
the tabernacle, that the pillar of cloud de-
scended and stood *at* the door of the taberna-
cle, and *the LORD* talked with Moses.
10 All the people saw the pillar of cloud
standing *at* the tabernacle door, and all the
people rose and worshiped, each man *in* his
tent door.
11 So the LORD spoke to Moses face to face,
as a man speaks to his friend. And he would
return to the camp, but his servant Joshua the
son of Nun, a young man, did not depart from
the tabernacle.

32:13 [a]Genesis 13:15 and 22:17

The Promise of God's Presence

12 Then Moses said to the LORD, "See, You say to me, 'Bring up this people.' But You have not let me know whom You will send with me. Yet You have said, 'I know you by name, and you have also found grace in My sight.'

13 "Now therefore, I pray, if I have found grace in Your sight, show me now Your way, that I may know You and that I may find grace in Your sight. And consider that this nation *is* Your people."

14 And He said, "My Presence will go *with you*, and I will give you rest."

15 Then he said to Him, "If Your Presence does not go *with us*, do not bring us up from here.

16 "For how then will it be known that Your people and I have found grace in Your sight, except You go with us? So we shall be separate, Your people and I, from all the people who *are* upon the face of the earth."

17 So the LORD said to Moses, "I will also do this thing that you have spoken; for you have found grace in My sight, and I know you by name."

18 And he said, "Please, show me Your glory."

19 Then He said, "I will make all My goodness pass before you, and I will proclaim the name of the LORD before you. I will be gracious to whom I will be gracious, and I will have compassion on whom I will have compassion."

20 But He said, "You cannot see My face; for no man shall see Me, and live."

21 And the LORD said, "Here is a place by Me, and you shall stand on the rock.

22 "So it shall be, while My glory passes by, that I will put you in the cleft of the rock, and will cover you with My hand while I pass by.

23 "Then I will take away My hand, and you shall see My back; but My face shall not be seen."

Moses Makes New Tablets

34 And the LORD said to Moses, "Cut two tablets of stone like the first *ones*, and I will write on *these* tablets the words that were on the first tablets which you broke.

2 "So be ready in the morning, and come up in the morning to Mount Sinai, and present yourself to Me there on the top of the mountain.

3 "And no man shall come up with you, and let no man be seen throughout all the mountain; let neither flocks nor herds feed before that mountain."

4 So he cut two tablets of stone like the first *ones*. Then Moses rose early in the morning and went up Mount Sinai, as the LORD had commanded him; and he took in his hand the two tablets of stone.

5 Now the LORD descended in the cloud and stood with him there, and proclaimed the name of the LORD.

6 And the LORD passed before him and proclaimed, "The LORD, the LORD God, merciful and gracious, longsuffering, and abounding in goodness and truth,

7 "keeping mercy for thousands, forgiving iniquity and transgression and sin, by no means clearing *the guilty*, visiting the iniquity of the fathers upon the children and the children's children to the third and the fourth generation."

8 So Moses made haste and bowed his head toward the earth, and worshiped.

9 Then he said, "If now I have found grace in Your sight, O Lord, let my Lord, I pray, go among us, even though we *are* a stiff-necked people; and pardon our iniquity and our sin, and take us as Your inheritance."

The Covenant Renewed

10 And He said: "Behold, I make a covenant. Before all your people I will do marvels such as have not been done in all the earth, nor in any nation; and all the people among whom you *are* shall see the work of the LORD. For it *is* an awesome thing that I will do with you.

11 "Observe what I command you this day. Behold, I am driving out from before you the Amorite and the Canaanite and the Hittite and the Perizzite and the Hivite and the Jebusite.

12 "Take heed to yourself, lest you make a covenant with the inhabitants of the land where you are going, lest it be a snare in your midst.

13 "But you shall destroy their altars, break their *sacred* pillars, and cut down their wooden images

14 "(for you shall worship no other god, for the LORD, whose name *is* Jealous, *is* a jealous God),

15 "lest you make a covenant with the inhabitants of the land, and they play the harlot with their gods and make sacrifice to their gods, and *one of them* invites you and you eat of his sacrifice,

16 "and you take of his daughters for your sons, and his daughters play the harlot with their gods and make your sons play the harlot with their gods.

17 "You shall make no molded gods for yourselves.

18 "The Feast of Unleavened Bread you shall keep. Seven days you shall eat unleavened bread, as I commanded you, in the appointed time of the month of Abib; for in the month of Abib you came out from Egypt.

19 "All that open the womb *are* Mine, and every male firstborn among your livestock, *whether* ox or sheep.

20 "But the firstborn of a donkey you shall redeem with a lamb. And if you will not redeem *him*, then you shall break his neck. All the firstborn of your sons you shall redeem. And none shall appear before Me empty-handed.

21 "Six days you shall work, but on the seventh day you shall rest; in plowing time and in harvest you shall rest.

22 "And you shall observe the Feast of Weeks, of the firstfruits of wheat harvest, and the Feast of Ingathering at the year's end.

23 "Three times in the year all your men shall appear before the Lord, the LORD God of Israel.

24 "For I will cast out the nations before you and enlarge your borders; neither will any man covet your land when you go up to appear before the LORD your God three times in the year.

25 "You shall not offer the blood of My sacrifice with leaven, nor shall the sacrifice of the Feast of the Passover be left until morning.

26 "The first of the firstfruits of your land you shall bring to the house of the LORD your God.

You shall not boil a young goat in its mother's milk."

27 Then the LORD said to Moses, "Write these words, for according to the tenor of these words I have made a covenant with you and with Israel."

28 So he was there with the LORD forty days and forty nights; he neither ate bread nor drank water. And He wrote on the tablets the words of the covenant, the Ten Commandments.[a]

The Shining Face of Moses

29 Now it was so, when Moses came down from Mount Sinai (and the two tablets of the Testimony *were* in Moses' hand when he came down from the mountain), that Moses did not know that the skin of his face shone while he talked with Him.

30 So when Aaron and all the children of Israel saw Moses, behold, the skin of his face shone, and they were afraid to come near him.

31 Then Moses called to them, and Aaron and all the rulers of the congregation returned to him; and Moses talked with them.

32 Afterward all the children of Israel came near, and he gave them as commandments all that the LORD had spoken with him on Mount Sinai.

33 And when Moses had finished speaking with them, he put a veil on his face.

34 But whenever Moses went in before the LORD to speak with Him, he would take the veil off until he came out; and he would come out and speak to the children of Israel whatever he had been commanded.

35 And whenever the children of Israel saw the face of Moses, that the skin of Moses' face shone, then Moses would put the veil on his face again, until he went in to speak with Him.

Sabbath Regulations

35 Then Moses gathered all the congregation of the children of Israel together, and said to them, "These *are* the words which the LORD has commanded *you* to do:

2 "Work shall be done for six days, but the seventh day shall be a holy day for you, a Sabbath of rest to the LORD. Whoever does any work on it shall be put to death.

3 "You shall kindle no fire throughout your dwellings on the Sabbath day."

Offerings for the Tabernacle

4 And Moses spoke to all the congregation of the children of Israel, saying, "This *is* the thing which the LORD commanded, saying:

5 'Take from among you an offering to the LORD. Whoever *is* of a willing heart, let him bring it as an offering to the LORD: gold, silver, and bronze;

6 'blue, purple, and scarlet *thread*, fine linen, and goats' *hair;*

7 'ram skins dyed red, badger skins, and acacia wood;

8 'oil for the light, and spices for the anointing oil and for the sweet incense;

9 'onyx stones, and stones to be set in the ephod and in the breastplate.

Articles of the Tabernacle

10 'All *who are* gifted artisans among you shall come and make all that the LORD has commanded:

11 'the tabernacle, its tent, its covering, its clasps, its boards, its bars, its pillars, and its sockets;

12 'the ark and its poles, *with* the mercy seat, and the veil of the covering;

13 'the table and its poles, all its utensils, and the showbread;

14 'also the lampstand for the light, its utensils, its lamps, and the oil for the light;

15 'the incense altar, its poles, the anointing oil, the sweet incense, and the screen for the door at the entrance of the tabernacle;

16 'the altar of burnt offering with its bronze grating, its poles, all its utensils, *and* the laver and its base;

17 'the hangings of the court, its pillars, their sockets, and the screen for the gate of the court;

18 'the pegs of the tabernacle, the pegs of the court, and their cords;

19 'the garments of ministry,[a] for ministering in the holy *place*—the holy garments for Aaron the priest and the garments of his sons, to minister as priests.'"

The Tabernacle Offerings Presented

20 And all the congregation of the children of Israel departed from the presence of Moses.

21 Then everyone came whose heart was stirred, and everyone whose spirit was willing, *and* they brought the LORD's offering for the work of the tabernacle of meeting, for all its service, and for the holy garments.

22 They came, both men and women, as many as had a willing heart, *and* brought earrings and nose rings, rings and necklaces, all jewelry of gold, that is, every man who *made* an offering of gold to the LORD.

23 And every man, with whom was found blue, purple, and scarlet *thread*, fine linen, and goats' *hair*, red skins of rams, and badger skins, brought *them*.

24 Everyone who offered an offering of silver or bronze brought the LORD's offering. And everyone with whom was found acacia wood for any work of the service, brought *it*.

25 All the women *who were* gifted artisans spun yarn with their hands, and brought what they had spun, of blue, purple, *and* scarlet, and fine linen.

26 And all the women whose hearts stirred with wisdom spun yarn of goats' *hair*.

27 The rulers brought onyx stones, and the stones to be set in the ephod and in the breastplate,

28 and spices and oil for the light, for the anointing oil, and for the sweet incense.

29 The children of Israel brought a freewill offering to the LORD, all the men and women whose hearts were willing to bring *material* for all kinds of work which the LORD, by the hand of Moses, had commanded to be done.

The Artisans Called by God

30 And Moses said to the children of Israel, "See, the LORD has called by name Bezalel the son of Uri, the son of Hur, of the tribe of Judah;

31 "and He has filled him with the Spirit of

34:28 [a]Literally *Ten Words* **35:19** [a]Or *woven garments*

God, in wisdom and understanding, in knowledge and all manner of workmanship,
32 "to design artistic works, to work in gold
and silver and bronze,
33 "in cutting jewels for setting, in carving
wood, and to work in all manner of artistic
workmanship.
34 "And He has put in his heart the ability to
teach, *in* him and Aholiab the son of Ahisamach, of the tribe of Dan.
35 "He has filled them with skill to do all
manner of work of the engraver and the designer and the tapestry maker, in blue, purple, and scarlet *thread,* and fine linen, and of the weaver—those who do every work and those who design artistic works.
36 "And Bezalel and Aholiab, and every
gifted artisan in whom the LORD has put wisdom and understanding, to know how to do all manner of work for the service of the sanctuary, shall do according to all that the LORD has commanded."

The People Give More than Enough

2 Then Moses called Bezalel and Aholiab,
and every gifted artisan in whose heart the LORD had put wisdom, everyone whose heart was stirred, to come and do the work.
3 And they received from Moses all the of-
fering which the children of Israel had brought for the work of the service of making the sanctuary. So they continued bringing to him freewill offerings every morning.
4 Then all the craftsmen who were doing all
the work of the sanctuary came, each from the work he was doing,
5 and they spoke to Moses, saying, "The
people bring much more than enough for the service of the work which the LORD commanded *us* to do."
6 So Moses gave a commandment, and they
caused it to be proclaimed throughout the camp, saying, "Let neither man nor woman do any more work for the offering of the sanctuary." And the people were restrained from bringing,
7 for the material they had was sufficient for
all the work to be done—indeed too much.

Building the Tabernacle

8 Then all the gifted artisans among them
who worked on the tabernacle made ten curtains woven of fine linen, and of blue, purple, and scarlet *thread; with* artistic designs of cherubim they made them.
9 The length of each curtain *was* twenty-
eight cubits, and the width of each curtain four cubits; the curtains *were* all the same size.
10 And he coupled five curtains to one an-
other, and *the other* five curtains he coupled to one another.
11 He made loops of blue *yarn* on the edge of
the curtain on the selvedge of one set; likewise he did on the outer edge of *the other* curtain of the second set.
12 Fifty loops he made on one curtain, and
fifty loops he made on the edge of the curtain on the end of the second set; the loops held one *curtain* to another.
13 And he made fifty clasps of gold, and cou-
pled the curtains to one another with the clasps, that it might be one tabernacle.
14 He made curtains of goats' *hair* for the tent
over the tabernacle; he made eleven curtains.
15 The length of each curtain *was* thirty cu-
bits, and the width of each curtain four cubits; the eleven curtains *were* the same size.
16 He coupled five curtains by themselves
and six curtains by themselves.
17 And he made fifty loops on the edge of the
curtain that is outermost in one set, and fifty loops he made on the edge of the curtain of the second set.
18 He also made fifty bronze clasps to couple
the tent together, that it might be one.
19 Then he made a covering for the tent of
ram skins dyed red, and a covering of badger skins above *that.*
20 For the tabernacle he made boards of aca-
cia wood, standing upright.
21 The length of each board *was* ten cubits,
and the width of each board a cubit and a half.
22 Each board had two tenons for binding
one to another. Thus he made for all the boards of the tabernacle.
23 And he made boards for the tabernacle,
twenty boards for the south side.
24 Forty sockets of silver he made to go under
the twenty boards: two sockets under each of the boards for its two tenons.
25 And for the other side of the tabernacle,
the north side, he made twenty boards
26 and their forty sockets of silver: two sock-
ets under each of the boards.
27 For the west side of the tabernacle he made
six boards.
28 He also made two boards for the two back
corners of the tabernacle.
29 And they were coupled at the bottom and
coupled together at the top by one ring. Thus he made both of them for the two corners.
30 So there were eight boards and their sock-
ets—sixteen sockets of silver—two sockets under each of the boards.
31 And he made bars of acacia wood: five for
the boards on one side of the tabernacle,
32 five bars for the boards on the other side
of the tabernacle, and five bars for the boards of the tabernacle on the far side westward.
33 And he made the middle bar to pass
through the boards from one end to the other.
34 He overlaid the boards with gold, made
their rings of gold *to be* holders for the bars, and overlaid the bars with gold.
35 And he made a veil of blue, purple, and
scarlet *thread,* and fine woven linen; it was worked *with* an artistic design of cherubim.
36 He made for it four pillars of acacia *wood,*
and overlaid them with gold, with their hooks of gold; and he cast four sockets of silver for them.
37 He also made a screen for the tabernacle
door, of blue, purple, and scarlet *thread,* and fine woven linen, made by a weaver,
38 and its five pillars with their hooks. And
he overlaid their capitals and their rings with gold, but their five sockets *were* bronze.

Making the Ark of the Testimony

37 Then Bezalel made the ark of acacia
wood; two and a half cubits *was* its length, a cubit and a half its width, and a cubit and a half its height.
2 He overlaid it with pure gold inside and
outside, and made a molding of gold all around it.
3 And he cast for it four rings of gold *to be*
set in its four corners: two rings on one side, and two rings on the other side of it.

4 He made poles of acacia wood, and overlaid them with gold.

5 And he put the poles into the rings at the sides of the ark, to bear the ark.

6 He also made the mercy seat of pure gold; two and a half cubits *was* its length and a cubit and a half its width.

7 He made two cherubim of beaten gold; he made them of one piece at the two ends of the mercy seat:

8 one cherub at one end on this side, and the other cherub at the *other* end on that side. He made the cherubim at the two ends *of one piece* with the mercy seat.

9 The cherubim spread out *their* wings above, *and* covered the mercy seat with their wings. They faced one another; the faces of the cherubim were toward the mercy seat.

Making the Table for the Showbread

10 He made the table of acacia wood; two cubits *was* its length, a cubit its width, and a cubit and a half its height.

11 And he overlaid it with pure gold, and made a molding of gold all around it.

12 Also he made a frame of a handbreadth all around it, and made a molding of gold for the frame all around it.

13 And he cast for it four rings of gold, and put the rings on the four corners that *were* at its four legs.

14 The rings were close to the frame, as holders for the poles to bear the table.

15 And he made the poles of acacia wood to bear the table, and overlaid them with gold.

16 He made of pure gold the utensils which were on the table: its dishes, its cups, its bowls, and its pitchers for pouring.

Making the Gold Lampstand

17 He also made the lampstand of pure gold; of hammered work he made the lampstand. Its shaft, its branches, its bowls, its *ornamental* knobs, and its flowers were of the same piece.

18 And six branches came out of its sides: three branches of the lampstand out of one side, and three branches of the lampstand out of the other side.

19 There were three bowls made like almond *blossoms* on one branch, with an *ornamental* knob and a flower, and three bowls made like almond *blossoms* on the other branch, with an *ornamental* knob and a flower—and so for the six branches coming out of the lampstand.

20 And on the lampstand itself *were* four bowls made like almond *blossoms, each with* its *ornamental* knob and flower.

21 *There was* a knob under the *first* two branches of the same, a knob under the *second* two branches of the same, and a knob under the *third* two branches of the same, according to the six branches extending from it.

22 Their knobs and their branches were of one piece; all of it *was* one hammered piece of pure gold.

23 And he made its seven lamps, its wick-trimmers, and its trays of pure gold.

24 Of a talent of pure gold he made it, with all its utensils.

Making the Altar of Incense

25 He made the incense altar of acacia wood. Its length *was* a cubit and its width a cubit—*it was* square—and two cubits *was* its height. Its horns were *of one piece* with it.

26 And he overlaid it with pure gold: its top, its sides all around, and its horns. He also made for it a molding of gold all around it.

27 He made two rings of gold for it under its molding, by its two corners on both sides, as holders for the poles with which to bear it.

28 And he made the poles of acacia wood, and overlaid them with gold.

Making the Anointing Oil and the Incense

29 He also made the holy anointing oil and the pure incense of sweet spices, according to the work of the perfumer.

Making the Altar of Burnt Offering

38 He made the altar of burnt offering of acacia wood; five cubits *was* its length and five cubits its width—*it was* square—and its height *was* three cubits.

2 He made its horns on its four corners; the horns were *of one piece* with it. And he overlaid it with bronze.

3 He made all the utensils for the altar: the pans, the shovels, the basins, the forks, and the firepans; all its utensils he made of bronze.

4 And he made a grate of bronze network for the altar, under its rim, midway from the bottom.

5 He cast four rings for the four corners of the bronze grating, *as* holders for the poles.

6 And he made the poles of acacia wood, and overlaid them with bronze.

7 Then he put the poles into the rings on the sides of the altar, with which to bear it. He made the altar hollow with boards.

Making the Bronze Laver

8 He made the laver of bronze and its base of bronze, from the bronze mirrors of the serving women who assembled at the door of the tabernacle of meeting.

Making the Court of the Tabernacle

9 Then he made the court on the south side; the hangings of the court *were of* fine woven linen, one hundred cubits long.

10 There *were* twenty pillars for them, with twenty bronze sockets. The hooks of the pillars and their bands *were* silver.

11 On the north side *the hangings were* one hundred cubits *long,* with twenty pillars and their twenty bronze sockets. The hooks of the pillars and their bands *were* silver.

12 And on the west side *there were* hangings of fifty cubits, with ten pillars and their ten sockets. The hooks of the pillars and their bands *were* silver.

13 For the east side *the hangings were* fifty cubits.

14 The hangings of one side *of the gate were* fifteen cubits *long, with* their three pillars and their three sockets,

15 and the same for the other side of the court gate; on this side and that *were* hangings of fifteen cubits, *with* their three pillars and their three sockets.

16 All the hangings of the court all around *were of* fine woven linen.

17 The sockets for the pillars *were* bronze, the hooks of the pillars and their bands *were* silver, and the overlay of their capitals *was* silver; and all the pillars of the court had bands of silver.

18 The screen for the gate of the court *was* woven of blue, purple, and scarlet *thread,* and

of fine woven linen. The length *was* twenty cubits, and the height along its width *was* five cubits, corresponding to the hangings of the court.
19 And *there were* four pillars *with* their four sockets of bronze; their hooks *were* silver, and the overlay of their capitals and their bands *was* silver.
20 All the pegs of the tabernacle, and of the court all around, *were* bronze.

Materials of the Tabernacle

21 This is the inventory of the tabernacle, the tabernacle of the Testimony, which was counted according to the commandment of Moses, for the service of the Levites, by the hand of Ithamar, son of Aaron the priest.
22 Bezalel the son of Uri, the son of Hur, of the tribe of Judah, made all that the LORD had commanded Moses.
23 And with him *was* Aholiab the son of Ahisamach, of the tribe of Dan, an engraver and designer, a weaver of blue, purple, and scarlet *thread,* and of fine linen.
24 All the gold that was used in all the work of the holy *place,* that is, the gold of the offering, was twenty-nine talents and seven hundred and thirty shekels, according to the shekel of the sanctuary.
25 And the silver from those who were numbered of the congregation *was* one hundred talents and one thousand seven hundred and seventy-five shekels, according to the shekel of the sanctuary:
26 a bekah for each man (*that is,* half a shekel, according to the shekel of the sanctuary), for everyone included in the numbering from twenty years old and above, for six hundred and three thousand, five hundred and fifty *men.*
27 And from the hundred talents of silver were cast the sockets of the sanctuary and the bases of the veil: one hundred sockets from the hundred talents, one talent for each socket.
28 Then from the one thousand seven hundred and seventy-five *shekels* he made hooks for the pillars, overlaid their capitals, and made bands for them.
29 The offering of bronze *was* seventy talents and two thousand four hundred shekels.
30 And with it he made the sockets for the door of the tabernacle of meeting, the bronze altar, the bronze grating for it, and all the utensils for the altar,
31 the sockets for the court all around, the bases for the court gate, all the pegs for the tabernacle, and all the pegs for the court all around.

Making the Garments of the Priesthood

39 Of the blue, purple, and scarlet *thread* they made garments of ministry,[a] for ministering in the holy *place,* and made the holy garments for Aaron, as the LORD had commanded Moses.

Making the Ephod

2 He made the ephod of gold, blue, purple, and scarlet *thread,* and of fine woven linen.
3 And they beat the gold into thin sheets and cut *it into* threads, to work *it* in *with* the blue, purple, and scarlet *thread,* and the fine linen, *into* artistic designs.
4 They made shoulder straps for it to couple *it* together; it was coupled together at its two edges.
5 And the intricately woven band of his ephod that *was* on it *was* of the same workmanship, *woven of* gold, blue, purple, and scarlet *thread,* and *of* fine woven linen, as the LORD had commanded Moses.
6 And they set onyx stones, enclosed in settings of gold; they were engraved, as signets are engraved, with the names of the sons of Israel.
7 He put them on the shoulders of the ephod *as* memorial stones for the sons of Israel, as the LORD had commanded Moses.

Making the Breastplate

8 And he made the breastplate, artistically woven like the workmanship of the ephod, of gold, blue, purple, and scarlet *thread,* and of fine woven linen.
9 They made the breastplate square by doubling it; a span *was* its length and a span its width when doubled.
10 And they set in it four rows of stones: a row with a sardius, a topaz, and an emerald was the first row;
11 the second row, a turquoise, a sapphire, and a diamond;
12 the third row, a jacinth, an agate, and an amethyst;
13 the fourth row, a beryl, an onyx, and a jasper. *They were* enclosed in settings of gold in their mountings.
14 *There were* twelve stones according to the names of the sons of Israel: according to their names, *engraved like* a signet, each one with its own name according to the twelve tribes.
15 And they made chains for the breastplate at the ends, like braided cords of pure gold.
16 They also made two settings of gold and two gold rings, and put the two rings on the two ends of the breastplate.
17 And they put the two braided *chains* of gold in the two rings on the ends of the breastplate.
18 The two ends of the two braided *chains* they fastened in the two settings, and put them on the shoulder straps of the ephod in the front.
19 And they made two rings of gold and put *them* on the two ends of the breastplate, on the edge of it, which *was* on the inward side of the ephod.
20 They made two *other* gold rings and put them on the two shoulder straps, underneath the ephod toward its front, right at the seam above the intricately woven band of the ephod.
21 And they bound the breastplate by means of its rings to the rings of the ephod with a blue cord, so that it would be above the intricately woven band of the ephod, and that the breastplate would not come loose from the ephod, as the LORD had commanded Moses.

Making the Other Priestly Garments

22 He made the robe of the ephod of woven work, all of blue.
23 And *there was* an opening in the middle of the robe, like the opening in a coat of mail, *with* a woven binding all around the opening, so that it would not tear.

39:1 [a]Or *woven garments*

24 They made on the hem of the robe pomegranates of blue, purple, and scarlet, and of fine woven *linen.*

25 And they made bells of pure gold, and put the bells between the pomegranates on the hem of the robe all around between the pomegranates:

26 a bell and a pomegranate, a bell and a pomegranate, all around the hem of the robe to minister in, as the LORD had commanded Moses.

27 They made tunics, artistically woven of fine linen, for Aaron and his sons,

28 a turban of fine linen, exquisite hats of fine linen, short trousers of fine woven linen,

29 and a sash of fine woven linen with blue, purple, and scarlet *thread,* made by a weaver, as the LORD had commanded Moses.

30 Then they made the plate of the holy crown of pure gold, and wrote on it an inscription *like* the engraving of a signet:

HOLINESS TO THE LORD.

31 And they tied to it a blue cord, to fasten *it* above on the turban, as the LORD had commanded Moses.

The Work Completed

32 Thus all the work of the tabernacle of the tent of meeting was finished. And the children of Israel did according to all that the LORD had commanded Moses; so they did.

33 And they brought the tabernacle to Moses, the tent and all its furnishings: its clasps, its boards, its bars, its pillars, and its sockets;

34 the covering of ram skins dyed red, the covering of badger skins, and the veil of the covering;

35 the ark of the Testimony with its poles, and the mercy seat;

36 the table, all its utensils, and the showbread;

37 the pure *gold* lampstand with its lamps (the lamps set in order), all its utensils, and the oil for light;

38 the gold altar, the anointing oil, and the sweet incense; the screen for the tabernacle door;

39 the bronze altar, its grate of bronze, its poles, and all its utensils; the laver with its base;

40 the hangings of the court, its pillars and its sockets, the screen for the court gate, its cords, and its pegs; all the utensils for the service of the tabernacle, for the tent of meeting;

41 and the garments of ministry,[a] to minister in the holy *place:* the holy garments for Aaron the priest, and his sons' garments, to minister as priests.

42 According to all that the LORD had commanded Moses, so the children of Israel did all the work.

43 Then Moses looked over all the work, and indeed they had done it; as the LORD had commanded, just so they had done it. And Moses blessed them.

The Tabernacle Erected and Arranged

40 Then the LORD spoke to Moses, saying:

2 "On the first day of the first month you shall set up the tabernacle of the tent of meeting.

3 "You shall put in it the ark of the Testimony, and partition off the ark with the veil.

4 "You shall bring in the table and arrange the things that are to be set in order on it; and you shall bring in the lampstand and light its lamps.

5 "You shall also set the altar of gold for the incense before the ark of the Testimony, and put up the screen for the door of the tabernacle.

6 "Then you shall set the altar of the burnt offering before the door of the tabernacle of the tent of meeting.

7 "And you shall set the laver between the tabernacle of meeting and the altar, and put water in it.

8 "You shall set up the court all around, and hang up the screen at the court gate.

9 "And you shall take the anointing oil, and anoint the tabernacle and all that *is* in it; and you shall hallow it and all its utensils, and it shall be holy.

10 "You shall anoint the altar of the burnt offering and all its utensils, and consecrate the altar. The altar shall be most holy.

11 "And you shall anoint the laver and its base, and consecrate it.

12 "Then you shall bring Aaron and his sons to the door of the tabernacle of meeting and wash them with water.

13 "You shall put the holy garments on Aaron, and anoint him and consecrate him, that he may minister to Me as priest.

14 "And you shall bring his sons and clothe them with tunics.

15 "You shall anoint them, as you anointed their father, that they may minister to Me as priests; for their anointing shall surely be an everlasting priesthood throughout their generations."

16 Thus Moses did; according to all that the LORD had commanded him, so he did.

17 And it came to pass in the first month of the second year, on the first *day* of the month, *that* the tabernacle was raised up.

18 So Moses raised up the tabernacle, fastened its sockets, set up its boards, put in its bars, and raised up its pillars.

19 And he spread out the tent over the tabernacle and put the covering of the tent on top of it, as the LORD had commanded Moses.

20 He took the Testimony and put *it* into the ark, inserted the poles through the rings of the ark, and put the mercy seat on top of the ark.

21 And he brought the ark into the tabernacle, hung up the veil of the covering, and partitioned off the ark of the Testimony, as the LORD had commanded Moses.

22 He put the table in the tabernacle of meeting, on the north side of the tabernacle, outside the veil;

23 and he set the bread in order upon it before the LORD, as the LORD had commanded Moses.

24 He put the lampstand in the tabernacle of meeting, across from the table, on the south side of the tabernacle;

25 and he lit the lamps before the LORD, as the LORD had commanded Moses.

26 He put the gold altar in the tabernacle of meeting in front of the veil;

27 and he burned sweet incense on it, as the LORD had commanded Moses.

28 He hung up the screen *at* the door of the tabernacle.

29 And he put the altar of burnt offering *be-*

39:41 [a]Or *woven garments*

fore the door of the tabernacle of the tent of meeting, and offered upon it the burnt offering and the grain offering, as the LORD had commanded Moses.

30 He set the laver between the tabernacle of meeting and the altar, and put water there for washing;

31 and Moses, Aaron, and his sons would wash their hands and their feet *with water* from it.

32 Whenever they went into the tabernacle of meeting, and when they came near the altar, they washed, as the LORD had commanded Moses.

33 And he raised up the court all around the tabernacle and the altar, and hung up the screen of the court gate. So Moses finished the work.

The Cloud and the Glory

34 Then the cloud covered the tabernacle of meeting, and the glory of the LORD filled the tabernacle.

35 And Moses was not able to enter the tabernacle of meeting, because the cloud rested above it, and the glory of the LORD filled the tabernacle.

36 Whenever the cloud was taken up from above the tabernacle, the children of Israel would go onward in all their journeys.

37 But if the cloud was not taken up, then they did not journey till the day that it was taken up.

38 For the cloud of the LORD *was* above the tabernacle by day, and fire was over it by night, in the sight of all the house of Israel, throughout all their journeys.

The Third Book of Moses Called

LEVITICUS

The Burnt Offering

1 Now the LORD called to Moses, and spoke to him from the tabernacle of meeting, saying,

2 "Speak to the children of Israel, and say to them: 'When any one of you brings an offering to the LORD, you shall bring your offering of the livestock—of the herd and of the flock.

3 'If his offering *is* a burnt sacrifice of the herd, let him offer a male without blemish; he shall offer it of his own free will at the door of the tabernacle of meeting before the LORD.

4 'Then he shall put his hand on the head of the burnt offering, and it will be accepted on his behalf to make atonement for him.

5 'He shall kill the bull before the LORD; and the priests, Aaron's sons, shall bring the blood and sprinkle the blood all around on the altar that *is by* the door of the tabernacle of meeting.

6 'And he shall skin the burnt offering and cut it into its pieces.

7 'The sons of Aaron the priest shall put fire on the altar, and lay the wood in order on the fire.

8 'Then the priests, Aaron's sons, shall lay the parts, the head, and the fat in order on the wood that *is* on the fire upon the altar;

9 'but he shall wash its entrails and its legs with water. And the priest shall burn all on the altar as a burnt sacrifice, an offering made by fire, a sweet aroma to the LORD.

10 'If his offering *is* of the flocks—of the sheep or of the goats—as a burnt sacrifice, he shall bring a male without blemish.

11 'He shall kill it on the north side of the altar before the LORD; and the priests, Aaron's sons, shall sprinkle its blood all around on the altar.

12 'And he shall cut it into its pieces, with its head and its fat; and the priest shall lay them in order on the wood that *is* on the fire upon the altar;

13 'but he shall wash the entrails and the legs with water. Then the priest shall bring *it* all and burn *it* on the altar; it *is* a burnt sacrifice, an offering made by fire, a sweet aroma to the LORD.

14 'And if the burnt sacrifice of his offering to the LORD *is* of birds, then he shall bring his offering of turtledoves or young pigeons.

15 'The priest shall bring it to the altar, wring off its head, and burn *it* on the altar; its blood shall be drained out at the side of the altar.

16 'And he shall remove its crop with its feathers and cast it beside the altar on the east side, into the place for ashes.

17 'Then he shall split it at its wings, *but* shall not divide *it* completely; and the priest shall burn it on the altar, on the wood that *is* on the fire. It *is* a burnt sacrifice, an offering made by fire, a sweet aroma to the LORD.

The Grain Offering

2 'When anyone offers a grain offering to the LORD, his offering shall be *of* fine flour. And he shall pour oil on it, and put frankincense on it.

2 'He shall bring it to Aaron's sons, the priests, one of whom shall take from it his handful of fine flour and oil with all the frankincense. And the priest shall burn *it as* a memorial on the altar, an offering made by fire, a sweet aroma to the LORD.

3 'The rest of the grain offering *shall be* Aaron's and his sons'. *It is* most holy of the offerings to the LORD made by fire.

4 'And if you bring as an offering a grain offering baked in the oven, *it shall be* unleavened cakes of fine flour mixed with oil, or unleavened wafers anointed with oil.

5 'But if your offering *is* a grain offering *baked* in a pan, *it shall be of* fine flour, unleavened, mixed with oil.

6 'You shall break it in pieces and pour oil on it; it *is* a grain offering.

7 'If your offering *is* a grain offering *baked* in a covered pan, it shall be made *of* fine flour with oil.

8 'You shall bring the grain offering that is made of these things to the LORD. And when it is presented to the priest, he shall bring it to the altar.

9 'Then the priest shall take from the grain offering a memorial portion, and burn *it* on the altar. *It is* an offering made by fire, a sweet aroma to the LORD.

10 'And what is left of the grain offering *shall*

be Aaron's and his sons'. *It is* most holy of the offerings to the LORD made by fire.

11 'No grain offering which you bring to the LORD shall be made with leaven, for you shall burn no leaven nor any honey in any offering to the LORD made by fire.

12 'As for the offering of the firstfruits, you shall offer them to the LORD, but they shall not be burned on the altar for a sweet aroma.

13 'And every offering of your grain offering you shall season with salt; you shall not allow the salt of the covenant of your God to be lacking from your grain offering. With all your offerings you shall offer salt.

14 'If you offer a grain offering of your firstfruits to the LORD, you shall offer for the grain offering of your firstfruits green heads of grain roasted on the fire, grain beaten from full heads.

15 'And you shall put oil on it, and lay frankincense on it. It *is* a grain offering.

16 'Then the priest shall burn the memorial portion: *part* of its beaten grain and *part* of its oil, with all the frankincense, as an offering made by fire to the LORD.

The Peace Offering

3 'When his offering *is* a sacrifice of a peace offering, if he offers *it* of the herd, whether male or female, he shall offer it without blemish before the LORD.

2 'And he shall lay his hand on the head of his offering, and kill it *at* the door of the tabernacle of meeting; and Aaron's sons, the priests, shall sprinkle the blood all around on the altar.

3 'Then he shall offer from the sacrifice of the peace offering an offering made by fire to the LORD. The fat that covers the entrails and all the fat that *is* on the entrails,

4 'the two kidneys and the fat that *is* on them by the flanks, and the fatty lobe *attached* to the liver above the kidneys, he shall remove;

5 'and Aaron's sons shall burn it on the altar upon the burnt sacrifice, which *is* on the wood that *is* on the fire, *as* an offering made by fire, a sweet aroma to the LORD.

6 'If his offering as a sacrifice of a peace offering to the LORD *is* of the flock, *whether* male or female, he shall offer it without blemish.

7 'If he offers a lamb as his offering, then he shall offer it before the LORD.

8 'And he shall lay his hand on the head of his offering, and kill it before the tabernacle of meeting; and Aaron's sons shall sprinkle its blood all around on the altar.

9 'Then he shall offer from the sacrifice of the peace offering, as an offering made by fire to the LORD, its fat *and* the whole fat tail which he shall remove close to the backbone. And the fat that covers the entrails and all the fat that *is* on the entrails,

10 'the two kidneys and the fat that *is* on them by the flanks, and the fatty lobe *attached* to the liver above the kidneys, he shall remove;

11 'and the priest shall burn *them* on the altar *as* food, an offering made by fire to the LORD.

12 'And if his offering *is* a goat, then he shall offer it before the LORD.

13 'He shall lay his hand on its head and kill it before the tabernacle of meeting; and the sons of Aaron shall sprinkle its blood all around on the altar.

14 'Then he shall offer from it his offering, as an offering made by fire to the LORD. The fat that covers the entrails and all the fat that *is* on the entrails,

15 'the two kidneys and the fat that *is* on them by the flanks, and the fatty lobe *attached* to the liver above the kidneys, he shall remove;

16 'and the priest shall burn them on the altar *as* food, an offering made by fire for a sweet aroma; all the fat *is* the LORD's.

17 '*This shall be* a perpetual statute throughout your generations in all your dwellings: you shall eat neither fat nor blood.'"

The Sin Offering

4 Now the LORD spoke to Moses, saying,
2 "Speak to the children of Israel, saying: 'If a person sins unintentionally against any of the commandments of the LORD *in anything* which ought not to be done, and does any of them,

3 'if the anointed priest sins, bringing guilt on the people, then let him offer to the LORD for his sin which he has sinned a young bull without blemish as a sin offering.

4 'He shall bring the bull to the door of the tabernacle of meeting before the LORD, lay his hand on the bull's head, and kill the bull before the LORD.

5 'Then the anointed priest shall take some of the bull's blood and bring it to the tabernacle of meeting.

6 'The priest shall dip his finger in the blood and sprinkle some of the blood seven times before the LORD, in front of the veil of the sanctuary.

7 'And the priest shall put some of the blood on the horns of the altar of sweet incense before the LORD, which is in the tabernacle of meeting; and he shall pour the remaining blood of the bull at the base of the altar of the burnt offering, which is at the door of the tabernacle of meeting.

8 'He shall take from it all the fat of the bull as the sin offering. The fat that covers the entrails and all the fat which *is* on the entrails,

9 'the two kidneys and the fat that *is* on them by the flanks, and the fatty lobe *attached* to the liver above the kidneys, he shall remove,

10 'as it was taken from the bull of the sacrifice of the peace offering; and the priest shall burn them on the altar of the burnt offering.

11 'But the bull's hide and all its flesh, with its head and legs, its entrails and offal—

12 'the whole bull he shall carry outside the camp to a clean place, where the ashes are poured out, and burn it on wood with fire; where the ashes are poured out it shall be burned.

13 'Now if the whole congregation of Israel sins unintentionally, and the thing is hidden from the eyes of the assembly, and they have done *something against* any of the commandments of the LORD *in anything* which should not be done, and are guilty;

14 'when the sin which they have committed becomes known, then the assembly shall offer a young bull for the sin, and bring it before the tabernacle of meeting.

15 'And the elders of the congregation shall lay their hands on the head of the bull before the LORD. Then the bull shall be killed before the LORD.

16 'The anointed priest shall bring some of the bull's blood to the tabernacle of meeting.

17 'Then the priest shall dip his finger in the blood and sprinkle *it* seven times before the LORD, in front of the veil.

18 'And he shall put *some* of the blood on the horns of the altar which *is* before the LORD,

which *is* in the tabernacle of meeting; and he
shall pour the remaining blood at the base of
the altar of burnt offering, which is at the door
of the tabernacle of meeting.
19 'He shall take all the fat from it and burn
it on the altar.
20 'And he shall do with the bull as he did
with the bull as a sin offering; thus he shall do
with it. So the priest shall make atonement for
them, and it shall be forgiven them.
21 'Then he shall carry the bull outside the
camp, and burn it as he burned the first bull. It
is a sin offering for the assembly.
22 'When a ruler has sinned, and done *some-
thing* unintentionally *against* any of the com-
mandments of the LORD his God *in anything*
which should not be done, and is guilty,
23 'or if his sin which he has committed comes
to his knowledge, he shall bring as his offering
a kid of the goats, a male without blemish.
24 'And he shall lay his hand on the head of
the goat, and kill it at the place where they kill
the burnt offering before the LORD. It *is* a sin
offering.
25 'The priest shall take some of the blood of
the sin offering with his finger, put *it* on the
horns of the altar of burnt offering, and pour
its blood at the base of the altar of burnt offering.
26 'And he shall burn all its fat on the altar, like
the fat of the sacrifice of the peace offering.
So the priest shall make atonement for him
concerning his sin, and it shall be forgiven
him.
27 'If anyone of the common people sins unin-
tentionally by doing *something against* any of
the commandments of the LORD *in anything*
which ought not to be done, and is guilty,
28 'or if his sin which he has committed
comes to his knowledge, then he shall bring as
his offering a kid of the goats, a female without
blemish, for his sin which he has committed.
29 'And he shall lay his hand on the head of
the sin offering, and kill the sin offering at the
place of the burnt offering.
30 'Then the priest shall take *some* of its
blood with his finger, put *it* on the horns of
the altar of burnt offering, and pour all *the
remaining* blood at the base of the altar.
31 'He shall remove all its fat, as fat is re-
moved from the sacrifice of the peace offering;
and the priest shall burn it on the altar for a
sweet aroma to the LORD. So the priest shall
make atonement for him, and it shall be for-
given him.
32 'If he brings a lamb as his sin offering, he
shall bring a female without blemish.
33 'Then he shall lay his hand on the head of
the sin offering, and kill it as a sin offering at
the place where they kill the burnt offering.
34 'The priest shall take *some* of the blood of
the sin offering with his finger, put *it* on the
horns of the altar of burnt offering, and pour
all *the remaining* blood at the base of the altar.
35 'He shall remove all its fat, as the fat of the
lamb is removed from the sacrifice of the peace
offering. Then the priest shall burn it on the
altar, according to the offerings made by fire
to the LORD. So the priest shall make atone-
ment for his sin that he has committed, and it
shall be forgiven him.

The Trespass Offering

5 'If a person sins in hearing the utterance of
an oath, and *is* a witness, whether he has
seen or known *of the matter*—if he does not
tell *it*, he bears guilt.
2 'Or if a person touches any unclean thing,
whether *it is* the carcass of an unclean beast,
or the carcass of unclean livestock, or the car-
cass of unclean creeping things, and he is un-
aware of it, he also shall be unclean and guilty.
3 'Or if he touches human uncleanness—
whatever uncleanness with which a man may
be defiled, and he is unaware of it—when he
realizes *it*, then he shall be guilty.
4 'Or if a person swears, speaking thought-
lessly with *his* lips to do evil or to do good,
whatever *it is* that a man may pronounce by
an oath, and he is unaware of it—when he real-
izes *it*, then he shall be guilty in any of these
matters.
5 'And it shall be, when he is guilty in any of
these *matters*, that he shall confess that he has
sinned in that *thing*;
6 'and he shall bring his trespass offering to
the LORD for his sin which he has committed,
a female from the flock, a lamb or a kid of the
goats as a sin offering. So the priest shall make
atonement for him concerning his sin.
7 'If he is not able to bring a lamb, then he
shall bring to the LORD, for his trespass which
he has committed, two turtledoves or two
young pigeons: one as a sin offering and the
other as a burnt offering.
8 'And he shall bring them to the priest, who
shall offer *that* which *is* for the sin offering
first, and wring off its head from its neck, but
shall not divide *it* completely.
9 'Then he shall sprinkle *some* of the blood
of the sin offering on the side of the altar, and
the rest of the blood shall be drained out at the
base of the altar. It *is* a sin offering.
10 'And he shall offer the second *as* a burnt
offering according to the prescribed manner.
So the priest shall make atonement on his be-
half for his sin which he has committed, and it
shall be forgiven him.
11 'But if he is not able to bring two turtle-
doves or two young pigeons, then he who
sinned shall bring for his offering one-tenth of
an ephah of fine flour as a sin offering. He
shall put no oil on it, nor shall he put frankin-
cense on it, for it *is* a sin offering.
12 'Then he shall bring it to the priest, and the
priest shall take his handful of it as a memorial
portion, and burn *it* on the altar according to
the offerings made by fire to the LORD. It *is* a
sin offering.
13 'The priest shall make atonement for him,
for his sin that he has committed in any of
these matters; and it shall be forgiven him. *The
rest* shall be the priest's as a grain offering.'"

Offerings with Restitution

14 Then the LORD spoke to Moses, saying:
15 "If a person commits a trespass, and sins
unintentionally in regard to the holy things of
the LORD, then he shall bring to the LORD as
his trespass offering a ram without blemish
from the flocks, with your valuation in shekels
of silver according to the shekel of the sanctu-
ary, as a trespass offering.
16 "And he shall make restitution for the harm
that he has done in regard to the holy thing,
and shall add one-fifth to it and give it to the

priest. So the priest shall make atonement for him with the ram of the trespass offering, and it shall be forgiven him.
17 "If a person sins, and commits any of these things which are forbidden to be done by the commandments of the LORD, though he does not know *it*, yet he is guilty and shall bear his iniquity.
18 "And he shall bring to the priest a ram without blemish from the flock, with your valuation, as a trespass offering. So the priest shall make atonement for him regarding his ignorance in which he erred and did not know *it*, and it shall be forgiven him.
19 "It is a trespass offering; he has certainly trespassed against the LORD."

6 And the LORD spoke to Moses, saying:
2 "If a person sins and commits a trespass against the LORD by lying to his neighbor about what was delivered to him for safekeeping, or about a pledge, or about a robbery, or if he has extorted from his neighbor,
3 "or if he has found what was lost and lies concerning it, and swears falsely—in any one of these things that a man may do in which he sins:
4 "then it shall be, because he has sinned and is guilty, that he shall restore what he has stolen, or the thing which he has extorted, or what was delivered to him for safekeeping, or the lost thing which he found,
5 "or all that about which he has sworn falsely. He shall restore its full value, add one-fifth more to it, *and* give it to whomever it belongs, on the day of his trespass offering.
6 "And he shall bring his trespass offering to the LORD, a ram without blemish from the flock, with your valuation, as a trespass offering, to the priest.
7 "So the priest shall make atonement for him before the LORD, and he shall be forgiven for any one of these things that he may have done in which he trespasses."

The Law of the Burnt Offering

8 Then the LORD spoke to Moses, saying,
9 "Command Aaron and his sons, saying, 'This *is* the law of the burnt offering: The burnt offering *shall be* on the hearth upon the altar all night until morning, and the fire of the altar shall be kept burning on it.
10 'And the priest shall put on his linen garment, and his linen trousers he shall put on his body, and take up the ashes of the burnt offering which the fire has consumed on the altar, and he shall put them beside the altar.
11 'Then he shall take off his garments, put on other garments, and carry the ashes outside the camp to a clean place.
12 'And the fire on the altar shall be kept burning on it; it shall not be put out. And the priest shall burn wood on it every morning, and lay the burnt offering in order on it; and he shall burn on it the fat of the peace offerings.
13 'A fire shall always be burning on the altar; it shall never go out.

The Law of the Grain Offering

14 'This *is* the law of the grain offering: The sons of Aaron shall offer it on the altar before the LORD.
15 'He shall take from it his handful of the fine flour of the grain offering, with its oil, and all the frankincense which *is* on the grain offering, and shall burn *it* on the altar *for* a sweet aroma, as a memorial to the LORD.
16 'And the remainder of it Aaron and his sons shall eat; with unleavened bread it shall be eaten in a holy place; in the court of the tabernacle of meeting they shall eat it.
17 'It shall not be baked with leaven. I have given it *as* their portion of My offerings made by fire; it *is* most holy, like the sin offering and the trespass offering.
18 'All the males among the children of Aaron may eat it. *It shall be* a statute forever in your generations concerning the offerings made by fire to the LORD. Everyone who touches them must be holy.' "[a]
19 And the LORD spoke to Moses, saying,
20 "This *is* the offering of Aaron and his sons, which they shall offer to the LORD, *beginning* on the day when he is anointed: one-tenth of an ephah of fine flour as a daily grain offering, half of it in the morning and half of it at night.
21 "It shall be made in a pan with oil. *When it is* mixed, you shall bring it in. The baked pieces of the grain offering you shall offer *for* a sweet aroma to the LORD.
22 "The priest from among his sons, who is anointed in his place, shall offer it. *It is* a statute forever to the LORD. It shall be wholly burned.
23 "For every grain offering for the priest shall be wholly burned. It shall not be eaten."

The Law of the Sin Offering

24 Also the LORD spoke to Moses, saying,
25 "Speak to Aaron and to his sons, saying, 'This *is* the law of the sin offering: In the place where the burnt offering is killed, the sin offering shall be killed before the LORD. It *is* most holy.
26 'The priest who offers it for sin shall eat it. In a holy place it shall be eaten, in the court of the tabernacle of meeting.
27 'Everyone who touches its flesh must be holy.[a] And when its blood is sprinkled on any garment, you shall wash that on which it was sprinkled, in a holy place.
28 'But the earthen vessel in which it is boiled shall be broken. And if it is boiled in a bronze pot, it shall be both scoured and rinsed in water.
29 'All the males among the priests may eat it. It *is* most holy.
30 'But no sin offering from which *any* of the blood is brought into the tabernacle of meeting, to make atonement in the holy *place*,[a] shall be eaten. It shall be burned in the fire.

The Law of the Trespass Offering

7 'Likewise this *is* the law of the trespass offering (it *is* most holy):
2 'In the place where they kill the burnt offering they shall kill the trespass offering. And its blood he shall sprinkle all around on the altar.
3 'And he shall offer from it all its fat. The fat tail and the fat that covers the entrails,
4 'the two kidneys and the fat that *is* on them by the flanks, and the fatty lobe *attached* to the liver above the kidneys, he shall remove;
5 'and the priest shall burn them on the altar

6:18 [a]Compare Numbers 4:15 and Haggai 2:11–13 **6:27** [a]Compare Numbers 4:15 and Haggai 2:11–13
6:30 [a]The Most Holy Place when capitalized

as an offering made by fire to the LORD. It *is* a
trespass offering.
6 'Every male among the priests may eat it.
It shall be eaten in a holy place. It *is* most holy.
7 'The trespass offering *is* like the sin offer-
ing; *there is* one law for them both: the priest
who makes atonement with it shall have *it.*
8 'And the priest who offers anyone's burnt
offering, that priest shall have for himself the
skin of the burnt offering which he has offered.
9 'Also every grain offering that is baked in
the oven and all that is prepared in the covered
pan, or in a pan, shall be the priest's who offers
it.
10 'Every grain offering, *whether* mixed with
oil or dry, shall belong to all the sons of Aaron,
to one *as much* as the other.

The Law of Peace Offerings

11 'This *is* the law of the sacrifice of peace
offerings which he shall offer to the LORD:
12 'If he offers it for a thanksgiving, then he
shall offer, with the sacrifice of thanksgiving,
unleavened cakes mixed with oil, unleavened
wafers anointed with oil, or cakes of blended
flour mixed with oil.
13 'Besides the cakes, *as* his offering he shall
offer leavened bread with the sacrifice of
thanksgiving of his peace offering.
14 'And from it he shall offer one cake from
each offering *as* a heave offering to the LORD.
It shall belong to the priest who sprinkles the
blood of the peace offering.
15 'The flesh of the sacrifice of his peace of-
fering for thanksgiving shall be eaten the same
day it is offered. He shall not leave any of it
until morning.
16 'But if the sacrifice of his offering *is* a vow
or a voluntary offering, it shall be eaten the same
day that he offers his sacrifice; but on the next
day the remainder of it also may be eaten;
17 'the remainder of the flesh of the sacrifice
on the third day must be burned with fire.
18 'And if *any* of the flesh of the sacrifice of
his peace offering is eaten at all on the third
day, it shall not be accepted, nor shall it be
imputed to him; it shall be an abomination *to*
him who offers it, and the person who eats of
it shall bear guilt.
19 'The flesh that touches any unclean thing
shall not be eaten. It shall be burned with fire.
And as for the *clean* flesh, all who are clean
may eat of it.
20 'But the person who eats the flesh of the
sacrifice of the peace offering that *belongs* to
the LORD, while he is unclean, that person
shall be cut off from his people.
21 'Moreover the person who touches any un-
clean thing, *such as* human uncleanness, *an*
unclean animal, or any abominable unclean
thing,[a] and who eats the flesh of the sacrifice
of the peace offering that *belongs* to the LORD,
that person shall be cut off from his people.' "

Fat and Blood May Not Be Eaten

22 And the LORD spoke to Moses, saying,
23 "Speak to the children of Israel, saying: 'You
shall not eat any fat, of ox or sheep or goat.
24 'And the fat of an animal that dies *natu-
rally,* and the fat of what is torn by wild beasts,
may be used in any other way; but you shall by
no means eat it.
25 'For whoever eats the fat of the animal of
which men offer an offering made by fire to
the LORD, the person who eats *it* shall be cut
off from his people.
26 'Moreover you shall not eat any blood in
any of your dwellings, *whether* of bird or beast.
27 'Whoever eats any blood, that person shall
be cut off from his people.' "

The Portion of Aaron and His Sons

28 Then the LORD spoke to Moses, saying,
29 "Speak to the children of Israel, saying:
'He who offers the sacrifice of his peace offer-
ing to the LORD shall bring his offering to the
LORD from the sacrifice of his peace offering.
30 'His own hands shall bring the offerings
made by fire to the LORD. The fat with the
breast he shall bring, that the breast may be
waved *as* a wave offering before the LORD.
31 'And the priest shall burn the fat on the
altar, but the breast shall be Aaron's and his
sons'.
32 'Also the right thigh you shall give to the
priest *as* a heave offering from the sacrifices
of your peace offerings.
33 'He among the sons of Aaron, who offers
the blood of the peace offering and the fat,
shall have the right thigh for *his* part.
34 'For the breast of the wave offering and the
thigh of the heave offering I have taken from
the children of Israel, from the sacrifices of
their peace offerings, and I have given them
to Aaron the priest and to his sons from the
children of Israel by a statute forever.' "
35 This *is* the consecrated portion for Aaron
and his sons, from the offerings made by fire
to the LORD, on the day when *Moses* presented
them to minister to the LORD as priests.
36 The LORD commanded this to be given to
them by the children of Israel, on the day that
He anointed them, *by* a statute forever
throughout their generations.
37 This *is* the law of the burnt offering, the
grain offering, the sin offering, the trespass
offering, the consecrations, and the sacrifice
of the peace offering,
38 which the LORD commanded Moses on
Mount Sinai, on the day when He commanded
the children of Israel to offer their offerings to
the LORD in the Wilderness of Sinai.

Aaron and His Sons Consecrated

8 And the LORD spoke to Moses, saying:
2 "Take Aaron and his sons with him,
and the garments, the anointing oil, a bull as
the sin offering, two rams, and a basket of un-
leavened bread;
3 "and gather all the congregation together
at the door of the tabernacle of meeting."
4 So Moses did as the LORD commanded
him. And the congregation was gathered to-
gether at the door of the tabernacle of meeting.
5 And Moses said to the congregation, "This
is what the LORD commanded to be done."
6 Then Moses brought Aaron and his sons
and washed them with water.
7 And he put the tunic on him, girded him with
the sash, clothed him with the robe, and put
the ephod on him; and he girded him with the
intricately woven band of the ephod, and with
it tied *the ephod* on him.
8 Then he put the breastplate on him, and he

7:21 [a]Following Masoretic Text, Septuagint, and Vulgate; Samaritan Pentateuch, Syriac, and Targum read *swarming thing* (compare 5:2).

put the Urim and the Thummim[a] in the breast-
plate.
9 And he put the turban on his head. Also
on the turban, on its front, he put the golden
plate, the holy crown, as the LORD had com-
manded Moses.
10 Also Moses took the anointing oil, and
anointed the tabernacle and all that *was* in it,
and consecrated them.
11 He sprinkled some of it on the altar seven
times, anointed the altar and all its utensils,
and the laver and its base, to consecrate them.
12 And he poured some of the anointing oil
on Aaron's head and anointed him, to conse-
crate him.
13 Then Moses brought Aaron's sons and put
tunics on them, girded them with sashes, and
put hats on them, as the LORD had commanded
Moses.
14 And he brought the bull for the sin offer-
ing. Then Aaron and his sons laid their hands
on the head of the bull for the sin offering,
15 and Moses killed *it*. Then he took the
blood, and put *some* on the horns of the altar
all around with his finger, and purified the al-
tar. And he poured the blood at the base of the
altar, and consecrated it, to make atonement
for it.
16 Then he took all the fat that *was* on the
entrails, the fatty lobe *attached to* the liver,
and the two kidneys with their fat, and Moses
burned *them* on the altar.
17 But the bull, its hide, its flesh, and its offal,
he burned with fire outside the camp, as the
LORD had commanded Moses.
18 Then he brought the ram as the burnt of-
fering. And Aaron and his sons laid their hands
on the head of the ram,
19 and Moses killed *it*. Then he sprinkled the
blood all around on the altar.
20 And he cut the ram into pieces; and Moses
burned the head, the pieces, and the fat.
21 Then he washed the entrails and the legs
in water. And Moses burned the whole ram on
the altar. It *was* a burnt sacrifice for a sweet
aroma, an offering made by fire to the LORD,
as the LORD had commanded Moses.
22 And he brought the second ram, the ram
of consecration. Then Aaron and his sons laid
their hands on the head of the ram,
23 and Moses killed *it*. Also he took *some* of
its blood and put it on the tip of Aaron's right
ear, on the thumb of his right hand, and on the
big toe of his right foot.
24 Then he brought Aaron's sons. And Moses
put *some* of the blood on the tips of their right
ears, on the thumbs of their right hands, and
on the big toes of their right feet. And Moses
sprinkled the blood all around on the altar.
25 Then he took the fat and the fat tail, all
the fat that *was* on the entrails, the fatty lobe
attached to the liver, the two kidneys and their
fat, and the right thigh;
26 and from the basket of unleavened bread
that was before the LORD he took one unleav-
ened cake, a cake of bread *anointed with* oil,
and one wafer, and put *them* on the fat and on
the right thigh;
27 and he put all *these* in Aaron's hands and
in his sons' hands, and waved them *as* a wave
offering before the LORD.
28 Then Moses took them from their hands
and burned *them* on the altar, on the burnt
offering. They *were* consecration offerings for
a sweet aroma. That *was* an offering made by
fire to the LORD.
29 And Moses took the breast and waved it
as a wave offering before the LORD. It was
Moses' part of the ram of consecration, as the
LORD had commanded Moses.
30 Then Moses took some of the anointing oil
and some of the blood which *was* on the altar,
and sprinkled *it* on Aaron, on his garments, on
his sons, and on the garments of his sons with
him; and he consecrated Aaron, his garments,
his sons, and the garments of his sons with
him.
31 And Moses said to Aaron and his sons,
"Boil the flesh *at* the door of the tabernacle of
meeting, and eat it there with the bread that *is*
in the basket of consecration offerings, as I
commanded, saying, 'Aaron and his sons shall
eat it.'
32 "What remains of the flesh and of the
bread you shall burn with fire.
33 "And you shall not go outside the door of
the tabernacle of meeting *for* seven days, until
the days of your consecration are ended. For
seven days he shall consecrate you.
34 "As he has done this day, *so* the LORD has
commanded to do, to make atonement for you.
35 "Therefore you shall stay *at* the door of
the tabernacle of meeting day and night for
seven days, and keep the charge of the LORD,
so that you may not die; for so I have been
commanded."
36 So Aaron and his sons did all the things
that the LORD had commanded by the hand of
Moses.

The Priestly Ministry Begins

9 It came to pass on the eighth day that Mo-
ses called Aaron and his sons and the el-
ders of Israel.
2 And he said to Aaron, "Take for yourself a
young bull as a sin offering and a ram as a
burnt offering, without blemish, and offer
them before the LORD.
3 "And to the children of Israel you shall
speak, saying, 'Take a kid of the goats as a sin
offering, and a calf and a lamb, *both* of the
first year, without blemish, as a burnt offering,
4 'also a bull and a ram as peace offerings, to
sacrifice before the LORD, and a grain offering
mixed with oil; for today the LORD will appear
to you.'"
5 So they brought what Moses commanded
before the tabernacle of meeting. And all the
congregation drew near and stood before the
LORD.
6 Then Moses said, "This *is* the thing which
the LORD commanded you to do, and the glory
of the LORD will appear to you."
7 And Moses said to Aaron, "Go to the altar,
offer your sin offering and your burnt offering,
and make atonement for yourself and for the
people. Offer the offering of the people, and
make atonement for them, as the LORD com-
manded."
8 Aaron therefore went to the altar and killed
the calf of the sin offering, which *was* for him-
self.
9 Then the sons of Aaron brought the blood
to him. And he dipped his finger in the blood,
put *it* on the horns of the altar, and poured the
blood at the base of the altar.

8:8 [a]Literally *the Lights and the Perfections* (compare Exodus 28:30)

10 But the fat, the kidneys, and the fatty lobe
from the liver of the sin offering he burned on
the altar, as the LORD had commanded Moses.
11 The flesh and the hide he burned with fire
outside the camp.
12 And he killed the burnt offering; and
Aaron's sons presented to him the blood,
which he sprinkled all around on the altar.
13 Then they presented the burnt offering to
him, with its pieces and head, and he burned
them on the altar.
14 And he washed the entrails and the legs,
and burned *them* with the burnt offering on
the altar.
15 Then he brought the people's offering, and
took the goat, which *was* the sin offering for
the people, and killed it and offered it for sin,
like the first one.
16 And he brought the burnt offering and of-
fered it according to the prescribed manner.
17 Then he brought the grain offering, took a
handful of it, and burned *it* on the altar, besides
the burnt sacrifice of the morning.
18 He also killed the bull and the ram *as* sacri-
fices of peace offerings, which *were* for the
people. And Aaron's sons presented to him
the blood, which he sprinkled all around on
the altar,
19 and the fat from the bull and the ram—
the fatty tail, what covers *the entrails* and the
kidneys, and the fatty lobe *attached to* the
liver;
20 and they put the fat on the breasts. Then
he burned the fat on the altar;
21 but the breasts and the right thigh Aaron
waved *as* a wave offering before the LORD, as
Moses had commanded.
22 Then Aaron lifted his hand toward the peo-
ple, blessed them, and came down from offer-
ing the sin offering, the burnt offering, and
peace offerings.
23 And Moses and Aaron went into the taber-
nacle of meeting, and came out and blessed
the people. Then the glory of the LORD ap-
peared to all the people,
24 and fire came out from before the LORD
and consumed the burnt offering and the fat
on the altar. When all the people saw *it*, they
shouted and fell on their faces.

The Profane Fire of Nadab and Abihu

10 Then Nadab and Abihu, the sons of
Aaron, each took his censer and put fire
in it, put incense on it, and offered profane fire
before the LORD, which He had not commanded
them.
2 So fire went out from the LORD and de-
voured them, and they died before the LORD.
3 And Moses said to Aaron, "This is what
the LORD spoke, saying:

'By those who come near Me
I must be regarded as holy;
And before all the people
I must be glorified.' "

So Aaron held his peace.
4 Then Moses called Mishael and Elzaphan,
the sons of Uzziel the uncle of Aaron, and said
to them, "Come near, carry your brethren from
before the sanctuary out of the camp."
5 So they went near and carried them by
their tunics out of the camp, as Moses had said.
6 And Moses said to Aaron, and to Eleazar
and Ithamar, his sons, "Do not uncover your
heads nor tear your clothes, lest you die, and
wrath come upon all the people. But let your
brethren, the whole house of Israel, bewail the
burning which the LORD has kindled.
7 "You shall not go out from the door of the
tabernacle of meeting, lest you die, for the
anointing oil of the LORD *is* upon you." And
they did according to the word of Moses.

Conduct Prescribed for Priests

8 Then the LORD spoke to Aaron, saying:
9 "Do not drink wine or intoxicating drink,
you, nor your sons with you, when you go into
the tabernacle of meeting, lest you die. *It shall
be* a statute forever throughout your genera-
tions,
10 "that you may distinguish between holy
and unholy, and between unclean and clean,
11 "and that you may teach the children of
Israel all the statutes which the LORD has spo-
ken to them by the hand of Moses."
12 And Moses spoke to Aaron, and to Eleazar
and Ithamar, his sons who were left: "Take the
grain offering that remains of the offerings
made by fire to the LORD, and eat it without
leaven beside the altar; for it *is* most holy.
13 "You shall eat it in a holy place, because it
is your due and your sons' due, of the sacrifices
made by fire to the LORD; for so I have been
commanded.
14 "The breast of the wave offering and the
thigh of the heave offering you shall eat in a
clean place, you, your sons, and your daugh-
ters with you; for *they are* your due and your
sons' due, *which* are given from the sacrifices
of peace offerings of the children of Israel.
15 "The thigh of the heave offering and the
breast of the wave offering they shall bring
with the offerings of fat made by fire, to offer
as a wave offering before the LORD. And it
shall be yours and your sons' with you, by a
statute forever, as the LORD has commanded."
16 Then Moses made careful inquiry about
the goat of the sin offering, and there it was—
burned up. And he was angry with Eleazar
and Ithamar, the sons of Aaron *who were* left,
saying,
17 "Why have you not eaten the sin offering
in a holy place, since it *is* most holy, and *God*
has given it to you to bear the guilt of the con-
gregation, to make atonement for them before
the LORD?
18 "See! Its blood was not brought inside the
holy *place*;[a] indeed you should have eaten it in
a holy *place*, as I commanded."
19 And Aaron said to Moses, "Look, this day
they have offered their sin offering and their
burnt offering before the LORD, and such
things have befallen me! *If* I had eaten the sin
offering today, would it have been accepted in
the sight of the LORD?"
20 So when Moses heard *that*, he was con-
tent.

Foods Permitted and Forbidden

11 Now the LORD spoke to Moses and Aaron,
saying to them,
2 "Speak to the children of Israel, saying,
'These *are* the animals which you may eat
among all the animals that *are* on the earth:
3 'Among the animals, whatever divides the

10:18 [a]The Most Holy Place when capitalized

hoof, having cloven hooves *and* chewing the cud—that you may eat.

4 'Nevertheless these you shall not eat among those that chew the cud or those that have cloven hooves: the camel, because it chews the cud but does not have cloven hooves, is unclean to you;

5 'the rock hyrax, because it chews the cud but does not have cloven hooves, *is* unclean to you;

6 'the hare, because it chews the cud but does not have cloven hooves, *is* unclean to you;

7 'and the swine, though it divides the hoof, having cloven hooves, yet does not chew the cud, *is* unclean to you.

8 'Their flesh you shall not eat, and their carcasses you shall not touch. They *are* unclean to you.

9 'These you may eat of all that *are* in the water: whatever in the water has fins and scales, whether in the seas or in the rivers—that you may eat.

10 'But all in the seas or in the rivers that do not have fins and scales, all that move in the water or any living thing which *is* in the water, they *are* an abomination to you.

11 'They shall be an abomination to you; you shall not eat their flesh, but you shall regard their carcasses as an abomination.

12 'Whatever in the water does not have fins or scales—that *shall be* an abomination to you.

13 'And these you shall regard as an abomination among the birds; they shall not be eaten, they *are* an abomination: the eagle, the vulture, the buzzard,

14 'the kite, and the falcon after its kind;

15 'every raven after its kind,

16 'the ostrich, the short-eared owl, the sea gull, and the hawk after its kind;

17 'the little owl, the fisher owl, and the screech owl;

18 'the white owl, the jackdaw, and the carrion vulture;

19 'the stork, the heron after its kind, the hoopoe, and the bat.

20 'All flying insects that creep on *all* fours *shall be* an abomination to you.

21 'Yet these you may eat of every flying insect that creeps on *all* fours: those which have jointed legs above their feet with which to leap on the earth.

22 'These you may eat: the locust after its kind, the destroying locust after its kind, the cricket after its kind, and the grasshopper after its kind.

23 'But all *other* flying insects which have four feet *shall be* an abomination to you.

Unclean Animals

24 'By these you shall become unclean; whoever touches the carcass of any of them shall be unclean until evening;

25 'whoever carries part of the carcass of any of them shall wash his clothes and be unclean until evening:

26 '*The carcass* of any animal which divides the foot, but is not cloven-hoofed or does not chew the cud, *is* unclean to you. Everyone who touches it shall be unclean.

27 'And whatever goes on its paws, among all kinds of animals that go on *all* fours, those *are* unclean to you. Whoever touches any such carcass shall be unclean until evening.

28 'Whoever carries *any such* carcass shall wash his clothes and be unclean until evening. It *is* unclean to you.

29 'These also *shall be* unclean to you among the creeping things that creep on the earth: the mole, the mouse, and the large lizard after its kind;

30 'the gecko, the monitor lizard, the sand reptile, the sand lizard, and the chameleon.

31 'These *are* unclean to you among all that creep. Whoever touches them when they are dead shall be unclean until evening.

32 'Anything on which *any* of them falls, when they are dead shall be unclean, whether *it is* any item of wood or clothing or skin or sack, whatever item *it is*, in which *any* work is done, it must be put in water. And it shall be unclean until evening; then it shall be clean.

33 'Any earthen vessel into which *any* of them falls you shall break; and whatever *is* in it shall be unclean:

34 'in such a vessel, any edible food upon which water falls becomes unclean, and any drink that may be drunk from it becomes unclean.

35 'And everything on which *a part* of *any such* carcass falls shall be unclean; *whether it is* an oven or cooking stove, it shall be broken down; *for* they *are* unclean, and shall be unclean to you.

36 'Nevertheless a spring or a cistern, *in which there is* plenty of water, shall be clean, but whatever touches any such carcass becomes unclean.

37 'And if a part of *any such* carcass falls on any planting seed which is to be sown, it *remains* clean.

38 'But if water is put on the seed, and if *a part* of *any such* carcass falls on it, it *becomes* unclean to you.

39 'And if any animal which you may eat dies, he who touches its carcass shall be unclean until evening.

40 'He who eats of its carcass shall wash his clothes and be unclean until evening. He also who carries its carcass shall wash his clothes and be unclean until evening.

41 'And every creeping thing that creeps on the earth *shall be* an abomination. It shall not be eaten.

42 'Whatever crawls on its belly, whatever goes on *all* fours, or whatever has many feet among all creeping things that creep on the earth—these you shall not eat, for they *are* an abomination.

43 'You shall not make yourselves abominable with any creeping thing that creeps; nor shall you make yourselves unclean with them, lest you be defiled by them.

44 'For I *am* the LORD your God. You shall therefore consecrate yourselves, and you shall be holy; for I *am* holy. Neither shall you defile yourselves with any creeping thing that creeps on the earth.

45 'For I *am* the LORD who brings you up out of the land of Egypt, to be your God. You shall therefore be holy, for I *am* holy.

46 'This *is* the law of the animals and the birds and every living creature that moves in the waters, and of every creature that creeps on the earth,

47 'to distinguish between the unclean and the clean, and between the animal that may be eaten and the animal that may not be eaten.' "

The Ritual After Childbirth

12 Then the LORD spoke to Moses, saying,
2 "Speak to the children of Israel, saying: 'If a woman has conceived, and borne a male child, then she shall be unclean seven days; as in the days of her customary impurity she shall be unclean.
3 'And on the eighth day the flesh of his foreskin shall be circumcised.
4 'She shall then continue in the blood of *her* purification thirty-three days. She shall not touch any hallowed thing, nor come into the sanctuary until the days of her purification are fulfilled.
5 'But if she bears a female child, then she shall be unclean two weeks, as in her customary impurity, and she shall continue in the blood of *her* purification sixty-six days.
6 'When the days of her purification are fulfilled, whether for a son or a daughter, she shall bring to the priest a lamb of the first year as a burnt offering, and a young pigeon or a turtledove as a sin offering, to the door of the tabernacle of meeting.
7 'Then he shall offer it before the LORD, and make atonement for her. And she shall be clean from the flow of her blood. This *is* the law for her who has borne a male or a female.
8 'And if she is not able to bring a lamb, then she may bring two turtledoves or two young pigeons—one as a burnt offering and the other as a sin offering. So the priest shall make atonement for her, and she will be clean.'"

The Law Concerning Leprosy

13 And the LORD spoke to Moses and Aaron, saying:
2 "When a man has on the skin of his body a swelling, a scab, or a bright spot, and it becomes on the skin of his body *like* a leprous[a] sore, then he shall be brought to Aaron the priest or to one of his sons the priests.
3 "The priest shall examine the sore on the skin of the body; and if the hair on the sore has turned white, and the sore appears *to be* deeper than the skin of his body, it *is* a leprous sore. Then the priest shall examine him, and pronounce him unclean.
4 "But if the bright spot *is* white on the skin of his body, and does not appear *to be* deeper than the skin, and its hair has not turned white, then the priest shall isolate *the one who has* the sore seven days.
5 "And the priest shall examine him on the seventh day; and indeed *if* the sore appears to be as it was, *and* the sore has not spread on the skin, then the priest shall isolate him another seven days.
6 "Then the priest shall examine him again on the seventh day; and indeed *if* the sore has faded, *and* the sore has not spread on the skin, then the priest shall pronounce him clean; it *is* *only* a scab, and he shall wash his clothes and be clean.
7 "But if the scab should at all spread over the skin, after he has been seen by the priest for his cleansing, he shall be seen by the priest again.
8 "And *if* the priest sees that the scab has indeed spread on the skin, then the priest shall pronounce him unclean. It *is* leprosy.
9 "When the leprous sore is on a person, then he shall be brought to the priest.
10 "And the priest shall examine *him;* and indeed *if* the swelling on the skin *is* white, and it has turned the hair white, and *there is* a spot of raw flesh in the swelling,
11 "it *is* an old leprosy on the skin of his body. The priest shall pronounce him unclean, and shall not isolate him, for he *is* unclean.
12 "And if leprosy breaks out all over the skin, and the leprosy covers all the skin of *the one who has* the sore, from his head to his foot, wherever the priest looks,
13 "then the priest shall consider; and indeed *if* the leprosy has covered all his body, he shall pronounce *him* clean *who has* the sore. It has all turned white. He *is* clean.
14 "But when raw flesh appears on him, he shall be unclean.
15 "And the priest shall examine the raw flesh and pronounce him to be unclean; *for* the raw flesh *is* unclean. It *is* leprosy.
16 "Or if the raw flesh changes and turns white again, he shall come to the priest.
17 "And the priest shall examine him; and indeed *if* the sore has turned white, then the priest shall pronounce *him* clean *who has* the sore. He *is* clean.
18 "If the body develops a boil in the skin, and it is healed,
19 "and in the place of the boil there comes a white swelling or a bright spot, reddish-white, then it shall be shown to the priest;
20 "and *if,* when the priest sees it, it indeed appears deeper than the skin, and its hair has turned white, the priest shall pronounce him unclean. It *is* a leprous sore which has broken out of the boil.
21 "But if the priest examines it, and indeed *there are* no white hairs in it, and it *is* not deeper than the skin, but has faded, then the priest shall isolate him seven days;
22 "and if it should at all spread over the skin, then the priest shall pronounce him unclean. It *is* a leprous sore.
23 "But if the bright spot stays in one place, *and* has not spread, it *is* the scar of the boil; and the priest shall pronounce him clean.
24 "Or if the body receives a burn on its skin by fire, and the raw *flesh* of the burn becomes a bright spot, reddish-white or white,
25 "then the priest shall examine it; and indeed *if* the hair of the bright spot has turned white, and it appears deeper than the skin, it *is* leprosy broken out in the burn. Therefore the priest shall pronounce him unclean. It *is* a leprous sore.
26 "But if the priest examines it, and indeed *there are* no white hairs in the bright spot, and it *is* not deeper than the skin, but has faded, then the priest shall isolate him seven days.
27 "And the priest shall examine him on the seventh day. If it has at all spread over the skin, then the priest shall pronounce him unclean. It *is* a leprous sore.
28 "But if the bright spot stays in one place, *and* has not spread on the skin, but has faded, it *is* a swelling from the burn. The priest shall pronounce him clean, for it *is* the scar from the burn.
29 "If a man or woman has a sore on the head or the beard,
30 "then the priest shall examine the sore; and

13:2 [a]Hebrew *saraath,* disfiguring skin diseases, including leprosy, and so in verses 2–46 and 14:1–32

indeed if it appears deeper than the skin, *and there is* in it thin yellow hair, then the priest shall pronounce him unclean. It *is* a scaly leprosy of the head or beard.

31 "But if the priest examines the scaly sore, and indeed it does not appear deeper than the skin, and *there is* no black hair in it, then the priest shall isolate *the one who has* the scale seven days.

32 "And on the seventh day the priest shall examine the sore; and indeed *if* the scale has not spread, and there is no yellow hair in it, and the scale does not appear deeper than the skin,

33 "he shall shave himself, but the scale he shall not shave. And the priest shall isolate *the one who has* the scale another seven days.

34 "On the seventh day the priest shall examine the scale; and indeed *if* the scale has not spread over the skin, and does not appear deeper than the skin, then the priest shall pronounce him clean. He shall wash his clothes and be clean.

35 "But if the scale should at all spread over the skin after his cleansing,

36 "then the priest shall examine him; and indeed *if* the scale has spread over the skin, the priest need not seek for yellow hair. He *is* unclean.

37 "But if the scale appears to be at a standstill, and there is black hair grown up in it, the scale has healed. He *is* clean, and the priest shall pronounce him clean.

38 "If a man or a woman has bright spots on the skin of the body, *specifically* white bright spots,

39 "then the priest shall look; and indeed *if* the bright spots on the skin of the body *are* dull white, it *is* a white spot *that* grows on the skin. He *is* clean.

40 "As for the man whose hair has fallen from his head, he *is* bald, *but* he *is* clean.

41 "He whose hair has fallen from his forehead, he *is* bald on the forehead, *but* he *is* clean.

42 "And if there is on the bald head or bald forehead a reddish-white sore, it *is* leprosy breaking out on his bald head or his bald forehead.

43 "Then the priest shall examine it; and indeed *if* the swelling of the sore *is* reddish-white on his bald head or on his bald forehead, as the appearance of leprosy on the skin of the body,

44 "he is a leprous man. He *is* unclean. The priest shall surely pronounce him unclean; his sore *is* on his head.

45 "Now the leper on whom the sore *is*, his clothes shall be torn and his head bare; and he shall cover his mustache, and cry, 'Unclean! Unclean!'

46 "He shall be unclean. All the days he has the sore he shall be unclean. He *is* unclean, and he shall dwell alone; his dwelling *shall be* outside the camp.

The Law Concerning Leprous Garments

47 "Also, if a garment has a leprous plague[a] in it, *whether it is* a woolen garment or a linen garment,

48 "whether *it is* in the warp or woof of linen or wool, whether in leather or in anything made of leather,

49 "and if the plague is greenish or reddish in the garment or in the leather, whether in the warp or in the woof, or in anything made of leather, it *is* a leprous plague and shall be shown to the priest.

50 "The priest shall examine the plague and isolate *that which has* the plague seven days.

51 "And he shall examine the plague on the seventh day. If the plague has spread in the garment, either in the warp or in the woof, in the leather *or* in anything made of leather, the plague *is* an active leprosy. It *is* unclean.

52 "He shall therefore burn that garment in which is the plague, whether warp or woof, in wool or in linen, or anything of leather, for it *is* an active leprosy; *the garment* shall be burned in the fire.

53 "But if the priest examines *it*, and indeed the plague has not spread in the garment, either in the warp or in the woof, or in anything made of leather,

54 "then the priest shall command that they wash *the thing* in which *is* the plague; and he shall isolate it another seven days.

55 "Then the priest shall examine the plague after it has been washed; and indeed *if* the plague has not changed its color, though the plague has not spread, it *is* unclean, and you shall burn it in the fire; it continues eating away, *whether* the damage *is* outside or inside.

56 "If the priest examines *it*, and indeed the plague has faded after washing it, then he shall tear it out of the garment, whether out of the warp or out of the woof, or out of the leather.

57 "But if it appears again in the garment, either in the warp or in the woof, or in anything made of leather, it *is* a spreading *plague*; you shall burn with fire that in which is the plague.

58 "And if you wash the garment, either warp or woof, or whatever is made of leather, if the plague has disappeared from it, then it shall be washed a second time, and shall be clean.

59 "This *is* the law of the leprous plague in a garment of wool or linen, either in the warp or woof, or in anything made of leather, to pronounce it clean or to pronounce it unclean."

The Ritual for Cleansing Healed Lepers

14 Then the LORD spoke to Moses, saying,

2 "This shall be the law of the leper for the day of his cleansing: He shall be brought to the priest.

3 "And the priest shall go out of the camp, and the priest shall examine *him;* and indeed, *if* the leprosy is healed in the leper,

4 "then the priest shall command to take for him who is to be cleansed two living *and* clean birds, cedar wood, scarlet, and hyssop.

5 "And the priest shall command that one of the birds be killed in an earthen vessel over running water.

6 "As for the living bird, he shall take it, the cedar wood and the scarlet and the hyssop, and dip them and the living bird in the blood of the bird *that was* killed over the running water.

7 "And he shall sprinkle it seven times on him who is to be cleansed from the leprosy, and shall pronounce him clean, and shall let the living bird loose in the open field.

8 "He who is to be cleansed shall wash his clothes, shave off all his hair, and wash himself in water, that he may be clean. After that he

13:47 [a]A mold, fungus, or similar infestation, and so in verses 47–59

shall come into the camp, and shall stay out-
side his tent seven days.
9 "But on the seventh day he shall shave all
the hair off his head and his beard and his
eyebrows—all his hair he shall shave off. He
shall wash his clothes and wash his body in
water, and he shall be clean.
10 "And on the eighth day he shall take two
male lambs without blemish, one ewe lamb of
the first year without blemish, three-tenths *of*
an ephah of fine flour mixed with oil as a grain
offering, and one log of oil.
11 "Then the priest who makes *him* clean
shall present the man who is to be made clean,
and those things, before the LORD, *at* the door
of the tabernacle of meeting.
12 "And the priest shall take one male lamb
and offer it as a trespass offering, and the log
of oil, and wave them *as* a wave offering before
the LORD.
13 "Then he shall kill the lamb in the place
where he kills the sin offering and the burnt
offering, in a holy place; for as the sin offering
is the priest's, so *is* the trespass offering. It *is*
most holy.
14 "The priest shall take *some* of the blood of
the trespass offering, and the priest shall put
it on the tip of the right ear of him who is to be
cleansed, on the thumb of his right hand, and
on the big toe of his right foot.
15 "And the priest shall take *some* of the log
of oil, and pour *it* into the palm of his own left
hand.
16 "Then the priest shall dip his right finger
in the oil that *is* in his left hand, and shall
sprinkle some of the oil with his finger seven
times before the LORD.
17 "And of the rest of the oil in his hand, the
priest shall put *some* on the tip of the right ear
of him who is to be cleansed, on the thumb of
his right hand, and on the big toe of his right
foot, on the blood of the trespass offering.
18 "The rest of the oil that *is* in the priest's
hand he shall put on the head of him who is to
be cleansed. So the priest shall make atone-
ment for him before the LORD.
19 "Then the priest shall offer the sin offer-
ing, and make atonement for him who is to be
cleansed from his uncleanness. Afterward he
shall kill the burnt offering.
20 "And the priest shall offer the burnt offer-
ing and the grain offering on the altar. So the
priest shall make atonement for him, and he
shall be clean.
21 "But if he *is* poor and cannot afford it, then
he shall take one male lamb *as* a trespass offer-
ing to be waved, to make atonement for him,
one-tenth *of an ephah* of fine flour mixed with
oil as a grain offering, a log of oil,
22 "and two turtledoves or two young pi-
geons, such as he is able to afford: one shall be
a sin offering and the other a burnt offering.
23 "He shall bring them to the priest on the
eighth day for his cleansing, to the door of the
tabernacle of meeting, before the LORD.
24 "And the priest shall take the lamb of the
trespass offering and the log of oil, and the
priest shall wave them *as* a wave offering be-
fore the LORD.
25 "Then he shall kill the lamb of the trespass
offering, and the priest shall take *some* of the
blood of the trespass offering and put *it* on the
tip of the right ear of him who is to be cleansed,
on the thumb of his right hand, and on the big
toe of his right foot.
26 "And the priest shall pour some of the oil
into the palm of his own left hand.
27 "Then the priest shall sprinkle with his
right finger *some* of the oil that *is* in his left
hand seven times before the LORD.
28 "And the priest shall put *some* of the oil
that *is* in his hand on the tip of the right ear of
him who is to be cleansed, on the thumb of the
right hand, and on the big toe of his right foot,
on the place of the blood of the trespass of-
fering.
29 "The rest of the oil that *is* in the priest's
hand he shall put on the head of him who is to
be cleansed, to make atonement for him before
the LORD.
30 "And he shall offer one of the turtledoves
or young pigeons, such as he can afford—
31 "such as he is able to afford, the one *as* a
sin offering and the other *as* a burnt offering,
with the grain offering. So the priest shall
make atonement for him who is to be cleansed
before the LORD.
32 "This *is* the law *for one* who had a leprous
sore, who cannot afford the usual cleansing."

The Law Concerning Leprous Houses

33 And the LORD spoke to Moses and Aaron,
saying:
34 "When you have come into the land of Ca-
naan, which I give you as a possession, and I
put the leprous plague[a] in a house in the land
of your possession,
35 "and he who owns the house comes and
tells the priest, saying, 'It seems to me that
there is some plague in the house,'
36 "then the priest shall command that they
empty the house, before the priest goes *into it*
to examine the plague, that all that *is* in the
house may not be made unclean; and afterward
the priest shall go in to examine the house.
37 "And he shall examine the plague; and in-
deed *if* the plague *is* on the walls of the house
with ingrained streaks, greenish or reddish,
which appear to be deep in the wall,
38 "then the priest shall go out of the house,
to the door of the house, and shut up the house
seven days.
39 "And the priest shall come again on the
seventh day and look; and indeed *if* the plague
has spread on the walls of the house,
40 "then the priest shall command that they
take away the stones in which *is* the plague,
and they shall cast them into an unclean place
outside the city.
41 "And he shall cause the house to be
scraped inside, all around, and the dust that
they scrape off they shall pour out in an un-
clean place outside the city.
42 "Then they shall take other stones and put
them in the place of *those* stones, and he shall
take other mortar and plaster the house.
43 "Now if the plague comes back and breaks
out in the house, after he has taken away the
stones, after he has scraped the house, and
after it is plastered,
44 "then the priest shall come and look; and
indeed *if* the plague has spread in the house, it
is an active leprosy in the house. It *is* unclean.
45 "And he shall break down the house, its
stones, its timber, and all the plaster of the

14:34 [a]Decomposition by mildew, mold, dry rot, etc., and so in verses 34–53

house, and he shall carry *them* outside the city to an unclean place.

46 "Moreover he who goes into the house at all while it is shut up shall be unclean until evening.

47 "And he who lies down in the house shall wash his clothes, and he who eats in the house shall wash his clothes.

48 "But if the priest comes in and examines *it*, and indeed the plague has not spread in the house after the house was plastered, then the priest shall pronounce the house clean, because the plague is healed.

49 "And he shall take, to cleanse the house, two birds, cedar wood, scarlet, and hyssop.

50 "Then he shall kill one of the birds in an earthen vessel over running water;

51 "and he shall take the cedar wood, the hyssop, the scarlet, and the living bird, and dip them in the blood of the slain bird and in the running water, and sprinkle the house seven times.

52 "And he shall cleanse the house with the blood of the bird and the running water and the living bird, with the cedar wood, the hyssop, and the scarlet.

53 "Then he shall let the living bird loose outside the city in the open field, and make atonement for the house, and it shall be clean.

54 "This *is* the law for any leprous sore and scale,

55 "for the leprosy of a garment and of a house,

56 "for a swelling and a scab and a bright spot,

57 "to teach when *it is* unclean and when *it is* clean. This *is* the law of leprosy."

The Law Concerning Bodily Discharges

15 And the LORD spoke to Moses and Aaron, saying,

2 "Speak to the children of Israel, and say to them: 'When any man has a discharge from his body, his discharge *is* unclean.

3 'And this shall be his uncleanness in regard to his discharge—whether his body runs with his discharge, or his body is stopped up by his discharge, it *is* his uncleanness.

4 'Every bed is unclean on which he who has the discharge lies, and everything on which he sits shall be unclean.

5 'And whoever touches his bed shall wash his clothes and bathe in water, and be unclean until evening.

6 'He who sits on anything on which he who has the discharge sat shall wash his clothes and bathe in water, and be unclean until evening.

7 'And he who touches the body of him who has the discharge shall wash his clothes and bathe in water, and be unclean until evening.

8 'If he who has the discharge spits on him who is clean, then he shall wash his clothes and bathe in water, and be unclean until evening.

9 'Any saddle on which he who has the discharge rides shall be unclean.

10 'Whoever touches anything that was under him shall be unclean until evening. He who carries *any of* those things shall wash his clothes and bathe in water, and be unclean until evening.

11 'And whomever the one who has the discharge touches, and has not rinsed his hands in water, he shall wash his clothes and bathe in water, and be unclean until evening.

12 'The vessel of earth that he who has the discharge touches shall be broken, and every vessel of wood shall be rinsed in water.

13 'And when he who has a discharge is cleansed of his discharge, then he shall count for himself seven days for his cleansing, wash his clothes, and bathe his body in running water; then he shall be clean.

14 'On the eighth day he shall take for himself two turtledoves or two young pigeons, and come before the LORD, to the door of the tabernacle of meeting, and give them to the priest.

15 'Then the priest shall offer them, the one *as* a sin offering and the other *as* a burnt offering. So the priest shall make atonement for him before the LORD because of his discharge.

16 'If any man has an emission of semen, then he shall wash all his body in water, and be unclean until evening.

17 'And any garment and any leather on which there is semen, it shall be washed with water, and be unclean until evening.

18 'Also, when a woman lies with a man, and *there is* an emission of semen, they shall bathe in water, and be unclean until evening.

19 'If a woman has a discharge, *and* the discharge from her body is blood, she shall be set apart seven days; and whoever touches her shall be unclean until evening.

20 'Everything that she lies on during her impurity shall be unclean; also everything that she sits on shall be unclean.

21 'Whoever touches her bed shall wash his clothes and bathe in water, and be unclean until evening.

22 'And whoever touches anything that she sat on shall wash his clothes and bathe in water, and be unclean until evening.

23 'If *anything* is on *her* bed or on anything on which she sits, when he touches it, he shall be unclean until evening.

24 'And if any man lies with her at all, so that her impurity is on him, he shall be unclean seven days; and every bed on which he lies shall be unclean.

25 'If a woman has a discharge of blood for many days, other than at the time of her *customary* impurity, or if it runs beyond her *usual time of* impurity, all the days of her unclean discharge shall be as the days of her *customary* impurity. She *shall be* unclean.

26 'Every bed on which she lies all the days of her discharge shall be to her as the bed of her impurity; and whatever she sits on shall be unclean, as the uncleanness of her impurity.

27 'Whoever touches those things shall be unclean; he shall wash his clothes and bathe in water, and be unclean until evening.

28 'But if she is cleansed of her discharge, then she shall count for herself seven days, and after that she shall be clean.

29 'And on the eighth day she shall take for herself two turtledoves or two young pigeons, and bring them to the priest, to the door of the tabernacle of meeting.

30 'Then the priest shall offer the one *as* a sin offering and the other *as* a burnt offering, and the priest shall make atonement for her before the LORD for the discharge of her uncleanness.

31 'Thus you shall separate the children of Israel from their uncleanness, lest they die in their uncleanness when they defile My tabernacle that *is* among them.

32 'This *is* the law for one who has a discharge, and *for him* who emits semen and is unclean thereby,

33 'and for her who is indisposed because of
her *customary* impurity, and for one who has
a discharge, either man or woman, and for him
who lies with her who is unclean.'"

The Day of Atonement

16 Now the LORD spoke to Moses after the
death of the two sons of Aaron, when
they offered *profane fire* before the LORD, and
died;
2 and the LORD said to Moses: "Tell Aaron
your brother not to come at *just* any time into
the Holy *Place* inside the veil, before the mercy
seat which *is* on the ark, lest he die; for I will
appear in the cloud above the mercy seat.
3 "Thus Aaron shall come into the Holy
Place: with *the blood of* a young bull as a sin
offering, and *of* a ram as a burnt offering.
4 "He shall put the holy linen tunic and the
linen trousers on his body; he shall be girded
with a linen sash, and with the linen turban
he shall be attired. These *are* holy garments.
Therefore he shall wash his body in water, and
put them on.
5 "And he shall take from the congregation
of the children of Israel two kids of the goats as
a sin offering, and one ram as a burnt offering.
6 "Aaron shall offer the bull as a sin offering,
which *is* for himself, and make atonement for
himself and for his house.
7 "He shall take the two goats and present
them before the LORD *at* the door of the taber-
nacle of meeting.
8 "Then Aaron shall cast lots for the two
goats: one lot for the LORD and the other lot
for the scapegoat.
9 "And Aaron shall bring the goat on which
the LORD's lot fell, and offer it *as* a sin offering.
10 "But the goat on which the lot fell to be the
scapegoat shall be presented alive before the
LORD, to make atonement upon it, *and* to let it
go as the scapegoat into the wilderness.
11 "And Aaron shall bring the bull of the sin
offering, which is for himself, and make atone-
ment for himself and for his house, and shall
kill the bull as the sin offering which *is* for
himself.
12 "Then he shall take a censer full of burn-
ing coals of fire from the altar before the LORD,
with his hands full of sweet incense beaten
fine, and bring *it* inside the veil.
13 "And he shall put the incense on the fire
before the LORD, that the cloud of incense may
cover the mercy seat that *is* on the Testimony,
lest he die.
14 "He shall take some of the blood of the
bull and sprinkle *it* with his finger on the
mercy seat on the east *side;* and before the
mercy seat he shall sprinkle some of the blood
with his finger seven times.
15 "Then he shall kill the goat of the sin offer-
ing, which *is* for the people, bring its blood
inside the veil, do with that blood as he did
with the blood of the bull, and sprinkle it on
the mercy seat and before the mercy seat.
16 "So he shall make atonement for the Holy
Place, because of the uncleanness of the chil-
dren of Israel, and because of their transgres-
sions, for all their sins; and so he shall do for
the tabernacle of meeting which remains
among them in the midst of their uncleanness.
17 "There shall be no man in the tabernacle
of meeting when he goes in to make atonement
in the Holy *Place,* until he comes out, that he
may make atonement for himself, for his
household, and for all the assembly of Israel.
18 "And he shall go out to the altar that *is*
before the LORD, and make atonement for it,
and shall take some of the blood of the bull
and some of the blood of the goat, and put it
on the horns of the altar all around.
19 "Then he shall sprinkle some of the blood
on it with his finger seven times, cleanse it,
and consecrate it from the uncleanness of the
children of Israel.
20 "And when he has made an end of atoning
for the Holy *Place,* the tabernacle of meeting,
and the altar, he shall bring the live goat.
21 "Aaron shall lay both his hands on the
head of the live goat, confess over it all the
iniquities of the children of Israel, and all their
transgressions, concerning all their sins, put-
ting them on the head of the goat, and shall
send *it* away into the wilderness by the hand
of a suitable man.
22 "The goat shall bear on itself all their iniq-
uities to an uninhabited land; and he shall re-
lease the goat in the wilderness.
23 "Then Aaron shall come into the taberna-
cle of meeting, shall take off the linen gar-
ments which he put on when he went into the
Holy *Place,* and shall leave them there.
24 "And he shall wash his body with water in
a holy place, put on his garments, come out
and offer his burnt offering and the burnt of-
fering of the people, and make atonement for
himself and for the people.
25 "The fat of the sin offering he shall burn
on the altar.
26 "And he who released the goat as the
scapegoat shall wash his clothes and bathe his
body in water, and afterward he may come into
the camp.
27 "The bull *for* the sin offering and the goat
for the sin offering, whose blood was brought
in to make atonement in the Holy *Place,* shall
be carried outside the camp. And they shall
burn in the fire their skins, their flesh, and
their offal.
28 "Then he who burns them shall wash his
clothes and bathe his body in water, and after-
ward he may come into the camp.
29 "*This* shall be a statute forever for you: In
the seventh month, on the tenth *day* of the
month, you shall afflict your souls, and do no
work at all, *whether* a native of your own coun-
try or a stranger who dwells among you.
30 "For on that day *the priest* shall make
atonement for you, to cleanse you, *that* you
may be clean from all your sins before the LORD.
31 "It *is* a sabbath of solemn rest for you,
and you shall afflict your souls. *It is* a statute
forever.
32 "And the priest, who is anointed and con-
secrated to minister as priest in his father's
place, shall make atonement, and put on the
linen clothes, the holy garments;
33 "then he shall make atonement for the
Holy Sanctuary,[a] and he shall make atonement
for the tabernacle of meeting and for the altar,
and he shall make atonement for the priests
and for all the people of the assembly.
34 "This shall be an everlasting statute for
you, to make atonement for the children of
Israel, for all their sins, once a year." And he
did as the LORD commanded Moses.

16:33 [a]That is, the Most Holy Place

The Sanctity of Blood

17 And the LORD spoke to Moses, saying,
2 "Speak to Aaron, to his sons, and to all the children of Israel, and say to them, 'This *is* the thing which the LORD has commanded, saying:
3 "Whatever man of the house of Israel who kills an ox or lamb or goat in the camp, or who kills *it* outside the camp,
4 "and does not bring it to the door of the tabernacle of meeting to offer an offering to the LORD before the tabernacle of the LORD, the guilt of bloodshed shall be imputed to that man. He has shed blood; and that man shall be cut off from among his people,
5 "to the end that the children of Israel may bring their sacrifices which they offer in the open field, that they may bring them to the LORD at the door of the tabernacle of meeting, to the priest, and offer them *as* peace offerings to the LORD.
6 "And the priest shall sprinkle the blood on the altar of the LORD *at* the door of the tabernacle of meeting, and burn the fat for a sweet aroma to the LORD.
7 "They shall no more offer their sacrifices to demons, after whom they have played the harlot. This shall be a statute forever for them throughout their generations." '
8 "Also you shall say to them: 'Whatever man of the house of Israel, or of the strangers who dwell among you, who offers a burnt offering or sacrifice,
9 'and does not bring it to the door of the tabernacle of meeting, to offer it to the LORD, that man shall be cut off from among his people.
10 'And whatever man of the house of Israel, or of the strangers who dwell among you, who eats any blood, I will set My face against that person who eats blood, and will cut him off from among his people.
11 'For the life of the flesh *is* in the blood, and I have given it to you upon the altar to make atonement for your souls; for it *is* the blood *that* makes atonement for the soul.'
12 "Therefore I said to the children of Israel, 'No one among you shall eat blood, nor shall any stranger who dwells among you eat blood.'
13 "Whatever man of the children of Israel, or of the strangers who dwell among you, who hunts and catches any animal or bird that may be eaten, he shall pour out its blood and cover it with dust;
14 "for *it is* the life of all flesh. Its blood sustains its life. Therefore I said to the children of Israel, 'You shall not eat the blood of any flesh, for the life of all flesh is its blood. Whoever eats it shall be cut off.'
15 "And every person who eats what died *naturally* or what was torn *by beasts, whether he is* a native of your own country or a stranger, he shall both wash his clothes and bathe in water, and be unclean until evening. Then he shall be clean.
16 "But if he does not wash *them* or bathe his body, then he shall bear his guilt."

Laws of Sexual Morality

18 Then the LORD spoke to Moses, saying,
2 "Speak to the children of Israel, and say to them: 'I am the LORD your God.
3 'According to the doings of the land of Egypt, where you dwelt, you shall not do; and according to the doings of the land of Canaan, where I am bringing you, you shall not do; nor shall you walk in their ordinances.
4 'You shall observe My judgments and keep My ordinances, to walk in them: I *am* the LORD your God.
5 'You shall therefore keep My statutes and My judgments, which if a man does, he shall live by them: I *am* the LORD.
6 'None of you shall approach anyone who is near of kin to him, to uncover his nakedness: I *am* the LORD.
7 'The nakedness of your father or the nakedness of your mother you shall not uncover. She *is* your mother; you shall not uncover her nakedness.
8 'The nakedness of your father's wife you shall not uncover; it *is* your father's nakedness.
9 'The nakedness of your sister, the daughter of your father, or the daughter of your mother, *whether* born at home or elsewhere, their nakedness you shall not uncover.
10 'The nakedness of your son's daughter or your daughter's daughter, their nakedness you shall not uncover; for theirs *is* your own nakedness.
11 'The nakedness of your father's wife's daughter, begotten by your father—she *is* your sister—you shall not uncover her nakedness.
12 'You shall not uncover the nakedness of your father's sister; she *is* near of kin to your father.
13 'You shall not uncover the nakedness of your mother's sister, for she *is* near of kin to your mother.
14 'You shall not uncover the nakedness of your father's brother. You shall not approach his wife; she *is* your aunt.
15 'You shall not uncover the nakedness of your daughter-in-law—she *is* your son's wife—you shall not uncover her nakedness.
16 'You shall not uncover the nakedness of your brother's wife; it *is* your brother's nakedness.
17 'You shall not uncover the nakedness of a woman and her daughter, nor shall you take her son's daughter or her daughter's daughter, to uncover her nakedness. They *are* near of kin to her. It *is* wickedness.
18 'Nor shall you take a woman as a rival to her sister, to uncover her nakedness while the other is alive.
19 'Also you shall not approach a woman to uncover her nakedness as long as she is in her *customary* impurity.
20 'Moreover you shall not lie carnally with your neighbor's wife, to defile yourself with her.
21 'And you shall not let any of your descendants pass through *the fire* to Molech, nor shall you profane the name of your God: I *am* the LORD.
22 'You shall not lie with a male as with a woman. It *is* an abomination.
23 'Nor shall you mate with any animal, to defile yourself with it. Nor shall any woman stand before an animal to mate with it. It *is* perversion.
24 'Do not defile yourselves with any of these things; for by all these the nations are defiled, which I am casting out before you.
25 'For the land is defiled; therefore I visit the punishment of its iniquity upon it, and the land vomits out its inhabitants.
26 'You shall therefore keep My statutes and My judgments, and shall not commit *any* of

these abominations, *either* any of your own
nation or any stranger who dwells among you
27 '(for all these abominations the men of the
land have done, who *were* before you, and thus
the land is defiled),
28 'lest the land vomit you out also when you
defile it, as it vomited out the nations that *were*
before you.
29 'For whoever commits any of these abomi-
nations, the persons who commit *them* shall
be cut off from among their people.
30 'Therefore you shall keep My ordinance,
so that *you* do not commit *any* of these abomi-
nable customs which were committed before
you, and that you do not defile yourselves by
them: I *am* the LORD your God.'"

Moral and Ceremonial Laws

19 And the LORD spoke to Moses, saying,
2 "Speak to all the congregation of
the children of Israel, and say to them: 'You
shall be holy, for I the LORD your God *am* holy.
3 'Every one of you shall revere his mother
and his father, and keep My Sabbaths: I *am*
the LORD your God.
4 'Do not turn to idols, nor make for your-
selves molded gods: I *am* the LORD your God.
5 'And if you offer a sacrifice of a peace of-
fering to the LORD, you shall offer it of your
own free will.
6 'It shall be eaten the same day you offer *it*,
and on the next day. And if any remains until
the third day, it shall be burned in the fire.
7 'And if it is eaten at all on the third day, it
is an abomination. It shall not be accepted.
8 'Therefore *everyone* who eats it shall bear
his iniquity, because he has profaned the hal-
lowed *offering* of the LORD; and that person
shall be cut off from his people.
9 'When you reap the harvest of your land,
you shall not wholly reap the corners of your
field, nor shall you gather the gleanings of your
harvest.
10 'And you shall not glean your vineyard,
nor shall you gather *every* grape of your vine-
yard; you shall leave them for the poor and the
stranger: I *am* the LORD your God.
11 'You shall not steal, nor deal falsely, nor
lie to one another.
12 'And you shall not swear by My name
falsely, nor shall you profane the name of your
God: I *am* the LORD.
13 'You shall not cheat your neighbor, nor rob
him. The wages of him who is hired shall not
remain with you all night until morning.
14 'You shall not curse the deaf, nor put a
stumbling block before the blind, but shall fear
your God: I *am* the LORD.
15 'You shall do no injustice in judgment. You
shall not be partial to the poor, nor honor the
person of the mighty. In righteousness you
shall judge your neighbor.
16 'You shall not go about *as* a talebearer
among your people; nor shall you take a stand
against the life of your neighbor: I *am* the
LORD.
17 'You shall not hate your brother in your
heart. You shall surely rebuke your neighbor,
and not bear sin because of him.
18 'You shall not take vengeance, nor bear
any grudge against the children of your peo-
ple, but you shall love your neighbor as your-
self: I *am* the LORD.
19 'You shall keep My statutes. You shall not
let your livestock breed with another kind. You
shall not sow your field with mixed seed. Nor
shall a garment of mixed linen and wool come
upon you.
20 'Whoever lies carnally with a woman who
is betrothed to a man as a concubine, and who
has not at all been redeemed nor given her
freedom, for this there shall be scourging; *but*
they shall not be put to death, because she was
not free.
21 'And he shall bring his trespass offering
to the LORD, to the door of the tabernacle of
meeting, a ram as a trespass offering.
22 'The priest shall make atonement for him
with the ram of the trespass offering before
the LORD for his sin which he has committed.
And the sin which he has committed shall be
forgiven him.
23 'When you come into the land, and have
planted all kinds of trees for food, then you
shall count their fruit as uncircumcised. Three
years it shall be as uncircumcised to you. *It*
shall not be eaten.
24 'But in the fourth year all its fruit shall be
holy, a praise to the LORD.
25 'And in the fifth year you may eat its fruit,
that it may yield to you its increase: I *am* the
LORD your God.
26 'You shall not eat *anything* with the blood,
nor shall you practice divination or sooth-
saying.
27 'You shall not shave around the sides of
your head, nor shall you disfigure the edges of
your beard.
28 'You shall not make any cuttings in your
flesh for the dead, nor tattoo any marks on
you: I *am* the LORD.
29 'Do not prostitute your daughter, to cause
her to be a harlot, lest the land fall into har-
lotry, and the land become full of wickedness.
30 'You shall keep My Sabbaths and rever-
ence My sanctuary: I *am* the LORD.
31 'Give no regard to mediums and familiar
spirits; do not seek after them, to be defiled by
them: I *am* the LORD your God.
32 'You shall rise before the gray headed and
honor the presence of an old man, and fear
your God: I *am* the LORD.
33 'And if a stranger dwells with you in your
land, you shall not mistreat him.
34 'The stranger who dwells among you shall
be to you as one born among you, and you shall
love him as yourself; for you were strangers in
the land of Egypt: I *am* the LORD your God.
35 'You shall do no injustice in judgment, in
measurement of length, weight, or volume.
36 'You shall have honest scales, honest
weights, an honest ephah, and an honest hin:
I *am* the LORD your God, who brought you out
of the land of Egypt.
37 'Therefore you shall observe all My stat-
utes and all My judgments, and perform them:
I *am* the LORD.'"

Penalties for Breaking the Law

20 Then the LORD spoke to Moses, saying,
2 "Again, you shall say to the children
of Israel: 'Whoever of the children of Israel, or
of the strangers who dwell in Israel, who gives
any of his descendants to Molech, he shall
surely be put to death. The people of the land
shall stone him with stones.
3 'I will set My face against that man, and
will cut him off from his people, because he
has given *some* of his descendants to Molech,

to defile My sanctuary and profane My holy
name.
4 'And if the people of the land should in any
way hide their eyes from the man, when he
gives *some* of his descendants to Molech, and
they do not kill him,
5 'then I will set My face against that man
and against his family; and I will cut him off
from his people, and all who prostitute them-
selves with him to commit harlotry with Mo-
lech.
6 'And the person who turns to mediums and
familiar spirits, to prostitute himself with
them, I will set My face against that person
and cut him off from his people.
7 'Consecrate yourselves therefore, and be
holy, for I *am* the LORD your God.
8 'And you shall keep My statutes, and per-
form them: I *am* the LORD who sanctifies you.
9 'For everyone who curses his father or his
mother shall surely be put to death. He has
cursed his father or his mother. His blood *shall*
be upon him.
10 'The man who commits adultery with *an-*
other man's wife, *he* who commits adultery
with his neighbor's wife, the adulterer and the
adulteress, shall surely be put to death.
11 'The man who lies with his father's wife
has uncovered his father's nakedness; both of
them shall surely be put to death. Their blood
shall be upon them.
12 'If a man lies with his daughter-in-law,
both of them shall surely be put to death. They
have committed perversion. Their blood *shall*
be upon them.
13 'If a man lies with a male as he lies with a
woman, both of them have committed an
abomination. They shall surely be put to death.
Their blood *shall be* upon them.
14 'If a man marries a woman and her mother,
it *is* wickedness. They shall be burned with
fire, both he and they, that there may be no
wickedness among you.
15 'If a man mates with an animal, he shall
surely be put to death, and you shall kill the
animal.
16 'If a woman approaches any animal and
mates with it, you shall kill the woman and the
animal. They shall surely be put to death. Their
blood *is* upon them.
17 'If a man takes his sister, his father's
daughter or his mother's daughter, and sees
her nakedness and she sees his nakedness, it
is a wicked thing. And they shall be cut off in
the sight of their people. He has uncovered his
sister's nakedness. He shall bear his guilt.
18 'If a man lies with a woman during her
sickness and uncovers her nakedness, he has
exposed her flow, and she has uncovered the
flow of her blood. Both of them shall be cut off
from their people.
19 'You shall not uncover the nakedness of
your mother's sister nor of your father's sister,
for that would uncover his near of kin. They
shall bear their guilt.
20 'If a man lies with his uncle's wife, he has
uncovered his uncle's nakedness. They shall
bear their sin; they shall die childless.
21 'If a man takes his brother's wife, it *is* an
unclean thing. He has uncovered his brother's
nakedness. They shall be childless.
22 'You shall therefore keep all My statutes
and all My judgments, and perform them, that
the land where I am bringing you to dwell may
not vomit you out.
23 'And you shall not walk in the statutes of
the nation which I am casting out before you;
for they commit all these things, and therefore
I abhor them.
24 'But I have said to you, "You shall inherit
their land, and I will give it to you to possess,
a land flowing with milk and honey." I *am* the
LORD your God, who has separated you from
the peoples.
25 'You shall therefore distinguish between
clean animals and unclean, between unclean
birds and clean, and you shall not make your-
selves abominable by beast or by bird, or by
any kind of living thing that creeps on the
ground, which I have separated from you as
unclean.
26 'And you shall be holy to Me, for I the
LORD *am* holy, and have separated you from
the peoples, that you should be Mine.
27 'A man or a woman who is a medium, or
who has familiar spirits, shall surely be put to
death; they shall stone them with stones. Their
blood *shall be* upon them.' "

Regulations for Conduct of Priests

21 And the LORD said to Moses, "Speak to
the priests, the sons of Aaron, and say
to them: 'None shall defile himself for the dead
among his people,
2 'except for his relatives who are nearest to
him: his mother, his father, his son, his daugh-
ter, and his brother;
3 'also his virgin sister who is near to him,
who has had no husband, for her he may defile
himself.
4 '*Otherwise* he shall not defile himself, *be-*
ing a chief man among his people, to profane
himself.
5 'They shall not make any bald *place* on
their heads, nor shall they shave the edges of
their beards nor make any cuttings in their
flesh.
6 'They shall be holy to their God and not
profane the name of their God, for they offer
the offerings of the LORD made by fire, *and* the
bread of their God; therefore they shall be holy.
7 'They shall not take a wife *who is* a harlot
or a defiled woman, nor shall they take a
woman divorced from her husband; for *the*
priest[a] is holy to his God.
8 'Therefore you shall consecrate him, for
he offers the bread of your God. He shall be
holy to you, for I the LORD, who sanctify you,
am holy.
9 'The daughter of any priest, if she profanes
herself by playing the harlot, she profanes her
father. She shall be burned with fire.
10 '*He who is* the high priest among his breth-
ren, on whose head the anointing oil was
poured and who is consecrated to wear the
garments, shall not uncover his head nor tear
his clothes;
11 'nor shall he go near any dead body, nor
defile himself for his father or his mother;
12 'nor shall he go out of the sanctuary, nor
profane the sanctuary of his God; for the con-
secration of the anointing oil of his God *is* upon
him: I *am* the LORD.
13 'And he shall take a wife in her virginity.
14 'A widow or a divorced woman or a defiled
woman *or* a harlot—these he shall not marry;

21:7 [a]Literally *he*

but he shall take a virgin of his own people as
wife.
15 'Nor shall he profane his posterity among
his people, for I the LORD sanctify him.'"
16 And the LORD spoke to Moses, saying,
17 "Speak to Aaron, saying: 'No man of your
descendants in *succeeding* generations, who
has *any* defect, may approach to offer the
bread of his God.
18 'For any man who has a defect shall not
approach: a man blind or lame, who has a
marred *face* or any *limb* too long,
19 'a man who has a broken foot or broken
hand,
20 'or is a hunchback or a dwarf, or *a man*
who has a defect in his eye, or eczema or scab,
or is a eunuch.
21 'No man of the descendants of Aaron the
priest, who has a defect, shall come near to
offer the offerings made by fire to the LORD.
He has a defect; he shall not come near to offer
the bread of his God.
22 'He may eat the bread of his God, *both* the
most holy and the holy;
23 'only he shall not go near the veil or ap-
proach the altar, because he has a defect, lest
he profane My sanctuaries; for I the LORD
sanctify them.'"
24 And Moses told *it* to Aaron and his sons,
and to all the children of Israel.
22 Then the LORD spoke to Moses, saying,
2 "Speak to Aaron and his sons, that
they separate themselves from the holy things
of the children of Israel, and that they do not
profane My holy name *by* what they dedicate
to Me: I *am* the LORD.
3 "Say to them: 'Whoever of all your descen-
dants throughout your generations, who goes
near the holy things which the children of Is-
rael dedicate to the LORD, while he has un-
cleanness upon him, that person shall be cut
off from My presence: I *am* the LORD.
4 'Whatever man of the descendants of
Aaron, who *is* a leper or has a discharge, shall
not eat the holy offerings until he is clean. And
whoever touches anything made unclean *by* a
corpse, or a man who has had an emission of
semen,
5 'or whoever touches any creeping thing by
which he would be made unclean, or any per-
son by whom he would become unclean, what-
ever his uncleanness may be—
6 'the person who has touched any such
thing shall be unclean until evening, and shall
not eat the holy *offerings* unless he washes his
body with water.
7 'And when the sun goes down he shall be
clean; and afterward he may eat the holy *offer-
ings*, because it *is* his food.
8 'Whatever dies *naturally* or is torn *by
beasts* he shall not eat, to defile himself with
it: I *am* the LORD.
9 'They shall therefore keep My ordinance,
lest they bear sin for it and die thereby, if they
profane it: I the LORD sanctify them.
10 'No outsider shall eat the holy *offering;* one
who dwells with the priest, or a hired servant,
shall not eat the holy thing.
11 'But if the priest buys a person with his
money, he may eat it; and one who is born in
his house may eat his food.
12 'If the priest's daughter is married to an
outsider, she may not eat of the holy offerings.
13 'But if the priest's daughter is a widow or
divorced, and has no child, and has returned
to her father's house as in her youth, she may
eat her father's food; but no outsider shall eat
it.
14 'And if a man eats the holy *offering* un-
intentionally, then he shall restore a holy *offer-
ing* to the priest, and add one-fifth to it.
15 'They shall not profane the holy *offerings*
of the children of Israel, which they offer to
the LORD,
16 'or allow them to bear the guilt of trespass
when they eat their holy *offerings;* for I the
LORD sanctify them.'"

Offerings Accepted and Not Accepted

17 And the LORD spoke to Moses, saying,
18 "Speak to Aaron and his sons, and to all
the children of Israel, and say to them: 'What-
ever man of the house of Israel, or of the
strangers in Israel, who offers his sacrifice for
any of his vows or for any of his freewill offer-
ings, which they offer to the LORD as a burnt
offering—
19 '*you shall offer* of your own free will a male
without blemish from the cattle, from the
sheep, or from the goats.
20 'Whatever has a defect, you shall not offer,
for it shall not be acceptable on your behalf.
21 'And whoever offers a sacrifice of a peace
offering to the LORD, to fulfill *his* vow, or a
freewill offering from the cattle or the sheep,
it must be perfect to be accepted; there shall
be no defect in it.
22 'Those *that are* blind or broken or
maimed, or have an ulcer or eczema or scabs,
you shall not offer to the LORD, nor make an
offering by fire of them on the altar to the
LORD.
23 'Either a bull or a lamb that has any limb
too long or too short you may offer *as* a freewill
offering, but for a vow it shall not be accepted.
24 'You shall not offer to the LORD what is
bruised or crushed, or torn or cut; nor shall
you make *any offering of them* in your land.
25 'Nor from a foreigner's hand shall you of-
fer any of these as the bread of your God, be-
cause their corruption *is* in them, *and* defects
are in them. They shall not be accepted on your
behalf.'"
26 And the LORD spoke to Moses, saying:
27 "When a bull or a sheep or a goat is born,
it shall be seven days with its mother; and from
the eighth day and thereafter it shall be ac-
cepted as an offering made by fire to the LORD.
28 "*Whether it is* a cow or ewe, do not kill
both her and her young on the same day.
29 "And when you offer a sacrifice of thanks-
giving to the LORD, offer *it* of your own free
will.
30 "On the same day it shall be eaten; you
shall leave none of it until morning: I *am* the
LORD.
31 "Therefore you shall keep My command-
ments, and perform them: I *am* the LORD.
32 "You shall not profane My holy name, but
I will be hallowed among the children of Israel.
I *am* the LORD who sanctifies you,
33 "who brought you out of the land of Egypt,
to be your God: I *am* the LORD."

Feasts of the LORD

23 And the LORD spoke to Moses, saying,
2 "Speak to the children of Israel, and
say to them: 'The feasts of the LORD, which you
shall proclaim *to be* holy convocations, these
are My feasts.

The Sabbath

3 'Six days shall work be done, but the seventh day *is* a Sabbath of solemn rest, a holy convocation. You shall do no work *on it;* it *is* the Sabbath of the LORD in all your dwellings.

The Passover and Unleavened Bread

4 'These *are* the feasts of the LORD, holy convocations which you shall proclaim at their appointed times.

5 'On the fourteenth *day* of the first month at twilight *is* the LORD's Passover.

6 'And on the fifteenth day of the same month *is* the Feast of Unleavened Bread to the LORD; seven days you must eat unleavened bread.

7 'On the first day you shall have a holy convocation; you shall do no customary work on it.

8 'But you shall offer an offering made by fire to the LORD for seven days. The seventh day *shall be* a holy convocation; you shall do no customary work *on it.'* "

The Feast of Firstfruits

9 And the LORD spoke to Moses, saying,

10 "Speak to the children of Israel, and say to them: 'When you come into the land which I give to you, and reap its harvest, then you shall bring a sheaf of the firstfruits of your harvest to the priest.

11 'He shall wave the sheaf before the LORD, to be accepted on your behalf; on the day after the Sabbath the priest shall wave it.

12 'And you shall offer on that day, when you wave the sheaf, a male lamb of the first year, without blemish, as a burnt offering to the LORD.

13 'Its grain offering *shall be* two-tenths *of an ephah* of fine flour mixed with oil, an offering made by fire to the LORD, for a sweet aroma; and its drink offering *shall be* of wine, one-fourth of a hin.

14 'You shall eat neither bread nor parched grain nor fresh grain until the same day that you have brought an offering to your God; *it shall be* a statute forever throughout your generations in all your dwellings.

The Feast of Weeks

15 'And you shall count for yourselves from the day after the Sabbath, from the day that you brought the sheaf of the wave offering: seven Sabbaths shall be completed.

16 'Count fifty days to the day after the seventh Sabbath; then you shall offer a new grain offering to the LORD.

17 'You shall bring from your dwellings two wave *loaves* of two-tenths *of an ephah.* They shall be of fine flour; they shall be baked with leaven. *They are* the firstfruits to the LORD.

18 'And you shall offer with the bread seven lambs of the first year, without blemish, one young bull, and two rams. They shall be *as* a burnt offering to the LORD, with their grain offering and their drink offerings, an offering made by fire for a sweet aroma to the LORD.

19 'Then you shall sacrifice one kid of the goats as a sin offering, and two male lambs of the first year as a sacrifice of a peace offering.

20 'The priest shall wave them with the bread of the firstfruits *as* a wave offering before the LORD, with the two lambs. They shall be holy to the LORD for the priest.

21 'And you shall proclaim on the same day *that* it is a holy convocation to you. You shall do no customary work *on it. It shall be* a statute forever in all your dwellings throughout your generations.

22 'When you reap the harvest of your land, you shall not wholly reap the corners of your field when you reap, nor shall you gather any gleaning from your harvest. You shall leave them for the poor and for the stranger: I *am* the LORD your God.' "

The Feast of Trumpets

23 Then the LORD spoke to Moses, saying,

24 "Speak to the children of Israel, saying: 'In the seventh month, on the first *day* of the month, you shall have a sabbath-*rest,* a memorial of blowing of trumpets, a holy convocation.

25 'You shall do no customary work *on it;* and you shall offer an offering made by fire to the LORD.' "

The Day of Atonement

26 And the LORD spoke to Moses, saying:

27 "Also the tenth *day* of this seventh month *shall be* the Day of Atonement. It shall be a holy convocation for you; you shall afflict your souls, and offer an offering made by fire to the LORD.

28 "And you shall do no work on that same day, for it *is* the Day of Atonement, to make atonement for you before the LORD your God.

29 "For any person who is not afflicted *in soul* on that same day shall be cut off from his people.

30 "And any person who does any work on that same day, that person I will destroy from among his people.

31 "You shall do no manner of work; *it shall be* a statute forever throughout your generations in all your dwellings.

32 "It *shall be* to you a sabbath of *solemn* rest, and you shall afflict your souls; on the ninth *day* of the month at evening, from evening to evening, you shall celebrate your sabbath."

The Feast of Tabernacles

33 Then the LORD spoke to Moses, saying,

34 "Speak to the children of Israel, saying: 'The fifteenth day of this seventh month *shall be* the Feast of Tabernacles *for* seven days to the LORD.

35 'On the first day *there shall be* a holy convocation. You shall do no customary work *on it.*

36 '*For* seven days you shall offer an offering made by fire to the LORD. On the eighth day you shall have a holy convocation, and you shall offer an offering made by fire to the LORD. It *is* a sacred assembly, *and* you shall do no customary work *on it.*

37 'These *are* the feasts of the LORD which you shall proclaim *to be* holy convocations, to offer an offering made by fire to the LORD, a burnt offering and a grain offering, a sacrifice and drink offerings, everything on its day—

38 'besides the Sabbaths of the LORD, besides your gifts, besides all your vows, and besides all your freewill offerings which you give to the LORD.

39 'Also on the fifteenth day of the seventh month, when you have gathered in the fruit of the land, you shall keep the feast of the LORD *for* seven days; on the first day *there shall be* a sabbath-*rest*, and on the eighth day a sabbath-*rest*.

40 'And you shall take for yourselves on the first day the fruit of beautiful trees, branches of palm trees, the boughs of leafy trees, and willows of the brook; and you shall rejoice before the LORD your God for seven days.

41 'You shall keep it as a feast to the LORD for seven days in the year. *It shall be* a statute forever in your generations. You shall celebrate it in the seventh month.

42 'You shall dwell in booths for seven days. All who are native Israelites shall dwell in booths,

43 'that your generations may know that I made the children of Israel dwell in booths when I brought them out of the land of Egypt: I *am* the LORD your God.' "

44 So Moses declared to the children of Israel the feasts of the LORD.

Care of the Tabernacle Lamps

24 Then the LORD spoke to Moses, saying:

2 "Command the children of Israel that they bring to you pure oil of pressed olives for the light, to make the lamps burn continually.

3 "Outside the veil of the Testimony, in the tabernacle of meeting, Aaron shall be in charge of it from evening until morning before the LORD continually; *it shall be* a statute forever in your generations.

4 "He shall be in charge of the lamps on the pure *gold* lampstand before the LORD continually.

The Bread of the Tabernacle

5 "And you shall take fine flour and bake twelve cakes with it. Two-tenths *of an ephah* shall be in each cake.

6 "You shall set them in two rows, six in a row, on the pure *gold* table before the LORD.

7 "And you shall put pure frankincense on *each* row, that it may be on the bread for a memorial, an offering made by fire to the LORD.

8 "Every Sabbath he shall set it in order before the LORD continually, *being taken* from the children of Israel by an everlasting covenant.

9 "And it shall be for Aaron and his sons, and they shall eat it in a holy place; for it *is* most holy to him from the offerings of the LORD made by fire, by a perpetual statute."

The Penalty for Blasphemy

10 Now the son of an Israelite woman, whose father *was* an Egyptian, went out among the children of Israel; and this Israelite *woman's* son and a man of Israel fought each other in the camp.

11 And the Israelite woman's son blasphemed the name *of the LORD* and cursed; and so they brought him to Moses. (His mother's name *was* Shelomith the daughter of Dibri, of the tribe of Dan.)

12 Then they put him in custody, that the mind of the LORD might be shown to them.

13 And the LORD spoke to Moses, saying,

14 "Take outside the camp him who has cursed; then let all who heard *him* lay their hands on his head, and let all the congregation stone him.

15 "Then you shall speak to the children of Israel, saying: 'Whoever curses his God shall bear his sin.

16 'And whoever blasphemes the name of the LORD shall surely be put to death. All the congregation shall certainly stone him, the stranger as well as him who is born in the land. When he blasphemes the name *of the LORD*, he shall be put to death.

17 'Whoever kills any man shall surely be put to death.

18 'Whoever kills an animal shall make it good, animal for animal.

19 'If a man causes disfigurement of his neighbor, as he has done, so shall it be done to him—

20 'fracture for fracture, eye for eye, tooth for tooth; as he has caused disfigurement of a man, so shall it be done to him.

21 'And whoever kills an animal shall restore it; but whoever kills a man shall be put to death.

22 'You shall have the same law for the stranger and for one from your own country; for I *am* the LORD your God.' "

23 Then Moses spoke to the children of Israel; and they took outside the camp him who had cursed, and stoned him with stones. So the children of Israel did as the LORD commanded Moses.

The Sabbath of the Seventh Year

25 And the LORD spoke to Moses on Mount Sinai, saying,

2 "Speak to the children of Israel, and say to them: 'When you come into the land which I give you, then the land shall keep a sabbath to the LORD.

3 'Six years you shall sow your field, and six years you shall prune your vineyard, and gather its fruit;

4 'but in the seventh year there shall be a sabbath of solemn rest for the land, a sabbath to the LORD. You shall neither sow your field nor prune your vineyard.

5 'What grows of its own accord of your harvest you shall not reap, nor gather the grapes of your untended vine, *for* it is a year of rest for the land.

6 'And the sabbath *produce* of the land shall be food for you: for you, your male and female servants, your hired man, and the stranger who dwells with you,

7 'for your livestock and the beasts that *are* in your land—all its produce shall be for food.

The Year of Jubilee

8 'And you shall count seven sabbaths of years for yourself, seven times seven years; and the time of the seven sabbaths of years shall be to you forty-nine years.

9 'Then you shall cause the trumpet of the Jubilee to sound on the tenth *day* of the seventh month; on the Day of Atonement you shall make the trumpet to sound throughout all your land.

10 'And you shall consecrate the fiftieth year, and proclaim liberty throughout *all* the land to all its inhabitants. It shall be a Jubilee for you; and each of you shall return to his possession, and each of you shall return to his family.

11 'That fiftieth year shall be a Jubilee to you; in it you shall neither sow nor reap what grows of its own accord, nor gather *the grapes* of your untended vine.

12 'For it *is* the Jubilee; it shall be holy to you;
you shall eat its produce from the field.
13 'In this Year of Jubilee, each of you shall
return to his possession.
14 'And if you sell anything to your neighbor
or buy from your neighbor's hand, you shall
not oppress one another.
15 'According to the number of years after the
Jubilee you shall buy from your neighbor, and
according to the number of years of crops he
shall sell to you.
16 'According to the multitude of years you
shall increase its price, and according to the
fewer number of years you shall diminish its
price; for he sells to you *according* to the number
of the years of the crops.
17 'Therefore you shall not oppress one another,
but you shall fear your God; for I *am* the
LORD your God.

Provisions for the Seventh Year

18 'So you shall observe My statutes and keep
My judgments, and perform them; and you will
dwell in the land in safety.
19 'Then the land will yield its fruit, and you
will eat your fill, and dwell there in safety.
20 'And if you say, "What shall we eat in the
seventh year, since we shall not sow nor gather
in our produce?"
21 'Then I will command My blessing on you
in the sixth year, and it will bring forth produce
enough for three years.
22 'And you shall sow in the eighth year, and
eat old produce until the ninth year; until its
produce comes in, you shall eat *of* the old *harvest*.

Redemption of Property

23 'The land shall not be sold permanently,
for the land *is* Mine; for you *are* strangers and
sojourners with Me.
24 'And in all the land of your possession you
shall grant redemption of the land.
25 'If one of your brethren becomes poor, and
has sold *some* of his possession, and if his redeeming
relative comes to redeem it, then he
may redeem what his brother sold.
26 'Or if the man has no one to redeem it, but
he himself becomes able to redeem it,
27 'then let him count the years since its sale,
and restore the remainder to the man to whom
he sold it, that he may return to his possession.
28 'But if he is not able to have *it* restored to
himself, then what was sold shall remain in the
hand of him who bought it until the Year of
Jubilee; and in the Jubilee it shall be released,
and he shall return to his possession.
29 'If a man sells a house in a walled city, then
he may redeem it within a whole year after it
is sold; *within* a full year he may redeem it.
30 'But if it is not redeemed within the space
of a full year, then the house in the walled city
shall belong permanently to him who bought
it, throughout his generations. It shall not be
released in the Jubilee.
31 'However the houses of villages which
have no wall around them shall be counted as
the fields of the country. They may be redeemed,
and they shall be released in the Jubilee.
32 'Nevertheless the cities of the Levites, *and*
the houses in the cities of their possession, the
Levites may redeem at any time.
33 'And if a man purchases a house from the
Levites, then the house that was sold in the
city of his possession shall be released in the
Jubilee; for the houses in the cities of the Levites
are their possession among the children
of Israel.
34 'But the field of the common-land of their
cities may not be sold, for it *is* their perpetual
possession.

Lending to the Poor

35 'If one of your brethren becomes poor, and
falls into poverty among you, then you shall
help him, like a stranger or a sojourner, that
he may live with you.
36 'Take no usury or interest from him; but
fear your God, that your brother may live with
you.
37 'You shall not lend him your money for
usury, nor lend him your food at a profit.
38 'I *am* the LORD your God, who brought
you out of the land of Egypt, to give you the
land of Canaan *and* to be your God.

The Law Concerning Slavery

39 'And if *one of* your brethren *who dwells* by
you becomes poor, and sells himself to you,
you shall not compel him to serve as a slave.
40 'As a hired servant *and* a sojourner he shall
be with you, *and* shall serve you until the Year
of Jubilee.
41 'And *then* he shall depart from you—he
and his children with him—and shall return to
his own family. He shall return to the possession
of his fathers.
42 'For they *are* My servants, whom I brought
out of the land of Egypt; they shall not be sold
as slaves.
43 'You shall not rule over him with rigor, but
you shall fear your God.
44 'And as for your male and female slaves
whom you may have—from the nations that
are around you, from them you may buy male
and female slaves.
45 'Moreover you may buy the children of the
strangers who dwell among you, and their
families who are with you, which they beget in
your land; and they shall become your property.
46 'And you may take them as an inheritance
for your children after you, to inherit *them*
as a possession; they shall be your permanent
slaves. But regarding your brethren, the children
of Israel, you shall not rule over one another
with rigor.
47 'Now if a sojourner or stranger close to
you becomes rich, and *one of* your brethren
who dwells by him becomes poor, and sells
himself to the stranger *or* sojourner close to
you, or to a member of the stranger's family,
48 'after he is sold he may be redeemed again.
One of his brothers may redeem him;
49 'or his uncle or his uncle's son may redeem
him; or *anyone* who is near of kin to him in his
family may redeem him; or if he is able he may
redeem himself.
50 'Thus he shall reckon with him who
bought him: The price of his release shall be
according to the number of years, from the
year that he was sold to him until the Year of
Jubilee; *it shall be* according to the time of a
hired servant for him.
51 'If *there are* still many years *remaining*,
according to them he shall repay the price of
his redemption from the money with which he
was bought.
52 'And if there remain but a few years until the

Year of Jubilee, then he shall reckon with him, *and* according to his years he shall repay him the price of his redemption.
53 'He shall be with him as a yearly hired servant, and he shall not rule with rigor over him in your sight.
54 'And if he is not redeemed in these *years*, then he shall be released in the Year of Jubilee—he and his children with him.
55 'For the children of Israel *are* servants to Me; they *are* My servants whom I brought out of the land of Egypt: I *am* the LORD your God.

Promise of Blessing and Retribution

26 'You shall not make idols for yourselves;
neither a carved image nor a *sacred* pillar shall you rear up for yourselves;
nor shall you set up an engraved stone in your land, to bow down to it;
for I *am* the LORD your God.
2 You shall keep My Sabbaths and reverence My sanctuary:
I *am* the LORD.

3 'If you walk in My statutes and keep My commandments, and perform them,
4 then I will give you rain in its season, the land shall yield its produce, and the trees of the field shall yield their fruit.
5 Your threshing shall last till the time of vintage, and the vintage shall last till the time of sowing;
you shall eat your bread to the full, and dwell in your land safely.
6 I will give peace in the land, and you shall lie down, and none will make *you* afraid;
I will rid the land of evil beasts,
and the sword will not go through your land.
7 You will chase your enemies, and they shall fall by the sword before you.
8 Five of you shall chase a hundred, and a hundred of you shall put ten thousand to flight;
your enemies shall fall by the sword before you.

9 'For I will look on you favorably and make you fruitful, multiply you and confirm My covenant with you.
10 You shall eat the old harvest, and clear out the old because of the new.
11 I will set My tabernacle among you, and My soul shall not abhor you.
12 I will walk among you and be your God, and you shall be My people.
13 I *am* the LORD your God, who brought you out of the land of Egypt, that *you* should not be their slaves;
I have broken the bands of your yoke and made you walk upright.

14 'But if you do not obey Me, and do not observe all these commandments,
15 and if you despise My statutes, or if your soul abhors My judgments, so that you do not perform all My commandments, *but* break My covenant,
16 I also will do this to you:
I will even appoint terror over you, wasting disease and fever which shall consume the eyes and cause sorrow of heart.
And you shall sow your seed in vain, for your enemies shall eat it.
17 I will set My face against you, and you shall be defeated by your enemies.
Those who hate you shall reign over you, and you shall flee when no one pursues you.

18 'And after all this, if you do not obey Me, then I will punish you seven times more for your sins.
19 I will break the pride of your power;
I will make your heavens like iron and your earth like bronze.
20 And your strength shall be spent in vain;
for your land shall not yield its produce, nor shall the trees of the land yield their fruit.

21 'Then, if you walk contrary to Me, and are not willing to obey Me, I will bring on you seven times more plagues, according to your sins.
22 I will also send wild beasts among you, which shall rob you of your children, destroy your livestock, and make you few in number;
and your highways shall be desolate.

23 'And if by these things you are not reformed by Me, but walk contrary to Me,
24 then I also will walk contrary to you, and I will punish you yet seven times for your sins.
25 And I will bring a sword against you that will execute the vengeance of the covenant;
when you are gathered together within your cities I will send pestilence among you;
and you shall be delivered into the hand of the enemy.
26 When I have cut off your supply of bread, ten women shall bake your bread in one oven, and they shall bring back your bread by weight, and you shall eat and not be satisfied.

27 'And after all this, if you do not obey Me, but walk contrary to Me,
28 then I also will walk contrary to you in fury;
and I, even I, will chastise you seven times for your sins.
29 You shall eat the flesh of your sons, and you shall eat the flesh of your daughters.
30 I will destroy your high places, cut down your incense altars, and cast your carcasses on the lifeless forms of your idols;
and My soul shall abhor you.
31 I will lay your cities waste and bring your sanctuaries to desolation, and I will not smell the fragrance of your sweet aromas.
32 I will bring the land to desolation, and your enemies who dwell in it shall be astonished at it.
33 I will scatter you among the nations and draw out a sword after you;
your land shall be desolate and your cities waste.
34 Then the land shall enjoy its sabbaths as long as it lies desolate and you *are* in your enemies' land;
then the land shall rest and enjoy its sabbaths.

35 As long as *it* lies desolate it shall rest—
for the time it did not rest on your sabbaths
when you dwelt in it.

36 'And as for those of you who are left, I will
send faintness into their hearts in the
lands of their enemies;
the sound of a shaken leaf shall cause
them to flee;
they shall flee as though fleeing from a
sword, and they shall fall when no one
pursues.
37 They shall stumble over one another, as it
were before a sword, when no one pur-
sues;
and you shall have no *power* to stand be-
fore your enemies.
38 You shall perish among the nations, and
the land of your enemies shall eat you
up.
39 And those of you who are left shall waste
away in their iniquity in your enemies'
lands;
also in their fathers' iniquities, which are
with them, they shall waste away.

40 '*But* if they confess their iniquity and the
iniquity of their fathers, with their un-
faithfulness in which they were unfaith-
ful to Me, and that they also have walked
contrary to Me,
41 and *that* I also have walked contrary to
them and have brought them into the
land of their enemies;
if their uncircumcised hearts are humbled,
and they accept their guilt—
42 then I will remember My covenant with
Jacob, and My covenant with Isaac and
My covenant with Abraham I will re-
member;
I will remember the land.
43 The land also shall be left empty by them,
and will enjoy its sabbaths while it lies
desolate without them;
they will accept their guilt, because they
despised My judgments and because
their soul abhorred My statutes.
44 Yet for all that, when they are in the land
of their enemies, I will not cast them
away, nor shall I abhor them, to utterly
destroy them and break My covenant
with them;
for I *am* the LORD their God.
45 But for their sake I will remember the cov-
enant of their ancestors, whom I
brought out of the land of Egypt in the
sight of the nations, that I might be their
God:
I *am* the LORD.'"

46 These *are* the statutes and judgments and
laws which the LORD made between Himself
and the children of Israel on Mount Sinai by
the hand of Moses.

Redeeming Persons and Property Dedicated to God

27 Now the LORD spoke to Moses, saying,
2 "Speak to the children of Israel, and
say to them: 'When a man consecrates by a
vow certain persons to the LORD, according to
your valuation,
3 'if your valuation is of a male from twenty
years old up to sixty years old, then your valua-
tion shall be fifty shekels of silver, according
to the shekel of the sanctuary.
4 'If it *is* a female, then your valuation shall
be thirty shekels;
5 'and if from five years old up to twenty
years old, then your valuation for a male shall
be twenty shekels, and for a female ten shekels;
6 'and if from a month old up to five years
old, then your valuation for a male shall be
five shekels of silver, and for a female your
valuation shall be three shekels of silver;
7 'and if from sixty years old and above, if *it*
is a male, then your valuation shall be fifteen
shekels, and for a female ten shekels.
8 'But if he is too poor to pay your valuation,
then he shall present himself before the priest,
and the priest shall set a value for him; accord-
ing to the ability of him who vowed, the priest
shall value him.
9 'If *it is* an animal that men may bring as
an offering to the LORD, all that *anyone* gives
to the LORD shall be holy.
10 'He shall not substitute it or exchange it,
good for bad or bad for good; and if he at all
exchanges animal for animal, then both it and
the one exchanged for it shall be holy.
11 'If *it is* an unclean animal which they do
not offer as a sacrifice to the LORD, then he
shall present the animal before the priest;
12 'and the priest shall set a value for it,
whether it is good or bad; as you, the priest,
value it, so it shall be.
13 'But if he *wants* at all *to* redeem it, then he
must add one-fifth to your valuation.
14 'And when a man dedicates his house *to*
be holy to the LORD, then the priest shall set a
value for it, whether it is good or bad; as the
priest values it, so it shall stand.
15 'If he who dedicated it *wants to* redeem
his house, then he must add one-fifth of the
money of your valuation to it, and it shall be
his.
16 'If a man dedicates to the LORD *part* of a
field of his possession, then your valuation
shall be according to the seed for it. A homer
of barley seed *shall be valued* at fifty shekels
of silver.
17 'If he dedicates his field from the Year of
Jubilee, according to your valuation it shall
stand.
18 'But if he dedicates his field after the Jubi-
lee, then the priest shall reckon to him the
money due according to the years that remain
till the Year of Jubilee, and it shall be deducted
from your valuation.
19 'And if he who dedicates the field ever
wishes to redeem it, then he must add one-fifth
of the money of your valuation to it, and it shall
belong to him.
20 'But if he does not want to redeem the field,
or if he has sold the field to another man, it
shall not be redeemed anymore;
21 'but the field, when it is released in the
Jubilee, shall be holy to the LORD, as a devoted
field; it shall be the possession of the priest.
22 'And if a man dedicates to the LORD a field
which he has bought, which is not the field of
his possession,
23 'then the priest shall reckon to him the
worth of your valuation, up to the Year of Jubi-
lee, and he shall give your valuation on that
day *as* a holy *offering* to the LORD.
24 'In the Year of Jubilee the field shall return
to him from whom it was bought, to the one
who *owned* the land as a possession.

25 'And all your valuations shall be according
to the shekel of the sanctuary: twenty gerahs
to the shekel.
26 'But the firstborn of the animals, which
should be the LORD's firstborn, no man shall
dedicate; whether *it is* an ox or sheep, it *is* the
LORD's.
27 'And if *it is* an unclean animal, then he
shall redeem *it* according to your valuation,
and shall add one-fifth to it; or if it is not re-
deemed, then it shall be sold according to your
valuation.
28 'Nevertheless no devoted *offering* that a
man may devote to the LORD of all that he has,
both man and beast, or the field of his posses-
sion, shall be sold or redeemed; every devoted
offering is most holy to the LORD.
29 'No person under the ban, who may be-
come doomed to destruction among men, shall
be redeemed, *but* shall surely be put to death.
30 'And all the tithe of the land, *whether* of
the seed of the land *or* of the fruit of the tree,
is the LORD's. It *is* holy to the LORD.
31 'If a man wants at all to redeem *any* of his
tithes, he shall add one-fifth to it.
32 'And concerning the tithe of the herd or
the flock, of whatever passes under the rod,
the tenth one shall be holy to the LORD.
33 'He shall not inquire whether it is good or
bad, nor shall he exchange it; and if he ex-
changes it at all, then both it and the one ex-
changed for it shall be holy; it shall not be
redeemed.'"
34 These *are* the commandments which the
LORD commanded Moses for the children of
Israel on Mount Sinai.

The Fourth Book of Moses Called NUMBERS

The First Census of Israel

1 Now the LORD spoke to Moses in the Wil-
derness of Sinai, in the tabernacle of meet-
ing, on the first *day* of the second month, in
the second year after they had come out of the
land of Egypt, saying:
2 "Take a census of all the congregation of
the children of Israel, by their families, by their
fathers' houses, according to the number of
names, every male individually,
3 "from twenty years old and above—all
who *are able to* go to war in Israel. You and
Aaron shall number them by their armies.
4 "And with you there shall be a man from
every tribe, each one the head of his father's
house.
5 "These are the names of the men who shall
stand with you: from Reuben, Elizur the son of
Shedeur;
6 "from Simeon, Shelumiel the son of Zuri-
shaddai;
7 "from Judah, Nahshon the son of Ammin-
adab;
8 "from Issachar, Nethanel the son of Zuar;
9 "from Zebulun, Eliab the son of Helon;
10 "from the sons of Joseph: from Ephraim,
Elishama the son of Ammihud; from Manas-
seh, Gamaliel the son of Pedahzur;
11 "from Benjamin, Abidan the son of Gideoni;
12 "from Dan, Ahiezer the son of Ammishad-
dai;
13 "from Asher, Pagiel the son of Ocran;
14 "from Gad, Eliasaph the son of Deuel;[a]
15 "from Naphtali, Ahira the son of Enan."
16 These *were* chosen from the congregation,
leaders of their fathers' tribes, heads of the divi-
sions in Israel.
17 Then Moses and Aaron took these men who
had been mentioned by name,
18 and they assembled all the congregation
together on the first *day* of the second month;
and they recited their ancestry by families, by
their fathers' houses, according to the number
of names, from twenty years old and above,
each one individually.
19 As the LORD commanded Moses, so he
numbered them in the Wilderness of Sinai.
20 Now the children of Reuben, Israel's oldest
son, their genealogies by their families, by
their fathers' house, according to the number of
names, every male individually, from twenty
years old and above, all who *were able to* go
to war:
21 those who were numbered of the tribe of
Reuben *were* forty-six thousand five hundred.
22 From the children of Simeon, their geneal-
ogies by their families, by their fathers' house,
of those who were numbered, according to the
number of names, every male individually, from
twenty years old and above, all who *were able
to* go to war:
23 those who were numbered of the tribe of
Simeon *were* fifty-nine thousand three hundred.
24 From the children of Gad, their genealo-
gies by their families, by their fathers' house,
according to the number of names, from
twenty years old and above, all who *were able
to* go to war:
25 those who were numbered of the tribe of
Gad *were* forty-five thousand six hundred and
fifty.
26 From the children of Judah, their genealo-
gies by their families, by their fathers' house,
according to the number of names, from
twenty years old and above, all who *were able
to* go to war:
27 those who were numbered of the tribe of
Judah *were* seventy-four thousand six hun-
dred.
28 From the children of Issachar, their geneal-
ogies by their families, by their fathers' house,
according to the number of names, from
twenty years old and above, all who *were able
to* go to war:
29 those who were numbered of the tribe of
Issachar *were* fifty-four thousand four hun-
dred.
30 From the children of Zebulun, their geneal-
ogies by their families, by their fathers' house,
according to the number of names, from twenty
years old and above, all who *were able to* go
to war:

1:14 [a]Spelled *Reuel* in 2:14

31 those who were numbered of the tribe of
Zebulun *were* fifty-seven thousand four hun-
dred.
32 From the sons of Joseph, the children of
Ephraim, their genealogies by their families,
by their fathers' house, according to the num-
ber of names, from twenty years old and
above, all who *were able to* go to war:
33 those who were numbered of the tribe of
Ephraim *were* forty thousand five hundred.
34 From the children of Manasseh, their ge-
nealogies by their families, by their fathers'
house, according to the number of names, from
twenty years old and above, all who *were able
to* go to war:
35 those who were numbered of the tribe of
Manasseh *were* thirty-two thousand two hun-
dred.
36 From the children of Benjamin, their ge-
nealogies by their families, by their fathers'
house, according to the number of names, from
twenty years old and above, all who *were able
to* go to war:
37 those who were numbered of the tribe of
Benjamin *were* thirty-five thousand four hun-
dred.
38 From the children of Dan, their genealo-
gies by their families, by their fathers' house,
according to the number of names, from
twenty years old and above, all who *were able
to* go to war:
39 those who were numbered of the tribe of
Dan *were* sixty-two thousand seven hundred.
40 From the children of Asher, their genealo-
gies by their families, by their fathers' house,
according to the number of names, from twenty
years old and above, all who *were able to* go
to war:
41 those who were numbered of the tribe of
Asher *were* forty-one thousand five hundred.
42 From the children of Naphtali, their ge-
nealogies by their families, by their fathers'
house, according to the number of names, from
twenty years old and above, all who *were able
to* go to war:
43 those who were numbered of the tribe of
Naphtali *were* fifty-three thousand four hun-
dred.
44 These are the ones who were numbered,
whom Moses and Aaron numbered, with the
leaders of Israel, twelve men, each one repre-
senting his father's house.
45 So all who were numbered of the children
of Israel, by their fathers' houses, from twenty
years old and above, all who *were able to* go
to war in Israel—
46 all who were numbered were six hundred
and three thousand five hundred and fifty.
47 But the Levites were not numbered among
them by their fathers' tribe;
48 for the LORD had spoken to Moses, saying:
49 "Only the tribe of Levi you shall not num-
ber, nor take a census of them among the chil-
dren of Israel;
50 "but you shall appoint the Levites over the
tabernacle of the Testimony, over all its fur-
nishings, and over all things that belong to it;
they shall carry the tabernacle and all its fur-
nishings; they shall attend to it and camp around
the tabernacle.
51 "And when the tabernacle is to go forward,
the Levites shall take it down; and when the
tabernacle is to be set up, the Levites shall set
it up. The outsider who comes near shall be
put to death.
52 "The children of Israel shall pitch their
tents, everyone by his own camp, everyone by
his own standard, according to their armies;
53 "but the Levites shall camp around the
tabernacle of the Testimony, that there may be
no wrath on the congregation of the children
of Israel; and the Levites shall keep charge of
the tabernacle of the Testimony."
54 Thus the children of Israel did; according
to all that the LORD commanded Moses, so they
did.

The Tribes and Leaders by Armies

2 And the LORD spoke to Moses and Aaron,
saying:
2 "Everyone of the children of Israel shall
camp by his own standard, beside the emblems
of his father's house; they shall camp some
distance from the tabernacle of meeting.
3 "On the east side, toward the rising of the
sun, those of the standard of the forces with
Judah shall camp according to their armies; and
Nahshon the son of Amminadab *shall be* the
leader of the children of Judah."
4 And his army was numbered at seventy-
four thousand six hundred.
5 "Those who camp next to him *shall be* the
tribe of Issachar, and Nethanel the son of Zuar
shall be the leader of the children of Issachar."
6 And his army was numbered at fifty-four
thousand four hundred.
7 "Then *comes* the tribe of Zebulun, and
Eliab the son of Helon *shall be* the leader of
the children of Zebulun."
8 And his army was numbered at fifty-seven
thousand four hundred.
9 "All who were numbered according to
their armies of the forces with Judah, one hun-
dred and eighty-six thousand four hundred—
these shall break camp first.
10 "On the south side *shall be* the standard
of the forces with Reuben according to their
armies, and the leader of the children of Reu-
ben *shall be* Elizur the son of Shedeur."
11 And his army was numbered at forty-six
thousand five hundred.
12 "Those who camp next to him *shall be* the
tribe of Simeon, and the leader of the children
of Simeon *shall be* Shelumiel the son of Zuri-
shaddai."
13 And his army was numbered at fifty-nine
thousand three hundred.
14 "Then *comes* the tribe of Gad, and the
leader of the children of Gad *shall be* Eliasaph
the son of Reuel."[a]
15 And his army was numbered at forty-five
thousand six hundred and fifty.
16 "All who were numbered according to
their armies of the forces with Reuben, one
hundred and fifty-one thousand four hundred
and fifty—they shall be the second to break
camp.
17 "And the tabernacle of meeting shall move
out with the camp of the Levites in the middle
of the camps; as they camp, so they shall move
out, everyone in his place, by their standards.
18 "On the west side *shall be* the standard of
the forces with Ephraim according to their ar-
mies, and the leader of the children of Ephraim
shall be Elishama the son of Ammihud."

2:14 [a]Spelled *Deuel* in 1:14 and 7:42

19 And his army was numbered at forty thou-
sand five hundred.
20 "Next to him *comes* the tribe of Manasseh,
and the leader of the children of Manasseh
shall be Gamaliel the son of Pedahzur."
21 And his army was numbered at thirty-two
thousand two hundred.
22 "Then *comes* the tribe of Benjamin, and
the leader of the children of Benjamin *shall be*
Abidan the son of Gideoni."
23 And his army was numbered at thirty-five
thousand four hundred.
24 "All who were numbered according to
their armies of the forces with Ephraim, one
hundred and eight thousand one hundred—
they shall be the third to break camp.
25 "The standard of the forces with Dan *shall*
be on the north side according to their armies,
and the leader of the children of Dan *shall be*
Ahiezer the son of Ammishaddai."
26 And his army was numbered at sixty-two
thousand seven hundred.
27 "Those who camp next to him *shall be* the
tribe of Asher, and the leader of the children
of Asher *shall be* Pagiel the son of Ocran."
28 And his army was numbered at forty-one
thousand five hundred.
29 "Then *comes* the tribe of Naphtali, and the
leader of the children of Naphtali *shall be* Ahira
the son of Enan."
30 And his army was numbered at fifty-three
thousand four hundred.
31 "All who were numbered of the forces with
Dan, one hundred and fifty-seven thousand six
hundred—they shall break camp last, with their
standards."
32 These *are* the ones who were numbered of
the children of Israel by their fathers' houses.
All who were numbered according to their ar-
mies of the forces *were* six hundred and three
thousand five hundred and fifty.
33 But the Levites were not numbered among
the children of Israel, just as the LORD com-
manded Moses.
34 Thus the children of Israel did according
to all that the LORD commanded Moses; so
they camped by their standards and so they
broke camp, each one by his family, according
to their fathers' houses.

The Sons of Aaron

3 Now these *are* the records of Aaron and Mo-
ses when the LORD spoke with Moses on
Mount Sinai.
2 And these *are* the names of the sons of
Aaron: Nadab, the firstborn, and Abihu, Elea-
zar, and Ithamar.
3 These *are* the names of the sons of Aaron,
the anointed priests, whom he consecrated to
minister as priests.
4 Nadab and Abihu had died before the LORD
when they offered profane fire before the
LORD in the Wilderness of Sinai; and they had
no children. So Eleazar and Ithamar minis-
tered as priests in the presence of Aaron their
father.

The Levites Serve in the Tabernacle

5 And the LORD spoke to Moses, saying:
6 "Bring the tribe of Levi near, and present
them before Aaron the priest, that they may
serve him.
7 "And they shall attend to his needs and the
needs of the whole congregation before the
tabernacle of meeting, to do the work of the
tabernacle.
8 "Also they shall attend to all the furnishings
of the tabernacle of meeting, and to the needs
of the children of Israel, to do the work of the
tabernacle.
9 "And you shall give the Levites to Aaron
and his sons; they *are* given entirely to him[a]
from among the children of Israel.
10 "So you shall appoint Aaron and his sons,
and they shall attend to their priesthood; but
the outsider who comes near shall be put to
death."
11 Then the LORD spoke to Moses, saying:
12 "Now behold, I Myself have taken the Le-
vites from among the children of Israel instead
of every firstborn who opens the womb among
the children of Israel. Therefore the Levites
shall be Mine,
13 "because all the firstborn *are* Mine. On the
day that I struck all the firstborn in the land of
Egypt, I sanctified to Myself all the firstborn
in Israel, both man and beast. They shall be
Mine: I *am* the LORD."

Census of the Levites Commanded

14 Then the LORD spoke to Moses in the Wil-
derness of Sinai, saying:
15 "Number the children of Levi by their fa-
thers' houses, by their families; you shall num-
ber every male from a month old and above."
16 So Moses numbered them according to the
word of the LORD, as he was commanded.
17 These were the sons of Levi by their names:
Gershon, Kohath, and Merari.
18 And these *are* the names of the sons of
Gershon by their families: Libni and Shimei.
19 And the sons of Kohath by their families:
Amram, Izehar, Hebron, and Uzziel.
20 And the sons of Merari by their families:
Mahli and Mushi. These *are* the families of the
Levites by their fathers' houses.
21 From Gershon *came* the family of the Lib-
nites and the family of the Shimites; these *were*
the families of the Gershonites.
22 Those who were numbered, according to
the number of all the males from a month old
and above—of those who were numbered *there*
were seven thousand five hundred.
23 The families of the Gershonites were to
camp behind the tabernacle westward.
24 And the leader of the father's house of the
Gershonites *was* Eliasaph the son of Lael.
25 The duties of the children of Gershon in
the tabernacle of meeting *included* the taber-
nacle, the tent with its covering, the screen for
the door of the tabernacle of meeting,
26 the screen for the door of the court, the
hangings of the court which *are* around the tab-
ernacle and the altar, and their cords, accord-
ing to all the work relating to them.
27 From Kohath *came* the family of the Am-
ramites, the family of the Izharites, the family
of the Hebronites, and the family of the Uzziel-
ites; these *were* the families of the Kohathites.
28 According to the number of all the males,
from a month old and above, *there were* eight
thousand six[a] hundred keeping charge of the
sanctuary.
29 The families of the children of Kohath
were to camp on the south side of the taber-
nacle.

3:9 [a]Samaritan Pentateuch and Septuagint read *Me.* **3:28** [a]Some manuscripts of the Septuagint read *three.*

30 And the leader of the fathers' house of the
families of the Kohathites *was* Elizaphan the
son of Uzziel.
31 Their duty *included* the ark, the table, the
lampstand, the altars, the utensils of the sanc-
tuary with which they ministered, the screen,
and all the work relating to them.
32 And Eleazar the son of Aaron the priest
was to be chief over the leaders of the Levites,
with oversight of those who kept charge of the
sanctuary.
33 From Merari *came* the family of the Mah-
lites and the family of the Mushites; these *were*
the families of Merari.
34 And those who were numbered, according
to the number of all the males from a month
old and above, *were* six thousand two hundred.
35 The leader of the fathers' house of the fam-
ilies of Merari *was* Zuriel the son of Abihail.
These *were* to camp on the north side of the
tabernacle.
36 And the appointed duty of the children of
Merari *included* the boards of the tabernacle,
its bars, its pillars, its sockets, its utensils, all
the work relating to them,
37 and the pillars of the court all around, with
their sockets, their pegs, and their cords.
38 Moreover those who were to camp before
the tabernacle on the east, before the taberna-
cle of meeting, *were* Moses, Aaron, and his
sons, keeping charge of the sanctuary, to meet
the needs of the children of Israel; but the out-
sider who came near was to be put to death.
39 All who were numbered of the Levites,
whom Moses and Aaron numbered at the com-
mandment of the LORD, by their families, all
the males from a month old and above, *were*
twenty-two thousand.

Levites Dedicated Instead of the Firstborn

40 Then the LORD said to Moses: "Number
all the firstborn males of the children of Israel
from a month old and above, and take the num-
ber of their names.
41 "And you shall take the Levites for Me—I
am the LORD—instead of all the firstborn
among the children of Israel, and the livestock
of the Levites instead of all the firstborn
among the livestock of the children of Israel."
42 So Moses numbered all the firstborn
among the children of Israel, as the LORD com-
manded him.
43 And all the firstborn males, according to
the number of names from a month old and
above, of those who were numbered of them,
were twenty-two thousand two hundred and
seventy-three.
44 Then the LORD spoke to Moses, saying:
45 "Take the Levites instead of all the first-
born among the children of Israel, and the live-
stock of the Levites instead of their livestock.
The Levites shall be Mine: I *am* the LORD.
46 "And for the redemption of the two hun-
dred and seventy-three of the firstborn of the
children of Israel, who are more than the num-
ber of the Levites,
47 "you shall take five shekels for each one
individually; you shall take *them* in the cur-
rency of the shekel of the sanctuary, the shekel
of twenty gerahs.
48 "And you shall give the money, with which
the excess number of them is redeemed, to
Aaron and his sons."
49 So Moses took the redemption money
from those who were over and above those
who were redeemed by the Levites.
50 From the firstborn of the children of Israel
he took the money, one thousand three hun-
dred and sixty-five *shekels*, according to the
shekel of the sanctuary.
51 And Moses gave their redemption money
to Aaron and his sons, according to the word
of the LORD, as the LORD commanded Moses.

Duties of the Sons of Kohath

4 Then the LORD spoke to Moses and Aaron,
saying:
2 "Take a census of the sons of Kohath from
among the children of Levi, by their families,
by their fathers' house,
3 "from thirty years old and above, even to
fifty years old, all who enter the service to do
the work in the tabernacle of meeting.
4 "This *is* the service of the sons of Kohath
in the tabernacle of meeting, *relating to* the
most holy things:
5 "When the camp prepares to journey,
Aaron and his sons shall come, and they shall
take down the covering veil and cover the ark
of the Testimony with it.
6 "Then they shall put on it a covering of
badger skins, and spread over *that* a cloth en-
tirely of blue; and they shall insert its poles.
7 "On the table of showbread they shall
spread a blue cloth, and put on it the dishes,
the pans, the bowls, and the pitchers for pour-
ing; and the showbread[a] shall be on it.
8 "They shall spread over them a scarlet
cloth, and cover the same with a covering of
badger skins; and they shall insert its poles.
9 "And they shall take a blue cloth and cover
the lampstand of the light, with its lamps, its
wick-trimmers, its trays, and all its oil vessels,
with which they service it.
10 "Then they shall put it with all its utensils
in a covering of badger skins, and put *it* on a
carrying beam.
11 "Over the golden altar they shall spread a
blue cloth, and cover it with a covering of bad-
ger skins; and they shall insert its poles.
12 "Then they shall take all the utensils of
service with which they minister in the sanctu-
ary, put *them* in a blue cloth, cover them with
a covering of badger skins, and put *them* on a
carrying beam.
13 "Also they shall take away the ashes from
the altar, and spread a purple cloth over it.
14 "They shall put on it all its implements with
which they minister there—the firepans, the
forks, the shovels, the basins, and all the uten-
sils of the altar—and they shall spread on it a
covering of badger skins, and insert its poles.
15 "And when Aaron and his sons have fin-
ished covering the sanctuary and all the fur-
nishings of the sanctuary, when the camp is
set to go, then the sons of Kohath shall come
to carry *them;* but they shall not touch any
holy thing, lest they die. These *are* the things
in the tabernacle of meeting which the sons of
Kohath are to carry.
16 "The appointed duty of Eleazar the son of
Aaron the priest *is* the oil for the light, the sweet
incense, the daily grain offering, the anointing
oil, the oversight of all the tabernacle, of all
that *is* in it, with the sanctuary and its furnish-
ings."

4:7 [a]Literally *the continual bread*

17 Then the LORD spoke to Moses and Aaron, saying:
18 "Do not cut off the tribe of the families of the Kohathites from among the Levites;
19 "but do this in regard to them, that they may live and not die when they approach the most holy things: Aaron and his sons shall go in and appoint each of them to his service and his task.
20 "But they shall not go in to watch while the holy things are being covered, lest they die."

Duties of the Sons of Gershon

21 Then the LORD spoke to Moses, saying:
22 "Also take a census of the sons of Gershon, by their fathers' house, by their families.
23 "From thirty years old and above, even to fifty years old, you shall number them, all who enter to perform the service, to do the work in the tabernacle of meeting.
24 "This *is* the service of the families of the Gershonites, in serving and carrying:
25 "They shall carry the curtains of the tabernacle and the tabernacle of meeting *with* its covering, the covering of badger skins that *is* on it, the screen for the door of the tabernacle of meeting,
26 "the screen for the door of the gate of the court, the hangings of the court which *are* around the tabernacle and altar, and their cords, all the furnishings for their service and all that is made for these things: so shall they serve.
27 "Aaron and his sons shall assign all the service of the sons of the Gershonites, all their tasks and all their service. And you shall appoint to them all their tasks as their duty.
28 "This *is* the service of the families of the sons of Gershon in the tabernacle of meeting. And their duties *shall be* under the authority[a] of Ithamar the son of Aaron the priest.

Duties of the Sons of Merari

29 "*As for* the sons of Merari, you shall number them by their families and by their fathers' house.
30 "From thirty years old and above, even to fifty years old, you shall number them, everyone who enters the service to do the work of the tabernacle of meeting.
31 "And this *is* what they must carry as all their service for the tabernacle of meeting: the boards of the tabernacle, its bars, its pillars, its sockets,
32 "and the pillars around the court with their sockets, pegs, and cords, with all their furnishings and all their service; and you shall assign *to each man* by name the items he must carry.
33 "This *is* the service of the families of the sons of Merari, as all their service for the tabernacle of meeting, under the authority[a] of Ithamar the son of Aaron the priest."

Census of the Levites

34 And Moses, Aaron, and the leaders of the congregation numbered the sons of the Kohathites by their families and by their fathers' house,
35 from thirty years old and above, even to fifty years old, everyone who entered the service for work in the tabernacle of meeting;
36 and those who were numbered by their families were two thousand seven hundred and fifty.
37 These *were* the ones who were numbered of the families of the Kohathites, all who might serve in the tabernacle of meeting, whom Moses and Aaron numbered according to the commandment of the LORD by the hand of Moses.
38 And those who were numbered of the sons of Gershon, by their families and by their fathers' house,
39 from thirty years old and above, even to fifty years old, everyone who entered the service for work in the tabernacle of meeting—
40 those who were numbered by their families, by their fathers' house, were two thousand six hundred and thirty.
41 These *are* the ones who were numbered of the families of the sons of Gershon, of all who might serve in the tabernacle of meeting, whom Moses and Aaron numbered according to the commandment of the LORD.
42 Those of the families of the sons of Merari who were numbered, by their families, by their fathers' house,
43 from thirty years old and above, even to fifty years old, everyone who entered the service for work in the tabernacle of meeting—
44 those who were numbered by their families were three thousand two hundred.
45 These *are* the ones who were numbered of the families of the sons of Merari, whom Moses and Aaron numbered according to the word of the LORD by the hand of Moses.
46 All who were numbered of the Levites, whom Moses, Aaron, and the leaders of Israel numbered, by their families and by their fathers' houses,
47 from thirty years old and above, even to fifty years old, everyone who came to do the work of service and the work of bearing burdens in the tabernacle of meeting—
48 those who were numbered were eight thousand five hundred and eighty.
49 According to the commandment of the LORD they were numbered by the hand of Moses, each according to his service and according to his task; thus were they numbered by him, as the LORD commanded Moses.

Ceremonially Unclean Persons Isolated

5 And the LORD spoke to Moses, saying:
2 "Command the children of Israel that they put out of the camp every leper, everyone who has a discharge, and whoever becomes defiled by a corpse.
3 "You shall put out both male and female; you shall put them outside the camp, that they may not defile their camps in the midst of which I dwell."
4 And the children of Israel did so, and put them outside the camp; as the LORD spoke to Moses, so the children of Israel did.

Confession and Restitution

5 Then the LORD spoke to Moses, saying,
6 "Speak to the children of Israel: 'When a man or woman commits any sin that men commit in unfaithfulness against the LORD, and that person is guilty,
7 'then he shall confess the sin which he has committed. He shall make restitution for his trespass in full, plus one-fifth of it, and give *it* to the one he has wronged.
8 'But if the man has no relative to whom

4:28 [a]Literally *hand* **4:33** [a]Literally *hand*

restitution may be made for the wrong, the
restitution for the wrong *must go* to the LORD
for the priest, in addition to the ram of the
atonement with which atonement is made for
him.
9 'Every offering of all the holy things of
the children of Israel, which they bring to the
priest, shall be his.
10 'And every man's holy things shall be his;
whatever any man gives the priest shall be
his.'"

Concerning Unfaithful Wives

11 And the LORD spoke to Moses, saying,
12 "Speak to the children of Israel, and say
to them: 'If any man's wife goes astray and
behaves unfaithfully toward him,
13 'and a man lies with her carnally, and it is
hidden from the eyes of her husband, and it is
concealed that she has defiled herself, and
there was no witness against her, nor was she
caught—
14 'if the spirit of jealousy comes upon him
and he becomes jealous of his wife, who has
defiled herself; or if the spirit of jealousy
comes upon him and he becomes jealous of his
wife, although she has not defiled herself—
15 'then the man shall bring his wife to the
priest. He shall bring the offering required for
her, one-tenth of an ephah of barley meal; he
shall pour no oil on it and put no frankincense
on it, because it *is* a grain offering of jealousy,
an offering for remembering, for bringing iniq-
uity to remembrance.
16 'And the priest shall bring her near, and
set her before the LORD.
17 'The priest shall take holy water in an
earthen vessel, and take some of the dust that
is on the floor of the tabernacle and put *it* into
the water.
18 'Then the priest shall stand the woman be-
fore the LORD, uncover the woman's head, and
put the offering for remembering in her hands,
which *is* the grain offering of jealousy. And the
priest shall have in his hand the bitter water
that brings a curse.
19 'And the priest shall put her under oath,
and say to the woman, "If no man has lain
with you, and if you have not gone astray to
uncleanness *while* under your husband's *au-
thority*, be free from this bitter water that brings
a curse.
20 "But if you have gone astray *while* under
your husband's *authority*, and if you have de-
filed yourself and some man other than your
husband has lain with you"—
21 'then the priest shall put the woman under
the oath of the curse, and he shall say to the
woman—"the LORD make you a curse and an
oath among your people, when the LORD
makes your thigh rot and your belly swell;
22 "and may this water that causes the curse
go into your stomach, and make *your* belly
swell and *your* thigh rot." Then the woman
shall say, "Amen, so be it."
23 'Then the priest shall write these curses in
a book, and he shall scrape *them* off into the
bitter water.
24 'And he shall make the woman drink the
bitter water that brings a curse, and the water
that brings the curse shall enter her *to become*
bitter.
25 'Then the priest shall take the grain offer-
ing of jealousy from the woman's hand, shall
wave the offering before the LORD, and bring
it to the altar;
26 'and the priest shall take a handful of the
offering, as its memorial portion, burn *it* on
the altar, and afterward make the woman drink
the water.
27 'When he has made her drink the water,
then it shall be, if she has defiled herself and
behaved unfaithfully toward her husband, that
the water that brings a curse will enter her
and become bitter, and her belly will swell, her
thigh will rot, and the woman will become a
curse among her people.
28 'But if the woman has not defiled herself,
and is clean, then she shall be free and may
conceive children.
29 'This *is* the law of jealousy, when a wife,
while under her husband's *authority*, goes
astray and defiles herself,
30 'or when the spirit of jealousy comes upon
a man, and he becomes jealous of his wife;
then he shall stand the woman before the LORD,
and the priest shall execute all this law upon
her.
31 'Then the man shall be free from iniquity,
but that woman shall bear her guilt.'"

The Law of the Nazirite

6 Then the LORD spoke to Moses, saying,
2 "Speak to the children of Israel, and
say to them: 'When either a man or woman
consecrates an offering to take the vow of a
Nazirite, to separate himself to the LORD,
3 'he shall separate himself from wine and
similar drink; he shall drink neither vinegar
made from wine nor vinegar made from *simi-
lar* drink; neither shall he drink any grape
juice, nor eat fresh grapes or raisins.
4 'All the days of his separation he shall eat
nothing that is produced by the grapevine,
from seed to skin.
5 'All the days of the vow of his separation
no razor shall come upon his head; until the
days are fulfilled for which he separated him-
self to the LORD, he shall be holy. *Then* he shall
let the locks of the hair of his head grow.
6 'All the days that he separates himself to
the LORD he shall not go near a dead body.
7 'He shall not make himself unclean even
for his father or his mother, for his brother or
his sister, when they die, because his separa-
tion to God *is* on his head.
8 'All the days of his separation he shall be
holy to the LORD.
9 'And if anyone dies very suddenly beside
him, and he defiles his consecrated head, then
he shall shave his head on the day of his cleans-
ing; on the seventh day he shall shave it.
10 'Then on the eighth day he shall bring two
turtledoves or two young pigeons to the priest,
to the door of the tabernacle of meeting;
11 'and the priest shall offer one as a sin offer-
ing and *the* other as a burnt offering, and make
atonement for him, because he sinned in regard
to the corpse; and he shall sanctify his head
that same day.
12 'He shall consecrate to the LORD the days
of his separation, and bring a male lamb in its
first year as a trespass offering; but the former
days shall be lost, because his separation was
defiled.
13 'Now this *is* the law of the Nazirite: When
the days of his separation are fulfilled, he shall
be brought to the door of the tabernacle of
meeting.

14 'And he shall present his offering to the
LORD: one male lamb in its first year without
blemish as a burnt offering, one ewe lamb in
its first year without blemish as a sin offering,
one ram without blemish as a peace offering,
15 'a basket of unleavened bread, cakes of
fine flour mixed with oil, unleavened wafers
anointed with oil, and their grain offering with
their drink offerings.
16 'Then the priest shall bring *them* before the
LORD and offer his sin offering and his burnt
offering;
17 'and he shall offer the ram as a sacrifice of
a peace offering to the LORD, with the basket
of unleavened bread; the priest shall also offer
its grain offering and its drink offering.
18 'Then the Nazirite shall shave his conse-
crated head *at* the door of the tabernacle of
meeting, and shall take the hair from his con-
secrated head and put *it* on the fire which is
under the sacrifice of the peace offering.
19 'And the priest shall take the boiled shoul-
der of the ram, one unleavened cake from the
basket, and one unleavened wafer, and put
them upon the hands of the Nazirite after he
has shaved his consecrated *hair,*
20 'and the priest shall wave them as a wave
offering before the LORD; they *are* holy for the
priest, together with the breast of the wave of-
fering and the thigh of the heave offering. Af-
ter that the Nazirite may drink wine.'
21 "This is the law of the Nazirite who vows
to the LORD the offering for his separation,
and besides that, whatever else his hand is able
to provide; according to the vow which he
takes, so he must do according to the law of
his separation."

The Priestly Blessing

22 And the LORD spoke to Moses, saying:
23 "Speak to Aaron and his sons, saying,
'This is the way you shall bless the children of
Israel. Say to them:

24 "The LORD bless you and keep you;
25 The LORD make His face shine upon you,
And be gracious to you;
26 The LORD lift up His countenance upon
you,
And give you peace." '

27 "So they shall put My name on the chil-
dren of Israel, and I will bless them."

Offerings of the Leaders

7 Now it came to pass, when Moses had fin-
ished setting up the tabernacle, that he
anointed it and consecrated it and all its fur-
nishings, and the altar and all its utensils; so he
anointed them and consecrated them.
2 Then the leaders of Israel, the heads of their
fathers' houses, who *were* the leaders of the
tribes and over those who were numbered,
made an offering.
3 And they brought their offering before the
LORD, six covered carts and twelve oxen, a
cart for *every* two of the leaders, and for each
one an ox; and they presented them before the
tabernacle.
4 Then the LORD spoke to Moses, saying,
5 "Accept *these* from them, that they may be
used in doing the work of the tabernacle of
meeting; and you shall give them to the Le-
vites, *to* every man according to his service."
6 So Moses took the carts and the oxen, and
gave them to the Levites.
7 Two carts and four oxen he gave to the
sons of Gershon, according to their service;
8 and four carts and eight oxen he gave to
the sons of Merari, according to their service,
under the authority[a] of Ithamar the son of
Aaron the priest.
9 But to the sons of Kohath he gave none,
because theirs *was* the service of the holy
things, *which* they carried on their shoulders.
10 Now the leaders offered the dedication *of-
fering* for the altar when it was anointed; so
the leaders offered their offering before the
altar.
11 For the LORD said to Moses, "They shall
offer their offering, one leader each day, for
the dedication of the altar."
12 And the one who offered his offering on
the first day *was* Nahshon the son of Ammina-
dab, from the tribe of Judah.
13 His offering *was* one silver platter, the
weight of which *was* one hundred and thirty
shekels, and one silver bowl of seventy shek-
els, according to the shekel of the sanctuary,
both of them full of fine flour mixed with oil
as a grain offering;
14 one gold pan of ten *shekels,* full of incense;
15 one young bull, one ram, and one male
lamb in its first year, as a burnt offering;
16 one kid of the goats as a sin offering;
17 and for the sacrifice of peace offerings: two
oxen, five rams, five male goats, and five male
lambs in their first year. This *was* the offering
of Nahshon the son of Amminadab.
18 On the second day Nethanel the son of
Zuar, leader of Issachar, presented *an offering.*
19 *For* his offering he offered one silver plat-
ter, the weight of which *was* one hundred and
thirty *shekels,* and one silver bowl of seventy
shekels, according to the shekel of the sanctu-
ary, both of them full of fine flour mixed with
oil as a grain offering;
20 one gold pan of ten *shekels,* full of incense;
21 one young bull, one ram, and one male
lamb in its first year, as a burnt offering;
22 one kid of the goats as a sin offering;
23 and as the sacrifice of peace offerings: two
oxen, five rams, five male goats, and five male
lambs in their first year. This *was* the offering
of Nethanel the son of Zuar.
24 On the third day Eliab the son of Helon,
leader of the children of Zebulun, *presented
an offering.*
25 His offering *was* one silver platter, the
weight of which *was* one hundred and thirty
shekels, and one silver bowl of seventy shek-
els, according to the shekel of the sanctuary,
both of them full of fine flour mixed with oil
as a grain offering;
26 one gold pan of ten *shekels,* full of incense;
27 one young bull, one ram, and one male lamb
in its first year, as a burnt offering;
28 one kid of the goats as a sin offering;
29 and for the sacrifice of peace offerings: two
oxen, five rams, five male goats, and five male
lambs in their first year. This *was* the offering
of Eliab the son of Helon.
30 On the fourth day Elizur the son of Shed-
eur, leader of the children of Reuben, *pre-
sented an offering.*
31 His offering *was* one silver platter, the
weight of which *was* one hundred and thirty

7:8 [a]Literally *hand*

shekels, and one silver bowl of seventy shek-
els, according to the shekel of the sanctuary,
both of them full of fine flour mixed with oil
as a grain offering;
32 one gold pan of ten *shekels,* full of incense;
33 one young bull, one ram, and one male lamb
in its first year, as a burnt offering;
34 one kid of the goats as a sin offering;
35 and as the sacrifice of peace offerings: two
oxen, five rams, five male goats, and five male
lambs in their first year. This *was* the offering
of Elizur the son of Shedeur.
36 On the fifth day Shelumiel the son of Zuri-
shaddai, leader of the children of Simeon, *pre-
sented an offering.*
37 His offering *was* one silver platter, the
weight of which *was* one hundred and thirty
shekels, and one silver bowl of seventy shek-
els, according to the shekel of the sanctuary,
both of them full of fine flour mixed with oil
as a grain offering;
38 one gold pan of ten *shekels,* full of incense;
39 one young bull, one ram, and one male lamb
in its first year, as a burnt offering;
40 one kid of the goats as a sin offering;
41 and as the sacrifice of peace offerings: two
oxen, five rams, five male goats, and five male
lambs in their first year. This *was* the offering
of Shelumiel the son of Zurishaddai.
42 On the sixth day Eliasaph the son of Deuel,[a]
leader of the children of Gad, *presented an
offering.*
43 His offering *was* one silver platter, the
weight of which *was* one hundred and thirty
shekels, and one silver bowl of seventy shek-
els, according to the shekel of the sanctuary,
both of them full of fine flour mixed with oil
as a grain offering;
44 one gold pan of ten *shekels,* full of incense;
45 one young bull, one ram, and one male lamb
in its first year, as a burnt offering;
46 one kid of the goats as a sin offering;
47 and as the sacrifice of peace offerings: two
oxen, five rams, five male goats, and five male
lambs in their first year. This *was* the offering
of Eliasaph the son of Deuel.
48 On the seventh day Elishama the son of
Ammihud, leader of the children of Ephraim,
presented an offering.
49 His offering *was* one silver platter, the
weight of which *was* one hundred and thirty
shekels, and one silver bowl of seventy shek-
els, according to the shekel of the sanctuary,
both of them full of fine flour mixed with oil
as a grain offering;
50 one gold pan of ten *shekels,* full of incense;
51 one young bull, one ram, and one male lamb
in its first year, as a burnt offering;
52 one kid of the goats as a sin offering;
53 and as the sacrifice of peace offerings: two
oxen, five rams, five male goats, and five male
lambs in their first year. This *was* the offering
of Elishama the son of Ammihud.
54 On the eighth day Gamaliel the son of Pe-
dahzur, leader of the children of Manasseh, *pre-
sented an offering.*
55 His offering *was* one silver platter, the weight
of which *was* one hundred and thirty *shekels,*
and one silver bowl of seventy shekels, accord-
ing to the shekel of the sanctuary, both of them
full of fine flour mixed with oil as a grain of-
fering;
56 one gold pan of ten *shekels,* full of incense;
57 one young bull, one ram, and one male lamb
in its first year, as a burnt offering;
58 one kid of the goats as a sin offering;
59 and as the sacrifice of peace offerings: two
oxen, five rams, five male goats, and five male
lambs in their first year. This *was* the offering
of Gamaliel the son of Pedahzur.
60 On the ninth day Abidan the son of Gide-
oni, leader of the children of Benjamin, *pre-
sented an offering.*
61 His offering *was* one silver platter, the
weight of which *was* one hundred and thirty
shekels, and one silver bowl of seventy shek-
els, according to the shekel of the sanctuary,
both of them full of fine flour mixed with oil
as a grain offering;
62 one gold pan of ten *shekels,* full of incense;
63 one young bull, one ram, and one male lamb
in its first year, as a burnt offering;
64 one kid of the goats as a sin offering;
65 and as the sacrifice of peace offerings: two
oxen, five rams, five male goats, and five male
lambs in their first year. This *was* the offering
of Abidan the son of Gideoni.
66 On the tenth day Ahiezer the son of Ammi-
shaddai, leader of the children of Dan, *pre-
sented an offering.*
67 His offering *was* one silver platter, the
weight of which *was* one hundred and thirty
shekels, and one silver bowl of seventy shekels,
according to the shekel of the sanctuary, both
of them full of fine flour mixed with oil as a
grain offering;
68 one gold pan of ten *shekels,* full of incense;
69 one young bull, one ram, and one male lamb
in its first year, as a burnt offering;
70 one kid of the goats as a sin offering;
71 and as the sacrifice of peace offerings: two
oxen, five rams, five male goats, and five male
lambs in their first year. This *was* the offering
of Ahiezer the son of Ammishaddai.
72 On the eleventh day Pagiel the son of Oc-
ran, leader of the children of Asher, *presented
an offering.*
73 His offering *was* one silver platter, the
weight of which *was* one hundred and thirty
shekels, and one silver bowl of seventy shek-
els, according to the shekel of the sanctuary,
both of them full of fine flour mixed with oil
as a grain offering;
74 one gold pan of ten *shekels,* full of incense;
75 one young bull, one ram, and one male lamb
in its first year, as a burnt offering;
76 one kid of the goats as a sin offering;
77 and as the sacrifice of peace offerings: two
oxen, five rams, five male goats, and five male
lambs in their first year. This *was* the offering
of Pagiel the son of Ocran.
78 On the twelfth day Ahira the son of Enan,
leader of the children of Naphtali, *presented
an offering.*
79 His offering *was* one silver platter, the weight
of which *was* one hundred and thirty *shekels,*
and one silver bowl of seventy shekels, accord-
ing to the shekel of the sanctuary, both of them
full of fine flour mixed with oil as a grain of-
fering;
80 one gold pan of ten *shekels,* full of incense;
81 one young bull, one ram, and one male lamb
in its first year, as a burnt offering;
82 one kid of the goats as a sin offering;
83 and as the sacrifice of peace offerings: two
oxen, five rams, five male goats, and five male

7:42 [a]Spelled *Reuel* in 2:14

lambs in their first year. This *was* the offering of Ahira the son of Enan.

84 This *was* the dedication *offering* for the altar from the leaders of Israel, when it was anointed: twelve silver platters, twelve silver bowls, and twelve gold pans.

85 Each silver platter *weighed* one hundred and thirty *shekels* and each bowl seventy *shekels.* All the silver of the vessels *weighed* two thousand four hundred *shekels,* according to the shekel of the sanctuary.

86 The twelve gold pans full of incense *weighed* ten *shekels* apiece, according to the shekel of the sanctuary; all the gold of the pans *weighed* one hundred and twenty *shekels.*

87 All the oxen for the burnt offering *were* twelve young bulls, the rams twelve, the male lambs in their first year twelve, with their grain offering, and the kids of the goats as a sin offering twelve.

88 And all the oxen for the sacrifice of peace offerings were twenty-four bulls, the rams sixty, the male goats sixty, and the lambs in their first year sixty. This *was* the dedication *offering* for the altar after it was anointed.

89 Now when Moses went into the tabernacle of meeting to speak with Him, he heard the voice of One speaking to him from above the mercy seat that *was* on the ark of the Testimony, from between the two cherubim; thus He spoke to him.

Arrangement of the Lamps

8 And the LORD spoke to Moses, saying:

2 "Speak to Aaron, and say to him, 'When you arrange the lamps, the seven lamps shall give light in front of the lampstand.'"

3 And Aaron did so; he arranged the lamps to face toward the front of the lampstand, as the LORD commanded Moses.

4 Now this workmanship of the lampstand *was* hammered gold; from its shaft to its flowers it *was* hammered work. According to the pattern which the LORD had shown Moses, so he made the lampstand.

Cleansing and Dedication of the Levites

5 Then the LORD spoke to Moses, saying:

6 "Take the Levites from among the children of Israel and cleanse them *ceremonially.*

7 "Thus you shall do to them to cleanse them: Sprinkle water of purification on them, and let them shave all their body, and let them wash their clothes, and *so* make themselves clean.

8 "Then let them take a young bull with its grain offering of fine flour mixed with oil, and you shall take another young bull as a sin offering.

9 "And you shall bring the Levites before the tabernacle of meeting, and you shall gather together the whole congregation of the children of Israel.

10 "So you shall bring the Levites before the LORD, and the children of Israel shall lay their hands on the Levites;

11 "and Aaron shall offer the Levites before the LORD, *like* a wave offering from the children of Israel, that they may perform the work of the LORD.

12 "Then the Levites shall lay their hands on the heads of the young bulls, and you shall offer one as a sin offering and the other as a burnt offering to the LORD, to make atonement for the Levites.

13 "And you shall stand the Levites before Aaron and his sons, and then offer them *like* a wave offering to the LORD.

14 "Thus you shall separate the Levites from among the children of Israel, and the Levites shall be Mine.

15 "After that the Levites shall go in to service the tabernacle of meeting. So you shall cleanse them and offer them *like* a wave offering.

16 "For they *are* wholly given to Me from among the children of Israel; I have taken them for Myself instead of all who open the womb, the firstborn of all the children of Israel.

17 "For all the firstborn among the children of Israel *are* Mine, *both* man and beast; on the day that I struck all the firstborn in the land of Egypt I sanctified them to Myself.

18 "I have taken the Levites instead of all the firstborn of the children of Israel.

19 "And I have given the Levites as a gift to Aaron and his sons from among the children of Israel, to do the work for the children of Israel in the tabernacle of meeting, and to make atonement for the children of Israel, that there be no plague among the children of Israel when the children of Israel come near the sanctuary."

20 Thus Moses and Aaron and all the congregation of the children of Israel did to the Levites; according to all that the LORD commanded Moses concerning the Levites, so the children of Israel did to them.

21 And the Levites purified themselves and washed their clothes; then Aaron presented them *like* a wave offering before the LORD, and Aaron made atonement for them to cleanse them.

22 After that the Levites went in to do their work in the tabernacle of meeting before Aaron and his sons; as the LORD commanded Moses concerning the Levites, so they did to them.

23 Then the LORD spoke to Moses, saying,

24 "This *is* what *pertains* to the Levites: From twenty-five years old and above one may enter to perform service in the work of the tabernacle of meeting;

25 "and at the age of fifty years they must cease performing this work, and shall work no more.

26 "They may minister with their brethren in the tabernacle of meeting, to attend to needs, but they *themselves* shall do no work. Thus you shall do to the Levites regarding their duties."

The Second Passover

9 Now the LORD spoke to Moses in the Wilderness of Sinai, in the first month of the second year after they had come out of the land of Egypt, saying:

2 "Let the children of Israel keep the Passover at its appointed time.

3 "On the fourteenth day of this month, at twilight, you shall keep it at its appointed time. According to all its rites and ceremonies you shall keep it."

4 So Moses told the children of Israel that they should keep the Passover.

5 And they kept the Passover on the fourteenth day of the first month, at twilight, in the Wilderness of Sinai; according to all that the LORD commanded Moses, so the children of Israel did.

6 Now there were *certain* men who were defiled by a human corpse, so that they could not

keep the Passover on that day; and they came
before Moses and Aaron that day.
7 And those men said to him, "We *became*
defiled by a human corpse. Why are we kept
from presenting the offering of the LORD at its
appointed time among the children of Israel?"
8 And Moses said to them, "Stand still, that
I may hear what the LORD will command con-
cerning you."
9 Then the LORD spoke to Moses, saying,
10 "Speak to the children of Israel, saying:
'If anyone of you or your posterity is unclean
because of a corpse, or *is* far away on a journey,
he may still keep the LORD's Passover.
11 'On the fourteenth day of the second
month, at twilight, they may keep it. They shall
eat it with unleavened bread and bitter herbs.
12 'They shall leave none of it until morning,
nor break one of its bones. According to all the
ordinances of the Passover they shall keep it.
13 'But the man who *is* clean and is not on a
journey, and ceases to keep the Passover, that
same person shall be cut off from among his
people, because he did not bring the offering
of the LORD at its appointed time; that man
shall bear his sin.
14 'And if a stranger dwells among you, and
would keep the LORD's Passover, he must do
so according to the rite of the Passover and
according to its ceremony; you shall have one
ordinance, both for the stranger and the native
of the land.'"

The Cloud and the Fire

15 Now on the day that the tabernacle was
raised up, the cloud covered the tabernacle,
the tent of the Testimony; from evening until
morning it was above the tabernacle like the
appearance of fire.
16 So it was always: the cloud covered it *by
day,* and the appearance of fire by night.
17 Whenever the cloud was taken up from
above the tabernacle, after that the children of
Israel would journey; and in the place where
the cloud settled, there the children of Israel
would pitch their tents.
18 At the command of the LORD the children
of Israel would journey, and at the command
of the LORD they would camp; as long as the
cloud stayed above the tabernacle they re-
mained encamped.
19 Even when the cloud continued long,
many days above the tabernacle, the children
of Israel kept the charge of the LORD and did
not journey.
20 So it was, when the cloud was above the
tabernacle a few days: according to the com-
mand of the LORD they would remain en-
camped, and according to the command of the
LORD they would journey.
21 So it was, when the cloud remained only
from evening until morning: when the cloud
was taken up in the morning, then they would
journey; whether by day or by night, whenever
the cloud was taken up, they would journey.
22 *Whether it was* two days, a month, or a
year that the cloud remained above the taber-
nacle, the children of Israel would remain en-
camped and not journey; but when it was taken
up, they would journey.
23 At the command of the LORD they re-
mained encamped, and at the command of the
LORD they journeyed; they kept the charge of
the LORD, at the command of the LORD by the
hand of Moses.

Two Silver Trumpets

10 And the LORD spoke to Moses, saying:
2 "Make two silver trumpets for your-
self; you shall make them of hammered work;
you shall use them for calling the congregation
and for directing the movement of the camps.
3 "When they blow both of them, all the con-
gregation shall gather before you at the door
of the tabernacle of meeting.
4 "But if they blow *only* one, then the lead-
ers, the heads of the divisions of Israel, shall
gather to you.
5 "When you sound the advance, the camps
that lie on the east side shall then begin their
journey.
6 "When you sound the advance the second
time, then the camps that lie on the south side
shall begin their journey; they shall sound the
call for them to begin their journeys.
7 "And when the assembly is to be gathered
together, you shall blow, but not sound the ad-
vance.
8 "The sons of Aaron, the priests, shall blow
the trumpets; and these shall be to you as an
ordinance forever throughout your genera-
tions.
9 "When you go to war in your land against
the enemy who oppresses you, then you shall
sound an alarm with the trumpets, and you
will be remembered before the LORD your
God, and you will be saved from your enemies.
10 "Also in the day of your gladness, in your
appointed feasts, and at the beginning of your
months, you shall blow the trumpets over
your burnt offerings and over the sacrifices
of your peace offerings; and they shall be a
memorial for you before your God: I *am* the
LORD your God."

Departure from Sinai

11 Now it came to pass on the twentieth *day*
of the second month, in the second year, that
the cloud was taken up from above the taber-
nacle of the Testimony.
12 And the children of Israel set out from the
Wilderness of Sinai on their journeys; then the
cloud settled down in the Wilderness of Paran.
13 So they started out for the first time ac-
cording to the command of the LORD by the
hand of Moses.
14 The standard of the camp of the children
of Judah set out first according to their armies;
over their army was Nahshon the son of Am-
minadab.
15 Over the army of the tribe of the children
of Issachar *was* Nethanel the son of Zuar.
16 And over the army of the tribe of the chil-
dren of Zebulun *was* Eliab the son of Helon.
17 Then the tabernacle was taken down; and
the sons of Gershon and the sons of Merari set
out, carrying the tabernacle.
18 And the standard of the camp of Reuben
set out according to their armies; over their
army *was* Elizur the son of Shedeur.
19 Over the army of the tribe of the children
of Simeon *was* Shelumiel the son of Zurishad-
dai.
20 And over the army of the tribe of the chil-
dren of Gad *was* Eliasaph the son of Deuel.
21 Then the Kohathites set out, carrying the
holy things. (The tabernacle would be pre-
pared for their arrival.)
22 And the standard of the camp of the chil-
dren of Ephraim set out according to their ar-

mies; over their army *was* Elishama the son of Ammihud.

23 Over the army of the tribe of the children of Manasseh *was* Gamaliel the son of Pedahzur.

24 And over the army of the tribe of the children of Benjamin *was* Abidan the son of Gideoni.

25 Then the standard of the camp of the children of Dan (the rear guard of all the camps) set out according to their armies; over their army *was* Ahiezer the son of Ammishaddai.

26 Over the army of the tribe of the children of Asher *was* Pagiel the son of Ocran.

27 And over the army of the tribe of the children of Naphtali *was* Ahira the son of Enan.

28 Thus *was* the order of march of the children of Israel, according to their armies, when they began their journey.

29 Now Moses said to Hobab the son of Reuel[a] the Midianite, Moses' father-in-law, "We are setting out for the place of which the LORD said, 'I will give it to you.' Come with us, and we will treat you well; for the LORD has promised good things to Israel."

30 And he said to him, "I will not go, but I will depart to my *own* land and to my relatives."

31 So *Moses* said, "Please do not leave, inasmuch as you know how we are to camp in the wilderness, and you can be our eyes.

32 "And it shall be, if you go with us—indeed it shall be—that whatever good the LORD will do to us, the same we will do to you."

33 So they departed from the mountain of the LORD on a journey of three days; and the ark of the covenant of the LORD went before them for the three days' journey, to search out a resting place for them.

34 And the cloud of the LORD *was* above them by day when they went out from the camp.

35 So it was, whenever the ark set out, that Moses said:

"Rise up, O LORD!
Let Your enemies be scattered,
And let those who hate You flee before
You."

36 And when it rested, he said:

"Return, O LORD,
To the many thousands of Israel."

The People Complain

11 Now *when* the people complained, it displeased the LORD; for the LORD heard *it,* and His anger was aroused. So the fire of the LORD burned among them, and consumed *some* in the outskirts of the camp.

2 Then the people cried out to Moses, and when Moses prayed to the LORD, the fire was quenched.

3 So he called the name of the place Taberah,[a] because the fire of the LORD had burned among them.

4 Now the mixed multitude who were among them yielded to intense craving; so the children of Israel also wept again and said: "Who will give us meat to eat?

5 "We remember the fish which we ate freely in Egypt, the cucumbers, the melons, the leeks, the onions, and the garlic;

6 "but now our whole being *is* dried up; *there is* nothing at all except this manna *before* our eyes!"

7 Now the manna *was* like coriander seed, and its color like the color of bdellium.

8 The people went about and gathered *it,* ground *it* on millstones or beat *it* in the mortar, cooked *it* in pans, and made cakes of it; and its taste was like the taste of pastry prepared with oil.

9 And when the dew fell on the camp in the night, the manna fell on it.

10 Then Moses heard the people weeping throughout their families, everyone at the door of his tent; and the anger of the LORD was greatly aroused; Moses also was displeased.

11 So Moses said to the LORD, "Why have You afflicted Your servant? And why have I not found favor in Your sight, that You have laid the burden of all these people on me?

12 "Did I conceive all these people? Did I beget them, that You should say to me, 'Carry them in your bosom, as a guardian carries a nursing child,' to the land which You swore to their fathers?

13 "Where am I to get meat to give to all these people? For they weep all over me, saying, 'Give us meat, that we may eat.'

14 "I am not able to bear all these people alone, because the burden *is* too heavy for me.

15 "If You treat me like this, please kill me here and now—if I have found favor in Your sight—and do not let me see my wretchedness!"

The Seventy Elders

16 So the LORD said to Moses: "Gather to Me seventy men of the elders of Israel, whom you know to be the elders of the people and officers over them; bring them to the tabernacle of meeting, that they may stand there with you.

17 "Then I will come down and talk with you there. I will take of the Spirit that *is* upon you and will put *the same* upon them; and they shall bear the burden of the people with you, that you may not bear *it* yourself alone.

18 "Then you shall say to the people, 'Consecrate yourselves for tomorrow, and you shall eat meat; for you have wept in the hearing of the LORD, saying, "Who will give us meat to eat? For *it was* well with us in Egypt." Therefore the LORD will give you meat, and you shall eat.

19 'You shall eat, not one day, nor two days, nor five days, nor ten days, nor twenty days,

20 'but *for* a whole month, until it comes out of your nostrils and becomes loathsome to you, because you have despised the LORD who is among you, and have wept before Him, saying, "Why did we ever come up out of Egypt?" ' "

21 And Moses said, "The people whom I *am* among *are* six hundred thousand men on foot; yet You have said, 'I will give them meat, that they may eat *for* a whole month.'

22 "Shall flocks and herds be slaughtered for them, to provide enough for them? Or shall all the fish of the sea be gathered together for them, to provide enough for them?"

23 And the LORD said to Moses, "Has the LORD's arm been shortened? Now you shall see whether what I say will happen to you or not."

24 So Moses went out and told the people the words of the LORD, and he gathered the seventy men of the elders of the people and placed them around the tabernacle.

10:29 [a]Septuagint reads *Raguel* (compare Exodus 2:18). **11:3** [a]Literally *Burning*

25 Then the LORD came down in the cloud, and spoke to him, and took of the Spirit that *was* upon him, and placed *the same* upon the seventy elders; and it happened, when the Spirit rested upon them, that they prophesied, although they never did *so* again.[a]

26 But two men had remained in the camp: the name of one *was* Eldad, and the name of the other Medad. And the Spirit rested upon them. Now they *were* among those listed, but who had not gone out to the tabernacle; yet they prophesied in the camp.

27 And a young man ran and told Moses, and said, "Eldad and Medad are prophesying in the camp."

28 So Joshua the son of Nun, Moses' assistant, *one* of his choice men, answered and said, "Moses my lord, forbid them!"

29 Then Moses said to him, "Are you zealous for my sake? Oh, that all the LORD's people were prophets *and* that the LORD would put His Spirit upon them!"

30 And Moses returned to the camp, *both* he and the elders of Israel.

The LORD Sends Quail

31 Now a wind went out from the LORD, and it brought quail from the sea and left *them* fluttering near the camp, about a day's journey on this side and about a day's journey on the other side, all around the camp, and about two cubits above the surface of the ground.

32 And the people stayed up all that day, all night, and all the next day, and gathered the quail (he who gathered least gathered ten homers); and they spread *them* out for themselves all around the camp.

33 But while the meat *was* still between their teeth, before it was chewed, the wrath of the LORD was aroused against the people, and the LORD struck the people with a very great plague.

34 So he called the name of that place Kibroth Hattaavah,[a] because there they buried the people who had yielded to craving.

35 From Kibroth Hattaavah the people moved to Hazeroth, and camped at Hazeroth.

Dissension of Aaron and Miriam

12 Then Miriam and Aaron spoke against Moses because of the Ethiopian woman whom he had married; for he had married an Ethiopian woman.

2 So they said, "Has the LORD indeed spoken only through Moses? Has He not spoken through us also?" And the LORD heard *it*.

3 (Now the man Moses *was* very humble, more than all men who *were* on the face of the earth.)

4 Suddenly the LORD said to Moses, Aaron, and Miriam, "Come out, you three, to the tabernacle of meeting!" So the three came out.

5 Then the LORD came down in the pillar of cloud and stood *in* the door of the tabernacle, and called Aaron and Miriam. And they both went forward.

6 Then He said,

"Hear now My words:
If there is a prophet among you,
I, the LORD, make Myself known to him
in a vision;
I speak to him in a dream.
7 Not so with My servant Moses;
He *is* faithful in all My house.
8 I speak with him face to face,
Even plainly, and not in dark sayings;
And he sees the form of the LORD.
Why then were you not afraid
To speak against My servant Moses?"

9 So the anger of the LORD was aroused against them, and He departed.

10 And when the cloud departed from above the tabernacle, suddenly Miriam *became* leprous, as *white as* snow. Then Aaron turned toward Miriam, and there she was, a leper.

11 So Aaron said to Moses, "Oh, my lord! Please do not lay *this* sin on us, in which we have done foolishly and in which we have sinned.

12 "Please do not let her be as one dead, whose flesh is half consumed when he comes out of his mother's womb!"

13 So Moses cried out to the LORD, saying, "Please heal her, O God, I pray!"

14 Then the LORD said to Moses, "If her father had but spit in her face, would she not be shamed seven days? Let her be shut out of the camp seven days, and afterward she may be received *again*."

15 So Miriam was shut out of the camp seven days, and the people did not journey till Miriam was brought in *again*.

16 And afterward the people moved from Hazeroth and camped in the Wilderness of Paran.

Spies Sent into Canaan

13 And the LORD spoke to Moses, saying,
2 "Send men to spy out the land of
Canaan, which I am giving to the children of Israel; from each tribe of their fathers you shall send a man, every one a leader among them."

3 So Moses sent them from the Wilderness of Paran according to the command of the LORD, all of them men who *were* heads of the children of Israel.

4 Now these *were* their names: from the tribe of Reuben, Shammua the son of Zaccur;

5 from the tribe of Simeon, Shaphat the son of Hori;

6 from the tribe of Judah, Caleb the son of Jephunneh;

7 from the tribe of Issachar, Igal the son of Joseph;

8 from the tribe of Ephraim, Hoshea[a] the son of Nun;

9 from the tribe of Benjamin, Palti the son of Raphu;

10 from the tribe of Zebulun, Gaddiel the son of Sodi;

11 from the tribe of Joseph, *that is*, from the tribe of Manasseh, Gaddi the son of Susi;

12 from the tribe of Dan, Ammiel the son of Gemalli;

13 from the tribe of Asher, Sethur the son of Michael;

14 from the tribe of Naphtali, Nahbi the son of Vophsi;

15 from the tribe of Gad, Geuel the son of Machi.

16 These *are* the names of the men whom Moses sent to spy out the land. And Moses called Hoshea[a] the son of Nun, Joshua.

17 Then Moses sent them to spy out the land

11:25 [a]Targum and Vulgate read *did not cease.* **11:34** [a]Literally *Graves of Craving* **13:8** [a]Septuagint and Vulgate read *Oshea.* **13:16** [a]Septuagint and Vulgate read *Oshea.*

of Canaan, and said to them, "Go up this *way*
into the South, and go up to the mountains,
18 "and see what the land is like: whether the
people who dwell in it *are* strong or weak, few
or many;
19 "whether the land they dwell in *is* good or
bad; whether the cities they inhabit *are* like
camps or strongholds;
20 "whether the land *is* rich or poor; and
whether there are forests there or not. Be of
good courage. And bring some of the fruit of
the land." Now the time *was* the season of the
first ripe grapes.
21 So they went up and spied out the land
from the Wilderness of Zin as far as Rehob,
near the entrance of Hamath.
22 And they went up through the South and
came to Hebron; Ahiman, Sheshai, and Tal-
mai, the descendants of Anak, *were* there.
(Now Hebron was built seven years before
Zoan in Egypt.)
23 Then they came to the Valley of Eshcol,
and there cut down a branch with one cluster
of grapes; they carried it between two of them
on a pole. *They* also *brought* some of the pome-
granates and figs.
24 The place was called the Valley of Eshcol,[a]
because of the cluster which the men of Israel
cut down there.
25 And they returned from spying out the
land after forty days.
26 Now they departed and came back to Mo-
ses and Aaron and all the congregation of the
children of Israel in the Wilderness of Paran,
at Kadesh; they brought back word to them
and to all the congregation, and showed them
the fruit of the land.
27 Then they told him, and said: "We went to
the land where you sent us. It truly flows with
milk and honey, and this *is* its fruit.
28 "Nevertheless the people who dwell in the
land *are* strong; the cities *are* fortified *and* very
large; moreover we saw the descendants of
Anak there.
29 "The Amalekites dwell in the land of the
South; the Hittites, the Jebusites, and the Amo-
rites dwell in the mountains; and the Canaan-
ites dwell by the sea and along the banks of
the Jordan."
30 Then Caleb quieted the people before Mo-
ses, and said, "Let us go up at once and take
possession, for we are well able to overcome
it."
31 But the men who had gone up with him
said, "We are not able to go up against the peo-
ple, for they *are* stronger than we."
32 And they gave the children of Israel a bad
report of the land which they had spied out,
saying, "The land through which we have gone
as spies *is* a land that devours its inhabitants,
and all the people whom we saw in it *are* men
of *great* stature.
33 "There we saw the giants[a] (the descen-
dants of Anak came from the giants); and we
were like grasshoppers in our own sight, and
so we were in their sight."

Israel Refuses to Enter Canaan

14 So all the congregation lifted up their
voices and cried, and the people wept that
night.
2 And all the children of Israel complained
against Moses and Aaron, and the whole con-
gregation said to them, "If only we had died in
the land of Egypt! Or if only we had died in
this wilderness!
3 "Why has the LORD brought us to this land
to fall by the sword, that our wives and chil-
dren should become victims? Would it not be
better for us to return to Egypt?"
4 So they said to one another, "Let us select
a leader and return to Egypt."
5 Then Moses and Aaron fell on their faces
before all the assembly of the congregation of
the children of Israel.
6 But Joshua the son of Nun and Caleb the
son of Jephunneh, *who were* among those who
had spied out the land, tore their clothes;
7 and they spoke to all the congregation of
the children of Israel, saying: "The land we
passed through to spy out *is* an exceedingly
good land.
8 "If the LORD delights in us, then He will
bring us into this land and give it to us, 'a land
which flows with milk and honey.'[a]
9 "Only do not rebel against the LORD, nor
fear the people of the land, for they *are* our
bread; their protection has departed from them,
and the LORD *is* with us. Do not fear them."
10 And all the congregation said to stone
them with stones. Now the glory of the LORD
appeared in the tabernacle of meeting before
all the children of Israel.

Moses Intercedes for the People

11 Then the LORD said to Moses: "How long
will these people reject Me? And how long will
they not believe Me, with all the signs which I
have performed among them?
12 "I will strike them with the pestilence and
disinherit them, and I will make of you a nation
greater and mightier than they."
13 And Moses said to the LORD: "Then the
Egyptians will hear *it*, for by Your might You
brought these people up from among them,
14 "and they will tell *it* to the inhabitants of
this land. They have heard that You, LORD, *are*
among these people; that You, LORD, are seen
face to face and Your cloud stands above them,
and You go before them in a pillar of cloud by
day and in a pillar of fire by night.
15 "Now *if* You kill these people as one man,
then the nations which have heard of Your fame
will speak, saying,
16 'Because the LORD was not able to bring
this people to the land which He swore to give
them, therefore He killed them in the wilder-
ness.'
17 "And now, I pray, let the power of my Lord
be great, just as You have spoken, saying,
18 'The LORD is longsuffering and abundant
in mercy, forgiving iniquity and transgression;
but He by no means clears *the guilty*, visiting
the iniquity of the fathers on the children to
the third and fourth *generation*.'[a]
19 "Pardon the iniquity of this people, I pray,
according to the greatness of Your mercy, just
as You have forgiven this people, from Egypt
even until now."
20 Then the LORD said: "I have pardoned, ac-
cording to your word;
21 "but truly, as I live, all the earth shall be
filled with the glory of the LORD—
22 "because all these men who have seen My
glory and the signs which I did in Egypt and
in the wilderness, and have put Me to the test

13:24 [a]Literally *Cluster* **13:33** [a]Hebrew *nephilim* **14:8** [a]Exodus 3:8 **14:18** [a]Exodus 34:6, 7

now these ten times, and have not heeded My
voice,
23 "they certainly shall not see the land of
which I swore to their fathers, nor shall any of
those who rejected Me see it.
24 "But My servant Caleb, because he has a
different spirit in him and has followed Me
fully, I will bring into the land where he went,
and his descendants shall inherit it.
25 "Now the Amalekites and the Canaanites
dwell in the valley; tomorrow turn and move
out into the wilderness by the Way of the Red
Sea."

Death Sentence on the Rebels

26 And the LORD spoke to Moses and Aaron,
saying,
27 "How long *shall I bear with* this evil con-
gregation who complain against Me? I have
heard the complaints which the children of Is-
rael make against Me.
28 "Say to them, 'As I live,' says the LORD, 'just
as you have spoken in My hearing, so I will do
to you:
29 'The carcasses of you who have com-
plained against Me shall fall in this wilderness,
all of you who were numbered, according to
your entire number, from twenty years old and
above.
30 'Except for Caleb the son of Jephunneh
and Joshua the son of Nun, you shall by no
means enter the land which I swore I would
make you dwell in.
31 'But your little ones, whom you said would
be victims, I will bring in, and they shall know
the land which you have despised.
32 'But *as for* you, your carcasses shall fall in
this wilderness.
33 'And your sons shall be shepherds in the
wilderness forty years, and bear the brunt of
your infidelity, until your carcasses are con-
sumed in the wilderness.
34 'According to the number of the days in
which you spied out the land, forty days, for
each day you shall bear your guilt one year,
namely forty years, and you shall know My re-
jection.
35 'I the LORD have spoken this. I will surely
do so to all this evil congregation who are gath-
ered together against Me. In this wilderness they
shall be consumed, and there they shall die.'"
36 Now the men whom Moses sent to spy out
the land, who returned and made all the con-
gregation complain against him by bringing a
bad report of the land,
37 those very men who brought the evil re-
port about the land, died by the plague before
the LORD.
38 But Joshua the son of Nun and Caleb the
son of Jephunneh remained alive, of the men
who went to spy out the land.

A Futile Invasion Attempt

39 Then Moses told these words to all the chil-
dren of Israel, and the people mourned greatly.
40 And they rose early in the morning and
went up to the top of the mountain, saying, "Here
we are, and we will go up to the place which
the LORD has promised, for we have sinned!"
41 And Moses said, "Now why do you trans-
gress the command of the LORD? For this will
not succeed.
42 "Do not go up, lest you be defeated by your
enemies, for the LORD *is* not among you.
43 "For the Amalekites and the Canaanites
are there before you, and you shall fall by the
sword; because you have turned away from the
LORD, the LORD will not be with you."
44 But they presumed to go up to the moun-
taintop. Nevertheless, neither the ark of the
covenant of the LORD nor Moses departed from
the camp.
45 Then the Amalekites and the Canaanites
who dwelt in that mountain came down and
attacked them, and drove them back as far as
Hormah.

Laws of Grain and Drink Offerings

15 And the LORD spoke to Moses, saying,
2 "Speak to the children of Israel, and
say to them: 'When you have come into the land
you are to inhabit, which I am giving to you,
3 'and you make an offering by fire to the
LORD, a burnt offering or a sacrifice, to fulfill
a vow or as a freewill offering or in your ap-
pointed feasts, to make a sweet aroma to the
LORD, from the herd or the flock,
4 'then he who presents his offering to the
LORD shall bring a grain offering of one-tenth
of an ephah of fine flour mixed with one-fourth
of a hin of oil;
5 'and one-fourth of a hin of wine as a drink
offering you shall prepare with the burnt offer-
ing or the sacrifice, for each lamb.
6 'Or for a ram you shall prepare as a grain
offering two-tenths *of an ephah* of fine flour
mixed with one-third of a hin of oil;
7 'and as a drink offering you shall offer one-
third of a hin of wine as a sweet aroma to the
LORD.
8 'And when you prepare a young bull as a
burnt offering, or as a sacrifice to fulfill a vow,
or as a peace offering to the LORD,
9 'then shall be offered with the young bull
a grain offering of three-tenths *of an ephah* of
fine flour mixed with half a hin of oil;
10 'and you shall bring as the drink offering
half a hin of wine as an offering made by fire,
a sweet aroma to the LORD.
11 'Thus it shall be done for each young bull,
for each ram, or for each lamb or young goat.
12 'According to the number that you pre-
pare, so you shall do with everyone according
to their number.
13 'All who are native-born shall do these
things in this manner, in presenting an offering
made by fire, a sweet aroma to the LORD.
14 'And if a stranger dwells with you, or who-
ever *is* among you throughout your genera-
tions, and would present an offering made by
fire, a sweet aroma to the LORD, just as you do,
so shall he do.
15 'One ordinance *shall be* for you of the as-
sembly and for the stranger who dwells *with
you*, an ordinance forever throughout your
generations; as you are, so shall the stranger
be before the LORD.
16 'One law and one custom shall be for you
and for the stranger who dwells with you.'"[a]
17 Again the LORD spoke to Moses, saying,
18 "Speak to the children of Israel, and say to
them: 'When you come into the land to which I
bring you,
19 'then it will be, when you eat of the bread

15:16 [a]Compare Exodus 12:49

of the land, that you shall offer up a heave
offering to the LORD.
20 'You shall offer up a cake of the first of
your ground meal *as* a heave offering; as a
heave offering of the threshing floor, so shall
you offer it up.
21 'Of the first of your ground meal you shall
give to the LORD a heave offering throughout
your generations.

Laws Concerning Unintentional Sin

22 'If you sin unintentionally, and do not ob-
serve all these commandments which the
LORD has spoken to Moses—
23 'all that the LORD has commanded you by
the hand of Moses, from the day the LORD gave
commandment and onward throughout your
generations—
24 'then it will be, if it is unintentionally com-
mitted, without the knowledge of the congre-
gation, that the whole congregation shall offer
one young bull as a burnt offering, as a sweet
aroma to the LORD, with its grain offering and
its drink offering, according to the ordinance,
and one kid of the goats as a sin offering.
25 'So the priest shall make atonement for the
whole congregation of the children of Israel,
and it shall be forgiven them, for it was un-
intentional; they shall bring their offering, an
offering made by fire to the LORD, and their sin
offering before the LORD, for their unintended
sin.
26 'It shall be forgiven the whole congrega-
tion of the children of Israel and the stranger
who dwells among them, because all the peo-
ple *did it* unintentionally.
27 'And if a person sins unintentionally, then
he shall bring a female goat in its first year as
a sin offering.
28 'So the priest shall make atonement for the
person who sins unintentionally, when he sins
unintentionally before the LORD, to make
atonement for him; and it shall be forgiven
him.
29 'You shall have one law for him who sins
unintentionally, *for* him who is native-born
among the children of Israel and for the
stranger who dwells among them.

Law Concerning Presumptuous Sin

30 'But the person who does *anything* pre-
sumptuously, *whether he is* native-born or a
stranger, that one brings reproach on the
LORD, and he shall be cut off from among his
people.
31 'Because he has despised the word of the
LORD, and has broken His commandment, that
person shall be completely cut off; his guilt
shall be upon him.'"

Penalty for Violating the Sabbath

32 Now while the children of Israel were in
the wilderness, they found a man gathering
sticks on the Sabbath day.
33 And those who found him gathering sticks
brought him to Moses and Aaron, and to all
the congregation.
34 They put him under guard, because it had
not been explained what should be done to
him.
35 Then the LORD said to Moses, "The man
must surely be put to death; all the congrega-
tion shall stone him with stones outside the
camp."
36 So, as the LORD commanded Moses, all
the congregation brought him outside the
camp and stoned him with stones, and he died.

Tassels on Garments

37 Again the LORD spoke to Moses, saying,
38 "Speak to the children of Israel: Tell them
to make tassels on the corners of their gar-
ments throughout their generations, and to put
a blue thread in the tassels of the corners.
39 "And you shall have the tassel, that you
may look upon it and remember all the com-
mandments of the LORD and do them, and that
you *may* not follow the harlotry to which your
own heart and your own eyes are inclined,
40 "and that you may remember and do all
My commandments, and be holy for your God.
41 "I *am* the LORD your God, who brought
you out of the land of Egypt, to be your God: I
am the LORD your God."

Rebellion Against Moses and Aaron

16 Now Korah the son of Izhar, the son of
Kohath, the son of Levi, with Dathan
and Abiram the sons of Eliab, and On the son
of Peleth, sons of Reuben, took *men;*
2 and they rose up before Moses with some
of the children of Israel, two hundred and fifty
leaders of the congregation, representatives of
the congregation, men of renown.
3 They gathered together against Moses and
Aaron, and said to them, "*You take* too much
upon yourselves, for all the congregation *is*
holy, every one of them, and the LORD *is*
among them. Why then do you exalt your-
selves above the assembly of the LORD?"
4 So when Moses heard *it*, he fell on his face;
5 and he spoke to Korah and all his com-
pany, saying, "Tomorrow morning the LORD
will show who *is* His and *who is* holy, and will
cause *him* to come near to Him. That one
whom He chooses He will cause to come near
to Him.
6 "Do this: Take censers, Korah and all your
company;
7 "put fire in them and put incense in them
before the LORD tomorrow, and it shall be *that*
the man whom the LORD chooses *is* the holy
one. *You take* too much upon yourselves, you
sons of Levi!"
8 Then Moses said to Korah, "Hear now, you
sons of Levi:
9 "*Is it* a small thing to you that the God of
Israel has separated you from the congrega-
tion of Israel, to bring you near to Himself, to
do the work of the tabernacle of the LORD, and
to stand before the congregation to serve them;
10 "and that He has brought you near *to Him-
self,* you and all your brethren, the sons of Levi,
with you? And are you seeking the priesthood
also?
11 "Therefore you and all your company *are*
gathered together against the LORD. And what
is Aaron that you complain against him?"
12 And Moses sent to call Dathan and Abiram
the sons of Eliab, but they said, "We will not
come up!
13 "*Is it* a small thing that you have brought
us up out of a land flowing with milk and
honey, to kill us in the wilderness, that you
should keep acting like a prince over us?
14 "Moreover you have not brought us into a
land flowing with milk and honey, nor given
us inheritance of fields and vineyards. Will you

put out the eyes of these men? We will not come up!"

15 Then Moses was very angry, and said to the LORD, "Do not respect their offering. I have not taken one donkey from them, nor have I hurt one of them."

16 And Moses said to Korah, "Tomorrow, you and all your company be present before the LORD—you and they, as well as Aaron.

17 "Let each take his censer and put incense in it, and each of you bring his censer before the LORD, two hundred and fifty censers; both you and Aaron, each *with* his censer."

18 So every man took his censer, put fire in it, laid incense on it, and stood at the door of the tabernacle of meeting with Moses and Aaron.

19 And Korah gathered all the congregation against them at the door of the tabernacle of meeting. Then the glory of the LORD appeared to all the congregation.

20 And the LORD spoke to Moses and Aaron, saying,

21 "Separate yourselves from among this congregation, that I may consume them in a moment."

22 Then they fell on their faces, and said, "O God, the God of the spirits of all flesh, shall one man sin, and You be angry with all the congregation?"

23 So the LORD spoke to Moses, saying,

24 "Speak to the congregation, saying, 'Get away from the tents of Korah, Dathan, and Abiram.'"

25 Then Moses rose and went to Dathan and Abiram, and the elders of Israel followed him.

26 And he spoke to the congregation, saying, "Depart now from the tents of these wicked men! Touch nothing of theirs, lest you be consumed in all their sins."

27 So they got away from around the tents of Korah, Dathan, and Abiram; and Dathan and Abiram came out and stood at the door of their tents, with their wives, their sons, and their little children.

28 And Moses said: "By this you shall know that the LORD has sent me to do all these works, for *I have* not *done them* of my own will.

29 "If these men die naturally like all men, or if they are visited by the common fate of all men, *then* the LORD has not sent me.

30 "But if the LORD creates a new thing, and the earth opens its mouth and swallows them up with all that belongs to them, and they go down alive into the pit, then you will understand that these men have rejected the LORD."

31 Now it came to pass, as he finished speaking all these words, that the ground split apart under them,

32 and the earth opened its mouth and swallowed them up, with their households and all the men with Korah, with all *their* goods.

33 So they and all those with them went down alive into the pit; the earth closed over them, and they perished from among the assembly.

34 Then all Israel who *were* around them fled at their cry, for they said, "Lest the earth swallow us up *also!*"

35 And a fire came out from the LORD and consumed the two hundred and fifty men who were offering incense.

36 Then the LORD spoke to Moses, saying:

37 "Tell Eleazar, the son of Aaron the priest, to pick up the censers out of the blaze, for they are holy, and scatter the fire some distance away.

38 "The censers of these men who sinned against their own souls, let them be made into hammered plates as a covering for the altar. Because they presented them before the LORD, therefore they are holy; and they shall be a sign to the children of Israel."

39 So Eleazar the priest took the bronze censers, which those who were burned up had presented, and they were hammered out as a covering on the altar,

40 *to be* a memorial to the children of Israel that no outsider, who *is* not a descendant of Aaron, should come near to offer incense before the LORD, that he might not become like Korah and his companions, just as the LORD had said to him through Moses.

Complaints of the People

41 On the next day all the congregation of the children of Israel complained against Moses and Aaron, saying, "You have killed the people of the LORD."

42 Now it happened, when the congregation had gathered against Moses and Aaron, that they turned toward the tabernacle of meeting; and suddenly the cloud covered it, and the glory of the LORD appeared.

43 Then Moses and Aaron came before the tabernacle of meeting.

44 And the LORD spoke to Moses, saying,

45 "Get away from among this congregation, that I may consume them in a moment." And they fell on their faces.

46 So Moses said to Aaron, "Take a censer and put fire in it from the altar, put incense *on it*, and take it quickly to the congregation and make atonement for them; for wrath has gone out from the LORD. The plague has begun."

47 Then Aaron took *it* as Moses commanded, and ran into the midst of the assembly; and already the plague had begun among the people. So he put in the incense and made atonement for the people.

48 And he stood between the dead and the living; so the plague was stopped.

49 Now those who died in the plague were fourteen thousand seven hundred, besides those who died in the Korah incident.

50 So Aaron returned to Moses at the door of the tabernacle of meeting, for the plague had stopped.

The Budding of Aaron's Rod

17 And the LORD spoke to Moses, saying:

2 "Speak to the children of Israel, and get from them a rod from each father's house, all their leaders according to their fathers' houses—twelve rods. Write each man's name on his rod.

3 "And you shall write Aaron's name on the rod of Levi. For there shall be one rod for the head of *each* father's house.

4 "Then you shall place them in the tabernacle of meeting before the Testimony, where I meet with you.

5 "And it shall be *that* the rod of the man whom I choose will blossom; thus I will rid Myself of the complaints of the children of Israel, which they make against you."

6 So Moses spoke to the children of Israel, and each of their leaders gave him a rod apiece, for each leader according to their fathers' houses, twelve rods; and the rod of Aaron *was* among their rods.

7 And Moses placed the rods before the
LORD in the tabernacle of witness.
8 Now it came to pass on the next day that
Moses went into the tabernacle of witness, and
behold, the rod of Aaron, of the house of Levi,
had sprouted and put forth buds, had produced
blossoms and yielded ripe almonds.
9 Then Moses brought out all the rods from
before the LORD to all the children of Israel;
and they looked, and each man took his rod.
10 And the LORD said to Moses, "Bring
Aaron's rod back before the Testimony, to be
kept as a sign against the rebels, that you may
put their complaints away from Me, lest they
die."
11 Thus did Moses; just as the LORD had com-
manded him, so he did.
12 So the children of Israel spoke to Moses,
saying, "Surely we die, we perish, we all
perish!
13 "Whoever even comes near the tabernacle
of the LORD must die. Shall we all utterly die?"

Duties of Priests and Levites

18 Then the LORD said to Aaron: "You and
your sons and your father's house with
you shall bear the iniquity *related to* the sanc-
tuary, and you and your sons with you shall
bear the iniquity *associated with* your priest-
hood.
2 "Also bring with you your brethren of the
tribe of Levi, the tribe of your father, that they
may be joined with you and serve you while
you and your sons *are* with you before the tab-
ernacle of witness.
3 "They shall attend to your needs and all
the needs of the tabernacle; but they shall not
come near the articles of the sanctuary and the
altar, lest they die—they and you also.
4 "They shall be joined with you and attend
to the needs of the tabernacle of meeting, for
all the work of the tabernacle; but an outsider
shall not come near you.
5 "And you shall attend to the duties of the
sanctuary and the duties of the altar, that there
may be no more wrath on the children of Israel.
6 "Behold, I Myself have taken your breth-
ren the Levites from among the children of
Israel; *they are* a gift to you, given by the LORD,
to do the work of the tabernacle of meeting.
7 "Therefore you and your sons with you
shall attend to your priesthood for everything
at the altar and behind the veil; and you shall
serve. I give your priesthood *to you* as a gift
for service, but the outsider who comes near
shall be put to death."

Offerings for Support of the Priests

8 And the LORD spoke to Aaron: "Here, I
Myself have also given you charge of My heave
offerings, all the holy gifts of the children of
Israel; I have given them as a portion to you
and your sons, as an ordinance forever.
9 "This shall be yours of the most holy
things *reserved* from the fire: every offering
of theirs, every grain offering and every sin
offering and every trespass offering which
they render to Me, *shall be* most holy for you
and your sons.
10 "In a most holy *place* you shall eat it; every
male shall eat it. It shall be holy to you.
11 "This also *is* yours: the heave offering of
their gift, with all the wave offerings of the chil-
dren of Israel; I have given them to you, and
your sons and daughters with you, as an ordi-
nance forever. Everyone who is clean in your
house may eat it.
12 "All the best of the oil, all the best of the
new wine and the grain, their firstfruits which
they offer to the LORD, I have given them to
you.
13 "Whatever first ripe fruit is in their land,
which they bring to the LORD, shall be yours.
Everyone who is clean in your house may eat
it.
14 "Every devoted thing in Israel shall be
yours.
15 "Everything that first opens the womb of
all flesh, which they bring to the LORD,
whether man or beast, shall be yours; never-
theless the firstborn of man you shall surely
redeem, and the firstborn of unclean animals
you shall redeem.
16 "And those redeemed of the devoted things
you shall redeem when one month old, accord-
ing to your valuation, for five shekels of silver,
according to the shekel of the sanctuary, which
is twenty gerahs.
17 "But the firstborn of a cow, the firstborn
of a sheep, or the firstborn of a goat you shall
not redeem; they *are* holy. You shall sprinkle
their blood on the altar, and burn their fat *as*
an offering made by fire for a sweet aroma to
the LORD.
18 "And their flesh shall be yours, just as the
wave breast and the right thigh are yours.
19 "All the heave offerings of the holy things,
which the children of Israel offer to the LORD, I
have given to you and your sons and daughters
with you as an ordinance forever; it *is* a cov-
enant of salt forever before the LORD with you
and your descendants with you."
20 Then the LORD said to Aaron: "You shall
have no inheritance in their land, nor shall you
have any portion among them; I *am* your por-
tion and your inheritance among the children
of Israel.

Tithes for Support of the Levites

21 "Behold, I have given the children of Levi
all the tithes in Israel as an inheritance in re-
turn for the work which they perform, the
work of the tabernacle of meeting.
22 "Hereafter the children of Israel shall not
come near the tabernacle of meeting, lest they
bear sin and die.
23 "But the Levites shall perform the work of
the tabernacle of meeting, and they shall bear
their iniquity; *it shall be* a statute forever,
throughout your generations, that among the
children of Israel they shall have no inheri-
tance.
24 "For the tithes of the children of Israel,
which they offer up *as* a heave offering to the
LORD, I have given to the Levites as an inheri-
tance; therefore I have said to them, 'Among
the children of Israel they shall have no inheri-
tance.'"

The Tithe of the Levites

25 Then the LORD spoke to Moses, saying,
26 "Speak thus to the Levites, and say to
them: 'When you take from the children of Is-
rael the tithes which I have given you from
them as your inheritance, then you shall offer
up a heave offering of it to the LORD, a tenth
of the tithe.
27 'And your heave offering shall be reckoned
to you as though *it were* the grain of the thresh-
ing floor and as the fullness of the winepress.

28 'Thus you shall also offer a heave offering to the LORD from all your tithes which you receive from the children of Israel, and you shall give the LORD's heave offering from it to Aaron the priest.

29 'Of all your gifts you shall offer up every heave offering due to the LORD, from all the best of them, the consecrated part of them.'

30 "Therefore you shall say to them: 'When you have lifted up the best of it, then *the rest* shall be accounted to the Levites as the produce of the threshing floor and as the produce of the winepress.

31 'You may eat it in any place, you and your households, for it *is* your reward for your work in the tabernacle of meeting.

32 'And you shall bear no sin because of it, when you have lifted up the best of it. But you shall not profane the holy gifts of the children of Israel, lest you die.' "

Laws of Purification

19 Now the LORD spoke to Moses and Aaron, saying,

2 "This *is* the ordinance of the law which the LORD has commanded, saying: 'Speak to the children of Israel, that they bring you a red heifer without blemish, in which there *is* no defect *and* on which a yoke has never come.

3 'You shall give it to Eleazar the priest, that he may take it outside the camp, and it shall be slaughtered before him;

4 'and Eleazar the priest shall take some of its blood with his finger, and sprinkle some of its blood seven times directly in front of the tabernacle of meeting.

5 'Then the heifer shall be burned in his sight: its hide, its flesh, its blood, and its offal shall be burned.

6 'And the priest shall take cedar wood and hyssop and scarlet, and cast *them* into the midst of the fire burning the heifer.

7 'Then the priest shall wash his clothes, he shall bathe in water, and afterward he shall come into the camp; the priest shall be unclean until evening.

8 'And the one who burns it shall wash his clothes in water, bathe in water, and shall be unclean until evening.

9 'Then a man *who is* clean shall gather up the ashes of the heifer, and store *them* outside the camp in a clean place; and they shall be kept for the congregation of the children of Israel for the water of purification;[a] it *is* for purifying from sin.

10 'And the one who gathers the ashes of the heifer shall wash his clothes, and be unclean until evening. It shall be a statute forever to the children of Israel and to the stranger who dwells among them.

11 'He who touches the dead body of anyone shall be unclean seven days.

12 'He shall purify himself with the water on the third day and on the seventh day; *then* he will be clean. But if he does not purify himself on the third day and on the seventh day, he will not be clean.

13 'Whoever touches the body of anyone who has died, and does not purify himself, defiles the tabernacle of the LORD. That person shall be cut off from Israel. He shall be unclean, because the water of purification was not sprinkled on him; his uncleanness *is* still on him.

14 'This *is* the law when a man dies in a tent: All who come into the tent and all who *are* in the tent shall be unclean seven days;

15 'and every open vessel, which has no cover fastened on it, *is* unclean.

16 'Whoever in the open field touches one who is slain by a sword or who has died, or a bone of a man, or a grave, shall be unclean seven days.

17 'And for an unclean *person* they shall take some of the ashes of the heifer burnt for purification from sin, and running water shall be put on them in a vessel.

18 'A clean person shall take hyssop and dip *it* in the water, sprinkle *it* on the tent, on all the vessels, on the persons who were there, or on the one who touched a bone, the slain, the dead, or a grave.

19 'The clean *person* shall sprinkle the unclean on the third day and on the seventh day; and on the seventh day he shall purify himself, wash his clothes, and bathe in water; and at evening he shall be clean.

20 'But the man who is unclean and does not purify himself, that person shall be cut off from among the assembly, because he has defiled the sanctuary of the LORD. The water of purification has not been sprinkled on him; he *is* unclean.

21 'It shall be a perpetual statute for them. He who sprinkles the water of purification shall wash his clothes; and he who touches the water of purification shall be unclean until evening.

22 'Whatever the unclean *person* touches shall be unclean; and the person who touches *it* shall be unclean until evening.' "

Moses' Error at Kadesh

20 Then the children of Israel, the whole congregation, came into the Wilderness of Zin in the first month, and the people stayed in Kadesh; and Miriam died there and was buried there.

2 Now there was no water for the congregation; so they gathered together against Moses and Aaron.

3 And the people contended with Moses and spoke, saying: "If only we had died when our brethren died before the LORD!

4 "Why have you brought up the assembly of the LORD into this wilderness, that we and our animals should die here?

5 "And why have you made us come up out of Egypt, to bring us to this evil place? It *is* not a place of grain or figs or vines or pomegranates; nor *is* there any water to drink."

6 So Moses and Aaron went from the presence of the assembly to the door of the tabernacle of meeting, and they fell on their faces. And the glory of the LORD appeared to them.

7 Then the LORD spoke to Moses, saying,

8 "Take the rod; you and your brother Aaron gather the congregation together. Speak to the rock before their eyes, and it will yield its water; thus you shall bring water for them out of the rock, and give drink to the congregation and their animals."

9 So Moses took the rod from before the LORD as He commanded him.

10 And Moses and Aaron gathered the assembly together before the rock; and he said to them, "Hear now, you rebels! Must we bring water for you out of this rock?"

19:9 [a]Literally *impurity*

11 Then Moses lifted his hand and struck the rock twice with his rod; and water came out abundantly, and the congregation and their animals drank.

12 Then the LORD spoke to Moses and Aaron, "Because you did not believe Me, to hallow Me in the eyes of the children of Israel, therefore you shall not bring this assembly into the land which I have given them."

13 This *was* the water of Meribah,[a] because the children of Israel contended with the LORD, and He was hallowed among them.

Passage Through Edom Refused

14 Now Moses sent messengers from Kadesh to the king of Edom. "Thus says your brother Israel: 'You know all the hardship that has befallen us,

15 'how our fathers went down to Egypt, and we dwelt in Egypt a long time, and the Egyptians afflicted us and our fathers.

16 'When we cried out to the LORD, He heard our voice and sent the Angel and brought us up out of Egypt; now here we are in Kadesh, a city on the edge of your border.

17 'Please let us pass through your country. We will not pass through fields or vineyards, nor will we drink water from wells; we will go along the King's Highway; we will not turn aside to the right hand or to the left until we have passed through your territory.' "

18 Then Edom said to him, "You shall not pass through my *land*, lest I come out against you with the sword."

19 So the children of Israel said to him, "We will go by the Highway, and if I or my livestock drink any of your water, then I will pay for it; let me only pass through on foot, nothing *more*."

20 Then he said, "You shall not pass through." So Edom came out against them with many men and with a strong hand.

21 Thus Edom refused to give Israel passage through his territory; so Israel turned away from him.

Death of Aaron

22 Now the children of Israel, the whole congregation, journeyed from Kadesh and came to Mount Hor.

23 And the LORD spoke to Moses and Aaron in Mount Hor by the border of the land of Edom, saying:

24 "Aaron shall be gathered to his people, for he shall not enter the land which I have given to the children of Israel, because you rebelled against My word at the water of Meribah.

25 "Take Aaron and Eleazar his son, and bring them up to Mount Hor;

26 "and strip Aaron of his garments and put them on Eleazar his son; for Aaron shall be gathered *to his people* and die there."

27 So Moses did just as the LORD commanded, and they went up to Mount Hor in the sight of all the congregation.

28 Moses stripped Aaron of his garments and put them on Eleazar his son; and Aaron died there on the top of the mountain. Then Moses and Eleazar came down from the mountain.

29 Now when all the congregation saw that Aaron was dead, all the house of Israel mourned for Aaron thirty days.

Canaanites Defeated at Hormah

21 The king of Arad, the Canaanite, who dwelt in the South, heard that Israel was coming on the road to Atharim. Then he fought against Israel and took *some* of them prisoners.

2 So Israel made a vow to the LORD, and said, "If You will indeed deliver this people into my hand, then I will utterly destroy their cities."

3 And the LORD listened to the voice of Israel and delivered up the Canaanites, and they utterly destroyed them and their cities. So the name of that place was called Hormah.[a]

The Bronze Serpent

4 Then they journeyed from Mount Hor by the Way of the Red Sea, to go around the land of Edom; and the soul of the people became very discouraged on the way.

5 And the people spoke against God and against Moses: "Why have you brought us up out of Egypt to die in the wilderness? For *there is* no food and no water, and our soul loathes this worthless bread."

6 So the LORD sent fiery serpents among the people, and they bit the people; and many of the people of Israel died.

7 Therefore the people came to Moses, and said, "We have sinned, for we have spoken against the LORD and against you; pray to the LORD that He take away the serpents from us." So Moses prayed for the people.

8 Then the LORD said to Moses, "Make a fiery *serpent*, and set it on a pole; and it shall be that everyone who is bitten, when he looks at it, shall live."

9 So Moses made a bronze serpent, and put it on a pole; and so it was, if a serpent had bitten anyone, when he looked at the bronze serpent, he lived.

From Mount Hor to Moab

10 Now the children of Israel moved on and camped in Oboth.

11 And they journeyed from Oboth and camped at Ije Abarim, in the wilderness which *is* east of Moab, toward the sunrise.

12 From there they moved and camped in the Valley of Zered.

13 From there they moved and camped on the other side of the Arnon, which *is* in the wilderness that extends from the border of the Amorites; for the Arnon *is* the border of Moab, between Moab and the Amorites.

14 Therefore it is said in the Book of the Wars of the LORD:

"Waheb in Suphah,[a]
The brooks of the Arnon,
15 And the slope of the brooks
That reaches to the dwelling of Ar,
And lies on the border of Moab."

16 From there *they went* to Beer, which *is* the well where the LORD said to Moses, "Gather the people together, and I will give them water."

17 Then Israel sang this song:

"Spring up, O well!
All of you sing to it—

20:13 [a]Literally *Contention* **21:3** [a]Literally *Utter Destruction* **21:14** [a]Ancient unknown places; Vulgate reads *What He did in the Red Sea.*

18 The well the leaders sank,
Dug by the nation's nobles,
By the lawgiver, with their staves."

And from the wilderness *they went* to Mattanah,
19 from Mattanah to Nahaliel, from Nahaliel
to Bamoth,
20 and from Bamoth, *in* the valley that *is* in
the country of Moab, to the top of Pisgah which
looks down on the wasteland.[a]

King Sihon Defeated

21 Then Israel sent messengers to Sihon king
of the Amorites, saying,
22 "Let me pass through your land. We will
not turn aside into fields or vineyards; we will
not drink water from wells. We will go by the
King's Highway until we have passed through
your territory."
23 But Sihon would not allow Israel to pass
through his territory. So Sihon gathered all his
people together and went out against Israel
in the wilderness, and he came to Jahaz and
fought against Israel.
24 Then Israel defeated him with the edge of
the sword, and took possession of his land
from the Arnon to the Jabbok, as far as the
people of Ammon; for the border of the people
of Ammon *was* fortified.
25 So Israel took all these cities, and Israel
dwelt in all the cities of the Amorites, in Heshbon and in all its villages.
26 For Heshbon *was* the city of Sihon king
of the Amorites, who had fought against the
former king of Moab, and had taken all his
land from his hand as far as the Arnon.
27 Therefore those who speak in proverbs
say:

"Come to Heshbon, let it be built;
Let the city of Sihon be repaired.

28 "For fire went out from Heshbon,
A flame from the city of Sihon;
It consumed Ar of Moab,
The lords of the heights of the Arnon.
29 Woe to you, Moab!
You have perished, O people of Chemosh!
He has given his sons as fugitives,
And his daughters into captivity,
To Sihon king of the Amorites.

30 "But we have shot at them;
Heshbon has perished as far as Dibon.
Then we laid waste as far as Nophah,
Which *reaches* to Medeba."

31 Thus Israel dwelt in the land of the Amorites.
32 Then Moses sent to spy out Jazer; and they
took its villages and drove out the Amorites
who *were* there.

King Og Defeated

33 And they turned and went up by the way
to Bashan. So Og king of Bashan went out
against them, he and all his people, to battle at
Edrei.
34 Then the LORD said to Moses, "Do not fear
him, for I have delivered him into your hand,
with all his people and his land; and you shall
do to him as you did to Sihon king of the Amorites, who dwelt at Heshbon."
35 So they defeated him, his sons, and all his
people, until there was no survivor left him;
and they took possession of his land.

Balak Sends for Balaam

22 Then the children of Israel moved, and
camped in the plains of Moab on the
side of the Jordan *across from* Jericho.
2 Now Balak the son of Zippor saw all that
Israel had done to the Amorites.
3 And Moab was exceedingly afraid of the
people because they *were* many, and Moab
was sick with dread because of the children of
Israel.
4 So Moab said to the elders of Midian,
"Now this company will lick up everything
around us, as an ox licks up the grass of the
field." And Balak the son of Zippor *was* king
of the Moabites at that time.
5 Then he sent messengers to Balaam the
son of Beor at Pethor, which *is* near the River[a]
in the land of the sons of his people,[b] to call
him, saying: "Look, a people has come from
Egypt. See, they cover the face of the earth,
and are settling next to me!
6 "Therefore please come at once, curse this
people for me, for they *are* too mighty for me.
Perhaps I shall be able to defeat them and drive
them out of the land, for I know that he whom
you bless *is* blessed, and he whom you curse is
cursed."
7 So the elders of Moab and the elders of
Midian departed with the diviner's fee in their
hand, and they came to Balaam and spoke to
him the words of Balak.
8 And he said to them, "Lodge here tonight,
and I will bring back word to you, as the LORD
speaks to me." So the princes of Moab stayed
with Balaam.
9 Then God came to Balaam and said, "Who
are these men with you?"
10 So Balaam said to God, "Balak the son of
Zippor, king of Moab, has sent to me, *saying,*
11 'Look, a people has come out of Egypt, and
they cover the face of the earth. Come now,
curse them for me; perhaps I shall be able to
overpower them and drive them out.'"
12 And God said to Balaam, "You shall not
go with them; you shall not curse the people,
for they *are* blessed."
13 So Balaam rose in the morning and said to
the princes of Balak, "Go back to your land, for
the LORD has refused to give me permission to
go with you."
14 And the princes of Moab rose and went to
Balak, and said, "Balaam refuses to come with
us."
15 Then Balak again sent princes, more numerous and more honorable than they.
16 And they came to Balaam and said to him,
"Thus says Balak the son of Zippor: 'Please let
nothing hinder you from coming to me;
17 'for I will certainly honor you greatly, and
I will do whatever you say to me. Therefore
please come, curse this people for me.'"
18 Then Balaam answered and said to the servants of Balak, "Though Balak were to give
me his house full of silver and gold, I could not
go beyond the word of the LORD my God, to
do less or more.
19 "Now therefore, please, you also stay here
tonight, that I may know what more the LORD
will say to me."

21:20 [a]Hebrew *Jeshimon* **22:5** [a]That is, the Euphrates [b]Or *the people of Amau*

20 And God came to Balaam at night and said to him, "If the men come to call you, rise *and* go with them; but only the word which I speak to you—that you shall do."

21 So Balaam rose in the morning, saddled his donkey, and went with the princes of Moab.

Balaam, the Donkey, and the Angel

22 Then God's anger was aroused because he went, and the Angel of the LORD took His stand in the way as an adversary against him. And he was riding on his donkey, and his two servants *were* with him.

23 Now the donkey saw the Angel of the LORD standing in the way with His drawn sword in His hand, and the donkey turned aside out of the way and went into the field. So Balaam struck the donkey to turn her back onto the road.

24 Then the Angel of the LORD stood in a narrow path between the vineyards, *with* a wall on this side and a wall on that side.

25 And when the donkey saw the Angel of the LORD, she pushed herself against the wall and crushed Balaam's foot against the wall; so he struck her again.

26 Then the Angel of the LORD went further, and stood in a narrow place where there *was* no way to turn either to the right hand or to the left.

27 And when the donkey saw the Angel of the LORD, she lay down under Balaam; so Balaam's anger was aroused, and he struck the donkey with his staff.

28 Then the LORD opened the mouth of the donkey, and she said to Balaam, "What have I done to you, that you have struck me these three times?"

29 And Balaam said to the donkey, "Because you have abused me. I wish there were a sword in my hand, for now I would kill you!"

30 So the donkey said to Balaam, "*Am* I not your donkey on which you have ridden, ever since *I became* yours, to this day? Was I ever disposed to do this to you?" And he said, "No."

31 Then the LORD opened Balaam's eyes, and he saw the Angel of the LORD standing in the way with His drawn sword in His hand; and he bowed his head and fell flat on his face.

32 And the Angel of the LORD said to him, "Why have you struck your donkey these three times? Behold, I have come out to stand against you, because *your* way is perverse before Me.

33 "The donkey saw Me and turned aside from Me these three times. If she had not turned aside from Me, surely I would also have killed you by now, and let her live."

34 And Balaam said to the Angel of the LORD, "I have sinned, for I did not know You stood in the way against me. Now therefore, if it displeases You, I will turn back."

35 Then the Angel of the LORD said to Balaam, "Go with the men, but only the word that I speak to you, that you shall speak." So Balaam went with the princes of Balak.

36 Now when Balak heard that Balaam was coming, he went out to meet him at the city of Moab, which *is* on the border at the Arnon, the boundary of the territory.

37 Then Balak said to Balaam, "Did I not earnestly send to you, calling for you? Why did you not come to me? Am I not able to honor you?"

38 And Balaam said to Balak, "Look, I have come to you! Now, have I any power at all to say anything? The word that God puts in my mouth, that I must speak."

39 So Balaam went with Balak, and they came to Kirjath Huzoth.

40 Then Balak offered oxen and sheep, and he sent *some* to Balaam and to the princes who *were* with him.

Balaam's First Prophecy

41 So it was, the next day, that Balak took Balaam and brought him up to the high places of Baal, that from there he might observe the extent of the people.

23 Then Balaam said to Balak, "Build seven altars for me here, and prepare for me here seven bulls and seven rams."

2 And Balak did just as Balaam had spoken, and Balak and Balaam offered a bull and a ram on *each* altar.

3 Then Balaam said to Balak, "Stand by your burnt offering, and I will go; perhaps the LORD will come to meet me, and whatever He shows me I will tell you." So he went to a desolate height.

4 And God met Balaam, and he said to Him, "I have prepared the seven altars, and I have offered on *each* altar a bull and a ram."

5 Then the LORD put a word in Balaam's mouth, and said, "Return to Balak, and thus you shall speak."

6 So he returned to him, and there he was, standing by his burnt offering, he and all the princes of Moab.

7 And he took up his oracle and said:

"Balak the king of Moab has brought me
from Aram,
From the mountains of the east.
'Come, curse Jacob for me,
And come, denounce Israel!'

8 "How shall I curse whom God has not
cursed?
And how shall I denounce *whom* the
LORD has not denounced?

9 For from the top of the rocks I see him,
And from the hills I behold him;
There! A people dwelling alone,
Not reckoning itself among the nations.

10 "Who can count the dust[a] of Jacob,
Or number one-fourth of Israel?
Let me die the death of the righteous,
And let my end be like his!"

11 Then Balak said to Balaam, "What have you done to me? I took you to curse my enemies, and look, you have blessed *them* bountifully!"

12 So he answered and said, "Must I not take heed to speak what the LORD has put in my mouth?"

Balaam's Second Prophecy

13 Then Balak said to him, "Please come with me to another place from which you may see them; you shall see only the outer part of them, and shall not see them all; curse them for me from there."

14 So he brought him to the field of Zophim, to the top of Pisgah, and built seven altars, and offered a bull and a ram on *each* altar.

15 And he said to Balak, "Stand here by your

23:10 [a]Or *dust cloud*

burnt offering while I meet[a] *the* LORD over
there."
16 Then the LORD met Balaam, and put a word
in his mouth, and said, "Go back to Balak, and
thus you shall speak."
17 So he came to him, and there he was,
standing by his burnt offering, and the princes
of Moab were with him. And Balak said to him,
"What has the LORD spoken?"
18 Then he took up his oracle and said:

"Rise up, Balak, and hear!
Listen to me, son of Zippor!

19 "God *is* not a man, that He should lie,
Nor a son of man, that He should repent.
Has He said, and will He not do?
Or has He spoken, and will He not make it good?
20 Behold, I have received *a command* to bless;
He has blessed, and I cannot reverse it.

21 "He has not observed iniquity in Jacob,
Nor has He seen wickedness in Israel.
The LORD his God *is* with him,
And the shout of a King *is* among them.
22 God brings them out of Egypt;
He has strength like a wild ox.

23 "For *there is* no sorcery against Jacob,
Nor any divination against Israel.
It now must be said of Jacob
And of Israel, 'Oh, what God has done!'
24 Look, a people rises like a lioness,
And lifts itself up like a lion;
It shall not lie down until it devours the prey,
And drinks the blood of the slain."

25 Then Balak said to Balaam, "Neither curse
them at all, nor bless them at all!"
26 So Balaam answered and said to Balak,
"Did I not tell you, saying, 'All that the LORD
speaks, that I must do'?"

Balaam's Third Prophecy

27 Then Balak said to Balaam, "Please come,
I will take you to another place; perhaps it will
please God that you may curse them for me
from there."
28 So Balak took Balaam to the top of Peor,
that overlooks the wasteland.[a]
29 Then Balaam said to Balak, "Build for me
here seven altars, and prepare for me here
seven bulls and seven rams."
30 And Balak did as Balaam had said, and
offered a bull and a ram on *every* altar.

24 Now when Balaam saw that it pleased
the LORD to bless Israel, he did not go
as at other times, to seek to use sorcery, but he
set his face toward the wilderness.
2 And Balaam raised his eyes, and saw Is-
rael encamped according to their tribes; and
the Spirit of God came upon him.
3 Then he took up his oracle and said:

"The utterance of Balaam the son of Beor,
The utterance of the man whose eyes are opened,
4 The utterance of him who hears the words of God,
Who sees the vision of the Almighty,
Who falls down, with eyes wide open:

5 "How lovely are your tents, O Jacob!
Your dwellings, O Israel!
6 Like valleys that stretch out,
Like gardens by the riverside,
Like aloes planted by the LORD,
Like cedars beside the waters.
7 He shall pour water from his buckets,
And his seed *shall be* in many waters.

"His king shall be higher than Agag,
And his kingdom shall be exalted.

8 "God brings him out of Egypt;
He has strength like a wild ox;
He shall consume the nations, his enemies;
He shall break their bones
And pierce *them* with his arrows.
9 'He bows down, he lies down as a lion;
And as a lion, who shall rouse him?'[a]

"Blessed *is* he who blesses you,
And cursed *is* he who curses you."

10 Then Balak's anger was aroused against
Balaam, and he struck his hands together; and
Balak said to Balaam, "I called you to curse
my enemies, and look, you have bountifully
blessed *them* these three times!
11 "Now therefore, flee to your place. I said I
would greatly honor you, but in fact, the LORD
has kept you back from honor."
12 So Balaam said to Balak, "Did I not also
speak to your messengers whom you sent to
me, saying,
13 'If Balak were to give me his house full of
silver and gold, I could not go beyond the word
of the LORD, to do good or bad of my own will.
What the LORD says, that I must speak'?
14 "And now, indeed, I am going to my peo-
ple. Come, I will advise you what this people
will do to your people in the latter days."

Balaam's Fourth Prophecy

15 So he took up his oracle and said:

"The utterance of Balaam the son of Beor,
And the utterance of the man whose eyes are opened;
16 The utterance of him who hears the words of God,
And has the knowledge of the Most High,
Who sees the vision of the Almighty,
Who falls down, with eyes wide open:

17 "I see Him, but not now;
I behold Him, but not near;
A Star shall come out of Jacob;
A Scepter shall rise out of Israel,
And batter the brow of Moab,
And destroy all the sons of tumult.[a]

18 "And Edom shall be a possession;
Seir also, his enemies, shall be a possession,
While Israel does valiantly.
19 Out of Jacob One shall have dominion,
And destroy the remains of the city."

20 Then he looked on Amalek, and he took
up his oracle and said:

"Amalek *was* first among the nations,
But *shall be* last until he perishes."

21 Then he looked on the Kenites, and he took
up his oracle and said:

23:15 [a]Following Masoretic Text, Targum, and Vulgate; Syriac reads *call;* Septuagint reads *go and ask God.* **23:28** [a]Hebrew *Jeshimon* **24:9** [a]Genesis 49:9 **24:17** [a]Hebrew *Sheth* (compare Jeremiah 48:45)

"Firm is your dwelling place,
And your nest is set in the rock;
22 Nevertheless Kain shall be burned.
How long until Asshur carries you away
captive?"

23 Then he took up his oracle and said:

"Alas! Who shall live when God does this?
24 But ships *shall come* from the coasts of
Cyprus,[a]
And they shall afflict Asshur and afflict
Eber,
And so shall *Amalek*,[b] until he perishes."

25 So Balaam rose and departed and returned
to his place; Balak also went his way.

Israel's Harlotry in Moab

25 Now Israel remained in Acacia Grove,[a]
and the people began to commit har-
lotry with the women of Moab.
2 They invited the people to the sacrifices of
their gods, and the people ate and bowed down
to their gods.
3 So Israel was joined to Baal of Peor, and the
anger of the LORD was aroused against Israel.
4 Then the LORD said to Moses, "Take all the
leaders of the people and hang the offenders
before the LORD, out in the sun, that the fierce
anger of the LORD may turn away from Israel."
5 So Moses said to the judges of Israel,
"Every one of you kill his men who were joined
to Baal of Peor."
6 And indeed, one of the children of Israel
came and presented to his brethren a Midian-
ite woman in the sight of Moses and in the
sight of all the congregation of the children of
Israel, who *were* weeping at the door of the
tabernacle of meeting.
7 Now when Phinehas the son of Eleazar,
the son of Aaron the priest, saw *it*, he rose from
among the congregation and took a javelin in
his hand;
8 and he went after the man of Israel into
the tent and thrust both of them through, the
man of Israel, and the woman through her
body. So the plague was stopped among the
children of Israel.
9 And those who died in the plague were
twenty-four thousand.
10 Then the LORD spoke to Moses, saying:
11 "Phinehas the son of Eleazar, the son of
Aaron the priest, has turned back My wrath from
the children of Israel, because he was zealous
with My zeal among them, so that I did not
consume the children of Israel in My zeal.
12 "Therefore say, 'Behold, I give to him My
covenant of peace;
13 'and it shall be to him and his descendants
after him a covenant of an everlasting priest-
hood, because he was zealous for his God, and
made atonement for the children of Israel.'"
14 Now the name of the Israelite who was
killed, who was killed with the Midianite
woman, *was* Zimri the son of Salu, a leader of
a father's house among the Simeonites.
15 And the name of the Midianite woman
who was killed *was* Cozbi the daughter of Zur;
he *was* head of the people of a father's house
in Midian.
16 Then the LORD spoke to Moses, saying:
17 "Harass the Midianites, and attack them;
18 "for they harassed you with their schemes
by which they seduced you in the matter of
Peor and in the matter of Cozbi, the daughter
of a leader of Midian, their sister, who was
killed in the day of the plague because of Peor."

The Second Census of Israel

26 And it came to pass, after the plague,
that the LORD spoke to Moses and Elea-
zar the son of Aaron the priest, saying:
2 "Take a census of all the congregation of
the children of Israel from twenty years old
and above, by their fathers' houses, all who
are able to go to war in Israel."
3 So Moses and Eleazar the priest spoke
with them in the plains of Moab by the Jordan,
across from Jericho, saying:
4 "*Take a census of the people* from twenty
years old and above, just as the LORD com-
manded Moses and the children of Israel who
came out of the land of Egypt."
5 Reuben *was* the firstborn of Israel. The
children of Reuben *were: of* Hanoch, the fam-
ily of the Hanochites; *of* Pallu, the family of the
Palluites;
6 *of* Hezron, the family of the Hezronites; *of*
Carmi, the family of the Carmites.
7 These *are* the families of the Reubenites:
those who were numbered of them were forty-
three thousand seven hundred and thirty.
8 And the son of Pallu *was* Eliab.
9 The sons of Eliab *were* Nemuel, Dathan,
and Abiram. These *are* the Dathan and Abi-
ram, representatives of the congregation, who
contended against Moses and Aaron in the
company of Korah, when they contended
against the LORD;
10 and the earth opened its mouth and swal-
lowed them up together with Korah when that
company died, when the fire devoured two hun-
dred and fifty men; and they became a sign.
11 Nevertheless the children of Korah did not
die.
12 The sons of Simeon according to their fam-
ilies *were: of* Nemuel,[a] the family of the Nemu-
elites; *of* Jamin, the family of the Jaminites; *of*
Jachin,[b] the family of the Jachinites;
13 *of* Zerah,[a] the family of the Zarhites; *of*
Shaul, the family of the Shaulites.
14 These *are* the families of the Simeonites:
twenty-two thousand two hundred.
15 The sons of Gad according to their families
were: of Zephon,[a] the family of the Zephonites;
of Haggi, the family of the Haggites; *of* Shuni,
the family of the Shunites;
16 *of* Ozni,[a] the family of the Oznites; *of* Eri,
the family of the Erites;
17 *of* Arod,[a] the family of the Arodites; *of*
Areli, the family of the Arelites.
18 These *are* the families of the sons of Gad
according to those who were numbered of
them: forty thousand five hundred.
19 The sons of Judah *were* Er and Onan; and
Er and Onan died in the land of Canaan.
20 And the sons of Judah according to their
families were: *of* Shelah, the family of the She-
lanites; *of* Perez, the family of the Parzites; *of*
Zerah, the family of the Zarhites.

24:24 [a]Hebrew *Kittim* [b]Literally *he* or *that one* **25:1** [a]Hebrew *Shittim* **26:12** [a]Spelled *Jemuel* in Genesis 46:10 and Exodus 6:15 [b]Called *Jarib* in 1 Chronicles 4:24 **26:13** [a]Called *Zohar* in Genesis 46:10 **26:15** [a]Called *Ziphion* in Genesis 46:16 **26:16** [a]Called *Ezbon* in Genesis 46:16 **26:17** [a]Spelled *Arodi* in Samaritan Pentateuch, Syriac, and Genesis 46:16

21 And the sons of Perez were: *of* Hezron, the family of the Hezronites; *of* Hamul, the family of the Hamulites.

22 These *are* the families of Judah according to those who were numbered of them: seventy-six thousand five hundred.

23 The sons of Issachar according to their families *were: of* Tola, the family of the Tolaites; of Puah,[a] the family of the Punites;[b]

24 of Jashub, the family of the Jashubites; of Shimron, the family of the Shimronites.

25 These *are* the families of Issachar according to those who were numbered of them: sixty-four thousand three hundred.

26 The sons of Zebulun according to their families *were:* of Sered, the family of the Sardites; of Elon, the family of the Elonites; of Jahleel, the family of the Jahleelites.

27 These *are* the families of the Zebulunites according to those who were numbered of them: sixty thousand five hundred.

28 The sons of Joseph according to their families, by Manasseh and Ephraim, *were:*

29 The sons of Manasseh: of Machir, the family of the Machirites; and Machir begot Gilead; of Gilead, the family of the Gileadites.

30 These *are* the sons of Gilead: *of* Jeezer,[a] the family of the Jeezerites; of Helek, the family of the Helekites;

31 *of* Asriel, the family of the Asrielites; *of* Shechem, the family of the Shechemites;

32 *of* Shemida, the family of the Shemidaites; *of* Hepher, the family of the Hepherites.

33 Now Zelophehad the son of Hepher had no sons, but daughters; and the names of the daughters of Zelophehad *were* Mahlah, Noah, Hoglah, Milcah, and Tirzah.

34 These *are* the families of Manasseh; and those who were numbered of them *were* fifty-two thousand seven hundred.

35 These *are* the sons of Ephraim according to their families: of Shuthelah, the family of the Shuthalhites; of Becher,[a] the family of the Bachrites; of Tahan, the family of the Tahanites.

36 And these *are* the sons of Shuthelah: of Eran, the family of the Eranites.

37 These *are* the families of the sons of Ephraim according to those who were numbered of them: thirty-two thousand five hundred. These *are* the sons of Joseph according to their families.

38 The sons of Benjamin according to their families were: of Bela, the family of the Belaites; of Ashbel, the family of the Ashbelites; of Ahiram, the family of the Ahiramites;

39 of Shupham,[a] the family of the Shuphamites; of Hupham,[b] the family of the Huphamites.

40 And the sons of Bela were Ard[a] and Naaman: *of Ard,* the family of the Ardites; of Naaman, the family of the Naamites.

41 These *are* the sons of Benjamin according to their families; and those who were numbered of them *were* forty-five thousand six hundred.

42 These *are* the sons of Dan according to their families: of Shuham,[a] the family of the Shuhamites. These *are* the families of Dan according to their families.

43 All the families of the Shuhamites, according to those who were numbered of them, *were* sixty-four thousand four hundred.

44 The sons of Asher according to their families *were:* of Jimna, the family of the Jimnites; of Jesui, the family of the Jesuites; of Beriah, the family of the Beriites.

45 Of the sons of Beriah: of Heber, the family of the Heberites; of Malchiel, the family of the Malchielites.

46 And the name of the daughter of Asher *was* Serah.

47 These *are* the families of the sons of Asher according to those who were numbered of them: fifty-three thousand four hundred.

48 The sons of Naphtali according to their families *were:* of Jahzeel,[a] the family of the Jahzeelites; of Guni, the family of the Gunites;

49 of Jezer, the family of the Jezerites; of Shillem, the family of the Shillemites.

50 These *are* the families of Naphtali according to their families; and those who were numbered of them *were* forty-five thousand four hundred.

51 These *are* those who were numbered of the children of Israel: six hundred and one thousand seven hundred and thirty.

52 Then the LORD spoke to Moses, saying:

53 "To these the land shall be divided as an inheritance, according to the number of names.

54 "To a large *tribe* you shall give a larger inheritance, and to a small *tribe* you shall give a smaller inheritance. Each shall be given its inheritance according to those who were numbered of them.

55 "But the land shall be divided by lot; they shall inherit according to the names of the tribes of their fathers.

56 "According to the lot their inheritance shall be divided between the larger and the smaller."

57 And these *are* those who were numbered of the Levites according to their families: of Gershon, the family of the Gershonites; of Kohath, the family of the Kohathites; of Merari, the family of the Merarites.

58 These *are* the families of the Levites: the family of the Libnites, the family of the Hebronites, the family of the Mahlites, the family of the Mushites, and the family of the Korathites. And Kohath begot Amram.

59 The name of Amram's wife *was* Jochebed the daughter of Levi, who was born to Levi in Egypt; and to Amram she bore Aaron and Moses and their sister Miriam.

60 To Aaron were born Nadab and Abihu, Eleazar and Ithamar.

61 And Nadab and Abihu died when they offered profane fire before the LORD.

62 Now those who were numbered of them were twenty-three thousand, every male from a month old and above; for they were not numbered among the other children of Israel, because there was no inheritance given to them among the children of Israel.

63 These *are* those who were numbered by Moses and Eleazar the priest, who numbered the children of Israel in the plains of Moab by the Jordan, *across from* Jericho.

64 But among these there was not a man of those who were numbered by Moses and

26:23 [a]Hebrew *Puvah* (compare Genesis 46:13 and 1 Chronicles 7:1); Samaritan Pentateuch, Septuagint, Syriac, and Vulgate read *Puah.* [b]Samaritan Pentateuch, Septuagint, Syriac, and Vulgate read *Puaites.* **26:30** [a]Called *Abiezer* in Joshua 17:2 **26:35** [a]Called *Bered* in 1 Chronicles 7:20 **26:39** [a]Masoretic Text reads *Shephupham,* spelled *Shephuphan* in 1 Chronicles 8:5. [b]Called *Huppim* in Genesis 46:21 **26:40** [a]Called *Addar* in 1 Chronicles 8:3 **26:42** [a]Called *Hushim* in Genesis 46:23 **26:48** [a]Spelled *Jahziel* in 1 Chronicles 7:13

Aaron the priest when they numbered the chil-
dren of Israel in the Wilderness of Sinai.
65 For the LORD had said of them, "They shall
surely die in the wilderness." So there was not
left a man of them, except Caleb the son of
Jephunneh and Joshua the son of Nun.

Inheritance Laws

27 Then came the daughters of Zelophehad
the son of Hepher, the son of Gilead, the
son of Machir, the son of Manasseh, from the
families of Manasseh the son of Joseph; and
these *were* the names of his daughters: Mah-
lah, Noah, Hoglah, Milcah, and Tirzah.
2 And they stood before Moses, before Elea-
zar the priest, and before the leaders and all
the congregation, *by* the doorway of the taber-
nacle of meeting, saying:
3 "Our father died in the wilderness; but he
was not in the company of those who gathered
together against the LORD, in company with
Korah, but he died in his own sin; and he had
no sons.
4 "Why should the name of our father be
removed from among his family because he
had no son? Give us a possession among our
father's brothers."
5 So Moses brought their case before the
LORD.
6 And the LORD spoke to Moses, saying:
7 "The daughters of Zelophehad speak *what*
is right; you shall surely give them a posses-
sion of inheritance among their father's
brothers, and cause the inheritance of their
father to pass to them.
8 "And you shall speak to the children of Is-
rael, saying: 'If a man dies and has no son, then
you shall cause his inheritance to pass to his
daughter.
9 'If he has no daughter, then you shall give
his inheritance to his brothers.
10 'If he has no brothers, then you shall give
his inheritance to his father's brothers.
11 'And if his father has no brothers, then you
shall give his inheritance to the relative closest
to him in his family, and he shall possess it.'"
And it shall be to the children of Israel a statute
of judgment, just as the LORD commanded
Moses.

Joshua the Next Leader of Israel

12 Now the LORD said to Moses: "Go up into
this Mount Abarim, and see the land which I
have given to the children of Israel.
13 "And when you have seen it, you also shall
be gathered to your people, as Aaron your
brother was gathered.
14 "For in the Wilderness of Zin, during the
strife of the congregation, you rebelled against
My command to hallow Me at the waters be-
fore their eyes." (These *are* the waters of Meri-
bah, at Kadesh in the Wilderness of Zin.)
15 Then Moses spoke to the LORD, saying:
16 "Let the LORD, the God of the spirits of all
flesh, set a man over the congregation,
17 "who may go out before them and go in
before them, who may lead them out and bring
them in, that the congregation of the LORD
may not be like sheep which have no shepherd."
18 And the LORD said to Moses: "Take Joshua
the son of Nun with you, a man in whom *is* the
Spirit, and lay your hand on him;
19 "set him before Eleazar the priest and be-
fore all the congregation, and inaugurate him
in their sight.
20 "And you shall give *some* of your authority
to him, that all the congregation of the children
of Israel may be obedient.
21 "He shall stand before Eleazar the priest,
who shall inquire before the LORD for him by
the judgment of the Urim. At his word they
shall go out, and at his word they shall come
in, he and all the children of Israel with him—
all the congregation."
22 So Moses did as the LORD commanded
him. He took Joshua and set him before Elea-
zar the priest and before all the congregation.
23 And he laid his hands on him and inaugu-
rated him, just as the LORD commanded by the
hand of Moses.

Daily Offerings

28 Now the LORD spoke to Moses, saying,
2 "Command the children of Israel,
and say to them, 'My offering, My food for My
offerings made by fire as a sweet aroma to
Me, you shall be careful to offer to Me at their
appointed time.'
3 "And you shall say to them, 'This *is* the
offering made by fire which you shall offer to
the LORD: two male lambs in their first year
without blemish, day by day, as a regular burnt
offering.
4 'The one lamb you shall offer in the morn-
ing, the other lamb you shall offer in the evening,
5 'and one-tenth of an ephah of fine flour as
a grain offering mixed with one-fourth of a hin
of pressed oil.
6 '*It is* a regular burnt offering which was
ordained at Mount Sinai for a sweet aroma, an
offering made by fire to the LORD.
7 'And its drink offering *shall be* one-fourth
of a hin for each lamb; in a holy *place* you shall
pour out the drink to the LORD as an offering.
8 'The other lamb you shall offer in the eve-
ning; as the morning grain offering and its
drink offering, you shall offer *it* as an offering
made by fire, a sweet aroma to the LORD.

Sabbath Offerings

9 'And on the Sabbath day two lambs in their
first year, without blemish, and two-tenths *of an*
ephah of fine flour as a grain offering, mixed
with oil, with its drink offering—
10 '*this is* the burnt offering for every Sabbath,
besides the regular burnt offering with its
drink offering.

Monthly Offerings

11 'At the beginnings of your months you
shall present a burnt offering to the LORD: two
young bulls, one ram, and seven lambs in their
first year, without blemish;
12 'three-tenths *of an ephah* of fine flour as a
grain offering, mixed with oil, for each bull; two-
tenths *of an ephah* of fine flour as a grain offer-
ing, mixed with oil, for the one ram;
13 'and one-tenth *of an ephah* of fine flour,
mixed with oil, as a grain offering for each
lamb, as a burnt offering of sweet aroma, an
offering made by fire to the LORD.
14 'Their drink offering shall be half a hin of
wine for a bull, one-third of a hin for a ram,
and one-fourth of a hin for a lamb; this *is* the
burnt offering for each month throughout the
months of the year.
15 'Also one kid of the goats as a sin offering
to the LORD shall be offered, besides the regu-
lar burnt offering and its drink offering.

Offerings at Passover

16 'On the fourteenth day of the first month *is* the Passover of the LORD.

17 'And on the fifteenth day of this month *is* the feast; unleavened bread shall be eaten for seven days.

18 'On the first day *you shall have* a holy convocation. You shall do no customary work.

19 'And you shall present an offering made by fire as a burnt offering to the LORD: two young bulls, one ram, and seven lambs in their first year. Be sure they are without blemish.

20 'Their grain offering shall be of fine flour mixed with oil: three-tenths *of an ephah* you shall offer for a bull, and two-tenths for a ram;

21 'you shall offer one-tenth *of an ephah* for each of the seven lambs;

22 'also one goat *as* a sin offering, to make atonement for you.

23 'You shall offer these besides the burnt offering of the morning, which *is* for a regular burnt offering.

24 'In this manner you shall offer the food of the offering made by fire daily for seven days, as a sweet aroma to the LORD; it shall be offered besides the regular burnt offering and its drink offering.

25 'And on the seventh day you shall have a holy convocation. You shall do no customary work.

Offerings at the Feast of Weeks

26 'Also on the day of the firstfruits, when you bring a new grain offering to the LORD at your *Feast of* Weeks, you shall have a holy convocation. You shall do no customary work.

27 'You shall present a burnt offering as a sweet aroma to the LORD: two young bulls, one ram, and seven lambs in their first year,

28 'with their grain offering of fine flour mixed with oil: three-tenths *of an ephah* for each bull, two-tenths for the one ram,

29 'and one-tenth for each of the seven lambs;

30 '*also* one kid of the goats, to make atonement for you.

31 'Be sure they are without blemish. You shall present *them* with their drink offerings, besides the regular burnt offering with its grain offering.

Offerings at the Feast of Trumpets

29 'And in the seventh month, on the first *day* of the month, you shall have a holy convocation. You shall do no customary work. For you it is a day of blowing the trumpets.

2 'You shall offer a burnt offering as a sweet aroma to the LORD: one young bull, one ram, *and* seven lambs in their first year, without blemish.

3 'Their grain offering *shall be* fine flour mixed with oil: three-tenths *of an ephah* for the bull, two-tenths for the ram,

4 'and one-tenth for each of the seven lambs;

5 'also one kid of the goats *as* a sin offering, to make atonement for you;

6 'besides the burnt offering with its grain offering for the New Moon, the regular burnt offering with its grain offering, and their drink offerings, according to their ordinance, as a sweet aroma, an offering made by fire to the LORD.

Offerings on the Day of Atonement

7 'On the tenth *day* of this seventh month you shall have a holy convocation. You shall afflict your souls; you shall not do any work.

8 'You shall present a burnt offering to the LORD *as* a sweet aroma: one young bull, one ram, *and* seven lambs in their first year. Be sure they are without blemish.

9 'Their grain offering *shall be of* fine flour mixed with oil: three-tenths *of an ephah* for the bull, two-tenths for the one ram,

10 'and one-tenth for each of the seven lambs;

11 'also one kid of the goats *as* a sin offering, besides the sin offering for atonement, the regular burnt offering with its grain offering, and their drink offerings.

Offerings at the Feast of Tabernacles

12 'On the fifteenth day of the seventh month you shall have a holy convocation. You shall do no customary work, and you shall keep a feast to the LORD seven days.

13 'You shall present a burnt offering, an offering made by fire as a sweet aroma to the LORD: thirteen young bulls, two rams, *and* fourteen lambs in their first year. They shall be without blemish.

14 'Their grain offering *shall be of* fine flour mixed with oil: three-tenths *of an ephah* for each of the thirteen bulls, two-tenths for each of the two rams,

15 'and one-tenth for each of the fourteen lambs;

16 'also one kid of the goats *as* a sin offering, besides the regular burnt offering, its grain offering, and its drink offering.

17 'On the second day *present* twelve young bulls, two rams, fourteen lambs in their first year without blemish,

18 'and their grain offering and their drink offerings for the bulls, for the rams, and for the lambs, by their number, according to the ordinance;

19 'also one kid of the goats *as* a sin offering, besides the regular burnt offering with its grain offering, and their drink offerings.

20 'On the third day *present* eleven bulls, two rams, fourteen lambs in their first year without blemish,

21 'and their grain offering and their drink offerings for the bulls, for the rams, and for the lambs, by their number, according to the ordinance;

22 'also one goat *as* a sin offering, besides the regular burnt offering, its grain offering, and its drink offering.

23 'On the fourth day *present* ten bulls, two rams, *and* fourteen lambs in their first year, without blemish,

24 'and their grain offering and their drink offerings for the bulls, for the rams, and for the lambs, by their number, according to the ordinance;

25 'also one kid of the goats *as* a sin offering, besides the regular burnt offering, its grain offering, and its drink offering.

26 'On the fifth day *present* nine bulls, two rams, *and* fourteen lambs in their first year without blemish,

27 'and their grain offering and their drink offerings for the bulls, for the rams, and for the lambs, by their number, according to the ordinance;

28 'also one goat *as* a sin offering, besides the

regular burnt offering, its grain offering, and
its drink offering.
29 'On the sixth day *present* eight bulls, two
rams, *and* fourteen lambs in their first year
without blemish,
30 'and their grain offering and their drink
offerings for the bulls, for the rams, and for
the lambs, by their number, according to the
ordinance;
31 'also one goat *as* a sin offering, besides the
regular burnt offering, its grain offering, and
its drink offering.
32 'On the seventh day *present* seven bulls,
two rams, *and* fourteen lambs in their first year
without blemish,
33 'and their grain offering and their drink
offerings for the bulls, for the rams, and for
the lambs, by their number, according to the
ordinance;
34 'also one goat *as* a sin offering, besides the
regular burnt offering, its grain offering, and
its drink offering.
35 'On the eighth day you shall have a sacred
assembly. You shall do no customary work.
36 'You shall present a burnt offering, an offering
made by fire as a sweet aroma to the
LORD: one bull, one ram, seven lambs in their
first year without blemish,
37 'and their grain offering and their drink
offerings for the bull, for the ram, and for the
lambs, by their number, according to the ordinance;
38 'also one goat *as* a sin offering, besides the
regular burnt offering, its grain offering, and
its drink offering.
39 'These you shall present to the LORD at your
appointed feasts (besides your vowed offerings
and your freewill offerings) as your burnt offerings
and your grain offerings, as your drink
offerings and your peace offerings.'"
40 So Moses told the children of Israel everything,
just as the LORD commanded Moses.

The Law Concerning Vows

30 Then Moses spoke to the heads of the
tribes concerning the children of Israel,
saying, "This *is* the thing which the LORD has
commanded:
2 "If a man makes a vow to the LORD, or
swears an oath to bind himself by some agreement,
he shall not break his word; he shall do
according to all that proceeds out of his mouth.
3 "Or if a woman makes a vow to the LORD,
and binds *herself* by some agreement while in
her father's house in her youth,
4 "and her father hears her vow and the
agreement by which she has bound herself,
and her father holds his peace, then all her
vows shall stand, and every agreement with
which she has bound herself shall stand.
5 "But if her father overrules her on the day
that he hears, then none of her vows nor her
agreements by which she has bound herself
shall stand; and the LORD will release her, because
her father overruled her.
6 "If indeed she takes a husband, while
bound by her vows or by a rash utterance from
her lips by which she bound herself,
7 "and her husband hears *it*, and makes no
response to her on the day that he hears, then
her vows shall stand, and her agreements by
which she bound herself shall stand.
8 "But if her husband overrules her on the
day that he hears *it*, he shall make void her
vow which she took and what she uttered with
her lips, by which she bound herself, and the
LORD will release her.
9 "Also any vow of a widow or a divorced
woman, by which she has bound herself, shall
stand against her.
10 "If she vowed in her husband's house, or
bound herself by an agreement with an oath,
11 "and her husband heard *it*, and made no
response to her *and* did not overrule her, then
all her vows shall stand, and every agreement
by which she bound herself shall stand.
12 "But if her husband truly made them void
on the day he heard *them*, then whatever proceeded
from her lips concerning her vows or
concerning the agreement binding her, it shall
not stand; her husband has made them void,
and the LORD will release her.
13 "Every vow and every binding oath to afflict
her soul, her husband may confirm it, or
her husband may make it void.
14 "Now if her husband makes no response
whatever to her from day to day, then he confirms
all her vows or all the agreements that
bind her; he confirms them, because he made
no response to her on the day that he heard
them.
15 "But if he does make them void after he
has heard *them*, then he shall bear her guilt."
16 These *are* the statutes which the LORD
commanded Moses, between a man and his
wife, and between a father and his daughter in
her youth in her father's house.

Vengeance on the Midianites

31 And the LORD spoke to Moses, saying:
2 "Take vengeance on the Midianites
for the children of Israel. Afterward you shall
be gathered to your people."
3 So Moses spoke to the people, saying,
"Arm some of yourselves for war, and let them
go against the Midianites to take vengeance
for the LORD on Midian.
4 "A thousand from each tribe of all the
tribes of Israel you shall send to the war."
5 So there were recruited from the divisions
of Israel one thousand from *each* tribe, twelve
thousand armed for war.
6 Then Moses sent them to the war, one
thousand from *each* tribe; he sent them to the
war with Phinehas the son of Eleazar the
priest, with the holy articles and the signal
trumpets in his hand.
7 And they warred against the Midianites,
just as the LORD commanded Moses, and they
killed all the males.
8 They killed the kings of Midian with *the
rest of* those who were killed—Evi, Rekem,
Zur, Hur, and Reba, the five kings of Midian.
Balaam the son of Beor they also killed with
the sword.
9 And the children of Israel took the women
of Midian captive, with their little ones, and
took as spoil all their cattle, all their flocks,
and all their goods.
10 They also burned with fire all the cities
where they dwelt, and all their forts.
11 And they took all the spoil and all the
booty—of man and beast.

Return from the War

12 Then they brought the captives, the booty,
and the spoil to Moses, to Eleazar the priest,
and to the congregation of the children of Israel,
to the camp in the plains of Moab by the
Jordan, *across from* Jericho.

13 And Moses, Eleazar the priest, and all the
leaders of the congregation, went to meet them
outside the camp.
14 But Moses was angry with the officers of
the army, *with* the captains over thousands and
captains over hundreds, who had come from
the battle.
15 And Moses said to them: "Have you kept
all the women alive?
16 "Look, these *women* caused the children
of Israel, through the counsel of Balaam, to
trespass against the LORD in the incident of
Peor, and there was a plague among the con-
gregation of the LORD.
17 "Now therefore, kill every male among the
little ones, and kill every woman who has
known a man intimately.
18 "But keep alive for yourselves all the young
girls who have not known a man intimately.
19 "And as for you, remain outside the camp
seven days; whoever has killed any person,
and whoever has touched any slain, purify
yourselves and your captives on the third day
and on the seventh day.
20 "Purify every garment, everything made
of leather, everything woven of goats' *hair*, and
everything made of wood."
21 Then Eleazar the priest said to the men of
war who had gone to the battle, "This *is* the
ordinance of the law which the LORD com-
manded Moses:
22 "Only the gold, the silver, the bronze, the
iron, the tin, and the lead,
23 "everything that can endure fire, you shall
put through the fire, and it shall be clean; and it
shall be purified with the water of purification.
But all that cannot endure fire you shall put
through water.
24 "And you shall wash your clothes on the
seventh day and be clean, and afterward you
may come into the camp."

Division of the Plunder

25 Now the LORD spoke to Moses, saying:
26 "Count up the plunder that was taken—of
man and beast—you and Eleazar the priest and
the chief fathers of the congregation;
27 "and divide the plunder into two parts, be-
tween those who took part in the war, who
went out to battle, and all the congregation.
28 "And levy a tribute for the LORD on the
men of war who went out to battle: one of every
five hundred of the persons, the cattle, the don-
keys, and the sheep;
29 "take *it* from their half, and give *it* to Elea-
zar the priest as a heave offering to the LORD.
30 "And from the children of Israel's half you
shall take one of every fifty, drawn from the
persons, the cattle, the donkeys, and the sheep,
from all the livestock, and give them to the
Levites who keep charge of the tabernacle of
the LORD."
31 So Moses and Eleazar the priest did as the
LORD commanded Moses.
32 The booty remaining from the plunder,
which the men of war had taken, was six hun-
dred and seventy-five thousand sheep,
33 seventy-two thousand cattle,
34 sixty-one thousand donkeys,
35 and thirty-two thousand persons in all, of
women who had not known a man intimately.
36 And the half, the portion for those who
had gone out to war, was in number three hun-
dred and thirty-seven thousand five hundred
sheep;
37 and the LORD's tribute of the sheep was six
hundred and seventy-five.
38 The cattle *were* thirty-six thousand, of
which the LORD's tribute *was* seventy-two.
39 The donkeys *were* thirty thousand five
hundred, of which the LORD's tribute *was*
sixty-one.
40 The persons *were* sixteen thousand, of
which the LORD's tribute *was* thirty-two per-
sons.
41 So Moses gave the tribute *which was* the
LORD's heave offering to Eleazar the priest, as
the LORD commanded Moses.
42 And from the children of Israel's half, which
Moses separated from the men who fought—
43 now the half belonging to the congrega-
tion was three hundred and thirty-seven thou-
sand five hundred sheep,
44 thirty-six thousand cattle,
45 thirty thousand five hundred donkeys,
46 and sixteen thousand persons—
47 and from the children of Israel's half Mo-
ses took one of every fifty, drawn from man
and beast, and gave them to the Levites, who
kept charge of the tabernacle of the LORD, as
the LORD commanded Moses.
48 Then the officers who *were* over thou-
sands of the army, the captains of thousands
and captains of hundreds, came near to Moses;
49 and they said to Moses, "Your servants
have taken a count of the men of war who *are*
under our command, and not a man of us is
missing.
50 "Therefore we have brought an offering
for the LORD, what every man found of orna-
ments of gold: armlets and bracelets and signet
rings and earrings and necklaces, to make
atonement for ourselves before the LORD."
51 So Moses and Eleazar the priest received
the gold from them, all the fashioned ornaments.
52 And all the gold of the offering that they
offered to the LORD, from the captains of thou-
sands and captains of hundreds, was sixteen
thousand seven hundred and fifty shekels.
53 (The men of war had taken spoil, every
man for himself.)
54 And Moses and Eleazar the priest received
the gold from the captains of thousands and of
hundreds, and brought it into the tabernacle
of meeting as a memorial for the children of
Israel before the LORD.

The Tribes Settling East of the Jordan

32 Now the children of Reuben and the
children of Gad had a very great multi-
tude of livestock; and when they saw the land
of Jazer and the land of Gilead, that indeed the
region *was* a place for livestock,
2 the children of Gad and the children of
Reuben came and spoke to Moses, to Eleazar
the priest, and to the leaders of the congrega-
tion, saying,
3 "Ataroth, Dibon, Jazer, Nimrah, Heshbon,
Elealeh, Shebam, Nebo, and Beon,
4 "the country which the LORD defeated be-
fore the congregation of Israel, *is* a land for
livestock, and your servants have livestock."
5 Therefore they said, "If we have found fa-
vor in your sight, let this land be given to your
servants as a possession. Do not take us over
the Jordan."
6 And Moses said to the children of Gad and
to the children of Reuben: "Shall your brethren
go to war while you sit here?
7 "Now why will you discourage the heart

of the children of Israel from going over into
the land which the LORD has given them?
8 "Thus your fathers did when I sent them
away from Kadesh Barnea to see the land.
9 "For when they went up to the Valley of
Eshcol and saw the land, they discouraged the
heart of the children of Israel, so that they did
not go into the land which the LORD had given
them.
10 "So the LORD's anger was aroused on that
day, and He swore an oath, saying,
11 'Surely none of the men who came up from
Egypt, from twenty years old and above, shall
see the land of which I swore to Abraham,
Isaac, and Jacob, because they have not wholly
followed Me,
12 'except Caleb the son of Jephunneh, the
Kenizzite, and Joshua the son of Nun, for they
have wholly followed the LORD.'
13 "So the LORD's anger was aroused against
Israel, and He made them wander in the wil-
derness forty years, until all the generation
that had done evil in the sight of the LORD was
gone.
14 "And look! You have risen in your fathers'
place, a brood of sinful men, to increase still
more the fierce anger of the LORD against Is-
rael.
15 "For if you turn away from following Him,
He will once again leave them in the wilderness,
and you will destroy all these people."
16 Then they came near to him and said: "We
will build sheepfolds here for our livestock,
and cities for our little ones,
17 "but we ourselves will be armed, ready *to*
go before the children of Israel until we have
brought them to their place; and our little ones
will dwell in the fortified cities because of the
inhabitants of the land.
18 "We will not return to our homes until
every one of the children of Israel has received
his inheritance.
19 "For we will not inherit with them on the
other side of the Jordan and beyond, because
our inheritance has fallen to us on this eastern
side of the Jordan."
20 Then Moses said to them: "If you do this
thing, if you arm yourselves before the LORD
for the war,
21 "and all your armed men cross over the
Jordan before the LORD until He has driven
out His enemies from before Him,
22 "and the land is subdued before the LORD,
then afterward you may return and be blame-
less before the LORD and before Israel; and
this land shall be your possession before the
LORD.
23 "But if you do not do so, then take note,
you have sinned against the LORD; and be sure
your sin will find you out.
24 "Build cities for your little ones and folds
for your sheep, and do what has proceeded out
of your mouth."
25 And the children of Gad and the children
of Reuben spoke to Moses, saying: "Your ser-
vants will do as my lord commands.
26 "Our little ones, our wives, our flocks, and
all our livestock will be there in the cities of
Gilead;
27 "but your servants will cross over, every
man armed for war, before the LORD to battle,
just as my lord says."
28 So Moses gave command concerning them
to Eleazar the priest, to Joshua the son of Nun,
and to the chief fathers of the tribes of the
children of Israel.
29 And Moses said to them: "If the children
of Gad and the children of Reuben cross over
the Jordan with you, every man armed for bat-
tle before the LORD, and the land is subdued
before you, then you shall give them the land
of Gilead as a possession.
30 "But if they do not cross over armed with
you, they shall have possessions among you in
the land of Canaan."
31 Then the children of Gad and the children
of Reuben answered, saying: "As the LORD has
said to your servants, so we will do.
32 "We will cross over armed before the
LORD into the land of Canaan, but the posses-
sion of our inheritance *shall remain* with us on
this side of the Jordan."
33 So Moses gave to the children of Gad, to
the children of Reuben, and to half the tribe of
Manasseh the son of Joseph, the kingdom of
Sihon king of the Amorites and the kingdom
of Og king of Bashan, the land with its cities
within the borders, the cities of the surround-
ing country.
34 And the children of Gad built Dibon and
Ataroth and Aroer,
35 Atroth and Shophan and Jazer and Jog-
behah,
36 Beth Nimrah and Beth Haran, fortified cit-
ies, and folds for sheep.
37 And the children of Reuben built Heshbon
and Elealeh and Kirjathaim,
38 Nebo and Baal Meon (*their* names being
changed) and Shibmah; and they gave *other*
names to the cities which they built.
39 And the children of Machir the son of
Manasseh went to Gilead and took it, and dis-
possessed the Amorites who *were* in it.
40 So Moses gave Gilead to Machir the son of
Manasseh, and he dwelt in it.
41 Also Jair the son of Manasseh went and
took its small towns, and called them Havoth
Jair.[a]
42 Then Nobah went and took Kenath and its
villages, and he called it Nobah, after his own
name.

Israel's Journey from Egypt Reviewed

33 These *are* the journeys of the children
of Israel, who went out of the land of
Egypt by their armies under the hand of Moses
and Aaron.
2 Now Moses wrote down the starting points
of their journeys at the command of the LORD.
And these *are* their journeys according to their
starting points:
3 They departed from Rameses in the first
month, on the fifteenth day of the first month;
on the day after the Passover the children of
Israel went out with boldness in the sight of all
the Egyptians.
4 For the Egyptians were burying all *their*
firstborn, whom the LORD had killed among
them. Also on their gods the LORD had exe-
cuted judgments.
5 Then the children of Israel moved from
Rameses and camped at Succoth.
6 They departed from Succoth and camped
at Etham, which *is* on the edge of the wilderness.
7 They moved from Etham and turned back

32:41 [a]Literally *Towns of Jair*

to Pi Hahiroth, which *is* east of Baal Zephon;
and they camped near Migdol.
8 They departed from before Hahiroth[a] and
passed through the midst of the sea into the
wilderness, went three days' journey in the
Wilderness of Etham, and camped at Marah.
9 They moved from Marah and came to
Elim. At Elim *were* twelve springs of water and
seventy palm trees; so they camped there.
10 They moved from Elim and camped by the
Red Sea.
11 They moved from the Red Sea and camped
in the Wilderness of Sin.
12 They journeyed from the Wilderness of Sin
and camped at Dophkah.
13 They departed from Dophkah and camped
at Alush.
14 They moved from Alush and camped at
Rephidim, where there was no water for the people to drink.
15 They departed from Rephidim and camped
in the Wilderness of Sinai.
16 They moved from the Wilderness of Sinai
and camped at Kibroth Hattaavah.
17 They departed from Kibroth Hattaavah
and camped at Hazeroth.
18 They departed from Hazeroth and camped
at Rithmah.
19 They departed from Rithmah and camped
at Rimmon Perez.
20 They departed from Rimmon Perez and
camped at Libnah.
21 They moved from Libnah and camped at
Rissah.
22 They journeyed from Rissah and camped
at Kehelathah.
23 They went from Kehelathah and camped
at Mount Shepher.
24 They moved from Mount Shepher and
camped at Haradah.
25 They moved from Haradah and camped at
Makheloth.
26 They moved from Makheloth and camped
at Tahath.
27 They departed from Tahath and camped at
Terah.
28 They moved from Terah and camped at Mithkah.
29 They went from Mithkah and camped at
Hashmonah.
30 They departed from Hashmonah and camped
at Moseroth.
31 They departed from Moseroth and camped
at Bene Jaakan.
32 They moved from Bene Jaakan and camped
at Hor Hagidgad.
33 They went from Hor Hagidgad and
camped at Jotbathah.
34 They moved from Jotbathah and camped
at Abronah.
35 They departed from Abronah and camped
at Ezion Geber.
36 They moved from Ezion Geber and camped
in the Wilderness of Zin, which *is* Kadesh.
37 They moved from Kadesh and camped at
Mount Hor, on the boundary of the land of
Edom.
38 Then Aaron the priest went up to Mount
Hor at the command of the LORD, and died
there in the fortieth year after the children of
Israel had come out of the land of Egypt, on
the first *day* of the fifth month.
39 Aaron *was* one hundred and twenty-three
years old when he died on Mount Hor.
40 Now the king of Arad, the Canaanite, who
dwelt in the South in the land of Canaan, heard
of the coming of the children of Israel.
41 So they departed from Mount Hor and
camped at Zalmonah.
42 They departed from Zalmonah and camped
at Punon.
43 They departed from Punon and camped at
Oboth.
44 They departed from Oboth and camped at
Ije Abarim, at the border of Moab.
45 They departed from Ijim[a] and camped at
Dibon Gad.
46 They moved from Dibon Gad and camped
at Almon Diblathaim.
47 They moved from Almon Diblathaim and
camped in the mountains of Abarim, before
Nebo.
48 They departed from the mountains of Abarim and camped in the plains of Moab by the
Jordan, *across from* Jericho.
49 They camped by the Jordan, from Beth
Jesimoth as far as the Abel Acacia Grove[a] in
the plains of Moab.

Instructions for the Conquest of Canaan

50 Now the LORD spoke to Moses in the
plains of Moab by the Jordan, *across from* Jericho, saying,
51 "Speak to the children of Israel, and say
to them: 'When you have crossed the Jordan
into the land of Canaan,
52 'then you shall drive out all the inhabitants
of the land from before you, destroy all their
engraved stones, destroy all their molded images, and demolish all their high places;
53 'you shall dispossess *the inhabitants of* the
land and dwell in it, for I have given you the
land to possess.
54 'And you shall divide the land by lot as an
inheritance among your families; to the larger
you shall give a larger inheritance, and to the
smaller you shall give a smaller inheritance;
there everyone's *inheritance* shall be whatever
falls to him by lot. You shall inherit according
to the tribes of your fathers.
55 'But if you do not drive out the inhabitants
of the land from before you, then it shall be that
those whom you let remain *shall be* irritants in
your eyes and thorns in your sides, and they
shall harass you in the land where you dwell.
56 'Moreover it shall be *that* I will do to you
as I thought to do to them.'"

The Appointed Boundaries of Canaan

34 Then the LORD spoke to Moses, saying,
2 "Command the children of Israel,
and say to them: 'When you come into the land
of Canaan, this *is* the land that shall fall to you
as an inheritance—the land of Canaan to its
boundaries.
3 'Your southern border shall be from the Wilderness of Zin along the border of Edom; then
your southern border shall extend eastward to
the end of the Salt Sea;
4 'your border shall turn from the southern
side of the Ascent of Akrabbim, continue to
Zin, and be on the south of Kadesh Barnea;
then it shall go on to Hazar Addar, and continue to Azmon;

33:8 [a]Many Hebrew manuscripts, Samaritan Pentateuch, Syriac, Targum, and Vulgate read *from Pi Hahiroth* (compare verse 7). **33:45** [a]Same as *Ije Abarim*, verse 44 **33:49** [a]Hebrew *Abel Shittim*

5 'the border shall turn from Azmon to the
Brook of Egypt, and it shall end at the Sea.
6 'As for the western border, you shall have
the Great Sea for a border; this shall be your
western border.
7 'And this shall be your northern border:
From the Great Sea you shall mark out your
border line to Mount Hor;
8 'from Mount Hor you shall mark out *your*
border to the entrance of Hamath; then the
direction of the border shall be toward Zedad;
9 'the border shall proceed to Ziphron, and
it shall end at Hazar Enan. This shall be your
northern border.
10 'You shall mark out your eastern border
from Hazar Enan to Shepham;
11 'the border shall go down from Shepham
to Riblah on the east side of Ain; the border
shall go down and reach to the eastern side of
the Sea of Chinnereth;
12 'the border shall go down along the Jor-
dan, and it shall end at the Salt Sea. This shall
be your land with its surrounding boundaries.' "
13 Then Moses commanded the children of
Israel, saying: "This *is* the land which you shall
inherit by lot, which the LORD has commanded
to give to the nine tribes and to the half-tribe.
14 "For the tribe of the children of Reuben
according to the house of their fathers, and the
tribe of the children of Gad according to the
house of their fathers, have received *their in-*
heritance; and the half-tribe of Manasseh has
received its inheritance.
15 "The two tribes and the half-tribe have re-
ceived their inheritance on this side of the Jor-
dan, *across from* Jericho eastward, toward the
sunrise."

The Leaders Appointed to Divide the Land

16 And the LORD spoke to Moses, saying,
17 "These *are* the names of the men who shall
divide the land among you as an inheritance:
Eleazar the priest and Joshua the son of Nun.
18 "And you shall take one leader of every
tribe to divide the land for the inheritance.
19 "These *are* the names of the men: from the
tribe of Judah, Caleb the son of Jephunneh;
20 "from the tribe of the children of Simeon,
Shemuel the son of Ammihud;
21 "from the tribe of Benjamin, Elidad the
son of Chislon;
22 "a leader from the tribe of the children of
Dan, Bukki the son of Jogli;
23 "from the sons of Joseph: a leader from the
tribe of the children of Manasseh, Hanniel the
son of Ephod,
24 "and a leader from the tribe of the children
of Ephraim, Kemuel the son of Shiphtan;
25 "a leader from the tribe of the children of
Zebulun, Elizaphan the son of Parnach;
26 "a leader from the tribe of the children of
Issachar, Paltiel the son of Azzan;
27 "a leader from the tribe of the children of
Asher, Ahihud the son of Shelomi;
28 "and a leader from the tribe of the children
of Naphtali, Pedahel the son of Ammihud."
29 These *are* the ones the LORD commanded
to divide the inheritance among the children
of Israel in the land of Canaan.

Cities for the Levites

35 And the LORD spoke to Moses in the
plains of Moab by the Jordan *across*
from Jericho, saying:
2 "Command the children of Israel that they
give the Levites cities to dwell in from the in-
heritance of their possession, and you shall
also give the Levites common-land around the
cities.
3 "They shall have the cities to dwell in; and
their common-land shall be for their cattle, for
their herds, and for all their animals.
4 "The common-land of the cities which you
will give the Levites *shall extend* from the wall
of the city outward a thousand cubits all around.
5 "And you shall measure outside the city on
the east side two thousand cubits, on the south
side two thousand cubits, on the west side two
thousand cubits, and on the north side two
thousand cubits. The city *shall be* in the mid-
dle. This shall belong to them as common-land
for the cities.
6 "Now among the cities which you will give
to the Levites *you shall appoint* six cities of
refuge, to which a manslayer may flee. And to
these you shall add forty-two cities.
7 "So all the cities you will give to the Le-
vites *shall be* forty-eight; these *you shall give*
with their common-land.
8 "And the cities which you will give *shall*
be from the possession of the children of Israel;
from the larger *tribe* you shall give many, from
the smaller you shall give few. Each shall give
some of its cities to the Levites, in proportion
to the inheritance that each receives."

Cities of Refuge

9 Then the LORD spoke to Moses, saying,
10 "Speak to the children of Israel, and say
to them: 'When you cross the Jordan into the
land of Canaan,
11 'then you shall appoint cities to be cities of
refuge for you, that the manslayer who kills
any person accidentally may flee there.
12 'They shall be cities of refuge for you from
the avenger, that the manslayer may not die
until he stands before the congregation in
judgment.
13 'And of the cities which you give, you shall
have six cities of refuge.
14 'You shall appoint three cities on this side
of the Jordan, and three cities you shall ap-
point in the land of Canaan, *which* will be cities
of refuge.
15 'These six cities shall be for refuge for the
children of Israel, for the stranger, and for the
sojourner among them, that anyone who kills
a person accidentally may flee there.
16 'But if he strikes him with an iron imple-
ment, so that he dies, he *is* a murderer; the
murderer shall surely be put to death.
17 'And if he strikes him with a stone in the
hand, by which one could die, and he does die,
he *is* a murderer; the murderer shall surely be
put to death.
18 'Or *if* he strikes him with a wooden hand
weapon, by which one could die, and he does
die, he *is* a murderer; the murderer shall surely
be put to death.
19 'The avenger of blood himself shall put the
murderer to death; when he meets him, he
shall put him to death.
20 'If he pushes him out of hatred or, while
lying in wait, hurls something at him so that
he dies,
21 'or in enmity he strikes him with his hand
so that he dies, the one who struck *him* shall
surely be put to death. He *is* a murderer. The
avenger of blood shall put the murderer to
death when he meets him.

22 'However, if he pushes him suddenly with-
out enmity, or throws anything at him without
lying in wait,
23 'or uses a stone, by which a man could die,
throwing *it* at him without seeing *him*, so that
he dies, while he was not his enemy or seeking
his harm,
24 'then the congregation shall judge be-
tween the manslayer and the avenger of blood
according to these judgments.
25 'So the congregation shall deliver the man-
slayer from the hand of the avenger of blood,
and the congregation shall return him to the
city of refuge where he had fled, and he shall
remain there until the death of the high priest
who was anointed with the holy oil.
26 'But if the manslayer at any time goes out-
side the limits of the city of refuge where he fled,
27 'and the avenger of blood finds him out-
side the limits of his city of refuge, and the
avenger of blood kills the manslayer, he shall
not be guilty of blood,
28 'because he should have remained in his
city of refuge until the death of the high priest.
But after the death of the high priest the man-
slayer may return to the land of his possession.
29 'And these *things* shall be a statute of judg-
ment to you throughout your generations in all
your dwellings.
30 'Whoever kills a person, the murderer shall
be put to death on the testimony of witnesses;
but one witness is not *sufficient* testimony
against a person for the death *penalty*.
31 'Moreover you shall take no ransom for
the life of a murderer who *is* guilty of death,
but he shall surely be put to death.
32 'And you shall take no ransom for him who
has fled to his city of refuge, that he may return
to dwell in the land before the death of the priest.
33 'So you shall not pollute the land where
you *are;* for blood defiles the land, and no
atonement can be made for the land, for the
blood that is shed on it, except by the blood of
him who shed it.
34 'Therefore do not defile the land which you
inhabit, in the midst of which I dwell; for I the
LORD dwell among the children of Israel.'"

Marriage of Female Heirs

36 Now the chief fathers of the families of
the children of Gilead the son of Machir,
the son of Manasseh, of the families of the sons
of Joseph, came near and spoke before Moses
and before the leaders, the chief fathers of the
children of Israel.
2 And they said: "The LORD commanded my
lord *Moses* to give the land as an inheritance
by lot to the children of Israel, and my lord was
commanded by the LORD to give the inheritance
of our brother Zelophehad to his daughters.
3 "Now if they are married to any of the sons
of the *other* tribes of the children of Israel,
then their inheritance will be taken from the
inheritance of our fathers, and it will be added
to the inheritance of the tribe into which they
marry; so it will be taken from the lot of our
inheritance.
4 "And when the Jubilee of the children of
Israel comes, then their inheritance will be
added to the inheritance of the tribe into which
they marry; so their inheritance will be taken
away from the inheritance of the tribe of our
fathers."
5 Then Moses commanded the children of
Israel according to the word of the LORD, say-
ing: "What the tribe of the sons of Joseph
speaks is right.
6 "This *is* what the LORD commands con-
cerning the daughters of Zelophehad, saying,
'Let them marry whom they think best, but
they may marry only within the family of their
father's tribe.'
7 "So the inheritance of the children of Is-
rael shall not change hands from tribe to tribe,
for every one of the children of Israel shall
keep the inheritance of the tribe of his fathers.
8 "And every daughter who possesses an in-
heritance in any tribe of the children of Israel
shall be the wife of one of the family of her
father's tribe, so that the children of Israel each
may possess the inheritance of his fathers.
9 "Thus no inheritance shall change hands
from *one* tribe to another, but every tribe of the
children of Israel shall keep its own inheritance."
10 Just as the LORD commanded Moses, so
did the daughters of Zelophehad;
11 for Mahlah, Tirzah, Hoglah, Milcah, and
Noah, the daughters of Zelophehad, were mar-
ried to the sons of their father's brothers.
12 They were married into the families of the
children of Manasseh the son of Joseph, and
their inheritance remained in the tribe of their
father's family.
13 These *are* the commandments and the judg-
ments which the LORD commanded the children
of Israel by the hand of Moses in the plains of
Moab by the Jordan, *across from* Jericho.

The Fifth Book of Moses Called DEUTERONOMY

The Previous Command to Enter Canaan

1 These *are* the words which Moses spoke to
all Israel on this side of the Jordan in the
wilderness, in the plain[a] opposite Suph,[b] between
Paran, Tophel, Laban, Hazeroth, and Dizahab.
2 *It is* eleven days' *journey* from Horeb by
way of Mount Seir to Kadesh Barnea.
3 Now it came to pass in the fortieth year,
in the eleventh month, on the first *day* of the
month, *that* Moses spoke to the children of Is-
rael according to all that the LORD had given
him as commandments to them,
4 after he had killed Sihon king of the Amo-
rites, who dwelt in Heshbon, and Og king of
Bashan, who dwelt at Ashtaroth in[a] Edrei.
5 On this side of the Jordan in the land of
Moab, Moses began to explain this law, saying,
6 "The LORD our God spoke to us in Horeb,
saying: 'You have dwelt long enough at this
mountain.

1:1 [a]Hebrew *arabah* [b]One manuscript of the Septuagint, also Targum and Vulgate, read *Red Sea*. **1:4** [a]Septuagint, Syriac, and Vulgate read *and* (compare Joshua 12:4).

7 'Turn and take your journey, and go to the mountains of the Amorites, to all the neighboring *places* in the plain,[a] in the mountains and in the lowland, in the South and on the seacoast, to the land of the Canaanites and to Lebanon, as far as the great river, the River Euphrates.
8 'See, I have set the land before you; go in and possess the land which the LORD swore to your fathers—to Abraham, Isaac, and Jacob—to give to them and their descendants after them.'

Tribal Leaders Appointed

9 "And I spoke to you at that time, saying: 'I alone am not able to bear you.
10 'The LORD your God has multiplied you, and here you *are* today, as the stars of heaven in multitude.
11 'May the LORD God of your fathers make you a thousand times more numerous than you are, and bless you as He has promised you!
12 'How can I alone bear your problems and your burdens and your complaints?
13 'Choose wise, understanding, and knowledgeable men from among your tribes, and I will make them heads over you.'
14 "And you answered me and said, 'The thing which you have told *us* to do *is* good.'
15 "So I took the heads of your tribes, wise and knowledgeable men, and made them heads over you, leaders of thousands, leaders of hundreds, leaders of fifties, leaders of tens, and officers for your tribes.
16 "Then I commanded your judges at that time, saying, 'Hear *the cases* between your brethren, and judge righteously between a man and his brother or the stranger who is with him.
17 'You shall not show partiality in judgment; you shall hear the small as well as the great; you shall not be afraid in any man's presence, for the judgment *is* God's. The case that is too hard for you, bring to me, and I will hear it.'
18 "And I commanded you at that time all the things which you should do.

Israel's Refusal to Enter the Land

19 "So we departed from Horeb, and went through all that great and terrible wilderness which you saw on the way to the mountains of the Amorites, as the LORD our God had commanded us. Then we came to Kadesh Barnea.
20 "And I said to you, 'You have come to the mountains of the Amorites, which the LORD our God is giving us.
21 'Look, the LORD your God has set the land before you; go up *and* possess *it*, as the LORD God of your fathers has spoken to you; do not fear or be discouraged.'
22 "And every one of you came near to me and said, 'Let us send men before us, and let them search out the land for us, and bring back word to us of the way by which we should go up, and of the cities into which we shall come.'
23 "The plan pleased me well; so I took twelve of your men, one man from *each* tribe.
24 "And they departed and went up into the mountains, and came to the Valley of Eshcol, and spied it out.
25 "They also took *some* of the fruit of the land in their hands and brought *it* down to us; and they brought back word to us, saying, '*It is* a good land which the LORD our God is giving us.'
26 "Nevertheless you would not go up, but rebelled against the command of the LORD your God;
27 "and you complained in your tents, and said, 'Because the LORD hates us, He has brought us out of the land of Egypt to deliver us into the hand of the Amorites, to destroy us.
28 'Where can we go up? Our brethren have discouraged our hearts, saying, "The people *are* greater and taller than we; the cities *are* great and fortified up to heaven; moreover we have seen the sons of the Anakim there." '
29 "Then I said to you, 'Do not be terrified, or afraid of them.
30 'The LORD your God, who goes before you, He will fight for you, according to all He did for you in Egypt before your eyes,
31 'and in the wilderness where you saw how the LORD your God carried you, as a man carries his son, in all the way that you went until you came to this place.'
32 "Yet, for all that, you did not believe the LORD your God,
33 "who went in the way before you to search out a place for you to pitch your tents, to show you the way you should go, in the fire by night and in the cloud by day.

The Penalty for Israel's Rebellion

34 "And the LORD heard the sound of your words, and was angry, and took an oath, saying,
35 'Surely not one of these men of this evil generation shall see that good land of which I swore to give to your fathers,
36 'except Caleb the son of Jephunneh; he shall see it, and to him and his children I am giving the land on which he walked, because he wholly followed the LORD.'
37 "The LORD was also angry with me for your sakes, saying, 'Even you shall not go in there.
38 'Joshua the son of Nun, who stands before you, he shall go in there. Encourage him, for he shall cause Israel to inherit it.
39 'Moreover your little ones and your children, who you say will be victims, who today have no knowledge of good and evil, they shall go in there; to them I will give it, and they shall possess it.
40 'But *as for* you, turn and take your journey into the wilderness by the Way of the Red Sea.'
41 "Then you answered and said to me, 'We have sinned against the LORD; we will go up and fight, just as the LORD our God commanded us.' And when everyone of you had girded on his weapons of war, you were ready to go up into the mountain.
42 "And the LORD said to me, 'Tell them, "Do not go up nor fight, for I *am* not among you; lest you be defeated before your enemies." '
43 "So I spoke to you; yet you would not listen, but rebelled against the command of the LORD, and presumptuously went up into the mountain.
44 "And the Amorites who dwelt in that mountain came out against you and chased you as bees do, and drove you back from Seir to Hormah.
45 "Then you returned and wept before the LORD, but the LORD would not listen to your voice nor give ear to you.
46 "So you remained in Kadesh many days, according to the days that you spent *there*.

1:7 [a]Hebrew *arabah*

The Desert Years

2 "Then we turned and journeyed into the wilderness of the Way of the Red Sea, as the LORD spoke to me, and we skirted Mount Seir for many days.
2 "And the LORD spoke to me, saying:
3 'You have skirted this mountain long enough; turn northward.
4 'And command the people, saying, "You *are about to* pass through the territory of your brethren, the descendants of Esau, who live in Seir; and they will be afraid of you. Therefore watch yourselves carefully.
5 "Do not meddle with them, for I will not give you *any* of their land, no, not so much as one footstep, because I have given Mount Seir to Esau *as* a possession.
6 "You shall buy food from them with money, that you may eat; and you shall also buy water from them with money, that you may drink.
7 "For the LORD your God has blessed you in all the work of your hand. He knows your trudging through this great wilderness. These forty years the LORD your God *has been* with you; you have lacked nothing." '
8 "And when we passed beyond our brethren, the descendants of Esau who dwell in Seir, away from the road of the plain, away from Elath and Ezion Geber, we turned and passed by way of the Wilderness of Moab.
9 "Then the LORD said to me, 'Do not harass Moab, nor contend with them in battle, for I will not give you *any* of their land *as* a possession, because I have given Ar to the descendants of Lot *as* a possession.' "
10 (The Emim had dwelt there in times past, a people as great and numerous and tall as the Anakim.
11 They were also regarded as giants,[a] like the Anakim, but the Moabites call them Emim.
12 The Horites formerly dwelt in Seir, but the descendants of Esau dispossessed them and destroyed them from before them, and dwelt in their place, just as Israel did to the land of their possession which the LORD gave them.)
13 " 'Now rise and cross over the Valley of the Zered.' So we crossed over the Valley of the Zered.
14 "And the time we took to come from Kadesh Barnea until we crossed over the Valley of the Zered *was* thirty-eight years, until all the generation of the men of war was consumed from the midst of the camp, just as the LORD had sworn to them.
15 "For indeed the hand of the LORD was against them, to destroy them from the midst of the camp until they were consumed.
16 "So it was, when all the men of war had finally perished from among the people,
17 "that the LORD spoke to me, saying:
18 'This day you are to cross over at Ar, the boundary of Moab.
19 'And *when* you come near the people of Ammon, do not harass them or meddle with them, for I will not give you *any* of the land of the people of Ammon *as* a possession, because I have given it to the descendants of Lot *as* a possession.' "
20 (That was also regarded as a land of giants;[a] giants formerly dwelt there. But the Ammonites call them Zamzummim,
21 a people as great and numerous and tall as the Anakim. But the LORD destroyed them before them, and they dispossessed them and dwelt in their place,
22 just as He had done for the descendants of Esau, who dwelt in Seir, when He destroyed the Horites from before them. They dispossessed them and dwelt in their place, even to this day.
23 And the Avim, who dwelt in villages as far as Gaza—the Caphtorim, who came from Caphtor, destroyed them and dwelt in their place.)
24 " 'Rise, take your journey, and cross over the River Arnon. Look, I have given into your hand Sihon the Amorite, king of Heshbon, and his land. Begin to possess *it*, and engage him in battle.
25 'This day I will begin to put the dread and fear of you upon the nations under the whole heaven, who shall hear the report of you, and shall tremble and be in anguish because of you.'

King Sihon Defeated

26 "And I sent messengers from the Wilderness of Kedemoth to Sihon king of Heshbon, with words of peace, saying,
27 'Let me pass through your land; I will keep strictly to the road, and I will turn neither to the right nor to the left.
28 'You shall sell me food for money, that I may eat, and give me water for money, that I may drink; only let me pass through on foot,
29 'just as the descendants of Esau who dwell in Seir and the Moabites who dwell in Ar did for me, until I cross the Jordan to the land which the LORD our God is giving us.'
30 "But Sihon king of Heshbon would not let us pass through, for the LORD your God hardened his spirit and made his heart obstinate, that He might deliver him into your hand, as *it is* this day.
31 "And the LORD said to me, 'See, I have begun to give Sihon and his land over to you. Begin to possess *it*, that you may inherit his land.'
32 "Then Sihon and all his people came out against us to fight at Jahaz.
33 "And the LORD our God delivered him over to us; so we defeated him, his sons, and all his people.
34 "We took all his cities at that time, and we utterly destroyed the men, women, and little ones of every city; we left none remaining.
35 "We took only the livestock as plunder for ourselves, with the spoil of the cities which we took.
36 "From Aroer, which *is* on the bank of the River Arnon, and *from* the city that *is* in the ravine, as far as Gilead, there was not one city too strong for us; the LORD our God delivered all to us.
37 "Only you did not go near the land of the people of Ammon—anywhere along the River Jabbok, or to the cities of the mountains, or wherever the LORD our God had forbidden us.

King Og Defeated

3 "Then we turned and went up the road to Bashan; and Og king of Bashan came out against us, he and all his people, to battle at Edrei.

2:11 [a]Hebrew *rephaim* **2:20** [a]Hebrew *rephaim*

2 "And the LORD said to me, 'Do not fear
him, for I have delivered him and all his people
and his land into your hand; you shall do to
him as you did to Sihon king of the Amorites,
who dwelt at Heshbon.'
3 "So the LORD our God also delivered into
our hands Og king of Bashan, with all his peo-
ple, and we attacked him until he had no survi-
vors remaining.
4 "And we took all his cities at that time;
there was not a city which we did not take from
them: sixty cities, all the region of Argob, the
kingdom of Og in Bashan.
5 "All these cities *were* fortified with high
walls, gates, and bars, besides a great many
rural towns.
6 "And we utterly destroyed them, as we did
to Sihon king of Heshbon, utterly destroying
the men, women, and children of every city.
7 "But all the livestock and the spoil of the
cities we took as booty for ourselves.
8 "And at that time we took the land from
the hand of the two kings of the Amorites who
were on this side of the Jordan, from the River
Arnon to Mount Hermon
9 "(the Sidonians call Hermon Sirion, and
the Amorites call it Senir),
10 "all the cities of the plain, all Gilead, and
all Bashan, as far as Salcah and Edrei, cities
of the kingdom of Og in Bashan.
11 "For only Og king of Bashan remained of
the remnant of the giants.[a] Indeed his bedstead
was an iron bedstead. (*Is* it not in Rabbah of
the people of Ammon?) Nine cubits *is* its length
and four cubits its width, according to the stan-
dard cubit.

The Land East of the Jordan Divided

12 "And this land, *which* we possessed at that
time, from Aroer, which *is* by the River Arnon,
and half the mountains of Gilead and its cities,
I gave to the Reubenites and the Gadites.
13 "The rest of Gilead, and all Bashan, the
kingdom of Og, I gave to half the tribe of Ma-
nasseh. (All the region of Argob, with all Ba-
shan, was called the land of the giants.[a]
14 "Jair the son of Manasseh took all the re-
gion of Argob, as far as the border of the Gesh-
urites and the Maachathites, and called
Bashan after his own name, Havoth Jair,[a] to
this day.)
15 "Also I gave Gilead to Machir.
16 "And to the Reubenites and the Gadites I
gave from Gilead as far as the River Arnon,
the middle of the river as *the* border, as far as
the River Jabbok, the border of the people of
Ammon;
17 "the plain also, with the Jordan as *the* bor-
der, from Chinnereth as far as the east side of
the Sea of the Arabah (the Salt Sea), below the
slopes of Pisgah.
18 "Then I commanded you at that time, say-
ing: 'The LORD your God has given you this
land to possess. All you men of valor shall
cross over armed before your brethren, the
children of Israel.
19 'But your wives, your little ones, and your
livestock (I know that you have much live-
stock) shall stay in your cities which I have
given you,
20 'until the LORD has given rest to your
brethren as to you, and they also possess the
land which the LORD your God is giving them
beyond the Jordan. Then each of you may re-
turn to his possession which I have given you.'
21 "And I commanded Joshua at that time,
saying, 'Your eyes have seen all that the LORD
your God has done to these two kings; so will
the LORD do to all the kingdoms through
which you pass.
22 'You must not fear them, for the LORD your
God Himself fights for you.'

Moses Forbidden to Enter the Land

23 "Then I pleaded with the LORD at that
time, saying:
24 'O Lord GOD, You have begun to show
Your servant Your greatness and Your mighty
hand, for what god *is there* in heaven or on
earth who can do *anything* like Your works
and Your mighty *deeds*?
25 "I pray, let me cross over and see the good
land beyond the Jordan, those pleasant moun-
tains, and Lebanon.'
26 "But the LORD was angry with me on your
account, and would not listen to me. So the
LORD said to me: 'Enough of that! Speak no
more to Me of this matter.
27 'Go up to the top of Pisgah, and lift your
eyes toward the west, the north, the south, and
the east; behold *it* with your eyes, for you shall
not cross over this Jordan.
28 'But command Joshua, and encourage him
and strengthen him; for he shall go over before
this people, and he shall cause them to inherit
the land which you will see.'
29 "So we stayed in the valley opposite Beth
Peor.

Moses Commands Obedience

4 "Now, O Israel, listen to the statutes and
the judgments which I teach you to ob-
serve, that you may live, and go in and possess
the land which the LORD God of your fathers
is giving you.
2 "You shall not add to the word which I
command you, nor take from it, that you may
keep the commandments of the LORD your
God which I command you.
3 "Your eyes have seen what the LORD did
at Baal Peor; for the LORD your God has de-
stroyed from among you all the men who fol-
lowed Baal of Peor.
4 "But you who held fast to the LORD your
God *are* alive today, every one of you.
5 "Surely I have taught you statutes and
judgments, just as the LORD my God com-
manded me, that you should act according *to*
them in the land which you go to possess.
6 "Therefore be careful to observe *them;* for
this *is* your wisdom and your understanding in
the sight of the peoples who will hear all these
statutes, and say, 'Surely this great nation *is* a
wise and understanding people.'
7 "For what great nation *is there* that has
God *so* near to it, as the LORD our God *is* to us,
for whatever *reason* we may call upon Him?
8 "And what great nation *is there* that has
such statutes and righteous judgments as are
in all this law which I set before you this day?
9 "Only take heed to yourself, and diligently
keep yourself, lest you forget the things your
eyes have seen, and lest they depart from your
heart all the days of your life. And teach them
to your children and your grandchildren,
10 "*especially concerning* the day you stood

3:11 [a]Hebrew *rephaim* **3:13** [a]Hebrew *rephaim* **3:14** [a]Literally *Towns of Jair*

before the LORD your God in Horeb, when the LORD said to me, 'Gather the people to Me, and I will let them hear My words, that they may learn to fear Me all the days they live on the earth, and *that* they may teach their children.'

11 "Then you came near and stood at the foot of the mountain, and the mountain burned with fire to the midst of heaven, with darkness, cloud, and thick darkness.

12 "And the LORD spoke to you out of the midst of the fire. You heard the sound of the words, but saw no form; *you* only *heard* a voice.

13 "So He declared to you His covenant which He commanded you to perform, the Ten Commandments; and He wrote them on two tablets of stone.

14 "And the LORD commanded me at that time to teach you statutes and judgments, that you might observe them in the land which you cross over to possess.

Beware of Idolatry

15 "Take careful heed to yourselves, for you saw no form when the LORD spoke to you at Horeb out of the midst of the fire,

16 "lest you act corruptly and make for yourselves a carved image in the form of any figure: the likeness of male or female,

17 "the likeness of any animal that *is* on the earth or the likeness of any winged bird that flies in the air,

18 "the likeness of anything that creeps on the ground or the likeness of any fish that *is* in the water beneath the earth.

19 "And *take heed,* lest you lift your eyes to heaven, and *when* you see the sun, the moon, and the stars, all the host of heaven, you feel driven to worship them and serve them, which the LORD your God has given to all the peoples under the whole heaven as a heritage.

20 "But the LORD has taken you and brought you out of the iron furnace, out of Egypt, to be His people, an inheritance, as you are this day.

21 "Furthermore the LORD was angry with me for your sakes, and swore that I would not cross over the Jordan, and that I would not enter the good land which the LORD your God is giving you as an inheritance.

22 "But I must die in this land, I must not cross over the Jordan; but you shall cross over and possess that good land.

23 "Take heed to yourselves, lest you forget the covenant of the LORD your God which He made with you, and make for yourselves a carved image in the form of anything which the LORD your God has forbidden you.

24 "For the LORD your God *is* a consuming fire, a jealous God.

25 "When you beget children and grandchildren and have grown old in the land, and act corruptly and make a carved image in the form of anything, and do evil in the sight of the LORD your God to provoke Him to anger,

26 "I call heaven and earth to witness against you this day, that you will soon utterly perish from the land which you cross over the Jordan to possess; you will not prolong *your* days in it, but will be utterly destroyed.

27 "And the LORD will scatter you among the peoples, and you will be left few in number among the nations where the LORD will drive you.

28 "And there you will serve gods, the work of men's hands, wood and stone, which neither see nor hear nor eat nor smell.

29 "But from there you will seek the LORD your God, and you will find *Him* if you seek Him with all your heart and with all your soul.

30 "When you are in distress, and all these things come upon you in the latter days, when you turn to the LORD your God and obey His voice

31 "(for the LORD your God *is* a merciful God), He will not forsake you nor destroy you, nor forget the covenant of your fathers which He swore to them.

32 "For ask now concerning the days that are past, which were before you, since the day that God created man on the earth, and *ask* from one end of heaven to the other, whether *any* great *thing* like this has happened, or *anything* like it has been heard.

33 "Did *any* people *ever* hear the voice of God speaking out of the midst of the fire, as you have heard, and live?

34 "Or did God *ever* try to go *and* take for Himself a nation from the midst of *another* nation, by trials, by signs, by wonders, by war, by a mighty hand and an outstretched arm, and by great terrors, according to all that the LORD your God did for you in Egypt before your eyes?

35 "To you it was shown, that you might know that the LORD Himself *is* God; *there is* none other besides Him.

36 "Out of heaven He let you hear His voice, that He might instruct you; on earth He showed you His great fire, and you heard His words out of the midst of the fire.

37 "And because He loved your fathers, therefore He chose their descendants after them; and He brought you out of Egypt with His Presence, with His mighty power,

38 "driving out from before you nations greater and mightier than you, to bring you in, to give you their land *as* an inheritance, as *it is* this day.

39 "Therefore know this day, and consider *it* in your heart, that the LORD Himself *is* God in heaven above and on the earth beneath; *there is* no other.

40 "You shall therefore keep His statutes and His commandments which I command you today, that it may go well with you and with your children after you, and that you may prolong *your* days in the land which the LORD your God is giving you for all time."

Cities of Refuge East of the Jordan

41 Then Moses set apart three cities on this side of the Jordan, toward the rising of the sun,

42 that the manslayer might flee there, who kills his neighbor unintentionally, without having hated him in time past, and that by fleeing to one of these cities he might live:

43 Bezer in the wilderness on the plateau for the Reubenites, Ramoth in Gilead for the Gadites, and Golan in Bashan for the Manassites.

Introduction to God's Law

44 Now this *is* the law which Moses set before the children of Israel.

45 These *are* the testimonies, the statutes, and the judgments which Moses spoke to the children of Israel after they came out of Egypt,

46 on this side of the Jordan, in the valley opposite Beth Peor, in the land of Sihon king of the Amorites, who dwelt at Heshbon, whom

Moses and the children of Israel defeated after
they came out of Egypt.
47 And they took possession of his land and
the land of Og king of Bashan, two kings of
the Amorites, who *were* on this side of the
Jordan, toward the rising of the sun,
48 from Aroer, which *is* on the bank of the
River Arnon, even to Mount Sion[a] (that is,
Hermon),
49 and all the plain on the east side of the
Jordan as far as the Sea of the Arabah, below
the slopes of Pisgah.

The Ten Commandments Reviewed

5 And Moses called all Israel, and said to
them: "Hear, O Israel, the statutes and
judgments which I speak in your hearing to-
day, that you may learn them and be careful to
observe them.
2 "The LORD our God made a covenant with
us in Horeb.
3 "The LORD did not make this covenant
with our fathers, but with us, those who *are*
here today, all of us who *are* alive.
4 "The LORD talked with you face to face on
the mountain from the midst of the fire.
5 "I stood between the LORD and you at that
time, to declare to you the word of the LORD;
for you were afraid because of the fire, and
you did not go up the mountain. *He* said:
6 'I *am* the LORD your God who brought you
out of the land of Egypt, out of the
house of bondage.
7 'You shall have no other gods before Me.
8 'You shall not make for yourself a carved
image—any likeness *of anything* that
is in heaven above, or that *is* in the
earth beneath, or that *is* in the water
under the earth;
9 you shall not bow down to them nor
serve them. For I, the LORD your God,
am a jealous God, visiting the iniquity
of the fathers upon the children to the
third and fourth *generations* of those
who hate Me,
10 but showing mercy to thousands, to
those who love Me and keep My com-
mandments.
11 'You shall not take the name of the LORD
your God in vain, for the LORD will not
hold *him* guiltless who takes His name
in vain.
12 'Observe the Sabbath day, to keep it holy,
as the LORD your God commanded
you.
13 Six days you shall labor and do all
your work,
14 but the seventh day *is* the Sabbath of
the LORD your God. *In it* you shall do
no work: you, nor your son, nor your
daughter, nor your male servant, nor
your female servant, nor your ox, nor
your donkey, nor any of your cattle,
nor your stranger who *is* within your
gates, that your male servant and
your female servant may rest as well
as you.
15 And remember that you were a slave
in the land of Egypt, and the LORD
your God brought you out from there
by a mighty hand and by an out-
stretched arm; therefore the LORD
your God commanded you to keep the
Sabbath day.
16 'Honor your father and your mother, as the
LORD your God has commanded you,
that your days may be long, and that
it may be well with you in the land
which the LORD your God is giving
you.
17 'You shall not murder.
18 'You shall not commit adultery.
19 'You shall not steal.
20 'You shall not bear false witness against
your neighbor.
21 'You shall not covet your neighbor's wife;
and you shall not desire your neigh-
bor's house, his field, his male servant,
his female servant, his ox, his donkey,
or anything that *is* your neighbor's.'
22 "These words the LORD spoke to all your
assembly, in the mountain from the midst of
the fire, the cloud, and the thick darkness, with
a loud voice; and He added no more. And He
wrote them on two tablets of stone and gave
them to me.

The People Afraid of God's Presence

23 "So it was, when you heard the voice from
the midst of the darkness, while the mountain
was burning with fire, that you came near to
me, all the heads of your tribes and your elders.
24 "And you said: 'Surely the LORD our God
has shown us His glory and His greatness, and
we have heard His voice from the midst of the
fire. We have seen this day that God speaks
with man; yet he *still* lives.
25 'Now therefore, why should we die? For
this great fire will consume us; if we hear the
voice of the LORD our God anymore, then we
shall die.
26 'For who *is there* of all flesh who has heard
the voice of the living God speaking from the
midst of the fire, as we *have*, and lived?
27 'You go near and hear all that the LORD
our God may say, and tell us all that the LORD
our God says to you, and we will hear and do
it.'
28 "Then the LORD heard the voice of your
words when you spoke to me, and the LORD
said to me: 'I have heard the voice of the words
of this people which they have spoken to you.
They are right *in* all that they have spoken.
29 'Oh, that they had such a heart in them
that they would fear Me and always keep all
My commandments, that it might be well with
them and with their children forever!
30 'Go and say to them, "Return to your
tents."
31 'But as for you, stand here by Me, and I
will speak to you all the commandments, the
statutes, and the judgments which you shall
teach them, that they may observe *them* in the
land which I am giving them to possess.'
32 "Therefore you shall be careful to do as
the LORD your God has commanded you; you
shall not turn aside to the right hand or to the
left.
33 "You shall walk in all the ways which the
LORD your God has commanded you, that you
may live and *that it may be* well with you, and
that you may prolong *your* days in the land
which you shall possess.

4:48 [a]Syriac reads *Sirion* (compare 3:9).

The Greatest Commandment

6 "Now this *is* the commandment, *and these are* the statutes and judgments which the LORD your God has commanded to teach you, that you may observe *them* in the land which you are crossing over to possess,

2 "that you may fear the LORD your God, to keep all His statutes and His commandments which I command you, you and your son and your grandson, all the days of your life, and that your days may be prolonged.

3 "Therefore hear, O Israel, and be careful to observe *it*, that it may be well with you, and that you may multiply greatly as the LORD God of your fathers has promised you—'a land flowing with milk and honey.'[a]

4 "Hear, O Israel: The LORD our God, the LORD *is* one![a]

5 "You shall love the LORD your God with all your heart, with all your soul, and with all your strength.

6 "And these words which I command you today shall be in your heart.

7 "You shall teach them diligently to your children, and shall talk of them when you sit in your house, when you walk by the way, when you lie down, and when you rise up.

8 "You shall bind them as a sign on your hand, and they shall be as frontlets between your eyes.

9 "You shall write them on the doorposts of your house and on your gates.

Caution Against Disobedience

10 "So it shall be, when the LORD your God brings you into the land of which He swore to your fathers, to Abraham, Isaac, and Jacob, to give you large and beautiful cities which you did not build,

11 "houses full of all good things, which you did not fill, hewn-out wells which you did not dig, vineyards and olive trees which you did not plant—when you have eaten and are full—

12 "*then* beware, lest you forget the LORD who brought you out of the land of Egypt, from the house of bondage.

13 "You shall fear the LORD your God and serve Him, and shall take oaths in His name.

14 "You shall not go after other gods, the gods of the peoples who *are* all around you

15 "(for the LORD your God *is* a jealous God among you), lest the anger of the LORD your God be aroused against you and destroy you from the face of the earth.

16 "You shall not tempt the LORD your God as you tempted *Him* in Massah.

17 "You shall diligently keep the commandments of the LORD your God, His testimonies, and His statutes which He has commanded you.

18 "And you shall do *what is* right and good in the sight of the LORD, that it may be well with you, and that you may go in and possess the good land of which the LORD swore to your fathers,

19 "to cast out all your enemies from before you, as the LORD has spoken.

20 "When your son asks you in time to come, saying, 'What *is the meaning of* the testimonies, the statutes, and the judgments which the LORD our God has commanded you?'

21 "then you shall say to your son: 'We were slaves of Pharaoh in Egypt, and the LORD brought us out of Egypt with a mighty hand;

22 'and the LORD showed signs and wonders before our eyes, great and severe, against Egypt, Pharaoh, and all his household.

23 'Then He brought us out from there, that He might bring us in, to give us the land of which He swore to our fathers.

24 'And the LORD commanded us to observe all these statutes, to fear the LORD our God, for our good always, that He might preserve us alive, as *it is* this day.

25 'Then it will be righteousness for us, if we are careful to observe all these commandments before the LORD our God, as He has commanded us.'

A Chosen People

7 "When the LORD your God brings you into the land which you go to possess, and has cast out many nations before you, the Hittites and the Girgashites and the Amorites and the Canaanites and the Perizzites and the Hivites and the Jebusites, seven nations greater and mightier than you,

2 "and when the LORD your God delivers them over to you, you shall conquer them *and* utterly destroy them. You shall make no covenant with them nor show mercy to them.

3 "Nor shall you make marriages with them. You shall not give your daughter to their son, nor take their daughter for your son.

4 "For they will turn your sons away from following Me, to serve other gods; so the anger of the LORD will be aroused against you and destroy you suddenly.

5 "But thus you shall deal with them: you shall destroy their altars, and break down their *sacred* pillars, and cut down their wooden images,[a] and burn their carved images with fire.

6 "For you *are* a holy people to the LORD your God; the LORD your God has chosen you to be a people for Himself, a special treasure above all the peoples on the face of the earth.

7 "The LORD did not set His love on you nor choose you because you were more in number than any other people, for you were the least of all peoples;

8 "but because the LORD loves you, and because He would keep the oath which He swore to your fathers, the LORD has brought you out with a mighty hand, and redeemed you from the house of bondage, from the hand of Pharaoh king of Egypt.

9 "Therefore know that the LORD your God, He *is* God, the faithful God who keeps covenant and mercy for a thousand generations with those who love Him and keep His commandments;

10 "and He repays those who hate Him to their face, to destroy them. He will not be slack with him who hates Him; He will repay him to his face.

11 "Therefore you shall keep the commandment, the statutes, and the judgments which I command you today, to observe them.

Blessings of Obedience

12 "Then it shall come to pass, because you listen to these judgments, and keep and do them, that the LORD your God will keep with

6:3 [a]Exodus 3:8 **6:4** [a]Or *The LORD is our God, the LORD alone* (that is, the only one) **7:5** [a]Hebrew *Asherim*, Canaanite deities

you the covenant and the mercy which He
swore to your fathers.
13 "And He will love you and bless you and
multiply you; He will also bless the fruit of
your womb and the fruit of your land, your
grain and your new wine and your oil, the in-
crease of your cattle and the offspring of your
flock, in the land of which He swore to your
fathers to give you.
14 "You shall be blessed above all peoples;
there shall not be a male or female barren
among you or among your livestock.
15 "And the LORD will take away from you
all sickness, and will afflict you with none of
the terrible diseases of Egypt which you have
known, but will lay *them* on all those who hate
you.
16 "Also you shall destroy all the peoples
whom the LORD your God delivers over to you;
your eye shall have no pity on them; nor shall
you serve their gods, for that *will be* a snare
to you.
17 "If you should say in your heart, 'These
nations are greater than I; how can I dispossess
them?'—
18 "you shall not be afraid of them, *but* you
shall remember well what the LORD your God
did to Pharaoh and to all Egypt:
19 "the great trials which your eyes saw, the
signs and the wonders, the mighty hand and
the outstretched arm, by which the LORD your
God brought you out. So shall the LORD your
God do to all the peoples of whom you are
afraid.
20 "Moreover the LORD your God will send
the hornet among them until those who are
left, who hide themselves from you, are de-
stroyed.
21 "You shall not be terrified of them; for the
LORD your God, the great and awesome God,
is among you.
22 "And the LORD your God will drive out
those nations before you little by little; you
will be unable to destroy them at once, lest the
beasts of the field become *too* numerous for
you.
23 "But the LORD your God will deliver them
over to you, and will inflict defeat upon them
until they are destroyed.
24 "And He will deliver their kings into your
hand, and you will destroy their name from
under heaven; no one shall be able to stand
against you until you have destroyed them.
25 "You shall burn the carved images of their
gods with fire; you shall not covet the silver or
gold *that is* on them, nor take *it* for yourselves,
lest you be snared by it; for it *is* an abomination
to the LORD your God.
26 "Nor shall you bring an abomination into
your house, lest you be doomed to destruction
like it. You shall utterly detest it and utterly
abhor it, for it *is* an accursed thing.

Remember the LORD Your God

8 "Every commandment which I command
you today you must be careful to observe,
that you may live and multiply, and go in and
possess the land of which the LORD swore to
your fathers.
2 "And you shall remember that the LORD
your God led you all the way these forty years
in the wilderness, to humble you *and* test you,
to know what *was* in your heart, whether you
would keep His commandments or not.
3 "So He humbled you, allowed you to hun-
ger, and fed you with manna which you did not
know nor did your fathers know, that He might
make you know that man shall not live by
bread alone; but man lives by every *word* that
proceeds from the mouth of the LORD.
4 "Your garments did not wear out on you,
nor did your foot swell these forty years.
5 "You should know in your heart that as a
man chastens his son, *so* the LORD your God
chastens you.
6 "Therefore you shall keep the command-
ments of the LORD your God, to walk in His
ways and to fear Him.
7 "For the LORD your God is bringing you
into a good land, a land of brooks of water, of
fountains and springs, that flow out of valleys
and hills;
8 "a land of wheat and barley, of vines and
fig trees and pomegranates, a land of olive oil
and honey;
9 "a land in which you will eat bread without
scarcity, in which you will lack nothing; a land
whose stones *are* iron and out of whose hills
you can dig copper.
10 "When you have eaten and are full, then
you shall bless the LORD your God for the good
land which He has given you.
11 "Beware that you do not forget the LORD
your God by not keeping His commandments,
His judgments, and His statutes which I com-
mand you today,
12 "lest—*when* you have eaten and are full,
and have built beautiful houses and dwell *in
them;*
13 "and *when* your herds and your flocks
multiply, and your silver and your gold are
multiplied, and all that you have is multiplied;
14 "when your heart is lifted up, and you for-
get the LORD your God who brought you out of
the land of Egypt, from the house of bondage;
15 "who led you through that great and terri-
ble wilderness, *in which were* fiery serpents
and scorpions and thirsty land where there
was no water; who brought water for you out
of the flinty rock;
16 "who fed you in the wilderness with
manna, which your fathers did not know, that
He might humble you and that He might test
you, to do you good in the end—
17 "then you say in your heart, 'My power
and the might of my hand have gained me this
wealth.'
18 "And you shall remember the LORD your
God, for *it is* He who gives you power to get
wealth, that He may establish His covenant
which He swore to your fathers, as *it is* this
day.
19 "Then it shall be, if you by any means for-
get the LORD your God, and follow other gods,
and serve them and worship them, I testify
against you this day that you shall surely
perish.
20 "As the nations which the LORD destroys
before you, so you shall perish, because you
would not be obedient to the voice of the LORD
your God.

Israel's Rebellions Reviewed

9 "Hear, O Israel: You *are* to cross over the
Jordan today, and go in to dispossess na-
tions greater and mightier than yourself, cities
great and fortified up to heaven,
2 "a people great and tall, the descendants
of the Anakim, whom you know, and *of whom*

you heard *it said,* 'Who can stand before the descendants of Anak?'

3 "Therefore understand today that the LORD your God *is* He who goes over before you *as* a consuming fire. He will destroy them and bring them down before you; so you shall drive them out and destroy them quickly, as the LORD has said to you.

4 "Do not think in your heart, after the LORD your God has cast them out before you, saying, 'Because of my righteousness the LORD has brought me in to possess this land'; but *it is* because of the wickedness of these nations *that* the LORD is driving them out from before you.

5 "*It is* not because of your righteousness or the uprightness of your heart *that* you go in to possess their land, but because of the wickedness of these nations *that* the LORD your God drives them out from before you, and that He may fulfill the word which the LORD swore to your fathers, to Abraham, Isaac, and Jacob.

6 "Therefore understand that the LORD your God is not giving you this good land to possess because of your righteousness, for you *are* a stiff-necked people.

7 "Remember! Do not forget how you provoked the LORD your God to wrath in the wilderness. From the day that you departed from the land of Egypt until you came to this place, you have been rebellious against the LORD.

8 "Also in Horeb you provoked the LORD to wrath, so that the LORD was angry *enough* with you to have destroyed you.

9 "When I went up into the mountain to receive the tablets of stone, the tablets of the covenant which the LORD made with you, then I stayed on the mountain forty days and forty nights. I neither ate bread nor drank water.

10 "Then the LORD delivered to me two tablets of stone written with the finger of God, and on them *were* all the words which the LORD had spoken to you on the mountain from the midst of the fire in the day of the assembly.

11 "And it came to pass, at the end of forty days and forty nights, *that* the LORD gave me the two tablets of stone, the tablets of the covenant.

12 "Then the LORD said to me, 'Arise, go down quickly from here, for your people whom you brought out of Egypt have acted corruptly; they have quickly turned aside from the way which I commanded them; they have made themselves a molded image.'

13 "Furthermore the LORD spoke to me, saying, 'I have seen this people, and indeed they are a stiff-necked people.

14 'Let Me alone, that I may destroy them and blot out their name from under heaven; and I will make of you a nation mightier and greater than they.'

15 "So I turned and came down from the mountain, and the mountain burned with fire; and the two tablets of the covenant *were* in my two hands.

16 "And I looked, and behold, you had sinned against the LORD your God—had made for yourselves a molded calf! You had turned aside quickly from the way which the LORD had commanded you.

17 "Then I took the two tablets and threw them out of my two hands and broke them before your eyes.

18 "And I fell down before the LORD, as at the first, forty days and forty nights; I neither ate bread nor drank water, because of all your sin which you committed in doing wickedly in the sight of the LORD, to provoke Him to anger.

19 "For I was afraid of the anger and hot displeasure with which the LORD was angry with you, to destroy you. But the LORD listened to me at that time also.

20 "And the LORD was very angry with Aaron *and* would have destroyed him; so I prayed for Aaron also at the same time.

21 "Then I took your sin, the calf which you had made, and burned it with fire and crushed it *and* ground *it* very small, until it was as fine as dust; and I threw its dust into the brook that descended from the mountain.

22 "Also at Taberah and Massah and Kibroth Hattaavah you provoked the LORD to wrath.

23 "Likewise, when the LORD sent you from Kadesh Barnea, saying, 'Go up and possess the land which I have given you,' then you rebelled against the commandment of the LORD your God, and you did not believe Him nor obey His voice.

24 "You have been rebellious against the LORD from the day that I knew you.

25 "Thus I prostrated myself before the LORD; forty days and forty nights I kept prostrating myself, because the LORD had said He would destroy you.

26 "Therefore I prayed to the LORD, and said: 'O Lord GOD, do not destroy Your people and Your inheritance whom You have redeemed through Your greatness, whom You have brought out of Egypt with a mighty hand.

27 'Remember Your servants, Abraham, Isaac, and Jacob; do not look on the stubbornness of this people, or on their wickedness or their sin,

28 'lest the land from which You brought us should say, "Because the LORD was not able to bring them to the land which He promised them, and because He hated them, He has brought them out to kill them in the wilderness."

29 'Yet they *are* Your people and Your inheritance, whom You brought out by Your mighty power and by Your outstretched arm.'

The Second Pair of Tablets

10 "At that time the LORD said to me, 'Hew for yourself two tablets of stone like the first, and come up to Me on the mountain and make yourself an ark of wood.

2 'And I will write on the tablets the words that were on the first tablets, which you broke; and you shall put them in the ark.'

3 "So I made an ark of acacia wood, hewed two tablets of stone like the first, and went up the mountain, having the two tablets in my hand.

4 "And He wrote on the tablets according to the first writing, the Ten Commandments, which the LORD had spoken to you in the mountain from the midst of the fire in the day of the assembly; and the LORD gave them to me.

5 "Then I turned and came down from the mountain, and put the tablets in the ark which I had made; and there they are, just as the LORD commanded me."

6 (Now the children of Israel journeyed from the wells of Bene Jaakan to Moserah, where Aaron died, and where he was buried; and Eleazar his son ministered as priest in his stead.

7 From there they journeyed to Gudgodah,

and from Gudgodah to Jotbathah, a land of
rivers of water.
8 At that time the LORD separated the tribe
of Levi to bear the ark of the covenant of the
LORD, to stand before the LORD to minister to
Him and to bless in His name, to this day.
9 Therefore Levi has no portion nor inheri-
tance with his brethren; the LORD *is* his inheri-
tance, just as the LORD your God promised
him.)
10 "As at the first time, I stayed in the moun-
tain forty days and forty nights; the LORD also
heard me at that time, *and* the LORD chose not
to destroy you.
11 "Then the LORD said to me, 'Arise, begin
your journey before the people, that they may
go in and possess the land which I swore to
their fathers to give them.'

The Essence of the Law

12 "And now, Israel, what does the LORD your
God require of you, but to fear the LORD your
God, to walk in all His ways and to love Him,
to serve the LORD your God with all your heart
and with all your soul,
13 "*and* to keep the commandments of the
LORD and His statutes which I command you
today for your good?
14 "Indeed heaven and the highest heavens
belong to the LORD your God, *also* the earth
with all that *is* in it.
15 "The LORD delighted only in your fathers,
to love them; and He chose their descendants
after them, you above all peoples, as *it is* this
day.
16 "Therefore circumcise the foreskin of your
heart, and be stiff-necked no longer.
17 "For the LORD your God *is* God of gods
and Lord of lords, the great God, mighty and
awesome, who shows no partiality nor takes a
bribe.
18 "He administers justice for the fatherless
and the widow, and loves the stranger, giving
him food and clothing.
19 "Therefore love the stranger, for you were
strangers in the land of Egypt.
20 "You shall fear the LORD your God; you
shall serve Him, and to Him you shall hold fast,
and take oaths in His name.
21 "He *is* your praise, and He *is* your God,
who has done for you these great and awesome
things which your eyes have seen.
22 "Your fathers went down to Egypt with
seventy persons, and now the LORD your God
has made you as the stars of heaven in multi-
tude.

Love and Obedience Rewarded

11 "Therefore you shall love the LORD your
God, and keep His charge, His statutes,
His judgments, and His commandments al-
ways.
2 "Know today that *I do* not *speak* with your
children, who have not known and who have
not seen the chastening of the LORD your God,
His greatness and His mighty hand and His
outstretched arm—
3 "His signs and His acts which He did in
the midst of Egypt, to Pharaoh king of Egypt,
and to all his land;
4 "what He did to the army of Egypt, to their
horses and their chariots: how He made the
waters of the Red Sea overflow them as they
pursued you, and *how* the LORD has destroyed
them to this day;
5 "what He did for you in the wilderness
until you came to this place;
6 "and what He did to Dathan and Abiram
the sons of Eliab, the son of Reuben: how the
earth opened its mouth and swallowed them
up, their households, their tents, and all the
substance that *was* in their possession, in the
midst of all Israel—
7 "but your eyes have seen every great act
of the LORD which He did.
8 "Therefore you shall keep every com-
mandment which I command you today, that
you may be strong, and go in and possess the
land which you cross over to possess,
9 "and that you may prolong *your* days in
the land which the LORD swore to give your
fathers, to them and their descendants, 'a land
flowing with milk and honey.'[a]
10 "For the land which you go to possess *is*
not like the land of Egypt from which you have
come, where you sowed your seed and watered
it by foot, as a vegetable garden;
11 "but the land which you cross over to pos-
sess *is* a land of hills and valleys, which drinks
water from the rain of heaven,
12 "a land for which the LORD your God
cares; the eyes of the LORD your God *are* al-
ways on it, from the beginning of the year to
the very end of the year.
13 'And it shall be that if you earnestly obey
My commandments which I command you to-
day, to love the LORD your God and serve Him
with all your heart and with all your soul,
14 'then I[a] will give *you* the rain for your land
in its season, the early rain and the latter rain,
that you may gather in your grain, your new
wine, and your oil.
15 'And I will send grass in your fields for
your livestock, that you may eat and be filled.'
16 "Take heed to yourselves, lest your heart
be deceived, and you turn aside and serve
other gods and worship them,
17 "lest the LORD's anger be aroused against
you, and He shut up the heavens so that there
be no rain, and the land yield no produce, and
you perish quickly from the good land which
the LORD is giving you.
18 "Therefore you shall lay up these words of
mine in your heart and in your soul, and bind
them as a sign on your hand, and they shall be
as frontlets between your eyes.
19 "You shall teach them to your children,
speaking of them when you sit in your house,
when you walk by the way, when you lie down,
and when you rise up.
20 "And you shall write them on the door-
posts of your house and on your gates,
21 "that your days and the days of your chil-
dren may be multiplied in the land of which
the LORD swore to your fathers to give them,
like the days of the heavens above the earth.
22 "For if you carefully keep all these com-
mandments which I command you to do—to
love the LORD your God, to walk in all His
ways, and to hold fast to Him—
23 "then the LORD will drive out all these na-
tions from before you, and you will dispossess
greater and mightier nations than yourselves.
24 "Every place on which the sole of your foot

11:9 [a]Exodus 3:8 **11:14** [a]Following Masoretic Text and Targum; Samaritan Pentateuch, Septuagint, and Vulgate read *He*.

treads shall be yours: from the wilderness and
Lebanon, from the river, the River Euphrates,
even to the Western Sea,[a] shall be your terri-
tory.
25 "No man shall be able to stand against
you; the LORD your God will put the dread of
you and the fear of you upon all the land
where you tread, just as He has said to you.
26 "Behold, I set before you today a blessing
and a curse:
27 "the blessing, if you obey the command-
ments of the LORD your God which I command
you today;
28 "and the curse, if you do not obey the com-
mandments of the LORD your God, but turn
aside from the way which I command you to-
day, to go after other gods which you have not
known.
29 "Now it shall be, when the LORD your God
has brought you into the land which you go
to possess, that you shall put the blessing on
Mount Gerizim and the curse on Mount Ebal.
30 "*Are* they not on the other side of the Jor-
dan, toward the setting sun, in the land of the
Canaanites who dwell in the plain opposite
Gilgal, beside the terebinth trees of Moreh?
31 "For you will cross over the Jordan and go
in to possess the land which the LORD your
God is giving you, and you will possess it and
dwell in it.
32 "And you shall be careful to observe all the
statutes and judgments which I set before you
today.

A Prescribed Place of Worship

12 "These *are* the statutes and judgments
which you shall be careful to observe in
the land which the LORD God of your fathers
is giving you to possess, all the days that you
live on the earth.
2 "You shall utterly destroy all the places
where the nations which you shall dispossess
served their gods, on the high mountains and
on the hills and under every green tree.
3 "And you shall destroy their altars, break
their *sacred* pillars, and burn their wooden im-
ages with fire; you shall cut down the carved
images of their gods and destroy their names
from that place.
4 "You shall not worship the LORD your God
with such *things*.
5 "But you shall seek the place where the
LORD your God chooses, out of all your tribes,
to put His name for His dwelling place; and
there you shall go.
6 "There you shall take your burnt offerings,
your sacrifices, your tithes, the heave offerings
of your hand, your vowed offerings, your free-
will offerings, and the firstborn of your herds
and flocks.
7 "And there you shall eat before the LORD
your God, and you shall rejoice in all to which
you have put your hand, you and your house-
holds, in which the LORD your God has blessed
you.
8 "You shall not at all do as we are doing
here today—every man doing whatever *is* right
in his own eyes—
9 "for as yet you have not come to the rest
and the inheritance which the LORD your God
is giving you.
10 "But *when* you cross over the Jordan and
dwell in the land which the LORD your God is
giving you to inherit, and He gives you rest
from all your enemies round about, so that you
dwell in safety,
11 "then there will be the place where the
LORD your God chooses to make His name
abide. There you shall bring all that I com-
mand you: your burnt offerings, your sacri-
fices, your tithes, the heave offerings of your
hand, and all your choice offerings which you
vow to the LORD.
12 "And you shall rejoice before the LORD
your God, you and your sons and your daugh-
ters, your male and female servants, and the
Levite who *is* within your gates, since he has
no portion nor inheritance with you.
13 "Take heed to yourself that you do not of-
fer your burnt offerings in every place that you
see;
14 "but in the place which the LORD chooses,
in one of your tribes, there you shall offer your
burnt offerings, and there you shall do all that
I command you.
15 "However, you may slaughter and eat
meat within all your gates, whatever your
heart desires, according to the blessing of the
LORD your God which He has given you; the
unclean and the clean may eat of it, of the
gazelle and the deer alike.
16 "Only you shall not eat the blood; you shall
pour it on the earth like water.
17 "You may not eat within your gates the
tithe of your grain or your new wine or your
oil, of the firstborn of your herd or your flock,
of any of your offerings which you vow, of your
freewill offerings, or of the heave offering of
your hand.
18 "But you must eat them before the LORD
your God in the place which the LORD your
God chooses, you and your son and your
daughter, your male servant and your female
servant, and the Levite who *is* within your
gates; and you shall rejoice before the LORD
your God in all to which you put your hands.
19 "Take heed to yourself that you do not for-
sake the Levite as long as you live in your land.
20 "When the LORD your God enlarges your
border as He has promised you, and you say,
'Let me eat meat,' because you long to eat meat,
you may eat as much meat as your heart de-
sires.
21 "If the place where the LORD your God
chooses to put His name is too far from you,
then you may slaughter from your herd and
from your flock which the LORD has given you,
just as I have commanded you, and you may
eat within your gates as much as your heart
desires.
22 "Just as the gazelle and the deer are eaten,
so you may eat them; the unclean and the clean
alike may eat them.
23 "Only be sure that you do not eat the
blood, for the blood *is* the life; you may not eat
the life with the meat.
24 "You shall not eat it; you shall pour it on
the earth like water.
25 "You shall not eat it, that it may go well
with you and your children after you, when
you do *what is* right in the sight of the LORD.
26 "Only the holy things which you have, and
your vowed offerings, you shall take and go to
the place which the LORD chooses.
27 "And you shall offer your burnt offerings,
the meat and the blood, on the altar of the

11:24 [a]That is, the Mediterranean

LORD your God; and the blood of your sacrifices shall be poured out on the altar of the LORD your God, and you shall eat the meat.
28 "Observe and obey all these words which I command you, that it may go well with you and your children after you forever, when you do *what is* good and right in the sight of the LORD your God.

Beware of False Gods

29 "When the LORD your God cuts off from before you the nations which you go to dispossess, and you displace them and dwell in their land,
30 "take heed to yourself that you are not ensnared to follow them, after they are destroyed from before you, and that you do not inquire after their gods, saying, 'How did these nations serve their gods? I also will do likewise.'
31 "You shall not worship the LORD your God in that way; for every abomination to the LORD which He hates they have done to their gods; for they burn even their sons and daughters in the fire to their gods.
32 "Whatever I command you, be careful to observe it; you shall not add to it nor take away from it.

Punishment of Apostates

13 "If there arises among you a prophet or a dreamer of dreams, and he gives you a sign or a wonder,
2 "and the sign or the wonder comes to pass, of which he spoke to you, saying, 'Let us go after other gods'—which you have not known—'and let us serve them,'
3 "you shall not listen to the words of that prophet or that dreamer of dreams, for the LORD your God is testing you to know whether you love the LORD your God with all your heart and with all your soul.
4 "You shall walk after the LORD your God and fear Him, and keep His commandments and obey His voice; you shall serve Him and hold fast to Him.
5 "But that prophet or that dreamer of dreams shall be put to death, because he has spoken in order to turn *you* away from the LORD your God, who brought you out of the land of Egypt and redeemed you from the house of bondage, to entice you from the way in which the LORD your God commanded you to walk. So you shall put away the evil from your midst.
6 "If your brother, the son of your mother, your son or your daughter, the wife of your bosom, or your friend who is as your own soul, secretly entices you, saying, 'Let us go and serve other gods,' which you have not known, neither you nor your fathers,
7 "of the gods of the people which *are* all around you, near to you or far off from you, from *one* end of the earth to the *other* end of the earth,
8 "you shall not consent to him or listen to him, nor shall your eye pity him, nor shall you spare him or conceal him;
9 "but you shall surely kill him; your hand shall be first against him to put him to death, and afterward the hand of all the people.
10 "And you shall stone him with stones until he dies, because he sought to entice you away from the LORD your God, who brought you out of the land of Egypt, from the house of bondage.
11 "So all Israel shall hear and fear, and not again do such wickedness as this among you.
12 "If you hear someone in one of your cities, which the LORD your God gives you to dwell in, saying,
13 'Corrupt men have gone out from among you and enticed the inhabitants of their city, saying, "Let us go and serve other gods"'—which you have not known—
14 "then you shall inquire, search out, and ask diligently. And *if it is* indeed true *and* certain *that* such an abomination was committed among you,
15 "you shall surely strike the inhabitants of that city with the edge of the sword, utterly destroying it, all that is in it and its livestock—with the edge of the sword.
16 "And you shall gather all its plunder into the middle of the street, and completely burn with fire the city and all its plunder, for the LORD your God. It shall be a heap forever; it shall not be built again.
17 "So none of the accursed things shall remain in your hand, that the LORD may turn from the fierceness of His anger and show you mercy, have compassion on you and multiply you, just as He swore to your fathers,
18 "because you have listened to the voice of the LORD your God, to keep all His commandments which I command you today, to do *what is* right in the eyes of the LORD your God.

Improper Mourning

14 "You *are* the children of the LORD your God; you shall not cut yourselves nor shave the front of your head for the dead.
2 "For you *are* a holy people to the LORD your God, and the LORD has chosen you to be a people for Himself, a special treasure above all the peoples who *are* on the face of the earth.

Clean and Unclean Meat

3 "You shall not eat any detestable thing.
4 "These *are* the animals which you may eat: the ox, the sheep, the goat,
5 "the deer, the gazelle, the roe deer, the wild goat, the mountain goat,[a] the antelope, and the mountain sheep.
6 "And you may eat every animal with cloven hooves, having the hoof split into two parts, *and that* chews the cud, among the animals.
7 "Nevertheless, of those that chew the cud or have cloven hooves, you shall not eat, *such as* these: the camel, the hare, and the rock hyrax; for they chew the cud but do not have cloven hooves; they *are* unclean for you.
8 "Also the swine is unclean for you, because it has cloven hooves, yet *does* not *chew* the cud; you shall not eat their flesh or touch their dead carcasses.
9 "These you may eat of all that *are* in the waters: you may eat all that have fins and scales.
10 "And whatever does not have fins and scales you shall not eat; it *is* unclean for you.
11 "All clean birds you may eat.
12 "But these you shall not eat: the eagle, the vulture, the buzzard,
13 "the red kite, the falcon, and the kite after their kinds;
14 "every raven after its kind;

14:5 [a]Or *addax*

15 "the ostrich, the short-eared owl, the sea
gull, and the hawk after their kinds;
16 "the little owl, the screech owl, the white
owl,
17 "the jackdaw, the carrion vulture, the
fisher owl,
18 "the stork, the heron after its kind, and the
hoopoe and the bat.
19 "Also every creeping thing that flies is un-
clean for you; they shall not be eaten.
20 "You may eat all clean birds.
21 "You shall not eat anything that dies *of
itself;* you may give it to the alien who *is* within
your gates, that he may eat it, or you may sell
it to a foreigner; for you *are* a holy people to
the LORD your God. You shall not boil a young
goat in its mother's milk.

Tithing Principles

22 "You shall truly tithe all the increase of
your grain that the field produces year by year.
23 "And you shall eat before the LORD your
God, in the place where He chooses to make
His name abide, the tithe of your grain and
your new wine and your oil, of the firstborn of
your herds and your flocks, that you may learn
to fear the LORD your God always.
24 "But if the journey is too long for you, so
that you are not able to carry *the tithe, or* if
the place where the LORD your God chooses
to put His name is too far from you, when the
LORD your God has blessed you,
25 "then you shall exchange *it* for money,
take the money in your hand, and go to the
place which the LORD your God chooses.
26 "And you shall spend that money for what-
ever your heart desires: for oxen or sheep, for
wine or similar drink, for whatever your heart
desires; you shall eat there before the LORD
your God, and you shall rejoice, you and your
household.
27 "You shall not forsake the Levite who *is*
within your gates, for he has no part nor inheri-
tance with you.
28 "At the end of *every* third year you shall
bring out the tithe of your produce of that year
and store *it* up within your gates.
29 "And the Levite, because he has no portion
nor inheritance with you, and the stranger and
the fatherless and the widow who *are* within
your gates, may come and eat and be satisfied,
that the LORD your God may bless you in all
the work of your hand which you do.

Debts Canceled Every Seven Years

15 "At the end of *every* seven years you
shall grant a release *of debts.*
2 "And this *is* the form of the release: Every
creditor who has lent *anything* to his neighbor
shall release *it;* he shall not require *it* of his
neighbor or his brother, because it is called the
LORD's release.
3 "Of a foreigner you may require *it;* but you
shall give up your claim to what is owed by
your brother,
4 "except when there may be no poor among
you; for the LORD will greatly bless you in the
land which the LORD your God is giving you
to possess *as* an inheritance—
5 "only if you carefully obey the voice of the
LORD your God, to observe with care all these
commandments which I command you today.
6 "For the LORD your God will bless you just
as He promised you; you shall lend to many
nations, but you shall not borrow; you shall
reign over many nations, but they shall not
reign over you.

Generosity to the Poor

7 "If there is among you a poor man of your
brethren, within any of the gates in your land
which the LORD your God is giving you, you
shall not harden your heart nor shut your hand
from your poor brother,
8 "but you shall open your hand wide to him
and willingly lend him sufficient for his need,
whatever he needs.
9 "Beware lest there be a wicked thought in
your heart, saying, 'The seventh year, the year
of release, is at hand,' and your eye be evil
against your poor brother and you give him
nothing, and he cry out to the LORD against
you, and it become sin among you.
10 "You shall surely give to him, and your
heart should not be grieved when you give to
him, because for this thing the LORD your God
will bless you in all your works and in all to
which you put your hand.
11 "For the poor will never cease from the
land; therefore I command you, saying, 'You
shall open your hand wide to your brother, to
your poor and your needy, in your land.'

The Law Concerning Bondservants

12 "If your brother, a Hebrew man, or a He-
brew woman, is sold to you and serves you six
years, then in the seventh year you shall let
him go free from you.
13 "And when you send him away free from
you, you shall not let him go away empty-
handed;
14 "you shall supply him liberally from your
flock, from your threshing floor, and from your
winepress. *From what* the LORD your God has
blessed you with, you shall give to him.
15 "You shall remember that you were a slave
in the land of Egypt, and the LORD your God
redeemed you; therefore I command you this
thing today.
16 "And if it happens that he says to you, 'I
will not go away from you,' because he loves
you and your house, since he prospers with
you,
17 "then you shall take an awl and thrust *it*
through his ear to the door, and he shall be
your servant forever. Also to your female ser-
vant you shall do likewise.
18 "It shall not seem hard to you when you
send him away free from you; for he has been
worth a double hired servant in serving you
six years. Then the LORD your God will bless
you in all that you do.

The Law Concerning Firstborn Animals

19 "All the firstborn males that come from
your herd and your flock you shall sanctify to
the LORD your God; you shall do no work with
the firstborn of your herd, nor shear the first-
born of your flock.
20 "You and your household shall eat *it* be-
fore the LORD your God year by year in the
place which the LORD chooses.
21 "But if there is a defect in it, *if it is* lame or
blind *or has* any serious defect, you shall not
sacrifice it to the LORD your God.
22 "You may eat it within your gates; the un-

clean and the clean *person* alike *may eat it*, as
if it were a gazelle or a deer.
23 "Only you shall not eat its blood; you shall
pour it on the ground like water.

The Passover Reviewed

16 "Observe the month of Abib, and keep
the Passover to the LORD your God, for
in the month of Abib the LORD your God
brought you out of Egypt by night.
2 "Therefore you shall sacrifice the Pass-
over to the LORD your God, from the flock and
the herd, in the place where the LORD chooses
to put His name.
3 "You shall eat no leavened bread with it;
seven days you shall eat unleavened bread
with it, *that is*, the bread of affliction (for you
came out of the land of Egypt in haste), that
you may remember the day in which you came
out of the land of Egypt all the days of your
life.
4 "And no leaven shall be seen among you
in all your territory for seven days, nor shall
any of the meat which you sacrifice the first
day at twilight remain overnight until morning.
5 "You may not sacrifice the Passover within
any of your gates which the LORD your God
gives you;
6 "but at the place where the LORD your God
chooses to make His name abide, there you
shall sacrifice the Passover at twilight, at the
going down of the sun, at the time you came
out of Egypt.
7 "And you shall roast and eat *it* in the place
which the LORD your God chooses, and in the
morning you shall turn and go to your tents.
8 "Six days you shall eat unleavened bread,
and on the seventh day there *shall be* a sacred
assembly to the LORD your God. You shall do
no work *on it*.

The Feast of Weeks Reviewed

9 "You shall count seven weeks for yourself;
begin to count the seven weeks from *the time*
you begin *to put* the sickle to the grain.
10 "Then you shall keep the Feast of Weeks
to the LORD your God with the tribute of a
freewill offering from your hand, which you
shall give as the LORD your God blesses you.
11 "You shall rejoice before the LORD your
God, you and your son and your daughter, your
male servant and your female servant, the Le-
vite who *is* within your gates, the stranger and
the fatherless and the widow who *are* among
you, at the place where the LORD your God
chooses to make His name abide.
12 "And you shall remember that you were
a slave in Egypt, and you shall be careful to
observe these statutes.

The Feast of Tabernacles Reviewed

13 "You shall observe the Feast of Taberna-
cles seven days, when you have gathered from
your threshing floor and from your winepress.
14 "And you shall rejoice in your feast, you
and your son and your daughter, your male
servant and your female servant and the Le-
vite, the stranger and the fatherless and the
widow, who *are* within your gates.
15 "Seven days you shall keep a sacred feast
to the LORD your God in the place which the
LORD chooses, because the LORD your God
will bless you in all your produce and in all the
work of your hands, so that you surely rejoice.
16 "Three times a year all your males shall
appear before the LORD your God in the place
which He chooses: at the Feast of Unleavened
Bread, at the Feast of Weeks, and at the Feast
of Tabernacles; and they shall not appear be-
fore the LORD empty-handed.
17 "Every man *shall give* as he is able, accord-
ing to the blessing of the LORD your God which
He has given you.

Justice Must Be Administered

18 "You shall appoint judges and officers in
all your gates, which the LORD your God gives
you, according to your tribes, and they shall
judge the people with just judgment.
19 "You shall not pervert justice; you shall
not show partiality, nor take a bribe, for a bribe
blinds the eyes of the wise and twists the words
of the righteous.
20 "You shall follow what is altogether just,
that you may live and inherit the land which
the LORD your God is giving you.
21 "You shall not plant for yourself any tree,
as a wooden image, near the altar which you
build for yourself to the LORD your God.
22 "You shall not set up a *sacred* pillar, which
the LORD your God hates.
17 "You shall not sacrifice to the LORD
your God a bull or sheep which has any
blemish *or* defect, for that *is* an abomination
to the LORD your God.
2 "If there is found among you, within any
of your gates which the LORD your God gives
you, a man or a woman who has been wicked
in the sight of the LORD your God, in trans-
gressing His covenant,
3 "who has gone and served other gods and
worshiped them, either the sun or moon or
any of the host of heaven, which I have not
commanded,
4 "and it is told you, and you hear *of it*, then
you shall inquire diligently. And if *it is* indeed
true *and* certain that such an abomination has
been committed in Israel,
5 "then you shall bring out to your gates that
man or woman who has committed that
wicked thing, and shall stone to death that man
or woman with stones.
6 "Whoever is deserving of death shall be
put to death on the testimony of two or three
witnesses; he shall not be put to death on the
testimony of one witness.
7 "The hands of the witnesses shall be the
first against him to put him to death, and after-
ward the hands of all the people. So you shall
put away the evil from among you.
8 "If a matter arises which is too hard for
you to judge, between degrees of guilt for
bloodshed, between one judgment or another,
or between one punishment or another, mat-
ters of controversy within your gates, then you
shall arise and go up to the place which the
LORD your God chooses.
9 "And you shall come to the priests, the Le-
vites, and to the judge *there* in those days, and
inquire *of them;* they shall pronounce upon
you the sentence of judgment.
10 "You shall do according to the sentence
which they pronounce upon you in that place
which the LORD chooses. And you shall be
careful to do according to all that they order
you.
11 "According to the sentence of the law in
which they instruct you, according to the judg-
ment which they tell you, you shall do; you
shall not turn aside *to* the right hand or *to* the

left from the sentence which they pronounce
upon you.
12 "Now the man who acts presumptuously
and will not heed the priest who stands to min-
ister there before the LORD your God, or the
judge, that man shall die. So you shall put away
the evil from Israel.
13 "And all the people shall hear and fear,
and no longer act presumptuously.

Principles Governing Kings

14 "When you come to the land which the
LORD your God is giving you, and possess it
and dwell in it, and say, 'I will set a king over
me like all the nations that *are* around me,'
15 "you shall surely set a king over you whom
the LORD your God chooses; *one* from among
your brethren you shall set as king over you;
you may not set a foreigner over you, who *is*
not your brother.
16 "But he shall not multiply horses for him-
self, nor cause the people to return to Egypt to
multiply horses, for the LORD has said to you,
'You shall not return that way again.'
17 "Neither shall he multiply wives for him-
self, lest his heart turn away; nor shall he
greatly multiply silver and gold for himself.
18 "Also it shall be, when he sits on the throne
of his kingdom, that he shall write for himself
a copy of this law in a book, from *the one*
before the priests, the Levites.
19 "And it shall be with him, and he shall read
it all the days of his life, that he may learn to
fear the LORD his God and be careful to ob-
serve all the words of this law and these stat-
utes,
20 "that his heart may not be lifted above his
brethren, that he may not turn aside from the
commandment *to* the right hand or *to* the left,
and that he may prolong *his* days in his king-
dom, he and his children in the midst of Israel.

The Portion of the Priests and Levites

18 "The priests, the Levites—all the tribe of
Levi—shall have no part nor inheritance
with Israel; they shall eat the offerings of the
LORD made by fire, and His portion.
2 "Therefore they shall have no inheritance
among their brethren; the LORD is their inheri-
tance, as He said to them.
3 "And this shall be the priest's due from
the people, from those who offer a sacrifice,
whether *it is* bull or sheep: they shall give to
the priest the shoulder, the cheeks, and the
stomach.
4 "The firstfruits of your grain and your new
wine and your oil, and the first of the fleece of
your sheep, you shall give him.
5 "For the LORD your God has chosen him
out of all your tribes to stand to minister in the
name of the LORD, him and his sons forever.
6 "So if a Levite comes from any of your
gates, from where he dwells among all Israel,
and comes with all the desire of his mind to
the place which the LORD chooses,
7 "then he may serve in the name of the
LORD his God as all his brethren the Levites
do, who stand there before the LORD.
8 "They shall have equal portions to eat, be-
sides what comes from the sale of his inheri-
tance.

Avoid Wicked Customs

9 "When you come into the land which the
LORD your God is giving you, you shall not
learn to follow the abominations of those na-
tions.
10 "There shall not be found among you *any-
one* who makes his son or his daughter pass
through the fire, *or one* who practices witch-
craft, *or* a soothsayer, or one who interprets
omens, or a sorcerer,
11 "or one who conjures spells, or a medium,
or a spiritist, or one who calls up the dead.
12 "For all who do these things *are* an abomi-
nation to the LORD, and because of these
abominations the LORD your God drives them
out from before you.
13 "You shall be blameless before the LORD
your God.
14 "For these nations which you will dis-
possess listened to soothsayers and diviners;
but as for you, the LORD your God has not
appointed such for you.

A New Prophet Like Moses

15 "The LORD your God will raise up for you
a Prophet like me from your midst, from your
brethren. Him you shall hear,
16 "according to all you desired of the LORD
your God in Horeb in the day of the assembly,
saying, 'Let me not hear again the voice of the
LORD my God, nor let me see this great fire
anymore, lest I die.'
17 "And the LORD said to me: 'What they have
spoken is good.
18 'I will raise up for them a Prophet like you
from among their brethren, and will put My
words in His mouth, and He shall speak to
them all that I command Him.
19 'And it shall be *that* whoever will not hear
My words, which He speaks in My name, I will
require *it* of him.
20 'But the prophet who presumes to speak a
word in My name, which I have not com-
manded him to speak, or who speaks in the
name of other gods, that prophet shall die.'
21 "And if you say in your heart, 'How shall
we know the word which the LORD has not
spoken?'—
22 "when a prophet speaks in the name of the
LORD, if the thing does not happen or come to
pass, that *is* the thing which the LORD has not
spoken; the prophet has spoken it presumptu-
ously; you shall not be afraid of him.

Three Cities of Refuge

19 "When the LORD your God has cut off
the nations whose land the LORD your
God is giving you, and you dispossess them
and dwell in their cities and in their houses,
2 "you shall separate three cities for yourself
in the midst of your land which the LORD your
God is giving you to possess.
3 "You shall prepare roads for yourself, and
divide into three parts the territory of your
land which the LORD your God is giving you
to inherit, that any manslayer may flee there.
4 "And this *is* the case of the manslayer who
flees there, that he may live: Whoever kills his
neighbor unintentionally, not having hated
him in time past—
5 "as when *a man* goes to the woods with
his neighbor to cut timber, and his hand swings
a stroke with the ax to cut down the tree, and
the head slips from the handle and strikes his
neighbor so that he dies—he shall flee to one
of these cities and live;
6 "lest the avenger of blood, while his anger
is hot, pursue the manslayer and overtake him,

because the way is long, and kill him, though
he *was* not deserving of death, since he had
not hated the victim in time past.
7 "Therefore I command you, saying, 'You
shall separate three cities for yourself.'
8 "Now if the LORD your God enlarges your
territory, as He swore to your fathers, and gives
you the land which He promised to give to your
fathers,
9 "and if you keep all these commandments
and do them, which I command you today, to
love the LORD your God and to walk always in
His ways, then you shall add three more cities
for yourself besides these three,
10 "lest innocent blood be shed in the midst
of your land which the LORD your God is giv-
ing you *as* an inheritance, and *thus* guilt of
bloodshed be upon you.
11 "But if anyone hates his neighbor, lies in
wait for him, rises against him and strikes him
mortally, so that he dies, and he flees to one of
these cities,
12 "then the elders of his city shall send and
bring him from there, and deliver him over to
the hand of the avenger of blood, that he may
die.
13 "Your eye shall not pity him, but you shall
put away *the guilt of* innocent blood from Is-
rael, that it may go well with you.

Property Boundaries

14 "You shall not remove your neighbor's
landmark, which the men of old have set, in
your inheritance which you will inherit in the
land that the LORD your God is giving you to
possess.

The Law Concerning Witnesses

15 "One witness shall not rise against a man
concerning any iniquity or any sin that he com-
mits; by the mouth of two or three witnesses
the matter shall be established.
16 "If a false witness rises against any man
to testify against him of wrongdoing,
17 "then both men in the controversy shall
stand before the LORD, before the priests and
the judges who serve in those days.
18 "And the judges shall make careful in-
quiry, and indeed, *if* the witness *is* a false wit-
ness, who has testified falsely against his
brother,
19 "then you shall do to him as he thought to
have done to his brother; so you shall put away
the evil from among you.
20 "And those who remain shall hear and
fear, and hereafter they shall not again commit
such evil among you.
21 "Your eye shall not pity: life *shall be* for
life, eye for eye, tooth for tooth, hand for hand,
foot for foot.

Principles Governing Warfare

20 "When you go out to battle against your
enemies, and see horses and chariots
and people more numerous than you, do not
be afraid of them; for the LORD your God *is*
with you, who brought you up from the land of
Egypt.
2 "So it shall be, when you are on the verge
of battle, that the priest shall approach and
speak to the people.
3 "And he shall say to them, 'Hear, O Israel:
Today you are on the verge of battle with your
enemies. Do not let your heart faint, do not
be afraid, and do not tremble or be terrified
because of them;
4 'for the LORD your God *is* He who goes
with you, to fight for you against your enemies,
to save you.'
5 "Then the officers shall speak to the peo-
ple, saying: 'What man *is there* who has built
a new house and has not dedicated it? Let him
go and return to his house, lest he die in the
battle and another man dedicate it.
6 'Also what man *is there* who has planted a
vineyard and has not eaten of it? Let him go
and return to his house, lest he die in the battle
and another man eat of it.
7 'And what man *is there* who is betrothed
to a woman and has not married her? Let him
go and return to his house, lest he die in the
battle and another man marry her.'
8 "The officers shall speak further to the
people, and say, 'What man *is there who is*
fearful and fainthearted? Let him go and re-
turn to his house, lest the heart of his brethren
faint[a] like his heart.'
9 "And so it shall be, when the officers have
finished speaking to the people, that they shall
make captains of the armies to lead the people.
10 "When you go near a city to fight against
it, then proclaim an offer of peace to it.
11 "And it shall be that if they accept your
offer of peace, and open to you, then all the
people *who are* found in it shall be placed un-
der tribute to you, and serve you.
12 "Now if *the city* will not make peace with
you, but makes war against you, then you shall
besiege it.
13 "And when the LORD your God delivers it
into your hands, you shall strike every male in
it with the edge of the sword.
14 "But the women, the little ones, the live-
stock, and all that is in the city, all its spoil, you
shall plunder for yourself; and you shall eat
the enemies' plunder which the LORD your
God gives you.
15 "Thus you shall do to all the cities *which
are* very far from you, which *are* not of the
cities of these nations.
16 "But of the cities of these peoples which
the LORD your God gives you *as* an inheri-
tance, you shall let nothing that breathes re-
main alive,
17 "but you shall utterly destroy them: the
Hittite and the Amorite and the Canaanite and
the Perizzite and the Hivite and the Jebusite,
just as the LORD your God has commanded
you,
18 "lest they teach you to do according to all
their abominations which they have done for
their gods, and you sin against the LORD your
God.
19 "When you besiege a city for a long time,
while making war against it to take it, you shall
not destroy its trees by wielding an ax against
them; if you can eat of them, do not cut them
down to use in the siege, for the tree of the
field *is* man's *food*.
20 "Only the trees which you know *are* not
trees for food you may destroy and cut down,
to build siegeworks against the city that makes
war with you, until it is subdued.

20:8 [a]Following Masoretic Text and Targum; Samaritan Pentateuch, Septuagint, Syriac, and Vulgate read *lest he make his brother's heart faint*.

The Law Concerning Unsolved Murder

21 "If *anyone* is found slain, lying in the field in the land which the LORD your God is giving you to possess, *and* it is not known who killed him,
2 "then your elders and your judges shall go out and measure *the distance* from the slain man to the surrounding cities.
3 "And it shall be *that* the elders of the city nearest to the slain man will take a heifer which has not been worked *and* which has not pulled with a yoke.
4 "The elders of that city shall bring the heifer down to a valley with flowing water, which is neither plowed nor sown, and they shall break the heifer's neck there in the valley.
5 "Then the priests, the sons of Levi, shall come near, for the LORD your God has chosen them to minister to Him and to bless in the name of the LORD; by their word every controversy and every assault shall be *settled.*
6 "And all the elders of that city nearest to the slain *man* shall wash their hands over the heifer whose neck was broken in the valley.
7 "Then they shall answer and say, 'Our hands have not shed this blood, nor have our eyes seen *it.*
8 'Provide atonement, O LORD, for Your people Israel, whom You have redeemed, and do not lay innocent blood to the charge of Your people Israel.' And atonement shall be provided on their behalf for the blood.
9 "So you shall put away the *guilt of* innocent blood from among you when you do *what is* right in the sight of the LORD.

Female Captives

10 "When you go out to war against your enemies, and the LORD your God delivers them into your hand, and you take them captive,
11 "and you see among the captives a beautiful woman, and desire her and would take her for your wife,
12 "then you shall bring her home to your house, and she shall shave her head and trim her nails.
13 "She shall put off the clothes of her captivity, remain in your house, and mourn her father and her mother a full month; after that you may go in to her and be her husband, and she shall be your wife.
14 "And it shall be, if you have no delight in her, then you shall set her free, but you certainly shall not sell her for money; you shall not treat her brutally, because you have humbled her.

Firstborn Inheritance Rights

15 "If a man has two wives, one loved and the other unloved, and they have borne him children, *both* the loved and the unloved, and *if* the firstborn son is of her who is unloved,
16 "then it shall be, on the day he bequeaths his possessions to his sons, *that* he must not bestow firstborn status on the son of the loved wife in preference to the son of the unloved, the *true* firstborn.
17 "But he shall acknowledge the son of the unloved wife *as* the firstborn by giving him a double portion of all that he has, for he *is* the beginning of his strength; the right of the firstborn *is* his.

The Rebellious Son

18 "If a man has a stubborn and rebellious son who will not obey the voice of his father or the voice of his mother, and *who,* when they have chastened him, will not heed them,
19 "then his father and his mother shall take hold of him and bring him out to the elders of his city, to the gate of his city.
20 "And they shall say to the elders of his city, 'This son of ours is stubborn and rebellious; he will not obey our voice; he is a glutton and a drunkard.'
21 "Then all the men of his city shall stone him to death with stones; so you shall put away the evil from among you, and all Israel shall hear and fear.

Miscellaneous Laws

22 "If a man has committed a sin deserving of death, and he is put to death, and you hang him on a tree,
23 "his body shall not remain overnight on the tree, but you shall surely bury him that day, so that you do not defile the land which the LORD your God is giving you *as* an inheritance; for he who is hanged *is* accursed of God.

22 "You shall not see your brother's ox or his sheep going astray, and hide yourself from them; you shall certainly bring them back to your brother.
2 "And if your brother *is* not near you, or if you do not know him, then you shall bring it to your own house, and it shall remain with you until your brother seeks it; then you shall restore it to him.
3 "You shall do the same with his donkey, and so shall you do with his garment; with any lost thing of your brother's, which he has lost and you have found, you shall do likewise; you must not hide yourself.
4 "You shall not see your brother's donkey or his ox fall down along the road, and hide yourself from them; you shall surely help him lift *them* up again.
5 "A woman shall not wear anything that pertains to a man, nor shall a man put on a woman's garment, for all who do so *are* an abomination to the LORD your God.
6 "If a bird's nest happens to be before you along the way, in any tree or on the ground, with young ones or eggs, with the mother sitting on the young or on the eggs, you shall not take the mother with the young;
7 "you shall surely let the mother go, and take the young for yourself, that it may be well with you and *that* you may prolong *your* days.
8 "When you build a new house, then you shall make a parapet for your roof, that you may not bring guilt of bloodshed on your household if anyone falls from it.
9 "You shall not sow your vineyard with different kinds of seed, lest the yield of the seed which you have sown and the fruit of your vineyard be defiled.
10 "You shall not plow with an ox and a donkey together.
11 "You shall not wear a garment of different sorts, *such as* wool and linen mixed together.
12 "You shall make tassels on the four corners of the clothing with which you cover *yourself.*

Laws of Sexual Morality

13 "If any man takes a wife, and goes in to her, and detests her,
14 "and charges her with shameful conduct, and brings a bad name on her, and says, 'I took this woman, and when I came to her I found she *was* not a virgin,'
15 "then the father and mother of the young woman shall take and bring out *the evidence of* the young woman's virginity to the elders of the city at the gate.
16 "And the young woman's father shall say to the elders, 'I gave my daughter to this man as wife, and he detests her.
17 'Now he has charged her with shameful conduct, saying, "I found your daughter *was* not a virgin," and yet these *are the evidences of* my daughter's virginity.' And they shall spread the cloth before the elders of the city.
18 "Then the elders of that city shall take that man and punish him;
19 "and they shall fine him one hundred *shekels* of silver and give *them* to the father of the young woman, because he has brought a bad name on a virgin of Israel. And she shall be his wife; he cannot divorce her all his days.
20 "But if the thing is true, *and evidences of* virginity are not found for the young woman,
21 "then they shall bring out the young woman to the door of her father's house, and the men of her city shall stone her to death with stones, because she has done a disgraceful thing in Israel, to play the harlot in her father's house. So you shall put away the evil from among you.
22 "If a man is found lying with a woman married to a husband, then both of them shall die—the man that lay with the woman, and the woman; so you shall put away the evil from Israel.
23 "If a young woman *who is* a virgin is betrothed to a husband, and a man finds her in the city and lies with her,
24 "then you shall bring them both out to the gate of that city, and you shall stone them to death with stones, the young woman because she did not cry out in the city, and the man because he humbled his neighbor's wife; so you shall put away the evil from among you.
25 "But if a man finds a betrothed young woman in the countryside, and the man forces her and lies with her, then only the man who lay with her shall die.
26 "But you shall do nothing to the young woman; *there is* in the young woman no sin *deserving* of death, for just as when a man rises against his neighbor and kills him, even so *is* this matter.
27 "For he found her in the countryside, *and* the betrothed young woman cried out, but *there was* no one to save her.
28 "If a man finds a young woman *who is* a virgin, who is not betrothed, and he seizes her and lies with her, and they are found out,
29 "then the man who lay with her shall give to the young woman's father fifty *shekels* of silver, and she shall be his wife because he has humbled her; he shall not be permitted to divorce her all his days.
30 "A man shall not take his father's wife, nor uncover his father's bed.

Those Excluded from the Congregation

23 "He who is emasculated by crushing or mutilation shall not enter the assembly of the LORD.
2 "One of illegitimate birth shall not enter the assembly of the LORD; even to the tenth generation none of his *descendants* shall enter the assembly of the LORD.
3 "An Ammonite or Moabite shall not enter the assembly of the LORD; even to the tenth generation none of his *descendants* shall enter the assembly of the LORD forever,
4 "because they did not meet you with bread and water on the road when you came out of Egypt, and because they hired against you Balaam the son of Beor from Pethor of Mesopotamia,[a] to curse you.
5 "Nevertheless the LORD your God would not listen to Balaam, but the LORD your God turned the curse into a blessing for you, because the LORD your God loves you.
6 "You shall not seek their peace nor their prosperity all your days forever.
7 "You shall not abhor an Edomite, for he *is* your brother. You shall not abhor an Egyptian, because you were an alien in his land.
8 "The children of the third generation born to them may enter the assembly of the LORD.

Cleanliness of the Campsite

9 "When the army goes out against your enemies, then keep yourself from every wicked thing.
10 "If there is any man among you who becomes unclean by some occurrence in the night, then he shall go outside the camp; he shall not come inside the camp.
11 "But it shall be, when evening comes, that he shall wash with water; and when the sun sets, he may come into the camp.
12 "Also you shall have a place outside the camp, where you may go out;
13 "and you shall have an implement among your equipment, and when you sit down outside, you shall dig with it and turn and cover your refuse.
14 "For the LORD your God walks in the midst of your camp, to deliver you and give your enemies over to you; therefore your camp shall be holy, that He may see no unclean thing among you, and turn away from you.

Miscellaneous Laws

15 "You shall not give back to his master the slave who has escaped from his master to you.
16 "He may dwell with you in your midst, in the place which he chooses within one of your gates, where it seems best to him; you shall not oppress him.
17 "There shall be no *ritual* harlot[a] of the daughters of Israel, or a perverted[b] one of the sons of Israel.
18 "You shall not bring the wages of a harlot or the price of a dog to the house of the LORD your God for any vowed offering, for both of these *are* an abomination to the LORD your God.
19 "You shall not charge interest to your brother—interest on money *or* food *or* anything that is lent out at interest.
20 "To a foreigner you may charge interest,

23:4 [a]Hebrew *Aram Naharaim* 23:17 [a]Hebrew *qedeshah,* feminine of *qadesh* (see following note) [b]Hebrew *qadesh,* that is, one practicing sodomy and prostitution in religious rituals

but to your brother you shall not charge interest, that the LORD your God may bless you in all to which you set your hand in the land which you are entering to possess.
21 "When you make a vow to the LORD your God, you shall not delay to pay it; for the LORD your God will surely require it of you, and it would be sin to you.
22 "But if you abstain from vowing, it shall not be sin to you.
23 "That which has gone from your lips you shall keep and perform, for you voluntarily vowed to the LORD your God what you have promised with your mouth.
24 "When you come into your neighbor's vineyard, you may eat your fill of grapes at your pleasure, but you shall not put *any* in your container.
25 "When you come into your neighbor's standing grain, you may pluck the heads with your hand, but you shall not use a sickle on your neighbor's standing grain.

Law Concerning Divorce

24 "When a man takes a wife and marries her, and it happens that she finds no favor in his eyes because he has found some uncleanness in her, and he writes her a certificate of divorce, puts *it* in her hand, and sends her out of his house,
2 "when she has departed from his house, and goes and becomes another man's *wife,*
3 "*if* the latter husband detests her and writes her a certificate of divorce, puts *it* in her hand, and sends her out of his house, or if the latter husband dies who took her as his wife,
4 "*then* her former husband who divorced her must not take her back to be his wife after she has been defiled; for that *is* an abomination before the LORD, and you shall not bring sin on the land which the LORD your God is giving you *as* an inheritance.

Miscellaneous Laws

5 "When a man has taken a new wife, he shall not go out to war or be charged with any business; he shall be free at home one year, and bring happiness to his wife whom he has taken.
6 "No man shall take the lower or the upper millstone in pledge, for he takes *one's* living in pledge.
7 "If a man is found kidnapping any of his brethren of the children of Israel, and mistreats him or sells him, then that kidnapper shall die; and you shall put away the evil from among you.
8 "Take heed in an outbreak of leprosy, that you carefully observe and do according to all that the priests, the Levites, shall teach you; just as I commanded them, *so* you shall be careful to do.
9 "Remember what the LORD your God did to Miriam on the way when you came out of Egypt!
10 "When you lend your brother anything, you shall not go into his house to get his pledge.
11 "You shall stand outside, and the man to whom you lend shall bring the pledge out to you.
12 "And if the man *is* poor, you shall not keep his pledge overnight.
13 "You shall in any case return the pledge to him again when the sun goes down, that he may sleep in his own garment and bless you; and it shall be righteousness to you before the LORD your God.
14 "You shall not oppress a hired servant *who is* poor and needy, *whether* one of your brethren or one of the aliens who *is* in your land within your gates.
15 "Each day you shall give *him* his wages, and not let the sun go down on it, for he *is* poor and has set his heart on it; lest he cry out against you to the LORD, and it be sin to you.
16 "Fathers shall not be put to death for *their* children, nor shall children be put to death for *their* fathers; a person shall be put to death for his own sin.
17 "You shall not pervert justice due the stranger or the fatherless, nor take a widow's garment as a pledge.
18 "But you shall remember that you were a slave in Egypt, and the LORD your God redeemed you from there; therefore I command you to do this thing.
19 "When you reap your harvest in your field, and forget a sheaf in the field, you shall not go back to get it; it shall be for the stranger, the fatherless, and the widow, that the LORD your God may bless you in all the work of your hands.
20 "When you beat your olive trees, you shall not go over the boughs again; it shall be for the stranger, the fatherless, and the widow.
21 "When you gather the grapes of your vineyard, you shall not glean *it* afterward; it shall be for the stranger, the fatherless, and the widow.
22 "And you shall remember that you were a slave in the land of Egypt; therefore I command you to do this thing.
25 "If there is a dispute between men, and they come to court, that *the judges* may judge them, and they justify the righteous and condemn the wicked,
2 "then it shall be, if the wicked man deserves to be beaten, that the judge will cause him to lie down and be beaten in his presence, according to his guilt, with a certain number of blows.
3 "Forty blows he may give him *and* no more, lest he should exceed this and beat him with many blows above these, and your brother be humiliated in your sight.
4 "You shall not muzzle an ox while it treads out *the grain.*

Marriage Duty of the Surviving Brother

5 "If brothers dwell together, and one of them dies and has no son, the widow of the dead man shall not be *married* to a stranger outside *the family;* her husband's brother shall go in to her, take her as his wife, and perform the duty of a husband's brother to her.
6 "And it shall be *that* the firstborn son which she bears will succeed to the name of his dead brother, that his name may not be blotted out of Israel.
7 "But if the man does not want to take his brother's wife, then let his brother's wife go up to the gate to the elders, and say, 'My husband's brother refuses to raise up a name to his brother in Israel; he will not perform the duty of my husband's brother.'
8 "Then the elders of his city shall call him and speak to him. But *if* he stands firm and says, 'I do not want to take her,'
9 "then his brother's wife shall come to him in the presence of the elders, remove his sandal from his foot, spit in his face, and answer and

say, 'So shall it be done to the man who will
not build up his brother's house.'
10 "And his name shall be called in Israel,
'The house of him who had his sandal re-
moved.'

Miscellaneous Laws

11 "If *two* men fight together, and the wife of
one draws near to rescue her husband from
the hand of the one attacking him, and puts
out her hand and seizes him by the genitals,
12 "then you shall cut off her hand; your eye
shall not pity *her.*
13 "You shall not have in your bag differing
weights, a heavy and a light.
14 "You shall not have in your house differing
measures, a large and a small.
15 "You shall have a perfect and just weight,
a perfect and just measure, that your days may
be lengthened in the land which the LORD your
God is giving you.
16 "For all who do such things, all who be-
have unrighteously, *are* an abomination to the
LORD your God.

Destroy the Amalekites

17 "Remember what Amalek did to you on
the way as you were coming out of Egypt,
18 "how he met you on the way and attacked
your rear ranks, all the stragglers at your rear,
when you *were* tired and weary; and he did not
fear God.
19 "Therefore it shall be, when the LORD your
God has given you rest from your enemies all
around, in the land which the LORD your God
is giving you to possess *as* an inheritance, *that*
you will blot out the remembrance of Amalek
from under heaven. You shall not forget.

Offerings of Firstfruits and Tithes

26 "And it shall be, when you come into the
land which the LORD your God is giving
you *as* an inheritance, and you possess it and
dwell in it,
2 "that you shall take some of the first of all
the produce of the ground, which you shall
bring from your land that the LORD your God
is giving you, and put *it* in a basket and go to
the place where the LORD your God chooses
to make His name abide.
3 "And you shall go to the one who is priest
in those days, and say to him, 'I declare today
to the LORD your[a] God that I have come to the
country which the LORD swore to our fathers
to give us.'
4 "Then the priest shall take the basket out
of your hand and set it down before the altar
of the LORD your God.
5 "And you shall answer and say before the
LORD your God: 'My father *was* a Syrian,[a]
about to perish, and he went down to Egypt
and dwelt there, few in number; and there he
became a nation, great, mighty, and populous.
6 'But the Egyptians mistreated us, afflicted
us, and laid hard bondage on us.
7 'Then we cried out to the LORD God of
our fathers, and the LORD heard our voice and
looked on our affliction and our labor and our
oppression.
8 'So the LORD brought us out of Egypt with
a mighty hand and with an outstretched arm,
with great terror and with signs and wonders.
9 'He has brought us to this place and has
given us this land, "a land flowing with milk
and honey";[a]
10 'and now, behold, I have brought the first-
fruits of the land which you, O LORD, have
given me.' Then you shall set it before the
LORD your God, and worship before the LORD
your God.
11 "So you shall rejoice in every good *thing*
which the LORD your God has given to you
and your house, you and the Levite and the
stranger who *is* among you.
12 "When you have finished laying aside all
the tithe of your increase in the third year—
the year of tithing—and have given *it* to the
Levite, the stranger, the fatherless, and the
widow, so that they may eat within your gates
and be filled,
13 "then you shall say before the LORD your
God: 'I have removed the holy *tithe* from *my*
house, and also have given them to the Levite,
the stranger, the fatherless, and the widow, ac-
cording to all Your commandments which You
have commanded me; I have not transgressed
Your commandments, nor have I forgotten
them.
14 'I have not eaten any of it when in mourn-
ing, nor have I removed *any* of it for an unclean
use, nor given *any* of it for the dead. I have
obeyed the voice of the LORD my God, and
have done according to all that You have com-
manded me.
15 'Look down from Your holy habitation,
from heaven, and bless Your people Israel and
the land which You have given us, just as You
swore to our fathers, "a land flowing with milk
and honey."'[a]

A Special People of God

16 "This day the LORD your God commands
you to observe these statutes and judgments;
therefore you shall be careful to observe them
with all your heart and with all your soul.
17 "Today you have proclaimed the LORD to
be your God, and that you will walk in His
ways and keep His statutes, His command-
ments, and His judgments, and that you will
obey His voice.
18 "Also today the LORD has proclaimed you
to be His special people, just as He promised
you, that *you* should keep all His command-
ments,
19 "and that He will set you high above all
nations which He has made, in praise, in name,
and in honor, and that you may be a holy peo-
ple to the LORD your God, just as He has
spoken."

The Law Inscribed on Stones

27 Now Moses, with the elders of Israel,
commanded the people, saying: "Keep
all the commandments which I command you
today.
2 "And it shall be, on the day when you cross
over the Jordan to the land which the LORD
your God is giving you, that you shall set up for
yourselves large stones, and whitewash them
with lime.
3 "You shall write on them all the words of
this law, when you have crossed over, that you
may enter the land which the LORD your God
is giving you, 'a land flowing with milk and
honey,'[a] just as the LORD God of your fathers
promised you.

26:3 [a]Septuagint reads *my.* **26:5** [a]Or *Aramean* **26:9** [a]Exodus 3:8 **26:15** [a]Exodus 3:8 **27:3** [a]Exodus 3:8

4 "Therefore it shall be, when you have
crossed over the Jordan, *that* on Mount Ebal
you shall set up these stones, which I command
you today, and you shall whitewash them with
lime.
5 "And there you shall build an altar to the
LORD your God, an altar of stones; you shall
not use an iron *tool* on them.
6 "You shall build with whole stones the al-
tar of the LORD your God, and offer burnt of-
ferings on it to the LORD your God.
7 "You shall offer peace offerings, and shall
eat there, and rejoice before the LORD your
God.
8 "And you shall write very plainly on the
stones all the words of this law."
9 Then Moses and the priests, the Levites,
spoke to all Israel, saying, "Take heed and lis-
ten, O Israel: This day you have become the
people of the LORD your God.
10 "Therefore you shall obey the voice of the
LORD your God, and observe His command-
ments and His statutes which I command you
today."

Curses Pronounced from Mount Ebal

11 And Moses commanded the people on the
same day, saying,
12 "These shall stand on Mount Gerizim to
bless the people, when you have crossed over
the Jordan: Simeon, Levi, Judah, Issachar, Jo-
seph, and Benjamin;
13 "and these shall stand on Mount Ebal to
curse: Reuben, Gad, Asher, Zebulun, Dan, and
Naphtali.
14 "And the Levites shall speak with a loud
voice and say to all the men of Israel:
15 'Cursed *is* the one who makes a carved or
molded image, an abomination to the LORD,
the work of the hands of the craftsman, and
sets *it* up in secret.'
"And all the people shall answer and say,
'Amen!'
16 'Cursed *is* the one who treats his father or
his mother with contempt.'
"And all the people shall say, 'Amen!'
17 'Cursed *is* the one who moves his neigh-
bor's landmark.'
"And all the people shall say, 'Amen!'
18 'Cursed *is* the one who makes the blind to
wander off the road.'
"And all the people shall say, 'Amen!'
19 'Cursed *is* the one who perverts the justice
due the stranger, the fatherless, and widow.'
"And all the people shall say, 'Amen!'
20 'Cursed *is* the one who lies with his fa-
ther's wife, because he has uncovered his fa-
ther's bed.'
"And all the people shall say, 'Amen!'
21 'Cursed *is* the one who lies with any kind
of animal.'
"And all the people shall say, 'Amen!'
22 'Cursed *is* the one who lies with his sister,
the daughter of his father or the daughter of
his mother.'
"And all the people shall say, 'Amen!'
23 'Cursed *is* the one who lies with his
mother-in-law.'
"And all the people shall say, 'Amen!'
24 'Cursed *is* the one who attacks his neigh-
bor secretly.'
"And all the people shall say, 'Amen!'
25 'Cursed *is* the one who takes a bribe to slay
an innocent person.'
"And all the people shall say, 'Amen!'
26 'Cursed *is* the one who does not confirm
all the words of this law by observing them.'
"And all the people shall say, 'Amen!'

Blessings on Obedience

28 "Now it shall come to pass, if you dili-
gently obey the voice of the LORD your
God, to observe carefully all His command-
ments which I command you today, that the
LORD your God will set you high above all
nations of the earth.
2 "And all these blessings shall come upon
you and overtake you, because you obey the
voice of the LORD your God:
3 "Blessed *shall* you *be* in the city, and
blessed *shall* you *be* in the country.
4 "Blessed *shall be* the fruit of your body,
the produce of your ground and the increase
of your herds, the increase of your cattle and
the offspring of your flocks.
5 "Blessed *shall be* your basket and your
kneading bowl.
6 "Blessed *shall* you *be* when you come in,
and blessed *shall* you *be* when you go out.
7 "The LORD will cause your enemies who
rise against you to be defeated before your
face; they shall come out against you one way
and flee before you seven ways.
8 "The LORD will command the blessing on
you in your storehouses and in all to which you
set your hand, and He will bless you in the land
which the LORD your God is giving you.
9 "The LORD will establish you as a holy
people to Himself, just as He has sworn to you,
if you keep the commandments of the LORD
your God and walk in His ways.
10 "Then all peoples of the earth shall see
that you are called by the name of the LORD,
and they shall be afraid of you.
11 "And the LORD will grant you plenty of
goods, in the fruit of your body, in the increase
of your livestock, and in the produce of your
ground, in the land of which the LORD swore
to your fathers to give you.
12 "The LORD will open to you His good trea-
sure, the heavens, to give the rain to your land
in its season, and to bless all the work of your
hand. You shall lend to many nations, but you
shall not borrow.
13 "And the LORD will make you the head
and not the tail; you shall be above only, and
not be beneath, if you heed the command-
ments of the LORD your God, which I com-
mand you today, and are careful to observe
them.
14 "So you shall not turn aside from any of
the words which I command you this day, *to*
the right or the left, to go after other gods to
serve them.

Curses on Disobedience

15 "But it shall come to pass, if you do not
obey the voice of the LORD your God, to ob-
serve carefully all His commandments and His
statutes which I command you today, that all
these curses will come upon you and overtake
you:
16 "Cursed *shall* you *be* in the city, and cursed
shall you *be* in the country.
17 "Cursed *shall be* your basket and your
kneading bowl.
18 "Cursed *shall be* the fruit of your body and
the produce of your land, the increase of your
cattle and the offspring of your flocks.

19 "Cursed *shall* you *be* when you come in,
and cursed *shall* you *be* when you go out.
20 "The LORD will send on you cursing, confusion, and rebuke in all that you set your hand to do, until you are destroyed and until you perish quickly, because of the wickedness of your doings in which you have forsaken Me.
21 "The LORD will make the plague cling to you until He has consumed you from the land which you are going to possess.
22 "The LORD will strike you with consumption, with fever, with inflammation, with severe burning fever, with the sword, with scorching, and with mildew; they shall pursue you until you perish.
23 "And your heavens which *are* over your head shall be bronze, and the earth which is under you *shall be* iron.
24 "The LORD will change the rain of your land to powder and dust; from the heaven it shall come down on you until you are destroyed.
25 "The LORD will cause you to be defeated before your enemies; you shall go out one way against them and flee seven ways before them; and you shall become troublesome to all the kingdoms of the earth.
26 "Your carcasses shall be food for all the birds of the air and the beasts of the earth, and no one shall frighten *them* away.
27 "The LORD will strike you with the boils of Egypt, with tumors, with the scab, and with the itch, from which you cannot be healed.
28 "The LORD will strike you with madness and blindness and confusion of heart.
29 "And you shall grope at noonday, as a blind man gropes in darkness; you shall not prosper in your ways; you shall be only oppressed and plundered continually, and no one shall save *you.*
30 "You shall betroth a wife, but another man shall lie with her; you shall build a house, but you shall not dwell in it; you shall plant a vineyard, but shall not gather its grapes.
31 "Your ox *shall be* slaughtered before your eyes, but you shall not eat of it; your donkey *shall be* violently taken away from before you, and shall not be restored to you; your sheep *shall be* given to your enemies, and you shall have no one to rescue *them.*
32 "Your sons and your daughters *shall be* given to another people, and your eyes shall look and fail *with longing* for them all day long; and *there shall be* no strength in your hand.
33 "A nation whom you have not known shall eat the fruit of your land and the produce of your labor, and you shall be only oppressed and crushed continually.
34 "So you shall be driven mad because of the sight which your eyes see.
35 "The LORD will strike you in the knees and on the legs with severe boils which cannot be healed, and from the sole of your foot to the top of your head.
36 "The LORD will bring you and the king whom you set over you to a nation which neither you nor your fathers have known, and there you shall serve other gods—wood and stone.
37 "And you shall become an astonishment, a proverb, and a byword among all nations where the LORD will drive you.
38 "You shall carry much seed out to the field but gather little in, for the locust shall consume it.
39 "You shall plant vineyards and tend *them,* but you shall neither drink *of* the wine nor gather the *grapes;* for the worms shall eat them.
40 "You shall have olive trees throughout all your territory, but you shall not anoint *yourself* with the oil; for your olives shall drop off.
41 "You shall beget sons and daughters, but they shall not be yours; for they shall go into captivity.
42 "Locusts shall consume all your trees and the produce of your land.
43 "The alien who *is* among you shall rise higher and higher above you, and you shall come down lower and lower.
44 "He shall lend to you, but you shall not lend to him; he shall be the head, and you shall be the tail.
45 "Moreover all these curses shall come upon you and pursue and overtake you, until you are destroyed, because you did not obey the voice of the LORD your God, to keep His commandments and His statutes which He commanded you.
46 "And they shall be upon you for a sign and a wonder, and on your descendants forever.
47 "Because you did not serve the LORD your God with joy and gladness of heart, for the abundance of everything,
48 "therefore you shall serve your enemies, whom the LORD will send against you, in hunger, in thirst, in nakedness, and in need of everything; and He will put a yoke of iron on your neck until He has destroyed you.
49 "The LORD will bring a nation against you from afar, from the end of the earth, *as swift* as the eagle flies, a nation whose language you will not understand,
50 "a nation of fierce countenance, which does not respect the elderly nor show favor to the young.
51 "And they shall eat the increase of your livestock and the produce of your land, until you are destroyed; they shall not leave you grain or new wine or oil, *or* the increase of your cattle or the offspring of your flocks, until they have destroyed you.
52 "They shall besiege you at all your gates until your high and fortified walls, in which you trust, come down throughout all your land; and they shall besiege you at all your gates throughout all your land which the LORD your God has given you.
53 "You shall eat the fruit of your own body, the flesh of your sons and your daughters whom the LORD your God has given you, in the siege and desperate straits in which your enemy shall distress you.
54 "The sensitive and very refined man among you will be hostile toward his brother, toward the wife of his bosom, and toward the rest of his children whom he leaves behind,
55 "so that he will not give any of them the flesh of his children whom he will eat, because he has nothing left in the siege and desperate straits in which your enemy shall distress you at all your gates.
56 "The tender and delicate woman among you, who would not venture to set the sole of her foot on the ground because of her delicateness and sensitivity, will refuse[a] to the husband of her bosom, and to her son and her daughter,

28:56 [a]Literally *her eye shall be evil toward*

57 "her placenta which comes out from be-
tween her feet and her children whom she
bears; for she will eat them secretly for lack of
everything in the siege and desperate straits in
which your enemy shall distress you at all your
gates.
58 "If you do not carefully observe all the
words of this law that are written in this book,
that you may fear this glorious and awesome
name, THE LORD YOUR GOD,
59 "then the LORD will bring upon you and
your descendants extraordinary plagues—
great and prolonged plagues—and serious and
prolonged sicknesses.
60 "Moreover He will bring back on you all
the diseases of Egypt, of which you were
afraid, and they shall cling to you.
61 "Also every sickness and every plague,
which *is* not written in this Book of the Law,
will the LORD bring upon you until you are
destroyed.
62 "You shall be left few in number, whereas
you were as the stars of heaven in multitude,
because you would not obey the voice of the
LORD your God.
63 "And it shall be, *that* just as the LORD re-
joiced over you to do you good and multiply
you, so the LORD will rejoice over you to de-
stroy you and bring you to nothing; and you
shall be plucked from off the land which you
go to possess.
64 "Then the LORD will scatter you among all
peoples, from one end of the earth to the other,
and there you shall serve other gods, which
neither you nor your fathers have known—
wood and stone.
65 And among those nations you shall find no
rest, nor shall the sole of your foot have a rest-
ing place; but there the LORD will give you a
trembling heart, failing eyes, and anguish of soul.
66 "Your life shall hang in doubt before you;
you shall fear day and night, and have no as-
surance of life.
67 "In the morning you shall say, 'Oh, that it
were evening!' And at evening you shall say,
'Oh, that it were morning!' because of the fear
which terrifies your heart, and because of the
sight which your eyes see.
68 "And the LORD will take you back to Egypt
in ships, by the way of which I said to you, 'You
shall never see it again.' And there you shall
be offered for sale to your enemies as male and
female slaves, but no one will buy *you*."

The Covenant Renewed in Moab

29 These *are* the words of the covenant
which the LORD commanded Moses to
make with the children of Israel in the land of
Moab, besides the covenant which He made
with them in Horeb.
2 Now Moses called all Israel and said to
them: "You have seen all that the LORD did
before your eyes in the land of Egypt, to Pha-
raoh and to all his servants and to all his land—
3 "the great trials which your eyes have
seen, the signs, and those great wonders.
4 "Yet the LORD has not given you a heart
to perceive and eyes to see and ears to hear, to
this *very* day.
5 "And I have led you forty years in the wil-
derness. Your clothes have not worn out on
you, and your sandals have not worn out on
your feet.
6 "You have not eaten bread, nor have you
drunk wine or *similar* drink, that you may
know that I *am* the LORD your God.
7 "And when you came to this place, Sihon
king of Heshbon and Og king of Bashan came
out against us to battle, and we conquered
them.
8 "We took their land and gave it as an inher-
itance to the Reubenites, to the Gadites, and to
half the tribe of Manasseh.
9 "Therefore keep the words of this cov-
enant, and do them, that you may prosper in
all that you do.
10 "All of you stand today before the LORD
your God: your leaders and your tribes and
your elders and your officers, all the men of
Israel,
11 "your little ones and your wives—also the
stranger who *is* in your camp, from the one
who cuts your wood to the one who draws your
water—
12 "that you may enter into covenant with the
LORD your God, and into His oath, which the
LORD your God makes with you today,
13 "that He may establish you today as a peo-
ple for Himself, and *that* He may be God to
you, just as He has spoken to you, and just as
He has sworn to your fathers, to Abraham,
Isaac, and Jacob.
14 "I make this covenant and this oath, not
with you alone,
15 "but with *him* who stands here with us
today before the LORD our God, as well as with
him who *is* not here with us today
16 (for you know that we dwelt in the land of
Egypt and that we came through the nations
which you passed by,
17 and you saw their abominations and their
idols which *were* among them—wood and
stone and silver and gold);
18 "so that there may not be among you man
or woman or family or tribe, whose heart turns
away today from the LORD our God, to go *and*
serve the gods of these nations, and that there
may not be among you a root bearing bitter-
ness or wormwood;
19 "and so it may not happen, when he hears
the words of this curse, that he blesses himself
in his heart, saying, 'I shall have peace, even
though I follow the dictates[a] of my heart'—as
though the drunkard could be included with
the sober.
20 "The LORD would not spare him; for then
the anger of the LORD and His jealousy would
burn against that man, and every curse that is
written in this book would settle on him, and
the LORD would blot out his name from under
heaven.
21 "And the LORD would separate him from
all the tribes of Israel for adversity, according
to all the curses of the covenant that are writ-
ten in this Book of the Law,
22 "so that the coming generation of your
children who rise up after you, and the for-
eigner who comes from a far land, would say,
when they see the plagues of that land and the
sicknesses which the LORD has laid on it:
23 'The whole land *is* brimstone, salt, and
burning; it is not sown, nor does it bear, nor
does any grass grow there, like the overthrow
of Sodom and Gomorrah, Admah, and Ze-
boiim, which the LORD overthrew in His anger
and His wrath.'

29:19 [a]Or *stubbornness*

24 "All nations would say, 'Why has the LORD
done so to this land? What does the heat of this
great anger mean?'
25 "Then *people* would say: 'Because they have
forsaken the covenant of the LORD God of their
fathers, which He made with them when He
brought them out of the land of Egypt;
26 'for they went and served other gods and
worshiped them, gods that they did not know
and that He had not given to them.
27 'Then the anger of the LORD was aroused
against this land, to bring on it every curse that
is written in this book.
28 'And the LORD uprooted them from their
land in anger, in wrath, and in great indigna-
tion, and cast them into another land, as *it is*
this day.'
29 "The secret *things belong* to the LORD our
God, but those *things which are* revealed *be-
long* to us and to our children forever, that *we*
may do all the words of this law.

The Blessing of Returning to God

30 "Now it shall come to pass, when all
these things come upon you, the bless-
ing and the curse which I have set before you,
and you call *them* to mind among all the na-
tions where the LORD your God drives you,
2 "and you return to the LORD your God and
obey His voice, according to all that I com-
mand you today, you and your children, with
all your heart and with all your soul,
3 "that the LORD your God will bring you
back from captivity, and have compassion on
you, and gather you again from all the nations
where the LORD your God has scattered you.
4 "If *any* of you are driven out to the farthest
parts under heaven, from there the LORD your
God will gather you, and from there He will
bring you.
5 "Then the LORD your God will bring you
to the land which your fathers possessed, and
you shall possess it. He will prosper you and
multiply you more than your fathers.
6 "And the LORD your God will circumcise
your heart and the heart of your descendants,
to love the LORD your God with all your heart
and with all your soul, that you may live.
7 "Also the LORD your God will put all these
curses on your enemies and on those who hate
you, who persecuted you.
8 "And you will again obey the voice of the
LORD and do all His commandments which I
command you today.
9 "The LORD your God will make you
abound in all the work of your hand, in the
fruit of your body, in the increase of your live-
stock, and in the produce of your land for good.
For the LORD will again rejoice over you for
good as He rejoiced over your fathers,
10 "if you obey the voice of the LORD your
God, to keep His commandments and His stat-
utes which are written in this Book of the Law,
and if you turn to the LORD your God with all
your heart and with all your soul.

The Choice of Life or Death

11 "For this commandment which I command
you today *is* not *too* mysterious for you, nor *is*
it far off.
12 "It *is* not in heaven, that you should say,
'Who will ascend into heaven for us and bring
it to us, that we may hear it and do it?'
13 "Nor *is* it beyond the sea, that you should
say, 'Who will go over the sea for us and bring
it to us, that we may hear it and do it?'
14 "But the word *is* very near you, in your
mouth and in your heart, that you may do it.
15 "See, I have set before you today life and
good, death and evil,
16 "in that I command you today to love the
LORD your God, to walk in His ways, and to
keep His commandments, His statutes, and His
judgments, that you may live and multiply; and
the LORD your God will bless you in the land
which you go to possess.
17 "But if your heart turns away so that you
do not hear, and are drawn away, and worship
other gods and serve them,
18 "I announce to you today that you shall
surely perish; you shall not prolong *your* days
in the land which you cross over the Jordan to
go in and possess.
19 "I call heaven and earth as witnesses today
against you, *that* I have set before you life and
death, blessing and cursing; therefore choose
life, that both you and your descendants may
live;
20 "that you may love the LORD your God,
that you may obey His voice, and that you may
cling to Him, for He *is* your life and the length
of your days; and that you may dwell in the
land which the LORD swore to your fathers, to
Abraham, Isaac, and Jacob, to give them."

Joshua the New Leader of Israel

31 Then Moses went and spoke these words
to all Israel.
2 And he said to them: "I *am* one hundred
and twenty years old today. I can no longer go
out and come in. Also the LORD has said to
me, 'You shall not cross over this Jordan.'
3 "The LORD your God Himself crosses over
before you; He will destroy these nations from
before you, and you shall dispossess them.
Joshua himself crosses over before you, just as
the LORD has said.
4 "And the LORD will do to them as He did
to Sihon and Og, the kings of the Amorites and
their land, when He destroyed them.
5 "The LORD will give them over to you, that
you may do to them according to every com-
mandment which I have commanded you.
6 "Be strong and of good courage, do not
fear nor be afraid of them; for the LORD your
God, He *is* the One who goes with you. He will
not leave you nor forsake you."
7 Then Moses called Joshua and said to him
in the sight of all Israel, "Be strong and of good
courage, for you must go with this people to
the land which the LORD has sworn to their
fathers to give them, and you shall cause them
to inherit it.
8 "And the LORD, He *is* the One who goes
before you. He will be with you, He will not
leave you nor forsake you; do not fear nor be
dismayed."

The Law to Be Read Every Seven Years

9 So Moses wrote this law and delivered it
to the priests, the sons of Levi, who bore the
ark of the covenant of the LORD, and to all the
elders of Israel.
10 And Moses commanded them, saying: "At
the end of *every* seven years, at the appointed
time in the year of release, at the Feast of Tab-
ernacles,
11 "when all Israel comes to appear before
the LORD your God in the place which He

chooses, you shall read this law before all Israel in their hearing.

12 "Gather the people together, men and women and little ones, and the stranger who *is* within your gates, that they may hear and that they may learn to fear the LORD your God and carefully observe all the words of this law,

13 "and *that* their children, who have not known it, may hear and learn to fear the LORD your God as long as you live in the land which you cross the Jordan to possess."

Prediction of Israel's Rebellion

14 Then the LORD said to Moses, "Behold, the days approach when you must die; call Joshua, and present yourselves in the tabernacle of meeting, that I may inaugurate him." So Moses and Joshua went and presented themselves in the tabernacle of meeting.

15 Now the LORD appeared at the tabernacle in a pillar of cloud, and the pillar of cloud stood above the door of the tabernacle.

16 And the LORD said to Moses: "Behold, you will rest with your fathers; and this people will rise and play the harlot with the gods of the foreigners of the land, where they go *to be* among them, and they will forsake Me and break My covenant which I have made with them.

17 "Then My anger shall be aroused against them in that day, and I will forsake them, and I will hide My face from them, and they shall be devoured. And many evils and troubles shall befall them, so that they will say in that day, 'Have not these evils come upon us because our God *is* not among us?'

18 "And I will surely hide My face in that day because of all the evil which they have done, in that they have turned to other gods.

19 "Now therefore, write down this song for yourselves, and teach it to the children of Israel; put it in their mouths, that this song may be a witness for Me against the children of Israel.

20 "When I have brought them to the land flowing with milk and honey, of which I swore to their fathers, and they have eaten and filled themselves and grown fat, then they will turn to other gods and serve them; and they will provoke Me and break My covenant.

21 "Then it shall be, when many evils and troubles have come upon them, that this song will testify against them as a witness; for it will not be forgotten in the mouths of their descendants, for I know the inclination of their behavior today, even before I have brought them to the land of which I swore *to give them.*"

22 Therefore Moses wrote this song the same day, and taught it to the children of Israel.

23 Then He inaugurated Joshua the son of Nun, and said, "Be strong and of good courage; for you shall bring the children of Israel into the land of which I swore to them, and I will be with you."

24 So it was, when Moses had completed writing the words of this law in a book, when they were finished,

25 that Moses commanded the Levites, who bore the ark of the covenant of the LORD, saying:

26 "Take this Book of the Law, and put it beside the ark of the covenant of the LORD your God, that it may be there as a witness against you;

27 "for I know your rebellion and your stiff neck. *If* today, while I am yet alive with you, you have been rebellious against the LORD, then how much more after my death?

28 "Gather to me all the elders of your tribes, and your officers, that I may speak these words in their hearing and call heaven and earth to witness against them.

29 "For I know that after my death you will become utterly corrupt, and turn aside from the way which I have commanded you. And evil will befall you in the latter days, because you will do evil in the sight of the LORD, to provoke Him to anger through the work of your hands."

The Song of Moses

30 Then Moses spoke in the hearing of all the assembly of Israel the words of this song until they were ended:

32 "Give ear, O heavens, and I will speak;
And hear, O earth, the words of my mouth.
2 Let my teaching drop as the rain,
My speech distill as the dew,
As raindrops on the tender herb,
And as showers on the grass.
3 For I proclaim the name of the LORD:
Ascribe greatness to our God.
4 *He is* the Rock, His work *is* perfect;
For all His ways *are* justice,
A God of truth and without injustice;
Righteous and upright *is* He.

5 "They have corrupted themselves;
They are not His children,
Because of their blemish:
A perverse and crooked generation.
6 Do you thus deal with the LORD,
O foolish and unwise people?
Is He not your Father, *who* bought you?
Has He not made you and established you?

7 "Remember the days of old,
Consider the years of many generations.
Ask your father, and he will show you;
Your elders, and they will tell you:
8 When the Most High divided their inheritance to the nations,
When He separated the sons of Adam,
He set the boundaries of the peoples
According to the number of the children of Israel.
9 For the LORD's portion *is* His people;
Jacob *is* the place of His inheritance.

10 "He found him in a desert land
And in the wasteland, a howling wilderness;
He encircled him, He instructed him,
He kept him as the apple of His eye.
11 As an eagle stirs up its nest,
Hovers over its young,
Spreading out its wings, taking them up,
Carrying them on its wings,
12 *So* the LORD alone led him,
And *there was* no foreign god with him.

13 "He made him ride in the heights of the earth,
That he might eat the produce of the fields;
He made him draw honey from the rock,
And oil from the flinty rock;
14 Curds from the cattle, and milk of the flock,
With fat of lambs;

And rams of the breed of Bashan, and goats,
With the choicest wheat;
And you drank wine, the blood of the grapes.

15 "But Jeshurun grew fat and kicked;
You grew fat, you grew thick,
You are obese!
Then he forsook God *who* made him,
And scornfully esteemed the Rock of his salvation.
16 They provoked Him to jealousy with foreign *gods;*
With abominations they provoked Him to anger.
17 They sacrificed to demons, not to God,
To gods they did not know,
To new *gods,* new arrivals
That your fathers did not fear.
18 Of the Rock *who* begot you, you are unmindful,
And have forgotten the God who fathered you.

19 "And when the LORD saw *it,* He spurned *them,*
Because of the provocation of His sons and His daughters.
20 And He said: 'I will hide My face from them,
I will see what their end *will be,*
For they *are* a perverse generation,
Children in whom *is* no faith.
21 They have provoked Me to jealousy by *what* is not God;
They have moved Me to anger by their foolish idols.
But I will provoke them to jealousy by *those who are* not a nation;
I will move them to anger by a foolish nation.
22 For a fire is kindled in My anger,
And shall burn to the lowest hell;
It shall consume the earth with her increase,
And set on fire the foundations of the mountains.

23 'I will heap disasters on them;
I will spend My arrows on them.
24 *They shall be* wasted with hunger,
Devoured by pestilence and bitter destruction;
I will also send against them the teeth of beasts,
With the poison of serpents of the dust.
25 The sword shall destroy outside;
There shall be terror within
For the young man and virgin,
The nursing child with the man of gray hairs.
26 I would have said, "I will dash them in pieces,
I will make the memory of them to cease from among men,"
27 Had I not feared the wrath of the enemy,
Lest their adversaries should misunderstand,
Lest they should say, "Our hand *is* high;
And it is not the LORD who has done all this."'

28 "For they *are* a nation void of counsel,
Nor *is there any* understanding in them.
29 Oh, that they were wise, *that* they understood this,
That they would consider their latter end!
30 How could one chase a thousand,
And two put ten thousand to flight,
Unless their Rock had sold them,
And the LORD had surrendered them?
31 For their rock *is* not like our Rock,
Even our enemies themselves *being* judges.
32 For their vine *is* of the vine of Sodom
And of the fields of Gomorrah;
Their grapes *are* grapes of gall,
Their clusters *are* bitter.
33 Their wine *is* the poison of serpents,
And the cruel venom of cobras.

34 '*Is* this not laid up in store with Me,
Sealed up among My treasures?
35 Vengeance is Mine, and recompense;
Their foot shall slip in *due* time;
For the day of their calamity *is* at hand,
And the things to come hasten upon them.'

36 "For the LORD will judge His people
And have compassion on His servants,
When He sees that *their* power is gone,
And *there is* no one *remaining,* bond or free.
37 He will say: 'Where *are* their gods,
The rock in which they sought refuge?
38 Who ate the fat of their sacrifices,
And drank the wine of their drink offering?
Let them rise and help you,
And be your refuge.

39 'Now see that I, *even* I, *am* He,
And *there is* no God besides Me;
I kill and I make alive;
I wound and I heal;
Nor *is there any* who can deliver from My hand.
40 For I raise My hand to heaven,
And say, "*As* I live forever,
41 If I whet My glittering sword,
And My hand takes hold on judgment,
I will render vengeance to My enemies,
And repay those who hate Me.
42 I will make My arrows drunk with blood,
And My sword shall devour flesh,
With the blood of the slain and the captives,
From the heads of the leaders of the enemy."'

43 "Rejoice, O Gentiles, *with* His people;[a]
For He will avenge the blood of His servants,
And render vengeance to His adversaries;
He will provide atonement for His land *and* His people."

44 So Moses came with Joshua[a] the son of
Nun and spoke all the words of this song in the
hearing of the people.
45 Moses finished speaking all these words
to all Israel,
46 and he said to them: "Set your hearts on
all the words which I testify among you today,

32:43 [a]A Dead Sea Scroll fragment adds *And let all the gods (angels) worship Him* (compare Septuagint and Hebrews 1:6). **32:44** [a]Hebrew *Hoshea* (compare Numbers 13:8, 16)

which you shall command your children to be
careful to observe—all the words of this law.
47 "For it *is* not a futile thing for you, because
it *is* your life, and by this word you shall pro-
long *your* days in the land which you cross
over the Jordan to possess."

Moses to Die on Mount Nebo

48 Then the LORD spoke to Moses that very
same day, saying:
49 "Go up this mountain of the Abarim,
Mount Nebo, which *is* in the land of Moab,
across from Jericho; view the land of Canaan,
which I give to the children of Israel as a pos-
session;
50 "and die on the mountain which you as-
cend, and be gathered to your people, just as
Aaron your brother died on Mount Hor and
was gathered to his people;
51 "because you trespassed against Me
among the children of Israel at the waters of
Meribah Kadesh, in the Wilderness of Zin, be-
cause you did not hallow Me in the midst of
the children of Israel.
52 "Yet you shall see the land before *you*,
though you shall not go there, into the land
which I am giving to the children of Israel."

Moses' Final Blessing on Israel

33 Now this *is* the blessing with which Mo-
ses the man of God blessed the children
of Israel before his death.
2 And he said:

"The LORD came from Sinai,
And dawned on them from Seir;
He shone forth from Mount Paran,
And He came with ten thousands of saints;
From His right hand
Came a fiery law for them.
3 Yes, He loves the people;
All His saints *are* in Your hand;
They sit down at Your feet;
Everyone receives Your words.
4 Moses commanded a law for us,
A heritage of the congregation of Jacob.
5 And He was King in Jeshurun,
When the leaders of the people were gathered,
All the tribes of Israel together.

6 "Let Reuben live, and not die,
Nor let his men be few."

7 And this he said of Judah:

"Hear, LORD, the voice of Judah,
And bring him to his people;
Let his hands be sufficient for him,
And may You be a help against his enemies."

8 And of Levi he said:

"*Let* Your Thummim and Your Urim *be* with Your holy one,
Whom You tested at Massah,
And with whom You contended at the waters of Meribah,
9 Who says of his father and mother,
'I have not seen them';
Nor did he acknowledge his brothers,
Or know his own children;
For they have observed Your word
And kept Your covenant.
10 They shall teach Jacob Your judgments,
And Israel Your law.
They shall put incense before You,
And a whole burnt sacrifice on Your altar.
11 Bless his substance, LORD,
And accept the work of his hands;
Strike the loins of those who rise against him,
And of those who hate him, that they rise not again."

12 Of Benjamin he said:

"The beloved of the LORD shall dwell in safety by Him,
Who shelters him all the day long;
And he shall dwell between His shoulders."

13 And of Joseph he said:

"Blessed of the LORD *is* his land,
With the precious things of heaven, with the dew,
And the deep lying beneath,
14 With the precious fruits of the sun,
With the precious produce of the months,
15 With the best things of the ancient mountains,
With the precious things of the everlasting hills,
16 With the precious things of the earth and its fullness,
And the favor of Him who dwelt in the bush.
Let *the blessing* come 'on the head of Joseph,
And on the crown of the head of him *who was* separate from his brothers.'[a]
17 His glory *is like* a firstborn bull,
And his horns *like* the horns of the wild ox;
Together with them
He shall push the peoples
To the ends of the earth;
They *are* the ten thousands of Ephraim,
And they *are* the thousands of Manasseh."

18 And of Zebulun he said:

"Rejoice, Zebulun, in your going out,
And Issachar in your tents!
19 They shall call the peoples *to* the mountain;
There they shall offer sacrifices of righteousness;
For they shall partake *of* the abundance of the seas
And *of* treasures hidden in the sand."

20 And of Gad he said:

"Blessed *is* he who enlarges Gad;
He dwells as a lion,
And tears the arm and the crown of his head.
21 He provided the first *part* for himself,
Because a lawgiver's portion was reserved there.
He came *with* the heads of the people;
He administered the justice of the LORD,
And His judgments with Israel."

22 And of Dan he said:

"Dan *is* a lion's whelp;
He shall leap from Bashan."

33:16 [a]Genesis 49:26

23 And of Naphtali he said:

"O Naphtali, satisfied with favor,
And full of the blessing of the LORD,
Possess the west and the south."

24 And of Asher he said:

"Asher *is* most blessed of sons;
Let him be favored by his brothers,
And let him dip his foot in oil.
25 Your sandals *shall be* iron and bronze;
As your days, *so shall* your strength *be*.

26 "*There is* no one like the God of Jeshurun,
Who rides the heavens to help you,
And in His excellency on the clouds.
27 The eternal God *is your* refuge,
And underneath *are* the everlasting arms;
He will thrust out the enemy from before
you,
And will say, 'Destroy!'
28 Then Israel shall dwell in safety,
The fountain of Jacob alone,
In a land of grain and new wine;
His heavens shall also drop dew.
29 Happy *are* you, O Israel!
Who *is* like you, a people saved by the
LORD,
The shield of your help
And the sword of your majesty!
Your enemies shall submit to you,
And you shall tread down their high
places."

Moses Dies on Mount Nebo

34 Then Moses went up from the plains of
Moab to Mount Nebo, to the top of Pis-
gah, which is across from Jericho. And the
LORD showed him all the land of Gilead as far
as Dan,
2 all Naphtali and the land of Ephraim and
Manasseh, all the land of Judah as far as the
Western Sea,[a]
3 the South, and the plain of the Valley of
Jericho, the city of palm trees, as far as Zoar.
4 Then the LORD said to him, "This *is* the
land of which I swore to give Abraham, Isaac,
and Jacob, saying, 'I will give it to your descen-
dants.' I have caused you to see *it* with your
eyes, but you shall not cross over there."
5 So Moses the servant of the LORD died there
in the land of Moab, according to the word of
the LORD.
6 And He buried him in a valley in the land
of Moab, opposite Beth Peor; but no one knows
his grave to this day.
7 Moses *was* one hundred and twenty years
old when he died. His eyes were not dim nor
his natural vigor diminished.
8 And the children of Israel wept for Moses
in the plains of Moab thirty days. So the days
of weeping *and* mourning for Moses ended.
9 Now Joshua the son of Nun was full of the
spirit of wisdom, for Moses had laid his hands
on him; so the children of Israel heeded him,
and did as the LORD had commanded Moses.
10 But since then there has not arisen in Israel
a prophet like Moses, whom the LORD knew
face to face,
11 in all the signs and wonders which the
LORD sent him to do in the land of Egypt, be-
fore Pharaoh, before all his servants, and in all
his land,
12 and by all that mighty power and all the
great terror which Moses performed in the
sight of all Israel.

34:2 [a]That is, the Mediterranean

THE HISTORICAL BOOKS

Joshua • Judges • Ruth • 1 Samuel • 2 Samuel • 1 Kings 2 Kings • 1 Chronicles • 2 Chronicles Ezra • Nehemiah • Esther

The historical books include Joshua, Judges, Ruth, 1 and 2 Samuel, 1 and 2 Kings, 1 and 2 Chronicles, Ezra, Nehemiah, and Esther. In the Jewish canon, the books are split into two categories. (1) Joshua, Judges, 1 and 2 Samuel, and 1 and 2 Kings are called "The Former Prophets." (2) All the rest are included in "The Writings," the third major collection of the Hebrew Scripture.

These books are history in the best sense, that is, they do more than present data about past events. They present the data in a form that tries to explain what the events mean and how God was working in them.

The Former Prophets (Joshua, Judges, 1 and 2 Samuel, and 1 and 2 Kings) record the history of the period from the death of Moses to the fall of the southern kingdom of Judah, from somewhere before 1400 B.C. to 586 B.C. This period includes the settlement of Israel in the land, the tribal government under the judges, the time of seeking a king, the golden age under David and Solomon, the division and downfall of the kingdoms. All through the narrative runs the understanding of God's judgment and redemption in political and social life.

First and 2 Chronicles cover much of the same history from a different perspective. The books of Ezra and Nehemiah pick up the account of Israel and Israel's God in the period after the Exile, the time of the rebuilding of Jerusalem and the renewing of the covenant in a harsh new time.

JOSHUA marks the end of the Exodus period. Israel enters the land under a new generation of leaders, conquers the hill country, and enters into a great ceremony of covenant in a harsh new time.

JUDGES is a collection of accounts of tribal heroes and heroines from the period between the time of Joshua and the time of Samuel. These are accounts of charismatic leaders who, in times of crisis, were called by God to save a part of the tribes from the oppression of an enemy. They teach an understanding of history in a pattern of faithfulness, unfaithfulness, judgment, and salvation in the political world.

RUTH emphasizes God working through a foreign woman to bring forth King David. It carries a strong warning against excluding anyone from a place among God's people.

FIRST AND 2 SAMUEL record the end of the period of the judges and the rise of the kingship in Israel, with all the accompanying tensions between old ways and new ways. The narratives include the lives and rules of Samuel, Saul, and David.

FIRST AND 2 KINGS are the history of the monarchy from Solomon to the Exile. Solomon's glory, the building of the temple, the division of the kingdom, the destruction of the two kingdoms, and the rise of prophecy (Elijah and Elisha) are important themes in these books. Faithfulness to God is defined in social and political terms as well as religious.

KINGDOM OF DAVID

FIRST AND 2 CHRONICLES were written after the destruction of Jerusalem to try to answer the question "Why did God choose to punish His people in such a way?" The answer is found in history. God's people were unfaithful and what happened in social and political history is an expression of God's judgment on an unfaithful people.

EZRA picks up the themes of Chronicles and argues for national purity and exclusiveness.

NEHEMIAH is the account of the rebuilding of the walls of Jerusalem and the reestablishment of the covenant. It, too, argues for exclusiveness.

ESTHER is a delightful account of a Jewish heroine whose faithfulness saved her people from certain death. ■

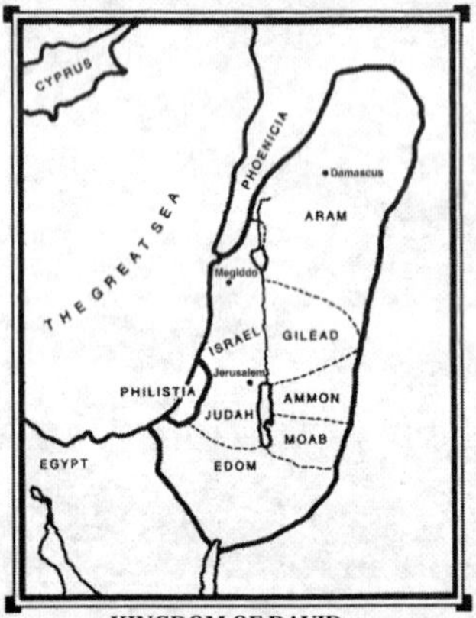

The Book of
JOSHUA

God's Commission to Joshua

1 After the death of Moses the servant of the
LORD, it came to pass that the LORD spoke
to Joshua the son of Nun, Moses' assistant,
saying:
2 "Moses My servant is dead. Now there-
fore, arise, go over this Jordan, you and all this
people, to the land which I am giving to them—
the children of Israel.
3 "Every place that the sole of your foot will
tread upon I have given you, as I said to Moses.
4 "From the wilderness and this Lebanon as
far as the great river, the River Euphrates, all
the land of the Hittites, and to the Great Sea
toward the going down of the sun, shall be
your territory.
5 "No man shall *be able to* stand before you
all the days of your life; as I was with Moses,
so I will be with you. I will not leave you nor
forsake you.
6 "Be strong and of good courage, for to this
people you shall divide as an inheritance the
land which I swore to their fathers to give them.
7 "Only be strong and very courageous, that
you may observe to do according to all the law
which Moses My servant commanded you; do
not turn from it to the right hand or to the left,
that you may prosper wherever you go.
8 "This Book of the Law shall not depart
from your mouth, but you shall meditate in
it day and night, that you may observe to do
according to all that is written in it. For then
you will make your way prosperous, and then
you will have good success.
9 "Have I not commanded you? Be strong
and of good courage; do not be afraid, nor be
dismayed, for the LORD your God *is* with you
wherever you go."

The Order to Cross the Jordan

10 Then Joshua commanded the officers of
the people, saying,
11 "Pass through the camp and command the
people, saying, 'Prepare provisions for your-
selves, for within three days you will cross over
this Jordan, to go in to possess the land which
the LORD your God is giving you to possess.'"
12 And to the Reubenites, the Gadites, and half
the tribe of Manasseh Joshua spoke, saying,
13 "Remember the word which Moses the
servant of the LORD commanded you, saying,
'The LORD your God is giving you rest and is
giving you this land.'
14 "Your wives, your little ones, and your
livestock shall remain in the land which Moses
gave you on this side of the Jordan. But you
shall pass before your brethren armed, all your
mighty men of valor, and help them,
15 "until the LORD has given your brethren
rest, as He *gave* you, and they also have taken
possession of the land which the LORD your
God is giving them. Then you shall return to
the land of your possession and enjoy it, which
Moses the LORD's servant gave you on this
side of the Jordan toward the sunrise."
16 So they answered Joshua, saying, "All that
you command us we will do, and wherever you
send us we will go.
17 "Just as we heeded Moses in all things, so
we will heed you. Only the LORD your God be
with you, as He was with Moses.
18 "Whoever rebels against your command
and does not heed your words, in all that you
command him, shall be put to death. Only be
strong and of good courage."

Rahab Hides the Spies

2 Now Joshua the son of Nun sent out two
men from Acacia Grove[a] to spy secretly,
saying, "Go, view the land, especially Jericho."
So they went, and came to the house of a harlot
named Rahab, and lodged there.
2 And it was told the king of Jericho, saying,
"Behold, men have come here tonight from the
children of Israel to search out the country."
3 So the king of Jericho sent to Rahab, say-
ing, "Bring out the men who have come to you,
who have entered your house, for they have
come to search out all the country."
4 Then the woman took the two men and hid
them. So she said, "Yes, the men came to me,
but I did not know where they *were* from.
5 "And it happened as the gate was being
shut, when it was dark, that the men went out.
Where the men went I do not know; pursue
them quickly, for you may overtake them."
6 (But she had brought them up to the roof
and hidden them with the stalks of flax, which
she had laid in order on the roof.)
7 Then the men pursued them by the road to
the Jordan, to the fords. And as soon as those
who pursued them had gone out, they shut the
gate.
8 Now before they lay down, she came up to
them on the roof,
9 and said to the men: "I know that the LORD
has given you the land, that the terror of you
has fallen on us, and that all the inhabitants of
the land are fainthearted because of you.
10 "For we have heard how the LORD dried
up the water of the Red Sea for you when you
came out of Egypt, and what you did to the two
kings of the Amorites who *were* on the other
side of the Jordan, Sihon and Og, whom you
utterly destroyed.
11 "And as soon as we heard *these things*,
our hearts melted; neither did there remain
any more courage in anyone because of you,
for the LORD your God, He *is* God in heaven
above and on earth beneath.
12 "Now therefore, I beg you, swear to me by
the LORD, since I have shown you kindness,
that you also will show kindness to my father's
house, and give me a true token,
13 "and spare my father, my mother, my
brothers, my sisters, and all that they have,
and deliver our lives from death."
14 So the men answered her, "Our lives for
yours, if none of you tell this business of ours.
And it shall be, when the LORD has given us
the land, that we will deal kindly and truly
with you."
15 Then she let them down by a rope through
the window, for her house *was* on the city wall;
she dwelt on the wall.
16 And she said to them, "Get to the mountain,
lest the pursuers meet you. Hide there three days,

2:1 [a]Hebrew *Shittim*

until the pursuers have returned. Afterward you
may go your way."
17 So the men said to her: "We *will be* blame-
less of this oath of yours which you have made
us swear,
18 "unless, *when* we come into the land, you
bind this line of scarlet cord in the window
through which you let us down, and unless you
bring your father, your mother, your brothers,
and all your father's household to your own
home.
19 "So it shall be *that* whoever goes outside
the doors of your house into the street, his
blood *shall be* on his own head, and we *will be*
guiltless. And whoever is with you in the
house, his blood *shall be* on our head if a hand
is laid on him.
20 "And if you tell this business of ours, then
we will be free from your oath which you made
us swear."
21 Then she said, "According to your words,
so *be* it." And she sent them away, and they
departed. And she bound the scarlet cord in
the window.
22 They departed and went to the mountain,
and stayed there three days until the pursuers
returned. The pursuers sought *them* all along
the way, but did not find *them*.
23 So the two men returned, descended from
the mountain, and crossed over; and they came
to Joshua the son of Nun, and told him all that
had befallen them.
24 And they said to Joshua, "Truly the LORD
has delivered all the land into our hands, for
indeed all the inhabitants of the country are
fainthearted because of us."

Israel Crosses the Jordan

3 Then Joshua rose early in the morning; and
they set out from Acacia Grove[a] and came
to the Jordan, he and all the children of Israel,
and lodged there before they crossed over.
2 So it was, after three days, that the officers
went through the camp;
3 and they commanded the people, saying,
"When you see the ark of the covenant of the
LORD your God, and the priests, the Levites,
bearing it, then you shall set out from your place
and go after it.
4 "Yet there shall be a space between you
and it, about two thousand cubits by measure.
Do not come near it, that you may know the
way by which you must go, for you have not
passed *this* way before."
5 And Joshua said to the people, "Sanctify
yourselves, for tomorrow the LORD will do
wonders among you."
6 Then Joshua spoke to the priests, saying,
"Take up the ark of the covenant and cross
over before the people." So they took up the
ark of the covenant and went before the people.
7 And the LORD said to Joshua, "This day I
will begin to exalt you in the sight of all Israel,
that they may know that, as I was with Moses,
so I will be with you.
8 "You shall command the priests who bear
the ark of the covenant, saying, 'When you
have come to the edge of the water of the Jor-
dan, you shall stand in the Jordan.'"
9 So Joshua said to the children of Israel,
"Come here, and hear the words of the LORD
your God."
10 And Joshua said, "By this you shall know
that the living God *is* among you, and *that* He
will without fail drive out from before you the
Canaanites and the Hittites and the Hivites
and the Perizzites and the Girgashites and the
Amorites and the Jebusites:
11 "Behold, the ark of the covenant of the Lord
of all the earth is crossing over before you into
the Jordan.
12 "Now therefore, take for yourselves twelve
men from the tribes of Israel, one man from
every tribe.
13 "And it shall come to pass, as soon as the
soles of the feet of the priests who bear the ark
of the LORD, the Lord of all the earth, shall rest
in the waters of the Jordan, *that* the waters of
the Jordan shall be cut off, the waters that
come down from upstream, and they shall stand
as a heap."
14 So it was, when the people set out from
their camp to cross over the Jordan, with the
priests bearing the ark of the covenant before
the people,
15 and as those who bore the ark came to the
Jordan, and the feet of the priests who bore
the ark dipped in the edge of the water (for the
Jordan overflows all its banks during the whole
time of harvest),
16 that the waters which came down from up-
stream stood *still, and* rose in a heap very far
away at Adam, the city that *is* beside Zaretan.
So the waters that went down into the Sea of
the Arabah, the Salt Sea, failed, *and* were cut
off; and the people crossed over opposite Jer-
icho.
17 Then the priests who bore the ark of the
covenant of the LORD stood firm on dry ground
in the midst of the Jordan; and all Israel
crossed over on dry ground, until all the people
had crossed completely over the Jordan.

The Memorial Stones

4 And it came to pass, when all the people
had completely crossed over the Jordan, that
the LORD spoke to Joshua, saying:
2 "Take for yourselves twelve men from the
people, one man from every tribe,
3 "and command them, saying, 'Take for your-
selves twelve stones from here, out of the midst
of the Jordan, from the place where the priests'
feet stood firm. You shall carry them over with
you and leave them in the lodging place where
you lodge tonight.'"
4 Then Joshua called the twelve men whom
he had appointed from the children of Israel,
one man from every tribe;
5 and Joshua said to them: "Cross over be-
fore the ark of the LORD your God into the midst
of the Jordan, and each one of you take up a
stone on his shoulder, according to the number
of the tribes of the children of Israel,
6 "that this may be a sign among you when
your children ask in time to come, saying, 'What
do these stones *mean* to you?'
7 "Then you shall answer them that the waters
of the Jordan were cut off before the ark of the
covenant of the LORD; when it crossed over the
Jordan, the waters of the Jordan were cut off.
And these stones shall be for a memorial to
the children of Israel forever."
8 And the children of Israel did so, just as
Joshua commanded, and took up twelve stones
from the midst of the Jordan, as the LORD had
spoken to Joshua, according to the number of

3:1 [a]Hebrew *Shittim*

the tribes of the children of Israel, and carried
them over with them to the place where they
lodged, and laid them down there.
9 Then Joshua set up twelve stones in the
midst of the Jordan, in the place where the feet
of the priests who bore the ark of the covenant
stood; and they are there to this day.
10 So the priests who bore the ark stood in
the midst of the Jordan until everything was
finished that the LORD had commanded
Joshua to speak to the people, according to all
that Moses had commanded Joshua; and the
people hurried and crossed over.
11 Then it came to pass, when all the people
had completely crossed over, that the ark of
the LORD and the priests crossed over in the
presence of the people.
12 And the men of Reuben, the men of Gad,
and half the tribe of Manasseh crossed over
armed before the children of Israel, as Moses
had spoken to them.
13 About forty thousand prepared for war
crossed over before the LORD for battle, to the
plains of Jericho.
14 On that day the LORD exalted Joshua in
the sight of all Israel; and they feared him, as
they had feared Moses, all the days of his life.
15 Then the LORD spoke to Joshua, saying,
16 "Command the priests who bear the ark
of the Testimony to come up from the Jordan."
17 Joshua therefore commanded the priests,
saying, "Come up from the Jordan."
18 And it came to pass, when the priests who
bore the ark of the covenant of the LORD had
come from the midst of the Jordan, *and* the
soles of the priests' feet touched the dry land,
that the waters of the Jordan returned to their
place and overflowed all its banks as before.
19 Now the people came up from the Jordan
on the tenth *day* of the first month, and they
camped in Gilgal on the east border of Jericho.
20 And those twelve stones which they took
out of the Jordan, Joshua set up in Gilgal.
21 Then he spoke to the children of Israel,
saying: "When your children ask their fathers
in time to come, saying, 'What *are* these stones?'
22 "then you shall let your children know,
saying, 'Israel crossed over this Jordan on dry
land';
23 "for the LORD your God dried up the wa-
ters of the Jordan before you until you had
crossed over, as the LORD your God did to the
Red Sea, which He dried up before us until we
had crossed over,
24 "that all the peoples of the earth may know
the hand of the LORD, that it *is* mighty, that you
may fear the LORD your God forever."

The Second Generation Circumcised

5 So it was, when all the kings of the Amo-
rites who *were* on the west side of the Jor-
dan, and all the kings of the Canaanites who
were by the sea, heard that the LORD had dried
up the waters of the Jordan from before the
children of Israel until we[a] had crossed over,
that their heart melted; and there was no spirit
in them any longer because of the children of
Israel.
2 At that time the LORD said to Joshua,
"Make flint knives for yourself, and circumcise
the sons of Israel again the second time."
3 So Joshua made flint knives for himself,
and circumcised the sons of Israel at the hill of
the foreskins.[a]
4 And this *is* the reason why Joshua circum-
cised them: All the people who came out of
Egypt *who were* males, all the men of war, had
died in the wilderness on the way, after they
had come out of Egypt.
5 For all the people who came out had been
circumcised, but all the people born in the wil-
derness, on the way as they came out of Egypt,
had not been circumcised.
6 For the children of Israel walked forty
years in the wilderness, till all the people *who
were* men of war, who came out of Egypt, were
consumed, because they did not obey the voice
of the LORD—to whom the LORD swore that
He would not show them the land which the
LORD had sworn to their fathers that He would
give us, "a land flowing with milk and honey."[a]
7 Then Joshua circumcised their sons *whom*
He raised up in their place; for they were un-
circumcised, because they had not been cir-
cumcised on the way.
8 So it was, when they had finished circum-
cising all the people, that they stayed in their
places in the camp till they were healed.
9 Then the LORD said to Joshua, "This day I
have rolled away the reproach of Egypt from
you." Therefore the name of the place is called
Gilgal[a] to this day.
10 Now the children of Israel camped in Gil-
gal, and kept the Passover on the fourteenth
day of the month at twilight on the plains of
Jericho.
11 And they ate of the produce of the land on
the day after the Passover, unleavened bread
and parched grain, on the very same day.
12 Then the manna ceased on the day after
they had eaten the produce of the land; and the
children of Israel no longer had manna, but
they ate the food of the land of Canaan that
year.

The Commander of the Army of the LORD

13 And it came to pass, when Joshua was by
Jericho, that he lifted his eyes and looked, and
behold, a Man stood opposite him with His
sword drawn in His hand. And Joshua went to
Him and said to Him, "*Are* You for us or for
our adversaries?"
14 So He said, "No, but *as* Commander of the
army of the LORD I have now come." And Joshua
fell on his face to the earth and worshiped, and
said to Him, "What does my Lord say to His
servant?"
15 Then the Commander of the LORD's army
said to Joshua, "Take your sandal off your foot,
for the place where you stand *is* holy." And
Joshua did so.

The Destruction of Jericho

6 Now Jericho was securely shut up because
of the children of Israel; none went out, and
none came in.
2 And the LORD said to Joshua: "See! I have
given Jericho into your hand, its king, *and* the
mighty men of valor.
3 "You shall march around the city, all *you*
men of war; you shall go all around the city once.
This you shall do six days.
4 "And seven priests shall bear seven trumpets
of rams' horns before the ark. But the seventh

5:1 [a]Following Kethib; Qere, some Hebrew manuscripts and editions, Septuagint, Syriac, Targum, and Vulgate read *they.* **5:3** [a]Hebrew *Gibeath Haaraloth* **5:6** [a]Exodus 3:8 **5:9** [a]Literally *Rolling*

day you shall march around the city seven
times, and the priests shall blow the trumpets.
5 "It shall come to pass, when they make a
long *blast* with the ram's horn, *and* when you
hear the sound of the trumpet, that all the people shall shout with a great shout; then the wall
of the city will fall down flat. And the people
shall go up every man straight before him."
6 Then Joshua the son of Nun called the
priests and said to them, "Take up the ark of
the covenant, and let seven priests bear seven
trumpets of rams' horns before the ark of the
LORD."
7 And he said to the people, "Proceed, and
march around the city, and let him who is
armed advance before the ark of the LORD."
8 So it was, when Joshua had spoken to the
people, that the seven priests bearing the seven
trumpets of rams' horns before the LORD advanced and blew the trumpets, and the ark of
the covenant of the LORD followed them.
9 The armed men went before the priests
who blew the trumpets, and the rear guard
came after the ark, while *the priests* continued
blowing the trumpets.
10 Now Joshua had commanded the people,
saying, "You shall not shout or make any noise
with your voice, nor shall a word proceed out
of your mouth, until the day I say to you,
'Shout!' Then you shall shout."
11 So he had the ark of the LORD circle the
city, going around *it* once. Then they came into
the camp and lodged in the camp.
12 And Joshua rose early in the morning, and
the priests took up the ark of the LORD.
13 Then seven priests bearing seven trumpets
of rams' horns before the ark of the LORD went
on continually and blew with the trumpets.
And the armed men went before them. But the
rear guard came after the ark of the LORD,
while *the priests* continued blowing the trumpets.
14 And the second day they marched around
the city once and returned to the camp. So they
did six days.
15 But it came to pass on the seventh day that
they rose early, about the dawning of the day,
and marched around the city seven times in the
same manner. On that day only they marched
around the city seven times.
16 And the seventh time it happened, when
the priests blew the trumpets, that Joshua said
to the people: "Shout, for the LORD has given
you the city!
17 "Now the city shall be doomed by the
LORD to destruction, it and all who *are* in it.
Only Rahab the harlot shall live, she and all
who *are* with her in the house, because she hid
the messengers that we sent.
18 "And you, by all means abstain from the
accursed things, lest you become accursed
when you take of the accursed things, and
make the camp of Israel a curse, and trouble
it.
19 "But all the silver and gold, and vessels of
bronze and iron, *are* consecrated to the LORD;
they shall come into the treasury of the LORD."
20 So the people shouted when *the priests*
blew the trumpets. And it happened when the
people heard the sound of the trumpet, and the
people shouted with a great shout, that the wall
fell down flat. Then the people went up into
the city, every man straight before him, and
they took the city.
21 And they utterly destroyed all that *was* in
the city, both man and woman, young and old,
ox and sheep and donkey, with the edge of the
sword.
22 But Joshua had said to the two men who
had spied out the country, "Go into the harlot's
house, and from there bring out the woman
and all that she has, as you swore to her."
23 And the young men who had been spies
went in and brought out Rahab, her father, her
mother, her brothers, and all that she had. So
they brought out all her relatives and left them
outside the camp of Israel.
24 But they burned the city and all that *was*
in it with fire. Only the silver and gold, and the
vessels of bronze and iron, they put into the
treasury of the house of the LORD.
25 And Joshua spared Rahab the harlot, her
father's household, and all that she had. So she
dwells in Israel to this day, because she hid
the messengers whom Joshua sent to spy out
Jericho.
26 Then Joshua charged *them* at that time,
saying, "Cursed *be* the man before the LORD
who rises up and builds this city Jericho; he
shall lay its foundation with his firstborn, and
with his youngest he shall set up its gates."
27 So the LORD was with Joshua, and his
fame spread throughout all the country.

Defeat at Ai

7 But the children of Israel committed a trespass regarding the accursed things, for
Achan the son of Carmi, the son of Zabdi,[a] the
son of Zerah, of the tribe of Judah, took of
the accursed things; so the anger of the LORD
burned against the children of Israel.
2 Now Joshua sent men from Jericho to Ai,
which *is* beside Beth Aven, on the east side of
Bethel, and spoke to them, saying, "Go up and
spy out the country." So the men went up and
spied out Ai.
3 And they returned to Joshua and said to
him, "Do not let all the people go up, but let
about two or three thousand men go up and
attack Ai. Do not weary all the people there,
for *the people of Ai are* few."
4 So about three thousand men went up
there from the people, but they fled before the
men of Ai.
5 And the men of Ai struck down about thirty-six men, for they chased them *from* before the
gate as far as Shebarim, and struck them down
on the descent; therefore the hearts of the people melted and became like water.
6 Then Joshua tore his clothes, and fell to
the earth on his face before the ark of the LORD
until evening, he and the elders of Israel; and
they put dust on their heads.
7 And Joshua said, "Alas, Lord GOD, why
have You brought this people over the Jordan
at all—to deliver us into the hand of the Amorites, to destroy us? Oh, that we had been content, and dwelt on the other side of the Jordan!
8 "O Lord, what shall I say when Israel turns
its back before its enemies?
9 For the Canaanites and all the inhabitants
of the land will hear *it*, and surround us, and
cut off our name from the earth. Then what will
You do for Your great name?"

7:1 [a]Called *Zimri* in 1 Chronicles 2:6

The Sin of Achan

10 So the LORD said to Joshua: "Get up! Why
do you lie thus on your face?
11 "Israel has sinned, and they have also
transgressed My covenant which I com-
manded them. For they have even taken some
of the accursed things, and have both stolen
and deceived; and they have also put *it* among
their own stuff.
12 "Therefore the children of Israel could not
stand before their enemies, *but* turned *their*
backs before their enemies, because they have
become doomed to destruction. Neither will I
be with you anymore, unless you destroy the
accursed from among you.
13 "Get up, sanctify the people, and say,
'Sanctify yourselves for tomorrow, because
thus says the LORD God of Israel: "*There is*
an accursed thing in your midst, O Israel; you
cannot stand before your enemies until you take
away the accursed thing from among you."
14 'In the morning therefore you shall be
brought according to your tribes. And it shall
be *that* the tribe which the LORD takes shall
come according to families; and the family
which the LORD takes shall come by house-
holds; and the household which the LORD
takes shall come man by man.
15 'Then it shall be *that* he who is taken with
the accursed thing shall be burned with fire,
he and all that he has, because he has trans-
gressed the covenant of the LORD, and because
he has done a disgraceful thing in Israel.'"
16 So Joshua rose early in the morning and
brought Israel by their tribes, and the tribe of
Judah was taken.
17 He brought the clan of Judah, and he took
the family of the Zarhites; and he brought the
family of the Zarhites man by man, and Zabdi
was taken.
18 Then he brought his household man by
man, and Achan the son of Carmi, the son of
Zabdi, the son of Zerah, of the tribe of Judah,
was taken.
19 Now Joshua said to Achan, "My son, I beg
you, give glory to the LORD God of Israel, and
make confession to Him, and tell me now what
you have done; do not hide *it* from me."
20 And Achan answered Joshua and said,
"Indeed I have sinned against the LORD God
of Israel, and this is what I have done:
21 "When I saw among the spoils a beautiful
Babylonian garment, two hundred shekels of
silver, and a wedge of gold weighing fifty shek-
els, I coveted them and took them. And there
they are, hidden in the earth in the midst of my
tent, with the silver under it."
22 So Joshua sent messengers, and they ran
to the tent; and there it was, hidden in his tent,
with the silver under it.
23 And they took them from the midst of the
tent, brought them to Joshua and to all the
children of Israel, and laid them out before the
LORD.
24 Then Joshua, and all Israel with him, took
Achan the son of Zerah, the silver, the gar-
ment, the wedge of gold, his sons, his daugh-
ters, his oxen, his donkeys, his sheep, his tent,
and all that he had, and they brought them to
the Valley of Achor.
25 And Joshua said, "Why have you troubled
us? The LORD will trouble you this day." So all
Israel stoned him with stones; and they burned
them with fire after they had stoned them with
stones.
26 Then they raised over him a great heap of
stones, still there to this day. So the LORD
turned from the fierceness of His anger. There-
fore the name of that place has been called the
Valley of Achor[a] to this day.

The Fall of Ai

8 Now the LORD said to Joshua: "Do not be
afraid, nor be dismayed; take all the people
of war with you, and arise, go up to Ai. See, I
have given into your hand the king of Ai, his
people, his city, and his land.
2 "And you shall do to Ai and its king as you
did to Jericho and its king. Only its spoil and
its cattle you shall take as booty for yourselves.
Lay an ambush for the city behind it."
3 So Joshua arose, and all the people of war,
to go up against Ai; and Joshua chose thirty
thousand mighty men of valor and sent them
away by night.
4 And he commanded them, saying: "Be-
hold, you shall lie in ambush against the city,
behind the city. Do not go very far from the
city, but all of you be ready.
5 "Then I and all the people who *are* with
me will approach the city; and it will come
about, when they come out against us as at the
first, that we shall flee before them.
6 "For they will come out after us till we
have drawn them from the city, for they will
say, '*They are* fleeing before us as at the first.'
Therefore we will flee before them.
7 "Then you shall rise from the ambush and
seize the city, for the LORD your God will de-
liver it into your hand.
8 "And it will be, when you have taken the
city, *that* you shall set the city on fire. Accord-
ing to the commandment of the LORD you shall
do. See, I have commanded you."
9 Joshua therefore sent them out; and they
went to lie in ambush, and stayed between
Bethel and Ai, on the west side of Ai; but
Joshua lodged that night among the people.
10 Then Joshua rose up early in the morning
and mustered the people, and went up, he and
the elders of Israel, before the people to Ai.
11 And all the people of war who *were* with
him went up and drew near; and they came
before the city and camped on the north side
of Ai. Now a valley *lay* between them and Ai.
12 So he took about five thousand men and
set them in ambush between Bethel and Ai, on
the west side of the city.
13 And when they had set the people, all the
army that *was* on the north of the city, and its
rear guard on the west of the city, Joshua went
that night into the midst of the valley.
14 Now it happened, when the king of Ai saw
it, that the men of the city hurried and rose
early and went out against Israel to battle, he
and all his people, at an appointed place before
the plain. But he did not know that *there was*
an ambush against him behind the city.
15 And Joshua and all Israel made as if they
were beaten before them, and fled by the way
of the wilderness.
16 So all the people who *were* in Ai were
called together to pursue them. And they pur-
sued Joshua and were drawn away from the
city.

7:26 [a]Literally *Trouble*

17 There was not a man left in Ai or Bethel
who did not go out after Israel. So they left the
city open and pursued Israel.
18 Then the LORD said to Joshua, "Stretch
out the spear that *is* in your hand toward Ai,
for I will give it into your hand." And Joshua
stretched out the spear that *was* in his hand
toward the city.
19 So *those in* ambush arose quickly out of
their place; they ran as soon as he had stretched
out his hand, and they entered the city and
took it, and hurried to set the city on fire.
20 And when the men of Ai looked behind
them, they saw, and behold, the smoke of the
city ascended to heaven. So they had no power
to flee this way or that way, and the people
who had fled to the wilderness turned back on
the pursuers.
21 Now when Joshua and all Israel saw that
the ambush had taken the city and that the
smoke of the city ascended, they turned back
and struck down the men of Ai.
22 Then the others came out of the city
against them; so they were *caught* in the midst
of Israel, some on this side and some on that
side. And they struck them down, so that they
let none of them remain or escape.
23 But the king of Ai they took alive, and
brought him to Joshua.
24 And it came to pass when Israel had made
an end of slaying all the inhabitants of Ai in
the field, in the wilderness where they pursued
them, and when they all had fallen by the edge
of the sword until they were consumed, that all
the Israelites returned to Ai and struck it with
the edge of the sword.
25 So it was *that* all who fell that day, both
men and women, *were* twelve thousand—all
the people of Ai.
26 For Joshua did not draw back his hand,
with which he stretched out the spear, until he
had utterly destroyed all the inhabitants of Ai.
27 Only the livestock and the spoil of that city
Israel took as booty for themselves, according
to the word of the LORD which He had com-
manded Joshua.
28 So Joshua burned Ai and made it a heap
forever, a desolation to this day.
29 And the king of Ai he hanged on a tree
until evening. And as soon as the sun was
down, Joshua commanded that they should
take his corpse down from the tree, cast it at
the entrance of the gate of the city, and raise
over it a great heap of stones *that remains* to
this day.

Joshua Renews the Covenant

30 Now Joshua built an altar to the LORD God
of Israel in Mount Ebal,
31 as Moses the servant of the LORD had com-
manded the children of Israel, as it is written
in the Book of the Law of Moses: "an altar of
whole stones over which no man has wielded
an iron *tool*."[a] And they offered on it burnt
offerings to the LORD, and sacrificed peace of-
ferings.
32 And there, in the presence of the children
of Israel, he wrote on the stones a copy of the
law of Moses, which he had written.
33 Then all Israel, with their elders and offi-
cers and judges, stood on either side of the ark
before the priests, the Levites, who bore the ark
of the covenant of the LORD, the stranger as
well as he who was born among them. Half of
them *were* in front of Mount Gerizim and half
of them in front of Mount Ebal, as Moses the
servant of the LORD had commanded before,
that they should bless the people of Israel.
34 And afterward he read all the words of the
law, the blessings and the cursings, according
to all that is written in the Book of the Law.
35 There was not a word of all that Moses had
commanded which Joshua did not read before
all the assembly of Israel, with the women, the
little ones, and the strangers who were living
among them.

The Treaty with the Gibeonites

9 And it came to pass when all the kings who
were on this side of the Jordan, in the hills
and in the lowland and in all the coasts of the
Great Sea toward Lebanon—the Hittite, the
Amorite, the Canaanite, the Perizzite, the Hi-
vite, and the Jebusite—heard *about it,*
2 that they gathered together to fight with
Joshua and Israel with one accord.
3 But when the inhabitants of Gibeon heard
what Joshua had done to Jericho and Ai,
4 they worked craftily, and went and pre-
tended to be ambassadors. And they took old
sacks on their donkeys, old wineskins torn and
mended,
5 old and patched sandals on their feet, and
old garments on themselves; and all the bread
of their provision was dry *and* moldy.
6 And they went to Joshua, to the camp at
Gilgal, and said to him and to the men of Israel,
"We have come from a far country; now there-
fore, make a covenant with us."
7 Then the men of Israel said to the Hivites,
"Perhaps you dwell among us; so how can we
make a covenant with you?"
8 But they said to Joshua, "We *are* your ser-
vants." And Joshua said to them, "Who *are*
you, and where do you come from?"
9 So they said to him: "From a very far coun-
try your servants have come, because of the
name of the LORD your God; for we have heard
of His fame, and all that He did in Egypt,
10 "and all that He did to the two kings of
the Amorites who *were* beyond the Jordan—to
Sihon king of Heshbon, and Og king of Ba-
shan, who was at Ashtaroth.
11 "Therefore our elders and all the inhab-
itants of our country spoke to us, saying, 'Take
provisions with you for the journey, and go to
meet them, and say to them, "We *are* your ser-
vants; now therefore, make a covenant with
us." '
12 "This bread of ours we took hot *for* our pro-
vision from our houses on the day we departed
to come to you. But now look, it is dry and moldy.
13 "And these wineskins which we filled *were*
new, and see, they are torn; and these our gar-
ments and our sandals have become old be-
cause of the very long journey."
14 Then the men of Israel took some of their
provisions; but they did not ask counsel of the
LORD.
15 So Joshua made peace with them, and made
a covenant with them to let them live; and the
rulers of the congregation swore to them.
16 And it happened at the end of three days,
after they had made a covenant with them, that
they heard that they *were* their neighbors who
dwelt near them.

8:31 [a]Deuteronomy 27:5, 6

17 Then the children of Israel journeyed and came to their cities on the third day. Now their cities *were* Gibeon, Chephirah, Beeroth, and Kirjath Jearim.

18 But the children of Israel did not attack them, because the rulers of the congregation had sworn to them by the LORD God of Israel. And all the congregation complained against the rulers.

19 Then all the rulers said to all the congregation, "We have sworn to them by the LORD God of Israel; now therefore, we may not touch them.

20 "This we will do to them: We will let them live, lest wrath be upon us because of the oath which we swore to them."

21 And the rulers said to them, "Let them live, but let them be woodcutters and water carriers for all the congregation, as the rulers had promised them."

22 Then Joshua called for them, and he spoke to them, saying, "Why have you deceived us, saying, 'We *are* very far from you,' when you dwell near us?

23 "Now therefore, you *are* cursed, and none of you shall be freed from being slaves—woodcutters and water carriers for the house of my God."

24 So they answered Joshua and said, "Because your servants were clearly told that the LORD your God commanded His servant Moses to give you all the land, and to destroy all the inhabitants of the land from before you; therefore we were very much afraid for our lives because of you, and have done this thing.

25 "And now, here we are, in your hands; do with us as it seems good and right to do to us."

26 So he did to them, and delivered them out of the hand of the children of Israel, so that they did not kill them.

27 And that day Joshua made them woodcutters and water carriers for the congregation and for the altar of the LORD, in the place which He would choose, even to this day.

The Sun Stands Still

10 Now it came to pass when Adoni-Zedek king of Jerusalem heard how Joshua had taken Ai and had utterly destroyed it—as he had done to Jericho and its king, so he had done to Ai and its king—and how the inhabitants of Gibeon had made peace with Israel and were among them,

2 that they feared greatly, because Gibeon *was* a great city, like one of the royal cities, and because it *was* greater than Ai, and all its men *were* mighty.

3 Therefore Adoni-Zedek king of Jerusalem sent to Hoham king of Hebron, Piram king of Jarmuth, Japhia king of Lachish, and Debir king of Eglon, saying,

4 "Come up to me and help me, that we may attack Gibeon, for it has made peace with Joshua and with the children of Israel."

5 Therefore the five kings of the Amorites, the king of Jerusalem, the king of Hebron, the king of Jarmuth, the king of Lachish, *and* the king of Eglon, gathered together and went up, they and all their armies, and camped before Gibeon and made war against it.

6 And the men of Gibeon sent to Joshua at the camp at Gilgal, saying, "Do not forsake your servants; come up to us quickly, save us and help us, for all the kings of the Amorites who dwell in the mountains have gathered together against us."

7 So Joshua ascended from Gilgal, he and all the people of war with him, and all the mighty men of valor.

8 And the LORD said to Joshua, "Do not fear them, for I have delivered them into your hand; not a man of them shall stand before you."

9 Joshua therefore came upon them suddenly, having marched all night from Gilgal.

10 So the LORD routed them before Israel, killed them with a great slaughter at Gibeon, chased them along the road that goes to Beth Horon, and struck them down as far as Azekah and Makkedah.

11 And it happened, as they fled before Israel *and* were on the descent of Beth Horon, that the LORD cast down large hailstones from heaven on them as far as Azekah, and they died. *There were* more who died from the hailstones than the children of Israel killed with the sword.

12 Then Joshua spoke to the LORD in the day when the LORD delivered up the Amorites before the children of Israel, and he said in the sight of Israel:

"Sun, stand still over Gibeon;
And Moon, in the Valley of Aijalon."
13 So the sun stood still,
And the moon stopped,
Till the people had revenge
Upon their enemies.

Is this not written in the Book of Jasher? So the sun stood still in the midst of heaven, and did not hasten to go *down* for about a whole day.

14 And there has been no day like that, before it or after it, that the LORD heeded the voice of a man; for the LORD fought for Israel.

15 Then Joshua returned, and all Israel with him, to the camp at Gilgal.

The Amorite Kings Executed

16 But these five kings had fled and hidden themselves in a cave at Makkedah.

17 And it was told Joshua, saying, "The five kings have been found hidden in the cave at Makkedah."

18 So Joshua said, "Roll large stones against the mouth of the cave, and set men by it to guard them.

19 "And do not stay *there* yourselves, *but* pursue your enemies, and attack their rear *guard*. Do not allow them to enter their cities, for the LORD your God has delivered them into your hand."

20 Then it happened, while Joshua and the children of Israel made an end of slaying them with a very great slaughter, till they had finished, that those who escaped entered fortified cities.

21 And all the people returned to the camp, to Joshua at Makkedah, in peace. No one moved his tongue against any of the children of Israel.

22 Then Joshua said, "Open the mouth of the cave, and bring out those five kings to me from the cave."

23 And they did so, and brought out those five kings to him from the cave: the king of Jerusalem, the king of Hebron, the king of Jarmuth, the king of Lachish, *and* the king of Eglon.

24 So it was, when they brought out those kings to Joshua, that Joshua called for all the men of Israel, and said to the captains of the men of war who went with him, "Come near, put your feet on the necks of these kings." And they drew near and put their feet on their necks.

25 Then Joshua said to them, "Do not be afraid, nor be dismayed; be strong and of good

courage, for thus the LORD will do to all your enemies against whom you fight."

26 And afterward Joshua struck them and killed them, and hanged them on five trees; and they were hanging on the trees until evening.

27 So it was at the time of the going down of the sun *that* Joshua commanded, and they took them down from the trees, cast them into the cave where they had been hidden, and laid large stones against the cave's mouth, *which remain* until this very day.

Conquest of the Southland

28 On that day Joshua took Makkedah, and struck it and its king with the edge of the sword. He utterly destroyed them[a]—all the people who *were* in it. He let none remain. He also did to the king of Makkedah as he had done to the king of Jericho.

29 Then Joshua passed from Makkedah, and all Israel with him, to Libnah; and they fought against Libnah.

30 And the LORD also delivered it and its king into the hand of Israel; he struck it and all the people who *were* in it with the edge of the sword. He let none remain in it, but did to its king as he had done to the king of Jericho.

31 Then Joshua passed from Libnah, and all Israel with him, to Lachish; and they encamped against it and fought against it.

32 And the LORD delivered Lachish into the hand of Israel, who took it on the second day, and struck it and all the people who *were* in it with the edge of the sword, according to all that he had done to Libnah.

33 Then Horam king of Gezer came up to help Lachish; and Joshua struck him and his people, until he left him none remaining.

34 From Lachish Joshua passed to Eglon, and all Israel with him; and they encamped against it and fought against it.

35 They took it on that day and struck it with the edge of the sword; all the people who *were* in it he utterly destroyed that day, according to all that he had done to Lachish.

36 So Joshua went up from Eglon, and all Israel with him, to Hebron; and they fought against it.

37 And they took it and struck it with the edge of the sword—its king, all its cities, and all the people who *were* in it; he left none remaining, according to all that he had done to Eglon, but utterly destroyed it and all the people who *were* in it.

38 Then Joshua returned, and all Israel with him, to Debir; and they fought against it.

39 And he took it and its king and all its cities; they struck them with the edge of the sword and utterly destroyed all the people who *were* in it. He left none remaining; as he had done to Hebron, so he did to Debir and its king, as he had done also to Libnah and its king.

40 So Joshua conquered all the land: the mountain country and the South[a] and the lowland and the wilderness slopes, and all their kings; he left none remaining, but utterly destroyed all that breathed, as the LORD God of Israel had commanded.

41 And Joshua conquered them from Kadesh Barnea as far as Gaza, and all the country of Goshen, even as far as Gibeon.

42 All these kings and their land Joshua took at one time, because the LORD God of Israel fought for Israel.

43 Then Joshua returned, and all Israel with him, to the camp at Gilgal.

The Northern Conquest

11 And it came to pass, when Jabin king of Hazor heard *these things,* that he sent to Jobab king of Madon, to the king of Shimron, to the king of Achshaph,

2 and to the kings who *were* from the north, in the mountains, in the plain south of Chinneroth, in the lowland, and in the heights of Dor on the west,

3 to the Canaanites in the east and in the west, the Amorite, the Hittite, the Perizzite, the Jebusite in the mountains, and the Hivite below Hermon in the land of Mizpah.

4 So they went out, they and all their armies with them, *as* many people *as* the sand that *is* on the seashore in multitude, with very many horses and chariots.

5 And when all these kings had met together, they came and camped together at the waters of Merom to fight against Israel.

6 But the LORD said to Joshua, "Do not be afraid because of them, for tomorrow about this time I will deliver all of them slain before Israel. You shall hamstring their horses and burn their chariots with fire."

7 So Joshua and all the people of war with him came against them suddenly by the waters of Merom, and they attacked them.

8 And the LORD delivered them into the hand of Israel, who defeated them and chased them to Greater Sidon, to the Brook Misrephoth,[a] and to the Valley of Mizpah eastward; they attacked them until they left none of them remaining.

9 So Joshua did to them as the LORD had told him: he hamstrung their horses and burned their chariots with fire.

10 Joshua turned back at that time and took Hazor, and struck its king with the sword; for Hazor was formerly the head of all those kingdoms.

11 And they struck all the people who *were* in it with the edge of the sword, utterly destroying *them.* There was none left breathing. Then he burned Hazor with fire.

12 So all the cities of those kings, and all their kings, Joshua took and struck with the edge of the sword. He utterly destroyed them, as Moses the servant of the LORD had commanded.

13 But *as for* the cities that stood on their mounds,[a] Israel burned none of them, except Hazor only, *which* Joshua burned.

14 And all the spoil of these cities and the livestock, the children of Israel took as booty for themselves; but they struck every man with the edge of the sword until they had destroyed them, and they left none breathing.

15 As the LORD had commanded Moses his servant, so Moses commanded Joshua, and so Joshua did. He left nothing undone of all that the LORD had commanded Moses.

Summary of Joshua's Conquests

16 Thus Joshua took all this land: the mountain country, all the South, all the land of Goshen,

10:28 [a]Following Masoretic Text and most authorities; many Hebrew manuscripts, some manuscripts of the Septuagint, and some manuscripts of the Targum read *it.* **10:40** [a]Hebrew *Negev,* and so throughout this book **11:8** [a]Hebrew *Misrephoth Maim* **11:13** [a]Hebrew *tel,* a heap of successive city ruins

the lowland, and the Jordan plain[a]—the moun-
tains of Israel and its lowlands,
17 from Mount Halak and the ascent to Seir,
even as far as Baal Gad in the Valley of Leba-
non below Mount Hermon. He captured all
their kings, and struck them down and killed
them.
18 Joshua made war a long time with all those
kings.
19 There was not a city that made peace with
the children of Israel, except the Hivites, the
inhabitants of Gibeon. All *the others* they took
in battle.
20 For it was of the LORD to harden their
hearts, that they should come against Israel in
battle, that He might utterly destroy them, *and*
that they might receive no mercy, but that He
might destroy them, as the LORD had com-
manded Moses.
21 And at that time Joshua came and cut off
the Anakim from the mountains: from Hebron,
from Debir, from Anab, from all the mountains
of Judah, and from all the mountains of Israel;
Joshua utterly destroyed them with their cities.
22 None of the Anakim were left in the land
of the children of Israel; they remained only in
Gaza, in Gath, and in Ashdod.
23 So Joshua took the whole land, according
to all that the LORD had said to Moses; and
Joshua gave it as an inheritance to Israel ac-
cording to their divisions by their tribes. Then
the land rested from war.

The Kings Conquered by Moses

12 These *are* the kings of the land whom
the children of Israel defeated, and
whose land they possessed on the other side
of the Jordan toward the rising of the sun, from
the River Arnon to Mount Hermon, and all the
eastern Jordan plain:
2 *One king was* Sihon king of the Amorites,
who dwelt in Heshbon *and* ruled half of Gilead,
from Aroer, which is on the bank of the River
Arnon, from the middle of that river, even as
far as the River Jabbok, *which is* the border of
the Ammonites,
3 and the eastern Jordan plain from the Sea
of Chinneroth as far as the Sea of the Arabah
(the Salt Sea), the road to Beth Jeshimoth, and
southward below the slopes of Pisgah.
4 *The other king was* Og king of Bashan and
his territory, *who was* of the remnant of the
giants, who dwelt at Ashtaroth and at Edrei,
5 and reigned over Mount Hermon, over Sal-
cah, over all Bashan, as far as the border of
the Geshurites and the Maachathites, and over
half of Gilead *to* the border of Sihon king of
Heshbon.
6 These Moses the servant of the LORD and
the children of Israel had conquered; and Mo-
ses the servant of the LORD had given it *as* a
possession to the Reubenites, the Gadites, and
half the tribe of Manasseh.

The Kings Conquered by Joshua

7 And these *are* the kings of the country
which Joshua and the children of Israel con-
quered on this side of the Jordan, on the west,
from Baal Gad in the Valley of Lebanon as far
as Mount Halak and the ascent to Seir, which
Joshua gave to the tribes of Israel *as* a posses-
sion according to their divisions,
8 in the mountain country, in the lowlands,
in the *Jordan* plain, in the slopes, in the wilder-
ness, and in the South—the Hittites, the Amo-
rites, the Canaanites, the Perizzites, the Hivites,
and the Jebusites:
9 the king of Jericho, one; the king of Ai,
which *is* beside Bethel, one;
10 the king of Jerusalem, one; the king of He-
bron, one;
11 the king of Jarmuth, one; the king of La-
chish, one;
12 the king of Eglon, one; the king of Gezer,
one;
13 the king of Debir, one; the king of Geder,
one;
14 the king of Hormah, one; the king of Arad,
one;
15 the king of Libnah, one; the king of Adul-
lam, one;
16 the king of Makkedah, one; the king of
Bethel, one;
17 the king of Tappuah, one; the king of Hepher,
one;
18 the king of Aphek, one; the king of Lasha-
ron, one;
19 the king of Madon, one; the king of Hazor,
one;
20 the king of Shimron Meron, one; the king
of Achshaph, one;
21 the king of Taanach, one; the king of Me-
giddo, one;
22 the king of Kedesh, one; the king of Jok-
neam in Carmel, one;
23 the king of Dor in the heights of Dor, one;
the king of the people of Gilgal, one;
24 the king of Tirzah, one—all the kings, thirty-
one.

Remaining Land to Be Conquered

13 Now Joshua was old, advanced in years.
And the LORD said to him: "You are old,
advanced in years, and there remains very
much land yet to be possessed.
2 "This is the land that yet remains: all the
territory of the Philistines and all *that of* the
Geshurites,
3 "from Sihor, which *is* east of Egypt, as far
as the border of Ekron northward (*which* is
counted as Canaanite); the five lords of the
Philistines—the Gazites, the Ashdodites, the
Ashkelonites, the Gittites, and the Ekronites;
also the Avites;
4 "from the south, all the land of the Canaan-
ites, and Mearah that belongs to the Sidonians
as far as Aphek, to the border of the Amorites;
5 "the land of the Gebalites,[a] and all Leba-
non, toward the sunrise, from Baal Gad below
Mount Hermon as far as the entrance to Hamath;
6 "all the inhabitants of the mountains from
Lebanon as far as the Brook Misrephoth,[a] *and*
all the Sidonians—them I will drive out from
before the children of Israel; only divide it by
lot to Israel as an inheritance, as I have com-
manded you.
7 "Now therefore, divide this land as an in-
heritance to the nine tribes and half the tribe
of Manasseh."

The Land Divided East of the Jordan

8 With the other half-tribe the Reubenites
and the Gadites received their inheritance,
which Moses had given them, beyond the Jordan
eastward, as Moses the servant of the LORD
had given them:

11:16 [a]Hebrew *arabah* **13:5** [a]Or *Giblites* **13:6** [a]Hebrew *Misrephoth Maim*

9 from Aroer which *is* on the bank of the River Arnon, and the town that *is* in the midst of the ravine, and all the plain of Medeba as far as Dibon;

10 all the cities of Sihon king of the Amorites, who reigned in Heshbon, as far as the border of the children of Ammon;

11 Gilead, and the border of the Geshurites and Maachathites, all Mount Hermon, and all Bashan as far as Salcah;

12 all the kingdom of Og in Bashan, who reigned in Ashtaroth and Edrei, who remained of the remnant of the giants; for Moses had defeated and cast out these.

13 Nevertheless the children of Israel did not drive out the Geshurites or the Maachathites, but the Geshurites and the Maachathites dwell among the Israelites until this day.

14 Only to the tribe of Levi he had given no inheritance; the sacrifices of the LORD God of Israel made by fire *are* their inheritance, as He said to them.

The Land of Reuben

15 And Moses had given to the tribe of the children of Reuben *an inheritance* according to their families.

16 Their territory was from Aroer, which *is* on the bank of the River Arnon, and the city that *is* in the midst of the ravine, and all the plain by Medeba;

17 Heshbon and all its cities that *are* in the plain: Dibon, Bamoth Baal, Beth Baal Meon,

18 Jahaza, Kedemoth, Mephaath,

19 Kirjathaim, Sibmah, Zereth Shahar on the mountain of the valley,

20 Beth Peor, the slopes of Pisgah, and Beth Jeshimoth—

21 all the cities of the plain and all the kingdom of Sihon king of the Amorites, who reigned in Heshbon, whom Moses had struck with the princes of Midian: Evi, Rekem, Zur, Hur, and Reba, who *were* princes of Sihon dwelling in the country.

22 The children of Israel also killed with the sword Balaam the son of Beor, the soothsayer, among those who were killed by them.

23 And the border of the children of Reuben was the bank of the Jordan. This *was* the inheritance of the children of Reuben according to their families, the cities and their villages.

The Land of Gad

24 Moses also had given *an inheritance* to the tribe of Gad, to the children of Gad according to their families.

25 Their territory was Jazer, and all the cities of Gilead, and half the land of the Ammonites as far as Aroer, which *is* before Rabbah,

26 and from Heshbon to Ramath Mizpah and Betonim, and from Mahanaim to the border of Debir,

27 and in the valley Beth Haram, Beth Nimrah, Succoth, and Zaphon, the rest of the kingdom of Sihon king of Heshbon, with the Jordan as *its* border, as far as the edge of the Sea of Chinnereth, on the other side of the Jordan eastward.

28 This *is* the inheritance of the children of Gad according to their families, the cities and their villages.

Half the Tribe of Manasseh (East)

29 Moses also had given *an inheritance* to half the tribe of Manasseh; it was for half the tribe of the children of Manasseh according to their families:

30 Their territory was from Mahanaim, all Bashan, all the kingdom of Og king of Bashan, and all the towns of Jair which are in Bashan, sixty cities;

31 half of Gilead, and Ashtaroth and Edrei, cities of the kingdom of Og in Bashan, *were* for the children of Machir the son of Manasseh, for half of the children of Machir according to their families.

32 These *are the areas* which Moses had distributed as an inheritance in the plains of Moab on the other side of the Jordan, by Jericho eastward.

33 But to the tribe of Levi Moses had given no inheritance; the LORD God of Israel *was* their inheritance, as He had said to them.

The Land Divided West of the Jordan

14 These *are the areas* which the children of Israel inherited in the land of Canaan, which Eleazar the priest, Joshua the son of Nun, and the heads of the fathers of the tribes of the children of Israel distributed as an inheritance to them.

2 Their inheritance *was* by lot, as the LORD had commanded by the hand of Moses, for the nine tribes and the half-tribe.

3 For Moses had given the inheritance of the two tribes and the half-tribe on the other side of the Jordan; but to the Levites he had given no inheritance among them.

4 For the children of Joseph were two tribes: Manasseh and Ephraim. And they gave no part to the Levites in the land, except cities to dwell *in,* with their common-lands for their livestock and their property.

5 As the LORD had commanded Moses, so the children of Israel did; and they divided the land.

Caleb Inherits Hebron

6 Then the children of Judah came to Joshua in Gilgal. And Caleb the son of Jephunneh the Kenizzite said to him: "You know the word which the LORD said to Moses the man of God concerning you and me in Kadesh Barnea.

7 "I *was* forty years old when Moses the servant of the LORD sent me from Kadesh Barnea to spy out the land, and I brought back word to him as *it was* in my heart.

8 "Nevertheless my brethren who went up with me made the heart of the people melt, but I wholly followed the LORD my God.

9 "So Moses swore on that day, saying, 'Surely the land where your foot has trodden shall be your inheritance and your children's forever, because you have wholly followed the LORD my God.'

10 "And now, behold, the LORD has kept me alive, as He said, these forty-five years, ever since the LORD spoke this word to Moses while Israel wandered in the wilderness; and now, here I am this day, eighty-five years old.

11 "As yet I *am as* strong this day as on the day that Moses sent me; just as my strength *was* then, so now *is* my strength for war, both for going out and for coming in.

12 "Now therefore, give me this mountain of which the LORD spoke in that day; for you heard in that day how the Anakim *were* there, and *that* the cities *were* great *and* fortified. It may be that the LORD *will be* with me, and I shall be able to drive them out as the LORD said."

13 And Joshua blessed him, and gave Hebron
to Caleb the son of Jephunneh as an inheri-
tance.
14 Hebron therefore became the inheritance
of Caleb the son of Jephunneh the Kenizzite to
this day, because he wholly followed the LORD
God of Israel.
15 And the name of Hebron formerly was Kir-
jath Arba (*Arba was* the greatest man among
the Anakim). Then the land had rest from war.

The Land of Judah

15 So *this* was the lot of the tribe of the
children of Judah according to their
families: The border of Edom at the Wilderness
of Zin southward *was* the extreme southern
boundary.
2 And their southern border began at the
shore of the Salt Sea, from the bay that faces
southward.
3 Then it went out to the southern side of
the Ascent of Akrabbim, passed along to Zin,
ascended on the south side of Kadesh Barnea,
passed along to Hezron, went up to Adar, and
went around to Karkaa.
4 *From there* it passed toward Azmon and
went out to the Brook of Egypt; and the border
ended at the sea. This shall be your southern
border.
5 The east border *was* the Salt Sea as far as
the mouth of the Jordan. And the border on
the northern quarter *began* at the bay of the
sea at the mouth of the Jordan.
6 The border went up to Beth Hoglah and
passed north of Beth Arabah; and the border
went up to the stone of Bohan the son of
Reuben.
7 Then the border went up toward Debir
from the Valley of Achor, and it turned north-
ward toward Gilgal, which *is* before the Ascent
of Adummim, which *is* on the south side of the
valley. The border continued toward the waters
of En Shemesh and ended at En Rogel.
8 And the border went up by the Valley of
the Son of Hinnom to the southern slope of the
Jebusite *city* (which *is* Jerusalem). The border
went up to the top of the mountain that *lies*
before the Valley of Hinnom westward, which
is at the end of the Valley of Rephaim[a] north-
ward.
9 Then the border went around from the top
of the hill to the fountain of the water of Neph-
toah, and extended to the cities of Mount
Ephron. And the border went around to Baalah
(which *is* Kirjath Jearim).
10 Then the border turned westward from Ba-
alah to Mount Seir, passed along to the side of
Mount Jearim on the north (which *is* Chesa-
lon), went down to Beth Shemesh, and passed
on to Timnah.
11 And the border went out to the side of Ek-
ron northward. Then the border went around
to Shicron, passed along to Mount Baalah, and
extended to Jabneel; and the border ended at
the sea.
12 The west border *was* the coastline of the
Great Sea. This *is* the boundary of the children
of Judah all around according to their families.

Caleb Occupies Hebron and Debir

13 Now to Caleb the son of Jephunneh he
gave a share among the children of Judah, ac-
cording to the commandment of the LORD to
Joshua, *namely*, Kirjath Arba, which *is* Hebron
(*Arba was* the father of Anak).
14 Caleb drove out the three sons of Anak
from there: Sheshai, Ahiman, and Talmai, the
children of Anak.
15 Then he went up from there to the inhab-
itants of Debir (formerly the name of Debir
was Kirjath Sepher).
16 And Caleb said, "He who attacks Kirjath
Sepher and takes it, to him I will give Achsah
my daughter as wife."
17 So Othniel the son of Kenaz, the brother
of Caleb, took it; and he gave him Achsah his
daughter as wife.
18 Now it was so, when she came *to him*, that
she persuaded him to ask her father for a field.
So she dismounted from *her* donkey, and Caleb
said to her, "What do you wish?"
19 She answered, "Give me a blessing; since
you have given me land in the South, give me
also springs of water." So he gave her the up-
per springs and the lower springs.

The Cities of Judah

20 This *was* the inheritance of the tribe of the
children of Judah according to their families:
21 The cities at the limits of the tribe of the
children of Judah, toward the border of Edom
in the South, were Kabzeel, Eder, Jagur,
22 Kinah, Dimonah, Adadah,
23 Kedesh, Hazor, Ithnan,
24 Ziph, Telem, Bealoth,
25 Hazor, Hadattah, Kerioth, Hezron (which
is Hazor),
26 Amam, Shema, Moladah,
27 Hazar Gaddah, Heshmon, Beth Pelet,
28 Hazar Shual, Beersheba, Bizjothjah,
29 Baalah, Ijim, Ezem,
30 Eltolad, Chesil, Hormah,
31 Ziklag, Madmannah, Sansannah,
32 Lebaoth, Shilhim, Ain, and Rimmon: all
the cities *are* twenty-nine, with their villages.
33 In the lowland: Eshtaol, Zorah, Ashnah,
34 Zanoah, En Gannim, Tappuah, Enam,
35 Jarmuth, Adullam, Socoh, Azekah,
36 Sharaim, Adithaim, Gederah, and Gedero-
thaim: fourteen cities with their villages;
37 Zenan, Hadashah, Migdal Gad,
38 Dilean, Mizpah, Joktheel,
39 Lachish, Bozkath, Eglon,
40 Cabbon, Lahmas,[a] Kithlish,
41 Gederoth, Beth Dagon, Naamah, and Mak-
kedah: sixteen cities with their villages;
42 Libnah, Ether, Ashan,
43 Jiphtah, Ashnah, Nezib,
44 Keilah, Achzib, and Mareshah: nine cities
with their villages;
45 Ekron, with its towns and villages;
46 from Ekron to the sea, all that *lay* near
Ashdod, with their villages;
47 Ashdod with its towns and villages, Gaza
with its towns and villages—as far as the Brook
of Egypt and the Great Sea with *its* coastline.
48 And in the mountain country: Shamir, Jat-
tir, Sochoh,
49 Dannah, Kirjath Sannah (which *is* Debir),
50 Anab, Eshtemoh, Anim,
51 Goshen, Holon, and Giloh: eleven cities
with their villages;
52 Arab, Dumah, Eshean,
53 Janum, Beth Tappuah, Aphekah,
54 Humtah, Kirjath Arba (which *is* Hebron),
and Zior: nine cities with their villages;

15:8 [a]Literally *Giants* **15:40** [a]Or *Lahmam*

55 Maon, Carmel, Ziph, Juttah,
56 Jezreel, Jokdeam, Zanoah,
57 Kain, Gibeah, and Timnah: ten cities with
their villages;
58 Halhul, Beth Zur, Gedor,
59 Maarath, Beth Anoth, and Eltekon: six cit-
ies with their villages;
60 Kirjath Baal (which *is* Kirjath Jearim) and
Rabbah: two cities with their villages.
61 In the wilderness: Beth Arabah, Middin,
Secacah,
62 Nibshan, the City of Salt, and En Gedi: six
cities with their villages.
63 As for the Jebusites, the inhabitants of Je-
rusalem, the children of Judah could not drive
them out; but the Jebusites dwell with the chil-
dren of Judah at Jerusalem to this day.

Ephraim and West Manasseh

16 The lot fell to the children of Joseph
from the Jordan, by Jericho, to the wa-
ters of Jericho on the east, to the wilderness
that goes up from Jericho through the moun-
tains to Bethel,
2 then went out from Bethel to Luz,[a] passed
along to the border of the Archites at Ataroth,
3 and went down westward to the boundary
of the Japhletites, as far as the boundary of
Lower Beth Horon to Gezer; and it ended at
the sea.
4 So the children of Joseph, Manasseh and
Ephraim, took their inheritance.

The Land of Ephraim

5 The border of the children of Ephraim, ac-
cording to their families, was *thus*: The border
of their inheritance on the east side was Ata-
roth Addar as far as Upper Beth Horon.
6 And the border went out toward the sea on
the north side of Michmethath; then the border
went around eastward to Taanath Shiloh, and
passed by it on the east of Janohah.
7 Then it went down from Janohah to Ata-
roth and Naarah,[a] reached to Jericho, and
came out at the Jordan.
8 The border went out from Tappuah west-
ward to the Brook Kanah, and it ended at the
sea. This *was* the inheritance of the tribe of the
children of Ephraim according to their families.
9 The separate cities for the children of
Ephraim *were* among the inheritance of the chil-
dren of Manasseh, all the cities with their vil-
lages.
10 And they did not drive out the Canaanites
who dwelt in Gezer; but the Canaanites dwell
among the Ephraimites to this day and have
become forced laborers.

The Other Half-Tribe of Manasseh (West)

17 There was also a lot for the tribe of Ma-
nasseh, for he *was* the firstborn of Joseph:
namely for Machir the firstborn of Manasseh,
the father of Gilead, because he was a man of
war; therefore he was given Gilead and Bashan.
2 And there was *a lot* for the rest of the chil-
dren of Manasseh according to their families:
for the children of Abiezer,[a] the children of
Helek, the children of Asriel, the children of
Shechem, the children of Hepher, and the chil-
dren of Shemida; these *were* the male children
of Manasseh the son of Joseph according to
their families.
3 But Zelophehad the son of Hepher, the son
of Gilead, the son of Machir, the son of Manas-
seh, had no sons, but only daughters. And
these *are* the names of his daughters: Mahlah,
Noah, Hoglah, Milcah, and Tirzah.
4 And they came near before Eleazar the
priest, before Joshua the son of Nun, and be-
fore the rulers, saying, "The LORD commanded
Moses to give us an inheritance among our
brothers." Therefore, according to the com-
mandment of the LORD, he gave them an inher-
itance among their father's brothers.
5 Ten shares fell to Manasseh, besides the
land of Gilead and Bashan, which *were* on the
other side of the Jordan,
6 because the daughters of Manasseh re-
ceived an inheritance among his sons; and the
rest of Manasseh's sons had the land of Gilead.
7 And the territory of Manasseh was from
Asher to Michmethath, that *lies* east of She-
chem; and the border went along south to the
inhabitants of En Tappuah.
8 Manasseh had the land of Tappuah, but
Tappuah on the border of Manasseh *belonged*
to the children of Ephraim.
9 And the border descended to the Brook
Kanah, southward to the brook. These cities of
Ephraim *are* among the cities of Manasseh.
The border of Manasseh *was* on the north side
of the brook; and it ended at the sea.
10 Southward *it was* Ephraim's, northward *it*
was Manasseh's, and the sea was its border.
Manasseh's territory was adjoining Asher on
the north and Issachar on the east.
11 And in Issachar and in Asher, Manasseh
had Beth Shean and its towns, Ibleam and its
towns, the inhabitants of Dor and its towns,
the inhabitants of En Dor and its towns, the
inhabitants of Taanach and its towns, and the
inhabitants of Megiddo and its towns—three
hilly regions.
12 Yet the children of Manasseh could not
drive out *the inhabitants of* those cities, but
the Canaanites were determined to dwell in that
land.
13 And it happened, when the children of Is-
rael grew strong, that they put the Canaanites
to forced labor, but did not utterly drive them
out.

More Land for Ephraim and Manasseh

14 Then the children of Joseph spoke to Joshua,
saying, "Why have you given us *only* one lot
and one share to inherit, since we *are* a great
people, inasmuch as the LORD has blessed us
until now?"
15 So Joshua answered them, "If you *are* a
great people, *then* go up to the forest *country*
and clear a place for yourself there in the land
of the Perizzites and the giants, since the
mountains of Ephraim are too confined for
you."
16 But the children of Joseph said, "The moun-
tain country is not enough for us; and all the
Canaanites who dwell in the land of the valley
have chariots of iron, *both those* who *are* of
Beth Shean and its towns and *those* who *are*
of the Valley of Jezreel."
17 And Joshua spoke to the house of Joseph—
to Ephraim and Manasseh—saying, "You *are*
a great people and have great power; you shall
not have *only* one lot,

16:2 [a]Septuagint reads *Bethel* (that is, Luz). **16:7** [a]Or *Naaran* (compare 1 Chronicles 7:28) **17:2** [a]Called *Jeezer* in Numbers 26:30

18 "but the mountain country shall be yours.
Although it *is* wooded, you shall cut it down,
and its farthest extent shall be yours; for you
shall drive out the Canaanites, though they
have iron chariots *and* are strong."

The Remainder of the Land Divided

18 Now the whole congregation of the chil-
dren of Israel assembled together at Shi-
loh, and set up the tabernacle of meeting there.
And the land was subdued before them.
2 But there remained among the children of
Israel seven tribes which had not yet received
their inheritance.
3 Then Joshua said to the children of Israel:
"How long will you neglect to go and possess
the land which the LORD God of your fathers
has given you?
4 "Pick out from among you three men for
each tribe, and I will send them; they shall rise
and go through the land, survey it according
to their inheritance, and come *back* to me.
5 "And they shall divide it into seven parts.
Judah shall remain in their territory on the
south, and the house of Joseph shall remain in
their territory on the north.
6 "You shall therefore survey the land in
seven parts and bring *the survey* here to me,
that I may cast lots for you here before the
LORD our God.
7 "But the Levites have no part among you,
for the priesthood of the LORD *is* their inheri-
tance. And Gad, Reuben, and half the tribe
of Manasseh have received their inheritance
beyond the Jordan on the east, which Moses
the servant of the LORD gave them."
8 Then the men arose to go away; and
Joshua charged those who went to survey the
land, saying, "Go, walk through the land, sur-
vey it, and come back to me, that I may cast
lots for you here before the LORD in Shiloh."
9 So the men went, passed through the land,
and wrote the survey in a book in seven parts
by cities; and they came to Joshua at the camp
in Shiloh.
10 Then Joshua cast lots for them in Shiloh
before the LORD, and there Joshua divided the
land to the children of Israel according to their
divisions.

The Land of Benjamin

11 Now the lot of the tribe of the children of
Benjamin came up according to their families,
and the territory of their lot came out between
the children of Judah and the children of Jo-
seph.
12 Their border on the north side began at the
Jordan, and the border went up to the side of
Jericho on the north, and went up through the
mountains westward; it ended at the Wilder-
ness of Beth Aven.
13 The border went over from there toward
Luz, to the side of Luz (which *is* Bethel) south-
ward; and the border descended to Ataroth Ad-
dar, near the hill that *lies* on the south side of
Lower Beth Horon.
14 Then the border extended around the west
side to the south, from the hill that *lies* before
Beth Horon southward; and it ended at Kirjath
Baal (which *is* Kirjath Jearim), a city of the
children of Judah. This *was* the west side.
15 The south side *began* at the end of Kirjath
Jearim, and the border extended on the west
and went out to the spring of the waters of
Nephtoah.
16 Then the border came down to the end of
the mountain that *lies* before the Valley of the
Son of Hinnom, which *is* in the Valley of the
Rephaim[a] on the north, descended to the Valley
of Hinnom, to the side of the Jebusite *city* on
the south, and descended to En Rogel.
17 And it went around from the north, went
out to En Shemesh, and extended toward Geli-
loth, which is before the Ascent of Adummim,
and descended to the stone of Bohan the son
of Reuben.
18 Then it passed along toward the north side
of Arabah,[a] and went down to Arabah.
19 And the border passed along to the north
side of Beth Hoglah; then the border ended at
the north bay at the Salt Sea, at the south end
of the Jordan. This *was* the southern boundary.
20 The Jordan was its border on the east side.
This *was* the inheritance of the children of
Benjamin, according to its boundaries all
around, according to their families.
21 Now the cities of the tribe of the children
of Benjamin, according to their families, were
Jericho, Beth Hoglah, Emek Keziz,
22 Beth Arabah, Zemaraim, Bethel,
23 Avim, Parah, Ophrah,
24 Chephar Haammoni, Ophni, and Gaba:
twelve cities with their villages;
25 Gibeon, Ramah, Beeroth,
26 Mizpah, Chephirah, Mozah,
27 Rekem, Irpeel, Taralah,
28 Zelah, Eleph, Jebus (which *is* Jerusalem),
Gibeath, *and* Kirjath: fourteen cities with their
villages. This was the inheritance of the chil-
dren of Benjamin according to their families.

Simeon's Inheritance with Judah

19 The second lot came out for Simeon, for
the tribe of the children of Simeon ac-
cording to their families. And their inheritance
was within the inheritance of the children of
Judah.
2 They had in their inheritance Beersheba
(Sheba), Moladah,
3 Hazar Shual, Balah, Ezem,
4 Eltolad, Bethul, Hormah,
5 Ziklag, Beth Marcaboth, Hazar Susah,
6 Beth Lebaoth, and Sharuhen: thirteen cit-
ies and their villages;
7 Ain, Rimmon, Ether, and Ashan: four cit-
ies and their villages;
8 and all the villages that *were* all around these
cities as far as Baalath Beer, Ramah of the South.
This *was* the inheritance of the tribe of the
children of Simeon according to their families.
9 The inheritance of the children of Simeon
was included in the share of the children of
Judah, for the share of the children of Judah
was too much for them. Therefore the children
of Simeon had *their* inheritance within the in-
heritance of that people.

The Land of Zebulun

10 The third lot came out for the children of
Zebulun according to their families, and the
border of their inheritance was as far as Sarid.
11 Their border went toward the west and to
Maralah, went to Dabbasheth, and extended
along the brook that is east of Jokneam.
12 Then from Sarid it went eastward toward
the sunrise along the border of Chisloth Tabor,

18:16 [a]Literally *Giants* 18:18 [a]Or *Beth Arabah* (compare 15:6 and 18:22)

and went out toward Daberath, bypassing Ja-
phia.
13 And from there it passed along on the east
of Gath Hepher, toward Eth Kazin, and ex-
tended to Rimmon, which borders on Neah.
14 Then the border went around it on the
north side of Hannathon, and it ended in the
Valley of Jiphthah El.
15 Included were Kattath, Nahallal, Shimron,
Idalah, and Bethlehem: twelve cities with their
villages.
16 This *was* the inheritance of the children
of Zebulun according to their families, these
cities with their villages.

The Land of Issachar

17 The fourth lot came out to Issachar, for the
children of Issachar according to their families.
18 And their territory went to Jezreel, and
included Chesulloth, Shunem,
19 Haphraim, Shion, Anaharath,
20 Rabbith, Kishion, Abez,
21 Remeth, En Gannim, En Haddah, and Beth
Pazzez.
22 And the border reached to Tabor, Shahazi-
mah, and Beth Shemesh; their border ended at
the Jordan: sixteen cities with their villages.
23 This *was* the inheritance of the tribe of the
children of Issachar according to their fami-
lies, the cities and their villages.

The Land of Asher

24 The fifth lot came out for the tribe of the
children of Asher according to their families.
25 And their territory included Helkath, Hali,
Beten, Achshaph,
26 Alammelech, Amad, and Mishal; it
reached to Mount Carmel westward, along *the
Brook* Shihor Libnath.
27 It turned toward the sunrise to Beth Da-
gon; and it reached to Zebulun and to the Val-
ley of Jiphthah El, then northward beyond
Beth Emek and Neiel, bypassing Cabul *which
was* on the left,
28 including Ebron,[a] Rehob, Hammon, and
Kanah, as far as Greater Sidon.
29 And the border turned to Ramah and to
the fortified city of Tyre; then the border turned
to Hosah, and ended at the sea by the region
of Achzib.
30 Also Ummah, Aphek, and Rehob *were in-
cluded:* twenty-two cities with their villages.
31 This *was* the inheritance of the tribe of the
children of Asher according to their families,
these cities with their villages.

The Land of Naphtali

32 The sixth lot came out to the children of
Naphtali, for the children of Naphtali accord-
ing to their families.
33 And their border began at Heleph, enclos-
ing the territory from the terebinth tree in Zaa-
nannim, Adami Nekeb, and Jabneel, as far as
Lakkum; it ended at the Jordan.
34 From Heleph the border extended westward
to Aznoth Tabor, and went out from there to-
ward Hukkok; it adjoined Zebulun on the south
side and Asher on the west side, and ended at
Judah by the Jordan toward the sunrise.
35 And the fortified cities *are* Ziddim, Zer,
Hammath, Rakkath, Chinnereth,
36 Adamah, Ramah, Hazor,
37 Kedesh, Edrei, En Hazor,
38 Iron, Migdal El, Horem, Beth Anath, and
Beth Shemesh: nineteen cities with their villages.
39 This *was* the inheritance of the tribe of the
children of Naphtali according to their fami-
lies, the cities and their villages.

The Land of Dan

40 The seventh lot came out for the tribe of
the children of Dan according to their families.
41 And the territory of their inheritance was
Zorah, Eshtaol, Ir Shemesh,
42 Shaalabbin, Aijalon, Jethlah,
43 Elon, Timnah, Ekron,
44 Eltekeh, Gibbethon, Baalath,
45 Jehud, Bene Berak, Gath Rimmon,
46 Me Jarkon, and Rakkon, with the region
near Joppa.
47 And the border of the children of Dan went
beyond these, because the children of Dan went
up to fight against Leshem and took it; and they
struck it with the edge of the sword, took pos-
session of it, and dwelt in it. They called Le-
shem, Dan, after the name of Dan their father.
48 This *is* the inheritance of the tribe of the
children of Dan according to their families,
these cities with their villages.

Joshua's Inheritance

49 When they had made an end of dividing
the land as an inheritance according to their
borders, the children of Israel gave an inheri-
tance among them to Joshua the son of Nun.
50 According to the word of the LORD they
gave him the city which he asked for, Timnath
Serah in the mountains of Ephraim; and he
built the city and dwelt in it.
51 These *were* the inheritances which Elea-
zar the priest, Joshua the son of Nun, and the
heads of the fathers of the tribes of the children
of Israel divided as an inheritance by lot in
Shiloh before the LORD, at the door of the tab-
ernacle of meeting. So they made an end of di-
viding the country.

The Cities of Refuge

20 The LORD also spoke to Joshua, saying,
2 "Speak to the children of Israel, say-
ing: 'Appoint for yourselves cities of refuge, of
which I spoke to you through Moses,
3 'that the slayer who kills a person acciden-
tally *or* unintentionally may flee there; and
they shall be your refuge from the avenger of
blood.
4 'And when he flees to one of those cities,
and stands at the entrance of the gate of the
city, and declares his case in the hearing of
the elders of that city, they shall take him into
the city as one of them, and give him a place,
that he may dwell among them.
5 'Then if the avenger of blood pursues him,
they shall not deliver the slayer into his hand,
because he struck his neighbor unintention-
ally, but did not hate him beforehand.
6 'And he shall dwell in that city until he
stands before the congregation for judgment,
and until the death of the one who is high priest
in those days. Then the slayer may return and
come to his own city and his own house, to the
city from which he fled.'"
7 So they appointed Kedesh in Galilee, in
the mountains of Naphtali, Shechem in the

19:28 [a]Following Masoretic Text, Targum, and Vulgate; a few Hebrew manuscripts read *Abdon* (compare
21:30 and 1 Chronicles 6:74).

mountains of Ephraim, and Kirjath Arba
(which *is* Hebron) in the mountains of Judah.
8 And on the other side of the Jordan, by Jeri-
cho eastward, they assigned Bezer in the wil-
derness on the plain, from the tribe of Reuben,
Ramoth in Gilead, from the tribe of Gad, and
Golan in Bashan, from the tribe of Manasseh.
9 These were the cities appointed for all the
children of Israel and for the stranger who
dwelt among them, that whoever killed a per-
son accidentally might flee there, and not die
by the hand of the avenger of blood until he
stood before the congregation.

Cities of the Levites

21 Then the heads of the fathers' *houses*
of the Levites came near to Eleazar the
priest, to Joshua the son of Nun, and to the heads
of the fathers' *houses* of the tribes of the chil-
dren of Israel.
2 And they spoke to them at Shiloh in the land
of Canaan, saying, "The LORD commanded
through Moses to give us cities to dwell in, with
their common-lands for our livestock."
3 So the children of Israel gave to the Levites
from their inheritance, at the commandment of
the LORD, these cities and their common-lands:
4 Now the lot came out for the families of
the Kohathites. And the children of Aaron the
priest, *who were* of the Levites, had thirteen
cities by lot from the tribe of Judah, from the
tribe of Simeon, and from the tribe of Benjamin.
5 The rest of the children of Kohath had ten
cities by lot from the families of the tribe of
Ephraim, from the tribe of Dan, and from the
half-tribe of Manasseh.
6 And the children of Gershon had thirteen
cities by lot from the families of the tribe of
Issachar, from the tribe of Asher, from the tribe
of Naphtali, and from the half-tribe of Manas-
seh in Bashan.
7 The children of Merari according to their
families had twelve cities from the tribe of Reu-
ben, from the tribe of Gad, and from the tribe
of Zebulun.
8 And the children of Israel gave these cities
with their common-lands by lot to the Levites,
as the LORD had commanded by the hand of
Moses.
9 So they gave from the tribe of the children
of Judah and from the tribe of the children of
Simeon these cities which are designated by
name,
10 which were for the children of Aaron, one
of the families of the Kohathites, *who were* of
the children of Levi; for the lot was theirs first.
11 And they gave them Kirjath Arba (*Arba was*
the father of Anak), which *is* Hebron, in the
mountains of Judah, with the common-land
surrounding it.
12 But the fields of the city and its villages they
gave to Caleb the son of Jephunneh as his pos-
session.
13 Thus to the children of Aaron the priest
they gave Hebron with its common-land (a city
of refuge for the slayer), Libnah with its common-
land,
14 Jattir with its common-land, Eshtemoa
with its common-land,
15 Holon with its common-land, Debir with
its common-land,
16 Ain with its common-land, Juttah with its
common-land, and Beth Shemesh with its
common-land: nine cities from those two
tribes;
17 and from the tribe of Benjamin, Gibeon with
its common-land, Geba with its common-land,
18 Anathoth with its common-land, and Al-
mon with its common-land: four cities.
19 All the cities of the children of Aaron, the
priests, *were* thirteen cities with their common-
lands.
20 And the families of the children of Kohath,
the Levites, the rest of the children of Kohath,
even they had the cities of their lot from the
tribe of Ephraim.
21 For they gave them Shechem with its
common-land in the mountains of Ephraim (a
city of refuge for the slayer), Gezer with its
common-land,
22 Kibzaim with its common-land, and Beth
Horon with its common-land: four cities;
23 and from the tribe of Dan, Eltekeh with its
common-land, Gibbethon with its common-
land,
24 Aijalon with its common-land, *and* Gath
Rimmon with its common-land: four cities;
25 and from the half-tribe of Manasseh, Ta-
nach with its common-land and Gath Rimmon
with its common-land: two cities.
26 All the ten cities with their common-lands
were for the rest of the families of the children
of Kohath.
27 Also to the children of Gershon, of the
families of the Levites, from the *other* half-
tribe of Manasseh, *they gave* Golan in Bashan
with its common-land (a city of refuge for the
slayer), and Be Eshterah with its common-
land: two cities;
28 and from the tribe of Issachar, Kishion with
its common-land, Daberath with its common-
land,
29 Jarmuth with its common-land, *and* En
Gannim with its common-land: four cities;
30 and from the tribe of Asher, Mishal with its
common-land, Abdon with its common-land,
31 Helkath with its common-land, and Rehob
with its common-land: four cities;
32 and from the tribe of Naphtali, Kedesh in
Galilee with its common-land (a city of ref-
uge for the slayer), Hammoth Dor with its
common-land, and Kartan with its common-
land: three cities.
33 All the cities of the Gershonites according
to their families *were* thirteen cities with their
common-lands.
34 And to the families of the children of Me-
rari, the rest of the Levites, from the tribe of
Zebulun, Jokneam with its common-land, Kar-
tah with its common-land,
35 Dimnah with its common-land, *and* Naha-
lal with its common-land: four cities;
36 and from the tribe of Reuben, Bezer with
its common-land, Jahaz with its common-land,
37 Kedemoth with its common-land, and
Mephaath with its common-land: four cities;[a]
38 and from the tribe of Gad, Ramoth in Gil-
ead with its common-land (a city of refuge for
the slayer), Mahanaim with its common-land,
39 Heshbon with its common-land, *and* Jazer
with its common-land: four cities in all.
40 So all the cities for the children of Merari
according to their families, the rest of the fami-
lies of the Levites, were *by* their lot twelve cities.

21:37 [a]Following Septuagint and Vulgate (compare 1 Chronicles 6:78, 79); Masoretic Text, Bomberg, and Targum omit verses 36 and 37.

41 All the cities of the Levites within the possession of the children of Israel *were* forty-eight cities with their common-lands.
42 Every one of these cities had its common-land surrounding it; thus *were* all these cities.

The Promise Fulfilled

43 So the LORD gave to Israel all the land of which He had sworn to give to their fathers, and they took possession of it and dwelt in it.
44 The LORD gave them rest all around, according to all that He had sworn to their fathers. And not a man of all their enemies stood against them; the LORD delivered all their enemies into their hand.
45 Not a word failed of any good thing which the LORD had spoken to the house of Israel. All came to pass.

Eastern Tribes Return to Their Lands

22 Then Joshua called the Reubenites, the Gadites, and half the tribe of Manasseh,
2 and said to them: "You have kept all that Moses the servant of the LORD commanded you, and have obeyed my voice in all that I commanded you.
3 "You have not left your brethren these many days, up to this day, but have kept the charge of the commandment of the LORD your God.
4 "And now the LORD your God has given rest to your brethren, as He promised them; now therefore, return and go to your tents *and* to the land of your possession, which Moses the servant of the LORD gave you on the other side of the Jordan.
5 "But take careful heed to do the commandment and the law which Moses the servant of the LORD commanded you, to love the LORD your God, to walk in all His ways, to keep His commandments, to hold fast to Him, and to serve Him with all your heart and with all your soul."
6 So Joshua blessed them and sent them away, and they went to their tents.
7 Now to half the tribe of Manasseh Moses had given a possession in Bashan, but to the *other* half of it Joshua gave *a possession* among their brethren on this side of the Jordan, westward. And indeed, when Joshua sent them away to their tents, he blessed them,
8 and spoke to them, saying, "Return with much riches to your tents, with very much livestock, with silver, with gold, with bronze, with iron, and with very much clothing. Divide the spoil of your enemies with your brethren."
9 So the children of Reuben, the children of Gad, and half the tribe of Manasseh returned, and departed from the children of Israel at Shiloh, which *is* in the land of Canaan, to go to the country of Gilead, to the land of their possession, which they had obtained according to the word of the LORD by the hand of Moses.

An Altar by the Jordan

10 And when they came to the region of the Jordan which *is* in the land of Canaan, the children of Reuben, the children of Gad, and half the tribe of Manasseh built an altar there by the Jordan—a great, impressive altar.
11 Now the children of Israel heard *someone* say, "Behold, the children of Reuben, the children of Gad, and half the tribe of Manasseh have built an altar on the frontier of the land of Canaan, in the region of the Jordan—on the children of Israel's side."
12 And when the children of Israel heard *of it*, the whole congregation of the children of Israel gathered together at Shiloh to go to war against them.
13 Then the children of Israel sent Phinehas the son of Eleazar the priest to the children of Reuben, to the children of Gad, and to half the tribe of Manasseh, into the land of Gilead,
14 and with him ten rulers, one ruler each from the chief house of every tribe of Israel; and each one *was* the head of the house of his father among the divisions[a] of Israel.
15 Then they came to the children of Reuben, to the children of Gad, and to half the tribe of Manasseh, to the land of Gilead, and they spoke with them, saying,
16 "Thus says the whole congregation of the LORD: 'What treachery *is* this that you have committed against the God of Israel, to turn away this day from following the LORD, in that you have built for yourselves an altar, that you might rebel this day against the LORD?
17 '*Is* the iniquity of Peor not enough for us, from which we are not cleansed till this day, although there was a plague in the congregation of the LORD,
18 'but that you must turn away this day from following the LORD? And it shall be, if you rebel today against the LORD, that tomorrow He will be angry with the whole congregation of Israel.
19 'Nevertheless, if the land of your possession *is* unclean, *then* cross over to the land of the possession of the LORD, where the LORD's tabernacle stands, and take possession among us; but do not rebel against the LORD, nor rebel against us, by building yourselves an altar besides the altar of the LORD our God.
20 'Did not Achan the son of Zerah commit a trespass in the accursed thing, and wrath fell on all the congregation of Israel? And that man did not perish alone in his iniquity.' "
21 Then the children of Reuben, the children of Gad, and half the tribe of Manasseh answered and said to the heads of the divisions[a] of Israel:
22 "The LORD God of gods, the LORD God of gods, He knows, and let Israel itself know—if *it is* in rebellion, or if in treachery against the LORD, do not save us this day.
23 "If we have built ourselves an altar to turn from following the LORD, or if to offer on it burnt offerings or grain offerings, or if to offer peace offerings on it, let the LORD Himself require *an account*.
24 "But in fact we have done it for fear, for a reason, saying, 'In time to come your descendants may speak to our descendants, saying, "What have you to do with the LORD God of Israel?
25 "For the LORD has made the Jordan a border between you and us, *you* children of Reuben and children of Gad. You have no part in the LORD." So your descendants would make our descendants cease fearing the LORD.'
26 "Therefore we said, 'Let us now prepare to build ourselves an altar, not for burnt offering nor for sacrifice,
27 'but *that* it *may be* a witness between you and us and our generations after us, that we may perform the service of the LORD before

22:14 [a]Literally *thousands* **22:21** [a]Literally *thousands*

Him with our burnt offerings, with our sacrifices, and with our peace offerings; that your descendants may not say to our descendants in time to come, "You have no part in the LORD." '
28 "Therefore we said that it will be, when they say *this* to us or to our generations in time to come, that we may say, 'Here is the replica of the altar of the LORD which our fathers made, though not for burnt offerings nor for sacrifices; but it *is* a witness between you and us.'
29 "Far be it from us that we should rebel against the LORD, and turn from following the LORD this day, to build an altar for burnt offerings, for grain offerings, or for sacrifices, besides the altar of the LORD our God which *is* before His tabernacle."
30 Now when Phinehas the priest and the rulers of the congregation, the heads of the divisions[a] of Israel who *were* with him, heard the words that the children of Reuben, the children of Gad, and the children of Manasseh spoke, it pleased them.
31 Then Phinehas the son of Eleazar the priest said to the children of Reuben, the children of Gad, and the children of Manasseh, "This day we perceive that the LORD *is* among us, because you have not committed this treachery against the LORD. Now you have delivered the children of Israel out of the hand of the LORD."
32 And Phinehas the son of Eleazar the priest, and the rulers, returned from the children of Reuben and the children of Gad, from the land of Gilead to the land of Canaan, to the children of Israel, and brought back word to them.
33 So the thing pleased the children of Israel, and the children of Israel blessed God; they spoke no more of going against them in battle, to destroy the land where the children of Reuben and Gad dwelt.
34 The children of Reuben and the children of Gad[a] called the altar, *Witness*, "For *it is* a witness between us that the LORD *is* God."

Joshua's Farewell Address

23 Now it came to pass, a long time after the LORD had given rest to Israel from all their enemies round about, that Joshua was old, advanced in age.
2 And Joshua called for all Israel, for their elders, for their heads, for their judges, and for their officers, and said to them: "I am old, advanced in age.
3 "You have seen all that the LORD your God has done to all these nations because of you, for the LORD your God *is* He who has fought for you.
4 "See, I have divided to you by lot these nations that remain, to be an inheritance for your tribes, from the Jordan, with all the nations that I have cut off, as far as the Great Sea westward.
5 "And the LORD your God will expel them from before you and drive them out of your sight. So you shall possess their land, as the LORD your God promised you.
6 "Therefore be very courageous to keep and to do all that is written in the Book of the Law of Moses, lest you turn aside from it to the right hand or to the left,
7 "*and* lest you go among these nations, these who remain among you. You shall not make mention of the name of their gods, nor cause *anyone* to swear *by them;* you shall not serve them nor bow down to them,
8 "but you shall hold fast to the LORD your God, as you have done to this day.
9 "For the LORD has driven out from before you great and strong nations; but *as for* you, no one has been able to stand against you to this day.
10 "One man of you shall chase a thousand, for the LORD your God *is* He who fights for you, as He promised you.
11 "Therefore take careful heed to yourselves, that you love the LORD your God.
12 "Or else, if indeed you do go back, and cling to the remnant of these nations—these that remain among you—and make marriages with them, and go in to them and they to you,
13 "know for certain that the LORD your God will no longer drive out these nations from before you. But they shall be snares and traps to you, and scourges on your sides and thorns in your eyes, until you perish from this good land which the LORD your God has given you.
14 "Behold, this day I *am* going the way of all the earth. And you know in all your hearts and in all your souls that not one thing has failed of all the good things which the LORD your God spoke concerning you. All have come to pass for you; not one word of them has failed.
15 "Therefore it shall come to pass, that as all the good things have come upon you which the LORD your God promised you, so the LORD will bring upon you all harmful things, until He has destroyed you from this good land which the LORD your God has given you.
16 "When you have transgressed the covenant of the LORD your God, which He commanded you, and have gone and served other gods, and bowed down to them, then the anger of the LORD will burn against you, and you shall perish quickly from the good land which He has given you."

The Covenant at Shechem

24 Then Joshua gathered all the tribes of Israel to Shechem and called for the elders of Israel, for their heads, for their judges, and for their officers; and they presented themselves before God.
2 And Joshua said to all the people, "Thus says the LORD God of Israel: 'Your fathers, *including* Terah, the father of Abraham and the father of Nahor, dwelt on the other side of the River[a] in old times; and they served other gods.
3 'Then I took your father Abraham from the other side of the River, led him throughout all the land of Canaan, and multiplied his descendants and gave him Isaac.
4 'To Isaac I gave Jacob and Esau. To Esau I gave the mountains of Seir to possess, but Jacob and his children went down to Egypt.
5 'Also I sent Moses and Aaron, and I plagued Egypt, according to what I did among them. Afterward I brought you out.
6 'Then I brought your fathers out of Egypt, and you came to the sea; and the Egyptians pursued your fathers with chariots and horsemen to the Red Sea.
7 'So they cried out to the LORD; and He put darkness between you and the Egyptians, brought the sea upon them, and covered them.

22:30 [a]Literally *thousands* **22:34** [a]Septuagint adds *and half the tribe of Manasseh.* **24:2** [a]Hebrew *Nahar,* the Euphrates, and so in verses 3, 14, and 15

And your eyes saw what I did in Egypt. Then you dwelt in the wilderness a long time.

8 'And I brought you into the land of the Amorites, who dwelt on the other side of the Jordan, and they fought with you. But I gave them into your hand, that you might possess their land, and I destroyed them from before you.

9 'Then Balak the son of Zippor, king of Moab, arose to make war against Israel, and sent and called Balaam the son of Beor to curse you.

10 'But I would not listen to Balaam; therefore he continued to bless you. So I delivered you out of his hand.

11 'Then you went over the Jordan and came to Jericho. And the men of Jericho fought against you—*also* the Amorites, the Perizzites, the Canaanites, the Hittites, the Girgashites, the Hivites, and the Jebusites. But I delivered them into your hand.

12 'I sent the hornet before you which drove them out from before you, *also* the two kings of the Amorites, *but* not with your sword or with your bow.

13 'I have given you a land for which you did not labor, and cities which you did not build, and you dwell in them; you eat of the vineyards and olive groves which you did not plant.'

14 "Now therefore, fear the LORD, serve Him in sincerity and in truth, and put away the gods which your fathers served on the other side of the River and in Egypt. Serve the LORD!

15 "And if it seems evil to you to serve the LORD, choose for yourselves this day whom you will serve, whether the gods which your fathers served that *were* on the other side of the River, or the gods of the Amorites, in whose land you dwell. But as for me and my house, we will serve the LORD."

16 So the people answered and said: "Far be it from us that we should forsake the LORD to serve other gods;

17 "for the LORD our God *is* He who brought us and our fathers up out of the land of Egypt, from the house of bondage, who did those great signs in our sight, and preserved us in all the way that we went and among all the people through whom we passed.

18 "And the LORD drove out from before us all the people, including the Amorites who dwelt in the land. We also will serve the LORD, for He *is* our God."

19 But Joshua said to the people, "You cannot serve the LORD, for He *is* a holy God. He *is* a jealous God; He will not forgive your transgressions nor your sins.

20 "If you forsake the LORD and serve foreign gods, then He will turn and do you harm and consume you, after He has done you good."

21 And the people said to Joshua, "No, but we will serve the LORD!"

22 So Joshua said to the people, "You *are* witnesses against yourselves that you have chosen the LORD for yourselves, to serve Him." And they said, "*We are* witnesses!"

23 "Now therefore," *he said*, "put away the foreign gods which *are* among you, and incline your heart to the LORD God of Israel."

24 And the people said to Joshua, "The LORD our God we will serve, and His voice we will obey!"

25 So Joshua made a covenant with the people that day, and made for them a statute and an ordinance in Shechem.

26 Then Joshua wrote these words in the Book of the Law of God. And he took a large stone, and set it up there under the oak that *was* by the sanctuary of the LORD.

27 And Joshua said to all the people, "Behold, this stone shall be a witness to us, for it has heard all the words of the LORD which He spoke to us. It shall therefore be a witness to you, lest you deny your God."

28 So Joshua let the people depart, each to his own inheritance.

Death of Joshua and Eleazar

29 Now it came to pass after these things that Joshua the son of Nun, the servant of the LORD, died, *being* one hundred and ten years old.

30 And they buried him within the border of his inheritance at Timnath Serah, which *is* in the mountains of Ephraim, on the north side of Mount Gaash.

31 Israel served the LORD all the days of Joshua, and all the days of the elders who outlived Joshua, who had known all the works of the LORD which He had done for Israel.

32 The bones of Joseph, which the children of Israel had brought up out of Egypt, they buried at Shechem, in the plot of ground which Jacob had bought from the sons of Hamor the father of Shechem for one hundred pieces of silver, and which had become an inheritance of the children of Joseph.

33 And Eleazar the son of Aaron died. They buried him in a hill *belonging to* Phinehas his son, which was given to him in the mountains of Ephraim.

The Book of JUDGES

The Continuing Conquest of Canaan

1 Now after the death of Joshua it came to pass that the children of Israel asked the LORD, saying, "Who shall be first to go up for us against the Canaanites to fight against them?"

2 And the LORD said, "Judah shall go up. Indeed I have delivered the land into his hand."

3 So Judah said to Simeon his brother, "Come up with me to my allotted territory, that we may fight against the Canaanites; and I will likewise go with you to your allotted territory." And Simeon went with him.

4 Then Judah went up, and the LORD delivered the Canaanites and the Perizzites into their hand; and they killed ten thousand men at Bezek.

5 And they found Adoni-Bezek in Bezek, and fought against him; and they defeated the Canaanites and the Perizzites.

6 Then Adoni-Bezek fled, and they pursued him and caught him and cut off his thumbs and big toes.

7 And Adoni-Bezek said, "Seventy kings with their thumbs and big toes cut off used to gather

scraps under my table; as I have done, so God
has repaid me." Then they brought him to Jeru-
salem, and there he died.
8 Now the children of Judah fought against
Jerusalem and took it; they struck it with the
edge of the sword and set the city on fire.
9 And afterward the children of Judah went
down to fight against the Canaanites who
dwelt in the mountains, in the South,[a] and in
the lowland.
10 Then Judah went against the Canaanites
who dwelt in Hebron. (Now the name of He-
bron *was* formerly Kirjath Arba.) And they
killed Sheshai, Ahiman, and Talmai.
11 From there they went against the inhab-
itants of Debir. (The name of Debir *was* for-
merly Kirjath Sepher.)
12 Then Caleb said, "Whoever attacks Kir-
jath Sepher and takes it, to him I will give my
daughter Achsah as wife."
13 And Othniel the son of Kenaz, Caleb's
younger brother, took it; so he gave him his
daughter Achsah as wife.
14 Now it happened, when she came *to him,*
that she urged him[a] to ask her father for a field.
And she dismounted from *her* donkey, and Ca-
leb said to her, "What do you wish?"
15 So she said to him, "Give me a blessing; since
you have given me land in the South, give me
also springs of water." And Caleb gave her the
upper springs and the lower springs.
16 Now the children of the Kenite, Moses' fa-
ther-in-law, went up from the City of Palms
with the children of Judah into the Wilderness
of Judah, which *lies* in the South *near* Arad;
and they went and dwelt among the people.
17 And Judah went with his brother Simeon,
and they attacked the Canaanites who inhab-
ited Zephath, and utterly destroyed it. So the
name of the city was called Hormah.
18 Also Judah took Gaza with its territory,
Ashkelon with its territory, and Ekron with its
territory.
19 So the LORD was with Judah. And they
drove out the mountaineers, but they could not
drive out the inhabitants of the lowland, be-
cause they had chariots of iron.
20 And they gave Hebron to Caleb, as Moses
had said. Then he expelled from there the three
sons of Anak.
21 But the children of Benjamin did not drive
out the Jebusites who inhabited Jerusalem; so
the Jebusites dwell with the children of Benja-
min in Jerusalem to this day.
22 And the house of Joseph also went up
against Bethel, and the LORD *was* with them.
23 So the house of Joseph sent men to spy out
Bethel. (The name of the city *was* formerly Luz.)
24 And when the spies saw a man coming out
of the city, they said to him, "Please show us
the entrance to the city, and we will show you
mercy."
25 So he showed them the entrance to the city,
and they struck the city with the edge of the
sword; but they let the man and all his family
go.
26 And the man went to the land of the Hit-
tites, built a city, and called its name Luz, which
is its name to this day.

Incomplete Conquest of the Land

27 However, Manasseh did not drive out *the
inhabitants of* Beth Shean and its villages, or
Taanach and its villages, or the inhabitants of
Dor and its villages, or the inhabitants of Ib-
leam and its villages, or the inhabitants of Me-
giddo and its villages; for the Canaanites were
determined to dwell in that land.
28 And it came to pass, when Israel was
strong, that they put the Canaanites under trib-
ute, but did not completely drive them out.
29 Nor did Ephraim drive out the Canaanites
who dwelt in Gezer; so the Canaanites dwelt
in Gezer among them.
30 Nor did Zebulun drive out the inhabitants
of Kitron or the inhabitants of Nahalol; so the
Canaanites dwelt among them, and were put
under tribute.
31 Nor did Asher drive out the inhabitants of
Acco or the inhabitants of Sidon, or of Ahlab,
Achzib, Helbah, Aphik, or Rehob.
32 So the Asherites dwelt among the Canaan-
ites, the inhabitants of the land; for they did
not drive them out.
33 Nor did Naphtali drive out the inhabitants
of Beth Shemesh or the inhabitants of Beth
Anath; but they dwelt among the Canaanites,
the inhabitants of the land. Nevertheless the
inhabitants of Beth Shemesh and Beth Anath
were put under tribute to them.
34 And the Amorites forced the children of
Dan into the mountains, for they would not
allow them to come down to the valley;
35 and the Amorites were determined to dwell
in Mount Heres, in Aijalon, and in Shaalbim;[a]
yet when the strength of the house of Joseph
became greater, they were put under tribute.
36 Now the boundary of the Amorites *was* from
the Ascent of Akrabbim, from Sela, and upward.

Israel's Disobedience

2 Then the Angel of the LORD came up from
Gilgal to Bochim, and said: "I led you up
from Egypt and brought you to the land of
which I swore to your fathers; and I said, 'I will
never break My covenant with you.
2 'And you shall make no covenant with the
inhabitants of this land; you shall tear down
their altars.' But you have not obeyed My voice.
Why have you done this?
3 "Therefore I also said, 'I will not drive
them out before you; but they shall be *thorns* in
your side,[a] and their gods shall be a snare to
you.' "
4 So it was, when the Angel of the LORD
spoke these words to all the children of Israel,
that the people lifted up their voices and wept.
5 Then they called the name of that place
Bochim;[a] and they sacrificed there to the LORD.
6 And when Joshua had dismissed the peo-
ple, the children of Israel went each to his own
inheritance to possess the land.

Death of Joshua

7 So the people served the LORD all the days
of Joshua, and all the days of the elders who
outlived Joshua, who had seen all the great
works of the LORD which He had done for
Israel.
8 Now Joshua the son of Nun, the servant of

1:9 [a]Hebrew *Negev,* and so throughout this book **1:14** [a]Septuagint and Vulgate read *he urged her.* **1:35** [a]Spelled *Shaalabbin* in Joshua 19:42 **2:3** [a]Septuagint, Targum, and Vulgate read *enemies to you.* **2:5** [a]Literally *Weeping*

the LORD, died *when he was* one hundred and
ten years old.
9 And they buried him within the border of
his inheritance at Timnath Heres, in the moun-
tains of Ephraim, on the north side of Mount
Gaash.
10 When all that generation had been gath-
ered to their fathers, another generation arose
after them who did not know the LORD nor the
work which He had done for Israel.

Israel's Unfaithfulness

11 Then the children of Israel did evil in the
sight of the LORD, and served the Baals;
12 and they forsook the LORD God of their
fathers, who had brought them out of the land
of Egypt; and they followed other gods from
among the gods of the people who *were* all
around them, and they bowed down to them;
and they provoked the LORD to anger.
13 They forsook the LORD and served Baal
and the Ashtoreths.[a]
14 And the anger of the LORD was hot against
Israel. So He delivered them into the hands of
plunderers who despoiled them; and He sold
them into the hands of their enemies all around,
so that they could no longer stand before their
enemies.
15 Wherever they went out, the hand of the
LORD was against them for calamity, as the
LORD had said, and as the LORD had sworn to
them. And they were greatly distressed.
16 Nevertheless, the LORD raised up judges
who delivered them out of the hand of those
who plundered them.
17 Yet they would not listen to their judges,
but they played the harlot with other gods, and
bowed down to them. They turned quickly
from the way in which their fathers walked, in
obeying the commandments of the LORD; they
did not do so.
18 And when the LORD raised up judges for
them, the LORD was with the judge and deliv-
ered them out of the hand of their enemies all
the days of the judge; for the LORD was moved
to pity by their groaning because of those who
oppressed them and harassed them.
19 And it came to pass, when the judge was
dead, that they reverted and behaved more
corruptly than their fathers, by following other
gods, to serve them and bow down to them.
They did not cease from their own doings nor
from their stubborn way.
20 Then the anger of the LORD was hot against
Israel; and He said, "Because this nation has
transgressed My covenant which I commanded
their fathers, and has not heeded My voice,
21 "I also will no longer drive out before them
any of the nations which Joshua left when he
died,
22 "so that through them I may test Israel,
whether they will keep the ways of the LORD,
to walk in them as their fathers kept *them*, or
not."
23 Therefore the LORD left those nations, with-
out driving them out immediately; nor did He
deliver them into the hand of Joshua.

The Nations Remaining in the Land

3 Now these *are* the nations which the LORD
left, that He might test Israel by them, *that
is*, all who had not known any of the wars in
Canaan
2 (*this was* only so that the generations of
the children of Israel might be taught to know
war, at least those who had not formerly known
it),
3 *namely*, five lords of the Philistines, all the
Canaanites, the Sidonians, and the Hivites
who dwelt in Mount Lebanon, from Mount
Baal Hermon to the entrance of Hamath.
4 And they were *left, that He might* test Is-
rael by them, to know whether they would
obey the commandments of the LORD, which
He had commanded their fathers by the hand
of Moses.
5 Thus the children of Israel dwelt among
the Canaanites, the Hittites, the Amorites, the
Perizzites, the Hivites, and the Jebusites.
6 And they took their daughters to be their
wives, and gave their daughters to their sons;
and they served their gods.

Othniel

7 So the children of Israel did evil in the
sight of the LORD. They forgot the LORD their
God, and served the Baals and Asherahs.[a]
8 Therefore the anger of the LORD was hot
against Israel, and He sold them into the hand
of Cushan-Rishathaim king of Mesopotamia;
and the children of Israel served Cushan-
Rishathaim eight years.
9 When the children of Israel cried out to the
LORD, the LORD raised up a deliverer for the
children of Israel, who delivered them: Othniel
the son of Kenaz, Caleb's younger brother.
10 The Spirit of the LORD came upon him,
and he judged Israel. He went out to war, and
the LORD delivered Cushan-Rishathaim king
of Mesopotamia into his hand; and his hand
prevailed over Cushan-Rishathaim.
11 So the land had rest for forty years. Then
Othniel the son of Kenaz died.

Ehud

12 And the children of Israel again did evil in
the sight of the LORD. So the LORD strength-
ened Eglon king of Moab against Israel, be-
cause they had done evil in the sight of the
LORD.
13 Then he gathered to himself the people of
Ammon and Amalek, went and defeated Is-
rael, and took possession of the City of Palms.
14 So the children of Israel served Eglon king
of Moab eighteen years.
15 But when the children of Israel cried out
to the LORD, the LORD raised up a deliverer
for them: Ehud the son of Gera, the Benjamite,
a left-handed man. By him the children of Is-
rael sent tribute to Eglon king of Moab.
16 Now Ehud made himself a dagger (it was
double-edged and a cubit in length) and fas-
tened it under his clothes on his right thigh.
17 So he brought the tribute to Eglon king of
Moab. (Now Eglon *was* a very fat man.)
18 And when he had finished presenting the
tribute, he sent away the people who had car-
ried the tribute.
19 But he himself turned back from the stone
images that *were* at Gilgal, and said, "I have a
secret message for you, O king." He said,
"Keep silence!" And all who attended him
went out from him.
20 So Ehud came to him (now he was sitting
upstairs in his cool private chamber). Then

2:13 [a]Canaanite goddesses 3:7 [a]Name or symbol for Canaanite goddesses

Ehud said, "I have a message from God for you." So he arose from *his* seat.
21 Then Ehud reached with his left hand, took the dagger from his right thigh, and thrust it into his belly.
22 Even the hilt went in after the blade, and the fat closed over the blade, for he did not draw the dagger out of his belly; and his entrails came out.
23 Then Ehud went out through the porch and shut the doors of the upper room behind him and locked them.
24 When he had gone out, *Eglon's*[a] servants came to look, and *to their* surprise, the doors of the upper room were locked. So they said, "He is probably attending to his needs in the cool chamber."
25 So they waited till they were embarrassed, and still he had not opened the doors of the upper room. Therefore they took the key and opened *them*. And there was their master, fallen dead on the floor.
26 But Ehud had escaped while they delayed, and passed beyond the stone images and escaped to Seirah.
27 And it happened, when he arrived, that he blew the trumpet in the mountains of Ephraim, and the children of Israel went down with him from the mountains; and he led them.
28 Then he said to them, "Follow *me*, for the LORD has delivered your enemies the Moabites into your hand." So they went down after him, seized the fords of the Jordan leading to Moab, and did not allow anyone to cross over.
29 And at that time they killed about ten thousand men of Moab, all stout men of valor; not a man escaped.
30 So Moab was subdued that day under the hand of Israel. And the land had rest for eighty years.

Shamgar

31 After him was Shamgar the son of Anath, who killed six hundred men of the Philistines with an ox goad; and he also delivered Israel.

Deborah

4 When Ehud was dead, the children of Israel again did evil in the sight of the LORD.
2 So the LORD sold them into the hand of Jabin king of Canaan, who reigned in Hazor. The commander of his army *was* Sisera, who dwelt in Harosheth Hagoyim.
3 And the children of Israel cried out to the LORD; for Jabin had nine hundred chariots of iron, and for twenty years he had harshly oppressed the children of Israel.
4 Now Deborah, a prophetess, the wife of Lapidoth, was judging Israel at that time.
5 And she would sit under the palm tree of Deborah between Ramah and Bethel in the mountains of Ephraim. And the children of Israel came up to her for judgment.
6 Then she sent and called for Barak the son of Abinoam from Kedesh in Naphtali, and said to him, "Has not the LORD God of Israel commanded, 'Go and deploy *troops* at Mount Tabor; take with you ten thousand men of the sons of Naphtali and of the sons of Zebulun;
7 'and against you I will deploy Sisera, the commander of Jabin's army, with his chariots and his multitude at the River Kishon; and I will deliver him into your hand'?"
8 And Barak said to her, "If you will go with me, then I will go; but if you will not go with me, I will not go!"
9 So she said, "I will surely go with you; nevertheless there will be no glory for you in the journey you are taking, for the LORD will sell Sisera into the hand of a woman." Then Deborah arose and went with Barak to Kedesh.
10 And Barak called Zebulun and Naphtali to Kedesh; he went up with ten thousand men under his command,[a] and Deborah went up with him.
11 Now Heber the Kenite, of the children of Hobab the father-in-law of Moses, had separated himself from the Kenites and pitched his tent near the terebinth tree at Zaanaim, which *is* beside Kedesh.
12 And they reported to Sisera that Barak the son of Abinoam had gone up to Mount Tabor.
13 So Sisera gathered together all his chariots, nine hundred chariots of iron, and all the people who *were* with him, from Harosheth Hagoyim to the River Kishon.
14 Then Deborah said to Barak, "Up! For this *is* the day in which the LORD has delivered Sisera into your hand. Has not the LORD gone out before you?" So Barak went down from Mount Tabor with ten thousand men following him.
15 And the LORD routed Sisera and all *his* chariots and all *his* army with the edge of the sword before Barak; and Sisera alighted from *his* chariot and fled away on foot.
16 But Barak pursued the chariots and the army as far as Harosheth Hagoyim, and all the army of Sisera fell by the edge of the sword; not a man was left.
17 However, Sisera had fled away on foot to the tent of Jael, the wife of Heber the Kenite; for *there was* peace between Jabin king of Hazor and the house of Heber the Kenite.
18 And Jael went out to meet Sisera, and said to him, "Turn aside, my lord, turn aside to me; do not fear." And when he had turned aside with her into the tent, she covered him with a blanket.
19 Then he said to her, "Please give me a little water to drink, for I am thirsty." So she opened a jug of milk, gave him a drink, and covered him.
20 And he said to her, "Stand at the door of the tent, and if any man comes and inquires of you, and says, 'Is there any man here?' you shall say, 'No.'"
21 Then Jael, Heber's wife, took a tent peg and took a hammer in her hand, and went softly to him and drove the peg into his temple, and it went down into the ground; for he was fast asleep and weary. So he died.
22 And then, as Barak pursued Sisera, Jael came out to meet him, and said to him, "Come, I will show you the man whom you seek." And when he went into her *tent*, there lay Sisera, dead with the peg in his temple.
23 So on that day God subdued Jabin king of Canaan in the presence of the children of Israel.
24 And the hand of the children of Israel grew stronger and stronger against Jabin king of Canaan, until they had destroyed Jabin king of Canaan.

3:24 [a]Literally *his* **4:10** [a]Literally *at his feet*

The Song of Deborah

5 Then Deborah and Barak the son of Abinoam sang on that day, saying:

2 "When leaders lead in Israel,
When the people willingly offer
themselves,
Bless the LORD!

3 "Hear, O kings! Give ear, O princes!
I, *even* I, will sing to the LORD;
I will sing praise to the LORD God of
Israel.

4 "LORD, when You went out from Seir,
When You marched from the field of
Edom,
The earth trembled and the heavens
poured,
The clouds also poured water;
5 The mountains gushed before the LORD,
This Sinai, before the LORD God of Israel.

6 "In the days of Shamgar, son of Anath,
In the days of Jael,
The highways were deserted,
And the travelers walked along the
byways.
7 Village life ceased, it ceased in Israel,
Until I, Deborah, arose,
Arose a mother in Israel.
8 They chose new gods;
Then *there was* war in the gates;
Not a shield or spear was seen among
forty thousand in Israel.
9 My heart *is* with the rulers of Israel
Who offered themselves willingly with
the people.
Bless the LORD!

10 "Speak, you who ride on white donkeys,
Who sit in judges' attire,
And who walk along the road.
11 Far from the noise of the archers, among
the watering places,
There they shall recount the righteous
acts of the LORD,
The righteous acts *for* His villagers in
Israel;
Then the people of the LORD shall go
down to the gates.

12 "Awake, awake, Deborah!
Awake, awake, sing a song!
Arise, Barak, and lead your captives
away,
O son of Abinoam!

13 "Then the survivors came down, the
people against the nobles;
The LORD came down for me against the
mighty.
14 From Ephraim *were* those whose roots
were in Amalek.
After you, Benjamin, with your peoples,
From Machir rulers came down,
And from Zebulun those who bear the
recruiter's staff.
15 And the princes of Issachar[a] *were* with
Deborah;
As Issachar, so *was* Barak
Sent into the valley under his command;[b]
Among the divisions of Reuben
There were great resolves of heart.
16 Why did you sit among the sheepfolds,
To hear the pipings for the flocks?
The divisions of Reuben have great
searchings of heart.
17 Gilead stayed beyond the Jordan,
And why did Dan remain on ships?[a]
Asher continued at the seashore,
And stayed by his inlets.
18 Zebulun *is* a people *who* jeopardized
their lives to the point of death,
Naphtali also, on the heights of the
battlefield.

19 "The kings came *and* fought,
Then the kings of Canaan fought
In Taanach, by the waters of Megiddo;
They took no spoils of silver.
20 They fought from the heavens;
The stars from their courses fought
against Sisera.
21 The torrent of Kishon swept them away,
That ancient torrent, the torrent of
Kishon.
O my soul, march on in strength!
22 Then the horses' hooves pounded,
The galloping, galloping of his steeds.
23 'Curse Meroz,' said the angel[a] of the
LORD,
'Curse its inhabitants bitterly,
Because they did not come to the help of
the LORD,
To the help of the LORD against the
mighty.'

24 "Most blessed among women is Jael,
The wife of Heber the Kenite;
Blessed is she among women in tents.
25 He asked for water, she gave milk;
She brought out cream in a lordly bowl.
26 She stretched her hand to the tent peg,
Her right hand to the workmen's
hammer;
She pounded Sisera, she pierced his
head,
She split and struck through his temple.
27 At her feet he sank, he fell, he lay still;
At her feet he sank, he fell;
Where he sank, there he fell dead.

28 "The mother of Sisera looked through the
window,
And cried out through the lattice,
'Why is his chariot *so* long in coming?
Why tarries the clatter of his chariots?'
29 Her wisest ladies answered her,
Yes, she answered herself,
30 'Are they not finding and dividing the
spoil:
To every man a girl *or* two;
For Sisera, plunder of dyed garments,
Plunder of garments embroidered and
dyed,
Two pieces of dyed embroidery for the
neck of the looter?'

31 "Thus let all Your enemies perish,
O LORD!
But *let* those who love Him *be* like the
sun
When it comes out in full strength."

So the land had rest for forty years.

Midianites Oppress Israel

6 Then the children of Israel did evil in the
sight of the LORD. So the LORD delivered
them into the hand of Midian for seven years,

5:15 [a]Following Septuagint, Syriac, Targum, and Vulgate; Masoretic Text reads *And my princes in Issachar.* [b]Literally *at his feet* **5:17** [a]Or *at ease* **5:23** [a]Or *Angel*

2 and the hand of Midian prevailed against
Israel. Because of the Midianites, the children
of Israel made for themselves the dens, the
caves, and the strongholds which *are* in the
mountains.
3 So it was, whenever Israel had sown, Midi-
anites would come up; also Amalekites and
the people of the East would come up against
them.
4 Then they would encamp against them
and destroy the produce of the earth as far
as Gaza, and leave no sustenance for Israel,
neither sheep nor ox nor donkey.
5 For they would come up with their live-
stock and their tents, coming in as numerous
as locusts; both they and their camels were
without number; and they would enter the land
to destroy it.
6 So Israel was greatly impoverished be-
cause of the Midianites, and the children of
Israel cried out to the LORD.
7 And it came to pass, when the children of
Israel cried out to the LORD because of the
Midianites,
8 that the LORD sent a prophet to the children
of Israel, who said to them, "Thus says the
LORD God of Israel: 'I brought you up from Egypt
and brought you out of the house of bondage;
9 'and I delivered you out of the hand of the
Egyptians and out of the hand of all who op-
pressed you, and drove them out before you
and gave you their land.
10 'Also I said to you, "I *am* the LORD your
God; do not fear the gods of the Amorites, in
whose land you dwell." But you have not
obeyed My voice.'"

Gideon

11 Now the Angel of the LORD came and sat
under the terebinth tree which *was* in Ophrah,
which *belonged* to Joash the Abiezrite, while
his son Gideon threshed wheat in the wine-
press, in order to hide *it* from the Midianites.
12 And the Angel of the LORD appeared to
him, and said to him, "The LORD *is* with you,
you mighty man of valor!"
13 Gideon said to Him, "O my lord,[a] if the
LORD is with us, why then has all this hap-
pened to us? And where *are* all His miracles
which our fathers told us about, saying, 'Did
not the LORD bring us up from Egypt?' But
now the LORD has forsaken us and delivered
us into the hands of the Midianites."
14 Then the LORD turned to him and said,
"Go in this might of yours, and you shall save
Israel from the hand of the Midianites. Have I
not sent you?"
15 So he said to Him, "O my Lord,[a] how can
I save Israel? Indeed my clan *is* the weakest in
Manasseh, and I *am* the least in my father's
house."
16 And the LORD said to him, "Surely I will
be with you, and you shall defeat the Midian-
ites as one man."
17 Then he said to Him, "If now I have found
favor in Your sight, then show me a sign that
it is You who talk with me.
18 "Do not depart from here, I pray, until I
come to You and bring out my offering and set
it before You." And He said, "I will wait until
you come back."
19 So Gideon went in and prepared a young
goat, and unleavened bread from an ephah of
flour. The meat he put in a basket, and he put
the broth in a pot; and he brought *them* out to
Him under the terebinth tree and presented
them.
20 The Angel of God said to him, "Take the
meat and the unleavened bread and lay *them*
on this rock, and pour out the broth." And he
did so.
21 Then the Angel of the LORD put out the
end of the staff that *was* in His hand, and
touched the meat and the unleavened bread;
and fire rose out of the rock and consumed the
meat and the unleavened bread. And the Angel
of the LORD departed out of his sight.
22 Now Gideon perceived that He *was* the
Angel of the LORD. So Gideon said, "Alas,
O Lord GOD! For I have seen the Angel of the
LORD face to face."
23 Then the LORD said to him, "Peace *be* with
you; do not fear, you shall not die."
24 So Gideon built an altar there to the LORD,
and called it The-LORD-*Is*-Peace.[a] To this day
it *is* still in Ophrah of the Abiezrites.
25 Now it came to pass the same night that
the LORD said to him, "Take your father's
young bull, the second bull of seven years old,
and tear down the altar of Baal that your father
has, and cut down the wooden image[a] that *is*
beside it;
26 "and build an altar to the LORD your God
on top of this rock in the proper arrangement,
and take the second bull and offer a burnt sac-
rifice with the wood of the image which you
shall cut down."
27 So Gideon took ten men from among his
servants and did as the LORD had said to him.
But because he feared his father's household
and the men of the city too much to do *it* by
day, he did *it* by night.

Gideon Destroys the Altar of Baal

28 And when the men of the city arose early
in the morning, there was the altar of Baal, torn
down; and the wooden image that *was* beside
it was cut down, and the second bull was being
offered on the altar *which had been* built.
29 So they said to one another, "Who has
done this thing?" And when they had inquired
and asked, they said, "Gideon the son of Joash
has done this thing."
30 Then the men of the city said to Joash,
"Bring out your son, that he may die, because
he has torn down the altar of Baal, and because
he has cut down the wooden image that *was*
beside it."
31 But Joash said to all who stood against
him, "Would you plead for Baal? Would you
save him? Let the one who would plead for him
be put to death by morning! If he *is* a god, let
him plead for himself, because his altar has
been torn down!"
32 Therefore on that day he called him Jerub-
baal,[a] saying, "Let Baal plead against him, be-
cause he has torn down his altar."
33 Then all the Midianites and Amalekites,
the people of the East, gathered together; and
they crossed over and encamped in the Valley
of Jezreel.
34 But the Spirit of the LORD came upon Gid-
eon; then he blew the trumpet, and the Abiez-
rites gathered behind him.

6:13 [a]Hebrew *adoni,* used of man **6:15** [a]Hebrew *Adonai,* used of God **6:24** [a]Hebrew *YHWH Shalom* **6:25** [a]Hebrew *Asherah,* a Canaanite goddess **6:32** [a]Literally *Let Baal Plead*

35 And he sent messengers throughout all
Manasseh, who also gathered behind him. He
also sent messengers to Asher, Zebulun, and
Naphtali; and they came up to meet them.

The Sign of the Fleece

36 So Gideon said to God, "If You will save
Israel by my hand as You have said—
37 "look, I shall put a fleece of wool on the
threshing floor; if there is dew on the fleece
only, and *it is* dry on all the ground, then I shall
know that You will save Israel by my hand, as
You have said."
38 And it was so. When he rose early the next
morning and squeezed the fleece together, he
wrung the dew out of the fleece, a bowlful of
water.
39 Then Gideon said to God, "Do not be angry
with me, but let me speak just once more:
Let me test, I pray, just once more with the
fleece; let it now be dry only on the fleece, but
on all the ground let there be dew."
40 And God did so that night. It was dry on
the fleece only, but there was dew on all the
ground.

Gideon's Valiant Three Hundred

7 Then Jerubbaal (that *is*, Gideon) and all the
people who *were* with him rose early and
encamped beside the well of Harod, so that the
camp of the Midianites was on the north side
of them by the hill of Moreh in the valley.
2 And the LORD said to Gideon, "The people
who *are* with you *are* too many for Me to give
the Midianites into their hands, lest Israel
claim glory for itself against Me, saying, 'My
own hand has saved me.'
3 "Now therefore, proclaim in the hearing
of the people, saying, 'Whoever *is* fearful and
afraid, let him turn and depart at once from
Mount Gilead.'" And twenty-two thousand of
the people returned, and ten thousand remained.
4 But the LORD said to Gideon, "The people
are still *too* many; bring them down to the
water, and I will test them for you there. Then
it will be, *that* of whom I say to you, 'This one
shall go with you,' the same shall go with you;
and of whomever I say to you, 'This one shall
not go with you,' the same shall not go."
5 So he brought the people down to the water.
And the LORD said to Gideon, "Everyone
who laps from the water with his tongue, as a
dog laps, you shall set apart by himself; likewise
everyone who gets down on his knees to
drink."
6 And the number of those who lapped, *putting*
their hand to their mouth, was three hundred
men; but all the rest of the people got
down on their knees to drink water.
7 Then the LORD said to Gideon, "By the
three hundred men who lapped I will save you,
and deliver the Midianites into your hand. Let
all the *other* people go, every man to his place."
8 So the people took provisions and their
trumpets in their hands. And he sent away all
the rest of Israel, every man to his tent, and
retained those three hundred men. Now the
camp of Midian was below him in the valley.
9 It happened on the same night that the
LORD said to him, "Arise, go down against the
camp, for I have delivered it into your hand.
10 "But if you are afraid to go down, go down
to the camp with Purah your servant,
11 "and you shall hear what they say; and
afterward your hands shall be strengthened to
go down against the camp." Then he went
down with Purah his servant to the outpost of
the armed men who *were* in the camp.
12 Now the Midianites and Amalekites, all
the people of the East, were lying in the valley
as numerous as locusts; and their camels *were*
without number, as the sand by the seashore
in multitude.
13 And when Gideon had come, there was a
man telling a dream to his companion. He said,
"I have had a dream: *To my* surprise, a loaf of
barley bread tumbled into the camp of Midian;
it came to a tent and struck it so that it fell and
overturned, and the tent collapsed."
14 Then his companion answered and said,
"This *is* nothing else but the sword of Gideon
the son of Joash, a man of Israel! Into his hand
God has delivered Midian and the whole
camp."
15 And so it was, when Gideon heard the telling
of the dream and its interpretation, that he
worshiped. He returned to the camp of Israel,
and said, "Arise, for the LORD has delivered
the camp of Midian into your hand."
16 Then he divided the three hundred men
into three companies, and he put a trumpet
into every man's hand, with empty pitchers,
and torches inside the pitchers.
17 And he said to them, "Look at me and do
likewise; watch, and when I come to the edge
of the camp you shall do as I do:
18 "When I blow the trumpet, I and all who
are with me, then you also blow the trumpets
on every side of the whole camp, and say, '*The
sword of* the LORD and of Gideon!'"
19 So Gideon and the hundred men who *were*
with him came to the outpost of the camp at
the beginning of the middle watch, just as they
had posted the watch; and they blew the trumpets
and broke the pitchers that *were* in their
hands.
20 Then the three companies blew the trumpets
and broke the pitchers—they held the
torches in their left hands and the trumpets in
their right hands for blowing—and they cried,
"The sword of the LORD and of Gideon!"
21 And every man stood in his place all
around the camp; and the whole army ran and
cried out and fled.
22 When the three hundred blew the trumpets,
the LORD set every man's sword against
his companion throughout the whole camp;
and the army fled to Beth Acacia,[a] toward Zererah,
as far as the border of Abel Meholah, by
Tabbath.
23 And the men of Israel gathered together
from Naphtali, Asher, and all Manasseh, and
pursued the Midianites.
24 Then Gideon sent messengers throughout
all the mountains of Ephraim, saying, "Come
down against the Midianites, and seize from
them the watering places as far as Beth Barah
and the Jordan." Then all the men of Ephraim
gathered together and seized the watering
places as far as Beth Barah and the Jordan.
25 And they captured two princes of the Midianites,
Oreb and Zeeb. They killed Oreb at the

7:22 [a]Hebrew *Beth Shittah*

rock of Oreb, and Zeeb they killed at the wine-
press of Zeeb. They pursued Midian and
brought the heads of Oreb and Zeeb to Gideon
on the other side of the Jordan.

Gideon Subdues the Midianites

8 Now the men of Ephraim said to him, "Why
have you done this to us by not calling us
when you went to fight with the Midianites?"
And they reprimanded him sharply.
2 So he said to them, "What have I done now
in comparison with you? *Is* not the gleaning *of
the grapes* of Ephraim better than the vintage
of Abiezer?
3 "God has delivered into your hands the
princes of Midian, Oreb and Zeeb. And what
was I able to do in comparison with you?"
Then their anger toward him subsided when
he said that.
4 When Gideon came to the Jordan, he and
the three hundred men who *were* with him
crossed over, exhausted but still in pursuit.
5 Then he said to the men of Succoth,
"Please give loaves of bread to the people who
follow me, for they are exhausted, and I am
pursuing Zebah and Zalmunna, kings of
Midian."
6 And the leaders of Succoth said, "*Are* the
hands of Zebah and Zalmunna now in your
hand, that we should give bread to your
army?"
7 So Gideon said, "For this cause, when the
LORD has delivered Zebah and Zalmunna into
my hand, then I will tear your flesh with the
thorns of the wilderness and with briers!"
8 Then he went up from there to Penuel and
spoke to them in the same way. And the men
of Penuel answered him as the men of Succoth
had answered.
9 So he also spoke to the men of Penuel,
saying, "When I come back in peace, I will tear
down this tower!"
10 Now Zebah and Zalmunna *were* at Karkor,
and their armies with them, about fifteen thou-
sand, all who were left of all the army of the
people of the East; for one hundred and twenty
thousand men who drew the sword had fallen.
11 Then Gideon went up by the road of those
who dwell in tents on the east of Nobah and
Jogbehah; and he attacked the army while the
camp felt secure.
12 When Zebah and Zalmunna fled, he pur-
sued them; and he took the two kings of Mid-
ian, Zebah and Zalmunna, and routed the
whole army.
13 Then Gideon the son of Joash returned
from battle, from the Ascent of Heres.
14 And he caught a young man of the men of
Succoth and interrogated him; and he wrote
down for him the leaders of Succoth and its
elders, seventy-seven men.
15 Then he came to the men of Succoth and
said, "Here are Zebah and Zalmunna, about
whom you ridiculed me, saying, '*Are* the hands
of Zebah and Zalmunna now in your hand,
that we should give bread to your weary
men?'"
16 And he took the elders of the city, and
thorns of the wilderness and briers, and with
them he taught the men of Succoth.
17 Then he tore down the tower of Penuel and
killed the men of the city.
18 And he said to Zebah and Zalmunna,
"What kind of men *were they* whom you killed
at Tabor?" So they answered, "As you *are*, so
were they; each one resembled the son of a
king."
19 Then he said, "They *were* my brothers, the
sons of my mother. *As* the LORD lives, if you
had let them live, I would not kill you."
20 And he said to Jether his firstborn, "Rise,
kill them!" But the youth would not draw his
sword; for he was afraid, because he *was* still
a youth.
21 So Zebah and Zalmunna said, "Rise your-
self, and kill us; for as a man *is*, *so is* his
strength." So Gideon arose and killed Zebah
and Zalmunna, and took the crescent orna-
ments that *were* on their camels' necks.

Gideon's Ephod

22 Then the men of Israel said to Gideon,
"Rule over us, both you and your son, and your
grandson also; for you have delivered us from
the hand of Midian."
23 But Gideon said to them, "I will not rule
over you, nor shall my son rule over you; the
LORD shall rule over you."
24 Then Gideon said to them, "I would like to
make a request of you, that each of you would
give me the earrings from his plunder." For
they had golden earrings, because they *were*
Ishmaelites.
25 So they answered, "We will gladly give
them." And they spread out a garment, and
each man threw into it the earrings from his
plunder.
26 Now the weight of the gold earrings that
he requested was one thousand seven hundred
shekels of gold, besides the crescent orna-
ments, pendants, and purple robes which *were*
on the kings of Midian, and besides the chains
that *were* around their camels' necks.
27 Then Gideon made it into an ephod and
set it up in his city, Ophrah. And all Israel
played the harlot with it there. It became a
snare to Gideon and to his house.
28 Thus Midian was subdued before the chil-
dren of Israel, so that they lifted their heads no
more. And the country was quiet for forty
years in the days of Gideon.

Death of Gideon

29 Then Jerubbaal the son of Joash went and
dwelt in his own house.
30 Gideon had seventy sons who were his
own offspring, for he had many wives.
31 And his concubine who *was* in Shechem
also bore him a son, whose name he called
Abimelech.
32 Now Gideon the son of Joash died at a
good old age, and was buried in the tomb of
Joash his father, in Ophrah of the Abiezrites.
33 So it was, as soon as Gideon was dead,
that the children of Israel again played the har-
lot with the Baals, and made Baal-Berith their
god.
34 Thus the children of Israel did not remem-
ber the LORD their God, who had delivered
them from the hands of all their enemies on
every side;
35 nor did they show kindness to the house
of Jerubbaal (Gideon) in accordance with the
good he had done for Israel.

Abimelech's Conspiracy

9 Then Abimelech the son of Jerubbaal went
to Shechem, to his mother's brothers, and
spoke with them and with all the family of the
house of his mother's father, saying,

2 "Please speak in the hearing of all the men
of Shechem: 'Which is better for you, that all
seventy of the sons of Jerubbaal reign over
you, or that one reign over you?' Remember
that I *am* your own flesh and bone."
3 And his mother's brothers spoke all these
words concerning him in the hearing of all the
men of Shechem; and their heart was inclined
to follow Abimelech, for they said, "He is our
brother."
4 So they gave him seventy *shekels* of silver
from the temple of Baal-Berith, with which
Abimelech hired worthless and reckless men;
and they followed him.
5 Then he went to his father's house at Oph-
rah and killed his brothers, the seventy sons
of Jerubbaal, on one stone. But Jotham the
youngest son of Jerubbaal was left, because he
hid himself.
6 And all the men of Shechem gathered to-
gether, all of Beth Millo, and they went and
made Abimelech king beside the terebinth tree
at the pillar that *was* in Shechem.

The Parable of the Trees

7 Now when they told Jotham, he went and
stood on top of Mount Gerizim, and lifted his
voice and cried out. And he said to them:

"Listen to me, you men of Shechem,
That God may listen to you!

8 "The trees once went forth to anoint a
king over them.
And they said to the olive tree,
'Reign over us!'
9 But the olive tree said to them,
'Should I cease giving my oil,
With which they honor God and men,
And go to sway over trees?'

10 "Then the trees said to the fig tree,
'You come *and* reign over us!'
11 But the fig tree said to them,
'Should I cease my sweetness and my
good fruit,
And go to sway over trees?'

12 "Then the trees said to the vine,
'You come *and* reign over us!'
13 But the vine said to them,
'Should I cease my new wine,
Which cheers *both* God and men,
And go to sway over trees?'

14 "Then all the trees said to the bramble,
'You come *and* reign over us!'
15 And the bramble said to the trees,
'If in truth you anoint me as king over
you,
Then come *and* take shelter in my shade;
But if not, let fire come out of the
bramble
And devour the cedars of Lebanon!'

16 "Now therefore, if you have acted in truth
and sincerity in making Abimelech king, and
if you have dealt well with Jerubbaal and his
house, and have done to him as he deserves—
17 "for my father fought for you, risked his
life, and delivered you out of the hand of
Midian;
18 "but you have risen up against my father's
house this day, and killed his seventy sons on
one stone, and made Abimelech, the son of his
female servant, king over the men of Shechem,
because he is your brother—
19 "if then you have acted in truth and sincer-
ity with Jerubbaal and with his house this day,
then rejoice in Abimelech, and let him also
rejoice in you.
20 "But if not, let fire come from Abimelech
and devour the men of Shechem and Beth
Millo; and let fire come from the men of She-
chem and from Beth Millo and devour Abime-
lech!"
21 And Jotham ran away and fled; and he
went to Beer and dwelt there, for fear of Abim-
elech his brother.

Downfall of Abimelech

22 After Abimelech had reigned over Israel
three years,
23 God sent a spirit of ill will between Abime-
lech and the men of Shechem; and the men of
Shechem dealt treacherously with Abimelech,
24 that the crime *done* to the seventy sons of
Jerubbaal might be settled and their blood be
laid on Abimelech their brother, who killed
them, and on the men of Shechem, who aided
him in the killing of his brothers.
25 And the men of Shechem set men in am-
bush against him on the tops of the mountains,
and they robbed all who passed by them along
that way; and it was told Abimelech.
26 Now Gaal the son of Ebed came with his
brothers and went over to Shechem; and the
men of Shechem put their confidence in him.
27 So they went out into the fields, and gath-
ered *grapes* from their vineyards and trod
them, and made merry. And they went into the
house of their god, and ate and drank, and
cursed Abimelech.
28 Then Gaal the son of Ebed said, "Who *is*
Abimelech, and who *is* Shechem, that we
should serve him? *Is he* not the son of Jerub-
baal, and *is not* Zebul his officer? Serve the
men of Hamor the father of Shechem; but why
should we serve him?
29 "If only this people were under my author-
ity![a] Then I would remove Abimelech." So he[b]
said to Abimelech, "Increase your army and
come out!"
30 When Zebul, the ruler of the city, heard
the words of Gaal the son of Ebed, his anger
was aroused.
31 And he sent messengers to Abimelech se-
cretly, saying, "Take note! Gaal the son of Ebed
and his brothers have come to Shechem; and
here they are, fortifying the city against you.
32 "Now therefore, get up by night, you and
the people who *are* with you, and lie in wait in
the field.
33 "And it shall be, as soon as the sun is up
in the morning, *that* you shall rise early and
rush upon the city; and *when* he and the people
who are with him come out against you, you
may then do to them as you find opportunity."
34 So Abimelech and all the people who *were*
with him rose by night, and lay in wait against
Shechem in four companies.
35 When Gaal the son of Ebed went out and
stood in the entrance to the city gate, Abime-
lech and the people who *were* with him rose
from lying in wait.
36 And when Gaal saw the people, he said to
Zebul, "Look, people are coming down from
the tops of the mountains!" But Zebul said to

9:29 [a]Literally *hand* [b]Following Masoretic Text and Targum; Dead Sea Scrolls read *they;* Septuagint reads *I.*

him, "You see the shadows of the mountains
as *if they were* men."
37 So Gaal spoke again and said, "See, people are coming down from the center of the land, and another company is coming from the Diviners'[a] Terebinth Tree."
38 Then Zebul said to him, "Where indeed *is* your mouth now, with which you said, 'Who is Abimelech, that we should serve him?' *Are* not these the people whom you despised? Go out, if you will, and fight with them now."
39 So Gaal went out, leading the men of Shechem, and fought with Abimelech.
40 And Abimelech chased him, and he fled from him; and many fell wounded, to the *very* entrance of the gate.
41 Then Abimelech dwelt at Arumah, and Zebul drove out Gaal and his brothers, so that they would not dwell in Shechem.
42 And it came about on the next day that the people went out into the field, and they told Abimelech.
43 So he took his people, divided them into three companies, and lay in wait in the field. And he looked, and there were the people, coming out of the city; and he rose against them and attacked them.
44 Then Abimelech and the company that *was* with him rushed forward and stood at the entrance of the gate of the city; and the *other* two companies rushed upon all who *were* in the fields and killed them.
45 So Abimelech fought against the city all that day; he took the city and killed the people who *were* in it; and he demolished the city and sowed it with salt.
46 Now when all the men of the tower of Shechem had heard *that,* they entered the stronghold of the temple of the god Berith.
47 And it was told Abimelech that all the men of the tower of Shechem were gathered together.
48 Then Abimelech went up to Mount Zalmon, he and all the people who *were* with him. And Abimelech took an ax in his hand and cut down a bough from the trees, and took it and laid *it* on his shoulder; then he said to the people who were with him, "What you have seen me do, make haste *and* do as I *have done.*"
49 So each of the people likewise cut down his own bough and followed Abimelech, put *them* against the stronghold, and set the stronghold on fire above them, so that all the people of the tower of Shechem died, about a thousand men and women.
50 Then Abimelech went to Thebez, and he encamped against Thebez and took it.
51 But there was a strong tower in the city, and all the men and women—all the people of the city—fled there and shut themselves in; then they went up to the top of the tower.
52 So Abimelech came as far as the tower and fought against it; and he drew near the door of the tower to burn it with fire.
53 But a certain woman dropped an upper millstone on Abimelech's head and crushed his skull.
54 Then he called quickly to the young man, his armorbearer, and said to him, "Draw your sword and kill me, lest men say of me, 'A woman killed him.'" So his young man thrust him through, and he died.
55 And when the men of Israel saw that Abimelech was dead, they departed, every man to his place.
56 Thus God repaid the wickedness of Abimelech, which he had done to his father by killing his seventy brothers.
57 And all the evil of the men of Shechem God returned on their own heads, and on them came the curse of Jotham the son of Jerubbaal.

Tola

10 After Abimelech there arose to save Israel Tola the son of Puah, the son of Dodo, a man of Issachar; and he dwelt in Shamir in the mountains of Ephraim.
2 He judged Israel twenty-three years; and he died and was buried in Shamir.

Jair

3 After him arose Jair, a Gileadite; and he judged Israel twenty-two years.
4 Now he had thirty sons who rode on thirty donkeys; they also had thirty towns, which are called "Havoth Jair"[a] to this day, which *are* in the land of Gilead.
5 And Jair died and was buried in Camon.

Israel Oppressed Again

6 Then the children of Israel again did evil in the sight of the LORD, and served the Baals and the Ashtoreths, the gods of Syria, the gods of Sidon, the gods of Moab, the gods of the people of Ammon, and the gods of the Philistines; and they forsook the LORD and did not serve Him.
7 So the anger of the LORD was hot against Israel; and He sold them into the hands of the Philistines and into the hands of the people of Ammon.
8 From that year they harassed and oppressed the children of Israel for eighteen years—all the children of Israel who *were* on the other side of the Jordan in the land of the Amorites, in Gilead.
9 Moreover the people of Ammon crossed over the Jordan to fight against Judah also, against Benjamin, and against the house of Ephraim, so that Israel was severely distressed.
10 And the children of Israel cried out to the LORD, saying, "We have sinned against You, because we have both forsaken our God and served the Baals!"
11 So the LORD said to the children of Israel, "*Did I* not *deliver you* from the Egyptians and from the Amorites and from the people of Ammon and from the Philistines?
12 "Also the Sidonians and Amalekites and Maonites[a] oppressed you; and you cried out to Me, and I delivered you from their hand.
13 "Yet you have forsaken Me and served other gods. Therefore I will deliver you no more.
14 "Go and cry out to the gods which you have chosen; let them deliver you in your time of distress."
15 And the children of Israel said to the LORD, "We have sinned! Do to us whatever seems best to You; only deliver us this day, we pray."
16 So they put away the foreign gods from among them and served the LORD. And His soul could no longer endure the misery of Israel.

9:37 [a]Hebrew *Meonenim* **10:4** [a]Literally *Towns of Jair* (compare Numbers 32:41 and Deuteronomy 3:14)
10:12 [a]Some Septuagint manuscripts read *Midianites.*

17 Then the people of Ammon gathered to-
gether and encamped in Gilead. And the
children of Israel assembled together and en-
camped in Mizpah.
18 And the people, the leaders of Gilead, said
to one another, "Who *is* the man who will be-
gin the fight against the people of Ammon?
He shall be head over all the inhabitants of
Gilead."

Jephthah

11 Now Jephthah the Gileadite was a mighty
man of valor, but he *was* the son of a
harlot; and Gilead begot Jephthah.
2 Gilead's wife bore sons; and when his
wife's sons grew up, they drove Jephthah out,
and said to him, "You shall have no inheritance
in our father's house, for you *are* the son of
another woman."
3 Then Jephthah fled from his brothers and
dwelt in the land of Tob; and worthless men
banded together with Jephthah and went out
raiding with him.
4 It came to pass after a time that the people
of Ammon made war against Israel.
5 And so it was, when the people of Ammon
made war against Israel, that the elders of Gil-
ead went to get Jephthah from the land of Tob.
6 Then they said to Jephthah, "Come and be
our commander, that we may fight against the
people of Ammon."
7 So Jephthah said to the elders of Gilead,
"Did you not hate me, and expel me from my
father's house? Why have you come to me now
when you are in distress?"
8 And the elders of Gilead said to Jephthah,
"That is why we have turned again to you now,
that you may go with us and fight against the
people of Ammon, and be our head over all the
inhabitants of Gilead."
9 So Jephthah said to the elders of Gilead,
"If you take me back home to fight against the
people of Ammon, and the LORD delivers them
to me, shall I be your head?"
10 And the elders of Gilead said to Jephthah,
"The LORD will be a witness between us, if we
do not do according to your words."
11 Then Jephthah went with the elders of Gil-
ead, and the people made him head and com-
mander over them; and Jephthah spoke all his
words before the LORD in Mizpah.
12 Now Jephthah sent messengers to the king
of the people of Ammon, saying, "What do you
have against me, that you have come to fight
against me in my land?"
13 And the king of the people of Ammon an-
swered the messengers of Jephthah, "Because
Israel took away my land when they came up
out of Egypt, from the Arnon as far as the
Jabbok, and to the Jordan. Now therefore, re-
store those *lands* peaceably."
14 So Jephthah again sent messengers to the
king of the people of Ammon,
15 and said to him, "Thus says Jephthah: 'Is-
rael did not take away the land of Moab, nor
the land of the people of Ammon;
16 'for when Israel came up from Egypt, they
walked through the wilderness as far as the Red
Sea and came to Kadesh.
17 'Then Israel sent messengers to the king
of Edom, saying, "Please let me pass through
your land." But the king of Edom would not
heed. And in like manner they sent to the king
of Moab, but he would not *consent*. So Israel
remained in Kadesh.
18 'And they went along through the wilder-
ness and bypassed the land of Edom and the
land of Moab, came to the east side of the land
of Moab, and encamped on the other side of
the Arnon. But they did not enter the border of
Moab, for the Arnon *was* the border of Moab.
19 'Then Israel sent messengers to Sihon king
of the Amorites, king of Heshbon; and Israel
said to him, "Please let us pass through your
land into our place."
20 'But Sihon did not trust Israel to pass
through his territory. So Sihon gathered all his
people together, encamped in Jahaz, and
fought against Israel.
21 'And the LORD God of Israel delivered Si-
hon and all his people into the hand of Israel,
and they defeated them. Thus Israel gained
possession of all the land of the Amorites, who
inhabited that country.
22 'They took possession of all the territory
of the Amorites, from the Arnon to the Jabbok
and from the wilderness to the Jordan.
23 'And now the LORD God of Israel has dis-
possessed the Amorites from before His people
Israel; should you then possess it?
24 'Will you not possess whatever Chemosh
your god gives you to possess? So whatever
the LORD our God takes possession of before
us, we will possess.
25 'And now, *are* you any better than Balak
the son of Zippor, king of Moab? Did he ever
strive against Israel? Did he ever fight against
them?
26 'While Israel dwelt in Heshbon and its vil-
lages, in Aroer and its villages, and in all the
cities along the banks of the Arnon, for three
hundred years, why did you not recover *them*
within that time?
27 'Therefore I have not sinned against you,
but you wronged me by fighting against me.
May the LORD, the Judge, render judgment
this day between the children of Israel and the
people of Ammon.'"
28 However, the king of the people of Ammon
did not heed the words which Jephthah sent
him.

Jephthah's Vow and Victory

29 Then the Spirit of the LORD came upon
Jephthah, and he passed through Gilead and
Manasseh, and passed through Mizpah of Gil-
ead; and from Mizpah of Gilead he advanced
toward the people of Ammon.
30 And Jephthah made a vow to the LORD,
and said, "If You will indeed deliver the people
of Ammon into my hands,
31 "then it will be that whatever comes out of
the doors of my house to meet me, when I re-
turn in peace from the people of Ammon, shall
surely be the LORD's, and I will offer it up as a
burnt offering."
32 So Jephthah advanced toward the people
of Ammon to fight against them, and the LORD
delivered them into his hands.
33 And he defeated them from Aroer as far
as Minnith—twenty cities—and to Abel Kera-
mim,[a] with a very great slaughter. Thus the
people of Ammon were subdued before the
children of Israel.

11:33 [a]Literally *Plain of Vineyards*

Jephthah's Daughter

34 When Jephthah came to his house at Miz-
pah, there was his daughter, coming out to
meet him with timbrels and dancing; and she
was his only child. Besides her he had neither
son nor daughter.
35 And it came to pass, when he saw her, that
he tore his clothes, and said, "Alas, my daugh-
ter! You have brought me very low! You are
among those who trouble me! For I have given
my word to the LORD, and I cannot go back on
it."
36 So she said to him, "My father, *if* you have
given your word to the LORD, do to me accord-
ing to what has gone out of your mouth, be-
cause the LORD has avenged you of your
enemies, the people of Ammon."
37 Then she said to her father, "Let this thing
be done for me: let me alone for two months,
that I may go and wander on the mountains
and bewail my virginity, my friends and I."
38 So he said, "Go." And he sent her away *for*
two months; and she went with her friends,
and bewailed her virginity on the mountains.
39 And it was so at the end of two months
that she returned to her father, and he carried
out his vow with her which he had vowed. She
knew no man. And it became a custom in Israel
40 *that* the daughters of Israel went four days
each year to lament the daughter of Jephthah
the Gileadite.

Jephthah's Conflict with Ephraim

12 Then the men of Ephraim gathered to-
gether, crossed over toward Zaphon,
and said to Jephthah, "Why did you cross over
to fight against the people of Ammon, and did
not call us to go with you? We will burn your
house down on you with fire!"
2 And Jephthah said to them, "My people
and I were in a great struggle with the people
of Ammon; and when I called you, you did not
deliver me out of their hands.
3 "So when I saw that you would not deliver
me, I took my life in my hands and crossed over
against the people of Ammon; and the LORD
delivered them into my hand. Why then have
you come up to me this day to fight against me?"
4 Now Jephthah gathered together all the
men of Gilead and fought against Ephraim.
And the men of Gilead defeated Ephraim, be-
cause they said, "You Gileadites *are* fugitives
of Ephraim among the Ephraimites *and* among
the Manassites."
5 The Gileadites seized the fords of the Jor-
dan before the Ephraimites *arrived.* And when
any Ephraimite who escaped said, "Let me
cross over," the men of Gilead would say to him,
"*Are* you an Ephraimite?" If he said, "No,"
6 then they would say to him, "Then say,
'Shibboleth'!" And he would say, "Sibboleth,"
for he could not pronounce *it* right. Then they
would take him and kill him at the fords of
the Jordan. There fell at that time forty-two
thousand Ephraimites.
7 And Jephthah judged Israel six years.
Then Jephthah the Gileadite died and was bur-
ied among the cities of Gilead.

Ibzan, Elon, and Abdon

8 After him, Ibzan of Bethlehem judged Is-
rael.
9 He had thirty sons. And he gave away thirty
daughters in marriage, and brought in thirty
daughters from elsewhere for his sons. He
judged Israel seven years.
10 Then Ibzan died and was buried at Beth-
lehem.
11 After him, Elon the Zebulunite judged Is-
rael. He judged Israel ten years.
12 And Elon the Zebulunite died and was bur-
ied at Aijalon in the country of Zebulun.
13 After him, Abdon the son of Hillel the Pira-
thonite judged Israel.
14 He had forty sons and thirty grandsons,
who rode on seventy young donkeys. He
judged Israel eight years.
15 Then Abdon the son of Hillel the Pirathon-
ite died and was buried in Pirathon in the land
of Ephraim, in the mountains of the Amalek-
ites.

The Birth of Samson

13 Again the children of Israel did evil in
the sight of the LORD, and the LORD de-
livered them into the hand of the Philistines
for forty years.
2 Now there was a certain man from Zorah,
of the family of the Danites, whose name *was*
Manoah; and his wife *was* barren and had no
children.
3 And the Angel of the LORD appeared to
the woman and said to her, "Indeed now, you
are barren and have borne no children, but you
shall conceive and bear a son.
4 "Now therefore, please be careful not to
drink wine or *similar* drink, and not to eat any-
thing unclean.
5 "For behold, you shall conceive and bear
a son. And no razor shall come upon his head,
for the child shall be a Nazirite to God from the
womb; and he shall begin to deliver Israel out
of the hand of the Philistines."
6 So the woman came and told her husband,
saying, "A Man of God came to me, and His
countenance *was* like the countenance of the
Angel of God, very awesome; but I did not ask
Him where He *was* from, and He did not tell
me His name.
7 "And He said to me, 'Behold, you shall con-
ceive and bear a son. Now drink no wine or
similar drink, nor eat anything unclean, for the
child shall be a Nazirite to God from the womb
to the day of his death.'"
8 Then Manoah prayed to the LORD, and said,
"O my Lord, please let the Man of God whom
You sent come to us again and teach us what
we shall do for the child who will be born."
9 And God listened to the voice of Manoah,
and the Angel of God came to the woman again
as she was sitting in the field; but Manoah her
husband *was* not with her.
10 Then the woman ran in haste and told her
husband, and said to him, "Look, the Man who
came to me the *other* day has just now appeared
to me!"
11 So Manoah arose and followed his wife.
When he came to the Man, he said to Him, "Are
You the Man who spoke to this woman?" And
He said, "I *am.*"
12 Manoah said, "Now let Your words come *to
pass!* What will be the boy's rule of life, and his
work?"
13 So the Angel of the LORD said to Manoah,
"Of all that I said to the woman let her be care-
ful.
14 "She may not eat anything that comes from
the vine, nor may she drink wine or *similar* drink,

nor eat anything unclean. All that I com-
manded her let her observe."
15 Then Manoah said to the Angel of the
LORD, "Please let us detain You, and we will
prepare a young goat for You."
16 And the Angel of the LORD said to Ma-
noah, "Though you detain Me, I will not eat
your food. But if you offer a burnt offering, you
must offer it to the LORD." (For Manoah did
not know He *was* the Angel of the LORD.)
17 Then Manoah said to the Angel of the
LORD, "What *is* Your name, that when Your
words come *to pass* we may honor You?"
18 And the Angel of the LORD said to him,
"Why do you ask My name, seeing it *is* won-
derful?"
19 So Manoah took the young goat with the
grain offering, and offered it upon the rock to
the LORD. And He did a wondrous thing while
Manoah and his wife looked on—
20 it happened as the flame went up toward
heaven from the altar—the Angel of the LORD
ascended in the flame of the altar! When Ma-
noah and his wife saw *this*, they fell on their
faces to the ground.
21 When the Angel of the LORD appeared no
more to Manoah and his wife, then Manoah
knew that He *was* the Angel of the LORD.
22 And Manoah said to his wife, "We shall
surely die, because we have seen God!"
23 But his wife said to him, "If the LORD had
desired to kill us, He would not have accepted
a burnt offering and a grain offering from our
hands, nor would He have shown us all these
things, nor would He have told us *such things*
as these at this time."
24 So the woman bore a son and called his
name Samson; and the child grew, and the
LORD blessed him.
25 And the Spirit of the LORD began to move
upon him at Mahaneh Dan[a] between Zorah
and Eshtaol.

Samson's Philistine Wife

14 Now Samson went down to Timnah, and
saw a woman in Timnah of the daugh-
ters of the Philistines.
2 So he went up and told his father and
mother, saying, "I have seen a woman in Tim-
nah of the daughters of the Philistines; now
therefore, get her for me as a wife."
3 Then his father and mother said to him,
"*Is there* no woman among the daughters of
your brethren, or among all my people, that
you must go and get a wife from the uncircum-
cised Philistines?" And Samson said to his fa-
ther, "Get her for me, for she pleases me well."
4 But his father and mother did not know
that it was of the LORD—that He was seeking
an occasion to move against the Philistines.
For at that time the Philistines had dominion
over Israel.
5 So Samson went down to Timnah with his
father and mother, and came to the vineyards
of Timnah.
Now *to his* surprise, a young lion *came* roar-
ing against him.
6 And the Spirit of the LORD came mightily
upon him, and he tore the lion apart as one
would have torn apart a young goat, though *he
had* nothing in his hand. But he did not tell his
father or his mother what he had done.
7 Then he went down and talked with the
woman; and she pleased Samson well.
8 After some time, when he returned to get
her, he turned aside to see the carcass of the
lion. And behold, a swarm of bees and honey
were in the carcass of the lion.
9 He took some of it in his hands and went
along, eating. When he came to his father and
mother, he gave *some* to them, and they also
ate. But he did not tell them that he had taken
the honey out of the carcass of the lion.
10 So his father went down to the woman.
And Samson gave a feast there, for young men
used to do so.
11 And it happened, when they saw him, that
they brought thirty companions to be with
him.
12 Then Samson said to them, "Let me pose
a riddle to you. If you can correctly solve and
explain it to me within the seven days of the
feast, then I will give you thirty linen garments
and thirty changes of clothing.
13 "But if you cannot explain *it* to me, then
you shall give me thirty linen garments and
thirty changes of clothing." And they said to him,
"Pose your riddle, that we may hear it."
14 So he said to them:

"Out of the eater came something to eat,
And out of the strong came something
sweet."

Now for three days they could not explain the
riddle.
15 But it came to pass on the seventh[a] day that
they said to Samson's wife, "Entice your hus-
band, that he may explain the riddle to us, or
else we will burn you and your father's house
with fire. Have you invited us in order to take
what is ours? *Is that* not *so?*"
16 Then Samson's wife wept on him, and said,
"You only hate me! You do not love me! You
have posed a riddle to the sons of my people,
but you have not explained *it* to me." And he
said to her, "Look, I have not explained *it* to
my father or my mother; so should I explain *it*
to you?"
17 Now she had wept on him the seven days
while their feast lasted. And it happened on
the seventh day that he told her, because she
pressed him so much. Then she explained the
riddle to the sons of her people.
18 So the men of the city said to him on the
seventh day before the sun went down:

"What *is* sweeter than honey?
And what *is* stronger than a lion?"

And he said to them:

"If you had not plowed with my heifer,
You would not have solved my riddle!"

19 Then the Spirit of the LORD came upon him
mightily, and he went down to Ashkelon and
killed thirty of their men, took their apparel,
and gave the changes *of clothing* to those who
had explained the riddle. So his anger was
aroused, and he went back up to his father's
house.
20 And Samson's wife was *given* to his com-
panion, who had been his best man.

13:25 [a]Literally *Camp of Dan* (compare 18:12) **14:15** [a]Following Masoretic Text, Targum, and Vulgate; Septuagint and Syriac read *fourth*.

Samson Defeats the Philistines

15 After a while, in the time of wheat har-
vest, it happened that Samson visited
his wife with a young goat. And he said, "Let
me go in to my wife, into *her* room." But her
father would not permit him to go in.
2 Her father said, "I really thought that you
thoroughly hated her; therefore I gave her to
your companion. *Is* not her younger sister bet-
ter than she? Please, take her instead."
3 And Samson said to them, "This time I
shall be blameless regarding the Philistines if
I harm them!"
4 Then Samson went and caught three hun-
dred foxes; and he took torches, turned *the
foxes* tail to tail, and put a torch between each
pair of tails.
5 When he had set the torches on fire, he
let *the foxes* go into the standing grain of the
Philistines, and burned up both the shocks and
the standing grain, as well as the vineyards *and*
olive groves.
6 Then the Philistines said, "Who has done
this?" And they answered, "Samson, the son-
in-law of the Timnite, because he has taken his
wife and given her to his companion." So the
Philistines came up and burned her and her
father with fire.
7 Samson said to them, "Since you would do
a thing like this, I will surely take revenge on
you, and after that I will cease."
8 So he attacked them hip and thigh with a
great slaughter; then he went down and dwelt
in the cleft of the rock of Etam.
9 Now the Philistines went up, encamped in
Judah, and deployed themselves against Lehi.
10 And the men of Judah said, "Why have
you come up against us?" So they answered,
"We have come up to arrest Samson, to do to
him as he has done to us."
11 Then three thousand men of Judah went
down to the cleft of the rock of Etam, and said
to Samson, "Do you not know that the Philis-
tines rule over us? What *is* this you have done
to us?" And he said to them, "As they did to
me, so I have done to them."
12 But they said to him, "We have come down
to arrest you, that we may deliver you into the
hand of the Philistines." Then Samson said to
them, "Swear to me that you will not kill me
yourselves."
13 So they spoke to him, saying, "No, but we
will tie you securely and deliver you into their
hand; but we will surely not kill you." And they
bound him with two new ropes and brought
him up from the rock.
14 When he came to Lehi, the Philistines
came shouting against him. Then the Spirit of
the LORD came mightily upon him; and the
ropes that *were* on his arms became like flax
that is burned with fire, and his bonds broke
loose from his hands.
15 He found a fresh jawbone of a donkey,
reached out his hand and took it, and killed a
thousand men with it.
16 Then Samson said:

"With the jawbone of a donkey,
Heaps upon heaps,
With the jawbone of a donkey
I have slain a thousand men!"

17 And so it was, when he had finished speak-
ing, that he threw the jawbone from his hand,
and called that place Ramath Lehi.[a]
18 Then he became very thirsty; so he cried
out to the LORD and said, "You have given this
great deliverance by the hand of Your servant;
and now shall I die of thirst and fall into the
hand of the uncircumcised?"
19 So God split the hollow place that *is* in
Lehi,[a] and water came out, and he drank; and
his spirit returned, and he revived. Therefore
he called its name En Hakkore,[b] which is in
Lehi to this day.
20 And he judged Israel twenty years in the
days of the Philistines.

Samson and Delilah

16 Now Samson went to Gaza and saw a
harlot there, and went in to her.
2 *When* the Gazites *were told,* "Samson has
come here!" they surrounded *the place* and lay
in wait for him all night at the gate of the city.
They were quiet all night, saying, "In the morn-
ing, when it is daylight, we will kill him."
3 And Samson lay *low* till midnight; then he
arose at midnight, took hold of the doors of the
gate of the city and the two gateposts, pulled
them up, bar and all, put *them* on his shoul-
ders, and carried them to the top of the hill that
faces Hebron.
4 Afterward it happened that he loved a
woman in the Valley of Sorek, whose name *was*
Delilah.
5 And the lords of the Philistines came up to
her and said to her, "Entice him, and find out
where his great strength *lies,* and by what
means we may overpower him, that we may
bind him to afflict him; and every one of us
will give you eleven hundred *pieces* of silver."
6 So Delilah said to Samson, "Please tell me
where your great strength *lies,* and with what
you may be bound to afflict you."
7 And Samson said to her, "If they bind me
with seven fresh bowstrings, not yet dried,
then I shall become weak, and be like any *other*
man."
8 So the lords of the Philistines brought up
to her seven fresh bowstrings, not yet dried,
and she bound him with them.
9 Now *men were* lying in wait, staying with
her in the room. And she said to him, "The
Philistines *are* upon you, Samson!" But he broke
the bowstrings as a strand of yarn breaks when
it touches fire. So the secret of his strength was
not known.
10 Then Delilah said to Samson, "Look, you
have mocked me and told me lies. Now, please
tell me what you may be bound with."
11 So he said to her, "If they bind me securely
with new ropes that have never been used, then
I shall become weak, and be like any *other* man."
12 Therefore Delilah took new ropes and
bound him with them, and said to him, "The
Philistines *are* upon you, Samson!" And *men
were* lying in wait, staying in the room. But he
broke them off his arms like a thread.
13 Delilah said to Samson, "Until now you
have mocked me and told me lies. Tell me what
you may be bound with." And he said to her,
"If you weave the seven locks of my head into
the web of the loom"—
14 So she wove *it* tightly with the batten of
the loom, and said to him, "The Philistines *are*

15:17 [a]Literally *Jawbone Height* **15:19** [a]Literally *Jawbone* (compare verse 14) [b]Literally *Spring of the Caller*

upon you, Samson!" But he awoke from his
sleep, and pulled out the batten and the web
from the loom.
15 Then she said to him, "How can you say, 'I
love you,' when your heart *is* not with me? You
have mocked me these three times, and have
not told me where your great strength *lies*."
16 And it came to pass, when she pestered
him daily with her words and pressed him, *so*
that his soul was vexed to death,
17 that he told her all his heart, and said to
her, "No razor has ever come upon my head, for
I *have been* a Nazirite to God from my mother's
womb. If I am shaven, then my strength will
leave me, and I shall become weak, and be like
any *other* man."
18 When Delilah saw that he had told her all
his heart, she sent and called for the lords of
the Philistines, saying, "Come up once more,
for he has told me all his heart." So the lords
of the Philistines came up to her and brought
the money in their hand.
19 Then she lulled him to sleep on her knees,
and called for a man and had him shave off the
seven locks of his head. Then she began to
torment him,[a] and his strength left him.
20 And she said, "The Philistines *are* upon you,
Samson!" So he awoke from his sleep, and
said, "I will go out as before, at other times, and
shake myself free!" But he did not know that
the LORD had departed from him.
21 Then the Philistines took him and put out
his eyes, and brought him down to Gaza. They
bound him with bronze fetters, and he became
a grinder in the prison.
22 However, the hair of his head began to
grow again after it had been shaven.

Samson Dies with the Philistines

23 Now the lords of the Philistines gathered
together to offer a great sacrifice to Dagon
their god, and to rejoice. And they said:

"Our god has delivered into our hands
Samson our enemy!"

24 When the people saw him, they praised
their god; for they said:

"Our god has delivered into our hands our
enemy,
The destroyer of our land,
And the one who multiplied our dead."

25 So it happened, when their hearts were
merry, that they said, "Call for Samson, that he
may perform for us." So they called for Sam-
son from the prison, and he performed for them.
And they stationed him between the pillars.
26 Then Samson said to the lad who held him
by the hand, "Let me feel the pillars which
support the temple, so that I can lean on them."
27 Now the temple was full of men and women.
All the lords of the Philistines *were* there—
about three thousand men and women on the
roof watching while Samson performed.
28 Then Samson called to the LORD, saying,
"O Lord GOD, remember me, I pray! Strengthen
me, I pray, just this once, O God, that I may
with one *blow* take vengeance on the Philis-
tines for my two eyes!"
29 And Samson took hold of the two middle
pillars which supported the temple, and he
braced himself against them, one on his right
and the other on his left.
30 Then Samson said, "Let me die with the
Philistines!" And he pushed with *all his* might,
and the temple fell on the lords and all the
people who *were* in it. So the dead that he killed
at his death were more than he had killed in
his life.
31 And his brothers and all his father's house-
hold came down and took him, and brought
him up and buried him between Zorah and
Eshtaol in the tomb of his father Manoah. He
had judged Israel twenty years.

Micah's Idolatry

17 Now there was a man from the moun-
tains of Ephraim, whose name *was*
Micah.
2 And he said to his mother, "The eleven
hundred *shekels* of silver that were taken from
you, and on which you put a curse, even saying
it in my ears—here *is* the silver with me; I took
it." And his mother said, "*May you be* blessed
by the LORD, my son!"
3 So when he had returned the eleven hun-
dred *shekels* of silver to his mother, his mother
said, "I had wholly dedicated the silver from
my hand to the LORD for my son, to make a
carved image and a molded image; now there-
fore, I will return it to you."
4 Thus he returned the silver to his mother.
Then his mother took two hundred *shekels* of
silver and gave them to the silversmith, and
he made it into a carved image and a molded
image; and they were in the house of Micah.
5 The man Micah had a shrine, and made an
ephod and household idols;[a] and he conse-
crated one of his sons, who became his priest.
6 In those days *there was* no king in Israel;
everyone did *what was* right in his own eyes.
7 Now there was a young man from Bethle-
hem in Judah, of the family of Judah; he *was*
a Levite, and was staying there.
8 The man departed from the city of Bethle-
hem in Judah to stay wherever he could find
a place. Then he came to the mountains of
Ephraim, to the house of Micah, as he journeyed.
9 And Micah said to him, "Where do you
come from?" So he said to him, "I *am* a Levite
from Bethlehem in Judah, and I am on my way
to find *a place* to stay."
10 Micah said to him, "Dwell with me, and be
a father and a priest to me, and I will give you
ten *shekels* of silver per year, a suit of clothes,
and your sustenance." So the Levite went in.
11 Then the Levite was content to dwell with
the man; and the young man became like one
of his sons to him.
12 So Micah consecrated the Levite, and the
young man became his priest, and lived in the
house of Micah.
13 Then Micah said, "Now I know that the
LORD will be good to me, since I have a Levite
as priest!"

The Danites Adopt Micah's Idolatry

18 In those days *there was* no king in Is-
rael. And in those days the tribe of the
Danites was seeking an inheritance for itself
to dwell in; for until that day *their* inheritance
among the tribes of Israel had not fallen to
them.

16:19 [a]Following Masoretic Text, Targum, and Vulgate; Septuagint reads *he began to be weak*.
17:5 [a]Hebrew *teraphim*

2 So the children of Dan sent five men of
their family from their territory, men of valor
from Zorah and Eshtaol, to spy out the land
and search it. They said to them, "Go, search
the land." So they went to the mountains of
Ephraim, to the house of Micah, and lodged
there.
3 While they *were* at the house of Micah,
they recognized the voice of the young Levite.
They turned aside and said to him, "Who
brought you here? What are you doing in this
place? What do you have here?"
4 He said to them, "Thus and so Micah did
for me. He has hired me, and I have become his
priest."
5 So they said to him, "Please inquire of
God, that we may know whether the journey
on which we go will be prosperous."
6 And the priest said to them, "Go in peace.
The presence of the LORD *be* with you on your
way."
7 So the five men departed and went to La-
ish. They saw the people who *were* there, how
they dwelt safely, in the manner of the Sidoni-
ans, quiet and secure. *There were* no rulers in
the land who might put *them* to shame for
anything. They *were* far from the Sidonians,
and they had no ties with anyone.[a]
8 Then *the spies* came back to their brethren
at Zorah and Eshtaol, and their brethren said
to them, "What *is* your *report?*"
9 So they said, "Arise, let us go up against
them. For we have seen the land, and indeed it
is very good. *Would* you *do* nothing? Do not
hesitate to go, *and* enter to possess the land.
10 "When you go, you will come to a secure
people and a large land. For God has given it
into your hands, a place where *there is* no lack
of anything that *is* on the earth."
11 And six hundred men of the family of the
Danites went from there, from Zorah and Esh-
taol, armed with weapons of war.
12 Then they went up and encamped in Kir-
jath Jearim in Judah. (Therefore they call that
place Mahaneh Dan[a] to this day. There *it is*,
west of Kirjath Jearim.)
13 And they passed from there to the moun-
tains of Ephraim, and came to the house of
Micah.
14 Then the five men who had gone to spy out
the country of Laish answered and said to their
brethren, "Do you know that there are in these
houses an ephod, household idols, a carved
image, and a molded image? Now therefore,
consider what you should do."
15 So they turned aside there, and came to
the house of the young Levite man—to the
house of Micah—and greeted him.
16 The six hundred men armed with their
weapons of war, who *were* of the children of
Dan, stood by the entrance of the gate.
17 Then the five men who had gone to spy out
the land went up. Entering there, they took the
carved image, the ephod, the household idols,
and the molded image. The priest stood at the
entrance of the gate with the six hundred men
who were armed with weapons of war.
18 When these went into Micah's house and
took the carved image, the ephod, the house-
hold idols, and the molded image, the priest
said to them, "What are you doing?"
19 And they said to him, "Be quiet, put your
hand over your mouth, and come with us; be a
father and a priest to us. *Is it* better for you to
be a priest to the household of one man, or that
you be a priest to a tribe and a family in Israel?"
20 So the priest's heart was glad; and he took
the ephod, the household idols, and the carved
image, and took his place among the people.
21 Then they turned and departed, and put
the little ones, the livestock, and the goods in
front of them.
22 When they were a good way from the
house of Micah, the men who *were* in the
houses near Micah's house gathered together
and overtook the children of Dan.
23 And they called out to the children of Dan.
So they turned around and said to Micah,
"What ails you, that you have gathered such a
company?"
24 So he said, "You have taken away my gods
which I made, and the priest, and you have
gone away. Now what more do I have? How
can you say to me, 'What ails you?' "
25 And the children of Dan said to him, "Do
not let your voice be heard among us, lest an-
gry men fall upon you, and you lose your life,
with the lives of your household!"
26 Then the children of Dan went their way.
And when Micah saw that they *were* too strong
for him, he turned and went back to his house.

Danites Settle in Laish

27 So they took *the things* Micah had made,
and the priest who had belonged to him, and
went to Laish, to a people quiet and secure; and
they struck them with the edge of the sword
and burned the city with fire.
28 *There was* no deliverer, because it *was* far
from Sidon, and they had no ties with anyone.
It was in the valley that belongs to Beth Rehob.
So they rebuilt the city and dwelt there.
29 And they called the name of the city Dan,
after the name of Dan their father, who was
born to Israel. However, the name of the city
formerly *was* Laish.
30 Then the children of Dan set up for them-
selves the carved image; and Jonathan the son
of Gershom, the son of Manasseh,[a] and his
sons were priests to the tribe of Dan until the
day of the captivity of the land.
31 So they set up for themselves Micah's
carved image which he made, all the time that
the house of God was in Shiloh.

The Levite's Concubine

19 And it came to pass in those days, when
there was no king in Israel, that there
was a certain Levite staying in the remote
mountains of Ephraim. He took for himself a
concubine from Bethlehem in Judah.
2 But his concubine played the harlot against
him, and went away from him to her father's
house at Bethlehem in Judah, and was there four
whole months.
3 Then her husband arose and went after her,
to speak kindly to her *and* bring her back, hav-
ing his servant and a couple of donkeys with
him. So she brought him into her father's house;
and when the father of the young woman saw
him, he was glad to meet him.
4 Now his father-in-law, the young woman's
father, detained him; and he stayed with him

18:7 [a]Following Masoretic Text, Targum, and Vulgate; Septuagint reads *with Syria.* **18:12** [a]Literally *Camp of Dan* **18:30** [a]Septuagint and Vulgate read *Moses.*

three days. So they ate and drank and lodged
there.
5 Then it came to pass on the fourth day that
they arose early in the morning, and he stood
to depart; but the young woman's father said
to his son-in-law, "Refresh your heart with a
morsel of bread, and afterward go your way."
6 So they sat down, and the two of them ate
and drank together. Then the young woman's
father said to the man, "Please be content to
stay all night, and let your heart be merry."
7 And when the man stood to depart, his
father-in-law urged him; so he lodged there again.
8 Then he arose early in the morning on the
fifth day to depart, but the young woman's fa-
ther said, "Please refresh your heart." So they
delayed until afternoon; and both of them ate.
9 And when the man stood to depart—he
and his concubine and his servant—his father-
in-law, the young woman's father, said to him,
"Look, the day is now drawing toward eve-
ning; please spend the night. See, the day is
coming to an end; lodge here, that your heart
may be merry. Tomorrow go your way early,
so that you may get home."
10 However, the man was not willing to spend
that night; so he rose and departed, and came
opposite Jebus (that *is*, Jerusalem). With him
were the two saddled donkeys; his concubine
was also with him.
11 They *were* near Jebus, and the day was
far spent; and the servant said to his master,
"Come, please, and let us turn aside into this
city of the Jebusites and lodge in it."
12 But his master said to him, "We will not
turn aside here into a city of foreigners, who
are not of the children of Israel; we will go on
to Gibeah."
13 So he said to his servant, "Come, let us
draw near to one of these places, and spend
the night in Gibeah or in Ramah."
14 And they passed by and went their way;
and the sun went down on them near Gibeah,
which belongs to Benjamin.
15 They turned aside there to go in to lodge
in Gibeah. And when he went in, he sat down
in the open square of the city, for no one would
take them into *his* house to spend the night.
16 Just then an old man came in from his
work in the field at evening, who also *was* from
the mountains of Ephraim; he was staying in
Gibeah, whereas the men of the place *were*
Benjamites.
17 And when he raised his eyes, he saw the
traveler in the open square of the city; and
the old man said, "Where are you going, and
where do you come from?"
18 So he said to him, "We *are* passing from
Bethlehem in Judah toward the remote moun-
tains of Ephraim; I *am* from there. I went to
Bethlehem in Judah; *now* I am going to the
house of the LORD. But there *is* no one who
will take me into his house,
19 "although we have both straw and fodder
for our donkeys, and bread and wine for my-
self, for your female servant, and for the young
man *who is* with your servant; *there is* no lack
of anything."
20 And the old man said, "Peace *be* with you!
However, *let* all your needs *be* my responsibil-
ity; only do not spend the night in the open
square."
21 So he brought him into his house, and gave
fodder to the donkeys. And they washed their
feet, and ate and drank.

Gibeah's Crime

22 As they were enjoying themselves, sud-
denly certain men of the city, perverted men,[a]
surrounded the house *and* beat on the door.
They spoke to the master of the house, the old
man, saying, "Bring out the man who came to
your house, that we may know him *carnally!*"
23 But the man, the master of the house, went
out to them and said to them, "No, my breth-
ren! I beg you, do not act *so* wickedly! Seeing
this man has come into my house, do not com-
mit this outrage.
24 "Look, *here is* my virgin daughter and *the
man's*[a] concubine; let me bring them out now.
Humble them, and do with them as you please;
but to this man do not do such a vile thing!"
25 But the men would not heed him. So the
man took his concubine and brought *her* out
to them. And they knew her and abused her
all night until morning; and when the day be-
gan to break, they let her go.
26 Then the woman came as the day was dawn-
ing, and fell down at the door of the man's
house where her master *was*, till it was light.
27 When her master arose in the morning,
and opened the doors of the house and went
out to go his way, there was his concubine,
fallen *at* the door of the house with her hands
on the threshold.
28 And he said to her, "Get up and let us be
going." But there was no answer. So the man
lifted her onto the donkey; and the man got up
and went to his place.
29 When he entered his house he took a knife,
laid hold of his concubine, and divided her into
twelve pieces, limb by limb,[a] and sent her
throughout all the territory of Israel.
30 And so it was that all who saw it said, "No
such deed has been done or seen from the day
that the children of Israel came up from the
land of Egypt until this day. Consider it, confer,
and speak up!"

Israel's War with the Benjamites

20 So all the children of Israel came out,
from Dan to Beersheba, as well as from
the land of Gilead, and the congregation gath-
ered together as one man before the LORD at
Mizpah.
2 And the leaders of all the people, all the
tribes of Israel, presented themselves in the
assembly of the people of God, four hundred
thousand foot soldiers who drew the sword.
3 (Now the children of Benjamin heard that
the children of Israel had gone up to Mizpah.)
Then the children of Israel said, "Tell *us*, how
did this wicked deed happen?"
4 So the Levite, the husband of the woman
who was murdered, answered and said, "My
concubine and I went into Gibeah, which be-
longs to Benjamin, to spend the night.
5 "And the men of Gibeah rose against me,
and surrounded the house at night because of
me. They intended to kill me, but instead they
ravished my concubine so that she died.
6 "So I took hold of my concubine, cut her
in pieces, and sent her throughout all the terri-
tory of the inheritance of Israel, because they
committed lewdness and outrage in Israel.

19:22 [a]Literally *sons of Belial* **19:24** [a]Literally *his* **19:29** [a]Literally *with her bones*

7 "Look! All of you *are* children of Israel;
give your advice and counsel here and now!"
8 So all the people arose as one man, saying,
"None of *us* will go to his tent, nor will any
turn back to his house;
9 "but now this *is* the thing which we will do
to Gibeah: *We will go up* against it by lot.
10 "We will take ten men out of *every* hun-
dred throughout all the tribes of Israel, a hun-
dred out of *every* thousand, and a thousand
out of *every* ten thousand, to make provisions
for the people, that when they come to Gibeah
in Benjamin, they may repay all the vileness
that they have done in Israel."
11 So all the men of Israel were gathered
against the city, united together as one man.
12 Then the tribes of Israel sent men through
all the tribe of Benjamin, saying, "What *is* this
wickedness that has occurred among you?
13 "Now therefore, deliver up the men, the
perverted men[a] who *are* in Gibeah, that we
may put them to death and remove the evil
from Israel!" But the children of Benjamin
would not listen to the voice of their brethren,
the children of Israel.
14 Instead, the children of Benjamin gathered
together from their cities to Gibeah, to go to
battle against the children of Israel.
15 And from their cities at that time the chil-
dren of Benjamin numbered twenty-six thou-
sand men who drew the sword, besides the
inhabitants of Gibeah, who numbered seven
hundred select men.
16 Among all this people *were* seven hundred
select men *who were* left-handed; every one
could sling a stone at a hair's *breadth* and not
miss.
17 Now besides Benjamin, the men of Israel
numbered four hundred thousand men who
drew the sword; all of these *were* men of war.
18 Then the children of Israel arose and went
up to the house of God[a] to inquire of God. They
said, "Which of us shall go up first to battle
against the children of Benjamin?" The LORD
said, "Judah first!"
19 So the children of Israel rose in the morn-
ing and encamped against Gibeah.
20 And the men of Israel went out to battle
against Benjamin, and the men of Israel put
themselves in battle array to fight against them
at Gibeah.
21 Then the children of Benjamin came out of
Gibeah, and on that day cut down to the ground
twenty-two thousand men of the Israelites.
22 And the people, that is, the men of Israel,
encouraged themselves and again formed the
battle line at the place where they had put
themselves in array on the first day.
23 Then the children of Israel went up and
wept before the LORD until evening, and asked
counsel of the LORD, saying, "Shall I again
draw near for battle against the children of my
brother Benjamin?" And the LORD said, "Go
up against him."
24 So the children of Israel approached the
children of Benjamin on the second day.
25 And Benjamin went out against them from
Gibeah on the second day, and cut down to the
ground eighteen thousand more of the chil-
dren of Israel; all these drew the sword.
26 Then all the children of Israel, that is, all
the people, went up and came to the house of
God[a] and wept. They sat there before the LORD
and fasted that day until evening; and they of-
fered burnt offerings and peace offerings be-
fore the LORD.
27 So the children of Israel inquired of the
LORD (the ark of the covenant of God *was*
there in those days,
28 and Phinehas the son of Eleazar, the son
of Aaron, stood before it in those days), saying,
"Shall I yet again go out to battle against the
children of my brother Benjamin, or shall I
cease?" And the LORD said, "Go up, for tomor-
row I will deliver them into your hand."
29 Then Israel set men in ambush all around
Gibeah.
30 And the children of Israel went up against
the children of Benjamin on the third day, and
put themselves in battle array against Gibeah
as at the other times.
31 So the children of Benjamin went out
against the people, *and* were drawn away from
the city. They began to strike down *and* kill
some of the people, as at the other times, in the
highways (one of which goes up to Bethel and
the other to Gibeah) and in the field, about
thirty men of Israel.
32 And the children of Benjamin said, "They
are defeated before us, as at first." But the chil-
dren of Israel said, "Let us flee and draw them
away from the city to the highways."
33 So all the men of Israel rose from their
place and put themselves in battle array at
Baal Tamar. Then Israel's men in ambush burst
forth from their position in the plain of Geba.
34 And ten thousand select men from all Is-
rael came against Gibeah, and the battle was
fierce. But *the Benjamites*[a] did not know that
disaster *was* upon them.
35 The LORD defeated Benjamin before Is-
rael. And the children of Israel destroyed that
day twenty-five thousand one hundred Benja-
mites; all these drew the sword.
36 So the children of Benjamin saw that they
were defeated. The men of Israel had given
ground to the Benjamites, because they relied
on the men in ambush whom they had set
against Gibeah.
37 And the men in ambush quickly rushed upon
Gibeah; the men in ambush spread out and struck
the whole city with the edge of the sword.
38 Now the appointed signal between the
men of Israel and the men in ambush was that
they would make a great cloud of smoke rise
up from the city,
39 whereupon the men of Israel would turn
in battle. Now Benjamin had begun to strike
and kill about thirty of the men of Israel. For
they said, "Surely they are defeated before us,
as *in* the first battle."
40 But when the cloud began to rise from the
city in a column of smoke, the Benjamites
looked behind them, and there was the whole
city going up *in smoke* to heaven.
41 And when the men of Israel turned back,
the men of Benjamin panicked, for they saw
that disaster had come upon them.
42 Therefore they turned *their backs* before
the men of Israel in the direction of the wilder-
ness; but the battle overtook them, and who-
ever *came* out of the cities they destroyed in
their midst.
43 They surrounded the Benjamites, chased
them, *and* easily trampled them down as far as
the front of Gibeah toward the east.

20:13 [a]Literally *sons of Belial* **20:18** [a]Or *Bethel* **20:26** [a]Or *Bethel* **20:34** [a]Literally *they*

44 And eighteen thousand men of Benjamin
fell; all these *were* men of valor.
45 Then they[a] turned and fled toward the wilderness to the rock of Rimmon; and they cut down five thousand of them on the highways. Then they pursued them relentlessly up to Gidom, and killed two thousand of them.
46 So all who fell of Benjamin that day were
twenty-five thousand men who drew the sword; all these *were* men of valor.
47 But six hundred men turned and fled toward
the wilderness to the rock of Rimmon, and they stayed at the rock of Rimmon for four months.
48 And the men of Israel turned back against
the children of Benjamin, and struck them down with the edge of the sword—from *every* city, men and beasts, all who were found. They also set fire to all the cities they came to.

Wives Provided for the Benjamites

21 Now the men of Israel had sworn an oath at Mizpah, saying, "None of us shall give his daughter to Benjamin as a wife."
2 Then the people came to the house of God,[a]
and remained there before God till evening. They lifted up their voices and wept bitterly,
3 and said, "O LORD God of Israel, why has
this come to pass in Israel, that today there should be one tribe *missing* in Israel?"
4 So it was, on the next morning, that the
people rose early and built an altar there, and offered burnt offerings and peace offerings.
5 The children of Israel said, "Who *is there*
among all the tribes of Israel who did not come up with the assembly to the LORD?" For they had made a great oath concerning anyone who had not come up to the LORD at Mizpah, saying, "He shall surely be put to death."
6 And the children of Israel grieved for Ben-
jamin their brother, and said, "One tribe is cut off from Israel today.
7 "What shall we do for wives for those who
remain, seeing we have sworn by the LORD that we will not give them our daughters as wives?"
8 And they said, "What one *is there* from the
tribes of Israel who did not come up to Mizpah to the LORD?" And, in fact, no one had come to the camp from Jabesh Gilead to the assembly.
9 For when the people were counted, indeed,
not one of the inhabitants of Jabesh Gilead *was* there.
10 So the congregation sent out there twelve
thousand of their most valiant men, and commanded them, saying, "Go and strike the inhabitants of Jabesh Gilead with the edge of the sword, including the women and children.
11 "And this *is* the thing that you shall do:
You shall utterly destroy every male, and every woman who has known a man intimately."
12 So they found among the inhabitants of
Jabesh Gilead four hundred young virgins who had not known a man intimately; and they brought them to the camp at Shiloh, which is in the land of Canaan.
13 Then the whole congregation sent *word* to
the children of Benjamin who *were* at the rock of Rimmon, and announced peace to them.
14 So Benjamin came back at that time, and
they gave them the women whom they had saved alive of the women of Jabesh Gilead; and yet they had not found enough for them.
15 And the people grieved for Benjamin, be-
cause the LORD had made a void in the tribes of Israel.
16 Then the elders of the congregation said,
"What shall we do for wives for those who remain, since the women of Benjamin have been destroyed?"
17 And they said, "*There must be* an inheri-
tance for the survivors of Benjamin, that a tribe may not be destroyed from Israel.
18 "However, we cannot give them wives
from our daughters, for the children of Israel have sworn an oath, saying, 'Cursed *be* the one who gives a wife to Benjamin.'"
19 Then they said, "In fact, *there is* a yearly
feast of the LORD in Shiloh, which *is* north of Bethel, on the east side of the highway that goes up from Bethel to Shechem, and south of Lebonah."
20 Therefore they instructed the children of
Benjamin, saying, "Go, lie in wait in the vineyards,
21 "and watch; and just when the daughters
of Shiloh come out to perform their dances, then come out from the vineyards, and every man catch a wife for himself from the daughters of Shiloh; then go to the land of Benjamin.
22 "Then it shall be, when their fathers or
their brothers come to us to complain, that we will say to them, 'Be kind to them for our sakes, because we did not take a wife for any of them in the war; for *it is* not *as though* you have given the *women* to them at this time, making yourselves guilty of your oath.'"
23 And the children of Benjamin did so; they
took enough wives for their number from those who danced, whom they caught. Then they went and returned to their inheritance, and they rebuilt the cities and dwelt in them.
24 So the children of Israel departed from
there at that time, every man to his tribe and family; they went out from there, every man to his inheritance.
25 In those days *there was* no king in Israel;
everyone did *what was* right in his own eyes.

The Book of RUTH

Elimelech's Family Goes to Moab

1 Now it came to pass, in the days when the judges ruled, that there was a famine in the land. And a certain man of Bethlehem, Judah, went to dwell in the country of Moab, he and his wife and his two sons.
2 The name of the man *was* Elimelech, the
name of his wife *was* Naomi, and the names of his two sons *were* Mahlon and Chilion—Ephrathites of Bethlehem, Judah. And they went to the country of Moab and remained there.
3 Then Elimelech, Naomi's husband, died;
and she was left, and her two sons.

20:45 [a]Septuagint reads *the rest.* 21:2 [a]Or *Bethel*

4 Now they took wives of the women of
Moab: the name of the one *was* Orpah, and the
name of the other Ruth. And they dwelt there
about ten years.
5 Then both Mahlon and Chilion also died;
so the woman survived her two sons and her
husband.

Naomi Returns with Ruth

6 Then she arose with her daughters-in-law
that she might return from the country of
Moab, for she had heard in the country of
Moab that the LORD had visited His people by
giving them bread.
7 Therefore she went out from the place
where she was, and her two daughters-in-law
with her; and they went on the way to return
to the land of Judah.
8 And Naomi said to her two daughters-in-
law, "Go, return each to her mother's house.
The LORD deal kindly with you, as you have
dealt with the dead and with me.
9 "The LORD grant that you may find rest,
each in the house of her husband." So she
kissed them, and they lifted up their voices and
wept.
10 And they said to her, "Surely we will re-
turn with you to your people."
11 But Naomi said, "Turn back, my daughters;
why will you go with me? *Are* there still sons
in my womb, that they may be your husbands?
12 "Turn back, my daughters, go—for I am too
old to have a husband. If I should say I have
hope, *if* I should have a husband tonight and
should also bear sons,
13 "would you wait for them till they were
grown? Would you restrain yourselves from
having husbands? No, my daughters; for it
grieves me very much for your sakes that the
hand of the LORD has gone out against me!"
14 Then they lifted up their voices and wept
again; and Orpah kissed her mother-in-law, but
Ruth clung to her.
15 And she said, "Look, your sister-in-law has
gone back to her people and to her gods; return
after your sister-in-law."
16 But Ruth said:

"Entreat me not to leave you,
Or to turn back from following after you;
For wherever you go, I will go;
And wherever you lodge, I will lodge;
Your people *shall be* my people,
And your God, my God.
17 Where you die, I will die,
And there will I be buried.
The LORD do so to me, and more also,
If *anything but* death parts you and me."

18 When she saw that she was determined to
go with her, she stopped speaking to her.
19 Now the two of them went until they came
to Bethlehem. And it happened, when they had
come to Bethlehem, that all the city was ex-
cited because of them; and the women said, "*Is*
this Naomi?"
20 But she said to them, "Do not call me Na-
omi;[a] call me Mara,[b] for the Almighty has dealt
very bitterly with me.
21 "I went out full, and the LORD has brought
me home again empty. Why do you call me
Naomi, since the LORD has testified against
me, and the Almighty has afflicted me?"
22 So Naomi returned, and Ruth the Moabit-
ess her daughter-in-law with her, who returned
from the country of Moab. Now they came to
Bethlehem at the beginning of barley harvest.

Ruth Meets Boaz

2 There was a relative of Naomi's husband,
a man of great wealth, of the family of Elime-
lech. His name *was* Boaz.
2 So Ruth the Moabitess said to Naomi,
"Please let me go to the field, and glean heads
of grain after *him* in whose sight I may find
favor." And she said to her, "Go, my daughter."
3 Then she left, and went and gleaned in the
field after the reapers. And she happened to
come to the part of the field *belonging* to Boaz,
who *was* of the family of Elimelech.
4 Now behold, Boaz came from Bethlehem,
and said to the reapers, "The LORD *be* with
you!" And they answered him, "The LORD bless
you!"
5 Then Boaz said to his servant who was in
charge of the reapers, "Whose young woman
is this?"
6 So the servant who was in charge of the
reapers answered and said, "It *is* the young
Moabite woman who came back with Naomi
from the country of Moab.
7 "And she said, 'Please let me glean and
gather after the reapers among the sheaves.'
So she came and has continued from morning
until now, though she rested a little in the house."
8 Then Boaz said to Ruth, "You will listen,
my daughter, will you not? Do not go to glean
in another field, nor go from here, but stay
close by my young women.
9 "*Let* your eyes *be* on the field which they
reap, and go after them. Have I not commanded
the young men not to touch you? And when
you are thirsty, go to the vessels and drink from
what the young men have drawn."
10 So she fell on her face, bowed down to the
ground, and said to him, "Why have I found
favor in your eyes, that you should take notice
of me, since I *am* a foreigner?"
11 And Boaz answered and said to her, "It
has been fully reported to me, all that you have
done for your mother-in-law since the death of
your husband, and *how* you have left your fa-
ther and your mother and the land of your birth,
and have come to a people whom you did not
know before.
12 "The LORD repay your work, and a full
reward be given you by the LORD God of Israel,
under whose wings you have come for refuge."
13 Then she said, "Let me find favor in your
sight, my lord; for you have comforted me, and
have spoken kindly to your maidservant, though
I am not like one of your maidservants."
14 Now Boaz said to her at mealtime, "Come
here, and eat of the bread, and dip your piece
of bread in the vinegar." So she sat beside the
reapers, and he passed parched *grain* to her;
and she ate and was satisfied, and kept some
back.
15 And when she rose up to glean, Boaz com-
manded his young men, saying, "Let her glean
even among the sheaves, and do not reproach
her.

1:20 [a]Literally *Pleasant* [b]Literally *Bitter*

16 "Also let *grain* from the bundles fall pur-
posely for her; leave *it* that she may glean, and
do not rebuke her."
17 So she gleaned in the field until evening,
and beat out what she had gleaned, and it was
about an ephah of barley.
18 Then she took *it* up and went into the city,
and her mother-in-law saw what she had
gleaned. So she brought out and gave to her
what she had kept back after she had been
satisfied.
19 And her mother-in-law said to her, "Where
have you gleaned today? And where did you
work? Blessed be the one who took notice of
you." So she told her mother-in-law with whom
she had worked, and said, "The man's name
with whom I worked today *is* Boaz."
20 Then Naomi said to her daughter-in-law,
"Blessed *be* he of the LORD, who has not for-
saken His kindness to the living and the dead!"
And Naomi said to her, "This man *is* a relation
of ours, one of our close relatives."
21 Ruth the Moabitess said, "He also said to
me, 'You shall stay close by my young men until
they have finished all my harvest.' "
22 And Naomi said to Ruth her daughter-in-
law, "*It is* good, my daughter, that you go out
with his young women, and that people do not
meet you in any other field."
23 So she stayed close by the young women
of Boaz, to glean until the end of barley harvest
and wheat harvest; and she dwelt with her
mother-in-law.

Ruth's Redemption Assured

3 Then Naomi her mother-in-law said to her,
"My daughter, shall I not seek security for
you, that it may be well with you?
2 "Now Boaz, whose young women you were
with, *is he* not our relative? In fact, he is win-
nowing barley tonight at the threshing floor.
3 "Therefore wash yourself and anoint your-
self, put on your *best* garment and go down to
the threshing floor; *but* do not make yourself
known to the man until he has finished eating
and drinking.
4 "Then it shall be, when he lies down, that
you shall notice the place where he lies; and
you shall go in, uncover his feet, and lie down;
and he will tell you what you should do."
5 And she said to her, "All that you say to
me I will do."
6 So she went down to the threshing floor
and did according to all that her mother-in-law
instructed her.
7 And after Boaz had eaten and drunk, and
his heart was cheerful, he went to lie down at
the end of the heap of grain; and she came
softly, uncovered his feet, and lay down.
8 Now it happened at midnight that the man
was startled, and turned himself; and there, a
woman was lying at his feet.
9 And he said, "Who *are* you?" So she an-
swered, "I *am* Ruth, your maidservant. Take
your maidservant under your wing,[a] for you
are a close relative."
10 Then he said, "Blessed *are* you of the
LORD, my daughter! For you have shown more
kindness at the end than at the beginning, in
that you did not go after young men, whether
poor or rich.
11 "And now, my daughter, do not fear. I will
do for you all that you request, for all the peo-
ple of my town know that you *are* a virtuous
woman.
12 "Now it is true that I *am* a close relative;
however, there is a relative closer than I.
13 "Stay this night, and in the morning it shall
be *that* if he will perform the duty of a close
relative for you—good; let him do it. But if he
does not want to perform the duty for you, then
I will perform the duty for you, *as* the LORD
lives! Lie down until morning."
14 So she lay at his feet until morning, and
she arose before one could recognize another.
Then he said, "Do not let it be known that the
woman came to the threshing floor."
15 Also he said, "Bring the shawl that *is* on
you and hold it." And when she held it, he
measured six *ephahs* of barley, and laid *it* on
her. Then she[a] went into the city.
16 When she came to her mother-in-law, she
said, "*Is* that you, my daughter?" Then she told
her all that the man had done for her.
17 And she said, "These six *ephahs* of barley
he gave me; for he said to me, 'Do not go
empty-handed to your mother-in-law.' "
18 Then she said, "Sit still, my daughter, until
you know how the matter will turn out; for the
man will not rest until he has concluded the
matter this day."

Boaz Redeems Ruth

4 Now Boaz went up to the gate and sat down
there; and behold, the close relative of
whom Boaz had spoken came by. So Boaz said,
"Come aside, friend,[a] sit down here." So he came
aside and sat down.
2 And he took ten men of the elders of the
city, and said, "Sit down here." So they sat down.
3 Then he said to the close relative, "Naomi,
who has come back from the country of Moab,
sold the piece of land which *belonged* to our
brother Elimelech.
4 "And I thought to inform you, saying, 'Buy
it back in the presence of the inhabitants and
the elders of my people. If you will redeem *it*,
redeem *it*; but if you[a] will not redeem *it*, *then*
tell me, that I may know; for *there is* no one
but you to redeem *it*, and I *am* next after you.' "
And he said, "I will redeem *it*."
5 Then Boaz said, "On the day you buy the
field from the hand of Naomi, you must also
buy *it* from Ruth the Moabitess, the wife of
the dead, to perpetuate[a] the name of the dead
through his inheritance."
6 And the close relative said, "I cannot re-
deem *it* for myself, lest I ruin my own inheri-
tance. You redeem my right of redemption for
yourself, for I cannot redeem *it*."
7 Now this *was the custom* in former times
in Israel concerning redeeming and exchang-
ing, to confirm anything: one man took off his

3:9 [a]Or *Spread the corner of your garment over your maidservant* **3:15** [a]Many Hebrew manuscripts, Syriac, and Vulgate read *she;* Masoretic Text, Septuagint, and Targum read *he.* **4:1** [a]Hebrew *peloni almoni;* literally *so and so*
4:4 [a]Following many Hebrew manuscripts, Septuagint, Syriac, Targum, and Vulgate; Masoretic Text reads *he.*
4:5 [a]Literally *raise up*

sandal and gave *it* to the other, and this *was* a confirmation in Israel.

8 Therefore the close relative said to Boaz, "Buy *it* for yourself." So he took off his sandal.

9 And Boaz said to the elders and all the people, "You *are* witnesses this day that I have bought all that was Elimelech's, and all that *was* Chilion's and Mahlon's, from the hand of Naomi.

10 "Moreover, Ruth the Moabitess, the widow of Mahlon, I have acquired as my wife, to perpetuate the name of the dead through his inheritance, that the name of the dead may not be cut off from among his brethren and from his position at the gate.[a] You *are* witnesses this day."

11 And all the people who *were* at the gate, and the elders, said, "*We are* witnesses. The LORD make the woman who is coming to your house like Rachel and Leah, the two who built the house of Israel; and may you prosper in Ephrathah and be famous in Bethlehem.

12 "May your house be like the house of Perez, whom Tamar bore to Judah, because of the offspring which the LORD will give you from this young woman."

Descendants of Boaz and Ruth

13 So Boaz took Ruth and she became his wife; and when he went in to her, the LORD gave her conception, and she bore a son.

14 Then the women said to Naomi, "Blessed *be* the LORD, who has not left you this day without a close relative; and may his name be famous in Israel!

15 "And may he be to you a restorer of life and a nourisher of your old age; for your daughter-in-law, who loves you, who is better to you than seven sons, has borne him."

16 Then Naomi took the child and laid him on her bosom, and became a nurse to him.

17 Also the neighbor women gave him a name, saying, "There is a son born to Naomi." And they called his name Obed. He *is* the father of Jesse, the father of David.

18 Now this *is* the genealogy of Perez: Perez begot Hezron;

19 Hezron begot Ram, and Ram begot Amminadab;

20 Amminadab begot Nahshon, and Nahshon begot Salmon;[a]

21 Salmon begot Boaz, and Boaz begot Obed;

22 Obed begot Jesse, and Jesse begot David.

The First Book of SAMUEL

The Family of Elkanah

1 Now there was a certain man of Ramathaim Zophim, of the mountains of Ephraim, and his name *was* Elkanah the son of Jeroham, the son of Elihu,[a] the son of Tohu,[b] the son of Zuph, an Ephraimite.

2 And he had two wives: the name of one *was* Hannah, and the name of the other Peninnah. Peninnah had children, but Hannah had no children.

3 This man went up from his city yearly to worship and sacrifice to the LORD of hosts in Shiloh. Also the two sons of Eli, Hophni and Phinehas, the priests of the LORD, *were* there.

4 And whenever the time came for Elkanah to make an offering, he would give portions to Peninnah his wife and to all her sons and daughters.

5 But to Hannah he would give a double portion, for he loved Hannah, although the LORD had closed her womb.

6 And her rival also provoked her severely, to make her miserable, because the LORD had closed her womb.

7 So it was, year by year, when she went up to the house of the LORD, that she provoked her; therefore she wept and did not eat.

Hannah's Vow

8 Then Elkanah her husband said to her, "Hannah, why do you weep? Why do you not eat? And why is your heart grieved? *Am* I not better to you than ten sons?"

9 So Hannah arose after they had finished eating and drinking in Shiloh. Now Eli the priest was sitting on the seat by the doorpost of the tabernacle[a] of the LORD.

10 And she *was* in bitterness of soul, and prayed to the LORD and wept in anguish.

11 Then she made a vow and said, "O LORD of hosts, if You will indeed look on the affliction of Your maidservant and remember me, and not forget Your maidservant, but will give Your maidservant a male child, then I will give him to the LORD all the days of his life, and no razor shall come upon his head."

12 And it happened, as she continued praying before the LORD, that Eli watched her mouth.

13 Now Hannah spoke in her heart; only her lips moved, but her voice was not heard. Therefore Eli thought she was drunk.

14 So Eli said to her, "How long will you be drunk? Put your wine away from you!"

15 But Hannah answered and said, "No, my lord, I *am* a woman of sorrowful spirit. I have drunk neither wine nor intoxicating drink, but have poured out my soul before the LORD.

16 "Do not consider your maidservant a wicked woman,[a] for out of the abundance of my complaint and grief I have spoken until now."

17 Then Eli answered and said, "Go in peace, and the God of Israel grant your petition which you have asked of Him."

18 And she said, "Let your maidservant find favor in your sight." So the woman went her way and ate, and her face was no longer *sad.*

Samuel Is Born and Dedicated

19 Then they rose early in the morning and worshiped before the LORD, and returned and came to their house at Ramah. And Elkanah knew Hannah his wife, and the LORD remembered her.

4:10 [a]Probably his civic office **4:20** [a]Hebrew *Salmah* **1:1** [a]Spelled *Eliel* in 1 Chronicles 6:34 [b]Spelled *Toah* in 1 Chronicles 6:34 **1:9** [a]Hebrew *heykal,* palace or temple **1:16** [a]Literally *daughter of Belial*

20 So it came to pass in the process of time
that Hannah conceived and bore a son, and
called his name Samuel,[a] *saying*, "Because I
have asked for him from the LORD."
21 Now the man Elkanah and all his house
went up to offer to the LORD the yearly sacri-
fice and his vow.
22 But Hannah did not go up, for she said to
her husband, "*Not* until the child is weaned;
then I will take him, that he may appear before
the LORD and remain there forever."
23 So Elkanah her husband said to her, "Do
what seems best to you; wait until you have
weaned him. Only let the LORD establish His[a]
word." Then the woman stayed and nursed her
son until she had weaned him.
24 Now when she had weaned him, she took
him up with her, with three bulls,[a] one ephah
of flour, and a skin of wine, and brought him
to the house of the LORD in Shiloh. And the
child *was* young.
25 Then they slaughtered a bull, and brought
the child to Eli.
26 And she said, "O my lord! As your soul
lives, my lord, I *am* the woman who stood by
you here, praying to the LORD.
27 "For this child I prayed, and the LORD has
granted me my petition which I asked of Him.
28 "Therefore I also have lent him to the
LORD; as long as he lives he shall be lent to the
LORD." So they worshiped the LORD there.

Hannah's Prayer

2 And Hannah prayed and said:

"My heart rejoices in the LORD;
My horn[a] is exalted in the LORD.
I smile at my enemies,
Because I rejoice in Your salvation.

2 "No one is holy like the LORD,
For *there is* none besides You,
Nor *is there* any rock like our God.

3 "Talk no more so very proudly;
Let no arrogance come from your mouth,
For the LORD *is* the God of knowledge;
And by Him actions are weighed.

4 "The bows of the mighty men *are* broken,
And those who stumbled are girded with strength.
5 *Those who were* full have hired themselves out for bread,
And the hungry have ceased *to hunger*.
Even the barren has borne seven,
And she who has many children has become feeble.

6 "The LORD kills and makes alive;
He brings down to the grave and brings up.
7 The LORD makes poor and makes rich;
He brings low and lifts up.
8 He raises the poor from the dust
And lifts the beggar from the ash heap,
To set *them* among princes
And make them inherit the throne of glory.

"For the pillars of the earth *are* the LORD's,
And He has set the world upon them.
9 He will guard the feet of His saints,
But the wicked shall be silent in darkness.

"For by strength no man shall prevail.
10 The adversaries of the LORD shall be broken in pieces;
From heaven He will thunder against them.
The LORD will judge the ends of the earth.

"He will give strength to His king,
And exalt the horn of His anointed."

11 Then Elkanah went to his house at Ramah.
But the child ministered to the LORD before Eli
the priest.

The Wicked Sons of Eli

12 Now the sons of Eli *were* corrupt;[a] they did
not know the LORD.
13 And the priests' custom with the people
was that when any man offered a sacrifice, the
priest's servant would come with a three-
pronged fleshhook in his hand while the meat
was boiling.
14 Then he would thrust *it* into the pan, or
kettle, or caldron, or pot; and the priest would
take for himself all that the fleshhook brought
up. So they did in Shiloh to all the Israelites who
came there.
15 Also, before they burned the fat, the priest's
servant would come and say to the man who
sacrificed, "Give meat for roasting to the priest,
for he will not take boiled meat from you, but
raw."
16 And *if* the man said to him, "They should
really burn the fat first; *then* you may take *as
much* as your heart desires," he would then
answer him, "*No*, but you must give *it* now;
and if not, I will take *it* by force."
17 Therefore the sin of the young men was
very great before the LORD, for men abhorred
the offering of the LORD.

Samuel's Childhood Ministry

18 But Samuel ministered before the LORD,
even as a child, wearing a linen ephod.
19 Moreover his mother used to make him a
little robe, and bring *it* to him year by year
when she came up with her husband to offer
the yearly sacrifice.
20 And Eli would bless Elkanah and his wife,
and say, "The LORD give you descendants from
this woman for the loan that was given to the
LORD." Then they would go to their own home.
21 And the LORD visited Hannah, so that she
conceived and bore three sons and two daugh-
ters. Meanwhile the child Samuel grew before
the LORD.

Prophecy Against Eli's Household

22 Now Eli was very old; and he heard every-
thing his sons did to all Israel,[a] and how they
lay with the women who assembled at the door
of the tabernacle of meeting.
23 So he said to them, "Why do you do such
things? For I hear of your evil dealings from
all the people.

1:20 [a]Literally *Heard by God* **1:23** [a]Following Masoretic Text, Targum, and Vulgate; Dead Sea Scrolls, Septuagint, and Syriac read *your*. **1:24** [a]Dead Sea Scrolls, Septuagint, and Syriac read *a three-year-old bull*. **2:1** [a]That is, strength **2:12** [a]Literally *sons of Belial* **2:22** [a]Following Masoretic Text, Targum, and Vulgate; Dead Sea Scrolls and Septuagint omit the rest of this verse.

24 "No, my sons! For *it is* not a good report that
I hear. You make the LORD's people transgress.
25 "If one man sins against another, God will
judge him. But if a man sins against the LORD,
who will intercede for him?" Nevertheless they
did not heed the voice of their father, because
the LORD desired to kill them.
26 And the child Samuel grew in stature, and
in favor both with the LORD and men.
27 Then a man of God came to Eli and said to
him, "Thus says the LORD: 'Did I not clearly
reveal Myself to the house of your father when
they were in Egypt in Pharaoh's house?
28 'Did I not choose him out of all the tribes
of Israel *to be* My priest, to offer upon My altar,
to burn incense, and to wear an ephod before
Me? And did I not give to the house of your
father all the offerings of the children of Israel
made by fire?
29 'Why do you kick at My sacrifice and My
offering which I have commanded *in My* dwell-
ing place, and honor your sons more than Me,
to make yourselves fat with the best of all the
offerings of Israel My people?'
30 "Therefore the LORD God of Israel says: 'I
said indeed *that* your house and the house of
your father would walk before Me forever.' But
now the LORD says: 'Far be it from Me; for
those who honor Me I will honor, and those
who despise Me shall be lightly esteemed.
31 'Behold, the days are coming that I will cut
off your arm and the arm of your father's
house, so that there will not be an old man in
your house.
32 'And you will see an enemy *in My* dwelling
place, *despite* all the good which God does for
Israel. And there shall not be an old man in
your house forever.
33 'But any of your men *whom* I do not cut
off from My altar shall consume your eyes and
grieve your heart. And all the descendants of
your house shall die in the flower of their age.
34 'Now this *shall be* a sign to you that will
come upon your two sons, on Hophni and
Phinehas: in one day they shall die, both of
them.
35 'Then I will raise up for Myself a faithful
priest *who* shall do according to what *is* in My
heart and in My mind. I will build him a sure
house, and he shall walk before My anointed
forever.
36 'And it shall come to pass that everyone
who is left in your house will come *and* bow
down to him for a piece of silver and a morsel
of bread, and say, "Please, put me in one of the
priestly positions, that I may eat a piece of
bread."'"

Samuel's First Prophecy

3 Now the boy Samuel ministered to the
LORD before Eli. And the word of the LORD
was rare in those days; *there was* no widespread
revelation.
2 And it came to pass at that time, while Eli
was lying down in his place, and when his eyes
had begun to grow so dim that he could not
see,
3 and before the lamp of God went out in the
tabernacle[a] of the LORD where the ark of God
was, and while Samuel was lying down,
4 that the LORD called Samuel. And he an-
swered, "Here I am!"
5 So he ran to Eli and said, "Here I am, for
you called me." And he said, "I did not call; lie
down again." And he went and lay down.
6 Then the LORD called yet again, "Sam-
uel!" So Samuel arose and went to Eli, and
said, "Here I am, for you called me." He an-
swered, "I did not call, my son; lie down
again."
7 (Now Samuel did not yet know the LORD,
nor was the word of the LORD yet revealed to
him.)
8 And the LORD called Samuel again the
third time. So he arose and went to Eli, and
said, "Here I am, for you did call me." Then Eli
perceived that the LORD had called the boy.
9 Therefore Eli said to Samuel, "Go, lie
down; and it shall be, if He calls you, that you
must say, 'Speak, LORD, for Your servant
hears.'" So Samuel went and lay down in his
place.
10 Now the LORD came and stood and called
as at other times, "Samuel! Samuel!" And
Samuel answered, "Speak, for Your servant
hears."
11 Then the LORD said to Samuel: "Behold, I
will do something in Israel at which both ears
of everyone who hears it will tingle.
12 "In that day I will perform against Eli all
that I have spoken concerning his house, from
beginning to end.
13 "For I have told him that I will judge his
house forever for the iniquity which he knows,
because his sons made themselves vile, and he
did not restrain them.
14 "And therefore I have sworn to the house
of Eli that the iniquity of Eli's house shall not
be atoned for by sacrifice or offering forever."
15 So Samuel lay down until morning,[a] and
opened the doors of the house of the LORD.
And Samuel was afraid to tell Eli the vision.
16 Then Eli called Samuel and said, "Samuel,
my son!" He answered, "Here I am."
17 And he said, "What *is* the word that *the
LORD* spoke to you? Please do not hide *it* from
me. God do so to you, and more also, if you
hide anything from me of all the things that He
said to you."
18 Then Samuel told him everything, and hid
nothing from him. And he said, "It *is* the LORD.
Let Him do what seems good to Him."
19 So Samuel grew, and the LORD was with
him and let none of his words fall to the ground.
20 And all Israel from Dan to Beersheba
knew that Samuel *had been* established as a
prophet of the LORD.
21 Then the LORD appeared again in Shiloh.
For the LORD revealed Himself to Samuel in
Shiloh by the word of the LORD.
4 And the word of Samuel came to all Is-
rael.[a]

The Ark of God Captured

Now Israel went out to battle against the
Philistines, and encamped beside Ebenezer;
and the Philistines encamped in Aphek.
2 Then the Philistines put themselves in bat-
tle array against Israel. And when they joined
battle, Israel was defeated by the Philistines,

3:3 [a]Hebrew *heykal*, palace or temple **3:15** [a]Following Masoretic Text, Targum, and Vulgate; Septuagint adds *and he arose in the morning.* **4:1** [a]Following Masoretic Text and Targum; Septuagint and Vulgate add *And it came to pass in those days that the Philistines gathered themselves together to fight;* Septuagint adds further *against Israel.*

who killed about four thousand men of the
army in the field.
3 And when the people had come into the
camp, the elders of Israel said, "Why has the
LORD defeated us today before the Philistines?
Let us bring the ark of the covenant of the
LORD from Shiloh to us, that when it comes
among us it may save us from the hand of our
enemies."
4 So the people sent to Shiloh, that they
might bring from there the ark of the covenant
of the LORD of hosts, who dwells *between* the
cherubim. And the two sons of Eli, Hophni and
Phinehas, *were* there with the ark of the cov-
enant of God.
5 And when the ark of the covenant of the
LORD came into the camp, all Israel shouted
so loudly that the earth shook.
6 Now when the Philistines heard the noise
of the shout, they said, "What *does* the sound
of this great shout in the camp of the Hebrews
mean?" Then they understood that the ark of
the LORD had come into the camp.
7 So the Philistines were afraid, for they
said, "God has come into the camp!" And they
said, "Woe to us! For such a thing has never
happened before.
8 "Woe to us! Who will deliver us from the
hand of these mighty gods? These *are* the gods
who struck the Egyptians with all the plagues
in the wilderness.
9 "Be strong and conduct yourselves like
men, you Philistines, that you do not become
servants of the Hebrews, as they have been to
you. Conduct yourselves like men, and fight!"
10 So the Philistines fought, and Israel was
defeated, and every man fled to his tent. There
was a very great slaughter, and there fell of
Israel thirty thousand foot soldiers.
11 Also the ark of God was captured; and the
two sons of Eli, Hophni and Phinehas, died.

Death of Eli

12 Then a man of Benjamin ran from the bat-
tle line the same day, and came to Shiloh with
his clothes torn and dirt on his head.
13 Now when he came, there was Eli, sitting
on a seat by the wayside watching,[a] for his
heart trembled for the ark of God. And when
the man came into the city and told *it*, all the
city cried out.
14 When Eli heard the noise of the outcry,
he said, "What *does* the sound of this tumult
mean?" And the man came quickly and told
Eli.
15 Eli was ninety-eight years old, and his eyes
were so dim that he could not see.
16 Then the man said to Eli, "I *am* he who
came from the battle. And I fled today from the
battle line." And he said, "What happened, my
son?"
17 So the messenger answered and said, "Is-
rael has fled before the Philistines, and there
has been a great slaughter among the people.
Also your two sons, Hophni and Phinehas, are
dead; and the ark of God has been captured."
18 Then it happened, when he made mention
of the ark of God, that Eli fell off the seat back-
ward by the side of the gate; and his neck was
broken and he died, for the man was old and
heavy. And he had judged Israel forty years.

Ichabod

19 Now his daughter-in-law, Phinehas' wife,
was with child, *due* to be delivered; and when
she heard the news that the ark of God was
captured, and that her father-in-law and her
husband were dead, she bowed herself and
gave birth, for her labor pains came upon her.
20 And about the time of her death the
women who stood by her said to her, "Do not
fear, for you have borne a son." But she did not
answer, nor did she regard *it*.
21 Then she named the child Ichabod,[a] say-
ing, "The glory has departed from Israel!" be-
cause the ark of God had been captured and
because of her father-in-law and her husband.
22 And she said, "The glory has departed
from Israel, for the ark of God has been cap-
tured."

The Philistines and the Ark

5 Then the Philistines took the ark of God
and brought it from Ebenezer to Ashdod.
2 When the Philistines took the ark of God,
they brought it into the house of Dagon[a] and
set it by Dagon.
3 And when the people of Ashdod arose
early in the morning, there was Dagon, fallen
on its face to the earth before the ark of the
LORD. So they took Dagon and set it in its
place again.
4 And when they arose early the next morn-
ing, there was Dagon, fallen on its face to the
ground before the ark of the LORD. The head
of Dagon and both the palms of its hands *were*
broken off on the threshold; only Dagon's
torso[a] was left of it.
5 Therefore neither the priests of Dagon nor
any who come into Dagon's house tread on the
threshold of Dagon in Ashdod to this day.
6 But the hand of the LORD was heavy on
the people of Ashdod, and He ravaged them
and struck them with tumors,[a] *both* Ashdod
and its territory.
7 And when the men of Ashdod saw how *it*
was, they said, "The ark of the God of Israel
must not remain with us, for His hand is harsh
toward us and Dagon our god."
8 Therefore they sent and gathered to them-
selves all the lords of the Philistines, and said,
"What shall we do with the ark of the God of
Israel?" And they answered, "Let the ark of
the God of Israel be carried away to Gath." So
they carried the ark of the God of Israel away.
9 So it was, after they had carried it away,
that the hand of the LORD was against the city
with a very great destruction; and He struck
the men of the city, both small and great, and
tumors broke out on them.
10 Therefore they sent the ark of God to Ek-
ron. So it was, as the ark of God came to Ekron,
that the Ekronites cried out, saying, "They
have brought the ark of the God of Israel to us,
to kill us and our people!"
11 So they sent and gathered together all the
lords of the Philistines, and said, "Send away

4:13 [a]Following Masoretic Text and Vulgate; Septuagint reads *beside the gate watching the road.* **4:21** [a]Literally *Inglorious* **5:2** [a]A Philistine idol **5:4** [a]Following Septuagint, Syriac, Targum, and Vulgate; Masoretic Text reads *Dagon.* **5:6** [a]Probably bubonic plague. Septuagint and Vulgate add here *And in the midst of their land rats sprang up, and there was a great death panic in the city.*

the ark of the God of Israel, and let it go back
to its own place, so that it does not kill us and
our people." For there was a deadly destruction
throughout all the city; the hand of God was
very heavy there.
12 And the men who did not die were stricken
with the tumors, and the cry of the city went
up to heaven.

The Ark Returned to Israel

6 Now the ark of the LORD was in the country
of the Philistines seven months.
2 And the Philistines called for the priests
and the diviners, saying, "What shall we do
with the ark of the LORD? Tell us how we
should send it to its place."
3 So they said, "If you send away the ark of
the God of Israel, do not send it empty; but
by all means return *it* to Him *with* a trespass
offering. Then you will be healed, and it will
be known to you why His hand is not removed
from you."
4 Then they said, "What *is* the trespass of-
fering which we shall return to Him?" They
answered, "Five golden tumors and five golden
rats, *according to* the number of the lords of
the Philistines. For the same plague *was* on all
of you and on your lords.
5 "Therefore you shall make images of your
tumors and images of your rats that ravage the
land, and you shall give glory to the God of
Israel; perhaps He will lighten His hand from
you, from your gods, and from your land.
6 "Why then do you harden your hearts as
the Egyptians and Pharaoh hardened their
hearts? When He did mighty things among
them, did they not let the people go, that they
might depart?
7 "Now therefore, make a new cart, take two
milk cows which have never been yoked, and
hitch the cows to the cart; and take their calves
home, away from them.
8 "Then take the ark of the LORD and set it
on the cart; and put the articles of gold which
you are returning to Him *as* a trespass offering
in a chest by its side. Then send it away, and
let it go.
9 "And watch: if it goes up the road to its
own territory, to Beth Shemesh, *then* He has
done us this great evil. But if not, then we shall
know that *it is* not His hand *that* struck us—it
happened to us by chance."
10 Then the men did so; they took two milk
cows and hitched them to the cart, and shut up
their calves at home.
11 And they set the ark of the LORD on the
cart, and the chest with the gold rats and the
images of their tumors.
12 Then the cows headed straight for the road
to Beth Shemesh, *and* went along the highway,
lowing as they went, and did not turn aside to
the right hand or the left. And the lords of the
Philistines went after them to the border of
Beth Shemesh.
13 Now *the people of* Beth Shemesh *were*
reaping their wheat harvest in the valley; and
they lifted their eyes and saw the ark, and re-
joiced to see *it*.
14 Then the cart came into the field of Joshua
of Beth Shemesh, and stood there; a large
stone *was* there. So they split the wood of the
cart and offered the cows as a burnt offering
to the LORD.
15 The Levites took down the ark of the LORD
and the chest that *was* with it, in which *were*
the articles of gold, and put *them* on the large
stone. Then the men of Beth Shemesh offered
burnt offerings and made sacrifices the same
day to the LORD.
16 So when the five lords of the Philistines
had seen *it*, they returned to Ekron the same
day.
17 These *are* the golden tumors which the
Philistines returned *as* a trespass offering to
the LORD: one for Ashdod, one for Gaza, one
for Ashkelon, one for Gath, one for Ekron;
18 and the golden rats, *according to* the num-
ber of all the cities of the Philistines *belonging*
to the five lords, *both* fortified cities and coun-
try villages, even as far as the large *stone of*
Abel on which they set the ark of the LORD,
which stone remains to this day in the field of
Joshua of Beth Shemesh.
19 Then He struck the men of Beth Shemesh,
because they had looked into the ark of the
LORD. He struck fifty thousand and seventy
men[a] of the people, and the people lamented
because the LORD had struck the people with
a great slaughter.

The Ark at Kirjath Jearim

20 And the men of Beth Shemesh said, "Who
is able to stand before this holy LORD God?
And to whom shall it go up from us?"
21 So they sent messengers to the inhabitants
of Kirjath Jearim, saying, "The Philistines
have brought back the ark of the LORD; come
down *and* take it up with you."
7 Then the men of Kirjath Jearim came and
took the ark of the LORD, and brought it
into the house of Abinadab on the hill, and
consecrated Eleazar his son to keep the ark of
the LORD.

Samuel Judges Israel

2 So it was that the ark remained in Kirjath
Jearim a long time; it was there twenty years.
And all the house of Israel lamented after the
LORD.
3 Then Samuel spoke to all the house of Is-
rael, saying, "If you return to the LORD with
all your hearts, *then* put away the foreign gods
and the Ashtoreths[a] from among you, and pre-
pare your hearts for the LORD, and serve Him
only; and He will deliver you from the hand of
the Philistines."
4 So the children of Israel put away the Ba-
als and the Ashtoreths,[a] and served the LORD
only.
5 And Samuel said, "Gather all Israel to Miz-
pah, and I will pray to the LORD for you."
6 So they gathered together at Mizpah, drew
water, and poured *it* out before the LORD. And
they fasted that day, and said there, "We have
sinned against the LORD." And Samuel judged
the children of Israel at Mizpah.
7 Now when the Philistines heard that the
children of Israel had gathered together at
Mizpah, the lords of the Philistines went up
against Israel. And when the children of Israel
heard *of it*, they were afraid of the Philistines.
8 So the children of Israel said to Samuel,
"Do not cease to cry out to the LORD our God

6:19 [a]Or *He struck seventy men of the people and fifty oxen of a man* **7:3** [a]Canaanite goddesses **7:4** [a]Canaanite goddesses

for us, that He may save us from the hand of the Philistines."

9 And Samuel took a suckling lamb and offered *it as* a whole burnt offering to the LORD. Then Samuel cried out to the LORD for Israel, and the LORD answered him.

10 Now as Samuel was offering up the burnt offering, the Philistines drew near to battle against Israel. But the LORD thundered with a loud thunder upon the Philistines that day, and so confused them that they were overcome before Israel.

11 And the men of Israel went out of Mizpah and pursued the Philistines, and drove them back as far as below Beth Car.

12 Then Samuel took a stone and set *it* up between Mizpah and Shen, and called its name Ebenezer,[a] saying, "Thus far the LORD has helped us."

13 So the Philistines were subdued, and they did not come anymore into the territory of Israel. And the hand of the LORD was against the Philistines all the days of Samuel.

14 Then the cities which the Philistines had taken from Israel were restored to Israel, from Ekron to Gath; and Israel recovered its territory from the hands of the Philistines. Also there was peace between Israel and the Amorites.

15 And Samuel judged Israel all the days of his life.

16 He went from year to year on a circuit to Bethel, Gilgal, and Mizpah, and judged Israel in all those places.

17 But he always returned to Ramah, for his home *was* there. There he judged Israel, and there he built an altar to the LORD.

Israel Demands a King

8 Now it came to pass when Samuel was old that he made his sons judges over Israel.

2 The name of his firstborn was Joel, and the name of his second, Abijah; *they were* judges in Beersheba.

3 But his sons did not walk in his ways; they turned aside after dishonest gain, took bribes, and perverted justice.

4 Then all the elders of Israel gathered together and came to Samuel at Ramah,

5 and said to him, "Look, you are old, and your sons do not walk in your ways. Now make us a king to judge us like all the nations."

6 But the thing displeased Samuel when they said, "Give us a king to judge us." So Samuel prayed to the LORD.

7 And the LORD said to Samuel, "Heed the voice of the people in all that they say to you; for they have not rejected you, but they have rejected Me, that I should not reign over them.

8 "According to all the works which they have done since the day that I brought them up out of Egypt, even to this day—with which they have forsaken Me and served other gods—so they are doing to you also.

9 "Now therefore, heed their voice. However, you shall solemnly forewarn them, and show them the behavior of the king who will reign over them."

10 So Samuel told all the words of the LORD to the people who asked him for a king.

11 And he said, "This will be the behavior of the king who will reign over you: He will take your sons and appoint *them* for his own chariots and *to be* his horsemen, and *some* will run before his chariots.

12 "He will appoint captains over his thousands and captains over his fifties, *will set some* to plow his ground and reap his harvest, and *some* to make his weapons of war and equipment for his chariots.

13 "He will take your daughters *to be* perfumers, cooks, and bakers.

14 "And he will take the best of your fields, your vineyards, and your olive groves, and give *them* to his servants.

15 "He will take a tenth of your grain and your vintage, and give it to his officers and servants.

16 "And he will take your male servants, your female servants, your finest young men,[a] and your donkeys, and put *them* to his work.

17 "He will take a tenth of your sheep. And you will be his servants.

18 "And you will cry out in that day because of your king whom you have chosen for yourselves, and the LORD will not hear you in that day."

19 Nevertheless the people refused to obey the voice of Samuel; and they said, "No, but we will have a king over us,

20 "that we also may be like all the nations, and that our king may judge us and go out before us and fight our battles."

21 And Samuel heard all the words of the people, and he repeated them in the hearing of the LORD.

22 So the LORD said to Samuel, "Heed their voice, and make them a king." And Samuel said to the men of Israel, "Every man go to his city."

Saul Chosen to Be King

9 There was a man of Benjamin whose name *was* Kish the son of Abiel, the son of Zeror, the son of Bechorath, the son of Aphiah, a Benjamite, a mighty man of power.

2 And he had a choice and handsome son whose name *was* Saul. *There was* not a more handsome person than he among the children of Israel. From his shoulders upward *he was* taller than any of the people.

3 Now the donkeys of Kish, Saul's father, were lost. And Kish said to his son Saul, "Please take one of the servants with you, and arise, go and look for the donkeys."

4 So he passed through the mountains of Ephraim and through the land of Shalisha, but they did not find *them*. Then they passed through the land of Shaalim, and *they were* not *there*. Then he passed through the land of the Benjamites, but they did not find *them*.

5 When they had come to the land of Zuph, Saul said to his servant who *was* with him, "Come, let us return, lest my father cease *caring* about the donkeys and become worried about us."

6 And he said to him, "Look now, *there is* in this city a man of God, and *he is* an honorable man; all that he says surely comes to pass. So let us go there; perhaps he can show us the way that we should go."

7 Then Saul said to his servant, "But look, *if* we go, what shall we bring the man? For the bread in our vessels is all gone, and *there is* no present to bring to the man of God. What do we have?"

8 And the servant answered Saul again and

7:12 [a]Literally *Stone of Help* **8:16** [a]Septuagint reads *cattle*.

said, "Look, I have here at hand one-fourth of a shekel of silver. I will give *that* to the man of God, to tell us our way."

9 (Formerly in Israel, when a man went to inquire of God, he spoke thus: "Come, let us go to the seer"; for *he who is* now *called* a prophet was formerly called a seer.)

10 Then Saul said to his servant, "Well said; come, let us go." So they went to the city where the man of God *was*.

11 As they went up the hill to the city, they met some young women going out to draw water, and said to them, "Is the seer here?"

12 And they answered them and said, "Yes, there he is, just ahead of you. Hurry now; for today he came to this city, because there is a sacrifice of the people today on the high place.

13 "As soon as you come into the city, you will surely find him before he goes up to the high place to eat. For the people will not eat until he comes, because he must bless the sacrifice; afterward those who are invited will eat. Now therefore, go up, for about this time you will find him."

14 So they went up to the city. As they were coming into the city, there was Samuel, coming out toward them on his way up to the high place.

15 Now the LORD had told Samuel in his ear the day before Saul came, saying,

16 "Tomorrow about this time I will send you a man from the land of Benjamin, and you shall anoint him commander over My people Israel, that he may save My people from the hand of the Philistines; for I have looked upon My people, because their cry has come to Me."

17 So when Samuel saw Saul, the LORD said to him, "There he is, the man of whom I spoke to you. This one shall reign over My people."

18 Then Saul drew near to Samuel in the gate, and said, "Please tell me, where *is* the seer's house?"

19 Samuel answered Saul and said, "I *am* the seer. Go up before me to the high place, for you shall eat with me today; and tomorrow I will let you go and will tell you all that *is* in your heart.

20 "But as for your donkeys that were lost three days ago, do not be anxious about them, for they have been found. And on whom *is* all the desire of Israel? *Is it* not on you and on all your father's house?"

21 And Saul answered and said, "*Am* I not a Benjamite, of the smallest of the tribes of Israel, and my family the least of all the families of the tribe[a] of Benjamin? Why then do you speak like this to me?"

22 Now Samuel took Saul and his servant and brought them into the hall, and had them sit in the place of honor among those who were invited; there *were* about thirty persons.

23 And Samuel said to the cook, "Bring the portion which I gave you, of which I said to you, 'Set it apart.'"

24 So the cook took up the thigh with its upper part and set *it* before Saul. And *Samuel* said, "Here it is, what was kept back. *It* was set apart for you. Eat; for until this time it has been kept for you, since I said I invited the people." So Saul ate with Samuel that day.

25 When they had come down from the high place into the city, *Samuel* spoke with Saul on the top of the house.[a]

26 They arose early; and it was about the dawning of the day that Samuel called to Saul on the top of the house, saying, "Get up, that I may send you on your way." And Saul arose, and both of them went outside, he and Samuel.

Saul Anointed King

27 As they were going down to the outskirts of the city, Samuel said to Saul, "Tell the servant to go on ahead of us." And he went on. "But you stand here awhile, that I may announce to you the word of God."

10 Then Samuel took a flask of oil and poured *it* on his head, and kissed him and said: "*Is it* not because the LORD has anointed you commander over His inheritance?[a]

2 "When you have departed from me today, you will find two men by Rachel's tomb in the territory of Benjamin at Zelzah; and they will say to you, 'The donkeys which you went to look for have been found. And now your father has ceased caring about the donkeys and is worrying about you, saying, "What shall I do about my son?"'

3 "Then you shall go on forward from there and come to the terebinth tree of Tabor. There three men going up to God at Bethel will meet you, one carrying three young goats, another carrying three loaves of bread, and another carrying a skin of wine.

4 "And they will greet you and give you two *loaves* of bread, which you shall receive from their hands.

5 "After that you shall come to the hill of God where the Philistine garrison *is*. And it will happen, when you have come there to the city, that you will meet a group of prophets coming down from the high place with a stringed instrument, a tambourine, a flute, and a harp before them; and they will be prophesying.

6 "Then the Spirit of the LORD will come upon you, and you will prophesy with them and be turned into another man.

7 "And let it be, when these signs come to you, *that* you do as the occasion demands; for God *is* with you.

8 "You shall go down before me to Gilgal; and surely I will come down to you to offer burnt offerings *and* make sacrifices of peace offerings. Seven days you shall wait, till I come to you and show you what you should do."

9 So it was, when he had turned his back to go from Samuel, that God gave him another heart; and all those signs came to pass that day.

10 When they came there to the hill, there was a group of prophets to meet him; then the Spirit of God came upon him, and he prophesied among them.

11 And it happened, when all who knew him formerly saw that he indeed prophesied among the prophets, that the people said to one another, "What *is* this *that* has come upon the son of Kish? *Is* Saul also among the prophets?"

12 Then a man from there answered and said, "But who *is* their father?" Therefore it became a proverb: "*Is* Saul also among the prophets?"

9:21 [a]Literally *tribes* **9:25** [a]Following Masoretic Text and Targum; Septuagint omits *He spoke with Saul on the top of the house;* Septuagint and Vulgate add *And he prepared a bed for Saul on the top of the house, and he slept.*
10:1 [a]Following Masoretic Text, Targum, and Vulgate; Septuagint reads *His people Israel; and you shall rule the people of the Lord;* Septuagint and Vulgate add *And you shall deliver His people from the hands of their enemies all around them. And this shall be a sign to you, that God has anointed you to be a prince.*

13 And when he had finished prophesying,
he went to the high place.
14 Then Saul's uncle said to him and his ser-
vant, "Where did you go?" So he said, "To look
for the donkeys. When we saw that *they were*
nowhere *to be found*, we went to Samuel."
15 And Saul's uncle said, "Tell me, please,
what Samuel said to you."
16 So Saul said to his uncle, "He told us plainly
that the donkeys had been found." But about
the matter of the kingdom, he did not tell him
what Samuel had said.

Saul Proclaimed King

17 Then Samuel called the people together to
the LORD at Mizpah,
18 and said to the children of Israel, "Thus
says the LORD God of Israel: 'I brought up Is-
rael out of Egypt, and delivered you from the
hand of the Egyptians *and* from the hand of all
kingdoms and from those who oppressed you.'
19 "But you have today rejected your God,
who Himself saved you from all your adversi-
ties and your tribulations; and you have said
to Him, 'No, set a king over us!' Now therefore,
present yourselves before the LORD by your
tribes and by your clans."[a]
20 And when Samuel had caused all the
tribes of Israel to come near, the tribe of Benja-
min was chosen.
21 When he had caused the tribe of Benjamin
to come near by their families, the family of
Matri was chosen. And Saul the son of Kish
was chosen. But when they sought him, he
could not be found.
22 Therefore they inquired of the LORD fur-
ther, "Has the man come here yet?" And the
LORD answered, "There he is, hidden among
the equipment."
23 So they ran and brought him from there;
and when he stood among the people, he was
taller than any of the people from his shoulders
upward.
24 And Samuel said to all the people, "Do you
see him whom the LORD has chosen, that *there*
is no one like him among all the people?" So
all the people shouted and said, "Long live the
king!"
25 Then Samuel explained to the people the
behavior of royalty, and wrote *it* in a book and
laid *it* up before the LORD. And Samuel sent
all the people away, every man to his house.
26 And Saul also went home to Gibeah; and
valiant *men* went with him, whose hearts God
had touched.
27 But some rebels said, "How can this man
save us?" So they despised him, and brought
him no presents. But he held his peace.

Saul Saves Jabesh Gilead

11 Then Nahash the Ammonite came up
and encamped against Jabesh Gilead;
and all the men of Jabesh said to Nahash, "Make
a covenant with us, and we will serve you."
2 And Nahash the Ammonite answered
them, "On this *condition* I will make *a cov-*
enant with you, that I may put out all your
right eyes, and bring reproach on all Israel."
3 Then the elders of Jabesh said to him,
"Hold off for seven days, that we may send
messengers to all the territory of Israel. And
then, if *there is* no one to save us, we will come
out to you."
4 So the messengers came to Gibeah of Saul
and told the news in the hearing of the people.
And all the people lifted up their voices and
wept.
5 Now there was Saul, coming behind the
herd from the field; and Saul said, "What *trou-*
bles the people, that they weep?" And they told
him the words of the men of Jabesh.
6 Then the Spirit of God came upon Saul
when he heard this news, and his anger was
greatly aroused.
7 So he took a yoke of oxen and cut them
in pieces, and sent *them* throughout all the
territory of Israel by the hands of messengers,
saying, "Whoever does not go out with Saul
and Samuel to battle, so it shall be done to his
oxen." And the fear of the LORD fell on the
people, and they came out with one consent.
8 When he numbered them in Bezek, the
children of Israel were three hundred thou-
sand, and the men of Judah thirty thousand.
9 And they said to the messengers who
came, "Thus you shall say to the men of Jabesh
Gilead: 'Tomorrow, by *the time* the sun is hot,
you shall have help.'" Then the messengers
came and reported *it* to the men of Jabesh, and
they were glad.
10 Therefore the men of Jabesh said, "Tomor-
row we will come out to you, and you may do
with us whatever seems good to you."
11 So it was, on the next day, that Saul put
the people in three companies; and they came
into the midst of the camp in the morning
watch, and killed Ammonites until the heat of
the day. And it happened that those who sur-
vived were scattered, so that no two of them
were left together.
12 Then the people said to Samuel, "Who *is*
he who said, 'Shall Saul reign over us?' Bring
the men, that we may put them to death."
13 But Saul said, "Not a man shall be put to
death this day, for today the LORD has accom-
plished salvation in Israel."
14 Then Samuel said to the people, "Come, let
us go to Gilgal and renew the kingdom there."
15 So all the people went to Gilgal, and there
they made Saul king before the LORD in Gilgal.
There they made sacrifices of peace offerings
before the LORD, and there Saul and all the
men of Israel rejoiced greatly.

Samuel's Address at Saul's Coronation

12 Now Samuel said to all Israel: "Indeed I
have heeded your voice in all that you
said to me, and have made a king over you.
2 "And now here is the king, walking before
you; and I am old and grayheaded, and look,
my sons *are* with you. I have walked before
you from my childhood to this day.
3 "Here I am. Witness against me before the
LORD and before His anointed: Whose ox have
I taken, or whose donkey have I taken, or
whom have I cheated? Whom have I op-
pressed, or from whose hand have I received
any bribe with which to blind my eyes? I will
restore *it* to you."
4 And they said, "You have not cheated us
or oppressed us, nor have you taken anything
from any man's hand."
5 Then he said to them, "The LORD *is* wit-
ness against you, and His anointed *is* witness
this day, that you have not found anything in

10:19 [a]Literally *thousands*

my hand." And they answered, "*He is* wit-
ness."
6 Then Samuel said to the people, "*It is* the
LORD who raised up Moses and Aaron, and
who brought your fathers up from the land of
Egypt.
7 "Now therefore, stand still, that I may rea-
son with you before the LORD concerning all
the righteous acts of the LORD which He did
to you and your fathers:
8 "When Jacob had gone into Egypt,[a] and
your fathers cried out to the LORD, then the
LORD sent Moses and Aaron, who brought
your fathers out of Egypt and made them dwell
in this place.
9 "And when they forgot the LORD their
God, He sold them into the hand of Sisera,
commander of the army of Hazor, into the
hand of the Philistines, and into the hand of the
king of Moab; and they fought against them.
10 "Then they cried out to the LORD, and said,
'We have sinned, because we have forsaken
the LORD and served the Baals and Ashto-
reths;[a] but now deliver us from the hand of our
enemies, and we will serve You.'
11 "And the LORD sent Jerubbaal,[a] Bedan,[b]
Jephthah, and Samuel,[c] and delivered you out
of the hand of your enemies on every side; and
you dwelt in safety.
12 "And when you saw that Nahash king of
the Ammonites came against you, you said to
me, 'No, but a king shall reign over us,' when
the LORD your God *was* your king.
13 "Now therefore, here is the king whom
you have chosen *and* whom you have desired.
And take note, the LORD has set a king over
you.
14 "If you fear the LORD and serve Him and
obey His voice, and do not rebel against the
commandment of the LORD, then both you and
the king who reigns over you will continue
following the LORD your God.
15 "However, if you do not obey the voice of
the LORD, but rebel against the commandment
of the LORD, then the hand of the LORD will
be against you, as *it was* against your fathers.
16 "Now therefore, stand and see this great
thing which the LORD will do before your eyes:
17 "*Is* today not the wheat harvest? I will call
to the LORD, and He will send thunder and
rain, that you may perceive and see that your
wickedness *is* great, which you have done in
the sight of the LORD, in asking a king for
yourselves."
18 So Samuel called to the LORD, and the
LORD sent thunder and rain that day; and all
the people greatly feared the LORD and
Samuel.
19 And all the people said to Samuel, "Pray
for your servants to the LORD your God, that
we may not die; for we have added to all our
sins the evil of asking a king for ourselves."
20 Then Samuel said to the people, "Do not
fear. You have done all this wickedness; yet do
not turn aside from following the LORD, but
serve the LORD with all your heart.
21 "And do not turn aside; for *then you would
go* after empty things which cannot profit or
deliver, for they *are* nothing.
22 "For the LORD will not forsake His people,
for His great name's sake, because it has
pleased the LORD to make you His people.
23 "Moreover, as for me, far be it from me
that I should sin against the LORD in ceasing
to pray for you; but I will teach you the good
and the right way.
24 "Only fear the LORD, and serve Him in
truth with all your heart; for consider what
great things He has done for you.
25 "But if you still do wickedly, you shall be
swept away, both you and your king."

Saul's Unlawful Sacrifice

13 Saul reigned one year; and when he had
reigned two years over Israel,[a]
2 Saul chose for himself three thousand *men*
of Israel. Two thousand were with Saul in
Michmash and in the mountains of Bethel, and
a thousand were with Jonathan in Gibeah of
Benjamin. The rest of the people he sent away,
every man to his tent.
3 And Jonathan attacked the garrison of the
Philistines that *was* in Geba, and the Philis-
tines heard *of it*. Then Saul blew the trumpet
throughout all the land, saying, "Let the He-
brews hear!"
4 Now all Israel heard it said *that* Saul had
attacked a garrison of the Philistines, and *that*
Israel had also become an abomination to the
Philistines. And the people were called to-
gether to Saul at Gilgal.
5 Then the Philistines gathered together to
fight with Israel, thirty[a] thousand chariots and
six thousand horsemen, and people as the sand
which *is* on the seashore in multitude. And
they came up and encamped in Michmash, to
the east of Beth Aven.
6 When the men of Israel saw that they were
in danger (for the people were distressed), then
the people hid in caves, in thickets, in rocks, in
holes, and in pits.
7 And *some of* the Hebrews crossed over the
Jordan to the land of Gad and Gilead. As for
Saul, he *was* still in Gilgal, and all the people
followed him trembling.
8 Then he waited seven days, according to
the time set by Samuel. But Samuel did not
come to Gilgal; and the people were scattered
from him.
9 So Saul said, "Bring a burnt offering and
peace offerings here to me." And he offered
the burnt offering.
10 Now it happened, as soon as he had fin-
ished presenting the burnt offering, that Sam-
uel came; and Saul went out to meet him, that
he might greet him.
11 And Samuel said, "What have you done?"
Saul said, "When I saw that the people were
scattered from me, and *that* you did not come
within the days appointed, and *that* the Philis-
tines gathered together at Michmash,
12 "then I said, 'The Philistines will now
come down on me at Gilgal, and I have not
made supplication to the LORD.' Therefore I
felt compelled, and offered a burnt offering."
13 And Samuel said to Saul, "You have done
foolishly. You have not kept the commandment
of the LORD your God, which He commanded

12:8 [a]Following Masoretic Text, Targum, and Vulgate; Septuagint adds *and the Egyptians afflicted them.*
12:10 [a]Canaanite goddesses **12:11** [a]Syriac reads *Deborah;* Targum reads *Gideon.* [b]Septuagint and Syriac read *Barak;* Targum reads *Simson.* [c]Syriac reads *Simson.* **13:1** [a]The Hebrew is difficult (compare 2 Samuel 5:4; 2 Kings 14:2; see also 2 Samuel 2:10; Acts 13:21). **13:5** [a]Following Masoretic Text, Septuagint, Targum, and Vulgate; Syriac and some manuscripts of the Septuagint read *three.*

you. For now the LORD would have established
your kingdom over Israel forever.
14 "But now your kingdom shall not continue.
The LORD has sought for Himself a man after
His own heart, and the LORD has commanded
him *to be* commander over His people, because
you have not kept what the LORD commanded
you."
15 Then Samuel arose and went up from Gil-
gal to Gibeah of Benjamin.[a] And Saul num-
bered the people present with him, about six
hundred men.

No Weapons for the Army

16 Saul, Jonathan his son, and the people
present with them remained in Gibeah of Ben-
jamin. But the Philistines encamped in Mich-
mash.
17 Then raiders came out of the camp of the
Philistines in three companies. One company
turned onto the road to Ophrah, to the land of
Shual,
18 another company turned to the road *to*
Beth Horon, and another company turned *to*
the road of the border that overlooksthe Valley
of Zeboim toward the wilderness.
19 Now there was no blacksmith to be found
throughout all the land of Israel, for the Philis-
tines said, "Lest the Hebrews make swords or
spears."
20 But all the Israelites would go down to the
Philistines to sharpen each man's plowshare,
his mattock, his ax, and his sickle;
21 and the charge for a sharpening was a pim[a]
for the plowshares, the mattocks, the forks,
and the axes, and to set the points of the goads.
22 So it came about, on the day of battle, that
there was neither sword nor spear found in the
hand of any of the people who *were* with Saul
and Jonathan. But they were found with Saul
and Jonathan his son.
23 And the garrison of the Philistines went
out to the pass of Michmash.

Jonathan Defeats the Philistines

14 Now it happened one day that Jonathan
the son of Saul said to the young man
who bore his armor, "Come, let us go over to
the Philistines' garrison that *is* on the other
side." But he did not tell his father.
2 And Saul was sitting in the outskirts of
Gibeah under a pomegranate tree which *is* in
Migron. The people who *were* with him *were*
about six hundred men.
3 Ahijah the son of Ahitub, Ichabod's brother,
the son of Phinehas, the son of Eli, the LORD's
priest in Shiloh, was wearing an ephod. But the
people did not know that Jonathan had gone.
4 Between the passes, by which Jonathan
sought to go over to the Philistines' garrison,
there was a sharp rock on one side and a sharp
rock on the other side. And the name of one
was Bozez, and the name of the other Seneh.
5 The front of one faced northward opposite
Michmash, and the other southward opposite
Gibeah.
6 Then Jonathan said to the young man who
bore his armor, "Come, let us go over to the
garrison of these uncircumcised; it may be that
the LORD will work for us. For nothing re-
strains the LORD from saving by many or by
few."
7 So his armorbearer said to him, "Do all that
is in your heart. Go then; here I am with you,
according to your heart."
8 Then Jonathan said, "Very well, let us
cross over to *these* men, and we will show our-
selves to them.
9 "If they say thus to us, 'Wait until we come
to you,' then we will stand still in our place and
not go up to them.
10 "But if they say thus, 'Come up to us,' then
we will go up. For the LORD has delivered them
into our hand, and this *will be* a sign to us."
11 So both of them showed themselves to the
garrison of the Philistines. And the Philistines
said, "Look, the Hebrews are coming out of
the holes where they have hidden."
12 Then the men of the garrison called to Jon-
athan and his armorbearer, and said, "Come
up to us, and we will show you something."
Jonathan said to his armorbearer, "Come up
after me, for the LORD has delivered them into
the hand of Israel."
13 And Jonathan climbed up on his hands
and knees with his armorbearer after him; and
they fell before Jonathan. And as he came after
him, his armorbearer killed them.
14 That first slaughter which Jonathan and
his armorbearer made was about twenty men
within about half an acre of land.[a]
15 And there was trembling in the camp, in
the field, and among all the people. The garri-
son and the raiders also trembled; and the
earth quaked, so that it was a very great trem-
bling.
16 Now the watchmen of Saul in Gibeah of
Benjamin looked, and *there* was the multitude,
melting away; and they went here and there.
17 Then Saul said to the people who *were*
with him, "Now call the roll and see who has
gone from us." And when they had called the
roll, surprisingly, Jonathan and his armor-
bearer *were* not *there*.
18 And Saul said to Ahijah, "Bring the ark[a]
of God here" (for at that time the ark[b] of God
was with the children of Israel).
19 Now it happened, while Saul talked to the
priest, that the noise which *was* in the camp of
the Philistines continued to increase; so Saul
said to the priest, "Withdraw your hand."
20 Then Saul and all the people who *were*
with him assembled, and they went to the bat-
tle; and indeed every man's sword was against
his neighbor, *and there was* very great confu-
sion.
21 Moreover the Hebrews *who* were with the
Philistines before that time, who went up with
them into the camp *from the* surrounding
country, they also joined the Israelites who
were with Saul and Jonathan.
22 Likewise all the men of Israel who had
hidden in the mountains of Ephraim, *when*
they heard that the Philistines fled, they also
followed hard after them in the battle.
23 So the LORD saved Israel that day, and the
battle shifted to Beth Aven.

13:15 [a]Following Masoretic Text and Targum; Septuagint and Vulgate add *And the rest of the people went up after Saul to meet the people who fought against them, going from Gilgal to Gibeah in the hill of Benjamin.* **13:21** [a]About two-thirds shekel weight **14:14** [a]Literally *half the area plowed by a yoke* (of oxen in a day) **14:18** [a]Following Masoretic Text, Targum, and Vulgate; Septuagint reads *ephod.* [b]Following Masoretic Text, Targum, and Vulgate; Septuagint reads *ephod.*

Saul's Rash Oath

24 And the men of Israel were distressed that day, for Saul had placed the people under oath, saying, "Cursed *is* the man who eats *any* food until evening, before I have taken vengeance on my enemies." So none of the people tasted food.

25 Now all *the people* of the land came to a forest; and there was honey on the ground.

26 And when the people had come into the woods, there was the honey, dripping; but no one put his hand to his mouth, for the people feared the oath.

27 But Jonathan had not heard his father charge the people with the oath; therefore he stretched out the end of the rod that *was* in his hand and dipped it in a honeycomb, and put his hand to his mouth; and his countenance brightened.

28 Then one of the people said, "Your father strictly charged the people with an oath, saying, 'Cursed *is* the man who eats food this day.'" And the people were faint.

29 But Jonathan said, "My father has troubled the land. Look now, how my countenance has brightened because I tasted a little of this honey.

30 "How much better if the people had eaten freely today of the spoil of their enemies which they found! For now would there not have been a much greater slaughter among the Philistines?"

31 Now they had driven back the Philistines that day from Michmash to Aijalon. So the people were very faint.

32 And the people rushed on the spoil, and took sheep, oxen, and calves, and slaughtered *them* on the ground; and the people ate *them* with the blood.

33 Then they told Saul, saying, "Look, the people are sinning against the LORD by eating with the blood!" So he said, "You have dealt treacherously; roll a large stone to me this day."

34 Then Saul said, "Disperse yourselves among the people, and say to them, 'Bring me here every man's ox and every man's sheep, slaughter *them* here, and eat; and do not sin against the LORD by eating with the blood.'" So every one of the people brought his ox with him that night, and slaughtered *it* there.

35 Then Saul built an altar to the LORD. This was the first altar that he built to the LORD.

36 Now Saul said, "Let us go down after the Philistines by night, and plunder them until the morning light; and let us not leave a man of them." And they said, "Do whatever seems good to you." Then the priest said, "Let us draw near to God here."

37 So Saul asked counsel of God, "Shall I go down after the Philistines? Will You deliver them into the hand of Israel?" But He did not answer him that day.

38 And Saul said, "Come over here, all you chiefs of the people, and know and see what this sin was today.

39 "For *as* the LORD lives, who saves Israel, though it be in Jonathan my son, he shall surely die." But not a man among all the people answered him.

40 Then he said to all Israel, "You be on one side, and my son Jonathan and I will be on the other side." And the people said to Saul, "Do what seems good to you."

41 Therefore Saul said to the LORD God of Israel, "Give a perfect *lot*."[a] So Saul and Jonathan were taken, but the people escaped.

42 And Saul said, "Cast *lots* between my son Jonathan and me." So Jonathan was taken.

43 Then Saul said to Jonathan, "Tell me what you have done." And Jonathan told him, and said, "I only tasted a little honey with the end of the rod that *was* in my hand. So now I must die!"

44 Saul answered, "God do so and more also; for you shall surely die, Jonathan."

45 But the people said to Saul, "Shall Jonathan die, who has accomplished this great deliverance in Israel? Certainly not! *As* the LORD lives, not one hair of his head shall fall to the ground, for he has worked with God this day." So the people rescued Jonathan, and he did not die.

46 Then Saul returned from pursuing the Philistines, and the Philistines went to their own place.

Saul's Continuing Wars

47 So Saul established his sovereignty over Israel, and fought against all his enemies on every side, against Moab, against the people of Ammon, against Edom, against the kings of Zobah, and against the Philistines. Wherever he turned, he harassed *them*.[a]

48 And he gathered an army and attacked the Amalekites, and delivered Israel from the hands of those who plundered them.

49 The sons of Saul were Jonathan, Jishui,[a] and Malchishua. And the names of his two daughters *were these:* the name of the firstborn Merab, and the name of the younger Michal.

50 The name of Saul's wife *was* Ahinoam the daughter of Ahimaaz. And the name of the commander of his army *was* Abner the son of Ner, Saul's uncle.

51 Kish *was* the father of Saul, and Ner the father of Abner *was* the son of Abiel.

52 Now there was fierce war with the Philistines all the days of Saul. And when Saul saw any strong man or any valiant man, he took him for himself.

Saul Spares King Agag

15 Samuel also said to Saul, "The LORD sent me to anoint you king over His people, over Israel. Now therefore, heed the voice of the words of the LORD.

2 "Thus says the LORD of hosts: 'I will punish Amalek *for* what he did to Israel, how he ambushed him on the way when he came up from Egypt.

3 'Now go and attack Amalek, and utterly destroy all that they have, and do not spare them. But kill both man and woman, infant and nursing child, ox and sheep, camel and donkey.'"

4 So Saul gathered the people together and numbered them in Telaim, two hundred

14:41 [a]Following Masoretic Text and Targum; Septuagint and Vulgate read *Why do You not answer Your servant today? If the injustice is with me or Jonathan my son, O LORD God of Israel, give proof; and if You say it is with Your people Israel, give holiness.* **14:47** [a]Septuagint and Vulgate read *prospered.* **14:49** [a]Called *Abinadab* in 1 Chronicles 8:33 and 9:39

thousand foot soldiers and ten thousand men of Judah.

5 And Saul came to a city of Amalek, and lay in wait in the valley.

6 Then Saul said to the Kenites, "Go, depart, get down from among the Amalekites, lest I destroy you with them. For you showed kindness to all the children of Israel when they came up out of Egypt." So the Kenites departed from among the Amalekites.

7 And Saul attacked the Amalekites, from Havilah all the way to Shur, which is east of Egypt.

8 He also took Agag king of the Amalekites alive, and utterly destroyed all the people with the edge of the sword.

9 But Saul and the people spared Agag and the best of the sheep, the oxen, the fatlings, the lambs, and all *that was* good, and were unwilling to utterly destroy them. But everything despised and worthless, that they utterly destroyed.

Saul Rejected as King

10 Now the word of the LORD came to Samuel, saying,

11 "I greatly regret that I have set up Saul *as* king, for he has turned back from following Me, and has not performed My commandments." And it grieved Samuel, and he cried out to the LORD all night.

12 So when Samuel rose early in the morning to meet Saul, it was told Samuel, saying, "Saul went to Carmel, and indeed, he set up a monument for himself; and he has gone on around, passed by, and gone down to Gilgal."

13 Then Samuel went to Saul, and Saul said to him, "Blessed *are* you of the LORD! I have performed the commandment of the LORD."

14 But Samuel said, "What then *is* this bleating of the sheep in my ears, and the lowing of the oxen which I hear?"

15 And Saul said, "They have brought them from the Amalekites; for the people spared the best of the sheep and the oxen, to sacrifice to the LORD your God; and the rest we have utterly destroyed."

16 Then Samuel said to Saul, "Be quiet! And I will tell you what the LORD said to me last night." And he said to him, "Speak on."

17 So Samuel said, "When you *were* little in your own eyes, *were* you not head of the tribes of Israel? And did not the LORD anoint you king over Israel?

18 "Now the LORD sent you on a mission, and said, 'Go, and utterly destroy the sinners, the Amalekites, and fight against them until they are consumed.'

19 "Why then did you not obey the voice of the LORD? Why did you swoop down on the spoil, and do evil in the sight of the LORD?"

20 And Saul said to Samuel, "But I have obeyed the voice of the LORD, and gone on the mission on which the LORD sent me, and brought back Agag king of Amalek; I have utterly destroyed the Amalekites.

21 "But the people took of the plunder, sheep and oxen, the best of the things which should have been utterly destroyed, to sacrifice to the LORD your God in Gilgal."

22 So Samuel said:

"Has the LORD *as great* delight in burnt
offerings and sacrifices,
As in obeying the voice of the LORD?
Behold, to obey is better than sacrifice,
And to heed than the fat of rams.

23 For rebellion *is as* the sin of witchcraft,
And stubbornness *is as* iniquity and
idolatry.
Because you have rejected the word of
the LORD,
He also has rejected you from *being*
king."

24 Then Saul said to Samuel, "I have sinned, for I have transgressed the commandment of the LORD and your words, because I feared the people and obeyed their voice.

25 "Now therefore, please pardon my sin, and return with me, that I may worship the LORD."

26 But Samuel said to Saul, "I will not return with you, for you have rejected the word of the LORD, and the LORD has rejected you from being king over Israel."

27 And as Samuel turned around to go away, *Saul* seized the edge of his robe, and it tore.

28 So Samuel said to him, "The LORD has torn the kingdom of Israel from you today, and has given it to a neighbor of yours, *who is* better than you.

29 "And also the Strength of Israel will not lie nor relent. For He *is* not a man, that He should relent."

30 Then he said, "I have sinned; *yet* honor me now, please, before the elders of my people and before Israel, and return with me, that I may worship the LORD your God."

31 So Samuel turned back after Saul, and Saul worshiped the LORD.

32 Then Samuel said, "Bring Agag king of the Amalekites here to me." So Agag came to him cautiously. And Agag said, "Surely the bitterness of death is past."

33 But Samuel said, "As your sword has made women childless, so shall your mother be childless among women." And Samuel hacked Agag in pieces before the LORD in Gilgal.

34 Then Samuel went to Ramah, and Saul went up to his house at Gibeah of Saul.

35 And Samuel went no more to see Saul until the day of his death. Nevertheless Samuel mourned for Saul, and the LORD regretted that He had made Saul king over Israel.

David Anointed King

16 Now the LORD said to Samuel, "How long will you mourn for Saul, seeing I have rejected him from reigning over Israel? Fill your horn with oil, and go; I am sending you to Jesse the Bethlehemite. For I have provided Myself a king among his sons."

2 And Samuel said, "How can I go? If Saul hears *it*, he will kill me." But the LORD said, "Take a heifer with you, and say, 'I have come to sacrifice to the LORD.'

3 "Then invite Jesse to the sacrifice, and I will show you what you shall do; you shall anoint for Me the one I name to you."

4 So Samuel did what the LORD said, and went to Bethlehem. And the elders of the town trembled at his coming, and said, "Do you come peaceably?"

5 And he said, "Peaceably; I have come to sacrifice to the LORD. Sanctify yourselves, and come with me to the sacrifice." Then he consecrated Jesse and his sons, and invited them to the sacrifice.

6 So it was, when they came, that he looked

at Eliab and said, "Surely the LORD's anointed *is* before Him!"
7 But the LORD said to Samuel, "Do not look at his appearance or at his physical stature, because I have refused him. For *the LORD does* not *see* as man sees;[a] for man looks at the outward appearance, but the LORD looks at the heart."
8 So Jesse called Abinadab, and made him pass before Samuel. And he said, "Neither has the LORD chosen this one."
9 Then Jesse made Shammah pass by. And he said, "Neither has the LORD chosen this one."
10 Thus Jesse made seven of his sons pass before Samuel. And Samuel said to Jesse, "The LORD has not chosen these."
11 And Samuel said to Jesse, "Are all the young men here?" Then he said, "There remains yet the youngest, and there he is, keeping the sheep." And Samuel said to Jesse, "Send and bring him. For we will not sit down[a] till he comes here."
12 So he sent and brought him in. Now he *was* ruddy, with bright eyes, and good-looking. And the LORD said, "Arise, anoint him; for this *is* the one!"
13 Then Samuel took the horn of oil and anointed him in the midst of his brothers; and the Spirit of the LORD came upon David from that day forward. So Samuel arose and went to Ramah.

A Distressing Spirit Troubles Saul

14 But the Spirit of the LORD departed from Saul, and a distressing spirit from the LORD troubled him.
15 And Saul's servants said to him, "Surely, a distressing spirit from God is troubling you.
16 "Let our master now command your servants, *who are* before you, to seek out a man *who is* a skillful player on the harp. And it shall be that he will play it with his hand when the distressing spirit from God is upon you, and you shall be well."
17 So Saul said to his servants, "Provide me now a man who can play well, and bring *him* to me."
18 Then one of the servants answered and said, "Look, I have seen a son of Jesse the Bethlehemite, *who is* skillful in playing, a mighty man of valor, a man of war, prudent in speech, and a handsome person; and the LORD *is* with him."
19 Therefore Saul sent messengers to Jesse, and said, "Send me your son David, who *is* with the sheep."
20 And Jesse took a donkey *loaded with* bread, a skin of wine, and a young goat, and sent *them* by his son David to Saul.
21 So David came to Saul and stood before him. And he loved him greatly, and he became his armorbearer.
22 Then Saul sent to Jesse, saying, "Please let David stand before me, for he has found favor in my sight."
23 And so it was, whenever the spirit from God was upon Saul, that David would take a harp and play *it* with his hand. Then Saul would become refreshed and well, and the distressing spirit would depart from him.

David and Goliath

17 Now the Philistines gathered their armies together to battle, and were gathered at Sochoh, which *belongs* to Judah; they encamped between Sochoh and Azekah, in Ephes Dammim.
2 And Saul and the men of Israel were gathered together, and they encamped in the Valley of Elah, and drew up in battle array against the Philistines.
3 The Philistines stood on a mountain on one side, and Israel stood on a mountain on the other side, with a valley between them.
4 And a champion went out from the camp of the Philistines, named Goliath, from Gath, whose height *was* six cubits and a span.
5 *He had* a bronze helmet on his head, and he *was* armed with a coat of mail, and the weight of the coat *was* five thousand shekels of bronze.
6 And *he had* bronze armor on his legs and a bronze javelin between his shoulders.
7 Now the staff of his spear *was* like a weaver's beam, and his iron spearhead *weighed* six hundred shekels; and a shield-bearer went before him.
8 Then he stood and cried out to the armies of Israel, and said to them, "Why have you come out to line up for battle? *Am* I not a Philistine, and you the servants of Saul? Choose a man for yourselves, and let him come down to me.
9 "If he is able to fight with me and kill me, then we will be your servants. But if I prevail against him and kill him, then you shall be our servants and serve us."
10 And the Philistine said, "I defy the armies of Israel this day; give me a man, that we may fight together."
11 When Saul and all Israel heard these words of the Philistine, they were dismayed and greatly afraid.
12 Now David *was* the son of that Ephrathite of Bethlehem Judah, whose name *was* Jesse, and who had eight sons. And the man was old, advanced *in years,* in the days of Saul.
13 The three oldest sons of Jesse had gone to follow Saul to the battle. The names of his three sons who went to the battle *were* Eliab the firstborn, next to him Abinadab, and the third Shammah.
14 David *was* the youngest. And the three oldest followed Saul.
15 But David occasionally went and returned from Saul to feed his father's sheep at Bethlehem.
16 And the Philistine drew near and presented himself forty days, morning and evening.
17 Then Jesse said to his son David, "Take now for your brothers an ephah of this dried *grain* and these ten loaves, and run to your brothers at the camp.
18 "And carry these ten cheeses to the captain of *their* thousand, and see how your brothers fare, and bring back news of them."
19 Now Saul and they and all the men of Israel *were* in the Valley of Elah, fighting with the Philistines.
20 So David rose early in the morning, left the sheep with a keeper, and took *the things* and

16:7 [a]Septuagint reads *For God does not see as man sees;* Targum reads *It is not by the appearance of a man;* Vulgate reads *Nor do I judge according to the looks of a man.* **16:11** [a]Following Septuagint and Vulgate; Masoretic Text reads *turn around;* Targum and Syriac read *turn away.*

went as Jesse had commanded him. And he
came to the camp as the army was going out
to the fight and shouting for the battle.
21 For Israel and the Philistines had drawn
up in battle array, army against army.
22 And David left his supplies in the hand of
the supply keeper, ran to the army, and came
and greeted his brothers.
23 Then as he talked with them, there was the
champion, the Philistine of Gath, Goliath by
name, coming up from the armies of the Philis-
tines; and he spoke according to the same
words. So David heard *them*.
24 And all the men of Israel, when they saw
the man, fled from him and were dreadfully
afraid.
25 So the men of Israel said, "Have you seen
this man who has come up? Surely he has
come up to defy Israel; and it shall be *that* the
man who kills him the king will enrich with
great riches, will give him his daughter, and
give his father's house exemption *from taxes*
in Israel."
26 Then David spoke to the men who stood
by him, saying, "What shall be done for the
man who kills this Philistine and takes away
the reproach from Israel? For who *is* this un-
circumcised Philistine, that he should defy the
armies of the living God?"
27 And the people answered him in this man-
ner, saying, "So shall it be done for the man
who kills him."
28 Now Eliab his oldest brother heard when
he spoke to the men; and Eliab's anger was
aroused against David, and he said, "Why did
you come down here? And with whom have
you left those few sheep in the wilderness? I
know your pride and the insolence of your
heart, for you have come down to see the
battle."
29 And David said, "What have I done now?
Is there not a cause?"
30 Then he turned from him toward another
and said the same thing; and these people an-
swered him as the first ones *did*.
31 Now when the words which David spoke
were heard, they reported *them* to Saul; and
he sent for him.
32 Then David said to Saul, "Let no man's
heart fail because of him; your servant will go
and fight with this Philistine."
33 And Saul said to David, "You are not able
to go against this Philistine to fight with him;
for you *are* a youth, and he a man of war from
his youth."
34 But David said to Saul, "Your servant used
to keep his father's sheep, and when a lion or
a bear came and took a lamb out of the flock,
35 "I went out after it and struck it, and deliv-
ered *the lamb* from its mouth; and when it
arose against me, I caught *it* by its beard, and
struck and killed it.
36 "Your servant has killed both lion and bear;
and this uncircumcised Philistine will be like
one of them, seeing he has defied the armies
of the living God."
37 Moreover David said, "The LORD, who de-
livered me from the paw of the lion and from
the paw of the bear, He will deliver me from
the hand of this Philistine." And Saul said to
David, "Go, and the LORD be with you!"
38 So Saul clothed David with his armor, and
he put a bronze helmet on his head; he also
clothed him with a coat of mail.
39 David fastened his sword to his armor and
tried to walk, for he had not tested *them*. And
David said to Saul, "I cannot walk with these,
for I have not tested *them*." So David took
them off.
40 Then he took his staff in his hand; and he
chose for himself five smooth stones from the
brook, and put them in a shepherd's bag, in a
pouch which he had, and his sling was in his
hand. And he drew near to the Philistine.
41 So the Philistine came, and began drawing
near to David, and the man who bore the shield
went before him.
42 And when the Philistine looked about and
saw David, he disdained him; for he was *only*
a youth, ruddy and good-looking.
43 So the Philistine said to David, "*Am* I a
dog, that you come to me with sticks?" And
the Philistine cursed David by his gods.
44 And the Philistine said to David, "Come to
me, and I will give your flesh to the birds of
the air and the beasts of the field!"
45 Then David said to the Philistine, "You
come to me with a sword, with a spear, and
with a javelin. But I come to you in the name
of the LORD of hosts, the God of the armies of
Israel, whom you have defied.
46 "This day the LORD will deliver you into
my hand, and I will strike you and take your
head from you. And this day I will give the
carcasses of the camp of the Philistines to the
birds of the air and the wild beasts of the earth,
that all the earth may know that there is a God
in Israel.
47 "Then all this assembly shall know that
the LORD does not save with sword and spear;
for the battle *is* the LORD's, and He will give
you into our hands."
48 So it was, when the Philistine arose and
came and drew near to meet David, that David
hurried and ran toward the army to meet the
Philistine.
49 Then David put his hand in his bag and
took out a stone; and he slung *it* and struck
the Philistine in his forehead, so that the stone
sank into his forehead, and he fell on his face
to the earth.
50 So David prevailed over the Philistine with
a sling and a stone, and struck the Philistine
and killed him. But *there was* no sword in the
hand of David.
51 Therefore David ran and stood over the
Philistine, took his sword and drew it out of its
sheath and killed him, and cut off his head
with it. And when the Philistines saw that their
champion was dead, they fled.
52 Now the men of Israel and Judah arose
and shouted, and pursued the Philistines as far
as the entrance of the valley[a] and to the gates
of Ekron. And the wounded of the Philistines
fell along the road to Shaaraim, even as far as
Gath and Ekron.
53 Then the children of Israel returned from
chasing the Philistines, and they plundered their
tents.
54 And David took the head of the Philistine
and brought it to Jerusalem, but he put his ar-
mor in his tent.
55 When Saul saw David going out against the
Philistine, he said to Abner, the commander of
the army, "Abner, whose son *is* this youth?" And

17:52 [a]Following Masoretic Text, Syriac, Targum, and Vulgate; Septuagint reads *Gath*.

Abner said, "As your soul lives, O king, I do not
know."
56 So the king said, "Inquire whose son this
young man *is*."
57 Then, as David returned from the slaughter of the Philistine, Abner took him and
brought him before Saul with the head of the
Philistine in his hand.
58 And Saul said to him, "Whose son *are* you,
young man?" So David answered, "*I am* the
son of your servant Jesse the Bethlehemite."

Saul Resents David

18 Now when he had finished speaking to
Saul, the soul of Jonathan was knit to
the soul of David, and Jonathan loved him as
his own soul.
2 Saul took him that day, and would not let
him go home to his father's house anymore.
3 Then Jonathan and David made a covenant, because he loved him as his own soul.
4 And Jonathan took off the robe that *was*
on him and gave it to David, with his armor,
even to his sword and his bow and his belt.
5 So David went out wherever Saul sent him,
and behaved wisely. And Saul set him over the
men of war, and he was accepted in the sight
of all the people and also in the sight of Saul's
servants.
6 Now it had happened as they were coming
home, when David was returning from the
slaughter of the Philistine, that the women had
come out of all the cities of Israel, singing and
dancing, to meet King Saul, with tambourines,
with joy, and with musical instruments.
7 So the women sang as they danced, and
said:

"Saul has slain his thousands,
And David his ten thousands."

8 Then Saul was very angry, and the saying
displeased him; and he said, "They have ascribed to David ten thousands, and to me they
have ascribed *only* thousands. Now *what* more
can he have but the kingdom?"
9 So Saul eyed David from that day forward.
10 And it happened on the next day that the
distressing spirit from God came upon Saul,
and he prophesied inside the house. So David
played *music* with his hand, as at other times;
but *there was* a spear in Saul's hand.
11 And Saul cast the spear, for he said, "I will
pin David to the wall!" But David escaped his
presence twice.
12 Now Saul was afraid of David, because the
LORD was with him, but had departed from
Saul.
13 Therefore Saul removed him from his presence, and made him his captain over a thousand; and he went out and came in before the
people.
14 And David behaved wisely in all his ways,
and the LORD *was* with him.
15 Therefore, when Saul saw that he behaved
very wisely, he was afraid of him.
16 But all Israel and Judah loved David, because he went out and came in before them.

David Marries Michal

17 Then Saul said to David, "Here is my older
daughter Merab; I will give her to you as a wife.
Only be valiant for me, and fight the LORD's
battles." For Saul thought, "Let my hand not
be against him, but let the hand of the Philistines be against him."
18 So David said to Saul, "Who *am* I, and
what *is* my life *or* my father's family in Israel,
that I should be son-in-law to the king?"
19 But it happened at the time when Merab,
Saul's daughter, should have been given to David, that she was given to Adriel the Meholathite as a wife.
20 Now Michal, Saul's daughter, loved David.
And they told Saul, and the thing pleased him.
21 So Saul said, "I will give her to him, that
she may be a snare to him, and that the hand of
the Philistines may be against him." Therefore
Saul said to David a second time, "You shall
be my son-in-law today."
22 And Saul commanded his servants, "Communicate with David secretly, and say, 'Look,
the king has delight in you, and all his servants
love you. Now therefore, become the king's
son-in-law.'"
23 So Saul's servants spoke those words in
the hearing of David. And David said, "Does
it seem to you *a* light *thing* to be a king's son-in-law, seeing I *am* a poor and lightly esteemed
man?"
24 And the servants of Saul told him, saying,
"In this manner David spoke."
25 Then Saul said, "Thus you shall say to David: 'The king does not desire any dowry but
one hundred foreskins of the Philistines, to
take vengeance on the king's enemies.'" But
Saul thought to make David fall by the hand
of the Philistines.
26 So when his servants told David these
words, it pleased David well to become the king's
son-in-law. Now the days had not expired;
27 therefore David arose and went, he and his
men, and killed two hundred men of the Philistines. And David brought their foreskins, and
they gave them in full count to the king, that
he might become the king's son-in-law. Then
Saul gave him Michal his daughter as a wife.
28 Thus Saul saw and knew that the LORD *was*
with David, and *that* Michal, Saul's daughter,
loved him;
29 and Saul was still more afraid of David. So
Saul became David's enemy continually.
30 Then the princes of the Philistines went
out *to war*. And so it was, whenever they went
out, *that* David behaved more wisely than all
the servants of Saul, so that his name became
highly esteemed.

Saul Persecutes David

19 Now Saul spoke to Jonathan his son and
to all his servants, that they should kill
David; but Jonathan, Saul's son, delighted
greatly in David.
2 So Jonathan told David, saying, "My father
Saul seeks to kill you. Therefore please be on
your guard until morning, and stay in a secret
place and hide.
3 "And I will go out and stand beside my
father in the field where you *are*, and I will
speak with my father about you. Then what I
observe, I will tell you."
4 Thus Jonathan spoke well of David to Saul
his father, and said to him, "Let not the king
sin against his servant, against David, because
he has not sinned against you, and because his
works *have been* very good toward you.
5 "For he took his life in his hands and killed
the Philistine, and the LORD brought about a
great deliverance for all Israel. You saw *it* and
rejoiced. Why then will you sin against innocent blood, to kill David without a cause?"

6 So Saul heeded the voice of Jonathan, and
Saul swore, "*As* the LORD lives, he shall not be
killed."
7 Then Jonathan called David, and Jonathan
told him all these things. So Jonathan brought
David to Saul, and he was in his presence as
in times past.
8 And there was war again; and David went
out and fought with the Philistines, and struck
them with a mighty blow, and they fled from
him.
9 Now the distressing spirit from the LORD
came upon Saul as he sat in his house with
his spear in his hand. And David was playing
music with *his* hand.
10 Then Saul sought to pin David to the wall
with the spear, but he slipped away from Saul's
presence; and he drove the spear into the wall.
So David fled and escaped that night.
11 Saul also sent messengers to David's
house to watch him and to kill him in the morn-
ing. And Michal, David's wife, told him, say-
ing, "If you do not save your life tonight,
tomorrow you will be killed."
12 So Michal let David down through a win-
dow. And he went and fled and escaped.
13 And Michal took an image and laid *it* in
the bed, put a cover of goats' *hair* for his head,
and covered *it* with clothes.
14 So when Saul sent messengers to take Da-
vid, she said, "He *is* sick."
15 Then Saul sent the messengers *back* to see
David, saying, "Bring him up to me in the bed,
that I may kill him."
16 And when the messengers had come in,
there was the image in the bed, with a cover of
goats' *hair* for his head.
17 Then Saul said to Michal, "Why have you
deceived me like this, and sent my enemy
away, so that he has escaped?" And Michal
answered Saul, "He said to me, 'Let me go!
Why should I kill you?'"
18 So David fled and escaped, and went to
Samuel at Ramah, and told him all that Saul
had done to him. And he and Samuel went and
stayed in Naioth.
19 Now it was told Saul, saying, "Take note,
David *is* at Naioth in Ramah!"
20 Then Saul sent messengers to take David.
And when they saw the group of prophets
prophesying, and Samuel standing *as* leader
over them, the Spirit of God came upon the
messengers of Saul, and they also prophesied.
21 And when Saul was told, he sent other
messengers, and they prophesied likewise.
Then Saul sent messengers again the third time,
and they prophesied also.
22 Then he also went to Ramah, and came to
the great well that *is* at Sechu. So he asked,
and said, "Where *are* Samuel and David?" And
someone said, "Indeed *they are* at Naioth in
Ramah."
23 So he went there to Naioth in Ramah. Then
the Spirit of God was upon him also, and he
went on and prophesied until he came to Nai-
oth in Ramah.
24 And he also stripped off his clothes and
prophesied before Samuel in like manner, and
lay down naked all that day and all that night.
Therefore they say, "*Is* Saul also among the
prophets?"[a]

Jonathan's Loyalty to David

20 Then David fled from Naioth in Ramah,
and went and said to Jonathan, "What
have I done? What *is* my iniquity, and what *is*
my sin before your father, that he seeks my
life?"
2 So Jonathan said to him, "By no means!
You shall not die! Indeed, my father will do
nothing either great or small without first tell-
ing me. And why should my father hide this
thing from me? It *is* not *so!*"
3 Then David took an oath again, and said,
"Your father certainly knows that I have found
favor in your eyes, and he has said, 'Do not let
Jonathan know this, lest he be grieved.' But
truly, *as* the LORD lives and *as* your soul lives,
there is but a step between me and death."
4 So Jonathan said to David, "Whatever you
yourself desire, I will do *it* for you."
5 And David said to Jonathan, "Indeed to-
morrow *is* the New Moon, and I should not fail
to sit with the king to eat. But let me go, that
I may hide in the field until the third *day* at
evening.
6 "If your father misses me at all, then say,
'David earnestly asked *permission* of me that
he might run over to Bethlehem, his city, for
there is a yearly sacrifice there for all the family.'
7 "If he says thus: '*It is* well,' your servant
will be safe. But if he is very angry, be sure that
evil is determined by him.
8 "Therefore you shall deal kindly with your
servant, for you have brought your servant into
a covenant of the LORD with you. Neverthe-
less, if there is iniquity in me, kill me yourself,
for why should you bring me to your father?"
9 But Jonathan said, "Far be it from you! For
if I knew certainly that evil was determined by
my father to come upon you, then would I not
tell you?"
10 Then David said to Jonathan, "Who will tell
me, or what *if* your father answers you roughly?"
11 And Jonathan said to David, "Come, let us
go out into the field." So both of them went out
into the field.
12 Then Jonathan said to David: "The LORD
God of Israel *is witness!* When I have sounded
out my father sometime tomorrow, *or* the third
day, and indeed *there is* good toward David,
and I do not send to you and tell you,
13 "may the LORD do so and much more to
Jonathan. But if it pleases my father *to do* you
evil, then I will report it to you and send you
away, that you may go in safety. And the LORD
be with you as He has been with my father.
14 "And you shall not only show me the kind-
ness of the LORD while I still live, that I may
not die;
15 "but you shall not cut off your kindness
from my house forever, no, not when the LORD
has cut off every one of the enemies of David
from the face of the earth."
16 So Jonathan made *a covenant* with the
house of David, *saying*, "Let the LORD require
it at the hand of David's enemies."
17 Now Jonathan again caused David to vow,
because he loved him; for he loved him as he
loved his own soul.
18 Then Jonathan said to David, "Tomorrow
is the New Moon; and you will be missed, be-
cause your seat will be empty.
19 "And *when* you have stayed three days, go

19:24 [a]Compare 1 Samuel 10:12

down quickly and come to the place where you hid on the day of the deed; and remain by the stone Ezel.

20 "Then I will shoot three arrows to the side, as though I shot at a target;

21 "and there I will send a lad, *saying,* 'Go, find the arrows.' If I expressly say to the lad, 'Look, the arrows *are* on this side of you; get them and come'—then, as the LORD lives, *there is* safety for you and no harm.

22 "But if I say thus to the young man, 'Look, the arrows *are* beyond you'—go your way, for the LORD has sent you away.

23 "And as for the matter which you and I have spoken of, indeed the LORD *be* between you and me forever."

24 Then David hid in the field. And when the New Moon had come, the king sat down to eat the feast.

25 Now the king sat on his seat, as at other times, on a seat by the wall. And Jonathan arose,[a] and Abner sat by Saul's side, but David's place was empty.

26 Nevertheless Saul did not say anything that day, for he thought, "Something has happened to him; he *is* unclean, surely he *is* unclean."

27 And it happened the next day, the second *day* of the month, that David's place was empty. And Saul said to Jonathan his son, "Why has the son of Jesse not come to eat, either yesterday or today?"

28 So Jonathan answered Saul, "David earnestly asked *permission* of me *to go* to Bethlehem.

29 "And he said, 'Please let me go, for our family has a sacrifice in the city, and my brother has commanded me *to be there.* And now, if I have found favor in your eyes, please let me get away and see my brothers.' Therefore he has not come to the king's table."

30 Then Saul's anger was aroused against Jonathan, and he said to him, "You son of a perverse, rebellious *woman!* Do I not know that you have chosen the son of Jesse to your own shame and to the shame of your mother's nakedness?

31 "For as long as the son of Jesse lives on the earth, you shall not be established, nor your kingdom. Now therefore, send and bring him to me, for he shall surely die."

32 And Jonathan answered Saul his father, and said to him, "Why should he be killed? What has he done?"

33 Then Saul cast a spear at him to kill him, by which Jonathan knew that it was determined by his father to kill David.

34 So Jonathan arose from the table in fierce anger, and ate no food the second day of the month, for he was grieved for David, because his father had treated him shamefully.

35 And so it was, in the morning, that Jonathan went out into the field at the time appointed with David, and a little lad *was* with him.

36 Then he said to his lad, "Now run, find the arrows which I shoot." As the lad ran, he shot an arrow beyond him.

37 When the lad had come to the place where the arrow was which Jonathan had shot, Jonathan cried out after the lad and said, "*Is* not the arrow beyond you?"

38 And Jonathan cried out after the lad, "Make haste, hurry, do not delay!" So Jonathan's lad gathered up the arrows and came back to his master.

39 But the lad did not know anything. Only Jonathan and David knew of the matter.

40 Then Jonathan gave his weapons to his lad, and said to him, "Go, carry *them* to the city."

41 As soon as the lad had gone, David arose from *a place* toward the south, fell on his face to the ground, and bowed down three times. And they kissed one another; and they wept together, but David more so.

42 Then Jonathan said to David, "Go in peace, since we have both sworn in the name of the LORD, saying, 'May the LORD be between you and me, and between your descendants and my descendants, forever.' " So he arose and departed, and Jonathan went into the city.

David and the Holy Bread

21 Now David came to Nob, to Ahimelech the priest. And Ahimelech was afraid when he met David, and said to him, "Why *are* you alone, and no one is with you?"

2 So David said to Ahimelech the priest, "The king has ordered me on some business, and said to me, 'Do not let anyone know anything about the business on which I send you, or what I have commanded you.' And I have directed *my* young men to such and such a place.

3 "Now therefore, what have you on hand? Give *me* five *loaves of* bread in my hand, or whatever can be found."

4 And the priest answered David and said, "*There is* no common bread on hand; but there is holy bread, if the young men have at least kept themselves from women."

5 Then David answered the priest, and said to him, "Truly, women *have been* kept from us about three days since I came out. And the vessels of the young men are holy, and *the bread is* in effect common, even though it was consecrated in the vessel this day."

6 So the priest gave him holy *bread;* for there was no bread there but the showbread which had been taken from before the LORD, in order to put hot bread *in its place* on the day when it was taken away.

7 Now a certain man of the servants of Saul *was* there that day, detained before the LORD. And his name *was* Doeg, an Edomite, the chief of the herdsmen who *belonged* to Saul.

8 And David said to Ahimelech, "Is there not here on hand a spear or a sword? For I have brought neither my sword nor my weapons with me, because the king's business required haste."

9 So the priest said, "The sword of Goliath the Philistine, whom you killed in the Valley of Elah, there it is, wrapped in a cloth behind the ephod. If you will take that, take *it.* For *there is* no other except that one here." And David said, "*There is* none like it; give it to me."

David Flees to Gath

10 Then David arose and fled that day from before Saul, and went to Achish the king of Gath.

11 And the servants of Achish said to him, "*Is* this not David the king of the land? Did they not sing of him to one another in dances, saying:

20:25 [a]Following Masoretic Text, Syriac, Targum, and Vulgate; Septuagint reads *he sat across from Jonathan.*

'Saul has slain his thousands,
And David his ten thousands'?"[a]

12 Now David took these words to heart, and was very much afraid of Achish the king of Gath.

13 So he changed his behavior before them, pretended madness in their hands, scratched on the doors of the gate, and let his saliva fall down on his beard.

14 Then Achish said to his servants, "Look, you see the man is insane. Why have you brought him to me?

15 "Have I need of madmen, that you have brought this *fellow* to play the madman in my presence? Shall this *fellow* come into my house?"

David's Four Hundred Men

22 David therefore departed from there and escaped to the cave of Adullam. So when his brothers and all his father's house heard *it*, they went down there to him.

2 And everyone *who was* in distress, everyone who *was* in debt, and everyone *who was* discontented gathered to him. So he became captain over them. And there were about four hundred men with him.

3 Then David went from there to Mizpah of Moab; and he said to the king of Moab, "Please let my father and mother come here with you, till I know what God will do for me."

4 So he brought them before the king of Moab, and they dwelt with him all the time that David was in the stronghold.

5 Now the prophet Gad said to David, "Do not stay in the stronghold; depart, and go to the land of Judah." So David departed and went into the forest of Hereth.

Saul Murders the Priests

6 When Saul heard that David and the men who *were* with him had been discovered—now Saul was staying in Gibeah under a tamarisk tree in Ramah, with his spear in his hand, and all his servants standing about him—

7 then Saul said to his servants who stood about him, "Hear now, you Benjamites! Will the son of Jesse give every one of you fields and vineyards, *and* make you all captains of thousands and captains of hundreds?

8 "All of you have conspired against me, and *there is* no one who reveals to me that my son has made a covenant with the son of Jesse; and *there is* not one of you who is sorry for me or reveals to me that my son has stirred up my servant against me, to lie in wait, as *it is* this day."

9 Then answered Doeg the Edomite, who was set over the servants of Saul, and said, "I saw the son of Jesse going to Nob, to Ahimelech the son of Ahitub.

10 "And he inquired of the LORD for him, gave him provisions, and gave him the sword of Goliath the Philistine."

11 So the king sent to call Ahimelech the priest, the son of Ahitub, and all his father's house, the priests who *were* in Nob. And they all came to the king.

12 And Saul said, "Hear now, son of Ahitub!" He answered, "Here I am, my lord."

13 Then Saul said to him, "Why have you conspired against me, you and the son of Jesse, in that you have given him bread and a sword, and have inquired of God for him, that he should rise against me, to lie in wait, as it is this day?"

14 So Ahimelech answered the king and said, "And who among all your servants *is as* faithful as David, who is the king's son-in-law, who goes at your bidding, and is honorable in your house?

15 "Did I then begin to inquire of God for him? Far be it from me! Let not the king impute anything to his servant, *or* to any in the house of my father. For your servant knew nothing of all this, little or much."

16 And the king said, "You shall surely die, Ahimelech, you and all your father's house!"

17 Then the king said to the guards who stood about him, "Turn and kill the priests of the LORD, because their hand also *is* with David, and because they knew when he fled and did not tell it to me." But the servants of the king would not lift their hands to strike the priests of the LORD.

18 And the king said to Doeg, "You turn and kill the priests!" So Doeg the Edomite turned and struck the priests, and killed on that day eighty-five men who wore a linen ephod.

19 Also Nob, the city of the priests, he struck with the edge of the sword, both men and women, children and nursing infants, oxen and donkeys and sheep—with the edge of the sword.

20 Now one of the sons of Ahimelech the son of Ahitub, named Abiathar, escaped and fled after David.

21 And Abiathar told David that Saul had killed the LORD's priests.

22 So David said to Abiathar, "I knew that day, when Doeg the Edomite *was* there, that he would surely tell Saul. I have caused *the death* of all the persons of your father's house.

23 "Stay with me; do not fear. For he who seeks my life seeks your life, but with me you *shall be* safe."

David Saves the City of Keilah

23 Then they told David, saying, "Look, the Philistines are fighting against Keilah, and they are robbing the threshing floors."

2 Therefore David inquired of the LORD, saying, "Shall I go and attack these Philistines?" And the LORD said to David, "Go and attack the Philistines, and save Keilah."

3 But David's men said to him, "Look, we are afraid here in Judah. How much more then if we go to Keilah against the armies of the Philistines?"

4 Then David inquired of the LORD once again. And the LORD answered him and said, "Arise, go down to Keilah. For I will deliver the Philistines into your hand."

5 And David and his men went to Keilah and fought with the Philistines, struck them with a mighty blow, and took away their livestock. So David saved the inhabitants of Keilah.

6 Now it happened, when Abiathar the son of Ahimelech fled to David at Keilah, *that* he went down *with* an ephod in his hand.

7 And Saul was told that David had gone to Keilah. So Saul said, "God has delivered him into my hand, for he has shut himself in by entering a town that has gates and bars."

8 Then Saul called all the people together for

21:11 [a]Compare 1 Samuel 18:7

war, to go down to Keilah to besiege David and
his men.
9 When David knew that Saul plotted evil
against him, he said to Abiathar the priest,
"Bring the ephod here."
10 Then David said, "O LORD God of Israel,
Your servant has certainly heard that Saul
seeks to come to Keilah to destroy the city for
my sake.
11 "Will the men of Keilah deliver me into his
hand? Will Saul come down, as Your servant
has heard? O LORD God of Israel, I pray, tell
Your servant." And the LORD said, "He will
come down."
12 Then David said, "Will the men of Keilah
deliver me and my men into the hand of Saul?"
And the LORD said, "They will deliver *you*."
13 So David and his men, about six hundred,
arose and departed from Keilah and went
wherever they could go. Then it was told Saul
that David had escaped from Keilah; so he
halted the expedition.

David in Wilderness Strongholds

14 And David stayed in strongholds in the
wilderness, and remained in the mountains in
the Wilderness of Ziph. Saul sought him every
day, but God did not deliver him into his hand.
15 So David saw that Saul had come out to
seek his life. And David *was* in the Wilderness
of Ziph in a forest.[a]
16 Then Jonathan, Saul's son, arose and went
to David in the woods and strengthened his
hand in God.
17 And he said to him, "Do not fear, for the
hand of Saul my father shall not find you. You
shall be king over Israel, and I shall be next to
you. Even my father Saul knows that."
18 So the two of them made a covenant before
the LORD. And David stayed in the woods, and
Jonathan went to his own house.
19 Then the Ziphites came up to Saul at Gib-
eah, saying, "Is David not hiding with us in
strongholds in the woods, in the hill of Hachi-
lah, which *is* on the south of Jeshimon?
20 "Now therefore, O king, come down ac-
cording to all the desire of your soul to come
down; and our part *shall be* to deliver him into
the king's hand."
21 And Saul said, "Blessed *are* you of the
LORD, for you have compassion on me.
22 "Please go and find out for sure, and see
the place where his hideout is, *and* who has
seen him there. For I am told he is very crafty.
23 "See therefore, and take knowledge of all
the lurking places where he hides; and come
back to me with certainty, and I will go with
you. And it shall be, if he is in the land, that I
will search for him throughout all the clans[a] of
Judah."
24 So they arose and went to Ziph before
Saul. But David and his men *were* in the Wil-
derness of Maon, in the plain on the south of
Jeshimon.
25 When Saul and his men went to seek *him*,
they told David. Therefore he went down to
the rock, and stayed in the Wilderness of
Maon. And when Saul heard *that*, he pursued
David in the Wilderness of Maon.
26 Then Saul went on one side of the moun-
tain, and David and his men on the other side
of the mountain. So David made haste to get
away from Saul, for Saul and his men were
encircling David and his men to take them.
27 But a messenger came to Saul, saying,
"Hurry and come, for the Philistines have in-
vaded the land!"
28 Therefore Saul returned from pursuing
David, and went against the Philistines; so
they called that place the Rock of Escape.[a]
29 Then David went up from there and dwelt
in strongholds at En Gedi.

David Spares Saul

24 Now it happened, when Saul had re-
turned from following the Philistines,
that it was told him, saying, "Take note! David
is in the Wilderness of En Gedi."
2 Then Saul took three thousand chosen
men from all Israel, and went to seek David
and his men on the Rocks of the Wild Goats.
3 So he came to the sheepfolds by the road,
where there *was* a cave; and Saul went in to
attend to his needs. (David and his men were
staying in the recesses of the cave.)
4 Then the men of David said to him, "This
is the day of which the LORD said to you, 'Be-
hold, I will deliver your enemy into your hand,
that you may do to him as it seems good to
you.'" And David arose and secretly cut off a
corner of Saul's robe.
5 Now it happened afterward that David's
heart troubled him because he had cut Saul's
robe.
6 And he said to his men, "The LORD forbid
that I should do this thing to my master, the
LORD's anointed, to stretch out my hand
against him, seeing he *is* the anointed of the
LORD."
7 So David restrained his servants with
these words, and did not allow them to rise
against Saul. And Saul got up from the cave
and went on *his* way.
8 David also arose afterward, went out of the
cave, and called out to Saul, saying, "My lord
the king!" And when Saul looked behind him,
David stooped with his face to the earth, and
bowed down.
9 And David said to Saul: "Why do you lis-
ten to the words of men who say, 'Indeed David
seeks your harm'?
10 "Look, this day your eyes have seen that
the LORD delivered you today into my hand in
the cave, and *someone* urged *me* to kill you.
But *my eye* spared you, and I said, 'I will not
stretch out my hand against my lord, for he *is*
the LORD's anointed.'
11 "Moreover, my father, see! Yes, see the cor-
ner of your robe in my hand! For in that I cut
off the corner of your robe, and did not kill
you, know and see that *there is* neither evil nor
rebellion in my hand, and I have not sinned
against you. Yet you hunt my life to take it.
12 "Let the LORD judge between you and me,
and let the LORD avenge me on you. But my
hand shall not be against you.
13 "As the proverb of the ancients says,
'Wickedness proceeds from the wicked.' But
my hand shall not be against you.
14 "After whom has the king of Israel come
out? Whom do you pursue? A dead dog? A flea?
15 "Therefore let the LORD be judge, and judge
between you and me, and see and plead my
case, and deliver me out of your hand."

23:15 [a]Or *in Horesh* **23:23** [a]Literally *thousands* **23:28** [a]Hebrew *Sela Hammahlekoth*

16 So it was, when David had finished speak-
ing these words to Saul, that Saul said, "*Is* this
your voice, my son David?" And Saul lifted up
his voice and wept.
17 Then he said to David: "You *are* more righ-
teous than I; for you have rewarded me with
good, whereas I have rewarded you with evil.
18 "And you have shown this day how you
have dealt well with me; for when the LORD
delivered me into your hand, you did not kill
me.
19 "For if a man finds his enemy, will he let
him get away safely? Therefore may the LORD
reward you with good for what you have done
to me this day.
20 "And now I know indeed that you shall
surely be king, and that the kingdom of Israel
shall be established in your hand.
21 "Therefore swear now to me by the LORD
that you will not cut off my descendants after
me, and that you will not destroy my name
from my father's house."
22 So David swore to Saul. And Saul went
home, but David and his men went up to the
stronghold.

Death of Samuel

25 Then Samuel died; and the Israelites
gathered together and lamented for
him, and buried him at his home in Ramah.
And David arose and went down to the Wilder-
ness of Paran.[a]

David and the Wife of Nabal

2 Now *there was* a man in Maon whose busi-
ness *was* in Carmel, and the man *was* very
rich. He had three thousand sheep and a thou-
sand goats. And he was shearing his sheep in
Carmel.
3 The name of the man *was* Nabal, and the
name of his wife Abigail. And *she was* a woman
of good understanding and beautiful appear-
ance; but the man *was* harsh and evil in *his*
doings. He *was of the house of* Caleb.
4 When David heard in the wilderness that
Nabal was shearing his sheep,
5 David sent ten young men; and David said
to the young men, "Go up to Carmel, go to
Nabal, and greet him in my name.
6 "And thus you shall say to him who lives
in prosperity: 'Peace *be* to you, peace to your
house, and peace to all that you have!
7 'Now I have heard that you have shearers.
Your shepherds were with us, and we did not
hurt them, nor was there anything missing
from them all the while they were in Carmel.
8 'Ask your young men, and they will tell
you. Therefore let *my* young men find favor in
your eyes, for we come on a feast day. Please
give whatever comes to your hand to your ser-
vants and to your son David.'"
9 So when David's young men came, they
spoke to Nabal according to all these words in
the name of David, and waited.
10 Then Nabal answered David's servants,
and said, "Who *is* David, and who *is* the son of
Jesse? There are many servants nowadays
who break away each one from his master.
11 "Shall I then take my bread and my water
and my meat that I have killed for my shearers,
and give *it* to men when I do not know where
they *are* from?"
12 So David's young men turned on their
heels and went back; and they came and told
him all these words.
13 Then David said to his men, "Every man
gird on his sword." So every man girded on his
sword, and David also girded on his sword.
And about four hundred men went with David,
and two hundred stayed with the supplies.
14 Now one of the young men told Abigail,
Nabal's wife, saying, "Look, David sent messen-
gers from the wilderness to greet our master;
and he reviled them.
15 "But the men *were* very good to us, and
we were not hurt, nor did we miss anything as
long as we accompanied them, when we were
in the fields.
16 "They were a wall to us both by night and
day, all the time we were with them keeping the
sheep.
17 "Now therefore, know and consider what
you will do, for harm is determined against our
master and against all his household. For he
is such a scoundrel[a] that *one* cannot speak to
him."
18 Then Abigail made haste and took two
hundred *loaves* of bread, two skins of wine,
five sheep already dressed, five seahs of
roasted *grain,* one hundred clusters of raisins,
and two hundred cakes of figs, and loaded
them on donkeys.
19 And she said to her servants, "Go on be-
fore me; see, I am coming after you." But she
did not tell her husband Nabal.
20 So it was, *as* she rode on the donkey, that
she went down under cover of the hill; and
there were David and his men, coming down
toward her, and she met them.
21 Now David had said, "Surely in vain I have
protected all that this *fellow* has in the wilder-
ness, so that nothing was missed of all that
belongs to him. And he has repaid me evil for
good.
22 "May God do so, and more also, to the
enemies of David, if I leave one male of all who
belong to him by morning light."
23 Now when Abigail saw David, she dis-
mounted quickly from the donkey, fell on her
face before David, and bowed down to the
ground.
24 So she fell at his feet and said: "On me, my
lord, *on* me *let* this iniquity *be!* And please let
your maidservant speak in your ears, and hear
the words of your maidservant.
25 "Please, let not my lord regard this scoun-
drel Nabal. For as his name *is,* so *is* he: Nabal[a]
is his name, and folly *is* with him! But I, your
maidservant, did not see the young men of my
lord whom you sent.
26 "Now therefore, my lord, *as* the LORD lives
and *as* your soul lives, since the LORD has held
you back from coming to bloodshed and from
avenging yourself with your own hand, now
then, let your enemies and those who seek
harm for my lord be as Nabal.
27 "And now this present which your maid-
servant has brought to my lord, let it be given
to the young men who follow my lord.
28 "Please forgive the trespass of your maid-
servant. For the LORD will certainly make for
my lord an enduring house, because my lord
fights the battles of the LORD, and evil is not
found in you throughout your days.

25:1 [a]Following Masoretic Text, Syriac, Targum, and Vulgate; Septuagint reads *Maon.* **25:17** [a]Literally *son of Belial* **25:25** [a]Literally *Fool*

29 "Yet a man has risen to pursue you and seek your life, but the life of my lord shall be bound in the bundle of the living with the LORD your God; and the lives of your enemies He shall sling out, *as from* the pocket of a sling.

30 "And it shall come to pass, when the LORD has done for my lord according to all the good that He has spoken concerning you, and has appointed you ruler over Israel,

31 "that this will be no grief to you, nor offense of heart to my lord, either that you have shed blood without cause, or that my lord has avenged himself. But when the LORD has dealt well with my lord, then remember your maidservant."

32 Then David said to Abigail: "Blessed *is* the LORD God of Israel, who sent you this day to meet me!

33 "And blessed *is* your advice and blessed *are* you, because you have kept me this day from coming to bloodshed and from avenging myself with my own hand.

34 "For indeed, *as* the LORD God of Israel lives, who has kept me back from hurting you, unless you had hurried and come to meet me, surely by morning light no males would have been left to Nabal!"

35 So David received from her hand what she had brought him, and said to her, "Go up in peace to your house. See, I have heeded your voice and respected your person."

36 Now Abigail went to Nabal, and there he was, holding a feast in his house, like the feast of a king. And Nabal's heart *was* merry within him, for he *was* very drunk; therefore she told him nothing, little or much, until morning light.

37 So it was, in the morning, when the wine had gone from Nabal, and his wife had told him these things, that his heart died within him, and he became *like* a stone.

38 Then it happened, *after* about ten days, that the LORD struck Nabal, and he died.

39 So when David heard that Nabal was dead, he said, "Blessed *be* the LORD, who has pleaded the cause of my reproach from the hand of Nabal, and has kept His servant from evil! For the LORD has returned the wickedness of Nabal on his own head." And David sent and proposed to Abigail, to take her as his wife.

40 When the servants of David had come to Abigail at Carmel, they spoke to her saying, "David sent us to you, to ask you to become his wife."

41 Then she arose, bowed her face to the earth, and said, "Here is your maidservant, a servant to wash the feet of the servants of my lord."

42 So Abigail rose in haste and rode on a donkey, attended by five of her maidens; and she followed the messengers of David, and became his wife.

43 David also took Ahinoam of Jezreel, and so both of them were his wives.

44 But Saul had given Michal his daughter, David's wife, to Palti[a] the son of Laish, who *was* from Gallim.

David Spares Saul a Second Time

26 Now the Ziphites came to Saul at Gibeah, saying, "Is David not hiding in the hill of Hachilah, opposite Jeshimon?"

2 Then Saul arose and went down to the Wilderness of Ziph, having three thousand chosen men of Israel with him, to seek David in the Wilderness of Ziph.

3 And Saul encamped in the hill of Hachilah, which *is* opposite Jeshimon, by the road. But David stayed in the wilderness, and he saw that Saul came after him into the wilderness.

4 David therefore sent out spies, and understood that Saul had indeed come.

5 So David arose and came to the place where Saul had encamped. And David saw the place where Saul lay, and Abner the son of Ner, the commander of his army. Now Saul lay within the camp, with the people encamped all around him.

6 Then David answered, and said to Ahimelech the Hittite and to Abishai the son of Zeruiah, brother of Joab, saying, "Who will go down with me to Saul in the camp?" And Abishai said, "I will go down with you."

7 So David and Abishai came to the people by night; and there Saul lay sleeping within the camp, with his spear stuck in the ground by his head. And Abner and the people lay all around him.

8 Then Abishai said to David, "God has delivered your enemy into your hand this day. Now therefore, please, let me strike him at once with the spear, right to the earth; and I will not *have to strike* him a second time!"

9 But David said to Abishai, "Do not destroy him; for who can stretch out his hand against the LORD's anointed, and be guiltless?"

10 David said furthermore, "*As* the LORD lives, the LORD shall strike him, or his day shall come to die, or he shall go out to battle and perish.

11 "The LORD forbid that I should stretch out my hand against the LORD's anointed. But please, take now the spear and the jug of water that *are* by his head, and let us go."

12 So David took the spear and the jug of water *by* Saul's head, and they got away; and no man saw or knew *it* or awoke. For they *were* all asleep, because a deep sleep from the LORD had fallen on them.

13 Now David went over to the other side, and stood on the top of a hill afar off, a great distance *being* between them.

14 And David called out to the people and to Abner the son of Ner, saying, "Do you not answer, Abner?" Then Abner answered and said, "Who *are* you, calling out to the king?"

15 So David said to Abner, "*Are* you not a man? And who *is* like you in Israel? Why then have you not guarded your lord the king? For one of the people came in to destroy your lord the king.

16 "This thing that you have done *is* not good. *As* the LORD lives, you deserve to die, because you have not guarded your master, the LORD's anointed. And now see where the king's spear *is,* and the jug of water that *was* by his head."

17 Then Saul knew David's voice, and said, "*Is* that your voice, my son David?" David said, "*It is* my voice, my lord, O king."

18 And he said, "Why does my lord thus pursue his servant? For what have I done, or what evil *is* in my hand?

19 "Now therefore, please, let my lord the king hear the words of his servant: If the LORD has stirred you up against me, let Him accept

25:44 [a]Spelled *Paltiel* in 2 Samuel 3:15

an offering. But if *it is* the children of men, *may* they *be* cursed before the LORD, for they have driven me out this day from sharing in the inheritance of the LORD, saying, 'Go, serve other gods.'
20 "So now, do not let my blood fall to the earth before the face of the LORD. For the king of Israel has come out to seek a flea, as when one hunts a partridge in the mountains."
21 Then Saul said, "I have sinned. Return, my son David. For I will harm you no more, because my life was precious in your eyes this day. Indeed I have played the fool and erred exceedingly."
22 And David answered and said, "Here is the king's spear. Let one of the young men come over and get it.
23 "May the LORD repay every man *for* his righteousness and his faithfulness; for the LORD delivered you into *my* hand today, but I would not stretch out my hand against the LORD's anointed.
24 "And indeed, as your life was valued much this day in my eyes, so let my life be valued much in the eyes of the LORD, and let Him deliver me out of all tribulation."
25 Then Saul said to David, "*May* you *be* blessed, my son David! You shall both do great things and also still prevail." So David went on his way, and Saul returned to his place.

David Allied with the Philistines

27 And David said in his heart, "Now I shall perish someday by the hand of Saul. *There is* nothing better for me than that I should speedily escape to the land of the Philistines; and Saul will despair of me, to seek me anymore in any part of Israel. So I shall escape out of his hand."
2 Then David arose and went over with the six hundred men who *were* with him to Achish the son of Maoch, king of Gath.
3 So David dwelt with Achish at Gath, he and his men, each man with his household, *and* David with his two wives, Ahinoam the Jezreelitess, and Abigail the Carmelitess, Nabal's widow.
4 And it was told Saul that David had fled to Gath; so he sought him no more.
5 Then David said to Achish, "If I have now found favor in your eyes, let them give me a place in some town in the country, that I may dwell there. For why should your servant dwell in the royal city with you?"
6 So Achish gave him Ziklag that day. Therefore Ziklag has belonged to the kings of Judah to this day.
7 Now the time that David dwelt in the country of the Philistines was one full year and four months.
8 And David and his men went up and raided the Geshurites, the Girzites,[a] and the Amalekites. For those *nations* were the inhabitants of the land from of old, as you go to Shur, even as far as the land of Egypt.
9 Whenever David attacked the land, he left neither man nor woman alive, but took away the sheep, the oxen, the donkeys, the camels, and the apparel, and returned and came to Achish.
10 Then Achish would say, "Where have you made a raid today?" And David would say, "Against the southern *area* of Judah, or against the southern *area* of the Jerahmeelites, or against the southern *area* of the Kenites."
11 David would save neither man nor woman alive, to bring *news* to Gath, saying, "Lest they should inform on us, saying, 'Thus David did.'" And thus *was* his behavior all the time he dwelt in the country of the Philistines.
12 So Achish believed David, saying, "He has made his people Israel utterly abhor him; therefore he will be my servant forever."

28 Now it happened in those days that the Philistines gathered their armies together for war, to fight with Israel. And Achish said to David, "You assuredly know that you will go out with me to battle, you and your men."
2 So David said to Achish, "Surely you know what your servant can do." And Achish said to David, "Therefore I will make you one of my chief guardians forever."

Saul Consults a Medium

3 Now Samuel had died, and all Israel had lamented for him and buried him in Ramah, in his own city. And Saul had put the mediums and the spiritists out of the land.
4 Then the Philistines gathered together, and came and encamped at Shunem. So Saul gathered all Israel together, and they encamped at Gilboa.
5 When Saul saw the army of the Philistines, he was afraid, and his heart trembled greatly.
6 And when Saul inquired of the LORD, the LORD did not answer him, either by dreams or by Urim or by the prophets.
7 Then Saul said to his servants, "Find me a woman who is a medium, that I may go to her and inquire of her." And his servants said to him, "In fact, *there is* a woman who is a medium at En Dor."
8 So Saul disguised himself and put on other clothes, and he went, and two men with him; and they came to the woman by night. And he said, "Please conduct a séance for me, and bring up for me the one I shall name to you."
9 Then the woman said to him, "Look, you know what Saul has done, how he has cut off the mediums and the spiritists from the land. Why then do you lay a snare for my life, to cause me to die?"
10 And Saul swore to her by the LORD, saying, "*As* the LORD lives, no punishment shall come upon you for this thing."
11 Then the woman said, "Whom shall I bring up for you?" And he said, "Bring up Samuel for me."
12 When the woman saw Samuel, she cried out with a loud voice. And the woman spoke to Saul, saying, "Why have you deceived me? For you *are* Saul!"
13 And the king said to her, "Do not be afraid. What did you see?" And the woman said to Saul, "I saw a spirit[a] ascending out of the earth."
14 So he said to her, "What *is* his form?" And she said, "An old man is coming up, and he *is* covered with a mantle." And Saul perceived that it *was* Samuel, and he stooped with *his* face to the ground and bowed down.
15 Now Samuel said to Saul, "Why have you disturbed me by bringing me up?" And Saul

27:8 [a]Or *Gezrites* **28:13** [a]Hebrew *elohim*

answered, "I am deeply distressed; for the Phi-
listines make war against me, and God has
departed from me and does not answer me
anymore, neither by prophets nor by dreams.
Therefore I have called you, that you may re-
veal to me what I should do."
16 Then Samuel said: "So why do you ask
me, seeing the LORD has departed from you
and has become your enemy?
17 "And the LORD has done for Himself[a] as
He spoke by me. For the LORD has torn the
kingdom out of your hand and given it to your
neighbor, David.
18 "Because you did not obey the voice of
the LORD nor execute His fierce wrath upon
Amalek, therefore the LORD has done this
thing to you this day.
19 "Moreover the LORD will also deliver Is-
rael with you into the hand of the Philistines.
And tomorrow you and your sons *will be* with
me. The LORD will also deliver the army of
Israel into the hand of the Philistines."
20 Immediately Saul fell full length on the
ground, and was dreadfully afraid because of
the words of Samuel. And there was no
strength in him, for he had eaten no food all
day or all night.
21 And the woman came to Saul and saw that
he was severely troubled, and said to him,
"Look, your maidservant has obeyed your
voice, and I have put my life in my hands and
heeded the words which you spoke to me.
22 "Now therefore, please, heed also the
voice of your maidservant, and let me set a
piece of bread before you; and eat, that you
may have strength when you go on *your* way."
23 But he refused and said, "I will not eat." So
his servants, together with the woman, urged
him; and he heeded their voice. Then he arose
from the ground and sat on the bed.
24 Now the woman had a fatted calf in the
house, and she hastened to kill it. And she took
flour and kneaded *it,* and baked unleavened
bread from it.
25 So she brought *it* before Saul and his ser-
vants, and they ate. Then they rose and went
away that night.

The Philistines Reject David

29 Then the Philistines gathered together
all their armies at Aphek, and the Israel-
ites encamped by a fountain which *is* in Jez-
reel.
2 And the lords of the Philistines passed in
review by hundreds and by thousands, but Da-
vid and his men passed in review at the rear
with Achish.
3 Then the princes of the Philistines said,
"What *are* these Hebrews *doing here?*" And
Achish said to the princes of the Philistines,
"*Is* this not David, the servant of Saul king of
Israel, who has been with me these days, or
these years? And to this day I have found no
fault in him since he defected *to me.*"
4 But the princes of the Philistines were an-
gry with him; so the princes of the Philistines
said to him, "Make this fellow return, that he
may go back to the place which you have ap-
pointed for him, and do not let him go down
with us to battle, lest in the battle he become
our adversary. For with what could he recon-
cile himself to his master, if not with the heads
of these men?
5 "*Is* this not David, of whom they sang to
one another in dances, saying:

'Saul has slain his thousands,
And David his ten thousands'?"[a]

6 Then Achish called David and said to him,
"Surely, *as* the LORD lives, you have been up-
right, and your going out and your coming in
with me in the army *is* good in my sight. For to
this day I have not found evil in you since the
day of your coming to me. Nevertheless the
lords do not favor you.
7 "Therefore return now, and go in peace,
that you may not displease the lords of the
Philistines."
8 So David said to Achish, "But what have I
done? And to this day what have you found in
your servant as long as I have been with you,
that I may not go and fight against the enemies
of my lord the king?"
9 Then Achish answered and said to David,
"I know that you *are* as good in my sight as an
angel of God; nevertheless the princes of the
Philistines have said, 'He shall not go up with
us to the battle.'
10 "Now therefore, rise early in the morning
with your master's servants who have come
with you.[a] And as soon as you are up early in
the morning and have light, depart."
11 So David and his men rose early to depart
in the morning, to return to the land of the
Philistines. And the Philistines went up to Jez-
reel.

David's Conflict with the Amalekites

30 Now it happened, when David and his
men came to Ziklag, on the third day,
that the Amalekites had invaded the South and
Ziklag, attacked Ziklag and burned it with fire,
2 and had taken captive the women and
those who *were* there, from small to great; they
did not kill anyone, but carried *them* away and
went their way.
3 So David and his men came to the city, and
there it was, burned with fire; and their wives,
their sons, and their daughters had been taken
captive.
4 Then David and the people who *were* with
him lifted up their voices and wept, until they
had no more power to weep.
5 And David's two wives, Ahinoam the Jez-
reelitess, and Abigail the widow of Nabal the
Carmelite, had been taken captive.
6 Now David was greatly distressed, for the
people spoke of stoning him, because the soul
of all the people was grieved, every man for
his sons and his daughters. But David
strengthened himself in the LORD his God.
7 Then David said to Abiathar the priest,
Ahimelech's son, "Please bring the ephod here
to me." And Abiathar brought the ephod to
David.
8 So David inquired of the LORD, saying,
"Shall I pursue this troop? Shall I overtake
them?" And He answered him, "Pursue, for
you shall surely overtake *them* and without
fail recover *all.*"
9 So David went, he and the six hundred men

28:17 [a]Or *him,* that is, David **29:5** [a]Compare 1 Samuel 18:7 **29:10** [a]Following Masoretic Text, Targum, and Vulgate; Septuagint adds *and go to the place which I have selected for you there; and set no bothersome word in your heart, for you are good before me. And rise on your way.*

who *were* with him, and came to the Brook
Besor, where those stayed who were left behind.
10 But David pursued, he and four hundred
men; for two hundred stayed *behind*, who were
so weary that they could not cross the Brook
Besor.
11 Then they found an Egyptian in the field,
and brought him to David; and they gave him
bread and he ate, and they let him drink water.
12 And they gave him a piece of a cake of figs
and two clusters of raisins. So when he had
eaten, his strength came back to him; for he
had eaten no bread nor drunk water for three
days and three nights.
13 Then David said to him, "To whom do you
belong, and where *are* you from?" And he said,
"I *am* a young man from Egypt, servant of
an Amalekite; and my master left me behind,
because three days ago I fell sick.
14 "We made an invasion of the southern *area*
of the Cherethites, in the *territory* which *belongs*
to Judah, and of the southern *area* of
Caleb; and we burned Ziklag with fire."
15 And David said to him, "Can you take me
down to this troop?" So he said, "Swear to me
by God that you will neither kill me nor deliver
me into the hands of my master, and I will take
you down to this troop."
16 And when he had brought him down, there
they were, spread out over all the land, eating
and drinking and dancing, because of all the
great spoil which they had taken from the land
of the Philistines and from the land of Judah.
17 Then David attacked them from twilight
until the evening of the next day. Not a man of
them escaped, except four hundred young men
who rode on camels and fled.
18 So David recovered all that the Amalekites
had carried away, and David rescued his two
wives.
19 And nothing of theirs was lacking, either
small or great, sons or daughters, spoil or anything
which they had taken from them; David
recovered all.
20 Then David took all the flocks and herds
they had driven before those *other* livestock,
and said, "This *is* David's spoil."
21 Now David came to the two hundred men
who had been so weary that they could not
follow David, whom they also had made to stay
at the Brook Besor. So they went out to meet
David and to meet the people who *were* with
him. And when David came near the people,
he greeted them.
22 Then all the wicked and worthless men[a] of
those who went with David answered and said,
"Because they did not go with us, we will not
give them *any* of the spoil that we have recovered,
except for every man's wife and children,
that they may lead *them* away and depart."
23 But David said, "My brethren, you shall
not do so with what the LORD has given us,
who has preserved us and delivered into our
hand the troop that came against us.
24 "For who will heed you in this matter? But
as his part *is* who goes down to the battle, so
shall his part *be* who stays by the supplies;
they shall share alike."
25 So it was, from that day forward; he made
it a statute and an ordinance for Israel to this
day.
26 Now when David came to Ziklag, he sent
some of the spoil to the elders of Judah, to his
friends, saying, "Here is a present for you from
the spoil of the enemies of the LORD"—
27 to *those* who *were* in Bethel, *those* who
were in Ramoth of the South, *those* who *were*
in Jattir,
28 *those* who *were* in Aroer, *those* who *were*
in Siphmoth, *those* who *were* in Eshtemoa,
29 *those* who *were* in Rachal, *those* who *were*
in the cities of the Jerahmeelites, *those* who
were in the cities of the Kenites,
30 *those* who *were* in Hormah, *those* who *were*
in Chorashan,[a] *those* who *were* in Athach,
31 *those* who *were* in Hebron, and to all the
places where David himself and his men were
accustomed to rove.

The Tragic End of Saul and His Sons

31 Now the Philistines fought against Israel;
and the men of Israel fled from before
the Philistines, and fell slain on Mount
Gilboa.
2 Then the Philistines followed hard after
Saul and his sons. And the Philistines killed
Jonathan, Abinadab, and Malchishua, Saul's
sons.
3 The battle became fierce against Saul. The
archers hit him, and he was severely wounded
by the archers.
4 Then Saul said to his armorbearer, "Draw
your sword, and thrust me through with it, lest
these uncircumcised men come and thrust me
through and abuse me." But his armorbearer
would not, for he was greatly afraid. Therefore
Saul took a sword and fell on it.
5 And when his armorbearer saw that Saul
was dead, he also fell on his sword, and died
with him.
6 So Saul, his three sons, his armorbearer,
and all his men died together that same day.
7 And when the men of Israel who *were* on
the other side of the valley, and *those* who *were*
on the other side of the Jordan, saw that the
men of Israel had fled and that Saul and his
sons were dead, they forsook the cities and
fled; and the Philistines came and dwelt in
them.
8 So it happened the next day, when the Philistines
came to strip the slain, that they found
Saul and his three sons fallen on Mount
Gilboa.
9 And they cut off his head and stripped off
his armor, and sent *word* throughout the land
of the Philistines, to proclaim *it in* the temple
of their idols and among the people.
10 Then they put his armor in the temple of
the Ashtoreths, and they fastened his body to
the wall of Beth Shan.[a]
11 Now when the inhabitants of Jabesh Gilead
heard what the Philistines had done to
Saul,
12 all the valiant men arose and traveled all
night, and took the body of Saul and the bodies
of his sons from the wall of Beth Shan; and
they came to Jabesh and burned them there.
13 Then they took their bones and buried
them under the tamarisk tree at Jabesh, and
fasted seven days.

30:22 [a]Literally *men of Belial* **30:30** [a]Or *Borashan* **31:10** [a]Spelled *Beth Shean* in Joshua 17:11 and elsewhere

The Second Book of

SAMUEL

The Report of Saul's Death

1 Now it came to pass after the death of Saul,
when David had returned from the slaugh-
ter of the Amalekites, and David had stayed
two days in Ziklag,
2 on the third day, behold, it happened that
a man came from Saul's camp with his clothes
torn and dust on his head. So it was, when he
came to David, that he fell to the ground and
prostrated himself.
3 And David said to him, "Where have you
come from?" So he said to him, "I have escaped
from the camp of Israel."
4 Then David said to him, "How did the mat-
ter go? Please tell me." And he answered, "The
people have fled from the battle, many of the
people are fallen and dead, and Saul and Jona-
than his son are dead also."
5 So David said to the young man who told
him, "How do you know that Saul and Jona-
than his son are dead?"
6 Then the young man who told him said,
"As I happened by chance *to be* on Mount Gil-
boa, there was Saul, leaning on his spear; and
indeed the chariots and horsemen followed
hard after him.
7 "Now when he looked behind him, he saw
me and called to me. And I answered, 'Here I
am.'
8 "And he said to me, 'Who *are* you?' So I
answered him, 'I *am* an Amalekite.'
9 "He said to me again, 'Please stand over
me and kill me, for anguish has come upon me,
but my life still *remains* in me.'
10 "So I stood over him and killed him, be-
cause I was sure that he could not live after he
had fallen. And I took the crown that *was* on
his head and the bracelet that *was* on his arm,
and have brought them here to my lord."
11 Therefore David took hold of his own clothes
and tore them, and *so did* all the men who *were*
with him.
12 And they mourned and wept and fasted
until evening for Saul and for Jonathan his
son, for the people of the LORD and for the
house of Israel, because they had fallen by the
sword.
13 Then David said to the young man who told
him, "Where *are* you from?" And he answered,
"I *am* the son of an alien, an Amalekite."
14 So David said to him, "How was it you
were not afraid to put forth your hand to de-
stroy the LORD's anointed?"
15 Then David called one of the young men
and said, "Go near, *and* execute him!" And he
struck him so that he died.
16 So David said to him, "Your blood *is* on your
own head, for your own mouth has testified
against you, saying, 'I have killed the LORD's
anointed.'"

The Song of the Bow

17 Then David lamented with this lamenta-
tion over Saul and over Jonathan his son,
18 and he told *them* to teach the children of
Judah *the Song of* the Bow; indeed *it is* written
in the Book of Jasher:

19 "The beauty of Israel is slain on your high
places!
How the mighty have fallen!
20 Tell *it* not in Gath,
Proclaim *it* not in the streets of
Ashkelon—
Lest the daughters of the Philistines
rejoice,
Lest the daughters of the uncircumcised
triumph.

21 "O mountains of Gilboa,
Let there be no dew nor rain upon you,
Nor fields of offerings.
For the shield of the mighty is cast away
there!
The shield of Saul, not anointed with oil.
22 From the blood of the slain,
From the fat of the mighty,
The bow of Jonathan did not turn back,
And the sword of Saul did not return
empty.

23 "Saul and Jonathan *were* beloved and
pleasant in their lives,
And in their death they were not divided;
They were swifter than eagles,
They were stronger than lions.

24 "O daughters of Israel, weep over Saul,
Who clothed you in scarlet, with luxury;
Who put ornaments of gold on your
apparel.

25 "How the mighty have fallen in the midst
of the battle!
Jonathan *was* slain in your high places.
26 I am distressed for you, my brother
Jonathan;
You have been very pleasant to me;
Your love to me was wonderful,
Surpassing the love of women.

27 "How the mighty have fallen,
And the weapons of war perished!"

David Anointed King of Judah

2 It happened after this that David inquired
of the LORD, saying, "Shall I go up to any
of the cities of Judah?" And the LORD said to
him, "Go up." David said, "Where shall I go up?"
And He said, "To Hebron."
2 So David went up there, and his two wives
also, Ahinoam the Jezreelitess, and Abigail the
widow of Nabal the Carmelite.
3 And David brought up the men who *were*
with him, every man with his household. So
they dwelt in the cities of Hebron.
4 Then the men of Judah came, and there they
anointed David king over the house of Judah.
And they told David, saying, "The men of Ja-
besh Gilead *were the ones* who buried Saul."
5 So David sent messengers to the men of
Jabesh Gilead, and said to them, "You *are*
blessed of the LORD, for you have shown this
kindness to your lord, to Saul, and have buried
him.
6 "And now may the LORD show kindness and
truth to you. I also will repay you this kindness,
because you have done this thing.
7 "Now therefore, let your hands be strength-
ened, and be valiant; for your master Saul is
dead, and also the house of Judah has anointed
me king over them."

Ishbosheth Made King of Israel

8 But Abner the son of Ner, commander of Saul's army, took Ishbosheth[a] the son of Saul and brought him over to Mahanaim;
9 and he made him king over Gilead, over the Ashurites, over Jezreel, over Ephraim, over Benjamin, and over all Israel.
10 Ishbosheth, Saul's son, *was* forty years old when he began to reign over Israel, and he reigned two years. Only the house of Judah followed David.
11 And the time that David was king in Hebron over the house of Judah was seven years and six months.

Israel and Judah at War

12 Now Abner the son of Ner, and the servants of Ishbosheth the son of Saul, went out from Mahanaim to Gibeon.
13 And Joab the son of Zeruiah, and the servants of David, went out and met them by the pool of Gibeon. So they sat down, one on one side of the pool and the other on the other side of the pool.
14 Then Abner said to Joab, "Let the young men now arise and compete before us." And Joab said, "Let them arise."
15 So they arose and went over by number, twelve from Benjamin, *followers* of Ishbosheth the son of Saul, and twelve from the servants of David.
16 And each one grasped his opponent by the head and *thrust* his sword in his opponent's side; so they fell down together. Therefore that place was called the Field of Sharp Swords,[a] which *is* in Gibeon.
17 So there was a very fierce battle that day, and Abner and the men of Israel were beaten before the servants of David.
18 Now the three sons of Zeruiah were there: Joab and Abishai and Asahel. And Asahel *was as* fleet of foot as a wild gazelle.
19 So Asahel pursued Abner, and in going he did not turn to the right hand or to the left from following Abner.
20 Then Abner looked behind him and said, "*Are* you Asahel?" He answered, "I *am*."
21 And Abner said to him, "Turn aside to your right hand or to your left, and lay hold on one of the young men and take his armor for yourself." But Asahel would not turn aside from following him.
22 So Abner said again to Asahel, "Turn aside from following me. Why should I strike you to the ground? How then could I face your brother Joab?"
23 However, he refused to turn aside. Therefore Abner struck him in the stomach with the blunt end of the spear, so that the spear came out of his back; and he fell down there and died on the spot. So it was *that* as many as came to the place where Asahel fell down and died, stood still.
24 Joab and Abishai also pursued Abner. And the sun was going down when they came to the hill of Ammah, which *is* before Giah by the road to the Wilderness of Gibeon.
25 Now the children of Benjamin gathered together behind Abner and became a unit, and took their stand on top of a hill.
26 Then Abner called to Joab and said, "Shall the sword devour forever? Do you not know that it will be bitter in the latter end? How long will it be then until you tell the people to return from pursuing their brethren?"
27 And Joab said, "*As* God lives, unless you had spoken, surely then by morning all the people would have given up pursuing their brethren."
28 So Joab blew a trumpet; and all the people stood still and did not pursue Israel anymore, nor did they fight anymore.
29 Then Abner and his men went on all that night through the plain, crossed over the Jordan, and went through all Bithron; and they came to Mahanaim.
30 So Joab returned from pursuing Abner. And when he had gathered all the people together, there were missing of David's servants nineteen men and Asahel.
31 But the servants of David had struck down, of Benjamin and Abner's men, three hundred and sixty men who died.
32 Then they took up Asahel and buried him in his father's tomb, which *was in* Bethlehem. And Joab and his men went all night, and they came to Hebron at daybreak.

3 Now there was a long war between the house of Saul and the house of David. But David grew stronger and stronger, and the house of Saul grew weaker and weaker.

Sons of David

2 Sons were born to David in Hebron: His firstborn was Amnon by Ahinoam the Jezreelitess;
3 his second, Chileab, by Abigail the widow of Nabal the Carmelite; the third, Absalom the son of Maacah, the daughter of Talmai, king of Geshur;
4 the fourth, Adonijah the son of Haggith; the fifth, Shephatiah the son of Abital;
5 and the sixth, Ithream, by David's wife Eglah. These were born to David in Hebron.

Abner Joins Forces with David

6 Now it was so, while there was war between the house of Saul and the house of David, that Abner was strengthening *his hold* on the house of Saul.
7 And Saul had a concubine, whose name *was* Rizpah, the daughter of Aiah. So *Ishbosheth* said to Abner, "Why have you gone in to my father's concubine?"
8 Then Abner became very angry at the words of Ishbosheth, and said, "*Am* I a dog's head that belongs to Judah? Today I show loyalty to the house of Saul your father, to his brothers, and to his friends, and have not delivered you into the hand of David; and you charge me today with a fault concerning this woman?
9 "May God do so to Abner, and more also, if I do not do for David as the LORD has sworn to him—
10 "to transfer the kingdom from the house of Saul, and set up the throne of David over Israel and over Judah, from Dan to Beersheba."
11 And he could not answer Abner another word, because he feared him.
12 Then Abner sent messengers on his behalf to David, saying, "Whose *is* the land?" saying *also*, "Make your covenant with me, and indeed

2:8 [a]Called *Esh-Baal* in 1 Chronicles 8:33 and 9:39 **2:16** [a]Hebrew *Helkath Hazzurim*

my hand *shall be* with you to bring all Israel to
you."
13 And *David* said, "Good, I will make a cov-
enant with you. But one thing I require of you:
you shall not see my face unless you first bring
Michal, Saul's daughter, when you come to see
my face."
14 So David sent messengers to Ishbosheth,
Saul's son, saying, "Give *me* my wife Michal,
whom I betrothed to myself for a hundred fore-
skins of the Philistines."
15 And Ishbosheth sent and took her from
her husband, from Paltiel[a] the son of Laish.
16 Then her husband went along with her to
Bahurim, weeping behind her. So Abner said
to him, "Go, return!" And he returned.
17 Now Abner had communicated with the
elders of Israel, saying, "In time past you were
seeking for David *to be* king over you.
18 "Now then, do *it!* For the LORD has spoken
of David, saying, 'By the hand of My servant
David, I[a] will save My people Israel from the
hand of the Philistines and the hand of all their
enemies.'"
19 And Abner also spoke in the hearing of
Benjamin. Then Abner also went to speak in
the hearing of David in Hebron all that seemed
good to Israel and the whole house of Ben-
jamin.
20 So Abner and twenty men with him came
to David at Hebron. And David made a feast
for Abner and the men who *were* with him.
21 Then Abner said to David, "I will arise and
go, and gather all Israel to my lord the king,
that they may make a covenant with you, and
that you may reign over all that your heart
desires." So David sent Abner away, and he
went in peace.

Joab Murders Abner

22 At that moment the servants of David and
Joab came from a raid and brought much spoil
with them. But Abner *was* not with David in
Hebron, for he had sent him away, and he had
gone in peace.
23 When Joab and all the troops that *were* with
him had come, they told Joab, saying, "Abner
the son of Ner came to the king, and he sent
him away, and he has gone in peace."
24 Then Joab came to the king and said,
"What have you done? Look, Abner came to
you; why *is* it *that* you sent him away, and he
has already gone?
25 "Surely you realize that Abner the son of
Ner came to deceive you, to know your going
out and your coming in, and to know all that
you are doing."
26 And when Joab had gone from David's
presence, he sent messengers after Abner, who
brought him back from the well of Sirah. But
David did not know *it.*
27 Now when Abner had returned to Hebron,
Joab took him aside in the gate to speak with
him privately, and there stabbed him in the
stomach, so that he died for the blood of Asa-
hel his brother.
28 Afterward, when David heard *it,* he said,
"My kingdom and I *are* guiltless before the
LORD forever of the blood of Abner the son of
Ner.
29 "Let it rest on the head of Joab and on all
his father's house; and let there never fail to
be in the house of Joab one who has a dis-
charge or is a leper, who leans on a staff or
falls by the sword, or who lacks bread."
30 So Joab and Abishai his brother killed Ab-
ner, because he had killed their brother Asahel
at Gibeon in the battle.

David's Mourning for Abner

31 Then David said to Joab and to all the peo-
ple who were with him, "Tear your clothes,
gird yourselves with sackcloth, and mourn for
Abner." And King David followed the coffin.
32 So they buried Abner in Hebron; and the
king lifted up his voice and wept at the grave
of Abner, and all the people wept.
33 And the king sang *a lament* over Abner
and said:

"Should Abner die as a fool dies?
34 Your hands were not bound
Nor your feet put into fetters;
As a man falls before wicked men, *so* you
fell."

Then all the people wept over him again.
35 And when all the people came to persuade
David to eat food while it was still day, David
took an oath, saying, "God do so to me, and
more also, if I taste bread or anything else till
the sun goes down!"
36 Now all the people took note *of it,* and
it pleased them, since whatever the king did
pleased all the people.
37 For all the people and all Israel understood
that day that it had not been the king's *intent*
to kill Abner the son of Ner.
38 Then the king said to his servants, "Do you
not know that a prince and a great man has
fallen this day in Israel?
39 "And I *am* weak today, though anointed
king; and these men, the sons of Zeruiah, *are*
too harsh for me. The LORD shall repay the
evildoer according to his wickedness."

Ishbosheth Is Murdered

4 When Saul's son[a] heard that Abner had
died in Hebron, he lost heart, and all Israel
was troubled.
2 Now Saul's son *had* two men *who were*
captains of troops. The name of one *was* Baa-
nah and the name of the other Rechab, the
sons of Rimmon the Beerothite, of the children
of Benjamin. (For Beeroth also was *part* of
Benjamin,
3 because the Beerothites fled to Gittaim
and have been sojourners there until this day.)
4 Jonathan, Saul's son, had a son *who was*
lame in *his* feet. He was five years old when
the news about Saul and Jonathan came from
Jezreel; and his nurse took him up and fled.
And it happened, as she made haste to flee,
that he fell and became lame. His name *was*
Mephibosheth.[a]
5 Then the sons of Rimmon the Beerothite,
Rechab and Baanah, set out and came at about
the heat of the day to the house of Ishbosheth,
who was lying on his bed at noon.
6 And they came there, all the way into the
house, *as though* to get wheat, and they
stabbed him in the stomach. Then Rechab and
Baanah his brother escaped.
7 For when they came into the house, he was
lying on his bed in his bedroom; then they

3:15 [a]Spelled *Palti* in 1 Samuel 25:44 3:18 [a]Following many Hebrew manuscripts, Septuagint, Syriac, and Targum; Masoretic Text reads *he.* 4:1 [a]That is, Ishbosheth 4:4 [a]Called *Merib-Baal* in 1 Chronicles 8:34 and 9:40

struck him and killed him, beheaded him and
took his head, and were all night escaping
through the plain.
8 And they brought the head of Ishbosheth
to David at Hebron, and said to the king, "Here
is the head of Ishbosheth, the son of Saul your
enemy, who sought your life; and the LORD has
avenged my lord the king this day of Saul and
his descendants."
9 But David answered Rechab and Baanah
his brother, the sons of Rimmon the Beerothite,
and said to them, "*As* the LORD lives, who has
redeemed my life from all adversity,
10 "when someone told me, saying, 'Look,
Saul is dead,' thinking to have brought good
news, I arrested him and had him executed in
Ziklag—the one who *thought* I would give him
a reward for *his* news.
11 "How much more, when wicked men have
killed a righteous person in his own house on
his bed? Therefore, shall I not now require his
blood at your hand and remove you from the
earth?"
12 So David commanded his young men, and
they executed them, cut off their hands and
feet, and hanged *them* by the pool in Hebron.
But they took the head of Ishbosheth and bur-
ied *it* in the tomb of Abner in Hebron.

David Reigns over All Israel

5 Then all the tribes of Israel came to David
at Hebron and spoke, saying, "Indeed we
are your bone and your flesh.
2 "Also, in time past, when Saul was king
over us, you were the one who led Israel out
and brought them in; and the LORD said to
you, 'You shall shepherd My people Israel, and
be ruler over Israel.'"
3 Therefore all the elders of Israel came to
the king at Hebron, and King David made a
covenant with them at Hebron before the
LORD. And they anointed David king over Is-
rael.
4 David *was* thirty years old when he began
to reign, *and* he reigned forty years.
5 In Hebron he reigned over Judah seven
years and six months, and in Jerusalem he
reigned thirty-three years over all Israel and
Judah.

The Conquest of Jerusalem

6 And the king and his men went to Jerusa-
lem against the Jebusites, the inhabitants of
the land, who spoke to David, saying, "You
shall not come in here; but the blind and the
lame will repel you," thinking, "David cannot
come in here."
7 Nevertheless David took the stronghold of
Zion (that *is*, the City of David).
8 Now David said on that day, "Whoever
climbs up by way of the water shaft and defeats
the Jebusites (the lame and the blind, *who are*
hated by David's soul), *he shall be chief and
captain*."[a] Therefore they say, "The blind and
the lame shall not come into the house."
9 Then David dwelt in the stronghold, and
called it the City of David. And David built all
around from the Millo[a] and inward.
10 So David went on and became great, and
the LORD God of hosts *was* with him.
11 Then Hiram king of Tyre sent messengers
to David, and cedar trees, and carpenters and
masons. And they built David a house.
12 So David knew that the LORD had estab-
lished him as king over Israel, and that He had
exalted His kingdom for the sake of His people
Israel.
13 And David took more concubines and
wives from Jerusalem, after he had come from
Hebron. Also more sons and daughters were
born to David.
14 Now these *are* the names of those who
were born to him in Jerusalem: Shammua,[a]
Shobab, Nathan, Solomon,
15 Ibhar, Elishua,[a] Nepheg, Japhia,
16 Elishama, Eliada, and Eliphelet.

The Philistines Defeated

17 Now when the Philistines heard that they
had anointed David king over Israel, all the
Philistines went up to search for David. And
David heard *of it* and went down to the strong-
hold.
18 The Philistines also went and deployed
themselves in the Valley of Rephaim.
19 So David inquired of the LORD, saying,
"Shall I go up against the Philistines? Will You
deliver them into my hand?" And the LORD
said to David, "Go up, for I will doubtless de-
liver the Philistines into your hand."
20 So David went to Baal Perazim, and David
defeated them there; and he said, "The LORD
has broken through my enemies before me,
like a breakthrough of water." Therefore he
called the name of that place Baal Perazim.[a]
21 And they left their images there, and Da-
vid and his men carried them away.
22 Then the Philistines went up once again
and deployed themselves in the Valley of
Rephaim.
23 Therefore David inquired of the LORD, and
He said, "You shall not go up; circle around
behind them, and come upon them in front of
the mulberry trees.
24 "And it shall be, when you hear the sound
of marching in the tops of the mulberry trees,
then you shall advance quickly. For then the
LORD will go out before you to strike the camp
of the Philistines."
25 And David did so, as the LORD com-
manded him; and he drove back the Philistines
from Geba[a] as far as Gezer.

The Ark Brought to Jerusalem

6 Again David gathered all *the* choice *men*
of Israel, thirty thousand.
2 And David arose and went with all the peo-
ple who *were* with him from Baale Judah to
bring up from there the ark of God, whose
name is called by the Name,[a] the LORD of
Hosts, who dwells *between* the cherubim.
3 So they set the ark of God on a new cart,
and brought it out of the house of Abinadab,
which *was* on the hill; and Uzzah and Ahio,
the sons of Abinadab, drove the new cart.[a]
4 And they brought it out of the house of
Abinadab, which *was* on the hill, accompany-
ing the ark of God; and Ahio went before the
ark.
5 Then David and all the house of Israel

5:8 [a]Compare 1 Chronicles 11:6 5:9 [a]Literally *The Landfill* 5:14 [a]Spelled *Shimea* in 1 Chronicles 3:5 5:15 [a]Spelled *Elishama* in 1 Chronicles 3:6 5:20 [a]Literally *Master of Breakthroughs* 5:25 [a]Following Masoretic Text, Targum, and Vulgate; Septuagint reads *Gibeon*. 6:2 [a]Septuagint, Targum, and Vulgate omit *by the Name*; many Hebrew manuscripts and Syriac read *there*. 6:3 [a]Septuagint adds *with the ark*.

played *music* before the LORD on all kinds of
instruments of fir wood, on harps, on stringed
instruments, on tambourines, on sistrums, and
on cymbals.
6 And when they came to Nachon's thresh-
ing floor, Uzzah put out *his hand* to the ark of
God and took hold of it, for the oxen stumbled.
7 Then the anger of the LORD was aroused
against Uzzah, and God struck him there for
his error; and he died there by the ark of God.
8 And David became angry because of the
LORD's outbreak against Uzzah; and he called
the name of the place Perez Uzzah[a] to this day.
9 David was afraid of the LORD that day;
and he said, "How can the ark of the LORD
come to me?"
10 So David would not move the ark of the
LORD with him into the City of David; but Da-
vid took it aside into the house of Obed-Edom
the Gittite.
11 The ark of the LORD remained in the house
of Obed-Edom the Gittite three months. And
the LORD blessed Obed-Edom and all his
household.
12 Now it was told King David, saying, "The
LORD has blessed the house of Obed-Edom
and all that *belongs* to him, because of the ark
of God." So David went and brought up the
ark of God from the house of Obed-Edom to
the City of David with gladness.
13 And so it was, when those bearing the ark
of the LORD had gone six paces, that he sacri-
ficed oxen and fatted sheep.
14 Then David danced before the LORD with
all *his* might; and David *was* wearing a linen
ephod.
15 So David and all the house of Israel
brought up the ark of the LORD with shouting
and with the sound of the trumpet.
16 Now as the ark of the LORD came into the
City of David, Michal, Saul's daughter, looked
through a window and saw King David leaping
and whirling before the LORD; and she de-
spised him in her heart.
17 So they brought the ark of the LORD, and
set it in its place in the midst of the tabernacle
that David had erected for it. Then David of-
fered burnt offerings and peace offerings be-
fore the LORD.
18 And when David had finished offering
burnt offerings and peace offerings, he blessed
the people in the name of the LORD of hosts.
19 Then he distributed among all the people,
among the whole multitude of Israel, both the
women and the men, to everyone a loaf of
bread, a piece *of meat,* and a cake of raisins. So
all the people departed, everyone to his house.
20 Then David returned to bless his house-
hold. And Michal the daughter of Saul came
out to meet David, and said, "How glorious
was the king of Israel today, uncovering him-
self today in the eyes of the maids of his ser-
vants, as one of the base fellows shamelessly
uncovers himself!"
21 So David said to Michal, "*It was* before
the LORD, who chose me instead of your father
and all his house, to appoint me ruler over the
people of the LORD, over Israel. Therefore I
will play *music* before the LORD.
22 "And I will be even more undignified than
this, and will be humble in my own sight. But
as for the maidservants of whom you have spo-
ken, by them I will be held in honor."
23 Therefore Michal the daughter of Saul had
no children to the day of her death.

God's Covenant with David

7 Now it came to pass when the king was
dwelling in his house, and the LORD had
given him rest from all his enemies all around,
2 that the king said to Nathan the prophet,
"See now, I dwell in a house of cedar, but the
ark of God dwells inside tent curtains."
3 Then Nathan said to the king, "Go, do all
that *is* in your heart, for the LORD *is* with you."
4 But it happened that night that the word of
the LORD came to Nathan, saying,
5 "Go and tell My servant David, 'Thus says
the LORD: "Would you build a house for Me to
dwell in?
6 "For I have not dwelt in a house since the
time that I brought the children of Israel up
from Egypt, even to this day, but have moved
about in a tent and in a tabernacle.
7 "Wherever I have moved about with all the
children of Israel, have I ever spoken a word
to anyone from the tribes of Israel, whom I
commanded to shepherd My people Israel,
saying, 'Why have you not built Me a house of
cedar?' " '
8 "Now therefore, thus shall you say to My
servant David, 'Thus says the LORD of hosts:
"I took you from the sheepfold, from following
the sheep, to be ruler over My people, over
Israel.
9 "And I have been with you wherever you
have gone, and have cut off all your enemies
from before you, and have made you a great
name, like the name of the great men who *are*
on the earth.
10 "Moreover I will appoint a place for My
people Israel, and will plant them, that they
may dwell in a place of their own and move no
more; nor shall the sons of wickedness oppress
them anymore, as previously,
11 "since the time that I commanded judges
to be over My people Israel, and have caused
you to rest from all your enemies. Also the
LORD tells you that He will make you a house.[a]
12 "When your days are fulfilled and you rest
with your fathers, I will set up your seed after
you, who will come from your body, and I will
establish his kingdom.
13 "He shall build a house for My name, and
I will establish the throne of his kingdom for-
ever.
14 "I will be his Father, and he shall be My
son. If he commits iniquity, I will chasten him
with the rod of men and with the blows of the
sons of men.
15 "But My mercy shall not depart from him,
as I took *it* from Saul, whom I removed from
before you.
16 "And your house and your kingdom shall
be established forever before you.[a] Your throne
shall be established forever." ' "
17 According to all these words and accord-
ing to all this vision, so Nathan spoke to David.

David's Thanksgiving to God

18 Then King David went in and sat before
the LORD; and he said: "Who *am* I, O Lord
GOD? And what is my house, that You have
brought me this far?

6:8 [a]Literally *Outburst Against Uzzah* **7:11** [a]That is, a royal dynasty **7:16** [a]Septuagint reads *Me.*

19 "And yet this was a small thing in Your
sight, O Lord GOD; and You have also spoken
of Your servant's house for a great while to
come. *Is* this the manner of man, O Lord GOD?
20 "Now what more can David say to You?
For You, Lord GOD, know Your servant.
21 "For Your word's sake, and according to
Your own heart, You have done all these great
things, to make Your servant know *them*.
22 "Therefore You are great, O Lord GOD.[a]
For *there is* none like You, nor *is there any*
God besides You, according to all that we have
heard with our ears.
23 "And who *is* like Your people, like Israel,
the one nation on the earth whom God went to
redeem for Himself as a people, to make for
Himself a name—and to do for Yourself great
and awesome deeds for Your land—before
Your people whom You redeemed for Yourself
from Egypt, the nations, and their gods?
24 "For You have made Your people Israel
Your very own people forever; and You, LORD,
have become their God.
25 "Now, O LORD God, the word which You
have spoken concerning Your servant and con-
cerning his house, establish *it* forever and do
as You have said.
26 "So let Your name be magnified forever,
saying, 'The LORD of hosts *is* the God over
Israel.' And let the house of Your servant David
be established before You.
27 "For You, O LORD of hosts, God of Israel,
have revealed *this* to Your servant, saying, 'I
will build you a house.' Therefore Your servant
has found it in his heart to pray this prayer to
You.
28 "And now, O Lord GOD, You are God, and
Your words are true, and You have promised
this goodness to Your servant.
29 "Now therefore, let it please You to bless
the house of Your servant, that it may continue
before You forever; for You, O Lord GOD, have
spoken *it*, and with Your blessing let the house
of Your servant be blessed forever."

David's Further Conquests

8 After this it came to pass that David at-
tacked the Philistines and subdued them.
And David took Metheg Ammah from the
hand of the Philistines.
2 Then he defeated Moab. Forcing them
down to the ground, he measured them off
with a line. With two lines he measured off
those to be put to death, and with one full
line those to be kept alive. So the Moabites
became David's servants, *and* brought tribute.
3 David also defeated Hadadezer the son of
Rehob, king of Zobah, as he went to recover
his territory at the River Euphrates.
4 David took from him one thousand *chari-
ots*, seven hundred[a] horsemen, and twenty
thousand foot soldiers. Also David hamstrung
all the chariot *horses*, except that he spared
enough of them for one hundred chariots.
5 When the Syrians of Damascus came to
help Hadadezer king of Zobah, David killed
twenty-two thousand of the Syrians.
6 Then David put garrisons in Syria of Da-
mascus; and the Syrians became David's ser-
vants, *and* brought tribute. So the LORD
preserved David wherever he went.
7 And David took the shields of gold that
had belonged to the servants of Hadadezer,
and brought them to Jerusalem.
8 Also from Betah[a] and from Berothai, cities
of Hadadezer, King David took a large amount
of bronze.
9 When Toi[a] king of Hamath heard that Da-
vid had defeated all the army of Hadadezer,
10 then Toi sent Joram[a] his son to King David,
to greet him and bless him, because he had
fought against Hadadezer and defeated him
(for Hadadezer had been at war with Toi); and
Joram brought with him articles of silver, arti-
cles of gold, and articles of bronze.
11 King David also dedicated these to the
LORD, along with the silver and gold that he
had dedicated from all the nations which he
had subdued—
12 from Syria,[a] from Moab, from the people
of Ammon, from the Philistines, from Amalek,
and from the spoil of Hadadezer the son of
Rehob, king of Zobah.
13 And David made *himself* a name when he
returned from killing eighteen thousand Syri-
ans[a] in the Valley of Salt.
14 He also put garrisons in Edom; throughout
all Edom he put garrisons, and all the Edom-
ites became David's servants. And the LORD
preserved David wherever he went.

David's Administration

15 So David reigned over all Israel; and David
administered judgment and justice to all his
people.
16 Joab the son of Zeruiah *was* over the army;
Jehoshaphat the son of Ahilud *was* recorder;
17 Zadok the son of Ahitub and Ahimelech
the son of Abiathar *were* the priests; Seraiah[a]
was the scribe;
18 Benaiah the son of Jehoiada *was over* both
the Cherethites and the Pelethites; and David's
sons were chief ministers.

David's Kindness to Mephibosheth

9 Now David said, "Is there still anyone who
is left of the house of Saul, that I may show
him kindness for Jonathan's sake?"
2 And *there was* a servant of the house of
Saul whose name *was* Ziba. So when they had
called him to David, the king said to him, "*Are*
you Ziba?" He said, "At your service!"
3 Then the king said, "*Is* there not still some-
one of the house of Saul, to whom I may show
the kindness of God?" And Ziba said to the
king, "There is still a son of Jonathan *who is*
lame in *his* feet."
4 So the king said to him, "Where *is* he?"
And Ziba said to the king, "Indeed he *is* in
the house of Machir the son of Ammiel, in Lo
Debar."
5 Then King David sent and brought him out
of the house of Machir the son of Ammiel, from
Lo Debar.
6 Now when Mephibosheth the son of Jona-
than, the son of Saul, had come to David, he
fell on his face and prostrated himself. Then

7:22 [a]Targum and Syriac read *O LORD God.* **8:4** [a]Or *seven thousand* (compare 1 Chronicles 18:4) **8:8** [a]Spelled *Tibhath* in 1 Chronicles 18:8 **8:9** [a]Spelled *Tou* in 1 Chronicles 18:9 **8:10** [a]Spelled *Hadoram* in 1 Chronicles 18:10 **8:12** [a]Septuagint, Syriac, and some Hebrew manuscripts read *Edom.* **8:13** [a]Septuagint, Syriac, and some Hebrew manuscripts read *Edomites* (compare 1 Chronicles 18:12). **8:17** [a]Spelled *Shavsha* in 1 Chronicles 18:16

David said, "Mephibosheth?" And he answered,
"Here is your servant!"
7 So David said to him, "Do not fear, for I
will surely show you kindness for Jonathan
your father's sake, and will restore to you all
the land of Saul your grandfather; and you
shall eat bread at my table continually."
8 Then he bowed himself, and said, "What
is your servant, that you should look upon such
a dead dog as I?"
9 And the king called to Ziba, Saul's servant,
and said to him, "I have given to your master's
son all that belonged to Saul and to all his
house.
10 "You therefore, and your sons and your
servants, shall work the land for him, and you
shall bring in *the harvest*, that your master's
son may have food to eat. But Mephibosheth
your master's son shall eat bread at my table
always." Now Ziba had fifteen sons and twenty
servants.
11 Then Ziba said to the king, "According to
all that my lord the king has commanded his
servant, so will your servant do." "As for Me-
phibosheth," *said the king*, "he shall eat at my
table[a] like one of the king's sons."
12 Mephibosheth had a young son whose
name *was* Micha. And all who dwelt in the
house of Ziba *were* servants of Mephibosheth.
13 So Mephibosheth dwelt in Jerusalem, for
he ate continually at the king's table. And he
was lame in both his feet.

The Ammonites and Syrians Defeated

10 It happened after this that the king of
the people of Ammon died, and Hanun
his son reigned in his place.
2 Then David said, "I will show kindness to
Hanun the son of Nahash, as his father showed
kindness to me." So David sent by the hand
of his servants to comfort him concerning his
father. And David's servants came into the
land of the people of Ammon.
3 And the princes of the people of Ammon
said to Hanun their lord, "Do you think that
David really honors your father because he
has sent comforters to you? Has David not
rather sent his servants to you to search the
city, to spy it out, and to overthrow it?"
4 Therefore Hanun took David's servants,
shaved off half of their beards, cut off their
garments in the middle, at their buttocks, and
sent them away.
5 When they told David, he sent to meet
them, because the men were greatly ashamed.
And the king said, "Wait at Jericho until your
beards have grown, and *then* return."
6 When the people of Ammon saw that they
had made themselves repulsive to David, the
people of Ammon sent and hired the Syrians
of Beth Rehob and the Syrians of Zoba, twenty
thousand foot soldiers; and from the king of
Maacah one thousand men, and from Ish-Tob
twelve thousand men.
7 Now when David heard *of it*, he sent Joab
and all the army of the mighty men.
8 Then the people of Ammon came out and
put themselves in battle array at the entrance
of the gate. And the Syrians of Zoba, Beth Re-
hob, Ish-Tob, and Maacah *were* by themselves
in the field.
9 When Joab saw that the battle line was
against him before and behind, he chose some
of Israel's best and put *them* in battle array
against the Syrians.
10 And the rest of the people he put under the
command of Abishai his brother, that he might
set *them* in battle array against the people of
Ammon.
11 Then he said, "If the Syrians are too strong
for me, then you shall help me; but if the people
of Ammon are too strong for you, then I will
come and help you.
12 "Be of good courage, and let us be strong
for our people and for the cities of our God. And
may the LORD do *what is* good in His sight."
13 So Joab and the people who *were* with him
drew near for the battle against the Syrians,
and they fled before him.
14 When the people of Ammon saw that the
Syrians were fleeing, they also fled before
Abishai, and entered the city. So Joab returned
from the people of Ammon and went to Jeru-
salem.
15 When the Syrians saw that they had been
defeated by Israel, they gathered together.
16 Then Hadadezer[a] sent and brought out the
Syrians who *were* beyond the River,[b] and they
came to Helam. And Shobach the commander
of Hadadezer's army *went* before them.
17 When it was told David, he gathered all
Israel, crossed over the Jordan, and came to
Helam. And the Syrians set themselves in bat-
tle array against David and fought with him.
18 Then the Syrians fled before Israel; and
David killed seven hundred charioteers and
forty thousand horsemen of the Syrians, and
struck Shobach the commander of their army,
who died there.
19 And when all the kings *who were* servants
to Hadadezer[a] saw that they were defeated by
Israel, they made peace with Israel and served
them. So the Syrians were afraid to help the
people of Ammon anymore.

David, Bathsheba, and Uriah

11 It happened in the spring of the year, at
the time when kings go out *to battle*,
that David sent Joab and his servants with him,
and all Israel; and they destroyed the people
of Ammon and besieged Rabbah. But David
remained at Jerusalem.
2 Then it happened one evening that David
arose from his bed and walked on the roof of
the king's house. And from the roof he saw
a woman bathing, and the woman *was* very
beautiful to behold.
3 So David sent and inquired about the
woman. And *someone* said, "*Is* this not Bath-
sheba, the daughter of Eliam, the wife of Uriah
the Hittite?"
4 Then David sent messengers, and took
her; and she came to him, and he lay with her,
for she was cleansed from her impurity; and
she returned to her house.
5 And the woman conceived; so she sent and
told David, and said, "I *am* with child."
6 Then David sent to Joab, *saying*, "Send
me Uriah the Hittite." And Joab sent Uriah to
David.
7 When Uriah had come to him, David asked
how Joab was doing, and how the people were
doing, and how the war prospered.
8 And David said to Uriah, "Go down to your
house and wash your feet." So Uriah departed

9:11 [a]Septuagint reads *David's table*. **10:16** [a]Hebrew *Hadarezer* [b]That is, the Euphrates **10:19** [a]Hebrew *Hadarezer*

from the king's house, and a gift *of food* from
the king followed him.
9 But Uriah slept at the door of the king's
house with all the servants of his lord, and did
not go down to his house.
10 So when they told David, saying, "Uriah
did not go down to his house," David said to
Uriah, "Did you not come from a journey? Why
did you not go down to your house?"
11 And Uriah said to David, "The ark and
Israel and Judah are dwelling in tents, and my
lord Joab and the servants of my lord are en-
camped in the open fields. Shall I then go to
my house to eat and drink, and to lie with my
wife? *As* you live, and *as* your soul lives, I will
not do this thing."
12 Then David said to Uriah, "Wait here to-
day also, and tomorrow I will let you depart."
So Uriah remained in Jerusalem that day and
the next.
13 Now when David called him, he ate and
drank before him; and he made him drunk.
And at evening he went out to lie on his bed
with the servants of his lord, but he did not go
down to his house.
14 In the morning it happened that David
wrote a letter to Joab and sent *it* by the hand
of Uriah.
15 And he wrote in the letter, saying, "Set
Uriah in the forefront of the hottest battle, and
retreat from him, that he may be struck down
and die."
16 So it was, while Joab besieged the city, that
he assigned Uriah to a place where he knew
there *were* valiant men.
17 Then the men of the city came out and
fought with Joab. And *some* of the people of
the servants of David fell; and Uriah the Hittite
died also.
18 Then Joab sent and told David all the
things concerning the war,
19 and charged the messenger, saying,
"When you have finished telling the matters of
the war to the king,
20 "if it happens that the king's wrath rises,
and he says to you: 'Why did you approach so
near to the city when you fought? Did you not
know that they would shoot from the wall?
21 'Who struck Abimelech the son of Jerub-
besheth?[a] Was it not a woman who cast a piece
of a millstone on him from the wall, so that
he died in Thebez? Why did you go near the
wall?'—then you shall say, 'Your servant Uriah
the Hittite is dead also.'"
22 So the messenger went, and came and told
David all that Joab had sent by him.
23 And the messenger said to David, "Surely
the men prevailed against us and came out to
us in the field; then we drove them back as far
as the entrance of the gate.
24 "The archers shot from the wall at your
servants; and *some* of the king's servants are
dead, and your servant Uriah the Hittite is
dead also."
25 Then David said to the messenger, "Thus
you shall say to Joab: 'Do not let this thing
displease you, for the sword devours one as
well as another. Strengthen your attack
against the city, and overthrow it.' So encour-
age him."
26 When the wife of Uriah heard that Uriah
her husband was dead, she mourned for her
husband.
27 And when her mourning was over, David
sent and brought her to his house, and she
became his wife and bore him a son. But the
thing that David had done displeased the
LORD.

Nathan's Parable and David's Confession

12 Then the LORD sent Nathan to David.
And he came to him, and said to him:
"There were two men in one city, one rich and
the other poor.
2 "The rich *man* had exceedingly many
flocks and herds.
3 "But the poor *man* had nothing, except one
little ewe lamb which he had bought and nour-
ished; and it grew up together with him and
with his children. It ate of his own food and
drank from his own cup and lay in his bosom;
and it was like a daughter to him.
4 "And a traveler came to the rich man, who
refused to take from his own flock and from
his own herd to prepare one for the wayfaring
man who had come to him; but he took the
poor man's lamb and prepared it for the man
who had come to him."
5 So David's anger was greatly aroused
against the man, and he said to Nathan, "*As*
the LORD lives, the man who has done this
shall surely die!
6 "And he shall restore fourfold for the lamb,
because he did this thing and because he had
no pity."
7 Then Nathan said to David, "You *are* the
man! Thus says the LORD God of Israel: 'I
anointed you king over Israel, and I delivered
you from the hand of Saul.
8 'I gave you your master's house and your
master's wives into your keeping, and gave
you the house of Israel and Judah. And if *that
had been* too little, I also would have given you
much more!
9 'Why have you despised the command-
ment of the LORD, to do evil in His sight? You
have killed Uriah the Hittite with the sword;
you have taken his wife *to be* your wife, and
have killed him with the sword of the people
of Ammon.
10 'Now therefore, the sword shall never de-
part from your house, because you have de-
spised Me, and have taken the wife of Uriah
the Hittite to be your wife.'
11 "Thus says the LORD: 'Behold, I will raise
up adversity against you from your own house;
and I will take your wives before your eyes and
give *them* to your neighbor, and he shall lie
with your wives in the sight of this sun.
12 'For you did *it* secretly, but I will do this
thing before all Israel, before the sun.'"
13 So David said to Nathan, "I have sinned
against the LORD." And Nathan said to David,
"The LORD also has put away your sin; you
shall not die.
14 "However, because by this deed you have
given great occasion to the enemies of the
LORD to blaspheme, the child also *who is* born
to you shall surely die."
15 Then Nathan departed to his house.

The Death of David's Son

And the LORD struck the child that Uriah's
wife bore to David, and it became ill.
16 David therefore pleaded with God for the

11:21 [a]Same as *Jerubbaal* (Gideon), Judges 6:32ff

child, and David fasted and went in and lay all
night on the ground.
17 So the elders of his house arose *and went*
to him, to raise him up from the ground. But
he would not, nor did he eat food with them.
18 Then on the seventh day it came to pass
that the child died. And the servants of David
were afraid to tell him that the child was dead.
For they said, "Indeed, while the child was
alive, we spoke to him, and he would not heed
our voice. How can we tell him that the child
is dead? He may do some harm!"
19 When David saw that his servants were
whispering, David perceived that the child was
dead. Therefore David said to his servants, "Is
the child dead?" And they said, "He is dead."
20 So David arose from the ground, washed
and anointed himself, and changed his clothes;
and he went into the house of the LORD and
worshiped. Then he went to his own house;
and when he requested, they set food before
him, and he ate.
21 Then his servants said to him, "What *is*
this that you have done? You fasted and wept
for the child *while he was* alive, but when the
child died, you arose and ate food."
22 And he said, "While the child was alive, I
fasted and wept; for I said, 'Who can tell
whether the LORD[a] will be gracious to me, that
the child may live?'
23 "But now he is dead; why should I fast?
Can I bring him back again? I shall go to him,
but he shall not return to me."

Solomon Is Born

24 Then David comforted Bathsheba his wife,
and went in to her and lay with her. So she
bore a son, and he[a] called his name Solomon.
Now the LORD loved him,
25 and He sent *word* by the hand of Nathan
the prophet: So he[a] called his name Jedidiah,[b]
because of the LORD.

Rabbah Is Captured

26 Now Joab fought against Rabbah of the
people of Ammon, and took the royal city.
27 And Joab sent messengers to David, and
said, "I have fought against Rabbah, and I have
taken the city's water *supply*.
28 "Now therefore, gather the rest of the peo-
ple together and encamp against the city and
take it, lest I take the city and it be called after
my name."
29 So David gathered all the people together
and went to Rabbah, fought against it, and
took it.
30 Then he took their king's crown from his
head. Its weight *was* a talent of gold, with pre-
cious stones. And it was *set* on David's head.
Also he brought out the spoil of the city in
great abundance.
31 And he brought out the people who *were*
in it, and put *them to work* with saws and iron
picks and iron axes, and made them cross over
to the brick works. So he did to all the cities of
the people of Ammon. Then David and all the
people returned to Jerusalem.

Amnon and Tamar

13 After this Absalom the son of David had
a lovely sister, whose name *was* Tamar;
and Amnon the son of David loved her.
2 Amnon was so distressed over his sister
Tamar that he became sick; for she *was* a vir-
gin. And it was improper for Amnon to do any-
thing to her.
3 But Amnon had a friend whose name *was*
Jonadab the son of Shimeah, David's brother.
Now Jonadab *was* a very crafty man.
4 And he said to him, "Why *are* you, the
king's son, becoming thinner day after day?
Will you not tell me?" Amnon said to him, "I
love Tamar, my brother Absalom's sister."
5 So Jonadab said to him, "Lie down on your
bed and pretend to be ill. And when your father
comes to see you, say to him, 'Please let my
sister Tamar come and give me food, and pre-
pare the food in my sight, that I may see *it* and
eat it from her hand.'"
6 Then Amnon lay down and pretended to
be ill; and when the king came to see him,
Amnon said to the king, "Please let Tamar my
sister come and make a couple of cakes for me
in my sight, that I may eat from her hand."
7 And David sent home to Tamar, saying,
"Now go to your brother Amnon's house, and
prepare food for him."
8 So Tamar went to her brother Amnon's
house; and he was lying down. Then she took
flour and kneaded *it*, made cakes in his sight,
and baked the cakes.
9 And she took the pan and placed *them* out
before him, but he refused to eat. Then Amnon
said, "Have everyone go out from me." And
they all went out from him.
10 Then Amnon said to Tamar, "Bring the
food into the bedroom, that I may eat from
your hand." And Tamar took the cakes which
she had made, and brought *them* to Amnon
her brother in the bedroom.
11 Now when she had brought *them* to him
to eat, he took hold of her and said to her,
"Come, lie with me, my sister."
12 But she answered him, "No, my brother,
do not force me, for no such thing should be
done in Israel. Do not do this disgraceful thing!
13 "And I, where could I take my shame? And
as for you, you would be like one of the fools
in Israel. Now therefore, please speak to the
king; for he will not withhold me from you."
14 However, he would not heed her voice; and
being stronger than she, he forced her and lay
with her.
15 Then Amnon hated her exceedingly, so
that the hatred with which he hated her *was*
greater than the love with which he had loved
her. And Amnon said to her, "Arise, be gone!"
16 So she said to him, "No, indeed! This evil
of sending me away *is* worse than the other
that you did to me." But he would not listen to
her.
17 Then he called his servant who attended
him, and said, "Here! Put this *woman* out,
away from me, and bolt the door behind her."
18 Now she had on a robe of many colors, for
the king's virgin daughters wore such apparel.
And his servant put her out and bolted the door
behind her.

12:22 [a]A few Hebrew manuscripts and Syriac read *God*. **12:24** [a]Following Kethib, Septuagint, and Vulgate; Qere, a few Hebrew manuscripts, Syriac, and Targum read *she*. **12:25** [a]Qere, some Hebrew manuscripts, Syriac, and Targum read *she*. [b]Literally *Beloved of the LORD*

19 Then Tamar put ashes on her head, and
tore her robe of many colors that *was* on her,
and laid her hand on her head and went away
crying bitterly.
20 And Absalom her brother said to her, "Has
Amnon your brother been with you? But now
hold your peace, my sister. He *is* your brother;
do not take this thing to heart." So Tamar re-
mained desolate in her brother Absalom's
house.
21 But when King David heard of all these
things, he was very angry.
22 And Absalom spoke to his brother Amnon
neither good nor bad. For Absalom hated Am-
non, because he had forced his sister Tamar.

Absalom Murders Amnon

23 And it came to pass, after two full years,
that Absalom had sheepshearers in Baal Ha-
zor, which *is* near Ephraim; so Absalom invited
all the king's sons.
24 Then Absalom came to the king and said,
"Kindly note, your servant has sheepshearers;
please, let the king and his servants go with
your servant."
25 But the king said to Absalom, "No, my son,
let us not all go now, lest we be a burden to
you." Then he urged him, but he would not go;
and he blessed him.
26 Then Absalom said, "If not, please let my
brother Amnon go with us." And the king said
to him, "Why should he go with you?"
27 But Absalom urged him; so he let Amnon
and all the king's sons go with him.
28 Now Absalom had commanded his ser-
vants, saying, "Watch now, when Amnon's
heart is merry with wine, and when I say to
you, 'Strike Amnon!' then kill him. Do not be
afraid. Have I not commanded you? Be coura-
geous and valiant."
29 So the servants of Absalom did to Amnon
as Absalom had commanded. Then all the
king's sons arose, and each one got on his mule
and fled.
30 And it came to pass, while they were on
the way, that news came to David, saying, "Ab-
salom has killed all the king's sons, and not
one of them is left!"
31 So the king arose and tore his garments
and lay on the ground, and all his servants
stood by with their clothes torn.
32 Then Jonadab the son of Shimeah, David's
brother, answered and said, "Let not my lord
suppose they have killed all the young men,
the king's sons, for only Amnon is dead. For
by the command of Absalom this has been de-
termined from the day that he forced his sister
Tamar.
33 "Now therefore, let not my lord the king
take the thing to his heart, to think that all the
king's sons are dead. For only Amnon is dead."

Absalom Flees to Geshur

34 Then Absalom fled. And the young man
who was keeping watch lifted his eyes and
looked, and there, many people were coming
from the road on the hillside behind him.[a]
35 And Jonadab said to the king, "Look, the
king's sons are coming; as your servant said,
so it is."
36 So it was, as soon as he had finished speak-
ing, that the king's sons indeed came, and they
lifted up their voice and wept. Also the king
and all his servants wept very bitterly.
37 But Absalom fled and went to Talmai the
son of Ammihud, king of Geshur. And *David*
mourned for his son every day.
38 So Absalom fled and went to Geshur, and
was there three years.
39 And King David[a] longed to go to[b] Absalom.
For he had been comforted concerning Am-
non, because he was dead.

Absalom Returns to Jerusalem

14 So Joab the son of Zeruiah perceived
that the king's heart *was* concerned
about Absalom.
2 And Joab sent to Tekoa and brought from
there a wise woman, and said to her, "Please
pretend to be a mourner, and put on mourning
apparel; do not anoint yourself with oil, but act
like a woman who has been mourning a long
time for the dead.
3 "Go to the king and speak to him in this
manner." So Joab put the words in her mouth.
4 And when the woman of Tekoa spoke[a] to
the king, she fell on her face to the ground and
prostrated herself, and said, "Help, O king!"
5 Then the king said to her, "What troubles
you?" And she answered, "Indeed I *am* a
widow, my husband is dead.
6 "Now your maidservant had two sons; and
the two fought with each other in the field, and
there was no one to part them, but the one
struck the other and killed him.
7 "And now the whole family has risen up
against your maidservant, and they said, 'De-
liver him who struck his brother, that we may
execute him for the life of his brother whom
he killed; and we will destroy the heir also.' So
they would extinguish my ember that is left,
and leave to my husband *neither* name nor
remnant on the earth."
8 Then the king said to the woman, "Go to
your house, and I will give orders concerning
you."
9 And the woman of Tekoa said to the king,
"My lord, O king, *let* the iniquity *be* on me and
on my father's house, and the king and his
throne *be* guiltless."
10 So the king said, "Whoever says *anything*
to you, bring him to me, and he shall not touch
you anymore."
11 Then she said, "Please let the king remem-
ber the LORD your God, and do not permit the
avenger of blood to destroy anymore, lest they
destroy my son." And he said, "As the LORD
lives, not one hair of your son shall fall to the
ground."
12 Therefore the woman said, "Please, let
your maidservant speak *another* word to my
lord the king." And he said, "Say on."
13 So the woman said: "Why then have you
schemed such a thing against the people of
God? For the king speaks this thing as one who
is guilty, *in that* the king does not bring his
banished one home again.
14 "For we will surely die and *become* like
water spilled on the ground, which cannot be
gathered up again. Yet God does not take away

13:34 [a]Septuagint adds *And the watchman went and told the king, and said, "I see men from the way of Horonaim, from the regions of the mountains."* **13:39** [a]Following Masoretic Text, Syriac, and Vulgate; Septuagint reads *the spirit of the king*; Targum reads *the soul of King David.* [b]Following Masoretic Text and Targum; Septuagint and Vulgate read *ceased to pursue after.* **14:4** [a]Many Hebrew manuscripts, Septuagint, Syriac, and Vulgate read *came.*

a life; but He devises means, so that His banished ones are not expelled from Him.

15 "Now therefore, I have come to speak of this thing to my lord the king because the people have made me afraid. And your maidservant said, 'I will now speak to the king; it may be that the king will perform the request of his maidservant.

16 'For the king will hear and deliver his maidservant from the hand of the man *who would* destroy me and my son together from the inheritance of God.'

17 "Your maidservant said, 'The word of my lord the king will now be comforting; for as the angel of God, so *is* my lord the king in discerning good and evil. And may the LORD your God be with you.'"

18 Then the king answered and said to the woman, "Please do not hide from me anything that I ask you." And the woman said, "Please, let my lord the king speak."

19 So the king said, "*Is* the hand of Joab with you in all this?" And the woman answered and said, "*As* you live, my lord the king, no one can turn to the right hand or to the left from anything that my lord the king has spoken. For your servant Joab commanded me, and he put all these words in the mouth of your maidservant.

20 "To bring about this change of affairs your servant Joab has done this thing; but my lord *is* wise, according to the wisdom of the angel of God, to know everything that *is* in the earth."

21 And the king said to Joab, "All right, I have granted this thing. Go therefore, bring back the young man Absalom."

22 Then Joab fell to the ground on his face and bowed himself, and thanked the king. And Joab said, "Today your servant knows that I have found favor in your sight, my lord, O king, in that the king has fulfilled the request of his servant."

23 So Joab arose and went to Geshur, and brought Absalom to Jerusalem.

24 And the king said, "Let him return to his own house, but do not let him see my face." So Absalom returned to his own house, but did not see the king's face.

David Forgives Absalom

25 Now in all Israel there was no one who was praised as much as Absalom for his good looks. From the sole of his foot to the crown of his head there was no blemish in him.

26 And when he cut the hair of his head—at the end of every year he cut *it* because it was heavy on him—when he cut it, he weighed the hair of his head at two hundred shekels according to the king's standard.

27 To Absalom were born three sons, and one daughter whose name *was* Tamar. She was a woman of beautiful appearance.

28 And Absalom dwelt two full years in Jerusalem, but did not see the king's face.

29 Therefore Absalom sent for Joab, to send him to the king, but he would not come to him. And when he sent again the second time, he would not come.

30 So he said to his servants, "See, Joab's field is near mine, and he has barley there; go and set it on fire." And Absalom's servants set the field on fire.

31 Then Joab arose and came to Absalom's house, and said to him, "Why have your servants set my field on fire?"

32 And Absalom answered Joab, "Look, I sent to you, saying, 'Come here, so that I may send you to the king, to say, "Why have I come from Geshur? *It would be* better for me *to be* there still."' Now therefore, let me see the king's face; but if there is iniquity in me, let him execute me."

33 So Joab went to the king and told him. And when he had called for Absalom, he came to the king and bowed himself on his face to the ground before the king. Then the king kissed Absalom.

Absalom's Treason

15 After this it happened that Absalom provided himself with chariots and horses, and fifty men to run before him.

2 Now Absalom would rise early and stand beside the way to the gate. *So* it was, whenever anyone who had a lawsuit came to the king for a decision, that Absalom would call to him and say, "What city *are* you from?" And he would say, "Your servant *is* from such and such a tribe of Israel."

3 Then Absalom would say to him, "Look, your case *is* good and right; but *there is* no deputy of the king to hear you."

4 Moreover Absalom would say, "Oh, that I were made judge in the land, and everyone who has any suit or cause would come to me; then I would give him justice."

5 And *so* it was, whenever anyone came near to bow down to him, that he would put out his hand and take him and kiss him.

6 In this manner Absalom acted toward all Israel who came to the king for judgment. So Absalom stole the hearts of the men of Israel.

7 Now it came to pass after forty[a] years that Absalom said to the king, "Please, let me go to Hebron and pay the vow which I made to the LORD.

8 "For your servant took a vow while I dwelt at Geshur in Syria, saying, 'If the LORD indeed brings me back to Jerusalem, then I will serve the LORD.'"

9 And the king said to him, "Go in peace." So he arose and went to Hebron.

10 Then Absalom sent spies throughout all the tribes of Israel, saying, "As soon as you hear the sound of the trumpet, then you shall say, 'Absalom reigns in Hebron!'"

11 And with Absalom went two hundred men invited from Jerusalem, and they went along innocently and did not know anything.

12 Then Absalom sent for Ahithophel the Gilonite, David's counselor, from his city—from Giloh—while he offered sacrifices. And the conspiracy grew strong, for the people with Absalom continually increased in number.

David Escapes from Jerusalem

13 Now a messenger came to David, saying, "The hearts of the men of Israel are with Absalom."

14 So David said to all his servants who *were* with him at Jerusalem, "Arise, and let us flee, or we shall not escape from Absalom. Make haste to depart, lest he overtake us suddenly and bring disaster upon us, and strike the city with the edge of the sword."

15 And the king's servants said to the king,

15:7 [a]Septuagint manuscripts, Syriac, and Josephus read *four*.

"We *are* your servants, *ready to do* whatever
my lord the king commands."
16 Then the king went out with all his house-
hold after him. But the king left ten women,
concubines, to keep the house.
17 And the king went out with all the people
after him, and stopped at the outskirts.
18 Then all his servants passed before him;
and all the Cherethites, all the Pelethites, and
all the Gittites, six hundred men who had fol-
lowed him from Gath, passed before the king.
19 Then the king said to Ittai the Gittite, "Why
are you also going with us? Return and remain
with the king. For you *are* a foreigner and also
an exile from your own place.
20 "In fact, you came *only* yesterday. Should
I make you wander up and down with us today,
since I go I know not where? Return, and take
your brethren back. Mercy and truth *be* with
you."
21 But Ittai answered the king and said, "As
the LORD lives, and *as* my lord the king lives,
surely in whatever place my lord the king shall
be, whether in death or life, even there also
your servant will be."
22 So David said to Ittai, "Go, and cross over."
Then Ittai the Gittite and all his men and all
the little ones who *were* with him crossed over.
23 And all the country wept with a loud voice,
and all the people crossed over. The king him-
self also crossed over the Brook Kidron, and
all the people crossed over toward the way of
the wilderness.
24 There was Zadok also, and all the Levites
with him, bearing the ark of the covenant of
God. And they set down the ark of God, and
Abiathar went up until all the people had fin-
ished crossing over from the city.
25 Then the king said to Zadok, "Carry the
ark of God back into the city. If I find favor in
the eyes of the LORD, He will bring me back
and show me *both* it and His dwelling place.
26 "But if He says thus: 'I have no delight in
you,' here I am, let Him do to me as seems good
to Him."
27 The king also said to Zadok the priest,
"*Are* you *not* a seer? Return to the city in peace,
and your two sons with you, Ahimaaz your
son, and Jonathan the son of Abiathar.
28 "See, I will wait in the plains of the wilder-
ness until word comes from you to inform me."
29 Therefore Zadok and Abiathar carried the
ark of God back to Jerusalem. And they re-
mained there.
30 So David went up by the Ascent of the
Mount of Olives, and wept as he went up; and
he had his head covered and went barefoot.
And all the people who *were* with him covered
their heads and went up, weeping as they went
up.
31 Then *someone* told David, saying, "Ahith-
ophel *is* among the conspirators with Absa-
lom." And David said, "O LORD, I pray, turn
the counsel of Ahithophel into foolishness!"
32 Now it happened when David had come to
the top *of the mountain,* where he worshiped
God—there was Hushai the Archite coming to
meet him with his robe torn and dust on his
head.
33 David said to him, "If you go on with me,
then you will become a burden to me.
34 "But if you return to the city, and say to
Absalom, 'I will be your servant, O king; *as* I
was your father's servant previously, so I *will*
now also *be* your servant,' then you may defeat
the counsel of Ahithophel for me.
35 "And *do* you not *have* Zadok and Abiathar
the priests with you there? Therefore it will be
that whatever you hear from the king's house,
you shall tell to Zadok and Abiathar the priests.
36 "Indeed *they have* there with them their
two sons, Ahimaaz, Zadok's *son,* and Jonathan,
Abiathar's *son;* and by them you shall send me
everything you hear."
37 So Hushai, David's friend, went into the
city. And Absalom came into Jerusalem.

Mephibosheth's Servant

16 When David was a little past the top *of
the mountain,* there was Ziba the ser-
vant of Mephibosheth, who met him with a
couple of saddled donkeys, and on them two
hundred *loaves* of bread, one hundred clusters
of raisins, one hundred summer fruits, and a
skin of wine.
2 And the king said to Ziba, "What do you
mean to do with these?" So Ziba said, "The don-
keys *are* for the king's household to ride on,
the bread and summer fruit for the young men
to eat, and the wine for those who are faint in
the wilderness to drink."
3 Then the king said, "And where *is* your
master's son?" And Ziba said to the king, "In-
deed he is staying in Jerusalem, for he said,
'Today the house of Israel will restore the king-
dom of my father to me.'"
4 So the king said to Ziba, "Here, all that
belongs to Mephibosheth *is* yours." And Ziba
said, "I humbly bow before you, *that* I may
find favor in your sight, my lord, O king!"

Shimei Curses David

5 Now when King David came to Bahurim,
there was a man from the family of the house
of Saul, whose name *was* Shimei the son of
Gera, coming from there. He came out, cursing
continuously as he came.
6 And he threw stones at David and at all
the servants of King David. And all the people
and all the mighty men *were* on his right hand
and on his left.
7 Also Shimei said thus when he cursed:
"Come out! Come out! You bloodthirsty man,
you rogue!
8 "The LORD has brought upon you all the
blood of the house of Saul, in whose place you
have reigned; and the LORD has delivered the
kingdom into the hand of Absalom your son.
So now you *are caught* in your own evil, be-
cause you are a bloodthirsty man!"
9 Then Abishai the son of Zeruiah said to
the king, "Why should this dead dog curse my
lord the king? Please, let me go over and take
off his head!"
10 But the king said, "What have I to do with
you, you sons of Zeruiah? So let him curse,
because the LORD has said to him, 'Curse Da-
vid.' Who then shall say, 'Why have you done
so?'"
11 And David said to Abishai and all his ser-
vants, "See how my son who came from my
own body seeks my life. How much more now
may this Benjamite? Let him alone, and let him
curse; for so the LORD has ordered him.
12 "It may be that the LORD will look on my

affliction,[a] and that the LORD will repay me
with good for his cursing this day."
13 And as David and his men went along the
road, Shimei went along the hillside opposite
him and cursed as he went, threw stones at
him and kicked up dust.
14 Now the king and all the people who *were*
with him became weary; so they refreshed
themselves there.

The Advice of Ahithophel

15 Meanwhile Absalom and all the people,
the men of Israel, came to Jerusalem; and
Ahithophel *was* with him.
16 And so it was, when Hushai the Archite,
David's friend, came to Absalom, that Hushai
said to Absalom, "*Long* live the king! *Long* live
the king!"
17 So Absalom said to Hushai, "*Is* this your
loyalty to your friend? Why did you not go with
your friend?"
18 And Hushai said to Absalom, "No, but
whom the LORD and this people and all the
men of Israel choose, his I will be, and with
him I will remain.
19 "Furthermore, whom should I serve?
Should I not *serve* in the presence of his son?
As I have served in your father's presence, so
will I be in your presence."
20 Then Absalom said to Ahithophel, "Give
advice as to what we should do."
21 And Ahithophel said to Absalom, "Go in
to your father's concubines, whom he has left
to keep the house; and all Israel will hear that
you are abhorred by your father. Then the
hands of all who are with you will be strong."
22 So they pitched a tent for Absalom on the
top of the house, and Absalom went in to his
father's concubines in the sight of all Israel.
23 Now the advice of Ahithophel, which he
gave in those days, *was* as if one had inquired
at the oracle of God. So *was* all the advice of
Ahithophel both with David and with Ab-
salom.

17 Moreover Ahithophel said to Absalom,
"Now let me choose twelve thousand
men, and I will arise and pursue David tonight.
2 "I will come upon him while he *is* weary
and weak, and make him afraid. And all the
people who *are* with him will flee, and I will
strike only the king.
3 "Then I will bring back all the people to
you. When all return except the man whom
you seek, all the people will be at peace."
4 And the saying pleased Absalom and all
the elders of Israel.

The Advice of Hushai

5 Then Absalom said, "Now call Hushai the
Archite also, and let us hear what he says too."
6 And when Hushai came to Absalom, Absa-
lom spoke to him, saying, "Ahithophel has spo-
ken in this manner. Shall we do as he says? If
not, speak up."
7 So Hushai said to Absalom: "The advice
that Ahithophel has given *is* not good at this
time.
8 "For," said Hushai, "you know your father
and his men, that they *are* mighty men, and
they *are* enraged in their minds, like a bear
robbed of her cubs in the field; and your father
is a man of war, and will not camp with the
people.
9 "Surely by now he is hidden in some pit,
or in some *other* place. And it will be, when
some of them are overthrown at the first, that
whoever hears *it* will say, 'There is a slaughter
among the people who follow Absalom.'
10 "And even he *who is* valiant, whose heart
is like the heart of a lion, will melt completely.
For all Israel knows that your father *is* a mighty
man, and *those* who *are* with him *are* valiant
men.
11 "Therefore I advise that all Israel be fully
gathered to you, from Dan to Beersheba, like
the sand that *is* by the sea for multitude, and
that you go to battle in person.
12 "So we will come upon him in some place
where he may be found, and we will fall on
him as the dew falls on the ground. And of him
and all the men who *are* with him there shall
not be left so much as one.
13 "Moreover, if he has withdrawn into a city,
then all Israel shall bring ropes to that city;
and we will pull it into the river, until there is
not one small stone found there."
14 So Absalom and all the men of Israel said,
"The advice of Hushai the Archite *is* better
than the advice of Ahithophel." For the LORD
had purposed to defeat the good advice of
Ahithophel, to the intent that the LORD might
bring disaster on Absalom.

Hushai Warns David to Escape

15 Then Hushai said to Zadok and Abiathar
the priests, "Thus and so Ahithophel advised
Absalom and the elders of Israel, and thus and
so I have advised.
16 "Now therefore, send quickly and tell Da-
vid, saying, 'Do not spend this night in the
plains of the wilderness, but speedily cross
over, lest the king and all the people who *are*
with him be swallowed up.'"
17 Now Jonathan and Ahimaaz stayed at En
Rogel, for they dared not be seen coming into
the city; so a female servant would come and
tell them, and they would go and tell King
David.
18 Nevertheless a lad saw them, and told Ab-
salom. But both of them went away quickly
and came to a man's house in Bahurim, who
had a well in his court; and they went down
into it.
19 Then the woman took and spread a cover-
ing over the well's mouth, and spread ground
grain on it; and the thing was not known.
20 And when Absalom's servants came to the
woman at the house, they said, "Where *are*
Ahimaaz and Jonathan?" So the woman said
to them, "They have gone over the water
brook." And when they had searched and could
not find *them*, they returned to Jerusalem.
21 Now it came to pass, after they had de-
parted, that they came up out of the well and
went and told King David, and said to David,
"Arise and cross over the water quickly. For
thus has Ahithophel advised against you."
22 So David and all the people who *were* with
him arose and crossed over the Jordan. By
morning light not one of them was left who
had not gone over the Jordan.
23 Now when Ahithophel saw that his advice
was not followed, he saddled a donkey, and
arose and went home to his house, to his city.
Then he put his household in order, and hanged

16:12 [a]Following Kethib, Septuagint, Syriac, and Vulgate; Qere reads *my eyes;* Targum reads *tears of my eyes.*

himself, and died; and he was buried in his
father's tomb.
24 Then David went to Mahanaim. And Absa-
lom crossed over the Jordan, he and all the
men of Israel with him.
25 And Absalom made Amasa captain of the
army instead of Joab. This Amasa *was* the son
of a man whose name *was* Jithra,[a] an Israelite,[b]
who had gone in to Abigail the daughter of
Nahash, sister of Zeruiah, Joab's mother.
26 So Israel and Absalom encamped in the
land of Gilead.
27 Now it happened, when David had come
to Mahanaim, that Shobi the son of Nahash
from Rabbah of the people of Ammon, Machir
the son of Ammiel from Lo Debar, and Barzil-
lai the Gileadite from Rogelim,
28 brought beds and basins, earthen vessels
and wheat, barley and flour, parched *grain* and
beans, lentils and parched *seeds*,
29 honey and curds, sheep and cheese of the
herd, for David and the people who *were* with
him to eat. For they said, "The people are hun-
gry and weary and thirsty in the wilderness."

Absalom's Defeat and Death

18 And David numbered the people who
were with him, and set captains of thou-
sands and captains of hundreds over them.
2 Then David sent out one third of the people
under the hand of Joab, one third under the
hand of Abishai the son of Zeruiah, Joab's
brother, and one third under the hand of Ittai
the Gittite. And the king said to the people, "I
also will surely go out with you myself."
3 But the people answered, "You shall not
go out! For if we flee away, they will not care
about us; nor if half of us die, will they care
about us. But *you are* worth ten thousand of us
now. For you are now more help to us in the
city."
4 Then the king said to them, "Whatever
seems best to you I will do." So the king stood
beside the gate, and all the people went out by
hundreds and by thousands.
5 Now the king had commanded Joab,
Abishai, and Ittai, saying, "*Deal* gently for my
sake with the young man Absalom." And all
the people heard when the king gave all the
captains orders concerning Absalom.
6 So the people went out into the field of
battle against Israel. And the battle was in the
woods of Ephraim.
7 The people of Israel were overthrown
there before the servants of David, and a great
slaughter of twenty thousand took place there
that day.
8 For the battle there was scattered over the
face of the whole countryside, and the woods
devoured more people that day than the sword
devoured.
9 Then Absalom met the servants of David.
Absalom rode on a mule. The mule went under
the thick boughs of a great terebinth tree, and
his head caught in the terebinth; so he was left
hanging between heaven and earth. And the
mule which *was* under him went on.
10 Now a certain man saw *it* and told Joab,
and said, "I just saw Absalom hanging in a
terebinth tree!"
11 So Joab said to the man who told him,
"You just saw *him!* And why did you not strike
him there to the ground? I would have given
you ten *shekels* of silver and a belt."
12 But the man said to Joab, "Though I were
to receive a thousand *shekels* of silver in my
hand, I would not raise my hand against the
king's son. For in our hearing the king com-
manded you and Abishai and Ittai, saying, 'Be-
ware lest anyone *touch* the young man
Absalom!'[a]
13 "Otherwise I would have dealt falsely
against my own life. For there is nothing hid-
den from the king, and you yourself would
have set yourself against *me*."
14 Then Joab said, "I cannot linger with you."
And he took three spears in his hand and
thrust them through Absalom's heart, while he
was *still* alive in the midst of the terebinth tree.
15 And ten young men who bore Joab's ar-
mor surrounded Absalom, and struck and
killed him.
16 So Joab blew the trumpet, and the people
returned from pursuing Israel. For Joab held
back the people.
17 And they took Absalom and cast him into
a large pit in the woods, and laid a very large
heap of stones over him. Then all Israel fled,
everyone to his tent.
18 Now Absalom in his lifetime had taken
and set up a pillar for himself, which *is* in the
King's Valley. For he said, "I have no son to
keep my name in remembrance." He called the
pillar after his own name. And to this day it is
called Absalom's Monument.

David Hears of Absalom's Death

19 Then Ahimaaz the son of Zadok said, "Let
me run now and take the news to the king, how
the LORD has avenged him of his enemies."
20 And Joab said to him, "You shall not take
the news this day, for you shall take the news
another day. But today you shall take no news,
because the king's son is dead."
21 Then Joab said to the Cushite, "Go, tell
the king what you have seen." So the Cushite
bowed himself to Joab and ran.
22 And Ahimaaz the son of Zadok said again
to Joab, "But whatever happens, please let me
also run after the Cushite." So Joab said, "Why
will you run, my son, since you have no news
ready?"
23 "But whatever happens," *he said*, "let me
run." So he said to him, "Run." Then Ahimaaz
ran by way of the plain, and outran the Cushite.
24 Now David was sitting between the two
gates. And the watchman went up to the roof
over the gate, to the wall, lifted his eyes and
looked, and there was a man, running alone.
25 Then the watchman cried out and told the
king. And the king said, "If he *is* alone, *there*
is news in his mouth." And he came rapidly
and drew near.
26 Then the watchman saw *another* man run-
ning, and the watchman called to the gate-
keeper and said, "There is *another* man,
running alone!" And the king said, "He also
brings news."
27 So the watchman said, "I think the run-
ning of the first is like the running of Ahimaaz
the son of Zadok." And the king said, "He *is* a
good man, and comes with good news."

17:25 [a]Spelled *Jether* in 1 Chronicles 2:17 and elsewhere [b]Following Masoretic Text, some manuscripts of the Septuagint, and Targum; some manuscripts of the Septuagint read *Ishmaelite* (compare 1 Chronicles 2:17); Vulgate reads *of Jezrael*. **18:12** [a]The ancient versions read *'Protect the young man Absalom for me!'*

28 So Ahimaaz called out and said to the
king, "All is well!" Then he bowed down with
his face to the earth before the king, and said,
"Blessed *be* the LORD your God, who has deliv-
ered up the men who raised their hand against
my lord the king!"
29 The king said, "Is the young man Absalom
safe?" Ahimaaz answered, "When Joab sent
the king's servant and *me* your servant, I saw
a great tumult, but I did not know what *it was*
about."
30 And the king said, "Turn aside *and* stand
here." So he turned aside and stood still.
31 Just then the Cushite came, and the Cush-
ite said, "There is good news, my lord the king!
For the LORD has avenged you this day of all
those who rose against you."
32 And the king said to the Cushite, "Is the
young man Absalom safe?" So the Cushite an-
swered, "May the enemies of my lord the king,
and all who rise against you to do harm, be
like *that* young man!"

David's Mourning for Absalom

33 Then the king was deeply moved, and
went up to the chamber over the gate, and
wept. And as he went, he said thus: "O my son
Absalom—my son, my son Absalom—if only I
had died in your place! O Absalom my son, my
son!"

19 And Joab was told, "Behold, the king is
weeping and mourning for Absalom."
2 So the victory that day was *turned* into
mourning for all the people. For the people
heard it said that day, "The king is grieved for
his son."
3 And the people stole back into the city that
day, as people who are ashamed steal away
when they flee in battle.
4 But the king covered his face, and the king
cried out with a loud voice, "O my son Absa-
lom! O Absalom, my son, my son!"
5 Then Joab came into the house to the king,
and said, "Today you have disgraced all your
servants who today have saved your life, the
lives of your sons and daughters, the lives of
your wives and the lives of your concubines,
6 "in that you love your enemies and hate
your friends. For you have declared today that
you regard neither princes nor servants; for
today I perceive that if Absalom had lived and
all of us had died today, then it would have
pleased you well.
7 "Now therefore, arise, go out and speak
comfort to your servants. For I swear by the
LORD, if you do not go out, not one will stay
with you this night. And that will be worse for
you than all the evil that has befallen you from
your youth until now."
8 Then the king arose and sat in the gate.
And they told all the people, saying, "There is
the king, sitting in the gate." So all the people
came before the king. For everyone of Israel
had fled to his tent.

David Returns to Jerusalem

9 Now all the people were in a dispute
throughout all the tribes of Israel, saying, "The
king saved us from the hand of our enemies,
he delivered us from the hand of the Philis-
tines, and now he has fled from the land be-
cause of Absalom.
10 "But Absalom, whom we anointed over us,
has died in battle. Now therefore, why do you
say nothing about bringing back the king?"
11 So King David sent to Zadok and Abiathar
the priests, saying, "Speak to the elders of Ju-
dah, saying, 'Why are you the last to bring the
king back to his house, since the words of all
Israel have come to the king, to his *very* house?
12 'You *are* my brethren, you *are* my bone
and my flesh. Why then are you the last to
bring back the king?'
13 "And say to Amasa, '*Are* you not my bone
and my flesh? God do so to me, and more also,
if you are not commander of the army before
me continually in place of Joab.'"
14 So he swayed the hearts of all the men of
Judah, just as *the heart of* one man, so that
they sent *this word* to the king: "Return, you
and all your servants!"
15 Then the king returned and came to the
Jordan. And Judah came to Gilgal, to go to
meet the king, to escort the king across the
Jordan.
16 And Shimei the son of Gera, a Benjamite,
who *was* from Bahurim, hurried and came
down with the men of Judah to meet King
David.
17 *There were* a thousand men of Benjamin
with him, and Ziba the servant of the house
of Saul, and his fifteen sons and his twenty
servants with him; and they went over the Jor-
dan before the king.
18 Then a ferryboat went across to carry over
the king's household, and to do what he
thought good.

David's Mercy to Shimei

Now Shimei the son of Gera fell down be-
fore the king when he had crossed the Jordan.
19 Then he said to the king, "Do not let my
lord impute iniquity to me, or remember what
wrong your servant did on the day that my lord
the king left Jerusalem, that the king should
take *it* to heart.
20 "For I, your servant, know that I have
sinned. Therefore here I am, the first to come
today of all the house of Joseph to go down to
meet my lord the king."
21 But Abishai the son of Zeruiah answered
and said, "Shall not Shimei be put to death for
this, because he cursed the LORD's anointed?"
22 And David said, "What have I to do with
you, you sons of Zeruiah, that you should be
adversaries to me today? Shall any man be put
to death today in Israel? For do I not know that
today I *am* king over Israel?"
23 Therefore the king said to Shimei, "You
shall not die." And the king swore to him.

David and Mephibosheth Meet

24 Now Mephibosheth the son of Saul came
down to meet the king. And he had not cared
for his feet, nor trimmed his mustache, nor
washed his clothes, from the day the king de-
parted until the day he returned in peace.
25 So it was, when he had come to Jerusalem
to meet the king, that the king said to him,
"Why did you not go with me, Mephibosheth?"
26 And he answered, "My lord, O king, my
servant deceived me. For your servant said, 'I
will saddle a donkey for myself, that I may ride
on it and go to the king,' because your servant
is lame.
27 "And he has slandered your servant to my
lord the king, but my lord the king *is* like the
angel of God. Therefore do *what is* good in
your eyes.
28 "For all my father's house were but dead

men before my lord the king. Yet you set your servant among those who eat at your own table. Therefore what right have I still to cry out anymore to the king?"
29 So the king said to him, "Why do you speak anymore of your matters? I have said, 'You and Ziba divide the land.'"
30 Then Mephibosheth said to the king, "Rather, let him take it all, inasmuch as my lord the king has come back in peace to his own house."

David's Kindness to Barzillai

31 And Barzillai the Gileadite came down from Rogelim and went across the Jordan with the king, to escort him across the Jordan.
32 Now Barzillai was a very aged man, eighty years old. And he had provided the king with supplies while he stayed at Mahanaim, for he *was* a very rich man.
33 And the king said to Barzillai, "Come across with me, and I will provide for you while you are with me in Jerusalem."
34 But Barzillai said to the king, "How long have I to live, that I should go up with the king to Jerusalem?
35 "I *am* today eighty years old. Can I discern between the good and bad? Can your servant taste what I eat or what I drink? Can I hear any longer the voice of singing men and singing women? Why then should your servant be a further burden to my lord the king?
36 "Your servant will go a little way across the Jordan with the king. And why should the king repay me *with* such a reward?
37 "Please let your servant turn back again, that I may die in my own city, near the grave of my father and mother. But here is your servant Chimham; let him cross over with my lord the king, and do for him what seems good to you."
38 And the king answered, "Chimham shall cross over with me, and I will do for him what seems good to you. Now whatever you request of me, I will do for you."
39 Then all the people went over the Jordan. And when the king had crossed over, the king kissed Barzillai and blessed him, and he returned to his own place.

The Quarrel About the King

40 Now the king went on to Gilgal, and Chimham[a] went on with him. And all the people of Judah escorted the king, and also half the people of Israel.
41 Just then all the men of Israel came to the king, and said to the king, "Why have our brethren, the men of Judah, stolen you away and brought the king, his household, and all David's men with him across the Jordan?"
42 So all the men of Judah answered the men of Israel, "Because the king *is* a close relative of ours. Why then are you angry over this matter? Have we ever eaten at the king's *expense*? Or has he given us any gift?"
43 And the men of Israel answered the men of Judah, and said, "We have ten shares in the king; therefore we also have more *right* to David than you. Why then do you despise us—were we not the first to advise bringing back our king?" Yet the words of the men of Judah were fiercer than the words of the men of Israel.

The Rebellion of Sheba

20 And there happened to be there a rebel,[a] whose name *was* Sheba the son of Bichri, a Benjamite. And he blew a trumpet, and said:

"We have no share in David,
Nor do we have inheritance in the son of Jesse;
Every man to his tents, O Israel!"

2 So every man of Israel deserted David, *and* followed Sheba the son of Bichri. But the men of Judah, from the Jordan as far as Jerusalem, remained loyal to their king.
3 Now David came to his house at Jerusalem. And the king took the ten women, his concubines whom he had left to keep the house, and put them in seclusion and supported them, but did not go in to them. So they were shut up to the day of their death, living in widowhood.
4 And the king said to Amasa, "Assemble the men of Judah for me within three days, and be present here yourself."
5 So Amasa went to assemble *the men of* Judah. But he delayed longer than the set time which David had appointed him.
6 And David said to Abishai, "Now Sheba the son of Bichri will do us more harm than Absalom. Take your lord's servants and pursue him, lest he find for himself fortified cities, and escape us."
7 So Joab's men, with the Cherethites, the Pelethites, and all the mighty men, went out after him. And they went out of Jerusalem to pursue Sheba the son of Bichri.
8 When they *were* at the large stone which *is* in Gibeon, Amasa came before them. Now Joab was dressed in battle armor; on it was a belt *with* a sword fastened in its sheath at his hips; and as he was going forward, it fell out.
9 Then Joab said to Amasa, "*Are* you in health, my brother?" And Joab took Amasa by the beard with his right hand to kiss him.
10 But Amasa did not notice the sword that *was* in Joab's hand. And he struck him with it in the stomach, and his entrails poured out on the ground; and he did not *strike* him again. Thus he died. Then Joab and Abishai his brother pursued Sheba the son of Bichri.
11 Meanwhile one of Joab's men stood near Amasa, and said, "Whoever favors Joab and whoever *is* for David—follow Joab!"
12 But Amasa wallowed in *his* blood in the middle of the highway. And when the man saw that all the people stood still, he moved Amasa from the highway to the field and threw a garment over him, when he saw that everyone who came upon him halted.
13 When he was removed from the highway, all the people went on after Joab to pursue Sheba the son of Bichri.
14 And he went through all the tribes of Israel to Abel and Beth Maachah and all the Berites. So they were gathered together and also went after *Sheba*.[a]
15 Then they came and besieged him in Abel of Beth Maachah; and they cast up a siege mound against the city, and it stood by the rampart. And all the people who *were* with Joab battered the wall to throw it down.
16 Then a wise woman cried out from the city,

19:40 [a]Masoretic Text reads *Chimhan*. **20:1** [a]Literally *man of Belial* **20:14** [a]Literally *him*

"Hear, hear! Please say to Joab, 'Come nearby,
that I may speak with you.'"
17 When he had come near to her, the woman
said, "*Are* you Joab?" He answered, "I *am*."
Then she said to him, "Hear the words of your
maidservant." And he answered, "I am lis-
tening."
18 So she spoke, saying, "They used to talk
in former times, saying, 'They shall surely seek
guidance at Abel,' and so they would end *dis-
putes*.
19 "I *am among the* peaceable *and* faithful in
Israel. You seek to destroy a city and a mother
in Israel. Why would you swallow up the inher-
itance of the LORD?"
20 And Joab answered and said, "Far be it,
far be it from me, that I should swallow up or
destroy!
21 "That *is* not so. But a man from the moun-
tains of Ephraim, Sheba the son of Bichri by
name, has raised his hand against the king,
against David. Deliver him only, and I will de-
part from the city." So the woman said to Joab,
"Watch, his head will be thrown to you over
the wall."
22 Then the woman in her wisdom went to all
the people. And they cut off the head of Sheba
the son of Bichri, and threw *it* out to Joab.
Then he blew a trumpet, and they withdrew
from the city, every man to his tent. So Joab
returned to the king at Jerusalem.

David's Government Officers

23 And Joab *was* over all the army of Israel;
Benaiah the son of Jehoiada *was* over the
Cherethites and the Pelethites;
24 Adoram *was* in charge of revenue; Jehosh-
aphat the son of Ahilud *was* recorder;
25 Sheva *was* scribe; Zadok and Abiathar
were the priests;
26 and Ira the Jairite was a chief minister un-
der David.

David Avenges the Gibeonites

21 Now there was a famine in the days of
David for three years, year after year;
and David inquired of the LORD. And the LORD
answered, "*It is* because of Saul and *his* blood-
thirsty house, because he killed the Gibeon-
ites."
2 So the king called the Gibeonites and
spoke to them. Now the Gibeonites *were* not
of the children of Israel, but of the remnant of
the Amorites; the children of Israel had sworn
protection to them, but Saul had sought to kill
them in his zeal for the children of Israel and
Judah.
3 Therefore David said to the Gibeonites,
"What shall I do for you? And with what shall
I make atonement, that you may bless the in-
heritance of the LORD?"
4 And the Gibeonites said to him, "We will
have no silver or gold from Saul or from his
house, nor shall you kill any man in Israel for
us." So he said, "Whatever you say, I will do
for you."
5 Then they answered the king, "As for the
man who consumed us and plotted against us,
that we should be destroyed from remaining
in any of the territories of Israel,
6 "let seven men of his descendants be deliv-
ered to us, and we will hang them before the
LORD in Gibeah of Saul, *whom* the LORD
chose." And the king said, "I will give *them*."
7 But the king spared Mephibosheth the son
of Jonathan, the son of Saul, because of the
LORD's oath that *was* between them, between
David and Jonathan the son of Saul.
8 So the king took Armoni and Mephibo-
sheth, the two sons of Rizpah the daughter of
Aiah, whom she bore to Saul, and the five sons
of Michal[a] the daughter of Saul, whom she
brought up for Adriel the son of Barzillai the
Meholathite;
9 and he delivered them into the hands of
the Gibeonites, and they hanged them on the
hill before the LORD. So they fell, *all* seven
together, and were put to death in the days of
harvest, in the first *days*, in the beginning of
barley harvest.
10 Now Rizpah the daughter of Aiah took
sackcloth and spread it for herself on the rock,
from the beginning of harvest until the late
rains poured on them from heaven. And she
did not allow the birds of the air to rest on
them by day nor the beasts of the field by night.
11 And David was told what Rizpah the
daughter of Aiah, the concubine of Saul, had
done.
12 Then David went and took the bones of
Saul, and the bones of Jonathan his son, from
the men of Jabesh Gilead who had stolen them
from the street of Beth Shan,[a] where the Philis-
tines had hung them up, after the Philistines
had struck down Saul in Gilboa.
13 So he brought up the bones of Saul and
the bones of Jonathan his son from there; and
they gathered the bones of those who had been
hanged.
14 They buried the bones of Saul and Jona-
than his son in the country of Benjamin in Ze-
lah, in the tomb of Kish his father. So they
performed all that the king commanded. And
after that God heeded the prayer for the land.

Philistine Giants Destroyed

15 When the Philistines were at war again
with Israel, David and his servants with him
went down and fought against the Philistines;
and David grew faint.
16 Then Ishbi-Benob, who *was* one of the
sons of the giant, the weight of whose bronze
spear *was* three hundred *shekels*, who was
bearing a new *sword*, thought he could kill
David.
17 But Abishai the son of Zeruiah came to his
aid, and struck the Philistine and killed him.
Then the men of David swore to him, saying,
"You shall go out no more with us to battle,
lest you quench the lamp of Israel."
18 Now it happened afterward that there was
again a battle with the Philistines at Gob. Then
Sibbechai the Hushathite killed Saph,[a] who
was one of the sons of the giant.
19 Again there was war at Gob with the Phi-
listines, where Elhanan the son of Jaare-
Oregim[a] the Bethlehemite killed *the brother of*
Goliath the Gittite, the shaft of whose spear
was like a weaver's beam.
20 Yet again there was war at Gath, where
there was a man of *great* stature, who had six
fingers on each hand and six toes on each foot,
twenty-four in number; and he also was born
to the giant.

21:8 [a]Or *Merab* (compare 1 Samuel 18:19 and 25:44; 2 Samuel 3:14 and 6:23) **21:12** [a]Spelled *Beth Shean* in Joshua 17:11 and elsewhere **21:18** [a]Spelled *Sippai* in 1 Chronicles 20:4 **21:19** [a]Spelled *Jair* in 1 Chronicles 20:5

21 So when he defied Israel, Jonathan the son
of Shimea,[a] David's brother, killed him.
22 These four were born to the giant in Gath,
and fell by the hand of David and by the hand
of his servants.

Praise for God's Deliverance

22 Then David spoke to the LORD the
words of this song, on the day when the
LORD had delivered him from the hand of all
his enemies, and from the hand of Saul.
2 And he said:[a]

"The LORD *is* my rock and my fortress and my deliverer;
3 The God of my strength, in whom I will trust;
My shield and the horn of my salvation,
My stronghold and my refuge;
My Savior, You save me from violence.
4 I will call upon the LORD, *who is worthy* to be praised;
So shall I be saved from my enemies.

5 "When the waves of death surrounded me,
The floods of ungodliness made me afraid.
6 The sorrows of Sheol surrounded me;
The snares of death confronted me.
7 In my distress I called upon the LORD,
And cried out to my God;
He heard my voice from His temple,
And my cry *entered* His ears.

8 "Then the earth shook and trembled;
The foundations of heaven[a] quaked and were shaken,
Because He was angry.
9 Smoke went up from His nostrils,
And devouring fire from His mouth;
Coals were kindled by it.
10 He bowed the heavens also, and came down
With darkness under His feet.
11 He rode upon a cherub, and flew;
And He was seen[a] upon the wings of the wind.
12 He made darkness canopies around Him,
Dark waters *and* thick clouds of the skies.
13 From the brightness before Him
Coals of fire were kindled.

14 "The LORD thundered from heaven,
And the Most High uttered His voice.
15 He sent out arrows and scattered them;
Lightning bolts, and He vanquished them.
16 Then the channels of the sea were seen,
The foundations of the world were uncovered,
At the rebuke of the LORD,
At the blast of the breath of His nostrils.

17 "He sent from above, He took me,
He drew me out of many waters.
18 He delivered me from my strong enemy,
From those who hated me;
For they were too strong for me.
19 They confronted me in the day of my calamity,
But the LORD was my support.
20 He also brought me out into a broad place;
He delivered me because He delighted in me.

21 "The LORD rewarded me according to my righteousness;
According to the cleanness of my hands
He has recompensed me.
22 For I have kept the ways of the LORD,
And have not wickedly departed from my God.
23 For all His judgments *were* before me;
And *as for* His statutes, I did not depart from them.
24 I was also blameless before Him,
And I kept myself from my iniquity.
25 Therefore the LORD has recompensed me according to my righteousness,
According to my cleanness in His eyes.[a]

26 "With the merciful You will show Yourself merciful;
With a blameless man You will show Yourself blameless;
27 With the pure You will show Yourself pure;
And with the devious You will show Yourself shrewd.
28 You will save the humble people;
But Your eyes *are* on the haughty, *that* You may bring *them* down.

29 "For You *are* my lamp, O LORD;
The LORD shall enlighten my darkness.
30 For by You I can run against a troop;
By my God I can leap over a wall.
31 *As for* God, His way *is* perfect;
The word of the LORD *is* proven;
He *is* a shield to all who trust in Him.

32 "For who *is* God, except the LORD?
And who *is* a rock, except our God?
33 God *is* my strength *and* power,[a]
And He makes my[b] way perfect.
34 He makes my[a] feet like the *feet* of deer,
And sets me on my high places.
35 He teaches my hands to make war,
So that my arms can bend a bow of bronze.

36 "You have also given me the shield of Your salvation;
Your gentleness has made me great.
37 You enlarged my path under me;
So my feet did not slip.

38 "I have pursued my enemies and destroyed them;
Neither did I turn back again till they were destroyed.
39 And I have destroyed them and wounded them,
So that they could not rise;
They have fallen under my feet.

21:21 [a]Spelled *Shammah* in 1 Samuel 16:9 and elsewhere **22:2** [a]Compare Psalm 18 **22:8** [a]Following Masoretic Text, Septuagint, and Targum; Syriac and Vulgate read *hills* (compare Psalm 18:7). **22:11** [a]Following Masoretic Text and Septuagint; many Hebrew manuscripts, Syriac, and Vulgate read *He flew* (compare Psalm 18:10); Targum reads *He spoke with power.* **22:25** [a]Septuagint, Syriac, and Vulgate read *the cleanness of my hands in His sight* (compare Psalm 18:24); Targum reads *my cleanness before His word.* **22:33** [a]Dead Sea Scrolls, Septuagint, Syriac, and Vulgate read *It is God who arms me with strength* (compare Psalm 18:32); Targum reads *It is God who sustains me with strength.* [b]Following Qere, Septuagint, Syriac, Targum, and Vulgate (compare Psalm 18:32); Kethib reads *His.* **22:34** [a]Following Qere, Septuagint, Syriac, Targum, and Vulgate (compare Psalm 18:33); Kethib reads *His.*

40 For You have armed me with strength for the battle;
You have subdued under me those who rose against me.
41 You have also given me the necks of my enemies,
So that I destroyed those who hated me.
42 They looked, but *there was* none to save;
Even to the LORD, but He did not answer them.
43 Then I beat them as fine as the dust of the earth;
I trod them like dirt in the streets,
And I spread them out.

44 "You have also delivered me from the strivings of my people;
You have kept me as the head of the nations.
A people I have not known shall serve me.
45 The foreigners submit to me;
As soon as they hear, they obey me.
46 The foreigners fade away,
And come frightened[a] from their hideouts.

47 "The LORD lives!
Blessed *be* my Rock!
Let God be exalted,
The Rock of my salvation!
48 *It is* God who avenges me,
And subdues the peoples under me;
49 He delivers me from my enemies.
You also lift me up above those who rise against me;
You have delivered me from the violent man.
50 Therefore I will give thanks to You,
O LORD, among the Gentiles,
And sing praises to Your name.

51 "*He is* the tower of salvation to His king,
And shows mercy to His anointed,
To David and his descendants forevermore."

David's Last Words

23 Now these *are* the last words of David.

Thus says David the son of Jesse;
Thus says the man raised up on high,
The anointed of the God of Jacob,
And the sweet psalmist of Israel:

2 "The Spirit of the LORD spoke by me,
And His word *was* on my tongue.
3 The God of Israel said,
The Rock of Israel spoke to me:
'He who rules over men *must be* just,
Ruling in the fear of God.
4 And *he shall be* like the light of the morning *when* the sun rises,
A morning without clouds,
Like the tender grass *springing* out of the earth,
By clear shining after rain.'

5 "Although my house *is* not so with God,
Yet He has made with me an everlasting covenant,
Ordered in all *things* and secure.
For *this is* all my salvation and all *my* desire;
Will He not make *it* increase?
6 But *the sons* of rebellion *shall* all *be* as thorns thrust away,
Because they cannot be taken with hands.
7 But the man *who* touches them
Must be armed with iron and the shaft of a spear,
And they shall be utterly burned with fire in *their* place."

David's Mighty Men

8 These *are* the names of the mighty men
whom David had: Josheb-Basshebeth[a] the
Tachmonite, chief among the captains.[b] He was
called Adino the Eznite, because he had killed
eight hundred men at one time.
9 And after him *was* Eleazar the son of Do-
do,[a] the Ahohite, *one* of the three mighty men
with David when they defied the Philistines
who were gathered there for battle, and the
men of Israel had retreated.
10 He arose and attacked the Philistines until
his hand was weary, and his hand stuck to the
sword. The LORD brought about a great victory
that day; and the people returned after him
only to plunder.
11 And after him *was* Shammah the son of
Agee the Hararite. The Philistines had gath-
ered together into a troop where there was a
piece of ground full of lentils. So the people
fled from the Philistines.
12 But he stationed himself in the middle of
the field, defended it, and killed the Philistines.
So the LORD brought about a great victory.
13 Then three of the thirty chief men went
down at harvest time and came to David at the
cave of Adullam. And the troop of Philistines
encamped in the Valley of Rephaim.
14 David *was* then in the stronghold, and the
garrison of the Philistines *was* then *in* Beth-
lehem.
15 And David said with longing, "Oh, that
someone would give me a drink of the water
from the well of Bethlehem, which *is* by the
gate!"
16 So the three mighty men broke through
the camp of the Philistines, drew water from
the well of Bethlehem that *was* by the gate,
and took it and brought *it* to David. Neverthe-
less he would not drink it, but poured it out to
the LORD.
17 And he said, "Far be it from me, O LORD,
that I should do this! Is *this not* the blood of
the men who went in *jeopardy of* their lives?"
Therefore he would not drink it. These things
were done by the three mighty men.
18 Now Abishai the brother of Joab, the son
of Zeruiah, was chief of *another* three.[a] He
lifted his spear against three hundred *men*,
killed *them*, and won a name among *these*
three.
19 Was he not the most honored of three?
Therefore he became their captain. However,
he did not attain to the *first* three.
20 Benaiah *was* the son of Jehoiada, the son
of a valiant man from Kabzeel, who had done

22:46 [a]Following Septuagint, Targum, and Vulgate (compare Psalm 18:45); Masoretic Text reads *gird themselves*.
23:8 [a]Literally *One Who Sits in the Seat* (compare 1 Chronicles 11:11) [b]Following Masoretic Text and Targum; Septuagint and Vulgate read *the three*. **23:9** [a]Spelled *Dodai* in 1 Chronicles 27:4 **23:18** [a]Following Masoretic Text, Septuagint, and Vulgate; some Hebrew manuscripts and Syriac read *thirty*; Targum reads *the mighty men*.

many deeds. He had killed two lion-like heroes
of Moab. He also had gone down and killed a
lion in the midst of a pit on a snowy day.
21 And he killed an Egyptian, a spectacular
man. The Egyptian *had* a spear in his hand; so
he went down to him with a staff, wrested the
spear out of the Egyptian's hand, and killed
him with his own spear.
22 These *things* Benaiah the son of Jehoiada
did, and won a name among three mighty men.
23 He was more honored than the thirty, but
he did not attain to the *first* three. And David
appointed him over his guard.
24 Asahel the brother of Joab *was* one of the
thirty; Elhanan the son of Dodo of Bethlehem,
25 Shammah the Harodite, Elika the Ha-
rodite,
26 Helez the Paltite, Ira the son of Ikkesh the
Tekoite,
27 Abiezer the Anathothite, Mebunnai the
Hushathite,
28 Zalmon the Ahohite, Maharai the Netoph-
athite,
29 Heleb the son of Baanah (the Netopha-
thite), Ittai the son of Ribai from Gibeah of the
children of Benjamin,
30 Benaiah a Pirathonite, Hiddai from the
brooks of Gaash,
31 Abi-Albon the Arbathite, Azmaveth the
Barhumite,
32 Eliahba the Shaalbonite (of the sons of Ja-
shen), Jonathan,
33 Shammah the Hararite, Ahiam the son of
Sharar the Hararite,
34 Eliphelet the son of Ahasbai, the son of the
Maachathite, Eliam the son of Ahithophel the
Gilonite,
35 Hezrai[a] the Carmelite, Paarai the Arbite,
36 Igal the son of Nathan of Zobah, Bani the
Gadite,
37 Zelek the Ammonite, Naharai the Beeroth-
ite (armorbearer of Joab the son of Zeruiah),
38 Ira the Ithrite, Gareb the Ithrite,
39 *and* Uriah the Hittite: thirty-seven in all.

David's Census of Israel and Judah

24 Again the anger of the LORD was
aroused against Israel, and He moved
David against them to say, "Go, number Israel
and Judah."
2 So the king said to Joab the commander
of the army who *was* with him, "Now go
throughout all the tribes of Israel, from Dan to
Beersheba, and count the people, that I may
know the number of the people."
3 And Joab said to the king, "Now may the
LORD your God add to the people a hundred
times more than there are, and may the eyes
of my lord the king see *it*. But why does my
lord the king desire this thing?"
4 Nevertheless the king's word prevailed
against Joab and against the captains of the
army. Therefore Joab and the captains of the
army went out from the presence of the king
to count the people of Israel.
5 And they crossed over the Jordan and
camped in Aroer, on the right side of the town
which *is* in the midst of the ravine of Gad, and
toward Jazer.
6 Then they came to Gilead and to the land
of Tahtim Hodshi; they came to Dan Jaan and
around to Sidon;
7 and they came to the stronghold of Tyre
and to all the cities of the Hivites and the Ca-
naanites. Then they went out to South Judah
as far as Beersheba.
8 So when they had gone through all the
land, they came to Jerusalem at the end of nine
months and twenty days.
9 Then Joab gave the sum of the number of
the people to the king. And there were in Israel
eight hundred thousand valiant men who drew
the sword, and the men of Judah were five
hundred thousand men.

The Judgment on David's Sin

10 And David's heart condemned him after
he had numbered the people. So David said to
the LORD, "I have sinned greatly in what I have
done; but now, I pray, O LORD, take away the
iniquity of Your servant, for I have done very
foolishly."
11 Now when David arose in the morning, the
word of the LORD came to the prophet Gad,
David's seer, saying,
12 "Go and tell David, 'Thus says the LORD:
"I offer you three *things;* choose one of them
for yourself, that I may do *it* to you." ' "
13 So Gad came to David and told him; and
he said to him, "Shall seven[a] years of famine
come to you in your land? Or shall you flee
three months before your enemies, while they
pursue you? Or shall there be three days'
plague in your land? Now consider and see
what answer I should take back to Him who
sent me."
14 And David said to Gad, "I am in great dis-
tress. Please let us fall into the hand of the
LORD, for His mercies *are* great; but do not let
me fall into the hand of man."
15 So the LORD sent a plague upon Israel
from the morning till the appointed time. From
Dan to Beersheba seventy thousand men of
the people died.
16 And when the angel[a] stretched out His
hand over Jerusalem to destroy it, the LORD
relented from the destruction, and said to the
angel who was destroying the people, "It is
enough; now restrain your hand." And the an-
gel of the LORD was by the threshing floor of
Araunah[b] the Jebusite.
17 Then David spoke to the LORD when he
saw the angel who was striking the people, and
said, "Surely I have sinned, and I have done
wickedly; but these sheep, what have they
done? Let Your hand, I pray, be against me and
against my father's house."

The Altar on the Threshing Floor

18 And Gad came that day to David and said
to him, "Go up, erect an altar to the LORD on
the threshing floor of Araunah the Jebusite."
19 So David, according to the word of Gad,
went up as the LORD commanded.
20 Now Araunah looked, and saw the king
and his servants coming toward him. So Arau-
nah went out and bowed before the king with
his face to the ground.
21 Then Araunah said, "Why has my lord the
king come to his servant?" And David said,
"To buy the threshing floor from you, to build
an altar to the LORD, that the plague may be
withdrawn from the people."
22 Now Araunah said to David, "Let my lord

23:35 [a]Spelled *Hezro* in 1 Chronicles 11:37 **24:13** [a]Following Masoretic Text, Syriac, Targum, and Vulgate; Septuagint reads *three* (compare 1 Chronicles 21:12). **24:16** [a]Or *Angel* [b]Spelled *Ornan* in 1 Chronicles 21:15

the king take and offer up whatever *seems*
good to him. Look, *here are* oxen for burnt
sacrifice, and threshing implements and the
yokes of the oxen for wood.
23 "All these, O king, Araunah has given to
the king." And Araunah said to the king, "May
the LORD your God accept you."
24 Then the king said to Araunah, "No, but I
will surely buy *it* from you for a price; nor will
I offer burnt offerings to the LORD my God
with that which costs me nothing." So David
bought the threshing floor and the oxen for
fifty shekels of silver.
25 And David built there an altar to the LORD,
and offered burnt offerings and peace offer-
ings. So the LORD heeded the prayers for the
land, and the plague was withdrawn from Is-
rael.

The First Book of the KINGS

Adonijah Presumes to Be King

1 Now King David was old, advanced in
years; and they put covers on him, but he
could not get warm.
2 Therefore his servants said to him, "Let a
young woman, a virgin, be sought for our lord
the king, and let her stand before the king, and
let her care for him; and let her lie in your
bosom, that our lord the king may be warm."
3 So they sought for a lovely young woman
throughout all the territory of Israel, and found
Abishag the Shunammite, and brought her to
the king.
4 The young woman *was* very lovely; and
she cared for the king, and served him; but the
king did not know her.
5 Then Adonijah the son of Haggith exalted
himself, saying, "I will be king"; and he pre-
pared for himself chariots and horsemen, and
fifty men to run before him.
6 (And his father had not rebuked him at
any time by saying, "Why have you done so?"
He *was* also very good-looking. *His mother*
had borne him after Absalom.)
7 Then he conferred with Joab the son of
Zeruiah and with Abiathar the priest, and they
followed and helped Adonijah.
8 But Zadok the priest, Benaiah the son of
Jehoiada, Nathan the prophet, Shimei, Rei,
and the mighty men who *belonged* to David
were not with Adonijah.
9 And Adonijah sacrificed sheep and oxen
and fattened cattle by the stone of Zoheleth,
which *is* by En Rogel; he also invited all his
brothers, the king's sons, and all the men of
Judah, the king's servants.
10 But he did not invite Nathan the prophet,
Benaiah, the mighty men, or Solomon his
brother.
11 So Nathan spoke to Bathsheba the mother
of Solomon, saying, "Have you not heard that
Adonijah the son of Haggith has become king,
and David our lord does not know *it?*
12 "Come, please, let me now give you advice,
that you may save your own life and the life of
your son Solomon.
13 "Go immediately to King David and say to
him, 'Did you not, my lord, O king, swear to
your maidservant, saying, "Assuredly your son
Solomon shall reign after me, and he shall sit
on my throne"? Why then has Adonijah be-
come king?'
14 "Then, while you are still talking there
with the king, I also will come in after you and
confirm your words."
15 So Bathsheba went into the chamber to
the king. (Now the king was very old, and Abi-
shag the Shunammite was serving the king.)
16 And Bathsheba bowed and did homage to
the king. Then the king said, "What is your
wish?"
17 Then she said to him, "My lord, you swore
by the LORD your God to your maidservant,
saying, 'Assuredly Solomon your son shall
reign after me, and he shall sit on my throne.'
18 "So now, look! Adonijah has become king;
and now, my lord the king, you do not know
about *it.*
19 "He has sacrificed oxen and fattened cattle
and sheep in abundance, and has invited all
the sons of the king, Abiathar the priest, and
Joab the commander of the army; but Solomon
your servant he has not invited.
20 "And as for you, my lord, O king, the eyes
of all Israel *are* on you, that you should tell
them who will sit on the throne of my lord the
king after him.
21 "Otherwise it will happen, when my lord
the king rests with his fathers, that I and my
son Solomon will be counted as offenders."
22 And just then, while she was still talking
with the king, Nathan the prophet also came
in.
23 So they told the king, saying, "Here is Na-
than the prophet." And when he came in be-
fore the king, he bowed down before the king
with his face to the ground.
24 And Nathan said, "My lord, O king, have
you said, 'Adonijah shall reign after me, and
he shall sit on my throne'?
25 "For he has gone down today, and has sac-
rificed oxen and fattened cattle and sheep in
abundance, and has invited all the king's sons,
and the commanders of the army, and Abia-
thar the priest; and look! They are eating and
drinking before him; and they say, '*Long* live
King Adonijah!'
26 "But he has not invited me—me your ser-
vant—nor Zadok the priest, nor Benaiah the
son of Jehoiada, nor your servant Solomon.
27 "Has this thing been done by my lord the
king, and you have not told your servant who
should sit on the throne of my lord the king
after him?"

David Proclaims Solomon King

28 Then King David answered and said, "Call
Bathsheba to me." So she came into the king's
presence and stood before the king.
29 And the king took an oath and said, "*As*
the LORD lives, who has redeemed my life from
every distress,
30 "just as I swore to you by the LORD God of
Israel, saying, 'Assuredly Solomon your son

shall be king after me, and he shall sit on my
throne in my place,' so I certainly will do this
day."
31 Then Bathsheba bowed with *her* face to
the earth, and paid homage to the king, and
said, "Let my lord King David live forever!"
32 And King David said, "Call to me Zadok
the priest, Nathan the prophet, and Benaiah
the son of Jehoiada." So they came before the
king.
33 The king also said to them, "Take with you
the servants of your lord, and have Solomon
my son ride on my own mule, and take him
down to Gihon.
34 "There let Zadok the priest and Nathan
the prophet anoint him king over Israel; and
blow the horn, and say, '*Long* live King Sol-
omon!'
35 "Then you shall come up after him, and he
shall come and sit on my throne, and he shall
be king in my place. For I have appointed him
to be ruler over Israel and Judah."
36 Benaiah the son of Jehoiada answered the
king and said, "Amen! May the LORD God of
my lord the king say so *too*.
37 "As the LORD has been with my lord the
king, even so may He be with Solomon, and
make his throne greater than the throne of my
lord King David."
38 So Zadok the priest, Nathan the prophet,
Benaiah the son of Jehoiada, the Cherethites,
and the Pelethites went down and had Sol-
omon ride on King David's mule, and took him
to Gihon.
39 Then Zadok the priest took a horn of oil
from the tabernacle and anointed Solomon.
And they blew the horn, and all the people
said, "*Long* live King Solomon!"
40 And all the people went up after him; and
the people played the flutes and rejoiced with
great joy, so that the earth *seemed to* split with
their sound.
41 Now Adonijah and all the guests who *were*
with him heard *it* as they finished eating. And
when Joab heard the sound of the horn, he
said, "Why *is* the city in such a noisy uproar?"
42 While he was still speaking, there came
Jonathan, the son of Abiathar the priest. And
Adonijah said to him, "Come in, for you *are* a
prominent man, and bring good news."
43 Then Jonathan answered and said to Ado-
nijah, "No! Our lord King David has made Sol-
omon king.
44 "The king has sent with him Zadok the
priest, Nathan the prophet, Benaiah the son of
Jehoiada, the Cherethites, and the Pelethites;
and they have made him ride on the king's
mule.
45 "So Zadok the priest and Nathan the
prophet have anointed him king at Gihon; and
they have gone up from there rejoicing, so that
the city is in an uproar. This *is* the noise that
you have heard.
46 "Also Solomon sits on the throne of the
kingdom.
47 "And moreover the king's servants have
gone to bless our lord King David, saying, 'May
God make the name of Solomon better than your
name, and may He make his throne greater
than your throne.' Then the king bowed him-
self on the bed.
48 "Also the king said thus, 'Blessed *be* the
LORD God of Israel, who has given *one* to sit
on my throne this day, while my eyes see *it!*'"
49 So all the guests who were with Adonijah
were afraid, and arose, and each one went his
way.
50 Now Adonijah was afraid of Solomon; so
he arose, and went and took hold of the horns
of the altar.
51 And it was told Solomon, saying, "Indeed
Adonijah is afraid of King Solomon; for look,
he has taken hold of the horns of the altar,
saying, 'Let King Solomon swear to me today
that he will not put his servant to death with the
sword.'"
52 Then Solomon said, "If he proves himself
a worthy man, not one hair of him shall fall to
the earth; but if wickedness is found in him, he
shall die."
53 So King Solomon sent them to bring him
down from the altar. And he came and fell
down before King Solomon; and Solomon said
to him, "Go to your house."

David's Instructions to Solomon

2 Now the days of David drew near that he
should die, and he charged Solomon his
son, saying:
2 "I go the way of all the earth; be strong,
therefore, and prove yourself a man.
3 "And keep the charge of the LORD your
God: to walk in His ways, to keep His statutes,
His commandments, His judgments, and His
testimonies, as it is written in the Law of Mo-
ses, that you may prosper in all that you do
and wherever you turn;
4 "that the LORD may fulfill His word which
He spoke concerning me, saying, 'If your sons
take heed to their way, to walk before Me in
truth with all their heart and with all their
soul,' He said, 'you shall not lack a man on the
throne of Israel.'
5 "Moreover you know also what Joab the
son of Zeruiah did to me, *and* what he did to
the two commanders of the armies of Israel, to
Abner the son of Ner and Amasa the son of
Jether, whom he killed. And he shed the blood
of war in peacetime, and put the blood of war
on his belt that *was* around his waist, and on
his sandals that *were* on his feet.
6 "Therefore do according to your wisdom,
and do not let his gray hair go down to the grave
in peace.
7 "But show kindness to the sons of Barzillai
the Gileadite, and let them be among those
who eat at your table, for so they came to me
when I fled from Absalom your brother.
8 "And see, *you have* with you Shimei the
son of Gera, a Benjamite from Bahurim, who
cursed me with a malicious curse in the day
when I went to Mahanaim. But he came down
to meet me at the Jordan, and I swore to him
by the LORD, saying, 'I will not put you to death
with the sword.'
9 "Now therefore, do not hold him guiltless,
for you *are* a wise man and know what you
ought to do to him; but bring his gray hair
down to the grave with blood."

Death of David

10 So David rested with his fathers, and was
buried in the City of David.
11 The period that David reigned over Israel
was forty years; seven years he reigned in He-
bron, and in Jerusalem he reigned thirty-three
years.
12 Then Solomon sat on the throne of his fa-
ther David; and his kingdom was firmly estab-
lished.

Solomon Executes Adonijah

13 Now Adonijah the son of Haggith came to
Bathsheba the mother of Solomon. So she said,
"Do you come peaceably?" And he said, "Peace-
ably."
14 Moreover he said, "I have something *to*
say to you." And she said, "Say it."
15 Then he said, "You know that the kingdom
was mine, and all Israel had set their expecta-
tions on me, that I should reign. However, the
kingdom has been turned over, and has be-
come my brother's; for it was his from the
LORD.
16 "Now I ask one petition of you; do not deny
me." And she said to him, "Say it."
17 Then he said, "Please speak to King Sol-
omon, for he will not refuse you, that he may
give me Abishag the Shunammite as wife."
18 So Bathsheba said, "Very well, I will speak
for you to the king."
19 Bathsheba therefore went to King Sol-
omon, to speak to him for Adonijah. And the
king rose up to meet her and bowed down to
her, and sat down on his throne and had a
throne set for the king's mother; so she sat at
his right hand.
20 Then she said, "I desire one small petition
of you; do not refuse me." And the king said to
her, "Ask it, my mother, for I will not refuse
you."
21 So she said, "Let Abishag the Shunammite
be given to Adonijah your brother as wife."
22 And King Solomon answered and said to
his mother, "Now why do you ask Abishag the
Shunammite for Adonijah? Ask for him the
kingdom also—for he *is* my older brother—for
him, and for Abiathar the priest, and for Joab
the son of Zeruiah."
23 Then King Solomon swore by the LORD,
saying, "May God do so to me, and more also,
if Adonijah has not spoken this word against
his own life!
24 "Now therefore, *as* the LORD lives, who
has confirmed me and set me on the throne of
David my father, and who has established a
house[a] for me, as He promised, Adonijah shall
be put to death today!"
25 So King Solomon sent by the hand of Be-
naiah the son of Jehoiada; and he struck him
down, and he died.

Abiathar Exiled, Joab Executed

26 And to Abiathar the priest the king said,
"Go to Anathoth, to your own fields, for you
are deserving of death; but I will not put you
to death at this time, because you carried the
ark of the Lord GOD before my father David,
and because you were afflicted every time my
father was afflicted."
27 So Solomon removed Abiathar from being
priest to the LORD, that he might fulfill the
word of the LORD which He spoke concerning
the house of Eli at Shiloh.
28 Then news came to Joab, for Joab had de-
fected to Adonijah, though he had not defected
to Absalom. So Joab fled to the tabernacle of
the LORD, and took hold of the horns of the
altar.
29 And King Solomon was told, "Joab has fled
to the tabernacle of the LORD; there *he is,* by
the altar." Then Solomon sent Benaiah the son
of Jehoiada, saying, "Go, strike him down."
30 So Benaiah went to the tabernacle of the
LORD, and said to him, "Thus says the king,
'Come out!'" And he said, "No, but I will die
here." And Benaiah brought back word to the
king, saying, "Thus said Joab, and thus he an-
swered me."
31 Then the king said to him, "Do as he has
said, and strike him down and bury him, that
you may take away from me and from the house
of my father the innocent blood which Joab
shed.
32 "So the LORD will return his blood on his
head, because he struck down two men more
righteous and better than he, and killed them
with the sword—Abner the son of Ner, the
commander of the army of Israel, and Amasa
the son of Jether, the commander of the army
of Judah—though my father David did not
know *it.*
33 "Their blood shall therefore return upon
the head of Joab and upon the head of his
descendants forever. But upon David and his
descendants, upon his house and his throne,
there shall be peace forever from the LORD."
34 So Benaiah the son of Jehoiada went up
and struck and killed him; and he was buried
in his own house in the wilderness.
35 The king put Benaiah the son of Jehoiada
in his place over the army, and the king put
Zadok the priest in the place of Abiathar.

Shimei Executed

36 Then the king sent and called for Shimei,
and said to him, "Build yourself a house in
Jerusalem and dwell there, and do not go out
from there anywhere.
37 "For it shall be, on the day you go out and
cross the Brook Kidron, know for certain you
shall surely die; your blood shall be on your
own head."
38 And Shimei said to the king, "The saying
is good. As my lord the king has said, so your
servant will do." So Shimei dwelt in Jerusalem
many days.
39 Now it happened at the end of three years,
that two slaves of Shimei ran away to Achish
the son of Maachah, king of Gath. And they
told Shimei, saying, "Look, your slaves *are* in
Gath!"
40 So Shimei arose, saddled his donkey, and
went to Achish at Gath to seek his slaves. And
Shimei went and brought his slaves from Gath.
41 And Solomon was told that Shimei had
gone from Jerusalem to Gath and had come
back.
42 Then the king sent and called for Shimei,
and said to him, "Did I not make you swear by
the LORD, and warn you, saying, 'Know for
certain that on the day you go out and travel
anywhere, you shall surely die'? And you said
to me, 'The word I have heard *is* good.'
43 "Why then have you not kept the oath of
the LORD and the commandment that I gave
you?"
44 The king said moreover to Shimei, "You
know, as your heart acknowledges, all the
wickedness that you did to my father David;
therefore the LORD will return your wickedness
on your own head.
45 "But King Solomon *shall be* blessed, and
the throne of David shall be established before
the LORD forever."

2:24 [a]That is, a royal dynasty

46 So the king commanded Benaiah the son
of Jehoiada; and he went out and struck him
down, and he died. Thus the kingdom was es-
tablished in the hand of Solomon.

Solomon Requests Wisdom

3 Now Solomon made a treaty with Pharaoh
king of Egypt, and married Pharaoh's
daughter; then he brought her to the City of
David until he had finished building his own
house, and the house of the LORD, and the wall
all around Jerusalem.
2 Meanwhile the people sacrificed at the
high places, because there was no house built
for the name of the LORD until those days.
3 And Solomon loved the LORD, walking in
the statutes of his father David, except that
he sacrificed and burned incense at the high
places.
4 Now the king went to Gibeon to sacrifice
there, for that *was* the great high place: Solomon
offered a thousand burnt offerings on that
altar.
5 At Gibeon the LORD appeared to Solomon
in a dream by night; and God said, "Ask! What
shall I give you?"
6 And Solomon said: "You have shown great
mercy to Your servant David my father, be-
cause he walked before You in truth, in righ-
teousness, and in uprightness of heart with
You; You have continued this great kindness
for him, and You have given him a son to sit
on his throne, as *it is* this day.
7 "Now, O LORD my God, You have made
Your servant king instead of my father David,
but I *am* a little child; I do not know *how* to go
out or come in.
8 "And Your servant *is* in the midst of Your
people whom You have chosen, a great people,
too numerous to be numbered or counted.
9 "Therefore give to Your servant an under-
standing heart to judge Your people, that I may
discern between good and evil. For who is able
to judge this great people of Yours?"
10 The speech pleased the Lord, that Solomon
had asked this thing.
11 Then God said to him: "Because you have
asked this thing, and have not asked long life
for yourself, nor have asked riches for yourself,
nor have asked the life of your enemies, but
have asked for yourself understanding to dis-
cern justice,
12 "behold, I have done according to your
words; see, I have given you a wise and under-
standing heart, so that there has not been any-
one like you before you, nor shall any like you
arise after you.
13 "And I have also given you what you have
not asked: both riches and honor, so that there
shall not be anyone like you among the kings
all your days.
14 "So if you walk in My ways, to keep My
statutes and My commandments, as your fa-
ther David walked, then I will lengthen your
days."
15 Then Solomon awoke; and indeed it had
been a dream. And he came to Jerusalem and
stood before the ark of the covenant of the
LORD, offered up burnt offerings, offered
peace offerings, and made a feast for all his
servants.

Solomon's Wise Judgment

16 Now two women *who were* harlots came
to the king, and stood before him.
17 And one woman said, "O my lord, this
woman and I dwell in the same house; and I
gave birth while she *was* in the house.
18 "Then it happened, the third day after I
had given birth, that this woman also gave
birth. And we *were* together; no one *was* with
us in the house, except the two of us in the house.
19 "And this woman's son died in the night,
because she lay on him.
20 "So she arose in the middle of the night
and took my son from my side, while your
maidservant slept, and laid him in her bosom,
and laid her dead child in my bosom.
21 "And when I rose in the morning to nurse
my son, there he was, dead. But when I had
examined him in the morning, indeed, he was
not my son whom I had borne."
22 Then the other woman said, "No! But the
living one *is* my son, and the dead one *is* your
son." And the first woman said, "No! But the
dead one *is* your son, and the living one *is* my
son." Thus they spoke before the king.
23 And the king said, "The one says, 'This *is*
my son, who lives, and your son *is* the dead
one'; and the other says, 'No! But your son *is*
the dead one, and my son *is* the living one.'"
24 Then the king said, "Bring me a sword."
So they brought a sword before the king.
25 And the king said, "Divide the living child
in two, and give half to one, and half to the other."
26 Then the woman whose son *was* living
spoke to the king, for she yearned with com-
passion for her son; and she said, "O my lord,
give her the living child, and by no means kill
him!" But the other said, "Let him be neither
mine nor yours, *but* divide *him*."
27 So the king answered and said, "Give the
first woman the living child, and by no means
kill him; she *is* his mother."
28 And all Israel heard of the judgment which
the king had rendered; and they feared the
king, for they saw that the wisdom of God *was*
in him to administer justice.

Solomon's Administration

4 So King Solomon was king over all Israel.
2 And these *were* his officials: Azariah
the son of Zadok, the priest;
3 Elihoreph and Ahijah, the sons of Shisha,
scribes; Jehoshaphat the son of Ahilud, the re-
corder;
4 Benaiah the son of Jehoiada, over the
army; Zadok and Abiathar, the priests;
5 Azariah the son of Nathan, over the offi-
cers; Zabud the son of Nathan, a priest *and* the
king's friend;
6 Ahishar, over the household; and Adoni-
ram the son of Abda, over the labor force.
7 And Solomon had twelve governors over
all Israel, who provided food for the king and
his household; each one made provision for
one month of the year.
8 These *are* their names: Ben-Hur,[a] in the
mountains of Ephraim;
9 Ben-Deker,[a] in Makaz, Shaalbim, Beth
Shemesh, and Elon Beth Hanan;
10 Ben-Hesed,[a] in Arubboth; to him *belonged*
Sochoh and all the land of Hepher;

4:8 [a]Literally *Son of Hur* **4:9** [a]Literally *Son of Deker* **4:10** [a]Literally *Son of Hesed*

11 Ben-Abinadab,[a] *in* all the regions of Dor; he had Taphath the daughter of Solomon as wife;
12 Baana the son of Ahilud, *in* Taanach, Megiddo, and all Beth Shean, which *is* beside Zaretan below Jezreel, from Beth Shean to Abel Meholah, as far as the other side of Jokneam;
13 Ben-Geber,[a] in Ramoth Gilead; to him *belonged* the towns of Jair the son of Manasseh, in Gilead; to him *also belonged* the region of Argob in Bashan—sixty large cities with walls and bronze gate-bars;
14 Ahinadab the son of Iddo, *in* Mahanaim;
15 Ahimaaz, in Naphtali; he also took Basemath the daughter of Solomon as wife;
16 Baanah the son of Hushai, in Asher and Aloth;
17 Jehoshaphat the son of Paruah, in Issachar;
18 Shimei the son of Elah, in Benjamin;
19 Geber the son of Uri, in the land of Gilead, *in* the country of Sihon king of the Amorites, and of Og king of Bashan. *He was* the only governor who *was* in the land.

Prosperity and Wisdom of Solomon's Reign

20 Judah and Israel *were* as numerous as the sand by the sea in multitude, eating and drinking and rejoicing.
21 So Solomon reigned over all kingdoms from the River[a] *to* the land of the Philistines, as far as the border of Egypt. *They* brought tribute and served Solomon all the days of his life.
22 Now Solomon's provision for one day was thirty kors of fine flour, sixty kors of meal,
23 ten fatted oxen, twenty oxen from the pastures, and one hundred sheep, besides deer, gazelles, roebucks, and fatted fowl.
24 For he had dominion over all *the region* on this side of the River[a] from Tiphsah even to Gaza, namely over all the kings on this side of the River; and he had peace on every side all around him.
25 And Judah and Israel dwelt safely, each man under his vine and his fig tree, from Dan as far as Beersheba, all the days of Solomon.
26 Solomon had forty[a] thousand stalls of horses for his chariots, and twelve thousand horsemen.
27 And these governors, each man in his month, provided food for King Solomon and for all who came to King Solomon's table. There was no lack in their supply.
28 They also brought barley and straw to the proper place, for the horses and steeds, each man according to his charge.
29 And God gave Solomon wisdom and exceedingly great understanding, and largeness of heart like the sand on the seashore.
30 Thus Solomon's wisdom excelled the wisdom of all the men of the East and all the wisdom of Egypt.
31 For he was wiser than all men—than Ethan the Ezrahite, and Heman, Chalcol, and Darda, the sons of Mahol; and his fame was in all the surrounding nations.
32 He spoke three thousand proverbs, and his songs were one thousand and five.
33 Also he spoke of trees, from the cedar tree of Lebanon even to the hyssop that springs out of the wall; he spoke also of animals, of birds, of creeping things, and of fish.
34 And men of all nations, from all the kings of the earth who had heard of his wisdom, came to hear the wisdom of Solomon.

Solomon Prepares to Build the Temple

5 Now Hiram king of Tyre sent his servants to Solomon, because he heard that they had anointed him king in place of his father, for Hiram had always loved David.
2 Then Solomon sent to Hiram, saying:

3 You know how my father David could not
build a house for the name of the LORD
his God because of the wars which were
fought against him on every side, until
the LORD put *his foes*[a] under the soles of
his feet.
4 But now the LORD my God has given me
rest on every side; *there is* neither
adversary nor evil occurrence.
5 And behold, I propose to build a house
for the name of the LORD my God, as the
LORD spoke to my father David, saying,
"Your son, whom I will set on your throne
in your place, he shall build the house for
My name."
6 Now therefore, command that they cut
down cedars for me from Lebanon; and
my servants will be with your servants,
and I will pay you wages for your
servants according to whatever you say.
For you know *there is* none among us
who has skill to cut timber like the
Sidonians.

7 So it was, when Hiram heard the words of Solomon, that he rejoiced greatly and said,

Blessed *be* the LORD this day, for He has
given David a wise son over this great
people!

8 Then Hiram sent to Solomon, saying:

I have considered *the message* which you
sent me, *and* I will do all you desire
concerning the cedar and cypress logs.
9 My servants shall bring *them* down from
Lebanon to the sea; I will float them in
rafts by sea to the place you indicate to
me, and will have them broken apart
there; then you can take *them* away. And
you shall fulfill my desire by giving food
for my household.

10 Then Hiram gave Solomon cedar and cypress logs *according to* all his desire.
11 And Solomon gave Hiram twenty thousand kors of wheat *as* food for his household, and twenty[a] kors of pressed oil. Thus Solomon gave to Hiram year by year.
12 So the LORD gave Solomon wisdom, as He had promised him; and there was peace between Hiram and Solomon, and the two of them made a treaty together.
13 Then King Solomon raised up a labor force out of all Israel; and the labor force was thirty thousand men.
14 And he sent them to Lebanon, ten thousand

4:11 [a]Literally *Son of Abinadab* **4:13** [a]Literally *Son of Geber* **4:21** [a]That is, the Euphrates **4:24** [a]That is, the Euphrates **4:26** [a]Following Masoretic Text and most other authorities; some manuscripts of the Septuagint read *four* (compare 2 Chronicles 9:25). **5:3** [a]Literally *them* **5:11** [a]Following Masoretic Text, Targum, and Vulgate; Septuagint and Syriac read *twenty thousand.*

a month in shifts: they were one month in Lebanon *and* two months at home; Adoniram *was* in charge of the labor force.

15 Solomon had seventy thousand who carried burdens, and eighty thousand who quarried *stone* in the mountains,

16 besides three thousand three hundred[a] from the chiefs of Solomon's deputies, who supervised the people who labored in the work.

17 And the king commanded them to quarry large stones, costly stones, *and* hewn stones, to lay the foundation of the temple.[a]

18 So Solomon's builders, Hiram's builders, and the Gebalites quarried *them;* and they prepared timber and stones to build the temple.

Solomon Builds the Temple

6 And it came to pass in the four hundred and eightieth[a] year after the children of Israel had come out of the land of Egypt, in the fourth year of Solomon's reign over Israel, in the month of Ziv, which *is* the second month, that he began to build the house of the LORD.

2 Now the house which King Solomon built for the LORD, its length *was* sixty cubits, its width twenty, and its height thirty cubits.

3 The vestibule in front of the sanctuary[a] of the house *was* twenty cubits long across the width of the house, *and* the width of *the vestibule*[b] *extended* ten cubits from the front of the house.

4 And he made for the house windows with beveled frames.

5 Against the wall of the temple he built chambers all around, *against* the walls of the temple, all around the sanctuary and the inner sanctuary.[a] Thus he made side chambers all around it.

6 The lowest chamber *was* five cubits wide, the middle *was* six cubits wide, and the third *was* seven cubits wide; for he made narrow ledges around the outside of the temple, so that *the support beams* would not be fastened into the walls of the temple.

7 And the temple, when it was being built, was built with stone finished at the quarry, so that no hammer or chisel *or* any iron tool was heard in the temple while it was being built.

8 The doorway for the middle story[a] *was* on the right side of the temple. They went up by stairs to the middle *story,* and from the middle to the third.

9 So he built the temple and finished it, and he paneled the temple with beams and boards of cedar.

10 And he built side chambers against the entire temple, each five cubits high; they were attached to the temple with cedar beams.

11 Then the word of the LORD came to Solomon, saying:

12 "*Concerning* this temple which you are building, if you walk in My statutes, execute My judgments, keep all My commandments, and walk in them, then I will perform My word with you, which I spoke to your father David.

13 "And I will dwell among the children of Israel, and will not forsake My people Israel."

14 So Solomon built the temple and finished it.

15 And he built the inside walls of the temple with cedar boards; from the floor of the temple to the ceiling he paneled the inside with wood; and he covered the floor of the temple with planks of cypress.

16 Then he built the twenty-cubit room at the rear of the temple, from floor to ceiling, with cedar boards; he built *it* inside as the inner sanctuary, as the Most Holy *Place.*

17 And in front of it the temple sanctuary was forty cubits *long.*

18 The inside of the temple was cedar, carved with ornamental buds and open flowers. All *was* cedar; there was no stone *to be* seen.

19 And he prepared the inner sanctuary inside the temple, to set the ark of the covenant of the LORD there.

20 The inner sanctuary *was* twenty cubits long, twenty cubits wide, and twenty cubits high. He overlaid it with pure gold, and overlaid the altar of cedar.

21 So Solomon overlaid the inside of the temple with pure gold. He stretched gold chains across the front of the inner sanctuary, and overlaid it with gold.

22 The whole temple he overlaid with gold, until he had finished all the temple; also he overlaid with gold the entire altar that *was* by the inner sanctuary.

23 Inside the inner sanctuary he made two cherubim *of* olive wood, *each* ten cubits high.

24 One wing of the cherub *was* five cubits, and the other wing of the cherub five cubits: ten cubits from the tip of one wing to the tip of the other.

25 And the other cherub *was* ten cubits; both cherubim *were* of the same size and shape.

26 The height of one cherub *was* ten cubits, and so *was* the other cherub.

27 Then he set the cherubim inside the inner room;[a] and they stretched out the wings of the cherubim so that the wing of the one touched *one* wall, and the wing of the other cherub touched the other wall. And their wings touched each other in the middle of the room.

28 Also he overlaid the cherubim with gold.

29 Then he carved all the walls of the temple all around, both the inner and outer *sanctuaries,* with carved figures of cherubim, palm trees, and open flowers.

30 And the floor of the temple he overlaid with gold, both the inner and outer *sanctuaries.*

31 For the entrance of the inner sanctuary he made doors *of* olive wood; the lintel *and* doorposts *were* one-fifth *of the wall.*

32 The two doors *were of* olive wood; and he carved on them figures of cherubim, palm trees, and open flowers, and overlaid *them* with gold; and he spread gold on the cherubim and on the palm trees.

33 So for the door of the sanctuary he also made doorposts *of* olive wood, one-fourth *of the wall.*

34 And the two doors *were of* cypress wood; two panels *comprised* one folding door, and two panels *comprised* the other folding door.

5:16 [a]Following Masoretic Text, Targum, and Vulgate; Septuagint reads *three thousand six hundred.* **5:17** [a]Literally *house,* and so frequently throughout this book **6:1** [a]Following Masoretic Text, Targum, and Vulgate; Septuagint reads *fortieth.* **6:3** [a]Hebrew *heykal;* here the main room of the temple, elsewhere called the holy place (compare Exodus 26:33 and Ezekiel 41:1) [b]Literally *it* **6:5** [a]Hebrew *debir;* here the inner room of the temple, elsewhere called the Most Holy Place (compare verse 16) **6:8** [a]Following Masoretic Text and Vulgate; Septuagint reads *upper story;* Targum reads *ground story.* **6:27** [a]Literally *house*

35 Then he carved cherubim, palm trees, and open flowers *on them*, and overlaid *them* with gold applied evenly on the carved work.

36 And he built the inner court with three rows of hewn stone and a row of cedar beams.

37 In the fourth year the foundation of the house of the LORD was laid, in the month of Ziv.

38 And in the eleventh year, in the month of Bul, which is the eighth month, the house was finished in all its details and according to all its plans. So he was seven years in building it.

Solomon's Other Buildings

7 But Solomon took thirteen years to build his own house; so he finished all his house.

2 He also built the House of the Forest of Lebanon; its length *was* one hundred cubits, its width fifty cubits, and its height thirty cubits, with four rows of cedar pillars, and cedar beams on the pillars.

3 And *it was* paneled with cedar above the beams that *were* on forty-five pillars, fifteen *to* a row.

4 *There were* windows *with beveled frames in* three rows, and window *was* opposite window *in* three tiers.

5 And all the doorways and doorposts *had* rectangular frames; and window *was* opposite window *in* three tiers.

6 He also made the Hall of Pillars: its length *was* fifty cubits, and its width thirty cubits; and in front of them *was* a portico with pillars, and a canopy *was* in front of them.

7 Then he made a hall for the throne, the Hall of Judgment, where he might judge; and *it was* paneled with cedar from floor to ceiling.[a]

8 And the house where he dwelt *had* another court inside the hall, of like workmanship. Solomon also made a house like this hall for Pharaoh's daughter, whom he had taken *as wife*.

9 All these *were of* costly stones cut to size, trimmed with saws, inside and out, from the foundation to the eaves, and also on the outside to the great court.

10 The foundation *was of* costly stones, large stones, some ten cubits and some eight cubits.

11 And above *were* costly stones, hewn to size, and cedar wood.

12 The great court *was* enclosed with three rows of hewn stones and a row of cedar beams. So were the inner court of the house of the LORD and the vestibule of the temple.

Hiram the Craftsman

13 Now King Solomon sent and brought Huram[a] from Tyre.

14 He *was* the son of a widow from the tribe of Naphtali, and his father *was* a man of Tyre, a bronze worker; he was filled with wisdom and understanding and skill in working with all kinds of bronze work. So he came to King Solomon and did all his work.

The Bronze Pillars for the Temple

15 And he cast two pillars of bronze, each one eighteen cubits high, and a line of twelve cubits measured the circumference of each.

16 Then he made two capitals *of* cast bronze, to set on the tops of the pillars. The height of one capital *was* five cubits, and the height of the other capital *was* five cubits.

17 *He made* a lattice network, with wreaths of chainwork, for the capitals which *were* on top of the pillars: seven chains for one capital and seven for the other capital.

18 So he made the pillars, and two rows of pomegranates above the network all around to cover the capitals that *were* on top; and thus he did for the other capital.

19 The capitals which *were* on top of the pillars in the hall *were* in the shape of lilies, four cubits.

20 The capitals on the two pillars also *had pomegranates* above, by the convex surface which *was* next to the network; and there *were* two hundred such pomegranates in rows on each of the capitals all around.

21 Then he set up the pillars by the vestibule of the temple; he set up the pillar on the right and called its name Jachin, and he set up the pillar on the left and called its name Boaz.

22 The tops of the pillars were in the shape of lilies. So the work of the pillars was finished.

The Sea and the Oxen

23 And he made the Sea of cast bronze, ten cubits from one brim to the other; *it was* completely round. Its height *was* five cubits, and a line of thirty cubits measured its circumference.

24 Below its brim *were* ornamental buds encircling it all around, ten to a cubit, all the way around the Sea. The ornamental buds *were* cast in two rows when it was cast.

25 It stood on twelve oxen: three looking toward the north, three looking toward the west, three looking toward the south, and three looking toward the east; the Sea *was set* upon them, and all their back parts *pointed* inward.

26 It *was* a handbreadth thick; and its brim was shaped like the brim of a cup, *like* a lily blossom. It contained two thousand[a] baths.

The Carts and the Lavers

27 He also made ten carts of bronze; four cubits *was* the length of each cart, four cubits its width, and three cubits its height.

28 And this *was* the design of the carts: They had panels, and the panels *were* between frames;

29 on the panels that *were* between the frames *were* lions, oxen, and cherubim. And on the frames *was* a pedestal on top. Below the lions and oxen *were* wreaths of plaited work.

30 Every cart had four bronze wheels and axles of bronze, and its four feet had supports. Under the laver *were* supports of cast *bronze* beside each wreath.

31 Its opening inside the crown at the top *was* one cubit in diameter; and the opening *was* round, shaped *like* a pedestal, one and a half cubits in outside diameter; and also on the opening *were* engravings, but the panels were square, not round.

32 Under the panels *were* the four wheels, and the axles of the wheels *were joined* to the cart. The height of a wheel *was* one and a half cubits.

33 The workmanship of the wheels *was* like the workmanship of a chariot wheel; their axle pins, their rims, their spokes, and their hubs *were* all of cast *bronze*.

34 And *there were* four supports at the four

7:7 [a]Literally *floor*, that is, of the upper level **7:13** [a]Hebrew *Hiram* (compare 2 Chronicles 2:13, 14) **7:26** [a]Or *three thousand* (compare 2 Chronicles 4:5)

corners of each cart; its supports *were* part of the cart itself.
35 On the top of the cart, at the height of half a cubit, *it was* perfectly round. And on the top of the cart, its flanges and its panels *were* of the same casting.
36 On the plates of its flanges and on its panels he engraved cherubim, lions, and palm trees, wherever there was a clear space on each, with wreaths all around.
37 Thus he made the ten carts. All of them were of the same mold, one measure, *and* one shape.
38 Then he made ten lavers of bronze; each laver contained forty baths, *and* each laver *was* four cubits. On each of the ten carts *was* a laver.
39 And he put five carts on the right side of the house, and five on the left side of the house. He set the Sea on the right side of the house, toward the southeast.

Furnishings of the Temple

40 Huram[a] made the lavers and the shovels and the bowls. So Huram finished doing all the work that he was to do for King Solomon *for* the house of the LORD:
41 the two pillars, the *two* bowl-shaped capitals that *were* on top of the two pillars; the two networks covering the two bowl-shaped capitals which *were* on top of the pillars;
42 four hundred pomegranates for the two networks (two rows of pomegranates for each network, to cover the two bowl-shaped capitals that *were* on top of the pillars);
43 the ten carts, and ten lavers on the carts;
44 one Sea, and twelve oxen under the Sea;
45 the pots, the shovels, and the bowls. All these articles which Huram[a] made for King Solomon *for* the house of the LORD *were of* burnished bronze.
46 In the plain of Jordan the king had them cast in clay molds, between Succoth and Zaretan.
47 And Solomon did not weigh all the articles, because *there were* so many; the weight of the bronze was not determined.
48 Thus Solomon had all the furnishings made for the house of the LORD: the altar of gold, and the table of gold on which *was* the showbread;
49 the lampstands of pure gold, five on the right *side* and five on the left in front of the inner sanctuary, with the flowers and the lamps and the wick-trimmers of gold;
50 the basins, the trimmers, the bowls, the ladles, and the censers of pure gold; and the hinges of gold, *both* for the doors of the inner room (the Most Holy *Place*) *and* for the doors of the main hall of the temple.
51 So all the work that King Solomon had done for the house of the LORD was finished; and Solomon brought in the things which his father David had dedicated: the silver and the gold and the furnishings. He put them in the treasuries of the house of the LORD.

The Ark Brought into the Temple

8 Now Solomon assembled the elders of Israel and all the heads of the tribes, the chief fathers of the children of Israel, to King Solomon in Jerusalem, that they might bring up the ark of the covenant of the LORD from the City of David, which *is* Zion.
2 Therefore all the men of Israel assembled with King Solomon at the feast in the month of Ethanim, which *is* the seventh month.
3 So all the elders of Israel came, and the priests took up the ark.
4 Then they brought up the ark of the LORD, the tabernacle of meeting, and all the holy furnishings that *were* in the tabernacle. The priests and the Levites brought them up.
5 Also King Solomon, and all the congregation of Israel who were assembled with him, *were* with him before the ark, sacrificing sheep and oxen that could not be counted or numbered for multitude.
6 Then the priests brought in the ark of the covenant of the LORD to its place, into the inner sanctuary of the temple, to the Most Holy *Place*, under the wings of the cherubim.
7 For the cherubim spread *their* two wings over the place of the ark, and the cherubim overshadowed the ark and its poles.
8 The poles extended so that the ends of the poles could be seen from the holy *place*, in front of the inner sanctuary; but they could not be seen from outside. And they are there to this day.
9 Nothing *was* in the ark except the two tablets of stone which Moses put there at Horeb, when the LORD made *a covenant* with the children of Israel, when they came out of the land of Egypt.
10 And it came to pass, when the priests came out of the holy *place*, that the cloud filled the house of the LORD,
11 so that the priests could not continue ministering because of the cloud; for the glory of the LORD filled the house of the LORD.
12 Then Solomon spoke:

"The LORD said He would dwell in the
dark cloud.
13 I have surely built You an exalted house,
And a place for You to dwell in forever."

Solomon's Speech at Completion of the Work

14 Then the king turned around and blessed the whole assembly of Israel, while all the assembly of Israel was standing.
15 And he said: "Blessed *be* the LORD God of Israel, who spoke with His mouth to my father David, and with His hand has fulfilled *it*, saying,
16 'Since the day that I brought My people Israel out of Egypt, I have chosen no city from any tribe of Israel *in which* to build a house, that My name might be there; but I chose David to be over My people Israel.'
17 "Now it was in the heart of my father David to build a temple[a] for the name of the LORD God of Israel.
18 "But the LORD said to my father David, 'Whereas it was in your heart to build a temple for My name, you did well that it was in your heart.
19 'Nevertheless you shall not build the temple, but your son who will come from your body, he shall build the temple for My name.'
20 "So the LORD has fulfilled His word which He spoke; and I have filled the position of my father David, and sit on the throne of Israel, as the LORD promised; and I have built a temple for the name of the LORD God of Israel.

7:40 [a]Hebrew *Hiram* (compare 2 Chronicles 2:13, 14) **7:45** [a]Hebrew *Hiram* (compare 2 Chronicles 2:13, 14) **8:17** [a]Literally *house*, and so in verses 18–20

21 "And there I have made a place for the ark,
in which *is* the covenant of the LORD which He
made with our fathers, when He brought them
out of the land of Egypt."

Solomon's Prayer of Dedication

22 Then Solomon stood before the altar of the
LORD in the presence of all the assembly of
Israel, and spread out his hands toward heaven;
23 and he said: "LORD God of Israel, *there is*
no God in heaven above or on earth below like
You, who keep *Your* covenant and mercy with
Your servants who walk before You with all
their hearts.
24 "You have kept what You promised Your
servant David my father; You have both spo-
ken with Your mouth and fulfilled *it* with Your
hand, as *it is* this day.
25 "Therefore, LORD God of Israel, now keep
what You promised Your servant David my fa-
ther, saying, 'You shall not fail to have a man
sit before Me on the throne of Israel, only if
your sons take heed to their way, that they
walk before Me as you have walked before Me.'
26 "And now I pray, O God of Israel, let Your
word come true, which You have spoken to
Your servant David my father.
27 "But will God indeed dwell on the earth?
Behold, heaven and the heaven of heavens
cannot contain You. How much less this tem-
ple which I have built!
28 "Yet regard the prayer of Your servant and
his supplication, O LORD my God, and listen
to the cry and the prayer which Your servant
is praying before You today:
29 "that Your eyes may be open toward this
temple night and day, toward the place of
which You said, 'My name shall be there,' that
You may hear the prayer which Your servant
makes toward this place.
30 "And may You hear the supplication of
Your servant and of Your people Israel, when
they pray toward this place. Hear in heaven
Your dwelling place; and when You hear, for-
give.
31 "When anyone sins against his neighbor,
and is forced to take an oath, and comes *and*
takes an oath before Your altar in this temple,
32 "then hear in heaven, and act, and judge
Your servants, condemning the wicked, bring-
ing his way on his head, and justifying the
righteous by giving him according to his righ-
teousness.
33 "When Your people Israel are defeated be-
fore an enemy because they have sinned
against You, and when they turn back to You
and confess Your name, and pray and make
supplication to You in this temple,
34 "then hear in heaven, and forgive the sin
of Your people Israel, and bring them back to
the land which You gave to their fathers.
35 "When the heavens are shut up and there
is no rain because they have sinned against You,
when they pray toward this place and confess
Your name, and turn from their sin because
You afflict them,
36 "then hear in heaven, and forgive the sin
of Your servants, Your people Israel, that You
may teach them the good way in which they
should walk; and send rain on Your land which
You have given to Your people as an inheritance.
37 "When there is famine in the land, pesti-
lence *or* blight *or* mildew, locusts *or* grass-
hoppers; when their enemy besieges them in the
land of their cities; whatever plague or what-
ever sickness *there is;*
38 "whatever prayer, whatever supplication
is made by anyone, *or* by all Your people Israel,
when each one knows the plague of his own
heart, and spreads out his hands toward this
temple:
39 "then hear in heaven Your dwelling place,
and forgive, and act, and give to everyone ac-
cording to all his ways, whose heart You know
(for You alone know the hearts of all the sons
of men),
40 "that they may fear You all the days that
they live in the land which You gave to our
fathers.
41 "Moreover, concerning a foreigner, who *is*
not of Your people Israel, but has come from a
far country for Your name's sake
42 "(for they will hear of Your great name and
Your strong hand and Your outstretched arm),
when he comes and prays toward this temple,
43 "hear in heaven Your dwelling place, and
do according to all for which the foreigner calls
to You, that all peoples of the earth may know
Your name and fear You, as *do* Your people Is-
rael, and that they may know that this temple
which I have built is called by Your name.
44 "When Your people go out to battle against
their enemy, wherever You send them, and when
they pray to the LORD toward the city which
You have chosen and the temple which I have
built for Your name,
45 "then hear in heaven their prayer and their
supplication, and maintain their cause.
46 "When they sin against You (for *there is*
no one who does not sin), and You become
angry with them and deliver them to the en-
emy, and they take them captive to the land of
the enemy, far or near;
47 "*yet* when they come to themselves in the
land where they were carried captive, and re-
pent, and make supplication to You in the land
of those who took them captive, saying, 'We
have sinned and done wrong, we have commit-
ted wickedness';
48 "and *when* they return to You with all their
heart and with all their soul in the land of their
enemies who led them away captive, and pray
to You toward their land which You gave to
their fathers, the city which You have chosen
and the temple which I have built for Your
name:
49 "then hear in heaven Your dwelling place
their prayer and their supplication, and main-
tain their cause,
50 "and forgive Your people who have sinned
against You, and all their transgressions which
they have transgressed against You; and grant
them compassion before those who took them
captive, that they may have compassion on them
51 "(for they *are* Your people and Your inheri-
tance, whom You brought out of Egypt, out of
the iron furnace),
52 "that Your eyes may be open to the suppli-
cation of Your servant and the supplication of
Your people Israel, to listen to them whenever
they call to You.
53 "For You separated them from among all
the peoples of the earth *to be* Your inheritance,
as You spoke by Your servant Moses, when
You brought our fathers out of Egypt, O Lord
GOD."

Solomon Blesses the Assembly

54 And so it was, when Solomon had finished praying all this prayer and supplication to the LORD, that he arose from before the altar of the LORD, from kneeling on his knees with his hands spread up to heaven.

55 Then he stood and blessed all the assembly of Israel with a loud voice, saying:

56 "Blessed *be* the LORD, who has given rest to His people Israel, according to all that He promised. There has not failed one word of all His good promise, which He promised through His servant Moses.

57 "May the LORD our God be with us, as He was with our fathers. May He not leave us nor forsake us,

58 "that He may incline our hearts to Himself, to walk in all His ways, and to keep His commandments and His statutes and His judgments, which He commanded our fathers.

59 "And may these words of mine, with which I have made supplication before the LORD, be near the LORD our God day and night, that He may maintain the cause of His servant and the cause of His people Israel, as each day may require,

60 "that all the peoples of the earth may know that the LORD *is* God; *there is* no other.

61 "Let your heart therefore be loyal to the LORD our God, to walk in His statutes and keep His commandments, as at this day."

Solomon Dedicates the Temple

62 Then the king and all Israel with him offered sacrifices before the LORD.

63 And Solomon offered a sacrifice of peace offerings, which he offered to the LORD, twenty-two thousand bulls and one hundred and twenty thousand sheep. So the king and all the children of Israel dedicated the house of the LORD.

64 On the same day the king consecrated the middle of the court that *was* in front of the house of the LORD; for there he offered burnt offerings, grain offerings, and the fat of the peace offerings, because the bronze altar that *was* before the LORD *was* too small to receive the burnt offerings, the grain offerings, and the fat of the peace offerings.

65 At that time Solomon held a feast, and all Israel with him, a great assembly from the entrance of Hamath to the Brook of Egypt, before the LORD our God, seven days and seven *more* days—fourteen days.

66 On the eighth day he sent the people away; and they blessed the king, and went to their tents joyful and glad of heart for all the good that the LORD had done for His servant David, and for Israel His people.

God's Second Appearance to Solomon

9 And it came to pass, when Solomon had finished building the house of the LORD and the king's house, and all Solomon's desire which he wanted to do,

2 that the LORD appeared to Solomon the second time, as He had appeared to him at Gibeon.

3 And the LORD said to him: "I have heard your prayer and your supplication that you have made before Me; I have consecrated this house which you have built to put My name there forever, and My eyes and My heart will be there perpetually.

4 "Now if you walk before Me as your father David walked, in integrity of heart and in uprightness, to do according to all that I have commanded you, *and* if you keep My statutes and My judgments,

5 "then I will establish the throne of your kingdom over Israel forever, as I promised David your father, saying, 'You shall not fail to have a man on the throne of Israel.'

6 "*But* if you or your sons at all turn from following Me, and do not keep My commandments *and* My statutes which I have set before you, but go and serve other gods and worship them,

7 "then I will cut off Israel from the land which I have given them; and this house which I have consecrated for My name I will cast out of My sight. Israel will be a proverb and a byword among all peoples.

8 "And *as for* this house, *which* is exalted, everyone who passes by it will be astonished and will hiss, and say, 'Why has the LORD done thus to this land and to this house?'

9 "Then they will answer, 'Because they forsook the LORD their God, who brought their fathers out of the land of Egypt, and have embraced other gods, and worshiped them and served them; therefore the LORD has brought all this calamity on them.' "

Solomon and Hiram Exchange Gifts

10 Now it happened at the end of twenty years, when Solomon had built the two houses, the house of the LORD and the king's house

11 (Hiram the king of Tyre had supplied Solomon with cedar and cypress and gold, as much as he desired), *that* King Solomon then gave Hiram twenty cities in the land of Galilee.

12 Then Hiram went from Tyre to see the cities which Solomon had given him, but they did not please him.

13 So he said, "What *kind of* cities *are* these which you have given me, my brother?" And he called them the land of Cabul,[a] as they are to this day.

14 Then Hiram sent the king one hundred and twenty talents of gold.

Solomon's Additional Achievements

15 And this *is* the reason for the labor force which King Solomon raised: to build the house of the LORD, his own house, the Millo,[a] the wall of Jerusalem, Hazor, Megiddo, and Gezer.

16 (Pharaoh king of Egypt had gone up and taken Gezer and burned it with fire, had killed the Canaanites who dwelt in the city, and had given it *as* a dowry to his daughter, Solomon's wife.)

17 And Solomon built Gezer, Lower Beth Horon,

18 Baalath, and Tadmor in the wilderness, in the land *of Judah*,

19 all the storage cities that Solomon had, cities for his chariots and cities for his cavalry, and whatever Solomon desired to build in Jerusalem, in Lebanon, and in all the land of his dominion.

20 All the people *who were* left of the Amorites, Hittites, Perizzites, Hivites, and Jebusites, who *were* not of the children of Israel—

21 that is, their descendants who were left in

9:13 [a]Literally *Good for Nothing* **9:15** [a]Literally *The Landfill*

the land after them, whom the children of Israel had not been able to destroy completely—from these Solomon raised forced labor, as it is to this day.

22 But of the children of Israel Solomon made no forced laborers, because they *were* men of war and his servants: his officers, his captains, commanders of his chariots, and his cavalry.

23 Others *were* chiefs of the officials who *were* over Solomon's work: five hundred and fifty, who ruled over the people who did the work.

24 But Pharaoh's daughter came up from the City of David to her house which *Solomon*[a] had built for her. Then he built the Millo.

25 Now three times a year Solomon offered burnt offerings and peace offerings on the altar which he had built for the LORD, and he burned incense with them *on the altar* that *was* before the LORD. So he finished the temple.

26 King Solomon also built a fleet of ships at Ezion Geber, which *is* near Elath[a] on the shore of the Red Sea, in the land of Edom.

27 Then Hiram sent his servants with the fleet, seamen who knew the sea, to work with the servants of Solomon.

28 And they went to Ophir, and acquired four hundred and twenty talents of gold from there, and brought *it* to King Solomon.

The Queen of Sheba's Praise of Solomon

10 Now when the queen of Sheba heard of the fame of Solomon concerning the name of the LORD, she came to test him with hard questions.

2 She came to Jerusalem with a very great retinue, with camels that bore spices, very much gold, and precious stones; and when she came to Solomon, she spoke with him about all that was in her heart.

3 So Solomon answered all her questions; there was nothing so difficult for the king that he could not explain *it* to her.

4 And when the queen of Sheba had seen all the wisdom of Solomon, the house that he had built,

5 the food on his table, the seating of his servants, the service of his waiters and their apparel, his cupbearers, and his entryway by which he went up to the house of the LORD, there was no more spirit in her.

6 Then she said to the king: "It was a true report which I heard in my own land about your words and your wisdom.

7 "However I did not believe the words until I came and saw with my own eyes; and indeed the half was not told me. Your wisdom and prosperity exceed the fame of which I heard.

8 "Happy *are* your men and happy *are* these your servants, who stand continually before you *and* hear your wisdom!

9 "Blessed be the LORD your God, who delighted in you, setting you on the throne of Israel! Because the LORD has loved Israel forever, therefore He made you king, to do justice and righteousness."

10 Then she gave the king one hundred and twenty talents of gold, spices in great quantity, and precious stones. There never again came such abundance of spices as the queen of Sheba gave to King Solomon.

11 Also, the ships of Hiram, which brought gold from Ophir, brought great quantities of almug[a] wood and precious stones from Ophir.

12 And the king made steps of the almug wood for the house of the LORD and for the king's house, also harps and stringed instruments for singers. There never again came such almug wood, nor has the like been seen to this day.

13 Now King Solomon gave the queen of Sheba all she desired, whatever she asked, besides what Solomon had given her according to the royal generosity. So she turned and went to her own country, she and her servants.

Solomon's Great Wealth

14 The weight of gold that came to Solomon yearly was six hundred and sixty-six talents of gold,

15 besides *that* from the traveling merchants, from the income of traders, from all the kings of Arabia, and from the governors of the country.

16 And King Solomon made two hundred large shields *of* hammered gold; six hundred *shekels* of gold went into each shield.

17 He also *made* three hundred shields *of* hammered gold; three minas of gold went into each shield. The king put them in the House of the Forest of Lebanon.

18 Moreover the king made a great throne of ivory, and overlaid it with pure gold.

19 The throne had six steps, and the top of the throne *was* round at the back; *there were* armrests on either side of the place of the seat, and two lions stood beside the armrests.

20 Twelve lions stood there, one on each side of the six steps; nothing like *this* had been made for any *other* kingdom.

21 All King Solomon's drinking vessels *were* gold, and all the vessels of the House of the Forest of Lebanon *were* pure gold. Not *one was* silver, for this was accounted as nothing in the days of Solomon.

22 For the king had merchant ships[a] at sea with the fleet of Hiram. Once every three years the merchant ships came bringing gold, silver, ivory, apes, and monkeys.[b]

23 So King Solomon surpassed all the kings of the earth in riches and wisdom.

24 Now all the earth sought the presence of Solomon to hear his wisdom, which God had put in his heart.

25 Each man brought his present: articles of silver and gold, garments, armor, spices, horses, and mules, at a set rate year by year.

26 And Solomon gathered chariots and horsemen; he had one thousand four hundred chariots and twelve thousand horsemen, whom he stationed[a] in the chariot cities and with the king at Jerusalem.

27 The king made silver *as common* in Jerusalem as stones, and he made cedar trees as abundant as the sycamores which *are* in the lowland.

28 Also Solomon had horses imported from Egypt and Keveh; the king's merchants bought them in Keveh at the *current* price.

29 Now a chariot that was imported from Egypt cost six hundred *shekels* of silver, and a horse one hundred and fifty; and thus, through their agents,[a] they exported *them* to all the kings of the Hittites and the kings of Syria.

9:24 [a]Literally *he* (compare 2 Chronicles 8:11) **9:26** [a]Hebrew *Eloth* (compare 2 Kings 14:22) **10:11** [a]Or *algum* (compare 2 Chronicles 9:10, 11) **10:22** [a]Literally *ships of Tarshish*, deep-sea vessels [b]Or *peacocks* **10:26** [a]Following Septuagint, Syriac, Targum, and Vulgate (compare 2 Chronicles 9:25); Masoretic Text reads *led.* **10:29** [a]Literally *by their hands*

Solomon's Heart Turns from the LORD

11 But King Solomon loved many foreign
women, as well as the daughter of Pha-
raoh: women of the Moabites, Ammonites,
Edomites, Sidonians, *and* Hittites—
2 from the nations of whom the LORD had
said to the children of Israel, "You shall not
intermarry with them, nor they with you. Surely
they will turn away your hearts after their
gods." Solomon clung to these in love.
3 And he had seven hundred wives, prin-
cesses, and three hundred concubines; and his
wives turned away his heart.
4 For it was so, when Solomon was old, that
his wives turned his heart after other gods; and
his heart was not loyal to the LORD his God, as
was the heart of his father David.
5 For Solomon went after Ashtoreth the god-
dess of the Sidonians, and after Milcom the
abomination of the Ammonites.
6 Solomon did evil in the sight of the LORD,
and did not fully follow the LORD, as *did* his
father David.
7 Then Solomon built a high place for Che-
mosh the abomination of Moab, on the hill that
is east of Jerusalem, and for Molech the abomi-
nation of the people of Ammon.
8 And he did likewise for all his foreign wives,
who burned incense and sacrificed to their
gods.
9 So the LORD became angry with Solomon,
because his heart had turned from the LORD
God of Israel, who had appeared to him twice,
10 and had commanded him concerning this
thing, that he should not go after other gods;
but he did not keep what the LORD had com-
manded.
11 Therefore the LORD said to Solomon, "Be-
cause you have done this, and have not kept
My covenant and My statutes, which I have
commanded you, I will surely tear the kingdom
away from you and give it to your servant.
12 "Nevertheless I will not do it in your days,
for the sake of your father David; I will tear it
out of the hand of your son.
13 "However I will not tear away the whole
kingdom; I will give one tribe to your son for
the sake of My servant David, and for the sake
of Jerusalem which I have chosen."

Adversaries of Solomon

14 Now the LORD raised up an adversary
against Solomon, Hadad the Edomite; he *was*
a descendant of the king in Edom.
15 For it happened, when David was in Edom,
and Joab the commander of the army had gone
up to bury the slain, after he had killed every
male in Edom
16 (because for six months Joab remained
there with all Israel, until he had cut down every
male in Edom),
17 that Hadad fled to go to Egypt, he and cer-
tain Edomites of his father's servants with him.
Hadad *was* still a little child.
18 Then they arose from Midian and came to
Paran; and they took men with them from Pa-
ran and came to Egypt, to Pharaoh king of Egypt,
who gave him a house, apportioned food for
him, and gave him land.
19 And Hadad found great favor in the sight
of Pharaoh, so that he gave him as wife the sister
of his own wife, that is, the sister of Queen
Tahpenes.
20 Then the sister of Tahpenes bore him Ge-
nubath his son, whom Tahpenes weaned in
Pharaoh's house. And Genubath was in Pha-
raoh's household among the sons of Pharaoh.
21 So when Hadad heard in Egypt that David
rested with his fathers, and that Joab the com-
mander of the army was dead, Hadad said to
Pharaoh, "Let me depart, that I may go to my
own country."
22 Then Pharaoh said to him, "But what have
you lacked with me, that suddenly you seek to
go to your own country?" So he answered,
"Nothing, but do let me go anyway."
23 And God raised up *another* adversary
against him, Rezon the son of Eliadah, who had
fled from his lord, Hadadezer king of Zobah.
24 So he gathered men to him and became
captain over a band *of raiders*, when David
killed those *of Zobah*. And they went to Damas-
cus and dwelt there, and reigned in Damascus.
25 He was an adversary of Israel all the days
of Solomon (besides the trouble that Hadad
caused); and he abhorred Israel, and reigned
over Syria.

Jeroboam's Rebellion

26 Then Solomon's servant, Jeroboam the
son of Nebat, an Ephraimite from Zereda, whose
mother's name *was* Zeruah, a widow, also re-
belled against the king.
27 And this *is* what caused him to rebel against
the king: Solomon had built the Millo *and* re-
paired the damages to the City of David his fa-
ther.
28 The man Jeroboam *was* a mighty man of
valor; and Solomon, seeing that the young man
was industrious, made him the officer over all
the labor force of the house of Joseph.
29 Now it happened at that time, when Jero-
boam went out of Jerusalem, that the prophet
Ahijah the Shilonite met him on the way; and
he had clothed himself with a new garment,
and the two *were* alone in the field.
30 Then Ahijah took hold of the new garment
that *was* on him, and tore it *into* twelve pieces.
31 And he said to Jeroboam, "Take for your-
self ten pieces, for thus says the LORD, the God
of Israel: 'Behold, I will tear the kingdom out
of the hand of Solomon and will give ten tribes
to you
32 '(but he shall have one tribe for the sake
of My servant David, and for the sake of Jeru-
salem, the city which I have chosen out of all
the tribes of Israel),
33 'because they have[a] forsaken Me, and wor-
shiped Ashtoreth the goddess of the Sidonians,
Chemosh the god of the Moabites, and Milcom
the god of the people of Ammon, and have not
walked in My ways to do *what is* right in My
eyes and *keep* My statutes and My judgments,
as *did* his father David.
34 'However I will not take the whole kingdom
out of his hand, because I have made him ruler
all the days of his life for the sake of My ser-
vant David, whom I chose because he kept My
commandments and My statutes.
35 'But I will take the kingdom out of his son's
hand and give it to you—ten tribes.
36 'And to his son I will give one tribe, that My
servant David may always have a lamp before

11:33 [a]Following Masoretic Text and Targum; Septuagint, Syriac, and Vulgate read *he has*.

Me in Jerusalem, the city which I have chosen
for Myself, to put My name there.
37 'So I will take you, and you shall reign over
all your heart desires, and you shall be king over
Israel.
38 'Then it shall be, if you heed all that I command you, walk in My ways, and do *what is*
right in My sight, to keep My statutes and My
commandments, as My servant David did, then
I will be with you and build for you an enduring
house, as I built for David, and will give Israel
to you.
39 'And I will afflict the descendants of David
because of this, but not forever.' "
40 Solomon therefore sought to kill Jeroboam. But Jeroboam arose and fled to Egypt,
to Shishak king of Egypt, and was in Egypt
until the death of Solomon.

Death of Solomon

41 Now the rest of the acts of Solomon, all
that he did, and his wisdom, *are* they not written in the book of the acts of Solomon?
42 And the period that Solomon reigned in
Jerusalem over all Israel *was* forty years.
43 Then Solomon rested with his fathers, and
was buried in the City of David his father. And
Rehoboam his son reigned in his place.

The Revolt Against Rehoboam

12 And Rehoboam went to Shechem, for all
Israel had gone to Shechem to make him
king.
2 So it happened, when Jeroboam the son of
Nebat heard *it* (he was still in Egypt, for he
had fled from the presence of King Solomon
and had been dwelling in Egypt),
3 that they sent and called him. Then Jeroboam and the whole assembly of Israel came
and spoke to Rehoboam, saying,
4 "Your father made our yoke heavy; now
therefore, lighten the burdensome service of
your father, and his heavy yoke which he put
on us, and we will serve you."
5 So he said to them, "Depart *for* three days,
then come back to me." And the people departed.
6 Then King Rehoboam consulted the elders
who stood before his father Solomon while he
still lived, and he said, "How do you advise *me*
to answer these people?"
7 And they spoke to him, saying, "If you will
be a servant to these people today, and serve
them, and answer them, and speak good words
to them, then they will be your servants forever."
8 But he rejected the advice which the elders
had given him, and consulted the young men
who had grown up with him, who stood before
him.
9 And he said to them, "What advice do you
give? How should we answer this people who
have spoken to me, saying, 'Lighten the yoke
which your father put on us'?"
10 Then the young men who had grown up
with him spoke to him, saying, "Thus you should
speak to this people who have spoken to you,
saying, 'Your father made our yoke heavy, but
you make *it* lighter on us'—thus you shall say
to them: 'My little *finger* shall be thicker than
my father's waist!
11 'And now, whereas my father put a heavy
yoke on you, I will add to your yoke; my father
chastised you with whips, but I will chastise
you with scourges!' "[a]

12 So Jeroboam and all the people came to
Rehoboam the third day, as the king had directed, saying, "Come back to me the third day."
13 Then the king answered the people roughly,
and rejected the advice which the elders had
given him;
14 and he spoke to them according to the advice of the young men, saying, "My father made
your yoke heavy, but I will add to your yoke;
my father chastised you with whips, but I will
chastise you with scourges!"[a]
15 So the king did not listen to the people; for
the turn *of events* was from the LORD, that He
might fulfill His word, which the LORD had
spoken by Ahijah the Shilonite to Jeroboam
the son of Nebat.
16 Now when all Israel saw that the king did
not listen to them, the people answered the
king, saying:

"What share have we in David?
We have no inheritance in the son of
Jesse.
To your tents, O Israel!
Now, see to your own house, O David!"

So Israel departed to their tents.
17 But Rehoboam reigned over the children
of Israel who dwelt in the cities of Judah.
18 Then King Rehoboam sent Adoram, who
was in charge of the revenue; but all Israel
stoned him with stones, and he died. Therefore
King Rehoboam mounted his chariot in haste
to flee to Jerusalem.
19 So Israel has been in rebellion against the
house of David to this day.
20 Now it came to pass when all Israel heard
that Jeroboam had come back, they sent for
him and called him to the congregation, and
made him king over all Israel. There was none
who followed the house of David, but the tribe
of Judah only.
21 And when Rehoboam came to Jerusalem,
he assembled all the house of Judah with the
tribe of Benjamin, one hundred and eighty
thousand chosen *men* who were warriors, to
fight against the house of Israel, that he might
restore the kingdom to Rehoboam the son of
Solomon.
22 But the word of God came to Shemaiah the
man of God, saying,
23 "Speak to Rehoboam the son of Solomon,
king of Judah, to all the house of Judah and
Benjamin, and to the rest of the people, saying,
24 'Thus says the LORD: "You shall not go up
nor fight against your brethren the children of
Israel. Let every man return to his house, for
this thing is from Me." ' " Therefore they obeyed
the word of the LORD, and turned back, according to the word of the LORD.

Jeroboam's Gold Calves

25 Then Jeroboam built Shechem in the mountains of Ephraim, and dwelt there. Also he
went out from there and built Penuel.
26 And Jeroboam said in his heart, "Now the
kingdom may return to the house of David:
27 "If these people go up to offer sacrifices in
the house of the LORD at Jerusalem, then the
heart of this people will turn back to their lord,
Rehoboam king of Judah, and they will kill me
and go back to Rehoboam king of Judah."
28 Therefore the king asked advice, made two
calves of gold, and said to the people, "It is too

12:11 [a]Literally *scorpions* **12:14** [a]Literally *scorpions*

much for you to go up to Jerusalem. Here are
your gods, O Israel, which brought you up from
the land of Egypt!"
29 And he set up one in Bethel, and the other
he put in Dan.
30 Now this thing became a sin, for the people
went *to worship* before the one as far as Dan.
31 He made shrines[a] on the high places, and
made priests from every class of people, who
were not of the sons of Levi.
32 Jeroboam ordained a feast on the fifteenth
day of the eighth month, like the feast that *was*
in Judah, and offered sacrifices on the altar. So
he did at Bethel, sacrificing to the calves that
he had made. And at Bethel he installed the
priests of the high places which he had made.
33 So he made offerings on the altar which
he had made at Bethel on the fifteenth day of
the eighth month, in the month which he had
devised in his own heart. And he ordained a
feast for the children of Israel, and offered sac-
rifices on the altar and burned incense.

The Message of the Man of God

13 And behold, a man of God went from Ju-
dah to Bethel by the word of the LORD,
and Jeroboam stood by the altar to burn in-
cense.
2 Then he cried out against the altar by the
word of the LORD, and said, "O altar, altar! Thus
says the LORD: 'Behold, a child, Josiah by name,
shall be born to the house of David; and on you
he shall sacrifice the priests of the high places
who burn incense on you, and men's bones shall
be burned on you.'"
3 And he gave a sign the same day, saying,
"This *is* the sign which the LORD has spoken:
Surely the altar shall split apart, and the ashes
on it shall be poured out."
4 So it came to pass when King Jeroboam
heard the saying of the man of God, who cried
out against the altar in Bethel, that he stretched
out his hand from the altar, saying, "Arrest
him!" Then his hand, which he stretched out
toward him, withered, so that he could not pull
it back to himself.
5 The altar also was split apart, and the ashes
poured out from the altar, according to the sign
which the man of God had given by the word
of the LORD.
6 Then the king answered and said to the
man of God, "Please entreat the favor of the
LORD your God, and pray for me, that my hand
may be restored to me." So the man of God
entreated the LORD, and the king's hand was
restored to him, and became as before.
7 Then the king said to the man of God,
"Come home with me and refresh yourself,
and I will give you a reward."
8 But the man of God said to the king, "If
you were to give me half your house, I would
not go in with you; nor would I eat bread nor
drink water in this place.
9 "For so it was commanded me by the word
of the LORD, saying, 'You shall not eat bread,
nor drink water, nor return by the same way
you came.'"
10 So he went another way and did not return
by the way he came to Bethel.

Death of the Man of God

11 Now an old prophet dwelt in Bethel, and
his sons came and told him all the works that
the man of God had done that day in Bethel;
they also told their father the words which he
had spoken to the king.
12 And their father said to them, "Which way
did he go?" For his sons had seen[a] which way
the man of God went who came from Judah.
13 Then he said to his sons, "Saddle the don-
key for me." So they saddled the donkey for
him; and he rode on it,
14 and went after the man of God, and found
him sitting under an oak. Then he said to him,
"*Are* you the man of God who came from Ju-
dah?" And he said, "I *am*."
15 Then he said to him, "Come home with me
and eat bread."
16 And he said, "I cannot return with you nor
go in with you; neither can I eat bread nor drink
water with you in this place.
17 "For I have been told by the word of the
LORD, 'You shall not eat bread nor drink water
there, nor return by going the way you came.'"
18 He said to him, "I too *am* a prophet as you
are, and an angel spoke to me by the word of
the LORD, saying, 'Bring him back with you to
your house, that he may eat bread and drink
water.'" (He was lying to him.)
19 So he went back with him, and ate bread
in his house, and drank water.
20 Now it happened, as they sat at the table,
that the word of the LORD came to the prophet
who had brought him back;
21 and he cried out to the man of God who
came from Judah, saying, "Thus says the LORD:
'Because you have disobeyed the word of the
LORD, and have not kept the commandment
which the LORD your God commanded you,
22 'but you came back, ate bread, and drank
water in the place of which *the LORD* said to
you, "Eat no bread and drink no water," your
corpse shall not come to the tomb of your fa-
thers.'"
23 So it was, after he had eaten bread and
after he had drunk, that he saddled the donkey
for him, the prophet whom he had brought back.
24 When he was gone, a lion met him on the
road and killed him. And his corpse was thrown
on the road, and the donkey stood by it. The lion
also stood by the corpse.
25 And there, men passed by and saw the
corpse thrown on the road, and the lion stand-
ing by the corpse. Then they went and told *it*
in the city where the old prophet dwelt.
26 Now when the prophet who had brought
him back from the way heard *it*, he said, "It *is*
the man of God who was disobedient to the
word of the LORD. Therefore the LORD has de-
livered him to the lion, which has torn him and
killed him, according to the word of the LORD
which He spoke to him."
27 And he spoke to his sons, saying, "Saddle
the donkey for me." So they saddled *it*.
28 Then he went and found his corpse thrown
on the road, and the donkey and the lion stand-
ing by the corpse. The lion had not eaten the
corpse nor torn the donkey.
29 And the prophet took up the corpse of the
man of God, laid it on the donkey, and brought
it back. So the old prophet came to the city to
mourn, and to bury him.
30 Then he laid the corpse in his own tomb;
and they mourned over him, *saying*, "Alas, my
brother!"
31 So it was, after he had buried him, that he

12:31 [a]Literally *a house* **13:12** [a]Septuagint, Syriac, Targum, and Vulgate read *showed him*.

spoke to his sons, saying, "When I am dead,
then bury me in the tomb where the man of
God *is* buried; lay my bones beside his bones.
32 "For the saying which he cried out by the
word of the LORD against the altar in Bethel,
and against all the shrines[a] on the high places
which *are* in the cities of Samaria, will surely
come to pass."
33 After this event Jeroboam did not turn
from his evil way, but again he made priests from
every class of people for the high places; who-
ever wished, he consecrated him, and he be-
came *one* of the priests of the high places.
34 And this thing was the sin of the house of
Jeroboam, so as to exterminate and destroy *it*
from the face of the earth.

Judgment on the House of Jeroboam

14 At that time Abijah the son of Jeroboam
became sick.
2 And Jeroboam said to his wife, "Please
arise, and disguise yourself, that they may not
recognize you as the wife of Jeroboam, and go
to Shiloh. Indeed, Ahijah the prophet *is* there,
who told me that *I would be* king over this
people.
3 "Also take with you ten loaves, *some* cakes,
and a jar of honey, and go to him; he will tell
you what will become of the child."
4 And Jeroboam's wife did so; she arose and
went to Shiloh, and came to the house of Ahi-
jah. But Ahijah could not see, for his eyes were
glazed by reason of his age.
5 Now the LORD had said to Ahijah, "Here
is the wife of Jeroboam, coming to ask you some-
thing about her son, for he *is* sick. Thus and
thus you shall say to her; for it will be, when
she comes in, that she will pretend *to be* an-
other *woman.*"
6 And so it was, when Ahijah heard the sound
of her footsteps as she came through the door,
he said, "Come in, wife of Jeroboam. Why do
you pretend *to be* another *person?* For I *have
been* sent to you *with* bad *news.*
7 "Go, tell Jeroboam, 'Thus says the LORD
God of Israel: "Because I exalted you from
among the people, and made you ruler over
My people Israel,
8 "and tore the kingdom away from the house
of David, and gave it to you; and *yet* you have
not been as My servant David, who kept My
commandments and who followed Me with all
his heart, to do only *what was* right in My eyes;
9 "but you have done more evil than all who
were before you, for you have gone and made
for yourself other gods and molded images to
provoke Me to anger, and have cast Me behind
your back—
10 "therefore behold! I will bring disaster on
the house of Jeroboam, and will cut off from
Jeroboam every male in Israel, bond and free;
I will take away the remnant of the house of
Jeroboam, as one takes away refuse until it is
all gone.
11 "The dogs shall eat whoever belongs to
Jeroboam and dies in the city, and the birds of
the air shall eat whoever dies in the field; for
the LORD has spoken!"'
12 "Arise therefore, go to your own house.
When your feet enter the city, the child shall
die.
13 "And all Israel shall mourn for him and bury
him, for he is the only one of Jeroboam who
shall come to the grave, because in him there
is found something good toward the LORD God
of Israel in the house of Jeroboam.
14 "Moreover the LORD will raise up for Him-
self a king over Israel who shall cut off the
house of Jeroboam; this is the day. What? Even
now!
15 "For the LORD will strike Israel, as a reed
is shaken in the water. He will uproot Israel
from this good land which He gave to their
fathers, and will scatter them beyond the Ri-
ver,[a] because they have made their wooden im-
ages,[b] provoking the LORD to anger.
16 "And He will give Israel up because of the
sins of Jeroboam, who sinned and who made
Israel sin."
17 Then Jeroboam's wife arose and departed,
and came to Tirzah. When she came to the
threshold of the house, the child died.
18 And they buried him; and all Israel mourned
for him, according to the word of the LORD
which He spoke through His servant Ahijah
the prophet.

Death of Jeroboam

19 Now the rest of the acts of Jeroboam, how
he made war and how he reigned, indeed they
are written in the book of the chronicles of the
kings of Israel.
20 The period that Jeroboam reigned *was*
twenty-two years. So he rested with his fa-
thers. Then Nadab his son reigned in his place.

Rehoboam Reigns in Judah

21 And Rehoboam the son of Solomon reigned
in Judah. Rehoboam *was* forty-one years old
when he became king. He reigned seventeen
years in Jerusalem, the city which the LORD
had chosen out of all the tribes of Israel, to
put His name there. His mother's name *was*
Naamah, an Ammonitess.
22 Now Judah did evil in the sight of the
LORD, and they provoked Him to jealousy with
their sins which they committed, more than all
that their fathers had done.
23 For they also built for themselves high
places, *sacred* pillars, and wooden images on
every high hill and under every green tree.
24 And there were also perverted persons[a] in
the land. They did according to all the abomi-
nations of the nations which the LORD had cast
out before the children of Israel.
25 It happened in the fifth year of King Reho-
boam *that* Shishak king of Egypt came up
against Jerusalem.
26 And he took away the treasures of the house
of the LORD and the treasures of the king's
house; he took away everything. He also took
away all the gold shields which Solomon had
made.
27 Then King Rehoboam made bronze shields
in their place, and committed *them* to the hands
of the captains of the guard, who guarded the
doorway of the king's house.
28 And whenever the king entered the house
of the LORD, the guards carried them, then
brought them back into the guardroom.
29 Now the rest of the acts of Rehoboam, and
all that he did, *are* they not written in the book
of the chronicles of the kings of Judah?

13:32 [a]Literally *houses* **14:15** [a]That is, the Euphrates [b]Hebrew *Asherim*, Canaanite deities **14:24** [a]Hebrew *qadesh*, that is, one practicing sodomy and prostitution in religious rituals

30 And there was war between Rehoboam
and Jeroboam all *their* days.
31 So Rehoboam rested with his fathers, and
was buried with his fathers in the City of David. His mother's name *was* Naamah, an Ammonitess. Then Abijam[a] his son reigned in his place.

Abijam Reigns in Judah

15 In the eighteenth year of King Jeroboam the son of Nebat, Abijam became king over Judah.
2 He reigned three years in Jerusalem. His mother's name *was* Maachah the granddaughter of Abishalom.
3 And he walked in all the sins of his father, which he had done before him; his heart was not loyal to the LORD his God, as was the heart of his father David.
4 Nevertheless for David's sake the LORD his God gave him a lamp in Jerusalem, by setting up his son after him and by establishing Jerusalem;
5 because David did *what was* right in the eyes of the LORD, and had not turned aside from anything that He commanded him all the days of his life, except in the matter of Uriah the Hittite.
6 And there was war between Rehoboam[a] and Jeroboam all the days of his life.
7 Now the rest of the acts of Abijam, and all that he did, *are* they not written in the book of the chronicles of the kings of Judah? And there was war between Abijam and Jeroboam.
8 So Abijam rested with his fathers, and they buried him in the City of David. Then Asa his son reigned in his place.

Asa Reigns in Judah

9 In the twentieth year of Jeroboam king of Israel, Asa became king over Judah.
10 And he reigned forty-one years in Jerusalem. His grandmother's name *was* Maachah the granddaughter of Abishalom.
11 Asa did *what was* right in the eyes of the LORD, as *did* his father David.
12 And he banished the perverted persons[a] from the land, and removed all the idols that his fathers had made.
13 Also he removed Maachah his grandmother from *being* queen mother, because she had made an obscene image of Asherah.[a] And Asa cut down her obscene image and burned *it* by the Brook Kidron.
14 But the high places were not removed. Nevertheless Asa's heart was loyal to the LORD all his days.
15 He also brought into the house of the LORD the things which his father had dedicated, and the things which he himself had dedicated: silver and gold and utensils.
16 Now there was war between Asa and Baasha king of Israel all their days.
17 And Baasha king of Israel came up against Judah, and built Ramah, that he might let none go out or come in to Asa king of Judah.
18 Then Asa took all the silver and gold *that was* left in the treasuries of the house of the LORD and the treasuries of the king's house, and delivered them into the hand of his servants. And King Asa sent them to Ben-Hadad the son of Tabrimmon, the son of Hezion, king of Syria, who dwelt in Damascus, saying,
19 "*Let there be* a treaty between you and me, as there was between my father and your father. See, I have sent you a present of silver and gold. Come and break your treaty with Baasha king of Israel, so that he will withdraw from me."
20 So Ben-Hadad heeded King Asa, and sent the captains of his armies against the cities of Israel. He attacked Ijon, Dan, Abel Beth Maachah, and all Chinneroth, with all the land of Naphtali.
21 Now it happened, when Baasha heard *it*, that he stopped building Ramah, and remained in Tirzah.
22 Then King Asa made a proclamation throughout all Judah; none *was* exempted. And they took away the stones and timber of Ramah, which Baasha had used for building; and with them King Asa built Geba of Benjamin, and Mizpah.
23 The rest of all the acts of Asa, all his might, all that he did, and the cities which he built, *are* they not written in the book of the chronicles of the kings of Judah? But in the time of his old age he was diseased in his feet.
24 So Asa rested with his fathers, and was buried with his fathers in the City of David his father. Then Jehoshaphat his son reigned in his place.

Nadab Reigns in Israel

25 Now Nadab the son of Jeroboam became king over Israel in the second year of Asa king of Judah, and he reigned over Israel two years.
26 And he did evil in the sight of the LORD, and walked in the way of his father, and in his sin by which he had made Israel sin.
27 Then Baasha the son of Ahijah, of the house of Issachar, conspired against him. And Baasha killed him at Gibbethon, which *belonged* to the Philistines, while Nadab and all Israel laid siege to Gibbethon.
28 Baasha killed him in the third year of Asa king of Judah, and reigned in his place.
29 And it was so, when he became king, *that* he killed all the house of Jeroboam. He did not leave to Jeroboam anyone that breathed, until he had destroyed him, according to the word of the LORD which He had spoken by His servant Ahijah the Shilonite,
30 because of the sins of Jeroboam, which he had sinned and by which he had made Israel sin, because of his provocation with which he had provoked the LORD God of Israel to anger.
31 Now the rest of the acts of Nadab, and all that he did, *are* they not written in the book of the chronicles of the kings of Israel?
32 And there was war between Asa and Baasha king of Israel all their days.

Baasha Reigns in Israel

33 In the third year of Asa king of Judah, Baasha the son of Ahijah became king over all Israel in Tirzah, and *reigned* twenty-four years.

14:31 [a]Spelled *Abijah* in 2 Chronicles 12:16ff **15:6** [a]Following Masoretic Text, Septuagint, Targum, and Vulgate; some Hebrew manuscripts and Syriac read *Abijam*. **15:12** [a]Hebrew *qedeshim*, that is, those practicing sodomy and prostitution in religious rituals **15:13** [a]A Canaanite goddess

34 He did evil in the sight of the LORD, and
walked in the way of Jeroboam, and in his sin
by which he had made Israel sin.

16 Then the word of the LORD came to Jehu
the son of Hanani, against Baasha, saying:
2 "Inasmuch as I lifted you out of the dust
and made you ruler over My people Israel, and
you have walked in the way of Jeroboam, and
have made My people Israel sin, to provoke Me
to anger with their sins,
3 "surely I will take away the posterity of
Baasha and the posterity of his house, and I will
make your house like the house of Jeroboam
the son of Nebat.
4 "The dogs shall eat whoever belongs to Baa-
sha and dies in the city, and the birds of the air
shall eat whoever dies in the fields."
5 Now the rest of the acts of Baasha, what he
did, and his might, *are* they not written in the
book of the chronicles of the kings of Israel?
6 So Baasha rested with his fathers and was
buried in Tirzah. Then Elah his son reigned in
his place.
7 And also the word of the LORD came by
the prophet Jehu the son of Hanani against Baa-
sha and his house, because of all the evil that
he did in the sight of the LORD in provoking
Him to anger with the work of his hands, in
being like the house of Jeroboam, and because
he killed them.

Elah Reigns in Israel

8 In the twenty-sixth year of Asa king of Ju-
dah, Elah the son of Baasha became king over
Israel, *and reigned* two years in Tirzah.
9 Now his servant Zimri, commander of half
his chariots, conspired against him as he was in
Tirzah drinking himself drunk in the house of
Arza, steward of *his* house in Tirzah.
10 And Zimri went in and struck him and killed
him in the twenty-seventh year of Asa king of
Judah, and reigned in his place.
11 Then it came to pass, when he began to
reign, as soon as he was seated on his throne,
that he killed all the household of Baasha; he
did not leave him one male, neither of his rela-
tives nor of his friends.
12 Thus Zimri destroyed all the household of
Baasha, according to the word of the LORD,
which He spoke against Baasha by Jehu the
prophet,
13 for all the sins of Baasha and the sins of
Elah his son, by which they had sinned and by
which they had made Israel sin, in provoking
the LORD God of Israel to anger with their idols.
14 Now the rest of the acts of Elah, and all that
he did, *are* they not written in the book of the
chronicles of the kings of Israel?

Zimri Reigns in Israel

15 In the twenty-seventh year of Asa king of
Judah, Zimri had reigned in Tirzah seven days.
And the people *were* encamped against Gibbe-
thon, which *belonged* to the Philistines.
16 Now the people *who were* encamped heard
it said, "Zimri has conspired and also has
killed the king." So all Israel made Omri, the
commander of the army, king over Israel that
day in the camp.
17 Then Omri and all Israel with him went up
from Gibbethon, and they besieged Tirzah.
18 And it happened, when Zimri saw that the
city was taken, that he went into the citadel of
the king's house and burned the king's house
down upon himself with fire, and died,
19 because of the sins which he had commit-
ted in doing evil in the sight of the LORD, in
walking in the way of Jeroboam, and in his sin
which he had committed to make Israel sin.
20 Now the rest of the acts of Zimri, and the
treason he committed, *are* they not written in
the book of the chronicles of the kings of Is-
rael?

Omri Reigns in Israel

21 Then the people of Israel were divided into
two parts: half of the people followed Tibni the
son of Ginath, to make him king, and half fol-
lowed Omri.
22 But the people who followed Omri pre-
vailed over the people who followed Tibni the
son of Ginath. So Tibni died and Omri reigned.
23 In the thirty-first year of Asa king of Ju-
dah, Omri became king over Israel, *and reigned*
twelve years. Six years he reigned in Tirzah.
24 And he bought the hill of Samaria from
Shemer for two talents of silver; then he built
on the hill, and called the name of the city
which he built, Samaria, after the name of She-
mer, owner of the hill.
25 Omri did evil in the eyes of the LORD, and
did worse than all who *were* before him.
26 For he walked in all the ways of Jeroboam
the son of Nebat, and in his sin by which he
had made Israel sin, provoking the LORD God
of Israel to anger with their idols.
27 Now the rest of the acts of Omri which he
did, and the might that he showed, *are* they not
written in the book of the chronicles of the
kings of Israel?
28 So Omri rested with his fathers and was
buried in Samaria. Then Ahab his son reigned
in his place.

Ahab Reigns in Israel

29 In the thirty-eighth year of Asa king of
Judah, Ahab the son of Omri became king over
Israel; and Ahab the son of Omri reigned over
Israel in Samaria twenty-two years.
30 Now Ahab the son of Omri did evil in the
sight of the LORD, more than all who *were*
before him.
31 And it came to pass, as though it had been
a trivial thing for him to walk in the sins of
Jeroboam the son of Nebat, that he took as
wife Jezebel the daughter of Ethbaal, king of
the Sidonians; and he went and served Baal and
worshiped him.
32 Then he set up an altar for Baal in the tem-
ple of Baal, which he had built in Samaria.
33 And Ahab made a wooden image.[a] Ahab
did more to provoke the LORD God of Israel to
anger than all the kings of Israel who were
before him.
34 In his days Hiel of Bethel built Jericho. He
laid its foundation with Abiram his firstborn,
and with his youngest *son* Segub he set up its
gates, according to the word of the LORD,
which He had spoken through Joshua the son
of Nun.[a]

Elijah Proclaims a Drought

17 And Elijah the Tishbite, of the inhabitants
of Gilead, said to Ahab, "*As* the LORD
God of Israel lives, before whom I stand, there

16:33 [a]Hebrew *Asherah,* a Canaanite goddess **16:34** [a]Compare Joshua 6:26

shall not be dew nor rain these years, except at my word."

2 Then the word of the LORD came to him, saying,

3 "Get away from here and turn eastward, and hide by the Brook Cherith, which flows into the Jordan.

4 "And it will be *that* you shall drink from the brook, and I have commanded the ravens to feed you there."

5 So he went and did according to the word of the LORD, for he went and stayed by the Brook Cherith, which flows into the Jordan.

6 The ravens brought him bread and meat in the morning, and bread and meat in the evening; and he drank from the brook.

7 And it happened after a while that the brook dried up, because there had been no rain in the land.

Elijah and the Widow

8 Then the word of the LORD came to him, saying,

9 "Arise, go to Zarephath, which *belongs* to Sidon, and dwell there. See, I have commanded a widow there to provide for you."

10 So he arose and went to Zarephath. And when he came to the gate of the city, indeed a widow *was* there gathering sticks. And he called to her and said, "Please bring me a little water in a cup, that I may drink."

11 And as she was going to get *it*, he called to her and said, "Please bring me a morsel of bread in your hand."

12 So she said, "As the LORD your God lives, I do not have bread, only a handful of flour in a bin, and a little oil in a jar; and see, I *am* gathering a couple of sticks that I may go in and prepare it for myself and my son, that we may eat it, and die."

13 And Elijah said to her, "Do not fear; go *and* do as you have said, but make me a small cake from it first, and bring *it* to me; and afterward make *some* for yourself and your son.

14 "For thus says the LORD God of Israel: 'The bin of flour shall not be used up, nor shall the jar of oil run dry, until the day the LORD sends rain on the earth.'"

15 So she went away and did according to the word of Elijah; and she and he and her household ate for *many* days.

16 The bin of flour was not used up, nor did the jar of oil run dry, according to the word of the LORD which He spoke by Elijah.

Elijah Revives the Widow's Son

17 Now it happened after these things *that* the son of the woman who owned the house became sick. And his sickness was so serious that there was no breath left in him.

18 So she said to Elijah, "What have I to do with you, O man of God? Have you come to me to bring my sin to remembrance, and to kill my son?"

19 And he said to her, "Give me your son." So he took him out of her arms and carried him to the upper room where he was staying, and laid him on his own bed.

20 Then he cried out to the LORD and said, "O LORD my God, have You also brought tragedy on the widow with whom I lodge, by killing her son?"

21 And he stretched himself out on the child three times, and cried out to the LORD and said, "O LORD my God, I pray, let this child's soul come back to him."

22 Then the LORD heard the voice of Elijah; and the soul of the child came back to him, and he revived.

23 And Elijah took the child and brought him down from the upper room into the house, and gave him to his mother. And Elijah said, "See, your son lives!"

24 Then the woman said to Elijah, "Now by this I know that you *are* a man of God, *and* that the word of the LORD in your mouth *is* the truth."

Elijah's Message to Ahab

18 And it came to pass *after* many days that the word of the LORD came to Elijah, in the third year, saying, "Go, present yourself to Ahab, and I will send rain on the earth."

2 So Elijah went to present himself to Ahab; and *there was* a severe famine in Samaria.

3 And Ahab had called Obadiah, who *was* in charge of *his* house. (Now Obadiah feared the LORD greatly.

4 For so it was, while Jezebel massacred the prophets of the LORD, that Obadiah had taken one hundred prophets and hidden them, fifty to a cave, and had fed them with bread and water.)

5 And Ahab had said to Obadiah, "Go into the land to all the springs of water and to all the brooks; perhaps we may find grass to keep the horses and mules alive, so that we will not have to kill any livestock."

6 So they divided the land between them to explore it; Ahab went one way by himself, and Obadiah went another way by himself.

7 Now as Obadiah was on his way, suddenly Elijah met him; and he recognized him, and fell on his face, and said, "*Is* that you, my lord Elijah?"

8 And he answered him, "*It is* I. Go, tell your master, 'Elijah *is here.*'"

9 So he said, "How have I sinned, that you are delivering your servant into the hand of Ahab, to kill me?

10 "*As* the LORD your God lives, there is no nation or kingdom where my master has not sent someone to hunt for you; and when they said, '*He is* not *here,*' he took an oath from the kingdom or nation that they could not find you.

11 "And now you say, 'Go, tell your master, "Elijah *is here*"'!

12 "And it shall come to pass, *as soon as* I am gone from you, that the Spirit of the LORD will carry you to a place I do not know; so when I go and tell Ahab, and he cannot find you, he will kill me. But I your servant have feared the LORD from my youth.

13 "Was it not reported to my lord what I did when Jezebel killed the prophets of the LORD, how I hid one hundred men of the LORD's prophets, fifty to a cave, and fed them with bread and water?

14 "And now you say, 'Go, tell your master, "Elijah *is here.*"' He will kill me!"

15 Then Elijah said, "*As* the LORD of hosts lives, before whom I stand, I will surely present myself to him today."

16 So Obadiah went to meet Ahab, and told him; and Ahab went to meet Elijah.

17 Then it happened, when Ahab saw Elijah, that Ahab said to him, "*Is that* you, O troubler of Israel?"

18 And he answered, "I have not troubled Is-

rael, but you and your father's house *have,* in
that you have forsaken the commandments of
the LORD and have followed the Baals.
19 "Now therefore, send *and* gather all Israel
to me on Mount Carmel, the four hundred and
fifty prophets of Baal, and the four hundred
prophets of Asherah,[a] who eat at Jezebel's table."

Elijah's Mount Carmel Victory

20 So Ahab sent for all the children of Israel,
and gathered the prophets together on Mount
Carmel.
21 And Elijah came to all the people, and said,
"How long will you falter between two opin-
ions? If the LORD *is* God, follow Him; but if
Baal, follow him." But the people answered him
not a word.
22 Then Elijah said to the people, "I alone am
left a prophet of the LORD; but Baal's prophets
are four hundred and fifty men.
23 "Therefore let them give us two bulls; and
let them choose one bull for themselves, cut it
in pieces, and lay *it* on the wood, but put no fire
under it; and I will prepare the other bull, and
lay *it* on the wood, but put no fire *under it.*
24 "Then you call on the name of your gods,
and I will call on the name of the LORD; and
the God who answers by fire, He is God." So
all the people answered and said, "It is well
spoken."
25 Now Elijah said to the prophets of Baal,
"Choose one bull for yourselves and prepare
it first, for you *are* many; and call on the name
of your god, but put no fire *under it.*"
26 So they took the bull which was given
them, and they prepared *it,* and called on the
name of Baal from morning even till noon, say-
ing, "O Baal, hear us!" But *there was* no voice;
no one answered. Then they leaped about the
altar which they had made.
27 And so it was, at noon, that Elijah mocked
them and said, "Cry aloud, for he *is* a god; either
he is meditating, or he is busy, or he is on a
journey, *or* perhaps he is sleeping and must be
awakened."
28 So they cried aloud, and cut themselves, as
was their custom, with knives and lances, until
the blood gushed out on them.
29 And when midday was past, they prophe-
sied until the *time* of the offering of the *evening*
sacrifice. But *there was* no voice; no one an-
swered, no one paid attention.
30 Then Elijah said to all the people, "Come
near to me." So all the people came near to him.
And he repaired the altar of the LORD *that was*
broken down.
31 And Elijah took twelve stones, according
to the number of the tribes of the sons of Jacob,
to whom the word of the LORD had come, say-
ing, "Israel shall be your name."[a]
32 Then with the stones he built an altar in
the name of the LORD; and he made a trench
around the altar large enough to hold two se-
ahs of seed.
33 And he put the wood in order, cut the bull
in pieces, and laid *it* on the wood, and said,
"Fill four waterpots with water, and pour *it* on
the burnt sacrifice and on the wood."
34 Then he said, "Do *it* a second time," and
they did *it* a second time; and he said, "Do *it* a
third time," and they did *it* a third time.
35 So the water ran all around the altar; and
he also filled the trench with water.
36 And it came to pass, at *the time of* the
offering of the *evening* sacrifice, that Elijah the
prophet came near and said, "LORD God of
Abraham, Isaac, and Israel, let it be known this
day that You *are* God in Israel and I *am* Your
servant, and *that* I have done all these things
at Your word.
37 "Hear me, O LORD, hear me, that this peo-
ple may know that You *are* the LORD God, and
that You have turned their hearts back *to You*
again."
38 Then the fire of the LORD fell and con-
sumed the burnt sacrifice, and the wood and
the stones and the dust, and it licked up the
water that *was* in the trench.
39 Now when all the people saw *it,* they fell
on their faces; and they said, "The LORD, He
is God! The LORD, He *is* God!"
40 And Elijah said to them, "Seize the proph-
ets of Baal! Do not let one of them escape!"
So they seized them; and Elijah brought them
down to the Brook Kishon and executed them
there.

The Drought Ends

41 Then Elijah said to Ahab, "Go up, eat and
drink; for *there is* the sound of abundance of
rain."
42 So Ahab went up to eat and drink. And
Elijah went up to the top of Carmel; then he
bowed down on the ground, and put his face
between his knees,
43 and said to his servant, "Go up now, look
toward the sea." So he went up and looked,
and said, "*There is* nothing." And seven times
he said, "Go again."
44 Then it came to pass the seventh *time,* that
he said, "There is a cloud, as small as a man's
hand, rising out of the sea!" So he said, "Go
up, say to Ahab, 'Prepare *your chariot,* and go
down before the rain stops you.'"
45 Now it happened in the meantime that the
sky became black with clouds and wind, and
there was a heavy rain. So Ahab rode away and
went to Jezreel.
46 Then the hand of the LORD came upon
Elijah; and he girded up his loins and ran
ahead of Ahab to the entrance of Jezreel.

Elijah Escapes from Jezebel

19 And Ahab told Jezebel all that Elijah had
done, also how he had executed all the
prophets with the sword.
2 Then Jezebel sent a messenger to Elijah,
saying, "So let the gods do *to me,* and more
also, if I do not make your life as the life of one
of them by tomorrow about this time."
3 And when he saw *that,* he arose and ran
for his life, and went to Beersheba, which *be-
longs* to Judah, and left his servant there.
4 But he himself went a day's journey into
the wilderness, and came and sat down under
a broom tree. And he prayed that he might die,
and said, "It is enough! Now, LORD, take my
life, for I *am* no better than my fathers!"
5 Then as he lay and slept under a broom
tree, suddenly an angel[a] touched him, and said
to him, "Arise *and* eat."
6 Then he looked, and there by his head *was*
a cake baked on coals, and a jar of water. So
he ate and drank, and lay down again.

18:19 [a]A Canaanite goddess **18:31** [a]Genesis 32:28 **19:5** [a]Or *Angel*

7 And the angel[a] of the LORD came back the
second time, and touched him, and said, "Arise
and eat, because the journey *is* too great for
you."
8 So he arose, and ate and drank; and he
went in the strength of that food forty days and
forty nights as far as Horeb, the mountain of
God.
9 And there he went into a cave, and spent
the night in that place; and behold, the word
of the LORD *came* to him, and He said to him,
"What are you doing here, Elijah?"
10 So he said, "I have been very zealous for
the LORD God of hosts; for the children of Is-
rael have forsaken Your covenant, torn down
Your altars, and killed Your prophets with the
sword. I alone am left; and they seek to take
my life."

God's Revelation to Elijah

11 Then He said, "Go out, and stand on the
mountain before the LORD." And behold, the
LORD passed by, and a great and strong wind
tore into the mountains and broke the rocks in
pieces before the LORD, *but* the LORD *was* not
in the wind; and after the wind an earthquake,
but the LORD *was* not in the earthquake;
12 and after the earthquake a fire, *but* the LORD
was not in the fire; and after the fire a still small
voice.
13 So it was, when Elijah heard *it,* that he
wrapped his face in his mantle and went out
and stood in the entrance of the cave. Suddenly
a voice *came* to him, and said, "What are you
doing here, Elijah?"
14 And he said, "I have been very zealous for
the LORD God of hosts; because the children
of Israel have forsaken Your covenant, torn
down Your altars, and killed Your prophets
with the sword. I alone am left; and they seek
to take my life."
15 Then the LORD said to him: "Go, return on
your way to the Wilderness of Damascus; and
when you arrive, anoint Hazael *as* king over
Syria.
16 "Also you shall anoint Jehu the son of Nim-
shi *as* king over Israel. And Elisha the son of
Shaphat of Abel Meholah you shall anoint *as*
prophet in your place.
17 "It shall be *that* whoever escapes the sword
of Hazael, Jehu will kill; and whoever escapes
the sword of Jehu, Elisha will kill.
18 "Yet I have reserved seven thousand in Is-
rael, all whose knees have not bowed to Baal,
and every mouth that has not kissed him."

Elisha Follows Elijah

19 So he departed from there, and found Eli-
sha the son of Shaphat, who *was* plowing *with*
twelve yoke *of oxen* before him, and he was with
the twelfth. Then Elijah passed by him and threw
his mantle on him.
20 And he left the oxen and ran after Elijah,
and said, "Please let me kiss my father and my
mother, and *then* I will follow you." And he
said to him, "Go back again, for what have I done
to you?"
21 So *Elisha* turned back from him, and took
a yoke of oxen and slaughtered them and boiled
their flesh, using the oxen's equipment, and
gave it to the people, and they ate. Then he arose
and followed Elijah, and became his servant.

Ahab Defeats the Syrians

20 Now Ben-Hadad the king of Syria gath-
ered all his forces together; thirty-two
kings *were* with him, with horses and chariots.
And he went up and besieged Samaria, and
made war against it.
2 Then he sent messengers into the city to
Ahab king of Israel, and said to him, "Thus says
Ben-Hadad:
3 'Your silver and your gold *are* mine; your
loveliest wives and children are mine.' "
4 And the king of Israel answered and said,
"My lord, O king, just as you say, I and all that
I have *are* yours."
5 Then the messengers came back and said,
"Thus speaks Ben-Hadad, saying, 'Indeed I
have sent to you, saying, "You shall deliver to
me your silver and your gold, your wives and
your children";
6 'but I will send my servants to you tomor-
row about this time, and they shall search your
house and the houses of your servants. And it
shall be, *that* whatever is pleasant in your eyes,
they will put in their hands and take *it.*' "
7 So the king of Israel called all the elders
of the land, and said, "Notice, please, and see
how this *man* seeks trouble, for he sent to me
for my wives, my children, my silver, and my
gold; and I did not deny him."
8 And all the elders and all the people said
to him, "Do not listen or consent."
9 Therefore he said to the messengers of
Ben-Hadad, "Tell my lord the king, 'All that
you sent for to your servant the first time I
will do, but this thing I cannot do.' " And the
messengers departed and brought back word
to him.
10 Then Ben-Hadad sent to him and said, "The
gods do so to me, and more also, if enough dust
is left of Samaria for a handful for each of the
people who follow me."
11 So the king of Israel answered and said,
"Tell *him,* 'Let not the one who puts on *his
armor* boast like the one who takes *it off.*' "
12 And it happened when *Ben-Hadad* heard
this message, as he and the kings *were* drinking
at the command post, that he said to his ser-
vants, "Get ready." And they got ready to attack
the city.
13 Suddenly a prophet approached Ahab king
of Israel, saying, "Thus says the LORD: 'Have
you seen all this great multitude? Behold, I will
deliver it into your hand today, and you shall
know that I *am* the LORD.' "
14 So Ahab said, "By whom?" And he said,
"Thus says the LORD: 'By the young leaders of
the provinces.' " Then he said, "Who will set the
battle in order?" And he answered, "You."
15 Then he mustered the young leaders of the
provinces, and there were two hundred and
thirty-two; and after them he mustered all the
people, all the children of Israel—seven thou-
sand.
16 So they went out at noon. Meanwhile Ben-
Hadad and the thirty-two kings helping him
were getting drunk at the command post.
17 The young leaders of the provinces went
out first. And Ben-Hadad sent out *a patrol,* and
they told him, saying, "Men are coming out of
Samaria!"
18 So he said, "If they have come out for peace,

19:7 [a]Or *Angel*

take them alive; and if they have come out for
war, take them alive."
19 Then these young leaders of the provinces
went out of the city with the army which fol-
lowed them.
20 And each one killed his man; so the Syri-
ans fled, and Israel pursued them; and Ben-
Hadad the king of Syria escaped on a horse
with the cavalry.
21 Then the king of Israel went out and at-
tacked the horses and chariots, and killed the
Syrians with a great slaughter.
22 And the prophet came to the king of Israel
and said to him, "Go, strengthen yourself; take
note, and see what you should do, for in the
spring of the year the king of Syria will come
up against you."

The Syrians Again Defeated

23 Then the servants of the king of Syria said
to him, "Their gods *are* gods of the hills. There-
fore they were stronger than we; but if we fight
against them in the plain, surely we will be
stronger than they.
24 "So do this thing: Dismiss the kings, each
from his position, and put captains in their
places;
25 "and you shall muster an army like the army
that you have lost, horse for horse and chariot
for chariot. Then we will fight against them in
the plain; surely we will be stronger than they."
And he listened to their voice and did so.
26 So it was, in the spring of the year, that
Ben-Hadad mustered the Syrians and went up
to Aphek to fight against Israel.
27 And the children of Israel were mustered
and given provisions, and they went against
them. Now the children of Israel encamped
before them like two little flocks of goats, while
the Syrians filled the countryside.
28 Then a man of God came and spoke to the
king of Israel, and said, "Thus says the LORD:
'Because the Syrians have said, "The LORD *is*
God of the hills, but He *is* not God of the val-
leys," therefore I will deliver all this great mul-
titude into your hand, and you shall know that
I *am* the LORD.'"
29 And they encamped opposite each other
for seven days. So it was that on the seventh
day the battle was joined; and the children of
Israel killed one hundred thousand foot sol-
diers *of* the Syrians in one day.
30 But the rest fled to Aphek, into the city;
then a wall fell on twenty-seven thousand of
the men *who were* left. And Ben-Hadad fled
and went into the city, into an inner chamber.

Ahab's Treaty with Ben-Hadad

31 Then his servants said to him, "Look now,
we have heard that the kings of the house of
Israel *are* merciful kings. Please, let us put
sackcloth around our waists and ropes around
our heads, and go out to the king of Israel;
perhaps he will spare your life."
32 So they wore sackcloth around their waists
and *put* ropes around their heads, and came
to the king of Israel and said, "Your servant
Ben-Hadad says, 'Please let me live.'" And he
said, "*Is* he still alive? He *is* my brother."
33 Now the men were watching closely to see
whether *any sign of mercy would come* from
him; and they quickly grasped *at this word* and
said, "Your brother Ben-Hadad." So he said,
"Go, bring him." Then Ben-Hadad came out to
him; and he had him come up into the chariot.
34 So *Ben-Hadad* said to him, "The cities
which my father took from your father I will
restore; and you may set up marketplaces for
yourself in Damascus, as my father did in Sa-
maria." Then *Ahab said,* "I will send you away
with this treaty." So he made a treaty with him
and sent him away.

Ahab Condemned

35 Now a certain man of the sons of the proph-
ets said to his neighbor by the word of the
LORD, "Strike me, please." And the man re-
fused to strike him.
36 Then he said to him, "Because you have
not obeyed the voice of the LORD, surely, as
soon as you depart from me, a lion shall kill
you." And as soon as he left him, a lion found
him and killed him.
37 And he found another man, and said, "Strike
me, please." So the man struck him, inflicting
a wound.
38 Then the prophet departed and waited for
the king by the road, and disguised himself
with a bandage over his eyes.
39 Now as the king passed by, he cried out to
the king and said, "Your servant went out into
the midst of the battle; and there, a man came
over and brought a man to me, and said,
'Guard this man; if by any means he is missing,
your life shall be for his life, or else you shall
pay a talent of silver.'
40 "While your servant was busy here and
there, he was gone." Then the king of Israel
said to him, "So *shall* your judgment *be;* you
yourself have decided *it.*"
41 And he hastened to take the bandage away
from his eyes; and the king of Israel recognized
him as one of the prophets.
42 Then he said to him, "Thus says the LORD:
'Because you have let slip out of *your* hand a
man whom I appointed to utter destruction,
therefore your life shall go for his life, and your
people for his people.'"
43 So the king of Israel went to his house sullen
and displeased, and came to Samaria.

Naboth Is Murdered for His Vineyard

21 And it came to pass after these things
that Naboth the Jezreelite had a vine-
yard which *was* in Jezreel, next to the palace
of Ahab king of Samaria.
2 So Ahab spoke to Naboth, saying, "Give
me your vineyard, that I may have it for a vege-
table garden, because it *is* near, next to my
house; and for it I will give you a vineyard
better than it. *Or,* if it seems good to you, I will
give you its worth in money."
3 But Naboth said to Ahab, "The LORD for-
bid that I should give the inheritance of my
fathers to you!"
4 So Ahab went into his house sullen and
displeased because of the word which Naboth
the Jezreelite had spoken to him; for he had
said, "I will not give you the inheritance of
my fathers." And he lay down on his bed, and
turned away his face, and would eat no food.
5 But Jezebel his wife came to him, and said
to him, "Why is your spirit so sullen that you
eat no food?"
6 He said to her, "Because I spoke to Naboth
the Jezreelite, and said to him, 'Give me your
vineyard for money; or else, if it pleases you, I
will give you *another* vineyard for it.' And he
answered, 'I will not give you my vineyard.'"
7 Then Jezebel his wife said to him, "You now

exercise authority over Israel! Arise, eat food,
and let your heart be cheerful; I will give you
the vineyard of Naboth the Jezreelite."
8 And she wrote letters in Ahab's name, sealed
them with his seal, and sent the letters to the
elders and the nobles who *were* dwelling in the
city with Naboth.
9 She wrote in the letters, saying,

Proclaim a fast, and seat Naboth with
high honor among the people;
10 and seat two men, scoundrels, before him
to bear witness against him, saying, "You
have blasphemed God and the king."
Then take him out, and stone him, that he
may die.

11 So the men of his city, the elders and no-
bles who were inhabitants of his city, did as
Jezebel had sent to them, as it *was* written in
the letters which she had sent to them.
12 They proclaimed a fast, and seated Naboth
with high honor among the people.
13 And two men, scoundrels, came in and sat
before him; and the scoundrels witnessed against
him, against Naboth, in the presence of the
people, saying, "Naboth has blasphemed God
and the king!" Then they took him outside the
city and stoned him with stones, so that he died.
14 Then they sent to Jezebel, saying, "Naboth
has been stoned and is dead."
15 And it came to pass, when Jezebel heard
that Naboth had been stoned and was dead,
that Jezebel said to Ahab, "Arise, take posses-
sion of the vineyard of Naboth the Jezreelite,
which he refused to give you for money; for
Naboth is not alive, but dead."
16 So it was, when Ahab heard that Naboth
was dead, that Ahab got up and went down to
take possession of the vineyard of Naboth the
Jezreelite.

The LORD Condemns Ahab

17 Then the word of the LORD came to Elijah
the Tishbite, saying,
18 "Arise, go down to meet Ahab king of Is-
rael, who *lives* in Samaria. There *he is,* in the
vineyard of Naboth, where he has gone down
to take possession of it.
19 "You shall speak to him, saying, 'Thus says
the LORD: "Have you murdered and also taken
possession?"' And you shall speak to him, say-
ing, 'Thus says the LORD: "In the place where
dogs licked the blood of Naboth, dogs shall lick
your blood, even yours."'"
20 So Ahab said to Elijah, "Have you found
me, O my enemy?" And he answered, "I have
found *you,* because you have sold yourself to
do evil in the sight of the LORD:
21 'Behold, I will bring calamity on you. I will
take away your posterity, and will cut off from
Ahab every male in Israel, both bond and free.
22 'I will make your house like the house of
Jeroboam the son of Nebat, and like the house
of Baasha the son of Ahijah, because of the
provocation with which you have provoked *Me*
to anger, and made Israel sin.'
23 "And concerning Jezebel the LORD also
spoke, saying, 'The dogs shall eat Jezebel by the
wall[a] of Jezreel.'
24 "The dogs shall eat whoever belongs to Ahab
and dies in the city, and the birds of the air
shall eat whoever dies in the field."
25 But there was no one like Ahab who sold
himself to do wickedness in the sight of the
LORD, because Jezebel his wife stirred him up.
26 And he behaved very abominably in fol-
lowing idols, according to all *that* the Amo-
rites had done, whom the LORD had cast out
before the children of Israel.
27 So it was, when Ahab heard those words,
that he tore his clothes and put sackcloth on
his body, and fasted and lay in sackcloth, and
went about mourning.
28 And the word of the LORD came to Elijah
the Tishbite, saying,
29 "See how Ahab has humbled himself be-
fore Me? Because he has humbled himself be-
fore Me, I will not bring the calamity in his
days. In the days of his son I will bring the
calamity on his house."

Micaiah Warns Ahab

22 Now three years passed without war be-
tween Syria and Israel.
2 Then it came to pass, in the third year, that
Jehoshaphat the king of Judah went down to
visit the king of Israel.
3 And the king of Israel said to his servants,
"Do you know that Ramoth in Gilead *is* ours,
but we hesitate to take it out of the hand of the
king of Syria?"
4 So he said to Jehoshaphat, "Will you go
with me to fight at Ramoth Gilead?" Jehosha-
phat said to the king of Israel, "I *am* as you *are,*
my people as your people, my horses as your
horses."
5 Also Jehoshaphat said to the king of Israel,
"Please inquire for the word of the LORD today."
6 Then the king of Israel gathered the proph-
ets together, about four hundred men, and said
to them, "Shall I go against Ramoth Gilead to
fight, or shall I refrain?" So they said, "Go up,
for the Lord will deliver *it* into the hand of the
king."
7 And Jehoshaphat said, "*Is there* not still a
prophet of the LORD here, that we may inquire
of Him?"[a]
8 So the king of Israel said to Jehoshaphat,
"*There is* still one man, Micaiah the son of
Imlah, by whom we may inquire of the LORD;
but I hate him, because he does not prophesy
good concerning me, but evil." And Jehosha-
phat said, "Let not the king say such things!"
9 Then the king of Israel called an officer and
said, "Bring Micaiah the son of Imlah quickly!"
10 The king of Israel and Jehoshaphat the
king of Judah, having put on *their* robes, sat
each on his throne, at a threshing floor at the
entrance of the gate of Samaria; and all the
prophets prophesied before them.
11 Now Zedekiah the son of Chenaanah had
made horns of iron for himself; and he said,
"Thus says the LORD: 'With these you shall gore
the Syrians until they are destroyed.'"
12 And all the prophets prophesied so, say-
ing, "Go up to Ramoth Gilead and prosper, for
the LORD will deliver *it* into the king's hand."
13 Then the messenger who had gone to call
Micaiah spoke to him, saying, "Now listen, the
words of the prophets with one accord encour-
age the king. Please, let your word be like the
word of one of them, and speak encouragement."
14 And Micaiah said, "*As* the LORD lives, what-
ever the LORD says to me, that I will speak."

21:23 [a]Following Masoretic Text and Septuagint; some Hebrew manuscripts, Syriac, Targum, and Vulgate read *plot of ground* (compare 2 Kings 9:36). **22:7** [a]Or *him*

15 Then he came to the king; and the king
said to him, "Micaiah, shall we go to war
against Ramoth Gilead, or shall we refrain?"
And he answered him, "Go and prosper, for
the LORD will deliver *it* into the hand of the
king!"
16 So the king said to him, "How many times
shall I make you swear that you tell me nothing
but the truth in the name of the LORD?"
17 Then he said, "I saw all Israel scattered on
the mountains, as sheep that have no shep-
herd. And the LORD said, 'These have no mas-
ter. Let each return to his house in peace.'"
18 And the king of Israel said to Jehoshaphat,
"Did I not tell you he would not prophesy good
concerning me, but evil?"
19 Then *Micaiah* said, "Therefore hear the
word of the LORD: I saw the LORD sitting on
His throne, and all the host of heaven standing
by, on His right hand and on His left.
20 "And the LORD said, 'Who will persuade
Ahab to go up, that he may fall at Ramoth
Gilead?' So one spoke in this manner, and an-
other spoke in that manner.
21 "Then a spirit came forward and stood be-
fore the LORD, and said, 'I will persuade him.'
22 "The LORD said to him, 'In what way?' So
he said, 'I will go out and be a lying spirit in
the mouth of all his prophets.' And the LORD
said, 'You shall persuade *him*, and also prevail.
Go out and do so.'
23 "Therefore look! The LORD has put a lying
spirit in the mouth of all these prophets of yours,
and the LORD has declared disaster against you."
24 Now Zedekiah the son of Chenaanah went
near and struck Micaiah on the cheek, and
said, "Which way did the spirit from the LORD
go from me to speak to you?"
25 And Micaiah said, "Indeed, you shall see
on that day when you go into an inner chamber
to hide!"
26 So the king of Israel said, "Take Micaiah,
and return him to Amon the governor of the
city and to Joash the king's son;
27 "and say, 'Thus says the king: "Put this
fellow in prison, and feed him with bread of
affliction and water of affliction, until I come
in peace."'"
28 But Micaiah said, "If you ever return in
peace, the LORD has not spoken by me." And
he said, "Take heed, all you people!"

Ahab Dies in Battle

29 So the king of Israel and Jehoshaphat the
king of Judah went up to Ramoth Gilead.
30 And the king of Israel said to Jehoshaphat,
"I will disguise myself and go into battle; but
you put on your robes." So the king of Israel
disguised himself and went into battle.
31 Now the king of Syria had commanded
the thirty-two captains of his chariots, saying,
"Fight with no one small or great, but only with
the king of Israel."
32 So it was, when the captains of the chariots
saw Jehoshaphat, that they said, "Surely it *is*
the king of Israel!" Therefore they turned aside
to fight against him, and Jehoshaphat cried out.
33 And it happened, when the captains of the
chariots saw that it *was* not the king of Israel,
that they turned back from pursuing him.
34 Now a *certain* man drew a bow at random,
and struck the king of Israel between the joints
of his armor. So he said to the driver of his
chariot, "Turn around and take me out of the
battle, for I am wounded."
35 The battle increased that day; and the king
was propped up in his chariot, facing the Syri-
ans, and died at evening. The blood ran out
from the wound onto the floor of the chariot.
36 Then, as the sun was going down, a shout
went throughout the army, saying, "Every man
to his city, and every man to his own country!"
37 So the king died, and was brought to Sa-
maria. And they buried the king in Samaria.
38 Then *someone* washed the chariot at a pool
in Samaria, and the dogs licked up his blood
while the harlots bathed,[a] according to the
word of the LORD which He had spoken.
39 Now the rest of the acts of Ahab, and all
that he did, the ivory house which he built and
all the cities that he built, *are* they not written
in the book of the chronicles of the kings of
Israel?
40 So Ahab rested with his fathers. Then
Ahaziah his son reigned in his place.

Jehoshaphat Reigns in Judah

41 Jehoshaphat the son of Asa had become
king over Judah in the fourth year of Ahab
king of Israel.
42 Jehoshaphat *was* thirty-five years old
when he became king, and he reigned twenty-
five years in Jerusalem. His mother's name
was Azubah the daughter of Shilhi.
43 And he walked in all the ways of his father
Asa. He did not turn aside from them, doing
what was right in the eyes of the LORD. Never-
theless the high places were not taken away,
for the people offered sacrifices and burned
incense on the high places.
44 Also Jehoshaphat made peace with the
king of Israel.
45 Now the rest of the acts of Jehoshaphat,
the might that he showed, and how he made
war, *are* they not written in the book of the
chronicles of the kings of Judah?
46 And the rest of the perverted persons,[a]
who remained in the days of his father Asa, he
banished from the land.
47 *There was* then no king in Edom, only a
deputy of the king.
48 Jehoshaphat made merchant ships[a] to go
to Ophir for gold; but they never sailed, for the
ships were wrecked at Ezion Geber.
49 Then Ahaziah the son of Ahab said to Je-
hoshaphat, "Let my servants go with your ser-
vants in the ships." But Jehoshaphat would not.
50 And Jehoshaphat rested with his fathers,
and was buried with his fathers in the City of
David his father. Then Jehoram his son reigned
in his place.

Ahaziah Reigns in Israel

51 Ahaziah the son of Ahab became king over
Israel in Samaria in the seventeenth year of
Jehoshaphat king of Judah, and reigned two
years over Israel.
52 He did evil in the sight of the LORD, and
walked in the way of his father and in the way
of his mother and in the way of Jeroboam the
son of Nebat, who had made Israel sin;
53 for he served Baal and worshiped him, and
provoked the LORD God of Israel to anger, ac-
cording to all that his father had done.

22:38 [a]Syriac and Targum read *they washed his armor.* **22:46** [a]Hebrew *qadesh,* that is, one practicing sodomy and prostitution in religious rituals **22:48** [a]Or *ships of Tarshish*

The Second Book of the KINGS

God Judges Ahaziah

1 Moab rebelled against Israel after the death
of Ahab.
2 Now Ahaziah fell through the lattice of his
upper room in Samaria, and was injured; so he
sent messengers and said to them, "Go, inquire
of Baal-Zebub, the god of Ekron, whether I
shall recover from this injury."
3 But the angel[a] of the LORD said to Elijah
the Tishbite, "Arise, go up to meet the messen-
gers of the king of Samaria, and say to them,
'*Is it* because *there is* no God in Israel *that* you
are going to inquire of Baal-Zebub, the god of
Ekron?'
4 "Now therefore, thus says the LORD: 'You
shall not come down from the bed to which
you have gone up, but you shall surely die.'"
So Elijah departed.
5 And when the messengers returned to him,
he said to them, "Why have you come back?"
6 So they said to him, "A man came up to meet
us, and said to us, 'Go, return to the king who
sent you, and say to him, "Thus says the LORD:
'*Is it* because *there is* no God in Israel *that* you
are sending to inquire of Baal-Zebub, the god
of Ekron? Therefore you shall not come down
from the bed to which you have gone up, but you
shall surely die.'" '"
7 Then he said to them, "What kind of man
was it who came up to meet you and told you
these words?"
8 So they answered him, "A hairy man wear-
ing a leather belt around his waist." And he said,
"It *is* Elijah the Tishbite."
9 Then the king sent to him a captain of fifty
with his fifty men. So he went up to him; and
there he was, sitting on the top of a hill. And
he spoke to him: "Man of God, the king has
said, 'Come down!'"
10 So Elijah answered and said to the captain
of fifty, "If I *am* a man of God, then let fire
come down from heaven and consume you and
your fifty men." And fire came down from heaven
and consumed him and his fifty.
11 Then he sent to him another captain of fifty
with his fifty men. And he answered and said
to him: "Man of God, thus has the king said,
'Come down quickly!'"
12 So Elijah answered and said to them, "If I
am a man of God, let fire come down from
heaven and consume you and your fifty men."
And the fire of God came down from heaven
and consumed him and his fifty.
13 Again, he sent a third captain of fifty with
his fifty men. And the third captain of fifty
went up, and came and fell on his knees before
Elijah, and pleaded with him, and said to him:
"Man of God, please let my life and the life of
these fifty servants of yours be precious in your
sight.
14 "Look, fire has come down from heaven
and burned up the first two captains of fifties
with their fifties. But let my life now be precious
in your sight."
15 And the angel[a] of the LORD said to Elijah,
"Go down with him; do not be afraid of him."
So he arose and went down with him to the
king.
16 Then he said to him, "Thus says the LORD:
'Because you have sent messengers to inquire
of Baal-Zebub, the god of Ekron, *is it* because
there is no God in Israel to inquire of His word?
Therefore you shall not come down from the
bed to which you have gone up, but you shall
surely die.'"
17 So *Ahaziah* died according to the word of
the LORD which Elijah had spoken. Because
he had no son, Jehoram[a] became king in his
place, in the second year of Jehoram the son
of Jehoshaphat, king of Judah.
18 Now the rest of the acts of Ahaziah which
he did, *are* they not written in the book of the
chronicles of the kings of Israel?

Elijah Ascends to Heaven

2 And it came to pass, when the LORD was
about to take up Elijah into heaven by a
whirlwind, that Elijah went with Elisha from
Gilgal.
2 Then Elijah said to Elisha, "Stay here,
please, for the LORD has sent me on to Bethel."
But Elisha said, "*As* the LORD lives, and *as*
your soul lives, I will not leave you!" So they
went down to Bethel.
3 Now the sons of the prophets who *were* at
Bethel came out to Elisha, and said to him, "Do
you know that the LORD will take away your
master from over you today?" And he said,
"Yes, I know; keep silent!"
4 Then Elijah said to him, "Elisha, stay here,
please, for the LORD has sent me on to Jericho."
But he said, "*As* the LORD lives, and *as* your
soul lives, I will not leave you!" So they came
to Jericho.
5 Now the sons of the prophets who *were* at
Jericho came to Elisha and said to him, "Do
you know that the LORD will take away your
master from over you today?" So he answered,
"Yes, I know; keep silent!"
6 Then Elijah said to him, "Stay here, please,
for the LORD has sent me on to the Jordan."
But he said, "*As* the LORD lives, and *as* your
soul lives, I will not leave you!" So the two of
them went on.
7 And fifty men of the sons of the prophets
went and stood facing *them* at a distance,
while the two of them stood by the Jordan.
8 Now Elijah took his mantle, rolled *it* up,
and struck the water; and it was divided this
way and that, so that the two of them crossed
over on dry ground.
9 And so it was, when they had crossed over,
that Elijah said to Elisha, "Ask! What may I do
for you, before I am taken away from you?"
Elisha said, "Please let a double portion of
your spirit be upon me."
10 So he said, "You have asked a hard thing.
Nevertheless, if you see me *when I am* taken
from you, it shall be so for you; but if not, it
shall not be *so*."
11 Then it happened, as they continued on and
talked, that suddenly a chariot of fire *appeared*
with horses of fire, and separated the two of
them; and Elijah went up by a whirlwind into
heaven.
12 And Elisha saw *it*, and he cried out, "My
father, my father, the chariot of Israel and its

1:3 [a]Or *Angel* 1:15 [a]Or *Angel* 1:17 [a]The son of Ahab king of Israel (compare 3:1)

horsemen!" So he saw him no more. And he
took hold of his own clothes and tore them into
two pieces.
13 He also took up the mantle of Elijah that
had fallen from him, and went back and stood
by the bank of the Jordan.
14 Then he took the mantle of Elijah that had
fallen from him, and struck the water, and said,
"Where *is* the LORD God of Elijah?" And when
he also had struck the water, it was divided this
way and that; and Elisha crossed over.
15 Now when the sons of the prophets who
were from Jericho saw him, they said, "The
spirit of Elijah rests on Elisha." And they came
to meet him, and bowed to the ground before
him.
16 Then they said to him, "Look now, there are
fifty strong men with your servants. Please let
them go and search for your master, lest per-
haps the Spirit of the LORD has taken him up
and cast him upon some mountain or into some
valley." And he said, "You shall not send
anyone."
17 But when they urged him till he was
ashamed, he said, "Send *them!*" Therefore
they sent fifty men, and they searched for three
days but did not find him.
18 And when they came back to him, for he
had stayed in Jericho, he said to them, "Did I
not say to you, 'Do not go'?"

Elisha Performs Miracles

19 Then the men of the city said to Elisha,
"Please notice, the situation of this city *is* pleas-
ant, as my lord sees; but the water *is* bad, and
the ground barren."
20 And he said, "Bring me a new bowl, and
put salt in it." So they brought *it* to him.
21 Then he went out to the source of the wa-
ter, and cast in the salt there, and said, "Thus
says the LORD: 'I have healed this water; from
it there shall be no more death or barrenness.'"
22 So the water remains healed to this day,
according to the word of Elisha which he
spoke.
23 Then he went up from there to Bethel; and
as he was going up the road, some youths came
from the city and mocked him, and said to him,
"Go up, you baldhead! Go up, you baldhead!"
24 So he turned around and looked at them,
and pronounced a curse on them in the name
of the LORD. And two female bears came out of
the woods and mauled forty-two of the youths.
25 Then he went from there to Mount Carmel,
and from there he returned to Samaria.

Moab Rebels Against Israel

3 Now Jehoram the son of Ahab became king
over Israel at Samaria in the eighteenth
year of Jehoshaphat king of Judah, and reigned
twelve years.
2 And he did evil in the sight of the LORD,
but not like his father and mother; for he put
away the *sacred* pillar of Baal that his father
had made.
3 Nevertheless he persisted in the sins of
Jeroboam the son of Nebat, who had made
Israel sin; he did not depart from them.
4 Now Mesha king of Moab was a sheep-
breeder, and he regularly paid the king of Is-
rael one hundred thousand lambs and the wool
of one hundred thousand rams.
5 But it happened, when Ahab died, that the
king of Moab rebelled against the king of Is-
rael.
6 So King Jehoram went out of Samaria at
that time and mustered all Israel.
7 Then he went and sent to Jehoshaphat king
of Judah, saying, "The king of Moab has re-
belled against me. Will you go with me to fight
against Moab?" And he said, "I will go up; I
am as you *are*, my people as your people, my
horses as your horses."
8 Then he said, "Which way shall we go up?"
And he answered, "By way of the Wilderness
of Edom."
9 So the king of Israel went with the king of
Judah and the king of Edom, and they marched
on that roundabout route seven days; and there
was no water for the army, nor for the animals
that followed them.
10 And the king of Israel said, "Alas! For the
LORD has called these three kings together to
deliver them into the hand of Moab."
11 But Jehoshaphat said, "*Is there* no prophet
of the LORD here, that we may inquire of the
LORD by him?" So one of the servants of the
king of Israel answered and said, "Elisha the son
of Shaphat *is* here, who poured water on the
hands of Elijah."
12 And Jehoshaphat said, "The word of the
LORD is with him." So the king of Israel and
Jehoshaphat and the king of Edom went down
to him.
13 Then Elisha said to the king of Israel,
"What have I to do with you? Go to the proph-
ets of your father and the prophets of your
mother." But the king of Israel said to him, "No,
for the LORD has called these three kings *to-
gether* to deliver them into the hand of Moab."
14 And Elisha said, "*As* the LORD of hosts lives,
before whom I stand, surely were it not that I
regard the presence of Jehoshaphat king of
Judah, I would not look at you, nor see you.
15 "But now bring me a musician." Then it
happened, when the musician played, that the
hand of the LORD came upon him.
16 And he said, "Thus says the LORD: 'Make
this valley full of ditches.'
17 "For thus says the LORD: 'You shall not see
wind, nor shall you see rain; yet that valley
shall be filled with water, so that you, your cattle,
and your animals may drink.'
18 "And this is a simple matter in the sight of
the LORD; He will also deliver the Moabites into
your hand.
19 "Also you shall attack every fortified city
and every choice city, and shall cut down every
good tree, and stop up every spring of water,
and ruin every good piece of land with stones."
20 Now it happened in the morning, when the
grain offering was offered, that suddenly water
came by way of Edom, and the land was filled
with water.
21 And when all the Moabites heard that the
kings had come up to fight against them, all
who were able to bear arms and older were
gathered; and they stood at the border.
22 Then they rose up early in the morning,
and the sun was shining on the water; and the
Moabites saw the water on the other side *as* red
as blood.
23 And they said, "This is blood; the kings have
surely struck swords and have killed one an-
other; now therefore, Moab, to the spoil!"
24 So when they came to the camp of Israel,
Israel rose up and attacked the Moabites, so
that they fled before them; and they entered
their land, killing the Moabites.
25 Then they destroyed the cities, and each man

threw a stone on every good piece of land and
filled it; and they stopped up all the springs of
water and cut down all the good trees. But they
left the stones of Kir Haraseth *intact*. However
the slingers surrounded and attacked it.
26 And when the king of Moab saw that the
battle was too fierce for him, he took with him
seven hundred men who drew swords, to break
through to the king of Edom, but they could
not.
27 Then he took his eldest son who would have
reigned in his place, and offered him *as* a burnt
offering upon the wall; and there was great in-
dignation against Israel. So they departed
from him and returned to *their own* land.

Elisha and the Widow's Oil

4 A certain woman of the wives of the sons
of the prophets cried out to Elisha, saying,
"Your servant my husband is dead, and you
know that your servant feared the LORD. And
the creditor is coming to take my two sons to
be his slaves."
2 So Elisha said to her, "What shall I do for
you? Tell me, what do you have in the house?"
And she said, "Your maidservant has nothing
in the house but a jar of oil."
3 Then he said, "Go, borrow vessels from
everywhere, from all your neighbors—empty
vessels; do not gather just a few.
4 "And when you have come in, you shall
shut the door behind you and your sons; then
pour it into all those vessels, and set aside the
full ones."
5 So she went from him and shut the door
behind her and her sons, who brought *the ves-
sels* to her; and she poured *it* out.
6 Now it came to pass, when the vessels were
full, that she said to her son, "Bring me another
vessel." And he said to her, "*There is* not an-
other vessel." So the oil ceased.
7 Then she came and told the man of God.
And he said, "Go, sell the oil and pay your debt;
and you *and* your sons live on the rest."

Elisha Raises the Shunammite's Son

8 Now it happened one day that Elisha went
to Shunem, where there *was* a notable woman,
and she persuaded him to eat some food. So it
was, as often as he passed by, he would turn in
there to eat some food.
9 And she said to her husband, "Look now,
I know that this *is* a holy man of God, who
passes by us regularly.
10 "Please, let us make a small upper room on
the wall; and let us put a bed for him there, and
a table and a chair and a lampstand; so it will
be, whenever he comes to us, he can turn in
there."
11 And it happened one day that he came there,
and he turned in to the upper room and lay
down there.
12 Then he said to Gehazi his servant, "Call
this Shunammite woman." When he had called
her, she stood before him.
13 And he said to him, "Say now to her, 'Look,
you have been concerned for us with all this
care. What *can I* do for you? Do you want me
to speak on your behalf to the king or to the
commander of the army?'" She answered, "I
dwell among my own people."
14 So he said, "What then *is* to be done for
her?" And Gehazi answered, "Actually, she
has no son, and her husband is old."
15 So he said, "Call her." When he had called
her, she stood in the doorway.
16 Then he said, "About this time next year
you shall embrace a son." And she said, "No,
my lord. Man of God, do not lie to your maid-
servant!"
17 But the woman conceived, and bore a son
when the appointed time had come, of which
Elisha had told her.
18 And the child grew. Now it happened one
day that he went out to his father, to the
reapers.
19 And he said to his father, "My head, my
head!" So he said to a servant, "Carry him to
his mother."
20 When he had taken him and brought him
to his mother, he sat on her knees till noon, and
then died.
21 And she went up and laid him on the bed
of the man of God, shut *the door* upon him,
and went out.
22 Then she called to her husband, and said,
"Please send me one of the young men and one
of the donkeys, that I may run to the man of
God and come back."
23 So he said, "Why are you going to him
today? *It is* neither the New Moon nor the Sab-
bath." And she said, "*It is* well."
24 Then she saddled a donkey, and said to
her servant, "Drive, and go forward; do not
slacken the pace for me unless I tell you."
25 And so she departed, and went to the man
of God at Mount Carmel.
So it was, when the man of God saw her
afar off, that he said to his servant Gehazi, "Look,
the Shunammite woman!
26 "Please run now to meet her, and say to
her, '*Is it* well with you? *Is it* well with your
husband? *Is it* well with the child?'" And she
answered, "*It is* well."
27 Now when she came to the man of God at
the hill, she caught him by the feet, but Gehazi
came near to push her away. But the man of
God said, "Let her alone; for her soul *is* in deep
distress, and the LORD has hidden *it* from me,
and has not told me."
28 So she said, "Did I ask a son of my lord?
Did I not say, 'Do not deceive me'?"
29 Then he said to Gehazi, "Get yourself ready,
and take my staff in your hand, and be on your
way. If you meet anyone, do not greet him; and
if anyone greets you, do not answer him; but
lay my staff on the face of the child."
30 And the mother of the child said, "*As* the
LORD lives, and *as* your soul lives, I will not
leave you." So he arose and followed her.
31 Now Gehazi went on ahead of them, and
laid the staff on the face of the child; but *there
was* neither voice nor hearing. Therefore he
went back to meet him, and told him, saying,
"The child has not awakened."
32 When Elisha came into the house, there was
the child, lying dead on his bed.
33 He went in therefore, shut the door behind
the two of them, and prayed to the LORD.
34 And he went up and lay on the child, and
put his mouth on his mouth, his eyes on his eyes,
and his hands on his hands; and he stretched
himself out on the child, and the flesh of the
child became warm.
35 He returned and walked back and forth in
the house, and again went up and stretched
himself out on him; then the child sneezed
seven times, and the child opened his eyes.
36 And he called Gehazi and said, "Call this

Shunammite woman." So he called her. And when she came in to him, he said, "Pick up your son."

37 So she went in, fell at his feet, and bowed to the ground; then she picked up her son and went out.

Elisha Purifies the Pot of Stew

38 And Elisha returned to Gilgal, and *there was* a famine in the land. Now the sons of the prophets *were* sitting before him; and he said to his servant, "Put on the large pot, and boil stew for the sons of the prophets."

39 So one went out into the field to gather herbs, and found a wild vine, and gathered from it a lapful of wild gourds, and came and sliced *them* into the pot of stew, though they did not know *what they were*.

40 Then they served it to the men to eat. Now it happened, as they were eating the stew, that they cried out and said, "Man of God, *there is* death in the pot!" And they could not eat *it*.

41 So he said, "Then bring some flour." And he put *it* into the pot, and said, "Serve *it* to the people, that they may eat." And there was nothing harmful in the pot.

Elisha Feeds One Hundred Men

42 Then a man came from Baal Shalisha, and brought the man of God bread of the firstfruits, twenty loaves of barley bread, and newly ripened grain in his knapsack. And he said, "Give *it* to the people, that they may eat."

43 But his servant said, "What? Shall I set this before one hundred men?" He said again, "Give it to the people, that they may eat; for thus says the LORD: 'They shall eat and have *some* left over.' "

44 So he set *it* before them; and they ate and had *some* left over, according to the word of the LORD.

Naaman's Leprosy Healed

5 Now Naaman, commander of the army of the king of Syria, was a great and honorable man in the eyes of his master, because by him the LORD had given victory to Syria. He was also a mighty man of valor, *but* a leper.

2 And the Syrians had gone out on raids, and had brought back captive a young girl from the land of Israel. She waited on Naaman's wife.

3 Then she said to her mistress, "If only my master *were* with the prophet who *is* in Samaria! For he would heal him of his leprosy."

4 And *Naaman* went in and told his master, saying, "Thus and thus said the girl who *is* from the land of Israel."

5 Then the king of Syria said, "Go now, and I will send a letter to the king of Israel." So he departed and took with him ten talents of silver, six thousand *shekels* of gold, and ten changes of clothing.

6 Then he brought the letter to the king of Israel, which said,

> Now be advised, when this letter comes to you, that I have sent Naaman my servant to you, that you may heal him of his leprosy.

7 And it happened, when the king of Israel read the letter, that he tore his clothes and said, "*Am* I God, to kill and make alive, that this man sends a man to me to heal him of his leprosy? Therefore please consider, and see how he seeks a quarrel with me."

8 So it was, when Elisha the man of God heard that the king of Israel had torn his clothes, that he sent to the king, saying, "Why have you torn your clothes? Please let him come to me, and he shall know that there is a prophet in Israel."

9 Then Naaman went with his horses and chariot, and he stood at the door of Elisha's house.

10 And Elisha sent a messenger to him, saying, "Go and wash in the Jordan seven times, and your flesh shall be restored to you, and *you shall* be clean."

11 But Naaman became furious, and went away and said, "Indeed, I said to myself, 'He will surely come out *to me*, and stand and call on the name of the LORD his God, and wave his hand over the place, and heal the leprosy.'

12 "*Are* not the Abanah[a] and the Pharpar, the rivers of Damascus, better than all the waters of Israel? Could I not wash in them and be clean?" So he turned and went away in a rage.

13 And his servants came near and spoke to him, and said, "My father, *if* the prophet had told you *to do* something great, would you not have done *it*? How much more then, when he says to you, 'Wash, and be clean'?"

14 So he went down and dipped seven times in the Jordan, according to the saying of the man of God; and his flesh was restored like the flesh of a little child, and he was clean.

15 And he returned to the man of God, he and all his aides, and came and stood before him; and he said, "Indeed, now I know that *there is* no God in all the earth, except in Israel; now therefore, please take a gift from your servant."

16 But he said, "*As* the LORD lives, before whom I stand, I will receive nothing." And he urged him to take *it*, but he refused.

17 So Naaman said, "Then, if not, please let your servant be given two mule-loads of earth; for your servant will no longer offer either burnt offering or sacrifice to other gods, but to the LORD.

18 "Yet in this thing may the LORD pardon your servant: when my master goes into the temple of Rimmon to worship there, and he leans on my hand, and I bow down in the temple of Rimmon—when I bow down in the temple of Rimmon, may the LORD please pardon your servant in this thing."

19 Then he said to him, "Go in peace." So he departed from him a short distance.

Gehazi's Greed

20 But Gehazi, the servant of Elisha the man of God, said, "Look, my master has spared Naaman this Syrian, while not receiving from his hands what he brought; but *as* the LORD lives, I will run after him and take something from him."

21 So Gehazi pursued Naaman. When Naaman saw *him* running after him, he got down from the chariot to meet him, and said, "*Is* all well?"

22 And he said, "All *is* well. My master has sent me, saying, 'Indeed, just now two young men of the sons of the prophets have come to me from the mountains of Ephraim. Please give them a talent of silver and two changes of garments.' "

5:12 [a]Following Kethib, Septuagint, and Vulgate; Qere, Syriac, and Targum read *Amanah*.

23 So Naaman said, "Please, take two talents."
And he urged him, and bound two talents of
silver in two bags, with two changes of garments,
and handed *them* to two of his servants; and
they carried *them* on ahead of him.
24 When he came to the citadel, he took *them*
from their hand, and stored *them* away in the
house; then he let the men go, and they departed.
25 Now he went in and stood before his mas-
ter. Elisha said to him, "Where *did you go*, Ge-
hazi?" And he said, "Your servant did not go
anywhere."
26 Then he said to him, "Did not my heart go
with you when the man turned back from his
chariot to meet you? *Is it* time to receive money
and to receive clothing, olive groves and vine-
yards, sheep and oxen, male and female ser-
vants?
27 "Therefore the leprosy of Naaman shall
cling to you and your descendants forever."
And he went out from his presence leprous, *as
white* as snow.

The Floating Ax Head

6 And the sons of the prophets said to Elisha,
"See now, the place where we dwell with
you is too small for us.
2 "Please, let us go to the Jordan, and let
every man take a beam from there, and let us
make there a place where we may dwell." So
he answered, "Go."
3 Then one said, "Please consent to go with
your servants." And he answered, "I will go."
4 So he went with them. And when they
came to the Jordan, they cut down trees.
5 But as one was cutting down a tree, the
iron *ax head* fell into the water; and he cried
out and said, "Alas, master! For it was borrowed."
6 So the man of God said, "Where did it fall?"
And he showed him the place. So he cut off a
stick, and threw *it* in there; and he made the iron
float.
7 Therefore he said, "Pick *it* up for yourself."
So he reached out his hand and took it.

The Blinded Syrians Captured

8 Now the king of Syria was making war
against Israel; and he consulted with his ser-
vants, saying, "My camp *will be* in such and
such a place."
9 And the man of God sent to the king of
Israel, saying, "Beware that you do not pass this
place, for the Syrians are coming down there."
10 Then the king of Israel sent *someone* to
the place of which the man of God had told
him. Thus he warned him, and he was watchful
there, not just once or twice.
11 Therefore the heart of the king of Syria
was greatly troubled by this thing; and he
called his servants and said to them, "Will you
not show me which of us *is* for the king of Is-
rael?"
12 And one of his servants said, "None, my
lord, O king; but Elisha, the prophet who *is* in
Israel, tells the king of Israel the words that you
speak in your bedroom."
13 So he said, "Go and see where he *is*, that I
may send and get him." And it was told him,
saying, "Surely *he is* in Dothan."
14 Therefore he sent horses and chariots and
a great army there, and they came by night and
surrounded the city.
15 And when the servant of the man of God
arose early and went out, there was an army,
surrounding the city with horses and chariots.
And his servant said to him, "Alas, my master!
What shall we do?"
16 So he answered, "Do not fear, for those
who *are* with us *are* more than those who *are*
with them."
17 And Elisha prayed, and said, "LORD, I pray,
open his eyes that he may see." Then the LORD
opened the eyes of the young man, and he saw.
And behold, the mountain *was* full of horses
and chariots of fire all around Elisha.
18 So when *the Syrians* came down to him,
Elisha prayed to the LORD, and said, "Strike this
people, I pray, with blindness." And He struck
them with blindness according to the word of
Elisha.
19 Now Elisha said to them, "This *is* not the
way, nor *is* this the city. Follow me, and I will
bring you to the man whom you seek." But he
led them to Samaria.
20 So it was, when they had come to Samaria,
that Elisha said, "LORD, open the eyes of these
men, that they may see." And the LORD opened
their eyes, and they saw; and there *they were*,
inside Samaria!
21 Now when the king of Israel saw them, he
said to Elisha, "My father, shall I kill *them*?
Shall I kill *them*?"
22 But he answered, "You shall not kill *them*.
Would you kill those whom you have taken cap-
tive with your sword and your bow? Set food and
water before them, that they may eat and drink
and go to their master."
23 Then he prepared a great feast for them;
and after they ate and drank, he sent them
away and they went to their master. So the
bands of Syrian *raiders* came no more into the
land of Israel.

Syria Besieges Samaria in Famine

24 And it happened after this that Ben-Hadad
king of Syria gathered all his army, and went
up and besieged Samaria.
25 And there was a great famine in Samaria;
and indeed they besieged it until a donkey's
head was *sold* for eighty *shekels* of silver, and
one-fourth of a kab of dove droppings for five
shekels of silver.
26 Then, as the king of Israel was passing by
on the wall, a woman cried out to him, saying,
"Help, my lord, O king!"
27 And he said, "If the LORD does not help
you, where can I find help for you? From the
threshing floor or from the winepress?"
28 Then the king said to her, "What is trou-
bling you?" And she answered, "This woman
said to me, 'Give your son, that we may eat him
today, and we will eat my son tomorrow.'
29 "So we boiled my son, and ate him. And I
said to her on the next day, 'Give your son, that
we may eat him'; but she has hidden her son."
30 Now it happened, when the king heard the
words of the woman, that he tore his clothes;
and as he passed by on the wall, the people
looked, and there underneath *he had* sackcloth
on his body.
31 Then he said, "God do so to me and more
also, if the head of Elisha the son of Shaphat
remains on him today!"
32 But Elisha was sitting in his house, and the
elders were sitting with him. And *the king* sent
a man ahead of him, but before the messenger
came to him, he said to the elders, "Do you see
how this son of a murderer has sent someone
to take away my head? Look, when the mes-
senger comes, shut the door, and hold him fast

at the door. *Is* not the sound of his master's feet
behind him?"
33 And while he was still talking with them,
there was the messenger, coming down to him;
and then *the king* said, "Surely this calamity
is from the LORD; why should I wait for the LORD
any longer?"
7 Then Elisha said, "Hear the word of the
LORD. Thus says the LORD: 'Tomorrow about
this time a seah of fine flour *shall be sold* for a
shekel, and two seahs of barley for a shekel, at
the gate of Samaria.'"
2 So an officer on whose hand the king
leaned answered the man of God and said,
"Look, *if* the LORD would make windows in
heaven, could this thing be?" And he said, "In
fact, you shall see *it* with your eyes, but you
shall not eat of it."

The Syrians Flee

3 Now there were four leprous men at the
entrance of the gate; and they said to one an-
other, "Why are we sitting here until we die?
4 "If we say, 'We will enter the city,' the fam-
ine *is* in the city, and we shall die there. And if
we sit here, we die also. Now therefore, come,
let us surrender to the army of the Syrians. If
they keep us alive, we shall live; and if they
kill us, we shall only die."
5 And they rose at twilight to go to the camp
of the Syrians; and when they had come to the
outskirts of the Syrian camp, to their surprise
no one *was* there.
6 For the Lord had caused the army of the
Syrians to hear the noise of chariots and the
noise of horses—the noise of a great army; so
they said to one another, "Look, the king of
Israel has hired against us the kings of the
Hittites and the kings of the Egyptians to at-
tack us!"
7 Therefore they arose and fled at twilight,
and left the camp intact—their tents, their
horses, and their donkeys—and they fled for
their lives.
8 And when these lepers came to the out-
skirts of the camp, they went into one tent and
ate and drank, and carried from it silver and
gold and clothing, and went and hid *them*; then
they came back and entered another tent, and
carried *some* from there *also*, and went and
hid *it*.
9 Then they said to one another, "We are not
doing right. This day *is* a day of good news,
and we remain silent. If we wait until morning
light, some punishment will come upon us.
Now therefore, come, let us go and tell the king's
household."
10 So they went and called to the gatekeepers
of the city, and told them, saying, "We went to
the Syrian camp, and surprisingly no one *was*
there, not a human sound—only horses and
donkeys tied, and the tents intact."
11 And the gatekeepers called out, and they
told *it* to the king's household inside.
12 So the king arose in the night and said to his
servants, "Let me now tell you what the Syrians
have done to us. They know that we *are* hun-
gry; therefore they have gone out of the camp
to hide themselves in the field, saying, 'When
they come out of the city, we shall catch them
alive, and get into the city.'"
13 And one of his servants answered and said,
"Please, let several *men* take five of the remain-
ing horses which are left in the city. Look, they
may either become like all the multitude of
Israel that are left in it; or indeed, *I say*, they
may become like all the multitude of Israel left
from those who are consumed; so let us send
them and see."
14 Therefore they took two chariots with
horses; and the king sent them in the direction
of the Syrian army, saying, "Go and see."
15 And they went after them to the Jordan;
and indeed all the road *was* full of garments
and weapons which the Syrians had thrown
away in their haste. So the messengers re-
turned and told the king.
16 Then the people went out and plundered the
tents of the Syrians. So a seah of fine flour was
sold for a shekel, and two seahs of barley for
a shekel, according to the word of the LORD.
17 Now the king had appointed the officer on
whose hand he leaned to have charge of the gate.
But the people trampled him in the gate, and
he died, just as the man of God had said, who
spoke when the king came down to him.
18 So it happened just as the man of God had
spoken to the king, saying, "Two seahs of bar-
ley for a shekel, and a seah of fine flour for a
shekel, shall be *sold* tomorrow about this time
in the gate of Samaria."
19 Then that officer had answered the man of
God, and said, "Now look, *if* the LORD would
make windows in heaven, could such a thing
be?" And he had said, "In fact, you shall see *it*
with your eyes, but you shall not eat of it."
20 And so it happened to him, for the people
trampled him in the gate, and he died.

The King Restores the Shunammite's Land

8 Then Elisha spoke to the woman whose son
he had restored to life, saying, "Arise and go,
you and your household, and stay wherever
you can; for the LORD has called for a famine,
and furthermore, it will come upon the land for
seven years."
2 So the woman arose and did according to
the saying of the man of God, and she went with
her household and dwelt in the land of the
Philistines seven years.
3 It came to pass, at the end of seven years,
that the woman returned from the land of the
Philistines; and she went to make an appeal to
the king for her house and for her land.
4 Then the king talked with Gehazi, the ser-
vant of the man of God, saying, "Tell me, please,
all the great things Elisha has done."
5 Now it happened, as he was telling the
king how he had restored the dead to life, that
there was the woman whose son he had restored
to life, appealing to the king for her house and
for her land. And Gehazi said, "My lord,
O king, this *is* the woman, and this *is* her son
whom Elisha restored to life."
6 And when the king asked the woman, she
told him. So the king appointed a certain offi-
cer for her, saying, "Restore all that *was* hers,
and all the proceeds of the field from the day
that she left the land until now."

Death of Ben-Hadad

7 Then Elisha went to Damascus, and Ben-
Hadad king of Syria was sick; and it was told
him, saying, "The man of God has come here."
8 And the king said to Hazael, "Take a present
in your hand, and go to meet the man of God,
and inquire of the LORD by him, saying, 'Shall
I recover from this disease?'"
9 So Hazael went to meet him and took a pres-
ent with him, of every good thing of Damascus,

forty camel-loads; and he came and stood before him, and said, "Your son Ben-Hadad king of Syria has sent me to you, saying, 'Shall I recover from this disease?' "
10 And Elisha said to him, "Go, say to him, 'You shall certainly recover.' However the LORD has shown me that he will really die."
11 Then he set his countenance in a stare until he was ashamed; and the man of God wept.
12 And Hazael said, "Why is my lord weeping?" He answered, "Because I know the evil that you will do to the children of Israel: Their strongholds you will set on fire, and their young men you will kill with the sword; and you will dash their children, and rip open their women with child."
13 So Hazael said, "But what *is* your servant—a dog, that he should do this gross thing?" And Elisha answered, "The LORD has shown me that you *will become* king over Syria."
14 Then he departed from Elisha, and came to his master, who said to him, "What did Elisha say to you?" And he answered, "He told me you would surely recover."
15 But it happened on the next day that he took a thick cloth and dipped *it* in water, and spread *it* over his face so that he died; and Hazael reigned in his place.

Jehoram Reigns in Judah

16 Now in the fifth year of Joram the son of Ahab, king of Israel, Jehoshaphat *having been* king of Judah, Jehoram the son of Jehoshaphat began to reign as king of Judah.
17 He was thirty-two years old when he became king, and he reigned eight years in Jerusalem.
18 And he walked in the way of the kings of Israel, just as the house of Ahab had done, for the daughter of Ahab was his wife; and he did evil in the sight of the LORD.
19 Yet the LORD would not destroy Judah, for the sake of his servant David, as He promised him to give a lamp to him *and* his sons forever.
20 In his days Edom revolted against Judah's authority, and made a king over themselves.
21 So Joram[a] went to Zair, and all his chariots with him. Then he rose by night and attacked the Edomites who had surrounded him and the captains of the chariots; and the troops fled to their tents.
22 Thus Edom has been in revolt against Judah's authority to this day. And Libnah revolted at that time.
23 Now the rest of the acts of Joram, and all that he did, *are* they not written in the book of the chronicles of the kings of Judah?
24 So Joram rested with his fathers, and was buried with his fathers in the City of David. Then Ahaziah his son reigned in his place.

Ahaziah Reigns in Judah

25 In the twelfth year of Joram the son of Ahab, king of Israel, Ahaziah the son of Jehoram, king of Judah, began to reign.
26 Ahaziah *was* twenty-two years old when he became king, and he reigned one year in Jerusalem. His mother's name *was* Athaliah the granddaughter of Omri, king of Israel.
27 And he walked in the way of the house of Ahab, and did evil in the sight of the LORD, like the house of Ahab, for he *was* the son-in-law of the house of Ahab.
28 Now he went with Joram the son of Ahab to war against Hazael king of Syria at Ramoth Gilead; and the Syrians wounded Joram.
29 Then King Joram went back to Jezreel to recover from the wounds which the Syrians had inflicted on him at Ramah, when he fought against Hazael king of Syria. And Ahaziah the son of Jehoram, king of Judah, went down to see Joram the son of Ahab in Jezreel, because he was sick.

Jehu Anointed King of Israel

9 And Elisha the prophet called one of the sons of the prophets, and said to him, "Get yourself ready, take this flask of oil in your hand, and go to Ramoth Gilead.
2 "Now when you arrive at that place, look there for Jehu the son of Jehoshaphat, the son of Nimshi, and go in and make him rise up from among his associates, and take him to an inner room.
3 "Then take the flask of oil, and pour *it* on his head, and say, 'Thus says the LORD: "I have anointed you king over Israel." ' Then open the door and flee, and do not delay."
4 So the young man, the servant of the prophet, went to Ramoth Gilead.
5 And when he arrived, there *were* the captains of the army sitting; and he said, "I have a message for you, Commander." Jehu said, "For which *one* of us?" And he said, "For you, Commander."
6 Then he arose and went into the house. And he poured the oil on his head, and said to him, "Thus says the LORD God of Israel: 'I have anointed you king over the people of the LORD, over Israel.
7 'You shall strike down the house of Ahab your master, that I may avenge the blood of My servants the prophets, and the blood of all the servants of the LORD, at the hand of Jezebel.
8 'For the whole house of Ahab shall perish; and I will cut off from Ahab all the males in Israel, both bond and free.
9 'So I will make the house of Ahab like the house of Jeroboam the son of Nebat, and like the house of Baasha the son of Ahijah.
10 'The dogs shall eat Jezebel on the plot *of ground* at Jezreel, and *there shall be* none to bury *her.*' " And he opened the door and fled.
11 Then Jehu came out to the servants of his master, and *one* said to him, "*Is* all well? Why did this madman come to you?" And he said to them, "You know the man and his babble."
12 And they said, "A lie! Tell us now." So he said, "Thus and thus he spoke to me, saying, 'Thus says the LORD: "I have anointed you king over Israel." ' "
13 Then each man hastened to take his garment and put *it* under him on the top of the steps; and they blew trumpets, saying, "Jehu is king!"

Joram of Israel Killed

14 So Jehu the son of Jehoshaphat, the son of Nimshi, conspired against Joram. (Now Joram had been defending Ramoth Gilead, he and all Israel, against Hazael king of Syria.
15 But King Joram had returned to Jezreel to recover from the wounds which the Syrians had inflicted on him when he fought with Hazael king of Syria.) And Jehu said, "If you are so

8:21 [a]Spelled *Jehoram* in verse 16

minded, let no one leave *or* escape from the city to go and tell *it* in Jezreel."

16 So Jehu rode in a chariot and went to Jezreel, for Joram was laid up there; and Ahaziah king of Judah had come down to see Joram.

17 Now a watchman stood on the tower in Jezreel, and he saw the company of Jehu as he came, and said, "I see a company of men." And Joram said, "Get a horseman and send him to meet them, and let him say, '*Is it* peace?' "

18 So the horseman went to meet him, and said, "Thus says the king: '*Is it* peace?' " And Jehu said, "What have you to do with peace? Turn around and follow me." So the watchman reported, saying, "The messenger went to them, but is not coming back."

19 Then he sent out a second horseman who came to them, and said, "Thus says the king: '*Is it* peace?' " And Jehu answered, "What have you to do with peace? Turn around and follow me."

20 So the watchman reported, saying, "He went up to them and is not coming back; and the driving *is* like the driving of Jehu the son of Nimshi, for he drives furiously!"

21 Then Joram said, "Make ready." And his chariot was made ready. Then Joram king of Israel and Ahaziah king of Judah went out, each in his chariot; and they went out to meet Jehu, and met him on the property of Naboth the Jezreelite.

22 Now it happened, when Joram saw Jehu, that he said, "*Is it* peace, Jehu?" So he answered, "What peace, as long as the harlotries of your mother Jezebel and her witchcraft *are so* many?"

23 Then Joram turned around and fled, and said to Ahaziah, "Treachery, Ahaziah!"

24 Now Jehu drew his bow with full strength and shot Jehoram between his arms; and the arrow came out at his heart, and he sank down in his chariot.

25 Then *Jehu* said to Bidkar his captain, "Pick *him* up, *and* throw him into the tract of the field of Naboth the Jezreelite; for remember, when you and I were riding together behind Ahab his father, that the LORD laid this burden upon him:

26 'Surely I saw yesterday the blood of Naboth and the blood of his sons,' says the LORD, 'and I will repay you in this plot,' says the LORD. Now therefore, take *and* throw him on the plot *of ground*, according to the word of the LORD."

Ahaziah of Judah Killed

27 But when Ahaziah king of Judah saw *this*, he fled by the road to Beth Haggan.[a] So Jehu pursued him, and said, "Shoot him also in the chariot." *And they shot him* at the Ascent of Gur, which is by Ibleam. Then he fled to Megiddo, and died there.

28 And his servants carried him in the chariot to Jerusalem, and buried him in his tomb with his fathers in the City of David.

29 In the eleventh year of Joram the son of Ahab, Ahaziah had become king over Judah.

Jezebel's Violent Death

30 Now when Jehu had come to Jezreel, Jezebel heard *of it;* and she put paint on her eyes and adorned her head, and looked through a window.

31 Then, as Jehu entered at the gate, she said, "*Is it* peace, Zimri, murderer of your master?"

32 And he looked up at the window, and said, "Who *is* on my side? Who?" So two *or* three eunuchs looked out at him.

33 Then he said, "Throw her down." So they threw her down, and *some* of her blood spattered on the wall and on the horses; and he trampled her underfoot.

34 And when he had gone in, he ate and drank. Then he said, "Go now, see to this accursed *woman*, and bury her, for she was a king's daughter."

35 So they went to bury her, but they found no more of her than the skull and the feet and the palms of *her* hands.

36 Therefore they came back and told him. And he said, "This *is* the word of the LORD, which He spoke by His servant Elijah the Tishbite, saying, 'On the plot *of ground* at Jezreel dogs shall eat the flesh of Jezebel;[a]

37 'and the corpse of Jezebel shall be as refuse on the surface of the field, in the plot at Jezreel, so that they shall not say, "Here *lies* Jezebel." ' "

Ahab's Seventy Sons Killed

10 Now Ahab had seventy sons in Samaria. And Jehu wrote and sent letters to Samaria, to the rulers of Jezreel,[a] to the elders, and to those who reared Ahab's *sons*, saying:

2 Now as soon as this letter comes to you,
since your master's sons *are* with you,
and you have chariots and horses, a
fortified city also, and weapons,
3 choose the best qualified of your master's
sons, set *him* on his father's throne, and
fight for your master's house.

4 But they were exceedingly afraid, and said, "Look, two kings could not stand up to him; how then can we stand?"

5 And he who *was* in charge of the house, and he who *was* in charge of the city, the elders also, and those who reared *the sons*, sent to Jehu, saying, "We *are* your servants, we will do all you tell us; but we will not make anyone king. Do *what is* good in your sight."

6 Then he wrote a second letter to them, saying:

If you *are* for me and will obey my voice,
take the heads of the men, your master's
sons, and come to me at Jezreel by this
time tomorrow.

Now the king's sons, seventy persons, *were* with the great men of the city, *who* were rearing them.

7 So it was, when the letter came to them, that they took the king's sons and slaughtered seventy persons, put their heads in baskets and sent *them* to him at Jezreel.

8 Then a messenger came and told him, saying, "They have brought the heads of the king's sons." And he said, "Lay them in two heaps at the entrance of the gate until morning."

9 So it was, in the morning, that he went out and stood, and said to all the people, "You *are* righteous. Indeed I conspired against my master and killed him; but who killed all these?

10 "Know now that nothing shall fall to the earth of the word of the LORD which the LORD spoke concerning the house of Ahab; for the

9:27 [a]Literally *The Garden House* **9:36** [a]1 Kings 21:23 **10:1** [a]Following Masoretic Text, Syriac, and Targum; Septuagint reads *Samaria;* Vulgate reads *city.*

LORD has done what He spoke by His servant
Elijah."
11 So Jehu killed all who remained of the house
of Ahab in Jezreel, and all his great men and
his close acquaintances and his priests, until
he left him none remaining.

Ahaziah's Forty-two Brothers Killed

12 And he arose and departed and went to
Samaria. On the way, at Beth Eked[a] of the Shep-
herds,
13 Jehu met with the brothers of Ahaziah
king of Judah, and said, "Who *are* you?" So
they answered, "We *are* the brothers of Ahaziah;
we have come down to greet the sons of the
king and the sons of the queen mother."
14 And he said, "Take them alive!" So they took
them alive, and killed them at the well of Beth
Eked, forty-two men; and he left none of them.

The Rest of Ahab's Family Killed

15 Now when he departed from there, he met
Jehonadab the son of Rechab, *coming* to meet
him; and he greeted him and said to him, "Is
your heart right, as my heart *is* toward your
heart?" And Jehonadab answered, "It is." *Jehu
said,* "If it is, give *me* your hand." So he gave
him his hand, and he took him up to him into
the chariot.
16 Then he said, "Come with me, and see my
zeal for the LORD." So they had him ride in his
chariot.
17 And when he came to Samaria, he killed all
who remained to Ahab in Samaria, till he had
destroyed them, according to the word of the
LORD which He spoke to Elijah.

Worshipers of Baal Killed

18 Then Jehu gathered all the people together,
and said to them, "Ahab served Baal a little,
Jehu will serve him much.
19 "Now therefore, call to me all the prophets
of Baal, all his servants, and all his priests. Let
no one be missing, for I have a great sacrifice
for Baal. Whoever is missing shall not live."
But Jehu acted deceptively, with the intent of
destroying the worshipers of Baal.
20 And Jehu said, "Proclaim a solemn assem-
bly for Baal." So they proclaimed *it*.
21 Then Jehu sent throughout all Israel; and
all the worshipers of Baal came, so that there
was not a man left who did not come. So they
came into the temple[a] of Baal, and the temple
of Baal was full from one end to the other.
22 And he said to the one in charge of the
wardrobe, "Bring out vestments for all the wor-
shipers of Baal." So he brought out vestments
for them.
23 Then Jehu and Jehonadab the son of Re-
chab went into the temple of Baal, and said to
the worshipers of Baal, "Search and see that
no servants of the LORD are here with you, but
only the worshipers of Baal."
24 So they went in to offer sacrifices and burnt
offerings. Now Jehu had appointed for himself
eighty men on the outside, and had said, "*If* any
of the men whom I have brought into your
hands escapes, *whoever lets him escape, it shall
be* his life for the life of the other."
25 Now it happened, as soon as he had made
an end of offering the burnt offering, that Jehu
said to the guard and to the captains, "Go in
and kill them; let no one come out!" And they
killed them with the edge of the sword; then the
guards and the officers threw *them* out, and
went into the inner room of the temple of Baal.
26 And they brought the *sacred* pillars out of
the temple of Baal and burned them.
27 Then they broke down the *sacred* pillar of
Baal, and tore down the temple of Baal and
made it a refuse dump to this day.
28 Thus Jehu destroyed Baal from Israel.
29 However Jehu did not turn away from the
sins of Jeroboam the son of Nebat, who had
made Israel sin, *that is,* from the golden calves
that *were* at Bethel and Dan.
30 And the LORD said to Jehu, "Because you
have done well in doing *what is* right in My
sight, *and* have done to the house of Ahab all
that *was* in My heart, your sons shall sit on the
throne of Israel to the fourth *generation.*"
31 But Jehu took no heed to walk in the law
of the LORD God of Israel with all his heart;
for he did not depart from the sins of Jero-
boam, who had made Israel sin.

Death of Jehu

32 In those days the LORD began to cut off
parts of Israel; and Hazael conquered them in
all the territory of Israel
33 from the Jordan eastward: all the land of
Gilead—Gad, Reuben, and Manasseh—from
Aroer, which *is* by the River Arnon, including
Gilead and Bashan.
34 Now the rest of the acts of Jehu, all that he
did, and all his might, *are* they not written in
the book of the chronicles of the kings of Is-
rael?
35 So Jehu rested with his fathers, and they
buried him in Samaria. Then Jehoahaz his son
reigned in his place.
36 And the period that Jehu reigned over Is-
rael in Samaria *was* twenty-eight years.

Athaliah Reigns in Judah

11 When Athaliah the mother of Ahaziah
saw that her son was dead, she arose and
destroyed all the royal heirs.
2 But Jehosheba, the daughter of King Jo-
ram, sister of Ahaziah, took Joash the son of
Ahaziah, and stole him away from among the
king's sons *who were* being murdered; and
they hid him and his nurse in the bedroom,
from Athaliah, so that he was not killed.
3 So he was hidden with her in the house of
the LORD for six years, while Athaliah reigned
over the land.

Joash Crowned King of Judah

4 In the seventh year Jehoiada sent and
brought the captains of hundreds—of the body-
guards and the escorts—and brought them into
the house of the LORD to him. And he made a
covenant with them and took an oath from them
in the house of the LORD, and showed them the
king's son.
5 Then he commanded them, saying, "This
is what you shall do: One-third of you who come
on duty on the Sabbath shall be keeping watch
over the king's house,
6 "one-third *shall be* at the gate of Sur, and
one-third at the gate behind the escorts. You shall
keep the watch of the house, lest it be broken
down.
7 "The two contingents of you who go off duty

10:12 [a]Or *The Shearing House* 10:21 [a]Literally *house*, and so elsewhere in this chapter

on the Sabbath shall keep the watch of the house of the LORD for the king.

8 "But you shall surround the king on all sides, every man with his weapons in his hand; and whoever comes within range, let him be put to death. You are to be with the king as he goes out and as he comes in."

9 So the captains of the hundreds did according to all that Jehoiada the priest commanded. Each of them took his men who were to be on duty on the Sabbath, with those who were going off duty on the Sabbath, and came to Jehoiada the priest.

10 And the priest gave the captains of hundreds the spears and shields which *had belonged* to King David, that were in the temple of the LORD.

11 Then the escorts stood, every man with his weapons in his hand, all around the king, from the right side of the temple to the left side of the temple, by the altar and the house.

12 And he brought out the king's son, put the crown on him, and *gave him* the Testimony;[a] they made him king and anointed him, and they clapped their hands and said, "Long live the king!"

Death of Athaliah

13 Now when Athaliah heard the noise of the escorts *and* the people, she came to the people *in* the temple of the LORD.

14 When she looked, there was the king standing by a pillar according to custom; and the leaders and the trumpeters were by the king. All the people of the land were rejoicing and blowing trumpets. So Athaliah tore her clothes and cried out, "Treason! Treason!"

15 And Jehoiada the priest commanded the captains of the hundreds, the officers of the army, and said to them, "Take her outside under guard, and slay with the sword whoever follows her." For the priest had said, "Do not let her be killed in the house of the LORD."

16 So they seized her; and she went by way of the horses' entrance *into* the king's house, and there she was killed.

17 Then Jehoiada made a covenant between the LORD, the king, and the people, that they should be the LORD's people, and *also* between the king and the people.

18 And all the people of the land went to the temple of Baal, and tore it down. They thoroughly broke in pieces its altars and images, and killed Mattan the priest of Baal before the altars. And the priest appointed officers over the house of the LORD.

19 Then he took the captains of hundreds, the bodyguards, the escorts, and all the people of the land; and they brought the king down from the house of the LORD, and went by way of the gate of the escorts to the king's house. Then he sat on the throne of the kings.

20 So all the people of the land rejoiced; and the city was quiet, for they had slain Athaliah with the sword *in* the king's house.

21 Jehoash *was* seven years old when he became king.

Jehoash Repairs the Temple

12 In the seventh year of Jehu, Jehoash[a] became king, and he reigned forty years in Jerusalem. His mother's name *was* Zibiah of Beersheba.

2 Jehoash did *what was* right in the sight of the LORD all the days in which Jehoiada the priest instructed him.

3 But the high places were not taken away; the people still sacrificed and burned incense on the high places.

4 And Jehoash said to the priests, "All the money of the dedicated gifts that are brought into the house of the LORD—each man's census money, each man's assessment money[a]—*and* all the money that a man purposes in his heart to bring into the house of the LORD,

5 "let the priests take *it* themselves, each from his constituency; and let them repair the damages of the temple, wherever any dilapidation is found."

6 Now it was so, by the twenty-third year of king Jehoash, *that* the priests had not repaired the damages of the temple.

7 So King Jehoash called Jehoiada the priest and the *other* priests, and said to them, "Why have you not repaired the damages of the temple? Now therefore, do not take *more* money from your constituency, but deliver it for repairing the damages of the temple."

8 And the priests agreed that they would neither receive *more* money from the people, nor repair the damages of the temple.

9 Then Jehoiada the priest took a chest, bored a hole in its lid, and set it beside the altar, on the right side as one comes into the house of the LORD; and the priests who kept the door put there all the money brought into the house of the LORD.

10 So it was, whenever they saw that *there was* much money in the chest, that the king's scribe and the high priest came up and put it in bags, and counted the money that was found in the house of the LORD.

11 Then they gave the money, which had been apportioned, into the hands of those who did the work, who had the oversight of the house of the LORD; and they paid it out to the carpenters and builders who worked on the house of the LORD,

12 and to masons and stonecutters, and for buying timber and hewn stone, to repair the damage of the house of the LORD, and for all that was paid out to repair the temple.

13 However there were not made for the house of the LORD basins of silver, trimmers, sprinkling-bowls, trumpets, any articles of gold or articles of silver, from the money brought into the house of the LORD.

14 But they gave that to the workmen, and they repaired the house of the LORD with it.

15 Moreover they did not require an account from the men into whose hand they delivered the money to be paid to workmen, for they dealt faithfully.

16 The money from the trespass offerings and the money from the sin offerings was not brought into the house of the LORD. It belonged to the priests.

11:12 [a]That is, the Law (compare Exodus 25:16, 21 and Deuteronomy 31:9) **12:1** [a]Spelled *Joash* in 11:2ff
12:4 [a]Compare Leviticus 27:2ff

Hazael Threatens Jerusalem

17 Hazael king of Syria went up and fought
against Gath, and took it; then Hazael set his
face to go up to Jerusalem.
18 And Jehoash king of Judah took all the
sacred things that his fathers, Jehoshaphat
and Jehoram and Ahaziah, kings of Judah, had
dedicated, and his own sacred things, and all
the gold found in the treasuries of the house of
the LORD and in the king's house, and sent
them to Hazael king of Syria. Then he went away
from Jerusalem.

Death of Joash

19 Now the rest of the acts of Joash,[a] and all
that he did, *are* they not written in the book of
the chronicles of the kings of Judah?
20 And his servants arose and formed a con-
spiracy, and killed Joash in the house of the
Millo,[a] which goes down to Silla.
21 For Jozachar[a] the son of Shimeath and Je-
hozabad the son of Shomer,[b] his servants, struck
him. So he died, and they buried him with his
fathers in the City of David. Then Amaziah his
son reigned in his place.

Jehoahaz Reigns in Israel

13 In the twenty-third year of Joash[a] the
son of Ahaziah, king of Judah, Jehoahaz
the son of Jehu became king over Israel in Sa-
maria, *and reigned* seventeen years.
2 And he did evil in the sight of the LORD,
and followed the sins of Jeroboam the son of
Nebat, who had made Israel sin. He did not de-
part from them.
3 Then the anger of the LORD was aroused
against Israel, and He delivered them into the
hand of Hazael king of Syria, and into the hand
of Ben-Hadad the son of Hazael, all *their* days.
4 So Jehoahaz pleaded with the LORD, and
the LORD listened to him; for He saw the op-
pression of Israel, because the king of Syria
oppressed them.
5 Then the LORD gave Israel a deliverer, so
that they escaped from under the hand of the
Syrians; and the children of Israel dwelt in
their tents as before.
6 Nevertheless they did not depart from the
sins of the house of Jeroboam, who had made
Israel sin, *but* walked in them; and the wooden
image[a] also remained in Samaria.
7 For He left of the army of Jehoahaz only
fifty horsemen, ten chariots, and ten thousand
foot soldiers; for the king of Syria had destroyed
them and made them like the dust at threshing.
8 Now the rest of the acts of Jehoahaz, all
that he did, and his might, *are* they not written
in the book of the chronicles of the kings of
Israel?
9 So Jehoahaz rested with his fathers, and
they buried him in Samaria. Then Joash his son
reigned in his place.

Jehoash Reigns in Israel

10 In the thirty-seventh year of Joash king of
Judah, Jehoash[a] the son of Jehoahaz became
king over Israel in Samaria, *and reigned* six-
teen years.
11 And he did evil in the sight of the LORD. He
did not depart from all the sins of Jeroboam the
son of Nebat, who made Israel sin, *but* walked
in them.
12 Now the rest of the acts of Joash, all that
he did, and his might with which he fought
against Amaziah king of Judah, *are* they not
written in the book of the chronicles of the
kings of Israel?
13 So Joash rested with his fathers. Then Jer-
oboam sat on his throne. And Joash was buried
in Samaria with the kings of Israel.

Death of Elisha

14 Elisha had become sick with the illness of
which he would die. Then Joash the king of
Israel came down to him, and wept over his face,
and said, "O my father, my father, the chariots
of Israel and their horsemen!"
15 And Elisha said to him, "Take a bow and
some arrows." So he took himself a bow and
some arrows.
16 Then he said to the king of Israel, "Put your
hand on the bow." So he put his hand *on it,*
and Elisha put his hands on the king's hands.
17 And he said, "Open the east window"; and
he opened *it.* Then Elisha said, "Shoot"; and he
shot. And he said, "The arrow of the LORD's
deliverance and the arrow of deliverance from
Syria; for you must strike the Syrians at Aphek
till you have destroyed *them.*"
18 Then he said, "Take the arrows"; so he
took *them.* And he said to the king of Israel,
"Strike the ground"; so he struck three times,
and stopped.
19 And the man of God was angry with him,
and said, "You should have struck five or six
times; then you would have struck Syria till you
had destroyed *it!* But now you will strike Syria
only three times."
20 Then Elisha died, and they buried him.
And the *raiding* bands from Moab invaded the
land in the spring of the year.
21 So it was, as they were burying a man, that
suddenly they spied a band *of raiders;* and they
put the man in the tomb of Elisha; and when
the man was let down and touched the bones
of Elisha, he revived and stood on his feet.

Israel Recaptures Cities from Syria

22 And Hazael king of Syria oppressed Israel
all the days of Jehoahaz.
23 But the LORD was gracious to them, had
compassion on them, and regarded them, be-
cause of His covenant with Abraham, Isaac,
and Jacob, and would not yet destroy them or
cast them from His presence.
24 Now Hazael king of Syria died. Then Ben-
Hadad his son reigned in his place.
25 And Jehoash[a] the son of Jehoahaz recap-
tured from the hand of Ben-Hadad, the son of
Hazael, the cities which he had taken out of
the hand of Jehoahaz his father by war. Three
times Joash defeated him and recaptured the
cities of Israel.

Amaziah Reigns in Judah

14 In the second year of Joash the son of
Jehoahaz, king of Israel, Amaziah the
son of Joash, king of Judah, became king.
2 He was twenty-five years old when he be-
came king, and he reigned twenty-nine years

12:19 [a]Spelled *Jehoash* in 12:1ff **12:20** [a]Literally *The Landfill* **12:21** [a]Called *Zabad* in 2 Chronicles 24:26 [b]Called *Shimrith* in 2 Chronicles 24:26 **13:1** [a]Spelled *Jehoash* in 12:1ff **13:6** [a]Hebrew *Asherah,* a Canaanite goddess **13:10** [a]Spelled *Joash* in verse 9 **13:25** [a]Spelled *Joash* in verses 12–14, 25

in Jerusalem. His mother's name was Jehoaddan of Jerusalem.

3 And he did *what was* right in the sight of the LORD, yet not like his father David; he did everything as his father Joash had done.

4 However the high places were not taken away, and the people still sacrificed and burned incense on the high places.

5 Now it happened, as soon as the kingdom was established in his hand, that he executed his servants who had murdered his father the king.

6 But the children of the murderers he did not execute, according to what is written in the Book of the Law of Moses, in which the LORD commanded, saying, "Fathers shall not be put to death for their children, nor shall children be put to death for their fathers; but a person shall be put to death for his own sin."[a]

7 He killed ten thousand Edomites in the Valley of Salt, and took Sela by war, and called its name Joktheel to this day.

8 Then Amaziah sent messengers to Jehoash[a] the son of Jehoahaz, the son of Jehu, king of Israel, saying, "Come, let us face one another *in battle*."

9 And Jehoash king of Israel sent to Amaziah king of Judah, saying, "The thistle that *was* in Lebanon sent to the cedar that *was* in Lebanon, saying, 'Give your daughter to my son as wife'; and a wild beast that *was* in Lebanon passed by and trampled the thistle.

10 "You have indeed defeated Edom, and your heart has lifted you up. Glory *in that*, and stay at home; for why should you meddle with trouble so that you fall—you and Judah with you?"

11 But Amaziah would not heed. Therefore Jehoash king of Israel went out; so he and Amaziah king of Judah faced one another at Beth Shemesh, which *belongs* to Judah.

12 And Judah was defeated by Israel, and every man fled to his tent.

13 Then Jehoash king of Israel captured Amaziah king of Judah, the son of Jehoash, the son of Ahaziah, at Beth Shemesh; and he went to Jerusalem, and broke down the wall of Jerusalem from the Gate of Ephraim to the Corner Gate—four hundred cubits.

14 And he took all the gold and silver, all the articles that were found in the house of the LORD and in the treasuries of the king's house, and hostages, and returned to Samaria.

15 Now the rest of the acts of Jehoash which he did—his might, and how he fought with Amaziah king of Judah—*are* they not written in the book of the chronicles of the kings of Israel?

16 So Jehoash rested with his fathers, and was buried in Samaria with the kings of Israel. Then Jeroboam his son reigned in his place.

17 Amaziah the son of Joash, king of Judah, lived fifteen years after the death of Jehoash the son of Jehoahaz, king of Israel.

18 Now the rest of the acts of Amaziah, *are* they not written in the book of the chronicles of the kings of Judah?

19 And they formed a conspiracy against him in Jerusalem, and he fled to Lachish; but they sent after him to Lachish and killed him there.

20 Then they brought him on horses, and he was buried at Jerusalem with his fathers in the City of David.

21 And all the people of Judah took Azariah,[a] who *was* sixteen years old, and made him king instead of his father Amaziah.

22 He built Elath and restored it to Judah, after the king rested with his fathers.

Jeroboam II Reigns in Israel

23 In the fifteenth year of Amaziah the son of Joash, king of Judah, Jeroboam the son of Joash, king of Israel, became king in Samaria, *and reigned* forty-one years.

24 And he did evil in the sight of the LORD; he did not depart from all the sins of Jeroboam the son of Nebat, who had made Israel sin.

25 He restored the territory of Israel from the entrance of Hamath to the Sea of the Arabah, according to the word of the LORD God of Israel, which He had spoken through His servant Jonah the son of Amittai, the prophet who *was* from Gath Hepher.

26 For the LORD saw *that* the affliction of Israel *was* very bitter; and whether bond or free, there was no helper for Israel.

27 And the LORD did not say that He would blot out the name of Israel from under heaven; but He saved them by the hand of Jeroboam the son of Joash.

28 Now the rest of the acts of Jeroboam, and all that he did—his might, how he made war, and how he recaptured for Israel, from Damascus and Hamath, *what had belonged* to Judah—*are* they not written in the book of the chronicles of the kings of Israel?

29 So Jeroboam rested with his fathers, the kings of Israel. Then Zechariah his son reigned in his place.

Azariah Reigns in Judah

15 In the twenty-seventh year of Jeroboam king of Israel, Azariah the son of Amaziah, king of Judah, became king.

2 He was sixteen years old when he became king, and he reigned fifty-two years in Jerusalem. His mother's name *was* Jecholiah of Jerusalem.

3 And he did *what was* right in the sight of the LORD, according to all that his father Amaziah had done,

4 except that the high places were not removed; the people still sacrificed and burned incense on the high places.

5 Then the LORD struck the king, so that he was a leper until the day of his death; so he dwelt in an isolated house. And Jotham the king's son *was* over the *royal* house, judging the people of the land.

6 Now the rest of the acts of Azariah, and all that he did, *are* they not written in the book of the chronicles of the kings of Judah?

7 So Azariah rested with his fathers, and they buried him with his fathers in the City of David. Then Jotham his son reigned in his place.

Zechariah Reigns in Israel

8 In the thirty-eighth year of Azariah king of Judah, Zechariah the son of Jeroboam reigned over Israel in Samaria six months.

9 And he did evil in the sight of the LORD, as his fathers had done; he did not depart from the sins of Jeroboam the son of Nebat, who had made Israel sin.

10 Then Shallum the son of Jabesh conspired

14:6 [a]Deuteronomy 24:16 **14:8** [a]Spelled *Joash* in 13:12ff and 2 Chronicles 25:17ff **14:21** [a]Called *Uzziah* in 2 Chronicles 26:1ff, Isaiah 6:1, and elsewhere

against him, and struck and killed him in front
of the people; and he reigned in his place.
11 Now the rest of the acts of Zechariah, in-
deed they *are* written in the book of the chroni-
cles of the kings of Israel.
12 This *was* the word of the LORD which He
spoke to Jehu, saying, "Your sons shall sit on
the throne of Israel to the fourth *generation*."[a]
And so it was.

Shallum Reigns in Israel

13 Shallum the son of Jabesh became king in
the thirty-ninth year of Uzziah[a] king of Judah;
and he reigned a full month in Samaria.
14 For Menahem the son of Gadi went up
from Tirzah, came to Samaria, and struck Shal-
lum the son of Jabesh in Samaria and killed
him; and he reigned in his place.
15 Now the rest of the acts of Shallum, and
the conspiracy which he led, indeed they *are*
written in the book of the chronicles of the
kings of Israel.
16 Then from Tirzah, Menahem attacked Tiph-
sah, all who *were* there, and its territory. Be-
cause they did not surrender, therefore he
attacked *it*. All the women there who were
with child he ripped open.

Menahem Reigns in Israel

17 In the thirty-ninth year of Azariah king of
Judah, Menahem the son of Gadi became king
over Israel, *and reigned* ten years in Samaria.
18 And he did evil in the sight of the LORD;
he did not depart all his days from the sins of
Jeroboam the son of Nebat, who had made
Israel sin.
19 Pul[a] king of Assyria came against the land;
and Menahem gave Pul a thousand talents of
silver, that his hand might be with him to
strengthen the kingdom under his control.
20 And Menahem exacted the money from
Israel, from all the very wealthy, from each man
fifty shekels of silver, to give to the king of
Assyria. So the king of Assyria turned back,
and did not stay there in the land.
21 Now the rest of the acts of Menahem, and
all that he did, *are* they not written in the book
of the chronicles of the kings of Israel?
22 So Menahem rested with his fathers. Then
Pekahiah his son reigned in his place.

Pekahiah Reigns in Israel

23 In the fiftieth year of Azariah king of Ju-
dah, Pekahiah the son of Menahem became
king over Israel in Samaria, *and reigned* two
years.
24 And he did evil in the sight of the LORD;
he did not depart from the sins of Jeroboam
the son of Nebat, who had made Israel sin.
25 Then Pekah the son of Remaliah, an officer
of his, conspired against him and killed him
in Samaria, in the citadel of the king's house,
along with Argob and Arieh; and with him
were fifty men of Gilead. He killed him and
reigned in his place.
26 Now the rest of the acts of Pekahiah, and
all that he did, indeed they *are* written in the
book of the chronicles of the kings of Israel.

Pekah Reigns in Israel

27 In the fifty-second year of Azariah king of
Judah, Pekah the son of Remaliah became king
over Israel in Samaria, *and reigned* twenty
years.
28 And he did evil in the sight of the LORD;
he did not depart from the sins of Jeroboam
the son of Nebat, who had made Israel sin.
29 In the days of Pekah king of Israel, Tiglath-
Pileser king of Assyria came and took Ijon,
Abel Beth Maachah, Janoah, Kedesh, Hazor,
Gilead, and Galilee, all the land of Naphtali;
and he carried them captive to Assyria.
30 Then Hoshea the son of Elah led a conspir-
acy against Pekah the son of Remaliah, and
struck and killed him; so he reigned in his place
in the twentieth year of Jotham the son of Uz-
ziah.
31 Now the rest of the acts of Pekah, and all
that he did, indeed they *are* written in the book
of the chronicles of the kings of Israel.

Jotham Reigns in Judah

32 In the second year of Pekah the son of Rem-
aliah, king of Israel, Jotham the son of Uzziah,
king of Judah, began to reign.
33 He was twenty-five years old when he be-
came king, and he reigned sixteen years in Je-
rusalem. His mother's name *was* Jerusha[a] the
daughter of Zadok.
34 And he did *what was* right in the sight of
the LORD; he did according to all that his father
Uzziah had done.
35 However the high places were not removed;
the people still sacrificed and burned incense
on the high places. He built the Upper Gate of
the house of the LORD.
36 Now the rest of the acts of Jotham, and all
that he did, *are* they not written in the book of
the chronicles of the kings of Judah?
37 In those days the LORD began to send Re-
zin king of Syria and Pekah the son of Rema-
liah against Judah.
38 So Jotham rested with his fathers, and was
buried with his fathers in the City of David his
father. Then Ahaz his son reigned in his place.

Ahaz Reigns in Judah

16 In the seventeenth year of Pekah the son
of Remaliah, Ahaz the son of Jotham,
king of Judah, began to reign.
2 Ahaz *was* twenty years old when he became
king, and he reigned sixteen years in Jerusa-
lem; and he did not do *what was* right in the
sight of the LORD his God, as his father David
had done.
3 But he walked in the way of the kings of
Israel; indeed he made his son pass through the
fire, according to the abominations of the na-
tions whom the LORD had cast out from before
the children of Israel.
4 And he sacrificed and burned incense on
the high places, on the hills, and under every
green tree.
5 Then Rezin king of Syria and Pekah the son
of Remaliah, king of Israel, came up to Jerusa-
lem to *make* war; and they besieged Ahaz but
could not overcome *him*.
6 At that time Rezin king of Syria captured
Elath for Syria, and drove the men of Judah
from Elath. Then the Edomites[a] went to Elath,
and dwell there to this day.
7 So Ahaz sent messengers to Tiglath-Pileser
king of Assyria, saying, "I *am* your servant
and your son. Come up and save me from the

15:12 [a]2 Kings 10:30 **15:13** [a]Called *Azariah* in 14:21ff and 15:1ff **15:19** [a]That is, Tiglath-Pileser III (compare verse 29) **15:33** [a]Spelled *Jerushah* in 2 Chronicles 27:1 **16:6** [a]Some ancient authorities read *Syrians*.

hand of the king of Syria and from the hand of
the king of Israel, who rise up against me."
8 And Ahaz took the silver and gold that
was found in the house of the LORD, and in the
treasuries of the king's house, and sent *it as* a
present to the king of Assyria.
9 So the king of Assyria heeded him; for the
king of Assyria went up against Damascus and
took it, carried *its people* captive to Kir, and
killed Rezin.
10 Now King Ahaz went to Damascus to meet
Tiglath-Pileser king of Assyria, and saw an al-
tar that *was* at Damascus; and King Ahaz sent
to Urijah the priest the design of the altar and
its pattern, according to all its workmanship.
11 Then Urijah the priest built an altar ac-
cording to all that King Ahaz had sent from
Damascus. So Urijah the priest made *it* before
King Ahaz came back from Damascus.
12 And when the king came back from Da-
mascus, the king saw the altar; and the king
approached the altar and made offerings on it.
13 So he burned his burnt offering and his
grain offering; and he poured his drink offer-
ing and sprinkled the blood of his peace offer-
ings on the altar.
14 He also brought the bronze altar which *was*
before the LORD, from the front of the temple—
from between the *new* altar and the house of
the LORD—and put it on the north side of the
new altar.
15 Then King Ahaz commanded Urijah the
priest, saying, "On the great *new* altar burn
the morning burnt offering, the evening grain
offering, the king's burnt sacrifice, and his
grain offering, with the burnt offering of all
the people of the land, their grain offering, and
their drink offerings; and sprinkle on it all the
blood of the burnt offering and all the blood of
the sacrifice. And the bronze altar shall be for
me to inquire *by*."
16 Thus did Urijah the priest, according to all
that King Ahaz commanded.
17 And King Ahaz cut off the panels of the
carts, and removed the lavers from them; and
he took down the Sea from the bronze oxen
that *were* under it, and put it on a pavement of
stones.
18 Also he removed the Sabbath pavilion which
they had built in the temple, and he removed
the king's outer entrance from the house of the
LORD, on account of the king of Assyria.
19 Now the rest of the acts of Ahaz which he
did, *are* they not written in the book of the
chronicles of the kings of Judah?
20 So Ahaz rested with his fathers, and was
buried with his fathers in the City of David.
Then Hezekiah his son reigned in his place.

Hoshea Reigns in Israel

17 In the twelfth year of Ahaz king of Ju-
dah, Hoshea the son of Elah became king
of Israel in Samaria, *and he reigned* nine years.
2 And he did evil in the sight of the LORD,
but not as the kings of Israel who were before
him.
3 Shalmaneser king of Assyria came up
against him; and Hoshea became his vassal,
and paid him tribute money.
4 And the king of Assyria uncovered a con-
spiracy by Hoshea; for he had sent messengers
to So, king of Egypt, and brought no tribute to
the king of Assyria, as *he had done* year by
year. Therefore the king of Assyria shut him
up, and bound him in prison.

Israel Carried Captive to Assyria

5 Now the king of Assyria went throughout
all the land, and went up to Samaria and be-
sieged it for three years.
6 In the ninth year of Hoshea, the king of
Assyria took Samaria and carried Israel away to
Assyria, and placed them in Halah and by the
Habor, the River of Gozan, and in the cities of
the Medes.
7 For so it was that the children of Israel had
sinned against the LORD their God, who had
brought them up out of the land of Egypt, from
under the hand of Pharaoh king of Egypt; and
they had feared other gods,
8 and had walked in the statutes of the na-
tions whom the LORD had cast out from before
the children of Israel, and of the kings of Israel,
which they had made.
9 Also the children of Israel secretly did
against the LORD their God things that *were*
not right, and they built for themselves high
places in all their cities, from watchtower to
fortified city.
10 They set up for themselves *sacred* pillars
and wooden images[a] on every high hill and
under every green tree.
11 There they burned incense on all the high
places, like the nations whom the LORD had
carried away before them; and they did wicked
things to provoke the LORD to anger,
12 for they served idols, of which the LORD
had said to them, "You shall not do this thing."
13 Yet the LORD testified against Israel and
against Judah, by all of His prophets, every
seer, saying, "Turn from your evil ways, and
keep My commandments *and* My statutes, ac-
cording to all the law which I commanded your
fathers, and which I sent to you by My servants
the prophets."
14 Nevertheless they would not hear, but stiff-
ened their necks, like the necks of their fathers,
who did not believe in the LORD their God.
15 And they rejected His statutes and His cov-
enant that He had made with their fathers, and
His testimonies which He had testified against
them; they followed idols, became idolaters, and
went after the nations who *were* all around
them, *concerning* whom the LORD had charged
them that they should not do like them.
16 So they left all the commandments of the
LORD their God, made for themselves a molded
image *and* two calves, made a wooden image
and worshiped all the host of heaven, and
served Baal.
17 And they caused their sons and daughters
to pass through the fire, practiced witchcraft
and soothsaying, and sold themselves to do
evil in the sight of the LORD, to provoke Him
to anger.
18 Therefore the LORD was very angry with
Israel, and removed them from His sight; there
was none left but the tribe of Judah alone.
19 Also Judah did not keep the command-
ments of the LORD their God, but walked in
the statutes of Israel which they made.
20 And the LORD rejected all the descendants
of Israel, afflicted them, and delivered them

17:10 [a]Hebrew *Asherim*, Canaanite deities

into the hand of plunderers, until He had cast
them from His sight.
21 For He tore Israel from the house of David,
and they made Jeroboam the son of Nebat
king. Then Jeroboam drove Israel from follow-
ing the LORD, and made them commit a great
sin.
22 For the children of Israel walked in all the
sins of Jeroboam which he did; they did not
depart from them,
23 until the LORD removed Israel out of His
sight, as He had said by all His servants the
prophets. So Israel was carried away from their
own land to Assyria, *as it is* to this day.

Assyria Resettles Samaria

24 Then the king of Assyria brought *people*
from Babylon, Cuthah, Ava, Hamath, and from
Sepharvaim, and placed *them* in the cities of
Samaria instead of the children of Israel; and
they took possession of Samaria and dwelt in
its cities.
25 And it was so, at the beginning of their dwell-
ing there, *that* they did not fear the LORD; there-
fore the LORD sent lions among them, which
killed *some* of them.
26 So they spoke to the king of Assyria, say-
ing, "The nations whom you have removed and
placed in the cities of Samaria do not know the
rituals of the God of the land; therefore He has
sent lions among them, and indeed, they are
killing them because they do not know the ritu-
als of the God of the land."
27 Then the king of Assyria commanded, say-
ing, "Send there one of the priests whom you
brought from there; let him go and dwell there,
and let him teach them the rituals of the God
of the land."
28 Then one of the priests whom they had car-
ried away from Samaria came and dwelt in
Bethel, and taught them how they should fear
the LORD.
29 However every nation continued to make
gods of its own, and put *them* in the shrines
on the high places which the Samaritans had
made, *every* nation in the cities where they dwelt.
30 The men of Babylon made Succoth Be-
noth, the men of Cuth made Nergal, the men
of Hamath made Ashima,
31 and the Avites made Nibhaz and Tartak;
and the Sepharvites burned their children in
fire to Adrammelech and Anammelech, the
gods of Sepharvaim.
32 So they feared the LORD, and from every
class they appointed for themselves priests of
the high places, who sacrificed for them in the
shrines of the high places.
33 They feared the LORD, yet served their own
gods—according to the rituals of the nations
from among whom they were carried away.
34 To this day they continue practicing the for-
mer rituals; they do not fear the LORD, nor do
they follow their statutes or their ordinances,
or the law and commandment which the LORD
had commanded the children of Jacob, whom
He named Israel,
35 with whom the LORD had made a covenant
and charged them, saying: "You shall not fear
other gods, nor bow down to them nor serve
them nor sacrifice to them;
36 "but the LORD, who brought you up from
the land of Egypt with great power and an
outstretched arm, Him you shall fear, Him you
shall worship, and to Him you shall offer sacri-
fice.
37 "And the statutes, the ordinances, the law,
and the commandment which He wrote for
you, you shall be careful to observe forever;
you shall not fear other gods.
38 "And the covenant that I have made with
you, you shall not forget, nor shall you fear
other gods.
39 "But the LORD your God you shall fear;
and He will deliver you from the hand of all
your enemies."
40 However they did not obey, but they fol-
lowed their former rituals.
41 So these nations feared the LORD, yet
served their carved images; also their children
and their children's children have continued
doing as their fathers did, even to this day.

Hezekiah Reigns in Judah

18 Now it came to pass in the third year of
Hoshea the son of Elah, king of Israel,
that Hezekiah the son of Ahaz, king of Judah,
began to reign.
2 He was twenty-five years old when he be-
came king, and he reigned twenty-nine years
in Jerusalem. His mother's name *was* Abi[a] the
daughter of Zechariah.
3 And he did *what was* right in the sight of
the LORD, according to all that his father David
had done.
4 He removed the high places and broke the
sacred pillars, cut down the wooden image[a]
and broke in pieces the bronze serpent that
Moses had made; for until those days the chil-
dren of Israel burned incense to it, and called
it Nehushtan.[b]
5 He trusted in the LORD God of Israel, so
that after him was none like him among all the
kings of Judah, nor who were before him.
6 For he held fast to the LORD; he did not
depart from following Him, but kept His com-
mandments, which the LORD had commanded
Moses.
7 The LORD was with him; he prospered
wherever he went. And he rebelled against the
king of Assyria and did not serve him.
8 He subdued the Philistines, as far as Gaza
and its territory, from watchtower to fortified
city.
9 Now it came to pass in the fourth year of
King Hezekiah, which *was* the seventh year of
Hoshea the son of Elah, king of Israel, *that*
Shalmaneser king of Assyria came up against
Samaria and besieged it.
10 And at the end of three years they took it.
In the sixth year of Hezekiah, that *is*, the ninth
year of Hoshea king of Israel, Samaria was
taken.
11 Then the king of Assyria carried Israel
away captive to Assyria, and put them in Halah
and by the Habor, the River of Gozan, and in
the cities of the Medes,
12 because they did not obey the voice of the
LORD their God, but transgressed His cov-
enant *and* all that Moses the servant of the
LORD had commanded; and they would nei-
ther hear nor do *them*.
13 And in the fourteenth year of King Heze-
kiah, Sennacherib king of Assyria came up
against all the fortified cities of Judah and took
them.
14 Then Hezekiah king of Judah sent to the

18:2 [a]Called *Abijah* in 2 Chronicles 29:1ff **18:4** [a]Hebrew *Asherah*, a Canaanite goddess [b]Literally *Bronze Thing*

king of Assyria at Lachish, saying, "I have
done wrong; turn away from me; whatever you
impose on me I will pay." And the king of As-
syria assessed Hezekiah king of Judah three
hundred talents of silver and thirty talents of
gold.
15 So Hezekiah gave *him* all the silver that
was found in the house of the LORD and in the
treasuries of the king's house.
16 At that time Hezekiah stripped *the gold*
from the doors of the temple of the LORD, and
from the pillars which Hezekiah king of Judah
had overlaid, and gave it to the king of Assyria.

Sennacherib Boasts Against the LORD

17 Then the king of Assyria sent *the* Tartan,[a]
the Rabsaris,[b] *and the* Rabshakeh[c] from La-
chish, with a great army against Jerusalem, to
King Hezekiah. And they went up and came to
Jerusalem. When they had come up, they went
and stood by the aqueduct from the upper pool,
which *was* on the highway to the Fuller's Field.
18 And when they had called to the king, Elia-
kim the son of Hilkiah, who *was* over the
household, Shebna the scribe, and Joah the
son of Asaph, the recorder, came out to them.
19 Then *the* Rabshakeh said to them, "Say
now to Hezekiah, 'Thus says the great king,
the king of Assyria: "What confidence *is* this
in which you trust?
20 "You speak of *having* plans and power for
war; but *they are* mere words. And in whom
do you trust, that you rebel against me?
21 "Now look! You are trusting in the staff of
this broken reed, Egypt, on which if a man
leans, it will go into his hand and pierce it. So
is Pharaoh king of Egypt to all who trust in
him.
22 "But if you say to me, 'We trust in the LORD
our God,' *is* it not He whose high places and
whose altars Hezekiah has taken away, and
said to Judah and Jerusalem, 'You shall wor-
ship before this altar in Jerusalem'?"'
23 "Now therefore, I urge you, give a pledge
to my master the king of Assyria, and I will
give you two thousand horses—if you are able
on your part to put riders on them!
24 "How then will you repel one captain of
the least of my master's servants, and put your
trust in Egypt for chariots and horsemen?
25 "Have I now come up without the LORD
against this place to destroy it? The LORD said
to me, 'Go up against this land, and destroy
it.'"
26 Then Eliakim the son of Hilkiah, Shebna,
and Joah said to *the* Rabshakeh, "Please speak
to your servants in Aramaic, for we understand
it; and do not speak to us in Hebrew[a] in the
hearing of the people who *are* on the wall."
27 But *the* Rabshakeh said to them, "Has my
master sent me to your master and to you to
speak these words, and not to the men who sit
on the wall, who will eat and drink their own
waste with you?"
28 Then *the* Rabshakeh stood and called out
with a loud voice in Hebrew, and spoke, say-
ing, "Hear the word of the great king, the king
of Assyria!
29 "Thus says the king: 'Do not let Hezekiah
deceive you, for he shall not be able to deliver
you from his hand;
30 'nor let Hezekiah make you trust in the
LORD, saying, "The LORD will surely deliver
us; this city shall not be given into the hand of
the king of Assyria."'
31 "Do not listen to Hezekiah; for thus says
the king of Assyria: 'Make *peace* with me by a
present and come out to me; and every one of
you eat from his own vine and every one from
his own fig tree, and every one of you drink
the waters of his own cistern;
32 'until I come and take you away to a land
like your own land, a land of grain and new
wine, a land of bread and vineyards, a land of
olive groves and honey, that you may live and
not die. But do not listen to Hezekiah, lest he
persuade you, saying, "The LORD will deliver
us."
33 'Has any of the gods of the nations at all
delivered its land from the hand of the king of
Assyria?
34 'Where *are* the gods of Hamath and Ar-
pad? Where *are* the gods of Sepharvaim and
Hena and Ivah? Indeed, have they delivered
Samaria from my hand?
35 'Who among all the gods of the lands have
delivered their countries from my hand, that
the LORD should deliver Jerusalem from my
hand?'"
36 But the people held their peace and an-
swered him not a word; for the king's com-
mandment was, "Do not answer him."
37 Then Eliakim the son of Hilkiah, who *was*
over the household, Shebna the scribe, and
Joah the son of Asaph, the recorder, came to
Hezekiah with *their* clothes torn, and told him
the words of *the* Rabshakeh.

Isaiah Assures Deliverance

19 And so it was, when King Hezekiah
heard *it,* that he tore his clothes, covered
himself with sackcloth, and went into the
house of the LORD.
2 Then he sent Eliakim, who *was* over the
household, Shebna the scribe, and the elders
of the priests, covered with sackcloth, to Isaiah
the prophet, the son of Amoz.
3 And they said to him, "Thus says Heze-
kiah: 'This day *is* a day of trouble, and rebuke,
and blasphemy; for the children have come to
birth, but *there is* no strength to bring them
forth.
4 'It may be that the LORD your God will
hear all the words of *the* Rabshakeh, whom his
master the king of Assyria has sent to reproach
the living God, and will rebuke the words
which the LORD your God has heard. There-
fore lift up *your* prayer for the remnant that is
left.'"
5 So the servants of King Hezekiah came to
Isaiah.
6 And Isaiah said to them, "Thus you shall
say to your master, 'Thus says the LORD: "Do
not be afraid of the words which you have
heard, with which the servants of the king of
Assyria have blasphemed Me.
7 "Surely I will send a spirit upon him, and
he shall hear a rumor and return to his own
land; and I will cause him to fall by the sword
in his own land."'"

18:17 [a]A title, probably *Commander in Chief* [b]A title, probably *Chief Officer* [c]A title, probably *Chief of Staff* or *Governor* **18:26** [a]Literally *Judean*

Sennacherib's Threat and Hezekiah's Prayer

8 Then *the* Rabshakeh returned and found
the king of Assyria warring against Libnah, for
he heard that he had departed from Lachish.
9 And the king heard concerning Tirhakah
king of Ethiopia, "Look, he has come out to
make war with you." So he again sent messen-
gers to Hezekiah, saying,
10 "Thus you shall speak to Hezekiah king of
Judah, saying: 'Do not let your God in whom
you trust deceive you, saying, "Jerusalem shall
not be given into the hand of the king of Assyria."
11 'Look! You have heard what the kings of
Assyria have done to all lands by utterly de-
stroying them; and shall you be delivered?
12 'Have the gods of the nations delivered
those whom my fathers have destroyed, Gozan
and Haran and Rezeph, and the people of Eden
who *were* in Telassar?
13 'Where *is* the king of Hamath, the king of
Arpad, and the king of the city of Sepharvaim,
Hena, and Ivah?'"
14 And Hezekiah received the letter from the
hand of the messengers, and read it; and Hez-
ekiah went up to the house of the LORD, and
spread it before the LORD.
15 Then Hezekiah prayed before the LORD,
and said: "O LORD God of Israel, *the One* who
dwells *between* the cherubim, You are God, You
alone, of all the kingdoms of the earth. You have
made heaven and earth.
16 "Incline Your ear, O LORD, and hear; open
Your eyes, O LORD, and see; and hear the words
of Sennacherib, which he has sent to reproach
the living God.
17 "Truly, LORD, the kings of Assyria have laid
waste the nations and their lands,
18 "and have cast their gods into the fire; for
they *were* not gods, but the work of men's
hands—wood and stone. Therefore they de-
stroyed them.
19 "Now therefore, O LORD our God, I pray,
save us from his hand, that all the kingdoms
of the earth may know that You *are* the LORD
God, You alone."

The Word of the LORD Concerning Sennacherib

20 Then Isaiah the son of Amoz sent to Heze-
kiah, saying, "Thus says the LORD God of Is-
rael: 'Because you have prayed to Me against
Sennacherib king of Assyria, I have heard.'
21 "This *is* the word which the LORD has spo-
ken concerning him:

'The virgin, the daughter of Zion,
Has despised you, laughed you to scorn;
The daughter of Jerusalem
Has shaken *her* head behind your back!

22 'Whom have you reproached and blasphemed?
Against whom have you raised *your* voice,
And lifted up your eyes on high?
Against the Holy *One* of Israel.
23 By your messengers you have reproached the Lord,
And said: "By the multitude of my chariots
I have come up to the height of the mountains,
To the limits of Lebanon;
I will cut down its tall cedars
And its choice cypress trees;
I will enter the extremity of its borders,
To its fruitful forest.
24 I have dug and drunk strange water,
And with the soles of my feet I have dried up
All the brooks of defense."

25 'Did you not hear long ago
How I made it,
From ancient times that I formed it?
Now I have brought it to pass,
That you should be
For crushing fortified cities *into* heaps of ruins.
26 Therefore their inhabitants had little power;
They were dismayed and confounded;
They were *as* the grass of the field
And the green herb,
As the grass on the housetops
And *grain* blighted before it is grown.

27 'But I know your dwelling place,
Your going out and your coming in,
And your rage against Me.
28 Because your rage against Me and your tumult
Have come up to My ears,
Therefore I will put My hook in your nose
And My bridle in your lips,
And I will turn you back
By the way which you came.

29 'This *shall be* a sign to you:

You shall eat this year such as grows of itself,
And in the second year what springs from the same;
Also in the third year sow and reap,
Plant vineyards and eat the fruit of them.
30 And the remnant who have escaped of the house of Judah
Shall again take root downward,
And bear fruit upward.
31 For out of Jerusalem shall go a remnant,
And those who escape from Mount Zion.
The zeal of the LORD of hosts[a] will do this.'

32 "Therefore thus says the LORD concerning
the king of Assyria:

'He shall not come into this city,
Nor shoot an arrow there,
Nor come before it with shield,
Nor build a siege mound against it.
33 By the way that he came,
By the same shall he return;
And he shall not come into this city,'
Says the LORD.
34 'For I will defend this city, to save it
For My own sake and for My servant David's sake.'"

Sennacherib's Defeat and Death

35 And it came to pass on a certain night that
the angel[a] of the LORD went out, and killed in the
camp of the Assyrians one hundred and eighty-
five thousand; and when *people* arose early in
the morning, there were the corpses—all dead.
36 So Sennacherib king of Assyria departed

19:31 [a]Following many Hebrew manuscripts and ancient versions (compare Isaiah 37:32); Masoretic Text omits *of hosts.* **19:35** [a]Or *Angel*

and went away, returned *home*, and remained
at Nineveh.
37 Now it came to pass, as he was worshiping
in the temple of Nisroch his god, that his sons
Adrammelech and Sharezer struck him down
with the sword; and they escaped into the land
of Ararat. Then Esarhaddon his son reigned in
his place.

Hezekiah's Life Extended

20 In those days Hezekiah was sick and
near death. And Isaiah the prophet, the
son of Amoz, went to him and said to him, "Thus
says the LORD: 'Set your house in order, for
you shall die, and not live.' "
2 Then he turned his face toward the wall,
and prayed to the LORD, saying,
3 "Remember now, O LORD, I pray, how I
have walked before You in truth and with a
loyal heart, and have done *what was* good in
Your sight." And Hezekiah wept bitterly.
4 And it happened, before Isaiah had gone
out into the middle court, that the word of the
LORD came to him, saying,
5 "Return and tell Hezekiah the leader of
My people, 'Thus says the LORD, the God of
David your father: "I have heard your prayer,
I have seen your tears; surely I will heal you.
On the third day you shall go up to the house
of the LORD.
6 "And I will add to your days fifteen years.
I will deliver you and this city from the hand
of the king of Assyria; and I will defend this
city for My own sake, and for the sake of My
servant David." ' "
7 Then Isaiah said, "Take a lump of figs."
So they took and laid *it* on the boil, and he
recovered.
8 And Hezekiah said to Isaiah, "What *is* the
sign that the LORD will heal me, and that I
shall go up to the house of the LORD the third
day?"
9 Then Isaiah said, "This is the sign to you
from the LORD, that the LORD will do the thing
which He has spoken: *shall* the shadow go for-
ward ten degrees or go backward ten de-
grees?"
10 And Hezekiah answered, "It is an easy
thing for the shadow to go down ten degrees;
no, but let the shadow go backward ten de-
grees."
11 So Isaiah the prophet cried out to the LORD,
and He brought the shadow ten degrees back-
ward, by which it had gone down on the sun-
dial of Ahaz.

The Babylonian Envoys

12 At that time Berodach-Baladan[a] the son of
Baladan, king of Babylon, sent letters and a
present to Hezekiah, for he heard that Heze-
kiah had been sick.
13 And Hezekiah was attentive to them, and
showed them all the house of his treasures—
the silver and gold, the spices and precious
ointment, and all[a] his armory—all that was
found among his treasures. There was nothing
in his house or in all his dominion that Heze-
kiah did not show them.
14 Then Isaiah the prophet went to King Hez-
ekiah, and said to him, "What did these men
say, and from where did they come to you?" So
Hezekiah said, "They came from a far country,
from Babylon."
15 And he said, "What have they seen in your
house?" So Hezekiah answered, "They have
seen all that *is* in my house; there is nothing
among my treasures that I have not shown
them."
16 Then Isaiah said to Hezekiah, "Hear the
word of the LORD:
17 'Behold, the days are coming when all that
is in your house, and what your fathers have
accumulated until this day, shall be carried to
Babylon; nothing shall be left,' says the LORD.
18 'And they shall take away some of your
sons who will descend from you, whom you
will beget; and they shall be eunuchs in the
palace of the king of Babylon.' "
19 So Hezekiah said to Isaiah, "The word of
the LORD which you have spoken *is* good!" For
he said, "Will there not be peace and truth at
least in my days?"

Death of Hezekiah

20 Now the rest of the acts of Hezekiah—all
his might, and how he made a pool and a tun-
nel and brought water into the city—*are* they
not written in the book of the chronicles of the
kings of Judah?
21 So Hezekiah rested with his fathers. Then
Manasseh his son reigned in his place.

Manasseh Reigns in Judah

21 Manasseh *was* twelve years old when he
became king, and he reigned fifty-five
years in Jerusalem. His mother's name *was*
Hephzibah.
2 And he did evil in the sight of the LORD,
according to the abominations of the nations
whom the LORD had cast out before the chil-
dren of Israel.
3 For he rebuilt the high places which Heze-
kiah his father had destroyed; he raised up
altars for Baal, and made a wooden image,[a] as
Ahab king of Israel had done; and he wor-
shiped all the host of heaven[b] and served them.
4 He also built altars in the house of the
LORD, of which the LORD had said, "In Jerusa-
lem I will put My name."
5 And he built altars for all the host of
heaven in the two courts of the house of the
LORD.
6 Also he made his son pass through the fire,
practiced soothsaying, used witchcraft, and
consulted spiritists and mediums. He did much
evil in the sight of the LORD, to provoke *Him*
to anger.
7 He even set a carved image of Asherah[a] that
he had made, in the house of which the LORD
had said to David and to Solomon his son, "In
this house and in Jerusalem, which I have cho-
sen out of all the tribes of Israel, I will put My
name forever;
8 "and I will not make the feet of Israel wan-
der anymore from the land which I gave their
fathers—only if they are careful to do accord-
ing to all that I have commanded them, and
according to all the law that My servant Moses
commanded them."
9 But they paid no attention, and Manasseh
seduced them to do more evil than the nations

20:12 [a]Spelled *Merodach-Baladan* in Isaiah 39:1 **20:13** [a]Following many Hebrew manuscripts, Syriac, and Targum; Masoretic Text omits *all*. **21:3** [a]Hebrew *Asherah*, a Canaanite goddess [b]The gods of the Assyrians
21:7 [a]A Canaanite goddess

whom the LORD had destroyed before the chil-
dren of Israel.
10 And the LORD spoke by His servants the
prophets, saying,
11 "Because Manasseh king of Judah has
done these abominations (he has acted more
wickedly than all the Amorites who *were* be-
fore him, and has also made Judah sin with his
idols),
12 "therefore thus says the LORD God of Is-
rael: 'Behold, *I* am bringing *such* calamity upon
Jerusalem and Judah, that whoever hears of it,
both his ears will tingle.
13 'And I will stretch over Jerusalem the mea-
suring line of Samaria and the plummet of the
house of Ahab; I will wipe Jerusalem as *one*
wipes a dish, wiping *it* and turning *it* upside
down.
14 'So I will forsake the remnant of My inheri-
tance and deliver them into the hand of their
enemies; and they shall become victims of plun-
der to all their enemies,
15 'because they have done evil in My sight,
and have provoked Me to anger since the day
their fathers came out of Egypt, even to this
day.' "
16 Moreover Manasseh shed very much inno-
cent blood, till he had filled Jerusalem from
one end to another, besides his sin by which
he made Judah sin, in doing evil in the sight of
the LORD.
17 Now the rest of the acts of Manasseh—all
that he did, and the sin that he committed—*are*
they not written in the book of the chronicles
of the kings of Judah?
18 So Manasseh rested with his fathers, and
was buried in the garden of his own house, in
the garden of Uzza. Then his son Amon
reigned in his place.

Amon's Reign and Death

19 Amon *was* twenty-two years old when he
became king, and he reigned two years in Jeru-
salem. His mother's name *was* Meshullemeth
the daughter of Haruz of Jotbah.
20 And he did evil in the sight of the LORD,
as his father Manasseh had done.
21 So he walked in all the ways that his father
had walked; and he served the idols that his
father had served, and worshiped them.
22 He forsook the LORD God of his fathers,
and did not walk in the way of the LORD.
23 Then the servants of Amon conspired
against him, and killed the king in his own
house.
24 But the people of the land executed all
those who had conspired against King Amon.
Then the people of the land made his son Jo-
siah king in his place.
25 Now the rest of the acts of Amon which he
did, *are* they not written in the book of the
chronicles of the kings of Judah?
26 And he was buried in his tomb in the gar-
den of Uzza. Then Josiah his son reigned in
his place.

Josiah Reigns in Judah

22 Josiah *was* eight years old when he be-
came king, and he reigned thirty-one
years in Jerusalem. His mother's name *was*
Jedidah the daughter of Adaiah of Bozkath.
2 And he did *what was* right in the sight of
the LORD, and walked in all the ways of his
father David; he did not turn aside to the right
hand or to the left.

Hilkiah Finds the Book of the Law

3 Now it came to pass, in the eighteenth year
of King Josiah, *that* the king sent Shaphan the
scribe, the son of Azaliah, the son of Meshul-
lam, to the house of the LORD, saying:
4 "Go up to Hilkiah the high priest, that he
may count the money which has been brought
into the house of the LORD, which the door-
keepers have gathered from the people.
5 "And let them deliver it into the hand of
those doing the work, who are the overseers in
the house of the LORD; let them give it to those
who *are* in the house of the LORD doing the
work, to repair the damages of the house—
6 "to carpenters and builders and masons—
and to buy timber and hewn stone to repair the
house.
7 "However there need be no accounting
made with them of the money delivered into
their hand, because they deal faithfully."
8 Then Hilkiah the high priest said to Sha-
phan the scribe, "I have found the Book of the
Law in the house of the LORD." And Hilkiah
gave the book to Shaphan, and he read it.
9 So Shaphan the scribe went to the king,
bringing the king word, saying, "Your servants
have gathered the money that was found in the
house, and have delivered it into the hand of
those who do the work, who oversee the house
of the LORD."
10 Then Shaphan the scribe showed the king,
saying, "Hilkiah the priest has given me a
book." And Shaphan read it before the king.
11 Now it happened, when the king heard the
words of the Book of the Law, that he tore his
clothes.
12 Then the king commanded Hilkiah the
priest, Ahikam the son of Shaphan, Achbor[a]
the son of Michaiah, Shaphan the scribe, and
Asaiah a servant of the king, saying,
13 "Go, inquire of the LORD for me, for the
people and for all Judah, concerning the words
of this book that has been found; for great *is*
the wrath of the LORD that is aroused against
us, because our fathers have not obeyed the
words of this book, to do according to all that
is written concerning us."
14 So Hilkiah the priest, Ahikam, Achbor,
Shaphan, and Asaiah went to Huldah the
prophetess, the wife of Shallum the son of Tik-
vah, the son of Harhas, keeper of the ward-
robe. (She dwelt in Jerusalem in the Second
Quarter.) And they spoke with her.
15 Then she said to them, "Thus says the LORD
God of Israel, 'Tell the man who sent you to
Me,
16 "Thus says the LORD: 'Behold, I will bring
calamity on this place and on its inhabitants—
all the words of the book which the king of
Judah has read—
17 'because they have forsaken Me and burned
incense to other gods, that they might provoke
Me to anger with all the works of their hands.
Therefore My wrath shall be aroused against
this place and shall not be quenched.' " '
18 "But as for the king of Judah, who sent you
to inquire of the LORD, in this manner you shall
speak to him, 'Thus says the LORD God of Is-

22:12 [a]*Abdon the son of Micah* in 2 Chronicles 34:20

rael: "*Concerning* the words which you have
heard—
19 "because your heart was tender, and you
humbled yourself before the LORD when you
heard what I spoke against this place and
against its inhabitants, that they would become a desolation and a curse, and you tore
your clothes and wept before Me, I also have
heard *you*," says the LORD.
20 "Surely, therefore, I will gather you to your
fathers, and you shall be gathered to your
grave in peace; and your eyes shall not see all
the calamity which I will bring on this place." ' "
So they brought back word to the king.

Josiah Restores True Worship

23 Now the king sent them to gather all the
elders of Judah and Jerusalem to him.
2 The king went up to the house of the LORD
with all the men of Judah, and with him all the
inhabitants of Jerusalem—the priests and the
prophets and all the people, both small and
great. And he read in their hearing all the
words of the Book of the Covenant which had
been found in the house of the LORD.
3 Then the king stood by a pillar and made
a covenant before the LORD, to follow the
LORD and to keep His commandments and His
testimonies and His statutes, with all *his* heart
and all *his* soul, to perform the words of this
covenant that were written in this book. And
all the people took a stand for the covenant.
4 And the king commanded Hilkiah the high
priest, the priests of the second order, and the
doorkeepers, to bring out of the temple of the
LORD all the articles that were made for Baal,
for Asherah,[a] and for all the host of heaven;[b]
and he burned them outside Jerusalem in the
fields of Kidron, and carried their ashes to
Bethel.
5 Then he removed the idolatrous priests
whom the kings of Judah had ordained to burn
incense on the high places in the cities of Judah
and in the places all around Jerusalem, and
those who burned incense to Baal, to the sun,
to the moon, to the constellations, and to all
the host of heaven.
6 And he brought out the wooden image[a]
from the house of the LORD, to the Brook Kidron outside Jerusalem, burned it at the Brook
Kidron and ground *it* to ashes, and threw its
ashes on the graves of the common people.
7 Then he tore down the *ritual* booths of the
perverted persons[a] that *were* in the house of
the LORD, where the women wove hangings
for the wooden image.
8 And he brought all the priests from the
cities of Judah, and defiled the high places
where the priests had burned incense, from
Geba to Beersheba; also he broke down the
high places at the gates which *were* at the entrance of the Gate of Joshua the governor of
the city, which *were* to the left of the city gate.
9 Nevertheless the priests of the high places
did not come up to the altar of the LORD in
Jerusalem, but they ate unleavened bread
among their brethren.
10 And he defiled Topheth, which *is* in the
Valley of the Son[a] of Hinnom, that no man
might make his son or his daughter pass
through the fire to Molech.
11 Then he removed the horses that the kings
of Judah had dedicated to the sun, at the entrance to the house of the LORD, by the chamber of Nathan-Melech, the officer who *was* in
the court; and he burned the chariots of the
sun with fire.
12 The altars that *were* on the roof, the upper
chamber of Ahaz, which the kings of Judah
had made, and the altars which Manasseh had
made in the two courts of the house of the
LORD, the king broke down and pulverized
there, and threw their dust into the Brook
Kidron.
13 Then the king defiled the high places that
were east of Jerusalem, which *were* on the
south of the Mount of Corruption, which Solomon king of Israel had built for Ashtoreth the
abomination of the Sidonians, for Chemosh
the abomination of the Moabites, and for Milcom the abomination of the people of Ammon.
14 And he broke in pieces the *sacred* pillars
and cut down the wooden images, and filled
their places with the bones of men.
15 Moreover the altar that *was* at Bethel, *and*
the high place which Jeroboam the son of Nebat, who made Israel sin, had made, both that
altar and the high place he broke down; and
he burned the high place *and* crushed *it* to
powder, and burned the wooden image.
16 As Josiah turned, he saw the tombs that
were there on the mountain. And he sent and
took the bones out of the tombs and burned
them on the altar, and defiled it according to
the word of the LORD which the man of God
proclaimed, who proclaimed these words.
17 Then he said, "What gravestone *is* this that
I see?" So the men of the city told him, "*It is*
the tomb of the man of God who came from
Judah and proclaimed these things which you
have done against the altar of Bethel."
18 And he said, "Let him alone; let no one
move his bones." So they let his bones alone,
with the bones of the prophet who came from
Samaria.
19 Now Josiah also took away all the shrines
of the high places that *were* in the cities of
Samaria, which the kings of Israel had made
to provoke the LORD[a] to anger; and he did to
them according to all the deeds he had done in
Bethel.
20 He executed all the priests of the high
places who *were* there, on the altars, and burned
men's bones on them; and he returned to Jerusalem.
21 Then the king commanded all the people,
saying, "Keep the Passover to the LORD your
God, as *it is* written in this Book of the Covenant."
22 Such a Passover surely had never been
held since the days of the judges who judged
Israel, nor in all the days of the kings of Israel
and the kings of Judah.
23 But in the eighteenth year of King Josiah
this Passover was held before the LORD in Jerusalem.
24 Moreover Josiah put away those who consulted mediums and spiritists, the household
gods and idols, all the abominations that were
seen in the land of Judah and in Jerusalem,
that he might perform the words of the law

23:4 [a]A Canaanite goddess [b]The gods of the Assyrians **23:6** [a]Hebrew *Asherah*, a Canaanite goddess **23:7** [a]Hebrew *qedeshim*, that is, those practicing sodomy and prostitution in religious rituals **23:10** [a]Kethib reads *Sons*.
23:19 [a]Following Septuagint, Syriac, and Vulgate; Masoretic Text and Targum omit *the LORD*.

which were written in the book that Hilkiah
the priest found in the house of the LORD.
25 Now before him there was no king like
him, who turned to the LORD with all his heart,
with all his soul, and with all his might, accord-
ing to all the Law of Moses; nor after him did
any arise like him.

Impending Judgment on Judah

26 Nevertheless the LORD did not turn from
the fierceness of His great wrath, with which
His anger was aroused against Judah, because
of all the provocations with which Manasseh
had provoked Him.
27 And the LORD said, "I will also remove
Judah from My sight, as I have removed Israel,
and will cast off this city Jerusalem which I
have chosen, and the house of which I said,
'My name shall be there.' "[a]

Josiah Dies in Battle

28 Now the rest of the acts of Josiah, and all
that he did, *are* they not written in the book of
the chronicles of the kings of Judah?
29 In his days Pharaoh Necho king of Egypt
went to the aid of the king of Assyria, to the
River Euphrates; and King Josiah went against
him. And *Pharaoh Necho* killed him at Me-
giddo when he confronted him.
30 Then his servants moved his body in a
chariot from Megiddo, brought him to Jerusa-
lem, and buried him in his own tomb. And the
people of the land took Jehoahaz the son of
Josiah, anointed him, and made him king in
his father's place.

The Reign and Captivity of Jehoahaz

31 Jehoahaz *was* twenty-three years old
when he became king, and he reigned three
months in Jerusalem. His mother's name *was*
Hamutal the daughter of Jeremiah of Libnah.
32 And he did evil in the sight of the LORD,
according to all that his fathers had done.
33 Now Pharaoh Necho put him in prison at
Riblah in the land of Hamath, that he might
not reign in Jerusalem; and he imposed on the
land a tribute of one hundred talents of silver
and a talent of gold.
34 Then Pharaoh Necho made Eliakim the
son of Josiah king in place of his father Josiah,
and changed his name to Jehoiakim. And *Pha-
raoh* took Jehoahaz and went to Egypt, and he[a]
died there.

Jehoiakim Reigns in Judah

35 So Jehoiakim gave the silver and gold to
Pharaoh; but he taxed the land to give money
according to the command of Pharaoh; he ex-
acted the silver and gold from the people of
the land, from every one according to his as-
sessment, to give *it* to Pharaoh Necho.
36 Jehoiakim *was* twenty-five years old when
he became king, and he reigned eleven years
in Jerusalem. His mother's name *was* Zebudah
the daughter of Pedaiah of Rumah.
37 And he did evil in the sight of the LORD,
according to all that his fathers had done.

Judah Overrun by Enemies

24 In his days Nebuchadnezzar king of
Babylon came up, and Jehoiakim be-
came his vassal *for* three years. Then he turned
and rebelled against him.
2 And the LORD sent against him *raiding*
bands of Chaldeans, bands of Syrians, bands
of Moabites, and bands of the people of Am-
mon; He sent them against Judah to destroy it,
according to the word of the LORD which He
had spoken by His servants the prophets.
3 Surely at the commandment of the LORD
this came upon Judah, to remove *them* from
His sight because of the sins of Manasseh, ac-
cording to all that he had done,
4 and also because of the innocent blood
that he had shed; for he had filled Jerusalem
with innocent blood, which the LORD would
not pardon.
5 Now the rest of the acts of Jehoiakim, and
all that he did, *are* they not written in the book
of the chronicles of the kings of Judah?
6 So Jehoiakim rested with his fathers. Then
Jehoiachin his son reigned in his place.
7 And the king of Egypt did not come out of
his land anymore, for the king of Babylon had
taken all that belonged to the king of Egypt
from the Brook of Egypt to the River Eu-
phrates.

The Reign and Captivity of Jehoiachin

8 Jehoiachin *was* eighteen years old when
he became king, and he reigned in Jerusalem
three months. His mother's name *was* Ne-
hushta the daughter of Elnathan of Jerusalem.
9 And he did evil in the sight of the LORD,
according to all that his father had done.
10 At that time the servants of Nebuchadnez-
zar king of Babylon came up against Jerusa-
lem, and the city was besieged.
11 And Nebuchadnezzar king of Babylon
came against the city, as his servants were be-
sieging it.
12 Then Jehoiachin king of Judah, his
mother, his servants, his princes, and his offi-
cers went out to the king of Babylon; and the
king of Babylon, in the eighth year of his reign,
took him prisoner.

The Captivity of Jerusalem

13 And he carried out from there all the trea-
sures of the house of the LORD and the trea-
sures of the king's house, and he cut in pieces
all the articles of gold which Solomon king of
Israel had made in the temple of the LORD, as
the LORD had said.
14 Also he carried into captivity all Jerusa-
lem: all the captains and all the mighty men of
valor, ten thousand captives, and all the crafts-
men and smiths. None remained except the
poorest people of the land.
15 And he carried Jehoiachin captive to Bab-
ylon. The king's mother, the king's wives, his
officers, and the mighty of the land he carried
into captivity from Jerusalem to Babylon.
16 All the valiant men, seven thousand, and
craftsmen and smiths, one thousand, all *who
were* strong *and* fit for war, these the king of
Babylon brought captive to Babylon.

Zedekiah Reigns in Judah

17 Then the king of Babylon made Mattaniah,
Jehoiachin's[a] uncle, king in his place, and
changed his name to Zedekiah.
18 Zedekiah *was* twenty-one years old when
he became king, and he reigned eleven years
in Jerusalem. His mother's name *was* Hamutal
the daughter of Jeremiah of Libnah.

23:27 [a]1 Kings 8:29 **23:34** [a]That is, Jehoahaz **24:17** [a]Literally *his*

19 He also did evil in the sight of the LORD,
according to all that Jehoiakim had done.
20 For because of the anger of the LORD *this*
happened in Jerusalem and Judah, that He fi-
nally cast them out from His presence. Then
Zedekiah rebelled against the king of Babylon.

The Fall and Captivity of Judah

25 Now it came to pass in the ninth year of
his reign, in the tenth month, on the
tenth *day* of the month, *that* Nebuchadnezzar
king of Babylon and all his army came against
Jerusalem and encamped against it; and they
built a siege wall against it all around.
2 So the city was besieged until the eleventh
year of King Zedekiah.
3 By the ninth *day* of the *fourth* month the
famine had become so severe in the city that
there was no food for the people of the land.
4 Then the city wall was broken through,
and all the men of war *fled* at night by way of
the gate between two walls, which was by the
king's garden, even though the Chaldeans
were still encamped all around against the city.
And *the king*[a] went by way of the plain.[b]
5 But the army of the Chaldeans pursued the
king, and they overtook him in the plains of
Jericho. All his army was scattered from him.
6 So they took the king and brought him
up to the king of Babylon at Riblah, and they
pronounced judgment on him.
7 Then they killed the sons of Zedekiah be-
fore his eyes, put out the eyes of Zedekiah,
bound him with bronze fetters, and took him
to Babylon.
8 And in the fifth month, on the seventh *day*
of the month (which *was* the nineteenth year
of King Nebuchadnezzar king of Babylon),
Nebuzaradan the captain of the guard, a ser-
vant of the king of Babylon, came to Jeru-
salem.
9 He burned the house of the LORD and the
king's house; all the houses of Jerusalem, that
is, all the houses of the great, he burned with
fire.
10 And all the army of the Chaldeans who
were with the captain of the guard broke down
the walls of Jerusalem all around.
11 Then Nebuzaradan the captain of the
guard carried away captive the rest of the peo-
ple *who* remained in the city and the defectors
who had deserted to the king of Babylon, with
the rest of the multitude.
12 But the captain of the guard left *some* of
the poor of the land as vinedressers and
farmers.
13 The bronze pillars that *were* in the house
of the LORD, and the carts and the bronze Sea
that *were* in the house of the LORD, the Chalde-
ans broke in pieces, and carried their bronze
to Babylon.
14 They also took away the pots, the shovels,
the trimmers, the spoons, and all the bronze
utensils with which the priests ministered.
15 The firepans and the basins, the things of
solid gold and solid silver, the captain of the
guard took away.
16 The two pillars, one Sea, and the carts,
which Solomon had made for the house of the
LORD, the bronze of all these articles was be-
yond measure.
17 The height of one pillar *was* eighteen cu-
bits, and the capital on it *was* of bronze. The
height of the capital was three cubits, and the
network and pomegranates all around the cap-
ital were all of bronze. The second pillar was
the same, with a network.
18 And the captain of the guard took Seraiah
the chief priest, Zephaniah the second priest,
and the three doorkeepers.
19 He also took out of the city an officer who
had charge of the men of war, five men of the
king's close associates who were found in the
city, the chief recruiting officer of the army,
who mustered the people of the land, and sixty
men of the people of the land *who were* found
in the city.
20 So Nebuzaradan, captain of the guard,
took these and brought them to the king of
Babylon at Riblah.
21 Then the king of Babylon struck them and
put them to death at Riblah in the land of Ha-
math. Thus Judah was carried away captive
from its own land.

Gedaliah Made Governor of Judah

22 Then he made Gedaliah the son of Ahi-
kam, the son of Shaphan, governor over the
people who remained in the land of Judah,
whom Nebuchadnezzar king of Babylon had
left.
23 Now when all the captains of the armies,
they and *their* men, heard that the king of Bab-
ylon had made Gedaliah governor, they came
to Gedaliah at Mizpah—Ishmael the son of
Nethaniah, Johanan the son of Careah, Sera-
iah the son of Tanhumeth the Netophathite,
and Jaazaniah[a] the son of a Maachathite, they
and their men.
24 And Gedaliah took an oath before them
and their men, and said to them, "Do not be
afraid of the servants of the Chaldeans. Dwell
in the land and serve the king of Babylon, and
it shall be well with you."
25 But it happened in the seventh month that
Ishmael the son of Nethaniah, the son of Elish-
ama, of the royal family, came with ten men
and struck and killed Gedaliah, the Jews, as
well as the Chaldeans who were with him at
Mizpah.
26 And all the people, small and great, and
the captains of the armies, arose and went to
Egypt; for they were afraid of the Chaldeans.

Jehoiachin Released from Prison

27 Now it came to pass in the thirty-seventh
year of the captivity of Jehoiachin king of Ju-
dah, in the twelfth month, on the twenty-
seventh *day* of the month, *that* Evil-Merodach[a]
king of Babylon, in the year that he began to
reign, released Jehoiachin king of Judah from
prison.
28 He spoke kindly to him, and gave him a
more prominent seat than those of the kings
who *were* with him in Babylon.
29 So Jehoiachin changed from his prison
garments, and he ate bread regularly before
the king all the days of his life.
30 And as for his provisions, *there was* a reg-
ular ration given him by the king, a portion for
each day, all the days of his life.

25:4 [a]Literally *he* [b]Or *Arabah*, that is, the Jordan Valley **25:23** [a]Spelled *Jezaniah* in Jeremiah 40:8 **25:27** [a]Literally *Man of Marduk*

The First Book of the CHRONICLES

The Family of Adam—Seth to Abraham

1 Adam, Seth, Enosh,

2 Cainan,[a] Mahalalel, Jared,

3 Enoch, Methuselah, Lamech,

4 Noah,[a] Shem, Ham, and Japheth.

5 The sons of Japheth *were* Gomer, Magog, Madai, Javan, Tubal, Meshech, and Tiras.

6 The sons of Gomer *were* Ashkenaz, Diphath,[a] and Togarmah.

7 The sons of Javan *were* Elishah, Tarshishah,[a] Kittim, and Rodanim.[b]

8 The sons of Ham *were* Cush, Mizraim, Put, and Canaan.

9 The sons of Cush *were* Seba, Havilah, Sabta,[a] Raama,[b] and Sabtecha. The sons of Raama *were* Sheba and Dedan.

10 Cush begot Nimrod; he began to be a mighty one on the earth.

11 Mizraim begot Ludim, Anamim, Lehabim, Naphtuhim,

12 Pathrusim, Casluhim (from whom came the Philistines and the Caphtorim).

13 Canaan begot Sidon, his firstborn, and Heth;

14 the Jebusite, the Amorite, and the Girgashite;

15 the Hivite, the Arkite, and the Sinite;

16 the Arvadite, the Zemarite, and the Hamathite.

17 The sons of Shem *were* Elam, Asshur, Arphaxad, Lud, Aram, Uz, Hul, Gether, and Meshech.[a]

18 Arphaxad begot Shelah, and Shelah begot Eber.

19 To Eber were born two sons: the name of one *was* Peleg,[a] for in his days the earth was divided; and his brother's name *was* Joktan.

20 Joktan begot Almodad, Sheleph, Hazarmaveth, Jerah,

21 Hadoram, Uzal, Diklah,

22 Ebal,[a] Abimael, Sheba,

23 Ophir, Havilah, and Jobab. All these *were* the sons of Joktan.

24 Shem, Arphaxad, Shelah,

25 Eber, Peleg, Reu,

26 Serug, Nahor, Terah,

27 and Abram, who *is* Abraham.

28 The sons of Abraham *were* Isaac and Ishmael.

The Family of Ishmael

29 These *are* their genealogies: The firstborn of Ishmael *was* Nebajoth; then Kedar, Adbeel, Mibsam,

30 Mishma, Dumah, Massa, Hadad,[a] Tema,

31 Jetur, Naphish, and Kedemah. These *were* the sons of Ishmael.

The Family of Keturah

32 Now the sons born to Keturah, Abraham's concubine, *were* Zimran, Jokshan, Medan, Midian, Ishbak, and Shuah. The sons of Jokshan *were* Sheba and Dedan.

33 The sons of Midian *were* Ephah, Epher, Hanoch, Abida, and Eldaah. All these were the children of Keturah.

The Family of Isaac

34 And Abraham begot Isaac. The sons of Isaac *were* Esau and Israel.

35 The sons of Esau *were* Eliphaz, Reuel, Jeush, Jaalam, and Korah.

36 And the sons of Eliphaz *were* Teman, Omar, Zephi,[a] Gatam, *and* Kenaz; and *by* Timna,[b] Amalek.

37 The sons of Reuel *were* Nahath, Zerah, Shammah, and Mizzah.

The Family of Seir

38 The sons of Seir *were* Lotan, Shobal, Zibeon, Anah, Dishon, Ezer, and Dishan.

39 And the sons of Lotan *were* Hori and Homam; Lotan's sister *was* Timna.

40 The sons of Shobal *were* Alian,[a] Manahath, Ebal, Shephi,[b] and Onam. The sons of Zibeon *were* Ajah and Anah.

41 The son of Anah *was* Dishon. The sons of Dishon *were* Hamran,[a] Eshban, Ithran, and Cheran.

42 The sons of Ezer *were* Bilhan, Zaavan, *and* Jaakan.[a] The sons of Dishan *were* Uz and Aran.

The Kings of Edom

43 Now these *were* the kings who reigned in the land of Edom before a king reigned over the children of Israel: Bela the son of Beor, and the name of his city was Dinhabah.

44 And when Bela died, Jobab the son of Zerah of Bozrah reigned in his place.

45 When Jobab died, Husham of the land of the Temanites reigned in his place.

46 And when Husham died, Hadad the son of Bedad, who attacked Midian in the field of Moab, reigned in his place. The name of his city *was* Avith.

47 When Hadad died, Samlah of Masrekah reigned in his place.

48 And when Samlah died, Saul of Rehoboth-by-the-River reigned in his place.

49 When Saul died, Baal-Hanan the son of Achbor reigned in his place.

50 And when Baal-Hanan died, Hadad[a] reigned in his place; and the name of his city was Pai.[b] His wife's name was Mehetabel the daughter of Matred, the daughter of Mezahab.

51 Hadad died also. And the chiefs of Edom were Chief Timnah, Chief Aliah,[a] Chief Jetheth,

52 Chief Aholibamah, Chief Elah, Chief Pinon,

53 Chief Kenaz, Chief Teman, Chief Mibzar,

54 Chief Magdiel, and Chief Iram. These *were* the chiefs of Edom.

1:2 [a]Hebrew *Qenan* **1:4** [a]Following Masoretic Text and Vulgate; Septuagint adds *the sons of Noah.* **1:6** [a]Spelled *Riphath* in Genesis 10:3 **1:7** [a]Spelled *Tarshish* in Genesis 10:4 [b]Spelled *Dodanim* in Genesis 10:4 **1:9** [a]Spelled *Sabtah* in Genesis 10:7 [b]Spelled *Raamah* in Genesis 10:7 **1:17** [a]Spelled *Mash* in Genesis 10:23 **1:19** [a]Literally *Division* **1:22** [a]Spelled *Obal* in Genesis 10:28 **1:30** [a]Spelled *Hadar* in Genesis 25:15 **1:36** [a]Spelled *Zepho* in Genesis 36:11 [b]Compare Genesis 36:12 **1:40** [a]Spelled *Alvan* in Genesis 36:23 [b]Spelled *Shepho* in Genesis 36:23 **1:41** [a]Spelled *Hemdan* in Genesis 36:26 **1:42** [a]Spelled *Akan* in Genesis 36:27 **1:50** [a]Spelled *Hadar* in Genesis 36:39 [b]Spelled *Pau* in Genesis 36:39 **1:51** [a]Spelled *Alvah* in Genesis 36:40

The Family of Israel

2 These *were* the sons of Israel: Reuben, Simeon, Levi, Judah, Issachar, Zebulun,
2 Dan, Joseph, Benjamin, Naphtali, Gad, and Asher.

From Judah to David

3 The sons of Judah *were* Er, Onan, and Shelah. *These* three were born to him by the daughter of Shua, the Canaanitess. Er, the firstborn of Judah, was wicked in the sight of the LORD; so He killed him.
4 And Tamar, his daughter-in-law, bore him Perez and Zerah. All the sons of Judah *were* five.
5 The sons of Perez *were* Hezron and Hamul.
6 The sons of Zerah *were* Zimri, Ethan, Heman, Calcol, and Dara—five of them in all.
7 The son of Carmi *was* Achar,[a] the troubler of Israel, who transgressed in the accursed thing.
8 The son of Ethan *was* Azariah.
9 Also the sons of Hezron who were born to him *were* Jerahmeel, Ram, and Chelubai.[a]
10 Ram begot Amminadab, and Amminadab begot Nahshon, leader of the children of Judah;
11 Nahshon begot Salma,[a] and Salma begot Boaz;
12 Boaz begot Obed, and Obed begot Jesse;
13 Jesse begot Eliab his firstborn, Abinadab the second, Shimea[a] the third,
14 Nethanel the fourth, Raddai the fifth,
15 Ozem the sixth, *and* David the seventh.
16 Now their sisters *were* Zeruiah and Abigail. And the sons of Zeruiah *were* Abishai, Joab, and Asahel—three.
17 Abigail bore Amasa; and the father of Amasa *was* Jether the Ishmaelite.[a]

The Family of Hezron

18 Caleb the son of Hezron had children by Azubah, *his* wife, and by Jerioth. Now these were her sons: Jesher, Shobab, and Ardon.
19 When Azubah died, Caleb took Ephrath[a] as his wife, who bore him Hur.
20 And Hur begot Uri, and Uri begot Bezalel.
21 Now afterward Hezron went in to the daughter of Machir the father of Gilead, whom he married when he *was* sixty years old; and she bore him Segub.
22 Segub begot Jair, who had twenty-three cities in the land of Gilead.
23 (Geshur and Syria took from them the towns of Jair, with Kenath and its towns—sixty towns.) All these *belonged to* the sons of Machir the father of Gilead.
24 After Hezron died in Caleb Ephrathah, Hezron's wife Abijah bore him Ashhur the father of Tekoa.

The Family of Jerahmeel

25 The sons of Jerahmeel, the firstborn of Hezron, *were* Ram, the firstborn, and Bunah, Oren, Ozem, *and* Ahijah.
26 Jerahmeel had another wife, whose name was Atarah; she was the mother of Onam.
27 The sons of Ram, the firstborn of Jerahmeel, were Maaz, Jamin, and Eker.
28 The sons of Onam were Shammai and Jada. The sons of Shammai *were* Nadab and Abishur.
29 And the name of the wife of Abishur *was* Abihail, and she bore him Ahban and Molid.
30 The sons of Nadab *were* Seled and Appaim; Seled died without children.
31 The son of Appaim *was* Ishi, the son of Ishi *was* Sheshan, and Sheshan's son *was* Ahlai.
32 The sons of Jada, the brother of Shammai, *were* Jether and Jonathan; Jether died without children.
33 The sons of Jonathan *were* Peleth and Zaza. These were the sons of Jerahmeel.
34 Now Sheshan had no sons, only daughters. And Sheshan had an Egyptian servant whose name *was* Jarha.
35 Sheshan gave his daughter to Jarha his servant as wife, and she bore him Attai.
36 Attai begot Nathan, and Nathan begot Zabad;
37 Zabad begot Ephlal, and Ephlal begot Obed;
38 Obed begot Jehu, and Jehu begot Azariah;
39 Azariah begot Helez, and Helez begot Eleasah;
40 Eleasah begot Sismai, and Sismai begot Shallum;
41 Shallum begot Jekamiah, and Jekamiah begot Elishama.

The Family of Caleb

42 The descendants of Caleb the brother of Jerahmeel *were* Mesha, his firstborn, who was the father of Ziph, and the sons of Mareshah the father of Hebron.
43 The sons of Hebron *were* Korah, Tappuah, Rekem, and Shema.
44 Shema begot Raham the father of Jorkoam, and Rekem begot Shammai.
45 And the son of Shammai *was* Maon, and Maon *was* the father of Beth Zur.
46 Ephah, Caleb's concubine, bore Haran, Moza, and Gazez; and Haran begot Gazez.
47 And the sons of Jahdai *were* Regem, Jotham, Geshan, Pelet, Ephah, and Shaaph.
48 Maachah, Caleb's concubine, bore Sheber and Tirhanah.
49 She also bore Shaaph the father of Madmannah, Sheva the father of Machbenah and the father of Gibea. And the daughter of Caleb *was* Achsah.
50 These were the descendants of Caleb: The sons of Hur, the firstborn of Ephrathah, *were* Shobal the father of Kirjath Jearim,
51 Salma the father of Bethlehem, *and* Hareph the father of Beth Gader.
52 And Shobal the father of Kirjath Jearim had descendants: Haroeh, *and* half of the *families of* Manuhoth.[a]
53 The families of Kirjath Jearim *were* the Ithrites, the Puthites, the Shumathites, and the Mishraites. From these came the Zorathites and the Eshtaolites.
54 The sons of Salma *were* Bethlehem, the Netophathites, Atroth Beth Joab, half of the Manahethites, and the Zorites.
55 And the families of the scribes who dwelt at Jabez *were* the Tirathites, the Shimeathites, *and* the Suchathites. These *were* the Kenites who came from Hammath, the father of the house of Rechab.

2:7 [a]Spelled *Achan* in Joshua 7:1 and elsewhere **2:9** [a]Spelled *Caleb* in 2:18, 42 **2:11** [a]Spelled *Salmon* in Ruth 4:21 and Luke 3:32 **2:13** [a]Spelled *Shammah* in 1 Samuel 16:9 and elsewhere **2:17** [a]Compare 2 Samuel 17:25 **2:19** [a]Spelled *Ephrathah* elsewhere **2:52** [a]Same as *the Manahethites,* verse 54

The Family of David

3 Now these were the sons of David who were born to him in Hebron: The firstborn *was* Amnon, by Ahinoam the Jezreelitess; the second, Daniel,[a] by Abigail the Carmelitess;
2 the third, Absalom the son of Maacah, the daughter of Talmai, king of Geshur; the fourth, Adonijah the son of Haggith;
3 the fifth, Shephatiah, by Abital; the sixth, Ithream, by his wife Eglah.
4 *These* six were born to him in Hebron. There he reigned seven years and six months, and in Jerusalem he reigned thirty-three years.
5 And these were born to him in Jerusalem: Shimea,[a] Shobab, Nathan, and Solomon—four by Bathshua[b] the daughter of Ammiel.[c]
6 Also *there* were Ibhar, Elishama,[a] Eliphelet,[b]
7 Nogah, Nepheg, Japhia,
8 Elishama, Eliada,[a] and Eliphelet—nine *in all.*
9 *These were* all the sons of David, besides the sons of the concubines, and Tamar their sister.

The Family of Solomon

10 Solomon's son *was* Rehoboam; Abijah[a] *was* his son, Asa his son, Jehoshaphat his son,
11 Joram[a] his son, Ahaziah his son, Joash[b] his son,
12 Amaziah his son, Azariah[a] his son, Jotham his son,
13 Ahaz his son, Hezekiah his son, Manasseh his son,
14 Amon his son, *and* Josiah his son.
15 The sons of Josiah *were* Johanan the firstborn, the second Jehoiakim, the third Zedekiah, and the fourth Shallum.[a]
16 The sons of Jehoiakim *were* Jeconiah his son *and* Zedekiah[a] his son.

The Family of Jeconiah

17 And the sons of Jeconiah[a] *were* Assir,[b] Shealtiel his son,
18 *and* Malchiram, Pedaiah, Shenazzar, Jecamiah, Hoshama, and Nedabiah.
19 The sons of Pedaiah *were* Zerubbabel and Shimei. The sons of Zerubbabel *were* Meshullam, Hananiah, Shelomith their sister,
20 and Hashubah, Ohel, Berechiah, Hasadiah, and Jushab-Hesed—five *in all.*
21 The sons of Hananiah *were* Pelatiah and Jeshaiah, the sons of Rephaiah, the sons of Arnan, the sons of Obadiah, and the sons of Shechaniah.
22 The son of Shechaniah was Shemaiah. The sons of Shemaiah *were* Hattush, Igal, Bariah, Neariah, and Shaphat—six *in all.*
23 The sons of Neariah *were* Elioenai, Hezekiah, and Azrikam—three *in all.*
24 The sons of Elioenai *were* Hodaviah, Eliashib, Pelaiah, Akkub, Johanan, Delaiah, and Anani—seven *in all.*

The Family of Judah

4 The sons of Judah *were* Perez, Hezron, Carmi, Hur, and Shobal.
2 And Reaiah the son of Shobal begot Jahath, and Jahath begot Ahumai and Lahad. These *were* the families of the Zorathites.
3 These *were the sons of* the father of Etam: Jezreel, Ishma, and Idbash; and the name of their sister *was* Hazelelponi;
4 and Penuel *was* the father of Gedor, and Ezer *was the* father of Hushah. These *were* the sons of Hur, the firstborn of Ephrathah the father of Bethlehem.
5 And Ashhur the father of Tekoa had two wives, Helah and Naarah.
6 Naarah bore him Ahuzzam, Hepher, Temeni, and Haahashtari. These *were* the sons of Naarah.
7 The sons of Helah *were* Zereth, Zohar, and Ethnan;
8 and Koz begot Anub, Zobebah, and the families of Aharhel the son of Harum.
9 Now Jabez was more honorable than his brothers, and his mother called his name Jabez,[a] saying, "Because I bore *him* in pain."
10 And Jabez called on the God of Israel saying, "Oh, that You would bless me indeed, and enlarge my territory, that Your hand would be with me, and that You would keep *me* from evil, that I may not cause pain!" So God granted him what he requested.
11 Chelub the brother of Shuhah begot Mehir, who *was* the father of Eshton.
12 And Eshton begot Beth-Rapha, Paseah, and Tehinnah the father of Ir-Nahash. These *were* the men of Rechah.
13 The sons of Kenaz *were* Othniel and Seraiah. The sons of Othniel *were* Hathath,[a]
14 and Meonothai *who* begot Ophrah. Seraiah begot Joab the father of Ge Harashim,[a] for they were craftsmen.
15 The sons of Caleb the son of Jephunneh *were* Iru, Elah, and Naam. The son of Elah *was* Kenaz.
16 The sons of Jehallelel *were* Ziph, Ziphah, Tiria, and Asarel.
17 The sons of Ezrah *were* Jether, Mered, Epher, and Jalon. And *Mered's wife*[a] bore Miriam, Shammai, and Ishbah the father of Eshtemoa.
18 (His wife Jehudijah[a] bore Jered the father of Gedor, Heber the father of Sochoh, and Jekuthiel the father of Zanoah.) And these were the sons of Bithiah the daughter of Pharaoh, whom Mered took.
19 The sons of Hodiah's wife, the sister of Naham, *were* the fathers of Keilah the Garmite and of Eshtemoa the Maachathite.
20 And the sons of Shimon *were* Amnon, Rinnah, Ben-Hanan, and Tilon. And the sons of Ishi *were* Zoheth and Ben-Zoheth.
21 The sons of Shelah the son of Judah *were* Er the father of Lecah, Laadah the father of Mareshah, and the families of the house of the linen workers of the house of Ashbea;
22 also Jokim, the men of Chozeba, and Joash;

3:1 [a]Called *Chileab* in 2 Samuel 3:3 **3:5** [a]Spelled *Shammua* in 14:4 and 2 Samuel 5:14 [b]Spelled *Bathsheba* in 2 Samuel 11:3 [c]Called *Eliam* in 2 Samuel 11:3 **3:6** [a]Spelled *Elishua* in 14:5 and 2 Samuel 5:15 [b]Spelled *Elpelet* in 14:5 **3:8** [a]Spelled *Beeliada* in 14:7 **3:10** [a]Spelled *Abijam* in 1 Kings 15:1 **3:11** [a]Spelled *Jehoram* in 2 Kings 1:17 and 8:16 [b]Spelled *Jehoash* in 2 Kings 12:1 **3:12** [a]Called *Uzziah* in Isaiah 6:1 **3:15** [a]Called *Jehoahaz* in 2 Kings 23:31 **3:16** [a]Compare 2 Kings 24:17 **3:17** [a]Also called *Coniah* in Jeremiah 22:24 and *Jehoiachin* in 2 Kings 24:8 [b]Or *Jeconiah the captive were* **4:9** [a]Literally *He Will Cause Pain* **4:13** [a]Septuagint and Vulgate add *and Meonothai.* **4:14** [a]Literally *Valley of Craftsmen* **4:17** [a]Literally *she* **4:18** [a]Or *His Judean wife*

Saraph, who ruled in Moab, and Jashubi-
Lehem. Now the records are ancient.
23 These *were* the potters and those who
dwell at Netaim[a] and Gederah;[b] there they
dwelt with the king for his work.

The Family of Simeon

24 The sons of Simeon *were* Nemuel, Jamin,
Jarib,[a] Zerah,[b] *and* Shaul,
25 Shallum his son, Mibsam his son, and
Mishma his son.
26 And the sons of Mishma *were* Hamuel his
son, Zacchur his son, and Shimei his son.
27 Shimei had sixteen sons and six daugh-
ters; but his brothers did not have many chil-
dren, nor did any of their families multiply as
much as the children of Judah.
28 They dwelt at Beersheba, Moladah, Hazar
Shual,
29 Bilhah, Ezem, Tolad,
30 Bethuel, Hormah, Ziklag,
31 Beth Marcaboth, Hazar Susim, Beth Biri,
and at Shaaraim. These *were* their cities until
the reign of David.
32 And their villages *were* Etam, Ain, Rim-
mon, Tochen, and Ashan—five cities—
33 and all the villages that *were* around these
cities as far as Baal.[a] These *were* their dwelling
places, and they maintained their genealogy:
34 Meshobab, Jamlech, and Joshah the son of
Amaziah;
35 Joel, and Jehu the son of Joshibiah, the
son of Seraiah, the son of Asiel;
36 Elioenai, Jaakobah, Jeshohaiah, Asaiah,
Adiel, Jesimiel, and Benaiah;
37 Ziza the son of Shiphi, the son of Allon,
the son of Jedaiah, the son of Shimri, the son
of Shemaiah—
38 these mentioned by name *were* leaders in
their families, and their father's house in-
creased greatly.
39 So they went to the entrance of Gedor, as
far as the east side of the valley, to seek pasture
for their flocks.
40 And they found rich, good pasture, and the
land *was* broad, quiet, and peaceful; for some
Hamites formerly lived there.
41 These recorded by name came in the days
of Hezekiah king of Judah; and they attacked
their tents and the Meunites who were found
there, and utterly destroyed them, as it is to this
day. So they dwelt in their place, because *there
was* pasture for their flocks there.
42 Now *some* of them, five hundred men of
the sons of Simeon, went to Mount Seir, having
as their captains Pelatiah, Neariah, Rephaiah,
and Uzziel, the sons of Ishi.
43 And they defeated the rest of the Amalek-
ites who had escaped. They have dwelt there
to this day.

The Family of Reuben

5 Now the sons of Reuben the firstborn of
Israel—he *was* indeed the firstborn, but be-
cause he defiled his father's bed, his birthright
was given to the sons of Joseph, the son of
Israel, so that the genealogy is not listed ac-
cording to the birthright;
2 yet Judah prevailed over his brothers, and
from him *came* a ruler, although the birthright
was Joseph's—
3 the sons of Reuben the firstborn of Israel
were Hanoch, Pallu, Hezron, and Carmi.
4 The sons of Joel *were* Shemaiah his son,
Gog his son, Shimei his son,
5 Micah his son, Reaiah his son, Baal his son,
6 and Beerah his son, whom Tiglath-Pileser[a]
king of Assyria carried into captivity. He *was*
leader of the Reubenites.
7 And his brethren by their families, when
the genealogy of their generations was regis-
tered: the chief, Jeiel, and Zechariah,
8 and Bela the son of Azaz, the son of Shema,
the son of Joel, who dwelt in Aroer, as far as
Nebo and Baal Meon.
9 Eastward they settled as far as the entrance
of the wilderness this side of the River Euphra-
tes, because their cattle had multiplied in the
land of Gilead.
10 Now in the days of Saul they made war with
the Hagrites, who fell by their hand; and they
dwelt in their tents throughout the entire *area*
east of Gilead.

The Family of Gad

11 And the children of Gad dwelt next to them
in the land of Bashan as far as Salcah:
12 Joel *was* the chief, Shapham the next, then
Jaanai and Shaphat in Bashan,
13 and their brethren of their father's house:
Michael, Meshullam, Sheba, Jorai, Jachan,
Zia, and Eber—seven *in all.*
14 These *were* the children of Abihail the son
of Huri, the son of Jaroah, the son of Gilead,
the son of Michael, the son of Jeshishai, the
son of Jahdo, the son of Buz;
15 Ahi the son of Abdiel, the son of Guni, *was*
chief of their father's house.
16 And *the Gadites* dwelt in Gilead, in Ba-
shan and in its villages, and in all the common-
lands of Sharon within their borders.
17 All these were registered by genealogies
in the days of Jotham king of Judah, and in the
days of Jeroboam king of Israel.
18 The sons of Reuben, the Gadites, and half
the tribe of Manasseh *had* forty-four thousand
seven hundred and sixty valiant men, men able
to bear shield and sword, to shoot with the
bow, and skillful in war, who went to war.
19 They made war with the Hagrites, Jetur,
Naphish, and Nodab.
20 And they were helped against them, and
the Hagrites were delivered into their hand,
and all who *were* with them, for they cried out
to God in the battle. He heeded their prayer,
because they put their trust in Him.
21 Then they took away their livestock—fifty
thousand of their camels, two hundred and
fifty thousand of their sheep, and two thousand
of their donkeys—also one hundred thousand
of their men;
22 for many fell dead, because the war *was*
God's. And they dwelt in their place until the
captivity.

The Family of Manasseh (East)

23 So the children of the half-tribe of Manas-
seh dwelt in the land. Their *numbers* increased
from Bashan to Baal Hermon, that is, to Senir,
or Mount Hermon.
24 These *were* the heads of their fathers'
houses: Epher, Ishi, Eliel, Azriel, Jeremiah,
Hodaviah, and Jahdiel. They were mighty men

4:23 [a]Literally *Plants* [b]Literally *Hedges* **4:24** [a]Called *Jachin* in Genesis 46:10 [b]Called *Zohar* in Genesis 46:10
4:33 [a]Or *Baalath Beer* (compare Joshua 19:8) **5:6** [a]Hebrew *Tilgath-Pilneser*

of valor, famous men, *and* heads of their fathers' houses.

25 And they were unfaithful to the God of their fathers, and played the harlot after the gods of the peoples of the land, whom God had destroyed before them.

26 So the God of Israel stirred up the spirit of Pul king of Assyria, that is, Tiglath-Pileser[a] king of Assyria. He carried the Reubenites, the Gadites, and the half-tribe of Manasseh into captivity. He took them to Halah, Habor, Hara, and the river of Gozan to this day.

The Family of Levi

6 The sons of Levi *were* Gershon, Kohath, and Merari.

2 The sons of Kohath *were* Amram, Izhar, Hebron, and Uzziel.

3 The children of Amram *were* Aaron, Moses, and Miriam. And the sons of Aaron *were* Nadab, Abihu, Eleazar, and Ithamar.

4 Eleazar begot Phinehas, *and* Phinehas begot Abishua;

5 Abishua begot Bukki, and Bukki begot Uzzi;

6 Uzzi begot Zerahiah, and Zerahiah begot Meraioth;

7 Meraioth begot Amariah, and Amariah begot Ahitub;

8 Ahitub begot Zadok, and Zadok begot Ahimaaz;

9 Ahimaaz begot Azariah, and Azariah begot Johanan;

10 Johanan begot Azariah (it was he who ministered as priest in the temple that Solomon built in Jerusalem);

11 Azariah begot Amariah, and Amariah begot Ahitub;

12 Ahitub begot Zadok, and Zadok begot Shallum;

13 Shallum begot Hilkiah, and Hilkiah begot Azariah;

14 Azariah begot Seraiah, and Seraiah begot Jehozadak.

15 Jehozadak went *into captivity* when the LORD carried Judah and Jerusalem into captivity by the hand of Nebuchadnezzar.

16 The sons of Levi *were* Gershon,[a] Kohath, and Merari.

17 These are the names of the sons of Gershon: Libni and Shimei.

18 The sons of Kohath *were* Amram, Izhar, Hebron, and Uzziel.

19 The sons of Merari *were* Mahli and Mushi. Now these *are* the families of the Levites according to their fathers:

20 Of Gershon *were* Libni his son, Jahath his son, Zimmah his son,

21 Joah his son, Iddo his son, Zerah his son, *and* Jeatherai his son.

22 The sons of Kohath *were* Amminadab his son, Korah his son, Assir his son,

23 Elkanah his son, Ebiasaph his son, Assir his son,

24 Tahath his son, Uriel his son, Uzziah his son, and Shaul his son.

25 The sons of Elkanah *were* Amasai and Ahimoth.

26 *As for* Elkanah,[a] the sons of Elkanah *were* Zophai[b] his son, Nahath[c] his son,

27 Eliab[a] his son, Jeroham his son, *and* Elkanah his son.

28 The sons of Samuel *were Joel*[a] the firstborn, and Abijah the second.[b]

29 The sons of Merari *were* Mahli, Libni his son, Shimei his son, Uzzah his son,

30 Shimea his son, Haggiah his son, *and* Asaiah his son.

Musicians in the House of the LORD

31 Now these are the men whom David appointed over the service of song in the house of the LORD, after the ark came to rest.

32 They were ministering with music before the dwelling place of the tabernacle of meeting, until Solomon had built the house of the LORD in Jerusalem, and they served in their office according to their order.

33 And these *are* the ones who ministered with their sons: Of the sons of the Kohathites *were* Heman the singer, the son of Joel, the son of Samuel,

34 the son of Elkanah, the son of Jeroham, the son of Eliel,[a] the son of Toah,[b]

35 the son of Zuph, the son of Elkanah, the son of Mahath, the son of Amasai,

36 the son of Elkanah, the son of Joel, the son of Azariah, the son of Zephaniah,

37 the son of Tahath, the son of Assir, the son of Ebiasaph, the son of Korah,

38 the son of Izhar, the son of Kohath, the son of Levi, the son of Israel.

39 And his brother Asaph, who stood at his right hand, *was* Asaph the son of Berachiah, the son of Shimea,

40 the son of Michael, the son of Baaseiah, the son of Malchijah,

41 the son of Ethni, the son of Zerah, the son of Adaiah,

42 the son of Ethan, the son of Zimmah, the son of Shimei,

43 the son of Jahath, the son of Gershon, the son of Levi.

44 Their brethren, the sons of Merari, on the left hand, *were* Ethan the son of Kishi, the son of Abdi, the son of Malluch,

45 the son of Hashabiah, the son of Amaziah, the son of Hilkiah,

46 the son of Amzi, the son of Bani, the son of Shamer,

47 the son of Mahli, the son of Mushi, the son of Merari, the son of Levi.

48 And their brethren, the Levites, *were* appointed to every kind of service of the tabernacle of the house of God.

The Family of Aaron

49 But Aaron and his sons offered sacrifices on the altar of burnt offering and on the altar of incense, for all the work of the Most Holy *Place*, and to make atonement for Israel, according to all that Moses the servant of God had commanded.

50 Now these *are* the sons of Aaron: Eleazar his son, Phinehas his son, Abishua his son,

51 Bukki his son, Uzzi his son, Zerahiah his son,

52 Meraioth his son, Amariah his son, Ahitub his son,

53 Zadok his son, *and* Ahimaaz his son.

5:26 [a]Hebrew *Tilgath-Pilneser* **6:16** [a]Hebrew *Gershom* (alternate spelling of *Gershon*, as in verses 1, 17, 20, 43, 62, and 71) **6:26** [a]Compare verse 35 [b]Spelled *Zuph* in verse 35 and 1 Samuel 1:1 [c]Compare verse 34 **6:27** [a]Compare verse 34 **6:28** [a]Following Septuagint, Syriac, and Arabic (compare verse 33 and 1 Samuel 8:2) [b]Hebrew *Vasheni* **6:34** [a]Spelled *Elihu* in 1 Samuel 1:1 [b]Spelled *Tohu* in 1 Samuel 1:1

Dwelling Places of the Levites

54 Now these *are* their dwelling places through-
out their settlements in their territory, for they
were *given* by lot to the sons of Aaron, of the
family of the Kohathites:
55 They gave them Hebron in the land of Ju-
dah, with its surrounding common-lands.
56 But the fields of the city and its villages
they gave to Caleb the son of Jephunneh.
57 And to the sons of Aaron they gave *one of*
the cities of refuge, Hebron; also Libnah with
its common-lands, Jattir, Eshtemoa with its
common-lands,
58 Hilen[a] with its common-lands, Debir with
its common-lands,
59 Ashan[a] with its common-lands, and Beth
Shemesh with its common-lands.
60 And from the tribe of Benjamin: Geba with
its common-lands, Alemeth[a] with its common-
lands, and Anathoth with its common-lands. All
their cities among their families *were* thirteen.
61 To the rest of the family of the tribe of the
Kohathites *they gave* by lot ten cities from half
the tribe of Manasseh.
62 And to the sons of Gershon, throughout
their families, *they gave* thirteen cities from
the tribe of Issachar, from the tribe of Asher,
from the tribe of Naphtali, and from the tribe
of Manasseh in Bashan.
63 To the sons of Merari, throughout their fam-
ilies, *they gave* twelve cities from the tribe of
Reuben, from the tribe of Gad, and from the
tribe of Zebulun.
64 So the children of Israel gave *these* cities
with their common-lands to the Levites.
65 And they gave by lot from the tribe of the
children of Judah, from the tribe of the children
of Simeon, and from the tribe of the children of
Benjamin these cities which are called by *their*
names.
66 Now some of the families of the sons of
Kohath *were given* cities as their territory from
the tribe of Ephraim.
67 And they gave them *one of* the cities of
refuge, Shechem with its common-lands, in the
mountains of Ephraim, also Gezer with its
common-lands,
68 Jokmeam with its common-lands, Beth
Horon with its common-lands,
69 Aijalon with its common-lands, and Gath
Rimmon with its common-lands.
70 And from the half-tribe of Manasseh: Aner
with its common-lands and Bileam with its
common-lands, for the rest of the family of the
sons of Kohath.
71 From the family of the half-tribe of Manas-
seh the sons of Gershon *were given* Golan in
Bashan with its common-lands and Ashtaroth
with its common-lands.
72 And from the tribe of Issachar: Kedesh with
its common-lands, Daberath with its common-
lands,
73 Ramoth with its common-lands, and Anem
with its common-lands.
74 And from the tribe of Asher: Mashal with
its common-lands, Abdon with its common-
lands,
75 Hukok with its common-lands, and Rehob
with its common-lands.
76 And from the tribe of Naphtali: Kedesh in
Galilee with its common-lands, Hammon with
its common-lands, and Kirjathaim with its
common-lands.
77 From the tribe of Zebulun the rest of the
children of Merari *were given* Rimmon[a] with
its common-lands and Tabor with its common-
lands.
78 And on the other side of the Jordan, across
from Jericho, on the east side of the Jordan,
they were given from the tribe of Reuben: Be-
zer in the wilderness with its common-lands,
Jahzah with its common-lands,
79 Kedemoth with its common-lands, and
Mephaath with its common-lands.
80 And from the tribe of Gad: Ramoth in Gil-
ead with its common-lands, Mahanaim with its
common-lands,
81 Heshbon with its common-lands, and Ja-
zer with its common-lands.

The Family of Issachar

7 The sons of Issachar *were* Tola, Puah,[a] Ja-
shub, and Shimron—four *in all.*
2 The sons of Tola *were* Uzzi, Rephaiah, Je-
riel, Jahmai, Jibsam, and Shemuel, heads of
their father's house. *The sons* of Tola *were*
mighty men of valor in their generations; their
number in the days of David *was* twenty-two
thousand six hundred.
3 The son of Uzzi *was* Izrahiah, and the sons
of Izrahiah *were* Michael, Obadiah, Joel, and
Ishiah. All five of them *were* chief men.
4 And with them, by their generations, ac-
cording to their fathers' houses, *were* thirty-six
thousand troops ready for war; for they had
many wives and sons.
5 Now their brethren among all the families
of Issachar *were* mighty men of valor, listed
by their genealogies, eighty-seven thousand in
all.

The Family of Benjamin

6 *The sons* of Benjamin *were* Bela, Becher,
and Jediael—three *in all.*
7 The sons of Bela were Ezbon, Uzzi, Uzziel,
Jerimoth, and Iri—five *in all.* They *were* heads
of *their* fathers' houses, and they were listed
by their genealogies, twenty-two thousand and
thirty-four mighty men of valor.
8 The sons of Becher *were* Zemirah, Joash,
Eliezer, Elioenai, Omri, Jerimoth, Abijah, Ana-
thoth, and Alemeth. All these *are* the sons of
Becher.
9 And they were recorded by genealogy ac-
cording to their generations, heads of their fa-
thers' houses, twenty thousand two hundred
mighty men of valor.
10 The son of Jediael *was* Bilhan, and the
sons of Bilhan *were* Jeush, Benjamin, Ehud,
Chenaanah, Zethan, Tharshish, and Ahish-
ahar.
11 All these sons of Jediael *were* heads of their
fathers' houses; *there were* seventeen thou-
sand two hundred mighty men of valor fit to
go out for war *and* battle.
12 Shuppim and Huppim[a] *were* the sons of Ir,
and Hushim *was* the son of Aher.

The Family of Naphtali

13 The sons of Naphtali *were* Jahziel,[a] Guni,
Jezer, and Shallum,[b] the sons of Bilhah.

6:58 [a]Spelled *Holon* in Joshua 21:15 **6:59** [a]Spelled *Ain* in Joshua 21:16 **6:60** [a]Spelled *Almon* in Joshua 21:18
6:77 [a]Hebrew *Rimmono,* alternate spelling of *Rimmon;* see 4:32 **7:1** [a]Spelled *Puvah* in Genesis 46:13 **7:12** [a]Called
Hupham in Numbers 26:39 **7:13** [a]Spelled *Jahzeel* in Genesis 46:24 [b]Spelled *Shillem* in Genesis 46:24

The Family of Manasseh (West)

14 The descendants of Manasseh: his Syrian concubine bore him Machir the father of Gilead, the father of Asriel.[a]
15 Machir took as his wife *the sister* of Huppim and Shuppim,[a] whose name *was* Maachah. The name of *Gilead's* grandson[b] *was* Zelophehad,[c] but Zelophehad begot only daughters.
16 (Maachah the wife of Machir bore a son, and she called his name Peresh. The name of his brother *was* Sheresh, and his sons *were* Ulam and Rakem.
17 The son of Ulam *was* Bedan.) These *were* the descendants of Gilead the son of Machir, the son of Manasseh.
18 His sister Hammoleketh bore Ishhod, Abiezer, and Mahlah.
19 And the sons of Shemida were Ahian, Shechem, Likhi, and Aniam.

The Family of Ephraim

20 The sons of Ephraim *were* Shuthelah, Bered his son, Tahath his son, Eladah his son, Tahath his son,
21 Zabad his son, Shuthelah his son, and Ezer and Elead. The men of Gath who were born in *that* land killed *them* because they came down to take away their cattle.
22 Then Ephraim their father mourned many days, and his brethren came to comfort him.
23 And when he went in to his wife, she conceived and bore a son; and he called his name Beriah,[a] because tragedy had come upon his house.
24 Now his daughter *was* Sheerah, who built Lower and Upper Beth Horon and Uzzen Sheerah;
25 and Rephah *was* his son, *as well* as Resheph, and Telah his son, Tahan his son,
26 Laadan his son, Ammihud his son, Elishama his son,
27 Nun[a] his son, and Joshua his son.
28 Now their possessions and dwelling places *were* Bethel and its towns: to the east Naaran, to the west Gezer and its towns, and Shechem and its towns, as far as Ayyah[a] and its towns;
29 and by the borders of the children of Manasseh *were* Beth Shean and its towns, Taanach and its towns, Megiddo and its towns, Dor and its towns. In these dwelt the children of Joseph, the son of Israel.

The Family of Asher

30 The sons of Asher *were* Imnah, Ishvah, Ishvi, Beriah, and their sister Serah.
31 The sons of Beriah *were* Heber and Malchiel, who was the father of Birzaith.[a]
32 And Heber begot Japhlet, Shomer,[a] Hotham,[b] and their sister Shua.
33 The sons of Japhlet *were* Pasach, Bimhal, and Ashvath. These *were* the children of Japhlet.
34 The sons of Shemer *were* Ahi, Rohgah, Jehubbah, and Aram.
35 And the sons of his brother Helem *were* Zophah, Imna, Shelesh, and Amal.
36 The sons of Zophah *were* Suah, Harnepher, Shual, Beri, Imrah,
37 Bezer, Hod, Shamma, Shilshah, Jithran,[a] and Beera.
38 The sons of Jether *were* Jephunneh, Pispah, and Ara.
39 The sons of Ulla *were* Arah, Haniel, and Rizia.
40 All these *were* the children of Asher, heads of *their* fathers' houses, choice men, mighty men of valor, chief leaders. And they were recorded by genealogies among the army fit for battle; their number *was* twenty-six thousand.

The Family Tree of King Saul of Benjamin

8 Now Benjamin begot Bela his firstborn, Ashbel the second, Aharah[a] the third,
2 Nohah the fourth, and Rapha the fifth.
3 The sons of Bela *were* Addar,[a] Gera, Abihud,
4 Abishua, Naaman, Ahoah,
5 Gera, Shephuphan, and Huram.
6 These *are* the sons of Ehud, who were the heads of the fathers' *houses* of the inhabitants of Geba, and who forced them to move to Manahath:
7 Naaman, Ahijah, and Gera who forced them to move. He begot Uzza and Ahihud.
8 Also Shaharaim had children in the country of Moab, after he had sent away Hushim and Baara his wives.
9 By Hodesh his wife he begot Jobab, Zibia, Mesha, Malcam,
10 Jeuz, Sachiah, and Mirmah. These *were* his sons, heads of their fathers' *houses*.
11 And by Hushim he begot Abitub and Elpaal.
12 The sons of Elpaal *were* Eber, Misham, and Shemed, who built Ono and Lod with its towns;
13 and Beriah and Shema, who *were* heads of their fathers' *houses* of the inhabitants of Aijalon, who drove out the inhabitants of Gath.
14 Ahio, Shashak, Jeremoth,
15 Zebadiah, Arad, Eder,
16 Michael, Ispah, and Joha *were* the sons of Beriah.
17 Zebadiah, Meshullam, Hizki, Heber,
18 Ishmerai, Jizliah, and Jobab *were* the sons of Elpaal.
19 Jakim, Zichri, Zabdi,
20 Elienai, Zillethai, Eliel,
21 Adaiah, Beraiah, and Shimrath *were* the sons of Shimei.
22 Ishpan, Eber, Eliel,
23 Abdon, Zichri, Hanan,
24 Hananiah, Elam, Antothijah,
25 Iphdeiah, and Penuel *were* the sons of Shashak.
26 Shamsherai, Shehariah, Athaliah,
27 Jaareshiah, Elijah, and Zichri *were* the sons of Jeroham.
28 These *were* heads of the fathers' *houses* by their generations, chief men. These dwelt in Jerusalem.
29 Now the father of Gibeon, whose wife's name *was* Maacah, dwelt at Gibeon.
30 And his firstborn son *was* Abdon, then Zur, Kish, Baal, Nadab,
31 Gedor, Ahio, Zecher,

7:14 [a]The son of Gilead (compare Numbers 26:30, 31) **7:15** [a]Compare verse 12 [b]Literally *the second* [c]Compare Numbers 26:30–33 **7:23** [a]Literally *In Tragedy* **7:27** [a]Hebrew *Non* **7:28** [a]Many Hebrew manuscripts, Bomberg, Septuagint, Targum, and Vulgate read *Gazza.* **7:31** [a]Or *Birzavith* or *Birzoth* **7:32** [a]Spelled *Shemer* in verse 34 [b]Spelled *Helem* in verse 35 **7:37** [a]Spelled *Jether* in verse 38 **8:1** [a]Spelled *Ahiram* in Numbers 26:38 **8:3** [a]Called *Ard* in Numbers 26:40

32 and Mikloth, *who* begot Shimeah.[a] They
also dwelt alongside their relatives in Jerusa-
lem, with their brethren.
33 Ner[a] begot Kish, Kish begot Saul, and Saul
begot Jonathan, Malchishua, Abinadab,[b] and
Esh-Baal.[c]
34 The son of Jonathan *was* Merib-Baal,[a] and
Merib-Baal begot Micah.
35 The sons of Micah *were* Pithon, Melech, Ta-
rea, and Ahaz.
36 And Ahaz begot Jehoaddah;[a] Jehoaddah
begot Alemeth, Azmaveth, and Zimri; and
Zimri begot Moza.
37 Moza begot Binea, Raphah[a] his son, Elea-
sah his son, *and* Azel his son.
38 Azel had six sons whose names *were* these:
Azrikam, Bocheru, Ishmael, Sheariah, Oba-
diah, and Hanan. All these *were* the sons of Azel.
39 And the sons of Eshek his brother *were*
Ulam his firstborn, Jeush the second, and
Eliphelet the third.
40 The sons of Ulam were mighty men of
valor—archers. *They* had many sons and grand-
sons, one hundred and fifty *in all.* These *were*
all sons of Benjamin.

9 So all Israel was recorded by genealogies,
and indeed, they *were* inscribed in the book
of the kings of Israel. But Judah was carried
away captive to Babylon because of their un-
faithfulness.
2 And the first inhabitants who *dwelt* in
their possessions in their cities *were* Israelites,
priests, Levites, and the Nethinim.

Dwellers in Jerusalem

3 Now in Jerusalem the children of Judah
dwelt, and some of the children of Benjamin,
and of the children of Ephraim and Manasseh:
4 Uthai the son of Ammihud, the son of Omri,
the son of Imri, the son of Bani, of the descen-
dants of Perez, the son of Judah.
5 Of the Shilonites: Asaiah the firstborn and
his sons.
6 Of the sons of Zerah: Jeuel, and their breth-
ren—six hundred and ninety.
7 Of the sons of Benjamin: Sallu the son of
Meshullam, the son of Hodaviah, the son of Has-
senuah;
8 Ibneiah the son of Jeroham; Elah the son
of Uzzi, the son of Michri; Meshullam the son
of Shephatiah, the son of Reuel, the son of Ib-
nijah;
9 and their brethren, according to their gen-
erations—nine hundred and fifty-six. All these
men *were* heads of a father's *house* in their fa-
thers' houses.

The Priests at Jerusalem

10 Of the priests: Jedaiah, Jehoiarib, and Ja-
chin;
11 Azariah the son of Hilkiah, the son of Me-
shullam, the son of Zadok, the son of Meraioth,
the son of Ahitub, the officer over the house of
God;
12 Adaiah the son of Jeroham, the son of
Pashur, the son of Malchijah; Maasai the son
of Adiel, the son of Jahzerah, the son of Me-
shullam, the son of Meshillemith, the son of
Immer;
13 and their brethren, heads of their fathers'
houses—one thousand seven hundred and
sixty. *They were* very able men for the work of
the service of the house of God.

The Levites at Jerusalem

14 Of the Levites: Shemaiah the son of Has-
shub, the son of Azrikam, the son of Hashabiah,
of the sons of Merari;
15 Bakbakkar, Heresh, Galal, and Mattaniah
the son of Micah, the son of Zichri, the son of
Asaph;
16 Obadiah the son of Shemaiah, the son of
Galal, the son of Jeduthun; and Berechiah the
son of Asa, the son of Elkanah, who lived in
the villages of the Netophathites.

The Levite Gatekeepers

17 And the gatekeepers *were* Shallum, Ak-
kub, Talmon, Ahiman, and their brethren.
Shallum *was* the chief.
18 Until then *they had been* gatekeepers for
the camps of the children of Levi at the King's
Gate on the east.
19 Shallum the son of Kore, the son of Ebia-
saph, the son of Korah, and his brethren, from
his father's house, the Korahites, *were* in charge
of the work of the service, gatekeepers of the
tabernacle. Their fathers had been keepers of
the entrance to the camp of the LORD.
20 And Phinehas the son of Eleazar had been
the officer over them in time past; the LORD *was*
with him.
21 Zechariah the son of Meshelemiah *was*
keeper of the door of the tabernacle of meeting.
22 All those chosen as gatekeepers *were* two
hundred and twelve. They were recorded by
their genealogy, in their villages. David and
Samuel the seer had appointed them to their
trusted office.
23 So they and their children *were* in charge
of the gates of the house of the LORD, the house
of the tabernacle, by assignment.
24 The gatekeepers were assigned to the four
directions: the east, west, north, and south.
25 And their brethren in their villages *had* to
come with them from time to time for seven
days.
26 For in this trusted office *were* four chief
gatekeepers; they were Levites. And they had
charge over the chambers and treasuries of the
house of God.
27 And they lodged *all* around the house of
God because they *had* the responsibility, and
they *were* in charge of opening *it* every morning.

Other Levite Responsibilities

28 Now *some* of them were in charge of the
serving vessels, for they brought them in and
took them out by count.
29 *Some* of them *were* appointed over the fur-
nishings and over all the implements of the
sanctuary, and over the fine flour and the wine
and the oil and the incense and the spices.
30 And *some* of the sons of the priests made
the ointment of the spices.
31 Mattithiah of the Levites, the firstborn of
Shallum the Korahite, had the trusted office
over the things that were baked in the pans.
32 And some of their brethren of the sons of

8:32 [a]Spelled *Shimeam* in 9:38 **8:33** [a]Also the son of Gibeon (compare 9:36, 39) [b]Called *Jishui* in 1 Samuel 14:49 [c]Called *Ishbosheth* in 2 Samuel 2:8 and elsewhere **8:34** [a]Called *Mephibosheth* in 2 Samuel 4:4 **8:36** [a]Spelled *Jarah* in 9:42 **8:37** [a]Spelled *Rephaiah* in 9:43

the Kohathites *were* in charge of preparing the showbread for every Sabbath.

33 These are the singers, heads of the fathers' *houses* of the Levites, *who lodged* in the chambers, *and were* free *from other duties;* for they were employed in *that* work day and night.

34 These heads of the fathers' *houses* of the Levites *were* heads throughout their generations. They dwelt at Jerusalem.

The Family of King Saul

35 Jeiel the father of Gibeon, whose wife's name *was* Maacah, dwelt at Gibeon.

36 His firstborn son *was* Abdon, then Zur, Kish, Baal, Ner, Nadab,

37 Gedor, Ahio, Zechariah,[a] and Mikloth.

38 And Mikloth begot Shimeam.[a] They also dwelt alongside their relatives in Jerusalem, with their brethren.

39 Ner begot Kish, Kish begot Saul, and Saul begot Jonathan, Malchishua, Abinadab, and Esh-Baal.

40 The son of Jonathan *was* Merib-Baal, and Merib-Baal begot Micah.

41 The sons of Micah *were* Pithon, Melech, Tahrea,[a] and Ahaz.[b]

42 And Ahaz begot Jarah;[a] Jarah begot Alemeth, Azmaveth, and Zimri; and Zimri begot Moza;

43 Moza begot Binea, Rephaiah[a] his son, Eleasah his son, and Azel his son.

44 And Azel had six sons whose names *were* these: Azrikam, Bocheru, Ishmael, Sheariah, Obadiah, and Hanan; these *were* the sons of Azel.

Tragic End of Saul and His Sons

10 Now the Philistines fought against Israel; and the men of Israel fled from before the Philistines, and fell slain on Mount Gilboa.

2 Then the Philistines followed hard after Saul and his sons. And the Philistines killed Jonathan, Abinadab, and Malchishua, Saul's sons.

3 The battle became fierce against Saul. The archers hit him, and he was wounded by the archers.

4 Then Saul said to his armorbearer, "Draw your sword, and thrust me through with it, lest these uncircumcised men come and abuse me." But his armorbearer would not, for he was greatly afraid. Therefore Saul took a sword and fell on it.

5 And when his armorbearer saw that Saul was dead, he also fell on his sword and died.

6 So Saul and his three sons died, and all his house died together.

7 And when all the men of Israel who *were* in the valley saw that they had fled and that Saul and his sons were dead, they forsook their cities and fled; then the Philistines came and dwelt in them.

8 So it happened the next day, when the Philistines came to strip the slain, that they found Saul and his sons fallen on Mount Gilboa.

9 And they stripped him and took his head and his armor, and sent word throughout the land of the Philistines to proclaim the news *in the temple* of their idols and among the people.

10 Then they put his armor in the temple of their gods, and fastened his head in the temple of Dagon.

11 And when all Jabesh Gilead heard all that the Philistines had done to Saul,

12 all the valiant men arose and took the body of Saul and the bodies of his sons; and they brought them to Jabesh, and buried their bones under the tamarisk tree at Jabesh, and fasted seven days.

13 So Saul died for his unfaithfulness which he had committed against the LORD, because he did not keep the word of the LORD, and also because he consulted a medium for guidance.

14 But *he* did not inquire of the LORD; therefore He killed him, and turned the kingdom over to David the son of Jesse.

David Made King over All Israel

11 Then all Israel came together to David at Hebron, saying, "Indeed we *are* your bone and your flesh.

2 "Also, in time past, even when Saul was king, you *were* the one who led Israel out and brought them in; and the LORD your God said to you, 'You shall shepherd My people Israel, and be ruler over My people Israel.' "

3 Therefore all the elders of Israel came to the king at Hebron, and David made a covenant with them at Hebron before the LORD. And they anointed David king over Israel, according to the word of the LORD by Samuel.

The City of David

4 And David and all Israel went to Jerusalem, which is Jebus, where the Jebusites *were*, the inhabitants of the land.

5 But the inhabitants of Jebus said to David, "You shall not come in here!" Nevertheless David took the stronghold of Zion (that is, the City of David).

6 Now David said, "Whoever attacks the Jebusites first shall be chief and captain." And Joab the son of Zeruiah went up first, and became chief.

7 Then David dwelt in the stronghold; therefore they called it the City of David.

8 And he built the city around it, from the Millo[a] to the surrounding area. Joab repaired the rest of the city.

9 So David went on and became great, and the LORD of hosts *was* with him.

The Mighty Men of David

10 Now these *were* the heads of the mighty men whom David had, who strengthened themselves with him in his kingdom, with all Israel, to make him king, according to the word of the LORD concerning Israel.

11 And this *is* the number of the mighty men whom David had: Jashobeam the son of a Hachmonite, chief of the captains;[a] he had lifted up his spear against three hundred, killed *by him* at one time.

12 After him *was* Eleazar the son of Dodo, the Ahohite, who *was one* of the three mighty men.

13 He was with David at Pasdammim. Now there the Philistines were gathered for battle, and there was a piece of ground full of barley. So the people fled from the Philistines.

14 But they stationed themselves in the mid-

9:37 [a]Called *Zecher* in 8:31 **9:38** [a]Spelled *Shimeah* in 8:32 **9:41** [a]Spelled *Tarea* in 8:35 [b]Following Arabic, Syriac, Targum, and Vulgate (compare 8:35); Masoretic Text and Septuagint omit *and Ahaz.* **9:42** [a]Spelled *Jehoaddah* in 8:36 **9:43** [a]Spelled *Raphah* in 8:37 **11:8** [a]Literally *The Landfill* **11:11** [a]Following Qere; Kethib, Septuagint, and Vulgate read *the thirty* (compare 2 Samuel 23:8).

dle of *that* field, defended it, and killed the Philistines. So the LORD brought about a great victory.
15 Now three of the thirty chief men went down to the rock to David, into the cave of Adullam; and the army of the Philistines encamped in the Valley of Rephaim.
16 David *was* then in the stronghold, and the garrison of the Philistines *was* then in Bethlehem.
17 And David said with longing, "Oh, that someone would give me a drink of water from the well of Bethlehem, which is by the gate!"
18 So the three broke through the camp of the Philistines, drew water from the well of Bethlehem that *was* by the gate, and took *it* and brought *it* to David. Nevertheless David would not drink it, but poured it out to the LORD.
19 And he said, "Far be it from me, O my God, that I should do this! Shall I drink the blood of these men *who have put* their lives *in jeopardy*? For at the risk of their lives they brought it." Therefore he would not drink it. These things were done by the three mighty men.
20 Abishai the brother of Joab was chief of *another* three.[a] He had lifted up his spear against three hundred *men*, killed *them*, and won a name among *these* three.
21 Of the three he was more honored than the other two men. Therefore he became their captain. However he did not attain to the *first* three.
22 Benaiah was the son of Jehoiada, the son of a valiant man from Kabzeel, who had done many deeds. He had killed two lion-like heroes of Moab. He also had gone down and killed a lion in the midst of a pit on a snowy day.
23 And he killed an Egyptian, a man of *great* height, five cubits tall. In the Egyptian's hand *there was* a spear like a weaver's beam; and he went down to him with a staff, wrested the spear out of the Egyptian's hand, and killed him with his own spear.
24 These *things* Benaiah the son of Jehoiada did, and won a name among three mighty men.
25 Indeed he was more honored than the thirty, but he did not attain to the *first* three. And David appointed him over his guard.
26 Also the mighty warriors *were* Asahel the brother of Joab, Elhanan the son of Dodo of Bethlehem,
27 Shammoth the Harorite,[a] Helez the Pelonite,[b]
28 Ira the son of Ikkesh the Tekoite, Abiezer the Anathothite,
29 Sibbechai the Hushathite, Ilai the Ahohite,
30 Maharai the Netophathite, Heled[a] the son of Baanah the Netophathite,
31 Ithai[a] the son of Ribai of Gibeah, of the sons of Benjamin, Benaiah the Pirathonite,
32 Hurai[a] of the brooks of Gaash, Abiel[b] the Arbathite,
33 Azmaveth the Baharumite,[a] Eliahba the Shaalbonite,
34 the sons of Hashem the Gizonite, Jonathan the son of Shageh the Hararite,
35 Ahiam the son of Sacar the Hararite, Eliphal the son of Ur,
36 Hepher the Mecherathite, Ahijah the Pelonite,
37 Hezro the Carmelite, Naarai the son of Ezbai,
38 Joel the brother of Nathan, Mibhar the son of Hagri,
39 Zelek the Ammonite, Naharai the Berothite[a] (the armorbearer of Joab the son of Zeruiah),
40 Ira the Ithrite, Gareb the Ithrite,
41 Uriah the Hittite, Zabad the son of Ahlai,
42 Adina the son of Shiza the Reubenite (a chief of the Reubenites) and thirty with him,
43 Hanan the son of Maachah, Joshaphat the Mithnite,
44 Uzzia the Ashterathite, Shama and Jeiel the sons of Hotham the Aroerite,
45 Jediael the son of Shimri, and Joha his brother, the Tizite,
46 Eliel the Mahavite, Jeribai and Joshaviah the sons of Elnaam, Ithmah the Moabite,
47 Eliel, Obed, and Jaasiel the Mezobaite.

The Growth of David's Army

12 Now these *were* the men who came to David at Ziklag while he was still a fugitive from Saul the son of Kish; and they *were* among the mighty men, helpers in the war,
2 armed with bows, using both the right hand and the left in *hurling* stones and *shooting* arrows with the bow. *They were* of Benjamin, Saul's brethren.
3 The chief *was* Ahiezer, then Joash, the sons of Shemaah the Gibeathite; Jeziel and Pelet the sons of Azmaveth; Berachah, and Jehu the Anathothite;
4 Ishmaiah the Gibeonite, a mighty man among the thirty, and over the thirty; Jeremiah, Jahaziel, Johanan, and Jozabad the Gederathite;
5 Eluzai, Jerimoth, Bealiah, Shemariah, and Shephatiah the Haruphite;
6 Elkanah, Jisshiah, Azarel, Joezer, and Jashobeam, the Korahites;
7 and Joelah and Zebadiah the sons of Jeroham of Gedor.
8 *Some* Gadites joined David at the stronghold in the wilderness, mighty men of valor, men trained for battle, who could handle shield and spear, whose faces *were like* the faces of lions, and *were* as swift as gazelles on the mountains:
9 Ezer the first, Obadiah the second, Eliab the third,
10 Mishmannah the fourth, Jeremiah the fifth,
11 Attai the sixth, Eliel the seventh,
12 Johanan the eighth, Elzabad the ninth,
13 Jeremiah the tenth, and Machbanai the eleventh.
14 These *were* from the sons of Gad, captains of the army; the least was over a hundred, and the greatest was over a thousand.
15 These *are* the ones who crossed the Jordan in the first month, when it had overflowed all its banks; and they put to flight all *those* in the valleys, to the east and to the west.
16 Then some of the sons of Benjamin and Judah came to David at the stronghold.
17 And David went out to meet them, and answered and said to them, "If you have come peaceably to me to help me, my heart will be united with you; but if to betray me to my enemies, since *there is* no wrong in my hands,

11:20 [a]Following Masoretic Text, Septuagint, and Vulgate; Syriac reads *thirty*. **11:27** [a]Spelled *Harodite* in 2 Samuel 23:25 [b]Called *Paltite* in 2 Samuel 23:26 **11:30** [a]Spelled *Heleb* in 2 Samuel 23:29 and *Heldai* in 1 Chronicles 27:15 **11:31** [a]Spelled *Ittai* in 2 Samuel 23:29 **11:32** [a]Spelled *Hiddai* in 2 Samuel 23:30 [b]Spelled *Abi-Albon* in 2 Samuel 23:31 **11:33** [a]Spelled *Barhumite* in 2 Samuel 23:31 **11:39** [a]Spelled *Beerothite* in 2 Samuel 23:37

may the God of our fathers look and bring judgment."
18 Then the Spirit came upon Amasai, chief of the captains, *and he said:*

"*We are* yours, O David;
We *are* on your side, O son of Jesse!
Peace, peace to you,
And peace to your helpers!
For your God helps you."

So David received them, and made them captains of the troop.
19 And *some* from Manasseh defected to David when he was going with the Philistines to battle against Saul; but they did not help them, for the lords of the Philistines sent him away by agreement, saying, "He may defect to his master Saul *and endanger* our heads."
20 When he went to Ziklag, those of Manasseh who defected to him were Adnah, Jozabad, Jediael, Michael, Jozabad, Elihu, and Zillethai, captains of the thousands who *were* from Manasseh.
21 And they helped David against the bands *of raiders*, for they *were* all mighty men of valor, and they were captains in the army.
22 For at *that* time they came to David day by day to help him, until *it was* a great army, like the army of God.

David's Army at Hebron

23 Now these *were* the numbers of the divisions *that were* equipped for war, *and* came to David at Hebron to turn *over* the kingdom of Saul to him, according to the word of the LORD:
24 of the sons of Judah bearing shield and spear, six thousand eight hundred armed for war;
25 of the sons of Simeon, mighty men of valor fit for war, seven thousand one hundred;
26 of the sons of Levi four thousand six hundred;
27 Jehoiada, the leader of the Aaronites, and with him three thousand seven hundred;
28 Zadok, a young man, a valiant warrior, and from his father's house twenty-two captains;
29 of the sons of Benjamin, relatives of Saul, three thousand (until then the greatest part of them had remained loyal to the house of Saul);
30 of the sons of Ephraim twenty thousand eight hundred, mighty men of valor, famous men throughout their father's house;
31 of the half-tribe of Manasseh eighteen thousand, who were designated by name to come and make David king;
32 of the sons of Issachar who had understanding of the times, to know what Israel ought to do, their chiefs were two hundred; and all their brethren were at their command;
33 of Zebulun there were fifty thousand who went out to battle, expert in war with all weapons of war, stouthearted men who could keep ranks;
34 of Naphtali one thousand captains, and with them thirty-seven thousand with shield and spear;
35 of the Danites who could keep battle formation, twenty-eight thousand six hundred;
36 of Asher, those who could go out to war, able to keep battle formation, forty thousand;
37 of the Reubenites and the Gadites and the half-tribe of Manasseh, from the other side of the Jordan, one hundred and twenty thousand armed for battle with every *kind* of weapon of war.
38 All these men of war, who could keep ranks, came to Hebron with a loyal heart, to make David king over all Israel; and all the rest of Israel *were* of one mind to make David king.
39 And they were there with David three days, eating and drinking, for their brethren had prepared for them.
40 Moreover those who were near to them, from as far away as Issachar and Zebulun and Naphtali, were bringing food on donkeys and camels, on mules and oxen—provisions of flour and cakes of figs and cakes of raisins, wine and oil and oxen and sheep abundantly, for *there was* joy in Israel.

The Ark Brought from Kirjath Jearim

13 Then David consulted with the captains of thousands and hundreds, *and* with every leader.
2 And David said to all the assembly of Israel, "If *it seems* good to you, and if it is of the LORD our God, let us send out to our brethren everywhere *who are* left in all the land of Israel, and with them to the priests and Levites *who are* in their cities *and* their common-lands, that they may gather together to us;
3 "and let us bring the ark of our God back to us, for we have not inquired at it since the days of Saul."
4 Then all the assembly said that they would do so, for the thing was right in the eyes of all the people.
5 So David gathered all Israel together, from Shihor in Egypt to as far as the entrance of Hamath, to bring the ark of God from Kirjath Jearim.
6 And David and all Israel went up to Baalah,[a] to Kirjath Jearim, which belonged to Judah, to bring up from there the ark of God the LORD, who dwells *between* the cherubim, where *His* name is proclaimed.
7 So they carried the ark of God on a new cart from the house of Abinadab, and Uzza and Ahio drove the cart.
8 Then David and all Israel played *music* before God with all *their* might, with singing, on harps, on stringed instruments, on tambourines, on cymbals, and with trumpets.
9 And when they came to Chidon's[a] threshing floor, Uzza put out his hand to hold the ark, for the oxen stumbled.
10 Then the anger of the LORD was aroused against Uzza, and He struck him because he put his hand to the ark; and he died there before God.
11 And David became angry because of the LORD's outbreak against Uzza; therefore that place is called Perez Uzza[a] to this day.
12 David was afraid of God that day, saying, "How can I bring the ark of God to me?"
13 So David would not move the ark with him into the City of David, but took it aside into the house of Obed-Edom the Gittite.
14 The ark of God remained with the family of Obed-Edom in his house three months. And the LORD blessed the house of Obed-Edom and all that he had.

13:6 [a]Called *Baale Judah* in 2 Samuel 6:2 **13:9** [a]Called *Nachon* in 2 Samuel 6:6 **13:11** [a]Literally *Outburst Against Uzza*

David Established at Jerusalem

14 Now Hiram king of Tyre sent messen-
gers to David, and cedar trees, with ma-
sons and carpenters, to build him a house.
2 So David knew that the LORD had estab-
lished him as king over Israel, for his kingdom
was highly exalted for the sake of His people
Israel.
3 Then David took more wives in Jerusalem,
and David begot more sons and daughters.
4 And these are the names of his children
whom he had in Jerusalem: Shammua,[a] Shobab,
Nathan, Solomon,
5 Ibhar, Elishua,[a] Elpelet,[b]
6 Nogah, Nepheg, Japhia,
7 Elishama, Beeliada,[a] and Eliphelet.

The Philistines Defeated

8 Now when the Philistines heard that David
had been anointed king over all Israel, all the
Philistines went up to search for David. And
David heard *of it* and went out against them.
9 Then the Philistines went and made a raid
on the Valley of Rephaim.
10 And David inquired of God, saying, "Shall
I go up against the Philistines? Will You deliver
them into my hand?" The LORD said to him,
"Go up, for I will deliver them into your hand."
11 So they went up to Baal Perazim, and Da-
vid defeated them there. Then David said, "God
has broken through my enemies by my hand
like a breakthrough of water." Therefore they
called the name of that place Baal Perazim.[a]
12 And when they left their gods there, David
gave a commandment, and they were burned
with fire.
13 Then the Philistines once again made a raid
on the valley.
14 Therefore David inquired again of God,
and God said to him, "You shall not go up after
them; circle around them, and come upon them
in front of the mulberry trees.
15 "And it shall be, when you hear a sound of
marching in the tops of the mulberry trees,
then you shall go out to battle, for God has gone
out before you to strike the camp of the Philis-
tines."
16 So David did as God commanded him, and
they drove back the army of the Philistines from
Gibeon as far as Gezer.
17 Then the fame of David went out into all
lands, and the LORD brought the fear of him
upon all nations.

The Ark Brought to Jerusalem

15 *David* built houses for himself in the
City of David; and he prepared a place
for the ark of God, and pitched a tent for it.
2 Then David said, "No one may carry the
ark of God but the Levites, for the LORD has
chosen them to carry the ark of God and to min-
ister before Him forever."
3 And David gathered all Israel together at
Jerusalem, to bring up the ark of the LORD to
its place, which he had prepared for it.
4 Then David assembled the children of
Aaron and the Levites:
5 of the sons of Kohath, Uriel the chief, and
one hundred and twenty of his brethren;
6 of the sons of Merari, Asaiah the chief, and
two hundred and twenty of his brethren;
7 of the sons of Gershom, Joel the chief, and
one hundred and thirty of his brethren;
8 of the sons of Elizaphan, Shemaiah the
chief, and two hundred of his brethren;
9 of the sons of Hebron, Eliel the chief, and
eighty of his brethren;
10 of the sons of Uzziel, Amminadab the chief,
and one hundred and twelve of his brethren.
11 And David called for Zadok and Abiathar
the priests, and for the Levites: for Uriel, Asa-
iah, Joel, Shemaiah, Eliel, and Amminadab.
12 He said to them, "You *are* the heads of the
fathers' *houses* of the Levites; sanctify your-
selves, you and your brethren, that you may
bring up the ark of the LORD God of Israel to
the place I have prepared for it.
13 "For because you *did* not *do it* the first *time,*
the LORD our God broke out against us, be-
cause we did not consult Him about the proper
order."
14 So the priests and the Levites sanctified
themselves to bring up the ark of the LORD God
of Israel.
15 And the children of the Levites bore the ark
of God on their shoulders, by its poles, as Mo-
ses had commanded according to the word of
the LORD.
16 Then David spoke to the leaders of the Le-
vites to appoint their brethren *to be* the singers
accompanied by instruments of music, stringed
instruments, harps, and cymbals, by raising the
voice with resounding joy.
17 So the Levites appointed Heman the son
of Joel; and of his brethren, Asaph the son of
Berechiah; and of their brethren, the sons of
Merari, Ethan the son of Kushaiah;
18 and with them their brethren of the second
rank: Zechariah, Ben,[a] Jaaziel, Shemiramoth,
Jehiel, Unni, Eliab, Benaiah, Maaseiah, Matti-
thiah, Elipheleh, Mikneiah, Obed-Edom, and Je-
iel, the gatekeepers;
19 the singers, Heman, Asaph, and Ethan,
were to sound the cymbals of bronze;
20 Zechariah, Aziel, Shemiramoth, Jehiel,
Unni, Eliab, Maaseiah, and Benaiah, with strings
according to Alamoth;
21 Mattithiah, Elipheleh, Mikneiah, Obed-
Edom, Jeiel, and Azaziah, to direct with harps
on the Sheminith;
22 Chenaniah, leader of the Levites, was in-
structor *in charge of* the music, because he *was*
skillful;
23 Berechiah and Elkanah *were* doorkeepers
for the ark;
24 Shebaniah, Joshaphat, Nethanel, Amasai,
Zechariah, Benaiah, and Eliezer, the priests,
were to blow the trumpets before the ark of God;
and Obed-Edom and Jehiah, doorkeepers for
the ark.
25 So David, the elders of Israel, and the cap-
tains over thousands went to bring up the ark
of the covenant of the LORD from the house of
Obed-Edom with joy.
26 And so it was, when God helped the Le-
vites who bore the ark of the covenant of the
LORD, that they offered seven bulls and seven
rams.
27 David was clothed with a robe of fine linen,
as were all the Levites who bore the ark, the
singers, and Chenaniah the music master *with*
the singers. David also wore a linen ephod.

14:4 [a]Spelled *Shimea* in 3:5 **14:5** [a]Spelled *Elishama* in 3:6 [b]Spelled *Eliphelet* in 3:6 **14:7** [a]Spelled *Eliada* in 3:8
14:11 [a]Literally *Master of Breakthroughs* **15:18** [a]Following Masoretic Text and Vulgate; Septuagint omits *Ben.*

28 Thus all Israel brought up the ark of the cov-
enant of the LORD with shouting and with the
sound of the horn, with trumpets and with
cymbals, making music with stringed instru-
ments and harps.
29 And it happened, *as* the ark of the covenant
of the LORD came to the City of David, that
Michal, Saul's daughter, looked through a win-
dow and saw King David whirling and playing
music; and she despised him in her heart.

The Ark Placed in the Tabernacle

16 So they brought the ark of God, and set
it in the midst of the tabernacle that Da-
vid had erected for it. Then they offered burnt
offerings and peace offerings before God.
2 And when David had finished offering the
burnt offerings and the peace offerings, he
blessed the people in the name of the LORD.
3 Then he distributed to everyone of Israel,
both man and woman, to everyone a loaf of
bread, a piece *of meat*, and a cake of raisins.
4 And he appointed some of the Levites to min-
ister before the ark of the LORD, to commemo-
rate, to thank, and to praise the LORD God of
Israel:
5 Asaph the chief, and next to him Zechariah,
then Jeiel, Shemiramoth, Jehiel, Mattithiah,
Eliab, Benaiah, and Obed-Edom: Jeiel with
stringed instruments and harps, but Asaph made
music with cymbals;
6 Benaiah and Jahaziel the priests regularly
blew the trumpets before the ark of the cov-
enant of God.

David's Song of Thanksgiving

7 On that day David first delivered *this
psalm* into the hand of Asaph and his brethren,
to thank the LORD:

8 Oh, give thanks to the LORD!
Call upon His name;
Make known His deeds among the peoples!
9 Sing to Him, sing psalms to Him;
Talk of all His wondrous works!
10 Glory in His holy name;
Let the hearts of those rejoice who seek the LORD!
11 Seek the LORD and His strength;
Seek His face evermore!
12 Remember His marvelous works which He has done,
His wonders, and the judgments of His mouth,
13 O seed of Israel His servant,
You children of Jacob, His chosen ones!

14 He *is* the LORD our God;
His judgments *are* in all the earth.
15 Remember His covenant forever,
The word which He commanded, for a thousand generations,
16 *The covenant which* He made with Abraham,
And His oath to Isaac,
17 And confirmed it to Jacob for a statute,
To Israel *for* an everlasting covenant,
18 Saying, "To you I will give the land of Canaan
As the allotment of your inheritance,"
19 When you were few in number,
Indeed very few, and strangers in it.
20 When they went from one nation to another,
And from *one* kingdom to another people,
21 He permitted no man to do them wrong;
Yes, He rebuked kings for their sakes,
22 *Saying*, "Do not touch My anointed ones,
And do My prophets no harm."[a]

23 Sing to the LORD, all the earth;
Proclaim the good news of His salvation from day to day.
24 Declare His glory among the nations,
His wonders among all peoples.
25 For the LORD *is* great and greatly to be praised;
He *is* also to be feared above all gods.
26 For all the gods of the peoples *are* idols,
But the LORD made the heavens.
27 Honor and majesty *are* before Him;
Strength and gladness are in His place.

28 Give to the LORD, O families of the peoples,
Give to the LORD glory and strength.
29 Give to the LORD the glory *due* His name;
Bring an offering, and come before Him.
Oh, worship the LORD in the beauty of holiness!
30 Tremble before Him, all the earth.
The world also is firmly established,
It shall not be moved.

31 Let the heavens rejoice, and let the earth be glad;
And let them say among the nations,
"The LORD reigns."
32 Let the sea roar, and all its fullness;
Let the field rejoice, and all that *is* in it.
33 Then the trees of the woods shall rejoice before the LORD,
For He is coming to judge the earth.[a]

34 Oh, give thanks to the LORD, for *He is* good!
For His mercy *endures* forever.[a]
35 And say, "Save us, O God of our salvation;
Gather us together, and deliver us from the Gentiles,
To give thanks to Your holy name,
To triumph in Your praise."

36 Blessed *be* the LORD God of Israel
From everlasting to everlasting![a]

And all the people said, "Amen!" and praised
the LORD.

Regular Worship Maintained

37 So he left Asaph and his brothers there be-
fore the ark of the covenant of the LORD to min-
ister before the ark regularly, as every day's
work required;
38 and Obed-Edom with his sixty-eight breth-
ren, including Obed-Edom the son of Jedu-
thun, and Hosah, *to be* gatekeepers;
39 and Zadok the priest and his brethren the
priests, before the tabernacle of the LORD at
the high place that *was* at Gibeon,
40 to offer burnt offerings to the LORD on the
altar of burnt offering regularly morning and
evening, and *to do* according to all that is writ-

16:22 [a]Compare verses 8–22 with Psalm 105:1–15 **16:33** [a]Compare verses 23–33 with Psalm 96:1–13
16:34 [a]Compare verse 34 with Psalm 106:1 **16:36** [a]Compare verses 35, 36 with Psalm 106:47, 48

ten in the Law of the LORD which He commanded Israel;
41 and with them Heman and Jeduthun and the rest who were chosen, who were designated by name, to give thanks to the LORD, because His mercy *endures* forever;
42 and with them Heman and Jeduthun, to sound aloud with trumpets and cymbals and the musical instruments of God. Now the sons of Jeduthun *were* gatekeepers.
43 Then all the people departed, every man to his house; and David returned to bless his house.

God's Covenant with David

17 Now it came to pass, when David was dwelling in his house, that David said to Nathan the prophet, "See now, I dwell in a house of cedar, but the ark of the covenant of the LORD *is* under tent curtains."
2 Then Nathan said to David, "Do all that *is* in your heart, for God *is* with you."
3 But it happened that night that the word of God came to Nathan, saying,
4 "Go and tell My servant David, 'Thus says the LORD: "You shall not build Me a house to dwell in.
5 "For I have not dwelt in a house since the time that I brought up Israel, even to this day, but have gone from tent to tent, and from *one* tabernacle *to another.*
6 "Wherever I have moved about with all Israel, have I ever spoken a word to any of the judges of Israel, whom I commanded to shepherd My people, saying, 'Why have you not built Me a house of cedar?' " '
7 "Now therefore, thus shall you say to My servant David, 'Thus says the LORD of hosts: "I took you from the sheepfold, from following the sheep, to be ruler over My people Israel.
8 "And I have been with you wherever you have gone, and have cut off all your enemies from before you, and have made you a name like the name of the great men who *are* on the earth.
9 "Moreover I will appoint a place for My people Israel, and will plant them, that they may dwell in a place of their own and move no more; nor shall the sons of wickedness oppress them anymore, as previously,
10 "since the time that I commanded judges *to be* over My people Israel. Also I will subdue all your enemies. Furthermore I tell you that the LORD will build you a house.[a]
11 "And it shall be, when your days are fulfilled, when you must go *to be* with your fathers, that I will set up your seed after you, who will be of your sons; and I will establish his kingdom.
12 "He shall build Me a house, and I will establish his throne forever.
13 "I will be his Father, and he shall be My son; and I will not take My mercy away from him, as I took *it* from *him* who was before you.
14 "And I will establish him in My house and in My kingdom forever; and his throne shall be established forever." ' "
15 According to all these words and according to all this vision, so Nathan spoke to David.
16 Then King David went in and sat before the LORD; and he said: "Who *am* I, O LORD God? And what is my house, that You have brought me this far?
17 "And *yet* this was a small thing in Your sight, O God; and You have *also* spoken of Your servant's house for a great while to come, and have regarded me according to the rank of a man of high degree, O LORD God.
18 "What more can David *say* to You for the honor of Your servant? For You know Your servant.
19 "O LORD, for Your servant's sake, and according to Your own heart, You have done all this greatness, in making known all these great things.
20 "O LORD, *there is* none like You, nor *is there any* God besides You, according to all that we have heard with our ears.
21 "And who *is* like Your people Israel, the one nation on the earth whom God went to redeem for Himself *as* a people—to make for Yourself a name by great and awesome deeds, by driving out nations from before Your people whom You redeemed from Egypt?
22 "For You have made Your people Israel Your very own people forever; and You, LORD, have become their God.
23 "And now, O LORD, the word which You have spoken concerning Your servant and concerning his house, *let it* be established forever, and do as You have said.
24 "So let it be established, that Your name may be magnified forever, saying, 'The LORD of hosts, the God of Israel, *is* Israel's God.' And let the house of Your servant David be established before You.
25 "For You, O my God, have revealed to Your servant that You will build him a house. Therefore Your servant has found it *in his heart* to pray before You.
26 "And now, LORD, You are God, and have promised this goodness to Your servant.
27 "Now You have been pleased to bless the house of Your servant, that it may continue before You forever; for You have blessed it, O LORD, and *it shall be* blessed forever."

David's Further Conquests

18 After this it came to pass that David attacked the Philistines, subdued them, and took Gath and its towns from the hand of the Philistines.
2 Then he defeated Moab, and the Moabites became David's servants, *and* brought tribute.
3 And David defeated Hadadezer[a] king of Zobah *as far as* Hamath, as he went to establish his power by the River Euphrates.
4 David took from him one thousand chariots, seven thousand[a] horsemen, and twenty thousand foot soldiers. Also David hamstrung all the chariot *horses,* except that he spared enough of them for one hundred chariots.
5 When the Syrians of Damascus came to help Hadadezer king of Zobah, David killed twenty-two thousand of the Syrians.
6 Then David put *garrisons* in Syria of Damascus; and the Syrians became David's servants, *and* brought tribute. So the LORD preserved David wherever he went.
7 And David took the shields of gold that were on the servants of Hadadezer, and brought them to Jerusalem.
8 Also from Tibhath[a] and from Chun, cities of Hadadezer, David brought a large amount of bronze, with which Solomon made the bronze Sea, the pillars, and the articles of bronze.

17:10 [a]That is, a royal dynasty **18:3** [a]Hebrew *Hadarezer,* and so throughout chapters 18 and 19 **18:4** [a]Or *seven hundred* (compare 2 Samuel 8:4) **18:8** [a]Spelled *Betah* in 2 Samuel 8:8

9 Now when Tou[a] king of Hamath heard that
David had defeated all the army of Hadadezer
king of Zobah,
10 he sent Hadoram[a] his son to King David, to
greet him and bless him, because he had fought
against Hadadezer and defeated him (for Had-
adezer had been at war with Tou); and *Hadoram*
brought with him all kinds of articles of gold,
silver, and bronze.
11 King David also dedicated these to the
LORD, along with the silver and gold that he had
brought from all *these* nations—from Edom,
from Moab, from the people of Ammon, from
the Philistines, and from Amalek.
12 Moreover Abishai the son of Zeruiah
killed eighteen thousand Edomites[a] in the Val-
ley of Salt.
13 He also put garrisons in Edom, and all the
Edomites became David's servants. And the
LORD preserved David wherever he went.

David's Administration

14 So David reigned over all Israel, and ad-
ministered judgment and justice to all his
people.
15 Joab the son of Zeruiah *was* over the army;
Jehoshaphat the son of Ahilud *was* recorder;
16 Zadok the son of Ahitub and Abimelech
the son of Abiathar *were* the priests; Shavsha[a]
was the scribe;
17 Benaiah the son of Jehoiada *was* over the
Cherethites and the Pelethites; and David's
sons *were* chief ministers at the king's side.

The Ammonites and Syrians Defeated

19 It happened after this that Nahash the
king of the people of Ammon died, and
his son reigned in his place.
2 Then David said, "I will show kindness to
Hanun the son of Nahash, because his father
showed kindness to me." So David sent mes-
sengers to comfort him concerning his father.
And David's servants came to Hanun in the
land of the people of Ammon to comfort him.
3 And the princes of the people of Ammon
said to Hanun, "Do you think that David really
honors your father because he has sent com-
forters to you? Did his servants not come to
you to search and to overthrow and to spy out
the land?"
4 Therefore Hanun took David's servants,
shaved them, and cut off their garments in the
middle, at their buttocks, and sent them away.
5 Then *some* went and told David about the
men; and he sent to meet them, because the
men were greatly ashamed. And the king said,
"Wait at Jericho until your beards have grown,
and *then* return."
6 When the people of Ammon saw that they
had made themselves repulsive to David, Ha-
nun and the people of Ammon sent a thousand
talents of silver to hire for themselves chariots
and horsemen from Mesopotamia,[a] from Syr-
ian Maacah, and from Zobah.[b]
7 So they hired for themselves thirty-two
thousand chariots, with the king of Maacah
and his people, who came and encamped be-
fore Medeba. Also the people of Ammon gath-
ered together from their cities, and came to
battle.
8 Now when David heard *of it*, he sent Joab
and all the army of the mighty men.
9 Then the people of Ammon came out and
put themselves in battle array before the gate
of the city, and the kings who had come *were*
by themselves in the field.
10 When Joab saw that the battle line was
against him before and behind, he chose some
of Israel's best, and put *them* in battle array
against the Syrians.
11 And the rest of the people he put under the
command of Abishai his brother, and they set
themselves in battle array against the people
of Ammon.
12 Then he said, "If the Syrians are too strong
for me, then you shall help me; but if the people
of Ammon are too strong for you, then I will
help you.
13 "Be of good courage, and let us be strong
for our people and for the cities of our God. And
may the LORD do *what is* good in His sight."
14 So Joab and the people who *were* with him
drew near for the battle against the Syrians,
and they fled before him.
15 When the people of Ammon saw that the
Syrians were fleeing, they also fled before
Abishai his brother, and entered the city. So
Joab went to Jerusalem.
16 Now when the Syrians saw that they had
been defeated by Israel, they sent messengers
and brought the Syrians who were beyond the
River,[a] and Shophach[b] the commander of Had-
adezer's army *went* before them.
17 When it was told David, he gathered all
Israel, crossed over the Jordan and came upon
them, and set up in *battle* array against them.
So when David had set up in battle array
against the Syrians, they fought with him.
18 Then the Syrians fled before Israel; and
David killed seven thousand[a] charioteers and
forty thousand foot soldiers[b] of the Syrians,
and killed Shophach the commander of the
army.
19 And when the servants of Hadadezer saw
that they were defeated by Israel, they made
peace with David and became his servants. So
the Syrians were not willing to help the people
of Ammon anymore.

Rabbah Is Conquered

20 It happened in the spring of the year, at
the time kings go out *to battle*, that Joab
led out the armed forces and ravaged the coun-
try of the people of Ammon, and came and
besieged Rabbah. But David stayed at Jerusa-
lem. And Joab defeated Rabbah and overthrew
it.
2 Then David took their king's crown from
his head, and found it to weigh a talent of gold,
and *there were* precious stones in it. And it
was set on David's head. Also he brought out
the spoil of the city in great abundance.
3 And he brought out the people who *were*
in it, and put *them* to work[a] with saws, with
iron picks, and with axes. So David did to all
the cities of the people of Ammon. Then David
and all the people returned *to* Jerusalem.

18:9 [a]Spelled *Toi* in 2 Samuel 8:9, 10 **18:10** [a]Spelled *Joram* in 2 Samuel 8:10 **18:12** [a]Or *Syrians* (compare 2 Samuel 8:13) **18:16** [a]Spelled *Seraiah* in 2 Samuel 8:17 **19:6** [a]Hebrew *Aram Naharaim* [b]Spelled *Zoba* in 2 Samuel 10:6 **19:16** [a]That is, the Euphrates [b]Spelled *Shobach* in 2 Samuel 10:16 **19:18** [a]Or *seven hundred* (compare 2 Samuel 10:18) [b]Or *horsemen* (compare 2 Samuel 10:18) **20:3** [a]Septuagint reads *cut them.*

Philistine Giants Destroyed

4 Now it happened afterward that war broke
out at Gezer with the Philistines, at which time
Sibbechai the Hushathite killed Sippai,[a] *who
was one* of the sons of the giant. And they were
subdued.
5 Again there was war with the Philistines,
and Elhanan the son of Jair[a] killed Lahmi the
brother of Goliath the Gittite, the shaft of whose
spear *was* like a weaver's beam.
6 Yet again there was war at Gath, where there
was a man of *great* stature, with twenty-four
fingers and toes, six *on each hand* and six *on
each foot;* and he also was born to the giant.
7 So when he defied Israel, Jonathan the son
of Shimea,[a] David's brother, killed him.
8 These were born to the giant in Gath, and
they fell by the hand of David and by the hand
of his servants.

The Census of Israel and Judah

21 Now Satan stood up against Israel, and
moved David to number Israel.
2 So David said to Joab and to the leaders
of the people, "Go, number Israel from Beer-
sheba to Dan, and bring the number of them
to me that I may know *it*."
3 And Joab answered, "May the LORD make
His people a hundred times more than they
are. But, my lord the king, *are* they not all my
lord's servants? Why then does my lord require
this thing? Why should he be a cause of guilt
in Israel?"
4 Nevertheless the king's word prevailed
against Joab. Therefore Joab departed and
went throughout all Israel and came to Jeru-
salem.
5 Then Joab gave the sum of the number of
the people to David. All Israel *had* one million
one hundred thousand men who drew the
sword, and Judah *had* four hundred and sev-
enty thousand men who drew the sword.
6 But he did not count Levi and Benjamin
among them, for the king's word was abomina-
ble to Joab.
7 And God was displeased with this thing;
therefore He struck Israel.
8 So David said to God, "I have sinned
greatly, because I have done this thing; but
now, I pray, take away the iniquity of Your
servant, for I have done very foolishly."
9 Then the LORD spoke to Gad, David's seer,
saying,
10 "Go and tell David, saying, 'Thus says the
LORD: "I offer you three *things;* choose one of
them for yourself, that I may do *it* to you." ' "
11 So Gad came to David and said to him,
"Thus says the LORD: 'Choose for yourself,
12 'either three[a] years of famine, or three
months to be defeated by your foes with the
sword of your enemies overtaking *you,* or else
for three days the sword of the LORD—the
plague in the land, with the angel[b] of the LORD
destroying throughout all the territory of Is-
rael.' Now consider what answer I should take
back to Him who sent me."
13 And David said to Gad, "I am in great dis-
tress. Please let me fall into the hand of the
LORD, for His mercies *are* very great; but do
not let me fall into the hand of man."
14 So the LORD sent a plague upon Israel, and
seventy thousand men of Israel fell.
15 And God sent an angel to Jerusalem to
destroy it. As he[a] was destroying, the LORD
looked and relented of the disaster, and said to
the angel who was destroying, "It is enough;
now restrain your[b] hand." And the angel of the
LORD stood by the threshing floor of Ornan[c]
the Jebusite.
16 Then David lifted his eyes and saw the an-
gel of the LORD standing between earth and
heaven, having in his hand a drawn sword
stretched out over Jerusalem. So David and
the elders, clothed in sackcloth, fell on their
faces.
17 And David said to God, "Was it not I who
commanded the people to be numbered? I am
the one who has sinned and done evil indeed;
but these sheep, what have they done? Let Your
hand, I pray, O LORD my God, be against me
and my father's house, but not against Your
people that they should be plagued."
18 Therefore, the angel of the LORD com-
manded Gad to say to David that David should
go and erect an altar to the LORD on the thresh-
ing floor of Ornan the Jebusite.
19 So David went up at the word of Gad,
which he had spoken in the name of the LORD.
20 Now Ornan turned and saw the angel; and
his four sons *who were* with him hid them-
selves, but Ornan continued threshing wheat.
21 So David came to Ornan, and Ornan looked
and saw David. And he went out from the
threshing floor, and bowed before David with
his face to the ground.
22 Then David said to Ornan, "Grant me the
place of *this* threshing floor, that I may build
an altar on it to the LORD. You shall grant it to
me at the full price, that the plague may be
withdrawn from the people."
23 But Ornan said to David, "Take *it* to your-
self, and let my lord the king do *what is* good
in his eyes. Look, I *also* give *you* the oxen for
burnt offerings, the threshing implements for
wood, and the wheat for the grain offering; I
give *it* all."
24 Then King David said to Ornan, "No, but I
will surely buy *it* for the full price, for I will
not take what is yours for the LORD, nor offer
burnt offerings with *that which* costs *me*
nothing."
25 So David gave Ornan six hundred shekels
of gold by weight for the place.
26 And David built there an altar to the LORD,
and offered burnt offerings and peace offer-
ings, and called on the LORD; and He answered
him from heaven by fire on the altar of burnt
offering.
27 So the LORD commanded the angel, and
he returned his sword to its sheath.
28 At that time, when David saw that the
LORD had answered him on the threshing floor
of Ornan the Jebusite, he sacrificed there.
29 For the tabernacle of the LORD and the
altar of the burnt offering, which Moses had
made in the wilderness, *were* at that time at
the high place in Gibeon.
30 But David could not go before it to inquire
of God, for he was afraid of the sword of the
angel of the LORD.

20:4 [a]Spelled *Saph* in 2 Samuel 21:18 **20:5** [a]Spelled *Jaare-Oregim* in 2 Samuel 21:19 **20:7** [a]Spelled *Shimeah* in 2 Samuel 21:21 and *Shammah* in 1 Samuel 16:9 **21:12** [a]Or *seven* (compare 2 Samuel 24:13) [b]Or *Angel,* and so elsewhere in this chapter **21:15** [a]Or *He* [b]Or *Your* [c]Spelled *Araunah* in 2 Samuel 24:16

David Prepares to Build the Temple

22 Then David said, "This *is* the house of
the LORD God, and this *is* the altar of
burnt offering for Israel."
2 So David commanded to gather the aliens
who *were* in the land of Israel; and he appointed masons to cut hewn stones to build the
house of God.
3 And David prepared iron in abundance for
the nails of the doors of the gates and for the
joints, and bronze in abundance beyond measure,
4 and cedar trees in abundance; for the Sidonians and those from Tyre brought much cedar
wood to David.
5 Now David said, "Solomon my son *is* young
and inexperienced, and the house to be built for
the LORD *must be* exceedingly magnificent,
famous and glorious throughout all countries.
I will now make preparation for it." So David
made abundant preparations before his death.
6 Then he called for his son Solomon, and
charged him to build a house for the LORD God
of Israel.
7 And David said to Solomon: "My son, as
for me, it was in my mind to build a house to
the name of the LORD my God;
8 "but the word of the LORD came to me,
saying, 'You have shed much blood and have
made great wars; you shall not build a house
for My name, because you have shed much
blood on the earth in My sight.
9 'Behold, a son shall be born to you, who
shall be a man of rest; and I will give him rest
from all his enemies all around. His name shall
be Solomon,[a] for I will give peace and quietness to Israel in his days.
10 'He shall build a house for My name, and
he shall be My son, and I *will be* his Father;
and I will establish the throne of his kingdom
over Israel forever.'
11 "Now, my son, may the LORD be with you;
and may you prosper, and build the house of
the LORD your God, as He has said to you.
12 "Only may the LORD give you wisdom and
understanding, and give you charge concerning Israel, that you may keep the law of the LORD
your God.
13 "Then you will prosper, if you take care to
fulfill the statutes and judgments with which
the LORD charged Moses concerning Israel. Be
strong and of good courage; do not fear nor be
dismayed.
14 "Indeed I have taken much trouble to prepare for the house of the LORD one hundred
thousand talents of gold and one million talents of silver, and bronze and iron beyond measure, for it is so abundant. I have prepared
timber and stone also, and you may add to them.
15 "Moreover *there are* workmen with you in
abundance: woodsmen and stonecutters, and
all types of skillful men for every kind of work.
16 "Of gold and silver and bronze and iron
there is no limit. Arise and begin working, and
the LORD be with you."
17 David also commanded all the leaders of
Israel to help Solomon his son, *saying,*
18 "*Is* not the LORD your God with you? And
has He *not* given you rest on every side? For
He has given the inhabitants of the land into
my hand, and the land is subdued before the
LORD and before His people.
19 "Now set your heart and your soul to seek
the LORD your God. Therefore arise and build
the sanctuary of the LORD God, to bring the
ark of the covenant of the LORD and the holy
articles of God into the house that is to be built
for the name of the LORD."

The Divisions of the Levites

23 So when David was old and full of days,
he made his son Solomon king over Israel.
2 And he gathered together all the leaders
of Israel, with the priests and the Levites.
3 Now the Levites were numbered from the
age of thirty years and above; and the number
of individual males was thirty-eight thousand.
4 Of these, twenty-four thousand *were* to
look after the work of the house of the LORD,
six thousand *were* officers and judges,
5 four thousand *were* gatekeepers, and four
thousand praised the LORD with *musical* instruments, "which I made," *said David,* "for giving praise."
6 Also David separated them into divisions
among the sons of Levi: Gershon, Kohath, and
Merari.
7 Of the Gershonites: Laadan[a] and Shimei.
8 The sons of Laadan: the first Jehiel, then
Zetham and Joel—three *in all.*
9 The sons of Shimei: Shelomith, Haziel, and
Haran—three *in all.* These were the heads of
the fathers' *houses* of Laadan.
10 And the sons of Shimei: Jahath, Zina,[a] Jeush, and Beriah. These *were* the four sons of
Shimei.
11 Jahath was the first and Zizah the second.
But Jeush and Beriah did not have many sons;
therefore they were assigned as one father's
house.
12 The sons of Kohath: Amram, Izhar, Hebron,
and Uzziel—four *in all.*
13 The sons of Amram: Aaron and Moses; and
Aaron was set apart, he and his sons forever,
that he should sanctify the most holy things,
to burn incense before the LORD, to minister
to Him, and to give the blessing in His name
forever.
14 Now the sons of Moses the man of God
were reckoned to the tribe of Levi.
15 The sons of Moses *were* Gershon[a] and Eliezer.
16 Of the sons of Gershon, Shebuel[a] *was* the
first.
17 Of the descendants of Eliezer, Rehabiah
was the first. And Eliezer had no other sons,
but the sons of Rehabiah were very many.
18 Of the sons of Izhar, Shelomith *was* the
first.
19 Of the sons of Hebron, Jeriah *was* the first,
Amariah the second, Jahaziel the third, and
Jekameam the fourth.
20 Of the sons of Uzziel, Michah *was* the first
and Jesshiah the second.
21 The sons of Merari *were* Mahli and Mushi.
The sons of Mahli *were* Eleazar and Kish.
22 And Eleazar died, and had no sons, but
only daughters; and their brethren, the sons of
Kish, took them *as wives.*
23 The sons of Mushi *were* Mahli, Eder, and
Jeremoth—three *in all.*

22:9 [a]Literally *Peaceful* **23:7** [a]Spelled *Libni* in Exodus 6:17 **23:10** [a]Septuagint and Vulgate read *Zizah* (compare verse 11). **23:15** [a]Hebrew *Gershom* (compare 6:16) **23:16** [a]Spelled *Shubael* in 24:20

24 These *were* the sons of Levi by their fathers' houses—the heads of the fathers' *houses* as they were counted individually by the number of their names, who did the work for the service of the house of the LORD, from the age of twenty years and above.
25 For David said, "The LORD God of Israel has given rest to His people, that they may dwell in Jerusalem forever";
26 and also to the Levites, "They shall no longer carry the tabernacle, or any of the articles for its service."
27 For by the last words of David the Levites *were* numbered from twenty years old and above;
28 because their duty *was* to help the sons of Aaron in the service of the house of the LORD, in the courts and in the chambers, in the purifying of all holy things and the work of the service of the house of God,
29 both with the showbread and the fine flour for the grain offering, with the unleavened cakes and *what is baked in* the pan, with what is mixed and with all kinds of measures and sizes;
30 to stand every morning to thank and praise the LORD, and likewise at evening;
31 and at every presentation of a burnt offering to the LORD on the Sabbaths and on the New Moons and on the set feasts, by number according to the ordinance governing them, regularly before the LORD;
32 and that they should attend to the needs of the tabernacle of meeting, the needs of the holy *place,* and the needs of the sons of Aaron their brethren in the work of the house of the LORD.

The Divisions of the Priests

24 Now *these are* the divisions of the sons of Aaron. The sons of Aaron *were* Nadab, Abihu, Eleazar, and Ithamar.
2 And Nadab and Abihu died before their father, and had no children; therefore Eleazar and Ithamar ministered as priests.
3 Then David with Zadok of the sons of Eleazar, and Ahimelech of the sons of Ithamar, divided them according to the schedule of their service.
4 There were more leaders found of the sons of Eleazar than of the sons of Ithamar, and *thus* they were divided. Among the sons of Eleazar *were* sixteen heads of *their* fathers' houses, and eight heads of their fathers' houses among the sons of Ithamar.
5 Thus they were divided by lot, one group as another, for there were officials of the sanctuary and officials *of the house* of God, from the sons of Eleazar and from the sons of Ithamar.
6 And the scribe, Shemaiah the son of Nethanel, *one of* the Levites, wrote them down before the king, the leaders, Zadok the priest, Ahimelech the son of Abiathar, and the heads of the fathers' *houses* of the priests and Levites, one father's house taken for Eleazar and *one* for Ithamar.
7 Now the first lot fell to Jehoiarib, the second to Jedaiah,
8 the third to Harim, the fourth to Seorim,
9 the fifth to Malchijah, the sixth to Mijamin,
10 the seventh to Hakkoz, the eighth to Abijah,
11 the ninth to Jeshua, the tenth to Shecaniah,
12 the eleventh to Eliashib, the twelfth to Jakim,
13 the thirteenth to Huppah, the fourteenth to Jeshebeab,
14 the fifteenth to Bilgah, the sixteenth to Immer,
15 the seventeenth to Hezir, the eighteenth to Happizzez,[a]
16 the nineteenth to Pethahiah, the twentieth to Jehezekel,[a]
17 the twenty-first to Jachin, the twenty-second to Gamul,
18 the twenty-third to Delaiah, the twenty-fourth to Maaziah.
19 This *was* the schedule of their service for coming into the house of the LORD according to their ordinance by the hand of Aaron their father, as the LORD God of Israel had commanded him.

Other Levites

20 And the rest of the sons of Levi: of the sons of Amram, Shubael;[a] of the sons of Shubael, Jehdeiah.
21 Concerning Rehabiah, of the sons of Rehabiah, the first *was* Isshiah.
22 Of the Izharites, Shelomoth;[a] of the sons of Shelomoth, Jahath.
23 Of the sons *of Hebron,*[a] Jeriah *was the first,*[b] Amariah the second, Jahaziel the third, *and* Jekameam the fourth.
24 *Of* the sons of Uzziel, Michah; of the sons of Michah, Shamir.
25 The brother of Michah, Isshiah; of the sons of Isshiah, Zechariah.
26 The sons of Merari *were* Mahli and Mushi; the son of Jaaziah, Beno.
27 The sons of Merari by Jaaziah *were* Beno, Shoham, Zaccur, and Ibri.
28 Of Mahli: Eleazar, who had no sons.
29 Of Kish: the son of Kish, Jerahmeel.
30 Also the sons of Mushi *were* Mahli, Eder, and Jerimoth. These *were* the sons of the Levites according to their fathers' houses.
31 These also cast lots just as their brothers the sons of Aaron did, in the presence of King David, Zadok, Ahimelech, and the heads of the fathers' *houses* of the priests and Levites. The chief fathers *did* just as their younger brethren.

The Musicians

25 Moreover David and the captains of the army separated for the service *some* of the sons of Asaph, of Heman, and of Jeduthun, who *should* prophesy with harps, stringed instruments, and cymbals. And the number of the skilled men performing their service was:
2 Of the sons of Asaph: Zaccur, Joseph, Nethaniah, and Asharelah;[a] the sons of Asaph *were* under the direction of Asaph, who prophesied according to the order of the king.
3 Of Jeduthun, the sons of Jeduthun: Gedaliah, Zeri,[a] Jeshaiah, *Shimei,* Hashabiah, and Mattithiah, six,[b] under the direction of their father Jeduthun, who prophesied with a harp to give thanks and to praise the LORD.

24:15 [a]Septuagint and Vulgate read *Aphses.* **24:16** [a]Masoretic Text reads *Jehezkel.* **24:20** [a]Spelled *Shebuel* in 23:16 **24:22** [a]Spelled *Shelomith* in 23:18 **24:23** [a]Supplied from 23:19 (following some Hebrew manuscripts and Septuagint manuscripts) [b]Supplied from 23:19 (following some Hebrew manuscripts and Septuagint manuscripts) **25:2** [a]Spelled *Jesharelah* in verse 14 **25:3** [a]Spelled *Jizri* in verse 11 [b]*Shimei,* appearing in one Hebrew and several Septuagint manuscripts, completes the total of six sons (compare verse 17).

4 Of Heman, the sons of Heman: Bukkiah, Mattaniah, Uzziel,[a] Shebuel,[b] Jerimoth,[c] Hananiah, Hanani, Eliathah, Giddalti, Romamti-Ezer, Joshbekashah, Mallothi, Hothir, *and* Mahazioth.

5 All these *were* the sons of Heman the king's seer in the words of God, to exalt his horn.[a] For God gave Heman fourteen sons and three daughters.

6 All these *were* under the direction of their father for the music *in* the house of the LORD, with cymbals, stringed instruments, and harps, for the service of the house of God. Asaph, Jeduthun, and Heman *were* under the authority of the king.

7 So the number of them, with their brethren who were instructed in the songs of the LORD, all who were skillful, *was* two hundred and eighty-eight.

8 And they cast lots for their duty, the small as well as the great, the teacher with the student.

9 Now the first lot for Asaph came out for Joseph; the second for Gedaliah, him with his brethren and sons, twelve;

10 the third for Zaccur, his sons and his brethren, twelve;

11 the fourth for Jizri,[a] his sons and his brethren, twelve;

12 the fifth for Nethaniah, his sons and his brethren, twelve;

13 the sixth for Bukkiah, his sons and his brethren, twelve;

14 the seventh for Jesharelah,[a] his sons and his brethren, twelve;

15 the eighth for Jeshaiah, his sons and his brethren, twelve;

16 the ninth for Mattaniah, his sons and his brethren, twelve;

17 the tenth for Shimei, his sons and his brethren, twelve;

18 the eleventh for Azarel,[a] his sons and his brethren, twelve;

19 the twelfth for Hashabiah, his sons and his brethren, twelve;

20 the thirteenth for Shubael,[a] his sons and his brethren, twelve;

21 the fourteenth for Mattithiah, his sons and his brethren, twelve;

22 the fifteenth for Jeremoth,[a] his sons and his brethren, twelve;

23 the sixteenth for Hananiah, his sons and his brethren, twelve;

24 the seventeenth for Joshbekashah, his sons and his brethren, twelve;

25 the eighteenth for Hanani, his sons and his brethren, twelve;

26 the nineteenth for Mallothi, his sons and his brethren, twelve;

27 the twentieth for Eliathah, his sons and his brethren, twelve;

28 the twenty-first for Hothir, his sons and his brethren, twelve;

29 the twenty-second for Giddalti, his sons and his brethren, twelve;

30 the twenty-third for Mahazioth, his sons and his brethren, twelve;

31 the twenty-fourth for Romamti-Ezer, his sons and his brethren, twelve.

The Gatekeepers

26 Concerning the divisions of the gatekeepers: of the Korahites, Meshelemiah the son of Kore, of the sons of Asaph.

2 And the sons of Meshelemiah *were* Zechariah the firstborn, Jediael the second, Zebadiah the third, Jathniel the fourth,

3 Elam the fifth, Jehohanan the sixth, Eliehoenai the seventh.

4 Moreover the sons of Obed-Edom *were* Shemaiah the firstborn, Jehozabad the second, Joah the third, Sacar the fourth, Nethanel the fifth,

5 Ammiel the sixth, Issachar the seventh, Peulthai the eighth; for God blessed him.

6 Also to Shemaiah his son were sons born who governed their fathers' houses, because they *were* men of great ability.

7 The sons of Shemaiah *were* Othni, Rephael, Obed, and Elzabad, whose brothers Elihu and Semachiah *were* able men.

8 All these *were* of the sons of Obed-Edom, they and their sons and their brethren, able men with strength for the work: sixty-two of Obed-Edom.

9 And Meshelemiah had sons and brethren, eighteen able men.

10 Also Hosah, of the children of Merari, had sons: Shimri the first (for *though* he was not the firstborn, his father made him the first),

11 Hilkiah the second, Tebaliah the third, Zechariah the fourth; all the sons and brethren of Hosah *were* thirteen.

12 Among these *were* the divisions of the gatekeepers, among the chief men, *having* duties just like their brethren, to serve in the house of the LORD.

13 And they cast lots for each gate, the small as well as the great, according to their father's house.

14 The lot for the East *Gate* fell to Shelemiah. Then they cast lots *for* his son Zechariah, a wise counselor, and his lot came out for the North Gate;

15 to Obed-Edom the South Gate, and to his sons the storehouse.[a]

16 To Shuppim and Hosah *the lot came out* for the West Gate, with the Shallecheth Gate on the ascending highway—watchman opposite watchman.

17 On the east *were* six Levites, on the north four each day, on the south four each day, and for the storehouse[a] two by two.

18 As for the Parbar[a] on the west, *there were* four on the highway *and* two at the Parbar.

19 These were the divisions of the gatekeepers among the sons of Korah and among the sons of Merari.

The Treasuries and Other Duties

20 Of the Levites, Ahijah *was* over the treasuries of the house of God and over the treasuries of the dedicated things.

21 The sons of Laadan, the descendants of the Gershonites of Laadan, heads of their fathers' *houses,* of Laadan the Gershonite: Jehieli.

22 The sons of Jehieli, Zetham and Joel his brother, *were* over the treasuries of the house of the LORD.

25:4 [a]Spelled *Azarel* in verse 18 [b]Spelled *Shubael* in verse 20 [c]Spelled *Jeremoth* in verse 22 **25:5** [a]That is, to increase his power or influence **25:11** [a]Spelled *Zeri* in verse 3 **25:14** [a]Spelled *Asharelah* in verse 2 **25:18** [a]Spelled *Uzziel* in verse 4 **25:20** [a]Spelled *Shebuel* in verse 4 **25:22** [a]Spelled *Jerimoth* in verse 4 **26:15** [a]Hebrew *asuppim* **26:17** [a]Hebrew *asuppim* **26:18** [a]Probably a court or colonnade extending west of the temple

23 Of the Amramites, the Izharites, the Hebronites, and the Uzzielites:
24 Shebuel the son of Gershom, the son of Moses, *was* overseer of the treasuries.
25 And his brethren by Eliezer *were* Rehabiah his son, Jeshaiah his son, Joram his son, Zichri his son, and Shelomith his son.
26 This Shelomith and his brethren *were* over all the treasuries of the dedicated things which King David and the heads of fathers' *houses,* the captains over thousands and hundreds, and the captains of the army, had dedicated.
27 Some of the spoils won in battles they dedicated to maintain the house of the LORD.
28 And all that Samuel the seer, Saul the son of Kish, Abner the son of Ner, and Joab the son of Zeruiah had dedicated, every dedicated *thing,* was under the hand of Shelomith and his brethren.
29 Of the Izharites, Chenaniah and his sons *performed* duties as officials and judges over Israel outside Jerusalem.
30 Of the Hebronites, Hashabiah and his brethren, one thousand seven hundred able men, had the oversight of Israel on the west side of the Jordan for all the business of the LORD, and in the service of the king.
31 Among the Hebronites, Jerijah *was* head of the Hebronites according to his genealogy of the fathers. In the fortieth year of the reign of David they were sought, and there were found among them capable men at Jazer of Gilead.
32 And his brethren *were* two thousand seven hundred able men, heads of fathers' *houses,* whom King David made officials over the Reubenites, the Gadites, and the half-tribe of Manasseh, for every matter pertaining to God and the affairs of the king.

The Military Divisions

27 And the children of Israel, according to their number, the heads of fathers' *houses,* the captains of thousands and hundreds and their officers, served the king in every matter of the *military* divisions. *These divisions* came in and went out month by month throughout all the months of the year, each division *having* twenty-four thousand.
2 Over the first division for the first month *was* Jashobeam the son of Zabdiel, and in his division *were* twenty-four thousand;
3 *he was* of the children of Perez, and the chief of all the captains of the army for the first month.
4 Over the division of the second month *was* Dodai[a] an Ahohite, and of his division Mikloth also *was* the leader; in his division *were* twenty-four thousand.
5 The third captain of the army for the third month *was* Benaiah, the son of Jehoiada the priest, who was chief; in his division *were* twenty-four thousand.
6 This was the Benaiah *who was* mighty *among* the thirty, and was over the thirty; in his division *was* Ammizabad his son.
7 The fourth *captain* for the fourth month *was* Asahel the brother of Joab, and Zebadiah his son after him; in his division *were* twenty-four thousand.
8 The fifth captain for the fifth month *was* Shamhuth[a] the Izrahite; in his division were twenty-four thousand.
9 The sixth *captain* for the sixth month *was* Ira the son of Ikkesh the Tekoite; in his division *were* twenty-four thousand.
10 The seventh *captain* for the seventh month *was* Helez the Pelonite, of the children of Ephraim; in his division *were* twenty-four thousand.
11 The eighth *captain* for the eighth month *was* Sibbechai the Hushathite, of the Zarhites; in his division *were* twenty-four thousand.
12 The ninth *captain* for the ninth month *was* Abiezer the Anathothite, of the Benjamites; in his division *were* twenty-four thousand.
13 The tenth *captain* for the tenth month *was* Maharai the Netophathite, of the Zarhites; in his division *were* twenty-four thousand.
14 The eleventh *captain* for the eleventh month *was* Benaiah the Pirathonite, of the children of Ephraim; in his division *were* twenty-four thousand.
15 The twelfth *captain* for the twelfth month *was* Heldai[a] the Netophathite, of Othniel; in his division *were* twenty-four thousand.

Leaders of Tribes

16 Furthermore, over the tribes of Israel: the officer over the Reubenites *was* Eliezer the son of Zichri; over the Simeonites, Shephatiah the son of Maachah;
17 *over* the Levites, Hashabiah the son of Kemuel; over the Aaronites, Zadok;
18 *over* Judah, Elihu, *one* of David's brothers; *over* Issachar, Omri the son of Michael;
19 *over* Zebulun, Ishmaiah the son of Obadiah; *over* Naphtali, Jerimoth the son of Azriel;
20 *over* the children of Ephraim, Hoshea the son of Azaziah; *over* the half-tribe of Manasseh, Joel the son of Pedaiah;
21 *over* the half-*tribe* of Manasseh in Gilead, Iddo the son of Zechariah; *over* Benjamin, Jaasiel the son of Abner;
22 *over* Dan, Azarel the son of Jeroham. These *were* the leaders of the tribes of Israel.
23 But David did not take the number of those twenty years old and under, because the LORD had said He would multiply Israel like the stars of the heavens.
24 Joab the son of Zeruiah began a census, but he did not finish, for wrath came upon Israel because of this census; nor was the number recorded in the account of the chronicles of King David.

Other State Officials

25 And Azmaveth the son of Adiel *was* over the king's treasuries; and Jehonathan the son of Uzziah was over the storehouses in the field, in the cities, in the villages, and in the fortresses.
26 Ezri the son of Chelub was over those who did the work of the field for tilling the ground.
27 And Shimei the Ramathite *was* over the vineyards, and Zabdi the Shiphmite was over the produce of the vineyards for the supply of wine.
28 Baal-Hanan the Gederite was over the olive trees and the sycamore trees that *were* in the lowlands, and Joash *was* over the store of oil.
29 And Shitrai the Sharonite *was* over the herds that fed in Sharon, and Shaphat the son of Adlai was over the herds *that were* in the valleys.

27:4 [a]Hebrew *Dodai,* usually spelled *Dodo* (compare 2 Samuel 23:9) **27:8** [a]Spelled *Shammoth* in 11:27 and *Shammah* in 2 Samuel 23:11 **27:15** [a]Spelled *Heled* in 11:30 and *Heleb* in 2 Samuel 23:29

30 Obil the Ishmaelite *was* over the camels, Jehdeiah the Meronothite *was* over the donkeys,

31 and Jaziz the Hagrite *was* over the flocks. All these *were* the officials over King David's property.

32 Also Jehonathan, David's uncle, *was* a counselor, a wise man, and a scribe; and Jehiel the son of Hachmoni *was* with the king's sons.

33 Ahithophel *was* the king's counselor, and Hushai the Archite *was* the king's companion.

34 After Ahithophel *was* Jehoiada the son of Benaiah, then Abiathar. And the general of the king's army *was* Joab.

Solomon Instructed to Build the Temple

28 Now David assembled at Jerusalem all the leaders of Israel: the officers of the tribes and the captains of the divisions who served the king, the captains over thousands and captains over hundreds, and the stewards over all the substance and possessions of the king and of his sons, with the officials, the valiant men, and all the mighty men of valor.

2 Then King David rose to his feet and said, "Hear me, my brethren and my people: I *had* it in my heart to build a house of rest for the ark of the covenant of the LORD, and for the footstool of our God, and had made preparations to build it.

3 "But God said to me, 'You shall not build a house for My name, because you *have been* a man of war and have shed blood.'

4 "However the LORD God of Israel chose me above all the house of my father to be king over Israel forever, for He has chosen Judah *to be* the ruler. And of the house of Judah, the house of my father, and among the sons of my father, He was pleased with me to make *me* king over all Israel.

5 "And of all my sons (for the LORD has given me many sons) He has chosen my son Solomon to sit on the throne of the kingdom of the LORD over Israel.

6 "Now He said to me, 'It is your son Solomon *who* shall build My house and My courts; for I have chosen him *to be* My son, and I will be his Father.

7 'Moreover I will establish his kingdom forever, if he is steadfast to observe My commandments and My judgments, as it is this day.'

8 "Now therefore, in the sight of all Israel, the assembly of the LORD, and in the hearing of our God, be careful to seek out all the commandments of the LORD your God, that you may possess this good land, and leave *it* as an inheritance for your children after you forever.

9 "As for you, my son Solomon, know the God of your father, and serve Him with a loyal heart and with a willing mind; for the LORD searches all hearts and understands all the intent of the thoughts. If you seek Him, He will be found by you; but if you forsake Him, He will cast you off forever.

10 "Consider now, for the LORD has chosen you to build a house for the sanctuary; be strong, and do it."

11 Then David gave his son Solomon the plans for the vestibule, its houses, its treasuries, its upper chambers, its inner chambers, and the place of the mercy seat;

12 and the plans for all that he had by the Spirit, of the courts of the house of the LORD, of all the chambers all around, of the treasuries of the house of God, and of the treasuries for the dedicated things;

13 also for the division of the priests and the Levites, for all the work of the service of the house of the LORD, and for all the articles of service in the house of the LORD.

14 *He gave* gold by weight for *things* of gold, for all articles used in every kind of service; also *silver* for all articles of silver by weight, for all articles used in every kind of service;

15 the weight for the lampstands of gold, and their lamps of gold, by weight for each lampstand and its lamps; for the lampstands of silver by weight, for the lampstand and its lamps, according to the use of each lampstand.

16 And by weight *he gave* gold for the tables of the showbread, for each table, and silver for the tables of silver;

17 also pure gold for the forks, the basins, the pitchers of pure gold, and the golden bowls—*he gave gold* by weight for every bowl; and for the silver bowls, *silver* by weight for every bowl;

18 and refined gold by weight for the altar of incense, and for the construction of the chariot, that is, the gold cherubim that spread *their wings* and overshadowed the ark of the covenant of the LORD.

19 "All *this," said David,* "the LORD made me understand in writing, by *His* hand upon me, all the works of these plans."

20 And David said to his son Solomon, "Be strong and of good courage, and do *it;* do not fear nor be dismayed, for the LORD God—my God—*will be* with you. He will not leave you nor forsake you, until you have finished all the work for the service of the house of the LORD.

21 "*Here are* the divisions of the priests and the Levites for all the service of the house of God; and every willing craftsman *will be* with you for all manner of workmanship, for every kind of service; also the leaders and all the people *will be* completely at your command."

Offerings for Building the Temple

29 Furthermore King David said to all the assembly: "My son Solomon, whom alone God has chosen, *is* young and inexperienced; and the work *is* great, because the temple[a] *is* not for man but for the LORD God.

2 "Now for the house of my God I have prepared with all my might: gold for *things to be made of* gold, silver for *things of* silver, bronze for *things of* bronze, iron for *things of* iron, wood for *things of* wood, onyx stones, *stones* to be set, glistening stones of various colors, all kinds of precious stones, and marble slabs in abundance.

3 "Moreover, because I have set my affection on the house of my God, I have given to the house of my God, over and above all that I have prepared for the holy house, my own special treasure of gold and silver:

4 "three thousand talents of gold, of the gold of Ophir, and seven thousand talents of refined silver, to overlay the walls of the houses;

5 "the gold for *things of* gold and the silver for *things of* silver, and for all kinds of work *to be done* by the hands of craftsmen. Who *then* is willing to consecrate himself this day to the LORD?"

6 Then the leaders of the fathers' *houses,* leaders of the tribes of Israel, the captains of

29:1 [a]Literally *palace*

thousands and of hundreds, with the officers
over the king's work, offered willingly.
7 They gave for the work of the house of God
five thousand talents and ten thousand darics
of gold, ten thousand talents of silver, eighteen
thousand talents of bronze, and one hundred
thousand talents of iron.
8 And whoever had *precious* stones gave
them to the treasury of the house of the LORD,
into the hand of Jehiel[a] the Gershonite.
9 Then the people rejoiced, for they had of-
fered willingly, because with a loyal heart they
had offered willingly to the LORD; and King
David also rejoiced greatly.

David's Praise to God

10 Therefore David blessed the LORD before
all the assembly; and David said:

"Blessed are You, LORD God of Israel, our
Father, forever and ever.
11 Yours, O LORD, *is* the greatness,
The power and the glory,
The victory and the majesty;
For all *that is* in heaven and in earth *is*
Yours;
Yours *is* the kingdom, O LORD,
And You are exalted as head over all.
12 Both riches and honor *come* from You,
And You reign over all.
In Your hand *is* power and might;
In Your hand *it is* to make great
And to give strength to all.

13 "Now therefore, our God,
We thank You
And praise Your glorious name.
14 But who *am* I, and who *are* my people,
That we should be able to offer so
willingly as this?
For all things *come* from You,
And of Your own we have given You.
15 For we *are* aliens and pilgrims before
You,
As *were* all our fathers;
Our days on earth *are* as a shadow,
And without hope.

16 "O LORD our God, all this abundance that
we have prepared to build You a house for Your
holy name is from Your hand, and *is* all Your
own.
17 "I know also, my God, that You test the heart
and have pleasure in uprightness. As for me,
in the uprightness of my heart I have willingly
offered all these *things;* and now with joy I
have seen Your people, who are present here
to offer willingly to You.
18 "O LORD God of Abraham, Isaac, and Is-
rael, our fathers, keep this forever in the intent
of the thoughts of the heart of Your people, and
fix their heart toward You.
19 "And give my son Solomon a loyal heart
to keep Your commandments and Your testi-
monies and Your statutes, to do all *these*
things, and to build the temple[a] for which I
have made provision."
20 Then David said to all the assembly, "Now
bless the LORD your God." So all the assembly
blessed the LORD God of their fathers, and
bowed their heads and prostrated themselves
before the LORD and the king.

Solomon Anointed King

21 And they made sacrifices to the LORD and
offered burnt offerings to the LORD on the next
day: a thousand bulls, a thousand rams, a thou-
sand lambs, with their drink offerings, and
sacrifices in abundance for all Israel.
22 So they ate and drank before the LORD
with great gladness on that day. And they
made Solomon the son of David king the sec-
ond time, and anointed *him* before the LORD
to be the leader, and Zadok *to be* priest.
23 Then Solomon sat on the throne of the
LORD as king instead of David his father, and
prospered; and all Israel obeyed him.
24 All the leaders and the mighty men, and
also all the sons of King David, submitted
themselves to King Solomon.
25 So the LORD exalted Solomon exceedingly
in the sight of all Israel, and bestowed on him
such royal majesty as had not been on any king
before him in Israel.

The Close of David's Reign

26 Thus David the son of Jesse reigned over
all Israel.
27 And the period that he reigned over Israel
was forty years; seven years he reigned in He-
bron, and thirty-three *years* he reigned in Jeru-
salem.
28 So he died in a good old age, full of days
and riches and honor; and Solomon his son
reigned in his place.
29 Now the acts of King David, first and last,
indeed they *are* written in the book of Samuel
the seer, in the book of Nathan the prophet,
and in the book of Gad the seer,
30 with all his reign and his might, and the
events that happened to him, to Israel, and to
all the kingdoms of the lands.

The Second Book of the CHRONICLES

Solomon Requests Wisdom

1 Now Solomon the son of David was strength-
ened in his kingdom, and the LORD his God
was with him and exalted him exceedingly.
2 And Solomon spoke to all Israel, to the
captains of thousands and of hundreds, to the
judges, and to every leader in all Israel, the heads
of the fathers' *houses.*
3 Then Solomon, and all the assembly with
him, went to the high place that *was* at Gibeon;
for the tabernacle of meeting with God was
there, which Moses the servant of the LORD
had made in the wilderness.
4 But David had brought up the ark of God
from Kirjath Jearim to *the place* David had
prepared for it, for he had pitched a tent for it
at Jerusalem.
5 Now the bronze altar that Bezalel the son

29:8 [a]Possibly the same as *Jehieli* (compare 26:21, 22) **29:19** [a]Literally *palace*

of Uri, the son of Hur, had made, he put[a] before
the tabernacle of the LORD; Solomon and the
assembly sought Him *there.*
6 And Solomon went up there to the bronze
altar before the LORD, which *was* at the taber-
nacle of meeting, and offered a thousand burnt
offerings on it.
7 On that night God appeared to Solomon,
and said to him, "Ask! What shall I give you?"
8 And Solomon said to God: "You have shown
great mercy to David my father, and have made
me king in his place.
9 "Now, O LORD God, let Your promise to
David my father be established, for You have
made me king over a people like the dust of
the earth in multitude.
10 "Now give me wisdom and knowledge,
that I may go out and come in before this peo-
ple; for who can judge this great people of
Yours?"
11 Then God said to Solomon: "Because this
was in your heart, and you have not asked
riches or wealth or honor or the life of your
enemies, nor have you asked long life—but
have asked wisdom and knowledge for your-
self, that you may judge My people over whom
I have made you king—
12 "wisdom and knowledge *are* granted to
you; and I will give you riches and wealth and
honor, such as none of the kings have had who
were before you, nor shall any after you have
the like."

Solomon's Military and Economic Power

13 So Solomon came to Jerusalem from the
high place that *was* at Gibeon, from before the
tabernacle of meeting, and reigned over Israel.
14 And Solomon gathered chariots and horse-
men; he had one thousand four hundred chari-
ots and twelve thousand horsemen, whom he
stationed in the chariot cities and with the king
in Jerusalem.
15 Also the king made silver and gold as com-
mon in Jerusalem as stones, and he made ce-
dars as abundant as the sycamores which *are*
in the lowland.
16 And Solomon had horses imported from
Egypt and Keveh; the king's merchants bought
them in Keveh at the *current* price.
17 They also acquired and imported from
Egypt a chariot for six hundred *shekels* of sil-
ver, and a horse for one hundred and fifty; thus,
through their agents,[a] they exported them to all
the kings of the Hittites and the kings of Syria.

Solomon Prepares to Build the Temple

2 Then Solomon determined to build a tem-
ple for the name of the LORD, and a royal
house for himself.
2 Solomon selected seventy thousand men
to bear burdens, eighty thousand to quarry
stone in the mountains, and three thousand six
hundred to oversee them.
3 Then Solomon sent to Hiram[a] king of Tyre,
saying:

As you have dealt with David my father,
and sent him cedars to build himself a
house to dwell in, *so deal with me.*
4 Behold, I am building a temple for the
name of the LORD my God, to dedicate *it*
to Him, to burn before Him sweet
incense, for the continual showbread, for
the burnt offerings morning and evening,
on the Sabbaths, on the New Moons, and
on the set feasts of the LORD our God.
This *is an ordinance* forever to Israel.
5 And the temple which I build *will be*
great, for our God is greater than all
gods.
6 But who is able to build Him a temple,
since heaven and the heaven of heavens
cannot contain Him? Who *am* I then, that
I should build Him a temple, except to
burn sacrifice before Him?
7 Therefore send me at once a man skillful
to work in gold and silver, in bronze and
iron, in purple and crimson and blue,
who has skill to engrave with the skillful
men who are with me in Judah and
Jerusalem, whom David my father
provided.
8 Also send me cedar and cypress and
algum logs from Lebanon, for I know that
your servants have skill to cut timber in
Lebanon; and indeed my servants *will be*
with your servants,
9 to prepare timber for me in abundance,
for the temple which I am about to build
shall be great and wonderful.
10 And indeed I will give to your servants,
the woodsmen who cut timber, twenty
thousand kors of ground wheat, twenty
thousand kors of barley, twenty thousand
baths of wine, and twenty thousand baths
of oil.

11 Then Hiram king of Tyre answered in writ-
ing, which he sent to Solomon:

Because the LORD loves His people, He
has made you king over them.

12 Hiram[a] also said:

Blessed *be* the LORD God of Israel, who
made heaven and earth, for He has given
King David a wise son, endowed with
prudence and understanding, who will
build a temple for the LORD and a royal
house for himself!
13 And now I have sent a skillful man,
endowed with understanding, Huram[a] my
master[b] *craftsman*
14 (the son of a woman of the daughters of
Dan, and his father was a man of Tyre),
skilled to work in gold and silver, bronze
and iron, stone and wood, purple and
blue, fine linen and crimson, and to make
any engraving and to accomplish any
plan which may be given to him, with
your skillful men and with the skillful
men of my lord David your father.
15 Now therefore, the wheat, the barley, the
oil, and the wine which my lord has
spoken of, let him send to his servants.
16 And we will cut wood from Lebanon, as
much as you need; we will bring it to you
in rafts by sea to Joppa, and you will
carry it up to Jerusalem.

17 Then Solomon numbered all the aliens
who *were* in the land of Israel, after the census
in which David his father had numbered them;

1:5 [a]Some authorities read *it was there.* **1:17** [a]Literally *by their hands* **2:3** [a]Hebrew *Huram* (compare 1 Kings 5:1) **2:12** [a]Hebrew *Huram* (compare 1 Kings 5:1) **2:13** [a]Spelled *Hiram* in 1 Kings 7:13 [b]Literally *father* (compare 1 Kings 7:13, 14)

and there were found to be one hundred and
fifty-three thousand six hundred.
18 And he made seventy thousand of them
bearers of burdens, eighty thousand stone-
cutters in the mountain, and three thousand
six hundred overseers to make the people
work.

Solomon Builds the Temple

3 Now Solomon began to build the house of
the LORD at Jerusalem on Mount Moriah,
where *the LORD*[a] had appeared to his father
David, at the place that David had prepared on
the threshing floor of Ornan[b] the Jebusite.
2 And he began to build on the second *day*
of the second month in the fourth year of his
reign.
3 This is the foundation which Solomon laid
for building the house of God: The length *was*
sixty cubits (by cubits according to the former
measure) and the width twenty cubits.
4 And the vestibule that *was* in front *of the*
sanctuary[a] was twenty cubits long across the
width of the house, and the height *was* one hun-
dred and[b] twenty. He overlaid the inside with
pure gold.
5 The larger room[a] he paneled with cypress
which he overlaid with fine gold, and he carved
palm trees and chainwork on it.
6 And he decorated the house with precious
stones for beauty, and the gold *was* gold from
Parvaim.
7 He also overlaid the house—the beams and
doorposts, its walls and doors—with gold; and
he carved cherubim on the walls.
8 And he made the Most Holy Place. Its length
was according to the width of the house, twenty
cubits, and its width twenty cubits. He overlaid
it with six hundred talents of fine gold.
9 The weight of the nails *was* fifty shekels of
gold; and he overlaid the upper area with gold.
10 In the Most Holy Place he made two cheru-
bim, fashioned by carving, and overlaid them
with gold.
11 The wings of the cherubim *were* twenty
cubits in *overall* length: one wing *of the one*
cherub was five cubits, touching the wall of
the room, and the other wing *was* five cubits,
touching the wing of the other cherub;
12 *one* wing of the other cherub *was* five cu-
bits, touching the wall of the room, and the other
wing *also was* five cubits, touching the wing
of the other cherub.
13 The wings of these cherubim spanned
twenty cubits overall. They stood on their feet,
and they faced inward.
14 And he made the veil of blue, purple, crim-
son, and fine linen, and wove cherubim into it.
15 Also he made in front of the temple[a] two
pillars thirty-five[b] cubits high, and the capital
that *was* on the top of each of *them* was five
cubits.
16 He made wreaths of chainwork, as in the
inner sanctuary, and put *them* on top of the
pillars; and he made one hundred pomegran-
ates, and put *them* on the wreaths of chainwork.
17 Then he set up the pillars before the temple,
one on the right hand and the other on the left;
he called the name of the one on the right hand
Jachin, and the name of the one on the left Boaz.

Furnishings of the Temple

4 Moreover he made a bronze altar: twenty
cubits was its length, twenty cubits its
width, and ten cubits its height.
2 Then he made the Sea of cast *bronze,* ten
cubits from one brim to the other; *it was* com-
pletely round. Its height *was* five cubits, and a
line of thirty cubits measured its circumfer-
ence.
3 And under it *was* the likeness of oxen en-
circling it all around, ten to a cubit, all the way
around the Sea. The oxen *were* cast in two rows,
when it was cast.
4 It stood on twelve oxen: three looking to-
ward the north, three looking toward the west,
three looking toward the south, and three look-
ing toward the east; the Sea *was set* upon
them, and all their back parts *pointed* inward.
5 It *was* a handbreadth thick; and its brim
was shaped like the brim of a cup, *like* a lily
blossom. It contained three thousand[a] baths.
6 He also made ten lavers, and put five on
the right side and five on the left, to wash in
them; such things as they offered for the burnt
offering they would wash in them, but the Sea
was for the priests to wash in.
7 And he made ten lampstands of gold ac-
cording to their design, and set *them* in the
temple, five on the right side and five on the
left.
8 He also made ten tables, and placed *them*
in the temple, five on the right side and five on
the left. And he made one hundred bowls of
gold.
9 Furthermore he made the court of the
priests, and the great court and doors for the
court; and he overlaid these doors with bronze.
10 He set the Sea on the right side, toward the
southeast.
11 Then Huram made the pots and the shov-
els and the bowls. So Huram finished doing
the work that he was to do for King Solomon
for the house of God:
12 the two pillars and the bowl-shaped capi-
tals *that were* on top of the two pillars; the
two networks covering the two bowl-shaped
capitals which *were* on top of the pillars;
13 four hundred pomegranates for the two
networks (two rows of pomegranates for each
network, to cover the two bowl-shaped capi-
tals that *were* on the pillars);
14 he also made carts and the lavers on the
carts;
15 one Sea and twelve oxen under it;
16 also the pots, the shovels, the forks—and
all their articles Huram his master[a] *craftsman*
made of burnished bronze for King Solomon
for the house of the LORD.
17 In the plain of Jordan the king had them
cast in clay molds, between Succoth and Zere-
dah.[a]
18 And Solomon had all these articles made
in such great abundance that the weight of the
bronze was not determined.
19 Thus Solomon had all the furnishings made

3:1 [a]Literally *He,* following Masoretic Text and Vulgate; Septuagint reads *the LORD;* Targum reads *the Angel of the LORD.* [b]Spelled *Araunah* in 2 Samuel 24:16ff **3:4** [a]The main room of the temple; elsewhere called the holy place (compare 1 Kings 6:3) [b]Following Masoretic Text, Septuagint, and Vulgate; Arabic, some manuscripts of the Septuagint, and Syriac omit *one hundred and.* **3:5** [a]Literally *house* **3:15** [a]Literally *house* [b]Or *eighteen* (compare 1 Kings 7:15; 2 Kings 25:17; and Jeremiah 52:21) **4:5** [a]Or *two thousand* (compare 1 Kings 7:26) **4:16** [a]Literally *father* **4:17** [a]Spelled *Zaretan* in 1 Kings 7:46

for the house of God: the altar of gold and the tables on which *was* the showbread;

20 the lampstands with their lamps of pure gold, to burn in the prescribed manner in front of the inner sanctuary,

21 with the flowers and the lamps and the wick-trimmers of gold, of purest gold;

22 the trimmers, the bowls, the ladles, and the censers of pure gold. As for the entry of the sanctuary, its inner doors to the Most Holy *Place,* and the doors of the main hall of the temple, *were* gold.

5 So all the work that Solomon had done for the house of the LORD was finished; and Solomon brought in the things which his father David had dedicated: the silver and the gold and all the furnishings. And he put *them* in the treasuries of the house of God.

The Ark Brought into the Temple

2 Now Solomon assembled the elders of Israel and all the heads of the tribes, the chief fathers of the children of Israel, in Jerusalem, that they might bring the ark of the covenant of the LORD up from the City of David, which *is* Zion.

3 Therefore all the men of Israel assembled with the king at the feast, which *was* in the seventh month.

4 So all the elders of Israel came, and the Levites took up the ark.

5 Then they brought up the ark, the tabernacle of meeting, and all the holy furnishings that *were* in the tabernacle. The priests and the Levites brought them up.

6 Also King Solomon, and all the congregation of Israel who were assembled with him before the ark, were sacrificing sheep and oxen that could not be counted or numbered for multitude.

7 Then the priests brought in the ark of the covenant of the LORD to its place, into the inner sanctuary of the temple,[a] to the Most Holy *Place,* under the wings of the cherubim.

8 For the cherubim spread *their* wings over the place of the ark, and the cherubim overshadowed the ark and its poles.

9 The poles extended so that the ends of the poles of the ark could be seen from *the holy place,* in front of the inner sanctuary; but they could not be seen from outside. And they are there to this day.

10 Nothing was in the ark except the two tablets which Moses put *there* at Horeb, when the LORD made *a covenant* with the children of Israel, when they had come out of Egypt.

11 And it came to pass when the priests came out of the *Most* Holy *Place* (for all the priests who *were* present had sanctified themselves, without keeping to their divisions),

12 and the Levites *who were* the singers, all those of Asaph and Heman and Jeduthun, with their sons and their brethren, stood at the east end of the altar, clothed in white linen, having cymbals, stringed instruments and harps, and with them one hundred and twenty priests sounding with trumpets—

13 indeed it came to pass, when the trumpeters and singers *were* as one, to make one sound to be heard in praising and thanking the LORD, and when they lifted up their voice with the trumpets and cymbals and instruments of music, and praised the LORD, *saying:*

> *"For He is* good,
> For His mercy *endures* forever,"[a]

that the house, the house of the LORD, was filled with a cloud,

14 so that the priests could not continue ministering because of the cloud; for the glory of the LORD filled the house of God.

6 Then Solomon spoke:

> "The LORD said He would dwell in the dark cloud.
> 2 I have surely built You an exalted house,
> And a place for You to dwell in forever."

Solomon's Speech upon Completion of the Work

3 Then the king turned around and blessed the whole assembly of Israel, while all the assembly of Israel was standing.

4 And he said: "Blessed *be* the LORD God of Israel, who has fulfilled with His hands *what* He spoke with His mouth to my father David, saying,

5 'Since the day that I brought My people out of the land of Egypt, I have chosen no city from any tribe of Israel *in which* to build a house, that My name might be there, nor did I choose any man to be a ruler over My people Israel.

6 'Yet I have chosen Jerusalem, that My name may be there, and I have chosen David to be over My people Israel.'

7 "Now it was in the heart of my father David to build a temple[a] for the name of the LORD God of Israel.

8 "But the LORD said to my father David, 'Whereas it was in your heart to build a temple for My name, you did well in that it was in your heart.

9 'Nevertheless you shall not build the temple, but your son who will come from your body, he shall build the temple for My name.'

10 "So the LORD has fulfilled His word which He spoke, and I have filled the position of my father David, and sit on the throne of Israel, as the LORD promised; and I have built the temple for the name of the LORD God of Israel.

11 "And there I have put the ark, in which *is* the covenant of the LORD which He made with the children of Israel."

Solomon's Prayer of Dedication

12 Then *Solomon*[a] stood before the altar of the LORD in the presence of all the assembly of Israel, and spread out his hands

13 (for Solomon had made a bronze platform five cubits long, five cubits wide, and three cubits high, and had set it in the midst of the court; and he stood on it, knelt down on his knees before all the assembly of Israel, and spread out his hands toward heaven);

14 and he said: "LORD God of Israel, *there is* no God in heaven or on earth like You, who keep *Your* covenant and mercy with Your servants who walk before You with all their hearts.

15 "You have kept what You promised Your servant David my father; You have both spoken with Your mouth and fulfilled *it* with Your hand, as *it is* this day.

5:7 [a]Literally *house* **5:13** [a]Compare Psalm 106:1 **6:7** [a]Literally *house,* and so in verses 8–10 **6:12** [a]Literally *he* (compare 1 Kings 8:22)

16 "Therefore, LORD God of Israel, now keep what You promised Your servant David my father, saying, 'You shall not fail to have a man sit before Me on the throne of Israel, only if your sons take heed to their way, that they walk in My law as you have walked before Me.'

17 "And now, O LORD God of Israel, let Your word come true, which You have spoken to Your servant David.

18 "But will God indeed dwell with men on the earth? Behold, heaven and the heaven of heavens cannot contain You. How much less this temple[a] which I have built!

19 "Yet regard the prayer of Your servant and his supplication, O LORD my God, and listen to the cry and the prayer which Your servant is praying before You:

20 "that Your eyes may be open toward this temple day and night, toward the place where *You* said *You would* put Your name, that You may hear the prayer which Your servant makes toward this place.

21 "And may You hear the supplications of Your servant and of Your people Israel, when they pray toward this place. Hear from heaven Your dwelling place, and when You hear, forgive.

22 "If anyone sins against his neighbor, and is forced to take an oath, and comes *and* takes an oath before Your altar in this temple,

23 "then hear from heaven, and act, and judge Your servants, bringing retribution on the wicked by bringing his way on his own head, and justifying the righteous by giving him according to his righteousness.

24 "Or if Your people Israel are defeated before an enemy because they have sinned against You, and return and confess Your name, and pray and make supplication before You in this temple,

25 "then hear from heaven and forgive the sin of Your people Israel, and bring them back to the land which You gave to them and their fathers.

26 "When the heavens are shut up and there is no rain because they have sinned against You, when they pray toward this place and confess Your name, and turn from their sin because You afflict them,

27 "then hear *in* heaven, and forgive the sin of Your servants, Your people Israel, that You may teach them the good way in which they should walk; and send rain on Your land which You have given to Your people as an inheritance.

28 "When there is famine in the land, pestilence or blight or mildew, locusts or grasshoppers; when their enemies besiege them in the land of their cities; whatever plague or whatever sickness *there is;*

29 "whatever prayer, whatever supplication is *made* by anyone, or by all Your people Israel, when each one knows his own burden and his own grief, and spreads out his hands to this temple:

30 "then hear from heaven Your dwelling place, and forgive, and give to everyone according to all his ways, whose heart You know (for You alone know the hearts of the sons of men),

31 "that they may fear You, to walk in Your ways as long as they live in the land which You gave to our fathers.

32 "Moreover, concerning a foreigner, who is not of Your people Israel, but has come from a far country for the sake of Your great name and Your mighty hand and Your outstretched arm, when they come and pray in this temple;

33 "then hear from heaven Your dwelling place, and do according to all for which the foreigner calls to You, that all peoples of the earth may know Your name and fear You, as *do* Your people Israel, and that they may know that this temple which I have built is called by Your name.

34 "When Your people go out to battle against their enemies, wherever You send them, and when they pray to You toward this city which You have chosen and the temple which I have built for Your name,

35 "then hear from heaven their prayer and their supplication, and maintain their cause.

36 "When they sin against You (for *there is* no one who does not sin), and You become angry with them and deliver them to the enemy, and they take them captive to a land far or near;

37 "*yet* when they come to themselves in the land where they were carried captive, and repent, and make supplication to You in the land of their captivity, saying, 'We have sinned, we have done wrong, and have committed wickedness';

38 "and *when* they return to You with all their heart and with all their soul in the land of their captivity, where they have been carried captive, and pray toward their land which You gave to their fathers, the city which You have chosen, and toward the temple which I have built for Your name:

39 "then hear from heaven Your dwelling place their prayer and their supplications, and maintain their cause, and forgive Your people who have sinned against You.

40 "Now, my God, I pray, let Your eyes be open and *let* Your ears *be* attentive to the prayer *made* in this place.

41 "Now therefore,
Arise, O LORD God, to Your resting place,
You and the ark of Your strength.
Let Your priests, O LORD God, be clothed
with salvation,
And let Your saints rejoice in goodness.

42 "O LORD God, do not turn away the face
of Your Anointed;
Remember the mercies of Your servant
David."[a]

Solomon Dedicates the Temple

7 When Solomon had finished praying, fire came down from heaven and consumed the burnt offering and the sacrifices; and the glory of the LORD filled the temple.[a]

2 And the priests could not enter the house of the LORD, because the glory of the LORD had filled the LORD's house.

3 When all the children of Israel saw how the fire came down, and the glory of the LORD on the temple, they bowed their faces to the ground on the pavement, and worshiped and praised the LORD, *saying:*

"For *He is* good,
For His mercy *endures* forever."[a]

6:18 [a]Literally *house* **6:42** [a]Compare Psalm 132:8–10 **7:1** [a]Literally *house* **7:3** [a]Compare Psalm 106:1

4 Then the king and all the people offered sac-
rifices before the LORD.
5 King Solomon offered a sacrifice of twenty-
two thousand bulls and one hundred and twenty
thousand sheep. So the king and all the people
dedicated the house of God.
6 And the priests attended to their services;
the Levites also with instruments of the music
of the LORD, which King David had made to
praise the LORD, saying, "For His mercy *en-
dures* forever,"[a] whenever David offered praise
by their ministry. The priests sounded trum-
pets opposite them, while all Israel stood.
7 Furthermore Solomon consecrated the
middle of the court that *was* in front of the
house of the LORD; for there he offered burnt
offerings and the fat of the peace offerings,
because the bronze altar which Solomon had
made was not able to receive the burnt offer-
ings, the grain offerings, and the fat.
8 At that time Solomon kept the feast seven
days, and all Israel with him, a very great as-
sembly from the entrance of Hamath to the
Brook of Egypt.[a]
9 And on the eighth day they held a sacred
assembly, for they observed the dedication of
the altar seven days, and the feast seven days.
10 On the twenty-third day of the seventh
month he sent the people away to their tents,
joyful and glad of heart for the good that the
LORD had done for David, for Solomon, and
for His people Israel.
11 Thus Solomon finished the house of the
LORD and the king's house; and Solomon suc-
cessfully accomplished all that came into his
heart to make in the house of the LORD and in
his own house.

God's Second Appearance to Solomon

12 Then the LORD appeared to Solomon by
night, and said to him: "I have heard your
prayer, and have chosen this place for Myself
as a house of sacrifice.
13 "When I shut up heaven and there is no
rain, or command the locusts to devour the
land, or send pestilence among My people,
14 "if My people who are called by My name
will humble themselves, and pray and seek My
face, and turn from their wicked ways, then I
will hear from heaven, and will forgive their
sin and heal their land.
15 "Now My eyes will be open and My ears
attentive to prayer *made* in this place.
16 "For now I have chosen and sanctified this
house, that My name may be there forever; and
My eyes and My heart will be there perpetu-
ally.
17 "As for you, if you walk before Me as your
father David walked, and do according to all
that I have commanded you, and if you keep
My statutes and My judgments,
18 "then I will establish the throne of your
kingdom, as I covenanted with David your fa-
ther, saying, 'You shall not fail *to have* a man
as ruler in Israel.'
19 "But if you turn away and forsake My stat-
utes and My commandments which I have set
before you, and go and serve other gods, and
worship them,
20 "then I will uproot them from My land
which I have given them; and this house which
I have sanctified for My name I will cast out of
My sight, and will make it a proverb and a by-
word among all peoples.
21 "And *as for* this house, which is exalted,
everyone who passes by it will be astonished
and say, 'Why has the LORD done thus to this
land and this house?'
22 "Then they will answer, 'Because they for-
sook the LORD God of their fathers, who brought
them out of the land of Egypt, and embraced
other gods, and worshiped them and served
them; therefore He has brought all this calam-
ity on them.'"

Solomon's Additional Achievements

8 It came to pass at the end of twenty years,
when Solomon had built the house of the
LORD and his own house,
2 that the cities which Hiram[a] had given to
Solomon, Solomon built them; and he settled
the children of Israel there.
3 And Solomon went to Hamath Zobah and
seized it.
4 He also built Tadmor in the wilderness,
and all the storage cities which he built in Ha-
math.
5 He built Upper Beth Horon and Lower
Beth Horon, fortified cities *with* walls, gates,
and bars,
6 also Baalath and all the storage cities that
Solomon had, and all the chariot cities and
the cities of the cavalry, and all that Solomon
desired to build in Jerusalem, in Lebanon, and
in all the land of his dominion.
7 All the people *who were* left of the Hittites,
Amorites, Perizzites, Hivites, and Jebusites,
who *were* not of Israel—
8 that is, their descendants who were left in
the land after them, whom the children of Is-
rael did not destroy—from these Solomon
raised forced labor, as it is to this day.
9 But Solomon did not make the children of
Israel servants for his work. Some *were* men
of war, captains of his officers, captains of his
chariots, and his cavalry.
10 And others *were* chiefs of the officials of
King Solomon: two hundred and fifty, who
ruled over the people.
11 Now Solomon brought the daughter of
Pharaoh up from the City of David to the house
he had built for her, for he said, "My wife shall
not dwell in the house of David king of Israel,
because *the places* to which the ark of the
LORD has come are holy."
12 Then Solomon offered burnt offerings to
the LORD on the altar of the LORD which he
had built before the vestibule,
13 according to the daily rate, offering ac-
cording to the commandment of Moses, for the
Sabbaths, the New Moons, and the three ap-
pointed yearly feasts—the Feast of Unleavened
Bread, the Feast of Weeks, and the Feast of
Tabernacles.
14 And, according to the order of David his
father, he appointed the divisions of the priests
for their service, the Levites for their duties (to
praise and serve before the priests) as the duty
of each day required, and the gatekeepers by
their divisions at each gate; for so David the man
of God had commanded.
15 They did not depart from the command of
the king to the priests and Levites concerning
any matter or concerning the treasuries.

7:6 [a]Compare Psalm 106:1 7:8 [a]That is, the Shihor (compare 1 Chronicles 13:5) 8:2 [a]Hebrew *Huram* (compare 2 Chronicles 2:3)

16 Now all the work of Solomon was well-ordered from[a] the day of the foundation of the house of the LORD until it was finished. So the house of the LORD was completed.

17 Then Solomon went to Ezion Geber and Elath[a] on the seacoast, in the land of Edom.

18 And Hiram sent him ships by the hand of his servants, and servants who knew the sea. They went with the servants of Solomon to Ophir, and acquired four hundred and fifty talents of gold from there, and brought it to King Solomon.

The Queen of Sheba's Praise of Solomon

9 Now when the queen of Sheba heard of the fame of Solomon, she came to Jerusalem to test Solomon with hard questions, *having* a very great retinue, camels that bore spices, gold in abundance, and precious stones; and when she came to Solomon, she spoke with him about all that was in her heart.

2 So Solomon answered all her questions; there was nothing so difficult for Solomon that he could not explain it to her.

3 And when the queen of Sheba had seen the wisdom of Solomon, the house that he had built,

4 the food on his table, the seating of his servants, the service of his waiters and their apparel, his cupbearers and their apparel, and his entryway by which he went up to the house of the LORD, there was no more spirit in her.

5 Then she said to the king: "*It was* a true report which I heard in my own land about your words and your wisdom.

6 "However I did not believe their words until I came and saw with my own eyes; and indeed the half of the greatness of your wisdom was not told me. You exceed the fame of which I heard.

7 "Happy *are* your men and happy *are* these your servants, who stand continually before you and hear your wisdom!

8 "Blessed be the LORD your God, who delighted in you, setting you on His throne *to be* king for the LORD your God! Because your God has loved Israel, to establish them forever, therefore He made you king over them, to do justice and righteousness."

9 And she gave the king one hundred and twenty talents of gold, spices in great abundance, and precious stones; there never were any spices such as those the queen of Sheba gave to King Solomon.

10 Also, the servants of Hiram and the servants of Solomon, who brought gold from Ophir, brought algum[a] wood and precious stones.

11 And the king made walkways *of* the algum[a] wood for the house of the LORD and for the king's house, also harps and stringed instruments for singers; and there were none such *as these* seen before in the land of Judah.

12 Now King Solomon gave to the queen of Sheba all she desired, whatever she asked, *much more* than she had brought to the king. So she turned and went to her own country, she and her servants.

Solomon's Great Wealth

13 The weight of gold that came to Solomon yearly was six hundred and sixty-six talents of gold,

14 besides *what* the traveling merchants and traders brought. And all the kings of Arabia and governors of the country brought gold and silver to Solomon.

15 And King Solomon made two hundred large shields of hammered gold; six hundred *shekels* of hammered gold went into each shield.

16 *He* also *made* three hundred shields of hammered gold; three hundred *shekels*[a] of gold went into each shield. The king put them in the House of the Forest of Lebanon.

17 Moreover the king made a great throne of ivory, and overlaid it with pure gold.

18 The throne *had* six steps, with a footstool of gold, *which were* fastened to the throne; there were armrests on either side of the place of the seat, and two lions stood beside the armrests.

19 Twelve lions stood there, one on each side of the six steps; nothing like *this* had been made for any *other* kingdom.

20 All King Solomon's drinking vessels *were* gold, and all the vessels of the House of the Forest of Lebanon *were* pure gold. Not *one was* silver, for this was accounted as nothing in the days of Solomon.

21 For the king's ships went to Tarshish with the servants of Hiram.[a] Once every three years the merchant ships[b] came, bringing gold, silver, ivory, apes, and monkeys.[c]

22 So King Solomon surpassed all the kings of the earth in riches and wisdom.

23 And all the kings of the earth sought the presence of Solomon to hear his wisdom, which God had put in his heart.

24 Each man brought his present: articles of silver and gold, garments, armor, spices, horses, and mules, at a set rate year by year.

25 Solomon had four thousand stalls for horses and chariots, and twelve thousand horsemen whom he stationed in the chariot cities and with the king at Jerusalem.

26 So he reigned over all the kings from the River[a] to the land of the Philistines, as far as the border of Egypt.

27 The king made silver *as common* in Jerusalem as stones, and he made cedar trees as abundant as the sycamores which *are* in the lowland.

28 And they brought horses to Solomon from Egypt and from all lands.

Death of Solomon

29 Now the rest of the acts of Solomon, first and last, *are* they not written in the book of Nathan the prophet, in the prophecy of Ahijah the Shilonite, and in the visions of Iddo the seer concerning Jeroboam the son of Nebat?

30 Solomon reigned in Jerusalem over all Israel forty years.

31 Then Solomon rested with his fathers, and was buried in the City of David his father. And Rehoboam his son reigned in his place.

8:16 [a]Following Septuagint, Syriac, and Vulgate; Masoretic Text reads *as far as.* **8:17** [a]Hebrew *Eloth* (compare 2 Kings 14:22) **9:10** [a]Or *almug* (compare 1 Kings 10:11, 12) **9:11** [a]Or *almug* (compare 1 Kings 10:11, 12) **9:16** [a]Or *three minas* (compare 1 Kings 10:17) **9:21** [a]Hebrew *Huram* (compare 1 Kings 10:22) [b]Literally *ships of Tarshish,* deep-sea vessels [c]Or *peacocks* **9:26** [a]That is, the Euphrates

The Revolt Against Rehoboam

10 And Rehoboam went to Shechem, for
all Israel had gone to Shechem to make
him king.
2 So it happened, when Jeroboam the son of
Nebat heard *it* (he was in Egypt, where he had
fled from the presence of King Solomon), that
Jeroboam returned from Egypt.
3 Then they sent for him and called him. And
Jeroboam and all Israel came and spoke to Re-
hoboam, saying,
4 "Your father made our yoke heavy; now
therefore, lighten the burdensome service of
your father and his heavy yoke which he put
on us, and we will serve you."
5 So he said to them, "Come back to me after
three days." And the people departed.
6 Then King Rehoboam consulted the elders
who stood before his father Solomon while he
still lived, saying, "How do you advise *me* to
answer these people?"
7 And they spoke to him, saying, "If you are
kind to these people, and please them, and
speak good words to them, they will be your
servants forever."
8 But he rejected the advice which the elders
had given him, and consulted the young men
who had grown up with him, who stood before
him.
9 And he said to them, "What advice do you
give? How should we answer this people who
have spoken to me, saying, 'Lighten the yoke
which your father put on us'?"
10 Then the young men who had grown up
with him spoke to him, saying, "Thus you
should speak to the people who have spoken to
you, saying, 'Your father made our yoke heavy,
but you make *it* lighter on us'—thus you shall
say to them: 'My little *finger* shall be thicker
than my father's waist!
11 'And now, whereas my father put a heavy
yoke on you, I will add to your yoke; my father
chastised you with whips, but I *will chastise
you* with scourges!'"[a]
12 So Jeroboam and all the people came to
Rehoboam on the third day, as the king had
directed, saying, "Come back to me the third
day."
13 Then the king answered them roughly.
King Rehoboam rejected the advice of the el-
ders,
14 and he spoke to them according to the ad-
vice of the young men, saying, "My father[a]
made your yoke heavy, but I will add to it;
my father chastised you with whips, but I *will
chastise you* with scourges!"[b]
15 So the king did not listen to the people; for
the turn *of events* was from God, that the LORD
might fulfill His word, which He had spoken
by the hand of Ahijah the Shilonite to Jero-
boam the son of Nebat.
16 Now when all Israel *saw* that the king did
not listen to them, the people answered the
king, saying:

"What share have we in David?
We have no inheritance in the son of
Jesse.
Every man to your tents, O Israel!
Now see to your own house, O David!"

So all Israel departed to their tents.
17 But Rehoboam reigned over the children
of Israel who dwelt in the cities of Judah.
18 Then King Rehoboam sent Hadoram, who
was in charge of revenue; but the children of
Israel stoned him with stones, and he died.
Therefore King Rehoboam mounted *his* char-
iot in haste to flee to Jerusalem.
19 So Israel has been in rebellion against the
house of David to this day.

11 Now when Rehoboam came to Jerusa-
lem, he assembled from the house of Ju-
dah and Benjamin one hundred and eighty
thousand chosen *men* who were warriors, to
fight against Israel, that he might restore the
kingdom to Rehoboam.
2 But the word of the LORD came to Shema-
iah the man of God, saying,
3 "Speak to Rehoboam the son of Solomon,
king of Judah, and to all Israel in Judah and
Benjamin, saying,
4 'Thus says the LORD: "You shall not go up
or fight against your brethren! Let every man
return to his house, for this thing is from
Me."'" Therefore they obeyed the words of the
LORD, and turned back from attacking Jero-
boam.

Rehoboam Fortifies the Cities

5 So Rehoboam dwelt in Jerusalem, and
built cities for defense in Judah.
6 And he built Bethlehem, Etam, Tekoa,
7 Beth Zur, Sochoh, Adullam,
8 Gath, Mareshah, Ziph,
9 Adoraim, Lachish, Azekah,
10 Zorah, Aijalon, and Hebron, which are in
Judah and Benjamin, fortified cities.
11 And he fortified the strongholds, and put
captains in them, and stores of food, oil, and
wine.
12 Also in every city *he put* shields and
spears, and made them very strong, having Ju-
dah and Benjamin on his side.

Priests and Levites Move to Judah

13 And from all their territories the priests
and the Levites who *were* in all Israel took
their stand with him.
14 For the Levites left their common-lands
and their possessions and came to Judah and
Jerusalem, for Jeroboam and his sons had re-
jected them from serving as priests to the
LORD.
15 Then he appointed for himself priests for
the high places, for the demons, and the calf
idols which he had made.
16 And after *the Levites left*,[a] those from all
the tribes of Israel, such as set their heart to
seek the LORD God of Israel, came to Jerusa-
lem to sacrifice to the LORD God of their fa-
thers.
17 So they strengthened the kingdom of Ju-
dah, and made Rehoboam the son of Solomon
strong for three years, because they walked in
the way of David and Solomon for three years.

The Family of Rehoboam

18 Then Rehoboam took for himself as wife
Mahalath the daughter of Jerimoth the son of
David, *and of* Abihail the daughter of Eliah the
son of Jesse.

10:11 [a]Literally *scorpions* **10:14** [a]Following many Hebrew manuscripts, Septuagint, Syriac, and Vulgate (compare verse 10 and 1 Kings 12:14); Masoretic Text reads *I*. [b]Literally *scorpions* **11:16** [a]Literally *after them*

19 And she bore him children: Jeush, Shama-
riah, and Zaham.
20 After her he took Maachah the grand-
daughter[a] of Absalom; and she bore him Abi-
jah, Attai, Ziza, and Shelomith.
21 Now Rehoboam loved Maachah the grand-
daughter of Absalom more than all his wives
and his concubines; for he took eighteen wives
and sixty concubines, and begot twenty-eight
sons and sixty daughters.
22 And Rehoboam appointed Abijah the son
of Maachah as chief, *to be* leader among his
brothers; for he *intended* to make him king.
23 He dealt wisely, and dispersed some of his
sons throughout all the territories of Judah and
Benjamin, to every fortified city; and he gave
them provisions in abundance. He also sought
many wives *for them.*

Egypt Attacks Judah

12 Now it came to pass, when Rehoboam
had established the kingdom and had
strengthened himself, that he forsook the law
of the LORD, and all Israel along with him.
2 And it happened in the fifth year of King
Rehoboam *that* Shishak king of Egypt came
up against Jerusalem, because they had trans-
gressed against the LORD,
3 with twelve hundred chariots, sixty thou-
sand horsemen, and people without number
who came with him out of Egypt—the Lubim
and the Sukkiim and the Ethiopians.
4 And he took the fortified cities of Judah and
came to Jerusalem.
5 Then Shemaiah the prophet came to Reho-
boam and the leaders of Judah, who were gath-
ered together in Jerusalem because of Shishak,
and said to them, "Thus says the LORD: 'You
have forsaken Me, and therefore I also have
left you in the hand of Shishak.' "
6 So the leaders of Israel and the king hum-
bled themselves; and they said, "The LORD *is*
righteous."
7 Now when the LORD saw that they hum-
bled themselves, the word of the LORD came
to Shemaiah, saying, "They have humbled
themselves; *therefore* I will not destroy them,
but I will grant them some deliverance. My
wrath shall not be poured out on Jerusalem by
the hand of Shishak.
8 "Nevertheless they will be his servants,
that they may distinguish My service from the
service of the kingdoms of the nations."
9 So Shishak king of Egypt came up against
Jerusalem, and took away the treasures of the
house of the LORD and the treasures of the
king's house; he took everything. He also car-
ried away the gold shields which Solomon had
made.
10 Then King Rehoboam made bronze shields
in their place, and committed *them* to the
hands of the captains of the guard, who guarded
the doorway of the king's house.
11 And whenever the king entered the house
of the LORD, the guard would go and bring
them out; then they would take them back into
the guardroom.
12 When he humbled himself, the wrath of
the LORD turned from him, so as not to destroy
him completely; and things also went well in
Judah.

The End of Rehoboam's Reign

13 Thus King Rehoboam strengthened him-
self in Jerusalem and reigned. Now Rehoboam
was forty-one years old when he became king;
and he reigned seventeen years in Jerusalem,
the city which the LORD had chosen out of all
the tribes of Israel, to put His name there. His
mother's name *was* Naamah, an Ammonitess.
14 And he did evil, because he did not prepare
his heart to seek the LORD.
15 The acts of Rehoboam, first and last, *are*
they not written in the book of Shemaiah the
prophet, and of Iddo the seer concerning ge-
nealogies? And *there were* wars between Re-
hoboam and Jeroboam all their days.
16 So Rehoboam rested with his fathers, and
was buried in the City of David. Then Abijah[a]
his son reigned in his place.

Abijah Reigns in Judah

13 In the eighteenth year of King Jero-
boam, Abijah became king over Judah.
2 He reigned three years in Jerusalem. His
mother's name *was* Michaiah[a] the daughter of
Uriel of Gibeah. And there was war between
Abijah and Jeroboam.
3 Abijah set the battle in order with an army
of valiant warriors, four hundred thousand
choice men. Jeroboam also drew up in battle
formation against him with eight hundred
thousand choice men, mighty men of valor.
4 Then Abijah stood on Mount Zemaraim,
which *is* in the mountains of Ephraim, and
said, "Hear me, Jeroboam and all Israel:
5 "Should you not know that the LORD God
of Israel gave the dominion over Israel to Da-
vid forever, to him and his sons, by a covenant
of salt?
6 "Yet Jeroboam the son of Nebat, the ser-
vant of Solomon the son of David, rose up and
rebelled against his lord.
7 "Then worthless rogues gathered to him,
and strengthened themselves against Reho-
boam the son of Solomon, when Rehoboam
was young and inexperienced and could not
withstand them.
8 "And now you think to withstand the king-
dom of the LORD, which is in the hand of the
sons of David; and you *are* a great multitude,
and with you are the gold calves which Jero-
boam made for you as gods.
9 "Have you not cast out the priests of the
LORD, the sons of Aaron, and the Levites, and
made for yourselves priests, like the peoples
of *other* lands, so that whoever comes to conse-
crate himself with a young bull and seven rams
may be a priest of *things that are* not gods?
10 "But as for us, the LORD *is* our God, and
we have not forsaken Him; and the priests who
minister to the LORD *are* the sons of Aaron,
and the Levites *attend* to *their* duties.
11 "And they burn to the LORD every morning
and every evening burnt sacrifices and sweet
incense; *they* also *set* the showbread *in order*
on the pure *gold* table, and the lampstand of
gold with its lamps to burn every evening; for
we keep the command of the LORD our God,
but you have forsaken Him.
12 "Now look, God Himself is with us as *our*
head, and His priests with sounding trumpets
to sound the alarm against you. O children of

11:20 [a]Literally *daughter,* but in the broader sense of granddaughter (compare 2 Chronicles 13:2) **12:16** [a]Spelled *Abijam* in 1 Kings 14:31 **13:2** [a]Spelled *Maachah* in 11:20, 21 and 1 Kings 15:2

Israel, do not fight against the LORD God of
your fathers, for you shall not prosper!"
13 But Jeroboam caused an ambush to go
around behind them; so they were in front of
Judah, and the ambush *was* behind them.
14 And when Judah looked around, to their
surprise the battle line *was* at both front and
rear; and they cried out to the LORD, and the
priests sounded the trumpets.
15 Then the men of Judah gave a shout; and
as the men of Judah shouted, it happened that
God struck Jeroboam and all Israel before Abi-
jah and Judah.
16 And the children of Israel fled before Ju-
dah, and God delivered them into their hand.
17 Then Abijah and his people struck them
with a great slaughter; so five hundred thou-
sand choice men of Israel fell slain.
18 Thus the children of Israel were subdued
at that time; and the children of Judah pre-
vailed, because they relied on the LORD God
of their fathers.
19 And Abijah pursued Jeroboam and took
cities from him: Bethel with its villages, Jesha-
nah with its villages, and Ephrain[a] with its vil-
lages.
20 So Jeroboam did not recover strength again
in the days of Abijah; and the LORD struck
him, and he died.
21 But Abijah grew mighty, married fourteen
wives, and begot twenty-two sons and sixteen
daughters.
22 Now the rest of the acts of Abijah, his ways,
and his sayings *are* written in the annals of the
prophet Iddo.

14 So Abijah rested with his fathers, and they
buried him in the City of David. Then
Asa his son reigned in his place. In his days
the land was quiet for ten years.

Asa Reigns in Judah

2 Asa did *what was* good and right in the
eyes of the LORD his God,
3 for he removed the altars of the foreign
gods and the high places, and broke down the
sacred pillars and cut down the wooden im-
ages.
4 He commanded Judah to seek the LORD
God of their fathers, and to observe the law
and the commandment.
5 He also removed the high places and the
incense altars from all the cities of Judah, and
the kingdom was quiet under him.
6 And he built fortified cities in Judah, for
the land had rest; he had no war in those years,
because the LORD had given him rest.
7 Therefore he said to Judah, "Let us build
these cities and make walls around *them,* and
towers, gates, and bars, *while* the land *is* yet
before us, because we have sought the LORD
our God; we have sought *Him,* and He has given
us rest on every side." So they built and pros-
pered.
8 And Asa had an army of three hundred thou-
sand from Judah who carried shields and spears,
and from Benjamin two hundred and eighty thou-
sand men who carried shields and drew bows;
all these *were* mighty men of valor.
9 Then Zerah the Ethiopian came out against
them with an army of a million men and three
hundred chariots, and he came to Mareshah.
10 So Asa went out against him, and they set
the troops in battle array in the Valley of Zeph-
athah at Mareshah.
11 And Asa cried out to the LORD his God,
and said, "LORD, *it is* nothing for You to help,
whether with many or with those who have no
power; help us, O LORD our God, for we rest
on You, and in Your name we go against this
multitude. O LORD, You *are* our God; do not let
man prevail against You!"
12 So the LORD struck the Ethiopians before
Asa and Judah, and the Ethiopians fled.
13 And Asa and the people who *were* with
him pursued them to Gerar. So the Ethiopians
were overthrown, and they could not recover,
for they were broken before the LORD and His
army. And they carried away very much spoil.
14 Then they defeated all the cities around Ge-
rar, for the fear of the LORD came upon them;
and they plundered all the cities, for there was
exceedingly much spoil in them.
15 They also attacked the livestock enclo-
sures, and carried off sheep and camels in
abundance, and returned to Jerusalem.

The Reforms of Asa

15 Now the Spirit of God came upon Aza-
riah the son of Oded.
2 And he went out to meet Asa, and said to
him: "Hear me, Asa, and all Judah and Benja-
min. The LORD *is* with you while you are with
Him. If you seek Him, He will be found by you;
but if you forsake Him, He will forsake you.
3 "For a long time Israel *has been* without
the true God, without a teaching priest, and
without law;
4 "but when in their trouble they turned to
the LORD God of Israel, and sought Him, He
was found by them.
5 "And in those times *there was* no peace to
the one who went out, nor to the one who came
in, but great turmoil *was* on all the inhabitants
of the lands.
6 "So nation was destroyed by nation, and
city by city, for God troubled them with every
adversity.
7 "But you, be strong and do not let your hands
be weak, for your work shall be rewarded!"
8 And when Asa heard these words and the
prophecy of Oded[a] the prophet, he took cour-
age, and removed the abominable idols from
all the land of Judah and Benjamin and from
the cities which he had taken in the mountains
of Ephraim; and he restored the altar of the
LORD that *was* before the vestibule of the LORD.
9 Then he gathered all Judah and Benjamin,
and those who dwelt with them from Ephraim,
Manasseh, and Simeon, for they came over to
him in great numbers from Israel when they
saw that the LORD his God was with him.
10 So they gathered together at Jerusalem in
the third month, in the fifteenth year of the reign
of Asa.
11 And they offered to the LORD at that time
seven hundred bulls and seven thousand sheep
from the spoil they had brought.
12 Then they entered into a covenant to seek
the LORD God of their fathers with all their
heart and with all their soul;
13 and whoever would not seek the LORD
God of Israel was to be put to death, whether
small or great, whether man or woman.
14 Then they took an oath before the LORD

13:19 [a]Or *Ephron* **15:8** [a]Following Masoretic Text and Septuagint; Syriac and Vulgate read *Azariah the son of Oded* (compare verse 1).

with a loud voice, with shouting and trumpets
and rams' horns.
15 And all Judah rejoiced at the oath, for they
had sworn with all their heart and sought Him
with all their soul; and He was found by them,
and the LORD gave them rest all around.
16 Also he removed Maachah, the mother of
Asa the king, from *being* queen mother, be-
cause she had made an obscene image of Ashe-
rah;[a] and Asa cut down her obscene image,
then crushed and burned *it* by the Brook Kidron.
17 But the high places were not removed from
Israel. Nevertheless the heart of Asa was loyal
all his days.
18 He also brought into the house of God the
things that his father had dedicated and that
he himself had dedicated: silver and gold and
utensils.
19 And there was no war until the thirty-fifth
year of the reign of Asa.

Asa's Treaty with Syria

16 In the thirty-sixth year of the reign of
Asa, Baasha king of Israel came up
against Judah and built Ramah, that he might
let none go out or come in to Asa king of Judah.
2 Then Asa brought silver and gold from the
treasuries of the house of the LORD and of the
king's house, and sent to Ben-Hadad king of
Syria, who dwelt in Damascus, saying,
3 "*Let there be* a treaty between you and me,
as there was between my father and your fa-
ther. See, I have sent you silver and gold; come,
break your treaty with Baasha king of Israel,
so that he will withdraw from me."
4 So Ben-Hadad heeded King Asa, and sent
the captains of his armies against the cities of
Israel. They attacked Ijon, Dan, Abel Maim, and
all the storage cities of Naphtali.
5 Now it happened, when Baasha heard *it*,
that he stopped building Ramah and ceased his
work.
6 Then King Asa took all Judah, and they
carried away the stones and timber of Ramah,
which Baasha had used for building; and with
them he built Geba and Mizpah.

Hanani's Message to Asa

7 And at that time Hanani the seer came to
Asa king of Judah, and said to him: "Because
you have relied on the king of Syria, and have
not relied on the LORD your God, therefore the
army of the king of Syria has escaped from
your hand.
8 "Were the Ethiopians and the Lubim not a
huge army with very many chariots and horse-
men? Yet, because you relied on the LORD, He
delivered them into your hand.
9 "For the eyes of the LORD run to and fro
throughout the whole earth, to show Himself
strong on behalf of *those* whose heart *is* loyal
to Him. In this you have done foolishly; there-
fore from now on you shall have wars."
10 Then Asa was angry with the seer, and put
him in prison, for *he was* enraged at him be-
cause of this. And Asa oppressed *some* of the
people at that time.

Illness and Death of Asa

11 Note that the acts of Asa, first and last, are
indeed written in the book of the kings of Ju-
dah and Israel.
12 And in the thirty-ninth year of his reign,
Asa became diseased in his feet, and his mal-
ady was severe; yet in his disease he did not
seek the LORD, but the physicians.
13 So Asa rested with his fathers; he died in
the forty-first year of his reign.
14 They buried him in his own tomb, which
he had made for himself in the City of David;
and they laid him in the bed which was filled
with spices and various ingredients prepared
in a mixture of ointments. They made a very
great burning for him.

Jehoshaphat Reigns in Judah

17 Then Jehoshaphat his son reigned in his
place, and strengthened himself against
Israel.
2 And he placed troops in all the fortified
cities of Judah, and set garrisons in the land of
Judah and in the cities of Ephraim which Asa
his father had taken.
3 Now the LORD was with Jehoshaphat, be-
cause he walked in the former ways of his fa-
ther David; he did not seek the Baals,
4 but sought the God[a] of his father, and
walked in His commandments and not accord-
ing to the acts of Israel.
5 Therefore the LORD established the king-
dom in his hand; and all Judah gave presents
to Jehoshaphat, and he had riches and honor
in abundance.
6 And his heart took delight in the ways of
the LORD; moreover he removed the high
places and wooden images from Judah.
7 Also in the third year of his reign he sent
his leaders, Ben-Hail, Obadiah, Zechariah, Ne-
thanel, and Michaiah, to teach in the cities of
Judah.
8 And with them *he sent* Levites: Shemaiah,
Nethaniah, Zebadiah, Asahel, Shemiramoth,
Jehonathan, Adonijah, Tobijah, and Tobadoni-
jah—the Levites; and with them Elishama and
Jehoram, the priests.
9 So they taught in Judah, and *had* the Book
of the Law of the LORD with them; they went
throughout all the cities of Judah and taught
the people.
10 And the fear of the LORD fell on all the
kingdoms of the lands that *were* around Judah,
so that they did not make war against Jehosha-
phat.
11 Also *some* of the Philistines brought Je-
hoshaphat presents and silver as tribute; and
the Arabians brought him flocks, seven thou-
sand seven hundred rams and seven thousand
seven hundred male goats.
12 So Jehoshaphat became increasingly pow-
erful, and he built fortresses and storage cities
in Judah.
13 He had much property in the cities of Ju-
dah; and the men of war, mighty men of valor,
were in Jerusalem.
14 These *are* their numbers, according to
their fathers' houses. Of Judah, the captains of
thousands: Adnah the captain, and with him
three hundred thousand mighty men of valor;
15 and next to him *was* Jehohanan the cap-
tain, and with him two hundred and eighty
thousand;
16 and next to him *was* Amasiah the son of
Zichri, who willingly offered himself to the
LORD, and with him two hundred thousand
mighty men of valor.
17 Of Benjamin: Eliada a mighty man of valor,

15:16 [a]A Canaanite deity **17:4** [a]Septuagint reads *LORD God.*

and with him two hundred thousand men
armed with bow and shield;
18 and next to him *was* Jehozabad, and with
him one hundred and eighty thousand pre-
pared for war.
19 These served the king, besides those the
king put in the fortified cities throughout all
Judah.

Micaiah Warns Ahab

18 Jehoshaphat had riches and honor in
abundance; and by marriage he allied
himself with Ahab.
2 After some years he went down to *visit*
Ahab in Samaria; and Ahab killed sheep and
oxen in abundance for him and the people who
were with him, and persuaded him to go up
with him to Ramoth Gilead.
3 So Ahab king of Israel said to Jehoshaphat
king of Judah, "Will you go with me *against*
Ramoth Gilead?" And he answered him, "I *am*
as you *are*, and my people as your people; *we*
will be with you in the war."
4 Also Jehoshaphat said to the king of Israel,
"Please inquire for the word of the LORD
today."
5 Then the king of Israel gathered the proph-
ets together, four hundred men, and said to
them, "Shall we go to war against Ramoth Gil-
ead, or shall I refrain?" So they said, "Go up,
for God will deliver it into the king's hand."
6 But Jehoshaphat said, "*Is there* not still a
prophet of the LORD here, that we may inquire
of Him?"[a]
7 So the king of Israel said to Jehoshaphat,
"*There is* still one man by whom we may in-
quire of the LORD; but I hate him, because he
never prophesies good concerning me, but al-
ways evil. He *is* Micaiah the son of Imla." And
Jehoshaphat said, "Let not the king say such
things!"
8 Then the king of Israel called one *of his*
officers and said, "Bring Micaiah the son of
Imla quickly!"
9 The king of Israel and Jehoshaphat king
of Judah, clothed in *their* robes, sat each on his
throne; and they sat at a threshing floor at the
entrance of the gate of Samaria; and all the
prophets prophesied before them.
10 Now Zedekiah the son of Chenaanah had
made horns of iron for himself; and he said,
"Thus says the LORD: 'With these you shall gore
the Syrians until they are destroyed.'"
11 And all the prophets prophesied so, say-
ing, "Go up to Ramoth Gilead and prosper, for
the LORD will deliver *it* into the king's hand."
12 Then the messenger who had gone to call
Micaiah spoke to him, saying, "Now listen, the
words of the prophets with one accord encour-
age the king. Therefore please let your word
be like *the word of* one of them, and speak en-
couragement."
13 And Micaiah said, "As the LORD lives, what-
ever my God says, that I will speak."
14 Then he came to the king; and the king
said to him, "Micaiah, shall we go to war
against Ramoth Gilead, or shall I refrain?"
And he said, "Go and prosper, and they shall
be delivered into your hand!"
15 So the king said to him, "How many times
shall I make you swear that you tell me nothing
but the truth in the name of the LORD?"
16 Then he said, "I saw all Israel scattered on
the mountains, as sheep that have no shep-
herd. And the LORD said, 'These have no mas-
ter. Let each return to his house in peace.'"
17 And the king of Israel said to Jehoshaphat,
"Did I not tell you he would not prophesy good
concerning me, but evil?"
18 Then *Micaiah* said, "Therefore hear the
word of the LORD: I saw the LORD sitting on
His throne, and all the host of heaven standing
on His right hand and His left.
19 "And the LORD said, 'Who will persuade
Ahab king of Israel to go up, that he may fall
at Ramoth Gilead?' So one spoke in this man-
ner, and another spoke in that manner.
20 "Then a spirit came forward and stood be-
fore the LORD, and said, 'I will persuade him.'
The LORD said to him, 'In what way?'
21 "So he said, 'I will go out and be a lying
spirit in the mouth of all his prophets.' And *the*
LORD said, 'You shall persuade *him* and also
prevail; go out and do so.'
22 "Therefore look! The LORD has put a lying
spirit in the mouth of these prophets of yours,
and the LORD has declared disaster against
you."
23 Then Zedekiah the son of Chenaanah
went near and struck Micaiah on the cheek,
and said, "Which way did the spirit from the
LORD go from me to speak to you?"
24 And Micaiah said, "Indeed you shall see
on that day when you go into an inner chamber
to hide!"
25 Then the king of Israel said, "Take Mica-
iah, and return him to Amon the governor of
the city and to Joash the king's son;
26 "and say, 'Thus says the king: "Put this
fellow in prison, and feed him with bread of
affliction and water of affliction, until I return
in peace." '"
27 But Micaiah said, "If you ever return in
peace, the LORD has not spoken by me." And
he said, "Take heed, all you people!"

Ahab Dies in Battle

28 So the king of Israel and Jehoshaphat the
king of Judah went up to Ramoth Gilead.
29 And the king of Israel said to Jehoshaphat,
"I will disguise myself and go into battle; but
you put on your robes." So the king of Israel
disguised himself, and they went into battle.
30 Now the king of Syria had commanded the
captains of the chariots who *were* with him,
saying, "Fight with no one small or great, but
only with the king of Israel."
31 So it was, when the captains of the chariots
saw Jehoshaphat, that they said, "It *is* the king
of Israel!" Therefore they surrounded him to
attack; but Jehoshaphat cried out, and the
LORD helped him, and God diverted them from
him.
32 For so it was, when the captains of the
chariots saw that it was not the king of Israel,
that they turned back from pursuing him.
33 Now a certain man drew a bow at random,
and struck the king of Israel between the joints
of his armor. So he said to the driver of his
chariot, "Turn around and take me out of the
battle, for I am wounded."
34 The battle increased that day, and the king

18:6 [a]Or *him*

of Israel propped *himself* up in *his* chariot facing the Syrians until evening; and about the time of sunset he died.

19 Then Jehoshaphat the king of Judah returned safely to his house in Jerusalem.
2 And Jehu the son of Hanani the seer went out to meet him, and said to King Jehoshaphat, "Should you help the wicked and love those who hate the LORD? Therefore the wrath of the LORD *is* upon you.
3 "Nevertheless good things are found in you, in that you have removed the wooden images from the land, and have prepared your heart to seek God."

The Reforms of Jehoshaphat

4 So Jehoshaphat dwelt at Jerusalem; and he went out again among the people from Beersheba to the mountains of Ephraim, and brought them back to the LORD God of their fathers.
5 Then he set judges in the land throughout all the fortified cities of Judah, city by city,
6 and said to the judges, "Take heed to what you are doing, for you do not judge for man but for the LORD, who *is* with you in the judgment.
7 "Now therefore, let the fear of the LORD be upon you; take care and do *it,* for *there is* no iniquity with the LORD our God, no partiality, nor taking of bribes."
8 Moreover in Jerusalem, for the judgment of the LORD and for controversies, Jehoshaphat appointed some of the Levites and priests, and some of the chief fathers of Israel, when they returned to Jerusalem.[a]
9 And he commanded them, saying, "Thus you shall act in the fear of the LORD, faithfully and with a loyal heart:
10 "Whatever case comes to you from your brethren who dwell in their cities, whether of bloodshed or offenses against law or commandment, against statutes or ordinances, you shall warn them, lest they trespass against the LORD and wrath come upon you and your brethren. Do this, and you will not be guilty.
11 "And take notice: Amariah the chief priest *is* over you in all matters of the LORD; and Zebadiah the son of Ishmael, the ruler of the house of Judah, for all the king's matters; also the Levites *will be* officials before you. Behave courageously, and the LORD will be with the good."

Ammon, Moab, and Mount Seir Defeated

20 It happened after this *that* the people of Moab with the people of Ammon, and *others* with them besides the Ammonites,[a] came to battle against Jehoshaphat.
2 Then some came and told Jehoshaphat, saying, "A great multitude is coming against you from beyond the sea, from Syria;[a] and they are in Hazazon Tamar" (which *is* En Gedi).
3 And Jehoshaphat feared, and set himself to seek the LORD, and proclaimed a fast throughout all Judah.
4 So Judah gathered together to ask *help* from the LORD; and from all the cities of Judah they came to seek the LORD.
5 Then Jehoshaphat stood in the assembly of Judah and Jerusalem, in the house of the LORD, before the new court,
6 and said: "O LORD God of our fathers, *are* You not God in heaven, and do You *not* rule over all the kingdoms of the nations, and in Your hand *is there not* power and might, so that no one is able to withstand You?
7 "*Are* You not our God, *who* drove out the inhabitants of this land before Your people Israel, and gave it to the descendants of Abraham Your friend forever?
8 "And they dwell in it, and have built You a sanctuary in it for Your name, saying,
9 'If disaster comes upon us—sword, judgment, pestilence, or famine—we will stand before this temple and in Your presence (for Your name *is* in this temple), and cry out to You in our affliction, and You will hear and save.'
10 "And now, here are the people of Ammon, Moab, and Mount Seir—whom You would not let Israel invade when they came out of the land of Egypt, but they turned from them and did not destroy them—
11 "here they are, rewarding us by coming to throw us out of Your possession which You have given us to inherit.
12 "O our God, will You not judge them? For we have no power against this great multitude that is coming against us; nor do we know what to do, but our eyes *are* upon You."
13 Now all Judah, with their little ones, their wives, and their children, stood before the LORD.
14 Then the Spirit of the LORD came upon Jahaziel the son of Zechariah, the son of Benaiah, the son of Jeiel, the son of Mattaniah, a Levite of the sons of Asaph, in the midst of the assembly.
15 And he said, "Listen, all you of Judah and you inhabitants of Jerusalem, and you, King Jehoshaphat! Thus says the LORD to you: 'Do not be afraid nor dismayed because of this great multitude, for the battle *is* not yours, but God's.
16 'Tomorrow go down against them. They will surely come up by the Ascent of Ziz, and you will find them at the end of the brook before the Wilderness of Jeruel.
17 'You will not *need* to fight in this *battle.* Position yourselves, stand still and see the salvation of the LORD, who is with you, O Judah and Jerusalem!' Do not fear or be dismayed; tomorrow go out against them, for the LORD *is* with you."
18 And Jehoshaphat bowed his head with *his* face to the ground, and all Judah and the inhabitants of Jerusalem bowed before the LORD, worshiping the LORD.
19 Then the Levites of the children of the Kohathites and of the children of the Korahites stood up to praise the LORD God of Israel with voices loud and high.
20 So they rose early in the morning and went out into the Wilderness of Tekoa; and as they went out, Jehoshaphat stood and said, "Hear me, O Judah and you inhabitants of Jerusalem: Believe in the LORD your God, and you shall be established; believe His prophets, and you shall prosper."
21 And when he had consulted with the people, he appointed those who should sing to the

19:8 [a]Septuagint and Vulgate read *for the inhabitants of Jerusalem.* **20:1** [a]Following Masoretic Text and Vulgate; Septuagint reads *Meunites* (compare 26:7). **20:2** [a]Following Masoretic Text, Septuagint, and Vulgate; some Hebrew manuscripts and Old Latin read *Edom.*

LORD, and who should praise the beauty of holiness, as they went out before the army and were saying:

> "Praise the LORD,
> For His mercy *endures* forever."[a]

22 Now when they began to sing and to praise, the LORD set ambushes against the people of Ammon, Moab, and Mount Seir, who had come against Judah; and they were defeated.
23 For the people of Ammon and Moab stood up against the inhabitants of Mount Seir to utterly kill and destroy *them*. And when they had made an end of the inhabitants of Seir, they helped to destroy one another.
24 So when Judah came to a place overlooking the wilderness, they looked toward the multitude; and there *were* their dead bodies, fallen on the earth. No one had escaped.
25 When Jehoshaphat and his people came to take away their spoil, they found among them an abundance of valuables on the dead bodies,[a] and precious jewelry, which they stripped off for themselves, more than they could carry away; and they were three days gathering the spoil because there was so much.
26 And on the fourth day they assembled in the Valley of Berachah, for there they blessed the LORD; therefore the name of that place was called The Valley of Berachah[a] until this day.
27 Then they returned, every man of Judah and Jerusalem, with Jehoshaphat in front of them, to go back to Jerusalem with joy, for the LORD had made them rejoice over their enemies.
28 So they came to Jerusalem, with stringed instruments and harps and trumpets, to the house of the LORD.
29 And the fear of God was on all the kingdoms of *those* countries when they heard that the LORD had fought against the enemies of Israel.
30 Then the realm of Jehoshaphat was quiet, for his God gave him rest all around.

The End of Jehoshaphat's Reign

31 So Jehoshaphat was king over Judah. *He was* thirty-five years old when he became king, and he reigned twenty-five years in Jerusalem. His mother's name *was* Azubah the daughter of Shilhi.
32 And he walked in the way of his father Asa, and did not turn aside from it, doing *what was* right in the sight of the LORD.
33 Nevertheless the high places were not taken away, for as yet the people had not directed their hearts to the God of their fathers.
34 Now the rest of the acts of Jehoshaphat, first and last, indeed they *are* written in the book of Jehu the son of Hanani, which *is* mentioned in the book of the kings of Israel.
35 After this Jehoshaphat king of Judah allied himself with Ahaziah king of Israel, who acted very wickedly.
36 And he allied himself with him to make ships to go to Tarshish, and they made the ships in Ezion Geber.
37 But Eliezer the son of Dodavah of Mareshah prophesied against Jehoshaphat, saying, "Because you have allied yourself with Ahaziah, the LORD has destroyed your works." Then the ships were wrecked, so that they were not able to go to Tarshish.

Jehoram Reigns in Judah

21 And Jehoshaphat rested with his fathers, and was buried with his fathers in the City of David. Then Jehoram his son reigned in his place.
2 He had brothers, the sons of Jehoshaphat: Azariah, Jehiel, Zechariah, Azaryahu, Michael, and Shephatiah; all these *were* the sons of Jehoshaphat king of Israel.
3 Their father gave them great gifts of silver and gold and precious things, with fortified cities in Judah; but he gave the kingdom to Jehoram, because he *was* the firstborn.
4 Now when Jehoram was established over the kingdom of his father, he strengthened himself and killed all his brothers with the sword, and also *others* of the princes of Israel.
5 Jehoram *was* thirty-two years old when he became king, and he reigned eight years in Jerusalem.
6 And he walked in the way of the kings of Israel, just as the house of Ahab had done, for he had the daughter of Ahab as a wife; and he did evil in the sight of the LORD.
7 Yet the LORD would not destroy the house of David, because of the covenant that He had made with David, and since He had promised to give a lamp to him and to his sons forever.
8 In his days Edom revolted against Judah's authority, and made a king over themselves.
9 So Jehoram went out with his officers, and all his chariots with him. And he rose by night and attacked the Edomites who had surrounded him and the captains of the chariots.
10 Thus Edom has been in revolt against Judah's authority to this day. At that time Libnah revolted against his rule, because he had forsaken the LORD God of his fathers.
11 Moreover he made high places in the mountains of Judah, and caused the inhabitants of Jerusalem to commit harlotry, and led Judah astray.
12 And a letter came to him from Elijah the prophet, saying,

> Thus says the LORD God of your father David:
> Because you have not walked in the ways of Jehoshaphat your father, or in the ways of Asa king of Judah,
> 13 but have walked in the way of the kings of Israel, and have made Judah and the inhabitants of Jerusalem to play the harlot like the harlotry of the house of Ahab, and also have killed your brothers, those of your father's household, *who were* better than yourself,
> 14 behold, the LORD will strike your people with a serious affliction—your children, your wives, and all your possessions;
> 15 and you *will become* very sick with a disease of your intestines, until your intestines come out by reason of the sickness, day by day.

16 Moreover the LORD stirred up against Jehoram the spirit of the Philistines and the Arabians who *were* near the Ethiopians.

20:21 [a]Compare Psalm 106:1 **20:25** [a]A few Hebrew manuscripts, Old Latin, and Vulgate read *garments;* Septuagint reads *armor.* **20:26** [a]Literally *Blessing*

17 And they came up into Judah and invaded
it, and carried away all the possessions that
were found in the king's house, and also his
sons and his wives, so that there was not a son
left to him except Jehoahaz,[a] the youngest of
his sons.
18 After all this the LORD struck him in his
intestines with an incurable disease.
19 Then it happened in the course of time,
after the end of two years, that his intestines
came out because of his sickness; so he died in
severe pain. And his people made no burning
for him, like the burning for his fathers.
20 He was thirty-two years old when he be-
came king. He reigned in Jerusalem eight
years and, to no one's sorrow, departed. How-
ever they buried him in the City of David, but
not in the tombs of the kings.

Ahaziah Reigns in Judah

22 Then the inhabitants of Jerusalem made
Ahaziah his youngest son king in his
place, for the raiders who came with the Arabi-
ans into the camp had killed all the older *sons*.
So Ahaziah the son of Jehoram, king of Judah,
reigned.
2 Ahaziah *was* forty-two[a] years old when he
became king, and he reigned one year in Jeru-
salem. His mother's name *was* Athaliah the
granddaughter of Omri.
3 He also walked in the ways of the house of
Ahab, for his mother advised him to do wick-
edly.
4 Therefore he did evil in the sight of the
LORD, like the house of Ahab; for they were
his counselors after the death of his father, to
his destruction.
5 He also followed their advice, and went with
Jehoram[a] the son of Ahab king of Israel to war
against Hazael king of Syria at Ramoth Gilead;
and the Syrians wounded Joram.
6 Then he returned to Jezreel to recover
from the wounds which he had received at Ra-
mah, when he fought against Hazael king of
Syria. And Azariah[a] the son of Jehoram, king
of Judah, went down to see Jehoram the son
of Ahab in Jezreel, because he was sick.
7 His going to Joram was God's occasion for
Ahaziah's downfall; for when he arrived, he
went out with Jehoram against Jehu the son of
Nimshi, whom the LORD had anointed to cut
off the house of Ahab.
8 And it happened, when Jehu was execut-
ing judgment on the house of Ahab, and found
the princes of Judah and the sons of Ahaziah's
brothers who served Ahaziah, that he killed
them.
9 Then he searched for Ahaziah; and they
caught him (he was hiding in Samaria), and
brought him to Jehu. When they had killed
him, they buried him, "because," they said, "he
is the son of Jehoshaphat, who sought the
LORD with all his heart." So the house of Aha-
ziah had no one to assume power over the
kingdom.

Athaliah Reigns in Judah

10 Now when Athaliah the mother of Ahaziah
saw that her son was dead, she arose and de-
stroyed all the royal heirs of the house of Judah.
11 But Jehoshabeath,[a] the daughter of the
king, took Joash the son of Ahaziah, and stole
him away from among the king's sons who
were being murdered, and put him and his
nurse in a bedroom. So Jehoshabeath, the
daughter of King Jehoram, the wife of Jehoi-
ada the priest (for she was the sister of Aha-
ziah), hid him from Athaliah so that she did
not kill him.
12 And he was hidden with them in the house
of God for six years, while Athaliah reigned
over the land.

Joash Crowned King of Judah

23 In the seventh year Jehoiada strength-
ened himself, *and made a* covenant with
the captains of hundreds: Azariah the son of
Jeroham, Ishmael the son of Jehohanan, Aza-
riah the son of Obed, Maaseiah the son of Ada-
iah, and Elishaphat the son of Zichri.
2 And they went throughout Judah and
gathered the Levites from all the cities of Ju-
dah, and the chief fathers of Israel, and they
came to Jerusalem.
3 Then all the assembly made a covenant
with the king in the house of God. And he said
to them, "Behold, the king's son shall reign, as
the LORD has said of the sons of David.
4 "This *is* what you shall do: One-third of
you entering on the Sabbath, of the priests and
the Levites, *shall be* keeping watch over the
doors;
5 "one-third *shall be* at the king's house; and
one-third at the Gate of the Foundation. All the
people *shall be* in the courts of the house of the
LORD.
6 "But let no one come into the house of
the LORD except the priests and those of the
Levites who serve. They may go in, for they *are*
holy; but all the people shall keep the watch of
the LORD.
7 "And the Levites shall surround the king
on all sides, every man with his weapons in his
hand; and whoever comes into the house, let
him be put to death. You are to be with the king
when he comes in and when he goes out."
8 So the Levites and all Judah did according
to all that Jehoiada the priest commanded.
And each man took his men who were to be
on duty on the Sabbath, with those who were
going *off duty* on the Sabbath; for Jehoiada the
priest had not dismissed the divisions.
9 And Jehoiada the priest gave to the cap-
tains of hundreds the spears and the large and
small shields which *had belonged* to King Da-
vid, that *were* in the temple of God.
10 Then he set all the people, every man with
his weapon in his hand, from the right side of
the temple to the left side of the temple, along
by the altar and by the temple, all around the
king.
11 And they brought out the king's son, put
the crown on him, *gave him* the Testimony,[a]
and made him king. Then Jehoiada and his sons
anointed him, and said, "*Long* live the king!"

Death of Athaliah

12 Now when Athaliah heard the noise of the
people running and praising the king, she came
to the people *in* the temple of the LORD.

21:17 [a]Elsewhere called *Ahaziah* (compare 2 Chronicles 22:1) **22:2** [a]Or *twenty-two* (compare 2 Kings 8:26) **22:5** [a]Also spelled *Joram* (compare verses 5 and 7; 2 Kings 8:28; and elsewhere) **22:6** [a]Some Hebrew manuscripts, Septuagint, Syriac, Vulgate, and 2 Kings 8:29 read *Ahaziah.* **22:11** [a]Spelled *Jehosheba* in 2 Kings 11:2 **23:11** [a]That is, the Law (compare Exodus 25:16, 21; 31:18)

13 *When* she looked, there was the king standing by his pillar at the entrance; and the leaders and the trumpeters *were* by the king. All the people of the land were rejoicing and blowing trumpets, also the singers with musical instruments, and those who led in praise. So Athaliah tore her clothes and said, "Treason! Treason!"
14 And Jehoiada the priest brought out the captains of hundreds who were set over the army, and said to them, "Take her outside under guard, and slay with the sword whoever follows her." For the priest had said, "Do not kill her in the house of the LORD."
15 So they seized her; and she went by way of the entrance of the Horse Gate *into* the king's house, and they killed her there.
16 Then Jehoiada made a covenant between himself, the people, and the king, that they should be the LORD's people.
17 And all the people went to the temple[a] of Baal, and tore it down. They broke in pieces its altars and images, and killed Mattan the priest of Baal before the altars.
18 Also Jehoiada appointed the oversight of the house of the LORD to the hand of the priests, the Levites, whom David had assigned in the house of the LORD, to offer the burnt offerings of the LORD, as *it is* written in the Law of Moses, with rejoicing and with singing, *as it was established* by David.
19 And he set the gatekeepers at the gates of the house of the LORD, so that no one *who was* in any way unclean should enter.
20 Then he took the captains of hundreds, the nobles, the governors of the people, and all the people of the land, and brought the king down from the house of the LORD; and they went through the Upper Gate to the king's house, and set the king on the throne of the kingdom.
21 So all the people of the land rejoiced; and the city was quiet, for they had slain Athaliah with the sword.

Joash Repairs the Temple

24 Joash *was* seven years old when he became king, and he reigned forty years in Jerusalem. His mother's name *was* Zibiah of Beersheba.
2 Joash did *what was* right in the sight of the LORD all the days of Jehoiada the priest.
3 And Jehoiada took two wives for him, and he had sons and daughters.
4 Now it happened after this *that* Joash set his heart on repairing the house of the LORD.
5 Then he gathered the priests and the Levites, and said to them, "Go out to the cities of Judah, and gather from all Israel money to repair the house of your God from year to year, and see that you do it quickly." However the Levites did not do it quickly.
6 So the king called Jehoiada the chief *priest,* and said to him, "Why have you not required the Levites to bring in from Judah and from Jerusalem the collection, *according to the commandment* of Moses the servant of the LORD and of the assembly of Israel, for the tabernacle of witness?"
7 For the sons of Athaliah, that wicked woman, had broken into the house of God, and had also presented all the dedicated things of the house of the LORD to the Baals.
8 Then at the king's command they made a chest, and set it outside at the gate of the house of the LORD.
9 And they made a proclamation throughout Judah and Jerusalem to bring to the LORD the collection *that* Moses the servant of God *had imposed* on Israel in the wilderness.
10 Then all the leaders and all the people rejoiced, brought their contributions, and put *them* into the chest until all had given.
11 So it was, at that time, when the chest was brought to the king's official by the hand of the Levites, and when they saw that *there was* much money, that the king's scribe and the high priest's officer came and emptied the chest, and took it and returned it to its place. Thus they did day by day, and gathered money in abundance.
12 The king and Jehoiada gave it to those who did the work of the service of the house of the LORD; and they hired masons and carpenters to repair the house of the LORD, and also those who worked in iron and bronze to restore the house of the LORD.
13 So the workmen labored, and the work was completed by them; they restored the house of God to its original condition and reinforced it.
14 When they had finished, they brought the rest of the money before the king and Jehoiada; they made from it articles for the house of the LORD, articles for serving and offering, spoons and vessels of gold and silver. And they offered burnt offerings in the house of the LORD continually all the days of Jehoiada.

Apostasy of Joash

15 But Jehoiada grew old and was full of days, and he died; *he was* one hundred and thirty years old when he died.
16 And they buried him in the City of David among the kings, because he had done good in Israel, both toward God and His house.
17 Now after the death of Jehoiada the leaders of Judah came and bowed down to the king. And the king listened to them.
18 Therefore they left the house of the LORD God of their fathers, and served wooden images and idols; and wrath came upon Judah and Jerusalem because of their trespass.
19 Yet He sent prophets to them, to bring them back to the LORD; and they testified against them, but they would not listen.
20 Then the Spirit of God came upon Zechariah the son of Jehoiada the priest, who stood above the people, and said to them, "Thus says God: 'Why do you transgress the commandments of the LORD, so that you cannot prosper? Because you have forsaken the LORD, He also has forsaken you.'"
21 So they conspired against him, and at the command of the king they stoned him with stones in the court of the house of the LORD.
22 Thus Joash the king did not remember the kindness which Jehoiada his father had done to him, but killed his son; and as he died, he said, "The LORD look on *it,* and repay!"

Death of Joash

23 So it happened in the spring of the year *that* the army of Syria came up against him; and they came to Judah and Jerusalem, and destroyed all the leaders of the people from among the people, and sent all their spoil to the king of Damascus.

23:17 [a]Literally *house*

24 For the army of the Syrians came with a
small company of men; but the LORD delivered
a very great army into their hand, because they
had forsaken the LORD God of their fathers.
So they executed judgment against Joash.
25 And when they had withdrawn from him
(for they left him severely wounded), his own
servants conspired against him because of the
blood of the sons[a] of Jehoiada the priest, and
killed him on his bed. So he died. And they
buried him in the City of David, but they did
not bury him in the tombs of the kings.
26 These are the ones who conspired against
him: Zabad[a] the son of Shimeath the Ammonit-
ess, and Jehozabad the son of Shimrith[b] the
Moabitess.
27 Now *concerning* his sons, and the many ora-
cles about him, and the repairing of the house
of God, indeed they *are* written in the annals
of the book of the kings. Then Amaziah his son
reigned in his place.

Amaziah Reigns in Judah

25 Amaziah *was* twenty-five years old *when*
he became king, and he reigned twenty-
nine years in Jerusalem. His mother's name *was*
Jehoaddan of Jerusalem.
2 And he did *what was* right in the sight of
the LORD, but not with a loyal heart.
3 Now it happened, as soon as the kingdom
was established for him, that he executed his
servants who had murdered his father the
king.
4 However he did not execute their children,
but *did* as *it is* written in the Law in the Book of
Moses, where the LORD commanded, saying,
"The fathers shall not be put to death for their
children, nor shall the children be put to death
for their fathers; but a person shall die for his
own sin."[a]

The War Against Edom

5 Moreover Amaziah gathered Judah to-
gether and set over them captains of thousands
and captains of hundreds, according to *their*
fathers' houses, throughout all Judah and Ben-
jamin; and he numbered them from twenty
years old and above, and found them to be three
hundred thousand choice *men, able* to go to
war, who could handle spear and shield.
6 He also hired one hundred thousand mighty
men of valor from Israel for one hundred tal-
ents of silver.
7 But a man of God came to him, saying,
"O king, do not let the army of Israel go with
you, for the LORD *is* not with Israel—*not with*
any of the children of Ephraim.
8 "But if you go, be gone! Be strong in battle!
Even so, God shall make you fall before the
enemy; for God has power to help and to over-
throw."
9 Then Amaziah said to the man of God, "But
what *shall we* do about the hundred talents
which I have given to the troops of Israel?"
And the man of God answered, "The LORD is
able to give you much more than this."
10 So Amaziah discharged the troops that
had come to him from Ephraim, to go back
home. Therefore their anger was greatly aroused
against Judah, and they returned home in great
anger.
11 Then Amaziah strengthened himself, and
leading his people, he went to the Valley of Salt
and killed ten thousand of the people of Seir.
12 Also the children of Judah took captive ten
thousand alive, brought them to the top of the
rock, and cast them down from the top of the
rock, so that they all were dashed in pieces.
13 But as for the soldiers of the army which
Amaziah had discharged, so that they would
not go with him to battle, they raided the cities
of Judah from Samaria to Beth Horon, killed
three thousand in them, and took much spoil.
14 Now it was so, after Amaziah came from
the slaughter of the Edomites, that he brought
the gods of the people of Seir, set them up *to
be* his gods, and bowed down before them and
burned incense to them.
15 Therefore the anger of the LORD was
aroused against Amaziah, and He sent him a
prophet who said to him, "Why have you
sought the gods of the people, which could not
rescue their own people from your hand?"
16 So it was, as he talked with him, that *the
king* said to him, "Have we made you the king's
counselor? Cease! Why should you be killed?"
Then the prophet ceased, and said, "I know
that God has determined to destroy you, be-
cause you have done this and have not heeded
my advice."

Israel Defeats Judah

17 Now Amaziah king of Judah asked advice
and sent to Joash[a] the son of Jehoahaz, the son
of Jehu, king of Israel, saying, "Come, let us
face one another *in battle*."
18 And Joash king of Israel sent to Amaziah
king of Judah, saying, "The thistle that *was* in
Lebanon sent to the cedar that was in Lebanon,
saying, 'Give your daughter to my son as wife';
and a wild beast that *was* in Lebanon passed
by and trampled the thistle.
19 "Indeed you say that you have defeated the
Edomites, and your heart is lifted up to boast.
Stay at home now; why should you meddle with
trouble, that you should fall—you and Judah
with you?"
20 But Amaziah would not heed, for it *came*
from God, that He might give them into the
hand *of their enemies,* because they sought the
gods of Edom.
21 So Joash king of Israel went out; and he
and Amaziah king of Judah faced one another
at Beth Shemesh, which *belongs* to Judah.
22 And Judah was defeated by Israel, and every
man fled to his tent.
23 Then Joash the king of Israel captured
Amaziah king of Judah, the son of Joash, the
son of Jehoahaz, at Beth Shemesh; and he
brought him to Jerusalem, and broke down the
wall of Jerusalem from the Gate of Ephraim to
the Corner Gate—four hundred cubits.
24 And *he took* all the gold and silver, all the
articles that were found in the house of God
with Obed-Edom, the treasures of the king's
house, and hostages, and returned to Samaria.

Death of Amaziah

25 Amaziah the son of Joash, king of Judah,
lived fifteen years after the death of Joash the
son of Jehoahaz, king of Israel.
26 Now the rest of the acts of Amaziah, from
first to last, indeed *are* they not written in the
book of the kings of Judah and Israel?

24:25 [a]Septuagint and Vulgate read *son* (compare verses 20–22). **24:26** [a]Or *Jozachar* (compare 2 Kings 12:21) [b]Or *Shomer* (compare 2 Kings 12:21) **25:4** [a]Deuteronomy 24:16 **25:17** [a]Spelled *Jehoash* in 2 Kings 14:8ff

27 After the time that Amaziah turned away
from following the LORD, they made a conspir-
acy against him in Jerusalem, and he fled to
Lachish; but they sent after him to Lachish and
killed him there.
28 Then they brought him on horses and bur-
ied him with his fathers in the City of Judah.

Uzziah Reigns in Judah

26 Now all the people of Judah took Uz-
ziah,[a] who *was* sixteen years old, and
made him king instead of his father Amaziah.
2 He built Elath[a] and restored it to Judah,
after the king rested with his fathers.
3 Uzziah *was* sixteen years old when he be-
came king, and he reigned fifty-two years in
Jerusalem. His mother's name was Jecholiah
of Jerusalem.
4 And he did *what was* right in the sight
of the LORD, according to all that his father
Amaziah had done.
5 He sought God in the days of Zechariah,
who had understanding in the visions[a] of God;
and as long as he sought the LORD, God made
him prosper.
6 Now he went out and made war against the
Philistines, and broke down the wall of Gath,
the wall of Jabneh, and the wall of Ashdod; and
he built cities *around* Ashdod and among the
Philistines.
7 God helped him against the Philistines,
against the Arabians who lived in Gur Baal,
and against the Meunites.
8 Also the Ammonites brought tribute to Uz-
ziah. His fame spread as far as the entrance of
Egypt, for he became exceedingly strong.
9 And Uzziah built towers in Jerusalem at
the Corner Gate, at the Valley Gate, and at the
corner buttress of the wall; then he fortified
them.
10 Also he built towers in the desert. He dug
many wells, for he had much livestock, both in
the lowlands and in the plains; *he also had*
farmers and vinedressers in the mountains
and in Carmel, for he loved the soil.
11 Moreover Uzziah had an army of fighting
men who went out to war by companies, ac-
cording to the number on their roll as prepared
by Jeiel the scribe and Maaseiah the officer,
under the hand of Hananiah, *one* of the king's
captains.
12 The total number of chief officers[a] of the
mighty men of valor *was* two thousand six
hundred.
13 And under their authority *was* an army of
three hundred and seven thousand five hun-
dred, that made war with mighty power, to
help the king against the enemy.
14 Then Uzziah prepared for them, for the
entire army, shields, spears, helmets, body ar-
mor, bows, and slings *to cast* stones.
15 And he made devices in Jerusalem, in-
vented by skillful men, to be on the towers and
the corners, to shoot arrows and large stones.
So his fame spread far and wide, for he was
marvelously helped till he became strong.

The Penalty for Uzziah's Pride

16 But when he was strong his heart was lifted
up, to *his* destruction, for he transgressed
against the LORD his God by entering the tem-
ple of the LORD to burn incense on the altar of
incense.
17 So Azariah the priest went in after him,
and with him were eighty priests of the LORD—
valiant men.
18 And they withstood King Uzziah, and said
to him, "*It is* not for you, Uzziah, to burn in-
cense to the LORD, but for the priests, the sons
of Aaron, who are consecrated to burn incense.
Get out of the sanctuary, for you have tres-
passed! You *shall have* no honor from the
LORD God."
19 Then Uzziah became furious; and he *had*
a censer in his hand to burn incense. And while
he was angry with the priests, leprosy broke
out on his forehead, before the priests in the
house of the LORD, beside the incense altar.
20 And Azariah the chief priest and all the
priests looked at him, and there, on his fore-
head, he *was* leprous; so they thrust him out of
that place. Indeed he also hurried to get out,
because the LORD had struck him.
21 King Uzziah was a leper until the day of
his death. He dwelt in an isolated house, because
he was a leper; for he was cut off from the house
of the LORD. Then Jotham his son *was* over the
king's house, judging the people of the land.
22 Now the rest of the acts of Uzziah, from
first to last, the prophet Isaiah the son of Amoz
wrote.
23 So Uzziah rested with his fathers, and they
buried him with his fathers in the field of burial
which *belonged* to the kings, for they said, "He
is a leper." Then Jotham his son reigned in his
place.

Jotham Reigns in Judah

27 Jotham *was* twenty-five years old when
he became king, and he reigned sixteen
years in Jerusalem. His mother's name *was*
Jerushah[a] the daughter of Zadok.
2 And he did *what was* right in the sight of
the LORD, according to all that his father Uz-
ziah had done (although he did not enter the
temple of the LORD). But still the people acted
corruptly.
3 He built the Upper Gate of the house of the
LORD, and he built extensively on the wall of
Ophel.
4 Moreover he built cities in the mountains
of Judah, and in the forests he built fortresses
and towers.
5 He also fought with the king of the Am-
monites and defeated them. And the people of
Ammon gave him in that year one hundred
talents of silver, ten thousand kors of wheat, and
ten thousand of barley. The people of Ammon
paid this to him in the second and third years
also.
6 So Jotham became mighty, because he
prepared his ways before the LORD his God.
7 Now the rest of the acts of Jotham, and all
his wars and his ways, indeed they *are* written
in the book of the kings of Israel and Judah.
8 He was twenty-five years old when he be-
came king, and he reigned sixteen years in Jeru-
salem.
9 So Jotham rested with his fathers, and they
buried him in the City of David. Then Ahaz his
son reigned in his place.

26:1 [a]Called *Azariah* in 2 Kings 14:21ff **26:2** [a]Hebrew *Eloth* **26:5** [a]Several Hebrew manuscripts, Septuagint, Syriac, Targum, and Arabic read *fear.* **26:12** [a]Literally *chief fathers* **27:1** [a]Spelled *Jerusha* in 2 Kings 15:33

Ahaz Reigns in Judah

28 Ahaz *was* twenty years old when he be-
came king, and he reigned sixteen years
in Jerusalem; and he did not do *what was* right
in the sight of the LORD, as his father David
had done.
2 For he walked in the ways of the kings of
Israel, and made molded images for the Baals.
3 He burned incense in the Valley of the Son
of Hinnom, and burned his children in the fire,
according to the abominations of the nations
whom the LORD had cast out before the chil-
dren of Israel.
4 And he sacrificed and burned incense on
the high places, on the hills, and under every
green tree.

Syria and Israel Defeat Judah

5 Therefore the LORD his God delivered him
into the hand of the king of Syria. They de-
feated him, and carried away a great multitude
of them as captives, and brought *them* to Da-
mascus. Then he was also delivered into the
hand of the king of Israel, who defeated him
with a great slaughter.
6 For Pekah the son of Remaliah killed one
hundred and twenty thousand in Judah in one
day, all valiant men, because they had for-
saken the LORD God of their fathers.
7 Zichri, a mighty man of Ephraim, killed
Maaseiah the king's son, Azrikam the officer
over the house, and Elkanah *who was* second
to the king.
8 And the children of Israel carried away
captive of their brethren two hundred thou-
sand women, sons, and daughters; and they
also took away much spoil from them, and
brought the spoil to Samaria.

Israel Returns the Captives

9 But a prophet of the LORD was there,
whose name *was* Oded; and he went out before
the army that came to Samaria, and said to
them: "Look, because the LORD God of your
fathers was angry with Judah, He has deliv-
ered them into your hand; but you have killed
them in a rage *that* reaches up to heaven.
10 "And now you propose to force the chil-
dren of Judah and Jerusalem to be your male
and female slaves; *but are* you not also guilty
before the LORD your God?
11 "Now hear me, therefore, and return the
captives, whom you have taken captive from
your brethren, for the fierce wrath of the LORD
is upon you."
12 Then some of the heads of the children of
Ephraim, Azariah the son of Johanan, Bere-
chiah the son of Meshillemoth, Jehizkiah the
son of Shallum, and Amasa the son of Hadlai,
stood up against those who came from the war,
13 and said to them, "You shall not bring the
captives here, for we *already* have offended
the LORD. You intend to add to our sins and to
our guilt; for our guilt is great, and *there is*
fierce wrath against Israel."
14 So the armed men left the captives and the
spoil before the leaders and all the assembly.
15 Then the men who were designated by
name rose up and took the captives, and from
the spoil they clothed all who were naked
among them, dressed them and gave them san-
dals, gave them food and drink, and anointed
them; and they let all the feeble ones ride on
donkeys. So they brought them to their breth-
ren at Jericho, the city of palm trees. Then they
returned to Samaria.

Assyria Refuses to Help Judah

16 At the same time King Ahaz sent to the
kings[a] of Assyria to help him.
17 For again the Edomites had come, attacked
Judah, and carried away captives.
18 The Philistines also had invaded the cities
of the lowland and of the South of Judah, and
had taken Beth Shemesh, Aijalon, Gederoth,
Sochoh with its villages, Timnah with its vil-
lages, and Gimzo with its villages; and they
dwelt there.
19 For the LORD brought Judah low because
of Ahaz king of Israel, for he had encouraged
moral decline in Judah and had been continu-
ally unfaithful to the LORD.
20 Also Tiglath-Pileser[a] king of Assyria came
to him and distressed him, and did not assist
him.
21 For Ahaz took part *of the treasures* from
the house of the LORD, from the house of the
king, and from the leaders, and he gave *it* to
the king of Assyria; but he did not help him.

Apostasy and Death of Ahaz

22 Now in the time of his distress King Ahaz
became increasingly unfaithful to the LORD.
This *is that* King Ahaz.
23 For he sacrificed to the gods of Damascus
which had defeated him, saying, "Because the
gods of the kings of Syria help them, I will
sacrifice to them that they may help me." But
they were the ruin of him and of all Israel.
24 So Ahaz gathered the articles of the house
of God, cut in pieces the articles of the house
of God, shut up the doors of the house of the
LORD, and made for himself altars in every
corner of Jerusalem.
25 And in every single city of Judah he made
high places to burn incense to other gods, and
provoked to anger the LORD God of his fathers.
26 Now the rest of his acts and all his ways,
from first to last, indeed they *are* written in the
book of the kings of Judah and Israel.
27 So Ahaz rested with his fathers, and they
buried him in the city, in Jerusalem; but they
did not bring him into the tombs of the kings
of Israel. Then Hezekiah his son reigned in his
place.

Hezekiah Reigns in Judah

29 Hezekiah became king *when he was*
twenty-five years old, and he reigned
twenty-nine years in Jerusalem. His mother's
name *was* Abijah[a] the daughter of Zechariah.
2 And he did *what was* right in the sight of
the LORD, according to all that his father David
had done.

Hezekiah Cleanses the Temple

3 In the first year of his reign, in the first
month, he opened the doors of the house of the
LORD and repaired them.
4 Then he brought in the priests and the Le-
vites, and gathered them in the East Square,
5 and said to them: "Hear me, Levites! Now
sanctify yourselves, sanctify the house of the

28:16 [a]Septuagint, Syriac, and Vulgate read *king* (compare verse 20). **28:20** [a]Hebrew *Tilgath-Pilneser* **29:1** [a]Spelled *Abi* in 2 Kings 18:2

LORD God of your fathers, and carry out the
rubbish from the holy *place*.
6 "For our fathers have trespassed and done
evil in the eyes of the LORD our God; they have
forsaken Him, have turned their faces away
from the dwelling place of the LORD, and
turned *their* backs *on Him*.
7 "They have also shut up the doors of the
vestibule, put out the lamps, and have not
burned incense or offered burnt offerings in
the holy *place* to the God of Israel.
8 "Therefore the wrath of the LORD fell
upon Judah and Jerusalem, and He has given
them up to trouble, to desolation, and to jeer-
ing, as you see with your eyes.
9 "For indeed, because of this our fathers
have fallen by the sword; and our sons, our
daughters, and our wives *are* in captivity.
10 "Now *it is* in my heart to make a covenant
with the LORD God of Israel, that His fierce
wrath may turn away from us.
11 "My sons, do not be negligent now, for the
LORD has chosen you to stand before Him, to
serve Him, and that you should minister to Him
and burn incense."
12 Then these Levites arose: Mahath the son
of Amasai and Joel the son of Azariah, of the
sons of the Kohathites; of the sons of Merari,
Kish the son of Abdi and Azariah the son of
Jehallelel; of the Gershonites, Joah the son of
Zimmah and Eden the son of Joah;
13 of the sons of Elizaphan, Shimri and Jeiel;
of the sons of Asaph, Zechariah and Mattaniah;
14 of the sons of Heman, Jehiel and Shimei;
and of the sons of Jeduthun, Shemaiah and
Uzziel.
15 And they gathered their brethren, sancti-
fied themselves, and went according to the
commandment of the king, at the words of the
LORD, to cleanse the house of the LORD.
16 Then the priests went into the inner part
of the house of the LORD to cleanse *it*, and
brought out all the debris that they found in the
temple of the LORD to the court of the house
of the LORD. And the Levites took *it* out and
carried *it* to the Brook Kidron.
17 Now they began to sanctify on the first *day*
of the first month, and on the eighth day of the
month they came to the vestibule of the LORD.
So they sanctified the house of the LORD in
eight days, and on the sixteenth day of the first
month they finished.
18 Then they went in to King Hezekiah and
said, "We have cleansed all the house of the
LORD, the altar of burnt offerings with all its
articles, and the table of the showbread with
all its articles.
19 "Moreover all the articles which King
Ahaz in his reign had cast aside in his trans-
gression we have prepared and sanctified; and
there they *are*, before the altar of the LORD."

Hezekiah Restores Temple Worship

20 Then King Hezekiah rose early, gathered
the rulers of the city, and went up to the house
of the LORD.
21 And they brought seven bulls, seven rams,
seven lambs, and seven male goats for a sin
offering for the kingdom, for the sanctuary, and
for Judah. Then he commanded the priests, the
sons of Aaron, to offer *them* on the altar of the
LORD.
22 So they killed the bulls, and the priests
received the blood and sprinkled *it* on the altar.
Likewise they killed the rams and sprinkled
the blood on the altar. They also killed the
lambs and sprinkled the blood on the altar.
23 Then they brought out the male goats *for*
the sin offering before the king and the assem-
bly, and they laid their hands on them.
24 And the priests killed them; and they pre-
sented their blood on the altar as a sin offering
to make an atonement for all Israel, for the king
commanded *that* the burnt offering and the
sin offering *be made* for all Israel.
25 And he stationed the Levites in the house
of the LORD with cymbals, with stringed instru-
ments, and with harps, according to the com-
mandment of David, of Gad the king's seer, and
of Nathan the prophet; for thus *was* the com-
mandment of the LORD by His prophets.
26 The Levites stood with the instruments of
David, and the priests with the trumpets.
27 Then Hezekiah commanded *them* to offer
the burnt offering on the altar. And when the
burnt offering began, the song of the LORD *also*
began, with the trumpets and with the instru-
ments of David king of Israel.
28 So all the assembly worshiped, the singers
sang, and the trumpeters sounded; all *this con-
tinued* until the burnt offering was finished.
29 And when they had finished offering, the
king and all who were present with him bowed
and worshiped.
30 Moreover King Hezekiah and the leaders
commanded the Levites to sing praise to the
LORD with the words of David and of Asaph
the seer. So they sang praises with gladness,
and they bowed their heads and worshiped.
31 Then Hezekiah answered and said, "Now
that you have consecrated yourselves to the
LORD, come near, and bring sacrifices and
thank offerings into the house of the LORD." So
the assembly brought in sacrifices and thank
offerings, and as many as were of a willing
heart *brought* burnt offerings.
32 And the number of the burnt offerings
which the assembly brought was seventy bulls,
one hundred rams, *and* two hundred lambs; all
these *were* for a burnt offering to the LORD.
33 The consecrated things *were* six hundred
bulls and three thousand sheep.
34 But the priests were too few, so that they
could not skin all the burnt offerings; therefore
their brethren the Levites helped them until
the work was ended and until the *other* priests
had sanctified themselves, for the Levites were
more diligent in sanctifying themselves than
the priests.
35 Also the burnt offerings *were* in abundance,
with the fat of the peace offerings and *with* the
drink offerings for *every* burnt offering. So the
service of the house of the LORD was set in order.
36 Then Hezekiah and all the people rejoiced
that God had prepared the people, since the
events took place so suddenly.

Hezekiah Keeps the Passover

30 And Hezekiah sent to all Israel and Ju-
dah, and also wrote letters to Ephraim
and Manasseh, that they should come to the
house of the LORD at Jerusalem, to keep the
Passover to the LORD God of Israel.
2 For the king and his leaders and all the
assembly in Jerusalem had agreed to keep the
Passover in the second month.
3 For they could not keep it at the regular

time,[a] because a sufficient number of priests
had not consecrated themselves, nor had the
people gathered together at Jerusalem.
4 And the matter pleased the king and all the
assembly.
5 So they resolved to make a proclamation
throughout all Israel, from Beersheba to Dan,
that they should come to keep the Passover to
the LORD God of Israel at Jerusalem, since they
had not done *it* for a long *time* in the *prescribed*
manner.
6 Then the runners went throughout all Israel
and Judah with the letters from the king and
his leaders, and spoke according to the command of the king: "Children of Israel, return
to the LORD God of Abraham, Isaac, and Israel;
then He will return to the remnant of you who
have escaped from the hand of the kings of Assyria.
7 "And do not be like your fathers and your
brethren, who trespassed against the LORD
God of their fathers, so that He gave them up
to desolation, as you see.
8 "Now do not be stiff-necked, as your fathers *were, but* yield yourselves to the LORD;
and enter His sanctuary, which He has sanctified forever, and serve the LORD your God,
that the fierceness of His wrath may turn away
from you.
9 "For if you return to the LORD, your brethren and your children *will be treated* with compassion by those who lead them captive, so
that they may come back to this land; for the
LORD your God *is* gracious and merciful, and
will not turn *His* face from you if you return to
Him."
10 So the runners passed from city to city
through the country of Ephraim and Manasseh,
as far as Zebulun; but they laughed at them
and mocked them.
11 Nevertheless some from Asher, Manasseh,
and Zebulun humbled themselves and came to
Jerusalem.
12 Also the hand of God was on Judah to give
them singleness of heart to obey the command
of the king and the leaders, at the word of the
LORD.
13 Now many people, a very great assembly,
gathered at Jerusalem to keep the Feast of Unleavened Bread in the second month.
14 They arose and took away the altars that
were in Jerusalem, and they took away all the
incense altars and cast *them* into the Brook
Kidron.
15 Then they slaughtered the Passover *lambs*
on the fourteenth *day* of the second month.
The priests and the Levites were ashamed, and
sanctified themselves, and brought the burnt
offerings to the house of the LORD.
16 They stood in their place according to their
custom, according to the Law of Moses the
man of God; the priests sprinkled the blood
received from the hand of the Levites.
17 For *there were* many in the assembly who
had not sanctified themselves; therefore the
Levites had charge of the slaughter of the Passover *lambs* for everyone *who was* not clean, to
sanctify *them* to the LORD.
18 For a multitude of the people, many from
Ephraim, Manasseh, Issachar, and Zebulun,
had not cleansed themselves, yet they ate the
Passover contrary to what was written. But
Hezekiah prayed for them, saying, "May the
good LORD provide atonement for everyone
19 "*who* prepares his heart to seek God, the
LORD God of his fathers, though *he is* not
cleansed according to the purification of the
sanctuary."
20 And the LORD listened to Hezekiah and
healed the people.
21 So the children of Israel who were present
at Jerusalem kept the Feast of Unleavened
Bread seven days with great gladness; and the
Levites and the priests praised the LORD day
by day, *singing* to the LORD, accompanied by
loud instruments.
22 And Hezekiah gave encouragement to all
the Levites who taught the good knowledge of
the LORD; and they ate throughout the feast
seven days, offering peace offerings and making confession to the LORD God of their fathers.
23 Then the whole assembly agreed to keep
the feast another seven days, and they kept it
another seven days with gladness.
24 For Hezekiah king of Judah gave to the
assembly a thousand bulls and seven thousand
sheep, and the leaders gave to the assembly a
thousand bulls and ten thousand sheep; and a
great number of priests sanctified themselves.
25 The whole assembly of Judah rejoiced,
also the priests and Levites, all the assembly
that came from Israel, the sojourners who
came from the land of Israel, and those who
dwelt in Judah.
26 So there was great joy in Jerusalem, for
since the time of Solomon the son of David,
king of Israel, *there had* been nothing like this
in Jerusalem.
27 Then the priests, the Levites, arose and
blessed the people, and their voice was heard;
and their prayer came *up* to His holy dwelling
place, to heaven.

The Reforms of Hezekiah

31 Now when all this was finished, all Israel who were present went out to the
cities of Judah and broke the *sacred* pillars in
pieces, cut down the wooden images, and threw
down the high places and the altars—from all
Judah, Benjamin, Ephraim, and Manasseh—
until they had utterly destroyed them all. Then
all the children of Israel returned to their own
cities, every man to his possession.
2 And Hezekiah appointed the divisions of
the priests and the Levites according to their
divisions, each man according to his service,
the priests and Levites for burnt offerings and
peace offerings, to serve, to give thanks, and to
praise in the gates of the camp[a] of the LORD.
3 The king also *appointed* a portion of his
possessions for the burnt offerings: for the
morning and evening burnt offerings, the
burnt offerings for the Sabbaths and the New
Moons and the set feasts, as *it is* written in the
Law of the LORD.
4 Moreover he commanded the people who
dwelt in Jerusalem to contribute support for the
priests and the Levites, that they might devote
themselves to the Law of the LORD.
5 As soon as the commandment was circulated, the children of Israel brought in abundance the firstfruits of grain and wine, oil and
honey, and of all the produce of the field; and

30:3 [a]That is, the first month (compare Leviticus 23:5); literally *at that time* **31:2** [a]That is, the temple

they brought in abundantly the tithe of everything.

6 And the children of Israel and Judah, who dwelt in the cities of Judah, brought the tithe of oxen and sheep; also the tithe of holy things which were consecrated to the LORD their God they laid in heaps.

7 In the third month they began laying them in heaps, and they finished in the seventh month.

8 And when Hezekiah and the leaders came and saw the heaps, they blessed the LORD and His people Israel.

9 Then Hezekiah questioned the priests and the Levites concerning the heaps.

10 And Azariah the chief priest, from the house of Zadok, answered him and said, "Since *the people* began to bring the offerings into the house of the LORD, we have had enough to eat and have plenty left, for the LORD has blessed His people; and what is left *is* this great abundance."

11 Now Hezekiah commanded *them* to prepare rooms in the house of the LORD, and they prepared them.

12 Then they faithfully brought in the offerings, the tithes, and the dedicated things; Cononiah the Levite had charge of them, and Shimei his brother *was* the next.

13 Jehiel, Azaziah, Nahath, Asahel, Jerimoth, Jozabad, Eliel, Ismachiah, Mahath, and Benaiah *were* overseers under the hand of Cononiah and Shimei his brother, at the commandment of Hezekiah the king and Azariah the ruler of the house of God.

14 Kore the son of Imnah the Levite, the keeper of the East Gate, *was* over the freewill offerings to God, to distribute the offerings of the LORD and the most holy things.

15 And under him *were* Eden, Miniamin, Jeshua, Shemaiah, Amariah, and Shecaniah, *his* faithful assistants in the cities of the priests, to distribute allotments to their brethren by divisions, to the great as well as the small.

16 Besides those males from three years old and up who were written in the genealogy, they distributed to everyone who entered the house of the LORD his daily portion for the work of his service, by his division,

17 and to the priests who were written in the genealogy according to their father's house, and to the Levites from twenty years old and up according to their work, by their divisions,

18 and to all who were written in the genealogy—their little ones and their wives, their sons and daughters, the whole company of them—for in their faithfulness they sanctified themselves in holiness.

19 Also for the sons of Aaron the priests, *who were* in the fields of the common-lands of their cities, in every single city, *there were* men who were designated by name to distribute portions to all the males among the priests and to all who were listed by genealogies among the Levites.

20 Thus Hezekiah did throughout all Judah, and he did what *was* good and right and true before the LORD his God.

21 And in every work that he began in the service of the house of God, in the law and in the commandment, to seek his God, he did *it* with all his heart. So he prospered.

Sennacherib Boasts Against the LORD

32 After these deeds of faithfulness, Sennacherib king of Assyria came and entered Judah; he encamped against the fortified cities, thinking to win them over to himself.

2 And when Hezekiah saw that Sennacherib had come, and that his purpose was to make war against Jerusalem,

3 he consulted with his leaders and commanders[a] to stop the water from the springs which *were* outside the city; and they helped him.

4 Thus many people gathered together who stopped all the springs and the brook that ran through the land, saying, "Why should the kings[a] of Assyria come and find much water?"

5 And he strengthened himself, built up all the wall that was broken, raised *it* up to the towers, and *built* another wall outside; also he repaired the Millo[a] *in* the City of David, and made weapons and shields in abundance.

6 Then he set military captains over the people, gathered them together to him in the open square of the city gate, and gave them encouragement, saying,

7 "Be strong and courageous; do not be afraid nor dismayed before the king of Assyria, nor before all the multitude that *is* with him; for *there are* more with us than with him.

8 "With him *is* an arm of flesh; but with us *is* the LORD our God, to help us and to fight our battles." And the people were strengthened by the words of Hezekiah king of Judah.

9 After this Sennacherib king of Assyria sent his servants to Jerusalem (but he and all the forces with him *laid siege* against Lachish), to Hezekiah king of Judah, and to all Judah who *were* in Jerusalem, saying,

10 "Thus says Sennacherib king of Assyria: 'In what do you trust, that you remain under siege in Jerusalem?

11 'Does not Hezekiah persuade you to give yourselves over to die by famine and by thirst, saying, "The LORD our God will deliver us from the hand of the king of Assyria"?

12 'Has not the same Hezekiah taken away His high places and His altars, and commanded Judah and Jerusalem, saying, "You shall worship before one altar and burn incense on it"?

13 'Do you not know what I and my fathers have done to all the peoples of *other* lands? Were the gods of the nations of those lands in any way able to deliver their lands out of my hand?

14 'Who *was there* among all the gods of those nations that my fathers utterly destroyed that could deliver his people from my hand, that your God should be able to deliver you from my hand?

15 'Now therefore, do not let Hezekiah deceive you or persuade you like this, and do not believe him; for no god of any nation or kingdom was able to deliver his people from my hand or the hand of my fathers. How much less will your God deliver you from my hand?'"

16 Furthermore, his servants spoke against the LORD God and against His servant Hezekiah.

17 He also wrote letters to revile the LORD God of Israel, and to speak against Him, saying, "As the gods of the nations of *other* lands have

32:3 [a]Literally *mighty men* **32:4** [a]Following Masoretic Text and Vulgate; Arabic, Septuagint, and Syriac read *king*.
32:5 [a]Literally *The Landfill*

not delivered their people from my hand, so the God of Hezekiah will not deliver His people from my hand."
18 Then they called out with a loud voice in Hebrew[a] to the people of Jerusalem who *were* on the wall, to frighten them and trouble them, that they might take the city.
19 And they spoke against the God of Jerusalem, as against the gods of the people of the earth—the work of men's hands.

Sennacherib's Defeat and Death

20 Now because of this King Hezekiah and the prophet Isaiah, the son of Amoz, prayed and cried out to heaven.
21 Then the LORD sent an angel who cut down every mighty man of valor, leader, and captain in the camp of the king of Assyria. So he returned shamefaced to his own land. And when he had gone into the temple of his god, some of his own offspring struck him down with the sword there.
22 Thus the LORD saved Hezekiah and the inhabitants of Jerusalem from the hand of Sennacherib the king of Assyria, and from the hand of all *others*, and guided them[a] on every side.
23 And many brought gifts to the LORD at Jerusalem, and presents to Hezekiah king of Judah, so that he was exalted in the sight of all nations thereafter.

Hezekiah Humbles Himself

24 In those days Hezekiah was sick and near death, and he prayed to the LORD; and He spoke to him and gave him a sign.
25 But Hezekiah did not repay according to the favor *shown* him, for his heart was lifted up; therefore wrath was looming over him and over Judah and Jerusalem.
26 Then Hezekiah humbled himself for the pride of his heart, he and the inhabitants of Jerusalem, so that the wrath of the LORD did not come upon them in the days of Hezekiah.

Hezekiah's Wealth and Honor

27 Hezekiah had very great riches and honor. And he made himself treasuries for silver, for gold, for precious stones, for spices, for shields, and for all kinds of desirable items;
28 storehouses for the harvest of grain, wine, and oil; and stalls for all kinds of livestock, and folds for flocks.[a]
29 Moreover he provided cities for himself, and possessions of flocks and herds in abundance; for God had given him very much property.
30 This same Hezekiah also stopped the water outlet of Upper Gihon, and brought the water by tunnel[a] to the west side of the City of David. Hezekiah prospered in all his works.
31 However, *regarding* the ambassadors of the princes of Babylon, whom they sent to him to inquire about the wonder that was *done* in the land, God withdrew from him, in order to test him, that He might know all *that was* in his heart.

Death of Hezekiah

32 Now the rest of the acts of Hezekiah, and his goodness, indeed they *are* written in the vision of Isaiah the prophet, the son of Amoz, *and* in the book of the kings of Judah and Israel.
33 So Hezekiah rested with his fathers, and they buried him in the upper tombs of the sons of David; and all Judah and the inhabitants of Jerusalem honored him at his death. Then Manasseh his son reigned in his place.

Manasseh Reigns in Judah

33 Manasseh *was* twelve years old when he became king, and he reigned fifty-five years in Jerusalem.
2 But he did evil in the sight of the LORD, according to the abominations of the nations whom the LORD had cast out before the children of Israel.
3 For he rebuilt the high places which Hezekiah his father had broken down; he raised up altars for the Baals, and made wooden images; and he worshiped all the host of heaven[a] and served them.
4 He also built altars in the house of the LORD, of which the LORD had said, "In Jerusalem shall My name be forever."
5 And he built altars for all the host of heaven in the two courts of the house of the LORD.
6 Also he caused his sons to pass through the fire in the Valley of the Son of Hinnom; he practiced soothsaying, used witchcraft and sorcery, and consulted mediums and spiritists. He did much evil in the sight of the LORD, to provoke Him to anger.
7 He even set a carved image, the idol which he had made, in the house of God, of which God had said to David and to Solomon his son, "In this house and in Jerusalem, which I have chosen out of all the tribes of Israel, I will put My name forever;
8 "and I will not again remove the foot of Israel from the land which I have appointed for your fathers—only if they are careful to do all that I have commanded them, according to the whole law and the statutes and the ordinances by the hand of Moses."
9 So Manasseh seduced Judah and the inhabitants of Jerusalem to do more evil than the nations whom the LORD had destroyed before the children of Israel.

Manasseh Restored After Repentance

10 And the LORD spoke to Manasseh and his people, but they would not listen.
11 Therefore the LORD brought upon them the captains of the army of the king of Assyria, who took Manasseh with hooks,[a] bound him with bronze *fetters*, and carried him off to Babylon.
12 Now when he was in affliction, he implored the LORD his God, and humbled himself greatly before the God of his fathers,
13 and prayed to Him; and He received his entreaty, heard his supplication, and brought him back to Jerusalem into his kingdom. Then Manasseh knew that the LORD *was* God.
14 After this he built a wall outside the City of David on the west side of Gihon, in the valley, as far as the entrance of the Fish Gate; and *it* enclosed Ophel, and he raised it to a very

32:18 [a]Literally *Judean* **32:22** [a]Septuagint reads *gave them rest;* Vulgate reads *gave them treasures.*
32:28 [a]Following Septuagint and Vulgate; Arabic and Syriac omit *folds for flocks;* Masoretic Text reads *flocks for sheepfolds.* **32:30** [a]Literally *brought it straight* (compare 2 Kings 20:20) **33:3** [a]The gods of the Assyrians
33:11 [a]That is, nose hooks (compare 2 Kings 19:28)

great height. Then he put military captains in
all the fortified cities of Judah.
15 He took away the foreign gods and the idol
from the house of the LORD, and all the altars
that he had built in the mount of the house of
the LORD and in Jerusalem; and he cast *them*
out of the city.
16 He also repaired the altar of the LORD,
sacrificed peace offerings and thank offerings
on it, and commanded Judah to serve the LORD
God of Israel.
17 Nevertheless the people still sacrificed on
the high places, *but* only to the LORD their God.

Death of Manasseh

18 Now the rest of the acts of Manasseh, his
prayer to his God, and the words of the seers
who spoke to him in the name of the LORD
God of Israel, indeed they *are written* in the
book[a] of the kings of Israel.
19 Also his prayer and *how God* received his
entreaty, and all his sin and trespass, and the
sites where he built high places and set up
wooden images and carved images, before he
was humbled, indeed they *are* written among
the sayings of Hozai.[a]
20 So Manasseh rested with his fathers, and
they buried him in his own house. Then his son
Amon reigned in his place.

Amon's Reign and Death

21 Amon *was* twenty-two years old when he
became king, and he reigned two years in Jeru-
salem.
22 But he did evil in the sight of the LORD,
as his father Manasseh had done; for Amon
sacrificed to all the carved images which his
father Manasseh had made, and served them.
23 And he did not humble himself before the
LORD, as his father Manasseh had humbled
himself; but Amon trespassed more and more.
24 Then his servants conspired against him,
and killed him in his own house.
25 But the people of the land executed all
those who had conspired against King Amon.
Then the people of the land made his son Jo-
siah king in his place.

Josiah Reigns in Judah

34 Josiah *was* eight years old when he be-
came king, and he reigned thirty-one
years in Jerusalem.
2 And he did *what was* right in the sight of
the LORD, and walked in the ways of his father
David; *he* did *not* turn aside to the right hand
or to the left.
3 For in the eighth year of his reign, while
he was still young, he began to seek the God of
his father David; and in the twelfth year he be-
gan to purge Judah and Jerusalem of the high
places, the wooden images, the carved images,
and the molded images.
4 They broke down the altars of the Baals in
his presence, and the incense altars which *were*
above them he cut down; and the wooden im-
ages, the carved images, and the molded im-
ages he broke in pieces, and made dust of them
and scattered *it* on the graves of those who had
sacrificed to them.
5 He also burned the bones of the priests on
their altars, and cleansed Judah and Jeru-
salem.
6 And so *he did* in the cities of Manasseh,
Ephraim, and Simeon, as far as Naphtali and
all around, with axes.[a]
7 When he had broken down the altars and
the wooden images, had beaten the carved im-
ages into powder, and cut down all the incense
altars throughout all the land of Israel, he re-
turned to Jerusalem.

Hilkiah Finds the Book of the Law

8 In the eighteenth year of his reign, when
he had purged the land and the temple,[a] he
sent Shaphan the son of Azaliah, Maaseiah the
governor of the city, and Joah the son of Joahaz
the recorder, to repair the house of the LORD
his God.
9 When they came to Hilkiah the high priest,
they delivered the money that was brought into
the house of God, which the Levites who kept the
doors had gathered from the hand of Manas-
seh and Ephraim, from all the remnant of Is-
rael, from all Judah and Benjamin, and *which*
they had brought back to Jerusalem.
10 Then they put *it* in the hand of the foremen
who had the oversight of the house of the
LORD; and they gave it to the workmen who
worked in the house of the LORD, to repair and
restore the house.
11 They gave *it* to the craftsmen and builders
to buy hewn stone and timber for beams, and
to floor the houses which the kings of Judah
had destroyed.
12 And the men did the work faithfully. Their
overseers *were* Jahath and Obadiah the Levites,
of the sons of Merari, and Zechariah and Me-
shullam, of the sons of the Kohathites, to su-
pervise. *Others of* the Levites, all of whom were
skillful with instruments of music,
13 *were* over the burden bearers and *were*
overseers of all who did work in any kind of
service. And *some* of the Levites *were* scribes,
officers, and gatekeepers.
14 Now when they brought out the money
that was brought into the house of the LORD,
Hilkiah the priest found the Book of the Law
of the LORD *given* by Moses.
15 Then Hilkiah answered and said to Sha-
phan the scribe, "I have found the Book of the
Law in the house of the LORD." And Hilkiah gave
the book to Shaphan.
16 So Shaphan carried the book to the king,
bringing the king word, saying, "All that was
committed to your servants they are doing.
17 "And they have gathered the money that
was found in the house of the LORD, and have
delivered it into the hand of the overseers and
the workmen."
18 Then Shaphan the scribe told the king, say-
ing, "Hilkiah the priest has given me a book."
And Shaphan read it before the king.
19 Thus it happened, when the king heard the
words of the Law, that he tore his clothes.
20 Then the king commanded Hilkiah, Ahi-
kam the son of Shaphan, Abdon[a] the son of
Micah, Shaphan the scribe, and Asaiah a servant
of the king, saying,
21 "Go, inquire of the LORD for me, and for
those who are left in Israel and Judah, concern-
ing the words of the book that is found; for
great *is* the wrath of the LORD that is poured
out on us, because our fathers have not kept

33:18 [a]Literally *words* **33:19** [a]Septuagint reads *the seers.* **34:20** [a]*Achbor the son of Michaiah* in 2 Kings 22:12

34:6 [a]Literally *swords* **34:8** [a]Literally *house*

the word of the LORD, to do according to all
that is written in this book."
22 So Hilkiah and those the king *had appointed* went to Huldah the prophetess, the
wife of Shallum the son of Tokhath,[a] the son of
Hasrah,[b] keeper of the wardrobe. (She dwelt in
Jerusalem in the Second Quarter.) And they
spoke to her to that *effect*.
23 Then she answered them, "Thus says the
LORD God of Israel, 'Tell the man who sent you
to Me,
24 "Thus says the LORD: 'Behold, I will bring
calamity on this place and on its inhabitants,
all the curses that are written in the book
which they have read before the king of Judah,
25 'because they have forsaken Me and burned
incense to other gods, that they might provoke
Me to anger with all the works of their hands.
Therefore My wrath will be poured out on this
place, and not be quenched.'"'
26 "But as for the king of Judah, who sent
you to inquire of the LORD, in this manner you
shall speak to him, 'Thus says the LORD God of
Israel: "*Concerning* the words which you have
heard—
27 "because your heart was tender, and you
humbled yourself before God when you heard
His words against this place and against its
inhabitants, and you humbled yourself before
Me, and you tore your clothes and wept before
Me, I also have heard *you*," says the LORD.
28 "Surely I will gather you to your fathers,
and you shall be gathered to your grave in peace;
and your eyes shall not see all the calamity
which I will bring on this place and its inhabitants."'" So they brought back word to the king.

Josiah Restores True Worship

29 Then the king sent and gathered all the
elders of Judah and Jerusalem.
30 The king went up to the house of the LORD,
with all the men of Judah and the inhabitants
of Jerusalem—the priests and the Levites, and
all the people, great and small. And he read in
their hearing all the words of the Book of the
Covenant which had been found in the house
of the LORD.
31 Then the king stood in his place and made
a covenant before the LORD, to follow the
LORD, and to keep His commandments and
His testimonies and His statutes with all his
heart and all his soul, to perform the words of
the covenant that were written in this book.
32 And he made all who were present in Jerusalem and Benjamin take a stand. So the inhabitants of Jerusalem did according to the
covenant of God, the God of their fathers.
33 Thus Josiah removed all the abominations
from all the country that *belonged* to the children of Israel, and made all who were present
in Israel diligently serve the LORD their God.
All his days they did not depart from following
the LORD God of their fathers.

Josiah Keeps the Passover

35 Now Josiah kept a Passover to the LORD
in Jerusalem, and they slaughtered the
Passover *lambs* on the fourteenth *day* of the first
month.
2 And he set the priests in their duties and
encouraged them for the service of the house
of the LORD.
3 Then he said to the Levites who taught all
Israel, who were holy to the LORD: "Put the
holy ark in the house which Solomon the son
of David, king of Israel, built. *It shall* no longer
be a burden on *your* shoulders. Now serve the
LORD your God and His people Israel.
4 "Prepare *yourselves* according to your fathers' houses, according to your divisions, following the written instruction of David king of
Israel and the written instruction of Solomon
his son.
5 "And stand in the holy *place* according to
the divisions of the fathers' houses of your
brethren the *lay* people, and *according to* the
division of the father's house of the Levites.
6 "So slaughter the Passover *offerings*, consecrate yourselves, and prepare *them* for your
brethren, that *they* may do according to the
word of the LORD by the hand of Moses."
7 Then Josiah gave the *lay* people lambs and
young goats from the flock, all for Passover
offerings for all who were present, to the number of thirty thousand, as well as three thousand
cattle; these *were* from the king's possessions.
8 And his leaders gave willingly to the people, to the priests, and to the Levites. Hilkiah,
Zechariah, and Jehiel, rulers of the house of
God, gave to the priests for the Passover *offerings* two thousand six hundred *from the flock*,
and three hundred cattle.
9 Also Conaniah, his brothers Shemaiah
and Nethanel, and Hashabiah and Jeiel and
Jozabad, chief of the Levites, gave to the Levites for Passover *offerings* five thousand *from
the flock* and five hundred cattle.
10 So the service was prepared, and the priests
stood in their places, and the Levites in their
divisions, according to the king's command.
11 And they slaughtered the Passover *offerings;* and the priests sprinkled *the blood* with
their hands, while the Levites skinned *the animals*.
12 Then they removed the burnt offerings
that *they* might give them to the divisions of
the fathers' houses of the *lay* people, to offer
to the LORD, as *it is* written in the Book of Moses. And so *they did* with the cattle.
13 Also they roasted the Passover *offerings*
with fire according to the ordinance; but the
other holy *offerings* they boiled in pots, in caldrons, and in pans, and divided *them* quickly
among all the *lay* people.
14 Then afterward they prepared portions for
themselves and for the priests, because the
priests, the sons of Aaron, *were busy* in offering
burnt offerings and fat until night; therefore
the Levites prepared portions for themselves
and for the priests, the sons of Aaron.
15 And the singers, the sons of Asaph, *were*
in their places, according to the command of
David, Asaph, Heman, and Jeduthun the king's
seer. Also the gatekeepers were at each gate;
they did not have to leave their position, because their brethren the Levites prepared portions for them.
16 So all the service of the LORD was prepared
the same day, to keep the Passover and to offer
burnt offerings on the altar of the LORD, according to the command of King Josiah.
17 And the children of Israel who were
present kept the Passover at that time, and the
Feast of Unleavened Bread for seven days.
18 There had been no Passover kept in Israel
like that since the days of Samuel the prophet;

34:22 [a]Spelled *Tikvah* in 2 Kings 22:14 [b]Spelled *Harhas* in 2 Kings 22:14

and none of the kings of Israel had kept such
a Passover as Josiah kept, with the priests and
the Levites, all Judah and Israel who were
present, and the inhabitants of Jerusalem.
19 In the eighteenth year of the reign of Josiah this Passover was kept.

Josiah Dies in Battle

20 After all this, when Josiah had prepared
the temple, Necho king of Egypt came up to
fight against Carchemish by the Euphrates;
and Josiah went out against him.
21 But he sent messengers to him, saying,
"What have I to do with you, king of Judah? *I
have* not *come* against you this day, but against
the house with which I have war; for God commanded me to make haste. Refrain *from meddling with* God, who *is* with me, lest He destroy
you."
22 Nevertheless Josiah would not turn his
face from him, but disguised himself so that he
might fight with him, and did not heed the
words of Necho from the mouth of God. So he
came to fight in the Valley of Megiddo.
23 And the archers shot King Josiah; and the
king said to his servants, "Take me away, for I
am severely wounded."
24 His servants therefore took him out of that
chariot and put him in the second chariot that
he had, and they brought him to Jerusalem.
So he died, and was buried in *one of* the tombs
of his fathers. And all Judah and Jerusalem
mourned for Josiah.
25 Jeremiah also lamented for Josiah. And to
this day all the singing men and the singing
women speak of Josiah in their lamentations.
They made it a custom in Israel; and indeed
they *are* written in the Laments.
26 Now the rest of the acts of Josiah and his
goodness, according to *what was* written in
the Law of the LORD,
27 and his deeds from first to last, indeed they
are written in the book of the kings of Israel
and Judah.

The Reign and Captivity of Jehoahaz

36 Then the people of the land took Jehoahaz the son of Josiah, and made him
king in his father's place in Jerusalem.
2 Jehoahaz[a] *was* twenty-three years old
when he became king, and he reigned three
months in Jerusalem.
3 Now the king of Egypt deposed him at Jerusalem; and he imposed on the land a tribute
of one hundred talents of silver and a talent of
gold.
4 Then the king of Egypt made *Jehoahaz's*[a]
brother Eliakim king over Judah and Jerusalem, and changed his name to Jehoiakim. And
Necho took Jehoahaz[b] his brother and carried
him off to Egypt.

The Reign and Captivity of Jehoiakim

5 Jehoiakim *was* twenty-five years old when
he became king, and he reigned eleven years
in Jerusalem. And he did evil in the sight of
the LORD his God.
6 Nebuchadnezzar king of Babylon came up
against him, and bound him in bronze *fetters*
to carry him off to Babylon.
7 Nebuchadnezzar also carried off *some* of
the articles from the house of the LORD to Babylon, and put them in his temple at Babylon.
8 Now the rest of the acts of Jehoiakim, the
abominations which he did, and what was
found against him, indeed they *are* written in
the book of the kings of Israel and Judah. Then
Jehoiachin his son reigned in his place.

The Reign and Captivity of Jehoiachin

9 Jehoiachin *was* eight[a] years old when he
became king, and he reigned in Jerusalem
three months and ten days. And he did evil in
the sight of the LORD.
10 At the turn of the year King Nebuchadnezzar summoned *him* and took him to Babylon,
with the costly articles from the house of the
LORD, and made Zedekiah, *Jehoiakim's*[a]
brother, king over Judah and Jerusalem.

Zedekiah Reigns in Judah

11 Zedekiah *was* twenty-one years old when
he became king, and he reigned eleven years
in Jerusalem.
12 He did evil in the sight of the LORD his
God, *and* did not humble himself before Jeremiah the prophet, *who spoke* from the mouth
of the LORD.
13 And he also rebelled against King Nebuchadnezzar, who had made him swear *an oath*
by God; but he stiffened his neck and hardened
his heart against turning to the LORD God of
Israel.
14 Moreover all the leaders of the priests and
the people transgressed more and more, *according* to all the abominations of the nations,
and defiled the house of the LORD which He
had consecrated in Jerusalem.

The Fall of Jerusalem

15 And the LORD God of their fathers sent
warnings to them by His messengers, rising
up early and sending *them*, because He had
compassion on His people and on His dwelling
place.
16 But they mocked the messengers of God,
despised His words, and scoffed at His prophets, until the wrath of the LORD arose against
His people, till *there was* no remedy.
17 Therefore He brought against them the
king of the Chaldeans, who killed their young
men with the sword in the house of their sanctuary, and had no compassion on young man
or virgin, on the aged or the weak; He gave
them all into his hand.
18 And all the articles from the house of God,
great and small, the treasures of the house of
the LORD, and the treasures of the king and of
his leaders, all *these* he took to Babylon.
19 Then they burned the house of God, broke
down the wall of Jerusalem, burned all its palaces with fire, and destroyed all its precious
possessions.
20 And those who escaped from the sword he
carried away to Babylon, where they became
servants to him and his sons until the rule of
the kingdom of Persia,
21 to fulfill the word of the LORD by the
mouth of Jeremiah, until the land had enjoyed
her Sabbaths. As long as she lay desolate she
kept Sabbath, to fulfill seventy years.

36:2 [a]Masoretic Text reads *Joahaz*. **36:4** [a]Literally *his* [b]Masoretic Text reads *Joahaz*. **36:9** [a]Some Hebrew manuscripts, Septuagint, Syriac, and 2 Kings 24:8 read *eighteen*. **36:10** [a]Literally *his* (compare 2 Kings 24:17)

The Proclamation of Cyrus

22 Now in the first year of Cyrus king of Persia, that the word of the LORD by the mouth of Jeremiah might be fulfilled, the LORD stirred up the spirit of Cyrus king of Persia, so that he made a proclamation throughout all his kingdom, and also *put it* in writing, saying,

23 Thus says Cyrus king of Persia: All the
kingdoms of the earth the LORD God of
heaven has given me. And He has
commanded me to build Him a house at
Jerusalem which is in Judah. Who *is* among
you of all His people? May the LORD his
God *be* with him, and let him go up!

The Book of EZRA

End of the Babylonian Captivity

1 Now in the first year of Cyrus king of Persia, that the word of the LORD by the mouth of Jeremiah might be fulfilled, the LORD stirred up the spirit of Cyrus king of Persia, so that he made a proclamation throughout all his kingdom, and also *put it* in writing, saying,

2 Thus says Cyrus king of Persia: All the
kingdoms of the earth the LORD God of
heaven has given me. And He has
commanded me to build Him a house at
Jerusalem which *is* in Judah.

3 Who *is* among you of all His people? May
his God be with him, and let him go up to
Jerusalem which *is* in Judah, and build
the house of the LORD God of Israel (He
is God), which *is* in Jerusalem.

4 And whoever is left in any place where
he dwells, let the men of his place help
him with silver and gold, with goods and
livestock, besides the freewill offerings
for the house of God which *is* in
Jerusalem.

5 Then the heads of the fathers' *houses* of Judah and Benjamin, and the priests and the Levites, with all whose spirits God had moved, arose to go up and build the house of the LORD which *is* in Jerusalem.

6 And all those who *were* around them encouraged them with articles of silver and gold, with goods and livestock, and with precious things, besides all *that* was willingly offered.

7 King Cyrus also brought out the articles of the house of the LORD, which Nebuchadnezzar had taken from Jerusalem and put in the temple of his gods;

8 and Cyrus king of Persia brought them out by the hand of Mithredath the treasurer, and counted them out to Sheshbazzar the prince of Judah.

9 This *is* the number of them: thirty gold platters, one thousand silver platters, twenty-nine knives,

10 thirty gold basins, four hundred and ten silver basins of a similar *kind, and* one thousand other articles.

11 All the articles of gold and silver *were* five thousand four hundred. All *these* Sheshbazzar took with the captives who were brought from Babylon to Jerusalem.

The Captives Who Returned to Jerusalem

2 Now[a] these *are* the people of the province who came back from the captivity, of those who had been carried away, whom Nebuchadnezzar the king of Babylon had carried away to Babylon, and who returned to Jerusalem and Judah, everyone to his *own* city.

2 *Those* who came with Zerubbabel *were* Jeshua, Nehemiah, Seraiah, Reelaiah, Mordecai, Bilshan, Mispar,[a] Bigvai, Rehum,[b] *and* Baanah. The number of the men of the people of Israel:

3 the people of Parosh, two thousand one hundred and seventy-two;

4 the people of Shephatiah, three hundred and seventy-two;

5 the people of Arah, seven hundred and seventy-five;

6 the people of Pahath-Moab, of the people of Jeshua *and* Joab, two thousand eight hundred and twelve;

7 the people of Elam, one thousand two hundred and fifty-four;

8 the people of Zattu, nine hundred and forty-five;

9 the people of Zaccai, seven hundred and sixty;

10 the people of Bani,[a] six hundred and forty-two;

11 the people of Bebai, six hundred and twenty-three;

12 the people of Azgad, one thousand two hundred and twenty-two;

13 the people of Adonikam, six hundred and sixty-six;

14 the people of Bigvai, two thousand and fifty-six;

15 the people of Adin, four hundred and fifty-four;

16 the people of Ater of Hezekiah, ninety-eight;

17 the people of Bezai, three hundred and twenty-three;

18 the people of Jorah,[a] one hundred and twelve;

19 the people of Hashum, two hundred and twenty-three;

20 the people of Gibbar,[a] ninety-five;

21 the people of Bethlehem, one hundred and twenty-three;

22 the men of Netophah, fifty-six;

23 the men of Anathoth, one hundred and twenty-eight;

24 the people of Azmaveth,[a] forty-two;

25 the people of Kirjath Arim,[a] Chephirah, and Beeroth, seven hundred and forty-three;

2:1 [a]Compare this chapter with Nehemiah 7:6–73. **2:2** [a]Spelled *Mispereth* in Nehemiah 7:7 [b]Spelled *Nehum* in Nehemiah 7:7 **2:10** [a]Spelled *Binnui* in Nehemiah 7:15 **2:18** [a]Called *Hariph* in Nehemiah 7:24 **2:20** [a]Called *Gibeon* in Nehemiah 7:25 **2:24** [a]Called *Beth Azmaveth* in Nehemiah 7:28 **2:25** [a]Called *Kirjath Jearim* in Nehemiah 7:29

26 the people of Ramah and Geba, six hundred
and twenty-one;
27 the men of Michmas, one hundred and
twenty-two;
28 the men of Bethel and Ai, two hundred and
twenty-three;
29 the people of Nebo, fifty-two;
30 the people of Magbish, one hundred and
fifty-six;
31 the people of the other Elam, one thousand
two hundred and fifty-four;
32 the people of Harim, three hundred and
twenty;
33 the people of Lod, Hadid, and Ono, seven
hundred and twenty-five;
34 the people of Jericho, three hundred and
forty-five;
35 the people of Senaah, three thousand six
hundred and thirty.
36 The priests: the sons of Jedaiah, of the
house of Jeshua, nine hundred and seventy-
three;
37 the sons of Immer, one thousand and fifty-
two;
38 the sons of Pashhur, one thousand two
hundred and forty-seven;
39 the sons of Harim, one thousand and sev-
enteen.
40 The Levites: the sons of Jeshua and Kad-
miel, of the sons of Hodaviah,[a] seventy-four.
41 The singers: the sons of Asaph, one hun-
dred and twenty-eight.
42 The sons of the gatekeepers: the sons of
Shallum, the sons of Ater, the sons of Talmon,
the sons of Akkub, the sons of Hatita, and the
sons of Shobai, one hundred and thirty-nine *in*
all.
43 The Nethinim: the sons of Ziha, the sons
of Hasupha, the sons of Tabbaoth,
44 the sons of Keros, the sons of Siaha,[a] the
sons of Padon,
45 the sons of Lebanah, the sons of Hagabah,
the sons of Akkub,
46 the sons of Hagab, the sons of Shalmai, the
sons of Hanan,
47 the sons of Giddel, the sons of Gahar, the
sons of Reaiah,
48 the sons of Rezin, the sons of Nekoda, the
sons of Gazzam,
49 the sons of Uzza, the sons of Paseah, the
sons of Besai,
50 the sons of Asnah, the sons of Meunim, the
sons of Nephusim,[a]
51 the sons of Bakbuk, the sons of Hakupha,
the sons of Harhur,
52 the sons of Bazluth,[a] the sons of Mehida,
the sons of Harsha,
53 the sons of Barkos, the sons of Sisera, the
sons of Tamah,
54 the sons of Neziah, and the sons of Hatipha.
55 The sons of Solomon's servants: the sons
of Sotai, the sons of Sophereth, the sons of
Peruda,[a]
56 the sons of Jaala, the sons of Darkon, the
sons of Giddel,
57 the sons of Shephatiah, the sons of Hattil,
the sons of Pochereth of Zebaim, and the sons
of Ami.[a]
58 All the Nethinim and the children of Sol-
omon's servants were three hundred and ninety-
two.
59 And these *were* the ones who came up from
Tel Melah, Tel Harsha, Cherub, Addan,[a] and
Immer; but they could not identify their fa-
ther's house or their genealogy,[b] whether they
were of Israel:
60 the sons of Delaiah, the sons of Tobiah,
and the sons of Nekoda, six hundred and
fifty-two;
61 and of the sons of the priests: the sons of
Habaiah, the sons of Koz,[a] and the sons of Bar-
zillai, who took a wife of the daughters of Bar-
zillai the Gileadite, and was called by their
name.
62 These sought their listing *among* those
who were registered by genealogy, but they
were not found; therefore they *were excluded*
from the priesthood as defiled.
63 And the governor[a] said to them that they
should not eat of the most holy things till a priest
could consult with the Urim and Thummim.
64 The whole assembly together *was* forty-
two thousand three hundred *and* sixty,
65 besides their male and female servants, of
whom *there were* seven thousand three hun-
dred and thirty-seven; and they had two hundred
men and women singers.
66 Their horses *were* seven hundred and thirty-
six, their mules two hundred and forty-five,
67 their camels four hundred and thirty-five,
and *their* donkeys six thousand seven hundred
and twenty.
68 *Some* of the heads of the fathers' *houses*,
when they came to the house of the LORD which
is in Jerusalem, offered freely for the house of
God, to erect it in its place:
69 According to their ability, they gave to the
treasury for the work sixty-one thousand gold
drachmas, five thousand minas of silver, and
one hundred priestly garments.
70 So the priests and the Levites, *some* of the
people, the singers, the gatekeepers, and the
Nethinim, dwelt in their cities, and all Israel in
their cities.

Worship Restored at Jerusalem

3 And when the seventh month had come, and
the children of Israel *were* in the cities, the
people gathered together as one man to Jeru-
salem.
2 Then Jeshua the son of Jozadak[a] and his
brethren the priests, and Zerubbabel the son
of Shealtiel and his brethren, arose and built
the altar of the God of Israel, to offer burnt offer-
ings on it, as *it is* written in the Law of Moses
the man of God.
3 Though fear *had come* upon them because
of the people of those countries, they set the
altar on its bases; and they offered burnt offer-
ings on it to the LORD, *both* the morning and
evening burnt offerings.
4 They also kept the Feast of Tabernacles, as
it is written, and *offered* the daily burnt offer-
ings in the number required by ordinance for
each day.
5 Afterwards *they offered* the regular burnt
offering, and *those* for New Moons and for all
the appointed feasts of the LORD that were

2:40 [a]Spelled *Hodevah* in Nehemiah 7:43 **2:44** [a]Spelled *Sia* in Nehemiah 7:47 **2:50** [a]Spelled *Nephishesim* in Nehemiah 7:52 **2:52** [a]Spelled *Bazlith* in Nehemiah 7:54 **2:55** [a]Spelled *Perida* in Nehemiah 7:57 **2:57** [a]Spelled *Amon* in Nehemiah 7:59 **2:59** [a]Spelled *Addon* in Nehemiah 7:61 [b]Literally *seed* **2:61** [a]Or *Hakkoz* **2:63** [a]Hebrew *Tirshatha*
3:2 [a]Spelled *Jehozadak* in 1 Chronicles 6:14

consecrated, and *those* of everyone who willingly offered a freewill offering to the LORD.
6 From the first day of the seventh month they
began to offer burnt offerings to the LORD, although the foundation of the temple of the LORD had not been laid.
7 They also gave money to the masons and
the carpenters, and food, drink, and oil to the people of Sidon and Tyre to bring cedar logs from Lebanon to the sea, to Joppa, according to the permission which they had from Cyrus king of Persia.

Restoration of the Temple Begins

8 Now in the second month of the second year
of their coming to the house of God at Jerusalem, Zerubbabel the son of Shealtiel, Jeshua the son of Jozadak,[a] and the rest of their brethren the priests and the Levites, and all those who had come out of the captivity to Jerusalem, began *work* and appointed the Levites from twenty years old and above to oversee the work of the house of the LORD.
9 Then Jeshua *with* his sons and brothers,
Kadmiel *with* his sons, and the sons of Judah,[a] arose as one to oversee those working on the house of God: the sons of Henadad *with* their sons and their brethren the Levites.
10 When the builders laid the foundation of
the temple of the LORD, the priests stood[a] in their apparel with trumpets, and the Levites, the sons of Asaph, with cymbals, to praise the LORD, according to the ordinance of David king of Israel.
11 And they sang responsively, praising and
giving thanks to the LORD:

"For *He is* good,
For His mercy *endures* forever toward
Israel."[a]

Then all the people shouted with a great shout, when they praised the LORD, because the foundation of the house of the LORD was laid.
12 But many of the priests and Levites and
heads of the fathers' *houses,* old men who had seen the first temple, wept with a loud voice when the foundation of this temple was laid before their eyes. Yet many shouted aloud for joy,
13 so that the people could not discern the
noise of the shout of joy from the noise of the weeping of the people, for the people shouted with a loud shout, and the sound was heard afar off.

Resistance to Rebuilding the Temple

4 Now when the adversaries of Judah and
Benjamin heard that the descendants of the captivity were building the temple of the LORD God of Israel,
2 they came to Zerubbabel and the heads of
the fathers' *houses,* and said to them, "Let us build with you, for we seek your God as you *do;* and we have sacrificed to Him since the days of Esarhaddon king of Assyria, who brought us here."
3 But Zerubbabel and Jeshua and the rest of
the heads of the fathers' *houses* of Israel said to them, "You may do nothing with us to build a house for our God; but we alone will build to the LORD God of Israel, as King Cyrus the king of Persia has commanded us."
4 Then the people of the land tried to discour-
age the people of Judah. They troubled them in building,
5 and hired counselors against them to frus-
trate their purpose all the days of Cyrus king of Persia, even until the reign of Darius king of Persia.

Rebuilding of Jerusalem Opposed

6 In the reign of Ahasuerus, in the beginning
of his reign, they wrote an accusation against the inhabitants of Judah and Jerusalem.
7 In the days of Artaxerxes also, Bishlam,
Mithredath, Tabel, and the rest of their companions wrote to Artaxerxes king of Persia; and the letter *was* written in Aramaic script, and translated into the Aramaic language.
8 Rehum[a] the commander and Shimshai the
scribe wrote a letter against Jerusalem to King Artaxerxes in this fashion:

9 From[a] Rehum the commander, Shimshai
the scribe, and the rest of their
companions—*representatives* of the
Dinaites, the Apharsathchites, the
Tarpelites, the people of Persia and Erech
and Babylon and Shushan,[b] the
Dehavites, the Elamites,
10 and the rest of the nations whom the
great and noble Osnapper took captive
and settled in the cities of Samaria and
the remainder beyond the River[a]—and so
forth.[b]

11 (This *is* a copy of the letter that they sent
him)

To King Artaxerxes from your servants,
the men *of the region* beyond the River,
and so forth:[a]

12 Let it be known to the king that the Jews
who came up from you have come to us
at Jerusalem, and are building the
rebellious and evil city, and are finishing
its walls and repairing the foundations.
13 Let it now be known to the king that, if
this city is built and the walls completed,
they will not pay tax, tribute, or custom,
and the king's treasury will be
diminished.
14 Now because we receive support from the
palace, it was not proper for us to see the
king's dishonor; therefore we have sent
and informed the king,
15 that search may be made in the book of
the records of your fathers. And you will
find in the book of the records and know
that this city *is* a rebellious city, harmful
to kings and provinces, and that they
have incited sedition within the city in
former times, for which cause this city
was destroyed.
16 We inform the king that if this city is
rebuilt and its walls are completed, the
result will be that you will have no
dominion beyond the River.

3:8 [a]Spelled *Jehozadak* in 1 Chronicles 6:14 **3:9** [a]Or *Hodaviah* (compare 2:40) **3:10** [a]Following Septuagint, Syriac, and Vulgate; Masoretic Text reads *they stationed the priests.* **3:11** [a]Compare Psalm 136:1 **4:8** [a]The original language of Ezra 4:8 through 6:18 is Aramaic. **4:9** [a]Literally *Then* [b]Or *Susa* **4:10** [a]That is, the Euphrates [b]Literally *and now* **4:11** [a]Literally *and now*

17 The king sent an answer:

To Rehum the commander, *to* Shimshai the scribe, *to* the rest of their companions who dwell in Samaria, and *to* the remainder beyond the River:

Peace, and so forth.[a]

18 The letter which you sent to us has been clearly read before me.
19 And I gave the command, and a search has been made, and it was found that this city in former times has revolted against kings, and rebellion and sedition have been fostered in it.
20 There have also been mighty kings over Jerusalem, who have ruled over all *the region* beyond the River; and tax, tribute, and custom were paid to them.
21 Now give the command to make these men cease, that this city may not be built until the command is given by me.
22 Take heed now that you do not fail to do this. Why should damage increase to the hurt of the kings?

23 Now when the copy of King Artaxerxes'
letter *was* read before Rehum, Shimshai the
scribe, and their companions, they went up in
haste to Jerusalem against the Jews, and by
force of arms made them cease.
24 Thus the work of the house of God which
is at Jerusalem ceased, and it was discontinued
until the second year of the reign of Darius
king of Persia.

Restoration of the Temple Resumed

5 Then the prophet Haggai and Zechariah
the son of Iddo, prophets, prophesied to the
Jews who *were* in Judah and Jerusalem, in the
name of the God of Israel, *who was* over them.
2 So Zerubbabel the son of Shealtiel and
Jeshua the son of Jozadak[a] rose up and began
to build the house of God which *is* in Jerusalem; and the prophets of God *were* with them,
helping them.
3 At the same time Tattenai the governor of
the region beyond the River[a] and Shethar-Boznai and their companions came to them and
spoke thus to them: "Who has commanded you
to build this temple and finish this wall?"
4 Then, accordingly, we told them the names
of the men who were constructing this building.
5 But the eye of their God was upon the elders
of the Jews, so that they could not make them
cease till a report could go to Darius. Then a
written answer was returned concerning this
matter.
6 This is a copy of the letter that Tattenai sent:

The governor of *the region* beyond the River, and Shethar-Boznai, and his companions, the Persians who *were in the region* beyond the River, to Darius the king.

7 (They sent a letter to him, in which was written thus)

To Darius the king:

All peace.

8 Let it be known to the king that we went into the province of Judea, to the temple of the great God, which is being built with heavy stones, and timber is being laid in the walls; and this work goes on diligently and prospers in their hands.
9 Then we asked those elders, *and* spoke thus to them: "Who commanded you to build this temple and to finish these walls?"
10 We also asked them their names to inform you, that we might write the names of the men who *were* chief among them.
11 And thus they returned us an answer, saying: "We are the servants of the God of heaven and earth, and we are rebuilding the temple that was built many years ago, which a great king of Israel built and completed.
12 "But because our fathers provoked the God of heaven to wrath, He gave them into the hand of Nebuchadnezzar king of Babylon, the Chaldean, *who* destroyed this temple and carried the people away to Babylon.
13 "However, in the first year of Cyrus king of Babylon, King Cyrus issued a decree to build this house of God.
14 "Also, the gold and silver articles of the house of God, which Nebuchadnezzar had taken from the temple that *was* in Jerusalem and carried into the temple of Babylon—those King Cyrus took from the temple of Babylon, and they were given to one named Sheshbazzar, whom he had made governor.
15 "And he said to him, 'Take these articles; go, carry them to the temple *site* that *is* in Jerusalem, and let the house of God be rebuilt on its former site.'
16 "Then the same Sheshbazzar came *and* laid the foundation of the house of God which *is* in Jerusalem; but from that time even until now it has been under construction, and it is not finished."
17 Now therefore, if *it seems* good to the king, let a search be made in the king's treasure house, which *is* there in Babylon, whether it is *so* that a decree was issued by King Cyrus to build this house of God at Jerusalem, and let the king send us his pleasure concerning this *matter.*

The Decree of Darius

6 Then King Darius issued a decree, and a
search was made in the archives,[a] where
the treasures were stored in Babylon.
2 And at Achmetha,[a] in the palace that *is* in
the province of Media, a scroll was found, and
in it a record *was* written thus:

3 In the first year of King Cyrus, King Cyrus issued a decree *concerning* the house of God at Jerusalem: "Let the house be rebuilt, the place where they offered sacrifices; and let the foundations of it be firmly laid, its height sixty cubits *and* its width sixty cubits,
4 *with* three rows of heavy stones and one row of new timber. Let the expenses be paid from the king's treasury.

4:17 [a]Literally *and now* **5:2** [a]Spelled *Jehozadak* in 1 Chronicles 6:14 **5:3** [a]That is, the Euphrates **6:1** [a]Literally *house of the scrolls* **6:2** [a]Probably *Ecbatana*, the ancient capital of Media

5 Also let the gold and silver articles of the
house of God, which Nebuchadnezzar
took from the temple which *is* in
Jerusalem and brought to Babylon, be
restored and taken back to the temple
which *is* in Jerusalem, *each* to its place;
and deposit *them* in the house of God"—
6 Now *therefore,* Tattenai, governor of *the
region* beyond the River, and
Shethar-Boznai, and your companions
the Persians who *are* beyond the River,
keep yourselves far from there.
7 Let the work of this house of God alone;
let the governor of the Jews and the
elders of the Jews build this house of God
on its site.
8 Moreover I issue a decree *as to* what you
shall do for the elders of these Jews, for
the building of this house of God: Let the
cost be paid at the king's expense from
taxes *on the region* beyond the River; this
is to be given immediately to these men,
so that they are not hindered.
9 And whatever they need—young bulls,
rams, and lambs for the burnt offerings
of the God of heaven, wheat, salt, wine,
and oil, according to the request of the
priests who *are* in Jerusalem—let it be
given them day by day without fail,
10 that they may offer sacrifices of sweet
aroma to the God of heaven, and pray for
the life of the king and his sons.
11 Also I issue a decree that whoever alters
this edict, let a timber be pulled from his
house and erected, and let him be hanged
on it; and let his house be made a refuse
heap because of this.
12 And may the God who causes His name
to dwell there destroy any king or people
who put their hand to alter it, or to
destroy this house of God which is in
Jerusalem. I Darius issue a decree; let it
be done diligently.

The Temple Completed and Dedicated

13 Then Tattenai, governor of *the region* be-
yond the River, Shethar-Boznai, and their com-
panions diligently did according to what King
Darius had sent.
14 So the elders of the Jews built, and they
prospered through the prophesying of Haggai
the prophet and Zechariah the son of Iddo. And
they built and finished *it,* according to the com-
mandment of the God of Israel, and according
to the command of Cyrus, Darius, and Artax-
erxes king of Persia.
15 Now the temple was finished on the third
day of the month of Adar, which was in the
sixth year of the reign of King Darius.
16 Then the children of Israel, the priests and
the Levites and the rest of the descendants of
the captivity, celebrated the dedication of this
house of God with joy.
17 And they offered sacrifices at the dedication
of this house of God, one hundred bulls, two hun-
dred rams, four hundred lambs, and as a sin
offering for all Israel twelve male goats, ac-
cording to the number of the tribes of Israel.
18 They assigned the priests to their divisions
and the Levites to their divisions, over the ser-
vice of God in Jerusalem, as it is written in the
Book of Moses.

The Passover Celebrated

19 And the descendants of the captivity kept
the Passover on the fourteenth *day* of the first
month.
20 For the priests and the Levites had purified
themselves; all of them *were ritually* clean.
And they slaughtered the Passover *lambs* for
all the descendants of the captivity, for their
brethren the priests, and for themselves.
21 Then the children of Israel who had re-
turned from the captivity ate together with all
who had separated themselves from the filth
of the nations of the land in order to seek the
LORD God of Israel.
22 And they kept the Feast of Unleavened
Bread seven days with joy; for the LORD made
them joyful, and turned the heart of the king
of Assyria toward them, to strengthen their
hands in the work of the house of God, the God
of Israel.

The Arrival of Ezra

7 Now after these things, in the reign of Ar-
taxerxes king of Persia, Ezra the son of
Seraiah, the son of Azariah, the son of Hilkiah,
2 the son of Shallum, the son of Zadok, the
son of Ahitub,
3 the son of Amariah, the son of Azariah, the
son of Meraioth,
4 the son of Zerahiah, the son of Uzzi, the son
of Bukki,
5 the son of Abishua, the son of Phinehas,
the son of Eleazar, the son of Aaron the chief
priest—
6 this Ezra came up from Babylon; and he
was a skilled scribe in the Law of Moses, which
the LORD God of Israel had given. The king
granted him all his request, according to the
hand of the LORD his God upon him.
7 *Some* of the children of Israel, the priests,
the Levites, the singers, the gatekeepers, and
the Nethinim came up to Jerusalem in the sev-
enth year of King Artaxerxes.
8 And Ezra came to Jerusalem in the fifth
month, which *was* in the seventh year of the
king.
9 On the first *day* of the first month he began
his journey from Babylon, and on the first *day*
of the fifth month he came to Jerusalem, ac-
cording to the good hand of his God upon him.
10 For Ezra had prepared his heart to seek
the Law of the LORD, and to do *it,* and to teach
statutes and ordinances in Israel.

The Letter of Artaxerxes to Ezra

11 This *is* a copy of the letter that King Artax-
erxes gave Ezra the priest, the scribe, expert
in the words of the commandments of the
LORD, and of His statutes to Israel:

12 Artaxerxes,[a] king of kings,

To Ezra the priest, a scribe of the Law of
the God of heaven:

Perfect *peace,* and so forth.[b]

13 I issue a decree that all those of the
people of Israel and the priests and
Levites in my realm, who volunteer to go
up to Jerusalem, may go with you.
14 And whereas you are being sent by the
king and his seven counselors to inquire
concerning Judah and Jerusalem, with

7:12 [a]The original language of Ezra 7:12–26 is Aramaic. [b]Literally *and now*

regard to the Law of your God which *is* in
your hand;
15 and *whereas you are* to carry the silver
and gold which the king and his
counselors have freely offered to the God
of Israel, whose dwelling *is* in Jerusalem;
16 and *whereas* all the silver and gold that
you may find in all the province of
Babylon, along with the freewill offering
of the people and the priests, *are to be*
freely offered for the house of their God
in Jerusalem—
17 now therefore, be careful to buy with this
money bulls, rams, and lambs, with their
grain offerings and their drink offerings,
and offer them on the altar of the house
of your God in Jerusalem.
18 And whatever seems good to you and
your brethren to do with the rest of the
silver and the gold, do it according to the
will of your God.
19 Also the articles that are given to you for
the service of the house of your God,
deliver in full before the God of
Jerusalem.
20 And whatever more may be needed for
the house of your God, which you may
have occasion to provide, pay *for it* from
the king's treasury.
21 And I, *even* I, Artaxerxes the king, issue a
decree to all the treasurers who *are in the*
region beyond the River, that whatever
Ezra the priest, the scribe of the Law of
the God of heaven, may require of you,
let it be done diligently,
22 up to one hundred talents of silver, one
hundred kors of wheat, one hundred
baths of wine, one hundred baths of oil,
and salt without prescribed limit.
23 Whatever is commanded by the God of
heaven, let it diligently be done for the
house of the God of heaven. For why
should there be wrath against the realm
of the king and his sons?
24 Also we inform you that it shall not be
lawful to impose tax, tribute, or custom
on any of the priests, Levites, singers,
gatekeepers, Nethinim, or servants of this
house of God.
25 And you, Ezra, according to your
God-given wisdom, set magistrates and
judges who may judge all the people who
are in the region beyond the River, all
such as know the laws of your God; and
teach those who do not know *them.*
26 Whoever will not observe the law of your
God and the law of the king, let judgment
be executed speedily on him, whether *it*
be death, or banishment, or confiscation
of goods, or imprisonment.

27 Blessed *be* the LORD God of our fathers,
who has put *such a thing* as this in the king's
heart, to beautify the house of the LORD which
is in Jerusalem,
28 and has extended mercy to me before the
king and his counselors, and before all the
king's mighty princes.
So I was encouraged, as the hand of the
LORD my God *was* upon me; and I gathered
leading men of Israel to go up with me.

Heads of Families Who Returned with Ezra

8 These *are* the heads of their fathers' *houses,*
and *this is* the genealogy of those who went
up with me from Babylon, in the reign of King
Artaxerxes:
2 of the sons of Phinehas, Gershom; of the
sons of Ithamar, Daniel; of the sons of David,
Hattush;
3 of the sons of Shecaniah, of the sons of
Parosh, Zechariah; and registered with him
were one hundred and fifty males;
4 of the sons of Pahath-Moab, Eliehoenai the
son of Zerahiah, and with him two hundred
males;
5 of the sons of Shechaniah,[a] Ben-Jahaziel,
and with him three hundred males;
6 of the sons of Adin, Ebed the son of Jona-
than, and with him fifty males;
7 of the sons of Elam, Jeshaiah the son of
Athaliah, and with him seventy males;
8 of the sons of Shephatiah, Zebadiah the
son of Michael, and with him eighty males;
9 of the sons of Joab, Obadiah the son of
Jehiel, and with him two hundred and eighteen
males;
10 of the sons of Shelomith,[a] Ben-Josiphiah,
and with him one hundred and sixty males;
11 of the sons of Bebai, Zechariah the son of
Bebai, and with him twenty-eight males;
12 of the sons of Azgad, Johanan the son of
Hakkatan, and with him one hundred and ten
males;
13 of the last sons of Adonikam, whose names
are these—Eliphelet, Jeiel, and Shemaiah—
and with them sixty males;
14 also of the sons of Bigvai, Uthai and Zab-
bud, and with them seventy males.

Servants for the Temple

15 Now I gathered them by the river that flows
to Ahava, and we camped there three days.
And I looked among the people and the priests,
and found none of the sons of Levi there.
16 Then I sent for Eliezer, Ariel, Shemaiah,
Elnathan, Jarib, Elnathan, Nathan, Zechariah,
and Meshullam, leaders; also for Joiarib and
Elnathan, men of understanding.
17 And I gave them a command for Iddo the
chief man at the place Casiphia, and I told them
what they should say to Iddo *and* his brethren[a]
the Nethinim at the place Casiphia—that they
should bring us servants for the house of our
God.
18 Then, by the good hand of our God upon
us, they brought us a man of understanding,
of the sons of Mahli the son of Levi, the son of
Israel, namely Sherebiah, with his sons and
brothers, eighteen men;
19 and Hashabiah, and with him Jeshaiah of
the sons of Merari, his brothers and their sons,
twenty men;
20 also of the Nethinim, whom David and the
leaders had appointed for the service of the
Levites, two hundred and twenty Nethinim. All
of them were designated by name.

Fasting and Prayer for Protection

21 Then I proclaimed a fast there at the river
of Ahava, that we might humble ourselves be-

8:5 [a]Following Masoretic Text and Vulgate; Septuagint reads *the sons of Zatho, Shechaniah.* 8:10 [a]Following Masoretic Text and Vulgate; Septuagint reads *the sons of Banni, Shelomith.* 8:17 [a]Following Vulgate; Masoretic Text reads *to Iddo his brother;* Septuagint reads *to their brethren.*

fore our God, to seek from Him the right way for
us and our little ones and all our possessions.
22 For I was ashamed to request of the king
an escort of soldiers and horsemen to help us
against the enemy on the road, because we had
spoken to the king, saying, "The hand of our
God *is* upon all those for good who seek Him,
but His power and His wrath *are* against all
those who forsake Him."
23 So we fasted and entreated our God for
this, and He answered our prayer.

Gifts for the Temple

24 And I separated twelve of the leaders of
the priests—Sherebiah, Hashabiah, and ten of
their brethren with them—
25 and weighed out to them the silver, the gold,
and the articles, the offering for the house of
our God which the king and his counselors and
his princes, and all Israel *who were* present,
had offered.
26 I weighed into their hand six hundred and
fifty talents of silver, silver articles *weighing*
one hundred talents, one hundred talents of
gold,
27 twenty gold basins *worth* a thousand drach-
mas, and two vessels of fine polished bronze,
precious as gold.
28 And I said to them, "You *are* holy to the
LORD; the articles *are* holy also; and the silver
and the gold *are* a freewill offering to the LORD
God of your fathers.
29 "Watch and keep *them* until you weigh
them before the leaders of the priests and the
Levites and heads of the fathers' *houses* of Is-
rael in Jerusalem, *in* the chambers of the house
of the LORD."
30 So the priests and the Levites received the
silver and the gold and the articles by weight,
to bring *them* to Jerusalem to the house of our
God.

The Return to Jerusalem

31 Then we departed from the river of Ahava
on the twelfth *day* of the first month, to go to
Jerusalem. And the hand of our God was upon
us, and He delivered us from the hand of the
enemy and from ambush along the road.
32 So we came to Jerusalem, and stayed there
three days.
33 Now on the fourth day the silver and the
gold and the articles were weighed in the house
of our God by the hand of Meremoth the son
of Uriah the priest, and with him *was* Eleazar
the son of Phinehas; with them *were* the Levites,
Jozabad the son of Jeshua and Noadiah the
son of Binnui,
34 with the number *and* weight of everything.
All the weight was written down at that time.
35 The children of those who had been car-
ried away captive, who had come from the cap-
tivity, offered burnt offerings to the God of
Israel: twelve bulls for all Israel, ninety-six rams,
seventy-seven lambs, and twelve male goats *as*
a sin offering. All *this was* a burnt offering to
the LORD.
36 And they delivered the king's orders to the
king's satraps and the governors *in the region*
beyond the River. So they gave support to the
people and the house of God.

Intermarriage with Pagans

9 When these things were done, the leaders
came to me, saying, "The people of Israel
and the priests and the Levites have not sepa-
rated themselves from the peoples of the lands,
with respect to the abominations of the Canaan-
ites, the Hittites, the Perizzites, the Jebusites,
the Ammonites, the Moabites, the Egyptians,
and the Amorites.
2 "For they have taken some of their daugh-
ters *as wives* for themselves and their sons, so
that the holy seed is mixed with the peoples of
those lands. Indeed, the hand of the leaders
and rulers has been foremost in this trespass."
3 So when I heard this thing, I tore my gar-
ment and my robe, and plucked out some of
the hair of my head and beard, and sat down
astonished.
4 Then everyone who trembled at the words
of the God of Israel assembled to me, because
of the transgression of those who had been
carried away captive, and I sat astonished until
the evening sacrifice.
5 At the evening sacrifice I arose from my fast-
ing; and having torn my garment and my robe,
I fell on my knees and spread out my hands to
the LORD my God.
6 And I said: "O my God, I am too ashamed
and humiliated to lift up my face to You, my
God; for our iniquities have risen higher than
our heads, and our guilt has grown up to the
heavens.
7 "Since the days of our fathers to this day
we *have been* very guilty, and for our iniquities
we, our kings, *and* our priests have been deliv-
ered into the hand of the kings of the lands,
to the sword, to captivity, to plunder, and to
humiliation, as *it is* this day.
8 "And now for a little while grace has been
shown from the LORD our God, to leave us a
remnant to escape, and to give us a peg in His
holy place, that our God may enlighten our eyes
and give us a measure of revival in our bondage.
9 "For we *were* slaves. Yet our God did not
forsake us in our bondage; but He extended
mercy to us in the sight of the kings of Persia,
to revive us, to repair the house of our God, to
rebuild its ruins, and to give us a wall in Judah
and Jerusalem.
10 "And now, O our God, what shall we say
after this? For we have forsaken Your command-
ments,
11 "which You commanded by Your servants
the prophets, saying, 'The land which you are
entering to possess is an unclean land, with
the uncleanness of the peoples of the lands,
with their abominations which have filled it
from one end to another with their impurity.
12 'Now therefore, do not give your daughters
as wives for their sons, nor take their daugh-
ters to your sons; and never seek their peace or
prosperity, that you may be strong and eat the
good of the land, and leave *it* as an inheritance
to your children forever.'
13 "And after all that has come upon us for our
evil deeds and for our great guilt, since You our
God have punished us less than our iniquities
deserve, and have given us *such* deliverance as
this,
14 "should we again break Your command-
ments, and join in marriage with the people
committing these abominations? Would You not
be angry with us until You had consumed *us*,
so that *there would be* no remnant or survivor?
15 "O LORD God of Israel, You *are* righteous,
for we are left as a remnant, as *it is* this day.
Here we *are* before You, in our guilt, though no
one can stand before You because of this!"

Confession of Improper Marriages

10 Now while Ezra was praying, and while he was confessing, weeping, and bowing down before the house of God, a very large assembly of men, women, and children gathered to him from Israel; for the people wept very bitterly.

2 And Shechaniah the son of Jehiel, *one* of the sons of Elam, spoke up and said to Ezra, "We have trespassed against our God, and have taken pagan wives from the peoples of the land; yet now there is hope in Israel in spite of this.

3 "Now therefore, let us make a covenant with our God to put away all these wives and those who have been born to them, according to the advice of my master and of those who tremble at the commandment of our God; and let it be done according to the law.

4 "Arise, for *this* matter *is* your *responsibility*. We also *are* with you. Be of good courage, and do *it*."

5 Then Ezra arose, and made the leaders of the priests, the Levites, and all Israel swear an oath that they would do according to this word. So they swore an oath.

6 Then Ezra rose up from before the house of God, and went into the chamber of Jehohanan the son of Eliashib; and *when* he came there, he ate no bread and drank no water, for he mourned because of the guilt of those from the captivity.

7 And they issued a proclamation throughout Judah and Jerusalem to all the descendants of the captivity, that they must gather at Jerusalem,

8 and that whoever would not come within three days, according to the instructions of the leaders and elders, all his property would be confiscated, and he himself would be separated from the assembly of those from the captivity.

9 So all the men of Judah and Benjamin gathered at Jerusalem within three days. It *was* the ninth month, on the twentieth of the month; and all the people sat in the open square of the house of God, trembling because of *this* matter and because of heavy rain.

10 Then Ezra the priest stood up and said to them, "You have transgressed and have taken pagan wives, adding to the guilt of Israel.

11 "Now therefore, make confession to the LORD God of your fathers, and do His will; separate yourselves from the peoples of the land, and from the pagan wives."

12 Then all the assembly answered and said with a loud voice, "Yes! As you have said, so we must do.

13 "But *there are* many people; *it is* the season for heavy rain, and we are not able to stand outside. Nor *is this* the work of one or two days, for *there are* many of us who have transgressed in this matter.

14 "Please, let the leaders of our entire assembly stand; and let all those in our cities who have taken pagan wives come at appointed times, together with the elders and judges of their cities, until the fierce wrath of our God is turned away from us in this matter."

15 Only Jonathan the son of Asahel and Jahaziah the son of Tikvah opposed this, and Meshullam and Shabbethai the Levite gave them support.

16 Then the descendants of the captivity did so. And Ezra the priest, *with* certain heads of the fathers' *households*, were set apart by the fathers' households, each of them by name; and they sat down on the first day of the tenth month to examine the matter.

17 By the first day of the first month they finished *questioning* all the men who had taken pagan wives.

Pagan Wives Put Away

18 And among the sons of the priests who had taken pagan wives *the following* were found of the sons of Jeshua the son of Jozadak,[a] and his brothers: Maaseiah, Eliezer, Jarib, and Gedaliah.

19 And they gave their promise that they would put away their wives; and *being* guilty, *they presented* a ram of the flock as their trespass offering.

20 Also of the sons of Immer: Hanani and Zebadiah;

21 of the sons of Harim: Maaseiah, Elijah, Shemaiah, Jehiel, and Uzziah;

22 of the sons of Pashhur: Elioenai, Maaseiah, Ishmael, Nethanel, Jozabad, and Elasah.

23 Also of the Levites: Jozabad, Shimei, Kelaiah (the same *is* Kelita), Pethahiah, Judah, and Eliezer.

24 Also of the singers: Eliashib; and of the gatekeepers: Shallum, Telem, and Uri.

25 And others of Israel: of the sons of Parosh: Ramiah, Jeziah, Malchiah, Mijamin, Eleazar, Malchijah, and Benaiah;

26 of the sons of Elam: Mattaniah, Zechariah, Jehiel, Abdi, Jeremoth, and Eliah;

27 of the sons of Zattu: Elioenai, Eliashib, Mattaniah, Jeremoth, Zabad, and Aziza;

28 of the sons of Bebai: Jehohanan, Hananiah, Zabbai, *and* Athlai;

29 of the sons of Bani: Meshullam, Malluch, Adaiah, Jashub, Sheal, *and* Ramoth;[a]

30 of the sons of Pahath-Moab: Adna, Chelal, Benaiah, Maaseiah, Mattaniah, Bezalel, Binnui, and Manasseh;

31 *of* the sons of Harim: Eliezer, Ishijah, Malchijah, Shemaiah, Shimeon,

32 Benjamin, Malluch, *and* Shemariah;

33 of the sons of Hashum: Mattenai, Mattattah, Zabad, Eliphelet, Jeremai, Manasseh, *and* Shimei;

34 of the sons of Bani: Maadai, Amram, Uel,

35 Benaiah, Bedeiah, Cheluh,[a]

36 Vaniah, Meremoth, Eliashib,

37 Mattaniah, Mattenai, Jaasai,[a]

38 Bani, Binnui, Shimei,

39 Shelemiah, Nathan, Adaiah,

40 Machnadebai, Shashai, Sharai,

41 Azarel, Shelemiah, Shemariah,

42 Shallum, Amariah, *and* Joseph;

43 of the sons of Nebo: Jeiel, Mattithiah, Zabad, Zebina, Jaddai,[a] Joel, *and* Benaiah.

44 All these had taken pagan wives, and *some* of them had wives *by whom* they had children.

10:18 [a]Spelled *Jehozadak* in 1 Chronicles 6:14 **10:29** [a]Or *Jeremoth* **10:35** [a]Or *Cheluhi*, or *Cheluhu* **10:37** [a]Or *Jaasu* **10:43** [a]Or *Jaddu*

The Book of

NEHEMIAH

Nehemiah Prays for His People

1 The words of Nehemiah the son of Hacha-
liah.
It came to pass in the month of Chislev, *in*
the twentieth year, as I was in Shushan[a] the
citadel,
2 that Hanani one of my brethren came with
men from Judah; and I asked them concerning
the Jews who had escaped, who had survived
the captivity, and concerning Jerusalem.
3 And they said to me, "The survivors who
are left from the captivity in the province *are*
there in great distress and reproach. The wall
of Jerusalem *is* also broken down, and its gates
are burned with fire."
4 So it was, when I heard these words, that
I sat down and wept, and mourned *for many*
days; I was fasting and praying before the God
of heaven.
5 And I said: "I pray, LORD God of heaven,
O great and awesome God, *You* who keep *Your*
covenant and mercy with those who love You[a]
and observe Your[b] commandments,
6 "please let Your ear be attentive and Your
eyes open, that You may hear the prayer of
Your servant which I pray before You now, day
and night, for the children of Israel Your ser-
vants, and confess the sins of the children of
Israel which we have sinned against You. Both
my father's house and I have sinned.
7 "We have acted very corruptly against You,
and have not kept the commandments, the
statutes, nor the ordinances which You com-
manded Your servant Moses.
8 "Remember, I pray, the word that You com-
manded Your servant Moses, saying, '*If* you are
unfaithful, I will scatter you among the nations;[a]
9 'but *if* you return to Me, and keep My com-
mandments and do them, though some of you
were cast out to the farthest part of the heavens,
yet I will gather them from there, and bring them
to the place which I have chosen as a dwelling
for My name.'[a]
10 "Now these *are* Your servants and Your
people, whom You have redeemed by Your
great power, and by Your strong hand.
11 "O Lord, I pray, please let Your ear be at-
tentive to the prayer of Your servant, and to the
prayer of Your servants who desire to fear Your
name; and let Your servant prosper this day, I
pray, and grant him mercy in the sight of this
man." For I was the king's cupbearer.

Nehemiah Sent to Judah

2 And it came to pass in the month of Nisan,
in the twentieth year of King Artaxerxes,
when wine *was* before him, that I took the wine
and gave it to the king. Now I had never been
sad in his presence before.
2 Therefore the king said to me, "Why *is* your
face sad, since you *are* not sick? This *is* nothing
but sorrow of heart." So I became dreadfully
afraid,
3 and said to the king, "May the king live
forever! Why should my face not be sad, when
the city, the place of my fathers' tombs, *lies*
waste, and its gates are burned with fire?"
4 Then the king said to me, "What do you
request?" So I prayed to the God of heaven.
5 And I said to the king, "If it pleases the
king, and if your servant has found favor in
your sight, I ask that you send me to Judah, to
the city of my fathers' tombs, that I may rebuild
it."
6 Then the king said to me (the queen also
sitting beside him), "How long will your journey
be? And when will you return?" So it pleased
the king to send me; and I set him a time.
7 Furthermore I said to the king, "If it pleases
the king, let letters be given to me for the gov-
ernors *of the region* beyond the River,[a] that
they must permit me to pass through till I come
to Judah,
8 "and a letter to Asaph the keeper of the
king's forest, that he must give me timber to
make beams for the gates of the citadel which
pertains to the temple,[a] for the city wall, and
for the house that I will occupy." And the king
granted *them* to me according to the good
hand of my God upon me.
9 Then I went to the governors *in the region*
beyond the River, and gave them the king's
letters. Now the king had sent captains of the
army and horsemen with me.
10 When Sanballat the Horonite and Tobiah
the Ammonite official[a] heard *of it*, they were
deeply disturbed that a man had come to seek
the well-being of the children of Israel.

Nehemiah Views the Wall of Jerusalem

11 So I came to Jerusalem and was there three
days.
12 Then I arose in the night, I and a few men
with me; I told no one what my God had put in
my heart to do at Jerusalem; nor was there any
animal with me, except the one on which I rode.
13 And I went out by night through the Valley
Gate to the Serpent Well and the Refuse Gate,
and viewed the walls of Jerusalem which were
broken down and its gates which were burned
with fire.
14 Then I went on to the Fountain Gate and
to the King's Pool, but *there was* no room for
the animal under me to pass.
15 So I went up in the night by the valley, and
viewed the wall; then I turned back and en-
tered by the Valley Gate, and so returned.
16 And the officials did not know where I had
gone or what I had done; I had not yet told the
Jews, the priests, the nobles, the officials, or the
others who did the work.
17 Then I said to them, "You see the distress
that we *are* in, how Jerusalem *lies* waste, and
its gates are burned with fire. Come and let us
build the wall of Jerusalem, that we may no
longer be a reproach."
18 And I told them of the hand of my God
which had been good upon me, and also of the
king's words that he had spoken to me. So they
said, "Let us rise up and build." Then they set
their hands to *this* good *work*.
19 But when Sanballat the Horonite, Tobiah
the Ammonite official, and Geshem the Arab
heard *of it*, they laughed at us and despised

1:1 [a]Or *Susa* **1:5** [a]Literally *Him* [b]Literally *His* **1:8** [a]Leviticus 26:33 **1:9** [a]Deuteronomy 30:2–5 **2:7** [a]That is, the Euphrates, and so elsewhere in this book **2:8** [a]Literally *house* **2:10** [a]Literally *servant*, and so elsewhere in this book

us, and said, "What *is* this thing that you are doing? Will you rebel against the king?"

20 So I answered them, and said to them, "The God of heaven Himself will prosper us; therefore we His servants will arise and build, but you have no heritage or right or memorial in Jerusalem."

Rebuilding the Wall

3 Then Eliashib the high priest rose up with his brethren the priests and built the Sheep Gate; they consecrated it and hung its doors. They built as far as the Tower of the Hundred,[a] *and* consecrated it, then as far as the Tower of Hananel.

2 Next to *Eliashib*[a] the men of Jericho built. And next to them Zaccur the son of Imri built.

3 Also the sons of Hassenaah built the Fish Gate; they laid its beams and hung its doors with its bolts and bars.

4 And next to them Meremoth the son of Urijah, the son of Koz,[a] made repairs. Next to them Meshullam the son of Berechiah, the son of Meshezabel, made repairs. Next to them Zadok the son of Baana made repairs.

5 Next to them the Tekoites made repairs; but their nobles did not put their shoulders[a] to the work of their Lord.

6 Moreover Jehoiada the son of Paseah and Meshullam the son of Besodeiah repaired the Old Gate; they laid its beams and hung its doors, with its bolts and bars.

7 And next to them Melatiah the Gibeonite, Jadon the Meronothite, the men of Gibeon and Mizpah, repaired the residence[a] of the governor *of the region* beyond the River.

8 Next to him Uzziel the son of Harhaiah, one of the goldsmiths, made repairs. Also next to him Hananiah, one[a] of the perfumers, made repairs; and they fortified Jerusalem as far as the Broad Wall.

9 And next to them Rephaiah the son of Hur, leader of half the district of Jerusalem, made repairs.

10 Next to them Jedaiah the son of Harumaph made repairs in front of his house. And next to him Hattush the son of Hashabniah made repairs.

11 Malchijah the son of Harim and Hashub the son of Pahath-Moab repaired another section, as well as the Tower of the Ovens.

12 And next to him was Shallum the son of Hallohesh, leader of half the district of Jerusalem; he and his daughters made repairs.

13 Hanun and the inhabitants of Zanoah repaired the Valley Gate. They built it, hung its doors with its bolts and bars, and *repaired* a thousand cubits of the wall as far as the Refuse Gate.

14 Malchijah the son of Rechab, leader of the district of Beth Haccerem, repaired the Refuse Gate; he built it and hung its doors with its bolts and bars.

15 Shallun the son of Col-Hozeh, leader of the district of Mizpah, repaired the Fountain Gate; he built it, covered it, hung its doors with its bolts and bars, and repaired the wall of the Pool of Shelah by the King's Garden, as far as the stairs that go down from the City of David.

16 After him Nehemiah the son of Azbuk, leader of half the district of Beth Zur, made repairs as far as *the place* in front of the tombs[a] of David, to the man-made pool, and as far as the House of the Mighty.

17 After him the Levites, *under* Rehum the son of Bani, made repairs. Next to him Hashabiah, leader of half the district of Keilah, made repairs for his district.

18 After him their brethren, *under* Bavai[a] the son of Henadad, leader of the *other* half of the district of Keilah, made repairs.

19 And next to him Ezer the son of Jeshua, the leader of Mizpah, repaired another section in front of the Ascent to the Armory at the buttress.

20 After him Baruch the son of Zabbai[a] carefully repaired the other section, from the buttress to the door of the house of Eliashib the high priest.

21 After him Meremoth the son of Urijah, the son of Koz,[a] repaired another section, from the door of the house of Eliashib to the end of the house of Eliashib.

22 And after him the priests, the men of the plain, made repairs.

23 After him Benjamin and Hasshub made repairs opposite their house. After them Azariah the son of Maaseiah, the son of Ananiah, made repairs by his house.

24 After him Binnui the son of Henadad repaired another section, from the house of Azariah to the buttress, even as far as the corner.

25 Palal the son of Uzai *made repairs* opposite the buttress, and on the tower which projects from the king's upper house that *was* by the court of the prison. After him Pedaiah the son of Parosh *made repairs.*

26 Moreover the Nethinim who dwelt in Ophel *made repairs* as far as *the place* in front of the Water Gate toward the east, and on the projecting tower.

27 After them the Tekoites repaired another section, next to the great projecting tower, and as far as the wall of Ophel.

28 Beyond the Horse Gate the priests made repairs, each in front of his *own* house.

29 After them Zadok the son of Immer made repairs in front of his *own* house. After him Shemaiah the son of Shechaniah, the keeper of the East Gate, made repairs.

30 After him Hananiah the son of Shelemiah, and Hanun, the sixth son of Zalaph, repaired another section. After him Meshullam the son of Berechiah made repairs in front of his dwelling.

31 After him Malchijah, one of the goldsmiths, made repairs as far as the house of the Nethinim and of the merchants, in front of the Miphkad[a] Gate, and as far as the upper room at the corner.

32 And between the upper room at the corner, as far as the Sheep Gate, the goldsmiths and the merchants made repairs.

3:1 [a]Hebrew *Hammeah,* also at 12:39 **3:2** [a]Literally *On his hand* **3:4** [a]Or *Hakkoz* **3:5** [a]Literally *necks* **3:7** [a]Literally *throne* **3:8** [a]Literally *the son* **3:16** [a]Septuagint, Syriac, and Vulgate read *tomb.* **3:18** [a]Following Masoretic Text and Vulgate; some Hebrew manuscripts, Septuagint, and Syriac read *Binnui* (compare verse 24). **3:20** [a]A few Hebrew manuscripts, Syriac, and Vulgate read *Zaccai.* **3:21** [a]Or *Hakkoz* **3:31** [a]Literally *Inspection* or *Recruiting*

The Wall Defended Against Enemies

4 But it so happened, when Sanballat heard
that we were rebuilding the wall, that he
was furious and very indignant, and mocked
the Jews.
2 And he spoke before his brethren and the
army of Samaria, and said, "What are these
feeble Jews doing? Will they fortify themselves?
Will they offer sacrifices? Will they complete
it in a day? Will they revive the stones from the
heaps of rubbish—*stones* that are burned?"
3 Now Tobiah the Ammonite *was* beside him,
and he said, "Whatever they build, if even a
fox goes up *on it,* he will break down their stone
wall."
4 Hear, O our God, for we are despised; turn
their reproach on their own heads, and give them
as plunder to a land of captivity!
5 Do not cover their iniquity, and do not let
their sin be blotted out from before You; for they
have provoked *You* to anger before the builders.
6 So we built the wall, and the entire wall was
joined together up to half its *height,* for the
people had a mind to work.
7 Now it happened, when Sanballat, Tobiah,
the Arabs, the Ammonites, and the Ashdodites
heard that the walls of Jerusalem were being
restored and the gaps were beginning to be
closed, that they became very angry,
8 and all of them conspired together to come
and attack Jerusalem and create confusion.
9 Nevertheless we made our prayer to our
God, and because of them we set a watch against
them day and night.
10 Then Judah said, "The strength of the la-
borers is failing, and *there is* so much rubbish
that we are not able to build the wall."
11 And our adversaries said, "They will nei-
ther know nor see anything, till we come into
their midst and kill them and cause the work
to cease."
12 So it was, when the Jews who dwelt near
them came, that they told us ten times, "From
whatever place you turn, *they will be* upon us."
13 Therefore I positioned *men* behind the
lower parts of the wall, at the openings; and I
set the people according to their families, with
their swords, their spears, and their bows.
14 And I looked, and arose and said to the
nobles, to the leaders, and to the rest of the
people, "Do not be afraid of them. Remember
the Lord, great and awesome, and fight for your
brethren, your sons, your daughters, your
wives, and your houses."
15 And it happened, when our enemies heard
that it was known to us, and *that* God had
brought their plot to nothing, that all of us re-
turned to the wall, everyone to his work.
16 So it was, from that time on, *that* half of
my servants worked at construction, while the
other half held the spears, the shields, the bows,
and *wore* armor; and the leaders *were* behind
all the house of Judah.
17 Those who built on the wall, and those who
carried burdens, loaded themselves so that
with one hand they worked at construction, and
with the other held a weapon.
18 Every one of the builders had his sword
girded at his side as he built. And the one who
sounded the trumpet *was* beside me.
19 Then I said to the nobles, the rulers, and
the rest of the people, "The work *is* great and
extensive, and we are separated far from one
another on the wall.
20 "Wherever you hear the sound of the trum-
pet, rally to us there. Our God will fight for us."
21 So we labored in the work, and half of *the
men*[a] held the spears from daybreak until the
stars appeared.
22 At the same time I also said to the people,
"Let each man and his servant stay at night in
Jerusalem, that they may be our guard by night
and a working party by day."
23 So neither I, my brethren, my servants, nor
the men of the guard who followed me took off
our clothes, *except* that everyone took them
off for washing.

Nehemiah Deals with Oppression

5 And there was a great outcry of the people
and their wives against their Jewish breth-
ren.
2 For there were those who said, "We, our
sons, and our daughters *are* many; therefore
let us get grain, that we may eat and live."
3 There were also *some* who said, "We have
mortgaged our lands and vineyards and houses,
that we might buy grain because of the famine."
4 There were also those who said, "We have
borrowed money for the king's tax *on* our lands
and vineyards.
5 "Yet now our flesh *is* as the flesh of our
brethren, our children as their children; and in-
deed we are forcing our sons and our daugh-
ters to be slaves, and *some* of our daughters have
been brought into slavery. *It is* not in our power
to redeem them, for other men have our lands
and vineyards."
6 And I became very angry when I heard their
outcry and these words.
7 After serious thought, I rebuked the nobles
and rulers, and said to them, "Each of you is
exacting usury from his brother." So I called a
great assembly against them.
8 And I said to them, "According to our abil-
ity we have redeemed our Jewish brethren who
were sold to the nations. Now indeed, will you
even sell your brethren? Or should they be sold
to us?" Then they were silenced and found
nothing *to say.*
9 Then I said, "What you are doing *is* not
good. Should you not walk in the fear of our
God because of the reproach of the nations,
our enemies?
10 "I also, *with* my brethren and my servants,
am lending them money and grain. Please, let
us stop this usury!
11 "Restore now to them, even this day, their
lands, their vineyards, their olive groves, and
their houses, also a hundredth of the money
and the grain, the new wine and the oil, that
you have charged them."
12 So they said, "We will restore *it,* and will
require nothing from them; we will do as you
say." Then I called the priests, and required an
oath from them that they would do according
to this promise.
13 Then I shook out the fold of my garment[a]
and said, "So may God shake out each man
from his house, and from his property, who does
not perform this promise. Even thus may he be
shaken out and emptied." And all the assembly
said, "Amen!" and praised the LORD. Then the
people did according to this promise.

4:21 [a]Literally *them* **5:13** [a]Literally *my lap*

The Generosity of Nehemiah

14 Moreover, from the time that I was appointed to be their governor in the land of Judah, from the twentieth year until the thirty-second year of King Artaxerxes, twelve years, neither I nor my brothers ate the governor's provisions.

15 But the former governors who *were* before me laid burdens on the people, and took from them bread and wine, besides forty shekels of silver. Yes, even their servants bore rule over the people, but I did not do so, because of the fear of God.

16 Indeed, I also continued the work on this wall, and we[a] did not buy any land. All my servants *were* gathered there for the work.

17 And at my table *were* one hundred and fifty Jews and rulers, besides those who came to us from the nations around us.

18 Now *that* which was prepared daily *was* one ox *and* six choice sheep. Also fowl were prepared for me, and once every ten days an abundance of all kinds of wine. Yet in spite of this I did not demand the governor's provisions, because the bondage was heavy on this people.

19 Remember me, my God, for good, *according to* all that I have done for this people.

Conspiracy Against Nehemiah

6 Now it happened when Sanballat, Tobiah, Geshem the Arab, and the rest of our enemies heard that I had rebuilt the wall, and *that* there were no breaks left in it (though at that time I had not hung the doors in the gates),

2 that Sanballat and Geshem sent to me, saying, "Come, let us meet together among the villages in the plain of Ono." But they thought to do me harm.

3 So I sent messengers to them, saying, "I *am* doing a great work, so that I cannot come down. Why should the work cease while I leave it and go down to you?"

4 But they sent me this message four times, and I answered them in the same manner.

5 Then Sanballat sent his servant to me as before, the fifth time, with an open letter in his hand.

6 In it *was* written:

> It is reported among the nations, and Geshem[a] says, *that* you and the Jews plan to rebel; therefore, according to these rumors, you are rebuilding the wall, that you may be their king.
>
> 7 And you have also appointed prophets to proclaim concerning you at Jerusalem, saying, "*There is* a king in Judah!" Now these matters will be reported to the king. So come, therefore, and let us consult together.

8 Then I sent to him, saying, "No such things as you say are being done, but you invent them in your own heart."

9 For they all *were trying to* make us afraid, saying, "Their hands will be weakened in the work, and it will not be done."

Now therefore, *O God*, strengthen my hands.

10 Afterward I came to the house of Shemaiah the son of Delaiah, the son of Mehetabel, who *was* a secret informer; and he said, "Let us meet together in the house of God, within the temple, and let us close the doors of the temple, for they are coming to kill you; indeed, at night they will come to kill you."

11 And I said, "Should such a man as I flee? And who *is there* such as I who would go into the temple to save his life? I will not go in!"

12 Then I perceived that God had not sent him at all, but that he pronounced *this* prophecy against me because Tobiah and Sanballat had hired him.

13 For this reason he *was* hired, that I should be afraid and act that way and sin, so *that* they might have *cause* for an evil report, that they might reproach me.

14 My God, remember Tobiah and Sanballat, according to these their works, and the prophetess Noadiah and the rest of the prophets who would have made me afraid.

The Wall Completed

15 So the wall was finished on the twenty-fifth *day* of Elul, in fifty-two days.

16 And it happened, when all our enemies heard *of it*, and all the nations around us saw *these things*, that they were very disheartened in their own eyes; for they perceived that this work was done by our God.

17 Also in those days the nobles of Judah sent many letters to Tobiah, and *the letters of* Tobiah came to them.

18 For many in Judah were pledged to him, because he was the son-in-law of Shechaniah the son of Arah, and his son Jehohanan had married the daughter of Meshullam the son of Berechiah.

19 Also they reported his good deeds before me, and reported my words to him. Tobiah sent letters to frighten me.

7 Then it was, when the wall was built and I had hung the doors, when the gatekeepers, the singers, and the Levites had been appointed,

2 that I gave the charge of Jerusalem to my brother Hanani, and Hananiah the leader of the citadel, for he *was* a faithful man and feared God more than many.

3 And I said to them, "Do not let the gates of Jerusalem be opened until the sun is hot; and while they stand *guard*, let them shut and bar the doors; and appoint guards from among the inhabitants of Jerusalem, one at his watch station and another in front of his own house."

The Captives Who Returned to Jerusalem

4 Now the city *was* large and spacious, but the people in it *were* few, and the houses *were* not rebuilt.

5 Then my God put it into my heart to gather the nobles, the rulers, and the people, that they might be registered by genealogy. And I found a register of the genealogy of those who had come up in the first *return*, and found written in it:

> 6 These[a] *are* the people of the province who came back from the captivity, of those who had been carried away, whom Nebuchadnezzar the king of Babylon had carried away, and who returned to Jerusalem and Judah, everyone to his city.
>
> 7 Those who came with Zerubbabel *were* Jeshua, Nehemiah, Azariah, Raamiah,

5:16 [a]Following Masoretic Text; Septuagint, Syriac, and Vulgate read *I*. **6:6** [a]Hebrew *Gashmu* **7:6** [a]Compare verses 6–72 with Ezra 2:1–70

Nahamani, Mordecai, Bilshan, Mispereth,[a] Bigvai, Nehum, and Baanah.

The number of the men of the people of Israel:

8 the sons of Parosh, two thousand one hundred and seventy-two;

9 the sons of Shephatiah, three hundred and seventy-two;

10 the sons of Arah, six hundred and fifty-two;

11 the sons of Pahath-Moab, of the sons of Jeshua and Joab, two thousand eight hundred and eighteen;

12 the sons of Elam, one thousand two hundred and fifty-four;

13 the sons of Zattu, eight hundred and forty-five;

14 the sons of Zaccai, seven hundred and sixty;

15 the sons of Binnui,[a] six hundred and forty-eight;

16 the sons of Bebai, six hundred and twenty-eight;

17 the sons of Azgad, two thousand three hundred and twenty-two;

18 the sons of Adonikam, six hundred and sixty-seven;

19 the sons of Bigvai, two thousand and sixty-seven;

20 the sons of Adin, six hundred and fifty-five;

21 the sons of Ater of Hezekiah, ninety-eight;

22 the sons of Hashum, three hundred and twenty-eight;

23 the sons of Bezai, three hundred and twenty-four;

24 the sons of Hariph,[a] one hundred and twelve;

25 the sons of Gibeon,[a] ninety-five;

26 the men of Bethlehem and Netophah, one hundred and eighty-eight;

27 the men of Anathoth, one hundred and twenty-eight;

28 the men of Beth Azmaveth,[a] forty-two;

29 the men of Kirjath Jearim, Chephirah, and Beeroth, seven hundred and forty-three;

30 the men of Ramah and Geba, six hundred and twenty-one;

31 the men of Michmas, one hundred and twenty-two;

32 the men of Bethel and Ai, one hundred and twenty-three;

33 the men of the other Nebo, fifty-two;

34 the sons of the other Elam, one thousand two hundred and fifty-four;

35 the sons of Harim, three hundred and twenty;

36 the sons of Jericho, three hundred and forty-five;

37 the sons of Lod, Hadid, and Ono, seven hundred and twenty-one;

38 the sons of Senaah, three thousand nine hundred and thirty.

39 The priests: the sons of Jedaiah, of the house of Jeshua, nine hundred and seventy-three;

40 the sons of Immer, one thousand and fifty-two;

41 the sons of Pashhur, one thousand two hundred and forty-seven;

42 the sons of Harim, one thousand and seventeen.

43 The Levites: the sons of Jeshua, of Kadmiel, *and* of the sons of Hodevah,[a] seventy-four.

44 The singers: the sons of Asaph, one hundred and forty-eight.

45 The gatekeepers: the sons of Shallum, the sons of Ater, the sons of Talmon, the sons of Akkub, the sons of Hatita, the sons of Shobai, one hundred and thirty-eight.

46 The Nethinim: the sons of Ziha, the sons of Hasupha, the sons of Tabbaoth,

47 the sons of Keros, the sons of Sia,[a] the sons of Padon,

48 the sons of Lebana,[a] the sons of Hagaba,[b] the sons of Salmai,[c]

49 the sons of Hanan, the sons of Giddel, the sons of Gahar,

50 the sons of Reaiah, the sons of Rezin, the sons of Nekoda,

51 the sons of Gazzam, the sons of Uzza, the sons of Paseah,

52 the sons of Besai, the sons of Meunim, the sons of Nephishesim,[a]

53 the sons of Bakbuk, the sons of Hakupha, the sons of Harhur,

54 the sons of Bazlith,[a] the sons of Mehida, the sons of Harsha,

55 the sons of Barkos, the sons of Sisera, the sons of Tamah,

56 the sons of Neziah, and the sons of Hatipha.

57 The sons of Solomon's servants: the sons of Sotai, the sons of Sophereth, the sons of Perida,[a]

58 the sons of Jaala, the sons of Darkon, the sons of Giddel,

59 the sons of Shephatiah, the sons of Hattil, the sons of Pochereth of Zebaim, and the sons of Amon.[a]

60 All the Nethinim, and the sons of Solomon's servants, *were* three hundred and ninety-two.

61 And these *were* the ones who came up from Tel Melah, Tel Harsha, Cherub, Addon,[a] and Immer, but they could not identify their father's house nor their lineage, whether they *were* of Israel:

62 the sons of Delaiah, the sons of Tobiah, the sons of Nekoda, six hundred and forty-two;

63 and of the priests: the sons of Habaiah, the sons of Koz,[a] the sons of Barzillai, who took a wife of the daughters of Barzillai the Gileadite, and was called by their name.

64 These sought their listing *among* those who were registered by genealogy, but it was not found; therefore they were excluded from the priesthood as defiled.

65 And the governor[a] said to them that they should not eat of the most holy things till

7:7 [a]Spelled *Mispar* in Ezra 2:2 **7:15** [a]Spelled *Bani* in Ezra 2:10 **7:24** [a]Called *Jorah* in Ezra 2:18 **7:25** [a]Called *Gibbar* in Ezra 2:20 **7:28** [a]Called *Azmaveth* in Ezra 2:24 **7:43** [a]Spelled *Hodaviah* in Ezra 2:40 **7:47** [a]Spelled *Siaha* in Ezra 2:44 **7:48** [a]Masoretic Text reads *Lebanah.* [b]Masoretic Text reads *Hogabah.* [c]Or *Shalmai*, or *Shamlai* **7:52** [a]Spelled *Nephusim* in Ezra 2:50 **7:54** [a]Spelled *Bazluth* in Ezra 2:52 **7:57** [a]Spelled *Peruda* in Ezra 2:55 **7:59** [a]Spelled *Ami* in Ezra 2:57 **7:61** [a]Spelled *Addan* in Ezra 2:59 **7:63** [a]Or *Hakkoz* **7:65** [a]Hebrew *Tirshatha*

a priest could consult with the Urim and
Thummim.
66 Altogether the whole assembly *was*
forty-two thousand three hundred and
sixty,
67 besides their male and female servants,
of whom *there were* seven thousand
three hundred and thirty-seven; and they
had two hundred and forty-five men and
women singers.
68 Their horses were seven hundred and
thirty-six, their mules two hundred and
forty-five,
69 *their* camels four hundred and thirty-five,
and donkeys six thousand seven hundred
and twenty.
70 And some of the heads of the fathers'
houses gave to the work. The governor[a]
gave to the treasury one thousand gold
drachmas, fifty basins, and five hundred
and thirty priestly garments.
71 Some of the heads of the fathers' *houses*
gave to the treasury of the work twenty
thousand gold drachmas, and two
thousand two hundred silver minas.
72 And that which the rest of the people
gave *was* twenty thousand gold
drachmas, two thousand silver minas,
and sixty-seven priestly garments.

73 So the priests, the Levites, the gatekeepers,
the singers, *some* of the people, the Nethinim,
and all Israel dwelt in their cities.

Ezra Reads the Law

When the seventh month came, the chil-
dren of Israel *were* in their cities.
8 Now all the people gathered together as one
man in the open square that *was* in front of
the Water Gate; and they told Ezra the scribe
to bring the Book of the Law of Moses, which
the LORD had commanded Israel.
2 So Ezra the priest brought the Law before
the assembly of men and women and all who
could hear with understanding on the first day
of the seventh month.
3 Then he read from it in the open square that
was in front of the Water Gate from morning
until midday, before the men and women and
those who could understand; and the ears of
all the people *were attentive* to the Book of
the Law.
4 So Ezra the scribe stood on a platform of
wood which they had made for the purpose; and
beside him, at his right hand, stood Mattithiah,
Shema, Anaiah, Urijah, Hilkiah, and Maaseiah;
and at his left hand Pedaiah, Mishael, Malchi-
jah, Hashum, Hashbadana, Zechariah, *and*
Meshullam.
5 And Ezra opened the book in the sight of
all the people, for he was *standing* above all the
people; and when he opened it, all the people
stood up.
6 And Ezra blessed the LORD, the great God.
Then all the people answered, "Amen, Amen!"
while lifting up their hands. And they bowed
their heads and worshiped the LORD with *their*
faces to the ground.
7 Also Jeshua, Bani, Sherebiah, Jamin, Ak-
kub, Shabbethai, Hodijah, Maaseiah, Kelita,
Azariah, Jozabad, Hanan, Pelaiah, and the Le-
vites, helped the people to understand the Law;
and the people *stood* in their place.
8 So they read distinctly from the book, in
the Law of God; and they gave the sense, and
helped *them* to understand the reading.
9 And Nehemiah, who *was* the governor,[a]
Ezra the priest *and* scribe, and the Levites who
taught the people said to all the people, "This
day *is* holy to the LORD your God; do not mourn
nor weep." For all the people wept, when they
heard the words of the Law.
10 Then he said to them, "Go your way, eat
the fat, drink the sweet, and send portions to
those for whom nothing is prepared; for *this*
day *is* holy to our Lord. Do not sorrow, for the
joy of the LORD is your strength."
11 So the Levites quieted all the people, say-
ing, "Be still, for the day *is* holy; do not be
grieved."
12 And all the people went their way to eat
and drink, to send portions and rejoice greatly,
because they understood the words that were
declared to them.

The Feast of Tabernacles

13 Now on the second day the heads of the
fathers' *houses* of all the people, with the
priests and Levites, were gathered to Ezra
the scribe, in order to understand the words of
the Law.
14 And they found written in the Law, which
the LORD had commanded by Moses, that the
children of Israel should dwell in booths dur-
ing the feast of the seventh month,
15 and that they should announce and pro-
claim in all their cities and in Jerusalem, say-
ing, "Go out to the mountain, and bring olive
branches, branches of oil trees, myrtle branches,
palm branches, and branches of leafy trees, to
make booths, as *it is* written."
16 Then the people went out and brought *them*
and made themselves booths, each one on the
roof of his house, or in their courtyards or the
courts of the house of God, and in the open
square of the Water Gate and in the open square
of the Gate of Ephraim.
17 So the whole assembly of those who had
returned from the captivity made booths and
sat under the booths; for since the days of
Joshua the son of Nun until that day the chil-
dren of Israel had not done so. And there was
very great gladness.
18 Also day by day, from the first day until
the last day, he read from the Book of the Law
of God. And they kept the feast seven days; and
on the eighth day *there was* a sacred assembly,
according to the *prescribed* manner.

The People Confess Their Sins

9 Now on the twenty-fourth day of this month
the children of Israel were assembled with
fasting, in sackcloth, and with dust on their
heads.[a]
2 Then those of Israelite lineage separated
themselves from all foreigners; and they stood
and confessed their sins and the iniquities of
their fathers.
3 And they stood up in their place and read
from the Book of the Law of the LORD their
God *for one*-fourth of the day; and *for another*
fourth they confessed and worshiped the LORD
their God.
4 Then Jeshua, Bani, Kadmiel, Shebaniah,
Bunni, Sherebiah, Bani, *and* Chenani stood on

7:70 [a]Hebrew *Tirshatha* **8:9** [a]Hebrew *Tirshatha* **9:1** [a]Literally *earth on them*

the stairs of the Levites and cried out with a
loud voice to the LORD their God.
5 And the Levites, Jeshua, Kadmiel, Bani,
Hashabniah, Sherebiah, Hodijah, Shebaniah,
and Pethahiah, said:

"Stand up *and* bless the LORD your God
Forever and ever!

"Blessed be Your glorious name,
Which is exalted above all blessing and praise!
6 You alone *are* the LORD;
You have made heaven,
The heaven of heavens, with all their host,
The earth and everything on it,
The seas and all that is in them,
And You preserve them all.
The host of heaven worships You.

7 "You *are* the LORD God,
Who chose Abram,
And brought him out of Ur of the Chaldeans,
And gave him the name Abraham;
8 You found his heart faithful before You,
And made a covenant with him
To give the land of the Canaanites,
The Hittites, the Amorites,
The Perizzites, the Jebusites,
And the Girgashites—
To give *it* to his descendants.
You have performed Your words,
For You *are* righteous.

9 "You saw the affliction of our fathers in Egypt,
And heard their cry by the Red Sea.
10 You showed signs and wonders against Pharaoh,
Against all his servants,
And against all the people of his land.
For You knew that they acted proudly against them.
So You made a name for Yourself, as *it is* this day.
11 And You divided the sea before them,
So that they went through the midst of the sea on the dry land;
And their persecutors You threw into the deep,
As a stone into the mighty waters.
12 Moreover You led them by day with a cloudy pillar,
And by night with a pillar of fire,
To give them light on the road
Which they should travel.

13 "You came down also on Mount Sinai,
And spoke with them from heaven,
And gave them just ordinances and true laws,
Good statutes and commandments.
14 You made known to them Your holy Sabbath,
And commanded them precepts, statutes and laws,
By the hand of Moses Your servant.
15 You gave them bread from heaven for their hunger,
And brought them water out of the rock for their thirst,
And told them to go in to possess the land
Which You had sworn to give them.

16 "But they and our fathers acted proudly,
Hardened their necks,
And did not heed Your commandments.
17 They refused to obey,
And they were not mindful of Your wonders
That You did among them.
But they hardened their necks,
And in their rebellion[a]
They appointed a leader
To return to their bondage.
But You *are* God,
Ready to pardon,
Gracious and merciful,
Slow to anger,
Abundant in kindness,
And did not forsake them.

18 "Even when they made a molded calf for themselves,
And said, 'This *is* your god
That brought you up out of Egypt,'
And worked great provocations,
19 Yet in Your manifold mercies
You did not forsake them in the wilderness.
The pillar of the cloud did not depart from them by day,
To lead them on the road;
Nor the pillar of fire by night,
To show them light,
And the way they should go.
20 You also gave Your good Spirit to instruct them,
And did not withhold Your manna from their mouth,
And gave them water for their thirst.
21 Forty years You sustained them in the wilderness;
They lacked nothing;
Their clothes did not wear out[a]
And their feet did not swell.

22 "Moreover You gave them kingdoms and nations,
And divided them into districts.[a]
So they took possession of the land of Sihon,
The land of[b] the king of Heshbon,
And the land of Og king of Bashan.
23 You also multiplied their children as the stars of heaven,
And brought them into the land
Which You had told their fathers
To go in and possess.
24 So the people went in
And possessed the land;
You subdued before them the inhabitants of the land,
The Canaanites,
And gave them into their hands,
With their kings
And the people of the land,
That they might do with them as they wished.
25 And they took strong cities and a rich land,
And possessed houses full of all goods,

9:17 [a]Following Masoretic Text and Vulgate; Septuagint reads *in Egypt*. **9:21** [a]Compare Deuteronomy 29:5
9:22 [a]Literally *corners* [b]Following Masoretic Text and Vulgate; Septuagint omits *The land of*.

Cisterns *already* dug, vineyards, olive groves,
And fruit trees in abundance.
So they ate and were filled and grew fat,
And delighted themselves in Your great goodness.

26 "Nevertheless they were disobedient
And rebelled against You,
Cast Your law behind their backs
And killed Your prophets, who testified against them
To turn them to Yourself;
And they worked great provocations.
27 Therefore You delivered them into the hand of their enemies,
Who oppressed them;
And in the time of their trouble,
When they cried to You,
You heard from heaven;
And according to Your abundant mercies
You gave them deliverers who saved them
From the hand of their enemies.

28 "But after they had rest,
They again did evil before You.
Therefore You left them in the hand of their enemies,
So that they had dominion over them;
Yet when they returned and cried out to You,
You heard from heaven;
And many times You delivered them according to Your mercies,
29 And testified against them,
That You might bring them back to Your law.
Yet they acted proudly,
And did not heed Your commandments,
But sinned against Your judgments,
'Which if a man does, he shall live by them.'[a]
And they shrugged their shoulders,
Stiffened their necks,
And would not hear.
30 Yet for many years You had patience with them,
And testified against them by Your Spirit in Your prophets.
Yet they would not listen;
Therefore You gave them into the hand of the peoples of the lands.
31 Nevertheless in Your great mercy
You did not utterly consume them nor forsake them;
For You *are* God, gracious and merciful.

32 "Now therefore, our God,
The great, the mighty, and awesome God,
Who keeps covenant and mercy:
Do not let all the trouble seem small before You
That has come upon us,
Our kings and our princes,
Our priests and our prophets,
Our fathers and on all Your people,
From the days of the kings of Assyria until this day.
33 However You *are* just in all that has befallen us;
For You have dealt faithfully,
But we have done wickedly.
34 Neither our kings nor our princes,
Our priests nor our fathers,
Have kept Your law,
Nor heeded Your commandments and Your testimonies,
With which You testified against them.
35 For they have not served You in their kingdom,
Or in the many good *things* that You gave them,
Or in the large and rich land which You set before them;
Nor did they turn from their wicked works.

36 "Here we *are*, servants today!
And the land that You gave to our fathers,
To eat its fruit and its bounty,
Here we *are*, servants in it!
37 And it yields much increase to the kings
You have set over us,
Because of our sins;
Also they have dominion over our bodies and our cattle
At their pleasure;
And we *are* in great distress.

38 "And because of all this,
We make a sure *covenant* and write *it*;
Our leaders, our Levites, *and* our priests seal *it*."

The People Who Sealed the Covenant

10 Now those who placed *their* seal on *the document were:*
Nehemiah the governor, the son of Hacaliah, and Zedekiah,
2 Seraiah, Azariah, Jeremiah,
3 Pashhur, Amariah, Malchijah,
4 Hattush, Shebaniah, Malluch,
5 Harim, Meremoth, Obadiah,
6 Daniel, Ginnethon, Baruch,
7 Meshullam, Abijah, Mijamin,
8 Maaziah, Bilgai, *and* Shemaiah. These *were*
the priests.
9 The Levites: Jeshua the son of Azaniah, Binnui of the sons of Henadad, *and* Kadmiel.
10 Their brethren: Shebaniah, Hodijah, Kelita,
Pelaiah, Hanan,
11 Micha, Rehob, Hashabiah,
12 Zaccur, Sherebiah, Shebaniah,
13 Hodijah, Bani, *and* Beninu.
14 The leaders of the people: Parosh, Pahath-
Moab, Elam, Zattu, Bani,
15 Bunni, Azgad, Bebai,
16 Adonijah, Bigvai, Adin,
17 Ater, Hezekiah, Azzur,
18 Hodijah, Hashum, Bezai,
19 Hariph, Anathoth, Nebai,
20 Magpiash, Meshullam, Hezir,
21 Meshezabel, Zadok, Jaddua,
22 Pelatiah, Hanan, Anaiah,
23 Hoshea, Hananiah, Hasshub,
24 Hallohesh, Pilha, Shobek,
25 Rehum, Hashabnah, Maaseiah,
26 Ahijah, Hanan, Anan,
27 Malluch, Harim, *and* Baanah.

The Covenant That Was Sealed

28 Now the rest of the people—the priests, the
Levites, the gatekeepers, the singers, the Neth-
inim, and all those who had separated them-
selves from the peoples of the lands to the Law
of God, their wives, their sons, and their daugh-

9:29 [a]Leviticus 18:5

ters, everyone who had knowledge and understanding—
29 these joined with their brethren, their nobles, and entered into a curse and an oath to walk in God's Law, which was given by Moses the servant of God, and to observe and do all the commandments of the LORD our Lord, and His ordinances and His statutes:
30 We would not give our daughters as wives to the peoples of the land, nor take their daughters for our sons;
31 *if* the peoples of the land brought wares or any grain to sell on the Sabbath day, we would not buy it from them on the Sabbath, or on a holy day; and we would forego the seventh year's *produce* and the exacting of every debt.
32 Also we made ordinances for ourselves, to exact from ourselves yearly one-third of a shekel for the service of the house of our God:
33 for the showbread, for the regular grain offering, for the regular burnt offering of the Sabbaths, the New Moons, and the set feasts; for the holy things, for the sin offerings to make atonement for Israel, and all the work of the house of our God.
34 We cast lots among the priests, the Levites, and the people, for bringing the wood offering into the house of our God, according to our fathers' houses, at the appointed times year by year, to burn on the altar of the LORD our God as *it is* written in the Law.
35 And *we made ordinances* to bring the firstfruits of our ground and the firstfruits of all fruit of all trees, year by year, to the house of the LORD;
36 to bring the firstborn of our sons and our cattle, as *it is* written in the Law, and the firstborn of our herds and our flocks, to the house of our God, to the priests who minister in the house of our God;
37 to bring the firstfruits of our dough, our offerings, the fruit from all kinds of trees, *the* new wine and oil, to the priests, to the storerooms of the house of our God; and to bring the tithes of our land to the Levites, for the Levites should receive the tithes in all our farming communities.
38 And the priest, the descendant of Aaron, shall be with the Levites when the Levites receive tithes; and the Levites shall bring up a tenth of the tithes to the house of our God, to the rooms of the storehouse.
39 For the children of Israel and the children of Levi shall bring the offering of the grain, of the new wine and the oil, to the storerooms where the articles of the sanctuary *are, where* the priests who minister and the gatekeepers and the singers *are;* and we will not neglect the house of our God.

The People Dwelling in Jerusalem

11 Now the leaders of the people dwelt at Jerusalem; the rest of the people cast lots to bring one out of ten to dwell in Jerusalem, the holy city, and nine-tenths *were to dwell* in *other* cities.
2 And the people blessed all the men who willingly offered themselves to dwell at Jerusalem.
3 These *are* the heads of the province who dwelt in Jerusalem. (But in the cities of Judah everyone dwelt in his own possession in their cities—Israelites, priests, Levites, Nethinim, and descendants of Solomon's servants.)
4 Also in Jerusalem dwelt *some* of the children of Judah and of the children of Benjamin.
The children of Judah: Athaiah the son of Uzziah, the son of Zechariah, the son of Amariah, the son of Shephatiah, the son of Mahalalel, of the children of Perez;
5 and Maaseiah the son of Baruch, the son of Col-Hozeh, the son of Hazaiah, the son of Adaiah, the son of Joiarib, the son of Zechariah, the son of Shiloni.
6 All the sons of Perez who dwelt at Jerusalem *were* four hundred and sixty-eight valiant men.
7 And these are the sons of Benjamin: Sallu the son of Meshullam, the son of Joed, the son of Pedaiah, the son of Kolaiah, the son of Maaseiah, the son of Ithiel, the son of Jeshaiah;
8 and after him Gabbai *and* Sallai, nine hundred and twenty-eight.
9 Joel the son of Zichri *was* their overseer, and Judah the son of Senuah[a] *was* second over the city.
10 Of the priests: Jedaiah the son of Joiarib, and Jachin;
11 Seraiah the son of Hilkiah, the son of Meshullam, the son of Zadok, the son of Meraioth, the son of Ahitub, *was* the leader of the house of God.
12 Their brethren who did the work of the house *were* eight hundred and twenty-two; and Adaiah the son of Jeroham, the son of Pelaliah, the son of Amzi, the son of Zechariah, the son of Pashhur, the son of Malchijah,
13 and his brethren, heads of the fathers' *houses, were* two hundred and forty-two; and Amashai the son of Azarel, the son of Ahzai, the son of Meshillemoth, the son of Immer,
14 and their brethren, mighty men of valor, *were* one hundred and twenty-eight. Their overseer *was* Zabdiel the son of *one of* the great men.[a]
15 Also of the Levites: Shemaiah the son of Hasshub, the son of Azrikam, the son of Hashabiah, the son of Bunni;
16 Shabbethai and Jozabad, of the heads of the Levites, *had* the oversight of the business outside of the house of God;
17 Mattaniah the son of Micha,[a] the son of Zabdi, the son of Asaph, the leader *who* began the thanksgiving with prayer; Bakbukiah, the second among his brethren; and Abda the son of Shammua, the son of Galal, the son of Jeduthun.
18 All the Levites in the holy city *were* two hundred and eighty-four.
19 Moreover the gatekeepers, Akkub, Talmon, and their brethren who kept the gates, *were* one hundred and seventy-two.
20 And the rest of Israel, of the priests *and* Levites, *were* in all the cities of Judah, everyone in his inheritance.
21 But the Nethinim dwelt in Ophel. And Ziha and Gishpa *were* over the Nethinim.
22 Also the overseer of the Levites at Jerusalem *was* Uzzi the son of Bani, the son of Hashabiah, the son of Mattaniah, the son of Micha, of the sons of Asaph, the singers in charge of the service of the house of God.
23 For *it was* the king's command concerning them that a certain portion should be for the singers, a quota day by day.

11:9 [a]Or *Hassenuah* **11:14** [a]Or *the son of Haggedolim* **11:17** [a]Or *Michah*

24 Pethahiah the son of Meshezabel, of the children of Zerah the son of Judah, *was* the king's deputy[a] in all matters concerning the people.

The People Dwelling Outside Jerusalem

25 And as for the villages with their fields, *some* of the children of Judah dwelt in Kirjath Arba and its villages, Dibon and its villages, Jekabzeel and its villages;
26 in Jeshua, Moladah, Beth Pelet,
27 Hazar Shual, and Beersheba and its villages;
28 in Ziklag and Meconah and its villages;
29 in En Rimmon, Zorah, Jarmuth,
30 Zanoah, Adullam, and their villages; in Lachish and its fields; in Azekah and its villages. They dwelt from Beersheba to the Valley of Hinnom.
31 Also the children of Benjamin from Geba *dwelt* in Michmash, Aija, and Bethel, and their villages;
32 in Anathoth, Nob, Ananiah;
33 in Hazor, Ramah, Gittaim;
34 in Hadid, Zeboim, Neballat;
35 in Lod, Ono, *and* the Valley of Craftsmen.
36 Some of the Judean divisions of Levites *were* in Benjamin.

The Priests and Levites

12 Now these *are* the priests and the Levites who came up with Zerubbabel the son of Shealtiel, and Jeshua: Seraiah, Jeremiah, Ezra,
2 Amariah, Malluch, Hattush,
3 Shechaniah, Rehum, Meremoth,
4 Iddo, Ginnethoi,[a] Abijah,
5 Mijamin, Maadiah, Bilgah,
6 Shemaiah, Joiarib, Jedaiah,
7 Sallu, Amok, Hilkiah, *and* Jedaiah.
These *were* the heads of the priests and their brethren in the days of Jeshua.
8 Moreover the Levites *were* Jeshua, Binnui, Kadmiel, Sherebiah, Judah, *and* Mattaniah *who led* the thanksgiving *psalms,* he and his brethren.
9 Also Bakbukiah and Unni, their brethren, *stood* across from them in *their* duties.
10 Jeshua begot Joiakim, Joiakim begot Eliashib, Eliashib begot Joiada,
11 Joiada begot Jonathan, and Jonathan begot Jaddua.
12 Now in the days of Joiakim, the priests, the heads of the fathers' *houses were:* of Seraiah, Meraiah; of Jeremiah, Hananiah;
13 of Ezra, Meshullam; of Amariah, Jehohanan;
14 of Melichu,[a] Jonathan; of Shebaniah,[b] Joseph;
15 of Harim,[a] Adna; of Meraioth,[b] Helkai;
16 of Iddo, Zechariah; of Ginnethon, Meshullam;
17 of Abijah, Zichri; *the son* of Minjamin;[a] of Moadiah,[b] Piltai;
18 of Bilgah, Shammua; of Shemaiah, Jehonathan;
19 of Joiarib, Mattenai; of Jedaiah, Uzzi;
20 of Sallai,[a] Kallai; of Amok, Eber;
21 of Hilkiah, Hashabiah; *and* of Jedaiah, Nethanel.
22 During the reign of Darius the Persian, a record *was also kept* of the Levites and priests *who had been* heads of their fathers' *houses* in the days of Eliashib, Joiada, Johanan, and Jaddua.
23 The sons of Levi, the heads of the fathers' *houses* until the days of Johanan the son of Eliashib, *were* written in the book of the chronicles.
24 And the heads of the Levites *were* Hashabiah, Sherebiah, and Jeshua the son of Kadmiel, with their brothers across from them, to praise *and* give thanks, group alternating with group, according to the command of David the man of God.
25 Mattaniah, Bakbukiah, Obadiah, Meshullam, Talmon, and Akkub *were* gatekeepers keeping the watch at the storerooms of the gates.
26 These *lived* in the days of Joiakim the son of Jeshua, the son of Jozadak,[a] and in the days of Nehemiah the governor, and of Ezra the priest, the scribe.

Nehemiah Dedicates the Wall

27 Now at the dedication of the wall of Jerusalem they sought out the Levites in all their places, to bring them to Jerusalem to celebrate the dedication with gladness, both with thanksgivings and singing, *with* cymbals and stringed instruments and harps.
28 And the sons of the singers gathered together from the countryside around Jerusalem, from the villages of the Netophathites,
29 from the house of Gilgal, and from the fields of Geba and Azmaveth; for the singers had built themselves villages all around Jerusalem.
30 Then the priests and Levites purified themselves, and purified the people, the gates, and the wall.
31 So I brought the leaders of Judah up on the wall, and appointed two large thanksgiving choirs. *One* went to the right hand on the wall toward the Refuse Gate.
32 After them went Hoshaiah and half of the leaders of Judah,
33 and Azariah, Ezra, Meshullam,
34 Judah, Benjamin, Shemaiah, Jeremiah,
35 and some of the priests' sons with trumpets—Zechariah the son of Jonathan, the son of Shemaiah, the son of Mattaniah, the son of Michaiah, the son of Zaccur, the son of Asaph,
36 and his brethren, Shemaiah, Azarel, Milalai, Gilalai, Maai, Nethanel, Judah, *and* Hanani, with the musical instruments of David the man of God. Ezra the scribe *went* before them.
37 By the Fountain Gate, in front of them, they went up the stairs of the City of David, on the stairway of the wall, beyond the house of David, as far as the Water Gate eastward.
38 The other thanksgiving choir went the opposite *way,* and I *was* behind them with half of the people on the wall, going past the Tower of the Ovens as far as the Broad Wall,
39 and above the Gate of Ephraim, above the Old Gate, above the Fish Gate, the Tower of Hananel, the Tower of the Hundred, as far as the Sheep Gate; and they stopped by the Gate of the Prison.
40 So the two thanksgiving choirs stood in the house of God, likewise I and the half of the rulers with me;
41 and the priests, Eliakim, Maaseiah, Minja-

11:24 [a]Literally *at the king's hand* **12:4** [a]Or *Ginnethon* (compare verse 16) **12:14** [a]Or *Malluch* (compare verse 2) [b]Or *Shechaniah* (compare verse 3) **12:15** [a]Or *Rehum* (compare verse 3) [b]Or *Meremoth* (compare verse 3) **12:17** [a]Or *Mijamin* (compare verse 5) [b]Or *Maadiah* (compare verse 5) **12:20** [a]Or *Sallu* (compare verse 7) **12:26** [a]Spelled *Jehozadak* in 1 Chronicles 6:14

min,[a] Michaiah, Elioenai, Zechariah, *and* Hananiah, with trumpets;
42 also Maaseiah, Shemaiah, Eleazar, Uzzi, Jehohanan, Malchijah, Elam, and Ezer. The singers sang loudly with Jezrahiah the director.
43 Also that day they offered great sacrifices, and rejoiced, for God had made them rejoice with great joy; the women and the children also rejoiced, so that the joy of Jerusalem was heard afar off.

Temple Responsibilities

44 And at the same time some were appointed over the rooms of the storehouse for the offerings, the firstfruits, and the tithes, to gather into them from the fields of the cities the portions specified by the Law for the priests and Levites; for Judah rejoiced over the priests and Levites who ministered.
45 Both the singers and the gatekeepers kept the charge of their God and the charge of the purification, according to the command of David *and* Solomon his son.
46 For in the days of David and Asaph of old *there were* chiefs of the singers, and songs of praise and thanksgiving to God.
47 In the days of Zerubbabel and in the days of Nehemiah all Israel gave the portions for the singers and the gatekeepers, a portion for each day. They also consecrated *holy things* for the Levites, and the Levites consecrated *them* for the children of Aaron.

Principles of Separation

13 On that day they read from the Book of Moses in the hearing of the people, and in it was found written that no Ammonite or Moabite should ever come into the assembly of God,
2 because they had not met the children of Israel with bread and water, but hired Balaam against them to curse them. However, our God turned the curse into a blessing.
3 So it was, when they had heard the Law, that they separated all the mixed multitude from Israel.

The Reforms of Nehemiah

4 Now before this, Eliashib the priest, having authority over the storerooms of the house of our God, *was* allied with Tobiah.
5 And he had prepared for him a large room, where previously they had stored the grain offerings, the frankincense, the articles, the tithes of grain, the new wine and oil, which were commanded *to be given* to the Levites and singers and gatekeepers, and the offerings for the priests.
6 But during all this I was not in Jerusalem, for in the thirty-second year of Artaxerxes king of Babylon I had returned to the king. Then after certain days I obtained leave from the king,
7 and I came to Jerusalem and discovered the evil that Eliashib had done for Tobiah, in preparing a room for him in the courts of the house of God.
8 And it grieved me bitterly; therefore I threw all the household goods of Tobiah out of the room.
9 Then I commanded them to cleanse the rooms; and I brought back into them the articles of the house of God, with the grain offering and the frankincense.
10 I also realized that the portions for the Levites had not been given *them;* for each of the Levites and the singers who did the work had gone back to his field.
11 So I contended with the rulers, and said, "Why is the house of God forsaken?" And I gathered them together and set them in their place.
12 Then all Judah brought the tithe of the grain and the new wine and the oil to the storehouse.
13 And I appointed as treasurers over the storehouse Shelemiah the priest and Zadok the scribe, and of the Levites, Pedaiah; and next to them *was* Hanan the son of Zaccur, the son of Mattaniah; for they were considered faithful, and their task *was* to distribute to their brethren.
14 Remember me, O my God, concerning this, and do not wipe out my good deeds that I have done for the house of my God, and for its services!
15 In those days I saw *people* in Judah treading wine presses on the Sabbath, and bringing in sheaves, and loading donkeys with wine, grapes, figs, and all *kinds of* burdens, which they brought into Jerusalem on the Sabbath day. And I warned *them* about the day on which they were selling provisions.
16 Men of Tyre dwelt there also, who brought in fish and all kinds of goods, and sold *them* on the Sabbath to the children of Judah, and in Jerusalem.
17 Then I contended with the nobles of Judah, and said to them, "What evil thing *is* this that you do, by which you profane the Sabbath day?
18 "Did not your fathers do thus, and did not our God bring all this disaster on us and on this city? Yet you bring added wrath on Israel by profaning the Sabbath."
19 So it was, at the gates of Jerusalem, as it began to be dark before the Sabbath, that I commanded the gates to be shut, and charged that they must not be opened till after the Sabbath. Then I posted *some* of my servants at the gates, *so that* no burdens would be brought in on the Sabbath day.
20 Now the merchants and sellers of all kinds of wares lodged outside Jerusalem once or twice.
21 Then I warned them, and said to them, "Why do you spend the night around the wall? If you do *so* again, I will lay hands on you!" From that time on they came no *more* on the Sabbath.
22 And I commanded the Levites that they should cleanse themselves, and that they should go and guard the gates, to sanctify the Sabbath day.

Remember me, O my God, *concerning* this also, and spare me according to the greatness of Your mercy!
23 In those days I also saw Jews *who* had married women of Ashdod, Ammon, *and* Moab.
24 And half of their children spoke the language of Ashdod, and could not speak the language of Judah, but spoke according to the language of one or the other people.
25 So I contended with them and cursed them, struck some of them and pulled out their hair, and made them swear by God, *saying,* "You shall

12:41 [a]Or *Mijamin* (compare verse 5)

not give your daughters as wives to their sons,
nor take their daughters for your sons or yourselves.
26 "Did not Solomon king of Israel sin by these
things? Yet among many nations there was no
king like him, who was beloved of his God;
and God made him king over all Israel. Nevertheless
pagan women caused even him to sin.
27 "Should we then hear of your doing all this
great evil, transgressing against our God by
marrying pagan women?"
28 And *one* of the sons of Joiada, the son of
Eliashib the high priest, *was* a son-in-law of
Sanballat the Horonite; therefore I drove him
from me.
29 Remember them, O my God, because they
have defiled the priesthood and the covenant
of the priesthood and the Levites.
30 Thus I cleansed them of everything pagan.
I also assigned duties to the priests and the
Levites, each to his service,
31 and *to bringing* the wood offering and the
firstfruits at appointed times.

Remember me, O my God, for good!

The Book of ESTHER

The King Dethrones Queen Vashti

1 Now it came to pass in the days of Ahasuerus[a]
(this *was* the Ahasuerus who reigned
over one hundred and twenty-seven provinces,
from India to Ethiopia),
2 in those days when King Ahasuerus sat
on the throne of his kingdom, which *was* in
Shushan[a] the citadel,
3 *that* in the third year of his reign he made
a feast for all his officials and servants—the
powers of Persia and Media, the nobles, and
the princes of the provinces *being* before him—
4 when he showed the riches of his glorious
kingdom and the splendor of his excellent majesty
for many days, one hundred and eighty
days *in all.*
5 And when these days were completed, the
king made a feast lasting seven days for all the
people who were present in Shushan the citadel,
from great to small, in the court of the garden
of the king's palace.
6 *There were* white and blue linen *curtains*
fastened with cords of fine linen and purple on
silver rods and marble pillars; *and the* couches
were of gold and silver on a *mosaic* pavement
of alabaster, turquoise, and white and black
marble.
7 And they served drinks in golden vessels,
each vessel being different from the other, with
royal wine in abundance, according to the generosity
of the king.
8 In accordance with the law, the drinking was
not compulsory; for so the king had ordered
all the officers of his household, that they
should do according to each man's pleasure.
9 Queen Vashti also made a feast for the
women *in* the royal palace which *belonged* to
King Ahasuerus.
10 On the seventh day, when the heart of the
king was merry with wine, he commanded Mehuman,
Biztha, Harbona, Bigtha, Abagtha, Zethar,
and Carcas, seven eunuchs who served in
the presence of King Ahasuerus,
11 to bring Queen Vashti before the king,
wearing her royal crown, in order to show her
beauty to the people and the officials, for she
was beautiful to behold.
12 But Queen Vashti refused to come at the
king's command *brought* by *his* eunuchs; therefore
the king was furious, and his anger burned
within him.
13 Then the king said to the wise men who
understood the times (for this *was* the king's
manner toward all who knew law and justice,
14 those closest to him *being* Carshena, Shethar,
Admatha, Tarshish, Meres, Marsena, and
Memucan, the seven princes of Persia and Media,
who had access to the king's presence, *and*
who ranked highest in the kingdom):
15 "What *shall we* do to Queen Vashti, according
to law, because she did not obey the command
of King Ahasuerus *brought to her* by the
eunuchs?"
16 And Memucan answered before the king
and the princes: "Queen Vashti has not only
wronged the king, but also all the princes, and
all the people who *are* in all the provinces of
King Ahasuerus.
17 "For the queen's behavior will become
known to all women, so that they will despise
their husbands in their eyes, when they report,
'King Ahasuerus commanded Queen Vashti to
be brought in before him, but she did not
come.'
18 "This very day the *noble* ladies of Persia and
Media will say to all the king's officials that they
have heard of the behavior of the queen. Thus
there will be excessive contempt and wrath.
19 "If it pleases the king, let a royal decree go
out from him, and let it be recorded in the laws
of the Persians and the Medes, so that it will
not be altered, that Vashti shall come no more
before King Ahasuerus; and let the king give
her royal position to another who is better than
she.
20 "When the king's decree which he will make
is proclaimed throughout all his empire (for it
is great), all wives will honor their husbands,
both great and small."
21 And the reply pleased the king and the
princes, and the king did according to the word
of Memucan.
22 Then he sent letters to all the king's provinces,
to each province in its own script, and to
every people in their own language, that each
man should be master in his own house, and
speak in the language of his own people.

Esther Becomes Queen

2 After these things, when the wrath of King
Ahasuerus subsided, he remembered Vashti,
what she had done, and what had been decreed
against her.

1:1 [a]Generally identified with Xerxes I (485–464 B.C.) **1:2** [a]Or *Susa,* and so throughout this book

2 Then the king's servants who attended him said: "Let beautiful young virgins be sought for the king;

3 "and let the king appoint officers in all the provinces of his kingdom, that they may gather all the beautiful young virgins to Shushan the citadel, into the women's quarters, under the custody of Hegai[a] the king's eunuch, custodian of the women. And let beauty preparations be given *them.*

4 "Then let the young woman who pleases the king be queen instead of Vashti." This thing pleased the king, and he did so.

5 In Shushan the citadel there was a certain Jew whose name *was* Mordecai the son of Jair, the son of Shimei, the son of Kish, a Benjamite.

6 *Kish*[a] had been carried away from Jerusalem with the captives who had been captured with Jeconiah[b] king of Judah, whom Nebuchadnezzar the king of Babylon had carried away.

7 And *Mordecai* had brought up Hadassah, that *is,* Esther, his uncle's daughter, for she had neither father nor mother. The young woman *was* lovely and beautiful. When her father and mother died, Mordecai took her as his own daughter.

8 So it was, when the king's command and decree were heard, and when many young women were gathered at Shushan the citadel, *under* the custody of Hegai, that Esther also was taken to the king's palace, into the care of Hegai the custodian of the women.

9 Now the young woman pleased him, and she obtained his favor; so he readily gave beauty preparations to her, besides her allowance. Then seven choice maidservants were provided for her from the king's palace, and he moved her and her maidservants to the best *place* in the house of the women.

10 Esther had not revealed her people or family, for Mordecai had charged her not to reveal *it.*

11 And every day Mordecai paced in front of the court of the women's quarters, to learn of Esther's welfare and what was happening to her.

12 Each young woman's turn came to go in to King Ahasuerus after she had completed twelve months' preparation, according to the regulations for the women, for thus were the days of their preparation apportioned: six months with oil of myrrh, and six months with perfumes and preparations for beautifying women.

13 Thus *prepared, each* young woman went to the king, and she was given whatever she desired to take with her from the women's quarters to the king's palace.

14 In the evening she went, and in the morning she returned to the second house of the women, to the custody of Shaashgaz, the king's eunuch who kept the concubines. She would not go in to the king again unless the king delighted in her and called for her by name.

15 Now when the turn came for Esther the daughter of Abihail the uncle of Mordecai, who had taken her as his daughter, to go in to the king, she requested nothing but what Hegai the king's eunuch, the custodian of the women, advised. And Esther obtained favor in the sight of all who saw her.

16 So Esther was taken to King Ahasuerus, into his royal palace, in the tenth month, which *is* the month of Tebeth, in the seventh year of his reign.

17 The king loved Esther more than all the *other* women, and she obtained grace and favor in his sight more than all the virgins; so he set the royal crown upon her head and made her queen instead of Vashti.

18 Then the king made a great feast, the Feast of Esther, for all his officials and servants; and he proclaimed a holiday in the provinces and gave gifts according to the generosity of a king.

Mordecai Discovers a Plot

19 When virgins were gathered together a second time, Mordecai sat within the king's gate.

20 *Now* Esther had not revealed her family and her people, just as Mordecai had charged her, for Esther obeyed the command of Mordecai as when she was brought up by him.

21 In those days, while Mordecai sat within the king's gate, two of the king's eunuchs, Bigthan and Teresh, doorkeepers, became furious and sought to lay hands on King Ahasuerus.

22 So the matter became known to Mordecai, who told Queen Esther, and Esther informed the king in Mordecai's name.

23 And when an inquiry was made into the matter, it was confirmed, and both were hanged on a gallows; and it was written in the book of the chronicles in the presence of the king.

Haman's Conspiracy Against the Jews

3 After these things King Ahasuerus promoted Haman, the son of Hammedatha the Agagite, and advanced him and set his seat above all the princes who *were* with him.

2 And all the king's servants who *were* within the king's gate bowed and paid homage to Haman, for so the king had commanded concerning him. But Mordecai would not bow or pay homage.

3 Then the king's servants who *were* within the king's gate said to Mordecai, "Why do you transgress the king's command?"

4 Now it happened, when they spoke to him daily and he would not listen to them, that they told *it* to Haman, to see whether Mordecai's words would stand; for *Mordecai* had told them that he *was* a Jew.

5 When Haman saw that Mordecai did not bow or pay him homage, Haman was filled with wrath.

6 But he disdained to lay hands on Mordecai alone, for they had told him of the people of Mordecai. Instead, Haman sought to destroy all the Jews who *were* throughout the whole kingdom of Ahasuerus—the people of Mordecai.

7 In the first month, which is the month of Nisan, in the twelfth year of King Ahasuerus, they cast Pur (that *is,* the lot), before Haman to determine the day and the month,[a] until *it fell on the* twelfth *month,*[b] which *is* the month of Adar.

8 Then Haman said to King Ahasuerus, "There is a certain people scattered and dispersed among the people in all the provinces of your kingdom; their laws *are* different from all *other* people's, and they do not keep the king's

2:3 [a]Hebrew *Hege* **2:6** [a]Literally *Who* [b]Same as *Jehoiachin,* 2 Kings 24:6 and elsewhere **3:7** [a]Septuagint adds *to destroy the people of Mordecai in one day;* Vulgate adds *the nation of the Jews should be destroyed.* [b]Following Masoretic Text and Vulgate; Septuagint reads *and the lot fell on the fourteenth of the month.*

laws. Therefore it *is* not fitting for the king to let them remain.

9 "If it pleases the king, let *a decree* be written that they be destroyed, and I will pay ten thousand talents of silver into the hands of those who do the work, to bring *it* into the king's treasuries."

10 So the king took his signet ring from his hand and gave it to Haman, the son of Hammedatha the Agagite, the enemy of the Jews.

11 And the king said to Haman, "The money and the people *are* given to you, to do with them as seems good to you."

12 Then the king's scribes were called on the thirteenth day of the first month, and *a decree* was written according to all that Haman commanded—to the king's satraps, to the governors who *were* over each province, to the officials of all people, to every province according to its script, and to every people in their language. In the name of King Ahasuerus it was written, and sealed with the king's signet ring.

13 And the letters were sent by couriers into all the king's provinces, to destroy, to kill, and to annihilate all the Jews, both young and old, little children and women, in one day, on the thirteenth *day* of the twelfth month, which *is* the month of Adar, and to plunder their possessions.[a]

14 A copy of the document was to be issued as law in every province, being published for all people, that they should be ready for that day.

15 The couriers went out, hastened by the king's command; and the decree was proclaimed in Shushan the citadel. So the king and Haman sat down to drink, but the city of Shushan was perplexed.

Esther Agrees to Help the Jews

4 When Mordecai learned all that had happened, he tore his clothes and put on sackcloth and ashes, and went out into the midst of the city. He cried out with a loud and bitter cry.

2 He went as far as the front of the king's gate, for no one *might* enter the king's gate clothed with sackcloth.

3 And in every province where the king's command and decree arrived, *there was* great mourning among the Jews, with fasting, weeping, and wailing; and many lay in sackcloth and ashes.

4 So Esther's maids and eunuchs came and told her, and the queen was deeply distressed. Then she sent garments to clothe Mordecai and take his sackcloth away from him, but he would not accept *them*.

5 Then Esther called Hathach, *one* of the king's eunuchs whom he had appointed to attend her, and she gave him a command concerning Mordecai, to learn what and why this *was*.

6 So Hathach went out to Mordecai in the city square that *was* in front of the king's gate.

7 And Mordecai told him all that had happened to him, and the sum of money that Haman had promised to pay into the king's treasuries to destroy the Jews.

8 He also gave him a copy of the written decree for their destruction, which was given at Shushan, that he might show it to Esther and explain it to her, and that he might command her to go in to the king to make supplication to him and plead before him for her people.

9 So Hathach returned and told Esther the words of Mordecai.

10 Then Esther spoke to Hathach, and gave him a command for Mordecai:

11 "All the king's servants and the people of the king's provinces know that any man or woman who goes into the inner court to the king, who has not been called, *he has* but one law: put *all* to death, except the one to whom the king holds out the golden scepter, that he may live. Yet I myself have not been called to go in to the king these thirty days."

12 So they told Mordecai Esther's words.

13 And Mordecai told *them* to answer Esther: "Do not think in your heart that you will escape in the king's palace any more than all the other Jews.

14 "For if you remain completely silent at this time, relief and deliverance will arise for the Jews from another place, but you and your father's house will perish. Yet who knows whether you have come to the kingdom for *such* a time as this?"

15 Then Esther told *them* to reply to Mordecai:

16 "Go, gather all the Jews who are present in Shushan, and fast for me; neither eat nor drink for three days, night or day. My maids and I will fast likewise. And so I will go to the king, which *is* against the law; and if I perish, I perish!"

17 So Mordecai went his way and did according to all that Esther commanded him.[a]

Esther's Banquet

5 Now it happened on the third day that Esther put on *her* royal *robes* and stood in the inner court of the king's palace, across from the king's house, while the king sat on his royal throne in the royal house, facing the entrance of the house.[a]

2 So it was, when the king saw Queen Esther standing in the court, *that* she found favor in his sight, and the king held out to Esther the golden scepter that *was* in his hand. Then Esther went near and touched the top of the scepter.

3 And the king said to her, "What do you wish, Queen Esther? What *is* your request? It shall be given to you—up to half the kingdom!"

4 So Esther answered, "If it pleases the king, let the king and Haman come today to the banquet that I have prepared for him."

5 Then the king said, "Bring Haman quickly, that he may do as Esther has said." So the king and Haman went to the banquet that Esther had prepared.

6 At the banquet of wine the king said to Esther, "What *is* your petition? It shall be granted you. What *is* your request, up to half the kingdom? It shall be done!"

7 Then Esther answered and said, "My petition and request *is this:*

8 "If I have found favor in the sight of the king, and if it pleases the king to grant my petition and fulfill my request, then let the king and Haman come to the banquet which I will prepare for them, and tomorrow I will do as the king has said."

Haman's Plot Against Mordecai

9 So Haman went out that day joyful and with a glad heart; but when Haman saw Mor-

3:13 [a]Septuagint adds the text of the letter here. **4:17** [a]Septuagint adds a prayer of Mordecai here. **5:1** [a]Septuagint adds many extra details in verses 1 and 2.

decai in the king's gate, and that he did not
stand or tremble before him, he was filled with
indignation against Mordecai.
10 Nevertheless Haman restrained himself
and went home, and he sent and called for his
friends and his wife Zeresh.
11 Then Haman told them of his great riches,
the multitude of his children, everything in
which the king had promoted him, and how
he had advanced him above the officials and
servants of the king.
12 Moreover Haman said, "Besides, Queen
Esther invited no one but me to come in with
the king to the banquet that she prepared; and
tomorrow I am again invited by her, along with
the king.
13 "Yet all this avails me nothing, so long as
I see Mordecai the Jew sitting at the king's gate."
14 Then his wife Zeresh and all his friends
said to him, "Let a gallows be made, fifty cubits
high, and in the morning suggest to the king
that Mordecai be hanged on it; then go merrily
with the king to the banquet." And the thing
pleased Haman; so he had the gallows made.

The King Honors Mordecai

6 That night the king could not sleep. So one
was commanded to bring the book of the
records of the chronicles; and they were read
before the king.
2 And it was found written that Mordecai had
told of Bigthana and Teresh, two of the king's
eunuchs, the doorkeepers who had sought to
lay hands on King Ahasuerus.
3 Then the king said, "What honor or dig-
nity has been bestowed on Mordecai for this?"
And the king's servants who attended him
said, "Nothing has been done for him."
4 So the king said, "Who *is* in the court?" Now
Haman had *just* entered the outer court of the
king's palace to suggest that the king hang Mor-
decai on the gallows that he had prepared for
him.
5 The king's servants said to him, "Haman is
there, standing in the court." And the king said,
"Let him come in."
6 So Haman came in, and the king asked him,
"What shall be done for the man whom the
king delights to honor?" Now Haman thought
in his heart, "Whom would the king delight to
honor more than me?"
7 And Haman answered the king, "*For* the
man whom the king delights to honor,
8 "let a royal robe be brought which the king
has worn, and a horse on which the king has
ridden, which has a royal crest placed on its
head.
9 "Then let this robe and horse be delivered
to the hand of one of the king's most noble
princes, that he may array the man whom the
king delights to honor. Then parade him on
horseback through the city square, and pro-
claim before him: 'Thus shall it be done to the
man whom the king delights to honor!' "
10 Then the king said to Haman, "Hurry, take
the robe and the horse, as you have suggested,
and do so for Mordecai the Jew who sits within
the king's gate! Leave nothing undone of all that
you have spoken."
11 So Haman took the robe and the horse, ar-
rayed Mordecai and led him on horseback
through the city square, and proclaimed before
him, "Thus shall it be done to the man whom
the king delights to honor!"
12 Afterward Mordecai went back to the king's
gate. But Haman hurried to his house, mourn-
ing and with his head covered.
13 When Haman told his wife Zeresh and all
his friends everything that had happened to
him, his wise men and his wife Zeresh said to
him, "If Mordecai, before whom you have be-
gun to fall, is of Jewish descent, you will not
prevail against him but will surely fall before
him."
14 While they *were* still talking with him, the
king's eunuchs came, and hastened to bring Ha-
man to the banquet which Esther had prepared.

Haman Hanged Instead of Mordecai

7 So the king and Haman went to dine with
Queen Esther.
2 And on the second day, at the banquet of
wine, the king again said to Esther, "What *is*
your petition, Queen Esther? It shall be granted
you. And what *is* your request, up to half the
kingdom? It shall be done!"
3 Then Queen Esther answered and said, "If
I have found favor in your sight, O king, and if
it pleases the king, let my life be given me at
my petition, and my people at my request.
4 "For we have been sold, my people and I,
to be destroyed, to be killed, and to be annihi-
lated. Had we been sold as male and female
slaves, I would have held my tongue, although
the enemy could never compensate for the king's
loss."
5 So King Ahasuerus answered and said to
Queen Esther, "Who is he, and where is he, who
would dare presume in his heart to do such a
thing?"
6 And Esther said, "The adversary and en-
emy *is* this wicked Haman!" So Haman was
terrified before the king and queen.
7 Then the king arose in his wrath from the
banquet of wine *and went* into the palace gar-
den; but Haman stood before Queen Esther,
pleading for his life, for he saw that evil was
determined against him by the king.
8 When the king returned from the palace
garden to the place of the banquet of wine, Ha-
man had fallen across the couch where Esther
was. Then the king said, "Will he also assault the
queen while I *am* in the house?" As the word
left the king's mouth, they covered Haman's
face.
9 Now Harbonah, one of the eunuchs, said
to the king, "Look! The gallows, fifty cubits
high, which Haman made for Mordecai, who
spoke good on the king's behalf, is standing at
the house of Haman." Then the king said,
"Hang him on it!"
10 So they hanged Haman on the gallows that
he had prepared for Mordecai. Then the king's
wrath subsided.

Esther Saves the Jews

8 On that day King Ahasuerus gave Queen
Esther the house of Haman, the enemy of
the Jews. And Mordecai came before the king,
for Esther had told how he *was related* to her.
2 So the king took off his signet ring, which
he had taken from Haman, and gave it to Mor-
decai; and Esther appointed Mordecai over the
house of Haman.
3 Now Esther spoke again to the king, fell
down at his feet, and implored him with tears
to counteract the evil of Haman the Agagite,
and the scheme which he had devised against
the Jews.
4 And the king held out the golden scepter

toward Esther. So Esther arose and stood be-
fore the king,
5 and said, "If it pleases the king, and if I have
found favor in his sight and the thing *seems*
right to the king and I am pleasing in his eyes,
let it be written to revoke the letters devised by
Haman, the son of Hammedatha the Agagite,
which he wrote to annihilate the Jews who *are*
in all the king's provinces.
6 "For how can I endure to see the evil that
will come to my people? Or how can I endure
to see the destruction of my countrymen?"
7 Then King Ahasuerus said to Queen Es-
ther and Mordecai the Jew, "Indeed, I have given
Esther the house of Haman, and they have
hanged him on the gallows because he *tried to*
lay his hand on the Jews.
8 "You yourselves write *a decree* concerning
the Jews, as you please, in the king's name,
and seal *it* with the king's signet ring; for what-
ever is written in the king's name and sealed
with the king's signet ring no one can revoke."
9 So the king's scribes were called at that time,
in the third month, which *is* the month of Sivan,
on the twenty-third *day;* and it was written,
according to all that Mordecai commanded, to
the Jews, the satraps, the governors, and the
princes of the provinces from India to Ethiopia,
one hundred and twenty-seven provinces *in
all,* to every province in its own script, to every
people in their own language, and to the Jews
in their own script and language.
10 And he wrote in the name of King Ahasue-
rus, sealed *it* with the king's signet ring, and
sent letters by couriers on horseback, riding on
royal horses bred from swift steeds.[a]
11 By these letters the king permitted the
Jews who *were* in every city to gather together
and protect their lives—to destroy, kill, and an-
nihilate all the forces of any people or province
that would assault them, *both* little children
and women, and to plunder their possessions,
12 on one day in all the provinces of King
Ahasuerus, on the thirteenth *day* of the twelfth
month, which *is* the month of Adar.[a]
13 A copy of the document was to be issued
as a decree in every province and published for
all people, so that the Jews would be ready on
that day to avenge themselves on their enemies.
14 The couriers who rode on royal horses
went out, hastened and pressed on by the king's
command. And the decree was issued in Shu-
shan the citadel.
15 So Mordecai went out from the presence
of the king in royal apparel of blue and white,
with a great crown of gold and a garment of
fine linen and purple; and the city of Shushan
rejoiced and was glad.
16 The Jews had light and gladness, joy and
honor.
17 And in every province and city, wherever
the king's command and decree came, the Jews
had joy and gladness, a feast and a holiday.
Then many of the people of the land became
Jews, because fear of the Jews fell upon them.

The Jews Destroy Their Tormentors

9 Now in the twelfth month, that *is,* the
month of Adar, on the thirteenth day, *the
time* came for the king's command and his
decree to be executed. On the day that the ene-
mies of the Jews had hoped to overpower them,
the opposite occurred, in that the Jews them-
selves overpowered those who hated them.
2 The Jews gathered together in their cities
throughout all the provinces of King Ahasue-
rus to lay hands on those who sought their
harm. And no one could withstand them, be-
cause fear of them fell upon all people.
3 And all the officials of the provinces, the
satraps, the governors, and all those doing the
king's work, helped the Jews, because the fear
of Mordecai fell upon them.
4 For Mordecai *was* great in the king's pal-
ace, and his fame spread throughout all the
provinces; for this man Mordecai became in-
creasingly prominent.
5 Thus the Jews defeated all their enemies
with the stroke of the sword, with slaughter and
destruction, and did what they pleased with those
who hated them.
6 And in Shushan the citadel the Jews killed
and destroyed five hundred men.
7 Also Parshandatha, Dalphon, Aspatha,
8 Poratha, Adalia, Aridatha,
9 Parmashta, Arisai, Aridai, and Vajezatha—
10 the ten sons of Haman the son of Hamme-
datha, the enemy of the Jews—they killed; but
they did not lay a hand on the plunder.
11 On that day the number of those who were
killed in Shushan the citadel was brought to
the king.
12 And the king said to Queen Esther, "The
Jews have killed and destroyed five hundred
men in Shushan the citadel, and the ten sons
of Haman. What have they done in the rest of
the king's provinces? Now what *is* your peti-
tion? It shall be granted to you. Or what *is* your
further request? It shall be done."
13 Then Esther said, "If it pleases the king, let
it be granted to the Jews who *are* in Shushan to
do again tomorrow according to today's de-
cree, and let Haman's ten sons be hanged on
the gallows."
14 So the king commanded this to be done;
the decree was issued in Shushan, and they
hanged Haman's ten sons.
15 And the Jews who *were* in Shushan gath-
ered together again on the fourteenth day of
the month of Adar and killed three hundred
men at Shushan; but they did not lay a hand
on the plunder.
16 The remainder of the Jews in the king's
provinces gathered together and protected
their lives, had rest from their enemies, and
killed seventy-five thousand of their enemies;
but they did not lay a hand on the plunder.
17 *This was* on the thirteenth day of the month
of Adar. And on the fourteenth of *the month*[a]
they rested and made it a day of feasting and
gladness.

The Feast of Purim

18 But the Jews who *were* at Shushan assem-
bled together on the thirteenth *day,* as well as
on the fourteenth; and on the fifteenth of *the
month*[a] they rested, and made it a day of feast-
ing and gladness.
19 Therefore the Jews of the villages who dwelt
in the unwalled towns celebrated the four-
teenth day of the month of Adar *with* gladness
and feasting, as a holiday, and for sending pres-
ents to one another.
20 And Mordecai wrote these things and sent

8:10 [a]Literally *sons of the swift horses* **8:12** [a]Septuagint adds the text of the letter here. **9:17** [a]Literally *it*
9:18 [a]Literally *it*

letters to all the Jews, near and far, who *were*
in all the provinces of King Ahasuerus,
21 to establish among them that they should
celebrate yearly the fourteenth and fifteenth
days of the month of Adar,
22 as the days on which the Jews had rest
from their enemies, as the month which was
turned from sorrow to joy for them, and from
mourning to a holiday; that they should make
them days of feasting and joy, of sending pres-
ents to one another and gifts to the poor.
23 So the Jews accepted the custom which they
had begun, as Mordecai had written to them,
24 because Haman, the son of Hammedatha
the Agagite, the enemy of all the Jews, had
plotted against the Jews to annihilate them, and
had cast Pur (that *is*, the lot), to consume them
and destroy them;
25 but when *Esther*[a] came before the king,
he commanded by letter that this[b] wicked plot
which *Haman* had devised against the Jews
should return on his own head, and that he
and his sons should be hanged on the gallows.
26 So they called these days Purim, after the
name Pur. Therefore, because of all the words
of this letter, what they had seen concerning
this matter, and what had happened to them,
27 the Jews established and imposed it upon
themselves and their descendants and all who
would join them, that without fail they should
celebrate these two days every year, according
to the written *instructions* and according to
the *prescribed* time,
28 *that* these days *should be* remembered
and kept throughout every generation, every
family, every province, and every city, that
these days of Purim should not fail *to be ob-
served* among the Jews, and *that* the memory
of them should not perish among their descen-
dants.
29 Then Queen Esther, the daughter of Abi-
hail, with Mordecai the Jew, wrote with full au-
thority to confirm this second letter about
Purim.
30 And *Mordecai* sent letters to all the Jews,
to the one hundred and twenty-seven prov-
inces of the kingdom of Ahasuerus, *with* words
of peace and truth,
31 to confirm these days of Purim at their *ap-
pointed* time, as Mordecai the Jew and Queen
Esther had prescribed for them, and as they
had decreed for themselves and their descen-
dants concerning matters of their fasting and
lamenting.
32 So the decree of Esther confirmed these
matters of Purim, and it was written in the book.

Mordecai's Advancement

10 And King Ahasuerus imposed tribute on
the land and *on* the islands of the sea.
2 Now all the acts of his power and his might,
and the account of the greatness of Mordecai,
to which the king advanced him, *are* they not
written in the book of the chronicles of the
kings of Media and Persia?
3 For Mordecai the Jew *was* second to King
Ahasuerus, and was great among the Jews and
well received by the multitude of his brethren,
seeking the good of his people and speaking
peace to all his countrymen.[a]

9:25 [a]Literally *she* or *it* [b]Literally *his* **10:3** [a]Literally *seed.* Septuagint and Vulgate add a dream of Mordecai here; Vulgate adds six more chapters.

POETICAL AND WISDOM BOOKS

Job • The Psalms • Proverbs • Ecclesiastes Song of Solomon • Lamentations

In the Hebrew canon, these books are included in the "Writings." The books of poetry include the Psalms, Song of Solomon, and Lamentations. The wisdom books are Job, Proverbs, and Ecclesiastes. This does not mean all poetry in the Bible is found in Psalms and Song of Solomon, nor that all wisdom is found in only three books. Poetry abounds in the Torah and the Prophets. Much of the wisdom literature is written in poetic form. On the other hand, wisdom is also found throughout the Bible.

THE PSALMS were the hymnbook and prayer book of the second temple, and they continue to be used in the same way by the Jewish community today. Traditionally, the Psalms were ascribed to David, but a reading of the subheads shows there are several collections of Psalms, including many by David, but also collections credited to the sons of Korah, to Asaph, to Solomon, even to Moses. There are also many kinds of Psalms, just as there are many types of hymns in a modern hymnal. There are songs of praise and thanksgiving, songs of ascent, which were sung going up to the temple, royal psalms, prayers, laments, and so on. The Psalms are one of the favorite books for Christians and many of the biblical passages that are most meaningful come from the Psalms.

SONG OF SOLOMON is a collection of love poems, which are beautiful expressions of human love at its best. They remind us that God is present in all of life.

LAMENTATIONS is a collection of poems of deep bitterness and grief over the destruction of Jerusalem and the temple by the Babylonians in 586 B.C. It is traditionally attributed to Jeremiah and is printed immediately after his book in most Bibles.

Wisdom literature also takes several different forms. Sometimes it is short sayings on how to cope with life. The theme is usually how virtue can triumph over wrong. Sometimes wisdom takes the form of riddles. Or wisdom can be reflections on the meaning of life or on the life of faith (what we might call philosophy).

The heart of wisdom literature is a theology of creation and life. God has made the world and everything in it; and He is reflected in all of life. Because of this, we are called to live joyfully as well as responsibly. A great deal of wisdom literature deals with how to live the good life, that is, the life God approves.

PROVERBS is a collection of sayings about how to live the good life. It also contains the great passage on the personification of wisdom as God's handmaid, delighting in the works of creation (8:27 and ch. 9).

ECCLESIASTES reads almost like a diary of a spiritual journey. The author deals with ultimate questions of life and death, while talking about the routines of daily life. He reflects on what his life has meant from youth to old age, and how God has played a part in that life.

JOB begins with the undeserved suffering of the patriarch Job and reflects on the meaning of suffering and God's relationship to one who suffers unjustly. ■

The Book of
JOB

Job and His Family in Uz

1 There was a man in the land of Uz, whose
name *was* Job; and that man was blameless
and upright, and one who feared God and
shunned evil.
2 And seven sons and three daughters were
born to him.
3 Also, his possessions were seven thousand
sheep, three thousand camels, five hundred
yoke of oxen, five hundred female donkeys,
and a very large household, so that this man
was the greatest of all the people of the East.
4 And his sons would go and feast *in their*
houses, each on his *appointed* day, and would
send and invite their three sisters to eat and drink
with them.
5 So it was, when the days of feasting had
run their course, that Job would send and sanc-
tify them, and he would rise early in the morn-
ing and offer burnt offerings *according to* the
number of them all. For Job said, "It may be
that my sons have sinned and cursed[a] God in
their hearts." Thus Job did regularly.

Satan Attacks Job's Character

6 Now there was a day when the sons of God
came to present themselves before the LORD,
and Satan[a] also came among them.
7 And the LORD said to Satan, "From where
do you come?" So Satan answered the LORD
and said, "From going to and fro on the earth,
and from walking back and forth on it."
8 Then the LORD said to Satan, "Have you
considered My servant Job, that *there is* none
like him on the earth, a blameless and upright
man, one who fears God and shuns evil?"
9 So Satan answered the LORD and said,
"Does Job fear God for nothing?
10 "Have You not made a hedge around him,
around his household, and around all that he
has on every side? You have blessed the work
of his hands, and his possessions have in-
creased in the land.
11 "But now, stretch out Your hand and touch
all that he has, and he will surely curse You to
Your face!"
12 And the LORD said to Satan, "Behold, all
that he has *is* in your power; only do not lay a
hand on his *person*." So Satan went out from
the presence of the LORD.

Job Loses His Property and Children

13 Now there was a day when his sons and
daughters *were* eating and drinking wine in
their oldest brother's house;
14 and a messenger came to Job and said,
"The oxen were plowing and the donkeys feed-
ing beside them,
15 "when the Sabeans[a] raided *them* and took
them away—indeed they have killed the ser-
vants with the edge of the sword; and I alone
have escaped to tell you!"
16 While he *was* still speaking, another also
came and said, "The fire of God fell from
heaven and burned up the sheep and the ser-
vants, and consumed them; and I alone have
escaped to tell you!"
17 While he *was* still speaking, another also
came and said, "The Chaldeans formed three
bands, raided the camels and took them away,
yes, and killed the servants with the edge of
the sword; and I alone have escaped to tell you!"
18 While he *was* still speaking, another also
came and said, "Your sons and daughters *were*
eating and drinking wine in their oldest brother's
house,
19 "and suddenly a great wind came from
across[a] the wilderness and struck the four cor-
ners of the house, and it fell on the young peo-
ple, and they are dead; and I alone have
escaped to tell you!"
20 Then Job arose, tore his robe, and shaved
his head; and he fell to the ground and wor-
shiped.
21 And he said:

"Naked I came from my mother's womb,
And naked shall I return there.
The LORD gave, and the LORD has taken
away;
Blessed be the name of the LORD."

22 In all this Job did not sin nor charge God
with wrong.

Satan Attacks Job's Health

2 Again there was a day when the sons of
God came to present themselves before the
LORD, and Satan came also among them to
present himself before the LORD.
2 And the LORD said to Satan, "From where
do you come?" So Satan answered the LORD
and said, "From going to and fro on the earth,
and from walking back and forth on it."
3 Then the LORD said to Satan, "Have you
considered My servant Job, that *there is* none
like him on the earth, a blameless and upright
man, one who fears God and shuns evil? And
still he holds fast to his integrity, although you
incited Me against him, to destroy him without
cause."
4 So Satan answered the LORD and said,
"Skin for skin! Yes, all that a man has he will
give for his life.
5 "But stretch out Your hand now, and touch
his bone and his flesh, and he will surely curse
You to Your face!"
6 And the LORD said to Satan, "Behold, he
is in your hand, but spare his life."
7 So Satan went out from the presence of
the LORD, and struck Job with painful boils
from the sole of his foot to the crown of his
head.
8 And he took for himself a potsherd with
which to scrape himself while he sat in the
midst of the ashes.
9 Then his wife said to him, "Do you still
hold fast to your integrity? Curse God and die!"
10 But he said to her, "You speak as one of the
foolish women speaks. Shall we indeed accept
good from God, and shall we not accept adver-
sity?" In all this Job did not sin with his lips.

Job's Three Friends

11 Now when Job's three friends heard of all
this adversity that had come upon him, each one

1:5 [a]Literally *blessed*, but used here in the evil sense, and so in verse 11 and 2:5, 9 **1:6** [a]Literally *the Adversary*, and so throughout this book **1:15** [a]Literally *Sheba* (compare 6:19) **1:19** [a]Septuagint omits *across*.

came from his own place—Eliphaz the Teman-
ite, Bildad the Shuhite, and Zophar the Naa-
mathite. For they had made an appointment
together to come and mourn with him, and to
comfort him.
12 And when they raised their eyes from afar,
and did not recognize him, they lifted their voices
and wept; and each one tore his robe and sprin-
kled dust on his head toward heaven.
13 So they sat down with him on the ground
seven days and seven nights, and no one spoke
a word to him, for they saw that *his* grief was
very great.

Job Deplores His Birth

3 After this Job opened his mouth and cursed the day of his *birth.*
2 And Job spoke, and said:

3 "May the day perish on which I was born,
And the night *in which* it was said,
'A male child is conceived.'
4 May that day be darkness;
May God above not seek it,
Nor the light shine upon it.
5 May darkness and the shadow of death claim it;
May a cloud settle on it;
May the blackness of the day terrify it.
6 *As for* that night, may darkness seize it;
May it not rejoice[a] among the days of the year,
May it not come into the number of the months.
7 Oh, may that night be barren!
May no joyful shout come into it!
8 May those curse it who curse the day,
Those who are ready to arouse Leviathan.
9 May the stars of its morning be dark;
May it look for light, but *have* none,
And not see the dawning of the day;
10 Because it did not shut up the doors of my *mother's* womb,
Nor hide sorrow from my eyes.

11 "Why did I not die at birth?
Why did I *not* perish when I came from the womb?
12 Why did the knees receive me?
Or why the breasts, that I should nurse?
13 For now I would have lain still and been quiet,
I would have been asleep;
Then I would have been at rest
14 With kings and counselors of the earth,
Who built ruins for themselves,
15 Or with princes who had gold,
Who filled their houses *with* silver;
16 Or *why* was I not hidden like a stillborn child,
Like infants who never saw light?
17 There the wicked cease *from* troubling,
And there the weary are at rest.
18 *There* the prisoners rest together;
They do not hear the voice of the oppressor.
19 The small and great are there,
And the servant *is* free from his master.

20 "Why is light given to him who is in misery,
And life to the bitter of soul,
21 Who long for death, but it does not *come,*
And search for it more than hidden treasures;
22 Who rejoice exceedingly,
And are glad when they can find the grave?
23 *Why is light given* to a man whose way is hidden,
And whom God has hedged in?
24 For my sighing comes before I eat,[a]
And my groanings pour out like water.
25 For the thing I greatly feared has come upon me,
And what I dreaded has happened to me.
26 I am not at ease, nor am I quiet;
I have no rest, for trouble comes."

Eliphaz: Job Has Sinned

4 Then Eliphaz the Temanite answered and said:

2 "*If* one attempts a word with you, will you become weary?
But who can withhold himself from speaking?
3 Surely you have instructed many,
And you have strengthened weak hands.
4 Your words have upheld him who was stumbling,
And you have strengthened the feeble knees;
5 But now it comes upon you, and you are weary;
It touches you, and you are troubled.
6 *Is* not your reverence your confidence?
And the integrity of your ways your hope?

7 "Remember now, who *ever* perished being innocent?
Or where were the upright *ever* cut off?
8 Even as I have seen,
Those who plow iniquity
And sow trouble reap the same.
9 By the blast of God they perish,
And by the breath of His anger they are consumed.
10 The roaring of the lion,
The voice of the fierce lion,
And the teeth of the young lions are broken.
11 The old lion perishes for lack of prey,
And the cubs of the lioness are scattered.

12 "Now a word was secretly brought to me,
And my ear received a whisper of it.
13 In disquieting thoughts from the visions of the night,
When deep sleep falls on men,
14 Fear came upon me, and trembling,
Which made all my bones shake.
15 Then a spirit passed before my face;
The hair on my body stood up.
16 It stood still,
But I could not discern its appearance.
A form *was* before my eyes;
There was silence;
Then I heard a voice *saying:*
17 'Can a mortal be more righteous than God?
Can a man be more pure than his Maker?
18 If He puts no trust in His servants,
If He charges His angels with error,

3:6 [a]Septuagint, Syriac, Targum, and Vulgate read *be joined.* **3:24** [a]Literally *my bread*

19 How much more those who dwell in
houses of clay,
Whose foundation is in the dust,
Who are crushed before a moth?
20 They are broken in pieces from morning
till evening;
They perish forever, with no one
regarding.
21 Does not their own excellence go away?
They die, even without wisdom.'

Eliphaz: Job Is Chastened by God

5 "Call out now;
Is there anyone who will answer you?
And to which of the holy ones will you
turn?
2 For wrath kills a foolish man,
And envy slays a simple one.
3 I have seen the foolish taking root,
But suddenly I cursed his dwelling place.
4 His sons are far from safety,
They are crushed in the gate,
And *there is* no deliverer.
5 Because the hungry eat up his harvest,
Taking it even from the thorns,[a]
And a snare snatches their substance.[b]
6 For affliction does not come from the
dust,
Nor does trouble spring from the ground;
7 Yet man is born to trouble,
As the sparks fly upward.

8 "But as for me, I would seek God,
And to God I would commit my cause—
9 Who does great things, and
unsearchable,
Marvelous things without number.
10 He gives rain on the earth,
And sends waters on the fields.
11 He sets on high those who are lowly,
And those who mourn are lifted to safety.
12 He frustrates the devices of the crafty,
So that their hands cannot carry out their
plans.
13 He catches the wise in their own
craftiness,
And the counsel of the cunning comes
quickly upon them.
14 They meet with darkness in the daytime,
And grope at noontime as in the night.
15 But He saves the needy from the sword,
From the mouth of the mighty,
And from their hand.
16 So the poor have hope,
And injustice shuts her mouth.

17 "Behold, happy *is* the man whom God
corrects;
Therefore do not despise the chastening
of the Almighty.
18 For He bruises, but He binds up;
He wounds, but His hands make whole.
19 He shall deliver you in six troubles,
Yes, in seven no evil shall touch you.
20 In famine He shall redeem you from
death,
And in war from the power of the sword.
21 You shall be hidden from the scourge of
the tongue,
And you shall not be afraid of destruction
when it comes.
22 You shall laugh at destruction and
famine,
And you shall not be afraid of the beasts
of the earth.
23 For you shall have a covenant with the
stones of the field,
And the beasts of the field shall be at
peace with you.
24 You shall know that your tent *is* in peace;
You shall visit your dwelling and find
nothing amiss.
25 You shall also know that your
descendants *shall be* many,
And your offspring like the grass of the
earth.
26 You shall come to the grave at a full age,
As a sheaf of grain ripens in its season.
27 Behold, this we have searched out;
It *is* true.
Hear it, and know for yourself."

Job: My Complaint Is Just

6 Then Job answered and said:
2 "Oh, that my grief were fully weighed,
And my calamity laid with it on the
scales!
3 For then it would be heavier than the
sand of the sea—
Therefore my words have been rash.
4 For the arrows of the Almighty *are* within
me;
My spirit drinks in their poison;
The terrors of God are arrayed against
me.
5 Does the wild donkey bray when it has
grass,
Or does the ox low over its fodder?
6 Can flavorless food be eaten without salt?
Or is there *any* taste in the white of an
egg?
7 My soul refuses to touch them;
They *are* as loathsome food to me.

8 "Oh, that I might have my request,
That God would grant *me* the thing that I
long for!
9 That it would please God to crush me,
That He would loose His hand and cut me
off!
10 Then I would still have comfort;
Though in anguish I would exult,
He will not spare;
For I have not concealed the words of the
Holy One.

11 "What strength do I have, that I should
hope?
And what *is* my end, that I should
prolong my life?
12 *Is* my strength the strength of stones?
Or is my flesh bronze?
13 *Is* my help not within me?
And is success driven from me?

14 "To him who is afflicted, kindness *should
be shown* by his friend,
Even though he forsakes the fear of the
Almighty.
15 My brothers have dealt deceitfully like a
brook,
Like the streams of the brooks that pass
away,
16 Which are dark because of the ice,
And into which the snow vanishes.

5:5 [a]Septuagint reads *They shall not be taken from evil men;* Vulgate reads *And the armed man shall take him by violence.* [b]Septuagint reads *The might shall draw them off;* Vulgate reads *And the thirsty shall drink up their riches.*

17 When it is warm, they cease to flow;
When it is hot, they vanish from their place.
18 The paths of their way turn aside,
They go nowhere and perish.
19 The caravans of Tema look,
The travelers of Sheba hope for them.
20 They are disappointed because they were confident;
They come there and are confused.
21 For now you are nothing,
You see terror and are afraid.
22 Did I ever say, 'Bring *something* to me'?
Or, 'Offer a bribe for me from your wealth'?
23 Or, 'Deliver me from the enemy's hand'?
Or, 'Redeem me from the hand of oppressors'?

24 "Teach me, and I will hold my tongue;
Cause me to understand wherein I have erred.
25 How forceful are right words!
But what does your arguing prove?
26 Do you intend to rebuke *my* words,
And the speeches of a desperate one, *which are* as wind?
27 Yes, you overwhelm the fatherless,
And you undermine your friend.
28 Now therefore, be pleased to look at me;
For I would never lie to your face.
29 Yield now, let there be no injustice!
Yes, concede, my righteousness still stands!
30 Is there injustice on my tongue?
Cannot my taste discern the unsavory?

Job: My Suffering Is Comfortless

7 "*Is there* not a time of hard service for man on earth?
Are not his days also like the days of a hired man?
2 Like a servant who earnestly desires the shade,
And like a hired man who eagerly looks for his wages,
3 So I have been allotted months of futility,
And wearisome nights have been appointed to me.
4 When I lie down, I say, 'When shall I arise,
And the night be ended?'
For I have had my fill of tossing till dawn.
5 My flesh is caked with worms and dust,
My skin is cracked and breaks out afresh.

6 "My days are swifter than a weaver's shuttle,
And are spent without hope.
7 Oh, remember that my life *is* a breath!
My eye will never again see good.
8 The eye of him who sees me will see me no *more;*
While your eyes *are* upon me, I shall no longer *be.*
9 *As* the cloud disappears and vanishes away,
So he who goes down to the grave does not come up.
10 He shall never return to his house,
Nor shall his place know him anymore.

11 "Therefore I will not restrain my mouth;
I will speak in the anguish of my spirit;
I will complain in the bitterness of my soul.
12 *Am* I a sea, or a sea serpent,
That You set a guard over me?
13 When I say, 'My bed will comfort me,
My couch will ease my complaint,'
14 Then You scare me with dreams
And terrify me with visions,
15 So that my soul chooses strangling
And death rather than my body.[a]
16 I loathe *my life;*
I would not live forever.
Let me alone,
For my days *are but* a breath.

17 "What *is* man, that You should exalt him,
That You should set Your heart on him,
18 That You should visit him every morning,
And test him every moment?
19 How long?
Will You not look away from me,
And let me alone till I swallow my saliva?
20 Have I sinned?
What have I done to You, O watcher of men?
Why have You set me as Your target,
So that I am a burden to myself?[a]
21 Why then do You not pardon my transgression,
And take away my iniquity?
For now I will lie down in the dust,
And You will seek me diligently,
But I *will* no longer *be.*"

Bildad: Job Should Repent

8 Then Bildad the Shuhite answered and said:

2 "How long will you speak these *things,*
And the words of your mouth *be like* a strong wind?
3 Does God subvert judgment?
Or does the Almighty pervert justice?
4 If your sons have sinned against Him,
He has cast them away for their transgression.
5 If you would earnestly seek God
And make your supplication to the Almighty,
6 If you *were* pure and upright,
Surely now He would awake for you,
And prosper your rightful dwelling place.
7 Though your beginning was small,
Yet your latter end would increase abundantly.

8 "For inquire, please, of the former age,
And consider the things discovered by their fathers;
9 For we *were born* yesterday, and know nothing,
Because our days on earth *are* a shadow.
10 Will they not teach you and tell you,
And utter words from their heart?

11 "Can the papyrus grow up without a marsh?
Can the reeds flourish without water?
12 While it *is* yet green *and* not cut down,
It withers before any *other* plant.

7:15 [a]Literally *my bones* **7:20** [a]Following Masoretic Text, Targum, and Vulgate; Septuagint and Jewish tradition read *to You.*

13 So *are* the paths of all who forget God;
And the hope of the hypocrite shall perish,
14 Whose confidence shall be cut off,
And whose trust *is* a spider's web.
15 He leans on his house, but it does not stand.
He holds it fast, but it does not endure.
16 He grows green in the sun,
And his branches spread out in his garden.
17 His roots wrap around the rock heap,
And look for a place in the stones.
18 If he is destroyed from his place,
Then *it* will deny him, *saying*, 'I have not seen you.'

19 "Behold, this is the joy of His way,
And out of the earth others will grow.
20 Behold, God will not cast away the blameless,
Nor will He uphold the evildoers.
21 He will yet fill your mouth with laughing,
And your lips with rejoicing.
22 Those who hate you will be clothed with shame,
And the dwelling place of the wicked will come to nothing."[a]

Job: There Is No Mediator

9 Then Job answered and said:
2 "Truly I know *it is* so,
But how can a man be righteous before God?
3 If one wished to contend with Him,
He could not answer Him one time out of a thousand.
4 *God is* wise in heart and mighty in strength.
Who has hardened *himself* against Him and prospered?
5 He removes the mountains, and they do not know
When He overturns them in His anger;
6 He shakes the earth out of its place,
And its pillars tremble;
7 He commands the sun, and it does not rise;
He seals off the stars;
8 He alone spreads out the heavens,
And treads on the waves of the sea;
9 He made the Bear, Orion, and the Pleiades,
And the chambers of the south;
10 He does great things past finding out,
Yes, wonders without number.
11 If He goes by me, I do not see *Him;*
If He moves past, I do not perceive Him;
12 If He takes away, who can hinder Him?
Who can say to Him, 'What are You doing?'
13 God will not withdraw His anger,
The allies of the proud[a] lie prostrate beneath Him.

14 "How then can I answer Him,
And choose my words *to reason* with Him?
15 For though I were righteous, I could not answer Him;
I would beg mercy of my Judge.
16 If I called and He answered me,
I would not believe that He was listening to my voice.
17 For He crushes me with a tempest,
And multiplies my wounds without cause.
18 He will not allow me to catch my breath,
But fills me with bitterness.
19 If *it is a matter* of strength, indeed *He is* strong;
And if of justice, who will appoint my day *in court?*
20 Though I were righteous, my own mouth would condemn me;
Though I *were* blameless, it would prove me perverse.

21 "I am blameless, yet I do not know myself;
I despise my life.
22 It *is* all one *thing;*
Therefore I say, 'He destroys the blameless and the wicked.'
23 If the scourge slays suddenly,
He laughs at the plight of the innocent.
24 The earth is given into the hand of the wicked.
He covers the faces of its judges.
If it is not *He*, who else could it be?

25 "Now my days are swifter than a runner;
They flee away, they see no good.
26 They pass by like swift ships,
Like an eagle swooping on its prey.
27 If I say, 'I will forget my complaint,
I will put off my sad face and wear a smile,'
28 I am afraid of all my sufferings;
I know that You will not hold me innocent.
29 *If* I am condemned,
Why then do I labor in vain?
30 If I wash myself with snow water,
And cleanse my hands with soap,
31 Yet You will plunge me into the pit,
And my own clothes will abhor me.

32 "For *He is* not a man, as I *am*,
That I may answer Him,
And that we should go to court together.
33 Nor is there any mediator between us,
Who may lay his hand on us both.
34 Let Him take His rod away from me,
And do not let dread of Him terrify me.
35 *Then* I would speak and not fear Him,
But it is not so with me.

Job: I Would Plead with God

10 "My soul loathes my life;
I will give free course to my complaint,
I will speak in the bitterness of my soul.
2 I will say to God, 'Do not condemn me;
Show me why You contend with me.
3 *Does it* seem good to You that You should oppress,
That You should despise the work of Your hands,
And smile on the counsel of the wicked?
4 Do You have eyes of flesh?
Or do You see as man sees?
5 *Are* Your days like the days of a mortal man?
Are Your years like the days of a mighty man,

8:22 [a]Literally *will not be* **9:13** [a]Hebrew *rahab*

6 That You should seek for my iniquity
And search out my sin,
7 Although You know that I am not wicked,
And *there is* no one who can deliver from
Your hand?

8 'Your hands have made me and fashioned
me,
An intricate unity;
Yet You would destroy me.
9 Remember, I pray, that You have made
me like clay.
And will You turn me into dust again?
10 Did You not pour me out like milk,
And curdle me like cheese,
11 Clothe me with skin and flesh,
And knit me together with bones and
sinews?
12 You have granted me life and favor,
And Your care has preserved my spirit.

13 'And these *things* You have hidden in
Your heart;
I know that this *was* with You:
14 If I sin, then You mark me,
And will not acquit me of my iniquity.
15 If I am wicked, woe to me;
Even *if* I am righteous, I cannot lift up my
head.
I am full of disgrace;
See my misery!
16 If *my head* is exalted,
You hunt me like a fierce lion,
And again You show Yourself awesome
against me.
17 You renew Your witnesses against me,
And increase Your indignation toward
me;
Changes and war are *ever* with me.

18 'Why then have You brought me out of the
womb?
Oh, that I had perished and no eye had
seen me!
19 I would have been as though I had not
been.
I would have been carried from the womb
to the grave.
20 Are not my days few?
Cease! Leave me alone, that I may take a
little comfort,
21 Before I go *to the place from which* I
shall not return,
To the land of darkness and the shadow
of death,
22 A land as dark as darkness *itself*,
As the shadow of death, without any
order,
Where even the light *is* like darkness.' "

Zophar Urges Job to Repent

11 Then Zophar the Naamathite answered
and said:

2 "Should not the multitude of words be
answered?
And should a man full of talk be
vindicated?
3 Should your empty talk make men hold
their peace?
And when you mock, should no one
rebuke you?
4 For you have said,
'My doctrine *is* pure,
And I am clean in your eyes.'
5 But oh, that God would speak,
And open His lips against you,
6 That He would show you the secrets of
wisdom!
For *they would* double *your* prudence.
Know therefore that God exacts from you
Less than your iniquity *deserves*.

7 "Can you search out the deep things of
God?
Can you find out the limits of the
Almighty?
8 *They are* higher than heaven—what can
you do?
Deeper than Sheol—what can you know?
9 Their measure *is* longer than the earth
And broader than the sea.

10 "If He passes by, imprisons, and gathers *to
judgment*,
Then who can hinder Him?
11 For He knows deceitful men;
He sees wickedness also.
Will He not then consider *it?*
12 For an empty-headed man will be wise,
When a wild donkey's colt is born a man.

13 "If you would prepare your heart,
And stretch out your hands toward Him;
14 If iniquity *were* in your hand, *and you* put
it far away,
And would not let wickedness dwell in
your tents;
15 Then surely you could lift up your face
without spot;
Yes, you could be steadfast, and not fear;
16 Because you would forget *your* misery,
And remember *it* as waters *that have*
passed away,
17 And *your* life would be brighter than
noonday.
Though you were dark, you would be like
the morning.
18 And you would be secure, because there
is hope;
Yes, you would dig *around you, and* take
your rest in safety.
19 You would also lie down, and no one
would make *you* afraid;
Yes, many would court your favor.
20 But the eyes of the wicked will fail,
And they shall not escape,
And their hope—loss of life!"

Job Answers His Critics

12 Then Job answered and said:

2 "No doubt you *are* the people,
And wisdom will die with you!
3 But I have understanding as well as you;
I *am* not inferior to you.
Indeed, who does not *know* such things
as these?

4 "I am one mocked by his friends,
Who called on God, and He answered
him,
The just and blameless *who is* ridiculed.
5 A lamp[a] is despised in the thought of one
who is at ease;
It is made ready for those whose feet slip.
6 The tents of robbers prosper,
And those who provoke God are secure—
In what God provides by His hand.

12:5 [a]Or *disaster*

7 "But now ask the beasts, and they will teach you;
And the birds of the air, and they will tell you;
8 Or speak to the earth, and it will teach you;
And the fish of the sea will explain to you.
9 Who among all these does not know
That the hand of the LORD has done this,
10 In whose hand *is* the life of every living thing,
And the breath of all mankind?
11 Does not the ear test words
And the mouth taste its food?
12 Wisdom *is* with aged men,
And with length of days, understanding.

13 "With Him *are* wisdom and strength,
He has counsel and understanding.
14 If He breaks *a thing* down, it cannot be rebuilt;
If He imprisons a man, there can be no release.
15 If He withholds the waters, they dry up;
If He sends them out, they overwhelm the earth.
16 With Him *are* strength and prudence.
The deceived and the deceiver *are* His.
17 He leads counselors away plundered,
And makes fools of the judges.
18 He loosens the bonds of kings,
And binds their waist with a belt.
19 He leads princes[a] away plundered,
And overthrows the mighty.
20 He deprives the trusted ones of speech,
And takes away the discernment of the elders.
21 He pours contempt on princes,
And disarms the mighty.
22 He uncovers deep things out of darkness,
And brings the shadow of death to light.
23 He makes nations great, and destroys them;
He enlarges nations, and guides them.
24 He takes away the understanding[a] of the chiefs of the people of the earth,
And makes them wander in a pathless wilderness.
25 They grope in the dark without light,
And He makes them stagger like a drunken *man*.

13 "Behold, my eye has seen all *this*,
My ear has heard and understood it.
2 What you know, I also know;
I *am* not inferior to you.
3 But I would speak to the Almighty,
And I desire to reason with God.
4 But you forgers of lies,
You *are* all worthless physicians.
5 Oh, that you would be silent,
And it would be your wisdom!
6 Now hear my reasoning,
And heed the pleadings of my lips.
7 Will you speak wickedly for God,
And talk deceitfully for Him?
8 Will you show partiality for Him?
Will you contend for God?
9 Will it be well when He searches you out?
Or can you mock Him as one mocks a man?
10 He will surely rebuke you
If you secretly show partiality.
11 Will not His excellence make you afraid,
And the dread of Him fall upon you?
12 Your platitudes *are* proverbs of ashes,
Your defenses are defenses of clay.

13 "Hold your peace with me, and let me speak,
Then let come on me what *may!*
14 Why do I take my flesh in my teeth,
And put my life in my hands?
15 Though He slay me, yet will I trust Him.
Even so, I will defend my own ways before Him.
16 He also *shall* be my salvation,
For a hypocrite could not come before Him.
17 Listen carefully to my speech,
And to my declaration with your ears.
18 See now, I have prepared *my* case,
I know that I shall be vindicated.
19 Who *is* he *who* will contend with me?
If now I hold my tongue, I perish.

Job's Despondent Prayer

20 "Only two *things* do not do to me,
Then I will not hide myself from You:
21 Withdraw Your hand far from me,
And let not the dread of You make me afraid.
22 Then call, and I will answer;
Or let me speak, then You respond to me.
23 How many *are* my iniquities and sins?
Make me know my transgression and my sin.
24 Why do You hide Your face,
And regard me as Your enemy?
25 Will You frighten a leaf driven to and fro?
And will You pursue dry stubble?
26 For You write bitter things against me,
And make me inherit the iniquities of my youth.
27 You put my feet in the stocks,
And watch closely all my paths.
You set a limit[a] for the soles of my feet.

28 "*Man*[a] decays like a rotten thing,
Like a garment that is moth-eaten.

14 "Man *who is* born of woman
Is of few days and full of trouble.
2 He comes forth like a flower and fades away;
He flees like a shadow and does not continue.
3 And do You open Your eyes on such a one,
And bring me[a] to judgment with Yourself?
4 Who can bring a clean *thing* out of an unclean?
No one!
5 Since his days *are* determined,
The number of his months *is* with You;
You have appointed his limits, so that he cannot pass.
6 Look away from him that he may rest,
Till like a hired man he finishes his day.

7 "For there is hope for a tree,
If it is cut down, that it will sprout again,
And that its tender shoots will not cease.

12:19 [a]Literally *priests*, but not in a technical sense **12:24** [a]Literally *heart* **13:27** [a]Literally *inscribe a print*
13:28 [a]Literally *He* **14:3** [a]Septuagint, Syriac, and Vulgate read *him*.

8 Though its root may grow old in the earth,
And its stump may die in the ground,
9 *Yet* at the scent of water it will bud
And bring forth branches like a plant.
10 But man dies and is laid away;
Indeed he breathes his last
And where *is* he?
11 *As* water disappears from the sea,
And a river becomes parched and dries up,
12 So man lies down and does not rise.
Till the heavens *are* no more,
They will not awake
Nor be roused from their sleep.

13 "Oh, that You would hide me in the grave,
That You would conceal me until Your wrath is past,
That You would appoint me a set time, and remember me!
14 If a man dies, shall he live *again*?
All the days of my hard service I will wait,
Till my change comes.
15 You shall call, and I will answer You;
You shall desire the work of Your hands.
16 For now You number my steps,
But do not watch over my sin.
17 My transgression *is* sealed up in a bag,
And You cover[a] my iniquity.

18 "But *as* a mountain falls *and* crumbles away,
And *as* a rock is moved from its place;
19 *As* water wears away stones,
And as torrents wash away the soil of the earth;
So You destroy the hope of man.
20 You prevail forever against him, and he passes on;
You change his countenance and send him away.
21 His sons come to honor, and he does not know *it*;
They are brought low, and he does not perceive *it*.
22 But his flesh will be in pain over it,
And his soul will mourn over it."

Eliphaz Accuses Job of Folly

15 Then Eliphaz the Temanite answered and said:

2 "Should a wise man answer with empty knowledge,
And fill himself with the east wind?
3 Should he reason with unprofitable talk,
Or by speeches with which he can do no good?
4 Yes, you cast off fear,
And restrain prayer before God.
5 For your iniquity teaches your mouth,
And you choose the tongue of the crafty.
6 Your own mouth condemns you, and not I;
Yes, your own lips testify against you.

7 "*Are* you the first man *who* was born?
Or were you made before the hills?
8 Have you heard the counsel of God?
Do you limit wisdom to yourself?
9 What do you know that we do not know?
What do you understand that *is* not in us?
10 Both the gray-haired and the aged *are* among us,
Much older than your father.
11 *Are* the consolations of God too small for you,
And the word *spoken* gently[a] with you?
12 Why does your heart carry you away,
And what do your eyes wink at,
13 That you turn your spirit against God,
And let *such* words go out of your mouth?

14 "What *is* man, that he could be pure?
And *he who is* born of a woman, that he could be righteous?
15 If *God* puts no trust in His saints,
And the heavens are not pure in His sight,
16 How much less man, *who is* abominable and filthy,
Who drinks iniquity like water!

17 "I will tell you, hear me;
What I have seen I will declare,
18 What wise men have told,
Not hiding *anything received* from their fathers,
19 To whom alone the land was given,
And no alien passed among them:
20 The wicked man writhes with pain all *his* days,
And the number of years is hidden from the oppressor.
21 Dreadful sounds *are* in his ears;
In prosperity the destroyer comes upon him.
22 He does not believe that he will return from darkness,
For a sword is waiting for him.
23 He wanders about for bread, *saying*, 'Where *is it?*'
He knows that a day of darkness is ready at his hand.
24 Trouble and anguish make him afraid;
They overpower him, like a king ready for battle.
25 For he stretches out his hand against God,
And acts defiantly against the Almighty,
26 Running stubbornly against Him
With his strong, embossed shield.

27 "Though he has covered his face with his fatness,
And made *his* waist heavy with fat,
28 He dwells in desolate cities,
In houses which no one inhabits,
Which are destined to become ruins.
29 He will not be rich,
Nor will his wealth continue,
Nor will his possessions overspread the earth.
30 He will not depart from darkness;
The flame will dry out his branches,
And by the breath of His mouth he will go away.
31 Let him not trust in futile *things*, deceiving himself,
For futility will be his reward.
32 It will be accomplished before his time,
And his branch will not be green.
33 He will shake off his unripe grape like a vine,
And cast off his blossom like an olive tree.

14:17 [a]Literally *plaster over* 15:11 [a]Septuagint reads *a secret thing.*

34 For the company of hypocrites *will be* barren,
And fire will consume the tents of bribery.
35 They conceive trouble and bring forth futility;
Their womb prepares deceit."

Job Reproaches His Pitiless Friends

16 Then Job answered and said:
2 "I have heard many such things;
Miserable comforters *are* you all!
3 Shall words of wind have an end?
Or what provokes you that you answer?
4 I also could speak as you *do,*
If your soul were in my soul's place.
I could heap up words against you,
And shake my head at you;
5 *But* I would strengthen you with my mouth,
And the comfort of my lips would relieve *your grief.*

6 "Though I speak, my grief is not relieved;
And *if* I remain silent, how am I eased?
7 But now He has worn me out;
You have made desolate all my company.
8 You have shriveled me up,
And it is a witness *against me;*
My leanness rises up against me
And bears witness to my face.
9 He tears *me* in His wrath, and hates me;
He gnashes at me with His teeth;
My adversary sharpens His gaze on me.
10 They gape at me with their mouth,
They strike me reproachfully on the cheek,
They gather together against me.
11 God has delivered me to the ungodly,
And turned me over to the hands of the wicked.
12 I was at ease, but He has shattered me;
He also has taken *me* by my neck, and shaken me to pieces;
He has set me up for His target,
13 His archers surround me.
He pierces my heart[a] and does not pity;
He pours out my gall on the ground.
14 He breaks me with wound upon wound;
He runs at me like a warrior.[a]

15 "I have sewn sackcloth over my skin,
And laid my head[a] in the dust.
16 My face is flushed from weeping,
And on my eyelids *is* the shadow of death;
17 Although no violence *is* in my hands,
And my prayer *is* pure.

18 "O earth, do not cover my blood,
And let my cry have no *resting* place!
19 Surely even now my witness *is* in heaven,
And my evidence *is* on high.
20 My friends scorn me;
My eyes pour out *tears* to God.
21 Oh, that one might plead for a man with God,
As a man *pleads* for his neighbor!
22 For when a few years are finished,
I shall go the way of no return.

Job Prays for Relief

17 "My spirit is broken,
My days are extinguished,
The grave *is ready* for me.
2 *Are* not mockers with me?
And does not my eye dwell on their provocation?

3 "Now put down a pledge for me with Yourself.
Who *is* he *who* will shake hands with me?
4 For You have hidden their heart from understanding;
Therefore You will not exalt *them.*
5 He who speaks flattery to *his* friends,
Even the eyes of his children will fail.

6 "But He has made me a byword of the people,
And I have become one in whose face men spit.
7 My eye has also grown dim because of sorrow,
And all my members *are* like shadows.
8 Upright *men* are astonished at this,
And the innocent stirs himself up against the hypocrite.
9 Yet the righteous will hold to his way,
And he who has clean hands will be stronger and stronger.

10 "But please, come back again, all of you,[a]
For I shall not find *one* wise *man* among you.
11 My days are past,
My purposes are broken off,
Even the thoughts of my heart.
12 They change the night into day;
'The light *is* near,' *they say,* in the face of darkness.
13 If I wait *for* the grave *as* my house,
If I make my bed in the darkness,
14 If I say to corruption, 'You *are* my father,'
And to the worm, 'You *are* my mother and my sister,'
15 Where then *is* my hope?
As for my hope, who can see it?
16 *Will* they go down to the gates of Sheol?
Shall *we have* rest together in the dust?"

Bildad: The Wicked Are Punished

18 Then Bildad the Shuhite answered and said:
2 "How long *till* you put an end to words?
Gain understanding, and afterward we will speak.
3 Why are we counted as beasts,
And regarded as stupid in your sight?
4 You who tear yourself in anger,
Shall the earth be forsaken for you?
Or shall the rock be removed from its place?

5 "The light of the wicked indeed goes out,
And the flame of his fire does not shine.
6 The light is dark in his tent,
And his lamp beside him is put out.
7 The steps of his strength are shortened,
And his own counsel casts him down.
8 For he is cast into a net by his own feet,
And he walks into a snare.
9 The net takes *him* by the heel,
And a snare lays hold of him.

16:13 [a]Literally *kidneys* **16:14** [a]Vulgate reads *giant.* **16:15** [a]Literally *horn* **17:10** [a]Following some Hebrew manuscripts, Septuagint, Syriac, and Vulgate; Masoretic Text and Targum read *all of them.*

10 A noose *is* hidden for him on the ground,
And a trap for him in the road.
11 Terrors frighten him on every side,
And drive him to his feet.
12 His strength is starved,
And destruction *is* ready at his side.
13 It devours patches of his skin;
The firstborn of death devours his limbs.
14 He is uprooted from the shelter of his tent,
And they parade him before the king of terrors.
15 They dwell in his tent *who are* none of his;
Brimstone is scattered on his dwelling.
16 His roots are dried out below,
And his branch withers above.
17 The memory of him perishes from the earth,
And he has no name among the renowned.[a]
18 He is driven from light into darkness,
And chased out of the world.
19 He has neither son nor posterity among his people,
Nor any remaining in his dwellings.
20 Those in the west are astonished at his day,
As those in the east are frightened.
21 Surely such *are* the dwellings of the wicked,
And this *is* the place *of him who* does not know God."

Job Trusts in His Redeemer

19 Then Job answered and said:

2 "How long will you torment my soul,
And break me in pieces with words?
3 These ten times you have reproached me;
You are not ashamed *that* you have wronged me.[a]
4 And if indeed I have erred,
My error remains with me.
5 If indeed you exalt *yourselves* against me,
And plead my disgrace against me,
6 Know then that God has wronged me,
And has surrounded me with His net.

7 "If I cry out concerning wrong, I am not heard.
If I cry aloud, *there is* no justice.
8 He has fenced up my way, so that I cannot pass;
And He has set darkness in my paths.
9 He has stripped me of my glory,
And taken the crown *from* my head.
10 He breaks me down on every side,
And I am gone;
My hope He has uprooted like a tree.
11 He has also kindled His wrath against me,
And He counts me as *one of* His enemies.
12 His troops come together
And build up their road against me;
They encamp all around my tent.

13 "He has removed my brothers far from me,
And my acquaintances are completely estranged from me.
14 My relatives have failed,
And my close friends have forgotten me.
15 Those who dwell in my house, and my maidservants,
Count me as a stranger;
I am an alien in their sight.
16 I call my servant, but he gives no answer;
I beg him with my mouth.
17 My breath is offensive to my wife,
And I am repulsive to the children of my own body.
18 Even young children despise me;
I arise, and they speak against me.
19 All my close friends abhor me,
And those whom I love have turned against me.
20 My bone clings to my skin and to my flesh,
And I have escaped by the skin of my teeth.

21 "Have pity on me, have pity on me, O you my friends,
For the hand of God has struck me!
22 Why do you persecute me as God *does,*
And are not satisfied with my flesh?

23 "Oh, that my words were written!
Oh, that they were inscribed in a book!
24 That they were engraved on a rock
With an iron pen and lead, forever!
25 For I know *that* my Redeemer lives,
And He shall stand at last on the earth;
26 And after my skin is destroyed, this *I know,*
That in my flesh I shall see God,
27 Whom I shall see for myself,
And my eyes shall behold, and not another.
How my heart yearns within me!
28 If you should say, 'How shall we persecute him?'—
Since the root of the matter is found in me,
29 Be afraid of the sword for yourselves;
For wrath *brings* the punishment of the sword,
That you may know *there is* a judgment."

Zophar's Sermon on the Wicked Man

20 Then Zophar the Naamathite answered and said:

2 "Therefore my anxious thoughts make me answer,
Because of the turmoil within me.
3 I have heard the rebuke that reproaches me,
And the spirit of my understanding causes me to answer.

4 "Do you *not* know this of old,
Since man was placed on earth,
5 That the triumphing of the wicked is short,
And the joy of the hypocrite is *but* for a moment?
6 Though his haughtiness mounts up to the heavens,
And his head reaches to the clouds,
7 *Yet* he will perish forever like his own refuse;
Those who have seen him will say, 'Where is he?'
8 He will fly away like a dream, and not be found;

18:17 [a]Literally *before the outside,* meaning distinguished, famous 19:3 [a]A Jewish tradition reads *make yourselves strange to me.*

Yes, he will be chased away like a vision
of the night.
9 The eye *that* saw him will *see him* no
more,
Nor will his place behold him anymore.
10 His children will seek the favor of the poor,
And his hands will restore his wealth.
11 His bones are full of his youthful vigor,
But it will lie down with him in the dust.

12 "Though evil is sweet in his mouth,
And he hides it under his tongue,
13 *Though* he spares it and does not forsake
it,
But still keeps it in his mouth,
14 *Yet* his food in his stomach turns sour;
It becomes cobra venom within him.
15 He swallows down riches
And vomits them up again;
God casts them out of his belly.
16 He will suck the poison of cobras;
The viper's tongue will slay him.
17 He will not see the streams,
The rivers flowing with honey and cream.
18 He will restore that for which he labored,
And will not swallow *it* down;
From the proceeds of business
He will get no enjoyment.
19 For he has oppressed *and* forsaken the
poor,
He has violently seized a house which he
did not build.

20 "Because he knows no quietness in his
heart,[a]
He will not save anything he desires.
21 Nothing is left for him to eat;
Therefore his well-being will not last.
22 In his self-sufficiency he will be in
distress;
Every hand of misery will come against
him.
23 *When* he is about to fill his stomach,
God will cast on him the fury of His
wrath,
And will rain *it* on him while he is eating.
24 He will flee from the iron weapon;
A bronze bow will pierce him through.
25 It is drawn, and comes out of the body;
Yes, the glittering *point comes* out of his
gall.
Terrors *come* upon him;
26 Total darkness *is* reserved for his
treasures.
An unfanned fire will consume him;
It shall go ill with him who is left in his
tent.
27 The heavens will reveal his iniquity,
And the earth will rise up against him.
28 The increase of his house will depart,
And his goods will flow away in the day
of His wrath.
29 This *is* the portion from God for a wicked
man,
The heritage appointed to him by God."

Job's Discourse on the Wicked

21 Then Job answered and said:
2 "Listen carefully to my speech,
And let this be your consolation.
3 Bear with me that I may speak,
And after I have spoken, keep mocking.
4 "As for me, *is* my complaint against man?
And if *it were*, why should I not be
impatient?
5 Look at me and be astonished;
Put *your* hand over *your* mouth.
6 Even when I remember I am terrified,
And trembling takes hold of my flesh.
7 Why do the wicked live *and* become old,
Yes, become mighty in power?
8 Their descendants are established with
them in their sight,
And their offspring before their eyes.
9 Their houses *are* safe from fear,
Neither *is* the rod of God upon them.
10 Their bull breeds without failure;
Their cow calves without miscarriage.
11 They send forth their little ones like a
flock,
And their children dance.
12 They sing to the tambourine and harp,
And rejoice to the sound of the flute.
13 They spend their days in wealth,
And in a moment go down to the grave.[a]
14 Yet they say to God, 'Depart from us,
For we do not desire the knowledge of
Your ways.
15 Who *is* the Almighty, that we should
serve Him?
And what profit do we have if we pray to
Him?'
16 Indeed their prosperity *is* not in their
hand;
The counsel of the wicked is far from me.

17 "How often is the lamp of the wicked put
out?
How often does their destruction come
upon them,
The sorrows *God* distributes in His
anger?
18 They are like straw before the wind,
And like chaff that a storm carries away.
19 *They say,* 'God lays up one's[a] iniquity for
his children';
Let Him recompense him, that he may
know *it*.
20 Let his eyes see his destruction,
And let him drink of the wrath of the
Almighty.
21 For what does he care about his
household after him,
When the number of his months is cut in
half?

22 "Can *anyone* teach God knowledge,
Since He judges those on high?
23 One dies in his full strength,
Being wholly at ease and secure;
24 His pails[a] are full of milk,
And the marrow of his bones is moist.
25 Another man dies in the bitterness of his
soul,
Never having eaten with pleasure.
26 They lie down alike in the dust,
And worms cover them.

27 "Look, I know your thoughts,
And the schemes *with which* you would
wrong me.
28 For you say,
'Where *is* the house of the prince?
And where *is* the tent,[a]
The dwelling place of the wicked?'

20:20 [a]Literally *belly* **21:13** [a]Or *Sheol* **21:19** [a]Literally *his* **21:24** [a]Septuagint and Vulgate read *bowels;* Syriac reads *sides;* Targum reads *breasts.* **21:28** [a]Vulgate omits *the tent.*

29 Have you not asked those who travel the road?
And do you not know their signs?
30 For the wicked are reserved for the day of doom;
They shall be brought out on the day of wrath.
31 Who condemns his way to his face?
And who repays him *for what* he has done?
32 Yet he shall be brought to the grave,
And a vigil kept over the tomb.
33 The clods of the valley shall be sweet to him;
Everyone shall follow him,
As countless *have gone* before him.
34 How then can you comfort me with empty words,
Since falsehood remains in your answers?"

Eliphaz Accuses Job of Wickedness

22 Then Eliphaz the Temanite answered and said:

2 "Can a man be profitable to God,
Though he who is wise may be profitable to himself?
3 *Is it* any pleasure to the Almighty that you are righteous?
Or *is it* gain *to Him* that you make your ways blameless?

4 "Is it because of your fear of Him that He corrects you,
And enters into judgment with you?
5 *Is* not your wickedness great,
And your iniquity without end?
6 For you have taken pledges from your brother for no reason,
And stripped the naked of their clothing.
7 You have not given the weary water to drink,
And you have withheld bread from the hungry.
8 But the mighty man possessed the land,
And the honorable man dwelt in it.
9 You have sent widows away empty,
And the strength of the fatherless was crushed.
10 Therefore snares *are* all around you,
And sudden fear troubles you,
11 Or darkness *so that* you cannot see;
And an abundance of water covers you.

12 "Is not God in the height of heaven?
And see the highest stars, how lofty they are!
13 And you say, 'What does God know?
Can He judge through the deep darkness?
14 Thick clouds cover Him, so that He cannot see,
And He walks above the circle of heaven.'
15 Will you keep to the old way
Which wicked men have trod,
16 Who were cut down before their time,
Whose foundations were swept away by a flood?
17 They said to God, 'Depart from us!
What can the Almighty do to them?'[a]
18 Yet He filled their houses with good *things;*
But the counsel of the wicked is far from me.

19 "The righteous see *it* and are glad,
And the innocent laugh at them:
20 'Surely our adversaries[a] are cut down,
And the fire consumes their remnant.'

21 "Now acquaint yourself with Him, and be at peace;
Thereby good will come to you.
22 Receive, please, instruction from His mouth,
And lay up His words in your heart.
23 If you return to the Almighty, you will be built up;
You will remove iniquity far from your tents.
24 Then you will lay your gold in the dust,
And the *gold* of Ophir among the stones of the brooks.
25 Yes, the Almighty will be your gold[a]
And your precious silver;
26 For then you will have your delight in the Almighty,
And lift up your face to God.
27 You will make your prayer to Him,
He will hear you,
And you will pay your vows.
28 You will also declare a thing,
And it will be established for you;
So light will shine on your ways.
29 When they cast *you* down, and you say,
'Exaltation *will come!*'
Then He will save the humble *person.*
30 He will *even* deliver one who is not innocent;
Yes, he will be delivered by the purity of your hands."

Job Proclaims God's Righteous Judgments

23 Then Job answered and said:

2 "Even today my complaint is bitter;
My[a] hand is listless because of my groaning.
3 Oh, that I knew where I might find Him,
That I might come to His seat!
4 I would present *my* case before Him,
And fill my mouth with arguments.
5 I would know the words *which* He would answer me,
And understand what He would say to me.
6 Would He contend with me in His great power?
No! But He would take *note* of me.
7 There the upright could reason with Him,
And I would be delivered forever from my Judge.

8 "Look, I go forward, but He is not *there,*
And backward, but I cannot perceive Him;
9 When He works on the left hand, I cannot behold *Him;*
When He turns to the right hand, I cannot see *Him.*
10 But He knows the way that I take;
When He has tested me, I shall come forth as gold.

22:17 [a]Septuagint and Syriac read *us.* **22:20** [a]Septuagint reads *substance.* **22:25** [a]The ancient versions suggest *defense;* Hebrew reads *gold* as in verse 24. **23:2** [a]Following Masoretic Text, Targum, and Vulgate; Septuagint and Syriac read *His.*

11 My foot has held fast to His steps;
I have kept His way and not turned aside.
12 I have not departed from the commandment of His lips;
I have treasured the words of His mouth
More than my necessary *food.*

13 "But He *is* unique, and who can make Him change?
And *whatever* His soul desires, *that* He does.
14 For He performs *what is* appointed for me,
And many such *things are* with Him.
15 Therefore I am terrified at His presence;
When I consider *this,* I am afraid of Him.
16 For God made my heart weak,
And the Almighty terrifies me;
17 Because I was not cut off from the presence of darkness,
And He did *not* hide deep darkness from my face.

Job Complains of Violence on the Earth

24 "*Since* times are not hidden from the Almighty,
Why do those who know Him see not His days?

2 "*Some* remove landmarks;
They seize flocks violently and feed *on them;*
3 They drive away the donkey of the fatherless;
They take the widow's ox as a pledge.
4 They push the needy off the road;
All the poor of the land are forced to hide.
5 Indeed, *like* wild donkeys in the desert,
They go out to their work, searching for food.
The wilderness *yields* food for them *and* for *their* children.
6 They gather their fodder in the field
And glean in the vineyard of the wicked.
7 They spend the night naked, without clothing,
And have no covering in the cold.
8 They are wet with the showers of the mountains,
And huddle around the rock for want of shelter.

9 "*Some* snatch the fatherless from the breast,
And take a pledge from the poor.
10 They cause *the poor* to go naked, without clothing;
And they take away the sheaves from the hungry.
11 They press out oil within their walls,
And tread winepresses, yet suffer thirst.
12 The dying groan in the city,
And the souls of the wounded cry out;
Yet God does not charge *them* with wrong.

13 "There are those who rebel against the light;
They do not know its ways
Nor abide in its paths.
14 The murderer rises with the light;
He kills the poor and needy;
And in the night he is like a thief.
15 The eye of the adulterer waits for the twilight,
Saying, 'No eye will see me';
And he disguises *his* face.
16 In the dark they break into houses
Which they marked for themselves in the daytime;
They do not know the light.
17 For the morning is the same to them as the shadow of death;
If *someone* recognizes *them,*
They are in the terrors of the shadow of death.

18 "They *should be* swift on the face of the waters,
Their portion *should be* cursed in the earth,
So that no *one would* turn into the way of their vineyards.
19 As drought and heat consume the snow waters,
So the grave[a] *consumes those who* have sinned.
20 The womb *should* forget him,
The worm *should* feed sweetly on him;
He *should* be remembered no more,
And wickedness *should* be broken like a tree.
21 For he preys on the barren *who* do not bear,
And does no good for the widow.

22 "But *God* draws the mighty away with His power;
He rises up, but no *man* is sure of life.
23 He gives them security, and they rely *on it;*
Yet His eyes *are* on their ways.
24 They are exalted for a little while,
Then they are gone.
They are brought low;
They are taken out of the way like all *others;*
They dry out like the heads of grain.

25 "Now if *it is* not so, who will prove me a liar,
And make my speech worth nothing?"

Bildad: How Can Man Be Righteous?

25 Then Bildad the Shuhite answered and said:

2 "Dominion and fear *belong* to Him;
He makes peace in His high places.
3 Is there any number to His armies?
Upon whom does His light not rise?
4 How then can man be righteous before God?
Or how can he be pure *who is* born of a woman?
5 If even the moon does not shine,
And the stars are not pure in His sight,
6 How much less man, *who is* a maggot,
And a son of man, *who is* a worm?"

Job: Man's Frailty and God's Majesty

26 But Job answered and said:
2 "How have you helped *him who is* without power?
How have you saved the arm *that has* no strength?

24:19 [a]Or *Sheol*

3 How have you counseled *one who has* no
wisdom?
And *how* have you declared sound advice
to many?
4 To whom have you uttered words?
And whose spirit came from you?

5 "The dead tremble,
Those under the waters and those
inhabiting them.
6 Sheol *is* naked before Him,
And Destruction has no covering.
7 He stretches out the north over empty
space;
He hangs the earth on nothing.
8 He binds up the water in His thick clouds,
Yet the clouds are not broken under it.
9 He covers the face of *His* throne,
And spreads His cloud over it.
10 He drew a circular horizon on the face of
the waters,
At the boundary of light and darkness.
11 The pillars of heaven tremble,
And are astonished at His rebuke.
12 He stirs up the sea with His power,
And by His understanding He breaks up
the storm.
13 By His Spirit He adorned the heavens;
His hand pierced the fleeing serpent.
14 Indeed these *are* the mere edges of His
ways,
And how small a whisper we hear of
Him!
But the thunder of His power who can
understand?"

Job Maintains His Integrity

27 Moreover Job continued his discourse,
and said:

2 "*As* God lives, *who* has taken away my
justice,
And the Almighty, *who* has made my soul
bitter,
3 As long as my breath *is* in me,
And the breath of God in my nostrils,
4 My lips will not speak wickedness,
Nor my tongue utter deceit.
5 Far be it from me
That I should say you are right;
Till I die I will not put away my integrity
from me.
6 My righteousness I hold fast, and will not
let it go;
My heart shall not reproach *me* as long
as I live.

7 "May my enemy be like the wicked,
And he who rises up against me like the
unrighteous.
8 For what is the hope of the hypocrite,
Though he may gain *much*,
If God takes away his life?
9 Will God hear his cry
When trouble comes upon him?
10 Will he delight himself in the Almighty?
Will he always call on God?

11 "I will teach you about the hand of God;
What *is* with the Almighty I will not
conceal.
12 Surely all of you have seen *it*;
Why then do you behave with complete
nonsense?

13 "This is the portion of a wicked man with
God,
And the heritage of oppressors, received
from the Almighty:
14 If his children are multiplied, *it is* for the
sword;
And his offspring shall not be satisfied
with bread.
15 Those who survive him shall be buried in
death,
And their[a] widows shall not weep,
16 Though he heaps up silver like dust,
And piles up clothing like clay—
17 He may pile *it* up, but the just will wear
it,
And the innocent will divide the silver.
18 He builds his house like a moth,[a]
Like a booth *which* a watchman makes.
19 The rich man will lie down,
But not be gathered *up*;[a]
He opens his eyes,
And he *is* no more.
20 Terrors overtake him like a flood;
A tempest steals him away in the night.
21 The east wind carries him away, and he is
gone;
It sweeps him out of his place.
22 It hurls against him and does not spare;
He flees desperately from its power.
23 *Men* shall clap their hands at him,
And shall hiss him out of his place.

Job's Discourse on Wisdom

28 "Surely there is a mine for silver,
And a place *where* gold is refined.
2 Iron is taken from the earth,
And copper *is* smelted *from* ore.
3 *Man* puts an end to darkness,
And searches every recess
For ore in the darkness and the shadow
of death.
4 He breaks open a shaft away from
people;
In places forgotten by feet
They hang far away from men;
They swing to and fro.
5 *As for* the earth, from it comes bread,
But underneath it is turned up as by fire;
6 Its stones *are* the source of sapphires,
And it contains gold dust.
7 *That* path no bird knows,
Nor has the falcon's eye seen it.
8 The proud lions[a] have not trodden it,
Nor has the fierce lion passed over it.
9 He puts his hand on the flint;
He overturns the mountains at the roots.
10 He cuts out channels in the rocks,
And his eye sees every precious thing.
11 He dams up the streams from trickling;
What is hidden he brings forth to light.

12 "But where can wisdom be found?
And where *is* the place of understanding?
13 Man does not know its value,
Nor is it found in the land of the living.
14 The deep says, '*It is* not in me';
And the sea says, '*It is* not with me.'

27:15 [a]Literally *his* **27:18** [a]Following Masoretic Text and Vulgate; Septuagint and Syriac read *spider* (compare 8:14); Targum reads *decay.* **27:19** [a]Following Masoretic Text and Targum; Septuagint and Syriac read *But shall not add* (that is, do it again); Vulgate reads *But take away nothing.* **28:8** [a]Literally *sons of pride,* figurative of the great lions

15 It cannot be purchased for gold,
Nor can silver be weighed *for* its price.
16 It cannot be valued in the gold of Ophir,
In precious onyx or sapphire.
17 Neither gold nor crystal can equal it,
Nor can it be exchanged for jewelry of fine gold.
18 No mention shall be made of coral or quartz,
For the price of wisdom *is* above rubies.
19 The topaz of Ethiopia cannot equal it,
Nor can it be valued in pure gold.

20 "From where then does wisdom come?
And where *is* the place of understanding?
21 It is hidden from the eyes of all living,
And concealed from the birds of the air.
22 Destruction and Death say,
'We have heard a report about it with our ears.'
23 God understands its way,
And He knows its place.
24 For He looks to the ends of the earth,
And sees under the whole heavens,
25 To establish a weight for the wind,
And apportion the waters by measure.
26 When He made a law for the rain,
And a path for the thunderbolt,
27 Then He saw *wisdom*[a] and declared it;
He prepared it, indeed, He searched it out.
28 And to man He said,
'Behold, the fear of the Lord, that *is* wisdom,
And to depart from evil *is* understanding.' "

Job's Summary Defense

29 Job further continued his discourse, and said:

2 "Oh, that I were as *in* months past,
As *in* the days *when* God watched over me;
3 When His lamp shone upon my head,
And when by His light I walked *through* darkness;
4 Just as I was in the days of my prime,
When the friendly counsel of God *was* over my tent;
5 When the Almighty *was* yet with me,
When my children *were* around me;
6 When my steps were bathed with cream,[a]
And the rock poured out rivers of oil for me!

7 "When I went out to the gate by the city,
When I took my seat in the open square,
8 The young men saw me and hid,
And the aged arose *and* stood;
9 The princes refrained from talking,
And put *their* hand on their mouth;
10 The voice of nobles was hushed,
And their tongue stuck to the roof of their mouth.
11 When the ear heard, then it blessed me,
And when the eye saw, then it approved me;
12 Because I delivered the poor who cried out,
The fatherless and *the one who* had no helper.
13 The blessing of a perishing *man* came upon me,
And I caused the widow's heart to sing for joy.
14 I put on righteousness, and it clothed me;
My justice *was* like a robe and a turban.
15 I *was* eyes to the blind,
And I *was* feet to the lame.
16 I *was* a father to the poor,
And I searched out the case *that* I did not know.
17 I broke the fangs of the wicked,
And plucked the victim from his teeth.

18 "Then I said, 'I shall die in my nest,
And multiply *my* days as the sand.
19 My root *is* spread out to the waters,
And the dew lies all night on my branch.
20 My glory *is* fresh within me,
And my bow is renewed in my hand.'

21 "*Men* listened to me and waited,
And kept silence for my counsel.
22 After my words they did not speak again,
And my speech settled on them *as dew.*
23 They waited for me *as* for the rain,
And they opened their mouth wide *as* for the spring rain.
24 *If* I mocked at them, they did not believe *it,*
And the light of my countenance they did not cast down.
25 I chose the way for them, and sat as chief;
So I dwelt as a king in the army,
As one *who* comforts mourners.

30 "But now they mock at me, *men* younger than I,
Whose fathers I disdained to put with the dogs of my flock.
2 Indeed, what *profit* is the strength of their hands to me?
Their vigor has perished.
3 *They are* gaunt from want and famine,
Fleeing late to the wilderness, desolate and waste,
4 Who pluck mallow by the bushes,
And broom tree roots *for* their food.
5 They were driven out from among *men,*
They shouted at them as *at* a thief.
6 *They had* to live in the clefts of the valleys,
In caves of the earth and the rocks.
7 Among the bushes they brayed,
Under the nettles they nestled.
8 *They were* sons of fools,
Yes, sons of vile men;
They were scourged from the land.

9 "And now I am their taunting song;
Yes, I am their byword.
10 They abhor me, they keep far from me;
They do not hesitate to spit in my face.
11 Because He has loosed my[a] bowstring and afflicted me,
They have cast off restraint before me.
12 At *my* right *hand* the rabble arises;
They push away my feet,
And they raise against me their ways of destruction.
13 They break up my path,
They promote my calamity;
They have no helper.

28:27 [a]Literally *it* **29:6** [a]Masoretic Text reads *wrath;* ancient versions and some Hebrew manuscripts read *cream* (compare 20:17). **30:11** [a]Following Masoretic Text, Syriac, and Targum; Septuagint and Vulgate read *His.*

14 They come as broad breakers;
Under the ruinous storm they roll along.
15 Terrors are turned upon me;
They pursue my honor as the wind,
And my prosperity has passed like a cloud.

16 "And now my soul is poured out because of my *plight;*
The days of affliction take hold of me.
17 My bones are pierced in me at night,
And my gnawing pains take no rest.
18 By great force my garment is disfigured;
It binds me about as the collar of my coat.
19 He has cast me into the mire,
And I have become like dust and ashes.

20 "I cry out to You, but You do not answer me;
I stand up, and You regard me.
21 *But* You have become cruel to me;
With the strength of Your hand You oppose me.
22 You lift me up to the wind and cause me to ride *on it;*
You spoil my success.
23 For I know *that* You will bring me *to* death,
And *to* the house appointed for all living.

24 "Surely He would not stretch out *His* hand against a heap of ruins,
If they cry out when He destroys *it.*
25 Have I not wept for him who was in trouble?
Has *not* my soul grieved for the poor?
26 But when I looked for good, evil came *to me;*
And when I waited for light, then came darkness.
27 My heart is in turmoil and cannot rest;
Days of affliction confront me.
28 I go about mourning, but not in the sun;
I stand up in the assembly *and* cry out for help.
29 I am a brother of jackals,
And a companion of ostriches.
30 My skin grows black and falls from me;
My bones burn with fever.
31 My harp is *turned* to mourning,
And my flute to the voice of those who weep.

31 "I have made a covenant with my eyes;
Why then should I look upon a young woman?
2 For what *is* the allotment of God from above,
And the inheritance of the Almighty from on high?
3 *Is* it not destruction for the wicked,
And disaster for the workers of iniquity?
4 Does He not see my ways,
And count all my steps?

5 "If I have walked with falsehood,
Or if my foot has hastened to deceit,
6 Let me be weighed on honest scales,
That God may know my integrity.
7 If my step has turned from the way,
Or my heart walked after my eyes,
Or if any spot adheres to my hands,
8 *Then* let me sow, and another eat;
Yes, let my harvest be rooted out.

9 "If my heart has been enticed by a woman,
Or *if* I have lurked at my neighbor's door,
10 *Then* let my wife grind for another,
And let others bow down over her.
11 For that *would be* wickedness;
Yes, it *would be* iniquity *deserving of* judgment.
12 For that *would be* a fire *that* consumes to destruction,
And would root out all my increase.

13 "If I have despised the cause of my male or female servant
When they complained against me,
14 What then shall I do when God rises up?
When He punishes, how shall I answer Him?
15 Did not He who made me in the womb make them?
Did not the same One fashion us in the womb?

16 "If I have kept the poor from *their* desire,
Or caused the eyes of the widow to fail,
17 Or eaten my morsel by myself,
So that the fatherless could not eat of it
18 (But from my youth I reared him as a father,
And from my mother's womb I guided *the widow*[a]);
19 If I have seen anyone perish for lack of clothing,
Or any poor *man* without covering;
20 If his heart[a] has not blessed me,
And *if* he was *not* warmed with the fleece of my sheep;
21 If I have raised my hand against the fatherless,
When I saw I had help in the gate;
22 *Then* let my arm fall from my shoulder,
Let my arm be torn from the socket.
23 For destruction *from* God *is* a terror to me,
And because of His magnificence I cannot endure.

24 "If I have made gold my hope,
Or said to fine gold, '*You are* my confidence';
25 If I have rejoiced because my wealth *was* great,
And because my hand had gained much;
26 If I have observed the sun[a] when it shines,
Or the moon moving *in* brightness,
27 So that my heart has been secretly enticed,
And my mouth has kissed my hand;
28 This also *would be* an iniquity *deserving of* judgment,
For I would have denied God *who is* above.

29 "If I have rejoiced at the destruction of him who hated me,
Or lifted myself up when evil found him
30 (Indeed I have not allowed my mouth to sin
By asking for a curse on his soul);
31 If the men of my tent have not said,
'Who is there that has not been satisfied with his meat?'
32 (*But* no sojourner had to lodge in the street,

31:18 [a]Literally *her* (compare verse 16) **31:20** [a]Literally *loins* **31:26** [a]Literally *light*

For I have opened my doors to the traveler[a]);
33 If I have covered my transgressions as Adam,
By hiding my iniquity in my bosom,
34 Because I feared the great multitude,
And dreaded the contempt of families,
So that I kept silence
And did not go out of the door—
35 Oh, that I had one to hear me!
Here is my mark.
Oh, that the Almighty would answer me,
That my Prosecutor had written a book!
36 Surely I would carry it on my shoulder,
And bind it on me *like* a crown;
37 I would declare to Him the number of my steps;
Like a prince I would approach Him.

38 "If my land cries out against me,
And its furrows weep together;
39 If I have eaten its fruit[a] without money,
Or caused its owners to lose their lives;
40 *Then* let thistles grow instead of wheat,
And weeds instead of barley."

The words of Job are ended.

Elihu Contradicts Job's Friends

32 So these three men ceased answering
Job, because he *was* righteous in his own
eyes.
2 Then the wrath of Elihu, the son of Bara-
chel the Buzite, of the family of Ram, was
aroused against Job; his wrath was aroused
because he justified himself rather than God.
3 Also against his three friends his wrath
was aroused, because they had found no an-
swer, and *yet* had condemned Job.
4 Now because they *were* years older than
he, Elihu had waited to speak to Job.[a]
5 When Elihu saw that *there was* no answer
in the mouth of these three men, his wrath was
aroused.
6 So Elihu, the son of Barachel the Buzite,
answered and said:

"I *am* young in years, and you *are* very old;
Therefore I was afraid,
And dared not declare my opinion to you.
7 I said, 'Age[a] should speak,
And multitude of years should teach wisdom.'
8 But *there is* a spirit in man,
And the breath of the Almighty gives him understanding.
9 Great men[a] are not *always* wise,
Nor do the aged *always* understand justice.

10 "Therefore I say, 'Listen to me,
I also will declare my opinion.'
11 Indeed I waited for your words,
I listened to your reasonings, while you searched out what to say.
12 I paid close attention to you;
And surely not one of you convinced Job,
Or answered his words—
13 Lest you say,
'We have found wisdom';
God will vanquish him, not man.
14 Now he has not directed *his* words against me;
So I will not answer him with your words.

15 "They are dismayed and answer no more;
Words escape them.
16 And I have waited, because they did not speak,
Because they stood still *and* answered no more.
17 I also will answer my part,
I too will declare my opinion.
18 For I am full of words;
The spirit within me compels me.
19 Indeed my belly *is* like wine *that* has no vent;
It is ready to burst like new wineskins.
20 I will speak, that I may find relief;
I must open my lips and answer.
21 Let me not, I pray, show partiality to anyone;
Nor let me flatter any man.
22 For I do not know how to flatter,
Else my Maker would soon take me away.

Elihu Contradicts Job

33 "But please, Job, hear my speech,
And listen to all my words.
2 Now, I open my mouth;
My tongue speaks in my mouth.
3 My words *come* from my upright heart;
My lips utter pure knowledge.
4 The Spirit of God has made me,
And the breath of the Almighty gives me life.
5 If you can answer me,
Set *your words* in order before me;
Take your stand.
6 Truly I *am* as your spokesman[a] before God;
I also have been formed out of clay.
7 Surely no fear of me will terrify you,
Nor will my hand be heavy on you.

8 "Surely you have spoken in my hearing,
And I have heard the sound of *your* words, *saying*,
9 'I *am* pure, without transgression;
I *am* innocent, and *there is* no iniquity in me.
10 Yet He finds occasions against me,
He counts me as His enemy;
11 He puts my feet in the stocks,
He watches all my paths.'

12 "Look, *in* this you are not righteous.
I will answer you,
For God is greater than man.
13 Why do you contend with Him?
For He does not give an accounting of any of His words.
14 For God may speak in one way, or in another,
Yet man does not perceive it.
15 In a dream, in a vision of the night,
When deep sleep falls upon men,
While slumbering on their beds,
16 Then He opens the ears of men,
And seals their instruction.
17 In order to turn man *from his* deed,
And conceal pride from man,

31:32 [a]Following Septuagint, Syriac, Targum, and Vulgate; Masoretic Text reads *road.* **31:39** [a]Literally *its strength*
32:4 [a]Vulgate reads *till Job had spoken.* **32:7** [a]Literally *Days,* that is, years **32:9** [a]Or *Men of many years*
33:6 [a]Literally *as your mouth*

18 He keeps back his soul from the Pit,
And his life from perishing by the sword.

19 "*Man* is also chastened with pain on his bed,
And with strong *pain* in many of his bones,
20 So that his life abhors bread,
And his soul succulent food.
21 His flesh wastes away from sight,
And his bones stick out *which once* were not seen.
22 Yes, his soul draws near the Pit,
And his life to the executioners.

23 "If there is a messenger for him,
A mediator, one among a thousand,
To show man His uprightness,
24 Then He is gracious to him, and says,
'Deliver him from going down to the Pit;
I have found a ransom';
25 His flesh shall be young like a child's,
He shall return to the days of his youth.
26 He shall pray to God, and He will delight in him,
He shall see His face with joy,
For He restores to man His righteousness.
27 Then he looks at men and says,
'I have sinned, and perverted *what was* right,
And it did not profit me.'
28 He will redeem his[a] soul from going down to the Pit,
And his[b] life shall see the light.

29 "Behold, God works all these *things*,
Twice, *in fact*, three *times* with a man,
30 To bring back his soul from the Pit,
That he may be enlightened with the light of life.

31 "Give ear, Job, listen to me;
Hold your peace, and I will speak.
32 If you have anything to say, answer me;
Speak, for I desire to justify you.
33 If not, listen to me;
Hold your peace, and I will teach you wisdom."

Elihu Proclaims God's Justice

34 Elihu further answered and said:

2 "Hear my words, you wise *men;*
Give ear to me, you who have knowledge.
3 For the ear tests words
As the palate tastes food.
4 Let us choose justice for ourselves;
Let us know among ourselves what *is* good.

5 "For Job has said, 'I am righteous,
But God has taken away my justice;
6 Should I lie concerning my right?
My wound *is* incurable, *though I am* without transgression.'
7 What man *is* like Job,
Who drinks scorn like water,
8 Who goes in company with the workers of iniquity,
And walks with wicked men?
9 For he has said, 'It profits a man nothing
That he should delight in God.'

10 "Therefore listen to me, you men of understanding:
Far be it from God *to do* wickedness,
And *from* the Almighty to *commit* iniquity.
11 For He repays man *according to* his work,
And makes man to find a reward according to *his* way.
12 Surely God will never do wickedly,
Nor will the Almighty pervert justice.
13 Who gave Him charge over the earth?
Or who appointed *Him over* the whole world?
14 If He should set His heart on it,
If He should gather to Himself His Spirit and His breath,
15 All flesh would perish together,
And man would return to dust.

16 "If *you have* understanding, hear this;
Listen to the sound of my words:
17 Should one who hates justice govern?
Will you condemn *Him who is* most just?
18 *Is it fitting* to say to a king, '*You are* worthless,'
And to nobles, '*You are* wicked'?
19 Yet He is not partial to princes,
Nor does He regard the rich more than the poor;
For they *are* all the work of His hands.
20 In a moment they die, in the middle of the night;
The people are shaken and pass away;
The mighty are taken away without a hand.

21 "For His eyes *are* on the ways of man,
And He sees all his steps.
22 There is no darkness nor shadow of death
Where the workers of iniquity may hide themselves.
23 For He need not further consider a man,
That he should go before God in judgment.
24 He breaks in pieces mighty men without inquiry,
And sets others in their place.
25 Therefore He knows their works;
He overthrows *them* in the night,
And they are crushed.
26 He strikes them as wicked *men*
In the open sight of others,
27 Because they turned back from Him,
And would not consider any of His ways,
28 So that they caused the cry of the poor to come to Him;
For He hears the cry of the afflicted.
29 When He gives quietness, who then can make trouble?
And when He hides *His* face, who then can see Him,
Whether *it is* against a nation or a man alone?—
30 That the hypocrite should not reign,
Lest the people be ensnared.

31 "For has *anyone* said to God,
'I have borne *chastening;*
I will offend no more;
32 Teach me *what* I do not see;
If I have done iniquity, I will do no more'?
33 Should He repay *it* according to your *terms*,
Just because you disavow it?

33:28 [a]Or *my* (Kethib) [b]Or *my* (Kethib)

You must choose, and not I;
Therefore speak what you know.

34 "Men of understanding say to me,
Wise men who listen to me:
35 'Job speaks without knowledge,
His words *are* without wisdom.'
36 Oh, that Job were tried to the utmost,
Because *his* answers *are like* those of wicked men!
37 For he adds rebellion to his sin;
He claps *his hands* among us,
And multiplies his words against God."

Elihu Condemns Self-Righteousness

35 Moreover Elihu answered and said:
2 "Do you think this is right?
Do you say,
'My righteousness is more than God's'?
3 For you say,
'What advantage will it be to You?
What profit shall I have, more than *if* I had sinned?'

4 "I will answer you,
And your companions with you.
5 Look to the heavens and see;
And behold the clouds—
They are higher than you.
6 If you sin, what do you accomplish against Him?
Or, *if* your transgressions are multiplied, what do you do to Him?
7 If you are righteous, what do you give Him?
Or what does He receive from your hand?
8 Your wickedness affects a man such as you,
And your righteousness a son of man.

9 "Because of the multitude of oppressions they cry out;
They cry out for help because of the arm of the mighty.
10 But no one says, 'Where *is* God my Maker,
Who gives songs in the night,
11 Who teaches us more than the beasts of the earth,
And makes us wiser than the birds of heaven?'
12 There they cry out, but He does not answer,
Because of the pride of evil men.
13 Surely God will not listen to empty *talk*,
Nor will the Almighty regard it.
14 Although you say you do not see Him,
Yet justice *is* before Him, and you must wait for Him.
15 And now, because He has not punished in His anger,
Nor taken much notice of folly,
16 Therefore Job opens his mouth in vain;
He multiplies words without knowledge."

Elihu Proclaims God's Goodness

36 Elihu also proceeded and said:
2 "Bear with me a little, and I will show you
That *there are* yet words to speak on God's behalf.
3 I will fetch my knowledge from afar;
I will ascribe righteousness to my Maker.
4 For truly my words *are* not false;
One who is perfect in knowledge *is* with you.

5 "Behold, God *is* mighty, but despises *no one;*
He is mighty in strength of understanding.
6 He does not preserve the life of the wicked,
But gives justice to the oppressed.
7 He does not withdraw His eyes from the righteous;
But *they are* on the throne with kings,
For He has seated them forever,
And they are exalted.
8 And if *they are* bound in fetters,
Held in the cords of affliction,
9 Then He tells them their work and their transgressions—
That they have acted defiantly.
10 He also opens their ear to instruction,
And commands that they turn from iniquity.
11 If they obey and serve *Him*,
They shall spend their days in prosperity,
And their years in pleasures.
12 But if they do not obey,
They shall perish by the sword,
And they shall die without knowledge.[a]

13 "But the hypocrites in heart store up wrath;
They do not cry for help when He binds them.
14 They die in youth,
And their life *ends* among the perverted persons.[a]
15 He delivers the poor in their affliction,
And opens their ears in oppression.

16 "Indeed He would have brought you out of dire distress,
Into a broad place where *there is* no restraint;
And what is set on your table *would be* full of richness.
17 But you are filled with the judgment due the wicked;
Judgment and justice take hold *of you*.
18 Because *there is* wrath, *beware* lest He take you away with *one* blow;
For a large ransom would not help you avoid *it*.
19 Will your riches,
Or all the mighty forces,
Keep you from distress?
20 Do not desire the night,
When people are cut off in their place.
21 Take heed, do not turn to iniquity,
For you have chosen this rather than affliction.

22 "Behold, God is exalted by His power;
Who teaches like Him?
23 Who has assigned Him His way,
Or who has said, 'You have done wrong'?

Elihu Proclaims God's Majesty

24 "Remember to magnify His work,
Of which men have sung.

36:12 [a]Masoretic Text reads *as one without knowledge.* **36:14** [a]Hebrew *qedeshim,* that is, those practicing sodomy and prostitution in religious rituals

25 Everyone has seen it;
Man looks on *it* from afar.
26 "Behold, God *is* great, and we do not know *Him;*
Nor can the number of His years *be* discovered.
27 For He draws up drops of water,
Which distill as rain from the mist,
28 Which the clouds drop down
And pour abundantly on man.
29 Indeed, can *anyone* understand the spreading of clouds,
The thunder from His canopy?
30 Look, He scatters His light upon it,
And covers the depths of the sea.
31 For by these He judges the peoples;
He gives food in abundance.
32 He covers *His* hands with lightning,
And commands it to strike.
33 His thunder declares it,
The cattle also, concerning the rising *storm.*

37 "At this also my heart trembles,
And leaps from its place.
2 Hear attentively the thunder of His voice,
And the rumbling *that* comes from His mouth.
3 He sends it forth under the whole heaven,
His lightning to the ends of the earth.
4 After it a voice roars;
He thunders with His majestic voice,
And He does not restrain them when His voice is heard.
5 God thunders marvelously with His voice;
He does great things which we cannot comprehend.
6 For He says to the snow, 'Fall *on* the earth';
Likewise to the gentle rain and the heavy rain of His strength.
7 He seals the hand of every man,
That all men may know His work.
8 The beasts go into dens,
And remain in their lairs.
9 From the chamber *of the south* comes the whirlwind,
And cold from the scattering winds *of the north.*
10 By the breath of God ice is given,
And the broad waters are frozen.
11 Also with moisture He saturates the thick clouds;
He scatters His bright clouds.
12 And they swirl about, being turned by His guidance,
That they may do whatever He commands them
On the face of the whole earth.[a]
13 He causes it to come,
Whether for correction,
Or for His land,
Or for mercy.

14 "Listen to this, O Job;
Stand still and consider the wondrous works of God.
15 Do you know when God dispatches them,
And causes the light of His cloud to shine?
16 Do you know how the clouds are balanced,
Those wondrous works of Him who is perfect in knowledge?
17 Why *are* your garments hot,
When He quiets the earth by the south *wind?*
18 With Him, have you spread out the skies,
Strong as a cast metal mirror?

19 "Teach us what we should say to Him,
For we can prepare nothing because of the darkness.
20 Should He be told that I *wish to* speak?
If a man were to speak, surely he would be swallowed up.
21 Even now *men* cannot look at the light *when it is* bright in the skies,
When the wind has passed and cleared them.
22 He comes from the north *as* golden *splendor;*
With God *is* awesome majesty.
23 *As for* the Almighty, we cannot find Him;
He is excellent in power,
In judgment and abundant justice;
He does not oppress.
24 Therefore men fear Him;
He shows no partiality to any *who are* wise of heart."

The LORD Reveals His Omnipotence to Job

38 Then the LORD answered Job out of the whirlwind, and said:

2 "Who *is* this who darkens counsel
By words without knowledge?
3 Now prepare yourself like a man;
I will question you, and you shall answer Me.

4 "Where were you when I laid the foundations of the earth?
Tell *Me,* if you have understanding.
5 Who determined its measurements?
Surely you know!
Or who stretched the line upon it?
6 To what were its foundations fastened?
Or who laid its cornerstone,
7 When the morning stars sang together,
And all the sons of God shouted for joy?

8 "Or *who* shut in the sea with doors,
When it burst forth *and* issued from the womb;
9 When I made the clouds its garment,
And thick darkness its swaddling band;
10 When I fixed My limit for it,
And set bars and doors;
11 When I said,
'This far you may come, but no farther,
And here your proud waves must stop!'

12 "Have you commanded the morning since your days *began,*
And caused the dawn to know its place,
13 That it might take hold of the ends of the earth,
And the wicked be shaken out of it?
14 It takes on form like clay *under* a seal,
And stands out like a garment.
15 From the wicked their light is withheld,
And the upraised arm is broken.

16 "Have you entered the springs of the sea?
Or have you walked in search of the depths?

37:12 [a]Literally *the world of the earth*

17 Have the gates of death been revealed to
you?
Or have you seen the doors of the shadow
of death?
18 Have you comprehended the breadth of
the earth?
Tell *Me*, if you know all this.

19 "Where *is* the way *to* the dwelling of light?
And darkness, where *is* its place,
20 That you may take it to its territory,
That you may know the paths *to* its
home?
21 Do you know *it*, because you were born
then,
Or *because* the number of your days *is*
great?

22 "Have you entered the treasury of snow,
Or have you seen the treasury of hail,
23 Which I have reserved for the time of
trouble,
For the day of battle and war?
24 By what way is light diffused,
Or the east wind scattered over the earth?

25 "Who has divided a channel for the
overflowing *water*,
Or a path for the thunderbolt,
26 To cause it to rain on a land *where there
is* no one,
A wilderness in which *there is* no man;
27 To satisfy the desolate waste,
And cause to spring forth the growth of
tender grass?
28 Has the rain a father?
Or who has begotten the drops of dew?
29 From whose womb comes the ice?
And the frost of heaven, who gives it
birth?
30 The waters harden like stone,
And the surface of the deep is frozen.

31 "Can you bind the cluster of the Pleiades,
Or loose the belt of Orion?
32 Can you bring out Mazzaroth[a] in its
season?
Or can you guide the Great Bear with its
cubs?
33 Do you know the ordinances of the
heavens?
Can you set their dominion over the
earth?

34 "Can you lift up your voice to the clouds,
That an abundance of water may cover
you?
35 Can you send out lightnings, that they
may go,
And say to you, 'Here we *are*!'?
36 Who has put wisdom in the mind?[a]
Or who has given understanding to the
heart?
37 Who can number the clouds by wisdom?
Or who can pour out the bottles of
heaven,
38 When the dust hardens in clumps,
And the clods cling together?

39 "Can you hunt the prey for the lion,
Or satisfy the appetite of the young lions,
40 When they crouch in *their* dens,
Or lurk in their lairs to lie in wait?
41 Who provides food for the raven,
When its young ones cry to God,
And wander about for lack of food?

39 "Do you know the time when the wild
mountain goats bear young?
Or can you mark when the deer gives
birth?
2 Can you number the months *that* they
fulfill?
Or do you know the time when they bear
young?
3 They bow down,
They bring forth their young,
They deliver their offspring.[a]
4 Their young ones are healthy,
They grow strong with grain;
They depart and do not return to them.

5 "Who set the wild donkey free?
Who loosed the bonds of the onager,
6 Whose home I have made the wilderness,
And the barren land his dwelling?
7 He scorns the tumult of the city;
He does not heed the shouts of the driver.
8 The range of the mountains *is* his
pasture,
And he searches after every green thing.

9 "Will the wild ox be willing to serve you?
Will he bed by your manger?
10 Can you bind the wild ox in the furrow
with ropes?
Or will he plow the valleys behind you?
11 Will you trust him because his strength *is*
great?
Or will you leave your labor to him?
12 Will you trust him to bring home your
grain,
And gather it to your threshing floor?

13 "The wings of the ostrich wave proudly,
But are her wings and pinions *like the*
kindly stork's?
14 For she leaves her eggs on the ground,
And warms them in the dust;
15 She forgets that a foot may crush them,
Or that a wild beast may break them.
16 She treats her young harshly, as though
they were not hers;
Her labor is in vain, without concern,
17 Because God deprived her of wisdom,
And did not endow her with
understanding.
18 When she lifts herself on high,
She scorns the horse and its rider.

19 "Have you given the horse strength?
Have you clothed his neck with thunder?[a]
20 Can you frighten him like a locust?
His majestic snorting strikes terror.
21 He paws in the valley, and rejoices in *his*
strength;
He gallops into the clash of arms.
22 He mocks at fear, and is not frightened;
Nor does he turn back from the sword.
23 The quiver rattles against him,
The glittering spear and javelin.
24 He devours the distance with fierceness
and rage;
Nor does he come to a halt because the
trumpet *has* sounded.

38:32 [a]Literally *Constellations* **38:36** [a]Literally *inward parts* **39:3** [a]Literally *pangs*, figurative of offspring
39:19 [a]Or *a mane*

25 At *the blast of* the trumpet he says, 'Aha!'
He smells the battle from afar,
The thunder of captains and shouting.

26 "Does the hawk fly by your wisdom,
And spread its wings toward the south?
27 Does the eagle mount up at your
command,
And make its nest on high?
28 On the rock it dwells and resides,
On the crag of the rock and the
stronghold.
29 From there it spies out the prey;
Its eyes observe from afar.
30 Its young ones suck up blood;
And where the slain *are*, there it *is*."

40 Moreover the LORD answered Job, and said:

2 "Shall the one who contends with the
Almighty correct *Him?*
He who rebukes God, let him answer it."

Job's Response to God

3 Then Job answered the LORD and said:

4 "Behold, I am vile;
What shall I answer You?
I lay my hand over my mouth.
5 Once I have spoken, but I will not
answer;
Yes, twice, but I will proceed no further."

God's Challenge to Job

6 Then the LORD answered Job out of the
whirlwind, and said:

7 "Now prepare yourself like a man;
I will question you, and you shall answer
Me:

8 "Would you indeed annul My judgment?
Would you condemn Me that you may be
justified?
9 Have you an arm like God?
Or can you thunder with a voice like His?
10 Then adorn yourself *with* majesty and
splendor,
And array yourself with glory and beauty.
11 Disperse the rage of your wrath;
Look on everyone *who is* proud, and
humble him.
12 Look on everyone *who is* proud, *and*
bring him low;
Tread down the wicked in their place.
13 Hide them in the dust together,
Bind their faces in hidden *darkness*.
14 Then I will also confess to you
That your own right hand can save you.

15 "Look now at the behemoth,[a] which I
made *along* with you;
He eats grass like an ox.
16 See now, his strength *is* in his hips,
And his power *is* in his stomach muscles.
17 He moves his tail like a cedar;
The sinews of his thighs are tightly knit.
18 His bones *are like* beams of bronze,
His ribs like bars of iron.
19 He *is* the first of the ways of God;
Only He who made him can bring near
His sword.
20 Surely the mountains yield food for him,
And all the beasts of the field play there.
21 He lies under the lotus trees,
In a covert of reeds and marsh.
22 The lotus trees cover him *with* their
shade;
The willows by the brook surround him.
23 Indeed the river may rage,
Yet he is not disturbed;
He is confident, though the Jordan
gushes into his mouth,
24 *Though* he takes it in his eyes,
Or one pierces *his* nose with a snare.

41 "Can you draw out Leviathan[a] with a
hook,
Or *snare* his tongue with a line *which* you
lower?
2 Can you put a reed through his nose,
Or pierce his jaw with a hook?
3 Will he make many supplications to you?
Will he speak softly to you?
4 Will he make a covenant with you?
Will you take him as a servant forever?
5 Will you play with him as *with* a bird,
Or will you leash him for your maidens?
6 Will *your* companions make a banquet[a] of
him?
Will they apportion him among the
merchants?
7 Can you fill his skin with harpoons,
Or his head with fishing spears?
8 Lay your hand on him;
Remember the battle—
Never do it again!
9 Indeed, *any* hope of *overcoming* him is
false;
Shall *one not* be overwhelmed at the
sight of him?
10 No one *is so* fierce that he would dare stir
him up.
Who then is able to stand against Me?
11 Who has preceded Me, that I should pay
him?
Everything under heaven is Mine.

12 "I will not conceal[a] his limbs,
His mighty power, or his graceful
proportions.
13 Who can remove his outer coat?
Who can approach *him* with a double
bridle?
14 Who can open the doors of his face,
With his terrible teeth all around?
15 *His* rows of scales are *his* pride,
Shut up tightly *as with* a seal;
16 One is so near another
That no air can come between them;
17 They are joined one to another,
They stick together and cannot be parted.
18 His sneezings flash forth light,
And his eyes *are* like the eyelids of the
morning.
19 Out of his mouth go burning lights;
Sparks of fire shoot out.
20 Smoke goes out of his nostrils,
As *from* a boiling pot and burning rushes.
21 His breath kindles coals,
And a flame goes out of his mouth.
22 Strength dwells in his neck,
And sorrow dances before him.
23 The folds of his flesh are joined together;
They are firm on him and cannot be
moved.

40:15 [a]A large animal, exact identity unknown **41:1** [a]A large sea creature, exact identity unknown **41:6** [a]Or *bargain over him* **41:12** [a]Literally *keep silent about*

24 His heart is as hard as stone,
Even as hard as the lower *millstone*.
25 When he raises himself up, the mighty are afraid;
Because of his crashings they are beside[a] themselves.
26 *Though* the sword reaches him, it cannot avail;
Nor does spear, dart, or javelin.
27 He regards iron as straw,
And bronze as rotten wood.
28 The arrow cannot make him flee;
Slingstones become like stubble to him.
29 Darts are regarded as straw;
He laughs at the threat of javelins.
30 His undersides *are* like sharp potsherds;
He spreads pointed *marks* in the mire.
31 He makes the deep boil like a pot;
He makes the sea like a pot of ointment.
32 He leaves a shining wake behind him;
One would think the deep had white hair.
33 On earth there is nothing like him,
Which is made without fear.
34 He beholds every high *thing*;
He *is* king over all the children of pride."

Job's Repentance and Restoration

42 Then Job answered the LORD and said:
2 "I know that You can do everything,
And that no purpose *of Yours* can be withheld from You.
3 *You asked*, 'Who *is* this who hides counsel without knowledge?'
Therefore I have uttered what I did not understand,
Things too wonderful for me, which I did not know.
4 Listen, please, and let me speak;
You said, 'I will question you, and you shall answer Me.'
5 "I have heard of You by the hearing of the ear,
But now my eye sees You.
6 Therefore I abhor *myself*,
And repent in dust and ashes."

7 And so it was, after the LORD had spoken
these words to Job, that the LORD said to Eli-
phaz the Temanite, "My wrath is aroused
against you and your two friends, for you have
not spoken of Me *what is* right, as My servant
Job *has*.
8 "Now therefore, take for yourselves seven
bulls and seven rams, go to My servant Job, and
offer up for yourselves a burnt offering; and
My servant Job shall pray for you. For I will
accept him, lest I deal with you *according to*
your folly; because you have not spoken of Me
what is right, as My servant Job *has*."
9 So Eliphaz the Temanite and Bildad the
Shuhite *and* Zophar the Naamathite went and
did as the LORD commanded them; for the
LORD had accepted Job.
10 And the LORD restored Job's losses[a] when
he prayed for his friends. Indeed the LORD
gave Job twice as much as he had before.
11 Then all his brothers, all his sisters, and all
those who had been his acquaintances before,
came to him and ate food with him in his house;
and they consoled him and comforted him for
all the adversity that the LORD had brought
upon him. Each one gave him a piece of silver
and each a ring of gold.
12 Now the LORD blessed the latter *days* of
Job more than his beginning; for he had four-
teen thousand sheep, six thousand camels, one
thousand yoke of oxen, and one thousand fe-
male donkeys.
13 He also had seven sons and three daughters.
14 And he called the name of the first Jemi-
mah, the name of the second Keziah, and the
name of the third Keren-Happuch.
15 In all the land were found no women *so*
beautiful as the daughters of Job; and their fa-
ther gave them an inheritance among their
brothers.
16 After this Job lived one hundred and forty
years, and saw his children and grandchildren
for four generations.
17 So Job died, old and full of days.

The Book of PSALMS

BOOK ONE
Psalms 1—41

PSALM 1

The Way of the Righteous and the End of the Ungodly

BLESSED *is* the man
Who walks not in the counsel of the ungodly,
Nor stands in the path of sinners,
Nor sits in the seat of the scornful;
2 But his delight *is* in the law of the LORD,
And in His law he meditates day and night.
3 He shall be like a tree
Planted by the rivers of water,
That brings forth its fruit in its season,
Whose leaf also shall not wither;
And whatever he does shall prosper.
4 The ungodly *are* not so,
But *are* like the chaff which the wind drives away.
5 Therefore the ungodly shall not stand in the judgment,
Nor sinners in the congregation of the righteous.
6 For the LORD knows the way of the righteous,
But the way of the ungodly shall perish.

PSALM 2

The Messiah's Triumph and Kingdom

WHY do the nations rage,
And the people plot a vain thing?
2 The kings of the earth set themselves,
And the rulers take counsel together,

41:25 [a]Or *purify themselves* 42:10 [a]Literally *Job's captivity*, that is, what was captured from Job

Against the LORD and against His
Anointed, *saying*,
3 "Let us break Their bonds in pieces
And cast away Their cords from us."

4 He who sits in the heavens shall laugh;
The Lord shall hold them in derision.
5 Then He shall speak to them in His
wrath,
And distress them in His deep
displeasure:
6 "Yet I have set My King
On My holy hill of Zion."

7 "I will declare the decree:
The LORD has said to Me,
'You *are* My Son,
Today I have begotten You.
8 Ask of Me, and I will give *You*
The nations *for* Your inheritance,
And the ends of the earth *for* Your
possession.
9 You shall break[a] them with a rod of iron;
You shall dash them to pieces like a
potter's vessel.'"

10 Now therefore, be wise, O kings;
Be instructed, you judges of the earth.
11 Serve the LORD with fear,
And rejoice with trembling.
12 Kiss the Son,[a] lest He[b] be angry,
And you perish *in* the way,
When His wrath is kindled but a little.
Blessed *are* all those who put their trust
in Him.

PSALM 3

The LORD Helps His Troubled People

A Psalm of David when he fled
from Absalom his son.

LORD, how they have increased who
trouble me!
Many *are* they who rise up against me.
2 Many *are* they who say of me,
"*There is* no help for him in God." Selah

3 But You, O LORD, *are* a shield for me,
My glory and the One who lifts up my
head.
4 I cried to the LORD with my voice,
And He heard me from His holy hill.
Selah

5 I lay down and slept;
I awoke, for the LORD sustained me.
6 I will not be afraid of ten thousands of
people
Who have set *themselves* against me all
around.

7 Arise, O LORD;
Save me, O my God!
For You have struck all my enemies on
the cheekbone;
You have broken the teeth of the ungodly.
8 Salvation *belongs* to the LORD.
Your blessing *is* upon Your people. Selah

PSALM 4

The Safety of the Faithful

To the Chief Musician. With stringed
instruments. A Psalm of David.

HEAR me when I call, O God of my
righteousness!
You have relieved me in *my* distress;
Have mercy on me, and hear my prayer.

2 How long, O you sons of men,
Will you turn my glory to shame?
How long will you love worthlessness
And seek falsehood? Selah
3 But know that the LORD has set apart[a] for
Himself him who is godly;
The LORD will hear when I call to Him.

4 Be angry, and do not sin.
Meditate within your heart on your bed,
and be still. Selah
5 Offer the sacrifices of righteousness,
And put your trust in the LORD.

6 *There are* many who say,
"Who will show us *any* good?"
LORD, lift up the light of Your
countenance upon us.
7 You have put gladness in my heart,
More than in the season that their grain
and wine increased.
8 I will both lie down in peace, and sleep;
For You alone, O LORD, make me dwell in
safety.

PSALM 5

A Prayer for Guidance

To the Chief Musician. With flutes.[a]
A Psalm of David.

GIVE ear to my words, O LORD,
Consider my meditation.
2 Give heed to the voice of my cry,
My King and my God,
For to You I will pray.
3 My voice You shall hear in the morning,
O LORD;
In the morning I will direct *it* to You,
And I will look up.

4 For You *are* not a God who takes pleasure
in wickedness,
Nor shall evil dwell with You.
5 The boastful shall not stand in Your sight;
You hate all workers of iniquity.
6 You shall destroy those who speak
falsehood;
The LORD abhors the bloodthirsty and
deceitful man.

7 But as for me, I will come into Your house
in the multitude of Your mercy;
In fear of You I will worship toward Your
holy temple.
8 Lead me, O LORD, in Your righteousness
because of my enemies;
Make Your way straight before my face.
9 For *there is* no faithfulness in their
mouth;
Their inward part *is* destruction;
Their throat *is* an open tomb;

2:9 [a]Following Masoretic Text and Targum; Septuagint, Syriac, and Vulgate read *rule* (compare Revelation 2:27). **2:12** [a]Septuagint and Vulgate read *Embrace discipline;* Targum reads *Receive instruction.* [b]Septuagint reads *the LORD.* **4:3** [a]Many Hebrew manuscripts, Septuagint, Targum, and Vulgate read *made wonderful.* **5:title** [a]Hebrew *nehiloth*

They flatter with their tongue.
10 Pronounce them guilty, O God!
Let them fall by their own counsels;
Cast them out in the multitude of their transgressions,
For they have rebelled against You.
11 But let all those rejoice who put their trust in You;
Let them ever shout for joy, because You defend them;
Let those also who love Your name
Be joyful in You.
12 For You, O LORD, will bless the righteous;
With favor You will surround him as *with* a shield.

PSALM 6

A Prayer of Faith in Time of Distress

To the Chief Musician. With stringed instruments. On an eight-stringed harp.[a]
A Psalm of David.

O LORD, do not rebuke me in Your anger,
Nor chasten me in Your hot displeasure.
2 Have mercy on me, O LORD, for I *am* weak;
O LORD, heal me, for my bones are troubled.
3 My soul also is greatly troubled;
But You, O LORD—how long?
4 Return, O LORD, deliver me!
Oh, save me for Your mercies' sake!
5 For in death *there is* no remembrance of You;
In the grave who will give You thanks?
6 I am weary with my groaning;
All night I make my bed swim;
I drench my couch with my tears.
7 My eye wastes away because of grief;
It grows old because of all my enemies.
8 Depart from me, all you workers of iniquity;
For the LORD has heard the voice of my weeping.
9 The LORD has heard my supplication;
The LORD will receive my prayer.
10 Let all my enemies be ashamed and greatly troubled;
Let them turn back *and* be ashamed suddenly.

PSALM 7

Prayer and Praise for Deliverance from Enemies

A Meditation[a] of David, which he sang to the LORD concerning the words of Cush, a Benjamite.

O LORD my God, in You I put my trust;
Save me from all those who persecute me;
And deliver me,
2 Lest they tear me like a lion,
Rending *me* in pieces, while *there is* none to deliver.
3 O LORD my God, if I have done this:
If there is iniquity in my hands,
4 If I have repaid evil to him who was at peace with me,
Or have plundered my enemy without cause,
5 Let the enemy pursue me and overtake *me;*
Yes, let him trample my life to the earth,
And lay my honor in the dust. Selah
6 Arise, O LORD, in Your anger;
Lift Yourself up because of the rage of my enemies;
Rise up for me[a] *to* the judgment You have commanded!
7 So the congregation of the peoples shall surround You;
For their sakes, therefore, return on high.
8 The LORD shall judge the peoples;
Judge me, O LORD, according to my righteousness,
And according to my integrity within me.
9 Oh, let the wickedness of the wicked come to an end,
But establish the just;
For the righteous God tests the hearts and minds.
10 My defense *is* of God,
Who saves the upright in heart.
11 God *is* a just judge,
And God is angry *with the wicked* every day.
12 If he does not turn back,
He will sharpen His sword;
He bends His bow and makes it ready.
13 He also prepares for Himself instruments of death;
He makes His arrows into fiery shafts.
14 Behold, *the wicked* brings forth iniquity;
Yes, he conceives trouble and brings forth falsehood.
15 He made a pit and dug it out,
And has fallen into the ditch *which* he made.
16 His trouble shall return upon his own head,
And his violent dealing shall come down on his own crown.
17 I will praise the LORD according to His righteousness,
And will sing praise to the name of the LORD Most High.

PSALM 8

The Glory of the LORD in Creation

To the Chief Musician. On the instrument of Gath.[a] A Psalm of David.

O LORD, our Lord,
How excellent *is* Your name in all the earth,
Who have set Your glory above the heavens!
2 Out of the mouth of babes and nursing infants
You have ordained strength,
Because of Your enemies,

6:title [a]Hebrew *sheminith* **7:title** [a]Hebrew *Shiggaion* **7:6** [a]Following Masoretic Text, Targum, and Vulgate; Septuagint reads *O LORD my God.* **8:title** [a]Hebrew *Al Gittith*

That You may silence the enemy and the avenger.
3 When I consider Your heavens, the work of Your fingers,
The moon and the stars, which You have ordained,
4 What is man that You are mindful of him,
And the son of man that You visit him?
5 For You have made him a little lower than the angels,[a]
And You have crowned him with glory and honor.

6 You have made him to have dominion over the works of Your hands;
You have put all *things* under his feet,
7 All sheep and oxen—
Even the beasts of the field,
8 The birds of the air,
And the fish of the sea
That pass through the paths of the seas.

9 O LORD, our Lord,
How excellent *is* Your name in all the earth!

PSALM 9

Prayer and Thanksgiving for the LORD's Righteous Judgments

To the Chief Musician. To *the tune of* "Death of the Son."[a] A Psalm of David.

I WILL praise *You,* O LORD, with my whole heart;
I will tell of all Your marvelous works.
2 I will be glad and rejoice in You;
I will sing praise to Your name, O Most High.

3 When my enemies turn back,
They shall fall and perish at Your presence.
4 For You have maintained my right and my cause;
You sat on the throne judging in righteousness.
5 You have rebuked the nations,
You have destroyed the wicked;
You have blotted out their name forever and ever.

6 O enemy, destructions are finished forever!
And you have destroyed cities;
Even their memory has perished.
7 But the LORD shall endure forever;
He has prepared His throne for judgment.
8 He shall judge the world in righteousness,
And He shall administer judgment for the peoples in uprightness.

9 The LORD also will be a refuge for the oppressed,
A refuge in times of trouble.
10 And those who know Your name will put their trust in You;
For You, LORD, have not forsaken those who seek You.

11 Sing praises to the LORD, who dwells in Zion!
Declare His deeds among the people.
12 When He avenges blood, He remembers them;
He does not forget the cry of the humble.

13 Have mercy on me, O LORD!
Consider my trouble from those who hate me,
You who lift me up from the gates of death,
14 That I may tell of all Your praise
In the gates of the daughter of Zion.
I will rejoice in Your salvation.

15 The nations have sunk down in the pit *which* they made;
In the net which they hid, their own foot is caught.
16 The LORD is known *by* the judgment He executes;
The wicked is snared in the work of his own hands.
Meditation.[a] Selah

17 The wicked shall be turned into hell,
And all the nations that forget God.
18 For the needy shall not always be forgotten;
The expectation of the poor shall *not* perish forever.

19 Arise, O LORD,
Do not let man prevail;
Let the nations be judged in Your sight.
20 Put them in fear, O LORD,
That the nations may know themselves *to be but* men. Selah

PSALM 10

A Song of Confidence in God's Triumph over Evil

WHY do You stand afar off, O LORD?
Why do You hide in times of trouble?
2 The wicked in *his* pride persecutes the poor;
Let them be caught in the plots which they have devised.

3 For the wicked boasts of his heart's desire;
He blesses the greedy *and* renounces the LORD.
4 The wicked in his proud countenance does not seek *God;*
God *is* in none of his thoughts.

5 His ways are always prospering;
Your judgments *are* far above, out of his sight;
As for all his enemies, he sneers at them.
6 He has said in his heart, "I shall not be moved;
I shall never be in adversity."
7 His mouth is full of cursing and deceit and oppression;
Under his tongue *is* trouble and iniquity.

8 He sits in the lurking places of the villages;
In the secret places he murders the innocent;
His eyes are secretly fixed on the helpless.
9 He lies in wait secretly, as a lion in his den;

8:5 [a]Hebrew *Elohim, God;* Septuagint, Syriac, Targum, and Jewish tradition translate as *angels.* **9:title** [a]Hebrew *Muth Labben* **9:16** [a]Hebrew *Higgaion*

He lies in wait to catch the poor;
He catches the poor when he draws him into his net.
10 So he crouches, he lies low,
That the helpless may fall by his strength.
11 He has said in his heart,
"God has forgotten;
He hides His face;
He will never see."

12 Arise, O LORD!
O God, lift up Your hand!
Do not forget the humble.
13 Why do the wicked renounce God?
He has said in his heart,
"You will not require *an account*."

14 But You have seen, for You observe trouble and grief,
To repay *it* by Your hand.
The helpless commits himself to You;
You are the helper of the fatherless.
15 Break the arm of the wicked and the evil *man;*
Seek out his wickedness *until* You find none.
16 The LORD *is* King forever and ever;
The nations have perished out of His land.
17 LORD, You have heard the desire of the humble;
You will prepare their heart;
You will cause Your ear to hear,
18 To do justice to the fatherless and the oppressed,
That the man of the earth may oppress no more.

PSALM 11

Faith in the LORD's Righteousness

To the Chief Musician. *A Psalm* of David.

IN the LORD I put my trust;
How can you say to my soul,
"Flee *as* a bird to your mountain"?
2 For look! The wicked bend *their* bow,
They make ready their arrow on the string,
That they may shoot secretly at the upright in heart.
3 If the foundations are destroyed,
What can the righteous do?

4 The LORD *is* in His holy temple,
The LORD's throne *is* in heaven;
His eyes behold,
His eyelids test the sons of men.
5 The LORD tests the righteous,
But the wicked and the one who loves violence His soul hates.
6 Upon the wicked He will rain coals;
Fire and brimstone and a burning wind
Shall be the portion of their cup.

7 For the LORD *is* righteous,
He loves righteousness;
His countenance beholds the upright.[a]

PSALM 12

Man's Treachery and God's Constancy

To the Chief Musician. On an eight-stringed harp.[a] A Psalm of David.

HELP, LORD, for the godly man ceases!
For the faithful disappear from among the sons of men.
2 They speak idly everyone with his neighbor;
With flattering lips *and* a double heart they speak.

3 May the LORD cut off all flattering lips,
And the tongue that speaks proud things,
4 Who have said,
"With our tongue we will prevail;
Our lips *are* our own;
Who *is* lord over us?"

5 "For the oppression of the poor, for the sighing of the needy,
Now I will arise," says the LORD;
"I will set *him* in the safety for which he yearns."

6 The words of the LORD *are* pure words,
Like silver tried in a furnace of earth,
Purified seven times.
7 You shall keep them, O LORD,
You shall preserve them from this generation forever.

8 The wicked prowl on every side,
When vileness is exalted among the sons of men.

PSALM 13

Trust in the Salvation of the LORD

To the Chief Musician. A Psalm of David.

HOW long, O LORD? Will You forget me forever?
How long will You hide Your face from me?
2 How long shall I take counsel in my soul,
Having sorrow in my heart daily?
How long will my enemy be exalted over me?

3 Consider *and* hear me, O LORD my God;
Enlighten my eyes,
Lest I sleep the *sleep of* death;
4 Lest my enemy say,
"I have prevailed against him";
Lest those who trouble me rejoice when I am moved.

5 But I have trusted in Your mercy;
My heart shall rejoice in Your salvation.
6 I will sing to the LORD,
Because He has dealt bountifully with me.

PSALM 14

Folly of the Godless, and God's Final Triumph

To the Chief Musician. *A Psalm* of David.

THE fool has said in his heart,
"*There is* no God."
They are corrupt,
They have done abominable works,
There is none who does good.

11:7 [a]Or *The upright beholds His countenance* **12:title** [a]Hebrew *sheminith*

2 The LORD looks down from heaven upon
the children of men,
To see if there are any who understand,
who seek God.
3 They have all turned aside,
They have together become corrupt;
There is none who does good,
No, not one.

4 Have all the workers of iniquity no
knowledge,
Who eat up my people *as* they eat bread,
And do not call on the LORD?
5 There they are in great fear,
For God *is* with the generation of the
righteous.
6 You shame the counsel of the poor,
But the LORD *is* his refuge.

7 Oh, that the salvation of Israel *would
come* out of Zion!
When the LORD brings back the captivity
of His people,
Let Jacob rejoice *and* Israel be glad.

PSALM 15

The Character of Those Who May Dwell with the LORD

A Psalm of David.

LORD, who may abide in Your
tabernacle?
Who may dwell in Your holy hill?

2 He who walks uprightly,
And works righteousness,
And speaks the truth in his heart;
3 He *who* does not backbite with his
tongue,
Nor does evil to his neighbor,
Nor does he take up a reproach against
his friend;
4 In whose eyes a vile person is despised,
But he honors those who fear the
LORD;
He *who* swears to his own hurt and does
not change;
5 He *who* does not put out his money at
usury,
Nor does he take a bribe against the
innocent.

He who does these *things* shall never be
moved.

PSALM 16

The Hope of the Faithful, and the Messiah's Victory

A Michtam of David.

PRESERVE me, O God, for in You I put my
trust.

2 *O my soul,* you have said to the LORD,
"You *are* my Lord,
My goodness is nothing apart from You."
3 As for the saints who *are* on the earth,
"They are the excellent ones, in whom is
all my delight."

4 Their sorrows shall be multiplied who
hasten *after* another *god;*
Their drink offerings of blood I will not
offer,
Nor take up their names on my lips.

5 O LORD, *You are* the portion of my
inheritance and my cup;
You maintain my lot.
6 The lines have fallen to me in pleasant
places;
Yes, I have a good inheritance.

7 I will bless the LORD who has given me
counsel;
My heart also instructs me in the night
seasons.
8 I have set the LORD always before me;
Because *He is* at my right hand I shall not
be moved.

9 Therefore my heart is glad, and my glory
rejoices;
My flesh also will rest in hope.
10 For You will not leave my soul in Sheol,
Nor will You allow Your Holy One to see
corruption.
11 You will show me the path of life;
In Your presence *is* fullness of joy;
At Your right hand *are* pleasures
forevermore.

PSALM 17

Prayer with Confidence in Final Salvation

A Prayer of David.

HEAR a just cause, O LORD,
Attend to my cry;
Give ear to my prayer *which is* not from
deceitful lips.
2 Let my vindication come from Your
presence;
Let Your eyes look on the things that are
upright.

3 You have tested my heart;
You have visited *me* in the night;
You have tried me and have found
nothing;
I have purposed that my mouth shall not
transgress.
4 Concerning the works of men,
By the word of Your lips,
I have kept away from the paths of the
destroyer.
5 Uphold my steps in Your paths,
That my footsteps may not slip.

6 I have called upon You, for You will hear
me, O God;
Incline Your ear to me, *and* hear my
speech.
7 Show Your marvelous lovingkindness by
Your right hand,
O You who save those who trust *in You*
From those who rise up *against them.*
8 Keep me as the apple of Your eye;
Hide me under the shadow of Your
wings,
9 From the wicked who oppress me,
From my deadly enemies who surround
me.

10 They have closed up their fat *hearts;*
With their mouths they speak proudly.
11 They have now surrounded us in our
steps;
They have set their eyes, crouching down
to the earth,
12 As a lion is eager to tear his prey,
And like a young lion lurking in secret
places.

13 Arise, O LORD,
Confront him, cast him down;
Deliver my life from the wicked with
Your sword,
14 With Your hand from men, O LORD,
From men of the world *who have* their
portion in *this* life,
And whose belly You fill with Your
hidden treasure.
They are satisfied with children,
And leave the rest of their *possession* for
their babes.

15 As for me, I will see Your face in
righteousness;
I shall be satisfied when I awake in Your
likeness.

PSALM 18

God the Sovereign Savior

To the Chief Musician. *A Psalm* of David the servant of the LORD, who spoke to the LORD the words of this song on the day that the LORD delivered him from the hand of all his enemies and from the hand of Saul. And he said:

I WILL love You, O LORD, my
strength.
2 The LORD is my rock and my fortress and
my deliverer;
My God, my strength, in whom I will
trust;
My shield and the horn of my salvation,
my stronghold.
3 I will call upon the LORD, *who is worthy*
to be praised;
So shall I be saved from my enemies.

4 The pangs of death surrounded me,
And the floods of ungodliness made me
afraid.
5 The sorrows of Sheol surrounded me;
The snares of death confronted me.
6 In my distress I called upon the LORD,
And cried out to my God;
He heard my voice from His temple,
And my cry came before Him, *even* to His
ears.

7 Then the earth shook and trembled;
The foundations of the hills also quaked
and were shaken,
Because He was angry.
8 Smoke went up from His nostrils,
And devouring fire from His mouth;
Coals were kindled by it.
9 He bowed the heavens also, and came
down
With darkness under His feet.
10 And He rode upon a cherub, and flew;
He flew upon the wings of the wind.
11 He made darkness His secret place;
His canopy around Him *was* dark waters
And thick clouds of the skies.
12 From the brightness before Him,
His thick clouds passed with hailstones
and coals of fire.

13 The LORD thundered from heaven,
And the Most High uttered His voice,
Hailstones and coals of fire.[a]
14 He sent out His arrows and scattered the
foe,
Lightnings in abundance, and He
vanquished them.
15 Then the channels of the sea were seen,
The foundations of the world were
uncovered
At Your rebuke, O LORD,
At the blast of the breath of Your nostrils.

16 He sent from above, He took me;
He drew me out of many waters.
17 He delivered me from my strong enemy,
From those who hated me,
For they were too strong for me.
18 They confronted me in the day of my
calamity,
But the LORD was my support.
19 He also brought me out into a broad
place;
He delivered me because He delighted in
me.

20 The LORD rewarded me according to my
righteousness;
According to the cleanness of my hands
He has recompensed me.
21 For I have kept the ways of the LORD,
And have not wickedly departed from my
God.
22 For all His judgments *were* before me,
And I did not put away His statutes from
me.
23 I was also blameless before Him,
And I kept myself from my iniquity.
24 Therefore the LORD has recompensed me
according to my righteousness,
According to the cleanness of my hands
in His sight.

25 With the merciful You will show Yourself
merciful;
With a blameless man You will show
Yourself blameless;
26 With the pure You will show Yourself
pure;
And with the devious You will show
Yourself shrewd.
27 For You will save the humble people,
But will bring down haughty looks.
28 For You will light my lamp;
The LORD my God will enlighten my
darkness.
29 For by You I can run against a troop,
By my God I can leap over a wall.
30 *As for* God, His way *is* perfect;
The word of the LORD is proven;
He *is* a shield to all who trust in Him.

31 For who *is* God, except the LORD?
And who *is* a rock, except our God?
32 *It is* God who arms me with strength,
And makes my way perfect.
33 He makes my feet like the *feet of* deer,
And sets me on my high places.
34 He teaches my hands to make war,
So that my arms can bend a bow of
bronze.

35 You have also given me the shield of Your
salvation;
Your right hand has held me up,
Your gentleness has made me great.

18:13 [a]Following Masoretic Text, Targum, and Vulgate; a few Hebrew manuscripts and Septuagint omit *Hailstones and coals of fire.*

36 You enlarged my path under me,
So my feet did not slip.

37 I have pursued my enemies and overtaken them;
Neither did I turn back again till they were destroyed.
38 I have wounded them,
So that they could not rise;
They have fallen under my feet.
39 For You have armed me with strength for the battle;
You have subdued under me those who rose up against me.
40 You have also given me the necks of my enemies,
So that I destroyed those who hated me.
41 They cried out, but *there was* none to save;
Even to the LORD, but He did not answer them.
42 Then I beat them as fine as the dust before the wind;
I cast them out like dirt in the streets.

43 You have delivered me from the strivings of the people;
You have made me the head of the nations;
A people I have not known shall serve me.
44 As soon as they hear of me they obey me;
The foreigners submit to me.
45 The foreigners fade away,
And come frightened from their hideouts.

46 The LORD lives!
Blessed *be* my Rock!
Let the God of my salvation be exalted.
47 *It is* God who avenges me,
And subdues the peoples under me;
48 He delivers me from my enemies.
You also lift me up above those who rise against me;
You have delivered me from the violent man.
49 Therefore I will give thanks to You,
O LORD, among the Gentiles,
And sing praises to Your name.

50 Great deliverance He gives to His king,
And shows mercy to His anointed,
To David and his descendants forevermore.

PSALM 19

The Perfect Revelation of the LORD

To the Chief Musician. A Psalm of David.

THE heavens declare the glory of God;
And the firmament shows His handiwork.
2 Day unto day utters speech,
And night unto night reveals knowledge.
3 *There is* no speech nor language
Where their voice is not heard.
4 Their line[a] has gone out through all the earth,
And their words to the end of the world.

In them He has set a tabernacle for the sun,
5 Which *is* like a bridegroom coming out of his chamber,
And rejoices like a strong man to run its race.
6 Its rising *is* from one end of heaven,
And its circuit to the other end;
And there is nothing hidden from its heat.

7 The law of the LORD *is* perfect, converting the soul;
The testimony of the LORD *is* sure, making wise the simple;
8 The statutes of the LORD *are* right, rejoicing the heart;
The commandment of the LORD *is* pure, enlightening the eyes;
9 The fear of the LORD *is* clean, enduring forever;
The judgments of the LORD *are* true *and* righteous altogether.
10 More to be desired *are they* than gold,
Yea, than much fine gold;
Sweeter also than honey and the honeycomb.
11 Moreover by them Your servant is warned,
And in keeping them *there is* great reward.

12 Who can understand *his* errors?
Cleanse me from secret *faults*.
13 Keep back Your servant also from presumptuous *sins;*
Let them not have dominion over me.
Then I shall be blameless,
And I shall be innocent of great transgression.

14 Let the words of my mouth and the meditation of my heart
Be acceptable in Your sight,
O LORD, my strength and my Redeemer.

PSALM 20

The Assurance of God's Saving Work

To the Chief Musician. A Psalm of David.

MAY the LORD answer you in the day of trouble;
May the name of the God of Jacob defend you;
2 May He send you help from the sanctuary,
And strengthen you out of Zion;
3 May He remember all your offerings,
And accept your burnt sacrifice. Selah

4 May He grant you according to your heart's *desire*,
And fulfill all your purpose.
5 We will rejoice in your salvation,
And in the name of our God we will set up *our* banners!
May the LORD fulfill all your petitions.

6 Now I know that the LORD saves His anointed;
He will answer him from His holy heaven
With the saving strength of His right hand.

7 Some *trust* in chariots, and some in horses;
But we will remember the name of the LORD our God.

19:4 [a]Septuagint, Syriac, and Vulgate read *sound;* Targum reads *business.*

8 They have bowed down and fallen;
But we have risen and stand upright.

9 Save, LORD!
May the King answer us when we call.

PSALM 21

Joy in the Salvation of the LORD

To the Chief Musician. A Psalm of David.

THE king shall have joy in Your strength, O LORD;
And in Your salvation how greatly shall he rejoice!
2 You have given him his heart's desire,
And have not withheld the request of his lips. Selah

3 For You meet him with the blessings of goodness;
You set a crown of pure gold upon his head.
4 He asked life from You, *and* You gave *it* to him—
Length of days forever and ever.
5 His glory *is* great in Your salvation;
Honor and majesty You have placed upon him.
6 For You have made him most blessed forever;
You have made him exceedingly glad with Your presence.
7 For the king trusts in the LORD,
And through the mercy of the Most High he shall not be moved.

8 Your hand will find all Your enemies;
Your right hand will find those who hate You.
9 You shall make them as a fiery oven in the time of Your anger;
The LORD shall swallow them up in His wrath,
And the fire shall devour them.
10 Their offspring You shall destroy from the earth,
And their descendants from among the sons of men.
11 For they intended evil against You;
They devised a plot *which* they are not able *to perform.*
12 Therefore You will make them turn their back;
You will make ready *Your arrows* on Your string toward their faces.

13 Be exalted, O LORD, in Your own strength!
We will sing and praise Your power.

PSALM 22

The Suffering, Praise, and Posterity of the Messiah

To the Chief Musician. Set to "The Deer of the Dawn."[a] A Psalm of David.

MY God, My God, why have You forsaken Me?
Why are You so far from helping Me,
And from the words of My groaning?
2 O My God, I cry in the daytime, but You do not hear;
And in the night season, and am not silent.

3 But You *are* holy,
Enthroned in the praises of Israel.
4 Our fathers trusted in You;
They trusted, and You delivered them.
5 They cried to You, and were delivered;
They trusted in You, and were not ashamed.

6 But I *am* a worm, and no man;
A reproach of men, and despised by the people.
7 All those who see Me ridicule Me;
They shoot out the lip, they shake the head, *saying,*
8 "He trusted[a] in the LORD, let Him rescue Him;
Let Him deliver Him, since He delights in Him!"

9 But You *are* He who took Me out of the womb;
You made Me trust *while* on My mother's breasts.
10 I was cast upon You from birth.
From My mother's womb
You *have been* My God.
11 Be not far from Me,
For trouble *is* near;
For *there is* none to help.

12 Many bulls have surrounded Me;
Strong *bulls* of Bashan have encircled Me.
13 They gape at Me *with* their mouths,
Like a raging and roaring lion.

14 I am poured out like water,
And all My bones are out of joint;
My heart is like wax;
It has melted within Me.
15 My strength is dried up like a potsherd,
And My tongue clings to My jaws;
You have brought Me to the dust of death.

16 For dogs have surrounded Me;
The congregation of the wicked has enclosed Me.
They pierced[a] My hands and My feet;
17 I can count all My bones.
They look *and* stare at Me.
18 They divide My garments among them,
And for My clothing they cast lots.

19 But You, O LORD, do not be far from Me;
O My Strength, hasten to help Me!
20 Deliver Me from the sword,
My precious *life* from the power of the dog.
21 Save Me from the lion's mouth
And from the horns of the wild oxen!

You have answered Me.

22 I will declare Your name to My brethren;
In the midst of the assembly I will praise You.
23 You who fear the LORD, praise Him!
All you descendants of Jacob, glorify Him,
And fear Him, all you offspring of Israel!
24 For He has not despised nor abhorred the affliction of the afflicted;

22:title [a]Hebrew *Aijeleth Hashahar* **22:8** [a]Septuagint, Syriac, and Vulgate read *hoped;* Targum reads *praised.* **22:16** [a]Following some Hebrew manuscripts, Septuagint, Syriac, Vulgate; Masoretic Text reads *Like a lion.*

Nor has He hidden His face from Him;
But when He cried to Him, He heard.

25 My praise *shall be* of You in the great assembly;
I will pay My vows before those who fear Him.
26 The poor shall eat and be satisfied;
Those who seek Him will praise the LORD.
Let your heart live forever!

27 All the ends of the world
Shall remember and turn to the LORD,
And all the families of the nations
Shall worship before You.[a]
28 For the kingdom *is* the LORD's,
And He rules over the nations.

29 All the prosperous of the earth
Shall eat and worship;
All those who go down to the dust
Shall bow before Him,
Even he who cannot keep himself alive.
30 A posterity shall serve Him.
It will be recounted of the Lord to the *next* generation,
31 They will come and declare His righteousness to a people who will be born,
That He has done *this*.

PSALM 23

The LORD the Shepherd of His People

A Psalm of David.

THE LORD *is* my shepherd;
I shall not want.
2 He makes me to lie down in green pastures;
He leads me beside the still waters.
3 He restores my soul;
He leads me in the paths of righteousness
For His name's sake.

4 Yea, though I walk through the valley of the shadow of death,
I will fear no evil;
For You *are* with me;
Your rod and Your staff, they comfort me.

5 You prepare a table before me in the presence of my enemies;
You anoint my head with oil;
My cup runs over.
6 Surely goodness and mercy shall follow me
All the days of my life;
And I will dwell[a] in the house of the LORD
Forever.

PSALM 24

The King of Glory and His Kingdom

A Psalm of David.

THE earth *is* the LORD's, and all its fullness,
The world and those who dwell therein.
2 For He has founded it upon the seas,
And established it upon the waters.

3 Who may ascend into the hill of the LORD?
Or who may stand in His holy place?
4 He who has clean hands and a pure heart,
Who has not lifted up his soul to an idol,
Nor sworn deceitfully.
5 He shall receive blessing from the LORD,
And righteousness from the God of his salvation.
6 This *is* Jacob, the generation of those who seek Him,
Who seek Your face. Selah

7 Lift up your heads, O you gates!
And be lifted up, you everlasting doors!
And the King of glory shall come in.
8 Who *is* this King of glory?
The LORD strong and mighty,
The LORD mighty in battle.
9 Lift up your heads, O you gates!
Lift up, you everlasting doors!
And the King of glory shall come in.
10 Who is this King of glory?
The LORD of hosts,
He *is* the King of glory. Selah

PSALM 25

A Plea for Deliverance and Forgiveness

A *Psalm* of David.

TO You, O LORD, I lift up my soul.
2 O my God, I trust in You;
Let me not be ashamed;
Let not my enemies triumph over me.
3 Indeed, let no one who waits on You be ashamed;
Let those be ashamed who deal treacherously without cause.

4 Show me Your ways, O LORD;
Teach me Your paths.
5 Lead me in Your truth and teach me,
For You *are* the God of my salvation;
On You I wait all the day.

6 Remember, O LORD, Your tender mercies and Your lovingkindnesses,
For they *are* from of old.
7 Do not remember the sins of my youth, nor my transgressions;
According to Your mercy remember me,
For Your goodness' sake, O LORD.

8 Good and upright *is* the LORD;
Therefore He teaches sinners in the way.
9 The humble He guides in justice,
And the humble He teaches His way.
10 All the paths of the LORD *are* mercy and truth,
To such as keep His covenant and His testimonies.
11 For Your name's sake, O LORD,
Pardon my iniquity, for it *is* great.

12 Who *is* the man that fears the LORD?
Him shall He[a] teach in the way He[b] chooses.
13 He himself shall dwell in prosperity,
And his descendants shall inherit the earth.
14 The secret of the LORD *is* with those who fear Him,

22:27 [a]Following Masoretic Text, Septuagint, and Targum; Arabic, Syriac, and Vulgate read *Him*. **23:6** [a]Following Septuagint, Syriac, Targum, and Vulgate; Masoretic Text reads *return*. **25:12** [a]Or *he* [b]Or *he*

And He will show them His covenant.
15 My eyes *are* ever toward the LORD,
For He shall pluck my feet out of the net.

16 Turn Yourself to me, and have mercy on me,
For I *am* desolate and afflicted.
17 The troubles of my heart have enlarged;
Bring me out of my distresses!
18 Look on my affliction and my pain,
And forgive all my sins.
19 Consider my enemies, for they are many;
And they hate me with cruel hatred.
20 Keep my soul, and deliver me;
Let me not be ashamed, for I put my trust in You.
21 Let integrity and uprightness preserve me,
For I wait for You.

22 Redeem Israel, O God,
Out of all their troubles!

PSALM 26

A Prayer for Divine Scrutiny and Redemption

A Psalm of David.

VINDICATE me, O LORD,
For I have walked in my integrity.
I have also trusted in the LORD;
I shall not slip.
2 Examine me, O LORD, and prove me;
Try my mind and my heart.
3 For Your lovingkindness *is* before my eyes,
And I have walked in Your truth.
4 I have not sat with idolatrous mortals,
Nor will I go in with hypocrites.
5 I have hated the assembly of evildoers,
And will not sit with the wicked.

6 I will wash my hands in innocence;
So I will go about Your altar, O LORD,
7 That I may proclaim with the voice of thanksgiving,
And tell of all Your wondrous works.
8 LORD, I have loved the habitation of Your house,
And the place where Your glory dwells.

9 Do not gather my soul with sinners,
Nor my life with bloodthirsty men,
10 In whose hands *is* a sinister scheme,
And whose right hand is full of bribes.

11 But as for me, I will walk in my integrity;
Redeem me and be merciful to me.
12 My foot stands in an even place;
In the congregations I will bless the LORD.

PSALM 27

An Exuberant Declaration of Faith

A Psalm of David.

THE LORD *is* my light and my salvation;
Whom shall I fear?
The LORD *is* the strength of my life;
Of whom shall I be afraid?
2 When the wicked came against me
To eat up my flesh,
My enemies and foes,
They stumbled and fell.
3 Though an army may encamp against me,
My heart shall not fear;
Though war may rise against me,
In this I *will be* confident.

4 One *thing* I have desired of the LORD,
That will I seek:
That I may dwell in the house of the LORD
All the days of my life,
To behold the beauty of the LORD,
And to inquire in His temple.
5 For in the time of trouble
He shall hide me in His pavilion;
In the secret place of His tabernacle
He shall hide me;
He shall set me high upon a rock.

6 And now my head shall be lifted up above my enemies all around me;
Therefore I will offer sacrifices of joy in His tabernacle;
I will sing, yes, I will sing praises to the LORD.

7 Hear, O LORD, *when* I cry with my voice!
Have mercy also upon me, and answer me.
8 *When You said,* "Seek My face,"
My heart said to You, "Your face, LORD, I will seek."
9 Do not hide Your face from me;
Do not turn Your servant away in anger;
You have been my help;
Do not leave me nor forsake me,
O God of my salvation.
10 When my father and my mother forsake me,
Then the LORD will take care of me.

11 Teach me Your way, O LORD,
And lead me in a smooth path, because of my enemies.
12 Do not deliver me to the will of my adversaries;
For false witnesses have risen against me,
And such as breathe out violence.
13 *I would have lost heart,* unless I had believed
That I would see the goodness of the LORD
In the land of the living.
14 Wait on the LORD;
Be of good courage,
And He shall strengthen your heart;
Wait, I say, on the LORD!

PSALM 28

Rejoicing in Answered Prayer

A Psalm of David.

TO You I will cry, O LORD my Rock:
Do not be silent to me,
Lest, if You *are* silent to me,
I become like those who go down to the pit.
2 Hear the voice of my supplications
When I cry to You,
When I lift up my hands toward Your holy sanctuary.

3 Do not take me away with the wicked
And with the workers of iniquity,
Who speak peace to their neighbors,
But evil *is* in their hearts.

4 Give them according to their deeds,
And according to the wickedness of their endeavors;
Give them according to the work of their hands;
Render to them what they deserve.
5 Because they do not regard the works of the LORD,
Nor the operation of His hands,
He shall destroy them
And not build them up.

6 Blessed *be* the LORD,
Because He has heard the voice of my supplications!
7 The LORD *is* my strength and my shield;
My heart trusted in Him, and I am helped;
Therefore my heart greatly rejoices,
And with my song I will praise Him.

8 The LORD *is* their strength,[a]
And He *is* the saving refuge of His anointed.
9 Save Your people,
And bless Your inheritance;
Shepherd them also,
And bear them up forever.

PSALM 29

Praise to God in His Holiness and Majesty

A Psalm of David.

GIVE unto the LORD, O you mighty ones,
Give unto the LORD glory and strength.
2 Give unto the LORD the glory due to His name;
Worship the LORD in the beauty of holiness.

3 The voice of the LORD *is* over the waters;
The God of glory thunders;
The LORD *is* over many waters.
4 The voice of the LORD *is* powerful;
The voice of the LORD *is* full of majesty.

5 The voice of the LORD breaks the cedars,
Yes, the LORD splinters the cedars of Lebanon.
6 He makes them also skip like a calf,
Lebanon and Sirion like a young wild ox.
7 The voice of the LORD divides the flames of fire.

8 The voice of the LORD shakes the wilderness;
The LORD shakes the Wilderness of Kadesh.
9 The voice of the LORD makes the deer give birth,
And strips the forests bare;
And in His temple everyone says, "Glory!"

10 The LORD sat *enthroned* at the Flood,
And the LORD sits as King forever.
11 The LORD will give strength to His people;
The LORD will bless His people with peace.

PSALM 30

The Blessedness of Answered Prayer

A Psalm. A Song at the dedication of the house of David.

I WILL extol You, O LORD, for You have lifted me up,
And have not let my foes rejoice over me.
2 O LORD my God, I cried out to You,
And You healed me.
3 O LORD, You brought my soul up from the grave;
You have kept me alive, that I should not go down to the pit.[a]

4 Sing praise to the LORD, you saints of His,
And give thanks at the remembrance of His holy name.[a]
5 For His anger *is but for* a moment,
His favor *is for* life;
Weeping may endure for a night,
But joy *comes* in the morning.

6 Now in my prosperity I said,
"I shall never be moved."
7 LORD, by Your favor You have made my mountain stand strong;
You hid Your face, *and* I was troubled.

8 I cried out to You, O LORD;
And to the LORD I made supplication:
9 "What profit *is there* in my blood,
When I go down to the pit?
Will the dust praise You?
Will it declare Your truth?
10 Hear, O LORD, and have mercy on me;
LORD, be my helper!"

11 You have turned for me my mourning into dancing;
You have put off my sackcloth and clothed me with gladness,
12 To the end that *my* glory may sing praise to You and not be silent.
O LORD my God, I will give thanks to You forever.

PSALM 31

The LORD a Fortress in Adversity

To the Chief Musician. A Psalm of David.

IN You, O LORD, I put my trust;
Let me never be ashamed;
Deliver me in Your righteousness.
2 Bow down Your ear to me,
Deliver me speedily;
Be my rock of refuge,
A fortress of defense to save me.

3 For You *are* my rock and my fortress;
Therefore, for Your name's sake,
Lead me and guide me.
4 Pull me out of the net which they have secretly laid for me,
For You *are* my strength.
5 Into Your hand I commit my spirit;
You have redeemed me, O LORD God of truth.

6 I have hated those who regard useless idols;
But I trust in the LORD.

28:8 [a]Following Masoretic Text and Targum; Septuagint, Syriac, and Vulgate read *the strength of His people.*
30:3 [a]Following Qere and Targum; Kethib, Septuagint, Syriac, and Vulgate read *from those who descend to the pit.*
30:4 [a]Or *His holiness*

7 I will be glad and rejoice in Your mercy,
For You have considered my trouble;
You have known my soul in adversities,
8 And have not shut me up into the hand of the enemy;
You have set my feet in a wide place.

9 Have mercy on me, O LORD, for I am in trouble;
My eye wastes away with grief,
Yes, my soul and my body!
10 For my life is spent with grief,
And my years with sighing;
My strength fails because of my iniquity,
And my bones waste away.
11 I am a reproach among all my enemies,
But especially among my neighbors,
And *am* repulsive to my acquaintances;
Those who see me outside flee from me.
12 I am forgotten like a dead man, out of mind;
I am like a broken vessel.
13 For I hear the slander of many;
Fear *is* on every side;
While they take counsel together against me,
They scheme to take away my life.

14 But as for me, I trust in You, O LORD;
I say, "You *are* my God."
15 My times *are* in Your hand;
Deliver me from the hand of my enemies,
And from those who persecute me.
16 Make Your face shine upon Your servant;
Save me for Your mercies' sake.
17 Do not let me be ashamed, O LORD, for I have called upon You;
Let the wicked be ashamed;
Let them be silent in the grave.
18 Let the lying lips be put to silence,
Which speak insolent things proudly and contemptuously against the righteous.

19 Oh, how great *is* Your goodness,
Which You have laid up for those who fear You,
Which You have prepared for those who trust in You
In the presence of the sons of men!
20 You shall hide them in the secret place of Your presence
From the plots of man;
You shall keep them secretly in a pavilion
From the strife of tongues.

21 Blessed *be* the LORD,
For He has shown me His marvelous kindness in a strong city!
22 For I said in my haste,
"I am cut off from before Your eyes";
Nevertheless You heard the voice of my supplications
When I cried out to You.

23 Oh, love the LORD, all you His saints!
For the LORD preserves the faithful,
And fully repays the proud person.
24 Be of good courage,
And He shall strengthen your heart,
All you who hope in the LORD.

PSALM 32

The Joy of Forgiveness

A Psalm of David. A Contemplation.[a]

BLESSED *is he whose* transgression *is* forgiven,
Whose sin *is* covered.
2 Blessed *is* the man to whom the LORD does not impute iniquity,
And in whose spirit *there is* no deceit.

3 When I kept silent, my bones grew old
Through my groaning all the day long.
4 For day and night Your hand was heavy upon me;
My vitality was turned into the drought of summer. Selah
5 I acknowledged my sin to You,
And my iniquity I have not hidden.
I said, "I will confess my transgressions to the LORD,"
And You forgave the iniquity of my sin. Selah

6 For this cause everyone who is godly shall pray to You
In a time when You may be found;
Surely in a flood of great waters
They shall not come near him.
7 You *are* my hiding place;
You shall preserve me from trouble;
You shall surround me with songs of deliverance. Selah

8 I will instruct you and teach you in the way you should go;
I will guide you with My eye.
9 Do not be like the horse *or* like the mule,
Which have no understanding,
Which must be harnessed with bit and bridle,
Else they will not come near you.

10 Many sorrows *shall be* to the wicked;
But he who trusts in the LORD, mercy shall surround him.
11 Be glad in the LORD and rejoice, you righteous;
And shout for joy, all *you* upright in heart!

PSALM 33

The Sovereignty of the LORD in Creation and History

REJOICE in the LORD, O you righteous!
For praise from the upright is beautiful.
2 Praise the LORD with the harp;
Make melody to Him with an instrument of ten strings.
3 Sing to Him a new song;
Play skillfully with a shout of joy.

4 For the word of the LORD *is* right,
And all His work *is done* in truth.
5 He loves righteousness and justice;
The earth is full of the goodness of the LORD.

6 By the word of the LORD the heavens were made,
And all the host of them by the breath of His mouth.

32:title [a]Hebrew *Maschil*

7 He gathers the waters of the sea together
as a heap;[a]
He lays up the deep in storehouses.

8 Let all the earth fear the LORD;
Let all the inhabitants of the world stand
in awe of Him.
9 For He spoke, and it was *done;*
He commanded, and it stood fast.

10 The LORD brings the counsel of the
nations to nothing;
He makes the plans of the peoples of no
effect.
11 The counsel of the LORD stands forever,
The plans of His heart to all generations.
12 Blessed *is* the nation whose God *is* the
LORD,
The people He has chosen as His own
inheritance.

13 The LORD looks from heaven;
He sees all the sons of men.
14 From the place of His dwelling He looks
On all the inhabitants of the earth;
15 He fashions their hearts individually;
He considers all their works.

16 No king *is* saved by the multitude of an
army;
A mighty man is not delivered by great
strength.
17 A horse *is* a vain hope for safety;
Neither shall it deliver *any* by its great
strength.

18 Behold, the eye of the LORD *is* on those
who fear Him,
On those who hope in His mercy,
19 To deliver their soul from death,
And to keep them alive in famine.

20 Our soul waits for the LORD;
He *is* our help and our shield.
21 For our heart shall rejoice in Him,
Because we have trusted in His holy
name.
22 Let Your mercy, O LORD, be upon us,
Just as we hope in You.

PSALM 34

The Happiness of Those Who Trust in God

A Psalm of David when he pretended madness before Abimelech, who drove him away, and he departed.

I WILL bless the LORD at all times;
His praise *shall* continually *be* in my
mouth.
2 My soul shall make its boast in the LORD;
The humble shall hear *of it* and be glad.
3 Oh, magnify the LORD with me,
And let us exalt His name together.

4 I sought the LORD, and He heard me,
And delivered me from all my fears.
5 They looked to Him and were radiant,
And their faces were not ashamed.
6 This poor man cried out, and the LORD
heard *him,*
And saved him out of all his troubles.
7 The angel[a] of the LORD encamps all
around those who fear Him,
And delivers them.

8 Oh, taste and see that the LORD *is* good;
Blessed *is* the man *who* trusts in Him!
9 Oh, fear the LORD, you His saints!
There is no want to those who fear Him.
10 The young lions lack and suffer hunger;
But those who seek the LORD shall not
lack any good *thing.*

11 Come, you children, listen to me;
I will teach you the fear of the LORD.
12 Who *is* the man *who* desires life,
And loves *many* days, that he may see
good?
13 Keep your tongue from evil,
And your lips from speaking deceit.
14 Depart from evil and do good;
Seek peace and pursue it.

15 The eyes of the LORD *are* on the
righteous,
And His ears *are open* to their cry.
16 The face of the LORD *is* against those
who do evil,
To cut off the remembrance of them from
the earth.

17 *The righteous* cry out, and the LORD
hears,
And delivers them out of all their
troubles.
18 The LORD *is* near to those who have a
broken heart,
And saves such as have a contrite spirit.

19 Many *are* the afflictions of the righteous,
But the LORD delivers him out of them
all.
20 He guards all his bones;
Not one of them is broken.
21 Evil shall slay the wicked,
And those who hate the righteous shall
be condemned.
22 The LORD redeems the soul of His
servants,
And none of those who trust in Him shall
be condemned.

PSALM 35

The LORD the Avenger of His People

A Psalm of David.

PLEAD *my cause,* O LORD, with those who
strive with me;
Fight against those who fight against me.
2 Take hold of shield and buckler,
And stand up for my help.
3 Also draw out the spear,
And stop those who pursue me.
Say to my soul,
"I *am* your salvation."

4 Let those be put to shame and brought to
dishonor
Who seek after my life;
Let those be turned back and brought to
confusion
Who plot my hurt.
5 Let them be like chaff before the wind,
And let the angel[a] of the LORD chase
them.
6 Let their way be dark and slippery,
And let the angel of the LORD pursue
them.
7 For without cause they have hidden their
net for me *in* a pit,

33:7 [a]Septuagint, Targum, and Vulgate read *in a vessel.* 34:7 [a]Or *Angel* 35:5 [a]Or *Angel*

Which they have dug without cause for
my life.
8 Let destruction come upon him
unexpectedly,
And let his net that he has hidden catch
himself;
Into that very destruction let him fall.
9 And my soul shall be joyful in the LORD;
It shall rejoice in His salvation.
10 All my bones shall say,
"LORD, who *is* like You,
Delivering the poor from him who is too
strong for him,
Yes, the poor and the needy from him
who plunders him?"
11 Fierce witnesses rise up;
They ask me *things* that I do not know.
12 They reward me evil for good,
To the sorrow of my soul.
13 But as for me, when they were sick,
My clothing *was* sackcloth;
I humbled myself with fasting;
And my prayer would return to my own
heart.
14 I paced about as though *he were* my
friend *or* brother;
I bowed down heavily, as one who
mourns *for his* mother.
15 But in my adversity they rejoiced
And gathered together;
Attackers gathered against me,
And I did not know *it;*
They tore *at me* and did not cease;
16 With ungodly mockers at feasts
They gnashed at me with their teeth.
17 Lord, how long will You look on?
Rescue me from their destructions,
My precious *life* from the lions.
18 I will give You thanks in the great
assembly;
I will praise You among many people.
19 Let them not rejoice over me who are
wrongfully my enemies;
Nor let them wink with the eye who hate
me without a cause.
20 For they do not speak peace,
But they devise deceitful matters
Against *the* quiet ones in the land.
21 They also opened their mouth wide
against me,
And said, "Aha, aha!
Our eyes have seen *it.*"
22 *This* You have seen, O LORD;
Do not keep silence.
O Lord, do not be far from me.
23 Stir up Yourself, and awake to my
vindication,
To my cause, my God and my Lord.
24 Vindicate me, O LORD my God, according
to Your righteousness;
And let them not rejoice over me.
25 Let them not say in their hearts, "Ah, so
we would have it!"
Let them not say, "We have swallowed
him up."
26 Let them be ashamed and brought to
mutual confusion
Who rejoice at my hurt;
Let them be clothed with shame and
dishonor
Who exalt themselves against me.
27 Let them shout for joy and be glad,
Who favor my righteous cause;
And let them say continually,
"Let the LORD be magnified,
Who has pleasure in the prosperity of His
servant."
28 And my tongue shall speak of Your
righteousness
And of Your praise all the day long.

PSALM 36

Man's Wickedness and God's Perfections

To the Chief Musician. *A Psalm* of David the
servant of the LORD.

AN oracle within my heart concerning the
transgression of the wicked:
There is no fear of God before his eyes.
2 For he flatters himself in his own eyes,
When he finds out his iniquity *and* when
he hates.
3 The words of his mouth *are* wickedness
and deceit;
He has ceased to be wise *and* to do good.
4 He devises wickedness on his bed;
He sets himself in a way *that is* not good;
He does not abhor evil.
5 Your mercy, O LORD, *is* in the heavens;
Your faithfulness *reaches* to the clouds.
6 Your righteousness *is* like the great
mountains;
Your judgments *are* a great deep;
O LORD, You preserve man and beast.
7 How precious *is* Your lovingkindness,
O God!
Therefore the children of men put their
trust under the shadow of Your wings.
8 They are abundantly satisfied with the
fullness of Your house,
And You give them drink from the river
of Your pleasures.
9 For with You *is* the fountain of life;
In Your light we see light.
10 Oh, continue Your lovingkindness to
those who know You,
And Your righteousness to the upright in
heart.
11 Let not the foot of pride come against me,
And let not the hand of the wicked drive
me away.
12 There the workers of iniquity have fallen;
They have been cast down and are not
able to rise.

PSALM 37

The Heritage of the Righteous and the Calamity of the Wicked

A Psalm of David.

DO not fret because of evildoers,
Nor be envious of the workers of
iniquity.
2 For they shall soon be cut down like the
grass,
And wither as the green herb.
3 Trust in the LORD, and do good;
Dwell in the land, and feed on His
faithfulness.
4 Delight yourself also in the LORD,
And He shall give you the desires of your
heart.

5 Commit your way to the LORD,
Trust also in Him,
And He shall bring *it* to pass.
6 He shall bring forth your righteousness
as the light,
And your justice as the noonday.

7 Rest in the LORD, and wait patiently for
Him;
Do not fret because of him who prospers
in his way,
Because of the man who brings wicked
schemes to pass.
8 Cease from anger, and forsake wrath;
Do not fret—*it* only *causes* harm.

9 For evildoers shall be cut off;
But those who wait on the LORD,
They shall inherit the earth.
10 For yet a little while and the wicked *shall
be* no *more;*
Indeed, you will look carefully for his
place,
But it *shall be* no *more.*
11 But the meek shall inherit the earth,
And shall delight themselves in the
abundance of peace.

12 The wicked plots against the just,
And gnashes at him with his teeth.
13 The Lord laughs at him,
For He sees that his day is coming.
14 The wicked have drawn the sword
And have bent their bow,
To cast down the poor and needy,
To slay those who are of upright conduct.
15 Their sword shall enter their own heart,
And their bows shall be broken.

16 A little that a righteous man has
Is better than the riches of many wicked.
17 For the arms of the wicked shall be
broken,
But the LORD upholds the righteous.

18 The LORD knows the days of the upright,
And their inheritance shall be forever.
19 They shall not be ashamed in the evil
time,
And in the days of famine they shall be
satisfied.
20 But the wicked shall perish;
And the enemies of the LORD,
Like the splendor of the meadows, shall
vanish.
Into smoke they shall vanish away.

21 The wicked borrows and does not repay,
But the righteous shows mercy and gives.
22 For *those* blessed by Him shall inherit the
earth,
But *those* cursed by Him shall be cut off.

23 The steps of a *good* man are ordered by
the LORD,
And He delights in his way.
24 Though he fall, he shall not be utterly
cast down;
For the LORD upholds *him with* His hand.

25 I have been young, and *now* am old;
Yet I have not seen the righteous
forsaken,
Nor his descendants begging bread.
26 *He is* ever merciful, and lends;
And his descendants *are* blessed.

27 Depart from evil, and do good;
And dwell forevermore.
28 For the LORD loves justice,
And does not forsake His saints;
They are preserved forever,
But the descendants of the wicked shall
be cut off.
29 The righteous shall inherit the land,
And dwell in it forever.

30 The mouth of the righteous speaks
wisdom,
And his tongue talks of justice.
31 The law of his God *is* in his heart;
None of his steps shall slide.

32 The wicked watches the righteous,
And seeks to slay him.
33 The LORD will not leave him in his hand,
Nor condemn him when he is judged.

34 Wait on the LORD,
And keep His way,
And He shall exalt you to inherit the
land;
When the wicked are cut off, you shall
see *it.*
35 I have seen the wicked in great power,
And spreading himself like a native green
tree.
36 Yet he passed away,[a] and behold, he *was*
no *more;*
Indeed I sought him, but he could not be
found.

37 Mark the blameless *man,* and observe the
upright;
For the future of *that* man *is* peace.
38 But the transgressors shall be destroyed
together;
The future of the wicked shall be cut off.

39 But the salvation of the righteous *is* from
the LORD;
He is their strength in the time of trouble.
40 And the LORD shall help them and
deliver them;
He shall deliver them from the wicked,
And save them,
Because they trust in Him.

PSALM 38

Prayer in Time of Chastening

A Psalm of David. To bring to remembrance.

O LORD, do not rebuke me in Your
wrath,
Nor chasten me in Your hot displeasure!
2 For Your arrows pierce me deeply,
And Your hand presses me down.

3 *There is* no soundness in my flesh
Because of Your anger,
Nor *any* health in my bones
Because of my sin.
4 For my iniquities have gone over my
head;
Like a heavy burden they are too heavy
for me.
5 My wounds are foul *and* festering
Because of my foolishness.
6 I am troubled, I am bowed down greatly;
I go mourning all the day long.
7 For my loins are full of inflammation,
And *there is* no soundness in my flesh.

37:36 [a]Following Masoretic Text, Septuagint, and Targum; Syriac and Vulgate read *I passed by.*

8 I am feeble and severely broken;
I groan because of the turmoil of my heart.
9 Lord, all my desire *is* before You;
And my sighing is not hidden from You.
10 My heart pants, my strength fails me;
As for the light of my eyes, it also has gone from me.
11 My loved ones and my friends stand aloof from my plague,
And my relatives stand afar off.
12 Those also who seek my life lay snares *for me;*
Those who seek my hurt speak of destruction,
And plan deception all the day long.
13 But I, like a deaf *man,* do not hear;
And *I am* like a mute *who* does not open his mouth.
14 Thus I am like a man who does not hear,
And in whose mouth *is* no response.
15 For in You, O LORD, I hope;
You will hear, O Lord my God.
16 For I said, *"Hear me,* lest they rejoice over me,
Lest, when my foot slips, they exalt *themselves* against me."
17 For I *am* ready to fall,
And my sorrow *is* continually before me.
18 For I will declare my iniquity;
I will be in anguish over my sin.
19 But my enemies *are* vigorous, *and* they are strong;
And those who hate me wrongfully have multiplied.
20 Those also who render evil for good,
They are my adversaries, because I follow *what is* good.
21 Do not forsake me, O LORD;
O my God, be not far from me!
22 Make haste to help me,
O Lord, my salvation!

PSALM 39

Prayer for Wisdom and Forgiveness

To the Chief Musician. To Jeduthun. A Psalm of David.

I SAID, "I will guard my ways,
Lest I sin with my tongue;
I will restrain my mouth with a muzzle,
While the wicked are before me."
2 I was mute with silence,
I held my peace *even* from good;
And my sorrow was stirred up.
3 My heart was hot within me;
While I was musing, the fire burned.
Then I spoke with my tongue:
4 "LORD, make me to know my end,
And what *is* the measure of my days,
That I may know how frail I *am.*
5 Indeed, You have made my days *as* handbreadths,
And my age *is* as nothing before You;
Certainly every man at his best state *is* but vapor. Selah
6 Surely every man walks about like a shadow;
Surely they busy themselves in vain;
He heaps up *riches,*
And does not know who will gather them.
7 "And now, Lord, what do I wait for?
My hope *is* in You.
8 Deliver me from all my transgressions;
Do not make me the reproach of the foolish.
9 I was mute, I did not open my mouth,
Because it was You who did *it.*
10 Remove Your plague from me;
I am consumed by the blow of Your hand.
11 When with rebukes You correct man for iniquity,
You make his beauty melt away like a moth;
Surely every man *is* vapor. Selah
12 "Hear my prayer, O LORD,
And give ear to my cry;
Do not be silent at my tears;
For I *am* a stranger with You,
A sojourner, as all my fathers *were.*
13 Remove Your gaze from me, that I may regain strength,
Before I go away and am no more."

PSALM 40

Faith Persevering in Trial

To the Chief Musician. A Psalm of David.

I WAITED patiently for the LORD;
And He inclined to me,
And heard my cry.
2 He also brought me up out of a horrible pit,
Out of the miry clay,
And set my feet upon a rock,
And established my steps.
3 He has put a new song in my mouth—
Praise to our God;
Many will see *it* and fear,
And will trust in the LORD.
4 Blessed *is* that man who makes the LORD his trust,
And does not respect the proud, nor such as turn aside to lies.
5 Many, O LORD my God, *are* Your wonderful works
Which You have done;
And Your thoughts toward us
Cannot be recounted to You in order;
If I would declare and speak *of them,*
They are more than can be numbered.
6 Sacrifice and offering You did not desire;
My ears You have opened.
Burnt offering and sin offering You did not require.
7 Then I said, "Behold, I come;
In the scroll of the book *it is* written of me.
8 I delight to do Your will, O my God,
And Your law *is* within my heart."
9 I have proclaimed the good news of righteousness
In the great assembly;
Indeed, I do not restrain my lips,
O LORD, You Yourself know.
10 I have not hidden Your righteousness within my heart;
I have declared Your faithfulness and Your salvation;

I have not concealed Your lovingkindness
and Your truth
From the great assembly.
11 Do not withhold Your tender mercies
from me, O LORD;
Let Your lovingkindness and Your truth
continually preserve me.
12 For innumerable evils have surrounded
me;
My iniquities have overtaken me, so that I
am not able to look up;
They are more than the hairs of my head;
Therefore my heart fails me.
13 Be pleased, O LORD, to deliver me;
O LORD, make haste to help me!
14 Let them be ashamed and brought to
mutual confusion
Who seek to destroy my life;
Let them be driven backward and
brought to dishonor
Who wish me evil.
15 Let them be confounded because of their
shame,
Who say to me, "Aha, aha!"
16 Let all those who seek You rejoice and be
glad in You;
Let such as love Your salvation say
continually,
"The LORD be magnified!"
17 But I *am* poor and needy;
Yet the LORD thinks upon me.
You *are* my help and my deliverer;
Do not delay, O my God.

PSALM 41

The Blessing and Suffering of the Godly

To the Chief Musician. A Psalm of David.

BLESSED *is* he who considers the poor;
The LORD will deliver him in time of
trouble.
2 The LORD will preserve him and keep
him alive,
And he will be blessed on the earth;
You will not deliver him to the will of his
enemies.
3 The LORD will strengthen him on his bed
of illness;
You will sustain him on his sickbed.
4 I said, "LORD, be merciful to me;
Heal my soul, for I have sinned against
You."
5 My enemies speak evil of me:
"When will he die, and his name perish?"
6 And if he comes to see *me*, he speaks lies;
His heart gathers iniquity to itself;
When he goes out, he tells *it*.
7 All who hate me whisper together against
me;
Against me they devise my hurt.
8 "An evil disease," *they say*, "clings to him.
And *now* that he lies down, he will rise
up no more."
9 Even my own familiar friend in whom I
trusted,
Who ate my bread,
Has lifted up *his* heel against me.
10 But You, O LORD, be merciful to me, and
raise me up,
That I may repay them.
11 By this I know that You are well pleased
with me,
Because my enemy does not triumph over
me.
12 As for me, You uphold me in my integrity,
And set me before Your face forever.
13 Blessed *be* the LORD God of Israel
From everlasting to everlasting!
Amen and Amen.

BOOK TWO

Psalms 42—72

PSALM 42

Yearning for God in the Midst of Distresses

To the Chief Musician. A Contemplation[a] of the sons of Korah.

AS the deer pants for the water
brooks,
So pants my soul for You, O God.
2 My soul thirsts for God, for the living
God.
When shall I come and appear before
God?[a]
3 My tears have been my food day and
night,
While they continually say to me,
"Where *is* your God?"
4 When I remember these *things*,
I pour out my soul within me.
For I used to go with the multitude;
I went with them to the house of God,
With the voice of joy and praise,
With a multitude that kept a pilgrim feast.
5 Why are you cast down, O my soul?
And *why* are you disquieted within me?
Hope in God, for I shall yet praise Him
For the help of His countenance.[a]
6 O my God,[a] my soul is cast down within
me;
Therefore I will remember You from the
land of the Jordan,
And from the heights of Hermon,
From the Hill Mizar.
7 Deep calls unto deep at the noise of Your
waterfalls;
All Your waves and billows have gone
over me.
8 The LORD will command His
lovingkindness in the daytime,
And in the night His song *shall be* with
me—
A prayer to the God of my life.
9 I will say to God my Rock,
"Why have You forgotten me?
Why do I go mourning because of the
oppression of the enemy?"
10 *As* with a breaking of my bones,
My enemies reproach me,
While they say to me all day long,
"Where *is* your God?"

42:title [a]Hebrew *Maschil* **42:2** [a]Following Masoretic Text and Vulgate; some Hebrew manuscripts, Septuagint, Syriac, and Targum read *I see the face of God.* **42:5** [a]Following Masoretic Text and Targum; a few Hebrew manuscripts, Septuagint, Syriac, and Vulgate read *The help of my countenance, my God.* **42:6** [a]Following Masoretic Text and Targum; a few Hebrew manuscripts, Septuagint, Syriac, and Vulgate put *my God* at the end of verse 5.

11 Why are you cast down, O my soul?
And why are you disquieted within me?
Hope in God;
For I shall yet praise Him,
The help of my countenance and my God.

PSALM 43

Prayer to God in Time of Trouble

VINDICATE me, O God,
And plead my cause against an ungodly nation;
Oh, deliver me from the deceitful and unjust man!
2 For You *are* the God of my strength;
Why do You cast me off?
Why do I go mourning because of the oppression of the enemy?

3 Oh, send out Your light and Your truth!
Let them lead me;
Let them bring me to Your holy hill
And to Your tabernacle.
4 Then I will go to the altar of God,
To God my exceeding joy;
And on the harp I will praise You,
O God, my God.

5 Why are you cast down, O my soul?
And why are you disquieted within me?
Hope in God;
For I shall yet praise Him,
The help of my countenance and my God.

PSALM 44

Redemption Remembered in Present Dishonor

To the Chief Musician. A Contemplation[a] of the sons of Korah.

WE have heard with our ears, O God,
Our fathers have told us,
The deeds You did in their days,
In days of old:
2 You drove out the nations with Your hand,
But them You planted;
You afflicted the peoples, and cast them out.
3 For they did not gain possession of the land by their own sword,
Nor did their own arm save them;
But it was Your right hand, Your arm, and the light of Your countenance,
Because You favored them.

4 You are my King, O God;[a]
Command[b] victories for Jacob.
5 Through You we will push down our enemies;
Through Your name we will trample those who rise up against us.
6 For I will not trust in my bow,
Nor shall my sword save me.
7 But You have saved us from our enemies,
And have put to shame those who hated us.
8 In God we boast all day long,
And praise Your name forever. Selah

9 But You have cast *us* off and put us to shame,
And You do not go out with our armies.
10 You make us turn back from the enemy,
And those who hate us have taken spoil for themselves.
11 You have given us up like sheep *intended* for food,
And have scattered us among the nations.
12 You sell Your people for *next to* nothing,
And are not enriched by selling them.

13 You make us a reproach to our neighbors,
A scorn and a derision to those all around us.
14 You make us a byword among the nations,
A shaking of the head among the peoples.
15 My dishonor *is* continually before me,
And the shame of my face has covered me,
16 Because of the voice of him who reproaches and reviles,
Because of the enemy and the avenger.

17 All this has come upon us;
But we have not forgotten You,
Nor have we dealt falsely with Your covenant.
18 Our heart has not turned back,
Nor have our steps departed from Your way;
19 But You have severely broken us in the place of jackals,
And covered us with the shadow of death.

20 If we had forgotten the name of our God,
Or stretched out our hands to a foreign god,
21 Would not God search this out?
For He knows the secrets of the heart.
22 Yet for Your sake we are killed all day long;
We are accounted as sheep for the slaughter.

23 Awake! Why do You sleep, O Lord?
Arise! Do not cast *us* off forever.
24 Why do You hide Your face,
And forget our affliction and our oppression?
25 For our soul is bowed down to the dust;
Our body clings to the ground.
26 Arise for our help,
And redeem us for Your mercies' sake.

PSALM 45

The Glories of the Messiah and His Bride

To the Chief Musician. Set to "The Lilies."[a] A Contemplation[b] of the sons of Korah. A Song of Love.

MY heart is overflowing with a good theme;
I recite my composition concerning the King;
My tongue *is* the pen of a ready writer.

2 You are fairer than the sons of men;
Grace is poured upon Your lips;
Therefore God has blessed You forever.
3 Gird Your sword upon *Your* thigh,
O Mighty One,

44:title [a]Hebrew *Maschil* **44:4** [a]Following Masoretic Text and Targum; Septuagint and Vulgate read *and my God.* [b]Following Masoretic Text and Targum; Septuagint, Syriac, and Vulgate read *Who commands.* **45:title** [a]Hebrew *Shoshannim* [b]Hebrew *Maschil*

With Your glory and Your majesty.
4 And in Your majesty ride prosperously because of truth, humility, *and* righteousness;
And Your right hand shall teach You awesome things.
5 Your arrows *are* sharp in the heart of the King's enemies;
The peoples fall under You.

6 Your throne, O God, *is* forever and ever;
A scepter of righteousness *is* the scepter of Your kingdom.
7 You love righteousness and hate wickedness;
Therefore God, Your God, has anointed You
With the oil of gladness more than Your companions.
8 All Your garments *are scented* with myrrh and aloes *and* cassia,
Out of the ivory palaces, by which they have made You glad.
9 Kings' daughters *are* among Your honorable women;
At Your right hand stands the queen in gold from Ophir.

10 Listen, O daughter,
Consider and incline your ear;
Forget your own people also, and your father's house;
11 So the King will greatly desire your beauty;
Because He *is* your Lord, worship Him.
12 And the daughter of Tyre *will come* with a gift;
The rich among the people will seek your favor.

13 The royal daughter *is* all glorious within *the palace*;
Her clothing *is* woven with gold.
14 She shall be brought to the King in robes of many colors;
The virgins, her companions who follow her, shall be brought to You.
15 With gladness and rejoicing they shall be brought;
They shall enter the King's palace.
16 Instead of Your fathers shall be Your sons,
Whom You shall make princes in all the earth.
17 I will make Your name to be remembered in all generations;
Therefore the people shall praise You forever and ever.

PSALM 46

God the Refuge of His People and Conqueror of the Nations

To the Chief Musician. *A Psalm* of the sons of Korah. A Song for Alamoth.

GOD *is* our refuge and strength,
A very present help in trouble.
2 Therefore we will not fear,
Even though the earth be removed,
And though the mountains be carried into the midst of the sea;
3 *Though* its waters roar *and* be troubled,
Though the mountains shake with its swelling. Selah

4 *There is* a river whose streams shall make glad the city of God,
The holy *place* of the tabernacle of the Most High.
5 God *is* in the midst of her, she shall not be moved;
God shall help her, just at the break of dawn.
6 The nations raged, the kingdoms were moved;
He uttered His voice, the earth melted.

7 The LORD of hosts *is* with us;
The God of Jacob *is* our refuge. Selah

8 Come, behold the works of the LORD,
Who has made desolations in the earth.
9 He makes wars cease to the end of the earth;
He breaks the bow and cuts the spear in two;
He burns the chariot in the fire.

10 Be still, and know that I *am* God;
I will be exalted among the nations,
I will be exalted in the earth!

11 The LORD of hosts *is* with us;
The God of Jacob *is* our refuge. Selah

PSALM 47

Praise to God, the Ruler of the Earth

To the Chief Musician. A Psalm of the sons of Korah.

OH, clap your hands, all you peoples!
Shout to God with the voice of triumph!
2 For the LORD Most High *is* awesome;
He is a great King over all the earth.
3 He will subdue the peoples under us,
And the nations under our feet.
4 He will choose our inheritance for us,
The excellence of Jacob whom He loves. Selah

5 God has gone up with a shout,
The LORD with the sound of a trumpet.
6 Sing praises to God, sing praises!
Sing praises to our King, sing praises!
7 For God *is* the King of all the earth;
Sing praises with understanding.

8 God reigns over the nations;
God sits on His holy throne.
9 The princes of the people have gathered together,
The people of the God of Abraham.
For the shields of the earth *belong* to God;
He is greatly exalted.

PSALM 48

The Glory of God in Zion

A Song. A Psalm of the sons of Korah.

GREAT *is* the LORD, and greatly to be praised
In the city of our God,
In His holy mountain.
2 Beautiful in elevation,
The joy of the whole earth,
Is Mount Zion *on* the sides of the north,
The city of the great King.
3 God *is* in her palaces;
He is known as her refuge.

4 For behold, the kings assembled,
They passed by together.
5 They saw *it, and* so they marveled;
They were troubled, they hastened away.
6 Fear took hold of them there,
And pain, as of a woman in birth pangs,
7 *As when* You break the ships of Tarshish
With an east wind.

8 As we have heard,
So we have seen
In the city of the LORD of hosts,
In the city of our God:
God will establish it forever. Selah

9 We have thought, O God, on Your lovingkindness,
In the midst of Your temple.
10 According to Your name, O God,
So *is* Your praise to the ends of the earth;
Your right hand is full of righteousness.
11 Let Mount Zion rejoice,
Let the daughters of Judah be glad,
Because of Your judgments.

12 Walk about Zion,
And go all around her.
Count her towers;
13 Mark well her bulwarks;
Consider her palaces;
That you may tell *it* to the generation following.
14 For this *is* God,
Our God forever and ever;
He will be our guide
Even to death.[a]

PSALM 49

The Confidence of the Foolish

To the Chief Musician. A Psalm of the sons of Korah.

HEAR this, all peoples;
Give ear, all inhabitants of the world,
2 Both low and high,
Rich and poor together.
3 My mouth shall speak wisdom,
And the meditation of my heart *shall give* understanding.
4 I will incline my ear to a proverb;
I will disclose my dark saying on the harp.

5 Why should I fear in the days of evil,
When the iniquity at my heels surrounds me?
6 Those who trust in their wealth
And boast in the multitude of their riches,
7 None *of them* can by any means redeem *his* brother,
Nor give to God a ransom for him—
8 For the redemption of their souls *is* costly,
And it shall cease forever—
9 That he should continue to live eternally,
And not see the Pit.

10 For he sees wise men die;
Likewise the fool and the senseless person perish,
And leave their wealth to others.
11 Their inner thought *is that* their houses *will last* forever,[a]
Their dwelling places to all generations;
They call *their* lands after their own names.
12 Nevertheless man, *though* in honor, does not remain;[a]
He is like the beasts *that* perish.

13 This is the way of those who *are* foolish,
And of their posterity who approve their sayings. Selah
14 Like sheep they are laid in the grave;
Death shall feed on them;
The upright shall have dominion over them in the morning;
And their beauty shall be consumed in the grave, far from their dwelling.
15 But God will redeem my soul from the power of the grave,
For He shall receive me. Selah

16 Do not be afraid when one becomes rich,
When the glory of his house is increased;
17 For when he dies he shall carry nothing away;
His glory shall not descend after him.
18 Though while he lives he blesses himself
(For *men* will praise you when you do well for yourself),
19 He shall go to the generation of his fathers;
They shall never see light.
20 A man *who is* in honor, yet does not understand,
Is like the beasts *that* perish.

PSALM 50

God the Righteous Judge

A Psalm of Asaph.

THE Mighty One, God the LORD,
Has spoken and called the earth
From the rising of the sun to its going down.
2 Out of Zion, the perfection of beauty,
God will shine forth.
3 Our God shall come, and shall not keep silent;
A fire shall devour before Him,
And it shall be very tempestuous all around Him.
4 He shall call to the heavens from above,
And to the earth, that He may judge His people:
5 "Gather My saints together to Me,
Those who have made a covenant with Me by sacrifice."
6 Let the heavens declare His righteousness,
For God Himself *is* Judge. Selah

7 "Hear, O My people, and I will speak,
O Israel, and I will testify against you;
I *am* God, your God!
8 I will not rebuke you for your sacrifices
Or your burnt offerings,
Which are continually before Me.
9 I will not take a bull from your house,
Nor goats out of your folds.
10 For every beast of the forest *is* Mine,
And the cattle on a thousand hills.
11 I know all the birds of the mountains,
And the wild beasts of the field *are* Mine.

48:14 [a]Following Masoretic Text and Syriac; Septuagint and Vulgate read *Forever.* **49:11** [a]Septuagint, Syriac, Targum, and Vulgate read *Their graves shall be their houses forever.* **49:12** [a]Following Masoretic Text and Targum; Septuagint, Syriac, and Vulgate read *understand* (compare verse 20).

12 "If I were hungry, I would not tell you;
For the world *is* Mine, and all its fullness.
13 Will I eat the flesh of bulls,
Or drink the blood of goats?
14 Offer to God thanksgiving,
And pay your vows to the Most High.
15 Call upon Me in the day of trouble;
I will deliver you, and you shall glorify
Me."

16 But to the wicked God says:
"What *right* have you to declare My
statutes,
Or take My covenant in your mouth,
17 Seeing you hate instruction
And cast My words behind you?
18 When you saw a thief, you consented[a]
with him,
And have been a partaker with
adulterers.
19 You give your mouth to evil,
And your tongue frames deceit.
20 You sit *and* speak against your brother;
You slander your own mother's son.
21 These *things* you have done, and I kept
silent;
You thought that I was altogether like
you;
But I will rebuke you,
And set *them* in order before your eyes.

22 "Now consider this, you who forget God,
Lest I tear *you* in pieces,
And *there be* none to deliver:
23 Whoever offers praise glorifies Me;
And to him who orders *his* conduct *aright*
I will show the salvation of God."

PSALM 51

A Prayer of Repentance

To the Chief Musician. A Psalm of David when Nathan the prophet went to him, after he had gone in to Bathsheba.

HAVE mercy upon me, O God,
According to Your lovingkindness;
According to the multitude of Your tender
mercies,
Blot out my transgressions.
2 Wash me thoroughly from my iniquity,
And cleanse me from my sin.

3 For I acknowledge my transgressions,
And my sin *is* always before me.
4 Against You, You only, have I sinned,
And done *this* evil in Your sight—
That You may be found just when You
speak,[a]
And blameless when You judge.

5 Behold, I was brought forth in iniquity,
And in sin my mother conceived me.
6 Behold, You desire truth in the inward
parts,
And in the hidden *part* You will make me
to know wisdom.

7 Purge me with hyssop, and I shall be
clean;
Wash me, and I shall be whiter than
snow.
8 Make me hear joy and gladness,
That the bones You have broken may
rejoice.
9 Hide Your face from my sins,
And blot out all my iniquities.

10 Create in me a clean heart, O God,
And renew a steadfast spirit within me.
11 Do not cast me away from Your presence,
And do not take Your Holy Spirit from
me.

12 Restore to me the joy of Your salvation,
And uphold me *by Your* generous Spirit.
13 *Then* I will teach transgressors Your
ways,
And sinners shall be converted to You.

14 Deliver me from the guilt of bloodshed,
O God,
The God of my salvation,
And my tongue shall sing aloud of Your
righteousness.
15 O Lord, open my lips,
And my mouth shall show forth Your
praise.
16 For You do not desire sacrifice, or else I
would give *it;*
You do not delight in burnt offering.
17 The sacrifices of God *are* a broken spirit,
A broken and a contrite heart—
These, O God, You will not despise.

18 Do good in Your good pleasure to Zion;
Build the walls of Jerusalem.
19 Then You shall be pleased with the
sacrifices of righteousness,
With burnt offering and whole burnt
offering;
Then they shall offer bulls on Your altar.

PSALM 52

The End of the Wicked and the Peace of the Godly

To the Chief Musician. A Contemplation[a] of David when Doeg the Edomite went and told Saul, and said to him, "David has gone to the house of Ahimelech."

WHY do you boast in evil, O mighty
man?
The goodness of God *endures* continually.
2 Your tongue devises destruction,
Like a sharp razor, working deceitfully.
3 You love evil more than good,
Lying rather than speaking
righteousness. Selah
4 You love all devouring words,
You deceitful tongue.

5 God shall likewise destroy you forever;
He shall take you away, and pluck you
out of *your* dwelling place,
And uproot you from the land of the
living. Selah
6 The righteous also shall see and fear,
And shall laugh at him, *saying,*
7 "Here is the man *who* did not make God
his strength,
But trusted in the abundance of his
riches,
And strengthened himself in his
wickedness."

8 But I *am* like a green olive tree in the
house of God;

50:18 [a]Septuagint, Syriac, Targum, and Vulgate read *ran.* **51:4** [a]Septuagint, Targum, and Vulgate read *in Your words.* **52:title** [a]Hebrew *Maschil*

I trust in the mercy of God forever and
ever.
9 I will praise You forever,
Because You have done *it;*
And in the presence of Your saints
I will wait on Your name, for *it is* good.

PSALM 53

Folly of the Godless, and the Restoration of Israel

To the Chief Musician. Set to "Mahalath." A Contemplation[a] of David.

THE fool has said in his heart,
"*There is* no God."
They are corrupt, and have done
abominable iniquity;
There is none who does good.

2 God looks down from heaven upon the
children of men,
To see if there are *any* who understand,
who seek God.
3 Every one of them has turned aside;
They have together become corrupt;
There is none who does good,
No, not one.

4 Have the workers of iniquity no
knowledge,
Who eat up my people *as* they eat bread,
And do not call upon God?
5 There they are in great fear
Where no fear was,
For God has scattered the bones of him
who encamps against you;
You have put *them* to shame,
Because God has despised them.

6 Oh, that the salvation of Israel would
come out of Zion!
When God brings back the captivity of
His people,
Let Jacob rejoice *and* Israel be glad.

PSALM 54

Answered Prayer for Deliverance from Adversaries

To the Chief Musician. With stringed instruments.[a] A Contemplation[b] of David when the Ziphites went and said to Saul, "Is David not hiding with us?"

SAVE me, O God, by Your name,
And vindicate me by Your strength.
2 Hear my prayer, O God;
Give ear to the words of my mouth.
3 For strangers have risen up against me,
And oppressors have sought after my life;
They have not set God before them. Selah

4 Behold, God *is* my helper;
The Lord *is* with those who uphold my
life.
5 He will repay my enemies for their evil.
Cut them off in Your truth.

6 I will freely sacrifice to You;
I will praise Your name, O LORD, for *it is*
good.
7 For He has delivered me out of all
trouble;
And my eye has seen *its desire* upon my
enemies.

PSALM 55

Trust in God Concerning the Treachery of Friends

To the Chief Musician. With stringed instruments.[a] A Contemplation[b] of David.

GIVE ear to my prayer, O God,
And do not hide Yourself from my
supplication.
2 Attend to me, and hear me;
I am restless in my complaint, and moan
noisily,
3 Because of the voice of the enemy,
Because of the oppression of the wicked;
For they bring down trouble upon me,
And in wrath they hate me.

4 My heart is severely pained within me,
And the terrors of death have fallen upon
me.
5 Fearfulness and trembling have come
upon me,
And horror has overwhelmed me.
6 So I said, "Oh, that I had wings like a
dove!
I would fly away and be at rest.
7 Indeed, I would wander far off,
And remain in the wilderness. Selah
8 I would hasten my escape
From the windy storm *and* tempest."

9 Destroy, O Lord, *and* divide their tongues,
For I have seen violence and strife in the
city.
10 Day and night they go around it on its
walls;
Iniquity and trouble *are* also in the midst
of it.
11 Destruction *is* in its midst;
Oppression and deceit do not depart from
its streets.
12 For *it is* not an enemy *who* reproaches
me;
Then I could bear *it*.
Nor *is it* one *who* hates me who has
exalted *himself* against me;
Then I could hide from him.
13 But *it was* you, a man my equal,
My companion and my acquaintance.
14 We took sweet counsel together,
And walked to the house of God in the
throng.

15 Let death seize them;
Let them go down alive into hell,
For wickedness *is* in their dwellings *and*
among them.

16 As for me, I will call upon God,
And the LORD shall save me.
17 Evening and morning and at noon
I will pray, and cry aloud,
And He shall hear my voice.
18 He has redeemed my soul in peace from
the battle *that was* against me,
For there were many against me.
19 God will hear, and afflict them,
Even He who abides from of old. Selah
Because they do not change,
Therefore they do not fear God.

20 He has put forth his hands against those
who were at peace with him;
He has broken his covenant.

53:title [a]Hebrew *Maschil* **54:title** [a]Hebrew *neginoth* [b]Hebrew *Maschil* **55:title** [a]Hebrew *neginoth* [b]Hebrew *Maschil*

21 *The words* of his mouth were smoother
than butter,
But war *was* in his heart;
His words were softer than oil,
Yet they *were* drawn swords.
22 Cast your burden on the LORD,
And He shall sustain you;
He shall never permit the righteous to be
moved.
23 But You, O God, shall bring them down to
the pit of destruction;
Bloodthirsty and deceitful men shall not
live out half their days;
But I will trust in You.

PSALM 56

Prayer for Relief from Tormentors

To the Chief Musician. Set to "The Silent Dove in Distant Lands."[a] A Michtam of David when the Philistines captured him in Gath.

BE merciful to me, O God, for man would
swallow me up;
Fighting all day he oppresses me.
2 My enemies would hound *me* all day,
For *there are* many who fight against me,
O Most High.
3 Whenever I am afraid,
I will trust in You.
4 In God (I will praise His word),
In God I have put my trust;
I will not fear.
What can flesh do to me?
5 All day they twist my words;
All their thoughts *are* against me for evil.
6 They gather together,
They hide, they mark my steps,
When they lie in wait for my life.
7 Shall they escape by iniquity?
In anger cast down the peoples, O God!
8 You number my wanderings;
Put my tears into Your bottle;
Are they not in Your book?
9 When I cry out *to You*,
Then my enemies will turn back;
This I know, because God *is* for me.
10 In God (I will praise *His* word),
In the LORD (I will praise *His* word),
11 In God I have put my trust;
I will not be afraid.
What can man do to me?
12 Vows *made* to You *are binding* upon me,
O God;
I will render praises to You,
13 For You have delivered my soul from
death.
Have You not *kept* my feet from falling,
That I may walk before God
In the light of the living?

PSALM 57

Prayer for Safety from Enemies

To the Chief Musician. Set to "Do Not Destroy."[a] A Michtam of David when he fled from Saul into the cave.

BE merciful to me, O God, be merciful to
me!
For my soul trusts in You;
And in the shadow of Your wings I will
make my refuge,
Until *these* calamities have passed by.
2 I will cry out to God Most High,
To God who performs *all things* for me.
3 He shall send from heaven and save me;
He reproaches the one who would
swallow me up. Selah
God shall send forth His mercy and His
truth.
4 My soul *is* among lions;
I lie *among* the sons of men
Who are set on fire,
Whose teeth *are* spears and arrows,
And their tongue a sharp sword.
5 Be exalted, O God, above the heavens;
Let Your glory *be* above all the earth.
6 They have prepared a net for my steps;
My soul is bowed down;
They have dug a pit before me;
Into the midst of it they *themselves* have
fallen. Selah
7 My heart is steadfast, O God, my heart is
steadfast;
I will sing and give praise.
8 Awake, my glory!
Awake, lute and harp!
I will awaken the dawn.
9 I will praise You, O Lord, among the
peoples;
I will sing to You among the nations.
10 For Your mercy reaches unto the heavens,
And Your truth unto the clouds.
11 Be exalted, O God, above the heavens;
Let Your glory *be* above all the earth.

PSALM 58

The Just Judgment of the Wicked

To the Chief Musician. Set to "Do Not Destroy."[a] A Michtam of David.

DO you indeed speak righteousness,
you silent ones?
Do you judge uprightly, you sons of men?
2 No, in heart you work wickedness;
You weigh out the violence of your hands
in the earth.
3 The wicked are estranged from the
womb;
They go astray as soon as they are born,
speaking lies.
4 Their poison *is* like the poison of a
serpent;
They are like the deaf cobra *that* stops its
ear,
5 Which will not heed the voice of
charmers,
Charming ever so skillfully.
6 Break their teeth in their mouth, O God!
Break out the fangs of the young lions,
O LORD!
7 Let them flow away as waters *which* run
continually;
When he bends *his bow*,
Let his arrows be as if cut in pieces.
8 *Let them be* like a snail which melts
away as it goes,

56:title [a]Hebrew *Jonath Elem Rechokim* **57:title** [a]Hebrew *Al Tashcheth* **58:title** [a]Hebrew *Al Tashcheth*

Like a stillborn child of a woman, that they may not see the sun.

9 Before your pots can feel *the burning* thorns,
He shall take them away as with a whirlwind,
As in His living and burning wrath.
10 The righteous shall rejoice when he sees the vengeance;
He shall wash his feet in the blood of the wicked,
11 So that men will say,
"Surely *there is* a reward for the righteous;
Surely He is God who judges in the earth."

PSALM 59

The Assured Judgment of the Wicked

To the Chief Musician. Set to "Do Not Destroy."[a] A Michtam of David when Saul sent men, and they watched the house in order to kill him.

DELIVER me from my enemies, O my God;
Defend me from those who rise up against me.
2 Deliver me from the workers of iniquity,
And save me from bloodthirsty men.

3 For look, they lie in wait for my life;
The mighty gather against me,
Not *for* my transgression nor *for* my sin, O LORD.
4 They run and prepare themselves through no fault *of mine.*

Awake to help me, and behold!
5 You therefore, O LORD God of hosts, the God of Israel,
Awake to punish all the nations;
Do not be merciful to any wicked transgressors. Selah

6 At evening they return,
They growl like a dog,
And go all around the city.
7 Indeed, they belch with their mouth;
Swords *are* in their lips;
For *they say,* "Who hears?"

8 But You, O LORD, shall laugh at them;
You shall have all the nations in derision.
9 I will wait for You, O You his Strength;[a]
For God *is* my defense.
10 My God of mercy[a] shall come to meet me;
God shall let me see *my desire* on my enemies.

11 Do not slay them, lest my people forget;
Scatter them by Your power,
And bring them down,
O Lord our shield.
12 *For* the sin of their mouth *and* the words of their lips,
Let them even be taken in their pride,
And for the cursing and lying *which* they speak.
13 Consume *them* in wrath, consume *them,*
That they *may* not *be;*
And let them know that God rules in Jacob
To the ends of the earth. Selah

14 And at evening they return,
They growl like a dog,
And go all around the city.
15 They wander up and down for food,
And howl[a] if they are not satisfied.

16 But I will sing of Your power;
Yes, I will sing aloud of Your mercy in the morning;
For You have been my defense
And refuge in the day of my trouble.
17 To You, O my Strength, I will sing praises;
For God *is* my defense,
My God of mercy.

PSALM 60

Urgent Prayer for the Restored Favor of God

To the Chief Musician. Set to "Lily of the Testimony."[a] A Michtam of David. For teaching. When he fought against Mesopotamia and Syria of Zobah, and Joab returned and killed twelve thousand Edomites in the Valley of Salt.

O GOD, You have cast us off;
You have broken us down;
You have been displeased;
Oh, restore us again!
2 You have made the earth tremble;
You have broken it;
Heal its breaches, for it is shaking.
3 You have shown Your people hard things;
You have made us drink the wine of confusion.

4 You have given a banner to those who fear You,
That it may be displayed because of the truth. Selah
5 That Your beloved may be delivered,
Save *with* Your right hand, and hear me.

6 God has spoken in His holiness:
"I will rejoice;
I will divide Shechem
And measure out the Valley of Succoth.
7 Gilead *is* Mine, and Manasseh *is* Mine;
Ephraim also *is* the helmet for My head;
Judah *is* My lawgiver.
8 Moab *is* My washpot;
Over Edom I will cast My shoe;
Philistia, shout in triumph because of Me."

9 Who will bring me *to* the strong city?
Who will lead me to Edom?
10 *Is it* not You, O God, *who* cast us off?
And You, O God, *who* did not go out with our armies?
11 Give us help from trouble,
For the help of man *is* useless.
12 Through God we will do valiantly,
For *it is* He *who* shall tread down our enemies.[a]

59:title [a]Hebrew *Al Tashcheth* **59:9** [a]Following Masoretic Text and Syriac; some Hebrew manuscripts, Septuagint, Targum, and Vulgate read *my Strength.* **59:10** [a]Following Qere; some Hebrew manuscripts, Septuagint, and Vulgate read *My God, His mercy;* Kethib, some Hebrew manuscripts and Targum read *O God, my mercy;* Syriac reads *O God, Your mercy.* **59:15** [a]Following Septuagint and Vulgate; Masoretic Text, Syriac, and Targum read *spend the night.* **60:title** [a]Hebrew *Shushan Eduth* **60:12** [a]Compare verses 5–12 with 108:6–13

PSALM 61

Assurance of God's Eternal Protection

To the Chief Musician. On a stringed instrument.[a] *A Psalm* of David.

HEAR my cry, O God;
Attend to my prayer.
2 From the end of the earth I will cry to You,
When my heart is overwhelmed;
Lead me to the rock that is higher than I.

3 For You have been a shelter for me,
A strong tower from the enemy.
4 I will abide in Your tabernacle forever;
I will trust in the shelter of Your wings. Selah

5 For You, O God, have heard my vows;
You have given *me* the heritage of those who fear Your name.
6 You will prolong the king's life,
His years as many generations.
7 He shall abide before God forever.
Oh, prepare mercy and truth, *which* may preserve him!

8 So I will sing praise to Your name forever,
That I may daily perform my vows.

PSALM 62

A Calm Resolve to Wait for the Salvation of God

To the Chief Musician. To Jeduthun. A Psalm of David.

TRULY my soul silently *waits* for God;
From Him *comes* my salvation.
2 He only *is* my rock and my salvation;
He is my defense;
I shall not be greatly moved.

3 How long will you attack a man?
You shall be slain, all of you,
Like a leaning wall and a tottering fence.
4 They only consult to cast *him* down from his high position;
They delight in lies;
They bless with their mouth,
But they curse inwardly. Selah

5 My soul, wait silently for God alone,
For my expectation *is* from Him.
6 He only *is* my rock and my salvation;
He is my defense;
I shall not be moved.
7 In God *is* my salvation and my glory;
The rock of my strength,
And my refuge, *is* in God.

8 Trust in Him at all times, you people;
Pour out your heart before Him;
God *is* a refuge for us. Selah

9 Surely men of low degree *are* a vapor,
Men of high degree *are* a lie;
If they are weighed on the scales,
They *are* altogether *lighter* than vapor.
10 Do not trust in oppression,
Nor vainly hope in robbery;
If riches increase,
Do not set *your* heart *on them.*

11 God has spoken once,
Twice I have heard this:
That power *belongs* to God.
12 Also to You, O Lord, *belongs* mercy;
For You render to each one according to his work.

PSALM 63

Joy in the Fellowship of God

A Psalm of David when he was in the wilderness of Judah.

O GOD, You *are* my God;
Early will I seek You;
My soul thirsts for You;
My flesh longs for You
In a dry and thirsty land
Where there is no water.
2 So I have looked for You in the sanctuary,
To see Your power and Your glory.

3 Because Your lovingkindness *is* better than life,
My lips shall praise You.
4 Thus I will bless You while I live;
I will lift up my hands in Your name.
5 My soul shall be satisfied as with marrow and fatness,
And my mouth shall praise *You* with joyful lips.

6 When I remember You on my bed,
I meditate on You in the *night* watches.
7 Because You have been my help,
Therefore in the shadow of Your wings I will rejoice.
8 My soul follows close behind You;
Your right hand upholds me.

9 But those *who* seek my life, to destroy *it,*
Shall go into the lower parts of the earth.
10 They shall fall by the sword;
They shall be a portion for jackals.

11 But the king shall rejoice in God;
Everyone who swears by Him shall glory;
But the mouth of those who speak lies shall be stopped.

PSALM 64

Oppressed by the Wicked but Rejoicing in the LORD

To the Chief Musician. A Psalm of David.

HEAR my voice, O God, in my meditation;
Preserve my life from fear of the enemy.
2 Hide me from the secret plots of the wicked,
From the rebellion of the workers of iniquity,
3 Who sharpen their tongue like a sword,
And bend *their bows to shoot* their arrows—bitter words,
4 That they may shoot in secret at the blameless;
Suddenly they shoot at him and do not fear.

5 They encourage themselves *in* an evil matter;
They talk of laying snares secretly;
They say, "Who will see them?"
6 They devise iniquities:
"We have perfected a shrewd scheme."
Both the inward thought and the heart of man are deep.

7 But God shall shoot at them *with* an arrow;
Suddenly they shall be wounded.

61:title [a]Hebrew *neginah*

8 So He will make them stumble over their own tongue;
All who see them shall flee away.
9 All men shall fear,
And shall declare the work of God;
For they shall wisely consider His doing.

10 The righteous shall be glad in the LORD, and trust in Him.
And all the upright in heart shall glory.

PSALM 65

Praise to God for His Salvation and Providence

To the Chief Musician. A Psalm of David. A Song.

PRAISE is awaiting You, O God, in Zion;
And to You the vow shall be performed.
2 O You who hear prayer,
To You all flesh will come.
3 Iniquities prevail against me;
As for our transgressions,
You will provide atonement for them.

4 Blessed *is the man* You choose,
And cause to approach *You*,
That he may dwell in Your courts.
We shall be satisfied with the goodness of Your house,
Of Your holy temple.

5 *By* awesome deeds in righteousness You will answer us,
O God of our salvation,
You who are the confidence of all the ends of the earth,
And of the far-off seas;
6 Who established the mountains by His strength,
Being clothed with power;
7 You who still the noise of the seas,
The noise of their waves,
And the tumult of the peoples.
8 They also who dwell in the farthest parts are afraid of Your signs;
You make the outgoings of the morning and evening rejoice.

9 You visit the earth and water it,
You greatly enrich it;
The river of God is full of water;
You provide their grain,
For so You have prepared it.
10 You water its ridges abundantly,
You settle its furrows;
You make it soft with showers,
You bless its growth.

11 You crown the year with Your goodness,
And Your paths drip *with* abundance.
12 They drop *on* the pastures of the wilderness,
And the little hills rejoice on every side.
13 The pastures are clothed with flocks;
The valleys also are covered with grain;
They shout for joy, they also sing.

PSALM 66

Praise to God for His Awesome Works

To the Chief Musician. A Song. A Psalm.

MAKE a joyful shout to God, all the earth!
2 Sing out the honor of His name;
Make His praise glorious.
3 Say to God,
"How awesome are Your works!
Through the greatness of Your power
Your enemies shall submit themselves to You.
4 All the earth shall worship You
And sing praises to You;
They shall sing praises *to* Your name."
Selah

5 Come and see the works of God;
He is awesome *in His* doing toward the sons of men.
6 He turned the sea into dry *land;*
They went through the river on foot.
There we will rejoice in Him.
7 He rules by His power forever;
His eyes observe the nations;
Do not let the rebellious exalt themselves.
Selah

8 Oh, bless our God, you peoples!
And make the voice of His praise to be heard,
9 Who keeps our soul among the living,
And does not allow our feet to be moved.
10 For You, O God, have tested us;
You have refined us as silver is refined.
11 You brought us into the net;
You laid affliction on our backs.
12 You have caused men to ride over our heads;
We went through fire and through water;
But You brought us out to rich *fulfillment*.

13 I will go into Your house with burnt offerings;
I will pay You my vows,
14 Which my lips have uttered
And my mouth has spoken when I was in trouble.
15 I will offer You burnt sacrifices of fat animals,
With the sweet aroma of rams;
I will offer bulls with goats. Selah

16 Come *and* hear, all you who fear God,
And I will declare what He has done for my soul.
17 I cried to Him with my mouth,
And He was extolled with my tongue.
18 If I regard iniquity in my heart,
The Lord will not hear.
19 *But* certainly God has heard *me;*
He has attended to the voice of my prayer.

20 Blessed *be* God,
Who has not turned away my prayer,
Nor His mercy from me!

PSALM 67

An Invocation and a Doxology

To the Chief Musician. On stringed instruments.[a] A Psalm. A Song.

GOD be merciful to us and bless us,
And cause His face to shine upon us,
Selah
2 That Your way may be known on earth,
Your salvation among all nations.

67:title [a]Hebrew *neginoth*

3 Let the peoples praise You, O God;
Let all the peoples praise You.
4 Oh, let the nations be glad and sing for joy!
For You shall judge the people righteously,
And govern the nations on earth. Selah
5 Let the peoples praise You, O God;
Let all the peoples praise You.
6 *Then* the earth shall yield her increase;
God, our own God, shall bless us.
7 God shall bless us,
And all the ends of the earth shall fear Him.

PSALM 68

The Glory of God in His Goodness to Israel

To the Chief Musician. A Psalm of David. A Song.

LET God arise,
Let His enemies be scattered;
Let those also who hate Him flee before Him.
2 As smoke is driven away,
So drive *them* away;
As wax melts before the fire,
So let the wicked perish at the presence of God.
3 But let the righteous be glad;
Let them rejoice before God;
Yes, let them rejoice exceedingly.
4 Sing to God, sing praises to His name;
Extol Him who rides on the clouds,[a]
By His name YAH,
And rejoice before Him.
5 A father of the fatherless, a defender of widows,
Is God in His holy habitation.
6 God sets the solitary in families;
He brings out those who are bound into prosperity;
But the rebellious dwell in a dry *land.*
7 O God, when You went out before Your people,
When You marched through the wilderness, Selah
8 The earth shook;
The heavens also dropped *rain* at the presence of God;
Sinai itself *was moved* at the presence of God, the God of Israel.
9 You, O God, sent a plentiful rain,
Whereby You confirmed Your inheritance,
When it was weary.
10 Your congregation dwelt in it;
You, O God, provided from Your goodness for the poor.
11 The Lord gave the word;
Great *was* the company of those who proclaimed *it:*
12 "Kings of armies flee, they flee,
And she who remains at home divides the spoil.
13 Though you lie down among the sheepfolds,
You will be like the wings of a dove covered with silver,
And her feathers with yellow gold."
14 When the Almighty scattered kings in it,
It was *white* as snow in Zalmon.
15 A mountain of God *is* the mountain of Bashan;
A mountain *of many* peaks *is* the mountain of Bashan.
16 Why do you fume with envy, you mountains of *many* peaks?
This is the mountain *which* God desires to dwell in;
Yes, the LORD will dwell *in it* forever.
17 The chariots of God *are* twenty thousand,
Even thousands of thousands;
The Lord is among them *as in* Sinai, in the Holy *Place.*
18 You have ascended on high,
You have led captivity captive;
You have received gifts among men,
Even *from* the rebellious,
That the LORD God might dwell *there.*
19 Blessed *be* the Lord,
Who daily loads us *with benefits,*
The God of our salvation! Selah
20 Our God *is* the God of salvation;
And to GOD the Lord *belong* escapes from death.
21 But God will wound the head of His enemies,
The hairy scalp of the one who still goes on in his trespasses.
22 The Lord said, "I will bring back from Bashan,
I will bring *them* back from the depths of the sea,
23 That your foot may crush *them*[a] in blood,
And the tongues of your dogs *may have* their portion from *your* enemies."
24 They have seen Your procession, O God,
The procession of my God, my King, into the sanctuary.
25 The singers went before, the players on instruments *followed* after;
Among *them were* the maidens playing timbrels.
26 Bless God in the congregations,
The Lord, from the fountain of Israel.
27 There *is* little Benjamin, their leader,
The princes of Judah *and* their company,
The princes of Zebulun *and* the princes of Naphtali.
28 Your God has commanded[a] your strength;
Strengthen, O God, what You have done for us.
29 Because of Your temple at Jerusalem,
Kings will bring presents to You.
30 Rebuke the beasts of the reeds,
The herd of bulls with the calves of the peoples,
Till everyone submits himself with pieces of silver.
Scatter the peoples *who* delight in war.
31 Envoys will come out of Egypt;
Ethiopia will quickly stretch out her hands to God.

68:4 [a]Masoretic Text reads *deserts;* Targum reads *heavens* (compare verse 34 and Isaiah 19:1). **68:23** [a]Septuagint, Syriac, Targum, and Vulgate read *you may dip your foot.* **68:28** [a]Septuagint, Syriac, Targum, and Vulgate read *Command, O God.*

32 Sing to God, you kingdoms of the earth;
Oh, sing praises to the Lord, Selah
33 To Him who rides on the heaven of heavens, *which were* of old!
Indeed, He sends out His voice, a mighty voice.
34 Ascribe strength to God;
His excellence *is* over Israel,
And His strength *is* in the clouds.
35 O God, *You are* more awesome than Your holy places.
The God of Israel *is* He who gives strength and power to *His* people.

Blessed *be* God!

PSALM 69

An Urgent Plea for Help in Trouble

To the Chief Musician. Set to "The Lilies."[a] *A Psalm* of David.

SAVE me, O God!
For the waters have come up to *my* neck.
2 I sink in deep mire,
Where *there is* no standing;
I have come into deep waters,
Where the floods overflow me.
3 I am weary with my crying;
My throat is dry;
My eyes fail while I wait for my God.

4 Those who hate me without a cause
Are more than the hairs of my head;
They are mighty who would destroy me,
Being my enemies wrongfully;
Though I have stolen nothing,
I *still* must restore *it*.
5 O God, You know my foolishness;
And my sins are not hidden from You.
6 Let not those who wait for You, O Lord GOD of hosts, be ashamed because of me;
Let not those who seek You be confounded because of me, O God of Israel.
7 Because for Your sake I have borne reproach;
Shame has covered my face.
8 I have become a stranger to my brothers,
And an alien to my mother's children;
9 Because zeal for Your house has eaten me up,
And the reproaches of those who reproach You have fallen on me.
10 When I wept *and chastened* my soul with fasting,
That became my reproach.
11 I also made sackcloth my garment;
I became a byword to them.
12 Those who sit in the gate speak against me,
And I *am* the song of the drunkards.

13 But as for me, my prayer *is* to You,
O LORD, *in* the acceptable time;
O God, in the multitude of Your mercy,
Hear me in the truth of Your salvation.
14 Deliver me out of the mire,
And let me not sink;
Let me be delivered from those who hate me,
And out of the deep waters.
15 Let not the floodwater overflow me,
Nor let the deep swallow me up;
And let not the pit shut its mouth on me.

16 Hear me, O LORD, for Your lovingkindness *is* good;
Turn to me according to the multitude of Your tender mercies.
17 And do not hide Your face from Your servant,
For I am in trouble;
Hear me speedily.
18 Draw near to my soul, *and* redeem it;
Deliver me because of my enemies.

19 You know my reproach, my shame, and my dishonor;
My adversaries *are* all before You.
20 Reproach has broken my heart,
And I am full of heaviness;
I looked *for someone* to take pity, but *there was* none;
And for comforters, but I found none.
21 They also gave me gall for my food,
And for my thirst they gave me vinegar to drink.

22 Let their table become a snare before them,
And their well-being a trap.
23 Let their eyes be darkened, so that they do not see;
And make their loins shake continually.
24 Pour out Your indignation upon them,
And let Your wrathful anger take hold of them.
25 Let their dwelling place be desolate;
Let no one live in their tents.
26 For they persecute the *ones* You have struck,
And talk of the grief of those You have wounded.
27 Add iniquity to their iniquity,
And let them not come into Your righteousness.
28 Let them be blotted out of the book of the living,
And not be written with the righteous.

29 But I *am* poor and sorrowful;
Let Your salvation, O God, set me up on high.
30 I will praise the name of God with a song,
And will magnify Him with thanksgiving.
31 *This* also shall please the LORD better than an ox *or* bull,
Which has horns and hooves.
32 The humble shall see *this and* be glad;
And you who seek God, your hearts shall live.
33 For the LORD hears the poor,
And does not despise His prisoners.

34 Let heaven and earth praise Him,
The seas and everything that moves in them.
35 For God will save Zion
And build the cities of Judah,
That they may dwell there and possess it.
36 Also, the descendants of His servants shall inherit it,
And those who love His name shall dwell in it.

69:title [a]Hebrew *Shoshannim*

PSALM 70

Prayer for Relief from Adversaries

To the Chief Musician. *A Psalm* of David. To bring to remembrance.

MAKE *haste,* O God, to deliver me!
Make haste to help me, O LORD!

2 Let them be ashamed and confounded
Who seek my life;
Let them be turned back[a] and confused
Who desire my hurt.
3 Let them be turned back because of their shame,
Who say, "Aha, aha!"

4 Let all those who seek You rejoice and be glad in You;
And let those who love Your salvation say continually,
"Let God be magnified!"

5 But I *am* poor and needy;
Make haste to me, O God!
You *are* my help and my deliverer;
O LORD, do not delay.

PSALM 71

God the Rock of Salvation

IN You, O LORD, I put my trust;
Let me never be put to shame.
2 Deliver me in Your righteousness, and cause me to escape;
Incline Your ear to me, and save me.
3 Be my strong refuge,
To which I may resort continually;
You have given the commandment to save me,
For You *are* my rock and my fortress.

4 Deliver me, O my God, out of the hand of the wicked,
Out of the hand of the unrighteous and cruel man.
5 For You are my hope, O Lord GOD;
You are my trust from my youth.
6 By You I have been upheld from birth;
You are He who took me out of my mother's womb.
My praise *shall be* continually of You.

7 I have become as a wonder to many,
But You *are* my strong refuge.
8 Let my mouth be filled *with* Your praise
And with Your glory all the day.

9 Do not cast me off in the time of old age;
Do not forsake me when my strength fails.
10 For my enemies speak against me;
And those who lie in wait for my life take counsel together,
11 Saying, "God has forsaken him;
Pursue and take him, for *there is* none to deliver *him.*"

12 O God, do not be far from me;
O my God, make haste to help me!
13 Let them be confounded *and* consumed
Who are adversaries of my life;
Let them be covered *with* reproach and dishonor
Who seek my hurt.

14 But I will hope continually,
And will praise You yet more and more.
15 My mouth shall tell of Your righteousness
And Your salvation all the day,
For I do not know *their* limits.
16 I will go in the strength of the Lord GOD;
I will make mention of Your righteousness, of Yours only.

17 O God, You have taught me from my youth;
And to this *day* I declare Your wondrous works.
18 Now also when *I am* old and grayheaded,
O God, do not forsake me,
Until I declare Your strength to *this* generation,
Your power to everyone *who* is to come.

19 Also Your righteousness, O God, *is* very high,
You who have done great things;
O God, who *is* like You?
20 *You,* who have shown me great and severe troubles,
Shall revive me again,
And bring me up again from the depths of the earth.
21 You shall increase my greatness,
And comfort me on every side.

22 Also with the lute I will praise You—
And Your faithfulness, O my God!
To You I will sing with the harp,
O Holy One of Israel.
23 My lips shall greatly rejoice when I sing to You,
And my soul, which You have redeemed.
24 My tongue also shall talk of Your righteousness all the day long;
For they are confounded,
For they are brought to shame
Who seek my hurt.

PSALM 72

Glory and Universality of the Messiah's Reign

A Psalm of Solomon.

GIVE the king Your judgments, O God,
And Your righteousness to the king's Son.
2 He will judge Your people with righteousness,
And Your poor with justice.
3 The mountains will bring peace to the people,
And the little hills, by righteousness.
4 He will bring justice to the poor of the people;
He will save the children of the needy,
And will break in pieces the oppressor.

5 They shall fear You[a]
As long as the sun and moon endure,
Throughout all generations.
6 He shall come down like rain upon the grass before mowing,
Like showers *that* water the earth.

70:2 [a]Following Masoretic Text, Septuagint, Targum, and Vulgate; some Hebrew manuscripts and Syriac read *be appalled* (compare 40:15). **72:5** [a]Following Masoretic Text and Targum; Septuagint and Vulgate read *They shall continue.*

7 In His days the righteous shall flourish,
And abundance of peace,
Until the moon is no more.
8 He shall have dominion also from sea to sea,
And from the River to the ends of the earth.
9 Those who dwell in the wilderness will bow before Him,
And His enemies will lick the dust.
10 The kings of Tarshish and of the isles
Will bring presents;
The kings of Sheba and Seba
Will offer gifts.
11 Yes, all kings shall fall down before Him;
All nations shall serve Him.

12 For He will deliver the needy when he cries,
The poor also, and *him* who has no helper.
13 He will spare the poor and needy,
And will save the souls of the needy.
14 He will redeem their life from oppression and violence;
And precious shall be their blood in His sight.

15 And He shall live;
And the gold of Sheba will be given to Him;
Prayer also will be made for Him continually,
And daily He shall be praised.

16 There will be an abundance of grain in the earth,
On the top of the mountains;
Its fruit shall wave like Lebanon;
And *those* of the city shall flourish like grass of the earth.
17 His name shall endure forever;
His name shall continue as long as the sun.
And *men* shall be blessed in Him;
All nations shall call Him blessed.

18 Blessed *be* the LORD God, the God of Israel,
Who only does wondrous things!
19 And blessed *be* His glorious name forever!
And let the whole earth be filled *with* His glory.
Amen and Amen.

20 The prayers of David the son of Jesse are ended.

BOOK THREE

Psalms 73—89

PSALM 73

The Tragedy of the Wicked, and the Blessedness of Trust in God

A Psalm of Asaph.

TRULY God *is* good to Israel,
To such as are pure in heart.
2 But as for me, my feet had almost stumbled;
My steps had nearly slipped.
3 For I *was* envious of the boastful,
When I saw the prosperity of the wicked.

4 For *there are* no pangs in their death,
But their strength *is* firm.
5 They *are* not in trouble *as other* men,
Nor are they plagued like *other* men.
6 Therefore pride serves as their necklace;
Violence covers them *like* a garment.
7 Their eyes bulge[a] with abundance;
They have more than heart could wish.
8 They scoff and speak wickedly
concerning oppression;
They speak loftily.
9 They set their mouth against the heavens,
And their tongue walks through the earth.

10 Therefore his people return here,
And waters of a full *cup* are drained by them.
11 And they say, "How does God know?
And is there knowledge in the Most High?"
12 Behold, these *are* the ungodly,
Who are always at ease;
They increase *in* riches.
13 Surely I have cleansed my heart *in* vain,
And washed my hands in innocence.
14 For all day long I have been plagued,
And chastened every morning.

15 If I had said, "I will speak thus,"
Behold, I would have been untrue to the generation of Your children.
16 When I thought *how* to understand this,
It *was* too painful for me—
17 Until I went into the sanctuary of God;
Then I understood their end.

18 Surely You set them in slippery places;
You cast them down to destruction.
19 Oh, how they are *brought* to desolation, as in a moment!
They are utterly consumed with terrors.
20 As a dream when *one* awakes,
So, Lord, when You awake,
You shall despise their image.

21 Thus my heart was grieved,
And I was vexed in my mind.
22 I *was* so foolish and ignorant;
I was *like* a beast before You.
23 Nevertheless I *am* continually with You;
You hold *me* by my right hand.
24 You will guide me with Your counsel,
And afterward receive me *to* glory.

25 Whom have I in heaven *but You?*
And *there is* none upon earth *that* I desire besides You.
26 My flesh and my heart fail;
But God *is* the strength of my heart and my portion forever.

27 For indeed, those who are far from You shall perish;
You have destroyed all those who desert You for harlotry.
28 But *it is* good for me to draw near to God;
I have put my trust in the Lord GOD,
That I may declare all Your works.

PSALM 74

A Plea for Relief from Oppressors

A Contemplation[a] of Asaph.

O GOD, why have You cast *us* off forever?

73:7 [a]Targum reads *face bulges;* Septuagint, Syriac, and Vulgate read *iniquity bulges.* **74:title** [a]Hebrew *Maschil*

Why does Your anger smoke against the
sheep of Your pasture?
2 Remember Your congregation, *which* You
have purchased of old,
The tribe of Your inheritance, *which* You
have redeemed—
This Mount Zion where You have dwelt.
3 Lift up Your feet to the perpetual
desolations.
The enemy has damaged everything in
the sanctuary.
4 Your enemies roar in the midst of Your
meeting place;
They set up their banners *for* signs.
5 They seem like men who lift up
Axes among the thick trees.
6 And now they break down its carved
work, all at once,
With axes and hammers.
7 They have set fire to Your sanctuary;
They have defiled the dwelling place of
Your name to the ground.
8 They said in their hearts,
"Let us destroy them altogether."
They have burned up all the meeting
places of God in the land.

9 We do not see our signs;
There is no longer any prophet;
Nor *is there* any among us who knows
how long.
10 O God, how long will the adversary
reproach?
Will the enemy blaspheme Your name
forever?
11 Why do You withdraw Your hand, even
Your right hand?
Take it out of Your bosom and destroy
them.
12 For God *is* my King from of old,
Working salvation in the midst of the
earth.
13 You divided the sea by Your strength;
You broke the heads of the sea serpents
in the waters.
14 You broke the heads of Leviathan in
pieces,
And gave him *as* food to the people
inhabiting the wilderness.
15 You broke open the fountain and the
flood;
You dried up mighty rivers.
16 The day *is* Yours, the night also *is* Yours;
You have prepared the light and the sun.
17 You have set all the borders of the earth;
You have made summer and winter.

18 Remember this, *that* the enemy has
reproached, O LORD,
And *that* a foolish people has
blasphemed Your name.
19 Oh, do not deliver the life of Your
turtledove to the wild beast!
Do not forget the life of Your poor
forever.
20 Have respect to the covenant;
For the dark places of the earth are full of
the haunts of cruelty.
21 Oh, do not let the oppressed return
ashamed!
Let the poor and needy praise Your name.

22 Arise, O God, plead Your own cause;
Remember how the foolish man
reproaches You daily.
23 Do not forget the voice of Your enemies;
The tumult of those who rise up against
You increases continually.

PSALM 75

Thanksgiving for God's Righteous Judgment

To the Chief Musician. Set to "Do Not Destroy."[a] A Psalm of Asaph. A Song.

WE give thanks to You, O God, we
give thanks!
For Your wondrous works declare *that*
Your name is near.

2 "When I choose the proper time,
I will judge uprightly.
3 The earth and all its inhabitants are
dissolved;
I set up its pillars firmly. Selah

4 "I said to the boastful, 'Do not deal
boastfully,'
And to the wicked, 'Do not lift up the
horn.
5 Do not lift up your horn on high;
Do *not* speak with a stiff neck.'"

6 For exaltation *comes* neither from the
east
Nor from the west nor from the south.
7 But God *is* the Judge:
He puts down one,
And exalts another.
8 For in the hand of the LORD *there is* a
cup,
And the wine is red;
It is fully mixed, and He pours it out;
Surely its dregs shall all the wicked of the
earth
Drain *and* drink down.

9 But I will declare forever,
I will sing praises to the God of Jacob.

10 "All the horns of the wicked I will also cut
off,
But the horns of the righteous shall be
exalted."

PSALM 76

The Majesty of God in Judgment

To the Chief Musician. On stringed instruments.[a] A Psalm of Asaph. A Song.

IN Judah God *is* known;
His name *is* great in Israel.
2 In Salem[a] also is His tabernacle,
And His dwelling place in Zion.
3 There He broke the arrows of the bow,
The shield and sword of battle. Selah

4 You *are* more glorious and excellent
Than the mountains of prey.
5 The stouthearted were plundered;
They have sunk into their sleep;
And none of the mighty men have found
the use of their hands.
6 At Your rebuke, O God of Jacob,
Both the chariot and horse were cast into
a dead sleep.

75:title [a]Hebrew *Al Tashcheth* **76:title** [a]Hebrew *neginoth* **76:2** [a]That is, Jerusalem

7 You, Yourself, *are* to be feared;
And who may stand in Your presence
When once You are angry?
8 You caused judgment to be heard from heaven;
The earth feared and was still,
9 When God arose to judgment,
To deliver all the oppressed of the earth. Selah

10 Surely the wrath of man shall praise You;
With the remainder of wrath You shall gird Yourself.

11 Make vows to the LORD your God, and pay *them;*
Let all who are around Him bring presents to Him who ought to be feared.
12 He shall cut off the spirit of princes;
He is awesome to the kings of the earth.

PSALM 77

The Consoling Memory of God's Redemptive Works

To the Chief Musician. To Jeduthun. A Psalm of Asaph.

I CRIED out to God with my voice—
To God with my voice;
And He gave ear to me.
2 In the day of my trouble I sought the Lord;
My hand was stretched out in the night without ceasing;
My soul refused to be comforted.
3 I remembered God, and was troubled;
I complained, and my spirit was overwhelmed. Selah

4 You hold my eyelids *open;*
I am so troubled that I cannot speak.
5 I have considered the days of old,
The years of ancient times.
6 I call to remembrance my song in the night;
I meditate within my heart,
And my spirit makes diligent search.

7 Will the Lord cast off forever?
And will He be favorable no more?
8 Has His mercy ceased forever?
Has *His* promise failed forevermore?
9 Has God forgotten to be gracious?
Has He in anger shut up His tender mercies? Selah

10 And I said, "This *is* my anguish;
But I will remember the years of the right hand of the Most High."
11 I will remember the works of the LORD;
Surely I will remember Your wonders of old.
12 I will also meditate on all Your work,
And talk of Your deeds.
13 Your way, O God, *is* in the sanctuary;
Who *is* so great a God as *our* God?
14 You *are* the God who does wonders;
You have declared Your strength among the peoples.
15 You have with *Your* arm redeemed Your people,
The sons of Jacob and Joseph. Selah

16 The waters saw You, O God;
The waters saw You, they were afraid;
The depths also trembled.
17 The clouds poured out water;
The skies sent out a sound;
Your arrows also flashed about.
18 The voice of Your thunder *was* in the whirlwind;
The lightnings lit up the world;
The earth trembled and shook.
19 Your way *was* in the sea,
Your path in the great waters,
And Your footsteps were not known.
20 You led Your people like a flock
By the hand of Moses and Aaron.

PSALM 78

God's Kindness to Rebellious Israel

A Contemplation[a] of Asaph.

GIVE ear, O my people, *to* my law;
Incline your ears to the words of my mouth.
2 I will open my mouth in a parable;
I will utter dark sayings of old,
3 Which we have heard and known,
And our fathers have told us.
4 We will not hide *them* from their children,
Telling to the generation to come the praises of the LORD,
And His strength and His wonderful works that He has done.

5 For He established a testimony in Jacob,
And appointed a law in Israel,
Which He commanded our fathers,
That they should make them known to their children;
6 That the generation to come might know *them,*
The children *who* would be born,
That they may arise and declare *them* to their children,
7 That they may set their hope in God,
And not forget the works of God,
But keep His commandments;
8 And may not be like their fathers,
A stubborn and rebellious generation,
A generation *that* did not set its heart aright,
And whose spirit was not faithful to God.

9 The children of Ephraim, *being* armed *and* carrying bows,
Turned back in the day of battle.
10 They did not keep the covenant of God;
They refused to walk in His law,
11 And forgot His works
And His wonders that He had shown them.

12 Marvelous things He did in the sight of their fathers,
In the land of Egypt, *in* the field of Zoan.
13 He divided the sea and caused them to pass through;
And He made the waters stand up like a heap.
14 In the daytime also He led them with the cloud,
And all the night with a light of fire.

78:title [a]Hebrew *Maschil*

15 He split the rocks in the wilderness,
And gave *them* drink in abundance like the depths.
16 He also brought streams out of the rock,
And caused waters to run down like rivers.

17 But they sinned even more against Him
By rebelling against the Most High in the wilderness.
18 And they tested God in their heart
By asking for the food of their fancy.
19 Yes, they spoke against God:
They said, "Can God prepare a table in the wilderness?
20 Behold, He struck the rock,
So that the waters gushed out,
And the streams overflowed.
Can He give bread also?
Can He provide meat for His people?"

21 Therefore the LORD heard *this* and was furious;
So a fire was kindled against Jacob,
And anger also came up against Israel,
22 Because they did not believe in God,
And did not trust in His salvation.
23 Yet He had commanded the clouds above,
And opened the doors of heaven,
24 Had rained down manna on them to eat,
And given them of the bread of heaven.
25 Men ate angels' food;
He sent them food to the full.

26 He caused an east wind to blow in the heavens;
And by His power He brought in the south wind.
27 He also rained meat on them like the dust,
Feathered fowl like the sand of the seas;
28 And He let *them* fall in the midst of their camp,
All around their dwellings.
29 So they ate and were well filled,
For He gave them their own desire.
30 They were not deprived of their craving;
But while their food *was* still in their mouths,
31 The wrath of God came against them,
And slew the stoutest of them,
And struck down the choice *men* of Israel.

32 In spite of this they still sinned,
And did not believe in His wondrous works.
33 Therefore their days He consumed in futility,
And their years in fear.

34 When He slew them, then they sought Him;
And they returned and sought earnestly for God.
35 Then they remembered that God *was* their rock,
And the Most High God their Redeemer.
36 Nevertheless they flattered Him with their mouth,
And they lied to Him with their tongue;
37 For their heart was not steadfast with Him,
Nor were they faithful in His covenant.
38 But He, *being* full of compassion, forgave *their* iniquity,
And did not destroy *them.*
Yes, many a time He turned His anger away,
And did not stir up all His wrath;
39 For He remembered that they *were but* flesh,
A breath that passes away and does not come again.

40 How often they provoked Him in the wilderness,
And grieved Him in the desert!
41 Yes, again and again they tempted God,
And limited the Holy One of Israel.
42 They did not remember His power:
The day when He redeemed them from the enemy,
43 When He worked His signs in Egypt,
And His wonders in the field of Zoan;
44 Turned their rivers into blood,
And their streams, that they could not drink.
45 He sent swarms of flies among them, which devoured them,
And frogs, which destroyed them.
46 He also gave their crops to the caterpillar,
And their labor to the locust.
47 He destroyed their vines with hail,
And their sycamore trees with frost.
48 He also gave up their cattle to the hail,
And their flocks to fiery lightning.
49 He cast on them the fierceness of His anger,
Wrath, indignation, and trouble,
By sending angels of destruction *among them.*
50 He made a path for His anger;
He did not spare their soul from death,
But gave their life over to the plague,
51 And destroyed all the firstborn in Egypt,
The first of *their* strength in the tents of Ham.
52 But He made His own people go forth like sheep,
And guided them in the wilderness like a flock;
53 And He led them on safely, so that they did not fear;
But the sea overwhelmed their enemies.
54 And He brought them to His holy border,
This mountain *which* His right hand had acquired.
55 He also drove out the nations before them,
Allotted them an inheritance by survey,
And made the tribes of Israel dwell in their tents.

56 Yet they tested and provoked the Most High God,
And did not keep His testimonies,
57 But turned back and acted unfaithfully like their fathers;
They were turned aside like a deceitful bow.
58 For they provoked Him to anger with their high places,
And moved Him to jealousy with their carved images.
59 When God heard *this,* He was furious,
And greatly abhorred Israel,
60 So that He forsook the tabernacle of Shiloh,
The tent He had placed among men,
61 And delivered His strength into captivity,
And His glory into the enemy's hand.

62 He also gave His people over to the sword,
And was furious with His inheritance.
63 The fire consumed their young men,
And their maidens were not given in marriage.
64 Their priests fell by the sword,
And their widows made no lamentation.

65 Then the Lord awoke as *from* sleep,
Like a mighty man who shouts because of wine.
66 And He beat back His enemies;
He put them to a perpetual reproach.

67 Moreover He rejected the tent of Joseph,
And did not choose the tribe of Ephraim,
68 But chose the tribe of Judah,
Mount Zion which He loved.
69 And He built His sanctuary like the heights,
Like the earth which He has established forever.
70 He also chose David His servant,
And took him from the sheepfolds;
71 From following the ewes that had young He brought him,
To shepherd Jacob His people,
And Israel His inheritance.
72 So he shepherded them according to the integrity of his heart,
And guided them by the skillfulness of his hands.

PSALM 79

A Dirge and a Prayer for Israel, Destroyed by Enemies

A Psalm of Asaph.

O GOD, the nations have come into Your inheritance;
Your holy temple they have defiled;
They have laid Jerusalem in heaps.
2 The dead bodies of Your servants
They have given *as* food for the birds of the heavens,
The flesh of Your saints to the beasts of the earth.
3 Their blood they have shed like water all around Jerusalem,
And *there was* no one to bury *them*.
4 We have become a reproach to our neighbors,
A scorn and derision to those who are around us.

5 How long, LORD?
Will You be angry forever?
Will Your jealousy burn like fire?
6 Pour out Your wrath on the nations that do not know You,
And on the kingdoms that do not call on Your name.
7 For they have devoured Jacob,
And laid waste his dwelling place.

8 Oh, do not remember former iniquities against us!
Let Your tender mercies come speedily to meet us,
For we have been brought very low.
9 Help us, O God of our salvation,
For the glory of Your name;
And deliver us, and provide atonement for our sins,
For Your name's sake!
10 Why should the nations say,
"Where *is* their God?"
Let there be known among the nations in our sight
The avenging of the blood of Your servants *which has been* shed.

11 Let the groaning of the prisoner come before You;
According to the greatness of Your power
Preserve those who are appointed to die;
12 And return to our neighbors sevenfold into their bosom
Their reproach with which they have reproached You, O Lord.

13 So we, Your people and sheep of Your pasture,
Will give You thanks forever;
We will show forth Your praise to all generations.

PSALM 80

Prayer for Israel's Restoration

To the Chief Musician. Set to "The Lilies."[a] A Testimony[b] of Asaph. A Psalm.

GIVE ear, O Shepherd of Israel,
You who lead Joseph like a flock;
You who dwell *between* the cherubim, shine forth!
2 Before Ephraim, Benjamin, and Manasseh,
Stir up Your strength,
And come *and* save us!

3 Restore us, O God;
Cause Your face to shine,
And we shall be saved!

4 O LORD God of hosts,
How long will You be angry
Against the prayer of Your people?
5 You have fed them with the bread of tears,
And given them tears to drink in great measure.
6 You have made us a strife to our neighbors,
And our enemies laugh among themselves.

7 Restore us, O God of hosts;
Cause Your face to shine,
And we shall be saved!

8 You have brought a vine out of Egypt;
You have cast out the nations, and planted it.
9 You prepared *room* for it,
And caused it to take deep root,
And it filled the land.
10 The hills were covered with its shadow,
And the mighty cedars with its boughs.
11 She sent out her boughs to the Sea,[a]
And her branches to the River.[b]
12 Why have You broken down her hedges,
So that all who pass by the way pluck her *fruit?*
13 The boar out of the woods uproots it,
And the wild beast of the field devours it.

80:title [a]Hebrew *Shoshannim* [b]Hebrew *Eduth* **80:11** [a]That is, the Mediterranean [b]That is, the Euphrates

14 Return, we beseech You, O God of hosts;
Look down from heaven and see,
And visit this vine
15 And the vineyard which Your right hand
has planted,
And the branch *that* You made strong for
Yourself.
16 *It is* burned with fire, *it is* cut down;
They perish at the rebuke of Your
countenance.
17 Let Your hand be upon the man of Your
right hand,
Upon the son of man *whom* You made
strong for Yourself.
18 Then we will not turn back from You;
Revive us, and we will call upon Your
name.

19 Restore us, O LORD God of hosts;
Cause Your face to shine,
And we shall be saved!

PSALM 81

An Appeal for Israel's Repentance

To the Chief Musician. On an instrument of
Gath.[a] *A Psalm* of Asaph.

SING aloud to God our strength;
Make a joyful shout to the God of Jacob.
2 Raise a song and strike the timbrel,
The pleasant harp with the lute.

3 Blow the trumpet at the time of the New
Moon,
At the full moon, on our solemn feast day.
4 For this *is* a statute for Israel,
A law of the God of Jacob.
5 This He established in Joseph *as* a
testimony,
When He went throughout the land of
Egypt,
Where I heard a language I did not
understand.

6 "I removed his shoulder from the burden;
His hands were freed from the baskets.
7 You called in trouble, and I delivered you;
I answered you in the secret place of
thunder;
I tested you at the waters of Meribah.
Selah

8 "Hear, O My people, and I will admonish
you!
O Israel, if you will listen to Me!
9 There shall be no foreign god among you;
Nor shall you worship any foreign god.
10 I *am* the LORD your God,
Who brought you out of the land of
Egypt;
Open your mouth wide, and I will fill it.

11 "But My people would not heed My voice,
And Israel would *have* none of Me.
12 So I gave them over to their own
stubborn heart,
To walk in their own counsels.

13 "Oh, that My people would listen to Me,
That Israel would walk in My ways!
14 I would soon subdue their enemies,
And turn My hand against their
adversaries.
15 The haters of the LORD would pretend
submission to Him,
But their fate would endure forever.
16 He would have fed them also with the
finest of wheat;
And with honey from the rock I would
have satisfied you."

PSALM 82

A Plea for Justice

A Psalm of Asaph.

GOD stands in the congregation of the
mighty;
He judges among the gods.[a]
2 How long will you judge unjustly,
And show partiality to the wicked? Selah
3 Defend the poor and fatherless;
Do justice to the afflicted and needy.
4 Deliver the poor and needy;
Free *them* from the hand of the wicked.

5 They do not know, nor do they
understand;
They walk about in darkness;
All the foundations of the earth are
unstable.

6 I said, "You *are* gods,[a]
And all of you *are* children of the Most
High.
7 But you shall die like men,
And fall like one of the princes."

8 Arise, O God, judge the earth;
For You shall inherit all nations.

PSALM 83

Prayer to Frustrate Conspiracy Against Israel

A Song. A Psalm of Asaph.

DO not keep silent, O God!
Do not hold Your peace,
And do not be still, O God!
2 For behold, Your enemies make a tumult;
And those who hate You have lifted up
their head.
3 They have taken crafty counsel against
Your people,
And consulted together against Your
sheltered ones.
4 They have said, "Come, and let us cut
them off from *being* a nation,
That the name of Israel may be
remembered no more."

5 For they have consulted together with
one consent;
They form a confederacy against You:
6 The tents of Edom and the Ishmaelites;
Moab and the Hagrites;
7 Gebal, Ammon, and Amalek;
Philistia with the inhabitants of Tyre;
8 Assyria also has joined with them;
They have helped the children of Lot.
Selah

9 Deal with them as *with* Midian,
As *with* Sisera,
As *with* Jabin at the Brook Kishon,
10 Who perished at En Dor,
Who became *as* refuse on the earth.

81:title [a]Hebrew *Al Gittith* **82:1** [a]Hebrew *elohim*, mighty *ones*; that is, the judges **82:6** [a]Hebrew *elohim*, mighty *ones*; that is, the judges

11 Make their nobles like Oreb and like Zeeb,
Yes, all their princes like Zebah and Zalmunna,
12 Who said, "Let us take for ourselves
The pastures of God for a possession."
13 O my God, make them like the whirling dust,
Like the chaff before the wind!
14 As the fire burns the woods,
And as the flame sets the mountains on fire,
15 So pursue them with Your tempest,
And frighten them with Your storm.
16 Fill their faces with shame,
That they may seek Your name, O LORD.
17 Let them be confounded and dismayed forever;
Yes, let them be put to shame and perish,
18 That they may know that You, whose name alone *is* the LORD,
Are the Most High over all the earth.

PSALM 84

The Blessedness of Dwelling in the House of God

To the Chief Musician. On an instrument of Gath.[a] A Psalm of the sons of Korah.

HOW lovely *is* Your tabernacle,
O LORD of hosts!
2 My soul longs, yes, even faints
For the courts of the LORD;
My heart and my flesh cry out for the living God.
3 Even the sparrow has found a home,
And the swallow a nest for herself,
Where she may lay her young—
Even Your altars, O LORD of hosts,
My King and my God.
4 Blessed *are* those who dwell in Your house;
They will still be praising You. Selah
5 Blessed *is* the man whose strength *is* in You,
Whose heart *is* set on pilgrimage.
6 *As they* pass through the Valley of Baca,
They make it a spring;
The rain also covers it with pools.
7 They go from strength to strength;
Each one appears before God in Zion.[a]
8 O LORD God of hosts, hear my prayer;
Give ear, O God of Jacob! Selah
9 O God, behold our shield,
And look upon the face of Your anointed.
10 For a day in Your courts *is* better than a thousand.
I would rather be a doorkeeper in the house of my God
Than dwell in the tents of wickedness.
11 For the LORD God *is* a sun and shield;
The LORD will give grace and glory;
No good *thing* will He withhold
From those who walk uprightly.
12 O LORD of hosts,
Blessed *is* the man who trusts in You!

PSALM 85

Prayer that the LORD Will Restore Favor to the Land

To the Chief Musician. A Psalm of the sons of Korah.

LORD, You have been favorable to Your land;
You have brought back the captivity of Jacob.
2 You have forgiven the iniquity of Your people;
You have covered all their sin. Selah
3 You have taken away all Your wrath;
You have turned from the fierceness of Your anger.
4 Restore us, O God of our salvation,
And cause Your anger toward us to cease.
5 Will You be angry with us forever?
Will You prolong Your anger to all generations?
6 Will You not revive us again,
That Your people may rejoice in You?
7 Show us Your mercy, LORD,
And grant us Your salvation.
8 I will hear what God the LORD will speak,
For He will speak peace
To His people and to His saints;
But let them not turn back to folly.
9 Surely His salvation *is* near to those who fear Him,
That glory may dwell in our land.
10 Mercy and truth have met together;
Righteousness and peace have kissed.
11 Truth shall spring out of the earth,
And righteousness shall look down from heaven.
12 Yes, the LORD will give *what is* good;
And our land will yield its increase.
13 Righteousness will go before Him,
And shall make His footsteps *our* pathway.

PSALM 86

Prayer for Mercy, with Meditation on the Excellencies of the LORD

A Prayer of David.

BOW down Your ear, O LORD, hear me;
For I *am* poor and needy.
2 Preserve my life, for I *am* holy;
You are my God;
Save Your servant who trusts in You!
3 Be merciful to me, O Lord,
For I cry to You all day long.
4 Rejoice the soul of Your servant,
For to You, O Lord, I lift up my soul.
5 For You, Lord, *are* good, and ready to forgive,
And abundant in mercy to all those who call upon You.
6 Give ear, O LORD, to my prayer;
And attend to the voice of my supplications.
7 In the day of my trouble I will call upon You,
For You will answer me.
8 Among the gods *there is* none like You, O Lord;

84:title [a]Hebrew *Al Gittith* **84:7** [a]Septuagint, Syriac, and Vulgate read *The God of gods shall be seen.*

Nor *are there any works* like Your works.
9 All nations whom You have made
Shall come and worship before You,
O Lord,
And shall glorify Your name.
10 For You *are* great, and do wondrous
things;
You alone *are* God.

11 Teach me Your way, O LORD;
I will walk in Your truth;
Unite my heart to fear Your name.
12 I will praise You, O Lord my God, with all
my heart,
And I will glorify Your name
forevermore.
13 For great *is* Your mercy toward me,
And You have delivered my soul from the
depths of Sheol.
14 O God, the proud have risen against me,
And a mob of violent *men* have sought
my life,
And have not set You before them.
15 But You, O Lord, *are* a God full of
compassion, and gracious,
Longsuffering and abundant in mercy
and truth.
16 Oh, turn to me, and have mercy on me!
Give Your strength to Your servant,
And save the son of Your maidservant.
17 Show me a sign for good,
That those who hate me may see *it* and
be ashamed,
Because You, LORD, have helped me and
comforted me.

PSALM 87

The Glories of the City of God

A Psalm of the sons of Korah. A Song.

HIS foundation *is* in the holy
mountains.
2 The LORD loves the gates of Zion
More than all the dwellings of Jacob.
3 Glorious things are spoken of you,
O city of God! Selah

4 "I will make mention of Rahab and
Babylon to those who know Me;
Behold, O Philistia and Tyre, with
Ethiopia:
'This *one* was born there.'"
5 And of Zion it will be said,
"This *one* and that *one* were born in her;
And the Most High Himself shall
establish her."
6 The LORD will record,
When He registers the peoples:
"This *one* was born there." Selah

7 Both the singers and the players on
instruments *say,*
"All my springs *are* in you."

PSALM 88

A Prayer for Help in Despondency

A Song. A Psalm of the sons of Korah. To the Chief Musician. Set to "Mahalath Leannoth." A Contemplation[a] of Heman the Ezrahite.

O LORD, God of my salvation,
I have cried out day and night before
You.
2 Let my prayer come before You;
Incline Your ear to my cry.

3 For my soul is full of troubles,
And my life draws near to the grave.
4 I am counted with those who go down to
the pit;
I am like a man *who has* no strength,
5 Adrift among the dead,
Like the slain who lie in the grave,
Whom You remember no more,
And who are cut off from Your hand.

6 You have laid me in the lowest pit,
In darkness, in the depths.
7 Your wrath lies heavy upon me,
And You have afflicted *me* with all Your
waves. Selah
8 You have put away my acquaintances far
from me;
You have made me an abomination to
them;
I am shut up, and I cannot get out;
9 My eye wastes away because of affliction.

LORD, I have called daily upon You;
I have stretched out my hands to You.
10 Will You work wonders for the dead?
Shall the dead arise *and* praise You? Selah
11 Shall Your lovingkindness be declared in
the grave?
Or Your faithfulness in the place of
destruction?
12 Shall Your wonders be known in the
dark?
And Your righteousness in the land of
forgetfulness?

13 But to You I have cried out, O LORD,
And in the morning my prayer comes
before You.
14 LORD, why do You cast off my soul?
Why do You hide Your face from me?
15 I *have been* afflicted and ready to die
from *my* youth;
I suffer Your terrors;
I am distraught.
16 Your fierce wrath has gone over me;
Your terrors have cut me off.
17 They came around me all day long like
water;
They engulfed me altogether.
18 Loved one and friend You have put far
from me,
And my acquaintances into darkness.

PSALM 89

Remembering the Covenant with David, and Sorrow for Lost Blessings

A Contemplation[a] of Ethan the Ezrahite.

I WILL sing of the mercies of the LORD
forever;
With my mouth will I make known Your
faithfulness to all generations.
2 For I have said, "Mercy shall be built up
forever;
Your faithfulness You shall establish in
the very heavens."

3 "I have made a covenant with My chosen,
I have sworn to My servant David:
4 'Your seed I will establish forever,

88:title [a]Hebrew *Maschil* **89:title** [a]Hebrew *Maschil*

And build up your throne to all
generations.'" Selah
5 And the heavens will praise Your
wonders, O LORD;
Your faithfulness also in the assembly of
the saints.
6 For who in the heavens can be compared
to the LORD?
Who among the sons of the mighty can
be likened to the LORD?
7 God is greatly to be feared in the
assembly of the saints,
And to be held in reverence by all *those*
around Him.
8 O LORD God of hosts,
Who *is* mighty like You, O LORD?
Your faithfulness also surrounds You.
9 You rule the raging of the sea;
When its waves rise, You still them.
10 You have broken Rahab in pieces, as one
who is slain;
You have scattered Your enemies with
Your mighty arm.

11 The heavens *are* Yours, the earth also *is*
Yours;
The world and all its fullness, You have
founded them.
12 The north and the south, You have
created them;
Tabor and Hermon rejoice in Your name.
13 You have a mighty arm;
Strong is Your hand, *and* high is Your
right hand.
14 Righteousness and justice *are* the
foundation of Your throne;
Mercy and truth go before Your face.
15 Blessed *are* the people who know the
joyful sound!
They walk, O LORD, in the light of Your
countenance.
16 In Your name they rejoice all day long,
And in Your righteousness they are
exalted.
17 For You *are* the glory of their strength,
And in Your favor our horn is exalted.
18 For our shield *belongs* to the LORD,
And our king to the Holy One of Israel.

19 Then You spoke in a vision to Your holy
one,[a]
And said: "I have given help to *one who*
is mighty;
I have exalted one chosen from the
people.
20 I have found My servant David;
With My holy oil I have anointed him,
21 With whom My hand shall be established;
Also My arm shall strengthen him.
22 The enemy shall not outwit him,
Nor the son of wickedness afflict him.
23 I will beat down his foes before his face,
And plague those who hate him.

24 "But My faithfulness and My mercy *shall*
be with him,
And in My name his horn shall be
exalted.
25 Also I will set his hand over the sea,
And his right hand over the rivers.
26 He shall cry to Me, 'You *are* my Father,
My God, and the rock of my salvation.'
27 Also I will make him *My* firstborn,
The highest of the kings of the earth.
28 My mercy I will keep for him forever,
And My covenant shall stand firm with
him.
29 His seed also I will make *to endure*
forever,
And his throne as the days of heaven.

30 "If his sons forsake My law
And do not walk in My judgments,
31 If they break My statutes
And do not keep My commandments,
32 Then I will punish their transgression
with the rod,
And their iniquity with stripes.
33 Nevertheless My lovingkindness I will
not utterly take from him,
Nor allow My faithfulness to fail.
34 My covenant I will not break,
Nor alter the word that has gone out of
My lips.
35 Once I have sworn by My holiness;
I will not lie to David:
36 His seed shall endure forever,
And his throne as the sun before Me;
37 It shall be established forever like the
moon,
Even *like* the faithful witness in the sky."
Selah

38 But You have cast off and abhorred,
You have been furious with Your
anointed.
39 You have renounced the covenant of Your
servant;
You have profaned his crown *by casting*
it to the ground.
40 You have broken down all his hedges;
You have brought his strongholds to ruin.
41 All who pass by the way plunder him;
He is a reproach to his neighbors.
42 You have exalted the right hand of his
adversaries;
You have made all his enemies rejoice.
43 You have also turned back the edge of his
sword,
And have not sustained him in the battle.
44 You have made his glory cease,
And cast his throne down to the ground.
45 The days of his youth You have
shortened;
You have covered him with shame. Selah

46 How long, LORD?
Will You hide Yourself forever?
Will Your wrath burn like fire?
47 Remember how short my time is;
For what futility have You created all the
children of men?
48 What man can live and not see death?
Can he deliver his life from the power of
the grave? Selah

49 Lord, where *are* Your former
lovingkindnesses,
Which You swore to David in Your truth?
50 Remember, Lord, the reproach of Your
servants—
How I bear in my bosom *the reproach of*
all the many peoples,
51 With which Your enemies have
reproached, O LORD,
With which they have reproached the
footsteps of Your anointed.

89:19 [a]Following many Hebrew manuscripts; Masoretic Text, Septuagint, Targum, and Vulgate read *holy ones*.

52 Blessed *be* the LORD forevermore!
Amen and Amen.

BOOK FOUR

Psalms 90—106

PSALM 90

The Eternity of God, and Man's Frailty

A Prayer of Moses the man of God.

LORD, You have been our dwelling
place[a] in all generations.
2 Before the mountains were brought forth,
Or ever You had formed the earth and the world,
Even from everlasting to everlasting, You *are* God.
3 You turn man to destruction,
And say, "Return, O children of men."
4 For a thousand years in Your sight
Are like yesterday when it is past,
And *like* a watch in the night.
5 You carry them away *like* a flood;
They are like a sleep.
In the morning they are like grass *which* grows up:
6 In the morning it flourishes and grows up;
In the evening it is cut down and withers.
7 For we have been consumed by Your anger,
And by Your wrath we are terrified.
8 You have set our iniquities before You,
Our secret *sins* in the light of Your countenance.
9 For all our days have passed away in Your wrath;
We finish our years like a sigh.
10 The days of our lives *are* seventy years;
And if by reason of strength *they are* eighty years,
Yet their boast *is* only labor and sorrow;
For it is soon cut off, and we fly away.
11 Who knows the power of Your anger?
For as the fear of You, *so is* Your wrath.
12 So teach *us* to number our days,
That we may gain a heart of wisdom.
13 Return, O LORD!
How long?
And have compassion on Your servants.
14 Oh, satisfy us early with Your mercy,
That we may rejoice and be glad all our days!
15 Make us glad according to the days *in which* You have afflicted us,
The years *in which* we have seen evil.
16 Let Your work appear to Your servants,
And Your glory to their children.
17 And let the beauty of the LORD our God be upon us,
And establish the work of our hands for us;
Yes, establish the work of our hands.

PSALM 91

Safety of Abiding in the Presence of God

HE who dwells in the secret place of the Most High
Shall abide under the shadow of the Almighty.
2 I will say of the LORD, "*He is* my refuge and my fortress;
My God, in Him I will trust."
3 Surely He shall deliver you from the snare of the fowler[a]
And from the perilous pestilence.
4 He shall cover you with His feathers,
And under His wings you shall take refuge;
His truth *shall be your* shield and buckler.
5 You shall not be afraid of the terror by night,
Nor of the arrow *that* flies by day,
6 *Nor* of the pestilence *that* walks in darkness,
Nor of the destruction *that* lays waste at noonday.
7 A thousand may fall at your side,
And ten thousand at your right hand;
But it shall not come near you.
8 Only with your eyes shall you look,
And see the reward of the wicked.
9 Because you have made the LORD, *who is* my refuge,
Even the Most High, your dwelling place,
10 No evil shall befall you,
Nor shall any plague come near your dwelling;
11 For He shall give His angels charge over you,
To keep you in all your ways.
12 In *their* hands they shall bear you up,
Lest you dash your foot against a stone.
13 You shall tread upon the lion and the cobra,
The young lion and the serpent you shall trample underfoot.
14 "Because he has set his love upon Me, therefore I will deliver him;
I will set him on high, because he has known My name.
15 He shall call upon Me, and I will answer him;
I *will be* with him in trouble;
I will deliver him and honor him.
16 With long life I will satisfy him,
And show him My salvation."

PSALM 92

Praise to the LORD for His Love and Faithfulness

A Psalm. A Song for the Sabbath day.

IT *is* good to give thanks to the LORD,
And to sing praises to Your name, O Most High;
2 To declare Your lovingkindness in the morning,
And Your faithfulness every night,
3 On an instrument of ten strings,
On the lute,
And on the harp,
With harmonious sound.
4 For You, LORD, have made me glad through Your work;
I will triumph in the works of Your hands.
5 O LORD, how great are Your works!
Your thoughts are very deep.

90:1 [a]Septuagint, Targum, and Vulgate read *refuge*. 91:3 [a]That is, one who catches birds in a trap or snare

6 A senseless man does not know,
Nor does a fool understand this.
7 When the wicked spring up like grass,
And when all the workers of iniquity flourish,
It is that they may be destroyed forever.

8 But You, LORD, *are* on high forevermore.
9 For behold, Your enemies, O LORD,
For behold, Your enemies shall perish;
All the workers of iniquity shall be scattered.

10 But my horn You have exalted like a wild ox;
I have been anointed with fresh oil.
11 My eye also has seen *my desire* on my enemies;
My ears hear *my desire* on the wicked
Who rise up against me.

12 The righteous shall flourish like a palm tree,
He shall grow like a cedar in Lebanon.
13 Those who are planted in the house of the LORD
Shall flourish in the courts of our God.
14 They shall still bear fruit in old age;
They shall be fresh and flourishing,
15 To declare that the LORD is upright;
He is my rock, and *there is* no unrighteousness in Him.

PSALM 93

The Eternal Reign of the LORD

THE LORD reigns, He is clothed with majesty;
The LORD is clothed,
He has girded Himself with strength.
Surely the world is established, so that it cannot be moved.
2 Your throne *is* established from of old;
You *are* from everlasting.

3 The floods have lifted up, O LORD,
The floods have lifted up their voice;
The floods lift up their waves.
4 The LORD on high *is* mightier
Than the noise of many waters,
Than the mighty waves of the sea.

5 Your testimonies are very sure;
Holiness adorns Your house,
O LORD, forever.

PSALM 94

God the Refuge of the Righteous

O LORD God, to whom vengeance belongs—
O God, to whom vengeance belongs, shine forth!
2 Rise up, O Judge of the earth;
Render punishment to the proud.
3 LORD, how long will the wicked,
How long will the wicked triumph?

4 They utter speech, *and* speak insolent things;
All the workers of iniquity boast in themselves.
5 They break in pieces Your people, O LORD,
And afflict Your heritage.
6 They slay the widow and the stranger,
And murder the fatherless.
7 Yet they say, "The LORD does not see,
Nor does the God of Jacob understand."

8 Understand, you senseless among the people;
And *you* fools, when will you be wise?
9 He who planted the ear, shall He not hear?
He who formed the eye, shall He not see?
10 He who instructs the nations, shall He not correct,
He who teaches man knowledge?
11 The LORD knows the thoughts of man,
That they *are* futile.

12 Blessed *is* the man whom You instruct, O LORD,
And teach out of Your law,
13 That You may give him rest from the days of adversity,
Until the pit is dug for the wicked.
14 For the LORD will not cast off His people,
Nor will He forsake His inheritance.
15 But judgment will return to righteousness,
And all the upright in heart will follow it.

16 Who will rise up for me against the evildoers?
Who will stand up for me against the workers of iniquity?
17 Unless the LORD *had been* my help,
My soul would soon have settled in silence.
18 If I say, "My foot slips,"
Your mercy, O LORD, will hold me up.
19 In the multitude of my anxieties within me,
Your comforts delight my soul.

20 Shall the throne of iniquity, which devises evil by law,
Have fellowship with You?
21 They gather together against the life of the righteous,
And condemn innocent blood.
22 But the LORD has been my defense,
And my God the rock of my refuge.
23 He has brought on them their own iniquity,
And shall cut them off in their own wickedness;
The LORD our God shall cut them off.

PSALM 95

A Call to Worship and Obedience

OH come, let us sing to the LORD!
Let us shout joyfully to the Rock of our salvation.
2 Let us come before His presence with thanksgiving;
Let us shout joyfully to Him with psalms.
3 For the LORD *is* the great God,
And the great King above all gods.
4 In His hand *are* the deep places of the earth;
The heights of the hills *are* His also.
5 The sea *is* His, for He made it;
And His hands formed the dry *land*.

6 Oh come, let us worship and bow down;
Let us kneel before the LORD our Maker.
7 For He *is* our God,
And we *are* the people of His pasture,
And the sheep of His hand.

Today, if you will hear His voice:
8 "Do not harden your hearts, as in the rebellion,[a]
As *in* the day of trial[b] in the wilderness,
9 When your fathers tested Me;
They tried Me, though they saw My work.
10 For forty years I was grieved with *that* generation,
And said, 'It *is* a people who go astray in their hearts,
And they do not know My ways.'
11 So I swore in My wrath,
'They shall not enter My rest.'"

PSALM 96

A Song of Praise to God Coming in Judgment

OH, sing to the LORD a new song!
Sing to the LORD, all the earth.
2 Sing to the LORD, bless His name;
Proclaim the good news of His salvation from day to day.
3 Declare His glory among the nations,
His wonders among all peoples.

4 For the LORD *is* great and greatly to be praised;
He *is* to be feared above all gods.
5 For all the gods of the peoples *are* idols,
But the LORD made the heavens.
6 Honor and majesty *are* before Him;
Strength and beauty *are* in His sanctuary.

7 Give to the LORD, O families of the peoples,
Give to the LORD glory and strength.
8 Give to the LORD the glory *due* His name;
Bring an offering, and come into His courts.
9 Oh, worship the LORD in the beauty of holiness!
Tremble before Him, all the earth.

10 Say among the nations, "The LORD reigns;
The world also is firmly established,
It shall not be moved;
He shall judge the peoples righteously."

11 Let the heavens rejoice, and let the earth be glad;
Let the sea roar, and all its fullness;
12 Let the field be joyful, and all that *is* in it.
Then all the trees of the woods will rejoice
13 before the LORD.
For He is coming, for He is coming to judge the earth.
He shall judge the world with righteousness,
And the peoples with His truth.

PSALM 97

A Song of Praise to the Sovereign LORD

THE LORD reigns;
Let the earth rejoice;
Let the multitude of isles be glad!
2 Clouds and darkness surround Him;
Righteousness and justice *are* the foundation of His throne.
3 A fire goes before Him,
And burns up His enemies round about.
4 His lightnings light the world;
The earth sees and trembles.
5 The mountains melt like wax at the presence of the LORD,
At the presence of the Lord of the whole earth.
6 The heavens declare His righteousness,
And all the peoples see His glory.

7 Let all be put to shame who serve carved images,
Who boast of idols.
Worship Him, all *you* gods.
8 Zion hears and is glad,
And the daughters of Judah rejoice
Because of Your judgments, O LORD.
9 For You, LORD, *are* most high above all the earth;
You are exalted far above all gods.

10 You who love the LORD, hate evil!
He preserves the souls of His saints;
He delivers them out of the hand of the wicked.
11 Light is sown for the righteous,
And gladness for the upright in heart.
12 Rejoice in the LORD, you righteous,
And give thanks at the remembrance of His holy name.[a]

PSALM 98

A Song of Praise to the LORD for His Salvation and Judgment

A Psalm.

OH, sing to the LORD a new song!
For He has done marvelous things;
His right hand and His holy arm have gained Him the victory.
2 The LORD has made known His salvation;
His righteousness He has revealed in the sight of the nations.
3 He has remembered His mercy and His faithfulness to the house of Israel;
All the ends of the earth have seen the salvation of our God.

4 Shout joyfully to the LORD, all the earth;
Break forth in song, rejoice, and sing praises.
5 Sing to the LORD with the harp,
With the harp and the sound of a psalm,
6 With trumpets and the sound of a horn;
Shout joyfully before the LORD, the King.

7 Let the sea roar, and all its fullness,
The world and those who dwell in it;
8 Let the rivers clap *their* hands;
Let the hills be joyful together
9 before the LORD,
for He is coming to judge the earth.
With righteousness He shall judge the world,
And the peoples with equity.

PSALM 99

Praise to the LORD for His Holiness

THE LORD reigns;
Let the peoples tremble!
He dwells *between* the cherubim;
Let the earth be moved!

95:8 [a]Or *Meribah* [b]Or *Massah* 97:12 [a]Or *His holiness*

2 The LORD *is* great in Zion,
And He *is* high above all the peoples.
3 Let them praise Your great and awesome name—
He *is* holy.

4 The King's strength also loves justice;
You have established equity;
You have executed justice and righteousness in Jacob.
5 Exalt the LORD our God,
And worship at His footstool—
He *is* holy.

6 Moses and Aaron were among His priests,
And Samuel was among those who called upon His name;
They called upon the LORD, and He answered them.
7 He spoke to them in the cloudy pillar;
They kept His testimonies and the ordinance He gave them.

8 You answered them, O LORD our God;
You were to them God-Who-Forgives,
Though You took vengeance on their deeds.
9 Exalt the LORD our God,
And worship at His holy hill;
For the LORD our God *is* holy.

PSALM 100

A Song of Praise for the LORD's Faithfulness to His People

A Psalm of Thanksgiving.

MAKE a joyful shout to the LORD, all you lands!
2 Serve the LORD with gladness;
Come before His presence with singing.
3 Know that the LORD, He *is* God;
It is He *who* has made us, and not we ourselves;[a]
We are His people and the sheep of His pasture.

4 Enter into His gates with thanksgiving,
And into His courts with praise.
Be thankful to Him, *and* bless His name.
5 For the LORD *is* good;
His mercy *is* everlasting,
And His truth *endures* to all generations.

PSALM 101

Promised Faithfulness to the LORD

A Psalm of David.

I WILL sing of mercy and justice;
To You, O LORD, I will sing praises.

2 I will behave wisely in a perfect way.
Oh, when will You come to me?
I will walk within my house with a perfect heart.

3 I will set nothing wicked before my eyes;
I hate the work of those who fall away;
It shall not cling to me.
4 A perverse heart shall depart from me;
I will not know wickedness.

5 Whoever secretly slanders his neighbor,
Him I will destroy;
The one who has a haughty look and a proud heart,
Him I will not endure.

6 My eyes *shall be* on the faithful of the land,
That they may dwell with me;
He who walks in a perfect way,
He shall serve me.
7 He who works deceit shall not dwell within my house;
He who tells lies shall not continue in my presence.
8 Early I will destroy all the wicked of the land,
That I may cut off all the evildoers from the city of the LORD.

PSALM 102

The LORD's Eternal Love

A Prayer of the afflicted, when he is overwhelmed and pours out his complaint before the LORD.

HEAR my prayer, O LORD,
And let my cry come to You.
2 Do not hide Your face from me in the day of my trouble;
Incline Your ear to me;
In the day that I call, answer me speedily.

3 For my days are consumed like smoke,
And my bones are burned like a hearth.
4 My heart is stricken and withered like grass,
So that I forget to eat my bread.
5 Because of the sound of my groaning
My bones cling to my skin.
6 I am like a pelican of the wilderness;
I am like an owl of the desert.
7 I lie awake,
And am like a sparrow alone on the housetop.

8 My enemies reproach me all day long;
Those who deride me swear an oath against me.
9 For I have eaten ashes like bread,
And mingled my drink with weeping,
10 Because of Your indignation and Your wrath;
For You have lifted me up and cast me away.
11 My days *are* like a shadow that lengthens,
And I wither away like grass.

12 But You, O LORD, shall endure forever,
And the remembrance of Your name to all generations.
13 You will arise *and* have mercy on Zion;
For the time to favor her,
Yes, the set time, has come.
14 For Your servants take pleasure in her stones,
And show favor to her dust.
15 So the nations shall fear the name of the LORD,
And all the kings of the earth Your glory.
16 For the LORD shall build up Zion;
He shall appear in His glory.
17 He shall regard the prayer of the destitute,
And shall not despise their prayer.

100:3 [a]Following Kethib, Septuagint, and Vulgate; Qere, many Hebrew manuscripts, and Targum read *we are His*.

18 This will be written for the generation to come,
That a people yet to be created may praise the LORD.
19 For He looked down from the height of His sanctuary;
From heaven the LORD viewed the earth,
20 To hear the groaning of the prisoner,
To release those appointed to death,
21 To declare the name of the LORD in Zion,
And His praise in Jerusalem,
22 When the peoples are gathered together,
And the kingdoms, to serve the LORD.

23 He weakened my strength in the way;
He shortened my days.
24 I said, "O my God,
Do not take me away in the midst of my days;
Your years *are* throughout all generations.
25 Of old You laid the foundation of the earth,
And the heavens *are* the work of Your hands.
26 They will perish, but You will endure;
Yes, they will all grow old like a garment;
Like a cloak You will change them,
And they will be changed.
27 But You *are* the same,
And Your years will have no end.
28 The children of Your servants will continue,
And their descendants will be established before You."

PSALM 103

Praise for the LORD's Mercies

A Psalm of David.

BLESS the LORD, O my soul;
And all that is within me, *bless* His holy name!
2 Bless the LORD, O my soul,
And forget not all His benefits:
3 Who forgives all your iniquities,
Who heals all your diseases,
4 Who redeems your life from destruction,
Who crowns you with lovingkindness and tender mercies,
5 Who satisfies your mouth with good *things*,
So that your youth is renewed like the eagle's.

6 The LORD executes righteousness
And justice for all who are oppressed.
7 He made known His ways to Moses,
His acts to the children of Israel.
8 The LORD *is* merciful and gracious,
Slow to anger, and abounding in mercy.
9 He will not always strive *with us*,
Nor will He keep *His anger* forever.
10 He has not dealt with us according to our sins,
Nor punished us according to our iniquities.

11 For as the heavens are high above the earth,
So great is His mercy toward those who fear Him;
12 As far as the east is from the west,
So far has He removed our transgressions from us.
13 As a father pities *his* children,
So the LORD pities those who fear Him.
14 For He knows our frame;
He remembers that we *are* dust.

15 *As for* man, his days *are* like grass;
As a flower of the field, so he flourishes.
16 For the wind passes over it, and it is gone,
And its place remembers it no more.[a]
17 But the mercy of the LORD *is* from everlasting to everlasting
On those who fear Him,
And His righteousness to children's children,
18 To such as keep His covenant,
And to those who remember His commandments to do them.

19 The LORD has established His throne in heaven,
And His kingdom rules over all.

20 Bless the LORD, you His angels,
Who excel in strength, who do His word,
Heeding the voice of His word.
21 Bless the LORD, all *you* His hosts,
You ministers of His, who do His pleasure.
22 Bless the LORD, all His works,
In all places of His dominion.

Bless the LORD, O my soul!

PSALM 104

Praise to the Sovereign LORD for His Creation and Providence

BLESS the LORD, O my soul!
O LORD my God, You are very great:
You are clothed with honor and majesty,
2 Who cover *Yourself* with light as *with* a garment,
Who stretch out the heavens like a curtain.

3 He lays the beams of His upper chambers in the waters,
Who makes the clouds His chariot,
Who walks on the wings of the wind,
4 Who makes His angels spirits,
His ministers a flame of fire.

5 *You who* laid the foundations of the earth,
So *that* it should not be moved forever,
6 You covered it with the deep as *with* a garment;
The waters stood above the mountains.
7 At Your rebuke they fled;
At the voice of Your thunder they hastened away.
8 They went up over the mountains;
They went down into the valleys,
To the place which You founded for them.
9 You have set a boundary that they may not pass over,
That they may not return to cover the earth.

103:16 [a]Compare Job 7:10

10 He sends the springs into the valleys;
They flow among the hills.
11 They give drink to every beast of the field;
The wild donkeys quench their thirst.
12 By them the birds of the heavens have their home;
They sing among the branches.
13 He waters the hills from His upper chambers;
The earth is satisfied with the fruit of Your works.

14 He causes the grass to grow for the cattle,
And vegetation for the service of man,
That he may bring forth food from the earth,
15 And wine *that* makes glad the heart of man,
Oil to make *his* face shine,
And bread *which* strengthens man's heart.
16 The trees of the LORD are full *of sap,*
The cedars of Lebanon which He planted,
17 Where the birds make their nests;
The stork has her home in the fir trees.
18 The high hills *are* for the wild goats;
The cliffs are a refuge for the rock badgers.[a]

19 He appointed the moon for seasons;
The sun knows its going down.
20 You make darkness, and it is night,
In which all the beasts of the forest creep about.
21 The young lions roar after their prey,
And seek their food from God.
22 *When* the sun rises, they gather together
And lie down in their dens.
23 Man goes out to his work
And to his labor until the evening.

24 O LORD, how manifold are Your works!
In wisdom You have made them all.
The earth is full of Your possessions—
25 This great and wide sea,
In which *are* innumerable teeming things,
Living things both small and great.
26 There the ships sail about;
There is that Leviathan
Which You have made to play there.

27 These all wait for You,
That You may give *them* their food in due season.
28 *What* You give them they gather in;
You open Your hand, they are filled with good.
29 You hide Your face, they are troubled;
You take away their breath, they die and return to their dust.
30 You send forth Your Spirit, they are created;
And You renew the face of the earth.

31 May the glory of the LORD endure forever;
May the LORD rejoice in His works.
32 He looks on the earth, and it trembles;
He touches the hills, and they smoke.

33 I will sing to the LORD as long as I live;
I will sing praise to my God while I have my being.
34 May my meditation be sweet to Him;
I will be glad in the LORD.
35 May sinners be consumed from the earth,
And the wicked be no more.

Bless the LORD, O my soul!
Praise the LORD!

PSALM 105

The Eternal Faithfulness of the LORD

OH, give thanks to the LORD!
Call upon His name;
Make known His deeds among the peoples!
2 Sing to Him, sing psalms to Him;
Talk of all His wondrous works!
3 Glory in His holy name;
Let the hearts of those rejoice who seek the LORD!
4 Seek the LORD and His strength;
Seek His face evermore!
5 Remember His marvelous works which He has done,
His wonders, and the judgments of His mouth,
6 O seed of Abraham His servant,
You children of Jacob, His chosen ones!

7 He *is* the LORD our God;
His judgments *are* in all the earth.
8 He remembers His covenant forever,
The word *which* He commanded, for a thousand generations,
9 *The covenant* which He made with Abraham,
And His oath to Isaac,
10 And confirmed it to Jacob for a statute,
To Israel *as* an everlasting covenant,
11 Saying, "To you I will give the land of Canaan
As the allotment of your inheritance,"
12 When they were few in number,
Indeed very few, and strangers in it.

13 When they went from one nation to another,
From *one* kingdom to another people,
14 He permitted no one to do them wrong;
Yes, He rebuked kings for their sakes,
15 *Saying,* "Do not touch My anointed ones,
And do My prophets no harm."

16 Moreover He called for a famine in the land;
He destroyed all the provision of bread.
17 He sent a man before them—
Joseph—*who* was sold as a slave.
18 They hurt his feet with fetters,
He was laid in irons.
19 Until the time that his word came to pass,
The word of the LORD tested him.
20 The king sent and released him,
The ruler of the people let him go free.
21 He made him lord of his house,
And ruler of all his possessions,
22 To bind his princes at his pleasure,
And teach his elders wisdom.

23 Israel also came into Egypt,
And Jacob dwelt in the land of Ham.
24 He increased His people greatly,
And made them stronger than their enemies.
25 He turned their heart to hate His people,
To deal craftily with His servants.

104:18 [a]Or *rock hyrax* (compare Leviticus 11:5)

26 He sent Moses His servant,
And Aaron whom He had chosen.
27 They performed His signs among them,
And wonders in the land of Ham.
28 He sent darkness, and made *it* dark;
And they did not rebel against His word.
29 He turned their waters into blood,
And killed their fish.
30 Their land abounded with frogs,
Even in the chambers of their kings.
31 He spoke, and there came swarms of flies,
And lice in all their territory.
32 He gave them hail for rain,
And flaming fire in their land.
33 He struck their vines also, and their fig trees,
And splintered the trees of their territory.
34 He spoke, and locusts came,
Young locusts without number,
35 And ate up all the vegetation in their land,
And devoured the fruit of their ground.
36 He also destroyed all the firstborn in their land,
The first of all their strength.

37 He also brought them out with silver and gold,
And *there was* none feeble among His tribes.
38 Egypt was glad when they departed,
For the fear of them had fallen upon them.
39 He spread a cloud for a covering,
And fire to give light in the night.
40 *The people* asked, and He brought quail,
And satisfied them with the bread of heaven.
41 He opened the rock, and water gushed out;
It ran in the dry places *like* a river.
42 For He remembered His holy promise,
And Abraham His servant.
43 He brought out His people with joy,
His chosen ones with gladness.
44 He gave them the lands of the Gentiles,
And they inherited the labor of the nations,
45 That they might observe His statutes
And keep His laws.
Praise the LORD!

PSALM 106

Joy in Forgiveness of Israel's Sins

PRAISE the LORD!
Oh, give thanks to the LORD, for *He is* good!
For His mercy *endures* forever.

2 Who can utter the mighty acts of the LORD?
Who can declare all His praise?
3 Blessed *are* those who keep justice,
And he who does[a] righteousness at all times!

4 Remember me, O LORD, with the favor
You have toward Your people.
Oh, visit me with Your salvation,
5 That I may see the benefit of Your chosen ones,
That I may rejoice in the gladness of Your nation,
That I may glory with Your inheritance.

6 We have sinned with our fathers,
We have committed iniquity,
We have done wickedly.
7 Our fathers in Egypt did not understand Your wonders;
They did not remember the multitude of Your mercies,
But rebelled by the sea—the Red Sea.
8 Nevertheless He saved them for His name's sake,
That He might make His mighty power known.
9 He rebuked the Red Sea also, and it dried up;
So He led them through the depths,
As through the wilderness.
10 He saved them from the hand of him who hated *them*,
And redeemed them from the hand of the enemy.
11 The waters covered their enemies;
There was not one of them left.
12 Then they believed His words;
They sang His praise.

13 They soon forgot His works;
They did not wait for His counsel,
14 But lusted exceedingly in the wilderness,
And tested God in the desert.
15 And He gave them their request,
But sent leanness into their soul.

16 When they envied Moses in the camp,
And Aaron the saint of the LORD,
17 The earth opened up and swallowed Dathan,
And covered the faction of Abiram.
18 A fire was kindled in their company;
The flame burned up the wicked.

19 They made a calf in Horeb,
And worshiped the molded image.
20 Thus they changed their glory
Into the image of an ox that eats grass.
21 They forgot God their Savior,
Who had done great things in Egypt,
22 Wondrous works in the land of Ham,
Awesome things by the Red Sea.
23 Therefore He said that He would destroy them,
Had not Moses His chosen one stood before Him in the breach,
To turn away His wrath, lest He destroy *them*.

24 Then they despised the pleasant land;
They did not believe His word,
25 But complained in their tents,
And did not heed the voice of the LORD.
26 Therefore He raised His hand *in an oath* against them,
To overthrow them in the wilderness,
27 To overthrow their descendants among the nations,
And to scatter them in the lands.

28 They joined themselves also to Baal of Peor,
And ate sacrifices made to the dead.

106:3 [a]Septuagint, Syriac, Targum, and Vulgate read *those who do.*

29 Thus they provoked *Him* to anger with
their deeds,
And the plague broke out among them.
30 Then Phinehas stood up and intervened,
And the plague was stopped.
31 And that was accounted to him for
righteousness
To all generations forevermore.
32 They angered *Him* also at the waters of
strife,[a]
So that it went ill with Moses on account
of them;
33 Because they rebelled against His Spirit,
So that he spoke rashly with his lips.
34 They did not destroy the peoples,
Concerning whom the LORD had
commanded them,
35 But they mingled with the Gentiles
And learned their works;
36 They served their idols,
Which became a snare to them.
37 They even sacrificed their sons
And their daughters to demons,
38 And shed innocent blood,
The blood of their sons and daughters,
Whom they sacrificed to the idols of
Canaan;
And the land was polluted with blood.
39 Thus they were defiled by their own
works,
And played the harlot by their own deeds.
40 Therefore the wrath of the LORD was
kindled against His people,
So that He abhorred His own inheritance.
41 And He gave them into the hand of the
Gentiles,
And those who hated them ruled over
them.
42 Their enemies also oppressed them,
And they were brought into subjection
under their hand.
43 Many times He delivered them;
But they rebelled in their counsel,
And were brought low for their iniquity.
44 Nevertheless He regarded their affliction,
When He heard their cry;
45 And for their sake He remembered His
covenant,
And relented according to the multitude
of His mercies.
46 He also made them to be pitied
By all those who carried them away
captive.
47 Save us, O LORD our God,
And gather us from among the Gentiles,
To give thanks to Your holy name,
To triumph in Your praise.
48 Blessed *be* the LORD God of Israel
From everlasting to everlasting!
And let all the people say, "Amen!"
Praise the LORD!

BOOK FIVE
Psalms 107—150

PSALM 107

Thanksgiving to the LORD for His Great Works of Deliverance

OH, give thanks to the LORD, for *He is*
good!
For His mercy *endures* forever.
2 Let the redeemed of the LORD say *so,*
Whom He has redeemed from the hand
of the enemy,
3 And gathered out of the lands,
From the east and from the west,
From the north and from the south.
4 They wandered in the wilderness in a
desolate way;
They found no city to dwell in.
5 Hungry and thirsty,
Their soul fainted in them.
6 Then they cried out to the LORD in their
trouble,
And He delivered them out of their
distresses.
7 And He led them forth by the right way,
That they might go to a city for a
dwelling place.
8 Oh, that *men* would give thanks to the
LORD *for* His goodness,
And *for* His wonderful works to the
children of men!
9 For He satisfies the longing soul,
And fills the hungry soul with goodness.
10 Those who sat in darkness and in the
shadow of death,
Bound in affliction and irons—
11 Because they rebelled against the words
of God,
And despised the counsel of the Most
High,
12 Therefore He brought down their heart
with labor;
They fell down, and *there was* none to
help.
13 Then they cried out to the LORD in their
trouble,
And He saved them out of their
distresses.
14 He brought them out of darkness and the
shadow of death,
And broke their chains in pieces.
15 Oh, that *men* would give thanks to the
LORD *for* His goodness,
And *for* His wonderful works to the
children of men!
16 For He has broken the gates of bronze,
And cut the bars of iron in two.
17 Fools, because of their transgression,
And because of their iniquities, were
afflicted.
18 Their soul abhorred all manner of food,
And they drew near to the gates of death.
19 Then they cried out to the LORD in their
trouble,
And He saved them out of their
distresses.
20 He sent His word and healed them,
And delivered *them* from their
destructions.
21 Oh, that *men* would give thanks to the
LORD *for* His goodness,
And *for* His wonderful works to the
children of men!
22 Let them sacrifice the sacrifices of
thanksgiving,
And declare His works with rejoicing.
23 Those who go down to the sea in ships,
Who do business on great waters,

106:32 [a]Or *Meribah*

24 They see the works of the LORD,
And His wonders in the deep.
25 For He commands and raises the stormy wind,
Which lifts up the waves of the sea.
26 They mount up to the heavens,
They go down again to the depths;
Their soul melts because of trouble.
27 They reel to and fro, and stagger like a drunken man,
And are at their wits' end.
28 Then they cry out to the LORD in their trouble,
And He brings them out of their distresses.
29 He calms the storm,
So that its waves are still.
30 Then they are glad because they are quiet;
So He guides them to their desired haven.
31 Oh, that *men* would give thanks to the LORD *for* His goodness,
And *for* His wonderful works to the children of men!
32 Let them exalt Him also in the assembly of the people,
And praise Him in the company of the elders.

33 He turns rivers into a wilderness,
And the watersprings into dry ground;
34 A fruitful land into barrenness,
For the wickedness of those who dwell in it.
35 He turns a wilderness into pools of water,
And dry land into watersprings.
36 There He makes the hungry dwell,
That they may establish a city for a dwelling place,
37 And sow fields and plant vineyards,
That they may yield a fruitful harvest.
38 He also blesses them, and they multiply greatly;
And He does not let their cattle decrease.

39 When they are diminished and brought low
Through oppression, affliction, and sorrow,
40 He pours contempt on princes,
And causes them to wander in the wilderness *where there is* no way;
41 Yet He sets the poor on high, far from affliction,
And makes *their* families like a flock.
42 The righteous see *it* and rejoice,
And all iniquity stops its mouth.

43 Whoever *is* wise will observe these *things*,
And they will understand the lovingkindness of the LORD.

PSALM 108

Assurance of God's Victory over Enemies

A Song. A Psalm of David.

O GOD, my heart is steadfast;
I will sing and give praise, even with my glory.
2 Awake, lute and harp!
I will awaken the dawn.
3 I will praise You, O LORD, among the peoples,
And I will sing praises to You among the nations.
4 For Your mercy *is* great above the heavens,
And Your truth *reaches* to the clouds.

5 Be exalted, O God, above the heavens,
And Your glory above all the earth;
6 That Your beloved may be delivered,
Save *with* Your right hand, and hear me.

7 God has spoken in His holiness:
"I will rejoice;
I will divide Shechem
And measure out the Valley of Succoth.
8 Gilead *is* Mine; Manasseh *is* Mine;
Ephraim also *is* the helmet for My head;
Judah *is* My lawgiver.
9 Moab *is* My washpot;
Over Edom I will cast My shoe;
Over Philistia I will triumph."

10 Who will bring me *into* the strong city?
Who will lead me to Edom?
11 *Is it* not *You*, O God, *who* cast us off?
And *You*, O God, *who* did not go out with our armies?
12 Give us help from trouble,
For the help of man is useless.
13 Through God we will do valiantly,
For *it is* He *who* shall tread down our enemies.[a]

PSALM 109

Plea for Judgment of False Accusers

To the Chief Musician. A Psalm of David.

DO not keep silent,
O God of my praise!
2 For the mouth of the wicked and the mouth of the deceitful
Have opened against me;
They have spoken against me with a lying tongue.
3 They have also surrounded me with words of hatred,
And fought against me without a cause.
4 In return for my love they are my accusers,
But I *give myself to* prayer.
5 Thus they have rewarded me evil for good,
And hatred for my love.

6 Set a wicked man over him,
And let an accuser[a] stand at his right hand.
7 When he is judged, let him be found guilty,
And let his prayer become sin.
8 Let his days be few,
And let another take his office.
9 Let his children be fatherless,
And his wife a widow.
10 Let his children continually be vagabonds, and beg;
Let them seek *their bread*[a] also from their desolate places.
11 Let the creditor seize all that he has,
And let strangers plunder his labor.
12 Let there be none to extend mercy to him,
Nor let there be any to favor his fatherless children.

108:13 [a]Compare verses 6–13 with 60:5–12 **109:6** [a]Hebrew *satan* **109:10** [a]Following Masoretic Text and Targum; Septuagint and Vulgate read *be cast out*.

13 Let his posterity be cut off,
And in the generation following let their name be blotted out.
14 Let the iniquity of his fathers be remembered before the LORD,
And let not the sin of his mother be blotted out.
15 Let them be continually before the LORD,
That He may cut off the memory of them from the earth;
16 Because he did not remember to show mercy,
But persecuted the poor and needy man,
That he might even slay the broken in heart.
17 As he loved cursing, so let it come to him;
As he did not delight in blessing, so let it be far from him.
18 As he clothed himself with cursing as with his garment,
So let it enter his body like water,
And like oil into his bones.
19 Let it be to him like the garment which covers him,
And for a belt with which he girds himself continually.
20 *Let* this *be* the LORD's reward to my accusers,
And to those who speak evil against my person.

21 But You, O GOD the Lord,
Deal with me for Your name's sake;
Because Your mercy *is* good, deliver me.
22 For I *am* poor and needy,
And my heart is wounded within me.
23 I am gone like a shadow when it lengthens;
I am shaken off like a locust.
24 My knees are weak through fasting,
And my flesh is feeble from lack of fatness.
25 I also have become a reproach to them;
When they look at me, they shake their heads.

26 Help me, O LORD my God!
Oh, save me according to Your mercy,
27 That they may know that this *is* Your hand—
That You, LORD, have done it!
28 Let them curse, but You bless;
When they arise, let them be ashamed,
But let Your servant rejoice.
29 Let my accusers be clothed with shame,
And let them cover themselves with their own disgrace as with a mantle.

30 I will greatly praise the LORD with my mouth;
Yes, I will praise Him among the multitude.
31 For He shall stand at the right hand of the poor,
To save *him* from those who condemn him.

PSALM 110

Announcement of the Messiah's Reign

A Psalm of David.

THE LORD said to my Lord,
"Sit at My right hand,
Till I make Your enemies Your footstool."
2 The LORD shall send the rod of Your strength out of Zion.
Rule in the midst of Your enemies!
3 Your people *shall be* volunteers
In the day of Your power;
In the beauties of holiness, from the womb of the morning,
You have the dew of Your youth.
4 The LORD has sworn
And will not relent,
"You *are* a priest forever
According to the order of Melchizedek."

5 The Lord *is* at Your right hand;
He shall execute kings in the day of His wrath.
6 He shall judge among the nations,
He shall fill *the places* with dead bodies,
He shall execute the heads of many countries.
7 He shall drink of the brook by the wayside;
Therefore He shall lift up the head.

PSALM 111

Praise to God for His Faithfulness and Justice

PRAISE the LORD!

I will praise the LORD with *my* whole heart,
In the assembly of the upright and *in* the congregation.

2 The works of the LORD *are* great,
Studied by all who have pleasure in them.
3 His work *is* honorable and glorious,
And His righteousness endures forever.
4 He has made His wonderful works to be remembered;
The LORD *is* gracious and full of compassion.
5 He has given food to those who fear Him;
He will ever be mindful of His covenant.
6 He has declared to His people the power of His works,
In giving them the heritage of the nations.

7 The works of His hands *are* verity and justice;
All His precepts *are* sure.
8 They stand fast forever and ever,
And are done in truth and uprightness.
9 He has sent redemption to His people;
He has commanded His covenant forever:
Holy and awesome *is* His name.

10 The fear of the LORD *is* the beginning of wisdom;
A good understanding have all those who do *His commandments.*
His praise endures forever.

PSALM 112

The Blessed State of the Righteous

PRAISE the LORD!

Blessed *is* the man *who* fears the LORD,
Who delights greatly in His commandments.

2 His descendants will be mighty on earth;
The generation of the upright will be blessed.
3 Wealth and riches *will be* in his house,
And his righteousness endures forever.
4 Unto the upright there arises light in the darkness;
He is gracious, and full of compassion, and righteous.

5 A good man deals graciously and lends;
He will guide his affairs with discretion.
6 Surely he will never be shaken;
The righteous will be in everlasting remembrance.
7 He will not be afraid of evil tidings;
His heart is steadfast, trusting in the LORD.
8 His heart *is* established;
He will not be afraid,
Until he sees *his desire* upon his enemies.

9 He has dispersed abroad,
He has given to the poor;
His righteousness endures forever;
His horn will be exalted with honor.
10 The wicked will see *it* and be grieved;
He will gnash his teeth and melt away;
The desire of the wicked shall perish.

PSALM 113

The Majesty and Condescension of God

PRAISE the LORD!

Praise, O servants of the LORD,
Praise the name of the LORD!
2 Blessed be the name of the LORD
From this time forth and forevermore!
3 From the rising of the sun to its going down
The LORD's name *is* to be praised.

4 The LORD *is* high above all nations,
His glory above the heavens.
5 Who *is* like the LORD our God,
Who dwells on high,
6 Who humbles Himself to behold
The things that are in the heavens and in the earth?
7 He raises the poor out of the dust,
And lifts the needy out of the ash heap,
8 That He may seat *him* with princes—
With the princes of His people.
9 He grants the barren woman a home,
Like a joyful mother of children.

Praise the LORD!

PSALM 114

The Power of God in His Deliverance of Israel

WHEN Israel went out of Egypt,
The house of Jacob from a people of strange language,
2 Judah became His sanctuary,
And Israel His dominion.

3 The sea saw *it* and fled;
Jordan turned back.
4 The mountains skipped like rams,
The little hills like lambs.
5 What ails you, O sea, that you fled?
O Jordan, *that* you turned back?
6 O mountains, *that* you skipped like rams?
O little hills, like lambs?

7 Tremble, O earth, at the presence of the Lord,
At the presence of the God of Jacob,
8 Who turned the rock *into* a pool of water,
The flint into a fountain of waters.

PSALM 115

The Futility of Idols and the Trustworthiness of God

NOT unto us, O LORD, not unto us,
But to Your name give glory,
Because of Your mercy,
Because of Your truth.
2 Why should the Gentiles say,
"So where *is* their God?"

3 But our God *is* in heaven;
He does whatever He pleases.
4 Their idols *are* silver and gold,
The work of men's hands.
5 They have mouths, but they do not speak;
Eyes they have, but they do not see;
6 They have ears, but they do not hear;
Noses they have, but they do not smell;
7 They have hands, but they do not handle;
Feet they have, but they do not walk;
Nor do they mutter through their throat.
8 Those who make them are like them;
So is everyone who trusts in them.

9 O Israel, trust in the LORD;
He *is* their help and their shield.
10 O house of Aaron, trust in the LORD;
He *is* their help and their shield.
11 You who fear the LORD, trust in the LORD;
He *is* their help and their shield.

12 The LORD has been mindful of *us;*
He will bless us;
He will bless the house of Israel;
He will bless the house of Aaron.
13 He will bless those who fear the LORD,
Both small and great.

14 May the LORD give you increase more and more,
You and your children.
15 *May* you *be* blessed by the LORD,
Who made heaven and earth.

16 The heaven, *even* the heavens, *are* the LORD's;
But the earth He has given to the children of men.
17 The dead do not praise the LORD,
Nor any who go down into silence.
18 But we will bless the LORD
From this time forth and forevermore.

Praise the LORD!

PSALM 116

Thanksgiving for Deliverance from Death

I LOVE the LORD, because He has heard
My voice *and* my supplications.
2 Because He has inclined His ear to me,
Therefore I will call *upon Him* as long as I live.

3 The pains of death surrounded me,
And the pangs of Sheol laid hold of me;
I found trouble and sorrow.
4 Then I called upon the name of the LORD:
"O LORD, I implore You, deliver my soul!"

5 Gracious *is* the LORD, and righteous;
Yes, our God *is* merciful.
6 The LORD preserves the simple;
I was brought low, and He saved me.

7 Return to your rest, O my soul,
For the LORD has dealt bountifully with you.
8 For You have delivered my soul from death,
My eyes from tears,
And my feet from falling.
9 I will walk before the LORD
In the land of the living.
10 I believed, therefore I spoke,
"I am greatly afflicted."
11 I said in my haste,
"All men *are* liars."
12 What shall I render to the LORD
For all His benefits toward me?
13 I will take up the cup of salvation,
And call upon the name of the LORD.
14 I will pay my vows to the LORD
Now in the presence of all His people.
15 Precious in the sight of the LORD
Is the death of His saints.
16 O LORD, truly I *am* Your servant;
I *am* Your servant, the son of Your maidservant;
You have loosed my bonds.
17 I will offer to You the sacrifice of thanksgiving,
And will call upon the name of the LORD.
18 I will pay my vows to the LORD
Now in the presence of all His people,
19 In the courts of the LORD's house,
In the midst of you, O Jerusalem.
Praise the LORD!

PSALM 117

Let All Peoples Praise the LORD

PRAISE the LORD, all you Gentiles!
Laud Him, all you peoples!
2 For His merciful kindness is great toward us,
And the truth of the LORD *endures* forever.
Praise the LORD!

PSALM 118

Praise to God for His Everlasting Mercy

OH, give thanks to the LORD, for *He is* good!
For His mercy *endures* forever.
2 Let Israel now say,
"His mercy *endures* forever."
3 Let the house of Aaron now say,
"His mercy *endures* forever."
4 Let those who fear the LORD now say,
"His mercy *endures* forever."
5 I called on the LORD in distress;
The LORD answered me *and set me* in a broad place.
6 The LORD *is* on my side;
I will not fear.
What can man do to me?
7 The LORD is for me among those who help me;
Therefore I shall see *my desire* on those who hate me.
8 *It is* better to trust in the LORD
Than to put confidence in man.
9 *It is* better to trust in the LORD
Than to put confidence in princes.
10 All nations surrounded me,
But in the name of the LORD I will destroy them.
11 They surrounded me,
Yes, they surrounded me;
But in the name of the LORD I will destroy them.
12 They surrounded me like bees;
They were quenched like a fire of thorns;
For in the name of the LORD I will destroy them.
13 You pushed me violently, that I might fall,
But the LORD helped me.
14 The LORD *is* my strength and song,
And He has become my salvation.[a]
15 The voice of rejoicing and salvation
Is in the tents of the righteous;
The right hand of the LORD does valiantly.
16 The right hand of the LORD is exalted;
The right hand of the LORD does valiantly.
17 I shall not die, but live,
And declare the works of the LORD.
18 The LORD has chastened me severely,
But He has not given me over to death.
19 Open to me the gates of righteousness;
I will go through them,
And I will praise the LORD.
20 This is the gate of the LORD,
Through which the righteous shall enter.
21 I will praise You,
For You have answered me,
And have become my salvation.
22 The stone *which* the builders rejected
Has become the chief cornerstone.
23 This was the LORD's doing;
It *is* marvelous in our eyes.
24 This *is* the day the LORD has made;
We will rejoice and be glad in it.
25 Save now, I pray, O LORD;
O LORD, I pray, send now prosperity.
26 Blessed *is* he who comes in the name of the LORD!
We have blessed you from the house of the LORD.
27 God *is* the LORD,
And He has given us light;
Bind the sacrifice with cords to the horns of the altar.
28 You *are* my God, and I will praise You;
You are my God, I will exalt You.
29 Oh, give thanks to the LORD, for *He is* good!
For His mercy *endures* forever.

PSALM 119

Meditations on the Excellencies of the Word of God

א ALEPH

BLESSED *are* the undefiled in the way,
Who walk in the law of the LORD!

118:14 [a]Compare Exodus 15:2

2 Blessed *are* those who keep His testimonies,
Who seek Him with the whole heart!
3 They also do no iniquity;
They walk in His ways.
4 You have commanded *us*
To keep Your precepts diligently.
5 Oh, that my ways were directed
To keep Your statutes!
6 Then I would not be ashamed,
When I look into all Your commandments.
7 I will praise You with uprightness of heart,
When I learn Your righteous judgments.
8 I will keep Your statutes;
Oh, do not forsake me utterly!

ב BETH

9 How can a young man cleanse his way?
By taking heed according to Your word.
10 With my whole heart I have sought You;
Oh, let me not wander from Your commandments!
11 Your word I have hidden in my heart,
That I might not sin against You.
12 Blessed *are* You, O LORD!
Teach me Your statutes.
13 With my lips I have declared
All the judgments of Your mouth.
14 I have rejoiced in the way of Your testimonies,
As *much as* in all riches.
15 I will meditate on Your precepts,
And contemplate Your ways.
16 I will delight myself in Your statutes;
I will not forget Your word.

ג GIMEL

17 Deal bountifully with Your servant,
That I may live and keep Your word.
18 Open my eyes, that I may see
Wondrous things from Your law.
19 I *am* a stranger in the earth;
Do not hide Your commandments from me.
20 My soul breaks with longing
For Your judgments at all times.
21 You rebuke the proud—the cursed,
Who stray from Your commandments.
22 Remove from me reproach and contempt,
For I have kept Your testimonies.
23 Princes also sit *and* speak against me,
But Your servant meditates on Your statutes.
24 Your testimonies also *are* my delight
And my counselors.

ד DALETH

25 My soul clings to the dust;
Revive me according to Your word.
26 I have declared my ways, and You answered me;
Teach me Your statutes.
27 Make me understand the way of Your precepts;
So shall I meditate on Your wonderful works.
28 My soul melts from heaviness;
Strengthen me according to Your word.
29 Remove from me the way of lying,
And grant me Your law graciously.
30 I have chosen the way of truth;
Your judgments I have laid *before me.*
31 I cling to Your testimonies;
O LORD, do not put me to shame!
32 I will run the course of Your commandments,
For You shall enlarge my heart.

ה HE

33 Teach me, O LORD, the way of Your statutes,
And I shall keep it *to* the end.
34 Give me understanding, and I shall keep Your law;
Indeed, I shall observe it with *my* whole heart.
35 Make me walk in the path of Your commandments,
For I delight in it.
36 Incline my heart to Your testimonies,
And not to covetousness.
37 Turn away my eyes from looking at worthless things,
And revive me in Your way.[a]
38 Establish Your word to Your servant,
Who *is devoted* to fearing You.
39 Turn away my reproach which I dread,
For Your judgments *are* good.
40 Behold, I long for Your precepts;
Revive me in Your righteousness.

ו WAW

41 Let Your mercies come also to me, O LORD—
Your salvation according to Your word.
42 So shall I have an answer for him who reproaches me,
For I trust in Your word.
43 And take not the word of truth utterly out of my mouth,
For I have hoped in Your ordinances.
44 So shall I keep Your law continually,
Forever and ever.
45 And I will walk at liberty,
For I seek Your precepts.
46 I will speak of Your testimonies also before kings,
And will not be ashamed.
47 And I will delight myself in Your commandments,
Which I love.
48 My hands also I will lift up to Your commandments,
Which I love,
And I will meditate on Your statutes.

ז ZAYIN

49 Remember the word to Your servant,
Upon which You have caused me to hope.
50 This *is* my comfort in my affliction,
For Your word has given me life.
51 The proud have me in great derision,
Yet I do not turn aside from Your law.
52 I remembered Your judgments of old, O LORD,
And have comforted myself.
53 Indignation has taken hold of me
Because of the wicked, who forsake Your law.

119:37 [a]Following Masoretic Text, Septuagint, and Vulgate; Targum reads *Your words.*

54 Your statutes have been my songs
In the house of my pilgrimage.
55 I remember Your name in the night,
O LORD,
And I keep Your law.
56 This has become mine,
Because I kept Your precepts.

ח HETH

57 *You are* my portion, O LORD;
I have said that I would keep Your
words.
58 I entreated Your favor with *my* whole
heart;
Be merciful to me according to Your
word.
59 I thought about my ways,
And turned my feet to Your testimonies.
60 I made haste, and did not delay
To keep Your commandments.
61 The cords of the wicked have bound me,
But I have not forgotten Your law.
62 At midnight I will rise to give thanks to
You,
Because of Your righteous judgments.
63 I *am* a companion of all who fear You,
And of those who keep Your precepts.
64 The earth, O LORD, is full of Your
mercy;
Teach me Your statutes.

ט TETH

65 You have dealt well with Your servant,
O LORD, according to Your word.
66 Teach me good judgment and
knowledge,
For I believe Your commandments.
67 Before I was afflicted I went astray,
But now I keep Your word.
68 You *are* good, and do good;
Teach me Your statutes.
69 The proud have forged a lie against me,
But I will keep Your precepts with *my*
whole heart.
70 Their heart is as fat as grease,
But I delight in Your law.
71 *It is* good for me that I have been
afflicted,
That I may learn Your statutes.
72 The law of Your mouth *is* better to me
Than thousands of *coins of* gold and
silver.

י YOD

73 Your hands have made me and
fashioned me;
Give me understanding, that I may learn
Your commandments.
74 Those who fear You will be glad when
they see me,
Because I have hoped in Your word.
75 I know, O LORD, that Your judgments
are right,
And *that* in faithfulness You have
afflicted me.
76 Let, I pray, Your merciful kindness be
for my comfort,
According to Your word to Your servant.
77 Let Your tender mercies come to me,
that I may live;
For Your law *is* my delight.
78 Let the proud be ashamed,
For they treated me wrongfully with
falsehood;
But I will meditate on Your precepts.
79 Let those who fear You turn to me,
Those who know Your testimonies.
80 Let my heart be blameless regarding
Your statutes,
That I may not be ashamed.

כ KAPH

81 My soul faints for Your salvation,
But I hope in Your word.
82 My eyes fail *from searching* Your word,
Saying, "When will You comfort me?"
83 For I have become like a wineskin in
smoke,
Yet I do not forget Your statutes.
84 How many *are* the days of Your servant?
When will You execute judgment on
those who persecute me?
85 The proud have dug pits for me,
Which *is* not according to Your law.
86 All Your commandments *are* faithful;
They persecute me wrongfully;
Help me!
87 They almost made an end of me on
earth,
But I did not forsake Your precepts.
88 Revive me according to Your
lovingkindness,
So that I may keep the testimony of
Your mouth.

ל LAMED

89 Forever, O LORD,
Your word is settled in heaven.
90 Your faithfulness *endures* to all
generations;
You established the earth, and it abides.
91 They continue this day according to
Your ordinances,
For all *are* Your servants.
92 Unless Your law *had been* my delight,
I would then have perished in my
affliction.
93 I will never forget Your precepts,
For by them You have given me life.
94 I *am* Yours, save me;
For I have sought Your precepts.
95 The wicked wait for me to destroy me,
But I will consider Your testimonies.
96 I have seen the consummation of all
perfection,
But Your commandment *is* exceedingly
broad.

מ MEM

97 Oh, how I love Your law!
It *is* my meditation all the day.
98 You, through Your commandments,
make me wiser than my enemies;
For they *are* ever with me.
99 I have more understanding than all my
teachers,
For Your testimonies *are* my meditation.
100 I understand more than the ancients,
Because I keep Your precepts.
101 I have restrained my feet from every evil
way,
That I may keep Your word.
102 I have not departed from Your
judgments,
For You Yourself have taught me.
103 How sweet are Your words to my taste,
Sweeter than honey to my mouth!
104 Through Your precepts I get
understanding;
Therefore I hate every false way.

ℕ NUN

105 Your word *is* a lamp to my feet
And a light to my path.
106 I have sworn and confirmed
That I will keep Your righteous
judgments.
107 I am afflicted very much;
Revive me, O LORD, according to Your
word.
108 Accept, I pray, the freewill offerings of
my mouth, O LORD,
And teach me Your judgments.
109 My life *is* continually in my hand,
Yet I do not forget Your law.
110 The wicked have laid a snare for me,
Yet I have not strayed from Your
precepts.
111 Your testimonies I have taken as a
heritage forever,
For they *are* the rejoicing of my heart.
112 I have inclined my heart to perform
Your statutes
Forever, to the very end.

ס SAMEK

113 I hate the double-minded,
But I love Your law.
114 You *are* my hiding place and my shield;
I hope in Your word.
115 Depart from me, you evildoers,
For I will keep the commandments of
my God!
116 Uphold me according to Your word, that
I may live;
And do not let me be ashamed of my
hope.
117 Hold me up, and I shall be safe,
And I shall observe Your statutes
continually.
118 You reject all those who stray from Your
statutes,
For their deceit *is* falsehood.
119 You put away all the wicked of the earth
like dross;
Therefore I love Your testimonies.
120 My flesh trembles for fear of You,
And I am afraid of Your judgments.

ע AYIN

121 I have done justice and righteousness;
Do not leave me to my oppressors.
122 Be surety for Your servant for good;
Do not let the proud oppress me.
123 My eyes fail *from seeking* Your salvation
And Your righteous word.
124 Deal with Your servant according to
Your mercy,
And teach me Your statutes.
125 I *am* Your servant;
Give me understanding,
That I may know Your testimonies.
126 *It is* time for *You* to act, O LORD,
For they have regarded Your law as
void.
127 Therefore I love Your commandments
More than gold, yes, than fine gold!
128 Therefore all *Your* precepts *concerning*
all *things*
I consider *to be* right;
I hate every false way.

פ PE

129 Your testimonies are wonderful;
Therefore my soul keeps them.
130 The entrance of Your words gives light;
It gives understanding to the simple.
131 I opened my mouth and panted,
For I longed for Your commandments.
132 Look upon me and be merciful to me,
As Your custom *is* toward those who
love Your name.
133 Direct my steps by Your word,
And let no iniquity have dominion over
me.
134 Redeem me from the oppression of man,
That I may keep Your precepts.
135 Make Your face shine upon Your
servant,
And teach me Your statutes.
136 Rivers of water run down from my eyes,
Because *men* do not keep Your law.

צ TSADDE

137 Righteous *are* You, O LORD,
And upright *are* Your judgments.
138 Your testimonies, *which* You have
commanded,
Are righteous and very faithful.
139 My zeal has consumed me,
Because my enemies have forgotten
Your words.
140 Your word *is* very pure;
Therefore Your servant loves it.
141 I *am* small and despised,
Yet I do not forget Your precepts.
142 Your righteousness *is* an everlasting
righteousness,
And Your law *is* truth.
143 Trouble and anguish have overtaken me,
Yet Your commandments *are* my
delights.
144 The righteousness of Your testimonies *is*
everlasting;
Give me understanding, and I shall live.

ק QOPH

145 I cry out with *my* whole heart;
Hear me, O LORD!
I will keep Your statutes.
146 I cry out to You;
Save me, and I will keep Your
testimonies.
147 I rise before the dawning of the
morning,
And cry for help;
I hope in Your word.
148 My eyes are awake through the *night*
watches,
That I may meditate on Your word.
149 Hear my voice according to Your
lovingkindness;
O LORD, revive me according to Your
justice.
150 They draw near who follow after
wickedness;
They are far from Your law.
151 You *are* near, O LORD,
And all Your commandments *are* truth.
152 Concerning Your testimonies,
I have known of old that You have
founded them forever.

ר RESH

153 Consider my affliction and deliver me,
For I do not forget Your law.
154 Plead my cause and redeem me;
Revive me according to Your word.
155 Salvation *is* far from the wicked,
For they do not seek Your statutes.

156 Great *are* Your tender mercies, O LORD;
Revive me according to Your judgments.
157 Many *are* my persecutors and my enemies,
Yet I do not turn from Your testimonies.
158 I see the treacherous, and am disgusted,
Because they do not keep Your word.
159 Consider how I love Your precepts;
Revive me, O LORD, according to Your lovingkindness.
160 The entirety of Your word *is* truth,
And every one of Your righteous judgments *endures* forever.

ש SHIN

161 Princes persecute me without a cause,
But my heart stands in awe of Your word.
162 I rejoice at Your word
As one who finds great treasure.
163 I hate and abhor lying,
But I love Your law.
164 Seven times a day I praise You,
Because of Your righteous judgments.
165 Great peace have those who love Your law,
And nothing causes them to stumble.
166 LORD, I hope for Your salvation,
And I do Your commandments.
167 My soul keeps Your testimonies,
And I love them exceedingly.
168 I keep Your precepts and Your testimonies,
For all my ways *are* before You.

ת TAU

169 Let my cry come before You, O LORD;
Give me understanding according to Your word.
170 Let my supplication come before You;
Deliver me according to Your word.
171 My lips shall utter praise,
For You teach me Your statutes.
172 My tongue shall speak of Your word,
For all Your commandments *are* righteousness.
173 Let Your hand become my help,
For I have chosen Your precepts.
174 I long for Your salvation, O LORD,
And Your law *is* my delight.
175 Let my soul live, and it shall praise You;
And let Your judgments help me.
176 I have gone astray like a lost sheep;
Seek Your servant,
For I do not forget Your commandments.

PSALM 120

Plea for Relief from Bitter Foes

A Song of Ascents.

IN my distress I cried to the LORD,
And He heard me.
2 Deliver my soul, O LORD, from lying lips
And from a deceitful tongue.

3 What shall be given to you,
Or what shall be done to you,
You false tongue?
4 Sharp arrows of the warrior,
With coals of the broom tree!

5 Woe is me, that I dwell in Meshech,
That I dwell among the tents of Kedar!
6 My soul has dwelt too long
With one who hates peace.
7 I *am for* peace;
But when I speak, they *are* for war.

PSALM 121

God the Help of Those Who Seek Him

A Song of Ascents.

I WILL lift up my eyes to the hills—
From whence comes my help?
2 My help *comes* from the LORD,
Who made heaven and earth.

3 He will not allow your foot to be moved;
He who keeps you will not slumber.
4 Behold, He who keeps Israel
Shall neither slumber nor sleep.

5 The LORD *is* your keeper;
The LORD *is* your shade at your right hand.
6 The sun shall not strike you by day,
Nor the moon by night.

7 The LORD shall preserve you from all evil;
He shall preserve your soul.
8 The LORD shall preserve your going out and your coming in
From this time forth, and even forevermore.

PSALM 122

The Joy of Going to the House of the LORD

A Song of Ascents. Of David.

I WAS glad when they said to me,
"Let us go into the house of the LORD."
2 Our feet have been standing
Within your gates, O Jerusalem!

3 Jerusalem is built
As a city that is compact together,
4 Where the tribes go up,
The tribes of the LORD,
To the Testimony of Israel,
To give thanks to the name of the LORD.
5 For thrones are set there for judgment,
The thrones of the house of David.

6 Pray for the peace of Jerusalem:
"May they prosper who love you.
7 Peace be within your walls,
Prosperity within your palaces."
8 For the sake of my brethren and companions,
I will now say, "Peace *be* within you."
9 Because of the house of the LORD our God
I will seek your good.

PSALM 123

Prayer for Relief from Contempt

A Song of Ascents.

UNTO You I lift up my eyes,
O You who dwell in the heavens.
2 Behold, as the eyes of servants *look* to the hand of their masters,
As the eyes of a maid to the hand of her mistress,
So our eyes *look* to the LORD our God,
Until He has mercy on us.

3 Have mercy on us, O LORD, have mercy on us!

For we are exceedingly filled with contempt.
4 Our soul is exceedingly filled
With the scorn of those who are at ease,
With the contempt of the proud.

PSALM 124

The LORD the Defense of His People

A Song of Ascents. Of David.

"IF it had not been the LORD who was on our side,"
Let Israel now say—
2 "If it had not been the LORD who was on our side,
When men rose up against us,
3 Then they would have swallowed us alive,
When their wrath was kindled against us;
4 Then the waters would have overwhelmed us,
The stream would have gone over our soul;
5 Then the swollen waters
Would have gone over our soul."

6 Blessed *be* the LORD,
Who has not given us *as* prey to their teeth.
7 Our soul has escaped as a bird from the snare of the fowlers;[a]
The snare is broken, and we have escaped.
8 Our help *is* in the name of the LORD,
Who made heaven and earth.

PSALM 125

The LORD the Strength of His People

A Song of Ascents.

THOSE who trust in the LORD
Are like Mount Zion,
Which cannot be moved, *but* abides forever.
2 As the mountains surround Jerusalem,
So the LORD surrounds His people
From this time forth and forever.

3 For the scepter of wickedness shall not rest
On the land allotted to the righteous,
Lest the righteous reach out their hands to iniquity.

4 Do good, O LORD, to *those who are* good,
And to *those who are* upright in their hearts.

5 As for such as turn aside to their crooked ways,
The LORD shall lead them away
With the workers of iniquity.

Peace *be* upon Israel!

PSALM 126

A Joyful Return to Zion

A Song of Ascents.

WHEN the LORD brought back the captivity of Zion,
We were like those who dream.
2 Then our mouth was filled with laughter,
And our tongue with singing.
Then they said among the nations,
"The LORD has done great things for them."
3 The LORD has done great things for us,
And we are glad.

4 Bring back our captivity, O LORD,
As the streams in the South.

5 Those who sow in tears
Shall reap in joy.
6 He who continually goes forth weeping,
Bearing seed for sowing,
Shall doubtless come again with rejoicing,
Bringing his sheaves *with him.*

PSALM 127

Laboring and Prospering with the LORD

A Song of Ascents. Of Solomon.

UNLESS the LORD builds the house,
They labor in vain who build it;
Unless the LORD guards the city,
The watchman stays awake in vain.
2 *It is* vain for you to rise up early,
To sit up late,
To eat the bread of sorrows;
For so He gives His beloved sleep.

3 Behold, children *are* a heritage from the LORD,
The fruit of the womb *is* a reward.
4 Like arrows in the hand of a warrior,
So *are* the children of one's youth.
5 Happy *is* the man who has his quiver full of them;
They shall not be ashamed,
But shall speak with their enemies in the gate.

PSALM 128

Blessings of Those Who Fear the LORD

A Song of Ascents.

BLESSED *is* every one who fears the LORD,
Who walks in His ways.
2 When you eat the labor of your hands,
You *shall be* happy, and *it shall be* well with you.
3 Your wife *shall be* like a fruitful vine
In the very heart of your house,
Your children like olive plants
All around your table.
4 Behold, thus shall the man be blessed
Who fears the LORD.

5 The LORD bless you out of Zion,
And may you see the good of Jerusalem
All the days of your life.
6 Yes, may you see your children's children.

Peace *be* upon Israel!

PSALM 129

Song of Victory over Zion's Enemies

A Song of Ascents.

"MANY a time they have afflicted me from my youth,"
Let Israel now say—
2 "Many a time they have afflicted me from my youth;

124:7 [a]That is, persons who catch birds in a trap or snare

Yet they have not prevailed against me.
3 The plowers plowed on my back;
They made their furrows long."
4 The LORD *is* righteous;
He has cut in pieces the cords of the wicked.
5 Let all those who hate Zion
Be put to shame and turned back.
6 Let them be as the grass *on* the housetops,
Which withers before it grows up,
7 With which the reaper does not fill his hand,
Nor he who binds sheaves, his arms.
8 Neither let those who pass by them say,
"The blessing of the LORD *be* upon you;
We bless you in the name of the LORD!"

PSALM 130

Waiting for the Redemption of the LORD

A Song of Ascents.

OUT of the depths I have cried to You, O LORD;
2 Lord, hear my voice!
Let Your ears be attentive
To the voice of my supplications.

3 If You, LORD, should mark iniquities,
O Lord, who could stand?
4 But *there is* forgiveness with You,
That You may be feared.

5 I wait for the LORD, my soul waits,
And in His word I do hope.
6 My soul *waits* for the Lord
More than those who watch for the morning—
Yes, more than those who watch for the morning.
7 O Israel, hope in the LORD;
For with the LORD *there is* mercy,
And with Him *is* abundant redemption.
8 And He shall redeem Israel
From all his iniquities.

PSALM 131

Simple Trust in the LORD

A Song of Ascents. Of David.

LORD, my heart is not haughty,
Nor my eyes lofty.
Neither do I concern myself with great matters,
Nor with things too profound for me.

2 Surely I have calmed and quieted my soul,
Like a weaned child with his mother;
Like a weaned child *is* my soul within me.

3 O Israel, hope in the LORD
From this time forth and forever.

PSALM 132

The Eternal Dwelling of God in Zion

A Song of Ascents.

LORD, remember David
And all his afflictions;
2 How he swore to the LORD,
And vowed to the Mighty One of Jacob:
3 "Surely I will not go into the chamber of my house,
Or go up to the comfort of my bed;
4 I will not give sleep to my eyes
Or slumber to my eyelids,
5 Until I find a place for the LORD,
A dwelling place for the Mighty One of Jacob."

6 Behold, we heard of it in Ephrathah;
We found it in the fields of the woods.[a]
7 Let us go into His tabernacle;
Let us worship at His footstool.
8 Arise, O LORD, to Your resting place,
You and the ark of Your strength.
9 Let Your priests be clothed with righteousness,
And let Your saints shout for joy.

10 For Your servant David's sake,
Do not turn away the face of Your Anointed.

11 The LORD has sworn *in* truth to David;
He will not turn from it:
"I will set upon your throne the fruit of your body.
12 If your sons will keep My covenant
And My testimony which I shall teach them,
Their sons also shall sit upon your throne forevermore."

13 For the LORD has chosen Zion;
He has desired *it* for His dwelling place:
14 "This *is* My resting place forever;
Here I will dwell, for I have desired it.
15 I will abundantly bless her provision;
I will satisfy her poor with bread.
16 I will also clothe her priests with salvation,
And her saints shall shout aloud for joy.
17 There I will make the horn of David grow;
I will prepare a lamp for My Anointed.
18 His enemies I will clothe with shame,
But upon Himself His crown shall flourish."

PSALM 133

Blessed Unity of the People of God

A Song of Ascents. Of David.

BEHOLD, how good and how pleasant *it is*
For brethren to dwell together in unity!
2 *It is* like the precious oil upon the head,
Running down on the beard,
The beard of Aaron,
Running down on the edge of his garments.
3 *It is* like the dew of Hermon,
Descending upon the mountains of Zion;
For there the LORD commanded the blessing—
Life forevermore.

PSALM 134

Praising the LORD in His House at Night

A Song of Ascents.

BEHOLD, bless the LORD,
All *you* servants of the LORD,
Who by night stand in the house of the LORD!

132:6 [a]Hebrew *Jaar*

2 Lift up your hands *in* the sanctuary,
And bless the LORD.

3 The LORD who made heaven and earth
Bless you from Zion!

PSALM 135

Praise to God in Creation and Redemption

PRAISE the LORD!
Praise the name of the LORD;
Praise *Him*, O you servants of the LORD!
2 You who stand in the house of the LORD,
In the courts of the house of our God,
3 Praise the LORD, for the LORD *is* good;
Sing praises to His name, for *it is* pleasant.
4 For the LORD has chosen Jacob for Himself,
Israel for His special treasure.

5 For I know that the LORD *is* great,
And our Lord *is* above all gods.
6 Whatever the LORD pleases He does,
In heaven and in earth,
In the seas and in all deep places.
7 He causes the vapors to ascend from the ends of the earth;
He makes lightning for the rain;
He brings the wind out of His treasuries.

8 He destroyed the firstborn of Egypt,
Both of man and beast.
9 He sent signs and wonders into the midst of you, O Egypt,
Upon Pharaoh and all his servants.
10 He defeated many nations
And slew mighty kings—
11 Sihon king of the Amorites,
Og king of Bashan,
And all the kingdoms of Canaan—
12 And gave their land *as* a heritage,
A heritage to Israel His people.

13 Your name, O LORD, *endures* forever,
Your fame, O LORD, throughout all generations.
14 For the LORD will judge His people,
And He will have compassion on His servants.

15 The idols of the nations *are* silver and gold,
The work of men's hands.
16 They have mouths, but they do not speak;
Eyes they have, but they do not see;
17 They have ears, but they do not hear;
Nor is there *any* breath in their mouths.
18 Those who make them are like them;
So is everyone who trusts in them.

19 Bless the LORD, O house of Israel!
Bless the LORD, O house of Aaron!
20 Bless the LORD, O house of Levi!
You who fear the LORD, bless the LORD!
21 Blessed be the LORD out of Zion,
Who dwells in Jerusalem!

Praise the LORD!

PSALM 136

Thanksgiving to God for His Enduring Mercy

OH, give thanks to the LORD, for *He is* good!
For His mercy *endures* forever.
2 Oh, give thanks to the God of gods!
For His mercy *endures* forever.
3 Oh, give thanks to the Lord of lords!
For His mercy *endures* forever:

4 To Him who alone does great wonders,
For His mercy *endures* forever;
5 To Him who by wisdom made the heavens,
For His mercy *endures* forever;
6 To Him who laid out the earth above the waters,
For His mercy *endures* forever;
7 To Him who made great lights,
For His mercy *endures* forever—
8 The sun to rule by day,
For His mercy *endures* forever;
9 The moon and stars to rule by night,
For His mercy *endures* forever.

10 To Him who struck Egypt in their firstborn,
For His mercy *endures* forever;
11 And brought out Israel from among them,
For His mercy *endures* forever;
12 With a strong hand, and with an outstretched arm,
For His mercy *endures* forever;
13 To Him who divided the Red Sea in two,
For His mercy *endures* forever;
14 And made Israel pass through the midst of it,
For His mercy *endures* forever;
15 But overthrew Pharaoh and his army in the Red Sea,
For His mercy *endures* forever;
16 To Him who led His people through the wilderness,
For His mercy *endures* forever;
17 To Him who struck down great kings,
For His mercy *endures* forever;
18 And slew famous kings,
For His mercy *endures* forever—
19 Sihon king of the Amorites,
For His mercy *endures* forever;
20 And Og king of Bashan,
For His mercy *endures* forever—
21 And gave their land as a heritage,
For His mercy *endures* forever;
22 A heritage to Israel His servant,
For His mercy *endures* forever.

23 Who remembered us in our lowly state,
For His mercy *endures* forever;
24 And rescued us from our enemies,
For His mercy *endures* forever;
25 Who gives food to all flesh,
For His mercy *endures* forever.

26 Oh, give thanks to the God of heaven!
For His mercy *endures* forever.

PSALM 137

Longing for Zion in a Foreign Land

BY the rivers of Babylon,
There we sat down, yea, we wept
When we remembered Zion.
2 We hung our harps
Upon the willows in the midst of it.
3 For there those who carried us away captive asked of us a song,
And those who plundered us *requested* mirth,

Saying, "Sing us *one* of the songs of
Zion!"
4 How shall we sing the LORD's song
In a foreign land?
5 If I forget you, O Jerusalem,
Let my right hand forget *its skill!*
6 If I do not remember you,
Let my tongue cling to the roof of my
mouth—
If I do not exalt Jerusalem
Above my chief joy.
7 Remember, O LORD, against the sons of
Edom
The day of Jerusalem,
Who said, "Raze *it,* raze *it,*
To its very foundation!"
8 O daughter of Babylon, who are to be
destroyed,
Happy the one who repays you as you
have served us!
9 Happy the one who takes and dashes
Your little ones against the rock!

PSALM 138

The LORD's Goodness to the Faithful

A Psalm of David.

I WILL praise You with my whole heart;
Before the gods I will sing praises to You.
2 I will worship toward Your holy temple,
And praise Your name
For Your lovingkindness and Your truth;
For You have magnified Your word above
all Your name.
3 In the day when I cried out, You
answered me,
And made me bold *with* strength in my
soul.
4 All the kings of the earth shall praise
You, O LORD,
When they hear the words of Your
mouth.
5 Yes, they shall sing of the ways of the
LORD,
For great *is* the glory of the LORD.
6 Though the LORD *is* on high,
Yet He regards the lowly;
But the proud He knows from afar.
7 Though I walk in the midst of trouble,
You will revive me;
You will stretch out Your hand
Against the wrath of my enemies,
And Your right hand will save me.
8 The LORD will perfect *that which*
concerns me;
Your mercy, O LORD, *endures* forever;
Do not forsake the works of Your hands.

PSALM 139

God's Perfect Knowledge of Man

For the Chief Musician. A Psalm of David.

O LORD, You have searched me and
known *me.*
2 You know my sitting down and my rising
up;
You understand my thought afar off.
3 You comprehend my path and my lying
down,
And are acquainted with all my ways.
4 For *there is* not a word on my tongue,
But behold, O LORD, You know it
altogether.
5 You have hedged me behind and before,
And laid Your hand upon me.
6 *Such* knowledge *is* too wonderful for me;
It is high, I cannot *attain* it.
7 Where can I go from Your Spirit?
Or where can I flee from Your presence?
8 If I ascend into heaven, You *are* there;
If I make my bed in hell, behold, You *are*
there.
9 *If* I take the wings of the morning,
And dwell in the uttermost parts of the
sea,
10 Even there Your hand shall lead me,
And Your right hand shall hold me.
11 If I say, "Surely the darkness shall fall[a]
on me,"
Even the night shall be light about me;
12 Indeed, the darkness shall not hide from
You,
But the night shines as the day;
The darkness and the light *are* both alike
to You.
13 For You formed my inward parts;
You covered me in my mother's womb.
14 I will praise You, for I am fearfully *and*
wonderfully made;[a]
Marvelous are Your works,
And *that* my soul knows very well.
15 My frame was not hidden from You,
When I was made in secret,
And skillfully wrought in the lowest parts
of the earth.
16 Your eyes saw my substance, being yet
unformed.
And in Your book they all were written,
The days fashioned for me,
When *as yet there were* none of them.
17 How precious also are Your thoughts to
me, O God!
How great is the sum of them!
18 *If* I should count them, they would be
more in number than the sand;
When I awake, I am still with You.
19 Oh, that You would slay the wicked,
O God!
Depart from me, therefore, you
bloodthirsty men.
20 For they speak against You wickedly;
Your enemies take *Your name* in vain.[a]
21 Do I not hate them, O LORD, who hate
You?
And do I not loathe those who rise up
against You?
22 I hate them with perfect hatred;
I count them my enemies.
23 Search me, O God, and know my heart;
Try me, and know my anxieties;
24 And see if *there is any* wicked way in me,
And lead me in the way everlasting.

139:11 [a]Vulgate and Symmachus read *cover.* **139:14** [a]Following Masoretic Text and Targum; Septuagint, Syriac, and Vulgate read *You are fearfully wonderful.* **139:20** [a]Septuagint and Vulgate read *They take your cities in vain.*

PSALM 140

Prayer for Deliverance from Evil Men

To the Chief Musician. A Psalm of David.

DELIVER me, O LORD, from evil men;
Preserve me from violent men,
2 Who plan evil things in *their* hearts;
They continually gather together *for* war.
3 They sharpen their tongues like a serpent;
The poison of asps *is* under their lips. Selah
4 Keep me, O LORD, from the hands of the wicked;
Preserve me from violent men,
Who have purposed to make my steps stumble.
5 The proud have hidden a snare for me, and cords;
They have spread a net by the wayside;
They have set traps for me. Selah
6 I said to the LORD: "You *are* my God;
Hear the voice of my supplications, O LORD.
7 O GOD the Lord, the strength of my salvation,
You have covered my head in the day of battle.
8 Do not grant, O LORD, the desires of the wicked;
Do not further his *wicked* scheme,
Lest they be exalted. Selah
9 "*As for* the head of those who surround me,
Let the evil of their lips cover them;
10 Let burning coals fall upon them;
Let them be cast into the fire,
Into deep pits, that they rise not up again.
11 Let not a slanderer be established in the earth;
Let evil hunt the violent man to overthrow *him*."
12 I know that the LORD will maintain
The cause of the afflicted,
And justice for the poor.
13 Surely the righteous shall give thanks to Your name;
The upright shall dwell in Your presence.

PSALM 141

Prayer for Safekeeping from Wickedness

A Psalm of David.

LORD, I cry out to You;
Make haste to me!
Give ear to my voice when I cry out to You.
2 Let my prayer be set before You *as* incense,
The lifting up of my hands *as* the evening sacrifice.

3 Set a guard, O LORD, over my mouth;
Keep watch over the door of my lips.
4 Do not incline my heart to any evil thing,
To practice wicked works
With men who work iniquity;
And do not let me eat of their delicacies.

5 Let the righteous strike me;
It shall be a kindness.
And let him rebuke me;
It shall be as excellent oil;
Let my head not refuse it.
For still my prayer *is* against the deeds of the wicked.
6 Their judges are overthrown by the sides of the cliff,
And they hear my words, for they are sweet.
7 Our bones are scattered at the mouth of the grave,
As when one plows and breaks up the earth.

8 But my eyes *are* upon You, O GOD the Lord;
In You I take refuge;
Do not leave my soul destitute.
9 Keep me from the snares they have laid for me,
And from the traps of the workers of iniquity.
10 Let the wicked fall into their own nets,
While I escape safely.

PSALM 142

A Plea for Relief from Persecutors

A Contemplation[a] of David. A Prayer when he was in the cave.

I CRY out to the LORD with my voice;
With my voice to the LORD I make my supplication.
2 I pour out my complaint before Him;
I declare before Him my trouble.

3 When my spirit was overwhelmed within me,
Then You knew my path.
In the way in which I walk
They have secretly set a snare for me.
4 Look on *my* right hand and see,
For *there is* no one who acknowledges me;
Refuge has failed me;
No one cares for my soul.

5 I cried out to You, O LORD:
I said, "You *are* my refuge,
My portion in the land of the living.
6 Attend to my cry,
For I am brought very low;
Deliver me from my persecutors,
For they are stronger than I.
7 Bring my soul out of prison,
That I may praise Your name;
The righteous shall surround me,
For You shall deal bountifully with me."

PSALM 143

An Earnest Appeal for Guidance and Deliverance

A Psalm of David.

HEAR my prayer, O LORD,
Give ear to my supplications!
In Your faithfulness answer me,
And in Your righteousness.
2 Do not enter into judgment with Your servant,
For in Your sight no one living is righteous.

142:title [a]Hebrew *Maschil*

3 For the enemy has persecuted my soul;
He has crushed my life to the ground;
He has made me dwell in darkness,
Like those who have long been dead.
4 Therefore my spirit is overwhelmed within me;
My heart within me is distressed.

5 I remember the days of old;
I meditate on all Your works;
I muse on the work of Your hands.
6 I spread out my hands to You;
My soul *longs* for You like a thirsty land. Selah

7 Answer me speedily, O LORD;
My spirit fails!
Do not hide Your face from me,
Lest I be like those who go down into the pit.
8 Cause me to hear Your lovingkindness in the morning,
For in You do I trust;
Cause me to know the way in which I should walk,
For I lift up my soul to You.

9 Deliver me, O LORD, from my enemies;
In You I take shelter.[a]
10 Teach me to do Your will,
For You *are* my God;
Your Spirit *is* good.
Lead me in the land of uprightness.

11 Revive me, O LORD, for Your name's sake!
For Your righteousness' sake bring my soul out of trouble.
12 In Your mercy cut off my enemies,
And destroy all those who afflict my soul;
For I *am* Your servant.

PSALM 144

A Song to the LORD Who Preserves and Prospers His People

A Psalm of David.

BLESSED *be* the LORD my Rock,
Who trains my hands for war,
And my fingers for battle—
2 My lovingkindness and my fortress,
My high tower and my deliverer,
My shield and *the One* in whom I take refuge,
Who subdues my people[a] under me.

3 LORD, what *is* man, that You take knowledge of him?
Or the son of man, that You are mindful of him?
4 Man is like a breath;
His days *are* like a passing shadow.

5 Bow down Your heavens, O LORD, and come down;
Touch the mountains, and they shall smoke.
6 Flash forth lightning and scatter them;
Shoot out Your arrows and destroy them.
7 Stretch out Your hand from above;
Rescue me and deliver me out of great waters,
From the hand of foreigners,
8 Whose mouth speaks lying words,
And whose right hand *is* a right hand of falsehood.

9 I will sing a new song to You, O God;
On a harp of ten strings I will sing praises to You,
10 *The One* who gives salvation to kings,
Who delivers David His servant
From the deadly sword.

11 Rescue me and deliver me from the hand of foreigners,
Whose mouth speaks lying words,
And whose right hand *is* a right hand of falsehood—
12 That our sons *may be* as plants grown up in their youth;
That our daughters *may be* as pillars,
Sculptured in palace style;
13 *That* our barns *may be* full,
Supplying all kinds of produce;
That our sheep may bring forth thousands
And ten thousands in our fields;
14 *That* our oxen *may be* well laden;
That there be no breaking in or going out;
That there be no outcry in our streets.
15 Happy *are* the people who are in such a state;
Happy *are* the people whose God *is* the LORD!

PSALM 145

A Song of God's Majesty and Love

A Praise of David.

I WILL extol You, my God, O King;
And I will bless Your name forever and ever.
2 Every day I will bless You,
And I will praise Your name forever and ever.
3 Great *is* the LORD, and greatly to be praised;
And His greatness *is* unsearchable.

4 One generation shall praise Your works to another,
And shall declare Your mighty acts.
5 I[a] will meditate on the glorious splendor of Your majesty,
And on Your wondrous works.[b]
6 *Men* shall speak of the might of Your awesome acts,
And I will declare Your greatness.
7 They shall utter the memory of Your great goodness,
And shall sing of Your righteousness.

8 The LORD *is* gracious and full of compassion,
Slow to anger and great in mercy.
9 The LORD *is* good to all,
And His tender mercies *are* over all His works.

10 All Your works shall praise You, O LORD,
And Your saints shall bless You.
11 They shall speak of the glory of Your kingdom,
And talk of Your power,

143:9 [a]Septuagint and Vulgate read *To You I flee.* **144:2** [a]Following Masoretic Text, Septuagint, and Vulgate; Syriac and Targum read *the peoples* (compare 18:47). **145:5** [a]Following Masoretic Text and Targum; Dead Sea Scrolls, Septuagint, Syriac, and Vulgate read *They.* [b]Literally *on the words of Your wondrous works*

12 To make known to the sons of men His mighty acts,
And the glorious majesty of His kingdom.
13 Your kingdom *is* an everlasting kingdom,
And Your dominion *endures* throughout all generations.[a]
14 The LORD upholds all who fall,
And raises up all *who are* bowed down.
15 The eyes of all look expectantly to You,
And You give them their food in due season.
16 You open Your hand
And satisfy the desire of every living thing.
17 The LORD *is* righteous in all His ways,
Gracious in all His works.
18 The LORD *is* near to all who call upon Him,
To all who call upon Him in truth.
19 He will fulfill the desire of those who fear Him;
He also will hear their cry and save them.
20 The LORD preserves all who love Him,
But all the wicked He will destroy.
21 My mouth shall speak the praise of the LORD,
And all flesh shall bless His holy name
Forever and ever.

PSALM 146

The Happiness of Those Whose Help Is the LORD

PRAISE the LORD!
Praise the LORD, O my soul!
2 While I live I will praise the LORD;
I will sing praises to my God while I have my being.

3 Do not put your trust in princes,
Nor in a son of man, in whom *there is* no help.
4 His spirit departs, he returns to his earth;
In that very day his plans perish.

5 Happy *is he* who *has* the God of Jacob for his help,
Whose hope *is* in the LORD his God,
6 Who made heaven and earth,
The sea, and all that *is* in them;
Who keeps truth forever,
7 Who executes justice for the oppressed,
Who gives food to the hungry.
The LORD gives freedom to the prisoners.
8 The LORD opens *the eyes of* the blind;
The LORD raises those who are bowed down;
The LORD loves the righteous.
9 The LORD watches over the strangers;
He relieves the fatherless and widow;
But the way of the wicked He turns upside down.

10 The LORD shall reign forever—
Your God, O Zion, to all generations.

Praise the LORD!

PSALM 147

Praise to God for His Word and Providence

PRAISE the LORD!
For *it is* good to sing praises to our God;
For *it is* pleasant, *and* praise is beautiful.
2 The LORD builds up Jerusalem;
He gathers together the outcasts of Israel.
3 He heals the brokenhearted
And binds up their wounds.
4 He counts the number of the stars;
He calls them all by name.
5 Great *is* our Lord, and mighty in power;
His understanding *is* infinite.
6 The LORD lifts up the humble;
He casts the wicked down to the ground.

7 Sing to the LORD with thanksgiving;
Sing praises on the harp to our God,
8 Who covers the heavens with clouds,
Who prepares rain for the earth,
Who makes grass to grow on the mountains.
9 He gives to the beast its food,
And to the young ravens that cry.

10 He does not delight in the strength of the horse;
He takes no pleasure in the legs of a man.
11 The LORD takes pleasure in those who fear Him,
In those who hope in His mercy.

12 Praise the LORD, O Jerusalem!
Praise your God, O Zion!
13 For He has strengthened the bars of your gates;
He has blessed your children within you.
14 He makes peace *in* your borders,
And fills you with the finest wheat.

15 He sends out His command *to the* earth;
His word runs very swiftly.
16 He gives snow like wool;
He scatters the frost like ashes;
17 He casts out His hail like morsels;
Who can stand before His cold?
18 He sends out His word and melts them;
He causes His wind to blow, *and* the waters flow.

19 He declares His word to Jacob,
His statutes and His judgments to Israel.
20 He has not dealt thus with any nation;
And *as for His* judgments, they have not known them.

Praise the LORD!

PSALM 148

Praise to the LORD from Creation

PRAISE the LORD!
Praise the LORD from the heavens;
Praise Him in the heights!
2 Praise Him, all His angels;
Praise Him, all His hosts!
3 Praise Him, sun and moon;
Praise Him, all you stars of light!
4 Praise Him, you heavens of heavens,
And you waters above the heavens!

5 Let them praise the name of the LORD,
For He commanded and they were created.
6 He also established them forever and ever;
He made a decree which shall not pass away.

145:13 [a]Following Masoretic Text and Targum; Dead Sea Scrolls, Septuagint, Syriac, and Vulgate add *The LORD is faithful in all His words, And holy in all His works.*

7 Praise the LORD from the earth,
You great sea creatures and all the depths;
8 Fire and hail, snow and clouds;
Stormy wind, fulfilling His word;
9 Mountains and all hills;
Fruitful trees and all cedars;
10 Beasts and all cattle;
Creeping things and flying fowl;
11 Kings of the earth and all peoples;
Princes and all judges of the earth;
12 Both young men and maidens;
Old men and children.

13 Let them praise the name of the LORD,
For His name alone is exalted;
His glory *is* above the earth and heaven.
14 And He has exalted the horn of His people,
The praise of all His saints—
Of the children of Israel,
A people near to Him.

Praise the LORD!

PSALM 149

Praise to God for His Salvation and Judgment

PRAISE the LORD!
Sing to the LORD a new song,
And His praise in the assembly of saints.

2 Let Israel rejoice in their Maker;
Let the children of Zion be joyful in their King.
3 Let them praise His name with the dance;
Let them sing praises to Him with the timbrel and harp.
4 For the LORD takes pleasure in His people;
He will beautify the humble with salvation.
5 Let the saints be joyful in glory;
Let them sing aloud on their beds.
6 *Let* the high praises of God *be* in their mouth,
And a two-edged sword in their hand,
7 To execute vengeance on the nations,
And punishments on the peoples;
8 To bind their kings with chains,
And their nobles with fetters of iron;
9 To execute on them the written judgment—
This honor have all His saints.

Praise the LORD!

PSALM 150

Let All Things Praise the LORD

PRAISE the LORD!
Praise God in His sanctuary;
Praise Him in His mighty firmament!
2 Praise Him for His mighty acts;
Praise Him according to His excellent greatness!

3 Praise Him with the sound of the trumpet;
Praise Him with the lute and harp!
4 Praise Him with the timbrel and dance;
Praise Him with stringed instruments and flutes!
5 Praise Him with loud cymbals;
Praise Him with clashing cymbals!

6 Let everything that has breath praise the LORD.
Praise the LORD!

The Book of PROVERBS

The Beginning of Knowledge

1 The proverbs of Solomon the son of David, king of Israel:

2 To know wisdom and instruction,
To perceive the words of understanding,
3 To receive the instruction of wisdom,
Justice, judgment, and equity;
4 To give prudence to the simple,
To the young man knowledge and discretion—
5 A wise *man* will hear and increase learning,
And a man of understanding will attain wise counsel,
6 To understand a proverb and an enigma,
The words of the wise and their riddles.

7 The fear of the LORD *is* the beginning of knowledge,
But fools despise wisdom and instruction.

Shun Evil Counsel

8 My son, hear the instruction of your father,
And do not forsake the law of your mother;
9 For they *will be* a graceful ornament on your head,
And chains about your neck.

10 My son, if sinners entice you,
Do not consent.
11 If they say, "Come with us,
Let us lie in wait to *shed* blood;
Let us lurk secretly for the innocent without cause;
12 Let us swallow them alive like Sheol,[a]
And whole, like those who go down to the Pit;
13 We shall find all *kinds* of precious possessions,
We shall fill our houses with spoil;
14 Cast in your lot among us,
Let us all have one purse"—
15 My son, do not walk in the way with them,
Keep your foot from their path;
16 For their feet run to evil,
And they make haste to shed blood.

1:12 [a]Or *the grave*

17 Surely, in vain the net is spread
In the sight of any bird;
18 But they lie in wait for their *own* blood,
They lurk secretly for their *own* lives.
19 So *are* the ways of everyone who is
greedy for gain;
It takes away the life of its owners.

The Call of Wisdom

20 Wisdom calls aloud outside;
She raises her voice in the open squares.
21 She cries out in the chief concourses,[a]
At the openings of the gates in the city
She speaks her words:
22 "How long, you simple ones, will you love
simplicity?
For scorners delight in their scorning,
And fools hate knowledge.
23 Turn at my rebuke;
Surely I will pour out my spirit on you;
I will make my words known to you.
24 Because I have called and you refused,
I have stretched out my hand and no one
regarded,
25 Because you disdained all my counsel,
And would have none of my rebuke,
26 I also will laugh at your calamity;
I will mock when your terror comes,
27 When your terror comes like a storm,
And your destruction comes like a
whirlwind,
When distress and anguish come upon
you.

28 "Then they will call on me, but I will not
answer;
They will seek me diligently, but they will
not find me.
29 Because they hated knowledge
And did not choose the fear of the LORD,
30 They would have none of my counsel
And despised my every rebuke.
31 Therefore they shall eat the fruit of their
own way,
And be filled to the full with their own
fancies.
32 For the turning away of the simple will
slay them,
And the complacency of fools will
destroy them;
33 But whoever listens to me will dwell
safely,
And will be secure, without fear of evil."

The Value of Wisdom

2 My son, if you receive my words,
And treasure my commands within you,
2 So that you incline your ear to wisdom,
And apply your heart to understanding;
3 Yes, if you cry out for discernment,
And lift up your voice for understanding,
4 If you seek her as silver,
And search for her as *for* hidden
treasures;
5 Then you will understand the fear of the
LORD,
And find the knowledge of God.
6 For the LORD gives wisdom;
From His mouth *come* knowledge and
understanding;
7 He stores up sound wisdom for the
upright;
He is a shield to those who walk
uprightly;
8 He guards the paths of justice,
And preserves the way of His saints.
9 Then you will understand righteousness
and justice,
Equity *and* every good path.

10 When wisdom enters your heart,
And knowledge is pleasant to your soul,
11 Discretion will preserve you;
Understanding will keep you,
12 To deliver you from the way of evil,
From the man who speaks perverse
things,
13 From those who leave the paths of
uprightness
To walk in the ways of darkness;
14 Who rejoice in doing evil,
And delight in the perversity of the
wicked;
15 Whose ways *are* crooked,
And *who are* devious in their paths;
16 To deliver you from the immoral woman,
From the seductress *who* flatters with her
words,
17 Who forsakes the companion of her
youth,
And forgets the covenant of her God.
18 For her house leads down to death,
And her paths to the dead;
19 None who go to her return,
Nor do they regain the paths of life—
20 So you may walk in the way of goodness,
And keep *to* the paths of righteousness.
21 For the upright will dwell in the land,
And the blameless will remain in it;
22 But the wicked will be cut off from the
earth,
And the unfaithful will be uprooted from
it.

Guidance for the Young

3 My son, do not forget my law,
But let your heart keep my commands;
2 For length of days and long life
And peace they will add to you.

3 Let not mercy and truth forsake you;
Bind them around your neck,
Write them on the tablet of your heart,
4 *And* so find favor and high esteem
In the sight of God and man.

5 Trust in the LORD with all your heart,
And lean not on your own understanding;
6 In all your ways acknowledge Him,
And He shall direct[a] your paths.

7 Do not be wise in your own eyes;
Fear the LORD and depart from evil.
8 It will be health to your flesh,[a]
And strength[b] to your bones.

9 Honor the LORD with your possessions,
And with the firstfruits of all your
increase;
10 So your barns will be filled with plenty,
And your vats will overflow with new
wine.

11 My son, do not despise the chastening of
the LORD,

1:21 [a]Septuagint, Syriac, and Targum read *top of the walls;* Vulgate reads *the head of multitudes.* **3:6** [a]Or *make smooth* or *straight* **3:8** [a]Literally *navel,* figurative of the body [b]Literally *drink* or *refreshment*

Nor detest His correction;
12 For whom the LORD loves He corrects,
Just as a father the son *in whom* he
delights.

13 Happy *is* the man *who* finds wisdom,
And the man *who* gains understanding;
14 For her proceeds *are* better than the
profits of silver,
And her gain than fine gold.
15 She *is* more precious than rubies,
And all the things you may desire cannot
compare with her.
16 Length of days *is* in her right hand,
In her left hand riches and honor.
17 Her ways *are* ways of pleasantness,
And all her paths *are* peace.
18 She *is* a tree of life to those who take hold
of her,
And happy *are all* who retain her.

19 The LORD by wisdom founded the earth;
By understanding He established the
heavens;
20 By His knowledge the depths were
broken up,
And clouds drop down the dew.

21 My son, let them not depart from your
eyes—
Keep sound wisdom and discretion;
22 So they will be life to your soul
And grace to your neck.
23 Then you will walk safely in your way,
And your foot will not stumble.
24 When you lie down, you will not be
afraid;
Yes, you will lie down and your sleep will
be sweet.
25 Do not be afraid of sudden terror,
Nor of trouble from the wicked when it
comes;
26 For the LORD will be your confidence,
And will keep your foot from being
caught.

27 Do not withhold good from those to
whom it is due,
When it is in the power of your hand to
do *so*.
28 Do not say to your neighbor,
"Go, and come back,
And tomorrow I will give *it*,"
When you have it with you.
29 Do not devise evil against your neighbor,
For he dwells by you for safety's sake.
30 Do not strive with a man without cause,
If he has done you no harm.

31 Do not envy the oppressor,
And choose none of his ways;
32 For the perverse *person is* an
abomination to the LORD,
But His secret counsel *is* with the upright.
33 The curse of the LORD *is* on the house of
the wicked,
But He blesses the home of the just.
34 Surely He scorns the scornful,
But gives grace to the humble.
35 The wise shall inherit glory,
But shame shall be the legacy of fools.

Security in Wisdom

4 Hear, *my* children, the instruction of a
father,
And give attention to know
understanding;
2 For I give you good doctrine:
Do not forsake my law.
3 When I was my father's son,
Tender and the only one in the sight of
my mother,
4 He also taught me, and said to me:
"Let your heart retain my words;
Keep my commands, and live.
5 Get wisdom! Get understanding!
Do not forget, nor turn away from the
words of my mouth.
6 Do not forsake her, and she will preserve
you;
Love her, and she will keep you.
7 Wisdom *is* the principal thing;
Therefore get wisdom.
And in all your getting, get
understanding.
8 Exalt her, and she will promote you;
She will bring you honor, when you
embrace her.
9 She will place on your head an ornament
of grace;
A crown of glory she will deliver to you."

10 Hear, my son, and receive my sayings,
And the years of your life will be many.
11 I have taught you in the way of wisdom;
I have led you in right paths.
12 When you walk, your steps will not be
hindered,
And when you run, you will not stumble.
13 Take firm hold of instruction, do not let
go;
Keep her, for she *is* your life.

14 Do not enter the path of the wicked,
And do not walk in the way of evil.
15 Avoid it, do not travel on it;
Turn away from it and pass on.
16 For they do not sleep unless they have
done evil;
And their sleep is taken away unless they
make *someone* fall.
17 For they eat the bread of wickedness,
And drink the wine of violence.

18 But the path of the just *is* like the shining
sun,[a]
That shines ever brighter unto the perfect
day.
19 The way of the wicked *is* like darkness;
They do not know what makes them
stumble.

20 My son, give attention to my words;
Incline your ear to my sayings.
21 Do not let them depart from your eyes;
Keep them in the midst of your heart;
22 For they *are* life to those who find them,
And health to all their flesh.
23 Keep your heart with all diligence,
For out of it *spring* the issues of life.
24 Put away from you a deceitful mouth,
And put perverse lips far from you.
25 Let your eyes look straight ahead,
And your eyelids look right before you.
26 Ponder the path of your feet,
And let all your ways be established.

4:18 [a]Literally *light*

27 Do not turn to the right or the left;
Remove your foot from evil.

The Peril of Adultery

5 My son, pay attention to my wisdom;
Lend your ear to my understanding,
2 That you may preserve discretion,
And your lips may keep knowledge.
3 For the lips of an immoral woman drip honey,
And her mouth *is* smoother than oil;
4 But in the end she is bitter as wormwood,
Sharp as a two-edged sword.
5 Her feet go down to death,
Her steps lay hold of hell.[a]
6 Lest you ponder *her* path of life—
Her ways are unstable;
You do not know *them*.

7 Therefore hear me now, *my* children,
And do not depart from the words of my mouth.
8 Remove your way far from her,
And do not go near the door of her house,
9 Lest you give your honor to others,
And your years to the cruel *one;*
10 Lest aliens be filled with your wealth,
And your labors *go* to the house of a foreigner;
11 And you mourn at last,
When your flesh and your body are consumed,
12 And say:
"How I have hated instruction,
And my heart despised correction!
13 I have not obeyed the voice of my teachers,
Nor inclined my ear to those who instructed me!
14 I was on the verge of total ruin,
In the midst of the assembly and congregation."

15 Drink water from your own cistern,
And running water from your own well.
16 Should your fountains be dispersed abroad,
Streams of water in the streets?
17 Let them be only your own,
And not for strangers with you.
18 Let your fountain be blessed,
And rejoice with the wife of your youth.
19 *As a* loving deer and a graceful doe,
Let her breasts satisfy you at all times;
And always be enraptured with her love.
20 For why should you, my son, be enraptured by an immoral woman,
And be embraced in the arms of a seductress?
21 For the ways of man *are* before the eyes of the LORD,
And He ponders all his paths.
22 His own iniquities entrap the wicked *man,*
And he is caught in the cords of his sin.
23 He shall die for lack of instruction,
And in the greatness of his folly he shall go astray.

Dangerous Promises

6 My son, if you become surety for your friend,
If you have shaken hands in pledge for a stranger,
2 You are snared by the words of your mouth;
You are taken by the words of your mouth.
3 So do this, my son, and deliver yourself;
For you have come into the hand of your friend:
Go and humble yourself;
Plead with your friend.
4 Give no sleep to your eyes,
Nor slumber to your eyelids.
5 Deliver yourself like a gazelle from the hand *of the hunter,*
And like a bird from the hand of the fowler.[a]

The Folly of Indolence

6 Go to the ant, you sluggard!
Consider her ways and be wise,
7 Which, having no captain,
Overseer or ruler,
8 Provides her supplies in the summer,
And gathers her food in the harvest.
9 How long will you slumber, O sluggard?
When will you rise from your sleep?
10 A little sleep, a little slumber,
A little folding of the hands to sleep—
11 So shall your poverty come on you like a prowler,
And your need like an armed man.

The Wicked Man

12 A worthless person, a wicked man,
Walks with a perverse mouth;
13 He winks with his eyes,
He shuffles his feet,
He points with his fingers;
14 Perversity *is* in his heart,
He devises evil continually,
He sows discord.
15 Therefore his calamity shall come suddenly;
Suddenly he shall be broken without remedy.

16 These six *things* the LORD hates,
Yes, seven *are* an abomination to Him:
17 A proud look,
A lying tongue,
Hands that shed innocent blood,
18 A heart that devises wicked plans,
Feet that are swift in running to evil,
19 A false witness *who* speaks lies,
And one who sows discord among brethren.

Beware of Adultery

20 My son, keep your father's command,
And do not forsake the law of your mother.
21 Bind them continually upon your heart;
Tie them around your neck.
22 When you roam, they[a] will lead you;
When you sleep, they will keep you;
And *when* you awake, they will speak with you.
23 For the commandment *is* a lamp,
And the law a light;
Reproofs of instruction *are* the way of life,

5:5 [a]Or *Sheol* 6:5 [a]That is, one who catches birds in a trap or snare 6:22 [a]Literally *it*

24 To keep you from the evil woman,
From the flattering tongue of a seductress.
25 Do not lust after her beauty in your heart,
Nor let her allure you with her eyelids.
26 For by means of a harlot
A man is reduced to a crust of bread;
And an adulteress[a] will prey upon his precious life.
27 Can a man take fire to his bosom,
And his clothes not be burned?
28 Can one walk on hot coals,
And his feet not be seared?
29 So *is* he who goes in to his neighbor's wife;
Whoever touches her shall not be innocent.

30 *People* do not despise a thief
If he steals to satisfy himself when he is starving.
31 Yet *when* he is found, he must restore sevenfold;
He may have to give up all the substance of his house.
32 Whoever commits adultery with a woman lacks understanding;
He *who* does so destroys his own soul.
33 Wounds and dishonor he will get,
And his reproach will not be wiped away.
34 For jealousy *is* a husband's fury;
Therefore he will not spare in the day of vengeance.
35 He will accept no recompense,
Nor will he be appeased though you give many gifts.

7 My son, keep my words,
And treasure my commands within you.
2 Keep my commands and live,
And my law as the apple of your eye.
3 Bind them on your fingers;
Write them on the tablet of your heart.
4 Say to wisdom, "You *are* my sister,"
And call understanding *your* nearest kin,
5 That they may keep you from the immoral woman,
From the seductress *who* flatters with her words.

The Crafty Harlot

6 For at the window of my house
I looked through my lattice,
7 And saw among the simple,
I perceived among the youths,
A young man devoid of understanding,
8 Passing along the street near her corner;
And he took the path to her house
9 In the twilight, in the evening,
In the black and dark night.

10 And there a woman met him,
With the attire of a harlot, and a crafty heart.
11 She *was* loud and rebellious,
Her feet would not stay at home.
12 At times *she was* outside, at times in the open square,
Lurking at every corner.
13 So she caught him and kissed him;
With an impudent face she said to him:
14 "*I have* peace offerings with me;
Today I have paid my vows.
15 So I came out to meet you,
Diligently to seek your face,
And I have found you.
16 I have spread my bed with tapestry,
Colored coverings of Egyptian linen.
17 I have perfumed my bed
With myrrh, aloes, and cinnamon.
18 Come, let us take our fill of love until morning;
Let us delight ourselves with love.
19 For my husband *is* not at home;
He has gone on a long journey;
20 He has taken a bag of money with him,
And will come home on the appointed day."

21 With her enticing speech she caused him to yield,
With her flattering lips she seduced him.
22 Immediately he went after her, as an ox goes to the slaughter,
Or as a fool to the correction of the stocks,[a]
23 Till an arrow struck his liver.
As a bird hastens to the snare,
He did not know it *would cost* his life.

24 Now therefore, listen to me, *my* children;
Pay attention to the words of my mouth:
25 Do not let your heart turn aside to her ways,
Do not stray into her paths;
26 For she has cast down many wounded,
And all who were slain by her were strong *men.*
27 Her house *is* the way to hell,[a]
Descending to the chambers of death.

The Excellence of Wisdom

8 Does not wisdom cry out,
And understanding lift up her voice?
2 She takes her stand on the top of the high hill,
Beside the way, where the paths meet.
3 She cries out by the gates, at the entry of the city,
At the entrance of the doors:
4 "To you, O men, I call,
And my voice *is* to the sons of men.
5 O you simple ones, understand prudence,
And you fools, be of an understanding heart.
6 Listen, for I will speak of excellent things,
And from the opening of my lips *will come* right things;
7 For my mouth will speak truth;
Wickedness *is* an abomination to my lips.
8 All the words of my mouth *are* with righteousness;
Nothing crooked or perverse *is* in them.
9 They *are* all plain to him who understands,
And right to those who find knowledge.
10 Receive my instruction, and not silver,
And knowledge rather than choice gold;
11 For wisdom *is* better than rubies,
And all the things one may desire cannot be compared with her.

12 "I, wisdom, dwell with prudence,
And find out knowledge *and* discretion.

6:26 [a]Literally *a man's wife,* that is, of another 7:22 [a]Septuagint, Syriac, and Targum read *as a dog to bonds;* Vulgate reads *as a lamb . . . to bonds.* 7:27 [a]Or *Sheol*

13 The fear of the LORD *is* to hate evil;
Pride and arrogance and the evil way
And the perverse mouth I hate.
14 Counsel *is* mine, and sound wisdom;
I *am* understanding, I have strength.
15 By me kings reign,
And rulers decree justice.
16 By me princes rule, and nobles,
All the judges of the earth.[a]
17 I love those who love me,
And those who seek me diligently will find me.
18 Riches and honor *are* with me,
Enduring riches and righteousness.
19 My fruit *is* better than gold, yes, than fine gold,
And my revenue than choice silver.
20 I traverse the way of righteousness,
In the midst of the paths of justice,
21 That I may cause those who love me to inherit wealth,
That I may fill their treasuries.

22 "The LORD possessed me at the beginning of His way,
Before His works of old.
23 I have been established from everlasting,
From the beginning, before there was ever an earth.
24 When *there were* no depths I was brought forth,
When *there were* no fountains abounding with water.
25 Before the mountains were settled,
Before the hills, I was brought forth;
26 While as yet He had not made the earth or the fields,
Or the primal dust of the world.
27 When He prepared the heavens, I *was* there,
When He drew a circle on the face of the deep,
28 When He established the clouds above,
When He strengthened the fountains of the deep,
29 When He assigned to the sea its limit,
So that the waters would not transgress His command,
When He marked out the foundations of the earth,
30 Then I was beside Him *as* a master craftsman;[a]
And I was daily *His* delight,
Rejoicing always before Him,
31 Rejoicing in His inhabited world,
And my delight *was* with the sons of men.

32 "Now therefore, listen to me, *my* children,
For blessed *are those who* keep my ways.
33 Hear instruction and be wise,
And do not disdain *it*.
34 Blessed is the man who listens to me,
Watching daily at my gates,
Waiting at the posts of my doors.
35 For whoever finds me finds life,
And obtains favor from the LORD;
36 But he who sins against me wrongs his own soul;
All those who hate me love death."

The Way of Wisdom

9 Wisdom has built her house,
She has hewn out her seven pillars;
2 She has slaughtered her meat,
She has mixed her wine,
She has also furnished her table.
3 She has sent out her maidens,
She cries out from the highest places of the city,
4 "Whoever *is* simple, let him turn in here!"
As for him who lacks understanding, she says to him,
5 "Come, eat of my bread
And drink of the wine I have mixed.
6 Forsake foolishness and live,
And go in the way of understanding.

7 "He who corrects a scoffer gets shame for himself,
And he who rebukes a wicked *man only* harms himself.
8 Do not correct a scoffer, lest he hate you;
Rebuke a wise *man*, and he will love you.
9 Give *instruction* to a wise *man*, and he will be still wiser;
Teach a just *man*, and he will increase in learning.

10 "The fear of the LORD *is* the beginning of wisdom,
And the knowledge of the Holy One *is* understanding.
11 For by me your days will be multiplied,
And years of life will be added to you.
12 If you are wise, you are wise for yourself,
And *if* you scoff, you will bear *it* alone."

The Way of Folly

13 A foolish woman is clamorous;
She is simple, and knows nothing.
14 For she sits at the door of her house,
On a seat *by* the highest places of the city,
15 To call to those who pass by,
Who go straight on their way:
16 "Whoever *is* simple, let him turn in here";
And *as for* him who lacks understanding, she says to him,
17 "Stolen water is sweet,
And bread *eaten* in secret is pleasant."
18 But he does not know that the dead *are* there,
That her guests *are* in the depths of hell.[a]

Wise Sayings of Solomon

10 The proverbs of Solomon:
A wise son makes a glad father,
But a foolish son *is* the grief of his mother.

2 Treasures of wickedness profit nothing,
But righteousness delivers from death.
3 The LORD will not allow the righteous soul to famish,
But He casts away the desire of the wicked.

4 He who has a slack hand becomes poor,
But the hand of the diligent makes rich.
5 He who gathers in summer *is* a wise son;
He who sleeps in harvest *is* a son who causes shame.

8:16 [a]Masoretic Text, Syriac, Targum, and Vulgate read *righteousness;* Septuagint, Bomberg, and some manuscripts and editions read *earth.* **8:30** [a]A Jewish tradition reads *one brought up.* **9:18** [a]Or *Sheol*

6 Blessings *are* on the head of the righteous,
But violence covers the mouth of the wicked.
7 The memory of the righteous *is* blessed,
But the name of the wicked will rot.

8 The wise in heart will receive commands,
But a prating fool will fall.

9 He who walks with integrity walks securely,
But he who perverts his ways will become known.

10 He who winks with the eye causes trouble,
But a prating fool will fall.

11 The mouth of the righteous *is* a well of life,
But violence covers the mouth of the wicked.

12 Hatred stirs up strife,
But love covers all sins.

13 Wisdom is found on the lips of him who has understanding,
But a rod *is* for the back of him who is devoid of understanding.

14 Wise *people* store up knowledge,
But the mouth of the foolish *is* near destruction.

15 The rich man's wealth *is* his strong city;
The destruction of the poor *is* their poverty.

16 The labor of the righteous *leads* to life,
The wages of the wicked to sin.

17 He who keeps instruction *is in* the way of life,
But he who refuses correction goes astray.

18 Whoever hides hatred *has* lying lips,
And whoever spreads slander *is* a fool.

19 In the multitude of words sin is not lacking,
But he who restrains his lips *is* wise.
20 The tongue of the righteous *is* choice silver;
The heart of the wicked *is worth* little.
21 The lips of the righteous feed many,
But fools die for lack of wisdom.[a]

22 The blessing of the LORD makes *one* rich,
And He adds no sorrow with it.

23 To do evil *is* like sport to a fool,
But a man of understanding has wisdom.
24 The fear of the wicked will come upon him,
And the desire of the righteous will be granted.
25 When the whirlwind passes by, the wicked *is* no *more,*
But the righteous *has* an everlasting foundation.

26 As vinegar to the teeth and smoke to the eyes,
So *is* the lazy *man* to those who send him.

27 The fear of the LORD prolongs days,
But the years of the wicked will be shortened.
28 The hope of the righteous *will be* gladness,
But the expectation of the wicked will perish.
29 The way of the LORD *is* strength for the upright,
But destruction *will come* to the workers of iniquity.

30 The righteous will never be removed,
But the wicked will not inhabit the earth.
31 The mouth of the righteous brings forth wisdom,
But the perverse tongue will be cut out.
32 The lips of the righteous know what is acceptable,
But the mouth of the wicked *what is* perverse.

11 Dishonest scales *are* an abomination to the LORD,
But a just weight *is* His delight.

2 When pride comes, then comes shame;
But with the humble *is* wisdom.

3 The integrity of the upright will guide them,
But the perversity of the unfaithful will destroy them.
4 Riches do not profit in the day of wrath,
But righteousness delivers from death.
5 The righteousness of the blameless will direct[a] his way aright,
But the wicked will fall by his own wickedness.
6 The righteousness of the upright will deliver them,
But the unfaithful will be caught by *their* lust.

7 When a wicked man dies, *his* expectation will perish,
And the hope of the unjust perishes.
8 The righteous is delivered from trouble,
And it comes to the wicked instead.
9 The hypocrite with *his* mouth destroys his neighbor,
But through knowledge the righteous will be delivered.
10 When it goes well with the righteous, the city rejoices;
And when the wicked perish, *there is* jubilation.
11 By the blessing of the upright the city is exalted,
But it is overthrown by the mouth of the wicked.

12 He who is devoid of wisdom despises his neighbor,
But a man of understanding holds his peace.

13 A talebearer reveals secrets,
But he who is of a faithful spirit conceals a matter.

14 Where *there is* no counsel, the people fall;
But in the multitude of counselors *there is* safety.

10:21 [a]Literally *heart* **11:5** [a]Or *make smooth* or *straight*

15 He who is surety for a stranger will suffer,
But one who hates being surety is secure.

16 A gracious woman retains honor,
But ruthless *men* retain riches.
17 The merciful man does good for his own soul,
But *he who is* cruel troubles his own flesh.
18 The wicked *man* does deceptive work,
But he who sows righteousness *will have* a sure reward.
19 As righteousness *leads* to life,
So he who pursues evil *pursues it* to his own death.
20 Those who are of a perverse heart *are* an abomination to the LORD,
But *the* blameless in their ways *are* His delight.
21 *Though they join* forces,[a] the wicked will not go unpunished;
But the posterity of the righteous will be delivered.

22 *As* a ring of gold in a swine's snout,
So is a lovely woman who lacks discretion.

23 The desire of the righteous *is* only good,
But the expectation of the wicked *is* wrath.

24 There is *one* who scatters, yet increases more;
And there is *one* who withholds more than is right,
But it *leads* to poverty.
25 The generous soul will be made rich,
And he who waters will also be watered himself.
26 The people will curse him who withholds grain,
But blessing *will be* on the head of him who sells *it*.

27 He who earnestly seeks good finds favor,
But trouble will come to him who seeks *evil*.

28 He who trusts in his riches will fall,
But the righteous will flourish like foliage.
29 He who troubles his own house will inherit the wind,
And the fool *will be* servant to the wise of heart.

30 The fruit of the righteous *is a* tree of life,
And he who wins souls *is* wise.

31 If the righteous will be recompensed on the earth,
How much more the ungodly and the sinner.

12

Whoever loves instruction loves knowledge,
But he who hates correction *is* stupid.

2 A good *man* obtains favor from the LORD,
But a man of wicked intentions He will condemn.

3 A man is not established by wickedness,
But the root of the righteous cannot be moved.

4 An excellent[a] wife *is* the crown of her husband,
But she who causes shame *is* like rottenness in his bones.

5 The thoughts of the righteous *are* right,
But the counsels of the wicked *are* deceitful.
6 The words of the wicked *are*, "Lie in wait for blood,"
But the mouth of the upright will deliver them.

7 The wicked are overthrown and *are* no more,
But the house of the righteous will stand.

8 A man will be commended according to his wisdom,
But he who is of a perverse heart will be despised.

9 Better *is the one* who is slighted but has a servant,
Than he who honors himself but lacks bread.

10 A righteous *man* regards the life of his animal,
But the tender mercies of the wicked *are* cruel.

11 He who tills his land will be satisfied with bread,
But he who follows frivolity *is* devoid of understanding.[a]

12 The wicked covet the catch of evil *men*,
But the root of the righteous yields *fruit*.
13 The wicked is ensnared by the transgression of *his* lips,
But the righteous will come through trouble.
14 A man will be satisfied with good by the fruit of *his* mouth,
And the recompense of a man's hands will be rendered to him.

15 The way of a fool *is* right in his own eyes,
But he who heeds counsel *is* wise.
16 A fool's wrath is known at once,
But a prudent *man* covers shame.

17 He *who* speaks truth declares righteousness,
But a false witness, deceit.
18 There is one who speaks like the piercings of a sword,
But the tongue of the wise *promotes* health.
19 The truthful lip shall be established forever,
But a lying tongue *is* but for a moment.
20 Deceit is in the heart of those who devise evil,
But counselors of peace have joy.
21 No grave trouble will overtake the righteous,
But the wicked shall be filled with evil.
22 Lying lips *are* an abomination to the LORD,
But those who deal truthfully *are* His delight.

11:21 [a]Literally *hand to hand* 12:4 [a]Literally *A wife of valor* 12:11 [a]Literally *heart*

23 A prudent man conceals knowledge,
But the heart of fools proclaims foolishness.

24 The hand of the diligent will rule,
But the lazy *man* will be put to forced labor.

25 Anxiety in the heart of man causes depression,
But a good word makes it glad.

26 The righteous should choose his friends carefully,
For the way of the wicked leads them astray.

27 The lazy *man* does not roast what he took in hunting,
But diligence *is* man's precious possession.

28 In the way of righteousness *is* life,
And in *its* pathway *there is* no death.

13 A wise son *heeds* his father's instruction,
But a scoffer does not listen to rebuke.

2 A man shall eat well by the fruit of *his* mouth,
But the soul of the unfaithful feeds on violence.

3 He who guards his mouth preserves his life,
But he who opens wide his lips shall have destruction.

4 The soul of a lazy *man* desires, and *has* nothing;
But the soul of the diligent shall be made rich.

5 A righteous *man* hates lying,
But a wicked *man* is loathsome and comes to shame.

6 Righteousness guards *him whose* way is blameless,
But wickedness overthrows the sinner.

7 There is one who makes himself rich, yet *has* nothing;
And one who makes himself poor, yet *has* great riches.

8 The ransom of a man's life *is* his riches,
But the poor does not hear rebuke.

9 The light of the righteous rejoices,
But the lamp of the wicked will be put out.

10 By pride comes nothing but strife,
But with the well-advised *is* wisdom.

11 Wealth *gained by* dishonesty will be diminished,
But he who gathers by labor will increase.

12 Hope deferred makes the heart sick,
But *when* the desire comes, *it is* a tree of life.

13 He who despises the word will be destroyed,
But he who fears the commandment will be rewarded.

14 The law of the wise *is* a fountain of life,
To turn *one* away from the snares of death.

15 Good understanding gains favor,
But the way of the unfaithful *is* hard.

16 Every prudent *man* acts with knowledge,
But a fool lays open *his* folly.

17 A wicked messenger falls into trouble,
But a faithful ambassador *brings* health.

18 Poverty and shame *will come* to him who disdains correction,
But he who regards a rebuke will be honored.

19 A desire accomplished is sweet to the soul,
But *it is* an abomination to fools to depart from evil.

20 He who walks with wise *men* will be wise,
But the companion of fools will be destroyed.

21 Evil pursues sinners,
But to the righteous, good shall be repaid.

22 A good *man* leaves an inheritance to his children's children,
But the wealth of the sinner is stored up for the righteous.

23 Much food *is in* the fallow *ground* of the poor,
And for lack of justice there is waste.[a]

24 He who spares his rod hates his son,
But he who loves him disciplines him promptly.

25 The righteous eats to the satisfying of his soul,
But the stomach of the wicked shall be in want.

14 The wise woman builds her house,
But the foolish pulls it down with her hands.

2 He who walks in his uprightness fears the LORD,
But *he who is* perverse in his ways despises Him.

3 In the mouth of a fool *is* a rod of pride,
But the lips of the wise will preserve them.

4 Where no oxen *are*, the trough *is* clean;
But much increase *comes* by the strength of an ox.

5 A faithful witness does not lie,
But a false witness will utter lies.

6 A scoffer seeks wisdom and does not *find it*,
But knowledge *is* easy to him who understands.

7 Go from the presence of a foolish man,
When you do not perceive *in him* the lips of knowledge.

8 The wisdom of the prudent *is* to understand his way,
But the folly of fools *is* deceit.

9 Fools mock at sin,
But among the upright *there is* favor.

13:23 [a]Literally *what is swept away*

10 The heart knows its own bitterness,
And a stranger does not share its joy.

11 The house of the wicked will be overthrown,
But the tent of the upright will flourish.

12 There is a way *that seems* right to a man,
But its end *is* the way of death.

13 Even in laughter the heart may sorrow,
And the end of mirth *may be* grief.

14 The backslider in heart will be filled with his own ways,
But a good man *will be satisfied* from above.[a]

15 The simple believes every word,
But the prudent considers well his steps.
16 A wise *man* fears and departs from evil,
But a fool rages and is self-confident.
17 A quick-tempered *man* acts foolishly,
And a man of wicked intentions is hated.
18 The simple inherit folly,
But the prudent are crowned with knowledge.
19 The evil will bow before the good,
And the wicked at the gates of the righteous.

20 The poor *man* is hated even by his own neighbor,
But the rich *has* many friends.
21 He who despises his neighbor sins;
But he who has mercy on the poor, happy *is* he.

22 Do they not go astray who devise evil?
But mercy and truth *belong* to those who devise good.

23 In all labor there is profit,
But idle chatter[a] *leads* only to poverty.
24 The crown of the wise is their riches,
But the foolishness of fools *is* folly.

25 A true witness delivers souls,
But a deceitful *witness* speaks lies.

26 In the fear of the LORD *there is* strong confidence,
And His children will have a place of refuge.
27 The fear of the LORD *is* a fountain of life,
To turn *one* away from the snares of death.

28 In a multitude of people *is* a king's honor,
But in the lack of people *is* the downfall of a prince.

29 *He who is* slow to wrath has great understanding,
But *he who is* impulsive[a] exalts folly.

30 A sound heart *is* life to the body,
But envy *is* rottenness to the bones.

31 He who oppresses the poor reproaches his Maker,
But he who honors Him has mercy on the needy.

32 The wicked is banished in his wickedness,
But the righteous has a refuge in his death.

33 Wisdom rests in the heart of him who has understanding,
But *what is* in the heart of fools is made known.

34 Righteousness exalts a nation,
But sin *is* a reproach to *any* people.

35 The king's favor *is* toward a wise servant,
But his wrath *is against* him who causes shame.

15 A soft answer turns away wrath,
But a harsh word stirs up anger.
2 The tongue of the wise uses knowledge rightly,
But the mouth of fools pours forth foolishness.

3 The eyes of the LORD *are* in every place,
Keeping watch on the evil and the good.

4 A wholesome tongue *is* a tree of life,
But perverseness in it breaks the spirit.

5 A fool despises his father's instruction,
But he who receives correction is prudent.

6 *In* the house of the righteous *there is* much treasure,
But in the revenue of the wicked is trouble.

7 The lips of the wise disperse knowledge,
But the heart of the fool *does* not *do* so.

8 The sacrifice of the wicked *is* an abomination to the LORD,
But the prayer of the upright *is* His delight.
9 The way of the wicked *is* an abomination to the LORD,
But He loves him who follows righteousness.

10 Harsh discipline *is* for him who forsakes the way,
And he who hates correction will die.

11 Hell[a] and Destruction[b] *are* before the LORD;
So how much more the hearts of the sons of men.

12 A scoffer does not love one who corrects him,
Nor will he go to the wise.

13 A merry heart makes a cheerful countenance,
But by sorrow of the heart the spirit is broken.

14 The heart of him who has understanding seeks knowledge,
But the mouth of fools feeds on foolishness.

15 All the days of the afflicted *are* evil,
But he who is of a merry heart *has* a continual feast.

16 Better *is* a little with the fear of the LORD,
Than great treasure with trouble.
17 Better *is* a dinner of herbs[a] where love is,
Than a fatted calf with hatred.

14:14 [a]Literally *from above himself* **14:23** [a]Literally *talk of the lips* **14:29** [a]Literally *short of spirit* **15:11** [a]Or *Sheol* [b]Hebrew *Abaddon* **15:17** [a]Or *vegetables*

18 A wrathful man stirs up strife,
But *he who is* slow to anger allays contention.

19 The way of the lazy *man is* like a hedge of thorns,
But the way of the upright *is* a highway.

20 A wise son makes a father glad,
But a foolish man despises his mother.

21 Folly *is* joy *to him who is* destitute of discernment,
But a man of understanding walks uprightly.

22 Without counsel, plans go awry,
But in the multitude of counselors they are established.

23 A man has joy by the answer of his mouth,
And a word *spoken* in due season, how good *it is!*

24 The way of life *winds* upward for the wise,
That he may turn away from hell[a] below.

25 The LORD will destroy the house of the proud,
But He will establish the boundary of the widow.

26 The thoughts of the wicked *are* an abomination to the LORD,
But the words of the pure *are* pleasant.

27 He who is greedy for gain troubles his own house,
But he who hates bribes will live.

28 The heart of the righteous studies how to answer,
But the mouth of the wicked pours forth evil.

29 The LORD *is* far from the wicked,
But He hears the prayer of the righteous.

30 The light of the eyes rejoices the heart,
And a good report makes the bones healthy.[a]

31 The ear that hears the rebukes of life
Will abide among the wise.

32 He who disdains instruction despises his own soul,
But he who heeds rebuke gets understanding.

33 The fear of the LORD *is* the instruction of wisdom,
And before honor *is* humility.

16 The preparations of the heart *belong* to man,
But the answer of the tongue *is* from the LORD.

2 All the ways of a man *are* pure in his own eyes,
But the LORD weighs the spirits.

3 Commit your works to the LORD,
And your thoughts will be established.

4 The LORD has made all for Himself,
Yes, even the wicked for the day of doom.

5 Everyone proud in heart *is* an abomination to the LORD;
Though they join forces,[a] none will go unpunished.

6 In mercy and truth
Atonement is provided for iniquity;
And by the fear of the LORD *one* departs from evil.

7 When a man's ways please the LORD,
He makes even his enemies to be at peace with him.

8 Better *is* a little with righteousness,
Than vast revenues without justice.

9 A man's heart plans his way,
But the LORD directs his steps.

10 Divination *is* on the lips of the king;
His mouth must not transgress in judgment.

11 Honest weights and scales *are* the LORD's;
All the weights in the bag *are* His work.

12 *It is* an abomination for kings to commit wickedness,
For a throne is established by righteousness.

13 Righteous lips *are* the delight of kings,
And they love him who speaks *what is* right.

14 As messengers of death *is* the king's wrath,
But a wise man will appease it.

15 In the light of the king's face *is* life,
And his favor *is* like a cloud of the latter rain.

16 How much better to get wisdom than gold!
And to get understanding is to be chosen rather than silver.

17 The highway of the upright *is* to depart from evil;
He who keeps his way preserves his soul.

18 Pride *goes* before destruction,
And a haughty spirit before a fall.

19 Better *to be* of a humble spirit with the lowly,
Than to divide the spoil with the proud.

20 He who heeds the word wisely will find good,
And whoever trusts in the LORD, happy *is* he.

21 The wise in heart will be called prudent,
And sweetness of the lips increases learning.

22 Understanding *is* a wellspring of life to him who has it.
But the correction of fools *is* folly.

23 The heart of the wise teaches his mouth,
And adds learning to his lips.

24 Pleasant words *are like* a honeycomb,
Sweetness to the soul and health to the bones.

25 There is a way *that seems* right to a man,
But its end *is* the way of death.

26 The person who labors, labors for himself,
For his *hungry* mouth drives him *on*.

15:24 [a]Or *Sheol* **15:30** [a]Literally *fat* **16:5** [a]Literally *hand to hand*

27 An ungodly man digs up evil,
And *it is* on his lips like a burning fire.
28 A perverse man sows strife,
And a whisperer separates the best of friends.
29 A violent man entices his neighbor,
And leads him in a way *that is* not good.
30 He winks his eye to devise perverse things;
He purses his lips *and* brings about evil.

31 The silver-haired head *is* a crown of glory,
If it is found in the way of righteousness.

32 *He who is* slow to anger *is* better than the mighty,
And he who rules his spirit than he who takes a city.

33 The lot is cast into the lap,
But its every decision *is* from the LORD.

17 Better *is* a dry morsel with quietness,
Than a house full of feasting[a] *with* strife.

2 A wise servant will rule over a son who causes shame,
And will share an inheritance among the brothers.

3 The refining pot *is* for silver and the furnace for gold,
But the LORD tests the hearts.

4 An evildoer gives heed to false lips;
A liar listens eagerly to a spiteful tongue.

5 He who mocks the poor reproaches his Maker;
He who is glad at calamity will not go unpunished.

6 Children's children *are* the crown of old men,
And the glory of children *is* their father.

7 Excellent speech is not becoming to a fool,
Much less lying lips to a prince.

8 A present *is* a precious stone in the eyes of its possessor;
Wherever he turns, he prospers.

9 He who covers a transgression seeks love,
But he who repeats a matter separates friends.

10 Rebuke is more effective for a wise *man*
Than a hundred blows on a fool.

11 An evil *man* seeks only rebellion;
Therefore a cruel messenger will be sent against him.

12 Let a man meet a bear robbed of her cubs,
Rather than a fool in his folly.

13 Whoever rewards evil for good,
Evil will not depart from his house.

14 The beginning of strife *is like* releasing water;
Therefore stop contention before a quarrel starts.

15 He who justifies the wicked, and he who condemns the just,
Both of them alike *are* an abomination to the LORD.

16 Why *is there* in the hand of a fool the purchase price of wisdom,
Since *he has* no heart *for it?*

17 A friend loves at all times,
And a brother is born for adversity.

18 A man devoid of understanding shakes hands in a pledge,
And becomes surety for his friend.

19 He who loves transgression loves strife,
And he who exalts his gate seeks destruction.

20 He who has a deceitful heart finds no good,
And he who has a perverse tongue falls into evil.

21 He who begets a scoffer *does so* to his sorrow,
And the father of a fool has no joy.

22 A merry heart does good, *like* medicine,[a]
But a broken spirit dries the bones.

23 A wicked *man* accepts a bribe behind the back[a]
To pervert the ways of justice.

24 Wisdom *is* in the sight of him who has understanding,
But the eyes of a fool *are* on the ends of the earth.

25 A foolish son *is* a grief to his father,
And bitterness to her who bore him.

26 Also, to punish the righteous *is* not good,
Nor to strike princes for *their* uprightness.

27 He who has knowledge spares his words,
And a man of understanding is of a calm spirit.

28 Even a fool is counted wise when he holds his peace;
When he shuts his lips, *he is considered* perceptive.

18 A man who isolates himself seeks his own desire;
He rages against all wise judgment.

2 A fool has no delight in understanding,
But in expressing his own heart.

3 When the wicked comes, contempt comes also;
And with dishonor *comes* reproach.

4 The words of a man's mouth *are* deep waters;
The wellspring of wisdom *is* a flowing brook.

5 *It is* not good to show partiality to the wicked,
Or to overthrow the righteous in judgment.

6 A fool's lips enter into contention,
And his mouth calls for blows.
7 A fool's mouth *is* his destruction,
And his lips *are* the snare of his soul.

17:1 [a]Or *sacrificial meals* 17:22 [a]Or *makes medicine even better* 17:23 [a]Literally *from the bosom*

8 The words of a talebearer *are* like tasty
trifles,[a]
And they go down into the inmost body.

9 He who is slothful in his work
Is a brother to him who is a great
destroyer.

10 The name of the LORD *is* a strong tower;
The righteous run to it and are safe.

11 The rich man's wealth *is* his strong city,
And like a high wall in his own esteem.

12 Before destruction the heart of a man is
haughty,
And before honor *is* humility.

13 He who answers a matter before he hears
it,
It *is* folly and shame to him.

14 The spirit of a man will sustain him in
sickness,
But who can bear a broken spirit?

15 The heart of the prudent acquires
knowledge,
And the ear of the wise seeks knowledge.

16 A man's gift makes room for him,
And brings him before great men.

17 The first *one* to plead his cause *seems*
right,
Until his neighbor comes and examines
him.

18 Casting lots causes contentions to cease,
And keeps the mighty apart.

19 A brother offended *is harder to win* than
a strong city,
And contentions *are* like the bars of a
castle.

20 A man's stomach shall be satisfied from
the fruit of his mouth;
From the produce of his lips he shall be
filled.

21 Death and life *are* in the power of the
tongue,
And those who love it will eat its fruit.

22 *He who* finds a wife finds a good *thing,*
And obtains favor from the LORD.

23 The poor *man* uses entreaties,
But the rich answers roughly.

24 A man *who has* friends must himself be
friendly,[a]
But there is a friend *who* sticks closer
than a brother.

19 Better *is* the poor who walks in his
integrity
Than *one who is* perverse in his lips, and
is a fool.

2 Also it is not good *for* a soul *to be*
without knowledge,
And he sins who hastens with *his* feet.

3 The foolishness of a man twists his way,
And his heart frets against the LORD.

4 Wealth makes many friends,
But the poor is separated from his friend.

5 A false witness will not go unpunished,
And *he who* speaks lies will not escape.

6 Many entreat the favor of the nobility,
And every man *is* a friend to one who
gives gifts.

7 All the brothers of the poor hate him;
How much more do his friends go far
from him!
He may pursue *them with* words, *yet*
they abandon *him.*

8 He who gets wisdom loves his own soul;
He who keeps understanding will find
good.

9 A false witness will not go unpunished,
And *he who* speaks lies shall perish.

10 Luxury is not fitting for a fool,
Much less for a servant to rule over
princes.

11 The discretion of a man makes him slow
to anger,
And his glory *is* to overlook a
transgression.

12 The king's wrath *is* like the roaring of a
lion,
But his favor *is* like dew on the grass.

13 A foolish son *is* the ruin of his father,
And the contentions of a wife *are* a
continual dripping.

14 Houses and riches *are* an inheritance
from fathers,
But a prudent wife *is* from the LORD.

15 Laziness casts *one* into a deep sleep,
And an idle person will suffer hunger.

16 He who keeps the commandment keeps
his soul,
But he who is careless[a] of his ways will
die.

17 He who has pity on the poor lends to the
LORD,
And He will pay back what he has given.

18 Chasten your son while there is hope,
And do not set your heart on his
destruction.[a]

19 *A man of* great wrath will suffer
punishment;
For if you rescue *him,* you will have to do
it again.

20 Listen to counsel and receive instruction,
That you may be wise in your latter days.

21 There are many plans in a man's heart,
Nevertheless the LORD's counsel—that
will stand.

22 What is desired in a man is kindness,
And a poor man is better than a liar.

23 The fear of the LORD *leads* to life,
And *he who has it* will abide in
satisfaction;
He will not be visited with evil.

24 A lazy *man* buries his hand in the bowl,[a]
And will not so much as bring it to his
mouth again.

18:8 [a]A Jewish tradition reads *wounds.* **18:24** [a]Following Greek manuscripts, Syriac, Targum, and Vulgate; Masoretic Text reads *may come to ruin.* **19:16** [a]Literally *despises,* figurative of recklessness or carelessness **19:18** [a]Literally *to put him to death;* a Jewish tradition reads *on his crying.* **19:24** [a]Septuagint and Syriac read *bosom;* Targum and Vulgate read *armpit.*

25 Strike a scoffer, and the simple will become wary;
Rebuke one who has understanding, *and* he will discern knowledge.

26 He who mistreats *his* father *and* chases away *his* mother
Is a son who causes shame and brings reproach.

27 Cease listening to instruction, my son,
And you will stray from the words of knowledge.

28 A disreputable witness scorns justice,
And the mouth of the wicked devours iniquity.

29 Judgments are prepared for scoffers,
And beatings for the backs of fools.

20 Wine *is* a mocker,
Strong drink *is* a brawler,
And whoever is led astray by it is not wise.

2 The wrath[a] of a king *is* like the roaring of a lion;
Whoever provokes him to anger sins *against* his own life.

3 *It is* honorable for a man to stop striving,
Since any fool can start a quarrel.

4 The lazy *man* will not plow because of winter;
He will beg during harvest and *have* nothing.

5 Counsel in the heart of man *is like* deep water,
But a man of understanding will draw it out.

6 Most men will proclaim each his own goodness,
But who can find a faithful man?

7 The righteous *man* walks in his integrity;
His children *are* blessed after him.

8 A king who sits on the throne of judgment
Scatters all evil with his eyes.

9 Who can say, "I have made my heart clean,
I am pure from my sin"?

10 Diverse weights *and* diverse measures,
They *are* both alike, an abomination to the LORD.

11 Even a child is known by his deeds,
Whether what he does *is* pure and right.

12 The hearing ear and the seeing eye,
The LORD has made them both.

13 Do not love sleep, lest you come to poverty;
Open your eyes, *and* you will be satisfied with bread.

14 "*It is* good for nothing,"[a] cries the buyer;
But when he has gone his way, then he boasts.

15 There is gold and a multitude of rubies,
But the lips of knowledge *are* a precious jewel.

16 Take the garment of one who is surety *for* a stranger,
And hold it as a pledge *when it* is for a seductress.

17 Bread gained by deceit *is* sweet to a man,
But afterward his mouth will be filled with gravel.

18 Plans are established by counsel;
By wise counsel wage war.

19 He who goes about *as* a talebearer reveals secrets;
Therefore do not associate with one who flatters with his lips.

20 Whoever curses his father or his mother,
His lamp will be put out in deep darkness.

21 An inheritance gained hastily at the beginning
Will not be blessed at the end.

22 Do not say, "I will recompense evil";
Wait for the LORD, and He will save you.

23 Diverse weights *are* an abomination to the LORD,
And dishonest scales *are* not good.

24 A man's steps *are* of the LORD;
How then can a man understand his own way?

25 *It is* a snare for a man to devote rashly *something as* holy,
And afterward to reconsider *his* vows.

26 A wise king sifts out the wicked,
And brings the threshing wheel over them.

27 The spirit of a man *is* the lamp of the LORD,
Searching all the inner depths of his heart.[a]

28 Mercy and truth preserve the king,
And by lovingkindness he upholds his throne.

29 The glory of young men *is* their strength,
And the splendor of old men *is* their gray head.

30 Blows that hurt cleanse away evil,
As *do* stripes the inner depths of the heart.[a]

21 The king's heart *is* in the hand of the LORD,
Like the rivers of water;
He turns it wherever He wishes.

2 Every way of a man *is* right in his own eyes,
But the LORD weighs the hearts.

3 To do righteousness and justice
Is more acceptable to the LORD than sacrifice.

4 A haughty look, a proud heart,
And the plowing[a] of the wicked *are* sin.

5 The plans of the diligent *lead* surely to plenty,
But *those of* everyone *who is* hasty, surely to poverty.

20:2 [a]Literally *fear* or *terror* which is produced by the king's wrath **20:14** [a]Literally *evil, evil* **20:27** [a]Literally *the rooms of the belly* **20:30** [a]Literally *the rooms of the belly* **21:4** [a]Or *lamp*

6 Getting treasures by a lying tongue
Is the fleeting fantasy of those who seek death.[a]

7 The violence of the wicked will destroy them,[a]
Because they refuse to do justice.

8 The way of a guilty man *is* perverse;[a]
But *as for* the pure, his work *is* right.

9 Better to dwell in a corner of a housetop,
Than in a house shared with a contentious woman.

10 The soul of the wicked desires evil;
His neighbor finds no favor in his eyes.

11 When the scoffer is punished, the simple is made wise;
But when the wise is instructed, he receives knowledge.

12 The righteous *God* wisely considers the house of the wicked,
Overthrowing the wicked for *their* wickedness.

13 Whoever shuts his ears to the cry of the poor
Will also cry himself and not be heard.

14 A gift in secret pacifies anger,
And a bribe behind the back,[a] strong wrath.

15 *It is* a joy for the just to do justice,
But destruction *will come* to the workers of iniquity.

16 A man who wanders from the way of understanding
Will rest in the assembly of the dead.

17 He who loves pleasure *will be* a poor man;
He who loves wine and oil will not be rich.

18 The wicked *shall be* a ransom for the righteous,
And the unfaithful for the upright.

19 Better to dwell in the wilderness,
Than with a contentious and angry woman.

20 *There is* desirable treasure,
And oil in the dwelling of the wise,
But a foolish man squanders it.

21 He who follows righteousness and mercy
Finds life, righteousness, and honor.

22 A wise *man* scales the city of the mighty,
And brings down the trusted stronghold.

23 Whoever guards his mouth and tongue
Keeps his soul from troubles.

24 A proud *and* haughty *man*—"Scoffer" *is* his name;
He acts with arrogant pride.

25 The desire of the lazy *man* kills him,
For his hands refuse to labor.

26 He covets greedily all day long,
But the righteous gives and does not spare.

27 The sacrifice of the wicked *is* an abomination;
How much more *when* he brings it with wicked intent!

28 A false witness shall perish,
But the man who hears *him* will speak endlessly.

29 A wicked man hardens his face,
But *as for* the upright, he establishes[a] his way.

30 *There is* no wisdom or understanding
Or counsel against the LORD.

31 The horse *is* prepared for the day of battle,
But deliverance *is* of the LORD.

22 A *good* name is to be chosen rather than great riches,
Loving favor rather than silver and gold.

2 The rich and the poor have this in common,
The LORD *is* the maker of them all.

3 A prudent *man* foresees evil and hides himself,
But the simple pass on and are punished.

4 By humility *and* the fear of the LORD
Are riches and honor and life.

5 Thorns *and* snares *are* in the way of the perverse;
He who guards his soul will be far from them.

6 Train up a child in the way he should go,
And when he is old he will not depart from it.

7 The rich rules over the poor,
And the borrower *is* servant to the lender.

8 He who sows iniquity will reap sorrow,
And the rod of his anger will fail.

9 He who has a generous eye will be blessed,
For he gives of his bread to the poor.

10 Cast out the scoffer, and contention will leave;
Yes, strife and reproach will cease.

11 He who loves purity of heart
And has grace on his lips,
The king *will be* his friend.

12 The eyes of the LORD preserve knowledge,
But He overthrows the words of the faithless.

13 The lazy *man* says, "*There is* a lion outside!
I shall be slain in the streets!"

14 The mouth of an immoral woman *is* a deep pit;
He who is abhorred by the LORD will fall there.

15 Foolishness *is* bound up in the heart of a child;

21:6 [a]Septuagint reads *Pursue vanity on the snares of death;* Vulgate reads *Is vain and foolish, and shall stumble on the snares of death;* Targum reads *They shall be destroyed, and they shall fall who seek death.* **21:7** [a]Literally *drag them away* **21:8** [a]Or *The way of a man is perverse and strange* **21:14** [a]Literally *in the bosom* **21:29** [a]Qere and Septuagint read *understands.*

The rod of correction will drive it far
from him.
16 He who oppresses the poor to increase
his *riches*,
And he who gives to the rich, *will* surely
come to poverty.

Sayings of the Wise

17 Incline your ear and hear the words of
the wise,
And apply your heart to my knowledge;
18 For *it is* a pleasant thing if you keep them
within you;
Let them all be fixed upon your lips,
19 So that your trust may be in the LORD;
I have instructed you today, even you.
20 Have I not written to you excellent things
Of counsels and knowledge,
21 That I may make you know the certainty
of the words of truth,
That you may answer words of truth
To those who send to you?

22 Do not rob the poor because he *is* poor,
Nor oppress the afflicted at the gate;
23 For the LORD will plead their cause,
And plunder the soul of those who
plunder them.

24 Make no friendship with an angry man,
And with a furious man do not go,
25 Lest you learn his ways
And set a snare for your soul.

26 Do not be one of those who shakes hands
in a pledge,
One of those who is surety for debts;
27 If you have nothing *with which* to pay,
Why should he take away your bed from
under you?

28 Do not remove the ancient landmark
Which your fathers have set.

29 Do you see a man *who* excels in his
work?
He will stand before kings;
He will not stand before unknown *men*.

23 When you sit down to eat with a ruler,
Consider carefully what *is* before you;
2 And put a knife to your throat
If you *are* a man given to appetite.
3 Do not desire his delicacies,
For they *are* deceptive food.

4 Do not overwork to be rich;
Because of your own understanding,
cease!
5 Will you set your eyes on that which is
not?
For *riches* certainly make themselves
wings;
They fly away like an eagle *toward*
heaven.

6 Do not eat the bread of a miser,[a]
Nor desire his delicacies;
7 For as he thinks in his heart, so *is* he.
"Eat and drink!" he says to you,
But his heart is not with you.
8 The morsel you have eaten, you will
vomit up,
And waste your pleasant words.

9 Do not speak in the hearing of a fool,
For he will despise the wisdom of your
words.

10 Do not remove the ancient landmark,
Nor enter the fields of the fatherless;
11 For their Redeemer *is* mighty;
He will plead their cause against you.

12 Apply your heart to instruction,
And your ears to words of knowledge.

13 Do not withhold correction from a child,
For *if* you beat him with a rod, he will not
die.
14 You shall beat him with a rod,
And deliver his soul from hell.[a]

15 My son, if your heart is wise,
My heart will rejoice—indeed, I myself;
16 Yes, my inmost being will rejoice
When your lips speak right things.

17 Do not let your heart envy sinners,
But *be zealous* for the fear of the LORD
all the day;
18 For surely there is a hereafter,
And your hope will not be cut off.

19 Hear, my son, and be wise;
And guide your heart in the way.
20 Do not mix with winebibbers,
Or with gluttonous eaters of meat;
21 For the drunkard and the glutton will
come to poverty,
And drowsiness will clothe *a man* with
rags.

22 Listen to your father who begot you,
And do not despise your mother when
she is old.

23 Buy the truth, and do not sell *it*,
Also wisdom and instruction and
understanding.

24 The father of the righteous will greatly
rejoice,
And he who begets a wise *child* will
delight in him.
25 Let your father and your mother be glad,
And let her who bore you rejoice.

26 My son, give me your heart,
And let your eyes observe my ways.
27 For a harlot *is* a deep pit,
And a seductress *is* a narrow well.
28 She also lies in wait as *for* a victim,
And increases the unfaithful among men.

29 Who has woe?
Who has sorrow?
Who has contentions?
Who has complaints?
Who has wounds without cause?
Who has redness of eyes?
30 Those who linger long at the wine,
Those who go in search of mixed wine.
31 Do not look on the wine when it is red,
When it sparkles in the cup,
When it swirls around smoothly;
32 At the last it bites like a serpent,
And stings like a viper.
33 Your eyes will see strange things,
And your heart will utter perverse things.
34 Yes, you will be like one who lies down in
the midst of the sea,

23:6 [a]Literally *one who has an evil eye* 23:14 [a]Or *Sheol*

Or like one who lies at the top of the
mast, *saying:*
35 "They have struck me, *but* I was not hurt;
They have beaten me, but I did not feel *it.*
When shall I awake, that I may seek
another *drink?*"

24 Do not be envious of evil men,
Nor desire to be with them;
2 For their heart devises violence,
And their lips talk of troublemaking.

3 Through wisdom a house is built,
And by understanding it is established;
4 By knowledge the rooms are filled
With all precious and pleasant riches.

5 A wise man *is* strong,
Yes, a man of knowledge increases
strength;
6 For by wise counsel you will wage your
own war,
And in a multitude of counselors *there is*
safety.

7 Wisdom *is* too lofty for a fool;
He does not open his mouth in the gate.

8 He who plots to do evil
Will be called a schemer.
9 The devising of foolishness *is* sin,
And the scoffer *is* an abomination to
men.

10 *If* you faint in the day of adversity,
Your strength *is* small.

11 Deliver *those who* are drawn toward
death,
And hold back *those* stumbling to the
slaughter.
12 If you say, "Surely we did not know this,"
Does not He who weighs the hearts
consider *it?*
He who keeps your soul, does He *not*
know *it?*
And will He *not* render to *each* man
according to his deeds?

13 My son, eat honey because *it is* good,
And the honeycomb *which is* sweet to
your taste;
14 So *shall* the knowledge of wisdom *be* to
your soul;
If you have found *it,* there is a prospect,
And your hope will not be cut off.

15 Do not lie in wait, O wicked *man,* against
the dwelling of the righteous;
Do not plunder his resting place;
16 For a righteous *man* may fall seven times
And rise again,
But the wicked shall fall by calamity.

17 Do not rejoice when your enemy falls,
And do not let your heart be glad when
he stumbles;
18 Lest the LORD see *it,* and it displease
Him,
And He turn away His wrath from him.

19 Do not fret because of evildoers,
Nor be envious of the wicked;
20 For there will be no prospect for the evil
man;
The lamp of the wicked will be put out.

21 My son, fear the LORD and the king;
Do not associate with those given to
change;
22 For their calamity will rise suddenly,
And who knows the ruin those two can
bring?

Further Sayings of the Wise

23 These *things* also *belong* to the wise:

It is not good to show partiality in
judgment.
24 He who says to the wicked, "You *are*
righteous,"
Him the people will curse;
Nations will abhor him.
25 But those who rebuke *the wicked* will
have delight,
And a good blessing will come upon
them.

26 He who gives a right answer kisses the
lips.

27 Prepare your outside work,
Make it fit for yourself in the field;
And afterward build your house.

28 Do not be a witness against your
neighbor without cause,
For would you deceive[a] with your lips?
29 Do not say, "I will do to him just as he
has done to me;
I will render to the man according to his
work."

30 I went by the field of the lazy *man,*
And by the vineyard of the man devoid of
understanding;
31 And there it was, all overgrown with
thorns;
Its surface was covered with nettles;
Its stone wall was broken down.
32 When I saw *it,* I considered *it* well;
I looked on *it and* received instruction:
33 A little sleep, a little slumber,
A little folding of the hands to rest;
34 So shall your poverty come *like* a
prowler,
And your need like an armed man.

Further Wise Sayings of Solomon

25 These also *are* proverbs of Solomon
which the men of Hezekiah king of Ju-
dah copied:

2 *It is* the glory of God to conceal a matter,
But the glory of kings *is* to search out a
matter.

3 *As* the heavens for height and the earth
for depth,
So the heart of kings *is* unsearchable.

4 Take away the dross from silver,
And it will go to the silversmith *for*
jewelry.
5 Take away the wicked from before the
king,
And his throne will be established in
righteousness.

6 Do not exalt yourself in the presence of
the king,
And do not stand in the place of the
great;

24:28 [a]Septuagint and Vulgate read *Do not deceive.*

7 For *it is* better that he say to you,
"Come up here,"
Than that you should be put lower in the presence of the prince,
Whom your eyes have seen.

8 Do not go hastily to court;
For what will you do in the end,
When your neighbor has put you to shame?
9 Debate your case with your neighbor,
And do not disclose the secret to another;
10 Lest he who hears *it* expose your shame,
And your reputation be ruined.

11 A word fitly spoken *is like* apples of gold
In settings of silver.
12 *Like* an earring of gold and an ornament of fine gold
Is a wise rebuker to an obedient ear.

13 Like the cold of snow in time of harvest
Is a faithful messenger to those who send him,
For he refreshes the soul of his masters.

14 Whoever falsely boasts of giving
Is like clouds and wind without rain.

15 By long forbearance a ruler is persuaded,
And a gentle tongue breaks a bone.
16 Have you found honey?
Eat only as much as you need,
Lest you be filled with it and vomit.

17 Seldom set foot in your neighbor's house,
Lest he become weary of you and hate you.

18 A man who bears false witness against his neighbor
Is like a club, a sword, and a sharp arrow.
19 Confidence in an unfaithful *man* in time of trouble
Is like a bad tooth and a foot out of joint.

20 *Like* one who takes away a garment in cold weather,
And like vinegar on soda,
Is one who sings songs to a heavy heart.
21 If your enemy is hungry, give him bread to eat;
And if he is thirsty, give him water to drink;
22 For *so* you will heap coals of fire on his head,
And the LORD will reward you.

23 The north wind brings forth rain,
And a backbiting tongue an angry countenance.

24 *It is* better to dwell in a corner of a housetop,
Than in a house shared with a contentious woman.

25 *As* cold water to a weary soul,
So *is* good news from a far country.

26 A righteous *man* who falters before the wicked
Is like a murky spring and a polluted well.

27 *It is* not good to eat much honey;
So to seek one's own glory *is not* glory.

28 Whoever *has* no rule over his own spirit
Is like a city broken down, without walls.

26 As snow in summer and rain in harvest,
So honor is not fitting for a fool.

2 Like a flitting sparrow, like a flying swallow,
So a curse without cause shall not alight.

3 A whip for the horse,
A bridle for the donkey,
And a rod for the fool's back.
4 Do not answer a fool according to his folly,
Lest you also be like him.
5 Answer a fool according to his folly,
Lest he be wise in his own eyes.
6 He who sends a message by the hand of a fool
Cuts off *his own* feet *and* drinks violence.
7 *Like* the legs of the lame that hang limp
Is a proverb in the mouth of fools.
8 Like one who binds a stone in a sling
Is he who gives honor to a fool.
9 *Like* a thorn *that* goes into the hand of a drunkard
Is a proverb in the mouth of fools.
10 The great *God* who formed everything
Gives the fool *his* hire and the transgressor *his* wages.[a]
11 As a dog returns to his own vomit,
So a fool repeats his folly.
12 Do you see a man wise in his own eyes?
There is more hope for a fool than for him.

13 The lazy *man* says, "*There is* a lion in the road!
A fierce lion *is* in the streets!"
14 *As* a door turns on its hinges,
So *does* the lazy *man* on his bed.
15 The lazy *man* buries his hand in the bowl;[a]
It wearies him to bring it back to his mouth.
16 The lazy *man is* wiser in his own eyes
Than seven men who can answer sensibly.

17 He who passes by *and* meddles in a quarrel not his own
Is like one who takes a dog by the ears.
18 Like a madman who throws firebrands, arrows, and death,
19 *Is* the man *who* deceives his neighbor,
And says, "I was only joking!"
20 Where *there is* no wood, the fire goes out;
And where *there is* no talebearer, strife ceases.
21 *As* charcoal *is* to burning coals, and wood to fire,
So *is* a contentious man to kindle strife.
22 The words of a talebearer *are* like tasty trifles,
And they go down into the inmost body.
23 Fervent lips with a wicked heart
Are like earthenware covered with silver dross.
24 He who hates, disguises *it* with his lips,
And lays up deceit within himself;

26:10 [a]The Hebrew is difficult; ancient and modern translators differ greatly. **26:15** [a]Compare 19:24

25 When he speaks kindly, do not believe him,
For *there are* seven abominations in his heart;
26 *Though his* hatred is covered by deceit,
His wickedness will be revealed before the assembly.

27 Whoever digs a pit will fall into it,
And he who rolls a stone will have it roll back on him.

28 A lying tongue hates *those who are* crushed by it,
And a flattering mouth works ruin.

27 Do not boast about tomorrow,
For you do not know what a day may bring forth.

2 Let another man praise you, and not your own mouth;
A stranger, and not your own lips.

3 A stone *is* heavy and sand *is* weighty,
But a fool's wrath *is* heavier than both of them.

4 Wrath *is* cruel and anger a torrent,
But who *is* able to stand before jealousy?

5 Open rebuke *is* better
Than love carefully concealed.

6 Faithful *are* the wounds of a friend,
But the kisses of an enemy *are* deceitful.

7 A satisfied soul loathes the honeycomb,
But to a hungry soul every bitter thing *is* sweet.

8 Like a bird that wanders from its nest
Is a man who wanders from his place.

9 Ointment and perfume delight the heart,
And the sweetness of a man's friend *gives delight* by hearty counsel.

10 Do not forsake your own friend or your father's friend,
Nor go to your brother's house in the day of your calamity;
Better *is* a neighbor nearby than a brother far away.

11 My son, be wise, and make my heart glad,
That I may answer him who reproaches me.

12 A prudent *man* foresees evil *and* hides himself;
The simple pass on *and* are punished.

13 Take the garment of him who is surety for a stranger,
And hold it in pledge *when* he is surety for a seductress.

14 He who blesses his friend with a loud voice, rising early in the morning,
It will be counted a curse to him.

15 A continual dripping on a very rainy day
And a contentious woman are alike;
16 Whoever restrains her restrains the wind,
And grasps oil with his right hand.

17 *As* iron sharpens iron,
So a man sharpens the countenance of his friend.

18 Whoever keeps the fig tree will eat its fruit;
So he who waits on his master will be honored.

19 As in water face *reflects* face,
So a man's heart *reveals* the man.

20 Hell[a] and Destruction[b] are never full;
So the eyes of man are never satisfied.

21 The refining pot *is* for silver and the furnace for gold,
And a man *is valued* by what others say of him.

22 Though you grind a fool in a mortar with a pestle along with crushed grain,
Yet his foolishness will not depart from him.

23 Be diligent to know the state of your flocks,
And attend to your herds;
24 For riches *are* not forever,
Nor does a crown *endure* to all generations.
25 *When* the hay is removed, and the tender grass shows itself,
And the herbs of the mountains are gathered in,
26 The lambs *will provide* your clothing,
And the goats the price of a field;
27 *You shall have* enough goats' milk for your food,
For the food of your household,
And the nourishment of your maidservants.

28 The wicked flee when no one pursues,
But the righteous are bold as a lion.

2 Because of the transgression of a land, many *are* its princes;
But by a man of understanding *and* knowledge
Right will be prolonged.

3 A poor man who oppresses the poor
Is like a driving rain which leaves no food.

4 Those who forsake the law praise the wicked,
But such as keep the law contend with them.

5 Evil men do not understand justice,
But those who seek the LORD understand all.

6 Better *is* the poor who walks in his integrity
Than one perverse *in his* ways, though he *be* rich.

7 Whoever keeps the law *is* a discerning son,
But a companion of gluttons shames his father.

8 One who increases his possessions by usury and extortion
Gathers it for him who will pity the poor.

9 One who turns away his ear from hearing the law,
Even his prayer *is* an abomination.

27:20 [a]Or *Sheol* [b]Hebrew *Abaddon*

10 Whoever causes the upright to go astray
in an evil way,
He himself will fall into his own pit;
But the blameless will inherit good.

11 The rich man *is* wise in his own eyes,
But the poor who has understanding
searches him out.

12 When the righteous rejoice, *there is* great
glory;
But when the wicked arise, men hide
themselves.

13 He who covers his sins will not prosper,
But whoever confesses and forsakes
them will have mercy.

14 Happy *is* the man who is always reverent,
But he who hardens his heart will fall
into calamity.

15 *Like* a roaring lion and a charging bear
Is a wicked ruler over poor people.

16 A ruler who lacks understanding *is* a
great oppressor,
But he who hates covetousness will
prolong *his* days.

17 A man burdened with bloodshed will flee
into a pit;
Let no one help him.

18 Whoever walks blamelessly will be
saved,
But *he who is* perverse *in his* ways will
suddenly fall.

19 He who tills his land will have plenty of
bread,
But he who follows frivolity will have
poverty enough!

20 A faithful man will abound with
blessings,
But he who hastens to be rich will not go
unpunished.

21 To show partiality *is* not good,
Because for a piece of bread a man will
transgress.

22 A man with an evil eye hastens after
riches,
And does not consider that poverty will
come upon him.

23 He who rebukes a man will find more
favor afterward
Than he who flatters with the tongue.

24 Whoever robs his father or his mother,
And says, "*It is* no transgression,"
The same *is* companion to a destroyer.

25 He who is of a proud heart stirs up strife,
But he who trusts in the LORD will be
prospered.

26 He who trusts in his own heart is a fool,
But whoever walks wisely will be
delivered.

27 He who gives to the poor will not lack,
But he who hides his eyes will have many
curses.

28 When the wicked arise, men hide
themselves;
But when they perish, the righteous
increase.

29 He who is often rebuked, *and* hardens
his neck,
Will suddenly be destroyed, and that
without remedy.

2 When the righteous are in authority, the
people rejoice;
But when a wicked *man* rules, the people
groan.

3 Whoever loves wisdom makes his father
rejoice,
But a companion of harlots wastes *his*
wealth.

4 The king establishes the land by justice,
But he who receives bribes overthrows it.

5 A man who flatters his neighbor
Spreads a net for his feet.

6 By transgression an evil man is snared,
But the righteous sings and rejoices.

7 The righteous considers the cause of the
poor,
But the wicked does not understand *such*
knowledge.

8 Scoffers set a city aflame,
But wise *men* turn away wrath.

9 *If* a wise man contends with a foolish
man,
Whether *the fool* rages or laughs, *there is*
no peace.

10 The bloodthirsty hate the blameless,
But the upright seek his well-being.[a]

11 A fool vents all his feelings,[a]
But a wise *man* holds them back.

12 If a ruler pays attention to lies,
All his servants *become* wicked.

13 The poor *man* and the oppressor have
this in common:
The LORD gives light to the eyes of both.

14 The king who judges the poor with truth,
His throne will be established forever.

15 The rod and rebuke give wisdom,
But a child left *to himself* brings shame to
his mother.

16 When the wicked are multiplied,
transgression increases;
But the righteous will see their fall.

17 Correct your son, and he will give you
rest;
Yes, he will give delight to your soul.

18 Where *there is* no revelation,[a] the people
cast off restraint;
But happy *is* he who keeps the law.

19 A servant will not be corrected by mere
words;
For though he understands, he will not
respond.

20 Do you see a man hasty in his words?
There is more hope for a fool than for
him.

29:10 [a]Literally *soul* 29:11 [a]Literally *spirit* 29:18 [a]Or *prophetic vision*

21 He who pampers his servant from childhood
Will have him as a son in the end.

22 An angry man stirs up strife,
And a furious man abounds in transgression.

23 A man's pride will bring him low,
But the humble in spirit will retain honor.

24 Whoever is a partner with a thief hates his own life;
He swears to tell the truth,[a] but reveals nothing.

25 The fear of man brings a snare,
But whoever trusts in the LORD shall be safe.

26 Many seek the ruler's favor,
But justice for man *comes* from the LORD.

27 An unjust man *is* an abomination to the righteous,
And *he who is* upright in the way *is* an abomination to the wicked.

The Wisdom of Agur

30 The words of Agur the son of Jakeh, *his*
utterance. This man declared to Ithiel—
to Ithiel and Ucal:

2 Surely I *am* more stupid than *any* man,
And do not have the understanding of a man.

3 I neither learned wisdom
Nor have knowledge of the Holy One.

4 Who has ascended into heaven, or descended?
Who has gathered the wind in His fists?
Who has bound the waters in a garment?
Who has established all the ends of the earth?
What *is* His name, and what *is* His Son's name,
If you know?

5 Every word of God *is* pure;
He *is* a shield to those who put their trust in Him.

6 Do not add to His words,
Lest He rebuke you, and you be found a liar.

7 Two *things* I request of You
(Deprive me not before I die):

8 Remove falsehood and lies far from me;
Give me neither poverty nor riches—
Feed me with the food allotted to me;

9 Lest I be full and deny *You*,
And say, "Who *is* the LORD?"
Or lest I be poor and steal,
And profane the name of my God.

10 Do not malign a servant to his master,
Lest he curse you, and you be found guilty.

11 *There is* a generation *that* curses its father,
And does not bless its mother.

12 *There is* a generation *that is* pure in its own eyes,
Yet is not washed from its filthiness.

13 *There is* a generation—oh, how lofty are their eyes!
And their eyelids are lifted up.

14 *There is* a generation whose teeth *are like* swords,
And whose fangs *are like* knives,
To devour the poor from off the earth,
And the needy from *among* men.

15 The leech has two daughters—
Give *and* Give!

There are three *things that* are never satisfied,
Four never say, "Enough!":

16 The grave,[a]
The barren womb,
The earth *that* is not satisfied with water—
And the fire never says, "Enough!"

17 The eye *that* mocks *his* father,
And scorns obedience to *his* mother,
The ravens of the valley will pick it out,
And the young eagles will eat it.

18 There are three *things which* are too wonderful for me,
Yes, four *which* I do not understand:

19 The way of an eagle in the air,
The way of a serpent on a rock,
The way of a ship in the midst of the sea,
And the way of a man with a virgin.

20 This *is* the way of an adulterous woman:
She eats and wipes her mouth,
And says, "I have done no wickedness."

21 For three *things* the earth is perturbed,
Yes, for four it cannot bear up:

22 For a servant when he reigns,
A fool when he is filled with food,

23 A hateful *woman* when she is married,
And a maidservant who succeeds her mistress.

24 There are four *things which* are little on the earth,
But they *are* exceedingly wise:

25 The ants *are* a people not strong,
Yet they prepare their food in the summer;

26 The rock badgers[a] are a feeble folk,
Yet they make their homes in the crags;

27 The locusts have no king,
Yet they all advance in ranks;

28 The spider[a] skillfully grasps with its hands,
And it is in kings' palaces.

29 There are three *things which* are majestic in pace,
Yes, four *which* are stately in walk:

30 A lion, *which is* mighty among beasts
And does not turn away from any;

31 A greyhound,[a]
A male goat also,
And a king *whose* troops *are* with him.[b]

32 If you have been foolish in exalting yourself,
Or if you have devised evil, *put your* hand on *your* mouth.

29:24 [a]Literally *hears the adjuration* **30:16** [a]Or *Sheol* **30:26** [a]Or *hyraxes* **30:28** [a]Or *lizard* **30:31** [a]Exact identity unknown [b]A Jewish tradition reads *a king against whom there is no uprising.*

33 For *as* the churning of milk produces butter,
And wringing the nose produces blood,
So the forcing of wrath produces strife.

The Words of King Lemuel's Mother

31 The words of King Lemuel, the utterance which his mother taught him:

2 What, my son?
And what, son of my womb?
And what, son of my vows?
3 Do not give your strength to women,
Nor your ways to that which destroys kings.

4 *It is* not for kings, O Lemuel,
It is not for kings to drink wine,
Nor for princes intoxicating drink;
5 Lest they drink and forget the law,
And pervert the justice of all the afflicted.
6 Give strong drink to him who is perishing,
And wine to those who are bitter of heart.
7 Let him drink and forget his poverty,
And remember his misery no more.

8 Open your mouth for the speechless,
In the cause of all *who are* appointed to die.[a]
9 Open your mouth, judge righteously,
And plead the cause of the poor and needy.

The Virtuous Wife

10 Who[a] can find a virtuous[b] wife?
For her worth *is* far above rubies.
11 The heart of her husband safely trusts her;
So he will have no lack of gain.
12 She does him good and not evil
All the days of her life.
13 She seeks wool and flax,
And willingly works with her hands.
14 She is like the merchant ships,
She brings her food from afar.
15 She also rises while it is yet night,
And provides food for her household,
And a portion for her maidservants.
16 She considers a field and buys it;
From her profits she plants a vineyard.
17 She girds herself with strength,
And strengthens her arms.
18 She perceives that her merchandise *is* good,
And her lamp does not go out by night.
19 She stretches out her hands to the distaff,
And her hand holds the spindle.
20 She extends her hand to the poor,
Yes, she reaches out her hands to the needy.
21 She is not afraid of snow for her household,
For all her household *is* clothed with scarlet.
22 She makes tapestry for herself;
Her clothing *is* fine linen and purple.
23 Her husband is known in the gates,
When he sits among the elders of the land.
24 She makes linen garments and sells *them*,
And supplies sashes for the merchants.
25 Strength and honor *are* her clothing;
She shall rejoice in time to come.
26 She opens her mouth with wisdom,
And on her tongue *is* the law of kindness.
27 She watches over the ways of her household,
And does not eat the bread of idleness.
28 Her children rise up and call her blessed;
Her husband *also*, and he praises her:
29 "Many daughters have done well,
But you excel them all."
30 Charm *is* deceitful and beauty *is* passing,
But a woman *who* fears the LORD, she shall be praised.
31 Give her of the fruit of her hands,
And let her own works praise her in the gates.

The Book of ECCLESIASTES

The Vanity of Life

1 The words of the Preacher, the son of David, king in Jerusalem.

2 "Vanity[a] of vanities," says the Preacher;
"Vanity of vanities, all *is* vanity."
3 What profit has a man from all his labor
In which he toils under the sun?
4 *One* generation passes away, and *another* generation comes;
But the earth abides forever.
5 The sun also rises, and the sun goes down,
And hastens to the place where it arose.
6 The wind goes toward the south,
And turns around to the north;
The wind whirls about continually,
And comes again on its circuit.
7 All the rivers run into the sea,
Yet the sea *is* not full;
To the place from which the rivers come,
There they return again.
8 All things *are* full of labor;
Man cannot express *it*.
The eye is not satisfied with seeing,
Nor the ear filled with hearing.

9 That which has been *is* what will be,
That which *is* done is what will be done,
And *there is* nothing new under the sun.
10 Is there anything of which it may be said,
"See, this *is* new"?
It has already been in ancient times before us.
11 *There is* no remembrance of former *things*,

31:8 [a]Literally *sons of passing away* **31:10** [a]Verses 10 through 31 are an alphabetic acrostic in Hebrew (compare Psalm 119). [b]Literally *a wife of valor*, in the sense of all forms of excellence **1:2** [a]Or *Absurdity, Frustration, Futility, Nonsense;* and so throughout this book

Nor will there be any remembrance of
things that are to come
By *those* who will come after.

The Grief of Wisdom

12 I, the Preacher, was king over Israel in Jerusalem.
13 And I set my heart to seek and search out
by wisdom concerning all that is done under
heaven; this burdensome task God has given
to the sons of man, by which they may be exercised.
14 I have seen all the works that are done
under the sun; and indeed, all *is* vanity and
grasping for the wind.

15 *What is* crooked cannot be made straight,
And what is lacking cannot be numbered.

16 I communed with my heart, saying, "Look,
I have attained greatness, and have gained
more wisdom than all who were before me
in Jerusalem. My heart has understood great
wisdom and knowledge."
17 And I set my heart to know wisdom and to
know madness and folly. I perceived that this
also is grasping for the wind.

18 For in much wisdom *is* much grief,
And he who increases knowledge
increases sorrow.

The Vanity of Pleasure

2 I said in my heart, "Come now, I will test
you with mirth; therefore enjoy pleasure";
but surely, this also *was* vanity.
2 I said of laughter—"Madness!"; and of
mirth, "What does it accomplish?"
3 I searched in my heart *how* to gratify my
flesh with wine, while guiding my heart with
wisdom, and how to lay hold on folly, till I
might see what *was* good for the sons of men
to do under heaven all the days of their lives.
4 I made my works great, I built myself
houses, and planted myself vineyards.
5 I made myself gardens and orchards, and
I planted all *kinds* of fruit trees in them.
6 I made myself water pools from which to
water the growing trees of the grove.
7 I acquired male and female servants, and
had servants born in my house. Yes, I had
greater possessions of herds and flocks than
all who were in Jerusalem before me.
8 I also gathered for myself silver and gold
and the special treasures of kings and of the
provinces. I acquired male and female singers,
the delights of the sons of men, *and* musical
instruments[a] of all kinds.
9 So I became great and excelled more than
all who were before me in Jerusalem. Also my
wisdom remained with me.

10 Whatever my eyes desired I did not keep
from them.
I did not withhold my heart from any
pleasure,
For my heart rejoiced in all my labor;
And this was my reward from all my
labor.
11 Then I looked on all the works that my
hands had done
And on the labor in which I had toiled;
And indeed all *was* vanity and grasping
for the wind.
There was no profit under the sun.

The End of the Wise and the Fool

12 Then I turned myself to consider wisdom
and madness and folly;
For what *can* the man *do* who succeeds
the king?—
Only what he has already done.
13 Then I saw that wisdom excels folly
As light excels darkness.
14 The wise man's eyes *are* in his head,
But the fool walks in darkness.
Yet I myself perceived
That the same event happens to them all.

15 So I said in my heart,
"As it happens to the fool,
It also happens to me,
And why was I then more wise?"
Then I said in my heart,
"This also *is* vanity."
16 For *there is* no more remembrance of the
wise than of the fool forever,
Since all that now *is* will be forgotten in
the days to come.
And how does a wise *man* die?
As the fool!

17 Therefore I hated life because the work that
was done under the sun *was* distressing to me,
for all *is* vanity and grasping for the wind.
18 Then I hated all my labor in which I had
toiled under the sun, because I must leave it to
the man who will come after me.
19 And who knows whether he will be wise
or a fool? Yet he will rule over all my labor in
which I toiled and in which I have shown myself wise under the sun. This also *is* vanity.
20 Therefore I turned my heart and despaired
of all the labor in which I had toiled under the
sun.
21 For there is a man whose labor *is* with wisdom, knowledge, and skill; yet he must leave
his heritage to a man who has not labored for
it. This also *is* vanity and a great evil.
22 For what has man for all his labor, and
for the striving of his heart with which he has
toiled under the sun?
23 For all his days *are* sorrowful, and his work
burdensome; even in the night his heart takes
no rest. This also is vanity.
24 Nothing *is* better for a man *than* that he
should eat and drink, and *that* his soul should
enjoy good in his labor. This also, I saw, was
from the hand of God.
25 For who can eat, or who can have enjoyment, more than I?[a]
26 For *God* gives wisdom and knowledge and
joy to a man who *is* good in His sight; but to
the sinner He gives the work of gathering and
collecting, that he may give to *him who is* good
before God. This also *is* vanity and grasping
for the wind.

Everything Has Its Time

3 To everything *there is* a season,
A time for every purpose under heaven:

2 A time to be born,
And a time to die;
A time to plant,
And a time to pluck *what is* planted;

2:8 [a]Exact meaning unknown **2:25** [a]Following Masoretic Text, Targum, and Vulgate; some Hebrew manuscripts, Septuagint, and Syriac read *without Him.*

3 A time to kill,
And a time to heal;
A time to break down,
And a time to build up;
4 A time to weep,
And a time to laugh;
A time to mourn,
And a time to dance;
5 A time to cast away stones,
And a time to gather stones;
A time to embrace,
And a time to refrain from embracing;
6 A time to gain,
And a time to lose;
A time to keep,
And a time to throw away;
7 A time to tear,
And a time to sew;
A time to keep silence,
And a time to speak;
8 A time to love,
And a time to hate;
A time of war,
And a time of peace.

The God-Given Task

9 What profit has the worker from that in
which he labors?
10 I have seen the God-given task with which
the sons of men are to be occupied.
11 He has made everything beautiful in its
time. Also He has put eternity in their hearts,
except that no one can find out the work that
God does from beginning to end.
12 I know that nothing *is* better for them than
to rejoice, and to do good in their lives,
13 and also that every man should eat and
drink and enjoy the good of all his labor—it *is*
the gift of God.

14 I know that whatever God does,
It shall be forever.
Nothing can be added to it,
And nothing taken from it.
God does *it*, that men should fear before
Him.
15 That which is has already been,
And what is to be has already been;
And God requires an account of what is
past.

Injustice Seems to Prevail

16 Moreover I saw under the sun:

In the place of judgment,
Wickedness *was* there;
And *in* the place of righteousness,
Iniquity *was* there.

17 I said in my heart,

"God shall judge the righteous and the
wicked,
For *there is* a time there for every
purpose and for every work."

18 I said in my heart, "Concerning the condi-
tion of the sons of men, God tests them, that
they may see that they themselves are *like* ani-
mals."
19 For what happens to the sons of men also
happens to animals; one thing befalls them: as
one dies, so dies the other. Surely, they all have
one breath; man has no advantage over animals,
for all *is* vanity.
20 All go to one place: all are from the dust, and
all return to dust.
21 Who knows the spirit of the sons of men,
which goes upward, and the spirit of the ani-
mal, which goes down to the earth?[a]
22 So I perceived that nothing *is* better than
that a man should rejoice in his own works,
for that *is* his heritage. For who can bring him
to see what will happen after him?

4 Then I returned and considered all the op-
pression that is done under the sun:

And look! The tears of the oppressed,
But they have no comforter—
On the side of their oppressors *there is*
power,
But they have no comforter.
2 Therefore I praised the dead who were
already dead,
More than the living who are still alive.
3 Yet, better than both *is he* who has never
existed,
Who has not seen the evil work that is
done under the sun.

The Vanity of Selfish Toil

4 Again, I saw that for all toil and every skill-
ful work a man is envied by his neighbor. This
also *is* vanity and grasping for the wind.

5 The fool folds his hands
And consumes his own flesh.
6 Better a handful *with* quietness
Than both hands full, *together with* toil
and grasping for the wind.

7 Then I returned, and I saw vanity under the
sun:

8 There is one alone, without companion:
He has neither son nor brother.
Yet *there is* no end to all his labors,
Nor is his eye satisfied with riches.
But he never asks,
"For whom do I toil and deprive myself of
good?"
This also *is* vanity and a grave
misfortune.

The Value of a Friend

9 Two *are* better than one,
Because they have a good reward for
their labor.
10 For if they fall, one will lift up his
companion.
But woe to him *who is* alone when he
falls,
For *he has* no one to help him up.
11 Again, if two lie down together, they will
keep warm;
But how can one be warm *alone*?
12 Though one may be overpowered by
another, two can withstand him.
And a threefold cord is not quickly
broken.

Popularity Passes Away

13 Better a poor and wise youth
Than an old and foolish king who will be
admonished no more.

3:21 [a]Septuagint, Syriac, Targum, and Vulgate read *Who knows whether the spirit . . . goes upward, and whether . . . goes downward to the earth?*

14 For he comes out of prison to be king,
Although he was born poor in his kingdom.
15 I saw all the living who walk under the sun;
They were with the second youth who stands in his place.
16 *There was* no end of all the people over whom he was made king;
Yet those who come afterward will not rejoice in him.
Surely this also *is* vanity and grasping for the wind.

Fear God, Keep Your Vows

5 Walk prudently when you go to the house
of God; and draw near to hear rather than
to give the sacrifice of fools, for they do not
know that they do evil.

2 Do not be rash with your mouth,
And let not your heart utter anything hastily before God.
For God *is* in heaven, and you on earth;
Therefore let your words be few.
3 For a dream comes through much activity,
And a fool's voice *is known* by *his* many words.

4 When you make a vow to God, do not delay to pay it;
For *He has* no pleasure in fools.
Pay what you have vowed—
5 Better not to vow than to vow and not pay.

6 Do not let your mouth cause your flesh to
sin, nor say before the messenger *of God* that
it *was* an error. Why should God be angry at
your excuse[a] and destroy the work of your hands?
7 For in the multitude of dreams and many
words *there is* also vanity. But fear God.

The Vanity of Gain and Honor

8 If you see the oppression of the poor, and
the violent perversion of justice and righteous-
ness in a province, do not marvel at the matter;
for high official watches over high official, and
higher officials are over them.
9 Moreover the profit of the land is for all;
even the king is served from the field.

10 He who loves silver will not be satisfied with silver;
Nor he who loves abundance, with increase.
This also *is* vanity.

11 When goods increase,
They increase who eat them;
So what profit have the owners
Except to see *them* with their eyes?

12 The sleep of a laboring man *is* sweet,
Whether he eats little or much;
But the abundance of the rich will not permit him to sleep.

13 There is a severe evil *which* I have seen under the sun:
Riches kept for their owner to his hurt.
14 But those riches perish through misfortune;
When he begets a son, *there is* nothing in his hand.

15 As he came from his mother's womb, naked shall he return,
To go as he came;
And he shall take nothing from his labor
Which he may carry away in his hand.

16 And this also *is* a severe evil—
Just exactly as he came, so shall he go.
And what profit has he who has labored for the wind?
17 All his days he also eats in darkness,
And *he has* much sorrow and sickness and anger.

18 Here is what I have seen: *It is* good and
fitting *for one* to eat and drink, and to enjoy
the good of all his labor in which he toils under
the sun all the days of his life which God gives
him; for it *is* his heritage.
19 As for every man to whom God has given
riches and wealth, and given him power to eat
of it, to receive his heritage and rejoice in his
labor—this *is* the gift of God.
20 For he will not dwell unduly on the days of
his life, because God keeps *him* busy with the
joy of his heart.

6 There is an evil which I have seen under
the sun, and it *is* common among men:
2 A man to whom God has given riches and
wealth and honor, so that he lacks nothing for
himself of all he desires; yet God does not give
him power to eat of it, but a foreigner con-
sumes it. This *is* vanity, and it *is* an evil afflic-
tion.
3 If a man begets a hundred *children* and
lives many years, so that the days of his years
are many, but his soul is not satisfied with
goodness, or indeed he has no burial, I say *that*
a stillborn child *is* better than he—
4 for it comes in vanity and departs in dark-
ness, and its name is covered with darkness.
5 Though it has not seen the sun or known
anything, this has more rest than that man,
6 even if he lives a thousand years twice—
but has not seen goodness. Do not all go to one
place?

7 All the labor of man *is* for his mouth,
And yet the soul is not satisfied.
8 For what more has the wise *man* than the fool?
What does the poor man have,
Who knows *how* to walk before the living?
9 Better *is* the sight of the eyes than the wandering of desire.
This also *is* vanity and grasping for the wind.

10 Whatever one is, he has been named already,
For it is known that he *is* man;
And he cannot contend with Him who is mightier than he.
11 Since there are many things that increase vanity,
How *is* man the better?

12 For who knows what *is* good for man in
life, all the days of his vain life which he passes
like a shadow? Who can tell a man what will
happen after him under the sun?

5:6 [a]Literally *voice*

The Value of Practical Wisdom

7 A good name *is* better than precious ointment,
And the day of death than the day of one's birth;
2 Better to go to the house of mourning
Than to go to the house of feasting,
For that *is* the end of all men;
And the living will take *it* to heart.
3 Sorrow *is* better than laughter,
For by a sad countenance the heart is made better.
4 The heart of the wise *is* in the house of mourning,
But the heart of fools *is* in the house of mirth.

5 *It is* better to hear the rebuke of the wise
Than for a man to hear the song of fools.
6 For like the crackling of thorns under a pot,
So *is* the laughter of the fool.
This also is vanity.
7 Surely oppression destroys a wise *man's* reason,
And a bribe debases the heart.

8 The end of a thing *is* better than its beginning;
The patient in spirit *is* better than the proud in spirit.
9 Do not hasten in your spirit to be angry,
For anger rests in the bosom of fools.
10 Do not say,
"Why were the former days better than these?"
For you do not inquire wisely concerning this.

11 Wisdom *is* good with an inheritance,
And profitable to those who see the sun.
12 For wisdom *is* a defense *as* money *is* a defense,
But the excellence of knowledge *is that* wisdom gives life to those who have it.

13 Consider the work of God;
For who can make straight what He has made crooked?
14 In the day of prosperity be joyful,
But in the day of adversity consider:
Surely God has appointed the one as well as the other,
So that man can find out nothing *that will come* after him.

15 I have seen everything in my days of vanity:

There is a just *man* who perishes in his righteousness,
And there is a wicked *man* who prolongs *life* in his wickedness.

16 Do not be overly righteous,
Nor be overly wise:
Why should you destroy yourself?
17 Do not be overly wicked,
Nor be foolish:
Why should you die before your time?
18 *It is* good that you grasp this,
And also not remove your hand from the other;
For he who fears God will escape them all.

19 Wisdom strengthens the wise
More than ten rulers of the city.
20 For *there is* not a just man on earth who does good
And does not sin.

21 Also do not take to heart everything people say,
Lest you hear your servant cursing you.
22 For many times, also, your own heart has known
That even you have cursed others.

23 All this I have proved by wisdom.
I said, "I will be wise";
But it *was* far from me.
24 As for that which is far off and exceedingly deep,
Who can find it out?
25 I applied my heart to know,
To search and seek out wisdom and the reason *of things,*
To know the wickedness of folly,
Even of foolishness *and* madness.
26 And I find more bitter than death
The woman whose heart *is* snares and nets,
Whose hands *are* fetters.
He who pleases God shall escape from her,
But the sinner shall be trapped by her.

27 "Here is what I have found," says the Preacher,
"*Adding* one thing to the other to find out the reason,
28 Which my soul still seeks but I cannot find:
One man among a thousand I have found,
But a woman among all these I have not found.
29 Truly, this only I have found:
That God made man upright,
But they have sought out many schemes."

8 Who *is* like a wise *man?*
And who knows the interpretation of a thing?
A man's wisdom makes his face shine,
And the sternness of his face is changed.

Obey Authorities for God's Sake

2 I *say,* "Keep the king's commandment for
the sake of your oath to God.
3 "Do not be hasty to go from his presence.
Do not take your stand for an evil thing, for he
does whatever pleases him."

4 Where the word of a king *is, there is* power;
And who may say to him, "What are you doing?"

5 He who keeps his command will experience nothing harmful;
And a wise man's heart discerns both time and judgment,
6 Because for every matter there is a time and judgment,
Though the misery of man increases greatly.
7 For he does not know what will happen;
So who can tell him when it will occur?
8 No one has power over the spirit to retain the spirit,
And no one has power in the day of death.
There is no release from that war,

And wickedness will not deliver those
who are given to it.

9 All this I have seen, and applied my heart to every work that is done under the sun: *There is* a time in which one man rules over another to his own hurt.

Death Comes to All

10 Then I saw the wicked buried, who had come and gone from the place of holiness, and they were forgotten[a] in the city where they had so done. This also *is* vanity.
11 Because the sentence against an evil work is not executed speedily, therefore the heart of the sons of men is fully set in them to do evil.
12 Though a sinner does evil a hundred *times*, and his *days* are prolonged, yet I surely know that it will be well with those who fear God, who fear before Him.
13 But it will not be well with the wicked; nor will he prolong *his* days, *which are* as a shadow, because he does not fear before God.
14 There is a vanity which occurs on earth, that there are just *men* to whom it happens according to the work of the wicked; again, there are wicked *men* to whom it happens according to the work of the righteous. I said that this also *is* vanity.
15 So I commended enjoyment, because a man has nothing better under the sun than to eat, drink, and be merry; for this will remain with him in his labor *all* the days of his life which God gives him under the sun.
16 When I applied my heart to know wisdom and to see the business that is done on earth, even though one sees no sleep day or night,
17 then I saw all the work of God, that a man cannot find out the work that is done under the sun. For though a man labors to discover *it*, yet he will not find *it;* moreover, though a wise *man* attempts to know *it*, he will not be able to find *it*.

9 For I considered all this in my heart, so that I could declare it all: that the righteous and the wise and their works *are* in the hand of God. People know neither love nor hatred *by* anything *they see* before them.
2 All things *come* alike to all:

One event *happens* to the righteous and
the wicked;
To the good,[a] the clean, and the unclean;
To him who sacrifices and him who does
not sacrifice.
As is the good, so *is* the sinner;
He who takes an oath as *he* who fears an
oath.

3 This *is* an evil in all that is done under the sun: that one thing *happens* to all. Truly the hearts of the sons of men are full of evil; madness *is* in their hearts while they live, and after that *they go* to the dead.
4 But for him who is joined to all the living there is hope, for a living dog is better than a dead lion.

5 For the living know that they will die;
But the dead know nothing,
And they have no more reward,
For the memory of them is forgotten.
6 Also their love, their hatred, and their
envy have now perished;
Nevermore will they have a share
In anything done under the sun.

7 Go, eat your bread with joy,
And drink your wine with a merry heart;
For God has already accepted your
works.
8 Let your garments always be white,
And let your head lack no oil.

9 Live joyfully with the wife whom you love all the days of your vain life which He has given you under the sun, all your days of vanity; for that *is* your portion in life, and in the labor which you perform under the sun.
10 Whatever your hand finds to do, do *it* with your might; for *there is* no work or device or knowledge or wisdom in the grave where you are going.
11 I returned and saw under the sun that—

The race *is* not to the swift,
Nor the battle to the strong,
Nor bread to the wise,
Nor riches to men of understanding,
Nor favor to men of skill;
But time and chance happen to them all.
12 For man also does not know his time:
Like fish taken in a cruel net,
Like birds caught in a snare,
So the sons of men *are* snared in an evil
time,
When it falls suddenly upon them.

Wisdom Superior to Folly

13 This wisdom I have also seen under the sun, and it *seemed* great to me:
14 *There was* a little city with few men in it; and a great king came against it, besieged it, and built great snares[a] around it.
15 Now there was found in it a poor wise man, and he by his wisdom delivered the city. Yet no one remembered that same poor man.
16 Then I said:

"Wisdom *is* better than strength.
Nevertheless the poor man's wisdom *is*
despised,
And his words are not heard.
17 Words of the wise, *spoken* quietly, *should
be* heard
Rather than the shout of a ruler of fools.
18 Wisdom *is* better than weapons of war;
But one sinner destroys much good."

10 Dead flies putrefy[a] the perfumer's
ointment,
And cause it to give off a foul odor;
So does a little folly to one respected for
wisdom *and* honor.
2 A wise man's heart *is* at his right hand,
But a fool's heart at his left.
3 Even when a fool walks along the way,
He lacks wisdom,
And he shows everyone *that* he *is* a fool.
4 If the spirit of the ruler rises against you,
Do not leave your post;
For conciliation pacifies great offenses.

5 There is an evil I have seen under the
sun,
As an error proceeding from the ruler:
6 Folly is set in great dignity,
While the rich sit in a lowly place.

8:10 [a]Some Hebrew manuscripts, Septuagint, and Vulgate read *praised.* **9:2** [a]Septuagint, Syriac, and Vulgate read *good and bad.* **9:14** [a]Septuagint, Syriac, and Vulgate read *bulwarks.* **10:1** [a]Targum and Vulgate omit *putrefy.*

7 I have seen servants on horses,
While princes walk on the ground like servants.
8 He who digs a pit will fall into it,
And whoever breaks through a wall will be bitten by a serpent.
9 He who quarries stones may be hurt by them,
And he who splits wood may be endangered by it.
10 If the ax is dull,
And one does not sharpen the edge,
Then he must use more strength;
But wisdom brings success.
11 A serpent may bite when *it is* not charmed;
The babbler is no different.
12 The words of a wise man's mouth *are* gracious,
But the lips of a fool shall swallow him up;
13 The words of his mouth begin with foolishness,
And the end of his talk *is* raving madness.
14 A fool also multiplies words.
No man knows what is to be;
Who can tell him what will be after him?
15 The labor of fools wearies them,
For they do not even know how to go to the city!
16 Woe to you, O land, when your king *is* a child,
And your princes feast in the morning!
17 Blessed *are* you, O land, when your king *is* the son of nobles,
And your princes feast at the proper time—
For strength and not for drunkenness!
18 Because of laziness the building decays,
And through idleness of hands the house leaks.
19 A feast is made for laughter,
And wine makes merry;
But money answers everything.
20 Do not curse the king, even in your thought;
Do not curse the rich, even in your bedroom;
For a bird of the air may carry your voice,
And a bird in flight may tell the matter.

The Value of Diligence

11 Cast your bread upon the waters,
For you will find it after many days.
2 Give a serving to seven, and also to eight,
For you do not know what evil will be on the earth.
3 If the clouds are full of rain,
They empty *themselves* upon the earth;
And if a tree falls to the south or the north,
In the place where the tree falls, there it shall lie.
4 He who observes the wind will not sow,
And he who regards the clouds will not reap.
5 As you do not know what *is* the way of the wind,[a]
Or how the bones *grow* in the womb of her who is with child,
So you do not know the works of God who makes everything.
6 In the morning sow your seed,
And in the evening do not withhold your hand;
For you do not know which will prosper,
Either this or that,
Or whether both alike *will be* good.
7 Truly the light is sweet,
And *it is* pleasant for the eyes to behold the sun;
8 But if a man lives many years
And rejoices in them all,
Yet let him remember the days of darkness,
For they will be many.
All that is coming *is* vanity.

Seek God in Early Life

9 Rejoice, O young man, in your youth,
And let your heart cheer you in the days of your youth;
Walk in the ways of your heart,
And in the sight of your eyes;
But know that for all these
God will bring you into judgment.
10 Therefore remove sorrow from your heart,
And put away evil from your flesh,
For childhood and youth *are* vanity.

12 Remember now your Creator in the days of your youth,
Before the difficult days come,
And the years draw near when you say,
"I have no pleasure in them":
2 While the sun and the light,
The moon and the stars,
Are not darkened,
And the clouds do not return after the rain;
3 In the day when the keepers of the house tremble,
And the strong men bow down;
When the grinders cease because they are few,
And those that look through the windows grow dim;
4 When the doors are shut in the streets,
And the sound of grinding is low;
When one rises up at the sound of a bird,
And all the daughters of music are brought low.
5 Also they are afraid of height,
And of terrors in the way;
When the almond tree blossoms,
The grasshopper is a burden,
And desire fails.
For man goes to his eternal home,
And the mourners go about the streets.
6 *Remember your Creator* before the silver cord is loosed,[a]
Or the golden bowl is broken,
Or the pitcher shattered at the fountain,
Or the wheel broken at the well.

11:5 [a]Or *spirit* 12:6 [a]Following Qere and Targum; Kethib reads *removed;* Septuagint and Vulgate read *broken.*

7 Then the dust will return to the earth as it was,
And the spirit will return to God who gave it.

8 "Vanity of vanities," says the Preacher,
"All *is* vanity."

The Whole Duty of Man

9 And moreover, because the Preacher was
wise, he still taught the people knowledge; yes,
he pondered and sought out *and* set in order
many proverbs.
10 The Preacher sought to find acceptable
words; and *what was* written *was* upright—
words of truth.
11 The words of the wise are like goads, and
the words of scholars[a] are like well-driven
nails, given by one Shepherd.
12 And further, my son, be admonished by
these. Of making many books *there is* no end,
and much study *is* wearisome to the flesh.
13 Let us hear the conclusion of the whole matter:

Fear God and keep His commandments,
For this is man's all.
14 For God will bring every work into judgment,
Including every secret thing,
Whether good or evil.

The SONG OF SOLOMON

1 The song of songs, which *is* Solomon's.

The Banquet

THE SHULAMITE[a]

2 Let him kiss me with the kisses of his mouth—
For your[b] love *is* better than wine.
3 Because of the fragrance of your good ointments,
Your name *is* ointment poured forth;
Therefore the virgins love you.
4 Draw me away!

THE DAUGHTERS OF JERUSALEM

We will run after you.[a]

THE SHULAMITE

The king has brought me into his chambers.

THE DAUGHTERS OF JERUSALEM

We will be glad and rejoice in you.[b]

We will remember your[c] love more than wine.

THE SHULAMITE

Rightly do they love you.[d]

5 I *am* dark, but lovely,
O daughters of Jerusalem,
Like the tents of Kedar,
Like the curtains of Solomon.
6 Do not look upon me, because I *am* dark,
Because the sun has tanned me.
My mother's sons were angry with me;
They made me the keeper of the vineyards,
But my own vineyard I have not kept.

(TO HER BELOVED)

7 Tell me, O you whom I love,
Where you feed *your flock,*
Where you make *it* rest at noon.
For why should I be as one who veils herself[a]
By the flocks of your companions?

THE BELOVED

8 If you do not know, O fairest among women,
Follow in the footsteps of the flock,
And feed your little goats
Beside the shepherds' tents.
9 I have compared you, my love,
To my filly among Pharaoh's chariots.
10 Your cheeks are lovely with ornaments,
Your neck with chains *of gold.*

THE DAUGHTERS OF JERUSALEM

11 We will make you[a] ornaments of gold
With studs of silver.

THE SHULAMITE

12 While the king *is* at his table,
My spikenard sends forth its fragrance.
13 A bundle of myrrh *is* my beloved to me,
That lies all night between my breasts.
14 My beloved *is* to me a cluster of henna *blooms*
In the vineyards of En Gedi.

THE BELOVED

15 Behold, you *are* fair, my love!
Behold, you *are* fair!
You *have* dove's eyes.

THE SHULAMITE

16 Behold, you *are* handsome, my beloved!
Yes, pleasant!
Also our bed *is* green.
17 The beams of our houses *are* cedar,
And our rafters of fir.

2 I *am* the rose of Sharon,
And the lily of the valleys.

THE BELOVED

2 Like a lily among thorns,
So is my love among the daughters.

12:11 [a]Literally *masters of the assemblies* **1:2** [a]A Palestinian young woman (compare 6:13). The speaker and audience are identified according to the number, gender, and person of the Hebrew words. Occasionally the identity is not certain. [b]Masculine singular, that is, the Beloved **1:4** [a]Masculine singular, that is, the Beloved [b]Feminine singular, that is, the Shulamite [c]Masculine singular, that is, the Beloved [d]Masculine singular, that is, the Beloved **1:7** [a]Septuagint, Syriac, and Vulgate read *wanders.* **1:11** [a]Feminine singular, that is, the Shulamite

THE SHULAMITE

3 Like an apple tree among the trees of the woods,
So *is* my beloved among the sons.
I sat down in his shade with great delight,
And his fruit *was* sweet to my taste.

THE SHULAMITE TO THE DAUGHTERS OF JERUSALEM

4 He brought me to the banqueting house,
And his banner over me *was* love.
5 Sustain me with cakes of raisins,
Refresh me with apples,
For I *am* lovesick.

6 His left hand *is* under my head,
And his right hand embraces me.
7 I charge you, O daughters of Jerusalem,
By the gazelles or by the does of the field,
Do not stir up nor awaken love
Until it pleases.

The Beloved's Request

THE SHULAMITE

8 The voice of my beloved!
Behold, he comes
Leaping upon the mountains,
Skipping upon the hills.
9 My beloved is like a gazelle or a young stag.
Behold, he stands behind our wall;
He is looking through the windows,
Gazing through the lattice.

10 My beloved spoke, and said to me:
"Rise up, my love, my fair one,
And come away.
11 For lo, the winter is past,
The rain is over *and* gone.
12 The flowers appear on the earth;
The time of singing has come,
And the voice of the turtledove
Is heard in our land.
13 The fig tree puts forth her green figs,
And the vines *with* the tender grapes
Give a *good* smell.
Rise up, my love, my fair one,
And come away!

14 "O my dove, in the clefts of the rock,
In the secret *places* of the cliff,
Let me see your face,
Let me hear your voice;
For your voice *is* sweet,
And your face *is* lovely."

HER BROTHERS

15 Catch us the foxes,
The little foxes that spoil the vines,
For our vines *have* tender grapes.

THE SHULAMITE

16 My beloved *is* mine, and I *am* his.
He feeds *his flock* among the lilies.

(TO HER BELOVED)

17 Until the day breaks
And the shadows flee away,
Turn, my beloved,
And be like a gazelle
Or a young stag
Upon the mountains of Bether.[a]

A Troubled Night

THE SHULAMITE

3 By night on my bed I sought the one I love;
I sought him, but I did not find him.
2 "I will rise now," *I said,*
"And go about the city;
In the streets and in the squares
I will seek the one I love."
I sought him, but I did not find him.
3 The watchmen who go about the city found me;
I said,
"Have you seen the one I love?"

4 Scarcely had I passed by them,
When I found the one I love.
I held him and would not let him go,
Until I had brought him to the house of my mother,
And into the chamber of her who conceived me.

5 I charge you, O daughters of Jerusalem,
By the gazelles or by the does of the field,
Do not stir up nor awaken love
Until it pleases.

The Coming of Solomon

THE SHULAMITE

6 Who *is* this coming out of the wilderness
Like pillars of smoke,
Perfumed with myrrh and frankincense,
With all the merchant's fragrant powders?
7 Behold, it *is* Solomon's couch,
With sixty valiant men around it,
Of the valiant of Israel.
8 They all hold swords,
Being expert in war.
Every man *has* his sword on his thigh
Because of fear in the night.

9 Of the wood of Lebanon
Solomon the King
Made himself a palanquin:[a]
10 He made its pillars *of* silver,
Its support *of* gold,
Its seat *of* purple,
Its interior paved *with* love
By the daughters of Jerusalem.
11 Go forth, O daughters of Zion,
And see King Solomon with the crown
With which his mother crowned him
On the day of his wedding,
The day of the gladness of his heart.

THE BELOVED

4 Behold, you *are* fair, my love!
Behold, you *are* fair!
You *have* dove's eyes behind your veil.
Your hair *is* like a flock of goats,
Going down from Mount Gilead.
2 Your teeth *are* like a flock of shorn *sheep*
Which have come up from the washing,
Every one of which bears twins,
And none *is* barren among them.
3 Your lips *are* like a strand of scarlet,
And your mouth is lovely.
Your temples behind your veil
Are like a piece of pomegranate.
4 Your neck *is* like the tower of David,
Built for an armory,

2:17 [a]Literally *Separation* 3:9 [a]A portable enclosed chair

On which hang a thousand bucklers,
All shields of mighty men.
5 Your two breasts *are* like two fawns,
Twins of a gazelle,
Which feed among the lilies.

6 Until the day breaks
And the shadows flee away,
I will go my way to the mountain of myrrh
And to the hill of frankincense.

7 You *are* all fair, my love,
And *there is* no spot in you.
8 Come with me from Lebanon, *my* spouse,
With me from Lebanon.
Look from the top of Amana,
From the top of Senir and Hermon,
From the lions' dens,
From the mountains of the leopards.

9 You have ravished my heart,
My sister, *my* spouse;
You have ravished my heart
With one *look* of your eyes,
With one link of your necklace.
10 How fair is your love,
My sister, *my* spouse!
How much better than wine is your love,
And the scent of your perfumes
Than all spices!
11 Your lips, O *my* spouse,
Drip as the honeycomb;
Honey and milk *are* under your tongue;
And the fragrance of your garments
Is like the fragrance of Lebanon.

12 A garden enclosed
Is my sister, *my* spouse,
A spring shut up,
A fountain sealed.
13 Your plants *are* an orchard of pomegranates
With pleasant fruits,
Fragrant henna with spikenard,
14 Spikenard and saffron,
Calamus and cinnamon,
With all trees of frankincense,
Myrrh and aloes,
With all the chief spices—
15 A fountain of gardens,
A well of living waters,
And streams from Lebanon.

THE SHULAMITE

16 Awake, O north *wind*,
And come, O south!
Blow upon my garden,
That its spices may flow out.
Let my beloved come to his garden
And eat its pleasant fruits.

THE BELOVED

5 I have come to my garden, my sister, *my* spouse;
I have gathered my myrrh with my spice;
I have eaten my honeycomb with my honey;
I have drunk my wine with my milk.

(TO HIS FRIENDS)

Eat, O friends!
Drink, yes, drink deeply,
O beloved ones!

The Shulamite's Troubled Evening

THE SHULAMITE

2 I sleep, but my heart is awake;
It is the voice of my beloved!
He knocks, *saying,*
"Open for me, my sister, my love,
My dove, my perfect one;
For my head is covered with dew,
My locks with the drops of the night."

3 I have taken off my robe;
How can I put it on *again?*
I have washed my feet;
How can I defile them?
4 My beloved put his hand
By the latch *of the door,*
And my heart yearned for him.
5 I arose to open for my beloved,
And my hands dripped *with* myrrh,
My fingers with liquid myrrh,
On the handles of the lock.

6 I opened for my beloved,
But my beloved had turned away *and* was gone.
My heart leaped up when he spoke.
I sought him, but I could not find him;
I called him, but he gave me no answer.
7 The watchmen who went about the city found me.
They struck me, they wounded me;
The keepers of the walls
Took my veil away from me.
8 I charge you, O daughters of Jerusalem,
If you find my beloved,
That you tell him I *am* lovesick!

THE DAUGHTERS OF JERUSALEM

9 What *is* your beloved
More than *another* beloved,
O fairest among women?
What *is* your beloved
More than *another* beloved,
That you so charge us?

THE SHULAMITE

10 My beloved *is* white and ruddy,
Chief among ten thousand.
11 His head *is like* the finest gold;
His locks *are* wavy,
And black as a raven.
12 His eyes *are* like doves
By the rivers of waters,
Washed with milk,
And fitly set.
13 His cheeks *are* like a bed of spices,
Banks of scented herbs.
His lips *are* lilies,
Dripping liquid myrrh.

14 His hands *are* rods of gold
Set with beryl.
His body *is* carved ivory
Inlaid *with* sapphires.
15 His legs *are* pillars of marble
Set on bases of fine gold.
His countenance *is* like Lebanon,
Excellent as the cedars.
16 His mouth *is* most sweet,
Yes, he *is* altogether lovely.
This *is* my beloved,
And this *is* my friend,
O daughters of Jerusalem!

THE DAUGHTERS OF JERUSALEM

6 Where has your beloved gone,
O fairest among women?
Where has your beloved turned aside,
That we may seek him with you?

THE SHULAMITE

2 My beloved has gone to his garden,
To the beds of spices,
To feed *his flock* in the gardens,
And to gather lilies.
3 I *am* my beloved's,
And my beloved *is* mine.
He feeds *his flock* among the lilies.

Praise of the Shulamite's Beauty

THE BELOVED

4 O my love, you *are as* beautiful as Tirzah,
Lovely as Jerusalem,
Awesome as *an army* with banners!
5 Turn your eyes away from me,
For they have overcome me.
Your hair *is* like a flock of goats
Going down from Gilead.
6 Your teeth *are* like a flock of sheep
Which have come up from the washing;
Every one bears twins,
And none *is* barren among them.
7 Like a piece of pomegranate
Are your temples behind your veil.

8 There are sixty queens
And eighty concubines,
And virgins without number.
9 My dove, my perfect one,
Is the only one,
The only one of her mother,
The favorite of the one who bore her.
The daughters saw her
And called her blessed,
The queens and the concubines,
And they praised her.

10 Who is she who looks forth as the morning,
Fair as the moon,
Clear as the sun,
Awesome as *an army* with banners?

THE SHULAMITE

11 I went down to the garden of nuts
To see the verdure of the valley,
To see whether the vine had budded
And the pomegranates had bloomed.
12 Before I was even aware,
My soul had made me
As the chariots of my noble people.[a]

THE BELOVED AND HIS FRIENDS

13 Return, return, O Shulamite;
Return, return, that we may look upon you!

THE SHULAMITE

What would you see in the Shulamite—
As it were, the dance of the two camps?[a]

Expressions of Praise

THE BELOVED

7 How beautiful are your feet in sandals,
O prince's daughter!
The curves of your thighs *are* like jewels,
The work of the hands of a skillful workman.
2 Your navel *is* a rounded goblet;
It lacks no blended beverage.
Your waist *is* a heap of wheat
Set about with lilies.
3 Your two breasts *are* like two fawns,
Twins of a gazelle.
4 Your neck *is* like an ivory tower,
Your eyes *like* the pools in Heshbon
By the gate of Bath Rabbim.
Your nose *is* like the tower of Lebanon
Which looks toward Damascus.
5 Your head *crowns* you like *Mount* Carmel,
And the hair of your head *is* like purple;
A king *is* held captive by *your* tresses.

6 How fair and how pleasant you are,
O love, with your delights!
7 This stature of yours is like a palm tree,
And your breasts *like* its clusters.
8 I said, "I will go up to the palm tree,
I will take hold of its branches."
Let now your breasts be like clusters of the vine,
The fragrance of your breath like apples,
9 And the roof of your mouth like the best wine.

THE SHULAMITE

The wine goes *down* smoothly for my beloved,
Moving gently the lips of sleepers.[a]
10 I *am* my beloved's,
And his desire *is* toward me.

11 Come, my beloved,
Let us go forth to the field;
Let us lodge in the villages.
12 Let us get up early to the vineyards;
Let us see if the vine has budded,
Whether the grape blossoms are open,
And the pomegranates are in bloom.
There I will give you my love.
13 The mandrakes give off a fragrance,
And at our gates *are* pleasant *fruits*,
All manner, new and old,
Which I have laid up for you, my beloved.

8 Oh, that you were like my brother,
Who nursed at my mother's breasts!
If I should find you outside,
I would kiss you;
I would not be despised.
2 I would lead you *and* bring you
Into the house of my mother,
She *who* used to instruct me.
I would cause you to drink of spiced wine,
Of the juice of my pomegranate.

(TO THE DAUGHTERS OF JERUSALEM)

3 His left hand *is* under my head,
And his right hand embraces me.
4 I charge you, O daughters of Jerusalem,
Do not stir up nor awaken love
Until it pleases.

6:12 [a]Hebrew *Ammi Nadib* 6:13 [a]Hebrew *Mahanaim* 7:9 [a]Septuagint, Syriac, and Vulgate read *lips and teeth.*

Love Renewed in Lebanon

A RELATIVE

5 Who *is* this coming up from the
wilderness,
Leaning upon her beloved?

I awakened you under the apple tree.
There your mother brought you forth;
There she *who* bore you brought *you*
forth.

THE SHULAMITE TO HER BELOVED

6 Set me as a seal upon your heart,
As a seal upon your arm;
For love *is as* strong as death,
Jealousy *as* cruel as the grave;[a]
Its flames *are* flames of fire,
A most vehement flame.[b]
7 Many waters cannot quench love,
Nor can the floods drown it.
If a man would give for love
All the wealth of his house,
It would be utterly despised.

THE SHULAMITE'S BROTHERS

8 We have a little sister,
And she has no breasts.
What shall we do for our sister
In the day when she is spoken for?
9 If she *is* a wall,
We will build upon her
A battlement of silver;
And if she *is* a door,
We will enclose her
With boards of cedar.

THE SHULAMITE

10 I *am* a wall,
And my breasts like towers;
Then I became in his eyes
As one who found peace.
11 Solomon had a vineyard at Baal Hamon;
He leased the vineyard to keepers;
Everyone was to bring for its fruit
A thousand silver *coins*.

(TO SOLOMON)

12 My own vineyard *is* before me.
You, O Solomon, *may have* a thousand,
And those who tend its fruit two hundred.

THE BELOVED

13 You who dwell in the gardens,
The companions listen for your voice—
Let me hear it!

THE SHULAMITE

14 Make haste, my beloved,
And be like a gazelle
Or a young stag
On the mountains of spices.

8:6 [a]Or *Sheol* [b]Literally *A flame of* YAH (a poetic form of *YHWH, the* LORD)

THE PROPHETS

**Isaiah • Jeremiah • Ezekiel • Daniel • Hosea • Joel
Amos • Obadiah • Jonah • Micah • Nahum • Habakkuk
Zephaniah • Haggai • Zechariah • Malachi**

Prophets in Israel were persons who proclaimed and interpreted the actions of God in the events of history. They tried to keep alive the memory of the Exodus and reinterpret the meaning of the ancient faith for new times, to declare God's will (based on the Sinai covenant) in national crises. After the national disasters of the fall of Israel (722 B.C.) and Judah (597–586 B.C.), they began to speak words of hope and comfort.

The written works of these men are called the Major and Minor Prophets. The terms "major" and "minor" have to do with the size of the books and not with the importance of the message. In the Hebrew canon (the list of books accepted as Holy Scripture), the Prophets are Isaiah, Jeremiah, Ezekiel, and the Book of the Twelve. Daniel is included among the Writings in the Jewish Scripture, but we list that book with the Prophets. (For more on "The Writings," see "The Historical Books," p. 193, and "Poetical and Wisdom Books," p. 450.)

In roughly chronological order, the prophets are:

AMOS preached in the northern kingdom of Israel around 760 B.C. His message included an emphasis on social justice as an expression of the covenant, the idea of the coming Day of the Lord, and the hope of a remnant. He emphasized that the covenant with God carried obligations as well as promises.

HOSEA was active from about 755 to perhaps 710 B.C. He described the relationship between God and Israel as a marriage. His social themes were the danger of injustice at home and reliance on military alliances abroad. He talked about the compassion of God and of God's tender longing for His people.

ISAIAH of Jerusalem was a counselor to kings from 740 to 680 B.C. During this time there were two major crises—the war with Syria in 734 and the Assyrian threats from 734 to 701. Isaiah saw those events as expressions of God's rule over the nations. The cause of the wars, he said, is social injustice. God is working out punishment for His people in the international arena. Some of the best-known passages in this book are those dealing with the longing for a Messiah and Isaiah's description of his own call.

The latter part of the Book of Isaiah is a collection of great hymns and poems about the hope of restoration at the end of the Exile. Included in the hymns are four about the Servant of God, who suffers for the sake of Israel.

MICAH preached in Jerusalem somewhere between 735 and 710 B.C. He cried out against the injustice practiced in both Samaria and Jerusalem but also lifted up the vision of a great day of peace and salvation, with Jerusalem as the center of God's kingdom. Micah 6:8 is a good summary of the teachings of the prophets of the eighth century.

THE DIVIDED KINGDOM

ZEPHANIAH—For sixty years after Micah the kings of Judah practiced idolatry and oppression. Zephaniah's preaching began the great reform that culminated in the finding of Deuteronomy and national covenant-renewal. His message was one of condemnation of idolatry and injustice.

JEREMIAH preached from 627 to 580; and over so long a career, his message changed as world events changed and called forth new understandings of the work of God. It was a time of trouble for Judah and Jerusalem, ending with the destruction of the city and the temple. Jeremiah continued the great themes of the earlier prophets, calling for true piety, social justice, and loyalty to God rather than military alliances. His teaching deepened the idea of repentance, and he introduced the vision of a new covenant written on the heart. After 598, he began to preach the hope and new beginnings following a time of punishment.

JOEL lived in a time of a great locust plague, which he saw as the beginning of the judgment of God. His message is primarily a call to national repentance.

HABAKKUK preached between 626 and 605, a time when the Babylonians were on the march and overrunning all the little kingdoms of the Middle East. He questioned the justice of God in allowing the Babylonians to triumph, and finally received the answer that "the righteous live by their faith."

NAHUM was written between 663 and the time of the fall of Nineveh in 612. His work includes a hymn about a God who is slow to anger but who will punish those who defy Him.

EZEKIEL was a priest taken to Babylon in 597. Before 586, he preached a message of judgment and doom. After 586 he focused on hope and salvation. The source of his hope is not in any of the political powers of his day but in God's own nature and purpose. The temple is destroyed, but God is not bound by a temple and has moved into exile with His people. The sins of the past will not keep the present generation from choosing life and salvation. The book ends with a great vision of the future restoration of the people and the temple.

HAGGAI and **ZECHARIAH** preached in Jerusalem around 520 B.C., in the reign of Darius of Persia. Their message was that the temple was to be rebuilt and the people were to come together into a purified and faithful community. The source of hope was that God does keep His promises. When work on the temple is begun, then God will raise up the glory of the house of David in Zerubbabel, the last known prince of David's line.

MALACHI told of the coming day of the Lord and accused the people and priests of indifference, doubt, and immorality.

Opinion is divided as to the chronological places of the following prophets:

OBADIAH is the shortest book in the Old Testament. It is a song of anger toward the Edomites for their part in the destruction of Jerusalem.

JONAH is the story of a prophet driven by God to proclaim salvation and mercy even to Israel's enemies.

DANIEL was written to offer hope and consolation to Jews who were suffering persecution. The accounts of Daniel and his friends in the first half of the book show how loyalty to God brings victory over one's persecutors. The second part of the book says, in a series of visions, that the fate of the righteous is in the hands of God and that God can be trusted to keep the future safe for His people. ■

The Book of
ISAIAH

1 The vision of Isaiah the son of Amoz, which he saw concerning Judah and Jerusalem in the days of Uzziah, Jotham, Ahaz, *and* Hezekiah, kings of Judah.

The Wickedness of Judah

2 Hear, O heavens, and give ear, O earth!
For the LORD has spoken:
"I have nourished and brought up children,
And they have rebelled against Me;
3 The ox knows its owner
And the donkey its master's crib;
But Israel does not know,
My people do not consider."
4 Alas, sinful nation,
A people laden with iniquity,
A brood of evildoers,
Children who are corrupters!
They have forsaken the LORD,
They have provoked to anger
The Holy One of Israel,
They have turned away backward.

5 Why should you be stricken again?
You will revolt more and more.
The whole head is sick,
And the whole heart faints.
6 From the sole of the foot even to the head,
There is no soundness in it,
But wounds and bruises and putrefying sores;
They have not been closed or bound up,
Or soothed with ointment.

7 Your country *is* desolate,
Your cities *are* burned with fire;
Strangers devour your land in your presence;
And *it is* desolate, as overthrown by strangers.
8 So the daughter of Zion is left as a booth in a vineyard,
As a hut in a garden of cucumbers,
As a besieged city.
9 Unless the LORD of hosts
Had left to us a very small remnant,
We would have become like Sodom,
We would have been made like Gomorrah.

10 Hear the word of the LORD,
You rulers of Sodom;
Give ear to the law of our God,
You people of Gomorrah:
11 "To what purpose *is* the multitude of your sacrifices to Me?"
Says the LORD.
"I have had enough of burnt offerings of rams
And the fat of fed cattle.
I do not delight in the blood of bulls,
Or of lambs or goats.

12 "When you come to appear before Me,
Who has required this from your hand,
To trample My courts?
13 Bring no more futile sacrifices;
Incense is an abomination to Me.
The New Moons, the Sabbaths, and the calling of assemblies—
I cannot endure iniquity and the sacred meeting.
14 Your New Moons and your appointed feasts
My soul hates;
They are a trouble to Me,
I am weary of bearing *them.*
15 When you spread out your hands,
I will hide My eyes from you;
Even though you make many prayers,
I will not hear.
Your hands are full of blood.

16 "Wash yourselves, make yourselves clean;
Put away the evil of your doings from before My eyes.
Cease to do evil,
17 Learn to do good;
Seek justice,
Rebuke the oppressor;[a]
Defend the fatherless,
Plead for the widow.

18 "Come now, and let us reason together,"
Says the LORD,
"Though your sins are like scarlet,
They shall be as white as snow;
Though they are red like crimson,
They shall be as wool.
19 If you are willing and obedient,
You shall eat the good of the land;
20 But if you refuse and rebel,
You shall be devoured by the sword";
For the mouth of the LORD has spoken.

The Degenerate City

21 How the faithful city has become a harlot!
It was full of justice;
Righteousness lodged in it,
But now murderers.
22 Your silver has become dross,
Your wine mixed with water.
23 Your princes *are* rebellious,
And companions of thieves;
Everyone loves bribes,
And follows after rewards.
They do not defend the fatherless,
Nor does the cause of the widow come before them.

24 Therefore the Lord says,
The LORD of hosts, the Mighty One of Israel,
"Ah, I will rid Myself of My adversaries,
And take vengeance on My enemies.
25 I will turn My hand against you,
And thoroughly purge away your dross,
And take away all your alloy.
26 I will restore your judges as at the first,
And your counselors as at the beginning.
Afterward you shall be called the city of righteousness, the faithful city."

27 Zion shall be redeemed with justice,
And her penitents with righteousness.
28 The destruction of transgressors and of sinners *shall be* together,

1:17 [a]Some ancient versions read *the oppressed.*

And those who forsake the LORD shall be consumed.
29 For they[a] shall be ashamed of the terebinth trees
Which you have desired;
And you shall be embarrassed because of the gardens
Which you have chosen.
30 For you shall be as a terebinth whose leaf fades,
And as a garden that has no water.
31 The strong shall be as tinder,
And the work of it as a spark;
Both will burn together,
And no one shall quench *them.*

The Future House of God

2 The word that Isaiah the son of Amoz saw concerning Judah and Jerusalem.

2 Now it shall come to pass in the latter days
That the mountain of the LORD's house
Shall be established on the top of the mountains,
And shall be exalted above the hills;
And all nations shall flow to it.
3 Many people shall come and say,
"Come, and let us go up to the mountain of the LORD,
To the house of the God of Jacob;
He will teach us His ways,
And we shall walk in His paths."
For out of Zion shall go forth the law,
And the word of the LORD from Jerusalem.
4 He shall judge between the nations,
And rebuke many people;
They shall beat their swords into plowshares,
And their spears into pruning hooks;
Nation shall not lift up sword against nation,
Neither shall they learn war anymore.

The Day of the LORD

5 O house of Jacob, come and let us walk
In the light of the LORD.

6 For You have forsaken Your people, the house of Jacob,
Because they are filled with eastern ways;
They *are* soothsayers like the Philistines,
And they are pleased with the children of foreigners.
7 Their land is also full of silver and gold,
And there is no end to their treasures;
Their land is also full of horses,
And there is no end to their chariots.
8 Their land is also full of idols;
They worship the work of their own hands,
That which their own fingers have made.
9 People bow down,
And each man humbles himself;
Therefore do not forgive them.

10 Enter into the rock, and hide in the dust,
From the terror of the LORD
And the glory of His majesty.
11 The lofty looks of man shall be humbled,
The haughtiness of men shall be bowed down,
And the LORD alone shall be exalted in that day.

12 For the day of the LORD of hosts
Shall come upon everything proud and lofty,
Upon everything lifted up—
And it shall be brought low—
13 Upon all the cedars of Lebanon *that are* high and lifted up,
And upon all the oaks of Bashan;
14 Upon all the high mountains,
And upon all the hills *that are* lifted up;
15 Upon every high tower,
And upon every fortified wall;
16 Upon all the ships of Tarshish,
And upon all the beautiful sloops.
17 The loftiness of man shall be bowed down,
And the haughtiness of men shall be brought low;
The LORD alone will be exalted in that day,
18 But the idols He shall utterly abolish.
19 They shall go into the holes of the rocks,
And into the caves of the earth,
From the terror of the LORD
And the glory of His majesty,
When He arises to shake the earth mightily.

20 In that day a man will cast away his idols of silver
And his idols of gold,
Which they made, *each* for himself to worship,
To the moles and bats,
21 To go into the clefts of the rocks,
And into the crags of the rugged rocks,
From the terror of the LORD
And the glory of His majesty,
When He arises to shake the earth mightily.

22 Sever yourselves from such a man,
Whose breath *is* in his nostrils;
For of what account is he?

Judgment on Judah and Jerusalem

3 For behold, the Lord, the LORD of hosts,
Takes away from Jerusalem and from Judah
The stock and the store,
The whole supply of bread and the whole supply of water;
2 The mighty man and the man of war,
The judge and the prophet,
And the diviner and the elder;
3 The captain of fifty and the honorable man,
The counselor and the skillful artisan,
And the expert enchanter.

4 "I will give children *to be* their princes,
And babes shall rule over them.
5 The people will be oppressed,
Every one by another and every one by his neighbor;
The child will be insolent toward the elder,
And the base toward the honorable."

6 When a man takes hold of his brother
In the house of his father, *saying,*
"You have clothing;

1:29 [a]Following Masoretic Text, Septuagint, and Vulgate; some Hebrew manuscripts and Targum read *you.*

You be our ruler,
And *let* these ruins *be* under your power,"[a]
7 In that day he will protest, saying,
"I cannot cure *your* ills,
For in my house *is* neither food nor clothing;
Do not make me a ruler of the people."
8 For Jerusalem stumbled,
And Judah is fallen,
Because their tongue and their doings
Are against the LORD,
To provoke the eyes of His glory.
9 The look on their countenance witnesses against them,
And they declare their sin as Sodom;
They do not hide *it*.
Woe to their soul!
For they have brought evil upon themselves.
10 "Say to the righteous that *it shall be* well *with them*,
For they shall eat the fruit of their doings.
11 Woe to the wicked! *It shall be* ill *with him*,
For the reward of his hands shall be given him.
12 *As for* My people, children *are* their oppressors,
And women rule over them.
O My people! Those who lead you cause *you* to err,
And destroy the way of your paths."

Oppression and Luxury Condemned

13 The LORD stands up to plead,
And stands to judge the people.
14 The LORD will enter into judgment
With the elders of His people
And His princes:
"For you have eaten up the vineyard;
The plunder of the poor *is* in your houses.
15 What do you mean by crushing My people
And grinding the faces of the poor?"
Says the Lord GOD of hosts.

16 Moreover the LORD says:

"Because the daughters of Zion are haughty,
And walk with outstretched necks
And wanton eyes,
Walking and mincing *as* they go,
Making a jingling with their feet,
17 Therefore the Lord will strike with a scab
The crown of the head of the daughters of Zion,
And the LORD will uncover their secret parts."

18 In that day the Lord will take away the finery:
The jingling anklets, the scarves, and the crescents;
19 The pendants, the bracelets, and the veils;
20 The headdresses, the leg ornaments, and the headbands;
The perfume boxes, the charms,
21 and the rings;
The nose jewels,
22 the festal apparel, and the mantles;
The outer garments, the purses,
23 and the mirrors;
The fine linen, the turbans, and the robes.

24 And so it shall be:

Instead of a sweet smell there will be a stench;
Instead of a sash, a rope;
Instead of well-set hair, baldness;
Instead of a rich robe, a girding of sackcloth;
And branding instead of beauty.
25 Your men shall fall by the sword,
And your mighty in the war.
26 Her gates shall lament and mourn,
And she *being* desolate shall sit on the ground.

4 And in that day seven women shall take hold of one man, saying,
"We will eat our own food and wear our own apparel;
Only let us be called by your name,
To take away our reproach."

The Renewal of Zion

2 In that day the Branch of the LORD shall be beautiful and glorious;
And the fruit of the earth *shall be* excellent and appealing
For those of Israel who have escaped.

3 And it shall come to pass that *he who is*
left in Zion and remains in Jerusalem will be
called holy—everyone who is recorded among
the living in Jerusalem.
4 When the Lord has washed away the filth
of the daughters of Zion, and purged the blood
of Jerusalem from her midst, by the spirit of
judgment and by the spirit of burning,
5 then the LORD will create above every dwell-
ing place of Mount Zion, and above her assem-
blies, a cloud and smoke by day and the shining
of a flaming fire by night. For over all the glory
there *will be* a covering.
6 And there will be a tabernacle for shade in
the daytime from the heat, for a place of refuge,
and for a shelter from storm and rain.

God's Disappointing Vineyard

5 Now let me sing to my Well-beloved
A song of my Beloved regarding His vineyard:

My Well-beloved has a vineyard
On a very fruitful hill.
2 He dug it up and cleared out its stones,
And planted it with the choicest vine.
He built a tower in its midst,
And also made a winepress in it;
So He expected *it* to bring forth *good* grapes,
But it brought forth wild grapes.

3 "And now, O inhabitants of Jerusalem and men of Judah,
Judge, please, between Me and My vineyard.
4 What more could have been done to My vineyard
That I have not done in it?
Why then, when I expected *it* to bring forth *good* grapes,
Did it bring forth wild grapes?

3:6 [a]Literally *hand*

5 And now, please let Me tell you what I
will do to My vineyard:
I will take away its hedge, and it shall be
burned;
And break down its wall, and it shall be
trampled down.
6 I will lay it waste;
It shall not be pruned or dug,
But there shall come up briers and
thorns.
I will also command the clouds
That they rain no rain on it."

7 For the vineyard of the LORD of hosts *is*
the house of Israel,
And the men of Judah are His pleasant
plant.
He looked for justice, but behold,
oppression;
For righteousness, but behold, a cry *for
help*.

Impending Judgment on Excesses

8 Woe to those who join house to house;
They add field to field,
Till *there is* no place
Where they may dwell alone in the midst
of the land!
9 In my hearing the LORD of hosts *said*,
"Truly, many houses shall be desolate,
Great and beautiful ones, without
inhabitant.
10 For ten acres of vineyard shall yield one
bath,
And a homer of seed shall yield one
ephah."

11 Woe to those who rise early in the
morning,
That they may follow intoxicating drink;
Who continue until night, *till* wine
inflames them!
12 The harp and the strings,
The tambourine and flute,
And wine are in their feasts;
But they do not regard the work of the
LORD,
Nor consider the operation of His hands.

13 Therefore my people have gone into
captivity,
Because *they have* no knowledge;
Their honorable men *are* famished,
And their multitude dried up with thirst.
14 Therefore Sheol has enlarged itself
And opened its mouth beyond measure;
Their glory and their multitude and their
pomp,
And he who is jubilant, shall descend into
it.
15 People shall be brought down,
Each man shall be humbled,
And the eyes of the lofty shall be
humbled.
16 But the LORD of hosts shall be exalted in
judgment,
And God who is holy shall be hallowed in
righteousness.
17 Then the lambs shall feed in their
pasture,
And in the waste places of the fat ones
strangers shall eat.

18 Woe to those who draw iniquity with
cords of vanity,
And sin as if with a cart rope;
19 That say, "Let Him make speed *and*
hasten His work,
That we may see *it*;
And let the counsel of the Holy One of
Israel draw near and come,
That we may know *it*."

20 Woe to those who call evil good, and
good evil;
Who put darkness for light, and light for
darkness;
Who put bitter for sweet, and sweet for
bitter!

21 Woe to *those who are* wise in their own
eyes,
And prudent in their own sight!

22 Woe to men mighty at drinking wine,
Woe to men valiant for mixing
intoxicating drink,
23 Who justify the wicked for a bribe,
And take away justice from the righteous
man!

24 Therefore, as the fire devours the stubble,
And the flame consumes the chaff,
So their root will be as rottenness,
And their blossom will ascend like dust;
Because they have rejected the law of the
LORD of hosts,
And despised the word of the Holy One
of Israel.
25 Therefore the anger of the LORD is
aroused against His people;
He has stretched out His hand against
them
And stricken them,
And the hills trembled.
Their carcasses *were* as refuse in the
midst of the streets.

For all this His anger is not turned away,
But His hand *is* stretched out still.

26 He will lift up a banner to the nations
from afar,
And will whistle to them from the end of
the earth;
Surely they shall come with speed,
swiftly.
27 No one will be weary or stumble among
them,
No one will slumber or sleep;
Nor will the belt on their loins be loosed,
Nor the strap of their sandals be broken;
28 Whose arrows *are* sharp,
And all their bows bent;
Their horses' hooves will seem like flint,
And their wheels like a whirlwind.
29 Their roaring *will be* like a lion,
They will roar like young lions;
Yes, they will roar
And lay hold of the prey;
They will carry *it* away safely,
And no one will deliver.
30 In that day they will roar against them
Like the roaring of the sea.
And if *one* looks to the land,
Behold, darkness *and* sorrow;
And the light is darkened by the clouds.

Isaiah Called to Be a Prophet

6 In the year that King Uzziah died, I saw the
Lord sitting on a throne, high and lifted up,
and the train of His *robe* filled the temple.
2 Above it stood seraphim; each one had six

wings: with two he covered his face, with two
he covered his feet, and with two he flew.
3 And one cried to another and said:

"Holy, holy, holy *is* the LORD of hosts;
The whole earth *is* full of His glory!"

4 And the posts of the door were shaken by
the voice of him who cried out, and the house
was filled with smoke.
5 So I said:

"Woe *is* me, for I am undone!
Because I *am* a man of unclean lips,
And I dwell in the midst of a people of
unclean lips;
For my eyes have seen the King,
The LORD of hosts."

6 Then one of the seraphim flew to me, hav-
ing in his hand a live coal *which* he had taken
with the tongs from the altar.
7 And he touched my mouth *with it*, and said:

"Behold, this has touched your lips;
Your iniquity is taken away,
And your sin purged."

8 Also I heard the voice of the Lord, saying:

"Whom shall I send,
And who will go for Us?"

Then I said, "Here *am* I! Send me."
9 And He said, "Go, and tell this people:

'Keep on hearing, but do not understand;
Keep on seeing, but do not perceive.'

10 "Make the heart of this people dull,
And their ears heavy,
And shut their eyes;
Lest they see with their eyes,
And hear with their ears,
And understand with their heart,
And return and be healed."

11 Then I said, "Lord, how long?" And He an-
swered:

"Until the cities are laid waste and without
inhabitant,
The houses are without a man,
The land is utterly desolate,
12 The LORD has removed men far away,
And the forsaken places *are* many in the
midst of the land.
13 But yet a tenth *will be* in it,
And will return and be for consuming,
As a terebinth tree or as an oak,
Whose stump *remains* when it is cut
down.
So the holy seed *shall be* its stump."

Isaiah Sent to King Ahaz

7 Now it came to pass in the days of Ahaz the
son of Jotham, the son of Uzziah, king of
Judah, *that* Rezin king of Syria and Pekah the
son of Remaliah, king of Israel, went up to
Jerusalem to *make* war against it, but could
not prevail against it.
2 And it was told to the house of David, say-
ing, "Syria's forces are deployed in Ephraim."
So his heart and the heart of his people were
moved as the trees of the woods are moved
with the wind.
3 Then the LORD said to Isaiah, "Go out now
to meet Ahaz, you and Shear-Jashub[a] your son,
at the end of the aqueduct from the upper pool,
on the highway to the Fuller's Field,
4 "and say to him: 'Take heed, and be quiet;
do not fear or be fainthearted for these two
stubs of smoking firebrands, for the fierce an-
ger of Rezin and Syria, and the son of Rema-
liah.
5 'Because Syria, Ephraim, and the son of
Remaliah have plotted evil against you, saying,
6 "Let us go up against Judah and trouble it,
and let us make a gap in its wall for ourselves,
and set a king over them, the son of Tabel"—
7 'thus says the Lord GOD:

"It shall not stand,
Nor shall it come to pass.
8 For the head of Syria *is* Damascus,
And the head of Damascus *is* Rezin.
Within sixty-five years Ephraim will be
broken,
So that it will not *be* a people.
9 The head of Ephraim *is* Samaria,
And the head of Samaria *is* Remaliah's
son.
If you will not believe,
Surely you shall not be established."'"

The Immanuel Prophecy

10 Moreover the LORD spoke again to Ahaz,
saying,
11 "Ask a sign for yourself from the LORD
your God; ask it either in the depth or in the
height above."
12 But Ahaz said, "I will not ask, nor will I
test the LORD!"
13 Then he said, "Hear now, O house of Da-
vid! *Is it* a small thing for you to weary men,
but will you weary my God also?
14 "Therefore the Lord Himself will give you
a sign: Behold, the virgin shall conceive and
bear a Son, and shall call His name Immanuel.[a]
15 "Curds and honey He shall eat, that He
may know to refuse the evil and choose the
good.
16 "For before the Child shall know to refuse
the evil and choose the good, the land that you
dread will be forsaken by both her kings.
17 "The LORD will bring the king of Assyria
upon you and your people and your father's
house—days that have not come since the day
that Ephraim departed from Judah."

18 And it shall come to pass in that day
That the LORD will whistle for the fly
That *is* in the farthest part of the rivers of
Egypt,
And for the bee that *is* in the land of
Assyria.
19 They will come, and all of them will rest
In the desolate valleys and in the clefts of
the rocks,
And on all thorns and in all pastures.

20 In the same day the Lord will shave with
a hired razor,
With those from beyond the River,[a] with
the king of Assyria,
The head and the hair of the legs,
And will also remove the beard.

21 It shall be in that day
That a man will keep alive a young cow
and two sheep;
22 So it shall be, from the abundance of milk
they give,

7:3 [a]Literally *A Remnant Shall Return* **7:14** [a]Literally *God-With-Us* **7:20** [a]That is, the Euphrates

That he will eat curds;
For curds and honey everyone will eat
who is left in the land.

23 It shall happen in that day,
That wherever there could be a thousand
vines
Worth a thousand *shekels* of silver,
It will be for briers and thorns.
24 With arrows and bows *men* will come
there,
Because all the land will become briers
and thorns.

25 And to any hill which could be dug with
the hoe,
You will not go there for fear of briers
and thorns;
But it will become a range for oxen
And a place for sheep to roam.

Assyria Will Invade the Land

8 Moreover the LORD said to me, "Take a large
scroll, and write on it with a man's pen
concerning Maher-Shalal-Hash-Baz.[a]
2 "And I will take for Myself faithful wit-
nesses to record, Uriah the priest and Zecha-
riah the son of Jeberechiah."
3 Then I went to the prophetess, and she con-
ceived and bore a son. Then the LORD said to
me, "Call his name Maher-Shalal-Hash-Baz;
4 "for before the child shall have knowledge
to cry 'My father' and 'My mother,' the riches
of Damascus and the spoil of Samaria will be
taken away before the king of Assyria."
5 The LORD also spoke to me again, saying:

6 "Inasmuch as these people refused
The waters of Shiloah that flow softly,
And rejoice in Rezin and in Remaliah's
son;
7 Now therefore, behold, the Lord brings
up over them
The waters of the River,[a] strong and
mighty—
The king of Assyria and all his glory;
He will go up over all his channels
And go over all his banks.
8 He will pass through Judah,
He will overflow and pass over,
He will reach up to the neck;
And the stretching out of his wings
Will fill the breadth of Your land,
O Immanuel.[a]

9 "Be shattered, O you peoples, and be
broken in pieces!
Give ear, all you from far countries.
Gird yourselves, but be broken in pieces;
Gird yourselves, but be broken in pieces.
10 Take counsel together, but it will come to
nothing;
Speak the word, but it will not stand,
For God *is* with us."[a]

Fear God, Heed His Word

11 For the LORD spoke thus to me with a strong
hand, and instructed me that I should not walk
in the way of this people, saying:

12 "Do not say, 'A conspiracy,'
Concerning all that this people call a
conspiracy,
Nor be afraid of their threats, nor be
troubled.
13 The LORD of hosts, Him you shall hallow;
Let Him *be* your fear,
And *let* Him *be* your dread.
14 He will be as a sanctuary,
But a stone of stumbling and a rock of
offense
To both the houses of Israel,
As a trap and a snare to the inhabitants
of Jerusalem.
15 And many among them shall stumble;
They shall fall and be broken,
Be snared and taken."

16 Bind up the testimony,
Seal the law among my disciples.
17 And I will wait on the LORD,
Who hides His face from the house of
Jacob;
And I will hope in Him.
18 Here am I and the children whom the
LORD has given me!
We are for signs and wonders in Israel
From the LORD of hosts,
Who dwells in Mount Zion.

19 And when they say to you, "Seek those who
are mediums and wizards, who whisper and
mutter," should not a people seek their God?
Should they seek the dead on behalf of the
living?
20 To the law and to the testimony! If they do
not speak according to this word, *it is* because
there is no light in them.
21 They will pass through it hard-pressed and
hungry; and it shall happen, when they are hun-
gry, that they will be enraged and curse their
king and their God, and look upward.
22 Then they will look to the earth, and see
trouble and darkness, gloom of anguish; and
they will be driven into darkness.

The Government of the Promised Son

9 Nevertheless the gloom *will* not *be* upon
her who *is* distressed,
As when at first He lightly esteemed
The land of Zebulun and the land of
Naphtali,
And afterward more heavily oppressed
her,
By the way of the sea, beyond the Jordan,
In Galilee of the Gentiles.
2 The people who walked in darkness
Have seen a great light;
Those who dwelt in the land of the
shadow of death,
Upon them a light has shined.

3 You have multiplied the nation
And increased its joy;[a]
They rejoice before You
According to the joy of harvest,
As *men* rejoice when they divide the
spoil.
4 For You have broken the yoke of his
burden
And the staff of his shoulder,
The rod of his oppressor,
As in the day of Midian.
5 For every warrior's sandal from the noisy
battle,

8:1 [a]Literally *Speed the Spoil, Hasten the Booty* **8:7** [a]That is, the Euphrates **8:8** [a]Literally *God-With-Us*
8:10 [a]Hebrew *Immanuel* **9:3** [a]Following Qere and Targum; Kethib and Vulgate read *not increased joy;* Septuagint reads *Most of the people You brought down in Your joy.*

And garments rolled in blood,
Will be used for burning *and* fuel of fire.
6 For unto us a Child is born,
Unto us a Son is given;
And the government will be upon His shoulder.
And His name will be called
Wonderful, Counselor, Mighty God,
Everlasting Father, Prince of Peace.
7 Of the increase of *His* government and peace
There will be no end,
Upon the throne of David and over His kingdom,
To order it and establish it with judgment and justice
From that time forward, even forever.
The zeal of the LORD of hosts will perform this.

The Punishment of Samaria

8 The Lord sent a word against Jacob,
And it has fallen on Israel.
9 All the people will know—
Ephraim and the inhabitant of Samaria—
Who say in pride and arrogance of heart:
10 "The bricks have fallen down,
But we will rebuild with hewn stones;
The sycamores are cut down,
But we will replace *them* with cedars."
11 Therefore the LORD shall set up
The adversaries of Rezin against him,
And spur his enemies on,
12 The Syrians before and the Philistines behind;
And they shall devour Israel with an open mouth.

For all this His anger is not turned away,
But His hand *is* stretched out still.

13 For the people do not turn to Him who strikes them,
Nor do they seek the LORD of hosts.
14 Therefore the LORD will cut off head and tail from Israel,
Palm branch and bulrush in one day.
15 The elder and honorable, he *is* the head;
The prophet who teaches lies, he *is* the tail.
16 For the leaders of this people cause *them* to err,
And *those who are* led by them are destroyed.
17 Therefore the Lord will have no joy in their young men,
Nor have mercy on their fatherless and widows;
For everyone *is* a hypocrite and an evildoer,
And every mouth speaks folly.

For all this His anger is not turned away,
But His hand *is* stretched out still.

18 For wickedness burns as the fire;
It shall devour the briers and thorns,
And kindle in the thickets of the forest;
They shall mount up *like* rising smoke.
19 Through the wrath of the LORD of hosts
The land is burned up,
And the people shall be as fuel for the fire;
No man shall spare his brother.
20 And he shall snatch on the right hand
And be hungry;
He shall devour on the left hand
And not be satisfied;
Every man shall eat the flesh of his own arm.
21 Manasseh *shall devour* Ephraim, and Ephraim Manasseh;
Together they *shall be* against Judah.

For all this His anger is not turned away,
But His hand *is* stretched out still.

10 "Woe to those who decree unrighteous decrees,
Who write misfortune,
Which they have prescribed
2 To rob the needy of justice,
And to take what is right from the poor of My people,
That widows may be their prey,
And *that* they may rob the fatherless.
3 What will you do in the day of punishment,
And in the desolation *which* will come from afar?
To whom will you flee for help?
And where will you leave your glory?
4 Without Me they shall bow down among the prisoners,
And they shall fall among the slain."

For all this His anger is not turned away,
But His hand *is* stretched out still.

Arrogant Assyria Also Judged

5 "Woe to Assyria, the rod of My anger
And the staff in whose hand is My indignation.
6 I will send him against an ungodly nation,
And against the people of My wrath
I will give him charge,
To seize the spoil, to take the prey,
And to tread them down like the mire of the streets.
7 Yet he does not mean so,
Nor does his heart think so;
But *it is* in his heart to destroy,
And cut off not a few nations.
8 For he says,
'*Are* not my princes altogether kings?
9 *Is* not Calno like Carchemish?
Is not Hamath like Arpad?
Is not Samaria like Damascus?
10 As my hand has found the kingdoms of the idols,
Whose carved images excelled those of Jerusalem and Samaria,
11 As I have done to Samaria and her idols,
Shall I not do also to Jerusalem and her idols?'"

12 Therefore it shall come to pass, when the
Lord has performed all His work on Mount
Zion and on Jerusalem, *that He will say*, "I will
punish the fruit of the arrogant heart of the
king of Assyria, and the glory of his haughty
looks."
13 For he says:

"By the strength of my hand I have done *it*,
And by my wisdom, for I am prudent;
Also I have removed the boundaries of the people,
And have robbed their treasuries;

So I have put down the inhabitants like a
valiant *man*.
14 My hand has found like a nest the riches
of the people,
And as one gathers eggs *that are* left,
I have gathered all the earth;
And there was no one who moved *his*
wing,
Nor opened *his* mouth with even a peep."

15 Shall the ax boast itself against him who
chops with it?
Or shall the saw exalt itself against him
who saws with it?
As if a rod could wield *itself* against
those who lift it up,
Or as if a staff could lift up, *as if it were*
not wood!
16 Therefore the Lord, the Lord[a] of hosts,
Will send leanness among his fat ones;
And under his glory
He will kindle a burning
Like the burning of a fire.
17 So the Light of Israel will be for a fire,
And his Holy One for a flame;
It will burn and devour
His thorns and his briers in one day.
18 And it will consume the glory of his
forest and of his fruitful field,
Both soul and body;
And they will be as when a sick man
wastes away.
19 Then the rest of the trees of his forest
Will be so few in number
That a child may write them.

The Returning Remnant of Israel

20 And it shall come to pass in that day
That the remnant of Israel,
And such as have escaped of the house of
Jacob,
Will never again depend on him who
defeated them,
But will depend on the LORD, the Holy
One of Israel, in truth.
21 The remnant will return, the remnant of
Jacob,
To the Mighty God.
22 For though your people, O Israel, be as
the sand of the sea,
A remnant of them will return;
The destruction decreed shall overflow
with righteousness.
23 For the Lord GOD of hosts
Will make a determined end
In the midst of all the land.

24 Therefore thus says the Lord GOD of hosts:
"O My people, who dwell in Zion, do not be
afraid of the Assyrian. He shall strike you with
a rod and lift up his staff against you, in the
manner of Egypt.
25 "For yet a very little while and the indigna-
tion will cease, as will My anger in their de-
struction."
26 And the LORD of hosts will stir up a
scourge for him like the slaughter of Midian at
the rock of Oreb; *as* His rod was on the sea, so
will He lift it up in the manner of Egypt.

27 It shall come to pass in that day
That his burden will be taken away from
your shoulder,
And his yoke from your neck,
And the yoke will be destroyed because
of the anointing oil.

28 He has come to Aiath,
He has passed Migron;
At Michmash he has attended to his
equipment.
29 They have gone along the ridge,
They have taken up lodging at Geba.
Ramah is afraid,
Gibeah of Saul has fled.
30 Lift up your voice,
O daughter of Gallim!
Cause it to be heard as far as Laish—
O poor Anathoth![a]
31 Madmenah has fled,
The inhabitants of Gebim seek refuge.
32 As yet he will remain at Nob that day;
He will shake his fist at the mount of the
daughter of Zion,
The hill of Jerusalem.

33 Behold, the Lord,
The LORD of hosts,
Will lop off the bough with terror;
Those of high stature *will be* hewn down,
And the haughty will be humbled.
34 He will cut down the thickets of the forest
with iron,
And Lebanon will fall by the Mighty One.

The Reign of Jesse's Offspring

11 There shall come forth a Rod from the
stem of Jesse,
And a Branch shall grow out of his roots.
2 The Spirit of the LORD shall rest upon
Him,
The Spirit of wisdom and understanding,
The Spirit of counsel and might,
The Spirit of knowledge and of the fear
of the LORD.

3 His delight *is* in the fear of the LORD,
And He shall not judge by the sight of His
eyes,
Nor decide by the hearing of His ears;
4 But with righteousness He shall judge the
poor,
And decide with equity for the meek of
the earth;
He shall strike the earth with the rod of
His mouth,
And with the breath of His lips He shall
slay the wicked.
5 Righteousness shall be the belt of His
loins,
And faithfulness the belt of His waist.

6 "The wolf also shall dwell with the lamb,
The leopard shall lie down with the
young goat,
The calf and the young lion and the
fatling together;
And a little child shall lead them.
7 The cow and the bear shall graze;
Their young ones shall lie down together;
And the lion shall eat straw like the ox.
8 The nursing child shall play by the
cobra's hole,
And the weaned child shall put his hand
in the viper's den.
9 They shall not hurt nor destroy in all My
holy mountain,

10:16 [a]Following Bomberg; Masoretic Text and Dead Sea Scrolls read *YHWH* (*the* LORD). **10:30** [a]Following Masoretic Text, Targum, and Vulgate; Septuagint and Syriac read *Listen to her, O Anathoth.*

For the earth shall be full of the
knowledge of the LORD
As the waters cover the sea.

10 "And in that day there shall be a Root of
Jesse,
Who shall stand as a banner to the
people;
For the Gentiles shall seek Him,
And His resting place shall be glorious."

11 It shall come to pass in that day
That the Lord shall set His hand again
the second time
To recover the remnant of His people who
are left,
From Assyria and Egypt,
From Pathros and Cush,
From Elam and Shinar,
From Hamath and the islands of the sea.

12 He will set up a banner for the nations,
And will assemble the outcasts of Israel,
And gather together the dispersed of
Judah
From the four corners of the earth.
13 Also the envy of Ephraim shall depart,
And the adversaries of Judah shall be cut
off;
Ephraim shall not envy Judah,
And Judah shall not harass Ephraim.
14 But they shall fly down upon the shoulder
of the Philistines toward the west;
Together they shall plunder the people of
the East;
They shall lay their hand on Edom and
Moab;
And the people of Ammon shall obey
them.
15 The LORD will utterly destroy[a] the tongue
of the Sea of Egypt;
With His mighty wind He will shake His
fist over the River,[b]
And strike it in the seven streams,
And make *men* cross over dry-shod.
16 There will be a highway for the remnant
of His people
Who will be left from Assyria,
As it was for Israel
In the day that he came up from the land
of Egypt.

A Hymn of Praise

12 And in that day you will say:
"O LORD, I will praise You;
Though You were angry with me,
Your anger is turned away, and You
comfort me.
2 Behold, God *is* my salvation,
I will trust and not be afraid;
'For YAH, the LORD, *is* my strength and
song;
He also has become my salvation.' "[a]

3 Therefore with joy you will draw water
From the wells of salvation.

4 And in that day you will say:

"Praise the LORD, call upon His name;
Declare His deeds among the peoples,
Make mention that His name is exalted.
5 Sing to the LORD,
For He has done excellent things;
This *is* known in all the earth.
6 Cry out and shout, O inhabitant of Zion,
For great *is* the Holy One of Israel in your
midst!"

Proclamation Against Babylon

13 The burden against Babylon which Isa-
iah the son of Amoz saw.

2 "Lift up a banner on the high mountain,
Raise your voice to them;
Wave your hand, that they may enter the
gates of the nobles.
3 I have commanded My sanctified ones;
I have also called My mighty ones for My
anger—
Those who rejoice in My exaltation."

4 The noise of a multitude in the
mountains,
Like that of many people!
A tumultuous noise of the kingdoms of
nations gathered together!
The LORD of hosts musters
The army for battle.
5 They come from a far country,
From the end of heaven—
The LORD and His weapons of
indignation,
To destroy the whole land.

6 Wail, for the day of the LORD *is* at hand!
It will come as destruction from the
Almighty.
7 Therefore all hands will be limp,
Every man's heart will melt,
8 And they will be afraid.
Pangs and sorrows will take hold of
them;
They will be in pain as a woman in
childbirth;
They will be amazed at one another;
Their faces *will be like* flames.

9 Behold, the day of the LORD comes,
Cruel, with both wrath and fierce anger,
To lay the land desolate;
And He will destroy its sinners from it.
10 For the stars of heaven and their
constellations
Will not give their light;
The sun will be darkened in its going
forth,
And the moon will not cause its light to
shine.

11 "I will punish the world for *its* evil,
And the wicked for their iniquity;
I will halt the arrogance of the proud,
And will lay low the haughtiness of the
terrible.
12 I will make a mortal more rare than fine
gold,
A man more than the golden wedge of
Ophir.
13 Therefore I will shake the heavens,
And the earth will move out of her place,
In the wrath of the LORD of hosts
And in the day of His fierce anger.
14 It shall be as the hunted gazelle,
And as a sheep that no man takes up;
Every man will turn to his own people,
And everyone will flee to his own land.

11:15 [a]Following Masoretic Text and Vulgate; Septuagint, Syriac, and Targum read *dry up.* [b]That is, the Euphrates
12:2 [a]Exodus 15:2

15 Everyone who is found will be thrust
through,
And everyone who is captured will fall by
the sword.
16 Their children also will be dashed to
pieces before their eyes;
Their houses will be plundered
And their wives ravished.

17 "Behold, I will stir up the Medes against
them,
Who will not regard silver;
And *as for* gold, they will not delight in it.
18 Also *their* bows will dash the young men
to pieces,
And they will have no pity on the fruit of
the womb;
Their eye will not spare children.
19 And Babylon, the glory of kingdoms,
The beauty of the Chaldeans' pride,
Will be as when God overthrew Sodom
and Gomorrah.
20 It will never be inhabited,
Nor will it be settled from generation to
generation;
Nor will the Arabian pitch tents there,
Nor will the shepherds make their
sheepfolds there.
21 But wild beasts of the desert will lie
there,
And their houses will be full of owls;
Ostriches will dwell there,
And wild goats will caper there.
22 The hyenas will howl in their citadels,
And jackals in their pleasant palaces.
Her time *is* near to come,
And her days will not be prolonged."

Mercy on Jacob

14 For the LORD will have mercy on Jacob,
and will still choose Israel, and settle them
in their own land. The strangers will be joined
with them, and they will cling to the house of
Jacob.
2 Then people will take them and bring them
to their place, and the house of Israel will pos-
sess them for servants and maids in the land
of the LORD; they will take them captive whose
captives they were, and rule over their oppres-
sors.

Fall of the King of Babylon

3 It shall come to pass in the day the LORD
gives you rest from your sorrow, and from your
fear and the hard bondage in which you were
made to serve,
4 that you will take up this proverb against
the king of Babylon, and say:

"How the oppressor has ceased,
The golden[a] city ceased!
5 The LORD has broken the staff of the
wicked,
The scepter of the rulers;
6 He who struck the people in wrath with a
continual stroke,
He who ruled the nations in anger,
Is persecuted *and* no one hinders.
7 The whole earth is at rest *and* quiet;
They break forth into singing.
8 Indeed the cypress trees rejoice over you,
And the cedars of Lebanon,
Saying, 'Since you were cut down,
No woodsman has come up against us.'
9 "Hell from beneath is excited about you,
To meet *you* at your coming;
It stirs up the dead for you,
All the chief ones of the earth;
It has raised up from their thrones
All the kings of the nations.
10 They all shall speak and say to you:
'Have you also become as weak as we?
Have you become like us?
11 Your pomp is brought down to Sheol,
And the sound of your stringed
instruments;
The maggot is spread under you,
And worms cover you.'

The Fall of Lucifer

12 "How you are fallen from heaven,
O Lucifer,[a] son of the morning!
How you are cut down to the ground,
You who weakened the nations!
13 For you have said in your heart:
'I will ascend into heaven,
I will exalt my throne above the stars of
God;
I will also sit on the mount of the
congregation
On the farthest sides of the north;
14 I will ascend above the heights of the
clouds,
I will be like the Most High.'
15 Yet you shall be brought down to Sheol,
To the lowest depths of the Pit.

16 "Those who see you will gaze at you,
And consider you, *saying:*
'*Is* this the man who made the earth
tremble,
Who shook kingdoms,
17 Who made the world as a wilderness
And destroyed its cities,
Who did not open the house of his
prisoners?'

18 "All the kings of the nations,
All of them, sleep in glory,
Everyone in his own house;
19 But you are cast out of your grave
Like an abominable branch,
Like the garment of those who are slain,
Thrust through with a sword,
Who go down to the stones of the pit,
Like a corpse trodden underfoot.
20 You will not be joined with them in
burial,
Because you have destroyed your land
And slain your people.
The brood of evildoers shall never be
named.
21 Prepare slaughter for his children
Because of the iniquity of their fathers,
Lest they rise up and possess the land,
And fill the face of the world with cities."

Babylon Destroyed

22 "For I will rise up against them," says the
LORD of hosts,
"And cut off from Babylon the name and
remnant,
And offspring and posterity," says the
LORD.
23 "I will also make it a possession for the
porcupine,
And marshes of muddy water;

14:4 [a]Or *insolent* **14:12** [a]Literally *Day Star*

I will sweep it with the broom of
destruction," says the LORD of hosts.

Assyria Destroyed

24 The LORD of hosts has sworn, saying,
"Surely, as I have thought, so it shall come
to pass,
And as I have purposed, *so* it shall stand:
25 That I will break the Assyrian in My land,
And on My mountains tread him
underfoot.
Then his yoke shall be removed from
them,
And his burden removed from their
shoulders.
26 This *is* the purpose that is purposed
against the whole earth,
And this *is* the hand that is stretched out
over all the nations.
27 For the LORD of hosts has purposed,
And who will annul *it?*
His hand *is* stretched out,
And who will turn it back?"

Philistia Destroyed

28 This is the burden which came in the year
that King Ahaz died.

29 "Do not rejoice, all you of Philistia,
Because the rod that struck you is
broken;
For out of the serpent's roots will come
forth a viper,
And its offspring *will be* a fiery flying
serpent.
30 The firstborn of the poor will feed,
And the needy will lie down in safety;
I will kill your roots with famine,
And it will slay your remnant.
31 Wail, O gate! Cry, O city!
All you of Philistia *are* dissolved;
For smoke will come from the north,
And no one *will be* alone in his appointed
times."

32 What will they answer the messengers of
the nation?
That the LORD has founded Zion,
And the poor of His people shall take
refuge in it.

Proclamation Against Moab

15 The burden against Moab.

Because in the night Ar of Moab is laid
waste
And destroyed,
Because in the night Kir of Moab is laid
waste
And destroyed,
2 He has gone up to the temple[a] and Dibon,
To the high places to weep.
Moab will wail over Nebo and over
Medeba;
On all their heads *will be* baldness,
And every beard cut off.
3 In their streets they will clothe
themselves with sackcloth;
On the tops of their houses
And in their streets
Everyone will wail, weeping bitterly.
4 Heshbon and Elealeh will cry out,
Their voice shall be heard as far as Jahaz;
Therefore the armed soldiers[a] of Moab
will cry out;
His life will be burdensome to him.

5 "My heart will cry out for Moab;
His fugitives *shall flee* to Zoar,
Like a three-year-old heifer.[a]
For by the Ascent of Luhith
They will go up with weeping;
For in the way of Horonaim
They will raise up a cry of destruction,
6 For the waters of Nimrim will be
desolate,
For the green grass has withered away;
The grass fails, there is nothing green.
7 Therefore the abundance they have
gained,
And what they have laid up,
They will carry away to the Brook of the
Willows.
8 For the cry has gone all around the
borders of Moab,
Its wailing to Eglaim
And its wailing to Beer Elim.
9 For the waters of Dimon[a] will be full of
blood;
Because I will bring more upon Dimon,[b]
Lions upon him who escapes from Moab,
And on the remnant of the land."

Moab Destroyed

16 Send the lamb to the ruler of the land,
From Sela to the wilderness,
To the mount of the daughter of Zion.
2 For it shall be as a wandering bird thrown
out of the nest;
So shall be the daughters of Moab at the
fords of the Arnon.

3 "Take counsel, execute judgment;
Make your shadow like the night in the
middle of the day;
Hide the outcasts,
Do not betray him who escapes.
4 Let My outcasts dwell with you, O Moab;
Be a shelter to them from the face of the
spoiler.
For the extortioner is at an end,
Devastation ceases,
The oppressors are consumed out of the
land.
5 In mercy the throne will be established;
And One will sit on it in truth, in the
tabernacle of David,
Judging and seeking justice and
hastening righteousness."

6 We have heard of the pride of Moab—
He is very proud—
Of his haughtiness and his pride and his
wrath;
But his lies *shall* not *be* so.
7 Therefore Moab shall wail for Moab;
Everyone shall wail.
For the foundations of Kir Hareseth you
shall mourn;
Surely *they are* stricken.

8 For the fields of Heshbon languish,
And the vine of Sibmah;

15:2 [a]Hebrew *bayith,* literally *house* **15:4** [a]Following Masoretic Text, Targum, and Vulgate; Septuagint and Syriac read *loins.* **15:5** [a]Or *The Third Eglath,* an unknown city (compare Jeremiah 48:34) **15:9** [a]Following Masoretic Text and Targum; Dead Sea Scrolls and Vulgate read *Dibon;* Septuagint reads *Rimon.* [b]Following Masoretic Text and Targum; Dead Sea Scrolls and Vulgate read *Dibon;* Septuagint reads *Rimon.*

The lords of the nations have broken
down its choice plants,
Which have reached to Jazer
And wandered through the wilderness.
Her branches are stretched out,
They are gone over the sea.
9 Therefore I will bewail the vine of
Sibmah,
With the weeping of Jazer;
I will drench you with my tears,
O Heshbon and Elealeh;
For battle cries have fallen
Over your summer fruits and your
harvest.

10 Gladness is taken away,
And joy from the plentiful field;
In the vineyards there will be no singing,
Nor will there be shouting;
No treaders will tread out wine in the
presses;
I have made their shouting cease.
11 Therefore my heart shall resound like a
harp for Moab,
And my inner being for Kir Heres.

12 And it shall come to pass,
When it is seen that Moab is weary on
the high place,
That he will come to his sanctuary to
pray;
But he will not prevail.

13 This *is* the word which the LORD has spo-
ken concerning Moab since that time.
14 But now the LORD has spoken, saying,
"Within three years, as the years of a hired
man, the glory of Moab will be despised with
all that great multitude, and the remnant *will
be* very small *and* feeble."

Proclamation Against Syria and Israel

17 The burden against Damascus.

"Behold, Damascus will cease from
being a city,
And it will be a ruinous heap.
2 The cities of Aroer *are* forsaken;[a]
They will be for flocks
Which lie down, and no one will make
them afraid.
3 The fortress also will cease from
Ephraim,
The kingdom from Damascus,
And the remnant of Syria;
They will be as the glory of the children
of Israel,"
Says the LORD of hosts.

4 "In that day it shall come to pass
That the glory of Jacob will wane,
And the fatness of his flesh grow lean.
5 It shall be as when the harvester gathers
the grain,
And reaps the heads with his arm;
It shall be as he who gathers heads of
grain
In the Valley of Rephaim.
6 Yet gleaning grapes will be left in it,
Like the shaking of an olive tree,
Two *or* three olives at the top of the
uppermost bough,
Four *or* five in its most fruitful branches,"
Says the LORD God of Israel.

7 In that day a man will look to his Maker,
And his eyes will have respect for the
Holy One of Israel.
8 He will not look to the altars,
The work of his hands;
He will not respect what his fingers have
made,
Nor the wooden images[a] nor the incense
altars.

9 In that day his strong cities will be as a
forsaken bough[a]
And an uppermost branch,[b]
Which they left because of the children of
Israel;
And there will be desolation.

10 Because you have forgotten the God of
your salvation,
And have not been mindful of the Rock of
your stronghold,
Therefore you will plant pleasant plants
And set out foreign seedlings;
11 In the day you will make your plant to
grow,
And in the morning you will make your
seed to flourish;
But the harvest *will be* a heap of ruins
In the day of grief and desperate sorrow.

12 Woe to the multitude of many people
Who make a noise like the roar of the
seas,
And to the rushing of nations
That make a rushing like the rushing of
mighty waters!
13 The nations will rush like the rushing of
many waters;
But *God* will rebuke them and they will
flee far away,
And be chased like the chaff of the
mountains before the wind,
Like a rolling thing before the whirlwind.
14 Then behold, at eventide, trouble!
And before the morning, he *is* no more.
This *is* the portion of those who plunder
us,
And the lot of those who rob us.

Proclamation Against Ethiopia

18 Woe to the land shadowed with
buzzing wings,
Which *is* beyond the rivers of Ethiopia,
2 Which sends ambassadors by sea,
Even in vessels of reed on the waters,
saying,
"Go, swift messengers, to a nation tall and
smooth *of skin,*
To a people terrible from their beginning
onward,
A nation powerful and treading down,
Whose land the rivers divide."

3 All inhabitants of the world and dwellers
on the earth:
When he lifts up a banner on the
mountains, you see *it;*
And when he blows a trumpet, you hear
it.

17:2 [a]Following Masoretic Text and Vulgate; Septuagint reads *It shall be forsaken forever;* Targum reads *Its cities shall be forsaken and desolate.* **17:8** [a]Hebrew *Asherim,* Canaanite deities **17:9** [a]Septuagint reads *Hivites;* Targum reads *laid waste;* Vulgate reads *as the plows.* [b]Septuagint reads *Amorites;* Targum reads *in ruins;* Vulgate reads *corn.*

4 For so the LORD said to me,
"I will take My rest,
And I will look from My dwelling place
Like clear heat in sunshine,
Like a cloud of dew in the heat of harvest."
5 For before the harvest, when the bud is perfect
And the sour grape is ripening in the flower,
He will both cut off the sprigs with pruning hooks
And take away *and* cut down the branches.
6 They will be left together for the mountain birds of prey
And for the beasts of the earth;
The birds of prey will summer on them,
And all the beasts of the earth will winter on them.

7 In that time a present will be brought to the LORD of hosts
From[a] a people tall and smooth *of skin,*
And from a people terrible from their beginning onward,
A nation powerful and treading down,
Whose land the rivers divide—
To the place of the name of the LORD of hosts,
To Mount Zion.

Proclamation Against Egypt

19 The burden against Egypt.

Behold, the LORD rides on a swift cloud,
And will come into Egypt;
The idols of Egypt will totter at His presence,
And the heart of Egypt will melt in its midst.

2 "I will set Egyptians against Egyptians;
Everyone will fight against his brother,
And everyone against his neighbor,
City against city, kingdom against kingdom.
3 The spirit of Egypt will fail in its midst;
I will destroy their counsel,
And they will consult the idols and the charmers,
The mediums and the sorcerers.
4 And the Egyptians I will give
Into the hand of a cruel master,
And a fierce king will rule over them,"
Says the Lord, the LORD of hosts.

5 The waters will fail from the sea,
And the river will be wasted and dried up.
6 The rivers will turn foul;
The brooks of defense will be emptied and dried up;
The reeds and rushes will wither.
7 The papyrus reeds by the River,[a] by the mouth of the River,
And everything sown by the River,
Will wither, be driven away, and be no more.
8 The fishermen also will mourn;
All those will lament who cast hooks into the River,
And they will languish who spread nets on the waters.
9 Moreover those who work in fine flax
And those who weave fine fabric will be ashamed;
10 And its foundations will be broken.
All who make wages *will be* troubled of soul.

11 Surely the princes of Zoan *are* fools;
Pharaoh's wise counselors give foolish counsel.
How do you say to Pharaoh, "I *am* the son of the wise,
The son of ancient kings?"
12 Where *are* they?
Where are your wise men?
Let them tell you now,
And let them know what the LORD of hosts has purposed against Egypt.
13 The princes of Zoan have become fools;
The princes of Noph[a] are deceived;
They have also deluded Egypt,
Those who are the mainstay of its tribes.
14 The LORD has mingled a perverse spirit in her midst;
And they have caused Egypt to err in all her work,
As a drunken man staggers in his vomit.
15 Neither will there be *any* work for Egypt,
Which the head or tail,
Palm branch or bulrush, may do.[a]

16 In that day Egypt will be like women, and
will be afraid and fear because of the waving
of the hand of the LORD of hosts, which He
waves over it.
17 And the land of Judah will be a terror to
Egypt; everyone who makes mention of it will
be afraid in himself, because of the counsel of
the LORD of hosts which He has determined
against it.

Egypt, Assyria, and Israel Blessed

18 In that day five cities in the land of Egypt
will speak the language of Canaan and swear
by the LORD of hosts; one will be called the
City of Destruction.[a]
19 In that day there will be an altar to the
LORD in the midst of the land of Egypt, and a
pillar to the LORD at its border.
20 And it will be for a sign and for a witness
to the LORD of hosts in the land of Egypt; for
they will cry to the LORD because of the op-
pressors, and He will send them a Savior and
a Mighty One, and He will deliver them.
21 Then the LORD will be known to Egypt, and
the Egyptians will know the LORD in that day,
and will make sacrifice and offering; yes, they
will make a vow to the LORD and perform *it.*
22 And the LORD will strike Egypt, He will
strike and heal *it;* they will return to the LORD,
and He will be entreated by them and heal them.
23 In that day there will be a highway from
Egypt to Assyria, and the Assyrian will come
into Egypt and the Egyptian into Assyria, and
the Egyptians will serve with the Assyrians.
24 In that day Israel will be one of three with
Egypt and Assyria—a blessing in the midst of
the land,

18:7 [a]Following Dead Sea Scrolls, Septuagint, and Vulgate; Masoretic Text omits *From;* Targum reads *To.* 19:7 [a]That is, the Nile 19:13 [a]That is, ancient Memphis 19:15 [a]Compare Isaiah 9:14–16 19:18 [a]Some Hebrew manuscripts, Arabic, Dead Sea Scrolls, Targum, and Vulgate read *Sun;* Septuagint reads *Asedek* (literally *Righteousness*).

25 whom the LORD of hosts shall bless, say-
ing, "Blessed *is* Egypt My people, and Assyria
the work of My hands, and Israel My inheri-
tance."

The Sign Against Egypt and Ethiopia

20 In the year that Tartan[a] came to Ashdod,
when Sargon the king of Assyria sent
him, and he fought against Ashdod and took
it,
2 at the same time the LORD spoke by Isaiah
the son of Amoz, saying, "Go, and remove the
sackcloth from your body, and take your san-
dals off your feet." And he did so, walking na-
ked and barefoot.
3 Then the LORD said, "Just as My servant
Isaiah has walked naked and barefoot three
years *for* a sign and a wonder against Egypt
and Ethiopia,
4 "so shall the king of Assyria lead away the
Egyptians as prisoners and the Ethiopians as
captives, young and old, naked and barefoot,
with their buttocks uncovered, to the shame of
Egypt.
5 "Then they shall be afraid and ashamed
of Ethiopia their expectation and Egypt their
glory.
6 "And the inhabitant of this territory will
say in that day, 'Surely such *is* our expectation,
wherever we flee for help to be delivered from
the king of Assyria; and how shall we es-
cape?'"

The Fall of Babylon Proclaimed

21 The burden against the Wilderness of the Sea.

As whirlwinds in the South pass through,
So it comes from the desert, from a terrible land.
2 A distressing vision is declared to me;
The treacherous dealer deals treacherously,
And the plunderer plunders.
Go up, O Elam!
Besiege, O Media!
All its sighing I have made to cease.

3 Therefore my loins are filled with pain;
Pangs have taken hold of me, like the pangs of a woman in labor.
I was distressed when *I* heard *it;*
I was dismayed when *I* saw *it.*
4 My heart wavered, fearfulness frightened me;
The night for which I longed He turned into fear for me.
5 Prepare the table,
Set a watchman in the tower,
Eat and drink.
Arise, you princes,
Anoint the shield!

6 For thus has the Lord said to me:
"Go, set a watchman,
Let him declare what he sees."
7 And he saw a chariot *with* a pair of horsemen,
A chariot of donkeys, *and* a chariot of camels,
And he listened earnestly with great care.
8 Then he cried, "A lion,[a] my Lord!
I stand continually on the watchtower in the daytime;
I have sat at my post every night.
9 And look, here comes a chariot of men *with* a pair of horsemen!"
Then he answered and said,
"Babylon is fallen, is fallen!
And all the carved images of her gods
He has broken to the ground."
10 Oh, my threshing and the grain of my floor!
That which I have heard from the LORD of hosts,
The God of Israel,
I have declared to you.

Proclamation Against Edom

11 The burden against Dumah.

He calls to me out of Seir,
"Watchman, what of the night?
Watchman, what of the night?"
12 The watchman said,
"The morning comes, and also the night.
If you will inquire, inquire;
Return! Come back!"

Proclamation Against Arabia

13 The burden against Arabia.

In the forest in Arabia you will lodge,
O you traveling companies of Dedanites.
14 O inhabitants of the land of Tema,
Bring water to him who is thirsty;
With their bread they met him who fled.
15 For they fled from the swords, from the drawn sword,
From the bent bow, and from the distress of war.

16 For thus the LORD has said to me: "Within
a year, according to the year of a hired man,
all the glory of Kedar will fail;
17 "and the remainder of the number of ar-
chers, the mighty men of the people of Kedar,
will be diminished; for the LORD God of Israel
has spoken *it.*"

Proclamation Against Jerusalem

22 The burden against the Valley of Vision.

What ails you now, that you have all gone up to the housetops,
2 You who are full of noise,
A tumultuous city, a joyous city?
Your slain *men are* not slain with the sword,
Nor dead in battle.
3 All your rulers have fled together;
They are captured by the archers.
All who are found in you are bound together;
They have fled from afar.
4 Therefore I said, "Look away from me,
I will weep bitterly;
Do not labor to comfort me
Because of the plundering of the daughter of my people."

5 For *it is* a day of trouble and treading down and perplexity
By the Lord GOD of hosts
In the Valley of Vision—
Breaking down the walls

20:1 [a]Or *the Commander in Chief* **21:8** [a]Dead Sea Scrolls read *Then the observer cried.*

And of crying to the mountain.
6 Elam bore the quiver
With chariots of men *and* horsemen,
And Kir uncovered the shield.
7 It shall come to pass *that* your choicest valleys
Shall be full of chariots,
And the horsemen shall set themselves in array at the gate.

8 He removed the protection of Judah.
You looked in that day to the armor of the House of the Forest;
9 You also saw the damage to the city of David,
That it was great;
And you gathered together the waters of the lower pool.
10 You numbered the houses of Jerusalem,
And the houses you broke down
To fortify the wall.
11 You also made a reservoir between the two walls
For the water of the old pool.
But you did not look to its Maker,
Nor did you have respect for Him who fashioned it long ago.

12 And in that day the Lord GOD of hosts
Called for weeping and for mourning,
For baldness and for girding with sackcloth.
13 But instead, joy and gladness,
Slaying oxen and killing sheep,
Eating meat and drinking wine:
"Let us eat and drink, for tomorrow we die!"

14 Then it was revealed in my hearing by the LORD of hosts,
"Surely for this iniquity there will be no atonement for you,
Even to your death," says the Lord GOD of hosts.

The Judgment on Shebna

15 Thus says the Lord GOD of hosts:

"Go, proceed to this steward,
To Shebna, who *is* over the house, *and say:*
16 'What have you here, and whom have you here,
That you have hewn a sepulcher here,
As he who hews himself a sepulcher on high,
Who carves a tomb for himself in a rock?
17 Indeed, the LORD will throw you away violently,
O mighty man,
And will surely seize you.
18 He will surely turn violently and toss you like a ball
Into a large country;
There you shall die, and there your glorious chariots
Shall be the shame of your master's house.
19 So I will drive you out of your office,
And from your position he will pull you down.[a]

20 'Then it shall be in that day,
That I will call My servant Eliakim the son of Hilkiah;
21 I will clothe him with your robe
And strengthen him with your belt;
I will commit your responsibility into his hand.
He shall be a father to the inhabitants of Jerusalem
And to the house of Judah.
22 The key of the house of David
I will lay on his shoulder;
So he shall open, and no one shall shut;
And he shall shut, and no one shall open.
23 I will fasten him *as* a peg in a secure place,
And he will become a glorious throne to his father's house.

24 'They will hang on him all the glory of his
father's house, the offspring and the posterity,
all vessels of small quantity, from the cups to
all the pitchers.
25 'In that day,' says the LORD of hosts, 'the
peg that is fastened in the secure place will be
removed and be cut down and fall, and the
burden that *was* on it will be cut off; for the
LORD has spoken.'"

Proclamation Against Tyre

23 The burden against Tyre.

Wail, you ships of Tarshish!
For it is laid waste,
So that there is no house, no harbor;
From the land of Cyprus[a] it is revealed to them.

2 Be still, you inhabitants of the coastland,
You merchants of Sidon,
Whom those who cross the sea have filled.[a]
3 And on great waters the grain of Shihor,
The harvest of the River,[a] *is* her revenue;
And she is a marketplace for the nations.

4 Be ashamed, O Sidon;
For the sea has spoken,
The strength of the sea, saying,
"I do not labor, nor bring forth children;
Neither do I rear young men,
Nor bring up virgins."
5 When the report *reaches* Egypt,
They also will be in agony at the report of Tyre.

6 Cross over to Tarshish;
Wail, you inhabitants of the coastland!
7 *Is* this your joyous *city,*
Whose antiquity *is* from ancient days,
Whose feet carried her far off to dwell?
8 Who has taken this counsel against Tyre, the crowning *city,*
Whose merchants *are* princes,
Whose traders *are* the honorable of the earth?
9 The LORD of hosts has purposed it,
To bring to dishonor the pride of all glory,
To bring into contempt all the honorable of the earth.

10 Overflow through your land like the River,[a]
O daughter of Tarshish;

22:19 [a]Septuagint omits *he will pull you down;* Syriac, Targum, and Vulgate read *I will pull you down.* **23:1** [a]Hebrew *Kittim,* western lands, especially Cyprus **23:2** [a]Following Masoretic Text and Vulgate; Septuagint and Targum read *Passing over the water;* Dead Sea Scrolls read *Your messengers passing over the sea.* **23:3** [a]That is, the Nile **23:10** [a]That is, the Nile

There is no more strength.
11 He stretched out His hand over the sea,
He shook the kingdoms;
The LORD has given a commandment against Canaan
To destroy its strongholds.
12 And He said, "You will rejoice no more,
O you oppressed virgin daughter of Sidon.
Arise, cross over to Cyprus;
There also you will have no rest."

13 Behold, the land of the Chaldeans,
This people *which* was not;
Assyria founded it for wild beasts of the desert.
They set up its towers,
They raised up its palaces,
And brought it to ruin.

14 Wail, you ships of Tarshish!
For your strength is laid waste.

15 Now it shall come to pass in that day that
Tyre will be forgotten seventy years, according
to the days of one king. At the end of seventy
years it will happen to Tyre as *in* the song of
the harlot:

16 "Take a harp, go about the city,
You forgotten harlot;
Make sweet melody, sing many songs,
That you may be remembered."

17 And it shall be, at the end of seventy years,
that the LORD will deal with Tyre. She will return
to her hire, and commit fornication with all the
kingdoms of the world on the face of the earth.
18 Her gain and her pay will be set apart for
the LORD; it will not be treasured nor laid up,
for her gain will be for those who dwell before
the LORD, to eat sufficiently, and for fine
clothing.

Impending Judgment on the Earth

24 Behold, the LORD makes the earth empty and makes it waste,
Distorts its surface
And scatters abroad its inhabitants.
2 And it shall be:
As with the people, so with the priest;
As with the servant, so with his master;
As with the maid, so with her mistress;
As with the buyer, so with the seller;
As with the lender, so with the borrower;
As with the creditor, so with the debtor.
3 The land shall be entirely emptied and utterly plundered,
For the LORD has spoken this word.

4 The earth mourns *and* fades away,
The world languishes *and* fades away;
The haughty people of the earth languish.
5 The earth is also defiled under its inhabitants,
Because they have transgressed the laws,
Changed the ordinance,
Broken the everlasting covenant.
6 Therefore the curse has devoured the earth,
And those who dwell in it are desolate.
Therefore the inhabitants of the earth are burned,
And few men *are* left.

7 The new wine fails, the vine languishes,
All the merry-hearted sigh.
8 The mirth of the tambourine ceases,
The noise of the jubilant ends,
The joy of the harp ceases.
9 They shall not drink wine with a song;
Strong drink is bitter to those who drink it.
10 The city of confusion is broken down;
Every house is shut up, so that none may go in.
11 *There is* a cry for wine in the streets,
All joy is darkened,
The mirth of the land is gone.
12 In the city desolation is left,
And the gate is stricken with destruction.
13 When it shall be thus in the midst of the land among the people,
It shall be like the shaking of an olive tree,
Like the gleaning of grapes when the vintage is done.

14 They shall lift up their voice, they shall sing;
For the majesty of the LORD
They shall cry aloud from the sea.
15 Therefore glorify the LORD in the dawning light,
The name of the LORD God of Israel in the coastlands of the sea.
16 From the ends of the earth we have heard songs:
"Glory to the righteous!"
But I said, "I am ruined, ruined!
Woe to me!
The treacherous dealers have dealt treacherously,
Indeed, the treacherous dealers have dealt very treacherously."

17 Fear and the pit and the snare
Are upon you, O inhabitant of the earth.
18 And it shall be
That he who flees from the noise of the fear
Shall fall into the pit,
And he who comes up from the midst of the pit
Shall be caught in the snare;
For the windows from on high are open,
And the foundations of the earth are shaken.

19 The earth is violently broken,
The earth is split open,
The earth is shaken exceedingly.
20 The earth shall reel to and fro like a drunkard,
And shall totter like a hut;
Its transgression shall be heavy upon it,
And it will fall, and not rise again.

21 It shall come to pass in that day
That the LORD will punish on high the host of exalted ones,
And on the earth the kings of the earth.
22 They will be gathered together,
As prisoners are gathered in the pit,
And will be shut up in the prison;
After many days they will be punished.
23 Then the moon will be disgraced
And the sun ashamed;
For the LORD of hosts will reign
On Mount Zion and in Jerusalem
And before His elders, gloriously.

Praise to God

25 O LORD, You *are* my God.
I will exalt You,
I will praise Your name,
For You have done wonderful *things;*
Your counsels of old *are* faithfulness *and* truth.
2 For You have made a city a ruin,
A fortified city a ruin,
A palace of foreigners to be a city no more;
It will never be rebuilt.
3 Therefore the strong people will glorify You;
The city of the terrible nations will fear You.
4 For You have been a strength to the poor,
A strength to the needy in his distress,
A refuge from the storm,
A shade from the heat;
For the blast of the terrible ones *is* as a storm *against* the wall.
5 You will reduce the noise of aliens,
As heat in a dry place;
As heat in the shadow of a cloud,
The song of the terrible ones will be diminished.

6 And in this mountain
The LORD of hosts will make for all people
A feast of choice pieces,
A feast of wines on the lees,
Of fat things full of marrow,
Of well-refined wines on the lees.
7 And He will destroy on this mountain
The surface of the covering cast over all people,
And the veil that is spread over all nations.
8 He will swallow up death forever,
And the Lord GOD will wipe away tears from all faces;
The rebuke of His people
He will take away from all the earth;
For the LORD has spoken.

9 And it will be said in that day:
"Behold, this *is* our God;
We have waited for Him, and He will save us.
This *is* the LORD;
We have waited for Him;
We will be glad and rejoice in His salvation."

10 For on this mountain the hand of the LORD will rest,
And Moab shall be trampled down under Him,
As straw is trampled down for the refuse heap.
11 And He will spread out His hands in their midst
As a swimmer reaches out to swim,
And He will bring down their pride
Together with the trickery of their hands.
12 The fortress of the high fort of your walls
He will bring down, lay low,
And bring to the ground, down to the dust.

A Song of Salvation

26 In that day this song will be sung in the land of Judah:

"We have a strong city;
God will appoint salvation *for* walls and bulwarks.
2 Open the gates,
That the righteous nation which keeps the truth may enter in.
3 You will keep *him* in perfect peace,
Whose mind *is* stayed *on You,*
Because he trusts in You.
4 Trust in the LORD forever,
For in YAH, the LORD, *is* everlasting strength.[a]
5 For He brings down those who dwell on high,
The lofty city;
He lays it low,
He lays it low to the ground,
He brings it down to the dust.
6 The foot shall tread it down—
The feet of the poor
And the steps of the needy."

7 The way of the just *is* uprightness;
O Most Upright,
You weigh the path of the just.
8 Yes, in the way of Your judgments,
O LORD, we have waited for You;
The desire of *our* soul *is* for Your name
And for the remembrance of You.
9 With my soul I have desired You in the night,
Yes, by my spirit within me I will seek You early;
For when Your judgments *are* in the earth,
The inhabitants of the world will learn righteousness.

10 Let grace be shown to the wicked,
Yet he will not learn righteousness;
In the land of uprightness he will deal unjustly,
And will not behold the majesty of the LORD.
11 LORD, *when* Your hand is lifted up, they will not see.
But they will see and be ashamed
For *their* envy of people;
Yes, the fire of Your enemies shall devour them.
12 LORD, You will establish peace for us,
For You have also done all our works in us.
13 O LORD our God, masters besides You
Have had dominion over us;
But by You only we make mention of Your name.
14 *They are* dead, they will not live;
They are deceased, they will not rise.
Therefore You have punished and destroyed them,
And made all their memory to perish.
15 You have increased the nation, O LORD,
You have increased the nation;
You are glorified;
You have expanded all the borders of the land.

26:4 [a]Or *Rock of Ages*

16 LORD, in trouble they have visited You,
They poured out a prayer *when* Your
chastening *was* upon them.
17 As a woman with child
Is in pain and cries out in her pangs,
When she draws near the time of her
delivery,
So have we been in Your sight, O LORD.
18 We have been with child, we have been in
pain;
We have, as it were, brought forth wind;
We have not accomplished any
deliverance in the earth,
Nor have the inhabitants of the world
fallen.
19 Your dead shall live;
Together with my dead body[a] they shall
arise.
Awake and sing, you who dwell in dust;
For your dew *is like* the dew of herbs,
And the earth shall cast out the dead.

Take Refuge from the Coming Judgment

20 Come, my people, enter your chambers,
And shut your doors behind you;
Hide yourself, as it were, for a little
moment,
Until the indignation is past.
21 For behold, the LORD comes out of His
place
To punish the inhabitants of the earth for
their iniquity;
The earth will also disclose her blood,
And will no more cover her slain.

27 In that day the LORD with His severe
sword, great and strong,
Will punish Leviathan the fleeing serpent,
Leviathan that twisted serpent;
And He will slay the reptile that *is* in the
sea.

The Restoration of Israel

2 In that day sing to her,
"A vineyard of red wine![a]
3 I, the LORD, keep it,
I water it every moment;
Lest any hurt it,
I keep it night and day.
4 Fury *is* not in Me.
Who would set briers *and* thorns
Against Me in battle?
I would go through them,
I would burn them together.
5 Or let him take hold of My strength,
That he may make peace with Me;
And he shall make peace with Me."
6 Those who come He shall cause to take
root in Jacob;
Israel shall blossom and bud,
And fill the face of the world with fruit.

7 Has He struck Israel as He struck those
who struck him?
Or has He been slain according to the
slaughter of those who were slain by
Him?
8 In measure, by sending it away,
You contended with it.
He removes *it* by His rough wind
In the day of the east wind.
9 Therefore by this the iniquity of Jacob
will be covered;
And this *is* all the fruit of taking away his
sin:
When he makes all the stones of the altar
Like chalkstones that are beaten to dust,
Wooden images[a] and incense altars shall
not stand.
10 Yet the fortified city *will be* desolate,
The habitation forsaken and left like a
wilderness;
There the calf will feed, and there it will
lie down
And consume its branches.
11 When its boughs are withered, they will
be broken off;
The women come *and* set them on fire.
For it *is* a people of no understanding;
Therefore He who made them will not
have mercy on them,
And He who formed them will show them
no favor.

12 And it shall come to pass in that day
That the LORD will thresh,
From the channel of the River[a] to the
Brook of Egypt;
And you will be gathered one by one,
O you children of Israel.
13 So it shall be in that day:
The great trumpet will be blown;
They will come, who are about to perish
in the land of Assyria,
And they who are outcasts in the land of
Egypt,
And shall worship the LORD in the holy
mount at Jerusalem.

Woe to Ephraim and Jerusalem

28 Woe to the crown of pride, to the
drunkards of Ephraim,
Whose glorious beauty *is* a fading flower
Which *is* at the head of the verdant
valleys,
To those who are overcome with wine!
2 Behold, the Lord has a mighty and strong
one,
Like a tempest of hail and a destroying
storm,
Like a flood of mighty waters
overflowing,
Who will bring *them* down to the earth
with *His* hand.
3 The crown of pride, the drunkards of
Ephraim,
Will be trampled underfoot;
4 And the glorious beauty is a fading
flower
Which *is* at the head of the verdant
valley,
Like the first fruit before the summer,
Which an observer sees;
He eats it up while it is still in his hand.
5 In that day the LORD of hosts will be
For a crown of glory and a diadem of
beauty
To the remnant of His people,

26:19 [a]Following Masoretic Text and Vulgate; Syriac and Targum read *their dead bodies;* Septuagint reads *those in the tombs.* **27:2** [a]Following Masoretic Text (Kittel's *Biblia Hebraica*), Bomberg, and Vulgate; Masoretic Text (*Biblia Hebraica Stuttgartensia*), some Hebrew manuscripts, and Septuagint read *delight;* Targum reads *choice vineyard.* **27:9** [a]Hebrew *Asherim,* Canaanite deities **27:12** [a]That is, the Euphrates

6 For a spirit of justice to him who sits in judgment,
And for strength to those who turn back the battle at the gate.

7 But they also have erred through wine,
And through intoxicating drink are out of the way;
The priest and the prophet have erred through intoxicating drink,
They are swallowed up by wine,
They are out of the way through intoxicating drink;
They err in vision, they stumble *in* judgment.
8 For all tables are full of vomit *and* filth;
No place *is clean.*

9 "Whom will he teach knowledge?
And whom will he make to understand the message?
Those *just* weaned from milk?
Those *just* drawn from the breasts?
10 For precept *must be* upon precept, precept upon precept,
Line upon line, line upon line,
Here a little, there a little."

11 For with stammering lips and another tongue
He will speak to this people,
12 To whom He said, "This *is* the rest *with which*
You may cause the weary to rest,"
And, "This *is* the refreshing";
Yet they would not hear.
13 But the word of the LORD was to them,
"Precept upon precept, precept upon precept,
Line upon line, line upon line,
Here a little, there a little,"
That they might go and fall backward, and be broken
And snared and caught.

14 Therefore hear the word of the LORD, you scornful men,
Who rule this people who *are* in Jerusalem,
15 Because you have said, "We have made a covenant with death,
And with Sheol we are in agreement.
When the overflowing scourge passes through,
It will not come to us,
For we have made lies our refuge,
And under falsehood we have hidden ourselves."

A Cornerstone in Zion

16 Therefore thus says the Lord GOD:

"Behold, I lay in Zion a stone for a foundation,
A tried stone, a precious cornerstone, a sure foundation;
Whoever believes will not act hastily.
17 Also I will make justice the measuring line,
And righteousness the plummet;
The hail will sweep away the refuge of lies,
And the waters will overflow the hiding place.
18 Your covenant with death will be annulled,
And your agreement with Sheol will not stand;
When the overflowing scourge passes through,
Then you will be trampled down by it.
19 As often as it goes out it will take you;
For morning by morning it will pass over,
And by day and by night;
It will be a terror just to understand the report."

20 For the bed is too short to stretch out *on,*
And the covering so narrow that one cannot wrap himself *in it.*
21 For the LORD will rise up as *at* Mount Perazim,
He will be angry as in the Valley of Gibeon—
That He may do His work, His awesome work,
And bring to pass His act, His unusual act.
22 Now therefore, do not be mockers,
Lest your bonds be made strong;
For I have heard from the Lord GOD of hosts,
A destruction determined even upon the whole earth.

Listen to the Teaching of God

23 Give ear and hear my voice,
Listen and hear my speech.
24 Does the plowman keep plowing all day to sow?
Does he keep turning his soil and breaking the clods?
25 When he has leveled its surface,
Does he not sow the black cummin
And scatter the cummin,
Plant the wheat in rows,
The barley in the appointed place,
And the spelt in its place?
26 For He instructs him in right judgment,
His God teaches him.

27 For the black cummin is not threshed with a threshing sledge,
Nor is a cartwheel rolled over the cummin;
But the black cummin is beaten out with a stick,
And the cummin with a rod.
28 Bread *flour* must be ground;
Therefore he does not thresh it forever,
Break *it with* his cartwheel,
Or crush it *with* his horsemen.
29 This also comes from the LORD of hosts,
Who is wonderful in counsel *and* excellent in guidance.

Woe to Jerusalem

29 "Woe to Ariel,[a] to Ariel, the city *where* David dwelt!
Add year to year;
Let feasts come around.
2 Yet I will distress Ariel;
There shall be heaviness and sorrow,
And it shall be to Me as Ariel.
3 I will encamp against you all around,
I will lay siege against you with a mound,
And I will raise siegeworks against you.

29:1 [a]That is, Jerusalem

4 You shall be brought down,
You shall speak out of the ground;
Your speech shall be low, out of the dust;
Your voice shall be like a medium's, out of the ground;
And your speech shall whisper out of the dust.

5 "Moreover the multitude of your foes
Shall be like fine dust,
And the multitude of the terrible ones
Like chaff that passes away;
Yes, it shall be in an instant, suddenly.
6 You will be punished by the LORD of hosts
With thunder and earthquake and great noise,
With storm and tempest
And the flame of devouring fire.
7 The multitude of all the nations who fight against Ariel,
Even all who fight against her and her fortress,
And distress her,
Shall be as a dream of a night vision.
8 It shall even be as when a hungry man dreams,
And look—he eats;
But he awakes, and his soul is still empty;
Or as when a thirsty man dreams,
And look—he drinks;
But he awakes, and indeed *he is* faint,
And his soul still craves:
So the multitude of all the nations shall be,
Who fight against Mount Zion."

The Blindness of Disobedience

9 Pause and wonder!
Blind yourselves and be blind!
They are drunk, but not with wine;
They stagger, but not with intoxicating drink.
10 For the LORD has poured out on you
The spirit of deep sleep,
And has closed your eyes, namely, the prophets;
And He has covered your heads, *namely,* the seers.

11 The whole vision has become to you like
the words of a book that is sealed, which *men*
deliver to one who is literate, saying, "Read
this, please." And he says, "I cannot, for it *is*
sealed."
12 Then the book is delivered to one who is
illiterate, saying, "Read this, please." And he
says, "I am not literate."
13 Therefore the Lord said:

"Inasmuch as these people draw near with their mouths
And honor Me with their lips,
But have removed their hearts far from Me,
And their fear toward Me is taught by the commandment of men,
14 Therefore, behold, I will again do a marvelous work
Among this people,
A marvelous work and a wonder;
For the wisdom of their wise *men* shall perish,
And the understanding of their prudent *men* shall be hidden."

15 Woe to those who seek deep to hide their counsel far from the LORD,
And their works are in the dark;
They say, "Who sees us?" and, "Who knows us?"
16 Surely you have things turned around!
Shall the potter be esteemed as the clay;
For shall the thing made say of him who made it,
"He did not make me"?
Or shall the thing formed say of him who formed it,
"He has no understanding"?

Future Recovery of Wisdom

17 *Is* it not yet a very little while
Till Lebanon shall be turned into a fruitful field,
And the fruitful field be esteemed as a forest?
18 In that day the deaf shall hear the words of the book,
And the eyes of the blind shall see out of obscurity and out of darkness.
19 The humble also shall increase *their* joy in the LORD,
And the poor among men shall rejoice
In the Holy One of Israel.
20 For the terrible one is brought to nothing,
The scornful one is consumed,
And all who watch for iniquity are cut off—
21 Who make a man an offender by a word,
And lay a snare for him who reproves in the gate,
And turn aside the just by empty words.

22 Therefore thus says the LORD, who re-
deemed Abraham, concerning the house of
Jacob:

"Jacob shall not now be ashamed,
Nor shall his face now grow pale;
23 But when he sees his children,
The work of My hands, in his midst,
They will hallow My name,
And hallow the Holy One of Jacob,
And fear the God of Israel.
24 These also who erred in spirit will come to understanding,
And those who complained will learn doctrine."

Futile Confidence in Egypt

30 "Woe to the rebellious children," says the LORD,
"Who take counsel, but not of Me,
And who devise plans, but not of My Spirit,
That they may add sin to sin;
2 Who walk to go down to Egypt,
And have not asked My advice,
To strengthen themselves in the strength of Pharaoh,
And to trust in the shadow of Egypt!
3 Therefore the strength of Pharaoh
Shall be your shame,
And trust in the shadow of Egypt
Shall be *your* humiliation.
4 For his princes were at Zoan,
And his ambassadors came to Hanes.
5 They were all ashamed of a people *who* could not benefit them,
Or be help or benefit,
But a shame and also a reproach."

6 The burden against the beasts of the South.

Through a land of trouble and anguish,
From which *came* the lioness and lion,
The viper and fiery flying serpent,
They will carry their riches on the backs
of young donkeys,
And their treasures on the humps of
camels,
To a people *who* shall not profit;
7 For the Egyptians shall help in vain and
to no purpose.
Therefore I have called her
Rahab-Hem-Shebeth.[a]

A Rebellious People

8 Now go, write it before them on a tablet,
And note it on a scroll,
That it may be for time to come,
Forever and ever:
9 That this *is* a rebellious people,
Lying children,
Children *who* will not hear the law of the
LORD;
10 Who say to the seers, "Do not see,"
And to the prophets, "Do not prophesy to
us right things;
Speak to us smooth things, prophesy
deceits.
11 Get out of the way,
Turn aside from the path,
Cause the Holy One of Israel
To cease from before us."

12 Therefore thus says the Holy One of Israel:

"Because you despise this word,
And trust in oppression and perversity,
And rely on them,
13 Therefore this iniquity shall be to you
Like a breach ready to fall,
A bulge in a high wall,
Whose breaking comes suddenly, in an
instant.
14 And He shall break it like the breaking of
the potter's vessel,
Which is broken in pieces;
He shall not spare.
So there shall not be found among its
fragments
A shard to take fire from the hearth,
Or to take water from the cistern."

15 For thus says the Lord GOD, the Holy One
of Israel:

"In returning and rest you shall be saved;
In quietness and confidence shall be your
strength."
But you would not,
16 And you said, "No, for we will flee on
horses"—
Therefore you shall flee!
And, "We will ride on swift *horses*"—
Therefore those who pursue you shall be
swift!

17 One thousand *shall flee* at the threat of
one,
At the threat of five you shall flee,
Till you are left as a pole on top of a
mountain
And as a banner on a hill.

God Will Be Gracious

18 Therefore the LORD will wait, that He
may be gracious to you;
And therefore He will be exalted, that He
may have mercy on you.
For the LORD *is* a God of justice;
Blessed *are* all those who wait for Him.

19 For the people shall dwell in Zion at
Jerusalem;
You shall weep no more.
He will be very gracious to you at the
sound of your cry;
When He hears it, He will answer you.
20 And *though* the Lord gives you
The bread of adversity and the water of
affliction,
Yet your teachers will not be moved into
a corner anymore,
But your eyes shall see your teachers.
21 Your ears shall hear a word behind you,
saying,
"This *is* the way, walk in it,"
Whenever you turn to the right hand
Or whenever you turn to the left.
22 You will also defile the covering of your
images of silver,
And the ornament of your molded images
of gold.
You will throw them away as an unclean
thing;
You will say to them, "Get away!"

23 Then He will give the rain for your seed
With which you sow the ground,
And bread of the increase of the earth;
It will be fat and plentiful.
In that day your cattle will feed
In large pastures.
24 Likewise the oxen and the young
donkeys that work the ground
Will eat cured fodder,
Which has been winnowed with the
shovel and fan.
25 There will be on every high mountain
And on every high hill
Rivers *and* streams of waters,
In the day of the great slaughter,
When the towers fall.
26 Moreover the light of the moon will be as
the light of the sun,
And the light of the sun will be sevenfold,
As the light of seven days,
In the day that the LORD binds up the
bruise of His people
And heals the stroke of their wound.

Judgment on Assyria

27 Behold, the name of the LORD comes
from afar,
Burning *with* His anger,
And *His* burden *is* heavy;
His lips are full of indignation,
And His tongue like a devouring fire.
28 His breath is like an overflowing stream,
Which reaches up to the neck,
To sift the nations with the sieve of
futility;
And *there shall be* a bridle in the jaws of
the people,
Causing *them* to err.

29 You shall have a song
As in the night *when* a holy festival is kept,

30:7 [a]Literally *Rahab Sits Idle*

And gladness of heart as when one goes with a flute,
To come into the mountain of the LORD,
To the Mighty One of Israel.
30 The LORD will cause His glorious voice to be heard,
And show the descent of His arm,
With the indignation of *His* anger
And the flame of a devouring fire,
With scattering, tempest, and hailstones.
31 For through the voice of the LORD
Assyria will be beaten down,
As He strikes with the rod.
32 And *in* every place where the staff of punishment passes,
Which the LORD lays on him,
It will be with tambourines and harps;
And in battles of brandishing He will fight with it.
33 For Tophet *was* established of old,
Yes, for the king it is prepared.
He has made *it* deep and large;
Its pyre *is* fire with much wood;
The breath of the LORD, like a stream of brimstone,
Kindles it.

The Folly of Not Trusting God

31 Woe to those who go down to Egypt for help,
And rely on horses,
Who trust in chariots because *they are* many,
And in horsemen because they are very strong,
But who do not look to the Holy One of Israel,
Nor seek the LORD!
2 Yet He also *is* wise and will bring disaster,
And will not call back His words,
But will arise against the house of evildoers,
And against the help of those who work iniquity.
3 Now the Egyptians *are* men, and not God;
And their horses are flesh, and not spirit.
When the LORD stretches out His hand,
Both he who helps will fall,
And he who is helped will fall down;
They all will perish together.

God Will Deliver Jerusalem

4 For thus the LORD has spoken to me:
"As a lion roars,
And a young lion over his prey
(When a multitude of shepherds is summoned against him,
He will not be afraid of their voice
Nor be disturbed by their noise),
So the LORD of hosts will come down
To fight for Mount Zion and for its hill.
5 Like birds flying about,
So will the LORD of hosts defend Jerusalem.
Defending, He will also deliver *it;*
Passing over, He will preserve *it.*"

6 Return *to Him* against whom the children
of Israel have deeply revolted.
7 For in that day every man shall throw away
his idols of silver and his idols of gold—sin,
which your own hands have made for yourselves.

8 "Then Assyria shall fall by a sword not of man,
And a sword not of mankind shall devour him.
But he shall flee from the sword,
And his young men shall become forced labor.
9 He shall cross over to his stronghold for fear,
And his princes shall be afraid of the banner,"
Says the LORD,
Whose fire *is* in Zion
And whose furnace *is* in Jerusalem.

A Reign of Righteousness

32 Behold, a king will reign in righteousness,
And princes will rule with justice.
2 A man will be as a hiding place from the wind,
And a cover from the tempest,
As rivers of water in a dry place,
As the shadow of a great rock in a weary land.
3 The eyes of those who see will not be dim,
And the ears of those who hear will listen.
4 Also the heart of the rash will understand knowledge,
And the tongue of the stammerers will be ready to speak plainly.

5 The foolish person will no longer be called generous,
Nor the miser said *to be* bountiful;
6 For the foolish person will speak foolishness,
And his heart will work iniquity:
To practice ungodliness,
To utter error against the LORD,
To keep the hungry unsatisfied,
And he will cause the drink of the thirsty to fail.
7 Also the schemes of the schemer *are* evil;
He devises wicked plans
To destroy the poor with lying words,
Even when the needy speaks justice.
8 But a generous man devises generous things,
And by generosity he shall stand.

Consequences of Complacency

9 Rise up, you women who are at ease,
Hear my voice;
You complacent daughters,
Give ear to my speech.
10 In a year and *some* days
You will be troubled, you complacent women;
For the vintage will fail,
The gathering will not come.
11 Tremble, you *women* who are at ease;
Be troubled, you complacent ones;
Strip yourselves, make yourselves bare,
And gird *sackcloth* on *your* waists.

12 People shall mourn upon their breasts
For the pleasant fields, for the fruitful vine.
13 On the land of my people will come up thorns *and* briers,
Yes, on all the happy homes *in* the joyous city;

14 Because the palaces will be forsaken,
The bustling city will be deserted.
The forts and towers will become lairs forever,
A joy of wild donkeys, a pasture of flocks—
15 Until the Spirit is poured upon us from on high,
And the wilderness becomes a fruitful field,
And the fruitful field is counted as a forest.

The Peace of God's Reign

16 Then justice will dwell in the wilderness,
And righteousness remain in the fruitful field.
17 The work of righteousness will be peace,
And the effect of righteousness, quietness and assurance forever.
18 My people will dwell in a peaceful habitation,
In secure dwellings, and in quiet resting places,
19 Though hail comes down on the forest,
And the city is brought low in humiliation.
20 Blessed *are* you who sow beside all waters,
Who send out freely the feet of the ox and the donkey.

A Prayer in Deep Distress

33 Woe to you who plunder, though you *have* not *been* plundered;
And you who deal treacherously, though they have not dealt treacherously with you!
When you cease plundering,
You will be plundered;
When you make an end of dealing treacherously,
They will deal treacherously with you.

2 O LORD, be gracious to us;
We have waited for You.
Be their[a] arm every morning,
Our salvation also in the time of trouble.
3 At the noise of the tumult the people shall flee;
When You lift Yourself up, the nations shall be scattered;
4 And Your plunder shall be gathered
Like the gathering of the caterpillar;
As the running to and fro of locusts,
He shall run upon them.

5 The LORD is exalted, for He dwells on high;
He has filled Zion with justice and righteousness.
6 Wisdom and knowledge will be the stability of your times,
And the strength of salvation;
The fear of the LORD *is* His treasure.

7 Surely their valiant ones shall cry outside,
The ambassadors of peace shall weep bitterly.
8 The highways lie waste,
The traveling man ceases.
He has broken the covenant,
He has despised the cities,[a]
He regards no man.
9 The earth mourns *and* languishes,
Lebanon is shamed *and* shriveled;
Sharon is like a wilderness,
And Bashan and Carmel shake off *their fruits.*

Impending Judgment on Zion

10 "Now I will rise," says the LORD;
"Now I will be exalted,
Now I will lift Myself up.
11 You shall conceive chaff,
You shall bring forth stubble;
Your breath, *as* fire, shall devour you.
12 And the people shall be *like* the burnings of lime;
Like thorns cut up they shall be burned in the fire.
13 Hear, you *who are* afar off, what I have done;
And you *who are* near, acknowledge My might."

14 The sinners in Zion are afraid;
Fearfulness has seized the hypocrites:
"Who among us shall dwell with the devouring fire?
Who among us shall dwell with everlasting burnings?"
15 He who walks righteously and speaks uprightly,
He who despises the gain of oppressions,
Who gestures with his hands, refusing bribes,
Who stops his ears from hearing of bloodshed,
And shuts his eyes from seeing evil:
16 He will dwell on high;
His place of defense *will be* the fortress of rocks;
Bread will be given him,
His water *will be* sure.

The Land of the Majestic King

17 Your eyes will see the King in His beauty;
They will see the land that is very far off.
18 Your heart will meditate on terror:
"Where *is* the scribe?
Where *is* he who weighs?
Where *is* he who counts the towers?"
19 You will not see a fierce people,
A people of obscure speech, beyond perception,
Of a stammering tongue *that you* cannot understand.

20 Look upon Zion, the city of our appointed feasts;
Your eyes will see Jerusalem, a quiet home,
A tabernacle *that* will not be taken down;
Not one of its stakes will ever be removed,
Nor will any of its cords be broken.
21 But there the majestic LORD *will be* for us
A place of broad rivers *and* streams,
In which no galley with oars will sail,
Nor majestic ships pass by
22 (For the LORD *is* our Judge,
The LORD *is* our Lawgiver,
The LORD *is* our King;

33:2 [a]Septuagint omits *their;* Syriac, Targum, and Vulgate read *our.* **33:8** [a]Following Masoretic Text and Vulgate; Dead Sea Scrolls read *witnesses;* Septuagint omits *cities;* Targum reads *They have been removed from their cities.*

He will save us);
23 Your tackle is loosed,
They could not strengthen their mast,
They could not spread the sail.

Then the prey of great plunder is divided;
The lame take the prey.
24 And the inhabitant will not say, "I am sick";
The people who dwell in it *will be* forgiven *their* iniquity.

Judgment on the Nations

34 Come near, you nations, to hear;
And heed, you people!
Let the earth hear, and all that is in it,
The world and all things that come forth from it.
2 For the indignation of the LORD *is* against all nations,
And *His* fury against all their armies;
He has utterly destroyed them,
He has given them over to the slaughter.
3 Also their slain shall be thrown out;
Their stench shall rise from their corpses,
And the mountains shall be melted with their blood.
4 All the host of heaven shall be dissolved,
And the heavens shall be rolled up like a scroll;
All their host shall fall down
As the leaf falls from the vine,
And as *fruit* falling from a fig tree.

5 "For My sword shall be bathed in heaven;
Indeed it shall come down on Edom,
And on the people of My curse, for judgment.
6 The sword of the LORD is filled with blood,
It is made overflowing with fatness,
With the blood of lambs and goats,
With the fat of the kidneys of rams.
For the LORD has a sacrifice in Bozrah,
And a great slaughter in the land of Edom.
7 The wild oxen shall come down with them,
And the young bulls with the mighty bulls;
Their land shall be soaked with blood,
And their dust saturated with fatness."

8 For *it is* the day of the LORD's vengeance,
The year of recompense for the cause of Zion.
9 Its streams shall be turned into pitch,
And its dust into brimstone;
Its land shall become burning pitch.
10 It shall not be quenched night or day;
Its smoke shall ascend forever.
From generation to generation it shall lie waste;
No one shall pass through it forever and ever.
11 But the pelican and the porcupine shall possess it,
Also the owl and the raven shall dwell in it.
And He shall stretch out over it
The line of confusion and the stones of emptiness.
12 They shall call its nobles to the kingdom,
But none *shall be* there, and all its princes shall be nothing.
13 And thorns shall come up in its palaces,
Nettles and brambles in its fortresses;
It shall be a habitation of jackals,
A courtyard for ostriches.
14 The wild beasts of the desert shall also meet with the jackals,
And the wild goat shall bleat to its companion;
Also the night creature shall rest there,
And find for herself a place of rest.
15 There the arrow snake shall make her nest and lay *eggs*
And hatch, and gather *them* under her shadow;
There also shall the hawks be gathered,
Every one with her mate.

16 "Search from the book of the LORD, and read:
Not one of these shall fail;
Not one shall lack her mate.
For My mouth has commanded it, and
His Spirit has gathered them.
17 He has cast the lot for them,
And His hand has divided it among them with a measuring line.
They shall possess it forever;
From generation to generation they shall dwell in it."

The Future Glory of Zion

35 The wilderness and the wasteland shall be glad for them,
And the desert shall rejoice and blossom as the rose;
2 It shall blossom abundantly and rejoice,
Even with joy and singing.
The glory of Lebanon shall be given to it,
The excellence of Carmel and Sharon.
They shall see the glory of the LORD,
The excellency of our God.

3 Strengthen the weak hands,
And make firm the feeble knees.
4 Say to those *who are* fearful-hearted,
"Be strong, do not fear!
Behold, your God will come *with* vengeance,
With the recompense of God;
He will come and save you."

5 Then the eyes of the blind shall be opened,
And the ears of the deaf shall be unstopped.
6 Then the lame shall leap like a deer,
And the tongue of the dumb sing.
For waters shall burst forth in the wilderness,
And streams in the desert.
7 The parched ground shall become a pool,
And the thirsty land springs of water;
In the habitation of jackals, where each lay,
There shall be grass with reeds and rushes.

8 A highway shall be there, and a road,
And it shall be called the Highway of Holiness.
The unclean shall not pass over it,
But it *shall be* for others.
Whoever walks the road, although a fool,
Shall not go astray.
9 No lion shall be there,
Nor shall *any* ravenous beast go up on it;

It shall not be found there.
But the redeemed shall walk *there,*
10 And the ransomed of the LORD shall
return,
And come to Zion with singing,
With everlasting joy on their heads.
They shall obtain joy and gladness,
And sorrow and sighing shall flee away.

Sennacherib Boasts Against the LORD

36 Now it came to pass in the fourteenth
year of King Hezekiah *that* Sennach-
erib king of Assyria came up against all the
fortified cities of Judah and took them.
2 Then the king of Assyria sent *the* Rabsha-
keh[a] with a great army from Lachish to King
Hezekiah at Jerusalem. And he stood by the
aqueduct from the upper pool, on the highway
to the Fuller's Field.
3 And Eliakim the son of Hilkiah, who was
over the household, Shebna the scribe, and
Joah the son of Asaph, the recorder, came out
to him.
4 Then *the* Rabshakeh said to them, "Say
now to Hezekiah, 'Thus says the great king,
the king of Assyria: "What confidence is this
in which you trust?
5 "I say you speak of having plans and
power for war; but *they are* mere words. Now
in whom do you trust, that you rebel against me?
6 "Look! You are trusting in the staff of this
broken reed, Egypt, on which if a man leans,
it will go into his hand and pierce it. So *is*
Pharaoh king of Egypt to all who trust in him.
7 "But if you say to me, 'We trust in the LORD
our God,' *is it* not He whose high places and
whose altars Hezekiah has taken away, and
said to Judah and Jerusalem, 'You shall wor-
ship before this altar'?"'
8 "Now therefore, I urge you, give a pledge
to my master the king of Assyria, and I will
give you two thousand horses—if you are able
on your part to put riders on them!
9 "How then will you repel one captain of
the least of my master's servants, and put your
trust in Egypt for chariots and horsemen?
10 "Have I now come up without the LORD
against this land to destroy it? The LORD said
to me, 'Go up against this land, and destroy it.'"
11 Then Eliakim, Shebna, and Joah said to
the Rabshakeh, "Please speak to your servants
in Aramaic, for we understand *it;* and do not
speak to us in Hebrew[a] in the hearing of the
people who *are* on the wall."
12 But *the* Rabshakeh said, "Has my master
sent me to your master and to you to speak
these words, and not to the men who sit on the
wall, who will eat and drink their own waste
with you?"
13 Then *the* Rabshakeh stood and called out
with a loud voice in Hebrew, and said, "Hear
the words of the great king, the king of Assyria!
14 "Thus says the king: 'Do not let Hezekiah
deceive you, for he will not be able to deliver
you;
15 'nor let Hezekiah make you trust in the
LORD, saying, "The LORD will surely deliver
us; this city will not be given into the hand of
the king of Assyria."'
16 "Do not listen to Hezekiah; for thus says
the king of Assyria: 'Make *peace* with me *by a*
present and come out to me; and every one of
you eat from his own vine and every one from
his own fig tree, and every one of you drink
the waters of his own cistern;
17 'until I come and take you away to a land
like your own land, a land of grain and new wine,
a land of bread and vineyards.
18 '*Beware* lest Hezekiah persuade you, say-
ing, "The LORD will deliver us." Has any one
of the gods of the nations delivered its land
from the hand of the king of Assyria?
19 'Where *are* the gods of Hamath and Ar-
pad? Where *are* the gods of Sepharvaim? In-
deed, have they delivered Samaria from my
hand?
20 'Who among all the gods of these lands
have delivered their countries from my hand,
that the LORD should deliver Jerusalem from
my hand?'"
21 But they held their peace and answered
him not a word; for the king's commandment
was, "Do not answer him."
22 Then Eliakim the son of Hilkiah, who *was*
over the household, Shebna the scribe, and
Joah the son of Asaph, the recorder, came to
Hezekiah with *their* clothes torn, and told him
the words of *the* Rabshakeh.

Isaiah Assures Deliverance

37 And so it was, when King Hezekiah
heard *it,* that he tore his clothes, covered
himself with sackcloth, and went into the
house of the LORD.
2 Then he sent Eliakim, who *was* over the
household, Shebna the scribe, and the elders
of the priests, covered with sackcloth, to Isaiah
the prophet, the son of Amoz.
3 And they said to him, "Thus says Heze-
kiah: 'This day *is* a day of trouble and rebuke
and blasphemy; for the children have come to
birth, but *there is* no strength to bring them
forth.
4 'It may be that the LORD your God will hear
the words of *the* Rabshakeh, whom his master
the king of Assyria has sent to reproach the
living God, and will rebuke the words which
the LORD your God has heard. Therefore lift
up *your* prayer for the remnant that is left.'"
5 So the servants of King Hezekiah came to
Isaiah.
6 And Isaiah said to them, "Thus you shall
say to your master, 'Thus says the LORD: "Do
not be afraid of the words which you have
heard, with which the servants of the king of
Assyria have blasphemed Me.
7 "Surely I will send a spirit upon him, and
he shall hear a rumor and return to his own
land; and I will cause him to fall by the sword
in his own land."'"

Sennacherib's Threat and Hezekiah's Prayer

8 Then *the* Rabshakeh returned, and found
the king of Assyria warring against Libnah, for
he heard that he had departed from Lachish.
9 And the king heard concerning Tirhakah
king of Ethiopia, "He has come out to make
war with you." So when he heard *it,* he sent
messengers to Hezekiah, saying,
10 "Thus you shall speak to Hezekiah king of
Judah, saying: 'Do not let your God in whom
you trust deceive you, saying, "Jerusalem shall
not be given into the hand of the king of As-
syria."
11 'Look! You have heard what the kings of

36:2 [a]A title, probably *Chief of Staff* or *Governor* **36:11** [a]Literally *Judean*

Assyria have done to all lands by utterly destroying them; and shall you be delivered?
12 'Have the gods of the nations delivered
those whom my fathers have destroyed, Gozan
and Haran and Rezeph, and the people of Eden
who *were* in Telassar?
13 'Where *is* the king of Hamath, the king of
Arpad, and the king of the city of Sepharvaim,
Hena, and Ivah?'"
14 And Hezekiah received the letter from the
hand of the messengers, and read it; and Hezekiah went up to the house of the LORD, and
spread it before the LORD.
15 Then Hezekiah prayed to the LORD,
saying:
16 "O LORD of hosts, God of Israel, *the One*
who dwells *between* the cherubim, You *are*
God, You alone, of all the kingdoms of the
earth. You have made heaven and earth.
17 "Incline Your ear, O LORD, and hear; open
Your eyes, O LORD, and see; and hear all the
words of Sennacherib, which he has sent to
reproach the living God.
18 "Truly, LORD, the kings of Assyria have
laid waste all the nations and their lands,
19 "and have cast their gods into the fire; for
they *were* not gods, but the work of men's
hands—wood and stone. Therefore they destroyed them.
20 "Now therefore, O LORD our God, save us
from his hand, that all the kingdoms of the
earth may know that You *are* the LORD, You
alone."

The Word of the LORD Concerning Sennacherib

21 Then Isaiah the son of Amoz sent to Hezekiah, saying, "Thus says the LORD God of Israel, 'Because you have prayed to Me against
Sennacherib king of Assyria,
22 'this *is* the word which the LORD has spoken concerning him:

"The virgin, the daughter of Zion,
Has despised you, laughed you to scorn;
The daughter of Jerusalem
Has shaken *her* head behind your back!

23 "Whom have you reproached and blasphemed?
Against whom have you raised *your* voice,
And lifted up your eyes on high?
Against the Holy One of Israel.
24 By your servants you have reproached the Lord,
And said, 'By the multitude of my chariots
I have come up to the height of the mountains,
To the limits of Lebanon;
I will cut down its tall cedars
And its choice cypress trees;
I will enter its farthest height,
To its fruitful forest.
25 I have dug and drunk water,
And with the soles of my feet I have dried up
All the brooks of defense.'

26 "Did you not hear long ago
How I made it,
From ancient times that I formed it?
Now I have brought it to pass,
That you should be
For crushing fortified cities *into* heaps of ruins.
27 Therefore their inhabitants *had* little power;
They were dismayed and confounded;
They were *as* the grass of the field
And the green herb,
As the grass on the housetops
And *grain* blighted before it is grown.

28 "But I know your dwelling place,
Your going out and your coming in,
And your rage against Me.
29 Because your rage against Me and your tumult
Have come up to My ears,
Therefore I will put My hook in your nose
And My bridle in your lips,
And I will turn you back
By the way which you came."'

30 "This *shall be* a sign to you:

You shall eat this year such as grows of itself,
And the second year what springs from the same;
Also in the third year sow and reap,
Plant vineyards and eat the fruit of them.
31 And the remnant who have escaped of the house of Judah
Shall again take root downward,
And bear fruit upward.
32 For out of Jerusalem shall go a remnant,
And those who escape from Mount Zion.
The zeal of the LORD of hosts will do this.

33 "Therefore thus says the LORD concerning
the king of Assyria:

'He shall not come into this city,
Nor shoot an arrow there,
Nor come before it with shield,
Nor build a siege mound against it.
34 By the way that he came,
By the same shall he return;
And he shall not come into this city,'
Says the LORD.
35 'For I will defend this city, to save it
For My own sake and for My servant David's sake.'"

Sennacherib's Defeat and Death

36 Then the angel[a] of the LORD went out, and
killed in the camp of the Assyrians one hundred and eighty-five thousand; and when *people* arose early in the morning, there were the
corpses—all dead.
37 So Sennacherib king of Assyria departed
and went away, returned *home*, and remained
at Nineveh.
38 Now it came to pass, as he was worshiping
in the house of Nisroch his god, that his sons
Adrammelech and Sharezer struck him down
with the sword; and they escaped into the land
of Ararat. Then Esarhaddon his son reigned in
his place.

Hezekiah's Life Extended

38 In those days Hezekiah was sick and
near death. And Isaiah the prophet, the
son of Amoz, went to him and said to him,
"Thus says the LORD: 'Set your house in order,
for you shall die and not live.'"

37:36 [a]Or *Angel*

2 Then Hezekiah turned his face toward the
wall, and prayed to the LORD,
3 and said, "Remember now, O LORD, I pray,
how I have walked before You in truth and
with a loyal heart, and have done *what is* good
in Your sight." And Hezekiah wept bitterly.
4 And the word of the LORD came to Isaiah,
saying,
5 "Go and tell Hezekiah, 'Thus says the
LORD, the God of David your father: "I have
heard your prayer, I have seen your tears;
surely I will add to your days fifteen years.
6 "I will deliver you and this city from the
hand of the king of Assyria, and I will defend
this city."'
7 "And this *is* the sign to you from the LORD,
that the LORD will do this thing which He has
spoken:
8 "Behold, I will bring the shadow on the
sundial, which has gone down with the sun on
the sundial of Ahaz, ten degrees backward."
So the sun returned ten degrees on the dial by
which it had gone down.
9 This is the writing of Hezekiah king of Ju-
dah, when he had been sick and had recovered
from his sickness:

10 I said,
"In the prime of my life
I shall go to the gates of Sheol;
I am deprived of the remainder of my
years."
11 I said,
"I shall not see YAH,
The LORD[a] in the land of the living;
I shall observe man no more among the
inhabitants of the world.[b]
12 My life span is gone,
Taken from me like a shepherd's tent;
I have cut off my life like a weaver.
He cuts me off from the loom;
From day until night You make an end of
me.
13 I have considered until morning—
Like a lion,
So He breaks all my bones;
From day until night You make an end of
me.
14 Like a crane *or* a swallow, so I chattered;
I mourned like a dove;
My eyes fail *from looking* upward.
O LORD,[a] I am oppressed;
Undertake for me!

15 "What shall I say?
He has both spoken to me,[a]
And He Himself has done *it*.
I shall walk carefully all my years
In the bitterness of my soul.
16 O Lord, by these *things men* live;
And in all these *things is* the life of my
spirit;
So You will restore me and make me live.
17 Indeed *it was* for *my own* peace
That I had great bitterness;
But You have lovingly *delivered* my soul
from the pit of corruption,
For You have cast all my sins behind Your
back.
18 For Sheol cannot thank You,
Death cannot praise You;
Those who go down to the pit cannot
hope for Your truth.
19 The living, the living man, he shall praise
You,
As I *do* this day;
The father shall make known Your truth
to the children.

20 "The LORD *was ready* to save me;
Therefore we will sing my songs with
stringed instruments
All the days of our life, in the house of
the LORD."

21 Now Isaiah had said, "Let them take a
lump of figs, and apply *it* as a poultice on the
boil, and he shall recover."
22 And Hezekiah had said, "What *is* the sign
that I shall go up to the house of the LORD?"

The Babylonian Envoys

39 At that time Merodach-Baladan[a] the son
of Baladan, king of Babylon, sent letters
and a present to Hezekiah, for he heard that
he had been sick and had recovered.
2 And Hezekiah was pleased with them, and
showed them the house of his treasures—the
silver and gold, the spices and precious oint-
ment, and all his armory—all that was found
among his treasures. There was nothing in his
house or in all his dominion that Hezekiah did
not show them.
3 Then Isaiah the prophet went to King Hez-
ekiah, and said to him, "What did these men
say, and from where did they come to you?"
So Hezekiah said, "They came to me from a
far country, from Babylon."
4 And he said, "What have they seen in your
house?" So Hezekiah answered, "They have
seen all that *is* in my house; there is nothing
among my treasures that I have not shown
them."
5 Then Isaiah said to Hezekiah, "Hear the
word of the LORD of hosts:
6 'Behold, the days are coming when all that
is in your house, and what your fathers have
accumulated until this day, shall be carried to
Babylon; nothing shall be left,' says the LORD.
7 'And they shall take away *some* of your
sons who will descend from you, whom you
will beget; and they shall be eunuchs in the
palace of the king of Babylon.'"
8 So Hezekiah said to Isaiah, "The word of
the LORD which you have spoken *is* good!" For
he said, "At least there will be peace and truth
in my days."

God's People Are Comforted

40 "Comfort, yes, comfort My people!"
Says your God.
2 "Speak comfort to Jerusalem, and cry out
to her,
That her warfare is ended,
That her iniquity is pardoned;
For she has received from the LORD's
hand
Double for all her sins."

3 The voice of one crying in the wilderness:
"Prepare the way of the LORD;

38:11 [a]Hebrew *YAH, YAH* [b]Following some Hebrew manuscripts; Masoretic Text and Vulgate read *rest;* Septuagint omits *among the inhabitants of the world;* Targum reads *land.* **38:14** [a]Following Bomberg; Masoretic Text and Dead Sea Scrolls read *Lord.* **38:15** [a]Following Masoretic Text and Vulgate; Dead Sea Scrolls and Targum read *And shall I say to Him;* Septuagint omits first half of this verse. **39:1** [a]Spelled *Berodach-Baladan* in 2 Kings 20:12

Make straight in the desert[a]
A highway for our God.
4 Every valley shall be exalted
And every mountain and hill brought low;
The crooked places shall be made straight
And the rough places smooth;
5 The glory of the LORD shall be revealed,
And all flesh shall see *it* together;
For the mouth of the LORD has spoken."

6 The voice said, "Cry out!"
And he[a] said, "What shall I cry?"

"All flesh *is* grass,
And all its loveliness *is* like the flower of the field.
7 The grass withers, the flower fades,
Because the breath of the LORD blows upon it;
Surely the people *are* grass.
8 The grass withers, the flower fades,
But the word of our God stands forever."

9 O Zion,
You who bring good tidings,
Get up into the high mountain;
O Jerusalem,
You who bring good tidings,
Lift up your voice with strength,
Lift *it* up, be not afraid;
Say to the cities of Judah, "Behold your God!"
10 Behold, the Lord GOD shall come with a strong *hand,*
And His arm shall rule for Him;
Behold, His reward *is* with Him,
And His work before Him.
11 He will feed His flock like a shepherd;
He will gather the lambs with His arm,
And carry *them* in His bosom,
And gently lead those who are with young.

12 Who has measured the waters[a] in the hollow of His hand,
Measured heaven with a span
And calculated the dust of the earth in a measure?
Weighed the mountains in scales
And the hills in a balance?
13 Who has directed the Spirit of the LORD,
Or *as* His counselor has taught Him?
14 With whom did He take counsel, and *who* instructed Him,
And taught Him in the path of justice?
Who taught Him knowledge,
And showed Him the way of understanding?

15 Behold, the nations *are* as a drop in a bucket,
And are counted as the small dust on the scales;
Look, He lifts up the isles as a very little thing.
16 And Lebanon *is* not sufficient to burn,
Nor its beasts sufficient for a burnt offering.
17 All nations before Him *are* as nothing,
And they are counted by Him less than nothing and worthless.

18 To whom then will you liken God?
Or what likeness will you compare to Him?
19 The workman molds an image,
The goldsmith overspreads it with gold,
And the silversmith casts silver chains.
20 Whoever *is* too impoverished for *such* a contribution
Chooses a tree *that* will not rot;
He seeks for himself a skillful workman
To prepare a carved image *that* will not totter.

21 Have you not known?
Have you not heard?
Has it not been told you from the beginning?
Have you not understood from the foundations of the earth?
22 *It is* He who sits above the circle of the earth,
And its inhabitants *are* like grasshoppers,
Who stretches out the heavens like a curtain,
And spreads them out like a tent to dwell in.
23 He brings the princes to nothing;
He makes the judges of the earth useless.

24 Scarcely shall they be planted,
Scarcely shall they be sown,
Scarcely shall their stock take root in the earth,
When He will also blow on them,
And they will wither,
And the whirlwind will take them away like stubble.

25 "To whom then will you liken Me,
Or *to whom* shall I be equal?" says the Holy One.
26 Lift up your eyes on high,
And see who has created these *things,*
Who brings out their host by number;
He calls them all by name,
By the greatness of His might
And the strength of *His* power;
Not one is missing.

27 Why do you say, O Jacob,
And speak, O Israel:
"My way is hidden from the LORD,
And my just claim is passed over by my God"?
28 Have you not known?
Have you not heard?
The everlasting God, the LORD,
The Creator of the ends of the earth,
Neither faints nor is weary.
His understanding is unsearchable.
29 He gives power to the weak,
And to *those who have* no might He increases strength.
30 Even the youths shall faint and be weary,
And the young men shall utterly fall,
31 But those who wait on the LORD
Shall renew *their* strength;
They shall mount up with wings like eagles,
They shall run and not be weary,
They shall walk and not faint.

40:3 [a]Following Masoretic Text, Targum, and Vulgate; Septuagint omits *in the desert.* **40:6** [a]Following Masoretic Text and Targum; Dead Sea Scrolls, Septuagint, and Vulgate read *I.* **40:12** [a]Following Masoretic Text, Septuagint, and Vulgate; Dead Sea Scrolls read *waters of the sea;* Targum reads *waters of the world.*

Israel Assured of God's Help

41 "Keep silence before Me, O coastlands,
And let the people renew *their* strength!
Let them come near, then let them speak;
Let us come near together for judgment.

2 "Who raised up one from the east?
Who in righteousness called him to His feet?
Who gave the nations before him,
And made *him* rule over kings?
Who gave *them* as the dust *to* his sword,
As driven stubble to his bow?
3 Who pursued them, *and* passed safely
By the way *that* he had not gone with his feet?
4 Who has performed and done *it*,
Calling the generations from the beginning?
'I, the LORD, am the first;
And with the last I *am* He.'"

5 The coastlands saw *it* and feared,
The ends of the earth were afraid;
They drew near and came.
6 Everyone helped his neighbor,
And said to his brother,
"Be of good courage!"
7 So the craftsman encouraged the goldsmith;
He who smooths *with* the hammer
inspired him who strikes the anvil,
Saying, "It *is* ready for the soldering";
Then he fastened it with pegs,
That it might not totter.

8 "But you, Israel, *are* My servant,
Jacob whom I have chosen,
The descendants of Abraham My friend.
9 *You* whom I have taken from the ends of the earth,
And called from its farthest regions,
And said to you,
'You *are* My servant,
I have chosen you and have not cast you away:
10 Fear not, for I *am* with you;
Be not dismayed, for I *am* your God.
I will strengthen you,
Yes, I will help you,
I will uphold you with My righteous right hand.'

11 "Behold, all those who were incensed against you
Shall be ashamed and disgraced;
They shall be as nothing,
And those who strive with you shall perish.
12 You shall seek them and not find them—
Those who contended with you.
Those who war against you
Shall be as nothing,
As a nonexistent thing.
13 For I, the LORD your God, will hold your right hand,
Saying to you, 'Fear not, I will help you.'

14 "Fear not, you worm Jacob,
You men of Israel!
I will help you," says the LORD
And your Redeemer, the Holy One of Israel.
15 "Behold, I will make you into a new
threshing sledge with sharp teeth;
You shall thresh the mountains and beat *them* small,
And make the hills like chaff.
16 You shall winnow them, the wind shall carry them away,
And the whirlwind shall scatter them;
You shall rejoice in the LORD,
And glory in the Holy One of Israel.

17 "The poor and needy seek water, but *there is* none,
Their tongues fail for thirst.
I, the LORD, will hear them;
I, the God of Israel, will not forsake them.
18 I will open rivers in desolate heights,
And fountains in the midst of the valleys;
I will make the wilderness a pool of water,
And the dry land springs of water.
19 I will plant in the wilderness the cedar
and the acacia tree,
The myrtle and the oil tree;
I will set in the desert the cypress tree
and the pine
And the box tree together,
20 That they may see and know,
And consider and understand together,
That the hand of the LORD has done this,
And the Holy One of Israel has created it.

The Futility of Idols

21 "Present your case," says the LORD.
"Bring forth your strong *reasons*," says the King of Jacob.
22 "Let them bring forth and show us what will happen;
Let them show the former things, what they *were*,
That we may consider them,
And know the latter end of them;
Or declare to us things to come.
23 Show the things that are to come hereafter,
That we may know that you *are* gods;
Yes, do good or do evil,
That we may be dismayed and see *it* together.
24 Indeed you *are* nothing,
And your work *is* nothing;
He who chooses you *is* an abomination.

25 "I have raised up one from the north,
And he shall come;
From the rising of the sun he shall call on My name;
And he shall come against princes as *though* mortar,
As the potter treads clay.
26 Who has declared from the beginning,
that we may know?
And former times, that we may say, '*He is* righteous'?
Surely *there is* no one who shows,
Surely *there is* no one who declares,
Surely *there is* no one who hears your words.
27 The first time *I said* to Zion,
'Look, there they are!'
And I will give to Jerusalem one who brings good tidings.
28 For I looked, and *there was* no man;
I looked among them, but *there was* no counselor,
Who, when I asked of them, could answer a word.

29 Indeed they *are* all worthless;[a]
Their works *are* nothing;
Their molded images *are* wind and confusion.

The Servant of the LORD

42 "Behold! My Servant whom I uphold,
My Elect One *in whom* My soul delights!
I have put My Spirit upon Him;
He will bring forth justice to the Gentiles.
2 He will not cry out, nor raise *His voice,*
Nor cause His voice to be heard in the street.
3 A bruised reed He will not break,
And smoking flax He will not quench;
He will bring forth justice for truth.
4 He will not fail nor be discouraged,
Till He has established justice in the earth;
And the coastlands shall wait for His law."

5 Thus says God the LORD,
Who created the heavens and stretched them out,
Who spread forth the earth and that which comes from it,
Who gives breath to the people on it,
And spirit to those who walk on it:
6 "I, the LORD, have called You in righteousness,
And will hold Your hand;
I will keep You and give You as a covenant to the people,
As a light to the Gentiles,
7 To open blind eyes,
To bring out prisoners from the prison,
Those who sit in darkness from the prison house.
8 I *am* the LORD, that *is* My name;
And My glory I will not give to another,
Nor My praise to carved images.
9 Behold, the former things have come to pass,
And new things I declare;
Before they spring forth I tell you of them."

Praise to the LORD

10 Sing to the LORD a new song,
And His praise from the ends of the earth,
You who go down to the sea, and all that is in it,
You coastlands and you inhabitants of them!
11 Let the wilderness and its cities lift up *their voice,*
The villages *that* Kedar inhabits.
Let the inhabitants of Sela sing,
Let them shout from the top of the mountains.
12 Let them give glory to the LORD,
And declare His praise in the coastlands.
13 The LORD shall go forth like a mighty man;
He shall stir up *His* zeal like a man of war.
He shall cry out, yes, shout aloud;
He shall prevail against His enemies.

Promise of the LORD's Help

14 "I have held My peace a long time,
I have been still and restrained Myself.
Now I will cry like a woman in labor,
I will pant and gasp at once.
15 I will lay waste the mountains and hills,
And dry up all their vegetation;
I will make the rivers coastlands,
And I will dry up the pools.
16 I will bring the blind by a way they did not know;
I will lead them in paths they have not known.
I will make darkness light before them,
And crooked places straight.
These things I will do for them,
And not forsake them.
17 They shall be turned back,
They shall be greatly ashamed,
Who trust in carved images,
Who say to the molded images,
'You *are* our gods.'

18 "Hear, you deaf;
And look, you blind, that you may see.
19 Who *is* blind but My servant,
Or deaf as My messenger *whom* I send?
Who *is* blind as *he who is* perfect,
And blind as the LORD's servant?
20 Seeing many things, but you do not observe;
Opening the ears, but he does not hear."

Israel's Obstinate Disobedience

21 The LORD is well pleased for His righteousness' sake;
He will exalt the law and make *it* honorable.
22 But this *is* a people robbed and plundered;
All of them are snared in holes,
And they are hidden in prison houses;
They are for prey, and no one delivers;
For plunder, and no one says, "Restore!"

23 Who among you will give ear to this?
Who will listen and hear for the time to come?
24 Who gave Jacob for plunder, and Israel to the robbers?
Was it not the LORD,
He against whom we have sinned?
For they would not walk in His ways,
Nor were they obedient to His law.
25 Therefore He has poured on him the fury of His anger
And the strength of battle;
It has set him on fire all around,
Yet he did not know;
And it burned him,
Yet he did not take *it* to heart.

The Redeemer of Israel

43 But now, thus says the LORD, who created you, O Jacob,
And He who formed you, O Israel:
"Fear not, for I have redeemed you;
I have called *you* by your name;
You *are* Mine.
2 When you pass through the waters, I *will be* with you;

41:29 [a]Following Masoretic Text and Vulgate; Dead Sea Scrolls, Syriac, and Targum read *nothing;* Septuagint omits the first line.

And through the rivers, they shall not overflow you.
When you walk through the fire, you shall not be burned,
Nor shall the flame scorch you.
3 For I *am* the LORD your God,
The Holy One of Israel, your Savior;
I gave Egypt for your ransom,
Ethiopia and Seba in your place.
4 Since you were precious in My sight,
You have been honored,
And I have loved you;
Therefore I will give men for you,
And people for your life.
5 Fear not, for I *am* with you;
I will bring your descendants from the east,
And gather you from the west;
6 I will say to the north, 'Give them up!'
And to the south, 'Do not keep them back!'
Bring My sons from afar,
And My daughters from the ends of the earth—
7 Everyone who is called by My name,
Whom I have created for My glory;
I have formed him, yes, I have made him."

8 Bring out the blind people who have eyes,
And the deaf who have ears.
9 Let all the nations be gathered together,
And let the people be assembled.
Who among them can declare this,
And show us former things?
Let them bring out their witnesses, that they may be justified;
Or let them hear and say, "*It is* truth."
10 "You *are* My witnesses," says the LORD,
"And My servant whom I have chosen,
That you may know and believe Me,
And understand that I *am* He.
Before Me there was no God formed,
Nor shall there be after Me.
11 I, *even* I, *am* the LORD,
And besides Me *there is* no savior.
12 I have declared and saved,
I have proclaimed,
And *there was* no foreign *god* among you;
Therefore you *are* My witnesses,"
Says the LORD, "that I *am* God.
13 Indeed before the day *was*, I *am* He;
And *there is* no one who can deliver out of My hand;
I work, and who will reverse it?"

14 Thus says the LORD, your Redeemer,
The Holy One of Israel:
"For your sake I will send to Babylon,
And bring them all down as fugitives—
The Chaldeans, who rejoice in their ships.
15 I *am* the LORD, your Holy One,
The Creator of Israel, your King."

16 Thus says the LORD, who makes a way in the sea
And a path through the mighty waters,
17 Who brings forth the chariot and horse,
The army and the power
(They shall lie down together, they shall not rise;
They are extinguished, they are quenched like a wick):
18 "Do not remember the former things,
Nor consider the things of old.
19 Behold, I will do a new thing,
Now it shall spring forth;
Shall you not know it?
I will even make a road in the wilderness
And rivers in the desert.
20 The beast of the field will honor Me,
The jackals and the ostriches,
Because I give waters in the wilderness
And rivers in the desert,
To give drink to My people, My chosen.
21 This people I have formed for Myself;
They shall declare My praise.

Pleading with Unfaithful Israel

22 "But you have not called upon Me, O Jacob;
And you have been weary of Me, O Israel.
23 You have not brought Me the sheep for your burnt offerings,
Nor have you honored Me with your sacrifices.
I have not caused you to serve with grain offerings,
Nor wearied you with incense.
24 You have bought Me no sweet cane with money,
Nor have you satisfied Me with the fat of your sacrifices;
But you have burdened Me with your sins,
You have wearied Me with your iniquities.

25 "I, *even* I, *am* He who blots out your transgressions for My own sake;
And I will not remember your sins.
26 Put Me in remembrance;
Let us contend together;
State your *case*, that you may be acquitted.
27 Your first father sinned,
And your mediators have transgressed against Me.
28 Therefore I will profane the princes of the sanctuary;
I will give Jacob to the curse,
And Israel to reproaches.

God's Blessing on Israel

44 "Yet hear now, O Jacob My servant,
And Israel whom I have chosen.
2 Thus says the LORD who made you
And formed you from the womb, *who* will help you:
'Fear not, O Jacob My servant;
And you, Jeshurun, whom I have chosen.
3 For I will pour water on him who is thirsty,
And floods on the dry ground;
I will pour My Spirit on your descendants,
And My blessing on your offspring;
4 They will spring up among the grass
Like willows by the watercourses.'
5 One will say, 'I *am* the LORD's';
Another will call *himself* by the name of Jacob;
Another will write *with* his hand, 'The LORD's,'
And name *himself* by the name of Israel.

There Is No Other God

6 "Thus says the LORD, the King of Israel,
And his Redeemer, the LORD of hosts:

'I *am* the First and I *am* the Last;
Besides Me *there is* no God.
7 And who can proclaim as I do?
Then let him declare it and set it in order for Me,
Since I appointed the ancient people.
And the things that are coming and shall come,
Let them show these to them.
8 Do not fear, nor be afraid;
Have I not told you from that time, and declared *it?*
You *are* My witnesses.
Is there a God besides Me?
Indeed *there is* no other Rock;
I know not *one.*' "

Idolatry Is Foolishness

9 Those who make an image, all of them *are* useless,
And their precious things shall not profit;
They *are* their own witnesses;
They neither see nor know, that they may be ashamed.
10 Who would form a god or mold an image
That profits him nothing?
11 Surely all his companions would be ashamed;
And the workmen, they *are* mere men.
Let them all be gathered together,
Let them stand up;
Yet they shall fear,
They shall be ashamed together.

12 The blacksmith with the tongs works one in the coals,
Fashions it with hammers,
And works it with the strength of his arms.
Even so, he is hungry, and his strength fails;
He drinks no water and is faint.

13 The craftsman stretches out *his* rule,
He marks one out with chalk;
He fashions it with a plane,
He marks it out with the compass,
And makes it like the figure of a man,
According to the beauty of a man, that it may remain in the house.
14 He cuts down cedars for himself,
And takes the cypress and the oak;
He secures *it* for himself among the trees of the forest.
He plants a pine, and the rain nourishes *it.*

15 Then it shall be for a man to burn,
For he will take some of it and warm himself;
Yes, he kindles *it* and bakes bread;
Indeed he makes a god and worships *it;*
He makes it a carved image, and falls down to it.
16 He burns half of it in the fire;
With this half he eats meat;
He roasts a roast, and is satisfied.
He even warms *himself* and says,
"Ah! I am warm,
I have seen the fire."
17 And the rest of it he makes into a god,
His carved image.
He falls down before it and worships *it,*
Prays to it and says,
"Deliver me, for you *are* my god!"

18 They do not know nor understand;
For He has shut their eyes, so that they cannot see,
And their hearts, so that they cannot understand.
19 And no one considers in his heart,
Nor *is there* knowledge nor understanding to say,
"I have burned half of it in the fire,
Yes, I have also baked bread on its coals;
I have roasted meat and eaten *it;*
And shall I make the rest of it an abomination?
Shall I fall down before a block of wood?"
20 He feeds on ashes;
A deceived heart has turned him aside;
And he cannot deliver his soul,
Nor say, "*Is there* not a lie in my right hand?"

Israel Is Not Forgotten

21 "Remember these, O Jacob,
And Israel, for you *are* My servant;
I have formed you, you *are* My servant;
O Israel, you will not be forgotten by Me!
22 I have blotted out, like a thick cloud, your transgressions,
And like a cloud, your sins.
Return to Me, for I have redeemed you."

23 Sing, O heavens, for the LORD has done *it!*
Shout, you lower parts of the earth;
Break forth into singing, you mountains,
O forest, and every tree in it!
For the LORD has redeemed Jacob,
And glorified Himself in Israel.

Judah Will Be Restored

24 Thus says the LORD, your Redeemer,
And He who formed you from the womb:
"I *am* the LORD, who makes all *things,*
Who stretches out the heavens all alone,
Who spreads abroad the earth by Myself;
25 Who frustrates the signs of the babblers,
And drives diviners mad;
Who turns wise men backward,
And makes their knowledge foolishness;
26 Who confirms the word of His servant,
And performs the counsel of His messengers;
Who says to Jerusalem, 'You shall be inhabited,'
To the cities of Judah, 'You shall be built,'
And I will raise up her waste places;
27 Who says to the deep, 'Be dry!
And I will dry up your rivers';
28 Who says of Cyrus, '*He is* My shepherd,
And he shall perform all My pleasure,
Saying to Jerusalem, "You shall be built,"
And to the temple, "Your foundation shall be laid." '

Cyrus, God's Instrument

45 "Thus says the LORD to His anointed,
To Cyrus, whose right hand I have held—
To subdue nations before him
And loose the armor of kings,
To open before him the double doors,
So that the gates will not be shut:
2 'I will go before you

And make the crooked places[a] straight;
I will break in pieces the gates of bronze
And cut the bars of iron.
3 I will give you the treasures of darkness
And hidden riches of secret places,
That you may know that I, the LORD,
Who call *you* by your name,
Am the God of Israel.
4 For Jacob My servant's sake,
And Israel My elect,
I have even called you by your name;
I have named you, though you have not known Me.
5 I *am* the LORD, and *there is* no other;
There is no God besides Me.
I will gird you, though you have not known Me,
6 That they may know from the rising of the sun to its setting
That *there is* none besides Me.
I *am* the LORD, and *there is* no other;
7 I form the light and create darkness,
I make peace and create calamity;
I, the LORD, do all these *things*.'

8 "Rain down, you heavens, from above,
And let the skies pour down righteousness;
Let the earth open, let them bring forth salvation,
And let righteousness spring up together.
I, the LORD, have created it.

9 "Woe to him who strives with his Maker!
Let the potsherd *strive* with the potsherds of the earth!
Shall the clay say to him who forms it,
'What are you making?'
Or shall your handiwork *say*, 'He has no hands'?
10 Woe to him who says to *his* father, 'What are you begetting?'
Or to the woman, 'What have you brought forth?'"

11 Thus says the LORD,
The Holy One of Israel, and his Maker:
"Ask Me of things to come concerning My sons;
And concerning the work of My hands, you command Me.
12 I have made the earth,
And created man on it.
I—My hands—stretched out the heavens,
And all their host I have commanded.
13 I have raised him up in righteousness,
And I will direct all his ways;
He shall build My city
And let My exiles go free,
Not for price nor reward,"
Says the LORD of hosts.

The LORD, the Only Savior

14 Thus says the LORD:

"The labor of Egypt and merchandise of Cush
And of the Sabeans, men of stature,
Shall come over to you, and they shall be yours;
They shall walk behind you,
They shall come over in chains;
And they shall bow down to you.
They will make supplication to you, *saying*, 'Surely God *is* in you,
And *there is* no other;
There is no other God.'"

15 Truly You *are* God, who hide Yourself,
O God of Israel, the Savior!
16 They shall be ashamed
And also disgraced, all of them;
They shall go in confusion together,
Who are makers of idols.
17 *But* Israel shall be saved by the LORD
With an everlasting salvation;
You shall not be ashamed or disgraced
Forever and ever.

18 For thus says the LORD,
Who created the heavens,
Who is God,
Who formed the earth and made it,
Who has established it,
Who did not create it in vain,
Who formed it to be inhabited:
"I *am* the LORD, and *there is* no other.
19 I have not spoken in secret,
In a dark place of the earth;
I did not say to the seed of Jacob,
'Seek Me in vain';
I, the LORD, speak righteousness,
I declare things that are right.

20 "Assemble yourselves and come;
Draw near together,
You *who have* escaped from the nations.
They have no knowledge,
Who carry the wood of their carved image,
And pray to a god *that* cannot save.
21 Tell and bring forth *your case*;
Yes, let them take counsel together.
Who has declared this from ancient time?
Who has told it from that time?
Have not I, the LORD?
And *there is* no other God besides Me,
A just God and a Savior;
There is none besides Me.

22 "Look to Me, and be saved,
All you ends of the earth!
For I *am* God, and *there is* no other.
23 I have sworn by Myself;
The word has gone out of My mouth *in* righteousness,
And shall not return,
That to Me every knee shall bow,
Every tongue shall take an oath.
24 He shall say,
'Surely in the LORD I have righteousness and strength.
To Him *men* shall come,
And all shall be ashamed
Who are incensed against Him.
25 In the LORD all the descendants of Israel
Shall be justified, and shall glory.'"

Dead Idols and the Living God

46 Bel bows down, Nebo stoops;
Their idols were on the beasts and on the cattle.
Your carriages *were* heavily loaded,
A burden to the weary *beast*.
2 They stoop, they bow down together;
They could not deliver the burden,
But have themselves gone into captivity.

45:2 [a]Dead Sea Scrolls and Septuagint read *mountains;* Targum reads *I will trample down the walls;* Vulgate reads *I will humble the great ones of the earth.*

3 "Listen to Me, O house of Jacob,
And all the remnant of the house of Israel,
Who have been upheld *by Me* from birth,
Who have been carried from the womb:
4 Even to *your* old age, I *am* He,
And *even* to gray hairs I will carry *you!*
I have made, and I will bear;
Even I will carry, and will deliver *you.*

5 "To whom will you liken Me, and make *Me* equal
And compare Me, that we should be alike?
6 They lavish gold out of the bag,
And weigh silver on the scales;
They hire a goldsmith, and he makes it a god;
They prostrate themselves, yes, they worship.
7 They bear it on the shoulder, they carry it
And set it in its place, and it stands;
From its place it shall not move.
Though *one* cries out to it, yet it cannot answer
Nor save him out of his trouble.

8 "Remember this, and show yourselves men;
Recall to mind, O you transgressors.
9 Remember the former things of old,
For I *am* God, and *there is* no other;
I am God, and *there is* none like Me,
10 Declaring the end from the beginning,
And from ancient times *things* that are not *yet* done,
Saying, 'My counsel shall stand,
And I will do all My pleasure,'
11 Calling a bird of prey from the east,
The man who executes My counsel, from a far country.
Indeed I have spoken *it;*
I will also bring it to pass.
I have purposed *it;*
I will also do it.

12 "Listen to Me, you stubborn-hearted,
Who *are* far from righteousness:
13 I bring My righteousness near, it shall not be far off;
My salvation shall not linger.
And I will place salvation in Zion,
For Israel My glory.

The Humiliation of Babylon

47 "Come down and sit in the dust,
O virgin daughter of Babylon;
Sit on the ground without a throne,
O daughter of the Chaldeans!
For you shall no more be called
Tender and delicate.
2 Take the millstones and grind meal.
Remove your veil,
Take off the skirt,
Uncover the thigh,
Pass through the rivers.
3 Your nakedness shall be uncovered,
Yes, your shame will be seen;
I will take vengeance,
And I will not arbitrate with a man."

4 *As for* our Redeemer, the LORD of hosts *is* His name,
The Holy One of Israel.

5 "Sit in silence, and go into darkness,
O daughter of the Chaldeans;
For you shall no longer be called
The Lady of Kingdoms.
6 I was angry with My people;
I have profaned My inheritance,
And given them into your hand.
You showed them no mercy;
On the elderly you laid your yoke very heavily.
7 And you said, 'I shall be a lady forever,'
So that you did not take these *things* to heart,
Nor remember the latter end of them.

8 "Therefore hear this now, *you who are* given to pleasures,
Who dwell securely,
Who say in your heart,
'I *am,* and *there is* no one else besides me;
I shall not sit *as* a widow,
Nor shall I know the loss of children';
9 But these two *things* shall come to you
In a moment, in one day:
The loss of children, and widowhood.
They shall come upon you in their fullness
Because of the multitude of your sorceries,
For the great abundance of your enchantments.

10 "For you have trusted in your wickedness;
You have said, 'No one sees me';
Your wisdom and your knowledge have warped you;
And you have said in your heart,
'I *am,* and *there is* no one else besides me.'
11 Therefore evil shall come upon you;
You shall not know from where it arises.
And trouble shall fall upon you;
You will not be able to put it off.
And desolation shall come upon you suddenly,
Which you shall not know.

12 "Stand now with your enchantments
And the multitude of your sorceries,
In which you have labored from your youth—
Perhaps you will be able to profit,
Perhaps you will prevail.
13 You are wearied in the multitude of your counsels;
Let now the astrologers, the stargazers,
And the monthly prognosticators
Stand up and save you
From what shall come upon you.
14 Behold, they shall be as stubble,
The fire shall burn them;
They shall not deliver themselves
From the power of the flame;
It shall not *be* a coal to be warmed by,
Nor a fire to sit before!
15 Thus shall they be to you
With whom you have labored,
Your merchants from your youth;
They shall wander each one to his quarter.
No one shall save you.

Israel Refined for God's Glory

48 "Hear this, O house of Jacob,
Who are called by the name of Israel,
And have come forth from the wellsprings of Judah;
Who swear by the name of the LORD,
And make mention of the God of Israel,

But not in truth or in righteousness;
2 For they call themselves after the holy city,
And lean on the God of Israel;
The LORD of hosts *is* His name:

3 "I have declared the former things from the beginning;
They went forth from My mouth, and I caused them to hear it.
Suddenly I did *them*, and they came to pass.
4 Because I knew that you *were* obstinate,
And your neck *was* an iron sinew,
And your brow bronze,
5 Even from the beginning I have declared *it* to you;
Before it came to pass I proclaimed *it* to you,
Lest you should say, 'My idol has done them,
And my carved image and my molded image
Have commanded them.'

6 "You have heard;
See all this.
And will you not declare *it*?
I have made you hear new things from this time,
Even hidden things, and you did not know them.
7 They are created now and not from the beginning;
And before this day you have not heard them,
Lest you should say, 'Of course I knew them.'
8 Surely you did not hear,
Surely you did not know;
Surely from long ago your ear was not opened.
For I knew that you would deal very treacherously,
And were called a transgressor from the womb.

9 "For My name's sake I will defer My anger,
And *for* My praise I will restrain it from you,
So that I do not cut you off.
10 Behold, I have refined you, but not as silver;
I have tested you in the furnace of affliction.
11 For My own sake, for My own sake, I will do *it*;
For how should *My name* be profaned?
And I will not give My glory to another.

God's Ancient Plan to Redeem Israel

12 "Listen to Me, O Jacob,
And Israel, My called:
I *am* He, I *am* the First,
I *am* also the Last.
13 Indeed My hand has laid the foundation of the earth,
And My right hand has stretched out the heavens;
When I call to them,
They stand up together.

14 "All of you, assemble yourselves, and hear!
Who among them has declared these *things*?
The LORD loves him;
He shall do His pleasure on Babylon,
And His arm *shall be against* the Chaldeans.
15 I, *even* I, have spoken;
Yes, I have called him,
I have brought him, and his way will prosper.

16 "Come near to Me, hear this:
I have not spoken in secret from the beginning;
From the time that it was, I *was* there.
And now the Lord GOD and His Spirit
Have[a] sent Me."

17 Thus says the LORD, your Redeemer,
The Holy One of Israel:
"I *am* the LORD your God,
Who teaches you to profit,
Who leads you by the way you should go.
18 Oh, that you had heeded My commandments!
Then your peace would have been like a river,
And your righteousness like the waves of the sea.
19 Your descendants also would have been like the sand,
And the offspring of your body like the grains of sand;
His name would not have been cut off
Nor destroyed from before Me."

20 Go forth from Babylon!
Flee from the Chaldeans!
With a voice of singing,
Declare, proclaim this,
Utter it to the end of the earth;
Say, "The LORD has redeemed
His servant Jacob!"
21 And they did not thirst
When He led them through the deserts;
He caused the waters to flow from the rock for them;
He also split the rock, and the waters gushed out.

22 "*There is* no peace," says the LORD, "for the wicked."

The Servant, the Light to the Gentiles

49 "Listen, O coastlands, to Me,
And take heed, you peoples from afar!
The LORD has called Me from the womb;
From the matrix of My mother He has made mention of My name.
2 And He has made My mouth like a sharp sword;
In the shadow of His hand He has hidden Me,
And made Me a polished shaft;
In His quiver He has hidden Me."

3 "And He said to me,
'You *are* My servant, O Israel,
In whom I will be glorified.'
4 Then I said, 'I have labored in vain,
I have spent my strength for nothing and in vain;
Yet surely my just reward *is* with the LORD,
And my work with my God.'"

48:16 [a]The Hebrew verb is singular.

5 "And now the LORD says,
Who formed Me from the womb *to be* His Servant,
To bring Jacob back to Him,
So that Israel is gathered to Him[a]
(For I shall be glorious in the eyes of the LORD,
And My God shall be My strength),
6 Indeed He says,
'It is too small a thing that You should be My Servant
To raise up the tribes of Jacob,
And to restore the preserved ones of Israel;
I will also give You as a light to the Gentiles,
That You should be My salvation to the ends of the earth.' "

7 Thus says the LORD,
The Redeemer of Israel, their Holy One,
To Him whom man despises,
To Him whom the nation abhors,
To the Servant of rulers:
"Kings shall see and arise,
Princes also shall worship,
Because of the LORD who is faithful,
The Holy One of Israel;
And He has chosen You."
8 Thus says the LORD:

"In an acceptable time I have heard You,
And in the day of salvation I have helped You;
I will preserve You and give You
As a covenant to the people,
To restore the earth,
To cause them to inherit the desolate heritages;
9 That You may say to the prisoners, 'Go forth,'
To those who *are* in darkness, 'Show yourselves.'

"They shall feed along the roads,
And their pastures *shall be* on all desolate heights.
10 They shall neither hunger nor thirst,
Neither heat nor sun shall strike them;
For He who has mercy on them will lead them,
Even by the springs of water He will guide them.
11 I will make each of My mountains a road,
And My highways shall be elevated.
12 Surely these shall come from afar;
Look! Those from the north and the west,
And these from the land of Sinim."

13 Sing, O heavens!
Be joyful, O earth!
And break out in singing, O mountains!
For the LORD has comforted His people,
And will have mercy on His afflicted.

God Will Remember Zion

14 But Zion said, "The LORD has forsaken me,
And my Lord has forgotten me."

15 "Can a woman forget her nursing child,
And not have compassion on the son of her womb?
Surely they may forget,
Yet I will not forget you.
16 See, I have inscribed you on the palms of *My hands;*
Your walls *are* continually before Me.
17 Your sons[a] shall make haste;
Your destroyers and those who laid you waste
Shall go away from you.
18 Lift up your eyes, look around and see;
All these gather together *and* come to you.
As I live," says the LORD,
"You shall surely clothe yourselves with them all as an ornament,
And bind them *on you* as a bride *does.*

19 "For your waste and desolate places,
And the land of your destruction,
Will even now be too small for the inhabitants;
And those who swallowed you up will be far away.
20 The children you will have,
After you have lost the others,
Will say again in your ears,
'The place *is* too small for me;
Give me a place where I may dwell.'
21 Then you will say in your heart,
'Who has begotten these for me,
Since I have lost my children and am desolate,
A captive, and wandering to and fro?
And who has brought these up?
There I was, left alone;
But these, where *were* they?' "

22 Thus says the Lord GOD:

"Behold, I will lift My hand in an oath to the nations,
And set up My standard for the peoples;
They shall bring your sons in *their* arms,
And your daughters shall be carried on *their* shoulders;
23 Kings shall be your foster fathers,
And their queens your nursing mothers;
They shall bow down to you with *their* faces to the earth,
And lick up the dust of your feet.
Then you will know that I *am* the LORD,
For they shall not be ashamed who wait for Me."

24 Shall the prey be taken from the mighty,
Or the captives of the righteous[a] be delivered?

25 But thus says the LORD:

"Even the captives of the mighty shall be taken away,
And the prey of the terrible be delivered;
For I will contend with him who contends with you,
And I will save your children.
26 I will feed those who oppress you with their own flesh,
And they shall be drunk with their own blood as with sweet wine.
All flesh shall know
That I, the LORD, *am* your Savior,
And your Redeemer, the Mighty One of Jacob."

49:5 [a]Qere, Dead Sea Scrolls, and Septuagint read *is gathered to Him;* Kethib reads *is not gathered.* **49:17** [a]Dead Sea Scrolls, Septuagint, Targum, and Vulgate read *builders.* **49:24** [a]Following Masoretic Text and Targum; Dead Sea Scrolls, Syriac, and Vulgate read *the mighty;* Septuagint reads *unjustly.*

The Servant, Israel's Hope

50 Thus says the LORD:
"Where *is* the certificate of your mother's divorce,
Whom I have put away?
Or which of My creditors *is it* to whom I have sold you?
For your iniquities you have sold yourselves,
And for your transgressions your mother has been put away.
2 Why, when I came, *was there* no man?
Why, when I called, *was there* none to answer?
Is My hand shortened at all that it cannot redeem?
Or have I no power to deliver?
Indeed with My rebuke I dry up the sea,
I make the rivers a wilderness;
Their fish stink because *there is* no water,
And die of thirst.
3 I clothe the heavens with blackness,
And I make sackcloth their covering."

4 "The Lord GOD has given Me
The tongue of the learned,
That I should know how to speak
A word in season to *him who is* weary.
He awakens Me morning by morning,
He awakens My ear
To hear as the learned.
5 The Lord GOD has opened My ear;
And I was not rebellious,
Nor did I turn away.
6 I gave My back to those who struck *Me,*
And My cheeks to those who plucked out the beard;
I did not hide My face from shame and spitting.

7 "For the Lord GOD will help Me;
Therefore I will not be disgraced;
Therefore I have set My face like a flint,
And I know that I will not be ashamed.
8 *He is* near who justifies Me;
Who will contend with Me?
Let us stand together.
Who *is* My adversary?
Let him come near Me.
9 Surely the Lord GOD will help Me;
Who *is* he *who* will condemn Me?
Indeed they will all grow old like a garment;
The moth will eat them up.

10 "Who among you fears the LORD?
Who obeys the voice of His Servant?
Who walks in darkness
And has no light?
Let him trust in the name of the LORD
And rely upon his God.
11 Look, all you who kindle a fire,
Who encircle *yourselves* with sparks:
Walk in the light of your fire and in the sparks you have kindled—
This you shall have from My hand:
You shall lie down in torment.

The LORD Comforts Zion

51 "Listen to Me, you who follow after righteousness,
You who seek the LORD:
Look to the rock *from which* you were hewn,
And to the hole of the pit *from which* you were dug.
2 Look to Abraham your father,
And to Sarah *who* bore you;
For I called him alone,
And blessed him and increased him."

3 For the LORD will comfort Zion,
He will comfort all her waste places;
He will make her wilderness like Eden,
And her desert like the garden of the LORD;
Joy and gladness will be found in it,
Thanksgiving and the voice of melody.

4 "Listen to Me, My people;
And give ear to Me, O My nation:
For law will proceed from Me,
And I will make My justice rest
As a light of the peoples.
5 My righteousness *is* near,
My salvation has gone forth,
And My arms will judge the peoples;
The coastlands will wait upon Me,
And on My arm they will trust.
6 Lift up your eyes to the heavens,
And look on the earth beneath.
For the heavens will vanish away like smoke,
The earth will grow old like a garment,
And those who dwell in it will die in like manner;
But My salvation will be forever,
And My righteousness will not be abolished.

7 "Listen to Me, you who know righteousness,
You people in whose heart *is* My law:
Do not fear the reproach of men,
Nor be afraid of their insults.
8 For the moth will eat them up like a garment,
And the worm will eat them like wool;
But My righteousness will be forever,
And My salvation from generation to generation."

9 Awake, awake, put on strength,
O arm of the LORD!
Awake as in the ancient days,
In the generations of old.
Are You not *the arm* that cut Rahab apart,
And wounded the serpent?
10 *Are* You not *the One* who dried up the sea,
The waters of the great deep;
That made the depths of the sea a road
For the redeemed to cross over?
11 So the ransomed of the LORD shall return,
And come to Zion with singing,
With everlasting joy on their heads.
They shall obtain joy and gladness;
Sorrow and sighing shall flee away.

12 "I, *even* I, *am* He who comforts you.
Who *are* you that you should be afraid
Of a man *who* will die,
And of the son of a man *who* will be made like grass?
13 And you forget the LORD your Maker,
Who stretched out the heavens
And laid the foundations of the earth;
You have feared continually every day

Because of the fury of the oppressor,
When *he has* prepared to destroy.
And where *is* the fury of the oppressor?
14 The captive exile hastens, that he may be loosed,
That he should not die in the pit,
And that his bread should not fail.
15 But I *am* the LORD your God,
Who divided the sea whose waves roared—
The LORD of hosts *is* His name.
16 And I have put My words in your mouth;
I have covered you with the shadow of My hand,
That I may plant the heavens,
Lay the foundations of the earth,
And say to Zion, 'You *are* My people.'"

God's Fury Removed

17 Awake, awake!
Stand up, O Jerusalem,
You who have drunk at the hand of the LORD
The cup of His fury;
You have drunk the dregs of the cup of trembling,
And drained *it* out.
18 *There is* no one to guide her
Among all the sons she has brought forth;
Nor *is there any* who takes her by the hand
Among all the sons she has brought up.
19 These two *things* have come to you;
Who will be sorry for you?—
Desolation and destruction, famine and sword—
By whom will I comfort you?
20 Your sons have fainted,
They lie at the head of all the streets,
Like an antelope in a net;
They are full of the fury of the LORD,
The rebuke of your God.

21 Therefore please hear this, you afflicted,
And drunk but not with wine.
22 Thus says your Lord,
The LORD and your God,
Who pleads the cause of His people:
"See, I have taken out of your hand
The cup of trembling,
The dregs of the cup of My fury;
You shall no longer drink it.
23 But I will put it into the hand of those who afflict you,
Who have said to you,[a]
'Lie down, that we may walk over you.'
And you have laid your body like the ground,
And as the street, for those who walk over."

God Redeems Jerusalem

52 Awake, awake!
Put on your strength, O Zion;
Put on your beautiful garments,
O Jerusalem, the holy city!
For the uncircumcised and the unclean
Shall no longer come to you.
2 Shake yourself from the dust, arise;
Sit down, O Jerusalem!
Loose yourself from the bonds of your neck,
O captive daughter of Zion!

3 For thus says the LORD:

"You have sold yourselves for nothing,
And you shall be redeemed without money."

4 For thus says the Lord GOD:

"My people went down at first
Into Egypt to dwell there;
Then the Assyrian oppressed them without cause.
5 Now therefore, what have I here," says the LORD,
"That My people are taken away for nothing?
Those who rule over them
Make them wail,"[a] says the LORD,
"And My name *is* blasphemed continually every day.
6 Therefore My people shall know My name;
Therefore *they shall know* in that day
That I *am* He who speaks:
'Behold, *it is* I.'"

7 How beautiful upon the mountains
Are the feet of him who brings good news,
Who proclaims peace,
Who brings glad tidings of good *things*,
Who proclaims salvation,
Who says to Zion,
"Your God reigns!"
8 Your watchmen shall lift up *their* voices,
With their voices they shall sing together;
For they shall see eye to eye
When the LORD brings back Zion.
9 Break forth into joy, sing together,
You waste places of Jerusalem!
For the LORD has comforted His people,
He has redeemed Jerusalem.
10 The LORD has made bare His holy arm
In the eyes of all the nations;
And all the ends of the earth shall see
The salvation of our God.

11 Depart! Depart! Go out from there,
Touch no unclean *thing;*
Go out from the midst of her,
Be clean,
You who bear the vessels of the LORD.
12 For you shall not go out with haste,
Nor go by flight;
For the LORD will go before you,
And the God of Israel *will be* your rear guard.

The Sin-Bearing Servant

13 Behold, My Servant shall deal prudently;
He shall be exalted and extolled and be very high.
14 Just as many were astonished at you,
So His visage was marred more than any man,
And His form more than the sons of men;
15 So shall He sprinkle[a] many nations.
Kings shall shut their mouths at Him;
For what had not been told them they shall see,

51:23 [a]Literally *your soul* 52:5 [a]Dead Sea Scrolls read *Mock;* Septuagint reads *Marvel and wail;* Targum reads *Boast themselves;* Vulgate reads *Treat them unjustly.* 52:15 [a]Or *startle*

And what they had not heard they shall consider.

53 Who has believed our report?
And to whom has the arm of the LORD been revealed?
2 For He shall grow up before Him as a tender plant,
And as a root out of dry ground.
He has no form or comeliness;
And when we see Him,
There is no beauty that we should desire Him.
3 He is despised and rejected by men,
A Man of sorrows and acquainted with grief.
And we hid, as it were, *our* faces from Him;
He was despised, and we did not esteem Him.

4 Surely He has borne our griefs
And carried our sorrows;
Yet we esteemed Him stricken,
Smitten by God, and afflicted.
5 But He *was* wounded for our transgressions,
He was bruised for our iniquities;
The chastisement for our peace *was* upon Him,
And by His stripes we are healed.
6 All we like sheep have gone astray;
We have turned, every one, to his own way;
And the LORD has laid on Him the iniquity of us all.

7 He was oppressed and He was afflicted,
Yet He opened not His mouth;
He was led as a lamb to the slaughter,
And as a sheep before its shearers is silent,
So He opened not His mouth.
8 He was taken from prison and from judgment,
And who will declare His generation?
For He was cut off from the land of the living;
For the transgressions of My people He was stricken.
9 And they[a] made His grave with the wicked—
But with the rich at His death,
Because He had done no violence,
Nor *was any* deceit in His mouth.

10 Yet it pleased the LORD to bruise Him;
He has put *Him* to grief.
When You make His soul an offering for sin,
He shall see *His* seed, He shall prolong *His* days,
And the pleasure of the LORD shall prosper in His hand.
11 He shall see the labor of His soul,[a] *and* be satisfied.
By His knowledge My righteous Servant shall justify many,
For He shall bear their iniquities.
12 Therefore I will divide Him a portion with the great,
And He shall divide the spoil with the strong,
Because He poured out His soul unto death,
And He was numbered with the transgressors,
And He bore the sin of many,
And made intercession for the transgressors.

A Perpetual Covenant of Peace

54 "Sing, O barren,
You *who* have not borne!
Break forth into singing, and cry aloud,
You *who* have not labored with child!
For more *are* the children of the desolate
Than the children of the married woman," says the LORD.
2 "Enlarge the place of your tent,
And let them stretch out the curtains of your dwellings;
Do not spare;
Lengthen your cords,
And strengthen your stakes.
3 For you shall expand to the right and to the left,
And your descendants will inherit the nations,
And make the desolate cities inhabited.

4 "Do not fear, for you will not be ashamed;
Neither be disgraced, for you will not be put to shame;
For you will forget the shame of your youth,
And will not remember the reproach of your widowhood anymore.
5 For your Maker *is* your husband,
The LORD of hosts *is* His name;
And your Redeemer *is* the Holy One of Israel;
He is called the God of the whole earth.
6 For the LORD has called you
Like a woman forsaken and grieved in spirit,
Like a youthful wife when you were refused,"
Says your God.
7 "For a mere moment I have forsaken you,
But with great mercies I will gather you.
8 With a little wrath I hid My face from you for a moment;
But with everlasting kindness I will have mercy on you,"
Says the LORD, your Redeemer.

9 "For this *is* like the waters of Noah to Me;
For as I have sworn
That the waters of Noah would no longer cover the earth,
So have I sworn
That I would not be angry with you, nor rebuke you.
10 For the mountains shall depart
And the hills be removed,
But My kindness shall not depart from you,
Nor shall My covenant of peace be removed,"
Says the LORD, who has mercy on you.

11 "O you afflicted one,
Tossed with tempest, *and* not comforted,
Behold, I will lay your stones with colorful gems,

53:9 [a]Literally *he* or *He* **53:11** [a]Following Masoretic Text, Targum, and Vulgate; Dead Sea Scrolls and Septuagint read *From the labor of His soul He shall see light.*

And lay your foundations with sapphires.
12 I will make your pinnacles of rubies,
Your gates of crystal,
And all your walls of precious stones.
13 All your children *shall be* taught by the LORD,
And great *shall be* the peace of your children.
14 In righteousness you shall be established;
You shall be far from oppression, for you shall not fear;
And from terror, for it shall not come near you.
15 Indeed they shall surely assemble, *but* not because of Me.
Whoever assembles against you shall fall for your sake.

16 "Behold, I have created the blacksmith
Who blows the coals in the fire,
Who brings forth an instrument for his work;
And I have created the spoiler to destroy.
17 No weapon formed against you shall prosper,
And every tongue *which* rises against you in judgment
You shall condemn.
This *is* the heritage of the servants of the LORD,
And their righteousness *is* from Me,"
Says the LORD.

An Invitation to Abundant Life

55 "Ho! Everyone who thirsts,
Come to the waters;
And you who have no money,
Come, buy and eat.
Yes, come, buy wine and milk
Without money and without price.
2 Why do you spend money for *what is* not bread,
And your wages for *what* does not satisfy?
Listen carefully to Me, and eat *what is* good,
And let your soul delight itself in abundance.
3 Incline your ear, and come to Me.
Hear, and your soul shall live;
And I will make an everlasting covenant with you—
The sure mercies of David.
4 Indeed I have given him *as* a witness to the people,
A leader and commander for the people.
5 Surely you shall call a nation you do not know,
And nations *who* do not know you shall run to you,
Because of the LORD your God,
And the Holy One of Israel;
For He has glorified you."

6 Seek the LORD while He may be found,
Call upon Him while He is near.
7 Let the wicked forsake his way,
And the unrighteous man his thoughts;
Let him return to the LORD,
And He will have mercy on him;
And to our God,
For He will abundantly pardon.

8 "For My thoughts *are* not your thoughts,
Nor *are* your ways My ways," says the LORD.
9 "For *as* the heavens are higher than the earth,
So are My ways higher than your ways,
And My thoughts than your thoughts.

10 "For as the rain comes down, and the snow from heaven,
And do not return there,
But water the earth,
And make it bring forth and bud,
That it may give seed to the sower
And bread to the eater,
11 So shall My word be that goes forth from My mouth;
It shall not return to Me void,
But it shall accomplish what I please,
And it shall prosper *in the thing* for which I sent it.

12 "For you shall go out with joy,
And be led out with peace;
The mountains and the hills
Shall break forth into singing before you,
And all the trees of the field shall clap *their* hands.
13 Instead of the thorn shall come up the cypress tree,
And instead of the brier shall come up the myrtle tree;
And it shall be to the LORD for a name,
For an everlasting sign *that* shall not be cut off."

Salvation for the Gentiles

56 Thus says the LORD:
"Keep justice, and do righteousness,
For My salvation *is* about to come,
And My righteousness to be revealed.
2 Blessed *is* the man *who* does this,
And the son of man *who* lays hold on it;
Who keeps from defiling the Sabbath,
And keeps his hand from doing any evil."

3 Do not let the son of the foreigner
Who has joined himself to the LORD
Speak, saying,
"The LORD has utterly separated me from His people";
Nor let the eunuch say,
"Here I am, a dry tree."
4 For thus says the LORD:
"To the eunuchs who keep My Sabbaths,
And choose what pleases Me,
And hold fast My covenant,
5 Even to them I will give in My house
And within My walls a place and a name
Better than that of sons and daughters;
I will give them[a] an everlasting name
That shall not be cut off.

6 "Also the sons of the foreigner
Who join themselves to the LORD, to serve Him,
And to love the name of the LORD, to be His servants—
Everyone who keeps from defiling the Sabbath,
And holds fast My covenant—
7 Even them I will bring to My holy mountain,
And make them joyful in My house of prayer.

56:5 [a]Literally *him*

Their burnt offerings and their sacrifices
Will be accepted on My altar;
For My house shall be called a house of prayer for all nations."
8 The Lord God, who gathers the outcasts of Israel, says,
"Yet I will gather to him
Others besides those who are gathered to him."

Israel's Irresponsible Leaders

9 All you beasts of the field, come to devour,
All you beasts in the forest.
10 His watchmen *are* blind,
They are all ignorant;
They *are* all dumb dogs,
They cannot bark;
Sleeping, lying down, loving to slumber.
11 Yes, *they are* greedy dogs
Which never have enough.
And they *are* shepherds
Who cannot understand;
They all look to their own way,
Every one for his own gain,
From his *own* territory.
12 "Come," *one says,* "I will bring wine,
And we will fill ourselves with intoxicating drink;
Tomorrow will be as today,
And much more abundant."

Israel's Futile Idolatry

57 The righteous perishes,
And no man takes *it* to heart;
Merciful men *are* taken away,
While no one considers
That the righteous is taken away from evil.
2 He shall enter into peace;
They shall rest in their beds,
Each one walking *in* his uprightness.

3 "But come here,
You sons of the sorceress,
You offspring of the adulterer and the harlot!
4 Whom do you ridicule?
Against whom do you make a wide mouth
And stick out the tongue?
Are you not children of transgression,
Offspring of falsehood,
5 Inflaming yourselves with gods under every green tree,
Slaying the children in the valleys,
Under the clefts of the rocks?
6 Among the smooth *stones* of the stream
Is your portion;
They, they, *are* your lot!
Even to them you have poured a drink offering,
You have offered a grain offering.
Should I receive comfort in these?

7 "On a lofty and high mountain
You have set your bed;
Even there you went up
To offer sacrifice.
8 Also behind the doors and their posts
You have set up your remembrance;
For you have uncovered yourself *to those other* than Me,
And have gone up to them;
You have enlarged your bed
And made *a covenant* with them;
You have loved their bed,
Where you saw *their* nudity.[a]
9 You went to the king with ointment,
And increased your perfumes;
You sent your messengers far off,
And *even* descended to Sheol.
10 You are wearied in the length of your way;
Yet you did not say, 'There is no hope.'
You have found the life of your hand;
Therefore you were not grieved.

11 "And of whom have you been afraid, or feared,
That you have lied
And not remembered Me,
Nor taken *it* to your heart?
Is it not because I have held My peace from of old
That you do not fear Me?
12 I will declare your righteousness
And your works,
For they will not profit you.
13 When you cry out,
Let your collection *of idols* deliver you.
But the wind will carry them all away,
A breath will take *them.*
But he who puts his trust in Me shall possess the land,
And shall inherit My holy mountain."

Healing for the Backslider

14 And one shall say,
"Heap it up! Heap it up!
Prepare the way,
Take the stumbling block out of the way of My people."

15 For thus says the High and Lofty One
Who inhabits eternity, whose name *is* Holy:
"I dwell in the high and holy *place,*
With him *who* has a contrite and humble spirit,
To revive the spirit of the humble,
And to revive the heart of the contrite ones.
16 For I will not contend forever,
Nor will I always be angry;
For the spirit would fail before Me,
And the souls *which* I have made.
17 For the iniquity of his covetousness
I was angry and struck him;
I hid and was angry,
And he went on backsliding in the way of his heart.
18 I have seen his ways, and will heal him;
I will also lead him,
And restore comforts to him
And to his mourners.

19 "I create the fruit of the lips:
Peace, peace to *him who is* far off and to *him who is* near,"
Says the Lord,
"And I will heal him."
20 But the wicked *are* like the troubled sea,
When it cannot rest,
Whose waters cast up mire and dirt.

21 "*There is* no peace,"
Says my God, "for the wicked."

57:8 [a]Literally *hand,* a euphemism

Fasting that Pleases God

58 "Cry aloud, spare not;
Lift up your voice like a trumpet;
Tell My people their transgression,
And the house of Jacob their sins.
2 Yet they seek Me daily,
And delight to know My ways,
As a nation that did righteousness,
And did not forsake the ordinance of their God.
They ask of Me the ordinances of justice;
They take delight in approaching God.
3 'Why have we fasted,' *they say,* 'and You have not seen?
Why have we afflicted our souls, and You take no notice?'

"In fact, in the day of your fast you find pleasure,
And exploit all your laborers.
4 Indeed you fast for strife and debate,
And to strike with the fist of wickedness.
You will not fast as *you do* this day,
To make your voice heard on high.
5 Is it a fast that I have chosen,
A day for a man to afflict his soul?
Is it to bow down his head like a bulrush,
And to spread out sackcloth and ashes?
Would you call this a fast,
And an acceptable day to the LORD?

6 "*Is* this not the fast that I have chosen:
To loose the bonds of wickedness,
To undo the heavy burdens,
To let the oppressed go free,
And that you break every yoke?
7 *Is it* not to share your bread with the hungry,
And that you bring to your house the poor who are cast out;
When you see the naked, that you cover him,
And not hide yourself from your own flesh?
8 Then your light shall break forth like the morning,
Your healing shall spring forth speedily,
And your righteousness shall go before you;
The glory of the LORD shall be your rear guard.
9 Then you shall call, and the LORD will answer;
You shall cry, and He will say, 'Here I *am.*'

"If you take away the yoke from your midst,
The pointing of the finger, and speaking wickedness,
10 *If* you extend your soul to the hungry
And satisfy the afflicted soul,
Then your light shall dawn in the darkness,
And your darkness shall *be* as the noonday.
11 The LORD will guide you continually,
And satisfy your soul in drought,
And strengthen your bones;
You shall be like a watered garden,
And like a spring of water, whose waters do not fail.
12 Those from among you
Shall build the old waste places;
You shall raise up the foundations of many generations;
And you shall be called the Repairer of the Breach,
The Restorer of Streets to Dwell In.

13 "If you turn away your foot from the Sabbath,
From doing your pleasure on My holy day,
And call the Sabbath a delight,
The holy *day* of the LORD honorable,
And shall honor Him, not doing your own ways,
Nor finding your own pleasure,
Nor speaking *your own* words,
14 Then you shall delight yourself in the LORD;
And I will cause you to ride on the high hills of the earth,
And feed you with the heritage of Jacob your father.
The mouth of the LORD has spoken."

Separated from God

59 Behold, the LORD's hand is not shortened,
That it cannot save;
Nor His ear heavy,
That it cannot hear.
2 But your iniquities have separated you from your God;
And your sins have hidden *His* face from you,
So that He will not hear.
3 For your hands are defiled with blood,
And your fingers with iniquity;
Your lips have spoken lies,
Your tongue has muttered perversity.
4 No one calls for justice,
Nor does *any* plead for truth.
They trust in empty words and speak lies;
They conceive evil and bring forth iniquity.
5 They hatch vipers' eggs and weave the spider's web;
He who eats of their eggs dies,
And *from* that which is crushed a viper breaks out.
6 Their webs will not become garments,
Nor will they cover themselves with their works;
Their works *are* works of iniquity,
And the act of violence *is* in their hands.
7 Their feet run to evil,
And they make haste to shed innocent blood;
Their thoughts *are* thoughts of iniquity;
Wasting and destruction *are* in their paths.
8 The way of peace they have not known,
And *there is* no justice in their ways;
They have made themselves crooked paths;
Whoever takes that way shall not know peace.

Sin Confessed

9 Therefore justice is far from us,
Nor does righteousness overtake us;
We look for light, but there is darkness!
For brightness, *but* we walk in blackness!
10 We grope for the wall like the blind,
And we grope as if *we had* no eyes;
We stumble at noonday as at twilight;
We are as dead *men* in desolate places.

11 We all growl like bears,
And moan sadly like doves;
We look for justice, but *there is* none;
For salvation, *but* it is far from us.
12 For our transgressions are multiplied before You,
And our sins testify against us;
For our transgressions *are* with us,
And *as for* our iniquities, we know them:
13 In transgressing and lying against the LORD,
And departing from our God,
Speaking oppression and revolt,
Conceiving and uttering from the heart words of falsehood.
14 Justice is turned back,
And righteousness stands afar off;
For truth is fallen in the street,
And equity cannot enter.
15 So truth fails,
And he *who* departs from evil makes himself a prey.

The Redeemer of Zion

Then the LORD saw *it*, and it displeased Him
That *there was* no justice.
16 He saw that *there was* no man,
And wondered that *there was* no intercessor;
Therefore His own arm brought salvation for Him;
And His own righteousness, it sustained Him.
17 For He put on righteousness as a breastplate,
And a helmet of salvation on His head;
He put on the garments of vengeance for clothing,
And was clad with zeal as a cloak.
18 According to *their* deeds, accordingly He will repay,
Fury to His adversaries,
Recompense to His enemies;
The coastlands He will fully repay.
19 So shall they fear
The name of the LORD from the west,
And His glory from the rising of the sun;
When the enemy comes in like a flood,
The Spirit of the LORD will lift up a standard against him.

20 "The Redeemer will come to Zion,
And to those who turn from transgression in Jacob,"
Says the LORD.

21 "As for Me," says the LORD, "this *is* My cov-
enant with them: My Spirit who *is* upon you,
and My words which I have put in your mouth,
shall not depart from your mouth, nor from
the mouth of your descendants, nor from the
mouth of your descendants' descendants," says
the LORD, "from this time and forevermore."

The Gentiles Bless Zion

60 Arise, shine;
For your light has come!
And the glory of the LORD is risen upon you.
2 For behold, the darkness shall cover the earth,
And deep darkness the people;
But the LORD will arise over you,
And His glory will be seen upon you.
3 The Gentiles shall come to your light,
And kings to the brightness of your rising.
4 "Lift up your eyes all around, and see:
They all gather together, they come to you;
Your sons shall come from afar,
And your daughters shall be nursed at *your* side.
5 Then you shall see and become radiant,
And your heart shall swell with joy;
Because the abundance of the sea shall be turned to you,
The wealth of the Gentiles shall come to you.
6 The multitude of camels shall cover your *land*,
The dromedaries of Midian and Ephah;
All those from Sheba shall come;
They shall bring gold and incense,
And they shall proclaim the praises of the LORD.
7 All the flocks of Kedar shall be gathered together to you,
The rams of Nebaioth shall minister to you;
They shall ascend with acceptance on My altar,
And I will glorify the house of My glory.
8 "Who *are* these *who* fly like a cloud,
And like doves to their roosts?
9 Surely the coastlands shall wait for Me;
And the ships of Tarshish *will come* first,
To bring your sons from afar,
Their silver and their gold with them,
To the name of the LORD your God,
And to the Holy One of Israel,
Because He has glorified you.

10 "The sons of foreigners shall build up your walls,
And their kings shall minister to you;
For in My wrath I struck you,
But in My favor I have had mercy on you.
11 Therefore your gates shall be open continually;
They shall not be shut day or night,
That *men* may bring to you the wealth of the Gentiles,
And their kings in procession.
12 For the nation and kingdom which will not serve you shall perish,
And *those* nations shall be utterly ruined.

13 "The glory of Lebanon shall come to you,
The cypress, the pine, and the box tree together,
To beautify the place of My sanctuary;
And I will make the place of My feet glorious.
14 Also the sons of those who afflicted you
Shall come bowing to you,
And all those who despised you shall fall prostrate at the soles of your feet;
And they shall call you The City of the LORD,
Zion of the Holy One of Israel.

15 "Whereas you have been forsaken and hated,
So that no one went through *you*,
I will make you an eternal excellence,
A joy of many generations.
16 You shall drink the milk of the Gentiles,
And milk the breast of kings;

You shall know that I, the LORD, *am* your Savior
And your Redeemer, the Mighty One of Jacob.

17 "Instead of bronze I will bring gold,
Instead of iron I will bring silver,
Instead of wood, bronze,
And instead of stones, iron.
I will also make your officers peace,
And your magistrates righteousness.
18 Violence shall no longer be heard in your land,
Neither wasting nor destruction within your borders;
But you shall call your walls Salvation,
And your gates Praise.

God the Glory of His People

19 "The sun shall no longer be your light by day,
Nor for brightness shall the moon give light to you;
But the LORD will be to you an everlasting light,
And your God your glory.
20 Your sun shall no longer go down,
Nor shall your moon withdraw itself;
For the LORD will be your everlasting light,
And the days of your mourning shall be ended.
21 Also your people *shall* all *be* righteous;
They shall inherit the land forever,
The branch of My planting,
The work of My hands,
That I may be glorified.
22 A little one shall become a thousand,
And a small one a strong nation.
I, the LORD, will hasten it in its time."

The Good News of Salvation

61 "The Spirit of the Lord GOD *is* upon Me,
Because the LORD has anointed Me
To preach good tidings to the poor;
He has sent Me to heal the brokenhearted,
To proclaim liberty to the captives,
And the opening of the prison to *those who are* bound;
2 To proclaim the acceptable year of the LORD,
And the day of vengeance of our God;
To comfort all who mourn,
3 To console those who mourn in Zion,
To give them beauty for ashes,
The oil of joy for mourning,
The garment of praise for the spirit of heaviness;
That they may be called trees of righteousness,
The planting of the LORD, that He may be glorified."

4 And they shall rebuild the old ruins,
They shall raise up the former desolations,
And they shall repair the ruined cities,
The desolations of many generations.
5 Strangers shall stand and feed your flocks,
And the sons of the foreigner
Shall be your plowmen and your vinedressers.
6 But you shall be named the priests of the LORD,
They shall call you the servants of our God.
You shall eat the riches of the Gentiles,
And in their glory you shall boast.
7 Instead of your shame *you shall have* double *honor*,
And *instead of* confusion they shall rejoice in their portion.
Therefore in their land they shall possess double;
Everlasting joy shall be theirs.

8 "For I, the LORD, love justice;
I hate robbery for burnt offering;
I will direct their work in truth,
And will make with them an everlasting covenant.
9 Their descendants shall be known among the Gentiles,
And their offspring among the people.
All who see them shall acknowledge them,
That they *are* the posterity *whom* the LORD has blessed."

10 I will greatly rejoice in the LORD,
My soul shall be joyful in my God;
For He has clothed me with the garments of salvation,
He has covered me with the robe of righteousness,
As a bridegroom decks *himself* with ornaments,
And as a bride adorns *herself* with her jewels.
11 For as the earth brings forth its bud,
As the garden causes the things that are sown in it to spring forth,
So the Lord GOD will cause righteousness and praise to spring forth before all the nations.

Assurance of Zion's Salvation

62 For Zion's sake I will not hold My peace,
And for Jerusalem's sake I will not rest,
Until her righteousness goes forth as brightness,
And her salvation as a lamp *that* burns.
2 The Gentiles shall see your righteousness,
And all kings your glory.
You shall be called by a new name,
Which the mouth of the LORD will name.
3 You shall also be a crown of glory
In the hand of the LORD,
And a royal diadem
In the hand of your God.
4 You shall no longer be termed Forsaken,
Nor shall your land any more be termed Desolate;
But you shall be called Hephzibah,[a] and your land Beulah;[b]
For the LORD delights in you,
And your land shall be married.
5 For *as* a young man marries a virgin,
So shall your sons marry you;
And *as* the bridegroom rejoices over the bride,
So shall your God rejoice over you.

62:4 [a]Literally *My Delight Is in Her* [b]Literally *Married*

6 I have set watchmen on your walls,
O Jerusalem;
They shall never hold their peace day or night.
You who make mention of the LORD, do not keep silent,
7 And give Him no rest till He establishes
And till He makes Jerusalem a praise in the earth.

8 The LORD has sworn by His right hand
And by the arm of His strength:
"Surely I will no longer give your grain
As food for your enemies;
And the sons of the foreigner shall not drink your new wine,
For which you have labored.
9 But those who have gathered it shall eat it,
And praise the LORD;
Those who have brought it together shall drink it in My holy courts."

10 Go through,
Go through the gates!
Prepare the way for the people;
Build up,
Build up the highway!
Take out the stones,
Lift up a banner for the peoples!

11 Indeed the LORD has proclaimed
To the end of the world:
"Say to the daughter of Zion,
'Surely your salvation is coming;
Behold, His reward *is* with Him,
And His work before Him.'"
12 And they shall call them The Holy People,
The Redeemed of the LORD;
And you shall be called Sought Out,
A City Not Forsaken.

The LORD in Judgment and Salvation

63 Who *is* this who comes from Edom,
With dyed garments from Bozrah,
This *One who is* glorious in His apparel,
Traveling in the greatness of His strength?—

"I who speak in righteousness, mighty to save."

2 Why *is* Your apparel red,
And Your garments like one who treads in the winepress?

3 "I have trodden the winepress alone,
And from the peoples no one *was* with Me.
For I have trodden them in My anger,
And trampled them in My fury;
Their blood is sprinkled upon My garments,
And I have stained all My robes.
4 For the day of vengeance *is* in My heart,
And the year of My redeemed has come.
5 I looked, but *there was* no one to help,
And I wondered
That *there was* no one to uphold;
Therefore My own arm brought salvation for Me;
And My own fury, it sustained Me.
6 I have trodden down the peoples in My anger,
Made them drunk in My fury,
And brought down their strength to the earth."

God's Mercy Remembered

7 I will mention the lovingkindnesses of the LORD
And the praises of the LORD,
According to all that the LORD has bestowed on us,
And the great goodness toward the house of Israel,
Which He has bestowed on them according to His mercies,
According to the multitude of His lovingkindnesses.
8 For He said, "Surely they *are* My people,
Children *who* will not lie."
So He became their Savior.
9 In all their affliction He was afflicted,
And the Angel of His Presence saved them;
In His love and in His pity He redeemed them;
And He bore them and carried them
All the days of old.
10 But they rebelled and grieved His Holy Spirit;
So He turned Himself against them as an enemy,
And He fought against them.

11 Then he remembered the days of old,
Moses *and* his people, *saying*:
"Where *is* He who brought them up out of the sea
With the shepherd of His flock?
Where *is* He who put His Holy Spirit within them,
12 Who led *them* by the right hand of Moses,
With His glorious arm,
Dividing the water before them
To make for Himself an everlasting name,
13 Who led them through the deep,
As a horse in the wilderness,
That they might not stumble?"

14 As a beast goes down into the valley,
And the Spirit of the LORD causes him to rest,
So You lead Your people,
To make Yourself a glorious name.

A Prayer of Penitence

15 Look down from heaven,
And see from Your habitation, holy and glorious.
Where *are* Your zeal and Your strength,
The yearning of Your heart and Your mercies toward me?
Are they restrained?
16 Doubtless You *are* our Father,
Though Abraham was ignorant of us,
And Israel does not acknowledge us.
You, O LORD, *are* our Father;
Our Redeemer from Everlasting *is* Your name.
17 O LORD, why have You made us stray from Your ways,
And hardened our heart from Your fear?
Return for Your servants' sake,
The tribes of Your inheritance.

18 Your holy people have possessed *it* but a
little while;
Our adversaries have trodden down Your
sanctuary.
19 We have become *like* those of old, over
whom You never ruled,
Those who were never called by Your
name.

64 Oh, that You would rend the heavens!
That You would come down!
That the mountains might shake at Your
presence—
2 As fire burns brushwood,
As fire causes water to boil—
To make Your name known to Your
adversaries,
That the nations may tremble at Your
presence!
3 When You did awesome things *for which*
we did not look,
You came down,
The mountains shook at Your presence.
4 For since the beginning of the world
Men have not heard nor perceived by the
ear,
Nor has the eye seen any God besides
You,
Who acts for the one who waits for Him.
5 You meet him who rejoices and does
righteousness,
Who remembers You in Your ways.
You are indeed angry, for we have
sinned—
In these ways we continue;
And we need to be saved.

6 But we are all like an unclean *thing*,
And all our righteousnesses *are* like filthy
rags;
We all fade as a leaf,
And our iniquities, like the wind,
Have taken us away.
7 And *there is* no one who calls on Your
name,
Who stirs himself up to take hold of You;
For You have hidden Your face from us,
And have consumed us because of our
iniquities.
8 But now, O LORD,
You *are* our Father;
We *are* the clay, and You our potter;
And all we *are* the work of Your hand.
9 Do not be furious, O LORD,
Nor remember iniquity forever;
Indeed, please look—we all *are* Your
people!
10 Your holy cities are a wilderness,
Zion is a wilderness,
Jerusalem a desolation.
11 Our holy and beautiful temple,
Where our fathers praised You,
Is burned up with fire;
And all our pleasant things are laid
waste.
12 Will You restrain Yourself because of
these *things*, O LORD?
Will You hold Your peace, and afflict us
very severely?

The Righteousness of God's Judgment

65 "I was sought by *those who* did not ask
for Me;
I was found by *those who* did not seek
Me.
I said, 'Here I am, here I am,'
To a nation *that* was not called by My
name.
2 I have stretched out My hands all day
long to a rebellious people,
Who walk in a way *that is* not good,
According to their own thoughts;
3 A people who provoke Me to anger
continually to My face;
Who sacrifice in gardens,
And burn incense on altars of brick;
4 Who sit among the graves,
And spend the night in the tombs;
Who eat swine's flesh,
And the broth of abominable things is *in*
their vessels;
5 Who say, 'Keep to yourself,
Do not come near me,
For I am holier than you!'
These *are* smoke in My nostrils,
A fire that burns all the day.

6 "Behold, *it is* written before Me:
I will not keep silence, but will repay—
Even repay into their bosom—
7 Your iniquities and the iniquities of your
fathers together,"
Says the LORD,
"Who have burned incense on the
mountains
And blasphemed Me on the hills;
Therefore I will measure their former
work into their bosom."

8 Thus says the LORD:

"As the new wine is found in the cluster,
And *one* says, 'Do not destroy it,
For a blessing *is* in it,'
So will I do for My servants' sake,
That I may not destroy them all.
9 I will bring forth descendants from Jacob,
And from Judah an heir of My
mountains;
My elect shall inherit it,
And My servants shall dwell there.
10 Sharon shall be a fold of flocks,
And the Valley of Achor a place for herds
to lie down,
For My people who have sought Me.
11 "But you *are* those who forsake the LORD,
Who forget My holy mountain,
Who prepare a table for Gad,[a]
And who furnish a drink offering for
Meni.[b]
12 Therefore I will number you for the
sword,
And you shall all bow down to the
slaughter;
Because, when I called, you did not
answer;
When I spoke, you did not hear,
But did evil before My eyes,
And chose *that* in which I do not
delight."

13 Therefore thus says the Lord GOD:

"Behold, My servants shall eat,
But you shall be hungry;
Behold, My servants shall drink,

65:11 [a]Literally *Troop* or *Fortune*, a pagan deity [b]Literally *Number* or *Destiny*, a pagan deity

But you shall be thirsty;
Behold, My servants shall rejoice,
But you shall be ashamed;
14 Behold, My servants shall sing for joy of heart,
But you shall cry for sorrow of heart,
And wail for grief of spirit.
15 You shall leave your name as a curse to My chosen;
For the Lord GOD will slay you,
And call His servants by another name;
16 So that he who blesses himself in the earth
Shall bless himself in the God of truth;
And he who swears in the earth
Shall swear by the God of truth;
Because the former troubles are forgotten,
And because they are hidden from My eyes.

The Glorious New Creation

17 "For behold, I create new heavens and a new earth;
And the former shall not be remembered or come to mind.
18 But be glad and rejoice forever in what I create;
For behold, I create Jerusalem *as* a rejoicing,
And her people a joy.
19 I will rejoice in Jerusalem,
And joy in My people;
The voice of weeping shall no longer be heard in her,
Nor the voice of crying.

20 "No more shall an infant from there *live but a few* days,
Nor an old man who has not fulfilled his days;
For the child shall die one hundred years old,
But the sinner *being* one hundred years old shall be accursed.
21 They shall build houses and inhabit *them;*
They shall plant vineyards and eat their fruit.
22 They shall not build and another inhabit;
They shall not plant and another eat;
For as the days of a tree, *so shall be* the days of My people,
And My elect shall long enjoy the work of their hands.
23 They shall not labor in vain,
Nor bring forth children for trouble;
For they *shall be* the descendants of the blessed of the LORD,
And their offspring with them.

24 "It shall come to pass
That before they call, I will answer;
And while they are still speaking, I will hear.
25 The wolf and the lamb shall feed together,
The lion shall eat straw like the ox,
And dust *shall be* the serpent's food.
They shall not hurt nor destroy in all My holy mountain,"
Says the LORD.

True Worship and False

66 Thus says the LORD:
"Heaven *is* My throne,
And earth *is* My footstool.
Where *is* the house that you will build Me?
And where *is* the place of My rest?
2 For all those *things* My hand has made,
And all those *things* exist,"
Says the LORD.
"But on this *one* will I look:
On *him who is* poor and of a contrite spirit,
And who trembles at My word.

3 "He who kills a bull *is as if* he slays a man;
He who sacrifices a lamb, *as if* he breaks a dog's neck;
He who offers a grain offering, *as if he offers* swine's blood;
He who burns incense, *as if* he blesses an idol.
Just as they have chosen their own ways,
And their soul delights in their abominations,
4 So will I choose their delusions,
And bring their fears on them;
Because, when I called, no one answered,
When I spoke they did not hear;
But they did evil before My eyes,
And chose *that* in which I do not delight."

The LORD Vindicates Zion

5 Hear the word of the LORD,
You who tremble at His word:
"Your brethren who hated you,
Who cast you out for My name's sake, said,
'Let the LORD be glorified,
That we may see your joy.'
But they shall be ashamed."
6 The sound of noise from the city!
A voice from the temple!
The voice of the LORD,
Who fully repays His enemies!

7 "Before she was in labor, she gave birth;
Before her pain came,
She delivered a male child.
8 Who has heard such a thing?
Who has seen such things?
Shall the earth be made to give birth in one day?
Or shall a nation be born at once?
For as soon as Zion was in labor,
She gave birth to her children.
9 Shall I bring to the time of birth, and not cause delivery?" says the LORD.
"Shall I who cause delivery shut up *the womb?*" says your God.
10 "Rejoice with Jerusalem,
And be glad with her, all you who love her;
Rejoice for joy with her, all you who mourn for her;
11 That you may feed and be satisfied
With the consolation of her bosom,

That you may drink deeply and be delighted
With the abundance of her glory."

12 For thus says the LORD:

"Behold, I will extend peace to her like a river,
And the glory of the Gentiles like a flowing stream.
Then you shall feed;
On *her* sides shall you be carried,
And be dandled on *her* knees.
13 As one whom his mother comforts,
So I will comfort you;
And you shall be comforted in Jerusalem."

The Reign and Indignation of God

14 When you see *this*, your heart shall rejoice,
And your bones shall flourish like grass;
The hand of the LORD shall be known to His servants,
And *His* indignation to His enemies.
15 For behold, the LORD will come with fire
And with His chariots, like a whirlwind,
To render His anger with fury,
And His rebuke with flames of fire.
16 For by fire and by His sword
The LORD will judge all flesh;
And the slain of the LORD shall be many.

17 "Those who sanctify themselves and purify themselves,
To go to the gardens
After an *idol* in the midst,
Eating swine's flesh and the abomination and the mouse,
Shall be consumed together," says the LORD.

18 "For I *know* their works and their
thoughts. It shall be that I will gather all na-
tions and tongues; and they shall come and see
My glory.
19 "I will set a sign among them; and those
among them who escape I will send to the na-
tions: *to* Tarshish and Pul[a] and Lud, who draw
the bow, and Tubal and Javan, *to* the coast-
lands afar off who have not heard My fame nor
seen My glory. And they shall declare My glory
among the Gentiles.
20 "Then they shall bring all your brethren
for an offering to the LORD out of all nations,
on horses and in chariots and in litters, on
mules and on camels, to My holy mountain
Jerusalem," says the LORD, "as the children of
Israel bring an offering in a clean vessel into
the house of the LORD.
21 "And I will also take some of them for
priests *and* Levites," says the LORD.

22 "For as the new heavens and the new earth
Which I will make shall remain before Me," says the LORD,
"So shall your descendants and your name remain.
23 And it shall come to pass
That from one New Moon to another,
And from one Sabbath to another,
All flesh shall come to worship before Me," says the LORD.

24 "And they shall go forth and look
Upon the corpses of the men
Who have transgressed against Me.
For their worm does not die,
And their fire is not quenched.
They shall be an abhorrence to all flesh."

The Book of JEREMIAH

1 The words of Jeremiah the son of Hilkiah,
of the priests who *were* in Anathoth in the
land of Benjamin,
2 to whom the word of the LORD came in the
days of Josiah the son of Amon, king of Judah,
in the thirteenth year of his reign.
3 It came also in the days of Jehoiakim the
son of Josiah, king of Judah, until the end of
the eleventh year of Zedekiah the son of Jo-
siah, king of Judah, until the carrying away of
Jerusalem captive in the fifth month.

The Prophet Is Called

4 Then the word of the LORD came to me,
saying:

5 "Before I formed you in the womb I knew you;
Before you were born I sanctified you;
I ordained you a prophet to the nations."

6 Then said I:

"Ah, Lord GOD!
Behold, I cannot speak, for I *am* a youth."

7 But the LORD said to me:

"Do not say, 'I *am* a youth,'
For you shall go to all to whom I send you,
And whatever I command you, you shall speak.
8 Do not be afraid of their faces,
For I *am* with you to deliver you," says the LORD.

9 Then the LORD put forth His hand and
touched my mouth, and the LORD said to me:

"Behold, I have put My words in your mouth.
10 See, I have this day set you over the nations and over the kingdoms,
To root out and to pull down,
To destroy and to throw down,
To build and to plant."

11 Moreover the word of the LORD came to
me, saying, "Jeremiah, what do you see?" And
I said, "I see a branch of an almond tree."
12 Then the LORD said to me, "You have seen
well, for I am ready to perform My word."

66:19 [a]Following Masoretic Text and Targum; Septuagint reads *Put* (compare Jeremiah 46:9).

13 And the word of the LORD came to me the
second time, saying, "What do you see?" And
I said, "I see a boiling pot, and it is facing away
from the north."
14 Then the LORD said to me:

"Out of the north calamity shall break forth
On all the inhabitants of the land.
15 For behold, I am calling
All the families of the kingdoms of the north," says the LORD;
"They shall come and each one set his throne
At the entrance of the gates of Jerusalem,
Against all its walls all around,
And against all the cities of Judah.
16 I will utter My judgments
Against them concerning all their wickedness,
Because they have forsaken Me,
Burned incense to other gods,
And worshiped the works of their own hands.

17 "Therefore prepare yourself and arise,
And speak to them all that I command you.
Do not be dismayed before their faces,
Lest I dismay you before them.
18 For behold, I have made you this day
A fortified city and an iron pillar,
And bronze walls against the whole land—
Against the kings of Judah,
Against its princes,
Against its priests,
And against the people of the land.
19 They will fight against you,
But they shall not prevail against you.
For I *am* with you," says the LORD, "to deliver you."

God's Case Against Israel

2 Moreover the word of the LORD came to
me, saying,
2 "Go and cry in the hearing of Jerusalem,
saying, 'Thus says the LORD:

"I remember you,
The kindness of your youth,
The love of your betrothal,
When you went after Me in the wilderness,
In a land not sown.
3 Israel *was* holiness to the LORD,
The firstfruits of His increase.
All that devour him will offend;
Disaster will come upon them," says the LORD.'"

4 Hear the word of the LORD, O house of
Jacob and all the families of the house of Israel.
5 Thus says the LORD:

"What injustice have your fathers found in Me,
That they have gone far from Me,
Have followed idols,
And have become idolaters?
6 Neither did they say, 'Where *is* the LORD,
Who brought us up out of the land of Egypt,
Who led us through the wilderness,
Through a land of deserts and pits,
Through a land of drought and the shadow of death,
Through a land that no one crossed
And where no one dwelt?'
7 I brought you into a bountiful country,
To eat its fruit and its goodness.
But when you entered, you defiled My land
And made My heritage an abomination.
8 The priests did not say, 'Where *is* the LORD?'
And those who handle the law did not know Me;
The rulers also transgressed against Me;
The prophets prophesied by Baal,
And walked after *things that* do not profit.

9 "Therefore I will yet bring charges against you," says the LORD,
"And against your children's children I will bring charges.
10 For pass beyond the coasts of Cyprus[a] and see,
Send to Kedar[b] and consider diligently,
And see if there has been such *a thing*.
11 Has a nation changed *its* gods,
Which *are* not gods?
But My people have changed their Glory
For *what* does not profit.
12 Be astonished, O heavens, at this,
And be horribly afraid;
Be very desolate," says the LORD.
13 "For My people have committed two evils:
They have forsaken Me, the fountain of living waters,
And hewn themselves cisterns—broken cisterns that can hold no water.

14 "*Is* Israel a servant?
Is he a homeborn *slave*?
Why is he plundered?
15 The young lions roared at him, *and* growled;
They made his land waste;
His cities are burned, without inhabitant.
16 Also the people of Noph[a] and Tahpanhes
Have broken the crown of your head.
17 Have you not brought this on yourself,
In that you have forsaken the LORD your God
When He led you in the way?
18 And now why take the road to Egypt,
To drink the waters of Sihor?
Or why take the road to Assyria,
To drink the waters of the River?[a]
19 Your own wickedness will correct you,
And your backslidings will rebuke you.
Know therefore and see that *it is* an evil and bitter *thing*
That you have forsaken the LORD your God,
And the fear of Me *is* not in you,"
Says the Lord GOD of hosts.

20 "For of old I have broken your yoke *and* burst your bonds;
And you said, 'I will not transgress,'
When on every high hill and under every green tree
You lay down, playing the harlot.

2:10 [a]Hebrew *Kittim*, western lands, especially Cyprus [b]In the northern Arabian desert, representative of the eastern cultures **2:16** [a]That is, Memphis in ancient Egypt **2:18** [a]That is, the Euphrates

21 Yet I had planted you a noble vine, a seed of highest quality.
How then have you turned before Me
Into the degenerate plant of an alien vine?
22 For though you wash yourself with lye, and use much soap,
Yet your iniquity is marked before Me,"
says the Lord GOD.

23 "How can you say, 'I am not polluted,
I have not gone after the Baals'?
See your way in the valley;
Know what you have done:
You are a swift dromedary breaking loose in her ways,
24 A wild donkey used to the wilderness,
That sniffs at the wind in her desire;
In her time of mating, who can turn her away?
All those who seek her will not weary themselves;
In her month they will find her.
25 Withhold your foot from being unshod,
and your throat from thirst.
But you said, 'There is no hope.
No! For I have loved aliens, and after them I will go.'

26 "As the thief is ashamed when he is found out,
So is the house of Israel ashamed;
They and their kings and their princes,
and their priests and their prophets,
27 Saying to a tree, 'You *are* my father,'
And to a stone, 'You gave birth to me.'
For they have turned *their* back to Me,
and not *their* face.
But in the time of their trouble
They will say, 'Arise and save us.'
28 But where *are* your gods that you have made for yourselves?
Let them arise,
If they can save you in the time of your trouble;
For *according to* the number of your cities
Are your gods, O Judah.

29 "Why will you plead with Me?
You all have transgressed against Me,"
says the LORD.
30 "In vain I have chastened your children;
They received no correction.
Your sword has devoured your prophets
Like a destroying lion.

31 "O generation, see the word of the LORD!
Have I been a wilderness to Israel,
Or a land of darkness?
Why do My people say, 'We are lords;
We will come no more to You'?
32 Can a virgin forget her ornaments,
Or a bride her attire?
Yet My people have forgotten Me days without number.

33 "Why do you beautify your way to seek love?
Therefore you have also taught
The wicked women your ways.
34 Also on your skirts is found
The blood of the lives of the poor innocents.
I have not found it by secret search,
But plainly on all these things.
35 Yet you say, 'Because I am innocent,
Surely His anger shall turn from me.'
Behold, I will plead My case against you,
Because you say, 'I have not sinned.'
36 Why do you gad about so much to change your way?
Also you shall be ashamed of Egypt as you were ashamed of Assyria.
37 Indeed you will go forth from him
With your hands on your head;
For the LORD has rejected your trusted allies,
And you will not prosper by them.

Israel Is Shameless

3 "They say, 'If a man divorces his wife,
And she goes from him
And becomes another man's,
May he return to her again?'
Would not that land be greatly polluted?
But you have played the harlot with many lovers;
Yet return to Me," says the LORD.

2 "Lift up your eyes to the desolate heights and see:
Where have you not lain *with men?*
By the road you have sat for them
Like an Arabian in the wilderness;
And you have polluted the land
With your harlotries and your wickedness.
3 Therefore the showers have been withheld,
And there has been no latter rain.
You have had a harlot's forehead;
You refuse to be ashamed.
4 Will you not from this time cry to Me,
'My Father, You *are* the guide of my youth?
5 Will He remain angry forever?
Will He keep it to the end?'
Behold, you have spoken and done evil things,
As you were able."

A Call to Repentance

6 The LORD said also to me in the days of
Josiah the king: "Have you seen what back-
sliding Israel has done? She has gone up on
every high mountain and under every green
tree, and there played the harlot.
7 "And I said, after she had done all these
things, 'Return to Me.' But she did not return.
And her treacherous sister Judah saw it.
8 "Then I saw that for all the causes for which
backsliding Israel had committed adultery, I
had put her away and given her a certificate of
divorce; yet her treacherous sister Judah did
not fear, but went and played the harlot also.
9 "So it came to pass, through her casual har-
lotry, that she defiled the land and committed
adultery with stones and trees.
10 "And yet for all this her treacherous sister
Judah has not turned to Me with her whole
heart, but in pretense," says the LORD.
11 Then the LORD said to me, "Backsliding
Israel has shown herself more righteous than
treacherous Judah.
12 "Go and proclaim these words toward the
north, and say:

'Return, backsliding Israel,' says the LORD;
'I will not cause My anger to fall on you.

For I *am* merciful,' says the LORD;
'I will not remain angry forever.
13 Only acknowledge your iniquity,
That you have transgressed against the
LORD your God,
And have scattered your charms
To alien deities under every green tree,
And you have not obeyed My voice,' says
the LORD.

14 "Return, O backsliding children," says the
LORD; "for I am married to you. I will take you,
one from a city and two from a family, and I
will bring you to Zion.
15 "And I will give you shepherds according
to My heart, who will feed you with knowledge
and understanding.
16 "Then it shall come to pass, when you are
multiplied and increased in the land in those
days," says the LORD, "that they will say no
more, 'The ark of the covenant of the LORD.' It
shall not come to mind, nor shall they remem-
ber it, nor shall they visit *it,* nor shall it be
made anymore.
17 "At that time Jerusalem shall be called The
Throne of the LORD, and all the nations shall
be gathered to it, to the name of the LORD,
to Jerusalem. No more shall they follow the
dictates of their evil hearts.
18 "In those days the house of Judah shall
walk with the house of Israel, and they shall
come together out of the land of the north to
the land that I have given as an inheritance
to your fathers.
19 "But I said:

'How can I put you among the children
And give you a pleasant land,
A beautiful heritage of the hosts of
nations?'

"And I said:

'You shall call Me, "My Father,"
And not turn away from Me.'
20 Surely, *as* a wife treacherously departs
from her husband,
So have you dealt treacherously with Me,
O house of Israel," says the LORD.

21 A voice was heard on the desolate
heights,
Weeping *and* supplications of the
children of Israel.
For they have perverted their way;
They have forgotten the LORD their God.

22 "Return, you backsliding children,
And I will heal your backslidings."

"Indeed we do come to You,
For You are the LORD our God.
23 Truly, in vain *is salvation hoped for* from
the hills,
And from the multitude of mountains;
Truly, in the LORD our God
Is the salvation of Israel.
24 For shame has devoured
The labor of our fathers from our youth—
Their flocks and their herds,
Their sons and their daughters.
25 We lie down in our shame,
And our reproach covers us.
For we have sinned against the LORD our
God,
We and our fathers,
From our youth even to this day,
And have not obeyed the voice of the
LORD our God."

4 "If you will return, O Israel," says the
LORD,
"Return to Me;
And if you will put away your
abominations out of My sight,
Then you shall not be moved.
2 And you shall swear, 'The LORD lives,'
In truth, in judgment, and in
righteousness;
The nations shall bless themselves in
Him,
And in Him they shall glory."

3 For thus says the LORD to the men of Judah
and Jerusalem:

"Break up your fallow ground,
And do not sow among thorns.
4 Circumcise yourselves to the LORD,
And take away the foreskins of your
hearts,
You men of Judah and inhabitants of
Jerusalem,
Lest My fury come forth like fire,
And burn so that no one can quench *it,*
Because of the evil of your doings."

An Imminent Invasion

5 Declare in Judah and proclaim in Jerusa-
lem, and say:

"Blow the trumpet in the land;
Cry, 'Gather together,'
And say, 'Assemble yourselves,
And let us go into the fortified cities.'
6 Set up the standard toward Zion.
Take refuge! Do not delay!
For I will bring disaster from the north,
And great destruction."

7 The lion has come up from his thicket,
And the destroyer of nations is on his
way.
He has gone forth from his place
To make your land desolate.
Your cities will be laid waste,
Without inhabitant.
8 For this, clothe yourself with sackcloth,
Lament and wail.
For the fierce anger of the LORD
Has not turned back from us.

9 "And it shall come to pass in that day,"
says the LORD,
"*That* the heart of the king shall perish,
And the heart of the princes;
The priests shall be astonished,
And the prophets shall wonder."

10 Then I said, "Ah, Lord GOD!
Surely You have greatly deceived this
people and Jerusalem,
Saying, 'You shall have peace,'
Whereas the sword reaches to the heart."

11 At that time it will be said
To this people and to Jerusalem,
"A dry wind of the desolate heights *blows*
in the wilderness
Toward the daughter of My people—
Not to fan or to cleanse—
12 A wind too strong for these will come for
Me;
Now I will also speak judgment against
them."

13 "Behold, he shall come up like clouds,
And his chariots like a whirlwind.
His horses are swifter than eagles.
Woe to us, for we are plundered!"

14 O Jerusalem, wash your heart from wickedness,
That you may be saved.
How long shall your evil thoughts lodge within you?
15 For a voice declares from Dan
And proclaims affliction from Mount Ephraim:
16 "Make mention to the nations,
Yes, proclaim against Jerusalem,
That watchers come from a far country
And raise their voice against the cities of Judah.
17 Like keepers of a field they are against her all around,
Because she has been rebellious against Me," says the LORD.
18 "Your ways and your doings
Have procured these *things* for you.
This *is* your wickedness,
Because it is bitter,
Because it reaches to your heart."

Sorrow for the Doomed Nation

19 O my soul, my soul!
I am pained in my very heart!
My heart makes a noise in me;
I cannot hold my peace,
Because you have heard, O my soul,
The sound of the trumpet,
The alarm of war.
20 Destruction upon destruction is cried,
For the whole land is plundered.
Suddenly my tents are plundered,
And my curtains in a moment.
21 How long will I see the standard,
And hear the sound of the trumpet?

22 "For My people *are* foolish,
They have not known Me.
They *are* silly children,
And they have no understanding.
They *are* wise to do evil,
But to do good they have no knowledge."

23 I beheld the earth, and indeed *it was* without form, and void;
And the heavens, they *had* no light.
24 I beheld the mountains, and indeed they trembled,
And all the hills moved back and forth.
25 I beheld, and indeed *there was* no man,
And all the birds of the heavens had fled.
26 I beheld, and indeed the fruitful land *was* a wilderness,
And all its cities were broken down
At the presence of the LORD,
By His fierce anger.

27 For thus says the LORD:

"The whole land shall be desolate;
Yet I will not make a full end.
28 For this shall the earth mourn,
And the heavens above be black,
Because I have spoken.
I have purposed and will not relent,
Nor will I turn back from it.
29 The whole city shall flee from the noise of the horsemen and bowmen.
They shall go into thickets and climb up on the rocks.
Every city *shall be* forsaken,
And not a man shall dwell in it.

30 "And *when* you *are* plundered,
What will you do?
Though you clothe yourself with crimson,
Though you adorn *yourself* with ornaments of gold,
Though you enlarge your eyes with paint,
In vain you will make yourself fair;
Your lovers will despise you;
They will seek your life.

31 "For I have heard a voice as of a woman in labor,
The anguish as of her who brings forth her first child,
The voice of the daughter of Zion bewailing herself;
She spreads her hands, *saying*,
'Woe *is* me now, for my soul is weary
Because of murderers!'

The Justice of God's Judgment

5 "Run to and fro through the streets of Jerusalem;
See now and know;
And seek in her open places
If you can find a man,
If there is *anyone* who executes judgment,
Who seeks the truth,
And I will pardon her.
2 Though they say, '*As* the LORD lives,'
Surely they swear falsely."

3 O LORD, *are* not Your eyes on the truth?
You have stricken them,
But they have not grieved;
You have consumed them,
But they have refused to receive correction.
They have made their faces harder than rock;
They have refused to return.

4 Therefore I said, "Surely these *are* poor.
They are foolish;
For they do not know the way of the LORD,
The judgment of their God.
5 I will go to the great men and speak to them,
For they have known the way of the LORD,
The judgment of their God."

But these have altogether broken the yoke
And burst the bonds.
6 Therefore a lion from the forest shall slay them,
A wolf of the deserts shall destroy them;
A leopard will watch over their cities.
Everyone who goes out from there shall be torn in pieces,
Because their transgressions are many;
Their backslidings have increased.

7 "How shall I pardon you for this?
Your children have forsaken Me
And sworn by *those that are* not gods.
When I had fed them to the full,
Then they committed adultery
And assembled themselves by troops in the harlots' houses.

8 They were *like* well-fed lusty stallions;
Every one neighed after his neighbor's wife.
9 Shall I not punish *them* for these *things?*" says the LORD.
"And shall I not avenge Myself on such a nation as this?

10 "Go up on her walls and destroy,
But do not make a complete end.
Take away her branches,
For they *are* not the LORD's.
11 For the house of Israel and the house of Judah
Have dealt very treacherously with Me," says the LORD.
12 They have lied about the LORD,
And said, "*It is* not He.
Neither will evil come upon us,
Nor shall we see sword or famine.
13 And the prophets become wind,
For the word *is* not in them.
Thus shall it be done to them."

14 Therefore thus says the LORD God of hosts:

"Because you speak this word,
Behold, I will make My words in your mouth fire,
And this people wood,
And it shall devour them.
15 Behold, I will bring a nation against you from afar,
O house of Israel," says the LORD.
"It *is* a mighty nation,
It *is* an ancient nation,
A nation whose language you do not know,
Nor can you understand what they say.
16 Their quiver *is* like an open tomb;
They *are* all mighty men.
17 And they shall eat up your harvest and your bread,
Which your sons and daughters should eat.
They shall eat up your flocks and your herds;
They shall eat up your vines and your fig trees;
They shall destroy your fortified cities,
In which you trust, with the sword.

18 "Nevertheless in those days," says the
LORD, "I will not make a complete end of you.
19 "And it will be when you say, 'Why does
the LORD our God do all these *things* to us?'
then you shall answer them, 'Just as you have
forsaken Me and served foreign gods in your
land, so you shall serve aliens in a land *that is*
not yours.'

20 "Declare this in the house of Jacob
And proclaim it in Judah, saying,
21 'Hear this now, O foolish people,
Without understanding,
Who have eyes and see not,
And who have ears and hear not:
22 Do you not fear Me?' says the LORD.
'Will you not tremble at My presence,
Who have placed the sand as the bound of the sea,
By a perpetual decree, that it cannot pass beyond it?
And though its waves toss to and fro,
Yet they cannot prevail;
Though they roar, yet they cannot pass over it.
23 But this people has a defiant and rebellious heart;
They have revolted and departed.
24 They do not say in their heart,
"Let us now fear the LORD our God,
Who gives rain, both the former and the latter, in its season.
He reserves for us the appointed weeks of the harvest."
25 Your iniquities have turned these *things* away,
And your sins have withheld good from you.

26 'For among My people are found wicked *men;*
They lie in wait as one who sets snares;
They set a trap;
They catch men.
27 As a cage is full of birds,
So their houses *are* full of deceit.
Therefore they have become great and grown rich.
28 They have grown fat, they are sleek;
Yes, they surpass the deeds of the wicked;
They do not plead the cause,
The cause of the fatherless;
Yet they prosper,
And the right of the needy they do not defend.
29 Shall I not punish *them* for these *things?*' says the LORD.
'Shall I not avenge Myself on such a nation as this?'

30 "An astonishing and horrible thing
Has been committed in the land:
31 The prophets prophesy falsely,
And the priests rule by their *own* power;
And My people love *to have it* so.
But what will you do in the end?

Impending Destruction from the North

6 "O you children of Benjamin,
Gather yourselves to flee from the midst of Jerusalem!
Blow the trumpet in Tekoa,
And set up a signal-fire in Beth Haccerem;
For disaster appears out of the north,
And great destruction.
2 I have likened the daughter of Zion
To a lovely and delicate woman.
3 The shepherds with their flocks shall come to her.
They shall pitch *their* tents against her all around.
Each one shall pasture in his own place."

4 "Prepare war against her;
Arise, and let us go up at noon.
Woe to us, for the day goes away,
For the shadows of the evening are lengthening.
5 Arise, and let us go by night,
And let us destroy her palaces."

6 For thus has the LORD of hosts said:

"Cut down trees,
And build a mound against Jerusalem.
This *is* the city to be punished.
She *is* full of oppression in her midst.

7 As a fountain wells up with water,
So she wells up with her wickedness.
Violence and plundering are heard in her.
Before Me continually *are* grief and
wounds.
8 Be instructed, O Jerusalem,
Lest My soul depart from you;
Lest I make you desolate,
A land not inhabited."

9 Thus says the LORD of hosts:

"They shall thoroughly glean as a vine the
remnant of Israel;
As a grape-gatherer, put your hand back
into the branches."

10 To whom shall I speak and give warning,
That they may hear?
Indeed their ear *is* uncircumcised,
And they cannot give heed.
Behold, the word of the LORD is a
reproach to them;
They have no delight in it.
11 Therefore I am full of the fury of the
LORD.
I am weary of holding *it* in.
"I will pour it out on the children outside,
And on the assembly of young men
together;
For even the husband shall be taken with
the wife,
The aged with *him who is* full of days.
12 And their houses shall be turned over to
others,
Fields and wives together;
For I will stretch out My hand
Against the inhabitants of the land," says
the LORD.
13 "Because from the least of them even to
the greatest of them,
Everyone *is* given to covetousness;
And from the prophet even to the priest,
Everyone deals falsely.
14 They have also healed the hurt of My
people slightly,
Saying, 'Peace, peace!'
When *there is* no peace.
15 Were they ashamed when they had
committed abomination?
No! They were not at all ashamed;
Nor did they know how to blush.
Therefore they shall fall among those
who fall;
At the time I punish them,
They shall be cast down," says the LORD.

16 Thus says the LORD:

"Stand in the ways and see,
And ask for the old paths, where the
good way *is*,
And walk in it;
Then you will find rest for your souls.
But they said, 'We will not walk *in it*.'
17 Also, I set watchmen over you, *saying*,
'Listen to the sound of the trumpet!'
But they said, 'We will not listen.'
18 Therefore hear, you nations,
And know, O congregation, what *is*
among them.
19 Hear, O earth!
Behold, I will certainly bring calamity on
this people—
The fruit of their thoughts,
Because they have not heeded My words
Nor My law, but rejected it.
20 For what purpose to Me
Comes frankincense from Sheba,
And sweet cane from a far country?
Your burnt offerings *are* not acceptable,
Nor your sacrifices sweet to Me."

21 Therefore thus says the LORD:

"Behold, I will lay stumbling blocks before
this people,
And the fathers and the sons together
shall fall on them.
The neighbor and his friend shall perish."

22 Thus says the LORD:

"Behold, a people comes from the north
country,
And a great nation will be raised from the
farthest parts of the earth.
23 They will lay hold on bow and spear;
They *are* cruel and have no mercy;
Their voice roars like the sea;
And they ride on horses,
As men of war set in array against you,
O daughter of Zion."

24 We have heard the report of it;
Our hands grow feeble.
Anguish has taken hold of us,
Pain as of a woman in labor.
25 Do not go out into the field,
Nor walk by the way.
Because of the sword of the enemy,
Fear *is* on every side.
26 O daughter of my people,
Dress in sackcloth
And roll about in ashes!
Make mourning *as for* an only son, most
bitter lamentation;
For the plunderer will suddenly come
upon us.

27 "I have set you *as* an assayer *and* a
fortress among My people,
That you may know and test their way.
28 They *are* all stubborn rebels, walking as
slanderers.
They are bronze and iron,
They *are* all corrupters;
29 The bellows blow fiercely,
The lead is consumed by the fire;
The smelter refines in vain,
For the wicked are not drawn off.
30 *People* will call them rejected silver,
Because the LORD has rejected them."

Trusting in Lying Words

7 The word that came to Jeremiah from the
LORD, saying,
2 "Stand in the gate of the LORD's house,
and proclaim there this word, and say, 'Hear
the word of the LORD, all *you of* Judah who enter
in at these gates to worship the LORD!'"
3 Thus says the LORD of hosts, the God of
Israel: "Amend your ways and your doings,
and I will cause you to dwell in this place.
4 "Do not trust in these lying words, saying,
'The temple of the LORD, the temple of the LORD,
the temple of the LORD *are* these.'
5 "For if you thoroughly amend your ways
and your doings, if you thoroughly execute
judgment between a man and his neighbor,
6 "*if* you do not oppress the stranger, the
fatherless, and the widow, and do not shed in-
nocent blood in this place, or walk after other
gods to your hurt,

7 "then I will cause you to dwell in this place,
in the land that I gave to your fathers forever
and ever.
8 "Behold, you trust in lying words that can-
not profit.
9 "Will you steal, murder, commit adultery,
swear falsely, burn incense to Baal, and walk
after other gods whom you do not know,
10 "and *then* come and stand before Me in
this house which is called by My name, and say,
'We are delivered to do all these abominations'?
11 "Has this house, which is called by My
name, become a den of thieves in your eyes?
Behold, I, even I, have seen *it*," says the LORD.
12 "But go now to My place which *was* in
Shiloh, where I set My name at the first, and
see what I did to it because of the wickedness
of My people Israel.
13 "And now, because you have done all these
works," says the LORD, "and I spoke to you,
rising up early and speaking, but you did not
hear, and I called you, but you did not answer,
14 "therefore I will do to the house which is
called by My name, in which you trust, and to
this place which I gave to you and your fathers,
as I have done to Shiloh.
15 "And I will cast you out of My sight, as
I have cast out all your brethren—the whole
posterity of Ephraim.
16 "Therefore do not pray for this people, nor
lift up a cry or prayer for them, nor make inter-
cession to Me; for I will not hear you.
17 "Do you not see what they do in the cities
of Judah and in the streets of Jerusalem?
18 "The children gather wood, the fathers
kindle the fire, and the women knead dough,
to make cakes for the queen of heaven; and *they*
pour out drink offerings to other gods, that they
may provoke Me to anger.
19 "Do they provoke Me to anger?" says the
LORD. "*Do they* not *provoke* themselves, to the
shame of their own faces?"
20 Therefore thus says the Lord GOD: "Be-
hold, My anger and My fury will be poured out
on this place—on man and on beast, on the
trees of the field and on the fruit of the ground.
And it will burn and not be quenched."
21 Thus says the LORD of hosts, the God of
Israel: "Add your burnt offerings to your sacri-
fices and eat meat.
22 "For I did not speak to your fathers, or
command them in the day that I brought them
out of the land of Egypt, concerning burnt of-
ferings or sacrifices.
23 "But this is what I commanded them, say-
ing, 'Obey My voice, and I will be your God,
and you shall be My people. And walk in all
the ways that I have commanded you, that it
may be well with you.'
24 "Yet they did not obey or incline their ear,
but followed the counsels *and* the dictates of
their evil hearts, and went backward and not
forward.
25 "Since the day that your fathers came out
of the land of Egypt until this day, I have even
sent to you all My servants the prophets, daily
rising up early and sending *them*.
26 "Yet they did not obey Me or incline their
ear, but stiffened their neck. They did worse
than their fathers.
27 "Therefore you shall speak all these words
to them, but they will not obey you. You shall
also call to them, but they will not answer you.

Judgment on Obscene Religion

28 "So you shall say to them, 'This *is* a nation
that does not obey the voice of the LORD their
God nor receive correction. Truth has perished
and has been cut off from their mouth.
29 'Cut off your hair and cast *it* away, and take
up a lamentation on the desolate heights; for
the LORD has rejected and forsaken the gener-
ation of His wrath.'
30 "For the children of Judah have done evil
in My sight," says the LORD. "They have set
their abominations in the house which is called
by My name, to pollute it.
31 "And they have built the high places of
Tophet, which *is* in the Valley of the Son of
Hinnom, to burn their sons and their daughters
in the fire, which I did not command, nor did
it come into My heart.
32 "Therefore behold, the days are coming,"
says the LORD, "when it will no more be called
Tophet, or the Valley of the Son of Hinnom, but
the Valley of Slaughter; for they will bury in
Tophet until there is no room.
33 "The corpses of this people will be food
for the birds of the heaven and for the beasts
of the earth. And no one will frighten *them*
away.
34 "Then I will cause to cease from the cities
of Judah and from the streets of Jerusalem the
voice of mirth and the voice of gladness, the
voice of the bridegroom and the voice of the
bride. For the land shall be desolate.

8 "At that time," says the LORD, "they shall
bring out the bones of the kings of Judah,
and the bones of its princes, and the bones of
the priests, and the bones of the prophets, and
the bones of the inhabitants of Jerusalem, out
of their graves.
2 "They shall spread them before the sun
and the moon and all the host of heaven, which
they have loved and which they have served
and after which they have walked, which they
have sought and which they have worshiped.
They shall not be gathered nor buried; they
shall be like refuse on the face of the earth.
3 "Then death shall be chosen rather than
life by all the residue of those who remain of
this evil family, who remain in all the places
where I have driven them," says the LORD of
hosts.

The Peril of False Teaching

4 "Moreover you shall say to them, 'Thus
says the LORD:

"Will they fall and not rise?
Will one turn away and not return?
5 Why has this people slidden back,
Jerusalem, in a perpetual backsliding?
They hold fast to deceit,
They refuse to return.
6 I listened and heard,
But they do not speak aright.
No man repented of his wickedness,
Saying, 'What have I done?'
Everyone turned to his own course,
As the horse rushes into the battle.

7 "Even the stork in the heavens
Knows her appointed times;
And the turtledove, the swift, and the
swallow
Observe the time of their coming.
But My people do not know the judgment
of the LORD.

8 "How can you say, 'We *are* wise,
And the law of the LORD *is* with us'?
Look, the false pen of the scribe certainly works falsehood.
9 The wise men are ashamed,
They are dismayed and taken.
Behold, they have rejected the word of the LORD;
So what wisdom do they have?
10 Therefore I will give their wives to others,
And their fields to those who will inherit *them;*
Because from the least even to the greatest
Everyone is given to covetousness;
From the prophet even to the priest
Everyone deals falsely.
11 For they have healed the hurt of the daughter of My people slightly,
Saying, 'Peace, peace!'
When *there is* no peace.
12 Were they ashamed when they had committed abomination?
No! They were not at all ashamed,
Nor did they know how to blush.
Therefore they shall fall among those who fall;
In the time of their punishment
They shall be cast down," says the LORD.

13 "I will surely consume them," says the LORD.
"No grapes *shall be* on the vine,
Nor figs on the fig tree,
And the leaf shall fade;
And *the things* I have given them shall pass away from them." ' "

14 "Why do we sit still?
Assemble yourselves,
And let us enter the fortified cities,
And let us be silent there.
For the LORD our God has put us to silence
And given us water of gall to drink,
Because we have sinned against the LORD.
15 "*We* looked for peace, but no good *came;*
And for a time of health, and there was trouble!
16 The snorting of His horses was heard from Dan.
The whole land trembled at the sound of the neighing of His strong ones;
For they have come and devoured the land and all that is in it,
The city and those who dwell in it."

17 "For behold, I will send serpents among you,
Vipers which cannot be charmed,
And they shall bite you," says the LORD.

The Prophet Mourns for the People

18 I would comfort myself in sorrow;
My heart *is* faint in me.
19 Listen! The voice,
The cry of the daughter of my people
From a far country:
"*Is* not the LORD in Zion?
Is not her King in her?"

"Why have they provoked Me to anger
With their carved images—
With foreign idols?"

20 "The harvest is past,
The summer is ended,
And we are not saved!"
21 For the hurt of the daughter of my people I am hurt.
I am mourning;
Astonishment has taken hold of me.
22 *Is there* no balm in Gilead,
Is there no physician there?
Why then is there no recovery
For the health of the daughter of my people?

9 Oh, that my head were waters,
And my eyes a fountain of tears,
That I might weep day and night
For the slain of the daughter of my people!
2 Oh, that I had in the wilderness
A lodging place for travelers;
That I might leave my people,
And go from them!
For they *are* all adulterers,
An assembly of treacherous men.

3 "And *like* their bow they have bent their tongues *for* lies.
They are not valiant for the truth on the earth.
For they proceed from evil to evil,
And they do not know Me," says the LORD.
4 "Everyone take heed to his neighbor,
And do not trust any brother;
For every brother will utterly supplant,
And every neighbor will walk with slanderers.
5 Everyone will deceive his neighbor,
And will not speak the truth;
They have taught their tongue to speak lies;
They weary themselves to commit iniquity.
6 Your dwelling place *is* in the midst of deceit;
Through deceit they refuse to know Me,"
says the LORD.

7 Therefore thus says the LORD of hosts:

"Behold, I will refine them and try them;
For how shall I deal with the daughter of My people?
8 Their tongue *is* an arrow shot out;
It speaks deceit;
One speaks peaceably to his neighbor with his mouth,
But in his heart he lies in wait.
9 Shall I not punish them for these *things?*"
says the LORD.
"Shall I not avenge Myself on such a nation as this?"

10 I will take up a weeping and wailing for the mountains,
And for the dwelling places of the wilderness a lamentation,
Because they are burned up,
So that no one can pass through;
Nor can *men* hear the voice of the cattle.
Both the birds of the heavens and the beasts have fled;
They are gone.

11 "I will make Jerusalem a heap of ruins, a den of jackals.

I will make the cities of Judah desolate,
without an inhabitant."

12 Who *is* the wise man who may understand
this? And *who is he* to whom the mouth of the
LORD has spoken, that he may declare it? Why
does the land perish *and* burn up like a wilder-
ness, so that no one can pass through?
13 And the LORD said, "Because they have
forsaken My law which I set before them, and
have not obeyed My voice, nor walked accord-
ing to it,
14 "but they have walked according to the
dictates of their own hearts and after the Baals,
which their fathers taught them,"
15 therefore thus says the LORD of hosts, the
God of Israel: "Behold, I will feed them, this
people, with wormwood, and give them water
of gall to drink.
16 "I will scatter them also among the Gen-
tiles, whom neither they nor their fathers have
known. And I will send a sword after them
until I have consumed them."

The People Mourn in Judgment

17 Thus says the LORD of hosts:

"Consider and call for the mourning
women,
That they may come;
And send for skillful *wailing* women,
That they may come.
18 Let them make haste
And take up a wailing for us,
That our eyes may run with tears,
And our eyelids gush with water.
19 For a voice of wailing is heard from Zion:
'How we are plundered!
We are greatly ashamed,
Because we have forsaken the land,
Because we have been cast out of our
dwellings.'"

20 Yet hear the word of the LORD, O women,
And let your ear receive the word of His
mouth;
Teach your daughters wailing,
And everyone her neighbor a
lamentation.
21 For death has come through our
windows,
Has entered our palaces,
To kill off the children—*no longer to be*
outside!
And the young men—*no longer* on the
streets!

22 Speak, "Thus says the LORD:

'Even the carcasses of men shall fall as
refuse on the open field,
Like cuttings after the harvester,
And no one shall gather *them.*'"

23 Thus says the LORD:

"Let not the wise *man* glory in his wisdom,
Let not the mighty *man* glory in his
might,
Nor let the rich *man* glory in his riches;
24 But let him who glories glory in this,
That he understands and knows Me,
That I *am* the LORD, exercising
lovingkindness, judgment, and
righteousness in the earth.
For in these I delight," says the LORD.

25 "Behold, the days are coming," says the
LORD, "that I will punish all *who are* circum-
cised with the uncircumcised—
26 "Egypt, Judah, Edom, the people of Am-
mon, Moab, and all *who are* in the farthest
corners, who dwell in the wilderness. For all
these nations *are* uncircumcised, and all the
house of Israel *are* uncircumcised in the heart."

Idols and the True God

10 Hear the word which the LORD speaks
to you, O house of Israel.
2 Thus says the LORD:

"Do not learn the way of the Gentiles;
Do not be dismayed at the signs of
heaven,
For the Gentiles are dismayed at them.
3 For the customs of the peoples *are* futile;
For *one* cuts a tree from the forest,
The work of the hands of the workman,
with the ax.
4 They decorate it with silver and gold;
They fasten it with nails and hammers
So that it will not topple.
5 They *are* upright, like a palm tree,
And they cannot speak;
They must be carried,
Because they cannot go *by themselves.*
Do not be afraid of them,
For they cannot do evil,
Nor can they do any good."

6 Inasmuch as *there is* none like You,
O LORD
(You *are* great, and Your name *is* great in
might),
7 Who would not fear You, O King of the
nations?
For this is Your rightful due.
For among all the wise *men* of the
nations,
And in all their kingdoms,
There is none like You.
8 But they are altogether dull-hearted and
foolish;
A wooden idol *is* a worthless doctrine.
9 Silver is beaten into plates;
It is brought from Tarshish,
And gold from Uphaz,
The work of the craftsman
And of the hands of the metalsmith;
Blue and purple *are* their clothing;
They *are* all the work of skillful *men.*
10 But the LORD *is* the true God;
He *is* the living God and the everlasting
King.
At His wrath the earth will tremble,
And the nations will not be able to
endure His indignation.

11 Thus you shall say to them: "The gods that
have not made the heavens and the earth shall
perish from the earth and from under these
heavens."

12 He has made the earth by His power,
He has established the world by His
wisdom,
And has stretched out the heavens at His
discretion.
13 When He utters His voice,
There is a multitude of waters in the
heavens:
"And He causes the vapors to ascend from
the ends of the earth.

He makes lightning for the rain,
He brings the wind out of His
treasuries."[a]

14 Everyone is dull-hearted, without
knowledge;
Every metalsmith is put to shame by an
image;
For his molded image *is* falsehood,
And *there is* no breath in them.
15 They *are* futile, a work of errors;
In the time of their punishment they shall
perish.
16 The Portion of Jacob *is* not like them,
For He *is* the Maker of all *things*,
And Israel *is* the tribe of His inheritance;
The LORD of hosts *is* His name.

The Coming Captivity of Judah

17 Gather up your wares from the land,
O inhabitant of the fortress!

18 For thus says the LORD:
"Behold, I will throw out at this time
The inhabitants of the land,
And will distress them,
That they may find *it so.*"

19 Woe is me for my hurt!
My wound is severe.
But I say, "Truly this *is* an infirmity,
And I must bear it."
20 My tent is plundered,
And all my cords are broken;
My children have gone from me,
And they *are* no more.
There is no one to pitch my tent anymore,
Or set up my curtains.
21 For the shepherds have become
dull-hearted,
And have not sought the LORD;
Therefore they shall not prosper,
And all their flocks shall be scattered.
22 Behold, the noise of the report has come,
And a great commotion out of the north
country,
To make the cities of Judah desolate, a
den of jackals.

23 O LORD, I know the way of man *is* not in
himself;
It is not in man who walks to direct his
own steps.
24 O LORD, correct me, but with justice;
Not in Your anger, lest You bring me to
nothing.
25 Pour out Your fury on the Gentiles, who
do not know You,
And on the families who do not call on
Your name;
For they have eaten up Jacob,
Devoured him and consumed him,
And made his dwelling place desolate.

The Broken Covenant

11 The word that came to Jeremiah from
the LORD, saying,
2 "Hear the words of this covenant, and
speak to the men of Judah and to the inhab-
itants of Jerusalem;
3 "and say to them, 'Thus says the LORD
God of Israel: "Cursed *is* the man who does
not obey the words of this covenant
4 "which I commanded your fathers in the
day I brought them out of the land of Egypt,
from the iron furnace, saying, 'Obey My voice,
and do according to all that I command you;
so shall you be My people, and I will be your
God,'
5 "that I may establish the oath which I have
sworn to your fathers, to give them 'a land
flowing with milk and honey,'[a] as *it is* this
day."'" And I answered and said, "So be it,
LORD."
6 Then the LORD said to me, "Proclaim all
these words in the cities of Judah and in the
streets of Jerusalem, saying: 'Hear the words
of this covenant and do them.
7 'For I earnestly exhorted your fathers in
the day I brought them up out of the land of
Egypt, until this day, rising early and exhort-
ing, saying, "Obey My voice."
8 'Yet they did not obey or incline their ear,
but everyone followed the dictates of his evil
heart; therefore I will bring upon them all the
words of this covenant, which I commanded
them to do, but *which* they have not done.'"
9 And the LORD said to me, "A conspiracy
has been found among the men of Judah and
among the inhabitants of Jerusalem.
10 "They have turned back to the iniquities
of their forefathers who refused to hear My
words, and they have gone after other gods to
serve them; the house of Israel and the house
of Judah have broken My covenant which I
made with their fathers."
11 Therefore thus says the LORD: "Behold, I
will surely bring calamity on them which they
will not be able to escape; and though they cry
out to Me, I will not listen to them.
12 "Then the cities of Judah and the inhab-
itants of Jerusalem will go and cry out to the
gods to whom they offer incense, but they will
not save them at all in the time of their trouble.
13 "For *according to* the number of your cit-
ies were your gods, O Judah; and *according to*
the number of the streets of Jerusalem you
have set up altars to *that* shameful thing, altars
to burn incense to Baal.
14 "So do not pray for this people, or lift up a
cry or prayer for them; for I will not hear *them*
in the time that they cry out to Me because of
their trouble.

15 "What has My beloved to do in My house,
Having done lewd deeds with many?
And the holy flesh has passed from you.
When you do evil, then you rejoice.
16 The LORD called your name,
Green Olive Tree, Lovely *and* of Good
Fruit.
With the noise of a great tumult
He has kindled fire on it,
And its branches are broken.

17 "For the LORD of hosts, who planted you,
has pronounced doom against you for the evil
of the house of Israel and of the house of Ju-
dah, which they have done against themselves
to provoke Me to anger in offering incense to
Baal."

Jeremiah's Life Threatened

18 Now the LORD gave me knowledge *of it*,
and I know *it;* for You showed me their doings.
19 But I *was* like a docile lamb brought to the
slaughter; and I did not know that they had

10:13 [a]Psalm 135:7 **11:5** [a]Exodus 3:8

devised schemes against me, *saying*, "Let us de-
stroy the tree with its fruit, and let us cut him
off from the land of the living, that his name
may be remembered no more."

20 But, O LORD of hosts,
You who judge righteously,
Testing the mind and the heart,
Let me see Your vengeance on them,
For to You I have revealed my cause.

21 "Therefore thus says the LORD concerning
the men of Anathoth who seek your life, say-
ing, 'Do not prophesy in the name of the LORD,
lest you die by our hand'—
22 "therefore thus says the LORD of hosts:
'Behold, I will punish them. The young men
shall die by the sword, their sons and their
daughters shall die by famine;
23 'and there shall be no remnant of them, for
I will bring catastrophe on the men of Ana-
thoth, *even* the year of their punishment.'"

Jeremiah's Question

12 Righteous *are* You, O LORD, when I
plead with You;
Yet let me talk with You about *Your*
judgments.
Why does the way of the wicked prosper?
Why are those happy who deal so
treacherously?
2 You have planted them, yes, they have
taken root;
They grow, yes, they bear fruit.
You *are* near in their mouth
But far from their mind.
3 But You, O LORD, know me;
You have seen me,
And You have tested my heart toward
You.
Pull them out like sheep for the slaughter,
And prepare them for the day of
slaughter.
4 How long will the land mourn,
And the herbs of every field wither?
The beasts and birds are consumed,
For the wickedness of those who dwell
there,
Because they said, "He will not see our
final end."

The LORD Answers Jeremiah

5 "If you have run with the footmen, and
they have wearied you,
Then how can you contend with horses?
And *if* in the land of peace,
In which you trusted, *they wearied you,*
Then how will you do in the floodplain[a] of
the Jordan?
6 For even your brothers, the house of your
father,
Even they have dealt treacherously with
you;
Yes, they have called a multitude after
you.
Do not believe them,
Even though they speak smooth words to
you.

7 "I have forsaken My house, I have left My
heritage;
I have given the dearly beloved of My
soul into the hand of her enemies.
8 My heritage is to Me like a lion in the
forest;
It cries out against Me;
Therefore I have hated it.
9 My heritage *is* to Me *like* a speckled
vulture;
The vultures all around *are* against her.
Come, assemble all the beasts of the field,
Bring them to devour!

10 "Many rulers[a] have destroyed My
vineyard,
They have trodden My portion underfoot;
They have made My pleasant portion a
desolate wilderness.
11 They have made it desolate;
Desolate, it mourns to Me;
The whole land is made desolate,
Because no one takes *it* to heart.
12 The plunderers have come
On all the desolate heights in the
wilderness,
For the sword of the LORD shall devour
From *one* end of the land to the *other* end
of the land;
No flesh shall have peace.
13 They have sown wheat but reaped thorns;
They have put themselves to pain *but* do
not profit.
But be ashamed of your harvest
Because of the fierce anger of the LORD."

14 Thus says the LORD: "Against all My evil
neighbors who touch the inheritance which I
have caused My people Israel to inherit—be-
hold, I will pluck them out of their land and
pluck out the house of Judah from among them.
15 "Then it shall be, after I have plucked them
out, that I will return and have compassion on
them and bring them back, everyone to his heri-
tage and everyone to his land.
16 "And it shall be, if they will learn carefully
the ways of My people, to swear by My name,
'As the LORD lives,' as they taught My people
to swear by Baal, then they shall be established
in the midst of My people.
17 "But if they do not obey, I will utterly pluck
up and destroy that nation," says the LORD.

Symbol of the Linen Sash

13 Thus the LORD said to me: "Go and get
yourself a linen sash, and put it around
your waist, but do not put it in water."
2 So I got a sash according to the word of
the LORD, and put *it* around my waist.
3 And the word of the LORD came to me the
second time, saying,
4 "Take the sash that you acquired, which *is*
around your waist, and arise, go to the Euphra-
tes,[a] and hide it there in a hole in the rock."
5 So I went and hid it by the Euphrates, as
the LORD commanded me.
6 Now it came to pass after many days that
the LORD said to me, "Arise, go to the Euphra-
tes, and take from there the sash which I com-
manded you to hide there."
7 Then I went to the Euphrates and dug, and
I took the sash from the place where I had
hidden it; and there was the sash, ruined. It was
profitable for nothing.
8 Then the word of the LORD came to me, say-
ing,
9 "Thus says the LORD: 'In this manner I will

12:5 [a]Or *thicket* **12:10** [a]Literally *shepherds* or *pastors* **13:4** [a]Hebrew *Perath*

ruin the pride of Judah and the great pride of
Jerusalem.
10 'This evil people, who refuse to hear My
words, who follow the dictates of their hearts,
and walk after other gods to serve them and
worship them, shall be just like this sash which
is profitable for nothing.
11 'For as the sash clings to the waist of a
man, so I have caused the whole house of Israel
and the whole house of Judah to cling to Me,'
says the LORD, 'that they may become My peo-
ple, for renown, for praise, and for glory; but
they would not hear.'

Symbol of the Wine Bottles

12 "Therefore you shall speak to them this
word: 'Thus says the LORD God of Israel:
"Every bottle shall be filled with wine."' And
they will say to you, 'Do we not certainly know
that every bottle will be filled with wine?'
13 "Then you shall say to them, 'Thus says
the LORD: "Behold, I will fill all the inhabitants
of this land—even the kings who sit on David's
throne, the priests, the prophets, and all the
inhabitants of Jerusalem—with drunkenness!
14 "And I will dash them one against another,
even the fathers and the sons together," says
the LORD. "I will not pity nor spare nor have
mercy, but will destroy them."'"

Pride Precedes Captivity

15 Hear and give ear:
Do not be proud,
For the LORD has spoken.
16 Give glory to the LORD your God
Before He causes darkness,
And before your feet stumble
On the dark mountains,
And while you are looking for light,
He turns it into the shadow of death
And makes *it* dense darkness.
17 But if you will not hear it,
My soul will weep in secret for *your*
pride;
My eyes will weep bitterly
And run down with tears,
Because the LORD's flock has been taken
captive.

18 Say to the king and to the queen mother,
"Humble yourselves;
Sit down,
For your rule shall collapse, the crown of
your glory."
19 The cities of the South shall be shut up,
And no one shall open *them;*
Judah shall be carried away captive, all
of it;
It shall be wholly carried away captive.

20 Lift up your eyes and see
Those who come from the north.
Where *is* the flock *that* was given to you,
Your beautiful sheep?
21 What will you say when He punishes
you?
For you have taught them
To be chieftains, to be head over you.
Will not pangs seize you,
Like a woman in labor?
22 And if you say in your heart,
"Why have these things come upon me?"
For the greatness of your iniquity
Your skirts have been uncovered,
Your heels made bare.
23 Can the Ethiopian change his skin or the
leopard its spots?
Then may you also do good who are
accustomed to do evil.

24 "Therefore I will scatter them like stubble
That passes away by the wind of the
wilderness.
25 This is your lot,
The portion of your measures from Me,"
says the LORD,
"Because you have forgotten Me
And trusted in falsehood.
26 Therefore I will uncover your skirts over
your face,
That your shame may appear.
27 I have seen your adulteries
And your *lustful* neighings,
The lewdness of your harlotry,
Your abominations on the hills in the
fields.
Woe to you, O Jerusalem!
Will you still not be made clean?"

Sword, Famine, and Pestilence

14 The word of the LORD that came to Jere-
miah concerning the droughts.

2 "Judah mourns,
And her gates languish;
They mourn for the land,
And the cry of Jerusalem has gone up.
3 Their nobles have sent their lads for
water;
They went to the cisterns *and* found no
water.
They returned with their vessels empty;
They were ashamed and confounded
And covered their heads.
4 Because the ground is parched,
For there was no rain in the land,
The plowmen were ashamed;
They covered their heads.
5 Yes, the deer also gave birth in the field,
But left because there was no grass.
6 And the wild donkeys stood in the
desolate heights;
They sniffed at the wind like jackals;
Their eyes failed because *there was* no
grass."

7 O LORD, though our iniquities testify
against us,
Do it for Your name's sake;
For our backslidings are many,
We have sinned against You.
8 O the Hope of Israel, his Savior in time of
trouble,
Why should You be like a stranger in the
land,
And like a traveler *who* turns aside to
tarry for a night?
9 Why should You be like a man
astonished,
Like a mighty one *who* cannot save?
Yet You, O LORD, *are* in our midst,
And we are called by Your name;
Do not leave us!

10 Thus says the LORD to this people:

"Thus they have loved to wander;
They have not restrained their feet.
Therefore the LORD does not accept
them;
He will remember their iniquity now,
And punish their sins."

11 Then the LORD said to me, "Do not pray
for this people, for *their* good.
12 "When they fast, I will not hear their cry;
and when they offer burnt offering and grain
offering, I will not accept them. But I will con-
sume them by the sword, by the famine, and
by the pestilence."
13 Then I said, "Ah, Lord GOD! Behold, the
prophets say to them, 'You shall not see the
sword, nor shall you have famine, but I will
give you assured peace in this place.'"
14 And the LORD said to me, "The prophets
prophesy lies in My name. I have not sent them,
commanded them, nor spoken to them; they
prophesy to you a false vision, divination, a
worthless thing, and the deceit of their heart.
15 "Therefore thus says the LORD concerning
the prophets who prophesy in My name, whom
I did not send, and who say, 'Sword and famine
shall not be in this land'—'By sword and fam-
ine those prophets shall be consumed!
16 'And the people to whom they prophesy
shall be cast out in the streets of Jerusalem
because of the famine and the sword; they will
have no one to bury them—them nor their
wives, their sons nor their daughters—for I will
pour their wickedness on them.'
17 "Therefore you shall say this word to them:

'Let my eyes flow with tears night and
day,
And let them not cease;
For the virgin daughter of my people
Has been broken with a mighty stroke,
with a very severe blow.
18 If I go out to the field,
Then behold, those slain with the sword!
And if I enter the city,
Then behold, those sick from famine!
Yes, both prophet and priest go about in a
land they do not know.'"

The People Plead for Mercy

19 Have You utterly rejected Judah?
Has Your soul loathed Zion?
Why have You stricken us so that *there is*
no healing for us?
We looked for peace, but *there was* no
good;
And for the time of healing, and there
was trouble.
20 We acknowledge, O LORD, our
wickedness
And the iniquity of our fathers,
For we have sinned against You.
21 Do not abhor *us*, for Your name's sake;
Do not disgrace the throne of Your glory.
Remember, do not break Your covenant
with us.
22 Are there any among the idols of the
nations that can cause rain?
Or can the heavens give showers?
Are You not He, O LORD our God?
Therefore we will wait for You,
Since You have made all these.

The LORD Will Not Relent

15 Then the LORD said to me, "*Even* if Mo-
ses and Samuel stood before Me, My
mind *would* not *be* favorable toward this peo-
ple. Cast *them* out of My sight, and let them
go forth.
2 "And it shall be, if they say to you, 'Where
should we go?' then you shall tell them, 'Thus
says the LORD:

"Such as *are* for death, to death;
And such as *are* for the sword, to the
sword;
And such as *are* for the famine, to the
famine;
And such as *are* for the captivity, to the
captivity."'
3 "And I will appoint over them four forms
of destruction," says the LORD: "the sword to
slay, the dogs to drag, the birds of the heavens
and the beasts of the earth to devour and de-
stroy.
4 "I will hand them over to trouble, to all
kingdoms of the earth, because of Manasseh
the son of Hezekiah, king of Judah, for what
he did in Jerusalem.

5 "For who will have pity on you,
O Jerusalem?
Or who will bemoan you?
Or who will turn aside to ask how you
are doing?
6 You have forsaken Me," says the LORD,
"You have gone backward.
Therefore I will stretch out My hand
against you and destroy you;
I am weary of relenting!
7 And I will winnow them with a
winnowing fan in the gates of the land;
I will bereave *them* of children;
I will destroy My people,
Since they do not return from their ways.
8 Their widows will be increased to Me
more than the sand of the seas;
I will bring against them,
Against the mother of the young men,
A plunderer at noonday;
I will cause anguish and terror to fall on
them suddenly.
9 "She languishes who has borne seven;
She has breathed her last;
Her sun has gone down
While *it was* yet day;
She has been ashamed and confounded.
And the remnant of them I will deliver to
the sword
Before their enemies," says the LORD.

Jeremiah's Dejection

10 Woe is me, my mother,
That you have borne me,
A man of strife and a man of contention
to the whole earth!
I have neither lent for interest,
Nor have men lent to me for interest.
Every one of them curses me.
11 The LORD said:

"Surely it will be well with your remnant;
Surely I will cause the enemy to intercede
with you
In the time of adversity and in the time of
affliction.
12 Can anyone break iron,
The northern iron and the bronze?
13 Your wealth and your treasures
I will give as plunder without price,
Because of all your sins,
Throughout your territories.
14 And I will make *you* cross over with[a] your
enemies

15:14 [a]Following Masoretic Text and Vulgate; Septuagint, Syriac, and Targum read *cause you to serve* (compare 17:4).

Into a land *which* you do not know;
For a fire is kindled in My anger,
Which shall burn upon you."

15 O LORD, You know;
Remember me and visit me,
And take vengeance for me on my
persecutors.
In Your enduring patience, do not take
me away.
Know that for Your sake I have suffered
rebuke.
16 Your words were found, and I ate them,
And Your word was to me the joy and
rejoicing of my heart;
For I am called by Your name,
O LORD God of hosts.
17 I did not sit in the assembly of the
mockers,
Nor did I rejoice;
I sat alone because of Your hand,
For You have filled me with indignation.
18 Why is my pain perpetual
And my wound incurable,
Which refuses to be healed?
Will You surely be to me like an
unreliable stream,
As waters *that* fail?

The LORD Reassures Jeremiah

19 Therefore thus says the LORD:

"If you return,
Then I will bring you back;
You shall stand before Me;
If you take out the precious from the vile,
You shall be as My mouth.
Let them return to you,
But you must not return to them.
20 And I will make you to this people a
fortified bronze wall;
And they will fight against you,
But they shall not prevail against you;
For I *am* with you to save you
And deliver you," says the LORD.
21 "I will deliver you from the hand of the
wicked,
And I will redeem you from the grip of
the terrible."

Jeremiah's Lifestyle and Message

16 The word of the LORD also came to me,
saying,
2 "You shall not take a wife, nor shall you
have sons or daughters in this place."
3 For thus says the LORD concerning the
sons and daughters who are born in this place,
and concerning their mothers who bore them
and their fathers who begot them in this land:
4 "They shall die gruesome deaths; they
shall not be lamented nor shall they be buried,
but they shall be like refuse on the face of the
earth. They shall be consumed by the sword
and by famine, and their corpses shall be meat
for the birds of heaven and for the beasts of
the earth."
5 For thus says the LORD: "Do not enter the
house of mourning, nor go to lament or bemoan
them; for I have taken away My peace from
this people," says the LORD, "lovingkindness
and mercies.
6 "Both the great and the small shall die in
this land. They shall not be buried; neither
shall men lament for them, cut themselves, nor
make themselves bald for them.
7 "Nor shall *men* break *bread* in mourning
for them, to comfort them for the dead; nor
shall *men* give them the cup of consolation to
drink for their father or their mother.
8 "Also you shall not go into the house of
feasting to sit with them, to eat and drink."
9 For thus says the LORD of hosts, the God
of Israel: "Behold, I will cause to cease from
this place, before your eyes and in your days,
the voice of mirth and the voice of gladness, the
voice of the bridegroom and the voice of the
bride.
10 "And it shall be, when you show this peo-
ple all these words, and they say to you, 'Why
has the LORD pronounced all this great disas-
ter against us? Or what *is* our iniquity? Or what
is our sin that we have committed against the
LORD our God?'
11 "then you shall say to them, 'Because your
fathers have forsaken Me,' says the LORD;
'they have walked after other gods and have
served them and worshiped them, and have
forsaken Me and not kept My law.
12 'And you have done worse than your fa-
thers, for behold, each one follows the dictates
of his own evil heart, so that no one listens to
Me.
13 'Therefore I will cast you out of this land
into a land that you do not know, neither you
nor your fathers; and there you shall serve
other gods day and night, where I will not show
you favor.'

God Will Restore Israel

14 "Therefore behold, the days are coming,"
says the LORD, "that it shall no more be said,
'The LORD lives who brought up the children
of Israel from the land of Egypt,'
15 "but, 'The LORD lives who brought up the
children of Israel from the land of the north
and from all the lands where He had driven
them.' For I will bring them back into their land
which I gave to their fathers.
16 "Behold, I will send for many fishermen,"
says the LORD, "and they shall fish them; and
afterward I will send for many hunters, and
they shall hunt them from every mountain and
every hill, and out of the holes of the rocks.
17 "For My eyes *are* on all their ways; they are
not hidden from My face, nor is their iniquity
hidden from My eyes.
18 "And first I will repay double for their iniq-
uity and their sin, because they have defiled
My land; they have filled My inheritance with
the carcasses of their detestable and abomina-
ble idols."

19 O LORD, my strength and my fortress,
My refuge in the day of affliction,
The Gentiles shall come to You
From the ends of the earth and say,
"Surely our fathers have inherited lies,
Worthlessness and unprofitable *things*."
20 Will a man make gods for himself,
Which *are* not gods?

21 "Therefore behold, I will this once cause
them to know,
I will cause them to know
My hand and My might;
And they shall know that My name *is* the
LORD.

Judah's Sin and Punishment

17 "The sin of Judah *is* written with a pen of iron;
With the point of a diamond *it is* engraved
On the tablet of their heart,
And on the horns of your altars,
2 While their children remember
Their altars and their wooden images[a]
By the green trees on the high hills.
3 O My mountain in the field,
I will give as plunder your wealth, all your treasures,
And your high places of sin within all your borders.
4 And you, even yourself,
Shall let go of your heritage which I gave you;
And I will cause you to serve your enemies
In the land which you do not know;
For you have kindled a fire in My anger
which shall burn forever."

5 Thus says the LORD:

"Cursed *is* the man who trusts in man
And makes flesh his strength,
Whose heart departs from the LORD.
6 For he shall be like a shrub in the desert,
And shall not see when good comes,
But shall inhabit the parched places in the wilderness,
In a salt land *which is* not inhabited.

7 "Blessed *is* the man who trusts in the LORD,
And whose hope is the LORD.
8 For he shall be like a tree planted by the waters,
Which spreads out its roots by the river,
And will not fear[a] when heat comes;
But its leaf will be green,
And will not be anxious in the year of drought,
Nor will cease from yielding fruit.

9 "The heart *is* deceitful above all *things*,
And desperately wicked;
Who can know it?
10 I, the LORD, search the heart,
I test the mind,
Even to give every man according to his ways,
According to the fruit of his doings.

11 "*As* a partridge that broods but does not hatch,
So is he who gets riches, but not by right;
It will leave him in the midst of his days,
And at his end he will be a fool."

12 A glorious high throne from the beginning
Is the place of our sanctuary.
13 O LORD, the hope of Israel,
All who forsake You shall be ashamed.

"Those who depart from Me
Shall be written in the earth,
Because they have forsaken the LORD,
The fountain of living waters."

Jeremiah Prays for Deliverance

14 Heal me, O LORD, and I shall be healed;
Save me, and I shall be saved,
For You *are* my praise.
15 Indeed they say to me,
"Where *is* the word of the LORD?
Let it come now!"
16 As for me, I have not hurried away from *being* a shepherd *who* follows You,
Nor have I desired the woeful day;
You know what came out of my lips;
It was right there before You.
17 Do not be a terror to me;
You *are* my hope in the day of doom.
18 Let them be ashamed who persecute me,
But do not let me be put to shame;
Let them be dismayed,
But do not let me be dismayed.
Bring on them the day of doom,
And destroy them with double destruction!

Hallow the Sabbath Day

19 Thus the LORD said to me: "Go and stand
in the gate of the children of the people, by
which the kings of Judah come in and by which
they go out, and in all the gates of Jerusalem;
20 "and say to them, 'Hear the word of the
LORD, you kings of Judah, and all Judah, and
all the inhabitants of Jerusalem, who enter by
these gates.
21 'Thus says the LORD: "Take heed to your-
selves, and bear no burden on the Sabbath day,
nor bring *it* in by the gates of Jerusalem;
22 "nor carry a burden out of your houses on
the Sabbath day, nor do any work, but hallow
the Sabbath day, as I commanded your fathers.
23 "But they did not obey nor incline their
ear, but made their neck stiff, that they might
not hear nor receive instruction.
24 "And it shall be, if you heed Me carefully,"
says the LORD, "to bring no burden through
the gates of this city on the Sabbath day, but
hallow the Sabbath day, to do no work in it,
25 "then shall enter the gates of this city
kings and princes sitting on the throne of Da-
vid, riding in chariots and on horses, they and
their princes, accompanied by the men of Ju-
dah and the inhabitants of Jerusalem; and this
city shall remain forever.
26 "And they shall come from the cities of
Judah and from the places around Jerusalem,
from the land of Benjamin and from the low-
land, from the mountains and from the South,
bringing burnt offerings and sacrifices, grain
offerings and incense, bringing sacrifices of
praise to the house of the LORD.
27 "But if you will not heed Me to hallow the
Sabbath day, such as not carrying a burden
when entering the gates of Jerusalem on the
Sabbath day, then I will kindle a fire in its
gates, and it shall devour the palaces of Jerusa-
lem, and it shall not be quenched." ' "

The Potter and the Clay

18 The word which came to Jeremiah from
the LORD, saying:
2 "Arise and go down to the potter's house,
and there I will cause you to hear My words."
3 Then I went down to the potter's house,
and there he was, making something at the
wheel.
4 And the vessel that he made of clay was
marred in the hand of the potter; so he made
it again into another vessel, as it seemed good
to the potter to make.

17:2 [a]Hebrew *Asherim*, Canaanite deities 17:8 [a]Qere and Targum read *see*.

5 Then the word of the LORD came to me,
saying:
6 "O house of Israel, can I not do with you
as this potter?" says the LORD. "Look, as the
clay *is* in the potter's hand, so *are* you in My
hand, O house of Israel!
7 "The instant I speak concerning a nation
and concerning a kingdom, to pluck up, to pull
down, and to destroy *it*,
8 "if that nation against whom I have spoken
turns from its evil, I will relent of the disaster
that I thought to bring upon it.
9 "And the instant I speak concerning a na-
tion and concerning a kingdom, to build and to
plant *it*,
10 "if it does evil in My sight so that it does
not obey My voice, then I will relent concern-
ing the good with which I said I would benefit
it.
11 "Now therefore, speak to the men of Judah
and to the inhabitants of Jerusalem, saying,
'Thus says the LORD: "Behold, I am fashioning
a disaster and devising a plan against you. Re-
turn now every one from his evil way, and
make your ways and your doings good." ' "

God's Warning Rejected

12 And they said, "That is hopeless! So we
will walk according to our own plans, and
we will every one obey the dictates of his evil
heart."
13 Therefore thus says the LORD:

"Ask now among the Gentiles,
Who has heard such things?
The virgin of Israel has done a very
horrible thing.
14 Will *a man* leave the snow water of
Lebanon,
Which comes from the rock of the field?
Will the cold flowing waters be forsaken
for strange waters?

15 "Because My people have forgotten Me,
They have burned incense to worthless
idols.
And they have caused themselves to
stumble in their ways,
From the ancient paths,
To walk in pathways and not on a
highway,
16 To make their land desolate *and* a
perpetual hissing;
Everyone who passes by it will be
astonished
And shake his head.
17 I will scatter them as with an east wind
before the enemy;
I will show them[a] the back and not the
face
In the day of their calamity."

Jeremiah Persecuted

18 Then they said, "Come and let us devise
plans against Jeremiah; for the law shall not
perish from the priest, nor counsel from the
wise, nor the word from the prophet. Come
and let us attack him with the tongue, and let
us not give heed to any of his words."
19 Give heed to me, O LORD,
And listen to the voice of those who
contend with me!
20 Shall evil be repaid for good?
For they have dug a pit for my life.
Remember that I stood before You
To speak good for them,
To turn away Your wrath from them.
21 Therefore deliver up their children to the
famine,
And pour out their *blood*
By the force of the sword;
Let their wives *become* widows
And bereaved of their children.
Let their men be put to death,
Their young men *be* slain
By the sword in battle.
22 Let a cry be heard from their houses,
When You bring a troop suddenly upon
them;
For they have dug a pit to take me,
And hidden snares for my feet.
23 Yet, LORD, You know all their counsel
Which is against me, to slay *me*.
Provide no atonement for their iniquity,
Nor blot out their sin from Your sight;
But let them be overthrown before You.
Deal *thus* with them
In the time of Your anger.

The Sign of the Broken Flask

19 Thus says the LORD: "Go and get a pot-
ter's earthen flask, and *take* some of the
elders of the people and some of the elders of
the priests.
2 "And go out to the Valley of the Son of
Hinnom, which *is* by the entry of the Potsherd
Gate; and proclaim there the words that I will
tell you,
3 "and say, 'Hear the word of the LORD,
O kings of Judah and inhabitants of Jerusalem.
Thus says the LORD of hosts, the God of Israel:
"Behold, I will bring such a catastrophe on this
place, that whoever hears of it, his ears will
tingle.
4 "Because they have forsaken Me and made
this an alien place, because they have burned
incense in it to other gods whom neither they,
their fathers, nor the kings of Judah have
known, and have filled this place with the blood
of the innocents
5 "(they have also built the high places of
Baal, to burn their sons with fire *for* burnt of-
ferings to Baal, which I did not command or
speak, nor did it come into My mind),
6 "therefore behold, the days are coming,"
says the LORD, "that this place shall no more
be called Tophet or the Valley of the Son of
Hinnom, but the Valley of Slaughter.
7 "And I will make void the counsel of Judah
and Jerusalem in this place, and I will cause
them to fall by the sword before their enemies
and by the hands of those who seek their lives;
their corpses I will give as meat for the birds
of the heaven and for the beasts of the earth.
8 "I will make this city desolate and a hiss-
ing; everyone who passes by it will be aston-
ished and hiss because of all its plagues.
9 "And I will cause them to eat the flesh of
their sons and the flesh of their daughters, and
everyone shall eat the flesh of his friend in the
siege and in the desperation with which their
enemies and those who seek their lives shall
drive them to despair." '
10 "Then you shall break the flask in the sight
of the men who go with you,

18:17 [a]Following Septuagint, Syriac, Targum, and Vulgate; Masoretic Text reads *look them in*.

11 "and say to them, 'Thus says the LORD of
hosts: "Even so I will break this people and
this city, as *one* breaks a potter's vessel, which
cannot be made whole again; and they shall
bury *them* in Tophet till *there is* no place to bury.
12 "Thus I will do to this place," says the
LORD, "and to its inhabitants, and make this
city like Tophet.
13 "And the houses of Jerusalem and the
houses of the kings of Judah shall be defiled
like the place of Tophet, because of all the
houses on whose roofs they have burned in-
cense to all the host of heaven, and poured out
drink offerings to other gods." ' "
14 Then Jeremiah came from Tophet, where
the LORD had sent him to prophesy; and he
stood in the court of the Lord's house and said
to all the people,
15 "Thus says the LORD of hosts, the God of
Israel: 'Behold, I will bring on this city and on
all her towns all the doom that I have pro-
nounced against it, because they have stiff-
ened their necks that they might not hear My
words.' "

The Word of God to Pashhur

20 Now Pashhur the son of Immer, the
priest who *was* also chief governor in the
house of the LORD, heard that Jeremiah proph-
esied these things.
2 Then Pashhur struck Jeremiah the prophet,
and put him in the stocks that *were* in the high
gate of Benjamin, which *was* by the house of
the LORD.
3 And it happened on the next day that Pash-
hur brought Jeremiah out of the stocks. Then
Jeremiah said to him, "The LORD has not called
your name Pashhur, but Magor-Missabib.[a]
4 "For thus says the LORD: 'Behold, I will
make you a terror to yourself and to all your
friends; and they shall fall by the sword of their
enemies, and your eyes shall see *it*. I will give
all Judah into the hand of the king of Babylon,
and he shall carry them captive to Babylon and
slay them with the sword.
5 'Moreover I will deliver all the wealth of this
city, all its produce, and all its precious things;
all the treasures of the kings of Judah I will
give into the hand of their enemies, who will
plunder them, seize them, and carry them to
Babylon.
6 'And you, Pashhur, and all who dwell in
your house, shall go into captivity. You shall
go to Babylon, and there you shall die, and be
buried there, you and all your friends, to whom
you have prophesied lies.' "

Jeremiah's Unpopular Ministry

7 O LORD, You induced me, and I was
persuaded;
You are stronger than I, and have
prevailed.
I am in derision daily;
Everyone mocks me.
8 For when I spoke, I cried out;
I shouted, "Violence and plunder!"
Because the word of the LORD was made
to me
A reproach and a derision daily.
9 Then I said, "I will not make mention of
Him,
Nor speak anymore in His name."
But *His word* was in my heart like a
burning fire
Shut up in my bones;
I was weary of holding *it* back,
And I could not.
10 For I heard many mocking:
"Fear on every side!"
"Report," *they say*, "and we will report it!"
All my acquaintances watched for my
stumbling, *saying*,
"Perhaps he can be induced;
Then we will prevail against him,
And we will take our revenge on him."
11 But the LORD *is* with me as a mighty,
awesome One.
Therefore my persecutors will stumble,
and will not prevail.
They will be greatly ashamed, for they
will not prosper.
Their everlasting confusion will never be
forgotten.
12 But, O LORD of hosts,
You who test the righteous,
And see the mind and heart,
Let me see Your vengeance on them;
For I have pleaded my cause before You.
13 Sing to the LORD! Praise the LORD!
For He has delivered the life of the poor
From the hand of evildoers.
14 Cursed *be* the day in which I was born!
Let the day not be blessed in which my
mother bore me!
15 Let the man *be* cursed
Who brought news to my father, saying,
"A male child has been born to you!"
Making him very glad.
16 And let that man be like the cities
Which the LORD overthrew, and did not
relent;
Let him hear the cry in the morning
And the shouting at noon,
17 Because he did not kill me from the
womb,
That my mother might have been my
grave,
And her womb always enlarged *with me*.
18 Why did I come forth from the womb to
see labor and sorrow,
That my days should be consumed with
shame?

Jerusalem's Doom Is Sealed

21 The word which came to Jeremiah from
the LORD when King Zedekiah sent to
him Pashhur the son of Melchiah, and Zepha-
niah the son of Maaseiah, the priest, saying,
2 "Please inquire of the LORD for us, for
Nebuchadnezzar[a] king of Babylon makes war
against us. Perhaps the LORD will deal with us
according to all His wonderful works, that *the
king* may go away from us."
3 Then Jeremiah said to them, "Thus you shall
say to Zedekiah,
4 'Thus says the LORD God of Israel: "Be-
hold, I will turn back the weapons of war that
are in your hands, with which you fight against
the king of Babylon and the Chaldeans[a] who
besiege you outside the walls; and I will assem-
ble them in the midst of this city.
5 "I Myself will fight against you with an out-

20:3 [a]Literally *Fear on Every Side* **21:2** [a]Hebrew *Nebuchadrezzar*, and so elsewhere **21:4** [a]Or *Babylonians*

stretched hand and with a strong arm, even in anger and fury and great wrath.
6 "I will strike the inhabitants of this city, both man and beast; they shall die of a great pestilence.
7 "And afterward," says the LORD, "I will deliver Zedekiah king of Judah, his servants and the people, and such as are left in this city from the pestilence and the sword and the famine, into the hand of Nebuchadnezzar king of Babylon, into the hand of their enemies, and into the hand of those who seek their life; and he shall strike them with the edge of the sword. He shall not spare them, or have pity or mercy."'
8 "Now you shall say to this people, 'Thus says the LORD: "Behold, I set before you the way of life and the way of death.
9 "He who remains in this city shall die by the sword, by famine, and by pestilence; but he who goes out and defects to the Chaldeans who besiege you, he shall live, and his life shall be as a prize to him.
10 "For I have set My face against this city for adversity and not for good," says the LORD. "It shall be given into the hand of the king of Babylon, and he shall burn it with fire."'

Message to the House of David

11 "And concerning the house of the king of Judah, *say*, 'Hear the word of the LORD,
12 'O house of David! Thus says the LORD:

"Execute judgment in the morning;
And deliver *him who is* plundered
Out of the hand of the oppressor,
Lest My fury go forth like fire
And burn so that no one can quench *it*,
Because of the evil of your doings.

13 "Behold, I *am* against you, O inhabitant of the valley,
And rock of the plain," says the LORD,
"Who say, 'Who shall come down against us?
Or who shall enter our dwellings?'
14 But I will punish you according to the fruit of your doings," says the LORD;
"I will kindle a fire in its forest,
And it shall devour all things around it." ' "

22 Thus says the LORD: "Go down to the house of the king of Judah, and there speak this word,
2 "and say, 'Hear the word of the LORD, O king of Judah, you who sit on the throne of David, you and your servants and your people who enter these gates!
3 'Thus says the LORD: "Execute judgment and righteousness, and deliver the plundered out of the hand of the oppressor. Do no wrong and do no violence to the stranger, the fatherless, or the widow, nor shed innocent blood in this place.
4 "For if you indeed do this thing, then shall enter the gates of this house, riding on horses and in chariots, accompanied by servants and people, kings who sit on the throne of David.
5 "But if you will not hear these words, I swear by Myself," says the LORD, "that this house shall become a desolation." ' "
6 For thus says the LORD to the house of the king of Judah:

"You *are* Gilead to Me,
The head of Lebanon;
Yet I surely will make you a wilderness,
Cities *which* are not inhabited.
7 I will prepare destroyers against you,
Everyone with his weapons;
They shall cut down your choice cedars
And cast *them* into the fire.

8 "And many nations will pass by this city; and everyone will say to his neighbor, 'Why has the LORD done so to this great city?'
9 "Then they will answer, 'Because they have forsaken the covenant of the LORD their God, and worshiped other gods and served them.' "

10 Weep not for the dead, nor bemoan him;
Weep bitterly for him who goes away,
For he shall return no more,
Nor see his native country.

Message to the Sons of Josiah

11 For thus says the LORD concerning Shallum[a] the son of Josiah, king of Judah, who reigned instead of Josiah his father, who went from this place: "He shall not return here anymore,
12 "but he shall die in the place where they have led him captive, and shall see this land no more.

13 "Woe to him who builds his house by unrighteousness
And his chambers by injustice,
Who uses his neighbor's service without wages
And gives him nothing for his work,
14 Who says, 'I will build myself a wide house with spacious chambers,
And cut out windows for it,
Paneling *it* with cedar
And painting *it* with vermilion.'

15 "Shall you reign because you enclose *yourself* in cedar?
Did not your father eat and drink,
And do justice and righteousness?
Then *it was* well with him.
16 He judged the cause of the poor and needy;
Then *it was* well.
Was not this knowing Me?" says the LORD.
17 "Yet your eyes and your heart *are* for nothing but your covetousness,
For shedding innocent blood,
And practicing oppression and violence."

18 Therefore thus says the LORD concerning Jehoiakim the son of Josiah, king of Judah:

"They shall not lament for him,
Saying, 'Alas, my brother!' or 'Alas, my sister!'
They shall not lament for him,
Saying, 'Alas, master!' or 'Alas, his glory!'
19 He shall be buried with the burial of a donkey,
Dragged and cast out beyond the gates of Jerusalem.

20 "Go up to Lebanon, and cry out,
And lift up your voice in Bashan;
Cry from Abarim,
For all your lovers are destroyed.

22:11 [a]Also called *Jehoahaz*

21 I spoke to you in your prosperity,
But you said, 'I will not hear.'
This *has been* your manner from your youth,
That you did not obey My voice.
22 The wind shall eat up all your rulers,
And your lovers shall go into captivity;
Surely then you will be ashamed and humiliated
For all your wickedness.
23 O inhabitant of Lebanon,
Making your nest in the cedars,
How gracious will you be when pangs come upon you,
Like the pain of a woman in labor?

Message to Coniah

24 "*As* I live," says the LORD, "though Co-
niah[a] the son of Jehoiakim, king of Judah, were
the signet on My right hand, yet I would pluck
you off;
25 "and I will give you into the hand of those
who seek your life, and into the hand *of those*
whose face you fear—the hand of Nebuchad-
nezzar king of Babylon and the hand of the
Chaldeans.
26 "So I will cast you out, and your mother
who bore you, into another country where you
were not born; and there you shall die.
27 "But to the land to which they desire to
return, there they shall not return.

28 "Is this man Coniah a despised, broken idol—
A vessel in which *is* no pleasure?
Why are they cast out, he and his descendants,
And cast into a land which they do not know?
29 O earth, earth, earth,
Hear the word of the LORD!
30 Thus says the LORD:
'Write this man down as childless,
A man *who* shall not prosper in his days;
For none of his descendants shall prosper,
Sitting on the throne of David,
And ruling anymore in Judah.'"

The Branch of Righteousness

23 "Woe to the shepherds who destroy and
scatter the sheep of My pasture!" says
the LORD.
2 Therefore thus says the LORD God of Is-
rael against the shepherds who feed My peo-
ple: "You have scattered My flock, driven them
away, and not attended to them. Behold, I will
attend to you for the evil of your doings," says
the LORD.
3 "But I will gather the remnant of My flock
out of all countries where I have driven them,
and bring them back to their folds; and they
shall be fruitful and increase.
4 "I will set up shepherds over them who
will feed them; and they shall fear no more,
nor be dismayed, nor shall they be lacking,"
says the LORD.

5 "Behold, *the* days are coming," says the LORD,
"That I will raise to David a Branch of righteousness;
A King shall reign and prosper,
And execute judgment and righteousness in the earth.
6 In His days Judah will be saved,
And Israel will dwell safely;
Now this *is* His name by which He will be called:

THE LORD OUR RIGHTEOUSNESS.[a]

7 "Therefore, behold, *the* days are coming,"
says the LORD, "that they shall no longer say,
'As the LORD lives who brought up the children
of Israel from the land of Egypt,'
8 "but, 'As the LORD lives who brought up
and led the descendants of the house of Israel
from the north country and from all the coun-
tries where I had driven them.' And they shall
dwell in their own land."

False Prophets and Empty Oracles

9 My heart within me is broken
Because of the prophets;
All my bones shake.
I am like a drunken man,
And like a man whom wine has overcome,
Because of the LORD,
And because of His holy words.
10 For the land is full of adulterers;
For because of a curse the land mourns.
The pleasant places of the wilderness are dried up.
Their course of life is evil,
And their might *is* not right.

11 "For both prophet and priest are profane;
Yes, in My house I have found their wickedness," says the LORD.
12 "Therefore their way shall be to them
Like slippery *ways;*
In the darkness they shall be driven on
And fall in them;
For I will bring disaster on them,
The year of their punishment," says the LORD.
13 "And I have seen folly in the prophets of Samaria:
They prophesied by Baal
And caused My people Israel to err.
14 Also I have seen a horrible thing in the prophets of Jerusalem:
They commit adultery and walk in lies;
They also strengthen the hands of evildoers,
So that no one turns back from his wickedness.
All of them are like Sodom to Me,
And her inhabitants like Gomorrah.

15 "Therefore thus says the LORD of hosts
concerning the prophets:

'Behold, I will feed them with wormwood,
And make them drink the water of gall;
For from the prophets of Jerusalem
Profaneness has gone out into all the land.'"

16 Thus says the LORD of hosts:

"Do not listen to the words of the prophets who prophesy to you.
They make you worthless;
They speak a vision of their own heart,
Not from the mouth of the LORD.

22:24 [a]Also called *Jeconiah* and *Jehoiachin* 23:6 [a]Hebrew *YHWH Tsidkenu*

17 They continually say to those who
despise Me,
'The LORD has said, "You shall have
peace" ';
And *to* everyone who walks according to
the dictates of his own heart, they say,
'No evil shall come upon you.' "

18 For who has stood in the counsel of the
LORD,
And has perceived and heard His word?
Who has marked His word and heard *it*?
19 Behold, a whirlwind of the LORD has
gone forth in fury—
A violent whirlwind!
It will fall violently on the head of the
wicked.
20 The anger of the LORD will not turn back
Until He has executed and performed the
thoughts of His heart.
In the latter days you will understand it
perfectly.

21 "I have not sent these prophets, yet they
ran.
I have not spoken to them, yet they
prophesied.
22 But if they had stood in My counsel,
And had caused My people to hear My
words,
Then they would have turned them from
their evil way
And from the evil of their doings.

23 "*Am* I a God near at hand," says the LORD,
"And not a God afar off?
24 Can anyone hide himself in secret places,
So I shall not see him?" says the LORD;
"Do I not fill heaven and earth?" says the
LORD.

25 "I have heard what the prophets have said who prophesy lies in My name, saying, 'I have dreamed, I have dreamed!'

26 "How long will *this* be in the heart of the prophets who prophesy lies? Indeed *they are* prophets of the deceit of their own heart,

27 "who try to make My people forget My name by their dreams which everyone tells his neighbor, as their fathers forgot My name for Baal.

28 "The prophet who has a dream, let him tell
a dream;
And he who has My word, let him speak
My word faithfully.
What *is* the chaff to the wheat?" says the
LORD.
29 "*Is* not My word like a fire?" says the
LORD,
"And like a hammer *that* breaks the rock
in pieces?

30 "Therefore behold, I *am* against the prophets," says the LORD, "who steal My words every one from his neighbor.

31 "Behold, I *am* against the prophets," says the LORD, "who use their tongues and say, 'He says.'

32 "Behold, I *am* against those who prophesy false dreams," says the LORD, "and tell them, and cause My people to err by their lies and by their recklessness. Yet I did not send them or command them; therefore they shall not profit this people at all," says the LORD.

33 "So when these people or the prophet or the priest ask you, saying, 'What is the oracle of the LORD?' you shall then say to them, 'What oracle?'[a] I will even forsake you," says the LORD.

34 "And *as for* the prophet and the priest and the people who say, 'The oracle of the LORD!' I will even punish that man and his house.

35 "Thus every one of you shall say to his neighbor, and every one to his brother, 'What has the LORD answered?' and, 'What has the LORD spoken?'

36 "And the oracle of the LORD you shall mention no more. For every man's word will be his oracle, for you have perverted the words of the living God, the LORD of hosts, our God.

37 "Thus you shall say to the prophet, 'What has the LORD answered you?' and, 'What has the LORD spoken?'

38 "But since you say, 'The oracle of the LORD!' therefore thus says the LORD: 'Because you say this word, "The oracle of the LORD!" and I have sent to you, saying, "Do not say, 'The oracle of the LORD!' "

39 'therefore behold, I, even I, will utterly forget you and forsake you, and the city that I gave you and your fathers, and *will cast you* out of My presence.

40 'And I will bring an everlasting reproach upon you, and a perpetual shame, which shall not be forgotten.' "

The Sign of Two Baskets of Figs

24 The LORD showed me, and there were two baskets of figs set before the temple of the LORD, after Nebuchadnezzar king of Babylon had carried away captive Jeconiah the son of Jehoiakim, king of Judah, and the princes of Judah with the craftsmen and smiths, from Jerusalem, and had brought them to Babylon.

2 One basket *had* very good figs, like the figs *that are* first ripe; and the other basket *had* very bad figs which could not be eaten, they were so bad.

3 Then the LORD said to me, "What do you see, Jeremiah?" And I said, "Figs, the good figs, very good; and the bad, very bad, which cannot be eaten, they are so bad."

4 Again the word of the LORD came to me, saying,

5 "Thus says the LORD, the God of Israel: 'Like these good figs, so will I acknowledge those who are carried away captive from Judah, whom I have sent out of this place for *their own* good, into the land of the Chaldeans.

6 'For I will set My eyes on them for good, and I will bring them back to this land; I will build them and not pull *them* down, and I will plant them and not pluck *them* up.

7 'Then I will give them a heart to know Me, that I *am* the LORD; and they shall be My people, and I will be their God, for they shall return to Me with their whole heart.

8 'And as the bad figs which cannot be eaten, they are so bad'—surely thus says the LORD—'so will I give up Zedekiah the king of Judah, his princes, the residue of Jerusalem who remain in this land, and those who dwell in the land of Egypt.

9 'I will deliver them to trouble into all the kingdoms of the earth, for *their* harm, *to be* a reproach and a byword, a taunt and a curse, in all places where I shall drive them.

23:33 [a]Septuagint, Targum, and Vulgate read '*You are the burden.*'

10 'And I will send the sword, the famine, and
the pestilence among them, till they are con-
sumed from the land that I gave to them and
their fathers.'"

Seventy Years of Desolation

25 The word that came to Jeremiah con-
cerning all the people of Judah, in the
fourth year of Jehoiakim the son of Josiah,
king of Judah (which *was* the first year of Neb-
uchadnezzar king of Babylon),
2 which Jeremiah the prophet spoke to all
the people of Judah and to all the inhabitants
of Jerusalem, saying:
3 "From the thirteenth year of Josiah the son
of Amon, king of Judah, even to this day, this
is the twenty-third year in which the word of
the LORD has come to me; and I have spoken
to you, rising early and speaking, but you have
not listened.
4 "And the LORD has sent to you all His ser-
vants the prophets, rising early and sending
them, but you have not listened nor inclined
your ear to hear.
5 "They said, 'Repent now everyone of his
evil way and his evil doings, and dwell in the
land that the LORD has given to you and your
fathers forever and ever.
6 'Do not go after other gods to serve them
and worship them, and do not provoke Me to
anger with the works of your hands; and I will
not harm you.'
7 "Yet you have not listened to Me," says the
LORD, "that you might provoke Me to anger
with the works of your hands to your own hurt.
8 "Therefore thus says the LORD of hosts:
'Because you have not heard My words,
9 'behold, I will send and take all the fami-
lies of the north,' says the LORD, 'and Nebu-
chadnezzar the king of Babylon, My servant,
and will bring them against this land, against
its inhabitants, and against these nations all
around, and will utterly destroy them, and
make them an astonishment, a hissing, and
perpetual desolations.
10 'Moreover I will take from them the voice
of mirth and the voice of gladness, the voice of
the bridegroom and the voice of the bride, the
sound of the millstones and the light of the
lamp.
11 'And this whole land shall be a desolation
and an astonishment, and these nations shall
serve the king of Babylon seventy years.
12 'Then it will come to pass, when seventy
years are completed, *that* I will punish the king
of Babylon and that nation, the land of the
Chaldeans, for their iniquity,' says the LORD;
'and I will make it a perpetual desolation.
13 'So I will bring on that land all My words
which I have pronounced against it, all that
is written in this book, which Jeremiah has
prophesied concerning all the nations.
14 '(For many nations and great kings shall
be served by them also; and I will repay them
according to their deeds and according to the
works of their own hands.)'"

Judgment on the Nations

15 For thus says the LORD God of Israel to
me: "Take this wine cup of fury from My hand,
and cause all the nations, to whom I send you,
to drink it.
16 "And they will drink and stagger and go mad
because of the sword that I will send among
them."
17 Then I took the cup from the LORD's hand,
and made all the nations drink, to whom the
LORD had sent me:
18 Jerusalem and the cities of Judah, its kings
and its princes, to make them a desolation, an
astonishment, a hissing, and a curse, as *it is*
this day;
19 Pharaoh king of Egypt, his servants, his
princes, and all his people;
20 all the mixed multitude, all the kings of the
land of Uz, all the kings of the land of the
Philistines (namely, Ashkelon, Gaza, Ekron,
and the remnant of Ashdod);
21 Edom, Moab, and the people of Ammon;
22 all the kings of Tyre, all the kings of Sidon,
and the kings of the coastlands which *are*
across the sea;
23 Dedan, Tema, Buz, and all *who are* in the
farthest corners;
24 all the kings of Arabia and all the kings of
the mixed multitude who dwell in the desert;
25 all the kings of Zimri, all the kings of Elam,
and all the kings of the Medes;
26 all the kings of the north, far and near,
one with another; and all the kingdoms of the
world which *are* on the face of the earth. Also
the king of Sheshach[a] shall drink after them.
27 "Therefore you shall say to them, 'Thus
says the LORD of hosts, the God of Israel:
"Drink, be drunk, and vomit! Fall and rise no
more, because of the sword which I will send
among you."'
28 "And it shall be, if they refuse to take the
cup from your hand to drink, then you shall
say to them, 'Thus says the LORD of hosts:
"You shall certainly drink!
29 "For behold, I begin to bring calamity on
the city which is called by My name, and
should you be utterly unpunished? You shall
not be unpunished, for I will call for a sword
on all the inhabitants of the earth," says the
LORD of hosts.'
30 "Therefore prophesy against them all
these words, and say to them:

'The LORD will roar from on high,
And utter His voice from His holy
habitation;
He will roar mightily against His fold.
He will give a shout, as those who tread
the grapes,
Against all the inhabitants of the earth.
31 A noise will come to the ends of the
earth—
For the LORD has a controversy with the
nations;
He will plead His case with all flesh.
He will give those *who are* wicked to the
sword,' says the LORD."

32 Thus says the LORD of hosts:

"Behold, disaster shall go forth
From nation to nation,
And a great whirlwind shall be raised up
From the farthest parts of the earth.

33 "And at that day the slain of the LORD shall
be from *one* end of the earth even to the *other*
end of the earth. They shall not be lamented,
or gathered, or buried; they shall become re-
fuse on the ground.

25:26 [a]A code word for Babylon (compare 51:41)

34 "Wail, shepherds, and cry!
Roll about *in the ashes,*
You leaders of the flock!
For the days of your slaughter and your
dispersions are fulfilled;
You shall fall like a precious vessel.
35 And the shepherds will have no way to
flee,
Nor the leaders of the flock to escape.
36 A voice of the cry of the shepherds,
And a wailing of the leaders to the flock
will be heard.
For the LORD has plundered their
pasture,
37 And the peaceful dwellings are cut down
Because of the fierce anger of the LORD.
38 He has left His lair like the lion;
For their land is desolate
Because of the fierceness of the
Oppressor,
And because of His fierce anger."

Jeremiah Saved from Death

26 In the beginning of the reign of Jehoia-
kim the son of Josiah, king of Judah, this
word came from the LORD, saying,
2 "Thus says the LORD: 'Stand in the court
of the LORD's house, and speak to all the cities
of Judah, which come to worship *in* the LORD's
house, all the words that I command you to
speak to them. Do not diminish a word.
3 'Perhaps everyone will listen and turn
from his evil way, that I may relent concerning
the calamity which I purpose to bring on them
because of the evil of their doings.'
4 "And you shall say to them, 'Thus says the
LORD: "If you will not listen to Me, to walk in
My law which I have set before you,
5 "to heed the words of My servants the
prophets whom I sent to you, both rising up early
and sending *them* (but you have not heeded),
6 "then I will make this house like Shiloh,
and will make this city a curse to all the nations
of the earth." ' "
7 So the priests and the prophets and all the
people heard Jeremiah speaking these words
in the house of the LORD.
8 Now it happened, when Jeremiah had
made an end of speaking all that the LORD had
commanded *him* to speak to all the people, that
the priests and the prophets and all the people
seized him, saying, "You will surely die!
9 "Why have you prophesied in the name
of the LORD, saying, 'This house shall be like
Shiloh, and this city shall be desolate, without
an inhabitant'?" And all the people were gath-
ered against Jeremiah in the house of the
LORD.
10 When the princes of Judah heard these
things, they came up from the king's house to
the house of the LORD and sat down in the
entry of the New Gate of the LORD's *house.*
11 And the priests and the prophets spoke to
the princes and all the people, saying, "This
man deserves to die! For he has prophesied
against this city, as you have heard with your
ears."
12 Then Jeremiah spoke to all the princes and
all the people, saying: "The LORD sent me to
prophesy against this house and against this
city with all the words that you have heard.
13 "Now therefore, amend your ways and
your doings, and obey the voice of the LORD
your God; then the LORD will relent concern-
ing the doom that He has pronounced against
you.
14 "As for me, here I am, in your hand; do
with me as seems good and proper to you.
15 "But know for certain that if you put me to
death, you will surely bring innocent blood on
yourselves, on this city, and on its inhabitants;
for truly the LORD has sent me to you to speak
all these words in your hearing."
16 So the princes and all the people said to
the priests and the prophets, "This man does
not deserve to die. For he has spoken to us in
the name of the LORD our God."
17 Then certain of the elders of the land rose
up and spoke to all the assembly of the people,
saying:
18 "Micah of Moresheth prophesied in the
days of Hezekiah king of Judah, and spoke to
all the people of Judah, saying, 'Thus says the
LORD of hosts:

"Zion shall be plowed *like* a field,
Jerusalem shall become heaps of ruins,
And the mountain of the temple[a]
Like the bare hills of the forest." '[b]

19 "Did Hezekiah king of Judah and all Judah
ever put him to death? Did he not fear the
LORD and seek the LORD's favor? And the
LORD relented concerning the doom which He
had pronounced against them. But we are do-
ing great evil against ourselves."
20 Now there was also a man who prophesied
in the name of the LORD, Urijah the son of
Shemaiah of Kirjath Jearim, who prophesied
against this city and against this land accord-
ing to all the words of Jeremiah.
21 And when Jehoiakim the king, with all his
mighty men and all the princes, heard his
words, the king sought to put him to death; but
when Urijah heard *it,* he was afraid and fled,
and went to Egypt.
22 Then Jehoiakim the king sent men to
Egypt: Elnathan the son of Achbor, and *other*
men *who went* with him to Egypt.
23 And they brought Urijah from Egypt and
brought him to Jehoiakim the king, who killed
him with the sword and cast his dead body into
the graves of the common people.
24 Nevertheless the hand of Ahikam the son
of Shaphan was with Jeremiah, so that they
should not give him into the hand of the people
to put him to death.

Symbol of the Bonds and Yokes

27 In the beginning of the reign of Jehoia-
kim[a] the son of Josiah, king of Judah,
this word came to Jeremiah from the LORD,
saying,[b]
2 "Thus says the LORD to me: 'Make for your-
selves bonds and yokes, and put them on your
neck,
3 'and send them to the king of Edom, the
king of Moab, the king of the Ammonites, the
king of Tyre, and the king of Sidon, by the hand
of the messengers who come to Jerusalem to
Zedekiah king of Judah.
4 'And command them to say to their mas-
ters, "Thus says the LORD of hosts, the God of
Israel—thus you shall say to your masters:
5 'I have made the earth, the man and the

26:18 [a]Literally *house* [b]Compare Micah 3:12 **27:1** [a]Following Masoretic Text, Targum, and Vulgate; some Hebrew manuscripts, Arabic, and Syriac read *Zedekiah* (compare 27:3, 12; 28:1). [b]Septuagint omits verse 1.

beast that *are* on the ground, by My great
power and by My outstretched arm, and have
given it to whom it seemed proper to Me.
6 'And now I have given all these lands into
the hand of Nebuchadnezzar the king of Bab-
ylon, My servant; and the beasts of the field I
have also given him to serve him.
7 'So all nations shall serve him and his son
and his son's son, until the time of his land
comes; and then many nations and great kings
shall make him serve them.
8 'And it shall be, *that* the nation and king-
dom which will not serve Nebuchadnezzar the
king of Babylon, and which will not put its
neck under the yoke of the king of Babylon,
that nation I will punish,' says the LORD, 'with
the sword, the famine, and the pestilence, until
I have consumed them by his hand.
9 'Therefore do not listen to your prophets,
your diviners, your dreamers, your sooth-
sayers, or your sorcerers, who speak to you,
saying, "You shall not serve the king of Bab-
ylon."
10 'For they prophesy a lie to you, to remove
you far from your land; and I will drive you
out, and you will perish.
11 'But the nations that bring their necks un-
der the yoke of the king of Babylon and serve
him, I will let them remain in their own land,'
says the LORD, 'and they shall till it and dwell
in it.'"'"
12 I also spoke to Zedekiah king of Judah
according to all these words, saying, "Bring
your necks under the yoke of the king of Bab-
ylon, and serve him and his people, and live!
13 "Why will you die, you and your people,
by the sword, by the famine, and by the pesti-
lence, as the LORD has spoken against the na-
tion that will not serve the king of Babylon?
14 "Therefore do not listen to the words of
the prophets who speak to you, saying, 'You
shall not serve the king of Babylon,' for they
prophesy a lie to you;
15 "for I have not sent them," says the LORD,
"yet they prophesy a lie in My name, that I
may drive you out, and that you may perish,
you and the prophets who prophesy to you."
16 Also I spoke to the priests and to all this
people, saying, "Thus says the LORD: 'Do not
listen to the words of your prophets who
prophesy to you, saying, "Behold, the vessels
of the LORD's house will now shortly be
brought back from Babylon"; for they proph-
esy a lie to you.
17 'Do not listen to them; serve the king of
Babylon, and live! Why should this city be laid
waste?
18 'But if they *are* prophets, and if the word
of the LORD is with them, let them now make
intercession to the LORD of hosts, that the ves-
sels which are left in the house of the LORD, *in*
the house of the king of Judah, and at Jerusa-
lem, do not go to Babylon.'
19 "For thus says the LORD of hosts concern-
ing the pillars, concerning the Sea, concerning
the carts, and concerning the remainder of the
vessels that remain in this city,
20 "which Nebuchadnezzar king of Babylon
did not take, when he carried away captive
Jeconiah the son of Jehoiakim, king of Judah,
from Jerusalem to Babylon, and all the nobles
of Judah and Jerusalem—
21 "yes, thus says the LORD of hosts, the God
of Israel, concerning the vessels that remain in
the house of the LORD, and in the house of the
king of Judah and of Jerusalem:
22 'They shall be carried to Babylon, and there
they shall be until the day that I visit them,'
says the LORD. 'Then I will bring them up and
restore them to this place.'"

Hananiah's Falsehood and Doom

28 And it happened in the same year, at the
beginning of the reign of Zedekiah king
of Judah, in the fourth year *and* in the fifth
month, *that* Hananiah the son of Azur the
prophet, who *was* from Gibeon, spoke to me
in the house of the LORD in the presence of the
priests and of all the people, saying,
2 "Thus speaks the LORD of hosts, the God
of Israel, saying: 'I have broken the yoke of the
king of Babylon.
3 'Within two full years I will bring back to
this place all the vessels of the LORD's house,
that Nebuchadnezzar king of Babylon took
away from this place and carried to Babylon.
4 'And I will bring back to this place Jeco-
niah the son of Jehoiakim, king of Judah, with
all the captives of Judah who went to Babylon,'
says the LORD, 'for I will break the yoke of the
king of Babylon.'"
5 Then the prophet Jeremiah spoke to the
prophet Hananiah in the presence of the
priests and in the presence of all the people
who stood in the house of the LORD,
6 and the prophet Jeremiah said, "Amen!
The LORD do so; the LORD perform your words
which you have prophesied, to bring back the
vessels of the LORD's house and all who were
carried away captive, from Babylon to this place.
7 "Nevertheless hear now this word that I
speak in your hearing and in the hearing of all
the people:
8 "The prophets who have been before me
and before you of old prophesied against many
countries and great kingdoms—of war and di-
saster and pestilence.
9 "As for the prophet who prophesies of
peace, when the word of the prophet comes to
pass, the prophet will be known *as* one whom
the LORD has truly sent."
10 Then Hananiah the prophet took the yoke
off the prophet Jeremiah's neck and broke it.
11 And Hananiah spoke in the presence of all
the people, saying, "Thus says the LORD: 'Even
so I will break the yoke of Nebuchadnezzar
king of Babylon from the neck of all nations
within the space of two full years.'" And the
prophet Jeremiah went his way.
12 Now the word of the LORD came to Jere-
miah, after Hananiah the prophet had broken
the yoke from the neck of the prophet Jere-
miah, saying,
13 "Go and tell Hananiah, saying, 'Thus says
the LORD: "You have broken the yokes of
wood, but you have made in their place yokes
of iron."
14 'For thus says the LORD of hosts, the God
of Israel: "I have put a yoke of iron on the
neck of all these nations, that they may serve
Nebuchadnezzar king of Babylon; and they
shall serve him. I have given him the beasts of
the field also."'"
15 Then the prophet Jeremiah said to Hana-
niah the prophet, "Hear now, Hananiah, the
LORD has not sent you, but you make this peo-
ple trust in a lie.
16 "Therefore thus says the LORD: 'Behold, I
will cast you from the face of the earth. This

year you shall die, because you have taught
rebellion against the LORD.'"
17 So Hananiah the prophet died the same
year in the seventh month.

Jeremiah's Letter to the Captives

29 Now these *are* the words of the letter
that Jeremiah the prophet sent from Je-
rusalem to the remainder of the elders who
were carried away captive—to the priests, the
prophets, and all the people whom Nebuchad-
nezzar had carried away captive from Jerusa-
lem to Babylon.
2 (This happened after Jeconiah the king,
the queen mother, the eunuchs, the princes of
Judah and Jerusalem, the craftsmen, and the
smiths had departed from Jerusalem.)
3 *The letter was sent* by the hand of Elasah
the son of Shaphan, and Gemariah the son of
Hilkiah, whom Zedekiah king of Judah sent to
Babylon, to Nebuchadnezzar king of Babylon,
saying,

4 Thus says the LORD of hosts, the God of Israel, to all who were carried away captive, whom I have caused to be carried away from Jerusalem to Babylon:
5 Build houses and dwell *in them;* plant gardens and eat their fruit.
6 Take wives and beget sons and daughters; and take wives for your sons and give your daughters to husbands, so that they may bear sons and daughters—that you may be increased there, and not diminished.
7 And seek the peace of the city where I have caused you to be carried away captive, and pray to the LORD for it; for in its peace you will have peace.
8 For thus says the LORD of hosts, the God of Israel: Do not let your prophets and your diviners who are in your midst deceive you, nor listen to your dreams which you cause to be dreamed.
9 For they prophesy falsely to you in My name; I have not sent them, says the LORD.
10 For thus says the LORD: After seventy years are completed at Babylon, I will visit you and perform My good word toward you, and cause you to return to this place.
11 For I know the thoughts that I think toward you, says the LORD, thoughts of peace and not of evil, to give you a future and a hope.
12 Then you will call upon Me and go and pray to Me, and I will listen to you.
13 And you will seek Me and find *Me,* when you search for Me with all your heart.
14 I will be found by you, says the LORD, and I will bring you back from your captivity; I will gather you from all the nations and from all the places where I have driven you, says the LORD, and I will bring you to the place from which I cause you to be carried away captive.
15 Because you have said, "The LORD has raised up prophets for us in Babylon"—
16 therefore thus says the LORD concerning the king who sits on the throne of David, concerning all the people who dwell in this city, and concerning your brethren who have not gone out with you into captivity—
17 thus says the LORD of hosts: Behold, I will send on them the sword, the famine, and the pestilence, and will make them like rotten figs that cannot be eaten, they are so bad.
18 And I will pursue them with the sword, with famine, and with pestilence; and I will deliver them to trouble among all the kingdoms of the earth—to be a curse, an astonishment, a hissing, and a reproach among all the nations where I have driven them,
19 because they have not heeded My words, says the LORD, which I sent to them by My servants the prophets, rising up early and sending *them;* neither would you heed, says the LORD.
20 Therefore hear the word of the LORD, all you of the captivity, whom I have sent from Jerusalem to Babylon.
21 Thus says the LORD of hosts, the God of Israel, concerning Ahab the son of Kolaiah, and Zedekiah the son of Maaseiah, who prophesy a lie to you in My name: Behold, I will deliver them into the hand of Nebuchadnezzar king of Babylon, and he shall slay them before your eyes.
22 And because of them a curse shall be taken up by all the captivity of Judah who *are* in Babylon, saying, "The LORD make you like Zedekiah and Ahab, whom the king of Babylon roasted in the fire";
23 because they have done disgraceful things in Israel, have committed adultery with their neighbors' wives, and have spoken lying words in My name, which I have not commanded them. Indeed I know, and *am* a witness, says the LORD.

24 You shall also speak to Shemaiah the Nehelamite, saying,
25 Thus speaks the LORD of hosts, the God of Israel, saying: You have sent letters in your name to all the people who *are* at Jerusalem, to Zephaniah the son of Maaseiah the priest, and to all the priests, saying,
26 "The LORD has made you priest instead of Jehoiada the priest, so that there should be officers *in* the house of the LORD over every man *who* is demented and considers himself a prophet, that you should put him in prison and in the stocks.
27 Now therefore, why have you not rebuked Jeremiah of Anathoth who makes himself a prophet to you?
28 For he has sent to us *in* Babylon, saying, 'This *captivity is* long; build houses and dwell *in them,* and plant gardens and eat their fruit.'"

29 Now Zephaniah the priest read this letter in the hearing of Jeremiah the prophet.
30 Then the word of the LORD came to Jeremiah, saying:
31 Send to all those in captivity, saying, Thus says the LORD concerning Shemaiah the Nehelamite: Because Shemaiah has prophesied to you, and I have not sent him, and he has caused you to trust in a lie—
32 therefore thus says the LORD: Behold, I will punish Shemaiah the Nehelamite and his family: he shall not have anyone

to dwell among this people, nor shall he
see the good that I will do for My people,
says the LORD, because he has taught
rebellion against the LORD.

Restoration of Israel and Judah

30 The word that came to Jeremiah from
the LORD, saying,
2 "Thus speaks the LORD God of Israel, saying:
'Write in a book for yourself all the words
that I have spoken to you.
3 'For behold, the days are coming,' says the
LORD, 'that I will bring back from captivity My
people Israel and Judah,' says the LORD. 'And
I will cause them to return to the land that I
gave to their fathers, and they shall possess it.'"
4 Now these *are* the words that the LORD
spoke concerning Israel and Judah.
5 "For thus says the LORD:

'We have heard a voice of trembling,
Of fear, and not of peace.
6 Ask now, and see,
Whether a man is ever in labor with child?
So why do I see every man *with* his hands on his loins
Like a woman in labor,
And all faces turned pale?
7 Alas! For that day *is* great,
So that none *is* like it;
And it *is* the time of Jacob's trouble,
But he shall be saved out of it.

8 'For it shall come to pass in that day,'
Says the LORD of hosts,
'*That* I will break his yoke from your neck,
And will burst your bonds;
Foreigners shall no more enslave them.
9 But they shall serve the LORD their God,
And David their king,
Whom I will raise up for them.

10 'Therefore do not fear, O My servant Jacob,' says the LORD,
'Nor be dismayed, O Israel;
For behold, I will save you from afar,
And your seed from the land of their captivity.
Jacob shall return, have rest and be quiet,
And no one shall make *him* afraid.
11 For I *am* with you,' says the LORD, 'to save you;
Though I make a full end of all nations where I have scattered you,
Yet I will not make a complete end of you.
But I will correct you in justice,
And will not let you go altogether unpunished.'

12 "For thus says the LORD:

'Your affliction *is* incurable,
Your wound *is* severe.
13 *There is* no one to plead your cause,
That you may be bound up;
You have no healing medicines.
14 All your lovers have forgotten you;
They do not seek you;
For I have wounded you with the wound of an enemy,
With the chastisement of a cruel one,
For the multitude of your iniquities,
Because your sins have increased.
15 Why do you cry about your affliction?
Your sorrow *is* incurable.
Because of the multitude of your iniquities,
Because your sins have increased,
I have done these things to you.

16 'Therefore all those who devour you shall be devoured;
And all your adversaries, every one of them, shall go into captivity;
Those who plunder you shall become plunder,
And all who prey upon you I will make a prey.
17 For I will restore health to you
And heal you of your wounds,' says the LORD,
'Because they called you an outcast *saying*:
"This *is* Zion;
No one seeks her."'

18 "Thus says the LORD:

'Behold, I will bring back the captivity of Jacob's tents,
And have mercy on his dwelling places;
The city shall be built upon its own mound,
And the palace shall remain according to its own plan.
19 Then out of them shall proceed thanksgiving
And the voice of those who make merry;
I will multiply them, and they shall not diminish;
I will also glorify them, and they shall not be small.
20 Their children also shall be as before,
And their congregation shall be established before Me;
And I will punish all who oppress them.
21 Their nobles shall be from among them,
And their governor shall come from their midst;
Then I will cause him to draw near,
And he shall approach Me;
For who *is* this who pledged his heart to approach Me?' says the LORD.
22 'You shall be My people,
And I will be your God.'"

23 Behold, the whirlwind of the LORD
Goes forth with fury,
A continuing whirlwind;
It will fall violently on the head of the wicked.
24 The fierce anger of the LORD will not return until He has done it,
And until He has performed the intents of His heart.

In the latter days you will consider it.

The Remnant of Israel Saved

31 "At the same time," says the LORD, "I will
be the God of all the families of Israel,
and they shall be My people."
2 Thus says the LORD:

"The people who survived the sword
Found grace in the wilderness—
Israel, when I went to give him rest."
3 The LORD has appeared of old to me, *saying*:

"Yes, I have loved you with an everlasting love;
Therefore with lovingkindness I have drawn you.
4 Again I will build you, and you shall be rebuilt,
O virgin of Israel!
You shall again be adorned with your tambourines,
And shall go forth in the dances of those who rejoice.
5 You shall yet plant vines on the mountains of Samaria;
The planters shall plant and eat *them* as ordinary food.
6 For there shall be a day
When the watchmen will cry on Mount Ephraim,
'Arise, and let us go up *to* Zion,
To the LORD our God.'"

7 For thus says the LORD:
"Sing with gladness for Jacob,
And shout among the chief of the nations;
Proclaim, give praise, and say,
'O LORD, save Your people,
The remnant of Israel!'
8 Behold, I will bring them from the north country,
And gather them from the ends of the earth,
Among them the blind and the lame,
The woman with child
And the one who labors with child, together;
A great throng shall return there.
9 They shall come with weeping,
And with supplications I will lead them.
I will cause them to walk by the rivers of waters,
In a straight way in which they shall not stumble;
For I am a Father to Israel,
And Ephraim *is* My firstborn.

10 "Hear the word of the LORD, O nations,
And declare *it* in the isles afar off, and say,
'He who scattered Israel will gather him,
And keep him as a shepherd *does* his flock.'
11 For the LORD has redeemed Jacob,
And ransomed him from the hand of one stronger than he.
12 Therefore they shall come and sing in the height of Zion,
Streaming to the goodness of the LORD—
For wheat and new wine and oil,
For the young of the flock and the herd;
Their souls shall be like a well-watered garden,
And they shall sorrow no more at all.

13 "Then shall the virgin rejoice in the dance,
And the young men and the old, together;
For I will turn their mourning to joy,
Will comfort them,
And make them rejoice rather than sorrow.
14 I will satiate the soul of the priests with abundance,
And My people shall be satisfied with My goodness, says the LORD."

Mercy on Ephraim

15 Thus says the LORD:
"A voice was heard in Ramah,
Lamentation *and* bitter weeping,
Rachel weeping for her children,
Refusing to be comforted for her children,
Because they *are* no more."

16 Thus says the LORD:
"Refrain your voice from weeping,
And your eyes from tears;
For your work shall be rewarded, says the LORD,
And they shall come back from the land of the enemy.
17 There is hope in your future, says the LORD,
That *your* children shall come back to their own border.

18 "I have surely heard Ephraim bemoaning himself:
'You have chastised me, and I was chastised,
Like an untrained bull;
Restore me, and I will return,
For You *are* the LORD my God.
19 Surely, after my turning, I repented;
And after I was instructed, I struck myself on the thigh;
I was ashamed, yes, even humiliated,
Because I bore the reproach of my youth.'
20 *Is* Ephraim My dear son?
Is he a pleasant child?
For though I spoke against him,
I earnestly remember him still;
Therefore My heart yearns for him;
I will surely have mercy on him, says the LORD.

21 "Set up signposts,
Make landmarks;
Set your heart toward the highway,
The way in *which* you went.
Turn back, O virgin of Israel,
Turn back to these your cities.
22 How long will you gad about,
O you backsliding daughter?
For the LORD has created a new thing in the earth—
A woman shall encompass a man."

Future Prosperity of Judah

23 Thus says the LORD of hosts, the God of
Israel: "They shall again use this speech in the
land of Judah and in its cities, when I bring back
their captivity: 'The LORD bless you, O home
of justice, *and* mountain of holiness!'
24 "And there shall dwell in Judah itself, and
in all its cities together, farmers and those go-
ing out with flocks.
25 "For I have satiated the weary soul, and I
have replenished every sorrowful soul."
26 After this I awoke and looked around, and
my sleep was sweet to me.
27 "Behold, the days are coming, says the
LORD, that I will sow the house of Israel and
the house of Judah with the seed of man and
the seed of beast.
28 "And it shall come to pass, *that* as I have
watched over them to pluck up, to break down,
to throw down, to destroy, and to afflict, so I
will watch over them to build and to plant, says
the LORD.

29 "In those days they shall say no more:

'The fathers have eaten sour grapes,
And the children's teeth are set on edge.'

30 "But every one shall die for his own iniq-
uity; every man who eats the sour grapes, his
teeth shall be set on edge.

A New Covenant

31 "Behold, the days are coming, says the
LORD, when I will make a new covenant with
the house of Israel and with the house of
Judah—
32 "not according to the covenant that I made
with their fathers in the day *that* I took them
by the hand to lead them out of the land of
Egypt, My covenant which they broke, though
I was a husband to them,[a] says the LORD.
33 "But this *is* the covenant that I will make
with the house of Israel after those days, says
the LORD: I will put My law in their minds, and
write it on their hearts; and I will be their God,
and they shall be My people.
34 "No more shall every man teach his neigh-
bor, and every man his brother, saying, 'Know
the LORD,' for they all shall know Me, from the
least of them to the greatest of them, says the
LORD. For I will forgive their iniquity, and their
sin I will remember no more."

35 Thus says the LORD,
Who gives the sun for a light by day,
The ordinances of the moon and the stars
for a light by night,
Who disturbs the sea,
And its waves roar
(The LORD of hosts *is* His name):

36 "If those ordinances depart
From before Me, says the LORD,
Then the seed of Israel shall also cease
From being a nation before Me forever."

37 Thus says the LORD:

"If heaven above can be measured,
And the foundations of the earth
searched out beneath,
I will also cast off all the seed of Israel
For all that they have done, says the
LORD.

38 "Behold, the days are coming, says the
LORD, that the city shall be built for the LORD
from the Tower of Hananel to the Corner Gate.
39 "The surveyor's line shall again extend
straight forward over the hill Gareb; then it
shall turn toward Goath.
40 "And the whole valley of the dead bodies
and of the ashes, and all the fields as far as the
Brook Kidron, to the corner of the Horse Gate
toward the east, *shall be* holy to the LORD. It
shall not be plucked up or thrown down any-
more forever."

Jeremiah Buys a Field

32 The word that came to Jeremiah from the
LORD in the tenth year of Zedekiah king
of Judah, which was the eighteenth year of
Nebuchadnezzar.
2 For then the king of Babylon's army be-
sieged Jerusalem, and Jeremiah the prophet was
shut up in the court of the prison, which *was*
in the king of Judah's house.
3 For Zedekiah king of Judah had shut him
up, saying, "Why do you prophesy and say,
'Thus says the LORD: "Behold, I will give this
city into the hand of the king of Babylon, and
he shall take it;
4 "and Zedekiah king of Judah shall not es-
cape from the hand of the Chaldeans, but shall
surely be delivered into the hand of the king
of Babylon, and shall speak with him face to
face,[a] and see him eye to eye;
5 "then he shall lead Zedekiah to Babylon,
and there he shall be until I visit him," says the
LORD; "though you fight with the Chaldeans,
you shall not succeed" '?"
6 And Jeremiah said, "The word of the LORD
came to me, saying,
7 'Behold, Hanamel the son of Shallum your
uncle will come to you, saying, "Buy my field
which *is* in Anathoth, for the right of redemp-
tion *is* yours to buy *it*." '
8 "Then Hanamel my uncle's son came to
me in the court of the prison according to the
word of the LORD, and said to me, 'Please buy
my field that *is* in Anathoth, which *is* in the
country of Benjamin; for the right of inheri-
tance *is* yours, and the redemption yours; buy
it for yourself.' Then I knew that this was the
word of the LORD.
9 "So I bought the field from Hanamel, the
son of my uncle who *was* in Anathoth, and
weighed *out to* him the money—seventeen
shekels of silver.
10 "And I signed the deed and sealed *it*, took
witnesses, and weighed the money on the scales.
11 "So I took the purchase deed, *both* that
which was sealed *according* to the law and
custom, and that which was open;
12 "and I gave the purchase deed to Baruch
the son of Neriah, son of Mahseiah, in the pres-
ence of Hanamel my uncle's *son*, and in the
presence of the witnesses who signed the pur-
chase deed, before all the Jews who sat in the
court of the prison.
13 "Then I charged Baruch before them,
saying,
14 'Thus says the LORD of hosts, the God of
Israel: "Take these deeds, both this purchase
deed which is sealed and this deed which is
open, and put them in an earthen vessel, that
they may last many days."
15 'For thus says the LORD of hosts, the God
of Israel: "Houses and fields and vineyards
shall be possessed again in this land." '

Jeremiah Prays for Understanding

16 "Now when I had delivered the purchase
deed to Baruch the son of Neriah, I prayed to
the LORD, saying:
17 'Ah, Lord GOD! Behold, You have made the
heavens and the earth by Your great power and
outstretched arm. There is nothing too hard for
You.
18 '*You* show lovingkindness to thousands,
and repay the iniquity of the fathers into the
bosom of their children after them—the Great,
the Mighty God, whose name *is* the LORD of
hosts.
19 '*You are* great in counsel and mighty in
work, for Your eyes *are* open to all the ways of
the sons of men, to give everyone according
to his ways and according to the fruit of his
doings.

31:32 [a]Following Masoretic Text, Targum, and Vulgate; Septuagint and Syriac read *and I turned away from them.* **32:4** [a]Literally *mouth to mouth*

20 'You have set signs and wonders in the
land of Egypt, to this day, and in Israel and
among *other* men; and You have made Yourself a name, as it is this day.
21 'You have brought Your people Israel out
of the land of Egypt with signs and wonders,
with a strong hand and an outstretched arm,
and with great terror;
22 'You have given them this land, of which
You swore to their fathers to give them—"a
land flowing with milk and honey."[a]
23 'And they came in and took possession of
it, but they have not obeyed Your voice or
walked in Your law. They have done nothing
of all that You commanded them to do; therefore You have caused all this calamity to come
upon them.
24 'Look, the siege mounds! They have come
to the city to take it; and the city has been
given into the hand of the Chaldeans who fight
against it, because of the sword and famine
and pestilence. What You have spoken has
happened; there You see *it!*
25 'And You have said to me, O Lord GOD,
"Buy the field for money, and take witnesses"!—yet the city has been given into the
hand of the Chaldeans.'"

God's Assurance of the People's Return

26 Then the word of the LORD came to Jeremiah, saying,
27 "Behold, I *am* the LORD, the God of all
flesh. Is there anything too hard for Me?
28 "Therefore thus says the LORD: 'Behold, I
will give this city into the hand of the Chaldeans, into the hand of Nebuchadnezzar king of
Babylon, and he shall take it.
29 'And the Chaldeans who fight against this
city shall come and set fire to this city and burn
it, with the houses on whose roofs they have
offered incense to Baal and poured out drink
offerings to other gods, to provoke Me to
anger;
30 'because the children of Israel and the children of Judah have done only evil before Me
from their youth. For the children of Israel
have provoked Me only to anger with the work
of their hands,' says the LORD.
31 'For this city has been to Me *a provocation
of* My anger and My fury from the day that
they built it, even to this day; so I will remove
it from before My face
32 'because of all the evil of the children of
Israel and the children of Judah, which they
have done to provoke Me to anger—they, their
kings, their princes, their priests, their prophets, the men of Judah, and the inhabitants of
Jerusalem.
33 'And they have turned to Me the back, and
not the face; though I taught them, rising up
early and teaching *them*, yet they have not
listened to receive instruction.
34 'But they set their abominations in the
house which is called by My name, to defile it.
35 'And they built the high places of Baal
which *are* in the Valley of the Son of Hinnom,
to cause their sons and their daughters to pass
through *the fire* to Molech, which I did not
command them, nor did it come into My mind
that they should do this abomination, to cause
Judah to sin.'
36 "Now therefore, thus says the LORD, the
God of Israel, concerning this city of which
you say, 'It shall be delivered into the hand of
the king of Babylon by the sword, by the famine, and by the pestilence':
37 'Behold, I will gather them out of all countries where I have driven them in My anger, in
My fury, and in great wrath; I will bring them
back to this place, and I will cause them to
dwell safely.
38 'They shall be My people, and I will be their
God;
39 'then I will give them one heart and one
way, that they may fear Me forever, for the
good of them and their children after them.
40 'And I will make an everlasting covenant
with them, that I will not turn away from doing
them good; but I will put My fear in their hearts
so that they will not depart from Me.
41 'Yes, I will rejoice over them to do them
good, and I will assuredly plant them in this
land, with all My heart and with all My soul.'
42 "For thus says the LORD: 'Just as I have
brought all this great calamity on this people,
so I will bring on them all the good that I have
promised them.
43 'And fields will be bought in this land of
which you say, "*It is* desolate, without man or
beast; it has been given into the hand of the
Chaldeans."
44 'Men will buy fields for money, sign deeds
and seal *them*, and take witnesses, in the land
of Benjamin, in the places around Jerusalem,
in the cities of Judah, in the cities of the mountains, in the cities of the lowland, and in the
cities of the South; for I will cause their captives to return,' says the LORD."

Excellence of the Restored Nation

33 Moreover the word of the LORD came to
Jeremiah a second time, while he was
still shut up in the court of the prison, saying,
2 "Thus says the LORD who made it, the
LORD who formed it to establish it (the LORD
is His name):
3 'Call to Me, and I will answer you, and show
you great and mighty things, which you do not
know.'
4 "For thus says the LORD, the God of Israel,
concerning the houses of this city and the
houses of the kings of Judah, which have been
pulled down *to fortify*[a] against the siege
mounds and the sword:
5 'They come to fight with the Chaldeans,
but *only* to fill their places[a] with the dead bodies of men whom I will slay in My anger and
My fury, all for whose wickedness I have hidden My face from this city.
6 'Behold, I will bring it health and healing;
I will heal them and reveal to them the abundance of peace and truth.
7 'And I will cause the captives of Judah and
the captives of Israel to return, and will rebuild
those places as at the first.
8 'I will cleanse them from all their iniquity
by which they have sinned against Me, and I
will pardon all their iniquities by which they
have sinned and by which they have transgressed against Me.
9 'Then it shall be to Me a name of joy, a praise,
and an honor before all nations of the earth,
who shall hear all the good that I do to them;
they shall fear and tremble for all the goodness
and all the prosperity that I provide for it.'
10 "Thus says the LORD: 'Again there shall be

32:22 [a]Exodus 3:8 **33:4** [a]Compare Isaiah 22:10 **33:5** [a]Compare 2 Kings 23:14

heard in this place—of which you say, "It *is*
desolate, without man and without beast"—in
the cities of Judah, in the streets of Jerusalem
that are desolate, without man and without
inhabitant and without beast,
11 'the voice of joy and the voice of gladness,
the voice of the bridegroom and the voice of the
bride, the voice of those who will say:

"Praise the LORD of hosts,
For the LORD *is* good,
For His mercy *endures* forever"—

and of those *who will* bring the sacrifice of
praise into the house of the LORD. For I will
cause the captives of the land to return as at
the first,' says the LORD.
12 "Thus says the LORD of hosts: 'In this
place which is desolate, without man and with-
out beast, and in all its cities, there shall again
be a dwelling place of shepherds causing *their*
flocks to lie down.
13 'In the cities of the mountains, in the cities
of the lowland, in the cities of the South, in the
land of Benjamin, in the places around Jerusa-
lem, and in the cities of Judah, the flocks shall
again pass under the hands of him who counts
them,' says the LORD.
14 'Behold, the days are coming,' says the
LORD, 'that I will perform that good thing
which I have promised to the house of Israel
and to the house of Judah:

15 'In those days and at that time
I will cause to grow up to David
A Branch of righteousness;
He shall execute judgment and
righteousness in the earth.
16 In those days Judah will be saved,
And Jerusalem will dwell safely.
And this *is the name* by which she will be
called:

THE LORD OUR
RIGHTEOUSNESS.'[a]

17 "For thus says the LORD: 'David shall
never lack a man to sit on the throne of the
house of Israel;
18 'nor shall the priests, the Levites, lack a
man to offer burnt offerings before Me, to kin-
dle grain offerings, and to sacrifice continu-
ally.'"

The Permanence of God's Covenant

19 And the word of the LORD came to Jere-
miah, saying,
20 "Thus says the LORD: 'If you can break My
covenant with the day and My covenant with
the night, so that there will not be day and
night in their season,
21 'then My covenant may also be broken
with David My servant, so that he shall not
have a son to reign on his throne, and with the
Levites, the priests, My ministers.
22 'As the host of heaven cannot be num-
bered, nor the sand of the sea measured, so
will I multiply the descendants of David My
servant and the Levites who minister to Me.'"
23 Moreover the word of the LORD came to
Jeremiah, saying,
24 "Have you not considered what these peo-
ple have spoken, saying, 'The two families
which the LORD has chosen, He has also cast
them off'? Thus they have despised My people,
as if they should no more be a nation before
them.
25 "Thus says the LORD: 'If My covenant *is*
not with day and night, *and if* I have not ap-
pointed the ordinances of heaven and earth,
26 'then I will cast away the descendants of
Jacob and David My servant, *so* that I will not
take *any* of his descendants *to be* rulers over
the descendants of Abraham, Isaac, and Jacob.
For I will cause their captives to return, and
will have mercy on them.'"

Zedekiah Warned by God

34 The word which came to Jeremiah from
the LORD, when Nebuchadnezzar king
of Babylon and all his army, all the kingdoms
of the earth under his dominion, and all the
people, fought against Jerusalem and all its
cities, saying,
2 "Thus says the LORD, the God of Israel:
'Go and speak to Zedekiah king of Judah and
tell him, "Thus says the LORD: 'Behold, I will
give this city into the hand of the king of Bab-
ylon, and he shall burn it with fire.
3 'And you shall not escape from his hand,
but shall surely be taken and delivered into his
hand; your eyes shall see the eyes of the king
of Babylon, he shall speak with you face to
face,[a] and you shall go to Babylon.'"'
4 "Yet hear the word of the LORD, O Ze-
dekiah king of Judah! Thus says the LORD con-
cerning you: 'You shall not die by the sword.
5 'You shall die in peace; as in the ceremo-
nies of your fathers, the former kings who
were before you, so they shall burn *incense* for
you and lament for you, *saying*, "Alas, lord!"
For I have pronounced the word, says the
LORD.'"
6 Then Jeremiah the prophet spoke all these
words to Zedekiah king of Judah in Jerusalem,
7 when the king of Babylon's army fought
against Jerusalem and all the cities of Judah
that were left, against Lachish and Azekah; for
only these fortified cities remained of the cities
of Judah.

Treacherous Treatment of Slaves

8 *This is* the word that came to Jeremiah
from the LORD, after King Zedekiah had made
a covenant with all the people who *were* at
Jerusalem to proclaim liberty to them:
9 that every man should set free his male
and female slave—a Hebrew man or woman—
that no one should keep a Jewish brother in
bondage.
10 Now when all the princes and all the peo-
ple, who had entered into the covenant, heard
that everyone should set free his male and fe-
male slaves, that no one should keep them in
bondage anymore, they obeyed and let *them*
go.
11 But afterward they changed their minds
and made the male and female slaves return,
whom they had set free, and brought them into
subjection as male and female slaves.
12 Therefore the word of the LORD came to
Jeremiah from the LORD, saying,
13 "Thus says the LORD, the God of Israel: 'I
made a covenant with your fathers in the day
that I brought them out of the land of Egypt,
out of the house of bondage, saying,
14 "At the end of seven years let every man
set free his Hebrew brother, who has been sold

33:16 [a]Compare 23:5, 6 **34:3** [a]Literally *mouth to mouth*

to him; and when he has served you six years, you shall let him go free from you." But your fathers did not obey Me nor incline their ear.
15 'Then you recently turned and did what was right in My sight—every man proclaiming liberty to his neighbor; and you made a covenant before Me in the house which is called by My name.
16 'Then you turned around and profaned My name, and every one of you brought back his male and female slaves, whom you had set at liberty, at their pleasure, and brought them back into subjection, to be your male and female slaves.'
17 "Therefore thus says the LORD: 'You have not obeyed Me in proclaiming liberty, every one to his brother and every one to his neighbor. Behold, I proclaim liberty to you,' says the LORD—'to the sword, to pestilence, and to famine! And I will deliver you to trouble among all the kingdoms of the earth.
18 'And I will give the men who have transgressed My covenant, who have not performed the words of the covenant which they made before Me, when they cut the calf in two and passed between the parts of it—
19 'the princes of Judah, the princes of Jerusalem, the eunuchs, the priests, and all the people of the land who passed between the parts of the calf—
20 'I will give them into the hand of their enemies and into the hand of those who seek their life. Their dead bodies shall be for meat for the birds of the heaven and the beasts of the earth.
21 'And I will give Zedekiah king of Judah and his princes into the hand of their enemies, into the hand of those who seek their life, and into the hand of the king of Babylon's army which has gone back from you.
22 'Behold, I will command,' says the LORD, 'and cause them to return to this city. They will fight against it and take it and burn it with fire; and I will make the cities of Judah a desolation without inhabitant.'"

The Obedient Rechabites

35 The word which came to Jeremiah from the LORD in the days of Jehoiakim the son of Josiah, king of Judah, saying,
2 "Go to the house of the Rechabites, speak to them, and bring them into the house of the LORD, into one of the chambers, and give them wine to drink."
3 Then I took Jaazaniah the son of Jeremiah, the son of Habazziniah, his brothers and all his sons, and the whole house of the Rechabites,
4 and I brought them into the house of the LORD, into the chamber of the sons of Hanan the son of Igdaliah, a man of God, which *was* by the chamber of the princes, above the chamber of Maaseiah the son of Shallum, the keeper of the door.
5 Then I set before the sons of the house of the Rechabites bowls full of wine, and cups; and I said to them, "Drink wine."
6 But they said, "We will drink no wine, for Jonadab the son of Rechab, our father, commanded us, saying, 'You shall drink no wine, you nor your sons, forever.
7 'You shall not build a house, sow seed, plant a vineyard, nor have *any of these;* but all your days you shall dwell in tents, that you may live many days in the land where you are sojourners.'
8 "Thus we have obeyed the voice of Jonadab the son of Rechab, our father, in all that he charged us, to drink no wine all our days, we, our wives, our sons, or our daughters,
9 "nor to build ourselves houses to dwell in; nor do we have vineyard, field, or seed.
10 "But we have dwelt in tents, and have obeyed and done according to all that Jonadab our father commanded us.
11 "But it came to pass, when Nebuchadnezzar king of Babylon came up into the land, that we said, 'Come, let us go to Jerusalem for fear of the army of the Chaldeans and for fear of the army of the Syrians.' So we dwell at Jerusalem."
12 Then came the word of the LORD to Jeremiah, saying,
13 "Thus says the LORD of hosts, the God of Israel: 'Go and tell the men of Judah and the inhabitants of Jerusalem, "Will you not receive instruction to obey My words?" says the LORD.
14 "The words of Jonadab the son of Rechab, which he commanded his sons, not to drink wine, are performed; for to this day they drink none, and obey their father's commandment. But although I have spoken to you, rising early and speaking, you did not obey Me.
15 "I have also sent to you all My servants the prophets, rising up early and sending *them,* saying, 'Turn now everyone from his evil way, amend your doings, and do not go after other gods to serve them; then you will dwell in the land which I have given you and your fathers.' But you have not inclined your ear, nor obeyed Me.
16 "Surely the sons of Jonadab the son of Rechab have performed the commandment of their father, which he commanded them, but this people has not obeyed Me."'
17 "Therefore thus says the LORD God of hosts, the God of Israel: 'Behold, I will bring on Judah and on all the inhabitants of Jerusalem all the doom that I have pronounced against them; because I have spoken to them but they have not heard, and I have called to them but they have not answered.'"
18 And Jeremiah said to the house of the Rechabites, "Thus says the LORD of hosts, the God of Israel: 'Because you have obeyed the commandment of Jonadab your father, and kept all his precepts and done according to all that he commanded you,
19 'therefore thus says the LORD of hosts, the God of Israel: "Jonadab the son of Rechab shall not lack a man to stand before Me forever."'"

The Scroll Read in the Temple

36 Now it came to pass in the fourth year of Jehoiakim the son of Josiah, king of Judah, *that* this word came to Jeremiah from the LORD, saying:
2 "Take a scroll of a book and write on it all the words that I have spoken to you against Israel, against Judah, and against all the nations, from the day I spoke to you, from the days of Josiah even to this day.
3 "It may be that the house of Judah will hear all the adversities which I purpose to bring upon them, that everyone may turn from his evil way, that I may forgive their iniquity and their sin."
4 Then Jeremiah called Baruch the son of Neriah; and Baruch wrote on a scroll of a book,

at the instruction of Jeremiah,[a] all the words of the LORD which He had spoken to him.
5 And Jeremiah commanded Baruch, saying, "I *am* confined, I cannot go into the house of the LORD.
6 "You go, therefore, and read from the scroll which you have written at my instruction,[a] the words of the LORD, in the hearing of the people in the LORD's house on the day of fasting. And you shall also read them in the hearing of all Judah who come from their cities.
7 "It may be that they will present their supplication before the LORD, and everyone will turn from his evil way. For great *is* the anger and the fury that the LORD has pronounced against this people."
8 And Baruch the son of Neriah did according to all that Jeremiah the prophet commanded him, reading from the book the words of the LORD in the LORD's house.
9 Now it came to pass in the fifth year of Jehoiakim the son of Josiah, king of Judah, in the ninth month, *that* they proclaimed a fast before the LORD to all the people in Jerusalem, and to all the people who came from the cities of Judah to Jerusalem.
10 Then Baruch read from the book the words of Jeremiah in the house of the LORD, in the chamber of Gemariah the son of Shaphan the scribe, in the upper court at the entry of the New Gate of the LORD's house, in the hearing of all the people.

The Scroll Read in the Palace

11 When Michaiah the son of Gemariah, the son of Shaphan, heard all the words of the LORD from the book,
12 he then went down to the king's house, into the scribe's chamber; and there all the princes were sitting—Elishama the scribe, Delaiah the son of Shemaiah, Elnathan the son of Achbor, Gemariah the son of Shaphan, Zedekiah the son of Hananiah, and all the princes.
13 Then Michaiah declared to them all the words that he had heard when Baruch read the book in the hearing of the people.
14 Therefore all the princes sent Jehudi the son of Nethaniah, the son of Shelemiah, the son of Cushi, to Baruch, saying, "Take in your hand the scroll from which you have read in the hearing of the people, and come." So Baruch the son of Neriah took the scroll in his hand and came to them.
15 And they said to him, "Sit down now, and read it in our hearing." So Baruch read *it* in their hearing.
16 Now it happened, when they had heard all the words, that they looked in fear from one to another, and said to Baruch, "We will surely tell the king of all these words."
17 And they asked Baruch, saying, "Tell us now, how did you write all these words—at his instruction?"[a]
18 So Baruch answered them, "He proclaimed with his mouth all these words to me, and I wrote *them* with ink in the book."
19 Then the princes said to Baruch, "Go and hide, you and Jeremiah; and let no one know where you are."

The King Destroys Jeremiah's Scroll

20 And they went to the king, into the court; but they stored the scroll in the chamber of Elishama the scribe, and told all the words in the hearing of the king.
21 So the king sent Jehudi to bring the scroll, and he took it from Elishama the scribe's chamber. And Jehudi read it in the hearing of the king and in the hearing of all the princes who stood beside the king.
22 Now the king was sitting in the winter house in the ninth month, with *a fire* burning on the hearth before him.
23 And it happened, when Jehudi had read three or four columns, *that the king* cut it with the scribe's knife and cast *it* into the fire that *was* on the hearth, until all the scroll was consumed in the fire that *was* on the hearth.
24 Yet they were not afraid, nor did they tear their garments, the king nor any of his servants who heard all these words.
25 Nevertheless Elnathan, Delaiah, and Gemariah implored the king not to burn the scroll; but he would not listen to them.
26 And the king commanded Jerahmeel the king's[a] son, Seraiah the son of Azriel, and Shelemiah the son of Abdeel, to seize Baruch the scribe and Jeremiah the prophet, but the LORD hid them.

Jeremiah Rewrites the Scroll

27 Now after the king had burned the scroll with the words which Baruch had written at the instruction of Jeremiah,[a] the word of the LORD came to Jeremiah, saying:
28 "Take yet another scroll, and write on it all the former words that were in the first scroll which Jehoiakim the king of Judah has burned.
29 "And you shall say to Jehoiakim king of Judah, 'Thus says the LORD: "You have burned this scroll, saying, 'Why have you written in it that the king of Babylon will certainly come and destroy this land, and cause man and beast to cease from here?'"
30 'Therefore thus says the LORD concerning Jehoiakim king of Judah: "He shall have no one to sit on the throne of David, and his dead body shall be cast out to the heat of the day and the frost of the night.
31 "I will punish him, his family, and his servants for their iniquity; and I will bring on them, on the inhabitants of Jerusalem, and on the men of Judah all the doom that I have pronounced against them; but they did not heed."'"
32 Then Jeremiah took another scroll and gave it to Baruch the scribe, the son of Neriah, who wrote on it at the instruction of Jeremiah[a] all the words of the book which Jehoiakim king of Judah had burned in the fire. And besides, there were added to them many similar words.

Zedekiah's Vain Hope

37 Now King Zedekiah the son of Josiah reigned instead of Coniah the son of Jehoiakim, whom Nebuchadnezzar king of Babylon made king in the land of Judah.
2 But neither he nor his servants nor the people of the land gave heed to the words of the LORD which He spoke by the prophet Jeremiah.

36:4 [a]Literally *from Jeremiah's mouth* **36:6** [a]Literally *from my mouth* **36:17** [a]Literally *with his mouth*
36:26 [a]Hebrew *Hammelech* **36:27** [a]Literally *from Jeremiah's mouth* **36:32** [a]Literally *from Jeremiah's mouth*

3 And Zedekiah the king sent Jehucal the
son of Shelemiah, and Zephaniah the son of
Maaseiah, the priest, to the prophet Jeremiah,
saying, "Pray now to the LORD our God for us."
4 Now Jeremiah was coming and going
among the people, for they had not *yet* put him
in prison.
5 Then Pharaoh's army came up from Egypt;
and when the Chaldeans who were besieging
Jerusalem heard news of them, they departed
from Jerusalem.
6 Then the word of the LORD came to the
prophet Jeremiah, saying,
7 "Thus says the LORD, the God of Israel,
'Thus you shall say to the king of Judah, who
sent you to Me to inquire of Me: "Behold, Pha-
raoh's army which has come up to help you
will return to Egypt, to their own land.
8 "And the Chaldeans shall come back and
fight against this city, and take it and burn it
with fire."'
9 "Thus says the LORD: 'Do not deceive
yourselves, saying, "The Chaldeans will surely
depart from us," for they will not depart.
10 'For though you had defeated the whole
army of the Chaldeans who fight against you,
and there remained *only* wounded men among
them, they would rise up, every man in his tent,
and burn the city with fire.'"

Jeremiah Imprisoned

11 And it happened, when the army of the
Chaldeans left *the siege* of Jerusalem for fear
of Pharaoh's army,
12 that Jeremiah went out of Jerusalem to go
into the land of Benjamin to claim his property
there among the people.
13 And when he was in the Gate of Benjamin,
a captain of the guard *was* there whose name
was Irijah the son of Shelemiah, the son of
Hananiah; and he seized Jeremiah the
prophet, saying, "You are defecting to the
Chaldeans!"
14 Then Jeremiah said, "False! I am not de-
fecting to the Chaldeans." But he did not listen
to him. So Irijah seized Jeremiah and brought
him to the princes.
15 Therefore the princes were angry with Jer-
emiah, and they struck him and put him in
prison in the house of Jonathan the scribe. For
they had made that the prison.
16 When Jeremiah entered the dungeon and
the cells, and Jeremiah had remained there
many days,
17 then Zedekiah the king sent and took him
out. The king asked him secretly in his house,
and said, "Is there *any* word from the LORD?"
And Jeremiah said, "There is." Then he said,
"You shall be delivered into the hand of the
king of Babylon!"
18 Moreover Jeremiah said to King Zedekiah,
"What offense have I committed against you,
against your servants, or against this people,
that you have put me in prison?
19 "Where now *are* your prophets who
prophesied to you, saying, 'The king of Bab-
ylon will not come against you or against this
land'?
20 "Therefore please hear now, O my lord the
king. Please, let my petition be accepted before
you, and do not make me return to the house
of Jonathan the scribe, lest I die there."
21 Then Zedekiah the king commanded that
they should commit Jeremiah to the court of
the prison, and that they should give him daily
a piece of bread from the bakers' street, until
all the bread in the city was gone. Thus Jere-
miah remained in the court of the prison.

Jeremiah in the Dungeon

38 Now Shephatiah the son of Mattan,
Gedaliah the son of Pashhur, Jucal[a] the
son of Shelemiah, and Pashhur the son of Mal-
chiah heard the words that Jeremiah had spo-
ken to all the people, saying,
2 "Thus says the LORD: 'He who remains in
this city shall die by the sword, by famine, and
by pestilence; but he who goes over to the
Chaldeans shall live; his life shall be as a prize
to him, and he shall live.'[a]
3 "Thus says the LORD: 'This city shall
surely be given into the hand of the king of
Babylon's army, which shall take it.'"
4 Therefore the princes said to the king,
"Please, let this man be put to death, for thus
he weakens the hands of the men of war who
remain in this city, and the hands of all the
people, by speaking such words to them. For
this man does not seek the welfare of this peo-
ple, but their harm."
5 Then Zedekiah the king said, "Look, he *is*
in your hand. For the king can *do* nothing
against you."
6 So they took Jeremiah and cast him into
the dungeon of Malchiah the king's[a] son,
which *was* in the court of the prison, and they
let Jeremiah down with ropes. And in the dun-
geon *there was* no water, but mire. So Jere-
miah sank in the mire.
7 Now Ebed-Melech the Ethiopian, one of
the eunuchs, who was in the king's house,
heard that they had put Jeremiah in the dun-
geon. When the king was sitting at the Gate of
Benjamin,
8 Ebed-Melech went out of the king's house
and spoke to the king, saying:
9 "My lord the king, these men have done
evil in all that they have done to Jeremiah the
prophet, whom they have cast into the dun-
geon, and he is likely to die from hunger in the
place where he is. For *there is* no more bread
in the city."
10 Then the king commanded Ebed-Melech
the Ethiopian, saying, "Take from here thirty
men with you, and lift Jeremiah the prophet
out of the dungeon before he dies."
11 So Ebed-Melech took the men with him
and went into the house of the king under the
treasury, and took from there old clothes and
old rags, and let them down by ropes into the
dungeon to Jeremiah.
12 Then Ebed-Melech the Ethiopian said to
Jeremiah, "Please put these old clothes and
rags under your armpits, under the ropes."
And Jeremiah did so.
13 So they pulled Jeremiah up with ropes and
lifted him out of the dungeon. And Jeremiah
remained in the court of the prison.

Zedekiah's Fears and Jeremiah's Advice

14 Then Zedekiah the king sent and had Jere-
miah the prophet brought to him at the third
entrance of the house of the LORD. And the
king said to Jeremiah, "I will ask you some-
thing. Hide nothing from me."
15 Jeremiah said to Zedekiah, "If I declare *it*

38:1 [a]Same as *Jehucal* (compare 37:3) **38:2** [a]Compare 21:9 **38:6** [a]Hebrew *Hammelech*

to you, will you not surely put me to death? And if I give you advice, you will not listen to me."
16 So Zedekiah the king swore secretly to Jeremiah, saying, "*As* the LORD lives, who made our very souls, I will not put you to death, nor will I give you into the hand of these men who seek your life."
17 Then Jeremiah said to Zedekiah, "Thus says the LORD, the God of hosts, the God of Israel: 'If you surely surrender to the king of Babylon's princes, then your soul shall live; this city shall not be burned with fire, and you and your house shall live.
18 'But if you do not surrender to the king of Babylon's princes, then this city shall be given into the hand of the Chaldeans; they shall burn it with fire, and you shall not escape from their hand.'"
19 And Zedekiah the king said to Jeremiah, "I am afraid of the Jews who have defected to the Chaldeans, lest they deliver me into their hand, and they abuse me."
20 But Jeremiah said, "They shall not deliver *you.* Please, obey the voice of the LORD which I speak to you. So it shall be well with you, and your soul shall live.
21 "But if you refuse to surrender, this *is* the word that the LORD has shown me:
22 'Now behold, all the women who are left in the king of Judah's house *shall be* surrendered to the king of Babylon's princes, and those *women* shall say:

"Your close friends have set upon you
And prevailed against you;
Your feet have sunk in the mire,
And they have turned away again."

23 'So they shall surrender all your wives and children to the Chaldeans. You shall not escape from their hand, but shall be taken by the hand of the king of Babylon. And you shall cause this city to be burned with fire.'"
24 Then Zedekiah said to Jeremiah, "Let no one know of these words, and you shall not die.
25 "But if the princes hear that I have talked with you, and they come to you and say to you, 'Declare to us now what you have said to the king, and also what the king said to you; do not hide *it* from us, and we will not put you to death,'
26 "then you shall say to them, 'I presented my request before the king, that he would not make me return to Jonathan's house to die there.'"
27 Then all the princes came to Jeremiah and asked him. And he told them according to all these words that the king had commanded. So they stopped speaking with him, for the conversation had not been heard.
28 Now Jeremiah remained in the court of the prison until the day that Jerusalem was taken. And he was *there* when Jerusalem was taken.

The Fall of Jerusalem

39 In the ninth year of Zedekiah king of Judah, in the tenth month, Nebuchadnezzar king of Babylon and all his army came against Jerusalem, and besieged it.
2 In the eleventh year of Zedekiah, in the fourth month, on the ninth *day* of the month, the city was penetrated.
3 Then all the princes of the king of Babylon came in and sat in the Middle Gate: Nergal-Sharezer, Samgar-Nebo, Sarsechim, Rabsaris,[a] Nergal-Sarezer, Rabmag,[b] with the rest of the princes of the king of Babylon.
4 So it was, when Zedekiah the king of Judah and all the men of war saw them, that they fled and went out of the city by night, by way of the king's garden, by the gate between the two walls. And he went out by way of the plain.[a]
5 But the Chaldean army pursued them and overtook Zedekiah in the plains of Jericho. And when they had captured him, they brought him up to Nebuchadnezzar king of Babylon, to Riblah in the land of Hamath, where he pronounced judgment on him.
6 Then the king of Babylon killed the sons of Zedekiah before his eyes in Riblah; the king of Babylon also killed all the nobles of Judah.
7 Moreover he put out Zedekiah's eyes, and bound him with bronze fetters to carry him off to Babylon.
8 And the Chaldeans burned the king's house and the houses of the people with fire, and broke down the walls of Jerusalem.
9 Then Nebuzaradan the captain of the guard carried away captive to Babylon the remnant of the people who remained in the city and those who defected to him, with the rest of the people who remained.
10 But Nebuzaradan the captain of the guard left in the land of Judah the poor people, who had nothing, and gave them vineyards and fields at the same time.

Jeremiah Goes Free

11 Now Nebuchadnezzar king of Babylon gave charge concerning Jeremiah to Nebuzaradan the captain of the guard, saying,
12 "Take him and look after him, and do him no harm; but do to him just as he says to you."
13 So Nebuzaradan the captain of the guard sent Nebushasban, Rabsaris, Nergal-Sharezer, Rabmag, and all the king of Babylon's chief officers;
14 then they sent *someone* to take Jeremiah from the court of the prison, and committed him to Gedaliah the son of Ahikam, the son of Shaphan, that he should take him home. So he dwelt among the people.
15 Meanwhile the word of the LORD had come to Jeremiah while he was shut up in the court of the prison, saying,
16 "Go and speak to Ebed-Melech the Ethiopian, saying, 'Thus says the LORD of hosts, the God of Israel: "Behold, I will bring My words upon this city for adversity and not for good, and they shall be *performed* in that day before you.
17 "But I will deliver you in that day," says the LORD, "and you shall not be given into the hand of the men of whom you *are* afraid.
18 "For I will surely deliver you, and you shall not fall by the sword; but your life shall be as a prize to you, because you have put your trust in Me," says the LORD.'"

39:3 [a]A title, probably *Chief Officer;* also verse 13 [b]A title, probably *Troop Commander;* also verse 13 **39:4** [a]Or *the Arabah,* that is, the Jordan Valley

Jeremiah with Gedaliah the Governor

40 The word that came to Jeremiah from the LORD after Nebuzaradan the captain of the guard had let him go from Ramah, when he had taken him bound in chains among all who were carried away captive from Jerusalem and Judah, who were carried away captive to Babylon.
2 And the captain of the guard took Jeremiah and said to him: "The LORD your God has pronounced this doom on this place.
3 "Now the LORD has brought *it,* and has done just as He said. Because you *people* have sinned against the LORD, and not obeyed His voice, therefore this thing has come upon you.
4 "And now look, I free you this day from the chains that *were* on your hand. If it seems good to you to come with me to Babylon, come, and I will look after you. But if it seems wrong for you to come with me to Babylon, remain here. See, all the land *is* before you; wherever it seems good and convenient for you to go, go there."
5 Now while Jeremiah had not yet gone back, *Nebuzaradan said,* "Go back to Gedaliah the son of Ahikam, the son of Shaphan, whom the king of Babylon has made governor over the cities of Judah, and dwell with him among the people. Or go wherever it seems convenient for you to go." So the captain of the guard gave him rations and a gift and let him go.
6 Then Jeremiah went to Gedaliah the son of Ahikam, to Mizpah, and dwelt with him among the people who were left in the land.
7 And when all the captains of the armies who *were* in the fields, they and their men, heard that the king of Babylon had made Gedaliah the son of Ahikam governor in the land, and had committed to him men, women, children, and the poorest of the land who had not been carried away captive to Babylon,
8 then they came to Gedaliah at Mizpah—Ishmael the son of Nethaniah, Johanan and Jonathan the sons of Kareah, Seraiah the son of Tanhumeth, the sons of Ephai the Netophathite, and Jezaniah[a] the son of a Maachathite, they and their men.
9 And Gedaliah the son of Ahikam, the son of Shaphan, took an oath before them and their men, saying, "Do not be afraid to serve the Chaldeans. Dwell in the land and serve the king of Babylon, and it shall be well with you.
10 "As for me, I will indeed dwell at Mizpah and serve the Chaldeans who come to us. But you, gather wine and summer fruit and oil, put *them* in your vessels, and dwell in your cities that you have taken."
11 Likewise, when all the Jews who *were* in Moab, among the Ammonites, in Edom, and who *were* in all the countries, heard that the king of Babylon had left a remnant of Judah, and that he had set over them Gedaliah the son of Ahikam, the son of Shaphan,
12 then all the Jews returned out of all places where they had been driven, and came to the land of Judah, to Gedaliah at Mizpah, and gathered wine and summer fruit in abundance.
13 Moreover Johanan the son of Kareah and all the captains of the forces that *were* in the fields came to Gedaliah at Mizpah,
14 and said to him, "Do you certainly know that Baalis the king of the Ammonites has sent Ishmael the son of Nethaniah to murder you?" But Gedaliah the son of Ahikam did not believe them.
15 Then Johanan the son of Kareah spoke secretly to Gedaliah in Mizpah, saying, "Let me go, please, and I will kill Ishmael the son of Nethaniah, and no one will know *it.* Why should he murder you, so that all the Jews who are gathered to you would be scattered, and the remnant in Judah perish?"
16 But Gedaliah the son of Ahikam said to Johanan the son of Kareah, "You shall not do this thing, for you speak falsely concerning Ishmael."

Insurrection Against Gedaliah

41 Now it came to pass in the seventh month *that* Ishmael the son of Nethaniah, the son of Elishama, of the royal family and of the officers of the king, came with ten men to Gedaliah the son of Ahikam, at Mizpah. And there they ate bread together in Mizpah.
2 Then Ishmael the son of Nethaniah, and the ten men who were with him, arose and struck Gedaliah the son of Ahikam, the son of Shaphan, with the sword, and killed him whom the king of Babylon had made governor over the land.
3 Ishmael also struck down all the Jews who were with him, *that is,* with Gedaliah at Mizpah, and the Chaldeans who were found there, the men of war.
4 And it happened, on the second day after he had killed Gedaliah, when as yet no one knew *it,*
5 that certain men came from Shechem, from Shiloh, and from Samaria, eighty men with their beards shaved and their clothes torn, having cut themselves, with offerings and incense in their hand, to bring *them* to the house of the LORD.
6 Now Ishmael the son of Nethaniah went out from Mizpah to meet them, weeping as he went along; and it happened as he met them that he said to them, "Come to Gedaliah the son of Ahikam!"
7 So it was, when they came into the midst of the city, that Ishmael the son of Nethaniah killed them *and cast them* into the midst of a pit, he and the men who were with him.
8 But ten men were found among them who said to Ishmael, "Do not kill us, for we have treasures of wheat, barley, oil, and honey in the field." So he desisted and did not kill them among their brethren.
9 Now the pit into which Ishmael had cast all the dead bodies of the men whom he had slain, because of Gedaliah, *was* the same one Asa the king had made for fear of Baasha king of Israel. Ishmael the son of Nethaniah filled it with *the* slain.
10 Then Ishmael carried away captive all the rest of the people who *were* in Mizpah, the king's daughters and all the people who remained in Mizpah, whom Nebuzaradan the captain of the guard had committed to Gedaliah the son of Ahikam. And Ishmael the son of Nethaniah carried them away captive and departed to go over to the Ammonites.
11 But when Johanan the son of Kareah and all the captains of the forces that *were* with him heard of all the evil that Ishmael the son of Nethaniah had done,

40:8 [a]Spelled *Jaazaniah* in 2 Kings 25:23

12 they took all the men and went to fight
with Ishmael the son of Nethaniah; and they
found him by the great pool that *is* in Gibeon.
13 So it was, when all the people who *were*
with Ishmael saw Johanan the son of Kareah,
and all the captains of the forces who *were*
with him, that they were glad.
14 Then all the people whom Ishmael had
carried away captive from Mizpah turned
around and came back, and went to Johanan
the son of Kareah.
15 But Ishmael the son of Nethaniah escaped
from Johanan with eight men and went to the
Ammonites.
16 Then Johanan the son of Kareah, and all
the captains of the forces that were with him,
took from Mizpah all the rest of the people
whom he had recovered from Ishmael the son
of Nethaniah after he had murdered Gedaliah
the son of Ahikam—the mighty men of war and
the women and the children and the eunuchs,
whom he had brought back from Gibeon.
17 And they departed and dwelt in the habita-
tion of Chimham, which is near Bethlehem, as
they went on their way to Egypt,
18 because of the Chaldeans; for they were
afraid of them, because Ishmael the son of
Nethaniah had murdered Gedaliah the son of
Ahikam, whom the king of Babylon had made
governor in the land.

The Flight to Egypt Forbidden

42 Now all the captains of the forces, Joha-
nan the son of Kareah, Jezaniah the son
of Hoshaiah, and all the people, from the least
to the greatest, came near
2 and said to Jeremiah the prophet, "Please,
let our petition be acceptable to you, and pray
for us to the LORD your God, for all this rem-
nant (since we are left *but* a few of many, as you
can see),
3 "that the LORD your God may show us the
way in which we should walk and the thing we
should do."
4 Then Jeremiah the prophet said to them,
"I have heard. Indeed, I will pray to the LORD
your God according to your words, and it shall
be, *that* whatever the LORD answers you, I will
declare *it* to you. I will keep nothing back from
you."
5 So they said to Jeremiah, "Let the LORD
be a true and faithful witness between us, if we
do not do according to everything which the
LORD your God sends us by you.
6 "Whether *it is* pleasing or displeasing, we
will obey the voice of the LORD our God to
whom we send you, that it may be well with us
when we obey the voice of the LORD our God."
7 And it happened after ten days that the
word of the LORD came to Jeremiah.
8 Then he called Johanan the son of Kareah,
all the captains of the forces which *were* with
him, and all the people from the least even to
the greatest,
9 and said to them, "Thus says the LORD,
the God of Israel, to whom you sent me to pre-
sent your petition before Him:
10 'If you will still remain in this land, then I
will build you and not pull *you* down, and I will
plant you and not pluck *you* up. For I relent
concerning the disaster that I have brought
upon you.
11 'Do not be afraid of the king of Babylon,
of whom you are afraid; do not be afraid of him,'
says the LORD, 'for I *am* with you, to save you
and deliver you from his hand.
12 'And I will show you mercy, that he may
have mercy on you and cause you to return to
your own land.'
13 "But if you say, 'We will not dwell in this
land,' disobeying the voice of the LORD your
God,
14 "saying, 'No, but we will go to the land of
Egypt where we shall see no war, nor hear the
sound of the trumpet, nor be hungry for bread,
and there we will dwell'—
15 "Then hear now the word of the LORD,
O remnant of Judah! Thus says the LORD of
hosts, the God of Israel: 'If you wholly set your
faces to enter Egypt, and go to dwell there,
16 'then it shall be *that* the sword which you
feared shall overtake you there in the land of
Egypt; the famine of which you were afraid
shall follow close after you there *in* Egypt; and
there you shall die.
17 'So shall it be with all the men who set
their faces to go to Egypt to dwell there. They
shall die by the sword, by famine, and by pesti-
lence. And none of them shall remain or es-
cape from the disaster that I will bring upon
them.'
18 "For thus says the LORD of hosts, the God
of Israel: 'As My anger and My fury have been
poured out on the inhabitants of Jerusalem, so
will My fury be poured out on you when you
enter Egypt. And you shall be an oath, an as-
tonishment, a curse, and a reproach; and you
shall see this place no more.'
19 "The LORD has said concerning you, O rem-
nant of Judah, 'Do not go to Egypt!' Know cer-
tainly that I have admonished you this day.
20 "For you were hypocrites in your hearts
when you sent me to the LORD your God, say-
ing, 'Pray for us to the LORD our God, and
according to all that the LORD your God says,
so declare to us and we will do *it*.'
21 "And I have this day declared *it* to you, but
you have not obeyed the voice of the LORD
your God, or anything which He has sent you
by me.
22 "Now therefore, know certainly that you
shall die by the sword, by famine, and by pesti-
lence in the place where you desire to go to
dwell."

Jeremiah Taken to Egypt

43 Now it happened, when Jeremiah had
stopped speaking to all the people all
the words of the LORD their God, for which the
LORD their God had sent him to them, all these
words,
2 that Azariah the son of Hoshaiah, Johanan
the son of Kareah, and all the proud men
spoke, saying to Jeremiah, "You speak falsely!
The LORD our God has not sent you to say, 'Do
not go to Egypt to dwell there.'
3 "But Baruch the son of Neriah has set you
against us, to deliver us into the hand of the
Chaldeans, that they may put us to death or
carry us away captive to Babylon."
4 So Johanan the son of Kareah, all the cap-
tains of the forces, and all the people would
not obey the voice of the LORD, to remain in
the land of Judah.
5 But Johanan the son of Kareah and all the
captains of the forces took all the remnant of
Judah who had returned to dwell in the land
of Judah, from all nations where they had been
driven—

6 men, women, children, the king's daugh-
ters, and every person whom Nebuzaradan the
captain of the guard had left with Gedaliah the
son of Ahikam, the son of Shaphan, and Jere-
miah the prophet and Baruch the son of Ne-
riah.
7 So they went to the land of Egypt, for they
did not obey the voice of the LORD. And they
went as far as Tahpanhes.
8 Then the word of the LORD came to Jere-
miah in Tahpanhes, saying,
9 "Take large stones in your hand, and hide
them in the sight of the men of Judah, in the
clay in the brick courtyard which *is* at the en-
trance to Pharaoh's house in Tahpanhes;
10 "and say to them, 'Thus says the LORD of
hosts, the God of Israel: "Behold, I will send
and bring Nebuchadnezzar the king of Bab-
ylon, My servant, and will set his throne above
these stones that I have hidden. And he will
spread his royal pavilion over them.
11 "When he comes, he shall strike the land
of Egypt *and deliver* to death *those appointed*
for death, and to captivity *those appointed* for
captivity, and to the sword *those appointed* for
the sword.
12 "I[a] will kindle a fire in the houses of the
gods of Egypt, and he shall burn them and
carry them away captive. And he shall array
himself with the land of Egypt, as a shepherd
puts on his garment, and he shall go out from
there in peace.
13 "He shall also break the *sacred* pillars of
Beth Shemesh[a] that *are* in the land of Egypt;
and the houses of the gods of the Egyptians he
shall burn with fire." ' "

Israelites Will Be Punished in Egypt

44 The word that came to Jeremiah concern-
ing all the Jews who dwell in the land of
Egypt, who dwell at Migdol, at Tahpanhes, at
Noph,[a] and in the country of Pathros, saying,
2 "Thus says the LORD of hosts, the God of
Israel: 'You have seen all the calamity that I
have brought on Jerusalem and on all the cities
of Judah; and behold, this day they *are* a deso-
lation, and no one dwells in them,
3 'because of their wickedness which they
have committed to provoke Me to anger, in that
they went to burn incense *and* to serve other
gods whom they did not know, they nor you
nor your fathers.
4 'However I have sent to you all My ser-
vants the prophets, rising early and sending
them, saying, "Oh, do not do this abominable
thing that I hate!"
5 'But they did not listen or incline their ear
to turn from their wickedness, to burn no in-
cense to other gods.
6 'So My fury and My anger were poured
out and kindled in the cities of Judah and in
the streets of Jerusalem; and they are wasted
and desolate, as it is this day.'
7 "Now therefore, thus says the LORD, the
God of hosts, the God of Israel: 'Why do you
commit *this* great evil against yourselves, to
cut off from you man and woman, child and
infant, out of Judah, leaving none to remain,
8 'in that you provoke Me to wrath with the
works of your hands, burning incense to other
gods in the land of Egypt where you have gone
to dwell, that you may cut yourselves off and be
a curse and a reproach among all the nations of
the earth?
9 'Have you forgotten the wickedness of
your fathers, the wickedness of the kings of
Judah, the wickedness of their wives, your own
wickedness, and the wickedness of your wives,
which they committed in the land of Judah and
in the streets of Jerusalem?
10 'They have not been humbled, to this day,
nor have they feared; they have not walked in
My law or in My statutes that I set before you
and your fathers.'
11 "Therefore thus says the LORD of hosts,
the God of Israel: 'Behold, I will set My face
against you for catastrophe and for cutting off
all Judah.
12 'And I will take the remnant of Judah who
have set their faces to go into the land of Egypt
to dwell there, and they shall all be consumed
and fall in the land of Egypt. They shall be
consumed by the sword *and* by famine. They
shall die, from the least to the greatest, by the
sword and by famine; and they shall be an
oath, an astonishment, a curse and a reproach!
13 'For I will punish those who dwell in the
land of Egypt, as I have punished Jerusalem,
by the sword, by famine, and by pestilence,
14 'so that none of the remnant of Judah who
have gone into the land of Egypt to dwell there
shall escape or survive, lest they return to the
land of Judah, to which they desire to return
and dwell. For none shall return except those
who escape.' "
15 Then all the men who knew that their
wives had burned incense to other gods, with
all the women who stood by, a great multitude,
and all the people who dwelt in the land of
Egypt, in Pathros, answered Jeremiah, saying:
16 "*As for* the word that you have spoken to
us in the name of the LORD, we will not listen
to you!
17 "But we will certainly do whatever has
gone out of our own mouth, to burn incense to
the queen of heaven and pour out drink offer-
ings to her, as we have done, we and our fa-
thers, our kings and our princes, in the cities
of Judah and in the streets of Jerusalem. For
then we had plenty of food, were well-off, and
saw no trouble.
18 "But since we stopped burning incense to
the queen of heaven and pouring out drink
offerings to her, we have lacked everything
and have been consumed by the sword and by
famine."
19 *The women also said,* "And when we
burned incense to the queen of heaven and
poured out drink offerings to her, did we make
cakes for her, to worship her, and pour out
drink offerings to her without our husbands'
permission?"
20 Then Jeremiah spoke to all the people—
the men, the women, and all the people who
had given him *that* answer—saying:
21 "The incense that you burned in the cities
of Judah and in the streets of Jerusalem, you
and your fathers, your kings and your princes,
and the people of the land, did not the LORD
remember them, and did it *not* come into His
mind?
22 "So the LORD could no longer bear *it,* be-
cause of the evil of your doings *and* because of

43:12 [a]Following Masoretic Text and Targum; Septuagint, Syriac, and Vulgate read *He.* **43:13** [a]Literally *House of the Sun,* ancient On; later called Heliopolis **44:1** [a]That is, ancient Memphis

the abominations which you committed. There-
fore your land is a desolation, an astonish-
ment, a curse, and without an inhabitant, as *it*
is this day.
23 "Because you have burned incense and be-
cause you have sinned against the LORD, and
have not obeyed the voice of the LORD or
walked in His law, in His statutes or in His
testimonies, therefore this calamity has hap-
pened to you, as *at* this day."
24 Moreover Jeremiah said to all the people
and to all the women, "Hear the word of the
LORD, all Judah who *are* in the land of Egypt!
25 "Thus says the LORD of hosts, the God of
Israel, saying: 'You and your wives have spo-
ken with your mouths and fulfilled with your
hands, saying, "We will surely keep our vows
that we have made, to burn incense to the
queen of heaven and pour out drink offerings
to her." You will surely keep your vows and
perform your vows!'
26 "Therefore hear the word of the LORD, all
Judah who dwell in the land of Egypt: 'Behold,
I have sworn by My great name,' says the
LORD, 'that My name shall no more be named
in the mouth of any man of Judah in all the
land of Egypt, saying, "The Lord GOD lives."
27 'Behold, I will watch over them for adver-
sity and not for good. And all the men of Judah
who *are* in the land of Egypt shall be consumed
by the sword and by famine, until there is an
end to them.
28 'Yet a small number who escape the sword
shall return from the land of Egypt to the land
of Judah; and all the remnant of Judah, who
have gone to the land of Egypt to dwell there,
shall know whose words will stand, Mine or
theirs.
29 'And this *shall be* a sign to you,' says the
LORD, 'that I will punish you in this place, that
you may know that My words will surely stand
against you for adversity.'
30 "Thus says the LORD: 'Behold, I will give
Pharaoh Hophra king of Egypt into the hand
of his enemies and into the hand of those who
seek his life, as I gave Zedekiah king of Judah
into the hand of Nebuchadnezzar king of Bab-
ylon, his enemy who sought his life.'"

Assurance to Baruch

45 The word that Jeremiah the prophet
spoke to Baruch the son of Neriah, when
he had written these words in a book at the
instruction of Jeremiah,[a] in the fourth year of
Jehoiakim the son of Josiah, king of Judah,
saying,
2 "Thus says the LORD, the God of Israel, to
you, O Baruch:
3 'You said, "Woe is me now! For the LORD
has added grief to my sorrow. I fainted in my
sighing, and I find no rest."'
4 "Thus you shall say to him, 'Thus says the
LORD: "Behold, what I have built I will break
down, and what I have planted I will pluck up,
that is, this whole land.
5 "And do you seek great things for your-
self? Do not seek *them;* for behold, I will bring
adversity on all flesh," says the LORD. "But I
will give your life to you as a prize in all places,
wherever you go."'"

45:1 [a]Literally *from Jeremiah's mouth*

Judgment on Egypt

46 The word of the LORD which came to
Jeremiah the prophet against the na-
tions.
2 Against Egypt.
Concerning the army of Pharaoh Necho,
king of Egypt, which was by the River Euphra-
tes in Carchemish, and which Nebuchadnez-
zar king of Babylon defeated in the fourth year
of Jehoiakim the son of Josiah, king of Judah:

3 "Order the buckler and shield,
And draw near to battle!
4 Harness the horses,
And mount up, you horsemen!
Stand forth with *your* helmets,
Polish the spears,
Put on the armor!
5 Why have I seen them dismayed *and*
turned back?
Their mighty ones are beaten down;
They have speedily fled,
And did not look back,
For fear *was* all around," says the LORD.
6 "Do not let the swift flee away,
Nor the mighty man escape;
They will stumble and fall
Toward the north, by the River
Euphrates.
7 "Who *is* this coming up like a flood,
Whose waters move like the rivers?
8 Egypt rises up like a flood,
And *its* waters move like the rivers;
And he says, 'I will go up *and* cover the
earth,
I will destroy the city and its inhabitants.'
9 Come up, O horses, and rage, O chariots!
And let the mighty men come forth:
The Ethiopians and the Libyans who
handle the shield,
And the Lydians who handle *and* bend
the bow.
10 For this *is* the day of the Lord GOD of
hosts,
A day of vengeance,
That He may avenge Himself on His
adversaries.
The sword shall devour;
It shall be satiated and made drunk with
their blood;
For the Lord GOD of hosts has a sacrifice
In the north country by the River
Euphrates.

11 "Go up to Gilead and take balm,
O virgin, the daughter of Egypt;
In vain you will use many medicines;
You shall not be cured.
12 The nations have heard of your shame,
And your cry has filled the land;
For the mighty man has stumbled against
the mighty;
They both have fallen together."

Babylonia Will Strike Egypt

13 The word that the LORD spoke to Jeremiah
the prophet, how Nebuchadnezzar king of Bab-
ylon would come *and* strike the land of Egypt.
14 "Declare in Egypt, and proclaim in
Migdol;

Proclaim in Noph[a] and in Tahpanhes;
Say, 'Stand fast and prepare yourselves,
For the sword devours all around you.'
15 Why are your valiant *men* swept away?
They did not stand
Because the LORD drove them away.
16 He made many fall;
Yes, one fell upon another.
And they said, 'Arise!
Let us go back to our own people
And to the land of our nativity
From the oppressing sword.'
17 They cried there,
'Pharaoh, king of Egypt, *is but* a noise.
He has passed by the appointed time!'

18 "*As* I live," says the King,
Whose name *is* the LORD of hosts,
"Surely as Tabor *is* among the mountains
And as Carmel by the sea, *so* he shall
come.
19 O you daughter dwelling in Egypt,
Prepare yourself to go into captivity!
For Noph[a] shall be waste and desolate,
without inhabitant.

20 "Egypt *is* a very pretty heifer,
But destruction comes, it comes from the
north.
21 Also her mercenaries are in her midst
like fat bulls,
For they also are turned back,
They have fled away together.
They did not stand,
For the day of their calamity had come
upon them,
The time of their punishment.
22 Her noise shall go like a serpent,
For they shall march with an army
And come against her with axes,
Like those who chop wood.

23 "They shall cut down her forest," says the
LORD,
"Though it cannot be searched,
Because they *are* innumerable,
And more numerous than grasshoppers.
24 The daughter of Egypt shall be ashamed;
She shall be delivered into the hand
Of the people of the north."
25 The LORD of hosts, the God of Israel, says:
"Behold, I will bring punishment on Amon[a] of
No,[b] and Pharaoh and Egypt, with their gods
and their kings—Pharaoh and those who trust
in him.
26 "And I will deliver them into the hand of
those who seek their lives, into the hand of
Nebuchadnezzar king of Babylon and the
hand of his servants. Afterward it shall be in-
habited as in the days of old," says the LORD.

God Will Preserve Israel

27 "But do not fear, O My servant Jacob,
And do not be dismayed, O Israel!
For behold, I will save you from afar,
And your offspring from the land of their
captivity;
Jacob shall return, have rest and be at
ease;
No one shall make *him* afraid.
28 Do not fear, O Jacob My servant," says
the LORD,
"For I *am* with you;
For I will make a complete end of all the
nations
To which I have driven you,
But I will not make a complete end of
you.
I will rightly correct you,
For I will not leave you wholly
unpunished."

Judgment on Philistia

47 The word of the LORD that came to Jere-
miah the prophet against the Philistines,
before Pharaoh attacked Gaza.
2 Thus says the LORD:

"Behold, waters rise out of the north,
And shall be an overflowing flood;
They shall overflow the land and all that
is in it,
The city and those who dwell within;
Then the men shall cry,
And all the inhabitants of the land shall
wail.
3 At the noise of the stamping hooves of
his strong horses,
At the rushing of his chariots,
At the rumbling of his wheels,
The fathers will not look back for *their*
children,
Lacking courage,
4 Because of the day that comes to plunder
all the Philistines,
To cut off from Tyre and Sidon every
helper who remains;
For the LORD shall plunder the
Philistines,
The remnant of the country of Caphtor.
5 Baldness has come upon Gaza,
Ashkelon is cut off
With the remnant of their valley.
How long will you cut yourself?

6 "O you sword of the LORD,
How long until you are quiet?
Put yourself up into your scabbard,
Rest and be still!
7 How can it be quiet,
Seeing the LORD has given it a charge
Against Ashkelon and against the
seashore?
There He has appointed it."

Judgment on Moab

48 Against Moab.
Thus says the LORD of hosts, the God of
Israel:

"Woe to Nebo!
For it is plundered,
Kirjathaim is shamed *and* taken;
The high stronghold[a] is shamed and
dismayed—
2 No more praise of Moab.
In Heshbon they have devised evil
against her:
'Come, and let us cut her off as a nation.'
You also shall be cut down, O Madmen![a]
The sword shall pursue you;
3 A voice of crying *shall be* from
Horonaim:
'Plundering and great destruction!'

46:14 [a]That is, ancient Memphis **46:19** [a]That is, ancient Memphis **46:25** [a]A sun god [b]That is, ancient Thebes
48:1 [a]Hebrew *Misgab* **48:2** [a]A city of Moab

4 "Moab is destroyed;
Her little ones have caused a cry to be heard;[a]
5 For in the Ascent of Luhith they ascend with continual weeping;
For in the descent of Horonaim the enemies have heard a cry of destruction.

6 "Flee, save your lives!
And be like the juniper[a] in the wilderness.
7 For because you have trusted in your works and your treasures,
You also shall be taken.
And Chemosh shall go forth into captivity,
His priests and his princes together.
8 And the plunderer shall come against every city;
No one shall escape.
The valley also shall perish,
And the plain shall be destroyed,
As the LORD has spoken.

9 "Give wings to Moab,
That she may flee and get away;
For her cities shall be desolate,
Without any to dwell in them.
10 Cursed *is* he who does the work of the LORD deceitfully,
And cursed *is* he who keeps back his sword from blood.

11 "Moab has been at ease from his[a] youth;
He has settled on his dregs,
And has not been emptied from vessel to vessel,
Nor has he gone into captivity.
Therefore his taste remained in him,
And his scent has not changed.

12 "Therefore behold, the days are coming," says the LORD,
"That I shall send him wine-workers
Who will tip him over
And empty his vessels
And break the bottles.
13 Moab shall be ashamed of Chemosh,
As the house of Israel was ashamed of Bethel, their confidence.

14 "How can you say, 'We *are* mighty
And strong men for the war'?
15 Moab is plundered and gone up *from* her cities;
Her chosen young men have gone down to the slaughter," says the King,
Whose name *is* the LORD of hosts.

16 "The calamity of Moab *is* near at hand,
And his affliction comes quickly.
17 Bemoan him, all you who are around him;
And all you who know his name,
Say, 'How the strong staff is broken,
The beautiful rod!'

18 "O daughter inhabiting Dibon,
Come down from *your* glory,
And sit in thirst;
For the plunderer of Moab has come against you,
He has destroyed your strongholds.
19 O inhabitant of Aroer,
Stand by the way and watch;
Ask him who flees
And her who escapes;
Say, 'What has happened?'
20 Moab is shamed, for he is broken down.
Wail and cry!
Tell it in Arnon, that Moab is plundered.

21 "And judgment has come on the plain country:
On Holon and Jahzah and Mephaath,
22 On Dibon and Nebo and Beth Diblathaim,
23 On Kirjathaim and Beth Gamul and Beth Meon,
24 On Kerioth and Bozrah,
On all the cities of the land of Moab,
Far or near.
25 The horn of Moab is cut off,
And his arm is broken," says the LORD.

26 "Make him drunk,
Because he exalted *himself* against the LORD.
Moab shall wallow in his vomit,
And he shall also be in derision.
27 For was not Israel a derision to you?
Was he found among thieves?
For whenever you speak of him,
You shake *your head in scorn.*
28 You who dwell in Moab,
Leave the cities and dwell in the rock,
And be like the dove *which* makes her nest
In the sides of the cave's mouth.

29 "We have heard the pride of Moab
(He *is* exceedingly proud),
Of his loftiness and arrogance and pride,
And of the haughtiness of his heart."

30 "I know his wrath," says the LORD,
"But it *is* not right;
His lies have made nothing right.
31 Therefore I will wail for Moab,
And I will cry out for all Moab;
I[a] will mourn for the men of Kir Heres.
32 O vine of Sibmah! I will weep for you with the weeping of Jazer.
Your plants have gone over the sea,
They reach to the sea of Jazer.
The plunderer has fallen on your summer fruit and your vintage.
33 Joy and gladness are taken
From the plentiful field
And from the land of Moab;
I have caused wine to fail from the winepresses;
No one will tread with joyous shouting—
Not joyous shouting!

34 "From the cry of Heshbon to Elealeh and to Jahaz
They have uttered their voice,
From Zoar to Horonaim,
Like a three-year-old heifer;[a]
For the waters of Nimrim also shall be desolate.

35 "Moreover," says the LORD,
"I will cause to cease in Moab
The one who offers *sacrifices* in the high places
And burns incense to his gods.

48:4 [a]Following Masoretic Text, Targum, and Vulgate; Septuagint reads *Proclaim it in Zoar.* **48:6** [a]Or *Aroer,* a city of Moab **48:11** [a]The Hebrew uses masculine and feminine pronouns interchangeably in this chapter. **48:31** [a]Following Dead Sea Scrolls, Septuagint, and Vulgate; Masoretic Text reads *He.* **48:34** [a]Or *The Third Eglath,* an unknown city (compare Isaiah 15:5)

36 Therefore My heart shall wail like flutes for Moab,
And like flutes My heart shall wail
For the men of Kir Heres.
Therefore the riches they have acquired have perished.
37 "For every head *shall be* bald, and every beard clipped;
On all the hands *shall be* cuts, and on the loins sackcloth—
38 A general lamentation
On all the housetops of Moab,
And in its streets;
For I have broken Moab like a vessel in which *is* no pleasure," says the LORD.
39 "They shall wail:
'How she is broken down!
How Moab has turned her back with shame!'
So Moab shall be a derision
And a dismay to all those about her."

40 For thus says the LORD:

"Behold, one shall fly like an eagle,
And spread his wings over Moab.
41 Kerioth is taken,
And the strongholds are surprised;
The mighty men's hearts in Moab on that day shall be
Like the heart of a woman in birth pangs.
42 And Moab shall be destroyed as a people,
Because he exalted *himself* against the LORD.
43 Fear and the pit and the snare *shall be* upon you,
O inhabitant of Moab," says the LORD.
44 "He who flees from the fear shall fall into the pit,
And he who gets out of the pit shall be caught in the snare.
For upon Moab, upon it I will bring
The year of their punishment," says the LORD.

45 "Those who fled stood under the shadow of Heshbon
Because of exhaustion.
But a fire shall come out of Heshbon,
A flame from the midst of Sihon,
And shall devour the brow of Moab,
The crown of the head of the sons of tumult.
46 Woe to you, O Moab!
The people of Chemosh perish;
For your sons have been taken captive,
And your daughters captive.

47 "Yet I will bring back the captives of Moab
In the latter days," says the LORD.

Thus far *is* the judgment of Moab.

Judgment on Ammon

49 Against the Ammonites.
Thus says the LORD:

"Has Israel no sons?
Has he no heir?
Why *then* does Milcom[a] inherit Gad,
And his people dwell in its cities?
2 Therefore behold, the days are coming," says the LORD,
"That I will cause to be heard an alarm of war
In Rabbah of the Ammonites;
It shall be a desolate mound,
And her villages shall be burned with fire.
Then Israel shall take possession of his inheritance," says the LORD.

3 "Wail, O Heshbon, for Ai is plundered!
Cry, you daughters of Rabbah,
Gird yourselves with sackcloth!
Lament and run to and fro by the walls;
For Milcom shall go into captivity
With his priests and his princes together.
4 Why do you boast in the valleys,
Your flowing valley, O backsliding daughter?
Who trusted in her treasures, *saying*,
'Who will come against me?'
5 Behold, I will bring fear upon you,"
Says the Lord GOD of hosts,
"From all those who are around you;
You shall be driven out, everyone headlong,
And no one will gather those who wander off.
6 But afterward I will bring back
The captives of the people of Ammon,"
says the LORD.

Judgment on Edom

7 Against Edom.
Thus says the LORD of hosts:

"*Is* wisdom no more in Teman?
Has counsel perished from the prudent?
Has their wisdom vanished?
8 Flee, turn back, dwell in the depths,
O inhabitants of Dedan!
For I will bring the calamity of Esau upon him,
The time *that* I will punish him.
9 If grape-gatherers came to you,
Would they not leave *some* gleaning grapes?
If thieves by night,
Would they not destroy until they have enough?
10 But I have made Esau bare;
I have uncovered his secret places,[a]
And he shall not be able to hide himself.
His descendants are plundered,
His brethren and his neighbors,
And he *is* no more.
11 Leave your fatherless children,
I will preserve *them* alive;
And let your widows trust in Me."

12 For thus says the LORD: "Behold, those
whose judgment *was* not to drink of the cup
have assuredly drunk. And *are* you the one
who will altogether go unpunished? You shall
not go unpunished, but you shall surely drink
of it.
13 "For I have sworn by Myself," says the
LORD, "that Bozrah shall become a desolation,
a reproach, a waste, and a curse. And all its
cities shall be perpetual wastes."

14 I have heard a message from the LORD,
And an ambassador has been sent to the nations:

49:1 [a]Hebrew *Malcam,* literally *their king,* a god of the Ammonites; also called *Molech* (compare verse 3)
49:10 [a]Compare Obadiah 5, 6

"Gather together, come against her,
And rise up to battle!
15 "For indeed, I will make you small among nations,
Despised among men.
16 Your fierceness has deceived you,
The pride of your heart,
O you who dwell in the clefts of the rock,
Who hold the height of the hill!
Though you make your nest as high as the eagle,
I will bring you down from there," says the LORD.[a]

17 "Edom also shall be an astonishment;
Everyone who goes by it will be astonished
And will hiss at all its plagues.
18 As in the overthrow of Sodom and Gomorrah
And their neighbors," says the LORD,
"No one shall remain there,
Nor shall a son of man dwell in it.

19 "Behold, he shall come up like a lion from the floodplain[a] of the Jordan
Against the dwelling place of the strong;
But I will suddenly make him run away from her.
And who *is* a chosen *man that* I may appoint over her?
For who *is* like Me?
Who will arraign Me?
And who *is* that shepherd
Who will withstand Me?"

20 Therefore hear the counsel of the LORD that He has taken against Edom,
And His purposes that He has proposed against the inhabitants of Teman:
Surely the least of the flock shall draw them out;
Surely He shall make their dwelling places desolate with them.
21 The earth shakes at the noise of their fall;
At the cry its noise is heard at the Red Sea.
22 Behold, He shall come up and fly like the eagle,
And spread His wings over Bozrah;
The heart of the mighty men of Edom in that day shall be
Like the heart of a woman in birth pangs.

Judgment on Damascus

23 Against Damascus.

"Hamath and Arpad are shamed,
For they have heard bad news.
They are fainthearted;
There is trouble on the sea;
It cannot be quiet.
24 Damascus has grown feeble;
She turns to flee,
And fear has seized *her.*
Anguish and sorrows have taken her like a woman in labor.
25 Why is the city of praise not deserted, the city of My joy?
26 Therefore her young men shall fall in her streets,
And all the men of war shall be cut off in that day," says the LORD of hosts.
27 "I will kindle a fire in the wall of Damascus,
And it shall consume the palaces of Ben-Hadad."[a]

Judgment on Kedar and Hazor

28 Against Kedar and against the kingdoms
of Hazor, which Nebuchadnezzar king of Bab-
ylon shall strike.
Thus says the LORD:

"Arise, go up to Kedar,
And devastate the men of the East!
29 Their tents and their flocks they shall take away.
They shall take for themselves their curtains,
All their vessels and their camels;
And they shall cry out to them,
'Fear *is* on every side!'

30 "Flee, get far away! Dwell in the depths,
O inhabitants of Hazor!" says the LORD.
"For Nebuchadnezzar king of Babylon has taken counsel against you,
And has conceived a plan against you.

31 "Arise, go up to the wealthy nation that dwells securely," says the LORD,
"Which has neither gates nor bars,
Dwelling alone.
32 Their camels shall be for booty,
And the multitude of their cattle for plunder.
I will scatter to all winds those in the farthest corners,
And I will bring their calamity from all its sides," says the LORD.
33 "Hazor shall be a dwelling for jackals, a desolation forever;
No one shall reside there,
Nor son of man dwell in it."

Judgment on Elam

34 The word of the LORD that came to Jere-
miah the prophet against Elam, in the begin-
ning of the reign of Zedekiah king of Judah,
saying,
35 "Thus says the LORD of hosts:

'Behold, I will break the bow of Elam,
The foremost of their might.
36 Against Elam I will bring the four winds
From the four quarters of heaven,
And scatter them toward all those winds;
There shall be no nations where the outcasts of Elam will not go.
37 For I will cause Elam to be dismayed before their enemies
And before those who seek their life.
I will bring disaster upon them,
My fierce anger,' says the LORD;
'And I will send the sword after them
Until I have consumed them.
38 I will set My throne in Elam,
And will destroy from there the king and the princes,' says the LORD.

39 'But it shall come to pass in the latter days:
I will bring back the captives of Elam,' says the LORD."

Judgment on Babylon and Babylonia

50 The word that the LORD spoke against
Babylon *and* against the land of the
Chaldeans by Jeremiah the prophet.

49:16 [a]Compare Obadiah 3, 4 49:19 [a]Or *thicket* 49:27 [a]Compare Amos 1:4

2 "Declare among the nations,
Proclaim, and set up a standard;
Proclaim—do not conceal *it*—
Say, 'Babylon is taken, Bel is shamed.
Merodach[a] is broken in pieces;
Her idols are humiliated,
Her images are broken in pieces.'
3 For out of the north a nation comes up against her,
Which shall make her land desolate,
And no one shall dwell therein.
They shall move, they shall depart,
Both man and beast.

4 "In those days and in that time," says the LORD,
"The children of Israel shall come,
They and the children of Judah together;
With continual weeping they shall come,
And seek the LORD their God.
5 They shall ask the way to Zion,
With their faces toward it, *saying*,
'Come and let us join ourselves to the LORD
In a perpetual covenant
That will not be forgotten.'

6 "My people have been lost sheep.
Their shepherds have led them astray;
They have turned them away *on* the mountains.
They have gone from mountain to hill;
They have forgotten their resting place.
7 All who found them have devoured them;
And their adversaries said, 'We have not offended,
Because they have sinned against the LORD, the habitation of justice,
The LORD, the hope of their fathers.'

8 "Move from the midst of Babylon,
Go out of the land of the Chaldeans;
And be like the rams before the flocks.
9 For behold, I will raise and cause to come up against Babylon
An assembly of great nations from the north country,
And they shall array themselves against her;
From there she shall be captured.
Their arrows *shall be* like *those* of an expert warrior;[a]
None shall return in vain.
10 And Chaldea shall become plunder;
All who plunder her shall be satisfied,"
says the LORD.

11 "Because you were glad, because you rejoiced,
You destroyers of My heritage,
Because you have grown fat like a heifer threshing grain,
And you bellow like bulls,
12 Your mother shall be deeply ashamed;
She who bore you shall be ashamed.
Behold, the least of the nations *shall be* a wilderness,
A dry land and a desert.
13 Because of the wrath of the LORD
She shall not be inhabited,
But she shall be wholly desolate.
Everyone who goes by Babylon shall be horrified
And hiss at all her plagues.

14 "Put yourselves in array against Babylon all around,
All you who bend the bow;
Shoot at her, spare no arrows,
For she has sinned against the LORD.
15 Shout against her all around;
She has given her hand,
Her foundations have fallen,
Her walls are thrown down;
For it *is* the vengeance of the LORD.
Take vengeance on her.
As she has done, so do to her.
16 Cut off the sower from Babylon,
And him who handles the sickle at harvest time.
For fear of the oppressing sword
Everyone shall turn to his own people,
And everyone shall flee to his own land.

17 "Israel *is* like scattered sheep;
The lions have driven *him* away.
First the king of Assyria devoured him;
Now at last this Nebuchadnezzar king of Babylon has broken his bones."

18 Therefore thus says the LORD of hosts, the God of Israel:

"Behold, I will punish the king of Babylon and his land,
As I have punished the king of Assyria.
19 But I will bring back Israel to his home,
And he shall feed on Carmel and Bashan;
His soul shall be satisfied on Mount Ephraim and Gilead.
20 In those days and in that time," says the LORD,
"The iniquity of Israel shall be sought, but *there shall be* none;
And the sins of Judah, but they shall not be found;
For I will pardon those whom I preserve.

21 "Go up against the land of Merathaim, against it,
And against the inhabitants of Pekod.
Waste and utterly destroy them," says the LORD,
"And do according to all that I have commanded you.
22 A sound of battle *is* in the land,
And of great destruction.
23 How the hammer of the whole earth has been cut apart and broken!
How Babylon has become a desolation among the nations!
24 I have laid a snare for you;
You have indeed been trapped,
O Babylon,
And you were not aware;
You have been found and also caught,
Because you have contended against the LORD.
25 The LORD has opened His armory,
And has brought out the weapons of His indignation;
For this *is* the work of the Lord GOD of hosts
In the land of the Chaldeans.
26 Come against her from the farthest border;
Open her storehouses;
Cast her up as heaps of ruins,
And destroy her utterly;

50:2 [a]A Babylonian god; sometimes spelled *Marduk* **50:9** [a]Following some Hebrew manuscripts, Septuagint, and Syriac; Masoretic Text, Targum, and Vulgate read *a warrior who makes childless*.

Let nothing of her be left.
27 Slay all her bulls,
Let them go down to the slaughter.
Woe to them!
For their day has come, the time of their punishment.
28 The voice of those who flee and escape from the land of Babylon
Declares in Zion the vengeance of the LORD our God,
The vengeance of His temple.

29 "Call together the archers against Babylon.
All you who bend the bow, encamp against it all around;
Let none of them escape.[a]
Repay her according to her work;
According to all she has done, do to her;
For she has been proud against the LORD,
Against the Holy One of Israel.
30 Therefore her young men shall fall in the streets,
And all her men of war shall be cut off in that day," says the LORD.
31 "Behold, I *am* against you,
O most haughty one!" says the Lord GOD of hosts;
"For your day has come,
The time *that* I will punish you.[a]
32 The most proud shall stumble and fall,
And no one will raise him up;
I will kindle a fire in his cities,
And it will devour all around him."

33 Thus says the LORD of hosts:

"The children of Israel *were* oppressed,
Along with the children of Judah;
All who took them captive have held them fast;
They have refused to let them go.
34 Their Redeemer *is* strong;
The LORD of hosts *is* His name.
He will thoroughly plead their case,
That He may give rest to the land,
And disquiet the inhabitants of Babylon.

35 "A sword *is* against the Chaldeans," says the LORD,
"Against the inhabitants of Babylon,
And against her princes and her wise men.
36 A sword *is* against the soothsayers, and they will be fools.
A sword *is* against her mighty men, and they will be dismayed.
37 A sword *is* against their horses,
Against their chariots,
And against all the mixed peoples who *are* in her midst;
And they will become like women.
A sword *is* against her treasures, and they will be robbed.
38 A drought[a] *is* against her waters, and they will be dried up.
For it *is* the land of carved images,
And they are insane with *their* idols.

39 "Therefore the wild desert beasts shall dwell *there* with the jackals,
And the ostriches shall dwell in it.
It shall be inhabited no more forever,
Nor shall it be dwelt in from generation to generation.
40 As God overthrew Sodom and Gomorrah
And their neighbors," says the LORD,
"*So* no one shall reside there,
Nor son of man dwell in it.

41 "Behold, a people shall come from the north,
And a great nation and many kings
Shall be raised up from the ends of the earth.
42 They shall hold the bow and the lance;
They *are* cruel and shall not show mercy.
Their voice shall roar like the sea;
They shall ride on horses,
Set in array, like a man for the battle,
Against you, O daughter of Babylon.

43 "The king of Babylon has heard the report about them,
And his hands grow feeble;
Anguish has taken hold of him,
Pangs as of a woman in childbirth.

44 "Behold, he shall come up like a lion from the floodplain[a] of the Jordan
Against the dwelling place of the strong;
But I will make them suddenly run away from her.
And who *is* a chosen *man that* I may appoint over her?
For who *is* like Me?
Who will arraign Me?
And who *is* that shepherd
Who will withstand Me?"

45 Therefore hear the counsel of the LORD that He has taken against Babylon,
And His purposes that He has proposed against the land of the Chaldeans:
Surely the least of the flock shall draw them out;
Surely He will make their dwelling place desolate with them.
46 At the noise of the taking of Babylon
The earth trembles,
And the cry is heard among the nations.

The Utter Destruction of Babylon

51 Thus says the LORD:

"Behold, I will raise up against Babylon,
Against those who dwell in Leb Kamai,[a]
A destroying wind.
2 And I will send winnowers to Babylon,
Who shall winnow her and empty her land.
For in the day of doom
They shall be against her all around.
3 Against *her* let the archer bend his bow,
And lift himself up against *her* in his armor.
Do not spare her young men;
Utterly destroy all her army.
4 Thus the slain shall fall in the land of the Chaldeans,
And *those* thrust through in her streets.
5 For Israel is not forsaken, nor Judah,
By his God, the LORD of hosts,

50:29 [a]Qere, some Hebrew manuscripts, Septuagint, and Targum add *to her.* **50:31** [a]Following Masoretic Text and Targum; Septuagint and Vulgate read *The time of your punishment.* **50:38** [a]Following Masoretic Text, Targum, and Vulgate; Syriac reads *sword;* Septuagint omits *A drought is.* **50:44** [a]Or *thicket* **51:1** [a]A code word for Chaldea (Babylonia); may be translated *The Midst of Those Who Rise Up Against Me*

Though their land was filled with sin
against the Holy One of Israel."

6 Flee from the midst of Babylon,
And every one save his life!
Do not be cut off in her iniquity,
For this *is* the time of the LORD's
vengeance;
He shall recompense her.
7 Babylon *was* a golden cup in the LORD's
hand,
That made all the earth drunk.
The nations drank her wine;
Therefore the nations are deranged.
8 Babylon has suddenly fallen and been
destroyed.
Wail for her!
Take balm for her pain;
Perhaps she may be healed.

9 We would have healed Babylon,
But she is not healed.
Forsake her, and let us go everyone to his
own country;
For her judgment reaches to heaven and
is lifted up to the skies.
10 The LORD has revealed our
righteousness.
Come and let us declare in Zion the work
of the LORD our God.

11 Make the arrows bright!
Gather the shields!
The LORD has raised up the spirit of the
kings of the Medes.
For His plan *is* against Babylon to destroy
it,
Because it *is* the vengeance of the LORD,
The vengeance for His temple.
12 Set up the standard on the walls of
Babylon;
Make the guard strong,
Set up the watchmen,
Prepare the ambushes.
For the LORD has both devised and done
What He spoke against the inhabitants of
Babylon.
13 O you who dwell by many waters,
Abundant in treasures,
Your end has come,
The measure of your covetousness.
14 The LORD of hosts has sworn by Himself:
"Surely I will fill you with men, as with
locusts,
And they shall lift up a shout against
you."

15 He has made the earth by His power;
He has established the world by His
wisdom,
And stretched out the heaven by His
understanding.
16 When He utters *His* voice—
There is a multitude of waters in the
heavens:
"He causes the vapors to ascend from the
ends of the earth;
He makes lightnings for the rain;
He brings the wind out of His
treasuries."[a]

17 Everyone is dull-hearted, without
knowledge;
Every metalsmith is put to shame by the
carved image;
For his molded image *is* falsehood,
And *there is* no breath in them.
18 They *are* futile, a work of errors;
In the time of their punishment they shall
perish.
19 The Portion of Jacob *is* not like them,
For He *is* the Maker of all things;
And *Israel is* the tribe of His inheritance.
The LORD of hosts *is* His name.

20 "You *are* My battle-ax *and* weapons of
war:
For with you I will break the nation in
pieces;
With you I will destroy kingdoms;
21 With you I will break in pieces the horse
and its rider;
With you I will break in pieces the chariot
and its rider;
22 With you also I will break in pieces man
and woman;
With you I will break in pieces old and
young;
With you I will break in pieces the young
man and the maiden;
23 With you also I will break in pieces the
shepherd and his flock;
With you I will break in pieces the farmer
and his yoke of oxen;
And with you I will break in pieces
governors and rulers.

24 "And I will repay Babylon
And all the inhabitants of Chaldea
For all the evil they have done
In Zion in your sight," says the LORD.

25 "Behold, I *am* against you, O destroying
mountain,
Who destroys all the earth," says the
LORD.
"And I will stretch out My hand against
you,
Roll you down from the rocks,
And make you a burnt mountain.
26 They shall not take from you a stone for a
corner
Nor a stone for a foundation,
But you shall be desolate forever," says
the LORD.

27 Set up a banner in the land,
Blow the trumpet among the nations!
Prepare the nations against her,
Call the kingdoms together against her:
Ararat, Minni, and Ashkenaz.
Appoint a general against her;
Cause the horses to come up like the
bristling locusts.
28 Prepare against her the nations,
With the kings of the Medes,
Its governors and all its rulers,
All the land of his dominion.
29 And the land will tremble and sorrow;
For every purpose of the LORD shall be
performed against Babylon,
To make the land of Babylon a desolation
without inhabitant.
30 The mighty men of Babylon have ceased
fighting,
They have remained in their strongholds;
Their might has failed,
They became *like* women;
They have burned her dwelling places,
The bars of her *gate* are broken.

51:16 [a]Psalm 135:7

31 One runner will run to meet another,
And one messenger to meet another,
To show the king of Babylon that his city
is taken on *all* sides;
32 The passages are blocked,
The reeds they have burned with fire,
And the men of war are terrified.

33 For thus says the LORD of hosts, the God
of Israel:

"The daughter of Babylon *is* like a
threshing floor
When it is time to thresh her;
Yet a little while
And the time of her harvest will come."

34 "Nebuchadnezzar the king of Babylon
Has devoured me, he has crushed me;
He has made me an empty vessel,
He has swallowed me up like a monster;
He has filled his stomach with my
delicacies,
He has spit me out.
35 Let the violence *done* to me and my flesh
be upon Babylon,"
The inhabitant of Zion will say;
"And my blood be upon the inhabitants of
Chaldea!"
Jerusalem will say.
36 Therefore thus says the LORD:

"Behold, I will plead your case and take
vengeance for you.
I will dry up her sea and make her
springs dry.
37 Babylon shall become a heap,
A dwelling place for jackals,
An astonishment and a hissing,
Without an inhabitant.
38 They shall roar together like lions,
They shall growl like lions' whelps.
39 In their excitement I will prepare their
feasts;
I will make them drunk,
That they may rejoice,
And sleep a perpetual sleep
And not awake," says the LORD.
40 "I will bring them down
Like lambs to the slaughter,
Like rams with male goats.

41 "Oh, how Sheshach[a] is taken!
Oh, how the praise of the whole earth is
seized!
How Babylon has become desolate
among the nations!
42 The sea has come up over Babylon;
She is covered with the multitude of its
waves.
43 Her cities are a desolation,
A dry land and a wilderness,
A land where no one dwells,
Through which no son of man passes.
44 I will punish Bel in Babylon,
And I will bring out of his mouth what he
has swallowed;
And the nations shall not stream to him
anymore.
Yes, the wall of Babylon shall fall.

45 "My people, go out of the midst of her!
And let everyone deliver himself from the
fierce anger of the LORD.
46 And lest your heart faint,
And you fear for the rumor that *will be*
heard in the land
(A rumor will come *one* year,
And after that, in *another* year
A rumor *will come*,
And violence in the land,
Ruler against ruler),
47 Therefore behold, the days are coming
That I will bring judgment on the carved
images of Babylon;
Her whole land shall be ashamed,
And all her slain shall fall in her midst.
48 Then the heavens and the earth and all
that *is* in them
Shall sing joyously over Babylon;
For the plunderers shall come to her from
the north," says the LORD.

49 As Babylon *has caused* the slain of Israel
to fall,
So at Babylon the slain of all the earth
shall fall.
50 You who have escaped the sword,
Get away! Do not stand still!
Remember the LORD afar off,
And let Jerusalem come to your mind.

51 We are ashamed because we have heard
reproach.
Shame has covered our faces,
For strangers have come into the
sanctuaries of the LORD's house.

52 "Therefore behold, the days are coming,"
says the LORD,
"That I will bring judgment on her carved
images,
And throughout all her land the wounded
shall groan.
53 Though Babylon were to mount up to
heaven,
And though she were to fortify the height
of her strength,
Yet from Me plunderers would come to
her," says the LORD.

54 The sound of a cry *comes* from Babylon,
And great destruction from the land of
the Chaldeans,
55 Because the LORD is plundering Babylon
And silencing her loud voice,
Though her waves roar like great waters,
And the noise of their voice is uttered,
56 Because the plunderer comes against her,
against Babylon,
And her mighty men are taken.
Every one of their bows is broken;
For the LORD *is* the God of recompense,
He will surely repay.

57 "And I will make drunk
Her princes and wise men,
Her governors, her deputies, and her
mighty men.
And they shall sleep a perpetual sleep
And not awake," says the King,
Whose name *is* the LORD of hosts.

58 Thus says the LORD of hosts:

"The broad walls of Babylon shall be
utterly broken,
And her high gates shall be burned with
fire;

51:41 [a]A code word for Babylon (compare 25:26)

The people will labor in vain,
And the nations, because of the fire;
And they shall be weary."

Jeremiah's Command to Seraiah

59 The word which Jeremiah the prophet
commanded Seraiah the son of Neriah, the son
of Mahseiah, when he went with Zedekiah the
king of Judah to Babylon in the fourth year of
his reign. And Seraiah *was* the quartermaster.
60 So Jeremiah wrote in a book all the evil
that would come upon Babylon, all these words
that are written against Babylon.
61 And Jeremiah said to Seraiah, "When you
arrive in Babylon and see it, and read all these
words,
62 "then you shall say, 'O LORD, You have
spoken against this place to cut it off, so that
none shall remain in it, neither man nor beast,
but it shall be desolate forever.'
63 "Now it shall be, when you have finished
reading this book, *that* you shall tie a stone to
it and throw it out into the Euphrates.
64 "Then you shall say, 'Thus Babylon shall
sink and not rise from the catastrophe that I
will bring upon her. And they shall be weary.'"
Thus far *are* the words of Jeremiah.

The Fall of Jerusalem Reviewed

52 Zedekiah *was* twenty-one years old when
he became king, and he reigned eleven
years in Jerusalem. His mother's name *was*
Hamutal the daughter of Jeremiah of Libnah.
2 He also did evil in the sight of the LORD,
according to all that Jehoiakim had done.
3 For because of the anger of the LORD *this*
happened in Jerusalem and Judah, till He fi-
nally cast them out from His presence. Then
Zedekiah rebelled against the king of Babylon.
4 Now it came to pass in the ninth year of
his reign, in the tenth month, on the tenth *day*
of the month, *that* Nebuchadnezzar king of
Babylon and all his army came against Jerusa-
lem and encamped against it; and *they* built a
siege wall against it all around.
5 So the city was besieged until the eleventh
year of King Zedekiah.
6 By the fourth month, on the ninth day of
the month, the famine had become so severe
in the city that there was no food for the people
of the land.
7 Then the city *wall* was broken through, and
all the men of war fled and went out of the city
at night by way of the gate between the two
walls, which *was* by the king's garden, even
though the Chaldeans *were* near the city all
around. And they went by way of the plain.[a]
8 But the army of the Chaldeans pursued the
king, and they overtook Zedekiah in the plains
of Jericho. All his army was scattered from him.
9 So they took the king and brought him up
to the king of Babylon at Riblah in the land of
Hamath, and he pronounced judgment on him.
10 Then the king of Babylon killed the sons
of Zedekiah before his eyes. And he killed all
the princes of Judah in Riblah.
11 He also put out the eyes of Zedekiah; and
the king of Babylon bound him in bronze fet-
ters, took him to Babylon, and put him in
prison till the day of his death.

The Temple and City Plundered and Burned

12 Now in the fifth month, on the tenth *day* of
the month (which *was* the nineteenth year of
King Nebuchadnezzar king of Babylon), Nebu-
zaradan, the captain of the guard, *who* served
the king of Babylon, came to Jerusalem.
13 He burned the house of the LORD and the
king's house; all the houses of Jerusalem, that is,
all the houses of the great, he burned with fire.
14 And all the army of the Chaldeans who
were with the captain of the guard broke down
all the walls of Jerusalem all around.
15 Then Nebuzaradan the captain of the guard
carried away captive *some* of the poor people,
the rest of the people who remained in the city,
the defectors who had deserted to the king of
Babylon, and the rest of the craftsmen.
16 But Nebuzaradan the captain of the guard
left *some* of the poor of the land as vinedressers
and farmers.
17 The bronze pillars that *were* in the house
of the LORD, and the carts and the bronze Sea
that *were* in the house of the LORD, the Chalde-
ans broke in pieces, and carried all their
bronze to Babylon.
18 They also took away the pots, the shovels,
the trimmers, the bowls, the spoons, and all
the bronze utensils with which the *priests* min-
istered.
19 The basins, the firepans, the bowls, the
pots, the lampstands, the spoons, and the cups,
whatever *was* solid gold and whatever *was*
solid silver, the captain of the guard took away.
20 The two pillars, one Sea, the twelve bronze
bulls which *were* under *it, and* the carts, which
King Solomon had made for the house of the
LORD—the bronze of all these articles was be-
yond measure.
21 Now *concerning* the pillars: the height of
one pillar *was* eighteen cubits, a measuring
line of twelve cubits could measure its circum-
ference, and its thickness *was* four fingers; *it*
was hollow.
22 A capital of bronze *was* on it; and the height
of one capital *was* five cubits, with a network
and pomegranates all around the capital, all of
bronze. The second pillar, with pomegranates
was the same.
23 There were ninety-six pomegranates on
the sides; all the pomegranates, all around on
the network, *were* one hundred.

The People Taken Captive to Babylonia

24 The captain of the guard took Seraiah the
chief priest, Zephaniah the second priest, and
the three doorkeepers.
25 He also took out of the city an officer who
had charge of the men of war, seven men of
the king's close associates who were found in
the city, the principal scribe of the army who
mustered the people of the land, and sixty men
of the people of the land who were found in
the midst of the city.
26 And Nebuzaradan the captain of the guard
took these and brought them to the king of
Babylon at Riblah.
27 Then the king of Babylon struck them and
put them to death at Riblah in the land of Ha-
math. Thus Judah was carried away captive
from its own land.

52:7 [a]Or *the Arabah,* that is, the Jordan Valley

28 These *are* the people whom Nebuchadnez-
zar carried away captive: in the seventh year,
three thousand and twenty-three Jews;
29 in the eighteenth year of Nebuchadnezzar
he carried away captive from Jerusalem eight
hundred and thirty-two persons;
30 in the twenty-third year of Nebuchadnez-
zar, Nebuzaradan the captain of the guard car-
ried away captive of the Jews seven hundred
and forty-five persons. All the persons *were*
four thousand six hundred.

Jehoiachin Released from Prison

31 Now it came to pass in the thirty-seventh
year of the captivity of Jehoiachin king of Ju-
dah, in the twelfth month, on the twenty-fifth
day of the month, *that* Evil-Merodach[a] king of
Babylon, in the *first* year of his reign, lifted up
the head of Jehoiachin king of Judah and
brought him out of prison.
32 And he spoke kindly to him and gave him
a more prominent seat than those of the kings
who *were* with him in Babylon.
33 So Jehoiachin changed from his prison
garments, and he ate bread regularly before
the *king* all the days of his life.
34 And as for his provisions, there was a regu-
lar ration given him by the king of Babylon, a
portion for each day until the day of his death,
all the days of his life.

The Book of LAMENTATIONS

Jerusalem in Affliction

1 How lonely sits the city
That was full of people!
How like a widow is she,
Who *was* great among the nations!
The princess among the provinces
Has become a slave!

2 She weeps bitterly in the night,
Her tears *are* on her cheeks;
Among all her lovers
She has none to comfort *her.*
All her friends have dealt treacherously with her;
They have become her enemies.

3 Judah has gone into captivity,
Under affliction and hard servitude;
She dwells among the nations,
She finds no rest;
All her persecutors overtake her in dire straits.

4 The roads to Zion mourn
Because no one comes to the set feasts.
All her gates are desolate;
Her priests sigh,
Her virgins are afflicted,
And she *is* in bitterness.

5 Her adversaries have become the master,
Her enemies prosper;
For the LORD has afflicted her
Because of the multitude of her transgressions.
Her children have gone into captivity before the enemy.

6 And from the daughter of Zion
All her splendor has departed.
Her princes have become like deer
That find no pasture,
That flee without strength
Before the pursuer.

7 In the days of her affliction and roaming,
Jerusalem remembers all her pleasant things
That she had in the days of old.
When her people fell into the hand of the enemy,
With no one to help her,
The adversaries saw her
And mocked at her downfall.[a]

8 Jerusalem has sinned gravely,
Therefore she has become vile.[a]
All who honored her despise her
Because they have seen her nakedness;
Yes, she sighs and turns away.

9 Her uncleanness *is* in her skirts;
She did not consider her destiny;
Therefore her collapse was awesome;
She had no comforter.
"O LORD, behold my affliction,
For *the* enemy is exalted!"

10 The adversary has spread his hand
Over all her pleasant things;
For she has seen the nations enter her sanctuary,
Those whom You commanded
Not to enter Your assembly.

11 All her people sigh,
They seek bread;
They have given their valuables for food to restore life.
"See, O LORD, and consider,
For I am scorned."

12 "*Is it* nothing to you, all you who pass by?
Behold and see
If there is any sorrow like my sorrow,
Which has been brought on me,
Which the LORD has inflicted
In the day of His fierce anger.

13 "From above He has sent fire into my bones,
And it overpowered them;
He has spread a net for my feet
And turned me back;
He has made me desolate
And faint all the day.

14 "The yoke of my transgressions was bound;[a]
They were woven together by His hands,
And thrust upon my neck.
He made my strength fail;
The Lord delivered me into the hands of *those whom* I am not able to withstand.

52:31 [a]Or *Awil-Marduk* 1:7 [a]Vulgate reads *her Sabbaths.* 1:8 [a]Septuagint and Vulgate read *moved* or *removed.* 1:14 [a]Following Masoretic Text and Targum; Septuagint, Syriac, and Vulgate read *watched over.*

15 "The Lord has trampled underfoot all my mighty *men* in my midst;
He has called an assembly against me
To crush my young men;
The Lord trampled *as* in a winepress
The virgin daughter of Judah.

16 "For these *things* I weep;
My eye, my eye overflows with water;
Because the comforter, who should restore my life,
Is far from me.
My children are desolate
Because the enemy prevailed."

17 Zion spreads out her hands,
But no one comforts her;
The LORD has commanded concerning Jacob
That those around him *become* his adversaries;
Jerusalem has become an unclean thing among them.

18 "The LORD is righteous,
For I rebelled against His commandment.
Hear now, all peoples,
And behold my sorrow;
My virgins and my young men
Have gone into captivity.

19 "I called for my lovers,
But they deceived me;
My priests and my elders
Breathed their last in the city,
While they sought food
To restore their life.

20 "See, O LORD, that I *am* in distress;
My soul is troubled;
My heart is overturned within me,
For I have been very rebellious.
Outside the sword bereaves,
At home *it is* like death.

21 "They have heard that I sigh,
But no one comforts me.
All my enemies have heard of my trouble;
They are glad that You have done *it*.
Bring on the day You have announced,
That they may become like me.

22 "Let all their wickedness come before You,
And do to them as You have done to me
For all my transgressions;
For my sighs *are* many,
And my heart *is* faint."

God's Anger with Jerusalem

2 How the Lord has covered the daughter of Zion
With a cloud in His anger!
He cast down from heaven to the earth
The beauty of Israel,
And did not remember His footstool
In the day of His anger.

2 The Lord has swallowed up and has not pitied
All the dwelling places of Jacob.
He has thrown down in His wrath
The strongholds of the daughter of Judah;
He has brought *them* down to the ground;
He has profaned the kingdom and its princes.

3 He has cut off in fierce anger
Every horn of Israel;
He has drawn back His right hand
From before the enemy.
He has blazed against Jacob like a flaming fire
Devouring all around.

4 Standing like an enemy, He has bent His bow;
With His right hand, like an adversary,
He has slain all *who were* pleasing to His eye;
On the tent of the daughter of Zion,
He has poured out His fury like fire.

5 The Lord was like an enemy.
He has swallowed up Israel,
He has swallowed up all her palaces;
He has destroyed her strongholds,
And has increased mourning and lamentation
In the daughter of Judah.

6 He has done violence to His tabernacle,
As if it were a garden;
He has destroyed His place of assembly;
The LORD has caused
The appointed feasts and Sabbaths to be forgotten in Zion.
In His burning indignation He has spurned the king and the priest.

7 The Lord has spurned His altar,
He has abandoned His sanctuary;
He has given up the walls of her palaces
Into the hand of the enemy.
They have made a noise in the house of the LORD
As on the day of a set feast.

8 The LORD has purposed to destroy
The wall of the daughter of Zion.
He has stretched out a line;
He has not withdrawn His hand from destroying;
Therefore He has caused the rampart and wall to lament;
They languished together.

9 Her gates have sunk into the ground;
He has destroyed and broken her bars.
Her king and her princes *are* among the nations;
The Law *is* no *more*,
And her prophets find no vision from the LORD.

10 The elders of the daughter of Zion
Sit on the ground *and* keep silence;
They throw dust on their heads
And gird themselves with sackcloth.
The virgins of Jerusalem
Bow their heads to the ground.

11 My eyes fail with tears,
My heart is troubled;
My bile is poured on the ground
Because of the destruction of the daughter of my people,
Because the children and the infants
Faint in the streets of the city.

12 They say to their mothers,
"Where *is* grain and wine?"
As they swoon like the wounded
In the streets of the city,
As their life is poured out
In their mothers' bosom.

13 How shall I console you?
To what shall I liken you,
O daughter of Jerusalem?
What shall I compare with you, that I
may comfort you,
O virgin daughter of Zion?
For your ruin *is* spread wide as the sea;
Who can heal you?

14 Your prophets have seen for you
False and deceptive visions;
They have not uncovered your iniquity,
To bring back your captives,
But have envisioned for you false
prophecies and delusions.

15 All who pass by clap *their* hands at you;
They hiss and shake their heads
At the daughter of Jerusalem:
"*Is* this the city that is called
'The perfection of beauty,
The joy of the whole earth'?"

16 All your enemies have opened their
mouth against you;
They hiss and gnash *their* teeth.
They say, "We have swallowed *her* up!
Surely this *is* the day we have waited for;
We have found *it*, we have seen *it!*"

17 The LORD has done what He purposed;
He has fulfilled His word
Which He commanded in days of old.
He has thrown down and has not pitied,
And He has caused an enemy to rejoice
over you;
He has exalted the horn of your
adversaries.

18 Their heart cried out to the Lord,
"O wall of the daughter of Zion,
Let tears run down like a river day and
night;
Give yourself no relief;
Give your eyes no rest.

19 "Arise, cry out in the night,
At the beginning of the watches;
Pour out your heart like water before the
face of the Lord.
Lift your hands toward Him
For the life of your young children,
Who faint from hunger at the head of
every street."

20 "See, O LORD, and consider!
To whom have You done this?
Should the women eat their offspring,
The children they have cuddled?[a]
Should the priest and prophet be slain
In the sanctuary of the Lord?

21 "Young and old lie
On the ground in the streets;
My virgins and my young men
Have fallen by the sword;
You have slain *them* in the day of Your
anger,
You have slaughtered *and* not pitied.

22 "You have invited as to a feast day
The terrors that surround me.
In the day of the LORD's anger
There was no refugee or survivor.
Those whom I have borne and brought up
My enemies have destroyed."

The Prophet's Anguish and Hope

3 I *am* the man *who* has seen affliction by
the rod of His wrath.
2 He has led me and made *me* walk
In darkness and not *in* light.
3 Surely He has turned His hand against me
Time and time again throughout the day.

4 He has aged my flesh and my skin,
And broken my bones.
5 He has besieged me
And surrounded *me* with bitterness and
woe.
6 He has set me in dark places
Like the dead of long ago.

7 He has hedged me in so that I cannot get
out;
He has made my chain heavy.
8 Even when I cry and shout,
He shuts out my prayer.
9 He has blocked my ways with hewn
stone;
He has made my paths crooked.

10 He *has been* to me a bear lying in wait,
Like a lion in ambush.
11 He has turned aside my ways and torn
me in pieces;
He has made me desolate.
12 He has bent His bow
And set me up as a target for the arrow.

13 He has caused the arrows of His quiver
To pierce my loins.[a]
14 I have become the ridicule of all my
people—
Their taunting song all the day.
15 He has filled me with bitterness,
He has made me drink wormwood.

16 He has also broken my teeth with gravel,
And covered me with ashes.
17 You have moved my soul far from peace;
I have forgotten prosperity.
18 And I said, "My strength and my hope
Have perished from the LORD."

19 Remember my affliction and roaming,
The wormwood and the gall.
20 My soul still remembers
And sinks within me.
21 This I recall to my mind,
Therefore I have hope.

22 *Through* the LORD's mercies we are not
consumed,
Because His compassions fail not.
23 *They are* new every morning;
Great *is* Your faithfulness.
24 "The LORD *is* my portion," says my soul,
"Therefore I hope in Him!"

25 The LORD *is* good to those who wait for
Him,
To the soul *who* seeks Him.
26 *It is* good that *one* should hope and wait
quietly
For the salvation of the LORD.
27 *It is* good for a man to bear
The yoke in his youth.

28 Let him sit alone and keep silent,
Because *God* has laid *it* on him;
29 Let him put his mouth in the dust—
There may yet be hope.

2:20 [a]Vulgate reads *a span long.* **3:13** [a]Literally *kidneys*

30 Let him give *his* cheek to the one who
strikes him,
And be full of reproach.

31 For the Lord will not cast off forever.
32 Though He causes grief,
Yet He will show compassion
According to the multitude of His
mercies.
33 For He does not afflict willingly,
Nor grieve the children of men.

34 To crush under one's feet
All the prisoners of the earth,
35 To turn aside the justice *due* a man
Before the face of the Most High,
36 Or subvert a man in his cause—
The Lord does not approve.

37 Who *is* he *who* speaks and it comes to
pass,
When the Lord has not commanded *it?*
38 *Is it* not from the mouth of the Most High
That woe and well-being proceed?
39 Why should a living man complain,
A man for the punishment of his sins?

40 Let us search out and examine our ways,
And turn back to the LORD;
41 Let us lift our hearts and hands
To God in heaven.
42 We have transgressed and rebelled;
You have not pardoned.

43 You have covered *Yourself* with anger
And pursued us;
You have slain *and* not pitied.
44 You have covered Yourself with a cloud,
That prayer should not pass through.
45 You have made us an offscouring and
refuse
In the midst of the peoples.

46 All our enemies
Have opened their mouths against us.
47 Fear and a snare have come upon us,
Desolation and destruction.
48 My eyes overflow with rivers of water
For the destruction of the daughter of my
people.

49 My eyes flow and do not cease,
Without interruption,
50 Till the LORD from heaven
Looks down and sees.
51 My eyes bring suffering to my soul
Because of all the daughters of my city.

52 My enemies without cause
Hunted me down like a bird.
53 They silenced[a] my life in the pit
And threw stones at me.
54 The waters flowed over my head;
I said, "I am cut off!"

55 I called on Your name, O LORD,
From the lowest pit.
56 You have heard my voice:
"Do not hide Your ear
From my sighing, from my cry for help."
57 You drew near on the day I called on You,
And said, "Do not fear!"

58 O Lord, You have pleaded the case for my
soul;
You have redeemed my life.
59 O LORD, You have seen *how* I am
wronged;
Judge my case.
60 You have seen all their vengeance,
All their schemes against me.

61 You have heard their reproach, O LORD,
All their schemes against me,
62 The lips of my enemies
And their whispering against me all the
day.
63 Look at their sitting down and their
rising up;
I *am* their taunting song.

64 Repay them, O LORD,
According to the work of their hands.
65 Give them a veiled[a] heart;
Your curse *be* upon them!
66 In Your anger,
Pursue and destroy them
From under the heavens of the LORD.

The Degradation of Zion

4 How the gold has become dim!
How changed the fine gold!
The stones of the sanctuary are scattered
At the head of every street.

2 The precious sons of Zion,
Valuable as fine gold,
How they are regarded as clay pots,
The work of the hands of the potter!

3 Even the jackals present their breasts
To nurse their young;
But the daughter of my people *is* cruel,
Like ostriches in the wilderness.

4 The tongue of the infant clings
To the roof of its mouth for thirst;
The young children ask for bread,
But no one breaks *it* for them.

5 Those who ate delicacies
Are desolate in the streets;
Those who were brought up in scarlet
Embrace ash heaps.

6 The punishment of the iniquity of the
daughter of my people
Is greater than the punishment of the sin
of Sodom,
Which was overthrown in a moment,
With no hand to help her!

7 Her Nazirites[a] were brighter than snow
And whiter than milk;
They were more ruddy in body than
rubies,
Like sapphire in their appearance.

8 *Now* their appearance is blacker than
soot;
They go unrecognized in the streets;
Their skin clings to their bones,
It has become as dry as wood.

9 *Those* slain by the sword are better off
Than *those* who die of hunger;
For these pine away,
Stricken *for lack* of the fruits of the field.

10 The hands of the compassionate women
Have cooked their own children;
They became food for them
In the destruction of the daughter of my
people.
11 The LORD has fulfilled His fury,
He has poured out His fierce anger.

3:53 [a]Septuagint reads *put to death.* 3:65 [a]A Jewish tradition reads *sorrow of.* 4:7 [a]Or *nobles*

He kindled a fire in Zion,
And it has devoured its foundations.

12 The kings of the earth,
And all inhabitants of the world,
Would not have believed
That the adversary and the enemy
Could enter the gates of Jerusalem—

13 Because of the sins of her prophets
And the iniquities of her priests,
Who shed in her midst
The blood of the just.

14 They wandered blind in the streets;
They have defiled themselves with blood,
So that no one would touch their garments.

15 They cried out to them,
"Go away, unclean!
Go away, go away,
Do not touch us!"
When they fled and wandered,
Those among the nations said,
"They shall no longer dwell *here.*"

16 The face[a] of the LORD scattered them;
He no longer regards them.
The people do not respect the priests
Nor show favor to the elders.

17 Still our eyes failed us,
Watching vainly for our help;
In our watching we watched
For a nation *that* could not save *us.*

18 They tracked our steps
So that we could not walk in our streets.
Our end was near;
Our days were over,
For our end had come.

19 Our pursuers were swifter
Than the eagles of the heavens.
They pursued us on the mountains
And lay in wait for us in the wilderness.

20 The breath of our nostrils, the anointed of the LORD,
Was caught in their pits,
Of whom we said, "Under his shadow
We shall live among the nations."

21 Rejoice and be glad, O daughter of Edom,
You who dwell in the land of Uz!
The cup shall also pass over to you
And you shall become drunk and make yourself naked.

22 *The punishment of* your iniquity is accomplished,
O daughter of Zion;
He will no longer send you into captivity.
He will punish your iniquity,
O daughter of Edom;
He will uncover your sins!

A Prayer for Restoration

5 Remember, O LORD, what has come upon us;
Look, and behold our reproach!
2 Our inheritance has been turned over to aliens,
And our houses to foreigners.
3 We have become orphans and waifs,
Our mothers *are* like widows.

4 We pay for the water we drink,
And our wood comes at a price.
5 *They* pursue at our heels;[a]
We labor *and* have no rest.
6 We have given our hand *to* the Egyptians
And the Assyrians, to be satisfied with bread.

7 Our fathers sinned *and are* no more,
But we bear their iniquities.
8 Servants rule over us;
There is none to deliver *us* from their hand.
9 We get our bread *at the risk* of our lives,
Because of the sword in the wilderness.

10 Our skin is hot as an oven,
Because of the fever of famine.
11 They ravished the women in Zion,
The maidens in the cities of Judah.
12 Princes were hung up by their hands,
And elders were not respected.
13 Young men ground at the millstones;
Boys staggered under *loads of* wood.
14 The elders have ceased *gathering at* the gate,
And the young men from their music.

15 The joy of our heart has ceased;
Our dance has turned into mourning.
16 The crown has fallen *from* our head.
Woe to us, for we have sinned!
17 Because of this our heart is faint;
Because of these *things* our eyes grow dim;
18 Because of Mount Zion which is desolate,
With foxes walking about on it.

19 You, O LORD, remain forever;
Your throne from generation to generation.
20 Why do You forget us forever,
And forsake us for so long a time?
21 Turn us back to You, O LORD, and we will be restored;
Renew our days as of old,
22 Unless You have utterly rejected us,
And are very angry with us!

The Book of EZEKIEL

Ezekiel's Vision of God

1 Now it came to pass in the thirtieth year, in the fourth *month,* on the fifth *day* of the month, as I *was* among the captives by the River Chebar, *that* the heavens were opened and I saw visions[a] of God.
2 On the fifth *day* of the month, which *was* in the fifth year of King Jehoiachin's captivity,
3 the word of the LORD came expressly to Ezekiel the priest, the son of Buzi, in the land of the Chaldeans[a] by the River Chebar; and the hand of the LORD was upon him there.

4:16 [a]Targum reads *anger.* **5:5** [a]Literally *necks* **1:1** [a]Following Masoretic Text, Septuagint, and Vulgate; Syriac and Targum read *a vision.* **1:3** [a]Or *Babylonians,* and so elsewhere in this book

4 Then I looked, and behold, a whirlwind was coming out of the north, a great cloud with raging fire engulfing itself; and brightness *was* all around it and radiating out of its midst like the color of amber, out of the midst of the fire.

5 Also from within it *came* the likeness of four living creatures. And this *was* their appearance: they had the likeness of a man.

6 Each one had four faces, and each one had four wings.

7 Their legs *were* straight, and the soles of their feet *were* like the soles of calves' feet. They sparkled like the color of burnished bronze.

8 The hands of a man *were* under their wings on their four sides; and each of the four had faces and wings.

9 Their wings touched one another. *The creatures* did not turn when they went, but each one went straight forward.

10 As for the likeness of their faces, *each* had the face of a man; each of the four had the face of a lion on the right side, each of the four had the face of an ox on the left side, and each of the four had the face of an eagle.

11 Thus *were* their faces. Their wings stretched upward; two *wings* of each one touched one another, and two covered their bodies.

12 And each one went straight forward; they went wherever the spirit wanted to go, and they did not turn when they went.

13 As for the likeness of the living creatures, their appearance *was* like burning coals of fire, like the appearance of torches going back and forth among the living creatures. The fire was bright, and out of the fire went lightning.

14 And the living creatures ran back and forth, in appearance like a flash of lightning.

15 Now as I looked at the living creatures, behold, a wheel *was* on the earth beside each living creature with its four faces.

16 The appearance of the wheels and their workings *was* like the color of beryl, and all four had the same likeness. The appearance of their workings *was*, as it were, a wheel in the middle of a wheel.

17 When they moved, they went toward any one of four directions; they did not turn aside when they went.

18 As for their rims, they were so high they were awesome; and their rims *were* full of eyes, all around the four of them.

19 When the living creatures went, the wheels went beside them; and when the living creatures were lifted up from the earth, the wheels were lifted up.

20 Wherever the spirit wanted to go, they went, *because* there the spirit went; and the wheels were lifted together with them, for the spirit of the living creatures[a] *was* in the wheels.

21 When those went, *these* went; when those stood, *these* stood; and when those were lifted up from the earth, the wheels were lifted up together with them, for the spirit of the living creatures[a] *was* in the wheels.

22 The likeness of the firmament above the heads of the living creatures[a] *was* like the color of an awesome crystal, stretched out over their heads.

23 And under the firmament their wings *spread out* straight, one toward another. Each one had two which covered one side, and each one had two which covered the other side of the body.

24 When they went, I heard the noise of their wings, like the noise of many waters, like the voice of the Almighty, a tumult like the noise of an army; and when they stood still, they let down their wings.

25 A voice came from above the firmament that *was* over their heads; whenever they stood, they let down their wings.

26 And above the firmament over their heads *was* the likeness of a throne, in appearance like a sapphire stone; on the likeness of the throne *was* a likeness with the appearance of a man high above it.

27 Also from the appearance of His waist and upward I saw, as it were, the color of amber with the appearance of fire all around within it; and from the appearance of His waist and downward I saw, as it were, the appearance of fire with brightness all around.

28 Like the appearance of a rainbow in a cloud on a rainy day, so *was* the appearance of the brightness all around it. This *was* the appearance of the likeness of the glory of the LORD.

Ezekiel Sent to Rebellious Israel

So when I saw *it*, I fell on my face, and I heard a voice of One speaking.

2 And He said to me, "Son of man, stand on your feet, and I will speak to you."

2 Then the Spirit entered me when He spoke to me, and set me on my feet; and I heard Him who spoke to me.

3 And He said to me: "Son of man, I am sending you to the children of Israel, to a rebellious nation that has rebelled against Me; they and their fathers have transgressed against Me to this very day.

4 "For *they are* impudent and stubborn children. I am sending you to them, and you shall say to them, 'Thus says the Lord GOD.'

5 "As for them, whether they hear or whether they refuse—for they *are* a rebellious house—yet they will know that a prophet has been among them.

6 "And you, son of man, do not be afraid of them nor be afraid of their words, though briers and thorns *are* with you and you dwell among scorpions; do not be afraid of their words or dismayed by their looks, though they *are* a rebellious house.

7 "You shall speak My words to them, whether they hear or whether they refuse, for they *are* rebellious.

8 "But you, son of man, hear what I say to you. Do not be rebellious like that rebellious house; open your mouth and eat what I give you."

9 Now when I looked, there was a hand stretched out to me; and behold, a scroll of a book *was* in it.

10 Then He spread it before me; and *there was* writing on the inside and on the outside, and written on it *were* lamentations and mourning and woe.

3 Moreover He said to me, "Son of man, eat what you find; eat this scroll, and go, speak to the house of Israel."

2 So I opened my mouth, and He caused me to eat that scroll.

1:20 [a]Literally *living creature;* Septuagint and Vulgate read *spirit of life;* Targum reads *creatures.* **1:21** [a]Literally *living creature;* Septuagint and Vulgate read *spirit of life;* Targum reads *creatures.* **1:22** [a]Following Septuagint, Targum, and Vulgate; Masoretic Text reads *living creature.*

3 And He said to me, "Son of man, feed your
belly, and fill your stomach with this scroll that
I give you." So I ate, and it was in my mouth
like honey in sweetness.
4 Then He said to me: "Son of man, go to
the house of Israel and speak with My words
to them.
5 "For you *are* not sent to a people of unfa-
miliar speech and of hard language, *but* to the
house of Israel,
6 "not to many people of unfamiliar speech
and of hard language, whose words you cannot
understand. Surely, had I sent you to them,
they would have listened to you.
7 "But the house of Israel will not listen to
you, because they will not listen to Me; for all
the house of Israel *are* impudent and hard-
hearted.
8 "Behold, I have made your face strong
against their faces, and your forehead strong
against their foreheads.
9 "Like adamant stone, harder than flint, I
have made your forehead; do not be afraid of
them, nor be dismayed at their looks, though
they *are* a rebellious house."
10 Moreover He said to me: "Son of man, re-
ceive into your heart all My words that I speak
to you, and hear with your ears.
11 "And go, get to the captives, to the children
of your people, and speak to them and tell
them, 'Thus says the Lord GOD,' whether they
hear, or whether they refuse."
12 Then the Spirit lifted me up, and I heard
behind me a great thunderous voice: "Blessed
is the glory of the LORD from His place!"
13 *I* also *heard* the noise of the wings of the
living creatures that touched one another, and
the noise of the wheels beside them, and a
great thunderous noise.
14 So the Spirit lifted me up and took me
away, and I went in bitterness, in the heat of
my spirit; but the hand of the LORD was strong
upon me.
15 Then I came to the captives at Tel Abib,
who dwelt by the River Chebar; and I sat where
they sat, and remained there astonished
among them seven days.

Ezekiel Is a Watchman

16 Now it came to pass at the end of seven days
that the word of the LORD came to me, saying,
17 "Son of man, I have made you a watchman
for the house of Israel; therefore hear a word
from My mouth, and give them warning from
Me:
18 "When I say to the wicked, 'You shall surely
die,' and you give him no warning, nor speak
to warn the wicked from his wicked way, to
save his life, that same wicked *man* shall die in
his iniquity; but his blood I will require at your
hand.
19 "Yet, if you warn the wicked, and he does
not turn from his wickedness, nor from his
wicked way, he shall die in his iniquity; but
you have delivered your soul.
20 "Again, when a righteous *man* turns from
his righteousness and commits iniquity, and I
lay a stumbling block before him, he shall die;
because you did not give him warning, he shall
die in his sin, and his righteousness which he
has done shall not be remembered; but his
blood I will require at your hand.
21 "Nevertheless if you warn the righteous *man*
that the righteous should not sin, and he does
not sin, he shall surely live because he took
warning; also you will have delivered your
soul."
22 Then the hand of the LORD was upon me
there, and He said to me, "Arise, go out into
the plain, and there I shall talk with you."
23 So I arose and went out into the plain, and
behold, the glory of the LORD stood there, like
the glory which I saw by the River Chebar; and
I fell on my face.
24 Then the Spirit entered me and set me on
my feet, and spoke with me and said to me:
"Go, shut yourself inside your house.
25 "And you, O son of man, surely they will
put ropes on you and bind you with them, so
that you cannot go out among them.
26 "I will make your tongue cling to the roof
of your mouth, so that you shall be mute and
not be one to rebuke them, for they *are* a rebel-
lious house.
27 "But when I speak with you, I will open
your mouth, and you shall say to them, 'Thus
says the Lord GOD.' He who hears, let him
hear; and he who refuses, let him refuse; for
they *are* a rebellious house.

The Siege of Jerusalem Portrayed

4 "You also, son of man, take a clay tablet and
lay it before you, and portray on it a city,
Jerusalem.
2 "Lay siege against it, build a siege wall
against it, and heap up a mound against it; set
camps against it also, and place battering rams
against it all around.
3 "Moreover take for yourself an iron plate,
and set it *as* an iron wall between you and the
city. Set your face against it, and it shall be be-
sieged, and you shall lay siege against it. This
will be a sign to the house of Israel.
4 "Lie also on your left side, and lay the iniq-
uity of the house of Israel upon it. *According*
to the number of the days that you lie on it, you
shall bear their iniquity.
5 "For I have laid on you the years of their
iniquity, according to the number of the days,
three hundred and ninety days; so you shall bear
the iniquity of the house of Israel.
6 "And when you have completed them, lie
again on your right side; then you shall bear
the iniquity of the house of Judah forty days. I
have laid on you a day for each year.
7 "Therefore you shall set your face toward
the siege of Jerusalem; your arm *shall be* un-
covered, and you shall prophesy against it.
8 "And surely I will restrain you so that you
cannot turn from one side to another till you
have ended the days of your siege.
9 "Also take for yourself wheat, barley, beans,
lentils, millet, and spelt; put them into one ves-
sel, and make bread of them for yourself. *Dur-
ing* the number of days that you lie on your
side, three hundred and ninety days, you shall
eat it.
10 "And your food which you eat *shall be* by
weight, twenty shekels a day; from time to time
you shall eat it.
11 "You shall also drink water by measure,
one-sixth of a hin; from time to time you shall
drink.
12 "And you shall eat it *as* barley cakes; and
bake it using fuel of human waste in their sight."
13 Then the LORD said, "So shall the children
of Israel eat their defiled bread among the Gen-
tiles, where I will drive them."
14 So I said, "Ah, Lord GOD! Indeed I have
never defiled myself from my youth till now; I

have never eaten what died of itself or was torn by beasts, nor has abominable flesh ever come into my mouth.”
15 Then He said to me, “See, I am giving you cow dung instead of human waste, and you shall prepare your bread over it.”
16 Moreover He said to me, “Son of man, surely I will cut off the supply of bread in Jerusalem; they shall eat bread by weight and with anxiety, and shall drink water by measure and with dread,
17 “that they may lack bread and water, and be dismayed with one another, and waste away because of their iniquity.

A Sword Against Jerusalem

5 “And you, son of man, take a sharp sword, take it as a barber’s razor, and pass *it* over your head and your beard; then take scales to weigh and divide the *hair.*
2 “You shall burn with fire one-third in the midst of the city, when the days of the siege are finished; then you shall take one-third and strike around *it* with the sword, and one-third you shall scatter in the wind: I will draw out a sword after them.
3 “You shall also take a small number of them and bind them in the edge of your *garment.*
4 “Then take some of them again and throw them into the midst of the fire, and burn them in the fire. From there a fire will go out into all the house of Israel.
5 “Thus says the Lord GOD: ‘This *is* Jerusalem; I have set her in the midst of the nations and the countries all around her.
6 ‘She has rebelled against My judgments by doing wickedness more than the nations, and against My statutes more than the countries that *are* all around her; for they have refused My judgments, and they have not walked in My statutes.’
7 “Therefore thus says the Lord GOD: ‘Because you have multiplied *disobedience* more than the nations that *are* all around you, have not walked in My statutes nor kept My judgments, nor even done[a] according to the judgments of the nations that *are* all around you’—
8 “therefore thus says the Lord GOD: ‘Indeed I, even I, *am* against you and will execute judgments in your midst in the sight of the nations.
9 ‘And I will do among you what I have never done, and the like of which I will never do again, because of all your abominations.
10 ‘Therefore fathers shall eat *their* sons in your midst, and sons shall eat their fathers; and I will execute judgments among you, and all of you who remain I will scatter to all the winds.
11 ‘Therefore, *as* I live,’ says the Lord GOD, ‘surely, because you have defiled My sanctuary with all your detestable things and with all your abominations, therefore I will also diminish *you;* My eye will not spare, nor will I have any pity.
12 ‘One-third of you shall die of the pestilence, and be consumed with famine in your midst; and one-third shall fall by the sword all around you; and I will scatter another third to all the winds, and I will draw out a sword after them.
13 ‘Thus shall My anger be spent, and I will cause My fury to rest upon them, and I will be avenged; and they shall know that I, the LORD, have spoken *it* in My zeal, when I have spent My fury upon them.
14 ‘Moreover I will make you a waste and a reproach among the nations that *are* all around you, in the sight of all who pass by.
15 ‘So it[a] shall be a reproach, a taunt, a lesson, and an astonishment to the nations that *are* all around you, when I execute judgments among you in anger and in fury and in furious rebukes. I, the LORD, have spoken.
16 ‘When I send against them the terrible arrows of famine which shall be for destruction, which I will send to destroy you, I will increase the famine upon you and cut off your supply of bread.
17 ‘So I will send against you famine and wild beasts, and they will bereave you. Pestilence and blood shall pass through you, and I will bring the sword against you. I, the LORD, have spoken.’ ”

Judgment on Idolatrous Israel

6 Now the word of the LORD came to me, saying:
2 “Son of man, set your face toward the mountains of Israel, and prophesy against them,
3 “and say, ‘O mountains of Israel, hear the word of the Lord GOD! Thus says the Lord GOD to the mountains, to the hills, to the ravines, and to the valleys: “Indeed I, *even* I, will bring a sword against you, and I will destroy your high places.
4 “Then your altars shall be desolate, your incense altars shall be broken, and I will cast down your slain *men* before your idols.
5 “And I will lay the corpses of the children of Israel before their idols, and I will scatter your bones all around your altars.
6 “In all your dwelling places the cities shall be laid waste, and the high places shall be desolate, so that your altars may be laid waste and made desolate, your idols may be broken and made to cease, your incense altars may be cut down, and your works may be abolished.
7 “The slain shall fall in your midst, and you shall know that I *am* the LORD.
8 “Yet I will leave a remnant, so that you may have *some* who escape the sword among the nations, when you are scattered through the countries.
9 “Then those of you who escape will remember Me among the nations where they are carried captive, because I was crushed by their adulterous heart which has departed from Me, and by their eyes which play the harlot after their idols; they will loathe themselves for the evils which they committed in all their abominations.
10 “And they shall know that I *am* the LORD; I have not said in vain that I would bring this calamity upon them.”
11 ‘Thus says the Lord GOD: “Pound your fists and stamp your feet, and say, ‘Alas, for all the evil abominations of the house of Israel! For they shall fall by the sword, by famine, and by pestilence.
12 ‘He who is far off shall die by the pestilence, he who is near shall fall by the sword, and he who remains and is besieged shall die by the famine. Thus will I spend My fury upon them.
13 ‘Then you shall know that I *am* the LORD,

5:7 [a]Following Masoretic Text, Septuagint, Targum, and Vulgate; many Hebrew manuscripts and Syriac read *but have done* (compare 11:12). **5:15** [a]Septuagint, Syriac, Targum, and Vulgate read *you.*

when their slain are among their idols all
around their altars, on every high hill, on all
the mountaintops, under every green tree, and
under every thick oak, wherever they offered
sweet incense to all their idols.
14 'So I will stretch out My hand against them
and make the land desolate, yes, more desolate
than the wilderness toward Diblah, in all their
dwelling places. Then they shall know that I
am the LORD.'"'"

Judgment on Israel Is Near

7 Moreover the word of the LORD came to
me, saying,
2 "And you, son of man, thus says the Lord
GOD to the land of Israel:

'An end! The end has come upon the four
corners of the land.
3 Now the end *has come* upon you,
And I will send My anger against you;
I will judge you according to your ways,
And I will repay you for all your
abominations.
4 My eye will not spare you,
Nor will I have pity;
But I will repay your ways,
And your abominations will be in your
midst;
Then you shall know that I *am* the LORD!'

5 "Thus says the Lord GOD:

'A disaster, a singular disaster;
Behold, it has come!
6 An end has come,
The end has come;
It has dawned for you;
Behold, it has come!
7 Doom has come to you, you who dwell in
the land;
The time has come,
A day of trouble *is* near,
And not of rejoicing in the mountains.
8 Now upon you I will soon pour out My
fury,
And spend My anger upon you;
I will judge you according to your ways,
And I will repay you for all your
abominations.

9 'My eye will not spare,
Nor will I have pity;
I will repay you according to your ways,
And your abominations will be in your
midst.
Then you shall know that I *am* the LORD
who strikes.

10 'Behold, the day!
Behold, it has come!
Doom has gone out;
The rod has blossomed,
Pride has budded.
11 Violence has risen up into a rod of
wickedness;
None of them *shall remain,*
None of their multitude,
None of them;
Nor *shall there be* wailing for them.
12 The time has come,
The day draws near.
'Let not the buyer rejoice,
Nor the seller mourn,
For wrath *is* on their whole multitude.
13 For the seller shall not return to what has
been sold,
Though he may still be alive;
For the vision concerns the whole
multitude,
And it shall not turn back;
No one will strengthen himself
Who lives in iniquity.

14 'They have blown the trumpet and made
everyone ready,
But no one goes to battle;
For My wrath *is* on all their multitude.
15 The sword *is* outside,
And the pestilence and famine within.
Whoever *is* in the field
Will die by the sword;
And whoever *is* in the city,
Famine and pestilence will devour him.

16 'Those who survive will escape and be on
the mountains
Like doves of the valleys,
All of them mourning,
Each for his iniquity.
17 Every hand will be feeble,
And every knee will be *as* weak *as* water.
18 They will also be girded with sackcloth;
Horror will cover them;
Shame *will be* on every face,
Baldness on all their heads.

19 'They will throw their silver into the
streets,
And their gold will be like refuse;
Their silver and their gold will not be
able to deliver them
In the day of the wrath of the LORD;
They will not satisfy their souls,
Nor fill their stomachs,
Because it became their stumbling block
of iniquity.

20 'As for the beauty of his ornaments,
He set it in majesty;
But they made from it
The images of their abominations—
Their detestable things;
Therefore I have made it
Like refuse to them.
21 I will give it as plunder
Into the hands of strangers,
And to the wicked of the earth as spoil;
And they shall defile it.
22 I will turn My face from them,
And they will defile My secret place;
For robbers shall enter it and defile it.

23 'Make a chain,
For the land is filled with crimes of blood,
And the city is full of violence.
24 Therefore I will bring the worst of the
Gentiles,
And they will possess their houses;
I will cause the pomp of the strong to
cease,
And their holy places shall be defiled.
25 Destruction comes;
They will seek peace, but *there shall be*
none.
26 Disaster will come upon disaster,
And rumor will be upon rumor.
Then they will seek a vision from a
prophet;
But the law will perish from the priest,
And counsel from the elders.

27 'The king will mourn,
The prince will be clothed with
desolation,
And the hands of the common people will
tremble.
I will do to them according to their way,
And according to what they deserve I will
judge them;
Then they shall know that I *am* the
LORD!' "

Abominations in the Temple

8 And it came to pass in the sixth year, in the
sixth *month,* on the fifth *day* of the month,
as I sat in my house with the elders of Judah
sitting before me, that the hand of the Lord
GOD fell upon me there.
2 Then I looked, and there was a likeness,
like the appearance of fire—from the appearance
of His waist and downward, fire; and from His
waist and upward, like the appearance of bright-
ness, like the color of amber.
3 He stretched out the form of a hand, and
took me by a lock of my hair; and the Spirit
lifted me up between earth and heaven, and
brought me in visions of God to Jerusalem, to
the door of the north gate of the inner *court,*
where the seat of the image of jealousy *was,*
which provokes to jealousy.
4 And behold, the glory of the God of Israel
was there, like the vision that I saw in the plain.
5 Then He said to me, "Son of man, lift your
eyes now toward the north." So I lifted my eyes
toward the north, and there, north of the altar
gate, was this image of jealousy in the entrance.
6 Furthermore He said to me, "Son of man,
do you see what they are doing, the great abomi-
nations that the house of Israel commits here,
to make Me go far away from My sanctuary?
Now turn again, you will see greater abomina-
tions."
7 So He brought me to the door of the court;
and when I looked, there was a hole in the wall.
8 Then He said to me, "Son of man, dig into
the wall"; and when I dug into the wall, there
was a door.
9 And He said to me, "Go in, and see the
wicked abominations which they are doing
there."
10 So I went in and saw, and there—every sort
of creeping thing, abominable beasts, and all
the idols of the house of Israel, portrayed all
around on the walls.
11 And there stood before them seventy men
of the elders of the house of Israel, and in their
midst stood Jaazaniah the son of Shaphan.
Each man had a censer in his hand, and a thick
cloud of incense went up.
12 Then He said to me, "Son of man, have
you seen what the elders of the house of Israel
do in the dark, every man in the room of his
idols? For they say, 'The LORD does not see us,
the LORD has forsaken the land.' "
13 And He said to me, "Turn again, *and* you
will see greater abominations that they are
doing."
14 So He brought me to the door of the north
gate of the LORD's house; and to my dismay,
women were sitting there weeping for Tammuz.
15 Then He said to me, "Have you seen *this,*
O son of man? Turn again, you will see greater
abominations than these."
16 So He brought me into the inner court of
the LORD's house; and there, at the door of the
temple of the LORD, between the porch and the
altar, *were* about twenty-five men with their
backs toward the temple of the LORD and their
faces toward the east, and they were worship-
ing the sun toward the east.
17 And He said to me, "Have you seen *this,*
O son of man? Is it a trivial thing to the house
of Judah to commit the abominations which
they commit here? For they have filled the land
with violence; then they have returned to pro-
voke Me to anger. Indeed they put the branch
to their nose.
18 "Therefore I also will act in fury. My eye
will not spare nor will I have pity; and though
they cry in My ears with a loud voice, I will not
hear them."

The Wicked Are Slain

9 Then He called out in my hearing with a
loud voice, saying, "Let those who have
charge over the city draw near, each *with* a
deadly weapon in his hand."
2 And suddenly six men came from the di-
rection of the upper gate, which faces north,
each with his battle-ax in his hand. One man
among them *was* clothed with linen and had a
writer's inkhorn at his side. They went in and
stood beside the bronze altar.
3 Now the glory of the God of Israel had gone
up from the cherub, where it had been, to the
threshold of the temple.[a] And He called to the
man clothed with linen, who *had* the writer's
inkhorn at his side;
4 and the LORD said to him, "Go through the
midst of the city, through the midst of Jerusa-
lem, and put a mark on the foreheads of the
men who sigh and cry over all the abomina-
tions that are done within it."
5 To the others He said in my hearing, "Go
after him through the city and kill; do not let
your eye spare, nor have any pity.
6 "Utterly slay old *and* young men, maidens
and little children and women; but do not come
near anyone on whom *is* the mark; and begin
at My sanctuary." So they began with the el-
ders who *were* before the temple.
7 Then He said to them, "Defile the temple,
and fill the courts with the slain. Go out!" And
they went out and killed in the city.
8 So it was, that while they were killing
them, I was left *alone;* and I fell on my face and
cried out, and said, "Ah, Lord GOD! Will You
destroy all the remnant of Israel in pouring out
Your fury on Jerusalem?"
9 Then He said to me, "The iniquity of the
house of Israel and Judah *is* exceedingly great,
and the land is full of bloodshed, and the city
full of perversity; for they say, 'The LORD has
forsaken the land, and the LORD does not see!'
10 "And as for Me also, My eye will neither
spare, nor will I have pity, *but* I will recom-
pense their deeds on their own head."
11 Just then, the man clothed with linen, who
had the inkhorn at his side, reported back and
said, "I have done as You commanded me."

The Glory Departs from the Temple

10 And I looked, and there in the firmament
that was above the head of the cheru-
bim, there appeared something like a sapphire
stone, having the appearance of the likeness
of a throne.

9:3 [a]Literally *house*

2 Then He spoke to the man clothed with
linen, and said, "Go in among the wheels, under the cherub, fill your hands with coals of fire
from among the cherubim, and scatter *them*
over the city." And he went in as I watched.
3 Now the cherubim were standing on the
south side of the temple[a] when the man went
in, and the cloud filled the inner court.
4 Then the glory of the LORD went up from
the cherub, *and paused* over the threshold of
the temple; and the house was filled with the
cloud, and the court was full of the brightness
of the LORD's glory.
5 And the sound of the wings of the cherubim was heard *even* in the outer court, like the
voice of Almighty God when He speaks.
6 Then it happened, when He commanded
the man clothed in linen, saying, "Take fire from
among the wheels, from among the cherubim,"
that he went in and stood beside the wheels.
7 And the cherub stretched out his hand from
among the cherubim to the fire that *was* among
the cherubim, and took *some of it* and put *it*
into the hands of the *man* clothed with linen,
who took *it* and went out.
8 The cherubim appeared to have the form
of a man's hand under their wings.
9 And when I looked, there were four wheels
by the cherubim, one wheel by one cherub and
another wheel by each other cherub; the wheels
appeared *to have* the color of a beryl stone.
10 *As for* their appearance, all four looked
alike—as it were, a wheel in the middle of a
wheel.
11 When they went, they went toward *any of*
their four directions; they did not turn aside
when they went, but followed in the direction
the head was facing. They did not turn aside
when they went.
12 And their whole body, with their back, their
hands, their wings, and the wheels that the four
had, *were* full of eyes all around.
13 As for the wheels, they were called in my
hearing, "Wheel."
14 Each one had four faces: the first face *was*
the face of a cherub, the second face the face
of a man, the third the face of a lion, and the
fourth the face of an eagle.
15 And the cherubim were lifted up. This *was*
the living creature I saw by the River Chebar.
16 When the cherubim went, the wheels went
beside them; and when the cherubim lifted
their wings to mount up from the earth, the
same wheels also did not turn from beside them.
17 When *the cherubim*[a] stood still, *the wheels*
stood still, and when *one*[b] was lifted up, *the
other*[c] lifted itself up, for the spirit of the living
creature *was* in them.
18 Then the glory of the LORD departed from
the threshold of the temple and stood over the
cherubim.
19 And the cherubim lifted their wings and
mounted up from the earth in my sight. When
they went out, the wheels *were* beside them;
and they stood at the door of the east gate of
the LORD's house, and the glory of the God of
Israel *was* above them.
20 This *is* the living creature I saw under the
God of Israel by the River Chebar, and I knew
they *were* cherubim.
21 Each one had four faces and each one four
wings, and the likeness of the hands of a man
was under their wings.
22 And the likeness of their faces *was* the
same *as* the faces which I had seen by the River
Chebar, their appearance and their persons.
They each went straight forward.

Judgment on Wicked Counselors

11 Then the Spirit lifted me up and brought
me to the East Gate of the LORD's house,
which faces eastward; and there at the door of
the gate were twenty-five men, among whom
I saw Jaazaniah the son of Azzur, and Pelatiah
the son of Benaiah, princes of the people.
2 And He said to me: "Son of man, these *are*
the men who devise iniquity and give wicked
counsel in this city,
3 "who say, '*The time is* not near to build
houses; this *city is* the caldron, and we *are* the
meat.'
4 "Therefore prophesy against them, prophesy, O son of man!"
5 Then the Spirit of the LORD fell upon me,
and said to me, "Speak! 'Thus says the LORD:
"Thus you have said, O house of Israel; for I
know the things that come into your mind.
6 "You have multiplied your slain in this city,
and you have filled its streets with the slain."
7 'Therefore thus says the Lord GOD: "Your
slain whom you have laid in its midst, they *are*
the meat, and this *city is* the caldron; but I shall
bring you out of the midst of it.
8 "You have feared the sword; and I will
bring a sword upon you," says the Lord GOD.
9 "And I will bring you out of its midst, and
deliver you into the hands of strangers, and
execute judgments on you.
10 "You shall fall by the sword. I will judge
you at the border of Israel. Then you shall
know that I *am* the LORD.
11 "This *city* shall not be your caldron, nor
shall you be the meat in its midst. I will judge
you at the border of Israel.
12 "And you shall know that I *am* the LORD;
for you have not walked in My statutes nor
executed My judgments, but have done according to the customs of the Gentiles which *are*
all around you." ' "
13 Now it happened, while I was prophesying, that Pelatiah the son of Benaiah died. Then
I fell on my face and cried with a loud voice,
and said, "Ah, Lord GOD! Will You make a
complete end of the remnant of Israel?"

God Will Restore Israel

14 Again the word of the LORD came to me,
saying,
15 "Son of man, your brethren, your relatives, your countrymen, and all the house of
Israel in its entirety, *are* those about whom the
inhabitants of Jerusalem have said, 'Get far
away from the LORD; this land has been given
to us as a possession.'
16 "Therefore say, 'Thus says the Lord GOD:
"Although I have cast them far off among the
Gentiles, and although I have scattered them
among the countries, yet I shall be a little sanctuary for them in the countries where they
have gone." '
17 Therefore say, 'Thus says the Lord GOD:
"I will gather you from the peoples, assemble
you from the countries where you have been
scattered, and I will give you the land of Israel." '
18 "And they will go there, and they will take

10:3 [a]Literally *house*, also in verses 4 and 18 **10:17** [a]Literally *they* [b]Literally *they* [c]Literally *they*

away all its detestable things and all its abomi-
nations from there.
19 "Then I will give them one heart, and I will
put a new spirit within them,[a] and take the stony
heart out of their flesh, and give them a heart
of flesh,
20 that they may walk in My statutes and keep
My judgments and do them; and they shall be
My people, and I will be their God.
21 "But *as for those* whose hearts follow the
desire for their detestable things and their
abominations, I will recompense their deeds
on their own heads," says the Lord GOD.
22 So the cherubim lifted up their wings, with
the wheels beside them, and the glory of the
God of Israel *was* high above them.
23 And the glory of the LORD went up from
the midst of the city and stood on the mountain,
which *is* on the east side of the city.
24 Then the Spirit took me up and brought me
in a vision by the Spirit of God into Chaldea,[a] to
those in captivity. And the vision that I had
seen went up from me.
25 So I spoke to those in captivity of all the
things the LORD had shown me.

Judah's Captivity Portrayed

12 Now the word of the LORD came to me,
saying:
2 "Son of man, you dwell in the midst of a
rebellious house, which has eyes to see but
does not see, and ears to hear but does not hear;
for they *are* a rebellious house.
3 "Therefore, son of man, prepare your be-
longings for captivity, and go into captivity by
day in their sight. You shall go from your place
into captivity to another place in their sight. It
may be that they will consider, though they *are*
a rebellious house.
4 "By day you shall bring out your belong-
ings in their sight, as though going into captiv-
ity; and at evening you shall go in their sight,
like those who go into captivity.
5 "Dig through the wall in their sight, and
carry *your belongings* out through it.
6 "In their sight you shall bear *them* on *your*
shoulders *and* carry *them* out at twilight; you
shall cover your face, so that you cannot see the
ground, for I have made you a sign to the house
of Israel."
7 So I did as I was commanded. I brought
out my belongings by day, as though going into
captivity, and at evening I dug through the wall
with my hand. I brought *them* out at twilight,
and I bore *them* on *my* shoulder in their sight.
8 And in the morning the word of the LORD
came to me, saying,
9 "Son of man, has not the house of Israel,
the rebellious house, said to you, 'What are you
doing?'
10 "Say to them, 'Thus says the Lord GOD:
"This burden *concerns* the prince in Jerusalem
and all the house of Israel who are among
them."'
11 "Say, 'I *am* a sign to you. As I have done,
so shall it be done to them; they shall be carried
away into captivity.'
12 "And the prince who *is* among them shall
bear *his belongings* on *his* shoulder at twilight
and go out. They shall dig through the wall to
carry *them* out through it. He shall cover his
face, so that he cannot see the ground with *his*
eyes.
13 "I will also spread My net over him, and
he shall be caught in My snare. I will bring him
to Babylon, *to* the land of the Chaldeans; yet
he shall not see it, though he shall die there.
14 "I will scatter to every wind all who *are*
around him to help him, and all his troops; and
I will draw out the sword after them.
15 "Then they shall know that I *am* the LORD,
when I scatter them among the nations and dis-
perse them throughout the countries.
16 "But I will spare a few of their men from
the sword, from famine, and from pestilence,
that they may declare all their abominations
among the Gentiles wherever they go. Then
they shall know that I *am* the LORD."

Judgment Not Postponed

17 Moreover the word of the LORD came to
me, saying,
18 "Son of man, eat your bread with quaking,
and drink your water with trembling and anx-
iety.
19 "And say to the people of the land, 'Thus
says the Lord GOD to the inhabitants of Jerusa-
lem *and* to the land of Israel: "They shall eat
their bread with anxiety, and drink their water
with dread, so that her land may be emptied of
all who are in it, because of the violence of all
those who dwell in it.
20 "Then the cities that are inhabited shall be
laid waste, and the land shall become desolate;
and you shall know that I *am* the LORD."'"
21 And the word of the LORD came to me,
saying,
22 "Son of man, what *is* this proverb *that* you
people have about the land of Israel, which
says, 'The days are prolonged, and every vision
fails'?
23 "Tell them therefore, 'Thus says the Lord
GOD: "I will lay this proverb to rest, and they
shall no more use it as a proverb in Israel." But
say to them, "The days are at hand, and the
fulfillment of every vision.
24 "For no more shall there be any false vi-
sion or flattering divination within the house
of Israel.
25 "For I *am* the LORD. I speak, and the word
which I speak will come to pass; it will no more
be postponed; for in your days, O rebellious
house, I will say the word and perform it," says
the Lord GOD.'"
26 Again the word of the LORD came to me,
saying,
27 "Son of man, look, the house of Israel is
saying, 'The vision that he sees *is* for many days
from now, and he prophesies of times far off.'
28 "Therefore say to them, 'Thus says the Lord
GOD: "None of My words will be postponed
any more, but the word which I speak will be
done," says the Lord GOD.'"

Woe to Foolish Prophets

13 And the word of the LORD came to me,
saying,
2 "Son of man, prophesy against the proph-
ets of Israel who prophesy, and say to those
who prophesy out of their own heart, 'Hear the
word of the LORD!'"
3 Thus says the Lord GOD: "Woe to the fool-
ish prophets, who follow their own spirit and
have seen nothing!
4 "O Israel, your prophets are like foxes in
the deserts.

11:19 [a]Literally *you* **11:24** [a]Or *Babylon,* and so elsewhere in this book

5 "You have not gone up into the gaps to
build a wall for the house of Israel to stand in
battle on the day of the LORD.
6 "They have envisioned futility and false
divination, saying, 'Thus says the LORD!' But
the LORD has not sent them; yet they hope that
the word may be confirmed.
7 "Have you not seen a futile vision, and
have you not spoken false divination? You say,
'The LORD says,' but I have not spoken."
8 Therefore thus says the Lord GOD: "Be-
cause you have spoken nonsense and envi-
sioned lies, therefore I *am* indeed against you,"
says the Lord GOD.
9 "My hand will be against the prophets who
envision futility and who divine lies; they shall
not be in the assembly of My people, nor be
written in the record of the house of Israel, nor
shall they enter into the land of Israel. Then
you shall know that I *am* the Lord GOD.
10 "Because, indeed, because they have se-
duced My people, saying, 'Peace!' when *there*
is no peace—and one builds a wall, and they
plaster it with untempered *mortar*—
11 "say to those who plaster *it* with untem-
pered *mortar*, that it will fall. There will be
flooding rain, and you, O great hailstones, shall
fall; and a stormy wind shall tear *it* down.
12 "Surely, when the wall has fallen, will it
not be said to you, 'Where *is* the mortar with
which you plastered *it*?' "
13 Therefore thus says the Lord GOD: "I will
cause a stormy wind to break forth in My fury;
and there shall be a flooding rain in My anger,
and great hailstones in fury to consume *it*.
14 "So I will break down the wall you have
plastered with untempered *mortar*, and bring
it down to the ground, so that its foundation
will be uncovered; it will fall, and you shall be
consumed in the midst of it. Then you shall
know that I *am* the LORD.
15 "Thus will I accomplish My wrath on the
wall and on those who have plastered it with
untempered *mortar*; and I will say to you, 'The
wall *is* no *more*, nor those who plastered it,
16 '*that is*, the prophets of Israel who proph-
esy concerning Jerusalem, and who see visions
of peace for her when *there is* no peace,' " says
the Lord GOD.
17 "Likewise, son of man, set your face against
the daughters of your people, who prophesy
out of their own heart; prophesy against them,
18 "and say, 'Thus says the Lord GOD: "Woe
to the *women* who sew *magic* charms on their
sleeves[a] and make veils for the heads of people
of every height to hunt souls! Will you hunt the
souls of My people, and keep yourselves alive?
19 "And will you profane Me among My peo-
ple for handfuls of barley and for pieces of
bread, killing people who should not die, and
keeping people alive who should not live, by
your lying to My people who listen to lies?"
20 'Therefore thus says the Lord GOD: "Be-
hold, I *am* against your *magic* charms by which
you hunt souls there like birds. I will tear them
from your arms, and let the souls go, the souls
you hunt like birds.
21 "I will also tear off your veils and deliver
My people out of your hand, and they shall no
longer be as prey in your hand. Then you shall
know that I *am* the LORD.
22 "Because with lies you have made the heart
of the righteous sad, whom I have not made
sad; and you have strengthened the hands of
the wicked, so that he does not turn from his
wicked way to save his life.
23 "Therefore you shall no longer envision
futility nor practice divination; for I will deliver
My people out of your hand, and you shall
know that I *am* the LORD." ' "

Idolatry Will Be Punished

14 Now some of the elders of Israel came
to me and sat before me.
2 And the word of the LORD came to me, say-
ing,
3 "Son of man, these men have set up their
idols in their hearts, and put before them that
which causes them to stumble into iniquity.
Should I let Myself be inquired of at all by them?
4 "Therefore speak to them, and say to them,
'Thus says the Lord GOD: "Everyone of the
house of Israel who sets up his idols in his heart,
and puts before him what causes him to stum-
ble into iniquity, and then comes to the prophet,
I the LORD will answer him who comes, ac-
cording to the multitude of his idols,
5 "that I may seize the house of Israel by
their heart, because they are all estranged from
Me by their idols." '
6 "Therefore say to the house of Israel, 'Thus
says the Lord GOD: "Repent, turn away from
your idols, and turn your faces away from all
your abominations.
7 "For anyone of the house of Israel, or of the
strangers who dwell in Israel, who separates
himself from Me and sets up his idols in his
heart and puts before him what causes him to
stumble into iniquity, then comes to a prophet
to inquire of him concerning Me, I the LORD
will answer him by Myself.
8 "I will set My face against that man and
make him a sign and a proverb, and I will cut
him off from the midst of My people. Then you
shall know that I *am* the LORD.
9 "And if the prophet is induced to speak any-
thing, I the LORD have induced that prophet,
and I will stretch out My hand against him and
destroy him from among My people Israel.
10 "And they shall bear their iniquity; the
punishment of the prophet shall be the same
as the punishment of the one who inquired,
11 "that the house of Israel may no longer
stray from Me, nor be profaned anymore with
all their transgressions, but that they may be
My people and I may be their God," says the
Lord GOD.' "

Judgment on Persistent Unfaithfulness

12 The word of the LORD came again to me,
saying:
13 "Son of man, when a land sins against Me
by persistent unfaithfulness, I will stretch out
My hand against it; I will cut off its supply of
bread, send famine on it, and cut off man and
beast from it.
14 "Even *if* these three men, Noah, Daniel, and
Job, were in it, they would deliver *only* them-
selves by their righteousness," says the Lord
GOD.
15 "If I cause wild beasts to pass through the
land, and they empty it, and make it so deso-
late that no man may pass through because of
the beasts,

13:18 [a]Literally *over all the joints of My hands*; Vulgate reads *under every elbow*; Septuagint and Targum read *on all elbows of the hands*.

16 "*even though* these three men *were* in it,
as I live," says the Lord GOD, "they would de-
liver neither sons nor daughters; only they
would be delivered, and the land would be des-
olate.
17 "Or *if* I bring a sword on that land, and say,
'Sword, go through the land,' and I cut off man
and beast from it,
18 "even *though* these three men *were* in it,
as I live," says the Lord GOD, "they would de-
liver neither sons nor daughters, but only they
themselves would be delivered.
19 "Or *if* I send a pestilence into that land and
pour out My fury on it in blood, and cut off
from it man and beast,
20 "even *though* Noah, Daniel, and Job *were*
in it, *as* I live," says the Lord GOD, "they would
deliver neither son nor daughter; they would
deliver *only* themselves by their righteous-
ness."
21 For thus says the Lord GOD: "How much
more it shall be when I send My four severe
judgments on Jerusalem—the sword and fam-
ine and wild beasts and pestilence—to cut off
man and beast from it?
22 "Yet behold, there shall be left in it a rem-
nant who will be brought out, *both* sons and
daughters; surely they will come out to you,
and you will see their ways and their doings.
Then you will be comforted concerning the di-
saster that I have brought upon Jerusalem, all
that I have brought upon it.
23 "And they will comfort you, when you see
their ways and their doings; and you shall
know that I have done nothing without cause
that I have done in it," says the Lord GOD.

The Outcast Vine

15 Then the word of the LORD came to me,
saying:
2 "Son of man, how is the wood of the vine
better than any other wood, the vine branch
which is among the trees of the forest?
3 "Is wood taken from it to make any object?
Or can *men* make a peg from it to hang any
vessel on?
4 "Instead, it is thrown into the fire for fuel;
the fire devours both ends of it, and its middle
is burned. Is it useful for *any* work?
5 "Indeed, when it was whole, no object
could be made from it. How much less will
it be useful for *any* work when the fire has
devoured it, and it is burned?
6 "Therefore thus says the Lord GOD: 'Like
the wood of the vine among the trees of the
forest, which I have given to the fire for fuel,
so I will give up the inhabitants of Jerusalem;
7 'and I will set My face against them. They
will go out from *one* fire, but *another* fire shall
devour them. Then you shall know that I *am*
the LORD, when I set My face against them.
8 'Thus I will make the land desolate, be-
cause they have persisted in unfaithfulness,'
says the Lord GOD."

God's Love for Jerusalem

16 Again the word of the LORD came to me,
saying,
2 "Son of man, cause Jerusalem to know her
abominations,
3 "and say, 'Thus says the Lord GOD to Jeru-
salem: "Your birth and your nativity *are* from
the land of Canaan; your father *was* an Amo-
rite and your mother a Hittite.
4 "*As for* your nativity, on the day you were
born your navel cord was not cut, nor were you
washed in water to cleanse *you;* you were not
rubbed with salt nor wrapped in swaddling
cloths.
5 "No eye pitied you, to do any of these
things for you, to have compassion on you; but
you were thrown out into the open field, when
you yourself were loathed on the day you were
born.
6 "And when I passed by you and saw you
struggling in your own blood, I said to you in
your blood, 'Live!' Yes, I said to you in your
blood, 'Live!'
7 "I made you thrive like a plant in the field;
and you grew, matured, and became very beau-
tiful. *Your* breasts were formed, your hair
grew, but you *were* naked and bare.
8 "When I passed by you again and looked
upon you, indeed your time *was* the time of
love; so I spread My wing over you and covered
your nakedness. Yes, I swore an oath to you
and entered into a covenant with you, and you
became Mine," says the Lord GOD.
9 "Then I washed you in water; yes, I thor-
oughly washed off your blood, and I anointed
you with oil.
10 "I clothed you in embroidered cloth and
gave you sandals of badger skin; I clothed you
with fine linen and covered you with silk.
11 "I adorned you with ornaments, put brace-
lets on your wrists, and a chain on your neck.
12 "And I put a jewel in your nose, earrings
in your ears, and a beautiful crown on your
head.
13 "Thus you were adorned with gold and sil-
ver, and your clothing *was of* fine linen, silk,
and embroidered cloth. You ate *pastry of* fine
flour, honey, and oil. You were exceedingly
beautiful, and succeeded to royalty.
14 "Your fame went out among the nations
because of your beauty, for it *was* perfect
through My splendor which I had bestowed on
you," says the Lord GOD.

Jerusalem's Harlotry

15 "But you trusted in your own beauty,
played the harlot because of your fame, and
poured out your harlotry on everyone passing
by who *would have* it.
16 "You took some of your garments and
adorned multicolored high places for yourself,
and played the harlot on them. *Such* things
should not happen, nor be.
17 "You have also taken your beautiful jew-
elry from My gold and My silver, which I had
given you, and made for yourself male images
and played the harlot with them.
18 "You took your embroidered garments
and covered them, and you set My oil and My
incense before them.
19 "Also My food which I gave you—the
pastry of fine flour, oil, and honey *which* I fed
you—you set it before them as sweet incense;
and *so* it was," says the Lord GOD.
20 "Moreover you took your sons and your
daughters, whom you bore to Me, and these
you sacrificed to them to be devoured. *Were*
your *acts* of harlotry a small matter,
21 "that you have slain My children and of-
fered them up to them by causing them to pass
through *the fire?*
22 "And in all your abominations and acts of
harlotry you did not remember the days of
your youth, when you were naked and bare,
struggling in your blood.

23 "Then it was so, after all your wickedness—'Woe, woe to you!' says the Lord GOD—
24 "*that* you also built for yourself a shrine, and made a high place for yourself in every street.
25 "You built your high places at the head of every road, and made your beauty to be abhorred. You offered yourself to everyone who passed by, and multiplied your acts of harlotry.
26 "You also committed harlotry with the Egyptians, your very fleshly neighbors, and increased your acts of harlotry to provoke Me to anger.
27 "Behold, therefore, I stretched out My hand against you, diminished your allotment, and gave you up to the will of those who hate you, the daughters of the Philistines, who were ashamed of your lewd behavior.
28 "You also played the harlot with the Assyrians, because you were insatiable; indeed you played the harlot with them and still were not satisfied.
29 "Moreover you multiplied your acts of harlotry as far as the land of the trader, Chaldea; and even then you were not satisfied.
30 "How degenerate is your heart!" says the Lord GOD, "seeing you do all these *things*, the deeds of a brazen harlot.

Jerusalem's Adultery

31 "You erected your shrine at the head of every road, and built your high place in every street. Yet you were not like a harlot, because you scorned payment.
32 "*You are* an adulterous wife, *who* takes strangers instead of her husband.
33 "Men make payment to all harlots, but you made your payments to all your lovers, and hired them to come to you from all around for your harlotry.
34 "You are the opposite of *other* women in your harlotry, because no one solicited you to be a harlot. In that you gave payment but no payment was given you, therefore you are the opposite."

Jerusalem's Lovers Will Abuse Her

35 'Now then, O harlot, hear the word of the LORD!
36 'Thus says the Lord GOD: "Because your filthiness was poured out and your nakedness uncovered in your harlotry with your lovers, and with all your abominable idols, and because of the blood of your children which you gave to them,
37 "surely, therefore, I will gather all your lovers with whom you took pleasure, all those you loved, *and* all those you hated; I will gather them from all around against you and will uncover your nakedness to them, that they may see all your nakedness.
38 "And I will judge you as women who break wedlock or shed blood are judged; I will bring blood upon you in fury and jealousy.
39 "I will also give you into their hand, and they shall throw down your shrines and break down your high places. They shall also strip you of your clothes, take your beautiful jewelry, and leave you naked and bare.
40 "They shall also bring up an assembly against you, and they shall stone you with stones and thrust you through with their swords.
41 "They shall burn your houses with fire, and execute judgments on you in the sight of many women; and I will make you cease playing the harlot, and you shall no longer hire lovers.
42 "So I will lay to rest My fury toward you, and My jealousy shall depart from you. I will be quiet, and be angry no more.
43 "Because you did not remember the days of your youth, but agitated Me[a] with all these *things*, surely I will also recompense your deeds on *your own* head," says the Lord GOD. "And you shall not commit lewdness in addition to all your abominations.

More Wicked than Samaria and Sodom

44 "Indeed everyone who quotes proverbs will use *this* proverb against you: 'Like mother, like daughter!'
45 "You *are* your mother's daughter, loathing husband and children; and you *are* the sister of your sisters, who loathed their husbands and children; your mother *was* a Hittite and your father an Amorite.
46 "Your elder sister *is* Samaria, who dwells with her daughters to the north of you; and your younger sister, who dwells to the south of you, *is* Sodom and her daughters.
47 "You did not walk in their ways nor act according to their abominations; but, as *if that were* too little, you became more corrupt than they in all your ways.
48 "As I live," says the Lord GOD, "neither your sister Sodom nor her daughters have done as you and your daughters have done.
49 "Look, this was the iniquity of your sister Sodom: She and her daughter had pride, fullness of food, and abundance of idleness; neither did she strengthen the hand of the poor and needy.
50 "And they were haughty and committed abomination before Me; therefore I took them away as I saw *fit*.[a]
51 "Samaria did not commit half of your sins; but you have multiplied your abominations more than they, and have justified your sisters by all the abominations which you have done.
52 "You who judged your sisters, bear your own shame also, because the sins which you committed were more abominable than theirs; they are more righteous than you. Yes, be disgraced also, and bear your own shame, because you justified your sisters.
53 "When I bring back their captives, the captives of Sodom and her daughters, and the captives of Samaria and her daughters, then *I will also bring back* the captives of your captivity among them,
54 "that you may bear your own shame and be disgraced by all that you did when you comforted them.
55 "When your sisters, Sodom and her daughters, return to their former state, and Samaria and her daughters return to their former state, then you and your daughters will return to your former state.
56 "For your sister Sodom was not a byword in your mouth in the days of your pride,
57 "before your wickedness was uncovered. It was like the time of the reproach of the daugh-

16:43 [a]Following Septuagint, Syriac, Targum, and Vulgate; Masoretic Text reads *were agitated with Me.*
16:50 [a]Vulgate reads *you saw;* Septuagint reads *he saw;* Targum reads *as was revealed to Me.*

ters of Syria[a] and all *those* around her, and of the daughters of the Philistines, who despise you everywhere.
58 "You have paid for your lewdness and your abominations," says the LORD.
59 'For thus says the Lord GOD: "I will deal with you as you have done, who despised the oath by breaking the covenant.

An Everlasting Covenant

60 "Nevertheless I will remember My covenant with you in the days of your youth, and I will establish an everlasting covenant with you.
61 "Then you will remember your ways and be ashamed, when you receive your older and your younger sisters; for I will give them to you for daughters, but not because of My covenant with you.
62 "And I will establish My covenant with you. Then you shall know that I *am* the LORD,
63 "that you may remember and be ashamed, and never open your mouth anymore because of your shame, when I provide you an atonement for all you have done," says the Lord GOD.' "

The Eagles and the Vine

17 And the word of the LORD came to me, saying,
2 "Son of man, pose a riddle, and speak a parable to the house of Israel,
3 "and say, 'Thus says the Lord GOD:

"A great eagle with large wings and long
pinions,
Full of feathers of various colors,
Came to Lebanon
And took from the cedar the highest
branch.
4 He cropped off its topmost young twig
And carried it to a land of trade;
He set it in a city of merchants.
5 Then he took some of the seed of the land
And planted it in a fertile field;
He placed *it* by abundant waters
And set it like a willow tree.
6 And it grew and became a spreading vine
of low stature;
Its branches turned toward him,
But its roots were under it.
So it became a vine,
Brought forth branches,
And put forth shoots.

7 "But there was another[a] great eagle with
large wings and many feathers;
And behold, this vine bent its roots
toward him,
And stretched its branches toward him,
From the garden terrace where it had
been planted,
That he might water it.
8 It was planted in good soil by many
waters,
To bring forth branches, bear fruit,
And become a majestic vine." '

9 "Say, 'Thus says the Lord GOD:

"Will it thrive?
Will he not pull up its roots,
Cut off its fruit,
And leave it to wither?
All of its spring leaves will wither,
And no great power or many people
Will be needed to pluck it up by its roots.
10 Behold, *it is* planted,
Will it thrive?
Will it not utterly wither when the east
wind touches it?
It will wither in the garden terrace where
it grew." ' "

11 Moreover the word of the LORD came to me, saying,
12 "Say now to the rebellious house: 'Do you not know what these *things mean?*' Tell *them,* 'Indeed the king of Babylon went to Jerusalem and took its king and princes, and led them with him to Babylon.
13 'And he took the king's offspring, made a covenant with him, and put him under oath. He also took away the mighty of the land,
14 'that the kingdom might be brought low and not lift itself up, *but* that by keeping his covenant it might stand.
15 'But he rebelled against him by sending his ambassadors to Egypt, that they might give him horses and many people. Will he prosper? Will he who does such *things* escape? Can he break a covenant and still be delivered?
16 '*As* I live,' says the Lord GOD, 'surely in the place *where* the king *dwells* who made him king, whose oath he despised and whose covenant he broke—with him in the midst of Babylon he shall die.
17 'Nor will Pharaoh with *his* mighty army and great company do anything in the war, when they heap up a siege mound and build a wall to cut off many persons.
18 'Since he despised the oath by breaking the covenant, and in fact gave his hand and still did all these *things,* he shall not escape.' "
19 Therefore thus says the Lord GOD: "*As* I live, surely My oath which he despised, and My covenant which he broke, I will recompense on his own head.
20 "I will spread My net over him, and he shall be taken in My snare. I will bring him to Babylon and try him there for the treason which he committed against Me.
21 "All his fugitives[a] with all his troops shall fall by the sword, and those who remain shall be scattered to every wind; and you shall know that I, the LORD, have spoken."

Israel Exalted at Last

22 Thus says the Lord GOD: "I will take also *one* of the highest branches of the high cedar and set *it* out. I will crop off from the topmost of its young twigs a tender one, and will plant *it* on a high and prominent mountain.
23 "On the mountain height of Israel I will plant it; and it will bring forth boughs, and bear fruit, and be a majestic cedar. Under it will dwell birds of every sort; in the shadow of its branches they will dwell.
24 "And all the trees of the field shall know that I, the LORD, have brought down the high tree and exalted the low tree, dried up the green tree and made the dry tree flourish; I, the LORD, have spoken and have done *it.*"

16:57 [a]Following Masoretic Text, Septuagint, Targum, and Vulgate; many Hebrew manuscripts and Syriac read *Edom.* **17:7** [a]Following Septuagint, Syriac, and Vulgate; Masoretic Text and Targum read *one.* **17:21** [a]Following Masoretic Text and Vulgate; many Hebrew manuscripts and Syriac read *choice men;* Targum reads *mighty men;* Septuagint omits *All his fugitives.*

A False Proverb Refuted

18 The word of the LORD came to me again,
saying,
2 "What do you mean when you use this prov-
erb concerning the land of Israel, saying:

'The fathers have eaten sour grapes,
And the children's teeth are set on edge'?

3 "*As* I live," says the Lord GOD, "you shall no
longer use this proverb in Israel.

4 "Behold, all souls are Mine;
The soul of the father
As well as the soul of the son is Mine;
The soul who sins shall die.
5 But if a man is just
And does what is lawful and right;
6 If he has not eaten on the mountains,
Nor lifted up his eyes to the idols of the
house of Israel,
Nor defiled his neighbor's wife,
Nor approached a woman during her
impurity;
7 If he has not oppressed anyone,
But has restored to the debtor his pledge;
Has robbed no one by violence,
But has given his bread to the hungry
And covered the naked with clothing;
8 If he has not exacted usury
Nor taken any increase,
But has withdrawn his hand from iniquity
And executed true judgment between man
and man;
9 *If* he has walked in My statutes
And kept My judgments faithfully—
He *is* just;
He shall surely live!"
Says the Lord GOD.

10 "If he begets a son *who is* a robber
Or a shedder of blood,
Who does any of these *things*
11 And does none of those *duties*,
But has eaten on the mountains
Or defiled his neighbor's wife;
12 If he has oppressed the poor and needy,
Robbed by violence,
Not restored the pledge,
Lifted his eyes to the idols,
Or committed abomination;
13 If he has exacted usury
Or taken increase—
Shall he then live?
He shall not live!
If he has done any of these abominations,
He shall surely die;
His blood shall be upon him.

14 "*If*, however, he begets a son
Who sees all the sins which his father has
done,
And considers but does not do likewise;
15 *Who* has not eaten on the mountains,
Nor lifted his eyes to the idols of the house
of Israel,
Nor defiled his neighbor's wife;
16 Has not oppressed anyone,
Nor withheld a pledge,
Nor robbed by violence,
But has given his bread to the hungry
And covered the naked with clothing;
17 *Who* has withdrawn his hand from the
poor[a]
And not received usury or increase,
But has executed My judgments
And walked in My statutes—
He shall not die for the iniquity of his
father;
He shall surely live!

18 "*As for* his father,
Because he cruelly oppressed,
Robbed his brother by violence,
And did what *is* not good among his
people,
Behold, he shall die for his iniquity.

Turn and Live

19 "Yet you say, 'Why should the son not bear
the guilt of the father?' Because the son has done
what is lawful and right, and has kept all My
statutes and observed them, he shall surely live.
20 "The soul who sins shall die. The son shall
not bear the guilt of the father, nor the father
bear the guilt of the son. The righteousness of
the righteous shall be upon himself, and the
wickedness of the wicked shall be upon himself.
21 "But if a wicked man turns from all his sins
which he has committed, keeps all My statutes,
and does what is lawful and right, he shall surely
live; he shall not die.
22 "None of the transgressions which he has
committed shall be remembered against him;
because of the righteousness which he has done,
he shall live.
23 "Do I have any pleasure at all that the wicked
should die?" says the Lord GOD, "*and* not that
he should turn from his ways and live?
24 "But when a righteous man turns away
from his righteousness and commits iniquity,
and does according to all the abominations
that the wicked *man* does, shall he live? All the
righteousness which he has done shall not be
remembered; because of the unfaithfulness of
which he is guilty and the sin which he has
committed, because of them he shall die.
25 "Yet you say, 'The way of the Lord is not
fair.' Hear now, O house of Israel, is it not My
way which is fair, and your ways which are not
fair?
26 "When a righteous *man* turns away from
his righteousness, commits iniquity, and dies
in it, it is because of the iniquity which he has
done that he dies.
27 "Again, when a wicked *man* turns away from
the wickedness which he committed, and does
what is lawful and right, he preserves himself
alive.
28 "Because he considers and turns away from
all the transgressions which he committed, he
shall surely live; he shall not die.
29 "Yet the house of Israel says, 'The way of
the Lord is not fair.' O house of Israel, is it not
My ways which are fair, and your ways which
are not fair?
30 "Therefore I will judge you, O house of
Israel, every one according to his ways," says
the Lord GOD. "Repent, and turn from all your
transgressions, so that iniquity will not be your
ruin.
31 "Cast away from you all the transgressions
which you have committed, and get yourselves
a new heart and a new spirit. For why should
you die, O house of Israel?
32 "For I have no pleasure in the death of one
who dies," says the Lord GOD. "Therefore turn
and live!"

18:17 [a]Following Masoretic Text, Targum, and Vulgate; Septuagint reads *iniquity* (compare verse 8).

Israel Degraded

19 "Moreover take up a lamentation for the princes of Israel,
2 "and say:
'What *is* your mother? A lioness:
She lay down among the lions;
Among the young lions she nourished her cubs.
3 She brought up one of her cubs,
And he became a young lion;
He learned to catch prey,
And he devoured men.
4 The nations also heard of him;
He was trapped in their pit,
And they brought him with chains to the land of Egypt.

5 'When she saw that she waited, *that* her hope was lost,
She took another of her cubs *and* made him a young lion.
6 He roved among the lions,
And became a young lion;
He learned to catch prey;
He devoured men.
7 He knew their desolate places,[a]
And laid waste their cities;
The land with its fullness was desolated
By the noise of his roaring.
8 Then the nations set against him from the provinces on every side,
And spread their net over him;
He was trapped in their pit.
9 They put him in a cage with chains,
And brought him to the king of Babylon;
They brought him in nets,
That his voice should no longer be heard on the mountains of Israel.

10 'Your mother *was* like a vine in your bloodline,[a]
Planted by the waters,
Fruitful and full of branches
Because of many waters.
11 She had strong branches for scepters of rulers.
She towered in stature above the thick branches,
And was seen in her height amid the dense foliage.
12 But she was plucked up in fury,
She was cast down to the ground,
And the east wind dried her fruit.
Her strong branches were broken and withered;
The fire consumed them.
13 And now she *is* planted in the wilderness,
In a dry and thirsty land.
14 Fire has come out from a rod of her branches
And devoured her fruit,
So that she has no strong branch—a scepter for ruling.'"

This *is* a lamentation, and has become a lamentation.

The Rebellions of Israel

20 It came to pass in the seventh year, in
the fifth *month,* on the tenth *day* of the
month, *that* certain of the elders of Israel came
to inquire of the LORD, and sat before me.
2 Then the word of the LORD came to me,
saying,
3 "Son of man, speak to the elders of Israel,
and say to them, 'Thus says the Lord GOD:
"Have you come to inquire of Me? *As* I live,"
says the Lord GOD, "I will not be inquired of
by you."'
4 "Will you judge them, son of man, will you
judge *them?* Then make known to them the
abominations of their fathers.
5 "Say to them, 'Thus says the Lord GOD:
"On the day when I chose Israel and raised My
hand in an oath to the descendants of the
house of Jacob, and made Myself known to
them in the land of Egypt, I raised My hand in
an oath to them, saying, 'I *am* the LORD your
God.'
6 "On that day I raised My hand in an oath
to them, to bring them out of the land of Egypt
into a land that I had searched out for them,
'flowing with milk and honey,'[a] the glory of all
lands.
7 "Then I said to them, 'Each of you, throw
away the abominations which are before his
eyes, and do not defile yourselves with the
idols of Egypt. I *am* the LORD your God.'
8 "But they rebelled against Me and would
not obey Me. They did not all cast away the
abominations which were before their eyes,
nor did they forsake the idols of Egypt. Then I
said, 'I will pour out My fury on them and fulfill
My anger against them in the midst of the land
of Egypt.'
9 "But I acted for My name's sake, that it
should not be profaned before the Gentiles
among whom they *were,* in whose sight I had
made Myself known to them, to bring them out
of the land of Egypt.
10 "Therefore I made them go out of the land
of Egypt and brought them into the wilderness.
11 "And I gave them My statutes and showed
them My judgments, 'which, *if* a man does, he
shall live by them.'[a]
12 "Moreover I also gave them My Sabbaths,
to be a sign between them and Me, that they
might know that I *am* the LORD who sanctifies
them.
13 "Yet the house of Israel rebelled against
Me in the wilderness; they did not walk in My
statutes; they despised My judgments, 'which,
if a man does, he shall live by them';[a] and they
greatly defiled My Sabbaths. Then I said I
would pour out My fury on them in the wilder-
ness, to consume them.
14 "But I acted for My name's sake, that it
should not be profaned before the Gentiles, in
whose sight I had brought them out.
15 "So I also raised My hand in an oath to
them in the wilderness, that I would not bring
them into the land which I had given *them,*
'flowing with milk and honey,'[a] the glory of all
lands,
16 "because they despised My judgments and

19:7 [a]Septuagint reads *He stood in insolence;* Targum reads *He destroyed its palaces;* Vulgate reads *He learned to make widows.* **19:10** [a]Literally *blood,* following Masoretic Text, Syriac, and Vulgate; Septuagint reads *like a flower on a pomegranate tree;* Targum reads *in your likeness.* **20:6** [a]Exodus 3:8 **20:11** [a]Leviticus 18:5 **20:13** [a]Leviticus 18:5 **20:15** [a]Exodus 3:8

did not walk in My statutes, but profaned My Sabbaths; for their heart went after their idols.

17 "Nevertheless My eye spared them from destruction. I did not make an end of them in the wilderness.

18 "But I said to their children in the wilderness, 'Do not walk in the statutes of your fathers, nor observe their judgments, nor defile yourselves with their idols.

19 'I *am* the LORD your God: Walk in My statutes, keep My judgments, and do them;

20 'hallow My Sabbaths, and they will be a sign between Me and you, that you may know that I *am* the LORD your God.'

21 "Notwithstanding, the children rebelled against Me; they did not walk in My statutes, and were not careful to observe My judgments, 'which, *if* a man does, he shall live by them';[a] but they profaned My Sabbaths. Then I said I would pour out My fury on them and fulfill My anger against them in the wilderness.

22 "Nevertheless I withdrew My hand and acted for My name's sake, that it should not be profaned in the sight of the Gentiles, in whose sight I had brought them out.

23 "Also I raised My hand in an oath to those in the wilderness, that I would scatter them among the Gentiles and disperse them throughout the countries,

24 "because they had not executed My judgments, but had despised My statutes, profaned My Sabbaths, and their eyes were fixed on their fathers' idols.

25 "Therefore I also gave them up to statutes *that were* not good, and judgments by which they could not live;

26 "and I pronounced them unclean because of their ritual gifts, in that they caused all their firstborn to pass through *the fire,* that I might make them desolate and that they might know that I am the LORD." '

27 "Therefore, son of man, speak to the house of Israel, and say to them, 'Thus says the Lord GOD: "In this too your fathers have blasphemed Me, by being unfaithful to Me.

28 "When I brought them into the land *concerning* which I had raised My hand in an oath to give them, and they saw all the high hills and all the thick trees, there they offered their sacrifices and provoked Me with their offerings. There they also sent up their sweet aroma and poured out their drink offerings.

29 "Then I said to them, 'What *is* this high place to which you go?' So its name is called Bamah[a] to this day." '

30 "Therefore say to the house of Israel, 'Thus says the Lord GOD: "Are you defiling yourselves in the manner of your fathers, and committing harlotry according to their abominations?

31 "For when you offer your gifts and make your sons pass through the fire, you defile yourselves with all your idols, even to this day. So shall I be inquired of by you, O house of Israel? *As* I live," says the Lord GOD, "I will not be inquired of by you.

32 "What you have in your mind shall never be, when you say, 'We will be like the Gentiles, like the families in other countries, serving wood and stone.'

God Will Restore Israel

33 "*As* I live," says the Lord GOD, "surely with a mighty hand, with an outstretched arm, and with fury poured out, I will rule over you.

34 "I will bring you out from the peoples and gather you out of the countries where you are scattered, with a mighty hand, with an outstretched arm, and with fury poured out.

35 "And I will bring you into the wilderness of the peoples, and there I will plead My case with you face to face.

36 "Just as I pleaded My case with your fathers in the wilderness of the land of Egypt, so I will plead My case with you," says the Lord GOD.

37 "I will make you pass under the rod, and I will bring you into the bond of the covenant;

38 "I will purge the rebels from among you, and those who transgress against Me; I will bring them out of the country where they dwell, but they shall not enter the land of Israel. Then you will know that I *am* the LORD.

39 "As for you, O house of Israel," thus says the Lord GOD: "Go, serve every one of you his idols—and hereafter—if you will not obey Me; but profane My holy name no more with your gifts and your idols.

40 "For on My holy mountain, on the mountain height of Israel," says the Lord GOD, "there all the house of Israel, all of them in the land, shall serve Me; there I will accept them, and there I will require your offerings and the firstfruits of your sacrifices, together with all your holy things.

41 "I will accept you as a sweet aroma when I bring you out from the peoples and gather you out of the countries where you have been scattered; and I will be hallowed in you before the Gentiles.

42 "Then you shall know that I *am* the LORD, when I bring you into the land of Israel, into the country *for* which I raised My hand in an oath to give to your fathers.

43 "And there you shall remember your ways and all your doings with which you were defiled; and you shall loathe yourselves in your own sight because of all the evils that you have committed.

44 "Then you shall know that I *am* the LORD, when I have dealt with you for My name's sake, not according to your wicked ways nor according to your corrupt doings, O house of Israel," says the Lord GOD.' "

Fire in the Forest

45 Furthermore the word of the LORD came to me, saying,

46 "Son of man, set your face toward the south; preach against the south and prophesy against the forest land, the South,[a]

47 "and say to the forest of the South, 'Hear the word of the LORD! Thus says the Lord GOD: "Behold, I will kindle a fire in you, and it shall devour every green tree and every dry tree in you; the blazing flame shall not be quenched, and all faces from the south to the north shall be scorched by it.

48 "All flesh shall see that I, the LORD, have kindled it; it shall not be quenched." ' "

49 Then I said, "Ah, Lord GOD! They say of me, 'Does he not speak parables?' "

20:21 [a]Leviticus 18:5 **20:29** [a]Literally *High Place* **20:46** [a]Hebrew *Negev*

Babylon, the Sword of God

21 And the word of the LORD came to me,
saying,
2 "Son of man, set your face toward Jerusa-
lem, preach against the holy places, and
prophesy against the land of Israel;
3 "and say to the land of Israel, 'Thus says
the LORD: "Behold, I *am* against you, and I will
draw My sword out of its sheath and cut off
both righteous and wicked from you.
4 "Because I will cut off both righteous and
wicked from you, therefore My sword shall go
out of its sheath against all flesh from south *to*
north,
5 "that all flesh may know that I, the LORD,
have drawn My sword out of its sheath; it shall
not return anymore." '
6 "Sigh therefore, son of man, with a break-
ing heart, and sigh with bitterness before their
eyes.
7 "And it shall be when they say to you, 'Why
are you sighing?' that you shall answer, 'Be-
cause of the news; when it comes, every heart
will melt, all hands will be feeble, every spirit
will faint, and all knees will be weak *as* water.
Behold, it is coming and shall be brought to
pass,' says the Lord GOD."
8 Again the word of the LORD came to me,
saying,
9 "Son of man, prophesy and say, 'Thus says
the LORD!' Say:

'A sword, a sword is sharpened
And also polished!
10 Sharpened to make a dreadful slaughter,
Polished to flash like lightning!
Should we then make mirth?
It despises the scepter of My son,
As it does all wood.
11 And He has given it to be polished,
That it may be handled;
This sword is sharpened, and it is
polished
To be given into the hand of the slayer.'

12 "Cry and wail, son of man;
For it will be against My people,
Against all the princes of Israel.
Terrors including the sword will be
against My people;
Therefore strike *your* thigh.

13 "Because *it is* a testing,
And what if *the sword* despises even the
scepter?
The scepter shall be no *more,"*

says the Lord GOD.

14 "You therefore, son of man, prophesy,
And strike *your* hands together.
The third time let the sword do double
damage.
It *is* the sword *that* slays,
The sword that slays the great *men,*
That enters their private chambers.
15 I have set the point of the sword against
all their gates,
That the heart may melt and many may
stumble.
Ah! *It is* made bright;
It is grasped for slaughter:

16 "Swords at the ready!
Thrust right!
Set your blade!
Thrust left—
Wherever your edge is ordered!
17 "I also will beat My fists together,
And I will cause My fury to rest;
I, the LORD, have spoken."

18 The word of the LORD came to me again,
saying:
19 "And son of man, appoint for yourself two
ways for the sword of the king of Babylon to
go; both of them shall go from the same land.
Make a sign; put *it* at the head of the road to
the city.
20 "Appoint a road for the sword to go to Rab-
bah of the Ammonites, and to Judah, into forti-
fied Jerusalem.
21 "For the king of Babylon stands at the part-
ing of the road, at the fork of the two roads, to
use divination: he shakes the arrows, he con-
sults the images, he looks at the liver.
22 "In his right hand is the divination for Je-
rusalem: to set up battering rams, to call for a
slaughter, to lift the voice with shouting, to set
battering rams against the gates, to heap up a
siege mound, and to build a wall.
23 "And it will be to them like a false divina-
tion in the eyes of those who have sworn oaths
with them; but he will bring their iniquity to
remembrance, that they may be taken.
24 "Therefore thus says the Lord GOD: 'Be-
cause you have made your iniquity to be re-
membered, in that your transgressions are
uncovered, so that in all your doings your sins
appear—because you have come to remem-
brance, you shall be taken in hand.
25 'Now to you, O profane, wicked prince of
Israel, whose day has come, whose iniquity
shall end,
26 'thus says the Lord GOD:

"Remove the turban, and take off the
crown;
Nothing *shall remain* the same.
Exalt the humble, and humble the
exalted.
27 Overthrown, overthrown,
I will make it overthrown!
It shall be no *longer,*
Until He comes whose right it is,
And I will give it *to Him."* '

A Sword Against the Ammonites

28 "And you, son of man, prophesy and say,
'Thus says the Lord GOD concerning the Am-
monites and concerning their reproach,' and
say:

'A sword, a sword *is* drawn,
Polished for slaughter,
For consuming, for flashing—
29 While they see false visions for you,
While they divine a lie to you,
To bring you on the necks of the wicked,
the slain
Whose day has come,
Whose iniquity *shall* end.
30 'Return *it* to its sheath.
I will judge you
In the place where you were created,
In the land of your nativity.

31 I will pour out My indignation on you;
I will blow against you with the fire of My wrath,
And deliver you into the hands of brutal men *who are* skillful to destroy.
32 You shall be fuel for the fire;
Your blood shall be in the midst of the land.
You shall not be remembered,
For I the LORD have spoken.' "

Sins of Jerusalem

22 Moreover the word of the LORD came to
me, saying,
2 "Now, son of man, will you judge, will you
judge the bloody city? Yes, show her all her
abominations!
3 "Then say, 'Thus says the Lord GOD: "The
city sheds blood in her own midst, that her time
may come; and she makes idols within herself
to defile herself.
4 "You have become guilty by the blood which
you have shed, and have defiled yourself with
the idols which you have made. You have caused
your days to draw near, and have come to *the*
end of your years; therefore I have made you a
reproach to the nations, and a mockery to all
countries.
5 "*Those* near and *those* far from you will
mock you as infamous *and* full of tumult.
6 "Look, the princes of Israel: each one has
used his power to shed blood in you.
7 "In you they have made light of father and
mother; in your midst they have oppressed the
stranger; in you they have mistreated the fa-
therless and the widow.
8 "You have despised My holy things and pro-
faned My Sabbaths.
9 "In you are men who slander to cause blood-
shed; in you are those who eat on the moun-
tains; in your midst they commit lewdness.
10 "In you men uncover their fathers' naked-
ness; in you they violate women who are set
apart during their impurity.
11 "One commits abomination with his neigh-
bor's wife; another lewdly defiles his daughter-
in-law; and another in you violates his sister,
his father's daughter.
12 "In you they take bribes to shed blood; you
take usury and increase; you have made profit
from your neighbors by extortion, and have for-
gotten Me," says the Lord GOD.
13 "Behold, therefore, I beat My fists at the dis-
honest profit which you have made, and at the
bloodshed which has been in your midst.
14 "Can your heart endure, or can your hands
remain strong, in the days when I shall deal
with you? I, the LORD, have spoken, and will
do *it*.
15 "I will scatter you among the nations, dis-
perse you throughout the countries, and remove
your filthiness completely from you.
16 "You shall defile yourself in the sight of
the nations; then you shall know that I *am* the
LORD." ' "

Israel in the Furnace

17 The word of the LORD came to me, saying,
18 "Son of man, the house of Israel has be-
come dross to Me; they *are* all bronze, tin, iron,
and lead, in the midst of a furnace; they have
become dross from silver.
19 "Therefore thus says the Lord GOD: 'Because
you have all become dross, therefore behold, I
will gather you into the midst of Jerusalem.
20 '*As men* gather silver, bronze, iron, lead,
and tin into the midst of a furnace, to blow fire
on it, to melt *it;* so I will gather *you* in My anger
and in My fury, and I will leave *you there* and
melt you.
21 'Yes, I will gather you and blow on you with
the fire of My wrath, and you shall be melted
in its midst.
22 'As silver is melted in the midst of a fur-
nace, so shall you be melted in its midst; then
you shall know that I, the LORD, have poured
out My fury on you.' "

Israel's Wicked Leaders

23 And the word of the LORD came to me, say-
ing,
24 "Son of man, say to her: 'You *are* a land
that is not cleansed[a] or rained on in the day of
indignation.'
25 "The conspiracy of her prophets[a] in her
midst is like a roaring lion tearing the prey;
they have devoured people; they have taken
treasure and precious things; they have made
many widows in her midst.
26 "Her priests have violated My law and pro-
faned My holy things; they have not distin-
guished between the holy and unholy, nor have
they made known *the difference* between the
unclean and the clean; and they have hidden
their eyes from My Sabbaths, so that I am pro-
faned among them.
27 "Her princes in her midst *are* like wolves
tearing the prey, to shed blood, to destroy peo-
ple, and to get dishonest gain.
28 "Her prophets plastered them with untem-
pered *mortar,* seeing false visions, and divin-
ing lies for them, saying, 'Thus says the Lord
GOD,' when the LORD had not spoken.
29 "The people of the land have used oppres-
sions, committed robbery, and mistreated the
poor and needy; and they wrongfully oppress
the stranger.
30 "So I sought for a man among them who
would make a wall, and stand in the gap before
Me on behalf of the land, that I should not de-
stroy it; but I found no one.
31 "Therefore I have poured out My indigna-
tion on them; I have consumed them with the
fire of My wrath; and I have recompensed their
deeds on their own heads," says the Lord GOD.

Two Harlot Sisters

23 The word of the LORD came again to me,
saying:

2 "Son of man, there were two women,
The daughters of one mother.
3 They committed harlotry in Egypt,
They committed harlotry in their youth;
Their breasts were there embraced,
Their virgin bosom was there pressed.
4 Their names: Oholah[a] the elder and Oholibah[b] her sister;
They were Mine,
And they bore sons and daughters.
As for their names,

22:24 [a]Following Masoretic Text, Syriac, and Vulgate; Septuagint reads *showered upon.* **22:25** [a]Following Masoretic Text and Vulgate; Septuagint reads *princes;* Targum reads *scribes.* **23:4** [a]Literally *Her Own Tabernacle* [b]Literally *My Tabernacle Is in Her*

Samaria *is* Oholah, and Jerusalem *is*
Oholibah.

The Older Sister, Samaria

5 "Oholah played the harlot even though she
was Mine;
And she lusted for her lovers, the
neighboring Assyrians,
6 *Who were* clothed in purple,
Captains and rulers,
All of them desirable young men,
Horsemen riding on horses.
7 Thus she committed her harlotry with
them,
All of them choice men of Assyria;
And with all for whom she lusted,
With all their idols, she defiled herself.
8 She has never given up her harlotry
brought from Egypt,
For in her youth they had lain with her,
Pressed her virgin bosom,
And poured out their immorality upon
her.

9 "Therefore I have delivered her
Into the hand of her lovers,
Into the hand of the Assyrians,
For whom she lusted.
10 They uncovered her nakedness,
Took away her sons and daughters,
And slew her with the sword;
She became a byword among women,
For they had executed judgment on her.

The Younger Sister, Jerusalem

11 "Now although her sister Oholibah saw *this*,
she became more corrupt in her lust than she,
and in her harlotry more corrupt than her sis-
ter's harlotry.

12 "She lusted for the neighboring Assyrians,
Captains and rulers,
Clothed most gorgeously,
Horsemen riding on horses,
All of them desirable young men.
13 Then I saw that she was defiled;
Both *took* the same way.
14 But she increased her harlotry;
She looked at men portrayed on the wall,
Images of Chaldeans portrayed in
vermilion,
15 Girded with belts around their waists,
Flowing turbans on their heads,
All of them looking like captains,
In the manner of the Babylonians of
Chaldea,
The land of their nativity.
16 As soon as her eyes saw them,
She lusted for them
And sent messengers to them in Chaldea.

17 "Then the Babylonians came to her, into
the bed of love,
And they defiled her with their
immorality;
So she was defiled by them, and alienated
herself from them.
18 She revealed her harlotry and uncovered
her nakedness.
Then I alienated Myself from her,
As I had alienated Myself from her sister.

19 "Yet she multiplied her harlotry
In calling to remembrance the days of her
youth,
When she had played the harlot in the
land of Egypt.
20 For she lusted for her paramours,
Whose flesh *is like* the flesh of donkeys,
And whose issue *is like* the issue of
horses.
21 Thus you called to remembrance the
lewdness of your youth,
When the Egyptians pressed your bosom
Because of your youthful breasts.

Judgment on Jerusalem

22 "Therefore, Oholibah, thus says the Lord
GOD:

'Behold, I will stir up your lovers against
you,
From whom you have alienated yourself,
And I will bring them against you from
every side:
23 The Babylonians,
All the Chaldeans,
Pekod, Shoa, Koa,
All the Assyrians with them,
All of them desirable young men,
Governors and rulers,
Captains and men of renown,
All of them riding on horses.
24 And they shall come against you
With chariots, wagons, and war-horses,
With a horde of people.
They shall array against you
Buckler, shield, and helmet all around.

'I will delegate judgment to them,
And they shall judge you according to
their judgments.
25 I will set My jealousy against you,
And they shall deal furiously with you;
They shall remove your nose and your
ears,
And your remnant shall fall by the sword;
They shall take your sons and your
daughters,
And your remnant shall be devoured by
fire.
26 They shall also strip you of your clothes
And take away your beautiful jewelry.

27 'Thus I will make you cease your
lewdness and your harlotry
Brought from the land of Egypt,
So that you will not lift your eyes to them,
Nor remember Egypt anymore.'

28 "For thus says the Lord GOD: 'Surely I will
deliver you into the hand of those you hate, into
the hand *of those* from whom you alienated
yourself.
29 'They will deal hatefully with you, take away
all you have worked for, and leave you naked
and bare. The nakedness of your harlotry shall
be uncovered, both your lewdness and your har-
lotry.
30 'I will do these *things* to you because you
have gone as a harlot after the Gentiles, be-
cause you have become defiled by their idols.
31 'You have walked in the way of your sister;
therefore I will put her cup in your hand.'
32 "Thus says the Lord GOD:

'You shall drink of your sister's cup,
The deep and wide one;
You shall be laughed to scorn
And held in derision;
It contains much.

33 You will be filled with drunkenness and
sorrow,
The cup of horror and desolation,
The cup of your sister Samaria.
34 You shall drink and drain it,
You shall break its shards,
And tear at your own breasts;
For I have spoken,'
Says the Lord GOD.

35 "Therefore thus says the Lord GOD:

'Because you have forgotten Me and cast
Me behind your back,
Therefore you shall bear the *penalty*
Of your lewdness and your harlotry.'"

Both Sisters Judged

36 The LORD also said to me: "Son of man,
will you judge Oholah and Oholibah? Then de-
clare to them their abominations.
37 "For they have committed adultery, and
blood *is* on their hands. They have committed
adultery with their idols, and even *sacrificed*
their sons whom they bore to Me, passing them
through *the fire,* to devour *them.*
38 "Moreover they have done this to Me: They
have defiled My sanctuary on the same day and
profaned My Sabbaths.
39 "For after they had slain their children for
their idols, on the same day they came into My
sanctuary to profane it; and indeed thus they
have done in the midst of My house.
40 "Furthermore you sent for men to come from
afar, to whom a messenger *was* sent; and there
they came. And you washed yourself for them,
painted your eyes, and adorned yourself with
ornaments.
41 "You sat on a stately couch, with a table
prepared before it, on which you had set My
incense and My oil.
42 "The sound of a carefree multitude *was* with
her, and Sabeans *were* brought from the wilder-
ness with men of the common sort, who put
bracelets on their wrists and beautiful crowns
on their heads.
43 "Then I said concerning *her who had grown*
old in adulteries, 'Will they commit harlotry with
her now, and she *with them?*'
44 "Yet they went in to her, as men go in to a
woman who plays the harlot; thus they went
in to Oholah and Oholibah, the lewd women.
45 "But righteous men will judge them after the
manner of adulteresses, and after the manner
of women who shed blood, because they *are*
adulteresses, and blood *is* on their hands.
46 "For thus says the Lord GOD: 'Bring up an
assembly against them, give them up to trouble
and plunder.
47 'The assembly shall stone them with stones
and execute them with their swords; they shall
slay their sons and their daughters, and burn
their houses with fire.
48 'Thus I will cause lewdness to cease from
the land, that all women may be taught not to
practice your lewdness.
49 'They shall repay you for your lewdness,
and you shall pay for your idolatrous sins.
Then you shall know that I *am* the Lord GOD.'"

Symbol of the Cooking Pot

24 Again, in the ninth year, in the tenth
month, on the tenth *day* of the month,
the word of the LORD came to me, saying,
2 "Son of man, write down the name of the
day, this very day—the king of Babylon started
his siege against Jerusalem this very day.
3 "And utter a parable to the rebellious house,
and say to them, 'Thus says the Lord GOD:

"Put on a pot, set *it* on,
And also pour water into it.
4 Gather pieces *of meat* in it,
Every good piece,
The thigh and the shoulder.
Fill *it* with choice cuts;
5 Take the choice of the flock.
Also pile *fuel* bones under it,
Make it boil well,
And let the cuts simmer in it."

6 'Therefore thus says the Lord GOD:

"Woe to the bloody city,
To the pot whose scum *is* in it,
And whose scum is not gone from it!
Bring it out piece by piece,
On which no lot has fallen.
7 For her blood is in her midst;
She set it on top of a rock;
She did not pour it on the ground,
To cover it with dust.
8 That it may raise up fury and take
vengeance,
I have set her blood on top of a rock,
That it may not be covered."

9 'Therefore thus says the Lord GOD:

"Woe to the bloody city!
I too will make the pyre great.
10 Heap on the wood,
Kindle the fire;
Cook the meat well,
Mix in the spices,
And let the cuts be burned up.

11 "Then set the pot empty on the coals,
That it may become hot and its bronze
may burn,
That its filthiness may be melted in it,
That its scum may be consumed.
12 She has grown weary with lies,
And her great scum has not gone from
her.
Let her scum *be* in the fire!
13 In your filthiness *is* lewdness.
Because I have cleansed you, and you
were not cleansed,
You will not be cleansed of your filthiness
anymore,
Till I have caused My fury to rest upon
you.
14 I, the LORD, have spoken *it;*
It shall come to pass, and I will do *it;*
I will not hold back,
Nor will I spare,
Nor will I relent;
According to your ways
And according to your deeds
They[a] will judge you,"
Says the Lord GOD.'"

The Prophet's Wife Dies

15 Also the word of the LORD came to me, say-
ing,
16 "Son of man, behold, I take away from you
the desire of your eyes with one stroke; yet you
shall neither mourn nor weep, nor shall your
tears run down.

24:14 [a]Septuagint, Syriac, Targum, and Vulgate read *I.*

17 "Sigh in silence, make no mourning for the dead; bind your turban on your head, and put your sandals on your feet; do not cover *your* lips, and do not eat man's bread *of sorrow*."
18 So I spoke to the people in the morning, and at evening my wife died; and the next morning I did as I was commanded.
19 And the people said to me, "Will you not tell us what these *things signify* to us, that you behave so?"
20 Then I answered them, "The word of the LORD came to me, saying,
21 'Speak to the house of Israel, "Thus says the Lord GOD: 'Behold, I will profane My sanctuary, your arrogant boast, the desire of your eyes, the delight of your soul; and your sons and daughters whom you left behind shall fall by the sword.
22 'And you shall do as I have done; you shall not cover *your* lips nor eat man's bread *of sorrow*.
23 'Your turbans shall be on your heads and your sandals on your feet; you shall neither mourn nor weep, but you shall pine away in your iniquities and mourn with one another.
24 'Thus Ezekiel is a sign to you; according to all that he has done you shall do; and when this comes, you shall know that I *am* the Lord GOD.'"
25 'And you, son of man—*will it* not *be* in the day when I take from them their stronghold, their joy and their glory, the desire of their eyes, and that on which they set their minds, their sons and their daughters:
26 '*that* on that day one who escapes will come to you to let *you* hear *it* with *your* ears?
27 'On that day your mouth will be opened to him who has escaped; you shall speak and no longer be mute. Thus you will be a sign to them, and they shall know that I *am* the LORD.'"

Proclamation Against Ammon

25 The word of the LORD came to me, saying,
2 "Son of man, set your face against the Ammonites, and prophesy against them.
3 "Say to the Ammonites, 'Hear the word of the Lord GOD! Thus says the Lord GOD: "Because you said, 'Aha!' against My sanctuary when it was profaned, and against the land of Israel when it was desolate, and against the house of Judah when they went into captivity,
4 "indeed, therefore, I will deliver you as a possession to the men of the East, and they shall set their encampments among you and make their dwellings among you; they shall eat your fruit, and they shall drink your milk.
5 "And I will make Rabbah a stable for camels and Ammon a resting place for flocks. Then you shall know that I *am* the LORD."
6 'For thus says the Lord GOD: "Because you clapped *your* hands, stamped your feet, and rejoiced in heart with all your disdain for the land of Israel,
7 "indeed, therefore, I will stretch out My hand against you, and give you as plunder to the nations; I will cut you off from the peoples, and I will cause you to perish from the countries; I will destroy you, and you shall know that I *am* the LORD."

Proclamation Against Moab

8 'Thus says the Lord GOD: "Because Moab and Seir say, 'Look! The house of Judah *is* like all the nations,'
9 "therefore, behold, I will clear the territory of Moab of cities, of the cities on its frontier, the glory of the country, Beth Jeshimoth, Baal Meon, and Kirjathaim.
10 "To the men of the East I will give it as a possession, together with the Ammonites, that the Ammonites may not be remembered among the nations.
11 "And I will execute judgments upon Moab, and they shall know that I *am* the LORD."

Proclamation Against Edom

12 'Thus says the Lord GOD: "Because of what Edom did against the house of Judah by taking vengeance, and has greatly offended by avenging itself on them,"
13 'therefore thus says the Lord GOD: "I will also stretch out My hand against Edom, cut off man and beast from it, and make it desolate from Teman; Dedan shall fall by the sword.
14 "I will lay My vengeance on Edom by the hand of My people Israel, that they may do in Edom according to My anger and according to My fury; and they shall know My vengeance," says the Lord GOD.

Proclamation Against Philistia

15 'Thus says the Lord GOD: "Because the Philistines dealt vengefully and took vengeance with a spiteful heart, to destroy because of the old hatred,"
16 'therefore thus says the Lord GOD: "I will stretch out My hand against the Philistines, and I will cut off the Cherethites and destroy the remnant of the seacoast.
17 "I will execute great vengeance on them with furious rebukes; and they shall know that I *am* the LORD, when I lay My vengeance upon them."'"

Proclamation Against Tyre

26 And it came to pass in the eleventh year, on the first *day* of the month, *that* the word of the LORD came to me, saying,
2 "Son of man, because Tyre has said against Jerusalem, 'Aha! She is broken who *was* the gateway of the peoples; now she is turned over to me; I shall be filled; she is laid waste.'
3 "Therefore thus says the Lord GOD: 'Behold, I *am* against you, O Tyre, and will cause many nations to come up against you, as the sea causes its waves to come up.
4 'And they shall destroy the walls of Tyre and break down her towers; I will also scrape her dust from her, and make her like the top of a rock.
5 'It shall be *a place for* spreading nets in the midst of the sea, for I have spoken,' says the Lord GOD; 'it shall become plunder for the nations.
6 'Also her daughter *villages* which *are* in the fields shall be slain by the sword. Then they shall know that I am the LORD.'
7 "For thus says the Lord GOD: 'Behold, I will bring against Tyre from the north Nebuchadnezzar[a] king of Babylon, king of kings, with horses, with chariots, and with horsemen, and an army with many people.
8 'He will slay with the sword your daughter

26:7 [a]Hebrew *Nebuchadrezzar*, and so elsewhere in this book

villages in the fields; he will heap up a siege
mound against you, build a wall against you,
and raise a defense against you.
9 'He will direct his battering rams against
your walls, and with his axes he will break
down your towers.
10 'Because of the abundance of his horses,
their dust will cover you; your walls will shake
at the noise of the horsemen, the wagons, and
the chariots, when he enters your gates, as men
enter a city that has been breached.
11 'With the hooves of his horses he will tram-
ple all your streets; he will slay your people by
the sword, and your strong pillars will fall to
the ground.
12 'They will plunder your riches and pillage
your merchandise; they will break down your
walls and destroy your pleasant houses; they
will lay your stones, your timber, and your soil
in the midst of the water.
13 'I will put an end to the sound of your songs,
and the sound of your harps shall be heard no
more.
14 'I will make you like the top of a rock; you
shall be *a place for* spreading nets, and you
shall never be rebuilt, for I the LORD have spo-
ken,' says the Lord GOD.
15 "Thus says the Lord GOD to Tyre: 'Will the
coastlands not shake at the sound of your fall,
when the wounded cry, when slaughter is made
in the midst of you?
16 'Then all the princes of the sea will come
down from their thrones, lay aside their robes,
and take off their embroidered garments; they
will clothe themselves with trembling; they
will sit on the ground, tremble *every* moment,
and be astonished at you.
17 'And they will take up a lamentation for
you, and say to you:

"How you have perished,
O one inhabited by seafaring men,
O renowned city,
Who was strong at sea,
She and her inhabitants,
Who caused their terror *to be* on all her
inhabitants!
18 Now the coastlands tremble on the day of
your fall;
Yes, the coastlands by the sea are
troubled at your departure." '

19 "For thus says the Lord GOD: 'When I make
you a desolate city, like cities that are not in-
habited, when I bring the deep upon you, and
great waters cover you,
20 'then I will bring you down with those who
descend into the Pit, to the people of old, and
I will make you dwell in the lowest part of the
earth, in places desolate from antiquity, with
those who go down to the Pit, so that you may
never be inhabited; and I shall establish glory
in the land of the living.
21 'I will make you a terror, and you *shall be*
no *more;* though you are sought for, you will
never be found again,' says the Lord GOD."

Lamentation for Tyre

27 The word of the LORD came again to me,
saying,
2 "Now, son of man, take up a lamentation for
Tyre,
3 "and say to Tyre, 'You who are situated at the
entrance of the sea, merchant of the peoples on
many coastlands, thus says the Lord GOD:

"O Tyre, you have said,
'I *am* perfect in beauty.'
4 Your borders *are* in the midst of the seas.
Your builders have perfected your beauty.
5 They made all *your* planks of fir trees
from Senir;
They took a cedar from Lebanon to make
you a mast.
6 *Of* oaks from Bashan they made your
oars;
The company of Ashurites have inlaid
your planks
With ivory from the coasts of Cyprus.[a]
7 Fine embroidered linen from Egypt was
what you spread for your sail;
Blue and purple from the coasts of
Elishah was what covered you.

8 "Inhabitants of Sidon and Arvad were
your oarsmen;
Your wise men, O Tyre, were in you;
They became your pilots.
9 Elders of Gebal and its wise men
Were in you to caulk your seams;
All the ships of the sea
And their oarsmen were in you
To market your merchandise.

10 "Those from Persia, Lydia,[a] and Libya[b]
Were in your army as men of war;
They hung shield and helmet in you;
They gave splendor to you.
11 Men of Arvad with your army *were* on
your walls *all* around,
And the men of Gammad were in your
towers;
They hung their shields on your walls *all*
around;
They made your beauty perfect.

12 "Tarshish *was* your merchant because of
your many luxury goods. They gave you silver,
iron, tin, and lead for your goods.
13 "Javan, Tubal, and Meshech *were* your
traders. They bartered human lives and vessels
of bronze for your merchandise.
14 "Those from the house of Togarmah traded
for your wares with horses, steeds, and mules.
15 "The men of Dedan *were* your traders;
many isles *were* the market of your hand. They
brought you ivory tusks and ebony as payment.
16 "Syria *was* your merchant because of the
abundance of goods you made. They gave you
for your wares emeralds, purple, embroidery,
fine linen, corals, and rubies.
17 "Judah and the land of Israel *were* your
traders. They traded for your merchandise
wheat of Minnith, millet, honey, oil, and balm.
18 "Damascus *was* your merchant because of
the abundance of goods you made, because of
your many luxury items, with the wine of Hel-
bon and with white wool.
19 "Dan and Javan paid for your wares, tra-
versing back and forth. Wrought iron, cassia,
and cane were among your merchandise.
20 "Dedan *was* your merchant in saddlecloths
for riding.
21 "Arabia and all the princes of Kedar *were*
your regular merchants. They traded with you
in lambs, rams, and goats.
22 "The merchants of Sheba and Raamah
were your merchants. They traded for your

27:6 [a]Hebrew *Kittim*, western lands, especially Cyprus **27:10** [a]Hebrew *Lud* [b]Hebrew *Put*

wares the choicest spices, all kinds of precious
stones, and gold.
23 "Haran, Canneh, Eden, the merchants of
Sheba, Assyria, *and* Chilmad *were* your mer-
chants.
24 "These *were* your merchants in choice
items—in purple clothes, in embroidered gar-
ments, in chests of multicolored apparel, in
sturdy woven cords, which were in your market-
place.

25 "The ships of Tarshish were carriers of
your merchandise.
You were filled and very glorious in the
midst of the seas.
26 Your oarsmen brought you into many
waters,
But the east wind broke you in the midst
of the seas.

27 "Your riches, wares, and merchandise,
Your mariners and pilots,
Your caulkers and merchandisers,
All your men of war who *are* in you,
And the entire company which *is* in your
midst,
Will fall into the midst of the seas on the
day of your ruin.
28 The common-land will shake at the sound
of the cry of your pilots.

29 "All who handle the oar,
The mariners,
All the pilots of the sea
Will come down from their ships *and*
stand on the shore.
30 They will make their voice heard because
of you;
They will cry bitterly and cast dust on
their heads;
They will roll about in ashes;
31 They will shave themselves completely
bald because of you,
Gird themselves with sackcloth,
And weep for you
With bitterness of heart *and* bitter
wailing.
32 In their wailing for you
They will take up a lamentation,
And lament for you:
'What *city is* like Tyre,
Destroyed in the midst of the sea?

33 'When your wares went out by sea,
You satisfied many people;
You enriched the kings of the earth
With your many luxury goods and your
merchandise.
34 But you are broken by the seas in the
depths of the waters;
Your merchandise and the entire
company will fall in your midst.
35 All the inhabitants of the isles will be
astonished at you;
Their kings will be greatly afraid,
And *their* countenance will be troubled.
36 The merchants among the peoples will
hiss at you;
You will become a horror, and *be* no
more forever.'""

Proclamation Against the King of Tyre

28 The word of the LORD came to me again,
saying,
2 "Son of man, say to the prince of Tyre, 'Thus
says the Lord GOD:

"Because your heart *is* lifted up,
And you say, 'I *am* a god,
I sit *in* the seat of gods,
In the midst of the seas,'
Yet you *are* a man, and not a god,
Though you set your heart as the heart of
a god
3 (Behold, you *are* wiser than Daniel!
There is no secret that can be hidden
from you!
4 With your wisdom and your
understanding
You have gained riches for yourself,
And gathered gold and silver into your
treasuries;
5 By your great wisdom in trade you have
increased your riches,
And your heart is lifted up because of
your riches),"

6 'Therefore thus says the Lord GOD:

"Because you have set your heart as the
heart of a god,
7 Behold, therefore, I will bring strangers
against you,
The most terrible of the nations;
And they shall draw their swords against
the beauty of your wisdom,
And defile your splendor.
8 They shall throw you down into the Pit,
And you shall die the death of the slain
In the midst of the seas.

9 "Will you still say before him who slays
you,
'I *am* a god'?
But you *shall be* a man, and not a god,
In the hand of him who slays you.
10 You shall die the death of the
uncircumcised
By the hand of aliens;
For I have spoken," says the Lord GOD.'"

Lamentation for the King of Tyre

11 Moreover the word of the LORD came to me,
saying,
12 "Son of man, take up a lamentation for the
king of Tyre, and say to him, 'Thus says the Lord
GOD:

"You *were* the seal of perfection,
Full of wisdom and perfect in beauty.
13 You were in Eden, the garden of God;
Every precious stone *was* your covering:
The sardius, topaz, and diamond,
Beryl, onyx, and jasper,
Sapphire, turquoise, and emerald with
gold.
The workmanship of your timbrels and
pipes
Was prepared for you on the day you
were created.

14 "You *were* the anointed cherub who
covers;
I established you;
You were on the holy mountain of God;
You walked back and forth in the midst
of fiery stones.
15 You *were* perfect in your ways from the
day you were created,
Till iniquity was found in you.

16 "By the abundance of your trading
You became filled with violence within,
And you sinned;

Therefore I cast you as a profane thing
Out of the mountain of God;
And I destroyed you, O covering cherub,
From the midst of the fiery stones.

17 "Your heart was lifted up because of your beauty;
You corrupted your wisdom for the sake of your splendor;
I cast you to the ground,
I laid you before kings,
That they might gaze at you.

18 "You defiled your sanctuaries
By the multitude of your iniquities,
By the iniquity of your trading;
Therefore I brought fire from your midst;
It devoured you,
And I turned you to ashes upon the earth
In the sight of all who saw you.
19 All who knew you among the peoples are astonished at you;
You have become a horror,
And *shall be* no more forever." ' "

Proclamation Against Sidon

20 Then the word of the LORD came to me, saying,
21 "Son of man, set your face toward Sidon, and prophesy against her,
22 "and say, 'Thus says the Lord GOD:

"Behold, I *am* against you, O Sidon;
I will be glorified in your midst;
And they shall know that I *am* the LORD,
When I execute judgments in her and am hallowed in her.
23 For I will send pestilence upon her,
And blood in her streets;
The wounded shall be judged in her midst
By the sword against her on every side;
Then they shall know that I *am* the LORD.

24 "And there shall no longer be a pricking
brier or a painful thorn for the house of Israel
from among all *who are* around them, who despise them. Then they shall know that I *am* the
Lord GOD."

Israel's Future Blessing

25 'Thus says the Lord GOD: "When I have
gathered the house of Israel from the peoples
among whom they are scattered, and am hallowed in them in the sight of the Gentiles, then
they will dwell in their own land which I gave
to My servant Jacob.
26 "And they will dwell safely there, build
houses, and plant vineyards; yes, they will
dwell securely, when I execute judgments on
all those around them who despise them. Then
they shall know that I *am* the LORD their
God." ' "

Proclamation Against Egypt

29 In the tenth year, in the tenth *month,* on the twelfth *day* of the month, the word
of the LORD came to me, saying,
2 "Son of man, set your face against Pharaoh
king of Egypt, and prophesy against him, and
against all Egypt.
3 "Speak, and say, 'Thus says the Lord GOD:

"Behold, I *am* against you,
O Pharaoh king of Egypt,
O great monster who lies in the midst of his rivers,
Who has said, 'My River[a] *is* my own;
I have made *it* for myself.'
4 But I will put hooks in your jaws,
And cause the fish of your rivers to stick to your scales;
I will bring you up out of the midst of your rivers,
And all the fish in your rivers will stick to your scales.
5 I will leave you in the wilderness,
You and all the fish of your rivers;
You shall fall on the open field;
You shall not be picked up or gathered.[a]
I have given you as food
To the beasts of the field
And to the birds of the heavens.

6 "Then all the inhabitants of Egypt
Shall know that I *am* the LORD,
Because they have been a staff of reed to the house of Israel.
7 When they took hold of you with the hand,
You broke and tore all their shoulders;[a]
When they leaned on you,
You broke and made all their backs quiver."

8 'Therefore thus says the Lord GOD: "Surely
I will bring a sword upon you and cut off from
you man and beast.
9 "And the land of Egypt shall become desolate and waste; then they will know that I *am*
the LORD, because he said, 'The River *is* mine,
and I have made *it.*'
10 "Indeed, therefore, I *am* against you and
against your rivers, and I will make the land
of Egypt utterly waste and desolate, from Migdol[a] *to* Syene, as far as the border of Ethiopia.
11 "Neither foot of man shall pass through it
nor foot of beast pass through it, and it shall be
uninhabited forty years.
12 "I will make the land of Egypt desolate in
the midst of the countries *that are* desolate; and
among the cities *that are* laid waste, her cities
shall be desolate forty years; and I will scatter
the Egyptians among the nations and disperse
them throughout the countries."
13 'Yet, thus says the Lord GOD: "At the end
of forty years I will gather the Egyptians from
the peoples among whom they were scattered.
14 "I will bring back the captives of Egypt
and cause them to return to the land of Pathros,
to the land of their origin, and there they shall
be a lowly kingdom.
15 "It shall be the lowliest of kingdoms; it shall
never again exalt itself above the nations, for
I will diminish them so that they will not rule
over the nations anymore.
16 "No longer shall it be the confidence of the
house of Israel, but will remind them of *their*
iniquity when they turned to follow them. Then
they shall know that I *am* the Lord GOD." ' "

Babylonia Will Plunder Egypt

17 And it came to pass in the twenty-seventh
year, in the first *month,* on the first *day* of the

29:3 [a]That is, the Nile **29:5** [a]Following Masoretic Text, Septuagint, and Vulgate; some Hebrew manuscripts and Targum read *buried.* **29:7** [a]Following Masoretic Text and Vulgate; Septuagint and Syriac read *hand.* **29:10** [a]Or *tower*

month, *that* the word of the LORD came to me,
saying,
18 "Son of man, Nebuchadnezzar king of
Babylon caused his army to labor strenuously
against Tyre; every head *was* made bald, and
every shoulder rubbed raw; yet neither he nor
his army received wages from Tyre, for the la-
bor which they expended on it.
19 "Therefore thus says the Lord GOD: 'Surely
I will give the land of Egypt to Nebuchadnez-
zar king of Babylon; he shall take away her
wealth, carry off her spoil, and remove her pil-
lage; and that will be the wages for his army.
20 'I have given him the land of Egypt *for* his
labor, because they worked for Me,' says the
Lord GOD.
21 'In that day I will cause the horn of the
house of Israel to spring forth, and I will open
your mouth to speak in their midst. Then they
shall know that I *am* the LORD.'"

Egypt and Her Allies Will Fall

30 The word of the LORD came to me again,
saying,
2 "Son of man, prophesy and say, 'Thus says
the Lord GOD:

"Wail, 'Woe to the day!'
3 For the day *is* near,
Even the day of the LORD *is* near;
It will be a day of clouds, the time of the
Gentiles.
4 The sword shall come upon Egypt,
And great anguish shall be in Ethiopia,
When the slain fall in Egypt,
And they take away her wealth,
And her foundations are broken down.

5 "Ethiopia, Libya,[a] Lydia,[b] all the mingled
people, Chub, and the men of the lands who
are allied, shall fall with them by the sword."
6 'Thus says the LORD:

"Those who uphold Egypt shall fall,
And the pride of her power shall come
down.
From Migdol *to* Syene
Those within her shall fall by the sword,"
Says the Lord GOD.

7 "They shall be desolate in the midst of the
desolate countries,
And her cities shall be in the midst of the
cities *that are* laid waste.
8 Then they will know that I *am* the LORD,
When I have set a fire in Egypt
And all her helpers are destroyed.
9 On that day messengers shall go forth
from Me in ships
To make the careless Ethiopians afraid,
And great anguish shall come upon them,
As on the day of Egypt;
For indeed it is coming!"

10 'Thus says the Lord GOD:

"I will also make a multitude of Egypt to
cease
By the hand of Nebuchadnezzar king of
Babylon.
11 He and his people with him, the most
terrible of the nations,
Shall be brought to destroy the land;
They shall draw their swords against
Egypt,
And fill the land with the slain.
12 I will make the rivers dry,
And sell the land into the hand of the
wicked;
I will make the land waste, and all that is
in it,
By the hand of aliens.
I, the LORD, have spoken."

13 'Thus says the Lord GOD:

"I will also destroy the idols,
And cause the images to cease from
Noph;[a]
There shall no longer be princes from the
land of Egypt;
I will put fear in the land of Egypt.
14 I will make Pathros desolate,
Set fire to Zoan,
And execute judgments in No.[a]
15 I will pour My fury on Sin,[a] the strength
of Egypt;
I will cut off the multitude of No,
16 And set a fire in Egypt;
Sin shall have great pain,
No shall be split open,
And Noph *shall be in* distress daily.
17 The young men of Aven[a] and Pi Beseth
shall fall by the sword,
And these *cities* shall go into captivity.
18 At Tehaphnehes[a] the day shall also be
darkened,[b]
When I break the yokes of Egypt there.
And her arrogant strength shall cease in
her;
As for her, a cloud shall cover her,
And her daughters shall go into captivity.
19 Thus I will execute judgments on Egypt,
Then they shall know that I *am* the
LORD."'"

Proclamation Against Pharaoh

20 And it came to pass in the eleventh year,
in the first *month*, on the seventh *day* of the
month, *that* the word of the LORD came to me,
saying,
21 "Son of man, I have broken the arm of Pha-
raoh king of Egypt; and see, it has not been
bandaged for healing, nor a splint put on to bind
it, to make it strong enough to hold a sword.
22 "Therefore thus says the Lord GOD: 'Surely
I *am* against Pharaoh king of Egypt, and will
break his arms, both the strong one and the
one that was broken; and I will make the sword
fall out of his hand.
23 'I will scatter the Egyptians among the na-
tions, and disperse them throughout the coun-
tries.
24 'I will strengthen the arms of the king of
Babylon and put My sword in his hand; but I
will break Pharaoh's arms, and he will groan
before him with the groanings of a mortally
wounded *man*.
25 'Thus I will strengthen the arms of the king
of Babylon, but the arms of Pharaoh shall fall
down; they shall know that I *am* the LORD, when
I put My sword into the hand of the king of
Babylon and he stretches it out against the
land of Egypt.

30:5 [a]Hebrew *Put* [b]Hebrew *Lud* **30:13** [a]That is, ancient Memphis **30:14** [a]That is, ancient Thebes **30:15** [a]That is, ancient Pelusium **30:17** [a]That is, ancient On (Heliopolis) **30:18** [a]Spelled *Tahpanhes* in Jeremiah 43:7 and elsewhere [b]Following many Hebrew manuscripts, Bomberg, Septuagint, Syriac, Targum, and Vulgate; Masoretic Text reads *refrained*.

26 'I will scatter the Egyptians among the na-
tions and disperse them throughout the coun-
tries. Then they shall know that I *am* the
LORD.'"

Egypt Cut Down Like a Great Tree

31 Now it came to pass in the eleventh year,
in the third *month,* on the first *day* of
the month, *that* the word of the LORD came to
me, saying,
2 "Son of man, say to Pharaoh king of Egypt
and to his multitude:

'Whom are you like in your greatness?
3 Indeed Assyria *was* a cedar in Lebanon,
With fine branches that shaded the forest,
And of high stature;
And its top was among the thick boughs.
4 The waters made it grow;
Underground waters gave it height,
With their rivers running around the
place where it was planted,
And sent out rivulets to all the trees of
the field.

5 'Therefore its height was exalted above all
the trees of the field;
Its boughs were multiplied,
And its branches became long because of
the abundance of water,
As it sent them out.
6 All the birds of the heavens made their
nests in its boughs;
Under its branches all the beasts of the
field brought forth their young;
And in its shadow all great nations made
their home.

7 'Thus it was beautiful in greatness and in
the length of its branches,
Because its roots reached to abundant
waters.
8 The cedars in the garden of God could
not hide it;
The fir trees were not like its boughs,
And the chestnut[a] trees were not like its
branches;
No tree in the garden of God was like it
in beauty.
9 I made it beautiful with a multitude of
branches,
So that all the trees of Eden envied it,
That *were* in the garden of God.'

10 "Therefore thus says the Lord GOD: 'Be-
cause you have increased in height, and it set
its top among the thick boughs, and its heart
was lifted up in its height,
11 'therefore I will deliver it into the hand of
the mighty one of the nations, and he shall
surely deal with it; I have driven it out for its
wickedness.
12 'And aliens, the most terrible of the na-
tions, have cut it down and left it; its branches
have fallen on the mountains and in all the
valleys; its boughs lie broken by all the rivers
of the land; and all the peoples of the earth
have gone from under its shadow and left it.

13 'On its ruin will remain all the birds of the
heavens,
And all the beasts of the field will come
to its branches—

14 'So that no trees by the waters may ever
again exalt themselves for their height, nor set
their tops among the thick boughs, that no tree
which drinks water may ever be high enough
to reach up to them.

'For they have all been delivered to death,
To the depths of the earth,
Among the children of men who go down
to the Pit.'

15 "Thus says the Lord GOD: 'In the day when
it went down to hell, I caused mourning. I cov-
ered the deep because of it. I restrained its
rivers, and the great waters were held back. I
caused Lebanon to mourn for it, and all the
trees of the field wilted because of it.
16 'I made the nations shake at the sound of
its fall, when I cast it down to hell together with
those who descend into the Pit; and all the
trees of Eden, the choice and best of Lebanon,
all that drink water, were comforted in the depths
of the earth.
17 'They also went down to hell with it, with
those slain by the sword; and *those who were*
its *strong* arm dwelt in its shadows among the
nations.
18 'To which of the trees in Eden will you then
be likened in glory and greatness? Yet you
shall be brought down with the trees of Eden
to the depths of the earth; you shall lie in the
midst of the uncircumcised, with *those* slain
by the sword. This *is* Pharaoh and all his multi-
tude,' says the Lord GOD."

Lamentation for Pharaoh and Egypt

32 And it came to pass in the twelfth year,
in the twelfth *month,* on the first *day* of
the month, *that* the word of the LORD came to
me, saying,
2 "Son of man, take up a lamentation for Pha-
raoh king of Egypt, and say to him:

'You are like a young lion among the
nations,
And you *are* like a monster in the seas,
Bursting forth in your rivers,
Troubling the waters with your feet,
And fouling their rivers.'

3 "Thus says the Lord GOD:

'I will therefore spread My net over you
with a company of many people,
And they will draw you up in My net.
4 Then I will leave you on the land;
I will cast you out on the open fields,
And cause to settle on you all the birds of
the heavens.
And with you I will fill the beasts of the
whole earth.
5 I will lay your flesh on the mountains,
And fill the valleys with your carcass.

6 'I will also water the land with the flow of
your blood,
Even to the mountains;
And the riverbeds will be full of you.
7 When *I* put out your light,
I will cover the heavens, and make its
stars dark;
I will cover the sun with a cloud,
And the moon shall not give her light.
8 All the bright lights of the heavens I will
make dark over you,
And bring darkness upon your land,'
Says the Lord GOD.

31:8 [a]Hebrew *armon*

9 'I will also trouble the hearts of many peo-
ples, when I bring your destruction among the
nations, into the countries which you have not
known.
10 'Yes, I will make many peoples astonished
at you, and their kings shall be horribly afraid
of you when I brandish My sword before them;
and they shall tremble *every* moment, every
man for his own life, in the day of your fall.'
11 "For thus says the Lord GOD: 'The sword
of the king of Babylon shall come upon you.
12 'By the swords of the mighty warriors, all
of them the most terrible of the nations, I will
cause your multitude to fall.

'They shall plunder the pomp of Egypt,
And all its multitude shall be destroyed.
13 Also I will destroy all its animals
From beside its great waters;
The foot of man shall muddy them no more,
Nor shall the hooves of animals muddy them.
14 Then I will make their waters clear,
And make their rivers run like oil,'
Says the Lord GOD.

15 'When I make the land of Egypt desolate,
And the country is destitute of all that once filled it,
When I strike all who dwell in it,
Then they shall know that I *am* the LORD.

16 'This *is* the lamentation
With which they shall lament her;
The daughters of the nations shall lament her;
They shall lament for her, for Egypt,
And for all her multitude,'
Says the Lord GOD."

Egypt and Others Consigned to the Pit

17 It came to pass also in the twelfth year, on
the fifteenth *day* of the month, *that* the word
of the LORD came to me, saying:

18 "Son of man, wail over the multitude of Egypt,
And cast them down to the depths of the earth,
Her and the daughters of the famous nations,
With those who go down to the Pit:
19 'Whom do you surpass in beauty?
Go down, be placed with the uncircumcised.'

20 "They shall fall in the midst of *those* slain by the sword;
She is delivered to the sword,
Drawing her and all her multitudes.
21 The strong among the mighty
Shall speak to him out of the midst of hell
With those who help him:
'They have gone down,
They lie with the uncircumcised, slain by the sword.'

22 "Assyria *is* there, and all her company,
With their graves all around her,
All of them slain, fallen by the sword.
23 Her graves are set in the recesses of the Pit,
And her company is all around her grave,
All of them slain, fallen by the sword,
Who caused terror in the land of the living.

24 "There *is* Elam and all her multitude,
All around her grave,
All of them slain, fallen by the sword,
Who have gone down uncircumcised to the lower parts of the earth,
Who caused their terror in the land of the living;
Now they bear their shame with those who go down to the Pit.
25 They have set her bed in the midst of the slain,
With all her multitude,
With her graves all around it,
All of them uncircumcised, slain by the sword;
Though their terror was caused
In the land of the living,
Yet they bear their shame
With those who go down to the Pit;
It was put in the midst of the slain.

26 "There *are* Meshech and Tubal and all their multitudes,
With all their graves around it,
All of them uncircumcised, slain by the sword,
Though they caused their terror in the land of the living.
27 They do not lie with the mighty
Who are fallen of the uncircumcised,
Who have gone down to hell with their weapons of war;
They have laid their swords under their heads,
But their iniquities will be on their bones,
Because of the terror of the mighty in the land of the living.
28 Yes, you shall be broken in the midst of the uncircumcised,
And lie with *those* slain by the sword.

29 "There *is* Edom,
Her kings and all her princes,
Who despite their might
Are laid beside *those* slain by the sword;
They shall lie with the uncircumcised,
And with those who go down to the Pit.
30 There *are* the princes of the north,
All of them, and all the Sidonians,
Who have gone down with the slain
In shame at the terror which they caused by their might;
They lie uncircumcised with *those* slain by the sword,
And bear their shame with those who go down to the Pit.

31 "Pharaoh will see them
And be comforted over all his multitude,
Pharaoh and all his army,
Slain by the sword,"
Says the Lord GOD.

32 "For I have caused My terror in the land of the living;
And he shall be placed in the midst of the uncircumcised
With *those* slain by the sword,
Pharaoh and all his multitude,"
Says the Lord GOD.

The Watchman and His Message

33 Again the word of the LORD came to me,
saying,
2 "Son of man, speak to the children of your
people, and say to them: 'When I bring the sword

upon a land, and the people of the land take a
man from their territory and make him their
watchman,
3 'when he sees the sword coming upon the
land, if he blows the trumpet and warns the
people,
4 'then whoever hears the sound of the trum-
pet and does not take warning, if the sword
comes and takes him away, his blood shall be
on his *own* head.
5 'He heard the sound of the trumpet, but
did not take warning; his blood shall be upon
himself. But he who takes warning will save
his life.
6 'But if the watchman sees the sword com-
ing and does not blow the trumpet, and the
people are not warned, and the sword comes
and takes *any* person from among them, he is
taken away in his iniquity; but his blood I will
require at the watchman's hand.'
7 "So you, son of man: I have made you a
watchman for the house of Israel; therefore
you shall hear a word from My mouth and warn
them for Me.
8 "When I say to the wicked, 'O wicked *man,*
you shall surely die!' and you do not speak to
warn the wicked from his way, that wicked
man shall die in his iniquity; but his blood I
will require at your hand.
9 "Nevertheless if you warn the wicked to
turn from his way, and he does not turn from
his way, he shall die in his iniquity; but you
have delivered your soul.
10 "Therefore you, O son of man, say to the
house of Israel: 'Thus you say, "If our trans-
gressions and our sins *lie* upon us, and we pine
away in them, how can we then live?"'
11 "Say to them: '*As* I live,' says the Lord GOD,
'I have no pleasure in the death of the wicked,
but that the wicked turn from his way and live.
Turn, turn from your evil ways! For why should
you die, O house of Israel?'

The Fairness of God's Judgment

12 "Therefore you, O son of man, say to the
children of your people: 'The righteousness of
the righteous man shall not deliver him in the
day of his transgression; as for the wickedness
of the wicked, he shall not fall because of it in
the day that he turns from his wickedness; nor
shall the righteous be able to live because of *his
righteousness* in the day that he sins.'
13 "When I say to the righteous *that* he shall
surely live, but he trusts in his own righteous-
ness and commits iniquity, none of his righ-
teous works shall be remembered; but because
of the iniquity that he has committed, he shall
die.
14 "Again, when I say to the wicked, 'You shall
surely die,' if he turns from his sin and does
what is lawful and right,
15 "*if* the wicked restores the pledge, gives
back what he has stolen, and walks in the stat-
utes of life without committing iniquity, he
shall surely live; he shall not die.
16 "None of his sins which he has committed
shall be remembered against him; he has done
what is lawful and right; he shall surely live.
17 "Yet the children of your people say, 'The
way of the Lord is not fair.' But it is their way
which is not fair!
18 "When the righteous turns from his righ-
teousness and commits iniquity, he shall die
because of it.
19 "But when the wicked turns from his wick-
edness and does what is lawful and right, he
shall live because of it.
20 "Yet you say, 'The way of the Lord is not
fair.' O house of Israel, I will judge every one
of you according to his own ways."

The Fall of Jerusalem

21 And it came to pass in the twelfth year of
our captivity, in the tenth *month,* on the fifth
day of the month, *that* one who had escaped
from Jerusalem came to me and said, "The city
has been captured!"
22 Now the hand of the LORD had been upon
me the evening before the man came who had
escaped. And He had opened my mouth; so
when he came to me in the morning, my mouth
was opened, and I was no longer mute.

The Cause of Judah's Ruin

23 Then the word of the LORD came to me, say-
ing:
24 "Son of man, they who inhabit those ruins
in the land of Israel are saying, 'Abraham was
only one, and he inherited the land. But we
are many; the land has been given to us as a
possession.'
25 "Therefore say to them, 'Thus says the
Lord GOD: "You eat *meat* with blood, you lift
up your eyes toward your idols, and shed
blood. Should you then possess the land?
26 "You rely on your sword, you commit abomi-
nations, and you defile one another's wives.
Should you then possess the land?"'
27 "Say thus to them, 'Thus says the Lord GOD:
"*As* I live, surely those who *are* in the ruins shall
fall by the sword, and the one who *is* in the
open field I will give to the beasts to be de-
voured, and those who *are* in the strongholds
and caves shall die of the pestilence.
28 "For I will make the land most desolate,
her arrogant strength shall cease, and the moun-
tains of Israel shall be so desolate that no one
will pass through.
29 "Then they shall know that I *am* the LORD,
when I have made the land most desolate be-
cause of all their abominations which they
have committed."'

Hearing and Not Doing

30 "As for you, son of man, the children of
your people are talking about you beside the
walls and in the doors of the houses; and they
speak to one another, everyone saying to his
brother, 'Please come and hear what the word
is that comes from the LORD.'
31 "So they come to you as people do, they
sit before you *as* My people, and they hear
your words, but they do not do them; for with
their mouth they show much love, *but* their
hearts pursue their *own* gain.
32 "Indeed you *are* to them as a very lovely
song of one who has a pleasant voice and can
play well on an instrument; for they hear your
words, but they do not do them.
33 "And when this comes to pass—surely it
will come—then they will know that a prophet
has been among them."

Irresponsible Shepherds

34 And the word of the LORD came to me,
saying,
2 "Son of man, prophesy against the shep-
herds of Israel, prophesy and say to them, 'Thus
says the Lord GOD to the shepherds: "Woe to

the shepherds of Israel who feed themselves!
Should not the shepherds feed the flocks?
3 "You eat the fat and clothe yourselves with
the wool; you slaughter the fatlings, *but* you
do not feed the flock.
4 "The weak you have not strengthened, nor
have you healed those who were sick, nor bound
up the broken, nor brought back what was
driven away, nor sought what was lost; but with
force and cruelty you have ruled them.
5 "So they were scattered because *there was*
no shepherd; and they became food for all the
beasts of the field when they were scattered.
6 "My sheep wandered through all the moun-
tains, and on every high hill; yes, My flock was
scattered over the whole face of the earth, and
no one was seeking or searching *for them.*"
7 'Therefore, you shepherds, hear the word
of the LORD:
8 "*As* I live," says the Lord GOD, "surely be-
cause My flock became a prey, and My flock
became food for every beast of the field, be-
cause *there was* no shepherd, nor did My shep-
herds search for My flock, but the shepherds
fed themselves and did not feed My flock"—
9 'therefore, O shepherds, hear the word of
the LORD!
10 'Thus says the Lord GOD: "Behold, I *am*
against the shepherds, and I will require My
flock at their hand; I will cause them to cease
feeding the sheep, and the shepherds shall feed
themselves no more; for I will deliver My flock
from their mouths, that they may no longer be
food for them."

God, the True Shepherd

11 'For thus says the Lord GOD: "Indeed I My-
self will search for My sheep and seek them
out.
12 "As a shepherd seeks out his flock on the
day he is among his scattered sheep, so will I
seek out My sheep and deliver them from all
the places where they were scattered on a
cloudy and dark day.
13 "And I will bring them out from the peo-
ples and gather them from the countries, and
will bring them to their own land; I will feed
them on the mountains of Israel, in the valleys
and in all the inhabited places of the country.
14 "I will feed them in good pasture, and their
fold shall be on the high mountains of Israel.
There they shall lie down in a good fold and
feed in rich pasture on the mountains of Israel.
15 "I will feed My flock, and I will make them
lie down," says the Lord GOD.
16 "I will seek what was lost and bring back
what was driven away, bind up the broken and
strengthen what was sick; but I will destroy the
fat and the strong, and feed them in judgment."
17 'And *as for* you, O My flock, thus says the
Lord GOD: "Behold, I shall judge between
sheep and sheep, between rams and goats.
18 "*Is it* too little for you to have eaten up the
good pasture, that you must tread down with
your feet the residue of your pasture—and to
have drunk of the clear waters, that you must
foul the residue with your feet?
19 "And *as for* My flock, they eat what you
have trampled with your feet, and they drink
what you have fouled with your feet."
20 'Therefore thus says the Lord GOD to
them: "Behold, I Myself will judge between the
fat and the lean sheep.
21 "Because you have pushed with side and
shoulder, butted all the weak ones with your
horns, and scattered them abroad,
22 "therefore I will save My flock, and they
shall no longer be a prey; and I will judge be-
tween sheep and sheep.
23 "I will establish one shepherd over them,
and he shall feed them—My servant David. He
shall feed them and be their shepherd.
24 "And I, the LORD, will be their God, and
My servant David a prince among them; I, the
LORD, have spoken.
25 "I will make a covenant of peace with them,
and cause wild beasts to cease from the land;
and they will dwell safely in the wilderness and
sleep in the woods.
26 "I will make them and the places all around
My hill a blessing; and I will cause showers
to come down in their season; there shall be
showers of blessing.
27 "Then the trees of the field shall yield their
fruit, and the earth shall yield her increase.
They shall be safe in their land; and they shall
know that I *am* the LORD, when I have broken
the bands of their yoke and delivered them
from the hand of those who enslaved them.
28 "And they shall no longer be a prey for the
nations, nor shall beasts of the land devour
them; but they shall dwell safely, and no one
shall make *them* afraid.
29 "I will raise up for them a garden of renown,
and they shall no longer be consumed with
hunger in the land, nor bear the shame of the
Gentiles anymore.
30 "Thus they shall know that I, the LORD
their God, *am* with them, and they, the house
of Israel, *are* My people," says the Lord GOD.'"
31 "You are My flock, the flock of My pasture;
you *are* men, *and* I *am* your God," says the Lord
GOD.

Judgment on Mount Seir

35 Moreover the word of the LORD came to
me, saying,
2 "Son of man, set your face against Mount
Seir and prophesy against it,
3 "and say to it, 'Thus says the Lord GOD:

"Behold, O Mount Seir, I *am* against you;
I will stretch out My hand against you,
And make you most desolate;
4 I shall lay your cities waste,
And you shall be desolate.
Then you shall know that I *am* the LORD.

5 "Because you have had an ancient hatred,
and have shed *the blood of* the children of Is-
rael by the power of the sword at the time of
their calamity, when their iniquity *came to an*
end,
6 "therefore, *as* I live," says the Lord GOD,
"I will prepare you for blood, and blood shall
pursue you; since you have not hated blood,
therefore blood shall pursue you.
7 "Thus I will make Mount Seir most deso-
late, and cut off from it the one who leaves and
the one who returns.
8 "And I will fill its mountains with the slain;
on your hills and in your valleys and in all your
ravines those who are slain by the sword shall
fall.
9 "I will make you perpetually desolate, and
your cities shall be uninhabited; then you shall
know that I *am* the LORD.
10 "Because you have said, 'These two nations
and these two countries shall be mine, and we
will possess them,' although the LORD was there,

11 "therefore, *as* I live," says the Lord GOD,
"I will do according to your anger and according to the envy which you showed in your hatred against them; and I will make Myself known among them when I judge you.
12 "Then you shall know that I *am* the LORD.
I have heard all your blasphemies which you have spoken against the mountains of Israel, saying, 'They are desolate; they are given to us to consume.'
13 "Thus with your mouth you have boasted against Me and multiplied your words against Me; I have heard *them.*"
14 'Thus says the Lord GOD: "The whole earth will rejoice when I make you desolate.
15 "As you rejoiced because the inheritance of the house of Israel was desolate, so I will do to you; you shall be desolate, O Mount Seir, as well as all of Edom—all of it! Then they shall know that I *am* the LORD."'

Blessing on Israel

36 "And you, son of man, prophesy to the mountains of Israel, and say, 'O mountains of Israel, hear the word of the LORD!
2 'Thus says the Lord GOD: "Because the enemy has said of you, 'Aha! The ancient heights have become our possession,'"'
3 "therefore prophesy, and say, 'Thus says the Lord GOD: "Because they made *you* desolate and swallowed you up on every side, so that you became the possession of the rest of the nations, and you are taken up by the lips of talkers and slandered by the people"—
4 'therefore, O mountains of Israel, hear the word of the Lord GOD! Thus says the Lord GOD to the mountains, the hills, the rivers, the valleys, the desolate wastes, and the cities that have been forsaken, which became plunder and mockery to the rest of the nations all around—
5 'therefore thus says the Lord GOD: "Surely I have spoken in My burning jealousy against the rest of the nations and against all Edom, who gave My land to themselves as a possession, with wholehearted joy *and* spiteful minds, in order to plunder its open country."'
6 "Therefore prophesy concerning the land of Israel, and say to the mountains, the hills, the rivers, and the valleys, 'Thus says the Lord GOD: "Behold, I have spoken in My jealousy and My fury, because you have borne the shame of the nations."
7 'Therefore thus says the Lord GOD: "I have raised My hand in an oath that surely the nations that *are* around you shall bear their own shame.
8 "But you, O mountains of Israel, you shall shoot forth your branches and yield your fruit to My people Israel, for they are about to come.
9 "For indeed I *am* for you, and I will turn to you, and you shall be tilled and sown.
10 "I will multiply men upon you, all the house of Israel, all of it; and the cities shall be inhabited and the ruins rebuilt.
11 "I will multiply upon you man and beast; and they shall increase and bear young; I will make you inhabited as in former times, and do better *for you* than at your beginnings. Then you shall know that I *am* the LORD.
12 "Yes, I will cause men to walk on you, My people Israel; they shall take possession of you, and you shall be their inheritance; no more shall you bereave them *of children.*"
13 'Thus says the Lord GOD: "Because they say to you, 'You devour men and bereave your nation *of children,*'
14 "therefore you shall devour men no more, nor bereave your nation anymore," says the Lord GOD.
15 Nor will I let you hear the taunts of the nations anymore, nor bear the reproach of the peoples anymore, nor shall you cause your nation to stumble anymore," says the Lord GOD.'"

The Renewal of Israel

16 Moreover the word of the LORD came to me, saying:
17 "Son of man, when the house of Israel dwelt in their own land, they defiled it by their own ways and deeds; to Me their way was like the uncleanness of a woman in her customary impurity.
18 "Therefore I poured out My fury on them for the blood they had shed on the land, and for their idols *with which* they had defiled it.
19 "So I scattered them among the nations, and they were dispersed throughout the countries; I judged them according to their ways and their deeds.
20 "When they came to the nations, wherever they went, they profaned My holy name— when they said of them, 'These *are* the people of the LORD, *and* yet they have gone out of His land.'
21 "But I had concern for My holy name, which the house of Israel had profaned among the nations wherever they went.
22 "Therefore say to the house of Israel, 'Thus says the Lord GOD: "I do not do *this* for your sake, O house of Israel, but for My holy name's sake, which you have profaned among the nations wherever you went.
23 "And I will sanctify My great name, which has been profaned among the nations, which you have profaned in their midst; and the nations shall know that I *am* the LORD," says the Lord GOD, "when I am hallowed in you before their eyes.
24 "For I will take you from among the nations, gather you out of all countries, and bring you into your own land.
25 "Then I will sprinkle clean water on you, and you shall be clean; I will cleanse you from all your filthiness and from all your idols.
26 "I will give you a new heart and put a new spirit within you; I will take the heart of stone out of your flesh and give you a heart of flesh.
27 "I will put My Spirit within you and cause you to walk in My statutes, and you will keep My judgments and do *them.*
28 "Then you shall dwell in the land that I gave to your fathers; you shall be My people, and I will be your God.
29 "I will deliver you from all your uncleannesses. I will call for the grain and multiply it, and bring no famine upon you.
30 "And I will multiply the fruit of your trees and the increase of your fields, so that you need never again bear the reproach of famine among the nations.
31 "Then you will remember your evil ways and your deeds that *were* not good; and you will loathe yourselves in your own sight, for your iniquities and your abominations.
32 "Not for your sake do I do *this,*" says the Lord GOD, "let it be known to you. Be ashamed and confounded for your own ways, O house of Israel!"
33 'Thus says the Lord GOD: "On the day that

I cleanse you from all your iniquities, I will
also enable *you* to dwell in the cities, and the
ruins shall be rebuilt.
34 "The desolate land shall be tilled instead
of lying desolate in the sight of all who pass
by.
35 "So they will say, 'This land that was deso-
late has become like the garden of Eden; and
the wasted, desolate, and ruined cities *are now*
fortified *and* inhabited.'
36 "Then the nations which are left all around
you shall know that I, the LORD, have rebuilt
the ruined places *and* planted what was deso-
late. I, the LORD, have spoken *it*, and I will do
it."
37 'Thus says the Lord GOD: "I will also let
the house of Israel inquire of Me to do this for
them: I will increase their men like a flock.
38 "Like a flock *offered as* holy *sacrifices*, like
the flock at Jerusalem on its feast days, so shall
the ruined cities be filled with flocks of men.
Then they shall know that I *am* the LORD." ' "

The Dry Bones Live

37 The hand of the LORD came upon me
and brought me out in the Spirit of the
LORD, and set me down in the midst of the val-
ley; and it *was* full of bones.
2 Then He caused me to pass by them all
around, and behold, *there were* very many in
the open valley; and indeed *they were* very dry.
3 And He said to me, "Son of man, can these
bones live?" So I answered, "O Lord GOD, You
know."
4 Again He said to me, "Prophesy to these
bones, and say to them, 'O dry bones, hear the
word of the LORD!
5 'Thus says the Lord GOD to these bones:
"Surely I will cause breath to enter into you,
and you shall live.
6 "I will put sinews on you and bring flesh
upon you, cover you with skin and put breath
in you; and you shall live. Then you shall know
that I *am* the LORD." ' "
7 So I prophesied as I was commanded; and
as I prophesied, there was a noise, and sud-
denly a rattling; and the bones came together,
bone to bone.
8 Indeed, as I looked, the sinews and the flesh
came upon them, and the skin covered them
over; but *there was* no breath in them.
9 Also He said to me, "Prophesy to the breath,
prophesy, son of man, and say to the breath,
'Thus says the Lord GOD: "Come from the four
winds, O breath, and breathe on these slain,
that they may live." ' "
10 So I prophesied as He commanded me, and
breath came into them, and they lived, and
stood upon their feet, an exceedingly great
army.
11 Then He said to me, "Son of man, these
bones are the whole house of Israel. They in-
deed say, 'Our bones are dry, our hope is lost,
and we ourselves are cut off!'
12 "Therefore prophesy and say to them,
'Thus says the Lord GOD: "Behold, O My peo-
ple, I will open your graves and cause you
to come up from your graves, and bring you
into the land of Israel.
13 "Then you shall know that I *am* the LORD,
when I have opened your graves, O My people,
and brought you up from your graves.
14 "I will put My Spirit in you, and you shall
live, and I will place you in your own land.
Then you shall know that I, the LORD, have
spoken *it* and performed *it*," says the LORD.' "

One Kingdom, One King

15 Again the word of the LORD came to me,
saying,
16 "As for you, son of man, take a stick for
yourself and write on it: 'For Judah and for the
children of Israel, his companions.' Then take
another stick and write on it, 'For Joseph, the
stick of Ephraim, and *for* all the house of Israel,
his companions.'
17 "Then join them one to another for your-
self into one stick, and they will become one
in your hand.
18 "And when the children of your people
speak to you, saying, 'Will you not show us
what you *mean* by these?'—
19 "say to them, 'Thus says the Lord GOD:
"Surely I will take the stick of Joseph, which
is in the hand of Ephraim, and the tribes of
Israel, his companions; and I will join them
with it, with the stick of Judah, and make them
one stick, and they will be one in My hand." '
20 "And the sticks on which you write will be
in your hand before their eyes.
21 "Then say to them, 'Thus says the Lord
GOD: "Surely I will take the children of Israel
from among the nations, wherever they have
gone, and will gather them from every side and
bring them into their own land;
22 "and I will make them one nation in the
land, on the mountains of Israel; and one king
shall be king over them all; they shall no longer
be two nations, nor shall they ever be divided
into two kingdoms again.
23 "They shall not defile themselves anymore
with their idols, nor with their detestable
things, nor with any of their transgressions;
but I will deliver them from all their dwelling
places in which they have sinned, and will
cleanse them. Then they shall be My people,
and I will be their God.
24 "David My servant *shall be* king over
them, and they shall all have one shepherd;
they shall also walk in My judgments and ob-
serve My statutes, and do them.
25 "Then they shall dwell in the land that I
have given to Jacob My servant, where your
fathers dwelt; and they shall dwell there, they,
their children, and their children's children,
forever; and My servant David *shall be* their
prince forever.
26 "Moreover I will make a covenant of peace
with them, and it shall be an everlasting cov-
enant with them; I will establish them and mul-
tiply them, and I will set My sanctuary in their
midst forevermore.
27 "My tabernacle also shall be with them;
indeed I will be their God, and they shall be
My people.
28 "The nations also will know that I, the
LORD, sanctify Israel, when My sanctuary is in
their midst forevermore." ' "

Gog and Allies Attack Israel

38 Now the word of the LORD came to me,
saying,
2 "Son of man, set your face against Gog, of

the land of Magog, the prince of Rosh,[a] Me-
shech, and Tubal, and prophesy against him,
3 "and say, 'Thus says the Lord GOD: "Be-
hold, I *am* against you, O Gog, the prince of
Rosh, Meshech, and Tubal.
4 "I will turn you around, put hooks into your
jaws, and lead you out, with all your army, horses,
and horsemen, all splendidly clothed, a great
company *with* bucklers and shields, all of them
handling swords.
5 "Persia, Ethiopia,[a] and Libya[b] are with
them, all of them *with* shield and helmet;
6 "Gomer and all its troops; the house of To-
garmah *from* the far north and all its troops—
many people *are* with you.
7 "Prepare yourself and be ready, you and
all your companies that are gathered about
you; and be a guard for them.
8 "After many days you will be visited. In
the latter years you will come into the land of
those brought back from the sword *and* gath-
ered from many people on the mountains of
Israel, which had long been desolate; they were
brought out of the nations, and now all of them
dwell safely.
9 "You will ascend, coming like a storm, cov-
ering the land like a cloud, you and all your
troops and many peoples with you."
10 'Thus says the Lord GOD: "On that day it
shall come to pass *that* thoughts will arise in
your mind, and you will make an evil plan:
11 "You will say, 'I will go up against a land of
unwalled villages; I will go to a peaceful people,
who dwell safely, all of them dwelling without
walls, and having neither bars nor gates'—
12 "to take plunder and to take booty, to stretch
out your hand against the waste places *that
are again* inhabited, and against a people gath-
ered from the nations, who have acquired live-
stock and goods, who dwell in the midst of the
land.
13 "Sheba, Dedan, the merchants of Tarshish,
and all their young lions will say to you, 'Have
you come to take plunder? Have you gathered
your army to take booty, to carry away silver and
gold, to take away livestock and goods, to take
great plunder?'"'
14 "Therefore, son of man, prophesy and say
to Gog, 'Thus says the Lord GOD: "On that day
when My people Israel dwell safely, will you
not know *it*?
15 "Then you will come from your place out
of the far north, you and many peoples with
you, all of them riding on horses, a great com-
pany and a mighty army.
16 "You will come up against My people Israel
like a cloud, to cover the land. It will be in the
latter days that I will bring you against My
land, so that the nations may know Me, when I
am hallowed in you, O Gog, before their eyes."
17 'Thus says the Lord GOD: "Are *you* he of
whom I have spoken in former days by My
servants the prophets of Israel, who prophe-
sied for years in those days that I would bring
you against them?

Judgment on Gog

18 "And it will come to pass at the same time,
when Gog comes against the land of Israel,"
says the Lord GOD, "*that* My fury will show in
My face.
19 "For in My jealousy *and* in the fire of My
wrath I have spoken: 'Surely in that day there
shall be a great earthquake in the land of Israel,
20 'so that the fish of the sea, the birds of the
heavens, the beasts of the field, all creeping
things that creep on the earth, and all men who
are on the face of the earth shall shake at My
presence. The mountains shall be thrown down,
the steep places shall fall, and every wall shall
fall to the ground.'
21 "I will call for a sword against Gog through-
out all My mountains," says the Lord GOD.
"Every man's sword will be against his brother.
22 "And I will bring him to judgment with
pestilence and bloodshed; I will rain down on
him, on his troops, and on the many peoples
who *are* with him, flooding rain, great hailstones,
fire, and brimstone.
23 "Thus I will magnify Myself and sanctify
Myself, and I will be known in the eyes of many
nations. Then they shall know that I *am* the
LORD."'

Gog's Armies Destroyed

39 "And you, son of man, prophesy against
Gog, and say, 'Thus says the Lord GOD:
"Behold, I *am* against you, O Gog, the prince
of Rosh,[a] Meshech, and Tubal;
2 "and I will turn you around and lead you
on, bringing you up from the far north, and
bring you against the mountains of Israel.
3 "Then I will knock the bow out of your left
hand, and cause the arrows to fall out of your
right hand.
4 "You shall fall upon the mountains of Israel,
you and all your troops and the peoples who
are with you; I will give you to birds of prey of
every sort and *to* the beasts of the field to be
devoured.
5 "You shall fall on the open field; for I have
spoken," says the Lord GOD.
6 "And I will send fire on Magog and on
those who live in security in the coastlands.
Then they shall know that I *am* the LORD.
7 "So I will make My holy name known in
the midst of My people Israel, and I will not *let
them* profane My holy name anymore. Then
the nations shall know that *I am* the LORD, the
Holy One in Israel.
8 "Surely it is coming, and it shall be done,"
says the Lord GOD. "This *is* the day of which I
have spoken.
9 "Then those who dwell in the cities of Is-
rael will go out and set on fire and burn the
weapons, both the shields and bucklers, the
bows and arrows, the javelins and spears; and
they will make fires with them for seven years.
10 "They will not take wood from the field
nor cut down *any* from the forests, because they
will make fires with the weapons; and they will
plunder those who plundered them, and pillage
those who pillaged them," says the Lord GOD.

The Burial of Gog

11 "It will come to pass in that day *that* I will
give Gog a burial place there in Israel, the val-
ley of those who pass by east of the sea; and it
will obstruct travelers, because there they will
bury Gog and all his multitude. Therefore they
will call *it* the Valley of Hamon Gog.[a]
12 "For seven months the house of Israel will
be burying them, in order to cleanse the land.
13 "Indeed all the people of the land will be

38:2 [a]Targum, Vulgate, and Aquila read *chief prince of* (also verse 3). **38:5** [a]Hebrew *Cush* [b]Hebrew *Put*
39:1 [a]Targum, Vulgate and Aquila read *chief prince of.* **39:11** [a]Literally *The Multitude of Gog*

burying, and they will gain renown for it on
the day that I am glorified," says the Lord GOD.
14 "They will set apart men regularly employed,
with the help of a search party,[a] to pass through
the land and bury those bodies remaining on
the ground, in order to cleanse it. At the end of
seven months they will make a search.
15 "The search party will pass through the
land; and *when anyone* sees a man's bone, he
shall set up a marker by it, till the buriers have
buried it in the Valley of Hamon Gog.
16 "*The* name of *the* city *will* also *be* Hamo-
nah. Thus they shall cleanse the land."'

A Triumphant Festival

17 "And as for you, son of man, thus says the
Lord GOD, 'Speak to every sort of bird and to
every beast of the field:

"Assemble yourselves and come;
Gather together from all sides to My
sacrificial meal
Which I am sacrificing for you,
A great sacrificial meal on the mountains
of Israel,
That you may eat flesh and drink blood.
18 You shall eat the flesh of the mighty,
Drink the blood of the princes of the
earth,
Of rams and lambs,
Of goats and bulls,
All of them fatlings of Bashan.
19 You shall eat fat till you are full,
And drink blood till you are drunk,
At My sacrificial meal
Which I am sacrificing for you.
20 You shall be filled at My table
With horses and riders,
With mighty men
And with all the men of war," says the
Lord GOD.

Israel Restored to the Land

21 "I will set My glory among the nations; all
the nations shall see My judgment which I have
executed, and My hand which I have laid on
them.
22 "So the house of Israel shall know that I
am the LORD their God from that day forward.
23 "The Gentiles shall know that the house
of Israel went into captivity for their iniquity;
because they were unfaithful to Me, therefore
I hid My face from them. I gave them into the
hand of their enemies, and they all fell by the
sword.
24 "According to their uncleanness and ac-
cording to their transgressions I have dealt
with them, and hidden My face from them."'
25 "Therefore thus says the Lord GOD: 'Now
I will bring back the captives of Jacob, and have
mercy on the whole house of Israel; and I will
be jealous for My holy name—
26 'after they have borne their shame, and all
their unfaithfulness in which they were unfaith-
ful to Me, when they dwelt safely in their *own*
land and no one made *them* afraid.
27 'When I have brought them back from the
peoples and gathered them out of their enemies'
lands, and I am hallowed in them in the sight
of many nations,
28 'then they shall know that I *am* the LORD
their God, who sent them into captivity among
the nations, but also brought them back to their
land, and left none of them captive any longer.
29 'And I will not hide My face from them
anymore; for I shall have poured out My Spirit
on the house of Israel,' says the Lord GOD."

A New City, a New Temple

40 In the twenty-fifth year of our captivity,
at the beginning of the year, on the tenth
day of the month, in the fourteenth year after
the city was captured, on the very same day
the hand of the LORD was upon me; and He
took me there.
2 In the visions of God He took me into the
land of Israel and set me on a very high moun-
tain; on it toward the south *was* something like
the structure of a city.
3 He took me there, and behold, *there was* a
man whose appearance *was* like the appear-
ance of bronze. He had a line of flax and a
measuring rod in his hand, and he stood in the
gateway.
4 And the man said to me, "Son of man, look
with your eyes and hear with your ears, and
fix your mind on everything I show you; for
you *were* brought here so that I might show
them to you. Declare to the house of Israel
everything you see."
5 Now there was a wall all around the out-
side of the temple.[a] In the man's hand was a
measuring rod six cubits *long, each being a*
cubit and a handbreadth; and he measured
the width of the wall structure, one rod; and
the height, one rod.

The Eastern Gateway of the Temple

6 Then he went to the gateway which faced
east; and he went up its stairs and measured
the threshold of the gateway, *which was* one
rod wide, and the other threshold *was* one rod
wide.
7 Each gate chamber *was* one rod long and
one rod wide; between the gate chambers *was
a space of* five cubits; and the threshold of the
gateway by the vestibule of the inside gate *was*
one rod.
8 He also measured the vestibule of the inside
gate, one rod.
9 Then he measured the vestibule of the
gateway, eight cubits; and the gateposts, two
cubits. The vestibule of the gate *was* on the in-
side.
10 In the eastern gateway *were* three gate
chambers on one side and three on the other;
the three *were* all the same size; also the gate-
posts were of the same size on this side and that
side.
11 He measured the width of the entrance to
the gateway, ten cubits; *and* the length of the
gate, thirteen cubits.
12 *There was* a space in front of the gate
chambers, one cubit *on this side* and one cubit
on that side; the gate chambers *were* six cubits
on this side and six cubits on that side.
13 Then he measured the gateway from the roof
of *one* gate chamber to the roof of the other;
the width *was* twenty-five cubits, as door faces
door.
14 He measured the gateposts, sixty cubits
high, and the court all around the gateway *ex-
tended* to the gatepost.
15 *From* the front of the entrance gate to the

39:14 [a]Literally *those who pass through* **40:5** [a]Literally *house,* and so elsewhere in this book

front of the vestibule of the inner gate *was* fifty cubits.
16 *There were* beveled window *frames* in the gate chambers and in their intervening archways on the inside of the gateway all around, and likewise in the vestibules. *There were* windows all around on the inside. And on each gatepost *were* palm trees.

The Outer Court

17 Then he brought me into the outer court; and *there were* chambers and a pavement made all around the court; thirty chambers faced the pavement.
18 The pavement was by the side of the gateways, corresponding to the length of the gateways; *this was* the lower pavement.
19 Then he measured the width from the front of the lower gateway to the front of the inner court exterior, one hundred cubits toward the east and the north.

The Northern Gateway

20 On the outer court was also a gateway facing north, and he measured its length and its width.
21 Its gate chambers, three on this side and three on that side, its gateposts and its archways, had the same measurements as the first gate; its length *was* fifty cubits and its width twenty-five cubits.
22 Its windows and those of its archways, and also its palm trees, *had* the same measurements as the gateway facing east; it was ascended by seven steps, and its archway *was* in front of it.
23 A gate of the inner court was opposite the northern gateway, just as the eastern *gateway;* and he measured from gateway to gateway, one hundred cubits.

The Southern Gateway

24 After that he brought me toward the south, and there a gateway was facing south; and he measured its gateposts and archways according to these same measurements.
25 *There were* windows in it and in its archways all around like those windows; its length *was* fifty cubits and its width twenty-five cubits.
26 Seven steps led up to it, and its archway *was* in front of them; and it had palm trees on its gateposts, one on this side and one on that side.
27 *There was* also a gateway on the inner court, facing south; and he measured from gateway to gateway toward the south, one hundred cubits.

Gateways of the Inner Court

28 Then he brought me to the inner court through the southern gateway; he measured the southern gateway according to these same measurements.
29 Also its gate chambers, its gateposts, and its archways *were* according to these same measurements; *there were* windows in it and in its archways all around; *it was* fifty cubits long and twenty-five cubits wide.
30 *There were* archways all around, twenty-five cubits long and five cubits wide.
31 Its archways faced the outer court, palm trees *were* on its gateposts, and going up to it *were* eight steps.
32 And he brought me into the inner court facing east; he measured the gateway according to these same measurements.
33 Also its gate chambers, its gateposts, and its archways *were* according to these same measurements; and *there were* windows in it and in its archways all around; *it was* fifty cubits long and twenty-five cubits wide.
34 Its archways faced the outer court, and palm trees *were* on its gateposts on this side and on that side; and going up to it *were* eight steps.
35 Then he brought me to the north gateway and measured *it* according to these same measurements—
36 also its gate chambers, its gateposts, and its archways. It had windows all around; its length *was* fifty cubits and its width twenty-five cubits.
37 Its gateposts faced the outer court, palm trees *were* on its gateposts on this side and on that side, and going up to it *were* eight steps.

Where Sacrifices Were Prepared

38 *There was* a chamber and its entrance by the gateposts of the gateway, where they washed the burnt offering.
39 In the vestibule of the gateway *were* two tables on this side and two tables on that side, on which to slay the burnt offering, the sin offering, and the trespass offering.
40 At the outer side of the *vestibule,* as one goes up to the entrance of the northern gateway, *were* two tables; and on the other side of the vestibule of the gateway *were* two tables.
41 Four tables *were* on this side and four tables on that side, by the side of the gateway, eight tables on which they slaughtered *the sacrifices.*
42 *There were* also four tables of hewn stone for the burnt offering, one cubit and a half long, one cubit and a half wide, and one cubit high; on these they laid the instruments with which they slaughtered the burnt offering and the sacrifice.
43 Inside *were* hooks, a handbreadth wide, fastened all around; and the flesh of the sacrifices *was* on the tables.

Chambers for Singers and Priests

44 Outside the inner gate *were* the chambers for the singers in the inner court, one facing south at the side of the northern gateway, and the other facing north at the side of the southern gateway.
45 Then he said to me, "This chamber which faces south *is* for the priests who have charge of the temple.
46 "The chamber which faces north *is* for the priests who have charge of the altar; these *are* the sons of Zadok, from the sons of Levi, who come near the LORD to minister to Him."

Dimensions of the Inner Court and Vestibule

47 And he measured the court, one hundred cubits long and one hundred cubits wide, foursquare. The altar *was* in front of the temple.
48 Then he brought me to the vestibule of the temple and measured the doorposts of the vestibule, five cubits on this side and five cubits on that side; and the width of the gateway was three cubits on this side and three cubits on that side.
49 The length of the vestibule *was* twenty cubits, and the width eleven cubits; and by the steps which led up to it *there were* pillars by the doorposts, one on this side and another on that side.

Dimensions of the Sanctuary

41 Then he brought me into the sanctuary[a]
and measured the doorposts, six cubits
wide on one side and six cubits wide on the
other side—the width of the tabernacle.
2 The width of the entryway *was* ten cubits,
and the side walls of the entrance *were* five
cubits on this side and five cubits on the other
side; and he measured its length, forty cubits,
and its width, twenty cubits.
3 Also he went inside and measured the
doorposts, two cubits; and the entrance, six cu-
bits *high;* and the width of the entrance, seven
cubits.
4 He measured the length, twenty cubits; and
the width, twenty cubits, beyond the sanctu-
ary; and he said to me, "This *is* the Most Holy
Place."

The Side Chambers on the Wall

5 Next, he measured the wall of the temple,
six cubits. The width of each side chamber all
around the temple *was* four cubits on every
side.
6 The side chambers *were* in three stories,
one above the other, thirty chambers in each
story; they rested on ledges which *were* for the
side chambers all around, that they might be
supported, but not fastened to the wall of the
temple.
7 As one went up from story to story, the side
chambers became wider all around, because
their supporting ledges in the wall of the tem-
ple ascended like steps; therefore the width of
the structure increased as one went up *from* the
lowest *story* to the highest by way of the mid-
dle one.
8 I also saw an elevation all around the tem-
ple; it was the foundation of the side chambers,
a full rod, *that is,* six cubits *high.*
9 The thickness of the outer wall of the side
chambers *was* five cubits, and so also the re-
maining terrace by the place of the side cham-
bers of the temple.
10 And between *it and* the *wall* chambers was
a width of twenty cubits all around the temple
on every side.
11 The doors of the side chambers opened
on the terrace, one door toward the north and
another toward the south; and the width of the
terrace *was* five cubits all around.

The Building at the Western End

12 The building that faced the separating court-
yard at its western end *was* seventy cubits
wide; the wall of the building *was* five cubits
thick all around, and its length ninety cubits.

Dimensions and Design of the Temple Area

13 So he measured the temple, one hundred
cubits long; and the separating courtyard with
the building and its walls *was* one hundred
cubits long;
14 also the width of the eastern face of the tem-
ple, including the separating courtyard, *was* one
hundred cubits.
15 He measured the length of the building be-
hind it, facing the separating courtyard, with
its galleries on the one side and on the other
side, one hundred cubits, as well as the inner
temple and the porches of the court,
16 their doorposts and the beveled window
frames. And the galleries all around their three
stories opposite the threshold were paneled
with wood from the ground to the windows—
the windows were covered—
17 from the space above the door, even to the
inner room,[a] as well as outside, and on every
wall all around, inside and outside, by measure.
18 And *it was* made with cherubim and palm
trees, a palm tree between cherub and cherub.
Each cherub had two faces,
19 so that the face of a man *was* toward a palm
tree on one side, and the face of a young lion
toward a palm tree on the other side; thus *it*
was made throughout the temple all around.
20 From the floor to the space above the door,
and on the wall of the sanctuary, cherubim and
palm trees *were* carved.
21 The doorposts of the temple *were* square,
as was the front of the sanctuary; their appear-
ance was similar.
22 The altar *was* of wood, three cubits high,
and its length two cubits. Its corners, its length,
and its sides *were* of wood; and he said to me,
"This *is* the table that *is* before the LORD."
23 The temple and the sanctuary had two doors.
24 The doors had two panels *apiece,* two fold-
ing panels: two *panels* for one door and two
panels for the other *door.*
25 Cherubim and palm trees *were* carved on
the doors of the temple just as they *were* carved
on the walls. A wooden canopy *was* on the front
of the vestibule outside.
26 *There were* beveled window *frames* and
palm trees on one side and on the other, on the
sides of the vestibule—also on the side cham-
bers of the temple and on the canopies.

The Chambers for the Priests

42 Then he brought me out into the outer
court, by the way toward the north; and
he brought me into the chamber which *was*
opposite the separating courtyard, and which
was opposite the building toward the north.
2 Facing the length, *which was* one hundred
cubits (the width was fifty cubits), was the north
door.
3 Opposite the inner court of twenty *cubits,*
and opposite the pavement of the outer court,
was gallery against gallery in three *stories.*
4 In front of the chambers, toward the in-
side, *was* a walk ten cubits wide, at a distance
of one cubit; and their doors faced north.
5 Now the upper chambers *were* shorter, be-
cause the galleries took away *space* from them
more than from the lower and middle stories
of the building.
6 For they *were* in three *stories* and did not
have pillars like the pillars of the courts; there-
fore *the upper level* was shortened more than
the lower and middle levels from the ground
up.
7 And a wall which *was* outside ran parallel
to the chambers, at the front of the chambers,
toward the outer court; its length *was* fifty cu-
bits.
8 The length of the chambers toward the outer
court *was* fifty cubits, whereas that facing the
temple *was* one hundred cubits.
9 At the lower chambers *was* the entrance
on the east side, as one goes into them from the
outer court.

41:1 [a]Hebrew *heykal,* here the main room of the temple, sometimes called the *holy place* (compare Exodus 26:33)
41:17 [a]Literally *house,* here *the Most Holy Place*

10 Also *there were* chambers in the thickness
of the wall of the court toward the east, oppo-
site the separating courtyard and opposite the
building.
11 *There was* a walk in front of them also, and
their appearance *was* like the chambers which
were toward the north; they *were* as long and
as wide as the others, and all their exits and
entrances *were* according to plan.
12 And corresponding to the doors of the
chambers that *were* facing south, as one enters
them, *there was* a door in front of the walk,
the way directly in front of the wall toward the
east.
13 Then he said to me, "The north chambers
and the south chambers, which *are* opposite
the separating courtyard, *are* the holy cham-
bers where the priests who approach the LORD
shall eat the most holy offerings. There they
shall lay the most holy offerings—the grain
offering, the sin offering, and the trespass of-
fering—for the place *is* holy.
14 "When the priests enter them, they shall
not go out of the holy *chamber* into the outer
court; but there they shall leave their garments
in which they minister, for they *are* holy. They
shall put on other garments; then they may
approach *that* which *is* for the people."

Outer Dimensions of the Temple

15 Now when he had finished measuring the
inner temple, he brought me out through the
gateway that faces toward the east, and mea-
sured it all around.
16 He measured the east side with the measur-
ing rod,[a] five hundred rods by the measuring
rod all around.
17 He measured the north side, five hundred
rods by the measuring rod all around.
18 He measured the south side, five hundred
rods by the measuring rod.
19 He came around to the west side *and* mea-
sured five hundred rods by the measuring rod.
20 He measured it on the four sides; it had a
wall all around, five hundred *cubits* long and
five hundred wide, to separate the holy areas
from the common.

The Temple, the LORD's Dwelling Place

43 Afterward he brought me to the gate, the
gate that faces toward the east.
2 And behold, the glory of the God of Israel
came from the way of the east. His voice *was*
like the sound of many waters; and the earth
shone with His glory.
3 *It was* like the appearance of the vision
which I saw—like the vision which I saw when
I[a] came to destroy the city. The visions *were*
like the vision which I saw by the River Che-
bar; and I fell on my face.
4 And the glory of the LORD came into the
temple by way of the gate which faces toward
the east.
5 The Spirit lifted me up and brought me
into the inner court; and behold, the glory of
the LORD filled the temple.
6 Then I heard *Him* speaking to me from the
temple, while a man stood beside me.
7 And He said to me, "Son of man, *this is*
the place of My throne and the place of the
soles of My feet, where I will dwell in the midst
of the children of Israel forever. No more shall
the house of Israel defile My holy name, they
nor their kings, by their harlotry or with the
carcasses of their kings on their high places.
8 "When they set their threshold by My
threshold, and their doorpost by My doorpost,
with a wall between them and Me, they defiled
My holy name by the abominations which they
committed; therefore I have consumed them in
My anger.
9 'Now let them put their harlotry and the
carcasses of their kings far away from Me, and
I will dwell in their midst forever.
10 "Son of man, describe the temple to the
house of Israel, that they may be ashamed of
their iniquities; and let them measure the pat-
tern.
11 "And if they are ashamed of all that they
have done, make known to them the design of
the temple and its arrangement, its exits and
its entrances, its entire design and all its ordi-
nances, all its forms and all its laws. Write *it*
down in their sight, so that they may keep its
whole design and all its ordinances, and per-
form them.
12 "This *is* the law of the temple: The whole
area surrounding the mountaintop *is* most
holy. Behold, this *is* the law of the temple.

Dimensions of the Altar

13 "These are the measurements of the altar
in cubits (the cubit *is* one cubit and a hand-
breadth): the base one cubit high and one cubit
wide, with a rim all around its edge of one
span. This *is* the height of the altar:
14 "from the base on the ground to the lower
ledge, two cubits; the width of the ledge, one
cubit; from the smaller ledge to the larger
ledge, four cubits; and the width of the ledge,
one cubit.
15 "The altar hearth *is* four cubits high, with
four horns extending upward from the hearth.
16 "The altar hearth *is* twelve *cubits* long,
twelve wide, square at its four corners;
17 "the ledge, fourteen *cubits* long and four-
teen wide on its four sides, with a rim of half a
cubit around it; its base, one cubit all around;
and its steps face toward the east."

Consecrating the Altar

18 And He said to me, "Son of man, thus says
the Lord GOD: 'These *are* the ordinances for
the altar on the day when it is made, for sacri-
ficing burnt offerings on it, and for sprinkling
blood on it.
19 'You shall give a young bull for a sin offer-
ing to the priests, the Levites, who are of the
seed of Zadok, who approach Me to minister
to Me,' says the Lord GOD.
20 'You shall take some of its blood and put
it on the four horns of the altar, on the four
corners of the ledge, and on the rim around it;
thus you shall cleanse it and make atonement
for it.
21 'Then you shall also take the bull of the sin
offering, and burn it in the appointed place of
the temple, outside the sanctuary.
22 'On the second day you shall offer a kid of
the goats without blemish for a sin offering;
and they shall cleanse the altar, as they
cleansed *it* with the bull.
23 'When you have finished cleansing *it*, you
shall offer a young bull without blemish, and
a ram from the flock without blemish.
24 'When you offer them before the LORD, the

42:16 [a]Compare 40:5 **43:3** [a]Some Hebrew manuscripts and Vulgate read *He*.

priests shall throw salt on them, and they will offer them up *as* a burnt offering to the LORD.

25 'Every day for seven days you shall prepare a goat *for* a sin offering; they shall also prepare a young bull and a ram from the flock, both without blemish.

26 'Seven days they shall make atonement for the altar and purify it, and so consecrate *it*.

27 'When these days are over it shall be, on the eighth day and thereafter, that the priests shall offer your burnt offerings and your peace offerings on the altar; and I will accept you,' says the Lord GOD."

The East Gate and the Prince

44 Then He brought me back to the outer gate of the sanctuary which faces toward the east, but it *was* shut.

2 And the LORD said to me, "This gate shall be shut; it shall not be opened, and no man shall enter by it, because the LORD God of Israel has entered by it; therefore it shall be shut.

3 "*As for* the prince, *because* he *is* the prince, he may sit in it to eat bread before the LORD; he shall enter by way of the vestibule of the gateway, and go out the same way."

Those Admitted to the Temple

4 Also He brought me by way of the north gate to the front of the temple; so I looked, and behold, the glory of the LORD filled the house of the LORD; and I fell on my face.

5 And the LORD said to me, "Son of man, mark well, see with your eyes and hear with your ears, all that I say to you concerning all the ordinances of the house of the LORD and all its laws. Mark well who may enter the house and all who go out from the sanctuary.

6 "Now say to the rebellious, to the house of Israel, 'Thus says the Lord GOD: "O house of Israel, let Us have no more of all your abominations.

7 "When you brought in foreigners, uncircumcised in heart and uncircumcised in flesh, to be in My sanctuary to defile it—My house—and when you offered My food, the fat and the blood, then they broke My covenant because of all your abominations.

8 "And you have not kept charge of My holy things, but you have set *others* to keep charge of My sanctuary for you."

9 'Thus says the Lord GOD: "No foreigner, uncircumcised in heart or uncircumcised in flesh, shall enter My sanctuary, including any foreigner who *is* among the children of Israel.

Laws Governing Priests

10 "And the Levites who went far from Me, when Israel went astray, who strayed away from Me after their idols, they shall bear their iniquity.

11 "Yet they shall be ministers in My sanctuary, *as* gatekeepers of the house and ministers of the house; they shall slay the burnt offering and the sacrifice for the people, and they shall stand before them to minister to them.

12 "Because they ministered to them before their idols and caused the house of Israel to fall into iniquity, therefore I have raised My hand in an oath against them," says the Lord GOD, "that they shall bear their iniquity.

13 "And they shall not come near Me to minister to Me as priest, nor come near any of My holy things, nor into the Most Holy *Place;* but they shall bear their shame and their abominations which they have committed.

14 "Nevertheless I will make them keep charge of the temple, for all its work, and for all that has to be done in it.

15 "But the priests, the Levites, the sons of Zadok, who kept charge of My sanctuary when the children of Israel went astray from Me, they shall come near Me to minister to Me; and they shall stand before Me to offer to Me the fat and the blood," says the Lord GOD.

16 "They shall enter My sanctuary, and they shall come near My table to minister to Me, and they shall keep My charge.

17 "And it shall be, whenever they enter the gates of the inner court, that they shall put on linen garments; no wool shall come upon them while they minister within the gates of the inner court or within the house.

18 "They shall have linen turbans on their heads and linen trousers on their bodies; they shall not clothe themselves with *anything that causes* sweat.

19 "When they go out to the outer court, to the outer court to the people, they shall take off their garments in which they have ministered, leave them in the holy chambers, and put on other garments; and in their holy garments they shall not sanctify the people.

20 "They shall neither shave their heads nor let their hair grow long, but they shall keep their hair well trimmed.

21 "No priest shall drink wine when he enters the inner court.

22 "They shall not take as wife a widow or a divorced woman, but take virgins of the descendants of the house of Israel, or widows of priests.

23 "And they shall teach My people *the difference* between the holy and the unholy, and cause them to discern between the unclean and the clean.

24 "In controversy they shall stand as judges, *and* judge it according to My judgments. They shall keep My laws and My statutes in all My appointed meetings, and they shall hallow My Sabbaths.

25 "They shall not defile *themselves* by coming near a dead person. Only for father or mother, for son or daughter, for brother or unmarried sister may they defile themselves.

26 "After he is cleansed, they shall count seven days for him.

27 "And on the day that he goes to the sanctuary to minister in the sanctuary, he must offer his sin offering in the inner court," says the Lord GOD.

28 "It shall be, in regard to their inheritance, *that* I *am* their inheritance. You shall give them no possession in Israel, for I *am* their possession.

29 "They shall eat the grain offering, the sin offering, and the trespass offering; every dedicated thing in Israel shall be theirs.

30 "The best of all firstfruits of any kind, and every sacrifice of any kind from all your sacrifices, shall be the priest's; also you shall give to the priest the first of your ground meal, to cause a blessing to rest on your house.

31 "The priests shall not eat anything, bird or beast, that died naturally or was torn *by wild beasts*.

The Holy District

45 "Moreover, when you divide the land by
lot into inheritance, you shall set apart
a district for the LORD, a holy section of the
land; its length *shall be* twenty-five thousand
cubits, and the width ten thousand. It *shall be*
holy throughout its territory all around.
2 "Of this there shall be a square plot for the
sanctuary, five hundred by five hundred *rods*,
with fifty cubits around it for an open space.
3 "So this is the district you shall measure:
twenty-five thousand *cubits* long and ten thou-
sand wide; in it shall be the sanctuary, the Most
Holy *Place*.
4 "It shall be a holy *section* of the land, be-
longing to the priests, the ministers of the sanc-
tuary, who come near to minister to the LORD;
it shall be a place for their houses and a holy
place for the sanctuary.
5 "*An area* twenty-five thousand *cubits* long
and ten thousand wide shall belong to the Le-
vites, the ministers of the temple; they shall
have twenty chambers as a possession.[a]

Properties of the City and the Prince

6 "You shall appoint as the property of the
city *an area* five thousand *cubits* wide and
twenty-five thousand long, adjacent to the dis-
trict of the holy *section*; it shall belong to the
whole house of Israel.
7 "The prince shall have *a section* on one side
and the other of the holy district and the city's
property; and bordering on the holy district
and the city's property, extending westward on
the west side and eastward on the east side,
the length *shall be* side by side with one of the
tribal portions, from the west border to the east
border.
8 "The land shall be his possession in Israel;
and My princes shall no more oppress My peo-
ple, but they shall give *the rest of* the land to
the house of Israel, according to their tribes."

Laws Governing the Prince

9 'Thus says the Lord GOD: "Enough, O princes
of Israel! Remove violence and plundering, ex-
ecute justice and righteousness, and stop dis-
possessing My people," says the Lord GOD.
10 "You shall have honest scales, an honest
ephah, and an honest bath.
11 "The ephah and the bath shall be of the
same measure, so that the bath contains one-
tenth of a homer, and the ephah one-tenth of a
homer; their measure shall be according to the
homer.
12 "The shekel *shall be* twenty gerahs; twenty
shekels, twenty-five shekels, *and* fifteen shek-
els shall be your mina.
13 "This *is* the offering which you shall offer:
you shall give one-sixth of an ephah from a
homer of wheat, and one-sixth of an ephah from
a homer of barley.
14 "The ordinance concerning oil, the bath of
oil, *is* one-tenth of a bath from a kor. *A kor is*
a homer or ten baths, for ten baths *are* a homer.
15 "And one lamb shall be given from a flock
of two hundred, from the rich pastures of Is-
rael. These shall be for grain offerings, burnt
offerings, and peace offerings, to make atone-
ment for them," says the Lord GOD.
16 "All the people of the land shall give this
offering for the prince in Israel.
17 "Then it shall be the prince's part *to give*
burnt offerings, grain offerings, and drink of-
ferings, at the feasts, the New Moons, the Sab-
baths, and at all the appointed seasons of the
house of Israel. He shall prepare the sin offer-
ing, the grain offering, the burnt offering, and
the peace offerings to make atonement for the
house of Israel."

Keeping the Feasts

18 'Thus says the Lord GOD: "In the first *month*,
on the first *day* of the month, you shall take a
young bull without blemish and cleanse the
sanctuary.
19 "The priest shall take some of the blood of
the sin offering and put *it* on the doorposts of
the temple, on the four corners of the ledge
of the altar, and on the gateposts of the gate of
the inner court.
20 "And so you shall do on the seventh *day* of
the month for everyone who has sinned unin-
tentionally or in ignorance. Thus you shall
make atonement for the temple.
21 "In the first *month*, on the fourteenth day
of the month, you shall observe the Passover,
a feast of seven days; unleavened bread shall
be eaten.
22 "And on that day the prince shall prepare
for himself and for all the people of the land a
bull *for* a sin offering.
23 "On the seven days of the feast he shall pre-
pare a burnt offering to the LORD, seven bulls
and seven rams without blemish, daily for
seven days, and a kid of the goats daily *for* a
sin offering.
24 "And he shall prepare a grain offering of
one ephah for each bull and one ephah for each
ram, together with a hin of oil for each ephah.
25 "In the seventh *month*, on the fifteenth day
of the month, at the feast, he shall do likewise
for seven days, according to the sin offering,
the burnt offering, the grain offering, and the
oil."

The Manner of Worship

46 'Thus says the Lord GOD: "The gateway
of the inner court that faces toward the
east shall be shut the six working days; but on
the Sabbath it shall be opened, and on the day
of the New Moon it shall be opened.
2 "The prince shall enter by way of the vesti-
bule of the gateway from the outside, and stand
by the gatepost. The priests shall prepare his
burnt offering and his peace offerings. He shall
worship at the threshold of the gate. Then he
shall go out, but the gate shall not be shut until
evening.
3 "Likewise the people of the land shall wor-
ship at the entrance to this gateway before the
LORD on the Sabbaths and the New Moons.
4 "The burnt offering that the prince offers
to the LORD on the Sabbath day *shall be* six
lambs without blemish, and a ram without blem-
ish;
5 "and the grain offering *shall be one* ephah
for a ram, and the grain offering for the lambs,
as much as he wants to give, as well as a hin
of oil with every ephah.
6 "On the day of the New Moon *it shall be* a
young bull without blemish, six lambs, and a
ram; they shall be without blemish.
7 "He shall prepare a grain offering of an
ephah for a bull, an ephah for a ram, as much

45:5 [a]Following Masoretic Text, Targum, and Vulgate; Septuagint reads *a possession, cities of dwelling*.

as he wants to give for the lambs, and a hin of
oil with every ephah.
8 "When the prince enters, he shall go in by
way of the vestibule of the gateway, and go out
the same way.
9 "But when the people of the land come be-
fore the LORD on the appointed feast days,
whoever enters by way of the north gate to
worship shall go out by way of the south gate;
and whoever enters by way of the south gate
shall go out by way of the north gate. He shall
not return by way of the gate through which
he came, but shall go out through the opposite
gate.
10 "The prince shall then be in their midst.
When they go in, he shall go in; and when they
go out, he shall go out.
11 "At the festivals and the appointed feast
days the grain offering shall be an ephah for a
bull, an ephah for a ram, as much as he wants
to give for the lambs, and a hin of oil with
every ephah.
12 "Now when the prince makes a voluntary
burnt offering or voluntary peace offering to
the LORD, the gate that faces toward the east
shall then be opened for him; and he shall pre-
pare his burnt offering and his peace offerings
as he did on the Sabbath day. Then he shall go
out, and after he goes out the gate shall be shut.
13 "You shall daily make a burnt offering to
the LORD *of* a lamb of the first year without blem-
ish; you shall prepare it every morning.
14 "And you shall prepare a grain offering
with it every morning, a sixth of an ephah, and
a third of a hin of oil to moisten the fine flour.
This grain offering is a perpetual ordinance, to
be made regularly to the LORD.
15 "Thus they shall prepare the lamb, the grain
offering, and the oil, *as* a regular burnt offering
every morning."

The Prince and Inheritance Laws

16 'Thus says the Lord GOD: "If the prince gives
a gift *of some* of his inheritance to any of his
sons, it shall belong to his sons; it is their pos-
session by inheritance.
17 "But if he gives a gift of some of his inheri-
tance to one of his servants, it shall be his until
the year of liberty, after which it shall return
to the prince. But his inheritance shall belong
to his sons; it shall become theirs.
18 "Moreover the prince shall not take any of
the people's inheritance by evicting them from
their property; he shall provide an inheritance
for his sons from his own property, so that
none of My people may be scattered from his
property." ' "

How the Offerings Were Prepared

19 Now he brought me through the entrance,
which *was* at the side of the gate, into the holy
chambers of the priests which face toward the
north; and there a place *was* situated at their
extreme western end.
20 And he said to me, "This *is* the place where
the priests shall boil the trespass offering and
the sin offering, *and* where they shall bake the
grain offering, so that they do not bring *them*
out into the outer court to sanctify the people."
21 Then he brought me out into the outer
court and caused me to pass by the four cor-
ners of the court; and in fact, in every corner
of the court *there was another* court.
22 In the four corners of the court *were* en-
closed courts, forty *cubits* long and thirty
wide; all four corners *were* the same size.
23 *There was* a row *of building stones* all around
in them, all around the four of them; and cook-
ing hearths were made under the rows of
stones all around.
24 And he said to me, "These *are* the kitchens
where the ministers of the temple shall boil the
sacrifices of the people."

The Healing Waters and Trees

47 Then he brought me back to the door of
the temple; and there was water, flowing
from under the threshold of the temple toward
the east, for the front of the temple faced east;
the water was flowing from under the right side
of the temple, south of the altar.
2 He brought me out by way of the north
gate, and led me around on the outside to the
outer gateway that faces east; and there was
water, running out on the right side.
3 And when the man went out to the east
with the line in his hand, he measured one thou-
sand cubits, and he brought me through the
waters; the water *came up to my* ankles.
4 Again he measured one thousand and
brought me through the waters; the water
came up to my knees. Again he measured one
thousand and brought me through; the water
came up to my waist.
5 Again he measured one thousand, *and it
was* a river that I could not cross; for the water
was too deep, water in which one must swim,
a river that could not be crossed.
6 He said to me, "Son of man, have you seen
this?" Then he brought me and returned me to
the bank of the river.
7 When I returned, there, along the bank of
the river, *were* very many trees on one side and
the other.
8 Then he said to me: "This water flows to-
ward the eastern region, goes down into the
valley, and enters the sea. *When it* reaches the
sea, *its* waters are healed.
9 "And it shall be *that* every living thing that
moves, wherever the rivers go, will live. There
will be a very great multitude of fish, because
these waters go there; for they will be healed, and
everything will live wherever the river goes.
10 "It shall be *that* fishermen will stand by it
from En Gedi to En Eglaim; they will be *places*
for spreading their nets. Their fish will be of
the same kinds as the fish of the Great Sea, ex-
ceedingly many.
11 "But its swamps and marshes will not be
healed; they will be given over to salt.
12 "Along the bank of the river, on this side
and that, will grow all *kinds of* trees used for
food; their leaves will not wither, and their fruit
will not fail. They will bear fruit every month,
because their water flows from the sanctuary.
Their fruit will be for food, and their leaves for
medicine."

Borders of the Land

13 Thus says the Lord GOD: "These *are* the bor-
ders by which you shall divide the land as an
inheritance among the twelve tribes of Israel.
Joseph *shall have two* portions.
14 "You shall inherit it equally with one an-
other; for I raised My hand in an oath to give
it to your fathers, and this land shall fall to you
as your inheritance.
15 "This *shall be* the border of the land on the

north: from the Great Sea, *by* the road to Heth-
lon, as one goes to Zedad,
16 "Hamath, Berothah, Sibraim (which *is* be-
tween the border of Damascus and the border
of Hamath), to Hazar Hatticon (which *is* on the
border of Hauran).
17 "Thus the boundary shall be from the Sea
to Hazar Enan, the border of Damascus; and
as for the north, northward, it is the border of
Hamath. *This is* the north side.
18 "On the east side you shall mark out the
border from between Hauran and Damascus,
and between Gilead and the land of Israel, along
the Jordan, and along the eastern side of the
sea. *This is* the east side.
19 "The south side, toward the South,[a] *shall be*
from Tamar to the waters of Meribah by Ka-
desh, along the brook to the Great Sea. *This is*
the south side, toward the South.
20 "The west side *shall be* the Great Sea, from
the *southern* boundary until one comes to a point
opposite Hamath. This *is* the west side.
21 "Thus you shall divide this land among your-
selves according to the tribes of Israel.
22 "It shall be that you will divide it by lot
as an inheritance for yourselves, and for the
strangers who dwell among you and who bear
children among you. They shall be to you as
native-born among the children of Israel; they
shall have an inheritance with you among the
tribes of Israel.
23 "And it shall be *that* in whatever tribe the
stranger dwells, there you shall give *him* his
inheritance," says the Lord GOD.

Division of the Land

48 "Now these *are* the names of the tribes:
From the northern border along the
road to Hethlon at the entrance of Hamath, to
Hazar Enan, the border of Damascus northward,
in the direction of Hamath, *there shall be* one
section for Dan from its east to its west side;
2 "by the border of Dan, from the east side
to the west, one *section for* Asher;
3 "by the border of Asher, from the east side
to the west, one *section for* Naphtali;
4 "by the border of Naphtali, from the east
side to the west, one *section for* Manasseh;
5 "by the border of Manasseh, from the east
side to the west, one *section for* Ephraim;
6 "by the border of Ephraim, from the east
side to the west, one *section for* Reuben;
7 "by the border of Reuben, from the east
side to the west, one *section for* Judah;
8 "by the border of Judah, from the east side
to the west, shall be the district which you shall
set apart, twenty-five thousand *cubits* in
width, and *in* length the same as one of the
other portions, from the east side to the west,
with the sanctuary in the center.
9 "The district that you shall set apart for
the LORD *shall be* twenty-five thousand *cubits*
in length and ten thousand in width.
10 "To these—to the priests—the holy district
shall belong: on the north twenty-five thousand
cubits in length, on the west ten thousand in
width, on the east ten thousand in width, and
on the south twenty-five thousand in length.
The sanctuary of the LORD shall be in the
center.
11 "*It shall be* for the priests of the sons of
Zadok, who are sanctified, who have kept My
charge, who did not go astray when the chil-
dren of Israel went astray, as the Levites went
astray.
12 "And *this* district of land that is set apart
shall be to them a thing most holy by the bor-
der of the Levites.
13 "Opposite the border of the priests, the Le-
vites *shall have an area* twenty-five thousand
cubits in length and ten thousand in width; its
entire length *shall be* twenty-five thousand and
its width ten thousand.
14 "And they shall not sell or exchange any
of it; they may not alienate this best *part* of the
land, for *it is* holy to the LORD.
15 "The five thousand *cubits* in width that
remain, along the edge of the twenty-five thou-
sand, shall be for general use by the city, for
dwellings and common-land; and the city shall
be in the center.
16 "These *shall be* its measurements: the
north side four thousand five hundred *cubits*,
the south side four thousand five hundred, the
east side four thousand five hundred, and the
west side four thousand five hundred.
17 "The common-land of the city shall be: to
the north two hundred and fifty *cubits*, to the
south two hundred and fifty, to the east two
hundred and fifty, and to the west two hundred
and fifty.
18 "The rest of the length, alongside the dis-
trict of the holy *section*, *shall be* ten thousand
cubits to the east and ten thousand to the west.
It shall be adjacent to the district of the holy
section, and its produce shall be food for the
workers of the city.
19 "The workers of the city, from all the tribes
of Israel, shall cultivate it.
20 "The entire district *shall be* twenty-five
thousand *cubits* by twenty-five thousand *cu-
bits*, foursquare. You shall set apart the holy
district with the property of the city.
21 "The rest *shall belong* to the prince, on one
side and on the other of the holy district and
of the city's property, next to the twenty-five
thousand *cubits* of the *holy* district as far as
the eastern border, and westward next to the
twenty-five thousand as far as the western bor-
der, adjacent to the *tribal* portions; *it shall be-
long* to the prince. It shall be the holy district,
and the sanctuary of the temple *shall be* in the
center.
22 "Moreover, apart from the possession of
the Levites and the possession of the city
which are in the midst of what *belongs* to the
prince, *the area* between the border of Judah
and the border of Benjamin shall belong to the
prince.
23 "As for the rest of the tribes, from the east
side to the west, Benjamin *shall have* one *sec-
tion;*
24 "by the border of Benjamin, from the east
side to the west, Simeon *shall have* one *section;*
25 "by the border of Simeon, from the east
side to the west, Issachar *shall have* one *section;*
26 "by the border of Issachar, from the east
side to the west, Zebulun *shall have* one *section;*
27 "by the border of Zebulun, from the east
side to the west, Gad *shall have* one *section;*
28 "by the border of Gad, on the south side,
toward the South,[a] the border shall be from
Tamar *to* the waters of Meribah *by* Kadesh,
along the brook to the Great Sea.

47:19 [a]Hebrew *Negev* **48:28** [a]Hebrew *Negev*

29 "This *is* the land which you shall divide by
lot as an inheritance among the tribes of Israel,
and these *are* their portions," says the Lord GOD.

The Gates of the City and Its Name

30 "These *are* the exits of the city. On the
north side, measuring four thousand five hun-
dred *cubits*
31 "(the gates of the city *shall be* named after
the tribes of Israel), the three gates northward:
one gate for Reuben, one gate for Judah, and
one gate for Levi;
32 "on the east side, four thousand five hun-
dred *cubits*, three gates: one gate for Joseph,
one gate for Benjamin, and one gate for Dan;
33 "on the south side, measuring four thou-
sand five hundred *cubits*, three gates: one gate
for Simeon, one gate for Issachar, and one gate
for Zebulun;
34 "on the west side, four thousand five hun-
dred *cubits* with their three gates: one gate
for Gad, one gate for Asher, and one gate for
Naphtali.
35 "All the way around *shall be* eighteen thou-
sand *cubits*; and the name of the city from *that*
day *shall be*: THE LORD *IS* THERE."[a]

The Book of DANIEL

Daniel and His Friends Obey God

1 In the third year of the reign of Jehoiakim
king of Judah, Nebuchadnezzar king of
Babylon came to Jerusalem and besieged it.
2 And the Lord gave Jehoiakim king of Ju-
dah into his hand, with some of the articles of
the house of God, which he carried into the land
of Shinar to the house of his god; and he
brought the articles into the treasure house of
his god.
3 Then the king instructed Ashpenaz, the
master of his eunuchs, to bring some of the
children of Israel and some of the king's de-
scendants and some of the nobles,
4 young men in whom *there was* no blemish,
but good-looking, gifted in all wisdom, pos-
sessing knowledge and quick to understand,
who *had* ability to serve in the king's palace,
and whom they might teach the language and
literature of the Chaldeans.
5 And the king appointed for them a daily
provision of the king's delicacies and of the
wine which he drank, and three years of train-
ing for them, so that at the end of *that time*
they might serve before the king.
6 Now from among those of the sons of Ju-
dah were Daniel, Hananiah, Mishael, and Aza-
riah.
7 To them the chief of the eunuchs gave
names: he gave Daniel *the name* Belteshazzar;
to Hananiah, Shadrach; to Mishael, Meshach;
and to Azariah, Abed-Nego.
8 But Daniel purposed in his heart that he
would not defile himself with the portion of the
king's delicacies, nor with the wine which he
drank; therefore he requested of the chief of
the eunuchs that he might not defile himself.
9 Now God had brought Daniel into the fa-
vor and goodwill of the chief of the eunuchs.
10 And the chief of the eunuchs said to Dan-
iel, "I fear my lord the king, who has appointed
your food and drink. For why should he see
your faces looking worse than the young men
who *are* your age? Then you would endanger
my head before the king."
11 So Daniel said to the steward[a] whom the
chief of the eunuchs had set over Daniel, Hana-
niah, Mishael, and Azariah,
12 "Please test your servants for ten days, and
let them give us vegetables to eat and water to
drink.
13 "Then let our appearance be examined be-
fore you, and the appearance of the young men
who eat the portion of the king's delicacies;
and as you see fit, *so* deal with your servants."
14 So he consented with them in this matter,
and tested them ten days.
15 And at the end of ten days their features
appeared better and fatter in flesh than all the
young men who ate the portion of the king's
delicacies.
16 Thus the steward took away their portion
of delicacies and the wine that they were to
drink, and gave them vegetables.
17 As for these four young men, God gave
them knowledge and skill in all literature and
wisdom; and Daniel had understanding in all
visions and dreams.
18 Now at the end of the days, when the king
had said that they should be brought in, the
chief of the eunuchs brought them in before
Nebuchadnezzar.
19 Then the king interviewed them,[a] and
among them all none was found like Daniel,
Hananiah, Mishael, and Azariah; therefore
they served before the king.
20 And in all matters of wisdom *and* under-
standing about which the king examined them,
he found them ten times better than all the
magicians *and* astrologers who *were* in all his
realm.
21 Thus Daniel continued until the first year
of King Cyrus.

Nebuchadnezzar's Dream

2 Now in the second year of Nebuchadnez-
zar's reign, Nebuchadnezzar had dreams;
and his spirit was *so* troubled that his sleep left
him.
2 Then the king gave the command to call
the magicians, the astrologers, the sorcerers,
and the Chaldeans to tell the king his dreams.
So they came and stood before the king.
3 And the king said to them, "I have had a
dream, and my spirit is anxious to know the
dream."
4 Then the Chaldeans spoke to the king in
Aramaic,[a] "O king, live forever! Tell your ser-

48:35 [a]Hebrew *YHWH Shammah* **1:11** [a]Hebrew *Melzar*, also in verse 16 **1:19** [a]Literally *talked with them*
2:4 [a]The original language of Daniel 2:4b through 7:28 is Aramaic.

vants the dream, and we will give the interpre-
tation."
5 The king answered and said to the Chalde-
ans, "My decision is firm: if you do not make
known the dream to me, and its interpretation,
you shall be cut in pieces, and your houses
shall be made an ash heap.
6 "However, if you tell the dream and its in-
terpretation, you shall receive from me gifts,
rewards, and great honor. Therefore tell me
the dream and its interpretation."
7 They answered again and said, "Let the king
tell his servants the dream, and we will give its
interpretation."
8 The king answered and said, "I know for
certain that you would gain time, because you
see that my decision is firm:
9 "if you do not make known the dream to
me, *there is only* one decree for you! For you
have agreed to speak lying and corrupt words
before me till the time has changed. Therefore
tell me the dream, and I shall know that you
can give me its interpretation."
10 The Chaldeans answered the king, and said,
"There is not a man on earth who can tell the
king's matter; therefore no king, lord, or ruler
has *ever* asked such things of any magician,
astrologer, or Chaldean.
11 "*It is* a difficult thing that the king requests,
and there is no other who can tell it to the king
except the gods, whose dwelling is not with
flesh."
12 For this reason the king was angry and very
furious, and gave the command to destroy all
the wise *men* of Babylon.
13 So the decree went out, and they began
killing the wise *men;* and they sought Daniel
and his companions, to kill *them.*

God Reveals Nebuchadnezzar's Dream

14 Then with counsel and wisdom Daniel an-
swered Arioch, the captain of the king's guard,
who had gone out to kill the wise *men* of Bab-
ylon;
15 he answered and said to Arioch the king's
captain, "Why is the decree from the king so
urgent?" Then Arioch made the decision known
to Daniel.
16 So Daniel went in and asked the king to
give him time, that he might tell the king the
interpretation.
17 Then Daniel went to his house, and made
the decision known to Hananiah, Mishael, and
Azariah, his companions,
18 that they might seek mercies from the God
of heaven concerning this secret, so that Dan-
iel and his companions might not perish with
the rest of the wise *men* of Babylon.
19 Then the secret was revealed to Daniel in
a night vision. So Daniel blessed the God of
heaven.
20 Daniel answered and said:

"Blessed be the name of God forever and
ever,
For wisdom and might are His.
21 And He changes the times and the
seasons;
He removes kings and raises up kings;
He gives wisdom to the wise
And knowledge to those who have
understanding.
22 He reveals deep and secret things;
He knows what *is* in the darkness,
And light dwells with Him.

23 "I thank You and praise You,
O God of my fathers;
You have given me wisdom and might,
And have now made known to me what
we asked of You,
For You have made known to us the
king's demand."

Daniel Explains the Dream

24 Therefore Daniel went to Arioch, whom
the king had appointed to destroy the wise *men*
of Babylon. He went and said thus to him: "Do
not destroy the wise *men* of Babylon; take me
before the king, and I will tell the king the
interpretation."
25 Then Arioch quickly brought Daniel be-
fore the king, and said thus to him, "I have
found a man of the captives[a] of Judah, who will
make known to the king the interpretation."
26 The king answered and said to Daniel,
whose name *was* Belteshazzar, "Are you able
to make known to me the dream which I have
seen, and its interpretation?"
27 Daniel answered in the presence of the
king, and said, "The secret which the king has
demanded, the wise *men,* the astrologers, the
magicians, and the soothsayers cannot declare
to the king.
28 "But there is a God in heaven who reveals
secrets, and He has made known to King Neb-
uchadnezzar what will be in the latter days.
Your dream, and the visions of your head upon
your bed, were these:
29 "As for you, O king, thoughts came *to* your
mind while on your bed, *about* what would
come to pass after this; and He who reveals
secrets has made known to you what will be.
30 "But as for me, this secret has not been
revealed to me because I have more wisdom
than anyone living, but for *our* sakes who make
known the interpretation to the king, and that
you may know the thoughts of your heart.
31 "You, O king, were watching; and behold,
a great image! This great image, whose splendor
was excellent, stood before you; and its form
was awesome.
32 "This image's head *was* of fine gold, its chest
and arms of silver, its belly and thighs[a] of
bronze,
33 "its legs of iron, its feet partly of iron and
partly of clay.[a]
34 "You watched while a stone was cut out
without hands, which struck the image on its
feet of iron and clay, and broke them in pieces.
35 "Then the iron, the clay, the bronze, the
silver, and the gold were crushed together, and
became like chaff from the summer threshing
floors; the wind carried them away so that no
trace of them was found. And the stone that
struck the image became a great mountain and
filled the whole earth.
36 "This *is* the dream. Now we will tell the in-
terpretation of it before the king.
37 "You, O king, *are* a king of kings. For the
God of heaven has given you a kingdom,
power, strength, and glory;
38 "and wherever the children of men dwell,
or the beasts of the field and the birds of the
heaven, He has given *them* into your hand, and

2:25 [a]Literally *of the sons of the captivity* 2:32 [a]Or *sides* 2:33 [a]Or *baked clay,* and so in verses 34, 35, and 42

has made you ruler over them all—you *are* this head of gold.
39 "But after you shall arise another kingdom inferior to yours; then another, a third kingdom of bronze, which shall rule over all the earth.
40 "And the fourth kingdom shall be as strong as iron, inasmuch as iron breaks in pieces and shatters everything; and like iron that crushes, *that kingdom* will break in pieces and crush all the others.
41 "Whereas you saw the feet and toes, partly of potter's clay and partly of iron, the kingdom shall be divided; yet the strength of the iron shall be in it, just as you saw the iron mixed with ceramic clay.
42 "And *as* the toes of the feet *were* partly of iron and partly of clay, *so* the kingdom shall be partly strong and partly fragile.
43 "As you saw iron mixed with ceramic clay, they will mingle with the seed of men; but they will not adhere to one another, just as iron does not mix with clay.
44 "And in the days of these kings the God of heaven will set up a kingdom which shall never be destroyed; and the kingdom shall not be left to other people; it shall break in pieces and consume all these kingdoms, and it shall stand forever.
45 "Inasmuch as you saw that the stone was cut out of the mountain without hands, and that it broke in pieces the iron, the bronze, the clay, the silver, and the gold—the great God has made known to the king what will come to pass after this. The dream is certain, and its interpretation is sure."

Daniel and His Friends Promoted

46 Then King Nebuchadnezzar fell on his face, prostrate before Daniel, and commanded that they should present an offering and incense to him.
47 The king answered Daniel, and said, "Truly your God *is* the God of gods, the Lord of kings, and a revealer of secrets, since you could reveal this secret."
48 Then the king promoted Daniel and gave him many great gifts; and he made him ruler over the whole province of Babylon, and chief administrator over all the wise *men* of Babylon.
49 Also Daniel petitioned the king, and he set Shadrach, Meshach, and Abed-Nego over the affairs of the province of Babylon; but Daniel *sat* in the gate[a] of the king.

The Image of Gold

3 Nebuchadnezzar the king made an image of gold, whose height *was* sixty cubits *and* its width six cubits. He set it up in the plain of Dura, in the province of Babylon.
2 And King Nebuchadnezzar sent *word* to gather together the satraps, the administrators, the governors, the counselors, the treasurers, the judges, the magistrates, and all the officials of the provinces, to come to the dedication of the image which King Nebuchadnezzar had set up.
3 So the satraps, the administrators, the governors, the counselors, the treasurers, the judges, the magistrates, and all the officials of the provinces gathered together for the dedication of the image that King Nebuchadnezzar had set up; and they stood before the image that Nebuchadnezzar had set up.
4 Then a herald cried aloud: "To you it is commanded, O peoples, nations, and languages,
5 "*that* at the time you hear the sound of the horn, flute, harp, lyre, *and* psaltery, in symphony with all kinds of music, you shall fall down and worship the gold image that King Nebuchadnezzar has set up;
6 "and whoever does not fall down and worship shall be cast immediately into the midst of a burning fiery furnace."
7 So at that time, when all the people heard the sound of the horn, flute, harp, *and* lyre, in symphony with all kinds of music, all the people, nations, and languages fell down *and* worshiped the gold image which King Nebuchadnezzar had set up.

Daniel's Friends Disobey the King

8 Therefore at that time certain Chaldeans came forward and accused the Jews.
9 They spoke and said to King Nebuchadnezzar, "O king, live forever!
10 "You, O king, have made a decree that everyone who hears the sound of the horn, flute, harp, lyre, *and* psaltery, in symphony with all kinds of music, shall fall down and worship the gold image;
11 "and whoever does not fall down and worship shall be cast into the midst of a burning fiery furnace.
12 "There are certain Jews whom you have set over the affairs of the province of Babylon: Shadrach, Meshach, and Abed-Nego; these men, O king, have not paid due regard to you. They do not serve your gods or worship the gold image which you have set up."
13 Then Nebuchadnezzar, in rage and fury, gave the command to bring Shadrach, Meshach, and Abed-Nego. So they brought these men before the king.
14 Nebuchadnezzar spoke, saying to them, "*Is it* true, Shadrach, Meshach, and Abed-Nego, *that* you do not serve my gods or worship the gold image which I have set up?
15 "Now if you are ready at the time you hear the sound of the horn, flute, harp, lyre, *and* psaltery, in symphony with all kinds of music, and you fall down and worship the image which I have made, *good!* But if you do not worship, you shall be cast immediately into the midst of a burning fiery furnace. And who *is* the god who will deliver you from my hands?"
16 Shadrach, Meshach, and Abed-Nego answered and said to the king, "O Nebuchadnezzar, we have no need to answer you in this matter.
17 "If that *is the case,* our God whom we serve is able to deliver us from the burning fiery furnace, and He will deliver *us* from your hand, O king.
18 "But if not, let it be known to you, O king, that we do not serve your gods, nor will we worship the gold image which you have set up."

Saved in Fiery Trial

19 Then Nebuchadnezzar was full of fury, and the expression on his face changed toward Shadrach, Meshach, and Abed-Nego. He spoke and commanded that they heat the furnace seven times more than it was usually heated.

2:49 [a]That is, the king's court

20 And he commanded certain mighty men of
valor who *were* in his army to bind Shadrach,
Meshach, and Abed-Nego, *and* cast *them* into
the burning fiery furnace.
21 Then these men were bound in their coats,
their trousers, their turbans, and their *other*
garments, and were cast into the midst of the
burning fiery furnace.
22 Therefore, because the king's command
was urgent, and the furnace exceedingly hot,
the flame of the fire killed those men who took
up Shadrach, Meshach, and Abed-Nego.
23 And these three men, Shadrach, Meshach,
and Abed-Nego, fell down bound into the midst
of the burning fiery furnace.
24 Then King Nebuchadnezzar was aston-
ished; and he rose in haste *and* spoke, saying
to his counselors, "Did we not cast three men
bound into the midst of the fire?" They answered
and said to the king, "True, O king."
25 "Look!" he answered, "I see four men
loose, walking in the midst of the fire; and they
are not hurt, and the form of the fourth is like
the Son of God."[a]

Nebuchadnezzar Praises God

26 Then Nebuchadnezzar went near the
mouth of the burning fiery furnace *and* spoke,
saying, "Shadrach, Meshach, and Abed-Nego,
servants of the Most High God, come out, and
come *here*." Then Shadrach, Meshach, and
Abed-Nego came from the midst of the fire.
27 And the satraps, administrators, gover-
nors, and the king's counselors gathered to-
gether, and they saw these men on whose bodies
the fire had no power; the hair of their head
was not singed nor were their garments affected,
and the smell of fire was not on them.
28 Nebuchadnezzar spoke, saying, "Blessed
be the God of Shadrach, Meshach, and Abed-
Nego, who sent His Angel[a] and delivered His
servants who trusted in Him, and they have
frustrated the king's word, and yielded their
bodies, that they should not serve nor worship
any god except their own God!
29 "Therefore I make a decree that any peo-
ple, nation, or language which speaks anything
amiss against the God of Shadrach, Meshach,
and Abed-Nego shall be cut in pieces, and their
houses shall be made an ash heap; because there
is no other God who can deliver like this."
30 Then the king promoted Shadrach, Me-
shach, and Abed-Nego in the province of Bab-
ylon.

Nebuchadnezzar's Second Dream

4 Nebuchadnezzar the king,

To all peoples, nations, and languages that dwell in all the earth:

Peace be multiplied to you.

2 I thought it good to declare the signs and wonders that the Most High God has worked for me.

3 How great *are* His signs,
And how mighty His wonders!
His kingdom *is* an everlasting kingdom,
And His dominion *is* from generation to generation.

4 I, Nebuchadnezzar, was at rest in my house, and flourishing in my palace.
5 I saw a dream which made me afraid, and the thoughts on my bed and the visions of my head troubled me.
6 Therefore I issued a decree to bring in all the wise *men* of Babylon before me, that they might make known to me the interpretation of the dream.
7 Then the magicians, the astrologers, the Chaldeans, and the soothsayers came in, and I told them the dream; but they did not make known to me its interpretation.
8 But at last Daniel came before me (his name *is* Belteshazzar, according to the name of my god; in him *is* the Spirit of the Holy God), and I told the dream before him, *saying:*
9 "Belteshazzar, chief of the magicians, because I know that the Spirit of the Holy God *is* in you, and no secret troubles you, explain to me the visions of my dream that I have seen, and its interpretation.
10 "These *were* the visions of my head *while* on my bed:

"I was looking, and behold,
A tree in the midst of the earth,
And its height was great.
11 The tree grew and became strong;
Its height reached to the heavens,
And it could be seen to the ends of all the earth.
12 Its leaves *were* lovely,
Its fruit abundant,
And in it *was* food for all.
The beasts of the field found shade under it,
The birds of the heavens dwelt in its branches,
And all flesh was fed from it.

13 "I saw in the visions of my head *while* on my bed, and there was a watcher, a holy one, coming down from heaven.
14 He cried aloud and said thus:

'Chop down the tree and cut off its branches,
Strip off its leaves and scatter its fruit.
Let the beasts get out from under it,
And the birds from its branches.
15 Nevertheless leave the stump and roots in the earth,
Bound with a band of iron and bronze,
In the tender grass of the field.
Let it be wet with the dew of heaven,
And *let* him graze with the beasts
On the grass of the earth.
16 Let his heart be changed from *that of* a man,
Let him be given the heart of a beast,
And let seven times[a] pass over him.

17 'This decision *is* by the decree of the watchers,
And the sentence by the word of the holy ones,
In order that the living may know
That the Most High rules in the kingdom of men,
Gives it to whomever He will,
And sets over it the lowest of men.'

18 "This dream I, King Nebuchadnezzar, have seen. Now you, Belteshazzar, declare its interpretation, since all the

3:25 [a]Or *a son of the gods* **3:28** [a]Or *angel* **4:16** [a]Possibly *seven years*, and so in verses 23, 25, and 32

wise *men* of my kingdom are not able to make known to me the interpretation; but you *are* able, for the Spirit of the Holy God *is* in you."

Daniel Explains the Second Dream

19 Then Daniel, whose name *was* Belteshazzar, was astonished for a time, and his thoughts troubled him. So the king spoke, and said, "Belteshazzar, do not let the dream or its interpretation trouble you." Belteshazzar answered and said, "My lord, *may* the dream concern those who hate you, and its interpretation concern your enemies!
20 The tree that you saw, which grew and became strong, whose height reached to the heavens and which *could be* seen by all the earth,
21 whose leaves *were* lovely and its fruit abundant, in which *was* food for all, under which the beasts of the field dwelt, and in whose branches the birds of the heaven had their home—
22 it *is* you, O king, who have grown and become strong; for your greatness has grown and reaches to the heavens, and your dominion to the end of the earth.
23 And inasmuch as the king saw a watcher, a holy one, coming down from heaven and saying, 'Chop down the tree and destroy it, but leave its stump and roots in the earth, *bound* with a band of iron and bronze in the tender grass of the field; let it be wet with the dew of heaven, and let him graze with the beasts of the field, till seven times pass over him';
24 this is the interpretation, O king, and this is the decree of the Most High, which has come upon my lord the king:
25 They shall drive you from men, your dwelling shall be with the beasts of the field, and they shall make you eat grass like oxen. They shall wet you with the dew of heaven, and seven times shall pass over you, till you know that the Most High rules in the kingdom of men, and gives it to whomever He chooses.
26 And inasmuch as they gave the command to leave the stump *and* roots of the tree, your kingdom shall be assured to you, after you come to know that Heaven rules.
27 Therefore, O king, let my advice be acceptable to you; break off your sins by *being* righteous, and your iniquities by showing mercy to *the* poor. Perhaps there may be a lengthening of your prosperity."

Nebuchadnezzar's Humiliation

28 All *this* came upon King Nebuchadnezzar.
29 At the end of the twelve months he was walking about the royal palace of Babylon.
30 The king spoke, saying, "Is not this great Babylon, that I have built for a royal dwelling by my mighty power and for the honor of my majesty?"
31 While the word *was still* in the king's mouth, a voice fell from heaven: "King Nebuchadnezzar, to you it is spoken: the kingdom has departed from you!
32 And they shall drive you from men, and your dwelling *shall be* with the beasts of the field. They shall make you eat grass like oxen; and seven times shall pass over you, until you know that the Most High rules in the kingdom of men, and gives it to whomever He chooses."
33 That very hour the word was fulfilled concerning Nebuchadnezzar; he was driven from men and ate grass like oxen; his body was wet with the dew of heaven till his hair had grown like eagles' *feathers* and his nails like birds' *claws*.

Nebuchadnezzar Praises God

34 And at the end of the time[a] I, Nebuchadnezzar, lifted my eyes to heaven, and my understanding returned to me; and I blessed the Most High and praised and honored Him who lives forever:

For His dominion *is* an everlasting dominion,
And His kingdom *is* from generation to generation.
35 All the inhabitants of the earth *are* reputed as nothing;
He does according to His will in the army of heaven
And *among* the inhabitants of the earth.
No one can restrain His hand
Or say to Him, "What have You done?"

36 At the same time my reason returned to me, and for the glory of my kingdom, my honor and splendor returned to me. My counselors and nobles resorted to me, I was restored to my kingdom, and excellent majesty was added to me.
37 Now I, Nebuchadnezzar, praise and extol and honor the King of heaven, all of whose works *are* truth, and His ways justice. And those who walk in pride He is able to put down.

Belshazzar's Feast

5 Belshazzar the king made a great feast for
a thousand of his lords, and drank wine in
the presence of the thousand.
2 While he tasted the wine, Belshazzar gave
the command to bring the gold and silver ves-
sels which his father Nebuchadnezzar had
taken from the temple which *had been* in Jeru-
salem, that the king and his lords, his wives,
and his concubines might drink from them.
3 Then they brought the gold vessels that had
been taken from the temple of the house of God
which *had been* in Jerusalem; and the king and
his lords, his wives, and his concubines drank
from them.
4 They drank wine, and praised the gods of
gold and silver, bronze and iron, wood and stone.
5 In the same hour the fingers of a man's hand
appeared and wrote opposite the lampstand
on the plaster of the wall of the king's palace;
and the king saw the part of the hand that wrote.
6 Then the king's countenance changed, and
his thoughts troubled him, so that the joints of
his hips were loosened and his knees knocked
against each other.
7 The king cried aloud to bring in the astrol-
ogers, the Chaldeans, and the soothsayers. The
king spoke, saying to the wise *men* of Babylon,

4:34 [a]Literally *days*

"Whoever reads this writing, and tells me its
interpretation, shall be clothed with purple
and *have* a chain of gold around his neck; and
he shall be the third ruler in the kingdom."
8 Now all the king's wise *men* came, but they
could not read the writing, or make known to
the king its interpretation.
9 Then King Belshazzar was greatly troubled,
his countenance was changed, and his lords
were astonished.
10 The queen, because of the words of the king
and his lords, came to the banquet hall. The
queen spoke, saying, "O king, live forever! Do
not let your thoughts trouble you, nor let your
countenance change.
11 "There is a man in your kingdom in whom
is the Spirit of the Holy God. And in the days
of your father, light and understanding and
wisdom, like the wisdom of the gods, were
found in him; and King Nebuchadnezzar your
father—your father the king—made him chief
of the magicians, astrologers, Chaldeans, *and*
soothsayers.
12 "Inasmuch as an excellent spirit, knowl-
edge, understanding, interpreting dreams, solv-
ing riddles, and explaining enigmas[a] were
found in this Daniel, whom the king named
Belteshazzar, now let Daniel be called, and he
will give the interpretation."

The Writing on the Wall Explained

13 Then Daniel was brought in before the
king. The king spoke, and said to Daniel, "*Are*
you that Daniel who is one of the captives[a]
from Judah, whom my father the king brought
from Judah?
14 "I have heard of you, that the Spirit of God
is in you, and *that* light and understanding and
excellent wisdom are found in you.
15 "Now the wise *men*, the astrologers, have
been brought in before me, that they should
read this writing and make known to me its
interpretation, but they could not give the in-
terpretation of the thing.
16 "And I have heard of you, that you can give
interpretations and explain enigmas. Now if
you can read the writing and make known to
me its interpretation, you shall be clothed with
purple and *have* a chain of gold around your
neck, and shall be the third ruler in the king-
dom."
17 Then Daniel answered, and said before the
king, "Let your gifts be for yourself, and give
your rewards to another; yet I will read the
writing to the king, and make known to him
the interpretation.
18 "O king, the Most High God gave Nebu-
chadnezzar your father a kingdom and majesty,
glory and honor.
19 "And because of the majesty that He gave
him, all peoples, nations, and languages trem-
bled and feared before him. Whomever he
wished, he executed; whomever he wished, he
kept alive; whomever he wished, he set up; and
whomever he wished, he put down.
20 "But when his heart was lifted up, and his
spirit was hardened in pride, he was deposed
from his kingly throne, and they took his glory
from him.
21 "Then he was driven from the sons of men,
his heart was made like the beasts, and his dwell-
ing *was* with the wild donkeys. They fed him
with grass like oxen, and his body was wet
with the dew of heaven, till he knew that the
Most High God rules in the kingdom of men,
and appoints over it whomever He chooses.
22 "But you his son, Belshazzar, have not
humbled your heart, although you knew all this.
23 "And you have lifted yourself up against
the Lord of heaven. They have brought the ves-
sels of His house before you, and you and your
lords, your wives and your concubines, have
drunk wine from them. And you have praised
the gods of silver and gold, bronze and iron,
wood and stone, which do not see or hear or
know; and the God who *holds* your breath in
His hand and owns all your ways, you have not
glorified.
24 "Then the fingers[a] of the hand were sent
from Him, and this writing was written.
25 "And this is the inscription that was
written:

MENE,[a] MENE, TEKEL,[b] UPHARSIN.[c]

26 "This *is* the interpretation of *each* word.
MENE: God has numbered your kingdom, and
finished it;
27 "TEKEL: You have been weighed in the bal-
ances, and found wanting;
28 "PERES: Your kingdom has been divided,
and given to the Medes and Persians."[a]
29 Then Belshazzar gave the command, and
they clothed Daniel with purple and *put* a
chain of gold around his neck, and made a
proclamation concerning him that he should
be the third ruler in the kingdom.

Belshazzar's Fall

30 That very night Belshazzar, king of the
Chaldeans, was slain.
31 And Darius the Mede received the king-
dom, *being* about sixty-two years old.

The Plot Against Daniel

6 It pleased Darius to set over the kingdom
one hundred and twenty satraps, to be over
the whole kingdom;
2 and over these, three governors, of whom
Daniel *was* one, that the satraps might give ac-
count to them, so that the king would suffer no
loss.
3 Then this Daniel distinguished himself
above the governors and satraps, because an
excellent spirit *was* in him; and the king gave
thought to setting him over the whole realm.
4 So the governors and satraps sought to
find *some* charge against Daniel concerning the
kingdom; but they could find no charge or
fault, because he *was* faithful; nor was there any
error or fault found in him.
5 Then these men said, "We shall not find
any charge against this Daniel unless we find
it against him concerning the law of his God."
6 So these governors and satraps thronged
before the king, and said thus to him: "King
Darius, live forever!
7 "All the governors of the kingdom, the ad-
ministrators and satraps, the counselors and
advisors, have consulted together to establish
a royal statute and to make a firm decree, that
whoever petitions any god or man for thirty

5:12 [a]Literally *untying knots*, and so in verse 16 **5:13** [a]Literally *of the sons of the captivity* **5:24** [a]Literally *palm*
5:25 [a]Literally *a mina* (50 shekels) from the verb "to number" [b]Literally *a shekel* from the verb "to weigh" [c]Literally *and half-shekels* from the verb "to divide" **5:28** [a]Aramaic *Paras*, consonant with *Peres*

days, except you, O king, shall be cast into the
den of lions.
8 "Now, O king, establish the decree and
sign the writing, so that it cannot be changed,
according to the law of the Medes and Per-
sians, which does not alter."
9 Therefore King Darius signed the written
decree.

Daniel in the Lions' Den

10 Now when Daniel knew that the writing
was signed, he went home. And in his upper
room, with his windows open toward Jerusa-
lem, he knelt down on his knees three times
that day, and prayed and gave thanks before
his God, as was his custom since early days.
11 Then these men assembled and found
Daniel praying and making supplication be-
fore his God.
12 And they went before the king, and spoke
concerning the king's decree: "Have you not
signed a decree that every man who petitions
any god or man within thirty days, except you,
O king, shall be cast into the den of lions?" The
king answered and said, "The thing *is* true, ac-
cording to the law of the Medes and Persians,
which does not alter."
13 So they answered and said before the king,
"That Daniel, who is one of the captives[a] from
Judah, does not show due regard for you,
O king, or for the decree that you have signed,
but makes his petition three times a day."
14 And the king, when he heard *these* words,
was greatly displeased with himself, and set
his heart on Daniel to deliver him; and he la-
bored till the going down of the sun to deliver
him.
15 Then these men approached the king, and
said to the king, "Know, O king, that *it is* the
law of the Medes and Persians that no decree
or statute which the king establishes may be
changed."
16 So the king gave the command, and they
brought Daniel and cast *him* into the den of
lions. *But* the king spoke, saying to Daniel,
"Your God, whom you serve continually, He
will deliver you."
17 Then a stone was brought and laid on the
mouth of the den, and the king sealed it with
his own signet ring and with the signets of
his lords, that the purpose concerning Daniel
might not be changed.

Daniel Saved from the Lions

18 Now the king went to his palace and spent
the night fasting; and no musicians[a] were
brought before him. Also his sleep went from
him.
19 Then the king arose very early in the
morning and went in haste to the den of lions.
20 And when he came to the den, he cried
out with a lamenting voice to Daniel. The king
spoke, saying to Daniel, "Daniel, servant of the
living God, has your God, whom you serve con-
tinually, been able to deliver you from the
lions?"
21 Then Daniel said to the king, "O king, live
forever!
22 "My God sent His angel and shut the lions'
mouths, so that they have not hurt me, because
I was found innocent before Him; and also,
O king, I have done no wrong before you."
23 Now the king was exceedingly glad for
him, and commanded that they should take
Daniel up out of the den. So Daniel was taken
up out of the den, and no injury whatever was
found on him, because he believed in his God.

Darius Honors God

24 And the king gave the command, and they
brought those men who had accused Daniel,
and they cast *them* into the den of lions—them,
their children, and their wives; and the lions
overpowered them, and broke all their bones
in pieces before they ever came to the bottom
of the den.

25 Then King Darius wrote:

To all peoples, nations, and languages
that dwell in all the earth:

Peace be multiplied to you.

26 I make a decree that in every dominion of
my kingdom *men must* tremble and fear
before the God of Daniel.

For He *is* the living God,
And steadfast forever;
His kingdom *is the one* which shall not
be destroyed,
And His dominion *shall endure* to the
end.
27 He delivers and rescues,
And He works signs and wonders
In heaven and on earth,
Who has delivered Daniel from the power
of the lions.

28 So this Daniel prospered in the reign of
Darius and in the reign of Cyrus the Persian.

Vision of the Four Beasts

7 In the first year of Belshazzar king of Bab-
ylon, Daniel had a dream and visions of his
head *while* on his bed. Then he wrote down the
dream, telling the main facts.[a]
2 Daniel spoke, saying, "I saw in my vision
by night, and behold, the four winds of heaven
were stirring up the Great Sea.
3 "And four great beasts came up from the
sea, each different from the other.
4 "The first *was* like a lion, and had eagle's
wings. I watched till its wings were plucked
off; and it was lifted up from the earth and
made to stand on two feet like a man, and a
man's heart was given to it.
5 "And suddenly another beast, a second, like
a bear. It was raised up on one side, and *had*
three ribs in its mouth between its teeth. And
they said thus to it: 'Arise, devour much flesh!'
6 "After this I looked, and there was another,
like a leopard, which had on its back four
wings of a bird. The beast also had four heads,
and dominion was given to it.
7 "After this I saw in the night visions, and
behold, a fourth beast, dreadful and terrible,
exceedingly strong. It had huge iron teeth; it
was devouring, breaking in pieces, and tram-
pling the residue with its feet. It *was* different
from all the beasts that *were* before it, and it
had ten horns.
8 "I was considering the horns, and there
was another horn, a little one, coming up among

6:13 [a]Literally *of the sons of the captivity* **6:18** [a]Exact meaning unknown **7:1** [a]Literally *the head* (or *chief*) *of the words*

them, before whom three of the first horns
were plucked out by the roots. And there, in
this horn, *were* eyes like the eyes of a man, and
a mouth speaking pompous words.

Vision of the Ancient of Days

9 "I watched till thrones were put in place,
And the Ancient of Days was seated;
His garment *was* white as snow,
And the hair of His head *was* like pure
wool.
His throne *was* a fiery flame,
Its wheels a burning fire;
10 A fiery stream issued
And came forth from before Him.
A thousand thousands ministered to Him;
Ten thousand times ten thousand stood
before Him.
The court[a] was seated,
And the books were opened.

11 "I watched then because of the sound of
the pompous words which the horn was speak-
ing; I watched till the beast was slain, and its
body destroyed and given to the burning flame.
12 "As for the rest of the beasts, they had
their dominion taken away, yet their lives were
prolonged for a season and a time.

13 "I was watching in the night visions,
And behold, *One* like the Son of Man,
Coming with the clouds of heaven!
He came to the Ancient of Days,
And they brought Him near before Him.
14 Then to Him was given dominion and
glory and a kingdom,
That all peoples, nations, and languages
should serve Him.
His dominion *is* an everlasting dominion,
Which shall not pass away,
And His kingdom *the one*
Which shall not be destroyed.

Daniel's Visions Interpreted

15 "I, Daniel, was grieved in my spirit within
my body, and the visions of my head troubled
me.
16 "I came near to one of those who stood by,
and asked him the truth of all this. So he told
me and made known to me the interpretation
of these things:
17 'Those great beasts, which are four, *are* four
kings[a] *which* arise out of the earth.
18 'But the saints of the Most High shall re-
ceive the kingdom, and possess the kingdom
forever, even forever and ever.'
19 "Then I wished to know the truth about the
fourth beast, which was different from all the
others, exceedingly dreadful, *with* its teeth of
iron and its nails of bronze, *which* devoured,
broke in pieces, and trampled the residue with
its feet;
20 "and the ten horns that *were* on its head,
and the other *horn* which came up, before which
three fell, namely, that horn which had eyes
and a mouth which spoke pompous words,
whose appearance *was* greater than his fellows.
21 "I was watching; and the same horn was
making war against the saints, and prevailing
against them,
22 "until the Ancient of Days came, and a judg-
ment was made *in favor* of the saints of the
Most High, and the time came for the saints to
possess the kingdom.
23 "Thus he said:

'The fourth beast shall be
A fourth kingdom on earth,
Which shall be different from all *other*
kingdoms,
And shall devour the whole earth,
Trample it and break it in pieces.
24 The ten horns *are* ten kings
Who shall arise from this kingdom.
And another shall rise after them;
He shall be different from the first *ones*,
And shall subdue three kings.
25 He shall speak *pompous* words against
the Most High,
Shall persecute[a] the saints of the Most
High,
And shall intend to change times and law.
Then *the saints* shall be given into his
hand
For a time and times and half a time.

26 'But the court shall be seated,
And they shall take away his dominion,
To consume and destroy *it* forever.
27 Then the kingdom and dominion,
And the greatness of the kingdoms under
the whole heaven,
Shall be given to the people, the saints of
the Most High.
His kingdom *is* an everlasting kingdom,
And all dominions shall serve and obey
Him.'

28 "This *is* the end of the account.[a] As for me,
Daniel, my thoughts greatly troubled me, and
my countenance changed; but I kept the matter
in my heart."

Vision of a Ram and a Goat

8 In the third year of the reign of King Bel-
shazzar a vision appeared *to* me—to me,
Daniel—after the one that appeared to me the
first time.
2 I saw in the vision, and it so happened while
I was looking, that I *was* in Shushan, the cita-
del, which *is* in the province of Elam; and I saw
in the vision that I was by the River Ulai.
3 Then I lifted my eyes and saw, and there,
standing beside the river, was a ram which had
two horns, and the two horns *were* high; but one
was higher than the other, and the higher *one*
came up last.
4 I saw the ram pushing westward, north-
ward, and southward, so that no animal could
withstand him; nor *was there any* that could
deliver from his hand, but he did according to
his will and became great.
5 And as I was considering, suddenly a male
goat came from the west, across the surface of
the whole earth, without touching the ground;
and the goat *had* a notable horn between his
eyes.
6 Then he came to the ram that had two horns,
which I had seen standing beside the river, and
ran at him with furious power.
7 And I saw him confronting the ram; he
was moved with rage against him, attacked the
ram, and broke his two horns. There was no
power in the ram to withstand him, but he cast
him down to the ground and trampled him; and

7:10 [a]Or *judgment* 7:17 [a]Representing their kingdoms (compare verse 23) 7:25 [a]Literally *wear out* 7:28 [a]Literally *the word*

there was no one that could deliver the ram
from his hand.
8 Therefore the male goat grew very great;
but when he became strong, the large horn was
broken, and in place of it four notable ones
came up toward the four winds of heaven.
9 And out of one of them came a little horn
which grew exceedingly great toward the
south, toward the east, and toward the Glori-
ous *Land.*
10 And it grew up to the host of heaven; and
it cast down *some* of the host and *some* of the
stars to the ground, and trampled them.
11 He even exalted *himself* as high as the Prince
of the host; and by him the daily *sacrifices*
were taken away, and the place of His sanctu-
ary was cast down.
12 Because of transgression, an army was
given over *to the horn* to oppose the daily *sac-
rifices;* and he cast truth down to the ground.
He did *all this* and prospered.
13 Then I heard a holy one speaking; and *an-
other* holy one said to that certain *one* who was
speaking, "How long *will* the vision *be, concern-
ing* the daily *sacrifices* and the transgression
of desolation, the giving of both the sanctuary
and the host to be trampled underfoot?"
14 And he said to me, "For two thousand
three hundred days;[a] then the sanctuary shall
be cleansed."

Gabriel Interprets the Vision

15 Then it happened, when I, Daniel, had seen
the vision and was seeking the meaning, that
suddenly there stood before me one having the
appearance of a man.
16 And I heard a man's voice between *the
banks of* the Ulai, who called, and said, "Ga-
briel, make this *man* understand the vision."
17 So he came near where I stood, and when
he came I was afraid and fell on my face; but he
said to me, "Understand, son of man, that the
vision *refers* to the time of the end."
18 Now, as he was speaking with me, I was in
a deep sleep with my face to the ground; but
he touched me, and stood me upright.
19 And he said, "Look, I am making known
to you what shall happen in the latter time of
the indignation; for at the appointed time the
end *shall be.*
20 "The ram which you saw, having the two
horns—*they are* the kings of Media and Persia.
21 "And the male goat *is* the kingdom[a] of
Greece. The large horn that *is* between its eyes
is the first king.
22 "As for the broken *horn* and the four that
stood up in its place, four kingdoms shall arise
out of that nation, but not with its power.

23 "And in the latter time of their kingdom,
When the transgressors have reached
their fullness,
A king shall arise,
Having fierce features,
Who understands sinister schemes.
24 His power shall be mighty, but not by his
own power;
He shall destroy fearfully,
And shall prosper and thrive;
He shall destroy the mighty, and *also* the
holy people.

25 "Through his cunning
He shall cause deceit to prosper under his
rule;[a]
And he shall exalt *himself* in his heart.
He shall destroy many in *their* prosperity.
He shall even rise against the Prince of
princes;
But he shall be broken without *human*
means.[b]

26 "And the vision of the evenings and
mornings
Which was told is true;
Therefore seal up the vision,
For *it refers* to many days *in the future.*"

27 And I, Daniel, fainted and was sick for
days; afterward I arose and went about the
king's business. I was astonished by the vision,
but no one understood it.

Daniel's Prayer for the People

9 In the first year of Darius the son of Ahasu-
erus, of the lineage of the Medes, who was
made king over the realm of the Chaldeans—
2 in the first year of his reign I, Daniel, un-
derstood by the books the number of the years
specified by the word of the LORD through Jer-
emiah the prophet, that He would accomplish
seventy years in the desolations of Jerusalem.
3 Then I set my face toward the Lord God to
make request by prayer and supplications, with
fasting, sackcloth, and ashes.
4 And I prayed to the LORD my God, and
made confession, and said, "O Lord, great and
awesome God, who keeps His covenant and
mercy with those who love Him, and with
those who keep His commandments,
5 "we have sinned and committed iniquity,
we have done wickedly and rebelled, even by
departing from Your precepts and Your judg-
ments.
6 "Neither have we heeded Your servants
the prophets, who spoke in Your name to our
kings and our princes, to our fathers and all
the people of the land.
7 "O Lord, righteousness *belongs* to You, but
to us shame of face, as *it is* this day—to the
men of Judah, to the inhabitants of Jerusalem
and all Israel, those near and those far off in all
the countries to which You have driven them,
because of the unfaithfulness which they have
committed against You.
8 "O Lord, to us *belongs* shame of face, to
our kings, our princes, and our fathers, because
we have sinned against You.
9 "To the Lord our God *belong* mercy and
forgiveness, though we have rebelled against
Him.
10 "We have not obeyed the voice of the LORD
our God, to walk in His laws, which He set be-
fore us by His servants the prophets.
11 "Yes, all Israel has transgressed Your law,
and has departed so as not to obey Your voice;
therefore the curse and the oath written in the
Law of Moses the servant of God have been
poured out on us, because we have sinned
against Him.
12 "And He has confirmed His words, which
He spoke against us and against our judges who
judged us, by bringing upon us a great disaster;
for under the whole heaven such has never
been done as what has been done to Jerusalem.

8:14 [a]Literally *evening-mornings* **8:21** [a]Literally *king,* representing his kingdom (compare 7:17, 23) **8:25** [a]Literally *hand* [b]Literally *hand*

13 "As *it is* written in the Law of Moses, all
this disaster has come upon us; yet we have
not made our prayer before the LORD our God,
that we might turn from our iniquities and un-
derstand Your truth.
14 "Therefore the LORD has kept the disaster
in mind, and brought it upon us; for the LORD
our God *is* righteous in all the works which He
does, though we have not obeyed His voice.
15 "And now, O Lord our God, who brought
Your people out of the land of Egypt with a
mighty hand, and made Yourself a name, as
it is this day—we have sinned, we have done
wickedly!
16 "O Lord, according to all Your righteous-
ness, I pray, let Your anger and Your fury be
turned away from Your city Jerusalem, Your
holy mountain; because for our sins, and for
the iniquities of our fathers, Jerusalem and
Your people *are* a reproach to all *those* around
us.
17 "Now therefore, our God, hear the prayer
of Your servant, and his supplications, and for
the Lord's sake cause Your face to shine on
Your sanctuary, which is desolate.
18 "O my God, incline Your ear and hear; open
Your eyes and see our desolations, and the city
which is called by Your name; for we do not
present our supplications before You because
of our righteous deeds, but because of Your great
mercies.
19 "O Lord, hear! O Lord, forgive! O Lord,
listen and act! Do not delay for Your own sake,
my God, for Your city and Your people are
called by Your name."

The Seventy-Weeks Prophecy

20 Now while I *was* speaking, praying, and
confessing my sin and the sin of my people
Israel, and presenting my supplication before
the LORD my God for the holy mountain of my
God,
21 yes, while I *was* speaking in prayer, the man
Gabriel, whom I had seen in the vision at the
beginning, being caused to fly swiftly, reached
me about the time of the evening offering.
22 And he informed *me,* and talked with me,
and said, "O Daniel, I have now come forth to
give you skill to understand.
23 "At the beginning of your supplications the
command went out, and I have come to tell
you, for you *are* greatly beloved; therefore con-
sider the matter, and understand the vision:

24 "Seventy weeks[a] are determined
For your people and for your holy city,
To finish the transgression,
To make an end of[b] sins,
To make reconciliation for iniquity,
To bring in everlasting righteousness,
To seal up vision and prophecy,
And to anoint the Most Holy.

25 "Know therefore and understand,
That from the going forth of the
command
To restore and build Jerusalem
Until Messiah the Prince,
There shall be seven weeks and sixty-two
weeks;
The street[a] shall be built again, and the
wall,[b]
Even in troublesome times.

26 "And after the sixty-two weeks
Messiah shall be cut off, but not for
Himself;
And the people of the prince who is to
come
Shall destroy the city and the sanctuary.
The end of it *shall be* with a flood,
And till the end of the war desolations
are determined.
27 Then he shall confirm a covenant with
many for one week;
But in the middle of the week
He shall bring an end to sacrifice and
offering.
And on the wing of abominations shall be
one who makes desolate,
Even until the consummation, which is
determined,
Is poured out on the desolate."

Vision of the Glorious Man

10 In the third year of Cyrus king of Persia
a message was revealed to Daniel, whose
name was called Belteshazzar. The message
was true, but the appointed time *was* long;[a] and
he understood the message, and had under-
standing of the vision.
2 In those days I, Daniel, was mourning three
full weeks.
3 I ate no pleasant food, no meat or wine came
into my mouth, nor did I anoint myself at all,
till three whole weeks were fulfilled.
4 Now on the twenty-fourth day of the first
month, as I was by the side of the great river,
that *is,* the Tigris,[a]
5 I lifted my eyes and looked, and behold, a
certain man clothed in linen, whose waist *was*
girded with gold of Uphaz!
6 His body *was* like beryl, his face like the
appearance of lightning, his eyes like torches
of fire, his arms and feet like burnished bronze
in color, and the sound of his words like the
voice of a multitude.
7 And I, Daniel, alone saw the vision, for the
men who were with me did not see the vision;
but a great terror fell upon them, so that they
fled to hide themselves.
8 Therefore I was left alone when I saw this
great vision, and no strength remained in me;
for my vigor was turned to frailty in me, and I
retained no strength.
9 Yet I heard the sound of his words; and while
I heard the sound of his words I was in a deep
sleep on my face, with my face to the ground.

Prophecies Concerning Persia and Greece

10 Suddenly, a hand touched me, which made
me tremble on my knees and *on* the palms of
my hands.
11 And he said to me, "O Daniel, man greatly
beloved, understand the words that I speak to
you, and stand upright, for I have now been sent
to you." While he was speaking this word to me,
I stood trembling.
12 Then he said to me, "Do not fear, Daniel,
for from the first day that you set your heart
to understand, and to humble yourself before
your God, your words were heard; and I have
come because of your words.
13 "But the prince of the kingdom of Persia
withstood me twenty-one days; and behold,
Michael, one of the chief princes, came to help

9:24 [a]Literally *sevens,* and so throughout the chapter [b]Following Qere, Septuagint, Syriac, and Vulgate; Kethib and Theodotion read *To seal up.* **9:25** [a]Or *open square* [b]Or *moat* **10:1** [a]Or *and of great conflict* **10:4** [a]Hebrew *Hiddekel*

me, for I had been left alone there with the
kings of Persia.
14 "Now I have come to make you understand
what will happen to your people in the latter
days, for the vision *refers* to *many* days yet *to*
come."
15 When he had spoken such words to me, I
turned my face toward the ground and became
speechless.
16 And suddenly, *one* having the likeness of
the sons[a] of men touched my lips; then I opened
my mouth and spoke, saying to him who stood
before me, "My lord, because of the vision my
sorrows have overwhelmed me, and I have retained no strength.
17 "For how can this servant of my lord talk
with you, my lord? As for me, no strength remains in me now, nor is any breath left in me."
18 Then again, *the one* having the likeness of
a man touched me and strengthened me.
19 And he said, "O man greatly beloved, fear
not! Peace *be* to you; be strong, yes, be strong!"
So when he spoke to me I was strengthened,
and said, "Let my lord speak, for you have
strengthened me."
20 Then he said, "Do you know why I have
come to you? And now I must return to fight
with the prince of Persia; and when I have gone
forth, indeed the prince of Greece will come.
21 "But I will tell you what is noted in the
Scripture of Truth. (No one upholds me against
these, except Michael your prince.
11 "Also in the first year of Darius the
Mede, I, *even* I, stood up to confirm and
strengthen him.)
2 "And now I will tell you the truth: Behold,
three more kings will arise in Persia, and the
fourth shall be far richer than *them* all; by his
strength, through his riches, he shall stir up all
against the realm of Greece.
3 "Then a mighty king shall arise, who shall
rule with great dominion, and do according to
his will.
4 "And when he has arisen, his kingdom
shall be broken up and divided toward the four
winds of heaven, but not among his posterity
nor according to his dominion with which he
ruled; for his kingdom shall be uprooted, even
for others besides these.

Warring Kings of North and South

5 "Also the king of the South shall become
strong, as well as *one* of his princes; and he
shall gain power over him and have dominion.
His dominion *shall be* a great dominion.
6 "And at the end of *some* years they shall
join forces, for the daughter of the king of the
South shall go to the king of the North to make
an agreement; but she shall not retain the
power of her authority,[a] and neither he nor his
authority[b] shall stand; but she shall be given
up, with those who brought her, and with him
who begot her, and with him who strengthened
her in *those* times.
7 "But from a branch of her roots *one* shall
arise in his place, who shall come with an army,
enter the fortress of the king of the North, and
deal with them and prevail.
8 "And he shall also carry their gods captive
to Egypt, with their princes[a] *and* their precious
articles of silver and gold; and he shall continue *more* years than the king of the North.
9 "Also *the king of the North* shall come to
the kingdom of the king of the South, but shall
return to his own land.
10 "However his sons shall stir up strife, and
assemble a multitude of great forces; and *one*
shall certainly come and overwhelm and pass
through; then he shall return to his fortress
and stir up strife.
11 "And the king of the South shall be moved
with rage, and go out and fight with him, with
the king of the North, who shall muster a great
multitude; but the multitude shall be given into
the hand of his *enemy.*
12 "When he has taken away the multitude,
his heart will be lifted up; and he will cast down
tens of thousands, but he will not prevail.
13 "For the king of the North will return and
muster a multitude greater than the former, and
shall certainly come at the end of some years
with a great army and much equipment.
14 "Now in those times many shall rise up
against the king of the South. Also, violent
men[a] of your people shall exalt themselves in
fulfillment of the vision, but they shall fall.
15 "So the king of the North shall come and
build a siege mound, and take a fortified city;
and the forces[a] of the South shall not withstand
him. Even his choice troops *shall have* no
strength to resist.
16 "But he who comes against him shall do
according to his own will, and no one shall
stand against him. He shall stand in the Glorious Land with destruction in his power.[a]
17 "He shall also set his face to enter with the
strength of his whole kingdom, and upright
ones[a] with him; thus shall he do. And he shall
give him the daughter of women to destroy it;
but she shall not stand *with him,* or be for him.
18 "After this he shall turn his face to the
coastlands, and shall take many. But a ruler
shall bring the reproach against them to an end;
and with the reproach removed, he shall turn
back on him.
19 "Then he shall turn his face toward the
fortress of his own land; but he shall stumble
and fall, and not be found.
20 "There shall arise in his place one who imposes taxes *on* the glorious kingdom; but within
a few days he shall be destroyed, but not in
anger or in battle.
21 "And in his place shall arise a vile person,
to whom they will not give the honor of royalty;
but he shall come in peaceably, and seize the
kingdom by intrigue.
22 "With the force[a] of a flood they shall be
swept away from before him and be broken,
and also the prince of the covenant.
23 "And after the league *is made* with him he
shall act deceitfully, for he shall come up and
become strong with a small *number of* people.
24 "He shall enter peaceably, even into the richest places of the province; and he shall do *what*
his fathers have not done, nor his forefathers:
he shall disperse among them the plunder, spoil,

10:16 [a]Theodotion and Vulgate read *the son;* Septuagint reads *a hand.* **11:6** [a]Literally *arm* [b]Literally *arm* **11:8** [a]Or *molded images* **11:14** [a]Or *robbers,* literally *sons of breakage* **11:15** [a]Literally *arms* **11:16** [a]Literally *hand* **11:17** [a]Or *bring equitable terms* **11:22** [a]Literally *arms*

and riches; and he shall devise his plans against the strongholds, but *only* for a time.

25 "He shall stir up his power and his courage against the king of the South with a great army. And the king of the South shall be stirred up to battle with a very great and mighty army; but he shall not stand, for they shall devise plans against him.

26 "Yes, those who eat of the portion of his delicacies shall destroy him; his army shall be swept away, and many shall fall down slain.

27 "Both these kings' hearts *shall be* bent on evil, and they shall speak lies at the same table; but it shall not prosper, for the end *will* still *be* at the appointed time.

28 "While returning to his land with great riches, his heart shall be *moved* against the holy covenant; so he shall do *damage* and return to his own land.

The Northern King's Blasphemies

29 "At the appointed time he shall return and go toward the south; but it shall not be like the former or the latter.

30 "For ships from Cyprus[a] shall come against him; therefore he shall be grieved, and return in rage against the holy covenant, and do *damage*. "So he shall return and show regard for those who forsake the holy covenant.

31 "And forces[a] shall be mustered by him, and they shall defile the sanctuary fortress; then they shall take away the daily *sacrifices*, and place *there* the abomination of desolation.

32 "Those who do wickedly against the covenant he shall corrupt with flattery; but the people who know their God shall be strong, and carry out *great exploits*.

33 "And those of the people who understand shall instruct many; yet *for many* days they shall fall by sword and flame, by captivity and plundering.

34 "Now when they fall, they shall be aided with a little help; but many shall join with them by intrigue.

35 "And *some* of those of understanding shall fall, to refine them, purify *them*, and make *them* white, *until* the time of the end; because *it is* still for the appointed time.

36 "Then the king shall do according to his own will: he shall exalt and magnify himself above every god, shall speak blasphemies against the God of gods, and shall prosper till the wrath has been accomplished; for what has been determined shall be done.

37 "He shall regard neither the God[a] of his fathers nor the desire of women, nor regard any god; for he shall exalt himself above *them* all.

38 "But in their place he shall honor a god of fortresses; and a god which his fathers did not know he shall honor with gold and silver, with precious stones and pleasant things.

39 "Thus he shall act against the strongest fortresses with a foreign god, which he shall acknowledge, *and* advance *its* glory; and he shall cause them to rule over many, and divide the land for gain.

The Northern King's Conquests

40 "At the time of the end the king of the South shall attack him; and the king of the North shall come against him like a whirlwind, with chariots, horsemen, and with many ships; and he shall enter the countries, overwhelm *them*, and pass through.

41 "He shall also enter the Glorious Land, and many *countries* shall be overthrown; but these shall escape from his hand: Edom, Moab, and the prominent people of Ammon.

42 "He shall stretch out his hand against the countries, and the land of Egypt shall not escape.

43 "He shall have power over the treasures of gold and silver, and over all the precious things of Egypt; also the Libyans and Ethiopians *shall follow* at his heels.

44 "But news from the east and the north shall trouble him; therefore he shall go out with great fury to destroy and annihilate many.

45 "And he shall plant the tents of his palace between the seas and the glorious holy mountain; yet he shall come to his end, and no one will help him.

Prophecy of the End Time

12 "At that time Michael shall stand up,
The great prince who stands *watch* over the sons of your people;
And there shall be a time of trouble,
Such as never was since there was a nation,
Even to that time.
And at that time your people shall be delivered,
Every one who is found written in the book.
2 And many of those who sleep in the dust of the earth shall awake,
Some to everlasting life,
Some to shame *and* everlasting contempt.
3 Those who are wise shall shine
Like the brightness of the firmament,
And those who turn many to righteousness
Like the stars forever and ever.

4 "But you, Daniel, shut up the words, and seal the book until the time of the end; many shall run to and fro, and knowledge shall increase."

5 Then I, Daniel, looked; and there stood two others, one on this riverbank and the other on that riverbank.

6 And *one* said to the man clothed in linen, who *was* above the waters of the river, "How long shall the fulfillment of these wonders *be?*"

7 Then I heard the man clothed in linen, who *was* above the waters of the river, when he held up his right hand and his left hand to heaven, and swore by Him who lives forever, that *it shall be* for a time, times, and half *a time;* and when the power of the holy people has been completely shattered, all these *things* shall be finished.

8 Although I heard, I did not understand. Then I said, "My lord, what *shall be* the end of these *things?*"

9 And he said, "Go *your way,* Daniel, for the words *are* closed up and sealed till the time of the end.

10 "Many shall be purified, made white, and refined, but the wicked shall do wickedly; and

11:30 [a]Hebrew *Kittim,* western lands, especially Cyprus **11:31** [a]Literally *arms* **11:37** [a]Or *gods*

none of the wicked shall understand, but the wise shall understand.
11 "And from the time *that* the daily *sacrifice* is taken away, and the abomination of desolation is set up, *there shall be* one thousand two hundred and ninety days.
12 "Blessed *is* he who waits, and comes to the one thousand three hundred and thirty-five days.
13 "But you, go *your way* till the end; for you shall rest, and will arise to your inheritance at the end of the days."

The Book of HOSEA

1 The word of the LORD that came to Hosea the son of Beeri, in the days of Uzziah, Jotham, Ahaz, *and* Hezekiah, kings of Judah, and in the days of Jeroboam the son of Joash, king of Israel.

The Family of Hosea

2 When the LORD began to speak by Hosea, the LORD said to Hosea:

"Go, take yourself a wife of harlotry
And children of harlotry,
For the land has committed great harlotry
By departing from the LORD."

3 So he went and took Gomer the daughter of Diblaim, and she conceived and bore him a son.
4 Then the LORD said to him:

"Call his name Jezreel,
For in a little *while*
I will avenge the bloodshed of Jezreel on the house of Jehu,
And bring an end to the kingdom of the house of Israel.
5 It shall come to pass in that day
That I will break the bow of Israel in the Valley of Jezreel."

6 And she conceived again and bore a daughter. Then *God* said to him:

"Call her name Lo-Ruhamah,[a]
For I will no longer have mercy on the house of Israel,
But I will utterly take them away.[b]
7 Yet I will have mercy on the house of Judah,
Will save them by the LORD their God,
And will not save them by bow,
Nor by sword or battle,
By horses or horsemen."

8 Now when she had weaned Lo-Ruhamah, she conceived and bore a son.
9 Then *God* said:

"Call his name Lo-Ammi,[a]
For you *are* not My people,
And I will not be your *God.*

The Restoration of Israel

10 "Yet the number of the children of Israel
Shall be as the sand of the sea,
Which cannot be measured or numbered.
And it shall come to pass
In the place where it was said to them,
'You *are* not My people,'[a]
There it shall be said to them,
'*You are* sons of the living God.'
11 Then the children of Judah and the children of Israel
Shall be gathered together,
And appoint for themselves one head;
And they shall come up out of the land,
For great *will be* the day of Jezreel!

2 Say to your brethren, 'My people,'[a]
And to your sisters, 'Mercy[b] *is shown.*'

God's Unfaithful People

2 "Bring charges against your mother, bring charges;
For she *is* not My wife, nor *am* I her Husband!
Let her put away her harlotries from her sight,
And her adulteries from between her breasts;
3 Lest I strip her naked
And expose her, as in the day she was born,
And make her like a wilderness,
And set her like a dry land,
And slay her with thirst.

4 "I will not have mercy on her children,
For they *are* the children of harlotry.
5 For their mother has played the harlot;
She who conceived them has behaved shamefully.
For she said, 'I will go after my lovers,
Who give *me* my bread and my water,
My wool and my linen,
My oil and my drink.'

6 "Therefore, behold,
I will hedge up your way with thorns,
And wall her in,
So that she cannot find her paths.
7 She will chase her lovers,
But not overtake them;
Yes, she will seek them, but not find *them.*
Then she will say,
'I will go and return to my first husband,
For then *it was* better for me than now.'
8 For she did not know
That I gave her grain, new wine, and oil,
And multiplied her silver and gold—
Which they prepared for Baal.

9 "Therefore I will return and take away
My grain in its time
And My new wine in its season,
And will take back My wool and My linen,
Given to cover her nakedness.
10 Now I will uncover her lewdness in the sight of her lovers,

1:6 [a]Literally *No-Mercy* [b]Or *That I may forgive them at all* 1:9 [a]Literally *Not-My-People* 1:10 [a]Hebrew *lo-ammi* (compare verse 9) 2:1 [a]Hebrew *Ammi* (compare 1:9, 10) [b]Hebrew *Ruhamah* (compare 1:6)

And no one shall deliver her from My hand.
11 I will also cause all her mirth to cease,
Her feast days,
Her New Moons,
Her Sabbaths—
All her appointed feasts.

12 "And I will destroy her vines and her fig trees,
Of which she has said,
'These *are* my wages that my lovers have given me.'
So I will make them a forest,
And the beasts of the field shall eat them.
13 I will punish her
For the days of the Baals to which she burned incense.
She decked herself with her earrings and jewelry,
And went after her lovers;
But Me she forgot," says the LORD.

God's Mercy on His People

14 "Therefore, behold, I will allure her,
Will bring her into the wilderness,
And speak comfort to her.
15 I will give her her vineyards from there,
And the Valley of Achor as a door of hope;
She shall sing there,
As in the days of her youth,
As in the day when she came up from the land of Egypt.

16 "And it shall be, in that day,"
Says the LORD,
"*That* you will call Me 'My Husband,'[a]
And no longer call Me 'My Master,'[b]
17 For I will take from her mouth the names of the Baals,
And they shall be remembered by their name no more.
18 In that day I will make a covenant for them
With the beasts of the field,
With the birds of the air,
And *with* the creeping things of the ground.
Bow and sword of battle I will shatter from the earth,
To make them lie down safely.
19 "I will betroth you to Me forever;
Yes, I will betroth you to Me
In righteousness and justice,
In lovingkindness and mercy;
20 I will betroth you to Me in faithfulness,
And you shall know the LORD.

21 "It shall come to pass in that day
That I will answer," says the LORD;
"I will answer the heavens,
And they shall answer the earth.
22 The earth shall answer
With grain,
With new wine,
And with oil;
They shall answer Jezreel.[a]
23 Then I will sow her for Myself in the earth,
And I will have mercy on *her who had* not obtained mercy;[a]
Then I will say to *those who were* not My people,[b]
'You *are* My people!'
And they shall say, '*You are* my God!'"

Israel Will Return to God

3 Then the LORD said to me, "Go again, love
a woman *who is* loved by a lover[a] and is
committing adultery, just like the love of the
LORD for the children of Israel, who look to
other gods and love *the* raisin cakes *of the*
pagans."
2 So I bought her for myself for fifteen *shek-*
els of silver, and one and one-half homers of
barley.
3 And I said to her, "You shall stay with me
many days; you shall not play the harlot, nor
shall you have a man—so, too, *will* I *be* toward
you."
4 For the children of Israel shall abide many
days without king or prince, without sacrifice
or *sacred* pillar, without ephod or teraphim.
5 Afterward the children of Israel shall re-
turn and seek the LORD their God and David
their king. They shall fear the LORD and His
goodness in the latter days.

God's Charge Against Israel

4 Hear the word of the LORD,
You children of Israel,
For the LORD *brings* a charge against the inhabitants of the land:

"There is no truth or mercy
Or knowledge of God in the land.
2 *By* swearing and lying,
Killing and stealing and committing adultery,
They break all restraint,
With bloodshed upon bloodshed.
3 Therefore the land will mourn;
And everyone who dwells there will waste away
With the beasts of the field
And the birds of the air;
Even the fish of the sea will be taken away.

4 "Now let no man contend, or rebuke another;
For your people *are* like those who contend with the priest.
5 Therefore you shall stumble in the day;
The prophet also shall stumble with you in the night;
And I will destroy your mother.
6 My people are destroyed for lack of knowledge.
Because you have rejected knowledge,
I also will reject you from being priest for Me;
Because you have forgotten the law of your God,
I also will forget your children.

7 "The more they increased,
The more they sinned against Me;
I will change[a] their glory[b] into shame.

2:16 [a]Hebrew *Ishi* [b]Hebrew *Baali* **2:22** [a]Literally *God Will Sow* **2:23** [a]Hebrew *lo-ruhamah* [b]Hebrew *lo-ammi*
3:1 [a]Literally *friend* or *husband* **4:7** [a]Following Masoretic Text, Septuagint, and Vulgate; scribal tradition, Syriac, and Targum read *They will change.* [b]Following Masoretic Text, Septuagint, Syriac, Targum, and Vulgate; scribal tradition reads *My glory.*

8 They eat up the sin of My people;
They set their heart on their iniquity.
9 And it shall be: like people, like priest.
So I will punish them for their ways,
And reward them for their deeds.
10 For they shall eat, but not have enough;
They shall commit harlotry, but not increase;
Because they have ceased obeying the LORD.

The Idolatry of Israel

11 "Harlotry, wine, and new wine enslave the heart.
12 My people ask counsel from their wooden *idols*,
And their staff informs them.
For the spirit of harlotry has caused *them* to stray,
And they have played the harlot against their God.
13 They offer sacrifices on the mountaintops,
And burn incense on the hills,
Under oaks, poplars, and terebinths,
Because their shade *is* good.
Therefore your daughters commit harlotry,
And your brides commit adultery.

14 "I will not punish your daughters when they commit harlotry,
Nor your brides when they commit adultery;
For *the men* themselves go apart with harlots,
And offer sacrifices with a ritual harlot.[a]
Therefore people *who* do not understand will be trampled.

15 "Though you, Israel, play the harlot,
Let not Judah offend.
Do not come up to Gilgal,
Nor go up to Beth Aven,
Nor swear an oath, *saying*, 'As the LORD lives'—

16 "For Israel is stubborn
Like a stubborn calf;
Now the LORD will let them forage
Like a lamb in open country.

17 "Ephraim *is* joined to idols,
Let him alone.
18 Their drink is rebellion,
They commit harlotry continually.
Her rulers dearly love dishonor.[a]
19 The wind has wrapped her up in its wings,
And they shall be ashamed because of their sacrifices.

Impending Judgment on Israel and Judah

5 "Hear this, O priests!
Take heed, O house of Israel!
Give ear, O house of the king!
For yours *is* the judgment,
Because you have been a snare to Mizpah
And a net spread on Tabor.
2 The revolters are deeply involved in slaughter,
Though I rebuke them all.
3 I know Ephraim,
And Israel is not hidden from Me;
For now, O Ephraim, you commit harlotry;
Israel is defiled.

4 "They do not direct their deeds
Toward turning to their God,
For the spirit of harlotry is in their midst,
And they do not know the LORD.
5 The pride of Israel testifies to his face;
Therefore Israel and Ephraim stumble in their iniquity;
Judah also stumbles with them.

6 "With their flocks and herds
They shall go to seek the LORD,
But they will not find *Him;*
He has withdrawn Himself from them.
7 They have dealt treacherously with the LORD,
For they have begotten pagan children.
Now a New Moon shall devour them and their heritage.

8 "Blow the ram's horn in Gibeah,
The trumpet in Ramah!
Cry aloud *at* Beth Aven,
'*Look* behind you, O Benjamin!'
9 Ephraim shall be desolate in the day of rebuke;
Among the tribes of Israel I make known what is sure.

10 "The princes of Judah are like those who remove a landmark;
I will pour out My wrath on them like water.
11 Ephraim is oppressed *and* broken in judgment,
Because he willingly walked by *human* precept.
12 Therefore I *will be* to Ephraim like a moth,
And to the house of Judah like rottenness.

13 "When Ephraim saw his sickness,
And Judah *saw* his wound,
Then Ephraim went to Assyria
And sent to King Jareb;
Yet he cannot cure you,
Nor heal you of your wound.
14 For I *will be* like a lion to Ephraim,
And like a young lion to the house of Judah.
I, *even* I, will tear *them* and go away;
I will take *them* away, and no one shall rescue.
15 I will return again to My place
Till they acknowledge their offense.
Then they will seek My face;
In their affliction they will earnestly seek Me."

A Call to Repentance

6 Come, and let us return to the LORD;
For He has torn, but He will heal us;
He has stricken, but He will bind us up.
2 After two days He will revive us;
On the third day He will raise us up,
That we may live in His sight.
3 Let us know,
Let us pursue the knowledge of the LORD.

4:14 [a]Compare Deuteronomy 23:18 4:18 [a]Hebrew is difficult; a Jewish tradition reads *Her rulers shamefully love, 'Give!'*

His going forth is established as the morning;
He will come to us like the rain,
Like the latter *and* former rain to the earth.

Impenitence of Israel and Judah

4 "O Ephraim, what shall I do to you?
O Judah, what shall I do to you?
For your faithfulness is like a morning cloud,
And like the early dew it goes away.
5 Therefore I have hewn *them* by the prophets,
I have slain them by the words of My mouth;
And your judgments *are like* light *that* goes forth.
6 For I desire mercy and not sacrifice,
And the knowledge of God more than burnt offerings.

7 "But like men[a] they transgressed the covenant;
There they dealt treacherously with Me.
8 Gilead *is* a city of evildoers
And defiled with blood.
9 As bands of robbers lie in wait for a man,
So the company of priests murder on the way to Shechem;
Surely they commit lewdness.
10 I have seen a horrible thing in the house of Israel:
There *is* the harlotry of Ephraim;
Israel is defiled.
11 Also, O Judah, a harvest is appointed for you,
When I return the captives of My people.

7 "When I would have healed Israel,
Then the iniquity of Ephraim was uncovered,
And the wickedness of Samaria.
For they have committed fraud;
A thief comes in;
A band of robbers takes spoil outside.
2 They do not consider in their hearts
That I remember all their wickedness;
Now their own deeds have surrounded them;
They are before My face.
3 They make a king glad with their wickedness,
And princes with their lies.

4 "They *are* all adulterers.
Like an oven heated by a baker—
He ceases stirring *the fire* after kneading the dough,
Until it is leavened.
5 In the day of our king
Princes have made *him* sick, inflamed with wine;
He stretched out his hand with scoffers.
6 They prepare their heart like an oven,
While they lie in wait;
Their baker[a] sleeps all night;
In the morning it burns like a flaming fire.
7 They are all hot, like an oven,
And have devoured their judges;
All their kings have fallen.
None among them calls upon Me.

8 "Ephraim has mixed himself among the peoples;
Ephraim is a cake unturned.
9 Aliens have devoured his strength,
But he does not know *it;*
Yes, gray hairs are here and there on him,
Yet he does not know *it.*
10 And the pride of Israel testifies to his face,
But they do not return to the LORD their God,
Nor seek Him for all this.

Futile Reliance on the Nations

11 "Ephraim also is like a silly dove, without sense—
They call to Egypt,
They go to Assyria.
12 Wherever they go, I will spread My net on them;
I will bring them down like birds of the air;
I will chastise them
According to what their congregation has heard.

13 "Woe to them, for they have fled from Me!
Destruction to them,
Because they have transgressed against Me!
Though I redeemed them,
Yet they have spoken lies against Me.
14 They did not cry out to Me with their heart
When they wailed upon their beds.

"They assemble together for[a] grain and new wine,
They rebel against Me;[b]
15 Though I disciplined *and* strengthened their arms,
Yet they devise evil against Me;
16 They return, *but* not to the Most High;[a]
They are like a treacherous bow.
Their princes shall fall by the sword
For the cursings of their tongue.
This *shall be* their derision in the land of Egypt.

The Apostasy of Israel

8 "*Set* the trumpet[a] to your mouth!
He shall come like an eagle against the house of the LORD,
Because they have transgressed My covenant
And rebelled against My law.
2 Israel will cry to Me,
'My God, we know You!'
3 Israel has rejected the good;
The enemy will pursue him.

4 "They set up kings, but not by Me;
They made princes, but I did not acknowledge *them.*
From their silver and gold
They made idols for themselves—
That they might be cut off.
5 Your calf is rejected, O Samaria!
My anger is aroused against them—

6:7 [a]Or *like Adam* **7:6** [a]Following Masoretic Text and Vulgate; Syriac and Targum read *Their anger;* Septuagint reads *Ephraim.* **7:14** [a]Following Masoretic Text and Targum; Vulgate reads *thought upon;* Septuagint reads *slashed themselves for* (compare 1 Kings 18:28). [b]Following Masoretic Text, Syriac, and Targum; Septuagint omits *They rebel against Me;* Vulgate reads *They departed from Me.* **7:16** [a]Or *upward* **8:1** [a]Hebrew *shophar,* ram's horn

How long until they attain to innocence?
6 For from Israel *is* even this:
A workman made it, and it *is* not God;
But the calf of Samaria shall be broken to pieces.

7 "They sow the wind,
And reap the whirlwind.
The stalk has no bud;
It shall never produce meal.
If it should produce,
Aliens would swallow it up.
8 Israel is swallowed up;
Now they are among the Gentiles
Like a vessel in which *is* no pleasure.
9 For they have gone up to Assyria,
Like a wild donkey alone by itself;
Ephraim has hired lovers.
10 Yes, though they have hired among the nations,
Now I will gather them;
And they shall sorrow a little,[a]
Because of the burden[b] of the king of princes.

11 "Because Ephraim has made many altars for sin,
They have become for him altars for sinning.
12 I have written for him the great things of My law,
But they were considered a strange thing.
13 *For* the sacrifices of My offerings they sacrifice flesh and eat *it*,
But the LORD does not accept them.
Now He will remember their iniquity and punish their sins.
They shall return to Egypt.

14 "For Israel has forgotten his Maker,
And has built temples;[a]
Judah also has multiplied fortified cities;
But I will send fire upon his cities,
And it shall devour his palaces."

Judgment of Israel's Sin

9 Do not rejoice, O Israel, with joy like *other* peoples,
For you have played the harlot against your God.
You have made love *for* hire on every threshing floor.
2 The threshing floor and the winepress
Shall not feed them,
And the new wine shall fail in her.

3 They shall not dwell in the LORD's land,
But Ephraim shall return to Egypt,
And shall eat unclean *things* in Assyria.
4 They shall not offer wine *offerings* to the LORD,
Nor shall their sacrifices be pleasing to Him.
It shall be like bread of mourners to them;
All who eat it shall be defiled.
For their bread *shall be* for their *own* life;
It shall not come into the house of the LORD.

5 What will you do in the appointed day,
And in the day of the feast of the LORD?
6 For indeed they are gone because of destruction.
Egypt shall gather them up;
Memphis shall bury them.
Nettles shall possess their valuables of silver;
Thorns *shall be* in their tents.

7 The days of punishment have come;
The days of recompense have come.
Israel knows!
The prophet *is* a fool,
The spiritual man *is* insane,
Because of the greatness of your iniquity and great enmity.
8 The watchman of Ephraim *is* with my God;
But the prophet *is* a fowler's[a] snare in all his ways—
Enmity in the house of his God.
9 They are deeply corrupted,
As in the days of Gibeah.
He will remember their iniquity;
He will punish their sins.

10 "I found Israel
Like grapes in the wilderness;
I saw your fathers
As the firstfruits on the fig tree in its first season.
But they went to Baal Peor,
And separated themselves *to that* shame;
They became an abomination like the thing they loved.
11 *As for* Ephraim, their glory shall fly away like a bird—
No birth, no pregnancy, and no conception!
12 Though they bring up their children,
Yet I will bereave them to the last man.
Yes, woe to them when I depart from them!
13 Just as I saw Ephraim like Tyre, planted in a pleasant place,
So Ephraim will bring out his children to the murderer."

14 Give them, O LORD—
What will You give?
Give them a miscarrying womb
And dry breasts!

15 "All their wickedness *is* in Gilgal,
For there I hated them.
Because of the evil of their deeds
I will drive them from My house;
I will love them no more.
All their princes *are* rebellious.
16 Ephraim is stricken,
Their root is dried up;
They shall bear no fruit.
Yes, were they to bear children,
I would kill the darlings of their womb."

17 My God will cast them away,
Because they did not obey Him;
And they shall be wanderers among the nations.

Israel's Sin and Captivity

10 Israel empties *his* vine;
He brings forth fruit for himself.
According to the multitude of his fruit
He has increased the altars;
According to the bounty of his land
They have embellished *his sacred* pillars.
2 Their heart is divided;
Now they are held guilty.
He will break down their altars;
He will ruin their *sacred* pillars.

8:10 [a]Or *begin to diminish* [b]Or *oracle* **8:14** [a]Or *palaces* **9:8** [a]That is, one who catches birds in a trap or snare

3 For now they say,
"We have no king,
Because we did not fear the LORD.
And as for a king, what would he do for us?"
4 They have spoken words,
Swearing falsely in making a covenant.
Thus judgment springs up like hemlock in the furrows of the field.

5 The inhabitants of Samaria fear
Because of the calf[a] of Beth Aven.
For its people mourn for it,
And its priests shriek for it—
Because its glory has departed from it.
6 *The idol* also shall be carried to Assyria
As a present for King Jareb.
Ephraim shall receive shame,
And Israel shall be ashamed of his own counsel.

7 *As for* Samaria, her king is cut off
Like a twig on the water.
8 Also the high places of Aven, the sin of Israel,
Shall be destroyed.
The thorn and thistle shall grow on their altars;
They shall say to the mountains, "Cover us!"
And to the hills, "Fall on us!"

9 "O Israel, you have sinned from the days of Gibeah;
There they stood.
The battle in Gibeah against the children of iniquity[a]
Did not overtake them.
10 When *it is* My desire, I will chasten them.
Peoples shall be gathered against them
When I bind them for their two transgressions.[a]
11 Ephraim *is* a trained heifer
That loves to thresh *grain;*
But I harnessed her fair neck,
I will make Ephraim pull *a plow.*
Judah shall plow;
Jacob shall break his clods."
12 Sow for yourselves righteousness;
Reap in mercy;
Break up your fallow ground,
For *it is* time to seek the LORD,
Till He comes and rains righteousness on you.

13 You have plowed wickedness;
You have reaped iniquity.
You have eaten the fruit of lies,
Because you trusted in your own way,
In the multitude of your mighty men.
14 Therefore tumult shall arise among your people,
And all your fortresses shall be plundered
As Shalman plundered Beth Arbel in the day of battle—
A mother dashed in pieces upon *her* children.
15 Thus it shall be done to you, O Bethel,
Because of your great wickedness.
At dawn the king of Israel
Shall be cut off utterly.

God's Continuing Love for Israel

11 "When Israel *was* a child, I loved him,
And out of Egypt I called My son.
2 *As* they called them,[a]
So they went from them;[b]
They sacrificed to the Baals,
And burned incense to carved images.

3 "I taught Ephraim to walk,
Taking them by their arms;[a]
But they did not know that I healed them.
4 I drew them with gentle cords,[a]
With bands of love,
And I was to them as those who take the yoke from their neck.[b]
I stooped *and* fed them.

5 "He shall not return to the land of Egypt;
But the Assyrian shall be his king,
Because they refused to repent.
6 And the sword shall slash in his cities,
Devour his districts,
And consume *them,*
Because of their own counsels.
7 My people are bent on backsliding from Me.
Though they call to the Most High,[a]
None at all exalt *Him.*

8 "How can I give you up, Ephraim?
How can I hand you over, Israel?
How can I make you like Admah?
How can I set you like Zeboiim?
My heart churns within Me;
My sympathy is stirred.
9 I will not execute the fierceness of My anger;
I will not again destroy Ephraim.
For I *am* God, and not man,
The Holy One in your midst;
And I will not come with terror.[a]

10 "They shall walk after the LORD.
He will roar like a lion.
When He roars,
Then *His* sons shall come trembling from the west;
11 They shall come trembling like a bird from Egypt,
Like a dove from the land of Assyria.
And I will let them dwell in their houses,"
Says the LORD.

God's Charge Against Ephraim

12 "Ephraim has encircled Me with lies,
And the house of Israel with deceit;
But Judah still walks with God,
Even with the Holy One[a] *who is* faithful.

12 "Ephraim feeds on the wind,
And pursues the east wind;
He daily increases lies and desolation.
Also they make a covenant with the Assyrians,
And oil is carried to Egypt.

10:5 [a]Literally *calves* **10:9** [a]So read many Hebrew manuscripts, Septuagint, and Vulgate; Masoretic Text reads *unruliness.* **10:10** [a]Or *in their two habitations* **11:2** [a]Following Masoretic Text and Vulgate; Septuagint reads *Just as I called them;* Targum interprets as *I sent prophets to a thousand of them.* [b]Following Masoretic Text, Targum, and Vulgate; Septuagint reads *from My face.* **11:3** [a]Some Hebrew manuscripts, Septuagint, Syriac, and Vulgate read *My arms.* **11:4** [a]Literally *cords of a man* [b]Literally *jaws* **11:7** [a]Or *upward* **11:9** [a]Or *I will not enter a city* **11:12** [a]Or *holy ones*

2 "The LORD also *brings* a charge against
Judah,
And will punish Jacob according to his
ways;
According to his deeds He will
recompense him.
3 He took his brother by the heel in the
womb,
And in his strength he struggled with
God.[a]
4 Yes, he struggled with the Angel and
prevailed;
He wept, and sought favor from Him.
He found Him *in* Bethel,
And there He spoke to us—
5 That is, the LORD God of hosts.
The LORD *is* His memorable name.
6 So you, by *the help of* your God, return;
Observe mercy and justice,
And wait on your God continually.

7 "A cunning Canaanite!
Deceitful scales *are* in his hand;
He loves to oppress.
8 And Ephraim said,
'Surely I have become rich,
I have found wealth for myself;
In all my labors
They shall find in me no iniquity that *is*
sin.'

9 "But I *am* the LORD your God,
Ever since the land of Egypt;
I will again make you dwell in tents,
As in the days of the appointed feast.
10 I have also spoken by the prophets,
And have multiplied visions;
I have given symbols through the witness
of the prophets."

11 Though Gilead *has* idols—
Surely they are vanity—
Though they sacrifice bulls in Gilgal,
Indeed their altars *shall be* heaps in the
furrows of the field.

12 Jacob fled to the country of Syria;
Israel served for a spouse,
And for a wife he tended *sheep.*
13 By a prophet the LORD brought Israel out
of Egypt,
And by a prophet he was preserved.
14 Ephraim provoked *Him* to anger most
bitterly;
Therefore his Lord will leave the guilt of
his bloodshed upon him,
And return his reproach upon him.

Relentless Judgment on Israel

13 When Ephraim spoke, trembling,
He exalted *himself* in Israel;
But when he offended through Baal
worship, he died.
2 Now they sin more and more,
And have made for themselves molded
images,
Idols of their silver, according to their skill;
All of it *is* the work of craftsmen.
They say of them,
"Let the men who sacrifice[a] kiss the calves!"
3 Therefore they shall be like the morning
cloud
And like the early dew that passes away,
Like chaff blown off from a threshing
floor
And like smoke from a chimney.

4 "Yet I *am* the LORD your God
Ever since the land of Egypt,
And you shall know no God but Me;
For *there is* no savior besides Me.
5 I knew you in the wilderness,
In the land of great drought.
6 When they had pasture, they were filled;
They were filled and their heart was
exalted;
Therefore they forgot Me.

7 "So I will be to them like a lion;
Like a leopard by the road I will lurk;
8 I will meet them like a bear deprived *of
her cubs;*
I will tear open their rib cage,
And there I will devour them like a lion.
The wild beast shall tear them.

9 "O Israel, you are destroyed,[a]
But your help[b] *is* from Me.
10 I will be your King;[a]
Where *is any other,*
That he may save you in all your cities?
And your judges to whom you said,
'Give me a king and princes'?
11 I gave you a king in My anger,
And took *him* away in My wrath.

12 "The iniquity of Ephraim *is* bound up;
His sin *is* stored up.
13 The sorrows of a woman in childbirth
shall come upon him.
He *is* an unwise son,
For he should not stay long where
children are born.

14 "I will ransom them from the power of the
grave;[a]
I will redeem them from death.
O Death, I will be your plagues![b]
O Grave,[c] I will be your destruction![d]
Pity is hidden from My eyes."

15 Though he is fruitful among *his* brethren,
An east wind shall come;
The wind of the LORD shall come up from
the wilderness.
Then his spring shall become dry,
And his fountain shall be dried up.
He shall plunder the treasury of every
desirable prize.
16 Samaria is held guilty,[a]
For she has rebelled against her God.
They shall fall by the sword,
Their infants shall be dashed in pieces,
And their women with child ripped open.

Israel Restored at Last

14 O Israel, return to the LORD your God,
For you have stumbled because of your
iniquity;
2 Take words with you,
And return to the LORD.
Say to Him,
"Take away all iniquity;
Receive *us* graciously,
For we will offer the sacrifices[a] of our lips.

12:3 [a]Compare Genesis 32:28 **13:2** [a]Or *those who offer human sacrifice* **13:9** [a]Literally *it* or *he destroyed you* [b]Literally *in your help* **13:10** [a]Septuagint, Syriac, Targum, and Vulgate read *Where is your king?* **13:14** [a]Or *Sheol* [b]Septuagint reads *where is your punishment?* [c]Or *Sheol* [d]Septuagint reads *where is your sting?* **13:16** [a]Septuagint reads *shall be disfigured.* **14:2** [a]Literally *bull calves;* Septuagint reads *fruit.*

3 Assyria shall not save us,
We will not ride on horses,
Nor will we say anymore to the work of our hands,
'*You are* our gods.'
For in You the fatherless finds mercy."
4 "I will heal their backsliding,
I will love them freely,
For My anger has turned away from him.
5 I will be like the dew to Israel;
He shall grow like the lily,
And lengthen his roots like Lebanon.
6 His branches shall spread;
His beauty shall be like an olive tree,
And his fragrance like Lebanon.
7 Those who dwell under his shadow shall return;
They shall be revived *like* grain,
And grow like a vine.
Their scent[a] *shall be* like the wine of Lebanon.
8 "Ephraim *shall say,*
'What have I to do anymore with idols?'
I have heard and observed him.
I *am* like a green cypress tree;
Your fruit is found in Me."
9 Who *is* wise?
Let him understand these things.
Who is prudent?
Let him know them.
For the ways of the LORD *are* right;
The righteous walk in them,
But transgressors stumble in them.

The Book of JOEL

1 The word of the LORD that came to Joel the son of Pethuel.

The Land Laid Waste

2 Hear this, you elders,
And give ear, all you inhabitants of the land!
Has *anything like* this happened in your days,
Or even in the days of your fathers?
3 Tell your children about it,
Let your children *tell* their children,
And their children another generation.
4 What the chewing locust[a] left, the swarming locust has eaten;
What the swarming locust left, the crawling locust has eaten;
And what the crawling locust left, the consuming locust has eaten.
5 Awake, you drunkards, and weep;
And wail, all you drinkers of wine,
Because of the new wine,
For it has been cut off from your mouth.
6 For a nation has come up against My land,
Strong, and without number;
His teeth *are* the teeth of a lion,
And he has the fangs of a fierce lion.
7 He has laid waste My vine,
And ruined My fig tree;
He has stripped it bare and thrown *it* away;
Its branches are made white.
8 Lament like a virgin girded with sackcloth
For the husband of her youth.
9 The grain offering and the drink offering
Have been cut off from the house of the LORD;
The priests mourn, who minister to the LORD.
10 The field is wasted,
The land mourns;
For the grain is ruined,
The new wine is dried up,
The oil fails.
11 Be ashamed, you farmers,
Wail, you vinedressers,
For the wheat and the barley;
Because the harvest of the field has perished.
12 The vine has dried up,
And the fig tree has withered;
The pomegranate tree,
The palm tree also,
And the apple tree—
All the trees of the field are withered;
Surely joy has withered away from the sons of men.

Mourning for the Land

13 Gird yourselves and lament, you priests;
Wail, you who minister before the altar;
Come, lie all night in sackcloth,
You who minister to my God;
For the grain offering and the drink offering
Are withheld from the house of your God.
14 Consecrate a fast,
Call a sacred assembly;
Gather the elders
And all the inhabitants of the land
Into the house of the LORD your God,
And cry out to the LORD.
15 Alas for the day!
For the day of the LORD *is* at hand;
It shall come as destruction from the Almighty.
16 Is not the food cut off before our eyes,
Joy and gladness from the house of our God?
17 The seed shrivels under the clods,
Storehouses are in shambles;
Barns are broken down,
For the grain has withered.
18 How the animals groan!
The herds of cattle are restless,

14:7 [a]Literally *remembrance* 1:4 [a]Exact identity of these locusts is unknown.

Because they have no pasture;
Even the flocks of sheep suffer
punishment.[a]
19 O LORD, to You I cry out;
For fire has devoured the open pastures,
And a flame has burned all the trees of
the field.
20 The beasts of the field also cry out to You,
For the water brooks are dried up,
And fire has devoured the open pastures.

The Day of the LORD

2 Blow the trumpet in Zion,
And sound an alarm in My holy
mountain!
Let all the inhabitants of the land
tremble;
For the day of the LORD is coming,
For it is at hand:
2 A day of darkness and gloominess,
A day of clouds and thick darkness,
Like the morning *clouds* spread over the
mountains.
A people *come*, great and strong,
The like of whom has never been;
Nor will there ever be any *such* after
them,
Even for many successive generations.

3 A fire devours before them,
And behind them a flame burns;
The land *is* like the Garden of Eden
before them,
And behind them a desolate wilderness;
Surely nothing shall escape them.
4 Their appearance is like the appearance
of horses;
And like swift steeds, so they run.
5 With a noise like chariots
Over mountaintops they leap,
Like the noise of a flaming fire that
devours the stubble,
Like a strong people set in battle array.

6 Before them the people writhe in pain;
All faces are drained of color.[a]
7 They run like mighty men,
They climb the wall like men of war;
Every one marches in formation,
And they do not break ranks.
8 They do not push one another;
Every one marches in his own column.[a]
Though they lunge between the weapons,
They are not cut down.[b]
9 They run to and fro in the city,
They run on the wall;
They climb into the houses,
They enter at the windows like a thief.

10 The earth quakes before them,
The heavens tremble;
The sun and moon grow dark,
And the stars diminish their brightness.
11 The LORD gives voice before His army,
For His camp is very great;
For strong *is the One* who executes His
word.
For the day of the LORD *is* great and very
terrible;
Who can endure it?

A Call to Repentance

12 "Now, therefore," says the LORD,
"Turn to Me with all your heart,
With fasting, with weeping, and with
mourning."
13 So rend your heart, and not your
garments;
Return to the LORD your God,
For He *is* gracious and merciful,
Slow to anger, and of great kindness;
And He relents from doing harm.
14 Who knows *if* He will turn and relent,
And leave a blessing behind Him—
A grain offering and a drink offering
For the LORD your God?

15 Blow the trumpet in Zion,
Consecrate a fast,
Call a sacred assembly;
16 Gather the people,
Sanctify the congregation,
Assemble the elders,
Gather the children and nursing babes;
Let the bridegroom go out from his
chamber,
And the bride from her dressing room.
17 Let the priests, who minister to the LORD,
Weep between the porch and the altar;
Let them say, "Spare Your people,
O LORD,
And do not give Your heritage to
reproach,
That the nations should rule over them.
Why should they say among the peoples,
'Where *is* their God?'"

The Land Refreshed

18 Then the LORD will be zealous for His
land,
And pity His people.
19 The LORD will answer and say to His
people,
"Behold, I will send you grain and new
wine and oil,
And you will be satisfied by them;
I will no longer make you a reproach
among the nations.

20 "But I will remove far from you the
northern *army*,
And will drive him away into a barren
and desolate land,
With his face toward the eastern sea
And his back toward the western sea;
His stench will come up,
And his foul odor will rise,
Because he has done monstrous things."

21 Fear not, O land;
Be glad and rejoice,
For the LORD has done marvelous things!
22 Do not be afraid, you beasts of the field;
For the open pastures are springing up,
And the tree bears its fruit;
The fig tree and the vine yield their
strength.
23 Be glad then, you children of Zion,
And rejoice in the LORD your God;
For He has given you the former rain
faithfully,[a]
And He will cause the rain to come down
for you—

1:18 [a]Septuagint and Vulgate read *are made desolate.* **2:6** [a]Septuagint, Targum, and Vulgate read *gather blackness.* **2:8** [a]Literally *his own highway* [b]That is, they are not halted by losses **2:23** [a]Or *the teacher of righteousness*

The former rain,
And the latter rain in the first *month*.
24 The threshing floors shall be full of wheat,
And the vats shall overflow with new wine and oil.

25 "So I will restore to you the years that the swarming locust has eaten,
The crawling locust,
The consuming locust,
And the chewing locust,[a]
My great army which I sent among you.
26 You shall eat in plenty and be satisfied,
And praise the name of the LORD your God,
Who has dealt wondrously with you;
And My people shall never be put to shame.
27 Then you shall know that I *am* in the midst of Israel:
I *am* the LORD your God
And there is no other.
My people shall never be put to shame.

God's Spirit Poured Out

28 "And it shall come to pass afterward
That I will pour out My Spirit on all flesh;
Your sons and your daughters shall prophesy,
Your old men shall dream dreams,
Your young men shall see visions.
29 And also on *My* menservants and on *My* maidservants
I will pour out My Spirit in those days.
30 "And I will show wonders in the heavens and in the earth:
Blood and fire and pillars of smoke.
31 The sun shall be turned into darkness,
And the moon into blood,
Before the coming of the great and awesome day of the LORD.
32 And it shall come to pass
That whoever calls on the name of the LORD
Shall be saved.
For in Mount Zion and in Jerusalem there shall be deliverance,
As the LORD has said,
Among the remnant whom the LORD calls.

God Judges the Nations

3 "For behold, in those days and at that time,
When I bring back the captives of Judah and Jerusalem,
2 I will also gather all nations,
And bring them down to the Valley of Jehoshaphat;
And I will enter into judgment with them there
On account of My people, My heritage Israel,
Whom they have scattered among the nations;
They have also divided up My land.
3 They have cast lots for My people,
Have given a boy *as payment* for a harlot,
And sold a girl for wine, that they may drink.

4 "Indeed, what have you to do with Me,
O Tyre and Sidon, and all the coasts of Philistia?
Will you retaliate against Me?
But if you retaliate against Me,
Swiftly and speedily I will return your retaliation upon your own head;
5 Because you have taken My silver and My gold,
And have carried into your temples My prized possessions.
6 Also the people of Judah and the people of Jerusalem
You have sold to the Greeks,
That you may remove them far from their borders.

7 "Behold, I will raise them
Out of the place to which you have sold them,
And will return your retaliation upon your own head.
8 I will sell your sons and your daughters
Into the hand of the people of Judah,
And they will sell them to the Sabeans,[a]
To a people far off;
For the LORD has spoken."

9 Proclaim this among the nations:
"Prepare for war!
Wake up the mighty men,
Let all the men of war draw near,
Let them come up.
10 Beat your plowshares into swords
And your pruning hooks into spears;
Let the weak say, 'I *am* strong.'"
11 Assemble and come, all you nations,
And gather together all around.
Cause Your mighty ones to go down there, O LORD.

12 "Let the nations be wakened, and come up to the Valley of Jehoshaphat;
For there I will sit to judge all the surrounding nations.
13 Put in the sickle, for the harvest is ripe.
Come, go down;
For the winepress is full,
The vats overflow—
For their wickedness *is* great."

14 Multitudes, multitudes in the valley of decision!
For the day of the LORD *is* near in the valley of decision.
15 The sun and moon will grow dark,
And the stars will diminish their brightness.
16 The LORD also will roar from Zion,
And utter His voice from Jerusalem;
The heavens and earth will shake;
But the LORD will be a shelter for His people,
And the strength of the children of Israel.
17 "So you shall know that I *am* the LORD your God,
Dwelling in Zion My holy mountain.
Then Jerusalem shall be holy,

2:25 [a]Compare 1:4 3:8 [a]Literally *Shebaites* (compare Isaiah 60:6 and Ezekiel 27:22)

And no aliens shall ever pass through her
again."

God Blesses His People

18 And it will come to pass in that day
That the mountains shall drip with new
wine,
The hills shall flow with milk,
And all the brooks of Judah shall be
flooded with water;
A fountain shall flow from the house of
the LORD
And water the Valley of Acacias.

19 "Egypt shall be a desolation,
And Edom a desolate wilderness,
Because of violence *against* the people of
Judah,
For they have shed innocent blood in
their land.
20 But Judah shall abide forever,
And Jerusalem from generation to
generation.
21 For I will acquit them of the guilt of
bloodshed, whom I had not acquitted;
For the LORD dwells in Zion."

The Book of AMOS

1 The words of Amos, who was among the
sheepbreeders[a] of Tekoa, which he saw con-
cerning Israel in the days of Uzziah king of
Judah, and in the days of Jeroboam the son of
Joash, king of Israel, two years before the earth-
quake.
2 And he said:

"The LORD roars from Zion,
And utters His voice from Jerusalem;
The pastures of the shepherds mourn,
And the top of Carmel withers."

Judgment on the Nations

3 Thus says the LORD:

"For three transgressions of Damascus,
and for four,
I will not turn away its *punishment*,
Because they have threshed Gilead with
implements of iron.
4 But I will send a fire into the house of
Hazael,
Which shall devour the palaces of
Ben-Hadad.
5 I will also break the *gate* bar of Damascus,
And cut off the inhabitant from the Valley
of Aven,
And the one who holds the scepter from
Beth Eden.
The people of Syria shall go captive to Kir,"
Says the LORD.

6 Thus says the LORD:

"For three transgressions of Gaza, and for
four,
I will not turn away its *punishment*,
Because they took captive the whole
captivity
To deliver *them* up to Edom.
7 But I will send a fire upon the wall of
Gaza,
Which shall devour its palaces.
8 I will cut off the inhabitant from
Ashdod,
And the one who holds the scepter from
Ashkelon;
I will turn My hand against Ekron,
And the remnant of the Philistines shall
perish,"
Says the Lord GOD.

9 Thus says the LORD:

"For three transgressions of Tyre, and for
four,
I will not turn away its *punishment*,
Because they delivered up the whole
captivity to Edom,
And did not remember the covenant of
brotherhood.
10 But I will send a fire upon the wall of
Tyre,
Which shall devour its palaces."

11 Thus says the LORD:

"For three transgressions of Edom, and for
four,
I will not turn away its *punishment*,
Because he pursued his brother with the
sword,
And cast off all pity;
His anger tore perpetually,
And he kept his wrath forever.
12 But I will send a fire upon Teman,
Which shall devour the palaces of
Bozrah."

13 Thus says the LORD:

"For three transgressions of the people of
Ammon, and for four,
I will not turn away its *punishment*,
Because they ripped open the women
with child in Gilead,
That they might enlarge their territory.
14 But I will kindle a fire in the wall of
Rabbah,
And it shall devour its palaces,
Amid shouting in the day of battle,
And a tempest in the day of the
whirlwind.
15 Their king shall go into captivity,
He and his princes together,"
Says the LORD.

2 Thus says the LORD:

"For three transgressions of Moab, and
for four,
I will not turn away its *punishment*,
Because he burned the bones of the king
of Edom to lime.
2 But I will send a fire upon Moab,
And it shall devour the palaces of
Kerioth;

1:1 [a]Compare 2 Kings 3:4

Moab shall die with tumult,
With shouting *and* trumpet sound.
3 And I will cut off the judge from its midst,
And slay all its princes with him,"
Says the LORD.

Judgment on Judah

4 Thus says the LORD:

"For three transgressions of Judah, and for four,
I will not turn away its *punishment*,
Because they have despised the law of the LORD,
And have not kept His commandments.
Their lies lead them astray,
Lies which their fathers followed.
5 But I will send a fire upon Judah,
And it shall devour the palaces of Jerusalem."

Judgment on Israel

6 Thus says the LORD:

"For three transgressions of Israel, and for four,
I will not turn away its *punishment*,
Because they sell the righteous for silver,
And the poor for a pair of sandals.
7 They pant after[a] the dust of the earth *which is* on the head of the poor,
And pervert the way of the humble.
A man and his father go in to the *same* girl,
To defile My holy name.
8 They lie down by every altar on clothes taken in pledge,
And drink the wine of the condemned *in* the house of their god.

9 "Yet *it was* I *who* destroyed the Amorite before them,
Whose height *was* like the height of the cedars,
And he *was as* strong as the oaks;
Yet I destroyed his fruit above
And his roots beneath.
10 Also *it was* I *who* brought you up from the land of Egypt,
And led you forty years through the wilderness,
To possess the land of the Amorite.
11 I raised up some of your sons as prophets,
And some of your young men as Nazirites.
Is it not so, O you children of Israel?"
Says the LORD.
12 "But you gave the Nazirites wine to drink,
And commanded the prophets saying,
'Do not prophesy!'

13 "Behold, I am weighed down by you,
As a cart full of sheaves is weighed down.
14 Therefore flight shall perish from the swift,
The strong shall not strengthen his power,
Nor shall the mighty deliver himself;
15 He shall not stand who handles the bow,
The swift of foot shall not escape,
Nor shall he who rides a horse deliver himself.
16 The most courageous men of might
Shall flee naked in that day,"
Says the LORD.

Authority of the Prophet's Message

3 Hear this word that the LORD has spoken against you, O children of Israel, against the whole family which I brought up from the land of Egypt, saying:

2 "You only have I known of all the families of the earth;
Therefore I will punish you for all your iniquities."
3 Can two walk together, unless they are agreed?
4 Will a lion roar in the forest, when he has no prey?
Will a young lion cry out of his den, if he has caught nothing?
5 Will a bird fall into a snare on the earth, where there is no trap for it?
Will a snare spring up from the earth, if it has caught nothing at all?
6 If a trumpet is blown in a city, will not the people be afraid?
If there is calamity in a city, will not the LORD have done *it*?
7 Surely the Lord GOD does nothing,
Unless He reveals His secret to His servants the prophets.
8 A lion has roared!
Who will not fear?
The Lord GOD has spoken!
Who can but prophesy?

Punishment of Israel's Sins

9 "Proclaim in the palaces at Ashdod,[a]
And in the palaces in the land of Egypt, and say:
'Assemble on the mountains of Samaria;
See great tumults in her midst,
And the oppressed within her.
10 For they do not know to do right,'
Says the LORD,
'Who store up violence and robbery in their palaces.'"

11 Therefore thus says the Lord GOD:

"An adversary *shall be* all around the land;
He shall sap your strength from you,
And your palaces shall be plundered."

12 Thus says the LORD:

"As a shepherd takes from the mouth of a lion
Two legs or a piece of an ear,
So shall the children of Israel be taken out
Who dwell in Samaria—
In the corner of a bed and on the edge[a] of a couch!
13 Hear and testify against the house of Jacob,"
Says the Lord GOD, the God of hosts,
14 "That in the day I punish Israel for their transgressions,
I will also visit *destruction* on the altars of Bethel;
And the horns of the altar shall be cut off
And fall to the ground.
15 I will destroy the winter house along with the summer house;
The houses of ivory shall perish,
And the great houses shall have an end,"
Says the LORD.

2:7 [a]Or *trample on* 3:9 [a]Following Masoretic Text; Septuagint reads *Assyria.* 3:12 [a]The Hebrew is uncertain.

4 Hear this word, you cows of Bashan, who
are on the mountain of Samaria,
Who oppress the poor,
Who crush the needy,
Who say to your husbands,[a] "Bring *wine*,
let us drink!"
2 The Lord GOD has sworn by His holiness:
"Behold, the days shall come upon you
When He will take you away with
fishhooks,
And your posterity with fishhooks.
3 You will go out *through* broken *walls*,
Each one straight ahead of her,
And you will be cast into Harmon,"
Says the LORD.

4 "Come to Bethel and transgress,
At Gilgal multiply transgression;
Bring your sacrifices every morning,
Your tithes every three days.[a]
5 Offer a sacrifice of thanksgiving with
leaven,
Proclaim *and* announce the freewill
offerings;
For this you love,
You children of Israel!"
Says the Lord GOD.

Israel Did Not Accept Correction

6 "Also I gave you cleanness of teeth in all
your cities.
And lack of bread in all your places;
Yet you have not returned to Me,"
Says the LORD.

7 "I also withheld rain from you,
When *there were* still three months to the
harvest.
I made it rain on one city,
I withheld rain from another city.
One part was rained upon,
And where it did not rain the part
withered.
8 So two *or* three cities wandered to
another city to drink water,
But they were not satisfied;
Yet you have not returned to Me,"
Says the LORD.

9 "I blasted you with blight and mildew.
When your gardens increased,
Your vineyards,
Your fig trees,
And your olive trees,
The locust devoured *them;*
Yet you have not returned to Me,"
Says the LORD.

10 "I sent among you a plague after the
manner of Egypt;
Your young men I killed with a sword,
Along with your captive horses;
I made the stench of your camps come up
into your nostrils;
Yet you have not returned to Me,"
Says the LORD.

11 "I overthrew *some* of you,
As God overthrew Sodom and Gomorrah,
And you were like a firebrand plucked
from the burning;
Yet you have not returned to Me,"
Says the LORD.

12 "Therefore thus will I do to you, O Israel;
Because I will do this to you,
Prepare to meet your God, O Israel!"

13 For behold,
He who forms mountains,
And creates the wind,
Who declares to man what his[a] thought
is,
And makes the morning darkness,
Who treads the high places of the earth—
The LORD God of hosts *is* His name.

A Lament for Israel

5 Hear this word which I take up against you,
a lamentation, O house of Israel:

2 The virgin of Israel has fallen;
She will rise no more.
She lies forsaken on her land;
There is no one to raise her up.

3 For thus says the Lord GOD:

"The city that goes out by a thousand
Shall have a hundred left,
And that which goes out by a hundred
Shall have ten left to the house of Israel."

A Call to Repentance

4 For thus says the LORD to the house of Is-
rael:

"Seek Me and live;
5 But do not seek Bethel,
Nor enter Gilgal,
Nor pass over to Beersheba;
For Gilgal shall surely go into captivity,
And Bethel shall come to nothing.
6 Seek the LORD and live,
Lest He break out like fire *in* the house of
Joseph,
And devour *it*,
With no one to quench *it* in Bethel—
7 You who turn justice to wormwood,
And lay righteousness to rest in the
earth!"

8 He made the Pleiades and Orion;
He turns the shadow of death into
morning
And makes the day dark as night;
He calls for the waters of the sea
And pours them out on the face of the
earth;
The LORD *is* His name.
9 He rains ruin upon the strong,
So that fury comes upon the fortress.
10 They hate the one who rebukes in the
gate,
And they abhor the one who speaks
uprightly.
11 Therefore, because you tread down the
poor
And take grain taxes from him,
Though you have built houses of hewn
stone,
Yet you shall not dwell in them;
You have planted pleasant vineyards,
But you shall not drink wine from them.
12 For I know your manifold transgressions
And your mighty sins:
Afflicting the just *and* taking bribes;
Diverting the poor *from justice* at the
gate.
13 Therefore the prudent keep silent at that
time,
For it *is* an evil time.

4:1 [a]Literally *their lords* or *their masters* 4:4 [a]Or *years* (compare Deuteronomy 14:28) 4:13 [a]Or *His*

14 Seek good and not evil,
That you may live;
So the LORD God of hosts will be with you,
As you have spoken.
15 Hate evil, love good;
Establish justice in the gate.
It may be that the LORD God of hosts
Will be gracious to the remnant of Joseph.

The Day of the LORD

16 Therefore the LORD God of hosts, the Lord, says this:

"*There shall be* wailing in all streets,
And they shall say in all the highways,
'Alas! Alas!'
They shall call the farmer to mourning,
And skillful lamenters to wailing.
17 In all vineyards *there shall be* wailing,
For I will pass through you,"
Says the LORD.

18 Woe to you who desire the day of the LORD!
For what good *is* the day of the LORD to you?
It *will be* darkness, and not light.
19 It *will be* as though a man fled from a lion,
And a bear met him!
Or *as though* he went into the house,
Leaned his hand on the wall,
And a serpent bit him!
20 *Is* not the day of the LORD darkness, and not light?
Is it not very dark, with no brightness in it?

21 "I hate, I despise your feast days,
And I do not savor your sacred assemblies.
22 Though you offer Me burnt offerings and your grain offerings,
I will not accept *them,*
Nor will I regard your fattened peace offerings.
23 Take away from Me the noise of your songs,
For I will not hear the melody of your stringed instruments.
24 But let justice run down like water,
And righteousness like a mighty stream.

25 "Did you offer Me sacrifices and offerings
In the wilderness forty years, O house of Israel?
26 You also carried Sikkuth[a] your king[b]
And Chiun,[c] your idols,
The star of your gods,
Which you made for yourselves.
27 Therefore I will send you into captivity beyond Damascus,"
Says the LORD, whose name *is* the God of hosts.

Warnings to Zion and Samaria

6 Woe to you *who are* at ease in Zion,
And trust in Mount Samaria,
Notable persons in the chief nation,
To whom the house of Israel comes!
2 Go over to Calneh and see;
And from there go to Hamath the great;
Then go down to Gath of the Philistines.
Are you better than these kingdoms?
Or is their territory greater than your territory?
3 *Woe to* you who put far off the day of doom,
Who cause the seat of violence to come near;
4 Who lie on beds of ivory,
Stretch out on your couches,
Eat lambs from the flock
And calves from the midst of the stall;
5 Who sing idly to the sound of stringed instruments,
And invent for yourselves musical instruments like David;
6 Who drink wine from bowls,
And anoint yourselves with the best ointments,
But are not grieved for the affliction of Joseph.
7 Therefore they shall now go captive as the first of the captives,
And those who recline at banquets shall be removed.

8 The Lord GOD has sworn by Himself,
The LORD God of hosts says:
"I abhor the pride of Jacob,
And hate his palaces;
Therefore I will deliver up *the* city
And all that is in it."

9 Then it shall come to pass, that if ten men
remain in one house, they shall die.
10 And when a relative *of the dead,* with one
who will burn *the bodies,* picks up the bodies[a]
to take them out of the house, he will say to
one inside the house, "*Are there* any more with
you?" Then someone will say, "None." And he
will say, "Hold your tongue! For we dare not
mention the name of the LORD."

11 For behold, the LORD gives a command:
He will break the great house into bits,
And the little house into pieces.

12 Do horses run on rocks?
Does *one* plow *there* with oxen?
Yet you have turned justice into gall,
And the fruit of righteousness into wormwood,
13 You who rejoice over Lo Debar,[a]
Who say, "Have we not taken Karnaim[b] for ourselves
By our own strength?"

14 "But, behold, I will raise up a nation against you,
O house of Israel,"
Says the LORD God of hosts;
"And they will afflict you from the entrance of Hamath
To the Valley of the Arabah."

Vision of the Locusts

7 Thus the Lord GOD showed me: Behold, He
formed locust swarms at the beginning of
the late crop; indeed *it was* the late crop after
the king's mowings.
2 And so it was, when they had finished eat-
ing the grass of the land, that I said:

"O Lord GOD, forgive, I pray!
Oh, that Jacob may stand,
For he *is* small!"

5:26 [a]A pagan deity [b]Septuagint and Vulgate read *tabernacle of Moloch.* [c]A pagan deity **6:10** [a]Literally *bones*
6:13 [a]Literally *Nothing* [b]Literally *Horns,* symbol of strength

3 *So* the LORD relented concerning this.
"It shall not be," said the LORD.

Vision of the Fire

4 Thus the Lord GOD showed me: Behold, the Lord GOD called for conflict by fire, and it consumed the great deep and devoured the territory.
5 Then I said:

"O Lord GOD, cease, I pray!
Oh, that Jacob may stand,
For he *is* small!"
6 *So* the LORD relented concerning this.
"This also shall not be," said the Lord GOD.

Vision of the Plumb Line

7 Thus He showed me: Behold, the Lord stood on a wall *made* with a plumb line, with a plumb line in His hand.
8 And the LORD said to me, "Amos, what do you see?" And I said, "A plumb line." Then the Lord said:

"Behold, I am setting a plumb line
In the midst of My people Israel;
I will not pass by them anymore.
9 The high places of Isaac shall be desolate,
And the sanctuaries of Israel shall be laid waste.
I will rise with the sword against the house of Jeroboam."

Amaziah's Complaint

10 Then Amaziah the priest of Bethel sent to Jeroboam king of Israel, saying, "Amos has conspired against you in the midst of the house of Israel. The land is not able to bear all his words.
11 "For thus Amos has said:

'Jeroboam shall die by the sword,
And Israel shall surely be led away captive
From their own land.'"

12 Then Amaziah said to Amos:

"Go, you seer!
Flee to the land of Judah.
There eat bread,
And there prophesy.
13 But never again prophesy at Bethel,
For it *is* the king's sanctuary,
And it *is* the royal residence."

14 Then Amos answered, and said to Amaziah:

"I *was* no prophet,
Nor *was* I a son of a prophet,
But I *was* a sheepbreeder[a]
And a tender of sycamore fruit.
15 Then the LORD took me as I followed the flock,
And the LORD said to me,
'Go, prophesy to My people Israel.'
16 Now therefore, hear the word of the LORD:
You say, 'Do not prophesy against Israel,
And do not spout against the house of Isaac.'

17 "Therefore thus says the LORD:

'Your wife shall be a harlot in the city;
Your sons and daughters shall fall by the sword;
Your land shall be divided by *survey* line;
You shall die in a defiled land;
And Israel shall surely be led away captive
From his own land.'"

Vision of the Summer Fruit

8 Thus the Lord GOD showed me: Behold, a basket of summer fruit.
2 And He said, "Amos, what do you see?" So
I said, "A basket of summer fruit." Then the
LORD said to me:

"The end has come upon My people Israel;
I will not pass by them anymore.
3 And the songs of the temple
Shall be wailing in that day,"
Says the Lord GOD—
"Many dead bodies everywhere,
They shall be thrown out in silence."

4 Hear this, you who swallow up[a] the needy,
And make the poor of the land fail,

5 Saying:

"When will the New Moon be past,
That we may sell grain?
And the Sabbath,
That we may trade wheat?
Making the ephah small and the shekel large,
Falsifying the scales by deceit,
6 That we may buy the poor for silver,
And the needy for a pair of sandals—
Even sell the bad wheat?"

7 The LORD has sworn by the pride of Jacob:
"Surely I will never forget any of their works.
8 Shall the land not tremble for this,
And everyone mourn who dwells in it?
All of it shall swell like the River,[a]
Heave and subside
Like the River of Egypt.

9 "And it shall come to pass in that day," says the Lord GOD,
"That I will make the sun go down at noon,
And I will darken the earth in broad daylight;
10 I will turn your feasts into mourning,
And all your songs into lamentation;
I will bring sackcloth on every waist,
And baldness on every head;
I will make it like mourning for an only *son*,
And its end like a bitter day.

11 "Behold, the days are coming," says the Lord GOD,
"That I will send a famine on the land,
Not a famine of bread,
Nor a thirst for water,
But of hearing the words of the LORD.
12 They shall wander from sea to sea,
And from north to east;
They shall run to and fro, seeking the word of the LORD,
But shall not find *it*.

13 "In that day the fair virgins
And strong young men

7:14 [a]Compare 2 Kings 3:4 8:4 [a]Or *trample on* (compare 2:7) 8:8 [a]That is, the Nile; some Hebrew manuscripts, Septuagint, Syriac, Targum, and Vulgate read *River*; Masoretic Text reads *the light*.

Shall faint from thirst.
14 Those who swear by the sin[a] of Samaria,
Who say,
'As your god lives, O Dan!'
And, 'As the way of Beersheba lives!'
They shall fall and never rise again."

The Destruction of Israel

9 I saw the Lord standing by the altar, and He said:

"Strike the doorposts, that the thresholds may shake,
And break them on the heads of them all.
I will slay the last of them with the sword.
He who flees from them shall not get away,
And he who escapes from them shall not be delivered.

2 "Though they dig into hell,[a]
From there My hand shall take them;
Though they climb up to heaven,
From there I will bring them down;
3 And though they hide themselves on top of Carmel,
From there I will search and take them;
Though they hide from My sight at the bottom of the sea,
From there I will command the serpent, and it shall bite them;
4 Though they go into captivity before their enemies,
From there I will command the sword,
And it shall slay them.
I will set My eyes on them for harm and not for good."

5 The Lord GOD of hosts,
He who touches the earth and it melts,
And all who dwell there mourn;
All of it shall swell like the River,[a]
And subside like the River of Egypt.
6 He who builds His layers in the sky,
And has founded His strata in the earth;
Who calls for the waters of the sea,
And pours them out on the face of the earth—
The LORD *is* His name.

7 "*Are* you not like the people of Ethiopia to Me,
O children of Israel?" says the LORD.
"Did I not bring up Israel from the land of Egypt,
The Philistines from Caphtor,
And the Syrians from Kir?

8 "Behold, the eyes of the Lord GOD *are* on the sinful kingdom,
And I will destroy it from the face of the earth;
Yet I will not utterly destroy the house of Jacob,"
Says the LORD.

9 "For surely I will command,
And will sift the house of Israel among all nations,
As *grain* is sifted in a sieve;
Yet not the smallest grain shall fall to the ground.
10 All the sinners of My people shall die by the sword,
Who say, 'The calamity shall not overtake nor confront us.'

Israel Will Be Restored

11 "On that day I will raise up
The tabernacle[a] of David, which has fallen down,
And repair its damages;
I will raise up its ruins,
And rebuild it as in the days of old;
12 That they may possess the remnant of Edom,[a]
And all the Gentiles who are called by My name,"
Says the LORD who does this thing.

13 "Behold, the days are coming," says the LORD,
"When the plowman shall overtake the reaper,
And the treader of grapes him who sows seed;
The mountains shall drip with sweet wine,
And all the hills shall flow *with it*.
14 I will bring back the captives of My people Israel;
They shall build the waste cities and inhabit *them;*
They shall plant vineyards and drink wine from them;
They shall also make gardens and eat fruit from them.
15 I will plant them in their land,
And no longer shall they be pulled up
From the land I have given them,"
Says the LORD your God.

The Book of OBADIAH

The Coming Judgment on Edom

The vision of Obadiah.

Thus says the Lord GOD concerning Edom
(We have heard a report from the LORD,
And a messenger has been sent among the nations, *saying,*
"Arise, and let us rise up against her for battle"):

2 "Behold, I will make you small among the nations;
You shall be greatly despised.
3 The pride of your heart has deceived you,
You who dwell in the clefts of the rock,
Whose habitation is high;
You who say in your heart,
'Who will bring me down to the ground?'
4 Though you ascend *as* high as the eagle,
And though you set your nest among the stars,
From there I will bring you down," says the LORD.

8:14 [a]Or *Ashima*, a Syrian goddess 9:2 [a]Or *Sheol* 9:5 [a]That is, the Nile 9:11 [a]Literally *booth*, figure of a deposed dynasty 9:12 [a]Septuagint reads *mankind*.

5 "If thieves had come to you,
If robbers by night—
Oh, how you will be cut off!—
Would they not have stolen till they had enough?
If grape-gatherers had come to you,
Would they not have left *some* gleanings?

6 "Oh, how Esau shall be searched out!
How his hidden treasures shall be sought after!
7 All the men in your confederacy
Shall force you to the border;
The men at peace with you
Shall deceive you *and* prevail against you.
Those who eat your bread shall lay a trap[a] for you.
No one is aware of it.

8 "Will I not in that day," says the LORD,
"Even destroy the wise *men* from Edom,
And understanding from the mountains of Esau?
9 Then your mighty men, O Teman, shall be dismayed,
To the end that everyone from the mountains of Esau
May be cut off by slaughter.

Edom Mistreated His Brother

10 "For violence against your brother Jacob,
Shame shall cover you,
And you shall be cut off forever.
11 In the day that you stood on the other side—
In the day that strangers carried captive his forces,
When foreigners entered his gates
And cast lots for Jerusalem—
Even you *were* as one of them.

12 "But you should not have gazed on the day of your brother
In the day of his captivity;[a]
Nor should you have rejoiced over the children of Judah
In the day of their destruction;
Nor should you have spoken proudly
In the day of distress.
13 You should not have entered the gate of My people
In the day of their calamity.
Indeed, you should not have gazed on their affliction
In the day of their calamity,
Nor laid *hands* on their substance
In the day of their calamity.
14 You should not have stood at the crossroads
To cut off those among them who escaped;
Nor should you have delivered up those among them who remained
In the day of distress.

15 "For the day of the LORD upon all the nations *is* near;
As you have done, it shall be done to you;
Your reprisal shall return upon your own head.
16 For as you drank on My holy mountain,
So shall all the nations drink continually;
Yes, they shall drink, and swallow,
And they shall be as though they had never been.

Israel's Final Triumph

17 "But on Mount Zion there shall be deliverance,
And there shall be holiness;
The house of Jacob shall possess their possessions.
18 The house of Jacob shall be a fire,
And the house of Joseph a flame;
But the house of Esau *shall be* stubble;
They shall kindle them and devour them,
And no survivor shall *remain* of the house of Esau,"
For the LORD has spoken.

19 The South[a] shall possess the mountains of Esau,
And the Lowland shall possess Philistia.
They shall possess the fields of Ephraim
And the fields of Samaria.
Benjamin *shall possess* Gilead.
20 And the captives of this host of the children of Israel
Shall possess the land of the Canaanites
As far as Zarephath.
The captives of Jerusalem who are in Sepharad
Shall possess the cities of the South.[a]
21 Then saviors[a] shall come to Mount Zion
To judge the mountains of Esau,
And the kingdom shall be the LORD's.

The Book of JONAH

Jonah's Disobedience

1 Now the word of the LORD came to Jonah
the son of Amittai, saying,
2 "Arise, go to Nineveh, that great city, and
cry out against it; for their wickedness has come
up before Me."
3 But Jonah arose to flee to Tarshish from the
presence of the LORD. He went down to Joppa,
and found a ship going to Tarshish; so he paid
the fare, and went down into it, to go with them
to Tarshish from the presence of the LORD.

The Storm at Sea

4 But the LORD sent out a great wind on the
sea, and there was a mighty tempest on the sea,
so that the ship was about to be broken up.
5 Then the mariners were afraid; and every
man cried out to his god, and threw the cargo
that *was* in the ship into the sea, to lighten the
load.[a] But Jonah had gone down into the lowest
parts of the ship, had lain down, and was fast
asleep.
6 So the captain came to him, and said to
him, "What do you mean, sleeper? Arise, call

7 [a]Or *wound, or plot* 12 [a]Literally *On the day he became a foreigner* 19 [a]Hebrew *Negev* 20 [a]Hebrew *Negev*
21 [a]Or *deliverers* 1:5 [a]Literally *from upon them*

on your God; perhaps your God will consider
us, so that we may not perish."
7 And they said to one another, "Come, let
us cast lots, that we may know for whose cause
this trouble *has come* upon us." So they cast
lots, and the lot fell on Jonah.
8 Then they said to him, "Please tell us! For
whose cause *is* this trouble upon us? What is
your occupation? And where do you come
from? What is your country? And of what peo-
ple are you?"
9 So he said to them, "I *am* a Hebrew; and I
fear the LORD, the God of heaven, who made the
sea and the dry *land*."

Jonah Thrown into the Sea

10 Then the men were exceedingly afraid, and
said to him, "Why have you done this?" For
the men knew that he fled from the presence
of the LORD, because he had told them.
11 Then they said to him, "What shall we do to
you that the sea may be calm for us?"—for the
sea was growing more tempestuous.
12 And he said to them, "Pick me up and throw
me into the sea; then the sea will become calm
for you. For I know that this great tempest *is*
because of me."
13 Nevertheless the men rowed hard to return
to land, but they could not, for the sea contin-
ued to grow more tempestuous against them.
14 Therefore they cried out to the LORD and
said, "We pray, O LORD, please do not let us
perish for this man's life, and do not charge us
with innocent blood; for You, O LORD, have done
as it pleased You."
15 So they picked up Jonah and threw him
into the sea, and the sea ceased from its raging.
16 Then the men feared the LORD exceed-
ingly, and offered a sacrifice to the LORD and
took vows.

Jonah's Prayer and Deliverance

17 Now the LORD had prepared a great fish
to swallow Jonah. And Jonah was in the belly
of the fish three days and three nights.
2 Then Jonah prayed to the LORD his God
from the fish's belly.
2 And he said:

"I cried out to the LORD because of my
affliction,
And He answered me.

"Out of the belly of Sheol I cried,
And You heard my voice.
3 For You cast me into the deep,
Into the heart of the seas,
And the floods surrounded me;
All Your billows and Your waves passed
over me.
4 Then I said, 'I have been cast out of Your
sight;
Yet I will look again toward Your holy
temple.'
5 The waters surrounded me, *even* to my
soul;
The deep closed around me;
Weeds were wrapped around my head.
6 I went down to the moorings of the
mountains;
The earth with its bars *closed* behind me
forever;
Yet You have brought up my life from the
pit,
O LORD, my God.

7 "When my soul fainted within me,
I remembered the LORD;
And my prayer went *up* to You,
Into Your holy temple.

8 "Those who regard worthless idols
Forsake their own Mercy.
9 But I will sacrifice to You
With the voice of thanksgiving;
I will pay what I have vowed.
Salvation *is* of the LORD."

10 So the LORD spoke to the fish, and it vom-
ited Jonah onto dry *land*.

Jonah Preaches at Nineveh

3 Now the word of the LORD came to Jonah
the second time, saying,
2 "Arise, go to Nineveh, that great city, and
preach to it the message that I tell you."
3 So Jonah arose and went to Nineveh, ac-
cording to the word of the LORD. Now Nineveh
was an exceedingly great city, a three-day jour-
ney[a] *in extent*.
4 And Jonah began to enter the city on the
first day's walk. Then he cried out and said,
"Yet forty days, and Nineveh shall be over-
thrown!"

The People of Nineveh Believe

5 So the people of Nineveh believed God, pro-
claimed a fast, and put on sackcloth, from the
greatest to the least of them.
6 Then word came to the king of Nineveh;
and he arose from his throne and laid aside his
robe, covered *himself* with sackcloth and sat
in ashes.
7 And he caused *it* to be proclaimed and
published throughout Nineveh by the decree
of the king and his nobles, saying,

Let neither man nor beast, herd nor flock,
taste anything; do not let them eat, or
drink water.
8 But let man and beast be covered with
sackcloth, and cry mightily to God; yes,
let every one turn from his evil way and
from the violence that is in his hands.
9 Who can tell *if* God will turn and relent,
and turn away from His fierce anger, so
that we may not perish?

10 Then God saw their works, that they turned
from their evil way; and God relented from the
disaster that He had said He would bring upon
them, and He did not do it.

Jonah's Anger and God's Kindness

4 But it displeased Jonah exceedingly, and
he became angry.
2 So he prayed to the LORD, and said, "Ah,
LORD, was not this what I said when I was still
in my country? Therefore I fled previously to
Tarshish; for I know that You *are* a gracious
and merciful God, slow to anger and abundant
in lovingkindness, One who relents from doing
harm.
3 "Therefore now, O LORD, please take my life
from me, for *it is* better for me to die than to
live!"

3:3 [a]Exact meaning unknown

4 Then the LORD said, "*Is it* right for you to
be angry?"
5 So Jonah went out of the city and sat on
the east side of the city. There he made himself
a shelter and sat under it in the shade, till he
might see what would become of the city.
6 And the LORD God prepared a plant[a] and
made it come up over Jonah, that it might be
shade for his head to deliver him from his mis-
ery. So Jonah was very grateful for the plant.
7 But as morning dawned the next day God
prepared a worm, and it *so* damaged the plant
that it withered.
8 And it happened, when the sun arose, that
God prepared a vehement east wind; and the
sun beat on Jonah's head, so that he grew faint.
Then he wished death for himself, and said, "*It
is* better for me to die than to live."
9 Then God said to Jonah, "*Is it* right for you
to be angry about the plant?" And he said, "*It
is* right for me to be angry, even to death!"
10 But the LORD said, "You have had pity on
the plant for which you have not labored, nor
made it grow, which came up in a night and
perished in a night.
11 "And should I not pity Nineveh, that great
city, in which are more than one hundred and
twenty thousand persons who cannot discern
between their right hand and their left—and
much livestock?"

The Book of MICAH

1 The word of the LORD that came to Micah of Moresheth in the days of Jotham, Ahaz, *and* Hezekiah, kings of Judah, which he saw concerning Samaria and Jerusalem.

The Coming Judgment on Israel

2 Hear, all you peoples!
Listen, O earth, and all that is in it!
Let the Lord GOD be a witness against you,
The Lord from His holy temple.

3 For behold, the LORD is coming out of His place;
He will come down
And tread on the high places of the earth.
4 The mountains will melt under Him,
And the valleys will split
Like wax before the fire,
Like waters poured down a steep place.
5 All this is for the transgression of Jacob
And for the sins of the house of Israel.
What *is* the transgression of Jacob?
Is it not Samaria?
And what *are* the high places of Judah?
Are they not Jerusalem?

6 "Therefore I will make Samaria a heap of ruins in the field,
Places for planting a vineyard;
I will pour down her stones into the valley,
And I will uncover her foundations.
7 All her carved images shall be beaten to pieces,
And all her pay as a harlot shall be burned with the fire;
All her idols I will lay desolate,
For she gathered *it* from the pay of a harlot,
And they shall return to the pay of a harlot."

Mourning for Israel and Judah

8 Therefore I will wail and howl,
I will go stripped and naked;
I will make a wailing like the jackals
And a mourning like the ostriches,
9 For her wounds *are* incurable.
For it has come to Judah;
It has come to the gate of My people—
To Jerusalem.

10 Tell *it* not in Gath,
Weep not at all;
In Beth Aphrah[a]
Roll yourself in the dust.
11 Pass by in naked shame, you inhabitant of Shaphir;
The inhabitant of Zaanan[a] does not go out.
Beth Ezel mourns;
Its place to stand is taken away from you.

12 For the inhabitant of Maroth pined[a] for good,
But disaster came down from the LORD
To the gate of Jerusalem.
13 O inhabitant of Lachish,
Harness the chariot to the swift steeds
(She *was* the beginning of sin to the daughter of Zion),
For the transgressions of Israel were found in you.

14 Therefore you shall give presents to Moresheth Gath;[a]
The houses of Achzib[b] *shall be* a lie to the kings of Israel.
15 I will yet bring an heir to you,
O inhabitant of Mareshah;[a]
The glory of Israel shall come to Adullam.
16 Make yourself bald and cut off your hair,
Because of your precious children;
Enlarge your baldness like an eagle,
For they shall go from you into captivity.

Woe to Evildoers

2 Woe to those who devise iniquity,
And work out evil on their beds!
At morning light they practice it,
Because it is in the power of their hand.
2 They covet fields and take *them* by violence,
Also houses, and seize *them*.
So they oppress a man and his house,
A man and his inheritance.

4:6 [a]Hebrew *kikayon*, exact identity unknown **1:10** [a]Literally *House of Dust* **1:11** [a]Literally *Going Out*
1:12 [a]Literally *was sick* **1:14** [a]Literally *Possession of Gath* [b]Literally *Lie* **1:15** [a]Literally *Inheritance*

3 Therefore thus says the LORD:
"Behold, against this family I am devising disaster,
From which you cannot remove your necks;
Nor shall you walk haughtily,
For this *is* an evil time.
4 In that day *one* shall take up a proverb against you,
And lament with a bitter lamentation, saying:
'We are utterly destroyed!
He has changed the heritage of my people;
How He has removed *it* from me!
To a turncoat He has divided our fields.'"
5 Therefore you will have no one to determine boundaries[a] by lot
In the assembly of the LORD.

Lying Prophets

6 "Do not prattle," *you say to those* who prophesy.
So they shall not prophesy to you;[a]
They shall not return insult for insult.[b]
7 *You who are* named the house of Jacob:
"Is the Spirit of the LORD restricted?
Are these His doings?
Do not My words do good
To him who walks uprightly?
8 "Lately My people have risen up as an enemy—
You pull off the robe with the garment
From those who trust *you*, as they pass by,
Like men returned from war.
9 The women of My people you cast out
From their pleasant houses;
From their children
You have taken away My glory forever.
10 "Arise and depart,
For this *is* not *your* rest;
Because it is defiled, it shall destroy,
Yes, with utter destruction.
11 If a man should walk in a false spirit
And speak a lie, *saying*,
'I will prophesy to you of wine and drink,'
Even he would be the prattler of this people.

Israel Restored

12 "I will surely assemble all of you, O Jacob,
I will surely gather the remnant of Israel;
I will put them together like sheep of the fold,[a]
Like a flock in the midst of their pasture;
They shall make a loud noise because of *so many* people.
13 The one who breaks open will come up before them;
They will break out,
Pass through the gate,
And go out by it;
Their king will pass before them,
With the LORD at their head."

Wicked Rulers and Prophets

3 And I said:
"Hear now, O heads of Jacob,
And you rulers of the house of Israel:
Is it not for you to know justice?
2 You who hate good and love evil;
Who strip the skin from My people,[a]
And the flesh from their bones;
3 Who also eat the flesh of My people,
Flay their skin from them,
Break their bones,
And chop *them* in pieces
Like *meat* for the pot,
Like flesh in the caldron."
4 Then they will cry to the LORD,
But He will not hear them;
He will even hide His face from them at that time,
Because they have been evil in their deeds.
5 Thus says the LORD concerning the prophets
Who make my people stray;
Who chant "Peace"
While they chew with their teeth,
But who prepare war against him
Who puts nothing into their mouths:
6 "Therefore you shall have night without vision,
And you shall have darkness without divination;
The sun shall go down on the prophets,
And the day shall be dark for them.
7 So the seers shall be ashamed,
And the diviners abashed;
Indeed they shall all cover their lips;
For *there is* no answer from God."
8 But truly I am full of power by the Spirit of the LORD,
And of justice and might,
To declare to Jacob his transgression
And to Israel his sin.
9 Now hear this,
You heads of the house of Jacob
And rulers of the house of Israel,
Who abhor justice
And pervert all equity,
10 Who build up Zion with bloodshed
And Jerusalem with iniquity:
11 Her heads judge for a bribe,
Her priests teach for pay,
And her prophets divine for money.
Yet they lean on the LORD, and say,
"Is not the LORD among us?
No harm can come upon us."
12 Therefore because of you
Zion shall be plowed *like* a field,
Jerusalem shall become heaps of ruins,
And the mountain of the temple[a]
Like the bare hills of the forest.

The LORD's Reign in Zion

4 Now it shall come to pass in the latter days
That the mountain of the LORD's house
Shall be established on the top of the mountains,
And shall be exalted above the hills;

2:5 [a]Literally *one casting a surveyor's line* 2:6 [a]Literally *to these* [b]Vulgate reads *He shall not take shame.*
2:12 [a]Hebrew *Bozrah* 3:2 [a]Literally *them* 3:12 [a]Literally *house*

And peoples shall flow to it.
2 Many nations shall come and say,
"Come, and let us go up to the mountain of the LORD,
To the house of the God of Jacob;
He will teach us His ways,
And we shall walk in His paths."
For out of Zion the law shall go forth,
And the word of the LORD from Jerusalem.
3 He shall judge between many peoples,
And rebuke strong nations afar off;
They shall beat their swords into plowshares,
And their spears into pruning hooks;
Nation shall not lift up sword against nation,
Neither shall they learn war anymore.[a]
4 But everyone shall sit under his vine and under his fig tree,
And no one shall make *them* afraid;
For the mouth of the LORD of hosts has spoken.
5 For all people walk each in the name of his god,
But we will walk in the name of the LORD our God
Forever and ever.

Zion's Future Triumph

6 "In that day," says the LORD,
"I will assemble the lame,
I will gather the outcast
And those whom I have afflicted;
7 I will make the lame a remnant,
And the outcast a strong nation;
So the LORD will reign over them in Mount Zion
From now on, even forever.
8 And you, O tower of the flock,
The stronghold of the daughter of Zion,
To you shall it come,
Even the former dominion shall come,
The kingdom of the daughter of Jerusalem."

9 Now why do you cry aloud?
Is there no king in your midst?
Has your counselor perished?
For pangs have seized you like a woman in labor.
10 Be in pain, and labor to bring forth,
O daughter of Zion,
Like a woman in birth pangs.
For now you shall go forth from the city,
You shall dwell in the field,
And to Babylon you shall go.
There you shall be delivered;
There the LORD will redeem you
From the hand of your enemies.

11 Now also many nations have gathered against you,
Who say, "Let her be defiled,
And let our eye look upon Zion."
12 But they do not know the thoughts of the LORD,
Nor do they understand His counsel;
For He will gather them like sheaves to the threshing floor.
13 "Arise and thresh, O daughter of Zion;
For I will make your horn iron,
And I will make your hooves bronze;
You shall beat in pieces many peoples;
I will consecrate their gain to the LORD,
And their substance to the Lord of the whole earth."

5 Now gather yourself in troops,
O daughter of troops;
He has laid siege against us;
They will strike the judge of Israel with a rod on the cheek.

The Coming Messiah

2 "But you, Bethlehem Ephrathah,
Though you are little among the thousands of Judah,
Yet out of you shall come forth to Me
The One to be Ruler in Israel,
Whose goings forth *are* from of old,
From everlasting."

3 Therefore He shall give them up,
Until the time *that* she who is in labor has given birth;
Then the remnant of His brethren
Shall return to the children of Israel.
4 And He shall stand and feed *His flock*
In the strength of the LORD,
In the majesty of the name of the LORD His God;
And they shall abide,
For now He shall be great
To the ends of the earth;
5 And this *One* shall be peace.

Judgment on Israel's Enemies

When the Assyrian comes into our land,
And when he treads in our palaces,
Then we will raise against him
Seven shepherds and eight princely men.
6 They shall waste with the sword the land of Assyria,
And the land of Nimrod at its entrances;
Thus He shall deliver *us* from the Assyrian,
When he comes into our land
And when he treads within our borders.

7 Then the remnant of Jacob
Shall be in the midst of many peoples,
Like dew from the LORD,
Like showers on the grass,
That tarry for no man
Nor wait for the sons of men.
8 And the remnant of Jacob
Shall be among the Gentiles,
In the midst of many peoples,
Like a lion among the beasts of the forest,
Like a young lion among flocks of sheep,
Who, if he passes through,
Both treads down and tears in pieces,
And none can deliver.
9 Your hand shall be lifted against your adversaries,
And all your enemies shall be cut off.

10 "And it shall be in that day," says the LORD,
"That I will cut off your horses from your midst
And destroy your chariots.
11 I will cut off the cities of your land
And throw down all your strongholds.
12 I will cut off sorceries from your hand,
And you shall have no soothsayers.

4:3 [a]Compare Isaiah 2:2–4

13 Your carved images I will also cut off,
And your *sacred* pillars from your midst;
You shall no more worship the work of your hands;
14 I will pluck your wooden images[a] from your midst;
Thus I will destroy your cities.
15 And I will execute vengeance in anger and fury
On the nations that have not heard."[a]

God Pleads with Israel

6 Hear now what the LORD says:
"Arise, plead your case before the mountains,
And let the hills hear your voice.
2 Hear, O you mountains, the LORD's complaint,
And you strong foundations of the earth;
For the LORD has a complaint against His people,
And He will contend with Israel.

3 "O My people, what have I done to you?
And how have I wearied you?
Testify against Me.
4 For I brought you up from the land of Egypt,
I redeemed you from the house of bondage;
And I sent before you Moses, Aaron, and Miriam.
5 O My people, remember now
What Balak king of Moab counseled,
And what Balaam the son of Beor answered him,
From Acacia Grove[a] to Gilgal,
That you may know the righteousness of the LORD."

6 With what shall I come before the LORD,
And bow myself before the High God?
Shall I come before Him with burnt offerings,
With calves a year old?
7 Will the LORD be pleased with thousands of rams,
Ten thousand rivers of oil?
Shall I give my firstborn *for* my transgression,
The fruit of my body *for* the sin of my soul?
8 He has shown you, O man, what *is* good;
And what does the LORD require of you
But to do justly,
To love mercy,
And to walk humbly with your God?

Punishment of Israel's Injustice

9 The LORD's voice cries to the city—
Wisdom shall see Your name:

"Hear the rod!
Who has appointed it?
10 Are there yet the treasures of wickedness
In the house of the wicked,
And the short measure *that is* an abomination?
11 Shall I count pure *those* with the wicked scales,
And with the bag of deceitful weights?
12 For her rich men are full of violence,
Her inhabitants have spoken lies,
And their tongue is deceitful in their mouth.

13 "Therefore I will also make *you* sick by striking you,
By making *you* desolate because of your sins.
14 You shall eat, but not be satisfied;
Hunger[a] *shall be* in your midst.
You may carry *some* away,[b] but shall not save *them;*
And what you do rescue I will give over to the sword.

15 "You shall sow, but not reap;
You shall tread the olives, but not anoint yourselves with oil;
And *make* sweet wine, but not drink wine.
16 For the statutes of Omri are kept;
All the works of Ahab's house *are done;*
And you walk in their counsels,
That I may make you a desolation,
And your inhabitants a hissing.
Therefore you shall bear the reproach of My people."[a]

Sorrow for Israel's Sins

7 Woe is me!
For I am like those who gather summer fruits,
Like those who glean vintage grapes;
There is no cluster to eat
Of the first-ripe fruit *which* my soul desires.
2 The faithful *man* has perished from the earth,
And *there is* no one upright among men.
They all lie in wait for blood;
Every man hunts his brother with a net.

3 That they may successfully do evil with both hands—
The prince asks *for gifts,*
The judge *seeks* a bribe,
And the great *man* utters his evil desire;
So they scheme together.
4 The best of them *is* like a brier;
The most upright *is sharper* than a thorn hedge;
The day of your watchman and your punishment comes;
Now shall be their perplexity.

5 Do not trust in a friend;
Do not put your confidence in a companion;
Guard the doors of your mouth
From her who lies in your bosom.
6 For son dishonors father,
Daughter rises against her mother,
Daughter-in-law against her mother-in-law;
A man's enemies *are* the men of his own household.
7 Therefore I will look to the LORD;
I will wait for the God of my salvation;
My God will hear me.

Israel's Confession and Comfort

8 Do not rejoice over me, my enemy;
When I fall, I will arise;

5:14 [a]Hebrew *Asherim*, Canaanite deities **5:15** [a]Or *obeyed* **6:5** [a]Hebrew *Shittim* (compare Numbers 25:1; Joshua 2:1; 3:1) **6:14** [a]Or *Emptiness* or *Humiliation* [b]Targum and Vulgate read *You shall take hold.* **6:16** [a]Following Masoretic Text, Targum, and Vulgate; Septuagint reads *of nations.*

When I sit in darkness,
The LORD *will be* a light to me.
9 I will bear the indignation of the LORD,
Because I have sinned against Him,
Until He pleads my case
And executes justice for me.
He will bring me forth to the light;
I will see His righteousness.
10 Then *she who is* my enemy will see,
And shame will cover her who said to me,
"Where is the LORD your God?"
My eyes will see her;
Now she will be trampled down
Like mud in the streets.

11 *In* the day when your walls are to be built,
In that day the decree shall go far and wide.[a]
12 *In* that day they[a] shall come to you
From Assyria and the fortified cities,[b]
From the fortress[c] to the River,[d]
From sea to sea,
And mountain *to* mountain.
13 Yet the land shall be desolate
Because of those who dwell in it,
And for the fruit of their deeds.

God Will Forgive Israel

14 Shepherd Your people with Your staff,
The flock of Your heritage,
Who dwell solitarily *in* a woodland,
In the midst of Carmel;
Let them feed *in* Bashan and Gilead,
As in days of old.

15 "As in the days when you came out of the land of Egypt,
I will show them[a] wonders."

16 The nations shall see and be ashamed of all their might;
They shall put *their* hand over *their* mouth;
Their ears shall be deaf.
17 They shall lick the dust like a serpent;
They shall crawl from their holes like snakes of the earth.
They shall be afraid of the LORD our God,
And shall fear because of You.
18 Who *is* a God like You,
Pardoning iniquity
And passing over the transgression of the remnant of His heritage?

He does not retain His anger forever,
Because He delights *in* mercy.
19 He will again have compassion on us,
And will subdue our iniquities.
You will cast all our[a] sins
Into the depths of the sea.
20 You will give truth to Jacob
And mercy to Abraham,
Which You have sworn to our fathers
From days of old.

The Book of NAHUM

1 The burden[a] against Nineveh. The book of the vision of Nahum the Elkoshite.

God's Wrath on His Enemies

2 God *is* jealous, and the LORD avenges;
The LORD avenges and *is* furious.
The LORD will take vengeance on His adversaries,
And He reserves *wrath* for His enemies;
3 The LORD *is* slow to anger and great in power,
And will not at all acquit *the wicked.*

The LORD has His way
In the whirlwind and in the storm,
And the clouds *are* the dust of His feet.
4 He rebukes the sea and makes it dry,
And dries up all the rivers.
Bashan and Carmel wither,
And the flower of Lebanon wilts.
5 The mountains quake before Him,
The hills melt,
And the earth heaves[a] at His presence,
Yes, the world and all who dwell in it.

6 Who can stand before His indignation?
And who can endure the fierceness of His anger?
His fury is poured out like fire,
And the rocks are thrown down by Him.

7 The LORD *is* good,
A stronghold in the day of trouble;
And He knows those who trust in Him.
8 But with an overflowing flood
He will make an utter end of its place,
And darkness will pursue His enemies.

9 What do you conspire against the LORD?
He will make an utter end *of it.*
Affliction will not rise up a second time.
10 For while tangled *like* thorns,
And while drunken *like* drunkards,
They shall be devoured like stubble fully dried.
11 From you comes forth *one*
Who plots evil against the LORD,
A wicked counselor.

12 Thus says the LORD:

"Though *they are* safe, and likewise many,
Yet in this manner they will be cut down
When he passes through.
Though I have afflicted you,
I will afflict you no more;
13 For now I will break off his yoke from you,
And burst your bonds apart."

14 The LORD has given a command concerning you:
"Your name shall be perpetuated no longer.

7:11 [a]Or *the boundary shall be extended* **7:12** [a]Literally *he,* collective of the captives [b]Hebrew *arey mazor,* possibly *cities of Egypt* [c]Hebrew *mazor,* possibly *Egypt* [d]That is, the Euphrates **7:15** [a]Literally *him,* collective for the captives **7:19** [a]Literally *their* **1:1** [a]Or *oracle* **1:5** [a]Targum reads *burns.*

Out of the house of your gods
I will cut off the carved image and the molded image.
I will dig your grave,
For you are vile."

15 Behold, on the mountains
The feet of him who brings good tidings,
Who proclaims peace!
O Judah, keep your appointed feasts,
Perform your vows.
For the wicked one shall no more pass through you;
He is utterly cut off.

The Destruction of Nineveh

2 He who scatters[a] has come up before your face.
Man the fort!
Watch the road!
Strengthen *your* flanks!
Fortify *your* power mightily.

2 For the LORD will restore the excellence of Jacob
Like the excellence of Israel,
For the emptiers have emptied them out
And ruined their vine branches.

3 The shields of his mighty men *are* made red,
The valiant men *are* in scarlet.
The chariots *come* with flaming torches
In the day of his preparation,
And the spears are brandished.[a]
4 The chariots rage in the streets,
They jostle one another in the broad roads;
They seem like torches,
They run like lightning.

5 He remembers his nobles;
They stumble in their walk;
They make haste to her walls,
And the defense is prepared.
6 The gates of the rivers are opened,
And the palace is dissolved.
7 It is decreed:[a]
She shall be led away captive,
She shall be brought up;
And her maidservants shall lead *her* as with the voice of doves,
Beating their breasts.
8 Though Nineveh of old *was* like a pool of water,
Now they flee away.
"Halt! Halt!" *they cry;*
But no one turns back.
9 Take spoil of silver!
Take spoil of gold!
There is no end of treasure,
Or wealth of every desirable prize.
10 She is empty, desolate, and waste!
The heart melts, and the knees shake;
Much pain *is* in every side,
And all their faces are drained of color.[a]

11 Where *is* the dwelling of the lions,
And the feeding place of the young lions,
Where the lion walked, the lioness *and* lion's cub,
And no one made *them* afraid?
12 The lion tore in pieces enough for his cubs,
Killed for his lionesses,
Filled his caves with prey,
And his dens with flesh.

13 "Behold, I *am* against you," says the LORD
of hosts, "I will burn your[a] chariots in smoke,
and the sword shall devour your young lions; I
will cut off your prey from the earth, and the
voice of your messengers shall be heard no
more."

The Woe of Nineveh

3 Woe to the bloody city!
It *is* all full of lies *and* robbery.
Its victim never departs.
2 The noise of a whip
And the noise of rattling wheels,
Of galloping horses,
Of clattering chariots!
3 Horsemen charge with bright sword and glittering spear.
There is a multitude of slain,
A great number of bodies,
Countless corpses—
They stumble over the corpses—
4 Because of the multitude of harlotries of the seductive harlot,
The mistress of sorceries,
Who sells nations through her harlotries,
And families through her sorceries.

5 "Behold, I *am* against you," says the LORD of hosts;
"I will lift your skirts over your face,
I will show the nations your nakedness,
And the kingdoms your shame.
6 I will cast abominable filth upon you,
Make you vile,
And make you a spectacle.
7 It shall come to pass *that* all who look upon you
Will flee from you, and say,
'Nineveh is laid waste!
Who will bemoan her?'
Where shall I seek comforters for you?"

8 Are you better than No Amon[a]
That was situated by the River,[b]
That had the waters around her,
Whose rampart *was* the sea,
Whose wall *was* the sea?
9 Ethiopia and Egypt *were* her strength,
And *it was* boundless;
Put and Lubim were your[a] helpers.
10 Yet she *was* carried away,
She went into captivity;
Her young children also were dashed to pieces
At the head of every street;
They cast lots for her honorable men,
And all her great men were bound in chains.
11 You also will be drunk;
You will be hidden;
You also will seek refuge from the enemy.

12 All your strongholds *are* fig trees with ripened figs:

2:1 [a]Vulgate reads *He who destroys.* **2:3** [a]Literally *the cypresses are shaken;* Septuagint and Syriac read *the horses rush about;* Vulgate reads *the drivers are stupefied.* **2:7** [a]Hebrew *Huzzab* **2:10** [a]Compare Joel 2:6 **2:13** [a]Literally *her* **3:8** [a]That is, ancient Thebes; Targum and Vulgate read *populous Alexandria.* [b]Literally *rivers,* that is, the Nile and the surrounding canals **3:9** [a]Septuagint reads *her.*

If they are shaken,
They fall into the mouth of the eater.
13 Surely, your people in your midst *are* women!
The gates of your land are wide open for your enemies;
Fire shall devour the bars of your *gates*.
14 Draw your water for the siege!
Fortify your strongholds!
Go into the clay and tread the mortar!
Make strong the brick kiln!
15 There the fire will devour you,
The sword will cut you off;
It will eat you up like a locust.
Make yourself many—like the locust!
Make yourself many—like the *swarming* locusts!
16 You have multiplied your merchants more than the stars of heaven.
The locust plunders and flies away.
17 Your commanders *are* like *swarming* locusts,
And your generals like great grasshoppers,
Which camp in the hedges on a cold day;
When the sun rises they flee away,
And the place where they *are* is not known.
18 Your shepherds slumber, O king of Assyria;
Your nobles rest *in the dust*.
Your people are scattered on the mountains,
And no one gathers them.
19 Your injury *has* no healing,
Your wound is severe.
All who hear news of you
Will clap *their* hands over you,
For upon whom has not your wickedness passed continually?

The Book of HABAKKUK

1 The burden[a] which the prophet Habakkuk saw.

The Prophet's Question

2 O LORD, how long shall I cry,
And You will not hear?
Even cry out to You, "Violence!"
And You will not save.
3 Why do You show me iniquity,
And cause *me* to see trouble?
For plundering and violence *are* before me;
There is strife, and contention arises.
4 Therefore the law is powerless,
And justice never goes forth.
For the wicked surround the righteous;
Therefore perverse judgment proceeds.

The LORD's Reply

5 "Look among the nations and watch—
Be utterly astounded!
For *I will* work a work in your days
Which you would not believe, though it were told *you*.
6 For indeed I am raising up the Chaldeans,
A bitter and hasty nation
Which marches through the breadth of the earth,
To possess dwelling places *that are* not theirs.
7 They are terrible and dreadful;
Their judgment and their dignity proceed from themselves.
8 Their horses also are swifter than leopards,
And more fierce than evening wolves.
Their chargers charge ahead;
Their cavalry comes from afar;
They fly as the eagle *that* hastens to eat.
9 "They all come for violence;
Their faces are set *like* the east wind.
They gather captives like sand.
10 They scoff at kings,
And princes are scorned by them.
They deride every stronghold,
For they heap up earthen *mounds* and seize it.
11 Then *his* mind[a] changes, and he transgresses;
He commits offense,
Ascribing this power to his god."

The Prophet's Second Question

12 Are You not from everlasting,
O LORD my God, my Holy One?
We shall not die.
O LORD, You have appointed them for judgment;
O Rock, You have marked them for correction.
13 *You are* of purer eyes than to behold evil,
And cannot look on wickedness.
Why do You look on those who deal treacherously,
And hold Your tongue when the wicked devours
A *person* more righteous than he?
14 *Why* do You make men like fish of the sea,
Like creeping things *that have* no ruler over them?
15 They take up all of them with a hook,
They catch them in their net,
And gather them in their dragnet.
Therefore they rejoice and are glad.
16 Therefore they sacrifice to their net,
And burn incense to their dragnet;
Because by them their share *is* sumptuous
And their food plentiful.
17 Shall they therefore empty their net,
And continue to slay nations without pity?

2 I will stand my watch
And set myself on the rampart,
And watch to see what He will say to me,
And what I will answer when I am corrected.

1:1 [a]Or *oracle* **1:11** [a]Literally *spirit* or *wind*

The Just Live by Faith

2 Then the LORD answered me and said:

"Write the vision
And make *it* plain on tablets,
That he may run who reads it.
3 For the vision *is* yet for an appointed time;
But at the end it will speak, and it will not lie.
Though it tarries, wait for it;
Because it will surely come,
It will not tarry.

4 "Behold the proud,
His soul is not upright in him;
But the just shall live by his faith.

Woe to the Wicked

5 "Indeed, because he transgresses by wine,
He is a proud man,
And he does not stay at home.
Because he enlarges his desire as hell,[a]
And he *is* like death, and cannot be satisfied,
He gathers to himself all nations
And heaps up for himself all peoples.

6 "Will not all these take up a proverb against him,
And a taunting riddle against him, and say,
'Woe to him who increases
What is not his—how long?
And to him who loads himself with many pledges'?[a]
7 Will not your creditors[a] rise up suddenly?
Will they not awaken who oppress you?
And you will become their booty.
8 Because you have plundered many nations,
All the remnant of the people shall plunder you,
Because of men's blood
And the violence of the land *and* the city,
And of all who dwell in it.

9 "Woe to him who covets evil gain for his house,
That he may set his nest on high,
That he may be delivered from the power of disaster!
10 You give shameful counsel to your house,
Cutting off many peoples,
And sin *against* your soul.
11 For the stone will cry out from the wall,
And the beam from the timbers will answer it.

12 "Woe to him who builds a town with bloodshed,
Who establishes a city by iniquity!
13 Behold, *is it* not of the LORD of hosts
That the peoples labor to feed the fire,[a]
And nations weary themselves in vain?
14 For the earth will be filled
With the knowledge of the glory of the LORD,
As the waters cover the sea.

15 "Woe to him who gives drink to his neighbor,
Pressing[a] *him to* your bottle,
Even to make *him* drunk,
That you may look on his nakedness!
16 You are filled with shame instead of glory.
You also—drink!
And be exposed as uncircumcised![a]
The cup of the LORD's right hand *will be* turned against you,
And utter shame will be on your glory.
17 For the violence *done to* Lebanon will cover you,
And the plunder of beasts *which* made them afraid,
Because of men's blood
And the violence of the land *and* the city,
And of all who dwell in it.

18 "What profit is the image, that its maker should carve it,
The molded image, a teacher of lies,
That the maker of its mold should trust in it,
To make mute idols?
19 Woe to him who says to wood, 'Awake!'
To silent stone, 'Arise! It shall teach!'
Behold, it is overlaid with gold and silver,
Yet in it there is no breath at all.

20 "But the LORD is in His holy temple.
Let all the earth keep silence before Him."

The Prophet's Prayer

3 A prayer of Habakkuk the prophet, on Shigionoth.[a]

2 O LORD, I have heard Your speech *and* was afraid;
O LORD, revive Your work in the midst of the years!
In the midst of the years make *it* known;
In wrath remember mercy.

3 God came from Teman,
The Holy One from Mount Paran. Selah

His glory covered the heavens,
And the earth was full of His praise.
4 *His* brightness was like the light;
He had rays *flashing* from His hand,
And there His power *was* hidden.
5 Before Him went pestilence,
And fever followed at His feet.
6 He stood and measured the earth;
He looked and startled the nations.
And the everlasting mountains were scattered,
The perpetual hills bowed.
His ways *are* everlasting.
7 I saw the tents of Cushan in affliction;
The curtains of the land of Midian trembled.
8 O LORD, were *You* displeased with the rivers,
Was Your anger against the rivers,
Was Your wrath against the sea,
That You rode on Your horses,
Your chariots of salvation?
9 Your bow was made quite ready;
Oaths were sworn over *Your* arrows.[a]
Selah

You divided the earth with rivers.
10 The mountains saw You *and* trembled;
The overflowing of the water passed by.
The deep uttered its voice,

2:5 [a]Or *Sheol* 2:6 [a]Syriac and Vulgate read *thick clay.* 2:7 [a]Literally *those who bite you* 2:13 [a]Literally *for what satisfies fire,* that is, for what is of no lasting value 2:15 [a]Literally *Attaching* or *Joining* 2:16 [a]Dead Sea Scrolls and Septuagint read *And reel!;* Syriac and Vulgate read *And fall fast asleep!* 3:1 [a]Exact meaning unknown
3:9 [a]Literally *rods* or *tribes* (compare verse 14)

And lifted its hands on high.
11 The sun and moon stood still in their habitation;
At the light of Your arrows they went,
At the shining of Your glittering spear.

12 You marched through the land in indignation;
You trampled the nations in anger.
13 You went forth for the salvation of Your people,
For salvation with Your Anointed.
You struck the head from the house of the wicked,
By laying bare from foundation to neck. Selah

14 You thrust through with his own arrows
The head of his villages.
They came out like a whirlwind to scatter me;
Their rejoicing was like feasting on the poor in secret.
15 You walked through the sea with Your horses,
Through the heap of great waters.

16 When I heard, my body trembled;
My lips quivered at *the* voice;
Rottenness entered my bones;
And I trembled in myself,
That I might rest in the day of trouble.
When he comes up to the people,
He will invade them with his troops.

A Hymn of Faith

17 Though the fig tree may not blossom,
Nor fruit be on the vines;
Though the labor of the olive may fail,
And the fields yield no food;
Though the flock may be cut off from the fold,
And there be no herd in the stalls—
18 Yet I will rejoice in the LORD,
I will joy in the God of my salvation.

19 The LORD God[a] is my strength;
He will make my feet like deer's *feet*,
And He will make me walk on my high hills.

To the Chief Musician. With my stringed instruments.

The Book of ZEPHANIAH

1 The word of the LORD which came to Zeph-
aniah the son of Cushi, the son of Gedaliah,
the son of Amariah, the son of Hezekiah, in
the days of Josiah the son of Amon, king of
Judah.

The Great Day of the LORD

2 "I will utterly consume everything
From the face of the land,"
Says the LORD;
3 "I will consume man and beast;
I will consume the birds of the heavens,
The fish of the sea,
And the stumbling blocks[a] along with the wicked.
I will cut off man from the face of the land,"
Says the LORD.

4 "I will stretch out My hand against Judah,
And against all the inhabitants of Jerusalem.
I will cut off every trace of Baal from this place,
The names of the idolatrous priests[a] with the *pagan* priests—
5 Those who worship the host of heaven on the housetops;
Those who worship and swear *oaths* by the LORD,
But who *also* swear by Milcom;[a]
6 Those who have turned back from *following* the LORD,
And have not sought the LORD, nor inquired of Him."

7 Be silent in the presence of the Lord GOD;
For the day of the LORD *is* at hand,
For the LORD has prepared a sacrifice;
He has invited[a] His guests.

8 "And it shall be,
In the day of the LORD's sacrifice,
That I will punish the princes and the king's children,
And all such as are clothed with foreign apparel.
9 In the same day I will punish
All those who leap over the threshold,[a]
Who fill their masters' houses with violence and deceit.

10 "And there shall be on that day," says the LORD,
"The sound of a mournful cry from the Fish Gate,
A wailing from the Second Quarter,
And a loud crashing from the hills.
11 Wail, you inhabitants of Maktesh![a]
For all the merchant people are cut down;
All those who handle money are cut off.

12 "And it shall come to pass at that time
That I will search Jerusalem with lamps,
And punish the men
Who are settled in complacency,[a]
Who say in their heart,
'The LORD will not do good,
Nor will He do evil.'
13 Therefore their goods shall become booty,
And their houses a desolation;
They shall build houses, but not inhabit *them*;
They shall plant vineyards, but not drink their wine."

3:19 [a]Hebrew *YHWH Adonai* **1:3** [a]Figurative of idols **1:4** [a]Hebrew *chemarim* **1:5** [a]Or *Malcam*, an Ammonite god, also called *Molech* (compare Leviticus 18:21) **1:7** [a]Literally *set apart, consecrated* **1:9** [a]Compare 1 Samuel 5:5 **1:11** [a]Literally *Mortar*, a market district of Jerusalem **1:12** [a]Literally *on their lees*, that is, settled like the dregs of wine

14 The great day of the LORD *is* near;
It is near and hastens quickly.
The noise of the day of the LORD is bitter;
There the mighty men shall cry out.
15 That day *is* a day of wrath,
A day of trouble and distress,
A day of devastation and desolation,
A day of darkness and gloominess,
A day of clouds and thick darkness,
16 A day of trumpet and alarm
Against the fortified cities
And against the high towers.

17 "I will bring distress upon men,
And they shall walk like blind men,
Because they have sinned against the LORD;
Their blood shall be poured out like dust,
And their flesh like refuse."

18 Neither their silver nor their gold
Shall be able to deliver them
In the day of the LORD's wrath;
But the whole land shall be devoured
By the fire of His jealousy,
For He will make speedy riddance
Of all those who dwell in the land.

A Call to Repentance

2 Gather yourselves together, yes, gather together,
O undesirable[a] nation,
2 Before the decree is issued,
Or the day passes like chaff,
Before the LORD's fierce anger comes upon you,
Before the day of the LORD's anger comes upon you!
3 Seek the LORD, all you meek of the earth,
Who have upheld His justice.
Seek righteousness, seek humility.
It may be that you will be hidden
In the day of the LORD's anger.

Judgment on Nations

4 For Gaza shall be forsaken,
And Ashkelon desolate;
They shall drive out Ashdod at noonday,
And Ekron shall be uprooted.
5 Woe to the inhabitants of the seacoast,
The nation of the Cherethites!
The word of the LORD *is* against you,
O Canaan, land of the Philistines:
"I will destroy you;
So there shall be no inhabitant."

6 The seacoast shall be pastures,
With shelters[a] for shepherds and folds for flocks.
7 The coast shall be for the remnant of the house of Judah;
They shall feed *their* flocks there;
In the houses of Ashkelon they shall lie down at evening.
For the LORD their God will intervene for them,
And return their captives.

8 "I have heard the reproach of Moab,
And the insults of the people of Ammon,
With which they have reproached My people,
And made arrogant threats against their borders.
9 Therefore, as I live,"
Says the LORD of hosts, the God of Israel,
"Surely Moab shall be like Sodom,
And the people of Ammon like Gomorrah—
Overrun with weeds and saltpits,
And a perpetual desolation.
The residue of My people shall plunder them,
And the remnant of My people shall possess them."

10 This they shall have for their pride,
Because they have reproached and made arrogant threats
Against the people of the LORD of hosts.
11 The LORD *will be* awesome to them,
For He will reduce to nothing all the gods of the earth;
People shall worship Him,
Each one from his place,
Indeed all the shores of the nations.

12 "You Ethiopians also,
You shall be slain by My sword."

13 And He will stretch out His hand against the north,
Destroy Assyria,
And make Nineveh a desolation,
As dry as the wilderness.
14 The herds shall lie down in her midst,
Every beast of the nation.
Both the pelican and the bittern
Shall lodge on the capitals *of her pillars;*
Their voice shall sing in the windows;
Desolation *shall be* at the threshold;
For He will lay bare the cedar work.
15 This is the rejoicing city
That dwelt securely,
That said in her heart,
"I *am it,* and *there is* none besides me."
How has she become a desolation,
A place for beasts to lie down!
Everyone who passes by her
Shall hiss and shake his fist.

The Wickedness of Jerusalem

3 Woe to her who is rebellious and polluted,
To the oppressing city!
2 She has not obeyed *His* voice,
She has not received correction;
She has not trusted in the LORD,
She has not drawn near to her God.

3 Her princes in her midst *are* roaring lions;
Her judges *are* evening wolves
That leave not a bone till morning.
4 Her prophets are insolent, treacherous people;
Her priests have polluted the sanctuary,
They have done violence to the law.
5 The LORD *is* righteous in her midst,
He will do no unrighteousness.
Every morning He brings His justice to light;
He never fails,
But the unjust knows no shame.

6 "I have cut off nations,
Their fortresses are devastated;
I have made their streets desolate,
With none passing by.
Their cities are destroyed;
There is no one, no inhabitant.

2:1 [a]Or *shameless* 2:6 [a]Literally *excavations,* either underground huts or cisterns

7 I said, 'Surely you will fear Me,
You will receive instruction'—
So that her dwelling would not be cut off,
Despite everything for which I punished her.
But they rose early and corrupted all their deeds.

A Faithful Remnant

8 "Therefore wait for Me," says the LORD,
"Until the day I rise up for plunder;[a]
My determination *is* to gather the nations
To My assembly of kingdoms,
To pour on them My indignation,
All My fierce anger;
All the earth shall be devoured
With the fire of My jealousy.

9 "For then I will restore to the peoples a pure language,
That they all may call on the name of the LORD,
To serve Him with one accord.
10 From beyond the rivers of Ethiopia
My worshipers,
The daughter of My dispersed ones,
Shall bring My offering.
11 In that day you shall not be shamed for any of your deeds
In which you transgress against Me;
For then I will take away from your midst
Those who rejoice in your pride,
And you shall no longer be haughty
In My holy mountain.
12 I will leave in your midst
A meek and humble people,
And they shall trust in the name of the LORD.
13 The remnant of Israel shall do no unrighteousness
And speak no lies,
Nor shall a deceitful tongue be found in their mouth;
For they shall feed *their* flocks and lie down,
And no one shall make *them* afraid."

Joy in God's Faithfulness

14 Sing, O daughter of Zion!
Shout, O Israel!
Be glad and rejoice with all *your* heart,
O daughter of Jerusalem!
15 The LORD has taken away your judgments,
He has cast out your enemy.
The King of Israel, the LORD, *is* in your midst;
You shall see[a] disaster no more.

16 In that day it shall be said to Jerusalem:
"Do not fear;
Zion, let not your hands be weak.
17 The LORD your God in your midst,
The Mighty One, will save;
He will rejoice over you with gladness,
He will quiet *you* with His love,
He will rejoice over you with singing."

18 "I will gather those who sorrow over the appointed assembly,
Who are among you,
To whom its reproach *is* a burden.
19 Behold, at that time
I will deal with all who afflict you;
I will save the lame,
And gather those who were driven out;
I will appoint them for praise and fame
In every land where they were put to shame.
20 At that time I will bring you back,
Even at the time I gather you;
For I will give you fame and praise
Among all the peoples of the earth,
When I return your captives before your eyes,"
Says the LORD.

The Book of HAGGAI

The Command to Build God's House

1 In the second year of King Darius, in the
sixth month, on the first day of the month,
the word of the LORD came by Haggai the
prophet to Zerubbabel the son of Shealtiel, gov-
ernor of Judah, and to Joshua the son of Jehoz-
adak, the high priest, saying,
2 "Thus speaks the LORD of hosts, saying:
'This people says, "The time has not come, the
time that the LORD's house should be built." ' "
3 Then the word of the LORD came by Hag-
gai the prophet, saying,
4 "*Is it* time for you yourselves to dwell in
your paneled houses, and this temple[a] *to lie* in
ruins?"
5 Now therefore, thus says the LORD of hosts:
"Consider your ways!

6 "You have sown much, and bring in little;
You eat, but do not have enough;
You drink, but you are not filled with drink;
You clothe yourselves, but no one is warm;
And he who earns wages,
Earns wages *to put* into a bag with holes."

7 Thus says the LORD of hosts: "Consider your
ways!
8 "Go up to the mountains and bring wood
and build the temple, that I may take pleasure
in it and be glorified," says the LORD.
9 "*You* looked for much, but indeed *it came*
to little; and when you brought it home, I blew
it away. Why?" says the LORD of hosts. "Because
of My house that *is in* ruins, while every one of
you runs to his own house.
10 "Therefore the heavens above you with-
hold the dew, and the earth withholds its fruit.
11 "For I called for a drought on the land and
the mountains, on the grain and the new wine
and the oil, on whatever the ground brings
forth, on men and livestock, and on all the
labor of *your* hands."

3:8 [a]Septuagint and Syriac read *for witness;* Targum reads *for the day of My revelation for judgment;* Vulgate reads *for the day of My resurrection that is to come.* 3:15 [a]Some Hebrew manuscripts, Septuagint, and Bomberg read *see;* Masoretic Text and Vulgate read *fear.* 1:4 [a]Literally *house,* and so in verse 8

The People's Obedience

12 Then Zerubbabel the son of Shealtiel, and
Joshua the son of Jehozadak, the high priest,
with all the remnant of the people, obeyed the
voice of the LORD their God, and the words of
Haggai the prophet, as the LORD their God had
sent him; and the people feared the presence
of the LORD.
13 Then Haggai, the LORD's messenger, spoke
the LORD's message to the people, saying, "I
am with you, says the LORD."
14 So the LORD stirred up the spirit of Zerub-
babel the son of Shealtiel, governor of Judah,
and the spirit of Joshua the son of Jehozadak,
the high priest, and the spirit of all the remnant
of the people; and they came and worked on
the house of the LORD of hosts, their God,
15 on the twenty-fourth day of the sixth month,
in the second year of King Darius.

The Coming Glory of God's House

2 In the seventh *month*, on the twenty-first of
the month, the word of the LORD came by
Haggai the prophet, saying:
2 "Speak now to Zerubbabel the son of She-
altiel, governor of Judah, and to Joshua the
son of Jehozadak, the high priest, and to the
remnant of the people, saying:
3 'Who is left among you who saw this tem-
ple[a] in its former glory? And how do you see it
now? In comparison with it, *is this* not in your
eyes as nothing?
4 'Yet now be strong, Zerubbabel,' says the
LORD; 'and be strong, Joshua, son of Jehoza-
dak, the high priest; and be strong, all you
people of the land,' says the LORD, 'and work;
for I *am* with you,' says the LORD of hosts.
5 '*According to* the word that I covenanted
with you when you came out of Egypt, so My
Spirit remains among you; do not fear!'
6 "For thus says the LORD of hosts: 'Once
more (it *is* a little while) I will shake heaven and
earth, the sea and dry land;
7 'and I will shake all nations, and they shall
come to the Desire of All Nations,[a] and I will fill
this temple with glory,' says the LORD of hosts.
8 'The silver *is* Mine, and the gold *is* Mine,'
says the LORD of hosts.
9 'The glory of this latter temple shall be
greater than the former,' says the LORD of hosts.
'And in this place I will give peace,' says the
LORD of hosts."

The People Are Defiled

10 On the twenty-fourth *day* of the ninth *month*,
in the second year of Darius, the word of the
LORD came by Haggai the prophet, saying,
11 "Thus says the LORD of hosts: 'Now, ask
the priests *concerning the* law, saying,
12 "If one carries holy meat in the fold of his
garment, and with the edge he touches bread
or stew, wine or oil, or any food, will it become
holy?"'" Then the priests answered and said,
"No."
13 And Haggai said, "If *one who is* unclean
because of a dead body touches any of these,
will it be unclean?" So the priests answered
and said, "It shall be unclean."
14 Then Haggai answered and said, "'So is
this people, and so is this nation before Me,'
says the LORD, 'and so is every work of their
hands; and what they offer there is unclean.

Promised Blessing

15 'And now, carefully consider from this day
forward: from before stone was laid upon stone
in the temple of the LORD—
16 'since those *days*, when *one* came to a heap
of twenty ephahs, there were *but* ten; when
one came to the wine vat to draw out fifty baths
from the press, there were *but* twenty.
17 'I struck you with blight and mildew and
hail in all the labors of your hands; yet you did
not *turn* to Me,' says the LORD.
18 'Consider now from this day forward, from
the twenty-fourth day of the ninth month, from
the day that the foundation of the LORD's tem-
ple was laid—consider it:
19 'Is the seed still in the barn? As yet the vine,
the fig tree, the pomegranate, and the olive
tree have not yielded *fruit*. *But* from this day I
will bless *you*.'"

Zerubbabel Chosen as a Signet

20 And again the word of the LORD came to
Haggai on the twenty-fourth day of the month,
saying,
21 "Speak to Zerubbabel, governor of Judah,
saying:

'I will shake heaven and earth.
22 I will overthrow the throne of kingdoms;
I will destroy the strength of the Gentile
kingdoms.
I will overthrow the chariots
And those who ride in them;
The horses and their riders shall come
down,
Every one by the sword of his brother.

23 'In that day,' says the LORD of hosts, 'I will
take you, Zerubbabel My servant, the son of
Shealtiel,' says the LORD, 'and will make you
like a signet *ring*; for I have chosen you,' says
the LORD of hosts."

The Book of ZECHARIAH

A Call to Repentance

1 In the eighth month of the second year of
Darius, the word of the LORD came to
Zechariah the son of Berechiah, the son of
Iddo the prophet, saying,
2 "The LORD has been very angry with your
fathers.
3 "Therefore say to them, 'Thus says the
LORD of hosts: "Return to Me," says the LORD
of hosts, "and I will return to you," says the
LORD of hosts.
4 "Do not be like your fathers, to whom the
former prophets preached, saying, 'Thus says
the LORD of hosts: "Turn now from your evil

2:3 [a]Literally *house*, and so in verses 7 and 9 2:7 [a]Or *the desire of all nations*

ways and your evil deeds."' But they did not
hear nor heed Me," says the LORD.

5 "Your fathers, where *are* they?
And the prophets, do they live forever?
6 Yet surely My words and My statutes,
Which I commanded My servants the prophets,
Did they not overtake your fathers?

"So they returned and said:

'Just as the LORD of hosts determined to do to us,
According to our ways and according to our deeds,
So He has dealt with us.'"'"

Vision of the Horses

7 On the twenty-fourth day of the eleventh
month, which is the month Shebat, in the sec-
ond year of Darius, the word of the LORD came
to Zechariah the son of Berechiah, the son of
Iddo the prophet:
8 I saw by night, and behold, a man riding
on a red horse, and it stood among the myrtle
trees in the hollow; and behind him *were* horses:
red, sorrel, and white.
9 Then I said, "My lord, what *are* these?" So
the angel who talked with me said to me, "I will
show you what they *are*."
10 And the man who stood among the myrtle
trees answered and said, "These *are the ones*
whom the LORD has sent to walk to and fro
throughout the earth."
11 So they answered the Angel of the LORD,
who stood among the myrtle trees, and said, "We
have walked to and fro throughout the earth,
and behold, all the earth is resting quietly."

The LORD Will Comfort Zion

12 Then the Angel of the LORD answered and
said, "O LORD of hosts, how long will You not
have mercy on Jerusalem and on the cities of
Judah, against which You were angry these sev-
enty years?"
13 And the LORD answered the angel who
talked to me, *with* good *and* comforting words.
14 So the angel who spoke with me said to
me, "Proclaim, saying, 'Thus says the LORD of
hosts:

"I am zealous for Jerusalem
And for Zion with great zeal.
15 I am exceedingly angry with the nations at ease;
For I was a little angry,
And they helped—*but* with evil *intent*."

16 'Therefore thus says the LORD:

"I am returning to Jerusalem with mercy;
My house shall be built in it," says the LORD of hosts,
"And a *surveyor's* line shall be stretched out over Jerusalem."'

17 "Again proclaim, saying, 'Thus says the
LORD of hosts:

"My cities shall again spread out through prosperity;
The LORD will again comfort Zion,
And will again choose Jerusalem."'"

Vision of the Horns

18 Then I raised my eyes and looked, and there
were four horns.
19 And I said to the angel who talked with
me, "What *are* these?" So he answered me,
"These *are* the horns that have scattered Ju-
dah, Israel, and Jerusalem."
20 Then the LORD showed me four craftsmen.
21 And I said, "What are these coming to do?"
So he said, "These *are* the horns that scattered
Judah, so that no one could lift up his head;
but the craftsmen[a] are coming to terrify them,
to cast out the horns of the nations that lifted
up *their* horn against the land of Judah to scat-
ter it."

Vision of the Measuring Line

2 Then I raised my eyes and looked, and be-
hold, a man with a measuring line in his
hand.
2 So I said, "Where are you going?" And he
said to me, "To measure Jerusalem, to see what
is its width and what *is* its length."
3 And there *was* the angel who talked with
me, going out; and another angel was coming
out to meet him,
4 who said to him, "Run, speak to this young
man, saying: 'Jerusalem shall be inhabited *as*
towns without walls, because of the multitude
of men and livestock in it.
5 'For I,' says the LORD, 'will be a wall of fire
all around her, and I will be the glory in her
midst.'"

Future Joy of Zion and Many Nations

6 "Up, up! Flee from the land of the north,"
says the LORD; "for I have spread you abroad
like the four winds of heaven," says the LORD.
7 "Up, Zion! Escape, you who dwell with the
daughter of Babylon."
8 For thus says the LORD of hosts: "He sent
Me after glory, to the nations which plunder you;
for he who touches you touches the apple of
His eye.
9 "For surely I will shake My hand against
them, and they shall become spoil for their
servants. Then you will know that the LORD of
hosts has sent Me.
10 "Sing and rejoice, O daughter of Zion! For
behold, I am coming and I will dwell in your
midst," says the LORD.
11 "Many nations shall be joined to the LORD
in that day, and they shall become My people.
And I will dwell in your midst. Then you will
know that the LORD of hosts has sent Me to you.
12 "And the LORD will take possession of Ju-
dah as His inheritance in the Holy Land, and
will again choose Jerusalem.
13 "Be silent, all flesh, before the LORD, for
He is aroused from His holy habitation!"

Vision of the High Priest

3 Then he showed me Joshua the high priest
standing before the Angel of the LORD, and
Satan standing at his right hand to oppose him.
2 And the LORD said to Satan, "The LORD
rebuke you, Satan! The LORD who has chosen
Jerusalem rebuke you! *Is* this not a brand
plucked from the fire?"
3 Now Joshua was clothed with filthy gar-
ments, and was standing before the Angel.
4 Then He answered and spoke to those who

1:21 [a]Literally *these*

stood before Him, saying, "Take away the
filthy garments from him." And to him He said,
"See, I have removed your iniquity from you,
and I will clothe you with rich robes."
5 And I said, "Let them put a clean turban
on his head." So they put a clean turban on his
head, and they put the clothes on him. And the
Angel of the LORD stood by.

The Coming Branch

6 Then the Angel of the LORD admonished
Joshua, saying,
7 "Thus says the LORD of hosts:

'If you will walk in My ways,
And if you will keep My command,
Then you shall also judge My house,
And likewise have charge of My courts;
I will give you places to walk
Among these who stand here.

8 'Hear, O Joshua, the high priest,
You and your companions who sit before
you,
For they are a wondrous sign;
For behold, I am bringing forth My
Servant the BRANCH.
9 For behold, the stone
That I have laid before Joshua:
Upon the stone *are* seven eyes.
Behold, I will engrave its inscription,'
Says the LORD of hosts,
'And I will remove the iniquity of that
land in one day.
10 In that day,' says the LORD of hosts,
'Everyone will invite his neighbor
Under his vine and under his fig tree.'"

Vision of the Lampstand and Olive Trees

4 Now the angel who talked with me came
back and wakened me, as a man who is wak-
ened out of his sleep.
2 And he said to me, "What do you see?" So
I said, "I am looking, and there *is* a lampstand
of solid gold with a bowl on top of it, and on
the *stand* seven lamps with seven pipes to the
seven lamps.
3 "Two olive trees *are* by it, one at the right
of the bowl and the other at its left."
4 So I answered and spoke to the angel who
talked with me, saying, "What *are* these, my
lord?"
5 Then the angel who talked with me an-
swered and said to me, "Do you not know what
these are?" And I said, "No, my lord."
6 So he answered and said to me:

"This *is* the word of the LORD to
Zerubbabel:
'Not by might nor by power, but by My
Spirit,'
Says the LORD of hosts.
7 'Who *are* you, O great mountain?
Before Zerubbabel *you shall become* a
plain!
And he shall bring forth the capstone
With shouts of "Grace, grace to it!"'"

8 Moreover the word of the LORD came to
me, saying:
9 "The hands of Zerubbabel
Have laid the foundation of this temple;[a]
His hands shall also finish *it*.
Then you will know
That the LORD of hosts has sent Me to
you.
10 For who has despised the day of small
things?
For these seven rejoice to see
The plumb line in the hand of
Zerubbabel.
They are the eyes of the LORD,
Which scan to and fro throughout the
whole earth."

11 Then I answered and said to him, "What
are these two olive trees—at the right of the
lampstand and at its left?"
12 And I further answered and said to him,
"What *are these* two olive branches that *drip*
into the receptacles[a] of the two gold pipes from
which the golden *oil* drains?"
13 Then he answered me and said, "Do you
not know what these *are*?" And I said, "No, my
lord."
14 So he said, "These *are* the two anointed
ones, who stand beside the Lord of the whole
earth."

Vision of the Flying Scroll

5 Then I turned and raised my eyes, and saw
there a flying scroll.
2 And he said to me, "What do you see?" So
I answered, "I see a flying scroll. Its length *is*
twenty cubits and its width ten cubits."
3 Then he said to me, "This *is* the curse that
goes out over the face of the whole earth: 'Every
thief shall be expelled,' according *to* this side
of *the scroll;* and, 'Every perjurer shall be ex-
pelled,' according *to* that side of it."

4 "I will send out *the curse*," says the LORD
of hosts;
"It shall enter the house of the thief
And the house of the one who swears
falsely by My name.
It shall remain in the midst of his house
And consume it, with its timber and
stones."

Vision of the Woman in a Basket

5 Then the angel who talked with me came
out and said to me, "Lift your eyes now, and see
what this *is* that goes forth."
6 So I asked, "What *is* it?" And he said, "It
is a basket[a] that is going forth." He also said,
"This *is* their resemblance throughout the earth:
7 "Here *is* a lead disc lifted up, and this *is* a
woman sitting inside the basket";
8 then he said, "This *is* Wickedness!" And he
thrust her down into the basket, and threw the
lead cover[a] over its mouth.
9 Then I raised my eyes and looked, and there
were two women, coming with the wind in
their wings; for they had wings like the wings
of a stork, and they lifted up the basket between
earth and heaven.
10 So I said to the angel who talked with me,
"Where are they carrying the basket?"

4:9 [a]Literally *house* 4:12 [a]Literally *into the hands of* 5:6 [a]Hebrew *ephah*, a measuring container, and so elsewhere 5:8 [a]Literally *stone*

11 And he said to me, "To build a house for it
in the land of Shinar;[a] when it is ready, *the*
basket will be set there on its base."

Vision of the Four Chariots

6 Then I turned and raised my eyes and
looked, and behold, four chariots *were*
coming from between two mountains, and the
mountains *were* mountains of bronze.
2 With the first chariot *were* red horses, with
the second chariot black horses,
3 with the third chariot white horses, and with
the fourth chariot dappled horses—strong *steeds*.
4 Then I answered and said to the angel who
talked with me, "What *are* these, my lord?"
5 And the angel answered and said to me,
"These *are* four spirits of heaven, who go out
from *their* station before the Lord of all the earth.
6 "The one with the black horses is going to
the north country, the white are going after them,
and the dappled are going toward the south coun-
try."
7 Then the strong *steeds* went out, eager to
go, that they might walk to and fro throughout
the earth. And He said, "Go, walk to and fro
throughout the earth." So they walked to and
fro throughout the earth.
8 And He called to me, and spoke to me, say-
ing, "See, those who go toward the north coun-
try have given rest to My Spirit in the north
country."

The Command to Crown Joshua

9 Then the word of the LORD came to me, say-
ing:
10 "Receive *the gift* from the captives—from
Heldai, Tobijah, and Jedaiah, who have come
from Babylon—and go the same day and enter
the house of Josiah the son of Zephaniah.
11 "Take the silver and gold, make an elabo-
rate crown, and set *it* on the head of Joshua the
son of Jehozadak, the high priest.
12 "Then speak to him, saying, 'Thus says the
LORD of hosts, saying:

"Behold, the Man whose name *is* the
BRANCH!
From His place He shall branch out,
And He shall build the temple of the
LORD;
13 Yes, He shall build the temple of the
LORD.
He shall bear the glory,
And shall sit and rule on His throne;
So He shall be a priest on His throne,
And the counsel of peace shall be
between them both."'

14 "Now the elaborate crown shall be for a
memorial in the temple of the LORD for He-
lem,[a] Tobijah, Jedaiah, and Hen the son of Zeph-
aniah.
15 "Even those from afar shall come and build
the temple of the LORD. Then you shall know
that the LORD of hosts has sent Me to you. And
this shall come to pass if you diligently obey
the voice of the LORD your God."

Obedience Better than Fasting

7 Now in the fourth year of King Darius it came
to pass *that* the word of the LORD came to
Zechariah, on the fourth *day* of the ninth
month, Chislev,
2 when *the people*[a] sent Sherezer,[b] with Re-
gem-Melech and his men, *to* the house of God,[c]
to pray before the LORD,
3 *and* to ask the priests who *were* in the house
of the LORD of hosts, and the prophets, saying,
"Should I weep in the fifth month and fast as I
have done for so many years?"
4 Then the word of the LORD of hosts came
to me, saying,
5 "Say to all the people of the land, and to
the priests: 'When you fasted and mourned in
the fifth and seventh *months* during those sev-
enty years, did you really fast for Me—for Me?
6 'When you eat and when you drink, do you
not eat and drink *for yourselves?*
7 '*Should you* not *have obeyed* the words
which the LORD proclaimed through the for-
mer prophets when Jerusalem and the cities
around it were inhabited and prosperous, and
the South[a] and the Lowland were inhabited?'"

Disobedience Resulted in Captivity

8 Then the word of the LORD came to Zecha-
riah, saying,
9 "Thus says the LORD of hosts:

'Execute true justice,
Show mercy and compassion
Everyone to his brother.
10 Do not oppress the widow or the
fatherless,
The alien or the poor.
Let none of you plan evil in his heart
Against his brother.'

11 "But they refused to heed, shrugged their
shoulders, and stopped their ears so that they
could not hear.
12 "Yes, they made their hearts like flint, re-
fusing to hear the law and the words which the
LORD of hosts had sent by His Spirit through
the former prophets. Thus great wrath came
from the LORD of hosts.
13 "Therefore it happened, *that* just as He
proclaimed and they would not hear, so they
called out and I would not listen," says the
LORD of hosts.
14 "But I scattered them with a whirlwind
among all the nations which they had not
known. Thus the land became desolate after
them, so that no one passed through or re-
turned; for they made the pleasant land deso-
late."

Jerusalem, Holy City of the Future

8 Again the word of the LORD of hosts came,
saying,
2 "Thus says the LORD of hosts:

'I am zealous for Zion with great zeal;
With great fervor I am zealous for her.'

3 "Thus says the LORD:

'I will return to Zion,
And dwell in the midst of Jerusalem.
Jerusalem shall be called the City of
Truth,

5:11 [a]That is, Babylon **6:14** [a]Following Masoretic Text, Targum, and Vulgate; Syriac reads *for Heldai* (compare verse 10); Septuagint reads *for the patient ones.* **7:2** [a]Literally *they* (compare verse 5) [b]Or *Sar-Ezer* [c]Hebrew *Bethel*
7:7 [a]Hebrew *Negev*

The Mountain of the LORD of hosts,
The Holy Mountain.'

4 "Thus says the LORD of hosts:

'Old men and old women shall again sit
In the streets of Jerusalem,
Each one with his staff in his hand
Because of great age.
5 The streets of the city
Shall be full of boys and girls
Playing in its streets.'

6 "Thus says the LORD of hosts:

'If it is marvelous in the eyes of the
remnant of this people in these days,
Will it also be marvelous in My eyes?'
Says the LORD of hosts.

7 "Thus says the LORD of hosts:

'Behold, I will save My people from the
land of the east
And from the land of the west;
8 I will bring them *back*,
And they shall dwell in the midst of
Jerusalem.
They shall be My people
And I will be their God,
In truth and righteousness.'

9 "Thus says the LORD of hosts:

'Let your hands be strong,
You who have been hearing in these days
These words by the mouth of the
prophets,
Who *spoke* in the day the foundation was
laid
For the house of the LORD of hosts,
That the temple might be built.
10 For before these days
There were no wages for man nor any
hire for beast;
There was no peace from the enemy for
whoever went out or came in;
For I set all men, everyone, against his
neighbor.

11 'But now I *will* not *treat* the remnant of this
people as in the former days,' says the LORD
of hosts.

12 'For the seed *shall be* prosperous,
The vine shall give its fruit,
The ground shall give her increase,
And the heavens shall give their dew—
I will cause the remnant of this people
To possess all these.
13 And it shall come to pass
That just as you were a curse among the
nations,
O house of Judah and house of Israel,
So I will save you, and you shall be a
blessing.
Do not fear,
Let your hands be strong.'

14 "For thus says the LORD of hosts:

'Just as I determined to punish you
When your fathers provoked Me to
wrath,'
Says the LORD of hosts,
'And I would not relent,
15 So again in these days
I am determined to do good
To Jerusalem and to the house of Judah.
Do not fear.
16 These *are* the things you shall do:
Speak each man the truth to his
neighbor;
Give judgment in your gates for truth,
justice, and peace;
17 Let none of you think evil in your[a] heart
against your neighbor;
And do not love a false oath.
For all these *are things* that I hate,'
Says the LORD."

18 Then the word of the LORD of hosts came
to me, saying,
19 "Thus says the LORD of hosts:

'The fast of the fourth *month*,
The fast of the fifth,
The fast of the seventh,
And the fast of the tenth,
Shall be joy and gladness and cheerful
feasts
For the house of Judah.
Therefore love truth and peace.'

20 "Thus says the LORD of hosts:

'Peoples shall yet come,
Inhabitants of many cities;
21 The inhabitants of one *city* shall go to
another, saying,
"Let us continue to go and pray before the
LORD,
And seek the LORD of hosts.
I myself will go also."
22 Yes, many peoples and strong nations
Shall come to seek the LORD of hosts in
Jerusalem,
And to pray before the LORD.'

23 "Thus says the LORD of hosts: 'In those days
ten men from every language of the nations
shall grasp the sleeve of a Jewish man, saying,
"Let us go with you, for we have heard *that*
God *is* with you." '"

Israel Defended Against Enemies

9 The burden[a] of the word of the LORD
Against the land of Hadrach,
And Damascus its resting place
(For the eyes of men
And all the tribes of Israel
Are on the LORD);
2 Also *against* Hamath, *which* borders on
it,
And *against* Tyre and Sidon, though they
are very wise.

3 For Tyre built herself a tower,
Heaped up silver like the dust,
And gold like the mire of the streets.
4 Behold, the Lord will cast her out;
He will destroy her power in the sea,
And she will be devoured by fire.

5 Ashkelon shall see *it* and fear;
Gaza also shall be very sorrowful;
And Ekron, for He dried up her
expectation.
The king shall perish from Gaza,
And Ashkelon shall not be inhabited.

6 "A mixed race shall settle in Ashdod,
And I will cut off the pride of the
Philistines.
7 I will take away the blood from his
mouth,

8:17 [a]Literally *his* **9:1** [a]Or *oracle*

And the abominations from between his teeth.
But he who remains, even he *shall be* for our God,
And shall be like a leader in Judah,
And Ekron like a Jebusite.
8 I will camp around My house
Because of the army,
Because of him who passes by and him who returns.
No more shall an oppressor pass through them,
For now I have seen with My eyes.

The Coming King

9 "Rejoice greatly, O daughter of Zion!
Shout, O daughter of Jerusalem!
Behold, your King is coming to you;
He *is* just and having salvation,
Lowly and riding on a donkey,
A colt, the foal of a donkey.
10 I will cut off the chariot from Ephraim
And the horse from Jerusalem;
The battle bow shall be cut off.
He shall speak peace to the nations;
His dominion *shall be* 'from sea to sea,
And from the River to the ends of the earth.'[a]

God Will Save His People

11 "As for you also,
Because of the blood of your covenant,
I will set your prisoners free from the waterless pit.
12 Return to the stronghold,
You prisoners of hope.
Even today I declare
That I will restore double to you.
13 For I have bent Judah, My *bow*,
Fitted the bow with Ephraim,
And raised up your sons, O Zion,
Against your sons, O Greece,
And made you like the sword of a mighty man."

14 Then the LORD will be seen over them,
And His arrow will go forth like lightning.
The Lord GOD will blow the trumpet,
And go with whirlwinds from the south.
15 The LORD of hosts will defend them;
They shall devour and subdue with slingstones.
They shall drink *and* roar as if with wine;
They shall be filled *with blood* like basins,
Like the corners of the altar.
16 The LORD their God will save them in that day,
As the flock of His people.
For they *shall be like* the jewels of a crown,
Lifted like a banner over His land—
17 For how great is its[a] goodness
And how great its[b] beauty!
Grain shall make the young men thrive,
And new wine the young women.

Restoration of Judah and Israel

10 Ask the LORD for rain
In the time of the latter rain.[a]
The LORD will make flashing clouds;
He will give them showers of rain,
Grass in the field for everyone.
2 For the idols[a] speak delusion;
The diviners envision lies,
And tell false dreams;
They comfort in vain.
Therefore *the people* wend their way like sheep;
They are in trouble because *there is* no shepherd.

3 "My anger is kindled against the shepherds,
And I will punish the goatherds.
For the LORD of hosts will visit His flock,
The house of Judah,
And will make them as His royal horse in the battle.
4 From him comes the cornerstone,
From him the tent peg,
From him the battle bow,
From him every ruler[a] together.
5 They shall be like mighty men,
Who tread down *their enemies*
In the mire of the streets in the battle.
They shall fight because the LORD is with them,
And the riders on horses shall be put to shame.

6 "I will strengthen the house of Judah,
And I will save the house of Joseph.
I will bring them back,
Because I have mercy on them.
They shall be as though I had not cast them aside;
For I *am* the LORD their God,
And I will hear them.
7 *Those of* Ephraim shall be like a mighty man,
And their heart shall rejoice as if with wine.
Yes, their children shall see *it* and be glad;
Their heart shall rejoice in the LORD.
8 I will whistle for them and gather them,
For I will redeem them;
And they shall increase as they once increased.

9 "I will sow them among the peoples,
And they shall remember Me in far countries;
They shall live, together with their children,
And they shall return.
10 I will also bring them back from the land of Egypt,
And gather them from Assyria.
I will bring them into the land of Gilead and Lebanon,
Until no *more room* is found for them.
11 He shall pass through the sea with affliction,
And strike the waves of the sea:
All the depths of the River[a] shall dry up.
Then the pride of Assyria shall be brought down,
And the scepter of Egypt shall depart.

12 "So I will strengthen them in the LORD,
And they shall walk up and down in His name,"
Says the LORD.

9:10 [a]Psalm 72:8 **9:17** [a]Or *His* [b]Or *His* **10:1** [a]That is, spring rain **10:2** [a]Hebrew *teraphim* **10:4** [a]Or *despot*
10:11 [a]That is, the Nile

Desolation of Israel

11 Open your doors, O Lebanon,
That fire may devour your cedars.
2 Wail, O cypress, for the cedar has fallen,
Because the mighty *trees* are ruined.
Wail, O oaks of Bashan,
For the thick forest has come down.
3 *There is* the sound of wailing shepherds!
For their glory is in ruins.
There is the sound of roaring lions!
For the pride[a] of the Jordan is in ruins.

Prophecy of the Shepherds

4 Thus says the LORD my God, "Feed the flock
for slaughter,
5 "whose owners slaughter them and feel no
guilt; those who sell them say, 'Blessed be the
LORD, for I am rich'; and their shepherds do
not pity them.
6 "For I will no longer pity the inhabitants
of the land," says the LORD. "But indeed I will
give everyone into his neighbor's hand and
into the hand of his king. They shall attack the
land, and I will not deliver *them* from their
hand."
7 So I fed the flock for slaughter, in particu-
lar the poor of the flock.[a] I took for myself two
staffs: the one I called Beauty,[b] and the other I
called Bonds;[c] and I fed the flock.
8 I dismissed the three shepherds in one
month. My soul loathed them, and their soul
also abhorred me.
9 Then I said, "I will not feed you. Let what
is dying die, and what is perishing perish. Let
those that are left eat each other's flesh."
10 And I took my staff, Beauty, and cut it in
two, that I might break the covenant which I had
made with all the peoples.
11 So it was broken on that day. Thus the
poor[a] of the flock, who were watching me, knew
that it *was* the word of the LORD.
12 Then I said to them, "If it is agreeable to
you, give *me* my wages; and if not, refrain." So
they weighed out for my wages thirty *pieces* of
silver.
13 And the LORD said to me, "Throw it to the
potter"—that princely price they set on me. So
I took the thirty *pieces* of silver and threw them
into the house of the LORD for the potter.
14 Then I cut in two my other staff, Bonds,
that I might break the brotherhood between
Judah and Israel.
15 And the LORD said to me, "Next, take for
yourself the implements of a foolish shepherd.
16 "For indeed I will raise up a shepherd in
the land *who* will not care for those who are cut
off, nor seek the young, nor heal those that are
broken, nor feed those that still stand. But he
will eat the flesh of the fat and tear their hooves
in pieces.

17 "Woe to the worthless shepherd,
Who leaves the flock!
A sword *shall be* against his arm
And against his right eye;
His arm shall completely wither,
And his right eye shall be totally
blinded."

The Coming Deliverance of Judah

12 The burden[a] of the word of the LORD
against Israel. Thus says the LORD, who
stretches out the heavens, lays the foundation
of the earth, and forms the spirit of man within
him:
2 "Behold, I will make Jerusalem a cup of
drunkenness to all the surrounding peoples,
when they lay siege against Judah and Jeru-
salem.
3 "And it shall happen in that day that I will
make Jerusalem a very heavy stone for all peo-
ples; all who would heave it away will surely
be cut in pieces, though all nations of the earth
are gathered against it.
4 "In that day," says the LORD, "I will strike
every horse with confusion, and its rider with
madness; I will open My eyes on the house of
Judah, and will strike every horse of the peo-
ples with blindness.
5 "And the governors of Judah shall say in
their heart, 'The inhabitants of Jerusalem *are*
my strength in the LORD of hosts, their God.'
6 "In that day I will make the governors of
Judah like a firepan in the woodpile, and like
a fiery torch in the sheaves; they shall devour
all the surrounding peoples on the right hand
and on the left, but Jerusalem shall be inhab-
ited again in her own place—Jerusalem.
7 "The LORD will save the tents of Judah
first, so that the glory of the house of David
and the glory of the inhabitants of Jerusalem
shall not become greater than that of Judah.
8 "In that day the LORD will defend the
inhabitants of Jerusalem; the one who is feeble
among them in that day shall be like David,
and the house of David *shall be* like God, like
the Angel of the LORD before them.
9 "It shall be in that day *that* I will seek
to destroy all the nations that come against
Jerusalem.

Mourning for the Pierced One

10 "And I will pour on the house of David and
on the inhabitants of Jerusalem the Spirit of
grace and supplication; then they will look on
Me whom they pierced. Yes, they will mourn
for Him as one mourns for *his* only *son,* and
grieve for Him as one grieves for a firstborn.
11 "In that day there shall be a great mourn-
ing in Jerusalem, like the mourning at Hadad
Rimmon in the plain of Megiddo.[a]
12 "And the land shall mourn, every family
by itself: the family of the house of David by
itself, and their wives by themselves; the fam-
ily of the house of Nathan by itself, and their
wives by themselves;
13 "the family of the house of Levi by itself,
and their wives by themselves; the family of
Shimei by itself, and their wives by themselves;
14 "all the families that remain, every family
by itself, and their wives by themselves.

Idolatry Cut Off

13 "In that day a fountain shall be opened
for the house of David and for the inhab-
itants of Jerusalem, for sin and for uncleanness.
2 "It shall be in that day," says the LORD of
hosts, "*that* I will cut off the names of the idols
from the land, and they shall no longer be re-

11:3 [a]Or *floodplain, thicket* 11:7 [a]Following Masoretic Text, Targum, and Vulgate; Septuagint reads *for the Canaanites.* [b]Or *Grace,* and so in verse 10 [c]Or *Unity,* and so in verse 14 11:11 [a]Following Masoretic Text, Targum, and Vulgate; Septuagint reads *the Canaanites.* 12:1 [a]Or *oracle* 12:11 [a]Hebrew *Megiddon*

membered. I will also cause the prophets and
the unclean spirit to depart from the land.
3 "It shall come to pass *that* if anyone still
prophesies, then his father and mother who
begot him will say to him, 'You shall not live,
because you have spoken lies in the name of
the LORD.' And his father and mother who be-
got him shall thrust him through when he
prophesies.
4 "And it shall be in that day *that* every
prophet will be ashamed of his vision when he
prophesies; they will not wear a robe of coarse
hair to deceive.
5 "But he will say, 'I *am* no prophet, I *am* a
farmer; for a man taught me to keep cattle
from my youth.'
6 "And *one* will say to him, 'What are these
wounds between your arms?'[a] Then he will an-
swer, '*Those* with which I was wounded in the
house of my friends.'

The Shepherd Savior

7 "Awake, O sword, against My Shepherd,
Against the Man who is My Companion,"
Says the LORD of hosts.
"Strike the Shepherd,
And the sheep will be scattered;
Then I will turn My hand against the little
ones.
8 And it shall come to pass in all the land,"
Says the LORD,
"*That* two-thirds in it shall be cut off *and*
die,
But *one*-third shall be left in it:
9 I will bring the *one*-third through the fire,
Will refine them as silver is refined,
And test them as gold is tested.
They will call on My name,
And I will answer them.
I will say, 'This *is* My people';
And each one will say, 'The LORD *is* my
God.'"

The Day of the LORD

14 Behold, the day of the LORD is coming,
And your spoil will be divided in your
midst.
2 For I will gather all the nations to battle
against Jerusalem;
The city shall be taken,
The houses rifled,
And the women ravished.
Half of the city shall go into captivity,
But the remnant of the people shall not
be cut off from the city.

3 Then the LORD will go forth
And fight against those nations,
As He fights in the day of battle.
4 And in that day His feet will stand on the
Mount of Olives,
Which faces Jerusalem on the east.
And the Mount of Olives shall be split in two,
From east to west,
Making a very large valley;
Half of the mountain shall move toward
the north
And half of it toward the south.

5 Then you shall flee *through* My mountain
valley,
For the mountain valley shall reach to
Azal.
Yes, you shall flee
As you fled from the earthquake
In the days of Uzziah king of Judah.

Thus the LORD my God will come,
And all the saints with You.[a]

6 It shall come to pass in that day
That there will be no light;
The lights will diminish.
7 It shall be one day
Which is known to the LORD—
Neither day nor night.
But at evening time it shall happen
That it will be light.

8 And in that day it shall be
That living waters shall flow from
Jerusalem,
Half of them toward the eastern sea
And half of them toward the western sea;
In both summer and winter it shall occur.
9 And the LORD shall be King over all the
earth.
In that day it shall be—
"The LORD *is* one,"[a]
And His name one.

10 All the land shall be turned into a plain
from Geba to Rimmon south of Jerusalem. *Je-
rusalem*[a] shall be raised up and inhabited in
her place from Benjamin's Gate to the place of
the First Gate and the Corner Gate, and *from* the
Tower of Hananel to the king's winepresses.

11 *The people* shall dwell in it;
And no longer shall there be utter
destruction,
But Jerusalem shall be safely inhabited.

12 And this shall be the plague with which
the LORD will strike all the people who fought
against Jerusalem:

Their flesh shall dissolve while they stand
on their feet,
Their eyes shall dissolve in their sockets,
And their tongues shall dissolve in their
mouths.

13 It shall come to pass in that day
That a great panic from the LORD will be
among them.
Everyone will seize the hand of his
neighbor,
And raise his hand against his neighbor's
hand;
14 Judah also will fight at Jerusalem.
And the wealth of all the surrounding
nations
Shall be gathered together:
Gold, silver, and apparel in great
abundance.

15 Such also shall be the plague
On the horse *and* the mule,
On the camel and the donkey,
And on all the cattle that will be in those
camps.
So *shall* this plague *be*.

The Nations Worship the King

16 And it shall come to pass *that* everyone who
is left of all the nations which came against Jeru-
salem shall go up from year to year to worship

13:6 [a]Or *hands* 14:5 [a]Or *you;* Septuagint, Targum, and Vulgate read *Him.* 14:9 [a]Compare Deuteronomy 6:4
14:10 [a]Literally *She*

the King, the LORD of hosts, and to keep the
Feast of Tabernacles.
17 And it shall be *that* whichever of the families of the earth do not come up to Jerusalem
to worship the King, the LORD of hosts, on
them there will be no rain.
18 If the family of Egypt will not come up and
enter in, they *shall have* no *rain;* they shall
receive the plague with which the LORD strikes
the nations who do not come up to keep the
Feast of Tabernacles.
19 This shall be the punishment of Egypt and
the punishment of all the nations that do not
come up to keep the Feast of Tabernacles.
20 In that day "HOLINESS TO THE LORD"
shall be *engraved* on the bells of the horses.
The pots in the LORD's house shall be like the
bowls before the altar.
21 Yes, every pot in Jerusalem and Judah
shall be holiness to the LORD of hosts.[a] Everyone who sacrifices shall come and take them
and cook in them. In that day there shall no
longer be a Canaanite in the house of the LORD
of hosts.

The Book of MALACHI

1 The burden[a] of the word of the LORD to
Israel by Malachi.

Israel Beloved of God

2 "I have loved you," says the LORD.
"Yet you say, 'In what way have You loved us?'
Was not Esau Jacob's brother?"
Says the LORD.
"Yet Jacob I have loved;
3 But Esau I have hated,
And laid waste his mountains and his heritage
For the jackals of the wilderness."

4 Even though Edom has said,
"We have been impoverished,
But we will return and build the desolate places,"
Thus says the LORD of hosts:

"They may build, but I will throw down;
They shall be called the Territory of Wickedness,
And the people against whom the LORD will have indignation forever.
5 Your eyes shall see,
And you shall say,
'The LORD is magnified beyond the border of Israel.'

Polluted Offerings

6 "A son honors *his* father,
And a servant *his* master.
If then I am the Father,
Where *is* My honor?
And if I *am* a Master,
Where *is* My reverence?
Says the LORD of hosts
To you priests who despise My name.
Yet you say, 'In what way have we despised Your name?'

7 "You offer defiled food on My altar,
But say,
'In what way have we defiled You?'
By saying,
'The table of the LORD is contemptible.'
8 And when you offer the blind as a sacrifice,
Is it not evil?
And when you offer the lame and sick,
Is it not evil?
Offer it then to your governor!
Would he be pleased with you?
Would he accept you favorably?"
Says the LORD of hosts.

9 "But now entreat God's favor,
That He may be gracious to us.
While this is being *done* by your hands,
Will He accept you favorably?"
Says the LORD of hosts.
10 "Who *is there* even among you who would shut the doors,
So that you would not kindle fire *on* My altar in vain?
I have no pleasure in you,"
Says the LORD of hosts,
"Nor will I accept an offering from your hands.
11 For from the rising of the sun, even to its going down,
My name *shall be* great among the Gentiles;
In every place incense *shall be* offered to My name,
And a pure offering;
For My name shall be great among the nations,"
Says the LORD of hosts.

12 "But you profane it,
In that you say,
'The table of the LORD[a] is defiled;
And its fruit, its food, *is* contemptible.'
13 You also say,
'Oh, what a weariness!'
And you sneer at it,"
Says the LORD of hosts.
"And you bring the stolen, the lame, and the sick;
Thus you bring an offering!
Should I accept this from your hand?"
Says the LORD.
14 "But cursed *be* the deceiver
Who has in his flock a male,
And takes a vow,
But sacrifices to the Lord what is blemished—
For I *am* a great King,"
Says the LORD of hosts,
"And My name *is to be* feared among the nations.

14:21 [a]Or *on every pot . . . shall be (engraved) "HOLINESS TO THE LORD OF HOSTS"* **1:1** [a]Or *oracle*
1:12 [a]Following Bomberg; Masoretic Text reads *Lord*.

Corrupt Priests

2 "And now, O priests, this commandment
is for you.
2 If you will not hear,
And if you will not take *it* to heart,
To give glory to My name,"
Says the LORD of hosts,
"I will send a curse upon you,
And I will curse your blessings.
Yes, I have cursed them already,
Because you do not take *it* to heart.

3 "Behold, I will rebuke your descendants
And spread refuse on your faces,
The refuse of your solemn feasts;
And *one* will take you away with it.
4 Then you shall know that I have sent this
commandment to you,
That My covenant with Levi may
continue,"
Says the LORD of hosts.

5 "My covenant was with him, *one* of life
and peace,
And I gave them to him *that he might*
fear *Me;*
So he feared Me
And was reverent before My name.
6 The law of truth[a] was in his mouth,
And injustice was not found on his lips.
He walked with Me in peace and equity,
And turned many away from iniquity.

7 "For the lips of a priest should keep
knowledge,
And *people* should seek the law from his
mouth;
For he is the messenger of the LORD of
hosts.
8 But you have departed from the way;
You have caused many to stumble at the
law.
You have corrupted the covenant of
Levi,"
Says the LORD of hosts.
9 "Therefore I also have made you
contemptible and base
Before all the people,
Because you have not kept My ways
But have shown partiality in the law."

Treachery of Infidelity

10 Have we not all one Father?
Has not one God created us?
Why do we deal treacherously with one
another
By profaning the covenant of the fathers?
11 Judah has dealt treacherously,
And an abomination has been committed
in Israel and in Jerusalem,
For Judah has profaned
The LORD's holy *institution* which He
loves:
He has married the daughter of a foreign
god.
12 May the LORD cut off from the tents of
Jacob
The man who does this, being awake and
aware,[a]
Yet who brings an offering to the LORD of
hosts!

13 And this is the second thing you do:
You cover the altar of the LORD with
tears,
With weeping and crying;
So He does not regard the offering
anymore,
Nor receive *it* with goodwill from your
hands.
14 Yet you say, "For what reason?"
Because the LORD has been witness
Between you and the wife of your youth,
With whom you have dealt treacherously;
Yet she is your companion
And your wife by covenant.
15 But did He not make *them* one,
Having a remnant of the Spirit?
And why one?
He seeks godly offspring.
Therefore take heed to your spirit,
And let none deal treacherously with the
wife of his youth.

16 "For the LORD God of Israel says
That He hates divorce,
For it covers one's garment with
violence,"
Says the LORD of hosts.
"Therefore take heed to your spirit,
That you do not deal treacherously."

17 You have wearied the LORD with your
words;
Yet you say,
"In what way have we wearied *Him?*"
In that you say,
"Everyone who does evil
Is good in the sight of the LORD,
And He delights in them,"
Or, "Where *is* the God of justice?"

The Coming Messenger

3 "Behold, I send My messenger,
And he will prepare the way
before Me.
And the Lord, whom you seek,
Will suddenly come to His temple,
Even the Messenger of the covenant,
In whom you delight.
Behold, He is coming,"
Says the LORD of hosts.

2 "But who can endure the day of His
coming?
And who can stand when He appears?
For He *is* like a refiner's fire
And like launderers' soap.
3 He will sit as a refiner and a purifier of
silver;
He will purify the sons of Levi,
And purge them as gold and silver,
That they may offer to the LORD
An offering in righteousness.

4 "Then the offering of Judah and Jerusalem
Will be pleasant to the LORD,
As in the days of old,
As in former years.
5 And I will come near you for judgment;
I will be a swift witness
Against sorcerers,
Against adulterers,
Against perjurers,
Against those who exploit wage earners
and widows and orphans,

2:6 [a]Or *true instruction* **2:12** [a]Talmud and Vulgate read *teacher and student.*

And against those who turn away an alien—
Because they do not fear Me,"
Says the LORD of hosts.
6 "For I *am* the LORD, I do not change;
Therefore you are not consumed, O sons of Jacob.
7 Yet from the days of your fathers
You have gone away from My ordinances
And have not kept *them.*
Return to Me, and I will return to you,"
Says the LORD of hosts.
"But you said,
'In what way shall we return?'

Do Not Rob God

8 "Will a man rob God?
Yet you have robbed Me!
But you say,
'In what way have we robbed You?'
In tithes and offerings.
9 You are cursed with a curse,
For you have robbed Me,
Even this whole nation.
10 Bring all the tithes into the storehouse,
That there may be food in My house,
And try Me now in this,"
Says the LORD of hosts,
"If I will not open for you the windows of heaven
And pour out for you *such* blessing
That *there will* not *be room* enough *to receive it.*
11 "And I will rebuke the devourer for your sakes,
So that he will not destroy the fruit of your ground,
Nor shall the vine fail to bear fruit for you in the field,"
Says the LORD of hosts;
12 "And all nations will call you blessed,
For you will be a delightful land,"
Says the LORD of hosts.

The People Complain Harshly

13 "Your words have been harsh against Me,"
Says the LORD,
"Yet you say,
'What have we spoken against You?'
14 You have said,
'It is useless to serve God;
What profit *is it* that we have kept His ordinance,
And that we have walked as mourners
Before the LORD of hosts?
15 So now we call the proud blessed,
For those who do wickedness are raised up;
They even tempt God and go free.'"

A Book of Remembrance

16 Then those who feared the LORD spoke to one another,
And the LORD listened and heard *them;*
So a book of remembrance was written before Him
For those who fear the LORD
And who meditate on His name.
17 "They shall be Mine," says the LORD of hosts,
"On the day that I make them My jewels.[a]
And I will spare them
As a man spares his own son who serves him."
18 Then you shall again discern
Between the righteous and the wicked,
Between one who serves God
And one who does not serve Him.

The Great Day of God

4 "For behold, the day is coming,
Burning like an oven,
And all the proud, yes, all who do wickedly will be stubble.
And the day which is coming shall burn them up,"
Says the LORD of hosts,
"That will leave them neither root nor branch.
2 But to you who fear My name
The Sun of Righteousness shall arise
With healing in His wings;
And you shall go out
And grow fat like stall-fed calves.
3 You shall trample the wicked,
For they shall be ashes under the soles of your feet
On the day that I do *this,*"
Says the LORD of hosts.
4 "Remember the Law of Moses, My servant,
Which I commanded him in Horeb for all Israel,
With the statutes and judgments.
5 Behold, I will send you Elijah the prophet
Before the coming of the great and dreadful day of the LORD.
6 And he will turn
The hearts of the fathers to the children,
And the hearts of the children to their fathers,
Lest I come and strike the earth with a curse."

3:17 [a]Literally *special treasure*

The

NEW TESTAMENT

of

OUR LORD AND SAVIOR JESUS CHRIST

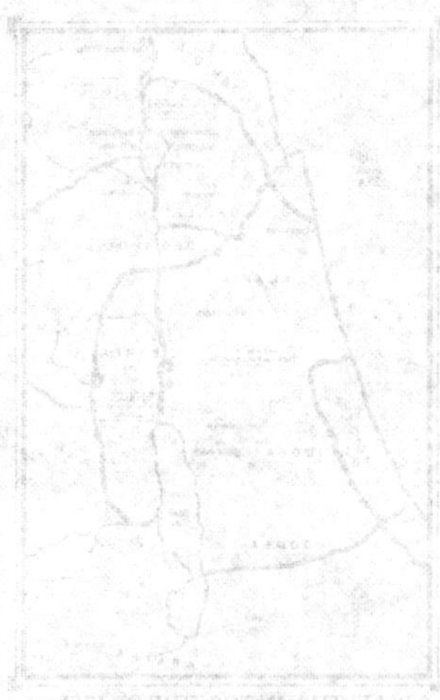

THE GOSPELS

Matthew • Mark • Luke • John

The word *Gospel* is from the Anglo-Saxon *godspell*, meaning "good news." Ultimately the word comes from the Greek *euangelion*, also meaning "good news." *Gospel* can mean the good news preached by Jesus, or the good news preached about Jesus. These two meanings are the ones found in the Bible. *Gospel* can also mean the books that contain the memories of Jesus, the Gospels we find in our New Testaments.

Gospels are not biographies. They are accounts of the life and teaching of Jesus, but they are also reflections on who Jesus is and what He means for the world. Each of the Gospel writers wanted to say something specific about the meaning of Jesus and each carefully selected materials and arranged them to carry his own particular emphasis. The Gospels contain a great deal of historical information, but that information is always used by the writers to show that Jesus is the Son of God and Savior of the world.

There are four Gospels. Matthew, Mark, and Luke are called *synoptic* Gospels because they follow a common synopsis, or outline. These three Gospels can be studied in parallel because they follow the same basic outline, use many of the same words, and the same order. Much of modern biblical study is based on the assumption that Matthew and Luke used Mark as a basic source and outline. The Gospel of John is entirely different from the other three. It does not follow the same outline, has a three-year ministry for Jesus instead of one year, and contains long reflections about the meaning of Jesus instead of short sayings and parables.

MARK is probably the oldest of the Gospels. Tradition says it was written in Rome by John Mark and contains the memories of Peter. The Crucifixion and Resurrection are the keys to understanding who Jesus is—nearly one-half of the Gospel deals with these events. Mark does not have any birth narratives but begins with the preaching of John the Baptist.

MATTHEW begins by placing Jesus within the whole story of salvation. Jesus is Son of Abraham and Son of David, the fulfillment of all the promises to God's people. The teaching material in Matthew is organized into five great sections, the best known of which is the Sermon on the Mount. Many have said Matthew saw Jesus as a second Moses, giving a new Torah to God's people.

LUKE's special interest is in the oppressed and outcasts of society, especially women and the poor. His Gospel begins with the births of John the Baptist and of Jesus. It has the only story of Jesus between His birth and ministry, the episode in the temple at the age of twelve. Some of the best-loved parables—the Good Samaritan, the Prodigal Son, the Rich Man and Lazarus—are found only in Luke's Gospel.

JOHN has less narrative and no parables, but a series of long reflections on Jesus as divine Son of God. The Gospel begins with a great hymn on the "Word" who was always God and became flesh for the salvation of the world. That word is Jesus. John also contains a series of miracles as signs pointing to Jesus, and the "I AM" sayings, which express what Jesus means in a series of striking metaphors. ■

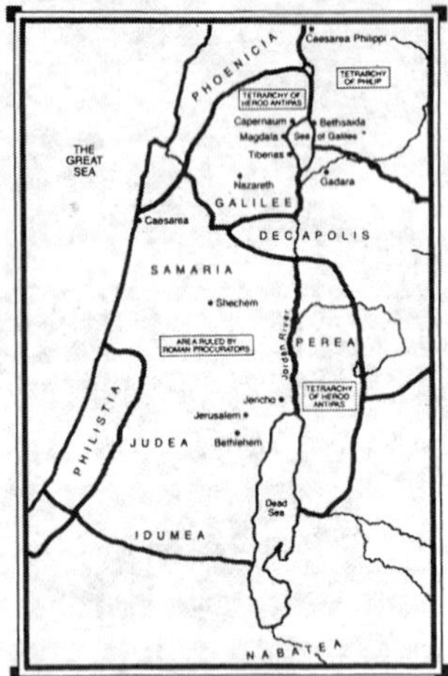

PALESTINE IN THE TIME OF JESUS

The Gospel According to
MATTHEW

The Genealogy of Jesus Christ

1 The book of the genealogy of Jesus Christ,
the Son of David, the Son of Abraham:
2 Abraham begot Isaac, Isaac begot Jacob,
and Jacob begot Judah and his brothers.
3 Judah begot Perez and Zerah by Tamar,
Perez begot Hezron, and Hezron begot Ram.
4 Ram begot Amminadab, Amminadab be-
got Nahshon, and Nahshon begot Salmon.
5 Salmon begot Boaz by Rahab, Boaz begot
Obed by Ruth, Obed begot Jesse,
6 and Jesse begot David the king.
David the king begot Solomon by her *who
had been the wife*[a] of Uriah.
7 Solomon begot Rehoboam, Rehoboam be-
got Abijah, and Abijah begot Asa.[a]
8 Asa begot Jehoshaphat, Jehoshaphat be-
got Joram, and Joram begot Uzziah.
9 Uzziah begot Jotham, Jotham begot Ahaz,
and Ahaz begot Hezekiah.
10 Hezekiah begot Manasseh, Manasseh be-
got Amon,[a] and Amon begot Josiah.
11 Josiah begot Jeconiah and his brothers
about the time they were carried away to Bab-
ylon.
12 And after they were brought to Babylon,
Jeconiah begot Shealtiel, and Shealtiel begot
Zerubbabel.
13 Zerubbabel begot Abiud, Abiud begot Eli-
akim, and Eliakim begot Azor.
14 Azor begot Zadok, Zadok begot Achim,
and Achim begot Eliud.
15 Eliud begot Eleazar, Eleazar begot Matthan,
and Matthan begot Jacob.
16 And Jacob begot Joseph the husband of
Mary, of whom was born Jesus who is called
Christ.
17 So all the generations from Abraham to
David *are* fourteen generations, from David
until the captivity in Babylon *are* fourteen gen-
erations, and from the captivity in Babylon un-
til the Christ *are* fourteen generations.

Christ Born of Mary

18 Now the birth of Jesus Christ was as fol-
lows: After His mother Mary was betrothed to
Joseph, before they came together, she was
found with child of the Holy Spirit.
19 Then Joseph her husband, being a just *man,*
and not wanting to make her a public example,
was minded to put her away secretly.
20 But while he thought about these things, be-
hold, an angel of the Lord appeared to him in
a dream, saying, "Joseph, son of David, do not
be afraid to take to you Mary your wife, for that
which is conceived in her is of the Holy Spirit.
21 "And she will bring forth a Son, and you
shall call His name JESUS, for He will save His
people from their sins."
22 So all this was done that it might be ful-
filled which was spoken by the Lord through the
prophet, saying:
23 *"Behold, the virgin shall be with child, and
bear a Son, and they shall call His name Im-
manuel,"*[a] which is translated, "God with us."
24 Then Joseph, being aroused from sleep, did
as the angel of the Lord commanded him and
took to him his wife,
25 and did not know her till she had brought
forth her firstborn Son.[a] And he called His name
JESUS.

Wise Men from the East

2 Now after Jesus was born in Bethlehem of
Judea in the days of Herod the king, behold,
wise men from the East came to Jerusalem,
2 saying, "Where is He who has been born
King of the Jews? For we have seen His star in
the East and have come to worship Him."
3 When Herod the king heard *this,* he was
troubled, and all Jerusalem with him.
4 And when he had gathered all the chief
priests and scribes of the people together, he
inquired of them where the Christ was to be
born.
5 So they said to him, "In Bethlehem of Ju-
dea, for thus it is written by the prophet:
6 *'But you, Bethlehem, in the land of Judah,*
Are not the least among the rulers of
Judah;
For out of you shall come a Ruler
Who will shepherd My people Israel.' "[a]
7 Then Herod, when he had secretly called
the wise men, determined from them what time
the star appeared.
8 And he sent them to Bethlehem and said,
"Go and search carefully for the young Child,
and when you have found *Him,* bring back
word to me, that I may come and worship Him
also."
9 When they heard the king, they departed;
and behold, the star which they had seen in the
East went before them, till it came and stood
over where the young Child was.
10 When they saw the star, they rejoiced with
exceedingly great joy.
11 And when they had come into the house,
they saw the young Child with Mary His mother,
and fell down and worshiped Him. And when
they had opened their treasures, they presented
gifts to Him: gold, frankincense, and myrrh.
12 Then, being divinely warned in a dream
that they should not return to Herod, they de-
parted for their own country another way.

The Flight into Egypt

13 Now when they had departed, behold, an
angel of the Lord appeared to Joseph in a dream,
saying, "Arise, take the young Child and His
mother, flee to Egypt, and stay there until I bring
you word; for Herod will seek the young Child
to destroy Him."
14 When he arose, he took the young Child and
His mother by night and departed for Egypt,
15 and was there until the death of Herod,
that it might be fulfilled which was spoken by
the Lord through the prophet, saying, *"Out of
Egypt I called My Son."*[a]

Massacre of the Innocents

16 Then Herod, when he saw that he was de-
ceived by the wise men, was exceedingly angry;

1:6 [a]Words in italic type have been added for clarity. They are not found in the original Greek. **1:7** [a]NU-Text reads *Asaph.* **1:10** [a]NU-Text reads *Amos.* **1:23** [a]Isaiah 7:14. Words in oblique type in the New Testament are quoted from the Old Testament. **1:25** [a]NU-Text reads *a Son.* **2:6** [a]Micah 5:2 **2:15** [a]Hosea 11:1

and he sent forth and put to death all the male children who were in Bethlehem and in all its districts, from two years old and under, according to the time which he had determined from the wise men.
17 Then was fulfilled what was spoken by Jeremiah the prophet, saying:

18 *"A voice was heard in Ramah,*
Lamentation, weeping, and great
mourning,
Rachel weeping for her children,
Refusing to be comforted,
Because they are no more."[a]

The Home in Nazareth

19 Now when Herod was dead, behold, an angel of the Lord appeared in a dream to Joseph in Egypt,
20 saying, "Arise, take the young Child and His mother, and go to the land of Israel, for those who sought the young Child's life are dead."
21 Then he arose, took the young Child and His mother, and came into the land of Israel.
22 But when he heard that Archelaus was reigning over Judea instead of his father Herod, he was afraid to go there. And being warned by God in a dream, he turned aside into the region of Galilee.
23 And he came and dwelt in a city called Nazareth, that it might be fulfilled which was spoken by the prophets, "He shall be called a Nazarene."

John the Baptist Prepares the Way

3 In those days John the Baptist came preaching in the wilderness of Judea,
2 and saying, "Repent, for the kingdom of heaven is at hand!"
3 For this is he who was spoken of by the prophet Isaiah, saying:

"The voice of one crying in the wilderness:
'Prepare the way of the LORD;
Make His paths straight.'"[a]

4 Now John himself was clothed in camel's hair, with a leather belt around his waist; and his food was locusts and wild honey.
5 Then Jerusalem, all Judea, and all the region around the Jordan went out to him
6 and were baptized by him in the Jordan, confessing their sins.
7 But when he saw many of the Pharisees and Sadducees coming to his baptism, he said to them, "Brood of vipers! Who warned you to flee from the wrath to come?
8 "Therefore bear fruits worthy of repentance,
9 "and do not think to say to yourselves, 'We have Abraham as *our* father.' For I say to you that God is able to raise up children to Abraham from these stones.
10 "And even now the ax is laid to the root of the trees. Therefore every tree which does not bear good fruit is cut down and thrown into the fire.
11 "I indeed baptize you with water unto repentance, but He who is coming after me is mightier than I, whose sandals I am not worthy to carry. He will baptize you with the Holy Spirit and fire.[a]
12 "His winnowing fan *is* in His hand, and He will thoroughly clean out His threshing floor, and gather His wheat into the barn; but He will burn up the chaff with unquenchable fire."

John Baptizes Jesus

13 Then Jesus came from Galilee to John at the Jordan to be baptized by him.
14 And John *tried to* prevent Him, saying, "I need to be baptized by You, and are You coming to me?"
15 But Jesus answered and said to him, "Permit *it to be so* now, for thus it is fitting for us to fulfill all righteousness." Then he allowed Him.
16 When He had been baptized, Jesus came up immediately from the water; and behold, the heavens were opened to Him, and He[a] saw the Spirit of God descending like a dove and alighting upon Him.
17 And suddenly a voice *came* from heaven, saying, "This is My beloved Son, in whom I am well pleased."

Satan Tempts Jesus

4 Then Jesus was led up by the Spirit into the wilderness to be tempted by the devil.
2 And when He had fasted forty days and forty nights, afterward He was hungry.
3 Now when the tempter came to Him, he said, "If You are the Son of God, command that these stones become bread."
4 But He answered and said, "It is written, *'Man shall not live by bread alone, but by every word that proceeds from the mouth of God.'*"[a]
5 Then the devil took Him up into the holy city, set Him on the pinnacle of the temple,
6 and said to Him, "If You are the Son of God, throw Yourself down. For it is written:

'He shall give His angels charge over you,'

and,

'In their hands they shall bear you up,
Lest you dash your foot against a
stone.'"[a]

7 Jesus said to him, "It is written again, *'You shall not tempt the LORD your God.'*"[a]
8 Again, the devil took Him up on an exceedingly high mountain, and showed Him all the kingdoms of the world and their glory.
9 And he said to Him, "All these things I will give You if You will fall down and worship me."
10 Then Jesus said to him, "Away with you,[a] Satan! For it is written, *'You shall worship the LORD your God, and Him only you shall serve.'*"[b]
11 Then the devil left Him, and behold, angels came and ministered to Him.

Jesus Begins His Galilean Ministry

12 Now when Jesus heard that John had been put in prison, He departed to Galilee.
13 And leaving Nazareth, He came and dwelt in Capernaum, which is by the sea, in the regions of Zebulun and Naphtali,
14 that it might be fulfilled which was spoken by Isaiah the prophet, saying:

15 *"The land of Zebulun and the land of*
Naphtali,
By the way of the sea, beyond the Jordan,
Galilee of the Gentiles:

2:18 [a]Jeremiah 31:15 **3:3** [a]Isaiah 40:3 **3:11** [a]M-Text omits *and fire.* **3:16** [a]Or *he* **4:4** [a]Deuteronomy 8:3
4:6 [a]Psalm 91:11, 12 **4:7** [a]Deuteronomy 6:16 **4:10** [a]M-Text reads *Get behind Me.* [b]Deuteronomy 6:13

16 *The people who sat in darkness have*
seen a great light,
And upon those who sat in the region and
shadow of death
Light has dawned."[a]

17 From that time Jesus began to preach and
to say, "Repent, for the kingdom of heaven is
at hand."

Four Fishermen Called as Disciples

18 And Jesus, walking by the Sea of Galilee,
saw two brothers, Simon called Peter, and An-
drew his brother, casting a net into the sea; for
they were fishermen.
19 Then He said to them, "Follow Me, and I
will make you fishers of men."
20 They immediately left *their* nets and fol-
lowed Him.
21 Going on from there, He saw two other
brothers, James *the son* of Zebedee, and John
his brother, in the boat with Zebedee their fa-
ther, mending their nets. He called them,
22 and immediately they left the boat and their
father, and followed Him.

Jesus Heals a Great Multitude

23 And Jesus went about all Galilee, teaching
in their synagogues, preaching the gospel of
the kingdom, and healing all kinds of sickness
and all kinds of disease among the people.
24 Then His fame went throughout all Syria;
and they brought to Him all sick people who
were afflicted with various diseases and tor-
ments, and those who were demon-possessed,
epileptics, and paralytics; and He healed them.
25 Great multitudes followed Him—from Gal-
ilee, and *from* Decapolis, Jerusalem, Judea,
and beyond the Jordan.

The Beatitudes

5 And seeing the multitudes, He went up on
a mountain, and when He was seated His
disciples came to Him.
2 Then He opened His mouth and taught
them, saying:
3 "Blessed *are* the poor in spirit,
For theirs is the kingdom of heaven.
4 Blessed *are* those who mourn,
For they shall be comforted.
5 Blessed *are* the meek,
For they shall inherit the earth.
6 Blessed *are* those who hunger and thirst
for righteousness,
For they shall be filled.
7 Blessed *are* the merciful,
For they shall obtain mercy.
8 Blessed *are* the pure in heart,
For they shall see God.
9 Blessed *are* the peacemakers,
For they shall be called sons of God.
10 Blessed are those who are persecuted for
righteousness' sake,
For theirs is the kingdom of heaven.

11 "Blessed are you when they revile and per-
secute you, and say all kinds of evil against
you falsely for My sake.
12 "Rejoice and be exceedingly glad, for
great *is* your reward in heaven, for so they
persecuted the prophets who were before you.

Believers Are Salt and Light

13 "You are the salt of the earth; but if the salt
loses its flavor, how shall it be seasoned? It is
then good for nothing but to be thrown out and
trampled underfoot by men.
14 "You are the light of the world. A city that
is set on a hill cannot be hidden.
15 "Nor do they light a lamp and put it under
a basket, but on a lampstand, and it gives light
to all *who are* in the house.
16 "Let your light so shine before men, that
they may see your good works and glorify your
Father in heaven.

Christ Fulfills the Law

17 "Do not think that I came to destroy the
Law or the Prophets. I did not come to destroy
but to fulfill.
18 "For assuredly, I say to you, till heaven and
earth pass away, one jot or one tittle will by no
means pass from the law till all is fulfilled.
19 "Whoever therefore breaks one of the
least of these commandments, and teaches
men so, shall be called least in the kingdom of
heaven; but whoever does and teaches *them*,
he shall be called great in the kingdom of
heaven.
20 "For I say to you, that unless your righ-
teousness exceeds *the righteousness* of the
scribes and Pharisees, you will by no means
enter the kingdom of heaven.

Murder Begins in the Heart

21 "You have heard that it was said to those
of old, *'You shall not murder,'*[a] and whoever
murders will be in danger of the judgment.'
22 "But I say to you that whoever is angry
with his brother without a cause[a] shall be in
danger of the judgment. And whoever says to
his brother, 'Raca!' shall be in danger of the
council. But whoever says, 'You fool!' shall be
in danger of hell fire.
23 "Therefore if you bring your gift to the
altar, and there remember that your brother
has something against you,
24 "leave your gift there before the altar, and
go your way. First be reconciled to your
brother, and then come and offer your gift.
25 "Agree with your adversary quickly, while
you are on the way with him, lest your adver-
sary deliver you to the judge, the judge hand
you over to the officer, and you be thrown into
prison.
26 "Assuredly, I say to you, you will by no
means get out of there till you have paid the
last penny.

Adultery in the Heart

27 "You have heard that it was said to those
of old,[a] *'You shall not commit adultery.'*[b]
28 "But I say to you that whoever looks at a
woman to lust for her has already committed
adultery with her in his heart.
29 "If your right eye causes you to sin, pluck
it out and cast *it* from you; for it is more profit-
able for you that one of your members perish,
than for your whole body to be cast into hell.
30 "And if your right hand causes you to sin,

4:16 [a]Isaiah 9:1, 2 **5:21** [a]Exodus 20:13; Deuteronomy 5:17 **5:22** [a]NU-Text omits *without a cause.* **5:27** [a]NU-Text and M-Text omit *to those of old.* [b]Exodus 20:14; Deuteronomy 5:18

cut it off and cast *it* from you; for it is more profitable for you that one of your members perish, than for your whole body to be cast into hell.

Marriage Is Sacred and Binding

31 "Furthermore it has been said, 'Whoever divorces his wife, let him give her a certificate of divorce.'
32 "But I say to you that whoever divorces his wife for any reason except sexual immorality[a] causes her to commit adultery; and whoever marries a woman who is divorced commits adultery.

Jesus Forbids Oaths

33 "Again you have heard that it was said to those of old, 'You shall not swear falsely, but shall perform your oaths to the Lord.'
34 "But I say to you, do not swear at all: neither by heaven, for it is God's throne;
35 "nor by the earth, for it is His footstool; nor by Jerusalem, for it is the city of the great King.
36 "Nor shall you swear by your head, because you cannot make one hair white or black.
37 "But let your 'Yes' be 'Yes,' and your 'No,' 'No.' For whatever is more than these is from the evil one.

Go the Second Mile

38 "You have heard that it was said, *'An eye for an eye and a tooth for a tooth.'*[a]
39 "But I tell you not to resist an evil person. But whoever slaps you on your right cheek, turn the other to him also.
40 "If anyone wants to sue you and take away your tunic, let him have *your* cloak also.
41 "And whoever compels you to go one mile, go with him two.
42 "Give to him who asks you, and from him who wants to borrow from you do not turn away.

Love Your Enemies

43 "You have heard that it was said, *'You shall love your neighbor*[a] and hate your enemy.'
44 "But I say to you, love your enemies, bless those who curse you, do good to those who hate you, and pray for those who spitefully use you and persecute you,[a]
45 "that you may be sons of your Father in heaven; for He makes His sun rise on the evil and on the good, and sends rain on the just and on the unjust.
46 "For if you love those who love you, what reward have you? Do not even the tax collectors do the same?
47 "And if you greet your brethren[a] only, what do you do more *than others?* Do not even the tax collectors[b] do so?
48 "Therefore you shall be perfect, just as your Father in heaven is perfect.

Do Good to Please God

6 "Take heed that you do not do your charitable deeds before men, to be seen by them. Otherwise you have no reward from your Father in heaven.
2 "Therefore, when you do a charitable deed, do not sound a trumpet before you as the hypocrites do in the synagogues and in the streets, that they may have glory from men. Assuredly, I say to you, they have their reward.
3 "But when you do a charitable deed, do not let your left hand know what your right hand is doing,
4 "that your charitable deed may be in secret; and your Father who sees in secret will Himself reward you openly.[a]

The Model Prayer

5 "And when you pray, you shall not be like the hypocrites. For they love to pray standing in the synagogues and on the corners of the streets, that they may be seen by men. Assuredly, I say to you, they have their reward.
6 "But you, when you pray, go into your room, and when you have shut your door, pray to your Father who *is* in the secret *place;* and your Father who sees in secret will reward you openly.[a]
7 "And when you pray, do not use vain repetitions as the heathen *do.* For they think that they will be heard for their many words.
8 "Therefore do not be like them. For your Father knows the things you have need of before you ask Him.
9 "In this manner, therefore, pray:

Our Father in heaven,
Hallowed be Your name.
10 Your kingdom come.
Your will be done
On earth as *it is* in heaven.
11 Give us this day our daily bread.
12 And forgive us our debts,
As we forgive our debtors.
13 And do not lead us into temptation,
But deliver us from the evil one.
For Yours is the kingdom and the power
and the glory forever. Amen.[a]

14 "For if you forgive men their trespasses, your heavenly Father will also forgive you.
15 "But if you do not forgive men their trespasses, neither will your Father forgive your trespasses.

Fasting to Be Seen Only by God

16 "Moreover, when you fast, do not be like the hypocrites, with a sad countenance. For they disfigure their faces that they may appear to men to be fasting. Assuredly, I say to you, they have their reward.
17 "But you, when you fast, anoint your head and wash your face,
18 "so that you do not appear to men to be fasting, but to your Father who *is* in the secret *place;* and your Father who sees in secret will reward you openly.[a]

Lay Up Treasures in Heaven

19 "Do not lay up for yourselves treasures on earth, where moth and rust destroy and where thieves break in and steal;
20 "but lay up for yourselves treasures in

5:32 [a]Or *fornication* **5:38** [a]Exodus 21:24; Leviticus 24:20; Deuteronomy 19:21 **5:43** [a]Compare Leviticus 19:18
5:44 [a]NU-Text omits three clauses from this verse, leaving, "*But I say to you, love your enemies and pray for those who persecute you.*" **5:47** [a]M-Text reads *friends.* [b]NU-Text reads *Gentiles.* **6:4** [a]NU-Text omits *openly.*
6:6 [a]NU-Text omits *openly.* **6:13** [a]NU-Text omits *For Yours* through *Amen.* **6:18** [a]NU-Text and M-Text omit *openly.*

heaven, where neither moth nor rust destroys and where thieves do not break in and steal.
21 “For where your treasure is, there your heart will be also.

The Lamp of the Body

22 “The lamp of the body is the eye. If therefore your eye is good, your whole body will be full of light.
23 “But if your eye is bad, your whole body will be full of darkness. If therefore the light that is in you is darkness, how great *is* that darkness!

You Cannot Serve God and Riches

24 “No one can serve two masters; for either he will hate the one and love the other, or else he will be loyal to the one and despise the other. You cannot serve God and mammon.

Do Not Worry

25 “Therefore I say to you, do not worry about your life, what you will eat or what you will drink; nor about your body, what you will put on. Is not life more than food and the body more than clothing?
26 “Look at the birds of the air, for they neither sow nor reap nor gather into barns; yet your heavenly Father feeds them. Are you not of more value than they?
27 “Which of you by worrying can add one cubit to his stature?
28 “So why do you worry about clothing? Consider the lilies of the field, how they grow: they neither toil nor spin;
29 “and yet I say to you that even Solomon in all his glory was not arrayed like one of these.
30 “Now if God so clothes the grass of the field, which today is, and tomorrow is thrown into the oven, *will He* not much more *clothe* you, O you of little faith?
31 “Therefore do not worry, saying, ‘What shall we eat?’ or ‘What shall we drink?’ or ‘What shall we wear?’
32 “For after all these things the Gentiles seek. For your heavenly Father knows that you need all these things.
33 “But seek first the kingdom of God and His righteousness, and all these things shall be added to you.
34 “Therefore do not worry about tomorrow, for tomorrow will worry about its own things. Sufficient for the day *is* its own trouble.

Do Not Judge

7 “Judge not, that you be not judged.
2 “For with what judgment you judge, you will be judged; and with the measure you use, it will be measured back to you.
3 “And why do you look at the speck in your brother’s eye, but do not consider the plank in your own eye?
4 “Or how can you say to your brother, ‘Let me remove the speck from your eye’; and look, a plank *is* in your own eye?
5 “Hypocrite! First remove the plank from your own eye, and then you will see clearly to remove the speck from your brother’s eye.
6 “Do not give what is holy to the dogs; nor cast your pearls before swine, lest they trample them under their feet, and turn and tear you in pieces.

Keep Asking, Seeking, Knocking

7 “Ask, and it will be given to you; seek, and you will find; knock, and it will be opened to you.
8 “For everyone who asks receives, and he who seeks finds, and to him who knocks it will be opened.
9 “Or what man is there among you who, if his son asks for bread, will give him a stone?
10 “Or if he asks for a fish, will he give him a serpent?
11 “If you then, being evil, know how to give good gifts to your children, how much more will your Father who is in heaven give good things to those who ask Him!
12 “Therefore, whatever you want men to do to you, do also to them, for this is the Law and the Prophets.

The Narrow Way

13 “Enter by the narrow gate; for wide *is* the gate and broad *is* the way that leads to destruction, and there are many who go in by it.
14 “Because[a] narrow *is* the gate and difficult *is* the way which leads to life, and there are few who find it.

You Will Know Them by Their Fruits

15 “Beware of false prophets, who come to you in sheep’s clothing, but inwardly they are ravenous wolves.
16 “You will know them by their fruits. Do men gather grapes from thornbushes or figs from thistles?
17 “Even so, every good tree bears good fruit, but a bad tree bears bad fruit.
18 “A good tree cannot bear bad fruit, nor *can* a bad tree bear good fruit.
19 “Every tree that does not bear good fruit is cut down and thrown into the fire.
20 “Therefore by their fruits you will know them.

I Never Knew You

21 “Not everyone who says to Me, ‘Lord, Lord,’ shall enter the kingdom of heaven, but he who does the will of My Father in heaven.
22 “Many will say to Me in that day, ‘Lord, Lord, have we not prophesied in Your name, cast out demons in Your name, and done many wonders in Your name?’
23 “And then I will declare to them, ‘I never knew you; depart from Me, you who practice lawlessness!’

Build on the Rock

24 “Therefore whoever hears these sayings of Mine, and does them, I will liken him to a wise man who built his house on the rock:
25 “and the rain descended, the floods came, and the winds blew and beat on that house; and it did not fall, for it was founded on the rock.
26 “But everyone who hears these sayings of Mine, and does not do them, will be like a foolish man who built his house on the sand:
27 “and the rain descended, the floods came, and the winds blew and beat on that house; and it fell. And great was its fall.”
28 And so it was, when Jesus had ended these

7:14 [a]NU-Text and M-Text read *How . . . !*

sayings, that the people were astonished at His teaching,
29 for He taught them as one having authority, and not as the scribes.

Jesus Cleanses a Leper

8 When He had come down from the mountain, great multitudes followed Him.
2 And behold, a leper came and worshiped Him, saying, "Lord, if You are willing, You can make me clean."
3 Then Jesus put out *His* hand and touched him, saying, "I am willing; be cleansed." Immediately his leprosy was cleansed.
4 And Jesus said to him, "See that you tell no one; but go your way, show yourself to the priest, and offer the gift that Moses commanded, as a testimony to them."

Jesus Heals a Centurion's Servant

5 Now when Jesus had entered Capernaum, a centurion came to Him, pleading with Him,
6 saying, "Lord, my servant is lying at home paralyzed, dreadfully tormented."
7 And Jesus said to him, "I will come and heal him."
8 The centurion answered and said, "Lord, I am not worthy that You should come under my roof. But only speak a word, and my servant will be healed.
9 "For I also am a man under authority, having soldiers under me. And I say to this *one*, 'Go,' and he goes; and to another, 'Come,' and he comes; and to my servant, 'Do this,' and he does *it*."
10 When Jesus heard *it*, He marveled, and said to those who followed, "Assuredly, I say to you, I have not found such great faith, not even in Israel!
11 "And I say to you that many will come from east and west, and sit down with Abraham, Isaac, and Jacob in the kingdom of heaven.
12 "But the sons of the kingdom will be cast out into outer darkness. There will be weeping and gnashing of teeth."
13 Then Jesus said to the centurion, "Go your way; and as you have believed, *so* let it be done for you." And his servant was healed that same hour.

Peter's Mother-in-Law Healed

14 Now when Jesus had come into Peter's house, He saw his wife's mother lying sick with a fever.
15 So He touched her hand, and the fever left her. And she arose and served them.[a]

Many Healed in the Evening

16 When evening had come, they brought to Him many who were demon-possessed. And He cast out the spirits with a word, and healed all who were sick,
17 that it might be fulfilled which was spoken by Isaiah the prophet, saying:

"He Himself took our infirmities
And bore our sicknesses."[a]

The Cost of Discipleship

18 And when Jesus saw great multitudes about Him, He gave a command to depart to the other side.
19 Then a certain scribe came and said to Him, "Teacher, I will follow You wherever You go."
20 And Jesus said to him, "Foxes have holes and birds of the air *have* nests, but the Son of Man has nowhere to lay *His* head."
21 Then another of His disciples said to Him, "Lord, let me first go and bury my father."
22 But Jesus said to him, "Follow Me, and let the dead bury their own dead."

Wind and Wave Obey Jesus

23 Now when He got into a boat, His disciples followed Him.
24 And suddenly a great tempest arose on the sea, so that the boat was covered with the waves. But He was asleep.
25 Then His disciples came to *Him* and awoke Him, saying, "Lord, save us! We are perishing!"
26 But He said to them, "Why are you fearful, O you of little faith?" Then He arose and rebuked the winds and the sea, and there was a great calm.
27 So the men marveled, saying, "Who can this be, that even the winds and the sea obey Him?"

Two Demon-Possessed Men Healed

28 When He had come to the other side, to the country of the Gergesenes,[a] there met Him two demon-possessed *men*, coming out of the tombs, exceedingly fierce, so that no one could pass that way.
29 And suddenly they cried out, saying, "What have we to do with You, Jesus, You Son of God? Have You come here to torment us before the time?"
30 Now a good way off from them there was a herd of many swine feeding.
31 So the demons begged Him, saying, "If You cast us out, permit us to go away[a] into the herd of swine."
32 And He said to them, "Go." So when they had come out, they went into the herd of swine. And suddenly the whole herd of swine ran violently down the steep place into the sea, and perished in the water.
33 Then those who kept *them* fled; and they went away into the city and told everything, including what *had happened* to the demon-possessed *men*.
34 And behold, the whole city came out to meet Jesus. And when they saw Him, they begged *Him* to depart from their region.

Jesus Forgives and Heals a Paralytic

9 So He got into a boat, crossed over, and came to His own city.
2 Then behold, they brought to Him a paralytic lying on a bed. When Jesus saw their faith, He said to the paralytic, "Son, be of good cheer; your sins are forgiven you."
3 And at once some of the scribes said within themselves, "This Man blasphemes!"
4 But Jesus, knowing their thoughts, said, "Why do you think evil in your hearts?
5 "For which is easier, to say, '*Your* sins are forgiven you,' or to say, 'Arise and walk'?
6 "But that you may know that the Son of Man has power on earth to forgive sins"—then He said to the paralytic, "Arise, take up your bed, and go to your house."
7 And he arose and departed to his house.

8:15 [a]NU-Text and M-Text read *Him*. **8:17** [a]Isaiah 53:4 **8:28** [a]NU-Text reads *Gadarenes*. **8:31** [a]NU-Text reads *send us*.

8 Now when the multitudes saw *it*, they mar-
veled[a] and glorified God, who had given such
power to men.

Matthew the Tax Collector

9 As Jesus passed on from there, He saw a
man named Matthew sitting at the tax office.
And He said to him, "Follow Me." So he arose
and followed Him.
10 Now it happened, as Jesus sat at the table
in the house, *that* behold, many tax collectors
and sinners came and sat down with Him and
His disciples.
11 And when the Pharisees saw *it*, they said
to His disciples, "Why does your Teacher eat
with tax collectors and sinners?"
12 When Jesus heard *that*, He said to them,
"Those who are well have no need of a physi-
cian, but those who are sick.
13 "But go and learn what *this* means: *'I de-
sire mercy and not sacrifice.'*[a] For I did not
come to call the righteous, but sinners, to re-
pentance."[b]

Jesus Is Questioned About Fasting

14 Then the disciples of John came to Him,
saying, "Why do we and the Pharisees fast
often,[a] but Your disciples do not fast?"
15 And Jesus said to them, "Can the friends
of the bridegroom mourn as long as the bride-
groom is with them? But the days will come
when the bridegroom will be taken away from
them, and then they will fast.
16 "No one puts a piece of unshrunk cloth on
an old garment; for the patch pulls away from
the garment, and the tear is made worse.
17 "Nor do they put new wine into old wine-
skins, or else the wineskins break, the wine is
spilled, and the wineskins are ruined. But they
put new wine into new wineskins, and both
are preserved."

A Girl Restored to Life and a Woman Healed

18 While He spoke these things to them, be-
hold, a ruler came and worshiped Him, saying,
"My daughter has just died, but come and lay
Your hand on her and she will live."
19 So Jesus arose and followed him, and so
did His disciples.
20 And suddenly, a woman who had a flow of
blood for twelve years came from behind and
touched the hem of His garment.
21 For she said to herself, "If only I may touch
His garment, I shall be made well."
22 But Jesus turned around, and when He
saw her He said, "Be of good cheer, daughter;
your faith has made you well." And the woman
was made well from that hour.
23 When Jesus came into the ruler's house,
and saw the flute players and the noisy crowd
wailing,
24 He said to them, "Make room, for the girl
is not dead, but sleeping." And they ridiculed
Him.
25 But when the crowd was put outside, He
went in and took her by the hand, and the girl
arose.
26 And the report of this went out into all that
land.

Two Blind Men Healed

27 When Jesus departed from there, two blind
men followed Him, crying out and saying, "Son
of David, have mercy on us!"
28 And when He had come into the house, the
blind men came to Him. And Jesus said to them,
"Do you believe that I am able to do this?"
They said to Him, "Yes, Lord."
29 Then He touched their eyes, saying, "Ac-
cording to your faith let it be to you."
30 And their eyes were opened. And Jesus
sternly warned them, saying, "See *that* no one
knows *it*."
31 But when they had departed, they spread
the news about Him in all that country.

A Mute Man Speaks

32 As they went out, behold, they brought to
Him a man, mute and demon-possessed.
33 And when the demon was cast out, the mute
spoke. And the multitudes marveled, saying,
"It was never seen like this in Israel!"
34 But the Pharisees said, "He casts out de-
mons by the ruler of the demons."

The Compassion of Jesus

35 Then Jesus went about all the cities and vil-
lages, teaching in their synagogues, preaching
the gospel of the kingdom, and healing every
sickness and every disease among the people.[a]
36 But when He saw the multitudes, He was
moved with compassion for them, because they
were weary[a] and scattered, like sheep having
no shepherd.
37 Then He said to His disciples, "The harvest
truly *is* plentiful, but the laborers *are* few.
38 "Therefore pray the Lord of the harvest to
send out laborers into His harvest."

The Twelve Apostles

10 And when He had called His twelve dis-
ciples to *Him*, He gave them power *over*
unclean spirits, to cast them out, and to heal
all kinds of sickness and all kinds of disease.
2 Now the names of the twelve apostles are
these: first, Simon, who is called Peter, and An-
drew his brother; James the *son* of Zebedee, and
John his brother;
3 Philip and Bartholomew; Thomas and Mat-
thew the tax collector; James the *son* of Al-
phaeus, and Lebbaeus, whose surname was[a]
Thaddaeus;
4 Simon the Cananite,[a] and Judas Iscariot,
who also betrayed Him.

Sending Out the Twelve

5 These twelve Jesus sent out and com-
manded them, saying: "Do not go into the way
of the Gentiles, and do not enter a city of the
Samaritans.
6 "But go rather to the lost sheep of the
house of Israel.
7 "And as you go, preach, saying, 'The king-
dom of heaven is at hand.'
8 "Heal the sick, cleanse the lepers, raise the
dead,[a] cast out demons. Freely you have re-
ceived, freely give.
9 "Provide neither gold nor silver nor cop-
per in your money belts,

9:8 [a]NU-Text reads *were afraid.* 9:13 [a]Hosea 6:6 [b]NU-Text omits *to repentance.* 9:14 [a]NU-Text brackets *often* as disputed. 9:35 [a]NU-Text omits *among the people.* 9:36 [a]NU-Text and M-Text read *harassed.* 10:3 [a]NU-Text omits *Lebbaeus, whose surname was.* 10:4 [a]NU-Text reads *Cananaean.* 10:8 [a]NU-Text reads *raise the dead, cleanse the lepers;* M-Text omits *raise the dead.*

10 "nor bag for *your* journey, nor two tunics,
nor sandals, nor staffs; for a worker is worthy
of his food.
11 "Now whatever city or town you enter, in-
quire who in it is worthy, and stay there till you
go out.
12 "And when you go into a household, greet
it.
13 "If the household is worthy, let your peace
come upon it. But if it is not worthy, let your
peace return to you.
14 "And whoever will not receive you nor
hear your words, when you depart from that
house or city, shake off the dust from your feet.
15 "Assuredly, I say to you, it will be more
tolerable for the land of Sodom and Gomorrah
in the day of judgment than for that city!

Persecutions Are Coming

16 "Behold, I send you out as sheep in the
midst of wolves. Therefore be wise as serpents
and harmless as doves.
17 "But beware of men, for they will deliver
you up to councils and scourge you in their
synagogues.
18 "You will be brought before governors and
kings for My sake, as a testimony to them and
to the Gentiles.
19 "But when they deliver you up, do not
worry about how or what you should speak.
For it will be given to you in that hour what
you should speak;
20 "for it is not you who speak, but the Spirit
of your Father who speaks in you.
21 "Now brother will deliver up brother to
death, and a father *his* child; and children will
rise up against parents and cause them to be
put to death.
22 "And you will be hated by all for My name's
sake. But he who endures to the end will be
saved.
23 "When they persecute you in this city, flee
to another. For assuredly, I say to you, you will
not have gone through the cities of Israel be-
fore the Son of Man comes.
24 "A disciple is not above *his* teacher, nor a
servant above his master.
25 "It is enough for a disciple that he be like
his teacher, and a servant like his master. If
they have called the master of the house Beel-
zebub,[a] how much more *will they call* those of
his household!
26 "Therefore do not fear them. For there is
nothing covered that will not be revealed, and
hidden that will not be known.

Jesus Teaches the Fear of God

27 "Whatever I tell you in the dark, speak in
the light; and what you hear in the ear, preach
on the housetops.
28 "And do not fear those who kill the body
but cannot kill the soul. But rather fear Him
who is able to destroy both soul and body in hell.
29 "Are not two sparrows sold for a copper
coin? And not one of them falls to the ground
apart from your Father's will.
30 "But the very hairs of your head are all num-
bered.
31 "Do not fear therefore; you are of more value
than many sparrows.

Confess Christ Before Men

32 "Therefore whoever confesses Me before
men, him I will also confess before My Father
who is in heaven.
33 "But whoever denies Me before men, him
I will also deny before My Father who is in
heaven.

Christ Brings Division

34 "Do not think that I came to bring peace
on earth. I did not come to bring peace but a
sword.
35 "For I have come to *'set a man against his
father, a daughter against her mother, and a
daughter-in-law against her mother-in-law'*;
36 "and *'a man's enemies will be those of his
own household.'*[a]
37 "He who loves father or mother more than
Me is not worthy of Me. And he who loves son
or daughter more than Me is not worthy of Me.
38 "And he who does not take his cross and
follow after Me is not worthy of Me.
39 "He who finds his life will lose it, and he
who loses his life for My sake will find it.

A Cup of Cold Water

40 "He who receives you receives Me, and he
who receives Me receives Him who sent Me.
41 "He who receives a prophet in the name of
a prophet shall receive a prophet's reward.
And he who receives a righteous man in the
name of a righteous man shall receive a righ-
teous man's reward.
42 "And whoever gives one of these little ones
only a cup of cold *water* in the name of a disci-
ple, assuredly, I say to you, he shall by no
means lose his reward."

John the Baptist Sends Messengers to Jesus

11 Now it came to pass, when Jesus finished
commanding His twelve disciples, that
He departed from there to teach and to preach
in their cities.
2 And when John had heard in prison about
the works of Christ, he sent two of[a] his disci-
ples
3 and said to Him, "Are You the Coming One,
or do we look for another?"
4 Jesus answered and said to them, "Go and
tell John the things which you hear and see:
5 "*The* blind see and *the* lame walk; *the* lep-
ers are cleansed and *the* deaf hear; *the* dead
are raised up and *the* poor have the gospel
preached to them.
6 "And blessed is he who is not offended be-
cause of Me."
7 As they departed, Jesus began to say to the
multitudes concerning John: "What did you go
out into the wilderness to see? A reed shaken
by the wind?
8 "But what did you go out to see? A man
clothed in soft garments? Indeed, those who
wear soft *clothing* are in kings' houses.
9 "But what did you go out to see? A prophet?
Yes, I say to you, and more than a prophet.
10 "For this is *he* of whom it is written:

'Behold, I send My messenger before
Your face,
Who will prepare Your way before You.'[a]

10:25 [a]NU-Text and M-Text read *Beelzebul.* **10:36** [a]Micah 7:6 **11:2** [a]NU-Text reads *by* for *two of.* **11:10** [a]Malachi 3:1

11 "Assuredly, I say to you, among those born of women there has not risen one greater than John the Baptist; but he who is least in the kingdom of heaven is greater than he.
12 "And from the days of John the Baptist until now the kingdom of heaven suffers violence, and the violent take it by force.
13 "For all the prophets and the law prophesied until John.
14 "And if you are willing to receive *it*, he is Elijah who is to come.
15 "He who has ears to hear, let him hear!
16 "But to what shall I liken this generation? It is like children sitting in the marketplaces and calling to their companions,
17 "and saying:

'We played the flute for you,
  And you did not dance;
We mourned to you,
  And you did not lament.'

18 "For John came neither eating nor drinking, and they say, 'He has a demon.'
19 "The Son of Man came eating and drinking, and they say, 'Look, a glutton and a winebibber, a friend of tax collectors and sinners!' But wisdom is justified by her children."[a]

Woe to the Impenitent Cities

20 Then He began to rebuke the cities in which most of His mighty works had been done, because they did not repent:
21 "Woe to you, Chorazin! Woe to you, Bethsaida! For if the mighty works which were done in you had been done in Tyre and Sidon, they would have repented long ago in sackcloth and ashes.
22 "But I say to you, it will be more tolerable for Tyre and Sidon in the day of judgment than for you.
23 "And you, Capernaum, who are exalted to heaven, will be[a] brought down to Hades; for if the mighty works which were done in you had been done in Sodom, it would have remained until this day.
24 "But I say to you that it shall be more tolerable for the land of Sodom in the day of judgment than for you."

Jesus Gives True Rest

25 At that time Jesus answered and said, "I thank You, Father, Lord of heaven and earth, that You have hidden these things from *the* wise and prudent and have revealed them to babes.
26 "Even so, Father, for so it seemed good in Your sight.
27 "All things have been delivered to Me by My Father, and no one knows the Son except the Father. Nor does anyone know the Father except the Son, and *the one* to whom the Son wills to reveal *Him*.
28 "Come to Me, all *you* who labor and are heavy laden, and I will give you rest.
29 "Take My yoke upon you and learn from Me, for I am gentle and lowly in heart, and you will find rest for your souls.
30 "For My yoke *is* easy and My burden is light."

Jesus Is Lord of the Sabbath

12 At that time Jesus went through the grainfields on the Sabbath. And His disciples were hungry, and began to pluck heads of grain and to eat.
2 And when the Pharisees saw *it*, they said to Him, "Look, Your disciples are doing what is not lawful to do on the Sabbath!"
3 But He said to them, "Have you not read what David did when he was hungry, he and those who were with him:
4 "how he entered the house of God and ate the showbread which was not lawful for him to eat, nor for those who were with him, but only for the priests?
5 "Or have you not read in the law that on the Sabbath the priests in the temple profane the Sabbath, and are blameless?
6 "Yet I say to you that in this place there is *One* greater than the temple.
7 "But if you had known what *this* means, *'I desire mercy and not sacrifice,'*[a] you would not have condemned the guiltless.
8 "For the Son of Man is Lord even[a] of the Sabbath."

Healing on the Sabbath

9 Now when He had departed from there, He went into their synagogue.
10 And behold, there was a man who had a withered hand. And they asked Him, saying, "Is it lawful to heal on the Sabbath?"—that they might accuse Him.
11 Then He said to them, "What man is there among you who has one sheep, and if it falls into a pit on the Sabbath, will not lay hold of it and lift *it* out?
12 "Of how much more value then is a man than a sheep? Therefore it is lawful to do good on the Sabbath."
13 Then He said to the man, "Stretch out your hand." And he stretched *it* out, and it was restored as whole as the other.
14 Then the Pharisees went out and plotted against Him, how they might destroy Him.

Behold, My Servant

15 But when Jesus knew *it*, He withdrew from there. And great multitudes[a] followed Him, and He healed them all.
16 Yet He warned them not to make Him known,
17 that it might be fulfilled which was spoken by Isaiah the prophet, saying:

18 *"Behold! My Servant whom I have chosen,*
  My Beloved in whom My soul is well pleased!
  I will put My Spirit upon Him,
  And He will declare justice to the Gentiles.
19 *He will not quarrel nor cry out,*
  Nor will anyone hear His voice in the streets.
20 *A bruised reed He will not break,*
  And smoking flax He will not quench,
  Till He sends forth justice to victory;
21 *And in His name Gentiles will trust."*[a]

A House Divided Cannot Stand

22 Then one was brought to Him who was demon-possessed, blind and mute; and He healed

11:19 [a]NU-Text reads *works*. **11:23** [a]NU-Text reads *will you be exalted to heaven? No, you will be.* **12:7** [a]Hosea 6:6
12:8 [a]NU-Text and M-Text omit *even*. **12:15** [a]NU-Text brackets *multitudes* as disputed. **12:21** [a]Isaiah 42:1–4

him, so that the blind and[a] mute man both spoke
and saw.
23 And all the multitudes were amazed and
said, "Could this be the Son of David?"
24 Now when the Pharisees heard *it* they
said, "This *fellow* does not cast out demons
except by Beelzebub,[a] the ruler of the demons."
25 But Jesus knew their thoughts, and said to
them: "Every kingdom divided against itself is
brought to desolation, and every city or house
divided against itself will not stand.
26 "If Satan casts out Satan, he is divided
against himself. How then will his kingdom
stand?
27 "And if I cast out demons by Beelzebub,
by whom do your sons cast *them* out? There-
fore they shall be your judges.
28 "But if I cast out demons by the Spirit of
God, surely the kingdom of God has come
upon you.
29 "Or how can one enter a strong man's
house and plunder his goods, unless he first
binds the strong man? And then he will plun-
der his house.
30 "He who is not with Me is against Me, and
he who does not gather with Me scatters abroad.

The Unpardonable Sin

31 "Therefore I say to you, every sin and blas-
phemy will be forgiven men, but the blas-
phemy *against* the Spirit will not be forgiven
men.
32 "Anyone who speaks a word against the Son
of Man, it will be forgiven him; but whoever
speaks against the Holy Spirit, it will not be
forgiven him, either in this age or in the *age* to
come.

A Tree Known by Its Fruit

33 "Either make the tree good and its fruit
good, or else make the tree bad and its fruit bad;
for a tree is known by *its* fruit.
34 "Brood of vipers! How can you, being evil,
speak good things? For out of the abundance
of the heart the mouth speaks.
35 "A good man out of the good treasure of
his heart[a] brings forth good things, and an evil
man out of the evil treasure brings forth evil
things.
36 "But I say to you that for every idle word
men may speak, they will give account of it in
the day of judgment.
37 "For by your words you will be justified,
and by your words you will be condemned."

The Scribes and Pharisees Ask for a Sign

38 Then some of the scribes and Pharisees an-
swered, saying, "Teacher, we want to see a sign
from You."
39 But He answered and said to them, "An
evil and adulterous generation seeks after a
sign, and no sign will be given to it except the
sign of the prophet Jonah.
40 "For as Jonah was three days and three
nights in the belly of the great fish, so will the
Son of Man be three days and three nights in
the heart of the earth.
41 "The men of Nineveh will rise up in the
judgment with this generation and condemn it,
because they repented at the preaching of Jo-
nah; and indeed a greater than Jonah *is* here.
42 "The queen of the South will rise up in the
judgment with this generation and condemn
it, for she came from the ends of the earth to
hear the wisdom of Solomon; and indeed a
greater than Solomon *is* here.

An Unclean Spirit Returns

43 "When an unclean spirit goes out of a man,
he goes through dry places, seeking rest, and
finds none.
44 "Then he says, 'I will return to my house
from which I came.' And when he comes, he
finds *it* empty, swept, and put in order.
45 "Then he goes and takes with him seven
other spirits more wicked than himself, and
they enter and dwell there; and the last *state*
of that man is worse than the first. So shall it
also be with this wicked generation."

Jesus' Mother and Brothers Send for Him

46 While He was still talking to the multitudes,
behold, His mother and brothers stood outside,
seeking to speak with Him.
47 Then one said to Him, "Look, Your mother
and Your brothers are standing outside, seek-
ing to speak with You."
48 But He answered and said to the one who
told Him, "Who is My mother and who are My
brothers?"
49 And He stretched out His hand toward His
disciples and said, "Here are My mother and
My brothers!
50 "For whoever does the will of My Father in
heaven is My brother and sister and mother."

The Parable of the Sower

13 On the same day Jesus went out of the
house and sat by the sea.
2 And great multitudes were gathered to-
gether to Him, so that He got into a boat and sat;
and the whole multitude stood on the shore.
3 Then He spoke many things to them in
parables, saying: "Behold, a sower went out to
sow.
4 "And as he sowed, some *seed* fell by the
wayside; and the birds came and devoured
them.
5 "Some fell on stony places, where they did
not have much earth; and they immediately
sprang up because they had no depth of earth.
6 "But when the sun was up they were
scorched, and because they had no root they
withered away.
7 "And some fell among thorns, and the
thorns sprang up and choked them.
8 "But others fell on good ground and yielded
a crop: some a hundredfold, some sixty, some
thirty.
9 "He who has ears to hear, let him hear!"

The Purpose of Parables

10 And the disciples came and said to Him,
"Why do You speak to them in parables?"
11 He answered and said to them, "Because
it has been given to you to know the mysteries
of the kingdom of heaven, but to them it has
not been given.
12 "For whoever has, to him more will be given,
and he will have abundance; but whoever does
not have, even what he has will be taken away
from him.
13 "Therefore I speak to them in parables, be-

12:22 [a]NU-Text omits *blind and.* **12:24** [a]NU-Text and M-Text read *Beelzebul.* **12:35** [a]NU-Text and M-Text omit *of his heart.*

cause seeing they do not see, and hearing they
do not hear, nor do they understand.
14 "And in them the prophecy of Isaiah is ful-
filled, which says:

'Hearing you will hear and shall not
understand,
And seeing you will see and not perceive;
15 *For the hearts of this people have grown*
dull.
Their ears are hard of hearing,
And their eyes they have closed,
Lest they should see with their eyes and
hear with their ears,
Lest they should understand with their
hearts and turn,
So that I should[a] *heal them.'*[b]

16 "But blessed *are* your eyes for they see, and
your ears for they hear;
17 "for assuredly, I say to you that many
prophets and righteous *men* desired to see
what you see, and did not see *it,* and to hear
what you hear, and did not hear *it.*

The Parable of the Sower Explained

18 "Therefore hear the parable of the sower:
19 "When anyone hears the word of the king-
dom, and does not understand *it,* then the
wicked *one* comes and snatches away what was
sown in his heart. This is he who received seed
by the wayside.
20 "But he who received the seed on stony
places, this is he who hears the word and im-
mediately receives it with joy;
21 "yet he has no root in himself, but endures
only for a while. For when tribulation or perse-
cution arises because of the word, immediately
he stumbles.
22 "Now he who received seed among the
thorns is he who hears the word, and the cares
of this world and the deceitfulness of riches
choke the word, and he becomes unfruitful.
23 "But he who received seed on the good
ground is he who hears the word and under-
stands *it,* who indeed bears fruit and produces:
some a hundredfold, some sixty, some thirty."

The Parable of the Wheat and the Tares

24 Another parable He put forth to them, say-
ing: "The kingdom of heaven is like a man who
sowed good seed in his field;
25 "but while men slept, his enemy came and
sowed tares among the wheat and went his way.
26 "But when the grain had sprouted and pro-
duced a crop, then the tares also appeared.
27 "So the servants of the owner came and
said to him, 'Sir, did you not sow good seed in
your field? How then does it have tares?'
28 "He said to them, 'An enemy has done this.'
The servants said to him, 'Do you want us then
to go and gather them up?'
29 "But he said, 'No, lest while you gather up
the tares you also uproot the wheat with them.
30 'Let both grow together until the harvest,
and at the time of harvest I will say to the reap-
ers, "First gather together the tares and bind
them in bundles to burn them, but gather the
wheat into my barn." ' "

The Parable of the Mustard Seed

31 Another parable He put forth to them, say-
ing: "The kingdom of heaven is like a mustard
seed, which a man took and sowed in his field,
32 "which indeed is the least of all the seeds;
but when it is grown it is greater than the herbs
and becomes a tree, so that the birds of the air
come and nest in its branches."

The Parable of the Leaven

33 Another parable He spoke to them: "The
kingdom of heaven is like leaven, which a
woman took and hid in three measures[a] of
meal till it was all leavened."

Prophecy and the Parables

34 All these things Jesus spoke to the multi-
tude in parables; and without a parable He did
not speak to them,
35 that it might be fulfilled which was spoken
by the prophet, saying:

"I will open My mouth in parables;
I will utter things kept secret from the
foundation of the world."[a]

The Parable of the Tares Explained

36 Then Jesus sent the multitude away and
went into the house. And His disciples came to
Him, saying, "Explain to us the parable of the
tares of the field."
37 He answered and said to them: "He who
sows the good seed is the Son of Man.
38 "The field is the world, the good seeds are
the sons of the kingdom, but the tares are the
sons of the wicked *one.*
39 "The enemy who sowed them is the devil,
the harvest is the end of the age, and the reap-
ers are the angels.
40 "Therefore as the tares are gathered and
burned in the fire, so it will be at the end of
this age.
41 "The Son of Man will send out His angels,
and they will gather out of His kingdom all
things that offend, and those who practice law-
lessness,
42 "and will cast them into the furnace of fire.
There will be wailing and gnashing of teeth.
43 "Then the righteous will shine forth as the
sun in the kingdom of their Father. He who has
ears to hear, let him hear!

The Parable of the Hidden Treasure

44 "Again, the kingdom of heaven is like trea-
sure hidden in a field, which a man found and
hid; and for joy over it he goes and sells all that
he has and buys that field.

The Parable of the Pearl of Great Price

45 "Again, the kingdom of heaven is like a
merchant seeking beautiful pearls,
46 "who, when he had found one pearl of
great price, went and sold all that he had and
bought it.

The Parable of the Dragnet

47 "Again, the kingdom of heaven is like a
dragnet that was cast into the sea and gathered
some of every kind,
48 "which, when it was full, they drew to shore;
and they sat down and gathered the good into
vessels, but threw the bad away.

13:15 [a]NU-Text and M-Text read *would.* [b]Isaiah 6:9, 10 **13:33** [a]Greek *sata,* approximately two pecks in all
13:35 [a]Psalm 78:2

49 "So it will be at the end of the age. The
angels will come forth, separate the wicked
from among the just,
50 "and cast them into the furnace of fire.
There will be wailing and gnashing of teeth."
51 Jesus said to them,[a] "Have you understood
all these things?" They said to Him, "Yes, Lord."[b]
52 Then He said to them, "Therefore every
scribe instructed concerning[a] the kingdom of
heaven is like a householder who brings out of
his treasure *things* new and old."

Jesus Rejected at Nazareth

53 Now it came to pass, when Jesus had fin-
ished these parables, that He departed from
there.
54 When He had come to His own country,
He taught them in their synagogue, so that
they were astonished and said, "Where did this
Man get this wisdom and *these* mighty works?
55 "Is this not the carpenter's son? Is not His
mother called Mary? And His brothers James,
Joses,[a] Simon, and Judas?
56 "And His sisters, are they not all with us?
Where then did this *Man* get all these things?"
57 So they were offended at Him. But Jesus
said to them, "A prophet is not without honor
except in his own country and in his own
house."
58 Now He did not do many mighty works
there because of their unbelief.

John the Baptist Beheaded

14 At that time Herod the tetrarch heard the
report about Jesus
2 and said to his servants, "This is John the
Baptist; he is risen from the dead, and there-
fore these powers are at work in him."
3 For Herod had laid hold of John and bound
him, and put *him* in prison for the sake of Hero-
dias, his brother Philip's wife.
4 Because John had said to him, "It is not law-
ful for you to have her."
5 And although he wanted to put him to death,
he feared the multitude, because they counted
him as a prophet.
6 But when Herod's birthday was cele-
brated, the daughter of Herodias danced be-
fore them and pleased Herod.
7 Therefore he promised with an oath to give
her whatever she might ask.
8 So she, having been prompted by her
mother, said, "Give me John the Baptist's head
here on a platter."
9 And the king was sorry; nevertheless, be-
cause of the oaths and because of those who
sat with him, he commanded *it* to be given to
her.
10 So he sent and had John beheaded in
prison.
11 And his head was brought on a platter and
given to the girl, and she brought *it* to her mother.
12 Then his disciples came and took away the
body and buried it, and went and told Jesus.

Feeding the Five Thousand

13 When Jesus heard *it*, He departed from
there by boat to a deserted place by Himself.
But when the multitudes heard it, they followed
Him on foot from the cities.
14 And when Jesus went out He saw a great
multitude; and He was moved with compas-
sion for them, and healed their sick.
15 When it was evening, His disciples came
to Him, saying, "This is a deserted place, and
the hour is already late. Send the multitudes
away, that they may go into the villages and
buy themselves food."
16 But Jesus said to them, "They do not need
to go away. You give them something to eat."
17 And they said to Him, "We have here only
five loaves and two fish."
18 He said, "Bring them here to Me."
19 Then He commanded the multitudes to sit
down on the grass. And He took the five loaves
and the two fish, and looking up to heaven, He
blessed and broke and gave the loaves to the
disciples; and the disciples gave to the multi-
tudes.
20 So they all ate and were filled, and they
took up twelve baskets full of the fragments
that remained.
21 Now those who had eaten were about five
thousand men, besides women and children.

Jesus Walks on the Sea

22 Immediately Jesus made His disciples get
into the boat and go before Him to the other
side, while He sent the multitudes away.
23 And when He had sent the multitudes
away, He went up on the mountain by Himself
to pray. Now when evening came, He was
alone there.
24 But the boat was now in the middle of the
sea,[a] tossed by the waves, for the wind was
contrary.
25 Now in the fourth watch of the night Jesus
went to them, walking on the sea.
26 And when the disciples saw Him walking
on the sea, they were troubled, saying, "It is a
ghost!" And they cried out for fear.
27 But immediately Jesus spoke to them, say-
ing, "Be of good cheer! It is I; do not be afraid."
28 And Peter answered Him and said, "Lord,
if it is You, command me to come to You on the
water."
29 So He said, "Come." And when Peter had
come down out of the boat, he walked on the
water to go to Jesus.
30 But when he saw that the wind *was* bois-
terous,[a] he was afraid; and beginning to sink
he cried out, saying, "Lord, save me!"
31 And immediately Jesus stretched out *His*
hand and caught him, and said to him, "O you
of little faith, why did you doubt?"
32 And when they got into the boat, the wind
ceased.
33 Then those who were in the boat came
and[a] worshiped Him, saying, "Truly You are
the Son of God."

Many Touch Him and Are Made Well

34 When they had crossed over, they came to
the land of[a] Gennesaret.
35 And when the men of that place recog-
nized Him, they sent out into all that surround-
ing region, brought to Him all who were sick,
36 and begged Him that they might only
touch the hem of His garment. And as many
as touched *it* were made perfectly well.

13:51 [a]NU-Text omits *Jesus said to them.* [b]NU-Text omits *Lord.* **13:52** [a]Or *for* **13:55** [a]NU-Text reads *Joseph.* **14:24** [a]NU-Text reads *many furlongs away from the land.* **14:30** [a]NU-Text brackets *that* and *boisterous* as disputed. **14:33** [a]NU-Text omits *came and.* **14:34** [a]NU-Text reads *came to land at.*

Defilement Comes from Within

15 Then the scribes and Pharisees who were from Jerusalem came to Jesus, saying,
2 "Why do Your disciples transgress the tradition of the elders? For they do not wash their hands when they eat bread."
3 He answered and said to them, "Why do you also transgress the commandment of God because of your tradition?
4 "For God commanded, saying, *'Honor your father and your mother'*;[a] and, *'He who curses father or mother, let him be put to death.'*[b]
5 "But you say, 'Whoever says to his father or mother, "Whatever profit you might have received from me *is* a gift *to God*"—
6 'then he need not honor his father or mother.'[a] Thus you have made the commandment[b] of God of no effect by your tradition.
7 "Hypocrites! Well did Isaiah prophesy about you, saying:

8 *'These people draw near to Me with their*
mouth,
And[a] *honor Me with their lips,*
But their heart is far from Me.
9 *And in vain they worship Me,*
Teaching as doctrines the
commandments of men.' "[a]

10 When He had called the multitude to *Himself,* He said to them, "Hear and understand:
11 "Not what goes into the mouth defiles a man; but what comes out of the mouth, this defiles a man."
12 Then His disciples came and said to Him, "Do You know that the Pharisees were offended when they heard this saying?"
13 But He answered and said, "Every plant which My heavenly Father has not planted will be uprooted.
14 "Let them alone. They are blind leaders of the blind. And if the blind leads the blind, both will fall into a ditch."
15 Then Peter answered and said to Him, "Explain this parable to us."
16 So Jesus said, "Are you also still without understanding?
17 "Do you not yet understand that whatever enters the mouth goes into the stomach and is eliminated?
18 "But those things which proceed out of the mouth come from the heart, and they defile a man.
19 "For out of the heart proceed evil thoughts, murders, adulteries, fornications, thefts, false witness, blasphemies.
20 "These are *the things* which defile a man, but to eat with unwashed hands does not defile a man."

A Gentile Shows Her Faith

21 Then Jesus went out from there and departed to the region of Tyre and Sidon.
22 And behold, a woman of Canaan came from that region and cried out to Him, saying, "Have mercy on me, O Lord, Son of David! My daughter is severely demon-possessed."
23 But He answered her not a word. And His disciples came and urged Him, saying, "Send her away, for she cries out after us."
24 But He answered and said, "I was not sent except to the lost sheep of the house of Israel."
25 Then she came and worshiped Him, saying, "Lord, help me!"
26 But He answered and said, "It is not good to take the children's bread and throw *it* to the little dogs."
27 And she said, "Yes, Lord, yet even the little dogs eat the crumbs which fall from their masters' table."
28 Then Jesus answered and said to her, "O woman, great *is* your faith! Let it be to you as you desire." And her daughter was healed from that very hour.

Jesus Heals Great Multitudes

29 Jesus departed from there, skirted the Sea of Galilee, and went up on the mountain and sat down there.
30 Then great multitudes came to Him, having with them *the* lame, blind, mute, maimed, and many others; and they laid them down at Jesus' feet, and He healed them.
31 So the multitude marveled when they saw *the* mute speaking, *the* maimed made whole, *the* lame walking, and *the* blind seeing; and they glorified the God of Israel.

Feeding the Four Thousand

32 Now Jesus called His disciples to *Himself* and said, "I have compassion on the multitude, because they have now continued with Me three days and have nothing to eat. And I do not want to send them away hungry, lest they faint on the way."
33 Then His disciples said to Him, "Where could we get enough bread in the wilderness to fill such a great multitude?"
34 Jesus said to them, "How many loaves do you have?" And they said, "Seven, and a few little fish."
35 So He commanded the multitude to sit down on the ground.
36 And He took the seven loaves and the fish and gave thanks, broke *them* and gave *them* to His disciples; and the disciples *gave* to the multitude.
37 So they all ate and were filled, and they took up seven large baskets full of the fragments that were left.
38 Now those who ate were four thousand men, besides women and children.
39 And He sent away the multitude, got into the boat, and came to the region of Magdala.[a]

The Pharisees and Sadducees Seek a Sign

16 Then the Pharisees and Sadducees came, and testing Him asked that He would show them a sign from heaven.
2 He answered and said to them, "When it is evening you say, *'It will be* fair weather, for the sky is red';
3 "and in the morning, *'It will be* foul weather today, for the sky is red and threatening.' Hypocrites![a] You know how to discern the face of the sky, but you cannot *discern* the signs of the times.

15:4 [a]Exodus 20:12; Deuteronomy 5:16 [b]Exodus 21:17 **15:6** [a]NU-Text omits *or mother.* [b]NU-Text reads *word.*
15:8 [a]NU-Text omits *draw near to Me with their mouth, And.* **15:9** [a]Isaiah 29:13 **15:39** [a]NU-Text reads *Magadan.*
16:3 [a]NU-Text omits *Hypocrites.*

4 "A wicked and adulterous generation
seeks after a sign, and no sign shall be given
to it except the sign of the prophet[a] Jonah."
And He left them and departed.

The Leaven of the Pharisees and Sadducees

5 Now when His disciples had come to the
other side, they had forgotten to take bread.
6 Then Jesus said to them, "Take heed and
beware of the leaven of the Pharisees and the
Sadducees."
7 And they reasoned among themselves,
saying, "*It is* because we have taken no bread."
8 But Jesus, being aware of *it*, said to them,
"O you of little faith, why do you reason among
yourselves because you have brought no bread?[a]
9 "Do you not yet understand, or remember
the five loaves of the five thousand and how
many baskets you took up?
10 "Nor the seven loaves of the four thousand
and how many large baskets you took up?
11 "How is it you do not understand that I did
not speak to you concerning bread?—*but* to
beware of the leaven of the Pharisees and Sad-
ducees."
12 Then they understood that He did not tell
them to beware of the leaven of bread, but of
the doctrine of the Pharisees and Sadducees.

Peter Confesses Jesus as the Christ

13 When Jesus came into the region of Caesa-
rea Philippi, He asked His disciples, saying,
"Who do men say that I, the Son of Man, am?"
14 So they said, "Some *say* John the Baptist,
some Elijah, and others Jeremiah or one of the
prophets."
15 He said to them, "But who do you say that
I am?"
16 Simon Peter answered and said, "You are
the Christ, the Son of the living God."
17 Jesus answered and said to him, "Blessed
are you, Simon Bar-Jonah, for flesh and blood
has not revealed *this* to you, but My Father who
is in heaven.
18 "And I also say to you that you are Peter,
and on this rock I will build My church, and
the gates of Hades shall not prevail against it.
19 "And I will give you the keys of the king-
dom of heaven, and whatever you bind on
earth will be bound in heaven, and whatever
you loose on earth will be loosed[a] in heaven."
20 Then He commanded His disciples that
they should tell no one that He was Jesus the
Christ.

Jesus Predicts His Death and Resurrection

21 From that time Jesus began to show to His
disciples that He must go to Jerusalem, and suf-
fer many things from the elders and chief
priests and scribes, and be killed, and be raised
the third day.
22 Then Peter took Him aside and began to
rebuke Him, saying, "Far be it from You, Lord;
this shall not happen to You!"
23 But He turned and said to Peter, "Get be-
hind Me, Satan! You are an offense to Me, for
you are not mindful of the things of God, but
the things of men."

Take Up the Cross and Follow Him

24 Then Jesus said to His disciples, "If anyone
desires to come after Me, let him deny himself,
and take up his cross, and follow Me.
25 "For whoever desires to save his life will
lose it, but whoever loses his life for My sake
will find it.
26 "For what profit is it to a man if he gains
the whole world, and loses his own soul? Or
what will a man give in exchange for his soul?
27 "For the Son of Man will come in the glory
of His Father with His angels, and then He will
reward each according to his works.

Jesus Transfigured on the Mount

28 "Assuredly, I say to you, there are some
standing here who shall not taste death till they
see the Son of Man coming in His kingdom."

17 Now after six days Jesus took Peter,
James, and John his brother, led them
up on a high mountain by themselves;
2 and He was transfigured before them. His
face shone like the sun, and His clothes became
as white as the light.
3 And behold, Moses and Elijah appeared to
them, talking with Him.
4 Then Peter answered and said to Jesus,
"Lord, it is good for us to be here; if You wish,
let us[a] make here three tabernacles: one for
You, one for Moses, and one for Elijah."
5 While he was still speaking, behold, a bright
cloud overshadowed them; and suddenly a
voice came out of the cloud, saying, "This is My
beloved Son, in whom I am well pleased. Hear
Him!"
6 And when the disciples heard *it*, they fell
on their faces and were greatly afraid.
7 But Jesus came and touched them and
said, "Arise, and do not be afraid."
8 When they had lifted up their eyes, they saw
no one but Jesus only.
9 Now as they came down from the moun-
tain, Jesus commanded them, saying, "Tell the
vision to no one until the Son of Man is risen
from the dead."
10 And His disciples asked Him, saying, "Why
then do the scribes say that Elijah must come
first?"
11 Jesus answered and said to them, "Indeed,
Elijah is coming first[a] and will restore all things.
12 "But I say to you that Elijah has come al-
ready, and they did not know him but did to
him whatever they wished. Likewise the Son
of Man is also about to suffer at their hands."
13 Then the disciples understood that He
spoke to them of John the Baptist.

A Boy Is Healed

14 And when they had come to the multitude,
a man came to Him, kneeling down to Him and
saying,
15 "Lord, have mercy on my son, for he is an
epileptic[a] and suffers severely; for he often
falls into the fire and often into the water.
16 "So I brought him to Your disciples, but
they could not cure him."
17 Then Jesus answered and said, "O faithless
and perverse generation, how long shall I be
with you? How long shall I bear with you?
Bring him here to Me."
18 And Jesus rebuked the demon, and it came

16:4 [a]NU-Text omits *the prophet.* **16:8** [a]NU-Text reads *you have no bread.* **16:19** [a]Or *will have been bound . . . will have been loosed* **17:4** [a]NU-Text reads *I will.* **17:11** [a]NU-Text omits *first.* **17:15** [a]Literally *moonstruck*

out of him; and the child was cured from that
very hour.
19 Then the disciples came to Jesus privately
and said, "Why could we not cast it out?"
20 So Jesus said to them, "Because of your
unbelief;[a] for assuredly, I say to you, if you have
faith as a mustard seed, you will say to this
mountain, 'Move from here to there,' and it will
move; and nothing will be impossible for you.
21 "However, this kind does not go out except
by prayer and fasting."[a]

Jesus Again Predicts His Death and Resurrection

22 Now while they were staying[a] in Galilee,
Jesus said to them, "The Son of Man is about
to be betrayed into the hands of men,
23 "and they will kill Him, and the third day
He will be raised up." And they were exceed-
ingly sorrowful.

Peter and His Master Pay Their Taxes

24 When they had come to Capernaum,[a] those
who received the *temple* tax came to Peter and
said, "Does your Teacher not pay the *temple*
tax?"
25 He said, "Yes." And when he had come
into the house, Jesus anticipated him, saying,
"What do you think, Simon? From whom do
the kings of the earth take customs or taxes,
from their sons or from strangers?"
26 Peter said to Him, "From strangers." Jesus
said to him, "Then the sons are free.
27 "Nevertheless, lest we offend them, go to
the sea, cast in a hook, and take the fish that
comes up first. And when you have opened its
mouth, you will find a piece of money;[a] take
that and give it to them for Me and you."

Who Is the Greatest?

18 At that time the disciples came to Jesus,
saying, "Who then is greatest in the
kingdom of heaven?"
2 Then Jesus called a little child to Him, set
him in the midst of them,
3 and said, "Assuredly, I say to you, unless
you are converted and become as little chil-
dren, you will by no means enter the kingdom
of heaven.
4 "Therefore whoever humbles himself as
this little child is the greatest in the kingdom
of heaven.
5 "Whoever receives one little child like this
in My name receives Me.

Jesus Warns of Offenses

6 "But whoever causes one of these little
ones who believe in Me to sin, it would be
better for him if a millstone were hung around
his neck, and he were drowned in the depth of
the sea.
7 "Woe to the world because of offenses! For
offenses must come, but woe to that man by
whom the offense comes!
8 "If your hand or foot causes you to sin, cut
it off and cast *it* from you. It is better for you
to enter into life lame or maimed, rather than
having two hands or two feet, to be cast into
the everlasting fire.
9 "And if your eye causes you to sin, pluck it
out and cast *it* from you. It is better for you to
enter into life with one eye, rather than having
two eyes, to be cast into hell fire.

The Parable of the Lost Sheep

10 "Take heed that you do not despise one of
these little ones, for I say to you that in heaven
their angels always see the face of My Father
who is in heaven.
11 "For the Son of Man has come to save that
which was lost.[a]
12 "What do you think? If a man has a hun-
dred sheep, and one of them goes astray, does
he not leave the ninety-nine and go to the
mountains to seek the one that is straying?
13 "And if he should find it, assuredly, I say
to you, he rejoices more over that *sheep* than
over the ninety-nine that did not go astray.
14 "Even so it is not the will of your Father
who is in heaven that one of these little ones
should perish.

Dealing with a Sinning Brother

15 "Moreover if your brother sins against
you, go and tell him his fault between you and
him alone. If he hears you, you have gained
your brother.
16 "But if he will not hear, take with you one
or two more, that *'by the mouth of two or three
witnesses every word may be established.'*[a]
17 "And if he refuses to hear them, tell *it* to
the church. But if he refuses even to hear the
church, let him be to you like a heathen and a
tax collector.
18 "Assuredly, I say to you, whatever you bind
on earth will be bound in heaven, and whatever
you loose on earth will be loosed in heaven.
19 "Again I say[a] to you that if two of you agree
on earth concerning anything that they ask, it
will be done for them by My Father in heaven.
20 "For where two or three are gathered to-
gether in My name, I am there in the midst of
them."

The Parable of the Unforgiving Servant

21 Then Peter came to Him and said, "Lord,
how often shall my brother sin against me, and
I forgive him? Up to seven times?"
22 Jesus said to him, "I do not say to you, up
to seven times, but up to seventy times seven.
23 "Therefore the kingdom of heaven is like
a certain king who wanted to settle accounts
with his servants.
24 "And when he had begun to settle ac-
counts, one was brought to him who owed him
ten thousand talents.
25 "But as he was not able to pay, his master
commanded that he be sold, with his wife and
children and all that he had, and that payment
be made.
26 "The servant therefore fell down before
him, saying, 'Master, have patience with me, and
I will pay you all.'
27 "Then the master of that servant was moved
with compassion, released him, and forgave him
the debt.
28 "But that servant went out and found one
of his fellow servants who owed him a hundred

17:20 [a]NU-Text reads *little faith.* **17:21** [a]NU-Text omits this verse. **17:22** [a]NU-Text reads *gathering together.* **17:24** [a]NU-Text reads *Capharnaum* (here and elsewhere). **17:27** [a]Greek *stater,* the exact amount to pay the temple tax (didrachma) for two **18:11** [a]NU-Text omits this verse. **18:16** [a]Deuteronomy 19:15 **18:19** [a]NU-Text and M-Text read *Again, assuredly, I say.*

denarii; and he laid hands on him and took *him*
by the throat, saying, 'Pay me what you owe!'
29 "So his fellow servant fell down at his feet[a]
and begged him, saying, 'Have patience with
me, and I will pay you all.'[b]
30 "And he would not, but went and threw
him into prison till he should pay the debt.
31 "So when his fellow servants saw what
had been done, they were very grieved, and
came and told their master all that had been
done.
32 "Then his master, after he had called him,
said to him, 'You wicked servant! I forgave you
all that debt because you begged me.
33 'Should you not also have had compassion
on your fellow servant, just as I had pity on
you?'
34 "And his master was angry, and delivered
him to the torturers until he should pay all that
was due to him.
35 "So My heavenly Father also will do to you
if each of you, from his heart, does not forgive
his brother his trespasses."[a]

Marriage and Divorce

19 Now it came to pass, when Jesus had fin-
ished these sayings, *that* He departed
from Galilee and came to the region of Judea
beyond the Jordan.
2 And great multitudes followed Him, and
He healed them there.
3 The Pharisees also came to Him, testing
Him, and saying to Him, "Is it lawful for a man
to divorce his wife for *just* any reason?"
4 And He answered and said to them, "Have
you not read that He who made[a] *them* at the
beginning *'made them male and female,'*[b]
5 "and said, *'For this reason a man shall
leave his father and mother and be joined to
his wife, and the two shall become one flesh'* ?[a]
6 "So then, they are no longer two but one
flesh. Therefore what God has joined together,
let not man separate."
7 They said to Him, "Why then did Moses
command to give a certificate of divorce, and
to put her away?"
8 He said to them, "Moses, because of the
hardness of your hearts, permitted you to di-
vorce your wives, but from the beginning it was
not so.
9 "And I say to you, whoever divorces his wife,
except for sexual immorality,[a] and marries an-
other, commits adultery; and whoever marries
her who is divorced commits adultery."
10 His disciples said to Him, "If such is the
case of the man with *his* wife, it is better not to
marry."

Jesus Teaches on Celibacy

11 But He said to them, "All cannot accept
this saying, but only *those* to whom it has been
given:
12 "For there are eunuchs who were born
thus from *their* mother's womb, and there are
eunuchs who were made eunuchs by men, and
there are eunuchs who have made themselves
eunuchs for the kingdom of heaven's sake. He
who is able to accept *it*, let him accept *it*."

Jesus Blesses Little Children

13 Then little children were brought to Him
that He might put *His* hands on them and pray,
but the disciples rebuked them.
14 But Jesus said, "Let the little children
come to Me, and do not forbid them; for of
such is the kingdom of heaven."
15 And He laid *His* hands on them and de-
parted from there.

Jesus Counsels the Rich Young Ruler

16 Now behold, one came and said to Him,
"Good[a] Teacher, what good thing shall I do that
I may have eternal life?"
17 So He said to him, "Why do you call Me
good?[a] No one *is* good but One, *that is*, God.[b]
But if you want to enter into life, keep the com-
mandments."
18 He said to Him, "Which ones?" Jesus said,
" *'You shall not murder,' 'You shall not commit
adultery,' 'You shall not steal,' 'You shall not
bear false witness,'*
19 *'Honor your father and your mother,'*[a] and,
'You shall love your neighbor as yourself.' "[b]
20 The young man said to Him, "All these
things I have kept from my youth.[a] What do I
still lack?"
21 Jesus said to him, "If you want to be per-
fect, go, sell what you have and give to the
poor, and you will have treasure in heaven; and
come, follow Me."
22 But when the young man heard that say-
ing, he went away sorrowful, for he had great
possessions.

With God All Things Are Possible

23 Then Jesus said to His disciples, "As-
suredly, I say to you that it is hard for a rich
man to enter the kingdom of heaven.
24 "And again I say to you, it is easier for a
camel to go through the eye of a needle than
for a rich man to enter the kingdom of God."
25 When His disciples heard *it*, they were
greatly astonished, saying, "Who then can be
saved?"
26 But Jesus looked at *them* and said to them,
"With men this is impossible, but with God all
things are possible."
27 Then Peter answered and said to Him,
"See, we have left all and followed You. There-
fore what shall we have?"
28 So Jesus said to them, "Assuredly I say to
you, that in the regeneration, when the Son of
Man sits on the throne of His glory, you who
have followed Me will also sit on twelve
thrones, judging the twelve tribes of Israel.
29 "And everyone who has left houses or
brothers or sisters or father or mother or wife[a]
or children or lands, for My name's sake, shall
receive a hundredfold, and inherit eternal life.
30 "But many *who are* first will be last, and
the last first.

The Parable of the Workers in the Vineyard

20 "For the kingdom of heaven is like a
landowner who went out early in the
morning to hire laborers for his vineyard.
2 "Now when he had agreed with the labor-

18:29 [a]NU-Text omits *at his feet.* [b]NU-Text and M-Text omit *all.* **18:35** [a]NU-Text omits *his trespasses.* **19:4** [a]NU-Text reads *created.* [b]Genesis 1:27; 5:2 **19:5** [a]Genesis 2:24 **19:9** [a]Or *fornication* **19:16** [a]NU-Text omits *Good.* **19:17** [a]NU-Text reads *Why do you ask Me about what is good?* [b]NU-Text reads *There is One who is good.* **19:19** [a]Exodus 20:12–16; Deuteronomy 5:16–20 [b]Leviticus 19:18 **19:20** [a]NU-Text omits *from my youth.* **19:29** [a]NU-Text omits *or wife.*

ers for a denarius a day, he sent them into his
vineyard.
3 "And he went out about the third hour and
saw others standing idle in the marketplace,
4 "and said to them, 'You also go into the
vineyard, and whatever is right I will give you.'
So they went.
5 "Again he went out about the sixth and the
ninth hour, and did likewise.
6 "And about the eleventh hour he went out
and found others standing idle,[a] and said to
them, 'Why have you been standing here idle
all day?'
7 "They said to him, 'Because no one hired
us.' He said to them, 'You also go into the vine-
yard, and whatever is right you will receive.'[a]
8 "So when evening had come, the owner of
the vineyard said to his steward, 'Call the la-
borers and give them *their* wages, beginning
with the last to the first.'
9 "And when those came who *were hired*
about the eleventh hour, they each received a
denarius.
10 "But when the first came, they supposed that
they would receive more; and they likewise
received each a denarius.
11 "And when they had received *it*, they com-
plained against the landowner,
12 "saying, 'These last *men* have worked *only*
one hour, and you made them equal to us who
have borne the burden and the heat of the day.'
13 "But he answered one of them and said,
'Friend, I am doing you no wrong. Did you not
agree with me for a denarius?
14 'Take *what is* yours and go your way. I wish
to give to this last man *the same* as to you.
15 'Is it not lawful for me to do what I wish
with my own things? Or is your eye evil be-
cause I am good?'
16 "So the last will be first, and the first last.
For many are called, but few chosen."[a]

Jesus a Third Time Predicts His Death and Resurrection

17 Now Jesus, going up to Jerusalem, took the
twelve disciples aside on the road and said to
them,
18 "Behold, we are going up to Jerusalem, and
the Son of Man will be betrayed to the chief
priests and to the scribes; and they will con-
demn Him to death,
19 "and deliver Him to the Gentiles to mock
and to scourge and to crucify. And the third
day He will rise again."

Greatness Is Serving

20 Then the mother of Zebedee's sons came
to Him with her sons, kneeling down and ask-
ing something from Him.
21 And He said to her, "What do you wish?"
She said to Him, "Grant that these two sons of
mine may sit, one on Your right hand and the
other on the left, in Your kingdom."
22 But Jesus answered and said, "You do not
know what you ask. Are you able to drink the
cup that I am about to drink, and be baptized
with the baptism that I am baptized with?"[a]
They said to Him, "We are able."
23 So He said to them, "You will indeed drink
My cup, and be baptized with the baptism that
I am baptized with;[a] but to sit on My right hand
and on My left is not Mine to give, but *it is for*
those for whom it is prepared by My Father."
24 And when the ten heard *it*, they were greatly
displeased with the two brothers.
25 But Jesus called them to *Himself* and said,
"You know that the rulers of the Gentiles lord
it over them, and those who are great exercise
authority over them.
26 "Yet it shall not be so among you; but who-
ever desires to become great among you, let him
be your servant.
27 "And whoever desires to be first among you,
let him be your slave—
28 "just as the Son of Man did not come to be
served, but to serve, and to give His life a ran-
som for many."

Two Blind Men Receive Their Sight

29 Now as they went out of Jericho, a great
multitude followed Him.
30 And behold, two blind men sitting by the
road, when they heard that Jesus was passing
by, cried out, saying, "Have mercy on us, O Lord,
Son of David!"
31 Then the multitude warned them that they
should be quiet; but they cried out all the more,
saying, "Have mercy on us, O Lord, Son of
David!"
32 So Jesus stood still and called them, and
said, "What do you want Me to do for you?"
33 They said to Him, "Lord, that our eyes may
be opened."
34 So Jesus had compassion and touched
their eyes. And immediately their eyes received
sight, and they followed Him.

The Triumphal Entry

21 Now when they drew near Jerusalem, and
came to Bethphage,[a] at the Mount of
Olives, then Jesus sent two disciples,
2 saying to them, "Go into the village oppo-
site you, and immediately you will find a don-
key tied, and a colt with her. Loose *them* and
bring *them* to Me.
3 "And if anyone says anything to you, you
shall say, 'The Lord has need of them,' and im-
mediately he will send them."
4 All[a] this was done that it might be fulfilled
which was spoken by the prophet, saying:

5 *"Tell the daughter of Zion,*
'Behold, your King is coming to you,
Lowly, and sitting on a donkey,
A colt, the foal of a donkey.'"[a]

6 So the disciples went and did as Jesus com-
manded them.
7 They brought the donkey and the colt, laid
their clothes on them, and set *Him*[a] on them.
8 And a very great multitude spread their
clothes on the road; others cut down branches
from the trees and spread *them* on the road.
9 Then the multitudes who went before and
those who followed cried out, saying:

"Hosanna to the Son of David!
'Blessed is He who comes in the name of
the LORD!'[a]
Hosanna in the highest!"

20:6 [a]NU-Text omits *idle*. **20:7** [a]NU-Text omits the last clause of this verse. **20:16** [a]NU-Text omits the last sentence of this verse. **20:22** [a]NU-Text omits *and be baptized with the baptism that I am baptized with*. **20:23** [a]NU-Text omits *and be baptized with the baptism that I am baptized with*. **21:1** [a]M-Text reads *Bethsphage*. **21:4** [a]NU-Text omits *All*. **21:5** [a]Zechariah 9:9 **21:7** [a]NU-Text reads *and He sat*. **21:9** [a]Psalm 118:26

10 And when He had come into Jerusalem,
all the city was moved, saying, "Who is this?"
11 So the multitudes said, "This is Jesus, the
prophet from Nazareth of Galilee."

Jesus Cleanses the Temple

12 Then Jesus went into the temple of God[a]
and drove out all those who bought and sold
in the temple, and overturned the tables of the
money changers and the seats of those who sold
doves.
13 And He said to them, "It is written, *'My
house shall be called a house of prayer,'*[a] but
you have made it a *'den of thieves.'*"[b]
14 Then *the* blind and *the* lame came to Him
in the temple, and He healed them.
15 But when the chief priests and scribes saw
the wonderful things that He did, and the chil-
dren crying out in the temple and saying, "Ho-
sanna to the Son of David!" they were indignant
16 and said to Him, "Do You hear what these
are saying?" And Jesus said to them, "Yes.
Have you never read,

*'Out of the mouth of babes and nursing
infants
You have perfected praise'?"*[a]

17 Then He left them and went out of the city
to Bethany, and He lodged there.

The Fig Tree Withered

18 Now in the morning, as He returned to the
city, He was hungry.
19 And seeing a fig tree by the road, He came
to it and found nothing on it but leaves, and
said to it, "Let no fruit grow on you ever again."
Immediately the fig tree withered away.

The Lesson of the Withered Fig Tree

20 And when the disciples saw *it,* they mar-
veled, saying, "How did the fig tree wither away
so soon?"
21 So Jesus answered and said to them, "As-
suredly, I say to you, if you have faith and do
not doubt, you will not only do what was done
to the fig tree, but also if you say to this moun-
tain, 'Be removed and be cast into the sea,' it will
be done.
22 "And whatever things you ask in prayer,
believing, you will receive."

Jesus' Authority Questioned

23 Now when He came into the temple, the
chief priests and the elders of the people con-
fronted Him as He was teaching, and said, "By
what authority are You doing these things?
And who gave You this authority?"
24 But Jesus answered and said to them, "I
also will ask you one thing, which if you tell
Me, I likewise will tell you by what authority I
do these things:
25 "The baptism of John—where was it from?
From heaven or from men?" And they rea-
soned among themselves, saying, "If we say,
'From heaven,' He will say to us, 'Why then did
you not believe him?'
26 "But if we say, 'From men,' we fear the
multitude, for all count John as a prophet."
27 So they answered Jesus and said, "We do
not know." And He said to them, "Neither will
I tell you by what authority I do these things.

The Parable of the Two Sons

28 "But what do you think? A man had two
sons, and he came to the first and said, 'Son,
go, work today in my vineyard.'
29 "He answered and said, 'I will not,' but
afterward he regretted it and went.
30 "Then he came to the second and said like-
wise. And he answered and said, 'I go, sir,' but
he did not go.
31 "Which of the two did the will of *his* fa-
ther?" They said to Him, "The first." Jesus said
to them, "Assuredly, I say to you that tax collec-
tors and harlots enter the kingdom of God be-
fore you.
32 "For John came to you in the way of righ-
teousness, and you did not believe him; but tax
collectors and harlots believed him; and when
you saw *it,* you did not afterward relent and
believe him.

The Parable of the Wicked Vinedressers

33 "Hear another parable: There was a cer-
tain landowner who planted a vineyard and set
a hedge around it, dug a winepress in it and
built a tower. And he leased it to vinedressers
and went into a far country.
34 "Now when vintage-time drew near, he sent
his servants to the vinedressers, that they
might receive its fruit.
35 "And the vinedressers took his servants,
beat one, killed one, and stoned another.
36 "Again he sent other servants, more than
the first, and they did likewise to them.
37 "Then last of all he sent his son to them,
saying, 'They will respect my son.'
38 "But when the vinedressers saw the son,
they said among themselves, 'This is the heir.
Come, let us kill him and seize his inheritance.'
39 "So they took him and cast *him* out of the
vineyard and killed *him.*
40 "Therefore, when the owner of the vineyard
comes, what will he do to those vinedressers?"
41 They said to Him, "He will destroy those
wicked men miserably, and lease *his* vineyard
to other vinedressers who will render to him
the fruits in their seasons."
42 Jesus said to them, "Have you never read
in the Scriptures:

*'The stone which the builders rejected
Has become the chief cornerstone.
This was the LORD's doing,
And it is marvelous in our eyes'?*[a]

43 "Therefore I say to you, the kingdom of God
will be taken from you and given to a nation
bearing the fruits of it.
44 "And whoever falls on this stone will be
broken; but on whomever it falls, it will grind
him to powder."
45 Now when the chief priests and Pharisees
heard His parables, they perceived that He was
speaking of them.
46 But when they sought to lay hands on Him,
they feared the multitudes, because they took
Him for a prophet.

The Parable of the Wedding Feast

22 And Jesus answered and spoke to them
again by parables and said:
2 "The kingdom of heaven is like a certain
king who arranged a marriage for his son,
3 "and sent out his servants to call those who

21:12 [a]NU-Text omits *of God.* **21:13** [a]Isaiah 56:7 [b]Jeremiah 7:11 **21:16** [a]Psalm 8:2 **21:42** [a]Psalm 118:22, 23

were invited to the wedding; and they were not
willing to come.
4 "Again, he sent out other servants, saying,
'Tell those who are invited, "See, I have pre-
pared my dinner; my oxen and fatted cattle *are*
killed, and all things *are* ready. Come to the
wedding." '
5 "But they made light of it and went their
ways, one to his own farm, another to his busi-
ness.
6 "And the rest seized his servants, treated
them spitefully, and killed *them*.
7 "But when the king heard *about it*, he was
furious. And he sent out his armies, destroyed
those murderers, and burned up their city.
8 "Then he said to his servants, 'The wed-
ding is ready, but those who were invited were
not worthy.
9 'Therefore go into the highways, and as
many as you find, invite to the wedding.'
10 "So those servants went out into the high-
ways and gathered together all whom they
found, both bad and good. And the wedding
hall was filled with guests.
11 "But when the king came in to see the
guests, he saw a man there who did not have
on a wedding garment.
12 "So he said to him, 'Friend, how did you
come in here without a wedding garment?'
And he was speechless.
13 "Then the king said to the servants, 'Bind
him hand and foot, take him away, and[a] cast *him*
into outer darkness; there will be weeping and
gnashing of teeth.'
14 "For many are called, but few *are* chosen."

The Pharisees: Is It Lawful to Pay Taxes to Caesar?

15 Then the Pharisees went and plotted how
they might entangle Him in *His* talk.
16 And they sent to Him their disciples with
the Herodians, saying, "Teacher, we know that
You are true, and teach the way of God in truth;
nor do You care about anyone, for You do not
regard the person of men.
17 "Tell us, therefore, what do You think? Is
it lawful to pay taxes to Caesar, or not?"
18 But Jesus perceived their wickedness, and
said, "Why do you test Me, *you* hypocrites?
19 "Show Me the tax money." So they brought
Him a denarius.
20 And He said to them, "Whose image and
inscription *is* this?"
21 They said to Him, "Caesar's." And He said
to them, "Render therefore to Caesar the
things that are Caesar's, and to God the things
that are God's."
22 When they had heard *these words*, they
marveled, and left Him and went their way.

The Sadducees: What About the Resurrection?

23 The same day the Sadducees, who say there
is no resurrection, came to Him and asked Him,
24 saying: "Teacher, Moses said that if a man
dies, having no children, his brother shall marry
his wife and raise up offspring for his brother.
25 "Now there were with us seven brothers.
The first died after he had married, and having
no offspring, left his wife to his brother.
26 "Likewise the second also, and the third,
even to the seventh.
27 "Last of all the woman died also.
28 "Therefore, in the resurrection, whose wife
of the seven will she be? For they all had her."
29 Jesus answered and said to them, "You are
mistaken, not knowing the Scriptures nor the
power of God.
30 "For in the resurrection they neither marry
nor are given in marriage, but are like angels
of God[a] in heaven.
31 "But concerning the resurrection of the
dead, have you not read what was spoken to
you by God, saying,
32 *'I am the God of Abraham, the God of
Isaac, and the God of Jacob'*?[a] God is not the
God of the dead, but of the living."
33 And when the multitudes heard *this*, they
were astonished at His teaching.

The Scribes: Which Is the First Commandment of All?

34 But when the Pharisees heard that He had
silenced the Sadducees, they gathered together.
35 Then one of them, a lawyer, asked *Him a
question*, testing Him, and saying,
36 "Teacher, which *is* the great commandment
in the law?"
37 Jesus said to him, " *'You shall love the
LORD your God with all your heart, with all your
soul, and with all your mind.'*[a]
38 "This is *the* first and great commandment.
39 "And *the* second *is* like it: *'You shall love
your neighbor as yourself.'*[a]
40 "On these two commandments hang all
the Law and the Prophets."

Jesus: How Can David Call His Descendant Lord?

41 While the Pharisees were gathered together,
Jesus asked them,
42 saying, "What do you think about the
Christ? Whose Son is He?" They said to Him,
"*The Son* of David."
43 He said to them, "How then does David in
the Spirit call Him *'Lord,'* saying:
44 *'The LORD said to my Lord,
"Sit at My right hand,
Till I make Your enemies Your
footstool" '*?[a]
45 "If David then calls Him *'Lord,'* how is He
his Son?"
46 And no one was able to answer Him a word,
nor from that day on did anyone dare question
Him anymore.

Woe to the Scribes and Pharisees

23 Then Jesus spoke to the multitudes and
to His disciples,
2 saying: "The scribes and the Pharisees sit
in Moses' seat.
3 "Therefore whatever they tell you to ob-
serve,[a] *that* observe and do, but do not do ac-
cording to their works; for they say, and do not
do.
4 "For they bind heavy burdens, hard to bear,
and lay *them* on men's shoulders; but they
themselves will not move them with one of their
fingers.
5 "But all their works they do to be seen by
men. They make their phylacteries broad and
enlarge the borders of their garments.

22:13 [a]NU-Text omits *take him away, and.* **22:30** [a]NU-Text omits *of God.* **22:32** [a]Exodus 3:6, 15
22:37 [a]Deuteronomy 6:5 **22:39** [a]Leviticus 19:18 **22:44** [a]Psalm 110:1 **23:3** [a]NU-Text omits *to observe.*

6 "They love the best places at feasts, the
best seats in the synagogues,
7 "greetings in the marketplaces, and to be
called by men, 'Rabbi, Rabbi.'
8 "But you, do not be called 'Rabbi'; for One
is your Teacher, the Christ,[a] and you are all
brethren.
9 "Do not call anyone on earth your father;
for One is your Father, He who is in heaven.
10 "And do not be called teachers; for One is
your Teacher, the Christ.
11 "But he who is greatest among you shall
be your servant.
12 "And whoever exalts himself will be hum-
bled, and he who humbles himself will be ex-
alted.
13 "But woe to you, scribes and Pharisees, hyp-
ocrites! For you shut up the kingdom of heaven
against men; for you neither go in *yourselves*,
nor do you allow those who are entering to go
in.
14 "Woe to you, scribes and Pharisees, hypo-
crites! For you devour widows' houses, and for
a pretense make long prayers. Therefore you
will receive greater condemnation.[a]
15 "Woe to you, scribes and Pharisees, hypo-
crites! For you travel land and sea to win one
proselyte, and when he is won, you make him
twice as much a son of hell as yourselves.
16 "Woe to you, blind guides, who say, 'Who-
ever swears by the temple, it is nothing; but
whoever swears by the gold of the temple, he
is obliged *to perform it*.'
17 "Fools and blind! For which is greater, the
gold or the temple that sanctifies[a] the gold?
18 "And, 'Whoever swears by the altar, it is
nothing; but whoever swears by the gift that is
on it, he is obliged *to perform it*.'
19 "Fools and blind! For which is greater, the
gift or the altar that sanctifies the gift?
20 "Therefore he who swears by the altar,
swears by it and by all things on it.
21 "He who swears by the temple, swears by
it and by Him who dwells[a] in it.
22 "And he who swears by heaven, swears by
the throne of God and by Him who sits on it.
23 "Woe to you, scribes and Pharisees, hypo-
crites! For you pay tithe of mint and anise and
cummin, and have neglected the weightier
matters of the law: justice and mercy and faith.
These you ought to have done, without leaving
the others undone.
24 "Blind guides, who strain out a gnat and
swallow a camel!
25 "Woe to you, scribes and Pharisees, hypo-
crites! For you cleanse the outside of the cup
and dish, but inside they are full of extortion
and self-indulgence.[a]
26 "Blind Pharisee, first cleanse the inside of
the cup and dish, that the outside of them may
be clean also.
27 "Woe to you, scribes and Pharisees, hypo-
crites! For you are like whitewashed tombs
which indeed appear beautiful outwardly, but
inside are full of dead *men's* bones and all un-
cleanness.
28 "Even so you also outwardly appear righ-
teous to men, but inside you are full of hypoc-
risy and lawlessness.
29 "Woe to you, scribes and Pharisees, hypo-
crites! Because you build the tombs of the
prophets and adorn the monuments of the
righteous,
30 "and say, 'If we had lived in the days of
our fathers, we would not have been partakers
with them in the blood of the prophets.'
31 "Therefore you are witnesses against your-
selves that you are sons of those who murdered
the prophets.
32 "Fill up, then, the measure of your fathers'
guilt.
33 "Serpents, brood of vipers! How can you
escape the condemnation of hell?
34 "Therefore, indeed, I send you prophets,
wise men, and scribes: *some* of them you will kill
and crucify, and *some* of them you will scourge
in your synagogues and persecute from city to
city,
35 "that on you may come all the righteous
blood shed on the earth, from the blood of righ-
teous Abel to the blood of Zechariah, son of
Berechiah, whom you murdered between the
temple and the altar.
36 "Assuredly, I say to you, all these things
will come upon this generation.

Jesus Laments over Jerusalem

37 "O Jerusalem, Jerusalem, the one who kills
the prophets and stones those who are sent to
her! How often I wanted to gather your chil-
dren together, as a hen gathers her chicks un-
der *her* wings, but you were not willing!
38 "See! Your house is left to you desolate;
39 "for I say to you, you shall see Me no more
till you say, *'Blessed is He who comes in the
name of the LORD!'* "[a]

Jesus Predicts the Destruction of the Temple

24 Then Jesus went out and departed from
the temple, and His disciples came up to
show Him the buildings of the temple.
2 And Jesus said to them, "Do you not see
all these things? Assuredly, I say to you, not
one stone shall be left here upon another, that
shall not be thrown down."

The Signs of the Times and the End of the Age

3 Now as He sat on the Mount of Olives, the
disciples came to Him privately, saying, "Tell us,
when will these things be? And what *will be*
the sign of Your coming, and of the end of the
age?"
4 And Jesus answered and said to them:
"Take heed that no one deceives you.
5 "For many will come in My name, saying,
'I am the Christ,' and will deceive many.
6 "And you will hear of wars and rumors of
wars. See that you are not troubled; for all[a]
these things must come to pass, but the end is
not yet.
7 "For nation will rise against nation, and
kingdom against kingdom. And there will be
famines, pestilences,[a] and earthquakes in vari-
ous places.
8 "All these *are* the beginning of sorrows.
9 "Then they will deliver you up to tribula-
tion and kill you, and you will be hated by all
nations for My name's sake.
10 "And then many will be offended, will be-
tray one another, and will hate one another.

23:8 [a]NU-Text omits *the Christ*. **23:14** [a]NU-Text omits this verse. **23:17** [a]NU-Text reads *sanctified*. **23:21** [a]M-Text reads *dwelt*. **23:25** [a]M-Text reads *unrighteousness*. **23:39** [a]Psalm 118:26 **24:6** [a]NU-Text omits *all*. **24:7** [a]NU-Text omits *pestilences*.

11 "Then many false prophets will rise up and
deceive many.
12 "And because lawlessness will abound, the
love of many will grow cold.
13 "But he who endures to the end shall be
saved.
14 "And this gospel of the kingdom will be
preached in all the world as a witness to all the
nations, and then the end will come.

The Great Tribulation

15 "Therefore when you see the *'abomination
of desolation,'*[a] spoken of by Daniel the
prophet, standing in the holy place" (whoever
reads, let him understand),
16 "then let those who are in Judea flee to the
mountains.
17 "Let him who is on the housetop not go
down to take anything out of his house.
18 "And let him who is in the field not go back
to get his clothes.
19 "But woe to those who are pregnant and
to those who are nursing babies in those days!
20 "And pray that your flight may not be in
winter or on the Sabbath.
21 "For then there will be great tribulation,
such as has not been since the beginning of the
world until this time, no, nor ever shall be.
22 "And unless those days were shortened,
no flesh would be saved; but for the elect's sake
those days will be shortened.
23 "Then if anyone says to you, 'Look, here *is*
the Christ!' or 'There!' do not believe *it*.
24 "For false christs and false prophets will
rise and show great signs and wonders to deceive, if possible, even the elect.
25 "See, I have told you beforehand.
26 "Therefore if they say to you, 'Look, He is
in the desert!' do not go out; *or* 'Look, *He is* in
the inner rooms!' do not believe *it*.
27 "For as the lightning comes from the east
and flashes to the west, so also will the coming
of the Son of Man be.
28 "For wherever the carcass is, there the eagles will be gathered together.

The Coming of the Son of Man

29 "Immediately after the tribulation of those
days the sun will be darkened, and the moon
will not give its light; the stars will fall from
heaven, and the powers of the heavens will be
shaken.
30 "Then the sign of the Son of Man will appear in heaven, and then all the tribes of the
earth will mourn, and they will see the Son
of Man coming on the clouds of heaven with
power and great glory.
31 "And He will send His angels with a great
sound of a trumpet, and they will gather together His elect from the four winds, from one
end of heaven to the other.

The Parable of the Fig Tree

32 "Now learn this parable from the fig tree:
When its branch has already become tender
and puts forth leaves, you know that summer
is near.
33 "So you also, when you see all these things,
know that it[a] is near—at the doors!
34 "Assuredly, I say to you, this generation will
by no means pass away till all these things take
place.
35 "Heaven and earth will pass away, but My
words will by no means pass away.

No One Knows the Day or Hour

36 "But of that day and hour no one knows,
not even the angels of heaven,[a] but My Father
only.
37 "But as the days of Noah *were*, so also will
the coming of the Son of Man be.
38 "For as in the days before the flood, they
were eating and drinking, marrying and giving
in marriage, until the day that Noah entered
the ark,
39 "and did not know until the flood came and
took them all away, so also will the coming of
the Son of Man be.
40 "Then two *men* will be in the field: one will
be taken and the other left.
41 "Two *women will be* grinding at the mill:
one will be taken and the other left.
42 "Watch therefore, for you do not know
what hour[a] your Lord is coming.
43 "But know this, that if the master of the
house had known what hour the thief would
come, he would have watched and not allowed
his house to be broken into.
44 "Therefore you also be ready, for the Son
of Man is coming at an hour you do not expect.

The Faithful Servant and the Evil Servant

45 "Who then is a faithful and wise servant,
whom his master made ruler over his household, to give them food in due season?
46 "Blessed *is* that servant whom his master,
when he comes, will find so doing.
47 "Assuredly, I say to you that he will make
him ruler over all his goods.
48 "But if that evil servant says in his heart,
'My master is delaying his coming,'[a]
49 "and begins to beat *his* fellow servants,
and to eat and drink with the drunkards,
50 "the master of that servant will come on a
day when he is not looking for *him* and at an
hour that he is not aware of,
51 "and will cut him in two and appoint *him*
his portion with the hypocrites. There shall be
weeping and gnashing of teeth.

The Parable of the Wise and Foolish Virgins

25 "Then the kingdom of heaven shall be
likened to ten virgins who took their
lamps and went out to meet the bridegroom.
2 "Now five of them were wise, and five
were foolish.
3 "Those who *were* foolish took their lamps
and took no oil with them,
4 "but the wise took oil in their vessels with
their lamps.
5 "But while the bridegroom was delayed,
they all slumbered and slept.
6 "And at midnight a cry was *heard:* 'Behold,
the bridegroom is coming;[a] go out to meet him!'
7 "Then all those virgins arose and trimmed
their lamps.
8 "And the foolish said to the wise, 'Give us
some of your oil, for our lamps are going out.'
9 "But the wise answered, saying, '*No*, lest
there should not be enough for us and you; but
go rather to those who sell, and buy for yourselves.'

24:15 [a]Daniel 11:31; 12:11 **24:33** [a]Or *He* **24:36** [a]NU-Text adds *nor the Son.* **24:42** [a]NU-Text reads *day.*
24:48 [a]NU-Text omits *his coming.* **25:6** [a]NU-Text omits *is coming.*

10 "And while they went to buy, the bridegroom came, and those who were ready went in with him to the wedding; and the door was shut.

11 "Afterward the other virgins came also, saying, 'Lord, Lord, open to us!'

12 "But he answered and said, 'Assuredly, I say to you, I do not know you.'

13 "Watch therefore, for you know neither the day nor the hour[a] in which the Son of Man is coming.

The Parable of the Talents

14 "For *the kingdom of heaven is* like a man traveling to a far country, *who* called his own servants and delivered his goods to them.

15 "And to one he gave five talents, to another two, and to another one, to each according to his own ability; and immediately he went on a journey.

16 "Then he who had received the five talents went and traded with them, and made another five talents.

17 "And likewise he who *had received* two gained two more also.

18 "But he who had received one went and dug in the ground, and hid his lord's money.

19 "After a long time the lord of those servants came and settled accounts with them.

20 "So he who had received five talents came and brought five other talents, saying, 'Lord, you delivered to me five talents; look, I have gained five more talents besides them.'

21 "His lord said to him, 'Well *done,* good and faithful servant; you were faithful over a few things, I will make you ruler over many things. Enter into the joy of your lord.'

22 "He also who had received two talents came and said, 'Lord, you delivered to me two talents; look, I have gained two more talents besides them.'

23 "His lord said to him, 'Well *done,* good and faithful servant; you have been faithful over a few things, I will make you ruler over many things. Enter into the joy of your lord.'

24 "Then he who had received the one talent came and said, 'Lord, I knew you to be a hard man, reaping where you have not sown, and gathering where you have not scattered seed.

25 'And I was afraid, and went and hid your talent in the ground. Look, *there* you have *what is* yours.'

26 "But his lord answered and said to him, 'You wicked and lazy servant, you knew that I reap where I have not sown, and gather where I have not scattered seed.

27 'So you ought to have deposited my money with the bankers, and at my coming I would have received back my own with interest.

28 'Therefore take the talent from him, and give *it* to him who has ten talents.

29 'For to everyone who has, more will be given, and he will have abundance; but from him who does not have, even what he has will be taken away.

30 'And cast the unprofitable servant into the outer darkness. There will be weeping and gnashing of teeth.'

The Son of Man Will Judge the Nations

31 "When the Son of Man comes in His glory, and all the holy[a] angels with Him, then He will sit on the throne of His glory.

32 "All the nations will be gathered before Him, and He will separate them one from another, as a shepherd divides *his* sheep from the goats.

33 "And He will set the sheep on His right hand, but the goats on the left.

34 "Then the King will say to those on His right hand, 'Come, you blessed of My Father, inherit the kingdom prepared for you from the foundation of the world:

35 'for I was hungry and you gave Me food; I was thirsty and you gave Me drink; I was a stranger and you took Me in;

36 'I *was* naked and you clothed Me; I was sick and you visited Me; I was in prison and you came to Me.'

37 "Then the righteous will answer Him, saying, 'Lord, when did we see You hungry and feed *You,* or thirsty and give *You* drink?

38 'When did we see You a stranger and take *You* in, or naked and clothe *You?*

39 'Or when did we see You sick, or in prison, and come to You?'

40 "And the King will answer and say to them, 'Assuredly, I say to you, inasmuch as you did *it* to one of the least of these My brethren, you did *it* to Me.'

41 "Then He will also say to those on the left hand, 'Depart from Me, you cursed, into the everlasting fire prepared for the devil and his angels:

42 'for I was hungry and you gave Me no food; I was thirsty and you gave Me no drink;

43 'I was a stranger and you did not take Me in, naked and you did not clothe Me, sick and in prison and you did not visit Me.'

44 "Then they also will answer Him,[a] saying, 'Lord, when did we see You hungry or thirsty or a stranger or naked or sick or in prison, and did not minister to You?'

45 "Then He will answer them, saying, 'Assuredly, I say to you, inasmuch as you did not do *it* to one of the least of these, you did not do *it* to Me.'

46 "And these will go away into everlasting punishment, but the righteous into eternal life."

The Plot to Kill Jesus

26 Now it came to pass, when Jesus had finished all these sayings, *that* He said to His disciples,

2 "You know that after two days is the Passover, and the Son of Man will be delivered up to be crucified."

3 Then the chief priests, the scribes,[a] and the elders of the people assembled at the palace of the high priest, who was called Caiaphas,

4 and plotted to take Jesus by trickery and kill *Him.*

5 But they said, "Not during the feast, lest there be an uproar among the people."

The Anointing at Bethany

6 And when Jesus was in Bethany at the house of Simon the leper,

7 a woman came to Him having an alabaster flask of very costly fragrant oil, and she poured *it* on His head as He sat *at the table.*

8 But when His disciples saw *it,* they were indignant, saying, "Why this waste?

9 "For this fragrant oil might have been sold for much and given to *the* poor."

10 But when Jesus was aware of *it,* He said to

25:13 [a]NU-Text omits the rest of this verse. **25:31** [a]NU-Text omits *holy.* **25:44** [a]NU-Text and M-Text omit *Him.*
26:3 [a]NU-Text omits *the scribes.*

them, "Why do you trouble the woman? For she has done a good work for Me.
11 "For you have the poor with you always, but Me you do not have always.
12 "For in pouring this fragrant oil on My body, she did *it* for My burial.
13 "Assuredly, I say to you, wherever this gospel is preached in the whole world, what this woman has done will also be told as a memorial to her."

Judas Agrees to Betray Jesus

14 Then one of the twelve, called Judas Iscariot, went to the chief priests
15 and said, "What are you willing to give me if I deliver Him to you?" And they counted out to him thirty pieces of silver.
16 So from that time he sought opportunity to betray Him.

Jesus Celebrates Passover with His Disciples

17 Now on the first *day of the Feast* of Unleavened Bread the disciples came to Jesus, saying to Him, "Where do You want us to prepare for You to eat the Passover?"
18 And He said, "Go into the city to a certain man, and say to him, 'The Teacher says, "My time is at hand; I will keep the Passover at your house with My disciples." ' "
19 So the disciples did as Jesus had directed them; and they prepared the Passover.
20 When evening had come, He sat down with the twelve.
21 Now as they were eating, He said, "Assuredly, I say to you, one of you will betray Me."
22 And they were exceedingly sorrowful, and each of them began to say to Him, "Lord, is it I?"
23 He answered and said, "He who dipped *his* hand with Me in the dish will betray Me.
24 "The Son of Man indeed goes just as it is written of Him, but woe to that man by whom the Son of Man is betrayed! It would have been good for that man if he had not been born."
25 Then Judas, who was betraying Him, answered and said, "Rabbi, is it I?" He said to him, "You have said it."

Jesus Institutes the Lord's Supper

26 And as they were eating, Jesus took bread, blessed[a] and broke *it*, and gave *it* to the disciples and said, "Take, eat; this is My body."
27 Then He took the cup, and gave thanks, and gave *it* to them, saying, "Drink from it, all of you.
28 "For this is My blood of the new[a] covenant, which is shed for many for the remission of sins.
29 "But I say to you, I will not drink of this fruit of the vine from now on until that day when I drink it new with you in My Father's kingdom."
30 And when they had sung a hymn, they went out to the Mount of Olives.

Jesus Predicts Peter's Denial

31 Then Jesus said to them, "All of you will be made to stumble because of Me this night, for it is written:

> *'I will strike the Shepherd,*
> *And the sheep of the flock will be*
> *scattered.'*[a]

32 "But after I have been raised, I will go before you to Galilee."
33 Peter answered and said to Him, "Even if all are made to stumble because of You, I will never be made to stumble."
34 Jesus said to him, "Assuredly, I say to you that this night, before the rooster crows, you will deny Me three times."
35 Peter said to Him, "Even if I have to die with You, I will not deny You!" And so said all the disciples.

The Prayer in the Garden

36 Then Jesus came with them to a place called Gethsemane, and said to the disciples, "Sit here while I go and pray over there."
37 And He took with Him Peter and the two sons of Zebedee, and He began to be sorrowful and deeply distressed.
38 Then He said to them, "My soul is exceedingly sorrowful, even to death. Stay here and watch with Me."
39 He went a little farther and fell on His face, and prayed, saying, "O My Father, if it is possible, let this cup pass from Me; nevertheless, not as I will, but as You *will*."
40 Then He came to the disciples and found them sleeping, and said to Peter, "What! Could you not watch with Me one hour?
41 "Watch and pray, lest you enter into temptation. The spirit indeed *is* willing, but the flesh *is* weak."
42 Again, a second time, He went away and prayed, saying, "O My Father, if this cup cannot pass away from Me unless[a] I drink it, Your will be done."
43 And He came and found them asleep again, for their eyes were heavy.
44 So He left them, went away again, and prayed the third time, saying the same words.
45 Then He came to His disciples and said to them, "Are *you* still sleeping and resting? Behold, the hour is at hand, and the Son of Man is being betrayed into the hands of sinners.
46 "Rise, let us be going. See, My betrayer is at hand."

Betrayal and Arrest in Gethsemane

47 And while He was still speaking, behold, Judas, one of the twelve, with a great multitude with swords and clubs, came from the chief priests and elders of the people.
48 Now His betrayer had given them a sign, saying, "Whomever I kiss, He is the One; seize Him."
49 Immediately he went up to Jesus and said, "Greetings, Rabbi!" and kissed Him.
50 But Jesus said to him, "Friend, why have you come?" Then they came and laid hands on Jesus and took Him.
51 And suddenly, one of those *who were* with Jesus stretched out *his* hand and drew his sword, struck the servant of the high priest, and cut off his ear.
52 But Jesus said to him, "Put your sword in its place, for all who take the sword will perish[a] by the sword.
53 "Or do you think that I cannot now pray to My Father, and He will provide Me with more than twelve legions of angels?
54 "How then could the Scriptures be fulfilled, that it must happen thus?"
55 In that hour Jesus said to the multitudes, "Have you come out, as against a robber, with swords and clubs to take Me? I sat daily with you,

26:26 [a]M-Text reads *gave thanks for.* **26:28** [a]NU-Text omits *new.* **26:31** [a]Zechariah 13:7 **26:42** [a]NU-Text reads *if this may not pass away unless.* **26:52** [a]M-Text reads *die.*

teaching in the temple, and you did not seize Me.
56 "But all this was done that the Scriptures of the prophets might be fulfilled." Then all the disciples forsook Him and fled.

Jesus Faces the Sanhedrin

57 And those who had laid hold of Jesus led *Him* away to Caiaphas the high priest, where the scribes and the elders were assembled.
58 But Peter followed Him at a distance to the high priest's courtyard. And he went in and sat with the servants to see the end.
59 Now the chief priests, the elders,[a] and all the council sought false testimony against Jesus to put Him to death,
60 but found none. Even though many false witnesses came forward, they found none.[a] But at last two false witnesses[b] came forward
61 and said, "This *fellow* said, 'I am able to destroy the temple of God and to build it in three days.' "
62 And the high priest arose and said to Him, "Do You answer nothing? What *is it* these men testify against You?"
63 But Jesus kept silent. And the high priest answered and said to Him, "I put You under oath by the living God: Tell us if You are the Christ, the Son of God!"
64 Jesus said to him, "*It is as* you said. Nevertheless, I say to you, hereafter you will see the Son of Man sitting at the right hand of the Power, and coming on the clouds of heaven."
65 Then the high priest tore his clothes, saying, "He has spoken blasphemy! What further need do we have of witnesses? Look, now you have heard His blasphemy!
66 "What do you think?" They answered and said, "He is deserving of death."
67 Then they spat in His face and beat Him; and others struck *Him* with the palms of their hands,
68 saying, "Prophesy to us, Christ! Who is the one who struck You?"

Peter Denies Jesus, and Weeps Bitterly

69 Now Peter sat outside in the courtyard. And a servant girl came to him, saying, "You also were with Jesus of Galilee."
70 But he denied it before *them* all, saying, "I do not know what you are saying."
71 And when he had gone out to the gateway, another *girl* saw him and said to those *who were* there, "This *fellow* also was with Jesus of Nazareth."
72 But again he denied with an oath, "I do not know the Man!"
73 And a little later those who stood by came up and said to Peter, "Surely you also are *one* of them, for your speech betrays you."
74 Then he began to curse and swear, *saying*, "I do not know the Man!" Immediately a rooster crowed.
75 And Peter remembered the word of Jesus who had said to him, "Before the rooster crows, you will deny Me three times." So he went out and wept bitterly.

Jesus Handed Over to Pontius Pilate

27 When morning came, all the chief priests and elders of the people plotted against Jesus to put Him to death.
2 And when they had bound Him, they led Him away and delivered Him to Pontius[a] Pilate the governor.

Judas Hangs Himself

3 Then Judas, His betrayer, seeing that He had been condemned, was remorseful and brought back the thirty pieces of silver to the chief priests and elders,
4 saying, "I have sinned by betraying innocent blood." And they said, "What *is that* to us? You see *to it!*"
5 Then he threw down the pieces of silver in the temple and departed, and went and hanged himself.
6 But the chief priests took the silver pieces and said, "It is not lawful to put them into the treasury, because they are the price of blood."
7 And they consulted together and bought with them the potter's field, to bury strangers in.
8 Therefore that field has been called the Field of Blood to this day.
9 Then was fulfilled what was spoken by Jeremiah the prophet, saying, *"And they took the thirty pieces of silver, the value of Him who was priced,* whom they of the children of Israel priced,
10 *"and gave them for the potter's field, as the LORD directed me."*[a]

Jesus Faces Pilate

11 Now Jesus stood before the governor. And the governor asked Him, saying, "Are You the King of the Jews?" Jesus said to him, "*It is as* you say."
12 And while He was being accused by the chief priests and elders, He answered nothing.
13 Then Pilate said to Him, "Do You not hear how many things they testify against You?"
14 But He answered him not one word, so that the governor marveled greatly.

Taking the Place of Barabbas

15 Now at the feast the governor was accustomed to releasing to the multitude one prisoner whom they wished.
16 And at that time they had a notorious prisoner called Barabbas.[a]
17 Therefore, when they had gathered together, Pilate said to them, "Whom do you want me to release to you? Barabbas, or Jesus who is called Christ?"
18 For he knew that they had handed Him over because of envy.
19 While he was sitting on the judgment seat, his wife sent to him, saying, "Have nothing to do with that just Man, for I have suffered many things today in a dream because of Him."
20 But the chief priests and elders persuaded the multitudes that they should ask for Barabbas and destroy Jesus.
21 The governor answered and said to them, "Which of the two do you want me to release to you?" They said, "Barabbas!"
22 Pilate said to them, "What then shall I do

26:59 [a]NU-Text omits *the elders.* **26:60** [a]NU-Text puts a comma after *but found none,* does not capitalize *Even,* and omits *they found none.* [b]NU-Text omits *false witnesses.* **27:2** [a]NU-Text omits *Pontius.* **27:10** [a]Jeremiah 32:6–9 **27:16** [a]NU-Text reads *Jesus Barabbas.*

with Jesus who is called Christ?" *They* all said
to him, "Let Him be crucified!"
23 Then the governor said, "Why, what evil has
He done?" But they cried out all the more, say-
ing, "Let Him be crucified!"
24 When Pilate saw that he could not prevail
at all, but rather *that* a tumult was rising, he
took water and washed *his* hands before the
multitude, saying, "I am innocent of the blood
of this just Person.[a] You see *to it*."
25 And all the people answered and said, "His
blood *be* on us and on our children."
26 Then he released Barabbas to them; and
when he had scourged Jesus, he delivered *Him*
to be crucified.

The Soldiers Mock Jesus

27 Then the soldiers of the governor took Jesus
into the Praetorium and gathered the whole gar-
rison around Him.
28 And they stripped Him and put a scarlet robe
on Him.
29 When they had twisted a crown of thorns,
they put *it* on His head, and a reed in His right
hand. And they bowed the knee before Him
and mocked Him, saying, "Hail, King of the
Jews!"
30 Then they spat on Him, and took the reed
and struck Him on the head.
31 And when they had mocked Him, they
took the robe off Him, put His *own* clothes on
Him, and led Him away to be crucified.

The King on a Cross

32 Now as they came out, they found a man
of Cyrene, Simon by name. Him they com-
pelled to bear His cross.
33 And when they had come to a place called
Golgotha, that is to say, Place of a Skull,
34 they gave Him sour[a] wine mingled with
gall to drink. But when He had tasted *it*, He
would not drink.
35 Then they crucified Him, and divided His
garments, casting lots,[a] that it might be fulfilled
which was spoken by the prophet:

"They divided My garments among them,
And for My clothing they cast lots."[b]

36 Sitting down, they kept watch over Him
there.
37 And they put up over His head the accusa-
tion written against Him:

THIS IS JESUS THE KING OF THE JEWS.

38 Then two robbers were crucified with Him,
one on the right and another on the left.
39 And those who passed by blasphemed Him,
wagging their heads
40 and saying, "You who destroy the temple
and build *it* in three days, save Yourself! If You
are the Son of God, come down from the cross."
41 Likewise the chief priests also, mocking with
the scribes and elders,[a] said,
42 "He saved others; Himself He cannot save.
If He is the King of Israel,[a] let Him now come
down from the cross, and we will believe Him.[b]
43 "He trusted in God; let Him deliver Him
now if He will have Him; for He said, 'I am the
Son of God.'"
44 Even the robbers who were crucified with
Him reviled Him with the same thing.

Jesus Dies on the Cross

45 Now from the sixth hour until the ninth hour
there was darkness over all the land.
46 And about the ninth hour Jesus cried out
with a loud voice, saying, "Eli, Eli, lama sa-
bachthani?" that is, *"My God, My God, why
have You forsaken Me?"*[a]
47 Some of those who stood there, when they
heard *that*, said, "This Man is calling for Elijah!"
48 Immediately one of them ran and took a
sponge, filled *it* with sour wine and put *it* on a
reed, and offered it to Him to drink.
49 The rest said, "Let Him alone; let us see if
Elijah will come to save Him."
50 And Jesus cried out again with a loud voice,
and yielded up His spirit.
51 Then, behold, the veil of the temple was torn
in two from top to bottom; and the earth quaked,
and the rocks were split,
52 and the graves were opened; and many bod-
ies of the saints who had fallen asleep were
raised;
53 and coming out of the graves after His res-
urrection, they went into the holy city and ap-
peared to many.
54 So when the centurion and those with him,
who were guarding Jesus, saw the earthquake
and the things that had happened, they feared
greatly, saying, "Truly this was the Son of God!"
55 And many women who followed Jesus from
Galilee, ministering to Him, were there look-
ing on from afar,
56 among whom were Mary Magdalene, Mary
the mother of James and Joses,[a] and the mother
of Zebedee's sons.

Jesus Buried in Joseph's Tomb

57 Now when evening had come, there came
a rich man from Arimathea, named Joseph, who
himself had also become a disciple of Jesus.
58 This man went to Pilate and asked for the
body of Jesus. Then Pilate commanded the body
to be given to him.
59 When Joseph had taken the body, he
wrapped it in a clean linen cloth,
60 and laid it in his new tomb which he had
hewn out of the rock; and he rolled a large
stone against the door of the tomb, and de-
parted.
61 And Mary Magdalene was there, and the
other Mary, sitting opposite the tomb.

Pilate Sets a Guard

62 On the next day, which followed the Day
of Preparation, the chief priests and Pharisees
gathered together to Pilate,
63 saying, "Sir, we remember, while He was
still alive, how that deceiver said, 'After three
days I will rise.'
64 "Therefore command that the tomb be
made secure until the third day, lest His disci-
ples come by night[a] and steal Him *away*, and
say to the people, 'He has risen from the dead.'
So the last deception will be worse than the first."

27:24 [a]NU-Text omits *just*. **27:34** [a]NU-Text omits *sour*. **27:35** [a]NU-Text and M-Text omit the rest of this verse. [b]Psalm 22:18 **27:41** [a]M-Text reads *with the scribes, the Pharisees, and the elders*. **27:42** [a]NU-Text reads *He is the King of Israel!* [b]NU-Text and M-Text read *we will believe in Him*. **27:46** [a]Psalm 22:1 **27:56** [a]NU-Text reads *Joseph*. **27:64** [a]NU-Text omits *by night*.

65 Pilate said to them, "You have a guard; go your way, make *it* as secure as you know how."

66 So they went and made the tomb secure, sealing the stone and setting the guard.

He Is Risen

28 Now after the Sabbath, as the first *day* of the week began to dawn, Mary Magdalene and the other Mary came to see the tomb.

2 And behold, there was a great earthquake; for an angel of the Lord descended from heaven, and came and rolled back the stone from the door,[a] and sat on it.

3 His countenance was like lightning, and his clothing as white as snow.

4 And the guards shook for fear of him, and became like dead *men.*

5 But the angel answered and said to the women, "Do not be afraid, for I know that you seek Jesus who was crucified.

6 "He is not here; for He is risen, as He said. Come, see the place where the Lord lay.

7 "And go quickly and tell His disciples that He is risen from the dead, and indeed He is going before you into Galilee; there you will see Him. Behold, I have told you."

8 So they went out quickly from the tomb with fear and great joy, and ran to bring His disciples word.

The Women Worship the Risen Lord

9 And as they went to tell His disciples,[a] behold, Jesus met them, saying, "Rejoice!" So they came and held Him by the feet and worshiped Him.

10 Then Jesus said to them, "Do not be afraid. Go *and* tell My brethren to go to Galilee, and there they will see Me."

The Soldiers Are Bribed

11 Now while they were going, behold, some of the guard came into the city and reported to the chief priests all the things that had happened.

12 When they had assembled with the elders and consulted together, they gave a large sum of money to the soldiers,

13 saying, "Tell them, 'His disciples came at night and stole Him *away* while we slept.'

14 "And if this comes to the governor's ears, we will appease him and make you secure."

15 So they took the money and did as they were instructed; and this saying is commonly reported among the Jews until this day.

The Great Commission

16 Then the eleven disciples went away into Galilee, to the mountain which Jesus had appointed for them.

17 When they saw Him, they worshiped Him; but some doubted.

18 And Jesus came and spoke to them, saying, "All authority has been given to Me in heaven and on earth.

19 "Go therefore[a] and make disciples of all the nations, baptizing them in the name of the Father and of the Son and of the Holy Spirit,

20 "teaching them to observe all things that I have commanded you; and lo, I am with you always, *even* to the end of the age." Amen.[a]

The Gospel According to MARK

John the Baptist Prepares the Way

1 The beginning of the gospel of Jesus Christ, the Son of God.

2 As it is written in the Prophets:[a]

"Behold, I send My messenger before Your face,
Who will prepare Your way before You."[b]

3 *"The voice of one crying in the wilderness:*
'Prepare the way of the LORD;
Make His paths straight.'"[a]

4 John came baptizing in the wilderness and preaching a baptism of repentance for the remission of sins.

5 Then all the land of Judea, and those from Jerusalem, went out to him and were all baptized by him in the Jordan River, confessing their sins.

6 Now John was clothed with camel's hair and with a leather belt around his waist, and he ate locusts and wild honey.

7 And he preached, saying, "There comes One after me who is mightier than I, whose sandal strap I am not worthy to stoop down and loose.

8 "I indeed baptized you with water, but He will baptize you with the Holy Spirit."

John Baptizes Jesus

9 It came to pass in those days *that* Jesus came from Nazareth of Galilee, and was baptized by John in the Jordan.

10 And immediately, coming up from[a] the water, He saw the heavens parting and the Spirit descending upon Him like a dove.

11 Then a voice came from heaven, "You are My beloved Son, in whom I am well pleased."

Satan Tempts Jesus

12 Immediately the Spirit drove Him into the wilderness.

13 And He was there in the wilderness forty days, tempted by Satan, and was with the wild beasts; and the angels ministered to Him.

Jesus Begins His Galilean Ministry

14 Now after John was put in prison, Jesus came to Galilee, preaching the gospel of the kingdom[a] of God,

15 and saying, "The time is fulfilled, and the kingdom of God is at hand. Repent, and believe in the gospel."

Four Fishermen Called as Disciples

16 And as He walked by the Sea of Galilee, He saw Simon and Andrew his brother casting a net into the sea; for they were fishermen.

28:2 [a]NU-Text omits *from the door.* **28:9** [a]NU-Text omits the first clause of this verse. **28:19** [a]M-Text omits *therefore.* **28:20** [a]NU-Text omits *Amen.* **1:2** [a]NU-Text reads *Isaiah the prophet.* [b]Malachi 3:1 **1:3** [a]Isaiah 40:3 **1:10** [a]NU-Text reads *out of.* **1:14** [a]NU-Text omits *of the kingdom.*

17 Then Jesus said to them, "Follow Me, and
I will make you become fishers of men."
18 They immediately left their nets and fol-
lowed Him.
19 When He had gone a little farther from
there, He saw James the *son* of Zebedee, and
John his brother, who also *were* in the boat
mending their nets.
20 And immediately He called them, and they
left their father Zebedee in the boat with the
hired servants, and went after Him.

Jesus Casts Out an Unclean Spirit

21 Then they went into Capernaum, and im-
mediately on the Sabbath He entered the syna-
gogue and taught.
22 And they were astonished at His teaching,
for He taught them as one having authority, and
not as the scribes.
23 Now there was a man in their synagogue
with an unclean spirit. And he cried out,
24 saying, "Let *us* alone! What have we to do
with You, Jesus of Nazareth? Did You come to
destroy us? I know who You are—the Holy One
of God!"
25 But Jesus rebuked him, saying, "Be quiet,
and come out of him!"
26 And when the unclean spirit had convulsed
him and cried out with a loud voice, he came out
of him.
27 Then they were all amazed, so that they
questioned among themselves, saying, "What
is this? What new doctrine *is* this? For with au-
thority[a] He commands even the unclean spir-
its, and they obey Him."
28 And immediately His fame spread through-
out all the region around Galilee.

Peter's Mother-in-Law Healed

29 Now as soon as they had come out of the
synagogue, they entered the house of Simon and
Andrew, with James and John.
30 But Simon's wife's mother lay sick with a
fever, and they told Him about her at once.
31 So He came and took her by the hand and
lifted her up, and immediately the fever left her.
And she served them.

Many Healed After Sabbath Sunset

32 At evening, when the sun had set, they
brought to Him all who were sick and those
who were demon-possessed.
33 And the whole city was gathered together
at the door.
34 Then He healed many who were sick with
various diseases, and cast out many demons;
and He did not allow the demons to speak, be-
cause they knew Him.

Preaching in Galilee

35 Now in the morning, having risen a long
while before daylight, He went out and departed
to a solitary place; and there He prayed.
36 And Simon and those *who were* with Him
searched for Him.
37 When they found Him, they said to Him,
"Everyone is looking for You."
38 But He said to them, "Let us go into the
next towns, that I may preach there also, be-
cause for this purpose I have come forth."
39 And He was preaching in their synagogues
throughout all Galilee, and casting out de-
mons.

Jesus Cleanses a Leper

40 Now a leper came to Him, imploring Him,
kneeling down to Him and saying to Him, "If
You are willing, You can make me clean."
41 Then Jesus, moved with compassion,
stretched out *His* hand and touched him, and
said to him, "I am willing; be cleansed."
42 As soon as He had spoken, immediately the
leprosy left him, and he was cleansed.
43 And He strictly warned him and sent him
away at once,
44 and said to him, "See that you say nothing
to anyone; but go your way, show yourself to
the priest, and offer for your cleansing those
things which Moses commanded, as a testimony
to them."
45 However, he went out and began to pro-
claim *it* freely, and to spread the matter, so that
Jesus could no longer openly enter the city, but
was outside in deserted places; and they came
to Him from every direction.

Jesus Forgives and Heals a Paralytic

2 And again He entered Capernaum after *some*
days, and it was heard that He was in the
house.
2 Immediately[a] many gathered together, so
that there was no longer room to receive *them*,
not even near the door. And He preached the
word to them.
3 Then they came to Him, bringing a paralytic
who was carried by four *men*.
4 And when they could not come near Him
because of the crowd, they uncovered the roof
where He was. So when they had broken
through, they let down the bed on which the para-
lytic was lying.
5 When Jesus saw their faith, He said to the
paralytic, "Son, your sins are forgiven you."
6 And some of the scribes were sitting there
and reasoning in their hearts,
7 "Why does this *Man* speak blasphemies like
this? Who can forgive sins but God alone?"
8 But immediately, when Jesus perceived in
His spirit that they reasoned thus within them-
selves, He said to them, "Why do you reason
about these things in your hearts?
9 "Which is easier, to say to the paralytic,
'*Your* sins are forgiven you,' or to say, 'Arise, take
up your bed and walk'?
10 "But that you may know that the Son of Man
has power on earth to forgive sins"—He said
to the paralytic,
11 "I say to you, arise, take up your bed, and
go to your house."
12 Immediately he arose, took up the bed, and
went out in the presence of them all, so that all
were amazed and glorified God, saying, "We
never saw *anything* like this!"

Matthew the Tax Collector

13 Then He went out again by the sea; and all
the multitude came to Him, and He taught them.
14 As He passed by, He saw Levi the *son* of
Alphaeus sitting at the tax office. And He said
to him, "Follow Me." So he arose and followed
Him.
15 Now it happened, as He was dining in *Le-
vi's* house, that many tax collectors and sinners
also sat together with Jesus and His disciples;
for there were many, and they followed Him.

1:27 [a]NU-Text reads *What is this? A new doctrine with authority.* **2:2** [a]NU-Text omits *Immediately.*

16 And when the scribes and[a] Pharisees saw
Him eating with the tax collectors and sinners,
they said to His disciples, "How *is it* that He eats
and drinks with tax collectors and sinners?"
17 When Jesus heard *it*, He said to them, "Those
who are well have no need of a physician, but
those who are sick. I did not come to call *the*
righteous, but sinners, to repentance."[a]

Jesus Is Questioned About Fasting

18 The disciples of John and of the Pharisees
were fasting. Then they came and said to Him,
"Why do the disciples of John and of the Phari-
sees fast, but Your disciples do not fast?"
19 And Jesus said to them, "Can the friends
of the bridegroom fast while the bridegroom is
with them? As long as they have the bridegroom
with them they cannot fast.
20 "But the days will come when the bride-
groom will be taken away from them, and then
they will fast in those days.
21 "No one sews a piece of unshrunk cloth on
an old garment; or else the new piece pulls away
from the old, and the tear is made worse.
22 "And no one puts new wine into old wine-
skins; or else the new wine bursts the wine-
skins, the wine is spilled, and the wineskins
are ruined. But new wine must be put into new
wineskins."

Jesus Is Lord of the Sabbath

23 Now it happened that He went through the
grainfields on the Sabbath; and as they went
His disciples began to pluck the heads of grain.
24 And the Pharisees said to Him, "Look, why
do they do what is not lawful on the Sabbath?"
25 But He said to them, "Have you never read
what David did when he was in need and hun-
gry, he and those with him:
26 "how he went into the house of God *in the*
days of Abiathar the high priest, and ate the
showbread, which is not lawful to eat except
for the priests, and also gave some to those
who were with him?"
27 And He said to them, "The Sabbath was
made for man, and not man for the Sabbath.
28 "Therefore the Son of Man is also Lord of
the Sabbath."

Healing on the Sabbath

3 And He entered the synagogue again, and
a man was there who had a withered hand.
2 So they watched Him closely, whether He
would heal him on the Sabbath, so that they
might accuse Him.
3 And He said to the man who had the with-
ered hand, "Step forward."
4 Then He said to them, "Is it lawful on the
Sabbath to do good or to do evil, to save life or
to kill?" But they kept silent.
5 And when He had looked around at them
with anger, being grieved by the hardness of
their hearts, He said to the man, "Stretch out
your hand." And he stretched *it* out, and his
hand was restored as whole as the other.[a]
6 Then the Pharisees went out and immedi-
ately plotted with the Herodians against Him,
how they might destroy Him.

A Great Multitude Follows Jesus

7 But Jesus withdrew with His disciples to the
sea. And a great multitude from Galilee fol-
lowed Him, and from Judea
8 and Jerusalem and Idumea and beyond the
Jordan; and those from Tyre and Sidon, a great
multitude, when they heard how many things
He was doing, came to Him.
9 So He told His disciples that a small boat
should be kept ready for Him because of the
multitude, lest they should crush Him.
10 For He healed many, so that as many as
had afflictions pressed about Him to touch Him.
11 And the unclean spirits, whenever they
saw Him, fell down before Him and cried out,
saying, "You are the Son of God."
12 But He sternly warned them that they
should not make Him known.

The Twelve Apostles

13 And He went up on the mountain and called
to *Him* those He Himself wanted. And they came
to Him.
14 Then He appointed twelve,[a] that they might
be with Him and that He might send them out
to preach,
15 and to have power to heal sicknesses and[a]
to cast out demons:
16 Simon,[a] to whom He gave the name Peter;
17 James the *son* of Zebedee and John the
brother of James, to whom He gave the name
Boanerges, that is, "Sons of Thunder";
18 Andrew, Philip, Bartholomew, Matthew,
Thomas, James the *son* of Alphaeus, Thaddaeus,
Simon the Cananite;
19 and Judas Iscariot, who also betrayed Him.
And they went into a house.

A House Divided Cannot Stand

20 Then the multitude came together again, so
that they could not so much as eat bread.
21 But when His own people heard *about this*,
they went out to lay hold of Him, for they said,
"He is out of His mind."
22 And the scribes who came down from Je-
rusalem said, "He has Beelzebub," and, "By
the ruler of the demons He casts out demons."
23 So He called them to *Himself* and said to
them in parables: "How can Satan cast out
Satan?
24 "If a kingdom is divided against itself, that
kingdom cannot stand.
25 "And if a house is divided against itself,
that house cannot stand.
26 "And if Satan has risen up against himself,
and is divided, he cannot stand, but has an end.
27 "No one can enter a strong man's house
and plunder his goods, unless he first binds the
strong man. And then he will plunder his house.

The Unpardonable Sin

28 "Assuredly, I say to you, all sins will be for-
given the sons of men, and whatever blasphe-
mies they may utter;
29 "but he who blasphemes against the Holy
Spirit never has forgiveness, but is subject to
eternal condemnation"—
30 because they said, "He has an unclean
spirit."

2:16 [a]NU-Text reads *of the*. **2:17** [a]NU-Text omits *to repentance*. **3:5** [a]NU-Text omits *as whole as the other*. **3:14** [a]NU-Text adds *whom He also named apostles*. **3:15** [a]NU-Text omits *to heal sicknesses and*. **3:16** [a]NU-Text reads *and He appointed the twelve: Simon, ...*

Jesus' Mother and Brothers Send for Him

31 Then His brothers and His mother came,
and standing outside they sent to Him, calling
Him.
32 And a multitude was sitting around Him;
and they said to Him, "Look, Your mother and
Your brothers[a] are outside seeking You."
33 But He answered them, saying, "Who is My
mother, or My brothers?"
34 And He looked around in a circle at those
who sat about Him, and said, "Here are My
mother and My brothers!
35 "For whoever does the will of God is My
brother and My sister and mother."

The Parable of the Sower

4 And again He began to teach by the sea. And
a great multitude was gathered to Him, so
that He got into a boat and sat *in it* on the sea;
and the whole multitude was on the land facing
the sea.
2 Then He taught them many things by para-
bles, and said to them in His teaching:
3 "Listen! Behold, a sower went out to sow.
4 "And it happened, as he sowed, *that* some
seed fell by the wayside; and the birds of the
air[a] came and devoured it.
5 "Some fell on stony ground, where it did
not have much earth; and immediately it sprang
up because it had no depth of earth.
6 "But when the sun was up it was scorched,
and because it had no root it withered away.
7 "And some *seed* fell among thorns; and the
thorns grew up and choked it, and it yielded no
crop.
8 "But other *seed* fell on good ground and
yielded a crop that sprang up, increased and
produced: some thirtyfold, some sixty, and some
a hundred."
9 And He said to them,[a] "He who has ears to
hear, let him hear!"

The Purpose of Parables

10 But when He was alone, those around Him
with the twelve asked Him about the parable.
11 And He said to them, "To you it has been
given to know the mystery of the kingdom of
God; but to those who are outside, all things
come in parables,
12 "so that

'Seeing they may see and not perceive,
And hearing they may hear and not
understand;
Lest they should turn,
And their sins be forgiven them.' "[a]

The Parable of the Sower Explained

13 And He said to them, "Do you not under-
stand this parable? How then will you under-
stand all the parables?
14 "The sower sows the word.
15 "And these are the ones by the wayside
where the word is sown. When they hear, Sa-
tan comes immediately and takes away the
word that was sown in their hearts.
16 "These likewise are the ones sown on stony
ground who, when they hear the word, imme-
diately receive it with gladness;
17 "and they have no root in themselves, and
so endure only for a time. Afterward, when trib-
ulation or persecution arises for the word's
sake, immediately they stumble.
18 "Now these are the ones sown among thorns;
they are the ones who hear the word,
19 "and the cares of this world, the deceitful-
ness of riches, and the desires for other things
entering in choke the word, and it becomes un-
fruitful.
20 "But these are the ones sown on good
ground, those who hear the word, accept *it*, and
bear fruit: some thirtyfold, some sixty, and
some a hundred."

Light Under a Basket

21 Also He said to them, "Is a lamp brought
to be put under a basket or under a bed? Is it
not to be set on a lampstand?
22 "For there is nothing hidden which will not
be revealed, nor has anything been kept secret
but that it should come to light.
23 "If anyone has ears to hear, let him hear."
24 Then He said to them, "Take heed what you
hear. With the same measure you use, it will
be measured to you; and to you who hear, more
will be given.
25 "For whoever has, to him more will be
given; but whoever does not have, even what
he has will be taken away from him."

The Parable of the Growing Seed

26 And He said, "The kingdom of God is as if
a man should scatter seed on the ground,
27 "and should sleep by night and rise by day,
and the seed should sprout and grow, he him-
self does not know how.
28 "For the earth yields crops by itself: first
the blade, then the head, after that the full grain
in the head.
29 "But when the grain ripens, immediately
he puts in the sickle, because the harvest has
come."

The Parable of the Mustard Seed

30 Then He said, "To what shall we liken the
kingdom of God? Or with what parable shall
we picture it?
31 "*It is* like a mustard seed which, when it is
sown on the ground, is smaller than all the
seeds on earth;
32 "but when it is sown, it grows up and be-
comes greater than all herbs, and shoots out
large branches, so that the birds of the air may
nest under its shade."

Jesus' Use of Parables

33 And with many such parables He spoke
the word to them as they were able to hear *it*.
34 But without a parable He did not speak to
them. And when they were alone, He ex-
plained all things to His disciples.

Wind and Wave Obey Jesus

35 On the same day, when evening had come,
He said to them, "Let us cross over to the other
side."
36 Now when they had left the multitude, they
took Him along in the boat as He was. And other
little boats were also with Him.
37 And a great windstorm arose, and the waves
beat into the boat, so that it was already filling.
38 But He was in the stern, asleep on a pillow.

3:32 [a]NU-Text and M-Text add *and Your sisters.* **4:4** [a]NU-Text and M-Text omit *of the air.* **4:9** [a]NU-Text and M-Text omit *to them.* **4:12** [a]Isaiah 6:9, 10

And they awoke Him and said to Him, "Teacher,
do You not care that we are perishing?"
39 Then He arose and rebuked the wind, and
said to the sea, "Peace, be still!" And the wind
ceased and there was a great calm.
40 But He said to them, "Why are you so fear-
ful? How *is it* that you have no faith?"[a]
41 And they feared exceedingly, and said to
one another, "Who can this be, that even the
wind and the sea obey Him!"

A Demon-Possessed Man Healed

5 Then they came to the other side of the sea,
to the country of the Gadarenes.[a]
2 And when He had come out of the boat,
immediately there met Him out of the tombs a
man with an unclean spirit,
3 who had *his* dwelling among the tombs;
and no one could bind him,[a] not even with
chains,
4 because he had often been bound with
shackles and chains. And the chains had been
pulled apart by him, and the shackles broken
in pieces; neither could anyone tame him.
5 And always, night and day, he was in the
mountains and in the tombs, crying out and cut-
ting himself with stones.
6 When he saw Jesus from afar, he ran and
worshiped Him.
7 And he cried out with a loud voice and said,
"What have I to do with You, Jesus, Son of the
Most High God? I implore You by God that You
do not torment me."
8 For He said to him, "Come out of the man,
unclean spirit!"
9 Then He asked him, "What *is* your name?"
And he answered, saying, "My name *is* Legion;
for we are many."
10 Also he begged Him earnestly that He would
not send them out of the country.
11 Now a large herd of swine was feeding there
near the mountains.
12 So all the demons begged Him, saying, "Send
us to the swine, that we may enter them."
13 And at once Jesus[a] gave them permission.
Then the unclean spirits went out and entered
the swine (there were about two thousand); and
the herd ran violently down the steep place into
the sea, and drowned in the sea.
14 So those who fed the swine fled, and they
told *it* in the city and in the country. And they
went out to see what it was that had happened.
15 Then they came to Jesus, and saw the one
who had been demon-possessed and had the
legion, sitting and clothed and in his right mind.
And they were afraid.
16 And those who saw it told them how it hap-
pened to him *who had been* demon-possessed,
and about the swine.
17 Then they began to plead with Him to de-
part from their region.
18 And when He got into the boat, he who had
been demon-possessed begged Him that he
might be with Him.
19 However, Jesus did not permit him, but said
to him, "Go home to your friends, and tell them
what great things the Lord has done for you,
and how He has had compassion on you."
20 And he departed and began to proclaim in
Decapolis all that Jesus had done for him; and
all marveled.

A Girl Restored to Life and a Woman Healed

21 Now when Jesus had crossed over again by
boat to the other side, a great multitude gath-
ered to Him; and He was by the sea.
22 And behold, one of the rulers of the syna-
gogue came, Jairus by name. And when he saw
Him, he fell at His feet
23 and begged Him earnestly, saying, "My lit-
tle daughter lies at the point of death. Come and
lay Your hands on her, that she may be healed,
and she will live."
24 So *Jesus* went with him, and a great multi-
tude followed Him and thronged Him.
25 Now a certain woman had a flow of blood
for twelve years,
26 and had suffered many things from many
physicians. She had spent all that she had and
was no better, but rather grew worse.
27 When she heard about Jesus, she came be-
hind *Him* in the crowd and touched His gar-
ment.
28 For she said, "If only I may touch His clothes,
I shall be made well."
29 Immediately the fountain of her blood was
dried up, and she felt in *her* body that she was
healed of the affliction.
30 And Jesus, immediately knowing in Him-
self that power had gone out of Him, turned
around in the crowd and said, "Who touched My
clothes?"
31 But His disciples said to Him, "You see the
multitude thronging You, and You say, 'Who
touched Me?' "
32 And He looked around to see her who had
done this thing.
33 But the woman, fearing and trembling,
knowing what had happened to her, came and
fell down before Him and told Him the whole
truth.
34 And He said to her, "Daughter, your faith
has made you well. Go in peace, and be healed
of your affliction."
35 While He was still speaking, *some* came
from the ruler of the synagogue's *house* who
said, "Your daughter is dead. Why trouble the
Teacher any further?"
36 As soon as Jesus heard the word that was
spoken, He said to the ruler of the synagogue,
"Do not be afraid; only believe."
37 And He permitted no one to follow Him ex-
cept Peter, James, and John the brother of James.
38 Then He came to the house of the ruler of
the synagogue, and saw a tumult and those who
wept and wailed loudly.
39 When He came in, He said to them, "Why
make this commotion and weep? The child is
not dead, but sleeping."
40 And they ridiculed Him. But when He had
put them all outside, He took the father and
the mother of the child, and those *who were*
with Him, and entered where the child was
lying.
41 Then He took the child by the hand, and
said to her, "Talitha, cumi," which is trans-
lated, "Little girl, I say to you, arise."
42 Immediately the girl arose and walked, for
she was twelve years *of age.* And they were
overcome with great amazement.
43 But He commanded them strictly that no
one should know it, and said that *something*
should be given her to eat.

4:40 [a]NU-Text reads *Have you still no faith?* **5:1** [a]NU-Text reads *Gerasenes.* **5:3** [a]NU-Text adds *anymore.*
5:13 [a]NU-Text reads *And He gave.*

Jesus Rejected at Nazareth

6 Then He went out from there and came to His own country, and His disciples followed Him.
2 And when the Sabbath had come, He began to teach in the synagogue. And many hearing *Him* were astonished, saying, "Where *did* this Man *get* these things? And what wisdom *is* this which is given to Him, that such mighty works are performed by His hands!
3 "Is this not the carpenter, the Son of Mary, and brother of James, Joses, Judas, and Simon? And are not His sisters here with us?" So they were offended at Him.
4 But Jesus said to them, "A prophet is not without honor except in his own country, among his own relatives, and in his own house."
5 Now He could do no mighty work there, except that He laid His hands on a few sick people and healed *them.*
6 And He marveled because of their unbelief. Then He went about the villages in a circuit, teaching.

Sending Out the Twelve

7 And He called the twelve to *Himself,* and began to send them out two *by* two, and gave them power over unclean spirits.
8 He commanded them to take nothing for the journey except a staff—no bag, no bread, no copper in *their* money belts—
9 but to wear sandals, and not to put on two tunics.
10 Also He said to them, "In whatever place you enter a house, stay there till you depart from that place.
11 "And whoever[a] will not receive you nor hear you, when you depart from there, shake off the dust under your feet as a testimony against them.[b] Assuredly, I say to you, it will be more tolerable for Sodom and Gomorrah in the day of judgment than for that city!"
12 So they went out and preached that *people* should repent.
13 And they cast out many demons, and anointed with oil many who were sick, and healed *them.*

John the Baptist Beheaded

14 Now King Herod heard *of Him,* for His name had become well known. And he said, "John the Baptist is risen from the dead, and therefore these powers are at work in him."
15 Others said, "It is Elijah." And others said, "It is the Prophet, or[a] like one of the prophets."
16 But when Herod heard, he said, "This is John, whom I beheaded; he has been raised from the dead!"
17 For Herod himself had sent and laid hold of John, and bound him in prison for the sake of Herodias, his brother Philip's wife; for he had married her.
18 Because John had said to Herod, "It is not lawful for you to have your brother's wife."
19 Therefore Herodias held it against him and wanted to kill him, but she could not;
20 for Herod feared John, knowing that he *was* a just and holy man, and he protected him. And when he heard him, he did many things, and heard him gladly.
21 Then an opportune day came when Herod on his birthday gave a feast for his nobles, the high officers, and the chief *men* of Galilee.
22 And when Herodias' daughter herself came in and danced, and pleased Herod and those who sat with him, the king said to the girl, "Ask me whatever you want, and I will give *it* to you."
23 He also swore to her, "Whatever you ask me, I will give you, up to half my kingdom."
24 So she went out and said to her mother, "What shall I ask?" And she said, "The head of John the Baptist!"
25 Immediately she came in with haste to the king and asked, saying, "I want you to give me at once the head of John the Baptist on a platter."
26 And the king was exceedingly sorry; *yet,* because of the oaths and because of those who sat with him, he did not want to refuse her.
27 Immediately the king sent an executioner and commanded his head to be brought. And he went and beheaded him in prison,
28 brought his head on a platter, and gave it to the girl; and the girl gave it to her mother.
29 When his disciples heard *of it,* they came and took away his corpse and laid it in a tomb.

Feeding the Five Thousand

30 Then the apostles gathered to Jesus and told Him all things, both what they had done and what they had taught.
31 And He said to them, "Come aside by yourselves to a deserted place and rest a while." For there were many coming and going, and they did not even have time to eat.
32 So they departed to a deserted place in the boat by themselves.
33 But the multitudes[a] saw them departing, and many knew Him and ran there on foot from all the cities. They arrived before them and came together to Him.
34 And Jesus, when He came out, saw a great multitude and was moved with compassion for them, because they were like sheep not having a shepherd. So He began to teach them many things.
35 When the day was now far spent, His disciples came to Him and said, "This is a deserted place, and already the hour *is* late.
36 "Send them away, that they may go into the surrounding country and villages and buy themselves bread;[a] for they have nothing to eat."
37 But He answered and said to them, "You give them something to eat." And they said to Him, "Shall we go and buy two hundred denarii worth of bread and give them *something* to eat?"
38 But He said to them, "How many loaves do you have? Go and see." And when they found out they said, "Five, and two fish."
39 Then He commanded them to make them all sit down in groups on the green grass.
40 So they sat down in ranks, in hundreds and in fifties.
41 And when He had taken the five loaves and the two fish, He looked up to heaven, blessed and broke the loaves, and gave *them* to His disciples to set before them; and the two fish He divided among *them* all.
42 So they all ate and were filled.

6:11 [a]NU-Text reads *whatever place.* [b]NU-Text omits the rest of this verse. **6:15** [a]NU-Text and M-Text omit *or.*
6:33 [a]NU-Text and M-Text read *they.* **6:36** [a]NU-Text reads *something to eat* and omits the rest of this verse.

43 And they took up twelve baskets full of
fragments and of the fish.
44 Now those who had eaten the loaves were
about[a] five thousand men.

Jesus Walks on the Sea

45 Immediately He made His disciples get into
the boat and go before Him to the other side, to
Bethsaida, while He sent the multitude away.
46 And when He had sent them away, He de-
parted to the mountain to pray.
47 Now when evening came, the boat was in
the middle of the sea; and He *was* alone on the
land.
48 Then He saw them straining at rowing, for
the wind was against them. Now about the fourth
watch of the night He came to them, walking
on the sea, and would have passed them by.
49 And when they saw Him walking on the
sea, they supposed it was a ghost, and cried out;
50 for they all saw Him and were troubled.
But immediately He talked with them and said
to them, "Be of good cheer! It is I; do not be
afraid."
51 Then He went up into the boat to them, and
the wind ceased. And they were greatly amazed
in themselves beyond measure, and marveled.
52 For they had not understood about the
loaves, because their heart was hardened.

Many Touch Him and Are Made Well

53 When they had crossed over, they came to
the land of Gennesaret and anchored there.
54 And when they came out of the boat, im-
mediately the people recognized Him,
55 ran through that whole surrounding re-
gion, and began to carry about on beds those
who were sick to wherever they heard He was.
56 Wherever He entered, into villages, cities,
or the country, they laid the sick in the market-
places, and begged Him that they might just
touch the hem of His garment. And as many
as touched Him were made well.

Defilement Comes from Within

7 Then the Pharisees and some of the scribes
came together to Him, having come from
Jerusalem.
2 Now when[a] they saw some of His disciples
eat bread with defiled, that is, with unwashed
hands, they found fault.
3 For the Pharisees and all the Jews do not
eat unless they wash *their* hands in a special
way, holding the tradition of the elders.
4 *When they come* from the marketplace, they
do not eat unless they wash. And there are
many other things which they have received
and hold, *like* the washing of cups, pitchers,
copper vessels, and couches.
5 Then the Pharisees and scribes asked Him,
"Why do Your disciples not walk according to
the tradition of the elders, but eat bread with
unwashed hands?"
6 He answered and said to them, "Well did
Isaiah prophesy of you hypocrites, as it is writ-
ten:

'This people honors Me with their lips,
But their heart is far from Me.
7 *And in vain they worship Me,*
Teaching as doctrines the
commandments of men.'[a]

8 "For laying aside the commandment of
God, you hold the tradition of men[a]—the wash-
ing of pitchers and cups, and many other such
things you do."
9 He said to them, "*All too* well you reject
the commandment of God, that you may keep
your tradition.
10 "For Moses said, *'Honor your father and
your mother'*;[a] and, *'He who curses father or
mother, let him be put to death.'*[b]
11 "But you say, 'If a man says to his father
or mother, "Whatever profit you might have
received from me *is* Corban"—' (that is, a gift
to God),
12 "then you no longer let him do anything
for his father or his mother,
13 "making the word of God of no effect
through your tradition which you have handed
down. And many such things you do."
14 When He had called all the multitude to
Himself, He said to them, "Hear Me, everyone,
and understand:
15 "There is nothing that enters a man from
outside which can defile him; but the things
which come out of him, those are the things that
defile a man.
16 "If anyone has ears to hear, let him hear!"[a]
17 When He had entered a house away from
the crowd, His disciples asked Him concerning
the parable.
18 So He said to them, "Are you thus without
understanding also? Do you not perceive that
whatever enters a man from outside cannot
defile him,
19 "because it does not enter his heart but his
stomach, and is eliminated, *thus* purifying all
foods?"[a]
20 And He said, "What comes out of a man,
that defiles a man.
21 "For from within, out of the heart of men,
proceed evil thoughts, adulteries, fornications,
murders,
22 "thefts, covetousness, wickedness, deceit,
lewdness, an evil eye, blasphemy, pride, fool-
ishness.
23 "All these evil things come from within and
defile a man."

A Gentile Shows Her Faith

24 From there He arose and went to the region
of Tyre and Sidon.[a] And He entered a house and
wanted no one to know *it*, but He could not be
hidden.
25 For a woman whose young daughter had
an unclean spirit heard about Him, and she came
and fell at His feet.
26 The woman was a Greek, a Syro-Phoenician
by birth, and she kept asking Him to cast the
demon out of her daughter.
27 But Jesus said to her, "Let the children be
filled first, for it is not good to take the chil-
dren's bread and throw *it* to the little dogs."
28 And she answered and said to Him, "Yes,
Lord, yet even the little dogs under the table
eat from the children's crumbs."
29 Then He said to her, "For this saying go

6:44 [a]NU-Text and M-Text omit *about*. **7:2** [a]NU-Text omits *when* and *they found fault*. **7:7** [a]Isaiah 29:13 **7:8** [a]NU-Text omits the rest of this verse. **7:10** [a]Exodus 20:12; Deuteronomy 5:16 [b]Exodus 21:17 **7:16** [a]NU-Text omits this verse. **7:19** [a]NU-Text ends quotation with *eliminated*, setting off the final clause as Mark's comment that Jesus has declared all foods clean. **7:24** [a]NU-Text omits *and Sidon*.

your way; the demon has gone out of your
daughter."
30 And when she had come to her house, she
found the demon gone out, and her daughter
lying on the bed.

Jesus Heals a Deaf-Mute

31 Again, departing from the region of Tyre
and Sidon, He came through the midst of the
region of Decapolis to the Sea of Galilee.
32 Then they brought to Him one who was deaf
and had an impediment in his speech, and they
begged Him to put His hand on him.
33 And He took him aside from the multitude,
and put His fingers in his ears, and He spat and
touched his tongue.
34 Then, looking up to heaven, He sighed, and
said to him, "Ephphatha," that is, "Be opened."
35 Immediately his ears were opened, and the
impediment of his tongue was loosed, and he
spoke plainly.
36 Then He commanded them that they should
tell no one; but the more He commanded them,
the more widely they proclaimed *it*.
37 And they were astonished beyond mea-
sure, saying, "He has done all things well. He
makes both the deaf to hear and the mute to
speak."

Feeding the Four Thousand

8 In those days, the multitude being very
great and having nothing to eat, Jesus called
His disciples *to Him* and said to them,
2 "I have compassion on the multitude, be-
cause they have now continued with Me three
days and have nothing to eat.
3 "And if I send them away hungry to their
own houses, they will faint on the way; for some
of them have come from afar."
4 Then His disciples answered Him, "How
can one satisfy these people with bread here
in the wilderness?"
5 He asked them, "How many loaves do you
have?" And they said, "Seven."
6 So He commanded the multitude to sit down
on the ground. And He took the seven loaves
and gave thanks, broke *them* and gave *them*
to His disciples to set before *them*; and they
set *them* before the multitude.
7 They also had a few small fish; and having
blessed them, He said to set them also before
them.
8 So they ate and were filled, and they took
up seven large baskets of leftover fragments.
9 Now those who had eaten were about four
thousand. And He sent them away,
10 immediately got into the boat with His dis-
ciples, and came to the region of Dalmanutha.

The Pharisees Seek a Sign

11 Then the Pharisees came out and began to
dispute with Him, seeking from Him a sign from
heaven, testing Him.
12 But He sighed deeply in His spirit, and said,
"Why does this generation seek a sign? As-
suredly, I say to you, no sign shall be given to
this generation."

Beware of the Leaven of the Pharisees and Herod

13 And He left them, and getting into the boat
again, departed to the other side.
14 Now the disciples[a] had forgotten to take
bread, and they did not have more than one
loaf with them in the boat.
15 Then He charged them, saying, "Take heed,
beware of the leaven of the Pharisees and the
leaven of Herod."
16 And they reasoned among themselves,
saying, "*It is* because we have no bread."
17 But Jesus, being aware of *it*, said to them,
"Why do you reason because you have no
bread? Do you not yet perceive nor under-
stand? Is your heart still[a] hardened?
18 "Having eyes, do you not see? And having
ears, do you not hear? And do you not re-
member?
19 "When I broke the five loaves for the five
thousand, how many baskets full of fragments
did you take up?" They said to Him, "Twelve."
20 "Also, when I broke the seven for the four
thousand, how many large baskets full of frag-
ments did you take up?" And they said, "Seven."
21 So He said to them, "How *is it* you do not
understand?"

A Blind Man Healed at Bethsaida

22 Then He came to Bethsaida; and they
brought a blind man to Him, and begged Him
to touch him.
23 So He took the blind man by the hand and
led him out of the town. And when He had spit
on his eyes and put His hands on him, He asked
him if he saw anything.
24 And he looked up and said, "I see men like
trees, walking."
25 Then He put *His* hands on his eyes again
and made him look up. And he was restored
and saw everyone clearly.
26 Then He sent him away to his house, say-
ing, "Neither go into the town, nor tell anyone
in the town."[a]

Peter Confesses Jesus as the Christ

27 Now Jesus and His disciples went out to
the towns of Caesarea Philippi; and on the
road He asked His disciples, saying to them,
"Who do men say that I am?"
28 So they answered, "John the Baptist; but
some *say*, Elijah; and others, one of the prophets."
29 He said to them, "But who do you say that
I am?" Peter answered and said to Him, "You
are the Christ."
30 Then He strictly warned them that they
should tell no one about Him.

Jesus Predicts His Death and Resurrection

31 And He began to teach them that the Son of
Man must suffer many things, and be rejected
by the elders and chief priests and scribes, and
be killed, and after three days rise again.
32 He spoke this word openly. Then Peter
took Him aside and began to rebuke Him.
33 But when He had turned around and
looked at His disciples, He rebuked Peter, say-
ing, "Get behind Me, Satan! For you are not
mindful of the things of God, but the things of
men."

Take Up the Cross and Follow Him

34 When He had called the people to *Himself*,
with His disciples also, He said to them, "Who-
ever desires to come after Me, let him deny
himself, and take up his cross, and follow Me.

8:14 [a]NU-Text and M-Text read *they*. **8:17** [a]NU-Text omits *still*. **8:26** [a]NU-Text reads *"Do not even go into the town."*

35 "For whoever desires to save his life will lose it, but whoever loses his life for My sake and the gospel's will save it.
36 "For what will it profit a man if he gains the whole world, and loses his own soul?
37 "Or what will a man give in exchange for his soul?
38 "For whoever is ashamed of Me and My words in this adulterous and sinful generation, of him the Son of Man also will be ashamed when He comes in the glory of His Father with the holy angels."

Jesus Transfigured on the Mount

9 And He said to them, "Assuredly, I say to you that there are some standing here who will not taste death till they see the kingdom of God present with power."
2 Now after six days Jesus took Peter, James, and John, and led them up on a high mountain apart by themselves; and He was transfigured before them.
3 His clothes became shining, exceedingly white, like snow, such as no launderer on earth can whiten them.
4 And Elijah appeared to them with Moses, and they were talking with Jesus.
5 Then Peter answered and said to Jesus, "Rabbi, it is good for us to be here; and let us make three tabernacles: one for You, one for Moses, and one for Elijah"—
6 because he did not know what to say, for they were greatly afraid.
7 And a cloud came and overshadowed them; and a voice came out of the cloud, saying, "This is My beloved Son. Hear Him!"
8 Suddenly, when they had looked around, they saw no one anymore, but only Jesus with themselves.
9 Now as they came down from the mountain, He commanded them that they should tell no one the things they had seen, till the Son of Man had risen from the dead.
10 So they kept this word to themselves, questioning what the rising from the dead meant.
11 And they asked Him, saying, "Why do the scribes say that Elijah must come first?"
12 Then He answered and told them, "Indeed, Elijah is coming first and restores all things. And how is it written concerning the Son of Man, that He must suffer many things and be treated with contempt?
13 "But I say to you that Elijah has also come, and they did to him whatever they wished, as it is written of him."

A Boy Is Healed

14 And when He came to the disciples, He saw a great multitude around them, and scribes disputing with them.
15 Immediately, when they saw Him, all the people were greatly amazed, and running to *Him,* greeted Him.
16 And He asked the scribes, "What are you discussing with them?"
17 Then one of the crowd answered and said, "Teacher, I brought You my son, who has a mute spirit.
18 "And wherever it seizes him, it throws him down; he foams at the mouth, gnashes his teeth, and becomes rigid. So I spoke to Your disciples, that they should cast it out, but they could not."
19 He answered him and said, "O faithless generation, how long shall I be with you? How long shall I bear with you? Bring him to Me."
20 Then they brought him to Him. And when he saw Him, immediately the spirit convulsed him, and he fell on the ground and wallowed, foaming at the mouth.
21 So He asked his father, "How long has this been happening to him?" And he said, "From childhood.
22 "And often he has thrown him both into the fire and into the water to destroy him. But if You can do anything, have compassion on us and help us."
23 Jesus said to him, "If you can believe,[a] all things *are* possible to him who believes."
24 Immediately the father of the child cried out and said with tears, "Lord, I believe; help my unbelief!"
25 When Jesus saw that the people came running together, He rebuked the unclean spirit, saying to it: "Deaf and dumb spirit, I command you, come out of him and enter him no more!"
26 Then *the spirit* cried out, convulsed him greatly, and came out of him. And he became as one dead, so that many said, "He is dead."
27 But Jesus took him by the hand and lifted him up, and he arose.
28 And when He had come into the house, His disciples asked Him privately, "Why could we not cast it out?"
29 So He said to them, "This kind can come out by nothing but prayer and fasting."[a]

Jesus Again Predicts His Death and Resurrection

30 Then they departed from there and passed through Galilee, and He did not want anyone to know *it.*
31 For He taught His disciples and said to them, "The Son of Man is being betrayed into the hands of men, and they will kill Him. And after He is killed, He will rise the third day."
32 But they did not understand this saying, and were afraid to ask Him.

Who Is the Greatest?

33 Then He came to Capernaum. And when He was in the house He asked them, "What was it you disputed among yourselves on the road?"
34 But they kept silent, for on the road they had disputed among themselves who *would be the* greatest.
35 And He sat down, called the twelve, and said to them, "If anyone desires to be first, he shall be last of all and servant of all."
36 Then He took a little child and set him in the midst of them. And when He had taken him in His arms, He said to them,
37 "Whoever receives one of these little children in My name receives Me; and whoever receives Me, receives not Me but Him who sent Me."

Jesus Forbids Sectarianism

38 Now John answered Him, saying, "Teacher, we saw someone who does not follow us casting out demons in Your name, and we forbade him because he does not follow us."
39 But Jesus said, "Do not forbid him, for no one who works a miracle in My name can soon afterward speak evil of Me.

9:23 [a]NU-Text reads "*'If You can!' All things* . . . ." **9:29** [a]NU-Text omits *and fasting.*

40 "For he who is not against us is on our[a] side.
41 "For whoever gives you a cup of water to
drink in My name, because you belong to
Christ, assuredly, I say to you, he will by no
means lose his reward.

Jesus Warns of Offenses

42 "But whoever causes one of these little
ones who believe in Me to stumble, it would be
better for him if a millstone were hung around
his neck, and he were thrown into the sea.
43 "If your hand causes you to sin, cut it off.
It is better for you to enter into life maimed,
rather than having two hands, to go to hell,
into the fire that shall never be quenched—
44 "where

'Their worm does not die,
And the fire is not quenched.'[a]

45 "And if your foot causes you to sin, cut it
off. It is better for you to enter life lame, rather
than having two feet, to be cast into hell, into
the fire that shall never be quenched—
46 "where

'Their worm does not die
And the fire is not quenched.'[a]

47 "And if your eye causes you to sin, pluck it
out. It is better for you to enter the kingdom of
God with one eye, rather than having two eyes,
to be cast into hell fire—
48 "where

'Their worm does not die,
And the fire is not quenched.'[a]

Tasteless Salt Is Worthless

49 "For everyone will be seasoned with fire,[a]
and every sacrifice will be seasoned with salt.
50 "Salt *is* good, but if the salt loses its flavor,
how will you season it? Have salt in yourselves,
and have peace with one another."

Marriage and Divorce

10 Then He arose from there and came to
the region of Judea by the other side of
the Jordan. And multitudes gathered to Him
again, and as He was accustomed, He taught
them again.
2 The Pharisees came and asked Him, "Is it
lawful for a man to divorce *his* wife?" testing
Him.
3 And He answered and said to them, "What
did Moses command you?"
4 They said, "Moses permitted *a man* to write
a certificate of divorce, and to dismiss *her*."
5 And Jesus answered and said to them,
"Because of the hardness of your heart he
wrote you this precept.
6 "But from the beginning of the creation,
God *'made them male and female.'*[a]
7 *'For this reason a man shall leave his fa-
ther and mother and be joined to his wife,*
8 *'and the two shall become one flesh'*;[a] so
then they are no longer two, but one flesh.
9 "Therefore what God has joined together,
let not man separate."
10 In the house His disciples also asked Him
again about the same *matter.*
11 So He said to them, "Whoever divorces his
wife and marries another commits adultery
against her.
12 "And if a woman divorces her husband
and marries another, she commits adultery."

Jesus Blesses Little Children

13 Then they brought little children to Him,
that He might touch them; but the disciples
rebuked those who brought *them.*
14 But when Jesus saw *it*, He was greatly dis-
pleased and said to them, "Let the little chil-
dren come to Me, and do not forbid them; for
of such is the kingdom of God.
15 "Assuredly, I say to you, whoever does not
receive the kingdom of God as a little child will
by no means enter it."
16 And He took them up in His arms, laid *His*
hands on them, and blessed them.

Jesus Counsels the Rich Young Ruler

17 Now as He was going out on the road, one
came running, knelt before Him, and asked Him,
"Good Teacher, what shall I do that I may in-
herit eternal life?"
18 So Jesus said to him, "Why do you call Me
good? No one *is* good but One, *that is,* God.
19 "You know the commandments: *'Do not
commit adultery,' 'Do not murder,' 'Do not
steal,' 'Do not bear false witness,'* 'Do not de-
fraud,' *'Honor your father and your mother.'* "[a]
20 And he answered and said to Him,
"Teacher, all these things I have kept from my
youth."
21 Then Jesus, looking at him, loved him, and
said to him, "One thing you lack: Go your way,
sell whatever you have and give to the poor,
and you will have treasure in heaven; and
come, take up the cross, and follow Me."
22 But he was sad at this word, and went away
sorrowful, for he had great possessions.

With God All Things Are Possible

23 Then Jesus looked around and said to His
disciples, "How hard it is for those who have
riches to enter the kingdom of God!"
24 And the disciples were astonished at His
words. But Jesus answered again and said to
them, "Children, how hard it is for those who
trust in riches[a] to enter the kingdom of God!
25 "It is easier for a camel to go through the
eye of a needle than for a rich man to enter the
kingdom of God."
26 And they were greatly astonished, saying
among themselves, "Who then can be saved?"
27 But Jesus looked at them and said, "With
men *it is* impossible, but not with God; for with
God all things are possible."
28 Then Peter began to say to Him, "See, we
have left all and followed You."
29 So Jesus answered and said, "Assuredly, I
say to you, there is no one who has left house
or brothers or sisters or father or mother or
wife[a] or children or lands, for My sake and the
gospel's,
30 "who shall not receive a hundredfold now
in this time—houses and brothers and sisters
and mothers and children and lands, with per-
secutions—and in the age to come, eternal life.
31 "But many *who are* first will be last, and
the last first."

9:40 [a]M-Text reads *against you is on your side.* **9:44** [a]NU-Text omits this verse. **9:46** [a]NU-Text omits the last clause of verse 45 and all of verse 46. **9:48** [a]Isaiah 66:24 **9:49** [a]NU-Text omits the rest of this verse. **10:6** [a]Genesis 1:27; 5:2 **10:8** [a]Genesis 2:24 **10:19** [a]Exodus 20:12–16; Deuteronomy 5:16–20 **10:24** [a]NU-Text omits *for those who trust in riches.* **10:29** [a]NU-Text omits *or wife.*

Jesus a Third Time Predicts His Death and Resurrection

32 Now they were on the road, going up to Jerusalem, and Jesus was going before them; and they were amazed. And as they followed they were afraid. Then He took the twelve aside again and began to tell them the things that would happen to Him:
33 "Behold, we are going up to Jerusalem, and the Son of Man will be betrayed to the chief priests and to the scribes; and they will condemn Him to death and deliver Him to the Gentiles;
34 "and they will mock Him, and scourge Him, and spit on Him, and kill Him. And the third day He will rise again."

Greatness Is Serving

35 Then James and John, the sons of Zebedee, came to Him, saying, "Teacher, we want You to do for us whatever we ask."
36 And He said to them, "What do you want Me to do for you?"
37 They said to Him, "Grant us that we may sit, one on Your right hand and the other on Your left, in Your glory."
38 But Jesus said to them, "You do not know what you ask. Are you able to drink the cup that I drink, and be baptized with the baptism that I am baptized with?"
39 They said to Him, "We are able." So Jesus said to them, "You will indeed drink the cup that I drink, and with the baptism I am baptized with you will be baptized;
40 "but to sit on My right hand and on My left is not Mine to give, but *it is for those* for whom it is prepared."
41 And when the ten heard *it*, they began to be greatly displeased with James and John.
42 But Jesus called them to *Himself* and said to them, "You know that those who are considered rulers over the Gentiles lord it over them, and their great ones exercise authority over them.
43 "Yet it shall not be so among you; but whoever desires to become great among you shall be your servant.
44 "And whoever of you desires to be first shall be slave of all.
45 "For even the Son of Man did not come to be served, but to serve, and to give His life a ransom for many."

Jesus Heals Blind Bartimaeus

46 Now they came to Jericho. As He went out of Jericho with His disciples and a great multitude, blind Bartimaeus, the son of Timaeus, sat by the road begging.
47 And when he heard that it was Jesus of Nazareth, he began to cry out and say, "Jesus, Son of David, have mercy on me!"
48 Then many warned him to be quiet; but he cried out all the more, "Son of David, have mercy on me!"
49 So Jesus stood still and commanded him to be called. Then they called the blind man, saying to him, "Be of good cheer. Rise, He is calling you."
50 And throwing aside his garment, he rose and came to Jesus.
51 So Jesus answered and said to him, "What do you want Me to do for you?" The blind man said to Him, "Rabboni, that I may receive my sight."
52 Then Jesus said to him, "Go your way; your faith has made you well." And immediately he received his sight and followed Jesus on the road.

The Triumphal Entry

11 Now when they drew near Jerusalem, to Bethphage[a] and Bethany, at the Mount of Olives, He sent two of His disciples;
2 and He said to them, "Go into the village opposite you; and as soon as you have entered it you will find a colt tied, on which no one has sat. Loose it and bring *it*.
3 "And if anyone says to you, 'Why are you doing this?' say, 'The Lord has need of it,' and immediately he will send it here."
4 So they went their way, and found the[a] colt tied by the door outside on the street, and they loosed it.
5 But some of those who stood there said to them, "What are you doing, loosing the colt?"
6 And they spoke to them just as Jesus had commanded. So they let them go.
7 Then they brought the colt to Jesus and threw their clothes on it, and He sat on it.
8 And many spread their clothes on the road, and others cut down leafy branches from the trees and spread *them* on the road.
9 Then those who went before and those who followed cried out, saying:

"Hosanna!
'Blessed is He who comes in the name of the LORD!'[a]
10 Blessed *is* the kingdom of our father David
That comes in the name of the Lord![a]
Hosanna in the highest!"

11 And Jesus went into Jerusalem and into the temple. So when He had looked around at all things, as the hour was already late, He went out to Bethany with the twelve.

The Fig Tree Withered

12 Now the next day, when they had come out from Bethany, He was hungry.
13 And seeing from afar a fig tree having leaves, He went to see if perhaps He would find something on it. When He came to it, He found nothing but leaves, for it was not the season for figs.
14 In response Jesus said to it, "Let no one eat fruit from you ever again." And His disciples heard *it*.

Jesus Cleanses the Temple

15 So they came to Jerusalem. Then Jesus went into the temple and began to drive out those who bought and sold in the temple, and overturned the tables of the money changers and the seats of those who sold doves.
16 And He would not allow anyone to carry wares through the temple.
17 Then He taught, saying to them, "Is it not written, *'My house shall be called a house of prayer for all nations'*?[a] But you have made it a *'den of thieves.'* "[b]
18 And the scribes and chief priests heard it and sought how they might destroy Him; for

11:1 [a]M-Text reads *Bethsphage.* **11:4** [a]NU-Text and M-Text read *a.* **11:9** [a]Psalm 118:26 **11:10** [a]NU-Text omits *in the name of the Lord.* **11:17** [a]Isaiah 56:7 [b]Jeremiah 7:11

they feared Him, because all the people were
astonished at His teaching.
19 When evening had come, He went out of
the city.

The Lesson of the Withered Fig Tree

20 Now in the morning, as they passed by, they
saw the fig tree dried up from the roots.
21 And Peter, remembering, said to Him,
"Rabbi, look! The fig tree which You cursed
has withered away."
22 So Jesus answered and said to them, "Have
faith in God.
23 "For assuredly, I say to you, whoever says
to this mountain, 'Be removed and be cast into
the sea,' and does not doubt in his heart, but
believes that those things he says will be done,
he will have whatever he says.
24 "Therefore I say to you, whatever things
you ask when you pray, believe that you receive *them*, and you will have *them*.

Forgiveness and Prayer

25 "And whenever you stand praying, if you
have anything against anyone, forgive him,
that your Father in heaven may also forgive
you your trespasses.
26 "But if you do not forgive, neither will your
Father in heaven forgive your trespasses."[a]

Jesus' Authority Questioned

27 Then they came again to Jerusalem. And
as He was walking in the temple, the chief priests,
the scribes, and the elders came to Him.
28 And they said to Him, "By what authority
are You doing these things? And who gave You
this authority to do these things?"
29 But Jesus answered and said to them, "I
also will ask you one question; then answer Me,
and I will tell you by what authority I do these
things:
30 "The baptism of John—was it from heaven
or from men? Answer Me."
31 And they reasoned among themselves, saying, "If we say, 'From heaven,' He will say, 'Why
then did you not believe him?'
32 "But if we say, 'From men' "—they feared
the people, for all counted John to have been a
prophet indeed.
33 So they answered and said to Jesus, "We
do not know." And Jesus answered and said to
them, "Neither will I tell you by what authority
I do these things."

The Parable of the Wicked Vinedressers

12 Then He began to speak to them in parables: "A man planted a vineyard and set
a hedge around *it*, dug *a place for* the wine vat
and built a tower. And he leased it to vinedressers and went into a far country.
2 "Now at vintage-time he sent a servant to
the vinedressers, that he might receive some of
the fruit of the vineyard from the vinedressers.
3 "And they took *him* and beat him and sent
him away empty-handed.
4 "Again he sent them another servant, and
at him they threw stones,[a] wounded *him* in the
head, and sent *him* away shamefully treated.
5 "And again he sent another, and him they
killed; and many others, beating some and killing some.
6 "Therefore still having one son, his beloved, he also sent him to them last, saying,
'They will respect my son.'
7 "But those vinedressers said among themselves, 'This is the heir. Come, let us kill him,
and the inheritance will be ours.'
8 "So they took him and killed *him* and cast
him out of the vineyard.
9 "Therefore what will the owner of the
vineyard do? He will come and destroy the
vinedressers, and give the vineyard to others.
10 "Have you not even read this Scripture:

'The stone which the builders rejected
Has become the chief cornerstone.
11 *This was the LORD's doing,*
And it is marvelous in our eyes'?"[a]

12 And they sought to lay hands on Him, but
feared the multitude, for they knew He had
spoken the parable against them. So they left
Him and went away.

The Pharisees: Is It Lawful to Pay Taxes to Caesar?

13 Then they sent to Him some of the Pharisees and the Herodians, to catch Him in *His*
words.
14 When they had come, they said to Him,
"Teacher, we know that You are true, and care
about no one; for You do not regard the person
of men, but teach the way of God in truth. Is it
lawful to pay taxes to Caesar, or not?
15 "Shall we pay, or shall we not pay?" But
He, knowing their hypocrisy, said to them,
"Why do you test Me? Bring Me a denarius that
I may see *it*."
16 So they brought *it*. And He said to them,
"Whose image and inscription *is* this?" They
said to Him, "Caesar's."
17 And Jesus answered and said to them,
"Render to Caesar the things that are Caesar's,
and to God the things that are God's." And they
marveled at Him.

The Sadducees: What About the Resurrection?

18 Then *some* Sadducees, who say there is
no resurrection, came to Him; and they asked
Him, saying:
19 "Teacher, Moses wrote to us that if a man's
brother dies, and leaves *his* wife behind, and
leaves no children, his brother should take his
wife and raise up offspring for his brother.
20 "Now there were seven brothers. The first
took a wife; and dying, he left no offspring.
21 "And the second took her, and he died; nor
did he leave any offspring. And the third likewise.
22 "So the seven had her and left no offspring.
Last of all the woman died also.
23 "Therefore, in the resurrection, when they
rise, whose wife will she be? For all seven had
her as wife."
24 Jesus answered and said to them, "Are you
not therefore mistaken, because you do not
know the Scriptures nor the power of God?
25 "For when they rise from the dead, they
neither marry nor are given in marriage, but
are like angels in heaven.
26 "But concerning the dead, that they rise,
have you not read in the book of Moses, in the
burning bush *passage*, how God spoke to him,

11:26 [a]NU-Text omits this verse. **12:4** [a]NU-Text omits *and at him they threw stones.* **12:11** [a]Psalm 118:22, 23

saying, *'I am the God of Abraham, the God of Isaac, and the God of Jacob'*?[a]
27 "He is not the God of the dead, but the God of the living. You are therefore greatly mistaken."

The Scribes: Which Is the First Commandment of All?

28 Then one of the scribes came, and having heard them reasoning together, perceiving[a] that He had answered them well, asked Him, "Which is the first commandment of all?"
29 Jesus answered him, "The first of all the commandments *is: 'Hear, O Israel, the LORD our God, the LORD is one.*
30 *'And you shall love the LORD your God with all your heart, with all your soul, with all your mind, and with all your strength.'*[a] This *is* the first commandment.[b]
31 "And the second, like *it, is* this: *'You shall love your neighbor as yourself.'*[a] There is no other commandment greater than these."
32 So the scribe said to Him, "Well *said,* Teacher. You have spoken the truth, for there is one God, and there is no other but He.
33 "And to love Him with all the heart, with all the understanding, with all the soul,[a] and with all the strength, and to love one's neighbor as oneself, is more than all the whole burnt offerings and sacrifices."
34 Now when Jesus saw that he answered wisely, He said to him, "You are not far from the kingdom of God." But after that no one dared question Him.

Jesus: How Can David Call His Descendant Lord?

35 Then Jesus answered and said, while He taught in the temple, "How *is it* that the scribes say that the Christ is the Son of David?
36 "For David himself said by the Holy Spirit:

'The LORD said to my Lord,
"Sit at My right hand,
Till I make Your enemies Your
footstool."'[a]

37 "Therefore David himself calls Him *'Lord'*; how is He *then* his Son?" And the common people heard Him gladly.

Beware of the Scribes

38 Then He said to them in His teaching, "Beware of the scribes, who desire to go around in long robes, *love* greetings in the marketplaces,
39 "the best seats in the synagogues, and the best places at feasts,
40 "who devour widows' houses, and for a pretense make long prayers. These will receive greater condemnation."

The Widow's Two Mites

41 Now Jesus sat opposite the treasury and saw how the people put money into the treasury. And many *who were* rich put in much.
42 Then one poor widow came and threw in two mites,[a] which make a quadrans.
43 So He called His disciples to *Himself* and said to them, "Assuredly, I say to you that this poor widow has put in more than all those who have given to the treasury;
44 "for they all put in out of their abundance, but she out of her poverty put in all that she had, her whole livelihood."

Jesus Predicts the Destruction of the Temple

13 Then as He went out of the temple, one of His disciples said to Him, "Teacher, see what manner of stones and what buildings *are here!*"
2 And Jesus answered and said to him, "Do you see these great buildings? Not *one* stone shall be left upon another, that shall not be thrown down."

The Signs of the Times and the End of the Age

3 Now as He sat on the Mount of Olives opposite the temple, Peter, James, John, and Andrew asked Him privately,
4 "Tell us, when will these things be? And what *will be* the sign when all these things will be fulfilled?"
5 And Jesus, answering them, began to say: "Take heed that no one deceives you.
6 "For many will come in My name, saying, 'I am *He,*' and will deceive many.
7 "But when you hear of wars and rumors of wars, do not be troubled; for *such things* must happen, but the end *is* not yet.
8 "For nation will rise against nation, and kingdom against kingdom. And there will be earthquakes in various places, and there will be famines and troubles.[a] These *are* the beginnings of sorrows.
9 "But watch out for yourselves, for they will deliver you up to councils, and you will be beaten in the synagogues. You will be brought[a] before rulers and kings for My sake, for a testimony to them.
10 "And the gospel must first be preached to all the nations.
11 "But when they arrest *you* and deliver you up, do not worry beforehand, or premeditate[a] what you will speak. But whatever is given you in that hour, speak that; for it is not you who speak, but the Holy Spirit.
12 "Now brother will betray brother to death, and a father *his* child; and children will rise up against parents and cause them to be put to death.
13 "And you will be hated by all for My name's sake. But he who endures to the end shall be saved.

The Great Tribulation

14 "So when you see the *'abomination of desolation,'*[a] spoken of by Daniel the prophet,[b] standing where it ought not" (let the reader understand), "then let those who are in Judea flee to the mountains.
15 "Let him who is on the housetop not go down into the house, nor enter to take anything out of his house.
16 "And let him who is in the field not go back to get his clothes.
17 "But woe to those who are pregnant and to those who are nursing babies in those days!
18 "And pray that your flight may not be in winter.

12:26 [a]Exodus 3:6, 15 **12:28** [a]NU-Text reads *seeing.* **12:30** [a]Deuteronomy 6:4, 5 [b]NU-Text omits this sentence. **12:31** [a]Leviticus 19:18 **12:33** [a]NU-Text omits *with all the soul.* **12:36** [a]Psalm 110:1 **12:42** [a]Greek *lepta,* very small copper coins worth a fraction of a penny **13:8** [a]NU-Text omits *and troubles.* **13:9** [a]NU-Text and M-Text read *will stand.* **13:11** [a]NU-Text omits *or premeditate.* **13:14** [a]Daniel 11:31; 12:11 [b]NU-Text omits *spoken of by Daniel the prophet.*

19 "For *in* those days there will be tribulation,
such as has not been since the beginning of
the creation which God created until this time,
nor ever shall be.
20 "And unless the Lord had shortened those
days, no flesh would be saved; but for the
elect's sake, whom He chose, He shortened the
days.
21 "Then if anyone says to you, 'Look, here *is*
the Christ!' or, 'Look, *He is* there!' do not be-
lieve it.
22 "For false christs and false prophets will
rise and show signs and wonders to deceive, if
possible, even the elect.
23 "But take heed; see, I have told you all
things beforehand.

The Coming of the Son of Man

24 "But in those days, after that tribulation,
the sun will be darkened, and the moon will
not give its light;
25 "the stars of heaven will fall, and the pow-
ers in the heavens will be shaken.
26 "Then they will see the Son of Man coming
in the clouds with great power and glory.
27 "And then He will send His angels, and
gather together His elect from the four winds,
from the farthest part of earth to the farthest
part of heaven.

The Parable of the Fig Tree

28 "Now learn this parable from the fig tree:
When its branch has already become tender,
and puts forth leaves, you know that summer
is near.
29 "So you also, when you see these things
happening, know that it[a] is near—at the doors!
30 "Assuredly, I say to you, this generation
will by no means pass away till all these things
take place.
31 "Heaven and earth will pass away, but My
words will by no means pass away.

No One Knows the Day or Hour

32 "But of that day and hour no one knows,
not even the angels in heaven, nor the Son, but
only the Father.
33 "Take heed, watch and pray; for you do not
know when the time is.
34 "*It is* like a man going to a far country,
who left his house and gave authority to his
servants, and to each his work, and com-
manded the doorkeeper to watch.
35 "Watch therefore, for you do not know
when the master of the house is coming—in
the evening, at midnight, at the crowing of the
rooster, or in the morning—
36 "lest, coming suddenly, he find you
sleeping.
37 "And what I say to you, I say to all: Watch!"

The Plot to Kill Jesus

14 After two days it was the Passover and
the Feast of Unleavened Bread. And the
chief priests and the scribes sought how they
might take Him by trickery and put *Him* to
death.
2 But they said, "Not during the feast, lest
there be an uproar of the people."

The Anointing at Bethany

3 And being in Bethany at the house of Si-
mon the leper, as He sat at the table, a woman
came having an alabaster flask of very costly
oil of spikenard. Then she broke the flask and
poured *it* on His head.
4 But there were some who were indignant
among themselves, and said, "Why was this
fragrant oil wasted?
5 "For it might have been sold for more than
three hundred denarii and given to the poor."
And they criticized her sharply.
6 But Jesus said, "Let her alone. Why do you
trouble her? She has done a good work for Me.
7 "For you have the poor with you always,
and whenever you wish you may do them
good; but Me you do not have always.
8 "She has done what she could. She has
come beforehand to anoint My body for burial.
9 "Assuredly, I say to you, wherever this gos-
pel is preached in the whole world, what this
woman has done will also be told as a memo-
rial to her."

Judas Agrees to Betray Jesus

10 Then Judas Iscariot, one of the twelve,
went to the chief priests to betray Him to them.
11 And when they heard *it*, they were glad,
and promised to give him money. So he sought
how he might conveniently betray Him.

Jesus Celebrates the Passover with His Disciples

12 Now on the first day of Unleavened Bread,
when they killed the Passover *lamb*, His disci-
ples said to Him, "Where do You want us to go
and prepare, that You may eat the Passover?"
13 And He sent out two of His disciples and
said to them, "Go into the city, and a man will
meet you carrying a pitcher of water; follow
him.
14 "Wherever he goes in, say to the master of
the house, 'The Teacher says, "Where is the
guest room in which I may eat the Passover
with My disciples?"'
15 "Then he will show you a large upper
room, furnished *and* prepared; there make
ready for us."
16 So His disciples went out, and came into
the city, and found it just as He had said to
them; and they prepared the Passover.
17 In the evening He came with the twelve.
18 Now as they sat and ate, Jesus said, "As-
suredly, I say to you, one of you who eats with
Me will betray Me."
19 And they began to be sorrowful, and to say
to Him one by one, "*Is* it I?" And another *said*,
"*Is* it I?"[a]
20 He answered and said to them, "*It is* one
of the twelve, who dips with Me in the dish.
21 "The Son of Man indeed goes just as it is
written of Him, but woe to that man by whom
the Son of Man is betrayed! It would have been
good for that man if he had never been born."

Jesus Institutes the Lord's Supper

22 And as they were eating, Jesus took bread,
blessed and broke *it*, and gave *it* to them and
said, "Take, eat;[a] this is My body."
23 Then He took the cup, and when He had
given thanks He gave *it* to them, and they all
drank from it.
24 And He said to them, "This is My blood of
the new[a] covenant, which is shed for many.
25 "Assuredly, I say to you, I will no longer

13:29 [a]Or *He* **14:19** [a]NU-Text omits this sentence. **14:22** [a]NU-Text omits *eat*. **14:24** [a]NU-Text omits *new*.

drink of the fruit of the vine until that day when I drink it new in the kingdom of God."

26 And when they had sung a hymn, they went out to the Mount of Olives.

Jesus Predicts Peter's Denial

27 Then Jesus said to them, "All of you will be made to stumble because of Me this night,[a] for it is written:

'I will strike the Shepherd,
And the sheep will be scattered.'[b]

28 "But after I have been raised, I will go before you to Galilee."

29 Peter said to Him, "Even if all are made to stumble, yet I *will* not *be.*"

30 Jesus said to him, "Assuredly, I say to you that today, *even* this night, before the rooster crows twice, you will deny Me three times."

31 But he spoke more vehemently, "If I have to die with You, I will not deny You!" And they all said likewise.

The Prayer in the Garden

32 Then they came to a place which was named Gethsemane; and He said to His disciples, "Sit here while I pray."

33 And He took Peter, James, and John with Him, and He began to be troubled and deeply distressed.

34 Then He said to them, "My soul is exceedingly sorrowful, *even* to death. Stay here and watch."

35 He went a little farther, and fell on the ground, and prayed that if it were possible, the hour might pass from Him.

36 And He said, "Abba, Father, all things *are* possible for You. Take this cup away from Me; nevertheless, not what I will, but what You will."

37 Then He came and found them sleeping, and said to Peter, "Simon, are you sleeping? Could you not watch one hour?

38 "Watch and pray, lest you enter into temptation. The spirit indeed *is* willing, but the flesh *is* weak."

39 Again He went away and prayed, and spoke the same words.

40 And when He returned, He found them asleep again, for their eyes were heavy; and they did not know what to answer Him.

41 Then He came the third time and said to them, "Are you still sleeping and resting? It is enough! The hour has come; behold, the Son of Man is being betrayed into the hands of sinners.

42 "Rise, let us be going. See, My betrayer is at hand."

Betrayal and Arrest in Gethsemane

43 And immediately, while He was still speaking, Judas, one of the twelve, with a great multitude with swords and clubs, came from the chief priests and the scribes and the elders.

44 Now His betrayer had given them a signal, saying, "Whomever I kiss, He is the One; seize Him and lead *Him* away safely."

45 As soon as he had come, immediately he went up to Him and said to Him, "Rabbi, Rabbi!" and kissed Him.

46 Then they laid their hands on Him and took Him.

47 And one of those who stood by drew his sword and struck the servant of the high priest, and cut off his ear.

48 Then Jesus answered and said to them, "Have you come out, as against a robber, with swords and clubs to take Me?

49 "I was daily with you in the temple teaching, and you did not seize Me. But the Scriptures must be fulfilled."

50 Then they all forsook Him and fled.

A Young Man Flees Naked

51 Now a certain young man followed Him, having a linen cloth thrown around *his* naked *body.* And the young men laid hold of him,

52 and he left the linen cloth and fled from them naked.

Jesus Faces the Sanhedrin

53 And they led Jesus away to the high priest; and with him were assembled all the chief priests, the elders, and the scribes.

54 But Peter followed Him at a distance, right into the courtyard of the high priest. And he sat with the servants and warmed himself at the fire.

55 Now the chief priests and all the council sought testimony against Jesus to put Him to death, but found none.

56 For many bore false witness against Him, but their testimonies did not agree.

57 Then some rose up and bore false witness against Him, saying,

58 "We heard Him say, 'I will destroy this temple made with hands, and within three days I will build another made without hands.' "

59 But not even then did their testimony agree.

60 And the high priest stood up in the midst and asked Jesus, saying, "Do You answer nothing? What *is it* these men testify against You?"

61 But He kept silent and answered nothing. Again the high priest asked Him, saying to Him, "Are You the Christ, the Son of the Blessed?"

62 Jesus said, "I am. And you will see the Son of Man sitting at the right hand of the Power, and coming with the clouds of heaven."

63 Then the high priest tore his clothes and said, "What further need do we have of witnesses?

64 "You have heard the blasphemy! What do you think?" And they all condemned Him to be deserving of death.

65 Then some began to spit on Him, and to blindfold Him, and to beat Him, and to say to Him, "Prophesy!" And the officers struck Him with the palms of their hands.[a]

Peter Denies Jesus, and Weeps

66 Now as Peter was below in the courtyard, one of the servant girls of the high priest came.

67 And when she saw Peter warming himself, she looked at him and said, "You also were with Jesus of Nazareth."

68 But he denied it, saying, "I neither know nor understand what you are saying." And he went out on the porch, and a rooster crowed.

69 And the servant girl saw him again, and began to say to those who stood by, "This is *one* of them."

70 But he denied it again. And a little later those who stood by said to Peter again, "Surely

14:27 [a]NU-Text omits *because of Me this night.* [b]Zechariah 13:7 **14:65** [a]NU-Text reads *received Him with slaps.*

you are *one* of them; for you are a Galilean,
and your speech shows *it*."[a]
71 Then he began to curse and swear, "I do
not know this Man of whom you speak!"
72 A second time *the* rooster crowed. Then
Peter called to mind the word that Jesus had
said to him, "Before the rooster crows twice,
you will deny Me three times." And when he
thought about it, he wept.

Jesus Faces Pilate

15 Immediately, in the morning, the chief
priests held a consultation with the el-
ders and scribes and the whole council; and
they bound Jesus, led *Him* away, and delivered
Him to Pilate.
2 Then Pilate asked Him, "Are You the King
of the Jews?" He answered and said to him, "*It
is as* you say."
3 And the chief priests accused Him of many
things, but He answered nothing.
4 Then Pilate asked Him again, saying, "Do
You answer nothing? See how many things
they testify against You!"[a]
5 But Jesus still answered nothing, so that Pi-
late marveled.

Taking the Place of Barabbas

6 Now at the feast he was accustomed to re-
leasing one prisoner to them, whomever they
requested.
7 And there was one named Barabbas, *who
was* chained with his fellow rebels; they had
committed murder in the rebellion.
8 Then the multitude, crying aloud,[a] began
to ask *him to do* just as he had always done for
them.
9 But Pilate answered them, saying, "Do you
want me to release to you the King of the Jews?"
10 For he knew that the chief priests had
handed Him over because of envy.
11 But the chief priests stirred up the crowd,
so that he should rather release Barabbas to
them.
12 Pilate answered and said to them again,
"What then do you want me to do *with Him*
whom you call the King of the Jews?"
13 So they cried out again, "Crucify Him!"
14 Then Pilate said to them, "Why, what evil
has He done?" But they cried out all the more,
"Crucify Him!"
15 So Pilate, wanting to gratify the crowd, re-
leased Barabbas to them; and he delivered
Jesus, after he had scourged *Him*, to be cruci-
fied.

The Soldiers Mock Jesus

16 Then the soldiers led Him away into the hall
called Praetorium, and they called together the
whole garrison.
17 And they clothed Him with purple; and they
twisted a crown of thorns, put it on His *head*,
18 and began to salute Him, "Hail, King of the
Jews!"
19 Then they struck Him on the head with a
reed and spat on Him; and bowing the knee,
they worshiped Him.
20 And when they had mocked Him, they took
the purple off Him, put His own clothes on
Him, and led Him out to crucify Him.

The King on a Cross

21 Then they compelled a certain man, Simon
a Cyrenian, the father of Alexander and Rufus,
as he was coming out of the country and pass-
ing by, to bear His cross.
22 And they brought Him to the place Golgo-
tha, which is translated, Place of a Skull.
23 Then they gave Him wine mingled with
myrrh to drink, but He did not take *it*.
24 And when they crucified Him, they divided
His garments, casting lots for them *to deter-
mine* what every man should take.
25 Now it was the third hour, and they cruci-
fied Him.
26 And the inscription of His accusation was
written above:

THE KING OF THE JEWS.

27 With Him they also crucified two robbers,
one on His right and the other on His left.
28 So the Scripture was fulfilled[a] which says,
*"And He was numbered with the transgres-
sors."*[b]
29 And those who passed by blasphemed Him,
wagging their heads and saying, "Aha! *You* who
destroy the temple and build *it* in three days,
30 "save Yourself, and come down from the
cross!"
31 Likewise the chief priests also, mocking
among themselves with the scribes, said, "He
saved others; Himself He cannot save.
32 "Let the Christ, the King of Israel, descend
now from the cross, that we may see and be-
lieve."[a] Even those who were crucified with Him
reviled Him.

Jesus Dies on the Cross

33 Now when the sixth hour had come, there
was darkness over the whole land until the ninth
hour.
34 And at the ninth hour Jesus cried out with
a loud voice, saying, "Eloi, Eloi, lama sabach-
thani?" which is translated, *"My God, My God,
why have You forsaken Me?"*[a]
35 Some of those who stood by, when they
heard *that*, said, "Look, He is calling for Elijah!"
36 Then someone ran and filled a sponge full
of sour wine, put *it* on a reed, and offered *it* to
Him to drink, saying, "Let Him alone; let us see
if Elijah will come to take Him down."
37 And Jesus cried out with a loud voice, and
breathed His last.
38 Then the veil of the temple was torn in two
from top to bottom.
39 So when the centurion, who stood oppo-
site Him, saw that He cried out like this and
breathed His last,[a] he said, "Truly this Man was
the Son of God!"
40 There were also women looking on from
afar, among whom were Mary Magdalene,
Mary the mother of James the Less and of Jo-
ses, and Salome,
41 who also followed Him and ministered to
Him when He was in Galilee, and many other
women who came up with Him to Jerusalem.

Jesus Buried in Joseph's Tomb

42 Now when evening had come, because it
was the Preparation Day, that is, the day before
the Sabbath,

14:70 [a]NU-Text omits *and your speech shows it.* **15:4** [a]NU-Text reads *of which they accuse You.* **15:8** [a]NU-Text reads *going up.* **15:28** [a]Isaiah 53:12 [b]NU-Text omits this verse. **15:32** [a]M-Text reads *believe Him.* **15:34** [a]Psalm 22:1 **15:39** [a]NU-Text reads *that He thus breathed His last.*

43 Joseph of Arimathea, a prominent council
member, who was himself waiting for the king-
dom of God, coming and taking courage, went
in to Pilate and asked for the body of Jesus.
44 Pilate marveled that He was already dead;
and summoning the centurion, he asked him if
He had been dead for some time.
45 So when he found out from the centurion,
he granted the body to Joseph.
46 Then he bought fine linen, took Him down,
and wrapped Him in the linen. And he laid Him
in a tomb which had been hewn out of the rock,
and rolled a stone against the door of the tomb.
47 And Mary Magdalene and Mary *the mother*
of Joses observed where He was laid.

He Is Risen

16 Now when the Sabbath was past, Mary
Magdalene, Mary *the mother* of James,
and Salome bought spices, that they might come
and anoint Him.
2 Very early in the morning, on the first *day*
of the week, they came to the tomb when the
sun had risen.
3 And they said among themselves, "Who will
roll away the stone from the door of the tomb
for us?"
4 But when they looked up, they saw that the
stone had been rolled away—for it was very
large.
5 And entering the tomb, they saw a young
man clothed in a long white robe sitting on the
right side; and they were alarmed.
6 But he said to them, "Do not be alarmed.
You seek Jesus of Nazareth, who was crucified.
He is risen! He is not here. See the place where
they laid Him.
7 "But go, tell His disciples—and Peter—that
He is going before you into Galilee; there you
will see Him, as He said to you."
8 So they went out quickly[a] and fled from
the tomb, for they trembled and were amazed.
And they said nothing to anyone, for they were
afraid.

Mary Magdalene Sees the Risen Lord

9 Now when *He* rose early on the first *day*
of the week, He appeared first to Mary Magda-
lene, out of whom He had cast seven demons.
10 She went and told those who had been
with Him, as they mourned and wept.
11 And when they heard that He was alive
and had been seen by her, they did not believe.

Jesus Appears to Two Disciples

12 After that, He appeared in another form to
two of them as they walked and went into the
country.
13 And they went and told *it* to the rest, *but*
they did not believe them either.

The Great Commission

14 Later He appeared to the eleven as they sat
at the table; and He rebuked their unbelief and
hardness of heart, because they did not believe
those who had seen Him after He had risen.
15 And He said to them, "Go into all the world
and preach the gospel to every creature.
16 "He who believes and is baptized will be
saved; but he who does not believe will be con-
demned.
17 "And these signs will follow those who be-
lieve: In My name they will cast out demons;
they will speak with new tongues;
18 "they[a] will take up serpents; and if they drink
anything deadly, it will by no means hurt them;
they will lay hands on the sick, and they will
recover."

Christ Ascends to God's Right Hand

19 So then, after the Lord had spoken to them,
He was received up into heaven, and sat down
at the right hand of God.
20 And they went out and preached every-
where, the Lord working with *them* and con-
firming the word through the accompanying
signs. Amen.[a]

The Gospel According to LUKE

Dedication to Theophilus

1 Inasmuch as many have taken in hand to set
in order a narrative of those things which
have been fulfilled[a] among us,
2 just as those who from the beginning were
eyewitnesses and ministers of the word deliv-
ered them to us,
3 it seemed good to me also, having had per-
fect understanding of all things from the very
first, to write to you an orderly account, most
excellent Theophilus,
4 that you may know the certainty of those
things in which you were instructed.

John's Birth Announced to Zacharias

5 There was in the days of Herod, the king of
Judea, a certain priest named Zacharias, of the
division of Abijah. His wife *was* of the daugh-
ters of Aaron, and her name *was* Elizabeth.
6 And they were both righteous before God,
walking in all the commandments and ordi-
nances of the Lord blameless.
7 But they had no child, because Elizabeth
was barren, and they were both well advanced
in years.
8 So it was, that while he was serving as
priest before God in the order of his division,
9 according to the custom of the priesthood,
his lot fell to burn incense when he went into
the temple of the Lord.
10 And the whole multitude of the people was
praying outside at the hour of incense.
11 Then an angel of the Lord appeared to
him, standing on the right side of the altar of
incense.

16:8 [a]NU-Text and M-Text omit *quickly.* 16:18 [a]NU-Text reads *and in their hands they will.* 16:20 [a]Verses 9–20 are bracketed in NU-Text as not original. They are lacking in Codex Sinaiticus and Codex Vaticanus, although nearly all other manuscripts of Mark contain them. 1:1 [a]Or *are most surely believed*

12 And when Zacharias saw *him*, he was trou-
bled, and fear fell upon him.
13 But the angel said to him, "Do not be afraid,
Zacharias, for your prayer is heard; and your
wife Elizabeth will bear you a son, and you shall
call his name John.
14 "And you will have joy and gladness, and
many will rejoice at his birth.
15 "For he will be great in the sight of the
Lord, and shall drink neither wine nor strong
drink. He will also be filled with the Holy Spirit,
even from his mother's womb.
16 "And he will turn many of the children of
Israel to the Lord their God.
17 "He will also go before Him in the spirit
and power of Elijah, *'to turn the hearts of the
fathers to the children,'*[a] and the disobedient
to the wisdom of the just, to make ready a people
prepared for the Lord."
18 And Zacharias said to the angel, "How shall
I know this? For I am an old man, and my wife
is well advanced in years."
19 And the angel answered and said to him,
"I am Gabriel, who stands in the presence of
God, and was sent to speak to you and bring
you these glad tidings.
20 "But behold, you will be mute and not able
to speak until the day these things take place,
because you did not believe my words which
will be fulfilled in their own time."
21 And the people waited for Zacharias, and
marveled that he lingered so long in the temple.
22 But when he came out, he could not speak
to them; and they perceived that he had seen a
vision in the temple, for he beckoned to them
and remained speechless.
23 So it was, as soon as the days of his service
were completed, that he departed to his own
house.
24 Now after those days his wife Elizabeth con-
ceived; and she hid herself five months, saying,
25 "Thus the Lord has dealt with me, in the
days when He looked on *me*, to take away my
reproach among people."

Christ's Birth Announced to Mary

26 Now in the sixth month the angel Gabriel
was sent by God to a city of Galilee named Naza-
reth,
27 to a virgin betrothed to a man whose name
was Joseph, of the house of David. The virgin's
name *was* Mary.
28 And having come in, the angel said to her,
"Rejoice, highly favored *one*, the Lord *is* with
you; blessed *are* you among women!"[a]
29 But when she saw *him*,[a] she was troubled
at his saying, and considered what manner of
greeting this was.
30 Then the angel said to her, "Do not be afraid,
Mary, for you have found favor with God.
31 "And behold, you will conceive in your
womb and bring forth a Son, and shall call His
name JESUS.
32 "He will be great, and will be called the
Son of the Highest; and the Lord God will give
Him the throne of His father David.
33 "And He will reign over the house of Jacob
forever, and of His kingdom there will be no
end."
34 Then Mary said to the angel, "How can this
be, since I do not know a man?"
35 And the angel answered and said to her,
"*The* Holy Spirit will come upon you, and the
power of the Highest will overshadow you; there-
fore, also, that Holy One who is to be born will
be called the Son of God.
36 "Now indeed, Elizabeth your relative has
also conceived a son in her old age; and this is
now the sixth month for her who was called bar-
ren.
37 "For with God nothing will be impossible."
38 Then Mary said, "Behold the maidservant
of the Lord! Let it be to me according to your
word." And the angel departed from her.

Mary Visits Elizabeth

39 Now Mary arose in those days and went
into the hill country with haste, to a city of Ju-
dah,
40 and entered the house of Zacharias and
greeted Elizabeth.
41 And it happened, when Elizabeth heard the
greeting of Mary, that the babe leaped in her
womb; and Elizabeth was filled with the Holy
Spirit.
42 Then she spoke out with a loud voice and
said, "Blessed *are* you among women, and
blessed *is* the fruit of your womb!
43 "But why *is* this *granted* to me, that the
mother of my Lord should come to me?
44 "For indeed, as soon as the voice of your
greeting sounded in my ears, the babe leaped
in my womb for joy.
45 "Blessed *is* she who believed, for there will
be a fulfillment of those things which were told
her from the Lord."

The Song of Mary

46 And Mary said:

"My soul magnifies the Lord,
47 And my spirit has rejoiced in God my
Savior.
48 For He has regarded the lowly state of
His maidservant;
For behold, henceforth all generations
will call me blessed.
49 For He who is mighty has done great
things for me,
And holy *is* His name.
50 And His mercy *is* on those who fear Him
From generation to generation.
51 He has shown strength with His arm;
He has scattered *the* proud in the
imagination of their hearts.
52 He has put down the mighty from *their*
thrones,
And exalted *the* lowly.
53 He has filled *the* hungry with good
things,
And *the* rich He has sent away empty.
54 He has helped His servant Israel,
In remembrance of *His* mercy,
55 As He spoke to our fathers,
To Abraham and to his seed forever."

56 And Mary remained with her about three
months, and returned to her house.

Birth of John the Baptist

57 Now Elizabeth's full time came for her to
be delivered, and she brought forth a son.
58 When her neighbors and relatives heard
how the Lord had shown great mercy to her,
they rejoiced with her.

1:17 [a]Malachi 4:5, 6 **1:28** [a]NU-Text omits *blessed are you among women.* **1:29** [a]NU-Text omits *when she saw him.*

Circumcision of John the Baptist

59 So it was, on the eighth day, that they came to circumcise the child; and they would have called him by the name of his father, Zacharias.
60 His mother answered and said, "No; he shall be called John."
61 But they said to her, "There is no one among your relatives who is called by this name."
62 So they made signs to his father—what he would have him called.
63 And he asked for a writing tablet, and wrote, saying, "His name is John." So they all marveled.
64 Immediately his mouth was opened and his tongue *loosed*, and he spoke, praising God.
65 Then fear came on all who dwelt around them; and all these sayings were discussed throughout all the hill country of Judea.
66 And all those who heard *them* kept *them* in their hearts, saying, "What kind of child will this be?" And the hand of the Lord was with him.

Zacharias' Prophecy

67 Now his father Zacharias was filled with the Holy Spirit, and prophesied, saying:

68 "Blessed *is* the Lord God of Israel,
For He has visited and redeemed His people,
69 And has raised up a horn of salvation for us
In the house of His servant David,
70 As He spoke by the mouth of His holy prophets,
Who *have been* since the world began,
71 That we should be saved from our enemies
And from the hand of all who hate us,
72 To perform the mercy *promised* to our fathers
And to remember His holy covenant,
73 The oath which He swore to our father Abraham:
74 To grant us that we,
Being delivered from the hand of our enemies,
Might serve Him without fear,
75 In holiness and righteousness before Him all the days of our life.

76 "And you, child, will be called the prophet of the Highest;
For you will go before the face of the Lord to prepare His ways,
77 To give knowledge of salvation to His people
By the remission of their sins,
78 Through the tender mercy of our God,
With which the Dayspring from on high has visited[a] us;
79 To give light to those who sit in darkness and the shadow of death,
To guide our feet into the way of peace."

80 So the child grew and became strong in spirit, and was in the deserts till the day of his manifestation to Israel.

Christ Born of Mary

2 And it came to pass in those days *that* a decree went out from Caesar Augustus that all the world should be registered.
2 This census first took place while Quirinius was governing Syria.
3 So all went to be registered, everyone to his own city.
4 Joseph also went up from Galilee, out of the city of Nazareth, into Judea, to the city of David, which is called Bethlehem, because he was of the house and lineage of David,
5 to be registered with Mary, his betrothed wife,[a] who was with child.
6 So it was, that while they were there, the days were completed for her to be delivered.
7 And she brought forth her firstborn Son, and wrapped Him in swaddling cloths, and laid Him in a manger, because there was no room for them in the inn.

Glory in the Highest

8 Now there were in the same country shepherds living out in the fields, keeping watch over their flock by night.
9 And behold,[a] an angel of the Lord stood before them, and the glory of the Lord shone around them, and they were greatly afraid.
10 Then the angel said to them, "Do not be afraid, for behold, I bring you good tidings of great joy which will be to all people.
11 "For there is born to you this day in the city of David a Savior, who is Christ the Lord.
12 "And this *will be* the sign to you: You will find a Babe wrapped in swaddling cloths, lying in a manger."
13 And suddenly there was with the angel a multitude of the heavenly host praising God and saying:

14 "Glory to God in the highest,
And on earth peace, goodwill toward men!"[a]

15 So it was, when the angels had gone away from them into heaven, that the shepherds said to one another, "Let us now go to Bethlehem and see this thing that has come to pass, which the Lord has made known to us."
16 And they came with haste and found Mary and Joseph, and the Babe lying in a manger.
17 Now when they had seen *Him*, they made widely[a] known the saying which was told them concerning this Child.
18 And all those who heard *it* marveled at those things which were told them by the shepherds.
19 But Mary kept all these things and pondered *them* in her heart.
20 Then the shepherds returned, glorifying and praising God for all the things that they had heard and seen, as it was told them.

Circumcision of Jesus

21 And when eight days were completed for the circumcision of the Child,[a] His name was called JESUS, the name given by the angel before He was conceived in the womb.

Jesus Presented in the Temple

22 Now when the days of her purification according to the law of Moses were completed, they brought Him to Jerusalem to present *Him* to the Lord
23 (as it is written in the law of the Lord, *"Every male who opens the womb shall be called holy to the* LORD*"*),[a]

1:78 [a]NU-Text reads *shall visit.* **2:5** [a]NU-Text omits *wife.* **2:9** [a]NU-Text omits *behold.* **2:14** [a]NU-Text reads *toward men of goodwill.* **2:17** [a]NU-Text omits *widely.* **2:21** [a]NU-Text reads *for His circumcision.* **2:23** [a]Exodus 13:2, 12, 15

24 and to offer a sacrifice according to what
is said in the law of the Lord, *"A pair of turtle-*
doves or two young pigeons."[a]

Simeon Sees God's Salvation

25 And behold, there was a man in Jerusalem
whose name *was* Simeon, and this man *was*
just and devout, waiting for the Consolation of
Israel, and the Holy Spirit was upon him.
26 And it had been revealed to him by the
Holy Spirit that he would not see death before
he had seen the Lord's Christ.
27 So he came by the Spirit into the temple.
And when the parents brought in the Child
Jesus, to do for Him according to the custom
of the law,
28 he took Him up in his arms and blessed
God and said:

29 "Lord, now You are letting Your servant
depart in peace,
According to Your word;
30 For my eyes have seen Your salvation
31 Which You have prepared before the face
of all peoples,
32 A light to *bring* revelation to the Gentiles,
And the glory of Your people Israel."

33 And Joseph and His mother[a] marveled at
those things which were spoken of Him.
34 Then Simeon blessed them, and said to Mary
His mother, "Behold, this *Child* is destined for
the fall and rising of many in Israel, and for a
sign which will be spoken against
35 "(yes, a sword will pierce through your own
soul also), that the thoughts of many hearts may
be revealed."

Anna Bears Witness to the Redeemer

36 Now there was one, Anna, a prophetess,
the daughter of Phanuel, of the tribe of Asher.
She was of a great age, and had lived with a
husband seven years from her virginity;
37 and this woman *was* a widow of about
eighty-four years,[a] who did not depart from the
temple, but served *God* with fastings and prayers
night and day.
38 And coming in that instant she gave thanks
to the Lord,[a] and spoke of Him to all those who
looked for redemption in Jerusalem.

The Family Returns to Nazareth

39 So when they had performed all things ac-
cording to the law of the Lord, they returned
to Galilee, to their *own* city, Nazareth.
40 And the Child grew and became strong in
spirit,[a] filled with wisdom; and the grace of God
was upon Him.

The Boy Jesus Amazes the Scholars

41 His parents went to Jerusalem every year
at the Feast of the Passover.
42 And when He was twelve years old, they
went up to Jerusalem according to the custom
of the feast.
43 When they had finished the days, as they
returned, the Boy Jesus lingered behind in Je-
rusalem. And Joseph and His mother[a] did not
know *it;*
44 but supposing Him to have been in the com-
pany, they went a day's journey, and sought Him
among *their* relatives and acquaintances.
45 So when they did not find Him, they re-
turned to Jerusalem, seeking Him.
46 Now so it was *that* after three days they
found Him in the temple, sitting in the midst of
the teachers, both listening to them and asking
them questions.
47 And all who heard Him were astonished at
His understanding and answers.
48 So when they saw Him, they were amazed;
and His mother said to Him, "Son, why have
You done this to us? Look, Your father and I
have sought You anxiously."
49 And He said to them, "Why did you seek
Me? Did you not know that I must be about My
Father's business?"
50 But they did not understand the statement
which He spoke to them.

Jesus Advances in Wisdom and Favor

51 Then He went down with them and came to
Nazareth, and was subject to them, but His
mother kept all these things in her heart.
52 And Jesus increased in wisdom and stat-
ure, and in favor with God and men.

John the Baptist Prepares the Way

3 Now in the fifteenth year of the reign of
Tiberius Caesar, Pontius Pilate being gov-
ernor of Judea, Herod being tetrarch of Gali-
lee, his brother Philip tetrarch of Iturea and the
region of Trachonitis, and Lysanias tetrarch of
Abilene,
2 while Annas and Caiaphas were high
priests,[a] the word of God came to John the son
of Zacharias in the wilderness.
3 And he went into all the region around the
Jordan, preaching a baptism of repentance for
the remission of sins,
4 as it is written in the book of the words of
Isaiah the prophet, saying:

"The voice of one crying in the wilderness:
'Prepare the way of the LORD;
Make His paths straight.
5 *Every valley shall be filled*
And every mountain and hill brought
low;
The crooked places shall be made
straight
And the rough ways smooth;
6 *And all flesh shall see the salvation of*
God.' "[a]

John Preaches to the People

7 Then he said to the multitudes that came out
to be baptized by him, "Brood of vipers! Who
warned you to flee from the wrath to come?
8 "Therefore bear fruits worthy of repentance,
and do not begin to say to yourselves, 'We have
Abraham as *our* father.' For I say to you that
God is able to raise up children to Abraham
from these stones.
9 "And even now the ax is laid to the root of
the trees. Therefore every tree which does not
bear good fruit is cut down and thrown into
the fire."
10 So the people asked him, saying, "What
shall we do then?"
11 He answered and said to them, "He who has
two tunics, let him give to him who has none;
and he who has food, let him do likewise."

2:24 [a]Leviticus 12:8 **2:33** [a]NU-Text reads *And His father and mother.* **2:37** [a]NU-Text reads *a widow until she was eighty-four.* **2:38** [a]NU-Text reads *to God.* **2:40** [a]NU-Text omits *in spirit.* **2:43** [a]NU-Text reads *And His parents.* **3:2** [a]NU-Text and M-Text read *in the high priesthood of Annas and Caiaphas.* **3:6** [a]Isaiah 40:3–5

12 Then tax collectors also came to be bap-
tized, and said to him, "Teacher, what shall we
do?"
13 And he said to them, "Collect no more than
what is appointed for you."
14 Likewise the soldiers asked him, saying,
"And what shall we do?" So he said to them,
"Do not intimidate anyone or accuse falsely, and
be content with your wages."
15 Now as the people were in expectation, and
all reasoned in their hearts about John, whether
he was the Christ *or* not,
16 John answered, saying to all, "I indeed
baptize you with water; but One mightier than
I is coming, whose sandal strap I am not wor-
thy to loose. He will baptize you with the Holy
Spirit and fire.
17 "His winnowing fan *is* in His hand, and He
will thoroughly clean out His threshing floor, and
gather the wheat into His barn; but the chaff
He will burn with unquenchable fire."
18 And with many other exhortations he
preached to the people.
19 But Herod the tetrarch, being rebuked by
him concerning Herodias, his brother Philip's
wife,[a] and for all the evils which Herod had
done,
20 also added this, above all, that he shut John
up in prison.

John Baptizes Jesus

21 When all the people were baptized, it came
to pass that Jesus also was baptized; and while
He prayed, the heaven was opened.
22 And the Holy Spirit descended in bodily
form like a dove upon Him, and a voice came
from heaven which said, "You are My beloved
Son; in You I am well pleased."

The Genealogy of Jesus Christ

23 Now Jesus Himself began *His ministry at*
about thirty years of age, being (as was sup-
posed) *the* son of Joseph, *the son* of Heli,
24 *the son* of Matthat,[a] *the son* of Levi, *the son*
of Melchi, *the son* of Janna, *the son* of Joseph,
25 *the son* of Mattathiah, *the son* of Amos,
the son of Nahum, *the son* of Esli, *the son* of
Naggai,
26 *the son* of Maath, *the son* of Mattathiah,
the son of Semei, *the son* of Joseph, *the son* of
Judah,
27 *the son* of Joannas, *the son* of Rhesa, *the
son* of Zerubbabel, *the son* of Shealtiel, *the son*
of Neri,
28 *the son* of Melchi, *the son* of Addi, *the son*
of Cosam, *the son* of Elmodam, *the son* of Er,
29 *the son* of Jose, *the son* of Eliezer, *the son*
of Jorim, *the son* of Matthat, *the son* of Levi,
30 *the son* of Simeon, *the son* of Judah, *the
son* of Joseph, *the son* of Jonan, *the son* of Eli-
akim,
31 *the son* of Melea, *the son* of Menan, *the
son* of Mattathah, *the son* of Nathan, *the son*
of David,
32 *the son* of Jesse, *the son* of Obed, *the son*
of Boaz, *the son* of Salmon, *the son* of Nah-
shon,
33 *the son* of Amminadab, *the son* of Ram, *the
son* of Hezron, *the son* of Perez, *the son* of Judah,
34 *the son* of Jacob, *the son* of Isaac, *the son*
of Abraham, *the son* of Terah, *the son* of Nahor,
35 *the son* of Serug, *the son* of Reu, *the son*
of Peleg, *the son* of Eber, *the son* of Shelah,
36 *the son* of Cainan, *the son* of Arphaxad,
the son of Shem, *the son* of Noah, *the son* of
Lamech,
37 *the son* of Methuselah, *the son* of Enoch,
the son of Jared, *the son* of Mahalalel, *the son*
of Cainan,
38 *the son* of Enosh, *the son* of Seth, *the son*
of Adam, *the son* of God.

Satan Tempts Jesus

4 Then Jesus, being filled with the Holy Spirit,
returned from the Jordan and was led by
the Spirit into[a] the wilderness,
2 being tempted for forty days by the devil.
And in those days He ate nothing, and after-
ward, when they had ended, He was hungry.
3 And the devil said to Him, "If You are the
Son of God, command this stone to become
bread."
4 But Jesus answered him, saying,[a] "It is writ-
ten, *'Man shall not live by bread alone, but by
every word of God.'* "[b]
5 Then the devil, taking Him up on a high
mountain, showed Him[a] all the kingdoms of
the world in a moment of time.
6 And the devil said to Him, "All this author-
ity I will give You, and their glory; for *this* has
been delivered to me, and I give it to whomever
I wish.
7 "Therefore, if You will worship before me,
all will be Yours."
8 And Jesus answered and said to him, "Get
behind Me, Satan![a] For[b] it is written, *'You shall
worship the LORD your God, and Him only you
shall serve.'* "[c]
9 Then he brought Him to Jerusalem, set Him
on the pinnacle of the temple, and said to Him,
"If You are the Son of God, throw Yourself down
from here.
10 "For it is written:

*'He shall give His angels charge over you,
To keep you,'*

11 "and,

*'In their hands they shall bear you up,
Lest you dash your foot against a
stone.'* "[a]

12 And Jesus answered and said to him, "It has
been said, *'You shall not tempt the LORD your
God.'* "[a]
13 Now when the devil had ended every temp-
tation, he departed from Him until an oppor-
tune time.

Jesus Begins His Galilean Ministry

14 Then Jesus returned in the power of the
Spirit to Galilee, and news of Him went out
through all the surrounding region.
15 And He taught in their synagogues, being
glorified by all.

3:19 [a]NU-Text reads *his brother's wife.* **3:24** [a]This and several other names in the genealogy are spelled somewhat differently in the NU-Text. Since the New King James Version uses the Old Testament spelling for persons mentioned in the New Testament, these variations, which come from the Greek, have not been footnoted. **4:1** [a]NU-Text reads *in.* **4:4** [a]Deuteronomy 8:3 [b]NU-Text omits *but by every word of God.* **4:5** [a]NU-Text reads *And taking Him up, he showed Him.* **4:8** [a]NU-Text omits *Get behind Me, Satan.* [b]NU-Text and M-Text omit *For.* [c]Deuteronomy 6:13
4:11 [a]Psalm 91:11, 12 **4:12** [a]Deuteronomy 6:16

Jesus Rejected at Nazareth

16 So He came to Nazareth, where He had
been brought up. And as His custom was, He
went into the synagogue on the Sabbath day,
and stood up to read.
17 And He was handed the book of the prophet
Isaiah. And when He had opened the book, He
found the place where it was written:

18 *"The Spirit of the LORD is upon Me,*
Because He has anointed Me
To preach the gospel to the poor;
He has sent Me to heal the
brokenhearted,[a]
To proclaim liberty to the captives
And recovery of sight to the blind,
To set at liberty those who are oppressed;
19 *To proclaim the acceptable year of the*
LORD."[a]

20 Then He closed the book, and gave *it* back
to the attendant and sat down. And the eyes of
all who were in the synagogue were fixed on
Him.
21 And He began to say to them, "Today this
Scripture is fulfilled in your hearing."
22 So all bore witness to Him, and marveled
at the gracious words which proceeded out of
His mouth. And they said, "Is this not Joseph's
son?"
23 He said to them, "You will surely say this
proverb to Me, 'Physician, heal yourself! What-
ever we have heard done in Capernaum,[a] do
also here in Your country.'"
24 Then He said, "Assuredly, I say to you, no
prophet is accepted in his own country.
25 "But I tell you truly, many widows were in
Israel in the days of Elijah, when the heaven
was shut up three years and six months, and
there was a great famine throughout all the land;
26 "but to none of them was Elijah sent ex-
cept to Zarephath,[a] *in the region* of Sidon, to a
woman *who was* a widow.
27 "And many lepers were in Israel in the time
of Elisha the prophet, and none of them was
cleansed except Naaman the Syrian."
28 So all those in the synagogue, when they
heard these things, were filled with wrath,
29 and rose up and thrust Him out of the city;
and they led Him to the brow of the hill on
which their city was built, that they might throw
Him down over the cliff.
30 Then passing through the midst of them,
He went His way.

Jesus Casts Out an Unclean Spirit

31 Then He went down to Capernaum, a city
of Galilee, and was teaching them on the Sab-
baths.
32 And they were astonished at His teaching,
for His word was with authority.
33 Now in the synagogue there was a man who
had a spirit of an unclean demon. And he cried
out with a loud voice,
34 saying, "Let *us* alone! What have we to do
with You, Jesus of Nazareth? Did You come to
destroy us? I know who You are—the Holy One
of God!"
35 But Jesus rebuked him, saying, "Be quiet,
and come out of him!" And when the demon
had thrown him in *their* midst, it came out of
him and did not hurt him.
36 Then they were all amazed and spoke among
themselves, saying, "What a word this *is!* For
with authority and power He commands the
unclean spirits, and they come out."
37 And the report about Him went out into
every place in the surrounding region.

Peter's Mother-in-Law Healed

38 Now He arose from the synagogue and en-
tered Simon's house. But Simon's wife's mother
was sick with a high fever, and they made re-
quest of Him concerning her.
39 So He stood over her and rebuked the fe-
ver, and it left her. And immediately she arose
and served them.

Many Healed After Sabbath Sunset

40 When the sun was setting, all those who had
any that were sick with various diseases brought
them to Him; and He laid His hands on every
one of them and healed them.
41 And demons also came out of many, crying
out and saying, "You are the Christ,[a] the Son
of God!" And He, rebuking *them,* did not allow
them to speak, for they knew that He was the
Christ.

Jesus Preaches in Galilee

42 Now when it was day, He departed and went
into a deserted place. And the crowd sought
Him and came to Him, and tried to keep Him
from leaving them;
43 but He said to them, "I must preach the
kingdom of God to the other cities also, be-
cause for this purpose I have been sent."
44 And He was preaching in the synagogues
of Galilee.[a]

Four Fishermen Called as Disciples

5 So it was, as the multitude pressed about
Him to hear the word of God, that He stood
by the Lake of Gennesaret,
2 and saw two boats standing by the lake;
but the fishermen had gone from them and were
washing *their* nets.
3 Then He got into one of the boats, which
was Simon's, and asked him to put out a little
from the land. And He sat down and taught the
multitudes from the boat.
4 When He had stopped speaking, He said
to Simon, "Launch out into the deep and let
down your nets for a catch."
5 But Simon answered and said to Him, "Mas-
ter, we have toiled all night and caught noth-
ing; nevertheless at Your word I will let down
the net."
6 And when they had done this, they caught
a great number of fish, and their net was break-
ing.
7 So they signaled to *their* partners in the
other boat to come and help them. And they
came and filled both the boats, so that they be-
gan to sink.
8 When Simon Peter saw *it,* he fell down at
Jesus' knees, saying, "Depart from me, for I
am a sinful man, O Lord!"
9 For he and all who were with him were as-
tonished at the catch of fish which they had
taken;
10 and so also *were* James and John, the sons
of Zebedee, who were partners with Simon. And

4:18 [a]NU-Text omits *to heal the brokenhearted.* **4:19** [a]Isaiah 61:1, 2 **4:23** [a]Here and elsewhere the NU-Text spelling is *Capharnaum.* **4:26** [a]Greek *Sarepta* **4:41** [a]NU-Text omits *the Christ.* **4:44** [a]NU-Text reads *Judea.*

Jesus said to Simon, "Do not be afraid. From now on you will catch men."

11 So when they had brought their boats to land, they forsook all and followed Him.

Jesus Cleanses a Leper

12 And it happened when He was in a certain city, that behold, a man who was full of leprosy saw Jesus; and he fell on *his* face and implored Him, saying, "Lord, if You are willing, You can make me clean."

13 Then He put out *His* hand and touched him, saying, "I am willing; be cleansed." Immediately the leprosy left him.

14 And He charged him to tell no one, "But go and show yourself to the priest, and make an offering for your cleansing, as a testimony to them, just as Moses commanded."

15 However, the report went around concerning Him all the more; and great multitudes came together to hear, and to be healed by Him of their infirmities.

16 So He Himself *often* withdrew into the wilderness and prayed.

Jesus Forgives and Heals a Paralytic

17 Now it happened on a certain day, as He was teaching, that there were Pharisees and teachers of the law sitting by, who had come out of every town of Galilee, Judea, and Jerusalem. And the power of the Lord was *present* to heal them.[a]

18 Then behold, men brought on a bed a man who was paralyzed, whom they sought to bring in and lay before Him.

19 And when they could not find how they might bring him in, because of the crowd, they went up on the housetop and let him down with *his* bed through the tiling into the midst before Jesus.

20 When He saw their faith, He said to him, "Man, your sins are forgiven you."

21 And the scribes and the Pharisees began to reason, saying, "Who is this who speaks blasphemies? Who can forgive sins but God alone?"

22 But when Jesus perceived their thoughts, He answered and said to them, "Why are you reasoning in your hearts?

23 "Which is easier, to say, 'Your sins are forgiven you,' or to say, 'Rise up and walk'?

24 "But that you may know that the Son of Man has power on earth to forgive sins"—He said to the man who was paralyzed, "I say to you, arise, take up your bed, and go to your house."

25 Immediately he rose up before them, took up what he had been lying on, and departed to his own house, glorifying God.

26 And they were all amazed, and they glorified God and were filled with fear, saying, "We have seen strange things today!"

Matthew the Tax Collector

27 After these things He went out and saw a tax collector named Levi, sitting at the tax office. And He said to him, "Follow Me."

28 So he left all, rose up, and followed Him.

29 Then Levi gave Him a great feast in his own house. And there were a great number of tax collectors and others who sat down with them.

30 And their scribes and the Pharisees[a] complained against His disciples, saying, "Why do You eat and drink with tax collectors and sinners?"

31 Jesus answered and said to them, "Those who are well have no need of a physician, but those who are sick.

32 "I have not come to call *the* righteous, but sinners, to repentance."

Jesus Is Questioned About Fasting

33 Then they said to Him, "Why do[a] the disciples of John fast often and make prayers, and likewise those of the Pharisees, but Yours eat and drink?"

34 And He said to them, "Can you make the friends of the bridegroom fast while the bridegroom is with them?

35 "But the days will come when the bridegroom will be taken away from them; then they will fast in those days."

36 Then He spoke a parable to them: "No one puts a piece from a new garment on an old one;[a] otherwise the new makes a tear, and also the piece that was *taken* out of the new does not match the old.

37 "And no one puts new wine into old wineskins; or else the new wine will burst the wineskins and be spilled, and the wineskins will be ruined.

38 "But new wine must be put into new wineskins, and both are preserved.[a]

39 "And no one, having drunk old *wine*, immediately[a] desires new; for he says, 'The old is better.'"[b]

Jesus Is Lord of the Sabbath

6 Now it happened on the second Sabbath after the first[a] that He went through the grainfields. And His disciples plucked the heads of grain and ate *them*, rubbing *them* in *their* hands.

2 And some of the Pharisees said to them, "Why are you doing what is not lawful to do on the Sabbath?"

3 But Jesus answering them said, "Have you not even read this, what David did when he was hungry, he and those who were with him:

4 "how he went into the house of God, took and ate the showbread, and also gave some to those with him, which is not lawful for any but the priests to eat?"

5 And He said to them, "The Son of Man is also Lord of the Sabbath."

Healing on the Sabbath

6 Now it happened on another Sabbath, also, that He entered the synagogue and taught. And a man was there whose right hand was withered.

7 So the scribes and Pharisees watched Him closely, whether He would heal on the Sabbath, that they might find an accusation against Him.

8 But He knew their thoughts, and said to the man who had the withered hand, "Arise and stand here." And he arose and stood.

9 Then Jesus said to them, "I will ask you one thing: Is it lawful on the Sabbath to do good or to do evil, to save life or to destroy?"[a]

10 And when He had looked around at them

5:17 [a]NU-Text reads *present with Him to heal.* **5:30** [a]NU-Text reads *But the Pharisees and their scribes.* **5:33** [a]NU-Text omits *Why do,* making the verse a statement. **5:36** [a]NU-Text reads *No one tears a piece from a new garment and puts it on an old one.* **5:38** [a]NU-Text omits *and both are preserved.* **5:39** [a]NU-Text omits *immediately.* [b]NU-Text reads *good.* **6:1** [a]NU-Text reads *on a Sabbath.* **6:9** [a]M-Text reads *to kill.*

all, He said to the man,[a] "Stretch out your hand."
And he did so, and his hand was restored as
whole as the other.[b]
11 But they were filled with rage, and discussed with one another what they might do to Jesus.

The Twelve Apostles

12 Now it came to pass in those days that He
went out to the mountain to pray, and continued all night in prayer to God.
13 And when it was day, He called His disciples to *Himself;* and from them He chose twelve
whom He also named apostles:
14 Simon, whom He also named Peter, and Andrew his brother; James and John; Philip and
Bartholomew;
15 Matthew and Thomas; James the *son* of Alphaeus, and Simon called the Zealot;
16 Judas *the son* of James, and Judas Iscariot
who also became a traitor.

Jesus Heals a Great Multitude

17 And He came down with them and stood
on a level place with a crowd of His disciples
and a great multitude of people from all Judea
and Jerusalem, and from the seacoast of Tyre
and Sidon, who came to hear Him and be healed
of their diseases,
18 as well as those who were tormented with
unclean spirits. And they were healed.
19 And the whole multitude sought to touch
Him, for power went out from Him and healed
them all.

The Beatitudes

20 Then He lifted up His eyes toward His disciples, and said:

"Blessed *are you* poor,
For yours is the kingdom of God.
21 Blessed *are you* who hunger now,
For you shall be filled.
Blessed *are you* who weep now,
For you shall laugh.
22 Blessed are you when men hate you,
And when they exclude you,
And revile *you,* and cast out your name as evil,
For the Son of Man's sake.
23 Rejoice in that day and leap for joy!
For indeed your reward *is* great in heaven,
For in like manner their fathers did to the prophets.

Jesus Pronounces Woes

24 "But woe to you who are rich,
For you have received your consolation.
25 Woe to you who are full,
For you shall hunger.
Woe to you who laugh now,
For you shall mourn and weep.
26 Woe to you[a] when all[b] men speak well of you,
For so did their fathers to the false prophets.

Love Your Enemies

27 "But I say to you who hear: Love your enemies, do good to those who hate you,
28 "bless those who curse you, and pray for
those who spitefully use you.
29 "To him who strikes you on the *one* cheek,
offer the other also. And from him who takes
away your cloak, do not withhold *your* tunic
either.
30 "Give to everyone who asks of you. And
from him who takes away your goods do not
ask *them* back.
31 "And just as you want men to do to you,
you also do to them likewise.
32 "But if you love those who love you, what
credit is that to you? For even sinners love those
who love them.
33 "And if you do good to those who do good
to you, what credit is that to you? For even sinners do the same.
34 "And if you lend *to those* from whom you
hope to receive back, what credit is that to you?
For even sinners lend to sinners to receive as
much back.
35 "But love your enemies, do good, and lend,
hoping for nothing in return; and your reward
will be great, and you will be sons of the Most
High. For He is kind to the unthankful and evil.
36 "Therefore be merciful, just as your Father
also is merciful.

Do Not Judge

37 "Judge not, and you shall not be judged.
Condemn not, and you shall not be condemned.
Forgive, and you will be forgiven.
38 "Give, and it will be given to you: good
measure, pressed down, shaken together, and
running over will be put into your bosom. For
with the same measure that you use, it will be
measured back to you."
39 And He spoke a parable to them: "Can the
blind lead the blind? Will they not both fall into
the ditch?
40 "A disciple is not above his teacher, but
everyone who is perfectly trained will be like
his teacher.
41 "And why do you look at the speck in your
brother's eye, but do not perceive the plank in
your own eye?
42 "Or how can you say to your brother,
'Brother, let me remove the speck that *is* in
your eye,' when you yourself do not see the
plank that *is* in your own eye? Hypocrite! First
remove the plank from your own eye, and then
you will see clearly to remove the speck that is
in your brother's eye.

A Tree Is Known by Its Fruit

43 "For a good tree does not bear bad fruit,
nor does a bad tree bear good fruit.
44 "For every tree is known by its own fruit.
For *men* do not gather figs from thorns, nor do
they gather grapes from a bramble bush.
45 "A good man out of the good treasure of
his heart brings forth good; and an evil man
out of the evil treasure of his heart[a] brings forth
evil. For out of the abundance of the heart his
mouth speaks.

Build on the Rock

46 "But why do you call Me 'Lord, Lord,' and
not do the things which I say?
47 "Whoever comes to Me, and hears My sayings and does them, I will show you whom he
is like:

6:10 [a]NU-Text and M-Text read *to him.* [b]NU-Text omits *as whole as the other.* **6:26** [a]NU-Text and M-Text omit *to you.* [b]M-Text omits *all.* **6:45** [a]NU-Text omits *treasure of his heart.*

48 "He is like a man building a house, who
dug deep and laid the foundation on the rock.
And when the flood arose, the stream beat ve-
hemently against that house, and could not shake
it, for it was founded on the rock.[a]
49 "But he who heard and did nothing is like
a man who built a house on the earth without
a foundation, against which the stream beat
vehemently; and immediately it fell.[a] And the
ruin of that house was great."

Jesus Heals a Centurion's Servant

7 Now when He concluded all His sayings in
the hearing of the people, He entered Caper-
naum.
2 And a certain centurion's servant, who was
dear to him, was sick and ready to die.
3 So when he heard about Jesus, he sent el-
ders of the Jews to Him, pleading with Him to
come and heal his servant.
4 And when they came to Jesus, they begged
Him earnestly, saying that the one for whom
He should do this was deserving,
5 "for he loves our nation, and has built us
a synagogue."
6 Then Jesus went with them. And when He
was already not far from the house, the centu-
rion sent friends to Him, saying to Him, "Lord,
do not trouble Yourself, for I am not worthy
that You should enter under my roof.
7 "Therefore I did not even think myself wor-
thy to come to You. But say the word, and my
servant will be healed.
8 "For I also am a man placed under author-
ity, having soldiers under me. And I say to one,
'Go,' and he goes; and to another, 'Come,' and
he comes; and to my servant, 'Do this,' and he
does *it*."
9 When Jesus heard these things, He mar-
veled at him, and turned around and said to
the crowd that followed Him, "I say to you, I
have not found such great faith, not even in
Israel!"
10 And those who were sent, returning to the
house, found the servant well who had been
sick.[a]

Jesus Raises the Son of the Widow of Nain

11 Now it happened, the day after, *that* He went
into a city called Nain; and many of His disci-
ples went with Him, and a large crowd.
12 And when He came near the gate of the city,
behold, a dead man was being carried out, the
only son of his mother; and she was a widow.
And a large crowd from the city was with her.
13 When the Lord saw her, He had compas-
sion on her and said to her, "Do not weep."
14 Then He came and touched the open cof-
fin, and those who carried *him* stood still. And
He said, "Young man, I say to you, arise."
15 So he who was dead sat up and began to
speak. And He presented him to his mother.
16 Then fear came upon all, and they glorified
God, saying, "A great prophet has risen up
among us"; and, "God has visited His people."
17 And this report about Him went through-
out all Judea and all the surrounding region.

John the Baptist Sends Messengers to Jesus

18 Then the disciples of John reported to him
concerning all these things.
19 And John, calling two of his disciples to
him, sent *them* to Jesus,[a] saying, "Are You the
Coming One, or do we look for another?"
20 When the men had come to Him, they said,
"John the Baptist has sent us to You, saying,
'Are You the Coming One, or do we look for
another?' "
21 And that very hour He cured many of infir-
mities, afflictions, and evil spirits; and to many
blind He gave sight.
22 Jesus answered and said to them, "Go and
tell John the things you have seen and heard:
that *the* blind see, *the* lame walk, *the* lepers are
cleansed, *the* deaf hear, *the* dead are raised,
the poor have the gospel preached to them.
23 "And blessed is *he* who is not offended be-
cause of Me."
24 When the messengers of John had departed,
He began to speak to the multitudes concern-
ing John: "What did you go out into the wilder-
ness to see? A reed shaken by the wind?
25 "But what did you go out to see? A man
clothed in soft garments? Indeed those who are
gorgeously appareled and live in luxury are in
kings' courts.
26 "But what did you go out to see? A prophet?
Yes, I say to you, and more than a prophet.
27 "This is *he* of whom it is written:

'Behold, I send My messenger before your face,
Who will prepare Your way before You.'[a]

28 "For I say to you, among those born of
women there is not a greater prophet than John
the Baptist;[a] but he who is least in the kingdom
of God is greater than he."
29 And when all the people heard *Him*, even
the tax collectors justified God, having been
baptized with the baptism of John.
30 But the Pharisees and lawyers rejected the
will of God for themselves, not having been
baptized by him.
31 And the Lord said,[a] "To what then shall I
liken the men of this generation, and what are
they like?
32 "They are like children sitting in the mar-
ketplace and calling to one another, saying:

'We played the flute for you,
And you did not dance;
We mourned to you,
And you did not weep.'

33 "For John the Baptist came neither eating
bread nor drinking wine, and you say, 'He has
a demon.'
34 "The Son of Man has come eating and drink-
ing, and you say, 'Look, a glutton and a wine-
bibber, a friend of tax collectors and sinners!'
35 "But wisdom is justified by all her chil-
dren."

A Sinful Woman Forgiven

36 Then one of the Pharisees asked Him to eat
with him. And He went to the Pharisee's house,
and sat down to eat.
37 And behold, a woman in the city who was
a sinner, when she knew that *Jesus* sat at the
table in the Pharisee's house, brought an ala-
baster flask of fragrant oil,
38 and stood at His feet behind *Him* weeping;
and she began to wash His feet with her tears,

6:48 [a]NU-Text reads *for it was well built.* **6:49** [a]NU-Text reads *collapsed.* **7:10** [a]NU-Text omits *who had been sick.* **7:19** [a]NU-Text reads *the Lord.* **7:27** [a]Malachi 3:1 **7:28** [a]NU-Text reads *there is none greater than John.* **7:31** [a]NU-Text and M-Text omit *And the Lord said.*

and wiped *them* with the hair of her head; and
she kissed His feet and anointed *them* with the
fragrant oil.
39 Now when the Pharisee who had invited
Him saw *this*, he spoke to himself, saying, "This
Man, if He were a prophet, would know who
and what manner of woman *this is* who is touch-
ing Him, for she is a sinner."
40 And Jesus answered and said to him, "Si-
mon, I have something to say to you." So he
said, "Teacher, say it."
41 "There was a certain creditor who had two
debtors. One owed five hundred denarii, and
the other fifty.
42 "And when they had nothing with which
to repay, he freely forgave them both. Tell Me,
therefore, which of them will love him more?"
43 Simon answered and said, "I suppose the
one whom he forgave more." And He said to
him, "You have rightly judged."
44 Then He turned to the woman and said to
Simon, "Do you see this woman? I entered
your house; you gave Me no water for My feet,
but she has washed My feet with her tears and
wiped *them* with the hair of her head.
45 "You gave Me no kiss, but this woman has
not ceased to kiss My feet since the time I came
in.
46 "You did not anoint My head with oil, but
this woman has anointed My feet with fragrant
oil.
47 "Therefore I say to you, her sins, which *are*
many, are forgiven, for she loved much. But to
whom little is forgiven, *the same* loves little."
48 Then He said to her, "Your sins are for-
given."
49 And those who sat at the table with Him
began to say to themselves, "Who is this who
even forgives sins?"
50 Then He said to the woman, "Your faith has
saved you. Go in peace."

Many Women Minister to Jesus

8 Now it came to pass, afterward, that He went
through every city and village, preaching
and bringing the glad tidings of the kingdom
of God. And the twelve *were* with Him,
2 and certain women who had been healed
of evil spirits and infirmities—Mary called Mag-
dalene, out of whom had come seven demons,
3 and Joanna the wife of Chuza, Herod's stew-
ard, and Susanna, and many others who pro-
vided for Him[a] from their substance.

The Parable of the Sower

4 And when a great multitude had gathered,
and they had come to Him from every city, He
spoke by a parable:
5 "A sower went out to sow his seed. And as
he sowed, some fell by the wayside; and it was
trampled down, and the birds of the air de-
voured it.
6 "Some fell on rock; and as soon as it sprang
up, it withered away because it lacked mois-
ture.
7 "And some fell among thorns, and the
thorns sprang up with it and choked it.
8 "But others fell on good ground, sprang
up, and yielded a crop a hundredfold." When
He had said these things He cried, "He who has
ears to hear, let him hear!"

The Purpose of Parables

9 Then His disciples asked Him, saying, "What
does this parable mean?"
10 And He said, "To you it has been given to
know the mysteries of the kingdom of God, but
to the rest *it is given* in parables, that

'Seeing they may not see,
And hearing they may not understand.'[a]

The Parable of the Sower Explained

11 "Now the parable is this: The seed is the
word of God.
12 "Those by the wayside are the ones who
hear; then the devil comes and takes away the
word out of their hearts, lest they should be-
lieve and be saved.
13 "But the ones on the rock *are those* who,
when they hear, receive the word with joy; and
these have no root, who believe for a while and
in time of temptation fall away.
14 "Now the ones *that* fell among thorns are
those who, when they have heard, go out and
are choked with cares, riches, and pleasures
of life, and bring no fruit to maturity.
15 "But the ones *that* fell on the good ground
are those who, having heard the word with a
noble and good heart, keep *it* and bear fruit
with patience.

The Parable of the Revealed Light

16 "No one, when he has lit a lamp, covers it
with a vessel or puts *it* under a bed, but sets *it*
on a lampstand, that those who enter may see
the light.
17 "For nothing is secret that will not be re-
vealed, nor *anything* hidden that will not be
known and come to light.
18 "Therefore take heed how you hear. For
whoever has, to him *more* will be given; and
whoever does not have, even what he seems to
have will be taken from him."

Jesus' Mother and Brothers Come to Him

19 Then His mother and brothers came to Him,
and could not approach Him because of the
crowd.
20 And it was told Him *by some*, who said,
"Your mother and Your brothers are standing
outside, desiring to see You."
21 But He answered and said to them, "My
mother and My brothers are these who hear
the word of God and do it."

Wind and Wave Obey Jesus

22 Now it happened, on a certain day, that He
got into a boat with His disciples. And He said
to them, "Let us cross over to the other side of
the lake." And they launched out.
23 But as they sailed He fell asleep. And a wind-
storm came down on the lake, and they were
filling *with water*, and were in jeopardy.
24 And they came to Him and awoke Him, say-
ing, "Master, Master, we are perishing!" Then
He arose and rebuked the wind and the raging
of the water. And they ceased, and there was a
calm.
25 But He said to them, "Where is your faith?"
And they were afraid, and marveled, saying to
one another, "Who can this be? For He com-
mands even the winds and water, and they obey
Him!"

8:3 [a]NU-Text and M-Text read *them*. 8:10 [a]Isaiah 6:9

A Demon-Possessed Man Healed

26 Then they sailed to the country of the Gad-
arenes,[a] which is opposite Galilee.
27 And when He stepped out on the land,
there met Him a certain man from the city who
had demons for a long time. And he wore no
clothes,[a] nor did he live in a house but in the
tombs.
28 When he saw Jesus, he cried out, fell down
before Him, and with a loud voice said, "What
have I to do with You, Jesus, Son of the Most
High God? I beg You, do not torment me!"
29 For He had commanded the unclean spirit
to come out of the man. For it had often seized
him, and he was kept under guard, bound with
chains and shackles; and he broke the bonds
and was driven by the demon into the wilder-
ness.
30 Jesus asked him, saying, "What is your
name?" And he said, "Legion," because many
demons had entered him.
31 And they begged Him that He would not
command them to go out into the abyss.
32 Now a herd of many swine was feeding there
on the mountain. So they begged Him that He
would permit them to enter them. And He per-
mitted them.
33 Then the demons went out of the man and
entered the swine, and the herd ran violently
down the steep place into the lake and drowned.
34 When those who fed *them* saw what had
happened, they fled and told *it* in the city and
in the country.
35 Then they went out to see what had hap-
pened, and came to Jesus, and found the man
from whom the demons had departed, sitting
at the feet of Jesus, clothed and in his right
mind. And they were afraid.
36 They also who had seen *it* told them by what
means he who had been demon-possessed was
healed.
37 Then the whole multitude of the surround-
ing region of the Gadarenes[a] asked Him to de-
part from them, for they were seized with great
fear. And He got into the boat and returned.
38 Now the man from whom the demons had
departed begged Him that he might be with Him.
But Jesus sent him away, saying,
39 "Return to your own house, and tell what
great things God has done for you." And he
went his way and proclaimed throughout the
whole city what great things Jesus had done
for him.

A Girl Restored to Life and a Woman Healed

40 So it was, when Jesus returned, that the
multitude welcomed Him, for they were all wait-
ing for Him.
41 And behold, there came a man named Jai-
rus, and he was a ruler of the synagogue. And
he fell down at Jesus' feet and begged Him to
come to his house,
42 for he had an only daughter about twelve
years of age, and she was dying. But as He went,
the multitudes thronged Him.
43 Now a woman, having a flow of blood for
twelve years, who had spent all her livelihood
on physicians and could not be healed by any,
44 came from behind and touched the border
of His garment. And immediately her flow of
blood stopped.
45 And Jesus said, "Who touched Me?" When
all denied it, Peter and those with him[a] said,
"Master, the multitudes throng and press You,
and You say, 'Who touched Me?' "[b]
46 But Jesus said, "Somebody touched Me, for
I perceived power going out from Me."
47 Now when the woman saw that she was not
hidden, she came trembling; and falling down
before Him, she declared to Him in the pres-
ence of all the people the reason she had
touched Him and how she was healed immedi-
ately.
48 And He said to her, "Daughter, be of good
cheer;[a] your faith has made you well. Go in
peace."
49 While He was still speaking, someone came
from the ruler of the synagogue's *house*, say-
ing to him, "Your daughter is dead. Do not
trouble the Teacher."[a]
50 But when Jesus heard *it*, He answered him,
saying, "Do not be afraid; only believe, and
she will be made well."
51 When He came into the house, He permit-
ted no one to go in[a] except Peter, James, and
John,[b] and the father and mother of the girl.
52 Now all wept and mourned for her; but
He said, "Do not weep; she is not dead, but
sleeping."
53 And they ridiculed Him, knowing that she
was dead.
54 But He put them all outside,[a] took her by
the hand and called, saying, "Little girl, arise."
55 Then her spirit returned, and she arose im-
mediately. And He commanded that she be
given *something* to eat.
56 And her parents were astonished, but He
charged them to tell no one what had happened.

Sending Out the Twelve

9 Then He called His twelve disciples together
and gave them power and authority over
all demons, and to cure diseases.
2 He sent them to preach the kingdom of God
and to heal the sick.
3 And He said to them, "Take nothing for the
journey, neither staffs nor bag nor bread nor
money; and do not have two tunics apiece.
4 "Whatever house you enter, stay there, and
from there depart.
5 "And whoever will not receive you, when
you go out of that city, shake off the very dust
from your feet as a testimony against them."
6 So they departed and went through the
towns, preaching the gospel and healing every-
where.

Herod Seeks to See Jesus

7 Now Herod the tetrarch heard of all that
was done by Him; and he was perplexed, be-
cause it was said by some that John had risen
from the dead,
8 and by some that Elijah had appeared, and
by others that one of the old prophets had risen
again.
9 Herod said, "John I have beheaded, but who
is this of whom I hear such things?" So he sought
to see Him.

8:26 [a]NU-Text reads *Gerasenes.* **8:27** [a]NU-Text reads *who had demons and for a long time wore no clothes.*
8:37 [a]NU-Text reads *Gerasenes.* **8:45** [a]NU-Text omits *and those with him.* [b]NU-Text omits *and You say, 'Who touched Me?'* **8:48** [a]NU-Text omits *be of good cheer.* **8:49** [a]NU-Text adds *anymore.* **8:51** [a]NU-Text adds *with Him.* [b]NU-Text and M-Text read *Peter, John, and James.* **8:54** [a]NU-Text omits *put them all outside.*

Feeding the Five Thousand

10 And the apostles, when they had returned,
told Him all that they had done. Then He took
them and went aside privately into a deserted
place belonging to the city called Bethsaida.
11 But when the multitudes knew *it,* they fol-
lowed Him; and He received them and spoke
to them about the kingdom of God, and healed
those who had need of healing.
12 When the day began to wear away, the twelve
came and said to Him, "Send the multitude away,
that they may go into the surrounding towns
and country, and lodge and get provisions; for
we are in a deserted place here."
13 But He said to them, "You give them some-
thing to eat." And they said, "We have no more
than five loaves and two fish, unless we go and
buy food for all these people."
14 For there were about five thousand men.
Then He said to His disciples, "Make them sit
down in groups of fifty."
15 And they did so, and made them all sit down.
16 Then He took the five loaves and the two
fish, and looking up to heaven, He blessed and
broke them, and gave *them* to the disciples to
set before the multitude.
17 So they all ate and were filled, and twelve
baskets of the leftover fragments were taken
up by them.

Peter Confesses Jesus as the Christ

18 And it happened, as He was alone praying,
that His disciples joined Him, and He asked
them, saying, "Who do the crowds say that I
am?"
19 So they answered and said, "John the Bap-
tist, but some *say* Elijah; and others *say* that
one of the old prophets has risen again."
20 He said to them, "But who do you say that
I am?" Peter answered and said, "The Christ
of God."

Jesus Predicts His Death and Resurrection

21 And He strictly warned and commanded
them to tell this to no one,
22 saying, "The Son of Man must suffer many
things, and be rejected by the elders and chief
priests and scribes, and be killed, and be raised
the third day."

Take Up the Cross and Follow Him

23 Then He said to *them* all, "If anyone de-
sires to come after Me, let him deny himself,
and take up his cross daily,[a] and follow Me.
24 "For whoever desires to save his life will
lose it, but whoever loses his life for My sake
will save it.
25 "For what profit is it to a man if he gains
the whole world, and is himself destroyed or
lost?
26 "For whoever is ashamed of Me and My
words, of him the Son of Man will be ashamed
when He comes in His *own* glory, and *in His*
Father's, and of the holy angels.
27 "But I tell you truly, there are some stand-
ing here who shall not taste death till they see
the kingdom of God."

Jesus Transfigured on the Mount

28 Now it came to pass, about eight days after
these sayings, that He took Peter, John, and
James and went up on the mountain to pray.
29 As He prayed, the appearance of His face
was altered, and His robe *became* white *and*
glistening.
30 And behold, two men talked with Him,
who were Moses and Elijah,
31 who appeared in glory and spoke of His
decease which He was about to accomplish at
Jerusalem.
32 But Peter and those with him were heavy
with sleep; and when they were fully awake,
they saw His glory and the two men who stood
with Him.
33 Then it happened, as they were parting from
Him, *that* Peter said to Jesus, "Master, it is
good for us to be here; and let us make three
tabernacles: one for You, one for Moses, and
one for Elijah"—not knowing what he said.
34 While he was saying this, a cloud came and
overshadowed them; and they were fearful as
they entered the cloud.
35 And a voice came out of the cloud, saying,
"This is My beloved Son.[a] Hear Him!"
36 When the voice had ceased, Jesus was found
alone. But they kept quiet, and told no one in
those days any of the things they had seen.

A Boy Is Healed

37 Now it happened on the next day, when
they had come down from the mountain, that
a great multitude met Him.
38 Suddenly a man from the multitude cried
out, saying, "Teacher, I implore You, look on
my son, for he is my only child.
39 "And behold, a spirit seizes him, and he sud-
denly cries out; it convulses him so that he
foams *at the mouth;* and it departs from him
with great difficulty, bruising him.
40 "So I implored Your disciples to cast it out,
but they could not."
41 Then Jesus answered and said, "O faithless
and perverse generation, how long shall I be
with you and bear with you? Bring your son
here."
42 And as he was still coming, the demon threw
him down and convulsed *him.* Then Jesus re-
buked the unclean spirit, healed the child, and
gave him back to his father.

Jesus Again Predicts His Death

43 And they were all amazed at the majesty of
God. But while everyone marveled at all the
things which Jesus did, He said to His disciples,
44 "Let these words sink down into your ears,
for the Son of Man is about to be betrayed into
the hands of men."
45 But they did not understand this saying,
and it was hidden from them so that they did
not perceive it; and they were afraid to ask
Him about this saying.

Who Is the Greatest?

46 Then a dispute arose among them as to
which of them would be greatest.
47 And Jesus, perceiving the thought of their
heart, took a little child and set him by Him,
48 and said to them, "Whoever receives this
little child in My name receives Me; and who-
ever receives Me receives Him who sent Me.
For he who is least among you all will be great."

Jesus Forbids Sectarianism

49 Now John answered and said, "Master, we
saw someone casting out demons in Your

9:23 [a]M-Text omits *daily.* **9:35** [a]NU-Text reads *This is My Son, the Chosen One.*

name, and we forbade him because he does not follow with us."

50 But Jesus said to him, "Do not forbid *him,* for he who is not against us[a] is on our[b] side."

A Samaritan Village Rejects the Savior

51 Now it came to pass, when the time had come for Him to be received up, that He steadfastly set His face to go to Jerusalem,

52 and sent messengers before His face. And as they went, they entered a village of the Samaritans, to prepare for Him.

53 But they did not receive Him, because His face was *set* for the journey to Jerusalem.

54 And when His disciples James and John saw *this,* they said, "Lord, do You want us to command fire to come down from heaven and consume them, just as Elijah did?"[a]

55 But He turned and rebuked them,[a] and said, "You do not know what manner of spirit you are of.

56 "For the Son of Man did not come to destroy men's lives but to save *them.*"[a] And they went to another village.

The Cost of Discipleship

57 Now it happened as they journeyed on the road, *that* someone said to Him, "Lord, I will follow You wherever You go."

58 And Jesus said to him, "Foxes have holes and birds of the air *have* nests, but the Son of Man has nowhere to lay *His* head."

59 Then He said to another, "Follow Me." But he said, "Lord, let me first go and bury my father."

60 Jesus said to him, "Let the dead bury their own dead, but you go and preach the kingdom of God."

61 And another also said, "Lord, I will follow You, but let me first go *and* bid them farewell who are at my house."

62 But Jesus said to him, "No one, having put his hand to the plow, and looking back, is fit for the kingdom of God."

The Seventy Sent Out

10 After these things the Lord appointed seventy others also,[a] and sent them two by two before His face into every city and place where He Himself was about to go.

2 Then He said to them, "The harvest truly *is* great, but the laborers *are* few; therefore pray the Lord of the harvest to send out laborers into His harvest.

3 "Go your way; behold, I send you out as lambs among wolves.

4 "Carry neither money bag, knapsack, nor sandals; and greet no one along the road.

5 "But whatever house you enter, first say, 'Peace to this house.'

6 "And if a son of peace is there, your peace will rest on it; if not, it will return to you.

7 "And remain in the same house, eating and drinking such things as they give, for the laborer is worthy of his wages. Do not go from house to house.

8 "Whatever city you enter, and they receive you, eat such things as are set before you.

9 "And heal the sick there, and say to them, 'The kingdom of God has come near to you.'

10 "But whatever city you enter, and they do not receive you, go out into its streets and say,

11 'The very dust of your city which clings to us[a] we wipe off against you. Nevertheless know this, that the kingdom of God has come near you.'

12 "But[a] I say to you that it will be more tolerable in that Day for Sodom than for that city.

Woe to the Impenitent Cities

13 "Woe to you, Chorazin! Woe to you, Bethsaida! For if the mighty works which were done in you had been done in Tyre and Sidon, they would have repented long ago, sitting in sackcloth and ashes.

14 "But it will be more tolerable for Tyre and Sidon at the judgment than for you.

15 "And you, Capernaum, who are exalted to heaven, will be brought down to Hades.[a]

16 "He who hears you hears Me, he who rejects you rejects Me, and he who rejects Me rejects Him who sent Me."

The Seventy Return with Joy

17 Then the seventy[a] returned with joy, saying, "Lord, even the demons are subject to us in Your name."

18 And He said to them, "I saw Satan fall like lightning from heaven.

19 "Behold, I give you the authority to trample on serpents and scorpions, and over all the power of the enemy, and nothing shall by any means hurt you.

20 "Nevertheless do not rejoice in this, that the spirits are subject to you, but rather[a] rejoice because your names are written in heaven."

Jesus Rejoices in the Spirit

21 In that hour Jesus rejoiced in the Spirit and said, "I thank You, Father, Lord of heaven and earth, that You have hidden these things from *the* wise and prudent and revealed them to babes. Even so, Father, for so it seemed good in Your sight.

22 "All[a] things have been delivered to Me by My Father, and no one knows who the Son is except the Father, and who the Father is except the Son, and *the one* to whom the Son wills to reveal *Him.*"

23 Then He turned to *His* disciples and said privately, "Blessed *are* the eyes which see the things you see;

24 "for I tell you that many prophets and kings have desired to see what you see, and have not seen *it,* and to hear what you hear, and have not heard *it.*"

The Parable of the Good Samaritan

25 And behold, a certain lawyer stood up and tested Him, saying, "Teacher, what shall I do to inherit eternal life?"

26 He said to him, "What is written in the law? What is your reading *of it?*"

27 So he answered and said, " *'You shall love the* LORD *your God with all your heart, with all your soul, with all your strength, and with*

9:50 [a]NU-Text reads *you.* [b]NU-Text reads *your.* **9:54** [a]NU-Text omits *just as Elijah did.* **9:55** [a]NU-Text omits the rest of this verse. **9:56** [a]NU-Text omits the first sentence of this verse. **10:1** [a]NU-Text reads *seventy-two others.* **10:11** [a]NU-Text reads *our feet.* **10:12** [a]NU-Text and M-Text omit *But.* **10:15** [a]NU-Text reads *will you be exalted to heaven? You will be thrust down to Hades!* **10:17** [a]NU-Text reads *seventy-two.* **10:20** [a]NU-Text and M-Text omit *rather.* **10:22** [a]M-Text reads *And turning to the disciples He said, "All . . . .*

all your mind,'[a] and *'your neighbor as your-*
self.' "[b]
28 And He said to him, "You have answered
rightly; do this and you will live."
29 But he, wanting to justify himself, said to
Jesus, "And who is my neighbor?"
30 Then Jesus answered and said: "A certain
man went down from Jerusalem to Jericho, and
fell among thieves, who stripped him of his
clothing, wounded *him*, and departed, leaving
him half dead.
31 "Now by chance a certain priest came
down that road. And when he saw him, he passed
by on the other side.
32 "Likewise a Levite, when he arrived at the
place, came and looked, and passed by on the
other side.
33 "But a certain Samaritan, as he journeyed,
came where he was. And when he saw him, he
had compassion.
34 "So he went to *him* and bandaged his
wounds, pouring on oil and wine; and he set
him on his own animal, brought him to an inn,
and took care of him.
35 "On the next day, when he departed,[a] he
took out two denarii, gave *them* to the inn-
keeper, and said to him, 'Take care of him; and
whatever more you spend, when I come again,
I will repay you.'
36 "So which of these three do you think was
neighbor to him who fell among the thieves?"
37 And he said, "He who showed mercy on
him." Then Jesus said to him, "Go and do like-
wise."

Mary and Martha Worship and Serve

38 Now it happened as they went that He en-
tered a certain village; and a certain woman
named Martha welcomed Him into her house.
39 And she had a sister called Mary, who also
sat at Jesus'[a] feet and heard His word.
40 But Martha was distracted with much serv-
ing, and she approached Him and said, "Lord,
do You not care that my sister has left me to
serve alone? Therefore tell her to help me."
41 And Jesus[a] answered and said to her, "Mar-
tha, Martha, you are worried and troubled
about many things.
42 "But one thing is needed, and Mary has
chosen that good part, which will not be taken
away from her."

The Model Prayer

11 Now it came to pass, as He was praying
in a certain place, when He ceased, *that*
one of His disciples said to Him, "Lord, teach
us to pray, as John also taught his disciples."
2 So He said to them, "When you pray, say:

Our Father in heaven,[a]
Hallowed be Your name.
Your kingdom come.[b]
Your will be done
On earth as *it is* in heaven.
3 Give us day by day our daily bread.
4 And forgive us our sins,
For we also forgive everyone who is
indebted to us.
And do not lead us into temptation,
But deliver us from the evil one." [a]

A Friend Comes at Midnight

5 And He said to them, "Which of you shall
have a friend, and go to him at midnight and
say to him, 'Friend, lend me three loaves;
6 'for a friend of mine has come to me on his
journey, and I have nothing to set before him';
7 "and he will answer from within and say,
'Do not trouble me; the door is now shut, and
my children are with me in bed; I cannot rise
and give to you'?
8 "I say to you, though he will not rise and
give to him because he is his friend, yet be-
cause of his persistence he will rise and give
him as many as he needs.

Keep Asking, Seeking, Knocking

9 "So I say to you, ask, and it will be given
to you; seek, and you will find; knock, and it
will be opened to you.
10 "For everyone who asks receives, and he
who seeks finds, and to him who knocks it will
be opened.
11 "If a son asks for bread[a] from any father
among you, will he give him a stone? Or if *he*
asks for a fish, will he give him a serpent in-
stead of a fish?
12 "Or if he asks for an egg, will he offer him
a scorpion?
13 "If you then, being evil, know how to give
good gifts to your children, how much more
will *your* heavenly Father give the Holy Spirit
to those who ask Him!"

A House Divided Cannot Stand

14 And He was casting out a demon, and it
was mute. So it was, when the demon had gone
out, that the mute spoke; and the multitudes mar-
veled.
15 But some of them said, "He casts out de-
mons by Beelzebub,[a] the ruler of the demons."
16 Others, testing *Him*, sought from Him a sign
from heaven.
17 But He, knowing their thoughts, said to
them: "Every kingdom divided against itself
is brought to desolation, and a house *divided*
against a house falls.
18 "If Satan also is divided against himself,
how will his kingdom stand? Because you say
I cast out demons by Beelzebub.
19 "And if I cast out demons by Beelzebub, by
whom do your sons cast *them* out? Therefore
they will be your judges.
20 "But if I cast out demons with the finger of
God, surely the kingdom of God has come
upon you.
21 "When a strong man, fully armed, guards
his own palace, his goods are in peace.
22 "But when a stronger than he comes upon
him and overcomes him, he takes from him all
his armor in which he trusted, and divides his
spoils.
23 "He who is not with Me is against Me, and
he who does not gather with Me scatters.

An Unclean Spirit Returns

24 "When an unclean spirit goes out of a man,
he goes through dry places, seeking rest; and
finding none, he says, 'I will return to my house
from which I came.'

10:27 [a]Deuteronomy 6:5 [b]Leviticus 19:18 **10:35** [a]NU-Text omits *when he departed.* **10:39** [a]NU-Text reads *the Lord's.* **10:41** [a]NU-Text reads *the Lord.* **11:2** [a]NU-Text omits *Our* and *in heaven.* [b]NU-Text omits the rest of this verse. **11:4** [a]NU-Text omits *But deliver us from the evil one.* **11:11** [a]NU-Text omits the words from *bread* through *for* in the next sentence. **11:15** [a]NU-Text and M-Text read *Beelzebul.*

25 "And when he comes, he finds *it* swept and put in order.

26 "Then he goes and takes with *him* seven other spirits more wicked than himself, and they enter and dwell there; and the last *state* of that man is worse than the first."

Keeping the Word

27 And it happened, as He spoke these things, that a certain woman from the crowd raised her voice and said to Him, "Blessed *is* the womb that bore You, and *the* breasts which nursed You!"

28 But He said, "More than that, blessed *are* those who hear the word of God and keep it!"

Seeking a Sign

29 And while the crowds were thickly gathered together, He began to say, "This is an evil generation. It seeks a sign, and no sign will be given to it except the sign of Jonah the prophet.[a]

30 "For as Jonah became a sign to the Ninevites, so also the Son of Man will be to this generation.

31 "The queen of the South will rise up in the judgment with the men of this generation and condemn them, for she came from the ends of the earth to hear the wisdom of Solomon; and indeed a greater than Solomon *is* here.

32 "The men of Nineveh will rise up in the judgment with this generation and condemn it, for they repented at the preaching of Jonah; and indeed a greater than Jonah *is* here.

The Lamp of the Body

33 "No one, when he has lit a lamp, puts *it* in a secret place or under a basket, but on a lampstand, that those who come in may see the light.

34 "The lamp of the body is the eye. Therefore, when your eye is good, your whole body also is full of light. But when *your eye* is bad, your body also *is* full of darkness.

35 "Therefore take heed that the light which is in you is not darkness.

36 "If then your whole body *is* full of light, having no part dark, *the* whole *body* will be full of light, as when the bright shining of a lamp gives you light."

Woe to the Pharisees and Lawyers

37 And as He spoke, a certain Pharisee asked Him to dine with him. So He went in and sat down to eat.

38 When the Pharisee saw *it*, he marveled that He had not first washed before dinner.

39 Then the Lord said to him, "Now you Pharisees make the outside of the cup and dish clean, but your inward part is full of greed and wickedness.

40 "Foolish ones! Did not He who made the outside make the inside also?

41 "But rather give alms of such things as you have; then indeed all things are clean to you.

42 "But woe to you Pharisees! For you tithe mint and rue and all manner of herbs, and pass by justice and the love of God. These you ought to have done, without leaving the others undone.

43 "Woe to you Pharisees! For you love the best seats in the synagogues and greetings in the marketplaces.

44 "Woe to you, scribes and Pharisees, hypocrites![a] For you are like graves which are not seen, and the men who walk over *them* are not aware *of them*."

45 Then one of the lawyers answered and said to Him, "Teacher, by saying these things You reproach us also."

46 And He said, "Woe to you also, lawyers! For you load men with burdens hard to bear, and you yourselves do not touch the burdens with one of your fingers.

47 "Woe to you! For you build the tombs of the prophets, and your fathers killed them.

48 "In fact, you bear witness that you approve the deeds of your fathers; for they indeed killed them, and you build their tombs.

49 "Therefore the wisdom of God also said, 'I will send them prophets and apostles, and *some* of them they will kill and persecute,'

50 "that the blood of all the prophets which was shed from the foundation of the world may be required of this generation,

51 "from the blood of Abel to the blood of Zechariah who perished between the altar and the temple. Yes, I say to you, it shall be required of this generation.

52 "Woe to you lawyers! For you have taken away the key of knowledge. You did not enter in yourselves, and those who were entering in you hindered."

53 And as He said these things to them,[a] the scribes and the Pharisees began to assail *Him* vehemently, and to cross-examine Him about many things,

54 lying in wait for Him, and seeking to catch Him in something He might say, that they might accuse Him.[a]

Beware of Hypocrisy

12 In the meantime, when an innumerable multitude of people had gathered together, so that they trampled one another, He began to say to His disciples first *of all*, "Beware of the leaven of the Pharisees, which is hypocrisy.

2 "For there is nothing covered that will not be revealed, nor hidden that will not be known.

3 "Therefore whatever you have spoken in the dark will be heard in the light, and what you have spoken in the ear in inner rooms will be proclaimed on the housetops.

Jesus Teaches the Fear of God

4 "And I say to you, My friends, do not be afraid of those who kill the body, and after that have no more that they can do.

5 "But I will show you whom you should fear: Fear Him who, after He has killed, has power to cast into hell; yes, I say to you, fear Him!

6 "Are not five sparrows sold for two copper coins?[a] And not one of them is forgotten before God.

7 "But the very hairs of your head are all numbered. Do not fear therefore; you are of more value than many sparrows.

11:29 [a]NU-Text omits *the prophet*. **11:44** [a]NU-Text omits *scribes and Pharisees, hypocrites*. **11:53** [a]NU-Text reads *And when He left there*. **11:54** [a]NU-Text omits *and seeking* and *that they might accuse Him*. **12:6** [a]Greek *assarion*, a coin of very small value

Confess Christ Before Men

8 "Also I say to you, whoever confesses Me
before men, him the Son of Man also will con-
fess before the angels of God.
9 "But he who denies Me before men will be
denied before the angels of God.
10 "And anyone who speaks a word against
the Son of Man, it will be forgiven him; but to
him who blasphemes against the Holy Spirit,
it will not be forgiven.
11 "Now when they bring you to the syna-
gogues and magistrates and authorities, do not
worry about how or what you should answer,
or what you should say.
12 "For the Holy Spirit will teach you in that
very hour what you ought to say."

The Parable of the Rich Fool

13 Then one from the crowd said to Him,
"Teacher, tell my brother to divide the inheri-
tance with me."
14 But He said to him, "Man, who made Me
a judge or an arbitrator over you?"
15 And He said to them, "Take heed and be-
ware of covetousness,[a] for one's life does not
consist in the abundance of the things he pos-
sesses."
16 Then He spoke a parable to them, saying:
"The ground of a certain rich man yielded
plentifully.
17 "And he thought within himself, saying,
'What shall I do, since I have no room to store
my crops?'
18 "So he said, 'I will do this: I will pull down
my barns and build greater, and there I will
store all my crops and my goods.
19 'And I will say to my soul, "Soul, you have
many goods laid up for many years; take your
ease; eat, drink, *and* be merry."'
20 "But God said to him, 'Fool! This night your
soul will be required of you; then whose will
those things be which you have provided?'
21 "So *is* he who lays up treasure for himself,
and is not rich toward God."

Do Not Worry

22 Then He said to His disciples, "Therefore
I say to you, do not worry about your life, what
you will eat; nor about the body, what you will
put on.
23 "Life is more than food, and the body *is more*
than clothing.
24 "Consider the ravens, for they neither sow
nor reap, which have neither storehouse nor
barn; and God feeds them. Of how much more
value are you than the birds?
25 "And which of you by worrying can add one
cubit to his stature?
26 "If you then are not able to do *the* least,
why are you anxious for the rest?
27 "Consider the lilies, how they grow: they
neither toil nor spin; and yet I say to you, even
Solomon in all his glory was not arrayed like
one of these.
28 "If then God so clothes the grass, which
today is in the field and tomorrow is thrown
into the oven, how much more *will He clothe*
you, O *you* of little faith?
29 "And do not seek what you should eat or
what you should drink, nor have an anxious
mind.
30 "For all these things the nations of the
world seek after, and your Father knows that
you need these things.
31 "But seek the kingdom of God, and all
these things[a] shall be added to you.
32 "Do not fear, little flock, for it is your Fa-
ther's good pleasure to give you the kingdom.
33 "Sell what you have and give alms; provide
yourselves money bags which do not grow old,
a treasure in the heavens that does not fail,
where no thief approaches nor moth destroys.
34 "For where your treasure is, there your
heart will be also.

The Faithful Servant and the Evil Servant

35 "Let your waist be girded and *your* lamps
burning;
36 "and you yourselves be like men who wait
for their master, when he will return from the
wedding, that when he comes and knocks they
may open to him immediately.
37 "Blessed *are* those servants whom the
master, when he comes, will find watching. As-
suredly, I say to you that he will gird himself
and have them sit down *to eat*, and will come
and serve them.
38 "And if he should come in the second
watch, or come in the third watch, and find
them so, blessed are those servants.
39 "But know this, that if the master of the
house had known what hour the thief would
come, he would have watched and[a] not allowed
his house to be broken into.
40 "Therefore you also be ready, for the Son
of Man is coming at an hour you do not ex-
pect."
41 Then Peter said to Him, "Lord, do You speak
this parable *only* to us, or to all *people*?"
42 And the Lord said, "Who then is that faith-
ful and wise steward, whom *his* master will
make ruler over his household, to give *them*
their portion of food in due season?
43 "Blessed *is* that servant whom his master
will find so doing when he comes.
44 "Truly, I say to you that he will make him
ruler over all that he has.
45 "But if that servant says in his heart, 'My
master is delaying his coming,' and begins to
beat the male and female servants, and to eat
and drink and be drunk,
46 "the master of that servant will come on a
day when he is not looking for *him*, and at an
hour when he is not aware, and will cut him
in two and appoint *him* his portion with the
unbelievers.
47 "And that servant who knew his master's
will, and did not prepare *himself* or do accord-
ing to his will, shall be beaten with many *stripes*.
48 "But he who did not know, yet committed
things deserving of stripes, shall be beaten with
few. For everyone to whom much is given, from
him much will be required; and to whom much
has been committed, of him they will ask the
more.

Christ Brings Division

49 "I came to send fire on the earth, and how
I wish it were already kindled!
50 "But I have a baptism to be baptized with,
and how distressed I am till it is accomplished!
51 "Do *you* suppose that I came to give peace

12:15 [a]NU-Text reads *all covetousness.* **12:31** [a]NU-Text reads *His kingdom, and these things.* **12:39** [a]NU-Text reads *he would not have allowed.*

on earth? I tell you, not at all, but rather divi-
sion.
52 "For from now on five in one house will
be divided: three against two, and two against
three.
53 "Father will be divided against son and son
against father, mother against daughter and
daughter against mother, mother-in-law against
her daughter-in-law and daughter-in-law against
her mother-in-law."

Discern the Time

54 Then He also said to the multitudes, "When-
ever you see a cloud rising out of the west,
immediately you say, 'A shower is coming'; and
so it is.
55 "And when *you see* the south wind blow,
you say, 'There will be hot weather'; and there
is.
56 "Hypocrites! You can discern the face of the
sky and of the earth, but how *is it* you do not
discern this time?

Make Peace with Your Adversary

57 "Yes, and why, even of yourselves, do you
not judge what is right?
58 "When you go with your adversary to the
magistrate, make every effort along the way to
settle with him, lest he drag you to the judge, the
judge deliver you to the officer, and the officer
throw you into prison.
59 "I tell you, you shall not depart from there
till you have paid the very last mite."

Repent or Perish

13 There were present at that season some
who told Him about the Galileans whose
blood Pilate had mingled with their sacrifices.
2 And Jesus answered and said to them, "Do
you suppose that these Galileans were worse
sinners than all *other* Galileans, because they
suffered such things?
3 "I tell you, no; but unless you repent you
will all likewise perish.
4 "Or those eighteen on whom the tower in
Siloam fell and killed them, do you think that
they were worse sinners than all *other* men
who dwelt in Jerusalem?
5 "I tell you, no; but unless you repent you
will all likewise perish."

The Parable of the Barren Fig Tree

6 He also spoke this parable: "A certain *man*
had a fig tree planted in his vineyard, and he
came seeking fruit on it and found none.
7 "Then he said to the keeper of his vine-
yard, 'Look, for three years I have come seek-
ing fruit on this fig tree and find none. Cut it
down; why does it use up the ground?'
8 "But he answered and said to him, 'Sir, let
it alone this year also, until I dig around it and
fertilize *it*.
9 'And if it bears fruit, *well*. But if not, after
that[a] you can cut it down.'"

A Spirit of Infirmity

10 Now He was teaching in one of the syna-
gogues on the Sabbath.
11 And behold, there was a woman who had
a spirit of infirmity eighteen years, and was
bent over and could in no way raise *herself* up.
12 But when Jesus saw her, He called *her* to
Him and said to her, "Woman, you are loosed
from your infirmity."
13 And He laid *His* hands on her, and immedi-
ately she was made straight, and glorified God.
14 But the ruler of the synagogue answered
with indignation, because Jesus had healed on
the Sabbath; and he said to the crowd, "There
are six days on which men ought to work; there-
fore come and be healed on them, and not on
the Sabbath day."
15 The Lord then answered him and said,
"Hypocrite![a] Does not each one of you on the
Sabbath loose his ox or donkey from the stall,
and lead *it* away to water it?
16 "So ought not this woman, being a daugh-
ter of Abraham, whom Satan has bound—
think of it—for eighteen years, be loosed from
this bond on the Sabbath?"
17 And when He said these things, all His ad-
versaries were put to shame; and all the multi-
tude rejoiced for all the glorious things that were
done by Him.

The Parable of the Mustard Seed

18 Then He said, "What is the kingdom of God
like? And to what shall I compare it?
19 "It is like a mustard seed, which a man
took and put in his garden; and it grew and be-
came a large[a] tree, and the birds of the air
nested in its branches."

The Parable of the Leaven

20 And again He said, "To what shall I liken
the kingdom of God?
21 "It is like leaven, which a woman took and
hid in three measures[a] of meal till it was all
leavened."

The Narrow Way

22 And He went through the cities and villages,
teaching, and journeying toward Jerusalem.
23 Then one said to Him, "Lord, are there few
who are saved?" And He said to them,
24 "Strive to enter through the narrow gate,
for many, I say to you, will seek to enter and
will not be able.
25 "When once the Master of the house has
risen up and shut the door, and you begin to
stand outside and knock at the door, saying,
'Lord, Lord, open for us,' and He will answer
and say to you, 'I do not know you, where you
are from,'
26 "then you will begin to say, 'We ate and
drank in Your presence, and You taught in our
streets.'
27 "But He will say, 'I tell you I do not know
you, where you are from. Depart from Me, all
you workers of iniquity.'
28 "There will be weeping and gnashing of
teeth, when you see Abraham and Isaac and
Jacob and all the prophets in the kingdom of
God, and yourselves thrust out.
29 "They will come from the east and the west,
from the north and the south, and sit down in
the kingdom of God.
30 "And indeed there are last who will be first,
and there are first who will be last."
31 On that very day[a] some Pharisees came,
saying to Him, "Get out and depart from here,
for Herod wants to kill You."

13:9 [a]NU-Text reads *And if it bears fruit after that, well. But if not, you can cut it down.* **13:15** [a]NU-Text and M-Text read *Hypocrites.* **13:19** [a]NU-Text omits *large.* **13:21** [a]Greek *sata*, approximately two pecks in all **13:31** [a]NU-Text reads *In that very hour.*

32 And He said to them, "Go, tell that fox,
'Behold, I cast out demons and perform cures
today and tomorrow, and the third *day* I shall
be perfected.'
33 "Nevertheless I must journey today, to-
morrow, and the *day* following; for it cannot
be that a prophet should perish outside of Jeru-
salem.

Jesus Laments over Jerusalem

34 "O Jerusalem, Jerusalem, the one who kills
the prophets and stones those who are sent to
her! How often I wanted to gather your chil-
dren together, as a hen *gathers* her brood un-
der *her* wings, but you were not willing!
35 "See! Your house is left to you desolate; and
assuredly,[a] I say to you, you shall not see Me
until *the time* comes when you say, *'Blessed is
He who comes in the name of the LORD!'* "[b]

A Man with Dropsy Healed on the Sabbath

14 Now it happened, as He went into the
house of one of the rulers of the Phari-
sees to eat bread on the Sabbath, that they
watched Him closely.
2 And behold, there was a certain man be-
fore Him who had dropsy.
3 And Jesus, answering, spoke to the lawyers
and Pharisees, saying, "Is it lawful to heal on
the Sabbath?"[a]
4 But they kept silent. And He took *him* and
healed him, and let him go.
5 Then He answered them, saying, "Which
of you, having a donkey[a] or an ox that has
fallen into a pit, will not immediately pull him
out on the Sabbath day?"
6 And they could not answer Him regarding
these things.

Take the Lowly Place

7 "So He told a parable to those who were
invited, when He noted how they chose the best
places, saying to them:
8 "When you are invited by anyone to a wed-
ding feast, do not sit down in the best place, lest
one more honorable than you be invited by him;
9 "and he who invited you and him come
and say to you, 'Give place to this man,' and
then you begin with shame to take the lowest
place.
10 "But when you are invited, go and sit down
in the lowest place, so that when he who in-
vited you comes he may say to you, 'Friend,
go up higher.' Then you will have glory in the
presence of those who sit at the table with you.
11 "For whoever exalts himself will be hum-
bled, and he who humbles himself will be ex-
alted."
12 Then He also said to him who invited Him,
"When you give a dinner or a supper, do not
ask your friends, your brothers, your relatives,
nor rich neighbors, lest they also invite you back,
and you be repaid.
13 "But when you give a feast, invite *the* poor,
the maimed, *the* lame, *the* blind.
14 "And you will be blessed, because they
cannot repay you; for you shall be repaid at
the resurrection of the just."

The Parable of the Great Supper

15 Now when one of those who sat at the table
with Him heard these things, he said to Him,
"Blessed *is* he who shall eat bread[a] in the king-
dom of God!"
16 Then He said to him, "A certain man gave
a great supper and invited many,
17 "and sent his servant at supper time to say
to those who were invited, 'Come, for all things
are now ready.'
18 "But they all with one *accord* began to make
excuses. The first said to him, 'I have bought a
piece of ground, and I must go and see it. I ask
you to have me excused.'
19 "And another said, 'I have bought five yoke
of oxen, and I am going to test them. I ask you
to have me excused.'
20 "Still another said, 'I have married a wife,
and therefore I cannot come.'
21 "So that servant came and reported these
things to his master. Then the master of the
house, being angry, said to his servant, 'Go out
quickly into the streets and lanes of the city,
and bring in here *the* poor and *the* maimed
and *the* lame and *the* blind.'
22 "And the servant said, 'Master, it is done
as you commanded, and still there is room.'
23 "Then the master said to the servant, 'Go
out into the highways and hedges, and compel
them to come in, that my house may be filled.
24 'For I say to you that none of those men
who were invited shall taste my supper.' "

Leaving All to Follow Christ

25 Now great multitudes went with Him. And
He turned and said to them,
26 "If anyone comes to Me and does not hate
his father and mother, wife and children,
brothers and sisters, yes, and his own life also,
he cannot be My disciple.
27 "And whoever does not bear his cross and
come after Me cannot be My disciple.
28 "For which of you, intending to build a tower,
does not sit down first and count the cost,
whether he has *enough* to finish *it*—
29 "lest, after he has laid the foundation, and
is not able to finish, all who see *it* begin to mock
him,
30 "saying, 'This man began to build and was
not able to finish.'
31 "Or what king, going to make war against
another king, does not sit down first and con-
sider whether he is able with ten thousand to
meet him who comes against him with twenty
thousand?
32 "Or else, while the other is still a great way
off, he sends a delegation and asks conditions
of peace.
33 "So likewise, whoever of you does not for-
sake all that he has cannot be My disciple.

Tasteless Salt Is Worthless

34 "Salt *is* good; but if the salt has lost its flavor,
how shall it be seasoned?
35 "It is neither fit for the land nor for the
dunghill, *but* men throw it out. He who has ears
to hear, let him hear!"

The Parable of the Lost Sheep

15 Then all the tax collectors and the sinners
drew near to Him to hear Him.
2 And the Pharisees and scribes complained,
saying, "This Man receives sinners and eats with
them."
3 So He spoke this parable to them, saying:

13:35 [a]NU-Text and M-Text omit *assuredly.* [b]Psalm 118:26 14:3 [a]NU-Text adds *or not.* 14:5 [a]NU-Text and M-Text read *son.* 14:15 [a]M-Text reads *dinner.*

4 "What man of you, having a hundred sheep,
if he loses one of them, does not leave the ninety-
nine in the wilderness, and go after the one which
is lost until he finds it?
5 "And when he has found *it*, he lays *it* on his
shoulders, rejoicing.
6 "And when he comes home, he calls together
his friends and neighbors, saying to them, 'Re-
joice with me, for I have found my sheep which
was lost!'
7 "I say to you that likewise there will be more
joy in heaven over one sinner who repents than
over ninety-nine just persons who need no re-
pentance.

The Parable of the Lost Coin

8 "Or what woman, having ten silver coins,[a]
if she loses one coin, does not light a lamp, sweep
the house, and search carefully until she finds
it?
9 "And when she has found *it*, she calls *her*
friends and neighbors together, saying, 'Re-
joice with me, for I have found the piece which
I lost!'
10 "Likewise, I say to you, there is joy in the
presence of the angels of God over one sinner
who repents."

The Parable of the Lost Son

11 Then He said: "A certain man had two sons.
12 "And the younger of them said to *his* fa-
ther, 'Father, give me the portion of goods that
falls *to me*.' So he divided to them *his* liveli-
hood.
13 "And not many days after, the younger son
gathered all together, journeyed to a far coun-
try, and there wasted his possessions with
prodigal living.
14 "But when he had spent all, there arose a
severe famine in that land, and he began to be
in want.
15 "Then he went and joined himself to a citi-
zen of that country, and he sent him into his
fields to feed swine.
16 "And he would gladly have filled his stom-
ach with the pods that the swine ate, and no
one gave him *anything*.
17 "But when he came to himself, he said,
'How many of my father's hired servants have
bread enough and to spare, and I perish with
hunger!
18 'I will arise and go to my father, and will
say to him, "Father, I have sinned against heaven
and before you,
19 "and I am no longer worthy to be called
your son. Make me like one of your hired ser-
vants." '
20 "And he arose and came to his father. But
when he was still a great way off, his father
saw him and had compassion, and ran and fell
on his neck and kissed him.
21 "And the son said to him, 'Father, I have
sinned against heaven and in your sight, and
am no longer worthy to be called your son.'
22 "But the father said to his servants, 'Bring[a]
out the best robe and put *it* on him, and put a
ring on his hand and sandals on *his* feet.
23 'And bring the fatted calf here and kill *it*,
and let us eat and be merry;
24 'for this my son was dead and is alive
again; he was lost and is found.' And they be-
gan to be merry.
25 "Now his older son was in the field. And
as he came and drew near to the house, he
heard music and dancing.
26 "So he called one of the servants and asked
what these things meant.
27 "And he said to him, 'Your brother has come,
and because he has received him safe and sound,
your father has killed the fatted calf.'
28 "But he was angry and would not go in.
Therefore his father came out and pleaded with
him.
29 "So he answered and said to *his* father,
'Lo, these many years I have been serving you;
I never transgressed your commandment at any
time; and yet you never gave me a young goat,
that I might make merry with my friends.
30 'But as soon as this son of yours came, who
has devoured your livelihood with harlots, you
killed the fatted calf for him.'
31 "And he said to him, 'Son, you are always
with me, and all that I have is yours.
32 'It was right that we should make merry
and be glad, for your brother was dead and is
alive again, and was lost and is found.' "

The Parable of the Unjust Steward

16 He also said to His disciples: "There was
a certain rich man who had a steward,
and an accusation was brought to him that this
man was wasting his goods.
2 "So he called him and said to him, 'What
is this I hear about you? Give an account of your
stewardship, for you can no longer be steward.'
3 "Then the steward said within himself,
'What shall I do? For my master is taking the
stewardship away from me. I cannot dig; I am
ashamed to beg.
4 'I have resolved what to do, that when I am
put out of the stewardship, they may receive
me into their houses.'
5 "So he called every one of his master's
debtors to *him*, and said to the first, 'How much
do you owe my master?'
6 "And he said, 'A hundred measures[a] of oil.'
So he said to him, 'Take your bill, and sit down
quickly and write fifty.'
7 "Then he said to another, 'And how much
do you owe?' So he said, 'A hundred measures[a]
of wheat.' And he said to him, 'Take your bill,
and write eighty.'
8 "So the master commended the unjust
steward because he had dealt shrewdly. For
the sons of this world are more shrewd in their
generation than the sons of light.
9 "And I say to you, make friends for your-
selves by unrighteous mammon, that when you
fail,[a] they may receive you into an everlasting
home.
10 "He who *is* faithful in *what is* least is faith-
ful also in much; and he who is unjust in *what*
is least is unjust also in much.
11 "Therefore if you have not been faithful in
the unrighteous mammon, who will commit to
your trust the true *riches?*
12 "And if you have not been faithful in what
is another man's, who will give you what is your
own?

15:8 [a]Greek *drachma*, a valuable coin often worn in a ten-piece garland by married women **15:22** [a]NU-Text reads *Quickly bring*. **16:6** [a]Greek *batos*, eight or nine gallons each (Old Testament *bath*) **16:7** [a]Greek *koros*, ten or twelve bushels each (Old Testament *kor*) **16:9** [a]NU-Text reads *it fails*.

13 "No servant can serve two masters; for ei-
ther he will hate the one and love the other, or
else he will be loyal to the one and despise the
other. You cannot serve God and mammon."

The Law, the Prophets, and the Kingdom

14 Now the Pharisees, who were lovers of
money, also heard all these things, and they
derided Him.
15 And He said to them, "You are those who
justify yourselves before men, but God knows
your hearts. For what is highly esteemed among
men is an abomination in the sight of God.
16 "The law and the prophets *were* until John.
Since that time the kingdom of God has been
preached, and everyone is pressing into it.
17 "And it is easier for heaven and earth to
pass away than for one tittle of the law to fail.
18 "Whoever divorces his wife and marries
another commits adultery; and whoever mar-
ries her who is divorced from *her* husband
commits adultery.

The Rich Man and Lazarus

19 "There was a certain rich man who was
clothed in purple and fine linen and fared
sumptuously every day.
20 "But there was a certain beggar named
Lazarus, full of sores, who was laid at his gate,
21 "desiring to be fed with the crumbs which
fell[a] from the rich man's table. Moreover the
dogs came and licked his sores.
22 "So it was that the beggar died, and was
carried by the angels to Abraham's bosom.
The rich man also died and was buried.
23 "And being in torments in Hades, he lifted
up his eyes and saw Abraham afar off, and
Lazarus in his bosom.
24 "Then he cried and said, 'Father Abraham,
have mercy on me, and send Lazarus that he
may dip the tip of his finger in water and cool
my tongue; for I am tormented in this flame.'
25 "But Abraham said, 'Son, remember that
in your lifetime you received your good things,
and likewise Lazarus evil things; but now he
is comforted and you are tormented.
26 'And besides all this, between us and you
there is a great gulf fixed, so that those who
want to pass from here to you cannot, nor can
those from there pass to us.'
27 "Then he said, 'I beg you therefore, father,
that you would send him to my father's house,
28 'for I have five brothers, that he may testify
to them, lest they also come to this place of
torment.'
29 "Abraham said to him, 'They have Moses
and the prophets; let them hear them.'
30 "And he said, 'No, father Abraham; but if
one goes to them from the dead, they will re-
pent.'
31 "But he said to him, 'If they do not hear
Moses and the prophets, neither will they be
persuaded though one rise from the dead.'"

Jesus Warns of Offenses

17 Then He said to the disciples, "It is im-
possible that no offenses should come,
but woe *to him* through whom they do come!
2 "It would be better for him if a millstone
were hung around his neck, and he were thrown
into the sea, than that he should offend one of
these little ones.
3 "Take heed to yourselves. If your brother
sins against you,[a] rebuke him; and if he re-
pents, forgive him.
4 "And if he sins against you seven times in
a day, and seven times in a day returns to you,[a]
saying, 'I repent,' you shall forgive him."

Faith and Duty

5 And the apostles said to the Lord, "Increase
our faith."
6 So the Lord said, "If you have faith as a
mustard seed, you can say to this mulberry tree,
'Be pulled up by the roots and be planted in
the sea,' and it would obey you.
7 "And which of you, having a servant plow-
ing or tending sheep, will say to him when he
has come in from the field, 'Come at once and
sit down to eat'?
8 "But will he not rather say to him, 'Prepare
something for my supper, and gird yourself
and serve me till I have eaten and drunk, and
afterward you will eat and drink'?
9 "Does he thank that servant because he
did the things that were commanded him? I think
not.[a]
10 "So likewise you, when you have done all
those things which you are commanded, say, 'We
are unprofitable servants. We have done what
was our duty to do.'"

Ten Lepers Cleansed

11 Now it happened as He went to Jerusalem
that He passed through the midst of Samaria
and Galilee.
12 Then as He entered a certain village, there
met Him ten men who were lepers, who stood
afar off.
13 And they lifted up *their* voices and said,
"Jesus, Master, have mercy on us!"
14 So when He saw *them,* He said to them,
"Go, show yourselves to the priests." And so it
was that as they went, they were cleansed.
15 And one of them, when he saw that he was
healed, returned, and with a loud voice glori-
fied God,
16 and fell down on *his* face at His feet, giving
Him thanks. And he was a Samaritan.
17 So Jesus answered and said, "Were there
not ten cleansed? But where *are* the nine?
18 "Were there not any found who returned
to give glory to God except this foreigner?"
19 And He said to him, "Arise, go your way.
Your faith has made you well."

The Coming of the Kingdom

20 Now when He was asked by the Pharisees
when the kingdom of God would come, He an-
swered them and said, "The kingdom of God
does not come with observation;
21 "nor will they say, 'See here!' or 'See there!'[a]
For indeed, the kingdom of God is within you."
22 Then He said to the disciples, "The days
will come when you will desire to see one of
the days of the Son of Man, and you will not
see *it.*
23 "And they will say to you, 'Look here!' or
'Look there!'[a] Do not go after *them* or follow
them.
24 "For as the lightning that flashes out of one

16:21 [a]NU-Text reads *with what fell.* **17:3** [a]NU-Text omits *against you.* **17:4** [a]M-Text omits *to you.* **17:9** [a]NU-Text ends verse with *commanded;* M-Text omits *him.* **17:21** [a]NU-Text reverses *here* and *there.* **17:23** [a]NU-Text reverses *here* and *there.*

part under heaven shines to the other *part* under heaven, so also the Son of Man will be in His day.
25 "But first He must suffer many things and be rejected by this generation.
26 "And as it was in the days of Noah, so it will be also in the days of the Son of Man:
27 "They ate, they drank, they married wives, they were given in marriage, until the day that Noah entered the ark, and the flood came and destroyed them all.
28 "Likewise as it was also in the days of Lot: They ate, they drank, they bought, they sold, they planted, they built;
29 "but on the day that Lot went out of Sodom it rained fire and brimstone from heaven and destroyed *them* all.
30 "Even so will it be in the day when the Son of Man is revealed.
31 "In that day, he who is on the housetop, and his goods *are* in the house, let him not come down to take them away. And likewise the one who is in the field, let him not turn back.
32 "Remember Lot's wife.
33 "Whoever seeks to save his life will lose it, and whoever loses his life will preserve it.
34 "I tell you, in that night there will be two *men* in one bed: the one will be taken and the other will be left.
35 "Two *women* will be grinding together: the one will be taken and the other left.
36 "Two *men* will be in the field: the one will be taken and the other left."[a]
37 And they answered and said to Him, "Where, Lord?" So He said to them, "Wherever the body is, there the eagles will be gathered together."

The Parable of the Persistent Widow

18 Then He spoke a parable to them, that men always ought to pray and not lose heart,
2 saying: "There was in a certain city a judge who did not fear God nor regard man.
3 "Now there was a widow in that city; and she came to him, saying, 'Get justice for me from my adversary.'
4 "And he would not for a while; but afterward he said within himself, 'Though I do not fear God nor regard man,
5 'yet because this widow troubles me I will avenge her, lest by her continual coming she weary me.'"
6 Then the Lord said, "Hear what the unjust judge said.
7 "And shall God not avenge His own elect who cry out day and night to Him, though He bears long with them?
8 "I tell you that He will avenge them speedily. Nevertheless, when the Son of Man comes, will He really find faith on the earth?"

The Parable of the Pharisee and the Tax Collector

9 Also He spoke this parable to some who trusted in themselves that they were righteous, and despised others:
10 "Two men went up to the temple to pray, one a Pharisee and the other a tax collector.
11 "The Pharisee stood and prayed thus with himself, 'God, I thank You that I am not like other men—extortioners, unjust, adulterers, or even as this tax collector.
12 'I fast twice a week; I give tithes of all that I possess.'
13 "And the tax collector, standing afar off, would not so much as raise *his* eyes to heaven, but beat his breast, saying, 'God, be merciful to me a sinner!'
14 "I tell you, this man went down to his house justified *rather* than the other; for everyone who exalts himself will be humbled, and he who humbles himself will be exalted."

Jesus Blesses Little Children

15 Then they also brought infants to Him that He might touch them; but when the disciples saw *it*, they rebuked them.
16 But Jesus called them to *Him* and said, "Let the little children come to Me, and do not forbid them; for of such is the kingdom of God.
17 "Assuredly, I say to you, whoever does not receive the kingdom of God as a little child will by no means enter it."

Jesus Counsels the Rich Young Ruler

18 Now a certain ruler asked Him, saying, "Good Teacher, what shall I do to inherit eternal life?"
19 So Jesus said to him, "Why do you call Me good? No one *is* good but One, *that is*, God.
20 "You know the commandments: *'Do not commit adultery,' 'Do not murder,' 'Do not steal,' 'Do not bear false witness,' 'Honor your father and your mother.'* "[a]
21 And he said, "All these things I have kept from my youth."
22 So when Jesus heard these things, He said to him, "You still lack one thing. Sell all that you have and distribute to the poor, and you will have treasure in heaven; and come, follow Me."
23 But when he heard this, he became very sorrowful, for he was very rich.

With God All Things Are Possible

24 And when Jesus saw that he became very sorrowful, He said, "How hard it is for those who have riches to enter the kingdom of God!
25 "For it is easier for a camel to go through the eye of a needle than for a rich man to enter the kingdom of God."
26 And those who heard it said, "Who then can be saved?"
27 But He said, "The things which are impossible with men are possible with God."
28 Then Peter said, "See, we have left all[a] and followed You."
29 So He said to them, "Assuredly, I say to you, there is no one who has left house or parents or brothers or wife or children, for the sake of the kingdom of God,
30 "who shall not receive many times more in this present time, and in the age to come eternal life."

Jesus a Third Time Predicts His Death and Resurrection

31 Then He took the twelve aside and said to them, "Behold, we are going up to Jerusalem, and all things that are written by the prophets concerning the Son of Man will be accomplished.

17:36 [a]NU-Text and M-Text omit verse 36. **18:20** [a]Exodus 20:12–16; Deuteronomy 5:16–20 **18:28** [a]NU-Text reads *our own.*

32 "For He will be delivered to the Gentiles and will be mocked and insulted and spit upon.
33 "They will scourge *Him* and kill Him. And the third day He will rise again."
34 But they understood none of these things; this saying was hidden from them, and they did not know the things which were spoken.

A Blind Man Receives His Sight

35 Then it happened, as He was coming near Jericho, that a certain blind man sat by the road begging.
36 And hearing a multitude passing by, he asked what it meant.
37 So they told him that Jesus of Nazareth was passing by.
38 And he cried out, saying, "Jesus, Son of David, have mercy on me!"
39 Then those who went before warned him that he should be quiet; but he cried out all the more, "Son of David, have mercy on me!"
40 So Jesus stood still and commanded him to be brought to Him. And when he had come near, He asked him,
41 saying, "What do you want Me to do for you?" He said, "Lord, that I may receive my sight."
42 Then Jesus said to him, "Receive your sight; your faith has made you well."
43 And immediately he received his sight, and followed Him, glorifying God. And all the people, when they saw *it*, gave praise to God.

Jesus Comes to Zacchaeus' House

19 Then *Jesus* entered and passed through Jericho.
2 Now behold, *there was* a man named Zacchaeus who was a chief tax collector, and he was rich.
3 And he sought to see who Jesus was, but could not because of the crowd, for he was of short stature.
4 So he ran ahead and climbed up into a sycamore tree to see Him, for He was going to pass that *way*.
5 And when Jesus came to the place, He looked up and saw him,[a] and said to him, "Zacchaeus, make haste and come down, for today I must stay at your house."
6 So he made haste and came down, and received Him joyfully.
7 But when they saw *it*, they all complained, saying, "He has gone to be a guest with a man who is a sinner."
8 Then Zacchaeus stood and said to the Lord, "Look, Lord, I give half of my goods to the poor; and if I have taken anything from anyone by false accusation, I restore fourfold."
9 And Jesus said to him, "Today salvation has come to this house, because he also is a son of Abraham;
10 "for the Son of Man has come to seek and to save that which was lost."

The Parable of the Minas

11 Now as they heard these things, He spoke another parable, because He was near Jerusalem and because they thought the kingdom of God would appear immediately.
12 Therefore He said: "A certain nobleman went into a far country to receive for himself a kingdom and to return.
13 "So he called ten of his servants, delivered to them ten minas,[a] and said to them, 'Do business till I come.'
14 "But his citizens hated him, and sent a delegation after him, saying, 'We will not have this *man* to reign over us.'
15 "And so it was that when he returned, having received the kingdom, he then commanded these servants, to whom he had given the money, to be called to him, that he might know how much every man had gained by trading.
16 "Then came the first, saying, 'Master, your mina has earned ten minas.'
17 "And he said to him, 'Well *done*, good servant; because you were faithful in a very little, have authority over ten cities.'
18 "And the second came, saying, 'Master, your mina has earned five minas.'
19 "Likewise he said to him, 'You also be over five cities.'
20 "Then another came, saying, 'Master, here is your mina, which I have kept put away in a handkerchief.
21 'For I feared you, because you are an austere man. You collect what you did not deposit, and reap what you did not sow.'
22 "And he said to him, 'Out of your own mouth I will judge you, *you* wicked servant. You knew that I was an austere man, collecting what I did not deposit and reaping what I did not sow.
23 'Why then did you not put my money in the bank, that at my coming I might have collected it with interest?'
24 "And he said to those who stood by, 'Take the mina from him, and give *it* to him who has ten minas.'
25 ("But they said to him, 'Master, he has ten minas.')
26 'For I say to you, that to everyone who has will be given; and from him who does not have, even what he has will be taken away from him.
27 'But bring here those enemies of mine, who did not want me to reign over them, and slay *them* before me.'"

The Triumphal Entry

28 When He had said this, He went on ahead, going up to Jerusalem.
29 And it came to pass, when He drew near to Bethphage[a] and Bethany, at the mountain called Olivet, *that* He sent two of His disciples,
30 saying, "Go into the village opposite *you*, where as you enter you will find a colt tied, on which no one has ever sat. Loose it and bring *it here*.
31 "And if anyone asks you, 'Why are you loosing *it?*' thus you shall say to him, 'Because the Lord has need of it.'"
32 So those who were sent went their way and found *it* just as He had said to them.
33 But as they were loosing the colt, the owners of it said to them, "Why are you loosing the colt?"
34 And they said, "The Lord has need of him."
35 Then they brought him to Jesus. And they threw their own clothes on the colt, and they set Jesus on him.
36 And as He went, *many* spread their clothes on the road.
37 Then, as He was now drawing near the descent of the Mount of Olives, the whole multitude

19:5 [a]NU-Text omits *and saw him*. **19:13** [a]The *mina* (Greek *mna*, Hebrew *minah*) was worth about three months' salary. **19:29** [a]M-Text reads *Bethsphage*.

of the disciples began to rejoice and praise God
with a loud voice for all the mighty works they
had seen,
38 saying:

" *'Blessed is the King who comes in the
name of the* LORD!'[a]
Peace in heaven and glory in the
highest!"

39 And some of the Pharisees called to Him
from the crowd, "Teacher, rebuke Your disci-
ples."
40 But He answered and said to them, "I tell
you that if these should keep silent, the stones
would immediately cry out."

Jesus Weeps over Jerusalem

41 Now as He drew near, He saw the city and
wept over it,
42 saying, "If you had known, even you, espe-
cially in this your day, the things *that make*
for your peace! But now they are hidden from
your eyes.
43 "For days will come upon you when your
enemies will build an embankment around
you, surround you and close you in on every
side,
44 "and level you, and your children within you,
to the ground; and they will not leave in you
one stone upon another, because you did not
know the time of your visitation."

Jesus Cleanses the Temple

45 Then He went into the temple and began
to drive out those who bought and sold in it,[a]
46 saying to them, "It is written, *'My house
is*[a] *a house of prayer,'*[b] but you have made it a
'den of thieves.' "[c]
47 And He was teaching daily in the temple.
But the chief priests, the scribes, and the lead-
ers of the people sought to destroy Him,
48 and were unable to do anything; for all the
people were very attentive to hear Him.

Jesus' Authority Questioned

20 Now it happened on one of those days,
as He taught the people in the temple
and preached the gospel, *that* the chief priests
and the scribes, together with the elders, con-
fronted *Him*
2 and spoke to Him, saying, "Tell us, by what
authority are You doing these things? Or who is
he who gave You this authority?"
3 But He answered and said to them, "I also
will ask you one thing, and answer Me:
4 "The baptism of John—was it from heaven
or from men?"
5 And they reasoned among themselves, say-
ing, "If we say, 'From heaven,' He will say, 'Why
then[a] did you not believe him?'
6 "But if we say, 'From men,' all the people
will stone us, for they are persuaded that John
was a prophet."
7 So they answered that they did not know
where *it was* from.
8 And Jesus said to them, "Neither will I tell
you by what authority I do these things."

The Parable of the Wicked Vinedressers

9 Then He began to tell the people this para-
ble: "A certain man planted a vineyard, leased
it to vinedressers, and went into a far country
for a long time.
10 "Now at vintage-time he sent a servant to
the vinedressers, that they might give him some
of the fruit of the vineyard. But the vinedressers
beat him and sent *him* away empty-handed.
11 "Again he sent another servant; and they
beat him also, treated *him* shamefully, and sent
him away empty-handed.
12 "And again he sent a third; and they wounded
him also and cast *him* out.
13 "Then the owner of the vineyard said, 'What
shall I do? I will send my beloved son. Probably
they will respect *him* when they see him.'
14 "But when the vinedressers saw him, they
reasoned among themselves, saying, 'This is the
heir. Come, let us kill him, that the inheritance
may be ours.'
15 "So they cast him out of the vineyard and
killed *him*. Therefore what will the owner of
the vineyard do to them?
16 "He will come and destroy those vinedress-
ers and give the vineyard to others." And when
they heard *it* they said, "Certainly not!"
17 Then He looked at them and said, "What
then is this that is written:

*'The stone which the builders rejected
Has become the chief cornerstone'* ?[a]

18 "Whoever falls on that stone will be broken;
but on whomever it falls, it will grind him to
powder."
19 And the chief priests and the scribes that
very hour sought to lay hands on Him, but they
feared the people[a]—for they knew He had spo-
ken this parable against them.

The Pharisees: Is It Lawful to Pay Taxes to Caesar?

20 So they watched *Him*, and sent spies who
pretended to be righteous, that they might
seize on His words, in order to deliver Him to
the power and the authority of the governor.
21 Then they asked Him, saying, "Teacher, we
know that You say and teach rightly, and You
do not show personal favoritism, but teach the
way of God in truth:
22 "Is it lawful for us to pay taxes to Caesar
or not?"
23 But He perceived their craftiness, and said
to them, "Why do you test Me?[a]
24 "Show Me a denarius. Whose image and
inscription does it have?" They answered and
said, "Caesar's."
25 And He said to them, "Render therefore to
Caesar the things that are Caesar's, and to God
the things that are God's."
26 But they could not catch Him in His words
in the presence of the people. And they mar-
veled at His answer and kept silent.

The Sadducees: What About the Resurrection?

27 Then some of the Sadducees, who deny that
there is a resurrection, came to *Him* and asked
Him,
28 saying: "Teacher, Moses wrote to us *that*
if a man's brother dies, having a wife, and he
dies without children, his brother should take
his wife and raise up offspring for his brother.

19:38 [a]Psalm 118:26 **19:45** [a]NU-Text reads *those who were selling.* **19:46** [a]NU-Text reads *shall be.* [b]Isaiah 56:7 [c]Jeremiah 7:11 **20:5** [a]NU-Text and M-Text omit *then.* **20:17** [a]Psalm 118:22 **20:19** [a]M-Text reads *but they were afraid.* **20:23** [a]NU-Text omits *Why do you test Me?*

29 "Now there were seven brothers. And the
first took a wife, and died without children.
30 "And the second[a] took her as wife, and he
died childless.
31 "Then the third took her, and in like manner the seven also; and they left no children,[a]
and died.
32 "Last of all the woman died also.
33 "Therefore, in the resurrection, whose wife
does she become? For all seven had her as wife."
34 Jesus answered and said to them, "The sons
of this age marry and are given in marriage.
35 "But those who are counted worthy to attain that age, and the resurrection from the dead, neither marry nor are given in marriage;
36 "nor can they die anymore, for they are equal to the angels and are sons of God, being sons of the resurrection.
37 "But even Moses showed in the *burning*
bush *passage* that the dead are raised, when he called the Lord *'the God of Abraham, the God of Isaac, and the God of Jacob.'*[a]
38 "For He is not the God of the dead but of
the living, for all live to Him."
39 Then some of the scribes answered and
said, "Teacher, You have spoken well."
40 But after that they dared not question Him
anymore.

Jesus: How Can David Call His Descendant Lord?

41 And He said to them, "How can they say
that the Christ is the Son of David?
42 "Now David himself said in the Book of
Psalms:

'The LORD said to my Lord,
"Sit at My right hand,
43 *Till I make Your enemies Your*
footstool."'[a]

44 "Therefore David calls Him *'Lord'*; how is
He then his Son?"

Beware of the Scribes

45 Then, in the hearing of all the people, He
said to His disciples,
46 "Beware of the scribes, who desire to go around in long robes, love greetings in the marketplaces, the best seats in the synagogues, and the best places at feasts,
47 "who devour widows' houses, and for a
pretense make long prayers. These will receive greater condemnation."

The Widow's Two Mites

21 And He looked up and saw the rich putting their gifts into the treasury,
2 and He saw also a certain poor widow putting in two mites.
3 So He said, "Truly I say to you that this
poor widow has put in more than all;
4 "for all these out of their abundance have
put in offerings for God,[a] but she out of her poverty put in all the livelihood that she had."

Jesus Predicts the Destruction of the Temple

5 Then, as some spoke of the temple, how it
was adorned with beautiful stones and donations, He said,
6 "These things which you see—the days
will come in which not *one* stone shall be left upon another that shall not be thrown down."

The Signs of the Times and the End of the Age

7 So they asked Him, saying, "Teacher, but
when will these things be? And what sign *will there be* when these things are about to take place?"
8 And He said: "Take heed that you not be
deceived. For many will come in My name, saying, 'I am *He*,' and, 'The time has drawn near.' Therefore[a] do not go after them.
9 "But when you hear of wars and commotions, do not be terrified; for these things must come to pass first, but the end *will* not *come* immediately."
10 Then He said to them, "Nation will rise
against nation, and kingdom against kingdom.
11 "And there will be great earthquakes in
various places, and famines and pestilences; and there will be fearful sights and great signs from heaven.
12 "But before all these things, they will lay
their hands on you and persecute *you*, delivering *you* up to the synagogues and prisons. You will be brought before kings and rulers for My name's sake.
13 "But it will turn out for you as an occasion
for testimony.
14 "Therefore settle *it* in your hearts not to
meditate beforehand on what you will answer;
15 "for I will give you a mouth and wisdom
which all your adversaries will not be able to contradict or resist.
16 "You will be betrayed even by parents and
brothers, relatives and friends; and they will put *some* of you to death.
17 "And you will be hated by all for My name's
sake.
18 "But not a hair of your head shall be lost.
19 "By your patience possess your souls.

The Destruction of Jerusalem

20 "But when you see Jerusalem surrounded
by armies, then know that its desolation is near.
21 "Then let those who are in Judea flee to
the mountains, let those who are in the midst of her depart, and let not those who are in the country enter her.
22 "For these are the days of vengeance, that
all things which are written may be fulfilled.
23 "But woe to those who are pregnant and to
those who are nursing babies in those days! For there will be great distress in the land and wrath upon this people.
24 "And they will fall by the edge of the sword,
and be led away captive into all nations. And Jerusalem will be trampled by Gentiles until the times of the Gentiles are fulfilled.

The Coming of the Son of Man

25 "And there will be signs in the sun, in the
moon, and in the stars; and on the earth distress of nations, with perplexity, the sea and the waves roaring;
26 "men's hearts failing them from fear and the
expectation of those things which are coming on the earth, for the powers of the heavens will be shaken.
27 "Then they will see the Son of Man coming
in a cloud with power and great glory.

20:30 [a]NU-Text ends verse 30 here. **20:31** [a]NU-Text and M-Text read *the seven also left no children.* **20:37** [a]Exodus 3:6, 15 **20:43** [a]Psalm 110:1 **21:4** [a]NU-Text omits *for God.* **21:8** [a]NU-Text omits *Therefore.*

28 "Now when these things begin to happen, look up and lift up your heads, because your redemption draws near."

The Parable of the Fig Tree

29 Then He spoke to them a parable: "Look at the fig tree, and all the trees.
30 "When they are already budding, you see and know for yourselves that summer is now near.
31 "So you also, when you see these things happening, know that the kingdom of God is near.
32 "Assuredly, I say to you, this generation will by no means pass away till all things take place.
33 "Heaven and earth will pass away, but My words will by no means pass away.

The Importance of Watching

34 "But take heed to yourselves, lest your hearts be weighed down with carousing, drunkenness, and cares of this life, and that Day come on you unexpectedly.
35 "For it will come as a snare on all those who dwell on the face of the whole earth.
36 "Watch therefore, and pray always that you may be counted worthy[a] to escape all these things that will come to pass, and to stand before the Son of Man."
37 And in the daytime He was teaching in the temple, but at night He went out and stayed on the mountain called Olivet.
38 Then early in the morning all the people came to Him in the temple to hear Him.

The Plot to Kill Jesus

22 Now the Feast of Unleavened Bread drew near, which is called Passover.
2 And the chief priests and the scribes sought how they might kill Him, for they feared the people.
3 Then Satan entered Judas, surnamed Iscariot, who was numbered among the twelve.
4 So he went his way and conferred with the chief priests and captains, how he might betray Him to them.
5 And they were glad, and agreed to give him money.
6 So he promised and sought opportunity to betray Him to them in the absence of the multitude.

Jesus and His Disciples Prepare the Passover

7 Then came the Day of Unleavened Bread, when the Passover must be killed.
8 And He sent Peter and John, saying, "Go and prepare the Passover for us, that we may eat."
9 So they said to Him, "Where do You want us to prepare?"
10 And He said to them, "Behold, when you have entered the city, a man will meet you carrying a pitcher of water; follow him into the house which he enters.
11 "Then you shall say to the master of the house, 'The Teacher says to you, "Where is the guest room where I may eat the Passover with My disciples?"'
12 "Then he will show you a large, furnished upper room; there make ready."
13 So they went and found it just as He had said to them, and they prepared the Passover.

Jesus Institutes the Lord's Supper

14 When the hour had come, He sat down, and the twelve[a] apostles with Him.
15 Then He said to them, "With *fervent* desire I have desired to eat this Passover with you before I suffer;
16 "for I say to you, I will no longer eat of it until it is fulfilled in the kingdom of God."
17 Then He took the cup, and gave thanks, and said, "Take this and divide *it* among yourselves;
18 "for I say to you,[a] I will not drink of the fruit of the vine until the kingdom of God comes."
19 And He took bread, gave thanks and broke *it*, and gave *it* to them, saying, "This is My body which is given for you; do this in remembrance of Me."
20 Likewise He also *took* the cup after supper, saying, "This cup *is* the new covenant in My blood, which is shed for you.
21 "But behold, the hand of My betrayer *is* with Me on the table.
22 "And truly the Son of Man goes as it has been determined, but woe to that man by whom He is betrayed!"
23 Then they began to question among themselves, which of them it was who would do this thing.

The Disciples Argue About Greatness

24 Now there was also a dispute among them, as to which of them should be considered the greatest.
25 And He said to them, "The kings of the Gentiles exercise lordship over them, and those who exercise authority over them are called 'benefactors.'
26 "But not so *among* you; on the contrary, he who is greatest among you, let him be as the younger, and he who governs as he who serves.
27 "For who *is* greater, he who sits at the table, or he who serves? *Is* it not he who sits at the table? Yet I am among you as the One who serves.
28 "But you are those who have continued with Me in My trials.
29 "And I bestow upon you a kingdom, just as My Father bestowed *one* upon Me,
30 "that you may eat and drink at My table in My kingdom, and sit on thrones judging the twelve tribes of Israel."

Jesus Predicts Peter's Denial

31 And the Lord said,[a] "Simon, Simon! Indeed, Satan has asked for you, that he may sift *you* as wheat.
32 "But I have prayed for you, that your faith should not fail; and when you have returned to *Me*, strengthen your brethren."
33 But he said to Him, "Lord, I am ready to go with You, both to prison and to death."
34 Then He said, "I tell you, Peter, the rooster shall not crow this day before you will deny three times that you know Me."

Supplies for the Road

35 And He said to them, "When I sent you without money bag, knapsack, and sandals, did you lack anything?" So they said, "Nothing."
36 Then He said to them, "But now, he who has a money bag, let him take *it*, and likewise

21:36 [a]NU-Text reads *may have strength.* **22:14** [a]NU-Text omits *twelve.* **22:18** [a]NU-Text adds *from now on.*
22:31 [a]NU-Text omits *And the Lord said.*

a knapsack; and he who has no sword, let him
sell his garment and buy one.
37 "For I say to you that this which is written
must still be accomplished in Me: *'And He was
numbered with the transgressors.'*[a] For the
things concerning Me have an end."
38 So they said, "Lord, look, here *are* two
swords." And He said to them, "It is enough."

The Prayer in the Garden

39 Coming out, He went to the Mount of Olives,
as He was accustomed, and His disciples also
followed Him.
40 When He came to the place, He said to
them, "Pray that you may not enter into temp-
tation."
41 And He was withdrawn from them about a
stone's throw, and He knelt down and prayed,
42 saying, "Father, if it is Your will, take this
cup away from Me; nevertheless not My will,
but Yours, be done."
43 Then an angel appeared to Him from heaven,
strengthening Him.
44 And being in agony, He prayed more ear-
nestly. Then His sweat became like great drops
of blood falling down to the ground.[a]
45 When He rose up from prayer, and had
come to His disciples, He found them sleeping
from sorrow.
46 Then He said to them, "Why do you sleep?
Rise and pray, lest you enter into temptation."

Betrayal and Arrest in Gethsemane

47 And while He was still speaking, behold,
a multitude; and he who was called Judas, one
of the twelve, went before them and drew near
to Jesus to kiss Him.
48 But Jesus said to him, "Judas, are you be-
traying the Son of Man with a kiss?"
49 When those around Him saw what was go-
ing to happen, they said to Him, "Lord, shall
we strike with the sword?"
50 And one of them struck the servant of the
high priest and cut off his right ear.
51 But Jesus answered and said, "Permit even
this." And He touched his ear and healed him.
52 Then Jesus said to the chief priests, cap-
tains of the temple, and the elders who had
come to Him, "Have you come out, as against
a robber, with swords and clubs?
53 "When I was with you daily in the temple,
you did not try to seize Me. But this is your
hour, and the power of darkness."

Peter Denies Jesus, and Weeps Bitterly

54 Having arrested Him, they led *Him* and
brought Him into the high priest's house. But
Peter followed at a distance.
55 Now when they had kindled a fire in the
midst of the courtyard and sat down together,
Peter sat among them.
56 And a certain servant girl, seeing him as
he sat by the fire, looked intently at him and
said, "This man was also with Him."
57 But he denied Him,[a] saying, "Woman, I do
not know Him."
58 And after a little while another saw him and
said, "You also are of them." But Peter said,
"Man, I am not!"
59 Then after about an hour had passed, an-
other confidently affirmed, saying, "Surely this
fellow also was with Him, for he is a Galilean."
60 But Peter said, "Man, I do not know what
you are saying!" Immediately, while he was
still speaking, the rooster[a] crowed.
61 And the Lord turned and looked at Peter.
Then Peter remembered the word of the Lord,
how He had said to him, "Before the rooster
crows,[a] you will deny Me three times."
62 So Peter went out and wept bitterly.

Jesus Mocked and Beaten

63 Now the men who held Jesus mocked Him
and beat Him.
64 And having blindfolded Him, they struck
Him on the face and asked Him,[a] saying, "Proph-
esy! Who is the one who struck You?"
65 And many other things they blasphemously
spoke against Him.

Jesus Faces the Sanhedrin

66 As soon as it was day, the elders of the peo-
ple, both chief priests and scribes, came to-
gether and led Him into their council, saying,
67 "If You are the Christ, tell us." But He said
to them, "If I tell you, you will by no means
believe.
68 "And if I also ask *you*, you will by no means
answer Me or let *Me* go.[a]
69 "Hereafter the Son of Man will sit on the
right hand of the power of God."
70 Then they all said, "Are You then the Son
of God?" So He said to them, "You *rightly* say
that I am."
71 And they said, "What further testimony do
we need? For we have heard it ourselves from
His own mouth."

Jesus Handed Over to Pontius Pilate

23 Then the whole multitude of them arose
and led Him to Pilate.
2 And they began to accuse Him, saying,
"We found this *fellow* perverting the[a] nation,
and forbidding to pay taxes to Caesar, saying
that He Himself is Christ, a King."
3 Then Pilate asked Him, saying, "Are You
the King of the Jews?" He answered him and
said, "*It is as* you say."
4 So Pilate said to the chief priests and the
crowd, "I find no fault in this Man."
5 But they were the more fierce, saying, "He
stirs up the people, teaching throughout all Ju-
dea, beginning from Galilee to this place."

Jesus Faces Herod

6 When Pilate heard of Galilee,[a] he asked if
the Man were a Galilean.
7 And as soon as he knew that He belonged
to Herod's jurisdiction, he sent Him to Herod,
who was also in Jerusalem at that time.
8 Now when Herod saw Jesus, he was ex-
ceedingly glad; for he had desired for a long
time to see Him, because he had heard many
things about Him, and he hoped to see some
miracle done by Him.
9 Then he questioned Him with many words,
but He answered him nothing.
10 And the chief priests and scribes stood and
vehemently accused Him.
11 Then Herod, with his men of war, treated

22:37 [a]Isaiah 53:12 **22:44** [a]NU-Text brackets verses 43 and 44 as not in the original text. **22:57** [a]NU-Text reads *denied it.* **22:60** [a]NU-Text and M-Text read *a rooster.* **22:61** [a]NU-Text adds *today.* **22:64** [a]NU-Text reads *And having blindfolded Him, they asked Him.* **22:68** [a]NU-Text omits *also* and *Me or let Me go.* **23:2** [a]NU-Text reads *our.* **23:6** [a]NU-Text omits *of Galilee.*

Him with contempt and mocked *Him,* arrayed Him in a gorgeous robe, and sent Him back to Pilate.

12 That very day Pilate and Herod became friends with each other, for previously they had been at enmity with each other.

Taking the Place of Barabbas

13 Then Pilate, when he had called together the chief priests, the rulers, and the people,

14 said to them, "You have brought this Man to me, as one who misleads the people. And indeed, having examined *Him* in your presence, I have found no fault in this Man concerning those things of which you accuse Him;

15 "no, neither did Herod, for I sent you back to him;[a] and indeed nothing deserving of death has been done by Him.

16 "I will therefore chastise Him and release *Him*"

17 (for it was necessary for him to release one to them at the feast).[a]

18 And they all cried out at once, saying, "Away with this *Man,* and release to us Barabbas"—

19 who had been thrown into prison for a certain rebellion made in the city, and for murder.

20 Pilate, therefore, wishing to release Jesus, again called out to them.

21 But they shouted, saying, "Crucify *Him,* crucify Him!"

22 Then he said to them the third time, "Why, what evil has He done? I have found no reason for death in Him. I will therefore chastise Him and let *Him* go."

23 But they were insistent, demanding with loud voices that He be crucified. And the voices of these men and of the chief priests prevailed.[a]

24 So Pilate gave sentence that it should be as they requested.

25 And he released to them[a] the one they requested, who for rebellion and murder had been thrown into prison; but he delivered Jesus to their will.

The King on a Cross

26 Now as they led Him away, they laid hold of a certain man, Simon a Cyrenian, who was coming from the country, and on him they laid the cross that he might bear *it* after Jesus.

27 And a great multitude of the people followed Him, and women who also mourned and lamented Him.

28 But Jesus, turning to them, said, "Daughters of Jerusalem, do not weep for Me, but weep for yourselves and for your children.

29 "For indeed the days are coming in which they will say, 'Blessed *are* the barren, wombs that never bore, and breasts which never nursed!'

30 "Then they will begin *'to say to the mountains, "Fall on us!" and to the hills, "Cover us!" '*[a]

31 "For if they do these things in the green wood, what will be done in the dry?"

32 There were also two others, criminals, led with Him to be put to death.

33 And when they had come to the place called Calvary, there they crucified Him, and the criminals, one on the right hand and the other on the left.

34 Then Jesus said, "Father, forgive them, for they do not know what they do."[a] And they divided His garments and cast lots.

35 And the people stood looking on. But even the rulers with them sneered, saying, "He saved others; let Him save Himself if He is the Christ, the chosen of God."

36 The soldiers also mocked Him, coming and offering Him sour wine,

37 and saying, "If You are the King of the Jews, save Yourself."

38 And an inscription also was written over Him in letters of Greek, Latin, and Hebrew:[a]

THIS IS THE KING OF THE JEWS.

39 Then one of the criminals who were hanged blasphemed Him, saying, "If You are the Christ,[a] save Yourself and us."

40 But the other, answering, rebuked him, saying, "Do you not even fear God, seeing you are under the same condemnation?

41 "And we indeed justly, for we receive the due reward of our deeds; but this Man has done nothing wrong."

42 Then he said to Jesus, "Lord,[a] remember me when You come into Your kingdom."

43 And Jesus said to him, "Assuredly, I say to you, today you will be with Me in Paradise."

Jesus Dies on the Cross

44 Now it was[a] about the sixth hour, and there was darkness over all the earth until the ninth hour.

45 Then the sun was darkened,[a] and the veil of the temple was torn in two.

46 And when Jesus had cried out with a loud voice, He said, "Father, *'into Your hands I commit My spirit.' "*[a] Having said this, He breathed His last.

47 So when the centurion saw what had happened, he glorified God, saying, "Certainly this was a righteous Man!"

48 And the whole crowd who came together to that sight, seeing what had been done, beat their breasts and returned.

49 But all His acquaintances, and the women who followed Him from Galilee, stood at a distance, watching these things.

Jesus Buried in Joseph's Tomb

50 Now behold, *there was* a man named Joseph, a council member, a good and just man.

51 He had not consented to their decision and deed. *He was* from Arimathea, a city of the Jews, who himself was also waiting[a] for the kingdom of God.

52 This man went to Pilate and asked for the body of Jesus.

53 Then he took it down, wrapped it in linen, and laid it in a tomb *that was* hewn out of the rock, where no one had ever lain before.

54 That day was the Preparation, and the Sabbath drew near.

55 And the women who had come with Him from Galilee followed after, and they observed the tomb and how His body was laid.

56 Then they returned and prepared spices and fragrant oils. And they rested on the Sabbath according to the commandment.

23:15 [a]NU-Text reads *for he sent Him back to us.* **23:17** [a]NU-Text omits verse 17. **23:23** [a]NU-Text omits *and of the chief priests.* **23:25** [a]NU-Text and M-Text omit *to them.* **23:30** [a]Hosea 10:8 **23:34** [a]NU-Text brackets the first sentence as a later addition. **23:38** [a]NU-Text omits *written* and *in letters of Greek, Latin, and Hebrew.* **23:39** [a]NU-Text reads *Are You not the Christ?* **23:42** [a]NU-Text reads *And he said, "Jesus, remember me.* **23:44** [a]NU-Text adds *already.* **23:45** [a]NU-Text reads *obscured.* **23:46** [a]Psalm 31:5 **23:51** [a]NU-Text reads *who was waiting.*

He Is Risen

24 Now on the first *day* of the week, very early in the morning, they, and certain *other women* with them,[a] came to the tomb bringing the spices which they had prepared.
2 But they found the stone rolled away from the tomb.
3 Then they went in and did not find the body of the Lord Jesus.
4 And it happened, as they were greatly[a] perplexed about this, that behold, two men stood by them in shining garments.
5 Then, as they were afraid and bowed *their* faces to the earth, they said to them, "Why do you seek the living among the dead?
6 "He is not here, but is risen! Remember how He spoke to you when He was still in Galilee,
7 "saying, 'The Son of Man must be delivered into the hands of sinful men, and be crucified, and the third day rise again.' "
8 And they remembered His words.
9 Then they returned from the tomb and told all these things to the eleven and to all the rest.
10 It was Mary Magdalene, Joanna, Mary *the mother* of James, and the other *women* with them, who told these things to the apostles.
11 And their words seemed to them like idle tales, and they did not believe them.
12 But Peter arose and ran to the tomb; and stooping down, he saw the linen cloths lying[a] by themselves; and he departed, marveling to himself at what had happened.

The Road to Emmaus

13 Now behold, two of them were traveling that same day to a village called Emmaus, which was seven miles[a] from Jerusalem.
14 And they talked together of all these things which had happened.
15 So it was, while they conversed and reasoned, that Jesus Himself drew near and went with them.
16 But their eyes were restrained, so that they did not know Him.
17 And He said to them, "What kind of conversation *is* this that you have with one another as you walk and are sad?"[a]
18 Then the one whose name was Cleopas answered and said to Him, "Are You the only stranger in Jerusalem, and have You not known the things which happened there in these days?"
19 And He said to them, "What things?" So they said to Him, "The things concerning Jesus of Nazareth, who was a Prophet mighty in deed and word before God and all the people,
20 "and how the chief priests and our rulers delivered Him to be condemned to death, and crucified Him.
21 "But we were hoping that it was He who was going to redeem Israel. Indeed, besides all this, today is the third day since these things happened.
22 "Yes, and certain women of our company, who arrived at the tomb early, astonished us.
23 "When they did not find His body, they came saying that they had also seen a vision of angels who said He was alive.
24 "And certain of those *who were* with us went to the tomb and found *it* just as the women had said; but Him they did not see."
25 Then He said to them, "O foolish ones, and slow of heart to believe in all that the prophets have spoken!
26 "Ought not the Christ to have suffered these things and to enter into His glory?"
27 And beginning at Moses and all the Prophets, He expounded to them in all the Scriptures the things concerning Himself.

The Disciples' Eyes Opened

28 Then they drew near to the village where they were going, and He indicated that He would have gone farther.
29 But they constrained Him, saying, "Abide with us, for it is toward evening, and the day is far spent." And He went in to stay with them.
30 Now it came to pass, as He sat at the table with them, that He took bread, blessed and broke *it*, and gave it to them.
31 Then their eyes were opened and they knew Him; and He vanished from their sight.
32 And they said to one another, "Did not our heart burn within us while He talked with us on the road, and while He opened the Scriptures to us?"
33 So they rose up that very hour and returned to Jerusalem, and found the eleven and those *who were* with them gathered together,
34 saying, "The Lord is risen indeed, and has appeared to Simon!"
35 And they told about the things *that had happened* on the road, and how He was known to them in the breaking of bread.

Jesus Appears to His Disciples

36 Now as they said these things, Jesus Himself stood in the midst of them, and said to them, "Peace to you."
37 But they were terrified and frightened, and supposed they had seen a spirit.
38 And He said to them, "Why are you troubled? And why do doubts arise in your hearts?
39 "Behold My hands and My feet, that it is I Myself. Handle Me and see, for a spirit does not have flesh and bones as you see I have."
40 When He had said this, He showed them His hands and His feet.[a]
41 But while they still did not believe for joy, and marveled, He said to them, "Have you any food here?"
42 So they gave Him a piece of a broiled fish and some honeycomb.[a]
43 And He took *it* and ate in their presence.

The Scriptures Opened

44 Then He said to them, "These *are* the words which I spoke to you while I was still with you, that all things must be fulfilled which were written in the Law of Moses and *the* Prophets and *the* Psalms concerning Me."
45 And He opened their understanding, that they might comprehend the Scriptures.

24:1 [a]NU-Text omits *and certain other women with them.* **24:4** [a]NU-Text omits *greatly.* **24:12** [a]NU-Text omits *lying.* **24:13** [a]Literally *sixty stadia* **24:17** [a]NU-Text reads *as you walk? And they stood still, looking sad.* **24:40** [a]Some printed New Testaments omit this verse. It is found in nearly all Greek manuscripts. **24:42** [a]NU-Text omits *and some honeycomb.*

46 Then He said to them, "Thus it is written, and thus it was necessary for the Christ to suffer and to rise[a] from the dead the third day,
47 "and that repentance and remission of sins should be preached in His name to all nations, beginning at Jerusalem.
48 "And you are witnesses of these things.
49 "Behold, I send the Promise of My Father upon you; but tarry in the city of Jerusalem[a] until you are endued with power from on high."

The Ascension

50 And He led them out as far as Bethany, and He lifted up His hands and blessed them.
51 Now it came to pass, while He blessed them, that He was parted from them and carried up into heaven.
52 And they worshiped Him, and returned to Jerusalem with great joy,
53 and were continually in the temple praising and[a] blessing God. Amen.[b]

The Gospel According to JOHN

The Eternal Word

1 In the beginning was the Word, and the Word was with God, and the Word was God.
2 He was in the beginning with God.
3 All things were made through Him, and without Him nothing was made that was made.
4 In Him was life, and the life was the light of men.
5 And the light shines in the darkness, and the darkness did not comprehend[a] it.

John's Witness: The True Light

6 There was a man sent from God, whose name *was* John.
7 This man came for a witness, to bear witness of the Light, that all through him might believe.
8 He was not that Light, but *was sent* to bear witness of that Light.
9 That was the true Light which gives light to every man coming into the world.[a]
10 He was in the world, and the world was made through Him, and the world did not know Him.
11 He came to His own,[a] and His own[b] did not receive Him.
12 But as many as received Him, to them He gave the right to become children of God, to those who believe in His name:
13 who were born, not of blood, nor of the will of the flesh, nor of the will of man, but of God.

The Word Becomes Flesh

14 And the Word became flesh and dwelt among us, and we beheld His glory, the glory as of the only begotten of the Father, full of grace and truth.
15 John bore witness of Him and cried out, saying, "This was He of whom I said, 'He who comes after me is preferred before me, for He was before me.' "
16 And[a] of His fullness we have all received, and grace for grace.
17 For the law was given through Moses, *but* grace and truth came through Jesus Christ.
18 No one has seen God at any time. The only begotten Son,[a] who is in the bosom of the Father, He has declared *Him.*

A Voice in the Wilderness

19 Now this is the testimony of John, when the Jews sent priests and Levites from Jerusalem to ask him, "Who are you?"
20 He confessed, and did not deny, but confessed, "I am not the Christ."
21 And they asked him, "What then? Are you Elijah?" He said, "I am not." "Are you the Prophet?" And he answered, "No."
22 Then they said to him, "Who are you, that we may give an answer to those who sent us? What do you say about yourself?"
23 He said: "I *am*

> *'The voice of one crying in the wilderness:*
> *"Make straight the way of the LORD," '*[a]

as the prophet Isaiah said."
24 Now those who were sent were from the Pharisees.
25 And they asked him, saying, "Why then do you baptize if you are not the Christ, nor Elijah, nor the Prophet?"
26 John answered them, saying, "I baptize with water, but there stands One among you whom you do not know.
27 "It is He who, coming after me, is preferred before me, whose sandal strap I am not worthy to loose."
28 These things were done in Bethabara[a] beyond the Jordan, where John was baptizing.

The Lamb of God

29 The next day John saw Jesus coming toward him, and said, "Behold! The Lamb of God who takes away the sin of the world!
30 "This is He of whom I said, 'After me comes a Man who is preferred before me, for He was before me.'
31 "I did not know Him; but that He should be revealed to Israel, therefore I came baptizing with water."
32 And John bore witness, saying, "I saw the Spirit descending from heaven like a dove, and He remained upon Him.
33 "I did not know Him, but He who sent me to baptize with water said to me, 'Upon whom you see the Spirit descending, and remaining

24:46 [a]NU-Text reads *written, that the Christ should suffer and rise.* **24:49** [a]NU-Text omits *of Jerusalem.* **24:53** [a]NU-Text omits *praising and,* [b]NU-Text omits *Amen.* **1:5** [a]Or *overcome* **1:9** [a]Or *That was the true Light which, coming into the world, gives light to every man.* **1:11** [a]That is, His own things or domain [b]That is, His own people **1:16** [a]NU-Text reads *For.* **1:18** [a]NU-Text reads *only begotten God.* **1:23** [a]Isaiah 40:3 **1:28** [a]NU-Text and M-Text read *Bethany.*

on Him, this is He who baptizes with the Holy
Spirit.'
34 "And I have seen and testified that this is
the Son of God."

The First Disciples

35 Again, the next day, John stood with two
of his disciples.
36 And looking at Jesus as He walked, he said,
"Behold the Lamb of God!"
37 The two disciples heard him speak, and they
followed Jesus.
38 Then Jesus turned, and seeing them follow-
ing, said to them, "What do you seek?" They
said to Him, "Rabbi" (which is to say, when
translated, Teacher), "where are You staying?"
39 He said to them, "Come and see." They
came and saw where He was staying, and re-
mained with Him that day (now it was about
the tenth hour).
40 One of the two who heard John *speak*, and
followed Him, was Andrew, Simon Peter's
brother.
41 He first found his own brother Simon, and
said to him, "We have found the Messiah" (which
is translated, the Christ).
42 And he brought him to Jesus. Now when
Jesus looked at him, He said, "You are Simon
the son of Jonah.[a] You shall be called Cephas"
(which is translated, A Stone).

Philip and Nathanael

43 The following day Jesus wanted to go to
Galilee, and He found Philip and said to him,
"Follow Me."
44 Now Philip was from Bethsaida, the city
of Andrew and Peter.
45 Philip found Nathanael and said to him, "We
have found Him of whom Moses in the law, and
also the prophets, wrote—Jesus of Nazareth,
the son of Joseph."
46 And Nathanael said to him, "Can anything
good come out of Nazareth?" Philip said to
him, "Come and see."
47 Jesus saw Nathanael coming toward Him,
and said of him, "Behold, an Israelite indeed,
in whom is no deceit!"
48 Nathanael said to Him, "How do You know
me?" Jesus answered and said to him, "Before
Philip called you, when you were under the fig
tree, I saw you."
49 Nathanael answered and said to Him,
"Rabbi, You are the Son of God! You are the
King of Israel!"
50 Jesus answered and said to him, "Because
I said to you, 'I saw you under the fig tree,' do
you believe? You will see greater things than
these."
51 And He said to him, "Most assuredly, I say
to you, hereafter[a] you shall see heaven open,
and the angels of God ascending and descend-
ing upon the Son of Man."

Water Turned to Wine

2 On the third day there was a wedding in
Cana of Galilee, and the mother of Jesus
was there.
2 Now both Jesus and His disciples were in-
vited to the wedding.
3 And when they ran out of wine, the mother
of Jesus said to Him, "They have no wine."
4 Jesus said to her, "Woman, what does your
concern have to do with Me? My hour has not
yet come."
5 His mother said to the servants, "Whatever
He says to you, do *it*."
6 Now there were set there six waterpots of
stone, according to the manner of purification
of the Jews, containing twenty or thirty gallons
apiece.
7 Jesus said to them, "Fill the waterpots with
water." And they filled them up to the brim.
8 And He said to them, "Draw *some* out now,
and take *it* to the master of the feast." And they
took *it*.
9 When the master of the feast had tasted the
water that was made wine, and did not know
where it came from (but the servants who had
drawn the water knew), the master of the feast
called the bridegroom.
10 And he said to him, "Every man at the be-
ginning sets out the good wine, and when the
guests have well drunk, then the inferior. You
have kept the good wine until now!"
11 This beginning of signs Jesus did in Cana
of Galilee, and manifested His glory; and His
disciples believed in Him.
12 After this He went down to Capernaum,
He, His mother, His brothers, and His disci-
ples; and they did not stay there many days.

Jesus Cleanses the Temple

13 Now the Passover of the Jews was at hand,
and Jesus went up to Jerusalem.
14 And He found in the temple those who sold
oxen and sheep and doves, and the money
changers doing business.
15 When He had made a whip of cords, He
drove them all out of the temple, with the sheep
and the oxen, and poured out the changers'
money and overturned the tables.
16 And He said to those who sold doves, "Take
these things away! Do not make My Father's
house a house of merchandise!"
17 Then His disciples remembered that it was
written, *"Zeal for Your house has eaten[a] Me
up."*[b]
18 So the Jews answered and said to Him,
"What sign do You show to us, since You do
these things?"
19 Jesus answered and said to them, "Destroy
this temple, and in three days I will raise it up."
20 Then the Jews said, "It has taken forty-six
years to build this temple, and will You raise it
up in three days?"
21 But He was speaking of the temple of His
body.
22 Therefore, when He had risen from the dead,
His disciples remembered that He had said this
to them;[a] and they believed the Scripture and
the word which Jesus had said.

The Discerner of Hearts

23 Now when He was in Jerusalem at the Pass-
over, during the feast, many believed in His
name when they saw the signs which He did.
24 But Jesus did not commit Himself to them,
because He knew all *men*,
25 and had no need that anyone should testify
of man, for He knew what was in man.

1:42 [a]NU-Text reads *John*. **1:51** [a]NU-Text omits *hereafter*. **2:17** [a]NU-Text and M-Text read *will eat*. [b]Psalm 69:9
2:22 [a]NU-Text and M-Text omit *to them*.

The New Birth

3 There was a man of the Pharisees named
Nicodemus, a ruler of the Jews.
2 This man came to Jesus by night and said
to Him, "Rabbi, we know that You are a teacher
come from God; for no one can do these signs
that You do unless God is with him."
3 Jesus answered and said to him, "Most as-
suredly, I say to you, unless one is born again,
he cannot see the kingdom of God."
4 Nicodemus said to Him, "How can a man
be born when he is old? Can he enter a second
time into his mother's womb and be born?"
5 Jesus answered, "Most assuredly, I say to
you, unless one is born of water and the Spirit,
he cannot enter the kingdom of God.
6 "That which is born of the flesh is flesh,
and that which is born of the Spirit is spirit.
7 "Do not marvel that I said to you, 'You
must be born again.'
8 "The wind blows where it wishes, and you
hear the sound of it, but cannot tell where it
comes from and where it goes. So is everyone
who is born of the Spirit."
9 Nicodemus answered and said to Him, "How
can these things be?"
10 Jesus answered and said to him, "Are you
the teacher of Israel, and do not know these
things?
11 "Most assuredly, I say to you, We speak what
We know and testify what We have seen, and
you do not receive Our witness.
12 "If I have told you earthly things and you
do not believe, how will you believe if I tell you
heavenly things?
13 "No one has ascended to heaven but He
who came down from heaven, *that is,* the Son
of Man who is in heaven.[a]
14 "And as Moses lifted up the serpent in the
wilderness, even so must the Son of Man be
lifted up,
15 "that whoever believes in Him should not
perish but[a] have eternal life.
16 "For God so loved the world that He gave
His only begotten Son, that whoever believes
in Him should not perish but have everlasting
life.
17 "For God did not send His Son into the
world to condemn the world, but that the world
through Him might be saved.
18 "He who believes in Him is not condemned;
but he who does not believe is condemned al-
ready, because he has not believed in the name
of the only begotten Son of God.
19 "And this is the condemnation, that the light
has come into the world, and men loved dark-
ness rather than light, because their deeds were
evil.
20 "For everyone practicing evil hates the light
and does not come to the light, lest his deeds
should be exposed.
21 "But he who does the truth comes to the
light, that his deeds may be clearly seen, that
they have been done in God."

John the Baptist Exalts Christ

22 After these things Jesus and His disciples
came into the land of Judea, and there He re-
mained with them and baptized.
23 Now John also was baptizing in Aenon near
Salim, because there was much water there.
And they came and were baptized.
24 For John had not yet been thrown into
prison.
25 Then there arose a dispute between *some*
of John's disciples and the Jews about purifica-
tion.
26 And they came to John and said to him,
"Rabbi, He who was with you beyond the Jor-
dan, to whom you have testified—behold, He
is baptizing, and all are coming to Him!"
27 John answered and said, "A man can re-
ceive nothing unless it has been given to him
from heaven.
28 "You yourselves bear me witness, that I
said, 'I am not the Christ,' but, 'I have been sent
before Him.'
29 "He who has the bride is the bridegroom;
but the friend of the bridegroom, who stands
and hears him, rejoices greatly because of the
bridegroom's voice. Therefore this joy of mine
is fulfilled.
30 "He must increase, but I *must* decrease.
31 "He who comes from above is above all;
he who is of the earth is earthly and speaks of
the earth. He who comes from heaven is above
all.
32 "And what He has seen and heard, that He
testifies; and no one receives His testimony.
33 "He who has received His testimony has
certified that God is true.
34 "For He whom God has sent speaks the
words of God, for God does not give the Spirit
by measure.
35 "The Father loves the Son, and has given
all things into His hand.
36 "He who believes in the Son has everlast-
ing life; and he who does not believe the Son
shall not see life, but the wrath of God abides
on him."

A Samaritan Woman Meets Her Messiah

4 Therefore, when the Lord knew that the
Pharisees had heard that Jesus made and
baptized more disciples than John
2 (though Jesus Himself did not baptize, but
His disciples),
3 He left Judea and departed again to Galilee.
4 But He needed to go through Samaria.
5 So He came to a city of Samaria which is
called Sychar, near the plot of ground that Ja-
cob gave to his son Joseph.
6 Now Jacob's well was there. Jesus there-
fore, being wearied from *His* journey, sat thus
by the well. It was about the sixth hour.
7 A woman of Samaria came to draw water.
Jesus said to her, "Give Me a drink."
8 For His disciples had gone away into the
city to buy food.
9 Then the woman of Samaria said to Him,
"How is it that You, being a Jew, ask a drink
from me, a Samaritan woman?" For Jews have
no dealings with Samaritans.
10 Jesus answered and said to her, "If you
knew the gift of God, and who it is who says
to you, 'Give Me a drink,' you would have
asked Him, and He would have given you liv-
ing water."
11 The woman said to Him, "Sir, You have
nothing to draw with, and the well is deep.
Where then do You get that living water?
12 "Are You greater than our father Jacob, who
gave us the well, and drank from it himself, as
well as his sons and his livestock?"

3:13 [a]NU-Text omits *who is in heaven.* **3:15** [a]NU-Text omits *not perish but.*

13 Jesus answered and said to her, "Whoever
drinks of this water will thirst again,
14 "but whoever drinks of the water that I shall
give him will never thirst. But the water that I
shall give him will become in him a fountain
of water springing up into everlasting life."
15 The woman said to Him, "Sir, give me this
water, that I may not thirst, nor come here to
draw."
16 Jesus said to her, "Go, call your husband,
and come here."
17 The woman answered and said, "I have no
husband." Jesus said to her, "You have well
said, 'I have no husband,'
18 "for you have had five husbands, and the
one whom you now have is not your husband;
in that you spoke truly."
19 The woman said to Him, "Sir, I perceive
that You are a prophet.
20 "Our fathers worshiped on this mountain,
and you *Jews* say that in Jerusalem is the place
where one ought to worship."
21 Jesus said to her, "Woman, believe Me, the
hour is coming when you will neither on this
mountain, nor in Jerusalem, worship the Father.
22 "You worship what you do not know; we
know what we worship, for salvation is of the
Jews.
23 "But the hour is coming, and now is, when
the true worshipers will worship the Father in
spirit and truth; for the Father is seeking such
to worship Him.
24 "God *is* Spirit, and those who worship Him
must worship in spirit and truth."
25 The woman said to Him, "I know that Mes-
siah is coming" (who is called Christ). "When
He comes, He will tell us all things."
26 Jesus said to her, "I who speak to you am
He."

The Whitened Harvest

27 And at this *point* His disciples came, and
they marveled that He talked with a woman;
yet no one said, "What do You seek?" or, "Why
are You talking with her?"
28 The woman then left her waterpot, went her
way into the city, and said to the men,
29 "Come, see a Man who told me all things
that I ever did. Could this be the Christ?"
30 Then they went out of the city and came to
Him.
31 In the meantime His disciples urged Him,
saying, "Rabbi, eat."
32 But He said to them, "I have food to eat of
which you do not know."
33 Therefore the disciples said to one another,
"Has anyone brought Him *anything* to eat?"
34 Jesus said to them, "My food is to do the
will of Him who sent Me, and to finish His
work.
35 "Do you not say, 'There are still four months
and *then* comes the harvest'? Behold, I say to
you, lift up your eyes and look at the fields, for
they are already white for harvest!
36 "And he who reaps receives wages, and
gathers fruit for eternal life, that both he who
sows and he who reaps may rejoice together.
37 "For in this the saying is true: 'One sows
and another reaps.'
38 "I sent you to reap that for which you have
not labored; others have labored, and you have
entered into their labors."

The Savior of the World

39 And many of the Samaritans of that city be-
lieved in Him because of the word of the woman
who testified, "He told me all that I *ever* did."
40 So when the Samaritans had come to Him,
they urged Him to stay with them; and He stayed
there two days.
41 And many more believed because of His
own word.
42 Then they said to the woman, "Now we be-
lieve, not because of what you said, for we our-
selves have heard *Him* and we know that this
is indeed the Christ,[a] the Savior of the world."

Welcome at Galilee

43 Now after the two days He departed from
there and went to Galilee.
44 For Jesus Himself testified that a prophet has
no honor in his own country.
45 So when He came to Galilee, the Galileans
received Him, having seen all the things He did
in Jerusalem at the feast; for they also had gone
to the feast.

A Nobleman's Son Healed

46 So Jesus came again to Cana of Galilee
where He had made the water wine. And there
was a certain nobleman whose son was sick at
Capernaum.
47 When he heard that Jesus had come out of
Judea into Galilee, he went to Him and implored
Him to come down and heal his son, for he was
at the point of death.
48 Then Jesus said to him, "Unless you *people*
see signs and wonders, you will by no means
believe."
49 The nobleman said to Him, "Sir, come down
before my child dies!"
50 Jesus said to him, "Go your way; your son
lives." So the man believed the word that Jesus
spoke to him, and he went his way.
51 And as he was now going down, his ser-
vants met him and told *him*, saying, "Your son
lives!"
52 Then he inquired of them the hour when
he got better. And they said to him, "Yesterday
at the seventh hour the fever left him."
53 So the father knew that *it was* at the same
hour in which Jesus said to him, "Your son
lives." And he himself believed, and his whole
household.
54 This again *is* the second sign Jesus did when
He had come out of Judea into Galilee.

A Man Healed at the Pool of Bethesda

5 After this there was a feast of the Jews, and
Jesus went up to Jerusalem.
2 Now there is in Jerusalem by the Sheep *Gate*
a pool, which is called in Hebrew, Bethesda,[a]
having five porches.
3 In these lay a great multitude of sick peo-
ple, blind, lame, paralyzed, waiting for the mov-
ing of the water.
4 For an angel went down at a certain time
into the pool and stirred up the water; then who-
ever stepped in first, after the stirring of the
water, was made well of whatever disease he
had.[a]
5 Now a certain man was there who had an
infirmity thirty-eight years.
6 When Jesus saw him lying there, and knew

4:42 [a]NU-Text omits *the Christ.* **5:2** [a]NU-Text reads *Bethzatha.* **5:4** [a]NU-Text omits *waiting for the moving of the water* at the end of verse 3, and all of verse 4.

that he already had been *in that condition* a
long time, He said to him, "Do you want to be
made well?"
7 The sick man answered Him, "Sir, I have
no man to put me into the pool when the water
is stirred up; but while I am coming, another
steps down before me."
8 Jesus said to him, "Rise, take up your bed
and walk."
9 And immediately the man was made well,
took up his bed, and walked. And that day was
the Sabbath.
10 The Jews therefore said to him who was
cured, "It is the Sabbath; it is not lawful for
you to carry your bed."
11 He answered them, "He who made me well
said to me, 'Take up your bed and walk.'"
12 Then they asked him, "Who is the Man
who said to you, 'Take up your bed and walk'?"
13 But the one who was healed did not know
who it was, for Jesus had withdrawn, a multi-
tude being in *that* place.
14 Afterward Jesus found him in the temple,
and said to him, "See, you have been made well.
Sin no more, lest a worse thing come upon you."
15 The man departed and told the Jews that
it was Jesus who had made him well.

Honor the Father and the Son

16 For this reason the Jews persecuted Jesus,
and sought to kill Him,[a] because He had done
these things on the Sabbath.
17 But Jesus answered them, "My Father has
been working until now, and I have been
working."
18 Therefore the Jews sought all the more to
kill Him, because He not only broke the Sab-
bath, but also said that God was His Father,
making Himself equal with God.
19 Then Jesus answered and said to them,
"Most assuredly, I say to you, the Son can do
nothing of Himself, but what He sees the Fa-
ther do; for whatever He does, the Son also
does in like manner.
20 "For the Father loves the Son, and shows
Him all things that He Himself does; and He
will show Him greater works than these, that
you may marvel.
21 "For as the Father raises the dead and gives
life to *them,* even so the Son gives life to whom
He will.
22 "For the Father judges no one, but has com-
mitted all judgment to the Son,
23 "that all should honor the Son just as they
honor the Father. He who does not honor the
Son does not honor the Father who sent Him.

Life and Judgment Are Through the Son

24 "Most assuredly, I say to you, he who hears
My word and believes in Him who sent Me
has everlasting life, and shall not come into
judgment, but has passed from death into life.
25 "Most assuredly, I say to you, the hour is
coming, and now is, when the dead will hear
the voice of the Son of God; and those who hear
will live.
26 "For as the Father has life in Himself, so
He has granted the Son to have life in Himself,
27 "and has given Him authority to execute
judgment also, because He is the Son of Man.
28 "Do not marvel at this; for the hour is com-
ing in which all who are in the graves will hear
His voice
29 "and come forth—those who have done
good, to the resurrection of life, and those who
have done evil, to the resurrection of condem-
nation.
30 "I can of Myself do nothing. As I hear, I
judge; and My judgment is righteous, because
I do not seek My own will but the will of the
Father who sent Me.

The Fourfold Witness

31 "If I bear witness of Myself, My witness is
not true.
32 "There is another who bears witness of Me,
and I know that the witness which He wit-
nesses of Me is true.
33 "You have sent to John, and he has borne
witness to the truth.
34 "Yet I do not receive testimony from man,
but I say these things that you may be saved.
35 "He was the burning and shining lamp, and
you were willing for a time to rejoice in his light.
36 "But I have a greater witness than John's;
for the works which the Father has given Me
to finish—the very works that I do—bear wit-
ness of Me, that the Father has sent Me.
37 "And the Father Himself, who sent Me, has
testified of Me. You have neither heard His
voice at any time, nor seen His form.
38 "But you do not have His word abiding in
you, because whom He sent, Him you do not
believe.
39 "You search the Scriptures, for in them you
think you have eternal life; and these are they
which testify of Me.
40 "But you are not willing to come to Me that
you may have life.
41 "I do not receive honor from men.
42 "But I know you, that you do not have the
love of God in you.
43 "I have come in My Father's name, and you
do not receive Me; if another comes in his own
name, him you will receive.
44 "How can you believe, who receive honor
from one another, and do not seek the honor
that *comes* from the only God?
45 "Do not think that I shall accuse you to the
Father; there is *one* who accuses you—Moses,
in whom you trust.
46 "For if you believed Moses, you would be-
lieve Me; for he wrote about Me.
47 "But if you do not believe his writings, how
will you believe My words?"

Feeding the Five Thousand

6 After these things Jesus went over the Sea
of Galilee, which is *the Sea* of Tiberias.
2 Then a great multitude followed Him, be-
cause they saw His signs which He performed
on those who were diseased.
3 And Jesus went up on the mountain, and
there He sat with His disciples.
4 Now the Passover, a feast of the Jews, was
near.
5 Then Jesus lifted up *His* eyes, and seeing
a great multitude coming toward Him, He said
to Philip, "Where shall we buy bread, that these
may eat?"
6 But this He said to test him, for He Himself
knew what He would do.
7 Philip answered Him, "Two hundred denarii
worth of bread is not sufficient for them, that
every one of them may have a little."

5:16 [a]NU-Text omits *and sought to kill Him.*

8 One of His disciples, Andrew, Simon Pe-
ter's brother, said to Him,
9 "There is a lad here who has five barley
loaves and two small fish, but what are they
among so many?"
10 Then Jesus said, "Make the people sit down."
Now there was much grass in the place. So the
men sat down, in number about five thousand.
11 And Jesus took the loaves, and when He
had given thanks He distributed *them* to the
disciples, and the disciples[a] to those sitting down;
and likewise of the fish, as much as they wanted.
12 So when they were filled, He said to His
disciples, "Gather up the fragments that remain,
so that nothing is lost."
13 Therefore they gathered *them* up, and filled
twelve baskets with the fragments of the five
barley loaves which were left over by those who
had eaten.
14 Then those men, when they had seen the
sign that Jesus did, said, "This is truly the
Prophet who is to come into the world."

Jesus Walks on the Sea

15 Therefore when Jesus perceived that they
were about to come and take Him by force
to make Him king, He departed again to the
mountain by Himself alone.
16 Now when evening came, His disciples went
down to the sea,
17 got into the boat, and went over the sea
toward Capernaum. And it was already dark,
and Jesus had not come to them.
18 Then the sea arose because a great wind was
blowing.
19 So when they had rowed about three or
four miles,[a] they saw Jesus walking on the sea
and drawing near the boat; and they were afraid.
20 But He said to them, "It is I; do not be afraid."
21 Then they willingly received Him into the
boat, and immediately the boat was at the land
where they were going.

The Bread from Heaven

22 On the following day, when the people who
were standing on the other side of the sea saw
that there was no other boat there, except that
one which His disciples had entered,[a] and that
Jesus had not entered the boat with His disci-
ples, but His disciples had gone away alone—
23 however, other boats came from Tiberias,
near the place where they ate bread after the
Lord had given thanks—
24 when the people therefore saw that Jesus
was not there, nor His disciples, they also got
into boats and came to Capernaum, seeking
Jesus.
25 And when they found Him on the other side
of the sea, they said to Him, "Rabbi, when did
You come here?"
26 Jesus answered them and said, "Most as-
suredly, I say to you, you seek Me, not because
you saw the signs, but because you ate of the
loaves and were filled.
27 "Do not labor for the food which perishes,
but for the food which endures to everlasting
life, which the Son of Man will give you, be-
cause God the Father has set His seal on Him."
28 Then they said to Him, "What shall we do,
that we may work the works of God?"
29 Jesus answered and said to them, "This is
the work of God, that you believe in Him whom
He sent."
30 Therefore they said to Him, "What sign will
You perform then, that we may see it and be-
lieve You? What work will You do?
31 "Our fathers ate the manna in the desert;
as it is written, *'He gave them bread from heaven
to eat.'* "[a]
32 Then Jesus said to them, "Most assuredly,
I say to you, Moses did not give you the bread
from heaven, but My Father gives you the true
bread from heaven.
33 "For the bread of God is He who comes
down from heaven and gives life to the world."
34 Then they said to Him, "Lord, give us this
bread always."
35 And Jesus said to them, "I am the bread of
life. He who comes to Me shall never hunger,
and he who believes in Me shall never thirst.
36 "But I said to you that you have seen Me
and yet do not believe.
37 "All that the Father gives Me will come to
Me, and the one who comes to Me I will by no
means cast out.
38 "For I have come down from heaven, not
to do My own will, but the will of Him who
sent Me.
39 "This is the will of the Father who sent Me,
that of all He has given Me I should lose noth-
ing, but should raise it up at the last day.
40 "And this is the will of Him who sent Me,
that everyone who sees the Son and believes
in Him may have everlasting life; and I will
raise him up at the last day."

Rejected by His Own

41 The Jews then complained about Him, be-
cause He said, "I am the bread which came
down from heaven."
42 And they said, "Is not this Jesus, the son
of Joseph, whose father and mother we know?
How is it then that He says, 'I have come down
from heaven'?"
43 Jesus therefore answered and said to them,
"Do not murmur among yourselves.
44 "No one can come to Me unless the Father
who sent Me draws him; and I will raise him
up at the last day.
45 "It is written in the prophets, *'And they shall
all be taught by God.'*[a] Therefore everyone who
has heard and learned[b] from the Father comes
to Me.
46 "Not that anyone has seen the Father, ex-
cept He who is from God; He has seen the Fa-
ther.
47 "Most assuredly, I say to you, he who be-
lieves in Me[a] has everlasting life.
48 "I am the bread of life.
49 "Your fathers ate the manna in the wilder-
ness, and are dead.
50 "This is the bread which comes down from
heaven, that one may eat of it and not die.
51 "I am the living bread which came down
from heaven. If anyone eats of this bread, he
will live forever; and the bread that I shall give
is My flesh, which I shall give for the life of the
world."
52 The Jews therefore quarreled among them-
selves, saying, "How can this Man give us *His*
flesh to eat?"
53 Then Jesus said to them, "Most assuredly,

6:11 [a]NU-Text omits *to the disciples, and the disciples.* **6:19** [a]Literally *twenty-five or thirty stadia* **6:22** [a]NU-Text omits *that* and *which His disciples had entered.* **6:31** [a]Exodus 16:4; Nehemiah 9:15; Psalm 78:24 **6:45** [a]Isaiah 54:13 [b]M-Text reads *hears and has learned.* **6:47** [a]NU-Text omits *in Me.*

I say to you, unless you eat the flesh of the Son of Man and drink His blood, you have no life in you.
54 "Whoever eats My flesh and drinks My blood has eternal life, and I will raise him up at the last day.
55 "For My flesh is food indeed,[a] and My blood is drink indeed.
56 "He who eats My flesh and drinks My blood abides in Me, and I in him.
57 "As the living Father sent Me, and I live because of the Father, so he who feeds on Me will live because of Me.
58 "This is the bread which came down from heaven—not as your fathers ate the manna, and are dead. He who eats this bread will live forever."
59 These things He said in the synagogue as He taught in Capernaum.

Many Disciples Turn Away

60 Therefore many of His disciples, when they heard *this*, said, "This is a hard saying; who can understand it?"
61 When Jesus knew in Himself that His disciples complained about this, He said to them, "Does this offend you?
62 "*What* then if you should see the Son of Man ascend where He was before?
63 "It is the Spirit who gives life; the flesh profits nothing. The words that I speak to you are spirit, and *they* are life.
64 "But there are some of you who do not believe." For Jesus knew from the beginning who they were who did not believe, and who would betray Him.
65 And He said, "Therefore I have said to you that no one can come to Me unless it has been granted to him by My Father."
66 From that *time* many of His disciples went back and walked with Him no more.
67 Then Jesus said to the twelve, "Do you also want to go away?"
68 But Simon Peter answered Him, "Lord, to whom shall we go? You have the words of eternal life.
69 "Also we have come to believe and know that You are the Christ, the Son of the living God."[a]
70 Jesus answered them, "Did I not choose you, the twelve, and one of you is a devil?"
71 He spoke of Judas Iscariot, *the son* of Simon, for it was he who would betray Him, being one of the twelve.

Jesus' Brothers Disbelieve

7 After these things Jesus walked in Galilee; for He did not want to walk in Judea, because the Jews[a] sought to kill Him.
2 Now the Jews' Feast of Tabernacles was at hand.
3 His brothers therefore said to Him, "Depart from here and go into Judea, that Your disciples also may see the works that You are doing.
4 "For no one does anything in secret while he himself seeks to be known openly. If You do these things, show Yourself to the world."
5 For even His brothers did not believe in Him.
6 Then Jesus said to them, "My time has not yet come, but your time is always ready.
7 "The world cannot hate you, but it hates Me because I testify of it that its works are evil.
8 "You go up to this feast. I am not yet[a] going up to this feast, for My time has not yet fully come."
9 When He had said these things to them, He remained in Galilee.

The Heavenly Scholar

10 But when His brothers had gone up, then He also went up to the feast, not openly, but as it were in secret.
11 Then the Jews sought Him at the feast, and said, "Where is He?"
12 And there was much complaining among the people concerning Him. Some said, "He is good"; others said, "No, on the contrary, He deceives the people."
13 However, no one spoke openly of Him for fear of the Jews.
14 Now about the middle of the feast Jesus went up into the temple and taught.
15 And the Jews marveled, saying, "How does this Man know letters, having never studied?"
16 Jesus[a] answered them and said, "My doctrine is not Mine, but His who sent Me.
17 "If anyone wills to do His will, he shall know concerning the doctrine, whether it is from God or *whether* I speak on My own *authority*.
18 "He who speaks from himself seeks his own glory; but He who seeks the glory of the One who sent Him is true, and no unrighteousness is in Him.
19 "Did not Moses give you the law, yet none of you keeps the law? Why do you seek to kill Me?"
20 The people answered and said, "You have a demon. Who is seeking to kill You?"
21 Jesus answered and said to them, "I did one work, and you all marvel.
22 "Moses therefore gave you circumcision (not that it is from Moses, but from the fathers), and you circumcise a man on the Sabbath.
23 "If a man receives circumcision on the Sabbath, so that the law of Moses should not be broken, are you angry with Me because I made a man completely well on the Sabbath?
24 "Do not judge according to appearance, but judge with righteous judgment."

Could This Be the Christ?

25 Now some of them from Jerusalem said, "Is this not He whom they seek to kill?
26 "But look! He speaks boldly, and they say nothing to Him. Do the rulers know indeed that this is truly[a] the Christ?
27 "However, we know where this Man is from; but when the Christ comes, no one knows where He is from."
28 Then Jesus cried out, as He taught in the temple, saying, "You both know Me, and you know where I am from; and I have not come of Myself, but He who sent Me is true, whom you do not know.
29 "But[a] I know Him, for I am from Him, and He sent Me."
30 Therefore they sought to take Him; but no one laid a hand on Him, because His hour had not yet come.

6:55 [a]NU-Text reads *true food* and *true drink*. **6:69** [a]NU-Text reads *You are the Holy One of God*. **7:1** [a]That is, the ruling authorities **7:8** [a]NU-Text omits *yet*. **7:16** [a]NU-Text and M-Text read *So Jesus*. **7:26** [a]NU-Text omits *truly*. **7:29** [a]NU-Text and M-Text omit *But*.

31 And many of the people believed in Him,
and said, "When the Christ comes, will He do
more signs than these which this *Man* has done?"

Jesus and the Religious Leaders

32 The Pharisees heard the crowd murmur-
ing these things concerning Him, and the Phar-
isees and the chief priests sent officers to take
Him.
33 Then Jesus said to them,[a] "I shall be with
you a little while longer, and *then* I go to Him
who sent Me.
34 "You will seek Me and not find *Me,* and
where I am you cannot come."
35 Then the Jews said among themselves,
"Where does He intend to go that we shall not
find Him? Does He intend to go to the Disper-
sion among the Greeks and teach the Greeks?
36 "What is this thing that He said, 'You will
seek Me and not find Me, and where I am you
cannot come'?"

The Promise of the Holy Spirit

37 On the last day, that great *day* of the feast,
Jesus stood and cried out, saying, "If anyone
thirsts, let him come to Me and drink.
38 "He who believes in Me, as the Scripture has
said, out of his heart will flow rivers of living
water."
39 But this He spoke concerning the Spirit,
whom those believing[a] in Him would receive;
for the Holy[b] Spirit was not yet *given,* because
Jesus was not yet glorified.

Who Is He?

40 Therefore many[a] from the crowd, when they
heard this saying, said, "Truly this is the Prophet."
41 Others said, "This is the Christ." But some
said, "Will the Christ come out of Galilee?
42 "Has not the Scripture said that the Christ
comes from the seed of David and from the town
of Bethlehem, where David was?"
43 So there was a division among the people
because of Him.
44 Now some of them wanted to take Him, but
no one laid hands on Him.

Rejected by the Authorities

45 Then the officers came to the chief priests
and Pharisees, who said to them, "Why have
you not brought Him?"
46 The officers answered, "No man ever spoke
like this Man!"
47 Then the Pharisees answered them, "Are
you also deceived?
48 "Have any of the rulers or the Pharisees
believed in Him?
49 "But this crowd that does not know the law
is accursed."
50 Nicodemus (he who came to Jesus by night,[a]
being one of them) said to them,
51 "Does our law judge a man before it hears
him and knows what he is doing?"
52 They answered and said to him, "Are you
also from Galilee? Search and look, for no
prophet has arisen[a] out of Galilee."

An Adulteress Faces the Light of the World

53 And everyone went to his *own* house.[a]

8 But Jesus went to the Mount of Olives.
2 Now early[a] in the morning He came
again into the temple, and all the people came
to Him; and He sat down and taught them.
3 Then the scribes and Pharisees brought to
Him a woman caught in adultery. And when they
had set her in the midst,
4 they said to Him, "Teacher, this woman was
caught[a] in adultery, in the very act.
5 "Now Moses, in the law, commanded[a] us
that such should be stoned.[b] But what do You
say?"[c]
6 This they said, testing Him, that they might
have *something* of which to accuse Him. But
Jesus stooped down and wrote on the ground
with *His* finger, as though He did not hear.[a]
7 So when they continued asking Him, He
raised Himself up[a] and said to them, "He who
is without sin among you, let him throw a stone
at her first."
8 And again He stooped down and wrote on
the ground.
9 Then those who heard *it,* being convicted
by *their* conscience,[a] went out one by one, be-
ginning with the oldest *even* to the last. And
Jesus was left alone, and the woman standing
in the midst.
10 When Jesus had raised Himself up and saw
no one but the woman, He said to her,[a] "Woman,
where are those accusers of yours?[b] Has no one
condemned you?"
11 She said, "No one, Lord." And Jesus said
to her, "Neither do I condemn you; go and[a] sin
no more."
12 Then Jesus spoke to them again, saying, "I
am the light of the world. He who follows Me
shall not walk in darkness, but have the light
of life."

Jesus Defends His Self-Witness

13 The Pharisees therefore said to Him, "You
bear witness of Yourself; Your witness is not
true."
14 Jesus answered and said to them, "Even if
I bear witness of Myself, My witness is true,
for I know where I came from and where I am
going; but you do not know where I come from
and where I am going.
15 "You judge according to the flesh; I judge
no one.
16 "And yet if I do judge, My judgment is true;
for I am not alone, but I *am* with the Father
who sent Me.
17 "It is also written in your law that the testi-
mony of two men is true.
18 "I am One who bears witness of Myself,
and the Father who sent Me bears witness of
Me."
19 Then they said to Him, "Where is Your
Father?" Jesus answered, "You know neither
Me nor My Father. If you had known Me, you
would have known My Father also."

7:33 [a]NU-Text and M-Text omit *to them.* **7:39** [a]NU-Text reads *who believed.* [b]NU-Text omits *Holy.* **7:40** [a]NU-Text reads *some.* **7:50** [a]NU-Text reads *before.* **7:52** [a]NU-Text reads *is to rise.* **7:53** [a]The words *And everyone* through *sin no more* (8:11) are bracketed by NU-Text as not original. They are present in over 900 manuscripts. **8:2** [a]M-Text reads *very early.* **8:4** [a]M-Text reads *we found this woman.* **8:5** [a]M-Text reads *in our law Moses commanded.* [b]NU-Text and M-Text read *to stone such.* [c]M-Text adds *about her.* **8:6** [a]NU-Text and M-Text omit *as though He did not hear.* **8:7** [a]M-Text reads *He looked up.* **8:9** [a]NU-Text and M-Text omit *being convicted by their conscience.* **8:10** [a]NU-Text omits *and saw no one but the woman;* M-Text reads *He saw her and said.* [b]NU-Text and M-Text omit *of yours.* **8:11** [a]NU-Text and M-Text add *from now on.*

20 These words Jesus spoke in the treasury, as He taught in the temple; and no one laid hands on Him, for His hour had not yet come.

Jesus Predicts His Departure

21 Then Jesus said to them again, "I am going away, and you will seek Me, and will die in your sin. Where I go you cannot come."
22 So the Jews said, "Will He kill Himself, because He says, 'Where I go you cannot come'?"
23 And He said to them, "You are from beneath; I am from above. You are of this world; I am not of this world.
24 "Therefore I said to you that you will die in your sins; for if you do not believe that I am *He*, you will die in your sins."
25 Then they said to Him, "Who are You?" And Jesus said to them, "Just what I have been saying to you from the beginning.
26 "I have many things to say and to judge concerning you, but He who sent Me is true; and I speak to the world those things which I heard from Him."
27 They did not understand that He spoke to them of the Father.
28 Then Jesus said to them, "When you lift up the Son of Man, then you will know that I am *He*, and *that* I do nothing of Myself; but as My Father taught Me, I speak these things.
29 "And He who sent Me is with Me. The Father has not left Me alone, for I always do those things that please Him."
30 As He spoke these words, many believed in Him.

The Truth Shall Make You Free

31 Then Jesus said to those Jews who believed Him, "If you abide in My word, you are My disciples indeed.
32 "And you shall know the truth, and the truth shall make you free."
33 They answered Him, "We are Abraham's descendants, and have never been in bondage to anyone. How *can* You say, 'You will be made free'?"
34 Jesus answered them, "Most assuredly, I say to you, whoever commits sin is a slave of sin.
35 "And a slave does not abide in the house forever, *but* a son abides forever.
36 "Therefore if the Son makes you free, you shall be free indeed.

Abraham's Seed and Satan's

37 "I know that you are Abraham's descendants, but you seek to kill Me, because My word has no place in you.
38 "I speak what I have seen with My Father, and you do what you have seen with[a] your father."
39 They answered and said to Him, "Abraham is our father." Jesus said to them, "If you were Abraham's children, you would do the works of Abraham.
40 "But now you seek to kill Me, a Man who has told you the truth which I heard from God. Abraham did not do this.
41 "You do the deeds of your father." Then they said to Him, "We were not born of fornication; we have one Father—God."
42 Jesus said to them, "If God were your Father, you would love Me, for I proceeded forth and came from God; nor have I come of Myself, but He sent Me.
43 "Why do you not understand My speech? Because you are not able to listen to My word.
44 "You are of *your* father the devil, and the desires of your father you want to do. He was a murderer from the beginning, and does not stand in the truth, because there is no truth in him. When he speaks a lie, he speaks from his own *resources*, for he is a liar and the father of it.
45 "But because I tell the truth, you do not believe Me.
46 "Which of you convicts Me of sin? And if I tell the truth, why do you not believe Me?
47 "He who is of God hears God's words; therefore you do not hear, because you are not of God."

Before Abraham Was, I AM

48 Then the Jews answered and said to Him, "Do we not say rightly that You are a Samaritan and have a demon?"
49 Jesus answered, "I do not have a demon; but I honor My Father, and you dishonor Me.
50 "And I do not seek My *own* glory; there is One who seeks and judges.
51 "Most assuredly, I say to you, if anyone keeps My word he shall never see death."
52 Then the Jews said to Him, "Now we know that You have a demon! Abraham is dead, and the prophets; and You say, 'If anyone keeps My word he shall never taste death.'
53 "Are You greater than our father Abraham, who is dead? And the prophets are dead. Who do You make Yourself out to be?"
54 Jesus answered, "If I honor Myself, My honor is nothing. It is My Father who honors Me, of whom you say that He is your[a] God.
55 "Yet you have not known Him, but I know Him. And if I say, 'I do not know Him,' I shall be a liar like you; but I do know Him and keep His word.
56 "Your father Abraham rejoiced to see My day, and he saw *it* and was glad."
57 Then the Jews said to Him, "You are not yet fifty years old, and have You seen Abraham?"
58 Jesus said to them, "Most assuredly, I say to you, before Abraham was, I AM."
59 Then they took up stones to throw at Him; but Jesus hid Himself and went out of the temple,[a] going through the midst of them, and so passed by.

A Man Born Blind Receives Sight

9 Now as *Jesus* passed by, He saw a man who was blind from birth.
2 And His disciples asked Him, saying, "Rabbi, who sinned, this man or his parents, that he was born blind?"
3 Jesus answered, "Neither this man nor his parents sinned, but that the works of God should be revealed in him.
4 "I[a] must work the works of Him who sent Me while it is day; *the* night is coming when no one can work.
5 "As long as I am in the world, I am the light of the world."
6 When He had said these things, He spat on the ground and made clay with the saliva; and He anointed the eyes of the blind man with the clay.

8:38 [a]NU-Text reads *heard from.* **8:54** [a]NU-Text and M-Text read *our.* **8:59** [a]NU-Text omits the rest of this verse.
9:4 [a]NU-Text reads *We.*

7 And He said to him, "Go, wash in the pool
of Siloam" (which is translated, Sent). So he
went and washed, and came back seeing.
8 Therefore the neighbors and those who pre-
viously had seen that he was blind[a] said, "Is
not this he who sat and begged?"
9 Some said, "This is he." Others *said*, "He is
like him."[a] He said, "I am *he*."
10 Therefore they said to him, "How were your
eyes opened?"
11 He answered and said, "A Man called Jesus
made clay and anointed my eyes and said to
me, 'Go to the pool of[a] Siloam and wash.' So I
went and washed, and I received sight."
12 Then they said to him, "Where is He?" He
said, "I do not know."

The Pharisees Excommunicate the Healed Man

13 They brought him who formerly was blind
to the Pharisees.
14 Now it was a Sabbath when Jesus made the
clay and opened his eyes.
15 Then the Pharisees also asked him again
how he had received his sight. He said to them,
"He put clay on my eyes, and I washed, and I
see."
16 Therefore some of the Pharisees said, "This
Man is not from God, because He does not
keep the Sabbath." Others said, "How can a
man who is a sinner do such signs?" And there
was a division among them.
17 They said to the blind man again, "What
do you say about Him because He opened your
eyes?" He said, "He is a prophet."
18 But the Jews did not believe concerning
him, that he had been blind and received his
sight, until they called the parents of him who
had received his sight.
19 And they asked them, saying, "Is this your
son, who you say was born blind? How then
does he now see?"
20 His parents answered them and said, "We
know that this is our son, and that he was born
blind;
21 "but by what means he now sees we do not
know, or who opened his eyes we do not know.
He is of age; ask him. He will speak for him-
self."
22 His parents said these *things* because they
feared the Jews, for the Jews had agreed al-
ready that if anyone confessed *that* He *was*
Christ, he would be put out of the synagogue.
23 Therefore his parents said, "He is of age;
ask him."
24 So they again called the man who was blind,
and said to him, "Give God the glory! We know
that this Man is a sinner."
25 He answered and said, "Whether He is a
sinner *or not* I do not know. One thing I know:
that though I was blind, now I see."
26 Then they said to him again, "What did He
do to you? How did He open your eyes?"
27 He answered them, "I told you already, and
you did not listen. Why do you want to hear *it*
again? Do you also want to become His disci-
ples?"
28 Then they reviled him and said, "You are
His disciple, but we are Moses' disciples.
29 "We know that God spoke to Moses; *as for*
this *fellow*, we do not know where He is from."
30 The man answered and said to them, "Why,
this is a marvelous thing, that you do not know
where He is from; yet He has opened my eyes!
31 "Now we know that God does not hear sin-
ners; but if anyone is a worshiper of God and
does His will, He hears him.
32 "Since the world began it has been unheard
of that anyone opened the eyes of one who was
born blind.
33 "If this Man were not from God, He could
do nothing."
34 They answered and said to him, "You were
completely born in sins, and are you teaching
us?" And they cast him out.

True Vision and True Blindness

35 Jesus heard that they had cast him out; and
when He had found him, He said to him, "Do
you believe in the Son of God?"[a]
36 He answered and said, "Who is He, Lord,
that I may believe in Him?"
37 And Jesus said to him, "You have both seen
Him and it is He who is talking with you."
38 Then he said, "Lord, I believe!" And he
worshiped Him.
39 And Jesus said, "For judgment I have come
into this world, that those who do not see may
see, and that those who see may be made blind."
40 Then *some* of the Pharisees who were with
Him heard these words, and said to Him, "Are
we blind also?"
41 Jesus said to them, "If you were blind, you
would have no sin; but now you say, 'We see.'
Therefore your sin remains.

Jesus the True Shepherd

10 "Most assuredly, I say to you, he who does
not enter the sheepfold by the door, but
climbs up some other way, the same is a thief
and a robber.
2 "But he who enters by the door is the shep-
herd of the sheep.
3 "To him the doorkeeper opens, and the
sheep hear his voice; and he calls his own
sheep by name and leads them out.
4 "And when he brings out his own sheep,
he goes before them; and the sheep follow him,
for they know his voice.
5 "Yet they will by no means follow a
stranger, but will flee from him, for they do not
know the voice of strangers."
6 Jesus used this illustration, but they did not
understand the things which He spoke to them.

Jesus the Good Shepherd

7 Then Jesus said to them again, "Most as-
suredly, I say to you, I am the door of the sheep.
8 "All who *ever* came before Me[a] are thieves
and robbers, but the sheep did not hear them.
9 "I am the door. If anyone enters by Me, he
will be saved, and will go in and out and find
pasture.
10 "The thief does not come except to steal,
and to kill, and to destroy. I have come that they
may have life, and that they may have *it* more
abundantly.
11 "I am the good shepherd. The good shep-
herd gives His life for the sheep.
12 "But a hireling, *he who is* not the shepherd,
one who does not own the sheep, sees the wolf
coming and leaves the sheep and flees; and the
wolf catches the sheep and scatters them.

9:8 [a]NU-Text reads *a beggar.* **9:9** [a]NU-Text reads *"No, but he is like him."* **9:11** [a]NU-Text omits *the pool of.* **9:35** [a]NU-Text reads *Son of Man.* **10:8** [a]M-Text omits *before Me.*

13 "The hireling flees because he is a hireling
and does not care about the sheep.
14 "I am the good shepherd; and I know My
sheep, and am known by My own.
15 "As the Father knows Me, even so I know
the Father; and I lay down My life for the sheep.
16 "And other sheep I have which are not of
this fold; them also I must bring, and they will
hear My voice; and there will be one flock *and*
one shepherd.
17 "Therefore My Father loves Me, because I
lay down My life that I may take it again.
18 "No one takes it from Me, but I lay it down
of Myself. I have power to lay it down, and I
have power to take it again. This command I
have received from My Father."
19 Therefore there was a division again among
the Jews because of these sayings.
20 And many of them said, "He has a demon
and is mad. Why do you listen to Him?"
21 Others said, "These are not the words of one
who has a demon. Can a demon open the eyes
of the blind?"

The Shepherd Knows His Sheep

22 Now it was the Feast of Dedication in Jeru-
salem, and it was winter.
23 And Jesus walked in the temple, in Solo-
mon's porch.
24 Then the Jews surrounded Him and said
to Him, "How long do You keep us in doubt? If
You are the Christ, tell us plainly."
25 Jesus answered them, "I told you, and you
do not believe. The works that I do in My Fa-
ther's name, they bear witness of Me.
26 "But you do not believe, because you are
not of My sheep, as I said to you.[a]
27 "My sheep hear My voice, and I know them,
and they follow Me.
28 "And I give them eternal life, and they shall
never perish; neither shall anyone snatch them
out of My hand.
29 "My Father, who has given *them* to Me, is
greater than all; and no one is able to snatch
them out of My Father's hand.
30 "I and *My* Father are one."

Renewed Efforts to Stone Jesus

31 Then the Jews took up stones again to stone
Him.
32 Jesus answered them, "Many good works
I have shown you from My Father. For which
of those works do you stone Me?"
33 The Jews answered Him, saying, "For a good
work we do not stone You, but for blasphemy,
and because You, being a Man, make Yourself
God."
34 Jesus answered them, "Is it not written in
your law, *'I said, "You are gods" '*?[a]
35 "If He called them gods, to whom the word
of God came (and the Scripture cannot be
broken),
36 "do you say of Him whom the Father sanc-
tified and sent into the world, 'You are blasphem-
ing,' because I said, 'I am the Son of God'?
37 "If I do not do the works of My Father, do
not believe Me;
38 "but if I do, though you do not believe Me,
believe the works, that you may know and be-
lieve[a] that the Father *is* in Me, and I in Him."
39 Therefore they sought again to seize Him,
but He escaped out of their hand.

The Believers Beyond Jordan

40 And He went away again beyond the Jor-
dan to the place where John was baptizing at
first, and there He stayed.
41 Then many came to Him and said, "John
performed no sign, but all the things that John
spoke about this Man were true."
42 And many believed in Him there.

The Death of Lazarus

11 Now a certain *man* was sick, Lazarus of
Bethany, the town of Mary and her sister
Martha.
2 It was *that* Mary who anointed the Lord
with fragrant oil and wiped His feet with her
hair, whose brother Lazarus was sick.
3 Therefore the sisters sent to Him, saying,
"Lord, behold, he whom You love is sick."
4 When Jesus heard *that,* He said, "This
sickness is not unto death, but for the glory
of God, that the Son of God may be glorified
through it."
5 Now Jesus loved Martha and her sister and
Lazarus.
6 So, when He heard that he was sick, He
stayed two more days in the place where He
was.
7 Then after this He said to *the* disciples, "Let
us go to Judea again."
8 *The* disciples said to Him, "Rabbi, lately the
Jews sought to stone You, and are You going
there again?"
9 Jesus answered, "Are there not twelve hours
in the day? If anyone walks in the day, he does
not stumble, because he sees the light of this
world.
10 "But if one walks in the night, he stumbles,
because the light is not in him."
11 These things He said, and after that He said
to them, "Our friend Lazarus sleeps, but I go
that I may wake him up."
12 Then His disciples said, "Lord, if he sleeps
he will get well."
13 However, Jesus spoke of his death, but they
thought that He was speaking about taking rest
in sleep.
14 Then Jesus said to them plainly, "Lazarus
is dead.
15 "And I am glad for your sakes that I was
not there, that you may believe. Nevertheless
let us go to him."
16 Then Thomas, who is called the Twin, said
to his fellow disciples, "Let us also go, that we
may die with Him."

I Am the Resurrection and the Life

17 So when Jesus came, He found that he had
already been in the tomb four days.
18 Now Bethany was near Jerusalem, about two
miles[a] away.
19 And many of the Jews had joined the women
around Martha and Mary, to comfort them
concerning their brother.
20 Now Martha, as soon as she heard that Jesus
was coming, went and met Him, but Mary was
sitting in the house.
21 Now Martha said to Jesus, "Lord, if You
had been here, my brother would not have died.
22 "But even now I know that whatever You
ask of God, God will give You."

10:26 [a]NU-Text omits *as I said to you.* **10:34** [a]Psalm 82:6 **10:38** [a]NU-Text reads *understand.* **11:18** [a]Literally *fifteen stadia*

23 Jesus said to her, "Your brother will rise
again."
24 Martha said to Him, "I know that he will rise
again in the resurrection at the last day."
25 Jesus said to her, "I am the resurrection and
the life. He who believes in Me, though he may
die, he shall live.
26 "And whoever lives and believes in Me shall
never die. Do you believe this?"
27 She said to Him, "Yes, Lord, I believe that
You are the Christ, the Son of God, who is to
come into the world."

Jesus and Death, the Last Enemy

28 And when she had said these things, she
went her way and secretly called Mary her sis-
ter, saying, "The Teacher has come and is call-
ing for you."
29 As soon as she heard *that*, she arose quickly
and came to Him.
30 Now Jesus had not yet come into the town,
but was[a] in the place where Martha met Him.
31 Then the Jews who were with her in the
house, and comforting her, when they saw that
Mary rose up quickly and went out, followed
her, saying, "She is going to the tomb to weep
there."[a]
32 Then, when Mary came where Jesus was,
and saw Him, she fell down at His feet, saying
to Him, "Lord, if You had been here, my brother
would not have died."
33 Therefore, when Jesus saw her weeping,
and the Jews who came with her weeping, He
groaned in the spirit and was troubled.
34 And He said, "Where have you laid him?"
They said to Him, "Lord, come and see."
35 Jesus wept.
36 Then the Jews said, "See how He loved him!"
37 And some of them said, "Could not this
Man, who opened the eyes of the blind, also
have kept this man from dying?"

Lazarus Raised from the Dead

38 Then Jesus, again groaning in Himself, came
to the tomb. It was a cave, and a stone lay against
it.
39 Jesus said, "Take away the stone." Martha,
the sister of him who was dead, said to Him,
"Lord, by this time there is a stench, for he has
been *dead* four days."
40 Jesus said to her, "Did I not say to you that
if you would believe you would see the glory
of God?"
41 Then they took away the stone *from the
place* where the dead man was lying.[a] And Jesus
lifted up *His* eyes and said, "Father, I thank
You that You have heard Me.
42 "And I know that You always hear Me, but
because of the people who are standing by I
said *this*, that they may believe that You sent Me."
43 Now when He had said these things, He
cried with a loud voice, "Lazarus, come forth!"
44 And he who had died came out bound hand
and foot with graveclothes, and his face was
wrapped with a cloth. Jesus said to them, "Loose
him, and let him go."

The Plot to Kill Jesus

45 Then many of the Jews who had come to
Mary, and had seen the things Jesus did, be-
lieved in Him.
46 But some of them went away to the Phari-
sees and told them the things Jesus did.
47 Then the chief priests and the Pharisees
gathered a council and said, "What shall we
do? For this Man works many signs.
48 "If we let Him alone like this, everyone will
believe in Him, and the Romans will come and
take away both our place and nation."
49 And one of them, Caiaphas, being high priest
that year, said to them, "You know nothing at all,
50 "nor do you consider that it is expedient
for us[a] that one man should die for the people,
and not that the whole nation should perish."
51 Now this he did not say on his own *author-
ity;* but being high priest that year he prophe-
sied that Jesus would die for the nation,
52 and not for that nation only, but also that
He would gather together in one the children
of God who were scattered abroad.
53 Then, from that day on, they plotted to put
Him to death.
54 Therefore Jesus no longer walked openly
among the Jews, but went from there into the
country near the wilderness, to a city called
Ephraim, and there remained with His disci-
ples.
55 And the Passover of the Jews was near, and
many went from the country up to Jerusalem
before the Passover, to purify themselves.
56 Then they sought Jesus, and spoke among
themselves as they stood in the temple, "What
do you think—that He will not come to the feast?"
57 Now both the chief priests and the Phari-
sees had given a command, that if anyone knew
where He was, he should report *it*, that they
might seize Him.

The Anointing at Bethany

12 Then, six days before the Passover, Jesus
came to Bethany, where Lazarus was
who had been dead,[a] whom He had raised from
the dead.
2 There they made Him a supper; and Mar-
tha served, but Lazarus was one of those who
sat at the table with Him.
3 Then Mary took a pound of very costly oil
of spikenard, anointed the feet of Jesus, and
wiped His feet with her hair. And the house
was filled with the fragrance of the oil.
4 But one of His disciples, Judas Iscariot,
Simon's *son*, who would betray Him, said,
5 "Why was this fragrant oil not sold for
three hundred denarii[a] and given to the poor?"
6 This he said, not that he cared for the poor,
but because he was a thief, and had the money
box; and he used to take what was put in it.
7 But Jesus said, "Let her alone; she has
kept[a] this for the day of My burial.
8 "For the poor you have with you always,
but Me you do not have always."

The Plot to Kill Lazarus

9 Now a great many of the Jews knew that
He was there; and they came, not for Jesus'
sake only, but that they might also see Lazarus,
whom He had raised from the dead.
10 But the chief priests plotted to put Lazarus
to death also,
11 because on account of him many of the
Jews went away and believed in Jesus.

11:30 [a]NU-Text adds *still.* **11:31** [a]NU-Text reads *supposing that she was going to the tomb to weep there.* **11:41** [a]NU-Text omits *from the place where the dead man was lying.* **11:50** [a]NU-Text reads *you.* **12:1** [a]NU-Text omits *who had been dead.* **12:5** [a]About one year's wages for a worker **12:7** [a]NU-Text reads *that she may keep.*

The Triumphal Entry

12 The next day a great multitude that had come
to the feast, when they heard that Jesus was
coming to Jerusalem,
13 took branches of palm trees and went out
to meet Him, and cried out:

"Hosanna!
'Blessed is He who comes in the name of
the LORD!'[a]
The King of Israel!"

14 Then Jesus, when He had found a young
donkey, sat on it; as it is written:

15 *"Fear not, daughter of Zion;*
Behold, your King is coming,
Sitting on a donkey's colt."[a]

16 His disciples did not understand these things
at first; but when Jesus was glorified, then they
remembered that these things were written about
Him and *that* they had done these things to Him.
17 Therefore the people, who were with Him
when He called Lazarus out of his tomb and
raised him from the dead, bore witness.
18 For this reason the people also met Him,
because they heard that He had done this sign.
19 The Pharisees therefore said among them-
selves, "You see that you are accomplishing
nothing. Look, the world has gone after Him!"

The Fruitful Grain of Wheat

20 Now there were certain Greeks among those
who came up to worship at the feast.
21 Then they came to Philip, who was from
Bethsaida of Galilee, and asked him, saying,
"Sir, we wish to see Jesus."
22 Philip came and told Andrew, and in turn
Andrew and Philip told Jesus.
23 But Jesus answered them, saying, "The hour
has come that the Son of Man should be glori-
fied.
24 "Most assuredly, I say to you, unless a grain
of wheat falls into the ground and dies, it re-
mains alone; but if it dies, it produces much
grain.
25 "He who loves his life will lose it, and he
who hates his life in this world will keep it for
eternal life.
26 "If anyone serves Me, let him follow Me;
and where I am, there My servant will be also.
If anyone serves Me, him *My* Father will honor.

Jesus Predicts His Death on the Cross

27 "Now My soul is troubled, and what shall
I say? 'Father, save Me from this hour'? But for
this purpose I came to this hour.
28 "Father, glorify Your name." Then a voice
came from heaven, *saying,* "I have both glori-
fied *it* and will glorify *it* again."
29 Therefore the people who stood by and
heard *it* said that it had thundered. Others said,
"An angel has spoken to Him."
30 Jesus answered and said, "This voice did
not come because of Me, but for your sake.
31 "Now is the judgment of this world; now
the ruler of this world will be cast out.
32 "And I, if I am lifted up from the earth, will
draw all *peoples* to Myself."
33 This He said, signifying by what death He
would die.
34 The people answered Him, "We have heard
from the law that the Christ remains forever;
and how *can* You say, 'The Son of Man must
be lifted up'? Who is this Son of Man?"
35 Then Jesus said to them, "A little while
longer the light is with you. Walk while you
have the light, lest darkness overtake you; he
who walks in darkness does not know where
he is going.
36 "While you have the light, believe in the
light, that you may become sons of light."
These things Jesus spoke, and departed, and
was hidden from them.

Who Has Believed Our Report?

37 But although He had done so many signs
before them, they did not believe in Him,
38 that the word of Isaiah the prophet might
be fulfilled, which he spoke:

"Lord, who has believed our report?
And to whom has the arm of the LORD
been revealed?"[a]

39 Therefore they could not believe, because
Isaiah said again:

40 *"He has blinded their eyes and hardened*
their hearts,
Lest they should see with their eyes,
Lest they should understand with their
hearts and turn,
So that I should heal them."[a]

41 These things Isaiah said when[a] he saw His
glory and spoke of Him.

Walk in the Light

42 Nevertheless even among the rulers many
believed in Him, but because of the Pharisees
they did not confess *Him,* lest they should be
put out of the synagogue;
43 for they loved the praise of men more than
the praise of God.
44 Then Jesus cried out and said, "He who
believes in Me, believes not in Me but in Him
who sent Me.
45 "And he who sees Me sees Him who sent
Me.
46 "I have come *as* a light into the world, that
whoever believes in Me should not abide in
darkness.
47 "And if anyone hears My words and does
not believe,[a] I do not judge him; for I did not
come to judge the world but to save the world.
48 "He who rejects Me, and does not receive
My words, has that which judges him—the
word that I have spoken will judge him in the
last day.
49 "For I have not spoken on My own *author-*
ity; but the Father who sent Me gave Me a
command, what I should say and what I should
speak.
50 "And I know that His command is everlast-
ing life. Therefore, whatever I speak, just as
the Father has told Me, so I speak."

Jesus Washes the Disciples' Feet

13 Now before the Feast of the Passover,
when Jesus knew that His hour had come
that He should depart from this world to the
Father, having loved His own who were in the
world, He loved them to the end.
2 And supper being ended,[a] the devil having

12:13 [a]Psalm 118:26 **12:15** [a]Zechariah 9:9 **12:38** [a]Isaiah 53:1 **12:40** [a]Isaiah 6:10 **12:41** [a]NU-Text reads *because.*
12:47 [a]NU-Text reads *keep them.* **13:2** [a]NU-Text reads *And during supper.*

already put it into the heart of Judas Iscariot, Simon's *son,* to betray Him,
3 Jesus, knowing that the Father had given all things into His hands, and that He had come from God and was going to God,
4 rose from supper and laid aside His garments, took a towel and girded Himself.
5 After that, He poured water into a basin and began to wash the disciples' feet, and to wipe *them* with the towel with which He was girded.
6 Then He came to Simon Peter. And *Peter* said to Him, "Lord, are You washing my feet?"
7 Jesus answered and said to him, "What I am doing you do not understand now, but you will know after this."
8 Peter said to Him, "You shall never wash my feet!" Jesus answered him, "If I do not wash you, you have no part with Me."
9 Simon Peter said to Him, "Lord, not my feet only, but also *my* hands and *my* head!"
10 Jesus said to him, "He who is bathed needs only to wash *his* feet, but is completely clean; and you are clean, but not all of you."
11 For He knew who would betray Him; therefore He said, "You are not all clean."
12 So when He had washed their feet, taken His garments, and sat down again, He said to them, "Do you know what I have done to you?
13 "You call Me Teacher and Lord, and you say well, for *so* I am.
14 "If I then, *your* Lord and Teacher, have washed your feet, you also ought to wash one another's feet.
15 "For I have given you an example, that you should do as I have done to you.
16 "Most assuredly, I say to you, a servant is not greater than his master; nor is he who is sent greater than he who sent him.
17 "If you know these things, blessed are you if you do them.

Jesus Identifies His Betrayer

18 "I do not speak concerning all of you. I know whom I have chosen; but that the Scripture may be fulfilled, *'He who eats bread with Me*[a] *has lifted up his heel against Me.'*[b]
19 "Now I tell you before it comes, that when it does come to pass, you may believe that I am *He.*
20 "Most assuredly, I say to you, he who receives whomever I send receives Me; and he who receives Me receives Him who sent Me."
21 When Jesus had said these things, He was troubled in spirit, and testified and said, "Most assuredly, I say to you, one of you will betray Me."
22 Then the disciples looked at one another, perplexed about whom He spoke.
23 Now there was leaning on Jesus' bosom one of His disciples, whom Jesus loved.
24 Simon Peter therefore motioned to him to ask who it was of whom He spoke.
25 Then, leaning back[a] on Jesus' breast, he said to Him, "Lord, who is it?"
26 Jesus answered, "It is he to whom I shall give a piece of bread when I have dipped *it.*" And having dipped the bread, He gave *it* to Judas Iscariot, *the son* of Simon.
27 Now after the piece of bread, Satan entered him. Then Jesus said to him, "What you do, do quickly."
28 But no one at the table knew for what reason He said this to him.
29 For some thought, because Judas had the money box, that Jesus had said to him, "Buy *those things* we need for the feast," or that he should give something to the poor.
30 Having received the piece of bread, he then went out immediately. And it was night.

The New Commandment

31 So, when he had gone out, Jesus said, "Now the Son of Man is glorified, and God is glorified in Him.
32 "If God is glorified in Him, God will also glorify Him in Himself, and glorify Him immediately.
33 "Little children, I shall be with you a little while longer. You will seek Me; and as I said to the Jews, 'Where I am going, you cannot come,' so now I say to you.
34 "A new commandment I give to you, that you love one another; as I have loved you, that you also love one another.
35 "By this all will know that you are My disciples, if you have love for one another."

Jesus Predicts Peter's Denial

36 Simon Peter said to Him, "Lord, where are You going?" Jesus answered him, "Where I am going you cannot follow Me now, but you shall follow Me afterward."
37 Peter said to Him, "Lord, why can I not follow You now? I will lay down my life for Your sake."
38 Jesus answered him, "Will you lay down your life for My sake? Most assuredly, I say to you, the rooster shall not crow till you have denied Me three times.

The Way, the Truth, and the Life

14 "Let not your heart be troubled; you believe in God, believe also in Me.
2 "In My Father's house are many mansions;[a] if *it were* not so, I would have told you. I go to prepare a place for you.[b]
3 "And if I go and prepare a place for you, I will come again and receive you to Myself; that where I am, *there* you may be also.
4 "And where I go you know, and the way you know."
5 Thomas said to Him, "Lord, we do not know where You are going, and how can we know the way?"
6 Jesus said to him, "I am the way, the truth, and the life. No one comes to the Father except through Me.

The Father Revealed

7 "If you had known Me, you would have known My Father also; and from now on you know Him and have seen Him."
8 Philip said to Him, "Lord, show us the Father, and it is sufficient for us."
9 Jesus said to him, "Have I been with you so long, and yet you have not known Me, Philip? He who has seen Me has seen the Father; so how can you say, 'Show us the Father'?
10 "Do you not believe that I am in the Father, and the Father in Me? The words that I speak

13:18 [a]NU-Text reads *My bread.* [b]Psalm 41:9 **13:25** [a]NU-Text and M-Text add *thus.* **14:2** [a]Literally *dwellings* [b]NU-Text adds a word which would cause the text to read either *if it were not so, would I have told you that I go to prepare a place for you?* or *if it were not so I would have told you; for I go to prepare a place for you.*

to you I do not speak on My own *authority;* but the Father who dwells in Me does the works.

11 "Believe Me that I *am* in the Father and the Father in Me, or else believe Me for the sake of the works themselves.

The Answered Prayer

12 "Most assuredly, I say to you, he who believes in Me, the works that I do he will do also; and greater *works* than these he will do, because I go to My Father.

13 "And whatever you ask in My name, that I will do, that the Father may be glorified in the Son.

14 "If you ask[a] anything in My name, I will do *it.*

Jesus Promises Another Helper

15 "If you love Me, keep[a] My commandments.

16 "And I will pray the Father, and He will give you another Helper, that He may abide with you forever—

17 "the Spirit of truth, whom the world cannot receive, because it neither sees Him nor knows Him; but you know Him, for He dwells with you and will be in you.

18 "I will not leave you orphans; I will come to you.

Indwelling of the Father and the Son

19 "A little while longer and the world will see Me no more, but you will see Me. Because I live, you will live also.

20 "At that day you will know that I *am* in My Father, and you in Me, and I in you.

21 "He who has My commandments and keeps them, it is he who loves Me. And he who loves Me will be loved by My Father, and I will love him and manifest Myself to him."

22 Judas (not Iscariot) said to Him, "Lord, how is it that You will manifest Yourself to us, and not to the world?"

23 Jesus answered and said to him, "If anyone loves Me, he will keep My word; and My Father will love him, and We will come to him and make Our home with him.

24 "He who does not love Me does not keep My words; and the word which you hear is not Mine but the Father's who sent Me.

The Gift of His Peace

25 "These things I have spoken to you while being present with you.

26 "But the Helper, the Holy Spirit, whom the Father will send in My name, He will teach you all things, and bring to your remembrance all things that I said to you.

27 "Peace I leave with you, My peace I give to you; not as the world gives do I give to you. Let not your heart be troubled, neither let it be afraid.

28 "You have heard Me say to you, 'I am going away and coming *back* to you.' If you loved Me, you would rejoice because I said,[a] 'I am going to the Father,' for My Father is greater than I.

29 "And now I have told you before it comes, that when it does come to pass, you may believe.

30 "I will no longer talk much with you, for the ruler of this world is coming, and he has nothing in Me.

31 "But that the world may know that I love the Father, and as the Father gave Me commandment, so I do. Arise, let us go from here.

The True Vine

15 "I am the true vine, and My Father is the vinedresser.

2 "Every branch in Me that does not bear fruit He takes away;[a] and every *branch* that bears fruit He prunes, that it may bear more fruit.

3 "You are already clean because of the word which I have spoken to you.

4 "Abide in Me, and I in you. As the branch cannot bear fruit of itself, unless it abides in the vine, neither can you, unless you abide in Me.

5 "I am the vine, you *are* the branches. He who abides in Me, and I in him, bears much fruit; for without Me you can do nothing.

6 "If anyone does not abide in Me, he is cast out as a branch and is withered; and they gather them and throw *them* into the fire, and they are burned.

7 "If you abide in Me, and My words abide in you, you will[a] ask what you desire, and it shall be done for you.

8 "By this My Father is glorified, that you bear much fruit; so you will be My disciples.

Love and Joy Perfected

9 "As the Father loved Me, I also have loved you; abide in My love.

10 "If you keep My commandments, you will abide in My love, just as I have kept My Father's commandments and abide in His love.

11 "These things I have spoken to you, that My joy may remain in you, and *that* your joy may be full.

12 "This is My commandment, that you love one another as I have loved you.

13 "Greater love has no one than this, than to lay down one's life for his friends.

14 "You are My friends if you do whatever I command you.

15 "No longer do I call you servants, for a servant does not know what his master is doing; but I have called you friends, for all things that I heard from My Father I have made known to you.

16 "You did not choose Me, but I chose you and appointed you that you should go and bear fruit, and *that* your fruit should remain, that whatever you ask the Father in My name He may give you.

17 "These things I command you, that you love one another.

The World's Hatred

18 "If the world hates you, you know that it hated Me before *it hated* you.

19 "If you were of the world, the world would love its own. Yet because you are not of the world, but I chose you out of the world, therefore the world hates you.

20 "Remember the word that I said to you, 'A servant is not greater than his master.' If they persecuted Me, they will also persecute you. If they kept My word, they will keep yours also.

21 "But all these things they will do to you for My name's sake, because they do not know Him who sent Me.

14:14 [a]NU-Text adds *Me.* **14:15** [a]NU-Text reads *you will keep.* **14:28** [a]NU-Text omits *I said.* **15:2** [a]Or *lifts up* **15:7** [a]NU-Text omits *you will.*

22 "If I had not come and spoken to them, they would have no sin, but now they have no excuse for their sin.
23 "He who hates Me hates My Father also.
24 "If I had not done among them the works which no one else did, they would have no sin; but now they have seen and also hated both Me and My Father.
25 "But *this happened* that the word might be fulfilled which is written in their law, *'They hated Me without a cause.'*[a]

The Coming Rejection

26 "But when the Helper comes, whom I shall send to you from the Father, the Spirit of truth who proceeds from the Father, He will testify of Me.
27 "And you also will bear witness, because you have been with Me from the beginning.

16 "These things I have spoken to you, that you should not be made to stumble.
2 "They will put you out of the synagogues; yes, the time is coming that whoever kills you will think that he offers God service.
3 "And these things they will do to you[a] because they have not known the Father nor Me.
4 "But these things I have told you, that when the[a] time comes, you may remember that I told you of them. And these things I did not say to you at the beginning, because I was with you.

The Work of the Holy Spirit

5 "But now I go away to Him who sent Me, and none of you asks Me, 'Where are You going?'
6 "But because I have said these things to you, sorrow has filled your heart.
7 "Nevertheless I tell you the truth. It is to your advantage that I go away; for if I do not go away, the Helper will not come to you; but if I depart, I will send Him to you.
8 "And when He has come, He will convict the world of sin, and of righteousness, and of judgment:
9 "of sin, because they do not believe in Me;
10 "of righteousness, because I go to My Father and you see Me no more;
11 "of judgment, because the ruler of this world is judged.
12 "I still have many things to say to you, but you cannot bear *them* now.
13 "However, when He, the Spirit of truth, has come, He will guide you into all truth; for He will not speak on His own *authority,* but whatever He hears He will speak; and He will tell you things to come.
14 "He will glorify Me, for He will take of what is Mine and declare *it* to you.
15 "All things that the Father has are Mine. Therefore I said that He will take of Mine and declare *it* to you.[a]

Sorrow Will Turn to Joy

16 "A little while, and you will not see Me; and again a little while, and you will see Me, because I go to the Father."
17 Then *some* of His disciples said among themselves, "What is this that He says to us, 'A little while, and you will not see Me; and again a little while, and you will see Me'; and, 'because I go to the Father'?"
18 They said therefore, "What is this that He says, 'A little while'? We do not know what He is saying."
19 Now Jesus knew that they desired to ask Him, and He said to them, "Are you inquiring among yourselves about what I said, 'A little while, and you will not see Me; and again a little while, and you will see Me'?
20 "Most assuredly, I say to you that you will weep and lament, but the world will rejoice; and you will be sorrowful, but your sorrow will be turned into joy.
21 "A woman, when she is in labor, has sorrow because her hour has come; but as soon as she has given birth to the child, she no longer remembers the anguish, for joy that a human being has been born into the world.
22 "Therefore you now have sorrow; but I will see you again and your heart will rejoice, and your joy no one will take from you.
23 "And in that day you will ask Me nothing. Most assuredly, I say to you, whatever you ask the Father in My name He will give you.
24 "Until now you have asked nothing in My name. Ask, and you will receive, that your joy may be full.

Jesus Christ Has Overcome the World

25 "These things I have spoken to you in figurative language; but the time is coming when I will no longer speak to you in figurative language, but I will tell you plainly about the Father.
26 "In that day you will ask in My name, and I do not say to you that I shall pray the Father for you;
27 "for the Father Himself loves you, because you have loved Me, and have believed that I came forth from God.
28 "I came forth from the Father and have come into the world. Again, I leave the world and go to the Father."
29 His disciples said to Him, "See, now You are speaking plainly, and using no figure of speech!
30 "Now we are sure that You know all things, and have no need that anyone should question You. By this we believe that You came forth from God."
31 Jesus answered them, "Do you now believe?
32 "Indeed the hour is coming, yes, has now come, that you will be scattered, each to his own, and will leave Me alone. And yet I am not alone, because the Father is with Me.
33 "These things I have spoken to you, that in Me you may have peace. In the world you will[a] have tribulation; but be of good cheer, I have overcome the world."

Jesus Prays for Himself

17 Jesus spoke these words, lifted up His eyes to heaven, and said: "Father, the hour has come. Glorify Your Son, that Your Son also may glorify You,
2 "as You have given Him authority over all flesh, that He should[a] give eternal life to as many as You have given Him.
3 "And this is eternal life, that they may know You, the only true God, and Jesus Christ whom You have sent.
4 "I have glorified You on the earth. I have finished the work which You have given Me to do.

15:25 [a]Psalm 69:4 **16:3** [a]NU-Text and M-Text omit *to you.* **16:4** [a]NU-Text reads *their.* **16:15** [a]NU-Text and M-Text read *He takes of Mine and will declare it to you.* **16:33** [a]NU-Text and M-Text omit *will.* **17:2** [a]M-Text reads *shall.*

5 "And now, O Father, glorify Me together with Yourself, with the glory which I had with You before the world was.

Jesus Prays for His Disciples

6 "I have manifested Your name to the men whom You have given Me out of the world. They were Yours, You gave them to Me, and they have kept Your word.

7 "Now they have known that all things which You have given Me are from You.

8 "For I have given to them the words which You have given Me; and they have received *them,* and have known surely that I came forth from You; and they have believed that You sent Me.

9 "I pray for them. I do not pray for the world but for those whom You have given Me, for they are Yours.

10 "And all Mine are Yours, and Yours are Mine, and I am glorified in them.

11 "Now I am no longer in the world, but these are in the world, and I come to You. Holy Father, keep through Your name those whom You have given Me,[a] that they may be one as We *are.*

12 "While I was with them in the world,[a] I kept them in Your name. Those whom You gave Me I have kept;[b] and none of them is lost except the son of perdition, that the Scripture might be fulfilled.

13 "But now I come to You, and these things I speak in the world, that they may have My joy fulfilled in themselves.

14 "I have given them Your word; and the world has hated them because they are not of the world, just as I am not of the world.

15 "I do not pray that You should take them out of the world, but that You should keep them from the evil one.

16 "They are not of the world, just as I am not of the world.

17 "Sanctify them by Your truth. Your word is truth.

18 "As You sent Me into the world, I also have sent them into the world.

19 "And for their sakes I sanctify Myself, that they also may be sanctified by the truth.

Jesus Prays for All Believers

20 "I do not pray for these alone, but also for those who will[a] believe in Me through their word;

21 "that they all may be one, as You, Father, *are* in Me, and I in You; that they also may be one in Us, that the world may believe that You sent Me.

22 "And the glory which You gave Me I have given them, that they may be one just as We are one:

23 "I in them, and You in Me; that they may be made perfect in one, and that the world may know that You have sent Me, and have loved them as You have loved Me.

24 "Father, I desire that they also whom You gave Me may be with Me where I am, that they may behold My glory which You have given Me; for You loved Me before the foundation of the world.

25 "O righteous Father! The world has not known You, but I have known You; and these have known that You sent Me.

26 "And I have declared to them Your name, and will declare *it,* that the love with which You loved Me may be in them, and I in them."

Betrayal and Arrest in Gethsemane

18 When Jesus had spoken these words, He went out with His disciples over the Brook Kidron, where there was a garden, which He and His disciples entered.

2 And Judas, who betrayed Him, also knew the place; for Jesus often met there with His disciples.

3 Then Judas, having received a detachment *of troops,* and officers from the chief priests and Pharisees, came there with lanterns, torches, and weapons.

4 Jesus therefore, knowing all things that would come upon Him, went forward and said to them, "Whom are you seeking?"

5 They answered Him, "Jesus of Nazareth." Jesus said to them, "I am *He.*" And Judas, who betrayed Him, also stood with them.

6 Now when He said to them, "I am *He,*" they drew back and fell to the ground.

7 Then He asked them again, "Whom are you seeking?" And they said, "Jesus of Nazareth."

8 Jesus answered, "I have told you that I am *He.* Therefore, if you seek Me, let these go their way,"

9 that the saying might be fulfilled which He spoke, "Of those whom You gave Me I have lost none."

10 Then Simon Peter, having a sword, drew it and struck the high priest's servant, and cut off his right ear. The servant's name was Malchus.

11 So Jesus said to Peter, "Put your sword into the sheath. Shall I not drink the cup which My Father has given Me?"

Before the High Priest

12 Then the detachment *of troops* and the captain and the officers of the Jews arrested Jesus and bound Him.

13 And they led Him away to Annas first, for he was the father-in-law of Caiaphas who was high priest that year.

14 Now it was Caiaphas who advised the Jews that it was expedient that one man should die for the people.

Peter Denies Jesus

15 And Simon Peter followed Jesus, and so *did* another[a] disciple. Now that disciple was known to the high priest, and went with Jesus into the courtyard of the high priest.

16 But Peter stood at the door outside. Then the other disciple, who was known to the high priest, went out and spoke to her who kept the door, and brought Peter in.

17 Then the servant girl who kept the door said to Peter, "You are not also *one* of this Man's disciples, are you?" He said, "I am not."

18 Now the servants and officers who had made a fire of coals stood there, for it was cold, and they warmed themselves. And Peter stood with them and warmed himself.

Jesus Questioned by the High Priest

19 The high priest then asked Jesus about His disciples and His doctrine.

20 Jesus answered him, "I spoke openly to the

17:11 [a]NU-Text and M-Text read *keep them through Your name which You have given Me.* **17:12** [a]NU-Text omits *in the world.* [b]NU-Text reads *in Your name which You gave me. And I guarded them;* (or *it;*). **17:20** [a]NU-Text and M-Text omit *will.* **18:15** [a]M-Text reads *the other.*

world. I always taught in synagogues and in
the temple, where the Jews always meet,[a] and
in secret I have said nothing.
21 "Why do you ask Me? Ask those who have
heard Me what I said to them. Indeed they know
what I said."
22 And when He had said these things, one
of the officers who stood by struck Jesus with
the palm of his hand, saying, "Do You answer
the high priest like that?"
23 Jesus answered him, "If I have spoken evil,
bear witness of the evil; but if well, why do you
strike Me?"
24 Then Annas sent Him bound to Caiaphas
the high priest.

Peter Denies Twice More

25 Now Simon Peter stood and warmed him-
self. Therefore they said to him, "You are not
also *one* of His disciples, are you?" He denied
it and said, "I am not!"
26 One of the servants of the high priest, a
relative *of him* whose ear Peter cut off, said,
"Did I not see you in the garden with Him?"
27 Peter then denied again; and immediately
a rooster crowed.

In Pilate's Court

28 Then they led Jesus from Caiaphas to the
Praetorium, and it was early morning. But they
themselves did not go into the Praetorium, lest
they should be defiled, but that they might eat
the Passover.
29 Pilate then went out to them and said, "What
accusation do you bring against this Man?"
30 They answered and said to him, "If He were
not an evildoer, we would not have delivered
Him up to you."
31 Then Pilate said to them, "You take Him
and judge Him according to your law." There-
fore the Jews said to him, "It is not lawful for
us to put anyone to death,"
32 that the saying of Jesus might be fulfilled
which He spoke, signifying by what death He
would die.
33 Then Pilate entered the Praetorium again,
called Jesus, and said to Him, "Are You the King
of the Jews?"
34 Jesus answered him, "Are you speaking for
yourself about this, or did others tell you this
concerning Me?"
35 Pilate answered, "Am I a Jew? Your own
nation and the chief priests have delivered You
to me. What have You done?"
36 Jesus answered, "My kingdom is not of this
world. If My kingdom were of this world, My
servants would fight, so that I should not be
delivered to the Jews; but now My kingdom is
not from here."
37 Pilate therefore said to Him, "Are You a
king then?" Jesus answered, "You say *rightly*
that I am a king. For this cause I was born, and
for this cause I have come into the world, that
I should bear witness to the truth. Everyone who
is of the truth hears My voice."
38 Pilate said to Him, "What is truth?" And
when he had said this, he went out again to the
Jews, and said to them, "I find no fault in Him
at all.

Taking the Place of Barabbas

39 "But you have a custom that I should re-
lease someone to you at the Passover. Do you
therefore want me to release to you the King
of the Jews?"
40 Then they all cried again, saying, "Not this
Man, but Barabbas!" Now Barabbas was a
robber.

The Soldiers Mock Jesus

19 So then Pilate took Jesus and scourged
Him.
2 And the soldiers twisted a crown of thorns
and put *it* on His head, and they put on Him a
purple robe.
3 Then they said,[a] "Hail, King of the Jews!"
And they struck Him with their hands.
4 Pilate then went out again, and said to them,
"Behold, I am bringing Him out to you, that
you may know that I find no fault in Him."

Pilate's Decision

5 Then Jesus came out, wearing the crown
of thorns and the purple robe. And *Pilate* said
to them, "Behold the Man!"
6 Therefore, when the chief priests and offi-
cers saw Him, they cried out, saying, "Crucify
Him, crucify *Him!*" Pilate said to them, "You take
Him and crucify *Him,* for I find no fault in Him."
7 The Jews answered him, "We have a law,
and according to our[a] law He ought to die, be-
cause He made Himself the Son of God."
8 Therefore, when Pilate heard that saying,
he was the more afraid,
9 and went again into the Praetorium, and
said to Jesus, "Where are You from?" But Jesus
gave him no answer.
10 Then Pilate said to Him, "Are You not
speaking to me? Do You not know that I have
power to crucify You, and power to release
You?"
11 Jesus answered, "You could have no power
at all against Me unless it had been given you
from above. Therefore the one who delivered
Me to you has the greater sin."
12 From then on Pilate sought to release Him,
but the Jews cried out, saying, "If you let this
Man go, you are not Caesar's friend. Whoever
makes himself a king speaks against Caesar."
13 When Pilate therefore heard that saying,
he brought Jesus out and sat down in the judg-
ment seat in a place that is called *The* Pave-
ment, but in Hebrew, Gabbatha.
14 Now it was the Preparation Day of the
Passover, and about the sixth hour. And he said
to the Jews, "Behold your King!"
15 But they cried out, "Away with *Him,* away
with *Him!* Crucify Him!" Pilate said to them,
"Shall I crucify your King?" The chief priests
answered, "We have no king but Caesar!"
16 Then he delivered Him to them to be cruci-
fied. So they took Jesus and led *Him* away.[a]

The King on a Cross

17 And He, bearing His cross, went out to a
place called *the Place* of a Skull, which is called
in Hebrew, Golgotha,
18 where they crucified Him, and two others
with Him, one on either side, and Jesus in the
center.

18:20 [a]NU-Text reads *where all the Jews meet.* **19:3** [a]NU-Text reads *And they came up to Him and said.*
19:7 [a]NU-Text reads *the law.* **19:16** [a]NU-Text omits *and led Him away.*

19 Now Pilate wrote a title and put *it* on the cross. And the writing was:

JESUS OF NAZARETH,
THE KING OF THE JEWS.

20 Then many of the Jews read this title, for the place where Jesus was crucified was near the city; and it was written in Hebrew, Greek, *and* Latin.
21 Therefore the chief priests of the Jews said to Pilate, "Do not write, 'The King of the Jews,' but, 'He said, "I am the King of the Jews." ' "
22 Pilate answered, "What I have written, I have written."
23 Then the soldiers, when they had crucified Jesus, took His garments and made four parts, to each soldier a part, and also the tunic. Now the tunic was without seam, woven from the top in one piece.
24 They said therefore among themselves, "Let us not tear it, but cast lots for it, whose it shall be," that the Scripture might be fulfilled which says:

"They divided My garments among them,
And for My clothing they cast lots."[a]

Therefore the soldiers did these things.

Behold Your Mother

25 Now there stood by the cross of Jesus His mother, and His mother's sister, Mary the *wife* of Clopas, and Mary Magdalene.
26 When Jesus therefore saw His mother, and the disciple whom He loved standing by, He said to His mother, "Woman, behold your son!"
27 Then He said to the disciple, "Behold your mother!" And from that hour that disciple took her to his own *home.*

It Is Finished

28 After this, Jesus, knowing[a] that all things were now accomplished, that the Scripture might be fulfilled, said, "I thirst!"
29 Now a vessel full of sour wine was sitting there; and they filled a sponge with sour wine, put *it* on hyssop, and put *it* to His mouth.
30 So when Jesus had received the sour wine, He said, "It is finished!" And bowing His head, He gave up His spirit.

Jesus' Side Is Pierced

31 Therefore, because it was the Preparation *Day,* that the bodies should not remain on the cross on the Sabbath (for that Sabbath was a high day), the Jews asked Pilate that their legs might be broken, and *that* they might be taken away.
32 Then the soldiers came and broke the legs of the first and of the other who was crucified with Him.
33 But when they came to Jesus and saw that He was already dead, they did not break His legs.
34 But one of the soldiers pierced His side with a spear, and immediately blood and water came out.
35 And he who has seen has testified, and his testimony is true; and he knows that he is telling the truth, so that you may believe.
36 For these things were done that the Scripture should be fulfilled, *"Not one of His bones shall be broken."*[a]
37 And again another Scripture says, *"They shall look on Him whom they pierced."*[a]

Jesus Buried in Joseph's Tomb

38 After this, Joseph of Arimathea, being a disciple of Jesus, but secretly, for fear of the Jews, asked Pilate that he might take away the body of Jesus; and Pilate gave *him* permission. So he came and took the body of Jesus.
39 And Nicodemus, who at first came to Jesus by night, also came, bringing a mixture of myrrh and aloes, about a hundred pounds.
40 Then they took the body of Jesus, and bound it in strips of linen with the spices, as the custom of the Jews is to bury.
41 Now in the place where He was crucified there was a garden, and in the garden a new tomb in which no one had yet been laid.
42 So there they laid Jesus, because of the Jews' Preparation *Day,* for the tomb was nearby.

The Empty Tomb

20 Now on the first *day* of the week Mary
Magdalene went to the tomb early, while
it was still dark, and saw *that* the stone had
been taken away from the tomb.
2 Then she ran and came to Simon Peter,
and to the other disciple, whom Jesus loved,
and said to them, "They have taken away the
Lord out of the tomb, and we do not know
where they have laid Him."
3 Peter therefore went out, and the other dis-
ciple, and were going to the tomb.
4 So they both ran together, and the other dis-
ciple outran Peter and came to the tomb first.
5 And he, stooping down and looking in, saw
the linen cloths lying *there;* yet he did not go
in.
6 Then Simon Peter came, following him, and
went into the tomb; and he saw the linen cloths
lying *there,*
7 and the handkerchief that had been around
His head, not lying with the linen cloths, but
folded together in a place by itself.
8 Then the other disciple, who came to the
tomb first, went in also; and he saw and be-
lieved.
9 For as yet they did not know the Scripture,
that He must rise again from the dead.
10 Then the disciples went away again to
their own homes.

Mary Magdalene Sees the Risen Lord

11 But Mary stood outside by the tomb weeping, and as she wept she stooped down *and looked* into the tomb.
12 And she saw two angels in white sitting, one at the head and the other at the feet, where the body of Jesus had lain.
13 Then they said to her, "Woman, why are you weeping?" She said to them, "Because they have taken away my Lord, and I do not know where they have laid Him."
14 Now when she had said this, she turned around and saw Jesus standing *there,* and did not know that it was Jesus.
15 Jesus said to her, "Woman, why are you weeping? Whom are you seeking?" She, supposing Him to be the gardener, said to Him, "Sir, if You have carried Him away, tell me

19:24 [a]Psalm 22:18 **19:28** [a]M-Text reads *seeing.* **19:36** [a]Exodus 12:46; Numbers 9:12; Psalm 34:20
19:37 [a]Zechariah 12:10

where You have laid Him, and I will take Him
away."
16 Jesus said to her, "Mary!" She turned and
said to Him,[a] "Rabboni!" (which is to say,
Teacher).
17 Jesus said to her, "Do not cling to Me, for
I have not yet ascended to My Father; but go
to My brethren and say to them, 'I am ascend-
ing to My Father and your Father, and *to* My
God and your God.'"
18 Mary Magdalene came and told the disci-
ples that she had seen the Lord,[a] and *that* He
had spoken these things to her.

The Apostles Commissioned

19 Then, the same day at evening, being the
first *day* of the week, when the doors were shut
where the disciples were assembled,[a] for fear
of the Jews, Jesus came and stood in the midst,
and said to them, "Peace *be* with you."
20 When He had said this, He showed them
His hands and His side. Then the disciples
were glad when they saw the Lord.
21 So Jesus said to them again, "Peace to you!
As the Father has sent Me, I also send you."
22 And when He had said this, He breathed
on *them*, and said to them, "Receive the Holy
Spirit.
23 "If you forgive the sins of any, they are for-
given them; if you retain the *sins* of any, they
are retained."

Seeing and Believing

24 Now Thomas, called the Twin, one of the
twelve, was not with them when Jesus came.
25 The other disciples therefore said to him,
"We have seen the Lord." So he said to them,
"Unless I see in His hands the print of the nails,
and put my finger into the print of the nails,
and put my hand into His side, I will not believe."
26 And after eight days His disciples were
again inside, and Thomas with them. Jesus
came, the doors being shut, and stood in the
midst, and said, "Peace to you!"
27 Then He said to Thomas, "Reach your fin-
ger here, and look at My hands; and reach your
hand *here*, and put *it* into My side. Do not be
unbelieving, but believing."
28 And Thomas answered and said to Him,
"My Lord and my God!"
29 Jesus said to him, "Thomas,[a] because you
have seen Me, you have believed. Blessed *are*
those who have not seen and *yet* have believed."

That You May Believe

30 And truly Jesus did many other signs in
the presence of His disciples, which are not
written in this book;
31 but these are written that you may believe
that Jesus is the Christ, the Son of God, and that
believing you may have life in His name.

Breakfast by the Sea

21 After these things Jesus showed Himself
again to the disciples at the Sea of Tibe-
rias, and in this way He showed *Himself:*
2 Simon Peter, Thomas called the Twin, Na-
thanael of Cana in Galilee, the *sons* of Zebedee,
and two others of His disciples were together.
3 Simon Peter said to them, "I am going fish-
ing." They said to him, "We are going with you
also." They went out and immediately[a] got into
the boat, and that night they caught nothing.
4 But when the morning had now come,
Jesus stood on the shore; yet the disciples did
not know that it was Jesus.
5 Then Jesus said to them, "Children, have
you any food?" They answered Him, "No."
6 And He said to them, "Cast the net on the
right side of the boat, and you will find *some.*"
So they cast, and now they were not able to
draw it in because of the multitude of fish.
7 Therefore that disciple whom Jesus loved
said to Peter, "It is the Lord!" Now when Simon
Peter heard that it was the Lord, he put on *his*
outer garment (for he had removed it), and
plunged into the sea.
8 But the other disciples came in the little boat
(for they were not far from land, but about two
hundred cubits), dragging the net with fish.
9 Then, as soon as they had come to land, they
saw a fire of coals there, and fish laid on it,
and bread.
10 Jesus said to them, "Bring some of the fish
which you have just caught."
11 Simon Peter went up and dragged the net
to land, full of large fish, one hundred and fifty-
three; and although there were so many, the
net was not broken.
12 Jesus said to them, "Come *and* eat break-
fast." Yet none of the disciples dared ask Him,
"Who are You?"—knowing that it was the Lord.
13 Jesus then came and took the bread and
gave it to them, and likewise the fish.
14 This *is* now the third time Jesus showed
Himself to His disciples after He was raised
from the dead.

Jesus Restores Peter

15 So when they had eaten breakfast, Jesus
said to Simon Peter, "Simon, *son* of Jonah,[a] do
you love Me more than these?" He said to Him,
"Yes, Lord; You know that I love You." He said
to him, "Feed My lambs."
16 He said to him again a second time, "Simon,
son of Jonah,[a] do you love Me?" He said to
Him, "Yes, Lord; You know that I love You."
He said to him, "Tend My sheep."
17 He said to him the third time, "Simon, *son*
of Jonah,[a] do you love Me?" Peter was grieved
because He said to him the third time, "Do you
love Me?" And he said to Him, "Lord, You
know all things; You know that I love You."
Jesus said to him, "Feed My sheep.
18 "Most assuredly, I say to you, when you
were younger, you girded yourself and walked
where you wished; but when you are old, you
will stretch out your hands, and another will
gird you and carry *you* where you do not wish."
19 This He spoke, signifying by what death
he would glorify God. And when He had spo-
ken this, He said to him, "Follow Me."

The Beloved Disciple and His Book

20 Then Peter, turning around, saw the disci-
ple whom Jesus loved following, who also had
leaned on His breast at the supper, and said,
"Lord, who is the one who betrays You?"
21 Peter, seeing him, said to Jesus, "But Lord,
what *about* this man?"
22 Jesus said to him, "If I will that he remain
till I come, what *is that* to you? You follow Me."

20:16 [a]NU-Text adds *in Hebrew.* **20:18** [a]NU-Text reads *disciples, "I have seen the Lord,"* . . . . **20:19** [a]NU-Text omits *assembled.* **20:29** [a]NU-Text and M-Text omit *Thomas.* **21:3** [a]NU-Text omits *immediately.* **21:15** [a]NU-Text reads *John.* **21:16** [a]NU-Text reads *John.* **21:17** [a]NU-Text reads *John.*

23 Then this saying went out among the
brethren that this disciple would not die. Yet
Jesus did not say to him that he would not die,
but, "If I will that he remain till I come, what
is that to you?"
24 This is the disciple who testifies of these
things, and wrote these things; and we know
that his testimony is true.
25 And there are also many other things that
Jesus did, which if they were written one by one,
I suppose that even the world itself could not
contain the books that would be written. Amen.

THE ACTS OF THE APOSTLES

ACTS is a unique book in the Scripture. It is really volume 2 of Luke's work and tells the story of the beginnings of the church. It begins with the ascension of Jesus, records the giving of the Spirit at Pentecost, and tells the life of the early church. It is not, however, the story of the whole church, or even of all the apostles. It focuses on the beginnings of the church, then on the work of Peter, and finally on the work of Paul. Luke wanted to show how the church spread from Jerusalem all over Palestine and then to the Gentiles.

Luke reports a series of episodes in the life and faith of the early church to show how Christianity rose out of Judaism and has deep roots in the Jewish faith. He shows something of the struggle the disciples felt in moving out in a mission to Gentiles. One of the major themes in the book is the role of the Holy Spirit in guiding and strengthening the church as it spread across the Mediterranean world. Another theme is the message that Christianity is not dangerous to the authority or power of the Roman Empire. (Luke-Acts may have been written as a legal document in Paul's defense.) More than one-half of Acts is devoted to the ministry of Paul and his travels to preach the good news. ■

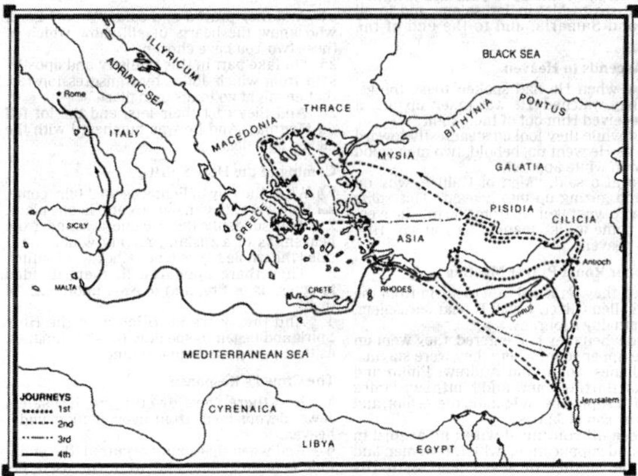

THE JOURNEYS OF PAUL

THE ACTS

of the Apostles

Prologue

1 The former account I made, O Theophilus,
of all that Jesus began both to do and teach,
2 until the day in which He was taken up,
after He through the Holy Spirit had given
commandments to the apostles whom He had
chosen,
3 to whom He also presented Himself alive
after His suffering by many infallible proofs,
being seen by them during forty days and
speaking of the things pertaining to the king-
dom of God.

The Holy Spirit Promised

4 And being assembled together with *them,*
He commanded them not to depart from Jeru-
salem, but to wait for the Promise of the Father,
"which," *He said,* "you have heard from Me;
5 "for John truly baptized with water, but
you shall be baptized with the Holy Spirit not
many days from now."
6 Therefore, when they had come together,
they asked Him, saying, "Lord, will You at this
time restore the kingdom to Israel?"
7 And He said to them, "It is not for you to
know times or seasons which the Father has
put in His own authority.
8 "But you shall receive power when the
Holy Spirit has come upon you; and you shall
be witnesses to Me[a] in Jerusalem, and in all
Judea and Samaria, and to the end of the
earth."

Jesus Ascends to Heaven

9 Now when He had spoken these things,
while they watched, He was taken up, and a
cloud received Him out of their sight.
10 And while they looked steadfastly toward
heaven as He went up, behold, two men stood
by them in white apparel,
11 who also said, "Men of Galilee, why do
you stand gazing up into heaven? This *same*
Jesus, who was taken up from you into heaven,
will so come in like manner as you saw Him
go into heaven."

The Upper Room Prayer Meeting

12 Then they returned to Jerusalem from the
mount called Olivet, which is near Jerusalem,
a Sabbath day's journey.
13 And when they had entered, they went up
into the upper room where they were staying:
Peter, James, John, and Andrew; Philip and
Thomas; Bartholomew and Matthew; James
the son of Alphaeus and Simon the Zealot; and
Judas *the son* of James.
14 These all continued with one accord in
prayer and supplication,[a] with the women and
Mary the mother of Jesus, and with His
brothers.

Matthias Chosen

15 And in those days Peter stood up in the
midst of the disciples[a] (altogether the number
of names was about a hundred and twenty),
and said,
16 "Men *and* brethren, this Scripture had to
be fulfilled, which the Holy Spirit spoke before
by the mouth of David concerning Judas, who
became a guide to those who arrested Jesus;
17 "for he was numbered with us and ob-
tained a part in this ministry."
18 (Now this man purchased a field with the
wages of iniquity; and falling headlong, he
burst open in the middle and all his entrails
gushed out.
19 And it became known to all those dwelling
in Jerusalem; so that field is called in their own
language, Akel Dama, that is, Field of Blood.)
20 "For it is written in the Book of Psalms:

> *'Let his dwelling place be desolate,*
> *And let no one live in it';*[a]

and,

> *'Let*[b] *another take his office.'*[c]

21 "Therefore, of these men who have accom-
panied us all the time that the Lord Jesus went
in and out among us,
22 "beginning from the baptism of John to
that day when He was taken up from us, one
of these must become a witness with us of His
resurrection."
23 And they proposed two: Joseph called Bar-
sabas, who was surnamed Justus, and Mat-
thias.
24 And they prayed and said, "You, O Lord,
who know the hearts of all, show which of
these two You have chosen
25 "to take part in this ministry and apostle-
ship from which Judas by transgression fell,
that he might go to his own place."
26 And they cast their lots, and the lot fell
on Matthias. And he was numbered with the
eleven apostles.

Coming of the Holy Spirit

2 When the Day of Pentecost had fully come,
they were all with one accord[a] in one place.
2 And suddenly there came a sound from
heaven, as of a rushing mighty wind, and it
filled the whole house where they were sitting.
3 Then there appeared to them divided
tongues, as of fire, and *one* sat upon each of
them.
4 And they were all filled with the Holy
Spirit and began to speak with other tongues,
as the Spirit gave them utterance.

The Crowd's Response

5 And there were dwelling in Jerusalem
Jews, devout men, from every nation under
heaven.
6 And when this sound occurred, the multi-
tude came together, and were confused, be-
cause everyone heard them speak in his own
language.
7 Then they were all amazed and marveled,
saying to one another, "Look, are not all these
who speak Galileans?
8 "And how *is it that* we hear, each in our
own language in which we were born?
9 "Parthians and Medes and Elamites, those

1:8 [a]NU-Text reads *My witnesses.* **1:14** [a]NU-Text omits *and supplication.* **1:15** [a]NU-Text reads *brethren.*
1:20 [a]Psalm 69:25 [b]Psalm 109:8 [c]Greek *episkopen,* position of overseer **2:1** [a]NU-Text reads *together.*

dwelling in Mesopotamia, Judea and Cappa-
docia, Pontus and Asia,
10 "Phrygia and Pamphylia, Egypt and the
parts of Libya adjoining Cyrene, visitors from
Rome, both Jews and proselytes,
11 "Cretans and Arabs—we hear them speak-
ing in our own tongues the wonderful works
of God."
12 So they were all amazed and perplexed,
saying to one another, "Whatever could this
mean?"
13 Others mocking said, "They are full of new
wine."

Peter's Sermon

14 But Peter, standing up with the eleven,
raised his voice and said to them, "Men of Ju-
dea and all who dwell in Jerusalem, let this be
known to you, and heed my words.
15 "For these are not drunk, as you suppose,
since it is *only* the third hour of the day.
16 "But this is what was spoken by the
prophet Joel:

17 *'And it shall come to pass in the last days, says God,*
That I will pour out of My Spirit on all flesh;
Your sons and your daughters shall prophesy,
Your young men shall see visions,
Your old men shall dream dreams.
18 *And on My menservants and on My maidservants*
I will pour out My Spirit in those days;
And they shall prophesy.
19 *I will show wonders in heaven above*
And signs in the earth beneath:
Blood and fire and vapor of smoke.
20 *The sun shall be turned into darkness,*
And the moon into blood,
Before the coming of the great and awesome day of the LORD.
21 *And it shall come to pass*
That whoever calls on the name of the LORD
Shall be saved.'[a]

22 "Men of Israel, hear these words: Jesus of
Nazareth, a Man attested by God to you by
miracles, wonders, and signs which God did
through Him in your midst, as you yourselves
also know—
23 "Him, being delivered by the determined
purpose and foreknowledge of God, you have
taken[a] by lawless hands, have crucified, and
put to death;
24 "whom God raised up, having loosed the
pains of death, because it was not possible that
He should be held by it.
25 "For David says concerning Him:

'I foresaw the LORD always before my face,
For He is at my right hand, that I may not be shaken.
26 *Therefore my heart rejoiced, and my tongue was glad;*
Moreover my flesh also will rest in hope.
27 *For You will not leave my soul in Hades,*
Nor will You allow Your Holy One to see corruption.
28 *You have made known to me the ways of life;*
You will make me full of joy in Your presence.'[a]

29 "Men *and* brethren, let *me* speak freely to
you of the patriarch David, that he is both dead
and buried, and his tomb is with us to this day.
30 "Therefore, being a prophet, and knowing
that God had sworn with an oath to him that
of the fruit of his body, according to the flesh,
He would raise up the Christ to sit on his
throne,[a]
31 "he, foreseeing this, spoke concerning the
resurrection of the Christ, that His soul was not
left in Hades, nor did His flesh see corruption.
32 "This Jesus God has raised up, of which
we are all witnesses.
33 "Therefore being exalted to the right hand
of God, and having received from the Father
the promise of the Holy Spirit, He poured out
this which you now see and hear.
34 "For David did not ascend into the heav-
ens, but he says himself:

'The LORD said to my Lord,
"Sit at My right hand,
35 *Till I make Your enemies Your footstool."'*[a]

36 "Therefore let all the house of Israel know
assuredly that God has made this Jesus, whom
you crucified, both Lord and Christ."
37 Now when they heard *this,* they were cut
to the heart, and said to Peter and the rest of
the apostles, "Men *and* brethren, what shall
we do?"
38 Then Peter said to them, "Repent, and let
every one of you be baptized in the name of
Jesus Christ for the remission of sins; and you
shall receive the gift of the Holy Spirit.
39 "For the promise is to you and to your chil-
dren, and to all who are afar off, as many as
the Lord our God will call."

A Vital Church Grows

40 And with many other words he testified
and exhorted them, saying, "Be saved from
this perverse generation."
41 Then those who gladly[a] received his word
were baptized; and that day about three thou-
sand souls were added *to them.*
42 And they continued steadfastly in the
apostles' doctrine and fellowship, in the break-
ing of bread, and in prayers.
43 Then fear came upon every soul, and many
wonders and signs were done through the
apostles.
44 Now all who believed were together, and
had all things in common,
45 and sold their possessions and goods, and
divided them among all, as anyone had need.
46 So continuing daily with one accord in the
temple, and breaking bread from house to
house, they ate their food with gladness and
simplicity of heart,
47 praising God and having favor with all the
people. And the Lord added to the church[a]
daily those who were being saved.

2:21 [a]Joel 2:28–32 **2:23** [a]NU-Text omits *have taken.* **2:28** [a]Psalm 16:8–11 **2:30** [a]NU-Text omits *according to the flesh, He would raise up the Christ* and completes the verse with *He would seat one on his throne.* **2:35** [a]Psalm 110:1 **2:41** [a]NU-Text omits *gladly.* **2:47** [a]NU-Text omits *to the church.*

A Lame Man Healed

3 Now Peter and John went up together to the temple at the hour of prayer, the ninth *hour.*

2 And a certain man lame from his mother's womb was carried, whom they laid daily at the gate of the temple which is called Beautiful, to ask alms from those who entered the temple;

3 who, seeing Peter and John about to go into the temple, asked for alms.

4 And fixing his eyes on him, with John, Peter said, "Look at us."

5 So he gave them his attention, expecting to receive something from them.

6 Then Peter said, "Silver and gold I do not have, but what I do have I give you: In the name of Jesus Christ of Nazareth, rise up and walk."

7 And he took him by the right hand and lifted *him* up, and immediately his feet and ankle bones received strength.

8 So he, leaping up, stood and walked and entered the temple with them—walking, leaping, and praising God.

9 And all the people saw him walking and praising God.

10 Then they knew that it was he who sat begging alms at the Beautiful Gate of the temple; and they were filled with wonder and amazement at what had happened to him.

Preaching in Solomon's Portico

11 Now as the lame man who was healed held on to Peter and John, all the people ran together to them in the porch which is called Solomon's, greatly amazed.

12 So when Peter saw *it,* he responded to the people: "Men of Israel, why do you marvel at this? Or why look so intently at us, as though by our own power or godliness we had made this man walk?

13 "The God of Abraham, Isaac, and Jacob, the God of our fathers, glorified His Servant Jesus, whom you delivered up and denied in the presence of Pilate, when he was determined to let *Him* go.

14 "But you denied the Holy One and the Just, and asked for a murderer to be granted to you,

15 "and killed the Prince of life, whom God raised from the dead, of which we are witnesses.

16 "And His name, through faith in His name, has made this man strong, whom you see and know. Yes, the faith which *comes* through Him has given him this perfect soundness in the presence of you all.

17 "Yet now, brethren, I know that you did *it* in ignorance, as *did* also your rulers.

18 "But those things which God foretold by the mouth of all His prophets, that the Christ would suffer, He has thus fulfilled.

19 "Repent therefore and be converted, that your sins may be blotted out, so that times of refreshing may come from the presence of the Lord,

20 "and that He may send Jesus Christ, who was preached to you before,[a]

21 "whom heaven must receive until the times of restoration of all things, which God has spoken by the mouth of all His holy prophets since the world began.

22 "For Moses truly said to the fathers, *'The* LORD *your God will raise up for you a Prophet like me from your brethren. Him you shall hear in all things, whatever He says to you.*

23 *'And it shall be that every soul who will not hear that Prophet shall be utterly destroyed from among the people.'*[a]

24 "Yes, and all the prophets, from Samuel and those who follow, as many as have spoken, have also foretold[a] these days.

25 "You are sons of the prophets, and of the covenant which God made with our fathers, saying to Abraham, *'And in your seed all the families of the earth shall be blessed.'*[a]

26 "To you first, God, having raised up His Servant Jesus, sent Him to bless you, in turning away every one *of you* from your iniquities."

Peter and John Arrested

4 Now as they spoke to the people, the priests, the captain of the temple, and the Sadducees came upon them,

2 being greatly disturbed that they taught the people and preached in Jesus the resurrection from the dead.

3 And they laid hands on them, and put *them* in custody until the next day, for it was already evening.

4 However, many of those who heard the word believed; and the number of the men came to be about five thousand.

Addressing the Sanhedrin

5 And it came to pass, on the next day, that their rulers, elders, and scribes,

6 as well as Annas the high priest, Caiaphas, John, and Alexander, and as many as were of the family of the high priest, were gathered together at Jerusalem.

7 And when they had set them in the midst, they asked, "By what power or by what name have you done this?"

8 Then Peter, filled with the Holy Spirit, said to them, "Rulers of the people and elders of Israel:

9 "If we this day are judged for a good deed *done* to a helpless man, by what means he has been made well,

10 "let it be known to you all, and to all the people of Israel, that by the name of Jesus Christ of Nazareth, whom you crucified, whom God raised from the dead, by Him this man stands here before you whole.

11 "This is the *'stone which was rejected by you builders, which has become the chief cornerstone.'*[a]

12 "Nor is there salvation in any other, for there is no other name under heaven given among men by which we must be saved."

The Name of Jesus Forbidden

13 Now when they saw the boldness of Peter and John, and perceived that they were uneducated and untrained men, they marveled. And they realized that they had been with Jesus.

14 And seeing the man who had been healed standing with them, they could say nothing against it.

15 But when they had commanded them to go aside out of the council, they conferred among themselves,

16 saying, "What shall we do to these men? For, indeed, that a notable miracle has been done

3:20 [a]NU-Text and M-Text read *Christ Jesus, who was ordained for you before.* **3:23** [a]Deuteronomy 18:15, 18, 19 **3:24** [a]NU-Text and M-Text read *proclaimed.* **3:25** [a]Genesis 22:18; 26:4; 28:14 **4:11** [a]Psalm 118:22

through them *is* evident to all who dwell in
Jerusalem, and we cannot deny *it.*
17 "But so that it spreads no further among
the people, let us severely threaten them, that
from now on they speak to no man in this name."
18 So they called them and commanded them
not to speak at all nor teach in the name of Jesus.
19 But Peter and John answered and said to
them, "Whether it is right in the sight of God
to listen to you more than to God, you judge.
20 "For we cannot but speak the things which
we have seen and heard."
21 So when they had further threatened them,
they let them go, finding no way of punishing
them, because of the people, since they all glo-
rified God for what had been done.
22 For the man was over forty years old on
whom this miracle of healing had been per-
formed.

Prayer for Boldness

23 And being let go, they went to their own
companions and reported all that the chief priests
and elders had said to them.
24 So when they heard that, they raised their
voice to God with one accord and said: "Lord,
You *are* God, who made heaven and earth and
the sea, and all that is in them,
25 "who by the mouth of Your servant David[a]
have said:

'Why did the nations rage,
And the people plot vain things?
26 *The kings of the earth took their stand,*
And the rulers were gathered together
Against the LORD *and against His*
Christ.'[a]

27 "For truly against Your holy Servant Jesus,
whom You anointed, both Herod and Pontius
Pilate, with the Gentiles and the people of Israel,
were gathered together
28 "to do whatever Your hand and Your pur-
pose determined before to be done.
29 "Now, Lord, look on their threats, and grant
to Your servants that with all boldness they
may speak Your word,
30 "by stretching out Your hand to heal, and
that signs and wonders may be done through
the name of Your holy Servant Jesus."
31 And when they had prayed, the place where
they were assembled together was shaken; and
they were all filled with the Holy Spirit, and they
spoke the word of God with boldness.

Sharing in All Things

32 Now the multitude of those who believed
were of one heart and one soul; neither did
anyone say that any of the things he possessed
was his own, but they had all things in common.
33 And with great power the apostles gave
witness to the resurrection of the Lord Jesus.
And great grace was upon them all.
34 Nor was there anyone among them who
lacked; for all who were possessors of lands or
houses sold them, and brought the proceeds of
the things that were sold,
35 and laid *them* at the apostles' feet; and they
distributed to each as anyone had need.
36 And Joses,[a] who was also named Barnabas
by the apostles (which is translated Son of En-
couragement), a Levite of the country of Cyprus,
37 having land, sold *it,* and brought the money
and laid *it* at the apostles' feet.

Lying to the Holy Spirit

5 But a certain man named Ananias, with Sap-
phira his wife, sold a possession.
2 And he kept back *part* of the proceeds,
his wife also being aware *of it,* and brought a
certain part and laid *it* at the apostles' feet.
3 But Peter said, "Ananias, why has Satan
filled your heart to lie to the Holy Spirit and
keep back *part* of the price of the land for your-
self?
4 "While it remained, was it not your own?
And after it was sold, was it not in your own
control? Why have you conceived this thing in
your heart? You have not lied to men but to
God."
5 Then Ananias, hearing these words, fell
down and breathed his last. So great fear came
upon all those who heard these things.
6 And the young men arose and wrapped him
up, carried *him* out, and buried *him.*
7 Now it was about three hours later when
his wife came in, not knowing what had hap-
pened.
8 And Peter answered her, "Tell me whether
you sold the land for so much?" She said, "Yes,
for so much."
9 Then Peter said to her, "How is it that you
have agreed together to test the Spirit of the
Lord? Look, the feet of those who have buried
your husband *are* at the door, and they will carry
you out."
10 Then immediately she fell down at his feet
and breathed her last. And the young men
came in and found her dead, and carrying *her*
out, buried *her* by her husband.
11 So great fear came upon all the church and
upon all who heard these things.

Continuing Power in the Church

12 And through the hands of the apostles many
signs and wonders were done among the peo-
ple. And they were all with one accord in Sol-
omon's Porch.
13 Yet none of the rest dared join them, but
the people esteemed them highly.
14 And believers were increasingly added to
the Lord, multitudes of both men and women,
15 so that they brought the sick out into the
streets and laid *them* on beds and couches, that
at least the shadow of Peter passing by might
fall on some of them.
16 Also a multitude gathered from the sur-
rounding cities to Jerusalem, bringing sick
people and those who were tormented by un-
clean spirits, and they were all healed.

Imprisoned Apostles Freed

17 Then the high priest rose up, and all those
who *were* with him (which is the sect of the
Sadducees), and they were filled with indigna-
tion,
18 and laid their hands on the apostles and put
them in the common prison.
19 But at night an angel of the Lord opened
the prison doors and brought them out, and said,
20 "Go, stand in the temple and speak to the
people all the words of this life."

4:25 [a]NU-Text reads *who through the Holy Spirit, by the mouth of our father, Your servant David.* **4:26** [a]Psalm 2:1, 2
4:36 [a]NU-Text reads *Joseph.*

21 And when they heard *that*, they entered
the temple early in the morning and taught.
But the high priest and those with him came
and called the council together, with all the
elders of the children of Israel, and sent to the
prison to have them brought.

Apostles on Trial Again

22 But when the officers came and did not find
them in the prison, they returned and reported,
23 saying, "Indeed we found the prison shut
securely, and the guards standing outside[a] be-
fore the doors; but when we opened them, we
found no one inside!"
24 Now when the high priest,[a] the captain of
the temple, and the chief priests heard these
things, they wondered what the outcome
would be.
25 So one came and told them, saying,[a] "Look,
the men whom you put in prison are standing
in the temple and teaching the people!"
26 Then the captain went with the officers and
brought them without violence, for they feared
the people, lest they should be stoned.
27 And when they had brought them, they set
them before the council. And the high priest
asked them,
28 saying, "Did we not strictly command you
not to teach in this name? And look, you have
filled Jerusalem with your doctrine, and intend
to bring this Man's blood on us!"
29 But Peter and the *other* apostles answered
and said: "We ought to obey God rather than
men.
30 "The God of our fathers raised up Jesus
whom you murdered by hanging on a tree.
31 "Him God has exalted to His right hand *to
be* Prince and Savior, to give repentance to Israel
and forgiveness of sins.
32 "And we are His witnesses to these things,
and *so* also *is* the Holy Spirit whom God has
given to those who obey Him."

Gamaliel's Advice

33 When they heard *this*, they were furious and
plotted to kill them.
34 Then one in the council stood up, a Phari-
see named Gamaliel, a teacher of the law held
in respect by all the people, and commanded
them to put the apostles outside for a little while.
35 And he said to them: "Men of Israel, take
heed to yourselves what you intend to do regard-
ing these men.
36 "For some time ago Theudas rose up, claim-
ing to be somebody. A number of men, about
four hundred, joined him. He was slain, and
all who obeyed him were scattered and came
to nothing.
37 "After this man, Judas of Galilee rose up in
the days of the census, and drew away many
people after him. He also perished, and all who
obeyed him were dispersed.
38 "And now I say to you, keep away from
these men and let them alone; for if this plan
or this work is of men, it will come to nothing;
39 "but if it is of God, you cannot overthrow
it—lest you even be found to fight against
God."
40 And they agreed with him, and when they
had called for the apostles and beaten *them*, they
commanded that they should not speak in the
name of Jesus, and let them go.
41 So they departed from the presence of the
council, rejoicing that they were counted wor-
thy to suffer shame for His[a] name.
42 And daily in the temple, and in every
house, they did not cease teaching and preach-
ing Jesus *as* the Christ.

Seven Chosen to Serve

6 Now in those days, when *the number of* the
disciples was multiplying, there arose a
complaint against the Hebrews by the Hellen-
ists,[a] because their widows were neglected in
the daily distribution.
2 Then the twelve summoned the multitude
of the disciples and said, "It is not desirable
that we should leave the word of God and serve
tables.
3 "Therefore, brethren, seek out from among
you seven men of *good* reputation, full of the
Holy Spirit and wisdom, whom we may appoint
over this business;
4 "but we will give ourselves continually to
prayer and to the ministry of the word."
5 And the saying pleased the whole multitude.
And they chose Stephen, a man full of faith
and the Holy Spirit, and Philip, Prochorus, Ni-
canor, Timon, Parmenas, and Nicolas, a prose-
lyte from Antioch,
6 whom they set before the apostles; and when
they had prayed, they laid hands on them.
7 Then the word of God spread, and the num-
ber of the disciples multiplied greatly in Jeru-
salem, and a great many of the priests were
obedient to the faith.

Stephen Accused of Blasphemy

8 And Stephen, full of faith[a] and power, did
great wonders and signs among the people.
9 Then there arose some from what is called
the Synagogue of the Freedmen (Cyrenians,
Alexandrians, and those from Cilicia and Asia),
disputing with Stephen.
10 And they were not able to resist the wis-
dom and the Spirit by which he spoke.
11 Then they secretly induced men to say,
"We have heard him speak blasphemous words
against Moses and God."
12 And they stirred up the people, the elders,
and the scribes; and they came upon *him*,
seized him, and brought *him* to the council.
13 They also set up false witnesses who said,
"This man does not cease to speak blasphe-
mous[a] words against this holy place and the law;
14 "for we have heard him say that this Jesus
of Nazareth will destroy this place and change
the customs which Moses delivered to us."
15 And all who sat in the council, looking
steadfastly at him, saw his face as the face of
an angel.

Stephen's Address: The Call of Abraham

7 Then the high priest said, "Are these things
so?"
2 And he said, "Brethren and fathers, listen:
The God of glory appeared to our father Abra-
ham when he was in Mesopotamia, before he
dwelt in Haran,
3 "and said to him, *'Get out of your country*

5:23 [a]NU-Text and M-Text omit *outside*. **5:24** [a]NU-Text omits *the high priest*. **5:25** [a]NU-Text and M-Text omit *saying*. **5:41** [a]NU-Text reads *the name*; M-Text reads *the name of Jesus*. **6:1** [a]That is, Greek-speaking Jews **6:8** [a]NU-Text reads *grace*. **6:13** [a]NU-Text omits *blasphemous*.

and from your relatives, and come to a land that I will show you.'[a]

4 "Then he came out of the land of the Chaldeans and dwelt in Haran. And from there, when his father was dead, He moved him to this land in which you now dwell.

5 "And *God* gave him no inheritance in it, not even *enough* to set his foot on. But even when *Abraham* had no child, He promised to give it to him for a possession, and to his descendants after him.

6 "But God spoke in this way: that his descendants would dwell in a foreign land, and that they would bring them into bondage and oppress *them* four hundred years.

7 *'And the nation to whom they will be in bondage I will judge,'*[a] said God, *'and after that they shall come out and serve Me in this place.'*[b]

8 "Then He gave him the covenant of circumcision; and so *Abraham* begot Isaac and circumcised him on the eighth day; and Isaac *begot* Jacob, and Jacob *begot* the twelve patriarchs.

The Patriarchs in Egypt

9 "And the patriarchs, becoming envious, sold Joseph into Egypt. But God was with him

10 "and delivered him out of all his troubles, and gave him favor and wisdom in the presence of Pharaoh, king of Egypt; and he made him governor over Egypt and all his house.

11 "Now a famine and great trouble came over all the land of Egypt and Canaan, and our fathers found no sustenance.

12 "But when Jacob heard that there was grain in Egypt, he sent out our fathers first.

13 "And the second *time* Joseph was made known to his brothers, and Joseph's family became known to the Pharaoh.

14 "Then Joseph sent and called his father Jacob and all his relatives to *him,* seventy-five[a] people.

15 "So Jacob went down to Egypt; and he died, he and our fathers.

16 "And they were carried back to Shechem and laid in the tomb that Abraham bought for a sum of money from the sons of Hamor, *the father* of Shechem.

God Delivers Israel by Moses

17 "But when the time of the promise drew near which God had sworn to Abraham, the people grew and multiplied in Egypt

18 "till another king arose who did not know Joseph.

19 "This man dealt treacherously with our people, and oppressed our forefathers, making them expose their babies, so that they might not live.

20 "At this time Moses was born, and was well pleasing to God; and he was brought up in his father's house for three months.

21 "But when he was set out, Pharaoh's daughter took him away and brought him up as her own son.

22 "And Moses was learned in all the wisdom of the Egyptians, and was mighty in words and deeds.

23 "Now when he was forty years old, it came into his heart to visit his brethren, the children of Israel.

24 "And seeing one of *them* suffer wrong, he defended and avenged him who was oppressed, and struck down the Egyptian.

25 "For he supposed that his brethren would have understood that God would deliver them by his hand, but they did not understand.

26 "And the next day he appeared to *two of* them as they were fighting, and *tried to* reconcile them, saying, 'Men, you are brethren; why do you wrong one another?'

27 "But he who did his neighbor wrong pushed him away, saying, *'Who made you a ruler and a judge over us?*

28 *'Do you want to kill me as you did the Egyptian yesterday?'*[a]

29 "Then, at this saying, Moses fled and became a dweller in the land of Midian, where he had two sons.

30 "And when forty years had passed, an Angel of the Lord[a] appeared to him in a flame of fire in a bush, in the wilderness of Mount Sinai.

31 "When Moses saw *it,* he marveled at the sight; and as he drew near to observe, the voice of the Lord came to him,

32 *"saying, 'I am the God of your fathers—the God of Abraham, the God of Isaac, and the God of Jacob.'*[a] And Moses trembled and dared not look.

33 *'Then the LORD said to him, "Take your sandals off your feet, for the place where you stand is holy ground.*

34 *"I have surely seen the oppression of My people who are in Egypt; I have heard their groaning and have come down to deliver them. And now come, I will send you to Egypt." '*[a]

35 "This Moses whom they rejected, saying, *'Who made you a ruler and a judge?'*[a] is the one God sent *to be* a ruler and a deliverer by the hand of the Angel who appeared to him in the bush.

36 "He brought them out, after he had shown wonders and signs in the land of Egypt, and in the Red Sea, and in the wilderness forty years.

Israel Rebels Against God

37 "This is that Moses who said to the children of Israel,[a] *'The LORD your God will raise up for you a Prophet like me from your brethren. Him you shall hear.'*[b]

38 "This is he who was in the congregation in the wilderness with the Angel who spoke to him on Mount Sinai, and *with* our fathers, the one who received the living oracles to give to us,

39 "whom our fathers would not obey, but rejected. And in their hearts they turned back to Egypt,

40 "saying to Aaron, *'Make us gods to go before us; as for this Moses who brought us out of the land of Egypt, we do not know what has become of him.'*[a]

41 "And they made a calf in those days, offered sacrifices to the idol, and rejoiced in the works of their own hands.

42 "Then God turned and gave them up to worship the host of heaven, as it is written in the book of the Prophets:

'Did you offer Me slaughtered animals
and sacrifices during forty years in the wilderness,
O house of Israel?

7:3 [a]Genesis 12:1 **7:7** [a]Genesis 15:14 [b]Exodus 3:12 **7:14** [a]Or *seventy* (compare Exodus 1:5) **7:28** [a]Exodus 2:14
7:30 [a]NU-Text omits *of the Lord.* **7:32** [a]Exodus 3:6, 15 **7:34** [a]Exodus 3:5, 7, 8, 10 **7:35** [a]Exodus 2:14
7:37 [a]Deuteronomy 18:15 [b]NU-Text and M-Text omit *Him you shall hear.* **7:40** [a]Exodus 32:1, 23

43 *You also took up the tabernacle of*
Moloch,
And the star of your god Remphan,
Images which you made to worship;
And I will carry you away beyond
Babylon.'[a]

God's True Tabernacle

44 "Our fathers had the tabernacle of witness in the wilderness, as He appointed, instructing Moses to make it according to the pattern that he had seen,

45 "which our fathers, having received it in turn, also brought with Joshua into the land possessed by the Gentiles, whom God drove out before the face of our fathers until the days of David,

46 "who found favor before God and asked to find a dwelling for the God of Jacob.

47 "But Solomon built Him a house.

48 "However, the Most High does not dwell in temples made with hands, as the prophet says:

49 *'Heaven is My throne,*
And earth is My footstool.
What house will you build for Me? says
the LORD,
Or what is the place of My rest?
50 *Has My hand not made all these things?'*[a]

Israel Resists the Holy Spirit

51 "*You* stiff-necked and uncircumcised in heart and ears! You always resist the Holy Spirit; as your fathers *did,* so *do* you.

52 "Which of the prophets did your fathers not persecute? And they killed those who foretold the coming of the Just One, of whom you now have become the betrayers and murderers,

53 "who have received the law by the direction of angels and have not kept *it.*"

Stephen the Martyr

54 When they heard these things they were cut to the heart, and they gnashed at him with *their* teeth.

55 But he, being full of the Holy Spirit, gazed into heaven and saw the glory of God, and Jesus standing at the right hand of God,

56 and said, "Look! I see the heavens opened and the Son of Man standing at the right hand of God!"

57 Then they cried out with a loud voice, stopped their ears, and ran at him with one accord;

58 and they cast *him* out of the city and stoned *him.* And the witnesses laid down their clothes at the feet of a young man named Saul.

59 And they stoned Stephen as he was calling on *God* and saying, "Lord Jesus, receive my spirit."

60 Then he knelt down and cried out with a loud voice, "Lord, do not charge them with this sin." And when he had said this, he fell asleep.

Saul Persecutes the Church

8 Now Saul was consenting to his death. At that time a great persecution arose against the church which was at Jerusalem; and they were all scattered throughout the regions of Judea and Samaria, except the apostles.

2 And devout men carried Stephen *to his burial,* and made great lamentation over him.

3 As for Saul, he made havoc of the church, entering every house, and dragging off men and women, committing *them* to prison.

Christ Is Preached in Samaria

4 Therefore those who were scattered went everywhere preaching the word.

5 Then Philip went down to the[a] city of Samaria and preached Christ to them.

6 And the multitudes with one accord heeded the things spoken by Philip, hearing and seeing the miracles which he did.

7 For unclean spirits, crying with a loud voice, came out of many who were possessed; and many who were paralyzed and lame were healed.

8 And there was great joy in that city.

The Sorcerer's Profession of Faith

9 But there was a certain man called Simon, who previously practiced sorcery in the city and astonished the people of Samaria, claiming that he was someone great,

10 to whom they all gave heed, from the least to the greatest, saying, "This man is the great power of God."

11 And they heeded him because he had astonished them with his sorceries for a long time.

12 But when they believed Philip as he preached the things concerning the kingdom of God and the name of Jesus Christ, both men and women were baptized.

13 Then Simon himself also believed; and when he was baptized he continued with Philip, and was amazed, seeing the miracles and signs which were done.

The Sorcerer's Sin

14 Now when the apostles who were at Jerusalem heard that Samaria had received the word of God, they sent Peter and John to them,

15 who, when they had come down, prayed for them that they might receive the Holy Spirit.

16 For as yet He had fallen upon none of them. They had only been baptized in the name of the Lord Jesus.

17 Then they laid hands on them, and they received the Holy Spirit.

18 And when Simon saw that through the laying on of the apostles' hands the Holy Spirit was given, he offered them money,

19 saying, "Give me this power also, that anyone on whom I lay hands may receive the Holy Spirit."

20 But Peter said to him, "Your money perish with you, because you thought that the gift of God could be purchased with money!

21 "You have neither part nor portion in this matter, for your heart is not right in the sight of God.

22 "Repent therefore of this your wickedness, and pray God if perhaps the thought of your heart may be forgiven you.

23 "For I see that you are poisoned by bitterness and bound by iniquity."

24 Then Simon answered and said, "Pray to the Lord for me, that none of the things which you have spoken may come upon me."

25 So when they had testified and preached the word of the Lord, they returned to Jerusalem, preaching the gospel in many villages of the Samaritans.

7:43 [a]Amos 5:25–27 7:50 [a]Isaiah 66:1, 2 8:5 [a]Or *a*

Christ Is Preached to an Ethiopian

26 Now an angel of the Lord spoke to Philip, saying, "Arise and go toward the south along the road which goes down from Jerusalem to Gaza." This is desert.
27 So he arose and went. And behold, a man of Ethiopia, a eunuch of great authority under Candace the queen of the Ethiopians, who had charge of all her treasury, and had come to Jerusalem to worship,
28 was returning. And sitting in his chariot, he was reading Isaiah the prophet.
29 Then the Spirit said to Philip, "Go near and overtake this chariot."
30 So Philip ran to him, and heard him reading the prophet Isaiah, and said, "Do you understand what you are reading?"
31 And he said, "How can I, unless someone guides me?" And he asked Philip to come up and sit with him.
32 The place in the Scripture which he read was this:

"He was led as a sheep to the slaughter;
And as a lamb before its shearer is silent,
So He opened not His mouth.
33 *In His humiliation His justice was taken away,*
And who will declare His generation?
For His life is taken from the earth."[a]

34 So the eunuch answered Philip and said, "I ask you, of whom does the prophet say this, of himself or of some other man?"
35 Then Philip opened his mouth, and beginning at this Scripture, preached Jesus to him.
36 Now as they went down the road, they came to some water. And the eunuch said, "See, *here is* water. What hinders me from being baptized?"
37 Then Philip said, "If you believe with all your heart, you may." And he answered and said, "I believe that Jesus Christ is the Son of God."[a]
38 So he commanded the chariot to stand still. And both Philip and the eunuch went down into the water, and he baptized him.
39 Now when they came up out of the water, the Spirit of the Lord caught Philip away, so that the eunuch saw him no more; and he went on his way rejoicing.
40 But Philip was found at Azotus. And passing through, he preached in all the cities till he came to Caesarea.

The Damascus Road: Saul Converted

9 Then Saul, still breathing threats and murder against the disciples of the Lord, went to the high priest
2 and asked letters from him to the synagogues of Damascus, so that if he found any who were of the Way, whether men or women, he might bring them bound to Jerusalem.
3 As he journeyed he came near Damascus, and suddenly a light shone around him from heaven.
4 Then he fell to the ground, and heard a voice saying to him, "Saul, Saul, why are you persecuting Me?"
5 And he said, "Who are You, Lord?" Then the Lord said, "I am Jesus, whom you are persecuting.[a] It *is* hard for you to kick against the goads."
6 So he, trembling and astonished, said, "Lord, what do You want me to do?" Then the Lord *said* to him, "Arise and go into the city, and you will be told what you must do."
7 And the men who journeyed with him stood speechless, hearing a voice but seeing no one.
8 Then Saul arose from the ground, and when his eyes were opened he saw no one. But they led him by the hand and brought *him* into Damascus.
9 And he was three days without sight, and neither ate nor drank.

Ananias Baptizes Saul

10 Now there was a certain disciple at Damascus named Ananias; and to him the Lord said in a vision, "Ananias." And he said, "Here I am, Lord."
11 So the Lord *said* to him, "Arise and go to the street called Straight, and inquire at the house of Judas for *one* called Saul of Tarsus, for behold, he is praying.
12 "And in a vision he has seen a man named Ananias coming in and putting *his* hand on him, so that he might receive his sight."
13 Then Ananias answered, "Lord, I have heard from many about this man, how much harm he has done to Your saints in Jerusalem.
14 "And here he has authority from the chief priests to bind all who call on Your name."
15 But the Lord said to him, "Go, for he is a chosen vessel of Mine to bear My name before Gentiles, kings, and the children of Israel.
16 "For I will show him how many things he must suffer for My name's sake."
17 And Ananias went his way and entered the house; and laying his hands on him he said, "Brother Saul, the Lord Jesus,[a] who appeared to you on the road as you came, has sent me that you may receive your sight and be filled with the Holy Spirit."
18 Immediately there fell from his eyes *something* like scales, and he received his sight at once; and he arose and was baptized.
19 So when he had received food, he was strengthened. Then Saul spent some days with the disciples at Damascus.

Saul Preaches Christ

20 Immediately he preached the Christ[a] in the synagogues, that He is the Son of God.
21 Then all who heard were amazed, and said, "Is this not he who destroyed those who called on this name in Jerusalem, and has come here for that purpose, so that he might bring them bound to the chief priests?"
22 But Saul increased all the more in strength, and confounded the Jews who dwelt in Damascus, proving that this *Jesus* is the Christ.

Saul Escapes Death

23 Now after many days were past, the Jews plotted to kill him.
24 But their plot became known to Saul. And they watched the gates day and night, to kill him.
25 Then the disciples took him by night and let *him* down through the wall in a large basket.

Saul at Jerusalem

26 And when Saul had come to Jerusalem, he tried to join the disciples; but they were all afraid

8:33 [a]Isaiah 53:7, 8 **8:37** [a]NU-Text and M-Text omit this verse. It is found in Western texts, including the Latin tradition. **9:5** [a]NU-Text and M-Text omit the last sentence of verse 5 and begin verse 6 with *But arise and go.* **9:17** [a]M-Text omits *Jesus.* **9:20** [a]NU-Text reads *Jesus.*

of him, and did not believe that he was a disciple.
27 But Barnabas took him and brought *him* to
the apostles. And he declared to them how he
had seen the Lord on the road, and that He had
spoken to him, and how he had preached boldly
at Damascus in the name of Jesus.
28 So he was with them at Jerusalem, coming
in and going out.
29 And he spoke boldly in the name of the
Lord Jesus and disputed against the Hellenists,
but they attempted to kill him.
30 When the brethren found out, they brought
him down to Caesarea and sent him out to
Tarsus.

The Church Prospers

31 Then the churches[a] throughout all Judea,
Galilee, and Samaria had peace and were edified. And walking in the fear of the Lord and
in the comfort of the Holy Spirit, they were
multiplied.

Aeneas Healed

32 Now it came to pass, as Peter went through
all *parts of the country,* that he also came
down to the saints who dwelt in Lydda.
33 There he found a certain man named Aeneas, who had been bedridden eight years and
was paralyzed.
34 And Peter said to him, "Aeneas, Jesus the
Christ heals you. Arise and make your bed."
Then he arose immediately.
35 So all who dwelt at Lydda and Sharon saw
him and turned to the Lord.

Dorcas Restored to Life

36 At Joppa there was a certain disciple
named Tabitha, which is translated Dorcas.
This woman was full of good works and charitable deeds which she did.
37 But it happened in those days that she became sick and died. When they had washed
her, they laid *her* in an upper room.
38 And since Lydda was near Joppa, and the
disciples had heard that Peter was there, they
sent two men to him, imploring *him* not to delay in coming to them.
39 Then Peter arose and went with them.
When he had come, they brought *him* to the
upper room. And all the widows stood by him
weeping, showing the tunics and garments
which Dorcas had made while she was with
them.
40 But Peter put them all out, and knelt down
and prayed. And turning to the body he said,
"Tabitha, arise." And she opened her eyes, and
when she saw Peter she sat up.
41 Then he gave her *his* hand and lifted her
up; and when he had called the saints and widows, he presented her alive.
42 And it became known throughout all
Joppa, and many believed on the Lord.
43 So it was that he stayed many days in
Joppa with Simon, a tanner.

Cornelius Sends a Delegation

10 There was a certain man in Caesarea
called Cornelius, a centurion of what
was called the Italian Regiment,
2 a devout *man* and one who feared God with
all his household, who gave alms generously
to the people, and prayed to God always.
3 About the ninth hour of the day he saw
clearly in a vision an angel of God coming in
and saying to him, "Cornelius!"
4 And when he observed him, he was afraid,
and said, "What is it, lord?" So he said to him,
"Your prayers and your alms have come up for
a memorial before God.
5 "Now send men to Joppa, and send for Simon whose surname is Peter.
6 "He is lodging with Simon, a tanner, whose
house is by the sea.[a] He will tell you what you
must do."
7 And when the angel who spoke to him had
departed, Cornelius called two of his household servants and a devout soldier from among
those who waited on him continually.
8 So when he had explained all *these* things
to them, he sent them to Joppa.

Peter's Vision

9 The next day, as they went on their journey
and drew near the city, Peter went up on the
housetop to pray, about the sixth hour.
10 Then he became very hungry and wanted
to eat; but while they made ready, he fell into
a trance
11 and saw heaven opened and an object like
a great sheet bound at the four corners, descending to him and let down to the earth.
12 In it were all kinds of four-footed animals
of the earth, wild beasts, creeping things, and
birds of the air.
13 And a voice came to him, "Rise, Peter; kill
and eat."
14 But Peter said, "Not so, Lord! For I have
never eaten anything common or unclean."
15 And a voice *spoke* to him again the second
time, "What God has cleansed you must not
call common."
16 This was done three times. And the object
was taken up into heaven again.

Summoned to Caesarea

17 Now while Peter wondered within himself
what this vision which he had seen meant, behold, the men who had been sent from Cornelius had made inquiry for Simon's house, and
stood before the gate.
18 And they called and asked whether Simon,
whose surname was Peter, was lodging there.
19 While Peter thought about the vision, the
Spirit said to him, "Behold, three men are seeking you.
20 "Arise therefore, go down and go with them,
doubting nothing; for I have sent them."
21 Then Peter went down to the men who had
been sent to him from Cornelius,[a] and said, "Yes,
I am he whom you seek. For what reason have
you come?"
22 And they said, "Cornelius *the* centurion, a
just man, one who fears God and has a good
reputation among all the nation of the Jews,
was divinely instructed by a holy angel to summon you to his house, and to hear words from
you."
23 Then he invited them in and lodged *them.*
On the next day Peter went away with them,
and some brethren from Joppa accompanied
him.

9:31 [a]NU-Text reads *church . . . was edified.* **10:6** [a]NU-Text and M-Text omit the last sentence of this verse.
10:21 [a]NU-Text and M-Text omit *who had been sent to him from Cornelius.*

Peter Meets Cornelius

24 And the following day they entered Caesarea. Now Cornelius was waiting for them, and had called together his relatives and close friends.

25 As Peter was coming in, Cornelius met him and fell down at his feet and worshiped *him.*

26 But Peter lifted him up, saying, "Stand up; I myself am also a man."

27 And as he talked with him, he went in and found many who had come together.

28 Then he said to them, "You know how unlawful it is for a Jewish man to keep company with or go to one of another nation. But God has shown me that I should not call any man common or unclean.

29 "Therefore I came without objection as soon as I was sent for. I ask, then, for what reason have you sent for me?"

30 So Cornelius said, "Four days ago I was fasting until this hour; and at the ninth hour[a] I prayed in my house, and behold, a man stood before me in bright clothing,

31 "and said, 'Cornelius, your prayer has been heard, and your alms are remembered in the sight of God.

32 'Send therefore to Joppa and call Simon here, whose surname is Peter. He is lodging in the house of Simon, a tanner, by the sea.[a] When he comes, he will speak to you.'

33 "So I sent to you immediately, and you have done well to come. Now therefore, we are all present before God, to hear all the things commanded you by God."

Preaching to Cornelius' Household

34 Then Peter opened *his* mouth and said: "In truth I perceive that God shows no partiality.

35 "But in every nation whoever fears Him and works righteousness is accepted by Him.

36 "The word which *God* sent to the children of Israel, preaching peace through Jesus Christ—He is Lord of all—

37 "that word you know, which was proclaimed throughout all Judea, and began from Galilee after the baptism which John preached:

38 "how God anointed Jesus of Nazareth with the Holy Spirit and with power, who went about doing good and healing all who were oppressed by the devil, for God was with Him.

39 "And we are witnesses of all things which He did both in the land of the Jews and in Jerusalem, whom they[a] killed by hanging on a tree.

40 "Him God raised up on the third day, and showed Him openly,

41 "not to all the people, but to witnesses chosen before by God, *even* to us who ate and drank with Him after He arose from the dead.

42 "And He commanded us to preach to the people, and to testify that it is He who was ordained by God *to be* Judge of the living and the dead.

43 "To Him all the prophets witness that, through His name, whoever believes in Him will receive remission of sins."

The Holy Spirit Falls on the Gentiles

44 While Peter was still speaking these words, the Holy Spirit fell upon all those who heard the word.

45 And those of the circumcision who believed were astonished, as many as came with Peter, because the gift of the Holy Spirit had been poured out on the Gentiles also.

46 For they heard them speak with tongues and magnify God. Then Peter answered,

47 "Can anyone forbid water, that these should not be baptized who have received the Holy Spirit just as we *have?*"

48 And he commanded them to be baptized in the name of the Lord. Then they asked him to stay a few days.

Peter Defends God's Grace

11 Now the apostles and brethren who were in Judea heard that the Gentiles had also received the word of God.

2 And when Peter came up to Jerusalem, those of the circumcision contended with him,

3 saying, "You went in to uncircumcised men and ate with them!"

4 But Peter explained *it* to them in order from the beginning, saying:

5 "I was in the city of Joppa praying; and in a trance I saw a vision, an object descending like a great sheet, let down from heaven by four corners; and it came to me.

6 "When I observed it intently and considered, I saw four-footed animals of the earth, wild beasts, creeping things, and birds of the air.

7 "And I heard a voice saying to me, 'Rise, Peter; kill and eat.'

8 "But I said, 'Not so, Lord! For nothing common or unclean has at any time entered my mouth.'

9 "But the voice answered me again from heaven, 'What God has cleansed you must not call common.'

10 "Now this was done three times, and all were drawn up again into heaven.

11 "At that very moment, three men stood before the house where I was, having been sent to me from Caesarea.

12 "Then the Spirit told me to go with them, doubting nothing. Moreover these six brethren accompanied me, and we entered the man's house.

13 "And he told us how he had seen an angel standing in his house, who said to him, 'Send men to Joppa, and call for Simon whose surname is Peter,

14 'who will tell you words by which you and all your household will be saved.'

15 "And as I began to speak, the Holy Spirit fell upon them, as upon us at the beginning.

16 "Then I remembered the word of the Lord, how He said, 'John indeed baptized with water, but you shall be baptized with the Holy Spirit.'

17 "If therefore God gave them the same gift as *He gave* us when we believed on the Lord Jesus Christ, who was I that I could withstand God?"

18 When they heard these things they became silent; and they glorified God, saying, "Then God has also granted to the Gentiles repentance to life."

Barnabas and Saul at Antioch

19 Now those who were scattered after the persecution that arose over Stephen traveled as far as Phoenicia, Cyprus, and Antioch, preaching the word to no one but the Jews only.

20 But some of them were men from Cyprus

10:30 [a]NU-Text reads *Four days ago to this hour, at the ninth hour.* **10:32** [a]NU-Text omits the last sentence of this verse. **10:39** [a]NU-Text and M-Text add *also.*

and Cyrene, who, when they had come to Anti-
och, spoke to the Hellenists, preaching the
Lord Jesus.
21 And the hand of the Lord was with them,
and a great number believed and turned to the
Lord.
22 Then news of these things came to the ears
of the church in Jerusalem, and they sent out
Barnabas to go as far as Antioch.
23 When he came and had seen the grace of
God, he was glad, and encouraged them all that
with purpose of heart they should continue
with the Lord.
24 For he was a good man, full of the Holy
Spirit and of faith. And a great many people were
added to the Lord.
25 Then Barnabas departed for Tarsus to seek
Saul.
26 And when he had found him, he brought
him to Antioch. So it was that for a whole year
they assembled with the church and taught a
great many people. And the disciples were first
called Christians in Antioch.

Relief to Judea

27 And in these days prophets came from Je-
rusalem to Antioch.
28 Then one of them, named Agabus, stood
up and showed by the Spirit that there was going
to be a great famine throughout all the world,
which also happened in the days of Claudius
Caesar.
29 Then the disciples, each according to his
ability, determined to send relief to the breth-
ren dwelling in Judea.
30 This they also did, and sent it to the elders
by the hands of Barnabas and Saul.

Herod's Violence to the Church

12 Now about that time Herod the king
stretched out *his* hand to harass some
from the church.
2 Then he killed James the brother of John
with the sword.
3 And because he saw that it pleased the
Jews, he proceeded further to seize Peter also.
Now it was *during* the Days of Unleavened
Bread.
4 So when he had arrested him, he put *him*
in prison, and delivered *him* to four squads of
soldiers to keep him, intending to bring him
before the people after Passover.

Peter Freed from Prison

5 Peter was therefore kept in prison, but con-
stant[a] prayer was offered to God for him by the
church.
6 And when Herod was about to bring him
out, that night Peter was sleeping, bound with
two chains between two soldiers; and the
guards before the door were keeping the
prison.
7 Now behold, an angel of the Lord stood by
him, and a light shone in the prison; and he
struck Peter on the side and raised him up,
saying, "Arise quickly!" And his chains fell off
his hands.
8 Then the angel said to him, "Gird yourself
and tie on your sandals"; and so he did. And
he said to him, "Put on your garment and fol-
low me."
9 So he went out and followed him, and did
not know that what was done by the angel was
real, but thought he was seeing a vision.
10 When they were past the first and the sec-
ond guard posts, they came to the iron gate
that leads to the city, which opened to them of
its own accord; and they went out and went
down one street, and immediately the angel de-
parted from him.
11 And when Peter had come to himself, he
said, "Now I know for certain that the Lord has
sent His angel, and has delivered me from the
hand of Herod and *from* all the expectation of
the Jewish people."
12 So, when he had considered *this*, he came
to the house of Mary, the mother of John whose
surname was Mark, where many were gathered
together praying.
13 And as Peter knocked at the door of the
gate, a girl named Rhoda came to answer.
14 When she recognized Peter's voice, because
of *her* gladness she did not open the gate, but
ran in and announced that Peter stood before
the gate.
15 But they said to her, "You are beside your-
self!" Yet she kept insisting that it was so. So
they said, "It is his angel."
16 Now Peter continued knocking; and when
they opened *the door* and saw him, they were
astonished.
17 But motioning to them with his hand to
keep silent, he declared to them how the Lord
had brought him out of the prison. And he said,
"Go, tell these things to James and to the breth-
ren." And he departed and went to another
place.
18 Then, as soon as it was day, there was no
small stir among the soldiers about what had
become of Peter.
19 But when Herod had searched for him and
not found him, he examined the guards and
commanded that *they* should be put to death.
And he went down from Judea to Caesarea, and
stayed *there*.

Herod's Violent Death

20 Now Herod had been very angry with the
people of Tyre and Sidon; but they came to him
with one accord, and having made Blastus the
king's personal aide their friend, they asked
for peace, because their country was supplied
with food by the king's *country*.
21 So on a set day Herod, arrayed in royal
apparel, sat on his throne and gave an oration
to them.
22 And the people kept shouting, "The voice
of a god and not of a man!"
23 Then immediately an angel of the Lord
struck him, because he did not give glory to
God. And he was eaten by worms and died.
24 But the word of God grew and multiplied.

Barnabas and Saul Appointed

25 And Barnabas and Saul returned from[a] Je-
rusalem when they had fulfilled *their* ministry,
and they also took with them John whose sur-
name was Mark.

13 Now in the church that was at Antioch
there were certain prophets and teachers:
Barnabas, Simeon who was called Niger, Lu-
cius of Cyrene, Manaen who had been brought
up with Herod the tetrarch, and Saul.
2 As they ministered to the Lord and fasted,
the Holy Spirit said, "Now separate to Me Bar-

12:5 [a]NU-Text reads *constantly* (or *earnestly*). 12:25 [a]NU-Text and M-Text read *to*.

nabas and Saul for the work to which I have called them."

3 Then, having fasted and prayed, and laid hands on them, they sent *them* away.

Preaching in Cyprus

4 So, being sent out by the Holy Spirit, they went down to Seleucia, and from there they sailed to Cyprus.

5 And when they arrived in Salamis, they preached the word of God in the synagogues of the Jews. They also had John as *their* assistant.

6 Now when they had gone through the island[a] to Paphos, they found a certain sorcerer, a false prophet, a Jew whose name *was* Bar-Jesus,

7 who was with the proconsul, Sergius Paulus, an intelligent man. This man called for Barnabas and Saul and sought to hear the word of God.

8 But Elymas the sorcerer (for so his name is translated) withstood them, seeking to turn the proconsul away from the faith.

9 Then Saul, who also *is called* Paul, filled with the Holy Spirit, looked intently at him

10 and said, "O full of all deceit and all fraud, *you* son of the devil, *you* enemy of all righteousness, will you not cease perverting the straight ways of the Lord?

11 "And now, indeed, the hand of the Lord *is* upon you, and you shall be blind, not seeing the sun for a time." And immediately a dark mist fell on him, and he went around seeking someone to lead him by the hand.

12 Then the proconsul believed, when he saw what had been done, being astonished at the teaching of the Lord.

At Antioch in Pisidia

13 Now when Paul and his party set sail from Paphos, they came to Perga in Pamphylia; and John, departing from them, returned to Jerusalem.

14 But when they departed from Perga, they came to Antioch in Pisidia, and went into the synagogue on the Sabbath day and sat down.

15 And after the reading of the Law and the Prophets, the rulers of the synagogue sent to them, saying, "Men *and* brethren, if you have any word of exhortation for the people, say on."

16 Then Paul stood up, and motioning with *his* hand said, "Men of Israel, and you who fear God, listen:

17 "The God of this people Israel[a] chose our fathers, and exalted the people when they dwelt as strangers in the land of Egypt, and with an uplifted arm He brought them out of it.

18 "Now for a time of about forty years He put up with their ways in the wilderness.

19 "And when He had destroyed seven nations in the land of Canaan, He distributed their land to them by allotment.

20 "After that He gave *them* judges for about four hundred and fifty years, until Samuel the prophet.

21 "And afterward they asked for a king; so God gave them Saul the son of Kish, a man of the tribe of Benjamin, for forty years.

22 "And when He had removed him, He raised up for them David as king, to whom also He gave testimony and said, *'I have found David*[a] the *son* of Jesse, *a man after My own heart,* who will do all My will.'[b]

23 "From this man's seed, according to *the* promise, God raised up for Israel a Savior—Jesus—[a]

24 "after John had first preached, before His coming, the baptism of repentance to all the people of Israel.

25 "And as John was finishing his course, he said, 'Who do you think I am? I am not *He.* But behold, there comes One after me, the sandals of whose feet I am not worthy to loose.'

26 "Men *and* brethren, sons of the family of Abraham, and those among you who fear God, to you the word of this salvation has been sent.

27 "For those who dwell in Jerusalem, and their rulers, because they did not know Him, nor even the voices of the Prophets which are read every Sabbath, have fulfilled *them* in condemning *Him.*

28 "And though they found no cause for death *in Him,* they asked Pilate that He should be put to death.

29 "Now when they had fulfilled all that was written concerning Him, they took *Him* down from the tree and laid *Him* in a tomb.

30 "But God raised Him from the dead.

31 "He was seen for many days by those who came up with Him from Galilee to Jerusalem, who are His witnesses to the people.

32 "And we declare to you glad tidings—that promise which was made to the fathers.

33 "God has fulfilled this for us their children, in that He has raised up Jesus. As it is also written in the second Psalm:

'You are My Son,
Today I have begotten You.'[a]

34 "And that He raised Him from the dead, no more to return to corruption, He has spoken thus:

'I will give you the sure mercies of
David.'[a]

35 "Therefore He also says in another *Psalm:*

'You will not allow Your Holy One to see
corruption.'[a]

36 "For David, after he had served his own generation by the will of God, fell asleep, was buried with his fathers, and saw corruption;

37 "but He whom God raised up saw no corruption.

38 "Therefore let it be known to you, brethren, that through this Man is preached to you the forgiveness of sins;

39 "and by Him everyone who believes is justified from all things from which you could not be justified by the law of Moses.

40 "Beware therefore, lest what has been spoken in the prophets come upon you:

41 *'Behold, you despisers,*
Marvel and perish!
For I work a work in your days,
A work which you will by no means
believe,
Though one were to declare it to you.' "[a]

13:6 [a]NU-Text reads *the whole island.* **13:17** [a]M-Text omits *Israel.* **13:22** [a]Psalm 89:20 [b]1 Samuel 13:14
13:23 [a]M-Text reads *for Israel salvation.* **13:33** [a]Psalm 2:7 **13:34** [a]Isaiah 55:3 **13:35** [a]Psalm 16:10
13:41 [a]Habakkuk 1:5

Blessing and Conflict at Antioch

42 So when the Jews went out of the synagogue,[a] the Gentiles begged that these words might be preached to them the next Sabbath.
43 Now when the congregation had broken up, many of the Jews and devout proselytes followed Paul and Barnabas, who, speaking to them, persuaded them to continue in the grace of God.
44 On the next Sabbath almost the whole city came together to hear the word of God.
45 But when the Jews saw the multitudes, they were filled with envy; and contradicting and blaspheming, they opposed the things spoken by Paul.
46 Then Paul and Barnabas grew bold and said, "It was necessary that the word of God should be spoken to you first; but since you reject it, and judge yourselves unworthy of everlasting life, behold, we turn to the Gentiles.
47 "For so the Lord has commanded us:

> *'I have set you as a light to the Gentiles,*
> *That you should be for salvation to the*
> *ends of the earth.'* "[a]

48 Now when the Gentiles heard this, they were glad and glorified the word of the Lord. And as many as had been appointed to eternal life believed.
49 And the word of the Lord was being spread throughout all the region.
50 But the Jews stirred up the devout and prominent women and the chief men of the city, raised up persecution against Paul and Barnabas, and expelled them from their region.
51 But they shook off the dust from their feet against them, and came to Iconium.
52 And the disciples were filled with joy and with the Holy Spirit.

At Iconium

14 Now it happened in Iconium that they went together to the synagogue of the Jews, and so spoke that a great multitude both of the Jews and of the Greeks believed.
2 But the unbelieving Jews stirred up the Gentiles and poisoned their minds against the brethren.
3 Therefore they stayed there a long time, speaking boldly in the Lord, who was bearing witness to the word of His grace, granting signs and wonders to be done by their hands.
4 But the multitude of the city was divided: part sided with the Jews, and part with the apostles.
5 And when a violent attempt was made by both the Gentiles and Jews, with their rulers, to abuse and stone them,
6 they became aware of it and fled to Lystra and Derbe, cities of Lycaonia, and to the surrounding region.
7 And they were preaching the gospel there.

Idolatry at Lystra

8 And in Lystra a certain man without strength in his feet was sitting, a cripple from his mother's womb, who had never walked.
9 *This* man heard Paul speaking. Paul, observing him intently and seeing that he had faith to be healed,
10 said with a loud voice, "Stand up straight on your feet!" And he leaped and walked.
11 Now when the people saw what Paul had done, they raised their voices, saying in the Lycaonian *language*, "The gods have come down to us in the likeness of men!"
12 And Barnabas they called Zeus, and Paul, Hermes, because he was the chief speaker.
13 Then the priest of Zeus, whose temple was in front of their city, brought oxen and garlands to the gates, intending to sacrifice with the multitudes.
14 But when the apostles Barnabas and Paul heard this, they tore their clothes and ran in among the multitude, crying out
15 and saying, "Men, why are you doing these things? We also are men with the same nature as you, and preach to you that you should turn from these useless things to the living God, who made the heaven, the earth, the sea, and all things that are in them,
16 "who in bygone generations allowed all nations to walk in their own ways.
17 "Nevertheless He did not leave Himself without witness, in that He did good, gave us rain from heaven and fruitful seasons, filling our hearts with food and gladness."
18 And with these sayings they could scarcely restrain the multitudes from sacrificing to them.

Stoning, Escape to Derbe

19 Then Jews from Antioch and Iconium came there; and having persuaded the multitudes, they stoned Paul *and* dragged *him* out of the city, supposing him to be dead.
20 However, when the disciples gathered around him, he rose up and went into the city. And the next day he departed with Barnabas to Derbe.

Strengthening the Converts

21 And when they had preached the gospel to that city and made many disciples, they returned to Lystra, Iconium, and Antioch,
22 strengthening the souls of the disciples, exhorting *them* to continue in the faith, and *saying*, "We must through many tribulations enter the kingdom of God."
23 So when they had appointed elders in every church, and prayed with fasting, they commended them to the Lord in whom they had believed.
24 And after they had passed through Pisidia, they came to Pamphylia.
25 Now when they had preached the word in Perga, they went down to Attalia.
26 From there they sailed to Antioch, where they had been commended to the grace of God for the work which they had completed.
27 Now when they had come and gathered the church together, they reported all that God had done with them, and that He had opened the door of faith to the Gentiles.
28 So they stayed there a long time with the disciples.

Conflict over Circumcision

15 And certain *men* came down from Judea and taught the brethren, "Unless you are circumcised according to the custom of Moses, you cannot be saved."

13:42 [a]Or *And when they went out of the synagogue of the Jews;* NU-Text reads *And when they went out, they begged.* **13:47** [a]Isaiah 49:6

2 Therefore, when Paul and Barnabas had
no small dissension and dispute with them, they
determined that Paul and Barnabas and cer-
tain others of them should go up to Jerusalem,
to the apostles and elders, about this question.
3 So, being sent on their way by the church,
they passed through Phoenicia and Samaria,
describing the conversion of the Gentiles; and
they caused great joy to all the brethren.
4 And when they had come to Jerusalem, they
were received by the church and the apostles
and the elders; and they reported all things
that God had done with them.
5 But some of the sect of the Pharisees who
believed rose up, saying, "It is necessary to
circumcise them, and to command *them* to
keep the law of Moses."

The Jerusalem Council

6 Now the apostles and elders came together
to consider this matter.
7 And when there had been much dispute,
Peter rose up *and* said to them: "Men *and*
brethren, you know that a good while ago God
chose among us, that by my mouth the Gentiles
should hear the word of the gospel and believe.
8 "So God, who knows the heart, acknowl-
edged them by giving them the Holy Spirit,
just as *He did* to us,
9 "and made no distinction between us and
them, purifying their hearts by faith.
10 "Now therefore, why do you test God by
putting a yoke on the neck of the disciples
which neither our fathers nor we were able to
bear?
11 "But we believe that through the grace of
the Lord Jesus Christ[a] we shall be saved in the
same manner as they."
12 Then all the multitude kept silent and lis-
tened to Barnabas and Paul declaring how
many miracles and wonders God had worked
through them among the Gentiles.
13 And after they had become silent, James
answered, saying, "Men *and* brethren, listen to
me:
14 "Simon has declared how God at the first
visited the Gentiles to take out of them a people
for His name.
15 "And with this the words of the prophets
agree, just as it is written:

16 *'After this I will return*
And will rebuild the tabernacle of David,
which has fallen down;
I will rebuild its ruins,
And I will set it up;
17 *So that the rest of mankind may seek the*
LORD,
Even all the Gentiles who are called by
My name,
Says the LORD who does all these
things.'[a]

18 "Known to God from eternity are all His
works.[a]
19 "Therefore I judge that we should not trou-
ble those from among the Gentiles who are
turning to God,
20 "but that we write to them to abstain from
things polluted by idols, *from* sexual immoral-
ity,[a] *from* things strangled, and *from* blood.
21 "For Moses has had throughout many gen-
erations those who preach him in every city,
being read in the synagogues every Sabbath."

The Jerusalem Decree

22 Then it pleased the apostles and elders, with
the whole church, to send chosen men of their
own company to Antioch with Paul and Barna-
bas, *namely,* Judas who was also named Barsa-
bas,[a] and Silas, leading men among the brethren.
23 They wrote this *letter* by them:

The apostles, the elders, and the
brethren,

To the brethren who are of the Gentiles in
Antioch, Syria, and Cilicia:

Greetings.

24 Since we have heard that some who went
out from us have troubled you with
words, unsettling your souls, saying,
"*You must* be circumcised and keep the
law"[a]—to whom we gave no *such*
commandment—
25 it seemed good to us, being assembled
with one accord, to send chosen men to
you with our beloved Barnabas and Paul,
26 men who have risked their lives for the
name of our Lord Jesus Christ.
27 We have therefore sent Judas and Silas,
who will also report the same things by
word of mouth.
28 For it seemed good to the Holy Spirit, and
to us, to lay upon you no greater burden
than these necessary things:
29 that you abstain from things offered to
idols, from blood, from things strangled,
and from sexual immorality.[a] If you keep
yourselves from these, you will do well.
Farewell.

Continuing Ministry in Syria

30 So when they were sent off, they came to
Antioch; and when they had gathered the mul-
titude together, they delivered the letter.
31 When they had read it, they rejoiced over
its encouragement.
32 Now Judas and Silas, themselves being
prophets also, exhorted and strengthened the
brethren with many words.
33 And after they had stayed *there* for a time,
they were sent back with greetings from the
brethren to the apostles.[a]
34 However, it seemed good to Silas to remain
there.[a]
35 Paul and Barnabas also remained in Anti-
och, teaching and preaching the word of the
Lord, with many others also.

Division over John Mark

36 Then after some days Paul said to Barna-
bas, "Let us now go back and visit our brethren
in every city where we have preached the word
of the Lord, *and see* how they are doing."
37 Now Barnabas was determined to take
with them John called Mark.
38 But Paul insisted that they should not take
with them the one who had departed from
them in Pamphylia, and had not gone with
them to the work.

15:11 [a]NU-Text and M-Text omit *Christ.* **15:17** [a]Amos 9:11, 12 **15:18** [a]NU-Text (combining with verse 17) reads *Says the Lord, who makes these things known from eternity (of old).* **15:20** [a]Or *fornication* **15:22** [a]NU-Text and M-Text read *Barsabbas.* **15:24** [a]NU-Text omits *saying, "You must be circumcised and keep the law."* **15:29** [a]Or *fornication* **15:33** [a]NU-Text reads *to those who had sent them.* **15:34** [a]NU-Text and M-Text omit this verse.

39 Then the contention became so sharp that
they parted from one another. And so Barna-
bas took Mark and sailed to Cyprus;
40 but Paul chose Silas and departed, being
commended by the brethren to the grace of God.
41 And he went through Syria and Cilicia,
strengthening the churches.

Timothy Joins Paul and Silas

16 Then he came to Derbe and Lystra. And
behold, a certain disciple was there, named
Timothy, *the* son of a certain Jewish woman
who believed, but his father *was* Greek.
2 He was well spoken of by the brethren who
were at Lystra and Iconium.
3 Paul wanted to have him go on with him.
And he took *him* and circumcised him because
of the Jews who were in that region, for they
all knew that his father was Greek.
4 And as they went through the cities, they
delivered to them the decrees to keep, which
were determined by the apostles and elders at
Jerusalem.
5 So the churches were strengthened in the
faith, and increased in number daily.

The Macedonian Call

6 Now when they had gone through Phrygia
and the region of Galatia, they were forbidden
by the Holy Spirit to preach the word in Asia.
7 After they had come to Mysia, they tried to
go into Bithynia, but the Spirit[a] did not permit
them.
8 So passing by Mysia, they came down to
Troas.
9 And a vision appeared to Paul in the night.
A man of Macedonia stood and pleaded with
him, saying, "Come over to Macedonia and help
us."
10 Now after he had seen the vision, immedi-
ately we sought to go to Macedonia, conclud-
ing that the Lord had called us to preach the
gospel to them.

Lydia Baptized at Philippi

11 Therefore, sailing from Troas, we ran a
straight course to Samothrace, and the next
day came to Neapolis,
12 and from there to Philippi, which is the
foremost city of that part of Macedonia, a col-
ony. And we were staying in that city for some
days.
13 And on the Sabbath day we went out of
the city to the riverside, where prayer was cus-
tomarily made; and we sat down and spoke to
the women who met *there.*
14 Now a certain woman named Lydia heard
us. She was a seller of purple from the city of
Thyatira, who worshiped God. The Lord
opened her heart to heed the things spoken by
Paul.
15 And when she and her household were
baptized, she begged *us,* saying, "If you have
judged me to be faithful to the Lord, come to
my house and stay." So she persuaded us.

Paul and Silas Imprisoned

16 Now it happened, as we went to prayer,
that a certain slave girl possessed with a spirit
of divination met us, who brought her masters
much profit by fortune-telling.
17 This girl followed Paul and us, and cried
out, saying, "These men are the servants of the
Most High God, who proclaim to us the way of
salvation."
18 And this she did for many days. But Paul,
greatly annoyed, turned and said to the spirit,
"I command you in the name of Jesus Christ
to come out of her." And he came out that very
hour.
19 But when her masters saw that their hope
of profit was gone, they seized Paul and Silas
and dragged *them* into the marketplace to the
authorities.
20 And they brought them to the magistrates,
and said, "These men, being Jews, exceedingly
trouble our city;
21 "and they teach customs which are not
lawful for us, being Romans, to receive or ob-
serve."
22 Then the multitude rose up together against
them; and the magistrates tore off their clothes
and commanded *them* to be beaten with rods.
23 And when they had laid many stripes on
them, they threw *them* into prison, command-
ing the jailer to keep them securely.
24 Having received such a charge, he put them
into the inner prison and fastened their feet in
the stocks.

The Philippian Jailer Saved

25 But at midnight Paul and Silas were pray-
ing and singing hymns to God, and the prison-
ers were listening to them.
26 Suddenly there was a great earthquake, so
that the foundations of the prison were shaken;
and immediately all the doors were opened and
everyone's chains were loosed.
27 And the keeper of the prison, awaking from
sleep and seeing the prison doors open, sup-
posing the prisoners had fled, drew his sword
and was about to kill himself.
28 But Paul called with a loud voice, saying,
"Do yourself no harm, for we are all here."
29 Then he called for a light, ran in, and fell
down trembling before Paul and Silas.
30 And he brought them out and said, "Sirs,
what must I do to be saved?"
31 So they said, "Believe on the Lord Jesus
Christ, and you will be saved, you and your
household."
32 Then they spoke the word of the Lord to
him and to all who were in his house.
33 And he took them the same hour of the
night and washed *their* stripes. And immedi-
ately he and all his *family* were baptized.
34 Now when he had brought them into his
house, he set food before them; and he rejoiced,
having believed in God with all his household.

Paul Refuses to Depart Secretly

35 And when it was day, the magistrates sent
the officers, saying, "Let those men go."
36 So the keeper of the prison reported these
words to Paul, saying, "The magistrates have
sent to let you go. Now therefore depart, and go
in peace."
37 But Paul said to them, "They have beaten
us openly, uncondemned Romans, *and* have
thrown *us* into prison. And now do they put us
out secretly? No indeed! Let them come them-
selves and get us out."
38 And the officers told these words to the
magistrates, and they were afraid when they
heard that they were Romans.
39 Then they came and pleaded with them and

16:7 [a]NU-Text adds *of Jesus.*

brought *them* out, and asked *them* to depart from the city.
40 So they went out of the prison and entered *the house of* Lydia; and when they had seen the brethren, they encouraged them and departed.

Preaching Christ at Thessalonica

17 Now when they had passed through Amphipolis and Apollonia, they came to Thessalonica, where there was a synagogue of the Jews.
2 Then Paul, as his custom was, went in to them, and for three Sabbaths reasoned with them from the Scriptures,
3 explaining and demonstrating that the Christ had to suffer and rise again from the dead, and *saying,* "This Jesus whom I preach to you is the Christ."
4 And some of them were persuaded; and a great multitude of the devout Greeks, and not a few of the leading women, joined Paul and Silas.

Assault on Jason's House

5 But the Jews who were not persuaded, becoming envious,[a] took some of the evil men from the marketplace, and gathering a mob, set all the city in an uproar and attacked the house of Jason, and sought to bring them out to the people.
6 But when they did not find them, they dragged Jason and some brethren to the rulers of the city, crying out, "These who have turned the world upside down have come here too.
7 "Jason has harbored them, and these are all acting contrary to the decrees of Caesar, saying there is another king—Jesus."
8 And they troubled the crowd and the rulers of the city when they heard these things.
9 So when they had taken security from Jason and the rest, they let them go.

Ministering at Berea

10 Then the brethren immediately sent Paul and Silas away by night to Berea. When they arrived, they went into the synagogue of the Jews.
11 These were more fair-minded than those in Thessalonica, in that they received the word with all readiness, and searched the Scriptures daily *to find out* whether these things were so.
12 Therefore many of them believed, and also not a few of the Greeks, prominent women as well as men.
13 But when the Jews from Thessalonica learned that the word of God was preached by Paul at Berea, they came there also and stirred up the crowds.
14 Then immediately the brethren sent Paul away, to go to the sea; but both Silas and Timothy remained there.
15 So those who conducted Paul brought him to Athens; and receiving a command for Silas and Timothy to come to him with all speed, they departed.

The Philosophers at Athens

16 Now while Paul waited for them at Athens, his spirit was provoked within him when he saw that the city was given over to idols.
17 Therefore he reasoned in the synagogue with the Jews and with the *Gentile* worshipers, and in the marketplace daily with those who happened to be there.
18 Then[a] certain Epicurean and Stoic philosophers encountered him. And some said, "What does this babbler want to say?" Others said, "He seems to be a proclaimer of foreign gods," because he preached to them Jesus and the resurrection.
19 And they took him and brought him to the Areopagus, saying, "May we know what this new doctrine *is* of which you speak?
20 "For you are bringing some strange things to our ears. Therefore we want to know what these things mean."
21 For all the Athenians and the foreigners who were there spent their time in nothing else but either to tell or to hear some new thing.

Addressing the Areopagus

22 Then Paul stood in the midst of the Areopagus and said, "Men of Athens, I perceive that in all things you are very religious;
23 "for as I was passing through and considering the objects of your worship, I even found an altar with this inscription:

TO THE UNKNOWN GOD.

Therefore, the One whom you worship without knowing, Him I proclaim to you:
24 "God, who made the world and everything in it, since He is Lord of heaven and earth, does not dwell in temples made with hands.
25 "Nor is He worshiped with men's hands, as though He needed anything, since He gives to all life, breath, and all things.
26 "And He has made from one blood[a] every nation of men to dwell on all the face of the earth, and has determined their preappointed times and the boundaries of their dwellings,
27 "so that they should seek the Lord, in the hope that they might grope for Him and find Him, though He is not far from each one of us;
28 "for in Him we live and move and have our being, as also some of your own poets have said, 'For we are also His offspring.'
29 "Therefore, since we are the offspring of God, we ought not to think that the Divine Nature is like gold or silver or stone, something shaped by art and man's devising.
30 "Truly, these times of ignorance God overlooked, but now commands all men everywhere to repent,
31 "because He has appointed a day on which He will judge the world in righteousness by the Man whom He has ordained. He has given assurance of this to all by raising Him from the dead."
32 And when they heard of the resurrection of the dead, some mocked, while others said, "We will hear you again on this *matter.*"
33 So Paul departed from among them.
34 However, some men joined him and believed, among them Dionysius the Areopagite, a woman named Damaris, and others with them.

Ministering at Corinth

18 After these things Paul departed from Athens and went to Corinth.
2 And he found a certain Jew named Aquila, born in Pontus, who had recently come from Italy with his wife Priscilla (because Claudius

17:5 [a]NU-Text omits *who were not persuaded;* M-Text omits *becoming envious.* **17:18** [a]NU-Text and M-Text add *also.* **17:26** [a]NU-Text omits *blood.*

had commanded all the Jews to depart from
Rome); and he came to them.
3 So, because he was of the same trade, he
stayed with them and worked; for by occupation
they were tentmakers.
4 And he reasoned in the synagogue every
Sabbath, and persuaded both Jews and Greeks.
5 When Silas and Timothy had come from
Macedonia, Paul was compelled by the Spirit,
and testified to the Jews *that* Jesus *is* the
Christ.
6 But when they opposed him and blas-
phemed, he shook *his* garments and said to
them, "Your blood *be* upon your *own* heads; I
am clean. From now on I will go to the Gen-
tiles."
7 And he departed from there and entered
the house of a certain *man* named Justus,[a] *one*
who worshiped God, whose house was next
door to the synagogue.
8 Then Crispus, the ruler of the synagogue,
believed on the Lord with all his household.
And many of the Corinthians, hearing, believed
and were baptized.
9 Now the Lord spoke to Paul in the night
by a vision, "Do not be afraid, but speak, and
do not keep silent;
10 "for I am with you, and no one will attack
you to hurt you; for I have many people in this
city."
11 And he continued *there* a year and six
months, teaching the word of God among
them.
12 When Gallio was proconsul of Achaia, the
Jews with one accord rose up against Paul and
brought him to the judgment seat,
13 saying, "This *fellow* persuades men to wor-
ship God contrary to the law."
14 And when Paul was about to open *his*
mouth, Gallio said to the Jews, "If it were a
matter of wrongdoing or wicked crimes,
O Jews, there would be reason why I should
bear with you.
15 "But if it is a question of words and names
and your own law, look *to it* yourselves; for I
do not want to be a judge of such *matters*."
16 And he drove them from the judgment
seat.
17 Then all the Greeks[a] took Sosthenes, the
ruler of the synagogue, and beat *him* before
the judgment seat. But Gallio took no notice of
these things.

Paul Returns to Antioch

18 So Paul still remained a good while. Then
he took leave of the brethren and sailed for
Syria, and Priscilla and Aquila *were* with him.
He had *his* hair cut off at Cenchrea, for he had
taken a vow.
19 And he came to Ephesus, and left them
there; but he himself entered the synagogue
and reasoned with the Jews.
20 When they asked *him* to stay a longer time
with them, he did not consent,
21 but took leave of them, saying, "I must by
all means keep this coming feast in Jerusalem;[a]
but I will return again to you, God willing."
And he sailed from Ephesus.
22 And when he had landed at Caesarea, and
gone up and greeted the church, he went down
to Antioch.
23 After he had spent some time *there,* he de-
parted and went over the region of Galatia and
Phrygia in order, strengthening all the disciples.

Ministry of Apollos

24 Now a certain Jew named Apollos, born at
Alexandria, an eloquent man *and* mighty in
the Scriptures, came to Ephesus.
25 This man had been instructed in the way
of the Lord; and being fervent in spirit, he spoke
and taught accurately the things of the Lord,
though he knew only the baptism of John.
26 So he began to speak boldly in the syna-
gogue. When Aquila and Priscilla heard him,
they took him aside and explained to him the
way of God more accurately.
27 And when he desired to cross to Achaia,
the brethren wrote, exhorting the disciples to
receive him; and when he arrived, he greatly
helped those who had believed through grace;
28 for he vigorously refuted the Jews publicly,
showing from the Scriptures that Jesus is the
Christ.

Paul at Ephesus

19 And it happened, while Apollos was at
Corinth, that Paul, having passed through
the upper regions, came to Ephesus. And find-
ing some disciples
2 he said to them, "Did you receive the Holy
Spirit when you believed?" So they said to him,
"We have not so much as heard whether there
is a Holy Spirit."
3 And he said to them, "Into what then were
you baptized?" So they said, "Into John's bap-
tism."
4 Then Paul said, "John indeed baptized with
a baptism of repentance, saying to the people
that they should believe on Him who would
come after him, that is, on Christ Jesus."
5 When they heard *this,* they were baptized
in the name of the Lord Jesus.
6 And when Paul had laid hands on them, the
Holy Spirit came upon them, and they spoke
with tongues and prophesied.
7 Now the men were about twelve in all.
8 And he went into the synagogue and spoke
boldly for three months, reasoning and per-
suading concerning the things of the kingdom
of God.
9 But when some were hardened and did not
believe, but spoke evil of the Way before the
multitude, he departed from them and withdrew
the disciples, reasoning daily in the school of
Tyrannus.
10 And this continued for two years, so that
all who dwelt in Asia heard the word of the
Lord Jesus, both Jews and Greeks.

Miracles Glorify Christ

11 Now God worked unusual miracles by the
hands of Paul,
12 so that even handkerchiefs or aprons were
brought from his body to the sick, and the dis-
eases left them and the evil spirits went out of
them.
13 Then some of the itinerant Jewish exor-
cists took it upon themselves to call the name
of the Lord Jesus over those who had evil spir-
its, saying, "We[a] exorcise you by the Jesus
whom Paul preaches."

18:7 [a]NU-Text reads *Titius Justus.* 18:17 [a]NU-Text reads *they all.* 18:21 [a]NU-Text omits *I must* through *Jerusalem.* 19:13 [a]NU-Text reads *I.*

14 Also there were seven sons of Sceva, a
Jewish chief priest, who did so.
15 And the evil spirit answered and said,
"Jesus I know, and Paul I know; but who are
you?"
16 Then the man in whom the evil spirit was
leaped on them, overpowered[a] them, and pre-
vailed against them,[b] so that they fled out of
that house naked and wounded.
17 This became known both to all Jews and
Greeks dwelling in Ephesus; and fear fell on
them all, and the name of the Lord Jesus was
magnified.
18 And many who had believed came confess-
ing and telling their deeds.
19 Also, many of those who had practiced
magic brought their books together and burned
them in the sight of all. And they counted up
the value of them, and *it* totaled fifty thousand
pieces of silver.
20 So the word of the Lord grew mightily and
prevailed.

The Riot at Ephesus

21 When these things were accomplished,
Paul purposed in the Spirit, when he had
passed through Macedonia and Achaia, to go
to Jerusalem, saying, "After I have been there,
I must also see Rome."
22 So he sent into Macedonia two of those
who ministered to him, Timothy and Erastus,
but he himself stayed in Asia for a time.
23 And about that time there arose a great com-
motion about the Way.
24 For a certain man named Demetrius, a sil-
versmith, who made silver shrines of Diana,[a]
brought no small profit to the craftsmen.
25 He called them together with the workers
of similar occupation, and said: "Men, you
know that we have our prosperity by this trade.
26 "Moreover you see and hear that not only
at Ephesus, but throughout almost all Asia, this
Paul has persuaded and turned away many
people, saying that they are not gods which are
made with hands.
27 "So not only is this trade of ours in danger
of falling into disrepute, but also the temple of
the great goddess Diana may be despised and
her magnificence destroyed,[a] whom all Asia and
the world worship."
28 Now when they heard *this*, they were full
of wrath and cried out, saying, "Great *is* Diana
of the Ephesians!"
29 So the whole city was filled with confu-
sion, and rushed into the theater with one ac-
cord, having seized Gaius and Aristarchus,
Macedonians, Paul's travel companions.
30 And when Paul wanted to go in to the peo-
ple, the disciples would not allow him.
31 Then some of the officials of Asia, who were
his friends, sent to him pleading that he would
not venture into the theater.
32 Some therefore cried one thing and some
another, for the assembly was confused, and
most of them did not know why they had come
together.
33 And they drew Alexander out of the multi-
tude, the Jews putting him forward. And Alex-
ander motioned with his hand, and wanted to
make his defense to the people.
34 But when they found out that he was a
Jew, all with one voice cried out for about two
hours, "Great *is* Diana of the Ephesians!"
35 And when the city clerk had quieted the
crowd, he said: "Men of Ephesus, what man is
there who does not know that the city of the
Ephesians is temple guardian of the great god-
dess Diana, and of the *image* which fell down
from Zeus?
36 "Therefore, since these things cannot be
denied, you ought to be quiet and do nothing
rashly.
37 "For you have brought these men here who
are neither robbers of temples nor blasphem-
ers of your[a] goddess.
38 "Therefore, if Demetrius and his fellow
craftsmen have a case against anyone, the courts
are open and there are proconsuls. Let them
bring charges against one another.
39 "But if you have any other inquiry to make,
it shall be determined in the lawful assembly.
40 "For we are in danger of being called in
question for today's uproar, there being no rea-
son which we may give to account for this dis-
orderly gathering."
41 And when he had said these things, he dis-
missed the assembly.

Journeys in Greece

20 After the uproar had ceased, Paul called
the disciples to *himself*, embraced *them*,
and departed to go to Macedonia.
2 Now when he had gone over that region
and encouraged them with many words, he
came to Greece
3 and stayed three months. And when the
Jews plotted against him as he was about to
sail to Syria, he decided to return through Mac-
edonia.
4 And Sopater of Berea accompanied him to
Asia—also Aristarchus and Secundus of the
Thessalonians, and Gaius of Derbe, and Timo-
thy, and Tychicus and Trophimus of Asia.
5 These men, going ahead, waited for us at
Troas.
6 But we sailed away from Philippi after the
Days of Unleavened Bread, and in five days
joined them at Troas, where we stayed seven
days.

Ministering at Troas

7 Now on the first *day* of the week, when the
disciples came together to break bread, Paul,
ready to depart the next day, spoke to them and
continued his message until midnight.
8 There were many lamps in the upper room
where they[a] were gathered together.
9 And in a window sat a certain young man
named Eutychus, who was sinking into a deep
sleep. He was overcome by sleep; and as Paul
continued speaking, he fell down from the
third story and was taken up dead.
10 But Paul went down, fell on him, and em-
bracing *him* said, "Do not trouble yourselves,
for his life is in him."
11 Now when he had come up, had broken
bread and eaten, and talked a long while, even
till daybreak, he departed.
12 And they brought the young man in alive,
and they were not a little comforted.

19:16 [a]M-Text reads *and they overpowered.* [b]NU-Text reads *both of them.* **19:24** [a]Greek *Artemis* **19:27** [a]NU-Text reads *she be deposed from her magnificence.* **19:37** [a]NU-Text reads *our.* **20:8** [a]NU-Text and M-Text read *we.*

From Troas to Miletus

13 Then we went ahead to the ship and sailed
to Assos, there intending to take Paul on board;
for so he had given orders, intending himself
to go on foot.
14 And when he met us at Assos, we took him
on board and came to Mitylene.
15 We sailed from there, and the next *day*
came opposite Chios. The following *day* we
arrived at Samos and stayed at Trogyllium.
The next *day* we came to Miletus.
16 For Paul had decided to sail past Ephesus,
so that he would not have to spend time in
Asia; for he was hurrying to be at Jerusalem,
if possible, on the Day of Pentecost.

The Ephesian Elders Exhorted

17 From Miletus he sent to Ephesus and
called for the elders of the church.
18 And when they had come to him, he said
to them: "You know, from the first day that I
came to Asia, in what manner I always lived
among you,
19 "serving the Lord with all humility, with
many tears and trials which happened to me
by the plotting of the Jews;
20 "how I kept back nothing that was helpful,
but proclaimed it to you, and taught you pub-
licly and from house to house,
21 "testifying to Jews, and also to Greeks, re-
pentance toward God and faith toward our
Lord Jesus Christ.
22 "And see, now I go bound in the spirit to
Jerusalem, not knowing the things that will
happen to me there,
23 "except that the Holy Spirit testifies in
every city, saying that chains and tribulations
await me.
24 "But none of these things move me; nor do
I count my life dear to myself,[a] so that I may
finish my race with joy, and the ministry which
I received from the Lord Jesus, to testify to the
gospel of the grace of God.
25 "And indeed, now I know that you all,
among whom I have gone preaching the king-
dom of God, will see my face no more.
26 "Therefore I testify to you this day that I
am innocent of the blood of all *men*.
27 "For I have not shunned to declare to you
the whole counsel of God.
28 "Therefore take heed to yourselves and to
all the flock, among which the Holy Spirit has
made you overseers, to shepherd the church of
God[a] which He purchased with His own blood.
29 "For I know this, that after my departure
savage wolves will come in among you, not
sparing the flock.
30 "Also from among yourselves men will rise
up, speaking perverse things, to draw away the
disciples after themselves.
31 "Therefore watch, and remember that for
three years I did not cease to warn everyone
night and day with tears.
32 "So now, brethren, I commend you to God
and to the word of His grace, which is able to
build you up and give you an inheritance
among all those who are sanctified.
33 "I have coveted no one's silver or gold or
apparel.
34 "Yes,[a] you yourselves know that these hands
have provided for my necessities, and for those
who were with me.
35 "I have shown you in every way, by labor-
ing like this, that you must support the weak.
And remember the words of the Lord Jesus,
that He said, 'It is more blessed to give than to
receive.' "
36 And when he had said these things, he
knelt down and prayed with them all.
37 Then they all wept freely, and fell on Paul's
neck and kissed him,
38 sorrowing most of all for the words which
he spoke, that they would see his face no more.
And they accompanied him to the ship.

Warnings on the Journey to Jerusalem

21 Now it came to pass, that when we had
departed from them and set sail, run-
ning a straight course we came to Cos, the
following *day* to Rhodes, and from there to
Patara.
2 And finding a ship sailing over to Phoe-
nicia, we went aboard and set sail.
3 When we had sighted Cyprus, we passed
it on the left, sailed to Syria, and landed at Tyre;
for there the ship was to unload her cargo.
4 And finding disciples,[a] we stayed there
seven days. They told Paul through the Spirit
not to go up to Jerusalem.
5 When we had come to the end of those
days, we departed and went on our way; and
they all accompanied us, with wives and chil-
dren, till *we were* out of the city. And we knelt
down on the shore and prayed.
6 When we had taken our leave of one an-
other, we boarded the ship, and they returned
home.
7 And when we had finished *our* voyage
from Tyre, we came to Ptolemais, greeted the
brethren, and stayed with them one day.
8 On the next *day* we who were Paul's com-
panions[a] departed and came to Caesarea, and
entered the house of Philip the evangelist, who
was *one* of the seven, and stayed with him.
9 Now this man had four virgin daughters
who prophesied.
10 And as we stayed many days, a certain
prophet named Agabus came down from Judea.
11 When he had come to us, he took Paul's
belt, bound his *own* hands and feet, and said,
"Thus says the Holy Spirit, 'So shall the Jews
at Jerusalem bind the man who owns this belt,
and deliver *him* into the hands of the Gen-
tiles.' "
12 Now when we heard these things, both we
and those from that place pleaded with him not
to go up to Jerusalem.
13 Then Paul answered, "What do you mean
by weeping and breaking my heart? For I am
ready not only to be bound, but also to die at
Jerusalem for the name of the Lord Jesus."
14 So when he would not be persuaded, we
ceased, saying, "The will of the Lord be done."

Paul Urged to Make Peace

15 And after those days we packed and went
up to Jerusalem.
16 Also some of the disciples from Caesarea
went with us and brought with them a certain
Mnason of Cyprus, an early disciple, with
whom we were to lodge.

20:24 [a]NU-Text reads *But I do not count my life of any value or dear to myself.* **20:28** [a]M-Text reads *of the Lord and God.* **20:34** [a]NU-Text and M-Text omit *Yes.* **21:4** [a]NU-Text reads *the disciples.* **21:8** [a]NU-Text omits *who were Paul's companions.*

17 And when we had come to Jerusalem, the
brethren received us gladly.
18 On the following *day* Paul went in with us
to James, and all the elders were present.
19 When he had greeted them, he told in detail those things which God had done among
the Gentiles through his ministry.
20 And when they heard *it*, they glorified the
Lord. And they said to him, "You see, brother,
how many myriads of Jews there are who have
believed, and they are all zealous for the law;
21 "but they have been informed about you that
you teach all the Jews who are among the Gentiles to forsake Moses, saying that they ought
not to circumcise *their* children nor to walk
according to the customs.
22 "What then? The assembly must certainly
meet, for they will[a] hear that you have come.
23 "Therefore do what we tell you: We have
four men who have taken a vow.
24 "Take them and be purified with them, and
pay their expenses so that they may shave *their*
heads, and that all may know that those things
of which they were informed concerning you
are nothing, but *that* you yourself also walk
orderly and keep the law.
25 "But concerning the Gentiles who believe,
we have written *and* decided that they should
observe no such thing, except[a] that they should
keep themselves from *things* offered to idols,
from blood, from things strangled, and from
sexual immorality."

Arrested in the Temple

26 Then Paul took the men, and the next day,
having been purified with them, entered the
temple to announce the expiration of the days
of purification, at which time an offering should
be made for each one of them.
27 Now when the seven days were almost
ended, the Jews from Asia, seeing him in the
temple, stirred up the whole crowd and laid
hands on him,
28 crying out, "Men of Israel, help! This is the
man who teaches all *men* everywhere against
the people, the law, and this place; and furthermore he also brought Greeks into the temple
and has defiled this holy place."
29 (For they had previously[a] seen Trophimus
the Ephesian with him in the city, whom they
supposed that Paul had brought into the temple.)
30 And all the city was disturbed; and the people ran together, seized Paul, and dragged him
out of the temple; and immediately the doors
were shut.
31 Now as they were seeking to kill him, news
came to the commander of the garrison that
all Jerusalem was in an uproar.
32 He immediately took soldiers and centurions, and ran down to them. And when they saw
the commander and the soldiers, they stopped
beating Paul.
33 Then the commander came near and took
him, and commanded *him* to be bound with
two chains; and he asked who he was and what
he had done.
34 And some among the multitude cried one
thing and some another. So when he could not
ascertain the truth because of the tumult, he
commanded him to be taken into the barracks.
35 When he reached the stairs, he had to be
carried by the soldiers because of the violence
of the mob.
36 For the multitude of the people followed
after, crying out, "Away with him!"

Addressing the Jerusalem Mob

37 Then as Paul was about to be led into the
barracks, he said to the commander, "May I
speak to you?" He replied, "Can you speak
Greek?
38 "Are you not the Egyptian who some time
ago stirred up a rebellion and led the four thousand assassins out into the wilderness?"
39 But Paul said, "I am a Jew from Tarsus, in
Cilicia, a citizen of no mean city; and I implore
you, permit me to speak to the people."
40 So when he had given him permission,
Paul stood on the stairs and motioned with his
hand to the people. And when there was a great
silence, he spoke to *them* in the Hebrew language, saying,

22 "Brethren and fathers, hear my defense
before you now."
2 And when they heard that he spoke to
them in the Hebrew language, they kept all the
more silent. Then he said:
3 "I am indeed a Jew, born in Tarsus of Cilicia, but brought up in this city at the feet of
Gamaliel, taught according to the strictness of
our fathers' law, and was zealous toward God
as you all are today.
4 "I persecuted this Way to the death, binding and delivering into prisons both men and
women,
5 "as also the high priest bears me witness,
and all the council of the elders, from whom I
also received letters to the brethren, and went
to Damascus to bring in chains even those who
were there to Jerusalem to be punished.
6 "Now it happened, as I journeyed and came
near Damascus at about noon, suddenly a great
light from heaven shone around me.
7 "And I fell to the ground and heard a voice
saying to me, 'Saul, Saul, why are you persecuting Me?'
8 "So I answered, 'Who are You, Lord?' And
He said to me, 'I am Jesus of Nazareth, whom
you are persecuting.'
9 "And those who were with me indeed saw
the light and were afraid,[a] but they did not hear
the voice of Him who spoke to me.
10 "So I said, 'What shall I do, Lord?' And the
Lord said to me, 'Arise and go into Damascus,
and there you will be told all things which are
appointed for you to do.'
11 "And since I could not see for the glory of
that light, being led by the hand of those who
were with me, I came into Damascus.
12 "Then a certain Ananias, a devout man according to the law, having a good testimony
with all the Jews who dwelt *there*,
13 "came to me; and he stood and said to me,
'Brother Saul, receive your sight.' And at that
same hour I looked up at him.
14 "Then he said, 'The God of our fathers has
chosen you that you should know His will, and
see the Just One, and hear the voice of His mouth.
15 'For you will be His witness to all men of
what you have seen and heard.
16 'And now why are you waiting? Arise and
be baptized, and wash away your sins, calling
on the name of the Lord.'

21:22 [a]NU-Text reads *What then is to be done? They will certainly.* **21:25** [a]NU-Text omits *that they should observe no such thing, except.* **21:29** [a]M-Text omits *previously.* **22:9** [a]NU-Text omits *and were afraid.*

17 "Now it happened, when I returned to Je-
rusalem and was praying in the temple, that I
was in a trance
18 "and saw Him saying to me, 'Make haste
and get out of Jerusalem quickly, for they will
not receive your testimony concerning Me.'
19 "So I said, 'Lord, they know that in every
synagogue I imprisoned and beat those who
believe on You.
20 'And when the blood of Your martyr Ste-
phen was shed, I also was standing by consent-
ing to his death,[a] and guarding the clothes of
those who were killing him.'
21 "Then He said to me, 'Depart, for I will
send you far from here to the Gentiles.'"

Paul's Roman Citizenship

22 And they listened to him until this word,
and *then* they raised their voices and said,
"Away with such a *fellow* from the earth, for he
is not fit to live!"
23 Then, as they cried out and tore off *their*
clothes and threw dust into the air,
24 the commander ordered him to be brought
into the barracks, and said that he should be
examined under scourging, so that he might
know why they shouted so against him.
25 And as they bound him with thongs, Paul
said to the centurion who stood by, "Is it lawful
for you to scourge a man who is a Roman, and
uncondemned?"
26 When the centurion heard *that*, he went
and told the commander, saying, "Take care
what you do, for this man is a Roman."
27 Then the commander came and said to him,
"Tell me, are you a Roman?" He said, "Yes."
28 The commander answered, "With a large
sum I obtained this citizenship." And Paul said,
"But I was born *a citizen*."
29 Then immediately those who were about
to examine him withdrew from him; and the
commander was also afraid after he found out
that he was a Roman, and because he had
bound him.

The Sanhedrin Divided

30 The next day, because he wanted to know
for certain why he was accused by the Jews,
he released him from *his* bonds, and com-
manded the chief priests and all their council
to appear, and brought Paul down and set him
before them.

23 Then Paul, looking earnestly at the
council, said, "Men *and* brethren, I have
lived in all good conscience before God until
this day."
2 And the high priest Ananias commanded
those who stood by him to strike him on the
mouth.
3 Then Paul said to him, "God will strike
you, *you* whitewashed wall! For you sit to judge
me according to the law, and do you command
me to be struck contrary to the law?"
4 And those who stood by said, "Do you re-
vile God's high priest?"
5 Then Paul said, "I did not know, brethren,
that he was the high priest; for it is written, *'You
shall not speak evil of a ruler of your people.'* "[a]
6 But when Paul perceived that one part were
Sadducees and the other Pharisees, he cried
out in the council, "Men *and* brethren, I am a
Pharisee, the son of a Pharisee; concerning the
hope and resurrection of the dead I am being
judged!"
7 And when he had said this, a dissension
arose between the Pharisees and the Saddu-
cees; and the assembly was divided.
8 For Sadducees say that there is no resur-
rection—and no angel or spirit; but the Phari-
sees confess both.
9 Then there arose a loud outcry. And the
scribes of the Pharisees' party arose and pro-
tested, saying, "We find no evil in this man; but
if a spirit or an angel has spoken to him, let us
not fight against God."[a]
10 Now when there arose a great dissension,
the commander, fearing lest Paul might be
pulled to pieces by them, commanded the sol-
diers to go down and take him by force from
among them, and bring *him* into the barracks.

The Plot Against Paul

11 But the following night the Lord stood by
him and said, "Be of good cheer, Paul; for as
you have testified for Me in Jerusalem, so you
must also bear witness at Rome."
12 And when it was day, some of the Jews
banded together and bound themselves under
an oath, saying that they would neither eat nor
drink till they had killed Paul.
13 Now there were more than forty who had
formed this conspiracy.
14 They came to the chief priests and elders,
and said, "We have bound ourselves under a
great oath that we will eat nothing until we have
killed Paul.
15 "Now you, therefore, together with the coun-
cil, suggest to the commander that he be
brought down to you tomorrow,[a] as though you
were going to make further inquiries concern-
ing him; but we are ready to kill him before he
comes near."
16 So when Paul's sister's son heard of their
ambush, he went and entered the barracks and
told Paul.
17 Then Paul called one of the centurions to
him and said, "Take this young man to the
commander, for he has something to tell him."
18 So he took him and brought *him* to the
commander and said, "Paul the prisoner called
me to *him* and asked *me* to bring this young
man to you. He has something to say to you."
19 Then the commander took him by the hand,
went aside, and asked privately, "What is it that
you have to tell me?"
20 And he said, "The Jews have agreed to ask
that you bring Paul down to the council tomor-
row, as though they were going to inquire more
fully about him.
21 "But do not yield to them, for more than
forty of them lie in wait for him, men who have
bound themselves by an oath that they will
neither eat nor drink till they have killed him;
and now they are ready, waiting for the prom-
ise from you."
22 So the commander let the young man de-
part, and commanded *him*, "Tell no one that
you have revealed these things to me."

Sent to Felix

23 And he called for two centurions, saying,
"Prepare two hundred soldiers, seventy horse-
men, and two hundred spearmen to go to Caes-
area at the third hour of the night;

22:20 [a]NU-Text omits *to his death.* **23:5** [a]Exodus 22:28 **23:9** [a]NU-Text omits last clause and reads *what if a spirit or an angel has spoken to him?* **23:15** [a]NU-Text omits *tomorrow.*

24 "and provide mounts to set Paul on, and
bring *him* safely to Felix the governor."
25 He wrote a letter in the following manner:

26 Claudius Lysias,

To the most excellent governor Felix:

Greetings.

27 This man was seized by the Jews and was
about to be killed by them. Coming with
the troops I rescued him, having learned
that he was a Roman.
28 And when I wanted to know the reason
they accused him, I brought him before
their council.
29 I found out that he was accused
concerning questions of their law, but
had nothing charged against him
deserving of death or chains.
30 And when it was told me that the Jews
lay in wait for the man,[a] I sent him
immediately to you, and also commanded
his accusers to state before you the
charges against him.

Farewell.

31 Then the soldiers, as they were commanded,
took Paul and brought *him* by night to Antipa-
tris.
32 The next day they left the horsemen to go
on with him, and returned to the barracks.
33 When they came to Caesarea and had de-
livered the letter to the governor, they also pre-
sented Paul to him.
34 And when the governor had read *it*, he
asked what province he was from. And when
he understood that *he was* from Cilicia,
35 he said, "I will hear you when your accus-
ers also have come." And he commanded him
to be kept in Herod's Praetorium.

Accused of Sedition

24 Now after five days Ananias the high
priest came down with the elders and
a certain orator *named* Tertullus. These gave
evidence to the governor against Paul.
2 And when he was called upon, Tertullus be-
gan his accusation, saying: "Seeing that through
you we enjoy great peace, and prosperity is
being brought to this nation by your foresight,
3 "we accept *it* always and in all places, most
noble Felix, with all thankfulness.
4 "Nevertheless, not to be tedious to you any
further, I beg you to hear, by your courtesy, a
few words from us.
5 "For we have found this man a plague, a
creator of dissension among all the Jews
throughout the world, and a ringleader of the
sect of the Nazarenes.
6 "He even tried to profane the temple, and
we seized him,[a] and wanted to judge him ac-
cording to our law.
7 "But the commander Lysias came by and
with great violence took *him* out of our hands,
8 "commanding his accusers to come to you.
By examining him yourself you may ascertain
all these things of which we accuse him."
9 And the Jews also assented,[a] maintaining
that these things were so.

The Defense Before Felix

10 Then Paul, after the governor had nodded
to him to speak, answered: "Inasmuch as I
know that you have been for many years a
judge of this nation, I do the more cheerfully
answer for myself,
11 "because you may ascertain that it is no
more than twelve days since I went up to Jeru-
salem to worship.
12 "And they neither found me in the temple
disputing with anyone nor inciting the crowd,
either in the synagogues or in the city.
13 "Nor can they prove the things of which
they now accuse me.
14 "But this I confess to you, that according
to the Way which they call a sect, so I worship
the God of my fathers, believing all things
which are written in the Law and in the
Prophets.
15 "I have hope in God, which they them-
selves also accept, that there will be a resurrec-
tion of *the* dead,[a] both of *the* just and *the*
unjust.
16 "This *being* so, I myself always strive to
have a conscience without offense toward God
and men.
17 "Now after many years I came to bring alms
and offerings to my nation,
18 "in the midst of which some Jews from
Asia found me purified in the temple, neither
with a mob nor with tumult.
19 "They ought to have been here before you
to object if they had anything against me.
20 "Or else let those who are *here* themselves
say if they found any wrongdoing[a] in me while
I stood before the council,
21 "unless *it is* for this one statement which I
cried out, standing among them, 'Concerning
the resurrection of the dead I am being judged
by you this day.' "

Felix Procrastinates

22 But when Felix heard these things, having
more accurate knowledge of *the* Way, he ad-
journed the proceedings and said, "When Lys-
ias the commander comes down, I will make a
decision on your case."
23 So he commanded the centurion to keep
Paul and to let *him* have liberty, and told him
not to forbid any of his friends to provide for
or visit him.
24 And after some days, when Felix came
with his wife Drusilla, who was Jewish, he sent
for Paul and heard him concerning the faith in
Christ.
25 Now as he reasoned about righteousness,
self-control, and the judgment to come, Felix
was afraid and answered, "Go away for now;
when I have a convenient time I will call for
you."
26 Meanwhile he also hoped that money would
be given him by Paul, that he might release
him.[a] Therefore he sent for him more often and
conversed with him.
27 But after two years Porcius Festus suc-
ceeded Felix; and Felix, wanting to do the Jews
a favor, left Paul bound.

23:30 [a]NU-Text reads *there would be a plot against the man.* **24:6** [a]NU-Text ends the sentence here and omits the rest of verse 6, all of verse 7, and the first clause of verse 8. **24:9** [a]NU-Text and M-Text read *joined the attack.* **24:15** [a]NU-Text omits *of the dead.* **24:20** [a]NU-Text and M-Text read *say what wrongdoing they found.* **24:26** [a]NU-Text omits *that he might release him.*

Paul Appeals to Caesar

25 Now when Festus had come to the province, after three days he went up from Caesarea to Jerusalem.
2 Then the high priest[a] and the chief men of the Jews informed him against Paul; and they petitioned him,
3 asking a favor against him, that he would summon him to Jerusalem—while *they* lay in ambush along the road to kill him.
4 But Festus answered that Paul should be kept at Caesarea, and that he himself was going *there* shortly.
5 "Therefore," he said, "let those who have authority among you go down with *me* and accuse this man, to see if there is any fault in him."
6 And when he had remained among them more than ten days, he went down to Caesarea. And the next day, sitting on the judgment seat, he commanded Paul to be brought.
7 When he had come, the Jews who had come down from Jerusalem stood about and laid many serious complaints against Paul, which they could not prove,
8 while he answered for himself, "Neither against the law of the Jews, nor against the temple, nor against Caesar have I offended in anything at all."
9 But Festus, wanting to do the Jews a favor, answered Paul and said, "Are you willing to go up to Jerusalem and there be judged before me concerning these things?"
10 So Paul said, "I stand at Caesar's judgment seat, where I ought to be judged. To the Jews I have done no wrong, as you very well know.
11 "For if I am an offender, or have committed anything deserving of death, I do not object to dying; but if there is nothing in these things of which these men accuse me, no one can deliver me to them. I appeal to Caesar."
12 Then Festus, when he had conferred with the council, answered, "You have appealed to Caesar? To Caesar you shall go!"

Paul Before Agrippa

13 And after some days King Agrippa and Bernice came to Caesarea to greet Festus.
14 When they had been there many days, Festus laid Paul's case before the king, saying: "There is a certain man left a prisoner by Felix,
15 "about whom the chief priests and the elders of the Jews informed *me*, when I was in Jerusalem, asking for a judgment against him.
16 "To them I answered, 'It is not the custom of the Romans to deliver any man to destruction[a] before the accused meets the accusers face to face, and has opportunity to answer for himself concerning the charge against him.'
17 "Therefore when they had come together, without any delay, the next day I sat on the judgment seat and commanded the man to be brought in.
18 "When the accusers stood up, they brought no accusation against him of such things as I supposed,
19 "but had some questions against him about their own religion and about a certain Jesus, who had died, whom Paul affirmed to be alive.
20 "And because I was uncertain of such questions, I asked whether he was willing to go to Jerusalem and there be judged concerning these matters.
21 "But when Paul appealed to be reserved for the decision of Augustus, I commanded him to be kept till I could send him to Caesar."
22 Then Agrippa said to Festus, "I also would like to hear the man myself." "Tomorrow," he said, "you shall hear him."
23 So the next day, when Agrippa and Bernice had come with great pomp, and had entered the auditorium with the commanders and the prominent men of the city, at Festus' command Paul was brought in.
24 And Festus said: "King Agrippa and all the men who are here present with us, you see this man about whom the whole assembly of the Jews petitioned me, both at Jerusalem and here, crying out that he was not fit to live any longer.
25 "But when I found that he had committed nothing deserving of death, and that he himself had appealed to Augustus, I decided to send him.
26 "I have nothing certain to write to my lord concerning him. Therefore I have brought him out before you, and especially before you, King Agrippa, so that after the examination has taken place I may have something to write.
27 "For it seems to me unreasonable to send a prisoner and not to specify the charges against him."

Paul's Early Life

26 Then Agrippa said to Paul, "You are permitted to speak for yourself." So Paul stretched out his hand and answered for himself:
2 "I think myself happy, King Agrippa, because today I shall answer for myself before you concerning all the things of which I am accused by the Jews,
3 "especially because you are expert in all customs and questions which have to do with the Jews. Therefore I beg you to hear me patiently.
4 "My manner of life from my youth, which was spent from the beginning among my own nation at Jerusalem, all the Jews know.
5 "They knew me from the first, if they were willing to testify, that according to the strictest sect of our religion I lived a Pharisee.
6 "And now I stand and am judged for the hope of the promise made by God to our fathers.
7 "To this *promise* our twelve tribes, earnestly serving *God* night and day, hope to attain. For this hope's sake, King Agrippa, I am accused by the Jews.
8 "Why should it be thought incredible by you that God raises the dead?
9 "Indeed, I myself thought I must do many things contrary to the name of Jesus of Nazareth.
10 "This I also did in Jerusalem, and many of the saints I shut up in prison, having received authority from the chief priests; and when they were put to death, I cast my vote against *them*.
11 "And I punished them often in every synagogue and compelled *them* to blaspheme; and being exceedingly enraged against them, I persecuted *them* even to foreign cities.

Paul Recounts His Conversion

12 "While thus occupied, as I journeyed to Damascus with authority and commission from the chief priests,

25:2 [a]NU-Text reads *chief priests.* 25:16 [a]NU-Text omits *to destruction,* although it is implied.

13 "at midday, O king, along the road I saw a
light from heaven, brighter than the sun, shin-
ing around me and those who journeyed with
me.
14 "And when we all had fallen to the ground,
I heard a voice speaking to me and saying in
the Hebrew language, 'Saul, Saul, why are you
persecuting Me? *It is* hard for you to kick
against the goads.'
15 "So I said, 'Who are You, Lord?' And He
said, 'I am Jesus, whom you are persecuting.
16 'But rise and stand on your feet; for I have
appeared to you for this purpose, to make you
a minister and a witness both of the things
which you have seen and of the things which I
will yet reveal to you.
17 'I will deliver you from the *Jewish* people,
as well as *from* the Gentiles, to whom I now[a]
send you,
18 'to open their eyes, *in order* to turn *them*
from darkness to light, and *from* the power of
Satan to God, that they may receive forgive-
ness of sins and an inheritance among those
who are sanctified by faith in Me.'

Paul's Post-Conversion Life

19 "Therefore, King Agrippa, I was not dis-
obedient to the heavenly vision,
20 "but declared first to those in Damascus
and in Jerusalem, and throughout all the re-
gion of Judea, and *then* to the Gentiles, that
they should repent, turn to God, and do works
befitting repentance.
21 "For these reasons the Jews seized me in
the temple and tried to kill *me*.
22 "Therefore, having obtained help from God,
to this day I stand, witnessing both to small and
great, saying no other things than those which
the prophets and Moses said would come—
23 "that the Christ would suffer, that He would
be the first to rise from the dead, and would
proclaim light to the *Jewish* people and to the
Gentiles."

Agrippa Parries Paul's Challenge

24 Now as he thus made his defense, Festus
said with a loud voice, "Paul, you are beside
yourself! Much learning is driving you mad!"
25 But he said, "I am not mad, most noble Fes-
tus, but speak the words of truth and reason.
26 "For the king, before whom I also speak
freely, knows these things; for I am convinced
that none of these things escapes his attention,
since this thing was not done in a corner.
27 "King Agrippa, do you believe the proph-
ets? I know that you do believe."
28 Then Agrippa said to Paul, "You almost
persuade me to become a Christian."
29 And Paul said, "I would to God that not
only you, but also all who hear me today, might
become both almost and altogether such as I
am, except for these chains."
30 When he had said these things, the king
stood up, as well as the governor and Bernice
and those who sat with them;
31 and when they had gone aside, they talked
among themselves, saying, "This man is doing
nothing deserving of death or chains."
32 Then Agrippa said to Festus, "This man
might have been set free if he had not appealed
to Caesar."

The Voyage to Rome Begins

27 And when it was decided that we should
sail to Italy, they delivered Paul and
some other prisoners to *one* named Julius, a
centurion of the Augustan Regiment.
2 So, entering a ship of Adramyttium, we put
to sea, meaning to sail along the coasts of Asia.
Aristarchus, a Macedonian of Thessalonica,
was with us.
3 And the next *day* we landed at Sidon. And
Julius treated Paul kindly and gave *him* liberty
to go to his friends and receive care.
4 When we had put to sea from there, we
sailed under *the shelter of* Cyprus, because the
winds were contrary.
5 And when we had sailed over the sea which
is off Cilicia and Pamphylia, we came to Myra,
a city of Lycia.
6 There the centurion found an Alexandrian
ship sailing to Italy, and he put us on board.
7 When we had sailed slowly many days,
and arrived with difficulty off Cnidus, the wind
not permitting us to proceed, we sailed under
the shelter of Crete off Salmone.
8 Passing it with difficulty, we came to a place
called Fair Havens, near the city of Lasea.

Paul's Warning Ignored

9 Now when much time had been spent, and
sailing was now dangerous because the Fast
was already over, Paul advised them,
10 saying, "Men, I perceive that this voyage
will end with disaster and much loss, not only
of the cargo and ship, but also our lives."
11 Nevertheless the centurion was more per-
suaded by the helmsman and the owner of the
ship than by the things spoken by Paul.
12 And because the harbor was not suitable
to winter in, the majority advised to set sail
from there also, if by any means they could reach
Phoenix, a harbor of Crete opening toward the
southwest and northwest, *and* winter *there*.

In the Tempest

13 When the south wind blew softly, suppos-
ing that they had obtained *their* desire, putting
out to sea, they sailed close by Crete.
14 But not long after, a tempestuous head wind
arose, called Euroclydon.[a]
15 So when the ship was caught, and could
not head into the wind, we let *her* drive.
16 And running under *the shelter of* an island
called Clauda,[a] we secured the skiff with diffi-
culty.
17 When they had taken it on board, they used
cables to undergird the ship; and fearing lest
they should run aground on the Syrtis[a] *Sands*,
they struck sail and so were driven.
18 And because we were exceedingly tempest-
tossed, the next *day* they lightened the ship.
19 On the third *day* we threw the ship's tackle
overboard with our own hands.
20 Now when neither sun nor stars appeared
for many days, and no small tempest beat on
us, all hope that we would be saved was finally
given up.
21 But after long abstinence from food, then
Paul stood in the midst of them and said, "Men,
you should have listened to me, and not have
sailed from Crete and incurred this disaster
and loss.

26:17 [a]NU-Text and M-Text omit *now*. **27:14** [a]NU-Text reads *Euraquilon*. **27:16** [a]NU-Text reads *Cauda*. **27:17** [a]M-Text reads *Syrtes*.

22 "And now I urge you to take heart, for
there will be no loss of life among you, but
only of the ship.
23 "For there stood by me this night an angel
of the God to whom I belong and whom I serve,
24 "saying, 'Do not be afraid, Paul; you must
be brought before Caesar; and indeed God has
granted you all those who sail with you.'
25 "Therefore take heart, men, for I believe
God that it will be just as it was told me.
26 "However, we must run aground on a cer-
tain island."
27 Now when the fourteenth night had come,
as we were driven up and down in the Adriatic
Sea, about midnight the sailors sensed that
they were drawing near some land.
28 And they took soundings and found *it* to
be twenty fathoms; and when they had gone a
little farther, they took soundings again and
found *it* to be fifteen fathoms.
29 Then, fearing lest we should run aground
on the rocks, they dropped four anchors from
the stern, and prayed for day to come.
30 And as the sailors were seeking to escape
from the ship, when they had let down the skiff
into the sea, under pretense of putting out an-
chors from the prow,
31 Paul said to the centurion and the soldiers,
"Unless these men stay in the ship, you cannot
be saved."
32 Then the soldiers cut away the ropes of the
skiff and let it fall off.
33 And as day was about to dawn, Paul im-
plored *them* all to take food, saying, "Today is
the fourteenth day you have waited and contin-
ued without food, and eaten nothing.
34 "Therefore I urge you to take nourish-
ment, for this is for your survival, since not a
hair will fall from the head of any of you."
35 And when he had said these things, he
took bread and gave thanks to God in the pres-
ence of them all; and when he had broken *it*
he began to eat.
36 Then they were all encouraged, and also
took food themselves.
37 And in all we were two hundred and sev-
enty-six persons on the ship.
38 So when they had eaten enough, they
lightened the ship and threw out the wheat into
the sea.

Shipwrecked on Malta

39 When it was day, they did not recognize
the land; but they observed a bay with a beach,
onto which they planned to run the ship if pos-
sible.
40 And they let go the anchors and left *them*
in the sea, meanwhile loosing the rudder
ropes; and they hoisted the mainsail to the
wind and made for shore.
41 But striking a place where two seas met,
they ran the ship aground; and the prow stuck
fast and remained immovable, but the stern
was being broken up by the violence of the
waves.
42 And the soldiers' plan was to kill the pris-
oners, lest any of them should swim away and
escape.
43 But the centurion, wanting to save Paul,
kept them from *their* purpose, and commanded
that those who could swim should jump *over-
board* first and get to land,
44 and the rest, some on boards and some on
parts of the ship. And so it was that they all
escaped safely to land.

Paul's Ministry on Malta

28 Now when they had escaped, they then
found out that the island was called
Malta.
2 And the natives showed us unusual kind-
ness; for they kindled a fire and made us all
welcome, because of the rain that was falling
and because of the cold.
3 But when Paul had gathered a bundle of
sticks and laid *them* on the fire, a viper came
out because of the heat, and fastened on his
hand.
4 So when the natives saw the creature hang-
ing from his hand, they said to one another,
"No doubt this man is a murderer, whom,
though he has escaped the sea, yet justice does
not allow to live."
5 But he shook off the creature into the fire
and suffered no harm.
6 However, they were expecting that he would
swell up or suddenly fall down dead. But after
they had looked for a long time and saw no
harm come to him, they changed their minds
and said that he was a god.
7 In that region there was an estate of the
leading citizen of the island, whose name was
Publius, who received us and entertained us
courteously for three days.
8 And it happened that the father of Publius
lay sick of a fever and dysentery. Paul went in
to him and prayed, and he laid his hands on
him and healed him.
9 So when this was done, the rest of those
on the island who had diseases also came and
were healed.
10 They also honored us in many ways; and
when we departed, they provided such things
as were necessary.

Arrival at Rome

11 After three months we sailed in an Alexan-
drian ship whose figurehead was the Twin
Brothers, which had wintered at the island.
12 And landing at Syracuse, we stayed three
days.
13 From there we circled round and reached
Rhegium. And after one day the south wind
blew; and the next day we came to Puteoli,
14 where we found brethren, and were in-
vited to stay with them seven days. And so we
went toward Rome.
15 And from there, when the brethren heard
about us, they came to meet us as far as Appii
Forum and Three Inns. When Paul saw them,
he thanked God and took courage.
16 Now when we came to Rome, the centu-
rion delivered the prisoners to the captain of
the guard; but Paul was permitted to dwell by
himself with the soldier who guarded him.

Paul's Ministry at Rome

17 And it came to pass after three days that
Paul called the leaders of the Jews together. So
when they had come together, he said to them:
"Men *and* brethren, though I have done noth-
ing against our people or the customs of our
fathers, yet I was delivered as a prisoner from
Jerusalem into the hands of the Romans,
18 "who, when they had examined me, wanted
to let *me* go, because there was no cause for
putting me to death.

19 "But when the Jews[a] spoke against *it,* I
was compelled to appeal to Caesar, not that I
had anything of which to accuse my nation.
20 "For this reason therefore I have called for
you, to see *you* and speak with *you,* because for
the hope of Israel I am bound with this chain."
21 Then they said to him, "We neither re-
ceived letters from Judea concerning you, nor
have any of the brethren who came reported
or spoken any evil of you.
22 "But we desire to hear from you what you
think; for concerning this sect, we know that
it is spoken against everywhere."
23 So when they had appointed him a day,
many came to him at *his* lodging, to whom he
explained and solemnly testified of the king-
dom of God, persuading them concerning
Jesus from both the Law of Moses and the
Prophets, from morning till evening.
24 And some were persuaded by the things
which were spoken, and some disbelieved.
25 So when they did not agree among them-
selves, they departed after Paul had said one
word: "The Holy Spirit spoke rightly through
Isaiah the prophet to our[a] fathers,
26 "saying,

'Go to this people and say:
"Hearing you will hear, and shall not
understand;
And seeing you will see, and not perceive;
27 *For the hearts of this people have grown*
dull.
Their ears are hard of hearing,
And their eyes they have closed,
Lest they should see with their eyes and
hear with their ears,
Lest they should understand with their
hearts and turn,
So that I should heal them."'[a]

28 "Therefore let it be known to you that the
salvation of God has been sent to the Gentiles,
and they will hear it!"
29 And when he had said these words, the
Jews departed and had a great dispute among
themselves.[a]
30 Then Paul dwelt two whole years in his
own rented house, and received all who came
to him,
31 preaching the kingdom of God and teaching
the things which concern the Lord Jesus Christ
with all confidence, no one forbidding him.

28:19 [a]That is, the ruling authorities **28:25** [a]NU-Text reads *your.* **28:27** [a]Isaiah 6:9, 10 **28:29** [a]NU-Text omits this verse.

THE LETTERS OF PAUL

Romans • 1 Corinthians • 2 Corinthians • Galatians Ephesians • Philippians • Colossians • 1 Thessalonians 2 Thessalonians • 1 Timothy • 2 Timothy • Titus • Philemon

Paul's letters are the oldest Christian documents we have. The first of them was written within twenty-five years of Jesus' death, and the last may have been written before any of the Gospels. These letters are also the largest collection of writings by any one person in the New Testament. They are in order of length, with the longest letter to the church first and the letters to individuals last.

We can learn from Paul's letters a great deal about Paul's faith and his understanding of what Jesus Christ means for the life of the ordinary Christian. We can learn some of the problems that churches and persons were facing because of their faith and what Paul said was an answer to the problems. We can learn a lot about Paul as a person and how his faith can help us as persons.

ROMANS was written to pave the way for Paul's visit to a church he had never seen, but whose help he needed as he began to preach the gospel in the western Mediterranean world. Romans is one of the fullest statements of Paul's faith. He tries to show how Christianity is rooted in Judaism, but is a faith for all of humanity. Romans is a book full of the power and grace of God and has been a source of inspiration and renewal in the church from earliest times to the present.

FIRST and **2 CORINTHIANS** are the most typical of Paul's letters. They were written in response to specific concerns, in this case to the division in the church and how Christians are called to live a way of life different from pagans. First Corinthians has great sections on love in the church (chs. 12—14) and the Resurrection (ch. 15). The accounts of the Resurrection and the Last Supper in 1 Corinthians are the oldest written accounts we have of those events. Second Corinthians is a combination of harsh differences and rejoicing over reconciliation. Because of the differences in tone, many scholars believe that parts of at least two letters are in our present 2 Corinthians. Chapters 3—5 are a meditation on what it means to be an apostle.

GALATIANS contains important information about Paul's own life and about the beginnings of the church. It is also a key to understanding Paul's faith in Christ, justification, and the relationship between Judaism and Christianity.

EPHESIANS is a meditation on the purpose of God in reconciling all things in Christ. The church is a part of the purpose of God, called to bring unity to the world, as Christ brought unity to the church.

PHILIPPIANS is a warm, personal letter, giving thanks for a gift from the church and encouraging the church to be faithful. The hymn quoted in 2:5–11 is a powerful statement about Christ coming into the world for salvation.

COLOSSIANS was written to a church confused by false teaching. Paul wrote to try to straighten out that confusion. He says that Christ is the ruling power in the universe. He also gives guidance for the true spiritual life.

FIRST and **2 THESSALONIANS** are among the earliest writings of the New Testament. Persecution had compelled Paul to leave Thessalonica, and in his letters he tells Christians there how they ought to live and to await the Lord's return with constant diligence.

FIRST and **2 TIMOTHY** and **TITUS** are known as the "Pastoral Epistles," since they are concerned about the care of the church. They reflect the beginnings of organizational life in the church. Paul wants to show how true faith results in a way of life in both the church and the world. There is guidance for the young pastors who are trying to lead the church.

PHILEMON is the only surviving private letter of Paul. It is a plea for Philemon to forgive the runaway slave Onesimus and receive him back as a brother in Christ. ■

The Epistle of Paul the Apostle to the

ROMANS

Greeting

1 Paul, a bondservant of Jesus Christ, called *to be* an apostle, separated to the gospel of God

2 which He promised before through His prophets in the Holy Scriptures,

3 concerning His Son Jesus Christ our Lord, who was born of the seed of David according to the flesh,

4 *and* declared *to be* the Son of God with power according to the Spirit of holiness, by the resurrection from the dead.

5 Through Him we have received grace and apostleship for obedience to the faith among all nations for His name,

6 among whom you also are the called of Jesus Christ;

7 To all who are in Rome, beloved of God, called *to be* saints:

Grace to you and peace from God our Father and the Lord Jesus Christ.

Desire to Visit Rome

8 First, I thank my God through Jesus Christ for you all, that your faith is spoken of throughout the whole world.

9 For God is my witness, whom I serve with my spirit in the gospel of His Son, that without ceasing I make mention of you always in my prayers,

10 making request if, by some means, now at last I may find a way in the will of God to come to you.

11 For I long to see you, that I may impart to you some spiritual gift, so that you may be established—

12 that is, that I may be encouraged together with you by the mutual faith both of you and me.

13 Now I do not want you to be unaware, brethren, that I often planned to come to you (but was hindered until now), that I might have some fruit among you also, just as among the other Gentiles.

14 I am a debtor both to Greeks and to barbarians, both to wise and to unwise.

15 So, as much as is in me, *I am* ready to preach the gospel to you who are in Rome also.

The Just Live by Faith

16 For I am not ashamed of the gospel of Christ,[a] for it is the power of God to salvation for everyone who believes, for the Jew first and also for the Greek.

17 For in it the righteousness of God is revealed from faith to faith; as it is written, *"The just shall live by faith."*[a]

God's Wrath on Unrighteousness

18 For the wrath of God is revealed from heaven against all ungodliness and unrighteousness of men, who suppress the truth in unrighteousness,

19 because what may be known of God is manifest in them, for God has shown *it* to them.

20 For since the creation of the world His invisible *attributes* are clearly seen, being understood by the things that are made, *even* His eternal power and Godhead, so that they are without excuse,

21 because, although they knew God, they did not glorify *Him* as God, nor were thankful, but became futile in their thoughts, and their foolish hearts were darkened.

22 Professing to be wise, they became fools,

23 and changed the glory of the incorruptible God into an image made like corruptible man—and birds and four-footed animals and creeping things.

24 Therefore God also gave them up to uncleanness, in the lusts of their hearts, to dishonor their bodies among themselves,

25 who exchanged the truth of God for the lie, and worshiped and served the creature rather than the Creator, who is blessed forever. Amen.

26 For this reason God gave them up to vile passions. For even their women exchanged the natural use for what is against nature.

27 Likewise also the men, leaving the natural use of the woman, burned in their lust for one another, men with men committing what is shameful, and receiving in themselves the penalty of their error which was due.

28 And even as they did not like to retain God in *their* knowledge, God gave them over to a debased mind, to do those things which are not fitting;

29 being filled with all unrighteousness, sexual immorality,[a] wickedness, covetousness, maliciousness; full of envy, murder, strife, deceit, evil-mindedness; *they are* whisperers,

30 backbiters, haters of God, violent, proud, boasters, inventors of evil things, disobedient to parents,

31 undiscerning, untrustworthy, unloving, unforgiving,[a] unmerciful;

32 who, knowing the righteous judgment of God, that those who practice such things are deserving of death, not only do the same but also approve of those who practice them.

God's Righteous Judgment

2 Therefore you are inexcusable, O man, whoever you are who judge, for in whatever you judge another you condemn yourself; for you who judge practice the same things.

2 But we know that the judgment of God is according to truth against those who practice such things.

3 And do you think this, O man, you who judge those practicing such things, and doing the same, that you will escape the judgment of God?

4 Or do you despise the riches of His goodness, forbearance, and longsuffering, not knowing that the goodness of God leads you to repentance?

5 But in accordance with your hardness and your impenitent heart you are treasuring up for yourself wrath in the day of wrath and revelation of the righteous judgment of God,

6 who *"will render to each one according to his deeds"*:[a]

1:16 [a]NU-Text omits *of Christ.* **1:17** [a]Habakkuk 2:4 **1:29** [a]NU-Text omits *sexual immorality.* **1:31** [a]NU-Text omits *unforgiving.* **2:6** [a]Psalm 62:12; Proverbs 24:12

7 eternal life to those who by patient contin-
uance in doing good seek for glory, honor, and
immortality;
8 but to those who are self-seeking and do
not obey the truth, but obey unrighteousness—
indignation and wrath,
9 tribulation and anguish, on every soul of
man who does evil, of the Jew first and also of
the Greek;
10 but glory, honor, and peace to everyone who
works what is good, to the Jew first and also
to the Greek.
11 For there is no partiality with God.
12 For as many as have sinned without law
will also perish without law, and as many as
have sinned in the law will be judged by the law
13 (for not the hearers of the law *are* just in
the sight of God, but the doers of the law will
be justified;
14 for when Gentiles, who do not have the
law, by nature do the things in the law, these,
although not having the law, are a law to them-
selves,
15 who show the work of the law written in
their hearts, their conscience also bearing wit-
ness, and between themselves *their* thoughts
accusing or else excusing *them*)
16 in the day when God will judge the secrets
of men by Jesus Christ, according to my gospel.

The Jews Guilty as the Gentiles

17 Indeed[a] you are called a Jew, and rest on
the law, and make your boast in God,
18 and know *His* will, and approve the things
that are excellent, being instructed out of the
law,
19 and are confident that you yourself are a
guide to the blind, a light to those who are in
darkness,
20 an instructor of the foolish, a teacher of
babes, having the form of knowledge and truth
in the law.
21 You, therefore, who teach another, do you
not teach yourself? You who preach that a man
should not steal, do you steal?
22 You who say, "Do not commit adultery,"
do you commit adultery? You who abhor idols,
do you rob temples?
23 You who make your boast in the law, do
you dishonor God through breaking the law?
24 For *"the name of God is blasphemed among
the Gentiles because of you,"*[a] as it is written.

Circumcision of No Avail

25 For circumcision is indeed profitable if you
keep the law; but if you are a breaker of the
law, your circumcision has become uncircum-
cision.
26 Therefore, if an uncircumcised man keeps
the righteous requirements of the law, will not
his uncircumcision be counted as circumcision?
27 And will not the physically uncircumcised,
if he fulfills the law, judge you who, *even* with
your written *code* and circumcision, *are* a
transgressor of the law?
28 For he is not a Jew who *is one* outwardly,
nor *is* circumcision that which *is* outward in
the flesh;
29 but *he is* a Jew who *is one* inwardly; and
circumcision *is that* of the heart, in the Spirit,
not in the letter; whose praise *is* not from men
but from God.

God's Judgment Defended

3 What advantage then has the Jew, or what
is the profit of circumcision?
2 Much in every way! Chiefly because to
them were committed the oracles of God.
3 For what if some did not believe? Will their
unbelief make the faithfulness of God without
effect?
4 Certainly not! Indeed, let God be true but
every man a liar. As it is written:

"That You may be justified in Your words,
And may overcome when You are judged."[a]

5 But if our unrighteousness demonstrates the
righteousness of God, what shall we say? *Is* God
unjust who inflicts wrath? (I speak as a man.)
6 Certainly not! For then how will God judge
the world?
7 For if the truth of God has increased through
my lie to His glory, why am I also still judged
as a sinner?
8 And *why* not *say*, "Let us do evil that good
may come"?—as we are slanderously reported
and as some affirm that we say. Their condem-
nation is just.

All Have Sinned

9 What then? Are we better *than they*? Not
at all. For we have previously charged both
Jews and Greeks that they are all under sin.
10 As it is written:

"There is none righteous, no, not one;
11 *There is none who understands;*
There is none who seeks after God.
12 *They have all turned aside;*
They have together become unprofitable;
There is none who does good, no, not
one."[a]
13 *"Their throat is an open tomb;*
With their tongues they have practiced
deceit";[a]
"The poison of asps is under their lips";[b]
14 *"Whose mouth is full of cursing and*
bitterness."[a]
15 *"Their feet are swift to shed blood;*
16 *Destruction and misery are in their ways;*
17 *And the way of peace they have not*
known."[a]
18 *"There is no fear of God before their*
eyes."[a]

19 Now we know that whatever the law says,
it says to those who are under the law, that every
mouth may be stopped, and all the world may
become guilty before God.
20 Therefore by the deeds of the law no flesh
will be justified in His sight, for by the law *is*
the knowledge of sin.

God's Righteousness Through Faith

21 But now the righteousness of God apart from
the law is revealed, being witnessed by the Law
and the Prophets,
22 even the righteousness of God, through faith
in Jesus Christ, to all and on all[a] who believe.
For there is no difference;

2:17 [a]NU-Text reads *But if.* **2:24** [a]Isaiah 52:5; Ezekiel 36:22 **3:4** [a]Psalm 51:4 **3:12** [a]Psalms 14:1–3; 53:1–3; Ecclesiastes 7:20 **3:13** [a]Psalm 5:9 [b]Psalm 140:3 **3:14** [a]Psalm 10:7 **3:17** [a]Isaiah 59:7, 8 **3:18** [a]Psalm 36:1 **3:22** [a]NU-Text omits *and on all.*

23 for all have sinned and fall short of the glory
of God,
24 being justified freely by His grace through
the redemption that is in Christ Jesus,
25 whom God set forth *as* a propitiation by His
blood, through faith, to demonstrate His righ-
teousness, because in His forbearance God had
passed over the sins that were previously com-
mitted,
26 to demonstrate at the present time His righ-
teousness, that He might be just and the justi-
fier of the one who has faith in Jesus.

Boasting Excluded

27 Where *is* boasting then? It is excluded. By
what law? Of works? No, but by the law of faith.
28 Therefore we conclude that a man is justi-
fied by faith apart from the deeds of the law.
29 Or *is He* the God of the Jews only? *Is He* not
also the God of the Gentiles? Yes, of the Gentiles
also,
30 since *there is* one God who will justify the
circumcised by faith and the uncircumcised
through faith.
31 Do we then make void the law through
faith? Certainly not! On the contrary, we estab-
lish the law.

Abraham Justified by Faith

4 What then shall we say that Abraham our
father has found according to the flesh?[a]
2 For if Abraham was justified by works, he
has *something* to boast about, but not before
God.
3 For what does the Scripture say? *"Abraham
believed God, and it was accounted to him for
righteousness."*[a]
4 Now to him who works, the wages are not
counted as grace but as debt.

David Celebrates the Same Truth

5 But to him who does not work but believes
on Him who justifies the ungodly, his faith is
accounted for righteousness,
6 just as David also describes the blessedness
of the man to whom God imputes righteousness
apart from works:

7 *"Blessed are those whose lawless deeds
are forgiven,
And whose sins are covered;*
8 *Blessed is the man to whom the* L*ORD*
shall not impute sin."[a]

Abraham Justified Before Circumcision

9 *Does* this blessedness then *come* upon the
circumcised *only,* or upon the uncircumcised
also? For we say that faith was accounted to
Abraham for righteousness.
10 How then was it accounted? While he was
circumcised, or uncircumcised? Not while cir-
cumcised, but while uncircumcised.
11 And he received the sign of circumcision,
a seal of the righteousness of the faith which
he had while still uncircumcised, that he might
be the father of all those who believe, though
they are uncircumcised, that righteousness
might be imputed to them also,
12 and the father of circumcision to those
who not only *are* of the circumcision, but who
also walk in the steps of the faith which our
father Abraham *had while still* uncircumcised.

The Promise Granted Through Faith

13 For the promise that he would be the heir
of the world *was* not to Abraham or to his seed
through the law, but through the righteousness
of faith.
14 For if those who are of the law *are* heirs,
faith is made void and the promise made of no
effect,
15 because the law brings about wrath; for
where there is no law *there is* no transgression.
16 Therefore *it is* of faith that *it might be*
according to grace, so that the promise might
be sure to all the seed, not only to those who
are of the law, but also to those who are of the
faith of Abraham, who is the father of us all
17 (as it is written, *"I have made you a father
of many nations"*[a]) in the presence of Him
whom he believed—God, who gives life to the
dead and calls those things which do not exist
as though they did;
18 who, contrary to hope, in hope believed,
so that he became the father of many nations,
according to what was spoken, *"So shall your
descendants be."*[a]
19 And not being weak in faith, he did not
consider his own body, already dead (since he
was about a hundred years old), and the dead-
ness of Sarah's womb.
20 He did not waver at the promise of God
through unbelief, but was strengthened in faith,
giving glory to God,
21 and being fully convinced that what He had
promised He was also able to perform.
22 And therefore *"it was accounted to him for
righteousness."*[a]
23 Now it was not written for his sake alone
that it was imputed to him,
24 but also for us. It shall be imputed to us
who believe in Him who raised up Jesus our
Lord from the dead,
25 who was delivered up because of our of-
fenses, and was raised because of our justifica-
tion.

Faith Triumphs in Trouble

5 Therefore, having been justified by faith,
we have[a] peace with God through our Lord
Jesus Christ,
2 through whom also we have access by faith
into this grace in which we stand, and rejoice
in hope of the glory of God.
3 And not only *that,* but we also glory in trib-
ulations, knowing that tribulation produces
perseverance;
4 and perseverance, character; and charac-
ter, hope.
5 Now hope does not disappoint, because the
love of God has been poured out in our hearts
by the Holy Spirit who was given to us.

Christ in Our Place

6 For when we were still without strength,
in due time Christ died for the ungodly.
7 For scarcely for a righteous man will one
die; yet perhaps for a good man someone would
even dare to die.
8 But God demonstrates His own love toward
us, in that while we were still sinners, Christ
died for us.
9 Much more then, having now been justified

4:1 [a]Or *Abraham our (fore)father according to the flesh has found?* **4:3** [a]Genesis 15:6 **4:8** [a]Psalm 32:1, 2
4:17 [a]Genesis 17:5 **4:18** [a]Genesis 15:5 **4:22** [a]Genesis 15:6 **5:1** [a]Another ancient reading is, *let us have peace.*

by His blood, we shall be saved from wrath through Him.

10 For if when we were enemies we were reconciled to God through the death of His Son, much more, having been reconciled, we shall be saved by His life.

11 And not only *that,* but we also rejoice in God through our Lord Jesus Christ, through whom we have now received the reconciliation.

Death in Adam, Life in Christ

12 Therefore, just as through one man sin entered the world, and death through sin, and thus death spread to all men, because all sinned—

13 (For until the law sin was in the world, but sin is not imputed when there is no law.

14 Nevertheless death reigned from Adam to Moses, even over those who had not sinned according to the likeness of the transgression of Adam, who is a type of Him who was to come.

15 But the free gift *is* not like the offense. For if by the one man's offense many died, much more the grace of God and the gift by the grace of the one Man, Jesus Christ, abounded to many.

16 And the gift *is* not like *that which came* through the one who sinned. For the judgment *which came* from one *offense resulted* in condemnation, but the free gift *which came* from many offenses *resulted* in justification.

17 For if by the one man's offense death reigned through the one, much more those who receive abundance of grace and of the gift of righteousness will reign in life through the One, Jesus Christ.)

18 Therefore, as through one man's offense *judgment came* to all men, resulting in condemnation, even so through one Man's righteous act *the free gift came* to all men, resulting in justification of life.

19 For as by one man's disobedience many were made sinners, so also by one Man's obedience many will be made righteous.

20 Moreover the law entered that the offense might abound. But where sin abounded, grace abounded much more,

21 so that as sin reigned in death, even so grace might reign through righteousness to eternal life through Jesus Christ our Lord.

Dead to Sin, Alive to God

6 What shall we say then? Shall we continue in sin that grace may abound?

2 Certainly not! How shall we who died to sin live any longer in it?

3 Or do you not know that as many of us as were baptized into Christ Jesus were baptized into His death?

4 Therefore we were buried with Him through baptism into death, that just as Christ was raised from the dead by the glory of the Father, even so we also should walk in newness of life.

5 For if we have been united together in the likeness of His death, certainly we also shall be *in the likeness* of *His* resurrection,

6 knowing this, that our old man was crucified with *Him,* that the body of sin might be done away with, that we should no longer be slaves of sin.

7 For he who has died has been freed from sin.

8 Now if we died with Christ, we believe that we shall also live with Him,

9 knowing that Christ, having been raised from the dead, dies no more. Death no longer has dominion over Him.

10 For *the death* that He died, He died to sin once for all; but *the life* that He lives, He lives to God.

11 Likewise you also, reckon yourselves to be dead indeed to sin, but alive to God in Christ Jesus our Lord.

12 Therefore do not let sin reign in your mortal body, that you should obey it in its lusts.

13 And do not present your members *as* instruments of unrighteousness to sin, but present yourselves to God as being alive from the dead, and your members *as* instruments of righteousness to God.

14 For sin shall not have dominion over you, for you are not under law but under grace.

From Slaves of Sin to Slaves of God

15 What then? Shall we sin because we are not under law but under grace? Certainly not!

16 Do you not know that to whom you present yourselves slaves to obey, you are that one's slaves whom you obey, whether of sin *leading* to death, or of obedience *leading* to righteousness?

17 But God be thanked that *though* you were slaves of sin, yet you obeyed from the heart that form of doctrine to which you were delivered.

18 And having been set free from sin, you became slaves of righteousness.

19 I speak in human *terms* because of the weakness of your flesh. For just as you presented your members *as* slaves of uncleanness, and of lawlessness *leading* to *more* lawlessness, so now present your members *as* slaves *of* righteousness for holiness.

20 For when you were slaves of sin, you were free in regard to righteousness.

21 What fruit did you have then in the things of which you are now ashamed? For the end of those things *is* death.

22 But now having been set free from sin, and having become slaves of God, you have your fruit to holiness, and the end, everlasting life.

23 For the wages of sin *is* death, but the gift of God *is* eternal life in Christ Jesus our Lord.

Freed from the Law

7 Or do you not know, brethren (for I speak to those who know the law), that the law has dominion over a man as long as he lives?

2 For the woman who has a husband is bound by the law to *her* husband as long as he lives. But if the husband dies, she is released from the law of *her* husband.

3 So then if, while *her* husband lives, she marries another man, she will be called an adulteress; but if her husband dies, she is free from that law, so that she is no adulteress, though she has married another man.

4 Therefore, my brethren, you also have become dead to the law through the body of Christ, that you may be married to another—to Him who was raised from the dead, that we should bear fruit to God.

5 For when we were in the flesh, the sinful passions which were aroused by the law were at work in our members to bear fruit to death.

6 But now we have been delivered from the law, having died to what we were held by, so that we should serve in the newness of the Spirit and not *in* the oldness of the letter.

Sin's Advantage in the Law

7 What shall we say then? *Is* the law sin? Certainly not! On the contrary, I would not have known sin except through the law. For I would not have known covetousness unless the law had said, *"You shall not covet."*[a]

8 But sin, taking opportunity by the commandment, produced in me all *manner of evil* desire. For apart from the law sin *was* dead.

9 I was alive once without the law, but when the commandment came, sin revived and I died.

10 And the commandment, which *was* to *bring* life, I found to *bring* death.

11 For sin, taking occasion by the commandment, deceived me, and by it killed *me*.

12 Therefore the law *is* holy, and the commandment holy and just and good.

Law Cannot Save from Sin

13 Has then what is good become death to me? Certainly not! But sin, that it might appear sin, was producing death in me through what is good, so that sin through the commandment might become exceedingly sinful.

14 For we know that the law is spiritual, but I am carnal, sold under sin.

15 For what I am doing, I do not understand. For what I will to do, that I do not practice; but what I hate, that I do.

16 If, then, I do what I will not to do, I agree with the law that *it is* good.

17 But now, *it is* no longer I who do it, but sin that dwells in me.

18 For I know that in me (that is, in my flesh) nothing good dwells; for to will is present with me, but *how* to perform what is good I do not find.

19 For the good that I will *to do*, I do not do; but the evil I will not *to do*, that I practice.

20 Now if I do what I will not *to do*, it is no longer I who do it, but sin that dwells in me.

21 I find then a law, that evil is present with me, the one who wills to do good.

22 For I delight in the law of God according to the inward man.

23 But I see another law in my members, warring against the law of my mind, and bringing me into captivity to the law of sin which is in my members.

24 O wretched man that I am! Who will deliver me from this body of death?

25 I thank God—through Jesus Christ our Lord! So then, with the mind I myself serve the law of God, but with the flesh the law of sin.

Free from Indwelling Sin

8 *There is* therefore now no condemnation to those who are in Christ Jesus,[a] who do not walk according to the flesh, but according to the Spirit.

2 For the law of the Spirit of life in Christ Jesus has made me free from the law of sin and death.

3 For what the law could not do in that it was weak through the flesh, God *did* by sending His own Son in the likeness of sinful flesh, on account of sin: He condemned sin in the flesh,

4 that the righteous requirement of the law might be fulfilled in us who do not walk according to the flesh but according to the Spirit.

5 For those who live according to the flesh set their minds on the things of the flesh, but those *who live* according to the Spirit, the things of the Spirit.

6 For to be carnally minded *is* death, but to be spiritually minded *is* life and peace.

7 Because the carnal mind *is* enmity against God; for it is not subject to the law of God, nor indeed can be.

8 So then, those who are in the flesh cannot please God.

9 But you are not in the flesh but in the Spirit, if indeed the Spirit of God dwells in you. Now if anyone does not have the Spirit of Christ, he is not His.

10 And if Christ *is* in you, the body *is* dead because of sin, but the Spirit *is* life because of righteousness.

11 But if the Spirit of Him who raised Jesus from the dead dwells in you, He who raised Christ from the dead will also give life to your mortal bodies through His Spirit who dwells in you.

Sonship Through the Spirit

12 Therefore, brethren, we are debtors—not to the flesh, to live according to the flesh.

13 For if you live according to the flesh you will die; but if by the Spirit you put to death the deeds of the body, you will live.

14 For as many as are led by the Spirit of God, these are sons of God.

15 For you did not receive the spirit of bondage again to fear, but you received the Spirit of adoption by whom we cry out, "Abba, Father."

16 The Spirit Himself bears witness with our spirit that we are children of God,

17 and if children, then heirs—heirs of God and joint heirs with Christ, if indeed we suffer with *Him*, that we may also be glorified together.

From Suffering to Glory

18 For I consider that the sufferings of this present time are not worthy *to be compared* with the glory which shall be revealed in us.

19 For the earnest expectation of the creation eagerly waits for the revealing of the sons of God.

20 For the creation was subjected to futility, not willingly, but because of Him who subjected *it* in hope;

21 because the creation itself also will be delivered from the bondage of corruption into the glorious liberty of the children of God.

22 For we know that the whole creation groans and labors with birth pangs together until now.

23 Not only *that*, but we also who have the firstfruits of the Spirit, even we ourselves groan within ourselves, eagerly waiting for the adoption, the redemption of our body.

24 For we were saved in this hope, but hope that is seen is not hope; for why does one still hope for what he sees?

25 But if we hope for what we do not see, we eagerly wait for *it* with perseverance.

26 Likewise the Spirit also helps in our weaknesses. For we do not know what we should pray for as we ought, but the Spirit Himself makes intercession for us[a] with groanings which cannot be uttered.

27 Now He who searches the hearts knows what the mind of the Spirit *is*, because He makes

7:7 [a]Exodus 20:17; Deuteronomy 5:21 **8:1** [a]NU-Text omits the rest of this verse. **8:26** [a]NU-Text omits *for us*.

intercession for the saints according to *the will* of God.
28 And we know that all things work together for good to those who love God, to those who are the called according to *His* purpose.
29 For whom He foreknew, He also predestined *to be* conformed to the image of His Son, that He might be the firstborn among many brethren.
30 Moreover whom He predestined, these He also called; whom He called, these He also justified; and whom He justified, these He also glorified.

God's Everlasting Love

31 What then shall we say to these things? If God *is* for us, who *can be* against us?
32 He who did not spare His own Son, but delivered Him up for us all, how shall He not with Him also freely give us all things?
33 Who shall bring a charge against God's elect? *It is* God who justifies.
34 Who *is* he who condemns? *It is* Christ who died, and furthermore is also risen, who is even at the right hand of God, who also makes intercession for us.
35 Who shall separate us from the love of Christ? *Shall* tribulation, or distress, or persecution, or famine, or nakedness, or peril, or sword?
36 As it is written:

"For Your sake we are killed all day long;
We are accounted as sheep for the
slaughter."[a]

37 Yet in all these things we are more than conquerors through Him who loved us.
38 For I am persuaded that neither death nor life, nor angels nor principalities nor powers, nor things present nor things to come,
39 nor height nor depth, nor any other created thing, shall be able to separate us from the love of God which is in Christ Jesus our Lord.

Israel's Rejection of Christ

9 I tell the truth in Christ, I am not lying, my conscience also bearing me witness in the Holy Spirit,
2 that I have great sorrow and continual grief in my heart.
3 For I could wish that I myself were accursed from Christ for my brethren, my countrymen[a] according to the flesh,
4 who are Israelites, to whom *pertain* the adoption, the glory, the covenants, the giving of the law, the service *of God,* and the promises;
5 of whom *are* the fathers and from whom, according to the flesh, Christ *came,* who is over all, *the* eternally blessed God. Amen.

Israel's Rejection and God's Purpose

6 But it is not that the word of God has taken no effect. For they *are* not all Israel who *are* of Israel,
7 nor *are they* all children because they are the seed of Abraham; but, *"In Isaac your seed shall be called."*[a]
8 That is, those who *are* the children of the flesh, these *are* not the children of God; but the children of the promise are counted as the seed.
9 For this *is* the word of promise: *"At this time I will come and Sarah shall have a son."*[a]
10 And not only *this,* but when Rebecca also had conceived by one man, *even* by our father Isaac
11 (for *the children* not yet being born, nor having done any good or evil, that the purpose of God according to election might stand, not of works but of Him who calls),
12 it was said to her, *"The older shall serve the younger."*[a]
13 As it is written, *"Jacob I have loved, but Esau I have hated."*[a]

Israel's Rejection and God's Justice

14 What shall we say then? *Is there* unrighteousness with God? Certainly not!
15 For He says to Moses, *"I will have mercy on whomever I will have mercy, and I will have compassion on whomever I will have compassion."*[a]
16 So then *it is* not of him who wills, nor of him who runs, but of God who shows mercy.
17 For the Scripture says to the Pharaoh, *"For this very purpose I have raised you up, that I may show My power in you, and that My name may be declared in all the earth."*[a]
18 Therefore He has mercy on whom He wills, and whom He wills He hardens.
19 You will say to me then, "Why does He still find fault? For who has resisted His will?"
20 But indeed, O man, who are you to reply against God? Will the thing formed say to him who formed *it,* "Why have you made me like this?"
21 Does not the potter have power over the clay, from the same lump to make one vessel for honor and another for dishonor?
22 *What* if God, wanting to show *His* wrath and to make His power known, endured with much longsuffering the vessels of wrath prepared for destruction,
23 and that He might make known the riches of His glory on the vessels of mercy, which He had prepared beforehand for glory,
24 even us whom He called, not of the Jews only, but also of the Gentiles?
25 As He says also in Hosea:

"I will call them My people, who were not
My people,
And her beloved, who was not beloved."[a]

26 *"And it shall come to pass in the place*
where it was said to them,
'You are not My people,'
There they shall be called sons of the
living God."[a]

27 Isaiah also cries out concerning Israel:[a]

"Though the number of the children of
Israel be as the sand of the sea,
The remnant will be saved.

28 *For He will finish the work and cut it*
short in righteousness,
Because the LORD will make a short
work upon the earth."[a]

8:36 [a]Psalm 44:22 **9:3** [a]Or *relatives* **9:7** [a]Genesis 21:12 **9:9** [a]Genesis 18:10, 14 **9:12** [a]Genesis 25:23 **9:13** [a]Malachi 1:2, 3 **9:15** [a]Exodus 33:19 **9:17** [a]Exodus 9:16 **9:25** [a]Hosea 2:23 **9:26** [a]Hosea 1:10 **9:27** [a]Isaiah 10:22, 23 **9:28** [a]NU-Text reads *For the LORD will finish the work and cut it short upon the earth.*

29 And as Isaiah said before:

"Unless the LORD of Sabaoth[a] *had left us*
a seed,
We would have become like Sodom,
And we would have been made like
Gomorrah."[b]

Present Condition of Israel

30 What shall we say then? That Gentiles,
who did not pursue righteousness, have at-
tained to righteousness, even the righteous-
ness of faith;
31 but Israel, pursuing the law of righteous-
ness, has not attained to the law of righteous-
ness.[a]
32 Why? Because *they did* not *seek it* by faith,
but as it were, by the works of the law.[a] For
they stumbled at that stumbling stone.
33 As it is written:

"Behold, I lay in Zion a stumbling stone
and rock of offense,
And whoever believes on Him will not be
put to shame."[a]

Israel Needs the Gospel

10 Brethren, my heart's desire and prayer
to God for Israel[a] is that they may be
saved.
2 For I bear them witness that they have a
zeal for God, but not according to knowledge.
3 For they being ignorant of God's righ-
teousness, and seeking to establish their own
righteousness, have not submitted to the righ-
teousness of God.
4 For Christ *is* the end of the law for righ-
teousness to everyone who believes.
5 For Moses writes about the righteousness
which is of the law, *"The man who does those
things shall live by them."*[a]
6 But the righteousness of faith speaks in
this way, *"Do not say in your heart, 'Who will
ascend into heaven?' "*[a] (that is, to bring Christ
down *from above*)
7 or, *" 'Who will descend into the abyss?' "*[a]
(that is, to bring Christ up from the dead).
8 But what does it say? *"The word is near
you, in your mouth and in your heart"*[a] (that
is, the word of faith which we preach):
9 that if you confess with your mouth the
Lord Jesus and believe in your heart that God
has raised Him from the dead, you will be saved.
10 For with the heart one believes unto righ-
teousness, and with the mouth confession is
made unto salvation.
11 For the Scripture says, *"Whoever believes
on Him will not be put to shame."*[a]
12 For there is no distinction between Jew
and Greek, for the same Lord over all is rich
to all who call upon Him.
13 For *"whoever calls on the name of the
LORD shall be saved."*[a]

Israel Rejects the Gospel

14 How then shall they call on Him in whom
they have not believed? And how shall they
believe in Him of whom they have not heard?
And how shall they hear without a preacher?
15 And how shall they preach unless they are
sent? As it is written:

"How beautiful are the feet of those who
preach the gospel of peace,[a]
Who bring glad tidings of good things!"[b]

16 But they have not all obeyed the gospel. For
Isaiah says, *"LORD, who has believed our re-
port?"*[a]
17 So then faith *comes* by hearing, and hear-
ing by the word of God.
18 But I say, have they not heard? Yes indeed:

"Their sound has gone out to all the earth,
And their words to the ends of the
world."[a]

19 But I say, did Israel not know? First Moses
says:

"I will provoke you to jealousy by those
who are not a nation,
I will move you to anger by a foolish
nation."[a]

20 But Isaiah is very bold and says:

"I was found by those who did not seek
Me;
I was made manifest to those who did not
ask for Me."[a]

21 But to Israel he says:

"All day long I have stretched out My
hands
To a disobedient and contrary people."[a]

Israel's Rejection Not Total

11 I say then, has God cast away His peo-
ple? Certainly not! For I also am an Isra-
elite, of the seed of Abraham, *of* the tribe of
Benjamin.
2 God has not cast away His people whom
He foreknew. Or do you not know what the
Scripture says of Elijah, how he pleads with
God against Israel, saying,
3 *"LORD, they have killed Your prophets and
torn down Your altars, and I alone am left, and
they seek my life"*?[a]
4 But what does the divine response say to
him? *"I have reserved for Myself seven thou-
sand men who have not bowed the knee to
Baal."*[a]
5 Even so then, at this present time there is
a remnant according to the election of grace.
6 And if by grace, then *it is* no longer of
works; otherwise grace is no longer grace.[a] But
if *it is* of works, it is no longer grace; otherwise
work is no longer work.
7 What then? Israel has not obtained what it
seeks; but the elect have obtained it, and the
rest were blinded.
8 Just as it is written:

"God has given them a spirit of stupor,
Eyes that they should not see
And ears that they should not hear,
To this very day."[a]

9:29 [a]Literally, in Hebrew, *Hosts* [b]Isaiah 1:9 **9:31** [a]NU-Text omits *of righteousness.* **9:32** [a]NU-Text reads *by works.* **9:33** [a]Isaiah 8:14; 28:16 **10:1** [a]NU-Text reads *them.* **10:5** [a]Leviticus 18:5 **10:6** [a]Deuteronomy 30:12 **10:7** [a]Deuteronomy 30:13 **10:8** [a]Deuteronomy 30:14 **10:11** [a]Isaiah 28:16 **10:13** [a]Joel 2:32 **10:15** [a]NU-Text omits *preach the gospel of peace, Who.* [b]Isaiah 52:7; Nahum 1:15 **10:16** [a]Isaiah 53:1 **10:18** [a]Psalm 19:4 **10:19** [a]Deuteronomy 32:21 **10:20** [a]Isaiah 65:1 **10:21** [a]Isaiah 65:2 **11:3** [a]1 Kings 19:10, 14 **11:4** [a]1 Kings 19:18 **11:6** [a]NU-Text omits the rest of this verse. **11:8** [a]Deuteronomy 29:4; Isaiah 29:10

9 And David says:

"Let their table become a snare and a trap,
A stumbling block and a recompense to them.
10 *Let their eyes be darkened, so that they do not see,*
And bow down their back always."[a]

Israel's Rejection Not Final

11 I say then, have they stumbled that they should fall? Certainly not! But through their fall, to provoke them to jealousy, salvation *has come* to the Gentiles.
12 Now if their fall *is* riches for the world, and their failure riches for the Gentiles, how much more their fullness!
13 For I speak to you Gentiles; inasmuch as I am an apostle to the Gentiles, I magnify my ministry,
14 if by any means I may provoke to jealousy *those who are* my flesh and save some of them.
15 For if their being cast away *is* the reconciling of the world, what *will* their acceptance *be* but life from the dead?
16 For if the firstfruit *is* holy, the lump *is* also *holy;* and if the root *is* holy, so *are* the branches.
17 And if some of the branches were broken off, and you, being a wild olive tree, were grafted in among them, and with them became a partaker of the root and fatness of the olive tree,
18 do not boast against the branches. But if you do boast, *remember that* you do not support the root, but the root *supports* you.
19 You will say then, "Branches were broken off that I might be grafted in."
20 Well *said.* Because of unbelief they were broken off, and you stand by faith. Do not be haughty, but fear.
21 For if God did not spare the natural branches, He may not spare you either.
22 Therefore consider the goodness and severity of God: on those who fell, severity; but toward you, goodness,[a] if you continue in *His* goodness. Otherwise you also will be cut off.
23 And they also, if they do not continue in unbelief, will be grafted in, for God is able to graft them in again.
24 For if you were cut out of the olive tree which is wild by nature, and were grafted contrary to nature into a cultivated olive tree, how much more will these, who *are* natural *branches,* be grafted into their own olive tree?
25 For I do not desire, brethren, that you should be ignorant of this mystery, lest you should be wise in your own opinion, that blindness in part has happened to Israel until the fullness of the Gentiles has come in.
26 And so all Israel will be saved,[a] as it is written:

"The Deliverer will come out of Zion,
And He will turn away ungodliness from Jacob;
27 *For this is My covenant with them,*
When I take away their sins."[a]

28 Concerning the gospel *they are* enemies for your sake, but concerning the election *they are* beloved for the sake of the fathers.
29 For the gifts and the calling of God *are* irrevocable.
30 For as you were once disobedient to God, yet have now obtained mercy through their disobedience,
31 even so these also have now been disobedient, that through the mercy shown you they also may obtain mercy.
32 For God has committed them all to disobedience, that He might have mercy on all.
33 Oh, the depth of the riches both of the wisdom and knowledge of God! How unsearchable *are* His judgments and His ways past finding out!

34 *"For who has known the mind of the LORD?*
Or who has become His counselor?"[a]
35 *"Or who has first given to Him*
And it shall be repaid to him?"[a]

36 For of Him and through Him and to Him *are* all things, to whom *be* glory forever. Amen.

Living Sacrifices to God

12 I beseech you therefore, brethren, by the mercies of God, that you present your bodies a living sacrifice, holy, acceptable to God, *which is* your reasonable service.
2 And do not be conformed to this world, but be transformed by the renewing of your mind, that you may prove what *is* that good and acceptable and perfect will of God.

Serve God with Spiritual Gifts

3 For I say, through the grace given to me, to everyone who is among you, not to think *of himself* more highly than he ought to think, but to think soberly, as God has dealt to each one a measure of faith.
4 For as we have many members in one body, but all the members do not have the same function,
5 so we, *being* many, are one body in Christ, and individually members of one another.
6 Having then gifts differing according to the grace that is given to us, *let us use them:* if prophecy, *let us prophesy* in proportion to our faith;
7 or ministry, *let us use it* in *our* ministering; he who teaches, in teaching;
8 he who exhorts, in exhortation; he who gives, with liberality; he who leads, with diligence; he who shows mercy, with cheerfulness.

Behave Like a Christian

9 *Let* love *be* without hypocrisy. Abhor what is evil. Cling to what is good.
10 *Be* kindly affectionate to one another with brotherly love, in honor giving preference to one another;
11 not lagging in diligence, fervent in spirit, serving the Lord;
12 rejoicing in hope, patient in tribulation, continuing steadfastly in prayer;
13 distributing to the needs of the saints, given to hospitality.
14 Bless those who persecute you; bless and do not curse.
15 Rejoice with those who rejoice, and weep with those who weep.
16 Be of the same mind toward one another. Do not set your mind on high things, but associate with the humble. Do not be wise in your own opinion.

11:10 [a]Psalm 69:22, 23 **11:22** [a]NU-Text adds *of God.* **11:26** [a]Or *delivered* **11:27** [a]Isaiah 59:20, 21 **11:34** [a]Isaiah 40:13; Jeremiah 23:18 **11:35** [a]Job 41:11

17 Repay no one evil for evil. Have regard for good things in the sight of all men.
18 If it is possible, as much as depends on you, live peaceably with all men.
19 Beloved, do not avenge yourselves, but *rather* give place to wrath; for it is written, *"Vengeance is Mine, I will repay,"*[a] says the Lord.
20 Therefore

"If your enemy is hungry, feed him;
If he is thirsty, give him a drink;
For in so doing you will heap coals of fire
on his head."[a]

21 Do not be overcome by evil, but overcome evil with good.

Submit to Government

13 Let every soul be subject to the governing authorities. For there is no authority except from God, and the authorities that exist are appointed by God.
2 Therefore whoever resists the authority resists the ordinance of God, and those who resist will bring judgment on themselves.
3 For rulers are not a terror to good works, but to evil. Do you want to be unafraid of the authority? Do what is good, and you will have praise from the same.
4 For he is God's minister to you for good. But if you do evil, be afraid; for he does not bear the sword in vain; for he is God's minister, an avenger to *execute* wrath on him who practices evil.
5 Therefore *you* must be subject, not only because of wrath but also for conscience' sake.
6 For because of this you also pay taxes, for they are God's ministers attending continually to this very thing.
7 Render therefore to all their due: taxes to whom taxes *are due,* customs to whom customs, fear to whom fear, honor to whom honor.

Love Your Neighbor

8 Owe no one anything except to love one another, for he who loves another has fulfilled the law.
9 For the commandments, *"You shall not commit adultery," "You shall not murder," "You shall not steal," "You shall not bear false witness,"*[a] *"You shall not covet,"*[b] and if *there is* any other commandment, are *all* summed up in this saying, namely, *"You shall love your neighbor as yourself."*[c]
10 Love does no harm to a neighbor; therefore love *is* the fulfillment of the law.

Put on Christ

11 And *do* this, knowing the time, that now *it is* high time to awake out of sleep; for now our salvation *is* nearer than when we *first* believed.
12 The night is far spent, the day is at hand. Therefore let us cast off the works of darkness, and let us put on the armor of light.
13 Let us walk properly, as in the day, not in revelry and drunkenness, not in lewdness and lust, not in strife and envy.
14 But put on the Lord Jesus Christ, and make no provision for the flesh, to *fulfill its* lusts.

The Law of Liberty

14 Receive one who is weak in the faith, *but* not to disputes over doubtful things.
2 For one believes he may eat all things, but he who is weak eats *only* vegetables.
3 Let not him who eats despise him who does not eat, and let not him who does not eat judge him who eats; for God has received him.
4 Who are you to judge another's servant? To his own master he stands or falls. Indeed, he will be made to stand, for God is able to make him stand.
5 One person esteems *one* day above another; another esteems every day *alike.* Let each be fully convinced in his own mind.
6 He who observes the day, observes *it* to the Lord;[a] and he who does not observe the day, to the Lord he does not observe *it.* He who eats, eats to the Lord, for he gives God thanks; and he who does not eat, to the Lord he does not eat, and gives God thanks.
7 For none of us lives to himself, and no one dies to himself.
8 For if we live, we live to the Lord; and if we die, we die to the Lord. Therefore, whether we live or die, we are the Lord's.
9 For to this end Christ died and rose[a] and lived again, that He might be Lord of both the dead and the living.
10 But why do you judge your brother? Or why do you show contempt for your brother? For we shall all stand before the judgment seat of Christ.[a]
11 For it is written:

"As I live, says the LORD,
Every knee shall bow to Me,
And every tongue shall confess to God."[a]

12 So then each of us shall give account of himself to God.
13 Therefore let us not judge one another anymore, but rather resolve this, not to put a stumbling block or a cause to fall in *our* brother's way.

The Law of Love

14 I know and am convinced by the Lord Jesus that *there is* nothing unclean of itself; but to him who considers anything to be unclean, to him *it is* unclean.
15 Yet if your brother is grieved because of *your* food, you are no longer walking in love. Do not destroy with your food the one for whom Christ died.
16 Therefore do not let your good be spoken of as evil;
17 for the kingdom of God is not eating and drinking, but righteousness and peace and joy in the Holy Spirit.
18 For he who serves Christ in these things[a] *is* acceptable to God and approved by men.
19 Therefore let us pursue the things *which make* for peace and the things by which one may edify another.
20 Do not destroy the work of God for the sake of food. All things indeed *are* pure, but *it is* evil for the man who eats with offense.
21 *It is* good neither to eat meat nor drink

12:19 [a]Deuteronomy 32:35 **12:20** [a]Proverbs 25:21, 22 **13:9** [a]NU-Text omits *"You shall not bear false witness."* [b]Exodus 20:13–15, 17; Deuteronomy 5:17–19, 21 [c]Leviticus 19:18 **14:6** [a]NU-Text omits the rest of this sentence. **14:9** [a]NU-Text omits *and rose.* **14:10** [a]NU-Text reads *of God.* **14:11** [a]Isaiah 45:23 **14:18** [a]NU-Text reads *this.*

wine nor *do anything* by which your brother stumbles or is offended or is made weak.[a]
22 Do you have faith? Have[a] *it* to yourself before God. Happy *is* he who does not condemn himself in what he approves.
23 But he who doubts is condemned if he eats, because *he does* not *eat* from faith; for whatever *is* not from faith is sin.[a]

Bearing Others' Burdens

15 We then who are strong ought to bear with the scruples of the weak, and not to please ourselves.
2 Let each of us please *his* neighbor for *his* good, leading to edification.
3 For even Christ did not please Himself; but as it is written, *"The reproaches of those who reproached You fell on Me."*[a]
4 For whatever things were written before were written for our learning, that we through the patience and comfort of the Scriptures might have hope.
5 Now may the God of patience and comfort grant you to be like-minded toward one another, according to Christ Jesus,
6 that you may with one mind *and* one mouth glorify the God and Father of our Lord Jesus Christ.

Glorify God Together

7 Therefore receive one another, just as Christ also received us,[a] to the glory of God.
8 Now I say that Jesus Christ has become a servant to the circumcision for the truth of God, to confirm the promises *made* to the fathers,
9 and that the Gentiles might glorify God for *His* mercy, as it is written:

> *"For this reason I will confess to You*
> *among the Gentiles,*
> *And sing to Your name."*[a]

10 And again he says:

> *"Rejoice, O Gentiles, with His people!"*[a]

11 And again:

> *"Praise the LORD, all you Gentiles!*
> *Laud Him, all you peoples!"*[a]

12 And again, Isaiah says:

> *"There shall be a root of Jesse;*
> *And He who shall rise to reign over the*
> *Gentiles,*
> *In Him the Gentiles shall hope."*[a]

13 Now may the God of hope fill you with all joy and peace in believing, that you may abound in hope by the power of the Holy Spirit.

From Jerusalem to Illyricum

14 Now I myself am confident concerning you, my brethren, that you also are full of goodness, filled with all knowledge, able also to admonish one another.[a]
15 Nevertheless, brethren, I have written more boldly to you on *some* points, as reminding you, because of the grace given to me by God,
16 that I might be a minister of Jesus Christ to the Gentiles, ministering the gospel of God, that the offering of the Gentiles might be acceptable, sanctified by the Holy Spirit.
17 Therefore I have reason to glory in Christ Jesus in the things *which pertain* to God.
18 For I will not dare to speak of any of those things which Christ has not accomplished through me, in word and deed, to make the Gentiles obedient—
19 in mighty signs and wonders, by the power of the Spirit of God, so that from Jerusalem and round about to Illyricum I have fully preached the gospel of Christ.
20 And so I have made it my aim to preach the gospel, not where Christ was named, lest I should build on another man's foundation,
21 but as it is written:

> *"To whom He was not announced, they*
> *shall see;*
> *And those who have not heard shall*
> *understand."*[a]

Plan to Visit Rome

22 For this reason I also have been much hindered from coming to you.
23 But now no longer having a place in these parts, and having a great desire these many years to come to you,
24 whenever I journey to Spain, I shall come to you.[a] For I hope to see you on my journey, and to be helped on my way there by you, if first I may enjoy your *company* for a while.
25 But now I am going to Jerusalem to minister to the saints.
26 For it pleased those from Macedonia and Achaia to make a certain contribution for the poor among the saints who are in Jerusalem.
27 It pleased them indeed, and they are their debtors. For if the Gentiles have been partakers of their spiritual things, their duty is also to minister to them in material things.
28 Therefore, when I have performed this and have sealed to them this fruit, I shall go by way of you to Spain.
29 But I know that when I come to you, I shall come in the fullness of the blessing of the gospel[a] of Christ.
30 Now I beg you, brethren, through the Lord Jesus Christ, and through the love of the Spirit, that you strive together with me in prayers to God for me,
31 that I may be delivered from those in Judea who do not believe, and that my service for Jerusalem may be acceptable to the saints,
32 that I may come to you with joy by the will of God, and may be refreshed together with you.
33 Now the God of peace *be* with you all. Amen.

Sister Phoebe Commended

16 I commend to you Phoebe our sister, who is a servant of the church in Cenchrea,
2 that you may receive her in the Lord in a manner worthy of the saints, and assist her in whatever business she has need of you; for indeed she has been a helper of many and of myself also.

14:21 [a]NU-Text omits *or is offended or is made weak.* **14:22** [a]NU-Text reads *The faith which you have—have.* **14:23** [a]M-Text puts Romans 16:25–27 here. **15:3** [a]Psalm 69:9 **15:7** [a]NU-Text and M-Text read *you.* **15:9** [a]2 Samuel 22:50; Psalm 18:49 **15:10** [a]Deuteronomy 32:43 **15:11** [a]Psalm 117:1 **15:12** [a]Isaiah 11:10 **15:14** [a]M-Text reads *others.* **15:21** [a]Isaiah 52:15 **15:24** [a]NU-Text omits *I shall come to you* (and joins *Spain* with the next sentence). **15:29** [a]NU-Text omits *of the gospel.*

Greeting Roman Saints

3 Greet Priscilla and Aquila, my fellow work-
ers in Christ Jesus,
4 who risked their own necks for my life, to
whom not only I give thanks, but also all the
churches of the Gentiles.
5 Likewise *greet* the church that is in their
house. Greet my beloved Epaenetus, who is the
firstfruits of Achaia[a] to Christ.
6 Greet Mary, who labored much for us.
7 Greet Andronicus and Junia, my country-
men and my fellow prisoners, who are of note
among the apostles, who also were in Christ be-
fore me.
8 Greet Amplias, my beloved in the Lord.
9 Greet Urbanus, our fellow worker in Christ,
and Stachys, my beloved.
10 Greet Apelles, approved in Christ. Greet
those who are of the *household* of Aristobulus.
11 Greet Herodion, my countryman.[a] Greet
those who are of the *household* of Narcissus
who are in the Lord.
12 Greet Tryphena and Tryphosa, who have
labored in the Lord. Greet the beloved Persis,
who labored much in the Lord.
13 Greet Rufus, chosen in the Lord, and his
mother and mine.
14 Greet Asyncritus, Phlegon, Hermas, Patro-
bas, Hermes, and the brethren who are with
them.
15 Greet Philologus and Julia, Nereus and his
sister, and Olympas, and all the saints who are
with them.
16 Greet one another with a holy kiss. The[a]
churches of Christ greet you.

Avoid Divisive Persons

17 Now I urge you, brethren, note those who
cause divisions and offenses, contrary to the
doctrine which you learned, and avoid them.
18 For those who are such do not serve our
Lord Jesus[a] Christ, but their own belly, and by
smooth words and flattering speech deceive the
hearts of the simple.
19 For your obedience has become known to
all. Therefore I am glad on your behalf; but I
want you to be wise in what is good, and simple
concerning evil.
20 And the God of peace will crush Satan un-
der your feet shortly. The grace of our Lord
Jesus Christ *be* with you. Amen.

Greetings from Paul's Friends

21 Timothy, my fellow worker, and Lucius, Ja-
son, and Sosipater, my countrymen, greet you.
22 I, Tertius, who wrote *this* epistle, greet you
in the Lord.
23 Gaius, my host and *the host* of the whole
church, greets you. Erastus, the treasurer of the
city, greets you, and Quartus, a brother.
24 The grace of our Lord Jesus Christ *be* with
you all. Amen.[a]

Benediction

25 Now to Him who is able to establish you
according to my gospel and the preaching of
Jesus Christ, according to the revelation of the
mystery kept secret since the world began
26 but now made manifest, and by the pro-
phetic Scriptures made known to all nations,
according to the commandment of the ever-
lasting God, for obedience to the faith—
27 to God, alone wise, *be* glory through Jesus
Christ forever. Amen.[a]

The First Epistle of Paul the Apostle to the CORINTHIANS

Greeting

1 Paul, called *to be* an apostle of Jesus Christ
through the will of God, and Sosthenes *our*
brother,
2 To the church of God which is at Corinth,
to those who are sanctified in Christ Jesus,
called *to be* saints, with all who in every place
call on the name of Jesus Christ our Lord, both
theirs and ours:
3 Grace to you and peace from God our Fa-
ther and the Lord Jesus Christ.

Spiritual Gifts at Corinth

4 I thank my God always concerning you for
the grace of God which was given to you by
Christ Jesus,
5 that you were enriched in everything by
Him in all utterance and all knowledge,
6 even as the testimony of Christ was con-
firmed in you,
7 so that you come short in no gift, eagerly
waiting for the revelation of our Lord Jesus
Christ,
8 who will also confirm you to the end, *that*
you may be blameless in the day of our Lord
Jesus Christ.
9 God *is* faithful, by whom you were called
into the fellowship of His Son, Jesus Christ our
Lord.

Sectarianism Is Sin

10 Now I plead with you, brethren, by the name
of our Lord Jesus Christ, that you all speak
the same thing, and *that* there be no divisions
among you, but *that* you be perfectly joined
together in the same mind and in the same
judgment.
11 For it has been declared to me concerning
you, my brethren, by those of Chloe's *house-*
hold, that there are contentions among you.
12 Now I say this, that each of you says, "I
am of Paul," or "I am of Apollos," or "I am of
Cephas," or "I am of Christ."
13 Is Christ divided? Was Paul crucified for
you? Or were you baptized in the name of Paul?
14 I thank God that I baptized none of you ex-
cept Crispus and Gaius,
15 lest anyone should say that I had baptized
in my own name.
16 Yes, I also baptized the household of

16:5 [a]NU-Text reads *Asia.* **16:11** [a]Or *relative* **16:16** [a]NU-Text reads *All the churches.* **16:18** [a]NU-Text and M-Text omit *Jesus.* **16:24** [a]NU-Text omits this verse. **16:27** [a]M-Text puts Romans 16:25–27 after Romans 14:23.

Stephanas. Besides, I do not know whether I
baptized any other.
17 For Christ did not send me to baptize, but to
preach the gospel, not with wisdom of words,
lest the cross of Christ should be made of no
effect.

Christ the Power and Wisdom of God

18 For the message of the cross is foolishness
to those who are perishing, but to us who are
being saved it is the power of God.
19 For it is written:

"I will destroy the wisdom of the wise,
And bring to nothing the understanding
of the prudent."[a]

20 Where *is* the wise? Where *is* the scribe?
Where *is* the disputer of this age? Has not God
made foolish the wisdom of this world?
21 For since, in the wisdom of God, the world
through wisdom did not know God, it pleased
God through the foolishness of the message
preached to save those who believe.
22 For Jews request a sign, and Greeks seek
after wisdom;
23 but we preach Christ crucified, to the Jews
a stumbling block and to the Greeks[a] foolish-
ness,
24 but to those who are called, both Jews and
Greeks, Christ the power of God and the wis-
dom of God.
25 Because the foolishness of God is wiser
than men, and the weakness of God is stronger
than men.

Glory Only in the Lord

26 For you see your calling, brethren, that not
many wise according to the flesh, not many
mighty, not many noble, *are called.*
27 But God has chosen the foolish things of the
world to put to shame the wise, and God has
chosen the weak things of the world to put to
shame the things which are mighty;
28 and the base things of the world and the
things which are despised God has chosen, and
the things which are not, to bring to nothing
the things that are,
29 that no flesh should glory in His presence.
30 But of Him you are in Christ Jesus, who
became for us wisdom from God—and righteous-
ness and sanctification and redemption—
31 that, as it is written, *"He who glories, let him*
glory in the LORD."[a]

Christ Crucified

2 And I, brethren, when I came to you, did
not come with excellence of speech or of
wisdom declaring to you the testimony[a] of
God.
2 For I determined not to know anything
among you except Jesus Christ and Him cruci-
fied.
3 I was with you in weakness, in fear, and in
much trembling.
4 And my speech and my preaching *were* not
with persuasive words of human[a] wisdom, but
in demonstration of the Spirit and of power,
5 that your faith should not be in the wisdom
of men but in the power of God.

Spiritual Wisdom

6 However, we speak wisdom among those
who are mature, yet not the wisdom of this age,
nor of the rulers of this age, who are coming to
nothing.
7 But we speak the wisdom of God in a mys-
tery, the hidden *wisdom* which God ordained
before the ages for our glory,
8 which none of the rulers of this age knew;
for had they known, they would not have cruci-
fied the Lord of glory.
9 But as it is written:

"Eye has not seen, nor ear heard,
Nor have entered into the heart of man
The things which God has prepared for
those who love Him."[a]

10 But God has revealed *them* to us through
His Spirit. For the Spirit searches all things, yes,
the deep things of God.
11 For what man knows the things of a man
except the spirit of the man which is in him?
Even so no one knows the things of God except
the Spirit of God.
12 Now we have received, not the spirit of the
world, but the Spirit who is from God, that we
might know the things that have been freely
given to us by God.
13 These things we also speak, not in words
which man's wisdom teaches but which the Holy[a]
Spirit teaches, comparing spiritual things with
spiritual.
14 But the natural man does not receive the
things of the Spirit of God, for they are foolish-
ness to him; nor can he know *them,* because
they are spiritually discerned.
15 But he who is spiritual judges all things, yet
he himself is *rightly* judged by no one.
16 For *"who has known the mind of the LORD*
that he may instruct Him?"[a] But we have the
mind of Christ.

Sectarianism Is Carnal

3 And I, brethren, could not speak to you as
to spiritual *people* but as to carnal, as to
babes in Christ.
2 I fed you with milk and not with solid food;
for until now you were not able *to receive it,*
and even now you are still not able;
3 for you are still carnal. For where *there are*
envy, strife, and divisions among you, are you
not carnal and behaving like *mere* men?
4 For when one says, "I am of Paul," and
another, "I *am* of Apollos," are you not carnal?

Watering, Working, Warning

5 Who then is Paul, and who *is* Apollos, but
ministers through whom you believed, as the
Lord gave to each one?
6 I planted, Apollos watered, but God gave
the increase.
7 So then neither he who plants is anything,
nor he who waters, but God who gives the in-
crease.
8 Now he who plants and he who waters are
one, and each one will receive his own reward
according to his own labor.
9 For we are God's fellow workers; you are
God's field, *you are* God's building.
10 According to the grace of God which was
given to me, as a wise master builder I have laid

1:19 [a]Isaiah 29:14 **1:23** [a]NU-Text reads *Gentiles.* **1:31** [a]Jeremiah 9:24 **2:1** [a]NU-Text reads *mystery.* **2:4** [a]NU-Text omits *human.* **2:9** [a]Isaiah 64:4 **2:13** [a]NU-Text omits *Holy.* **2:16** [a]Isaiah 40:13

the foundation, and another builds on it. But
let each one take heed how he builds on it.
11 For no other foundation can anyone lay
than that which is laid, which is Jesus Christ.
12 Now if anyone builds on this foundation
with gold, silver, precious stones, wood, hay,
straw,
13 each one's work will become clear; for the
Day will declare it, because it will be revealed
by fire; and the fire will test each one's work,
of what sort it is.
14 If anyone's work which he has built on *it*
endures, he will receive a reward.
15 If anyone's work is burned, he will suffer
loss; but he himself will be saved, yet so as
through fire.
16 Do you not know that you are the temple
of God and *that* the Spirit of God dwells in
you?
17 If anyone defiles the temple of God, God
will destroy him. For the temple of God is holy,
which *temple* you are.

Avoid Worldly Wisdom

18 Let no one deceive himself. If anyone
among you seems to be wise in this age, let
him become a fool that he may become wise.
19 For the wisdom of this world is foolishness
with God. For it is written, *"He catches the wise
in their own craftiness"*;[a]
20 and again, *"The* LORD *knows the thoughts
of the wise, that they are futile."*[a]
21 Therefore let no one boast in men. For all
things are yours:
22 whether Paul or Apollos or Cephas, or the
world or life or death, or things present or
things to come—all are yours.
23 And you *are* Christ's, and Christ *is* God's.

Stewards of the Mysteries of God

4 Let a man so consider us, as servants of
Christ and stewards of the mysteries of
God.
2 Moreover it is required in stewards that
one be found faithful.
3 But with me it is a very small thing that I
should be judged by you or by a human court.[a]
In fact, I do not even judge myself.
4 For I know of nothing against myself, yet I
am not justified by this; but He who judges me
is the Lord.
5 Therefore judge nothing before the time,
until the Lord comes, who will both bring to
light the hidden things of darkness and reveal
the counsels of the hearts. Then each one's
praise will come from God.

Fools for Christ's Sake

6 Now these things, brethren, I have figura-
tively transferred to myself and Apollos for
your sakes, that you may learn in us not to think
beyond what is written, that none of you may
be puffed up on behalf of one against the other.
7 For who makes you differ *from another?*
And what do you have that you did not receive?
Now if you did indeed receive *it,* why do you
boast as if you had not received *it?*
8 You are already full! You are already rich!
You have reigned as kings without us—and in-
deed I could wish you did reign, that we also
might reign with you!
9 For I think that God has displayed us, the
apostles, last, as men condemned to death; for
we have been made a spectacle to the world,
both to angels and to men.
10 We *are* fools for Christ's sake, but you *are*
wise in Christ! We *are* weak, but you *are*
strong! You *are* distinguished, but we *are* dis-
honored!
11 To the present hour we both hunger and
thirst, and we are poorly clothed, and beaten,
and homeless.
12 And we labor, working with our own
hands. Being reviled, we bless; being perse-
cuted, we endure;
13 being defamed, we entreat. We have been
made as the filth of the world, the offscouring
of all things until now.

Paul's Paternal Care

14 I do not write these things to shame you,
but as my beloved children I warn *you.*
15 For though you might have ten thousand
instructors in Christ, yet *you do* not *have* many
fathers; for in Christ Jesus I have begotten you
through the gospel.
16 Therefore I urge you, imitate me.
17 For this reason I have sent Timothy to you,
who is my beloved and faithful son in the Lord,
who will remind you of my ways in Christ, as
I teach everywhere in every church.
18 Now some are puffed up, as though I were
not coming to you.
19 But I will come to you shortly, if the Lord
wills, and I will know, not the word of those
who are puffed up, but the power.
20 For the kingdom of God *is* not in word but
in power.
21 What do you want? Shall I come to you
with a rod, or in love and a spirit of gentleness?

Immorality Defiles the Church

5 It is actually reported *that there is* sexual
immorality among you, and such sexual
immorality as is not even named[a] among the
Gentiles—that a man has his father's wife!
2 And you are puffed up, and have not rather
mourned, that he who has done this deed
might be taken away from among you.
3 For I indeed, as absent in body but present
in spirit, have already judged (as though I were
present) him who has so done this deed.
4 In the name of our Lord Jesus Christ, when
you are gathered together, along with my
spirit, with the power of our Lord Jesus Christ,
5 deliver such a one to Satan for the destruc-
tion of the flesh, that his spirit may be saved in
the day of the Lord Jesus.[a]
6 Your glorying *is* not good. Do you not
know that a little leaven leavens the whole
lump?
7 Therefore purge out the old leaven, that you
may be a new lump, since you truly are unleav-
ened. For indeed Christ, our Passover, was sac-
rificed for us.[a]
8 Therefore let us keep the feast, not with old
leaven, nor with the leaven of malice and wick-
edness, but with the unleavened *bread* of sin-
cerity and truth.

Immorality Must Be Judged

9 I wrote to you in my epistle not to keep
company with sexually immoral people.

3:19 [a]Job 5:13 **3:20** [a]Psalm 94:11 **4:3** [a]Literally *day* **5:1** [a]NU-Text omits *named.* **5:5** [a]NU-Text omits *Jesus.*
5:7 [a]NU-Text omits *for us.*

10 Yet *I* certainly *did* not *mean* with the sexually immoral people of this world, or with the covetous, or extortioners, or idolaters, since then you would need to go out of the world.
11 But now I have written to you not to keep company with anyone named a brother, who is sexually immoral, or covetous, or an idolater, or a reviler, or a drunkard, or an extortioner—not even to eat with such a person.
12 For what *have* I *to do* with judging those also who are outside? Do you not judge those who are inside?
13 But those who are outside God judges. Therefore *"put away from yourselves the evil person."*[a]

Do Not Sue the Brethren

6 Dare any of you, having a matter against another, go to law before the unrighteous, and not before the saints?
2 Do you not know that the saints will judge the world? And if the world will be judged by you, are you unworthy to judge the smallest matters?
3 Do you not know that we shall judge angels? How much more, things that pertain to this life?
4 If then you have judgments concerning things pertaining to this life, do you appoint those who are least esteemed by the church to judge?
5 I say this to your shame. Is it so, that there is not a wise man among you, not even one, who will be able to judge between his brethren?
6 But brother goes to law against brother, and that before unbelievers!
7 Now therefore, it is already an utter failure for you that you go to law against one another. Why do you not rather accept wrong? Why do you not rather *let yourselves* be cheated?
8 No, you yourselves do wrong and cheat, and *you do* these things *to your* brethren!
9 Do you not know that the unrighteous will not inherit the kingdom of God? Do not be deceived. Neither fornicators, nor idolaters, nor adulterers, nor homosexuals,[a] nor sodomites,
10 nor thieves, nor covetous, nor drunkards, nor revilers, nor extortioners will inherit the kingdom of God.
11 And such were some of you. But you were washed, but you were sanctified, but you were justified in the name of the Lord Jesus and by the Spirit of our God.

Glorify God in Body and Spirit

12 All things are lawful for me, but all things are not helpful. All things are lawful for me, but I will not be brought under the power of any.
13 Foods for the stomach and the stomach for foods, but God will destroy both it and them. Now the body *is* not for sexual immorality but for the Lord, and the Lord for the body.
14 And God both raised up the Lord and will also raise us up by His power.
15 Do you not know that your bodies are members of Christ? Shall I then take the members of Christ and make *them* members of a harlot? Certainly not!
16 Or do you not know that he who is joined to a harlot is one body *with her*? For *"the two,"* He says, *"shall become one flesh."*[a]
17 But he who is joined to the Lord is one spirit *with Him.*
18 Flee sexual immorality. Every sin that a man does is outside the body, but he who commits sexual immorality sins against his own body.
19 Or do you not know that your body is the temple of the Holy Spirit *who is* in you, whom you have from God, and you are not your own?
20 For you were bought at a price; therefore glorify God in your body[a] and in your spirit, which are God's.

Principles of Marriage

7 Now concerning the things of which you wrote to me: *It is* good for a man not to touch a woman.
2 Nevertheless, because of sexual immorality, let each man have his own wife, and let each woman have her own husband.
3 Let the husband render to his wife the affection due her, and likewise also the wife to her husband.
4 The wife does not have authority over her own body, but the husband *does.* And likewise the husband does not have authority over his own body, but the wife *does.*
5 Do not deprive one another except with consent for a time, that you may give yourselves to fasting and prayer; and come together again so that Satan does not tempt you because of your lack of self-control.
6 But I say this as a concession, not as a commandment.
7 For I wish that all men were even as I myself. But each one has his own gift from God, one in this manner and another in that.
8 But I say to the unmarried and to the widows: It is good for them if they remain even as I am;
9 but if they cannot exercise self-control, let them marry. For it is better to marry than to burn *with passion.*

Keep Your Marriage Vows

10 Now to the married I command, *yet* not I but the Lord: A wife is not to depart from *her* husband.
11 But even if she does depart, let her remain unmarried or be reconciled to *her* husband. And a husband is not to divorce *his* wife.
12 But to the rest I, not the Lord, say: If any brother has a wife who does not believe, and she is willing to live with him, let him not divorce her.
13 And a woman who has a husband who does not believe, if he is willing to live with her, let her not divorce him.
14 For the unbelieving husband is sanctified by the wife, and the unbelieving wife is sanctified by the husband; otherwise your children would be unclean, but now they are holy.
15 But if the unbeliever departs, let him depart; a brother or a sister is not under bondage in such *cases.* But God has called us to peace.
16 For how do you know, O wife, whether you will save *your* husband? Or how do you know, O husband, whether you will save *your* wife?

5:13 [a]Deuteronomy 17:7; 19:19; 22:21, 24; 24:7 **6:9** [a]That is, catamites **6:16** [a]Genesis 2:24 **6:20** [a]NU-Text ends the verse at *body.*

Live as You Are Called

17 But as God has distributed to each one, as the Lord has called each one, so let him walk. And so I ordain in all the churches.

18 Was anyone called while circumcised? Let him not become uncircumcised. Was anyone called while uncircumcised? Let him not be circumcised.

19 Circumcision is nothing and uncircumcision is nothing, but keeping the commandments of God *is what matters.*

20 Let each one remain in the same calling in which he was called.

21 Were you called *while* a slave? Do not be concerned about it; but if you can be made free, rather use *it.*

22 For he who is called in the Lord *while* a slave is the Lord's freedman. Likewise he who is called *while* free is Christ's slave.

23 You were bought at a price; do not become slaves of men.

24 Brethren, let each one remain with God in that *state* in which he was called.

To the Unmarried and Widows

25 Now concerning virgins: I have no commandment from the Lord; yet I give judgment as one whom the Lord in His mercy has made trustworthy.

26 I suppose therefore that this is good because of the present distress—that *it is* good for a man to remain as he is:

27 Are you bound to a wife? Do not seek to be loosed. Are you loosed from a wife? Do not seek a wife.

28 But even if you do marry, you have not sinned; and if a virgin marries, she has not sinned. Nevertheless such will have trouble in the flesh, but I would spare you.

29 But this I say, brethren, the time *is* short, so that from now on even those who have wives should be as though they had none,

30 those who weep as though they did not weep, those who rejoice as though they did not rejoice, those who buy as though they did not possess,

31 and those who use this world as not misusing *it.* For the form of this world is passing away.

32 But I want you to be without care. He who is unmarried cares for the things of the Lord—how he may please the Lord.

33 But he who is married cares about the things of the world—how he may please *his* wife.

34 There is[a] a difference between a wife and a virgin. The unmarried woman cares about the things of the Lord, that she may be holy both in body and in spirit. But she who is married cares about the things of the world—how she may please *her* husband.

35 And this I say for your own profit, not that I may put a leash on you, but for what is proper, and that you may serve the Lord without distraction.

36 But if any man thinks he is behaving improperly toward his virgin, if she is past the flower of youth, and thus it must be, let him do what he wishes. He does not sin; let them marry.

37 Nevertheless he who stands steadfast in his heart, having no necessity, but has power over his own will, and has so determined in his heart that he will keep his virgin,[a] does well.

38 So then he who gives *her*[a] in marriage does well, but he who does not give *her* in marriage does better.

39 A wife is bound by law as long as her husband lives; but if her husband dies, she is at liberty to be married to whom she wishes, only in the Lord.

40 But she is happier if she remains as she is, according to my judgment—and I think I also have the Spirit of God.

Be Sensitive to Conscience

8 Now concerning things offered to idols: We know that we all have knowledge. Knowledge puffs up, but love edifies.

2 And if anyone thinks that he knows anything, he knows nothing yet as he ought to know.

3 But if anyone loves God, this one is known by Him.

4 Therefore concerning the eating of things offered to idols, we know that an idol *is* nothing in the world, and that *there is* no other God but one.

5 For even if there are so-called gods, whether in heaven or on earth (as there are many gods and many lords),

6 yet for us *there is* one God, the Father, of whom *are* all things, and we for Him; and one Lord Jesus Christ, through whom *are* all things, and through whom we *live.*

7 However, *there is* not in everyone that knowledge; for some, with consciousness of the idol, until now eat *it* as a thing offered to an idol; and their conscience, being weak, is defiled.

8 But food does not commend us to God; for neither if we eat are we the better, nor if we do not eat are we the worse.

9 But beware lest somehow this liberty of yours become a stumbling block to those who are weak.

10 For if anyone sees you who have knowledge eating in an idol's temple, will not the conscience of him who is weak be emboldened to eat those things offered to idols?

11 And because of your knowledge shall the weak brother perish, for whom Christ died?

12 But when you thus sin against the brethren, and wound their weak conscience, you sin against Christ.

13 Therefore, if food makes my brother stumble, I will never again eat meat, lest I make my brother stumble.

A Pattern of Self-Denial

9 Am I not an apostle? Am I not free? Have I not seen Jesus Christ our Lord? Are you not my work in the Lord?

2 If I am not an apostle to others, yet doubtless I am to you. For you are the seal of my apostleship in the Lord.

3 My defense to those who examine me is this:

4 Do we have no right to eat and drink?

5 Do we have no right to take along a believing wife, as *do* also the other apostles, the brothers of the Lord, and Cephas?

6 Or *is it* only Barnabas and I *who* have no right to refrain from working?

7 Who ever goes to war at his own expense? Who plants a vineyard and does not eat of its fruit? Or who tends a flock and does not drink of the milk of the flock?

8 Do I say these things as a *mere* man? Or does not the law say the same also?

7:34 [a]M-Text adds *also.* **7:37** [a]Or *virgin daughter* **7:38** [a]NU-Text reads *his own virgin.*

9 For it is written in the law of Moses, *"You shall not muzzle an ox while it treads out the grain."*[a] Is it oxen God is concerned about?
10 Or does He say *it* altogether for our sakes? For our sakes, no doubt, *this* is written, that he who plows should plow in hope, and he who threshes in hope should be partaker of his hope.
11 If we have sown spiritual things for you, *is it* a great thing if we reap your material things?
12 If others are partakers of *this* right over you, *are* we not even more? Nevertheless we have not used this right, but endure all things lest we hinder the gospel of Christ.
13 Do you not know that those who minister the holy things eat *of the things* of the temple, and those who serve at the altar partake of *the offerings of* the altar?
14 Even so the Lord has commanded that those who preach the gospel should live from the gospel.
15 But I have used none of these things, nor have I written these things that it should be done so to me; for it *would be* better for me to die than that anyone should make my boasting void.
16 For if I preach the gospel, I have nothing to boast of, for necessity is laid upon me; yes, woe is me if I do not preach the gospel!
17 For if I do this willingly, I have a reward; but if against my will, I have been entrusted with a stewardship.
18 What is my reward then? That when I preach the gospel, I may present the gospel of Christ[a] without charge, that I may not abuse my authority in the gospel.

Serving All Men

19 For though I am free from all *men,* I have made myself a servant to all, that I might win the more;
20 and to the Jews I became as a Jew, that I might win Jews; to those *who are* under the law, as under the law,[a] that I might win those *who are* under the law;
21 to those *who are* without law, as without law (not being without law toward God,[a] but under law toward Christ[b]), that I might win those *who are* without law;
22 to the weak I became as[a] weak, that I might win the weak. I have become all things to all *men,* that I might by all means save some.
23 Now this I do for the gospel's sake, that I may be partaker of it with *you.*

Striving for a Crown

24 Do you not know that those who run in a race all run, but one receives the prize? Run in such a way that you may obtain *it.*
25 And everyone who competes *for the prize* is temperate in all things. Now they *do it* to obtain a perishable crown, but we *for* an imperishable *crown.*
26 Therefore I run thus: not with uncertainty. Thus I fight: not as *one who* beats the air.
27 But I discipline my body and bring *it* into subjection, lest, when I have preached to others, I myself should become disqualified.

Old Testament Examples

10 Moreover, brethren, I do not want you to be unaware that all our fathers were under the cloud, all passed through the sea,
2 all were baptized into Moses in the cloud and in the sea,
3 all ate the same spiritual food,
4 and all drank the same spiritual drink. For they drank of that spiritual Rock that followed them, and that Rock was Christ.
5 But with most of them God was not well pleased, for *their bodies* were scattered in the wilderness.
6 Now these things became our examples, to the intent that we should not lust after evil things as they also lusted.
7 And do not become idolaters as *were* some of them. As it is written, *"The people sat down to eat and drink, and rose up to play."*[a]
8 Nor let us commit sexual immorality, as some of them did, and in one day twenty-three thousand fell;
9 nor let us tempt Christ, as some of them also tempted, and were destroyed by serpents;
10 nor complain, as some of them also complained, and were destroyed by the destroyer.
11 Now all[a] these things happened to them as examples, and they were written for our admonition, upon whom the ends of the ages have come.
12 Therefore let him who thinks he stands take heed lest he fall.
13 No temptation has overtaken you except such as is common to man; but God *is* faithful, who will not allow you to be tempted beyond what you are able, but with the temptation will also make the way of escape, that you may be able to bear *it.*

Flee from Idolatry

14 Therefore, my beloved, flee from idolatry.
15 I speak as to wise men; judge for yourselves what I say.
16 The cup of blessing which we bless, is it not the communion of the blood of Christ? The bread which we break, is it not the communion of the body of Christ?
17 For we, *though* many, are one bread *and* one body; for we all partake of that one bread.
18 Observe Israel after the flesh: Are not those who eat of the sacrifices partakers of the altar?
19 What am I saying then? That an idol is anything, or what is offered to idols is anything?
20 Rather, that the things which the Gentiles sacrifice they sacrifice to demons and not to God, and I do not want you to have fellowship with demons.
21 You cannot drink the cup of the Lord and the cup of demons; you cannot partake of the Lord's table and of the table of demons.
22 Or do we provoke the Lord to jealousy? Are we stronger than He?

All to the Glory of God

23 All things are lawful for me,[a] but not all things are helpful; all things are lawful for me,[b] but not all things edify.
24 Let no one seek his own, but each one the other's *well-being.*

9:9 [a]Deuteronomy 25:4 **9:18** [a]NU-Text omits *of Christ.* **9:20** [a]NU-Text adds *though not being myself under the law.* **9:21** [a]NU-Text reads *God's law.* [b]NU-Text reads *Christ's law.* **9:22** [a]NU-Text omits *as.* **10:7** [a]Exodus 32:6 **10:11** [a]NU-Text omits *all.* **10:23** [a]NU-Text omits *for me.* [b]NU-Text omits *for me.*

25 Eat whatever is sold in the meat market,
asking no questions for conscience' sake;
26 for *"the earth is the LORD's, and all its full-
ness."*[a]
27 If any of those who do not believe invites
you *to dinner*, and you desire to go, eat what-
ever is set before you, asking no question for
conscience' sake.
28 But if anyone says to you, "This was of-
fered to idols," do not eat it for the sake of the
one who told you, and for conscience' sake;[a]
for *"the earth is the LORD's, and all its fullness."*[b]
29 "Conscience," I say, not your own, but that
of the other. For why is my liberty judged by
another *man's* conscience?
30 But if I partake with thanks, why am I evil
spoken of for *the food* over which I give thanks?
31 Therefore, whether you eat or drink, or
whatever you do, do all to the glory of God.
32 Give no offense, either to the Jews or to
the Greeks or to the church of God,
33 just as I also please all *men* in all *things*,
not seeking my own profit, but the *profit* of
many, that they may be saved.

11 Imitate me, just as I also *imitate* Christ.

Head Coverings

2 Now I praise you, brethren, that you re-
member me in all things and keep the tradi-
tions just as I delivered *them* to you.
3 But I want you to know that the head of
every man is Christ, the head of woman *is* man,
and the head of Christ *is* God.
4 Every man praying or prophesying, hav-
ing *his* head covered, dishonors his head.
5 But every woman who prays or prophesies
with *her* head uncovered dishonors her head,
for that is one and the same as if her head were
shaved.
6 For if a woman is not covered, let her also
be shorn. But if it is shameful for a woman to
be shorn or shaved, let her be covered.
7 For a man indeed ought not to cover *his*
head, since he is the image and glory of God;
but woman is the glory of man.
8 For man is not from woman, but woman
from man.
9 Nor was man created for the woman, but
woman for the man.
10 For this reason the woman ought to have
a symbol of authority on *her* head, because of
the angels.
11 Nevertheless, neither *is* man independent
of woman, nor woman independent of man, in
the Lord.
12 For as woman *came* from man, even so
man also *comes* through woman; but all things
are from God.
13 Judge among yourselves. Is it proper for a
woman to pray to God with her head uncovered?
14 Does not even nature itself teach you that
if a man has long hair, it is a dishonor to him?
15 But if a woman has long hair, it is a glory to
her; for *her* hair is given to her[a] for a covering.
16 But if anyone seems to be contentious, we
have no such custom, nor *do* the churches of God.

Conduct at the Lord's Supper

17 Now in giving these instructions I do not
praise *you*, since you come together not for the
better but for the worse.
18 For first of all, when you come together as
a church, I hear that there are divisions among
you, and in part I believe it.
19 For there must also be factions among you,
that those who are approved may be recog-
nized among you.
20 Therefore when you come together in one
place, it is not to eat the Lord's Supper.
21 For in eating, each one takes his own sup-
per ahead of *others;* and one is hungry and
another is drunk.
22 What! Do you not have houses to eat and
drink in? Or do you despise the church of God
and shame those who have nothing? What
shall I say to you? Shall I praise you in this? I
do not praise *you*.

Institution of the Lord's Supper

23 For I received from the Lord that which I
also delivered to you: that the Lord Jesus on
the *same* night in which He was betrayed took
bread;
24 and when He had given thanks, He broke
it and said, "Take, eat;[a] this is My body which
is broken[b] for you; do this in remembrance of
Me."
25 In the same manner *He* also *took* the cup
after supper, saying, "This cup is the new cov-
enant in My blood. This do, as often as you
drink *it*, in remembrance of Me."
26 For as often as you eat this bread and drink
this cup, you proclaim the Lord's death till He
comes.

Examine Yourself

27 Therefore whoever eats this bread or drinks
this cup of the Lord in an unworthy manner
will be guilty of the body and blood[a] of the Lord.
28 But let a man examine himself, and so let
him eat of the bread and drink of the cup.
29 For he who eats and drinks in an unworthy
manner[a] eats and drinks judgment to himself,
not discerning the Lord's[b] body.
30 For this reason many *are* weak and sick
among you, and many sleep.
31 For if we would judge ourselves, we would
not be judged.
32 But when we are judged, we are chastened
by the Lord, that we may not be condemned
with the world.
33 Therefore, my brethren, when you come
together to eat, wait for one another.
34 But if anyone is hungry, let him eat at
home, lest you come together for judgment.
And the rest I will set in order when I come.

Spiritual Gifts: Unity in Diversity

12 Now concerning spiritual *gifts*, breth-
ren, I do not want you to be ignorant:
2 You know that[a] you were Gentiles, carried
away to these dumb idols, however you were
led.
3 Therefore I make known to you that no one
speaking by the Spirit of God calls Jesus ac-
cursed, and no one can say that Jesus is Lord
except by the Holy Spirit.

10:26 [a]Psalm 24:1 **10:28** [a]NU-Text omits the rest of this verse. [b]Psalm 24:1 **11:15** [a]M-Text omits *to her.*
11:24 [a]NU-Text omits *Take, eat.* [b]NU-Text omits *broken.* **11:27** [a]NU-Text and M-Text read *the blood.*
11:29 [a]NU-Text omits *in an unworthy manner.* [b]NU-Text omits *Lord's.* **12:2** [a]NU-Text and M-Text add *when.*

4 There are diversities of gifts, but the same
Spirit.
5 There are differences of ministries, but the
same Lord.
6 And there are diversities of activities, but
it is the same God who works all in all.
7 But the manifestation of the Spirit is given
to each one for the profit *of all:*
8 for to one is given the word of wisdom
through the Spirit, to another the word of
knowledge through the same Spirit,
9 to another faith by the same Spirit, to an-
other gifts of healings by the same[a] Spirit,
10 to another the working of miracles, to an-
other prophecy, to another discerning of spir-
its, to another *different* kinds of tongues, to
another the interpretation of tongues.
11 But one and the same Spirit works all
these things, distributing to each one individu-
ally as He wills.

Unity and Diversity in One Body

12 For as the body is one and has many mem-
bers, but all the members of that one body,
being many, are one body, so also *is* Christ.
13 For by one Spirit we were all baptized into
one body—whether Jews or Greeks, whether
slaves or free—and have all been made to
drink into[a] one Spirit.
14 For in fact the body is not one member but
many.
15 If the foot should say, "Because I am not a
hand, I am not of the body," is it therefore not
of the body?
16 And if the ear should say, "Because I am
not an eye, I am not of the body," is it therefore
not of the body?
17 If the whole body *were* an eye, where *would
be* the hearing? If the whole *were* hearing,
where *would be* the smelling?
18 But now God has set the members, each one
of them, in the body just as He pleased.
19 And if they were all one member, where
would the body *be?*
20 But now indeed *there are* many members,
yet one body.
21 And the eye cannot say to the hand, "I have
no need of you"; nor again the head to the feet,
"I have no need of you."
22 No, much rather, those members of the
body which seem to be weaker are necessary.
23 And those *members* of the body which we
think to be less honorable, on these we bestow
greater honor; and our unpresentable *parts*
have greater modesty,
24 but our presentable *parts* have no need.
But God composed the body, having given
greater honor to that *part* which lacks it,
25 that there should be no schism in the body,
but *that* the members should have the same
care for one another.
26 And if one member suffers, all the mem-
bers suffer with *it;* or if one member is hon-
ored, all the members rejoice with *it.*
27 Now you are the body of Christ, and mem-
bers individually.
28 And God has appointed these in the church:
first apostles, second prophets, third teachers,
after that miracles, then gifts of healings, helps,
administrations, varieties of tongues.
29 *Are* all apostles? *Are* all prophets? *Are* all
teachers? *Are* all workers of miracles?
30 Do all have gifts of healings? Do all speak
with tongues? Do all interpret?
31 But earnestly desire the best[a] gifts. And yet
I show you a more excellent way.

The Greatest Gift

13 Though I speak with the tongues of men
and of angels, but have not love, I have
become sounding brass or a clanging cymbal.
2 And though I have *the gift of* prophecy, and
understand all mysteries and all knowledge,
and though I have all faith, so that I could re-
move mountains, but have not love, I am nothing.
3 And though I bestow all my goods to feed
the poor, and though I give my body to be
burned,[a] but have not love, it profits me nothing.
4 Love suffers long *and* is kind; love does not
envy; love does not parade itself, is not puffed
up;
5 does not behave rudely, does not seek its
own, is not provoked, thinks no evil;
6 does not rejoice in iniquity, but rejoices in
the truth;
7 bears all things, believes all things, hopes
all things, endures all things.
8 Love never fails. But whether *there are*
prophecies, they will fail; whether *there are*
tongues, they will cease; whether *there is* knowl-
edge, it will vanish away.
9 For we know in part and we prophesy in
part.
10 But when that which is perfect has come,
then that which is in part will be done away.
11 When I was a child, I spoke as a child, I
understood as a child, I thought as a child; but
when I became a man, I put away childish things.
12 For now we see in a mirror, dimly, but then
face to face. Now I know in part, but then I
shall know just as I also am known.
13 And now abide faith, hope, love, these
three; but the greatest of these *is* love.

Prophecy and Tongues

14 Pursue love, and desire spiritual *gifts,*
but especially that you may prophesy.
2 For he who speaks in a tongue does not
speak to men but to God, for no one under-
stands *him;* however, in the spirit he speaks
mysteries.
3 But he who prophesies speaks edification
and exhortation and comfort to men.
4 He who speaks in a tongue edifies himself,
but he who prophesies edifies the church.
5 I wish you all spoke with tongues, but even
more that you prophesied; for[a] he who prophe-
sies *is* greater than he who speaks with tongues,
unless indeed he interprets, that the church may
receive edification.

Tongues Must Be Interpreted

6 But now, brethren, if I come to you speak-
ing with tongues, what shall I profit you unless
I speak to you either by revelation, by knowl-
edge, by prophesying, or by teaching?
7 Even things without life, whether flute or
harp, when they make a sound, unless they make
a distinction in the sounds, how will it be
known what is piped or played?
8 For if the trumpet makes an uncertain
sound, who will prepare for battle?
9 So likewise you, unless you utter by the
tongue words easy to understand, how will it

12:9 [a]NU-Text reads *one.* **12:13** [a]NU-Text omits *into.* **12:31** [a]NU-Text reads *greater.* **13:3** [a]NU-Text reads *so I may boast.* **14:5** [a]NU-Text reads *and.*

be known what is spoken? For you will be
speaking into the air.
10 There are, it may be, so many kinds of languages in the world, and none of them *is* without significance.
11 Therefore, if I do not know the meaning of the language, I shall be a foreigner to him who speaks, and he who speaks *will be* a foreigner to me.
12 Even so you, since you are zealous for spiritual *gifts, let it be* for the edification of the church *that* you seek to excel.
13 Therefore let him who speaks in a tongue pray that he may interpret.
14 For if I pray in a tongue, my spirit prays, but my understanding is unfruitful.
15 What is *the conclusion* then? I will pray with the spirit, and I will also pray with the understanding. I will sing with the spirit, and I will also sing with the understanding.
16 Otherwise, if you bless with the spirit, how will he who occupies the place of the uninformed say "Amen" at your giving of thanks, since he does not understand what you say?
17 For you indeed give thanks well, but the other is not edified.
18 I thank my God I speak with tongues more than you all;
19 yet in the church I would rather speak five words with my understanding, that I may teach others also, than ten thousand words in a tongue.

Tongues a Sign to Unbelievers

20 Brethren, do not be children in understanding; however, in malice be babes, but in understanding be mature.
21 In the law it is written:

> *"With men of other tongues and other lips*
> *I will speak to this people;*
> *And yet, for all that, they will not hear*
> *Me,"*[a]

says the Lord.
22 Therefore tongues are for a sign, not to those who believe but to unbelievers; but prophesying is not for unbelievers but for those who believe.
23 Therefore if the whole church comes together in one place, and all speak with tongues, and there come in *those who are* uninformed or unbelievers, will they not say that you are out of your mind?
24 But if all prophesy, and an unbeliever or an uninformed person comes in, he is convinced by all, he is convicted by all.
25 And thus[a] the secrets of his heart are revealed; and so, falling down on *his* face, he will worship God and report that God is truly among you.

Order in Church Meetings

26 How is it then, brethren? Whenever you come together, each of you has a psalm, has a teaching, has a tongue, has a revelation, has an interpretation. Let all things be done for edification.
27 If anyone speaks in a tongue, *let there be* two or at the most three, *each* in turn, and let one interpret.
28 But if there is no interpreter, let him keep
silent in church, and let him speak to himself and to God.
29 Let two or three prophets speak, and let the others judge.
30 But if *anything* is revealed to another who sits by, let the first keep silent.
31 For you can all prophesy one by one, that all may learn and all may be encouraged.
32 And the spirits of the prophets are subject to the prophets.
33 For God is not *the author* of confusion but of peace, as in all the churches of the saints.
34 Let your[a] women keep silent in the churches, for they are not permitted to speak; but *they are* to be submissive, as the law also says.
35 And if they want to learn something, let them ask their own husbands at home; for it is shameful for women to speak in church.
36 Or did the word of God come *originally* from you? Or *was it* you only that it reached?
37 If anyone thinks himself to be a prophet or spiritual, let him acknowledge that the things which I write to you are the commandments of the Lord.
38 But if anyone is ignorant, let him be ignorant.[a]
39 Therefore, brethren, desire earnestly to prophesy, and do not forbid to speak with tongues.
40 Let all things be done decently and in order.

The Risen Christ, Faith's Reality

15 Moreover, brethren, I declare to you the gospel which I preached to you, which also you received and in which you stand,
2 by which also you are saved, if you hold fast that word which I preached to you—unless you believed in vain.
3 For I delivered to you first of all that which I also received: that Christ died for our sins according to the Scriptures,
4 and that He was buried, and that He rose again the third day according to the Scriptures,
5 and that He was seen by Cephas, then by the twelve.
6 After that He was seen by over five hundred brethren at once, of whom the greater part remain to the present, but some have fallen asleep.
7 After that He was seen by James, then by all the apostles.
8 Then last of all He was seen by me also, as by one born out of due time.
9 For I am the least of the apostles, who am not worthy to be called an apostle, because I persecuted the church of God.
10 But by the grace of God I am what I am, and His grace toward me was not in vain; but I labored more abundantly than they all, yet not I, but the grace of God *which was* with me.
11 Therefore, whether *it was* I or they, so we preach and so you believed.

The Risen Christ, Our Hope

12 Now if Christ is preached that He has been raised from the dead, how do some among you say that there is no resurrection of the dead?
13 But if there is no resurrection of the dead, then Christ is not risen.
14 And if Christ is not risen, then our preaching *is* empty and your faith *is* also empty.

14:21 [a]Isaiah 28:11, 12 **14:25** [a]NU-Text omits *And thus.* **14:34** [a]NU-Text omits *your.* **14:38** [a]NU-Text reads *if anyone does not recognize this, he is not recognized.*

15 Yes, and we are found false witnesses of God, because we have testified of God that He raised up Christ, whom He did not raise up—if in fact the dead do not rise.
16 For if *the* dead do not rise, then Christ is not risen.
17 And if Christ is not risen, your faith *is* futile; you are still in your sins!
18 Then also those who have fallen asleep in Christ have perished.
19 If in this life only we have hope in Christ, we are of all men the most pitiable.

The Last Enemy Destroyed

20 But now Christ is risen from the dead, *and* has become the firstfruits of those who have fallen asleep.
21 For since by man *came* death, by Man also *came* the resurrection of the dead.
22 For as in Adam all die, even so in Christ all shall be made alive.
23 But each one in his own order: Christ the firstfruits, afterward those *who are* Christ's at His coming.
24 Then *comes* the end, when He delivers the kingdom to God the Father, when He puts an end to all rule and all authority and power.
25 For He must reign till He has put all enemies under His feet.
26 The last enemy *that* will be destroyed *is* death.
27 For *"He has put all things under His feet."*[a] But when He says "all things are put under *Him," it is* evident that He who put all things under Him is excepted.
28 Now when all things are made subject to Him, then the Son Himself will also be subject to Him who put all things under Him, that God may be all in all.

Effects of Denying the Resurrection

29 Otherwise, what will they do who are baptized for the dead, if the dead do not rise at all? Why then are they baptized for the dead?
30 And why do we stand in jeopardy every hour?
31 I affirm, by the boasting in you which I have in Christ Jesus our Lord, I die daily.
32 If, in the manner of men, I have fought with beasts at Ephesus, what advantage *is it* to me? If *the* dead do not rise, *"Let us eat and drink, for tomorrow we die!"*[a]
33 Do not be deceived: "Evil company corrupts good habits."
34 Awake to righteousness, and do not sin; for some do not have the knowledge of God. I speak *this* to your shame.

A Glorious Body

35 But someone will say, "How are the dead raised up? And with what body do they come?"
36 Foolish one, what you sow is not made alive unless it dies.
37 And what you sow, you do not sow that body that shall be, but mere grain—perhaps wheat or some other *grain.*
38 But God gives it a body as He pleases, and to each seed its own body.
39 All flesh *is* not the same flesh, but *there is* one *kind of* flesh[a] of men, another flesh of animals, another of fish, *and* another of birds.
40 *There are* also celestial bodies and terrestrial bodies; but the glory of the celestial *is* one, and the *glory* of the terrestrial *is* another.
41 *There is* one glory of the sun, another glory of the moon, and another glory of the stars; for *one* star differs from *another* star in glory.
42 So also *is* the resurrection of the dead. *The body* is sown in corruption, it is raised in incorruption.
43 It is sown in dishonor, it is raised in glory. It is sown in weakness, it is raised in power.
44 It is sown a natural body, it is raised a spiritual body. There is a natural body, and there is a spiritual body.
45 And so it is written, *"The first man Adam became a living being."*[a] The last Adam *became* a life-giving spirit.
46 However, the spiritual is not first, but the natural, and afterward the spiritual.
47 The first man *was* of the earth, *made* of dust; the second Man *is* the Lord[a] from heaven.
48 As *was* the *man* of dust, so also *are* those *who are made* of dust; and as *is* the heavenly *Man,* so also *are* those *who are* heavenly.
49 And as we have borne the image of the *man* of dust, we shall also bear[a] the image of the heavenly *Man.*

Our Final Victory

50 Now this I say, brethren, that flesh and blood cannot inherit the kingdom of God; nor does corruption inherit incorruption.
51 Behold, I tell you a mystery: We shall not all sleep, but we shall all be changed—
52 in a moment, in the twinkling of an eye, at the last trumpet. For the trumpet will sound, and the dead will be raised incorruptible, and we shall be changed.
53 For this corruptible must put on incorruption, and this mortal *must* put on immortality.
54 So when this corruptible has put on incorruption, and this mortal has put on immortality, then shall be brought to pass the saying that is written: *"Death is swallowed up in victory."*[a]

55 *"O Death, where is your sting?*[a]
O Hades, where is your victory?"[b]

56 The sting of death *is* sin, and the strength of sin *is* the law.
57 But thanks *be* to God, who gives us the victory through our Lord Jesus Christ.
58 Therefore, my beloved brethren, be steadfast, immovable, always abounding in the work of the Lord, knowing that your labor is not in vain in the Lord.

Collection for the Saints

16 Now concerning the collection for the saints, as I have given orders to the churches of Galatia, so you must do also:
2 On the first *day* of the week let each one of you lay something aside, storing up as he may prosper, that there be no collections when I come.
3 And when I come, whomever you approve

15:27 [a]Psalm 8:6 **15:32** [a]Isaiah 22:13 **15:39** [a]NU-Text and M-Text omit *of flesh.* **15:45** [a]Genesis 2:7
15:47 [a]NU-Text omits *the Lord.* **15:49** [a]M-Text reads *let us also bear.* **15:54** [a]Isaiah 25:8 **15:55** [a]Hosea 13:14
[b]NU-Text reads *O Death, where is your victory? O Death, where is your sting?*

by *your* letters I will send to bear your gift to Jerusalem.
4 But if it is fitting that I go also, they will go with me.

Personal Plans

5 Now I will come to you when I pass through Macedonia (for I am passing through Macedonia).
6 And it may be that I will remain, or even spend the winter with you, that you may send me on my journey, wherever I go.
7 For I do not wish to see you now on the way; but I hope to stay a while with you, if the Lord permits.
8 But I will tarry in Ephesus until Pentecost.
9 For a great and effective door has opened to me, and *there are* many adversaries.
10 And if Timothy comes, see that he may be with you without fear; for he does the work of the Lord, as I also *do*.
11 Therefore let no one despise him. But send him on his journey in peace, that he may come to me; for I am waiting for him with the brethren.
12 Now concerning *our* brother Apollos, I strongly urged him to come to you with the brethren, but he was quite unwilling to come at this time; however, he will come when he has a convenient time.

Final Exhortations

13 Watch, stand fast in the faith, be brave, be strong.
14 Let all *that* you *do* be done with love.
15 I urge you, brethren—you know the household of Stephanas, that it is the firstfruits of Achaia, and *that* they have devoted themselves to the ministry of the saints—
16 that you also submit to such, and to everyone who works and labors with *us*.
17 I am glad about the coming of Stephanas, Fortunatus, and Achaicus, for what was lacking on your part they supplied.
18 For they refreshed my spirit and yours. Therefore acknowledge such men.

Greetings and a Solemn Farewell

19 The churches of Asia greet you. Aquila and Priscilla greet you heartily in the Lord, with the church that is in their house.
20 All the brethren greet you. Greet one another with a holy kiss.
21 The salutation with my own hand—Paul's.
22 If anyone does not love the Lord Jesus Christ, let him be accursed.[a] O Lord, come![b]
23 The grace of our Lord Jesus Christ *be* with you.
24 My love *be* with you all in Christ Jesus. Amen.

The Second Epistle of Paul the Apostle to the CORINTHIANS

Greeting

1 Paul, an apostle of Jesus Christ by the will of God, and Timothy *our* brother,
To the church of God which is at Corinth, with all the saints who are in all Achaia:

2 Grace to you and peace from God our Father and the Lord Jesus Christ.

Comfort in Suffering

3 Blessed *be* the God and Father of our Lord Jesus Christ, the Father of mercies and God of all comfort,
4 who comforts us in all our tribulation, that we may be able to comfort those who are in any trouble, with the comfort with which we ourselves are comforted by God.
5 For as the sufferings of Christ abound in us, so our consolation also abounds through Christ.
6 Now if we are afflicted, *it is* for your consolation and salvation, which is effective for enduring the same sufferings which we also suffer. Or if we are comforted, *it is* for your consolation and salvation.
7 And our hope for you *is* steadfast, because we know that as you are partakers of the sufferings, so also *you will partake* of the consolation.

Delivered from Suffering

8 For we do not want you to be ignorant, brethren, of our trouble which came to us in Asia: that we were burdened beyond measure, above strength, so that we despaired even of life.
9 Yes, we had the sentence of death in ourselves, that we should not trust in ourselves but in God who raises the dead,
10 who delivered us from so great a death, and does[a] deliver us; in whom we trust that He will still deliver *us*,
11 you also helping together in prayer for us, that thanks may be given by many persons on our[a] behalf for the gift *granted* to us through many.

Paul's Sincerity

12 For our boasting is this: the testimony of our conscience that we conducted ourselves in the world in simplicity and godly sincerity, not with fleshly wisdom but by the grace of God, and more abundantly toward you.
13 For we are not writing any other things to you than what you read or understand. Now I trust you will understand, even to the end
14 (as also you have understood us in part), that we are your boast as you also *are* ours, in the day of the Lord Jesus.

Sparing the Church

15 And in this confidence I intended to come to you before, that you might have a second benefit—
16 to pass by way of you to Macedonia, to come again from Macedonia to you, and be helped by you on my way to Judea.
17 Therefore, when I was planning this, did I do it lightly? Or the things I plan, do I plan

16:22 [a]Greek *anathema* [b]Aramaic *Maranatha* **1:10** [a]NU-Text reads *shall.* **1:11** [a]M-Text reads *your behalf.*

according to the flesh, that with me there should be Yes, Yes, and No, No?
18 But *as* God *is* faithful, our word to you was not Yes and No.
19 For the Son of God, Jesus Christ, who was preached among you by us—by me, Silvanus, and Timothy—was not Yes and No, but in Him was Yes.
20 For all the promises of God in Him *are* Yes, and in Him Amen, to the glory of God through us.
21 Now He who establishes us with you in Christ and has anointed us *is* God,
22 who also has sealed us and given us the Spirit in our hearts as a guarantee.
23 Moreover I call God as witness against my soul, that to spare you I came no more to Corinth.
24 Not that we have dominion over your faith, but are fellow workers for your joy; for by faith you stand.

2 But I determined this within myself, that I would not come again to you in sorrow.
2 For if I make you sorrowful, then who is he who makes me glad but the one who is made sorrowful by me?

Forgive the Offender

3 And I wrote this very thing to you, lest, when I came, I should have sorrow over those from whom I ought to have joy, having confidence in you all that my joy is *the joy* of you all.
4 For out of much affliction and anguish of heart I wrote to you, with many tears, not that you should be grieved, but that you might know the love which I have so abundantly for you.
5 But if anyone has caused grief, he has not grieved me, but all of you to some extent—not to be too severe.
6 This punishment which *was inflicted* by the majority *is* sufficient for such a man,
7 so that, on the contrary, you *ought* rather to forgive and comfort *him,* lest perhaps such a one be swallowed up with too much sorrow.
8 Therefore I urge you to reaffirm *your* love to him.
9 For to this end I also wrote, that I might put you to the test, whether you are obedient in all things.
10 Now whom you forgive anything, I also *forgive.* For if indeed I have forgiven anything, I have forgiven that one[a] for your sakes in the presence of Christ,
11 lest Satan should take advantage of us; for we are not ignorant of his devices.

Triumph in Christ

12 Furthermore, when I came to Troas to *preach* Christ's gospel, and a door was opened to me by the Lord,
13 I had no rest in my spirit, because I did not find Titus my brother; but taking my leave of them, I departed for Macedonia.
14 Now thanks *be* to God who always leads us in triumph in Christ, and through us diffuses the fragrance of His knowledge in every place.
15 For we are to God the fragrance of Christ among those who are being saved and among those who are perishing.
16 To the one *we are* the aroma of death *leading* to death, and to the other the aroma of life *leading* to life. And who *is* sufficient for these things?
17 For we are not, as so many,[a] peddling the word of God; but as of sincerity, but as from God, we speak in the sight of God in Christ.

Christ's Epistle

3 Do we begin again to commend ourselves? Or do we need, as some *others,* epistles of commendation to you or *letters* of commendation from you?
2 You are our epistle written in our hearts, known and read by all men;
3 clearly you are an epistle of Christ, ministered by us, written not with ink but by the Spirit of the living God, not on tablets of stone but on tablets of flesh, *that is,* of the heart.

The Spirit, Not the Letter

4 And we have such trust through Christ toward God.
5 Not that we are sufficient of ourselves to think of anything as *being* from ourselves, but our sufficiency *is* from God,
6 who also made us sufficient as ministers of the new covenant, not of the letter but of the Spirit;[a] for the letter kills, but the Spirit gives life.

Glory of the New Covenant

7 But if the ministry of death, written *and* engraved on stones, was glorious, so that the children of Israel could not look steadily at the face of Moses because of the glory of his countenance, which *glory* was passing away,
8 how will the ministry of the Spirit not be more glorious?
9 For if the ministry of condemnation *had* glory, the ministry of righteousness exceeds much more in glory.
10 For even what was made glorious had no glory in this respect, because of the glory that excels.
11 For if what is passing away *was* glorious, what remains *is* much more glorious.
12 Therefore, since we have such hope, we use great boldness of speech—
13 unlike Moses, *who* put a veil over his face so that the children of Israel could not look steadily at the end of what was passing away.
14 But their minds were blinded. For until this day the same veil remains unlifted in the reading of the Old Testament, because the *veil* is taken away in Christ.
15 But even to this day, when Moses is read, a veil lies on their heart.
16 Nevertheless when one turns to the Lord, the veil is taken away.
17 Now the Lord is the Spirit; and where the Spirit of the Lord *is,* there *is* liberty.
18 But we all, with unveiled face, beholding as in a mirror the glory of the Lord, are being transformed into the same image from glory to glory, just as by the Spirit of the Lord.

The Light of Christ's Gospel

4 Therefore, since we have this ministry, as we have received mercy, we do not lose heart.
2 But we have renounced the hidden things of shame, not walking in craftiness nor handling the word of God deceitfully, but by mani-

2:10 [a]NU-Text reads *For indeed, what I have forgiven, if I have forgiven anything, I did it.* **2:17** [a]M-Text reads *the rest.* **3:6** [a]Or *spirit*

festation of the truth commending ourselves to every man's conscience in the sight of God.

3 But even if our gospel is veiled, it is veiled to those who are perishing,

4 whose minds the god of this age has blinded, who do not believe, lest the light of the gospel of the glory of Christ, who is the image of God, should shine on them.

5 For we do not preach ourselves, but Christ Jesus the Lord, and ourselves your bondservants for Jesus' sake.

6 For it is the God who commanded light to shine out of darkness, who has shone in our hearts to *give* the light of the knowledge of the glory of God in the face of Jesus Christ.

Cast Down but Unconquered

7 But we have this treasure in earthen vessels, that the excellence of the power may be of God and not of us.

8 *We are* hard-pressed on every side, yet not crushed; *we are* perplexed, but not in despair;

9 persecuted, but not forsaken; struck down, but not destroyed—

10 always carrying about in the body the dying of the Lord Jesus, that the life of Jesus also may be manifested in our body.

11 For we who live are always delivered to death for Jesus' sake, that the life of Jesus also may be manifested in our mortal flesh.

12 So then death is working in us, but life in you.

13 And since we have the same spirit of faith, according to what is written, *"I believed and therefore I spoke,"*[a] we also believe and therefore speak,

14 knowing that He who raised up the Lord Jesus will also raise us up with Jesus, and will present *us* with you.

15 For all things *are* for your sakes, that grace, having spread through the many, may cause thanksgiving to abound to the glory of God.

Seeing the Invisible

16 Therefore we do not lose heart. Even though our outward man is perishing, yet the inward *man* is being renewed day by day.

17 For our light affliction, which is but for a moment, is working for us a far more exceeding *and* eternal weight of glory,

18 while we do not look at the things which are seen, but at the things which are not seen. For the things which are seen *are* temporary, but the things which are not seen *are* eternal.

Assurance of the Resurrection

5 For we know that if our earthly house, *this* tent, is destroyed, we have a building from God, a house not made with hands, eternal in the heavens.

2 For in this we groan, earnestly desiring to be clothed with our habitation which is from heaven,

3 if indeed, having been clothed, we shall not be found naked.

4 For we who are in *this* tent groan, being burdened, not because we want to be unclothed, but further clothed, that mortality may be swallowed up by life.

5 Now He who has prepared us for this very thing *is* God, who also has given us the Spirit as a guarantee.

6 So *we are* always confident, knowing that while we are at home in the body we are absent from the Lord.

7 For we walk by faith, not by sight.

8 We are confident, yes, well pleased rather to be absent from the body and to be present with the Lord.

The Judgment Seat of Christ

9 Therefore we make it our aim, whether present or absent, to be well pleasing to Him.

10 For we must all appear before the judgment seat of Christ, that each one may receive the things *done* in the body, according to what he has done, whether good or bad.

11 Knowing, therefore, the terror of the Lord, we persuade men; but we are well known to God, and I also trust are well known in your consciences.

Be Reconciled to God

12 For we do not commend ourselves again to you, but give you opportunity to boast on our behalf, that you may have *an answer* for those who boast in appearance and not in heart.

13 For if we are beside ourselves, *it is* for God; or if we are of sound mind, *it is* for you.

14 For the love of Christ compels us, because we judge thus: that if One died for all, then all died;

15 and He died for all, that those who live should live no longer for themselves, but for Him who died for them and rose again.

16 Therefore, from now on, we regard no one according to the flesh. Even though we have known Christ according to the flesh, yet now we know *Him thus* no longer.

17 Therefore, if anyone *is* in Christ, *he is* a new creation; old things have passed away; behold, all things have become new.

18 Now all things *are* of God, who has reconciled us to Himself through Jesus Christ, and has given us the ministry of reconciliation,

19 that is, that God was in Christ reconciling the world to Himself, not imputing their trespasses to them, and has committed to us the word of reconciliation.

20 Now then, we are ambassadors for Christ, as though God were pleading through us: we implore *you* on Christ's behalf, be reconciled to God.

21 For He made Him who knew no sin *to be* sin for us, that we might become the righteousness of God in Him.

Marks of the Ministry

6 We then, *as* workers together *with Him* also plead with *you* not to receive the grace of God in vain.

2 For He says:

> *"In an acceptable time I have heard you,*
> *And in the day of salvation I have helped you."*[a]

Behold, now *is* the accepted time; behold, now *is* the day of salvation.

3 We give no offense in anything, that our ministry may not be blamed.

4 But in all *things* we commend ourselves as ministers of God: in much patience, in tribulations, in needs, in distresses,

5 in stripes, in imprisonments, in tumults, in labors, in sleeplessness, in fastings;

4:13 [a]Psalm 116:10 **6:2** [a]Isaiah 49:8

6 by purity, by knowledge, by longsuffering,
by kindness, by the Holy Spirit, by sincere love,
7 by the word of truth, by the power of God,
by the armor of righteousness on the right
hand and on the left,
8 by honor and dishonor, by evil report and
good report; as deceivers, and *yet* true;
9 as unknown, and *yet* well known; as dy-
ing, and behold we live; as chastened, and *yet*
not killed;
10 as sorrowful, yet always rejoicing; as poor,
yet making many rich; as having nothing, and
yet possessing all things.

Be Holy

11 O Corinthians! We have spoken openly to
you, our heart is wide open.
12 You are not restricted by us, but you are
restricted by your *own* affections.
13 Now in return for the same (I speak as to
children), you also be open.
14 Do not be unequally yoked together with
unbelievers. For what fellowship has righ-
teousness with lawlessness? And what com-
munion has light with darkness?
15 And what accord has Christ with Belial?
Or what part has a believer with an unbeliever?
16 And what agreement has the temple of
God with idols? For you[a] are the temple of the
living God. As God has said:

"I will dwell in them
And walk among them.
I will be their God,
And they shall be My people."[b]

17 Therefore

"Come out from among them
And be separate, says the Lord.
Do not touch what is unclean,
And I will receive you."[a]

18 *"I will be a Father to you,*
And you shall be My sons and daughters,
Says the LORD Almighty."[a]

7 Therefore, having these promises, beloved,
let us cleanse ourselves from all filthiness
of the flesh and spirit, perfecting holiness in
the fear of God.

The Corinthians' Repentance

2 Open *your hearts* to us. We have wronged
no one, we have corrupted no one, we have
cheated no one.
3 I do not say *this* to condemn; for I have
said before that you are in our hearts, to die
together and to live together.
4 Great *is* my boldness of speech toward
you, great *is* my boasting on your behalf. I am
filled with comfort. I am exceedingly joyful in
all our tribulation.
5 For indeed, when we came to Macedonia,
our bodies had no rest, but we were troubled on
every side. Outside *were* conflicts, inside *were*
fears.
6 Nevertheless God, who comforts the down-
cast, comforted us by the coming of Titus,
7 and not only by his coming, but also by the
consolation with which he was comforted in
you, when he told us of your earnest desire,
your mourning, your zeal for me, so that I re-
joiced even more.
8 For even if I made you sorry with my letter,
I do not regret it; though I did regret it. For I
perceive that the same epistle made you sorry,
though only for a while.
9 Now I rejoice, not that you were made sorry,
but that your sorrow led to repentance. For you
were made sorry in a godly manner, that you
might suffer loss from us in nothing.
10 For godly sorrow produces repentance
leading to salvation, not to be regretted; but the
sorrow of the world produces death.
11 For observe this very thing, that you sor-
rowed in a godly manner: What diligence it
produced in you, *what* clearing *of yourselves,*
what indignation, *what* fear, *what* vehement
desire, *what* zeal, *what* vindication! In all *things*
you proved yourselves to be clear in this matter.
12 Therefore, although I wrote to you, *I did*
not *do it* for the sake of him who had done the
wrong, nor for the sake of him who suffered
wrong, but that our care for you in the sight of
God might appear to you.

The Joy of Titus

13 Therefore we have been comforted in your
comfort. And we rejoiced exceedingly more for
the joy of Titus, because his spirit has been re-
freshed by you all.
14 For if in anything I have boasted to him
about you, I am not ashamed. But as we spoke
all things to you in truth, even so our boasting
to Titus was found true.
15 And his affections are greater for you as
he remembers the obedience of you all, how
with fear and trembling you received him.
16 Therefore I rejoice that I have confidence
in you in everything.

Excel in Giving

8 Moreover, brethren, we make known to you
the grace of God bestowed on the churches
of Macedonia:
2 that in a great trial of affliction the abun-
dance of their joy and their deep poverty
abounded in the riches of their liberality.
3 For I bear witness that according to *their*
ability, yes, and beyond *their* ability, *they were*
freely willing,
4 imploring us with much urgency that we
would receive[a] the gift and the fellowship of
the ministering to the saints.
5 And not *only* as we had hoped, but they first
gave themselves to the Lord, and *then* to us by
the will of God.
6 So we urged Titus, that as he had begun,
so he would also complete this grace in you as
well.
7 But as you abound in everything—in faith,
in speech, in knowledge, in all diligence, and
in your love for us—*see* that you abound in this
grace also.

Christ Our Pattern

8 I speak not by commandment, but I am test-
ing the sincerity of your love by the diligence
of others.
9 For you know the grace of our Lord Jesus
Christ, that though He was rich, yet for your

6:16 [a]NU-Text reads *we.* [b]Leviticus 26:12; Jeremiah 32:38; Ezekiel 37:27 **6:17** [a]Isaiah 52:11; Ezekiel 20:34, 41 **6:18** [a]2 Samuel 7:14 **8:4** [a]NU-Text and M-Text omit *that we would receive,* thus changing text to *urgency for the favor and fellowship . . . .*

sakes He became poor, that you through His
poverty might become rich.
10 And in this I give advice: It is to your advantage not only to be doing what you began
and were desiring to do a year ago;
11 but now you also must complete the doing
of it; that as *there was* a readiness to desire *it,*
so *there* also *may be* a completion out of what
you have.
12 For if there is first a willing mind, *it is*
accepted according to what one has, *and* not
according to what he does not have.
13 For *I do* not *mean* that others should be
eased and you burdened;
14 but by an equality, *that* now at this time
your abundance *may supply* their lack, that
their abundance also may *supply* your lack—
that there may be equality.
15 As it is written, *"He who gathered much
had nothing left over, and he who gathered
little had no lack."*[a]

Collection for the Judean Saints

16 But thanks *be* to God who puts[a] the same
earnest care for you into the heart of Titus.
17 For he not only accepted the exhortation,
but being more diligent, he went to you of his
own accord.
18 And we have sent with him the brother
whose praise *is* in the gospel throughout all the
churches,
19 and not only *that,* but who was also chosen
by the churches to travel with us with this gift,
which is administered by us to the glory of the
Lord Himself and *to show* your ready mind,
20 avoiding this: that anyone should blame us
in this lavish gift which is administered by us—
21 providing honorable things, not only in the
sight of the Lord, but also in the sight of men.
22 And we have sent with them our brother
whom we have often proved diligent in many
things, but now much more diligent, because
of the great confidence which *we have* in you.
23 If *anyone inquires* about Titus, *he is* my partner and fellow worker concerning you. Or if
our brethren *are inquired about, they are* messengers of the churches, the glory of Christ.
24 Therefore show to them, and[a] before the
churches, the proof of your love and of our boasting on your behalf.

Administering the Gift

9 Now concerning the ministering to the
saints, it is superfluous for me to write to
you;
2 for I know your willingness, about which
I boast of you to the Macedonians, that Achaia
was ready a year ago; and your zeal has stirred
up the majority.
3 Yet I have sent the brethren, lest our boasting of you should be in vain in this respect, that,
as I said, you may be ready;
4 lest if *some* Macedonians come with me
and find you unprepared, we (not to mention
you!) should be ashamed of this confident boasting.[a]
5 Therefore I thought it necessary to exhort
the brethren to go to you ahead of time, and prepare your generous gift beforehand, which *you
had* previously promised, that it may be ready
as *a matter of* generosity and not as a grudging
obligation.

The Cheerful Giver

6 But this *I say:* He who sows sparingly will
also reap sparingly, and he who sows bountifully will also reap bountifully.
7 *So let* each one *give* as he purposes in his
heart, not grudgingly or of necessity; for God
loves a cheerful giver.
8 And God *is* able to make all grace abound
toward you, that you, always having all sufficiency in all *things,* may have an abundance
for every good work.
9 As it is written:

"He has dispersed abroad,
He has given to the poor;
His righteousness endures forever."[a]

10 Now may[a] He who supplies seed to the
sower, and bread for food, supply and multiply
the seed you have *sown* and increase the fruits
of your righteousness,
11 while *you are* enriched in everything for all
liberality, which causes thanksgiving through us
to God.
12 For the administration of this service not
only supplies the needs of the saints, but also
is abounding through many thanksgivings to
God,
13 while, through the proof of this ministry,
they glorify God for the obedience of your confession to the gospel of Christ, and for *your*
liberal sharing with them and all *men,*
14 and by their prayer for you, who long for
you because of the exceeding grace of God in
you.
15 Thanks *be* to God for His indescribable gift!

The Spiritual War

10 Now I, Paul, myself am pleading with
you by the meekness and gentleness of
Christ—who in presence *am* lowly among you,
but being absent am bold toward you.
2 But I beg *you* that when I am present I may
not be bold with that confidence by which I
intend to be bold against some, who think of
us as if we walked according to the flesh.
3 For though we walk in the flesh, we do not
war according to the flesh.
4 For the weapons of our warfare *are* not
carnal but mighty in God for pulling down
strongholds,
5 casting down arguments and every high
thing that exalts itself against the knowledge
of God, bringing every thought into captivity
to the obedience of Christ,
6 and being ready to punish all disobedience
when your obedience is fulfilled.

Reality of Paul's Authority

7 Do you look at things according to the outward appearance? If anyone is convinced in
himself that he is Christ's, let him again consider this in himself, that just as he *is* Christ's,
even so we *are* Christ's.[a]
8 For even if I should boast somewhat more
about our authority, which the Lord gave us[a] for

8:15 [a]Exodus 16:18 **8:16** [a]NU-Text reads *has put.* **8:24** [a]NU-Text and M-Text omit *and.* **9:4** [a]NU-Text reads *this confidence.* **9:9** [a]Psalm 112:9 **9:10** [a]NU-Text reads *Now He who supplies . . . will supply . . . .* **10:7** [a]NU-Text reads *even as we are.* **10:8** [a]NU-Text omits *us.*

edification and not for your destruction, I shall
not be ashamed—
9 lest I seem to terrify you by letters.
10 "For *his* letters," they say, "*are* weighty
and powerful, but *his* bodily presence *is* weak,
and *his* speech contemptible."
11 Let such a person consider this, that what
we are in word by letters when we are absent,
such *we will* also *be* in deed when we are
present.

Limits of Paul's Authority

12 For we dare not class ourselves or compare
ourselves with those who commend them-
selves. But they, measuring themselves by
themselves, and comparing themselves among
themselves, are not wise.
13 We, however, will not boast beyond mea-
sure, but within the limits of the sphere which
God appointed us—a sphere which especially
includes you.
14 For we are not overextending ourselves (as
though *our authority* did not extend to you),
for it was to you that we came with the gospel
of Christ;
15 not boasting of things beyond measure,
that is, in other men's labors, but having hope,
that as your faith is increased, we shall be
greatly enlarged by you in our sphere,
16 to preach the gospel in the *regions* beyond
you, *and* not to boast in another man's sphere
of accomplishment.
17 But *"he who glories, let him glory in the*
LORD."[a]
18 For not he who commends himself is ap-
proved, but whom the Lord commends.

Concern for Their Faithfulness

11 Oh, that you would bear with me in a
little folly—and indeed you do bear with
me.
2 For I am jealous for you with godly jeal-
ousy. For I have betrothed you to one husband,
that I may present *you as* a chaste virgin to
Christ.
3 But I fear, lest somehow, as the serpent de-
ceived Eve by his craftiness, so your minds
may be corrupted from the simplicity[a] that is
in Christ.
4 For if he who comes preaches another Jesus
whom we have not preached, or *if* you receive
a different spirit which you have not received,
or a different gospel which you have not ac-
cepted—you may well put up with it!

Paul and False Apostles

5 For I consider that I am not at all inferior
to the most eminent apostles.
6 Even though *I am* untrained in speech, yet
I am not in knowledge. But we have been thor-
oughly manifested[a] among you in all things.
7 Did I commit sin in humbling myself that
you might be exalted, because I preached the
gospel of God to you free of charge?
8 I robbed other churches, taking wages *from*
them to minister to you.
9 And when I was present with you, and in
need, I was a burden to no one, for what I
lacked the brethren who came from Macedo-
nia supplied. And in everything I kept myself
from being burdensome to you, and so I will
keep *myself.*
10 As the truth of Christ is in me, no one shall
stop me from this boasting in the regions of
Achaia.
11 Why? Because I do not love you? God knows!
12 But what I do, I will also continue to do,
that I may cut off the opportunity from those
who desire an opportunity to be regarded just
as we are in the things of which they boast.
13 For such *are* false apostles, deceitful work-
ers, transforming themselves into apostles of
Christ.
14 And no wonder! For Satan himself trans-
forms himself into an angel of light.
15 Therefore *it is* no great thing if his minis-
ters also transform themselves into ministers
of righteousness, whose end will be according
to their works.

Reluctant Boasting

16 I say again, let no one think me a fool. If
otherwise, at least receive me as a fool, that I
also may boast a little.
17 What I speak, I speak not according to the
Lord, but as it were, foolishly, in this confi-
dence of boasting.
18 Seeing that many boast according to the
flesh, I also will boast.
19 For you put up with fools gladly, since you
yourselves are wise!
20 For you put up with it if one brings you
into bondage, if one devours *you,* if one takes
from you, if one exalts himself, if one strikes
you on the face.
21 To *our* shame I say that we were too weak
for that! But in whatever anyone is bold—I
speak foolishly—I am bold also.

Suffering for Christ

22 Are they Hebrews? So *am* I. Are they Isra-
elites? So *am* I. Are they the seed of Abraham?
So *am* I.
23 Are they ministers of Christ?—I speak as
a fool—I *am* more: in labors more abundant,
in stripes above measure, in prisons more fre-
quently, in deaths often.
24 From the Jews five times I received forty
stripes minus one.
25 Three times I was beaten with rods; once I
was stoned; three times I was shipwrecked; a
night and a day I have been in the deep;
26 *in* journeys often, *in* perils of waters, *in* per-
ils of robbers, *in* perils of *my own* countrymen,
in perils of the Gentiles, *in* perils in the city, *in*
perils in the wilderness, *in* perils in the sea, *in*
perils among false brethren;
27 in weariness and toil, in sleeplessness of-
ten, in hunger and thirst, in fastings often, in
cold and nakedness—
28 besides the other things, what comes upon
me daily: my deep concern for all the churches.
29 Who is weak, and I am not weak? Who is
made to stumble, and I do not burn *with indigna-*
tion?
30 If I must boast, I will boast in the things
which concern my infirmity.
31 The God and Father of our Lord Jesus
Christ, who is blessed forever, knows that I am
not lying.
32 In Damascus the governor, under Aretas
the king, was guarding the city of the Dama-
scenes with a garrison, desiring to arrest me;
33 but I was let down in a basket through a
window in the wall, and escaped from his hands.

10:17 [a]Jeremiah 9:24 **11:3** [a]NU-Text adds *and purity.* **11:6** [a]NU-Text omits *been.*

The Vision of Paradise

12 It is doubtless[a] not profitable for me to
boast. I will come to visions and revela-
tions of the Lord:
2 I know a man in Christ who fourteen years
ago—whether in the body I do not know, or
whether out of the body I do not know, God
knows—such a one was caught up to the third
heaven.
3 And I know such a man—whether in the
body or out of the body I do not know, God
knows—
4 how he was caught up into Paradise and
heard inexpressible words, which it is not law-
ful for a man to utter.
5 Of such a one I will boast; yet of myself I
will not boast, except in my infirmities.
6 For though I might desire to boast, I will
not be a fool; for I will speak the truth. But I
refrain, lest anyone should think of me above
what he sees me *to be* or hears from me.

The Thorn in the Flesh

7 And lest I should be exalted above mea-
sure by the abundance of the revelations, a
thorn in the flesh was given to me, a messenger
of Satan to buffet me, lest I be exalted above
measure.
8 Concerning this thing I pleaded with the
Lord three times that it might depart from me.
9 And He said to me, "My grace is sufficient
for you, for My strength is made perfect in
weakness." Therefore most gladly I will rather
boast in my infirmities, that the power of
Christ may rest upon me.
10 Therefore I take pleasure in infirmities, in
reproaches, in needs, in persecutions, in dis-
tresses, for Christ's sake. For when I am weak,
then I am strong.

Signs of an Apostle

11 I have become a fool in boasting;[a] you have
compelled me. For I ought to have been com-
mended by you; for in nothing was I behind the
most eminent apostles, though I am nothing.
12 Truly the signs of an apostle were accom-
plished among you with all perseverance, in
signs and wonders and mighty deeds.
13 For what is it in which you were inferior to
other churches, except that I myself was not
burdensome to you? Forgive me this wrong!

Love for the Church

14 Now *for* the third time I am ready to come
to you. And I will not be burdensome to you;
for I do not seek yours, but you. For the chil-
dren ought not to lay up for the parents, but
the parents for the children.
15 And I will very gladly spend and be spent
for your souls; though the more abundantly I
love you, the less I am loved.
16 But be that *as it may,* I did not burden you.
Nevertheless, being crafty, I caught you by
cunning!
17 Did I take advantage of you by any of those
whom I sent to you?
18 I urged Titus, and sent our brother with
him. Did Titus take advantage of you? Did we
not walk in the same spirit? Did *we* not *walk*
in the same steps?
19 Again, do you think[a] that we excuse our-
selves to you? We speak before God in Christ.
But *we do* all things, beloved, for your edifica-
tion.
20 For I fear lest, when I come, I shall not find
you such as I wish, and *that* I shall be found
by you such as you do not wish; lest *there be*
contentions, jealousies, outbursts of wrath,
selfish ambitions, backbitings, whisperings,
conceits, tumults;
21 lest, when I come again, my God will hum-
ble me among you, and I shall mourn for many
who have sinned before and have not repented
of the uncleanness, fornication, and lewdness
which they have practiced.

Coming with Authority

13 This *will be* the third *time* I am coming
to you. *"By the mouth of two or three
witnesses every word shall be established."*[a]
2 I have told you before, and foretell as if I
were present the second time, and now being
absent I write[a] to those who have sinned be-
fore, and to all the rest, that if I come again I
will not spare—
3 since you seek a proof of Christ speaking
in me, who is not weak toward you, but mighty
in you.
4 For though He was crucified in weakness,
yet He lives by the power of God. For we also
are weak in Him, but we shall live with Him
by the power of God toward you.
5 Examine yourselves *as to* whether you are
in the faith. Test yourselves. Do you not know
yourselves, that Jesus Christ is in you?—unless
indeed you are disqualified.
6 But I trust that you will know that we are
not disqualified.

Paul Prefers Gentleness

7 Now I[a] pray to God that you do no evil, not
that we should appear approved, but that you
should do what is honorable, though we may
seem disqualified.
8 For we can do nothing against the truth,
but for the truth.
9 For we are glad when we are weak and
you are strong. And this also we pray, that you
may be made complete.
10 Therefore I write these things being ab-
sent, lest being present I should use sharpness,
according to the authority which the Lord has
given me for edification and not for destruc-
tion.

Greetings and Benediction

11 Finally, brethren, farewell. Become com-
plete. Be of good comfort, be of one mind, live
in peace; and the God of love and peace will
be with you.
12 Greet one another with a holy kiss.
13 All the saints greet you.
14 The grace of the Lord Jesus Christ, and the
love of God, and the communion of the Holy
Spirit *be* with you all. Amen.

12:1 [a]NU-Text reads *necessary, though not profitable, to boast.* **12:11** [a]NU-Text omits *in boasting.* **12:19** [a]NU-Text reads *You have been thinking for a long time . . . .* **13:1** [a]Deuteronomy 19:15 **13:2** [a]NU-Text omits *I write.* **13:7** [a]NU-Text reads *we.*

The Epistle of Paul the Apostle to the

GALATIANS

Greeting

1 Paul, an apostle (not from men nor through
man, but through Jesus Christ and God the
Father who raised Him from the dead),
2 and all the brethren who are with me,

To the churches of Galatia:

3 Grace to you and peace from God the Fa-
ther and our Lord Jesus Christ,
4 who gave Himself for our sins, that He
might deliver us from this present evil age,
according to the will of our God and Father,
5 to whom *be* glory forever and ever. Amen.

Only One Gospel

6 I marvel that you are turning away so soon
from Him who called you in the grace of Christ,
to a different gospel,
7 which is not another; but there are some
who trouble you and want to pervert the gospel
of Christ.
8 But even if we, or an angel from heaven,
preach any other gospel to you than what we
have preached to you, let him be accursed.
9 As we have said before, so now I say again,
if anyone preaches any other gospel to you
than what you have received, let him be ac-
cursed.
10 For do I now persuade men, or God? Or do
I seek to please men? For if I still pleased men,
I would not be a bondservant of Christ.

Call to Apostleship

11 But I make known to you, brethren, that
the gospel which was preached by me is not
according to man.
12 For I neither received it from man, nor was
I taught *it*, but *it came* through the revelation
of Jesus Christ.
13 For you have heard of my former conduct
in Judaism, how I persecuted the church of
God beyond measure and *tried to* destroy it.
14 And I advanced in Judaism beyond many
of my contemporaries in my own nation, being
more exceedingly zealous for the traditions of
my fathers.
15 But when it pleased God, who separated
me from my mother's womb and called *me*
through His grace,
16 to reveal His Son in me, that I might preach
Him among the Gentiles, I did not immediately
confer with flesh and blood,
17 nor did I go up to Jerusalem to those *who
were* apostles before me; but I went to Arabia,
and returned again to Damascus.

Contacts at Jerusalem

18 Then after three years I went up to Jerusa-
lem to see Peter,[a] remained with him fifteen days.
19 But I saw none of the other apostles except
James, the Lord's brother.
20 (Now *concerning* the things which I write
to you, indeed, before God, I do not lie.)
21 Afterward I went into the regions of Syria
and Cilicia.
22 And I was unknown by face to the churches
of Judea which *were* in Christ.
23 But they were hearing only, "He who for-
merly persecuted us now preaches the faith
which he once *tried to* destroy."
24 And they glorified God in me.

Defending the Gospel

2 Then after fourteen years I went up again
to Jerusalem with Barnabas, and also took
Titus with *me*.
2 And I went up by revelation, and commu-
nicated to them that gospel which I preach
among the Gentiles, but privately to those who
were of reputation, lest by any means I might
run, or had run, in vain.
3 Yet not even Titus who *was* with me, being
a Greek, was compelled to be circumcised.
4 And *this occurred* because of false breth-
ren secretly brought in (who came in by stealth
to spy out our liberty which we have in Christ
Jesus, that they might bring us into bondage),
5 to whom we did not yield submission even
for an hour, that the truth of the gospel might
continue with you.
6 But from those who seemed to be some-
thing—whatever they were, it makes no differ-
ence to me; God shows personal favoritism to
no man—for those who seemed *to be some-
thing* added nothing to me.
7 But on the contrary, when they saw that the
gospel for the uncircumcised had been com-
mitted to me, as *the gospel* for the circumcised
was to Peter
8 (for He who worked effectively in Peter for
the apostleship to the circumcised also worked
effectively in me toward the Gentiles),
9 and when James, Cephas, and John, who
seemed to be pillars, perceived the grace that
had been given to me, they gave me and Barna-
bas the right hand of fellowship, that we *should
go* to the Gentiles and they to the circumcised.
10 *They desired* only that we should remem-
ber the poor, the very thing which I also was
eager to do.

No Return to the Law

11 Now when Peter[a] had come to Antioch, I
withstood him to his face, because he was to
be blamed;
12 for before certain men came from James,
he would eat with the Gentiles; but when they
came, he withdrew and separated himself, fear-
ing those who were of the circumcision.
13 And the rest of the Jews also played the
hypocrite with him, so that even Barnabas was
carried away with their hypocrisy.
14 But when I saw that they were not straight-
forward about the truth of the gospel, I said to
Peter before *them* all, "If you, being a Jew, live
in the manner of Gentiles and not as the Jews,
why do you[a] compel Gentiles to live as Jews?[b]
15 "We *who are* Jews by nature, and not sin-
ners of the Gentiles,
16 "knowing that a man is not justified by the
works of the law but by faith in Jesus Christ,
even we have believed in Christ Jesus, that we
might be justified by faith in Christ and not by
the works of the law; for by the works of the
law no flesh shall be justified.

1:18 [a]NU-Text reads *Cephas.* **2:11** [a]NU-Text reads *Cephas.* **2:14** [a]NU-Text reads *how can you.* [b]Some interpreters stop the quotation here.

17 "But if, while we seek to be justified by Christ, we ourselves also are found sinners, *is* Christ therefore a minister of sin? Certainly not!

18 "For if I build again those things which I destroyed, I make myself a transgressor.

19 "For I through the law died to the law that I might live to God.

20 "I have been crucified with Christ; it is no longer I who live, but Christ lives in me; and the *life* which I now live in the flesh I live by faith in the Son of God, who loved me and gave Himself for me.

21 "I do not set aside the grace of God; for if righteousness *comes* through the law, then Christ died in vain."

Justification by Faith

3 O foolish Galatians! Who has bewitched you that you should not obey the truth,[a] before whose eyes Jesus Christ was clearly portrayed among you[b] as crucified?

2 This only I want to learn from you: Did you receive the Spirit by the works of the law, or by the hearing of faith?

3 Are you so foolish? Having begun in the Spirit, are you now being made perfect by the flesh?

4 Have you suffered so many things in vain—if indeed *it was* in vain?

5 Therefore He who supplies the Spirit to you and works miracles among you, *does He do it* by the works of the law, or by the hearing of faith?—

6 just as Abraham *"believed God, and it was accounted to him for righteousness."*[a]

7 Therefore know that *only* those who are of faith are sons of Abraham.

8 And the Scripture, foreseeing that God would justify the Gentiles by faith, preached the gospel to Abraham beforehand, *saying, "In you all the nations shall be blessed."*[a]

9 So then those who *are* of faith are blessed with believing Abraham.

The Law Brings a Curse

10 For as many as are of the works of the law are under the curse; for it is written, *"Cursed is everyone who does not continue in all things which are written in the book of the law, to do them."*[a]

11 But that no one is justified by the law in the sight of God *is* evident, for *"the just shall live by faith."*[a]

12 Yet the law is not of faith, but *"the man who does them shall live by them."*[a]

13 Christ has redeemed us from the curse of the law, having become a curse for us (for it is written, *"Cursed is everyone who hangs on a tree"*[a]),

14 that the blessing of Abraham might come upon the Gentiles in Christ Jesus, that we might receive the promise of the Spirit through faith.

The Changeless Promise

15 Brethren, I speak in the manner of men: Though *it is* only a man's covenant, yet *if it is* confirmed, no one annuls or adds to it.

16 Now to Abraham and his Seed were the promises made. He does not say, "And to seeds," as of many, but as of one, *"And to your Seed,"*[a] who is Christ.

17 And this I say, *that* the law, which was four hundred and thirty years later, cannot annul the covenant that was confirmed before by God in Christ,[a] that it should make the promise of no effect.

18 For if the inheritance *is* of the law, *it is* no longer of promise; but God gave *it* to Abraham by promise.

Purpose of the Law

19 What purpose then *does* the law *serve?* It was added because of transgressions, till the Seed should come to whom the promise was made; *and it was* appointed through angels by the hand of a mediator.

20 Now a mediator does not *mediate* for one *only,* but God is one.

21 *Is* the law then against the promises of God? Certainly not! For if there had been a law given which could have given life, truly righteousness would have been by the law.

22 But the Scripture has confined all under sin, that the promise by faith in Jesus Christ might be given to those who believe.

23 But before faith came, we were kept under guard by the law, kept for the faith which would afterward be revealed.

24 Therefore the law was our tutor *to bring us* to Christ, that we might be justified by faith.

25 But after faith has come, we are no longer under a tutor.

Sons and Heirs

26 For you are all sons of God through faith in Christ Jesus.

27 For as many of you as were baptized into Christ have put on Christ.

28 There is neither Jew nor Greek, there is neither slave nor free, there is neither male nor female; for you are all one in Christ Jesus.

29 And if you *are* Christ's, then you are Abraham's seed, and heirs according to the promise.

4 Now I say *that* the heir, as long as he is a child, does not differ at all from a slave, though he is master of all,

2 but is under guardians and stewards until the time appointed by the father.

3 Even so we, when we were children, were in bondage under the elements of the world.

4 But when the fullness of the time had come, God sent forth His Son, born[a] of a woman, born under the law,

5 to redeem those who were under the law, that we might receive the adoption as sons.

6 And because you are sons, God has sent forth the Spirit of His Son into your hearts, crying out, "Abba, Father!"

7 Therefore you are no longer a slave but a son, and if a son, then an heir of[a] God through Christ.

Fears for the Church

8 But then, indeed, when you did not know God, you served those which by nature are not gods.

9 But now after you have known God, or rather are known by God, how *is it that* you turn again to the weak and beggarly elements, to which you desire again to be in bondage?

3:1 [a]NU-Text omits *that you should not obey the truth.* [b]NU-Text omits *among you.* **3:6** [a]Genesis 15:6 **3:8** [a]Genesis 12:3; 18:18; 22:18; 26:4; 28:14 **3:10** [a]Deuteronomy 27:26 **3:11** [a]Habakkuk 2:4 **3:12** [a]Leviticus 18:5 **3:13** [a]Deuteronomy 21:23 **3:16** [a]Genesis 12:7; 13:15; 24:7 **3:17** [a]NU-Text omits *in Christ.* **4:4** [a]Or *made* **4:7** [a]NU-Text reads *through God* and omits *through Christ.*

10 You observe days and months and seasons
and years.
11 I am afraid for you, lest I have labored for
you in vain.
12 Brethren, I urge you to become like me, for
I *became* like you. You have not injured me at
all.
13 You know that because of physical infir-
mity I preached the gospel to you at the first.
14 And my trial which was in my flesh you
did not despise or reject, but you received me
as an angel of God, *even* as Christ Jesus.
15 What[a] then was the blessing you *enjoyed?*
For I bear you witness that, if possible, you
would have plucked out your own eyes and
given them to me.
16 Have I therefore become your enemy be-
cause I tell you the truth?
17 They zealously court you, *but* for no good;
yes, they want to exclude you, that you may be
zealous for them.
18 But it is good to be zealous in a good thing
always, and not only when I am present with
you.
19 My little children, for whom I labor in birth
again until Christ is formed in you,
20 I would like to be present with you now
and to change my tone; for I have doubts about
you.

Two Covenants

21 Tell me, you who desire to be under the law,
do you not hear the law?
22 For it is written that Abraham had two sons:
the one by a bondwoman, the other by a free-
woman.
23 But he *who was* of the bondwoman was
born according to the flesh, and he of the free-
woman through promise,
24 which things are symbolic. For these are the[a]
two covenants: the one from Mount Sinai which
gives birth to bondage, which is Hagar—
25 for this Hagar is Mount Sinai in Arabia,
and corresponds to Jerusalem which now is,
and is in bondage with her children—
26 but the Jerusalem above is free, which is
the mother of us all.
27 For it is written:

> *"Rejoice, O barren,*
> *You who do not bear!*
> *Break forth and shout,*
> *You who are not in labor!*
> *For the desolate has many more children*
> *Than she who has a husband."*[a]

28 Now we, brethren, as Isaac *was*, are chil-
dren of promise.
29 But, as he who was born according to the
flesh then persecuted him *who was born* ac-
cording to the Spirit, even so *it is* now.
30 Nevertheless what does the Scripture say?
"Cast out the bondwoman and her son, for the
son of the bondwoman shall not be heir with
the son of the freewoman."[a]
31 So then, brethren, we are not children of
the bondwoman but of the free.

Christian Liberty

5 Stand fast therefore in the liberty by which
Christ has made us free,[a] and do not be
entangled again with a yoke of bondage.
2 Indeed I, Paul, say to you that if you be-
come circumcised, Christ will profit you nothing.
3 And I testify again to every man who be-
comes circumcised that he is a debtor to keep
the whole law.
4 You have become estranged from Christ,
you who *attempt to* be justified by law; you
have fallen from grace.
5 For we through the Spirit eagerly wait for
the hope of righteousness by faith.
6 For in Christ Jesus neither circumcision
nor uncircumcision avails anything, but faith
working through love.

Love Fulfills the Law

7 You ran well. Who hindered you from
obeying the truth?
8 This persuasion does not *come* from Him
who calls you.
9 A little leaven leavens the whole lump.
10 I have confidence in you, in the Lord, that
you will have no other mind; but he who trou-
bles you shall bear his judgment, whoever he is.
11 And I, brethren, if I still preach circumci-
sion, why do I still suffer persecution? Then
the offense of the cross has ceased.
12 I could wish that those who trouble you
would even cut themselves off!
13 For you, brethren, have been called to lib-
erty; only do not *use* liberty as an opportunity
for the flesh, but through love serve one another.
14 For all the law is fulfilled in one word, *even*
in this: *"You shall love your neighbor as your-*
self."[a]
15 But if you bite and devour one another,
beware lest you be consumed by one another!

Walking in the Spirit

16 I say then: Walk in the Spirit, and you shall
not fulfill the lust of the flesh.
17 For the flesh lusts against the Spirit, and
the Spirit against the flesh; and these are con-
trary to one another, so that you do not do the
things that you wish.
18 But if you are led by the Spirit, you are not
under the law.
19 Now the works of the flesh are evident,
which are: adultery,[a] fornication, uncleanness,
lewdness,
20 idolatry, sorcery, hatred, contentions, jeal-
ousies, outbursts of wrath, selfish ambitions,
dissensions, heresies,
21 envy, murders,[a] drunkenness, revelries, and
the like; of which I tell you beforehand, just as
I also told *you* in time past, that those who
practice such things will not inherit the king-
dom of God.
22 But the fruit of the Spirit is love, joy, peace,
longsuffering, kindness, goodness, faithfulness,
23 gentleness, self-control. Against such there
is no law.
24 And those *who are* Christ's have crucified
the flesh with its passions and desires.
25 If we live in the Spirit, let us also walk in
the Spirit.
26 Let us not become conceited, provoking
one another, envying one another.

Bear and Share the Burdens

6 Brethren, if a man is overtaken in any tres-
pass, you who *are* spiritual restore such a

4:15 [a]NU-Text reads *Where.* **4:24** [a]NU-Text and M-Text omit *the.* **4:27** [a]Isaiah 54:1 **4:30** [a]Genesis 21:10
5:1 [a]NU-Text reads *For freedom Christ has made us free; stand fast therefore.* **5:14** [a]Leviticus 19:18 **5:19** [a]NU-Text omits *adultery.* **5:21** [a]NU-Text omits *murders.*

one in a spirit of gentleness, considering yourself lest you also be tempted.

2 Bear one another's burdens, and so fulfill the law of Christ.

3 For if anyone thinks himself to be something, when he is nothing, he deceives himself.

4 But let each one examine his own work, and then he will have rejoicing in himself alone, and not in another.

5 For each one shall bear his own load.

Be Generous and Do Good

6 Let him who is taught the word share in all good things with him who teaches.

7 Do not be deceived, God is not mocked; for whatever a man sows, that he will also reap.

8 For he who sows to his flesh will of the flesh reap corruption, but he who sows to the Spirit will of the Spirit reap everlasting life.

9 And let us not grow weary while doing good, for in due season we shall reap if we do not lose heart.

10 Therefore, as we have opportunity, let us do good to all, especially to those who are of the household of faith.

Glory Only in the Cross

11 See with what large letters I have written to you with my own hand!

12 As many as desire to make a good showing in the flesh, these *would* compel you to be circumcised, only that they may not suffer persecution for the cross of Christ.

13 For not even those who are circumcised keep the law, but they desire to have you circumcised that they may boast in your flesh.

14 But God forbid that I should boast except in the cross of our Lord Jesus Christ, by whom[a] the world has been crucified to me, and I to the world.

15 For in Christ Jesus neither circumcision nor uncircumcision avails anything, but a new creation.

Blessing and a Plea

16 And as many as walk according to this rule, peace and mercy *be* upon them, and upon the Israel of God.

17 From now on let no one trouble me, for I bear in my body the marks of the Lord Jesus.

18 Brethren, the grace of our Lord Jesus Christ *be* with your spirit. Amen.

The Epistle of Paul the Apostle to the EPHESIANS

Greeting

1 Paul, an apostle of Jesus Christ by the will of God,

To the saints who are in Ephesus, and faithful in Christ Jesus:

2 Grace to you and peace from God our Father and the Lord Jesus Christ.

Redemption in Christ

3 Blessed *be* the God and Father of our Lord Jesus Christ, who has blessed us with every spiritual blessing in the heavenly *places* in Christ,

4 just as He chose us in Him before the foundation of the world, that we should be holy and without blame before Him in love,

5 having predestined us to adoption as sons by Jesus Christ to Himself, according to the good pleasure of His will,

6 to the praise of the glory of His grace, by which He made us accepted in the Beloved.

7 In Him we have redemption through His blood, the forgiveness of sins, according to the riches of His grace

8 which He made to abound toward us in all wisdom and prudence,

9 having made known to us the mystery of His will, according to His good pleasure which He purposed in Himself,

10 that in the dispensation of the fullness of the times He might gather together in one all things in Christ, both[a] which are in heaven and which are on earth—in Him.

11 In Him also we have obtained an inheritance, being predestined according to the purpose of Him who works all things according to the counsel of His will,

12 that we who first trusted in Christ should be to the praise of His glory.

13 In Him you also *trusted,* after you heard the word of truth, the gospel of your salvation; in whom also, having believed, you were sealed with the Holy Spirit of promise,

14 who[a] is the guarantee of our inheritance until the redemption of the purchased possession, to the praise of His glory.

Prayer for Spiritual Wisdom

15 Therefore I also, after I heard of your faith in the Lord Jesus and your love for all the saints,

16 do not cease to give thanks for you, making mention of you in my prayers:

17 that the God of our Lord Jesus Christ, the Father of glory, may give to you the spirit of wisdom and revelation in the knowledge of Him,

18 the eyes of your understanding[a] being enlightened; that you may know what is the hope of His calling, what are the riches of the glory of His inheritance in the saints,

19 and what *is* the exceeding greatness of His power toward us who believe, according to the working of His mighty power

20 which He worked in Christ when He raised Him from the dead and seated *Him* at His right hand in the heavenly *places,*

21 far above all principality and power and might and dominion, and every name that is named, not only in this age but also in that which is to come.

22 And He put all *things* under His feet, and gave Him *to be* head over all *things* to the church,

23 which is His body, the fullness of Him who fills all in all.

6:14 [a]Or *by which* (the cross) **1:10** [a]NU-Text and M-Text omit *both.* **1:14** [a]NU-Text reads *which.* **1:18** [a]NU-Text and M-Text read *hearts.*

By Grace Through Faith

2 And you *He made alive*, who were dead in
trespasses and sins,
2 in which you once walked according to the
course of this world, according to the prince of
the power of the air, the spirit who now works
in the sons of disobedience,
3 among whom also we all once conducted
ourselves in the lusts of our flesh, fulfilling the
desires of the flesh and of the mind, and were
by nature children of wrath, just as the others.
4 But God, who is rich in mercy, because of
His great love with which He loved us,
5 even when we were dead in trespasses, made
us alive together with Christ (by grace you
have been saved),
6 and raised *us* up together, and made *us* sit
together in the heavenly *places* in Christ Jesus,
7 that in the ages to come He might show the
exceeding riches of His grace in *His* kindness
toward us in Christ Jesus.
8 For by grace you have been saved through
faith, and that not of yourselves; *it is* the gift
of God,
9 not of works, lest anyone should boast.
10 For we are His workmanship, created in
Christ Jesus for good works, which God prepared beforehand that we should walk in them.

Brought Near by His Blood

11 Therefore remember that you, once Gentiles in the flesh—who are called Uncircumcision by what is called the Circumcision made
in the flesh by hands—
12 that at that time you were without Christ,
being aliens from the commonwealth of Israel
and strangers from the covenants of promise,
having no hope and without God in the world.
13 But now in Christ Jesus you who once were
far off have been brought near by the blood of
Christ.

Christ Our Peace

14 For He Himself is our peace, who has made
both one, and has broken down the middle wall
of separation,
15 having abolished in His flesh the enmity,
that is, the law of commandments *contained*
in ordinances, so as to create in Himself one new
man *from* the two, *thus* making peace,
16 and that He might reconcile them both to
God in one body through the cross, thereby putting to death the enmity.
17 And He came and preached peace to you
who were afar off and to those who were near.
18 For through Him we both have access by
one Spirit to the Father.

Christ Our Cornerstone

19 Now, therefore, you are no longer strangers and foreigners, but fellow citizens with the
saints and members of the household of God,
20 having been built on the foundation of the
apostles and prophets, Jesus Christ Himself being the chief corner*stone*,
21 in whom the whole building, being fitted
together, grows into a holy temple in the Lord,
22 in whom you also are being built together
for a dwelling place of God in the Spirit.

The Mystery Revealed

3 For this reason I, Paul, the prisoner of
Christ Jesus for you Gentiles—
2 if indeed you have heard of the dispensation of the grace of God which was given to me
for you,
3 how that by revelation He made known to
me the mystery (as I have briefly written already,
4 by which, when you read, you may understand my knowledge in the mystery of Christ),
5 which in other ages was not made known
to the sons of men, as it has now been revealed
by the Spirit to His holy apostles and prophets:
6 that the Gentiles should be fellow heirs, of
the same body, and partakers of His promise
in Christ through the gospel,
7 of which I became a minister according to
the gift of the grace of God given to me by the
effective working of His power.

Purpose of the Mystery

8 To me, who am less than the least of all the
saints, this grace was given, that I should preach
among the Gentiles the unsearchable riches of
Christ,
9 and to make all see what *is* the fellowship[a]
of the mystery, which from the beginning of
the ages has been hidden in God who created
all things through Jesus Christ;[b]
10 to the intent that now the manifold wisdom
of God might be made known by the church to
the principalities and powers in the heavenly
places,
11 according to the eternal purpose which He
accomplished in Christ Jesus our Lord,
12 in whom we have boldness and access with
confidence through faith in Him.
13 Therefore I ask that you do not lose heart
at my tribulations for you, which is your glory.

Appreciation of the Mystery

14 For this reason I bow my knees to the Father of our Lord Jesus Christ,[a]
15 from whom the whole family in heaven and
earth is named,
16 that He would grant you, according to the
riches of His glory, to be strengthened with
might through His Spirit in the inner man,
17 that Christ may dwell in your hearts through
faith; that you, being rooted and grounded in love,
18 may be able to comprehend with all the
saints what *is* the width and length and depth
and height—
19 to know the love of Christ which passes
knowledge; that you may be filled with all the
fullness of God.
20 Now to Him who is able to do exceedingly
abundantly above all that we ask or think, according to the power that works in us,
21 to Him *be* glory in the church by Christ
Jesus to all generations, forever and ever. Amen.

Walk in Unity

4 I, therefore, the prisoner of the Lord, beseech you to walk worthy of the calling
with which you were called,
2 with all lowliness and gentleness, with longsuffering, bearing with one another in love,
3 endeavoring to keep the unity of the Spirit
in the bond of peace.
4 *There is* one body and one Spirit, just as
you were called in one hope of your calling;
5 one Lord, one faith, one baptism;
6 one God and Father of all, who *is* above all,
and through all, and in you[a] all.

3:9 [a]NU-Text and M-Text read *stewardship* (dispensation). [b]NU-Text omits *through Jesus Christ*. **3:14** [a]NU-Text omits *of our Lord Jesus Christ*. **4:6** [a]NU-Text omits *you;* M-Text reads *us*.

Spiritual Gifts

7 But to each one of us grace was given according to the measure of Christ's gift.
8 Therefore He says:

"When He ascended on high,
He led captivity captive,
And gave gifts to men."[a]

9 (Now this, *"He ascended"*—what does it mean but that He also first[a] descended into the lower parts of the earth?
10 He who descended is also the One who ascended far above all the heavens, that He might fill all things.)
11 And He Himself gave some *to be* apostles, some prophets, some evangelists, and some pastors and teachers,
12 for the equipping of the saints for the work of ministry, for the edifying of the body of Christ,
13 till we all come to the unity of the faith and of the knowledge of the Son of God, to a perfect man, to the measure of the stature of the fullness of Christ;
14 that we should no longer be children, tossed to and fro and carried about with every wind of doctrine, by the trickery of men, in the cunning craftiness of deceitful plotting,
15 but, speaking the truth in love, may grow up in all things into Him who is the head—Christ—
16 from whom the whole body, joined and knit together by what every joint supplies, according to the effective working by which every part does its share, causes growth of the body for the edifying of itself in love.

The New Man

17 This I say, therefore, and testify in the Lord, that you should no longer walk as the rest of[a] the Gentiles walk, in the futility of their mind,
18 having their understanding darkened, being alienated from the life of God, because of the ignorance that is in them, because of the blindness of their heart;
19 who, being past feeling, have given themselves over to lewdness, to work all uncleanness with greediness.
20 But you have not so learned Christ,
21 if indeed you have heard Him and have been taught by Him, as the truth is in Jesus:
22 that you put off, concerning your former conduct, the old man which grows corrupt according to the deceitful lusts,
23 and be renewed in the spirit of your mind,
24 and that you put on the new man which was created according to God, in true righteousness and holiness.

Do Not Grieve the Spirit

25 Therefore, putting away lying, *"Let each one of you speak truth with his neighbor,"*[a] for we are members of one another.
26 *"Be angry, and do not sin"*:[a] do not let the sun go down on your wrath,
27 nor give place to the devil.
28 Let him who stole steal no longer, but rather let him labor, working with *his* hands what is good, that he may have something to give him who has need.
29 Let no corrupt word proceed out of your mouth, but what is good for necessary edification, that it may impart grace to the hearers.
30 And do not grieve the Holy Spirit of God, by whom you were sealed for the day of redemption.
31 Let all bitterness, wrath, anger, clamor, and evil speaking be put away from you, with all malice.
32 And be kind to one another, tenderhearted, forgiving one another, even as God in Christ forgave you.

Walk in Love

5 Therefore be imitators of God as dear children.
2 And walk in love, as Christ also has loved us and given Himself for us, an offering and a sacrifice to God for a sweet-smelling aroma.
3 But fornication and all uncleanness or covetousness, let it not even be named among you, as is fitting for saints;
4 neither filthiness, nor foolish talking, nor coarse jesting, which are not fitting, but rather giving of thanks.
5 For this you know,[a] that no fornicator, unclean person, nor covetous man, who is an idolater, has any inheritance in the kingdom of Christ and God.
6 Let no one deceive you with empty words, for because of these things the wrath of God comes upon the sons of disobedience.
7 Therefore do not be partakers with them.

Walk in Light

8 For you were once darkness, but now *you are* light in the Lord. Walk as children of light
9 (for the fruit of the Spirit[a] *is* in all goodness, righteousness, and truth),
10 finding out what is acceptable to the Lord.
11 And have no fellowship with the unfruitful works of darkness, but rather expose *them.*
12 For it is shameful even to speak of those things which are done by them in secret.
13 But all things that are exposed are made manifest by the light, for whatever makes manifest is light.
14 Therefore He says:

"Awake, you who sleep,
Arise from the dead,
And Christ will give you light."

Walk in Wisdom

15 See then that you walk circumspectly, not as fools but as wise,
16 redeeming the time, because the days are evil.
17 Therefore do not be unwise, but understand what the will of the Lord *is.*
18 And do not be drunk with wine, in which is dissipation; but be filled with the Spirit,
19 speaking to one another in psalms and hymns and spiritual songs, singing and making melody in your heart to the Lord,
20 giving thanks always for all things to God the Father in the name of our Lord Jesus Christ,
21 submitting to one another in the fear of God.[a]

Marriage—Christ and the Church

22 Wives, submit to your own husbands, as to the Lord.
23 For the husband is head of the wife, as also

4:8 [a]Psalm 68:18 4:9 [a]NU-Text omits *first.* 4:17 [a]NU-Text omits *the rest of.* 4:25 [a]Zechariah 8:16 4:26 [a]Psalm 4:4
5:5 [a]NU-Text reads *For know this.* 5:9 [a]NU-Text reads *light.* 5:21 [a]NU-Text reads *Christ.*

Christ is head of the church; and He is the Savior of the body.
24 Therefore, just as the church is subject to Christ, so *let* the wives *be* to their own husbands in everything.
25 Husbands, love your wives, just as Christ also loved the church and gave Himself for her,
26 that He might sanctify and cleanse her with the washing of water by the word,
27 that He might present her to Himself a glorious church, not having spot or wrinkle or any such thing, but that she should be holy and without blemish.
28 So husbands ought to love their own wives as their own bodies; he who loves his wife loves himself.
29 For no one ever hated his own flesh, but nourishes and cherishes it, just as the Lord *does* the church.
30 For we are members of His body,[a] of His flesh and of His bones.
31 *"For this reason a man shall leave his father and mother and be joined to his wife, and the two shall become one flesh."*[a]
32 This is a great mystery, but I speak concerning Christ and the church.
33 Nevertheless let each one of you in particular so love his own wife as himself, and let the wife *see* that she respects *her* husband.

Children and Parents

6 Children, obey your parents in the Lord, for this is right.
2 *"Honor your father and mother,"* which is the first commandment with promise:
3 *"that it may be well with you and you may live long on the earth."*[a]
4 And you, fathers, do not provoke your children to wrath, but bring them up in the training and admonition of the Lord.

Bondservants and Masters

5 Bondservants, be obedient to those who are your masters according to the flesh, with fear and trembling, in sincerity of heart, as to Christ;
6 not with eyeservice, as men-pleasers, but as bondservants of Christ, doing the will of God from the heart,
7 with goodwill doing service, as to the Lord, and not to men,
8 knowing that whatever good anyone does, he will receive the same from the Lord, whether *he is* a slave or free.
9 And you, masters, do the same things to them, giving up threatening, knowing that your own Master also[a] is in heaven, and there is no partiality with Him.

The Whole Armor of God

10 Finally, my brethren, be strong in the Lord and in the power of His might.
11 Put on the whole armor of God, that you may be able to stand against the wiles of the devil.
12 For we do not wrestle against flesh and blood, but against principalities, against powers, against the rulers of the darkness of this age,[a] against spiritual *hosts* of wickedness in the heavenly *places*.
13 Therefore take up the whole armor of God, that you may be able to withstand in the evil day, and having done all, to stand.
14 Stand therefore, having girded your waist with truth, having put on the breastplate of righteousness,
15 and having shod your feet with the preparation of the gospel of peace;
16 above all, taking the shield of faith with which you will be able to quench all the fiery darts of the wicked one.
17 And take the helmet of salvation, and the sword of the Spirit, which is the word of God;
18 praying always with all prayer and supplication in the Spirit, being watchful to this end with all perseverance and supplication for all the saints—
19 and for me, that utterance may be given to me, that I may open my mouth boldly to make known the mystery of the gospel,
20 for which I am an ambassador in chains; that in it I may speak boldly, as I ought to speak.

A Gracious Greeting

21 But that you also may know my affairs *and* how I am doing, Tychicus, a beloved brother and faithful minister in the Lord, will make all things known to you;
22 whom I have sent to you for this very purpose, that you may know our affairs, and *that* he may comfort your hearts.
23 Peace to the brethren, and love with faith, from God the Father and the Lord Jesus Christ.
24 Grace *be* with all those who love our Lord Jesus Christ in sincerity. Amen.

The Epistle of Paul the Apostle to the

PHILIPPIANS

Greeting

1 Paul and Timothy, bondservants of Jesus Christ,

To all the saints in Christ Jesus who are in Philippi, with the bishops[a] and deacons:

2 Grace to you and peace from God our Father and the Lord Jesus Christ.

Thankfulness and Prayer

3 I thank my God upon every remembrance of you,
4 always in every prayer of mine making request for you all with joy,
5 for your fellowship in the gospel from the first day until now,
6 being confident of this very thing, that He who has begun a good work in you will complete *it* until the day of Jesus Christ;
7 just as it is right for me to think this of you all, because I have you in my heart, inasmuch as both in my chains and in the defense and confirmation of the gospel, you all are partakers with me of grace.

5:30 [a]NU-Text omits the rest of this verse. **5:31** [a]Genesis 2:24 **6:3** [a]Deuteronomy 5:16 **6:9** [a]NU-Text reads *He who is both their Master and yours.* **6:12** [a]NU-Text reads *rulers of this darkness.* **1:1** [a]Literally *overseers*

8 For God is my witness, how greatly I long for you all with the affection of Jesus Christ.

9 And this I pray, that your love may abound still more and more in knowledge and all discernment,

10 that you may approve the things that are excellent, that you may be sincere and without offense till the day of Christ,

11 being filled with the fruits of righteousness which *are* by Jesus Christ, to the glory and praise of God.

Christ Is Preached

12 But I want you to know, brethren, that the things *which happened* to me have actually turned out for the furtherance of the gospel,

13 so that it has become evident to the whole palace guard, and to all the rest, that my chains are in Christ;

14 and most of the brethren in the Lord, having become confident by my chains, are much more bold to speak the word without fear.

15 Some indeed preach Christ even from envy and strife, and some also from goodwill:

16 The former[a] preach Christ from selfish ambition, not sincerely, supposing to add affliction to my chains;

17 but the latter out of love, knowing that I am appointed for the defense of the gospel.

18 What then? Only *that* in every way, whether in pretense or in truth, Christ is preached; and in this I rejoice, yes, and will rejoice.

To Live Is Christ

19 For I know that this will turn out for my deliverance through your prayer and the supply of the Spirit of Jesus Christ,

20 according to my earnest expectation and hope that in nothing I shall be ashamed, but with all boldness, as always, so now also Christ will be magnified in my body, whether by life or by death.

21 For to me, to live *is* Christ, and to die *is* gain.

22 But if *I* live on in the flesh, this *will mean* fruit from *my* labor; yet what I shall choose I cannot tell.

23 For[a] I am hard-pressed between the two, having a desire to depart and be with Christ, *which is* far better.

24 Nevertheless to remain in the flesh *is* more needful for you.

25 And being confident of this, I know that I shall remain and continue with you all for your progress and joy of faith,

26 that your rejoicing for me may be more abundant in Jesus Christ by my coming to you again.

Striving and Suffering for Christ

27 Only let your conduct be worthy of the gospel of Christ, so that whether I come and see you or am absent, I may hear of your affairs, that you stand fast in one spirit, with one mind striving together for the faith of the gospel,

28 and not in any way terrified by your adversaries, which is to them a proof of perdition, but to you of salvation,[a] and that from God.

29 For to you it has been granted on behalf of Christ, not only to believe in Him, but also to suffer for His sake,

30 having the same conflict which you saw in me and now hear *is* in me.

Unity Through Humility

2 Therefore if *there is* any consolation in Christ, if any comfort of love, if any fellowship of the Spirit, if any affection and mercy,

2 fulfill my joy by being like-minded, having the same love, *being* of one accord, of one mind.

3 *Let* nothing *be done* through selfish ambition or conceit, but in lowliness of mind let each esteem others better than himself.

4 Let each of you look out not only for his own interests, but also for the interests of others.

The Humbled and Exalted Christ

5 Let this mind be in you which was also in Christ Jesus,

6 who, being in the form of God, did not consider it robbery to be equal with God,

7 but made Himself of no reputation, taking the form of a bondservant, *and* coming in the likeness of men.

8 And being found in appearance as a man, He humbled Himself and became obedient to *the point of* death, even the death of the cross.

9 Therefore God also has highly exalted Him and given Him the name which is above every name,

10 that at the name of Jesus every knee should bow, of those in heaven, and of those on earth, and of those under the earth,

11 and *that* every tongue should confess that Jesus Christ *is* Lord, to the glory of God the Father.

Light Bearers

12 Therefore, my beloved, as you have always obeyed, not as in my presence only, but now much more in my absence, work out your own salvation with fear and trembling;

13 for it is God who works in you both to will and to do for *His* good pleasure.

14 Do all things without complaining and disputing,

15 that you may become blameless and harmless, children of God without fault in the midst of a crooked and perverse generation, among whom you shine as lights in the world,

16 holding fast the word of life, so that I may rejoice in the day of Christ that I have not run in vain or labored in vain.

17 Yes, and if I am being poured out *as a drink offering* on the sacrifice and service of your faith, I am glad and rejoice with you all.

18 For the same reason you also be glad and rejoice with me.

Timothy Commended

19 But I trust in the Lord Jesus to send Timothy to you shortly, that I also may be encouraged when I know your state.

20 For I have no one like-minded, who will sincerely care for your state.

21 For all seek their own, not the things which are of Christ Jesus.

22 But you know his proven character, that as a son with *his* father he served with me in the gospel.

23 Therefore I hope to send him at once, as soon as I see how it goes with me.

24 But I trust in the Lord that I myself shall also come shortly.

1:16 [a]NU-Text reverses the contents of verses 16 and 17. **1:23** [a]NU-Text and M-Text read *But.* **1:28** [a]NU-Text reads *of your salvation.*

Epaphroditus Praised

25 Yet I considered it necessary to send to you Epaphroditus, my brother, fellow worker, and fellow soldier, but your messenger and the one who ministered to my need;
26 since he was longing for you all, and was distressed because you had heard that he was sick.
27 For indeed he was sick almost unto death; but God had mercy on him, and not only on him but on me also, lest I should have sorrow upon sorrow.
28 Therefore I sent him the more eagerly, that when you see him again you may rejoice, and I may be less sorrowful.
29 Receive him therefore in the Lord with all gladness, and hold such men in esteem;
30 because for the work of Christ he came close to death, not regarding his life, to supply what was lacking in your service toward me.

All for Christ

3 Finally, my brethren, rejoice in the Lord. For me to write the same things to you *is* not tedious, but for you *it is* safe.
2 Beware of dogs, beware of evil workers, beware of the mutilation!
3 For we are the circumcision, who worship God in the Spirit,[a] rejoice in Christ Jesus, and have no confidence in the flesh,
4 though I also might have confidence in the flesh. If anyone else thinks he may have confidence in the flesh, I more so:
5 circumcised the eighth day, of the stock of Israel, *of* the tribe of Benjamin, a Hebrew of the Hebrews; concerning the law, a Pharisee;
6 concerning zeal, persecuting the church; concerning the righteousness which is in the law, blameless.
7 But what things were gain to me, these I have counted loss for Christ.
8 Yet indeed I also count all things loss for the excellence of the knowledge of Christ Jesus my Lord, for whom I have suffered the loss of all things, and count them as rubbish, that I may gain Christ
9 and be found in Him, not having my own righteousness, which *is* from the law, but that which *is* through faith in Christ, the righteousness which is from God by faith;
10 that I may know Him and the power of His resurrection, and the fellowship of His sufferings, being conformed to His death,
11 if, by any means, I may attain to the resurrection from the dead.

Pressing Toward the Goal

12 Not that I have already attained, or am already perfected; but I press on, that I may lay hold of that for which Christ Jesus has also laid hold of me.
13 Brethren, I do not count myself to have apprehended; but one thing *I do,* forgetting those things which are behind and reaching forward to those things which are ahead,
14 I press toward the goal for the prize of the upward call of God in Christ Jesus.
15 Therefore let us, as many as are mature, have this mind; and if in anything you think otherwise, God will reveal even this to you.
16 Nevertheless, to *the degree* that we have already attained, let us walk by the same rule,[a] let us be of the same mind.

Our Citizenship in Heaven

17 Brethren, join in following my example, and note those who so walk, as you have us for a pattern.
18 For many walk, of whom I have told you often, and now tell you even weeping, *that they are* the enemies of the cross of Christ:
19 whose end *is* destruction, whose god *is their* belly, and *whose* glory *is* in their shame—who set their mind on earthly things.
20 For our citizenship is in heaven, from which we also eagerly wait for the Savior, the Lord Jesus Christ,
21 who will transform our lowly body that it may be conformed to His glorious body, according to the working by which He is able even to subdue all things to Himself.

4 Therefore, my beloved and longed-for brethren, my joy and crown, so stand fast in the Lord, beloved.

Be United, Joyful, and in Prayer

2 I implore Euodia and I implore Syntyche to be of the same mind in the Lord.
3 And[a] I urge you also, true companion, help these women who labored with me in the gospel, with Clement also, and the rest of my fellow workers, whose names *are* in the Book of Life.
4 Rejoice in the Lord always. Again I will say, rejoice!
5 Let your gentleness be known to all men. The Lord *is* at hand.
6 Be anxious for nothing, but in everything by prayer and supplication, with thanksgiving, let your requests be made known to God;
7 and the peace of God, which surpasses all understanding, will guard your hearts and minds through Christ Jesus.

Meditate on These Things

8 Finally, brethren, whatever things are true, whatever things *are* noble, whatever things *are* just, whatever things *are* pure, whatever things *are* lovely, whatever things *are* of good report, if *there is* any virtue and if *there is* anything praiseworthy—meditate on these things.
9 The things which you learned and received and heard and saw in me, these do, and the God of peace will be with you.

Philippian Generosity

10 But I rejoiced in the Lord greatly that now at last your care for me has flourished again; though you surely did care, but you lacked opportunity.
11 Not that I speak in regard to need, for I have learned in whatever state I am, to be content:
12 I know how to be abased, and I know how to abound. Everywhere and in all things I have learned both to be full and to be hungry, both to abound and to suffer need.
13 I can do all things through Christ[a] who strengthens me.
14 Nevertheless you have done well that you shared in my distress.

3:3 [a]NU-Text and M-Text read *who worship in the Spirit of God.* **3:16** [a]NU-Text omits *rule* and the rest of the verse.
4:3 [a]NU-Text and M-Text read *Yes.* **4:13** [a]NU-Text reads *Him who.*

15 Now you Philippians know also that in the
beginning of the gospel, when I departed from
Macedonia, no church shared with me con-
cerning giving and receiving but you only.
16 For even in Thessalonica you sent *aid* once
and again for my necessities.
17 Not that I seek the gift, but I seek the fruit
that abounds to your account.
18 Indeed I have all and abound. I am full,
having received from Epaphroditus the things
sent from you, a sweet-smelling aroma, an ac-
ceptable sacrifice, well pleasing to God.
19 And my God shall supply all your need ac-
cording to His riches in glory by Christ Jesus.
20 Now to our God and Father *be* glory for-
ever and ever. Amen.

Greeting and Blessing

21 Greet every saint in Christ Jesus. The breth-
ren who are with me greet you.
22 All the saints greet you, but especially
those who are of Caesar's household.
23 The grace of our Lord Jesus Christ be with
you all.[a] Amen.

The Epistle of Paul the Apostle to the COLOSSIANS

Greeting

1 Paul, an apostle of Jesus Christ by the will
of God, and Timothy our brother,
2 To the saints and faithful brethren in
Christ *who are* in Colosse:

Grace to you and peace from God our Fa-
ther and the Lord Jesus Christ.[a]

Their Faith in Christ

3 We give thanks to the God and Father of
our Lord Jesus Christ, praying always for you,
4 since we heard of your faith in Christ Jesus
and of your love for all the saints;
5 because of the hope which is laid up for
you in heaven, of which you heard before in
the word of the truth of the gospel,
6 which has come to you, as *it has* also in all
the world, and is bringing forth fruit,[a] as *it is*
also among you since the day you heard and
knew the grace of God in truth;
7 as you also learned from Epaphras, our dear
fellow servant, who is a faithful minister of
Christ on your behalf,
8 who also declared to us your love in the
Spirit.

Preeminence of Christ

9 For this reason we also, since the day we
heard it, do not cease to pray for you, and to
ask that you may be filled with the knowledge
of His will in all wisdom and spiritual under-
standing;
10 that you may walk worthy of the Lord,
fully pleasing *Him*, being fruitful in every good
work and increasing in the knowledge of God;
11 strengthened with all might, according to
His glorious power, for all patience and long-
suffering with joy;
12 giving thanks to the Father who has qual-
ified us to be partakers of the inheritance of the
saints in the light.
13 He has delivered us from the power of dark-
ness and conveyed *us* into the kingdom of the
Son of His love,
14 in whom we have redemption through His
blood,[a] the forgiveness of sins.
15 He is the image of the invisible God, the first-
born over all creation.
16 For by Him all things were created that are
in heaven and that are on earth, visible and in-
visible, whether thrones or dominions or prin-
cipalities or powers. All things were created
through Him and for Him.
17 And He is before all things, and in Him all
things consist.
18 And He is the head of the body, the church,
who is the beginning, the firstborn from the
dead, that in all things He may have the preem-
inence.

Reconciled in Christ

19 For it pleased *the Father that* in Him all the
fullness should dwell,
20 and by Him to reconcile all things to Him-
self, by Him, whether things on earth or things
in heaven, having made peace through the blood
of His cross.
21 And you, who once were alienated and en-
emies in your mind by wicked works, yet now
He has reconciled
22 in the body of His flesh through death, to
present you holy, and blameless, and above
reproach in His sight—
23 if indeed you continue in the faith, grounded
and steadfast, and are not moved away from
the hope of the gospel which you heard, which
was preached to every creature under heaven,
of which I, Paul, became a minister.

Sacrificial Service for Christ

24 I now rejoice in my sufferings for you, and
fill up in my flesh what is lacking in the afflic-
tions of Christ, for the sake of His body, which
is the church,
25 of which I became a minister according to
the stewardship from God which was given to
me for you, to fulfill the word of God,
26 the mystery which has been hidden from
ages and from generations, but now has been
revealed to His saints.
27 To them God willed to make known what
are the riches of the glory of this mystery among
the Gentiles: which[a] is Christ in you, the hope
of glory.
28 Him we preach, warning every man and
teaching every man in all wisdom, that we may
present every man perfect in Christ Jesus.
29 To this *end* I also labor, striving according
to His working which works in me mightily.

4:23 [a]NU-Text reads *your spirit.* **1:2** [a]NU-Text omits *and the Lord Jesus Christ.* **1:6** [a]NU-Text and M-Text add *and growing.* **1:14** [a]NU-Text and M-Text omit *through His blood.* **1:27** [a]M-Text reads *who.*

Not Philosophy but Christ

2 For I want you to know what a great conflict
I have for you and those in Laodicea, and
for as many as have not seen my face in the flesh,
2 that their hearts may be encouraged, being
knit together in love, and *attaining* to all riches
of the full assurance of understanding, to the
knowledge of the mystery of God, both of the
Father and[a] of Christ,
3 in whom are hidden all the treasures of wis-
dom and knowledge.
4 Now this I say lest anyone should deceive
you with persuasive words.
5 For though I am absent in the flesh, yet I
am with you in spirit, rejoicing to see your *good*
order and the steadfastness of your faith in
Christ.
6 As you therefore have received Christ Jesus
the Lord, so walk in Him,
7 rooted and built up in Him and established
in the faith, as you have been taught, abound-
ing in it[a] with thanksgiving.
8 Beware lest anyone cheat you through phi-
losophy and empty deceit, according to the tra-
dition of men, according to the basic principles
of the world, and not according to Christ.
9 For in Him dwells all the fullness of the
Godhead bodily;
10 and you are complete in Him, who is the
head of all principality and power.

Not Legalism but Christ

11 In Him you were also circumcised with the
circumcision made without hands, by putting
off the body of the sins[a] of the flesh, by the cir-
cumcision of Christ,
12 buried with Him in baptism, in which you
also were raised with *Him* through faith in the
working of God, who raised Him from the dead.
13 And you, being dead in your trespasses and
the uncircumcision of your flesh, He has made
alive together with Him, having forgiven you
all trespasses,
14 having wiped out the handwriting of re-
quirements that was against us, which was con-
trary to us. And He has taken it out of the way,
having nailed it to the cross.
15 Having disarmed principalities and powers,
He made a public spectacle of them, triumphing
over them in it.
16 So let no one judge you in food or in drink,
or regarding a festival or a new moon or sab-
baths,
17 which are a shadow of things to come, but
the substance is of Christ.
18 Let no one cheat you of your reward, tak-
ing delight in *false* humility and worship of
angels, intruding into those things which he has
not[a] seen, vainly puffed up by his fleshly mind,
19 and not holding fast to the Head, from whom
all the body, nourished and knit together by joints
and ligaments, grows with the increase *that is*
from God.
20 Therefore,[a] if you died with Christ from the
basic principles of the world, why, as *though*
living in the world, do you subject yourselves
to regulations—
21 "Do not touch, do not taste, do not handle,"
22 which all concern things which perish with
the using—according to the commandments
and doctrines of men?
23 These things indeed have an appearance
of wisdom in self-imposed religion, *false* hu-
mility, and neglect of the body, *but are* of no value
against the indulgence of the flesh.

Not Carnality but Christ

3 If then you were raised with Christ, seek
those things which are above, where Christ
is, sitting at the right hand of God.
2 Set your mind on things above, not on things
on the earth.
3 For you died, and your life is hidden with
Christ in God.
4 When Christ *who is* our life appears, then
you also will appear with Him in glory.
5 Therefore put to death your members which
are on the earth: fornication, uncleanness, pas-
sion, evil desire, and covetousness, which is
idolatry.
6 Because of these things the wrath of God
is coming upon the sons of disobedience,
7 in which you yourselves once walked when
you lived in them.
8 But now you yourselves are to put off all
these: anger, wrath, malice, blasphemy, filthy
language out of your mouth.
9 Do not lie to one another, since you have
put off the old man with his deeds,
10 and have put on the new *man* who is re-
newed in knowledge according to the image of
Him who created him,
11 where there is neither Greek nor Jew, cir-
cumcised nor uncircumcised, barbarian, Scyth-
ian, slave *nor* free, but Christ *is* all and in all.

Character of the New Man

12 Therefore, as *the* elect of God, holy and be-
loved, put on tender mercies, kindness, humil-
ity, meekness, longsuffering;
13 bearing with one another, and forgiving
one another, if anyone has a complaint against
another; even as Christ forgave you, so you also
must do.
14 But above all these things put on love, which
is the bond of perfection.
15 And let the peace of God rule in your hearts,
to which also you were called in one body; and
be thankful.
16 Let the word of Christ dwell in you richly
in all wisdom, teaching and admonishing one
another in psalms and hymns and spiritual
songs, singing with grace in your hearts to the
Lord.
17 And whatever you do in word or deed, *do*
all in the name of the Lord Jesus, giving thanks
to God the Father through Him.

The Christian Home

18 Wives, submit to your own husbands, as is
fitting in the Lord.
19 Husbands, love your wives and do not be
bitter toward them.
20 Children, obey your parents in all things,
for this is well pleasing to the Lord.
21 Fathers, do not provoke your children, lest
they become discouraged.
22 Bondservants, obey in all things your mas-
ters according to the flesh, not with eyeservice,
as men-pleasers, but in sincerity of heart, fear-
ing God.
23 And whatever you do, do it heartily, as to
the Lord and not to men,

2:2 [a]NU-Text omits *both of the Father and*. **2:7** [a]NU-Text omits *in it*. **2:11** [a]NU-Text omits *of the sins*.
2:18 [a]NU-Text omits *not*. **2:20** [a]NU-Text and M-Text omit *Therefore*.

24 knowing that from the Lord you will receive the reward of the inheritance; for[a] you serve the Lord Christ.
25 But he who does wrong will be repaid for what he has done, and there is no partiality.
4 Masters, give your bondservants what is just and fair, knowing that you also have a Master in heaven.

Christian Graces

2 Continue earnestly in prayer, being vigilant in it with thanksgiving;
3 meanwhile praying also for us, that God would open to us a door for the word, to speak the mystery of Christ, for which I am also in chains,
4 that I may make it manifest, as I ought to speak.
5 Walk in wisdom toward those *who are* outside, redeeming the time.
6 *Let* your speech always *be* with grace, seasoned with salt, that you may know how you ought to answer each one.

Final Greetings

7 Tychicus, a beloved brother, faithful minister, and fellow servant in the Lord, will tell you all the news about me.
8 I am sending him to you for this very purpose, that he[a] may know your circumstances and comfort your hearts,
9 with Onesimus, a faithful and beloved brother, who is *one* of you. They will make known to you all things which *are happening* here.
10 Aristarchus my fellow prisoner greets you, with Mark the cousin of Barnabas (about whom you received instructions: if he comes to you, welcome him),
11 and Jesus who is called Justus. These *are my* only fellow workers for the kingdom of God who are of the circumcision; they have proved to be a comfort to me.
12 Epaphras, who is *one* of you, a bondservant of Christ, greets you, always laboring fervently for you in prayers, that you may stand perfect and complete[a] in all the will of God.
13 For I bear him witness that he has a great zeal[a] for you, and those who are in Laodicea, and those in Hierapolis.
14 Luke the beloved physician and Demas greet you.
15 Greet the brethren who are in Laodicea, and Nymphas and the church that *is* in his[a] house.

Closing Exhortations and Blessing

16 Now when this epistle is read among you, see that it is read also in the church of the Laodiceans, and that you likewise read the *epistle* from Laodicea.
17 And say to Archippus, "Take heed to the ministry which you have received in the Lord, that you may fulfill it."
18 This salutation by my own hand—Paul. Remember my chains. Grace *be* with you. Amen.

The First Epistle of Paul the Apostle to the THESSALONIANS

Greeting

1 Paul, Silvanus, and Timothy,
To the church of the Thessalonians in God the Father and the Lord Jesus Christ:

Grace to you and peace from God our Father and the Lord Jesus Christ.[a]

Their Good Example

2 We give thanks to God always for you all, making mention of you in our prayers,
3 remembering without ceasing your work of faith, labor of love, and patience of hope in our Lord Jesus Christ in the sight of our God and Father,
4 knowing, beloved brethren, your election by God.
5 For our gospel did not come to you in word only, but also in power, and in the Holy Spirit and in much assurance, as you know what kind of men we were among you for your sake.
6 And you became followers of us and of the Lord, having received the word in much affliction, with joy of the Holy Spirit,
7 so that you became examples to all in Macedonia and Achaia who believe.
8 For from you the word of the Lord has sounded forth, not only in Macedonia and Achaia, but also in every place. Your faith toward God has gone out, so that we do not need to say anything.
9 For they themselves declare concerning us what manner of entry we had to you, and how you turned to God from idols to serve the living and true God,
10 and to wait for His Son from heaven, whom He raised from the dead, *even* Jesus who delivers us from the wrath to come.

Paul's Conduct

2 For you yourselves know, brethren, that our coming to you was not in vain.
2 But even[a] after we had suffered before and were spitefully treated at Philippi, as you know, we were bold in our God to speak to you the gospel of God in much conflict.
3 For our exhortation *did* not *come* from error or uncleanness, nor *was it* in deceit.
4 But as we have been approved by God to be entrusted with the gospel, even so we speak, not as pleasing men, but God who tests our hearts.
5 For neither at any time did we use flattering words, as you know, nor a cloak for covetousness—God *is* witness.
6 Nor did we seek glory from men, either from you or from others, when we might have made demands as apostles of Christ.
7 But we were gentle among you, just as a nursing *mother* cherishes her own children.
8 So, affectionately longing for you, we were well pleased to impart to you not only the gospel

4:12 [a]NU-Text reads *fully assured.* **4:13** [a]NU-Text reads *concern.* **4:15** [a]NU-Text reads *Nympha . . . her house.*
1:1 [a]NU-Text omits *from God our Father and the Lord Jesus Christ.* **2:2** [a]NU-Text and M-Text omit *even.*

of God, but also our own lives, because you had become dear to us.

9 For you remember, brethren, our labor and toil; for laboring night and day, that we might not be a burden to any of you, we preached to you the gospel of God.

10 You *are* witnesses, and God *also*, how devoutly and justly and blamelessly we behaved ourselves among you who believe;

11 as you know how we exhorted, and comforted, and charged[a] every one of you, as a father *does* his own children,

12 that you would walk worthy of God who calls you into His own kingdom and glory.

Their Conversion

13 For this reason we also thank God without ceasing, because when you received the word of God which you heard from us, you welcomed *it* not *as* the word of men, but as it is in truth, the word of God, which also effectively works in you who believe.

14 For you, brethren, became imitators of the churches of God which are in Judea in Christ Jesus. For you also suffered the same things from your own countrymen, just as they *did* from the Judeans,

15 who killed both the Lord Jesus and their own prophets, and have persecuted us; and they do not please God and are contrary to all men,

16 forbidding us to speak to the Gentiles that they may be saved, so as always to fill up *the measure of* their sins; but wrath has come upon them to the uttermost.

Longing to See Them

17 But we, brethren, having been taken away from you for a short time in presence, not in heart, endeavored more eagerly to see your face with great desire.

18 Therefore we wanted to come to you—even I, Paul, time and again—but Satan hindered us.

19 For what *is* our hope, or joy, or crown of rejoicing? *Is it* not even you in the presence of our Lord Jesus Christ at His coming?

20 For you are our glory and joy.

Concern for Their Faith

3 Therefore, when we could no longer endure it, we thought it good to be left in Athens alone,

2 and sent Timothy, our brother and minister of God, and our fellow laborer in the gospel of Christ, to establish you and encourage you concerning your faith,

3 that no one should be shaken by these afflictions; for you yourselves know that we are appointed to this.

4 For, in fact, we told you before when we were with you that we would suffer tribulation, just as it happened, and you know.

5 For this reason, when I could no longer endure it, I sent to know your faith, lest by some means the tempter had tempted you, and our labor might be in vain.

Encouraged by Timothy

6 But now that Timothy has come to us from you, and brought us good news of your faith and love, and that you always have good remembrance of us, greatly desiring to see us, as we also *to see* you—

7 therefore, brethren, in all our affliction and distress we were comforted concerning you by your faith.

8 For now we live, if you stand fast in the Lord.

9 For what thanks can we render to God for you, for all the joy with which we rejoice for your sake before our God,

10 night and day praying exceedingly that we may see your face and perfect what is lacking in your faith?

Prayer for the Church

11 Now may our God and Father Himself, and our Lord Jesus Christ, direct our way to you.

12 And may the Lord make you increase and abound in love to one another and to all, just as we *do* to you,

13 so that He may establish your hearts blameless in holiness before our God and Father at the coming of our Lord Jesus Christ with all His saints.

Plea for Purity

4 Finally then, brethren, we urge and exhort in the Lord Jesus that you should abound more and more, just as you received from us how you ought to walk and to please God;

2 for you know what commandments we gave you through the Lord Jesus.

3 For this is the will of God, your sanctification: that you should abstain from sexual immorality;

4 that each of you should know how to possess his own vessel in sanctification and honor,

5 not in passion of lust, like the Gentiles who do not know God;

6 that no one should take advantage of and defraud his brother in this matter, because the Lord *is* the avenger of all such, as we also forewarned you and testified.

7 For God did not call us to uncleanness, but in holiness.

8 Therefore he who rejects *this* does not reject man, but God, who has also given[a] us His Holy Spirit.

A Brotherly and Orderly Life

9 But concerning brotherly love you have no need that I should write to you, for you yourselves are taught by God to love one another;

10 and indeed you do so toward all the brethren who are in all Macedonia. But we urge you, brethren, that you increase more and more;

11 that you also aspire to lead a quiet life, to mind your own business, and to work with your own hands, as we commanded you,

12 that you may walk properly toward those who are outside, and *that* you may lack nothing.

The Comfort of Christ's Coming

13 But I do not want you to be ignorant, brethren, concerning those who have fallen asleep, lest you sorrow as others who have no hope.

14 For if we believe that Jesus died and rose again, even so God will bring with Him those who sleep in Jesus.[a]

15 For this we say to you by the word of the

2:11 [a]NU-Text and M-Text read *implored.* **4:8** [a]NU-Text reads *who also gives.* **4:14** [a]Or *those who through Jesus sleep*

Lord, that we who are alive *and* remain until the
coming of the Lord will by no means precede
those who are asleep.
16 For the Lord Himself will descend from
heaven with a shout, with the voice of an arch-
angel, and with the trumpet of God. And the
dead in Christ will rise first.
17 Then we who are alive *and* remain shall
be caught up together with them in the clouds
to meet the Lord in the air. And thus we shall
always be with the Lord.
18 Therefore comfort one another with these
words.

The Day of the Lord

5 But concerning the times and the seasons,
brethren, you have no need that I should
write to you.
2 For you yourselves know perfectly that the
day of the Lord so comes as a thief in the night.
3 For when they say, "Peace and safety!" then
sudden destruction comes upon them, as labor
pains upon a pregnant woman. And they shall
not escape.
4 But you, brethren, are not in darkness, so
that this Day should overtake you as a thief.
5 You are all sons of light and sons of the day.
We are not of the night nor of darkness.
6 Therefore let us not sleep, as others *do*, but
let us watch and be sober.
7 For those who sleep, sleep at night, and those
who get drunk are drunk at night.
8 But let us who are of the day be sober, put-
ting on the breastplate of faith and love, and
as a helmet the hope of salvation.
9 For God did not appoint us to wrath, but to
obtain salvation through our Lord Jesus Christ,
10 who died for us, that whether we wake or
sleep, we should live together with Him.
11 Therefore comfort each other and edify
one another, just as you also are doing.

Various Exhortations

12 And we urge you, brethren, to recognize
those who labor among you, and are over you
in the Lord and admonish you,
13 and to esteem them very highly in love for
their work's sake. Be at peace among yourselves.
14 Now we exhort you, brethren, warn those
who are unruly, comfort the fainthearted, up-
hold the weak, be patient with all.
15 See that no one renders evil for evil to any-
one, but always pursue what is good both for
yourselves and for all.
16 Rejoice always,
17 pray without ceasing,
18 in everything give thanks; for this is the will
of God in Christ Jesus for you.
19 Do not quench the Spirit.
20 Do not despise prophecies.
21 Test all things; hold fast what is good.
22 Abstain from every form of evil.

Blessing and Admonition

23 Now may the God of peace Himself sanc-
tify you completely; and may your whole spirit,
soul, and body be preserved blameless at the
coming of our Lord Jesus Christ.
24 He who calls you *is* faithful, who also will
do *it*.
25 Brethren, pray for us.
26 Greet all the brethren with a holy kiss.
27 I charge you by the Lord that this epistle
be read to all the holy[a] brethren.
28 The grace of our Lord Jesus Christ *be* with
you. Amen.

The Second Epistle of Paul the Apostle to the THESSALONIANS

Greeting

1 Paul, Silvanus, and Timothy,
To the church of the Thessalonians in God
our Father and the Lord Jesus Christ:

2 Grace to you and peace from God our Fa-
ther and the Lord Jesus Christ.

God's Final Judgment and Glory

3 We are bound to thank God always for you,
brethren, as it is fitting, because your faith
grows exceedingly, and the love of every one
of you all abounds toward each other,
4 so that we ourselves boast of you among
the churches of God for your patience and faith
in all your persecutions and tribulations that
you endure,
5 *which is* manifest evidence of the righteous
judgment of God, that you may be counted
worthy of the kingdom of God, for which you
also suffer;
6 since *it is* a righteous thing with God to
repay with tribulation those who trouble you,
7 and to *give* you who are troubled rest with
us when the Lord Jesus is revealed from
heaven with His mighty angels,
8 in flaming fire taking vengeance on those
who do not know God, and on those who do
not obey the gospel of our Lord Jesus Christ.
9 These shall be punished with everlasting
destruction from the presence of the Lord and
from the glory of His power,
10 when He comes, in that Day, to be glorified
in His saints and to be admired among all those
who believe,[a] because our testimony among
you was believed.
11 Therefore we also pray always for you that
our God would count you worthy of *this* call-
ing, and fulfill all the good pleasure of *His*
goodness and the work of faith with power,
12 that the name of our Lord Jesus Christ may
be glorified in you, and you in Him, according
to the grace of our God and the Lord Jesus
Christ.

The Great Apostasy

2 Now, brethren, concerning the coming of our
Lord Jesus Christ and our gathering to-
gether to Him, we ask you,
2 not to be soon shaken in mind or troubled,
either by spirit or by word or by letter, as if
from us, as though the day of Christ[a] had come.

5:27 [a]NU-Text omits *holy.* **1:10** [a]NU-Text and M-Text read *have believed.* **2:2** [a]NU-Text reads *the Lord.*

3 Let no one deceive you by any means; for *that Day will not come* unless the falling away comes first, and the man of sin[a] is revealed, the son of perdition,

4 who opposes and exalts himself above all that is called God or that is worshiped, so that he sits as God[a] in the temple of God, showing himself that he is God.

5 Do you not remember that when I was still with you I told you these things?

6 And now you know what is restraining, that he may be revealed in his own time.

7 For the mystery of lawlessness is already at work; only He[a] who now restrains *will do so* until He[b] is taken out of the way.

8 And then the lawless one will be revealed, whom the Lord will consume with the breath of His mouth and destroy with the brightness of His coming.

9 The coming of the *lawless one* is according to the working of Satan, with all power, signs, and lying wonders,

10 and with all unrighteous deception among those who perish, because they did not receive the love of the truth, that they might be saved.

11 And for this reason God will send them strong delusion, that they should believe the lie,

12 that they all may be condemned who did not believe the truth but had pleasure in unrighteousness.

Stand Fast

13 But we are bound to give thanks to God always for you, brethren beloved by the Lord, because God from the beginning chose you for salvation through sanctification by the Spirit and belief in the truth,

14 to which He called you by our gospel, for the obtaining of the glory of our Lord Jesus Christ.

15 Therefore, brethren, stand fast and hold the traditions which you were taught, whether by word or our epistle.

16 Now may our Lord Jesus Christ Himself, and our God and Father, who has loved us and given *us* everlasting consolation and good hope by grace,

17 comfort your hearts and establish you in every good word and work.

Pray for Us

3 Finally, brethren, pray for us, that the word of the Lord may run *swiftly* and be glorified, just as *it is* with you,

2 and that we may be delivered from unreasonable and wicked men; for not all have faith.

3 But the Lord is faithful, who will establish you and guard *you* from the evil one.

4 And we have confidence in the Lord concerning you, both that you do and will do the things we command you.

5 Now may the Lord direct your hearts into the love of God and into the patience of Christ.

Warning Against Idleness

6 But we command you, brethren, in the name of our Lord Jesus Christ, that you withdraw from every brother who walks disorderly and not according to the tradition which he[a] received from us.

7 For you yourselves know how you ought to follow us, for we were not disorderly among you;

8 nor did we eat anyone's bread free of charge, but worked with labor and toil night and day, that we might not be a burden to any of you,

9 not because we do not have authority, but to make ourselves an example of how you should follow us.

10 For even when we were with you, we commanded you this: If anyone will not work, neither shall he eat.

11 For we hear that there are some who walk among you in a disorderly manner, not working at all, but are busybodies.

12 Now those who are such we command and exhort through our Lord Jesus Christ that they work in quietness and eat their own bread.

13 But *as for* you, brethren, do not grow weary *in* doing good.

14 And if anyone does not obey our word in this epistle, note that person and do not keep company with him, that he may be ashamed.

15 Yet do not count *him* as an enemy, but admonish *him* as a brother.

Benediction

16 Now may the Lord of peace Himself give you peace always in every way. The Lord *be* with you all.

17 The salutation of Paul with my own hand, which is a sign in every epistle; so I write.

18 The grace of our Lord Jesus Christ *be* with you all. Amen.

The First Epistle of Paul the Apostle to

TIMOTHY

Greeting

1 Paul, an apostle of Jesus Christ, by the commandment of God our Savior and the Lord Jesus Christ, our hope,

2 To Timothy, a true son in the faith:

Grace, mercy, *and* peace from God our Father and Jesus Christ our Lord.

No Other Doctrine

3 As I urged you when I went into Macedonia—remain in Ephesus that you may charge some that they teach no other doctrine,

4 nor give heed to fables and endless genealogies, which cause disputes rather than godly edification which is in faith.

5 Now the purpose of the commandment is love from a pure heart, *from* a good conscience, and *from* sincere faith,

6 from which some, having strayed, have turned aside to idle talk,

7 desiring to be teachers of the law, understanding neither what they say nor the things which they affirm.

8 But we know that the law *is* good if one uses it lawfully,

2:3 [a]NU-Text reads *lawlessness.* 2:4 [a]NU-Text omits *as God.* 2:7 [a]Or *he* [b]Or *he* 3:6 [a]NU-Text and M-Text read *they.*

9 knowing this: that the law is not made for
a righteous person, but for *the* lawless and insub-
ordinate, for *the* ungodly and for sinners, for
the unholy and profane, for murderers of fa-
thers and murderers of mothers, for manslayers,
10 for fornicators, for sodomites, for kidnap-
pers, for liars, for perjurers, and if there is any
other thing that is contrary to sound doctrine,
11 according to the glorious gospel of the
blessed God which was committed to my trust.

Glory to God for His Grace

12 And I thank Christ Jesus our Lord who has
enabled me, because He counted me faithful,
putting *me* into the ministry,
13 although I was formerly a blasphemer, a per-
secutor, and an insolent man; but I obtained
mercy because I did *it* ignorantly in unbelief.
14 And the grace of our Lord was exceedingly
abundant, with faith and love which are in Christ
Jesus.
15 This *is* a faithful saying and worthy of all
acceptance, that Christ Jesus came into the
world to save sinners, of whom I am chief.
16 However, for this reason I obtained mercy,
that in me first Jesus Christ might show all long-
suffering, as a pattern to those who are going
to believe on Him for everlasting life.
17 Now to the King eternal, immortal, invisi-
ble, to God who alone is wise,[a] *be* honor and
glory forever and ever. Amen.

Fight the Good Fight

18 This charge I commit to you, son Timothy,
according to the prophecies previously made
concerning you, that by them you may wage
the good warfare,
19 having faith and a good conscience, which
some having rejected, concerning the faith have
suffered shipwreck,
20 of whom are Hymenaeus and Alexander,
whom I delivered to Satan that they may learn
not to blaspheme.

Pray for All Men

2 Therefore I exhort first of all that supplica-
tions, prayers, intercessions, *and* giving of
thanks be made for all men,
2 for kings and all who are in authority, that
we may lead a quiet and peaceable life in all
godliness and reverence.
3 For this *is* good and acceptable in the sight
of God our Savior,
4 who desires all men to be saved and to
come to the knowledge of the truth.
5 For *there is* one God and one Mediator
between God and men, *the* Man Christ Jesus,
6 who gave Himself a ransom for all, to be
testified in due time,
7 for which I was appointed a preacher and
an apostle—I am speaking the truth in Christ[a]
and not lying—a teacher of the Gentiles in faith
and truth.

Men and Women in the Church

8 I desire therefore that the men pray every-
where, lifting up holy hands, without wrath and
doubting;
9 in like manner also, that the women adorn
themselves in modest apparel, with propriety
and moderation, not with braided hair or gold
or pearls or costly clothing,
10 but, which is proper for women professing
godliness, with good works.
11 Let a woman learn in silence with all sub-
mission.
12 And I do not permit a woman to teach or to
have authority over a man, but to be in silence.
13 For Adam was formed first, then Eve.
14 And Adam was not deceived, but the woman
being deceived, fell into transgression.
15 Nevertheless she will be saved in child-
bearing if they continue in faith, love, and holi-
ness, with self-control.

Qualifications of Overseers

3 This *is* a faithful saying: If a man desires
the position of a bishop,[a] he desires a good
work.
2 A bishop then must be blameless, the hus-
band of one wife, temperate, sober-minded, of
good behavior, hospitable, able to teach;
3 not given to wine, not violent, not greedy
for money,[a] but gentle, not quarrelsome, not cov-
etous;
4 one who rules his own house well, having
his children in submission with all reverence
5 (for if a man does not know how to rule his
own house, how will he take care of the church
of God?);
6 not a novice, lest being puffed up with pride
he fall into the *same* condemnation as the
devil.
7 Moreover he must have a good testimony
among those who are outside, lest he fall into
reproach and the snare of the devil.

Qualifications of Deacons

8 Likewise deacons *must be* reverent, not
double-tongued, not given to much wine, not
greedy for money,
9 holding the mystery of the faith with a pure
conscience.
10 But let these also first be tested; then let
them serve as deacons, being *found* blameless.
11 Likewise, *their* wives *must be* reverent,
not slanderers, temperate, faithful in all things.
12 Let deacons be the husbands of one wife,
ruling *their* children and their own houses
well.
13 For those who have served well as deacons
obtain for themselves a good standing and great
boldness in the faith which is in Christ Jesus.

The Great Mystery

14 These things I write to you, though I hope
to come to you shortly;
15 but if I am delayed, *I write* so that you may
know how you ought to conduct yourself in the
house of God, which is the church of the living
God, the pillar and ground of the truth.
16 And without controversy great is the mys-
tery of godliness:

> God[a] was manifested in the flesh,
> Justified in the Spirit,
> Seen by angels,
> Preached among the Gentiles,
> Believed on in the world,
> Received up in glory.

1:17 [a]NU-Text reads *to the only God.* **2:7** [a]NU-Text omits *in Christ.* **3:1** [a]Literally *overseer* **3:3** [a]NU-Text omits *not greedy for money.* **3:16** [a]NU-Text reads *Who.*

The Great Apostasy

4 Now the Spirit expressly says that in latter times some will depart from the faith, giving heed to deceiving spirits and doctrines of demons,
2 speaking lies in hypocrisy, having their own conscience seared with a hot iron,
3 forbidding to marry, *and commanding* to abstain from foods which God created to be received with thanksgiving by those who believe and know the truth.
4 For every creature of God *is* good, and nothing is to be refused if it is received with thanksgiving;
5 for it is sanctified by the word of God and prayer.

A Good Servant of Jesus Christ

6 If you instruct the brethren in these things, you will be a good minister of Jesus Christ, nourished in the words of faith and of the good doctrine which you have carefully followed.
7 But reject profane and old wives' fables, and exercise yourself toward godliness.
8 For bodily exercise profits a little, but godliness is profitable for all things, having promise of the life that now is and of that which is to come.
9 This *is* a faithful saying and worthy of all acceptance.
10 For to this *end* we both labor and suffer reproach,[a] because we trust in the living God, who is *the* Savior of all men, especially of those who believe.
11 These things command and teach.

Take Heed to Your Ministry

12 Let no one despise your youth, but be an example to the believers in word, in conduct, in love, in spirit,[a] in faith, in purity.
13 Till I come, give attention to reading, to exhortation, to doctrine.
14 Do not neglect the gift that is in you, which was given to you by prophecy with the laying on of the hands of the eldership.
15 Meditate on these things; give yourself entirely to them, that your progress may be evident to all.
16 Take heed to yourself and to the doctrine. Continue in them, for in doing this you will save both yourself and those who hear you.

Treatment of Church Members

5 Do not rebuke an older man, but exhort *him* as a father, younger men as brothers,
2 older women as mothers, younger women as sisters, with all purity.

Honor True Widows

3 Honor widows who are really widows.
4 But if any widow has children or grandchildren, let them first learn to show piety at home and to repay their parents; for this is good and[a] acceptable before God.
5 Now she who is really a widow, and left alone, trusts in God and continues in supplications and prayers night and day.
6 But she who lives in pleasure is dead while she lives.
7 And these things command, that they may be blameless.
8 But if anyone does not provide for his own, and especially for those of his household, he has denied the faith and is worse than an unbeliever.
9 Do not let a widow under sixty years old be taken into the number, *and not unless* she has been the wife of one man,
10 well reported for good works: if she has brought up children, if she has lodged strangers, if she has washed the saints' feet, if she has relieved the afflicted, if she has diligently followed every good work.
11 But refuse *the* younger widows; for when they have begun to grow wanton against Christ, they desire to marry,
12 having condemnation because they have cast off their first faith.
13 And besides they learn *to be* idle, wandering about from house to house, and not only idle but also gossips and busybodies, saying things which they ought not.
14 Therefore I desire that *the* younger *widows* marry, bear children, manage the house, give no opportunity to the adversary to speak reproachfully.
15 For some have already turned aside after Satan.
16 If any believing man or[a] woman has widows, let them relieve them, and do not let the church be burdened, that it may relieve those who are really widows.

Honor the Elders

17 Let the elders who rule well be counted worthy of double honor, especially those who labor in the word and doctrine.
18 For the Scripture says, *"You shall not muzzle an ox while it treads out the grain,"*[a] and, "The laborer *is* worthy of his wages."[b]
19 Do not receive an accusation against an elder except from two or three witnesses.
20 Those who are sinning rebuke in the presence of all, that the rest also may fear.
21 I charge *you* before God and the Lord Jesus Christ and the elect angels that you observe these things without prejudice, doing nothing with partiality.
22 Do not lay hands on anyone hastily, nor share in other people's sins; keep yourself pure.
23 No longer drink only water, but use a little wine for your stomach's sake and your frequent infirmities.
24 Some men's sins are clearly evident, preceding *them* to judgment, but those of some *men* follow later.
25 Likewise, the good works *of some* are clearly evident, and those that are otherwise cannot be hidden.

Honor Masters

6 Let as many bondservants as are under the yoke count their own masters worthy of all honor, so that the name of God and *His* doctrine may not be blasphemed.
2 And those who have believing masters, let them not despise *them* because they are brethren, but rather serve *them* because those who are benefited are believers and beloved. Teach and exhort these things.

4:10 [a]NU-Text reads *we labor and strive.* **4:12** [a]NU-Text omits *in spirit.* **5:4** [a]NU-Text and M-Text omit *good and.*
5:16 [a]NU-Text omits *man or.* **5:18** [a]Deuteronomy 25:4 [b]Luke 10:7

Error and Greed

3 If anyone teaches otherwise and does not
consent to wholesome words, *even* the words
of our Lord Jesus Christ, and to the doctrine
which accords with godliness,
4 he is proud, knowing nothing, but is ob-
sessed with disputes and arguments over words,
from which come envy, strife, reviling, evil sus-
picions,
5 useless wranglings[a] of men of corrupt minds
and destitute of the truth, who suppose that
godliness is a *means of* gain. From such withdraw
yourself.[b]
6 Now godliness with contentment is great
gain.
7 For we brought nothing into *this* world, *and
it is* certain[a] we can carry nothing out.
8 And having food and clothing, with these
we shall be content.
9 But those who desire to be rich fall into
temptation and a snare, and *into* many foolish
and harmful lusts which drown men in de-
struction and perdition.
10 For the love of money is a root of all *kinds
of* evil, for which some have strayed from the
faith in their greediness, and pierced them-
selves through with many sorrows.

The Good Confession

11 But you, O man of God, flee these things
and pursue righteousness, godliness, faith,
love, patience, gentleness.
12 Fight the good fight of faith, lay hold on
eternal life, to which you were also called and
have confessed the good confession in the
presence of many witnesses.
13 I urge you in the sight of God who gives
life to all things, and *before* Christ Jesus who
witnessed the good confession before Pontius
Pilate,
14 that you keep *this* commandment without
spot, blameless until our Lord Jesus Christ's
appearing,
15 which He will manifest in His own time,
He who is the blessed and only Potentate, the
King of kings and Lord of lords,
16 who alone has immortality, dwelling in un-
approachable light, whom no man has seen or
can see, to whom *be* honor and everlasting
power. Amen.

Instructions to the Rich

17 Command those who are rich in this pres-
ent age not to be haughty, nor to trust in uncer-
tain riches but in the living God, who gives us
richly all things to enjoy.
18 *Let them* do good, that they be rich in good
works, ready to give, willing to share,
19 storing up for themselves a good founda-
tion for the time to come, that they may lay hold
on eternal life.

Guard the Faith

20 O Timothy! Guard what was committed to
your trust, avoiding the profane *and* idle bab-
blings and contradictions of what is falsely
called knowledge—
21 by professing it some have strayed concern-
ing the faith. Grace *be* with you. Amen.

The Second Epistle of Paul the Apostle to
TIMOTHY

Greeting

1 Paul, an apostle of Jesus Christ[a] by the will
of God, according to the promise of life
which is in Christ Jesus,

2 To Timothy, a beloved son:

Grace, mercy, *and* peace from God the Fa-
ther and Christ Jesus our Lord.

Timothy's Faith and Heritage

3 I thank God, whom I serve with a pure con-
science, as *my* forefathers *did*, as without ceas-
ing I remember you in my prayers night and day,
4 greatly desiring to see you, being mindful
of your tears, that I may be filled with joy,
5 when I call to remembrance the genuine faith
that is in you, which dwelt first in your grand-
mother Lois and your mother Eunice, and I am
persuaded is in you also.
6 Therefore I remind you to stir up the gift of
God which is in you through the laying on of
my hands.
7 For God has not given us a spirit of fear, but
of power and of love and of a sound mind.

Not Ashamed of the Gospel

8 Therefore do not be ashamed of the testi-
mony of our Lord, nor of me His prisoner, but
share with me in the sufferings for the gospel
according to the power of God,
9 who has saved us and called *us* with a holy
calling, not according to our works, but accord-
ing to His own purpose and grace which was
given to us in Christ Jesus before time began,
10 but has now been revealed by the appearing
of our Savior Jesus Christ, *who* has abolished
death and brought life and immortality to light
through the gospel,
11 to which I was appointed a preacher, an
apostle, and a teacher of the Gentiles.[a]
12 For this reason I also suffer these things;
nevertheless I am not ashamed, for I know whom
I have believed and am persuaded that He is
able to keep what I have committed to Him until
that Day.

Be Loyal to the Faith

13 Hold fast the pattern of sound words which
you have heard from me, in faith and love which
are in Christ Jesus.
14 That good thing which was committed to
you, keep by the Holy Spirit who dwells in us.
15 This you know, that all those in Asia have
turned away from me, among whom are Phy-
gellus and Hermogenes.
16 The Lord grant mercy to the household of

6:5 [a]NU-Text and M-Text read *constant friction.* [b]NU-Text omits this sentence. **6:7** [a]NU-Text omits *and it is certain.* **1:1** [a]NU-Text and M-Text read *Christ Jesus.* **1:11** [a]NU-Text omits *of the Gentiles.*

Onesiphorus, for he often refreshed me, and was
not ashamed of my chain;
17 but when he arrived in Rome, he sought
me out very zealously and found *me*.
18 The Lord grant to him that he may find
mercy from the Lord in that Day—and you
know very well how many ways he ministered
to me[a] at Ephesus.

Be Strong in Grace

2 You therefore, my son, be strong in the grace
that is in Christ Jesus.
2 And the things that you have heard from
me among many witnesses, commit these to
faithful men who will be able to teach others also.
3 You therefore must endure[a] hardship as a
good soldier of Jesus Christ.
4 No one engaged in warfare entangles him-
self with the affairs of *this* life, that he may
please him who enlisted him as a soldier.
5 And also if anyone competes in athletics,
he is not crowned unless he competes according
to the rules.
6 The hardworking farmer must be first to
partake of the crops.
7 Consider what I say, and may[a] the Lord give
you understanding in all things.
8 Remember that Jesus Christ, of the seed
of David, was raised from the dead according
to my gospel,
9 for which I suffer trouble as an evildoer,
even to the point of chains; but the word of God
is not chained.
10 Therefore I endure all things for the sake
of the elect, that they also may obtain the salva-
tion which is in Christ Jesus with eternal glory.
11 *This is* a faithful saying:

For if we died with *Him*,
We shall also live with *Him*.
12 If we endure,
We shall also reign with *Him*.
If we deny *Him*,
He also will deny us.
13 If we are faithless,
He remains faithful;
He cannot deny Himself.

Approved and Disapproved Workers

14 Remind *them* of these things, charging
them before the Lord not to strive about words
to no profit, to the ruin of the hearers.
15 Be diligent to present yourself approved to
God, a worker who does not need to be ashamed,
rightly dividing the word of truth.
16 But shun profane *and* idle babblings, for
they will increase to more ungodliness.
17 And their message will spread like cancer.
Hymenaeus and Philetus are of this sort,
18 who have strayed concerning the truth,
saying that the resurrection is already past; and
they overthrow the faith of some.
19 Nevertheless the solid foundation of God
stands, having this seal: "The Lord knows those
who are His," and, "Let everyone who names
the name of Christ[a] depart from iniquity."
20 But in a great house there are not only
vessels of gold and silver, but also of wood and
clay, some for honor and some for dishonor.
21 Therefore if anyone cleanses himself from
the latter, he will be a vessel for honor, sancti-
fied and useful for the Master, prepared for
every good work.
22 Flee also youthful lusts; but pursue righ-
teousness, faith, love, peace with those who
call on the Lord out of a pure heart.
23 But avoid foolish and ignorant disputes,
knowing that they generate strife.
24 And a servant of the Lord must not quarrel
but be gentle to all, able to teach, patient,
25 in humility correcting those who are in op-
position, if God perhaps will grant them repen-
tance, so that they may know the truth,
26 and *that* they may come to their senses
and escape the snare of the devil, having been
taken captive by him to *do* his will.

Perilous Times and Perilous Men

3 But know this, that in the last days perilous
times will come:
2 For men will be lovers of themselves, lov-
ers of money, boasters, proud, blasphemers,
disobedient to parents, unthankful, unholy,
3 unloving, unforgiving, slanderers, without
self-control, brutal, despisers of good,
4 traitors, headstrong, haughty, lovers of plea-
sure rather than lovers of God,
5 having a form of godliness but denying its
power. And from such people turn away!
6 For of this sort are those who creep into
households and make captives of gullible women
loaded down with sins, led away by various lusts,
7 always learning and never able to come to
the knowledge of the truth.
8 Now as Jannes and Jambres resisted Mo-
ses, so do these also resist the truth: men of cor-
rupt minds, disapproved concerning the faith;
9 but they will progress no further, for their
folly will be manifest to all, as theirs also was.

The Man of God and the Word of God

10 But you have carefully followed my doctrine,
manner of life, purpose, faith, longsuffering,
love, perseverance,
11 persecutions, afflictions, which happened to
me at Antioch, at Iconium, at Lystra—what per-
secutions I endured. And out of *them* all the
Lord delivered me.
12 Yes, and all who desire to live godly in Christ
Jesus will suffer persecution.
13 But evil men and impostors will grow worse
and worse, deceiving and being deceived.
14 But you must continue in the things which
you have learned and been assured of, know-
ing from whom you have learned *them*,
15 and that from childhood you have known
the Holy Scriptures, which are able to make you
wise for salvation through faith which is in
Christ Jesus.
16 All Scripture *is* given by inspiration of God,
and *is* profitable for doctrine, for reproof, for
correction, for instruction in righteousness,
17 that the man of God may be complete,
thoroughly equipped for every good work.

Preach the Word

4 I charge *you* therefore before God and the
Lord Jesus Christ, who will judge the living
and the dead at[a] His appearing and His king-
dom:
2 Preach the word! Be ready in season *and*

1:18 [a]*To me* is from the Vulgate and a few Greek manuscripts. **2:3** [a]NU-Text reads *You must share.* **2:7** [a]NU-Text reads *the Lord will give you.* **2:19** [a]NU-Text and M-Text read *the Lord.* **4:1** [a]NU-Text omits *therefore* and reads *and by* for *at*.

out of season. Convince, rebuke, exhort, with all longsuffering and teaching.

3 For the time will come when they will not endure sound doctrine, but according to their own desires, *because* they have itching ears, they will heap up for themselves teachers;

4 and they will turn *their* ears away from the truth, and be turned aside to fables.

5 But you be watchful in all things, endure afflictions, do the work of an evangelist, fulfill your ministry.

Paul's Valedictory

6 For I am already being poured out as a drink offering, and the time of my departure is at hand.

7 I have fought the good fight, I have finished the race, I have kept the faith.

8 Finally, there is laid up for me the crown of righteousness, which the Lord, the righteous Judge, will give to me on that Day, and not to me only but also to all who have loved His appearing.

The Abandoned Apostle

9 Be diligent to come to me quickly;

10 for Demas has forsaken me, having loved this present world, and has departed for Thessalonica—Crescens for Galatia, Titus for Dalmatia.

11 Only Luke is with me. Get Mark and bring him with you, for he is useful to me for ministry.

12 And Tychicus I have sent to Ephesus.

13 Bring the cloak that I left with Carpus at Troas when you come—and the books, especially the parchments.

14 Alexander the coppersmith did me much harm. May the Lord repay him according to his works.

15 You also must beware of him, for he has greatly resisted our words.

16 At my first defense no one stood with me, but all forsook me. May it not be charged against them.

The Lord Is Faithful

17 But the Lord stood with me and strengthened me, so that the message might be preached fully through me, and *that* all the Gentiles might hear. Also I was delivered out of the mouth of the lion.

18 And the Lord will deliver me from every evil work and preserve *me* for His heavenly kingdom. To Him *be* glory forever and ever. Amen!

Come Before Winter

19 Greet Prisca and Aquila, and the household of Onesiphorus.

20 Erastus stayed in Corinth, but Trophimus I have left in Miletus sick.

21 Do your utmost to come before winter. Eubulus greets you, as well as Pudens, Linus, Claudia, and all the brethren.

Farewell

22 The Lord Jesus Christ[a] be with your spirit. Grace be with you. Amen.

The Epistle of Paul the Apostle to TITUS

Greeting

1 Paul, a bondservant of God and an apostle of Jesus Christ, according to the faith of God's elect and the acknowledgment of the truth which accords with godliness,

2 in hope of eternal life which God, who cannot lie, promised before time began,

3 but has in due time manifested His word through preaching, which was committed to me according to the commandment of God our Savior;

4 To Titus, a true son in *our* common faith:

Grace, mercy, *and* peace from God the Father and the Lord Jesus Christ[a] our Savior.

Qualified Elders

5 For this reason I left you in Crete, that you should set in order the things that are lacking, and appoint elders in every city as I commanded you—

6 if a man is blameless, the husband of one wife, having faithful children not accused of dissipation or insubordination.

7 For a bishop[a] must be blameless, as a steward of God, not self-willed, not quick-tempered, not given to wine, not violent, not greedy for money,

8 but hospitable, a lover of what is good, sober-minded, just, holy, self-controlled,

9 holding fast the faithful word as he has been taught, that he may be able, by sound doctrine, both to exhort and convict those who contradict.

The Elders' Task

10 For there are many insubordinate, both idle talkers and deceivers, especially those of the circumcision,

11 whose mouths must be stopped, who subvert whole households, teaching things which they ought not, for the sake of dishonest gain.

12 One of them, a prophet of their own, said, "Cretans *are* always liars, evil beasts, lazy gluttons."

13 This testimony is true. Therefore rebuke them sharply, that they may be sound in the faith,

14 not giving heed to Jewish fables and commandments of men who turn from the truth.

15 To the pure all things are pure, but to those who are defiled and unbelieving nothing is pure; but even their mind and conscience are defiled.

16 They profess to know God, but in works they deny *Him*, being abominable, disobedient, and disqualified for every good work.

Qualities of a Sound Church

2 But as for you, speak the things which are proper for sound doctrine:

2 that the older men be sober, reverent, temperate, sound in faith, in love, in patience;

4:22 [a]NU-Text omits *Jesus Christ.* **1:4** [a]NU-Text reads *and Christ Jesus.* **1:7** [a]Literally *overseer*

3 the older women likewise, that they be reverent in behavior, not slanderers, not given to much wine, teachers of good things—

4 that they admonish the young women to love their husbands, to love their children,

5 *to be* discreet, chaste, homemakers, good, obedient to their own husbands, that the word of God may not be blasphemed.

6 Likewise, exhort the young men to be sober-minded,

7 in all things showing yourself *to be* a pattern of good works; in doctrine *showing* integrity, reverence, incorruptibility,[a]

8 sound speech that cannot be condemned, that one who is an opponent may be ashamed, having nothing evil to say of you.[a]

9 *Exhort* bondservants to be obedient to their own masters, to be well pleasing in all *things*, not answering back,

10 not pilfering, but showing all good fidelity, that they may adorn the doctrine of God our Savior in all things.

Trained by Saving Grace

11 For the grace of God that brings salvation has appeared to all men,

12 teaching us that, denying ungodliness and worldly lusts, we should live soberly, righteously, and godly in the present age,

13 looking for the blessed hope and glorious appearing of our great God and Savior Jesus Christ,

14 who gave Himself for us, that He might redeem us from every lawless deed and purify for Himself *His* own special people, zealous for good works.

15 Speak these things, exhort, and rebuke with all authority. Let no one despise you.

Graces of the Heirs of Grace

3 Remind them to be subject to rulers and authorities, to obey, to be ready for every good work,

2 to speak evil of no one, to be peaceable, gentle, showing all humility to all men.

3 For we ourselves were also once foolish, disobedient, deceived, serving various lusts and pleasures, living in malice and envy, hateful and hating one another.

4 But when the kindness and the love of God our Savior toward man appeared,

5 not by works of righteousness which we have done, but according to His mercy He saved us, through the washing of regeneration and renewing of the Holy Spirit,

6 whom He poured out on us abundantly through Jesus Christ our Savior,

7 that having been justified by His grace we should become heirs according to the hope of eternal life.

8 This is a faithful saying, and these things I want you to affirm constantly, that those who have believed in God should be careful to maintain good works. These things are good and profitable to men.

Avoid Dissension

9 But avoid foolish disputes, genealogies, contentions, and strivings about the law; for they are unprofitable and useless.

10 Reject a divisive man after the first and second admonition,

11 knowing that such a person is warped and sinning, being self-condemned.

Final Messages

12 When I send Artemas to you, or Tychicus, be diligent to come to me at Nicopolis, for I have decided to spend the winter there.

13 Send Zenas the lawyer and Apollos on their journey with haste, that they may lack nothing.

14 And let our *people* also learn to maintain good works, to *meet* urgent needs, that they may not be unfruitful.

Farewell

15 All who *are* with me greet you. Grace *be* with you all. Amen.

The Epistle of Paul the Apostle to

PHILEMON

Greeting

Paul, a prisoner of Christ Jesus, and Timothy *our* brother,

To Philemon our beloved *friend* and fellow laborer,

2 to the beloved[a] Apphia, Archippus our fellow soldier, and to the church in your house:

3 Grace to you and peace from God our Father and the Lord Jesus Christ.

Philemon's Love and Faith

4 I thank my God, making mention of you always in my prayers,

5 hearing of your love and faith which you have toward the Lord Jesus and toward all the saints,

6 that the sharing of your faith may become effective by the acknowledgment of every good thing which is in you[a] in Christ Jesus.

7 For we have[a] great joy[b] and consolation in your love, because the hearts of the saints have been refreshed by you, brother.

The Plea for Onesimus

8 Therefore, though I might be very bold in Christ to command you what is fitting,

9 *yet* for love's sake I rather appeal *to you*—being such a one as Paul, the aged, and now also a prisoner of Jesus Christ—

10 I appeal to you for my son Onesimus, whom I have begotten *while* in my chains,

11 who once was unprofitable to you, but now is profitable to you and to me.

12 I am sending him back.[a] You therefore receive him, that is, my own heart,

2:7 [a]NU-Text omits *incorruptibility.* **2:8** [a]NU-Text and M-Text read *us.* **2** [a]NU-Text reads *to our sister Apphia.* **6** [a]NU-Text and M-Text read *us.* **7** [a]NU-Text reads *had.* [b]M-Text reads *thanksgiving.* **12** [a]NU-Text reads *back to you in person, that is, my own heart.*

13 whom I wished to keep with me, that on
your behalf he might minister to me in my
chains for the gospel.
14 But without your consent I wanted to do
nothing, that your good deed might not be by
compulsion, as it were, but voluntary.
15 For perhaps he departed for a while for
this *purpose*, that you might receive him for-
ever,
16 no longer as a slave but more than a slave—
a beloved brother, especially to me but how
much more to you, both in the flesh and in the
Lord.

Philemon's Obedience Encouraged

17 If then you count me as a partner, receive
him as *you would* me.
18 But if he has wronged you or owes any-
thing, put that on my account.
19 I, Paul, am writing with my own hand. I
will repay—not to mention to you that you owe
me even your own self besides.
20 Yes, brother, let me have joy from you in
the Lord; refresh my heart in the Lord.
21 Having confidence in your obedience, I
write to you, knowing that you will do even
more than I say.
22 But, meanwhile, also prepare a guest room
for me, for I trust that through your prayers I
shall be granted to you.

Farewell

23 Epaphras, my fellow prisoner in Christ
Jesus, greets you,
24 *as do* Mark, Aristarchus, Demas, Luke, my
fellow laborers.
25 The grace of our Lord Jesus Christ *be* with
your spirit. Amen.

THE GENERAL EPISTLES AND REVELATION

Hebrews • James • 1 Peter • 2 Peter • 1 John 2 John • 3 John • Jude • Revelation

HEBREWS was written to Jewish Christians, saying that Christ is the perfect sacrifice and the true High Priest. Hebrews emphasizes the humanity of Jesus more than any other book in the New Testament, except the Gospels. It also emphasizes the role of Jesus as the mediator between God and humanity, the One who brings forgiveness once and for all.

JAMES was also written to Jewish Christians to remind them that faith, if it is real faith, leads to faithful living. We are to show our faith in the little acts of daily living. Church tradition says the book was written by James the Lord's half brother.

FIRST PETER was written to encourage the church in Asia Minor in a time of persecution. The key idea of the book is hope in Christ. It is this hope that sees us through tough times. Because we have hope in Christ, we are called to live a life of hope and love in the world.

SECOND PETER is a reflection of the belief in the early church that Jesus would return at any moment. It calls the church to be faithful and to continue to expect Jesus to return.

FIRST, 2, and **3 JOHN** are (1) a sermon, (2) a letter to a church, and (3) a letter to an individual. First John urges Christians to return to fundamental loyalties. It stresses that Jesus came in the flesh, probably against heretics who were teaching that Jesus only seemed to be human. The writer says that believers experience eternal life now, that to know God is to obey God's commandments, and that the mark of eternal life is love. Second John was written to a church to emphasize the commandment of love. Third John is a letter to a church leader warning against a false teacher.

JUDE was written to warn against a doctrine that said God's grace is an excuse for immoral living.

REVELATION is a book written about the struggle between good and evil and the ultimate triumph of Christ and the church. It was written in a time of persecution, probably around A.D. 95. Writing in code, the apostle John encourages his readers to stand fast in the face of persecution, for only the faithful will share in the final triumph of Christ. Yes, he says, things are bad and they will get worse, but Christ will triumph. Some of the great hymns and prayers of the early church are found in this book. ■

THE CHURCH AT THE END OF THE FIRST CENTURY

The Epistle to the

HEBREWS

God's Supreme Revelation

1 God, who at various times and in various
ways spoke in time past to the fathers by
the prophets,
2 has in these last days spoken to us by *His*
Son, whom He has appointed heir of all things,
through whom also He made the worlds;
3 who being the brightness of *His* glory and
the express image of His person, and upholding all things by the word of His power, when
He had by Himself[a] purged our[b] sins, sat down
at the right hand of the Majesty on high,
4 having become so much better than the angels, as He has by inheritance obtained a more
excellent name than they.

The Son Exalted Above Angels

5 For to which of the angels did He ever say:

"You are My Son,
Today I have begotten You"?[a]

And again:

"I will be to Him a Father,
And He shall be to Me a Son"?[b]

6 But when He again brings the firstborn into
the world, He says:

"Let all the angels of God worship Him."[a]

7 And of the angels He says:

"Who makes His angels spirits
And His ministers a flame of fire."[a]

8 But to the Son *He says:*

"Your throne, O God, is forever and ever;
A scepter of righteousness is the scepter of Your kingdom.
9 *You have loved righteousness and hated lawlessness;*
Therefore God, Your God, has anointed You
With the oil of gladness more than Your companions."[a]

10 And:

"You, LORD, in the beginning laid the foundation of the earth,
And the heavens are the work of Your hands.
11 *They will perish, but You remain;*
And they will all grow old like a garment;
12 *Like a cloak You will fold them up,*
And they will be changed.
But You are the same,
And Your years will not fail."[a]

13 But to which of the angels has He ever said:

"Sit at My right hand,
Till I make Your enemies Your footstool"?[a]

14 Are they not all ministering spirits sent
forth to minister for those who will inherit salvation?

Do Not Neglect Salvation

2 Therefore we must give the more earnest
heed to the things we have heard, lest we
drift away.
2 For if the word spoken through angels
proved steadfast, and every transgression and
disobedience received a just reward,
3 how shall we escape if we neglect so great
a salvation, which at the first began to be spoken by the Lord, and was confirmed to us by
those who heard *Him,*
4 God also bearing witness both with signs
and wonders, with various miracles, and gifts
of the Holy Spirit, according to His own will?

The Son Made Lower than Angels

5 For He has not put the world to come, of
which we speak, in subjection to angels.
6 But one testified in a certain place, saying:

"What is man that You are mindful of him,
Or the son of man that You take care of him?
7 *You have made him a little lower than the angels;*
You have crowned him with glory and honor,[a]
And set him over the works of Your hands.
8 *You have put all things in subjection under his feet."*[a]

For in that He put all in subjection under him,
He left nothing *that is* not put under him. But
now we do not yet see all things put under him.
9 But we see Jesus, who was made a little
lower than the angels, for the suffering of death
crowned with glory and honor, that He, by the
grace of God, might taste death for everyone.

Bringing Many Sons to Glory

10 For it was fitting for Him, for whom *are* all
things and by whom *are* all things, in bringing
many sons to glory, to make the captain of their
salvation perfect through sufferings.
11 For both He who sanctifies and those who
are being sanctified *are* all of one, for which
reason He is not ashamed to call them brethren,
12 saying:

"I will declare Your name to My brethren;
In the midst of the assembly I will sing praise to You."[a]

13 And again:

"I will put My trust in Him."[a]

And again:

"Here am I and the children whom God has given Me."[b]

14 Inasmuch then as the children have partaken of flesh and blood, He Himself likewise
shared in the same, that through death He might
destroy him who had the power of death, that
is, the devil,

1:3 [a]NU-Text omits *by Himself.* [b]NU-Text omits *our.* **1:5** [a]Psalm 2:7 [b]2 Samuel 7:14 **1:6** [a]Deuteronomy 32:43 (Septuagint, Dead Sea Scrolls); Psalm 97:7 **1:7** [a]Psalm 104:4 **1:9** [a]Psalm 45:6, 7 **1:12** [a]Psalm 102:25–27 **1:13** [a]Psalm 110:1 **2:7** [a]NU-Text and M-Text omit the rest of verse 7. **2:8** [a]Psalm 8:4–6 **2:12** [a]Psalm 22:22 **2:13** [a]2 Samuel 22:3; Isaiah 8:17 [b]Isaiah 8:18

15 and release those who through fear of death
were all their lifetime subject to bondage.
16 For indeed He does not give aid to angels,
but He does give aid to the seed of Abraham.
17 Therefore, in all things He had to be made
like *His* brethren, that He might be a merciful
and faithful High Priest in things *pertaining* to
God, to make propitiation for the sins of the
people.
18 For in that He Himself has suffered, being
tempted, He is able to aid those who are tempted.

The Son Was Faithful

3 Therefore, holy brethren, partakers of the
heavenly calling, consider the Apostle and
High Priest of our confession, Christ Jesus,
2 who was faithful to Him who appointed
Him, as Moses also *was faithful* in all His house.
3 For this One has been counted worthy of
more glory than Moses, inasmuch as He who
built the house has more honor than the house.
4 For every house is built by someone, but
He who built all things *is* God.
5 And Moses indeed *was* faithful in all His
house as a servant, for a testimony of those
things which would be spoken *afterward,*
6 but Christ as a Son over His own house,
whose house we are if we hold fast the confi-
dence and the rejoicing of the hope firm to the
end.[a]

Be Faithful

7 Therefore, as the Holy Spirit says:

"Today, if you will hear His voice,
8 *Do not harden your hearts as in the*
rebellion,
In the day of trial in the wilderness,
9 *Where your fathers tested Me, tried Me,*
And saw My works forty years.
10 *Therefore I was angry with that*
generation,
And said, 'They always go astray in their
heart,
And they have not known My ways.'
11 *So I swore in My wrath,*
'They shall not enter My rest.' "[a]

12 Beware, brethren, lest there be in any of you
an evil heart of unbelief in departing from the
living God;
13 but exhort one another daily, while it is called
"Today," lest any of you be hardened through
the deceitfulness of sin.
14 For we have become partakers of Christ if
we hold the beginning of our confidence stead-
fast to the end,
15 while it is said:

"Today, if you will hear His voice,
Do not harden your hearts as in the
rebellion."[a]

Failure of the Wilderness Wanderers

16 For who, having heard, rebelled? Indeed,
was it not all who came out of Egypt, *led* by
Moses?
17 Now with whom was He angry forty years?
Was it not with those who sinned, whose corpses
fell in the wilderness?
18 And to whom did He swear that they would
not enter His rest, but to those who did not obey?
19 So we see that they could not enter in be-
cause of unbelief.

The Promise of Rest

4 Therefore, since a promise remains of en-
tering His rest, let us fear lest any of you
seem to have come short of it.
2 For indeed the gospel was preached to us
as well as to them; but the word which they
heard did not profit them,[a] not being mixed
with faith in those who heard *it.*
3 For we who have believed do enter that rest,
as He has said:

"So I swore in My wrath,
'They shall not enter My rest,' "[a]

although the works were finished from the
foundation of the world.
4 For He has spoken in a certain place of the
seventh *day* in this way: *"And God rested on*
the seventh day from all His works";[a]
5 and again in this *place: "They shall not en-*
ter My rest."[a]
6 Since therefore it remains that some *must*
enter it, and those to whom it was first preached
did not enter because of disobedience,
7 again He designates a certain day, saying
in David, *"Today,"* after such a long time, as it
has been said:

"Today, if you will hear His voice,
Do not harden your hearts."[a]

8 For if Joshua had given them rest, then He
would not afterward have spoken of another
day.
9 There remains therefore a rest for the peo-
ple of God.
10 For he who has entered His rest has him-
self also ceased from his works as God *did* from
His.

The Word Discovers Our Condition

11 Let us therefore be diligent to enter that rest,
lest anyone fall according to the same example
of disobedience.
12 For the word of God *is* living and powerful,
and sharper than any two-edged sword, pierc-
ing even to the division of soul and spirit, and
of joints and marrow, and is a discerner of the
thoughts and intents of the heart.
13 And there is no creature hidden from His
sight, but all things *are* naked and open to the
eyes of Him to whom we *must give* account.

Our Compassionate High Priest

14 Seeing then that we have a great High Priest
who has passed through the heavens, Jesus the
Son of God, let us hold fast *our* confession.
15 For we do not have a High Priest who can-
not sympathize with our weaknesses, but was
in all *points* tempted as *we are, yet* without sin.
16 Let us therefore come boldly to the throne
of grace, that we may obtain mercy and find
grace to help in time of need.

Qualifications for High Priesthood

5 For every high priest taken from among men
is appointed for men in things *pertaining*
to God, that he may offer both gifts and sacri-
fices for sins.
2 He can have compassion on those who are

3:6 [a]NU-Text omits *firm to the end.* **3:11** [a]Psalm 95:7–11 **3:15** [a]Psalm 95:7, 8 **4:2** [a]NU-Text and M-Text read *profit them, since they were not united by faith with those who heeded it.* **4:3** [a]Psalm 95:11 **4:4** [a]Genesis 2:2 **4:5** [a]Psalm 95:11 **4:7** [a]Psalm 95:7, 8

ignorant and going astray, since he himself is also subject to weakness.

3 Because of this he is required as for the people, so also for himself, to offer *sacrifices* for sins.

4 And no man takes this honor to himself, but he who is called by God, just as Aaron *was.*

A Priest Forever

5 So also Christ did not glorify Himself to become High Priest, but *it was* He who said to Him:

"You are My Son,
Today I have begotten You."[a]

6 As *He* also says in another *place:*

"You *are a priest forever*
According to the order of Melchizedek";[a]

7 who, in the days of His flesh, when He had offered up prayers and supplications, with vehement cries and tears to Him who was able to save Him from death, and was heard because of His godly fear,

8 though He was a Son, *yet* He learned obedience by the things which He suffered.

9 And having been perfected, He became the author of eternal salvation to all who obey Him,

10 called by God as High Priest *"according to the order of Melchizedek,"*

11 of whom we have much to say, and hard to explain, since you have become dull of hearing.

Spiritual Immaturity

12 For though by this time you ought to be teachers, you need *someone* to teach you again the first principles of the oracles of God; and you have come to need milk and not solid food.

13 For everyone who partakes *only* of milk *is* unskilled in the word of righteousness, for he is a babe.

14 But solid food belongs to those who are of full age, *that is,* those who by reason of use have their senses exercised to discern both good and evil.

The Peril of Not Progressing

6 Therefore, leaving the discussion of the elementary *principles* of Christ, let us go on to perfection, not laying again the foundation of repentance from dead works and of faith toward God,

2 of the doctrine of baptisms, of laying on of hands, of resurrection of the dead, and of eternal judgment.

3 And this we will[a] do if God permits.

4 For *it is* impossible for those who were once enlightened, and have tasted the heavenly gift, and have become partakers of the Holy Spirit,

5 and have tasted the good word of God and the powers of the age to come,

6 if they fall away,[a] to renew them again to repentance, since they crucify again for themselves the Son of God, and put *Him* to an open shame.

7 For the earth which drinks in the rain that often comes upon it, and bears herbs useful for those by whom it is cultivated, receives blessing from God;

8 but if it bears thorns and briers, *it is* rejected and near to being cursed, whose end *is* to be burned.

A Better Estimate

9 But, beloved, we are confident of better things concerning you, yes, things that accompany salvation, though we speak in this manner.

10 For God *is* not unjust to forget your work and labor of[a] love which you have shown toward His name, *in that* you have ministered to the saints, and do minister.

11 And we desire that each one of you show the same diligence to the full assurance of hope until the end,

12 that you do not become sluggish, but imitate those who through faith and patience inherit the promises.

God's Infallible Purpose in Christ

13 For when God made a promise to Abraham, because He could swear by no one greater, He swore by Himself,

14 saying, *"Surely blessing I will bless you, and multiplying I will multiply you."*[a]

15 And so, after he had patiently endured, he obtained the promise.

16 For men indeed swear by the greater, and an oath for confirmation *is* for them an end of all dispute.

17 Thus God, determining to show more abundantly to the heirs of promise the immutability of His counsel, confirmed *it* by an oath,

18 that by two immutable things, in which it *is* impossible for God to lie, we might[a] have strong consolation, who have fled for refuge to lay hold of the hope set before *us.*

19 This *hope* we have as an anchor of the soul, both sure and steadfast, and which enters the *Presence* behind the veil,

20 where the forerunner has entered for us, *even* Jesus, having become High Priest forever according to the order of Melchizedek.

The King of Righteousness

7 For this Melchizedek, king of Salem, priest of the Most High God, who met Abraham returning from the slaughter of the kings and blessed him,

2 to whom also Abraham gave a tenth part of all, first being translated "king of righteousness," and then also king of Salem, meaning "king of peace,"

3 without father, without mother, without genealogy, having neither beginning of days nor end of life, but made like the Son of God, remains a priest continually.

4 Now consider how great this man *was,* to whom even the patriarch Abraham gave a tenth of the spoils.

5 And indeed those who are of the sons of Levi, who receive the priesthood, have a commandment to receive tithes from the people according to the law, that is, from their brethren, though they have come from the loins of Abraham;

6 but he whose genealogy is not derived from them received tithes from Abraham and blessed him who had the promises.

7 Now beyond all contradiction the lesser is blessed by the better.

8 Here mortal men receive tithes, but there he *receives them,* of whom it is witnessed that he lives.

5:5 [a]Psalm 2:7 **5:6** [a]Psalm 110:4 **6:3** [a]M-Text reads *let us do.* **6:6** [a]Or *and have fallen away* **6:10** [a]NU-Text omits *labor of.* **6:14** [a]Genesis 22:17 **6:18** [a]M-Text omits *might.*

9 Even Levi, who receives tithes, paid tithes through Abraham, so to speak,
10 for he was still in the loins of his father when Melchizedek met him.

Need for a New Priesthood

11 Therefore, if perfection were through the Levitical priesthood (for under it the people received the law), what further need *was there* that another priest should rise according to the order of Melchizedek, and not be called according to the order of Aaron?
12 For the priesthood being changed, of necessity there is also a change of the law.
13 For He of whom these things are spoken belongs to another tribe, from which no man has officiated at the altar.
14 For *it is* evident that our Lord arose from Judah, of which tribe Moses spoke nothing concerning priesthood.[a]
15 And it is yet far more evident if, in the likeness of Melchizedek, there arises another priest
16 who has come, not according to the law of a fleshly commandment, but according to the power of an endless life.
17 For He testifies:[a]

"You are a priest forever
According to the order of Melchizedek."[b]

18 For on the one hand there is an annulling of the former commandment because of its weakness and unprofitableness,
19 for the law made nothing perfect; on the other hand, *there is the* bringing in of a better hope, through which we draw near to God.

Greatness of the New Priest

20 And inasmuch as *He was* not *made priest* without an oath
21 (for they have become priests without an oath, but He with an oath by Him who said to Him:

"The LORD has sworn
And will not relent,
'You are a priest forever[a]
According to the order of
Melchizedek'"),[b]

22 by so much more Jesus has become a surety of a better covenant.
23 Also there were many priests, because they were prevented by death from continuing.
24 But He, because He continues forever, has an unchangeable priesthood.
25 Therefore He is also able to save to the uttermost those who come to God through Him, since He always lives to make intercession for them.
26 For such a High Priest was fitting for us, *who is* holy, harmless, undefiled, separate from sinners, and has become higher than the heavens;
27 who does not need daily, as those high priests, to offer up sacrifices, first for His own sins and then for the people's, for this He did once for all when He offered up Himself.
28 For the law appoints as high priests men who have weakness, but the word of the oath, which came after the law, *appoints* the Son who has been perfected forever.

The New Priestly Service

8 Now *this is* the main point of the things we are saying: We have such a High Priest, who is seated at the right hand of the throne of the Majesty in the heavens,
2 a Minister of the sanctuary and of the true tabernacle which the Lord erected, and not man.
3 For every high priest is appointed to offer both gifts and sacrifices. Therefore *it is* necessary that this One also have something to offer.
4 For if He were on earth, He would not be a priest, since there are priests who offer the gifts according to the law;
5 who serve the copy and shadow of the heavenly things, as Moses was divinely instructed when he was about to make the tabernacle. For He said, *"See that you make all things according to the pattern shown you on the mountain."*[a]
6 But now He has obtained a more excellent ministry, inasmuch as He is also Mediator of a better covenant, which was established on better promises.

A New Covenant

7 For if that first *covenant* had been faultless, then no place would have been sought for a second.
8 Because finding fault with them, He says: *"Behold, the days are coming, says the LORD, when I will make a new covenant with the house of Israel and with the house of Judah—*
9 *"not according to the covenant that I made with their fathers in the day when I took them by the hand to lead them out of the land of Egypt; because they did not continue in My covenant, and I disregarded them, says the LORD.*
10 *"For this is the covenant that I will make with the house of Israel after those days, says the LORD: I will put My laws in their mind and write them on their hearts; and I will be their God, and they shall be My people.*
11 *"None of them shall teach his neighbor, and none his brother, saying, 'Know the LORD,' for all shall know Me, from the least of them to the greatest of them.*
12 *"For I will be merciful to their unrighteousness, and their sins and their lawless deeds*[a] *I will remember no more."*[b]
13 In that He says, *"A new covenant,"* He has made the first obsolete. Now what is becoming obsolete and growing old is ready to vanish away.

The Earthly Sanctuary

9 Then indeed, even the first *covenant* had ordinances of divine service and the earthly sanctuary.
2 For a tabernacle was prepared: the first *part,* in which *was* the lampstand, the table, and the showbread, which is called the sanctuary;
3 and behind the second veil, the part of the tabernacle which is called the Holiest of All,
4 which had the golden censer and the ark of the covenant overlaid on all sides with gold, in which *were* the golden pot that had the manna, Aaron's rod that budded, and the tablets of the covenant;
5 and above it were the cherubim of glory overshadowing the mercy seat. Of these things we cannot now speak in detail.

7:14 [a]NU-Text reads *priests.* **7:17** [a]NU-Text reads *it is testified.* [b]Psalm 110:4 **7:21** [a]NU-Text ends the quotation here. [b]Psalm 110:4 **8:5** [a]Exodus 25:40 **8:12** [a]NU-Text omits *and their lawless deeds.* [b]Jeremiah 31:31–34

Limitations of the Earthly Service

6 Now when these things had been thus prepared, the priests always went into the first part of the tabernacle, performing the services.
7 But into the second part the high priest *went* alone once a year, not without blood, which he offered for himself and *for* the people's sins *committed* in ignorance;
8 the Holy Spirit indicating this, that the way into the Holiest of All was not yet made manifest while the first tabernacle was still standing.
9 It *was* symbolic for the present time in which both gifts and sacrifices are offered which cannot make him who performed the service perfect in regard to the conscience—
10 *concerned* only with foods and drinks, various washings, and fleshly ordinances imposed until the time of reformation.

The Heavenly Sanctuary

11 But Christ came *as* High Priest of the good things to come,[a] with the greater and more perfect tabernacle not made with hands, that is, not of this creation.
12 Not with the blood of goats and calves, but with His own blood He entered the Most Holy Place once for all, having obtained eternal redemption.
13 For if the blood of bulls and goats and the ashes of a heifer, sprinkling the unclean, sanctifies for the purifying of the flesh,
14 how much more shall the blood of Christ, who through the eternal Spirit offered Himself without spot to God, cleanse your conscience from dead works to serve the living God?
15 And for this reason He is the Mediator of the new covenant, by means of death, for the redemption of the transgressions under the first covenant, that those who are called may receive the promise of the eternal inheritance.

The Mediator's Death Necessary

16 For where there *is* a testament, there must also of necessity be the death of the testator.
17 For a testament *is* in force after men are dead, since it has no power at all while the testator lives.
18 Therefore not even the first *covenant* was dedicated without blood.
19 For when Moses had spoken every precept to all the people according to the law, he took the blood of calves and goats, with water, scarlet wool, and hyssop, and sprinkled both the book itself and all the people,
20 saying, *"This is the blood of the covenant which God has commanded you."*[a]
21 Then likewise he sprinkled with blood both the tabernacle and all the vessels of the ministry.
22 And according to the law almost all things are purified with blood, and without shedding of blood there is no remission.

Greatness of Christ's Sacrifice

23 Therefore *it was* necessary that the copies of the things in the heavens should be purified with these, but the heavenly things themselves with better sacrifices than these.
24 For Christ has not entered the holy places made with hands, *which are* copies of the true, but into heaven itself, now to appear in the presence of God for us;
25 not that He should offer Himself often, as the high priest enters the Most Holy Place every year with blood of another—
26 He then would have had to suffer often since the foundation of the world; but now, once at the end of the ages, He has appeared to put away sin by the sacrifice of Himself.
27 And as it is appointed for men to die once, but after this the judgment,
28 so Christ was offered once to bear the sins of many. To those who eagerly wait for Him He will appear a second time, apart from sin, for salvation.

Animal Sacrifices Insufficient

10 For the law, having a shadow of the good things to come, *and* not the very image of the things, can never with these same sacrifices, which they offer continually year by year, make those who approach perfect.
2 For then would they not have ceased to be offered? For the worshipers, once purified, would have had no more consciousness of sins.
3 But in those *sacrifices there is* a reminder of sins every year.
4 For *it is* not possible that the blood of bulls and goats could take away sins.

Christ's Death Fulfills God's Will

5 Therefore, when He came into the world, He said:

"Sacrifice and offering You did not desire,
But a body You have prepared for Me.
6 *In burnt offerings and sacrifices for sin*
You had no pleasure.
7 *Then I said, 'Behold, I have come—*
In the volume of the book it is written of Me—
To do Your will, O God.' "[a]

8 Previously saying, *"Sacrifice and offering, burnt offerings, and offerings for sin You did not desire, nor had pleasure in them"* (which are offered according to the law),
9 then He said, *"Behold, I have come to do Your will, O God."*[a] He takes away the first that He may establish the second.
10 By that will we have been sanctified through the offering of the body of Jesus Christ once *for all.*

Christ's Death Perfects the Sanctified

11 And every priest stands ministering daily and offering repeatedly the same sacrifices, which can never take away sins.
12 But this Man, after He had offered one sacrifice for sins forever, sat down at the right hand of God,
13 from that time waiting till His enemies are made His footstool.
14 For by one offering He has perfected forever those who are being sanctified.
15 But the Holy Spirit also witnesses to us; for after He had said before,
16 *"This is the covenant that I will make with them after those days, says the* LORD: *I will put My laws into their hearts, and in their minds I will write them,"*[a]

9:11 [a]NU-Text reads *that have come.* **9:20** [a]Exodus 24:8 **10:7** [a]Psalm 40:6–8 **10:9** [a]NU-Text and M-Text omit *O God.* **10:16** [a]Jeremiah 31:33

17 *then He adds, "Their sins and their lawless deeds I will remember no more."*[a]

18 Now where there is remission of these, *there is* no longer an offering for sin.

Hold Fast Your Confession

19 Therefore, brethren, having boldness to enter the Holiest by the blood of Jesus,

20 by a new and living way which He consecrated for us, through the veil, that is, His flesh,

21 and *having* a High Priest over the house of God,

22 let us draw near with a true heart in full assurance of faith, having our hearts sprinkled from an evil conscience and our bodies washed with pure water.

23 Let us hold fast the confession of *our* hope without wavering, for He who promised *is* faithful.

24 And let us consider one another in order to stir up love and good works,

25 not forsaking the assembling of ourselves together, as *is* the manner of some, but exhorting *one another,* and so much the more as you see the Day approaching.

The Just Live by Faith

26 For if we sin willfully after we have received the knowledge of the truth, there no longer remains a sacrifice for sins,

27 but a certain fearful expectation of judgment, and fiery indignation which will devour the adversaries.

28 Anyone who has rejected Moses' law dies without mercy on *the testimony of* two or three witnesses.

29 Of how much worse punishment, do you suppose, will he be thought worthy who has trampled the Son of God underfoot, counted the blood of the covenant by which he was sanctified a common thing, and insulted the Spirit of grace?

30 For we know Him who said, *"Vengeance is Mine, I will repay,"*[a] says the Lord.[b] And again, *"The LORD will judge His people."*[c]

31 It is a fearful thing to fall into the hands of the living God.

32 But recall the former days in which, after you were illuminated, you endured a great struggle with sufferings:

33 partly while you were made a spectacle both by reproaches and tribulations, and partly while you became companions of those who were so treated;

34 for you had compassion on me[a] in my chains, and joyfully accepted the plundering of your goods, knowing that you have a better and an enduring possession for yourselves in heaven.[b]

35 Therefore do not cast away your confidence, which has great reward.

36 For you have need of endurance, so that after you have done the will of God, you may receive the promise:

37 *"For yet a little while,*
And He[a] *who is coming will come and*
will not tarry.

38 *Now the*[a] *just shall live by faith;*
But if anyone draws back,
My soul has no pleasure in him."[b]

39 But we are not of those who draw back to perdition, but of those who believe to the saving of the soul.

By Faith We Understand

11 Now faith is the substance of things hoped for, the evidence of things not seen.

2 For by it the elders obtained a *good* testimony.

3 By faith we understand that the worlds were framed by the word of God, so that the things which are seen were not made of things which are visible.

Faith at the Dawn of History

4 By faith Abel offered to God a more excellent sacrifice than Cain, through which he obtained witness that he was righteous, God testifying of his gifts; and through it he being dead still speaks.

5 By faith Enoch was taken away so that he did not see death, *"and was not found, because God had taken him"*;[a] for before he was taken he had this testimony, that he pleased God.

6 But without faith *it is* impossible to please *Him,* for he who comes to God must believe that He is, and *that* He is a rewarder of those who diligently seek Him.

7 By faith Noah, being divinely warned of things not yet seen, moved with godly fear, prepared an ark for the saving of his household, by which he condemned the world and became heir of the righteousness which is according to faith.

Faithful Abraham

8 By faith Abraham obeyed when he was called to go out to the place which he would receive as an inheritance. And he went out, not knowing where he was going.

9 By faith he dwelt in the land of promise as *in* a foreign country, dwelling in tents with Isaac and Jacob, the heirs with him of the same promise;

10 for he waited for the city which has foundations, whose builder and maker *is* God.

11 By faith Sarah herself also received strength to conceive seed, and she bore a child[a] when she was past the age, because she judged Him faithful who had promised.

12 Therefore from one man, and him as good as dead, were born *as many* as the stars of the sky in multitude—innumerable as the sand which is by the seashore.

The Heavenly Hope

13 These all died in faith, not having received the promises, but having seen them afar off were assured of them,[a] embraced *them* and confessed that they were strangers and pilgrims on the earth.

14 For those who say such things declare plainly that they seek a homeland.

15 And truly if they had called to mind that

10:17 [a]Jeremiah 31:34 **10:30** [a]Deuteronomy 32:35 [b]NU-Text omits *says the Lord.* [c]Deuteronomy 32:36
10:34 [a]NU-Text reads *the prisoners* instead of *me in my chains.* [b]NU-Text omits *in heaven.* **10:37** [a]Or *that which*
10:38 [a]NU-Text reads *My just one.* [b]Habakkuk 2:3, 4 **11:5** [a]Genesis 5:24 **11:11** [a]NU-Text omits *she bore a child.*
11:13 [a]NU-Text and M-Text omit *were assured of them.*

country from which they had come out, they would have had opportunity to return.
16 But now they desire a better, that is, a heavenly *country.* Therefore God is not ashamed to be called their God, for He has prepared a city for them.

The Faith of the Patriarchs

17 By faith Abraham, when he was tested, offered up Isaac, and he who had received the promises offered up his only begotten *son,*
18 of whom it was said, *"In Isaac your seed shall be called,"*[a]
19 concluding that God *was* able to raise *him* up, even from the dead, from which he also received him in a figurative sense.
20 By faith Isaac blessed Jacob and Esau concerning things to come.
21 By faith Jacob, when he was dying, blessed each of the sons of Joseph, and worshiped, *leaning* on the top of his staff.
22 By faith Joseph, when he was dying, made mention of the departure of the children of Israel, and gave instructions concerning his bones.

The Faith of Moses

23 By faith Moses, when he was born, was hidden three months by his parents, because they saw *he was* a beautiful child; and they were not afraid of the king's command.
24 By faith Moses, when he became of age, refused to be called the son of Pharaoh's daughter,
25 choosing rather to suffer affliction with the people of God than to enjoy the passing pleasures of sin,
26 esteeming the reproach of Christ greater riches than the treasures in[a] Egypt; for he looked to the reward.
27 By faith he forsook Egypt, not fearing the wrath of the king; for he endured as seeing Him who is invisible.
28 By faith he kept the Passover and the sprinkling of blood, lest he who destroyed the firstborn should touch them.
29 By faith they passed through the Red Sea as by dry *land, whereas* the Egyptians, attempting to do so, were drowned.

By Faith They Overcame

30 By faith the walls of Jericho fell down after they were encircled for seven days.
31 By faith the harlot Rahab did not perish with those who did not believe, when she had received the spies with peace.
32 And what more shall I say? For the time would fail me to tell of Gideon and Barak and Samson and Jephthah, also *of* David and Samuel and the prophets:
33 who through faith subdued kingdoms, worked righteousness, obtained promises, stopped the mouths of lions,
34 quenched the violence of fire, escaped the edge of the sword, out of weakness were made strong, became valiant in battle, turned to flight the armies of the aliens.
35 Women received their dead raised to life again. Others were tortured, not accepting deliverance, that they might obtain a better resurrection.
36 Still others had trial of mockings and scourgings, yes, and of chains and imprisonment.
37 They were stoned, they were sawn in two, were tempted,[a] were slain with the sword. They wandered about in sheepskins and goatskins, being destitute, afflicted, tormented—
38 of whom the world was not worthy. They wandered in deserts and mountains, *in* dens and caves of the earth.
39 And all these, having obtained a good testimony through faith, did not receive the promise,
40 God having provided something better for us, that they should not be made perfect apart from us.

The Race of Faith

12 Therefore we also, since we are surrounded by so great a cloud of witnesses, let us lay aside every weight, and the sin which so easily ensnares *us,* and let us run with endurance the race that is set before us,
2 looking unto Jesus, the author and finisher of *our* faith, who for the joy that was set before Him endured the cross, despising the shame, and has sat down at the right hand of the throne of God.

The Discipline of God

3 For consider Him who endured such hostility from sinners against Himself, lest you become weary and discouraged in your souls.
4 You have not yet resisted to bloodshed, striving against sin.
5 And you have forgotten the exhortation which speaks to you as to sons:

"My son, do not despise the chastening of the LORD,
Nor be discouraged when you are rebuked by Him;
6 *For whom the LORD loves He chastens,*
And scourges every son whom He receives."[a]

7 If[a] you endure chastening, God deals with you as with sons; for what son is there whom a father does not chasten?
8 But if you are without chastening, of which all have become partakers, then you are illegitimate and not sons.
9 Furthermore, we have had human fathers who corrected *us,* and we paid *them* respect. Shall we not much more readily be in subjection to the Father of spirits and live?
10 For they indeed for a few days chastened *us* as seemed *best* to them, but He for *our* profit, that *we* may be partakers of His holiness.
11 Now no chastening seems to be joyful for the present, but painful; nevertheless, afterward it yields the peaceable fruit of righteousness to those who have been trained by it.

Renew Your Spiritual Vitality

12 Therefore strengthen the hands which hang down, and the feeble knees,
13 and make straight paths for your feet, so that what is lame may not be dislocated, but rather be healed.
14 Pursue peace with all *people,* and holiness, without which no one will see the Lord:
15 looking carefully lest anyone fall short of

11:18 [a]Genesis 21:12 **11:26** [a]NU-Text and M-Text read *of.* **11:37** [a]NU-Text omits *were tempted.* **12:6** [a]Proverbs 3:11, 12 **12:7** [a]NU-Text and M-Text read *It is for discipline that you endure: God . . . .*

the grace of God; lest any root of bitterness springing up cause trouble, and by this many become defiled;

16 lest there *be* any fornicator or profane person like Esau, who for one morsel of food sold his birthright.

17 For you know that afterward, when he wanted to inherit the blessing, he was rejected, for he found no place for repentance, though he sought it diligently with tears.

The Glorious Company

18 For you have not come to the mountain that[a] may be touched and that burned with fire, and to blackness and darkness[b] and tempest,

19 and the sound of a trumpet and the voice of words, so that those who heard *it* begged that the word should not be spoken to them anymore.

20 (For they could not endure what was commanded: *"And if so much as a beast touches the mountain, it shall be stoned*[a] *or shot with an arrow."*[b]

21 And so terrifying was the sight *that* Moses said, *"I am exceedingly afraid* and trembling."[a])

22 But you have come to Mount Zion and to the city of the living God, the heavenly Jerusalem, to an innumerable company of angels,

23 to the general assembly and church of the firstborn *who are* registered in heaven, to God the Judge of all, to the spirits of just men made perfect,

24 to Jesus the Mediator of the new covenant, and to the blood of sprinkling that speaks better things than *that of* Abel.

Hear the Heavenly Voice

25 See that you do not refuse Him who speaks. For if they did not escape who refused Him who spoke on earth, much more *shall we not escape* if we turn away from Him who *speaks* from heaven,

26 whose voice then shook the earth; but now He has promised, saying, *"Yet once more I shake*[a] *not only the earth, but also heaven."*[b]

27 Now this, *"Yet once more,"* indicates the removal of those things that are being shaken, as of things that are made, that the things which cannot be shaken may remain.

28 Therefore, since we are receiving a kingdom which cannot be shaken, let us have grace, by which we may[a] serve God acceptably with reverence and godly fear.

29 For our God *is* a consuming fire.

Concluding Moral Directions

13 Let brotherly love continue.

2 Do not forget to entertain strangers, for by so *doing* some have unwittingly entertained angels.

3 Remember the prisoners as if chained with them—those who are mistreated—since you yourselves are in the body also.

4 Marriage *is* honorable among all, and the bed undefiled; but fornicators and adulterers God will judge.

5 *Let your* conduct *be* without covetousness; *be* content with such things as you have. For He Himself has said, *"I will never leave you nor forsake you."*[a]

6 So we may boldly say:

"The LORD is my helper;
I will not fear.
What can man do to me?"[a]

Concluding Religious Directions

7 Remember those who rule over you, who have spoken the word of God to you, whose faith follow, considering the outcome of *their* conduct.

8 Jesus Christ *is* the same yesterday, today, and forever.

9 Do not be carried about[a] with various and strange doctrines. For *it is* good that the heart be established by grace, not with foods which have not profited those who have been occupied with them.

10 We have an altar from which those who serve the tabernacle have no right to eat.

11 For the bodies of those animals, whose blood is brought into the sanctuary by the high priest for sin, are burned outside the camp.

12 Therefore Jesus also, that He might sanctify the people with His own blood, suffered outside the gate.

13 Therefore let us go forth to Him, outside the camp, bearing His reproach.

14 For here we have no continuing city, but we seek the one to come.

15 Therefore by Him let us continually offer the sacrifice of praise to God, that is, the fruit of *our* lips, giving thanks to His name.

16 But do not forget to do good and to share, for with such sacrifices God is well pleased.

17 Obey those who rule over you, and be submissive, for they watch out for your souls, as those who must give account. Let them do so with joy and not with grief, for that would be unprofitable for you.

Prayer Requested

18 Pray for us; for we are confident that we have a good conscience, in all things desiring to live honorably.

19 But I especially urge *you* to do this, that I may be restored to you the sooner.

Benediction, Final Exhortation, Farewell

20 Now may the God of peace who brought up our Lord Jesus from the dead, that great Shepherd of the sheep, through the blood of the everlasting covenant,

21 make you complete in every good work to do His will, working in you[a] what is well pleasing in His sight, through Jesus Christ, to whom *be* glory forever and ever. Amen.

22 And I appeal to you, brethren, bear with the word of exhortation, for I have written to you in few words.

23 Know that *our* brother Timothy has been set free, with whom I shall see you if he comes shortly.

24 Greet all those who rule over you, and all the saints. Those from Italy greet you.

25 Grace *be* with you all. Amen.

12:18 [a]NU-Text reads *to that which.* [b]NU-Text reads *gloom.* **12:20** [a]NU-Text and M-Text omit the rest of this verse. [b]Exodus 19:12, 13 **12:21** [a]Deuteronomy 9:19 **12:26** [a]NU-Text reads *will shake.* [b]Haggai 2:6 **12:28** [a]M-Text omits *may.* **13:5** [a]Deuteronomy 31:6, 8; Joshua 1:5 **13:6** [a]Psalm 118:6 **13:9** [a]NU-Text and M-Text read *away.* **13:21** [a]NU-Text and M-Text read *us.*

The Epistle of JAMES

Greeting to the Twelve Tribes

1 James, a bondservant of God and of the
Lord Jesus Christ,

To the twelve tribes which are scattered
abroad:

Greetings.

Profiting from Trials

2 My brethren, count it all joy when you fall
into various trials,
3 knowing that the testing of your faith pro-
duces patience.
4 But let patience have *its* perfect work, that
you may be perfect and complete, lacking
nothing.
5 If any of you lacks wisdom, let him ask of
God, who gives to all liberally and without re-
proach, and it will be given to him.
6 But let him ask in faith, with no doubting,
for he who doubts is like a wave of the sea driven
and tossed by the wind.
7 For let not that man suppose that he will
receive anything from the Lord;
8 *he is* a double-minded man, unstable in all
his ways.

The Perspective of Rich and Poor

9 Let the lowly brother glory in his exaltation,
10 but the rich in his humiliation, because as
a flower of the field he will pass away.
11 For no sooner has the sun risen with a burn-
ing heat than it withers the grass; its flower
falls, and its beautiful appearance perishes. So
the rich man also will fade away in his pursuits.

Loving God Under Trials

12 Blessed *is* the man who endures temptation;
for when he has been approved, he will receive
the crown of life which the Lord has promised
to those who love Him.
13 Let no one say when he is tempted, "I am
tempted by God"; for God cannot be tempted
by evil, nor does He Himself tempt anyone.
14 But each one is tempted when he is drawn
away by his own desires and enticed.
15 Then, when desire has conceived, it gives
birth to sin; and sin, when it is full-grown, brings
forth death.
16 Do not be deceived, my beloved brethren.
17 Every good gift and every perfect gift is
from above, and comes down from the Father
of lights, with whom there is no variation or
shadow of turning.
18 Of His own will He brought us forth by the
word of truth, that we might be a kind of first-
fruits of His creatures.

Qualities Needed in Trials

19 So then,[a] my beloved brethren, let every man
be swift to hear, slow to speak, slow to wrath;
20 for the wrath of man does not produce the
righteousness of God.

Doers—Not Hearers Only

21 Therefore lay aside all filthiness and over-
flow of wickedness, and receive with meek-
ness the implanted word, which is able to save
your souls.
22 But be doers of the word, and not hearers
only, deceiving yourselves.
23 For if anyone is a hearer of the word and
not a doer, he is like a man observing his natu-
ral face in a mirror;
24 for he observes himself, goes away, and im-
mediately forgets what kind of man he was.
25 But he who looks into the perfect law of
liberty and continues *in it*, and is not a forget-
ful hearer but a doer of the work, this one will
be blessed in what he does.
26 If anyone among you[a] thinks he is religious,
and does not bridle his tongue but deceives his
own heart, this one's religion *is* useless.
27 Pure and undefiled religion before God
and the Father is this: to visit orphans and wid-
ows in their trouble, *and* to keep oneself un-
spotted from the world.

Beware of Personal Favoritism

2 My brethren, do not hold the faith of our
Lord Jesus Christ, *the Lord* of glory, with
partiality.
2 For if there should come into your assem-
bly a man with gold rings, in fine apparel, and
there should also come in a poor man in filthy
clothes,
3 and you pay attention to the one wearing
the fine clothes and say to him, "You sit here
in a good place," and say to the poor man, "You
stand there," or, "Sit here at my footstool,"
4 have you not shown partiality among your-
selves, and become judges with evil thoughts?
5 Listen, my beloved brethren: Has God not
chosen the poor of this world *to be* rich in faith
and heirs of the kingdom which He promised
to those who love Him?
6 But you have dishonored the poor man. Do
not the rich oppress you and drag you into the
courts?
7 Do they not blaspheme that noble name by
which you are called?
8 If you really fulfill *the* royal law according
to the Scripture, *"You shall love your neighbor
as yourself,"*[a] you do well;
9 but if you show partiality, you commit sin,
and are convicted by the law as transgressors.
10 For whoever shall keep the whole law, and
yet stumble in one *point*, he is guilty of all.
11 For He who said, *"Do not commit adul-
tery,"*[a] also said, *"Do not murder."*[b] Now if you
do not commit adultery, but you do murder,
you have become a transgressor of the law.
12 So speak and so do as those who will be
judged by the law of liberty.
13 For judgment is without mercy to the one
who has shown no mercy. Mercy triumphs over
judgment.

Faith Without Works Is Dead

14 What *does it* profit, my brethren, if some-
one says he has faith but does not have works?
Can faith save him?

1:19 [a]NU-Text reads *Know this* or *This you know.* **1:26** [a]NU-Text omits *among you.* **2:8** [a]Leviticus 19:18
2:11 [a]Exodus 20:14; Deuteronomy 5:18 [b]Exodus 20:13; Deuteronomy 5:17

15 If a brother or sister is naked and destitute
of daily food,
16 and one of you says to them, "Depart in
peace, be warmed and filled," but you do not
give them the things which are needed for the
body, what *does it* profit?
17 Thus also faith by itself, if it does not have
works, is dead.
18 But someone will say, "You have faith, and
I have works." Show me your faith without your[a]
works, and I will show you my faith by my[b] works.
19 You believe that there is one God. You do
well. Even the demons believe—and tremble!
20 But do you want to know, O foolish man,
that faith without works is dead?[a]
21 Was not Abraham our father justified by
works when he offered Isaac his son on the altar?
22 Do you see that faith was working together
with his works, and by works faith was made
perfect?
23 And the Scripture was fulfilled which says,
*"Abraham believed God, and it was accounted
to him for righteousness."*[a] And he was called
the friend of God.
24 You see then that a man is justified by
works, and not by faith only.
25 Likewise, was not Rahab the harlot also
justified by works when she received the mes-
sengers and sent *them* out another way?
26 For as the body without the spirit is dead,
so faith without works is dead also.

The Untamable Tongue

3 My brethren, let not many of you become
teachers, knowing that we shall receive a
stricter judgment.
2 For we all stumble in many things. If any-
one does not stumble in word, he *is* a perfect
man, able also to bridle the whole body.
3 Indeed,[a] we put bits in horses' mouths that
they may obey us, and we turn their whole body.
4 Look also at ships: although they are so large
and are driven by fierce winds, they are turned
by a very small rudder wherever the pilot de-
sires.
5 Even so the tongue is a little member and
boasts great things. See how great a forest a little
fire kindles!
6 And the tongue *is* a fire, a world of iniquity.
The tongue is so set among our members that
it defiles the whole body, and sets on fire the
course of nature; and it is set on fire by hell.
7 For every kind of beast and bird, of reptile
and creature of the sea, is tamed and has been
tamed by mankind.
8 But no man can tame the tongue. *It is* an
unruly evil, full of deadly poison.
9 With it we bless our God and Father, and
with it we curse men, who have been made in
the similitude of God.
10 Out of the same mouth proceed blessing
and cursing. My brethren, these things ought
not to be so.
11 Does a spring send forth fresh *water* and
bitter from the same opening?
12 Can a fig tree, my brethren, bear olives, or
a grapevine bear figs? Thus no spring yields
both salt water and fresh.[a]

Heavenly Versus Demonic Wisdom

13 Who *is* wise and understanding among you?
Let him show by good conduct *that* his works
are done in the meekness of wisdom.
14 But if you have bitter envy and self-seeking
in your hearts, do not boast and lie against the
truth.
15 This wisdom does not descend from above,
but *is* earthly, sensual, demonic.
16 For where envy and self-seeking *exist*,
confusion and every evil thing *are* there.
17 But the wisdom that is from above is first
pure, then peaceable, gentle, willing to yield,
full of mercy and good fruits, without partiality
and without hypocrisy.
18 Now the fruit of righteousness is sown in
peace by those who make peace.

Pride Promotes Strife

4 Where do wars and fights *come* from among
you? Do *they* not *come* from your *desires
for* pleasure that war in your members?
2 You lust and do not have. You murder and
covet and cannot obtain. You fight and war.
Yet[a] you do not have because you do not ask.
3 You ask and do not receive, because you
ask amiss, that you may spend *it* on your plea-
sures.
4 Adulterers and[a] adulteresses! Do you not
know that friendship with the world is enmity
with God? Whoever therefore wants to be a
friend of the world makes himself an enemy of
God.
5 Or do you think that the Scripture says in
vain, "The Spirit who dwells in us yearns jeal-
ously"?
6 But He gives more grace. Therefore He
says:

> *"God resists the proud,*
> *But gives grace to the humble."*[a]

Humility Cures Worldliness

7 Therefore submit to God. Resist the devil
and he will flee from you.
8 Draw near to God and He will draw near
to you. Cleanse *your* hands, *you* sinners; and
purify *your* hearts, *you* double-minded.
9 Lament and mourn and weep! Let your
laughter be turned to mourning and *your* joy
to gloom.
10 Humble yourselves in the sight of the Lord,
and He will lift you up.

Do Not Judge a Brother

11 Do not speak evil of one another, brethren.
He who speaks evil of a brother and judges his
brother, speaks evil of the law and judges the
law. But if you judge the law, you are not a doer
of the law but a judge.
12 There is one Lawgiver,[a] who is able to save
and to destroy. Who[b] are you to judge another?[c]

Do Not Boast About Tomorrow

13 Come now, you who say, "Today or tomor-
row we will[a] go to such and such a city, spend
a year there, buy and sell, and make a profit";

2:18 [a]NU-Text omits *your.* [b]NU-Text omits *my.* **2:20** [a]NU-Text reads *useless.* **2:23** [a]Genesis 15:6 **3:3** [a]NU-Text reads *Now if.* **3:12** [a]NU-Text reads *Neither can a salty spring produce fresh water.* **4:2** [a]NU-Text and M-Text omit *Yet.* **4:4** [a]NU-Text omits *Adulterers and.* **4:6** [a]Proverbs 3:34 **4:12** [a]NU-Text adds *and Judge.* [b]NU-Text and M-Text read *But who.* [c]NU-Text reads *a neighbor.* **4:13** [a]M-Text reads *let us.*

14 whereas you do not know what *will hap-*
pen tomorrow. For what *is* your life? It is even
a vapor that appears for a little time and then
vanishes away.
15 Instead you *ought* to say, "If the Lord wills,
we shall live and do this or that."
16 But now you boast in your arrogance. All
such boasting is evil.
17 Therefore, to him who knows to do good
and does not do *it*, to him it is sin.

Rich Oppressors Will Be Judged

5 Come now, *you* rich, weep and howl for your
miseries that are coming upon *you!*
2 Your riches are corrupted, and your gar-
ments are moth-eaten.
3 Your gold and silver are corroded, and
their corrosion will be a witness against you
and will eat your flesh like fire. You have
heaped up treasure in the last days.
4 Indeed the wages of the laborers who
mowed your fields, which you kept back by
fraud, cry out; and the cries of the reapers have
reached the ears of the Lord of Sabaoth.[a]
5 You have lived on the earth in pleasure and
luxury; you have fattened your hearts as[a] in a
day of slaughter.
6 You have condemned, you have murdered
the just; he does not resist you.

Be Patient and Persevering

7 Therefore be patient, brethren, until the
coming of the Lord. See *how* the farmer waits
for the precious fruit of the earth, waiting pa-
tiently for it until it receives the early and latter
rain.
8 You also be patient. Establish your hearts,
for the coming of the Lord is at hand.
9 Do not grumble against one another, breth-
ren, lest you be condemned.[a] Behold, the Judge
is standing at the door!
10 My brethren, take the prophets, who spoke
in the name of the Lord, as an example of suf-
fering and patience.
11 Indeed we count them blessed who en-
dure. You have heard of the perseverance of
Job and seen the end *intended by* the Lord—
that the Lord is very compassionate and mer-
ciful.
12 But above all, my brethren, do not swear,
either by heaven or by earth or with any other
oath. But let your "Yes" be "Yes," and *your*
"No," "No," lest you fall into judgment.[a]

Meeting Specific Needs

13 Is anyone among you suffering? Let him
pray. Is anyone cheerful? Let him sing psalms.
14 Is anyone among you sick? Let him call for
the elders of the church, and let them pray over
him, anointing him with oil in the name of the
Lord.
15 And the prayer of faith will save the sick,
and the Lord will raise him up. And if he has
committed sins, he will be forgiven.
16 Confess *your* trespasses[a] to one another, and
pray for one another, that you may be healed.
The effective, fervent prayer of a righteous
man avails much.
17 Elijah was a man with a nature like ours,
and he prayed earnestly that it would not rain;
and it did not rain on the land for three years
and six months.
18 And he prayed again, and the heaven gave
rain, and the earth produced its fruit.

Bring Back the Erring One

19 Brethren, if anyone among you wanders
from the truth, and someone turns him back,
20 let him know that he who turns a sinner
from the error of his way will save a soul[a] from
death and cover a multitude of sins.

The First Epistle of PETER

Greeting to the Elect Pilgrims

1 Peter, an apostle of Jesus Christ,

To the pilgrims of the Dispersion in Pontus,
Galatia, Cappadocia, Asia, and Bithynia,
2 elect according to the foreknowledge of God
the Father, in sanctification of the Spirit, for
obedience and sprinkling of the blood of Jesus
Christ:

Grace to you and peace be multiplied.

A Heavenly Inheritance

3 Blessed *be* the God and Father of our Lord
Jesus Christ, who according to His abundant
mercy has begotten us again to a living hope
through the resurrection of Jesus Christ from
the dead,
4 to an inheritance incorruptible and unde-
filed and that does not fade away, reserved in
heaven for you,
5 who are kept by the power of God through
faith for salvation ready to be revealed in the
last time.
6 In this you greatly rejoice, though now for
a little while, if need be, you have been grieved
by various trials,
7 that the genuineness of your faith, *being*
much more precious than gold that perishes,
though it is tested by fire, may be found to praise,
honor, and glory at the revelation of Jesus
Christ,
8 whom having not seen[a] you love. Though
now you do not see *Him*, yet believing, you
rejoice with joy inexpressible and full of glory,
9 receiving the end of your faith—the salva-
tion of *your* souls.
10 Of this salvation the prophets have inquired
and searched carefully, who prophesied of the
grace *that would come* to you,
11 searching what, or what manner of time,
the Spirit of Christ who was in them was indi-
cating when He testified beforehand the suffer-
ings of Christ and the glories that would follow.

5:4 [a]Literally, in Hebrew, *Hosts* **5:5** [a]NU-Text omits *as.* **5:9** [a]NU-Text and M-Text read *judged.* **5:12** [a]M-Text reads *hypocrisy.* **5:16** [a]NU-Text reads *Therefore confess your sins.* **5:20** [a]NU-Text reads *his soul.* **1:8** [a]M-Text reads *known.*

12 To them it was revealed that, not to them-
selves, but to us[a] they were ministering the
things which now have been reported to you
through those who have preached the gospel
to you by the Holy Spirit sent from heaven—
things which angels desire to look into.

Living Before God Our Father

13 Therefore gird up the loins of your mind,
be sober, and rest *your* hope fully upon the
grace that is to be brought to you at the revela-
tion of Jesus Christ;
14 as obedient children, not conforming your-
selves to the former lusts, *as* in your ignorance;
15 but as He who called you *is* holy, you also
be holy in all *your* conduct,
16 because it is written, *"Be holy, for I am
holy."*[a]
17 And if you call on the Father, who without
partiality judges according to each one's work,
conduct yourselves throughout the time of
your stay *here* in fear;
18 knowing that you were not redeemed with
corruptible things, *like* silver or gold, from
your aimless conduct *received* by tradition
from your fathers,
19 but with the precious blood of Christ, as of
a lamb without blemish and without spot.
20 He indeed was foreordained before the
foundation of the world, but was manifest in
these last times for you
21 who through Him believe in God, who
raised Him from the dead and gave Him glory,
so that your faith and hope are in God.

The Enduring Word

22 Since you have purified your souls in obey-
ing the truth through the Spirit[a] in sincere love
of the brethren, love one another fervently
with a pure heart,
23 having been born again, not of corruptible
seed but incorruptible, through the word of
God which lives and abides forever,[a]
24 because

"All flesh is as grass,
And all the glory of man[a] *as the flower of the grass.*
The grass withers,
And its flower falls away,
25 *But the word of the LORD endures forever."*[a]

Now this is the word which by the gospel was
preached to you.

2 Therefore, laying aside all malice, all de-
ceit, hypocrisy, envy, and all evil speaking,
2 as newborn babes, desire the pure milk of
the word, that you may grow thereby,[a]
3 if indeed you have tasted that the Lord *is*
gracious.

The Chosen Stone and His Chosen People

4 Coming to Him *as to* a living stone, rejected
indeed by men, but chosen by God *and* pre-
cious,
5 you also, as living stones, are being built
up a spiritual house, a holy priesthood, to offer
up spiritual sacrifices acceptable to God through
Jesus Christ.
6 Therefore it is also contained in the Scrip-
ture,

"Behold, I lay in Zion
A chief cornerstone, elect, precious,
And he who believes on Him will by no means be put to shame."[a]

7 Therefore, to you who believe, *He is* pre-
cious; but to those who are disobedient,[a]

"The stone which the builders rejected
Has become the chief cornerstone,"[b]

8 and

"A stone of stumbling
And a rock of offense."[a]

They stumble, being disobedient to the word,
to which they also were appointed.
9 But you *are* a chosen generation, a royal
priesthood, a holy nation, His own special peo-
ple, that you may proclaim the praises of Him
who called you out of darkness into His mar-
velous light;
10 who once *were* not a people but *are* now
the people of God, who had not obtained mercy
but now have obtained mercy.

Living Before the World

11 Beloved, I beg *you* as sojourners and pil-
grims, abstain from fleshly lusts which war
against the soul,
12 having your conduct honorable among the
Gentiles, that when they speak against you as
evildoers, they may, by *your* good works which
they observe, glorify God in the day of visita-
tion.

Submission to Government

13 Therefore submit yourselves to every ordi-
nance of man for the Lord's sake, whether to
the king as supreme,
14 or to governors, as to those who are sent
by him for the punishment of evildoers and *for
the* praise of those who do good.
15 For this is the will of God, that by doing
good you may put to silence the ignorance of
foolish men—
16 as free, yet not using liberty as a cloak for
vice, but as bondservants of God.
17 Honor all *people.* Love the brotherhood.
Fear God. Honor the king.

Submission to Masters

18 Servants, *be* submissive to *your* masters
with all fear, not only to the good and gentle,
but also to the harsh.
19 For this *is* commendable, if because of con-
science toward God one endures grief, suffer-
ing wrongfully.
20 For what credit *is it* if, when you are beaten
for your faults, you take it patiently? But when
you do good and suffer, if you take it patiently,
this *is* commendable before God.
21 For to this you were called, because Christ
also suffered for us,[a] leaving us[b] an example,
that you should follow His steps:

22 *"Who committed no sin,*
Nor was deceit found in His mouth";[a]

1:12 [a]NU-Text and M-Text read *you.* **1:16** [a]Leviticus 11:44, 45; 19:2; 20:7 **1:22** [a]NU-Text omits *through the Spirit.* **1:23** [a]NU-Text omits *forever.* **1:24** [a]NU-Text reads *all its glory.* **1:25** [a]Isaiah 40:6–8 **2:2** [a]NU-Text adds *up to salvation.* **2:6** [a]Isaiah 28:16 **2:7** [a]NU-Text reads *to those who disbelieve.* [b]Psalm 118:22 **2:8** [a]Isaiah 8:14 **2:21** [a]NU-Text reads *you.* [b]NU-Text and M-Text read *you.* **2:22** [a]Isaiah 53:9

23 who, when He was reviled, did not revile in return; when He suffered, He did not threaten, but committed *Himself* to Him who judges righteously;
24 who Himself bore our sins in His own body on the tree, that we, having died to sins, might live for righteousness—by whose stripes you were healed.
25 For you were like sheep going astray, but have now returned to the Shepherd and Overseer[a] of your souls.

Submission to Husbands

3 Wives, likewise, *be* submissive to your own husbands, that even if some do not obey the word, they, without a word, may be won by the conduct of their wives,
2 when they observe your chaste conduct *accompanied* by fear.
3 Do not let your adornment be *merely* outward—arranging the hair, wearing gold, or putting on *fine* apparel—
4 rather *let it be* the hidden person of the heart, with the incorruptible *beauty* of a gentle and quiet spirit, which is very precious in the sight of God.
5 For in this manner, in former times, the holy women who trusted in God also adorned themselves, being submissive to their own husbands,
6 as Sarah obeyed Abraham, calling him lord, whose daughters you are if you do good and are not afraid with any terror.

A Word to Husbands

7 Husbands, likewise, dwell with *them* with understanding, giving honor to the wife, as to the weaker vessel, and as *being* heirs together of the grace of life, that your prayers may not be hindered.

Called to Blessing

8 Finally, all *of you be* of one mind, having compassion for one another; love as brothers, *be* tenderhearted, *be* courteous;[a]
9 not returning evil for evil or reviling for reviling, but on the contrary blessing, knowing that you were called to this, that you may inherit a blessing.
10 For

"He who would love life
And see good days,
Let him refrain his tongue from evil,
And his lips from speaking deceit.
11 *Let him turn away from evil and do good;*
Let him seek peace and pursue it.
12 *For the eyes of the* LORD *are on the righteous,*
And His ears are open to their prayers;
But the face of the LORD *is against those who do evil."*[a]

Suffering for Right and Wrong

13 And who *is* he who will harm you if you become followers of what is good?
14 But even if you should suffer for righteousness' sake, *you are* blessed. *"And do not be afraid of their threats, nor be troubled."*[a]
15 But sanctify the Lord God[a] in your hearts, and always *be* ready to *give* a defense to everyone who asks you a reason for the hope that is in you, with meekness and fear;
16 having a good conscience, that when they defame you as evildoers, those who revile your good conduct in Christ may be ashamed.
17 For *it is* better, if it is the will of God, to suffer for doing good than for doing evil.

Christ's Suffering and Ours

18 For Christ also suffered once for sins, the just for the unjust, that He might bring us[a] to God, being put to death in the flesh but made alive by the Spirit,
19 by whom also He went and preached to the spirits in prison,
20 who formerly were disobedient, when once the Divine longsuffering waited[a] in the days of Noah, while *the* ark was being prepared, in which a few, that is, eight souls, were saved through water.
21 There is also an antitype which now saves us—baptism (not the removal of the filth of the flesh, but the answer of a good conscience toward God), through the resurrection of Jesus Christ,
22 who has gone into heaven and is at the right hand of God, angels and authorities and powers having been made subject to Him.

4 Therefore, since Christ suffered for us[a] in the flesh, arm yourselves also with the same mind, for he who has suffered in the flesh has ceased from sin,
2 that he no longer should live the rest of *his* time in the flesh for the lusts of men, but for the will of God.
3 For we *have spent* enough of our past lifetime[a] in doing the will of the Gentiles—when we walked in lewdness, lusts, drunkenness, revelries, drinking parties, and abominable idolatries.
4 In regard to these, they think it strange that you do not run with *them* in the same flood of dissipation, speaking evil of *you.*
5 They will give an account to Him who is ready to judge the living and the dead.
6 For this reason the gospel was preached also to those who are dead, that they might be judged according to men in the flesh, but live according to God in the spirit.

Serving for God's Glory

7 But the end of all things is at hand; therefore be serious and watchful in your prayers.
8 And above all things have fervent love for one another, for *"love will cover a multitude of sins."*[a]
9 *Be* hospitable to one another without grumbling.
10 As each one has received a gift, minister it to one another, as good stewards of the manifold grace of God.
11 If anyone speaks, *let him speak* as the oracles of God. If anyone ministers, *let him do it* as with the ability which God supplies, that in all things God may be glorified through Jesus Christ, to whom belong the glory and the dominion forever and ever. Amen.

2:25 [a]Greek *Episkopos* **3:8** [a]NU-Text reads *humble.* **3:12** [a]Psalm 34:12–16 **3:14** [a]Isaiah 8:12 **3:15** [a]NU-Text reads *Christ as Lord.* **3:18** [a]NU-Text and M-Text read *you.* **3:20** [a]NU-Text and M-Text read *when the longsuffering of God waited patiently.* **4:1** [a]NU-Text omits *for us.* **4:3** [a]NU-Text reads *time.* **4:8** [a]Proverbs 10:12

Suffering for God's Glory

12 Beloved, do not think it strange concern-
ing the fiery trial which is to try you, as though
some strange thing happened to you;
13 but rejoice to the extent that you partake
of Christ's sufferings, that when His glory is
revealed, you may also be glad with exceeding
joy.
14 If you are reproached for the name of
Christ, blessed *are you,* for the Spirit of glory
and of God rests upon you.[a] On their part He
is blasphemed, but on your part He is glorified.
15 But let none of you suffer as a murderer, a
thief, an evildoer, or as a busybody in other
people's matters.
16 Yet if *anyone suffers* as a Christian, let him
not be ashamed, but let him glorify God in this
matter.[a]
17 For the time *has come* for judgment to be-
gin at the house of God; and if *it begins* with
us first, what will *be* the end of those who do
not obey the gospel of God?
18 Now

"If the righteous one is scarcely saved,
Where will the ungodly and the sinner
appear?"[a]

19 Therefore let those who suffer according to
the will of God commit their souls *to Him* in
doing good, as to a faithful Creator.

Shepherd the Flock

5 The elders who are among you I exhort, I
who am a fellow elder and a witness of the
sufferings of Christ, and also a partaker of the
glory that will be revealed:
2 Shepherd the flock of God which is among
you, serving as overseers, not by compulsion
but willingly,[a] not for dishonest gain but eagerly;
3 nor as being lords over those entrusted to
you, but being examples to the flock;
4 and when the Chief Shepherd appears,
you will receive the crown of glory that does
not fade away.

Submit to God, Resist the Devil

5 Likewise you younger people, submit your-
selves to *your* elders. Yes, all of *you* be submissive
to one another, and be clothed with humility, for

"God resists the proud,
But gives grace to the humble."[a]

6 Therefore humble yourselves under the
mighty hand of God, that He may exalt you in
due time,
7 casting all your care upon Him, for He cares
for you.
8 Be sober, be vigilant; because[a] your adver-
sary the devil walks about like a roaring lion,
seeking whom he may devour.
9 Resist him, steadfast in the faith, knowing
that the same sufferings are experienced by
your brotherhood in the world.
10 But may[a] the God of all grace, who called
us[b] to His eternal glory by Christ Jesus, after
you have suffered a while, perfect, establish,
strengthen, and settle *you.*
11 To Him *be* the glory and the dominion for-
ever and ever. Amen.

Farewell and Peace

12 By Silvanus, our faithful brother as I con-
sider him, I have written to you briefly, exhort-
ing and testifying that this is the true grace of
God in which you stand.
13 She who is in Babylon, elect together with
you, greets you; and *so does* Mark my son.
14 Greet one another with a kiss of love.
Peace to you all who are in Christ Jesus. Amen.

The Second Epistle of PETER

Greeting the Faithful

1 Simon Peter, a bondservant and apostle of
Jesus Christ,

To those who have obtained like precious
faith with us by the righteousness of our God
and Savior Jesus Christ:

2 Grace and peace be multiplied to you in the
knowledge of God and of Jesus our Lord,
3 as His divine power has given to us all things
that *pertain* to life and godliness, through the
knowledge of Him who called us by glory and
virtue,
4 by which have been given to us exceedingly
great and precious promises, that through these
you may be partakers of the divine nature, hav-
ing escaped the corruption *that is* in the world
through lust.

Fruitful Growth in the Faith

5 But also for this very reason, giving all dili-
gence, add to your faith virtue, to virtue knowl-
edge,
6 to knowledge self-control, to self-control
perseverance, to perseverance godliness,
7 to godliness brotherly kindness, and to
brotherly kindness love.
8 For if these things are yours and abound,
you will be neither barren nor unfruitful in the
knowledge of our Lord Jesus Christ.
9 For he who lacks these things is shortsighted,
even to blindness, and has forgotten that he
was cleansed from his old sins.
10 Therefore, brethren, be even more diligent
to make your call and election sure, for if you
do these things you will never stumble;
11 for so an entrance will be supplied to you
abundantly into the everlasting kingdom of
our Lord and Savior Jesus Christ.

Peter's Approaching Death

12 For this reason I will not be negligent to
remind you always of these things, though you
know and are established in the present truth.

4:14 [a]NU-Text omits the rest of this verse. **4:16** [a]NU-Text reads *name.* **4:18** [a]Proverbs 11:31 **5:2** [a]NU-Text adds *according to God.* **5:5** [a]Proverbs 3:34 **5:8** [a]NU-Text and M-Text omit *because.* **5:10** [a]NU-Text reads *But the God of all grace . . . will perfect, establish, strengthen, and settle you.* [b]NU-Text and M-Text read *you.*

13 Yes, I think it is right, as long as I am in this tent, to stir you up by reminding *you,*

14 knowing that shortly I *must* put off my tent, just as our Lord Jesus Christ showed me.

15 Moreover I will be careful to ensure that you always have a reminder of these things after my decease.

The Trustworthy Prophetic Word

16 For we did not follow cunningly devised fables when we made known to you the power and coming of our Lord Jesus Christ, but were eyewitnesses of His majesty.

17 For He received from God the Father honor and glory when such a voice came to Him from the Excellent Glory: "This is My beloved Son, in whom I am well pleased."

18 And we heard this voice which came from heaven when we were with Him on the holy mountain.

19 And so we have the prophetic word confirmed,[a] which you do well to heed as a light that shines in a dark place, until the day dawns and the morning star rises in your hearts;

20 knowing this first, that no prophecy of Scripture is of any private interpretation,[a]

21 for prophecy never came by the will of man, but holy men of God[a] spoke *as they were* moved by the Holy Spirit.

Destructive Doctrines

2 But there were also false prophets among the people, even as there will be false teachers among you, who will secretly bring in destructive heresies, even denying the Lord who bought them, *and* bring on themselves swift destruction.

2 And many will follow their destructive ways, because of whom the way of truth will be blasphemed.

3 By covetousness they will exploit you with deceptive words; for a long time their judgment has not been idle, and their destruction does[a] not slumber.

Doom of False Teachers

4 For if God did not spare the angels who sinned, but cast *them* down to hell and delivered *them* into chains of darkness, to be reserved for judgment;

5 and did not spare the ancient world, but saved Noah, *one of* eight *people,* a preacher of righteousness, bringing in the flood on the world of the ungodly;

6 and turning the cities of Sodom and Gomorrah into ashes, condemned *them* to destruction, making *them* an example to those who afterward would live ungodly;

7 and delivered righteous Lot, *who was* oppressed by the filthy conduct of the wicked

8 (for that righteous man, dwelling among them, tormented *his* righteous soul from day to day by seeing and hearing *their* lawless deeds)—

9 *then* the Lord knows how to deliver the godly out of temptations and to reserve the unjust under punishment for the day of judgment,

10 and especially those who walk according to the flesh in the lust of uncleanness and despise authority. *They are* presumptuous, self-willed. They are not afraid to speak evil of dignitaries,

11 whereas angels, who are greater in power and might, do not bring a reviling accusation against them before the Lord.

Depravity of False Teachers

12 But these, like natural brute beasts made to be caught and destroyed, speak evil of the things they do not understand, and will utterly perish in their own corruption,

13 *and* will receive the wages of unrighteousness, *as* those who count it pleasure to carouse in the daytime. *They are* spots and blemishes, carousing in their own deceptions while they feast with you,

14 having eyes full of adultery and that cannot cease from sin, enticing unstable souls. They have a heart trained in covetous practices, *and are* accursed children.

15 They have forsaken the right way and gone astray, following the way of Balaam the *son* of Beor, who loved the wages of unrighteousness;

16 but he was rebuked for his iniquity: a dumb donkey speaking with a man's voice restrained the madness of the prophet.

17 These are wells without water, clouds[a] carried by a tempest, for whom is reserved the blackness of darkness forever.[b]

Deceptions of False Teachers

18 For when they speak great swelling *words* of emptiness, they allure through the lusts of the flesh, through lewdness, the ones who have actually escaped[a] from those who live in error.

19 While they promise them liberty, they themselves are slaves of corruption; for by whom a person is overcome, by him also he is brought into bondage.

20 For if, after they have escaped the pollutions of the world through the knowledge of the Lord and Savior Jesus Christ, they are again entangled in them and overcome, the latter end is worse for them than the beginning.

21 For it would have been better for them not to have known the way of righteousness, than having known *it,* to turn from the holy commandment delivered to them.

22 But it has happened to them according to the true proverb: *"A dog returns to his own vomit,"*[a] and, "a sow, having washed, to her wallowing in the mire."

God's Promise Is Not Slack

3 Beloved, I now write to you this second epistle (in *both of* which I stir up your pure minds by way of reminder),

2 that you may be mindful of the words which were spoken before by the holy prophets, and of the commandment of us,[a] the apostles of the Lord and Savior,

3 knowing this first: that scoffers will come in the last days, walking according to their own lusts,

4 and saying, "Where is the promise of His coming? For since the fathers fell asleep, all things continue as *they were* from the beginning of creation."

5 For this they willfully forget: that by the word of God the heavens were of old, and the earth standing out of water and in the water,

1:19 [a]Or *We also have the more sure prophetic word.* **1:20** [a]Or *origin* **1:21** [a]NU-Text reads *but men spoke from God.* **2:3** [a]M-Text reads *will not.* **2:17** [a]NU-Text reads *and mists.* [b]NU-Text omits *forever.* **2:18** [a]NU-Text reads *are barely escaping.* **2:22** [a]Proverbs 26:11 **3:2** [a]NU-Text and M-Text read *commandment of the apostles of your Lord and Savior* or *commandment of your apostles of the Lord and Savior.*

6 by which the world *that* then existed per-
ished, being flooded with water.
7 But the heavens and the earth *which* are now
preserved by the same word, are reserved for
fire until the day of judgment and perdition of
ungodly men.
8 But, beloved, do not forget this one thing,
that with the Lord one day *is* as a thousand years,
and a thousand years as one day.
9 The Lord is not slack concerning *His* prom-
ise, as some count slackness, but is longsuffer-
ing toward us,[a] not willing that any should
perish but that all should come to repentance.

The Day of the Lord

10 But the day of the Lord will come as a thief
in the night, in which the heavens will pass
away with a great noise, and the elements will
melt with fervent heat; both the earth and the
works that are in it will be burned up.[a]
11 Therefore, since all these things will be dis-
solved, what manner *of persons* ought you to
be in holy conduct and godliness,
12 looking for and hastening the coming of the
day of God, because of which the heavens will
be dissolved, being on fire, and the elements
will melt with fervent heat?
13 Nevertheless we, according to His promise,
look for new heavens and a new earth in which
righteousness dwells.

Be Steadfast

14 Therefore, beloved, looking forward to
these things, be diligent to be found by Him in
peace, without spot and blameless;
15 and consider *that* the longsuffering of our
Lord *is* salvation—as also our beloved brother
Paul, according to the wisdom given to him,
has written to you,
16 as also in all his epistles, speaking in them
of these things, in which are some things hard
to understand, which untaught and unstable
people twist to their own destruction, as *they do*
also the rest of the Scriptures.
17 You therefore, beloved, since you know
this beforehand, beware lest you also fall from
your own steadfastness, being led away with
the error of the wicked;
18 but grow in the grace and knowledge of
our Lord and Savior Jesus Christ. To Him *be*
the glory both now and forever. Amen.

The First Epistle of JOHN

What Was Heard, Seen, and Touched

1 That which was from the beginning, which
we have heard, which we have seen with
our eyes, which we have looked upon, and our
hands have handled, concerning the Word of
life—
2 the life was manifested, and we have seen,
and bear witness, and declare to you that eter-
nal life which was with the Father and was
manifested to us—
3 that which we have seen and heard we de-
clare to you, that you also may have fellowship
with us; and truly our fellowship *is* with the
Father and with His Son Jesus Christ.
4 And these things we write to you that your[a]
joy may be full.

Fellowship with Him and One Another

5 This is the message which we have heard
from Him and declare to you, that God is light
and in Him is no darkness at all.
6 If we say that we have fellowship with
Him, and walk in darkness, we lie and do not
practice the truth.
7 But if we walk in the light as He is in the
light, we have fellowship with one another, and
the blood of Jesus Christ His Son cleanses us
from all sin.
8 If we say that we have no sin, we deceive
ourselves, and the truth is not in us.
9 If we confess our sins, He is faithful and
just to forgive us *our* sins and to cleanse us from
all unrighteousness.
10 If we say that we have not sinned, we make
Him a liar, and His word is not in us.
2 My little children, these things I write to you,
so that you may not sin. And if anyone sins,
we have an Advocate with the Father, Jesus
Christ the righteous.
2 And He Himself is the propitiation for our
sins, and not for ours only but also for the
whole world.

The Test of Knowing Him

3 Now by this we know that we know Him,
if we keep His commandments.
4 He who says, "I know Him," and does not
keep His commandments, is a liar, and the
truth is not in him.
5 But whoever keeps His word, truly the love
of God is perfected in him. By this we know
that we are in Him.
6 He who says he abides in Him ought him-
self also to walk just as He walked.
7 Brethren,[a] I write no new commandment
to you, but an old commandment which you
have had from the beginning. The old com-
mandment is the word which you heard from
the beginning.[b]
8 Again, a new commandment I write to you,
which thing is true in Him and in you, because
the darkness is passing away, and the true light
is already shining.
9 He who says he is in the light, and hates
his brother, is in darkness until now.
10 He who loves his brother abides in the light,
and there is no cause for stumbling in him.
11 But he who hates his brother is in darkness
and walks in darkness, and does not know
where he is going, because the darkness has
blinded his eyes.

Their Spiritual State

12 I write to you, little children,
Because your sins are forgiven you for
His name's sake.

3:9 [a]NU-Text reads *you.* **3:10** [a]NU-Text reads *laid bare* (literally *found*). **1:4** [a]NU-Text and M-Text read *our.*
2:7 [a]NU-Text reads *Beloved.* [b]NU-Text omits *from the beginning.*

13 I write to you, fathers,
Because you have known Him *who is* from the beginning.
I write to you, young men,
Because you have overcome the wicked one.
I write to you, little children,
Because you have known the Father.
14 I have written to you, fathers,
Because you have known Him *who is* from the beginning.
I have written to you, young men,
Because you are strong, and the word of God abides in you,
And you have overcome the wicked one.

Do Not Love the World

15 Do not love the world or the things in the
world. If anyone loves the world, the love of
the Father is not in him.
16 For all that *is* in the world—the lust of the
flesh, the lust of the eyes, and the pride of life—
is not of the Father but is of the world.
17 And the world is passing away, and the lust
of it; but he who does the will of God abides
forever.

Deceptions of the Last Hour

18 Little children, it is the last hour; and as
you have heard that the[a] Antichrist is coming,
even now many antichrists have come, by which
we know that it is the last hour.
19 They went out from us, but they were not
of us; for if they had been of us, they would
have continued with us; but *they went out* that
they might be made manifest, that none of
them were of us.
20 But you have an anointing from the Holy
One, and you know all things.[a]
21 I have not written to you because you do
not know the truth, but because you know it,
and that no lie is of the truth.
22 Who is a liar but he who denies that Jesus
is the Christ? He is antichrist who denies the
Father and the Son.
23 Whoever denies the Son does not have the
Father either; he who acknowledges the Son
has the Father also.

Let Truth Abide in You

24 Therefore let that abide in you which you
heard from the beginning. If what you heard
from the beginning abides in you, you also will
abide in the Son and in the Father.
25 And this is the promise that He has prom-
ised us—eternal life.
26 These things I have written to you concern-
ing those who *try to* deceive you.
27 But the anointing which you have received
from Him abides in you, and you do not need
that anyone teach you; but as the same anoint-
ing teaches you concerning all things, and is
true, and is not a lie, and just as it has taught
you, you will[a] abide in Him.

The Children of God

28 And now, little children, abide in Him, that
when[a] He appears, we may have confidence
and not be ashamed before Him at His coming.
29 If you know that He is righteous, you know
that everyone who practices righteousness is
born of Him.

3 Behold what manner of love the Father has
bestowed on us, that we should be called
children of God![a] Therefore the world does not
know us,[b] because it did not know Him.
2 Beloved, now we are children of God; and
it has not yet been revealed what we shall be,
but we know that when He is revealed, we shall
be like Him, for we shall see Him as He is.
3 And everyone who has this hope in Him
purifies himself, just as He is pure.

Sin and the Child of God

4 Whoever commits sin also commits law-
lessness, and sin is lawlessness.
5 And you know that He was manifested to
take away our sins, and in Him there is no sin.
6 Whoever abides in Him does not sin. Who-
ever sins has neither seen Him nor known Him.
7 Little children, let no one deceive you. He
who practices righteousness is righteous, just
as He is righteous.
8 He who sins is of the devil, for the devil has
sinned from the beginning. For this purpose
the Son of God was manifested, that He might
destroy the works of the devil.
9 Whoever has been born of God does not
sin, for His seed remains in him; and he cannot
sin, because he has been born of God.

The Imperative of Love

10 In this the children of God and the children
of the devil are manifest: Whoever does not
practice righteousness is not of God, nor *is* he
who does not love his brother.
11 For this is the message that you heard from
the beginning, that we should love one an-
other,
12 not as Cain *who* was of the wicked one and
murdered his brother. And why did he murder
him? Because his works were evil and his
brother's righteous.
13 Do not marvel, my brethren, if the world
hates you.
14 We know that we have passed from death
to life, because we love the brethren. He who
does not love *his* brother[a] abides in death.
15 Whoever hates his brother is a murderer,
and you know that no murderer has eternal
life abiding in him.

The Outworking of Love

16 By this we know love, because He laid down
His life for us. And we also ought to lay down
our lives for the brethren.
17 But whoever has this world's goods, and
sees his brother in need, and shuts up his heart
from him, how does the love of God abide in
him?
18 My little children, let us not love in word
or in tongue, but in deed and in truth.
19 And by this we know[a] that we are of the
truth, and shall assure our hearts before Him.
20 For if our heart condemns us, God is
greater than our heart, and knows all things.
21 Beloved, if our heart does not condemn us,
we have confidence toward God.
22 And whatever we ask we receive from Him,

2:18 [a]NU-Text omits *the.* **2:20** [a]NU-Text reads *you all know.* **2:27** [a]NU-Text reads *you abide.* **2:28** [a]NU-Text reads *if.* **3:1** [a]NU-Text adds *And we are.* [b]M-Text reads *you.* **3:14** [a]NU-Text omits *his brother.* **3:19** [a]NU-Text reads *we shall know.*

because we keep His commandments and do
those things that are pleasing in His sight.
23 And this is His commandment: that we
should believe on the name of His Son Jesus
Christ and love one another, as He gave us[a] com-
mandment.

The Spirit of Truth and the Spirit of Error

24 Now he who keeps His commandments
abides in Him, and He in him. And by this we
know that He abides in us, by the Spirit whom
He has given us.
4 Beloved, do not believe every spirit, but test
the spirits, whether they are of God; be-
cause many false prophets have gone out into
the world.
2 By this you know the Spirit of God: Every
spirit that confesses that Jesus Christ has come
in the flesh is of God,
3 and every spirit that does not confess that[a]
Jesus Christ has come in the flesh is not of God.
And this is the *spirit* of the Antichrist, which
you have heard was coming, and is now already
in the world.
4 You are of God, little children, and have over-
come them, because He who is in you is greater
than he who is in the world.
5 They are of the world. Therefore they speak
as of the world, and the world hears them.
6 We are of God. He who knows God hears
us; he who is not of God does not hear us. By
this we know the spirit of truth and the spirit
of error.

Knowing God Through Love

7 Beloved, let us love one another, for love
is of God; and everyone who loves is born of
God and knows God.
8 He who does not love does not know God,
for God is love.
9 In this the love of God was manifested to-
ward us, that God has sent His only begotten
Son into the world, that we might live through
Him.
10 In this is love, not that we loved God, but
that He loved us and sent His Son *to be* the
propitiation for our sins.
11 Beloved, if God so loved us, we also ought
to love one another.

Seeing God Through Love

12 No one has seen God at any time. If we love
one another, God abides in us, and His love has
been perfected in us.
13 By this we know that we abide in Him, and
He in us, because He has given us of His Spirit.
14 And we have seen and testify that the Fa-
ther has sent the Son *as* Savior of the world.
15 Whoever confesses that Jesus is the Son
of God, God abides in him, and he in God.
16 And we have known and believed the love
that God has for us. God is love, and he who
abides in love abides in God, and God in him.

The Consummation of Love

17 Love has been perfected among us in this:
that we may have boldness in the day of judg-
ment; because as He is, so are we in this world.
18 There is no fear in love; but perfect love
casts out fear, because fear involves torment.
But he who fears has not been made perfect in
love.
19 We love Him[a] because He first loved us.

Obedience by Faith

20 If someone says, "I love God," and hates his
brother, he is a liar; for he who does not love
his brother whom he has seen, how can[a] he love
God whom he has not seen?
21 And this commandment we have from Him:
that he who loves God *must* love his brother
also.
5 Whoever believes that Jesus is the Christ is
born of God, and everyone who loves Him
who begot also loves him who is begotten of
Him.
2 By this we know that we love the children
of God, when we love God and keep His com-
mandments.
3 For this is the love of God, that we keep His
commandments. And His commandments are
not burdensome.
4 For whatever is born of God overcomes the
world. And this is the victory that has over-
come the world—our[a] faith.
5 Who is he who overcomes the world, but
he who believes that Jesus is the Son of God?

The Certainty of God's Witness

6 This is He who came by water and blood—
Jesus Christ; not only by water, but by water
and blood. And it is the Spirit who bears wit-
ness, because the Spirit is truth.
7 For there are three that bear witness in
heaven: the Father, the Word, and the Holy Spirit;
and these three are one.
8 And there are three that bear witness on
earth:[a] the Spirit, the water, and the blood; and
these three agree as one.
9 If we receive the witness of men, the wit-
ness of God is greater; for this is the witness
of God which[a] He has testified of His Son.
10 He who believes in the Son of God has the
witness in himself; he who does not believe
God has made Him a liar, because he has not
believed the testimony that God has given of
His Son.
11 And this is the testimony: that God has given
us eternal life, and this life is in His Son.
12 He who has the Son has life; he who does
not have the Son of God does not have life.
13 These things I have written to you who
believe in the name of the Son of God, that you
may know that you have eternal life,[a] and that
you may *continue to* believe in the name of the
Son of God.

Confidence and Compassion in Prayer

14 Now this is the confidence that we have in
Him, that if we ask anything according to His
will, He hears us.
15 And if we know that He hears us, whatever
we ask, we know that we have the petitions that
we have asked of Him.
16 If anyone sees his brother sinning a sin
which does not *lead* to death, he will ask, and
He will give him life for those who commit sin

3:23 [a]M-Text omits *us.* **4:3** [a]NU-Text omits *that* and *Christ has come in the flesh.* **4:19** [a]NU-Text omits *Him.*
4:20 [a]NU-Text reads *he cannot.* **5:4** [a]M-Text reads *your.* **5:8** [a]NU-Text and M-Text omit the words from *in heaven* (verse 7) through *on earth* (verse 8). Only four or five very late manuscripts contain these words in Greek.
5:9 [a]NU-Text reads *God, that.* **5:13** [a]NU-Text omits the rest of this verse.

not *leading* to death. There is sin *leading* to death.
I do not say that he should pray about that.
17 All unrighteousness is sin, and there is sin
not *leading* to death.

Knowing the True—Rejecting the False

18 We know that whoever is born of God does
not sin; but he who has been born of God keeps
himself,[a] and the wicked one does not touch him.
19 We know that we are of God, and the whole
world lies *under the sway of* the wicked one.
20 And we know that the Son of God has
come and has given us an understanding, that
we may know Him who is true; and we are in
Him who is true, in His Son Jesus Christ. This
is the true God and eternal life.
21 Little children, keep yourselves from idols.
Amen.

The Second Epistle of JOHN

Greeting the Elect Lady

The Elder,
To the elect lady and her children, whom I
love in truth, and not only I, but also all those
who have known the truth,
2 because of the truth which abides in us and
will be with us forever:

3 Grace, mercy, *and* peace will be with you[a]
from God the Father and from the Lord Jesus
Christ, the Son of the Father, in truth and love.

Walk in Christ's Commandments

4 I rejoiced greatly that I have found *some* of
your children walking in truth, as we received
commandment from the Father.
5 And now I plead with you, lady, not as
though I wrote a new commandment to you,
but that which we have had from the begin-
ning: that we love one another.
6 This is love, that we walk according to His
commandments. This is the commandment,
that as you have heard from the beginning, you
should walk in it.

Beware of Antichrist Deceivers

7 For many deceivers have gone out into the
world who do not confess Jesus Christ *as* com-
ing in the flesh. This is a deceiver and an anti-
christ.
8 Look to yourselves, that we[a] do not lose
those things we worked for, but *that* we[b] may
receive a full reward.
9 Whoever transgresses[a] and does not abide
in the doctrine of Christ does not have God. He
who abides in the doctrine of Christ has both
the Father and the Son.
10 If anyone comes to you and does not bring
this doctrine, do not receive him into your house
nor greet him;
11 for he who greets him shares in his evil
deeds.

John's Farewell Greeting

12 Having many things to write to you, I did
not wish *to do so* with paper and ink; but I
hope to come to you and speak face to face,
that our joy may be full.
13 The children of your elect sister greet you.
Amen.

The Third Epistle of JOHN

Greeting to Gaius

The Elder,
To the beloved Gaius, whom I love in truth:

2 Beloved, I pray that you may prosper in
all things and be in health, just as your soul
prospers.
3 For I rejoiced greatly when brethren came
and testified of the truth *that is* in you, just as
you walk in the truth.
4 I have no greater joy than to hear that my
children walk in truth.[a]

Gaius Commended for Generosity

5 Beloved, you do faithfully whatever you do
for the brethren and[a] for strangers,
6 who have borne witness of your love be-
fore the church. *If* you send them forward on
their journey in a manner worthy of God, you
will do well,
7 because they went forth for His name's
sake, taking nothing from the Gentiles.
8 We therefore ought to receive[a] such, that
we may become fellow workers for the truth.

Diotrephes and Demetrius

9 I wrote to the church, but Diotrephes, who
loves to have the preeminence among them,
does not receive us.
10 Therefore, if I come, I will call to mind his
deeds which he does, prating against us with
malicious words. And not content with that, he
himself does not receive the brethren, and for-
bids those who wish to, putting *them* out of the
church.
11 Beloved, do not imitate what is evil, but

5:18 [a]NU-Text reads *him.* **3** [a]NU-Text and M-Text read *us.* **8** [a]NU-Text reads *you.* [b]NU-Text reads *you.* **9** [a]NU-Text reads *goes ahead.* **4** [a]NU-Text reads *the truth.* **5** [a]NU-Text adds *especially.* **8** [a]NU-Text reads *support.*

what is good. He who does good is of God, but[a] he who does evil has not seen God.
12 Demetrius has a *good* testimony from all, and from the truth itself. And we also bear witness, and you know that our testimony is true.

Farewell Greeting

13 I had many things to write, but I do not wish to write to you with pen and ink;
14 but I hope to see you shortly, and we shall speak face to face. Peace to you. Our friends greet you. Greet the friends by name.

The Epistle of JUDE

Greeting to the Called

Jude, a bondservant of Jesus Christ, and brother of James,

To those who are called, sanctified[a] by God the Father, and preserved in Jesus Christ:

2 Mercy, peace, and love be multiplied to you.

Contend for the Faith

3 Beloved, while I was very diligent to write
to you concerning our common salvation, I found
it necessary to write to you exhorting you to
contend earnestly for the faith which was once
for all delivered to the saints.
4 For certain men have crept in unnoticed,
who long ago were marked out for this condemnation, ungodly men, who turn the grace of our God into lewdness and deny the only Lord God[a] and our Lord Jesus Christ.

Old and New Apostates

5 But I want to remind you, though you once
knew this, that the Lord, having saved the people out of the land of Egypt, afterward destroyed those who did not believe.
6 And the angels who did not keep their
proper domain, but left their own abode, He has reserved in everlasting chains under darkness for the judgment of the great day;
7 as Sodom and Gomorrah, and the cities
around them in a similar manner to these, having given themselves over to sexual immorality and gone after strange flesh, are set forth as an example, suffering the vengeance of eternal fire.
8 Likewise also these dreamers defile the
flesh, reject authority, and speak evil of dignitaries.
9 Yet Michael the archangel, in contending
with the devil, when he disputed about the body of Moses, dared not bring against him a reviling accusation, but said, "The Lord rebuke you!"
10 But these speak evil of whatever they do
not know; and whatever they know naturally, like brute beasts, in these things they corrupt themselves.
11 Woe to them! For they have gone in the
way of Cain, have run greedily in the error of Balaam for profit, and perished in the rebellion of Korah.

Apostates Depraved and Doomed

12 These are spots in your love feasts, while
they feast with you without fear, serving *only* themselves. *They are* clouds without water, carried about[a] by the winds; late autumn trees without fruit, twice dead, pulled up by the roots;
13 raging waves of the sea, foaming up their
own shame; wandering stars for whom is reserved the blackness of darkness forever.
14 Now Enoch, the seventh from Adam,
prophesied about these men also, saying, "Behold, the Lord comes with ten thousands of His saints,
15 "to execute judgment on all, to convict all
who are ungodly among them of all their ungodly deeds which they have committed in an ungodly way, and of all the harsh things which ungodly sinners have spoken against Him."

Apostates Predicted

16 These are grumblers, complainers, walk-
ing according to their own lusts; and they mouth great swelling *words*, flattering people to gain advantage.
17 But you, beloved, remember the words
which were spoken before by the apostles of our Lord Jesus Christ:
18 how they told you that there would be
mockers in the last time who would walk according to their own ungodly lusts.
19 These are sensual persons, who cause divi-
sions, not having the Spirit.

Maintain Your Life with God

20 But you, beloved, building yourselves up
on your most holy faith, praying in the Holy Spirit,
21 keep yourselves in the love of God, looking
for the mercy of our Lord Jesus Christ unto eternal life.
22 And on some have compassion, making a
distinction;[a]
23 but others save with fear, pulling *them* out
of the fire,[a] hating even the garment defiled by the flesh.

Glory to God

24 Now to Him who is able to keep you[a]
from stumbling,
And to present *you* faultless
Before the presence of His glory with
exceeding joy,
25 To God our Savior,[a]
Who alone is wise,[b]
Be glory and majesty,
Dominion and power,[c]
Both now and forever.
Amen.

11 [a]NU-Text and M-Text omit *but*. 1 [a]NU-Text reads *beloved*. 4 [a]NU-Text omits *God*. 12 [a]NU-Text and M-Text read *along*. 22 [a]NU-Text reads *who are doubting* (or *making distinctions*). 23 [a]NU-Text adds *and on some have mercy with fear* and omits *with fear* in first clause. 24 [a]M-Text reads *them*. 25 [a]NU-Text reads *To the only God our Savior*. [b]NU-Text omits *Who . . . is wise* and adds *Through Jesus Christ our Lord*. [c]NU-Text adds *Before all time*.

THE REVELATION

of Jesus Christ

Introduction and Benediction

1 The Revelation of Jesus Christ, which God gave Him to show His servants—things which must shortly take place. And He sent and signified *it* by His angel to His servant John,
2 who bore witness to the word of God, and to the testimony of Jesus Christ, to all things that he saw.
3 Blessed *is* he who reads and those who hear the words of this prophecy, and keep those things which are written in it; for the time *is* near.

Greeting the Seven Churches

4 John, to the seven churches which are in Asia:

Grace to you and peace from Him who is and who was and who is to come, and from the seven Spirits who are before His throne,
5 and from Jesus Christ, the faithful witness, the firstborn from the dead, and the ruler over the kings of the earth. To Him who loved us and washed[a] us from our sins in His own blood,
6 and has made us kings[a] and priests to His God and Father, to Him *be* glory and dominion forever and ever. Amen.
7 Behold, He is coming with clouds, and every eye will see Him, even they who pierced Him. And all the tribes of the earth will mourn because of Him. Even so, Amen.
8 "I am the Alpha and the Omega, *the* Beginning and *the* End,"[a] says the Lord,[b] "who is and who was and who is to come, the Almighty."

Vision of the Son of Man

9 I, John, both[a] your brother and companion in the tribulation and kingdom and patience of Jesus Christ, was on the island that is called Patmos for the word of God and for the testimony of Jesus Christ.
10 I was in the Spirit on the Lord's Day, and I heard behind me a loud voice, as of a trumpet,
11 saying, "I am the Alpha and the Omega, the First and the Last," and,[a] "What you see, write in a book and send *it* to the seven churches which are in Asia:[b] to Ephesus, to Smyrna, to Pergamos, to Thyatira, to Sardis, to Philadelphia, and to Laodicea."
12 Then I turned to see the voice that spoke with me. And having turned I saw seven golden lampstands,
13 and in the midst of the seven lampstands *One* like the Son of Man, clothed with a garment down to the feet and girded about the chest with a golden band.
14 His head and hair *were* white like wool, as white as snow, and His eyes like a flame of fire;
15 His feet *were* like fine brass, as if refined in a furnace, and His voice as the sound of many waters;
16 He had in His right hand seven stars, out of His mouth went a sharp two-edged sword, and His countenance *was* like the sun shining in its strength.
17 And when I saw Him, I fell at His feet as dead. But He laid His right hand on me, saying to me,[a] "Do not be afraid; I am the First and the Last.
18 "I *am* He who lives, and was dead, and behold, I am alive forevermore. Amen. And I have the keys of Hades and of Death.
19 "Write[a] the things which you have seen, and the things which are, and the things which will take place after this.
20 "The mystery of the seven stars which you saw in My right hand, and the seven golden lampstands: The seven stars are the angels of the seven churches, and the seven lampstands which you saw[a] are the seven churches.

The Loveless Church

2 "To the angel of the church of Ephesus write,

'These things says He who holds the seven stars in His right hand, who walks in the midst of the seven golden lampstands:
2 "I know your works, your labor, your patience, and that you cannot bear those who are evil. And you have tested those who say they are apostles and are not, and have found them liars;
3 "and you have persevered and have patience, and have labored for My name's sake and have not become weary.
4 "Nevertheless I have *this* against you, that you have left your first love.
5 "Remember therefore from where you have fallen; repent and do the first works, or else I will come to you quickly and remove your lampstand from its place—unless you repent.
6 "But this you have, that you hate the deeds of the Nicolaitans, which I also hate.
7 "He who has an ear, let him hear what the Spirit says to the churches. To him who overcomes I will give to eat from the tree of life, which is in the midst of the Paradise of God." '

The Persecuted Church

8 "And to the angel of the church in Smyrna write,

'These things says the First and the Last, who was dead, and came to life:
9 "I know your works, tribulation, and poverty (but you are rich); and *I know* the blasphemy of those who say they are Jews and are not, but *are* a synagogue of Satan.
10 "Do not fear any of those things which you are about to suffer. Indeed, the devil is about to throw *some* of you into prison, that you may be tested, and you will have tribulation ten days. Be faithful until death, and I will give you the crown of life.
11 "He who has an ear, let him hear what the Spirit says to the churches. He who overcomes shall not be hurt by the second death." '

1:5 [a]NU-Text reads *loves us and freed;* M-Text reads *loves us and washed.* **1:6** [a]NU-Text and M-Text read *a kingdom.* **1:8** [a]NU-Text and M-Text omit *the Beginning and the End.* [b]NU-Text and M-Text add *God.* **1:9** [a]NU-Text and M-Text omit *both.* **1:11** [a]NU-Text and M-Text omit *I am* through third *and.* [b]NU-Text and M-Text omit *which are in Asia.* **1:17** [a]NU-Text and M-Text omit *to me.* **1:19** [a]NU-Text and M-Text read *Therefore, write.* **1:20** [a]NU-Text and M-Text omit *which you saw.*

The Compromising Church

12 "And to the angel of the church in Pergamos write,

'These things says He who has the sharp two-edged sword:

13 "I know your works, and where you dwell, where Satan's throne *is.* And you hold fast to My name, and did not deny My faith even in the days in which Antipas *was* My faithful martyr, who was killed among you, where Satan dwells.

14 "But I have a few things against you, because you have there those who hold the doctrine of Balaam, who taught Balak to put a stumbling block before the children of Israel, to eat things sacrificed to idols, and to commit sexual immorality.

15 "Thus you also have those who hold the doctrine of the Nicolaitans, which thing I hate.[a]

16 "Repent, or else I will come to you quickly and will fight against them with the sword of My mouth.

17 "He who has an ear, let him hear what the Spirit says to the churches. To him who overcomes I will give some of the hidden manna to eat. And I will give him a white stone, and on the stone a new name written which no one knows except him who receives *it.*"'

The Corrupt Church

18 "And to the angel of the church in Thyatira write,

'These things says the Son of God, who has eyes like a flame of fire, and His feet like fine brass:

19 "I know your works, love, service, faith,[a] and your patience; and *as* for your works, the last *are* more than the first.

20 "Nevertheless I have a few things against you, because you allow[a] that woman[b] Jezebel, who calls herself a prophetess, to teach and seduce[c] My servants to commit sexual immorality and eat things sacrificed to idols.

21 "And I gave her time to repent of her sexual immorality, and she did not repent.[a]

22 "Indeed I will cast her into a sickbed, and those who commit adultery with her into great tribulation, unless they repent of their[a] deeds.

23 "I will kill her children with death, and all the churches shall know that I am He who searches the minds and hearts. And I will give to each one of you according to your works.

24 "Now to you I say, and[a] to the rest in Thyatira, as many as do not have this doctrine, who have not known the depths of Satan, as they say, I will[b] put on you no other burden.

25 "But hold fast what you have till I come.

26 "And he who overcomes, and keeps My works until the end, to him I will give power over the nations—

27 *'He shall rule them with a rod of iron;*
They shall be dashed to pieces like the potter's vessels'[a]—

as I also have received from My Father;

28 "and I will give him the morning star.

29 "He who has an ear, let him hear what the Spirit says to the churches."'

The Dead Church

3 "And to the angel of the church in Sardis write,

'These things says He who has the seven Spirits of God and the seven stars: "I know your works, that you have a name that you are alive, but you are dead.

2 "Be watchful, and strengthen the things which remain, that are ready to die, for I have not found your works perfect before God.[a]

3 "Remember therefore how you have received and heard; hold fast and repent. Therefore if you will not watch, I will come upon you as a thief, and you will not know what hour I will come upon you.

4 "You[a] have a few names even in Sardis who have not defiled their garments; and they shall walk with Me in white, for they are worthy.

5 "He who overcomes shall be clothed in white garments, and I will not blot out his name from the Book of Life; but I will confess his name before My Father and before His angels.

6 "He who has an ear, let him hear what the Spirit says to the churches."'

The Faithful Church

7 "And to the angel of the church in Philadelphia write,

'These things says He who is holy, He who is true, *"He who has the key of David, He who opens and no one shuts, and shuts and no one opens"*:[a]

8 "I know your works. See, I have set before you an open door, and no one can shut it;[a] for you have a little strength, have kept My word, and have not denied My name.

9 "Indeed I will make *those* of the synagogue of Satan, who say they are Jews and are not, but lie—indeed I will make them come and worship before your feet, and to know that I have loved you.

10 "Because you have kept My command to persevere, I also will keep you from the hour of trial which shall come upon the whole world, to test those who dwell on the earth.

11 "Behold,[a] I am coming quickly! Hold fast what you have, that no one may take your crown.

12 "He who overcomes, I will make him a pillar in the temple of My God, and he shall go out no more. I will write on him the name of My God and the name of the city of My God, the New Jerusalem, which comes down out of heaven from My God. And *I will write on him* My new name.

13 "He who has an ear, let him hear what the Spirit says to the churches."'

2:15 [a]NU-Text and M-Text read *likewise* for *which thing I hate.* **2:19** [a]NU-Text and M-Text read *faith, service.* **2:20** [a]NU-Text and M-Text read *I have against you that you tolerate.* [b]M-Text reads *your wife Jezebel.* [c]NU-Text and M-Text read *and teaches and seduces.* **2:21** [a]NU-Text and M-Text read *time to repent, and she does not want to repent of her sexual immorality.* **2:22** [a]NU-Text and M-Text read *her.* **2:24** [a]NU-Text and M-Text omit *and.* [b]NU-Text and M-Text omit *will.* **2:27** [a]Psalm 2:9 **3:2** [a]NU-Text and M-Text read *My God.* **3:4** [a]NU-Text and M-Text read *Nevertheless you have a few names in Sardis.* **3:7** [a]Isaiah 22:22 **3:8** [a]NU-Text and M-Text read *which no one can shut.* **3:11** [a]NU-Text and M-Text omit *Behold.*

The Lukewarm Church

14 "And to the angel of the church of the Laodiceans[a] write,

'These things says the Amen, the Faithful and True Witness, the Beginning of the creation of God:

15 "I know your works, that you are neither cold nor hot. I could wish you were cold or hot.
16 "So then, because you are lukewarm, and neither cold nor hot,[a] I will vomit you out of My mouth.
17 "Because you say, 'I am rich, have become wealthy, and have need of nothing'—and do not know that you are wretched, miserable, poor, blind, and naked—
18 "I counsel you to buy from Me gold refined in the fire, that you may be rich; and white garments, that you may be clothed, *that* the shame of your nakedness may not be revealed; and anoint your eyes with eye salve, that you may see.
19 "As many as I love, I rebuke and chasten. Therefore be zealous and repent.
20 "Behold, I stand at the door and knock. If anyone hears My voice and opens the door, I will come in to him and dine with him, and he with Me.
21 "To him who overcomes I will grant to sit with Me on My throne, as I also overcame and sat down with My Father on His throne.
22 "He who has an ear, let him hear what the Spirit says to the churches." ' "

The Throne Room of Heaven

4 After these things I looked, and behold, a door *standing* open in heaven. And the first voice which I heard *was* like a trumpet speaking with me, saying, "Come up here, and I will show you things which must take place after this."
2 Immediately I was in the Spirit; and behold, a throne set in heaven, and *One* sat on the throne.
3 And He who sat there was[a] like a jasper and a sardius stone in appearance; and *there was* a rainbow around the throne, in appearance like an emerald.
4 Around the throne *were* twenty-four thrones, and on the thrones I saw twenty-four elders sitting, clothed in white robes; and they had crowns[a] of gold on their heads.
5 And from the throne proceeded lightnings, thunderings, and voices.[a] Seven lamps of fire *were* burning before the throne, which are the[b] seven Spirits of God.
6 Before the throne *there was*[a] a sea of glass, like crystal. And in the midst of the throne, and around the throne, *were* four living creatures full of eyes in front and in back.
7 The first living creature *was* like a lion, the second living creature like a calf, the third living creature had a face like a man, and the fourth living creature *was* like a flying eagle.
8 *The* four living creatures, each having six wings, were full of eyes around and within. And they do not rest day or night, saying:

"Holy, holy, holy,[a]
Lord God Almighty,
Who was and is and is to come!"

9 Whenever the living creatures give glory and honor and thanks to Him who sits on the throne, who lives forever and ever,
10 the twenty-four elders fall down before Him who sits on the throne and worship Him who lives forever and ever, and cast their crowns before the throne, saying:

11 "You are worthy, O Lord,[a]
To receive glory and honor and power;
For You created all things,
And by Your will they exist[b] and were created."

The Lamb Takes the Scroll

5 And I saw in the right *hand* of Him who sat on the throne a scroll written inside and on the back, sealed with seven seals.
2 Then I saw a strong angel proclaiming with a loud voice, "Who is worthy to open the scroll and to loose its seals?"
3 And no one in heaven or on the earth or under the earth was able to open the scroll, or to look at it.
4 So I wept much, because no one was found worthy to open and read[a] the scroll, or to look at it.
5 But one of the elders said to me, "Do not weep. Behold, the Lion of the tribe of Judah, the Root of David, has prevailed to open the scroll and to loose[a] its seven seals."
6 And I looked, and behold,[a] in the midst of the throne and of the four living creatures, and in the midst of the elders, stood a Lamb as though it had been slain, having seven horns and seven eyes, which are the seven Spirits of God sent out into all the earth.
7 Then He came and took the scroll out of the right hand of Him who sat on the throne.

Worthy Is the Lamb

8 Now when He had taken the scroll, the four living creatures and the twenty-four elders fell down before the Lamb, each having a harp, and golden bowls full of incense, which are the prayers of the saints.
9 And they sang a new song, saying:

"You are worthy to take the scroll,
And to open its seals;
For You were slain,
And have redeemed us to God by Your blood
Out of every tribe and tongue and people and nation,
10 And have made us[a] kings[b] and priests to our God;
And we[c] shall reign on the earth."

11 Then I looked, and I heard the voice of many angels around the throne, the living creatures, and the elders; and the number of them was ten thousand times ten thousand, and thousands of thousands,
12 saying with a loud voice:

3:14 [a]NU-Text and M-Text read *in Laodicea*. **3:16** [a]NU-Text and M-Text read *hot nor cold*. **4:3** [a]M-Text omits *And He who sat there was* (which makes the description in verse 3 modify the throne rather than God). **4:4** [a]NU-Text and M-Text read *robes, with crowns*. **4:5** [a]NU-Text and M-Text read *voices, and thunderings*. [b]M-Text omits *the*. **4:6** [a]NU-Text and M-Text add *something like*. **4:8** [a]M-Text has *holy* nine times. **4:11** [a]NU-Text and M-Text read *our Lord and God*. [b]NU-Text and M-Text read *existed*. **5:4** [a]NU-Text and M-Text omit *and read*. **5:5** [a]NU-Text and M-Text omit *to loose*. **5:6** [a]NU-Text and M-Text read *I saw in the midst . . . a Lamb standing*. **5:10** [a]NU-Text and M-Text read *them*. [b]NU-Text reads *a kingdom*. [c]NU-Text and M-Text read *they*.

"Worthy is the Lamb who was slain
To receive power and riches and wisdom,
And strength and honor and glory and
blessing!"

13 And every creature which is in heaven and
on the earth and under the earth and such as
are in the sea, and all that are in them, I heard
saying:

"Blessing and honor and glory and power
Be to Him who sits on the throne,
And to the Lamb, forever and ever!"[a]

14 Then the four living creatures said, "Amen!"
And the twenty-four[a] elders fell down and wor-
shiped Him who lives forever and ever.[b]

First Seal: The Conqueror

6 Now I saw when the Lamb opened one of
the seals;[a] and I heard one of the four liv-
ing creatures saying with a voice like thunder,
"Come and see."
2 And I looked, and behold, a white horse.
He who sat on it had a bow; and a crown was
given to him, and he went out conquering and
to conquer.

Second Seal: Conflict on Earth

3 When He opened the second seal, I heard
the second living creature saying, "Come and
see."[a]
4 Another horse, fiery red, went out. And it
was granted to the one who sat on it to take
peace from the earth, and that *people* should
kill one another; and there was given to him a
great sword.

Third Seal: Scarcity on Earth

5 When He opened the third seal, I heard the
third living creature say, "Come and see." So I
looked, and behold, a black horse, and he who
sat on it had a pair of scales in his hand.
6 And I heard a voice in the midst of the four
living creatures saying, "A quart[a] of wheat for
a denarius,[b] and three quarts of barley for a
denarius; and do not harm the oil and the wine."

Fourth Seal: Widespread Death on Earth

7 When He opened the fourth seal, I heard
the voice of the fourth living creature saying,
"Come and see."
8 So I looked, and behold, a pale horse. And
the name of him who sat on it was Death, and
Hades followed with him. And power was given
to them over a fourth of the earth, to kill with
sword, with hunger, with death, and by the beasts
of the earth.

Fifth Seal: The Cry of the Martyrs

9 When He opened the fifth seal, I saw under
the altar the souls of those who had been slain
for the word of God and for the testimony which
they held.
10 And they cried with a loud voice, saying,
"How long, O Lord, holy and true, until You judge
and avenge our blood on those who dwell on
the earth?"
11 Then a white robe was given to each of them;
and it was said to them that they should rest a
little while longer, until both *the number of*
their fellow servants and their brethren, who
would be killed as they *were*, was completed.

Sixth Seal: Cosmic Disturbances

12 I looked when He opened the sixth seal,
and behold,[a] there was a great earthquake; and
the sun became black as sackcloth of hair, and
the moon[b] became like blood.
13 And the stars of heaven fell to the earth,
as a fig tree drops its late figs when it is shaken
by a mighty wind.
14 Then the sky receded as a scroll when it is
rolled up, and every mountain and island was
moved out of its place.
15 And the kings of the earth, the great men,
the rich men, the commanders,[a] the mighty
men, every slave and every free man, hid them-
selves in the caves and in the rocks of the moun-
tains,
16 and said to the mountains and rocks, "Fall
on us and hide us from the face of Him who sits
on the throne and from the wrath of the Lamb!
17 "For the great day of His wrath has come,
and who is able to stand?"

The Sealed of Israel

7 After these things I saw four angels stand-
ing at the four corners of the earth, holding
the four winds of the earth, that the wind should
not blow on the earth, on the sea, or on any tree.
2 Then I saw another angel ascending from
the east, having the seal of the living God. And
he cried with a loud voice to the four angels to
whom it was granted to harm the earth and the
sea,
3 saying, "Do not harm the earth, the sea, or
the trees till we have sealed the servants of our
God on their foreheads."
4 And I heard the number of those who were
sealed. One hundred *and* forty-four thousand
of all the tribes of the children of Israel *were*
sealed:

5 of the tribe of Judah
twelve thousand *were* sealed;[a]
of the tribe of Reuben
twelve thousand *were* sealed;
of the tribe of Gad
twelve thousand *were* sealed;
6 of the tribe of Asher
twelve thousand *were* sealed;
of the tribe of Naphtali
twelve thousand *were* sealed;
of the tribe of Manasseh
twelve thousand *were* sealed;
7 of the tribe of Simeon
twelve thousand *were* sealed;
of the tribe of Levi
twelve thousand *were* sealed;
of the tribe of Issachar
twelve thousand *were* sealed;
8 of the tribe of Zebulun
twelve thousand *were* sealed;

5:13 [a]M-Text adds *Amen.* **5:14** [a]NU-Text and M-Text omit *twenty-four.* [b]NU-Text and M-Text omit *Him who lives forever and ever.* **6:1** [a]NU-Text and M-Text read *seven seals.* **6:3** [a]NU-Text and M-Text omit *and see.* **6:6** [a]Greek *choinix;* that is, approximately one quart [b]This was approximately one day's wage for a worker. **6:12** [a]NU-Text and M-Text omit *behold.* [b]NU-Text and M-Text read *the whole moon.* **6:15** [a]NU-Text and M-Text read *the commanders, the rich men.* **7:5** [a]In NU-Text and M-Text *were sealed* is stated only in verses 5a and 8c; the words are understood in the remainder of the passage.

of the tribe of Joseph
twelve thousand *were* sealed;
of the tribe of Benjamin
twelve thousand *were* sealed.

A Multitude from the Great Tribulation

9 After these things I looked, and behold, a
great multitude which no one could number, of
all nations, tribes, peoples, and tongues, stand-
ing before the throne and before the Lamb,
clothed with white robes, with palm branches
in their hands,
10 and crying out with a loud voice, saying,
"Salvation *belongs* to our God who sits on the
throne, and to the Lamb!"
11 All the angels stood around the throne and
the elders and the four living creatures, and
fell on their faces before the throne and wor-
shiped God,
12 saying:

"Amen! Blessing and glory and wisdom,
Thanksgiving and honor and power and
might,
Be to our God forever and ever.
Amen."

13 Then one of the elders answered, saying to
me, "Who are these arrayed in white robes, and
where did they come from?"
14 And I said to him, "Sir,[a] you know." So he
said to me, "These are the ones who come out
of the great tribulation, and washed their robes
and made them white in the blood of the Lamb.
15 "Therefore they are before the throne of
God, and serve Him day and night in His tem-
ple. And He who sits on the throne will dwell
among them.
16 "They shall neither hunger anymore nor
thirst anymore; the sun shall not strike them, nor
any heat;
17 "for the Lamb who is in the midst of the
throne will shepherd them and lead them to
living fountains of waters.[a] And God will wipe
away every tear from their eyes."

Seventh Seal: Prelude to the Seven Trumpets

8 When He opened the seventh seal, there
was silence in heaven for about half an
hour.
2 And I saw the seven angels who stand be-
fore God, and to them were given seven trum-
pets.
3 Then another angel, having a golden cen-
ser, came and stood at the altar. He was given
much incense, that he should offer *it* with the
prayers of all the saints upon the golden altar
which was before the throne.
4 And the smoke of the incense, with the
prayers of the saints, ascended before God from
the angel's hand.
5 Then the angel took the censer, filled it with
fire from the altar, and threw *it* to the earth.
And there were noises, thunderings, light-
nings, and an earthquake.
6 So the seven angels who had the seven
trumpets prepared themselves to sound.

First Trumpet: Vegetation Struck

7 The first angel sounded: And hail and fire
followed, mingled with blood, and they were
thrown to the earth.[a] And a third of the trees
were burned up, and all green grass was burned
up.

Second Trumpet: The Seas Struck

8 Then the second angel sounded: And *some-
thing* like a great mountain burning with fire
was thrown into the sea, and a third of the sea
became blood.
9 And a third of the living creatures in the
sea died, and a third of the ships were de-
stroyed.

Third Trumpet: The Waters Struck

10 Then the third angel sounded: And a great
star fell from heaven, burning like a torch, and
it fell on a third of the rivers and on the springs
of water.
11 The name of the star is Wormwood. A third
of the waters became wormwood, and many
men died from the water, because it was made
bitter.

Fourth Trumpet: The Heavens Struck

12 Then the fourth angel sounded: And a third
of the sun was struck, a third of the moon, and
a third of the stars, so that a third of them were
darkened. A third of the day did not shine, and
likewise the night.
13 And I looked, and I heard an angel[a] flying
through the midst of heaven, saying with a
loud voice, "Woe, woe, woe to the inhabitants
of the earth, because of the remaining blasts
of the trumpet of the three angels who are about
to sound!"

Fifth Trumpet: The Locusts from the Bottomless Pit

9 Then the fifth angel sounded: And I saw a
star fallen from heaven to the earth. To him
was given the key to the bottomless pit.
2 And he opened the bottomless pit, and
smoke arose out of the pit like the smoke of a
great furnace. So the sun and the air were dark-
ened because of the smoke of the pit.
3 Then out of the smoke locusts came upon
the earth. And to them was given power, as the
scorpions of the earth have power.
4 They were commanded not to harm the
grass of the earth, or any green thing, or any
tree, but only those men who do not have the
seal of God on their foreheads.
5 And they were not given *authority* to kill
them, but to torment them *for* five months. Their
torment *was* like the torment of a scorpion
when it strikes a man.
6 In those days men will seek death and will
not find it; they will desire to die, and death
will flee from them.
7 The shape of the locusts was like horses pre-
pared for battle. On their heads were crowns
of something like gold, and their faces *were*
like the faces of men.
8 They had hair like women's hair, and their
teeth were like lions' *teeth.*
9 And they had breastplates like breastplates
of iron, and the sound of their wings *was* like

7:14 [a]NU-Text and M-Text read *My lord.* **7:17** [a]NU-Text and M-Text read *to fountains of the waters of life.*
8:7 [a]NU-Text and M-Text add *and a third of the earth was burned up.* **8:13** [a]NU-Text and M-Text read *eagle.*

the sound of chariots with many horses running into battle.

10 They had tails like scorpions, and there were stings in their tails. Their power *was* to hurt men five months.

11 And they had as king over them the angel of the bottomless pit, whose name in Hebrew *is* Abaddon, but in Greek he has the name Apollyon.

12 One woe is past. Behold, still two more woes are coming after these things.

Sixth Trumpet: The Angels from the Euphrates

13 Then the sixth angel sounded: And I heard a voice from the four horns of the golden altar which is before God,

14 saying to the sixth angel who had the trumpet, "Release the four angels who are bound at the great river Euphrates."

15 So the four angels, who had been prepared for the hour and day and month and year, were released to kill a third of mankind.

16 Now the number of the army of the horsemen *was* two hundred million; I heard the number of them.

17 And thus I saw the horses in the vision: those who sat on them had breastplates of fiery red, hyacinth blue, and sulfur yellow; and the heads of the horses *were* like the heads of lions; and out of their mouths came fire, smoke, and brimstone.

18 By these three *plagues* a third of mankind was killed—by the fire and the smoke and the brimstone which came out of their mouths.

19 For their power[a] is in their mouth and in their tails; for their tails *are* like serpents, having heads; and with them they do harm.

20 But the rest of mankind, who were not killed by these plagues, did not repent of the works of their hands, that they should not worship demons, and idols of gold, silver, brass, stone, and wood, which can neither see nor hear nor walk.

21 And they did not repent of their murders or their sorceries[a] or their sexual immorality or their thefts.

The Mighty Angel with the Little Book

10 I saw still another mighty angel coming down from heaven, clothed with a cloud. And a rainbow *was* on his head, his face *was* like the sun, and his feet like pillars of fire.

2 He had a little book open in his hand. And he set his right foot on the sea and *his* left *foot* on the land,

3 and cried with a loud voice, as *when* a lion roars. When he cried out, seven thunders uttered their voices.

4 Now when the seven thunders uttered their voices,[a] I was about to write; but I heard a voice from heaven saying to me,[b] "Seal up the things which the seven thunders uttered, and do not write them."

5 The angel whom I saw standing on the sea and on the land raised up his hand[a] to heaven

6 and swore by Him who lives forever and ever, who created heaven and the things that are in it, the earth and the things that are in it, and the sea and the things that are in it, that there should be delay no longer,

7 but in the days of the sounding of the seventh angel, when he is about to sound, the mystery of God would be finished, as He declared to His servants the prophets.

John Eats the Little Book

8 Then the voice which I heard from heaven spoke to me again and said, "Go, take the little book which is open in the hand of the angel who stands on the sea and on the earth."

9 So I went to the angel and said to him, "Give me the little book." And he said to me, "Take and eat it; and it will make your stomach bitter, but it will be as sweet as honey in your mouth."

10 Then I took the little book out of the angel's hand and ate it, and it was as sweet as honey in my mouth. But when I had eaten it, my stomach became bitter.

11 And he[a] said to me, "You must prophesy again about many peoples, nations, tongues, and kings."

The Two Witnesses

11 Then I was given a reed like a measuring rod. And the angel stood,[a] saying, "Rise and measure the temple of God, the altar, and those who worship there.

2 "But leave out the court which is outside the temple, and do not measure it, for it has been given to the Gentiles. And they will tread the holy city underfoot *for* forty-two months.

3 "And I will give *power* to my two witnesses, and they will prophesy one thousand two hundred and sixty days, clothed in sackcloth."

4 These are the two olive trees and the two lampstands standing before the God[a] of the earth.

5 And if anyone wants to harm them, fire proceeds from their mouth and devours their enemies. And if anyone wants to harm them, he must be killed in this manner.

6 These have power to shut heaven, so that no rain falls in the days of their prophecy; and they have power over waters to turn them to blood, and to strike the earth with all plagues, as often as they desire.

The Witnesses Killed

7 When they finish their testimony, the beast that ascends out of the bottomless pit will make war against them, overcome them, and kill them.

8 And their dead bodies *will lie* in the street of the great city which spiritually is called Sodom and Egypt, where also our[a] Lord was crucified.

9 Then *those* from the peoples, tribes, tongues, and nations will see their dead bodies three-and-a-half days, and not allow[a] their dead bodies to be put into graves.

10 And those who dwell on the earth will rejoice over them, make merry, and send gifts to one another, because these two prophets tormented those who dwell on the earth.

The Witnesses Resurrected

11 Now after the three-and-a-half days the breath of life from God entered them, and they

9:19 [a]NU-Text and M-Text read *the power of the horses.* **9:21** [a]NU-Text and M-Text read *drugs.* **10:4** [a]NU-Text and M-Text read *sounded.* [b]NU-Text and M-Text omit *to me.* **10:5** [a]NU-Text and M-Text read *right hand.* **10:11** [a]NU-Text and M-Text read *they.* **11:1** [a]NU-Text and M-Text omit *And the angel stood.* **11:4** [a]NU-Text and M-Text read *Lord.* **11:8** [a]NU-Text and M-Text read *their.* **11:9** [a]NU-Text and M-Text read *nations see . . . and will not allow.*

stood on their feet, and great fear fell on those who saw them.

12 And they[a] heard a loud voice from heaven saying to them, "Come up here." And they ascended to heaven in a cloud, and their enemies saw them.

13 In the same hour there was a great earthquake, and a tenth of the city fell. In the earthquake seven thousand people were killed, and the rest were afraid and gave glory to the God of heaven.

14 The second woe is past. Behold, the third woe is coming quickly.

Seventh Trumpet: The Kingdom Proclaimed

15 Then the seventh angel sounded: And there were loud voices in heaven, saying, "The kingdoms[a] of this world have become *the kingdoms* of our Lord and of His Christ, and He shall reign forever and ever!"

16 And the twenty-four elders who sat before God on their thrones fell on their faces and worshiped God,

17 saying:

"We give You thanks, O Lord God
Almighty,
The One who is and who was and who is
to come,[a]
Because You have taken Your great
power and reigned.
18 The nations were angry, and Your wrath
has come,
And the time of the dead, that they
should be judged,
And that You should reward Your
servants the prophets and the saints,
And those who fear Your name, small
and great,
And should destroy those who destroy
the earth."

19 Then the temple of God was opened in heaven, and the ark of His covenant[a] was seen in His temple. And there were lightnings, noises, thunderings, an earthquake, and great hail.

The Woman, the Child, and the Dragon

12 Now a great sign appeared in heaven: a woman clothed with the sun, with the moon under her feet, and on her head a garland of twelve stars.

2 Then being with child, she cried out in labor and in pain to give birth.

3 And another sign appeared in heaven: behold, a great, fiery red dragon having seven heads and ten horns, and seven diadems on his heads.

4 His tail drew a third of the stars of heaven and threw them to the earth. And the dragon stood before the woman who was ready to give birth, to devour her Child as soon as it was born.

5 She bore a male Child who was to rule all nations with a rod of iron. And her Child was caught up to God and His throne.

6 Then the woman fled into the wilderness, where she has a place prepared by God, that they should feed her there one thousand two hundred and sixty days.

Satan Thrown Out of Heaven

7 And war broke out in heaven: Michael and his angels fought with the dragon; and the dragon and his angels fought,

8 but they did not prevail, nor was a place found for them[a] in heaven any longer.

9 So the great dragon was cast out, that serpent of old, called the Devil and Satan, who deceives the whole world; he was cast to the earth, and his angels were cast out with him.

10 Then I heard a loud voice saying in heaven, "Now salvation, and strength, and the kingdom of our God, and the power of His Christ have come, for the accuser of our brethren, who accused them before our God day and night, has been cast down.

11 "And they overcame him by the blood of the Lamb and by the word of their testimony, and they did not love their lives to the death.

12 "Therefore rejoice, O heavens, and you who dwell in them! Woe to the inhabitants of the earth and the sea! For the devil has come down to you, having great wrath, because he knows that he has a short time."

The Woman Persecuted

13 Now when the dragon saw that he had been cast to the earth, he persecuted the woman who gave birth to the male *Child*.

14 But the woman was given two wings of a great eagle, that she might fly into the wilderness to her place, where she is nourished for a time and times and half a time, from the presence of the serpent.

15 So the serpent spewed water out of his mouth like a flood after the woman, that he might cause her to be carried away by the flood.

16 But the earth helped the woman, and the earth opened its mouth and swallowed up the flood which the dragon had spewed out of his mouth.

17 And the dragon was enraged with the woman, and he went to make war with the rest of her offspring, who keep the commandments of God and have the testimony of Jesus Christ.[a]

The Beast from the Sea

13 Then I[a] stood on the sand of the sea. And I saw a beast rising up out of the sea, having seven heads and ten horns,[b] and on his horns ten crowns, and on his heads a blasphemous name.

2 Now the beast which I saw was like a leopard, his feet were like *the feet of* a bear, and his mouth like the mouth of a lion. The dragon gave him his power, his throne, and great authority.

3 And I saw one of his heads as if it had been mortally wounded, and his deadly wound was healed. And all the world marveled and followed the beast.

4 So they worshiped the dragon who gave authority to the beast; and they worshiped the beast, saying, "Who *is* like the beast? Who is able to make war with him?"

5 And he was given a mouth speaking great things and blasphemies, and he was given authority to continue[a] for forty-two months.

6 Then he opened his mouth in blasphemy

11:12 [a]M-Text reads *I*. **11:15** [a]NU-Text and M-Text read *kingdom . . . has become*. **11:17** [a]NU-Text and M-Text omit *and who is to come*. **11:19** [a]M-Text reads *the covenant of the Lord*. **12:8** [a]M-Text reads *him*. **12:17** [a]NU-Text and M-Text omit *Christ*. **13:1** [a]NU-Text reads *he*. [b]NU-Text and M-Text read *ten horns and seven heads*. **13:5** [a]M-Text reads *make war*.

against God, to blaspheme His name, His tab-
ernacle, and those who dwell in heaven.
7 It was granted to him to make war with
the saints and to overcome them. And author-
ity was given him over every tribe,[a] tongue,
and nation.
8 All who dwell on the earth will worship
him, whose names have not been written in
the Book of Life of the Lamb slain from the
foundation of the world.
9 If anyone has an ear, let him hear.
10 He who leads into captivity shall go into
captivity; he who kills with the sword must be
killed with the sword. Here is the patience and
the faith of the saints.

The Beast from the Earth

11 Then I saw another beast coming up out of
the earth, and he had two horns like a lamb
and spoke like a dragon.
12 And he exercises all the authority of the
first beast in his presence, and causes the earth
and those who dwell in it to worship the first
beast, whose deadly wound was healed.
13 He performs great signs, so that he even
makes fire come down from heaven on the
earth in the sight of men.
14 And he deceives those[a] who dwell on the
earth by those signs which he was granted to
do in the sight of the beast, telling those who
dwell on the earth to make an image to the
beast who was wounded by the sword and
lived.
15 He was granted *power* to give breath to
the image of the beast, that the image of the
beast should both speak and cause as many as
would not worship the image of the beast to be
killed.
16 He causes all, both small and great, rich and
poor, free and slave, to receive a mark on their
right hand or on their foreheads,
17 and that no one may buy or sell except one
who has the mark or[a] the name of the beast, or
the number of his name.
18 Here is wisdom. Let him who has under-
standing calculate the number of the beast, for
it is the number of a man: His number *is* 666.

The Lamb and the 144,000

14 Then I looked, and behold, a[a] Lamb
standing on Mount Zion, and with Him
one hundred *and* forty-four thousand, having[b]
His Father's name written on their foreheads.
2 And I heard a voice from heaven, like the
voice of many waters, and like the voice of loud
thunder. And I heard the sound of harpists
playing their harps.
3 They sang as it were a new song before
the throne, before the four living creatures,
and the elders; and no one could learn that
song except the hundred *and* forty-four thou-
sand who were redeemed from the earth.
4 These are the ones who were not defiled
with women, for they are virgins. These are
the ones who follow the Lamb wherever He
goes. These were redeemed[a] from *among* men,
being firstfruits to God and to the Lamb.
5 And in their mouth was found no deceit,[a]
for they are without fault before the throne of
God.[b]

The Proclamations of Three Angels

6 Then I saw another angel flying in the midst
of heaven, having the everlasting gospel to
preach to those who dwell on the earth—to every
nation, tribe, tongue, and people—
7 saying with a loud voice, "Fear God and
give glory to Him, for the hour of His judgment
has come; and worship Him who made heaven
and earth, the sea and springs of water."
8 And another angel followed, saying, "Bab-
ylon[a] is fallen, is fallen, that great city, because
she has made all nations drink of the wine of
the wrath of her fornication."
9 Then a third angel followed them, saying
with a loud voice, "If anyone worships the
beast and his image, and receives *his* mark on
his forehead or on his hand,
10 "he himself shall also drink of the wine
of the wrath of God, which is poured out full
strength into the cup of His indignation. He
shall be tormented with fire and brimstone in
the presence of the holy angels and in the pres-
ence of the Lamb.
11 "And the smoke of their torment ascends
forever and ever; and they have no rest day or
night, who worship the beast and his image, and
whoever receives the mark of his name."
12 Here is the patience of the saints; here *are*
those[a] who keep the commandments of God
and the faith of Jesus.
13 Then I heard a voice from heaven saying
to me,[a] "Write: 'Blessed *are* the dead who die
in the Lord from now on.'" "Yes," says the
Spirit, "that they may rest from their labors,
and their works follow them."

Reaping the Earth's Harvest

14 Then I looked, and behold, a white cloud,
and on the cloud sat *One* like the Son of Man,
having on His head a golden crown, and in His
hand a sharp sickle.
15 And another angel came out of the temple,
crying with a loud voice to Him who sat on the
cloud, "Thrust in Your sickle and reap, for the
time has come for You[a] to reap, for the harvest
of the earth is ripe."
16 So He who sat on the cloud thrust in His
sickle on the earth, and the earth was reaped.

Reaping the Grapes of Wrath

17 Then another angel came out of the temple
which is in heaven, he also having a sharp sickle.
18 And another angel came out from the altar,
who had power over fire, and he cried with a
loud cry to him who had the sharp sickle, say-
ing, "Thrust in your sharp sickle and gather
the clusters of the vine of the earth, for her
grapes are fully ripe."
19 So the angel thrust his sickle into the earth
and gathered the vine of the earth, and threw
it into the great winepress of the wrath of God.

13:7 [a]NU-Text and M-Text add *and people.* **13:14** [a]M-Text reads *my own people.* **13:17** [a]NU-Text and M-Text omit *or.* **14:1** [a]NU-Text and M-Text read *the.* [b]NU-Text and M-Text add *His name and.* **14:4** [a]M-Text adds *by Jesus.* **14:5** [a]NU-Text and M-Text read *falsehood.* [b]NU-Text and M-Text omit *before the throne of God.* **14:8** [a]NU-Text reads *Babylon the great is fallen, is fallen, which has made;* M-Text reads *Babylon the great is fallen. She has made.* **14:12** [a]NU-Text and M-Text omit *here are those.* **14:13** [a]NU-Text and M-Text omit *to me.* **14:15** [a]NU-Text and M-Text omit *for You.*

20 And the winepress was trampled outside
the city, and blood came out of the winepress,
up to the horses' bridles, for one thousand six
hundred furlongs.

Prelude to the Bowl Judgments

15 Then I saw another sign in heaven, great
and marvelous: seven angels having the
seven last plagues, for in them the wrath of God
is complete.
2 And I saw *something* like a sea of glass min-
gled with fire, and those who have the victory
over the beast, over his image and over his
mark[a] *and* over the number of his name, stand-
ing on the sea of glass, having harps of God.
3 They sing the song of Moses, the servant
of God, and the song of the Lamb, saying:

"Great and marvelous *are* Your works,
Lord God Almighty!
Just and true *are* Your ways,
O King of the saints![a]
4 Who shall not fear You, O Lord, and
glorify Your name?
For *You* alone *are* holy.
For all nations shall come and worship
before You,
For Your judgments have been
manifested."

5 After these things I looked, and behold,[a] the
temple of the tabernacle of the testimony in
heaven was opened.
6 And out of the temple came the seven an-
gels having the seven plagues, clothed in pure
bright linen, and having their chests girded with
golden bands.
7 Then one of the four living creatures gave
to the seven angels seven golden bowls full of
the wrath of God who lives forever and ever.
8 The temple was filled with smoke from the
glory of God and from His power, and no one
was able to enter the temple till the seven
plagues of the seven angels were completed.

16 Then I heard a loud voice from the tem-
ple saying to the seven angels, "Go and
pour out the bowls[a] of the wrath of God on the
earth."

First Bowl: Loathsome Sores

2 So the first went and poured out his bowl
upon the earth, and a foul and loathsome sore
came upon the men who had the mark of the
beast and those who worshiped his image.

Second Bowl: The Sea Turns to Blood

3 Then the second angel poured out his bowl
on the sea, and it became blood as of a dead
man; and every living creature in the sea died.

Third Bowl: The Waters Turn to Blood

4 Then the third angel poured out his bowl
on the rivers and springs of water, and they
became blood.
5 And I heard the angel of the waters saying:

"You are righteous, O Lord,[a]
The One who is and who was and who is
to be,[b]
Because You have judged these things.
6 For they have shed the blood of saints
and prophets,
And You have given them blood to drink.
For[a] it is their just due."

7 And I heard another from[a] the altar saying,
"Even so, Lord God Almighty, true and righ-
teous *are* Your judgments."

Fourth Bowl: Men Are Scorched

8 Then the fourth angel poured out his bowl
on the sun, and power was given to him to scorch
men with fire.
9 And men were scorched with great heat,
and they blasphemed the name of God who
has power over these plagues; and they did not
repent and give Him glory.

Fifth Bowl: Darkness and Pain

10 Then the fifth angel poured out his bowl
on the throne of the beast, and his kingdom
became full of darkness; and they gnawed
their tongues because of the pain.
11 They blasphemed the God of heaven be-
cause of their pains and their sores, and did
not repent of their deeds.

Sixth Bowl: Euphrates Dried Up

12 Then the sixth angel poured out his bowl
on the great river Euphrates, and its water was
dried up, so that the way of the kings from the
east might be prepared.
13 And I saw three unclean spirits like frogs
coming out of the mouth of the dragon, out of
the mouth of the beast, and out of the mouth
of the false prophet.
14 For they are spirits of demons, performing
signs, *which* go out to the kings of the earth
and[a] of the whole world, to gather them to the
battle of that great day of God Almighty.
15 "Behold, I am coming as a thief. Blessed *is*
he who watches, and keeps his garments, lest
he walk naked and they see his shame."
16 And they gathered them together to the
place called in Hebrew, Armageddon.[a]

Seventh Bowl: The Earth Utterly Shaken

17 Then the seventh angel poured out his bowl
into the air, and a loud voice came out of the
temple of heaven, from the throne, saying, "It
is done!"
18 And there were noises and thunderings
and lightnings; and there was a great earth-
quake, such a mighty and great earthquake as
had not occurred since men were on the earth.
19 Now the great city was divided into three
parts, and the cities of the nations fell. And
great Babylon was remembered before God, to
give her the cup of the wine of the fierceness
of His wrath.
20 Then every island fled away, and the moun-
tains were not found.
21 And great hail from heaven fell upon men,
each hailstone about the weight of a talent.
Men blasphemed God because of the plague
of the hail, since that plague was exceedingly
great.

15:2 [a]NU-Text and M-Text omit *over his mark.* **15:3** [a]NU-Text and M-Text read *nations.* **15:5** [a]NU-Text and M-Text omit *behold.* **16:1** [a]NU-Text and M-Text read *seven bowls.* **16:5** [a]NU-Text and M-Text omit *O Lord.* [b]NU-Text and M-Text read *who was, the Holy One.* **16:6** [a]NU-Text and M-Text omit *For.* **16:7** [a]NU-Text and M-Text omit *another from.* **16:14** [a]NU-Text and M-Text omit *of the earth and.* **16:16** [a]M-Text reads *Megiddo.*

The Scarlet Woman and the Scarlet Beast

17 Then one of the seven angels who had
the seven bowls came and talked with
me, saying to me,[a] "Come, I will show you the
judgment of the great harlot who sits on many
waters,
2 "with whom the kings of the earth commit-
ted fornication, and the inhabitants of the
earth were made drunk with the wine of her
fornication."
3 So he carried me away in the Spirit into the
wilderness. And I saw a woman sitting on a
scarlet beast *which was* full of names of blas-
phemy, having seven heads and ten horns.
4 The woman was arrayed in purple and scar-
let, and adorned with gold and precious stones
and pearls, having in her hand a golden cup
full of abominations and the filthiness of her
fornication.[a]
5 And on her forehead a name *was* written:

MYSTERY,
BABYLON THE GREAT,
THE MOTHER OF HARLOTS AND OF THE
ABOMINATIONS OF THE EARTH.

6 I saw the woman, drunk with the blood of
the saints and with the blood of the martyrs of
Jesus. And when I saw her, I marveled with great
amazement.

The Meaning of the Woman and the Beast

7 But the angel said to me, "Why did you
marvel? I will tell you the mystery of the
woman and of the beast that carries her, which
has the seven heads and the ten horns.
8 "The beast that you saw was, and is not, and
will ascend out of the bottomless pit and go to
perdition. And those who dwell on the earth
will marvel, whose names are not written in
the Book of Life from the foundation of the
world, when they see the beast that was, and
is not, and yet is.[a]
9 "Here *is* the mind which has wisdom: The
seven heads are seven mountains on which the
woman sits.
10 "There are also seven kings. Five have
fallen, one is, *and* the other has not yet come.
And when he comes, he must continue a short
time.
11 "The beast that was, and is not, is himself
also the eighth, and is of the seven, and is going
to perdition.
12 "The ten horns which you saw are ten kings
who have received no kingdom as yet, but they
receive authority for one hour as kings with the
beast.
13 "These are of one mind, and they will give
their power and authority to the beast.
14 "These will make war with the Lamb, and
the Lamb will overcome them, for He is Lord
of lords and King of kings; and those *who are*
with Him *are* called, chosen, and faithful."
15 Then he said to me, "The waters which you
saw, where the harlot sits, are peoples, multi-
tudes, nations, and tongues.
16 "And the ten horns which you saw on[a] the
beast, these will hate the harlot, make her des-
olate and naked, eat her flesh and burn her
with fire.
17 "For God has put it into their hearts to
fulfill His purpose, to be of one mind, and to
give their kingdom to the beast, until the words
of God are fulfilled.
18 "And the woman whom you saw is that great
city which reigns over the kings of the earth."

The Fall of Babylon the Great

18 After these things I saw another angel
coming down from heaven, having great
authority, and the earth was illuminated with
his glory.
2 And he cried mightily[a] with a loud voice,
saying, "Babylon the great is fallen, is fallen,
and has become a dwelling place of demons, a
prison for every foul spirit, and a cage for every
unclean and hated bird!
3 "For all the nations have drunk of the wine
of the wrath of her fornication, the kings of the
earth have committed fornication with her, and
the merchants of the earth have become rich
through the abundance of her luxury."
4 And I heard another voice from heaven say-
ing, "Come out of her, my people, lest you share
in her sins, and lest you receive of her plagues.
5 "For her sins have reached[a] to heaven, and
God has remembered her iniquities.
6 "Render to her just as she rendered to you,[a]
and repay her double according to her works;
in the cup which she has mixed, mix double for
her.
7 "In the measure that she glorified herself
and lived luxuriously, in the same measure give
her torment and sorrow; for she says in her
heart, 'I sit *as* queen, and am no widow, and
will not see sorrow.'
8 "Therefore her plagues will come in one
day—death and mourning and famine. And
she will be utterly burned with fire, for strong
is the Lord God who judges[a] her.

The World Mourns Babylon's Fall

9 "The kings of the earth who committed for-
nication and lived luxuriously with her will
weep and lament for her, when they see the
smoke of her burning,
10 "standing at a distance for fear of her tor-
ment, saying, 'Alas, alas, that great city Bab-
ylon, that mighty city! For in one hour your
judgment has come.'
11 "And the merchants of the earth will weep
and mourn over her, for no one buys their mer-
chandise anymore:
12 "merchandise of gold and silver, precious
stones and pearls, fine linen and purple, silk
and scarlet, every kind of citron wood, every
kind of object of ivory, every kind of object of
most precious wood, bronze, iron, and marble;
13 "and cinnamon and incense, fragrant oil
and frankincense, wine and oil, fine flour and
wheat, cattle and sheep, horses and chariots,
and bodies and souls of men.
14 "The fruit that your soul longed for has
gone from you, and all the things which are rich

17:1 [a]NU-Text and M-Text omit *to me.* **17:4** [a]M-Text reads *the filthiness of the fornication of the earth.* **17:8** [a]NU-Text and M-Text read *and shall be present.* **17:16** [a]NU-Text and M-Text read *saw, and the beast.* **18:2** [a]NU-Text and M-Text omit *mightily.* **18:5** [a]NU-Text and M-Text read *have been heaped up.* **18:6** [a]NU-Text and M-Text omit *to you.* **18:8** [a]NU-Text and M-Text read *has judged.*

and splendid have gone from you,[a] and you
shall find them no more at all.
15 "The merchants of these things, who be-
came rich by her, will stand at a distance for
fear of her torment, weeping and wailing,
16 "and saying, 'Alas, alas, that great city that
was clothed in fine linen, purple, and scarlet,
and adorned with gold and precious stones
and pearls!
17 'For in one hour such great riches came to
nothing.' Every shipmaster, all who travel by
ship, sailors, and as many as trade on the sea,
stood at a distance
18 "and cried out when they saw the smoke
of her burning, saying, 'What *is* like this great
city?'
19 "They threw dust on their heads and cried
out, weeping and wailing, and saying, 'Alas,
alas, that great city, in which all who had ships
on the sea became rich by her wealth! For in
one hour she is made desolate.'
20 "Rejoice over her, O heaven, and *you* holy
apostles[a] and prophets, for God has avenged
you on her!"

Finality of Babylon's Fall

21 Then a mighty angel took up a stone like
a great millstone and threw *it* into the sea,
saying, "Thus with violence the great city Bab-
ylon shall be thrown down, and shall not be
found anymore.
22 "The sound of harpists, musicians, flutists,
and trumpeters shall not be heard in you any-
more. No craftsman of any craft shall be found
in you anymore, and the sound of a millstone
shall not be heard in you anymore.
23 "The light of a lamp shall not shine in you
anymore, and the voice of bridegroom and
bride shall not be heard in you anymore. For
your merchants were the great men of the
earth, for by your sorcery all the nations were
deceived.
24 "And in her was found the blood of proph-
ets and saints, and of all who were slain on the
earth."

Heaven Exults over Babylon

19 After these things I heard[a] a loud voice
of a great multitude in heaven, saying,
"Alleluia! Salvation and glory and honor and
power *belong* to the Lord[b] our God!
2 "For true and righteous *are* His judgments,
because He has judged the great harlot who
corrupted the earth with her fornication; and
He has avenged on her the blood of His servants
shed by her."
3 Again they said, "Alleluia! Her smoke rises
up forever and ever!"
4 And the twenty-four elders and the four liv-
ing creatures fell down and worshiped God who
sat on the throne, saying, "Amen! Alleluia!"
5 Then a voice came from the throne, saying,
"Praise our God, all you His servants and those
who fear Him, both[a] small and great!"
6 And I heard, as it were, the voice of a great
multitude, as the sound of many waters and as
the sound of mighty thunderings, saying, "Al-
leluia! For the[a] Lord God Omnipotent reigns!
7 "Let us be glad and rejoice and give Him
glory, for the marriage of the Lamb has come,
and His wife has made herself ready."
8 And to her it was granted to be arrayed in
fine linen, clean and bright, for the fine linen
is the righteous acts of the saints.
9 Then he said to me, "Write: 'Blessed *are*
those who are called to the marriage supper of
the Lamb!'" And he said to me, "These are the
true sayings of God."
10 And I fell at his feet to worship him. But
he said to me, "See *that you do* not *do that!* I
am your fellow servant, and of your brethren
who have the testimony of Jesus. Worship God!
For the testimony of Jesus is the spirit of
prophecy."

Christ on a White Horse

11 Now I saw heaven opened, and behold, a
white horse. And He who sat on him *was* called
Faithful and True, and in righteousness He
judges and makes war.
12 His eyes *were* like a flame of fire, and on
His head *were* many crowns. He had[a] a name
written that no one knew except Himself.
13 He *was* clothed with a robe dipped in
blood, and His name is called The Word of God.
14 And the armies in heaven, clothed in fine
linen, white and clean,[a] followed Him on white
horses.
15 Now out of His mouth goes a sharp[a] sword,
that with it He should strike the nations. And
He Himself will rule them with a rod of iron. He
Himself treads the winepress of the fierceness
and wrath of Almighty God.
16 And He has on *His* robe and on His thigh
a name written:

KING OF KINGS
AND LORD OF LORDS.

The Beast and His Armies Defeated

17 Then I saw an angel standing in the sun;
and he cried with a loud voice, saying to all the
birds that fly in the midst of heaven, "Come and
gather together for the supper of the great
God,[a]
18 "that you may eat the flesh of kings, the flesh
of captains, the flesh of mighty men, the flesh
of horses and of those who sit on them, and
the flesh of all *people,* free[a] and slave, both small
and great."
19 And I saw the beast, the kings of the earth,
and their armies, gathered together to make
war against Him who sat on the horse and
against His army.
20 Then the beast was captured, and with him
the false prophet who worked signs in his pres-
ence, by which he deceived those who received
the mark of the beast and those who worshiped
his image. These two were cast alive into the
lake of fire burning with brimstone.
21 And the rest were killed with the sword
which proceeded from the mouth of Him who
sat on the horse. And all the birds were filled
with their flesh.

18:14 [a]NU-Text and M-Text read *been lost to you.* **18:20** [a]NU-Text and M-Text read *saints and apostles.*
19:1 [a]NU-Text and M-Text add *something like.* [b]NU-Text and M-Text omit *the Lord.* **19:5** [a]NU-Text and M-Text omit *both.* **19:6** [a]NU-Text and M-Text read *our.* **19:12** [a]M-Text adds *names written, and.* **19:14** [a]NU-Text and M-Text read *pure white linen.* **19:15** [a]M-Text adds *two-edged.* **19:17** [a]NU-Text and M-Text read *the great supper of God.*
19:18 [a]NU-Text and M-Text read *both free.*

Satan Bound 1000 Years

20 Then I saw an angel coming down from
heaven, having the key to the bottom-
less pit and a great chain in his hand.
2 He laid hold of the dragon, that serpent of
old, who is *the* Devil and Satan, and bound
him for a thousand years;
3 and he cast him into the bottomless pit, and
shut him up, and set a seal on him, so that he
should deceive the nations no more till the
thousand years were finished. But after these
things he must be released for a little while.

The Saints Reign with Christ 1000 Years

4 And I saw thrones, and they sat on them,
and judgment was committed to them. Then *I*
saw the souls of those who had been beheaded
for their witness to Jesus and for the word of
God, who had not worshiped the beast or his
image, and had not received *his* mark on their
foreheads or on their hands. And they lived
and reigned with Christ for a[a] thousand years.
5 But the rest of the dead did not live again
until the thousand years were finished. This *is*
the first resurrection.
6 Blessed and holy *is* he who has part in the
first resurrection. Over such the second death
has no power, but they shall be priests of God
and of Christ, and shall reign with Him a thou-
sand years.

Satanic Rebellion Crushed

7 Now when the thousand years have ex-
pired, Satan will be released from his prison
8 and will go out to deceive the nations which
are in the four corners of the earth, Gog and
Magog, to gather them together to battle, whose
number *is* as the sand of the sea.
9 They went up on the breadth of the earth
and surrounded the camp of the saints and the
beloved city. And fire came down from God
out of heaven and devoured them.
10 The devil, who deceived them, was cast into
the lake of fire and brimstone where[a] the beast
and the false prophet *are*. And they will be
tormented day and night forever and ever.

The Great White Throne Judgment

11 Then I saw a great white throne and Him
who sat on it, from whose face the earth and
the heaven fled away. And there was found no
place for them.
12 And I saw the dead, small and great, stand-
ing before God,[a] and books were opened. And
another book was opened, which is *the Book*
of Life. And the dead were judged according
to their works, by the things which were writ-
ten in the books.
13 The sea gave up the dead who were in it,
and Death and Hades delivered up the dead
who were in them. And they were judged, each
one according to his works.
14 Then Death and Hades were cast into the
lake of fire. This is the second death.[a]
15 And anyone not found written in the Book
of Life was cast into the lake of fire.

All Things Made New

21 Now I saw a new heaven and a new
earth, for the first heaven and the first
earth had passed away. Also there was no more
sea.
2 Then I, John,[a] saw the holy city, New Jeru-
salem, coming down out of heaven from God,
prepared as a bride adorned for her husband.
3 And I heard a loud voice from heaven say-
ing, "Behold, the tabernacle of God *is* with men,
and He will dwell with them, and they shall be
His people. God Himself will be with them *and*
be their God.
4 "And God will wipe away every tear from
their eyes; there shall be no more death, nor
sorrow, nor crying. There shall be no more pain,
for the former things have passed away."
5 Then He who sat on the throne said, "Be-
hold, I make all things new." And He said to me,[a]
"Write, for these words are true and faithful."
6 And He said to me, "It is done![a] I am the
Alpha and the Omega, the Beginning and the
End. I will give of the fountain of the water of
life freely to him who thirsts.
7 "He who overcomes shall inherit all things,[a]
and I will be his God and he shall be My son.
8 "But the cowardly, unbelieving,[a] abomina-
ble, murderers, sexually immoral, sorcerers,
idolaters, and all liars shall have their part in
the lake which burns with fire and brimstone,
which is the second death."

The New Jerusalem

9 Then one of the seven angels who had the
seven bowls filled with the seven last plagues
came to me[a] and talked with me, saying, "Come,
I will show you the bride, the Lamb's wife."[b]
10 And he carried me away in the Spirit to a
great and high mountain, and showed me the
great city, the holy[a] Jerusalem, descending out
of heaven from God,
11 having the glory of God. Her light *was* like
a most precious stone, like a jasper stone, clear
as crystal.
12 Also she had a great and high wall with
twelve gates, and twelve angels at the gates, and
names written on them, which are *the names*
of the twelve tribes of the children of Israel:
13 three gates on the east, three gates on the
north, three gates on the south, and three gates
on the west.
14 Now the wall of the city had twelve foun-
dations, and on them were the names[a] of the
twelve apostles of the Lamb.
15 And he who talked with me had a gold reed
to measure the city, its gates, and its wall.
16 The city is laid out as a square; its length
is as great as its breadth. And he measured the
city with the reed: twelve thousand furlongs.
Its length, breadth, and height are equal.
17 Then he measured its wall: one hundred *and*
forty-four cubits, *according* to the measure of
a man, that is, of an angel.
18 The construction of its wall was *of* jasper;
and the city *was* pure gold, like clear glass.

20:4 [a]M-Text reads *the*. **20:10** [a]NU-Text and M-Text add *also*. **20:12** [a]NU-Text and M-Text read *the throne*. **20:14** [a]NU-Text and M-Text add *the lake of fire*. **21:2** [a]NU-Text and M-Text omit *John*. **21:5** [a]NU-Text and M-Text omit *to me*. **21:6** [a]M-Text omits *It is done*. **21:7** [a]M-Text reads *overcomes, I shall give him these things*. **21:8** [a]M-Text adds *and sinners*. **21:9** [a]NU-Text and M-Text omit *to me*. [b]M-Text reads *I will show you the woman, the Lamb's bride*. **21:10** [a]NU-Text and M-Text omit *the great* and read *the holy city, Jerusalem*. **21:14** [a]NU-Text and M-Text read *twelve names*.

19 The foundations of the wall of the city *were* adorned with all kinds of precious stones: the first foundation *was* jasper, the second sapphire, the third chalcedony, the fourth emerald,
20 the fifth sardonyx, the sixth sardius, the seventh chrysolite, the eighth beryl, the ninth topaz, the tenth chrysoprase, the eleventh jacinth, and the twelfth amethyst.
21 The twelve gates *were* twelve pearls: each individual gate was of one pearl. And the street of the city *was* pure gold, like transparent glass.

The Glory of the New Jerusalem

22 But I saw no temple in it, for the Lord God Almighty and the Lamb are its temple.
23 The city had no need of the sun or of the moon to shine in it,[a] for the glory[b] of God illuminated it. The Lamb *is* its light.
24 And the nations of those who are saved[a] shall walk in its light, and the kings of the earth bring their glory and honor into it.[b]
25 Its gates shall not be shut at all by day (there shall be no night there).
26 And they shall bring the glory and the honor of the nations into it.[a]
27 But there shall by no means enter it anything that defiles, or causes[a] an abomination or a lie, but only those who are written in the Lamb's Book of Life.

The River of Life

22 And he showed me a pure[a] river of water of life, clear as crystal, proceeding from the throne of God and of the Lamb.
2 In the middle of its street, and on either side of the river, *was* the tree of life, which bore twelve fruits, each *tree* yielding its fruit every month. The leaves of the tree *were* for the healing of the nations.
3 And there shall be no more curse, but the throne of God and of the Lamb shall be in it, and His servants shall serve Him.
4 They shall see His face, and His name *shall be* on their foreheads.
5 There shall be no night there: They need no lamp nor light of the sun, for the Lord God gives them light. And they shall reign forever and ever.

The Time Is Near

6 Then he said to me, "These words *are* faithful and true." And the Lord God of the holy[a] prophets sent His angel to show His servants the things which must shortly take place.
7 "Behold, I am coming quickly! Blessed *is* he who keeps the words of the prophecy of this book."
8 Now I, John, saw and heard[a] these things. And when I heard and saw, I fell down to worship before the feet of the angel who showed me these things.
9 Then he said to me, "See *that you do* not *do that.* For[a] I am your fellow servant, and of your brethren the prophets, and of those who keep the words of this book. Worship God."
10 And he said to me, "Do not seal the words of the prophecy of this book, for the time is at hand.
11 "He who is unjust, let him be unjust still; he who is filthy, let him be filthy still; he who is righteous, let him be righteous[a] still; he who is holy, let him be holy still."

Jesus Testifies to the Churches

12 "And behold, I am coming quickly, and My reward *is* with Me, to give to every one according to his work.
13 "I am the Alpha and the Omega, *the* Beginning and *the* End, the First and the Last."[a]
14 Blessed *are* those who do His commandments,[a] that they may have the right to the tree of life, and may enter through the gates into the city.
15 But[a] outside *are* dogs and sorcerers and sexually immoral and murderers and idolaters, and whoever loves and practices a lie.
16 "I, Jesus, have sent My angel to testify to you these things in the churches. I am the Root and the Offspring of David, the Bright and Morning Star."
17 And the Spirit and the bride say, "Come!" And let him who hears say, "Come!" And let him who thirsts come. Whoever desires, let him take the water of life freely.

A Warning

18 For[a] I testify to everyone who hears the words of the prophecy of this book: If anyone adds to these things, God will add[b] to him the plagues that are written in this book;
19 and if anyone takes away from the words of the book of this prophecy, God shall take away[a] his part from the Book[b] of Life, from the holy city, and *from* the things which are written in this book.

I Am Coming Quickly

20 He who testifies to these things says, "Surely I am coming quickly." Amen. Even so, come, Lord Jesus!
21 The grace of our Lord Jesus Christ *be* with you all.[a] Amen.

21:23 [a]NU-Text and M-Text omit *in it.* [b]M-Text reads *the very glory.* **21:24** [a]NU-Text and M-Text omit *of those who are saved.* [b]M-Text reads *the glory and honor of the nations to Him.* **21:26** [a]M-Text adds *that they may enter in.* **21:27** [a]NU-Text and M-Text read *anything profane, nor one who causes.* **22:1** [a]NU-Text and M-Text omit *pure.* **22:6** [a]NU-Text and M-Text read *spirits of the prophets.* **22:8** [a]NU-Text and M-Text read *am the one who heard and saw.* **22:9** [a]NU-Text and M-Text omit *For.* **22:11** [a]NU-Text and M-Text read *do right.* **22:13** [a]NU-Text and M-Text read *the First and the Last, the Beginning and the End.* **22:14** [a]NU-Text reads *wash their robes.* **22:15** [a]NU-Text and M-Text omit *But.* **22:18** [a]NU-Text and M-Text omit *For.* [b]M-text reads *may God add.* **22:19** [a]M-Text reads *may God take away.* [b]NU-Text and M-Text read *tree of life.* **22:21** [a]NU-Text reads *with all;* M-Text reads *with all the saints.*

Read Your Bible Through in a Year

A systematic division of the books of the Bible, primarily for reading.

JANUARY

Date	MORNING	EVENING
	MATT.	GEN.
1	1	1, 2, 3
2	2	4, 5, 6
3	3	7, 8, 9
4	4	10, 11, 12
5	5: 1–26	13, 14, 15
6	5:27–48	16, 17
7	6: 1–18	18, 19
8	6:19–34	20, 21, 22
9	7	23, 24
10	8: 1–17	25, 26
11	8:18–34	27, 28
12	9: 1–17	29, 30
13	9:18–38	31, 32
14	10: 1–20	33, 34, 35
15	10:21–42	36, 37, 38
16	11	39, 40
17	12: 1–23	41, 42
18	12:24–50	43, 44, 45
19	13: 1–30	46, 47, 48
20	13:31–58	49, 50
		EX.
21	14: 1–21	1, 2, 3
22	14:22–36	4, 5, 6
23	15: 1–20	7, 8
24	15:21–39	9, 10, 11
25	16	12, 13
26	17	14, 15
27	18: 1–20	16, 17, 18
28	18:21–35	19, 20
29	19	21, 22
30	20: 1–16	23, 24
31	20:17–34	25, 26

FEBRUARY

Date	MORNING	EVENING
	MATT.	EX.
1	21: 1–22	27, 28
2	21:23–46	29, 30
3	22: 1–22	31, 32, 33
4	22:23–46	34, 35
5	23: 1–22	36, 37, 38
6	23:23–39	39, 40
		LEV.
7	24: 1–28	1, 2, 3
8	24:29–51	4, 5
9	25: 1–30	6, 7
10	25:31–46	8, 9, 10
11	26: 1–25	11, 12
12	26:26–50	13
13	26:51–75	14
14	27: 1–26	15, 16
15	27:27–50	17, 18
16	27:51–66	19, 20
17	28	21, 22
	MARK	
18	1: 1–22	23, 24
19	1:23–45	25
20	2	26, 27
		NUM.
21	3: 1–19	1, 2
22	3:20–35	3, 4
23	4: 1–20	5, 6
24	4:21–41	7, 8
25	5: 1–20	9, 10, 11
26	5:21–43	12, 13, 14
27	6: 1–29	15, 16
28	6:30–56	17, 18, 19
29	7: 1–13	20, 21, 22

MARCH

Date	MORNING	EVENING
	MARK	NUM.
1	7:14–37	23, 24, 25
2	8: 1–21	26, 27
3	8:22–38	28, 29, 30
4	9: 1–29	31, 32, 33
5	9:30–50	34, 35, 36
		DEUT.
6	10: 1–31	1, 2
7	10:32–52	3, 4
8	11: 1–18	5, 6, 7
9	11:19–33	8, 9, 10
10	12: 1–27	11, 12, 13
11	12:28–44	14, 15, 16
12	13: 1–20	17, 18, 19
13	13:21–37	20, 21, 22
14	14: 1–26	23, 24, 25
15	14:27–53	26, 27
16	14:54–72	28, 29
17	15: 1–25	30, 31
18	15:26–47	32, 33, 34
		JOSH.
19	16	1, 2, 3
	LUKE	
20	1: 1–20	4, 5, 6
21	1:21–38	7, 8, 9
22	1:39–56	10, 11, 12
23	1:57–80	13, 14, 15
24	2: 1–24	16, 17, 18
25	2:25–52	19, 20, 21
26	3	22, 23, 24
		JUDG.
27	4: 1–30	1, 2, 3
28	4:31–44	4, 5, 6
29	5: 1–16	7, 8
30	5:17–39	9, 10
31	6: 1–26	11, 12

APRIL

Date	MORNING	EVENING
	LUKE	JUDG.
1	6:27–49	13, 14, 15
2	7: 1–30	16, 17, 18
3	7:31–50	19, 20, 21
		RUTH
4	8: 1–25	1, 2, 3, 4
		1 SAM.
5	8:26–56	1, 2, 3
6	9: 1–17	4, 5, 6
7	9:18–36	7, 8, 9
8	9:37–62	10, 11, 12
9	10: 1–24	13, 14
10	10:25–42	15, 16
11	11: 1–28	17, 18
12	11:29–54	19, 20, 21
13	12: 1–31	22, 23, 24
14	12:32–59	25, 26
15	13: 1–22	27, 28, 29
16	13:23–35	30, 31
		2 SAM.
17	14: 1–24	1, 2
18	14:25–35	3, 4, 5
19	15: 1–10	6, 7, 8
20	15:11–32	9, 10, 11
21	16	12, 13
22	17: 1–19	14, 15
23	17:20–37	16, 17, 18
24	18: 1–23	19, 20
25	18:24–43	21, 22
26	19: 1–27	23, 24
		1 KIN.
27	19:28–48	1, 2
28	20: 1–26	3, 4, 5
29	20:27–47	6, 7
30	21: 1–19	8, 9

MAY

Date	MORNING	EVENING
	LUKE	1 KIN.
1	21:20–38	10, 11
2	22: 1–20	12, 13
3	22:21–46	14, 15
4	22:47–71	16, 17, 18
5	23: 1–25	19, 20
6	23:26–56	21, 22
		2 KIN.
7	24: 1–35	1, 2, 3
8	24:36–53	4, 5, 6
	JOHN	
9	1: 1–28	7, 8, 9
10	1:29–51	10, 11, 12
11	2	13, 14
12	3: 1–18	15, 16
13	3:19–38	17, 18
14	4: 1–30	19, 20, 21
15	4:31–54	22, 23
16	5: 1–24	24, 25
		1 CHR.
17	5:25–47	1, 2, 3
18	6: 1–21	4, 5, 6
19	6:22–44	7, 8, 9
20	6:45–71	10, 11, 12
21	7: 1–27	13, 14, 15
22	7:28–53	16, 17, 18
23	8: 1–27	19, 20, 21
24	8:28–59	22, 23, 24
25	9: 1–23	25, 26, 27
26	9:24–41	28, 29
		2 CHR.
27	10: 1–23	1, 2, 3
28	10:24–42	4, 5, 6
29	11: 1–29	7, 8, 9
30	11:30–57	10, 11, 12
31	12: 1–26	13, 14

JUNE

Date	MORNING	EVENING
	JOHN	2 CHR.
1	12:27–50	15, 16
2	13: 1–20	17, 18
3	13:21–38	19, 20
4	14	21, 22
5	15	23, 24
6	16	25, 26, 27
7	17	28, 29
8	18: 1–18	30, 31
9	18:19–40	32, 33
10	19: 1–22	34, 35, 36
		EZRA
11	19:23–42	1, 2
12	20	3, 4, 5
13	21	6, 7, 8
	ACTS	
14	1	9, 10
		NEH.
15	2: 1–21	1, 2, 3
16	2:22–47	4, 5, 6
17	3	7, 8, 9
18	4: 1–22	10, 11
19	4:23–37	12, 13
		ESTH.
20	5: 1–21	1, 2
21	5:22–42	3, 4, 5
22	6	6, 7, 8
23	7: 1–21	9, 10
		JOB
24	7:22–43	1, 2
25	7:44–60	3, 4
26	8: 1–25	5, 6, 7
27	8:26–40	8, 9, 10
28	9: 1–21	11, 12, 13
29	9:22–43	14, 15, 16
30	10: 1–23	17, 18, 19

JULY

Date	MORNING	EVENING
	ACTS	JOB
1	10:24–48	20, 21
2	11	22, 23, 24
3	12	25, 26, 27
4	13: 1–25	28, 29
5	13:26–52	30, 31
6	14	32, 33
7	15: 1–21	34, 35
8	15:22–41	36, 37
9	16: 1–21	38, 39, 40
10	16:22–40	41, 42
		PS.
11	17: 1–15	1, 2, 3
12	17:16–34	4, 5, 6
13	18	7, 8, 9
14	19: 1–20	10, 11, 12
15	19:21–41	13, 14, 15
16	20: 1–16	16, 17
17	20:17–38	18, 19
18	21: 1–17	20, 21, 22
19	21:18–40	23, 24, 25
20	22	26, 27, 28
21	23: 1–15	29, 30
22	23:16–35	31, 32
23	24	33, 34
24	25	35, 36
25	26	37, 38, 39
26	27: 1–26	40, 41, 42
27	27:27–44	43, 44, 45
28	28	46, 47, 48
	ROM.	
29	1	49, 50
30	2	51, 52, 53
31	3	54, 55, 56

AUGUST

Date	MORNING	EVENING
	ROM.	PS.
1	4	57, 58, 59
2	5	60, 61, 62
3	6	63, 64, 65
4	7	66, 67
5	8: 1–21	68, 69
6	8:22–39	70, 71
7	9: 1–15	72, 73
8	9:16–33	74, 75, 76
9	10	77, 78
10	11: 1–18	79, 80
11	11:19–36	81, 82, 83
12	12	84, 85, 86
13	13	87, 88
14	14	89, 90
15	15: 1–13	91, 92, 93
16	15:14–33	94, 95, 96
17	16	97, 98, 99
	1 COR.	
18	1	100, 101, 102
19	2	103, 104
20	3	105, 106
21	4	107, 108, 109
22	5	110, 111, 112
23	6	113, 114, 115
24	7: 1–19	116, 117, 118
25	7:20–40	119: 1– 88
26	8	119: 89–176
27	9	120, 121, 122
28	10: 1–18	123, 124, 125
29	10:19–33	126, 127, 128
30	11: 1–16	129, 130, 131
31	11:17–34	132, 133, 134

SEPTEMBER

Date	MORNING	EVENING
	1 COR.	PS.
1	12	135, 136
2	13	137, 138, 139
3	14: 1–20	140, 141, 142
4	14:21–40	143, 144, 145
5	15: 1–28	146, 147
6	15:29–58	148, 149, 150
		PROV.
7	16	1, 2
	2 COR.	
8	1	3, 4, 5
9	2	6, 7
10	3	8, 9
11	4	10, 11, 12
12	5	13, 14, 15
13	6	16, 17, 18
14	7	19, 20, 21
15	8	22, 23, 24
16	9	25, 26
17	10	27, 28, 29
18	11: 1–15	30, 31
		ECCL.
19	11:16–33	1, 2, 3
20	12	4, 5, 6
21	13	7, 8, 9
	GAL.	
22	1	10, 11, 12
		SONG
23	2	1, 2, 3
24	3	4, 5
25	4	6, 7, 8
		IS.
26	5	1, 2
27	6	3, 4
	EPH.	
28	1	5, 6
29	2	7, 8
30	3	9, 10

OCTOBER

Date	MORNING	EVENING
	EPH.	IS.
1	4	11, 12, 13
2	5: 1–16	14, 15, 16
3	5:17–33	17, 18, 19
4	6	20, 21, 22
	PHIL.	
5	1	23, 24, 25
6	2	26, 27
7	3	28, 29
8	4	30, 31
	COL.	
9	1	32, 33
10	2	34, 35, 36
11	3	37, 38
12	4	39, 40
	1 THESS.	
13	1	41, 42
14	2	43, 44
15	3	45, 46
16	4	47, 48, 49
17	5	50, 51, 52
	2 THESS.	
18	1	53, 54, 55
19	2	56, 57, 58
20	3	59, 60, 61
	1 TIM.	
21	1	62, 63, 64
22	2	65, 66
		JER.
23	3	1, 2
24	4	3, 4, 5
25	5	6, 7, 8
26	6	9, 10, 11
	2 TIM.	
27	1	12, 13, 14
28	2	15, 16, 17
29	3	18, 19
30	4	20, 21
	TITUS	
31	1	22, 23

NOVEMBER

Date	MORNING	EVENING
	TITUS	JER.
1	2	24, 25, 26
2	3	27, 28, 29
3	PHILEM.	30, 31
	HEB.	
4	1	32, 33
5	2	34, 35, 36
6	3	37, 38, 39
7	4	40, 41, 42
8	5	43, 44, 45
9	6	46, 47
10	7	48, 49
11	8	50
12	9	51, 52
		LAM.
13	10: 1–18	1, 2
14	10:19–39	3, 4, 5
		EZEK.
15	11: 1–19	1, 2
16	11:20–40	3, 4
17	12	5, 6, 7
18	13	8, 9, 10
	JAMES	
19	1	11, 12, 13
20	2	14, 15
21	3	16, 17
22	4	18, 19
23	5	20, 21
	1 PET.	
24	1	22, 23
25	2	24, 25, 26
26	3	27, 28, 29
27	4	30, 31, 32
28	5	33, 34
	2 PET.	
29	1	35, 36
30	2	37, 38, 39

DECEMBER

Date	MORNING	EVENING
	2 PET.	EZEK.
1	3	40, 41
	1 JOHN	
2	1	42, 43, 44
3	2	45, 46
4	3	47, 48
		DAN.
5	4	1, 2
6	5	3, 4
7	2 JOHN	5, 6, 7
8	3 JOHN	8, 9, 10
9	JUDE	11, 12
	REV.	HOS.
10	1	1, 2, 3, 4
11	2	5, 6, 7, 8
12	3	9, 10, 11
13	4	12, 13, 14
14	5	JOEL
		AMOS
15	6	1, 2, 3
16	7	4, 5, 6
17	8	7, 8, 9
18	9	OBAD.
19	10	JON.
		MIC.
20	11	1, 2, 3
21	12	4, 5
22	13	6, 7
23	14	NAH.
24	15	HAB.
25	16	ZEPH.
26	17	HAG.
		ZECH.
27	18	1, 2, 3, 4
28	19	5, 6, 7, 8
29	20	9, 10, 11, 12
30	21	13, 14
31	22	MAL.

CONCORDANCE

New King James Version

A

ABASED
I know how to be *a* .... Phil 4:12

ABBA
And He said, "*A* .... Mark 14:36
whom we cry out, "*A* ..... Rom 8:15

ABHOR
Therefore I *a* myself ...... Job 42:6

ABHORRED
a His own inheritance .... Ps 106:40

ABIDE
the Most High Shall *a* ...... Ps 91:1
Him, "If you *a* .... John 8:31
"If you *a* in Me .... John 15:7
a in My love .... John 15:9

ABIDES
He who *a* in Me .... John 15:5
will of God *a* forever ... 1 John 2:17

ABIDING
not have His word *a* ...... John 5:38

ABILITY
to his own *a* .... Matt 25:15
a which God supplies .... 1 Pet 4:11

ABLE
shall give as he is *a* ..... Deut 16:17
whom we serve is *a* .... Dan 3:17
God is *a* to raise up ...... Matt 3:9
fear Him who is *a* ..... Matt 10:28
you *a* to drink the .... Matt 20:22
that He is *a* .... 2 Tim 1:12
learning and never *a* ..... 2 Tim 3:7
that God was *a* to .... Heb 11:19

ABOLISHED
having *a* in His flesh ..... Eph 2:15
Christ, who has *a* .... 2 Tim 1:10

ABOMINABLE
deny Him, being *a* .... Titus 1:16
unbelieving, *a* .... Rev 21:8

ABOMINATION
Yes, seven are an *a* ...... Prov 6:16
the scoffer is an *a* .... Prov 24:9
prayer is an *a* .... Prov 28:9
and place there the *a* .... Dan 11:31
the *a* of desolation ...... Dan 12:11
the '*a* of desolation,' ..... Matt 24:15

ABOMINATIONS
delights in their *a* .... Is 66:3
a golden cup full of *a* ...... Rev 17:4

ABOUND
the offense might *a* .... Rom 5:20
sin that grace may *a* .... Rom 6:1
to make all grace *a* .... 2 Cor 9:8
and I know how to *a* ...... Phil 4:12

ABOUNDED
But where sin *a* .... Rom 5:20

ABOUNDING
immovable, always *a* ... 1 Cor 15:58

ABOVE
that is in heaven *a* .... Ex 20:4
A it stood seraphim .... Is 6:2
"He who comes from *a* ... John 3:31
I am from *a* .... John 8:23
given you from *a* .... John 19:11
things which are *a* .... Col 3:1
perfect gift is from *a* .... James 1:17

ABSENT
in the body we are *a* ..... 2 Cor 5:6

ABSTAIN
we write to them to *a* .... Acts 15:20
A from every form .... 1 Thess 5:22

ABUNDANCE
put in out of their *a* .... Mark 12:44
not consist in the *a* ...... Luke 12:15

ABUNDANT
in labors more *a* .... 2 Cor 11:23

ABUNDANTLY
a satisfied with the .... Ps 36:8
may have it more *a* ...... John 10:10
to do exceedingly *a* .... Eph 3:20

ACCEPT
offering, I will not *a* .... Jer 14:12
Should I *a* this from .... Mal 1:13

ACCEPTABLE
a time I have heard .... Is 49:8
proclaim the *a* year .... Is 61:2
proclaim the *a* year ...... Luke 4:19
is that good and *a* .... Rom 12:2

ACCEPTABLY
we may serve God *a* ...... Heb 12:28

ACCEPTED
Behold, now is the *a* ..... 2 Cor 6:2
which He made us *a* .... Eph 1:6

ACCESS
whom also we have *a* ..... Rom 5:2

ACCOMPLISHED
all things were now *a* ... John 19:28

ACCORD
continued with one *a* ..... Acts 1:14

ACCOUNT
they will give *a* .... Matt 12:36
put that on my *a* .... Philem 18

ACCOUNTED
in the LORD, and He *a* ..... Gen 15:6
his faith is *a* .... Rom 4:5
God, and it was *a* .... Gal 3:6
God, and it was *a* .... James 2:23

ACCURSED
not know the law is *a* .... John 7:49
of God calls Jesus *a* ..... 1 Cor 12:3
to you, let him be *a* .... Gal 1:8

ACCUSATION
over His head the *a* ..... Matt 27:37
they might find an *a* .... Luke 6:7

ACCUSE
they began to *a* Him ..... Luke 23:2

ACCUSED
while He was being *a* ... Matt 27:12

ACCUSER
a of our brethren .... Rev 12:10

ACCUSING
their thoughts *a* .... Rom 2:15

ACKNOWLEDGE
a my transgressions .... Ps 51:3
In all your ways *a* .... Prov 3:6

ACKNOWLEDGES
a the Son has the .... 1 John 2:23

ACQUAINT
a yourself with Him ...... Job 22:21

ACQUAINTED
A Man of sorrows and *a* ..... Is 53:3

ACQUIT
at all *a* the wicked .... Nah 1:3

ACT
in the very *a* .... John 8:4

ACTIONS
by Him *a* are weighed .... 1 Sam 2:3

ACTS
of Your awesome *a* .... Ps 145:6

ADD
Do not *a* to His words .... Prov 30:6

ADDED
And the Lord *a* to the .... Acts 2:47
It was *a* because of .... Gal 3:19

ADMONISH
a him as a .... 2 Thess 3:15

ADMONITION
written for our *a* .... 1 Cor 10:11
in the training and *a* .... Eph 6:4

ADOPTION
the Spirit of *a* .... Rom 8:15
waiting for the *a* .... Rom 8:23
to whom pertain the *a* ..... Rom 9:4

ADORN
also, that the women *a* ... 1 Tim 2:9

ADORNED
God also *a* themselves .... 1 Pet 3:5
prepared as a bride *a* ...... Rev 21:2

ADRIFT
A among the dead .... Ps 88:5

ADULTERER
The eye of the *a* .... Job 24:15

ADULTERERS
nor idolaters, nor *a* .... 1 Cor 6:9
a God will judge .... Heb 13:4

ADULTEROUS
a generation .... Matt 12:39

ADULTERY
You shall not commit *a* .... Ex 20:14
already committed *a* ..... Matt 5:28
is divorced commits *a* .... Matt 5:32
another commits *a* ..... Mark 10:11
those who commit *a* .... Rev 2:22

ADVANTAGE
a that I go away .... John 16:7
Satan should take *a* ..... 2 Cor 2:11

ADVERSARIES
and there are many *a* ... 1 Cor 16:9
terrified by your *a* .... Phil 1:28

ADVERSARY
"Agree with your *a* .... Matt 5:25
opportunity to the *a* ..... 1 Tim 5:14
a the devil walks .... 1 Pet 5:8

ADVERSITY
I shall never be in *a* .... Ps 10:6
the day of *a* consider ...... Eccl 7:14

ADVICE
in this I give my *a* ...... 2 Cor 8:10

ADVOCATE
sins, we have an *A* ...... 1 John 2:1

AFAR
and not a God *a* .... Jer 23:23
to you who were *a* .... Eph 2:17
having seen them *a* ...... Heb 11:13

AFFAIRS
himself with the *a* .... 2 Tim 2:4

AFFECTION
to his wife the *a* .... 1 Cor 7:3

AFFECTIONATE
Be kindly *a* to one .... Rom 12:10

AFFIRM
you to *a* constantly .... Titus 3:8

AFFLICT
a Your heritage .... Ps 94:5
For He does not *a* .... Lam 3:33

AFFLICTED
To him who is *a* .... Job 6:14
hears the cry of the *a* ..... Job 34:28
days of the *a* are evil .... Prov 15:15
Smitten by God, and *a* ...... Is 53:4
"O you *a* one .... Is 54:11
being destitute, *a* .... Heb 11:37

AFFLICTING
A the just and taking .... Amos 5:12

Concordance copyright © 1995 by Thomas Nelson, Inc.

AFFLICTION
is, the bread of *a* ... Deut 16:3
a take hold of me ... Job 30:16
and it is an evil *a* ... Eccl 6:2
For our light *a* ... 2 Cor 4:17
supposing to add *a* ... Phil 1:16

AFRAID
garden, and I was *a* ... Gen 3:10
saying, "Do not be *a* ... Gen 15:1
none will make you *a* ... Lev 26:6
ungodliness made me *a* ... Ps 18:4
Whenever I am *a* ... Ps 56:3
one will make them *a* ... Is 17:2
do not be *a* ... Matt 14:27
if you do evil, be *a* ... Rom 13:4
do good and are not *a* ... 1 Pet 3:6

AFTERWARD
a receive me to glory ... Ps 73:24
you shall follow Me *a* ... John 13:36

AGAIN
'You must be born *a* ... John 3:7
having been born *a* ... 1 Pet 1:23

AGAINST
come to 'set a man *a* ... Matt 10:35
or house divided *a* ... Matt 12:25
Me is *a* Me ... Matt 12:30
a the Spirit will not ... Matt 12:31
lifted up his heel *a* ... John 13:18
LORD and *a* His Christ ... Acts 4:26
to kick *a* the goads ... Acts 9:5
a the promises of God ... Gal 3:21
we do not wrestle *a* ... Eph 6:12
I have a few things *a* ... Rev 2:20

AGE
the grave at a full *a* ... Job 5:26
and in the *a* to come ... Mark 10:30

AGED
a one as Paul, the *a* ... Philem 9

AGES
ordained before the *a* ... 1 Cor 2:7

AGONY
And being in *a* ... Luke 22:44

AGREE
that if two of you *a* ... Matt 18:19

AGREED
unless they are *a* ... Amos 3:3

AGREEMENT
what *a* has the temple ... 2 Cor 6:16

AIR
the birds of the *a* ... Gen 1:26
of the *a* have nests ... Luke 9:58
of the power of the *a* ... Eph 2:2
the Lord in the *a* ... 1 Thess 4:17

ALIENATED
darkened, being *a* ... Eph 4:18
you, who once were *a* ... Col 1:21

ALIENS
A have devoured his ... Hos 7:9
Christ, being *a* ... Eph 2:12

ALIKE
esteems every day *a* ... Rom 14:5

ALIVE
I kill and I make *a* ... Deut 32:39
was dead and is *a* ... Luke 15:24
presented Himself *a* ... Acts 1:3
indeed to sin, but *a* ... Rom 6:11
all shall be made *a* ... 1 Cor 15:22
that we who are *a* ... 1 Thess 4:15
and behold, I am *a* ... Rev 1:18
These two were cast *a* ... Rev 19:20

ALLELUIA
Again they said, "*A* ... Rev 19:3

ALLOW
a Your Holy One ... Ps 16:10
a My faithfulness ... Ps 89:33
a Your Holy One ... Acts 2:27

ALLURE
of emptiness, they *a* ... 2 Pet 2:18

ALMOND
a tree blossoms ... Eccl 12:5

ALMOST
a persuade me to ... Acts 26:28

ALOES
of myrrh and *a* ... John 19:39

ALPHA
"I am the *A* and the ... Rev 1:8
"I am the *A* and the ... Rev 22:13

ALTAR
Then Noah built an *a* ... Gen 8:20
'An *a* of earth you ... Ex 20:24
it to you upon the *a* ... Lev 17:11
your gift to the *a* ... Matt 5:23
swears by the *a* ... Matt 23:18
I even found an *a* ... Acts 17:23
We have an *a* from ... Heb 13:10

ALTARS
Even Your *a*, O LORD ... Ps 84:3
and torn down Your *a* ... Rom 11:3

ALTERED
of His face was *a* ... Luke 9:29

ALWAYS
delight, Rejoicing *a* ... Prov 8:30
the poor with you *a* ... Matt 26:11
lo, I am with you *a* ... Matt 28:20
to them, that men *a* ... Luke 18:1
immovable, *a* ... 1 Cor 15:58
Rejoice in the Lord *a* ... Phil 4:4
thus we shall *a* ... 1 Thess 4:17
a be ready to give a ... 1 Pet 3:15

AM
to Moses, "I A WHO I ... Ex 3:14
First and I *a* the Last ... Is 44:6
in My name, I *a* ... Matt 18:20
a the bread of life ... John 6:35
a the light of the ... John 8:12
I *a* from above ... John 8:23
Abraham was, I *A* ... John 8:58
"I *a* the door ... John 10:9
a the good shepherd ... John 10:11
a the resurrection ... John 11:25
to him, "I *a* the way ... John 14:6
of God I *a* what I *a* ... 1 Cor 15:10

AMBASSADOR
for which I am an *a* ... Eph 6:20

AMBASSADORS
we are *a* for Christ ... 2 Cor 5:20

AMBITION
Christ from selfish *a* ... Phil 1:16

AMEN
are Yes, and in Him *A* ... 2 Cor 1:20
creatures said, "*A* ... Rev 5:14

ANCHOR
hope we have as an *a* ... Heb 6:19

ANCIENT
Do not remove the *a* ... Prov 23:10
"until the *A* of Days ... Dan 7:22

ANGEL
"Behold, I send an *A* ... Ex 23:20
Manoah said to the *A* ... Judg 13:17
the *A* of His Presence ... Is 63:9
things, behold, an *a* ... Matt 1:20
for an *a* of the Lord ... Matt 28:2
Then an *a* of the Lord ... Luke 1:11
And behold, an *a* ... Luke 2:9
a appeared to Him ... Luke 22:43
For an *a* went down at ... John 5:4
a has spoken to Him ... John 12:29
But at night an *a* ... Acts 5:19
A who appeared to him ... Acts 7:35
immediately an *a* ... Acts 12:23
himself into an *a* ... 2 Cor 11:14
even if we, or an *a* ... Gal 1:8
Then I saw a strong *a* ... Rev 5:2
Jesus, have sent My *a* ... Rev 22:16

ANGELS
If He charges His *a* ... Job 4:18
lower than the *a* ... Ps 8:5
He shall give His *a* ... Ps 91:11
He shall give His *a* ... Matt 4:6
not even the *a* ... Matt 24:36
and all the holy *a* ... Matt 25:31
twelve legions of *a* ... Matt 26:53
And she saw two *a* ... John 20:12
and worship of *a* ... Col 2:18
much better than the *a* ... Heb 1:4
entertained *a* ... Heb 13:2
things which *a* desire ... 1 Pet 1:12
did not spare the *a* ... 2 Pet 2:4
a who did not keep ... Jude 6

ANGER
For His *a* is but for a ... Ps 30:5
gracious, Slow to *a* ... Ps 103:8
Nor will He keep His *a* ... Ps 103:9
around at them with *a* ... Mark 3:5
bitterness, wrath, *a* ... Eph 4:31

ANGRY
Cain, "Why are you *a* ... Gen 4:6
"Let not the Lord be *a* ... Gen 18:30
the Son, lest He be *a* ... Ps 2:12
a man stirs up strife ... Prov 29:22
right for you to be *a* ... Jon 4:4
you that whoever is *a* ... Matt 5:22
"Be *a*, and do not ... Eph 4:26

ANGUISH
remembers the *a* ... John 16:21
tribulation and *a* ... Rom 2:9

ANIMAL
of every clean *a* ... Gen 7:2
set him on his own *a* ... Luke 10:34

ANIMALS
of *a* after their kind ... Gen 6:20
of four-footed *a* ... Acts 10:12

ANNUL
years later, cannot *a* ... Gal 3:17

ANNULS
is confirmed, no one *a* ... Gal 3:15

ANOINT
a my head with oil ... Ps 23:5
when you fast, *a* ... Matt 6:17
a My body for burial ... Mark 14:8
a your eyes with eye ... Rev 3:18

ANOINTED
"Surely the LORD's *a* ... 1 Sam 16:6
destroy the LORD's *a* ... 2 Sam 1:14
"Do not touch My *a* ... 1 Chr 16:22
Because He has *a* ... Luke 4:18
but this woman has *a* ... Luke 7:46
a the eyes of the ... John 9:6
that Mary who *a* ... John 11:2
Jesus, whom You *a* ... Acts 4:27
and has *a* us is God ... 2 Cor 1:21

ANOINTING
But you have an *a* ... 1 John 2:20

ANOTHER
that you love one *a* ... John 13:34

ANSWER
Call, and I will *a* ... Job 13:22
How shall I *a* Him ... Job 31:14
the day that I call, *a* ... Ps 102:2
In Your faithfulness *a* ... Ps 143:1
a turns away wrath ... Prov 15:1
a a fool according ... Prov 26:4
or what you should *a* ... Luke 12:11
you may have an *a* ... 2 Cor 5:12

ANT
Go to the *a* ... Prov 6:6

ANTICHRIST
heard that the *A* ... 1 John 2:18
a who denies the ... 1 John 2:22
is a deceiver and an *a* ... 2 John 7

ANTITYPE
a which now saves us ... 1 Pet 3:21

ANXIETIES
the multitude of my *a* ... Ps 94:19

ANXIETY
A in the heart of man ... Prov 12:25

ANXIOUS
Be *a* for nothing ... Phil 4:6

APART
justified by faith *a* ... Rom 3:28

APOSTLE
called to be an *a* ... Rom 1:1
consider the *A* ... Heb 3:1

APOSTLES
of the twelve *a* ... Matt 10:2
He also named *a* ... Luke 6:13
am the least of the *a* ... 1 Cor 15:9
none of the other *a* ... Gal 1:19
gave some to be *a* ... Eph 4:11

APOSTLESHIP
in this ministry and *a* ... Acts 1:25
are the seal of my *a* ... 1 Cor 9:2

APPAREL
gold rings, in fine *a* ... James 2:2
or putting on fine *a* ... 1 Pet 3:3

APPEAL
love's sake I rather *a* ... Philem 9

APPEAR
and let the dry land *a* ... Gen 1:9
also outwardly *a* ... Matt 23:28
God would *a* ... Luke 19:11
For we must all *a* ... 2 Cor 5:10

APPEARANCE
Do not look at his *a* ... 1 Sam 16:7
judge according to *a* ... John 7:24
those who boast in *a* ... 2 Cor 5:12
found in *a* as a man ... Phil 2:8

APPEARED
an angel of the Lord *a* ... Luke 1:11
who *a* in glory and ... Luke 9:31
brings salvation has *a* ... Titus 2:11
of the ages, He has *a* ... Heb 9:26

APPEARING
Lord Jesus Christ's *a* ... 1 Tim 6:14
and the dead at His *a* ... 2 Tim 4:1
who have loved His *a* ... 2 Tim 4:8

APPEARS
can stand when He *a* ... Mal 3:2
who is our life *a* ... Col 3:4
the Chief Shepherd *a* ... 1 Pet 5:4
that when He *a* ... 1 John 2:28

APPETITE
are a man given to *a* ... Prov 23:2

APPLE
And my law as the *a* ... Prov 7:2

APPLES
fitly spoken is like *a* ... Prov 25:11

APPLIED
a my heart to know ... Eccl 7:25

APPOINT
For God did not *a* ... 1 Thess 5:9

APPOINTED
And as it is *a* for men ... Heb 9:27

APPROACH
year, make those who *a* ... Heb 10:1

APPROACHING
as you see the Day *a* ... Heb 10:25

APPROVE
do the same but also *a* ... Rom 1:32

APPROVED
to God and *a* by men ... Rom 14:18
to present yourself *a* ... 2 Tim 2:15

ARBITRATOR
Me a judge or an *a* ... Luke 12:14

ARCHANGEL
the voice of an *a* ... 1 Thess 4:16

ARGUMENTS
casting down *a* and ... 2 Cor 10:5

ARISE
A, shine ... Is 60:1
But the LORD will *a* ... Is 60:2
you who sleep, *A* ... Eph 5:14

ARK
"Make yourself an *a* ... Gen 6:14
him, she took an *a* ... Ex 2:3
Bezalel made the *a* ... Ex 37:1
in heaven, and the *a* ... Rev 11:19

ARM
with an outstretched *a* ... Ex 6:6
Have you an *a* like God ... Job 40:9
strength with His *a* ... Luke 1:51
a yourselves also with ... 1 Pet 4:1

ARMED
a strong man, fully *a* ... Luke 11:21

ARMIES
And he sent out his *a* ... Matt 22:7
surrounded by *a* ... Luke 21:20
And the *a* in heaven ... Rev 19:14
the earth, and their *a* ... Rev 19:19

ARMOR
Put on the whole *a* ... Eph 6:11

ARMS
are the everlasting *a* ... Deut 33:27
took Him up in his *a* ... Luke 2:28

AROMA
the one we are the *a* ... 2 Cor 2:16
for a sweet-smelling *a* ... Eph 5:2

AROUSED
LORD was greatly *a* ... Num 11:10
Then Joseph, being *a* ... Matt 1:24

ARRAYED
his glory was not *a* ... Matt 6:29
"Who are these *a* ... Rev 7:13

ARROGANCE
Pride and *a* and the ... Prov 8:13

ARROW
a that flies by day ... Ps 91:5

ARROWS
a pierce me deeply ... Ps 38:2
Like *a* in the hand of ... Ps 127:4

ASCEND
Who may *a* into the ... Ps 24:3
If I *a* into heaven ... Ps 139:8
'I will *a* into heaven ... Is 14:13
see the Son of Man *a* ... John 6:62

ASCENDED
You have *a* on high ... Ps 68:18
"No one has *a* ... John 3:13
"When He *a* on high ... Eph 4:8

ASCENDING
the angels of God *a* ... John 1:51

ASCRIBE
A strength to God ... Ps 68:34

ASHAMED
Let me not be *a* ... Ps 25:2
And Israel shall be *a* ... Hos 10:6
For whoever is *a* ... Mark 8:38
am not *a* of the gospel ... Rom 1:16
Therefore God is not *a* ... Heb 11:16

ASHES
become like dust and *a* ... Job 30:19
in sackcloth and *a* ... Luke 10:13

ASIDE
lay something *a* ... 1 Cor 16:2
lay *a* all filthiness ... James 1:21
Therefore, laying *a* ... 1 Pet 2:1

ASK
when your children *a* ... Josh 4:6
"*A* a sign for yourself ... Is 7:11
whatever things you *a* ... Matt 21:22
a, and it will be ... Luke 11:9
that whatever You *a* ... John 11:22
a anything in My ... John 14:14
in that day you will *a* ... John 16:23
above all that we *a* ... Eph 3:20
wisdom, let him *a* ... James 1:5
But let him *a* in faith ... James 1:6
because you do not *a* ... James 4:2

ASKS
For everyone who *a* ... Matt 7:8
you who, if his son *a* ... Matt 7:9
Or if he *a* for a fish ... Luke 11:11

ASLEEP
But He was *a* ... Matt 8:24
some have fallen *a* ... 1 Cor 15:6
those who are *a* ... 1 Thess 4:15

ASSEMBLING
not forsaking the *a* ... Heb 10:25

ASSEMBLY
a I will praise You ... Ps 22:22
fast, Call a sacred *a* ... Joel 1:14
a I will sing praise ... Heb 2:12
to the general *a* ... Heb 12:23

ASSURANCE
riches of the full *a* ... Col 2:2
Spirit and in much *a* ... 1 Thess 1:5
to the full *a* of hope ... Heb 6:11

ASSURE
a our heats before ... 1 John 3:19

ASSURED
learned and been *a* ... 2 Tim 3:14

ASTONISHED
Just as many were *a* ... Is 52:14
who heard Him were *a* ... Luke 2:47

ASTRAY
one of them goes *a* ... Matt 18:12
like sheep going *a* ... 1 Pet 2:25

ATONEMENT
the blood that makes *a* ... Lev 17:11
for it is the Day of *A* ... Lev 23:28
there will be no *a* ... Is 22:14

ATTAIN
It is high, I cannot *a* ... Ps 139:6
worthy to *a* that age ... Luke 20:35
by any means, I may *a* ... Phil 3:11

ATTENTION
My son, give *a* to my ... Prov 4:20

ATTENTIVE
Let Your ears be *a* ... Ps 130:2

ATTESTED
a Man *a* by God to you ... Acts 2:22

AUSTERE
because you are an *a* ... Luke 19:21

AUTHOR
For God is not the *a* ... 1 Cor 14:33
unto Jesus, the *a* ... Heb 12:2

AUTHORITIES
a that exist are ... Rom 13:1

AUTHORITY
them as one having *a* ... Matt 7:29
"All *a* has been given ... Matt 28:18
a I will give You ... Luke 4:6
and has given Him *a* ... John 5:27
You have given Him *a* ... John 17:2
the flesh, reject *a* ... Jude 8

AUTUMN
a trees without fruit ... Jude 12

AVAILS
of a righteous man *a* ... James 5:16

AVENGE
Beloved, do not *a* ... Rom 12:19
a our blood on those ... Rev 6:10

AVENGER
the Lord is the *a* ... 1 Thess 4:6

AWAKE
be satisfied when I *a* ... Ps 17:15
it is high time to *a* ... Rom 13:11
A to righteousness ... 1 Cor 15:34

AWAY
the wind drives *a* ... Ps 1:4
Do not cast me *a* ... Ps 51:11
A time to cast *a* ... Eccl 3:5
fait one, And come *a* ... Song 2:10
minded to put her *a* ... Matt 1:19
and earth will pass *a* ... Matt 24:35
"I am going *a* ... John 8:21
they cried out, "*A* ... John 19:15
unless the falling *a* ... 2 Thess 2:3
in Asia have turned *a* ... 2 Tim 1:15
heard, lest we drift *a* ... Heb 2:1
if they fall *a* ... Heb 6:6
can never take *a* ... Heb 10:11
world is passing *a* ... 1 John 2:17
if anyone takes *a* ... Rev 22:19

AWESOME
a is this place ... Gen 28:17
God, the great and *a* ... Deut 7:21
By *a* deeds in ... Ps 65:5
O God, You are more *a* ... Ps 68:35
Your great and *a* name ... Ps 99:3

AWL
his ear with an *a* ... Ex 21:6

AX
If the *a* is dull ... Eccl 10:10
And even now the *a* ... Matt 3:10

B

BABBLER
"What does this *b* ... Acts 17:18

BABBLINGS
the profane and idle *b* ... 1 Tim 6:20

BABE
the *b* leaped in my ... Luke 1:44
You will find a *B* ... Luke 2:12
for he is a *b* ... Heb 5:13

BABES
Out of the mouth of *b* ... Ps 8:2
revealed them to *b* ... Matt 11:25
of the mouth of *b* ... Matt 21:16
as to carnal, as to *b* ... 1 Cor 3:1
as newborn *b* ... 1 Pet 2:2

BACK
for the fool's *b* .... Prov 26:3
I gave My *b* to those .... Is 50:6
plow, and looking *b* .... Luke 9:62
of those who draw *b* ..... Heb 10:39
someone turns him *b* .... James 5:19

BACKBITERS
b, haters of God .... Rom 1:30

BACKBITING
b tongue an angry .... Prov 25:23

BACKSLIDER
The *b* in heart will be ... Prov 14:14

BACKSLIDINGS
And I will heal your *b* ...... Jer 3:22

BACKWARD
ten degrees *b* .... 2 Kin 20:11

BAD
b trees bears *b* fruit ...... Matt 7:17

BAG
"nor *b* for your .... Matt 10:10

BAKED
b unleavened cakes .... Ex 12:39

BAKER
the butler and the *b* .... Gen 40:1

BALANCES
Falsifying the *b* .... Amos 8:5

BALD
every head shall be *b* ...... Jer 48:37

BALDHEAD
Go up, you *b* .... 2 Kin 2:23

BALM
no *b* in Gilead .... Jer 8:22

BANDAGED
and *b* his wounds .... Luke 10:34

BANKERS
my money with the *b* .... Matt 25:27

BANNERS
we will set up our *b* .... Ps 20:5
as an army with *b* .... Song 6:4

BANQUET
b that I have prepared ..... Esth 5:4

BANQUETING
He brought me to the *b* .... Song 2:4

BAPTISM
coming to his *b* .... Matt 3:7
b that I am baptized ..... Matt 20:22
"But I have a *b* .... Luke 12:50
said, "Into John's *b* ...... Acts 19:3
Lord, one faith, one *b* ...... Eph 4:5
buried with Him in *b* ...... Col 2:12

BAPTISMS
of the doctrine of *b* .... Heb 6:2

BAPTIZE
"I indeed *b* you with ..... Matt 3:11
Himself did not *b* .... John 4:2

BAPTIZED
b will be saved .... Mark 16:16
every one of you be *b* .... Acts 2:38
all his family were *b* .... Acts 16:33
Arise and be *b* .... Acts 22:16
were *b* into Christ .... Rom 6:3
I thank God that I *b* ..... 1 Cor 1:14
Spirit we were all *b* .... 1 Cor 12:13

BAPTIZING
b them in the name of ... Matt 28:19

BARBARIAN
nor uncircumcised, *b* ...... Col 3:11

BARLEY
here who has five *b* .... John 6:9

BARN
the wheat into my *b* ..... Matt 13:30

BARNS
reap nor gather into *b* .... Matt 6:26
I will pull down my *b* .... Luke 12:18

BARREN
But Sarai was *b* .... Gen 11:30
"Sing, O *b* .... Is 54:1

BASE
and the *b* things of ...... 1 Cor 1:28

BASIN
poured water into a *b* .... John 13:5

BASKET
and put it under a *b* ...... Matt 5:15
I was let down in a *b* ... 2 Cor 11:33

BASKETS
they took up twelve *b* ... Matt 14:20

BATHED
to him, "He who is *b* .... John 13:10

BATS
To the moles and *b* .... Is 2:20

BATTLE
b is the LORD's .... 1 Sam 17:47
the *b* to the strong .... Eccl 9:11
became valiant in *b* ...... Heb 11:34

BEAR
greater than I can *b* .... Gen 4:13
whom Sarah shall *b* ...... Gen 17:21
not *b* false witness .... Ex 20:16
b their iniquities .... Is 53:11
child, and *b* a Son .... Matt 1:23
A good tree cannot *b* ..... Matt 7:18
how long shall I *b* .... Matt 17:17
by, to *b* His cross .... Mark 15:21
whoever does not *b* ..... Luke 14:27
are strong ought to *b* ..... Rom 15:1
B one another's .... Gal 6:2
b the sins of many .... Heb 9:28

BEARD
the edges of your *b* ...... Lev 19:27
Running down on the *b* ... Ps 133:2

BEARING
goes forth weeping, *B* ..... Ps 126:6
And He, *b* His cross ..... John 19:17
b His reproach .... Heb 13:13

BEARS
Every branch that *b* ...... John 15:2

BEAST
You preserve man and *b* ... Ps 36:6
And I saw a *b* rising .... Rev 13:1
the mark of the *b* .... Rev 19:20

BEASTS
like brute *b* .... Jude 10

BEAT
b their swords into .... Is 2:4
spat in His face and *b* ... Matt 26:67

BEATEN
Three times I was *b* .... 2 Cor 11:25

BEAUTIFUL
B in elevation .... Ps 48:2
has made everything *b* .... Eccl 3:11
my love, you are as *b* ...... Song 6:4
How *b* upon the .... Is 52:7
indeed appear *b* .... Matt 23:27

BEAUTIFY
b the place of My .... Is 60:13

BEAUTY
"The *b* of Israel is .... 2 Sam 1:19
To behold the *b* .... Ps 27:4
see the King in His *b* .... Is 33:17
no *b* that we should .... Is 53:2

BECAME
b a living being .... Gen 2:7
to the Jews I *b* .... 1 Cor 9:20

BED
I remember You on my *b* ... Ps 63:6
if I make my *b* in hell ..... Ps 139:8
"Arise; take up your *b* ..... Matt 9:6
be two men in one *b* ..... Luke 17:34
and the *b* undefiled .... Heb 13:4

BEDS
sing aloud on their *b* ...... Ps 149:5

BEFOREHAND
up, do not worry *b* ..... Mark 43:11
told you all things *b* .... Mark 13:23
when He testified *b* ...... 1 Pet 1:11

BEG
b you as sojourners ...... 1 Pet 2:11

BEGAN
since the world *b* .... Luke 1:70

BEGGAR
there was a certain *b* .... Luke 16:20

BEGGARLY
weak and *b* elements .... Gal 4:9

BEGINNING
b God created the .... Gen 1:1
In the *b* was the Word ..... John 1:1
a murderer from the *b* .... John 8:44
True Witness, the *B* .... Rev 3:14
and the Omega, the *B* ..... Rev 21:6

BEGOTTEN
I have *b* You .... Ps 2:7
glory as of the only *b* ..... John 1:14
loves him who is *b* ...... 1 John 5:1

BEGUILING
b unstable souls .... 2 Pet 2:14

BEGUN
Having *b* in the Spirit ...... Gal 3:3

BEHALF
you on Christ's *b* .... 2 Cor 5:20

BEHAVE
does not *b* rudely .... 1 Cor 13:5

BEHAVED
blamelessly we *b* ...... 1 Thess 2:10

BEHAVIOR
of good *b*, hospitable ..... 1 Tim 3:2

BEHEADED
and had John *b* .... Matt 14:10

BEHOLD
B, the virgin shall .... Is 7:14
Judah, "*B* your God .... Is 40:9
*"*B* the Lamb of God ..... John 1:36
to them, "*B* the Man ..... John 19:5
B what manner of .... 1 John 3:1

BEHOLDING
with unveiled face, *b* .... 2 Cor 3:18

BEING
move and have our *b* .... Acts 17:28
who, *b* in the form of .... Phil 2:6

BELIEVE
tears, "Lord, I *b* .... Mark 9:24
have no root, who *b* ...... Luke 8:13
slow of heart to *b* .... Luke 24:25
to those who *b* .... John 1:12
this, that they may *b* .... John 11:42
that you may *b* .... John 20:31
the Lord Jesus and *b* ..... Rom 10:9
Christ, not only to *b* .... Phil 1:29
comes to God must *b* ...... Heb 11:6
b that there is one .... James 2:19
Even the demons *b* ...... James 2:19

BELIEVED
And he *b* in the LORD ..... Gen 15:6
Who has *b* our report .... Is 53:1
seen Me, you have *b* ..... John 20:29
"Abraham *b* God .... Rom 4:3
whom I have *b* .... 2 Tim 1:12

BELIEVERS
example to the *b* .... 1 Tim 4:12

BELIEVES
The simple *b* every ...... Prov 14:15
that whoever *b* in Him ... John 3:16
"He who *b* in the Son .... John 3:36
with the heart brie *b* .... Rom 10:10

BELIEVING
you ask in prayer, *b* ..... Matt 21:22

BELLY
On your *b* you shall go .... Gen 3:14
and Jonah was in the *b* .... Jon 1:17
whose god is their *b* .... Phil 3:19

BELOVED
so He gives His *b* .... Ps 127:2
My *b* is mine .... Song 2:16
"This is My *b* .... Matt 3:17
us accepted in the *B* .... Eph 1:6
Luke the *b* physician ...... Col 4:14
"This is My *b* .... 2 Pet 1:17

BELT
with a leather *b* .... Matt 3:4

BEND
The wicked *b* their bow .... Ps 11:2

BENEATH
"You are from *b* .... John 8:23

BENEFACTORS
them are called '*b* .... Luke 22:25

BENEFIT
have a second *b* .... 2 Cor 1:15

BESEECH
b you therefore ... Rom 12:1

BESIDE
He leads me *b* the ... Ps 23:2
"Paul, you are *b* ... Acts 26:24

BEST
desire the *b* ... 1 Cor 12:31

BESTOWED
love the Father has *b* ... 1 John 3:1

BETRAY
you, one of you will *b* ... Matt 26:21

BETRAYED
Man is about to be *b* ... Matt 17:22

BETRAYER
See, My *b* is at ... Matt 26:46

BETRAYING
"Judas, are you *b* ... Luke 22:48

BETRAYS
who is the one who *b* ... John 21:20

BETROTH
"I will *b* you to Me ... Hos 2:19

BETROTHED
to a virgin *b* to a man ... Luke 1:27

BETTER
b than sacrifice ... 1 Sam 15:22
It is *b* to trust in ... Ps 118:8
For it is *b* to marry ... 1 Cor 7:9
Christ, which is far *b* ... Phil 1:23
b than the angels ... Heb 1:4
b things concerning ... Heb 6:9

BEWARE
"*B* of false prophets ... Matt 7:15

BEWITCHED
b you that you should ... Gal 3:1

BEYOND
advanced in Judaism *b* ... Gal 1:14

BILLOWS
b have gone over me ... Ps 42:7

BIND
and whatever you *b* ... Matt 16:19
'*B* him hand and foot ... Matt 22:13

BIRD
soul, "Flee as a *b* ... Ps 11:1

BIRDS
b make their nests ... Ps 104:17
"Look at the *b* ... Matt 6:26
have holes and *b* ... Matt 8:20

BIRTH
the day of one's *b* ... Eccl 7:1
Now the *b* of Jesus ... Matt 1:18
will rejoice at his *b* ... Luke 1:14
conceived, it gives *b* ... James 1:15

BIRTHDAY
was Pharaoh's *b* ... Gen 40:20

BIRTHRIGHT
Esau despised his *b* ... Gen 25:34

BISHOP
the position of a *b* ... 1 Tim 3:1
b must be blameless ... Titus 1:7

BIT
and they *b* the people ... Num 21:6

BITE
A serpent may *b* ... Eccl 10:11
But if you *b* and ... Gal 5:15

BITTER
b herbs they ... Ex 12:8
and do not be *b* ... Col 3:19
But if you have *b* ... James 3:14

BITTERLY
And Hezekiah wept *b* ... 2 Kin 20:3
went out and wept *b* ... Matt 26:75

BITTERNESS
you are poisoned by *b* ... Acts 8:23
b springing up cause ... Heb 12:15

BLACK
one hair white or *b* ... Matt 5:36
a *b* horse ... Rev 6:5
and the sun became *b* ... Rev 6:12

BLACKNESS
whom is reserved the *b* ... Jude 13

BLACKSMITH
I have created the *b* ... Is 54:16

BLADE
first the *b* ... Mark 4:28

BLAME
be holy and without *b* ... Eph 1:4

BLAMELESS
and that man was *b* ... Job 1:1
body be preserved *b* ... 1 Thess 5:23

BLAMELESSLY
b we behaved ... 1 Thess 2:10

BLASPHEME
b Your name forever ... Ps 74:10
compelled them to *b* ... Acts 26:11
b that noble name ... James 2:7

BLASPHEMED
who passed by *b* Him ... Matt 27:39
great heat, and they *b* ... Rev 16:9

BLASPHEMER
I was formerly a *b* ... 1 Tim 1:13

BLASPHEMES
b the name of the ... Lev 24:16
"This Man *b* ... Matt 9:3

BLASPHEMIES
is this who speaks *b* ... Luke 5:21

BLASPHEMY
but the *b* against ... Matt 12:31
was full of names of *b* ... Rev 17:3

BLEATING
"What then is this *b* ... 1 Sam 15:14

BLEMISH
be holy and without *b* ... Eph 5:27
as of a lamb without *b* ... 1 Pet 1:19

BLEMISHED
to the Lord what is *b* ... Mal 1:14

BLESS
b those who *b* you ... Gen 12:3
You go unless You *b* ... Gen 32:26
"The LORD *b* you and ... Num 6:24
b the LORD at all ... Ps 34:1
b You while I live ... Ps 63:4
b His holy name ... Ps 103:1
b those who curse ... Luke 6:28
B those who ... Rom 12:14
Being reviled, we *b* ... 1 Cor 4:12

BLESSED
B is the man who walks ... Ps 1:1
B is the man to whom ... Ps 32:2
B is the nation whose ... Ps 33:12
B is he who comes ... Ps 118:26
rise up and call her *b* ... Prov 31:28
"*B* are the poor in ... Matt 5:3
B are those who mourn ... Matt 5:4
B are the meek ... Matt 5:5
B are those who hunger ... Matt 5:6
B are the merciful ... Matt 5:7
B are the pure in ... Matt 5:8
B are the peacemakers ... Matt 5:9
B are those who are ... Matt 5:10
B is He who comes ... Matt 21:9
'It is more *b* to give ... Acts 20:35
B be the God and ... Eph 1:3
"*B* are the dead who ... Rev 14:13

BLESSING
And you shall be a *b* ... Gen 12:2
before you today a *b* ... Deut 11:26
shall be showers of *b* ... Ezek 34:26
and you shall be a *b* ... Zech 8:13
that the *b* of Abraham ... Gal 3:14
with every spiritual *b* ... Eph 1:3

BLIND
To open *b* eyes ... Is 42:7
His watchmen are *b* ... Is 56:10
b leads the *b* ... Matt 15:14
to Him, "Are we *b* ... John 9:40
miserable, poor, *b* ... Rev 3:17

BLINDED
and the rest were *b* ... Rom 11:7

BLINDS
a bribe, for a bribe *b* ... Deut 16:19

BLOOD
of your brother's *b* ... Gen 4:10
b shall be shed ... Gen 9:6
b that makes ... Lev 17:11
hands are full of *b* ... Is 1:15
And the moon into *b* ... Joel 2:31
For this is My *b* ... Matt 26:28
"His *b* be on us and ... Matt 27:25
covenant in My *b* ... Luke 22:20
were born, not of *b* ... John 1:13
b has eternal life ... John 6:54
with His own *b* ... Acts 20:28
propitiation by His *b* ... Rom 3:25
justified by His *b* ... Rom 5:9
through His *b* ... Eph 1:7
brought near by the *b* ... Eph 2:13
against flesh and *b* ... Eph 6:12
peace through the *b* ... Col 1:20
with the precious *b* ... 1 Pet 1:19
b of Jesus Christ His ... 1 John 1:7
our sins in His own *b* ... Rev 1:5
us to God by Your *b* ... Rev 5:9
them white in the *b* ... Rev 7:14
overcame him by the *b* ... Rev 12:11
a robe dipped in *b* ... Rev 19:13

BLOODSHED
me from the guilt of *b* ... Ps 51:14

BLOODTHIRSTY
The LORD abhors the *b* ... Ps 5:6

BLOSSOM
and *b* as the rose ... Is 35:1

BLOT
from my sins, and *b* ... Ps 51:9
and I will not *b* ... Rev 3:5

BLOTTED
your sins may be *b* ... Acts 3:19

BLOW
with a very severe *b* ... Jer 14:17

BLOWS
"The wind *b* where it ... John 3:8

BOAST
puts on his armor *b* ... 1 Kin 20:11
and make your *b* ... Rom 2:17
lest anyone should *b* ... Eph 2:9

BOASTERS
God, violent, proud, *b* ... Rom 1:30

BOASTING
Where is *b* then ... Rom 3:27

BODIES
b a living sacrifice ... Rom 12:1
not know that your *b* ... 1 Cor 6:15
wives as their own *b* ... Eph 5:28

BODILY
b form like a dove ... Luke 3:22
of the Godhead *b* ... Col 2:9

BODY
of the *b* is the eye ... Matt 6:22
those who kill the *b* ... Matt 10:28
this is My *b* ... Matt 26:26
of the temple of His *b* ... John 2:21
deliver me from this *b* ... Rom 7:24
redemption of our *b* ... Rom 8:23
members in one *b* ... Rom 12:4
But I discipline my *b* ... 1 Cor 9:27
b which is broken ... 1 Cor 11:24
baptized into one *b* ... 1 Cor 12:13
are the *b* of Christ ... 1 Cor 12:27
though I give my *b* ... 1 Cor 13:3
It is sown a natural *b* ... 1 Cor 15:44
in the *b* of His flesh ... Col 1:22
our sins in His own *b* ... 1 Pet 2:24

BOILS
Job with painful *b* ... Job 2:7

BOLDLY
therefore come *b* ... Heb 4:16

BOLDNESS
in whom we have *b* ... Eph 3:12
that we may have *b* ... 1 John 4:17

BOND
love, which is the *b* ... Col 3:14

BONDAGE
out of the house of *b* ... Ex 13:14
again with a yoke of *b* ... Gal 5:1

BONDS
"Let us break Their *b* ... Ps 2:3

BONDSERVANTS
B, be obedient to ... Eph 6:5
Masters, give your *b* ... Col 4:1

BONDWOMAN
the one by a *b* ... Gal 4:22

BONE
b clings to my skin . . . . Job 19:20

BONES
I can count all My *b* . . . . Ps 22:17
and my *b* waste away . . . . . Ps 31:10
I kept silent, my *b* . . . . Ps 32:3
the wind, Or how the *b* . . . .Eccl 11:5
say to them, 'O dry *b* . . . . .Ezek 37:4
of dead men's *b* . . . . Matt 23:27
b shall be broken . . . . .John 19:36

BOOK
are written in the *b* . . . . Gal 3:10
in the Lamb's *B* . . . . .Rev 21:27
the prophecy of this *b* . . . .Rev 22:18

BOOKS
b there is no end . . . . Eccl 12:12
not contain the *b* . . . . .John 21:25
and *b* were opened . . . . . . .Rev 20:12

BOOTH
of Zion is left as a *b* . . . . Is 1:8

BORDERS
and enlarge the *b* . . . . Matt 23:5

BORE
And to Sarah who *b* . . . . Is 51:2
b the sin of many . . . . .Is 53:12
b our sicknesses . . . . Matt 8:17
Himself *b* our sins . . . . 1 Pet 2:24
b a male Child who was . . . Rev 12:5

BORN
A time to be *b* . . . . .Eccl 3:2
unto us a Child is *b* . . . . Is 9:6
b Jesus who is called . . . . . Matt 1:16
unless one is *b* again . . . . . . John 3:3
"That which is *b* . . . . John 3:6
having been *b* again . . . . . . 1 Pet 1:23
who loves Is *b* of God . . . 1 John 4:7

BORROWER
b is servant to the . . . . Prov 22:7

BORROWS
The wicked *b* and does . . . . Ps 37:21

BOSOM
to Abraham's *b* . . . . .Luke 16:22
Son, who is in the *b* . . . . . . .John 1:18

BOTTOMLESS
ascend out of the *b* . . . . Rev 17:8
the key to the *b* . . . . Rev 20:1

BOUGHT
b the threshing floor . . 2 Sam 24:24
all that he had and *b* . . . . Matt 13:46
For you were *b* at a . . . . . . 1 Cor 6:20
denying the Lord who *b* . . . 2 Pet 2:1

BOUND
on earth will be *b* . . . . Matt 16:19
And see, now I go *b* . . . . . Acts 20:22
who has a husband is *b* . . . Rom 7:2
Are you *b* to a wife . . . . . . 1 Cor 7:27
Devil and Satan, and *b* . . . . Rev 20:2

BOUNTIFULLY
and he who sows *b* . . . . 2 Cor 9:6

BOW
"You shall not *b* . . . . Ex 23:24
let us worship and *b* . . . . Ps 95:6
who sat on it had a *b* . . . . Rev 6:2

BOWED
stood all around and *b* . . . .Gen 37:7
And they *b* the knee . . . . . Matt 27:29

BOWL
and poured out his *b* . . . . . Rev 16:2

BOWLS
Go and pour out the *b* . . . . . Rev 16:1

BOX
had the money *b* . . . . .John 13:29

BOYS
Shall be full of *b* . . . . Zech 8:5

BRAIDED
not with *b* hair or . . . . 1 Tim 2:9

BRANCH
raise to David a *B* . . . . .Jer 23:5
forth My Servant the *B* . . . . Zech 3:8
b that bears fruit He . . . . . . John 15:2

BRANCHES
vine, you are the *b* . . . . . . .John 15:5

BRASS
become sounding *b* . . . . . 1 Cor 13:1

BRAVE
in the faith, be *b* . . . . 1 Cor 16:13

BREAD
brought out *b* . . . . .Gen 14:18
shall eat unleavened *b* . . . . Ex 23:15
not live by *b* alone . . . . Deut 8:3
b eaten in secret is . . . . Prov 9:17
B gained by deceit is . . . . Prov 20:17
Cast your *b* upon the . . . . . .Eccl 11:1
for what is not *b* . . . . Is 55:2
these stones become *b* . . . . . Matt 4:3
not live by *b* alone . . . . Matt 4:4
this day our daily *b* . . . . . . Matt 6:11
eating, Jesus took *b* . . . . . Matt 26:26
"I am the *b* of life . . . . .John 6:48
betrayed took *b* . . . . 1 Cor 11:23

BREADTH
is as great as its *b* . . . . .Rev 21:16

BREAK
covenant I will not *b* . . . . . . Ps 89:34
together to *b* bread . . . . Acts 20:7

BREAKING
in the *b* of bread . . . . Acts 2:42
b bread from house to . . . . . Acts 2:46

BREAKS
Until the day *b* . . . . .Song 2:17

BREAST
back on Jesus' *b* . . . . .John 13:25

BREASTPLATE
righteousness as a *b* . . . . Is 59:17
having put on the *b* . . . . .Eph 6:14

BREASTS
Your two *b* are like . . . . .Song 4:5
b which nursed You . . . . .Luke 11:27

BREATH
nostrils the *b* of life . . . . Gen 2:7
that there was no *b* . . . . . 1 Kin 17:17
Man is like a *b* . . . . Ps 144:4
everything that has *b* . . . . . . Ps 150:6
"Surely I will cause *b* . . . . Ezek 37:5
gives to all life, *b* . . . . Acts 17:25
power to give *b* . . . . Rev 13:15

BREATHES
indeed he *b* his last . . . . . . Job 14:10

BRETHREN
and you are all *b* . . . . Matt 23:8
least of these My *b* . . . . . . Matt 25:40
among many *b* . . . . Rom 8:29
thus sin against the *b* . . . . 1 Cor 8:12
over five hundred *b* . . . . . . 1 Cor 15:6
perils among false *b* . . . . 2 Cor 11:26
sincere love of the *b* . . . . . . 1 Pet 1:22
we love the *b* . . . . 1 John 3:14
our lives for the *b* . . . . . . 1 John 3:16

BRIBE
you shall take no *b* . . . . Ex 23:8
b blinds the eyes . . . . .Deut 16:19

BRIBES
hand is full of *b* . . . . Ps 26:10

BRICK
people straw to make *b* . . . . . . Ex 5:7

BRICKS
"Come, let us make *b* . . . . . .Gen 11:3

BRIDE
I will show you the *b* . . . . . . Rev 21:9
the Spirit and the *b* . . . . . . .Rev 22:17

BRIDEGROOM
And as the *b* rejoices . . . . Is 62:5
mourn as long as the *b* . . . Matt 9:15
went out to meet the *b* . . . Matt 25:1
the friend of the *b* . . . . John 3:29

BRIDLE
b the whole body . . . . .James 3:2

BRIER
b shall come up the . . . . Is 55:13

BRIERS
there shall come up *b* . . . . Is 5:6

BRIGHTER
a light from heaven, *b* . . . Acts 26:13

BRIGHTNESS
And kings to the *b* . . . . Is 60:3
who being the *b* . . . . .Heb 1:3

BRIMSTONE
the lake of fire and *b* . . . . .Rev 20:10

BRING
b back his soul . . . . Job 33:30
b My righteousness . . . . Is 46:13
Who shall *b* a charge . . . . . Rom 8:33
b Christ down from . . . . . . Rom 10:6
even so God will *b* . . . . 1 Thess 4:14

BROAD
b is the way that . . . . Matt 7:13

BROKE
b them at the foot of . . . . Ex 32:19
He blessed and *b* . . . . Matt 14:19
b the legs of the . . . . .John 19:32

BROKEN
this stone will be *b* . . . . . . Matt 21:44
Scripture cannot be *b* . . . .John 10:35
body which is *b* . . . . 1 Cor 11:24

BROKENHEARTED
He heals the *b* And . . . . Ps 147:3

BRONZE
So Moses made a *b* . . . . . . Num 21:9
b walls against the . . . . .Jer 1:18
a third kingdom of *b* . . . . . .Dan 2:39

BROOD
"*B* of vipers . . . . Matt 12:34
hen gathers her *b* . . . . . . .Luke 13:34

BROOK
disciples over the *B* . . . . . . John 18:1

BROOKS
for the water *b* . . . . Ps 42:1

BROTHER
"Where is Abel your *b* . . . . . Gen 4:9
b offended is harder . . . . . Prov 18:19
b will deliver up . . . . Matt 10:21
how often shall my *b* . . . . Matt 18:21
b will rise again . . . . .John 11:23
b goes to law against . . . . . 1 Cor 6:6
Whoever hates his *b* . . . 1 John 3:15

BROTHERHOOD
Love the *b* . . . . 1 Pet 2:17

BROTHERLY
b love continue . . . . .Heb 13:1

BROTHER'S
Am I my *b* keeper . . . . .Gen 4:9
at the speck in your *b* . . . . . Matt 7:3

BROTHERS
is My mother, or My *b* . . . Mark 3:33
b are these who hear . . . . .Luke 8:21

BRUISE
He shall *b* your head . . . . . .Gen 3:15
the LORD to *b* Him . . . . .Is 53:10

BRUISED
He was *b* for our . . . . Is 53:5
b reed He will not . . . . Matt 12:20

BUCKLER
be your shield and *b* . . . . Ps 91:4

BUFFET
of Satan to *b* me . . . . 2 Cor 12:7

BUILD
b ourselves a city . . . . .Gen 11:4
"Would you *b* a house . . . .2 Sam 7:5
labor in vain who *b* . . . . Ps 127:1
down, And a time to *b* . . . . . .Eccl 3:3
'This man began to *b* . . . .Luke 14:30
What house will you *b* . . . Acts 7:49
"For if I *b* again . . . . Gal 2:18

BUILDER
foundations, whose *b* . . . .Heb 11:10

BUILDING
in whom the whole *b* . . . . . .Eph 2:21

BUILDS
take heed how he *b* . . . . . 1 Cor 3:10

BUILT
has *b* her house . . . . Prov 9:1
to a wise man who *b* . . . . . Matt 7:24
having been *b* on the . . . . . .Eph 2:20

BULLS
For if the blood of *b* . . . . . . .Heb 9:13

BULWARKS
Mark well her *b* . . . . Ps 48:13

BUNDLE
man's *b* of money ....Gen 42:35

BURDEN
Cast your *b* on the .... Ps 55:22
easy and My *b* is light ... Matt 11:30
we might not be a *b* .... 1 Thess 2:9
on you no other *b* ....Rev 2:24

BURDENS
"For they bind heavy *b* ... Matt 23:4
Bear one another's *b* .... Gal 6:2

BURDENSOME
I myself was not *b* ...... 2 Cor 12:13
are not *b* .... 1 John 5:3

BURIAL
she did it for My *b* ...... Matt 26:12
for the day of My *b* ....John 12:7

BURIED
Therefore we were *b* ...... Rom 6:4
and that He was *b* .... 1 Cor 15:4
b with Him in baptism .... Col 2:12

BURN
the bush does not *b* .... Ex 3:3
"Did not our heart *b* ....Luke 24:32

BURNED
If anyone's work is *b* .... 1 Cor 3:15
my body to be *b* .... 1 Cor 13:3

BURNING
b torch that passed ....Gen 15:17
b fire shut up in my ....Jer 20:9
plucked from the *b* ...... Amos 4:11

BURNT
lamb for a *b* offering ......Gen 22:7
delight in *b* offering .... Ps 51:16

BURST
the new wine will *b* ......Luke 5:37

BURY
and let the dead *b* .... Matt 8:22

BUSH
from the midst of a *b* .... Ex 3:2

BUSINESS
about My Father's *b* ......Luke 2:49

BUSYBODIES
at all, but are *b* .... 2 Thess 3:11

BUTLER
b did not remember ......Gen 40:23

BUTTER
were smoother than *b* ..... Ps 55:21

BUY
Yes, come, *b* wine and .... Is 55:1
"I counsel you to *b* ....Rev 3:18
and that no one may *b* ...Rev 13:17

BUYS
has and *b* that field ...... Matt 13:44

BYWORD
has made me a *b* .... Job 17:6

C

CAGE
foul spirit, and a *c* ....Rev 18:2

CAKE
Ephraim is a *c* ....Hos 7:8

CAKES
and love the raisin *c* ....Hos 3: I

CALAMITY
will laugh at your *c* ...... Prov 1:26

CALCULATED
c the dust of the ....Is 40:12

CALDRON
this city is the *c* ....Ezek 11:3

CALF
and made a molded *c* ...... Ex 32:4
bring the fatted *c* ....Luke 15:23

CALL
C upon Him while He .... Is 55:6
c His name JESUS .... Matt 1:21
c the righteous .... Matt 9:13
Lord our God will *c* ...... Acts 2:39
c them My people .... Rom 9:25
c and election sure .... 2 Pet 1:10

CALLED
c the light Day .... Gen 1:5
c his wife's name Eve .....Gen 3:20
I have *c* you by your .... Is 43:1
"Out of Egypt I *c* .... Matt 2:15
city *c* Nazareth .... Matt 2:23
For many are *c* ....Matt 20:16
to those who are the *c* .... Rom 8:28
these He also *c* .... Rom 8:30
c children of God .... 1 John 3:1

CALLING
the gifts and the *c* ....Rom 11:29
For you see your *c* ...... 1 Cor 1:26
remain in the same *c* .... 1 Cor 7:20

CALLS
c them all by name .... Ps 147:4
David himself *c* .... Mark 12:37
c his own sheep ....John 10:3

CALM
there was a great *c* .... Matt 8:26

CAMEL
it is easier for a *c* .... Matt 19:24

CAMP
to Him, outside the *c* .....Heb 13:13

CAN
I *c* do all things ....Phil 4:13

CANCER
will spread like *c* .... 2 Tim 2:17

CANOPY
His *c* around Him was ..... Ps 18:11

CAPSTONE
bring forth the *c* .... Zech 4:7

CAPTAIN
Which, having no *c* .... Prov 6:7

CAPTIVE
and be led away *c* ....Luke 21:24
He led captivity *c* ....Eph 4:8

CAPTIVES
and make *c* .... 2 Tim 3:6

CAPTIVITY
every thought into *c* ..... 2 Cor 10:5

CARCASS
"For wherever the *c* ..... Matt 24:28

CARE
"Lord, do You not *c* .....Luke 10:40
how will he take *c* .... 1 Tim 3:5

CARED
he said, not that he *c* ..... John 12:6

CAREFULLY
I shall walk *c* all my ....Is 38:15

CARELESS
But, he who is *c* .... Prov 19:16

CARES
No one *c* for my soul ...... Ps 142:4
for He *c* for you .... 1 Pet 5:7

CARNAL
c mind is enmity .... Rom 8:7

CARNALLY
c minded is death .... Rom 8:6

CAROUSE
count it pleasure to *c* .....2 Pet 2:13

CARPENTER
"Is this not the *c* ....Mark 6:3

CARRIED
And *c* our sorrows .... Is 53:4

CARRY
for you to *c* your bed .....John 5:10
it is certain we can *c* ..... 1 Tim 6:7

CARRYING
will meet you *c* .... Mark 14:13

CASE
Festus laid Paul's *c* ...... Acts 25:14

CASSIA
myrrh and aloes and *c* ..... Ps 45:8

CAST
Why are you *c* down .... Ps 42:5
whole body to be *c* .... Matt 5:29
My name they will *c* ... Mark 16:17
by no means *c* out ....John 6:37
c their crowns before ...... Rev 4:10
the great dragon was *c* .... Rev 12:9

CASTING
c down arguments ...... 2 Cor 10:5
c all your care .... 1 Pet 5:7

CASTS
perfect love *c* out .... 1 John 4:18

CATCH
c Him in His words ..... Mark 12:13
now on you will *c* ....Luke 5:10

CATCHES
and the wolf *c* the ....John 10:12
c the wise in their .... 1 Cor 3:19

CAUGHT
him was a ram *c* ....Gen 22:13
her Child was *c* up .... Rev 12:5

CAUSE
hated Me without a *c* ....John 15:25
For this *c* I was born ....John 18:37

CAVES
in dens and *c* of the ......Heb 11:38

CEASE
and night Shall not *c* ......Gen 8:22
He makes wars *c* .... Ps 46:9
tongues, they will *c* ..... 1 Cor 13:8

CEASING
pray without *c* .... 1 Thess 5:17

CEDAR
dwell in a house of *c* .....2 Sam 7:2

CEDARS
the LORD breaks the *c* ...... Ps 29:5

CELESTIAL
but the glory of the *c* ... 1 Cor 15:40

CENSER
Aaron, each took his *c* .... Lev 10:1

CERTAINTY
you may know the *c* ....Luke 1:4

CERTIFICATE
a man to write a *c* .... Mark 10:4

CHAFF
be chased like the *c* ....Is 17:13
He will burn up the *c* ..... Matt 3:12

CHAIN
pit and a great *c* .... Rev 20:1

CHAINED
of God is not *c* .... 2 Tim 2:9

CHAINS
And his *c* fell off .... Acts 12:7
am, except for these *c* ... Acts 26:29

CHAMBERS
brought me into his *c* .....Song 1:4

CHAMPION
And a *c* went out ....1 Sam 17:4

CHANGE
now and to *c* my tone ..... Gal 4:20
there is also a *c* ....Heb 7:12

CHANGED
c the glory of the .... Rom 1:23
but we shall all be *c* .... 1 Cor 15:51

CHANGERS'
and poured out the *c* .....John 2:15

CHANGES
c the times and the ....Dan 2:21

CHANNELS
c of the sea were seen ..... Ps 18:15

CHARIOT
that suddenly a *c* .... 2 Kin 2:11

CHARIOTS
Some trust in *c* .... Ps 20:7

CHARITABLE
you do not do your *c* ...... Matt 6:1
c deeds which she .... Acts 9:36

CHARM
C is deceitful and .... Prov 31:30

CHARMS
who sew magic *c* ....Ezek 13:18

CHASE
Five of you shall *c* .... Lev 26:8

CHASTE
present you as a *c* .... 2 Cor 11:2

CHASTEN
a father does not c ....Heb 12:7
I love, I rebuke and c ...... Rev 3:19

CHASTENED
c us as seemed best ......Heb 12:10

CHASTENING
do not despise the c ....Job 5:17
Now no c seems to be ....Heb 12:11

CHASTENS
the LORD loves He c ....Heb 12:6

CHASTISEMENT
The c for our peace ....Is 53:5

CHATTER
c leads only to ....Prov 14:23

CHEAT
Beware lest anyone c ....Col 2:8

CHEATED
let yourselves be c .... 1 Cor 6:7

CHEEK
on your right c .... Matt 5:39

CHEEKBONE
my enemies on the c ....Ps 3:7

CHEEKS
His c are like a bed ....Song 5:13

CHEER
"Son, be of good c .... Matt 9:2

CHEERFUL
for God loves a c .... 2 Cor 9:7

CHEERFULNESS
shows mercy, with c ...... Rom 12:8

CHEESE
And curdle me like c ..... Job 10:10

CHERISHES
but nourishes and c ....Eph 5:29

CHERUBIM
above it were the c ....Heb 9:5

CHIEF
of whom I am c .... 1 Tim 1:15
Zion a c cornerstone ...... 1 Pet 2:6

CHILD
Train up a c in the .... Prov 22:6
For unto us a C .... Is 9:6
virgin shall be with c ..... Matt 1:23
of God as a little c ...... Mark 10:15
So the c grew and ....Luke 1:80
When I was a c .... 1 Cor 13:11
She bore a male C .... Rev 12:5

CHILDBEARING
she will be saved in c .... 1 Tim 2:15

CHILDBIRTH
pain as a woman in c .... Is 13:8

CHILDHOOD
c you have known .... 2 Tim 3:15

CHILDLESS
give me, seeing I go c .....Gen 15:2
this man down as c ....Jer 22:30

CHILDREN
c are a heritage .... Ps 127:3
c rise up and call her .... Prov 31:28
and become as little c .... Matt 18:3
"Let the little c ....Matt 19:14
the right to become c .....John 1:12
now we are c of God .... 1 John 3:2

CHOOSE
therefore c life ....Deut 30:19
"You did not c ....John 15:16

CHOSE
Just as He c us in Him ...... Eph 1:4

CHOSEN
servant whom I have c .....Is 43:10
whom I have c ....John 13:18
c the foolish things ...... 1 Cor 1:27
Has God not c the ....James 2:5

CHRIST
Jesus who is called C ..... Matt 1:16
"You are the C ....Matt 16:16
a Savior, who is C ....Luke 2:11
It is C who died .... Rom 8:34
to be justified by C .... Gal 2:17
been crucified with C ..... Gal 2:20
C is head of the ....Eph 5:23
to me, to live is C ....Phil 1:21
which is C in you .... Col 1:27
C who is our ....Col 3:4
Jesus C is the same ....Heb 13:8
C His Son cleanses us ... 1 John 1:7
that Jesus is the C .... 1 John 5:1

CHRISTIAN
anyone suffers as a C .... 1 Pet 4:16

CHRISTIANS
were first called C .... Acts 11:26

CHRISTS
"For false c and .... Matt 24:24

CHURCH
rock I will build My c ... Matt 16:18
c daily those who were ... Acts 2:47
Himself a glorious c ....Eph 5:27
as the Lord does the c .....Eph 5:29
body, which is the c .... Col 1:24
assembly and c ....Heb 12:23

CHURCHES
these things in the c ......Rev 22:16

CIRCLE
who sits above the c ....Is 40:22

CIRCUMCISE
is necessary to c them .... Acts 15:5

CIRCUMCISED
among you shall be c .....Gen 17:10
who will justify the c ..... Rom 3:30
if you become c .... Gal 5:2

CIRCUMCISION
c is that of the heart ...... Rom 2:29
C is nothing and .... 1 Cor 7:19
Christ Jesus neither c ...... Gal 5:6

CIRCUMSPECTLY
then that you walk c ......Eph 5:15

CISTERN
from your own c .... Prov 5:15

CITIES
He overthrew those c ....Gen 19:25
three parts, and the c .....Rev 16:19

CITIZEN
But I was born a c .... Acts 22:28

CITIZENS
but fellow c with the ......Eph 2:19

CITIZENSHIP
For our c is in heaven .....Phil 3:20

CITY
shall make glad the c .... Ps 46:4
c has become a harlot .... Is 1:21
How lonely sits the c ...... Lam 1:1
c that is set on a .... Matt 5:14
He has prepared a c ......Heb 11:16
have no continuing c .....Heb 13:14
John, saw the holy c ...... Rev 21:2

CLAP
of the field shall c ....Is 55:12

CLAY
pit, out of the miry c .... Ps 40:2
We are the c .... Is 64:8
blind man with the c ...... John 9:6
have power over the c .... Rom 9:21

CLEAN
He who has c hands and ... Ps 24:4
make yourselves c .... Is 1:16
c out His threshing .... Matt 3:12
You can make me c .... Matt 8:2
"You are not all c ....John 13:11
"You are already c ....John 15:3

CLEANSE
C me from secret .... Ps 19:12
And c me from my sin .... Ps 51:2
How can a young man c ... Ps 119:9
might sanctify and c ......Eph 5:26
us our sins and to c ..... 1 John 1:9

CLEANSED
"Were there not ten c ...Luke 17:17

CLEANSES
Christ His Son c .... 1 John 1:7

CLEAR
of life, c as crystal .... Rev 22:1

CLIFF
secret places of the c .....Song 2:14

CLIMBS
c up some other way .....John 10:1

CLING
C to what is good .... Rom 12:9

CLINGS
And My tongue c .... Ps 22:15

CLOAK
let him have your c .... Matt 5:40
using liberty as a c .... 1 Pet 2:16

CLODS
The c of the valley .... Job 21:33

CLOSE
c friends abhor me .... Job 19:19

CLOSED
The deep c around me ...... Jon 2:5

CLOTH
a piece of unshrunk c .... Matt 9:16

CLOTHE
He not much more c ..... Matt 6:30

CLOTHED
of skin, and c them ....Gen 3:21
A man c in soft .... Matt 11:8
naked and you c ....Matt 25:36
legion, sitting and c ..... Mark 5:15
desiring to be c .... 2 Cor 5:2
that you may be c .... Rev 3:18

CLOTHES
c became shining ....Mark 9:3
many spread their c .....Luke 19:36
a poor man in filthy c ....James 2:2

CLOTHING
c they cast lots .... Ps 22:18
do you worry about c .... Matt 6:28
to you in sheep's c .... Matt 7:15
c they cast lots ....John 19:24

CLOTHS
in swaddling c ....Luke 2:12

CLOUD
My rainbow in the c ....Gen 9:13
day in a pillar of c ....Ex 13:21
He led them with the c .... Ps 78:14
behold, a bright c .... Matt 17:5
of Man coming in a c ....Luke 21:27
c received Him out of ..... Acts 1:9
by so great a c ....Heb 12:1

CLOUDS
Man coming on the c .... Matt 24:30
with them in the c ..... 1 Thess 4:17
are c without water ....Jude 12
He is coming with c .... Rev 1:7

CLOUDY
them by day with a c ......Neh 9:12

CLOVEN
chew the cud or have c ... Deut 14:7

CLUSTER
beloved is to me a c ......Song 1:14

COAL
in his hand a live c .... Is 6:6

COALS
doing you will heap c ... Rom 12:20

COBRA
the lion and the c .... Ps 91:13

COBRA'S
shall play by the c .... Is 11:8

COFFIN
and he was put in a c .....Gen 50:26
touched the open c ....Luke 7:14

COIN
if she loses one c ....Luke 15:8

COLD
and harvest, C and ....Gen 8:22
of many will grow c ..... Matt 24:12
that you are neither c ..... Rev 3:15

COLLECTION
concerning the c .... 1 Cor 16:1

COLT
on a donkey, A c ....Zech 9:9
on a donkey, A c .... Matt 21:5

COME
He will c and save you ...... Is 35:4
who have no money, C ...... Is 55:1
Your kingdom c .... Matt 6:10
"C to Me ....Matt 11:28
I have c in My ....John 5:43

thirsts, let him *c* .... John 7:37
c as a light into the ...... John 12:46
O Lord, *c* .... 1 Cor 16:22
the door, I will *c* .... Rev 3:20

COMELINESS
He has no form or *c* .... Is 53:2

COMES
Lord's death till He *c* ... 1 Cor 11:26

COMFORT
and Your staff, they *c* ...... Ps 23:4
yes, *c* My people .... Is 40:1
c each other .... 1 Thess 5:11

COMFORTED
So Isaac was *c* after ...... Gen 24:67
Refusing to be *c* .... Jer 31:15

COMFORTER
She had no *c* .... Lam 1:9

COMFORTS
I, even I, am He who *c* ...... Is 51:12

COMING
see the Son of Man *c* ... Mark 13:26
mightier than I is *c* .... Luke 3:16
are Christ's at His *c* .... 1 Cor 15:23
Behold, I am *c* .... Rev 3:11
"Surely I am *c* .... Rev 22:20

COMMAND
c I have received .... John 10:18
and I know that His *c* ... John 12:50
If you do whatever I *c* ... John 15:14

COMMANDED
not endure what was *c* ... Heb 12:20

COMMANDMENT
c of the LORD is pure .... Ps 19:8
which is the great *c* ..... Matt 22:36
"A new *c* I give to .... John 13:34
which is the first *c* .... Eph 6:2
And this is His *c* .... 1 John 3:23

COMMANDMENTS
covenant, the Ten *C* .... Ex 34:28
as doctrines the *c* .... Matt 15:9
c hang all the Law ...... Matt 22:40
He who has My *c* .... John 14:21

COMMANDS
with authority He *c* ..... Mark 1:27

COMMEND
But food does not *c* ...... 1 Cor 8:8

COMMENDABLE
patiently, this is *c* .... 1 Pet 2:20

COMMENDED
c the unjust steward ...... Luke 16:8

COMMENDS
but whom the Lord *c* ... 2 Cor 10:18

COMMIT
"You shall not *c* .... Ex 20:14
into Your hands I *c* ...... Luke 23:46

COMMITS
sin also *c* lawlessness ... 1 John 3:4

COMMITTED
c Himself to Him who .... 1 Pet 2:23

COMMON
c people heard Him .... Mark 12:37
had all things in *c* .... Acts 2:44
concerning our *c* .... Jude 3

COMMOTION
there arose a great *c* .... Acts 19:23

COMMUNED
I *c* with my heart .... Eccl 1:16

COMMUNION
c of the Holy Spirit ..... 2 Cor 13:14

COMPANION
a man my equal, My *c* ..... Ps 55:13

COMPANIONS
while you became *c* ...... Heb 10:33

COMPANY
Great was the *c* .... Ps 68:11
to an innumerable *c* ...... Heb 12:22

COMPARE
c ourselves with .... 2 Cor 10:12

COMPARED
are not worthy to be *c* .... Rom 8:18

COMPASSION
are a God full of *c* .... Ps 86:15
He was moved with *c* .... Matt 9:36
whomever I will have *c* ... Rom 9:15
He can have *c* on those ..... Heb 5:2

COMPASSIONATE
the Lord is very *c* .... James 5:11

COMPASSIONS
because His *c* fail not .... Lam 3:22

COMPEL
c them to come in .... Luke 14:23

COMPELS
the love of Christ *c* ...... 2 Cor 5:14

COMPLAINED
some of them also *c* .... 1 Cor 10:10

COMPLAINERS
These are grumblers, *c* ..... Jude 16

COMPLAINING
all things without *c* .... Phil 2:14

COMPLAINT
For the LORD has a *c* .... Mic 6:2

COMPLETE
work in you will *c* .... Phil 1:6
and you are *c* in Him ...... Col 2:10
of God may be *c* .... 2 Tim 3:17

COMPLETELY
sanctify you *c* .... 1 Thess 5:23

COMPOSED
But God *c* the body ..... 1 Cor 12:24

COMPREHEND
which we cannot *c* .... Job 37:5
the darkness did not *c* ..... John 1:5

CONCEAL
of God to *c* a matter ...... Prov 25:2

CONCEALED
Than love carefully *c* ..... Prov 27:5

CONCEIT
selfish ambition or *c* .... Phil 2:3

CONCEITED
Let us not become *c* .... Gal 5:26

CONCEIVE
the virgin shall *c* .... Is 7:14
And behold, you will *c* ... Luke 1:31

CONCEIVED
in sin my mother *c* .... Ps 51:5

CONCERN
Neither do I *c* myself ...... Ps 131:1

CONCERNED
Is it oxen God is *c* .... 1 Cor 9:9

CONCESSION
But I say this as a *c* ...... 1 Cor 7:6

CONCLUSION
Let us hear the *c* .... Eccl 12:13

CONDEMN
world to *c* the world ...... John 3:17

CONDEMNATION
can you escape the *c* .... Matt 23:33
"And this is the *c* .... John 3:19
Their *c* is just .... Rom 3:8
therefore now no *c* .... Rom 8:1

CONDEMNED
does not believe is *c* ...... John 3:18
c sin in the flesh .... Rom 8:3

CONDEMNS
Who is he who *c* .... Rom 8:34

CONDUCT
from your aimless *c* .... 1 Pet 1:8
may be won by the *c* ...... 1 Pet 3:1

CONFESS
c my transgressions .... Ps 32:5
that if you *c* with .... Rom 10:9
every tongue shall *c* ..... Rom 14:11
If we *c* our sins .... 1 John 1:9

CONFESSED
c that He was Christ ..... John 9:22

CONFESSES
c that Jesus is the ...... 1 John 4:15

CONFESSION
with the mouth *c* .... Rom 10:10
High Priest of our *c* .... Heb 3:1
let us hold fast our *c* ...... Heb 4:14

CONFIDENCE
c shall be Your .... Is 30:15
Jesus, and have no *c* .... Phil 3:3

CONFINED
the Scripture has *c* .... Gal 3:22

CONFIRM
who will also *c* .... 1 Cor 1:8

CONFIRMED
covenant that was *c* .... Gal 3:17
c it by an oath .... Heb 6:17

CONFIRMING
c the word through ..... Mark 16:20

CONFLICT
to know what a great *c* ...... Col 2:1

CONFLICTS
Outside were *c* .... 2 Cor 7:5

CONFORMED
predestined to be *c* .... Rom 8:29
And do not be *c* .... Rom 12:2

CONFUSE
c their language .... Gen 11:7

CONFUSED
the assembly was *c* ..... Acts 19:32

CONGREGATION
Nor sinners in the *c* .... Ps 1:5
God stands in the *c* .... Ps 82:1

CONQUER
conquering and to *c* .... Rev 6:2

CONQUERORS
we are more than *c* .... Rom 8:37

CONSCIENCE
convicted by their *c* .... John 8:9
strive to have a *c* .... Acts 24:16

CONSECRATED
c this house which you .... 1 Kin 9:3

CONSENT
and does not *c* to .... 1 Tim 6:3

CONSENTED
He had not *c* to their .... Luke 23:51

CONSENTING
Now Saul was *c* to his ..... Acts 8:1

CONSIDER
When I *c* Your heavens .... Ps 8:3
My people do not *c* .... Is 1:3
C the lilies of the .... Matt 6:28
"*C* the ravens .... Luke 12:24
c Him who endured .... Heb 12:3

CONSIST
in Him all things *c* .... Col 1:17

CONSOLATION
if there is any *c* .... Phil 2:1
us everlasting *c* .... 2 Thess 2:16

CONSOLE
c those who mourn .... Is 61:3

CONSTANT
c prayer was .... Acts 12:5

CONSUME
whom the Lord will *c* .. 2 Thess 2:8

CONSUMED
but the bush was not *c* ...... Ex 3:2
mercies we are not *c* ..... Lam 3:22
beware lest you be *c* ...... Gal 5:15

CONSUMING
our God is a *c* fire .... Heb 12:29

CONTAIN
of heavens cannot *c* ...... 2 Chr 2:6
c the books that .... John 21:25

CONTEMPT
and be treated with *c* .... Mark 9:12

CONTEMPTIBLE
and his speech *c* .... 2 Cor 10:10

CONTEND
c earnestly for the .... Jude 3

CONTENT
state I am, to be *c* .... Phil 4:11
covetousness: be *c* .... Heb 13:5

CRUCIFY
out again, "*C* Him ... Mark 15:13

CRUEL
hate me with *c* hatred ... Ps 25:19

CRUELTY
the haunts of *c* ... Ps 74:20

CRUSH
of peace will *c* ... Rom 16:20

CRUSHED
every side, yet not *c* ... 2 Cor 4:8

CRUST
man is reduced to a *c* ... Prov 6:26

CRY
and their *c* came up to ... Ex 2:23
Does not wisdom *c* ... Prov 8:1
at midnight a *c* ... Matt 25:6
His own elect who *c* ... Luke 18:7

CRYING
nor sorrow, nor *c* ... Rev 21:4

CRYSTAL
a sea of glass, like *c* ... Rev 4:6

CUBIT
can add one *c* ... Matt 6:27

CUNNING
the serpent was more *c* ... Gen 3:1
c craftiness of deceitful ... Eph 4:14

CUP
My *c* runs over ... Ps 23:5
Then He took the *c* ... Matt 26:27
possible, let this *c* ... Matt 26:39
c is the new covenant ... Luke 22:20
cannot drink the *c* ... 1 Cor 10:21
c is the new ... 1 Cor 11:25

CURE
and to *c* diseases ... Luke 9:1

CURES
and perform *c* ... Luke 13:32

CURSE
c the ground for man's ... Gen 8:21
C God and die ... Job 2:9
"I will send a *c* ... Mal 2:2
law are under the *c* ... Gal 3:10

CURSED
c more than all cattle ... Gen 3:14
from Me, you *c* ... Man 25:41

CURSES
I will curse him who *c* ... Gen 12:3

CURTAIN
the heavens like a *c* ... Ps 104:2

CUSTOM
according to the *c* ... Acts 15:1

CUT
evildoers shall be *c* ... Ps 37:9
the wicked will be *c* ... Prov 2:22

CYMBAL
or a clanging *c* ... 1 Cor 13:1

D

DAILY
Give us this day our *d* ... Matt 6:11
take up his cross *d* ... Luke 9:23
the Scriptures *d* ... Acts 17:11

DANCE
mourn, And a time to *d* ... Eccl 3:4
And you did not *d* ... Matt 11:17

DANCED
Then David *d* before ... 2 Sam 6:14

DANCING
saw the calf and the *d* ... Ex 32:19
he heard music and *d* ... Luke 15:25

DARE
someone would even *d* ... Rom 5:7

DARK
I tell you in the *d* ... Matt 10:27
shines in a *d* place ... 2 Pet 1:19

DARKENED
their understanding *d* ... Eph 4:18

DARKNESS
d He called Night ... Gen 1:5
Those who sat in *d* ... Ps 107:10
d Have seen a ... Is 9:2
And deep *d* the people ... Is 60:2
body will be full of *d* ... Matt 6:23
cast out into outer *d* ... Matt 8:12
d rather than light ... John 3:19
For you were once *d* ... Eph 5:8
called you out of *d* ... 1 Pet 2:9
d is reserved ... 2 Pet 2:17
and in Him is no *d* ... 1 John 1:5
d is passing away ... 1 John 2:8

DARTS
quench all the fiery *d* ... Eph 6:16

DASH
You shall *d* them to ... Ps 2:9
Lest you *d* your foot ... Matt 4:6

DASHED
infants shall be *d* ... Hos 13:16

DAUGHTER
"Rejoice greatly, O *d* ... Zech 9:9
"Fear not, *d* of Zion ... John 12:15
the son of Pharaoh's *d* ... Heb 11:24

DAUGHTERS
of God saw the *d* ... Gen 6:2
d shall prophesy ... Acts 2:17

DAY
God called the light *D* ... Gen 1:5
And *d* and night ... Gen 8:22
the Sabbath *d* ... Ex 20:8
For a *d* in Your courts ... Ps 84:10
d the LORD has ... Ps 118:24
not strike you by *d* ... Ps 121:6
For the *d* of the LORD ... Joel 2:11
who can endure the *d* ... Mal 3:2
d our daily bread ... Matt 6:11
sent Me while it is *d* ... John 9:4
person esteems one *d* ... Rom 14:5
D will declare it ... 1 Cor 3:13
again the third *d* ... 1 Cor 15:4
with the Lord one *d* ... 2 Pet 3:8

DAYS
d are swifter than a ... Job 7:6
of woman is of few *d* ... Job 14:1
The *d* of our lives are ... Ps 90:10
Before the difficult *d* ... Eccl 12:1
shortened those *d* ... Mark 13:20
raise it up in three *d* ... John 2:20

DAYSPRING
With which the *D* ... Luke 1:78

DEACONS
with the bishops and *d* ... Phil 1:1
d must be reverent ... 1 Tim 3:8
d be the husbands ... 1 Tim 3:12

DEAD
But the *d* know nothing ... Eccl 9:5
d bury their own *d* ... Matt 8:22
not the God of the *d* ... Matt 22:32
this my son was *d* ... Luke 15:24
d will hear the voice ... John 5:25
was raised from the *d* ... Rom 6:4
yourselves to be *d* ... Rom 6:11
be Lord of both the *d* ... Rom 14:9
resurrection of the *d* ... 1 Cor 15:12
And the *d* in Christ ... 1 Thess 4:16
without works is *d* ... James 2:26
And the *d* were judged ... Rev 20:12

DEADLY
drink anything *d* ... Mark 16:18
evil, full of *d* poison ... James 3:8

DEADNESS
the *d* of Sarah's womb ... Rom 4:19

DEAF
d shall be unstopped ... Is 35:5
are cleansed and the *d* ... Matt 11:5

DEAL
My Servant shall *d* ... Is 52:13

DEATH
d parts you and me ... Ruth 1:17
and the shadow of *d* ... Job 10:21
I sleep the sleep of *d* ... Ps 13:3
of the shadow of *d* ... Ps 23:4
house leads down to *d* ... Prov 2:18
who hate me love *d* ... Prov 8:36
swallow up *d* forever ... Is 25:8
no pleasure in the *d* ... Ezek 18:32
who shall not taste *d* ... Matt 16:28
but has passed from *d* ... John 5:24
Nevertheless *d* reigned ... Rom 5:14
D no longer has ... Rom 6:9
the wages of sin is *d* ... Rom 6:23
the Lord's *d* ... 1 Cor 11:26
since by man came *d* ... 1 Cor 15:21
D is swallowed up in ... 1 Cor 15:54
The sting of *d* is sin ... 1 Cor 15:56
is sin leading to *d* ... 1 John 5:16
Be faithful until *d* ... Rev 2:10
shall be no more *d* ... Rev 21:4
which is the second *d* ... Rev 21:8

DEBTOR
I am a *d* both to ... Rom 1:14
that he is a *d* to keep ... Gal 5:3

DEBTORS
as we forgive our *d* ... Matt 6:12
of his master's *d* ... Luke 16:5
brethren, we are *d* ... Rom. 8:12

DECEIT
Nor was any *d* in His ... Is 53:9
philosophy and empty *d* ... Col 2:8
no sin, nor was *d* ... 1 Pet 2:22
mouth was found no *d* ... Rev 14:5

DECEITFUL
deliver me from the *d* ... Ps 43:1
"The heart is *d* ... Jer 17:9
are false apostles, *d* ... 2 Cor 11:13

DECEITFULLY
an idol, Nor sworn *d* ... Ps 24:4
the word of God *d* ... 2 Cor 4:2

DECEITFULNESS
this world and the *d* ... Matt 13:22

DECEIVE
rise up and *d* many ... Matt 24:11
Let no one *d* you with ... Eph 5:6
we have no sin, we *d* ... 1 John 1:8

DECEIVED
"The serpent *d* ... Gen 3:13
the commandment, *d* ... Rom 7:11
deceiving and being *d* ... 2 Tim 3:13

DECEIVER
how that *d* said ... Matt 27:63
This is a *d* and an ... 2 John 7

DECEIVES
heed that no one *d* ... Matt 24:4

DECENTLY
all things be done *d* ... 1 Cor 14:40

DECEPTIVE
you with *d* words ... 2 Pet 2:3

DECISION
in the valley of *d* ... Joel 3:14

DECLARE
The heavens *d* the ... Ps 19:1
d Your name to My ... Ps 22:22
seen and heard we *d* ... 1 John 1:3

DECLARED
and *d* to be the Son of ... Rom 1:4

DECREE
"I will declare the *d* ... Ps 2:7
in those days that a *d* ... Luke 2:1

DEDICATION
it was the Feast of *D* ... John 10:22

DEED
you do in word or *d* ... Col 3:17

DEEDS
because their *d* ... John 3:19
"You do the *d* ... John 8:41
one according to his *d* ... Rom 2:6
you put to death the *d* ... Rom 8:13

DEEP
LORD God caused a *d* ... Gen 2:21
d uttered its voice ... Hab 3:10
"Launch out into the *d* ... Luke 5:4
I have been in the *d* ... 2 Cor 11:25

DEEPER
D than Sheol ... Job 11:8

DEEPLY
But He sighed *d* ... Mark 8:12

DEER
As the *d* pants for the ... Ps 42:1
shall leap like a *d* ... Is 35:6

DEFEATED
and Israel was *d* ... 1 Sam 4:10

DEFEND
D the fatherless ... Is 1:17

DEFENSE
For wisdom is a *d* ... Eccl 7:12
am appointed for the *d* ... Phil 1:17
be ready to give a *d* ... 1 Pet 3:15

DEFILE
also these dreamers *d* ... Jude 8

DEFILED
lest they should be *d* ... John 18:28
and conscience are *d* ... Titus 1:15

DEFILES
mouth, this *d* a man ... Matt 15:11
it anything that *d* ... Rev 21:27

DEFRAUD
d his brother in this ... 1 Thess 4:6

DEGREES
go forward ten *d* ... 2 Kin 20:9

DELICACIES
of the king's *d* ... Dan 1:5

DELICATE
a lovely and *d* woman ... Jer 6:2

DELIGHT
But his *d* is in the ... Ps 1:2
I *d* to do Your will ... Ps 40:8
And I was daily His *d* ... Prov 8:30
And let your soul *d* ... Is 55:2
call the Sabbath a *d* ... Is 58:13
For I *d* in the law of ... Rom 7:22

DELIGHTS
For the LORD *d* in you ... Is 62:4

DELIVER
Let Him *d* Him ... Ps 22:8
I will *d* him and honor ... Ps 91:15
into temptation, But *d* ... Matt 6:13
let Him *d* Him now if ... Matt 27:43
And the Lord will *d* ... 2 Tim 4:18
d the godly out of ... 2 Pet 2:9

DELIVERANCE
not accepting *d* ... Heb 11:35

DELIVERED
who was *d* up because ... Rom 4:25
was once for all *d* ... Jude 3

DELIVERER
D will come out of ... Rom 11:26

DELIVERS
even Jesus who *d* ... 1 Thess 1:10

DELUSION
send them strong *d* ... 2 Thess 2:11

DEMON
Jesus rebuked the *d* ... Matt 17:18
and have a *d* ... John 8:48

DEMONIC
is earthly, sensual, *d* ... James 3:15

DEMONS
authority over all *d* ... Luke 9:1
the *d* are subject ... Luke 10:17
Even the *d* believe ... James 2:19

DEMONSTRATE
faith, to *d* His ... Rom 3:25

DEMONSTRATES
d His own love toward ... Rom 5:8

DEN
cast him Into the *d* ... Dan 6:16
it a '*d* of thieves ... Matt 21:13

DENARIUS
the laborers for a *d* ... Matt 20:2

DENIED
before men will be *d* ... Luke 12:9
Peter then *d* again ... John 18:27
d the Holy One and the ... Acts 3:14
things cannot be *d* ... Acts 19:36
household, he has *d* ... 1 Tim 5:8

DENIES
But whoever *d* ... Matt 10:33
d that Jesus is the ... 1 John 2:22

DENY
let him *d* himself ... Matt 16:24
He cannot *d* Himself ... 2 Tim 2:13

DENYING
but *d* its power ... 2 Tim 3:5
d the Lord who bought ... 2 Pet 2:1

DEPART
scepter shall not *d* ... Gen 49:10
on the left hand, '*D* ... Matt 25:41
will *d* from the faith ... 1 Tim 4:1

DEPARTING
heart of unbelief in *d* ... Heb 3:12

DEPARTURE
d savage wolves will ... Acts 20:29
and the time of my *d* ... 2 Tim 4:6

DEPRESSION
of man causes *d* ... Prov 12:25

DEPTH
nor height nor *d* ... Rom 8:39
Oh, the *d* of the ... Rom 11:33

DEPTHS
our sins Into the *d* ... Mic 7:19

DERISION
shall hold them in *d* ... Ps 2:4

DESCEND
d now from the cross ... Mark 15:32
Lord Himself will *d* ... 1 Thess 4:16

DESCENDANTS
"We are Abraham's *d* ... John 8:33

DESCENDED
He who *d* is also the ... Eph 4:10

DESCENDING
God ascending and *d* ... John 1:51
the holy Jerusalem, *d* ... Rev 21:10

DESERT
d shall rejoice ... Is 35:1
'Look, He is in the *d* ... Matt 24:26

DESERTED
d place by Himself ... Matt 14:13

DESERTS
They wandered in *d* ... Heb 11:38

DESIGN
with an artistic *d* ... Ex 26:31

DESIRABLE
the eyes, and a tree *d* ... Gen 3:6

DESIRE
d shall be for your ... Gen 3:16
Behold, You *d* truth in ... Ps 51:6
"Father, I *d* that ... John 17:24
all manner of evil *d* ... Rom 7:8
Brethren, my heart's *d* ... Rom 10:1
d the best gifts ... 1 Cor 12:31
the two, having a *d* ... Phil 1:23

DESIRED
d are they than gold ... Ps 19:10
One thing I have *d* ... Ps 27:4

DESIRES
shall give you the *d* ... Ps 37:4
the devil, and the *d* ... John 8:44
not come from your *d* ... James 4:1

DESOLATE
any more be termed *D* ... Is 62:4
house is left to you *d* ... Matt 23:38

DESOLATION
the 'abomination of *d* ... Matt 24:15

DESPAIRED
strength, so that we *d* ... 2 Cor 1:8

DESPISE
one and *d* the other ... Matt 6:24
d the riches of His ... Rom 2:4

DESPISED
He is *d* and rejected ... Is 53:3
the things which are *d* ... 1 Cor 1:28

DESPISES
d his neighbor sins ... Prov 14:21

DESPISING
the cross, *d* the shame ... Heb 12:2

DESTITUTE
of corrupt minds and *d* ... 1 Tim 6:5

DESTROY
Why should you *d* ... Eccl 7:16
shall not hurt nor *d* ... Is 11:9
I did not come to *d* ... Matt 5:17
Him who is able to *d* ... Matt 10:28
Barabbas and *d* Jesus ... Matt 27:20
to save life or to *d* ... Luke 6:9
d men's lives but to ... Luke 9:56
d the wisdom of the ... 1 Cor 1:19
able to save and to *d* ... James 4:12

DESTROYED
d all living things ... Gen 7:23
house, this tent, is *d* ... 2 Cor 5:1

DESTRUCTION
You turn man to *d* ... Ps 90:3
d that lays waste ... Ps 91:6
your life from *d* ... Ps 103:4
Pride goes before *d* ... Prov 16:18
whose end is *d* ... Phil 3:19
with everlasting *d* ... 2 Thess 1:9

DESTRUCTIVE
bring in *d* heresies ... 2 Pet 2:1

DETERMINED
d their preappointed ... Acts 17:26
For I *d* not to know ... 1 Cor 2:2

DEVICE
there is no work or *d* ... Eccl 9:10

DEVICES
not ignorant of his *d* ... 2 Cor 2:11

DEVIL
to be tempted by the *d* ... Matt 4:1
prepared for the *d* ... Matt 25:41
of your father the *d* ... John 8:44
give place to the *d* ... Eph 4:27
the snare of the *d* ... 2 Tim 2:26
the works of the *d* ... 1 John 3:8

DEVIOUS
And who are *d* ... Prov 2:15

DEVISES
d wickedness on his ... Ps 36:4
But a generous man *d* ... Is 32:8

DEVOID
who is *d* of wisdom ... Prov 11:12

DEVOTED
Your servant, who is *d* ... Ps 119:38

DEVOUR
For you *d* widows' ... Matt 23:14
bite and *d* one another ... Gal 5:15
whom he may *d* ... 1 Pet 5:8
d her Child as ... Rev 12:4

DEVOURED
wild beast has *d* ... Gen 37:20
birds came and *d* them ... Matt 13:4
of heaven and *d* them ... Rev 20:9

DEVOUT
man was just and *d* ... Luke 2:25
d soldier from among ... Acts 10:7

DEW
God give you Of the *d* ... Gen 27:28

DIADEMS
ten horns, and seven *d* ... Rev 12:3

DIAMOND
d it is engraved ... Jer 17:1

DICTATES
according to the *d* ... Jer 23:17

DIE
it you shall surely *d* ... Gen 2:17
but a person shall *d* ... 2 Chr 25:4
I shall not *d* ... Ps 118:17
born, And a time to *d* ... Eccl 3:2
eat of it and not *d* ... John 6:50
to you that you will *d* ... John 8:24
though he may *d* ... John 11:25
one man should *d* ... John 11:50
the flesh you will *d* ... Rom 8:13
For as in Adam all *d* ... 1 Cor 15:22
and to *d* is gain ... Phil 1:21
for men to *d* once ... Heb 9:27
are the dead who *d* ... Rev 14:13

DIED
And all flesh *d* ... Gen 7:21
in due time Christ *d* ... Rom 5:6
Christ *d* for us ... Rom 5:8
Now if we *d* with ... Rom 6:8
and He *d* for all ... 2 Cor 5:15
for if we *d* with Him ... 2 Tim 2:11

DIES
alive unless it *d* ... 1 Cor 15:36

DIFFERS
for one star *d* from ... 1 Cor 15:41

DILIGENCE
d it produced in you ..... 2 Cor 7:11

DILIGENT
d makes rich .... Prov 10:4

DILIGENTLY
d lest anyone fall ....Heb 12:15

DIM
His eyes were not *d* ......Dent 34:7

DIMLY
we see in a mirror, *d* ... 1 Cor 13:12

DINE
come in to him and *d* ...... Rev 3:20

DINNER
invites you to *d* .... 1 Cor 10:27

DIP
d your piece of bread ..... Ruth 2:14

DIPPED
clothed with a robe *d* .....Rev 19:13

DIRECT
Now may the Lord *d* ... 2 Thess 3:5

DIRT
cast up mire and *d* ....Is 57:20

DISARMED
d principalities .... Col 2:15

DISASTER
will end with *d* .... Acts 27:10

DISCERN
d the face of the sky ...... Matt 16:3
senses exercised to *d* ......Heb 5:14

DISCERNED
they are spiritually *d* .... 1 Cor 2:14

DISCERNER
d of the thoughts ....Heb 4:12

DISCERNS
a wise man's heart *d* ....Eccl 8:5

DISCIPLE
he cannot be My *d* ......Luke 14:26
d whom Jesus loved ...... John 21:7

DISCIPLES
word, you are My *d* ......John 8:31
but we are Moses' *d* ...... John 9:28

DISCIPLINES
he who loves him *d* ...... Prov 13:24

DISCORD
And one who sows *d* ..... Prov 6:19

DISCOURAGED
lest they became *d* .... Col 3:21
become weary and *d* ......Heb 12:3

DISCRETION
D will preserve you ...... Prov 2:11

DISFIGURE
d their faces that .... Matt 6:16

DISGUISES
And he *d* his face .... Job 24:15

DISHONOR
Father, and you *d* Me ..... John 8:49
d their bodies among ..... Rom 1:24
It is sown in *d* .... 1 Cor 15:43

DISHONORED
But you have *d* the ....James 2:6

DISHONORS
For son *d* father .... Mic 7:6

DISOBEDIENT
out My hands To a *d* ....Rom 10:21

DISORDERLY
for this *d* gathering ...... Acts 19:40

DISPENSATION
d of the fullness of ....Eph 1:10

DISPERSION
the pilgrims of the *D* ......1 Pet 1:1

DISPLEASE
LORD see it, and it *d* ..... Prov 24:18

DISPLEASED
they were greatly *d* ...... Matt 20:24
it, He was greatly *d* .... Mark 10:14

DISPUTE
there was also a *d* ....Luke 22:24

DISPUTER
Where is the *d* of this ... 1 Cor 1:20

DISPUTES
But avoid foolish *d* .... Titus 3:9

DISQUALIFIED
should become *d* .... 1 Cor 9:27

DISQUIETED
And why are you *d* .... Ps 42:5

DISSENSION
had no small *d* and .... Acts 15:2

DISSIPATION
not accused of *d* .... Titus 1:6

DISSOLVED
the heavens will be *d* ..... 2 Pet 3:12

DISTINCTION
compassion, making a *d* .... Jude 22

DISTRESS
d them in His deep ....Ps 2:5
tribulation, or *d* .... Rom 8:35

DISTRESSED
and deeply *d* .... Mark 14:33

DISTRESSES
Bring me out of my *d* ...... Ps 25:17

DISTRIBUTED
and they *d* to each as ..... Acts 4:35

DISTRIBUTING
d to the needs of the ..... Rom 12:13

DITCH
will fall into a *d* .... Matt 15:14

DIVERSITIES
There are *d* .... 1 Cor 12:4

DIVIDE
d the spoil with the ...... Prov 16:19
"Take this and *d* ....Luke 22:17

DIVIDED
and the waters were *d* ..... Ex 14:21
they were not *d* ....2 Sam 1:23
"Every kingdom *d* ...... Matt 12:25
Is Christ *d* .... 1 Cor 1:13

DIVIDES
at home *d* the spoil .... Ps 68:12

DIVIDING
rightly *d* the word of .... 2 Tim 2:15

DIVINATION
shall you practice *d* ...... Lev 19:26
a spirit of *d* met us ...... Acts 16:16

DIVINE
d service and the .... Heb 9:1

DIVISION
So there was a *d* .... John 7:43

DIVISIONS
those who cause *d* .... Rom 16:17
persons, who cause *d* ...... Jude 19

DIVISIVE
Reject a *d* man after ...... Titus 3:10

DIVORCE
her a certificate of *d* ...... Deut 24:1
a certificate of *d* .... Mark 10:4

DO
men to *d* to you, *d* .... Matt 7:12
He sees the Father *d* ...... John 5:19
without Me you can *d* .... John 15:5
"Sirs, what must I *d* ..... Acts 16:30
d evil that good may ...... Rom 3:8
or whatever you *d*, *d* ... 1 Cor 10:31

DOCTRINE
What new *d* is this ...... Mark 1:27
"My *d* is not Mine .... John 7:16
with every wind of *d* ...... Eph 4:14
is contrary to sound *d* ... 1 Tim 1:10
is profitable for *d* .... 2 Tim 3:16
not endure sound *d* ...... 2 Tim 4:3

DOCTRINES
commandments and *d* ..... Col 2:22
various and strange *d* .....Heb 13:9

DOERS
But be *d* of the word ....James 1:22

DOG
d is better than a ....Eccl 9:4
d returns to his own ......2 Pet 2:22

DOGS
what is holy to the *d* .... Matt 7:6
d eat the crumbs .... Matt 15:27
But outside are *d* ....Rev 22:15

DOMINION
let them have *d* ....Gen 1:26
d is an everlasting ....Dan 4:34
sin shall not have *d* ...... Rom 6:14
glory and majesty, *D* .... Jude 25

DONKEY
d its master's crib .... Is 1:3
and riding on a *d* .... Zech 9:9
colt, the foal of a *d* .... Matt 21:5
d speaking with a ....2 Pet 2:16

DOOM
for the day of *d* .... Prov 16:4

DOOR
stone against the *d* ...... Matt 27:60
to you, I am the *d* ....John 10:7
before you an open *d* .... Rev 3:8
I stand at the *d* ....Rev 3:20

DOORKEEPER
I would rather be a *d* ...... Ps 84:10

DOORPOSTS
write them on the *d* .... Deut 6:9

DOORS
up, you everlasting *d* .... Ps 24:7

DOUBLE
from the LORD's hand *D* ..... Is 40:2
worthy of *d* honor .... 1 Tim 5:17

DOUBLE-MINDED
he is a *d* man ....James 1:8

DOUBT
faith, why did you *d* ..... Matt 14:31

DOUBTING
in faith, with no *d* ....James 1:6

DOUBTS
why do *d* arise in ....Luke 24:38
for I have *d* about you ..... Gal 4:20

DOVE
d found no resting ....Gen 8:9
descending like a *d* .... Matt 3:16

DOVES
and harmless as *d* .... Matt 10:16

DOWNCAST
who comforts the *d* .... 2 Cor 7:6

DRAGNET
d that was cast .... Matt 13:47

DRAGON
they worshiped the *d* ...... Rev 13:4
He laid hold of the *d* ...... Rev 20:2

DRAINED
All faces are *d* .... Joel 2:6

DRANK
them, and they all *d* .... Mark 14:23

DRAW
d honey from the ....Deut 32:13
me to *d* near to God .... Ps 73:28
And the years *d* ....Eccl 12:1
will *d* all peoples ....John 12:32
D near to God and He ....James 4:8

DRAWS
your redemption *d* ......Luke 21:28

DREAM
Now Joseph had a *d* ....Gen 37:5
Your old men shall *d* ......Joel 2:28
to Joseph in a *d* .... Matt 2:13
things today in a *d* ...... Matt 27:19

DREAMERS
d defile the flesh .... Jude 8

DREAMS
Nebuchadnezzar had *d* .....Dan 2:1

DRIED
of her blood was *d* ...... Mark 5:29
saw the fig tree *d* .... Mark 11:20

DRIFT
have heard, lest we *d* ....Heb 2:1

DRINK
gave me vinegar to *d* ...... Ps 69:21
Lest they *d* and forget .... Prov 31:5
follow intoxicating *d* .... Is 5:11
d the milk of the ....Is 60:16

bosom, That you may *d* ... Is 66:11
"Bring wine, let us *d* ... Amos 4:1
that day when I *d* ... Matt 26:29
mingled with gall to *d* ... Matt 27:34
with myrrh to *d* ... Mark 15:23
to her, "Give Me a *d* ... John 4:7
him come to Me and *d* ... John 7:37
do, as often as you *d* ... 1 Cor 11:25
No longer *d* only ... 1 Tim 5:23

DRINKS
to her, "Whoever *d* ... John 4:13
d My blood has ... John 6:54
he who eats and *d* ... 1 Cor 11:29

DRIPPING
His lips are lilies, *D* ... Song 5:13

DROSS
purge away your *d* ... Is 1:25

DROUGHT
in the year of *d* ... Jer 17:8
"For I called for a *d* ... Hag 1:11

DROVE
So He *d* out the man ... Gen 3:24
temple of God and *d* ... Matt 21:12

DROWN
Nor can the floods *d* ... Song 8:7
harmful lusts which *d* ... 1 Tim 6:9

DROWSINESS
d will clothe a ... Prov 23:21

DRUNK
of the wine and was *d* ... Gen 9:21
the guests have well *d* ... John 2:10
"For these are not *d* ... Acts 2:15
and another is *d* ... 1 Cor 11:21
I saw the woman, *d* ... Rev 17:6

DRUNKARD
to and fro like a *d* ... Is 24:20
or a reviler, or a *d* ... 1 Cor 5:11

DRUNKEN
I am like a *d* man ... Jer 23:9

DRUNKENNESS
will be filled with *d* ... Ezek 23:33
not in revelry and *d* ... Rom 13:13
envy, murders, *d* ... Gal 5:21

DRY
place, and let the *d* ... Gen 1:9
made the sea into *d* ... Ex 14:21
It was *d* on the fleece ... Judg 6:40
will be done in the *d* ... Luke 23:31

DUE
pay all that was *d* ... Matt 18:34
d time Christ died ... Rom 5:6
d season we shall ... Gal 6:9
exalt you in *d* time ... 1 Pet 5:6

DULL
heart of this people *d* ... Is 6:10
people have grown *d* ... Matt 13:15

DUMB
the tongue of the *d* ... Is 35:6

DUST
formed man of the *d* ... Gen 2:7
d you shall return ... Gen 3:19
And repent in *d* ... Job 42:6
that we are *d* ... Ps 103:14
counted as the small *d* ... Is 40:15
city, shake off the *d* ... Matt 10:14
of the man of *d* ... 1 Cor 15:49

DUTY
done what was our *d* ... Luke 17:10

DWELL
Who may *d* in Your holy ... Ps 15:1
"I *d* in the high and ... Is 57:15
"I will *d* in them ... 2 Cor 6:16
that Christ may *d* ... Eph 3:17
men, and He will *d* ... Rev 21:3

DWELLING
built together for a *d* ... Eph 2:22
a foreign country, *d* ... Heb 11:9

DWELLS
He who *d* in the secret ... Ps 91:1
but the Father who *d* ... John 14:10
d all the fullness ... Col 2:9
which righteousness *d* ... 2 Pet 3:13
you, where Satan *d* ... Rev 2:13

DWELT
became flesh and *d* ... John 1:14
By faith he *d* in the ... Heb 11:9

DYING
in the body the *d* ... 2 Cor 4:10

E

EAGLE
fly away like an *e* ... Prov 23:5
The way of an *e* ... Prov 30:19
like a flying *e* ... Rev 4:7

EAGLES
up with wings like *e* ... Is 40:31
e will be gathered ... Matt 24:28

EAGLES'
how I bore you on *e* ... Ex 19:4

EAR
shall pierce his *e* ... Ex 21:6
And the *e* of the wise ... Prov 18:15
e is uncircumcised ... Jer 6:10
you hear in the *e* ... Matt 10:27
cut off his right *e* ... John 18:10
not seen, nor *e* heard ... 1 Cor 2:9
"He who has an *e* ... Rev 2:7

EARLY
Very *e* in the morning ... Mark 16:2
arrived at the tomb *e* ... Luke 24:22

EARNESTLY
He prayed more *e* ... Luke 22:44
e that it would not ... James 5:17
you to contend *e* ... Jude 3

EARS
And hear with their *e* ... Is 6:10
"He who has *e* ... Matt 11:15
they have itching *e* ... 2 Tim 4:3

EARTH
to judge the *e* ... 1 Chr 16:33
foundations of the *e* ... Job 38:4
e is the LORD's ... Ps 24:1
You had formed the *e* ... Ps 90:2
there was ever an *e* ... Prov 8:23
e abides forever ... Eccl 1:4
for the meek of the *e* ... Is 11:4
e is My footstool ... Is 66:1
I will darken the *e* ... Amos 8:9
shall inherit the *e* ... Matt 5:5
heaven and *e* pass ... Matt 5:18
e as it is in heaven ... Matt 6:10
treasures on *e* ... Matt 6:19
then shook the *e* ... Heb 12:26
heaven and a new *e* ... Rev 21:1

EARTHLY
"If I have told you *e* ... John 3:12
that if our *e* house ... 2 Cor 5:1
their mind on *e* things ... Phil 3:19
from above, but is *e* ... James 3:15

EARTHQUAKE
after the wind an *e* ... 1 Kin 19:11
there was a great *e* ... Matt 28:2

EARTHQUAKES
And there will be *e* ... Mark 13:8

EASIER
"Which is *e*, to say ... Mark 2:9
"It is *e* for a camel ... Mark 10:25

EAST
goes toward the *e* ... Gen 2:14
wise men from the *E* ... Matt 2:1
many will come from *e* ... Matt 8:11
wilt come from the *e* ... Luke 13:29

EAT
you may freely *e* ... Gen 2:16
'You shall not *e* ... Gen 3:17
e this scroll ... Ezek 3:1
life, what you will *e* ... Matt 6:25
give us His flesh to *e* ... John 6:52
one believes he may *e* ... Rom 14:2
e meat nor drink wine ... Rom 14:21
I will never again *e* ... 1 Cor 8:13
neither shall he *e* ... 2 Thess 3:10

EATEN
Have you *e* from the ... Gen 3:11
he was *e* by worms ... Acts 12:23

EATS
receives sinners and *e* ... Luke 15:2
"Whoever *e* My flesh ... John 6:54
e this bread will live ... John 6:58
He who *e*, *e* to the ... Rom 14:6
unworthy manner *e* ... 1 Cor 11:29

EDIFICATION
has given me for *e* ... 2 Cor 13:10
rather than godly *e* ... 1 Tim 1:4

EDIFIES
puffs up, but love *e* ... 1 Cor 8:1

EDIFY
but not all things *e* ... 1 Cor 10:23

EDIFYING
of the body for the *e* ... Eph 4:16

ELDER
against an *e* except ... 1 Tim 5:19

ELDERS
the tradition of the *e* ... Matt 15:2
be rejected by the *e* ... Luke 9:22
they had appointed *e* ... Acts 14:23
e who rule well be ... 1 Tim 5:17
lacking, and appoint *e* ... Titus 1:5
e obtained a good ... Heb 11:2
e who are among you I ... 1 Pet 5:1
I saw twenty-four *e* ... Rev 4:4

ELDERSHIP
of the hands of the *e* ... 1 Tim 4:14

ELECT
gather together His *e* ... Matt 24:31
e have obtained it ... Rom 11:7
e according to the ... 1 Pet 1:2
A chief cornerstone, *e* ... 1 Pet 2:6

ELECTION
call and *e* sure ... 2 Pet 1:10

ELEMENTS
weak and beggarly *e* ... Gal 4:9
e will melt with ... 2 Pet 3:10

ELEVEN
numbered with the *e* ... Acts 1:26

ELOQUENT
an *e* man and mighty ... Acts 18:24

EMBALM
to *e* his father ... Gen 50:2

ENCOURAGED
is, that I may be *e* ... Rom 1:12
and all may be *e* ... 1 Cor 14:31

END
make me to know my *e* ... Ps 39:4
shall keep it to the *e* ... Ps 119:33
e is the way of death ... Prov 14:12
Declaring the *e* ... Is 46:10
what shall be the *e* ... Dan 12:8
the harvest is the *e* ... Matt 13:39
always, even to the *e* ... Matt 28:20
He loved them to the *e* ... John 13:1
For Christ is the *e* ... Rom 10:4
But the *e* of all ... 1 Pet 4:7
the latter *e* is worse ... 2 Pet 2:20
My works until the *e* ... Rev 2:26
Beginning and the *E* ... Rev 22:13

ENDLESS
and *e* genealogies ... 1 Tim 1:4
to the power of an *e* ... Heb 7:16

ENDURANCE
e the race that ... Heb 12:1

ENDURE
as the sun and moon *e* ... Ps 72:5
His name shall *e* ... Ps 72:17
persecuted, we *e* ... 1 Cor 4:12

ENDURED
he had patiently *e* ... Heb 6:15
e as seeing Him who ... Heb 11:27
consider Him who *e* ... Heb 12:3

ENDURES
And His truth *e* ... Ps 100:5
For His mercy *e* ... Ps 136:1
But he who *e* to the ... Matt 10:22
e only for a while ... Matt 13:21
for the food which *e* ... John 6:27
he has built on it *e* ... 1 Cor 3:14
hopes all things, *e* ... 1 Cor 13:7
word of the LORD *e* ... 1 Pet 1:25

ENDURING
the LORD is clean, *e* ... Ps 19:9

ENEMIES
- the presence of my *e* … Ps 23:5
- *e* will lick the dust … Ps 72:9
- to you, love your *e* … Matt 5:44
- *e* will be those … Matt 10:36
- *e* we were reconciled … Rom 5:10
- till He has put all *e* … 1 Cor 15:25
- were alienated and *e* … Col 1:21
- His *e* are made His … Heb 10:13

ENEMY
- If your *e* is hungry … Prov 25:21
- rejoice over me, my *e* … Mic 7:8
- and hate your *e* … Matt 5:43
- last *e* that will be … 1 Cor 15:26
- become your *e* because … Gal 4:16
- count him as an *e* … 2 Thess 3:15
- makes himself an *e* … James 4:4

ENJOY
- richly all things to *e* … 1 Tim 6:17
- than to *e* the passing … Heb 11:25

ENJOYMENT
- So I commended *e* … Eccl 8:15

ENLIGHTEN
- *E* my eyes … Ps 13:3

ENLIGHTENED
- those who were once *e* … Heb 6:4

ENMITY
- And I will put *e* … Gen 3:15
- the carnal mind is *e* … Rom 8:7
- in His flesh the *e* … Eph 2:15

ENRAPTURED
- And always be *e* … Prov 5:19

ENRICHED
- while you are *e* … 2 Cor 9:11

ENSNARED
- The wicked is *e* … Prov 12:13

ENSNARES
- sin which so easily *e* … Heb 12:1

ENTER
- *E* into His gates … Ps 100:4
- you will by no means *e* … Matt 5:20
- "*E* by the narrow … Matt 7:13
- *e* the kingdom of God … Matt 19:24
- *E* into the joy of your … Matt 25:21
- and pray, lest you *e* … Matt 26:41
- "Strive to *e* through … Luke 13:24
- who have believed do *e* … Heb 4:3
- *e* the temple till the … Rev 15:8

ENTERED
- Then Satan *e* Judas … Luke 22:3
- through one man sin *e* … Rom 5:12
- ear heard, Nor have *e* … 1 Cor 2:9
- the forerunner has *e* … Heb 6:20
- *e* the Most Holy Place … Heb 9:12

ENTERS
- If anyone *e* by Me … John 10:9

ENTHRONED
- You are holy, *E* in … Ps 22:3

ENTIRELY
- give yourself *e* … 1 Tim 4:15

ENTREAT
- being defamed, we *e* … 1 Cor 4:13

ENTREATED
- *e* our God for this … Ezra 8:23

ENVIOUS
- patriarchs, becoming *e* … Acts 7:9

ENVY
- *e* slays a simple … Job 5:2
- *e* is rottenness … Prov 14:30
- not let your heart *e* … Prov 23:17
- full of *e* … Rom 1:29
- not in strife and *e* … Rom 13:13
- love does not *e* … 1 Cor 13:4
- *e*, murders … Gal 5:21
- living in malice and *e* … Titus 3:3

EPISTLE
- You are our *e* written … 2 Cor 3:2

EPISTLES
- as also in all his *e* … 2 Pet 3:16

ERR
- My people Israel to *e* … Jer 23:13

ERROR
- a sinner from the *e* … James 5:20
- led away with the *e* … 2 Pet 3:17
- run greedily in the *e* … Jude 11

ERRORS
- can understand his *e* … Ps 19:12

ESCAPE
- *e* all these things … Luke 21:36
- same, that you will *e* … Rom 2:3
- make the way of *e* … 1 Cor 10:13
- how shall we *e* if we … Heb 2:3

ESCAPED
- after they have *e* … 2 Pet 2:20

ESTABLISH
- seeking to *e* their own … Rom 10:3
- faithful, who will *e* … 2 Thess 3:3
- *E* your hearts … James 5:8
- a while, perfect, *e* … 1 Pet 5:10

ESTABLISHED
- Your throne is *e* … Ps 93:2
- built up In Him and *e* … Col 2:7
- covenant, which was *e* … Heb 8:6

ESTEEM
- and we did not *e* … Is 53:3
- *e* others better than … Phil 2:3

ESTEEMED
- For what is highly *e* … Luke 16:15

ESTEEMS
- One person *e* one day … Rom 14:5

ETERNAL
- *e* God is your refuge … Deut 33:27
- For man goes to his *e* … Eccl 12:5
- and inherit *e* life … Matt 19:29
- in the age to come, *e* … Mark 10:30
- not perish but have *e* … John 3:15
- you think you have *e* … John 5:39
- I give them *e* life … John 10:28
- "And this is *e* life … John 17:3
- the gift of God is *e* … Rom 6:23
- are not seen are *e* … 2 Cor 4:18
- lay hold on *e* life … 1 Tim 6:12
- *e* life which was … 1 John 1:2

ETERNITY
- Also He has put *e* … Eccl 3:11
- One who inhabits *e* … Is 57:15

EUNUCH
- of Ethiopia, a *e* … Acts 8:27

EUNUCHS
- made themselves *e* … Matt 19:12

EVANGELIST
- of Philip the *e* … Acts 21:8
- do the work of an *e* … 2 Tim 4:5

EVANGELISTS
- some prophets, some *e* … Eph 4:11

EVERLASTING
- from *E* is Your name … Is 63:16
- awake, Some to *e* life … Dan 12:2
- not perish but have *e* … John 3:16
- who sent Me has *e* … John 5:24
- endures to *e* life … John 6:27
- in Him may have *e* … John 6:40
- believes in Me has *e* … John 6:47
- *e* destruction from … 2 Thess 1:9

EVIDENCE
- *e* of things not seen … Heb 11:1

EVIDENT
- *e* that our Lord arose … Heb 7:14

EVIL
- of good and *e* … Gen 2:9
- knowing good and *e* … Gen 3:5
- his heart was only *e* … Gen 6:5
- I will fear no *e* … Ps 23:4
- *e* more than good … Ps 52:3
- To do *e* is like sport … Prov 10:23
- *e* will bow before the … Prov 14:19
- Keeping watch on the *e* … Prov 15:3
- *e* All the days of her … Prov 31:12
- to those who call *e* … Is 5:20
- of peace and not of *e* … Jer 29:11
- Seek good and not *e* … Amos 5:14
- deliver us from the *e* … Matt 6:13
- "If you then, being *e* … Matt 7:11
- *e* treasure brings … Matt 12:35
- everyone practicing *e* … John 3:20
- done any good or *e* … Rom 9:11
- Repay no one *e* for … Rom 12:17
- provoked, thinks no *e* … 1 Cor 13:5

EVILDOER
- "If He were not an *e* … John 18:30
- suffer trouble as an *e* … 2 Tim 2:9

EVILDOERS
- *e* shall be cut off … Ps 37:9
- from me, you *e* … Ps 119:115
- iniquity, A brood of *e* … Is 1:4
- against you as *e* … 1 Pet 2:12

EXALT
- *e* His name together … Ps 34:3
- *E* the humble … Ezek 21:26
- And he shall *e* himself … Dan 8:25

EXALTATION
- who rejoice in My *e* … Is 13:3
- brother glory in his *e* … James 1:9

EXALTED
- Let God be *e* … 2 Sam 22:47
- I will be *e* among the … Ps 46:10
- You are *e* far above … Ps 97:9
- His name alone is *e* … Ps 148:13
- valley shall be *e* … Is 40:4
- "Him God has *e* … Acts 5:31
- And lest I should be *e* … 2 Cor 12:7
- also has highly *e* … Phil 2:9

EXALTS
- Righteousness *e* … Prov 14:34
- high thing that *e* … 2 Cor 10:5
- *e* himself above all … 2 Thess 2:4

EXAMINE
- But let a man *e* … 1 Cor 11:28
- But let each one *e* … Gal 6:4

EXAMPLE
- to make her a public *e* … Matt 1:19
- I have given you an *e* … John 13:15
- youth, but be an *e* … 1 Tim 4:12
- us, leaving us an *e* … 1 Pet 2:21
- are set forth as an *e* … Jude 7

EXAMPLES
- to them as *e* … 1 Cor 10:11
- to you, but being *e* … 1 Pet 5:3

EXCHANGE
- give in *e* for his soul … Matt 16:26

EXCHANGED
- Nor can it be *e* … Job 28:17
- *e* the truth of God for … Rom 1:25

EXCUSE
- now they have no *e* … John 15:22
- they are without *e* … Rom 1:20

EXCUSES
- began to make *e* … Luke 14:18

EXECUTE
- *e* judgment also … John 5:27
- *e* wrath on him who … Rom 13:4

EXECUTES
- *e* justice for me … Mic 7:9

EXERCISE
- *e* yourself toward … 1 Tim 4:7

EXHORT
- *e* him as a father … 1 Tim 5:1
- Speak these things, *e* … Titus 2:15
- *e* one another … Heb 3:13

EXHORTATION
- he who exhorts, in *e* … Rom 12:8
- to reading, to *e* … 1 Tim 4:13

EXHORTED
- know how we *e* … 1 Thess 2:11

EXIST
- by Your will they *e* … Rev 4:11

EXPECT
- an hour you do not *e* … Luke 12:40

EXPECTATION
- the people were in *e* … Luke 3:15
- a certain fearful *e* … Heb 10:27

EXPLAIN
- no one who could *e* … Gen 41:24
- "*E* this parable to us … Matt 15:15
- to say, and hard to *e* … Heb 5:11

EXPLAINED
- He *e* all things to His … Mark 4:34

EXPOSED
his deeds should be e ... John 3:20

EXPOUNDED
He e to them in all ... Luke 24:27

EXPRESS
of His glory and the e ... Heb 1:3

EXTORTION
they are full of e ... Matt 23:25

EXTORTIONERS
e will inherit ... 1 Cor 6:10

EYE
the ear, But now my e ... Job 42:5
guide you with My e ... Ps 32:8
e is not satisfied ... Eccl 1:8
the apple of His e ... Zech 2:8
if your right e ... Matt 5:29
it was said, 'An e ... Matt 5:38
plank in your own e ... Matt 7:3
e causes you to sin ... Matt 18:9
Or is your e evil ... Matt 20:15
the e of a needle ... Luke 18:25
the twinkling of an e ... 1 Cor 15:52
every e will see Him ... Rev 1:7
your eyes with e salve ... Rev 3:18

EYES
e will be opened ... Gen 3:5
And my e shall behold ... Job 19:27
e are ever toward the ... Ps 25:15
The e of the LORD are ... Ps 34:15
I will lift up my e ... Ps 121:1
but the e of a fool ... Prov 17:24
be wise in his own e ... Prov 26:5
You have dove's e ... Song 1:15
e have seen the King ... Is 6:5
Who have e and see ... Jer 5:21
rims were full of e ... Ezek 1:18
You are of purer e ... Hab 1:13
blessed are your e ... Matt 13:16
"He put clay on my e ... John 9:15
e they have closed ... Acts 28:27
E that they should not ... Rom 11:8
have seen with our e ... 1 John 1:1
the lust of the e ... 1 John 2:16
as snow, and His e ... Rev 1:14
creatures full of e ... Rev 4:6
horns and seven e ... Rev 5:6

EYESERVICE
not with e ... Eph 6:6

EYEWITNESSES
the beginning were e ... Luke 1:2
e of His majesty ... 2 Pet 1:16

F

FABLES
nor give heed to f ... 1 Tim 1:4
cunningly devised f ... 2 Pet 1:16

FACE
"For I have seen God f ... Gen 32:30
f shone while he ... Ex 34:29
sins have hidden His f ... Is 59:2
f shone like the sun ... Matt 17:2
dimly, but then f ... 1 Cor 13:12
with unveiled f ... 2 Cor 3:18
withstood him to his f ... Gal 2:11
They shall see His f ... Rev 22:4

FADE
We all f as a leaf ... Is 64:6
rich man also will f ... James 1:11
and that does not f ... 1 Pet 1:4

FADES
withers, the flower f ... Is 40:7

FAIL
tittle of the law to f ... Luke 16:17
faith should not f ... Luke 22:32
they will f ... 1 Cor 13:8
Your years will not f ... Heb 1:12

FAILING
"men's hearts f ... Luke 21:26

FAILS
Love never f ... 1 Cor 13:8

FAINT
shall walk and not f ... Is 40:31

FAINTS
My soul f for Your ... Ps 119:81
And the whole heart f ... Is 1:5
the earth, Neither f ... Is 40:28

FAITH
shall live by his f ... Hab 2:4
you, O you of little f ... Matt 6:30
not found such great f ... Matt 8:10
that you have no f ... Mark 4:40
"Increase our f ... Luke 17:5
will He really find f ... Luke 18:8
are sanctified by f ... Acts 26:18
God is revealed from f ... Rom 1:17
f apart from the deeds ... Rom 3:28
his f is accounted for ... Rom 4:5
those who are of the f ... Rom 4:16
f which we preach ... Rom 10:8
f comes by hearing ... Rom 10:17
and you stand by f ... Rom 11:20
in proportion to our f ... Rom 12:6
Do you have f ... Rom 14:22
though I have all f ... 1 Cor 13:2
And now abide f ... 1 Cor 13:13
For we walk by f ... 2 Cor 5:7
the flesh I live by f ... Gal 2:20
f are sons of Abraham ... Gal 3:7
But after f has come ... Gal 3:25
of the household of f ... Gal 6:10
been saved through f ... Eph 2:8
one Lord, one f ... Eph 4:5
taking the shield of f ... Eph 6:16
your work of f ... 1 Thess 1:3
for not all have f ... 2 Thess 3:2
the mystery of the f ... 1 Tim 3:9
I have kept the f ... 2 Tim 4:7
in our common f ... Titus 1:4
not being mixed with f ... Heb 4:2
f is the substance ... Heb 11:1
without f it is ... Heb 11:6
says he has f ... James 2:14
Show me your f ... James 2:18
and not by f only ... James 2:24
f will save the sick ... James 5:15
add to your f virtue ... 2 Pet 1:5
the patience and the f ... Rev 13:10

FAITHFUL
God, He Is God, the f ... Deut 7:9
LORD preserves the f ... Ps 31:23
eyes shall be on the f ... Ps 101:6
But who can find a f ... Prov 20:6
the Holy One who is f ... Hos 11:12
"Who then is a f ... Matt 24:45
good and f servant ... Matt 25:23
"He who is f in what ... Luke 16:10
Judged me to be f ... Acts 16:15
God is f ... 1 Cor 1:9
is my beloved and f ... 1 Cor 4:17
But as God is f ... 2 Cor 1:18
f brethren in Christ ... Col 1:2
who calls you is f ... 1 Thess 5:24
This is a f saying and ... 1 Tim 1:15
f High Priest in ... Heb 2:17
He who promised is f ... Heb 10:23
He is f and just to ... 1 John 1:9
Be f until death ... Rev 2:10
words are true and f ... Rev 21:5

FAITHFULNESS
I have declared Your f ... Ps 40:10
Your f also surrounds ... Ps 89:8
f endures to all ... Ps 119:90
Great is Your f ... Lam 3:23
unbelief make the f ... Rom 3:3

FAITHLESS
"O f generation ... Mark 9:19
If we are f ... 2 Tim 2:13

FALL
a deep sleep to f ... Gen 2:21
Let them f by their ... Ps 5:10
righteous man may f ... Prov 24:16
But the wicked shall f ... Prov 24:16
the blind, both will f ... Matt 15:14
the stars will f ... Matt 24:29
"I saw Satan f ... Luke 10:18
take heed lest he f ... 1 Cor 10:12
if they f away ... Heb 6:6
lest anyone f short of ... Heb 12:15
and rocks, "F on us ... Rev 6:16

FALLEN
"Babylon is f ... Is 21:9
you have f from grace ... Gal 5:4
"Babylon is f ... Rev 14:8

FALLING
great drops of blood f ... Luke 22:44
f away comes first ... 2 Thess 2:3

FALSE
"You shall not bear f ... Ex 20:16
I hate every f way ... Ps 119:104
f witness shall perish ... Prov 21:28
"Beware of f prophets ... Matt 7:15
f christs and f ... Matt 24:24
and we are found f ... 1 Cor 15:15
of f brethren ... Gal 2:4
f prophets have gone ... 1 John 4:1
mouth of the f prophet ... Rev 16:13

FALSEHOOD
For their deceit is f ... Ps 119:118
Offspring of f ... Is 57:4

FALSELY
of evil against you f ... Matt 5:11
f called knowledge ... 1 Tim 6:20

FAMILIES
in you all the f ... Gen 12:3
the God of all the f ... Jer 31:1
in your seed all the f ... Acts 3:25

FAMILY
shall mourn, every f ... Zech 12:12
f were baptized ... Acts 16:33

FAMINES
And there will be f ... Matt 24:7

FAMISH
righteous soul to f ... Prov 10:3

FAMISHED
honorable men are f ... Is 5:13

FAR
Your judgments are f ... Ps 10:5
Be not f from Me ... Ps 22:11
The LORD is f from ... Prov 15:29
their heart is f from ... Matt 15:8
going to a f country ... Mark 13:34
though He is not f ... Acts 17:27
you who once were f ... Eph 2:13

FARMER
The hard-working f ... 2 Tim 2:6
See how the f waits ... James 5:7

FASHIONED
have made me and f ... Job 10:8

FASHIONS
He f their hearts ... Ps 33:15

FAST
f as you do this day ... Is 58:4
f that I have chosen ... Is 58:5
"Moreover, when you f ... Matt 6:16
disciples do not f ... Matt 9:14
I f twice a week ... Luke 18:12

FASTED
'When you f and ... Zech 7:5
And when He had f ... Matt 4:2

FASTING
by prayer and f ... Matt 17:21
give yourselves to f ... 1 Cor 7:5

FASTINGS
in sleeplessness, in f ... 2 Cor 6:5

FAT
and you will eat the f ... Gen 45:18
f is the LORD's ... Lev 3:16

FATHER
man shall leave his f ... Gen 2:24
and you shall be a f ... Gen 17:4
I was a f to the poor ... Job 29:16
A f of the fatherless ... Ps 68:5
f pities his children ... Ps 103:13
God, Everlasting F ... Is 9:6
You, O LORD, are our F ... Is 63:16
time cry to Me, 'My F ... Jer 3:4
For I am a F to Israel ... Jer 31:9
"A son honors his f ... Mal 1:6
Have we not all one F ... Mal 2:10
Our F in heaven ... Matt 6:9
"He who loves f ... Matt 10:37
know the F ... Matt 11:27
'He who curses f ... Matt 15:4
for One is your F ... Matt 23:9
"F will be divided ... Luke 12:53
F loves the Son ... John 3:35
F raises the dead ... John 5:21
F judges no one ... John 5:22
He has seen the F ... John 6:46
F who sent Me bears ... John 8:18
we have one F ... John 8:41
of your f the devil ... John 8:44

FIRM
of the hope *f* to the ... Heb 3:6

FIRMAMENT
Thus God made the *f* ... Gen 1:7
f shows His handiwork ... Ps 19:1

FIRST
f father sinned ... Is 43:27
desires to be *f* ... Matt 20:27
f shall be slave ... Mark 10:44
the gospel must *f* ... Mark 13:10
evil, of the Jew *f* ... Rom 2:9
f man Adam became ... 1 Cor 15:45
that we who *f* trusted ... Eph 1:12
Him because He *f* ... 1 John 4:19
I am the *F* and the ... Rev 1:17
you have left your *f* ... Rev 2:4
is the *f* resurrection ... Rev 20:5

FIRSTBORN
LORD struck all the *f* ... Ex 12:29
brought forth her *f* ... Matt 1:25
that He might be the *f* ... Rom 8:29
invisible God, the *f* ... Col 1:15
the beginning, the *f* ... Col 1:18
witness, the *f* from ... Rev 1:5

FIRSTFRUITS
also who have the *f* ... Rom 8:23
and has become the *f* ... 1 Cor 15:20
Christ the *f* ... 1 Cor 15:23

FISH
had prepared a great *f* ... Jon 1:17
belly of the great *f* ... Matt 12:40
five loaves and two *f* ... Matt 14:17
and likewise the *f* ... John 21:13

FISHERS
and I will make you *f* ... Matt 4:19

FIVE
f smooth stones ... 1 Sam 17:40
about *f* thousand men ... Matt 14:21
and *f* were foolish ... Matt 25:2

FIXED
is a great gulf *f* ... Luke 16:26

FLAME
appeared to him in a *f* ... Ex 3:2
tormented in this *f* ... Luke 16:24
and His ministers *a f* ... Heb 1:7
and His eyes like a *f* ... Rev 1:14

FLAMES
the LORD divides the *f* ... Ps 29:7

FLAMING
f sword which turned ... Gen 3:24
in *f* fire taking ... 2 Thess 1:8

FLATTER
They *f* with their ... Ps 5:9

FLATTERED
Nevertheless they *f* ... Ps 78:36

FLATTERING
f speech deceive ... Rom 16:18
swelling words, *f* ... Jude 16

FLATTERS
f his neighbor Spreads ... Prov 29:5

FLATTERY
shall corrupt with *f* ... Dan 11:32

FLAVOR
the salt loses its *f* ... Matt 5:13

FLAX
f He will not quench ... Matt 12:20

FLEE
Or where can I *f* ... Ps 139:7
And the shadows *f* ... Song 2:17
who are in Judea *f* ... Matt 24:16
F sexual immorality ... 1 Cor 6:18
f these things and ... 1 Tim 6:11
devil and he will *f* ... James 4:7

FLESH
bone of my bones And *f* ... Gen 2:23
shall become one *f* ... Gen 2:24
f had corrupted their ... Gen 6:12
f I shall see God ... Job 19:26
My *f* also will rest in ... Ps 16:9
is wearisome to the *f* ... Eccl 12:12
And all *f* shall see it ... Is 40:5
"All *f* is grass ... Is 40:6
out My Spirit on all *f* ... Joel 2:28
two shall become one *f* ... Matt 19:5
were shortened, no *f* ... Matt 24:22
shall become one *f* ... Mark 10:8
the Word became *f* ... John 1:14
I shall give is My *f* ... John 6:51
f profits nothing ... John 6:63
of God, but with the *f* ... Rom 7:25
on the things of the *f* ... Rom 8:5
to the *f* you will die ... Rom 8:13
f should glory in His ... 1 Cor 1:29
"shall become one *f* ... 1 Cor 6:16
For the *f* lusts ... Gal 5:17
have crucified the *f* ... Gal 5:24
may boast in your *f* ... Gal 6:13
the lust of the *f* ... 1 John 2:16
has come in the *f* ... 1 John 4:2

FLESHLY
f wisdom but by the ... 2 Cor 1:12
f lusts which ... 1 Pet 2:11

FLIES
Dead *f* putrefy the ... Eccl 10:1

FLOAT
and he made the iron *f* ... 2 Kin 6:6

FLOCK
lead Joseph like a *f* ... Ps 80:1
He will feed His *f* ... Is 40:11
you do not feed the *f* ... Ezek 34:3
my God, "Feed the *f* ... Zech 11:4
sheep of the *f* ... Matt 26:31
"Do not fear, little *f* ... Luke 12:32
there will be one *f* ... John 10:16
Shepherd the *f* of God ... 1 Pet 5:2
examples to the *f* ... 1 Pet 5:3

FLOOD
the waters of the *f* ... Gen 7:10
them away like a *f* ... Ps 90:5
the days before the *f* ... Matt 24:38
bringing in the *f* ... 2 Pet 2:5
of his mouth like a *f* ... Rev 12:15

FLOODS
me, And the *f* of ... Ps 18:4
f on the dry ground ... Is 44:3
rain descended, the *f* ... Matt 7:25

FLOURISH
the righteous shall *f* ... Ps 72:7

FLOW
of his heart will *f* ... John 7:38

FLOWER
As a *f* of the field ... Ps 103:15
beauty is a fading *f* ... Is 28:4
grass withers, the *f* ... Is 40:7
of man as the *f* ... 1 Pet 1:24

FLOWERS
f appear on the earth ... Song 2:12

FLOWING
'a land *f* with milk ... Deut 6:3
the Gentiles like a *f* ... Is 66:12

FLUTE
play the harp and *f* ... Gen 4:21

FLUTES
instruments and *f* ... Ps 150:4

FLUTISTS
harpists, musicians, *f* ... Rev 18:22

FLY
soon cut off, and we *f* ... Ps 90:10

FOLLOW
f You wherever You go ... Matt 8:19
He said to him, "*F* ... Matt 9:9
up his cross, and *f* ... Mark 8:34
will by no means *f* ... John 10:5
serves Me, let him *f* ... John 12:26
that you should *f* ... 1 Pet 2:21
f the Lamb wherever ... Rev 14:4
and their works *f* ... Rev 14:13

FOLLOWED
f the LORD my God ... Josh 14:8
we have left all and *f* ... Mark 10:28

FOLLOWS
f Me shall not walk ... John 8:12

FOLLY
taken much notice of *f* ... Job 35:15
not turn back to *f* ... Ps 85:8
F is joy to him who is ... Prov 15:21
F is set in great ... Eccl 10:6

FOOD
you it shall be for *f* ... Gen 1:29
that lives shall be *f* ... Gen 9:3
f which you eat shall ... Ezek 4:10
the fields yield no *f* ... Hab 3:17
That there may be *f* ... Mal 3:10
to give them *f* ... Matt 24:45
and you gave Me *f* ... Matt 25:35
and he who has *f* ... Luke 3:11
have you any *f* ... John 21:5
they ate their *f* ... Acts 2:46
our hearts with *f* ... Acts 14:17
destroy with your *f* ... Rom 14:15
f makes my brother ... 1 Cor 8:13
the same spiritual *f* ... 1 Cor 10:3
sower, and bread for *f* ... 2 Cor 9:10
And having *f* and ... 1 Tim 6:8
and not solid *f* ... Heb 5:12
But solid *f* belongs to ... Heb 5:14
of *f* sold his ... Heb 12:16
destitute of daily *f* ... James 2:15

FOODS
f which God ... 1 Tim 4:3

FOOL
f has said in his ... Ps 14:1
is like sport to a *f* ... Prov 10:23
f is right in his own ... Prov 12:15
is too lofty for a *f* ... Prov 24:7
whoever says, 'You *f* ... Matt 5:22
I have become a *f* ... 2 Cor 12:11

FOOLISH
I was so *f* and ... Ps 73:22
f pulls it down with ... Prov 14:1
f man squanders it ... Prov 21:20
Has not God made *f* ... 1 Cor 1:20
O *f* Galatians ... Gal 3:1
were also once *f* ... Titus 3:3
But avoid *f* disputes ... Titus 3:9

FOOLISHLY
I speak *f* ... 2 Cor 11:21

FOOLISHNESS
F is bound up in the ... Prov 22:15
devising of *f* is sin ... Prov 24:9
of the cross is *f* ... 1 Cor 1:18
Because the *f* of God ... 1 Cor 1:25

FOOLS
f despise wisdom ... Prov 1:7
folly of *f* is deceit ... Prov 14:8
F mock at sin ... Prov 14:9
We are *f* for Christ's ... 1 Cor 4:10

FOOT
will not allow your *f* ... Ps 121:3
f will not stumble ... Prov 3:23
From the sole of the *f* ... Is 1:6
f causes you to sin ... Matt 18:8
you dash your *f* ... Luke 4:11
If the *f* should say ... 1 Cor 12:15

FOOTSTOOL
Your enemies Your *f* ... Ps 110:1
Your enemies Your *f* ... Matt 22:44

FORBID
said, "Do not *f* ... Mark 9:39
"Can anyone *f* ... Acts 10:47
f that I should boast ... Gal 6:14

FORBIDDING
f to marry ... 1 Tim 4:3

FOREFATHERS
conscience, as my *f* ... 2 Tim 1:3

FOREHEADS
put a mark on the *f* ... Ezek 9:4
seal of God on their *f* ... Rev 9:4
his mark on their *f* ... Rev 20:4

FOREIGNER
"I am a *f* and a ... Gen 23:4
of me, since I am a *f* ... Ruth 2:10
to God except this *f* ... Luke 17:18

FOREIGNERS
f who were there ... Acts 17:21
longer strangers and *f* ... Eph 2:19

FOREKNEW
For whom He *f* ... Rom 8:29
His people whom He *f* ... Rom 11:2

FOREKNOWLEDGE
purpose and *f* of God ... Acts 2:23

FOREORDAINED
He indeed was *f* ... 1 Pet 1:20

FORESAW
'I *f* the LORD ... Acts 2:25

FORESEEING
f that God would ... Gal 3:8

FORESEES
A prudent man *f* ... Prov 223

FORETOLD
have also *f* these days ... Acts 3:24
killed those who *f* ... Acts 7:52

FOREVER
and eat, and live *f* ... Gen 3:22
to our children *f* ... Deut 29:29
LORD sits as King *f* ... Ps 29:10
Do not cast us off *f* ... Ps 44:23
throne, O God, is *f* ... Ps 45:6
"You are a priest *f* ... Ps 110:4
His mercy endures *f* ... Ps 136:1
of our God stands *f* ... Is 40:8
My salvation will be *f* ... Is 51:6
will not cast off *f* ... Lam 3:31
Like the stars *f* ... Dan 12:3
and the glory *f* ... Matt 6:13
the Christ remains *f* ... John 12:34
who is blessed *f* ... 2 Cor 11:31
to whom be glory *f* ... Gal 1:5
generation, *f* and ever ... Eph 3:21
and Father be glory *f* ... Phil 4:20
throne, O God, is *f* ... Heb 1:8
lives and abides *f* ... 1 Pet 1:23
of darkness *f* ... Jude 13
power, Both now and *f* ... Jude 25
And they shall reign *f* ... Rev 22:5

FOREVERMORE
Blessed be the LORD *f* ... Ps 89:52
this time forth and *f* ... Ps 113:2
behold, I am alive *f* ... Rev 1:18

FORGAVE
to repay, he freely *f* ... Luke 7:42
God in Christ *f* ... Eph 4:32
even as Christ *f* ... Col 3:13

FORGET
f the LORD who ... Deut 6:12
I will not *f* Your word ... Ps 119:16
If I *f* you ... Ps 137:5
My son, do not *f* ... Prov 3:1
f the LORD your Maker ... Is 51:13
f your work and labor ... Heb 6:10

FORGETFULNESS
in the land of *f* ... Ps 88:12

FORGETS
and immediately *f* ... James 1:24

FORGETTING
f those things which ... Phil 3:13

FORGIVE
f their sin and heal ... 2 Chr 7:14
good, and ready to *f* ... Ps 86:5
And *f* us our debts ... Matt 6:12
Father will also *f* ... Matt 6:14
his heart, does not *f* ... Matt 18:35
Who can *f* sins but God ... Mark 2:7
f the sins of any ... John 20:23
you ought rather to *f* ... 2 Cor 2:7
F me this wrong ... 2 Cor 12:13
f us our sins and to ... 1 John 1:9

FORGIVEN
sins be *f* them ... Mark 4:12
to whom little is *f* ... Luke 7:47
f you all trespasses ... Col 2:13
your sins are *f* ... 1 John 2:12

FORGIVENESS
But there is *f* with ... Ps 130:4
preached to you the *f* ... Acts 13:38
they may receive *f* ... Acts 26:18
His blood, the *f* ... Eph 1:7

FORGIVES
f all your iniquities ... Ps 103:3
is this who even *f* ... Luke 7:49

FORGIVING
tenderhearted, *f* ... Eph 4:32
and *f* one another ... Col 3:13

FORGOT
Joseph, but *f* ... Gen 40:23
They soon *f* His works ... Ps 106:13

FORGOTTEN
f the God who ... Deut 32:18
not one of them is *f* ... Luke 12:6
f the exhortation ... Heb 12:5
f that he was ... 2 Pet 1:9

FORM
earth was without *f* ... Gen 1:2
Who would *f* a god or ... Is 44:10
f the light and create ... Is 45:7
descended in bodily *f* ... Luke 3:22
time, nor seen His *f* ... John 5:37
For the *f* of this ... 1 Cor 7:31
Who, being in the *f* ... Phil 2:6
having a *f* of ... 2 Tim 3:5

FORMED
And the LORD God *f* ... Gen 2:7
f my inward parts ... Ps 139:13
say of him who *f* ... Is 29:16
"Before I *f* you in ... Jer 1:5
Will the thing *f* ... Rom 9:20
until Christ is *f* ... Gal 4:19

FORMER
f days better than ... Eccl 7:10
f rain to the earth ... Hos 6:3
f prophets preached ... Zech 1:4
your *f* conduct ... Eph 4:22
f things have passed ... Rev 21:4

FORMS
clay say to him who *f* ... Is 45:9
f the spirit of man ... Zech 12:1

FORNICATION
"We were not born of *f* ... John 8:41
of the wrath of her *f* ... Rev 14:8

FORNICATOR
you know, that no *f* ... Eph 5:5
lest there be any *f* ... Heb 12:16

FORNICATORS
but *f* and adulterers ... Heb 13:4

FORSAKE
But I did not *f* ... Ps 119:87
father, And do not *f* ... Prov 1:8
of you does not *f* ... Luke 14:33
never leave you nor *f* ... Heb 13:5

FORSAKEN
My God, why have You *f* ... Ps 22:1
seen the righteous *f* ... Ps 37:25
a mere moment I have *f* ... Is 54:7
God, why have You *f* ... Matt 27:46
persecuted, but not *f* ... 2 Cor 4:9
for Demas has *f* ... 2 Tim 4:10

FORSAKING
f the assembling ... Heb 10:25

FORSOOK
f God who made him ... Deut 32:15
all the disciples *f* ... Matt 26:56
with me, but all *f* ... 2 Tim 4:16

FORTRESS
is my rock, my *f* ... 2 Sam 22:2
my rock of refuge, a *f* ... Ps 31:2

FOUND
f a helper comparable ... Gen 2:20
a thousand I have *f* ... Eccl 7:28
LORD while He may be *f* ... Is 55:6
fruit on it and *f* none ... Luke 13:6
he was lost and is *f* ... Luke 15:24
f the Messiah" (which ... John 1:41
and be *f* in Him ... Phil 3:9

FOUNDATION
Of old You laid the *f* ... Ps 102:25
the earth without a *f* ... Luke 6:49
loved Me before the *f* ... John 17:24
I have laid the *f* ... 1 Cor 3:10
f can anyone lay than ... 1 Cor 3:11
us in Him before the *f* ... Eph 1:4
not laying again the *f* ... Heb 6:1
Lamb slain from the *f* ... Rev 13:8

FOUNDATIONS
when I laid the *f* ... Job 38:4
And the *f* of the wall ... Rev 21:19

FOUNTAIN
will become in him a *f* ... John 4:14

FOUNTAINS
on that day all the *f* ... Gen 7:11
lead them to living *f* ... Rev 7:17

FRAGRANCE
was filled with the *f* ... John 12:3
we are to God the *f* ... 2 Cor 2:15

FREE
'You will be made *f* ... John 8:33
And having been set *f* ... Rom 6:18
Jesus has made me *f* ... Rom 8:2
is neither slave nor *f* ... Gal 3:28
Christ has made us *f* ... Gal 5:1
he is a slave or *f* ... Eph 6:8

FREED
has died has been *f* ... Rom 6:7

FREEDMAN
slave is the Lord's *f* ... 1 Cor 7:22

FREELY
the garden you may *f* ... Gen 2:16
F you have received ... Matt 10:8
f give us all ... Rom 8:32
the water of life *f* ... Rev 22:17

FRIEND
of Abraham Your *f* ... 2 Chr 20:7
f who sticks closer ... Prov 18:24
a *f* of tax collectors ... Matt 11:19
of you shall have a *f* ... Luke 11:5
f Lazarus sleeps ... John 11:11
he was called the *f* ... James 2:23
wants to be a *f* ... James 4:4

FRIENDS
My *f* scorn me ... Job 16:20
the rich has many *f* ... Prov 14:20
one's life for his *f* ... John 15:13
I have called you *f* ... John 15:15
to forbid any of his *f* ... Acts 24:23

FROGS
your territory with *f* ... Ex 8:2
f coming out of the ... Rev 16:13

FRUIT
showed them the *f* ... Num 13:26
brings forth its *f* ... Ps 1:3
f is better than gold ... Prov 8:19
with good by the *f* ... Prov 12:14
like the first *f* ... Is 28:4
does not bear good *f* ... Matt 3:10
good tree bears good *f* ... Matt 7:17
not drink of this *f* ... Matt 26:29
and blessed is the *f* ... Luke 1:42
life, and bring no *f* ... Luke 8:14
and he came seeking *f* ... Luke 13:6
'And if it bears *f* ... Luke 13:9
branch that bears *f* ... John 15:2
that you bear much *f* ... John 15:8
should go and bear *f* ... John 15:16
God, you have your *f* ... Rom 6:22
that we should bear *f* ... Rom 7:4
But the *f* of the ... Gal 5:22
yields the peaceable *f* ... Heb 12:11
Now the *f* of ... James 3:18
autumn trees without *f* ... Jude 12
tree yielding its *f* ... Rev 22:2

FRUITFUL
them, saying, "Be *f* ... Gen 1:22
wife shall be like a *f* ... Ps 128:3
pleasing Him, being *f* ... Col 1:10

FRUITS
Therefore bear *f* ... Matt 3:8
know them by their *f* ... Matt 7:16
of mercy and good *f* ... James 3:17
which bore twelve *f* ... Rev 22:2

FULFILL
for us to *f* all ... Matt 3:15
f the law of Christ ... Gal 6:2
f my joy by being ... Phil 2:2
and *f* all the good ... 2 Thess 1:11
If you really *f* ... James 2:8

FULFILLED
the law till all is *f* ... Matt 5:18
of the Gentiles are *f* ... Luke 21:24
all things must be *f* ... Luke 24:44
of the law might be *f* ... Rom 8:4
loves another has *f* ... Rom 13:8
For all the law is *f* ... Gal 5:14

FULFILLMENT
love is the *f* of the ... Rom 13:10

FULL
- and it was *f* of bones ... Ezek 37:1
- whole body will be *f* ... Matt 6:22
- your joy may be *f* ... John 15:11
- You are already *f* ... 1 Cor 4:8
- learned both to be *f* ... Phil 4:12

FULLNESS
- *f* we have all received ... John 1:16
- But when the *f* of the ... Gal 4:4
- filled with all the *f* ... Eph 3:19
- Him dwells all the *f* ... Col 2:9

FURNACE
- you out of the iron *f* ... Deut 4:20
- of a burning fiery *f* ... Dan 3:6
- cast them into the *f* ... Matt 13:42
- the smoke of a great *f* ... Rev 9:2

FURY
- Thus will I spend My *f* ... Ezek 6:12
- in anger and *f* On the ... Mic 5:15

G

GAIN
- and to die is *g* ... Phil 1:21
- rubbish, that I may *g* ... Phil 3:8
- is a means of *g* ... 1 Tim 6:5
- contentment is great *g* ... 1 Tim 6:6
- for dishonest *g* ... 1 Pet 5:2

GAINED
- *g* five more talents ... Matt 25:20

GAINS
- *g* the whole world ... Matt 16:26

GALL
- They also gave me *g* ... Ps 69:21
- wine mingled with *g* ... Matt 27:34

GAP
- and stand in the *g* ... Ezek 22:30

GARDEN
- Lord God planted a *g* ... Gen 2:8
- *g* enclosed Is my ... Song 4:12
- Eden, the *g* of God ... Ezek 28:13
- where there was a *g* ... John 18:1
- *g* a new tomb in ... John 19:41

GARMENT
- the hem of His *g* ... Matt 9:20
- on a wedding *g* ... Matt 22:11
- cloth on an old *g* ... Mark 2:21
- all grow old like a *g* ... Heb 1:11
- hating even the *g* ... Jude 23

GARMENTS
- *g* did not wear out on ... Deut 8:4
- They divide My *g* ... Ps 22:18
- from Edom, With dyed *g* ... Is 63:1
- "Take away the filthy *g* ... Zech 3:4
- man clothed in soft *g* ... Matt 11:8
- spread their *g* on the ... Matt 21:8
- and divided His *g* ... Matt 27:35
- by them in shining *g* ... Luke 24:4
- *g* are moth-eaten ... James 5:2
- be clothed in white *g* ... Rev 3:5

GATE
- by the narrow *g* ... Matt 7:13
- by the Sheep G a pool ... John 5:2
- laid daily at the *g* ... Acts 3:2
- suffered outside the *g* ... Heb 13:12

GATES
- up your heads, O you *g* ... Ps 24:7
- The Lord loves the *g* ... Ps 87:2
- is known in the *g* ... Prov 31:23
- Go through the *g* ... Is 62:10
- and the *g* of Hades ... Matt 16:18
- wall with twelve *g* ... Rev 21:12
- *g* were twelve pearls ... Rev 21:21
- *g* shall not be shut ... Rev 21:25

GATHER
- And a time to *g* stones ... Eccl 3:5
- *g* the lambs with His ... Is 40:11
- *g* His wheat into the ... Matt 3:12
- sow nor reap nor *g* ... Matt 6:26
- Do men *g* grapes from ... Matt 7:16
- *g* where I have not ... Matt 25:26
- *g* together His ... Mark 13:27

GATHERED
- *g* some of every kind ... Matt 13:47
- the nations will be *g* ... Matt 25:32

GATHERING
- *g* together of the ... Gen 1:10
- *g* together to Him ... 2 Thess 2:1

GATHERS
- The Lord God, who *g* ... Is 56:8
- together, as a hen *g* ... Matt 23:37

GAVE
- to be with me, she *g* ... Gen 3:12
- *g* You this authority ... Matt 21:23
- that He *g* His only ... John 3:16
- Those whom You *g* ... John 17:12
- but God *g* the increase ... 1 Cor 3:6
- *g* Himself for our sins ... Gal 1:4
- *g* Himself for me ... Gal 2:20
- *g* Himself for it ... Eph 5:25

GENERATION
- One *g* passes away ... Eccl 1:4
- who will declare His *g* ... Is 53:8
- and adulterous *g* ... Matt 12:39
- this *g* will by no ... Matt 24:34
- from this perverse *g* ... Acts 2:40
- But you are a chosen *g* ... 1 Pet 2:9

GENERATIONS
- be remembered in all *g* ... Ps 45:17
- *g* will call me blessed ... Luke 1:48

GENEROUS
- no longer be called *g* ... Is 32:5

GENTILES
- G were separated ... Gen 10:5
- As a light to the G ... Is 42:6
- G shall come to your ... Is 60:3
- all these things the G ... Matt 6:32
- into the way of the G ... Matt 10:5
- revelation to the G ... Luke 2:32
- G are fulfilled ... Luke 21:24
- My name before G ... Acts 9:15
- poured out on the G ... Acts 10:45
- a light to the G ... Acts 13:47
- also the God of the G ... Rom 3:29
- mystery among the G ... Col 1:27
- a teacher of the G ... 1 Tim 2:7

GENTLE
- from Me, for I am *g* ... Matt 11:29
- we were *g* among ... 1 Thess 2:7
- to be peaceable, *g* ... Titus 3:2
- only to the good and *g* ... 1 Pet 2:18
- ornament of a *g* ... 1 Pet 3:4

GENTLENESS
- love and a spirit of *g* ... 1 Cor 4:21
- *g*, self-control ... Gal 5:23
- all lowliness and *g* ... Eph 4:2
- Let your *g* be known to ... Phil 4:5
- love, patience, *g* ... 1 Tim 6:11

GHOST
- supposed it was a *g* ... Mark 6:49

GIFT
- it is the *g* of God ... Eccl 3:13
- "If you knew the *g* ... John 4:10
- but the *g* of God is ... Rom 6:23
- each one has his own *g* ... 1 Cor 7:7
- though I have the *g* ... 1 Cor 13:2
- it is the *g* of God ... Eph 2:8
- Do not neglect the *g* ... 1 Tim 4:14
- you to stir up the *g* ... 2 Tim 1:6
- tasted the heavenly *g* ... Heb 6:4
- Every good *g* and ... James 1:17

GIFTS
- You have received *g* ... Ps 68:18
- and Seba Will offer *g* ... Ps 72:10
- how to give good *g* ... Matt 7:11
- rich putting their *g* ... Luke 21:1
- *g* differing ... Rom 12:6
- are diversities of *g* ... 1 Cor 12:4
- and desire spiritual *g* ... 1 Cor 14:1
- captive, And gave *g* ... Eph 4:8

GIRD
- G Your sword upon Your ... Ps 45:3
- and another will *g* ... John 21:18
- Therefore *g* up the ... 1 Pet 1:13

GIRDED
- a towel and *g* Himself ... John 13:4

GIVE
- *g* you the desires ... Ps 37:4
- Yes, the Lord will *g* ... Ps 85:12
- G me understanding ... Ps 119:34
- "G to him who asks ... Matt 5:42
- G us this day our ... Matt 6:11
- what you have and *g* ... Matt 19:21
- authority I will *g* ... Luke 4:6
- *g* them eternal life ... John 10:28
- commandment I *g* ... John 13:34
- but what I do have I *g* ... Acts 3:6
- *g* us all things ... Rom 8:32
- G no offense ... 1 Cor 10:32
- *g* him who has need ... Eph 4:28
- *g* thanks to God ... 2 Thess 2:13
- *g* yourself entirely ... 1 Tim 4:15

GIVEN
- to him more will be *g* ... Matt 13:12
- has, more will be *g* ... Matt 25:29
- to whom much is *g* ... Luke 12:48
- *g* Me I should lose ... John 6:39
- Spirit was not yet *g* ... John 7:39

GIVES
- *g* life to the world ... John 6:33
- "All that the Father *g* ... John 6:37
- The good shepherd *g* ... John 10:11
- not as the world *g* ... John 14:27
- *g* us richly all things ... 1 Tim 6:17
- who *g* to all liberally ... James 1:5
- *g* grace to the humble ... James 4:6

GLAD
- streams shall make *g* ... Ps 46:4
- I was *g* when they said ... Ps 122:1
- make merry and be *g* ... Luke 15:32
- he saw it and was *g* ... John 8:56

GLADNESS
- me hear joy and *g* ... Ps 51:8
- Serve the Lord with *g* ... Ps 100:2

GLORIFIED
- and they *g* the God of ... Matt 15:31
- Jesus was not yet *g* ... John 7:39
- when Jesus was *g* ... John 12:16
- this My Father is *g* ... John 15:8
- "I have *g* You on the ... John 17:4
- *g* His Servant Jesus ... Acts 3:13
- these He also *g* ... Rom 8:30
- things God may be *g* ... 1 Pet 4:11

GLORIFY
- *g* your Father in ... Matt 5:16
- "Father, *g* Your name ... John 12:28
- "He will *g* Me ... John 16:14
- "And now, O Father, *g* ... John 17:5
- death he would *g* ... John 21:19
- therefore *g* God in ... 1 Cor 6:20
- also Christ did not *g* ... Heb 5:5
- ashamed, but let him *g* ... 1 Pet 4:16

GLORIOUS
- G things are spoken ... Ps 87:3
- *g* splendor of Your ... Ps 145:5
- habitation, holy and *g* ... Is 63:15
- it to Himself a *g* ... Eph 5:27
- be conformed to His *g* ... Phil 3:21
- *g* appearing of our ... Titus 2:13

GLORY
- show me Your *g* ... Ex 33:18
- *g* has departed from ... 1 Sam 4:21
- Who is this King of *g* ... Ps 24:8
- Your power and Your *g* ... Ps 63:2
- wise shall inherit *g* ... Prov 3:35
- It is the *g* of God to ... Prov 25:2
- *g* I will not give ... Is 42:8
- that they may have *g* ... Matt 6:2
- the power and the *g* ... Matt 6:13
- *g* was not arrayed ... Matt 6:29
- will come in the *g* ... Matt 16:27
- power and great *g* ... Matt 24:30
- "G to God in the ... Luke 2:14
- and we beheld His *g* ... John 1:14
- and manifested His *g* ... John 2:11
- not seek My own *g* ... John 8:50
- "Give God the *g* ... John 9:24
- *g* which I had with ... John 17:5
- *g* which You gave Me ... John 17:22
- he did not give *g* ... Acts 12:23
- doing good seek for *g* ... Rom 2:7
- fall short of the *g* ... Rom 3:23
- in faith, giving *g* ... Rom 4:20
- the adoption, the *g* ... Rom 9:4
- the riches of His *g* ... Rom 9:23
- God, alone wise, be *g* ... Rom 16:27
- who glories, let him *g* ... 1 Cor 1:31
- to His riches in *g* ... Phil 4:19
- appear with Him in *g* ... Col 3:4
- For you are our *g* ... 1 Thess 2:20
- many sons to *g* ... Heb 2:10
- grass, And all the *g* ... 1 Pet 1:24

to whom belong the *g* ... 1 Pet 4:11
for the Spirit of *g* ... 1 Pet 4:14
the presence of His *g* ... Jude 24
O Lord, to receive *g* ... Rev 4:11
g of God illuminated ... Rev 21:23

GLORYING
Your *g* is not good ... 1 Cor 5:6

GLUTTON
you say, 'Look, a *g* ... Luke 7:34

GLUTTONS
g shames his ... Prov 28:7
evil beasts, lazy *g* ... Titus 1:12

GNASHING
will be weeping and *g* ... Matt 8:12

GO
'Let My people *g* ... Ex 5:1
For wherever you *g* ... Ruth 1:16
Those who *g* down to ... Ps 107:23
Where can I *g* from ... Ps 139:7
to whom shall we *g* ... John 6:68
g you cannot come ... John 8:21
I *g* to prepare a place ... John 14:2
shall *g* out no more ... Rev 3:12

GOADS
to kick against the *g* ... Acts 9:5

GOAL
I press toward the *g* ... Phil 3:14

GOATS
his sheep from the *g* ... Matt 25:32
with the blood of *g* ... Heb 9:12
g could take away ... Heb 10:4

GOD
G created the heavens ... Gen 1:1
Abram of *G* Most ... Gen 14:19
and I will be their *G* ... Gen 17:8
"I am the LORD your *G* ... Ex 20:2
G is a consuming fire ... Deut 4:24
If the LORD is *G* ... 1 Kin 18:21
G is greater than all ... 2 Chr 2:5
You have been My *G* ... Ps 22:10
G is our refuge ... Ps 46:1
G is in the midst of ... Ps 46:5
me a clean heart, O *G* ... Ps 51:10
Our *G* is the *G* ... Ps 68:20
Who is so great a *G* ... Ps 77:13
Restore us, O *G* ... Ps 80:7
You alone are *G* ... Ps 86:10
Exalt the LORD our G ... Ps 99:9
Yes, our *G* is merciful ... Ps 116:5
For *G* is in heaven ... Eccl 5:2
Counselor, Mighty *G* ... Is 9:6
G is my salvation ... Is 12:2
stricken, Smitten by *G* ... Is 53:4
"*G* with us ... Matt 1:23
in G my Savior ... Luke 1:47
the Word was with *G* ... John 1:1
"For *G* so loved the ... John 3:16
"*G* is Spirit ... John 4:24
"My Lord and my *G* ... John 20:28
Christ Is the Son of *G* ... Acts 8:37
Indeed, let *G* be true ... Rom 3:4
If *G* is for us ... Rom 8:31
G is faithful ... 1 Cor 1:9
G shall supply all ... Phil 4:19
and I will be their *G* ... Heb 8:10
G is a consuming fire ... Heb 12:29
for *G* is love ... 1 John 4:8
No one has seen G ... 1 John 4:12
G Himself will be ... Rev 21:3
and I will be his *G* ... Rev 21:7

GODDESS
after Ashtoreth the *g* ... 1 Kin 11:5
of the great *g* Diana ... Acts 19:35

GODHEAD
eternal power and *G* ... Rom 1:20
the fullness of the *G* ... Col 2:9

GODLINESS
is the mystery of *g* ... 1 Tim 3:16
g with contentment ... 1 Tim 6:6
having a form of *g* ... 2 Tim 3:5
to perseverance *g* ... 2 Pet 1:6

GODLY
who desire to live *g* ... 2 Tim 3:12
reverence and *g* fear ... Heb 12:28
to deliver the *g* ... 2 Pet 2:9

GODS
God is God of *g* ... Deut 10:17
I said, "You are *g* ... Ps 82:6
yourselves with *g* ... Is 57:5
If He called them *g* ... John 10:35
g have come down to ... Acts 14:11

GOLD
g I do not have ... Acts 3:6
with braided hair or *g* ... 1 Tim 2:9
a man with *g* rings ... James 2:2
Your *g* and silver are ... James 5:3
more precious than *g* ... 1 Pet 1:7
like silver or *g* ... 1 Pet 1:18
of the city was pure *g* ... Rev 21:21

GONE
like sheep have *g* ... Is 53:6

GOOD
God saw that it was *g* ... Gen 1:10
but God meant it for *g* ... Gen 50:20
indeed accept *g* ... Job 2:10
is none who does *g* ... Ps 14:1
Truly God is *g* to ... Ps 73:1
g word makes it glad ... Prov 12:25
on the evil and the *g* ... Prov 15:3
A merry heart does *g* ... Prov 17:22
Learn to do *g* ... Is 1:17
talked to me, with *g* ... Zech 1:13
they may see your *g* ... Matt 5:16
"A *g* man out of the ... Matt 12:35
No one is *g* but One ... Matt 19:17
For she has done a *g* ... Matt 26:10
g works I have shown ... John 10:32
went about doing *g* ... Acts 10:38
g man someone would ... Rom 5:7
in my flesh) nothing *g* ... Rom 7:18
overcome evil with *g* ... Rom 12:21
Jesus for *g* works ... Eph 2:10
fruitful in every *g* ... Col 1:10
know that the law is *g* ... 1 Tim 1:8
For this is *g* and ... 1 Tim 2:3
bishop, he desires a *g* ... 1 Tim 3:1
for this is *g* and ... 1 Tim 5:4
prepared for every *g* ... 2 Tim 2:21
Every *g* gift and ... James 1:17

GOODNESS
"I will make all My *g* ... Ex 33:19
and abounding in *g* ... Ex 34:6
"You are my Lord, My *g* ... Ps 16:2
Surely *g* and mercy ... Ps 23:6
That I would see the *g* ... Ps 27:13
the riches of His *g* ... Rom 2:4
consider the *g* and ... Rom 11:22
kindness, *g* ... Gal 5:22

GOSPEL
The beginning of the *g* ... Mark 1:1
and believe in the *g* ... Mark 1:15
g must first be ... Mark 13:10
separated to the *g* ... Rom 1:1
not ashamed of the *g* ... Rom 1:16
to a different *g* ... Gal 1:6
the everlasting *g* ... Rev 14:6

GOVERNMENT
And the *g* will be upon ... Is 9:6

GRACE
But Noah found *g* ... Gen 6:8
G is poured upon Your ... Ps 45:2
The LORD will give *g* ... Ps 84:11
the Spirit of *g* ... Zech 12:10
and the *g* of God was ... Luke 2:40
g and truth came ... John 1:17
And great *g* was upon ... Acts 4:33
receive abundance of *g* ... Rom 5:17
g is no longer *g* ... Rom 11:6
For you know the *g* ... 2 Cor 8:9
g is sufficient ... 2 Cor 12:9
The *g* of the Lord ... 2 Cor 13:14
you have fallen from *g* ... Gal 5:4
to the riches of His *g* ... Eph 1:7
g you have been ... Eph 2:8
g was given according ... Eph 4:7
G be with all those ... Eph 6:24
shaken, let us have *g* ... Heb 12:28
But He gives more *g* ... James 4:6
but grow in the *g* ... 2 Pet 3:18

GRACIOUS
he said, "God be *g* ... Gen 43:29
I will be *g* to whom I ... Ex 33:19
at the *g* words which ... Luke 4:22
that the Lord is *g* ... 1 Pet 2:3

GRAFTED
In unbelief, will be *g* ... Rom 11:23

GRAIN
it treads out the *g* ... Deut 25:4
be revived like *g* ... Hos 14:7
to pluck heads of *g* ... Matt 12:1
unless a *g* of wheat ... John 12:24

GRAPES
brought forth wild *g* ... Is 5:2
have eaten sour *g* ... Ezek 18:2
Do men gather *g* ... Matt 7:16
g are fully ripe ... Rev 14:18

GRASS
The *g* withers ... Is 40:7
so clothes the *g* ... Matt 6:30
"All Flesh is as *g* ... 1 Pet 1:24

GRAVE
my soul up from the *g* ... Ps 30:3
And they made His *g* ... Is 53:9
the power of the *g* ... Hos 13:14

GRAVES
g were opened ... Matt 27:52
g which are not ... Luke 11:44
g will hear His voice ... John 5:28

GRAY
the man of *g* hairs ... Deut 32:25

GREAT
and make your name *g* ... Gen 12:2
For the LORD is *g* ... 1 Chr 16:25
Who does *g* things ... Job 5:9
g is the Holy One ... Is 12:6
G is Your faithfulness ... Lam 3:23
he shall be called *g* ... Matt 5:19
one pearl of *g* price ... Matt 13:46
desires to become *g* ... Matt 20:26
g drops of blood ... Luke 22:44
appearing of our *g* ... Titus 2:13
g men, the rich men ... Rev 6:15
Mystery, Babylon the *G* ... Rev 17:5
the dead, small and *g* ... Rev 20:12

GREATER
of heaven is *g* ... Matt 11:11
place there is One *g* ... Matt 12:6
g than Jonah is here ... Matt 12:41
g than Solomon is ... Matt 12:42
a servant is not *g* ... John 13:16
"*G* love has no one ... John 15:13
'A servant is not *g* ... John 15:20
who prophesies is *g* ... 1 Cor 14:5
God is *g* ... 1 John 3:20
witness of God is *g* ... 1 John 5:9

GREATEST
little child is the *g* ... Matt 18:4
but the *g* of these is ... 1 Cor 13:13

GREATNESS
is the exceeding *g* ... Eph 1:19

GREED
part is full of *g* ... Luke 11:39

GREEDINESS
all uncleanness with *g* ... Eph 4:19

GREEDY
of everyone who is *g* ... Prov 1:19
not violent, not *g* ... 1 Tim 3:3

GREEK
written in Hebrew, *G* ... John 19:20
and also for the *G* ... Rom 1:16
is neither Jew not *G* ... Gal 3:28

GREEN
lie down in *g* pastures ... Ps 23:2

GRIEF
and acquainted with *g* ... Is 53:3
joy and not with *g* ... Heb 13:17

GRIEVE
g the Holy Spirit ... Eph 4:30

GRIEVED
earth, and He was *g* ... Gen 6:6
g His Holy Spirit ... Is 63:10
with anger, being *g* ... Mark 3:5

GROAN
even we ourselves *g* ... Rom 8:23
who are in this tent *g* ... 2 Cor 5:4

GROANING
I am weary with my *g* ... Ps 6:6
Then Jesus, again *g* ... John 11:38

who is of the truth *h* ..... John 18:37
He who knows God *h* ... 1 John 4:6
And let him who *h* .... Rev 22:17

HEART
h was only evil .... Gen 6:5
h rejoices in the LORD .... 1 Sam 2:1
gave him another *h* ..... 1 Sam 10:9
LORD looks at the *h* ..... 1 Sam 16:7
his wives turned his *h* ... 1 Kin 11:4
He pierces my *h* .... Job 16:13
My *h* also instructs me ..... Ps 16:7
h is overflowing .... Ps 45:1
h shall depart from me .... Ps 101:4
look and a proud *h* .... Ps 101:5
with my whole *h* .... Ps 111:1
as he thinks in his *h* ...... Prov 23:7
h reveals the man .... Prov 27:19
trusts in his own *h* ...... Prov 28:26
The *h* of the wise is .... Eccl 7:4
And a wise man's *h* .... Eccl 8:5
h yearned for him .... Song 5:4
And the whole *h* .... Is 1:5
The yearning of Your *h* ..... Is 63:15
h is deceitful above .... Jer 17:9
I will give them a *h* .... Jer 24:7
and take the stony *h* .... Ezek 11:19
yourselves a new *h* ...... Ezek 18:31
are the pure in *h* .... Matt 5:8
is, there your *h* .... Matt 6:21
of the *h* proceed evil .... Matt 15:19
h will flow rivers .... John 7:38
"Let not your *h* .... John 14:1
Satan filled your *h* .... Acts 5:3
h that God has raised .... Rom 10:9
refresh my *h* in the .... Philem 20
and shuts up his *h* ...... 1 John 3:17

HEARTILY
you do, do it *h* .... Col 3:23

HEARTS
God tests the *h* .... Ps 7:9
And he will turn The *h* ..... Mal 4:6
h failing them from ..... Luke 21:26
will guard your *h* .... Phil 4:7
of God rule in your *h* ...... Col 3:15

HEATHEN
repetitions as the *h* .... Matt 6:7

HEAVEN
called the firmament *H* ..... Gen 1:8
LORD looks down from *h* ... Ps 14:2
word is settled in *h* .... Ps 119:89
For God is in *h* .... Eccl 5:2
"*H* is My throne .... Is 66:1
for the kingdom of *h* ...... Matt 3:2
your Father in *h* .... Matt 5:16
On earth as it is in *h* ...... Matt 6:10
"*H* and earth will .... Matt 24:35
Him a sign from *h* .... Mark 8:11
have sinned against *h* ... Luke 15:18
you shall see *h* .... John 1:51
one has ascended to *h* .... John 3:13
the true bread from *h* .... John 6:32
a voice came from *h* ..... John 12:28
sheet, let down from *h* ... Acts 11:5
laid up for you in *h* .... Col 1:5
there was silence in *h* ...... Rev 8:1
Now I saw a new *h* .... Rev 21:1

HEAVENLY
your *h* Father will .... Matt 6:14
h host praising God .... Luke 2:13
if I tell you *h* things .... John 3:12
blessing in the *h* .... Eph 1:3
a better, that is, a *h* .... Heb 11:16
the living God, the *h* ..... Heb 12:22

HEAVENS
and the highest *h* .... Deut 10:14
h cannot contain .... 1 Kin 8:27
h declare the glory .... Ps 19:1
For as the *h* are high ..... Ps 103:11
behold, I create new *h* ...... Is 65:17
and behold, the *h* .... Matt 3:16
h will be shaken .... Matt 24:29
h are the work of Your .... Heb 1:10
h will pass away .... 2 Pet 3:10

HEEDS
h counsel is wise .... Prov 12:15

HEEL
you shall bruise His *h* ..... Gen 3:15
has lifted up his *h* .... Ps 41:9
Me has lifted up his *h* ... John 13:18

HEIGHT
nor *h* nor depth .... Rom 8:39
length and depth and *h* .... Eph 3:18

HEIR
He has appointed *h* .... Heb 1:2
world and became *h* .... Heb 11:7

HEIRS
if children, then *h* .... Rom 8:17
should be fellow *h* .... Eph 3:6

HELL
shall be turned into *h* ...... Ps 9:17
go down alive into *h* .... Ps 55:15
H and Destruction are ... Prov 27:20
be in danger of *h* fire ..... Matt 5:22
to be cast into *h* .... Matt 18:9
condemnation of *h* ...... Matt 23:33
power to cast into *h* ...... Luke 12:5

HELMET
And take the *h* of .... Eph 6:17
and love, and as a *h* .... 1 Thess 5:8

HELP
May He send you *h* .... Ps 20:2
A very present *h* .... Ps 46:1
He is their *h* and .... Ps 115:9
Our *h* is in the name ...... Ps 124:8
h my unbelief .... Mark 9:24
and find grace to *h* .... Heb 4:16

HELPED
fall, but the LORD *h* ...... Ps 118:13
of salvation I have *h* .... Is 49:8
h His servant Israel .... Luke 1:54

HELPER
I will make him a *h* .... Gen 2:18
Behold, God is my *h* .... Ps 54:4
give you another *H* ...... John 14:16
"But when the *H* .... John 15:26
"The LORD is my *h* .... Heb 13:6

HELPFUL
all things are not *h* ...... 1 Cor 6:12

HELPS
the Spirit also *h* .... Rom 8:26

HEM
and touched the *h* .... Matt 9:20

HERE
Then I said, "*H* am I .... Is 6:8

HERESIES
dissensions, *h* .... Gal 5:20

HERITAGE
for that is his *h* .... Eccl 3:22
This is the *h* of the .... Is 54:17
of My people, My *h* .... Joel 3:2
The flock of Your *h* .... Mic 7:14

HIDDEN
And my sins are not *h* ...... Ps 69:5
Your word I have *h* .... Ps 119:11
h that will not .... Matt 10:26
the *h* wisdom which ...... 1 Cor 2:7
bring to light the *h* .... 1 Cor 4:5
have renounced the *h* .... 2 Cor 4:2
rather let it be the *h* .... 1 Pet 3:4
give some of the *h* .... Rev 2:17

HIDE
H me under the shadow .... Ps 17:8
You shall *h* them in .... Ps 31:20
You *h* Your face .... Ps 104:29
darkness shall not *h* ...... Ps 139:12
You are God, who *h* .... Is 45:15
"Fall on us and *h* .... Rev 6:16

HIDES
He *h* His face .... Ps 10:11

HIDING
You are my *h* place .... Ps 32:7

HIGH
priest of God Most *H* ..... Gen 14:18
For the LORD Most *H* .... Ps 47:2
"I dwell in the *h* .... Is 57:15
know That the Most *H* .... Dan 4:17
up on a *h* mountain by ... Matt 17:1
your mind on *h* things ... Rom 12:16
h thing that exalts .... 2 Cor 10:5
and faithful *H* Priest ...... Heb 2:17

HIGHER
you, 'Friend, go up *h* .... Luke 14:10

HIGHWAY
in the desert A *h* .... Is 40:3

HIGHWAYS
h shall be elevated .... Is 49:11
go into the *h* .... Matt 22:9

HILL
My King on My holy *h* .... Ps 2:6
h cannot be hidden .... Matt 5:14
and *h* brought low .... Luke 3:5

HILLS
of the everlasting *h* .... Gen 49:26
of the *h* are His also .... Ps 95:4
up my eyes to the *h* .... Ps 121:1

HINDER
all things lest we *h* ...... 1 Cor 9:12

HINDERED
Who *h* you from obeying ... Gal 5:7
prayers may not be *h* ...... 1 Pet 3:7

HOLD
right hand shall *h* .... Ps 139:10
h fast that word .... 1 Cor 15:2
h fast and repent .... Rev 3:3

HOLIER
near me, For I am *h* .... Is 65:5

HOLIEST
the way into the *H* .... Heb 9:8

HOLINESS
You, glorious in *h* .... Ex 15:11
I have sworn by My *h* ..... Ps 89:35
the Highway of *H* .... Is 35:8
to the Spirit of *h* .... Rom 1:4
spirit, perfecting *h* .... 2 Cor 7:1
uncleanness, but in *h* ... 1 Thess 4:7
be partakers of His *h* ..... Heb 12:10

HOLY
where you stand is *h* .... Ex 3:5
day, to keep it *h* .... Ex 20:8
LORD your God am *h* ...... Lev 19:2
h seed is mixed .... Ezra 9:2
God sits on His *h* .... Ps 47:8
God, in His *h* mountain .... Ps 48:1
"*H*, *h*, *h* .... Is 6:3
child of the *H* Spirit ..... Mark 1:18
baptize you with the *H* .... Mark 1:8
who speak, but the *H* ... Mark 13:11
H Spirit will come .... Luke 1:35
H Spirit descended .... Luke 3:22
Father give the *H* .... Luke 11:3
H Spirit will teach .... Luke 12:12
H Spirit was not .... John 7:39
H Spirit has come .... Acts 1:8
all filled with the *H* .... Acts 2:4
receive the *H* Spirit ...... Acts 19:2
joy in the *H* .... Rom 14:17
H Spirit teaches .... 1 Cor 2:13
that we should be *h* .... Eph 1:4
were sealed with the *H* ..... Eph 1:13
partakers of the *H* .... Heb 6:4
H Spirit sent from .... 1 Pet 1:12
it is written, "Be *h* .... 1 Pet 1:16
moved by the *H* Spirit .... 2 Pet 1:21
anointing from the *H* .... 1 John 2:20
says He who is *h* .... Rev 3:7
For You alone are *h* .... Rev 15:4
is *h*, let him be *h* .... Rev 22:11

HOME
sparrow has found a *h* ..... Ps 84:3
to his eternal *h* .... Eccl 12:5
that while we are at *h* .... 2 Cor 5:6
to show piety at *h* .... 1 Tim 5:4

HOMEMAKERS
be discreet, chaste, *h* ...... Titus 2:5

HONEY
and with *h* from the .... Ps 81:16
was locusts and wild *h* .... Matt 3:4

HONEYCOMB
than honey and the *h* ..... Ps 19:10
fish and some *h* .... Luke 24:42

HONOR
"*H* your father and your ... Ex 20:12
will deliver him and *h* ..... Ps 91:15
H and majesty are .... Ps 96:6
H the LORD with your ..... Prov 3:9
before *h* is humility ..... Prov 15:33
spirit will retain *h* .... Prov 29:23
Father, where is My *h* ...... Mal 1:6
is not without *h* .... Matt 13:57
'*H* your father and .... Matt 15:4
h the Son Just as they .... John 5:23

“I do not receive *h* .... John 5:41
but I *h* My Father .... John 8:49
“If I *h* Myself .... John 8:54
him My Father will *h* .... John 12:26
to whom fear, *h* .... Rom 13:7
sanctification and *h* .... 1 Thess 4:4
alone is wise, be *h* .... 1 Tim 1:17
and clay, some for *h* ..... 2 Tim 2:20
no man takes this *h* .... Heb 5:4
from God the Father *h* ..... 2 Pet 1:17
give glory and *h* .... Rev 4:9

HONORABLE
His work is *h* and .... Ps 111:3
holy day of the LORD *h* ..... Is 58:13
providing *h* things ...... 2 Cor 8:21
Marriage is *h* among ...... Heb 13:4
having your conduct *h* ... 1 Pet 2:12

HONORS
‘This people *h* Me .... Mark 7:6
It is My Father who *h* .... John 8:54

HOPE
h He has uprooted .... Job 19:10
also will rest in *h* .... Ps 16:9
My *h* is in You .... Ps 39:7
For You are my *h* .... Ps 71:5
I *h* in Your word .... Ps 119:147
good that one should *h* ... Lam 3:26
to *h*, in *h* believed .... Rom 4:18
h does not disappoint ..... Rom 5:5
were saved in this *h* ...... Rom 8:24
now abide faith, *h* .... 1 Cor 13:13
life only we have *h* ...... 1 Cor 15:19
may know what is the *h* ... Eph 1:18
were called in one *h* .... Eph 4:4
Christ in you, the *h* .... Col 1:27
Jesus Christ, our *h* .... 1 Tim 1:1
for the blessed *h* .... Titus 2:13
to lay hold of the *h* .... Heb 6:18
in of a better *h* .... Heb 7:19
who has this *h* in Him ... 1 John 3:3

HOPED
substance of things *h* ...... Heb 11:1

HORSE
and behold, a white *h* ...... Rev 6:2
and behold, a white *h* .... Rev 19:11

HOSANNA
H in the highest .... Matt 21:9

HOSPITABLE
Be *h* to one another .... 1 Pet 4:9

HOSTS
The LORD of *h* is with ...... Ps 46:7
Praise Him, all His *h* .... Ps 148:2
against spiritual *h* .... Eph 6:12

HOUR
is coming at an *h* .... Matt 24:44
“But the *h* is coming ...... John 4:23
save Me from this *h* ..... John 12:27
keep you from the *h* .... Rev 3:10

HOUSE
as for me and my *h* ...... Josh 24:15
Through wisdom a *h* ..... Prov 24:3
better to go to the *h* .... Eccl 7:2
h was filled with .... Is 6:4
h divided against .... Matt 12:25
h shall be called a .... Matt 21:13
make My Father's *h* ...... John 2:16
h are many mansions .... John 14:2
publicly and from *h* ...... Acts 20:20
who rules his own *h* ...... 1 Tim 3:4
the church in your *h* .... Philem 2
For every *h* is built .... Heb 3:4
His own *h*, whose *h* .... Heb 3:6

HOUSEHOLD
the ways of her *h* .... Prov 31:27
be those of his own *h* .... Matt 10:36
h were baptized .... Acts 16:15
saved, you and your *h* ... Acts 16:31
who are of Caesar's *h* ..... Phil 4:22

HOUSEHOLDER
h who brings out of ..... Matt 13:52

HOUSES
H and riches are an ..... Prov 19:14
who has left *h* or .... Matt 19:29
you devour widows' *h* ... Matt 23:14

HOVERING
Spirit of God was *h* .... Gen 1:2

HUMBLE
man Moses was very *h* ... Num 12:3
the cry of the *h* .... Ps 9:12
h shall hear of it and .... Ps 34:2
contrite and *h* spirit .... Is 57:15
A meek and *h* people ..... Zeph 3:12
associate with the *h* ..... Rom 12:16
gives grace to the *h* ...... James 4:6
H yourselves in the ...... James 4:10
gives grace to the *h* .... 1 Pet 5:5
h yourselves under the .... 1 Pet 5:6

HUMBLED
as a man, He *h* Himself .... Phil 2:8

HUMBLES
h Himself to behold .... Ps 113:6

HUMILITY
the Lord with all *h* ...... Acts 20:19
delight in false *h* .... Col 2:18
mercies, kindness, *h* .... Col 3:12
h correcting those .... 2 Tim 2:25
gentle, showing all *h* ...... Titus 3:2
and be clothed with *h* ...... 1 Pet 5:5

HUNGER
They shall neither *h* .... Is 49:10
are those who *h* .... Matt 5:6
for you shall *h* .... Luke 6:25
to Me shall never *h* .... John 6:35
hour we both *h* .... 1 Cor 4:11
“They shall neither *h* ...... Rev 7:16

HUNGRY
and fills the *h* .... Ps 107:9
gives food to the *h* .... Ps 146:7
‘for I was *h* and you ..... Matt 25:35
did we see You *h* .... Matt 25:37
to be full and to be *h* .... Phil 4:12

HUNTER
Nimrod the mighty *h* .... Gen 10:9
Esau was a skillful *h* ..... Gen 25:27

HURT
h a woman with child ..... Ex 21:22
but I was not *h* .... Prov 23:35
another to his own *h* .... Eccl 8:9
They shall not *h* .... Is 11:9
it will by no means *h* ... Mark 16:18
shall not be *h* by the .... Rev 2:11

HUSBAND
She also gave to her *h* ..... Gen 3:6
h safely trusts her .... Prov 31:11
your Maker is your *h* .... Is 54:5
now have is not your *h* ... John 4:18
you will save your *h* ..... 1 Cor 7:16
the *h* of one wife .... 1 Tim 12

HUSBANDS
H, love your wives .... Eph 5:25
Let deacons be the *h* .... 1 Tim 3:12

HYMN
they had sung a *h* .... Matt 26:30

HYMNS
praying and singing *h* ... Acts 16:25
in psalms and *h* .... Eph 5:19

HYPOCRISY
you are full of *h* .... Matt 23:28
Pharisees, which is *h* ..... Luke 12:1
Let love be without *h* ..... Rom 12:9
away with their *h* .... Gal 2:13
and without *h* .... James 3:17
malice, all deceit, *h* .... 1 Pet 2:1

HYPOCRITE
and the joy of the *h* .... Job 20:5
For everyone is a *h* .... Is 9:17
also played the *h* .... Gal 2:13

HYPOCRITES
not be like the *h* .... Matt 6:5
do you test Me, you *h* ... Matt 22:18
and Pharisees, *h* .... Matt 23:13

I

IDLE
i Person will suffer ...... Prov 19:15
i word men may .... Matt 12:36
saw others standing *i* .... Matt 20:3
they learn to be *i* .... 1 Tim 5:13

IDOL
thing offered to an *i* ...... 1 Cor 8:7
That an *i* is anything ... 1 Cor 10:19

IDOLATER
or covetous, or an *i* ...... 1 Cor 5:11

IDOLATERS
fornicators, nor *i* .... 1 Cor 6:9
and murderers and *i* ..... Rev 22:15

IDOLATRIES
and abominable *i* .... 1 Pet 4:3

IDOLATRY
beloved, flee from *i* ..... 1 Cor 10:14
i, sorcery .... Gal 5:20

IDOLS
land is also full of *i* .... Is 2:8
in the room of his *i* .... Ezek 8:12
who regard worthless *i* ...... Jon 2:8
You who abhor *i* .... Rom 2:22
yourselves from *i* .... 1 John 5:21
worship demons, and *i* .... Rev 9:20

IGNORANCE
that you did it in *i* .... Acts 3:17
i God overlooked .... Acts 17:30
sins committed in *i* .... Heb 9:7

IGNORANTLY
because I did it *i* .... 1 Tim 1:13

ILLUMINATED
after you were *i* .... Heb 10:32
and the earth was *i* .... Rev 18:1
for the glory of God *i* ..... Rev 21:23

IMAGE
Us make man in Our *i* ..... Gen 1:26
since he is the *i* .... 1 Cor 11:7
He is the *i* of the .... Col 1:15
and not the very *i* .... Heb 10:1
the beast and his *i* .... Rev 14:9

IMAGINATION
the proud in the *i* .... Luke 1:51

IMITATE
as I also *i* Christ .... 1 Cor 11:1

IMMANUEL
shall call His name *I* .... Is 7:14
shall call His name *I* ..... Matt 1:23

IMMORAL
murderers, sexually *i* ...... Rev 21:8

IMMORALITY
except sexual *i* .... Matt 5:32
abstain from sexual *i* ... 1 Thess 4:3

IMMORTAL
to the King eternal, *i* .... 1 Tim 1:17

IMMORTALITY
mortal must put on *i* ... 1 Cor 15:53
who alone has *i* .... 1 Tim 6:16

IMMOVABLE
be steadfast, *i* .... 1 Cor 15:58

IMMUTABLE
that by two *i* things .... Heb 6:18

IMPART
that it may *i* grace .... Eph 4:29

IMPENITENT
i heart you are .... Rom 2:5

IMPOSSIBLE
God nothing will be *i* ..... Luke 1:37
without faith it is *i* .... Heb 11:6

IMPUTE
the LORD does not *i* .... Ps 32:2

IMPUTED
might be *i* to them .... Rom 4:11
but sin is not *i* .... Rom 5:13

IMPUTES
i righteousness apart ...... Rom 4:6

INCORRUPTIBLE
the glory of the *i* .... Rom 1:23
dead will be raised *i* ..... 1 Cor 15:52
to an inheritance *i* .... 1 Pet 1:4

INCORRUPTION
corruption inherit *i* ..... 1 Cor 15:50

INCREASE
Of the *i* of His .... Is 9:7
Lord “*I* our faith .... Luke 17:5
“He must *i* .... John 3:30
but God gave the *i* .... 1 Cor 3:6

INCREASES
who have no might He *i* .... Is 40:29

INCURABLE
Your sorrow is *i* ....Jer 30:15

INDIGNATION
i which will devour ....Heb 10:27
into the cup of His *i* ......Rev 14:10

INEXCUSABLE
Therefore you are *i* .... Rom 2:1

INEXPRESSIBLE
Paradise and heard *i* .... 2 Cor 12:4
you rejoice with joy *i* ...... 1 Pet 1:8

INFALLIBLE
suffering by many *i* .... Acts 1:3

INFIRMITIES
"He Himself took our *i* ... Matt 8:17

INHERIT
love me to *i* wealth .... Prov 8:21
i the kingdom .... Matt 25:34
unrighteous will not *i* .... 1 Cor 6:9
who overcomes shall *i* ..... Rev 21:7

INHERITANCE
"You shall have no *i* .....Num 18:20
is the place of His *i* .... Deut 32:9
the portion of my *i* .... Ps 16:5
i shall be forever .... Ps 37:18
He will choose our *i* .... Ps 47:4
will arise to your *i* .... Dan 12:13
God gave him no *i* .... Acts 7:5
and give you an *i* .... Acts 20:32
For if the *i* is of the .... Gal 3:18
we have obtained an *i* .....Eph 1:11
be partakers of the *i* .... Col 1:12
receive as an *i* ....Heb 11:8
i incorruptible .... 1 Pet 1:4

INIQUITIES
i have overtaken me .... Ps 40:12
forgives all your *i* .... Ps 103:3
LORD, should mark *i* ...... Ps 130:3
was bruised for our *i* .... Is 53:5
He shall bear their *i* .... Is 53:11
i have separated you .... Is 59:2

INIQUITY
God, visiting the *i* of the .... Ex 20:5
was brought forth in *i* ...... Ps 51:5
If I regard *i* in my .... Ps 66:18
i have dominion .... Ps 119:133
i will reap sorrow .... Prov 22:8
A people laden with *i* .... Is 1:4
i is taken away .... Is 6:7
has laid on Him the *i* .... Is 53:6
will remember their *i* .... Hos 9:9
to those who devise *i* .... Mic 2:1
like You, Pardoning *i* .... Mic 7:18
all you workers of *i* .....Luke 13:27
a fire, a world of *i* ....James 3:6

INJUSTICE
i have your fathers ....Jer 2:5

INN
room for them in the *i* ..... Luke 2:7
brought him to an *i* ......Luke 10:34

INNOCENCE
washed my hands in *i* ..... Ps 73:13

INNOCENT
because I was found *i* .....Dan 6:22
saying, "I am *i* .... Matt 27:24
this day that I am *i* ...... Acts 20:26

INQUIRED
Therefore David *i* ....1 Sam 23:2
the prophets have *i* .... 1 Pet 1:10

INQUIRY
shall make careful *i* .....Deut 19:18

INSANE
images, And they are *i* ....Jer 50:38

INSPIRATION
is given by *i* of God ...... 2 Tim 3:16

INSTRUCT
I will *i* you and teach .... Ps 32:8
LORD that he may *i* ...... 1 Cor 2:16

INSTRUCTED
This man had been *i* .... Acts 18:25
are excellent, being *i* ..... Rom 2:18
Moses was divinely *i* ....Heb 8:5

INSTRUCTION
seeing you hate *i* .... Ps 50:17
Hear *i* and be wise .... Prov 8:33
Give *i* to a wise man .... Prov 9:9
for correction, for *i* ...... 2 Tim 3:16

INSTRUCTS
My heart also *i* .... Ps 16:7

INSTRUMENTS
your members as *i* .... Rom 6:13

INSUBORDINATE
for the lawless and *i* ...... 1 Tim 1:9

INSUBORDINATION
of dissipation or *i* .... Titus 1:6

INSULTED
will be mocked and *i* ....Luke 18:32
i the Spirit of grace ....Heb 10:29

INSULTS
nor be afraid of their *i* .... Is 51:7

INTEGRITY
in the *i* of my heart ....Gen 20:5
in doctrine showing *i* ...... Titus 2:7

INTERCEDE
the LORD, who will *i* .....1 Sam 2:25

INTERCESSION
of many, And made *i* .... Is 53:12
Spirit Himself makes *i* ... Rom 8:26
always lives to make *i* .....Heb 7:25

INTERCESSOR
that there was no *i* .... Is 59:16

INTEREST
collected it with *i* ....Luke 19:23

INTERPRET
Do all *i*? .... 1 Cor 12:30
pray that he may *i* ...... 1 Cor 14:13

INTERPRETATION
to another the *i* .... 1 Cor 12:10
of any private *i* ....2 Pet 1:20

INTERPRETATIONS
"Do not *i* belong to ....Gen 40:8

INVISIBLE
of the world His *i* .... Rom 1:20
is the image of the *i* .... Col 1:15
eternal, immortal, *i* .... 1 Tim 1:17
as seeing Him who is *i* ...Heb 11:27

INWARD
You have formed my *i* .... Ps 139:13
God according to the *i* .... Rom 7:22
i man is being .... 2 Cor 4:16

INWARDLY
i they are .... Matt 7:15
is a Jew who is one *i* ..... Rom 2:29

IRON
i sharpens *i* .... Prov 27:17
its feet partly of *i* ....Dan 2:33

ISRAEL
"Hear, O *I* .... Deut 6:4
For they are not all *I* ...... Rom 9:6
and upon the *I* of God ..... Gal 6:16

ITCHING
they have *i* ears .... 2 Tim 4:3

J

JEALOUS
God, am a *j* God .... Ex 20:5
a consuming fire, a *j* ..... Deut 4:24
For I am *j* for you .... 2 Cor 11:2

JEALOUSY
provoked Him to *j* ....Deut 32:16
as strong as death, *j* ....Song 8:6
for you with godly *j* ..... 2 Cor 11:2

JEOPARDY
stand in *j* every hour ... 1 Cor 15:30

JESTING
talking, nor coarse *j* .... Eph 5:4

JESUS
J Christ was as .... Matt 1:18
shall call His name *J* ..... Matt 1:21
J was led up by the .... Matt 4:1
and laid hands on *J* ..... Matt 26:50
and destroy *J* .... Matt 27:20
J withdrew with His ....Mark 3:7
J went into .... Mark 11:11
they were eating, *J* ..... Mark 14:22
and he delivered *J* ...... Mark 15:15
truth came through *J* ..... John 1:17
J lifted up His eyes .... John 6:5
J wept ....John 11:35
J was crucified ....John 19:20
"This *J* God has raised ... Acts 2:32
of Your holy Servant *J* ... Acts 4:30
believed on the Lord *J* ... Acts 11:17
your mouth the Lord *J* ... Rom 10:9
among you except *J* ...... 1 Cor 2:2
perfect in Christ *J* .... Col 1:28
But we see *J* ....Heb 2:9
looking unto *J* ....Heb 12:2
Revelation of *J* Christ ...... Rev 1:1
so, come, Lord *J* ....Rev 22:20

JOIN
of the rest dared *j* .... Acts 5:13

JOINED
and mother and be *j* ....Gen 2:24
what God has *j* .... Matt 19:6
the whole body, *j* ....Eph 4:16

JOINT
j as He wrestled ....Gen 32:25
My bones are out of *j* ...... Ps 22:14
j heirs with Christ .... Rom 8:17

JOINTS
and knit together by *j* ..... Col 2:19
and spirit, and of *j* ....Heb 4:12

JOT
one *j* or one tittle .... Matt 5:18

JOY
is fullness of *j* .... Ps 16:11
j comes in the morning ..... Ps 30:5
j you will draw .... Is 12:3
ashes, The oil of *j* .... Is 61:3
shall sing for *j* .... Is 65:14
receives it with *j* .... Matt 13:20
Enter into the *j* .... Matt 25:21
in my womb for *j* ....Luke 1:44
there will be more *j* ......Luke 15:7
did not believe for *j* .....Luke 24:41
My *j* may remain in ......John 15:11
they may have My *j* .....John 17:13
the Spirit is love, *j* .... Gal 5:22
are our glory and *j* .... 1 Thess 2:20
j that was set before ....Heb 12:2
count it all *j* ....James 1:2
with exceeding *j* .... 1 Pet 4:13

JOYFUL
Make a *j* shout to the ...... Ps 100:1
And make them *j* .... Is 56:7

JUDGE
The LORD *j* between ....Gen 16:5
coming to *j* the earth ... 1 Chr 16:33
sword The LORD will *j* ...... Is 66:16
deliver you to the *j* .... Matt 5:25
"*J* not .... Matt 7:1
who made Me a *j* ....Luke 12:14
j who did not fear God ...Luke 18:2
As I hear, I *j* .... John 5:30
"Do not *j* according ......John 7:24
I *j* no one .... John 8:15
j the world but to ....John 12:47
this, O man, you who *j* .... Rom 2:3
Therefore let us not *j* ....Rom 14:13
Christ, who will *j* .... 2 Tim 4:1
But if you *j* the law ......James 4:11

JUDGES
He makes the *j* of the .... Is 40:23
For the Father *j* .... John 5:22
he who is spiritual *j* ..... 1 Cor 2:15
j me is the Lord .... 1 Cor 4:4
Him who *j* righteously ... 1 Pet 2:23

JUDGMENT
Teach me good *j* .... Ps 119:66
from prison and from *j* ...... Is 53:8
be in danger of the *j* ...... Matt 5:21
shall not come into *j* ..... John 5:24
and My *j* is righteous ..... John 5:30
if I do judge, My *j* .... John 8:16
"Now is the *j* .... John 12:31
the righteous *j* .... Rom 1:32
j which came from one ... Rom 5:16
appear before the *j* ...... 2 Cor 5:10
after this the *j* ....Heb 9:27
time has come for *j* .... 1 Pet 4:17
a long time their *j* .... 2 Pet 2:3
darkness for the *j* .... Jude 6

JUDGMENTS
The *j* of the LORD are — Ps 19:9
unsearchable are His *j* — Rom 11:33

JUST
Noah was a *j* man — Gen 6:9
j man who perishes — Eccl 7:15
j shall live by his — Hab 2:4
her husband, being a *j* — Matt 1:19
resurrection of the *j* — Luke 14:14
j persons who need no — Luke 15:7
the Holy One and the *J* — Acts 3:14
dead, both of the *j* — Acts 24:15
j shall live by faith — Rom 1:17
that He might be *j* — Rom 3:26
j men made perfect — Heb 12:23
have murdered the *j* — James 5:6
He is faithful and *j* — 1 John 1:9

JUSTICE
j as the noonday — Ps 37:6
And Your poor with *j* — Ps 72:2
j the measuring line — Is 28:17
the LORD is a God of *j* — Is 30:18
He will bring forth *j* — Is 42:1
J is turned back — Is 59:14
I, the LORD, love *j* — Is 61:8
truth, and His ways *j* — Dan 4:37
'Execute true *j* — Zech 7:9
"Where is the God of *j* — Mal 2:17
And He will declare *j* — Matt 12:18
His humiliation His *j* — Acts 8:33

JUSTIFICATION
because of our *j* — Rom 4:25
offenses resulted in *j* — Rom 5:16

JUSTIFIED
Me that you may be *j* — Job 40:8
words you will be *j* — Matt 12:37
"But wisdom is *j* — Luke 7:35
j rather than the — Luke 18:14
who believes is *j* — Acts 13:39
"That You may be *j* — Rom 3:4
law no flesh will be *j* — Rom 3:20
j freely by His grace — Rom 3:24
having been *j* by — Rom 5:1
these He also *j* — Rom 8:30
that we might be *j* — Gal 2:16
no flesh shall be *j* — Gal 2:16
the harlot also *j* — James 2:25

JUSTIFIES
He who *j* the wicked — Prov 17:15
It is God who *j* — Rom 8:33

JUSTIFY
wanting to *j* himself — Luke 10:29
"You are those who *j* — Luke 16:15
is one God who will *j* — Rom 3:30

K

KEEP
k you wherever you — Gen 28:15
day, to *k* it holy — Ex 20:8
Let all the earth *k* — Hab 2:20
k the commandments — Matt 19:17
"If you love Me, *k* — John 14:15
k through Your name — John 17:11
orderly and *k* the law — Acts 21:24
k the unity of the — Eph 4:3
k His commandments — 1 John 2:3

KEEPER
Am I my brother's *k* — Gen 4:9
The LORD is your *k* — Ps 121:5

KEEPS
k truth forever — Ps 146:6
k the commandment — Prov 19:16
none of you *k* the law — John 7:19
born of God *k* — 1 John 5:18
and *k* his garments — Rev 16:15

KEPT
For I have *k* the — 2 Sam 22:22
these things I have *k* — Matt 19:20
love, just as I have *k* — John 15:10
k back part of the — Acts 5:2
I have *k* the faith — 2 Tim 4:7
who are *k* by the power — 1 Pet 1:5

KEY
taken away the *k* — Luke 11:52
"He who has the *k* — Rev 3:7

KEYS
I will give you the *k* — Matt 16:19
And I have the *k* — Rev 1:18

KILL
k the Passover — Ex 12:21
I *k* and I make alive — Deut 32:39
"Am I God, to *k* — 2 Kin 5:7
A time to *k* — Eccl 3:3
of them they will *k* — Luke 11:49
afraid of those who *k* — Luke 12:4
Why do you seek to *k* — John 7:19
k and eat — Acts 10:13

KILLED
Abel his brother and *k* — Gen 4:8
for Your sake we are *k* — Ps 44:22
and scribes, and be *k* — Matt 16:21
Siloam fell and *k* them — Luke 13:4
k the Prince of life — Acts 3:15
Your sake we are *k* — Rom 8:36
k both the Lord — 1 Thess 2:15

KILLS
the one who *k* the — Matt 23:37
for the letter *k* — 2 Cor 3:6

KIND
animals after their *k* — Gen 6:20
k can come out by — Mark 9:29
suffers long and is *k* — 1 Cor 13:4
And be *k* to one — Eph 4:32

KINDLY
Julius treated Paul *k* — Acts 27:3
k affectionate to one — Rom 12:10

KINDNESS
For His merciful *k* — Ps 117:2
k shall not depart — Is 54:10
I remember you, The *k* — Jer 2:2
by longsuffering, by *k* — 2 Cor 6:6
longsuffering, *k* — Gal 5:22
and to brotherly *k* — 2 Pet 1:7

KING
"Yet I have set My *K* — Ps 2:6
The LORD is *K* forever — Ps 10:16
And the *K* of glory — Ps 24:7
For God is my *K* — Ps 74:12
when your *k* is a child — Eccl 10:16
and the everlasting *K* — Jer 10:10
the LORD shall be *K* — Zech 14:9
who has been born *K* — Matt 2:2
This Is Jesus The *K* — Matt 27:37
"Behold your *K* — John 19:14
Now to the *K* eternal — 1 Tim 1:17
only Potentate, the *K* — 1 Tim 6:15
this Melchizedek, *k* — Heb 7:1
K of Kings and Lord — Rev 19:16

KINGDOM
Yours is the *k* — 1 Chr 29:11
k is the LORD's — Ps 22:28
the scepter of Your *k* — Ps 45:6
is an everlasting *k* — Ps 145:13
k which shall never be — Dan 2:44
High rules in the *k* — Dan 4:17
"Repent, for the *k* — Matt 3:2
for Yours is the *k* — Matt 6:13
"But seek first the *k* — Matt 6:33
the mysteries of the *k* — Matt 13:11
are the sons of the *k* — Matt 13:38
of such is the *k* — Matt 19:14
back, is fit for the *k* — Luke 9:62
against nation, and *k* — Luke 21:10
he cannot see the *k* — John 3:3
he cannot enter the *k* — John 3:5
If My *k* were of this — John 18:36
for the *k* of God is — Rom 14:17
will not inherit the *k* — Gal 5:21
the scepter of Your *k* — Heb 1:8
we are receiving a *k* — Heb 12:28

KINGDOMS
the *k* were moved — Ps 46:6
showed Him all the *k* — Matt 4:8
have become the *k* — Rev 11:15

KINGS
The *k* of the earth set — Ps 2:2
By me *k* reign — Prov 8:15
governors and *k* — Matt 10:18
k have desired to see — Luke 10:24
You have reigned as *k* — 1 Cor 4:8
and has made us *k* — Rev 1:6
that the way of the *k* — Rev 16:12

KISS
K the Son — Ps 2:12
"You gave Me no *k* — Luke 7:45
one another with a *k* — 1 Pet 5:14

KISSED
they *k* one another — 1 Sam 20:41
and *k* Him — Matt 26:49
and she *k* His feet and — Luke 7:38

KNEE
That to Me every *k* — Is 45:23
have not bowed the *k* — Rom 11:4
of Jesus every *k* — Phil 2:10

KNEES
make firm the feeble *k* — Is 35:3
this reason I bow my *k* — Eph 3:14
and the feeble *k* — Heb 12:12

KNEW
in the womb I *k* — Jer 1:5
to them, 'I never *k* — Matt 7:23
k what was in man — John 2:25
He made Him who *k* — 2 Cor 5:21

KNIT
be encouraged, being *k* — Col 2:2

KNOCK
k, and it will be — Matt 7:7
at the door and *k* — Rev 3:20

KNOW
k good and evil — Gen 3:22
k that I am the LORD — Ex 6:7
k that my Redeemer — Job 19:25
make me to *k* wisdom — Ps 51:6
Who can *k* it — Jer 17:9
saying, '*K* the LORD — Jer 31:34
k what hour your — Matt 24:42
an oath, "I do not *k* — Matt 26:72
the world did not *k* — John 1:10
We speak what We *k* — John 3:11
k that You are — John 6:69
My voice, and I *k* — John 10:27
If you *k* these things — John 13:17
k whom I have — John 13:18
are sure that You *k* — John 16:30
k that I love You — John 21:15
k times or seasons — Acts 1:7
and said, "Jesus I *k* — Acts 19:15
wisdom did not *k* — 1 Cor 1:21
nor can he *k* them — 1 Cor 2:14
For we *k* in part and — 1 Cor 13:9
k the love of Christ — Eph 3:19
k whom I have — 2 Tim 1:12
we *k* that we *k* Him — 1 John 2:3
and you *k* all things — 1 John 2:20
By this we *k* love — 1 John 3:16
k that He abides — 1 John 3:24
k that we are of God — 1 John 5:19
"I *k* your works — Rev 2:2

KNOWLEDGE
and the tree of the *k* — Gen 2:9
unto night reveals *k* — Ps 19:2
k is too wonderful — Ps 139:6
people store up *k* — Prov 10:14
k spares his words — Prov 17:27
and he who increases *k* — Eccl 1:18
k is that wisdom — Eccl 7:12
k shall increase — Dan 12:4
more accurate *k* — Acts 24:22
having the form of *k* — Rom 2:20
law is the *k* of sin — Rom 3:20
whether there is *k* — 1 Cor 13:8
Christ which passes *k* — Eph 3:19
is falsely called *k* — 1 Tim 6:20
in the grace and *k* — 2 Pet 3:18

KNOWN
If you had *k* Me — John 8:19
My sheep, and am *k* — John 10:14
The world has not *k* — John 17:25
peace they have not *k* — Rom 3:17
"For who has *k* — Rom 11:34
after you have *k* — Gal 4:9
requests be made *k* — Phil 4:6
k the Holy Scriptures — 2 Tim 3:15

KNOWS
"For God *k* that in — Gen 3:5
k what is in the — Dan 2:22
k the things you have — Matt 6:8
and hour no one *k* — Matt 24:36
God *k* your hearts — Luke 16:15
searches the hearts *k* — Rom 8:27
k the things of God — 1 Cor 2:11
k those who are His — 2 Tim 2:19
to him who *k* to do — James 4:17
and *k* all things — 1 John 3:20

L

LABOR
Six days you shall *l* .... Ex 20:9
things are full of *l* .... Eccl 1:8
has man for all his *l* .... Eccl 2:22
He shall see the *l* .... Is 53:11
to Me, all you who *l* ..... Matt 11:28
"Do not *l* for the .... John 6:27
knowing that your *l* .... 1 Cor 15:58
but rather let him *l* .... Eph 4:28
mean fruit from my *l* ...... Phil 1:22
your work of faith, *l* .... 1 Thess 1:3
forget your work and *l* .... Heb 6:10
your works, your *l* .... Rev 2:2

LABORED
l more abundantly ..... 1 Cor 15:10
for you, lest I have *l* .... Gal 4:11

LABORERS
but the *l* are few .... Matt 9:37

LABORING
l night and day .... 1 Thess 2:9

LABORS
entered into their *l* .... John 4:38
creation groans and *l* ..... Rom 8:22
l more abundant .... 2 Cor 11:23
may rest from their *l* ..... Rev 14:13

LACK
What do I still *l* .... Matt 19:20
"One thing you *l* .... Mark 10:21

LADDER
and behold, a *l* .... Gen 28:12

LAID
the place where they *l* ... Mark 16:6
"Where have you *l* ..... John 11:34

LAKE
cast alive into the *l* .... Rev 19:20

LAMB
but where is the *l* .... Gen 22:7
He was led as a *l* .... Is 53:7
The *L* of God who .... John 1:29
the elders, stood a *L* .... Rev 5:6
"Worthy is the *L* .... Rev 5:12
by the blood of the *L* ..... Rev 12:11

LAME
l shall leap like a .... Is 35:6
blind see and the *l* .... Matt 11:5
And a certain man *l* .... Acts 3:2

LAMENTATION
was heard in Ramah, *l* ... Matt 2:18
and made great *l* .... Acts 8:2

LAMP
Your word is a *l* .... Ps 119:105
the *l* of the wicked .... Prov 13:9
his *l* will be put out ...... Prov 20:20
"Nor do they light a *l* ..... Matt 5:15
"The *l* of the body .... Matt 6:22
when he has lit a *l* .... Luke 8:16
l gives you light .... Luke 11:36
does not light a *l* .... Luke 15:8
burning and shining *l* .... John 5:35

LAMPS
he made its seven *l* .... Ex 37:23
and trimmed their *l* ...... Matt 25:7

LAMPSTAND
branches of the *l* .... Ex 25:32
a basket, but on a *l* .... Matt 5:15
and remove your *l* .... Rev 2:5

LAND
l that I will show you ...... Gen 12:1
l flowing with milk .... Ex 3:8
They will see the *l* .... Is 33:17
Bethlehem, in the *l* .... Matt 2:6

LANGUAGE
whole earth had one *l* ..... Gen 11:1
speak in his own *l* .... Acts 2:6
blasphemy, filthy *l* .... Col 3:8

LANGUAGES
according to their *l* .... Gen 10:20

LAST
He shall stand at *l* .... Job 19:25
First and I am the *L* .... Is 44:6
l will be first .... Matt 20:16
the First and the *L* .... Rev 1:11

LATTER
l times some will .... 1 Tim 4:1

LAUGH
"Why did Sarah *l* .... Gen 18:13
Woe to you who *l* .... Luke 6:25

LAUGHS
The Lord *l* at him .... Ps 37:13

LAUGHTER
your *l* be turned to .... James 4:9

LAW
stones a copy of the *l* ..... Josh 8:32
The *l* of the LORD is .... Ps 19:7
I delight in Your *l* .... Ps 119:70
Oh, how I love Your *l* ..... Ps 119:97
And Your *l* is truth ...... Ps 119:142
l will proceed from Me ...... Is 51:4
in whose heart is My *l* .... Is 51:7
The *L* is no more .... Lam 2:9
The *l* of truth was in .... Mal 2:6
to destroy the *L* .... Matt 5:17
for this is the *L* .... Matt 7:12
hang all the *L* and the ... Matt 22:40
"The *l* and the .... Luke 16:16
l was given through ...... John 1:17
"Does our *l* judge a .... John 7:51
l is the knowledge .... Rom 3:20
because the *l* brings ...... Rom 4:15
when there is no *l* .... Rom 5:13
you are not under *l* .... Rom 6:14
For what the *l* could .... Rom 8:3
l that I might live .... Gal 2:19
under guard by the *l* .... Gal 3:23
born under the *l* .... Gal 4:4
l is fulfilled in one .... Gal 5:14
into the perfect *l* .... James 1:25
fulfill the royal *l* .... James 2:8

LAWFUL
Is it *l* to pay taxes .... Matt 22:17
All things are *l* .... 1 Cor 6:12

LAWGIVER
There is one *L* .... James 4:12

LAWLESS
l one will be revealed ... 2 Thess 2:8

LAWLESSNESS
Me, you who practice *l* ... Matt 7:23
l is already at work ..... 2 Thess 2:7

LAWYERS
"Woe to you also, *l* .... Luke 11:46

LAY
nowhere to *l* His head .... Matt 8:20
l hands may receive ...... Acts 8:19

LAZINESS
l the building decays .... Eccl 10:18

LAZY
l man will be put to ..... Prov 12:24
wicked and *l* servant .... Matt 25:26
liars, evil beasts, *l* .... Titus 1:12

LEAD
L me in Your truth and ..... Ps 25:5
And do not *l* us into .... Matt 6:13
"Can the blind *l* .... Luke 6:39

LEADS
He *l* me in the paths .... Ps 23:3
And if the blind *l* .... Matt 15:14

LEAF
plucked olive *l* .... Gen 8:11

LEAN
all your heart, And *l* .... Prov 3:5

LEAP
Then the lame shall *l* .... Is 35:6

LEARN
L to do good .... Is 1:17
yoke upon you and *l* .... Matt 11:29

LEARNED
Me The tongue of the *l* ...... Is 50:4
have not so *l* Christ .... Eph 4:20
in all things I have *l* .... Phil 4:12

LEARNING
l is driving you mad ..... Acts 26:24

LEAST
so, shall be called *l* .... Matt 5:19

LEAVE
a man shall *l* his .... Gen 2:24
For You will not *l* .... Ps 16:10
"I will never *l* .... Heb 13:5

LEAVEN
of heaven is like *l* .... Matt 13:33
l leavens the whole .... Gal 5:9

LEAVES
and they sewed fig *l* .... Gen 3:7
The *l* of the tree .... Rev 22:2

LED
l them forth by the .... Ps 107:7
For as many as are *l* ...... Rom 8:14

LEFT
l hand know what your .... Matt 6:3

LEND
"And if you *l* .... Luke 6:34

LENDER
is servant to the *l* .... Prov 22:7

LENDS
ever merciful, and *l* .... Ps 37:26

LENGTH
is your life and the *l* ..... Deut 30:20

LEOPARD
or the *l* its spots .... Jer 13:23

LEPERS
"And many *l* were in ..... Luke 4:27

LET
"*L* there be light .... Gen 1:3

LETTER
for the *l* kills .... 2 Cor 3:6
or by word or by *l* ...... 2 Thess 2:2

LETTERS
does this Man know *l* .... John 7:15

LEVIATHAN
"Can you draw out *L* ...... Job 41:1

LEVITE
"Likewise a *L* .... Luke 10:32

LEWDNESS
wickedness, deceit, *l* .... Mark 7:22

LIAR
for he is a *l* and the .... John 8:44
but every man a *l* .... Rom 3:4
we make Him a *l* .... 1 John 1:10
his brother, he is a *l* .... 1 John 4:20

LIARS
"All men are *l* .... Ps 116:11
l shall have their .... Rev 21:8

LIBERALITY
he who gives, with *l* ...... Rom 12:8

LIBERALLY
who gives to all *l* .... James 1:5

LIBERTY
year, and proclaim *l* ...... Lev 25:10
'To proclaim *l* to the ...... Luke 4:18
into the glorious *l* .... Rom 8:21
Lord is, there is *l* .... 2 Cor 3:17
therefore in the *l* .... Gal 5:1

LIE
Do not *l* to one .... Col 3:9
God, who cannot *l* .... Titus 1:2
an abomination or a *l* .... Rev 21:27

LIED
You have not *l* to men ..... Acts 5:4

LIES
sin *l* at the door .... Gen 4:7
speaking *l* in .... 1 Tim 4:2

LIFE
the breath of *l* .... Gen 2:7
'For the *l* of the .... Lev 17:11
before you today *l* .... Deut 30:15
He will redeem their *l* ..... Ps 72:14
word has given me *l* ...... Ps 119:50
She is a tree of *l* .... Prov 3:18
finds me finds *l* .... Prov 8:35
L is more than .... Luke 12:23
l was the light .... John 1:4
so the Son gives *l* .... John 5:21
spirit, and they are *l* ...... John 6:63
have the light of *l* .... John 8:12
and I lay down My *l* ..... John 10:15
resurrection and the *l* ... John 11:25
you lay down your *l* ..... John 13:38
l which I now live .... Gal 2:20
l is hidden with .... Col 3:3
For what is your *l* .... James 4:14
l was manifested .... 1 John 1:2

and the pride of *l* ... 1 John 2:16
has given us eternal *l* ... 1 John 5:11
the Lamb's Book of *L* ... Rev 21:27
right to the tree of *l* ... Rev 22:14
the water of *l* freely ... Rev22:17
from the Book of *L* ... Rev 22:19

LIFT
I will *l* up my eyes to ... Ps 121:1
Lord, and He will *l* ... James 4:10

LIFTED
your heart is *l* ... Ezek 28:2
in Hades, he *l* up his ... Luke 16:23
the Son of Man be *l* ... John 3:14
"And I, if I am *l* ... John 12:32

LIGHT
"Let there be *l* ... Gen 1:3
The LORD is my *l* ... Ps 27:1
and a *l* to my path ... Ps 119:105
The *l* of the righteous ... Prov 13:9
The LORD gives *l* ... Prov 29:13
Truly the *l* is sweet ... Eccl 11:7
let us walk in the *l* ... Is 2:5
l shall break forth ... Is 58:8
"You are the *l* ... Matt 5:14
"Let your *l* so shine ... Matt 5:16
than the sons of *l* ... Luke 16:8
and the life was the *l* ... John 1:4
darkness rather than *l* ... John 3:19
saying, "I am the *l* ... John 8:12
God who commanded *l* ... 2 Cor 4:6
Walk as children of *l* ... Eph 5:8
You are all sons of *l* ... 1 Thess 5:5
into His marvelous *l* ... 1 Pet 2:9
to you, that God is *l* ... 1 John 1:5
l as He is in the ... 1 John 1:7
says he is in the *l* ... 1 John 2:9
The Lamb is its *l* ... Rev 21:23

LIGHTNING
"For as the *l* ... Matt 24:27
countenance was like *l* ... Matt 283

LIGHTNINGS
the throne proceeded *l* ... Rev 4:5

LIGHTS
"Let there be *l* ... Gen 1:14
whom you shine as *l* ... Phil 2:15

LIKENESS
according to Our *l* ... Gen 1:26
carved image—any *l* ... Ex 20:4
when I awake in Your *l* ... Ps 17:15
and coming in the *l* ... Phil 2:7

LILY
the *l* of the valleys ... Song 2:1

LIMIT
to the sea its *l* ... Prov 8:29

LINE
upon precept, *L* upon ... Is 28:10
I am setting a plumb *l* ... Amos 7:8

LINEN
wrapped Him in the *l* ... Mark 15:46

LINGER
salvation shall not *l* ... Is 46:13

LION
l shall eat straw ... Is 11:7

LIONS
the mouths of *l* ... Heb 11:33

LIPS
off all flattering *l* ... Ps 12:3
The *l* of the righteous ... Prov 10:21
But the *l* of ... Prov 20:15
am a man of unclean *l* ... Is 6:5
other *l* I will speak ... 1 Cor 14:21
from evil, And his *l* ... 1 Pet 3:10

LISTEN
you are not able to *l* ... John 8:43
you who fear God, *l* ... Acts 13:16

LISTENS
But whoever *l* to me ... Prov 1:33

LITTLE
Though you are *l* ... Mic 5:2
l ones only a cup ... Matt 10:42
"O you of *l* faith ... Matt 14:31
to whom *l* is forgiven ... Luke 7:47
faithful in a very *l* ... Luke 19:17

LIVE
eat, and *l* forever ... Gen 3:22
a man does, he shall *l* ... Lev 18:5
"Seek Me and *l* ... Amos 5:4
But the just shall *l* ... Hab 2:4
l by bread alone ... Matt 4:4
"for in Him we *l* ... Acts 17:28
l peaceably with all ... Rom 12:18
the life which I now *l* ... Gal 2:20
If we *l* in the Spirit ... Gal 5:25
to me, to *l* is Christ ... Phil 1:21

LIVED
died and rose and *l* ... Rom 14:9
And they *l* and reigned ... Rev 20:4

LIVES
but man *l* by every ... Deut 8:3
but Christ *l* in me ... Gal 2:20
to lay down our *l* ... 1 John 3:16
"I am He who *l* ... Rev 1:18

LIVING
and man became a *l* ... Gen 2:7
in the light of the *l* ... Ps 56:13
the dead, but of the *l* ... Matt 22:32
do you seek the *l* ... Luke 24:5
the word of God is *l* ... Heb 4:12
l creature was like a ... Rev 4:7

LOATHSOME
But a wicked man is *l* ... Prov 13:5

LOAVES
have here only five *l* ... Matt 14:17
you ate of the *l* ... John 6:26

LOCUST
What the chewing *l* ... Joel 1:4

LOCUSTS
and his food was *l* ... Matt 3:4

LOFTY
Wisdom is too *l* ... Prov 24:7

LONG
your days may be *l* ... Deut 5:16
Who *l* for death ... Job 3:21
I *l* for Your salvation ... Ps 119:174
go around in *l* robes ... Mark 12:38

LONGSUFFERING
is love, joy, peace, *l* ... Gal 5:22
and gentleness, with *l* ... Eph 4:2
for all patience and *l* ... Col 1:11
might show all *l* ... 1 Tim 1:16
once the Divine *l* ... 1 Pet 3:20
and consider that the *l* ... 2 Pet 3:15

LOOK
A proud *l* ... Prov 6:17
"*L* to Me ... Is 45:22
l on Me whom they ... Zech 12:10
say to you, '*L* here ... Luke 17:23
while we do not *l* ... 2 Cor 4:18

LOOKED
For He *l* down from ... Ps 102:19
He *l* for justice ... Is 5:7
the Lord turned and *l* ... Luke 22:61
for he *l* to the reward ... Heb 11:26

LOOKING
the plow, and *l* back ... Luke 9:62
l for the blessed hope ... Titus 2:13
l unto Jesus ... Heb 12:2
l carefully lest ... Heb 12:15
l for the mercy of ... Jude 21

LOOKS
The lofty *l* of man ... Is 2:11
to you that whoever *l* ... Matt 5:28

LOOSE
and whatever you *l* ... Matt 16:19
said to them, "*L* him ... John 11:44

LOOSED
the silver cord is *l* ... Eccl 12:6

LORD
L is my strength ... Ex 15:2
L our God, the *L* ... Deut 6:4
You alone are the *L* ... Neh 9:6
The *L* of hosts ... Ps 24:10
Gracious is the *L* ... Ps 116:5
L surrounds His people ... Ps 125:2
The *L* is righteous ... Ps 129:4
L is near to all who ... Ps 145:18
L is a God of justice ... Is 30:18
L Our Righteousness ... Jer 23:6
"The *L* is one ... Zech 14:9

shall not tempt the *L* ... Matt 4:7
shall worship the *L* ... Matt 4:10
Son of Man is also *L* ... Mark 2:28
who is Christ the *L* ... Luke 2:11
L is risen indeed ... Luke 24:34
Me Teacher and *L* ... John 13:13
He is *L* of all ... Acts 10:36
with your mouth the *L* ... Rom 10:9
say that Jesus is *L* ... 1 Cor 12:3
second Man is the *L* ... 1 Cor 15:47
the Spirit of the *L* ... 2 Cor 3:17
that Jesus Christ is *L* ... Phil 2:11
and deny the only *L* ... Jude 4
L God Omnipotent ... Rev 19:6

LORDS
for He is Lord of *l* ... Rev 17:14

LOSE
save his life will *l* ... Matt 16:25

LOSES
but if the salt *l* ... Matt 5:13
and *l* his own soul ... Matt 16:26

LOSS
count all things *l* ... Phil 3:8

LOST
save that which was *l* ... Matt 18:11
and none of them is *l* ... John 17:12
You gave Me I have *l* ... John 18:9

LOTS
garments, casting *l* ... Mark 15:24
And they cast their *l* ... Acts 1:26

LOUD
cried out with a *l* ... Matt 27:46
I heard behind me a *l* ... Rev 1:10

LOVE
l your neighbor as ... Lev 19:18
l the LORD your God ... Deut 6:5
Oh, *l* the LORD ... Ps 31:23
he has set his *l* ... Ps 91:14
Oh, how I *l* Your law ... Ps 119:97
l covers all sins ... Prov 10:12
A time to *l* ... Eccl 3:8
banner over me was *l* ... Song 2:4
l is as strong as ... Song 8:6
do justly, To *l* mercy ... Mic 6:8
to you, *l* your enemies ... Matt 5:44
which of them will *l* ... Luke 7:42
you do not have the *l* ... John 5:42
If you have *l* for one ... John 13:35
"If you *l* Me ... John 14:15
and My Father will *l* ... John 14:23
l one another as I ... John 15:12
l has no one than this ... John 15:13
because the *l* of God ... Rom 5:5
to *l* one another ... Rom 13:8
L suffers long and is ... 1 Cor 13:4
L never fails ... 1 Cor 13:8
greatest of these is *l* ... 1 Cor 13:13
For the *l* of Christ ... 2 Cor 5:14
of the Spirit is *l* ... Gal 5:22
Husbands, *l* your wives ... Eph 5:25
the commandment is *l* ... 1 Tim 1:5
For the *l* of money is ... 1 Tim 6:10
Let brotherly *l* ... Heb 13:1
having not seen you *l* ... 1 Pet 1:8
for "*l* will cover a ... 1 Pet 4:8
brotherly kindness *l* ... 2 Pet 1:7
By this we know *l* ... 1 John 3:16
Beloved, let us *l* ... 1 John 4:7
for God is *l* ... 1 John 4:8
There is no fear in *l* ... 1 John 4:18
l Him because He ... 1 John 4:19
loves God must *l* ... 1 John 4:21
For this is the *l* ... 1 John 5:3
have left your first *l* ... Rev 2:4

LOVED
L one and friend You ... Ps 88:18
Yet Jacob I have *l* ... Mal 1:2
forgiven, for she *l* ... Luke 7:47
so *l* the world that ... John 3:16
whom Jesus *l* ... John 13:23
"As the Father *l* ... John 15:9
l them as You have ... John 17:23
the Son of God, who *l* ... Gal 2:20
l the church and gave ... Eph 5:25
Beloved, if God so *l* ... 1 John 4:11
To Him who *l* us and ... Rev 1:5

LOVELY
he is altogether *l* ... Song 5:16
whatever things are *l* ... Phil 4:8

LOVES
"He who *l* father or ..... Matt 10:37
l his life will lose .... John 12:25
l Me will be loved .... John 14:21
l a cheerful giver .... 2 Cor 9:7
If anyone *l* the world ... 1 John 2:15
l God must love his ..... 1 John 4:21

LOVINGKINDNESS
To declare Your *l* .... Ps 92:2

LOWER
made him a little *l* .... Heb 2:7

LOWLINESS
with all *l* and .... Eph 4:2

LOWLY
for I am gentle and *l* ..... Matt 11:29
in presence am *l* .... 2 Cor 10:1
l brother glory .... James 1:9

LUKEWARM
because you are *l* .... Rev 3:16

LUST
looks at a woman to *l* .... Matt 5:28
not fulfill the *l* .... Gal 5:16
You *l* and do not have ..... James 4:2
the *l* of the flesh .... 1 John 2:16

LUSTS
to fulfill its *l* .... Rom 13:14
also youthful *l* .... 2 Tim 2:22
and worldly *l* .... Titus 2:12
to the former *l* .... 1 Pet 1:14
abstain from fleshly *l* ..... 1 Pet 2:11
to their own ungodly *l* ...... Jude 18

LUTE
Praise Him with the *l* ...... Ps 150:3

LUXURY
in pleasure and *l* .... James 5:5
the abundance of her *l* .... Rev 18:3

LYING
I hate and abhor *l* .... Ps 119:163
righteous man hates *l* .... Prov 13:5
not trust in these *l* .... Jer 7:4
signs, and *l* wonders ... 2 Thess 2:9

M

MADE
m the stars also .... Gen 1:16
things My hand has *m* .... Is 66:2
All things were *m* .... John 1:3

MADNESS
m is in their hearts .... Eccl 9:3

MAGIC
m brought their books .. Acts 19:19

MAGNIFIED
let Your name be *m* ..... 2 Sam 7:26
the Lord Jesus was *m* ... Acts 19:17
also Christ will be *m* ...... Phil 1:20

MAGNIFIES
"My soul *m* the Lord ..... Luke 1:46

MAGNIFY
m the LORD with me .... Ps 34:3

MAIDSERVANT
"Behold the *m* .... Luke 1:38

MAIDSERVANTS
m I will pour out My ..... Acts 2:18

MAJESTY
right hand of the *M* .... Heb 1:3
eyewitnesses of His *m* ..... 2 Pet 1:16
wise, Be glory and *m* .... Jude 25

MAKE
"Let Us *m* man in Our ..... Gen 1:26
m you a great nation ...... Gen 12:2
"You shall not *m* .... Ex 20:4
m Our home with .... John 14:23

MAKER
M is your husband .... Is 54:5
has forgotten his *M* .... Hos 8:14
builder and *m* is God ..... Heb 11:10

MALICE
in *m* be babes .... 1 Cor 14:20
laying aside all *m* .... 1 Pet 2:1

MAN
"Let Us make *m* .... Gen 1:26
m that You are mindful .... Ps 8:4
of the Son of *M* .... Matt 24:27

"Behold the *M* .... John 19:5
by *m* came death .... 1 Cor 15:21
our outward *m* .... 2 Cor 4:16
the *m* of God may .... 2 Tim 3:17
is the number of a *m* ..... Rev 13:18

MANGER
and laid Him in a *m* .... Luke 2:7

MANIFEST
m Myself to him .... John 14:21

MANIFESTATION
But the *m* of the .... 1 Cor 12:7

MANIFESTED
"I have *m* Your name ..... John 17:6
God was *m* in the .... 1 Tim 3:16
the life was *m* .... 1 John 1:2

MANIFOLD
the *m* wisdom of God ..... Eph 3:10

MANNA
of Israel ate *m* .... Ex 16:35
"Our fathers ate the *m* ... John 6:31

MANNER
Is this the *m* of man ..... 2 Sam 7:19
in an unworthy *m* ...... 1 Cor 11:27
what *m* of love .... 1 John 3:1

MANSIONS
house are many *m* .... John 14:2

MANTLE
Then he took the *m* ..... 2 Kin 2:14

MARK
And the LORD set a *m* ..... Gen 4:15
receives the *m* .... Rev 14:11

MARRED
So His visage was *m* .... Is 52:14

MARRIAGE
M is honorable among .... Heb 13:4

MARRIED
But he who is *m* .... 1 Cor 7:33

MARRY
they neither *m* nor ...... Matt 22:30
forbidding to *m* .... 1 Tim 4:3

MARRYING
and drinking, *m* .... Matt 24:38

MARTYRS
the blood of the *m* .... Rev 17:6

MARVELED
Jesus heard it, He *m* ...... Matt 8:10
so that Pilate *m* .... Mark 15:5

MARVELOUS
It is *m* in our eyes .... Ps 118:23
of darkness into His *m* .... 1 Pet 2:9

MASTER
a servant like his *m* ..... Matt 10:25
greater than his *m* ...... John 15:20
and useful for the *M* .... 2 Tim 2:21

MASTERS
can serve two *m* .... Luke 16:13
who have believing *m* .... 1 Tim 6:2

MATTERS
the weightier *m* .... Matt 23:23

MATURE
understanding be *m* .... 1 Cor 14:20
us, as many as are *m* .... Phil 3:15

MEANT
but God *m* it for good .... Gen 50:20

MEASURE
a perfect and just *m* ..... Deut 25:15
give the Spirit by *m* .... John 3:34
to each one a *m* .... Rom 12:3

MEASURED
m the waters in the .... Is 40:12
you use, it will be *m* .... Matt 7:2

MEASURES
house differing *m* .... Deut 25:14

MEASURING
behold, a man with a *m* ... Zech 2:1
m themselves by .... 2 Cor 10:12

MEAT
will never again eat *m* ... 1 Cor 8:13

MEDIATOR
by the hand of a *m* .... Gal 3:19
is one God and one *M* .... 1 Tim 2:5
to Jesus the *M* of the ..... Heb 12:24

MEDICINE
does good , like *m* .... Prov 17:22

MEDICINES
you will use many *m* ...... Jer 46:11

MEDITATE
but you shall *m* .... Josh 1:8
M within your heart on .... Ps 4:4
I will *m* on Your .... Ps 119:15
m beforehand on .... Luke 21:14
m on these things .... Phil 4:8

MEDITATES
in His law he *m* .... Ps 1:2

MEDITATION
of my mouth and the *m* ... Ps 19:14
It is my *m* all the day ..... Ps 119:97

MEDIUM
a woman who is a *m* ..... Lev 20:27

MEDIUM'S
shall be like a *m* .... Is 29:4

MEDIUMS
"Seek those who are *m* ...... Is 8:19

MEEK
with equity for the *m* .... Is 11:4
Blessed are the *m* .... Matt 5:5

MEEKNESS
are done in the *m* .... James 3:13

MEET
prepare to *m* your .... Amos 4:12
m the Lord in the ..... 1 Thess 4:17

MELODY
singing and making *m* .... Eph 5:19

MELT
the elements will *m* ...... 2 Pet 3:10

MEMBER
body is not one *m* ...... 1 Cor 12:14

MEMBERS
you that one of your *m* ... Matt 5:29
do not present your *m* .... Rom 6:13
neighbor, for we are *m* .... Eph 4:25

MEMORIAL
and this is My *m* .... Ex 3:15
also be told as a *m* ...... Matt 26:13

MEMORY
The *m* of the righteous ... Prov 10:7

MEN
m began to call on the ..... Gen 4:26
make you fishers of *m* .... Matt 4:19
goodwill toward *m* .... Luke 2:14
heaven or from *m* .... Luke 20:4
Likewise also the *m* ...... Rom 1:27
the Lord, and not to *m* ..... Eph 6:7
between God and *m* ...... 1 Tim 2:5

MENSERVANTS
And also on My *m* .... Joel 2:29
And on My *m* and on ..... Acts 2:18

MERCHANDISE
house a house of *m* ...... John 2:16

MERCIES
give you the sure *m* ..... Acts 13:34

MERCIFUL
LORD, the LORD God, *m* .... Ex 34:6
He is ever *m* .... Ps 37:26
Blessed are the *m* .... Matt 5:7
saying, 'God be *m* .... Luke 18:13
"For I will be *m* .... Heb 8:12

MERCY
but showing *m* to .... Ex 20:6
and abundant in *m* ...... Num 14:18
m endures forever ...... 1 Chr 16:34
M and truth have met ..... Ps 85:10
m is everlasting .... Ps 100:5
Let not *m* and truth .... Prov 3:3
For I desire *m* and not ...... Hos 6:6
do justly, To love *m* .... Mic 6:8
'I desire *m* and not .... Matt 9:13
And His *m* is on those .... Luke 1:50
"I will have *m* .... Rom 9:15
that He might have *m* ... Rom 11:32
m has made .... 1 Cor 7:25
as we have received *m* ... 2 Cor 4:1

God, who is rich in *m* ..... Eph 2:4
but I obtained *m* .... 1 Tim 1:13
that he may find *m* ...... 2 Tim 1:18
to His *m* He saved us ...... Titus 3:5
that we may obtain *m* ..... Heb 4:16

MERRY
m heart makes a .... Prov 15:13
we should make *m* ...... Luke 15:32

MESSENGER
"Behold, I send My *m* ...... Mal 3:1
'Behold, I send My *m* .... Matt 11:10

MESSIAH
Until *M* the Prince .... Dan 9:25
"We have found the *M* ... John 1:41

MIDST
God is in the *m* .... Ps 46:5
I am there in the *m* ...... Matt 18:20

MIGHT
'My power and the *m* ..... Deut 8:17
'Not by *m* nor by .... Zech 4:6
in the power of His *m* ..... Eph 6:10
honor and power and *m* ... Rev 7:12

MIGHTIER
coming after me is *m* ..... Matt 3:11

MIGHTY
He was a *m* hunter .... Gen 10:9
m have fallen .... 2 Sam 1:19
The LORD *m* in battle ...... Ps 24:8
their Redeemer is *m* ..... Prov 23:11
m has done great .... Luke 1:49
the flesh, not many *m* ... 1 Cor 1:26
the working of His *m* ...... Eph 1:19

MILK
come, buy wine and *m* ...... Is 55:1
shall flow with *m* .... Joel 3:18
have come to need *m* ...... Heb 5:12
desire the pure *m* .... 1 Pet 2:2

MILLSTONE
m were hung around ..... Matt 18:6
a stone like a great *m* .... Rev 18:21

MIND
put wisdom in the *m* ..... Job 38:36
perfect peace, Whose *m* ...... Is 26:3
have an anxious *m* ...... Luke 12:29
m I myself serve the .... Rom 7:25
who has known the *m* ... Rom 11:34
Be of the same *m* .... Rom 12:16
in his own *m* .... Rom 14:5
has known the *m* .... 1 Cor 2:16
are out of your *m* ...... 1 Cor 14:23
Let this *m* be in you .... Phil 2:5
love and of a sound *m* .... 2 Tim 1:7

MINDFUL
is man that You are *m* .... Ps 8:4
for you are not *m* .... Matt 16:23
is man that You are *m* ...... Heb 2:6

MINDS
put My law in their *m* ...... Jer 31:33
I stir up your pure *m* .... 2 Pet 3:1

MINISTER
For he is God's *m* .... Rom 13:4
you will be a good *m* ..... 1 Tim 4:6

MINISTERS
for they are God's *m* ..... Rom 13:6
If anyone *m* .... 1 Pet 4:11

MINISTRIES
are differences of *m* ..... 1 Cor 12:5

MINISTRY
But if the *m* of death ..... 2 Cor 3:7
since we have this *m* ..... 2 Cor 4:1
has given us the *m* ...... 2 Cor 5:18
for the work of *m* .... Eph 4:12
fulfill your *m* .... 2 Tim 4:5
a more excellent *m* .... Heb 8:6

MIRACLE
one who works a *m* ..... Mark 9:39

MIRACLES
worked unusual *m* ...... Acts 19:11
the working of *m* .... 1 Cor 12:10

MISERY
And remember his *m* ..... Prov 31:7

MITES
putting in two *m* .... Luke 21:2

MOCK
Fools *m* at sin .... Prov 14:9
to the Gentiles to *m* ..... Matt 20:19

MOCKED
noon, that Elijah *m* ..... 1 Kin 18:27
deceived, God is not *m* ...... Gal 6:7

MOCKER
Wine is a *m* .... Prov 20:1

MOCKS
He who *m* the poor .... Prov 17:5

MODERATION
with propriety and *m* ...... 1 Tim 2:9

MOMENT
in a *m* they die .... Job 34:20
in a *m*, in the .... 1 Cor 15:52

MONEY
be redeemed without *m* ..... Is 52:3
And you who have no *m* .... Is 55:1
and hid his lord's *m* ..... Matt 25:18
to give him *m* .... Mark 14:11
"Carry neither *m* .... Luke 10:4
I sent you without *m* .... Luke 22:35
be purchased with *m* ..... Acts 8:20
not greedy for *m* .... 1 Tim 3:3
m is a root of all .... 1 Tim 6:10

MONEYCHANGERS
the tables of the *m* ...... Matt 21:12

MOON
until the *m* is no more ...... Ps 72:7
m will not give its ...... Mark 13:24

MORNING
Evening and *m* and at ...... Ps 55:17
Lucifer, son of the *m* .... Is 14:12
very early in the *m* .... Luke 24:1
the Bright and *M* Star .... Rev 22:16

MORTAL
sin reign in your *m* .... Rom 6:12
and this *m* must put .... 1 Cor 15:53

MORTALITY
m may be swallowed ..... 2 Cor 5:4

MOTH
where *m* and rust .... Matt 6:19

MOTHER
because she was the *m* .... Gen 3:20
leave his father and *m* .... Matt 19:5
"Behold your *m* .... John 19:27
The *M* of Harlots .... Rev 17:5

MOUNT
come up to *M* Sinai .... Ex 19:23
They shall *m* up with .... Is 40:31

MOUNTAIN
to Horeb, the *m* .... Ex 3:1
let us go up to the *m* .... Is 2:3
became a great *m* .... Dan 2:35
are you, O great *m* .... Zech 4:7
you will say to this *m* .... Matt 17:20
Him on the holy *m* .... 2 Pet 1:18

MOUNTAINS
m were brought forth ...... Ps 90:2
m shall depart And the ..... Is 54:10
in Judea flee to the *m* ... Matt 24:16
that I could remove *m* ... 1 Cor 13:2

MOURN
A time to *m* .... Eccl 3:4
are those who *m* .... Matt 5:4
of the earth will *m* .... Rev 1:7

MOURNED
and have not rather *m* .... 1 Cor 5:2

MOURNING
shall be a great *m* .... Zech 12:11
be turned to *m* and .... James 4:9

MOUTH
"Who has made man's *m* ... Ex 4:11
Out of the *m* of babes .... Ps 8:2
knowledge, But the *m* ... Prov 10:14
The *m* of an immoral .... Prov 22:14
And a flattering *m* ...... Prov 26:28
m speaking pompous ...... Dan 7:8
m defiles a man .... Matt 15:11
m I will judge you .... Luke 19:22
I will give you a *m* .... Luke 21:15
m confession is made ... Rom 10:10
m great swelling words .... Jude 16
vomit you out of My *m* .... Rev 3:16

MOVED
she shall not be *m* .... Ps 46:5
spoke as they were *m* .... 2 Pet 1:21

MUCH
m study is .... Eccl 12:12
to whom *m* is given ..... Luke 12:48

MULTIPLIED
of the disciples *m* .... Acts 6:7
of God grew and *m* ...... Acts 12:24

MULTIPLY
"Be fruitful and *m* .... Gen 1:22
m the descendants .... Jer 33:22

MULTITUDE
stars of heaven in *m* ...... Deut 1:10
In the *m* of words sin .... Prov 10:19
compassion on the *m* .... Matt 15:32
with the angel a *m* .... Luke 2:13
"love will cover a *m* .... 1 Pet 4:8
and behold, a great *m* ...... Rev 7:9

MURDER
"You shall not *m* .... Ex 20:13
'You shall not *m* .... Matt 5:21
You *m* and covet and ...... James 4:2

MURDERED
up Jesus whom you *m* .... Acts 5:30

MURDERER
He was a *m* from the ..... John 8:44
his brother is a *m* ...... 1 John 3:15

MURDERERS
and profane, for *m* .... 1 Tim 1:9
abominable, *m* .... Rev 21:8

MURDERS
evil thoughts, *m* .... Matt 15:19

MUSING
while I was *m* .... Ps 39:3

MUTILATION
beware of the *m* .... Phil 3:2

MUZZLE
"You shall not *m* .... 1 Tim 5:18

MYSTERIES
to you to know the *m* .... Matt 13:11
and understand all *m* ... 1 Cor 13:2

MYSTERY
given to know the *m* ...... Mark 4:11
wisdom of God in a *m* .... 1 Cor 2:7
I tell you a *m* .... 1 Cor 15:51
made known to us the *m* ... Eph 1:9
the *m* of godliness .... 1 Tim 3:16

N

NAILED
n it to the cross .... Col 2:14

NAKED
And they were both *n* ..... Gen 2:25
knew that they were *n* .... Gen 3:7
"*N* I came from my .... Job 1:21
'I was *n* and you .... Matt 25:36
but all things are *n* .... Heb 4:13
brother or sister is *n* .... James 2:15
poor, blind, and *n* .... Rev 3:17

NAKEDNESS
or famine, or *n* .... Rom 8:35
n may not be revealed ..... Rev 3:18

NAME
Abram called on the *n* .... Gen 13:4
Israel shall be your *n* ..... Gen 35:10
This is My *n* forever .... Ex 3:15
shall not take the *n* .... Ex 20:7
and awesome *n* .... Deut 28:58
excellent is Your *n* .... Ps 8:1
n will put their trust .... Ps 9:10
be His glorious *n* .... Ps 72:19
do not call on Your *n* .... Ps 79:6
to Your *n* give glory .... Ps 115:1
above all Your *n* .... Ps 138:2
A good *n* is to be .... Prov 22:1
what is His Son's *n* .... Prov 30:4
be called by a new *n* .... Is 62:2
Everlasting is Your *n* .... Is 63:16
They will call on My *n* ... Zech 13:9
to you who fear My *n* .... Mal 4:2
Hallowed be Your *n* .... Matt 6:9
prophesied in Your *n* ...... Matt 7:22
n Gentiles will trust ..... Matt 12:21
together in My *n* .... Matt 18:20

will come in My *n* .... Matt 24:5
who believe in His *n* ...... John 1:12
comes in his own *n* .... John 5:43
his own sheep by *n* .... John 10:3
through faith in His *n* .... Acts 3:16
there is no other *n* .... Acts 4:12
which is above every *n* ..... Phil 2:9
deed, do all in the *n* .... Col 3:17
a more excellent *n* .... Heb 1:4
you hold fast to My *n* ...... Rev 2:13
n that you are alive .... Rev 3:1
having His Father's *n* .... Rev 14:1
and glorify Your *n* .... Rev 15:4
n written that no one ..... Rev 19:12

NAMED
I have *n* you .... Is 45:4

NAME'S
saved them for His *n* ...... Ps 106:8

NARROW
"Enter by the *n* gate ...... Matt 7:13

NATION
make you a great *n* .... Gen 12:2
exalts a *n* .... Prov 14:34
n that was not called .... Is 65:1
make them one *n* .... Ezek 37:22
since there was a *n* .... Dan 12:1
n will rise against .... Matt 24:7
"for he loves our *n* .... Luke 7:5
those who are not a *n* ... Rom 10:19
tribe, tongue, and *n* .... Rev 13:7

NATIONS
Why do the *n* rage .... Ps 2:1
I will give You the *n* .... Ps 2:8
n shall serve Him .... Ps 72:11
disciples of all the *n* ..... Matt 28:19
who was to rule all *n* ...... Rev 12:5
the healing of the *n* .... Rev 22:2

NATURAL
exchanged the *n* .... Rom 1:26
the men, leaving the *n* .... Rom 1:27
did not spare the *n* ...... Rom 11:21
n man does not .... 1 Cor 2:14
It is sown a *n* body ..... 1 Cor 15:44

NATURE
"We who are Jews by *n* ... Gal 2:15
by *n* children of wrath ...... Eph 2:3
of the divine *n* .... 2 Pet 1:4

NEAR
the word is very *n* .... Deut 30:14
upon Him while He is *n* ..... Is 55:6
know that it is *n* .... Matt 24:33
kingdom of God is *n* .... Luke 21:31
"The word is *n* .... Rom 10:8
to those who were *n* .... Eph 2:17
for the time is *n* .... Rev 1:3

NEARER
now our salvation is *n* ... Rom 13:11

NEED
the things you have *n* ..... Mart 6:8
supply all your *n* .... Phil 4:19
to help in time of *n* .... Heb 4:16

NEGLECT
if we *n* so great a .... Heb 2:3

NEGLECTED
n the weightier .... Matt 23:23

NEIGHBOR
'you shall love your *n* .... Lev 19:18
"You shall love your *n* .... Matt 5:43
"And who is my *n* .... Luke 10:29
"You shall love your *n* .... Rom 13:9

NEVER
in Me shall *n* thirst .... John 6:35
in Me shall *n* die .... John 11:26
Love *n* fails .... 1 Cor 13:8
n take away sins .... Heb 10:11
"I will *n* leave you .... Heb 13:5
prophecy *n* came by ...... 2 Pet 1:21

NEW
And there is nothing *n* ..... Eccl 1:9
"For behold, I create *n* ..... Is 65:17
n every morning .... Lam 3:23
wine into *n* wineskins .... Matt 9:17
of the *n* covenant .... Matt 26:28
n commandment I .... John 13:34
he is a *n* creation .... 2 Cor 5:17
when I will make a *n* .... Heb 8:8
n heavens and a *n* .... 2 Pet 3:13

n name written which ..... Rev 2:17
And they sang a *n* .... Rev 5:9
And I saw a *n* heaven ..... Rev 21:1
I make all things *n* .... Rev 21:5

NEWNESS
also should walk in *n* ...... Rom 6:4

NIGHT
darkness He called *N* ...... Gen 1:5
It is a *n* of solemn .... Ex 12:42
pillar of fire by *n* .... Ex 13:22
gives songs in the *n* ...... Job 35:10
and continued all *n* .... Luke 6:12
man came to Jesus by *n* ... John 3:2
n is coming when no ...... John 9:4
came to Jesus by *n* ...... John 19:39
as a thief in the *n* .... 1 Thess 5:2
there shall be no *n* .... Rev 21:25

NINETY-NINE
he not leave the *n* .... Matt 18:12

NOTHING
"I can of Myself do *n* ..... John 5:30
Me you can do *n* .... John 15:5
men, it will come to *n* ..... Acts 5:38
have not love, I am *n* .... 1 Cor 13:2
Be anxious for *n* .... Phil 4:6
For we brought *n* .... 1 Tim 6:7

NOURISHED
"I have *n* and .... Is 1:2

NOURISHES
n and cherishes it .... Eph 5:29

NUMBER
if a man could *n* .... Gen 13:16
teach us to *n* our days ..... Ps 90:12
which no one could *n* ...... Rev 7:9
His *n* is 666 .... Rev 13:18

O

OATH
for the sake of your *o* ...... Eccl 8:2
he denied with an *o* ..... Matt 26:72
o which He swore .... Luke 1:73

OATHS
shall perform your *o* ..... Matt 5:33

OBEDIENCE
o many will be made ..... Rom 5:19
captivity to the *o* .... 2 Cor 10:5
yet He learned *o* .... Heb 5:8

OBEDIENT
you are willing and *o* .... Is 1:19
of the priests were *o* .... Acts 6:7
make the Gentiles *o* ..... Rom 15:18
Himself and became *o* ..... Phil 2:8
as *o* children .... 1 Pet 1:14

OBEY
God and *o* His voice ...... Deut 4:30
His voice we will *o* ...... Josh 24:24
o is better than .... 1 Sam 15:22
o God rather than men ... Acts 5:29
and do not *o* the truth ..... Rom 2:8
yourselves slaves to *o* .... Rom 6:16
o your parents in all .... Col 3:20
Bondservants, *o* in all ..... Col 3:22
those who do not *o* ..... 2 Thess 1:8
O those who rule .... Heb 13:17

OBEYED
of sin, yet you *o* .... Rom 6:17
they have not all *o* ...... Rom 10:16
By faith Abraham *o* .... Heb 11:8

OBSERVATION
does not come with *o* .... Luke 17:20

OBSERVE
teaching them to *o* all ... Matt 28:20

OBTAIN
also may *o* mercy .... Rom 11:31
o salvation through .... 1 Thess 5:9

OBTAINED
o a part in this .... Acts 1:17
yet have now *o* mercy ... Rom 11:30
endured, he *o* the .... Heb 6:15

OBTAINS
o favor from the LORD ... Prov 8:35

OFFEND
lest we *o* them .... Matt 17:27
than that he should *o* ..... Luke 17:2
them, "Does this *o* .... John 6:61

OFFENDED
they were *o* at Him ...... Matt 13:57

OFFENSE
and a rock of *o* .... Is 8:14
You are an *o* to Me ...... Matt 16:23
by the one man's *o* .... Rom 5:17
the *o* of the cross .... Gal 5:11
sincere and without *o* ..... Phil 1:10
And a rock of *o* .... 1 Pet 2:8

OFFENSES
For *o* must come .... Matt 18:7
impossible that no *o* ...... Luke 17:1

OFFER
come and *o* your gift ..... Matt 5:24
let us continually *o* .... Heb 13:15

OFFERED
to eat those things *o* ..... 1 Cor 8:10
so Christ was *o* .... Heb 9:28
o one sacrifice .... Heb 10:12

OFFERING
o You did not require .... Ps 40:6
You make His soul an *o* .... Is 53:10
Himself for us, an *o* .... Eph 5:2
o You did not .... Heb 10:5
o He has perfected .... Heb 10:14

OFFERINGS
and offered burnt *o* .... Gen 8:20
In burnt *o* .... Heb 10:6

OFFICE
sitting at the tax *o* .... Matt 9:9

OFFSPRING
wife and raise up *o* ...... Matt 22:24
we are also His *o* .... Acts 17:28
am the Root and the *O* ... Rev 22:16

OFTEN
o I wanted to gather ..... Luke 13:34
as *o* as you eat this ..... 1 Cor 11:26

OIL
a bin, and a little *o* ..... 1 Kin 17:12
very costly fragrant *o* .... Matt 26:7
anointing him with *o* .... James 5:14
and do not harm the *o* ...... Rev 6:6

OLD
young, and now am *o* ..... Ps 37:25
was said to those of *o* .... Matt 5:21
but when you are *o* ...... John 21:18
Your *o* men shall dream .. Acts 2:17
o man was crucified .... Rom 6:6
o things have passed .... 2 Cor 5:17
have put off the *o* man ...... Col 3:9
that serpent of *o* .... Rev 20:2

OLDER
o shall serve the .... Gen 25:23
not rebuke an *o* man ..... 1 Tim 5:1

OLDEST
beginning with the *o* ...... John 8:9

OLIVE
a freshly plucked *o* .... Gen 8:11
o tree which is wild ..... Rom 11:24

OMNIPOTENT
For the Lord God *O* .... Rev 19:6

ONCE
died, He died to sin *o* ..... Rom 6:10
for men to die *o* .... Heb 9:27
also suffered *o* .... 1 Pet 3:18

ONE
"*O* thing you lack .... Mark 10:21
o thing is needed .... Luke 10:42
I and My Father are *o* ... John 10:30
that they may be *o* ...... John 17:11
o accord in the temple .... Acts 2:46
for you are all *o* .... Gal 3:28
to create in Himself *o* ..... Eph 2:15
o Lord .... Eph 4:5
o faith .... Eph 4:5
o baptism .... Eph 4:5
o God and Father of .... Eph 4:6
For there is *o* God and ... 1 Tim 2:5
o Mediator between ...... 1 Tim 2:5
a thousand years as *o* ..... 2 Pet 3:8

OPENED
o not His mouth .... Is 53:7
o the Scriptures .... Luke 24:32
o their understanding ... Luke 24:45
Now I saw heaven *o* ...... Rev 19:11

OPENS
him the doorkeeper *o* .... John 10:3
and shuts and no one *o* ..... Rev 3:7

OPINION
be wise in your own *o* ... Rom 11:25

OPINIONS
falter between two *o* ... 1 Kin 18:21

OPPORTUNITY
But sin, taking *o* .... Rom 7:8
as we have *o* .... Gal 6:10
but you lacked *o* .... Phil 4:10

OPPRESS
he loves to *o* .... Hos 12:7
o the widow or the .... Zech 7:10
Do not the rich *o* .... James 2:6

OPPRESSED
for all who are *o* .... Ps 103:6
The tears of the *o* .... Eccl 4:1
He was *o* and He was .... Is 53:7
all who were *o* .... Acts 10:38

OPPRESSES
o the poor reproaches ... Prov 14:31

OPPRESSION
have surely seen the *o* .... Ex 3:7
their life from *o* .... Ps 72:14
brought low through *o* ... Ps 107:39
me from the *o* .... Ps 119:134
considered all the *o* .... Eccl 4:1
o destroys a wise .... Eccl 7:7
justice, but behold, *o* .... Is 5:7
surely seen the *o* .... Acts 7:34

ORACLES
received the living *o* ...... Acts 7:38
were committed the *o* ..... Rom 3:2
principles of the *o* .... Heb 5:12

ORDAINED
o you a prophet .... Jer 1:5
whom He has *o* .... Acts 17:31

ORDER
decently and in *o* .... 1 Cor 14:40

ORDERS
o his conduct aright I ..... Ps 50:23

ORDINANCE
resists the *o* of God ...... Rom 13:2

ORDINANCES
and fleshly *o* imposed ..... Heb 9:10

ORPHANS
will not leave you *o* ..... John 14:18
to visit *o* and widows ... James 1:27

OUGHT
These you *o* to have ..... Matt 23:23
pray for as we *o* .... Rom 8:26
persons *o* you to be ...... 2 Pet 3:11

OUTCAST
they called you an *o* .... Jer 30:17

OUTCASTS
will assemble the *o* .... Is 11:12

OUTRAN
the other disciple *o* .... John 20:4

OUTSIDE
and dish, that the *o* ...... Matt 23:26
Pharisees make the *o* ... Luke 11:39
toward those who are *o* ..... Col 4:5
to Him, *o* the camp .... Heb 13:13
But *o* are dogs and .... Rev 22:15

OUTSTRETCHED
and with an *o* arm .... Deut 26:8

OUTWARD
at the *o* appearance ..... 1 Sam 16:7
adornment be merely *o* ... 1 Pet 3:3

OUTWARDLY
not a Jew who is one *o* ... Rom 2:28

OVERCAME
My throne, as I also *o* ..... Rev 3:21
"And they *o* him by ...... Rev 12:11

OVERCOME
good cheer, I have *o* ..... John 16:33
and the Lamb will *o* ...... Rev 17:14

OVERCOMES
of God *o* the world ...... 1 John 5:4
o I will give to eat .... Rev 2:7
o shall not be hurt .... Rev 2:11
o shall inherit all .... Rev 21:7

OVERSEER
to the Shepherd and *O* ... 1 Pet 2:25

OVERSEERS
you, serving as *o* .... 1 Pet 5:2

OVERSHADOW
of the Highest will *o* ...... Luke 1:35

OVERTHREW
As God *o* Sodom and ...... Jer 50:40

OVERTHROW
o the faith of some ...... 2 Tim 2:18

OVERTHROWN
and Nineveh shall be *o* ..... Jon 3:4

OVERTHROWS
And *o* the mighty .... Job 12:19
o them in the night .... Job 34:25
o the words of the .... Prov 22:12

OVERWHELM
o the fatherless .... Job 6:27

OVERWHELMED
and my spirit was *o* .... Ps 77:3
my spirit is *o* within .... Ps 143:4

OVERWORK
Do not *o* to be rich .... Prov 23:4

OWE
O no one anything .... Rom 13:8

OWED
o him ten thousand ..... Matt 18:24

OWN
He came to His *o* .... John 1:11
having loved His *o* .... John 13:1
would love its *o* .... John 15:19
you are not your *o* ...... 1 Cor 6:19
But each one has his *o* ... 1 Cor 7:7
For all seek their *o* .... Phil 2:21
from our sins in His *o* ...... Rev 1:5

OX
shall not muzzle an *o* .... Deut 25:4
o knows its owner .... Is 1:3
Sabbath loose his *o* ..... Luke 13:15
shall not muzzle an *o* .... 1 Cor 9:9

P

PACIFIES
A gift in secret *p* .... Prov 21:14

PAIN
p you shall bring .... Gen 3:16
p as a woman in .... Is 13:8
Why is my *p* perpetual .... Jer 15:18
shall be no more *p* .... Rev 21:4

PAINED
My heart is severely *p* ...... Ps 55:4
I am *p* in my very .... Jer 4:19

PAINFUL
for the present, but *p* ..... Heb 12:11

PAINS
The *p* of death .... Ps 116:3
having loosed the *p* ...... Acts 2:24

PAINT
your eyes with *p* .... Jer 4:30

PALACE
enter the King's *p* .... Ps 45:15
guards his own *p* .... Luke 11:21
evident to the whole *p* ..... Phil 1:13

PALACES
Out of the ivory *p* .... Ps 45:8

PALE
behold, a *p* horse .... Rev 6:8

PALM
p branches in their .... Rev 7:9

PALMS
struck Him with the *p* ... Matt 26:67

PAMPERS
p his servant from .... Prov 29:21

PANGS
The *p* of death .... Ps 18:4
labors with birth *p* .... Rom 8:22

PARABLE
do You speak this *p* ..... Luke 12:41

PARABLES
rest it is given in *p* ...... Luke 8:10

PARADISE
will be with Me in *P* ..... Luke 23:43
in the midst of the *P* .... Rev 2:7

PARDON
He will abundantly *p* .... Is 55:7
p all their iniquities .... Jer 33:8

PARDONING
is a God like You, *p* .... Mic 7:18

PARENTS
will rise up against *p* .... Matt 10:21
has left house or *p* ...... Luke 18:29
disobedient to *p* .... Rom 1:30

PART
chosen that good *p* ...... Luke 10:42
you, you have no *p* .... John 13:8
For we know in *p* .... 1 Cor 13:9
shall take away his *p* ..... Rev 22:19

PARTAKE
for we all *p* of that ..... 1 Cor 10:17

PARTAKER
in hope should be *p* ..... 1 Cor 9:10
Christ, and also a *p* .... 1 Pet 5:1

PARTAKERS
Gentiles have been *p* .... Rom 15:27
know that as you are *p* ... 2 Cor 1:7
qualified us to be *p* .... Col 1:12

PARTIAL
You shall not be *p* .... Lev 19:15

PARTIALITY
that God shows no *p* .... Acts 10:34
doing nothing with *p* .... 1 Tim 5:21
good fruits, without *p* ... James 3:17

PASS
I will *p* over you .... Ex 12:13
When you *p* through the .... Is 43:2
and earth will *p* .... Matt 24:35

PASSED
forbearance God had *p* ... Rom 3:25
High Priest who has *p* ..... Heb 4:14
know that we have *p* ... 1 John 3:14

PASSES
of Christ which *p* .... Eph 3:19

PASSION
uncleanness, *p* .... Col 3:5

PASSIONS
gave them up to vile *p* .... Rom 1:26

PASSOVER
It is the LORD's *P* .... Ex 12:11
I will keep the *P* .... Matt 26:18
indeed Christ, our *P* ...... 1 Cor 5:7
By faith he kept the *P* .... Heb 11:28

PASTORS
and some *p* and .... Eph 4:11

PASTURE
the sheep of Your *p* .... Ps 74:1
in and out and find *p* ..... John 10:9

PASTURES
to lie down in green *p* ...... Ps 23:2

PATH
You will show me the *p* .... Ps 16:11

PATHS
He leads me in the *p* .... Ps 23:3
Make His *p* straight .... Matt 3:3
and make straight *p* ...... Heb 12:13

PATIENCE
'Master, have *p* .... Matt 18:26
and bear fruit with *p* ..... Luke 8:15
labor of love, and *p* .... 1 Thess 1:3
faith, love, *p* .... 1 Tim 6:11
your faith produces *p* .... James 1:3
p have its perfect .... James 1:4
in the kingdom and *p* ...... Rev 1:9

PATIENT
rejoicing in hope, *p* ..... Rom 12:12
the weak, be *p* .... 1 Thess 5:14

PATIENTLY
if you take it *p* .... 1 Pet 2:20

PATRIARCHS
begot the twelve *p* .... Acts 7:8

PATTERN
p which you were .... Ex 26:30
as you have us for a *p* ..... Phil 3:17
p shown you on the .... Heb 8:5

PEACE
you, And give you *p* ... Num 6:26
both lie down in *p* ... Ps 4:8
p have those who ... Ps 119:165
I am for *p* ... Ps 120:7
war, And a time of *p* ... Eccl 3:8
Father, Prince of *P* ... Is 9:6
keep him in perfect *p* ... Is 26:3
p they have not ... Is 59:8
slightly, Saying, '*P* ... Jer 6:14
place I will give *p* ... Hag 2:9
is worthy, let your *p* ... Matt 10:13
that I came to bring *p* ... Matt 10:34
And on earth *p* ... Luke 2:14
if a son of *p* is there ... Luke 10:6
that make for your *p* ... Luke 19:42
leave with you, My *p* ... John 14:27
Me you may have *p* ... John 16:33
Grace to you and *p* ... Rom 1:7
by faith, we have *p* ... Rom 5:1
God has called us to *p* ... 1 Cor 7:15
p will be with you ... 2 Cor 13:11
Spirit is love, joy, *p* ... Gal 5:22
He Himself is our *p* ... Eph 2:14
and the *p* of God ... Phil 4:7
And let the *p* of God ... Col 3:15
faith, love, *p* ... 2 Tim 2:22
meaning "king of *p*," ... Heb 7:2

PEACEABLE
is first pure, then *p* ... James 3:17

PEACEABLY
on you, live *p* ... Rom 12:18

PEACEFUL
in a *p* habitation ... Is 32:18

PEACEMAKERS
Blessed are the *p* ... Matt 5:9

PEARL
had found one *p* ... Matt 13:46

PEARLS
nor cast your *p* ... Matt 7:6
gates were twelve *p* ... Rev 21:21

PENTECOST
P had fully come ... Acts 2:1

PEOPLE
will take you as My *p* ... Ex 6:7
p shall be my *p* ... Ruth 1:16
p who know the joyful ... Ps 89:15
We are His *p* and the ... Ps 100:3
"Blessed is Egypt My *p* ... Is 19:25
to make ready a *p* ... Luke 1:17
take out of them a *p* ... Acts 15:14
who were not My *p* ... Rom 9:25
they shall be My *p* ... 2 Cor 6:16
LORD will judge His *p* ... Heb 10:30
but are now the *p* ... 1 Pet 2:10
tribe and tongue and *p* ... Rev 5:9
they shall be His *p* ... Rev 21:3

PERCEIVE
seeing, but do not *p* ... Is 6:9
may see and not *p* ... Mark 4:12

PERDITION
except the son of *p* ... John 17:12
revealed, the son of *p* ... 2 Thess 2:3
who draw back to *p* ... Heb 10:39

PERFECT
Noah was a just man, *p* ... Gen 6:9
Father in heaven is *p* ... Matt 5:48
they may be made *p* ... John 17:23
and *p* will of God ... Rom 12:2
when that which is *p* ... 1 Cor 13:10
present every man *p* ... Col 1:28
good gift and every *p* ... James 1:17
in word, he is a *p* ... James 3:2
p love casts out fear ... 1 John 4:18

PERFECTED
third day I shall be *p* ... Luke 13:32
or am already *p* ... Phil 3:12
Son who has been *p* ... Heb 7:28

PERFECTION
let us go on to *p* ... Heb 6:1

PERISH
so that we may not *p* ... Jon 1:6
little ones should *p* ... Matt 18:14
in Him should not *p* ... John 3:16
they shall never *p* ... John 10:28
among those who *p* ... 2 Thess 2:10
that any should *p* ... 2 Pet 3:9

PERISHABLE
do it to obtain a *p* ... 1 Cor 9:25

PERISHED
Truth has *p* and has ... Jer 7:28

PERISHING
We are *p* ... Matt 8:25

PERMIT
do not *p* a woman ... 1 Tim 2:12

PERMITS
we will do if God *p* ... Heb 6:3

PERMITTED
p no one to do them ... Ps 105:14
we are *p* ... 2 Cor 4:8

PERSECUTE
when they revile and *p* ... Matt 5:11

PERSECUTED
If they *p* Me ... John 15:20
p, but not forsaken ... 2 Cor 4:9

PERSECUTES
wicked in his pride *p* ... Ps 10:2

PERSECUTION
p arises because of ... Matt 13:21
At that time a great *p* ... Acts 8:1
do I still suffer *p* ... Gal 5:11

PERSECUTOR
a blasphemer, a *p* ... 1 Tim 1:13

PERSEVERANCE
tribulation produces *p* ... Rom 5:3

PERSEVERE
kept My command to *p* ... Rev 3:10

PERSISTENCE
p he will rise and ... Luke 11:8

PERSON
do not regard the *p* ... Matt 22:16
express image of His *p* ... Heb 1:3

PERSUADE
"You almost *p* me ... Acts 26:28

PERSUADED
neither will they be *p* ... Luke 16:31
p that He is able ... 2 Tim 1:12

PERSUASIVE
p words of human ... 1 Cor 2:4

PERVERSE
your way is *p* ... Num 22:32
p man sows strife ... Prov 16:28
from this *p* generation ... Acts 2:40

PERVERT
"You shall not *p* ... Deut 16:19
p the gospel of Christ ... Gal 1:7

PERVERTING
will you not cease *p* ... Acts 13:10

PERVERTS
p his ways will become ... Prov 10:9

PESTILENCE
from the perilous *p* ... Ps 91:3
Before Him went *p* ... Hab 3:5

PESTILENCES
will be famines, *p* ... Matt 24:7

PETITIONS
p that we have asked ... 1 John 5:15

PHARISEE
to pray, one a *P* ... Luke 18:10

PHILOSOPHERS
p encountered him ... Acts 17:18

PHILOSOPHY
cheat you through *p* ... Col 2:8

PHYSICIAN
have no need of a *p* ... Matt 9:12

PHYSICIANS
her livelihood on *p* ... Luke 8:43

PIECES
they took the thirty *p* ... Matt 27:9

PIERCE
a sword will *p* ... Luke 2:35

PIERCED
p My hands and My feet ... Ps 22:16
whom they have *p* ... Zech 12:10
of the soldiers *p* ... John 19:34
p themselves through ... 1 Tim 6:10
and they also who *p* ... Rev 1:7

PIERCING
p even to the division ... Heb 4:12

PILGRIMAGE
heart is set on *p* ... Ps 84:5
In the house of my *p* ... Ps 119:54

PILGRIMS
we are aliens and *p* ... 1 Chr 29:15
were strangers and *p* ... Heb 11:13

PILLAR
and she became a *p* ... Gen 19:26
and by night in a *p* ... Ex 13:21
the living God, the *p* ... 1 Tim 3:15

PILLARS
break their sacred *p* ... Ex 34:13
Blood and fire and *p* ... Joel 2:30
and his feet like *p* ... Rev 10:1

PIT
who go down to the *p* ... Ps 28:1
a harlot is a deep *p* ... Prov 23:27
my life in the *p* ... Lam 3:53
up my life from the *p* ... Jon 2:6
into the bottomless *p* ... Rev 20:3

PITIABLE
of all men the most *p* ... 1 Cor 15:19

PITS
The proud have dug *p* ... Ps 119:85

PITY
for someone to take *p* ... Ps 69:20
p He redeemed them ... Is 63:9
just as I had *p* ... Matt 18:33

PLACE
Come, see the *p* ... Matt 28:6
My word has no *p* ... John 8:37
I go to prepare a *p* ... John 14:2
might go to his own *p* ... Acts 1:25

PLACES
And the rough *p* ... Is 40:4
They love the best *p* ... Matt 23:6
in the heavenly *p* ... Eph 1:3

PLAGUE
bring yet one more *p* ... Ex 11:1

PLAGUES
p that are written ... Rev 22:18

PLANK
First remove the *p* ... Matt 7:5

PLANS
He makes the *p* of the ... Ps 33:10
that devises wicked *p* ... Prov 6:18

PLANT
A time to *p* ... Eccl 3:2
Him as a tender *p* ... Is 53:2
p of an alien vine ... Jer 2:21
p which My heavenly ... Matt 15:13

PLANTED
shall be like a tree *p* ... Ps 1:3
by the roots and be *p* ... Luke 17:6
I *p*, Apollos watered ... 1 Cor 3:6

PLANTS
neither he who *p* ... 1 Cor 3:7

PLATTER
head here on a *p* ... Matt 14:8

PLEASANT
food, that it was *p* ... Gen 3:6
how good and how *p* ... Ps 133:1

PLEASANTNESS
ways are ways of *p* ... Prov 3:17

PLEASE
in the flesh cannot *p* ... Rom 8:8
p his neighbor for his ... Rom 15:2
he may *p* the Lord ... 1 Cor 7:32
is impossible to *p* Him ... Heb 11:6

PLEASED
Then You shall be *p* ... Ps 51:19
in whom I am well *p* ... Matt 3:17
God was not well *p* ... 1 Cor 10:5
testimony, that he *p* ... Heb 11:5

PLEASES
Whatever the LORD *p* ... Ps 135:6

PLEASING
sacrifice, well *p* ... Phil 4:18
for this is well *p* ... Col 3:20
in you what is well *p* ... Heb 13:21

PLEASURE
Do good in Your good *p* . . . Ps 51:18
p will be a poor man . . . . Prov 21:17
shall perform all My *p* . . . . Is 44:28
your Father's good *p* . . . . Luke 12:32
to the good *p* of His . . . . Eph 1:5
for sin You had no *p* . . . . Heb 10:6
My soul has no *p* . . . . Heb 10:38
p that war in your . . . . James 4:1

PLEASURES
Your right hand are *p* . . . . . Ps 16:11
cares, riches, and *p* . . . . . Luke 8:14
to enjoy the passing *p* . . . . Heb 11:25

PLOW
put his hand to the *p* . . . . . Luke 9:62

PLOWED
You have *p* . . . . Hos 10:13

PLOWMAN
p shall overtake the . . . . . Amos 9:13

PLUCK
p the heads of grain . . . . . Mark 2:23

PLUCKED
cheeks to those who *p* . . . . . . Is 50:6
And His disciples *p* . . . . Luke 6:1
you would have *p* . . . . Gal 4:15

PLUNDER
p the Egyptians . . . . Ex 3:22
The *p* of the poor is . . . . Is 3:14
house and *p* his goods . . . Matt 12:29

PLUNDERED
a people robbed and *p* . . . . . Is 42:22
"And when you are *p* . . . . Jer 4:30

PLUNDERING
me Because of the *p* . . . . Is 22:4
accepted the *p* of your . . . . Heb 10:34

POETS
some of your own *p* . . . . Acts 171:28

POISON
"The *p* of asps is . . . . Rom 3:13

POISONED
p by bitterness . . . . Acts 8:23

POLLUTIONS
have escaped the *p* . . . . 2 Pet 2:20

POMP
had come with great *p* . . Acts 25:23

POMPOUS
and a mouth speaking *p* . . . . Dan 7:8

PONDER
P the path of your . . . . Prov 4:26

PONDERED
p them in her heart . . . . Luke 2:19

PONDERS
p all his paths . . . . Prov 5:21

POOR
p will never cease . . . . Deut 15:11
So the *p* have hope . . . . Job 5:16
I delivered the *p* . . . . Job 29:12
p shall eat and be . . . . Ps 22:26
But I am *p* and needy . . . . . Ps 40:17
Let the *p* and needy . . . . Ps 74:21
He raises the *p* . . . . Ps 113:7
slack hand becomes *p* . . . . Prov 10:4
p man is hated even . . . . . Prov 14:20
has mercy on the *p* . . . . Prov 14:21
who oppresses the *p* . . . . Prov 14:31
p reproaches his . . . . Prov 17:5
Do not rob the *p* . . . . Prov 22:22
that same *p* man . . . . Eccl 9:15
The alien or the *p* . . . . Zech 7:10
"Blessed are the *p* . . . . Matt 5:3
p have the gospel . . . . Matt 11:5
"For you have the *p* . . . . . Matt 26:11
sakes He became *p* . . . . 2 Cor 8:9
should remember the *p* . . . . Gal 2:10
God not chosen the *p* . . . . . James 2:5
wretched, miserable, *p* . . . . Rev 3:17

PORTION
O LORD, You, are the *p* . . . . . Ps 16:5
heart and my *p* forever . . . . Ps 73:26
You are my *p* . . . . Ps 119:57
I will divide Him a *p* . . . . Is 53:12
rejoice in their *p* . . . . Is 61:7
The *P* of Jacob is not . . . . . . Jer 10:16
"The LORD is my *p* . . . . Lam 3:24
and appoint him his *p* . . . Matt 24:51
to give them their *p* . . . . . Luke 12:42
give me the *p* . . . . Luke 15:12

POSSESS
descendants shall *p* . . . . . . Gen 22:17
p the land which . . . . Josh 1:11
"By your patience *p* . . . . . Luke 21:19
p his own vessel . . . . 1 Thess 4:4

POSSESSED
"The LORD *p* me at . . . . Prov 8:22

POSSESSING
and yet *p* all things . . . . . . 2 Cor 6:10

POSSESSION
as an everlasting *p* . . . . Gen 17:8
and an enduring *p* . . . . Heb 10:34

POSSESSIONS
and sold their *p* . . . . Acts 2:45

POSSIBLE
God all things are *p* . . . . . Matt 19:26
p that the blood . . . . Heb 10:4

POUR
p My Spirit on your . . . . Is 44:3
P out Your fury . . . . Jer 10:25
That I will *p* out My . . . . Joel 2:28
"And I will *p* . . . . Zech 12:10
angels, "Go and *p* . . . . Rev 16:1

POURED
I am *p* out like water . . . . . . Ps 22:14
grace is *p* upon Your . . . . Ps 45:2
strong, Because He *p* . . . . Is 53:12
and My fury will be *p* . . . . Jer 7:20
broke the flask and *p* . . . . Mark 14:3
I am already being *p* . . . . . 2 Tim 4:6
whom He *p* out on us . . . . . . Titus 3:6

POVERTY
leads only to *p* . . . . Prov 14:23
p put in all the . . . . Luke 21:4
and their deep *p* . . . . 2 Cor 8:2
p might become rich . . . . . 2 Cor 8:9
tribulation, and *p* . . . . Rev 2:9

POWER
that I may show My *p* . . . . . . Ex 9:16
him who is without *p* . . . . . . Job 26:2
p who can understand . . . . Job 26:14
p belongs to God . . . . Ps 62:11
p Your enemies shall . . . . Ps 66:3
gives strength and *p* . . . . Ps 68:35
a king is, there is *p* . . . . Eccl 8:4
No one has *p* over the . . . . . . Eccl 8:8
'Not by might nor by *p* . . . . Zech 4:6
the kingdom and the *p* . . . Matt 6:13
the Son of Man has *p* . . . . . Matt 9:6
Scriptures nor the *p* . . . . . Matt 22:29
p went out from Him . . . . . . Luke 6:19
are endued with *p* . . . . Luke 24:49
I have *p* to lay it . . . . John 10:18
"You could have no *p* . . . John 19:11
you shall receive *p* . . . . Acts 1:8
though by our own *p* . . . . Acts 3:12
man is the great *p* . . . . Acts 8:10
"Give me this *p* . . . . Acts 8:19
for it is the *p* . . . . Rom 1:16
saved it is the *p* . . . . 1 Cor 1:18
Greeks, Christ the *p* . . . . 1 Cor 1:24
that the *p* of Christ . . . . . . 2 Cor 12:9
greatness of His *p* . . . . Eph 1:19
the Lord and in the *p* . . . . . . Eph 6:10
to His glorious *p* . . . . Col 1:11
the glory of His *p* . . . . 2 Thess 1:9
of fear, but of *p* . . . . 2 Tim 1:7
by the word of His *p* . . . . Heb 1:3
p of death, that . . . . Heb 2:14
as His divine *p* . . . . 2 Pet 1:3
Dominion and *p* . . . . Jude 25
to him I will give *p* . . . . Rev 2:26
honor and glory and *p* . . . . Rev 5:13

POWERFUL
of the LORD is *p* . . . . Ps 29:4
of God is living and *p* . . . . . Heb 4:12

POWERS
principalities and *p* . . . . Col 2:15
word of God and the *p* . . . . . Heb 6:5

PRAISE
p shall be of You in . . . . Ps 22:25
the people shall *p* . . . . Ps 45:17
P is awaiting You . . . . Ps 65:1
Let all the peoples *p* . . . . Ps 67:3
p shall be continually . . . . Ps 71:6
And the heavens will *p* . . . . . . Ps 89:5
Seven times a day I *p* . . . . Ps 119:164
that has breath *p* . . . . Ps 150:6
Let another man *p* . . . . Prov 27:2
let her own works *p* . . . . . . Prov 31:31
And your gates *P* . . . . Is 60:18
He makes Jerusalem a *p* . . . . . Is 62:7
For You are my *p* . . . . Jer 17:14
Me a name of joy, a *p* . . . . Jer 33:9
give you fame and *p* . . . . Zeph 3:20
You have perfected *p* . . . . Matt 21:16
men more than the *p* . . . . . John 12:43
p is not from men but . . . . . Rom 2:29
Then each one's *p* . . . . 1 Cor 4:5
should be to the *p* . . . . Eph 1:12
to the glory and *p* . . . . Phil 1:11
I will sing *p* to You . . . . Heb 2:12
the sacrifice of *p* . . . . Heb 13:15
and for the *p* of those . . . . 1 Pet 2:14
saying, "*P* our God . . . . Rev 19:5

PRAISED
daily He shall be *p* . . . . Ps 72:15
LORD's name is to be *p* . . . . Ps 113:3
and greatly to be *p* . . . . Ps 145:3
the Most High and *p* . . . . Dan 4:34

PRAISES
it is good to sing *p* . . . . Ps 147:1
and he *p* . . . . Prov 31:28

PRAISEWORTHY
If there is anything *p* . . . . Phil 4:8

PRAISING
They will still be *p* . . . . Ps 84:4
of the heavenly host *p* . . . . . Luke 2:13
in the temple *p* . . . . Luke 24:53

PRAY
at noon I will *p* . . . . Ps 55:17
who hate you, and *p* . . . . Matt 5:44
"And when you *p* . . . . Matt 6:5
manner, therefore, *p* . . . . Matt 6:9
"Watch and *p* . . . . Matt 26:41
"Lord, teach us to *p* . . . . Luke 11:1
"And I will *p* . . . . John 14:16
I do not *p* for the . . . . John 17:9
"I do not *p* for . . . . John 17:20
p without ceasing . . . . . . 1 Thess 5:17
Brethren, *p* for us . . . . . . 1 Thess 5:25
Let him *p* . . . . James 5:13
to one another, and *p* . . . . James 5:16
say that he should *p* . . . . . 1 John 5:16

PRAYED
p more earnestly . . . . Luke 22:44
p earnestly that it . . . . James 5:17

PRAYER
p made in this place . . . . . 2 Chr 7:15
And my *p* is pure . . . . Job 16:17
A *p* to the God of my . . . . Ps 42:8
P also will be made . . . . Ps 72:15
He shall regard the *p* . . . . . Ps 102:17
to the LORD, But the *p* . . . . Prov 15:8
go out except by *p* . . . . Matt 17:21
all night in *p* to God . . . . . . Luke 6:12
continually to *p* . . . . Acts 6:4
where *p* was . . . . Acts 16:13
steadfastly in *p* . . . . Rom 12:12
to fasting and *p* . . . . 1 Cor 7:5
always with all *p* . . . . Eph 6:18
but in everything by *p* . . . . Phil 4:6
the word of God and *p* . . . . 1 Tim 4:5
And the *p* of faith . . . . James 5:15

PRAYERS
though You make many *p* . . . Is 1:15
pretense make long *p* . . . Matt 23:14
fervently for you in *p* . . . . Col 4:12
p may not be hindered . . . . 1 Pet 3:7
which are the *p* . . . . Rev 5:8

PREACH
time Jesus began to *p* . . . . Matt 4:17
you hear in the ear, *p* . . . . Matt 10:27
P the gospel to the . . . . Luke 4:18
And how shall they *p* . . . Rom 10:15
p Christ crucified . . . . 1 Cor 1:23
I or they, so we *p* . . . . 1 Cor 15:11
P the word . . . . 2 Tim 4:2

PREACHED
p that people . . . . Mark 6:12
out and *p* . . . . Mark 16:20
of sins should be *p* . . . . . . Luke 24:47
p Christ to them . . . . Acts 8:5
lest, when I have *p* . . . . . . 1 Cor 9:27

than what we have *p* ...... Gal 1:8
the gospel was *p* .... Heb 4:2
also He went and *p* ...... 1 Pet 3:19

PREACHER
they hear without a *p* ... Rom 10:14
I was appointed a *p* ...... 1 Tim 2:7

PREACHES
the Jesus whom Paul *p* .. Acts 19:13
p another Jesus .... 2 Cor 11:4
p any other gospel .... Gal 1:9
p the faith which he .... Gal 1:23

PREACHING
p Jesus as the .... Acts 5:42
not risen, then our *p* ... 1 Cor 15:14

PRECEPTS
all His *p* are sure .... Ps 111:7
how I love Your *p* .... Ps 119:159

PRECIOUS
P in the sight of the ...... Ps 116:15
She is more *p* than .... Prov 3:15
p things shall not .... Is 44:9
if you take out the *p* .... Jer 15:19
farmer waits for the *p* .... James 5:7
more *p* than gold .... 1 Pet 1:7
who believe, He is *p* .... 1 Pet 2:7
p in the sight of .... 1 Pet 3:4

PREDESTINED
foreknew, He also *p* ...... Rom 8:29
having *p* us to .... Eph 1:5
inheritance, being *p* .... Eph 1:11

PREEMINENCE
He may have the *p* .... Col 1:18
loves to have the *p* .... 3 John 9

PREFERENCE
in honor giving *p* .... Rom 12:10

PREJUDICE
these things without *p* ... 1 Tim 5:21

PREMEDITATE
p what you will .... Mark 13:11

PREPARATION
Now it was the *P* .... John 19:14
your feet with the *p* .... Eph 6:15

PREPARE
p a table before me in ...... Ps 23:5
P the way of the LORD .... Mark 1:3
p a place for you .... John 14:2

PREPARED
for whom it is *p* .... Matt 20:23
Which You have *p* .... Luke 2:31
mercy, which He had *p* ... Rom 9:23
things which God has *p* .. 1 Cor 2:9
Now He who has *p* .... 2 Cor 5:5
p beforehand that we ..... Eph 2:10
God, for He has *p* .... Heb 11:16

PRESENCE
themselves from the *p* ...... Gen 3:8
went out from the *p* ...... Gen 4:16
P will go with you .... Ex 33:14
afraid in any man's *p* ..... Deut 1:17
p is fullness of joy .... Ps 16:11
shall dwell in Your *p* ..... Ps 140:13
not tremble at My *p* .... Jer 5:22
shall shake at My *p* ...... Ezek 38:20
and drank in Your *p* ..... Luke 13:26
full of joy in Your *p* .... Acts 2:28
but his bodily *p* .... 2 Cor 10:10
obeyed, not as in my *p* .... Phil 2:12

PRESENT
we are all *p* before ...... Acts 10:33
evil is *p* with me .... Rom 7:21
p your bodies a living .... Rom 12:1
or death, or things *p* .... 1 Cor 3:22
absent in body but *p* ...... 1 Cor 5:3
that He might *p* .... Eph 5:27
p you faultless .... Jude 24

PRESERVE
He shall *p* your soul .... Ps 121:7
The LORD shall *p* .... Ps 121:8
loses his life will *p* ...... Luke 17:33
every evil work and *p* ... 2 Tim 4:18

PRESERVED
soul, and body be *p* ... 1 Thess 5:23

PRESERVES
For the LORD *p* the .... Ps 31:23
p the souls of His .... Ps 97:10
who keeps his way *p* .... Prov 16:17

PRETENSE
p make long prayers .... Matt 23:14

PRICE
one pearl of great *p* ..... Matt 13:46
were bought at a *p* ...... 1 Cor 6:20

PRIDE
p serves as .... Ps 73:6
By *p* comes nothing ..... Prov 13:10
P goes before .... Prov 16:18
her daughter had *p* ...... Ezek 16:49
was hardened in *p* .... Dan 5:20
For the *p* of the .... Zech 11:3
evil eye, blasphemy, *p* ... Mark 7:22
p he fall into the .... 1 Tim 3:6
eyes, and the *p* .... 1 John 2:16

PRIEST
he was the *p* of God ...... Gen 14:18
p forever According .... Ps 110:4
So He shall be a *p* .... Zech 6:13
and faithful High *P* .... Heb 2:17
we have a great High *P* .... Heb 4:14
p forever according .... Heb 5:6
Christ came as High *P* .... Heb 9:11

PRIESTHOOD
p being changed .... Heb 7:12
has an unchangeable *p* .... Heb 7:24
generation, a royal *p* ...... 1 Pet 2:9

PRIESTS
to Me a kingdom of *p* ...... Ex 19:6
Her *p* teach for pay .... Mic 3:11
made us kings and *p* .... Rev 1:6

PRINCE
is the house of the *p* ...... Job 21:28
Everlasting Father, *P* .... Is 9:6
Until Messiah the *P* .... Dan 9:25
days without king or *p* ...... Hos 3:4
p asks for gifts .... Mic 7:3
"and killed the *P* .... Acts 3:15
His right hand to be *P* .... Acts 5:31
the *p* of the power .... Eph 2:2

PRINCES
to put confidence in *p* ..... Ps 118:9
He brings the *p* .... Is 40:23

PRISON
and put him into the *p* .... Gen 39:20
Bring my soul out of *p* .... Ps 142:7
in darkness from the *p* ...... Is 42:7
the opening of the *p* .... Is 61:1
John had heard in *p* ...... Matt 11:2
I was in *p* and you ...... Matt 25:36

PRIZE
the goal for the *p* .... Phil 3:14

PROCEED
of the same mouth *p* .... James 3:10

PROCEEDED
for I *p* forth .... John 8:42

PROCEEDS
by every word that *p* ...... Deut 8:3
by every word that *p* ...... Matt 4:4
Spirit of truth who *p* .... John 15:26

PROCLAIM
began to *p* it freely ...... Mark 1:45
knowing, Him I *p* .... Acts 17:23
drink this cup, you *p* ... 1 Cor 11:26

PROCLAIMED
p the good news .... Ps 40:9
he went his way and *p* ... Luke 8:39

PROCLAIMER
"He seems to be a *p* ..... Acts 17:18

PROCLAIMS
good news, Who *p* .... Is 52:7

PRODIGAL
with *p* living .... Luke 15:13

PROFANE
and priest are *p* .... Jer 23:11
tried to *p* the temple ...... Acts 24:6
But reject *p* and old ...... 1 Tim 4:7

PROFANED
and *p* My Sabbaths ...... Ezek 22:8

PROFANENESS
of Jerusalem *p* has .... Jer 23:15

PROFANING
p the covenant of the ...... Mal 2:10

PROFESS
They *p* to know God ...... Titus 1:16

PROFIT
For what *p* is it to .... Matt 16:26
"For what will it *p* .... Mark 8:36
"For what *p* is it to .... Luke 9:25
her masters much *p* ..... Acts 16:16
brought no small *p* ...... Acts 19:24
what is the *p* of .... Rom 3:1
seeking my own *p* ...... 1 Cor 10:33
Christ will *p* you .... Gal 5:2
about words to no *p* ..... 2 Tim 2:14
them, but He for our *p* ... Heb 12:10
What does it *p* .... James 2:14
sell, and make a *p* .... James 4:13

PROFITABLE
It is doubtless not *p* ..... 1 Cor 12:1
of God, and is *p* .... 2 Tim 3:16

PROFITS
have not love, it *p* .... 1 Cor 13:3

PROMISE
"Behold, I send the *P* .... Luke 24:49
but to wait for the *P* .... Acts 1:4
"For the *p* is to you .... Acts 2:39
for the hope of the *p* ..... Acts 26:6
p might be sure .... Rom 4:16
Therefore, since a *p* .... Heb 4:1
to the heirs of *p* .... Heb 6:17
did not receive the *p* ..... Heb 11:39

PROMISED
faithful who had *p* .... Heb 11:11

PROMISES
For all the *p* of God ..... 2 Cor 1:20
his Seed were the *p* .... Gal 3:16
having received the *p* .... Heb 11:13
great and precious *p* .... 2 Pet 1:4

PROPER
you, but for what is *p* .... 1 Cor 7:35
but, which is *p* .... 1 Tim 2:10

PROPERLY
Let us walk *p* .... Rom 13:13

PROPHECY
to another *p* .... 1 Cor 12:10
for *p* never came by ...... 2 Pet 1:21
is the spirit of *p* .... Rev 19:10
of the book of this *p* ...... Rev 22:19

PROPHESIED
Lord, have we not *p* ...... Matt 7:22
and the law *p* .... Matt 11:13

PROPHESIES
p edifies the church ..... 1 Cor 14:4

PROPHESY
prophets, "Do not *p* .... Is 30:10
The prophets *p* falsely ...... Jer 5:31
your daughters shall *p* ..... Joel 2:28
Who can but *p* .... Amos 3:8
saying, "*P* to us .... Matt 26:68
your daughters shall *p* ... Acts 2:17
in part and we *p* .... 1 Cor 13:9

PROPHET
raise up for you a *P* ..... Deut 18:15
"I alone am left a *p* ..... 1 Kin 18:22
I ordained you a *p* .... Jer 1:5
The *p* is a fool .... Hos 9:7
Nor was I a son of a *p* ... Amos 7:14
send you Elijah the *p* .... Mal 4:5
p shall receive a .... Matt 10:41
p is not without honor ... Matt 13:57
by Daniel the *p* .... Mark 13:14
is not a greater *p* .... Luke 7:28
it cannot be that a *p* ...... Luke 13:33
who was a *P* .... Luke 24:19
"Are you the *P* .... John 1:21
"This is truly the *P* .... John 6:14
with him the false *p* ...... Rev 19:20

PROPHETIC
p word confirmed .... 2 Pet 1:19

PROPHETS
the Law or the *P* .... Matt 5:17
is the Law and the *P* ..... Matt 7:12
or one of the *p* .... Matt 16:14
the tombs of the *p* .... Matt 23:29
indeed, I send you *p* ...... Matt 23:34
one who kills the *p* ...... Matt 23:37
Then many false *p* ...... Matt 24:11
Moses and the *p* .... Luke 16:29
are sons of the *p* .... Acts 3:25

p did your fathers not .... Acts 7:52
"To Him all the *p* .... Acts 10:43
do you believe the *p* ...... Acts 26:27
by the Law and the *P* ..... Rom 3:21
have killed Your *p* .... Rom 11:3
to be apostles, some *p* ..... Eph 4:11
this salvation the *p* .... 1 Pet 1:10
because many false *p* ..... 1 John 4:1
found the blood of *p* ...... Rev 18:24

PROPITIATION
set forth as a *p* .... Rom 3:25
to God, to make *p* .... Heb 2:17
He Himself is the *p* ...... 1 John 2:2
His Son to be the *p* ..... 1 John 4:10

PROPRIETY
modest apparel, with *p* ... 1 Tim 2:9

PROSPER
they *p* who love you .... Ps 122:6
of the LORD shall *p* .... Is 53:10
against you shall *p* .... Is 54:17
up as he may *p* .... 1 Cor 16:2
I pray that you may *p* ..... 3 John 2

PROSPERED
since the LORD has *p* .....Gen 24:56

PROSPERING
His ways are always *p* ...... Ps 10:5

PROSPERITY
p all your days .... Deut 23:6
p the destroyer .... Job 15:21
Now in my *p* I said .... Ps 30:6
has pleasure in the *p* ...... Ps 35:27
When I saw the *p* .... Ps 73:3
I pray, send now *p* .... Ps 118:25
that we have our *p* ...... Acts 19:25

PROSPEROUS
will make your way *p* ...... Josh 1:8

PROSPERS
just as your soul *p* .... 3 John 2

PROUD
tongue that speaks *p* .... Ps 12:3
And fully repays the *p* ..... Ps 31:23
does not respect the *p* .... Ps 40:4
a haughty look and a *p* .... Ps 101:5
p He knows from afar ..... Ps 138:6
Everyone *p* .... Prov 16:5
by wine, He is a *p* .... Hab 2:5
He has scattered the *p* ....Luke 1:51
"God resists the *p* .... 1 Pet 5:5

PROVERB
of a drunkard Is a *p* ...... Prov 26:9
one shall take up a *p* .... Mic 2:4
to the true *p* .... 2 Pet 2:22

PROVERBS
three thousand *p* .... 1 Kin 4:32
in order many *p* ....Eccl 12:9

PROVIDE
"My son, God will *p* ....Gen 22:8
"*P* neither gold nor .... Matt 10:9
if anyone does not *p* .... 1 Tim 5:8

PROVIDED
these hands have *p* ...... Acts 20:34
p something better .... Heb 11:40

PROVISION
no *p* for the flesh ....Rom 13:14

PROVOKE
"Do they *p* Me to ....Jer 7:19
you, fathers, do not *p* .... Eph 6:4

PROVOKED
p the Most High .... Ps 78:56
his spirit was *p* .... Acts 17:16
seek its own, is not *p* .... 1 Cor 13:5

PRUDENCE
To give *p* to the .... Prov 1:4
wisdom, dwell with *p* .... Prov 8:12
us in all wisdom and *p* ..... Eph 1:8

PRUDENT
p man covers shame .... Prov 12:16
A *p* man conceals .... Prov 12:23
The wisdom of the *p* ..... Prov 14:8
p considers well .... Prov 14:15
heart will be called *p* .... Prov 16:21
p man foresees evil ...... Prov 22:3
Therefore the *p* .... Amos 5:13
from the wise and *p* ..... Matt 11:25

PRUDENTLY
Servant shall deal *p* .... Is 52:13

PRUNES
that bears fruit He *p* ...... John 15:2

PSALM
each of you has a *p* ..... 1 Cor 14:26

PSALMIST
And the sweet *p* ....2 Sam 23:1

PSALMS
to one another in *p* ....Eph 5:19
Let him sing *p* ....James 5:13

PUNISH
p the righteous is .... Prov 17:26
Shall I not *p* them for .... Jer 5:9

PUNISHED
p them often in every .... Acts 26:11
These shall be *p* .... 2 Thess 1:9

PUNISHES
will you say when He *p* ...Jer 13:21

PUNISHMENT
p is greater than I ....Gen 4:13
you do in the day of *p* .... Is 10:3
p they shall perish ....Jer 10:15
not turn away its *p* .... Amos 1:3
into everlasting *p* .... Matt 25:46
p which was inflicted ..... 2 Cor 2:6
Of how much worse *p* ....Heb 10:29
sent by him for the *p* ..... 1 Pet 2:14
the unjust under *p* .... 2 Pet 2:9

PURE
a mercy seat of *p* gold ..... Ex 25:17
'My doctrine is *p* .... Job 11:4
that he could be *p* .... Job 15:14
of the LORD are *p* .... Ps 12:6
ways of a man are *p* ...... Prov 16:2
a generation that is *p* .... Prov 30:12
things indeed are *p* ...... Rom 14:20
whatever things are *p* .... Phil 4:8
keep yourself *p* .... 1 Tim 5:22
p all things are *p* .... Titus 1:15
above is first *p* ....James 3:17
babes, desire the *p* .... 1 Pet 2:2
just as He is *p* .... 1 John 3:3

PURER
p eyes than to behold .....Hab 1:13

PURGE
P me with hyssop .... Ps 51:7

PURGED
away, And your sin *p* .... Is 6:7

PURIFICATION
with the water of *p* ......Num 31:23

PURIFIED
all things are *p* ....Heb 9:22
Since you have *p* .... 1 Pet 1:22

PURIFIES
hope in Him *p* himself ... 1 John 3:3

PURIFY
and *p* your hearts ....James 4:8

PURIFYING
p their hearts by .... Acts 15:9
sanctifies for the *p* ....Heb 9:13

PURIM
called these days *P* .... Esth 9:26

PURITY
spirit, in faith, in *p* ...... 1 Tim 4:12

PURPOSE
A time for every *p* ....Eccl 3:1
But for this *p* I came ....John 12:27
by the determined *p* ...... Acts 2:23
to fulfill His *p* ....Rev 17:17

PURSUE
p righteousness .... Rom 9:30
P love .... 1 Cor 14:1

PURSUES
flee when no one *p* .... Prov 28:1

Q

QUAIL
and it brought *q* ....Num 11:31

QUARREL
He will not *q* nor cry .... Matt 12:19
the Lord must not *q* ...... 2 Tim 2:24

QUARRELSOME
but gentle, not *q* .... 1 Tim 3:3

QUEEN
heart, 'I sit as *q* ....Rev 18:7

QUENCH
Many waters cannot *q* .....Song 8:7
flax He will not *q* .... Matt 12:20
q all the fiery ....Eph 6:16
Do not *q* the Spirit .... 1 Thess 5:19

QUENCHED
that shall never be *q* .... Mark 9:43

QUESTIONS
and asking them *q* ....Luke 2:46

QUICKLY
with your adversary *q* .... Matt 5:25
"Surely I am coming *q* ...Rev 22:20

QUIET
aspire to lead a *q* ...... 1 Thess 4:11
a gentle and *q* spirit .... 1 Pet 3:4

QUIETNESS
a handful with *q* ....Eccl 4:6
In *q* and confidence .... Is 30:15
of righteousness, *q* .... Is 32:17
that they work in *q* .... 2 Thess 3:12

R

RABBI
be called by men, '*R* ...... Matt 23:7

RACA
to his brother, '*R* .... Matt 5:22

RACE
man to run its *r* .... Ps 19:5
r is not to the swift ....Eccl 9:11
I have finished the *r* ...... 2 Tim 4:7
with endurance the *r* ......Heb 12:1

RAGE
Why do the nations *r* ....Ps 2:1
'Why did the nations *r* .... Acts 4:25

RAIN
had not caused it to *r* ....Gen 2:5
And the *r* was on the ....Gen 7:12
I will *r* down on him .....Ezek 38:22
given you the former *r* .... Joel 2:23
the good, and sends *r* .... Matt 5:45
"and the *r* descended ..... Matt 7:25
r that often comes .... Heb 6:7
that it would not *r* ....James 5:17

RAINBOW
"I set My *r* in the ....Gen 9:13
and there was a *r* .... Rev 4:3

RAINED
r fire and brimstone .....Luke 17:29

RAINS
r righteousness ....Hos 10:12

RAISE
third day He will *r* .... Hos 6:2
in three days I will *r* .... John 2:19
and I will *r* him up at ..... John 6:40
and the Lord will *r* ......James 5:15

RAISED
be killed, and be *r* ....Matt 16:21
Just as Christ was *r* .... Rom 6:4
Spirit of Him who *r* .... Rom 8:11
"How are the dead *r* ... 1 Cor 15:35
the dead will be *r* ...... 1 Cor 15:52
and *r* us up together .... Eph 2:6

RAISES
"For as the Father *r* ....John 5:21
but in God who *r* .... 2 Cor 1:9

RAN
You *r* well .... Gal 5:7

RANSOM
to give His life a *r* ...... Mark 10:45
who gave Himself a *r* ..... 1 Tim 2:6

RANSOMED
And the *r* of the LORD .... Is 35:10
redeemed Jacob, And *r* ....Jer 31:11

RASH
Do not be *r* with your ......Eccl 5:2

RASHLY
and do nothing *r* .... Acts 19:36

RAVENOUS
inwardly they are *r* .... Matt 7:15

RAVENS
“Consider the *r* .... Luke 12:24

REACHING
r forward to those .... Phil 3:13

READ
day, and stood up to *r* .... Luke 4:16
hearts, known and *r* ...... 2 Cor 3:2

READER
the *r* understand .... Mark 13:14

READINESS
the word with all *r* ...... Acts 17:11

READING
r the prophet Isaiah ...... Acts 8:30

READS
Blessed is he who *r* .... Rev 1:3

READY
and those who were *r* ... Matt 25:10
“Lord, I am *r* .... Luke 22:33
Be *r* in season and out .... 2 Tim 4:2
and always be *r* .... 1 Pet 3:15

REAP
they neither sow nor *r* .... Matt 6:26
you knew that I *r* .... Matt 25:26

REAPED
You have *r* iniquity .... Hos 10:13

REAPERS
r are the angels .... Matt 13:39

REAPING
r what I did not .... Luke 19:22

REAPS
sows and another *r* .... John 4:37

REASON
“Come now, and let us *r* ..... Is 1:18
who asks you a *r* .... 1 Pet 3:15

REASONED
for three Sabbaths *r* ...... Acts 17:2

REBEL
if you refuse and *r* .... Is 1:20

REBELLING
more against Him By *r* .... Ps 78:17

REBELLION
hearts as in the *r* .... Heb 3:8

REBELLIOUS
day long to a *r* people .... Is 65:2

REBUILD
God, to *r* its ruins .... Ezra 9:9
r it as in the days of ..... Amos 9:11

REBUKE
Turn at my *r* .... Prov 1:23
R a wise man .... Prov 9:8
r is better Than love ...... Prov 27:5
R the oppressor .... Is 1:17
sins against you, *r* .... Luke 17:3
Do not *r* an older man .... 1 Tim 5:1
who are sinning *r* .... 1 Tim 5:20
“The Lord *r* you .... Jude 9
“As many as I love, I *r* ..... Rev 3:19

REBUKED
r the winds and the .... Matt 8:26
r their unbelief .... Mark 16:14
but he was *r* for his ...... 2 Pet 2:16

REBUKES
ear that hears the *r* ...... Prov 15:31

RECEIVE
believing, you will *r* ..... Matt 21:22
and His own did not *r* .... John 1:11
will come again and *r* .... John 14:3
the world cannot *r* ...... John 14:17
Ask, and you will *r* ...... John 16:24
“*R* the Holy Spirit .... John 20:22
“Lord Jesus, *r* .... Acts 7:59
r the Holy Spirit .... Acts 19:2
R one who is weak .... Rom 14:1
r the Spirit by the .... Gal 3:2
suppose that he will *r* .... James 1:7

RECEIVED
But as many as *r* .... John 1:12
for God has *r* him .... Rom 14:3
For I *r* from the Lord ... 1 Cor 11:23
r Christ .... Col 2:6
R up in glory .... 1 Tim 3:16

RECEIVES
r you *r* Me .... Matt 10:40
and whoever *r* Me .... Mark 9:37

RECONCILE
and that He might *r* .... Eph 2:16

RECONCILED
First be *r* to your .... Matt 5:24
we were *r* .... Rom 5:10
Christ's behalf, be *r* ...... 2 Cor 5:20

RECONCILIATION
now received the *r* .... Rom 5:11
to us the word of *r* ...... 2 Cor 5:19

RECONCILING
cast away is the *r* .... Rom 11:15
God was in Christ *r* ..... 2 Cor 5:19

REDEEM
But God will *r* my soul .... Ps 49:15
r their life from .... Ps 72:14
was going to *r* Israel .... Luke 24:21
r those who were .... Gal 4:5
us, that He might *r* .... Titus 2:14

REDEEMED
Let the *r* of the LORD ...... Ps 107:2
r shall walk there .... Is 35:9
sea a road For the *r* .... Is 51:10
And you shall be *r* .... Is 52:3
and *r* His people .... Luke 1:68
Christ has *r* us from .... Gal 3:13
that you were not *r* .... 1 Pet 1:18
were slain, And have *r* ..... Rev 5:9

REDEEMER
For I know that my *R* ..... Job 19:25
Our *R* from Everlasting .... Is 63:16

REDEEMING
r the time .... Eph 5:16

REDEMPTION
those who looked for *r* ... Luke 2:38
your *r* draws near .... Luke 21:28
grace through the *r* .... Rom 3:24
the adoption, the *r* .... Rom 8:23
sanctification and *r* ..... 1 Cor 1:30
In Him we have *r* .... Eph 1:7
for the day of *r* .... Eph 4:30
obtained eternal *r* .... Heb 9:12

REED
r He will not break .... Is 42:3
r shaken by the wind ..... Matt 11:7

REFINED
us as silver is *r* .... Ps 66:10

REFINER
He will sit as a *r* .... Mal 3:3

REFORMATION
until the time of *r* .... Heb 9:10

REFRESH
r my heart in the Lord .... Philem 20

REFRESHED
his spirit has been *r* ..... 2 Cor 7:13
for he often *r* .... 2 Tim 1:16

REFRESHES
r the soul of his .... Prov 25:13

REFRESHING
r may come from the ..... Acts 3:19

REFUGE
eternal God is your *r* .... Deut 33:27
God is our *r* and .... Ps 46:1
who have fled for *r* .... Heb 6:18

REGARD
r iniquity in my heart ..... Ps 66:18
did not fear God nor *r* .... Luke 18:2

REGARDED
my hand and no one *r* .... Prov 1:24
r the lowly state .... Luke 1:48

REGARDS
r a rebuke will be .... Prov 13:18

REGENERATION
to you, that in the *r* ...... Matt 19:28
the washing of *r* .... Titus 3:5

REGISTERED
So all went to be *r* .... Luke 2:3

REGRETTED
but afterward he *r* .... Matt 21:29

REGULATIONS
yourselves to *r* .... Col 2:20

REIGN
“And He will *r* .... Luke 1:33
righteousness will *r* ...... Rom 5:17
so grace might *r* .... Rom 5:21
do not let sin *r* .... Rom 6:12
For He must *r* till He ... 1 Cor 15:25
of Christ, and shall *r* ...... Rev 20:6

REIGNED
so that as sin *r* .... Rom 5:21
You have *r* as kings ...... 1 Cor 4:8
And they lived and *r* ...... Rev 20:4

REIGNS
to Zion, “Your God *r* .... Is 52:7
Lord God Omnipotent *r* ... Rev 19:6

REJECT
“All too well you *r* .... Mark 7:9
R a divisive man .... Titus 3:10

REJECTED
He is despised and *r* .... Is 53:3
r Has become the .... Matt 21:42
many things and be *r* .... Luke 17:25
Moses whom they *r* ...... Acts 7:35
to a living stone, *r* .... 1 Pet 2:4

REJECTION
you shall know My *r* .... Num 14:34

REJECTS
he who *r* Me *r* .... Luke 10:16

REJOICE
R in the LORD .... Ps 33:1
of Your wings I will *r* .... Ps 63:7
Let them *r* before God ...... Ps 68:3
Let the heavens *r* .... Ps 96:11
Let the earth *r* .... Ps 97:1
We will *r* and be glad .... Ps 118:24
She shall *r* in time to .... Prov 31:25
R, O young man .... Eccl 11:9
your heart shall *r* .... Is 66:14
Do not *r* over me .... Mic 7:8
do not *r* .... Luke 10:20
you would *r* .... John 14:28
but the world will *r* ...... John 16:20
and your heart will *r* .... John 16:22
R with those who .... Rom 12:15
and in this I *r* .... Phil 1:18
faith, I am glad and *r* ...... Phil 2:17
R in the Lord always .... Phil 4:4
R always .... 1 Thess 5:16
yet believing, you *r* .... 1 Pet 1:8

REJOICED
And my spirit has *r* ...... Luke 1:47
In that hour Jesus *r* ..... Luke 10:21
Abraham *r* .... John 8:56

REJOICES
glad, and my glory *r* .... Ps 16:9
but *r* in the truth .... 1 Cor 13:6

REJOICING
come again with *r* .... Ps 126:6
he went on his way *r* ..... Acts 8:39
confidence and the *r* .... Heb 3:6

RELENT
sworn And will not *r* ...... Ps 110:4
sworn And will not *r* ...... Heb 7:21

RELENTED
and God *r* from the .... Jon 3:10

RELENTING
I am weary of *r* .... Jer 15:6

RELIGION
in self-imposed *r* .... Col 2:23
and undefiled *r* .... James 1:27

RELIGIOUS
things you are very *r* .... Acts 17:22

REMAIN
that My joy may *r* .... John 15:11
your fruit should *r* .... John 15:16
“If I will that he *r* .... John 21:22
the greater part *r* .... 1 Cor 15:6
are alive and *r* .... 1 Thess 4:15
the things which *r* .... Rev 3:2

REMAINS
“While the earth *r* .... Gen 8:22
Therefore your sin *r* .... John 9:41
There *r* therefore a .... Heb 4:9

REMEMBER
“*R* the Sabbath day .... Ex 20:8
But we will *r* the name ...... Ps 20:7
r Your name in the .... Ps 119:55

R now your Creator .... Eccl 12:1
r the former things .... Is 43:18
and their sin I will *r* .... Jer 31:34
In wrath *r* mercy .... Hab 3:2
And to *r* His holy .... Luke 1:72
"*R* Lot's wife .... Luke 17:32
r the words of the .... Acts 20:35
R that Jesus Christ .... 2 Tim 2:8
R those who rule .... Heb 13:7

REMEMBERED
Then God *r* Noah .... Gen 8:1
r His covenant with .... Ex 2:24
r His covenant forever .... Ps 105:8
yea, we wept When we *r* .. Ps 137:1
And Peter *r* the word .... Matt 26:75
r the word of the Lord ... Acts 11:16

REMEMBRANCE
r my song in the night ...... Ps 77:6
Put Me in *r* .... Is 43:26
do this in *r* of Me .... Luke 22:19
do this in *r* of Me ...... 1 Cor 11:24

REMISSION
for the *r* .... Mark 1:4
Jesus Christ for the *r* ..... Acts 2:38
where there is *r* .... Heb 10:18

REMNANT
The *r* will return .... Is 10:21
time there is a *r* .... Rom 11:5

REMORSEFUL
condemned, was *r* .... Matt 27:3

REMOVE
r this cup from Me ...... Luke 22:42
r your lampstand .... Rev 2:5

REMOVED
Though the earth be *r* ...... Ps 46:2
And the hills be *r* .... Is 54:10
this mountain, 'Be *r* ..... Matt 21:21

REND
So *r* your heart .... Joel 2:13

RENDER
What shall I *r* to the ...... Ps 116:12
"*R* therefore to Caesar .. Matt 22:21

RENEW
r a steadfast .... Ps 51:10
on the LORD Shall *r* .... Is 40:31

RENEWED
that your youth is *r* .... Ps 103:5
inward man is being *r* ... 2 Cor 4:16
and be *r* in the spirit ...... Eph 4:23

RENEWING
transformed by the *r* ..... Rom 12:2

RENOWN
were of old, men of *r* .... Gen 6:4

REPAID
Shall evil be *r* .... Jer 18:20

REPAY
again, I will *r* .... Luke 10:35
they cannot *r* .... Luke 14:14
R no one evil for evil .... Rom 12:17
is Mine, I will *r* .... Rom 12:19
r their parents .... 1 Tim 5:4

REPAYS
the LORD, Who fully *r* .... Is 66:6

REPENT
I abhor myself, And *r* ...... Job 42:6
"*R*, for the kingdom .... Matt 3:2
you *r* you will all .... Luke 13:3
said to them, "*R* .... Acts 2:38
men everywhere to *r* .... Acts 17:30
be zealous and *r* .... Rev 3:19

REPENTANCE
you with water unto *r* .... Matt 3:11
a baptism of *r* for the ...... Mark 1:4
persons who need no *r* ... Luke 15:7
renew them again to *r* ...... Heb 6:6
found no place for *r* ...... Heb 12:17
all should come to *r* .... 2 Pet 3:9

REPENTED
it, because they *r* .... Matt 12:41

REPETITIONS
r as the heathen do .... Matt 6:7

REPORT
Who has believed our *r* ...... Is 53:1
things are of good *r* .... Phil 4:8

REPROACH
R has broken my heart .... Ps 69:20
with dishonor comes *r* .... Prov 18:3
not remember the *r* .... Is 54:4
Because I bore the *r* .... Jer 31:19
these things You *r* .... Luke 11:45
lest he fall into *r* .... 1 Tim 3:7
esteeming the *r* .... Heb 11:26
and without *r* .... James 1:5

REPROACHED
If you are *r* for the .... 1 Pet 4:14

REPROACHES
is not an enemy who *r* ..... Ps 55:12
in infirmities, in *r* ...... 2 Cor 12:10

REPROOF
for doctrine, for *r* .... 2 Tim 3:16

REPROOFS
R of instruction are ...... Prov 6:23

REPUTATION
seven men of good *r* .... Acts 6:3
made Himself of no *r* .... Phil 2:7

REQUEST
He gave them their *r* ..... Ps 106:15
For Jews *r* a sign .... 1 Cor 1:22

REQUESTS
r be made known .... Phil 4:6

REQUIRE
offering You did not *r* .... Ps 40:6
what does the LORD *r* ...... Mic 6:8

REQUIRED
your soul will be *r* .... Luke 12:20
him much will be *r* ...... Luke 12:48

REQUIREMENTS
keeps the righteous *r* ..... Rom 2:26
r that was against us ...... Col 2:14

RESERVED
"I have *r* for Myself ...... Rom 11:4
r in heaven for you .... 1 Pet 1:4
habitation, He has *r* .... Jude 6

RESIST
r an evil person .... Matt 5:39
r the Holy Spirit .... Acts 7:51
R the devil and he .... James 4:7

RESISTED
For who has *r* His will .... Rom 9:19
for he has greatly *r* ...... 2 Tim 4:15
You have not yet *r* .... Heb 12:4

RESISTS
"God *r* the proud .... James 4:6
for "God *r* the proud .... 1 Pet 5:5

RESPECT
of the law held in *r* .... Acts 5:34
and we paid them *r* .... Heb 12:9

RESPECTED
And the LORD *r* Abel .... Gen 4:4

REST
is the Sabbath of *r* .... Ex 31:15
to build a house of *r* ...... 1 Chr 28:2
R in the LORD .... Ps 37:7
fly away and be at *r* .... Ps 55:6
"This is the *r* .... Is 28:12
is the place of My *r* .... Is 66:1
and I will give you *r* ..... Matt 11:28
shall not enter My *r* .... Heb 3:11
remains therefore a *r* .... Heb 4:9
that they should *r* .... Rev 6:11
"that they may *r* .... Rev 14:13
But the *r* of the dead .... Rev 20:5

RESTED
He had done, and He *r* ...... Gen 2:2
"And God *r* on the .... Heb 4:4

RESTORATION
until the times of *r* .... Acts 3:21

RESTORE
R to me the joy .... Ps 51:12
"So I will *r* to you .... Joel 2:25
and will *r* all things ..... Matt 17:11
You at this time *r* .... Acts 1:6
who are spiritual *r* .... Gal 6:1

RESTORES
He *r* my soul .... Ps 23:3

RESTRAINS
only He who now *r* ..... 2 Thess 2:7

RESTRAINT
They break all *r* .... Hos 4:2

RESTS
r quietly in the heart .... Prov 14:33

RESURRECTION
to her, "I am the *r* .... John 11:25
them Jesus and the *r* ..... Acts 17:18
the likeness of His *r* .... Rom 6:5
say that there is no *r* ... 1 Cor 15:12
and the power of His *r* .... Phil 3:10
obtain a better *r* .... Heb 11:35
This is the first *r* .... Rev 20:5

RETAIN
r the sins of any .... John 20:23

RETURN
womb, naked shall he *r* ... Eccl 5:15
Let him *r* to the LORD .... Is 55:7
me, and I will *r* .... Jer 31:18
"*R* to Me .... Zech 1:3
he says, 'I will *r* .... Matt 12:44

RETURNED
astray, but have now *r* .... 1 Pet 2:25

RETURNING
r evil for evil or .... 1 Pet 3:9

RETURNS
As a dog *r* to his own .... Prov 26:11
"A dog *r* to his own ...... 2 Pet 2:22

REVEAL
the Son wills to *r* Him ... Matt 11:27
r His Son in me .... Gal 1:16

REVEALED
things which are *r* .... Deut 29:29
righteousness to be *r* .... Is 56:1
the Son of Man is *r* ...... Luke 17:30
the wrath of God is *r* ..... Rom 1:18
glory which shall be *r* .... Rom 8:18
the Lord Jesus is *r* ..... 2 Thess 1:7
lawless one will be *r* ... 2 Thess 2:8
ready to be *r* in the .... 1 Pet 1:5
when His glory is *r* .... 1 Pet 4:13
r what we shall be .... 1 John 3:2

REVEALER
Lord of kings, and a *r* ..... Dan 2:47

REVEALING
waits for the *r* .... Rom 8:19

REVEALS
as a talebearer *r* .... Prov 20:19
r His secret to His .... Amos 3:7

REVELATION
Where there is no *r* ...... Prov 29:18
it came through the *r* ...... Gal 1:12
spirit of wisdom and *r* ..... Eph 1:17
r He made known to .... Eph 3:3
and glory at the *r* .... 1 Pet 1:7

REVERENCE
and *r* My sanctuary ...... Lev 19:30
God acceptably with *r* .... Heb 12:28

REVERENT
man who is always *r* ...... Prov 28:14
their wives must be *r* ..... 1 Tim 3:11

REVILE
are you when they *r* ...... Matt 5:11
r God's high priest .... Acts 23:4

REVILED
crucified with Him *r* ... Mark 15:32
who, when He was *r* ...... 1 Pet 2:23

REVIVAL
give us a measure of *r* ..... Ezra 9:8

REVIVE
Will You not *r* us .... Ps 85:6
two days He will *r* .... Hos 6:2

REVIVED
came, sin *r* and I died ..... Rom 7:9

REWARD
exceedingly great *r* .... Gen 15:1
look, And see the *r* .... Ps 91:8
Behold, His *r* is with .... Is 40:10
for great is your *r* .... Matt 5:12
you, they have their *r* ..... Matt 6:2
no means lose his *r* ..... Matt 10:42
we receive the due *r* ..... Luke 23:41
will receive his own *r* .... 1 Cor 3:8
cheat you of your *r* .... Col 2:18
for he looked to the *r* ..... Heb 11:26
quickly, and My *r* .... Rev 22:12

REWARDS
Whoever *r* evil for ...... Prov 17:13
And follows after *r* .... Is 1:23

RICH
Abram was very *r* ....Gen 13:2
The *r* and the poor .... Prov 22:2
r rules over the poor ..... Prov 22:7
r man is wise in his .... Prov 28:11
Do not curse the *r* .... Eccl 10:20
it is hard for a *r* .... Matt 19:23
to you who are *r* ....Luke 6:24
the *r* man's table ....Luke 16:21
for he was very *r* ....Luke 18:23
You are already *r* .... 1 Cor 4:8
though He was *r* .... 2 Cor 8:9
who desire to be *r* .... 1 Tim 6:9
of this world to be *r* ......James 2:5
you say, 'I am *r* .... Rev 3:17

RICHES
R and honor are .... Prov 8:18
R do not profit .... Prov 11:4
in his *r* will fall .... Prov 11:28
of the wise is their *r* ...... Prov 14:24
and *r* are an .... Prov 19:14
of the LORD Are *r* .... Prov 22:4
r are not forever ....Prov 27:24
do you despise the *r* .... Rom 2:4
make known the *r* .... Rom 9:23
what are the *r* ....Eph 1:18
show the exceeding *r* .... Eph 2:7
the unsearchable *r* ....Eph 3:8
r than the treasures ......Heb 11:26
To receive power and *r* .... Rev 5:12

RICHLY
Christ dwell in you *r* ...... Col 3:16
God, who gives us *r* ......1 Tim 6:17

RIGHT
the *r* of the firstborn ....Deut 21:17
"Is your heart *r* .... 2 Kin 10:15
Lord, "Sit at My *r* .... Ps 110:1
a way which seems *r* .... Prov 14:12
clothed and in his *r* ..... Mark 5:15
to them He gave the *r* .... John 1:12
your heart is not *r* .... Acts 8:21
seven stars in His *r* .... Rev 2:1

RIGHTEOUS
also destroy the *r* ....Gen 18:23
and they justify the *r* ..... Deut 25:1
that he could be *r* .... Job 15:14
"The *r* see it and .... Job 22:19
r shows mercy and .... Ps 37:21
I have not seen the *r* .... Ps 37:25
The LORD loves the *r* ...... Ps 146:8
r is a well of life .... Prov 10:11
r will be gladness .... Prov 10:28
r will be delivered .... Prov 11:21
r will be recompensed ... Prov 11:31
the prayer of the *r* .... Prov 15:29
r are bold as a lion .... Prov 28:1
r considers the cause ..... Prov 29:7
Do not be overly *r* ....Eccl 7:16
event happens to the *r* ......Eccl 9:2
with My *r* right hand .... Is 41:10
By His knowledge My *r* .... Is 53:11
The *r* perishes .... Is 57:1
they sell the *r* .... Amos 2:6
not come to call the *r* ...... Matt 9:13
r men desired to see ..... Matt 13:17
r will shine forth as ..... Matt 13:43
that they were *r* ....Luke 18:9
this was a *r* ....Luke 23:47
"There is none *r* .... Rom 3:10
r man will one die .... Rom 5:7
Jesus Christ the *r* .... 1 John 2:1

RIGHTEOUSLY
should live soberly, *r* ..... Titus 2:12
to Him who judges *r* ..... 1 Pet 2:23

RIGHTEOUSNESS
it to him for *r* ....Gen 15:6
I put on *r* .... Job 29:14
I call, O God of my *r* ....Ps 4:1
from the LORD, And *r* ...... Ps 24:5
shall speak of Your *r* ...... Ps 35:28
the good news of *r* .... Ps 40:9
heavens declare His *r* ...... Ps 50:6
R and peace have .... Ps 85:10
R will go before Him ...... Ps 85:13
r endures forever .... Ps 111:3
r delivers from death ..... Prov 10:2
The *r* of the blameless .... Prov 11:5
the way of *r* is life .... Prov 12:28
R exalts a nation .... Prov 14:34
He who follows *r* .... Prov 21:21
R lodged in it .... Is 1:21
in the LORD I have *r* .... Is 45:24
r will be forever .... Is 51:8
I will declare your *r* .... Is 57:12
r as a breastplate .... Is 59:17
r goes forth as .... Is 62:1
The Lord Our *R* ....Jer 23:6
to David A Branch of *r* ....Jer 33:15
The *r* of the righteous ...Ezek 18:20
who turn many to *r* ....Dan 12:3
to fulfill all *r* .... Matt 3:15
exceeds the *r* of the .... Matt 5:20
to you in the way of *r* .... Matt 21:32
For in it the *r* .... Rom 1:17
even the *r* of God .... Rom 3:22
accounted to him for *r* .... Rom 4:22
r will reign in life .... Rom 5:17
might reign through *r* .... Rom 5:21
ignorant of God's *r* .... Rom 10:3
might become the *r* ...... 2 Cor 5:21
the breastplate of *r* ....Eph 6:14
not having my own *r* .... Phil 3:9
r which we have .... Titus 3:5
not produce the *r* ....James 1:20
a preacher of *r* .... 2 Pet 2:5
a new earth in which *r* ... 2 Pet 3:13
who practices *r* .... 1 John 2:29
He who practices *r* ...... 1 John 3:7

RIGHTLY
wise uses knowledge *r* ... Prov 15:2
r dividing the word ...... 2 Tim 2:15

RISE
for He makes His sun *r* ... Matt 5:45
third day He will *r* .... Matt 20:19
third day He will *r* ....Luke 18:33
be the first to *r* .... Acts 26:23
in Christ will *r* .... 1 Thess 4:16

RISEN
there has not *r* .... Matt 11:11
disciples that He is *r* ..... Matt 28:7
"The Lord is *r* ....Luke 24:34
then Christ is not *r* ..... 1 Cor 15:13
if Christ is not *r* .... 1 Cor 15:17
But now Christ is *r* ..... 1 Cor 15:20

RIVER
peace to her like a *r* .... Is 66:12
he showed me a pure *r* .... Rev 22:1

RIVERS
By the *r* of Babylon .... Ps 137:1
All the *r* run into the ....Eccl 1:7
his heart will flow *r* ...... John 7:38

ROAR
The LORD also will *r* ......Joel 3:16

ROARING
and the waves *r* ....Luke 21:25
walks about like a *r* .... 1 Pet 5:8

ROARS
"The LORD *r* from .... Amos 1:2
as when a lion *r* .... Rev 10:3

ROB
"Will a man *r* God .... Mal 3:8

ROBBED
r other churches .... 2 Cor 11:8

ROBBER
is a thief and a *r* .... John 10:1
Barabbas was a *r* ....John 18:40

ROBBERS
also crucified two *r* ..... Mark 15:27
Me are thieves and *r* ..... John 10:8

ROBBERY
did not consider it *r* .... Phil 2:6

ROBE
'Bring out the best *r* .....Luke 15:22
on Him a purple *r* ....John 19:2
Then a white *r* was .... Rev 6:11

ROBES
have stained all My *r* .... Is 63:3
go around in long *r* ......Luke 20:46
clothed with white *r* .... Rev 7:9

ROCK
you shall strike the *r* .... Ex 17:6
and struck the *r* ....Num 20:11
For their *r* is not ....Deut 32:31
"The LORD is my *r* ......2 Sam 22:2
And who is a *r* .... 2 Sam 22:32
Blessed be my *R* ...... 2 Sam 22:47
For You are my *r* .... Ps 31:3
r that is higher than .... Ps 61:2
been mindful of the *R* ...... Is 17:10
shadow of a great *r* .... Is 32:2
his house on the *r* .... Matt 7:24
r I will build My .... Matt 16:18
stumbling stone and *r* .... Rom 9:33
R that followed them .... 1 Cor 10:4

ROD
Your *r* and Your staff .... Ps 23:4
shall come forth a *R* .... Is 11:1
rule them with a *r* .... Rev 2:27

ROOM
you a large upper *r* ..... Mark 14:15
no *r* for them in the .... Luke 2:7
into the upper *r* .... Acts 1:13

ROOT
day there shall be a *R* ...... Is 11:10
because they had no *r* .... Matt 13:6
of money is a *r* .... 1 Tim 6:10
lest any *r* of ....Heb 12:15
I am the *R* and the ....Rev 22:16

ROOTED
r and built up in Him ....Col 2:7

ROSE
end Christ died and *r* ..... Rom 14:9
buried, and that He *r* ..... 1 Cor 15:4
Jesus died and *r* .... 1 Thess 4:14

RULE
And he shall *r* ....Gen 3:16
puts an end to all *r* ..... 1 Cor 15:24
let the peace of God *r* ..... Col 3:15
Let the elders who *r* ..... 1 Tim 5:17
Remember those who *r* ....Heb 13:7

RULER
to Me The One to be *r* ...... Mic 5:2
by Beelzebub, the *r* ...... Matt 12:24
the *r* of this world ....John 12:31
'Who made you a *r* .... Acts 7:27

RULERS
And the *r* take counsel ....Ps 2:2
"You know that the *r* .... Matt 20:25
which none of the *r* ...... 1 Cor 2:8
powers, against the *r* ......Eph 6:12

RULES
That the Most High *r* ....Dan 4:17
that the Most High *r* ....Dan 4:32
r his own house well ..... 1 Tim 3:4

RULING
r their children .... 1 Tim 3:12

RUMORS
hear of wars and *r* .... Matt 24:6

RUN
r and not be weary ....Is 40:31
us, and let us *r* ....Heb 12:1

S

SABAOTH
S had left us a ....Rom 9:29
ears of the Lord of *S* .....James 5:4

SABBATH
"Remember the *S* .... Ex 20:8
S was made for man .... Mark 2:27

SABBATHS
S you shall keep .... Ex 31:13

SACRIFICE
to the LORD than *s* .... Prov 21:3
For the LORD has a *s* .... Is 34:6
of My offerings they *s* ..... Hos 8:13
LORD has prepared a *s* .... Zeph 1:7
desire mercy and not *s* ... Matt 9:13
an offering and a *s* .... Eph 5:2
put away sin by the *s* ......Heb 9:26
no longer remains a *s* ....Heb 10:26
offer the *s* of praise ......Heb 13:15

SACRIFICED
s their sons And their .... Ps 106:37

SACRIFICES
The *s* of God are a .... Ps 51:17
multitude of your *s* .... Is 1:11
priests, to offer up *s* ....Heb 7:27
s God is well pleased .....Heb 13:16

SAFE
he has received him *s* ...Luke 15:27

SAFELY
make them lie down *s* .....Hos 2:18

SAFETY
say, "Peace and *s* .... 1 Thess 5:3

SAINTS
s who are on the earth ...... Ps 16:3
does not forsake His *s* ..... Ps 37:28
Is the death of His *s* ...... Ps 116:15
war against the *s* ....Dan 7:21
Jesus, called to be *s* ...... 1 Cor 1:2
the least of all the *s* .... Eph 3:8
be glorified in His *s* ... 2 Thess 1:10
all delivered to the *s* ....Jude 3
shed the blood of *s* .... Rev 16:6

SALT
shall season with *s* .... Lev 2:13
"You are the *s* .... Matt 5:13
s loses its flavor .... Mark 9:50

SALVATION
still, and see the *s* .... Ex 14:13
S belongs to the LORD ....Ps 3:8
is my light and my *s* .... Ps 27:1
God is the God of *s* .... Ps 68:20
joy in the God of my *s* .....Hab 3:18
raised up a horn of *s* .....Luke 1:69
"Nor is there *s* .... Acts 4:12
the power of God to *s* .... Rom 1:16
now is the day of *s* .... 2 Cor 6:2
work out your own *s* ......Phil 2:12
chose you for *s* .... 2 Thess 2:13
neglect so great a *s* ....Heb 2:3

SAMARITAN
a drink from me, a *S* ...... John 4:9

SANCTIFICATION
will of God, your *s* ..... 1 Thess 4:3

SANCTIFIED
they also may be *s* ......John 17:19
but you were *s* .... 1 Cor 6:11
for it is *s* by the .... 1 Tim 4:5

SANCTIFIES
For both He who *s* ....Heb 2:11

SANCTIFY
s My great name ....Ezek 36:23
"*S* them by Your ....John 17:17
that He might *s* ....Eph 5:26

SANCTUARY
let them make Me a *s* ...... Ex 25:8
and the earthly *s* ....Heb 9:1

SAND
descendants as the *s* .....Gen 32:12
innumerable as the *s* .....Heb 11:12

SAT
into heaven, and *S* ..... Mark 16:19
And He who *s* there was ... Rev 4:3

SATAN
before the LORD, and *S* ..... Job 1:6
"Away with you, *S* .... Matt 4:10
"Get behind Me, *S* ...... Matt 16:23
"How can *S* cast out .... Mark 3:23
S has asked for you .....Luke 22:31
to the working of *S* ..... 2 Thess 2:9
known the depths of *S* .... Rev 2:24
years have expired, *S* ..... Rev 20:7

SATIATED
s the weary soul ....Jer 31:25

SATISFIED
I shall be *s* when I .... Ps 17:15
that are never *s* ....Prov 30:15
of His soul, and be *s* ....Is 53:11

SATISFIES
s the longing soul .... Ps 107:9

SATISFY
s us early with Your .... Ps 90:14
long life I will *s* .... Ps 91:16
for what does not *s* .... Is 55:2

SAVE
Oh, *s* me for Your ....Ps 6:4
s the children of the .... Ps 72:4
s the souls of the .... Ps 72:13
That it cannot *s* .... Is 59:1
s you And deliver you .....Jer 15:20
other, That he may *s* .....Hos 13:10
JESUS, for He will *s* ...... Matt 1:21
s his life will .... Matt 16:25
s that which was .... Matt 18:11
let Him *s* Himself if ......Luke 23:35
but to *s* the world ....John 12:47
the world to *s* sinners .... 1 Tim 1:15

SAVED
"He *s* others .... Matt 27:42
That we should be *s* ......Luke 1:71
"Your faith has *s* ....Luke 7:50
might be *s* ....John 3:17
them, saying, "Be *s* ...... Acts 2:40
what must I do to be *s* ... Acts 16:30
which also you are *s* ..... 1 Cor 15:2
grace you have been *s* ...... Eph 2:8
to His mercy He *s* .... Titus 3:5
of those who are *s* ....Rev 21:24

SAVES
antitype which now *s* .... 1 Pet 3:21

SAVIOR
I, the LORD, am your *S* ..... Is 60:16
rejoiced in God my *S* .....Luke 1:47
the city of David a *S* ......Luke 2:11
up for Israel a *S* .... Acts 13:23
God, who is the *S* .... 1 Tim 4:10
and *S* Jesus Christ .... Titus 2:13

SAWN
stoned, they were *s* ....Heb 11:37

SAY
"But I *s* to you that .... Matt 5:22
"But who do you *s* ...... Matt 16:15

SAYING
This is a faithful *s* .... 1 Tim 1:15

SAYINGS
whoever hears these *s* .... Matt 7:24

SCALES
on it had a pair of *s* .... Rev 6:5

SCARLET
your sins are like *s* .... Is 1:18

SCATTER
I will *s* you among the .... Lev 26:33

SCATTERED
"Israel is like *s* sheep ......Jer 50:17
the sheep will be *s* ..... Mark 14:27

SCATTERS
not gather with Me *s* .... Matt 12:30

SCEPTER
s shall not depart ....Gen 49:10

SCHEMER
Will be called a *s* .... Prov 24:8

SCHEMES
sought out many *s* ....Eccl 7:29

SCHISM
there should be no *s* .... 1 Cor 12:25

SCHOOL
daily in the *s* of .... Acts 19:9

SCOFF
They *s* at kings ....Hab 1:10

SCOFFER
"He who corrects a *s* ...... Prov 9:7
s is an abomination ...... Prov 24:9

SCOFFERS
s will come in the .... 2 Pet 3:3

SCORCHED
And men were *s* with ..... Rev 16:9

SCORN
My friends *s* me .... Job 16:20

SCORNS
He *s* the scornful .... Prov 3:34

SCORPIONS
on serpents and *s* ....Luke 10:19
They had tails like *s* .... Rev 9:10

SCOURGE
will mock Him, and *s* ... Mark 10:34

SCOURGES
s every son whom ....Heb 12:6

SCRIBES
"Beware of the *s* .... Mark 12:38

SCRIPTURE
S cannot be broken .....John 10:35
All *S* is given by .... 2 Tim 3:16

SCRIPTURES
S must be fulfilled ...... Mark 14:49

SCROLL
eat this *s* .... Ezek 3:1
the sky receded as a *s* ..... Rev 6:14

SEA
drowned in the Red *S* ...... Ex 15:4
who go down to the *s* .... Ps 107:23
and the *s* obey Him ...... Matt 8:27
throne there was a *s* .... Rev 4:6
there was no more *s* .... Rev 21:1

SEAL
stands, having this *s* .... 2 Tim 2:19

SEALED
by whom you were *s* ......Eph 4:30

SEAM
tunic was without *s* .....John 19:23

SÉANCE
"Please conduct a *s* .....1 Sam 28:8

SEARCH
glory of kings is to *s* ...... Prov 25:2
s the Scriptures .... John 5:39

SEARCHED
s the Scriptures .... Acts 17:11

SEARCHES
For the Spirit *s* .... 1 Cor 2:10

SEASON
Be ready in *s* and out ..... 2 Tim 4:2

SEASONED
how shall it be *s* .... Matt 5:13

SEASONS
the times and the *s* ..... 1 Thess 5:1

SEAT
shall make a mercy *s* ...... Ex 25:17
before the judgment *s* ... 2 Cor 5:10

SEATS
at feasts, the best *s* .... Matt 23:6

SECRET
s things belong ....Deut 29:29
In the *s* place of His .... Ps 27:5
Father who is in the *s* ..... Matt 6:6

SECRETLY
He lies in wait *s* .... Ps 10:9

SECRETS
For He knows the *s* .... Ps 44:21
God will judge the *s* ...... Rom 2:16

SECT
to the strictest *s* .... Acts 26:5

SECURELY
nation that dwells *s* ....Jer 49:31

SEDUCED
flattering lips she *s* .... Prov 7:21

SEE
in my flesh I shall *s* ...... Job 19:26
For they shall *s* God .... Matt 5:8
seeing they do not *s* ..... Matt 13:13
rejoiced to *s* My day ...... John 8:56
They shall *s* His face .... Rev 22:4

SEED
He shall see His *s* .... Is 53:10
S were the promises .... Gal 3:16
you are Abraham's *s* ...... Gal 3:29

SEEDS
the good *s* are the .... Matt 13:38

SEEK
pray and *s* My face ...... 2 Chr 7:14
S the LORD while He .... Is 55:6
s, and you will find .... Matt 7:7
of Man has come to *s* ....Luke 19:10
"You will *s* Me and .... John 7:34
For all *s* their own ....Phil 2:21
s those things which ....Col 3:1

SEEKING
like a roaring lion, *s* .... 1 Pet 5:8

SEEKS
There is none who *s* ...... Rom 3:11

SEEMS
is a way which *s* .... Prov 14:12

SEEN
s God face to face ....Gen 32:30
No one has *s* God at ......John 1:18
s Me has *s* the ....John 14:9
things which are not *s* ... 2 Cor 4:18

SEES
s his brother in need ... 1 John 3:17

SELF-CONFIDENT
a fool rages and is *s* ..... Prov 14:16

SELF-CONTROL
gentleness, *s* .... Gal 5:23
to knowledge *s* .... 2 Pet 1:6

SELF-CONTROLLED
just, holy, *s* .... Titus 1:8

SELF-SEEKING
envy and *s* exist ....James 3:16

SELL
s whatever you have ... Mark 10:21

SEND
"Behold, I *s* you out ..... Matt 10:16
has sent Me, I also *s* .....John 20:21

SENSES
of use have their *s* ....Heb 5:14

SENSIBLY
who can answer *s* .... Prov 26:16

SENSUAL
but is earthly, *s* ....James 3:15

SENT
unless they are *s* ....Rom 10:15

SEPARATED
it pleased God, who *s* ..... Gal 1:15

SEPARATES
who repeats a matter *s* ... Prov 17:9

SEPARATION
the middle wall of *s* ....Eph 2:14

SERAPHIM
Above it stood *s* .... Is 6:2

SERIOUS
therefore be *s* and .... 1 Pet 4:7

SERPENT
s was more cunning ....Gen 3:1
"Make a fiery *s* ....Num 21:8
Moses lifted up the *s* .....John 3:14

SERPENTS
be wise as *s* .... Matt 10:16

SERVANT
s will rule over a son ..... Prov 17:2
good and faithful *s* ...... Matt 25:21

SERVANTS
are unprofitable *s* ....Luke 17:10

SERVE
to be served, but to *s* .... Matt 20:28
but through love *s* .... Gal 5:13

SERVES
"If anyone *s* Me ....John 12:26

SERVICE
is your reasonable *s* ...... Rom 12:1
with good will doing *s* ......Eph 6:7

SERVING
fervent in spirit, *s* ....Rom 12:11

SET
"See, I have *s* ....Deut 30:15
s aside the grace .... Gal 2:21

SETTLE
"Therefore *s* it in ....Luke 21:14

SETTLED
O LORD, Your word is *s* ... Ps 119:89

SEVEN
s churches which are .... Rev 1:4

SEVENTY
"*S* weeks are ....Dan 9:24

SEVERE
not to be too *s* .... 2 Cor 2:5

SEVERITY
the goodness and *s* ......Rom 11:22

SHADE
may nest under its *s* ..... Mark 4:32

SHADOW
In the *s* of His hand .... Is 49:2
the law, having a *s* ....Heb 10:1

SHAKE
s the earth .... Is 2:19
I will *s* all nations ....Hag 2:7

SHAKEN
not to be soon *s* .... 2 Thess 2:2

SHAKES
s the Wilderness .... Ps 29:8

SHAME
never be put to *s* ....Joel 2:26
to put to *s* the wise ...... 1 Cor 1:27
glory is in their *s* ....Phil 3:19

SHAMEFUL
For it is *s* even to ....Eph 5:12

SHARE
to do good and to *s* ....Heb 13:16

SHARING
for your liberal *s* .... 2 Cor 9:13

SHARP
S as a two-edged sword ... Prov 5:4

SHARPEN
s their tongue like a .... Ps 64:3

SHARPENS
My adversary *s* His .... Job 16:9

SHARPNESS
I should use *s* .... 2 Cor 13:10

SHEATH
your sword into the *s* ....John 18:11

SHEAVES
Bringing his *s* .... Ps 126:6
gather them like *s* .... Mic 4:12

SHED
which is *s* for many ..... Matt 26:28

SHEDDING
blood, and without *s* ......Heb 9:22

SHEEP
s will be scattered ....Zech 13:7
having a hundred *s* ....Luke 15:4
and I know My *s* ....John 10:14
"He was led as a *s* ....Acts 8:32

SHEEPFOLDS
lie down among the *s* ..... Ps 68:13

SHEET
object like a great *s* ..... Acts 10:11

SHELTER
the LORD will be a *s* ....Joel 3:16

SHELTERS
s him all the day long ...Deut 33:12

SHEOL
not leave my soul in *S* ..... Ps 16:10
the belly of *S* I cried ....Jon 2:2

SHEPHERD
The LORD is my *S* .... Ps 23:1
His flock like a *s* ....Is 40:11
'I will strike the *S* .... Matt 26:31
"I am the good *s* ....John 10:11
the dead, that great *S* .....Heb 13:20
S the flock of God .... 1 Pet 5:2
when the Chief *S* .... 1 Pet 5:4

SHEPHERDS
"And I will give you *s* ......Jer 3:15
s have led them astray .....Jer 50:6

SHIELD
I am your *s* ....Gen 15:1
truth shall be your *s* .... Ps 91:4
all, taking the *s* ....Eph 6:16

SHINE
LORD make His face *s* ....Num 6:25
among whom you *s* ....Phil 2:15

SHINED
them a light has *s* .... Is 9:2

SHINES
heed as a light that *s* .....2 Pet 1:19

SHINING
light is already *s* .... 1 John 2:8

SHIPS
down to the sea in *s* ...... Ps 107:23

SHIPWRECK
faith have suffered *s* .... 1 Tim 1:19

SHOOT
They *s* out the lip .... Ps 22:7

SHORT
have sinned and fall *s* .... Rom 3:23

SHORTENED
those days were *s* .... Matt 24:22

SHOUT
heaven with a *s* .... 1 Thess 4:16

SHOW
a land that I will *s* ....Gen 12:1
s Him greater works .....John 5:20

SHOWBREAD
s which was not lawful ... Matt 12:4

SHOWERS
make it soft with *s* .... Ps 65:10

SHREWDLY
because he had dealt *s* ...Luke 16:8

SHRINES
who made silver *s* .... Acts 19:24

SHRIVELED
You have *s* me up .... Job 16:8

SHUFFLES
with his eyes, He *s* .... Prov 6:13

SHUNNED
feared God and *s* evil .... Job 1:1

SHUT
For you *s* up the .... Matt 23:13

SHUTS
s his eyes from seeing ...... Is 33:15
who opens and no one *s* .... Rev 3:7

SICK
I was *s* and you .... Matt 25:36
faith will save the *s* ......James 5:15

SICKLE
"Thrust in Your *s* ....Rev 14:15

SICKNESS
will sustain him in *s* ..... Prov 18:14
"This *s* is not unto ....John 11:4

SICKNESSES
And bore our *s* .... Matt 8:17

SIDE
The LORD is on my *s* ...... Ps 118:6

SIFT
s the nations with the ...... Is 30:28

SIGH
our years like a *s* .... Ps 90:9

SIGHING
For my *s* comes before .... Job 3:24

SIGHT
and see this great *s* .... Ex 3:3
by faith, not by *s* .... 2 Cor 5:7

SIGN
will give you a *s* .... Is 7:14
seeks after a *s* .... Matt 12:39
For Jews request a *s* ..... 1 Cor 1:22

SIGNS
and let them be for *s* ......Gen 1:14
cannot discern the *s* ...... Matt 16:3
did many other *s* ....John 20:30

SILENCE
That You may *s* ....Ps 8:2
seal, there was *s* .... Rev 8:1

SILENT
season, and am not *s* .... Ps 22:2

SILK
covered you with *s* ......Ezek 16:10

SILLY
They are *s* children ....Jer 4:22

SILVER
may buy the poor for *s* ... Amos 8:6
him thirty pieces of *s* .... Matt 26:15

SIMILITUDE
been made in the *s* ....James 3:9

SIMPLE
making wise the *s* .... Ps 19:7

SIMPLICITY
corrupted from the *s* .... 2 Cor 11:3

SIN
and be sure your *s* ......Num 32:23
Be angry, and do not *s* ....Ps 4:4
s is always before me ...... Ps 51:3
soul an offering for *s* .... Is 53:10

And He bore the *s* .... Is 53:12
who takes away the *s* ..... John 1:29
"He who is without *s* ...... John 8:7
convict the world of *s* .... John 16:8
s entered the world ...... Rom 5:12
s is not imputed .... Rom 5:13
s shall not have .... Rom 6:14
Shall we *s* because we ... Rom 6:15
Him who knew no *s* ..... 2 Cor 5:21
man of *s* is revealed .... 2 Thess 2:3
we are, yet without *s* ...... Heb 4:15
do it, to him it is *s* .... James 4:17
say that we have no *s* ... 1 John 1:8
and he cannot *s* .... 1 John 3:9

SINCERE
and from *s* faith .... 1 Tim 1:5

SINCERITY
simplicity and godly *s* ... 2 Cor 1:12

SINFUL
from me, for I am a *s* ...... Luke 5:8
become exceedingly *s* .... Rom 7:13

SING
Let him *s* psalms .... James 5:13

SINGERS
The *s* went before .... Ps 68:25

SINGING
His presence with *s* .... Ps 100:2
and spiritual songs, *s* ...... Eph 5:19

SINISTER
Who understands *s* .... Dan 8:23

SINK
I *s* in deep mire .... Ps 69:2
to *s* he cried out .... Matt 14:30

SINNED
You only, have I *s* .... Ps 51:4
"Father, I have *s* .... Luke 15:18
for all have *s* and .... Rom 3:23
that we have not *s* ...... 1 John 1:10

SINNER
s who repents than .... Luke 15:7
the ungodly and the *s* .... 1 Pet 4:18

SINNERS
in the path of *s* .... Ps 1:1
the righteous, but *s* .... Matt 9:13
while we were still *s* .... Rom 5:8
many were made *s* .... Rom 5:19
the world to save *s* ...... 1 Tim 1:15
such hostility from *s* ...... Heb 12:3

SINS
from presumptuous *s* ...... Ps 19:13
You, Our secret *s* .... Ps 90:8
The soul who *s* shall ...... Ezek 18:4
if your brother *s* .... Matt 18:15
s according to the .... 1 Cor 15:3
the forgiveness of *s* .... Eph 1:7
If we confess our *s* ...... 1 John 1:9
propitiation for our *s* .... 1 John 2:2

SISTER
is My brother and *s* ..... Matt 12:50

SIT
but to *s* on My right ..... Matt 20:23
"*S* at My right hand .... Heb 1:13
I will grant to *s* .... Rev 3:21

SITS
It is He who *s* above .... Is 40:22
so that he *s* as God ..... 2 Thess 2:4

SITTING
where Christ is, *s* .... Col 3:1

SKILL
hand forget its *s* .... Ps 137:5

SKILLFULNESS
guided them by the *s* ...... Ps 78:72

SKIN
God made tunics of *s* ...... Gen 3:21
LORD and said, "*S* .... Job 2:4
Ethiopian change his *s* .... Jer 13:23

SKIP
He makes them also *s* ...... Ps 29:6

SKIPPING
upon the mountains, *S* .... Song 2:8

SKULL
to say, Place of a *S* ...... Matt 27:33

SKY
s receded as a scroll .... Rev 6:14

SLACK
The Lord is not *s* .... 2 Pet 3:9

SLAIN
is the Lamb who was *s* .... Rev 5:12

SLANDER
whoever spreads *s* ...... Prov 10:18

SLANDERERS
be reverent, not *s* .... 1 Tim 3:11

SLANDEROUSLY
as we are *s* reported .... Rom 3:8

SLAUGHTER
led as a lamb to the *s* .... Is 53:7
as sheep for the *s* .... Rom 8:36

SLAVE
commits sin is a *s* .... John 8:34

SLAVES
should no longer be *s* ..... Rom 6:6

SLAY
s the righteous .... Gen 18:25

SLEEP
God caused a deep *s* ...... Gen 2:21
neither slumber nor *s* ..... Ps 121:4
He gives His beloved *s* .... Ps 127:2
and many *s* .... 1 Cor 11:30
We shall not all *s* ...... 1 Cor 15:51

SLEEPERS
gently the lips of *s* .... Song 7:9

SLEEPING
"Are you still *s* .... Matt 26:45

SLEEPLESSNESS
in labors, in *s* .... 2 Cor 6.5

SLEEPS
"Our friend Lazarus *s* ... John 11:11

SLEPT
I lay down and *s* .... Ps 3:5

SLIGHTED
is the one who is *s* .... Prov 12:9

SLING
he had, and his *s* ...... 1 Sam 17:40

SLIP
Their foot shall *s* .... Deut 32:35

SLIPPERY
set them in *s* places .... Ps 73:18

SLOOPS
all the beautiful *s* .... Is 2:16

SLOW
hear, *s* to speak, *s* ...... James 1:19

SLUGGARD
will you slumber, O *s* ...... Prov 6:9

SLUMBERING
upon men, While *s* .... Job 33:15

SMALL
And I saw the dead, *s* .... Rev 20:12

SMELL
and he smelled the *s* ..... Gen 27:27

SMELLS
s the battle from afar ..... Job 39:25

SMITTEN
Him stricken, *S* .... Is 53:4

SMOKE
was filled with *s* .... Rev 15:8

SMOOTH
And the rough places *s* ...... Is 40:4

SMOOTH-SKINNED
man, and I am a *s* .... Gen 27:11

SNAIL
s which melts away as ..... Ps 58:8

SNARE
is a fowler's *s* .... Hos 9:8
it will come as a *s* .... Luke 21:35
and escape the *s* .... 2 Tim 2:26

SNARED
All of them are *s* .... Is 42:22

SNARES
who seek my life lay *s* ..... Ps 38:12

SNATCH
neither shall anyone *s* ... John 10:28

SNATCHES
s away what was .... Matt 13:19

SNEER
And you *s* at it .... Mal 1:13

SNIFFED
They *s* at the wind .... Jer 14:6

SNORTING
s strikes terror .... Job 39:20

SNOW
shall be whiter than *s* .... Ps 51:7
shall be as white as *s* .... Is 1:18

SOAKED
Their land shall be *s* .... Is 34:7

SOAP
lye, and use much *s* .... Jer 2:22

SOBER
the older men be *s* .... Titus 2:2

SOBERLY
think, but to think *s* ...... Rom 12:3

SODA
And like vinegar on *s* ... Prov 25:20

SODOMITES
nor homosexuals, nor *s* .. 1 Cor 6:9

SOJOURNER
no *s* had to lodge .... Job 31:32

SOJOURNERS
are strangers and *s* .... Lev 25:23

SOLD
s his birthright .... Gen 25:33
s all that he had .... Matt 13:46
but I am carnal, *s* .... Rom 7:14

SOLDIER
hardship as a good *s* ..... 2 Tim 2:3

SOLDIERS
s twisted a crown .... John 19:2

SOLITARILY
heritage, Who dwell *s* ..... Mic 7:14

SOLITARY
God sets the *s* in .... Ps 68:6

SOMEBODY
up, claiming to be *s* ...... Acts 5:36

SOMETHING
thinks himself to be *s* ...... Gal 6:3

SON
Me, 'You are My *S* .... Ps 2:7
is born, Unto us a *S* .... Is 9:6
fourth is like the *S* .... Dan 3:25
will bring forth a *S* .... Matt 1:21
"This is My beloved *S* .... Matt 3:17
Jesus, You *S* of God ...... Matt 8:29
are the Christ, the *S* ..... Matt 16:16
Whose *S* is He .... Matt 22:42
of the *S* of Man .... Matt 24:37
'I am the *S* of God .... Matt 27:43
of Jesus Christ, the *S* ...... Mark 1:1
out, the only *s* .... Luke 7:12
The only begotten *S* ...... John 1:18
that this is the *S* .... John 1:34
of the only begotten *S* .... John 3:18
S can do nothing .... John 5:19
s abides forever .... John 8:35
you believe in the *S* .... John 9:35
I said, 'I am the *S* .... John 10:36
behold your *s* .... John 19:26
Jesus Christ is the *S* ...... Acts 8:37
by sending His own *S* ..... Rom 8:3
not spare His own *S* ...... Rom 8:32
live by faith in the *S* ...... Gal 2:20
God sent forth His *S* .... Gal 4:4
the knowledge of the *S* .... Eph 4:13
"You are My *S* .... Heb 1:5
though He was a *S* .... Heb 5:8
but made like the *S* .... Heb 7:3
"This is My beloved *S* .... 2 Pet 1:17
denies the *S* .... 1 John 2:23
One like the *S* of Man ..... Rev 1:13

SONG
Sing to Him a new *s* .... Ps 33:3
He has put a new *s* .... Ps 40:3
I will sing a new *s* .... Ps 144:9
they sang a new *s* .... Rev 5:9

SONGS
my Maker, Who gives *s* .. Job 35:10
and spiritual *s* .... Eph 5:19

SONS
s shall come from afar ...... Is 60:4
He will purify the *s* .... Mal 3:3
you may become *s* ......John 12:36
who are of faith are *s* ...... Gal 3:7
the adoption as *s* .... Gal 4:5
in bringing many *s* ....Heb 2:10
speaks to you as to *s* ......Heb 12:5

SOON
For it is *s* cut off .... Ps 90:10

SOOTHED
or bound up, Or *s* .... Is 1:6

SORCERER
But Elymas the *s* .... Acts 13:8

SORCERERS
outside are dogs and *s* ...Rev 22:15

SORCERESS
shall not permit a *s* ....Ex 22:18

SORCERY
idolatry, *s* .... Gal 5:20

SORES
and putrefying *s* .... Is 1:6

SORROW
multiply your *s* ....Gen 3:16
s is continually .... Ps 38:17
And He adds no *s* .... Prov 10:22
Your *s* is incurable ....Jer 30:15
them sleeping from *s* ....Luke 22:45
s will be turned ....John 16:20
s produces repentance .. 2 Cor 7:10
s as others who .... 1 Thess 4:13
no more death, nor *s* ...... Rev 21:4

SORROWFUL
But I am poor and *s* ...... Ps 69:29
he went away *s* .... Matt 19:22
soul is exceedingly *s* .... Matt 26:38
and I may be less *s* ....Phil 2:28

SORROWS
s shall be multiplied .... Ps 16:4
by men, A Man of *s* .... Is 53:3
are the beginning of *s* .... Matt 24:8

SORRY
s that He had made man ...Gen 6:6
For you were made *s* ..... 2 Cor 7:9

SOUGHT
I *s* the LORD .... Ps 34:4
s what was lost ....Ezek 34:4

SOUL
with all your *s* .... Deut 6:5
"My *s* loathes my life ...... Job 10:1
s draws near the Pit ...... Job 33:22
will not leave my *s* .... Ps 16:10
converting the *s* .... Ps 19:7
He restores my *s* .... Ps 23:3
you cast down, O my *s* ..... Ps 42:5
Let my *s* live ....Ps 119:175
No one cares for my *s* ..... Ps 142:4
me wrongs his own *s* ..... Prov 8:36
When You make His *s* ...... Is 53:10
s delight itself .... Is 55:2
The *s* of the father As .... Ezek 18:4
able to destroy both *s* ... Matt 10:28
and loses his own *s* ..... Matt 16:26
with all your *s* .... Matt 22:37
your whole spirit, *s* .... 1 Thess 5:23
to the saving of the *s* .....Heb 10:39
his way will save a *s* ....James 5:20
health, just as your *s* .... 3 John 2

SOULS
And will save the *s* .... Ps 72:13
And he who wins *s* ...... Prov 11:30
unsettling your *s* .... Acts 15:24
is able to save your *s* ....James 1:21

SOUND
voice was like the *s* ......Ezek 43:2
do not *s* a trumpet .... Matt 6:2
s words which you ...... 2 Tim 1:13

SOUNDNESS
him this perfect *s* .... Acts 3:16

SOUNDS
a distinction in the *s* ..... 1 Cor 14:7

SOW
s trouble reap .... Job 4:8
Those who *s* in tears ...... Ps 126:5
Blessed are you who *s* ...... Is 32:20
"They *s* the wind .... Hos 8:7
s is not made alive ..... 1 Cor 15:36

SOWER
"Behold, a *s* went .... Matt 13:3

SOWN
s spiritual things .... 1 Cor 9:11
of righteousness is *s* ....James 3:18

SOWS
s the good seed is the ... Matt 13:37
'One *s* and another ....John 4:37
for whatever a man *s* .... Gal 6:7

SPARE
He who did not *s* .... Rom 8:32
if God did not *s* .... 2 Pet 2:4

SPARES
s his rod hates his .... Prov 13:24

SPARK
the work of it as a *s* .... Is 1:31

SPARKLES
it is red, When it *s* .... Prov 23:31

SPARKS
to trouble, As the *s* .... Job 5:7

SPARROW
s has found a home .... Ps 84:3

SPARROWS
than many *s* .... Matt 10:31

SPAT
Then they *s* on Him ..... Matt 27:30

SPEAK
only the word that I *s* ...Num 22:35
oh, that God would *s* ...... Job 11:5
And a time to *s* ....Eccl 3:7
s anymore in His name .....Jer 20:9
or what you should *s* ..... Matt 10:19
to you when all men *s* ....Luke 6:26
s what I have seen ....John 8:38
He hears He will *s* ......John 16:13
Spirit and began to *s* ...... Acts 2:4

SPEAKING
envy, and all evil *s* .... 1 Pet 2:1

SPEAKS
to face, as a man *s* ....Ex 33:11
God has sent *s* ....John 3:34
When he *s* a lie ....John 8:44
he being dead still *s* ....Heb 11:4
of sprinkling that *s* ....Heb 12:24

SPEAR
His side with a *s* ....John 19:34

SPEARS
And their *s* into .... Is 2:4

SPECK
do you look at the *s* .... Matt 7:3

SPECTACLE
you were made a *s* ....Heb 10:33

SPEECH
one language and one *s* ...Gen 11:1
his *s* contemptible .... 2 Cor 10:10
s always be with grace ......Col 4:6

SPEECHLESS
your mouth for the *s* ..... Prov 31:8

SPEED
they shall come with *s* ...... Is 5:26

SPEEDILY
I call, answer me *s* .... Ps 102:2

SPEND
you *s* money for .... Is 55:2
amiss, that you may *s* ....James 4:3

SPENT
"But when he had *s* .....Luke 15:14

SPEW
nor hot, I will *s* ....Rev 3:16

SPIDER
s skillfully grasps .... Prov 30:28

SPIES
men who had been *s* ..... Josh 6:23

SPIN
neither toil nor *s* .... Matt 6:28

SPINDLE
her hand holds the *s* .... Prov 31:19

SPIRIT
And the *S* of God was ......Gen 1:2
S shall not strive ....Gen 6:3
S that is upon you ....Num 11:17
portion of your *s* ....2 Kin 2:9
Then a *s* passed .... Job 4:15
hand I commit my *s* .... Ps 31:5
The *s* of a man is the .... Prov 20:27
s will return to God ....Eccl 12:7
S has gathered them .... Is 34:16
I have put My *S* .... Is 42:1
"The *S* of the Lord .... Is 61:1
S entered me when He .... Ezek 2:2
and a new *s* ....Ezek 18:31
"I will put My *S* ....Ezek 36:27
walk in a false *s* .... Mic 2:11
and He saw the *S* .... Matt 3:16
I will put My *S* .... Matt 12:18
S descending upon ...... Mark 1:10
s indeed is willing ...... Mark 14:38
go before Him in the *s* ....Luke 1:17
manner of *s* you are of ...Luke 9:55
hands I commit My *s* ....Luke 23:46
they had seen a *s* ....Luke 24:37
"God is *S* ....John 4:24
I speak to you are *s* ......John 6:63
"the *S* of truth ....John 14:17
but if a *s* or an angel ..... Acts 23:9
the flesh but in the *S* ...... Rom 8:9
does not have the *S* .... Rom 8:9
s that we are children .... Rom 8:16
what the mind of the *S* ... Rom 8:27
to us through His *S* ...... 1 Cor 2:10
gifts, but the same *S* .... 1 Cor 12:4
but the *S* gives life .... 2 Cor 3:6
Now the Lord is the *S* ... 2 Cor 3:17
Having begun in the *S* ..... Gal 3:3
has sent forth the *S* .... Gal 4:6
with the Holy *S* ....Eph 1:13
the unity of the *S* ....Eph 4:3
stand fast in one *s* ....Phil 1:27
S expressly says that ..... 1 Tim 4:1
S who dwells in us ....James 4:5
made alive by the *S* ...... 1 Pet 3:18
do not believe every *s* ... 1 John 4:1
you know the *S* .... 1 John 4:2
has given us of His *S* ... 1 John 4:13
S who bears witness .... 1 John 5:6
not having the *S* .... Jude 19
I was in the *S* on the ...... Rev 1:10
him hear what the *S* .... Rev 2:7
And the *S* and the ....Rev 22:17

SPIRITS
Who makes His angels *s* .. Ps 104:4
heed to deceiving *s* .... 1 Tim 4:1

SPIRITUAL
s judges all things .... 1 Cor 2:15
However, the *s* is not ... 1 Cor 15:46
s restore such a one .... Gal 6:1

SPIRITUALLY
s minded is life .... Rom 8:6

SPITEFULLY
for those who *s* .... Matt 5:44

SPITTING
face from shame and *s* ...... Is 50:6

SPLENDOR
on the glorious *s* .... Ps 145:5

SPOIL
He shall divide the *s* ....Is 53:12

SPOILER
I have created the *s* ....Is 54:16

SPOKE
"No man ever *s* ....John 7:46
I was a child, I *s* .... 1 Cor 13:11
in various ways *s* .... Heb 1:1
s as they were moved .... 2 Pet 1:21

SPOKEN
I have not *s* in secret ....Is 45:19
why am I evil *s* .... 1 Cor 10:30

SPOKESMAN
"So he shall be your *s* ...... Ex 4:16

SPONGE
them ran and took a *s* ... Matt 27:48

SPOT
church, not having *s* ...... Eph 5:27
Himself without *s* .... Heb 9:14

SPOTS
These are *s* in your .... Jude 12

SPREAD
Then the word of God *s* ... Acts 6:7

SPREADS
s them out like a tent .... Is 40:22

SPRING
Truth shall *s* out of .... Ps 85:11
s send forth fresh .... James 3:11

SPRINGING
a fountain of water *s* ..... John 4:14

SPRINGS
And the thirsty land *s* .... Is 35:7

SPRINKLE
"Then I will *s* .... Ezek 36:25

SPRINKLED
having our hearts *s* .... Heb 10:22

SPRINKLING
s that speaks .... Heb 12:24

SPROUT
and the seed should *s* ... Mark 4:27

SQUARES
voice in the open *s* .... Prov 1:20

STAFF
this Jordan with my *s* .... Gen 32:10
Your rod and Your *s* .... Ps 23:4
on the top of his *s* .... Heb 11:21

STAGGER
they will drink and *s* ...... Jer 25:16

STAGGERS
As a drunken man *s* .... Is 19:14

STAKES
s will ever be removed ..... Is 33:20

STALLS
be no herd in the *s* .... Hab 3:17

STAMMERERS
s will be ready .... Is 32:4

STAMMERING
s tongue that you .... Is 33:19

STAMPING
At the noise of the *s* .... Jer 47:3

STAND
one shall be able to *s* ..... Deut 7:24
lives, And He shall *s* ..... Job 19:25
ungodly shall not *s* .... Ps 1:5
not lack a man to *s* .... Jer 35:19
And who can *s* when He ... Mal 3:2
that kingdom cannot *s* .. Mark 3:24
he will be made to *s* ...... Rom 14:4
Watch, *s* fast in the ...... 1 Cor 16:13
for by faith you *s* .... 2 Cor 1:24
having done all, to *s* .... Eph 6:13
S therefore .... Eph 6:14
of God in which you *s* .... 1 Pet 5:12
"Behold, I *s* at the .... Rev 3:20

STANDARD
LORD will lift up a *s* .... Is 59:19

STANDING
they love to pray *s* .... Matt 6:5
and the Son of Man *s* .... Acts 7:56

STANDS
him who thinks he *s* .... 1 Cor 10:12

STAR
For we have seen His *s* .... Matt 2:2
Bright and Morning *S* .... Rev 22:16

STARS
He made the *s* also .... Gen 1:16
born as many as the *s* .... Heb 11:12

STATE
learned in whatever *s* ..... Phil 4:11

STATURE
in wisdom and *s* .... Luke 2:52

STATUTE
shall be a perpetual *s* ...... Lev 3:17

STATUTES
the *s* of the LORD are .... Ps 19:8
Teach me Your *s* .... Ps 119:12

STAY
S here and watch .... Matt 26:38

STEADFAST
brethren, be *s* .... 1 Cor 15:58
soul, both sure and *s* ...... Heb 6:19
Resist him, *s* in the .... 1 Pet 5:9

STEADFASTLY
s set His face to go .... Luke 9:51
And they continued *s* .... Acts 2:42

STEADFASTNESS
good order and the *s* .... Col 2:5

STEADILY
could not look *s* .... 2 Cor 3:13

STEADY
and his hands were *s* ...... Ex 17:12

STEAL
"You shall not *s* .... Ex 20:15
thieves break in and *s* .... Matt 6:19
night and *s* Him away ... Matt 27:64

STEM
forth a Rod from the *s* .... Is 11:1

STENCH
there will be a *s* .... Is 3:24
this time there is a *s* ..... John 11:39

STEP
s has turned from the ..... Job 31:7

STEPS
The *s* of a good man ...... Ps 37:23
And established my *s* ...... Ps 40:2
the LORD directs his *s* .... Prov 16:9
should follow His *s* .... 1 Pet 2:21

STEWARD
be blameless, as a *s* .... Titus 1:7

STEWARDS
of Christ and *s* .... 1 Cor 4:1

STEWARDSHIP
entrusted with a *s* .... 1 Cor 9:17

STICK
'For Joseph, the *s* .... Ezek 37:16

STICKS
a man gathering *s* .... Num 15:32

STIFF
rebellion and your *s* ..... Deut 31:27

STIFF-NECKED
"You *s* and .... Acts 7:51

STILL
When I awake, I am *s* .... Ps 139:18
sea, "Peace, be *s* .... Mark 4:39

STILLBORN
burial, I say that a *s* .... Eccl 6:3

STINGS
like a serpent, And *s* .... Prov 23:32

STIR
I remind you to *s* .... 2 Tim 1:6

STIRRED
So the LORD *s* up the ...... Hag 1:14

STIRS
It *s* up the dead for .... Is 14:9

STOCKS
s that were in the .... Jer 20:2

STOIC
and *S* philosophers ...... Acts 17:18

STOMACH
Foods for the *s* .... 1 Cor 6:13

STOMACH'S
little wine for your *s* ..... 1 Tim 5:23

STONE
him, a pillar of *s* .... Gen 35:14
s shall be a witness ..... Josh 24:27
s which the builders ...... Ps 118:22
I lay in Zion a *s* .... Is 28:16
take the heart of *s* .... Ezek 36:26
will give him a *s* .... Matt 7:9
s will be broken .... Matt 21:44
s which the builders ..... Luke 20:17
those works do you *s* .... John 10:32
Him as to a living *s* .... 1 Pet 2:4

STONED
s Stephen as he was ...... Acts 7:59
They were *s* .... Heb 11:37

STONES
Abraham from these *s* .... Matt 3:9
command that these *s* ..... Matt 4:3

STONY
fell on *s* ground .... Mark 4:5

STOOPED
And again He *s* down ..... John 8:8

STOPPED
her flow of blood *s* .... Luke 8:44

STORE
exist are kept in *s* .... 2 Pet 3:7

STORK
s has her home in the .... Ps 104:17

STORM
He calms the *s* .... Ps 107:29
for a shelter from *s* .... Is 4:6

STRAIGHT
Make *s* in the desert A ...... Is 40:3
and make *s* paths for ..... Heb 12:13

STRAIGHTFORWARD
that they were not *s* .... Gal 2:14

STRAIN
"Blind guides, who *s* .... Matt 23:24

STRAITS
and desperate *s* .... Deut 28:53

STRANGE
s thing happened .... 1 Pet 4:12

STRANGER
and loves the *s* .... Deut 10:18
I was a *s* and you .... Matt 25:35

STRANGERS
know the voice of *s* ...... John 10:5
you are no longer *s* .... Eph 2:19

STRANGLING
that my soul chooses *s* .... Job 7:15

STRAP
than I, whose sandal *s* ..... Mark 1:7

STRAW
stones, wood, hay, *s* ..... 1 Cor 3:12

STRAY
Who make my people *s* .... Mic 3:5

STRAYED
Yet I have not *s* .... Ps 119:110
some have *s* .... 1 Tim 6:10

STREAM
like a flowing *s* .... Is 66:12

STREAMS
He also brought *s* .... Ps 78:16

STREET
In the middle of its *s* ...... Rev 22:2

STREETS
You taught in our *s* ...... Luke 13:26

STRENGTH
s no man shall .... 1 Sam 2:9
The LORD is the *s* .... Ps 27:1
is our refuge and *s* .... Ps 46:1
They go from *s* to .... Ps 84:7
S and honor are her ..... Prov 31:25
might He increases *s* .... Is 40:29
O LORD, my *s* and my ..... Jer 16:19
were still without *s* .... Rom 5:6
s is made perfect .... 2 Cor 12:9

STRENGTHEN
And He shall *s* .... Ps 27:14
S the weak hands .... Is 35:3
s your brethren .... Luke 22:32
s the things .... Rev 3:2

STRENGTHENED
unbelief, but was *s* .... Rom 4:20
stood with me and *s* ..... 2 Tim 4:17

STRENGTHENING
s the souls of the .... Acts 14:22

STRENGTHENS
through Christ who *s* ...... Phil 4:13

STRETCH
are old, you will *s* .... John 21:18

STRETCHED
I have *s* out my hands ...... Ps 88:9
"All day long I have *s* ... Rom 10:21

STRETCHES
For he *s* out his hand ...... Job 15:25

STRICKEN
of My people He was *s* ...... Is 53:8

STRIFE
man stirs up *s* .... Prov 15:18
even from envy and *s* ..... Phil 1:15
which come envy, *s* ...... 1 Tim 6:4

STRIKE
The sun shall not *s* .... Ps 121:6
"*S* the Shepherd .... Zech 13:7
'I will *s* the Shepherd .... Matt 26:31

STRINGED
of your *s* instruments ... Amos 5:23

STRIP
S yourselves .... Is 32:11

STRIPES
s we are healed .... Is 53:5
s you were healed .... 1 Pet 2:24

STRIVE
"My Spirit shall not *s* ...... Gen 6:3
"*S* to enter through ..... Luke 13:24
the Lord not to *s* .... 2 Tim 2:14

STRIVING
for a man to stop *s* .... Prov 20:3

STROKE
with a mighty *s* .... Jer 14:17

STRONG
The LORD *s* and mighty .... Ps 24:8
S is Your hand .... Ps 89:13
"When a *s* man .... Luke 11:21
We then who are *s* .... Rom 15:1
weak, then I am *s* ...... 2 Cor 12:10
my brethren, be *s* .... Eph 6:10
were made *s* .... Heb 11:34

STRONGHOLD
of my salvation, my *s* .... Ps 18:2

STRUCK
s the rock twice .... Num 20:11
the hand of God has *s* .... Job 19:21
Behold, He *s* the rock ..... Ps 78:20
in My wrath I *s* .... Is 60:10
s the head from the .... Hab 3:13
took the reed and *s* ...... Matt 27:30

STUBBLE
do wickedly will be *s* .... Mal 4:1

STUBBORN
"If a man has a *s* .... Deut 21:18

STUBBORN-HEARTED
"Listen to Me, you *s* .... Is 46:12

STUBBORNNESS
do not look on the *s* ...... Deut 9:27

STUDIED
having never *s* .... John 7:15

STUMBLE
have caused many to *s* ..... Mal 2:8
you will be made to *s* .... Matt 26:31
immediately they *s* .... Mark 4:17
who believe in Me to *s* .. Mark 9:42
For we all *s* in many ...... James 3:2

STUMBLED
s that they should .... Rom 11:11

STUMBLES
immediately he *s* .... Matt 13:21

STUMBLING
the deaf, nor put a *s* ...... Lev 19:14
But a stone of *s* .... Is 8:14
Behold, I will lay *s* .... Jer 6:21
I lay in Zion a *s* .... Rom 9:33
this, not to put a *s* .... Rom 14:13
of yours become a *s* ...... 1 Cor 8:9
and "A stone of *s* .... 1 Pet 2:8
to keep you from *s* .... Jude 24

STUPID
hates correction is *s* ...... Prov 12:1

SUBDUE
s all things to .... Phil 3:21

SUBJECT
for it is not *s* .... Rom 8:7
Let every soul be *s* .... Rom 13:1
all their lifetime *s* .... Heb 2:15

SUBJECTED
because of Him who *s* .... Rom 8:20

SUBJECTION
put all things in *s* .... Heb 2:8

SUBMISSION
his children in *s* .... 1 Tim 3:4

SUBMISSIVE
Yes, all of you be *s* .... 1 Pet 5:5

SUBMIT
Therefore *s* to God .... James 4:7
s yourselves to every ..... 1 Pet 2:13

SUBSIDED
and the waters *s* .... Gen 8:1

SUBSTANCE
Bless his *s* .... Deut 33:11

SUCCESS
please give me *s* .... Gen 24:12
But wisdom brings *s* .... Eccl 10:10

SUCCESSFUL
Joseph, and he was a *s* .... Gen 39:2

SUDDENLY
s there was with the ...... Luke 2:13

SUE
s you and take away ..... Matt 5:40

SUFFER
for the Christ to *s* .... Luke 24:46
Christ, if indeed we *s* ..... Rom 8:17
in Him, but also to *s* .... Phil 1:29

SUFFERED
s these things and to .... Luke 24:26
for whom I have *s* .... Phil 3:8
after you have *s* .... 1 Pet 5:10

SUFFERING
anyone among you *s* .... James 5:13

SUFFERINGS
I consider that the *s* ...... Rom 8:18
perfect through *s* .... Heb 2:10

SUFFERS
Love *s* long and is .... 1 Cor 13:4

SUFFICIENCY
but our *s* is from God ...... 2 Cor 3:5

SUFFICIENT
S for the day is Its .... Matt 6:34

SUM
How great is the *s* .... Ps 139:17

SUMMER
and heat, Winter and *s* .... Gen 8:22

SUMPTUOUSLY
fine linen and fared *s* .... Luke 16:19

SUN
So the *s* stood still .... Josh 10:13
s shall not strike you ...... Ps 121:6
s returned ten degrees ...... Is 38:8
The *s* and moon grow .... Joel 2:10
s shall go down on the ..... Mic 3:6
for He makes His *s* .... Matt 5:45
the *s* was darkened ..... Luke 23:45
do not let the *s* .... Eph 4:26
s became black as .... Rev 6:12
had no need of the *s* ...... Rev 21:23

SUPPER
to eat the Lord's *S* ...... 1 Cor 11:20
took the cup after *s* .... 1 Cor 11:25
together for the *s* .... Rev 19:17

SUPPLICATION
by prayer and *s* .... Phil 4:6

SUPPLIES
by what every joint *s* ...... Eph 4:16

SUPPLY
And my God shall *s* .... Phil 4:19

SUPPORT
this, that you must *s* ..... Acts 20:35

SUPREME
to the king as *s* .... 1 Pet 2:13

SURE
s your sin will find ...... Num 32:23
call and election *s* .... 2 Pet 1:10

SURETY
Be *s* for Your servant .... Ps 119:122
Jesus has become a *s* ...... Heb 7:22

SURROUND
LORD, mercy shall *s* .... Ps 32:10

SURROUNDED
also, since we are *s* .... Heb 12:1

SURVIVOR
was no refugee or *s* ...... Lam 2:22

SUSPICIONS
reviling, evil *s* .... 1 Tim 6:4

SUSTAIN
S me with cakes of .... Song 2:5

SWADDLING
Him in *s* cloths .... Luke 2:7

SWALLOW
a gnat and *s* a camel .... Matt 23:24

SWEAR
'You shall not *s* .... Matt 5:33
began to curse and *s* .... Matt 26:74

SWEARING
By *s* and lying .... Hos 4:2

SWEARS
but whoever *s* by the .... Matt 23:18

SWEAT
His *s* became like .... Luke 22:44

SWEET
s are Your words .... Ps 119:103
but it will be as *s* .... Rev 10:9

SWEETNESS
mouth like honey in *s* ..... Ezek 3:3

SWELLING
they speak great *s* .... 2 Pet 2:18

SWIFT
let every man be *s* .... James 1:19

SWIM
night I make my bed *s* .... Ps 6:6

SWOON
As they *s* like the .... Lam 2:12

SWORD
s which turned every ...... Gen 3:24
The *s* of the LORD is .... Is 34:6
'A *s* is sharpened .... Ezek 21:9
Bow and *s* of battle I ...... Hos 2:18
to bring peace but a *s* ... Matt 10:34
for all who take the *s* .... Matt 26:52
the *s* of the Spirit .... Eph 6:17
than any two-edged *s* ...... Heb 4:12
mouth goes a sharp *s* ..... Rev 19:15

SWORDS
shall beat their *s* .... Is 2:4

SWORE
So I *s* in My wrath .... Heb 3:11

SWORN
"By Myself I have *s* ...... Gen 22:16
"The LORD has *s* .... Heb 7:21

SYMBOLIC
which things are *s* .... Gal 4:24

SYMPATHIZE
Priest who cannot *s* .... Heb 4:15

SYMPATHY
My *s* is stirred .... Hos 11:8

SYNAGOGUE
but are a *s* of Satan .... Rev 2:9

T

TABERNACLE
t He shall hide me .... Ps 27:5
I will abide in Your *t* .... Ps 61:4
And will rebuild the *t* ... Acts 15:16
and more perfect *t* .... Heb 9:11

TABERNACLES
Feast of *T* was at hand .... John 7:2

TABLE
prepare a *t* before me ...... Ps 23:5
dogs under the *t* .... Mark 7:28
of the Lord's *t* .... 1 Cor 10:21

TABLES
and overturned the *t* .... Matt 21:12

TABLET
is engraved On the *t* .... Jer 17:1

TAIL
t drew a third of the .... Rev 12:4

TAKE
t Your Holy Spirit .... Ps 51:11
"*T* My yoke upon .... Matt 11:29
and *t* up his cross .... Mark 8:34
My life that I may *t* ...... John 10:17

TAKEN
He was *t* from prison .... Is 53:8
one will be *t* and the .... Matt 24:40
until He is *t* out of ...... 2 Thess 2:7

TALEBEARER
t reveals secrets .... Prov 11:13

TALENT
went and hid your *t* ..... Matt 25:25

TALK
shall *t* of them when ...... Deut 6:7

TALKED
within us while He *t* .....Luke 24:32

TALKERS
both idle *t* and .... Titus 1:10

TAMBOURINE
The mirth of the *t* .... Is 24:8

TARES
the *t* also appeared ...... Matt 13:26

TARGET
You set me as Your *t* ...... Job 7:20

TARRY
come and will not *t* ......Heb 10:37

TASK
this burdensome *t* ....Eccl 1:13

TASTE
Oh, *t* and see that the ...... Ps 34:8
might *t* death for .... Heb 2:9

TASTED
t the heavenly gift .... Heb 6:4

TAUGHT
as His counselor has *t* ...... Is 40:13
from man, nor was I *t* ..... Gal 1:12

TAUNT
and a byword, a *t* ....Jer 24:9

TAX
t collectors do the .... Matt 5:46

TAXES
t to whom *t* .... Rom 13:7

TEACH
"Can anyone *t* .... Job 21:22
T me Your paths .... Ps 25:4
t you the fear of the .... Ps 34:11
t transgressors Your ...... Ps 51:13
So *t* us to number our ..... Ps 90:12
t you again the first ....Heb 5:12

TEACHER
for One is your *T* .... Matt 23:8
know that You are a *t* ...... John 3:2
named Gamaliel, a *t* ..... Acts 5:34
a *t* of the Gentiles in ..... 1 Tim 2:7

TEACHERS
than all my *t* .... Ps 119:99
prophets, third *t* .... 1 Cor 12:28
and some pastors and *t* ... Eph 4:11
desiring to be *t* .... 1 Tim 1:7
there will be false *t* .... 2 Pet 2:1

TEACHES
the Holy Spirit *t* .... 1 Cor 2:13
the same anointing *t* ... 1 John 2:27

TEACHING
"*t* them to observe all ... Matt 28:20
t every man in all .... Col 1:28

TEAR
I, even I, will *t* ....Hos 5:14
will wipe away every *t* .... Rev 21:4

TEARS
my couch with my *t* ....Ps 6:6
mindful of your *t* .... 2 Tim 1:4
it diligently with *t* ....Heb 12:17

TEETH
You have broken the *t* ....Ps 3:7

TELL
"Who can *t* if God .... Jon 3:9
t him his fault .... Matt 18:15
whatever they *t* .... Matt 23:3
He comes, He will *t* .... John 4:25

TEMPERATE
prize is *t* in all .... 1 Cor 9:25
husband of one wife, *t* ... 1 Tim 3:2

TEMPEST
And suddenly a great *t* ... Matt 8:24

TEMPLE
So Solomon built the *t* .. 1 Kin 6:14
LORD is in His holy *t* .... Ps 11:4
One greater than the *t* .... Matt 12:6
"Destroy this *t* .... John 2:19
your body is the *t* .... 1 Cor 6:19
grows into a holy *t* ....Eph 2:21
sits as God in the *t* ..... 2 Thess 2:4
and the Lamb are its *t* .... Rev 21:22

TEMPLES
t made with hands .... Acts 7:48

TEMPORARY
which are seen are *t* .... 2 Cor 4:18

TEMPT
t the LORD your God ...... Matt 4:7
does He Himself *t* ....James 1:13

TEMPTATION
do not lead us into *t* ...... Matt 6:13
man who endures *t* ....James 1:12

TEMPTED
forty days, *t* by Satan ... Mark 1:13
lest you also be *t* .... Gal 6:1
in all points *t* ....Heb 4:15

TEMPTER
Now when the *t* came ..... Matt 4:3

TENDER
your heart was *t* .... 2 Kin 22:19

TENDERHEARTED
to one another, *t* ....Eph 4:32

TENDS
t a flock and does not .... 1 Cor 9:7

TENT
earthly house, this *t* ...... 2 Cor 5:1

TENTMAKERS
occupation they were *t* ... Acts 18:3

TENTS
Than dwell in the *t* ....Ps 84:10

TERRESTRIAL
bodies and *t* bodies .... 1 Cor 15:40

TERRIBLE
is great and very *t* ....Joel 2:11

TERRIFIED
and not in any way *t* ......Phil 1:28

TERRIFY
me with dreams And *t* .... Job 7:14

TERRIFYING
t was the sight ....Heb 12:21

TERROR
are nothing, You see *t* ..... Job 6:21
not be afraid of the *t* .... Ps 91:5

TERRORS
consumed with *t* .... Ps 73:19

TEST
said, "Why do you *t* ..... Matt 22:18
T all things .... 1 Thess 5:21
but *t* the spirits .... 1 John 4:1

TESTAMENT
where there is a *t* ....Heb 9:16

TESTED
God *t* Abraham ....Gen 22:1
Where your fathers *t* ....Heb 3:9
though it is *t* by fire .... 1 Pet 1:7

TESTIFIED
who has seen has *t* ......John 19:35
which He has *t* .... 1 John 5:9

TESTIFIES
that the Holy Spirit *t* .... Acts 20:23

TESTIFY
t what We have ....John 3:11
t that the Father .... 1 John 4:14

TESTIFYING
was righteous, God *t* ......Heb 11:4

TESTIMONIES
those who keep His *t* ..... Ps 119:2
t are my meditation ...... Ps 119:99

TESTIMONY
two tablets of the *T* .... Ex 31:18
under your feet as a *t* ... Mark 6:11
no one receives His *t* .....John 3:32
not believed the *t* .... 1 John 5:10
For the *t* of Jesus is ......Rev 19:10

TESTING
came to Him, *t* Him ...... Matt 19:3

TESTS
men, but God who *t* .... 1 Thess 2:4

THANK
"I *t* You, Father .... Matt 11:25
t You that I am not ......Luke 18:11

THANKFUL
as God, nor were *t* .... Rom 1:21

THANKFULNESS
Felix, with all *t* .... Acts 24:3

THANKS
the cup, and gave *t* ...... Matt 26:27
T be to God for His ...... 2 Cor 9:15

THANKSGIVING
His presence with *t* .... Ps 95:2
into His gates with *t* .... Ps 100:4
supplication, with *t* .... Phil 4:6

THEATER
and rushed into the *t* .... Acts 19:29

THIEF
do not despise a *t* .... Prov 6:30
because he was a *t* .... John 12:6
Lord will come as a *t* ..... 2 Pet 3:10

THIEVES
And companions of *t* .... Is 1:23

THINGS
in heaven give good *t* .... Matt 7:11
kept all these *t* ....Luke 2:51
share in all good *t* .... Gal 6:6

THINK
t you have eternal ....John 5:39
not to *t* of himself ....Rom 12:3

THINKS
Yet the LORD *t* upon me ... Ps 40:17
For as he *t* in his .... Prov 23:7
t he stands take heed .. 1 Cor 10:12

THIRST
those who hunger and *t* ... Matt 5:6
in Me shall never *t* ......John 6:35
anymore nor *t* anymore ... Rev 7:16

THIRSTS
My soul *t* for God .... Ps 42:2
saying, "If anyone *t* ......John 7:37
freely to him who *t* .... Rev 21:6

THIRSTY
I was *t* and you gave .... Matt 25:35

THISTLES
or figs from *t* .... Matt 7:16

THORN
a *t* in the flesh was ...... 2 Cor 12:7

THORNBUSHES
gather grapes from *t* ..... Matt 7:16

THORNS
Both *t* and thistles it ......Gen 3:18
some fell among *t* .... Matt 13:7
wearing the crown of *t* ...John 19:5

THOUGHT
You understand my *t* ...... Ps 139:2
I *t* as a child .... 1 Cor 13:11

THOUGHTS
The LORD knows the *t* .... Ps 94:11
unrighteous man his *t* .... Is 55:7
"For My *t* are not your ...... Is 55:8
Jesus, knowing their *t* ..... Matt 9:4
heart proceed evil *t* ..... Matt 15:19
The LORD knows the *t* .. 1 Cor 3:20

THREAT
shall flee at the *t* .... Is 30:17

THREATEN
suffered, He did not *t* .... 1 Pet 2:23

THREATENING
to them, giving up *t* .... Eph 6:9

THREATS
still breathing *t* .... Acts 9:1

THREE
hope, love, these *t* ...... 1 Cor 13:13

THRESH
It is time to *t* her ....Jer 51:33

THRESHING
t shall last till the .... Lev 26:5

TRIBES
t which are scattered ... James 1:1

TRIBULATION
there will be great *t* ... Matt 24:21
world you will have *t* ... John 16:33
with her into great *t* ... Rev 2:22
out of the great *t* ... Rev 7:14

TRIBULATIONS
t enter the kingdom ... Acts 14:22
but we also glory in *t* ... Rom 5:3
t that you endure ... 2 Thess 1:4

TRIED
A *t* stone, a precious ... Is 28:16

TRIMMED
and *t* their lamps ... Matt 25:7

TRIUMPH
always leads us in *t* ... 2 Cor 2:14

TRIUMPHED
the LORD, For He has *t* ... Ex 15:1

TRODDEN
t the winepress alone ... Is 63:3

TROUBLE
few days and full of *t* ... Job 14:1
t He shall hide me ... Ps 27:5
not in *t* as other men ... Ps 73:5
will be with him in *t* ... Ps 91:15
Savior in time of *t* ... Jer 14:8
there are some who *t* ... Gal 1:7

TROUBLED
worried and *t* ... Luke 10:41
shaken in mind or *t* ... 2 Thess 2:2

TROUBLES
Out of all their *t* ... Ps 25:22
will be famines and *t* ... Mark 13:8
him out of all his *t* ... Acts 7:10

TROUBLING
wicked cease from *t* ... Job 3:17

TRUE
He who sent Me is *t* ... John 7:28
Indeed, let God be *t* ... Rom 3:4
whatever things are *t* ... Phil 4:8
Him who is *t* ... 1 John 5:20
for these words are *t* ... Rev 21:5

TRUMPET
deed, do not sound a *t* ... Matt 6:2
t makes an uncertain ... 1 Cor 14:8
For the *t* will sound ... 1 Cor 15:52

TRUST
T in the LORD ... Ps 37:3
T in the LORD with all ... Prov 3:5
Do not *t* in a friend ... Mic 7:5
who *t* in riches ... Mark 10:24

TRUSTED
"He *t* in the LORD ... Ps 22:8
"He *t* in God ... Matt 27:43

TRUSTS
But he who *t* in the ... Ps 32:10

TRUTH
led me in the way of *t* ... Gen 24:48
Behold, You desire *t* ... Ps 51:6
t shall be your shield ... Ps 91:4
And Your law is *t* ... Ps 119:142
t is fallen in the ... Is 59:14
called the City of *T* ... Zech 8:3
you shall know the *t* ... John 8:32
"I am the way, the *t* ... John 14:6
He, the Spirit of *t* ... John 16:13
to Him. "What is *t* ... John 18:38
who suppress the *t* ... Rom 1:18
but, speaking the *t* ... Eph 4:15
your waist with *t* ... Eph 6:14
I am speaking the *t* ... 1 Tim 2:7
they may know the *t* ... 2 Tim 2:25
the knowledge of the *t* ... 2 Tim 3:7
that we are of the *t* ... 1 John 3:19
the Spirit is *t* ... 1 John 5:6

TRY
which is to *t* you ... 1 Pet 4:12

TUMULT
Your enemies make a *t* ... Ps 83:2

TUNIC
Also he made him a *t* ... Gen 37:3

TUNICS
the LORD God made *t* ... Gen 3:21

TURBAN
"Remove the *t* ... Ezek 21:26

TURN
you shall not *t* ... Deut 17:11
"Repent, *t* away from ... Ezek 14:6
on your right cheek, *t* ... Matt 5:39
t them from darkness ... Acts 26:18

TURNED
The wicked shall be *t* ... Ps 9:17
of Israel, They have *t* ... Is 1:4
and how you *t* ... 1 Thess 1:9

TURNING
marvel that you are *t* ... Gal 1:6
or shadow of *t* ... James 1:17

TURNS
A soft answer *t* ... Prov 15:1
that he who *t* ... James 5:20

TURTLEDOVE
t Is heard in our land ... Song 2:12

TUTOR
the law was our *t* ... Gal 3:24

TWIST
unstable people *t* to ... 2 Pet 3:16

TWO
T are better than one ... Eccl 4:9
t shall become one ... Matt 19:5
new man from the *t* ... Eph 2:15

TYPE
of Adam, who is a *t* ... Rom 5:14

U

UNAFRAID
Do you want to be *u* ... Rom 13:3

UNBELIEF
because of their *u* ... Matt 13:58
help my *u* ... Mark 9:24
did it ignorantly in *u* ... 1 Tim 1:13
enter in because of *u* ... Heb 3:19

UNBELIEVERS
yoked together with *u* ... 2 Cor 6:14

UNBELIEVING
Do not be *u* ... John 20:27
u nothing is pure ... Titus 1:15
"But the cowardly, *u* ... Rev 21:8

UNCIRCUMCISED
not the physically *u* ... Rom 2:27

UNCLEAN
I am a man of *u* lips ... Is 6:5
man common or *u* ... Acts 10:28
there is nothing *u* ... Rom 14:14
that no fornicator, *u* ... Eph 5:5

UNCLEANNESS
men's bones and all *u* ... Matt 23:27
flesh in the lust of *u* ... 2 Pet 2:10

UNCLOTHED
we want to be *u* ... 2 Cor 5:4

UNCOVERS
u deep things out of ... Job 12:22

UNDEFILED
incorruptible and *u* ... 1 Pet 1:4

UNDERMINE
And you *u* your friend ... Job 6:27

UNDERSTAND
if there are any who *u* ... Ps 14:2
hearing, but do not *u* ... Is 6:9
"Why do you not *u* ... John 8:43
lest they should *u* ... Acts 28:27
some things hard to *u* ... 2 Pet 3:16

UNDERSTANDING
His *u* is infinite ... Ps 147:5
lean not on your own *u* ... Prov 3:5
u will find good ... Prov 19:8
His *u* is unsearchable ... Is 40:28
also still without *u* ... Matt 15:16
also pray with the *u* ... 1 Cor 14:15
the Lord give you *u* ... 2 Tim 2:7
Who is wise and *u* ... James 3:13

UNDERSTANDS
There is none who *u* ... Rom 3:11

UNDERSTOOD
Then I *u* their end ... Ps 73:17
clearly seen, being *u* ... Rom 1:20

UNDESIRABLE
gather together, O *u* ... Zeph 2:1

UNDIGNIFIED
I will be even more *u* ... 2 Sam 6:22

UNDISCERNING
u, untrustworthy ... Rom 1:31

UNDONE
"Woe is me, for I am *u* ... Is 6:5

UNEDUCATED
that they were *u* ... Acts 4:13

UNFAITHFUL
way of the *u* is hard ... Prov 13:15

UNFAITHFULLY
back and acted *u* ... Ps 78:57

UNFORGIVING
unloving, *u* ... Rom 1:31

UNFORMED
substance, being yet *u* ... Ps 139:16

UNFRUITFUL
and it becomes *u* ... Mark 4:19

UNGODLINESS
heaven against all *u* ... Rom 1:18

UNGODLY
u shall not stand ... Ps 1:5
Christ died for the *u* ... Rom 5:6

UNHOLY
the holy and *u* ... Ezek 22:26

UNINFORMED
the place of the *u* ... 1 Cor 14:16

UNINTENTIONALLY
kills his neighbor *u* ... Deut 4:42

UNITE
U my heart to fear ... Ps 86:11

UNITY
to dwell together in *u* ... Ps 133:1
to keep the *u* of the ... Eph 4:3

UNJUST
commended the *u* ... Luke 16:8
of the just and the *u* ... Acts 24:15
For God is not *u* ... Heb 6:10

UNJUSTLY
long will you judge *u* ... Ps 82:2

UNKNOWN
To The *U* God ... Acts 17:23

UNLEAVENED
the Feast of *U* Bread ... Ex 12:17

UNLOVING
untrustworthy, *u* ... Rom 1:31

UNMERCIFUL
unforgiving, *u* ... Rom 1:31

UNPREPARED
with me and find you *u* ... 2 Cor 9:4

UNPRESENTABLE
u parts have greater ... 1 Cor 12:23

UNPROFITABLE
'We are *u* servants ... Luke 17:10
for that would be *u* ... Heb 13:17

UNPUNISHED
wicked will not go *u* ... Prov 11:21

UNQUENCHABLE
up the chaff with *u* ... Matt 3:12

UNRESTRAINED
that the people were *u* ... Ex 32:25

UNRIGHTEOUS
u man his thoughts ... Is 55:7
u will not inherit the ... 1 Cor 6:9

UNRIGHTEOUSNESS
all ungodliness and *u* ... Rom 1:18
cleanse us from all *u* ... 1 John 1:9
All *u* is sin ... 1 John 5:17

UNRULY
those who are *u* ... 1 Thess 5:14

UNSEARCHABLE
u are His judgments ... Rom 11:33

UNSKILLED
only of milk is *u* ... Heb 5:13

UNSPOTTED
to keep oneself *u* ... James 1:27

UNSTABLE
U as water ....Gen 49:4

UNSTOPPED
of the deaf shall be *u* .... Is 35:5

UNTAUGHT
which *u* and unstable ....2 Pet 3:16

UNTRUSTWORTHY
undiscerning, *u* .... Rom 1:31

UNWASHED
eat bread with *u* hands ....Mark 7:5

UNWISE
Therefore do not be *u* .....Eph 5:17

UNWORTHY
u manner will be .... 1 Cor 11:27

UPHOLD
U me according to ......Ps 119:116

UPHOLDING
u all things by the ....Heb 1:3

UPHOLDS
LORD *u* all who fall .... Ps 145:14

UPPER
show you a large *u* ..... Mark 14:15

UPRIGHT
u is His delight .... Prov 15:8

UPRIGHTNESS
princes for their *u* .... Prov 17:26

UPROOT
u the wheat with .... Matt 13:29

URIM
Thummim and Your *U* ... Deut 33:8

US
"God with *u* .... Matt 1:23
If God is for *u* .... Rom 8:31
of them were of *u* ...... 1 John 2:19

USE
who spitefully *u* you ..... Matt 5:44
u liberty as an .... Gal 5:13

USELESS
one's religion is *u* ....James 1:26

USES
if one *u* it lawfully .... 1 Tim 1:8

USING
u liberty as a .... 1 Pet 2:16

USURY
'Take no *u* or .... Lev 25:36

UTTER
u dark sayings of old .... Ps 78:2

UTTERANCE
the Spirit gave them *u* ..... Acts 2:4

UTTERED
which cannot be *u* .... Rom 8:26

UTTERMOST
u those who come ....Heb 7:25

UTTERS
Day unto day *u* speech ..... Ps 19:2

V

VAGABOND
v you shall be on the ......Gen 4:12

VAIN
the people plot a *v* ....Ps 2:1
you believed in *v* .... 1 Cor 15:2

VALIANT
They are not *v* for the ....Jer 9:3

VALIANTLY
God we will do *v* .... Ps 60:12

VALLEY
v shall be exalted .... Is 40:4

VALOR
a mighty man of *v* ..... 1 Sam 16:18

VALUE
of more *v* than they ...... Matt 6:26

VALUED
It cannot be *v* in the ...... Job 28:16

VANISH
knowledge, it will *v* ..... 1 Cor 13:8

VANISHED
and He *v* from their .....Luke 24:31

VANITY
of vanities, all is *v* ....Eccl 1:2

VAPOR
best state is but *v* .... Ps 39:5
It is even a *v* that ....James 4:14

VARIATION
whom there is no *v* ......James 1:17

VEGETABLES
and let them give us *v* .....Dan 1:12
is weak eats only *v* .... Rom 14:2

VEHEMENT
of fire, A most *v* ....Song 8:6

VEIL
v of the temple was ..... Matt 27:51
Presence behind the *v* .....Heb 6:19

VENGEANCE
V is Mine ....Deut 32:35

VENOM
It becomes cobra *v* .... Job 20:14

VESSEL
like a potter's *v* ....Ps 2:9
for he is a chosen *v* .... Acts 9:15

VESSELS
treasure in earthen *v* ..... 2 Cor 4:7

VEXED
grieved, and I was *v* .... Ps 73:21

VICE
as a cloak for *v* .... 1 Pet 2:16

VICTIM
And plucked the *v* .... Job 29:17

VICTORY
v that has overcome ..... 1 John 5:4

VIEW
"Go, *v* the land .... Josh 2:1

VIGILANT
Be sober, be *v* .... 1 Pet 5:8

VIGOR
nor his natural *v* .... Deut 34:7

VILE
them up to *v* passions .... Rom 1:26

VINDICATED
know that I shall be *v* .... Job 13:18

VINDICATION
Let my *v* come from .... Ps 17:2

VINE
"I am the true *v* ....John 15:1

VINEDRESSER
and My Father is the *v* ...John 15:1

VINEGAR
As *v* to the teeth and .... Prov 10:26

VINES
foxes that spoil the *v* .....Song 2:15

VINEYARD
Who plants a *v* and ...... 1 Cor 9:7

VIOLENCE
was filled with *v* ....Gen 6:11
of heaven suffers *v* ...... Matt 11:12

VIOLENT
haters of God, *v* .... Rom 1:30

VIPER
And stings like a *v* ...... Prov 23:32

VIPERS
to them, "Brood of *v* ...... Matt 3:7

VIRGIN
v shall conceive .... Is 7:14
"Behold, the *v* shall ...... Matt 1:23

VIRGINS
v who took their lamps ... Matt 25:1

VIRTUE
to your faith *v* .... 2 Pet 1:5

VISAGE
v was marred more than ... Is 52:14

VISIBLE
that are on earth, *v* .... Col 1:16

VISION
in a trance I saw a *v* ...... Acts 11:5
to the heavenly *v* .... Acts 26:19

VISIONS
young men shall see *v* ..... Joel 2:28

VISIT
v orphans and ....James 1:27

VISITATION
God in the day of *v* .... 1 Pet 2:12

VISITED
Israel, for He has *v* ....Luke 1:68

VISITING
v the iniquity of the .... Ex 20:5

VISITOR
am a foreigner and a *v* ....Gen 23:4

VITALITY
v was turned into the .... Ps 32:4

VOICE
fire a still small *v* .... 1 Kin 19:12
if you will hear His *v* .... Ps 95:7
"The *v* of one crying ...... Matt 3:3
And suddenly a *v* .... Matt 3:17
for they know his *v* ...... John 10:4
the truth hears My *v* ....John 18:37
If anyone hears My *v* ...... Rev 3:20

VOICES
And there were loud *v* .... Rev 11:15

VOID
they are a nation *v* ......Deut 32:28
heirs, faith is made *v* ..... Rom 4:14

VOLUME
In the *v* of the book ....Heb 10:7

VOLUNTEERS
Your people shall be *v* ..... Ps 110:3

VOMIT
returns to his own *v* ...... 2 Pet 2:22

VOW
for he had taken a *v* ..... Acts 18:18

VOWS
to reconsider his *v* ...... Prov 20:25

W

WAGE
w the good warfare ..... 1 Tim 1:18

WAGES
For the *w* of sin is .... Rom 6:23
Indeed the *w* of the ....James 5:4

WAIL
"Son of man, *w* ....Ezek 32:18

WAILING
There will be *w* .... Matt 13:42

WAIT
w patiently for Him .... Ps 37:7
those who *w* on the .... Is 40:31
To those who eagerly *w* ...Heb 9:28

WAITED
w patiently for the .... Ps 40:1
Divine longsuffering *w* ... 1 Pet 3:20

WAITING
ourselves, eagerly *w* ..... Rom 8:23
from that time *w* ....Heb 10:13

WAITS
the creation eagerly *w* ... Rom 8:19

WAKE
that whether we *w* .... 1 Thess 5:10

WALK
w before Me and be ....Gen 17:1
Yea, though I *w* .... Ps 23:4
W prudently when you .....Eccl 5:1
"This is the way, *w* .... Is 30:21
be weary, they shall *w* ...... Is 40:31
w humbly with your God ... Mic 6:8
W while you have the ...John 12:35
so we also should *w* .... Rom 6:4
For we *w* by faith .... 2 Cor 5:7
W in the Spirit .... Gal 5:16
And *w* in love
Eph 5:2
that you may *w* worthy .... Col 1:10
and they shall *w* .... Rev 3:4

WALKED
Methuselah, Enoch *w* .....Gen 5:22
The people who *w* .... Is 9:2
in which you once *w* .... Eph 2:2

WALKING
not *w* in craftiness .... 2 Cor 4:2

WALKS
the LORD your God *w* ... Deut 23:14
is the man Who *w* ... Ps 1:1
he who *w* in darkness ... John 12:35
adversary the devil *w* ... 1 Pet 5:8

WALL
then the *w* of the city ... Josh 6:5
you whitewashed *w* ... Acts 23:3
a window in the *w* ... 2 Cor 11:33
Now the *w* of the city ... Rev 21:14

WALLS
By faith the *w* of ... Heb 11:30

WANDER
they have loved to *w* ... Jer 14:10

WANDERED
They *w* in deserts and ... Heb 11:38

WANDERERS
And they shall be *w* ... Hos 9:17

WANDERING
w stars for whom is ... Jude 13

WANDERS
among you *w* ... James 5:19

WANT
I shall not *w* ... Ps 23:1

WANTING
balances, and found *w* ... Dan 5:27

WANTON
have begun to grow *w* ... 1 Tim 5:11

WAR
"There is a noise of *w* ... Ex 32:17
w may rise against ... Ps 27:3
shall they learn *w* ... Is 2:4
going to make *w* ... Luke 14:31
You fight and *w* ... James 4:2
fleshly lusts which *w* ... 1 Pet 2:11
judges and makes *w* ... Rev 19:11

WARFARE
to her, That her *w* ... Is 40:2
w entangles ... 2 Tim 2:4

WARMED
in peace, be *w* ... James 2:16

WARMING
she saw Peter *w* ... Mark 14:67

WARMS
w them in the dust ... Job 39:14

WARN
w those who are ... 1 Thess 5:14

WARNED
Then, being divinely *w* ... Matt 2:12
Who *w* you to flee ... Matt 3:7

WARNING
w every man and ... Col 1:28

WARPED
such a person is *w* ... Titus 3:11

WARRING
w against the law of ... Rom 7:23

WARRIOR
He runs at me like a *w* ... Job 16:14

WARS
you will hear of *w* ... Matt 24:6
Where do *w* and fights ... James 4:1

WASH
w myself with snow ... Job 9:30
W me thoroughly ... Ps 51:2
w His feet with her ... Luke 7:38
said to him, "Go, *w* ... John 9:7
w the disciples' ... John 13:5
w away your sins ... Acts 22:16

WASHED
w his hands before ... Matt 27:24
But you were *w* ... 1 Cor 6:11
Him who loved us and *w* ... Rev 1:5

WASHING
us, through the *w* ... Titus 3:5

WASHINGS
and drinks, various *w* ... Heb 9:10

WASTE
the cities are laid *w* ... Is 6:11
"Why this *w* ... Matt 26:8

WASTED
this fragrant oil *w* ... Mark 14:4

WASTELAND
w shall be glad ... Is 35:1

WASTING
that this man was *w* ... Luke 16:1

WATCH
is past, And like a *w* ... Ps 90:4
"*W* therefore ... Matt 24:42

WATCHED
he would have *w* ... Matt 24:43

WATCHES
Blessed is he who *w* ... Rev 16:15

WATCHFUL
But you be *w* in all ... 2 Tim 4:5

WATCHING
he comes, will find *w* ... Luke 12:37

WATCHMAN
I have made you a *w* ... Ezek 3:17

WATCHMEN
I have set *w* on your ... Is 62:6

WATER
Eden to *w* the garden ... Gen 2:10
I am poured out like *w* ... Ps 22:14
For I will pour *w* ... Is 44:3
given you living *w* ... John 4:10
rivers of living *w* ... John 7:38
can yield both salt *w* ... James 3:12
the Spirit, the *w* ... 1 John 5:8
are clouds without *w* ... Jude 12
let him take the *w* ... Rev 22:17

WATERED
I planted, Apollos *w* ... 1 Cor 3:6

WATERS
me beside the still *w* ... Ps 23:2
Though its *w* roar and ... Ps 46:3
your bread upon the *w* ... Eccl 11:1
thirsts, Come to the *w* ... Is 55:1
fountain of living *w* ... Jer 2:13
living fountains of *w* ... Rev 7:17

WAVE
Its fruit shall *w* ... Ps 72:16

WAVER
He did not *w* at the ... Rom 4:20

WAVERING
of our hope without *w* ... Heb 10:23

WAVES
sea, tossed by the *w* ... Matt 14:24

WAX
My heart is like *w* ... Ps 22:14

WAY
As for God, His *w* ... 2 Sam 22:31
the LORD knows the *w* ... Ps 1:6
Teach me Your *w* ... Ps 27:11
in the *w* everlasting ... Ps 139:24
w that seems right ... Prov 14:12
The *w* of the just is ... Is 26:7
wicked forsake his *w* ... Is 55:7
And pervert the *w* ... Amos 2:7
he will prepare the *w* ... Mal 3:1
and broad is the *w* ... Matt 7:13
will prepare Your *w* ... Matt 11:10
to him, "I am the *w* ... John 14:6
to him the *w* ... Acts 18:26
to have known the *w* ... 2 Pet 2:21

WAYS
For all His *w* are ... Deut 32:4
transgressors Your *w* ... Ps 51:13
w please the LORD ... Prov 16:7
"Stand in the *w* ... Jer 6:16
and owns all your *w* ... Dan 5:23
w are everlasting ... Hab 3:6
unstable in all his *w* ... James 1:8
and true are Your *w* ... Rev 15:3

WEAK
gives power to the *w* ... Is 40:29
knee will be as *w* ... Ezek 7:17
but the flesh is *w* ... Matt 26:41
Receive one who is *w* ... Rom 14:1
God has chosen the *w* ... 1 Cor 1:27
We are *w* ... 1 Cor 4:10
w I became as *w* ... 1 Cor 9:22
For when I am *w* ... 2 Cor 12:10

WEAKENED
w my strength in the ... Ps 102:23

WEAKENS
w the hands of the men ... Jer 38:4

WEAKER
the wife, as to the *w* ... 1 Pet 3:7

WEAKNESS
w were made strong ... Heb 11:34

WEAKNESSES
also helps in our *w* ... Rom 8:26

WEALTH
W gained by ... Prov 13:11

WEALTHY
rich, have become *w* ... Rev 3:17

WEANED
w child shall put his ... Is 11:8

WEAPON
w formed against you ... Is 54:17

WEAPONS
For the *w* of our ... 2 Cor 10:4

WEAR
'What shall we *w* ... Matt 6:31

WEARIED
You have *w* Me with ... Is 43:24
therefore, being *w* ... John 4:6

WEARINESS
say, 'Oh, what a *w* ... Mal 1:13

WEARISOME
and much study is *w* ... Eccl 12:12

WEARY
shall run and not be *w* ... Is 40:31
And let us not grow *w* ... Gal 6:9
do not grow *w* in ... 2 Thess 3:13

WEATHER
'It will be fair *w* ... Matt 16:2

WEDDING
day there was a *w* ... John 2:1

WEEK
the first day of the *w* ... Matt 28:1

WEEKS
w are determined ... Dan 9:24

WEEP
A time to *w* ... Eccl 3:4
You shall *w* no more ... Is 30:19
are you who *w* ... Luke 6:21
do not *w* ... Luke 23:28
w with those who *w* ... Rom 12:15

WEEPING
the noise of the *w* ... Ezra 3:13
They shall come with *w* ... Jer 31:9
There will be *w* ... Matt 8:12
by the tomb *w* ... John 20:11

WEIGH
O Most Upright, You *w* ... Is 26:7

WEIGHED
You have been *w* ... Dan 5:27

WEIGHS
eyes, But the LORD *w* ... Prov 16:2

WEIGHT
us lay aside every *w* ... Heb 12:1

WEIGHTIER
have neglected the *w* ... Matt 23:23

WELFARE
does not seek the *w* ... Jer 38:4

WELL
have done *w* ... Prov 31:29
wheel broken at the *w* ... Eccl 12:6
"Those who are *w* ... Matt 9:12
said to him, '*W* done ... Matt 25:21

WELLS
These are *w* without ... 2 Pet 2:17

WENT
They *w* out from us ... 1 John 2:19

WEPT
out and *w* bitterly ... Matt 26:75
saw the city and *w* ... Luke 19:41
Jesus *w* ... John 11:35

WET
his body was *w* with ... Dan 4:33

WHEAT
w falls into the ... John 12:24

WHEEL
in the middle of a *w* ... Ezek 1:16

WHEELS
noise of rattling *w* .... Nah 3:2

WHERE
not knowing *w* he was .... Heb 11:8

WHIP
A *w* for the horse .... Prov 26:3

WHIRLWIND
Job out of the *w* .... Job 38:1
has His way in the *w* .... Nah 1:3

WHISPER
my ear received a *w* .... Job 4:12

WHISPERER
w separates the best ..... Prov 16:28

WHISPERERS
they are *w* .... Rom 1:29

WHISPERINGS
backbitings, *w* .... 2 Cor 12:20

WHITE
clothed in *w* garments ..... Rev 3:5
behold, a *w* horse .... Rev 6:2
and made them *w* .... Rev 7:14

WHOLE
w body were an eye .... 1 Cor 12:17

WHOLESOME
not consent to *w* words ... 1 Tim 6:3

WHOLLY
w followed the LORD ..... Deut 1:36

WICKED
w shall be silent .... 1 Sam 2:9
w shall be no more .... Ps 37:10
if there is any *w* .... Ps 139:24
w forsake his way .... Is 55:7
And desperately *w* .... Jer 17:9
the sway of the *w* ...... 1 John 5:19

WICKEDLY
God will never do *w* .... Job 34:12

WICKEDNESS
LORD saw that the *w* .... Gen 6:5
in the tents of *w* .... Ps 84:10
man repented of his *w* .... Jer 8:6
is full of greed and *w* .... Luke 11:39
sexual immorality, *w* ..... Rom 1:29
and overflow of *w* .... James 1:21

WIDE
open your hand *w* .... Deut 15:8
w is the gate and .... Matt 7:13
to you, our heart is *w* .... 2 Cor 6:11

WIDOW
the fatherless and *w* .... Ps 146:9
How like a *w* is she .... Lam 1:1
Then one poor *w* .... Mark 12:42
w has children or .... 1 Tim 5:4

WIDOW'S
And I caused the *w* .... Job 29:13

WIDOWS
w were neglected .... Acts 6:1
visit orphans and *w* ..... James 1:27

WIFE
and be joined to his *w* ..... Gen 2:24
w finds a good thing ..... Prov 18:22
But a prudent *w* .... Prov 19:14
"Go, take yourself a *w* ...... Hos 1:2
divorces his *w* .... Mark 10:11
'I have married a *w* ..... Luke 14:20
"Remember Lot's *w* ..... Luke 17:32
so love his own *w* .... Eph 5:33
the husband of one *w* ..... Titus 1:6
bride, the Lamb's *w* .... Rev 21:9

WILD
olive tree which is *w* .... Rom 11:24

WILDERNESS
I will make the *w* .... Is 41:18
of one crying in the *w* ..... Matt 3:3
the serpent in the *w* ...... John 3:14

WILES
to stand against the *w* ..... Eph 6:11

WILL
w be done On earth as ... Matt 6:10
but he who does the *w* ... Matt 7:21
not My *w* .... Luke 22:42
flesh, nor of the *w* .... John 1:13
not to do My own *w* ...... John 6:38
w is present with me ..... Rom 7:18
and perfect *w* of God ..... Rom 12:2
works in you both to *w* .... Phil 2:13
according to His own *w* .... Heb 2:4
work to do His *w* .... Heb 13:21

WILLFULLY
For if we sin *w* .... Heb 10:26
For this they *w* .... 2 Pet 3:5

WILLING
If you are *w* and .... Is 1:19
The spirit indeed is *w* ... Matt 26:41
w that any should .... 2 Pet 3:9

WILLINGLY
by compulsion but *w* ...... 1 Pet 5:2

WILLOWS
our harps Upon the *w* ..... Ps 137:2

WILLS
to whom the Son *w* ..... Matt 11:27
it is not of him who *w* .... Rom 9:16
say, "If the Lord *w* ...... James 4:15

WIN
to all, that I might *w* ..... 1 Cor 9:19

WIND
the chaff which the *w* .... Ps 1:4
reed shaken by the *w* .... Matt 11:7
"The *w* blows where ...... John 3:8
of a rushing mighty *w* ..... Acts 2:2

WINDOWS
not open for you the *w* .... Mal 3:10

WINDS
be, that even the *w* ...... Matt 8:27

WINDSTORM
And a great *w* arose ...... Mark 4:37

WINE
W is a mocker .... Prov 20:1
love is better than *w* ...... Song 1:2
Yes, come, buy *w* .... Is 55:1
they gave Him sour *w* ... Matt 27:34
do not be drunk with *w* .... Eph 5:18
not given to much *w* ...... Titus 2:3

WINEBIBBERS
Do not mix with *w* ...... Prov 23:20

WINEPRESS
"I have trodden the *w* .... Is 63:3
into the great *w* .... Rev 14:19
Himself treads the *w* ..... Rev 19:15

WINESKINS
new wine into old *w* ...... Matt 9:17

WING
One *w* of the cherub .... 1 Kin 6:24

WINGS
the shadow of Your *w* ...... Ps 36:7
With healing in His *w* ...... Mal 4:2

WINNOW
You shall *w* them .... Is 41:16

WINS
w souls is wise .... Prov 11:30

WINTER
For lo, the *w* is past ...... Song 2:11
flight may not be in *w* ... Matt 24:20

WIPE
w away every tear .... Rev 21:4

WISDOM
for this is your *w* .... Deut 4:6
man who finds *w* .... Prov 3:13
Get *w* .... Prov 4:5
is the beginning of *w* .... Prov 9:10
w is justified by her ..... Matt 11:19
Jesus increased in *w* ...... Luke 2:52
riches both of the *w* ..... Rom 11:33
the gospel, not with *w* ... 1 Cor 1:17
w of this world .... 1 Cor 3:19
not with fleshly *w* .... 2 Cor 1:12
all the treasures of *w* .... Col 2:3
If any of you lacks *w* ..... James 1:5
power and riches and *w* ... Rev 5:12

WISE
Do not be *w* in your .... Prov 3:7
who wins souls is *w* ..... Prov 11:30
Therefore be *w* as .... Matt 10:16
five of them were *w* ...... Matt 25:2
to God, alone *w* .... Rom 16:27
Where is the *w* .... 1 Cor 1:20
not as fools but as *w* .... Eph 5:15
able to make you *w* ..... 2 Tim 3:15

WISELY
you do not inquire *w* ...... Eccl 7:10

WISER
he was *w* than all men .. 1 Kin 4:31
of God is *w* than men ... 1 Cor 1:25

WISH
w it were already .... Luke 12:49

WISHED
Then he *w* death for .... Jon 4:8

WITCHCRAFT
is as the sin of *w* ...... 1 Sam 15:23

WITHDRAW
From such *w* yourself .... 1 Tim 6:5

WITHER
also shall not *w* .... Ps 1:3

WITHERS
The grass *w* .... Is 40:7
The grass *w* .... 1 Pet 1:24

WITHHELD
And your sins have *w* ...... Jer 5:25

WITHHOLD
good thing will He *w* ...... Ps 84:11

WITHOUT
pray *w* ceasing .... 1 Thess 5:17
w works is dead .... James 2:26

WITHSTAND
you may be able to *w* ...... Eph 6:13

WITHSTOOD
I *w* him to his face ...... Gal 2:11

WITNESS
all the world as a *w* ..... Matt 24:14
This man came for a *w* .... John 1:7
do not receive Our *w* ..... John 3:11
Christ, the faithful *w* .... Rev 1:5
beheaded for their *w* ...... Rev 20:4

WITNESSED
is revealed, being *w* ...... Rom 3:21

WITNESSES
"You are My *w* .... Is 43:10
presence of many *w* ..... 1 Tim 6:12
so great a cloud of *w* .... Heb 12:1

WIVES
Husbands, love your *w* .... Eph 5:25
w must be reverent ...... 1 Tim 3:11

WOLF
The *w* and the lamb .... Is 65:25

WOLVES
out as lambs among *w* .... Luke 10:3
savage *w* .... Acts 20:29

WOMAN
She shall be called *W* ..... Gen 2:23
whoever looks at a *w* ..... Matt 5:28
Then the *w* of Samaria .... John 4:9
"*W*, behold your .... John 19:26
natural use of the *w* .... Rom 1:27
His Son, born of a *w* .... Gal 4:4
w being deceived .... 1 Tim 2:14
w clothed with the sun .... Rev 12:1

WOMB
nations are in your *w* .... Gen 25:23
in the *w* I knew you .... Jer 1:5
is the fruit of your *w* ..... Luke 1:42

WOMEN
O fairest among *w* .... Song 1:8
w will be grinding .... Matt 24:41
are you among *w* .... Luke 1:28
admonish the young *w* .... Titus 2:4
times, the holy *w* .... 1 Pet 3:5

WONDER
marvelous work and a *w* ... Is 29:14

WONDERFUL
Things too *w* for me .... Job 42:3
name will be called *W* .... Is 9:6

WONDERIFULLY
fearfully and *w* made .... Ps 139:14

WONDERS
"And I will show *w* .... Joel 2:30
signs, and lying *w* .... 2 Thess 2:9

WONDROUS
w works declare that .... Ps 75:1

WONDROUSLY
God, Who has dealt *w* ..... Joel 2:26

John 10:28–30
Nahum 1:
Ps. 18:17
Ps. 25:1 & 2
Ps. 34:19
Ps. 42:3, 10
Jer. 17:14
It is time for increase.
Isaiah 54:2–4
Ps. 40:2 (God will pull you out)
1st Corinth. 3:6 & 7
2nd Thess. 3:10
Ps. 32:8
Job. 32:8
Prov. 20:12
2nd Chron. 25 (1–9)
Gen 33:8–9
Ps. 115:14
Ps. 71:21
1 Tim. 1:18
Acts 16:16
Nahum 2:2

Lam. 3:36–37
Ps. 18:17
Job 5:12–13
Isaiah 54:15 & 17

Dec. 2 2018
2 Chron 26:15
2 Chron 18:31
1st Chron 12:21–22